THE NEW YORK PUBLIC LIBRARY DESK REFERENCE

Third Edition

A STONESONG PRESS BOOK

MACMILLAN • USA

Macmillan General Reference
A Simon & Schuster Macmillan Company
1633 Broadway
New York NY 10019-6785

Library of Congress Cataloging-in-Publication Data

The New York Public Library desk reference.—3rd ed.
  p. cm.
 "A Stonesong Press Book."
 Includes bibliographical references and index.
 ISBN 0-02-862169-7
 1. Encyclopedia and dictionaries. I. New York Public Library.
AG6.N49 1933
031—dc20   93-18299
                                    CIP

Printed in the United States of America on acid-free paper.

1 2 3 4 5 6 7 8 9 10   98 99 00 01 02

Third Edition

NEW YORK PUBLIC LIBRARY PROJECT SPONSOR

To Alison

A Note from the Editors

Every attempt has been made to ensure that this publication is as accurate as possible and as comprehensive as space would allow. We are grateful to the many researchers, librarians, teachers, reference editors, and friends who contributed facts, figures, time, energy, ideas, and opinions. Our choice of what to include was aided by their advice and their voices of experience. The contents, however, remain subjective to some extent, because we could not possibly cover everything that one might look for in basic information. If errors or omissions are discovered, we would appreciate hearing from you, the user, as we prepare future editions. Please address suggestions and comments to The Stonesong Press, 11 East 47th Street, New York, NY 10017.

We hope you find our work useful.

CONTENTS

PREFACE	XV

I THE PHYSICAL WORLD — 1

1 TIMES AND DATES — 3

Reckoning Days and Hours	4
The Length of the Day	4
How Is the Day Subdivided?	4
Clocks—Measuring Time	*5*
Ship's Bell Time Signals	*6*
Universal and Standard Time	6
U.S. and Canadian Time Zones	8
International Date Line	8
Standard Time for Major	9
Foreign Cities	
Time Adjustments	9
Daylight Savings Time in	9
the United States	
International Time Adjustments	10
Calendars	10
Names of the Days	10
Definitions of a Year	10
The Lunar Calendar	*11*
The Seasons	11
The Development of the Roman/	12
Julian/Gregorian Calendar	
Perpetual Calendar, 1775-2098	13
Words Describing Periods of Time	18
Major Holidays	18
American	18
Canadian	19
Other	19
Additional Sources of Information	21

2 WEIGHTS AND MEASURES — 23

U.S. Customary System of	
Weights and Measures	24
Length	24
Area	24
Volume	24
Capacity (Dry Measure)	24
Capacity (Liquid Measure)	25
Mass (Avoirdupois)	25
Mass (Troy and Apothecaries)	25
Angle	25
Six Quick Ways to Measure	*25*
When You Don't Have a Ruler	
Metric System of Measurement	26
Basic Units	26
Derived Units	26

Metric Prefixes	27
Tables of Metric Weights and Measures	27
Common Conversion Factors	28
Mile/Kilometer Conversions	*29*
Temperature Conversions	29
Special Weights and Measures	30
Historic Weights and Measures	*31*
Additional Sources of Information	32
Organizations and Services	32
Books	32

3 THE BIOLOGICAL WORLD — 33

Anatomical Drawings	34
of the Human body	
The Skeletal System	34
Skull Bones	34
The Ear	34
The Eye	34
The Brain	35
The Muscle System	35
The Digestive System	36
The Respiratory System	36
The Animal Kingdom	37
The Orders of Mammals	37
The Phyla of Invertebrates	40
Extinct Animals	40
Pets	42
Choosing a Pet	42
Training	43
Spaying and Neutering	43
Pets and Children	44
Nutrition	44
Pet Stains	44
Immunization	44
Animal First Aid	45
Broken Bones	45
Burns	45
Cat Diseases	46
Constipation	46
Dental Disorders	46
Diarrhea	47
Dog Diseases	47
Parasites, External	47
Parasites, Internal	47
Rabies	48
Respiratory Infections	48
Shock	48
Skin Problems	48

Sprains	49
Wounds	49
The Plant Kingdom	**49**
Orders of Plants	49
Botanical Names of Plants	51
Ground Covers	56
Vines for Special Uses	*56*
Poisonous Cultivated and Wild Plants	57
Plant Cultivation	**58**
When to Plant	58
USDA Hardiness Zones	59
Frost Dates	60
Germination Tables	**61**
Annual Flowers	61
Vegetable Garden Plants	61
Common Biological Terms	**62**
Additional Sources of Information	**65**
Organizations and Services	65
Books	65

4 THE PHYSICAL SCIENCES, MATHEMATICS, AND TECHNOLOGY   67

Astronomy	**68**
Phases of the Moon	68
Lunar and Solar Eclipses	68
Total Eclipses of the Sun, 1900-2010	70
The Planets	72
The Life of a Star	73
Types of Stars	73
Understanding the Invisible	*74*
Constellations	75
The 25 Nearest Star Systems	76
Common Astronomy Terms	76
Chemistry	**80**
Elements and Their Symbols	80
The Periodic Table of the Elements	81
Common Chemistry Terms	82
Geology and Geophysics	**84**
Layers of the Earth	84
Geological Time Chart	85
Plate Tectonics	87
Measuring an Earthquake	*89*
Earthquakes	90
Some Important Minerals and Their Uses	90
Igneous, Sedimentary, and Metamorphic Rocks	91
Common Geology and Cartography Terms	92

Meteorology	**96**
Cloud Types	96
Beaufort Scale of Wind Force	97
Windchill Factor	98
Physics	**99**
Basic Formulas and Laws of Physics	99
Common Physics Terms	99
Mathematics	**102**
Basic Rules of Mathematics	102
Decimal and Percent Equivalents of Common Fractions	103
Geometric Shapes and Their Area, Circumference, and Volume Formulas	103
Triangles	105
Roman Numerals	106
Computers	**107**
Personal Computer Components	107
Macs and PCs	107
Growth of the Internet	*108*
Internet Search Engines	108
National Internet Service Providers	108
Common Computer Terms	109
Space Exploration	**115**
Manned Spacecraft	115
Human Missions to the Moon	116
Common Engineering Terms	**117**
Additional Sources of Information	**119**
Organizations and Services	119
Magazines	119
Books	119

5 INVENTIONS AND SCIENTIFIC DISCOVERIES   121

Significant Inventions, Technological Advances, and Discoveries	**122**
The Kite	*122*
Leonardo da Vinci	*123*
Quarks	*139*
Major Scientists and Engineers	**141**
Aerospace Engineers	141
Astronomers	141
Biologists	143
Chemists	144
Computer Scientists	146
Earth Scientists and Environmentalists	146
Mathematicians	148
Medical Scientists	149
Physicists	151
Schrodinger's Cat Paradox	*152*
Additional Sources of Information	**153**

II THE WORLD OF IDEAS   155

6 PERFORMANCE AND ENTERTAINMENT ARTS   157

Illustrated List of Musical Instruments	158
Stringed Instruments	158
Wind Instruments	159
Percussion Instruments	162
Electronic Instruments and Devices	163
The Makeup of a Symphony Orchestra	*163*
Major Composers of Classical Music	164
American	164
Austrian	166
British	167
French	168
German	170
Italian	171
Russian	173
Other	174
Major Jazz Composers and Performers	175
Common Music Terms	178
Basic Positions for Ballet	188
Feet	188
Arms	189
Major Dancers and Choreographers	190
American	190
British	192
French	193
Russian	193
Other	195
Common Dance Terms	195
Major Playwrights	198
American	198
British	199
French	201
German	202
Greek	203
Irish	203
Roman	203
Russian	203
Spanish	204
Other	204
Major Film Directors	204
American	204
A Brief History of Film	*205*
Asian	207
British	207
French	208
German	208
Italian	208
Other	209
The Academy Awards	209
Additional Sources of Information	216
Magazines	216
Books	216

7 THE VISUAL ARTS   217

Major Painters and Sculptors	218
American	218
Belgian/Flemish	221
British	221
Dutch	222
Flemish	223
French	223
German	225
Italian	226
Mexican	228
Russian	228
Spanish	229
Other European	230
Art Movements and Styles	230
Common Art Terms	233
Major Architects	235
American	235
British	237
French	238
Italian	239
Other	240
Architectural Movements and Styles	240
Illustrations of Architectural Elements	242
Common Architectural Terms	244
Additional Sources of Information	246

8 LITERATURE   247

Important Authors	248
American	248
African	253
Asian	254
Australian	254
British	255
Canadian	257
French	258
German	259
Italian	259
Latin American	259
Russian	260
Other European	261
Literary Movements, Periods, and Styles	261
Pseudonyms of Famous Authors	264
Poet Laureates	266
English	266
American	267

Book Awards and Their Recipients   267
  Nobel Prize in Literature   267
  Pulitzer Prize in Letters   268
  National Book Award   269
The Great Books: A Reading List   271
The New York Public Library's Books   272
  of the Century
  Landmarks of Modern Literature   272
  Nature's Realm   273
  Protest and Progress   273
  Colonialism and Its Aftermath   273
  Mind and Spirit   274
  Popular Culture and Mass Entertainment   274
  Women Rise   274
  Economics and Technology   275
  Utopias and Dystopias   275
  War, Holocaust, Totalitarianism   275
  Optimism, Joy, Gentility   276
  Favorites of Childhood and Youth   276
Common Literary Terms   276
Additional Sources of Information   279

9 RELIGIONS   281

The Greek and Roman Deities   282
The World's Major Religions   283
  Baha'i   284
  Buddhism   284
  Confucianism   284
  Hinduism   284
  Islam   284
  Judaism   285
  Orthodox Church   285
  Protestantism   285
  Roman Catholicism   290
  Rosicrucianism   291
  Shinto   291
  Taoism   291
  Zoroastrianism   291
Significant Dates in the History   292
  of Religion
  The Ten Commandments   293
Holy Books of the World   294
  The Seven Canonical Hours   294
  The Four Horsemen of the Apocalypse   294
  The Books of the Bible   295
  The Twelve Apostles   296
Roman Catholic Patron Saints   296
The Roman Catholic Popes   297
Major Religious Holidays   304
  in the United States
Additional Sources of Information   306

10 PHILOSOPHY   309

Major World Philosophers   310
  How to Argue Logically   313
Philosophical Movements and Schools   317
  of Thought
  Famous Philosophical Quotes   319
Common Philosophical Terms   322
  More Than Just Philosophers   324
  God's Existence—Proofs For   328
  God's Existence—Proofs Against   329
Additional Sources of Information   333
  Organizations and Services   333
  Books   333

11 LIBRARIES AND MUSEUMS   335

Major Libraries and Their Special   336
  Collections
  United States   336
  Canada   344
The Dewey Decimal System and How   345
  to use It
The Library of Congress Subject Headings   345
  Cataloging in Publication Data   346
Libraries Online   346
Data Banks Available for Computer   347
  Research
  Getting Started in Genealogy   348
  Major Genealogical Libraries   349
Information Centers   349
Reference Works for General Information   351
  General Reference Works   351
  Anthropology and Ethnology   352
  Applied Arts   352
  Art and Architecture   353
  Astronomy   354
  Business   354
  Communications   355
  Education   356
  Ethnic Studies   356
  Film   356
  Geography and Travel Guides   356
  History   357
  Law   357
  Linguistics   357
  Literature   357
  Medical Science   358
  Music   359
  Mythology, Folklore, and Popular   359
    Customs
  Philosophy   359
  Political Science   359

Recreation and Sports 360
Religion 360
Science and Technology 361
Social Science 361
Sociology 361
Statistics and Demography 361
Theater and Performing Arts 361
Major Art Museums and Their Special 362
Collections
United States 362
Canada 369
Major Science and Technology Museums 370
and Their Special Collections
Children's Museums 371
Major Zoos and Aquariums 372
United States 372
Canada 379
Major Botanical Gardens and Arboretums 379
Additional Sources of Information 384

III THE WAY WE COMMUNICATE 385

12 SYMBOLS AND SIGNS 387

Symbols Used in Science, Mathematics,
and Technology 388
Astronomy Symbols 388
Biology Symbols 389
Chemistry Symbols 389
Electronics Symbols 389
Mathematics Symbols 390
Medicine and Pharmacology Symbols 391
Physics Symbols 392
Weather Symbols 392
Cultural Symbols 393
Music Symbols 393
Religion Symbols 394
Zodiac Signs 395
Birthstones and Flowers 396
Symbols to Guide the Traveler 396
Map and Chart Symbols 396
Distress Signals 397
Road Signs 397
Symbolic Alphabets 399
Semaphore Code 399
International Radio Alphabet 399
and Morse Code
Sign Language 400
Braille Alphabet, Numbers, 400
and Punctuation
Business and Monetary Symbols 401

Proofreaders' Marks 401
Smileys 402
Additional Sources of Information 402

13 ALPHABETS AND WORDS 403

Alphabetization 404
Acronyms 404
Recurrent Letters of the Alphabet 405
Common Abbreviations 407
Commonly Misused Words 412
Spelling Guidelines 413
Commonly Misspelled Words 413
Phonetic Symbols 415
Vowels 415
Consonants 415
American English and British English: 415
Spelling and Name Differences
Diacritical Marks 415
The Indo-European Family of Languages 416
Frequently Used Foreign Words 417
and Phrases
Common Phrases: Major World 421
Languages
Greek Prefixes and Suffixes 422
Latin Prefixes and Suffixes 424
Common Crossword-Puzzle Words 425
Oxymoron: A Pairing of Contradictory 427
or Incongruous Words
Palidromes 428
Foreign Alphabets 432
Arabic 432
Greek 432
Hebrew 432
Cyrillic 432
Additional Sources of Information 433
Web Sites 433
Books 433

14 GRAMMAR AND PUNCTUATION 435

The Parts of Speech 436
Modifiers 437
Sentence Structure 437
Simple Sentences 438
Compound, Complex, and Compound- 438
Complex Sentences
Subject-Verb Agreement 439
Tense, Voice, and Mood 439
Verbals 440
Four Common Grammatical Problems 440

Punctuation   441
    Terminating Punctuation   441
    Pause Punctuation   441
    Brackets and Parentheses   442
    Apostrophes, Single Quotation Marks,   443
      and Double Quotation Marks
American English and British English: 443
    Punctuation Differences
Additional Sources of Information   444

15 LETTERS AND FORMS OF ADDRESS   445

Personal Letters   446
Business Protocol and Forms of Address   446
    Business Letters   446
    How to Prepare a Résumé   447
    Work Experience   448
    Spoken and Written Forms of Address   454
    Grades and Ranks for U.S. Military   455
      Personnel
    Abbreviated Titles That Follow Names   455
Additional Sources of Information   455

IV DAILY LIFE   457

16 ETIQUETTE   459

Wedding Etiquette   460
    Invitations and Announcements   460
    Showers   461
    Bachelor Dinner   461
    Rehearsal Dinner   461
    Ceremony   463
    Reception   463
    Gifts and Thank-You Notes   465
      Division of Wedding Expenses   465
    Anniversary Gifts   466
Business Etiquette   466
    Appointments   466
    Entertainment   467
    Gifts   467
    The Telephone   467
Network Etiquette (Netiquette)   468
Parties   468
    General Aspects   468
    Formal Dinner Parties   469
    Informal Dinner Parties   471
Deaths and Funerals   471
    Funeral Arrangements   471
    Wakes   471
    Flowers   471
    Funeral Services   472
    Burial   472

    Letters or Calls of Condolence   472
    After Burial   472
Additional Sources of Information   472

17 FIRST AID   473

Lifesaving Procedures   474
    Maintaining Breathing and Circulation   474
      Methods of Cardiopulmonary   474
        Resuscitation (CPR)
    Preventing Loss of Blood   475
      Pressure Points   476
    Preventing Further Injury   478
    Preventing Shock   478
      First-Aid Kits   479
Treatment for Health Emergencies   480
    Abrasions   480
    Animal Bites   480
    Black Eyes and Bruises   480
    Boils and Blisters   480
    Burns   480
    Choking   481
    Concussions   482
    Convulsions   482
    Drowning   482
    Electric Shock   483
    Fractures, Dislocations, and Sprains   483
    Frostbite   485
    Heat Cramps, Heat Exhaustion,   485
      Heat Stroke
    Insect Bites   485
    Nosebleeds   486
    Poisoning   486
Directory of Poison Control Centers   488
    United States   489
      The Signs and Signals of Heart   491
        Attacks and Strokes
    Canada   492
Additional Sources of Information   493
    Organizations and Services   493
    Books   493

18 HEALTH AND NUTRITION   495

Questions to Ask Your Doctor   496
    Shelf Life of Medicine   497
The Patient's Bill of Rights   498
Approximate Dates of Childbirth   500
Precautions During Pregnancy   500
    Alcohol   500
    Caffeine   501
    Chemicals   501
    Chicken Pox (Varicella)   501
    Drugs and Medications   501
    Fifth Disease (Erythema Infectiosum)   501

Hot Tubs, Saunas, and Steam Baths 501
Measles 501
Radiation 501
Vaccines *502*
Smoking 502
Toxoplasmosis 502
Immunization Schedule for Infants, 502
Children, and Adults
Expected Number of Deaths at Given 503
Periods of Life per 100,000 Infants
Born Alive in 1995
Life Expectancy in 1995 by Race, Sex, 504
and Age
Recommended Weights 504
For Adults Only: Calculating the Body 504
Mass Index
Height and Weight Charts for Children 505
Home Remedies **506**
Allergies, Seasonal 506
Back Pain from Muscle Strain 507
Burns, First-Degree 507
Colds, Sore Throats, and Coughs Due 507
to Colds
Constipation 507
Flu (Influenza) 508
Headaches 508
Hiccups 508
Hyperventilation 509
Indigestion 509
Insect Bites 509
Insomnia 509
Premenstrual Syndrome (PMS) 510
Rashes, Plant-Allergy 510
Rashes, Heat 510
Sprains and Strains of the Ankle, Foot, 510
Hand, Wrist, or Elbow
Strep Throat 511
Looking for Signs of Breast Cancer **511**
Ask for a Breast Exam 511
Practice Breast Self-Examination (BSE) 511
When to Examine Your Breasts 511
When to Get a Mammogram 513
Infectious Diseases and How They **513**
Are Spread
Dental Care **514**
Osteopathy *514*
Chiropractic *514*
Homeopathy *515*
Living Wills **515**
Deaths and Death Rates from Selected **516**
Causes, 1970 to 1996
Combining Forms of Medical Terms **519**

Recommended Daily (or Dietary) 520
Allowances
Proteins 520
Fat-Soluble Vitamins 520
Water-Soluble Vitamins 521
Minerals 521
Vitamin/Mineral Food Chart **522**
Activities and the Calories They Consume **530**
Safe Alcohol Consumption **531**
Drinking and Driving 531
Additional Sources of Information **532**
Organizations and Services 532
Hot Lines and Information Services *533*
Magazines 534
Books 534

19 HOUSEHOLD TIPS **535**

Food **536**
Cooking Equivalents and Substitutions 536
Cooking Times and Serving Sizes 539
Carving a Turkey *541*
Refrigeration Food Storage Times *544*
Temperature of Food for Control of *544*
Bacteria
Food Hot Lines 545
Pantry Basics 545
Herbs and Spices 545
Herbal Salt Substitutes *546*
Chemical Additives **547**
Common Additive Terms 547
Types of Additives 547
Outlawed Additives 552
Beverages **553**
Amount of Liquor Needed for Number 553
of Drinks Served
Champagne Bottle Sizes *553*
Mixing Drinks 554
Alcoholic Drink Recipes 554
Wines and Their Service 556
Selecting Wines to Go With Foods 556
How to Store Coffee *557*
Prime Wine Vintages by Region/Variety 557
Clothing **557**
Water Temperatures *558*
Stain Removal 559
Clothing Size Conversion Tables 565
Standard Sizes of Materials and Tools **566**
Interior Materials 566
Exterior Materials 567
Disposal of Hazardous Household **568**
Chemicals
Recycling **567**

Composting   567
How to Build a Fire   567
Baby-Sitter Checklist   570
Car-Maintenance Checklist   570
Additional Sources of Information   570
   Organizations and Services   570
   Magazines   571
   Books   572

20 PERSONAL FINANCES   573

Tables of Common Interest   574
   Simple Interest   574
   Compound Interest   574
   Mortgage Amortization Factors   575
Making a Budget   575
How Much Can You Spend on Housing?   576
Average Cost of Raising a Child   576
Calculating Your Net Worth   576
Insurance   578
   Health Insurance   578
   Life Insurance   579
   Disability Insurance   580
   Property and Liability Insurance   580
   Automobile Insurance   581
Credit and Loans   582
Real Estate and Mortgages   583
   The Decision to Buy a Home   583
   Affordability   583
   An Old Home or a New One?   584
   The Down Payment   584
   The Mortgage   584
   Going to Contract   585
   Common Real-Estate Terms   585
Investments and Retirement   586
   Setting Goals   586
   Choosing Your Investments   587
   Worth the Risk?   589
   Mutual Funds   589
   Major Mutual Fund Companies   590
   Planning for Retirement   591
Common Investment Terms   592
Tipping   595
Additional Sources of Information   596
   Organizations and Services   596
   Magazines and Newspapers   596
   Books   596

21 LEGAL INFORMATION   597

Forms and Contracts   598
   Bill of Sale   598
   Certificate of Notary   599
   Contract   600

Declaration of a Gift   604
Leases   605
Living Will   613
Power of Attorney   614
Privacy Act/Freedom of Information   615
   Act Request
Promissory Note   616
Request for Reason for Adverse   616
   Credit Action
Security Agreement   617
Statute of Limitations   618
   Federal Statute of Limitations   618
   State Statute of Limitations   618
Copyrights   618
   The Death Penalty   *619*
Patents   620
Federal Judicial System   622
Supreme Court Justices   622
Supreme Court Decisions   623
Common Legal Terms   626
Additional Sources of Information   ·615
   Organizations and Services   633
   Books   634

22 USEFUL ADDRESSES AND   637
PHONE NUMBERS

Aging   638
   Private Organizations   638
   State Commissions and Offices   638
Alcoholism and Drug Abuse   643
Children   644
   Child Abuse   644
   Disabled Children   644
   Runaways   644
Consumer Information and Protection   645
   Better Business Bureaus   645
   State, County, and City Government   645
      Consumer Protection Offices
Disabilities   668
   Telecommunications Device for the Deaf 668
   Books for Blind and Physically   668
      Handicapped Persons
Domestic Violence Resources   668
Family Planning   671
Federal Government Agencies and   671
   Bureaus
Federal Information Centers   673
Parenting   674
   Adoption   674
   Single-Parent Families   674
      Hot Lines and Information Services *675*
Radio and Television Networks   674

United States Service Academies 677
Additional Sources of Information 678
Magazines 678
Books 680

V RECREATION 681

23 SPORTS AND GAMES 683

Auto Racing 684
Indianapolis 500 685
Baseball 686
U.S. and Canadian Major League 688
Baseball Teams
World Series 688
Basketball 690
National Basketball Association (NBA) 691
Teams
National Basketball Association 691
Champions
Bicycle Racing 693
Tour de France 693
Bowling 694
Football 694
National Football League (NFL) Teams 698
The Super Bowl 698
Golf 699
The Masters 700
Horse Racing 700
The Triple Crown 701
Winning Horses in the Kentucky Derby 701
Ice Hockey 702
National Hockey League (NHL) Teams 703
The Stanley Cup 703
Soccer 705
The World Cup 706
Tennis 707
Wimbledon 708
Volleyball 709
Olympic Games 710
Locations 710
1996 Summer Olympic Events 711
1998 Winter Olympic Games 712
Major Sports Figures 713
Board Games 719
Backgammon 719
Checkers 720
Chess 721
Monopoly® 722
The Most Landed-On Spaces on the 723
Monopoly® Game Board
Scrabble® 723
94 Acceptable Two-Letter Scrabble® 723
Words

Card Games 724
Blackjack 724
Bridge 724
Pinochle 725
Poker 725
Rummy 726
Solitaire 726
Additional Sources of Information 727
Organizations and Services 727
Magazines 729
Books 729

24 TRAVEL 733

Basic Information 734
Travelers' Checklist 734
Travelers' First-Aid Kit 734
Tips for Travelers with Disabilities 734
Traveling with Pets 735
Car-Rental Agency Toll-Free Numbers 736
and Web Sites
Hotel/Motel Chain Toll-Free Numbers 737
and Web Sites
Airline Codes and Toll-Free Numbers, 738
and Web Sites
Airport Codes, Names, and Locations 742
Domestic Travel 747
State Tourism Offices 747
Weather Charts 751
Air Mileage from New York City— 758
Domestic
National Park Directory 758
National Wildlife Refuges Locations 762
and Facilities
Animal Highlights of the Most Popular 778
National Wildlife Refuges
Best Vacation Bets 778
Best Theme Parks 779
International Travel 780
Government Tourist Information Centers 780
International Auto Registration Marks 786
Average Temperatures (°F) For 787
International Cities
International Currencies 788
Air Mileage From New York—International 788
Requirements Before Proceeding Abroad 793
Customs Information 818
Additional Sources of Information 818
Web Sites 818
Magazines 819
Books 819

25 THE UNITED STATES 823

Culture and History 824
Important Dates in American History 824
Admission of 13 Original States 825
Secession of American States 827
Readmission of American States 828
Historic Documents and 838
Pronouncements
The U.S. Flag 856
Federal Government 859
Federal Government Structure 859
Presidents and Vice Presidents of the 861
United States
The Sequence of Presidential 862
Succession
Where to Write Your Senators and 862
Representatives
Common Legislative Terms 863
The Electoral College 863
How a Bill Becomes Law 865
Finances 866
Federal Civilian Employment, by Branch 870
and Agency: 1990-1995
Government Benefits 872
States and Territories 875
Government 875
Flowers, Birds, Mottos, and Nicknames 877
Name Origins 879
Statistics 881
U.S. Population 881
Immigrant Admissions to the 884
United States
U.S. Economy 888
Crime in the United States 891
U.S. Postal Service 898
ZIP Codes 898
Two-Letter State and Territory 904
Abbreviations
Geographic Directional Abbreviations 904
Street Designators (Street Suffixes) 905
Major Daily Newspapers 906
National 906
Local (by State) 906
Additional Sources of Information 911
Magazines 911
Books 911

VI THE POLITICAL WORLD 821

26 THE WORLD 913

Countries of the World 914
Great Events in World History 931
Major Wars, Battles, and Other Armed 940
Conflicts
World Exploration and Discovery 947
Population of Major World Cities 954
The United Nations 958
The Six Official Languages of the 958
United Nations
The United Nations System 959
Secretaries-General of the United 958
Nations
United Nations Member States 960
International Organizations 961
Seven Wonders of the Ancient World 962
Royal Rulers of Europe and Asia 963
China 963
England/Great Britain 964
France 965
Germany 965
Japan 965
Russia 965
Order of British Peerage 966
The Six Wives of Henry VIII 966
Genealogy Charts of the British 966
Monarchy
Connections Between Royal Families 969
England, Denmark, and Russia 969
England, Germany, and Spain 970
Prime Ministers 970
Australia 970
Canada 970
England/Great Britain 970
Foreign Dialing Codes 972
Additional Sources of Information 974
Organizations and Services 974
Books 974

ATLAS 975

INDEX 985

PREFACE

The New York Public Library, through its Research and Branch Libraries, provides free and open access to information on a scale unmatched by any other library in the world. Consisting of four major research libraries—the Center for the Humanities, The New York Public Library for the Performing Arts, The Schomburg Center for Research in Black Culture, and The Science, Industry and Business Library—and 85 neighborhood libraries throughout the Bronx, Manhattan and Staten Island, it has more material than any other public library system in the nation.

The Library's collections themselves reflect the profoundly democratic and all-encompassing nature of the institution. Numbering over 55 million items, its holdings range from the most venerable monuments of human culture—such as the Gutenberg Bible and Jefferson's manuscript copy of the Declaration of Independence—to materials which document the everyday lives of otherwise anonymous people. The collections grow at a rate of approximately 10,000 items per week in dozens of languages. These collections have contributed to innovations ranging from Ripley's *Believe It Or Not* to the splitting of the atom, from the creation of the Xerox photocopying machine to Robert Caro's biography of Robert Moses. Its holdings have also played a vital role in the creation of innumerable works in the arts, science, literature and history.

The New York Public Library officially opened its doors on May 23, 1911, when on one day over 30,000 visitors streamed past the guardian lions on Fifth Avenue; today the Library system is visited and used annually by more than 15 million people, from neighborhood children and general readers to researchers and scholars from around the world. There are 2.5 million cardholders; over 6 million reference questions were answered last year either in person or by phone. As the new century approaches, the global use of its resources is dramatically increasing through access to catalogs and digitized collections via the Library's Web site.

Yet, as the Library embraces the new technologies of the 21st century, the technology that has stood the test of time—the book—remains very much at the heart of what the Library does. Among these extraordinary collections are over 18 million books, a format that remains convenient, easy-to-use tool for obtaining information. Back in 1989 when *The New York Public Library Desk Reference* was originally published, we felt that "a book fills a unique need for portability, individuality and beauty." We still do. And it has been gratifying to find that this particular book seems to have very much filled the needs for our using public, as a home and library reference, as well as an online resource. Our librarians handle the questions of thousands of users every day, but this book has provided the opportunity to extend their service well beyond the walls of the institution.

Like the first two editions, this third edition reflects the experience of librarians, professional researchers and reference editors in handling a wide range of questions in many subject areas. It retains the unique characteristic of the previous editions—a compendium of basic information about a variety of subjects that allows readers to efficiently find answers to their questions. It has been thoroughly revised and updated to help the general reader handle the explosion of information, which fills our world. In a sense, this is more than a revision. In response to many suggestions from users, changes in computer access to information and improvements in graphic technologies, we have added whole new sections to the book and taken advantage of color printing advances to devise easy-to-follow charts, graphs, and sidebars. All text has been revised, the index has been generously expanded and more than 300 new text entries have been written to maintain the "browsability" factor of the book that readers enjoy so much. All bibliographies have been complied with works probably available in smaller libraries in mind. Numerous Web sites and phone numbers for further information have been added. These tools will serve as a springboard for further inquiry. Revising and updating a project such as this one is a major undertaking and has involved many people within the institution and beyond, including readers who have taken the time to write to us about omissions or errors in the earlier editions. Our special thanks to the staff of The Stonesong Press who have provided steady guidance and direction through all the editions.

Paul LeClerc
President, The New York Public Library

I

THE PHYSICAL WORLD

CHAPTER ONE   3
TIMES AND DATES

CHAPTER TWO   23
WEIGHTS AND MEASURES

CHAPTER THREE   33
THE BIOLOGICAL WORLD

CHAPTER FOUR   67
THE PHYSICAL SCIENCES, MATH, AND TECHNOLOGY

CHAPTER FIVE   121
INVENTIONS AND SCIENTIFIC DISCOVERIES

1

TIMES AND DATES

RECKONING DAYS AND HOURS	4
UNIVERSAL AND STANDARD TIME	6
TIME ADJUSTMENTS	9
CALENDARS	10
WORDS DESCRIBING PERIODS OF TIME	18
MAJOR HOLIDAYS	18
ADDITIONAL SOURCES OF INFORMATION	21

RECKONING DAYS AND HOURS

THE LENGTH OF THE DAY

The length of the *sidereal day* (Latin: *sider*—star) is determined by the rotation of the Earth, which causes the stars, to any observer, to appear to make one revolution each sidereal day from east to west. The length of a *true solar day* is determined by noting one passage of the Sun across the meridian of an observer and calculating the time that it takes for the Sun to cross the same point in the sky a second time. Because the Earth moves along its orbit around the Sun during the time it makes a single rotation, the solar day is slightly longer than the sidereal day (on average, by 3 minutes and 56 seconds of solar time [defined below]).

The phrase "a red-letter day" dates back to 1704, when holy days were marked in red letters in church calendars.

Over the course of a year (the time it takes the Earth to make one revolution around the Sun), the length of the true solar day varies because of (1) the eccentricity of the Earth's elliptical orbit and (2) the inclination of the equator (the plane running through the Earth's center and perpendicular to the Earth's axis of rotation) to the ecliptic (the plane of the Earth's orbit). The uniform length of our 24-hour calendar day, the *mean solar day,* is based on the average length of the true solar day over a whole year.

HOW IS THE DAY SUBDIVIDED?

The division of the day into hours is an arbitrary standard, as is the uniform length of the hour. Different cultures divided their days in different ways. The ancient Egyptians, Greeks, and Romans had a 24-hour day; but they divided it into 10 hours of light, 10 hours of dark, and 1 hour each of dawn and dusk (the twilight hours), which meant that the length of the hours depended on the seasons. Only after the invention of mechanical clocks in the late Middle Ages (see the sidebar "Clocks— Measuring Time") did a need develop for days, hours, and smaller units of time of uniform length. The mean solar day, under the common system of solar time, is thus divided as follows:

1 mean solar day = 24 mean solar hours

1 mean solar hour = 60 mean solar minutes

1 mean solar minute = 60 mean solar seconds

One mean solar day is thus equal to 86,400 (= 24 × 60 × 60) mean solar seconds.

For civil purposes, the time when the Sun crosses the local meridian is defined as noon, the midpoint between successive noons is defined as midnight,

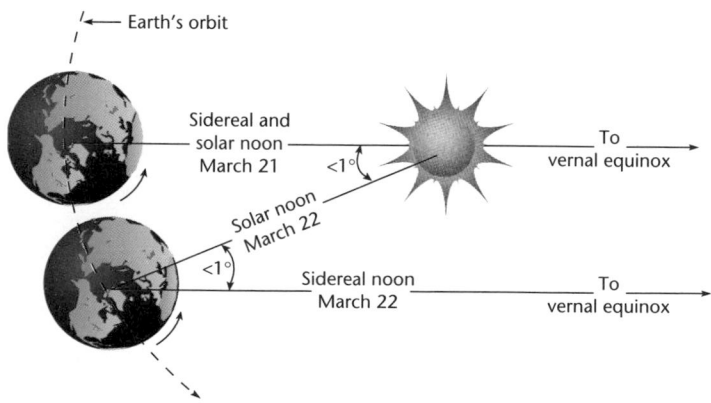

Sidereal and solar days

and the standard measurement of the day is from midnight to midnight. (Some ancient peoples, however, counted the day from dawn to dawn; others, such as the Jews, count their days from sunset to sunset.)

Under the 12-hour system of counting hours, the day is divided into two equal portions denoted by A.M. (before noon) and P.M. (after noon), which are derived from the Latin terms *ante meridiem* and *post meridiem*. The instant of time that is 4 hours and 15 minutes after midnight is thus designated 4:15 A.M.; the instant of time that is 5 hours and 23 minutes after noon is thus 5:23 P.M. Because the use of A.M. and P.M. with noon and midnight would cause confusion, they are designated, respectively, 12 N and 12 M.

A Closer Look

Clocks—Measuring Time

The sundial may be the oldest device for measuring time, going back to the Fertile Crescent of about 2000 B.C. Its operation is based on the fact that the shadow of a fixed object will move around it from one side to the other as the Sun moves from east to west. Naturally, the duration of the hours marked off by a sundial changes according to the seasons of the year. Along with sundials, ancient peoples used water clocks that measured time by a constant rate of flow of water through a bowl-like device with an outlet. Sand flowing from one compartment into another also was used in late medieval Europe to measure time. These last two methods could be used at night; they also counted more uniform units of time.

With the invention of mechanical clocks, the hours became uniform. The first mechanical clocks appeared in Europe in the 14th century (mechanical timepieces existed in China at least two centuries earlier, though the Chinese never developed them highly). The earliest ones were driven by weights strung around a drum. As the weight fell, the mechanism was activated. Next came spring-driven clocks, although they had the disadvantage of running differently when the spring was just wound and at its most tense position and after it had unwound somewhat. The workings of all clocks depend on a motion or vibration that is constant and regular.

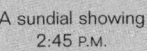

A sundial showing
2:45 P.M.

Circa 1581 the great Italian physicist Galileo (1564–1642) observed that the time it took for a pendulum to complete one total swing (called the period of oscillation) was almost independent of its magnitude—that is, how far it swung from side to side. He understood that this phenomenon could be used as a frequency mechanism for regulating a clock. In 1656, a Dutch physicist, Christian Huygens (1629–95), working independently, constructed the first pendulum clock. Pendulum clocks remained the most precise means of measuring time into the 20th century. Pendulums could be constructed to oscillate at specified frequencies once such factors as latitude, the pull of gravity, and weather and its effect on the materials used to make the clock had been compensated for.

With each swing of the pendulum, the escape wheel moves one notch as the pallet moves back and forth. Notch by notch, the escapement moves the clock's mechanism to a regular rhythm.

Pallet

Escapement

Escape wheel   Pendulum

Quartz clocks, introduced in the 1930s, improved on the pendulum, though only after years of development. By controlling the frequency of an electric circuit through the regular mechanical vibration of the quartz crystal, high degrees of constancy in vibration can be achieved, making a quartz clock even more accurate than a pendulum.

In the 1940s, atomic clocks were introduced. Their frequencies are based on the vibrations of certain atoms and molecules that vibrate the same number of times per second. Atomic clocks are constant to within a few seconds every 100,000 years.

A Closer Look

Ship's Bell Time Signals

On most ships, a day consists of six 4-hour watches. The watches change at 8 A.M., noon, 4 P.M., 8 P.M., midnight, and 4 A.M. A chime indicates each half hour. During a 4-hour watch, one bell chimes at the first half hour, two bells at the second, and so on, up to eight, when the next watch begins and the sequence starts over again.

1 bell	12:30 or	4:30 or	8:30 A.M. or P.M.
2 bells	1:00	5:00	9:00
3 bells	1:30	5:30	9:30
4 bells	2:00	6:00	10:00
5 bells	2:30	6:30	10:30
6 bells	3:00	7:00	11:00
7 bells	3:30	7:30	11:30
8 bells	4:00	8:00	12:00

On many vessels, the ship's whistle is blown at noon. On some ships, a lightly struck 1 bell announces 15 minutes before the change of watch.

A 24-hour system, which avoids repeating numbers and clearly distinguishes between midnight and noon, is used by the U.S. military and generally throughout continental Europe. Under this system, midnight (the beginning of the day) is designated 0000, the following noon is 1200, and the following midnight is 2400. (The designation 2400 of one day is thus the same instant of time as that of 0000 of the following day.) The times 4:15 A.M. and 5:23 P.M. are designated, respectively, as 0415 and 1723 under the 24-hour counting system.

UNIVERSAL AND STANDARD TIME

The mean solar time determined by the meridian that runs through Greenwich, England (where that country's Royal Observatory was originally located), is called *universal time.* It is used all over the world in navigation (at sea and in the air), in the precise determination of longitude, in geodesy, and in the tracking of artificial satellites and space probes. From Greenwich, too, longitudes are measured around the world. Greenwich, having a 0° longitude, is called the *prime meridian.*

Standard time, which for most localities differs from universal time by an integral number of hours, was created by international agreement in 1883 to avoid the continuous changes in mean solar time with longitude. Lines at every 15° longitude were drawn down a map of the Earth to create 24 international time zones. Within each zone, all localities keep the same standard time (i.e., the same minutes and seconds). The time in each zone differs from that in each neighboring zone by exactly 1 hour. (Because of political boundaries, the boundary lines between time zones often zigzag.) A few areas keep time that differs from universal time by a nonintegral number of hours (such an area might have, for example, a 30-minute difference from an adjoining zone).

Many years ago, a British king wrongly corrected a clockmaker and told him to use the Roman numeral IIII instead of IV for the number four. Rather than offend the king, the clockmaker obeyed. That tradition is still used for some clocks today.

Times and Dates

SYMBOLS TO SHOW TIME ZONE DIVISIONS

HALF-HOUR ZONES

NO ZONE SYSTEM ADOPTED

GREENLAND -3

CANADA

UNITED STATES

ALASKA -9

ALEUTIAN IS. -11

NEWFOUNDLAND -3.30

BERMUDA

BRAZIL -3

ARGENTINA

FALKLAND IS. -3

JUAN FERNANDEZ IS. -4

GALAPAGOS IS. -5

MIDWAY IS. -11

HAWAIIAN IS. -10

CHRISTMAS I. -10

LINE IS. -10

TOKELAU IS. -11

COOK IS. -10.30

TUAMOTU ARCH. -10

PITCAIRN IS. -8.30

TONGA -11

NORFOLK IS. -12

NAURU +11.30

MARSHALL IS. -12

WAKE I. -12

INTERNATIONAL DATE LINE

+1 Day / -1 Day

180°

172° 30'W

AUSTRALIA +9.30

JAPAN

PHILIPPINES

BURMA +6.30

ANDAMAN AND NICOBAR IS. +5.30

COCOS IS. +5.30

MADAGASCAR

ICELAND 0

BRITISH IS. I.E.S -1

CANARY IS. 0

AZORES -1

CAPE VERDE IS. -1

ASCENSION I. 0

TRISTAN DE CUNHA 0

PRIME MERIDIAN

+7.30

-0.45

-3.45

AM NOON PM MIDNIGHT

U.S. AND CANADIAN TIME ZONES

The continental United States has four standard time zones centered on the meridians 75° (Eastern Standard Time or EST), 90° (Central Standard Time or CST), 105° (Mountain Standard Time or MST), and 120° (Pacific Standard Time or PST) west of Greenwich; they are, respectively, 5, 6, 7, and 8 hours behind universal time. Alaska Standard Time is determined by the meridian at 135° west of Greenwich, and Hawaii-Aleutian Standard Time by the meridian at 150° west of Greenwich; they are 9 and 10 hours behind universal time. American Samoa and the Midway Islands use Samoan Standard Time, centered on the 165° W meridian and 11 hours behind universal time.

Canada has a total of six time zones: the four that apply to the continental United States and an additional two in the east. Atlantic Standard Time (which Puerto Rico and the U.S. Virgin Islands also keep) is determined by the meridian 60° west of Greenwich and is thus 4 hours behind universal time. Newfoundland Standard Time is determined by the meridian 52° 30' west of Greenwich and is thus 3½ hours behind universal time.

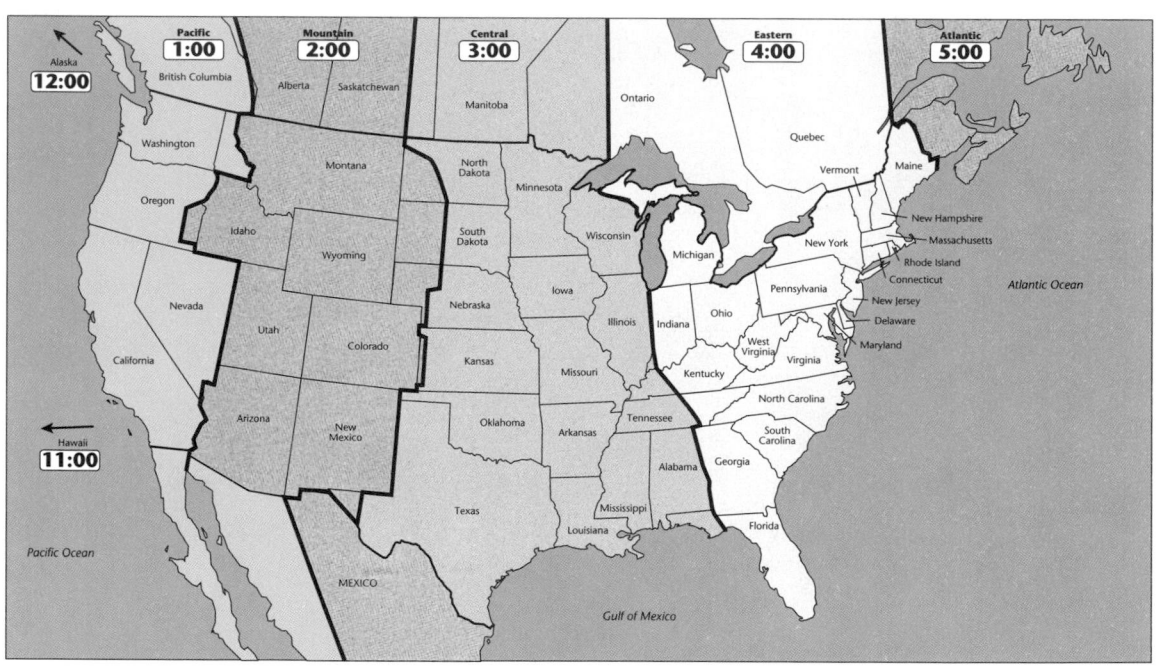

INTERNATIONAL DATE LINE

An imaginary line set at 180° longitude runs down the Earth. When someone crosses the line traveling to the west, one day is added—that is, Sunday on the east side of the line becomes Monday as one crosses westward. The line, of course, was fixed at the longitude exactly opposite Greenwich, England, on the other side of the Earth, but it zigzags for political reasons so that parts of countries do not find themselves on the wrong side—for instance, all of Siberia (west of the line), and all of Alaska (east of the line).

When written in Roman numerals, the year 1666 is the only date in history that is written from the highest to the lowest value, MDCLXVI (1000 + 500 + 100 + 50 + 10 + 5 + 1).

STANDARD TIME FOR MAJOR FOREIGN CITIES

The following list gives the time in cities around the world when it is 12 noon Eastern Standard Time. An asterisk (*) indicates the morning of the following day.

City	Time	City	Time	City	Time
Addis Ababa	8 P.M.	Geneva	6 P.M.	Ottawa	12 N
Alexandria	7 P.M.	Glasgow	5 P.M.	Panama	12 N
Amsterdam	6 P.M.	Halifax	1 P.M.	Paris	6 P.M.
Athens	7 P.M.	Hanoi	1 A.M.*	Prague	6 P.M.
Baghdad	8 P.M.	Havana	12 N	Quebec	12 N
Bangkok	12 M	Helsinki	7 P.M.	Rio de Janeiro	2 P.M.
Barcelona	6 P.M.	Ho Chi Minh City	1 A.M.*	Riyadh	8 P.M.
Beijing	1 A.M.*	Hong Kong	1 A.M.*	Rome	6 P.M.
Belfast	5 P.M.	Istanbul	7 P.M.	St. Petersburg	8 P.M.
Belgrade	6 P.M.	Jakarta	12 M	San Juan	1 P.M.
Berlin	6 P.M.	Jerusalem	7 P.M.	Santiago	1 P.M.
Bogotá	12 N	Johannesburg	7 P.M.	Seoul	2 A.M.*
Bombay	10:30 P.M.	Karachi	10 P.M.	Shanghai	1 A.M.*
Brasília	2 P.M.	Kuala Lumpur	1 A.M.*	Stockholm	6 P.M.
Brussels	6 P.M.	Lima	12 N	Sydney	4 A.M.*
Bucharest	7 P.M.	Lisbon	6 P.M.	Tangiers	5 P.M.
Budapest	6 P.M.	Liverpool	4 P.M.	Teheran	8:30 P.M.
Buenos Aires	2 P.M.	London	5 P.M.	Tel Aviv	7 P.M.
Cairo	7 P.M.	Madrid	6 P.M.	Tokyo	2 A.M.*
Calcutta	10:30 P.M.	Managua	11 A.M.	Toronto	12 N
Calgary	10 A.M.	Manila	1 A.M.*	Tripoli	7 P.M.
Cape Town	7 P.M.	Marseilles	6 P.M.	Vancouver	9 A.M.
Caracas	1 P.M.	Mecca	8 P.M.	Venice	6 P.M.
Casablanca	5 P.M.	Melbourne	4 A.M.*	Vienna	6 P.M.
Copenhagen	6 P.M.	Mexico City	11 A.M.	Vladivostock	3 A.M.*
Delhi	10:30 P.M.	Montreal	12 N	Warsaw	6 P.M.
Dublin	5 P.M.	Moscow	8 P.M.	Winnipeg	11 A.M.
Edinburgh	5 P.M.	Munich	6 P.M.	Yangon	11:30 P.M.
Florence	6 P.M.	Naples	6 P.M.	Yokohama	2 A.M.*
Frankfurt	6 P.M.	Oslo	6 P.M.	Zurich	6 P.M.

TIME ADJUSTMENTS

DAYLIGHT SAVING TIME IN THE UNITED STATES

Daylight Saving Time is attained by advancing the clock 1 hour. In 1967, the Uniform Time Act went into effect in the United States. It proclaimed that all states, the District of Columbia, and U.S. possessions were to observe Daylight Saving Time starting at 2 A.M. on the last Sunday in April and ending at 2 A.M. on the last Sunday in October. Any state could exempt itself by law, and a 1972 amendment to the act authorized the states split by time zones to consider that split in exempting themselves. Arizona, Hawaii, part of Indiana, Puerto Rico, the Virgin Islands, and American Samoa are now exempt. The Department of Transportation, which oversees the act, has modified some local zone boundaries in Alaska, Florida, Kansas, Michigan, and Texas over the last several years. Daylight Saving Time was extended by Congress during 1974 and 1975 to conserve energy, but the country then returned to the previous end-of-April to end-of-October system until 1987, when new legislation went into effect. The new bill, signed by President Ronald Reagan on July 8, 1986, moved the start of Daylight Saving Time up to the first Sunday in April, but it did not change the end from the last Sunday in October.

INTERNATIONAL TIME ADJUSTMENTS

It is common throughout the world for clock time to be adjusted to use added daylight during summer.

Generally, Western Europe goes on daylight time on the last Sunday in March and changes back on the last Sunday in September. Most regions of the Commonwealth of Independent States stay on "advanced time" year-round. China, by government order, operates as one time zone even though it should, geographically, be in five different zones. For religious reasons, Israel is approximately 2 hours behind the rest of its time zone. Thus, the Sun may be setting there as early as 3:30 P.M.

Paraguay, Ireland, and the Dominican Republic adjust their clock time in winter instead of summer. Thus, their time is aptly known as winter time.

CALENDARS

NAMES OF THE DAYS

The names of the days in English derive from either ancient Latin or Saxon systems of naming days after gods or astrological planets.

English	Latin	Saxon
Sunday	Dies Solis (Sun)	Sun's Day
Monday	Dies Lunae (Moon)	Moon's Day
Tuesday	Dies Martis (Mars)	Tiw's Day
Wednesday	Dies Mercurii (Mercury)	Woden's Day
Thursday	Dies Jovis (Jupiter)	Thor's Day
Friday	Dies Veneris (Venus)	Frigg's Day
Saturday	Dies Saturni (Saturn)	Saterne's Day

DEFINITIONS OF A YEAR

A year can be defined in several ways.

The *tropical/equinoctial/solar year* is the period (365 days, 5 hours, 48 minutes, and 46 seconds of mean solar time) spent by the Sun in making its apparent passage from vernal equinox to vernal equinox (defined in "The Seasons" section in this chapter).

The *sidereal year* is the period (365 days, 6 hours, 9 minutes, and 9.54 seconds) spent by the Sun in its apparent passage from a fixed star and back to the same position again. It is the true period of the Earth's revolution, and the difference in time between this and the tropical year is due to the precession of the equinoxes.

The *anomalistic year* is the period of time occupied by any planet in making one complete revolution from perihelion (the point in its orbit when it is closest to the Sun) to perihelion. For the Earth, this period is 365 days, 6 hours, 13 minutes, and 53 seconds. It is slightly longer than the sidereal year because of the extra time needed to reach an advancing perihelion, the lag being caused by the gravitational pull of the other planets.

Because the tropical year does not contain an integral number of days, the modern Gregorian *calendar year* (extending from January 1 to December 31) normally consists of 365 days (divided into 12 months). Because such a year is equivalent to 52 seven-day weeks plus one day, a given date normally advances by one day each year (for example, from Monday to Tuesday).

To avoid having the seasons move around the calendar, an extra leap day (February 29) is inserted in the calendar of a leap year, which thus has 366 days. A *leap year* is a year (e.g., 1992 and 1996) whose number is exactly divisible by 4, or, in case of the final year of a century, by 400. Thus, 1700, 1800, and 1900 were not leap years, but 2000 will be.

A *fiscal year* is an accounting period of 12 months. The U.S. government's fiscal year (FY) ends on September 30; thus, its FY 2000 extends from October 1, 1999, to September 30, 2000. A business firm's fiscal year, however, may end on the last day of any month.

Some cultures have used or continue to use a *lunar year* (defined in "The Lunar Calendar" sidebar above) of 12 lunar or synodic months.

The Lunar Calendar

A Closer Look

Calendars based on the movements of the moon and Sun have been used since ancient times. Whereas today most calendars are based on the solar year of 365.25 days, in ancient times the lunar calendar was the one most commonly used. Notches in bones dating back to 15,000 to 10,000 B.C. have been discovered in what are now Israel and Jordan; their recordings of number sequences are thought to be the first lunar calendars.

In the lunar system, time is based on the number of days between two moons, or 29.5306 days, resulting in a lunar year of 354.3672 days. The lunar year is thus approximately 11 days shorter than the solar year.

The ancient Chinese synchronized their lunar calendar with the solar year by intercalating, or adding, extra months at fixed intervals on a 60-year cycle. This calendar, along with the modern Western one, is still used today in China.

The ancient Hebrews also intercalated months into the lunar calendar to keep it in agreement with the solar year. This calendar of 12 lunar months, with an intercalary month added seven times in every 19-year cycle, is used today in Israel and by Jews throughout the world for religious purposes.

The traditional lunar calendar, without regard to the solar year, is still used today by Muslims. In order to establish agreement between lunar and civil, or calendar, months, they intercalate 11 days in each 30 years.

THE SEASONS

The beginnings of the four seasons occur when the Sun reaches certain points in its apparent path around the Earth.

Spring in the Northern Hemisphere (fall or autumn in the Southern Hemisphere) begins at the *vernal equinox* (about March 21), when the Sun crosses the equator as it ascends from a southerly to a northerly declination (its angular distance north or south of the celestial equator). On this day, the hours of daylight and darkness are equal in length (approximately 12 hours each) everywhere on Earth.

Summer in the Northern Hemisphere (winter in the Southern Hemisphere) begins at the *summer solstice* (about June 21), when the Sun reaches its most northerly declination (approximately 23.5° N). On this day, locations in the Northern (Southern) Hemisphere have their maximum (minimum) number of hours of daylight.

Fall or autumn in the Northern Hemisphere (spring in the Southern Hemisphere) begins at the *autumnal equinox* (about September 21), when the Sun crosses the equator as it descends from a northerly to a southerly declination. On this day, the hours of daylight and darkness are equal in

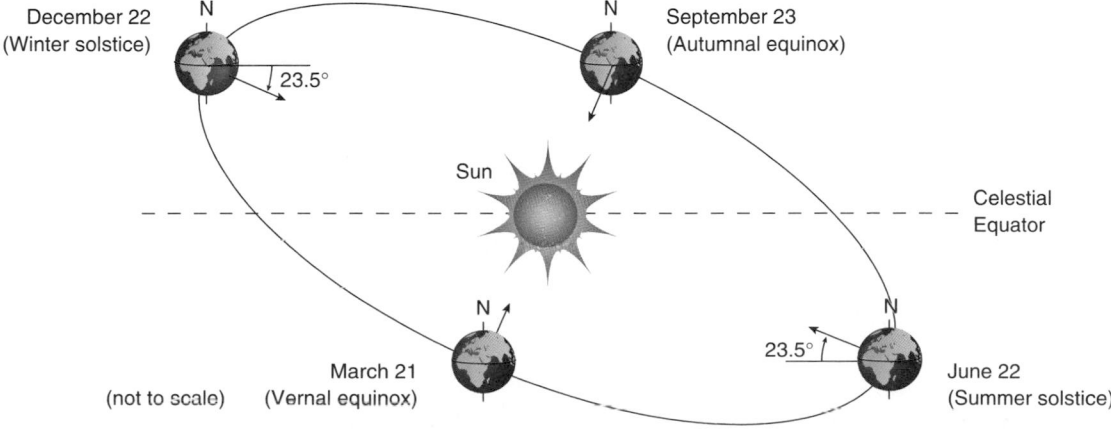

length (approximately 12 hours each) everywhere on Earth.

Winter in the Northern Hemisphere (summer in the Southern Hemisphere) begins at the *winter solstice* (about December 21), when the Sun reaches its most southerly declination (approximately 23.5° S). On this day, locations in the Northern (Southern) Hemisphere have their minimum (maximum) number of hours of daylight.

THE DEVELOPMENT OF THE ROMAN/JULIAN/GREGORIAN CALENDAR

According to legend, Romulus, one of the founders of the city of Rome, established the Roman calendar—most likely a version of the Greek lunar calendar—circa 738 B.C. King Numa Pompilius later added January at the beginning and February at the end to create a 12-month calendar year. In 46 B.C. Emperor Julius Caesar rejected the Roman lunar calendar in favor of a solar one, thus establishing a new dating system known as the Julian calendar. The solar year was made up of 365¼ days. A leap day was added every 4 years to maintain balance between the calendar and the seasons. However, because the Earth moves 11 minutes and 14 seconds faster every year than Caesar calculated, the calendar dates of the seasons regressed almost 1 day per century. In 1572 Pope Gregory XIII ordained that the calendar be decreased by 10 days that year and that no century year could be a leap year unless its date is evenly divisible by 400. (European nations adopted the Gregorian calendar at different dates, leading to some confusion regarding the 10 missing days in 1572.) See "Additional Sources of Information" at the end of this chapter to find out more about the development of the calendar.

Romulus 738 B.C.	King Numa Pompilius 713 B.C.	Council of Decemvirs 451 B.C.	Julius Caesar 47 B.C.	Augustus Caesar 8 B.C.	Gregory XIII Europe A.D. 1582 England A.D. 1752
Martius 31	Januarius 29	Januarius 29	Januarius 31	Januarius 31	January 31
Aprilis 30	Martius 31	Februarius 28	Februarius 29-30	Februarius 28-29	February 28-29
Maius 31	Aprilis 29	Martius 31	Martius 31	Martius 31	March 31
Junius 30	Maius 31	Aprilis 29	Aprilis 30	Aprilis 30	April 30
Quintilis 31	Junius 29	Maius 31	Maius 31	Maius 31	May 31
Sextilis 30	Quintilis 31	Junius 29	Junius 30	Junius 30	June 30
Septembris 31	Sextilis 29	Quintilis 31	Julius 31	Julius 31	July 31
Octobris 30	Septembris 29	Sextilis 29	Sextilis 30	Augustus 31	August 31
Novembris 31	Octobris 31	Septembris 29	Septembris 31	Septembris 30	September 30
Decembris 29	Novembris 29	Octobris 31	Octobris 30	Octobris 31	October 31
	Decembris 29	Novembris 29	Novembris 31	Novembris 30	November 30
	Februarius 28	Decembris 29	Decembris 30	Decembris 31	December 31
304 days	**355 days**	**355 days**	**348¼ days**	**365¼ days**	**365.2422 days**

PERPETUAL CALENDAR, 1775–2098

Look for the year you want in the following list. The number opposite each year is the number of the calendar on pages 14–17 to use for that year.

Year	No.	Year	No.	Year	No.	Year	No.	Year	No.
1775	1	1823	4	1871	1	1919	4	1967	1
1776	9	1824	12	1872	9	1920	12	1968	9
1777	4	1825	7	1873	4	1921	7	1969	4
1778	5	1826	1	1874	5	1922	1	1970	5
1779	6	1827	2	1875	6	1923	2	1971	6
1780	14	1828	10	1876	14	1924	10	1972	14
1781	2	1829	5	1877	2	1925	5	1973	2
1782	3	1830	6	1878	3	1926	6	1974	3
1783	4	1831	7	1879	4	1927	7	1975	4
1784	12	1832	8	1880	12	1928	8	1976	12
1785	7	1833	3	1881	7	1929	3	1977	7
1786	1	1834	4	1882	1	1930	4	1978	1
1787	2	1835	5	1883	2	1931	5	1979	2
1788	10	1836	13	1884	10	1932	13	1980	10
1789	5	1837	1	1885	5	1933	1	1981	5
1790	6	1838	2	1886	6	1934	2	1982	6
1791	7	1839	3	1887	7	1935	3	1983	7
1792	8	1840	11	1888	8	1936	11	1984	8
1793	3	1841	6	1889	3	1937	6	1985	3
1794	4	1842	7	1890	4	1938	7	1986	4
1795	5	1843	1	1891	5	1939	1	1987	5
1796	13	1844	9	1892	13	1940	9	1988	13
1797	1	1845	4	1893	1	1941	4	1989	1
1798	2	1846	5	1894	2	1942	5	1990	2
1799	3	1847	6	1895	3	1943	6	1991	3
1800	4	1848	14	1896	11	1944	14	1992	11
1801	5	1849	2	1897	6	1945	2	1993	6
1802	6	1850	3	1898	7	1946	3	1994	7
1803	7	1851	4	1899	1	1947	4	1995	1
1804	8	1852	12	1900	2	1948	12	1996	9
1805	3	1853	7	1901	3	1949	7	1997	4
1806	4	1854	1	1902	4	1950	1	1998	5
1807	5	1855	2	1903	5	1951	2	1999	6
1808	13	1856	10	1904	13	1952	10	2000	14
1809	1	1857	5	1905	1	1953	5	2001	2
1810	2	1858	6	1906	2	1954	6	2002	3
1811	3	1859	7	1907	3	1955	7	2003	4
1812	11	1860	8	1908	11	1956	8	2004	12
1813	6	1861	3	1909	6	1957	3	2005	7
1814	7	1862	4	1910	7	1958	4	2006	1
1815	1	1863	5	1911	1	1959	5	2007	2
1816	9	1864	13	1912	9	1960	13	2008	10
1817	4	1865	1	1913	4	1961	1	2009	5
1818	5	1866	2	1914	5	1962	2	2010	6
1819	6	1867	3	1915	6	1963	3	2011	7
1820	14	1868	11	1916	14	1964	11	2012	8
1821	2	1869	6	1917	2	1965	6	2013	3
1822	3	1870	7	1918	3	1966	7	2014	4

continues

Perpetual Calendar, Continued

Year		Year		Year		Year		Year	
2015	5	2032	12	2049	6	2066	6	2083	6
2016	13	2033	7	2050	7	2067	7	2084	14
2017	1	2034	1	2051	1	2068	8	2085	2
2018	2	2035	2	2052	9	2069	3	2086	3
2019	3	2036	10	2053	4	2070	4	2087	4
2020	11	2037	5	2054	5	2071	5	2088	12
2021	6	2038	6	2055	6	2072	13	2089	7
2022	7	2039	7	2056	14	2073	1	2090	1
2023	1	2040	8	2057	2	2074	2	2091	2
2024	9	2041	3	2058	3	2075	3	2092	10
2025	4	2042	4	2059	4	2076	11	2093	5
2026	5	2043	5	2060	12	2077	6	2094	6
2027	6	2044	13	2061	7	2078	7	2095	7
2028	14	2045	1	2062	1	2079	1	2096	8
2029	2	2046	2	2063	2	2080	9	2097	3
2030	3	2047	3	2064	10	2081	4	2098	4
2031	4	2048	11	2065	5	2082	5		

Calendar 1

JANUARY
```
 S  M  T  W  T  F  S
 1  2  3  4  5  6  7
 8  9 10 11 12 13 14
15 16 17 18 19 20 21
22 23 24 25 26 27 28
29 30 31
```

FEBRUARY
```
 S  M  T  W  T  F  S
             1  2  3  4
 5  6  7  8  9 10 11
12 13 14 15 16 17 18
19 20 21 22 23 24 25
26 27 28
```

MARCH
```
 S  M  T  W  T  F  S
             1  2  3  4
 5  6  7  8  9 10 11
12 13 14 15 16 17 18
19 20 21 22 23 24 25
26 27 28 29 30 31
```

APRIL
```
 S  M  T  W  T  F  S
                      1
 2  3  4  5  6  7  8
 9 10 11 12 13 14 15
16 17 18 19 20 21 22
23 24 25 26 27 28 29
30
```

MAY
```
 S  M  T  W  T  F  S
    1  2  3  4  5  6
 7  8  9 10 11 12 13
14 15 16 17 18 19 20
21 22 23 24 25 26 27
28 29 30 31
```

JUNE
```
 S  M  T  W  T  F  S
             1  2  3
 4  5  6  7  8  9 10
11 12 13 14 15 16 17
18 19 20 21 22 23 24
25 26 27 28 29 30
```

JULY
```
 S  M  T  W  T  F  S
                      1
 2  3  4  5  6  7  8
 9 10 11 12 13 14 15
16 17 18 19 20 21 22
23 24 25 26 27 28 29
30 31
```

AUGUST
```
 S  M  T  W  T  F  S
       1  2  3  4  5
 6  7  8  9 10 11 12
13 14 15 16 17 18 19
20 21 22 23 24 25 26
27 28 29 30 31
```

SEPTEMBER
```
 S  M  T  W  T  F  S
                   1  2
 3  4  5  6  7  8  9
10 11 12 13 14 15 16
17 18 19 20 21 22 23
24 25 26 27 28 29 30
```

OCTOBER
```
 S  M  T  W  T  F  S
 1  2  3  4  5  6  7
 8  9 10 11 12 13 14
15 16 17 18 19 20 21
22 23 24 25 26 27 28
29 30 31
```

NOVEMBER
```
 S  M  T  W  T  F  S
             1  2  3  4
 5  6  7  8  9 10 11
12 13 14 15 16 17 18
19 20 21 22 23 24 25
26 27 28 29 30
```

DECEMBER
```
 S  M  T  W  T  F  S
                   1  2
 3  4  5  6  7  8  9
10 11 12 13 14 15 16
17 18 19 20 21 22 23
24 25 26 27 28 29 30
31
```

Calendar 2

JANUARY
```
 S  M  T  W  T  F  S
 1  2  3  4  5  6
 7  8  9 10 11 12 13
14 15 16 17 18 19 20
21 22 23 24 25 26 27
28 29 30 31
```

FEBRUARY
```
 S  M  T  W  T  F  S
          1  2  3
 4  5  6  7  8  9 10
11 12 13 14 15 16 17
18 19 20 21 22 23 24
25 26 27 28
```

MARCH
```
 S  M  T  W  T  F  S
          1  2  3
 4  5  6  7  8  9 10
11 12 13 14 15 16 17
18 19 20 21 22 23 24
25 26 27 28 29 30 31
```

APRIL
```
 S  M  T  W  T  F  S
 1  2  3  4  5  6  7
 8  9 10 11 12 13 14
15 16 17 18 19 20 21
22 23 24 25 26 27 28
29 30
```

MAY
```
 S  M  T  W  T  F  S
       1  2  3  4  5
 6  7  8  9 10 11 12
13 14 15 16 17 18 19
20 21 22 23 24 25 26
27 28 29 30 31
```

JUNE
```
 S  M  T  W  T  F  S
                1  2
 3  4  5  6  7  8  9
10 11 12 13 14 15 16
17 18 19 20 21 22 23
24 25 26 27 28 29 30
```

JULY
```
 S  M  T  W  T  F  S
 1  2  3  4  5  6  7
 8  9 10 11 12 13 14
15 16 17 18 19 20 21
22 23 24 25 26 27 28
29 30 31
```

AUGUST
```
 S  M  T  W  T  F  S
          1  2  3  4
 5  6  7  8  9 10 11
12 13 14 15 16 17 18
19 20 21 22 23 24 25
26 27 28 29 30 31
```

SEPTEMBER
```
 S  M  T  W  T  F  S
                      1
 2  3  4  5  6  7  8
 9 10 11 12 13 14 15
16 17 18 19 20 21 22
23 24 25 26 27 28 29
30
```

OCTOBER
```
 S  M  T  W  T  F  S
    1  2  3  4  5  6
 7  8  9 10 11 12 13
14 15 16 17 18 19 20
21 22 23 24 25 26 27
28 29 30 31
```

NOVEMBER
```
 S  M  T  W  T  F  S
                1  2  3
 4  5  6  7  8  9 10
11 12 13 14 15 16 17
18 19 20 21 22 23 24
25 26 27 28 29 30
```

DECEMBER
```
 S  M  T  W  T  F  S
                      1
 2  3  4  5  6  7  8
 9 10 11 12 13 14 15
16 17 18 19 20 21 22
23 24 25 26 27 28 29
30 31
```

Calendar 3

JANUARY

S	M	T	W	T	F	S
		1	2	3	4	5
6	7	8	9	10	11	12
13	14	15	16	17	18	19
20	21	22	23	24	25	26
27	28	29	30	31		

FEBRUARY

S	M	T	W	T	F	S
					1	2
3	4	5	6	7	8	9
10	11	12	13	14	15	16
17	18	19	20	21	22	23
24	25	26	27	28		

MARCH

S	M	T	W	T	F	S
					1	2
3	4	5	6	7	8	9
10	11	12	13	14	15	16
17	18	19	20	21	22	23
24	25	26	27	28	29	30
31						

APRIL

S	M	T	W	T	F	S
	1	2	3	4	5	6
7	8	9	10	11	12	13
14	15	16	17	18	19	20
21	22	23	24	25	26	27
28	29	30				

MAY

S	M	T	W	T	F	S
			1	2	3	4
5	6	7	8	9	10	11
12	13	14	15	16	17	18
19	20	21	22	23	24	25
26	27	28	29	30	31	

JUNE

S	M	T	W	T	F	S
						1
2	3	4	5	6	7	8
9	10	11	12	13	14	15
16	17	18	19	20	21	22
23	24	25	26	27	28	29
30						

JULY

S	M	T	W	T	F	S
	1	2	3	4	5	6
7	8	9	10	11	12	13
14	15	16	17	18	19	20
21	22	23	24	25	26	27
28	29	30	31			

AUGUST

S	M	T	W	T	F	S
				1	2	3
4	5	6	7	8	9	10
11	12	13	14	15	16	17
18	19	20	21	22	23	24
25	26	27	28	29	30	31

SEPTEMBER

S	M	T	W	T	F	S
1	2	3	4	5	6	7
8	9	10	11	12	13	14
15	16	17	18	19	20	21
22	23	24	25	26	27	28
29	30					

OCTOBER

S	M	T	W	T	F	S
		1	2	3	4	5
6	7	8	9	10	11	12
13	14	15	16	17	18	19
20	21	22	23	24	25	26
27	28	29	30	31		

NOVEMBER

S	M	T	W	T	F	S
					1	2
3	4	5	6	7	8	9
10	11	12	13	14	15	16
17	18	19	20	21	22	23
24	25	26	27	28	29	30

DECEMBER

S	M	T	W	T	F	S
1	2	3	4	5	6	7
8	9	10	11	12	13	14
15	16	17	18	19	20	21
22	23	24	25	26	27	28
29	30	31				

Calendar 4

JANUARY

S	M	T	W	T	F	S
			1	2	3	4
5	6	7	8	9	10	11
12	13	14	15	16	17	18
19	20	21	22	23	24	25
26	27	28	29	30	31	

FEBRUARY

S	M	T	W	T	F	S
						1
2	3	4	5	6	7	8
9	10	11	12	13	14	15
16	17	18	19	20	21	22
23	24	25	26	27	28	

MARCH

S	M	T	W	T	F	S
						1
2	3	4	5	6	7	8
9	10	11	12	13	14	15
16	17	18	19	20	21	22
23	24	25	26	27	28	29
30	31					

APRIL

S	M	T	W	T	F	S
	1	2	3	4	5	
6	7	8	9	10	11	12
13	14	15	16	17	18	19
20	21	22	23	24	25	26
27	28	29	30			

MAY

S	M	T	W	T	F	S
				1	2	3
4	5	6	7	8	9	10
11	12	13	14	15	16	17
18	19	20	21	22	23	24
25	26	27	28	29	30	31

JUNE

S	M	T	W	T	F	S
1	2	3	4	5	6	7
8	9	10	11	12	13	14
15	16	17	18	19	20	21
22	23	24	25	26	27	28
29	30					

JULY

S	M	T	W	T	F	S
		1	2	3	4	5
6	7	8	9	10	11	12
13	14	15	16	17	18	19
20	21	22	23	24	25	26
27	28	29	30	31		

AUGUST

S	M	T	W	T	F	S
					1	2
3	4	5	6	7	8	9
10	11	12	13	14	15	16
17	18	19	20	21	22	23
24	25	26	27	28	29	30
31						

SEPTEMBER

S	M	T	W	T	F	S
	1	2	3	4	5	6
7	8	9	10	11	12	13
14	15	16	17	18	19	20
21	22	23	24	25	26	27
28	29	30				

OCTOBER

S	M	T	W	T	F	S
			1	2	3	4
5	6	7	8	9	10	11
12	13	14	15	16	17	18
19	20	21	22	23	24	25
26	27	28	29	30	31	

NOVEMBER

S	M	T	W	T	F	S
						1
2	3	4	5	6	7	8
9	10	11	12	13	14	15
16	17	18	19	20	21	22
23	24	25	26	27	28	29
30						

DECEMBER

S	M	T	W	T	F	S
	1	2	3	4	5	6
7	8	9	10	11	12	13
14	15	16	17	18	19	20
21	22	23	24	25	26	27
28	29	30	31			

Calendar 5

JANUARY

S	M	T	W	T	F	S
				1	2	3
4	5	6	7	8	9	10
11	12	13	14	15	16	17
18	19	20	21	22	23	24
25	26	27	28	29	30	31

FEBRUARY

S	M	T	W	T	F	S
1	2	3	4	5	6	7
8	9	10	11	12	13	14
15	16	17	18	19	20	21
22	23	24	25	26	27	28

MARCH

S	M	T	W	T	F	S
1	2	3	4	5	6	7
8	9	10	11	12	13	14
15	16	17	18	19	20	21
22	23	24	25	26	27	28
29	30	31				

APRIL

S	M	T	W	T	F	S
			1	2	3	4
5	6	7	8	9	10	11
12	13	14	15	16	17	18
19	20	21	22	23	24	25
26	27	28	29	30		

MAY

S	M	T	W	T	F	S
					1	2
3	4	5	6	7	8	9
10	11	12	13	14	15	16
17	18	19	20	21	22	23
24	25	26	27	28	29	30
31						

JUNE

S	M	T	W	T	F	S
	1	2	3	4	5	6
7	8	9	10	11	12	13
14	15	16	17	18	19	20
21	22	23	24	25	26	27
28	29	30				

JULY

S	M	T	W	T	F	S
			1	2	3	4
5	6	7	8	9	10	11
12	13	14	15	16	17	18
19	20	21	22	23	24	25
26	27	28	29	30	31	

AUGUST

S	M	T	W	T	F	S
						1
2	3	4	5	6	7	8
9	10	11	12	13	14	15
16	17	18	19	20	21	22
23	24	25	26	27	28	29
30	31					

SEPTEMBER

S	M	T	W	T	F	S
		1	2	3	4	5
6	7	8	9	10	11	12
13	14	15	16	17	18	19
20	21	22	23	24	25	26
27	28	29	30			

OCTOBER

S	M	T	W	T	F	S
				1	2	3
4	5	6	7	8	9	10
11	12	13	14	15	16	17
18	19	20	21	22	23	24
25	26	27	28	29	30	31

NOVEMBER

S	M	T	W	T	F	S
1	2	3	4	5	6	7
8	9	10	11	12	13	14
15	16	17	18	19	20	21
22	23	24	25	26	27	28
29	30					

DECEMBER

S	M	T	W	T	F	S
		1	2	3	4	5
6	7	8	9	10	11	12
13	14	15	16	17	18	19
20	21	22	23	24	25	26
27	28	29	30	31		

Calendar 6

JANUARY

S	M	T	W	T	F	S
					1	2
3	4	5	6	7	8	9
10	11	12	13	14	15	16
17	18	19	20	21	22	23
24	25	26	27	28	29	30
31						

FEBRUARY

S	M	T	W	T	F	S
	1	2	3	4	5	6
7	8	9	10	11	12	13
14	15	16	17	18	19	20
21	22	23	24	25	26	27
28						

MARCH

S	M	T	W	T	F	S
	1	2	3	4	5	6
7	8	9	10	11	12	13
14	15	16	17	18	19	20
21	22	23	24	25	26	27
28	29	30	31			

APRIL

S	M	T	W	T	F	S
				1	2	3
4	5	6	7	8	9	10
11	12	13	14	15	16	17
18	19	20	21	22	23	24
25	26	27	28	29	30	

MAY

S	M	T	W	T	F	S
						1
2	3	4	5	6	7	8
9	10	11	12	13	14	15
16	17	18	19	20	21	22
23	24	25	26	27	28	29
30	31					

JUNE

S	M	T	W	T	F	S
		1	2	3	4	5
6	7	8	9	10	11	12
13	14	15	16	17	18	19
20	21	22	23	24	25	26
27	28	29	30			

JULY

S	M	T	W	T	F	S
				1	2	3
4	5	6	7	8	9	10
11	12	13	14	15	16	17
18	19	20	21	22	23	24
25	26	27	28	29	30	31

AUGUST

S	M	T	W	T	F	S
1	2	3	4	5	6	7
8	9	10	11	12	13	14
15	16	17	18	19	20	21
22	23	24	25	26	27	28
29	30	31				

SEPTEMBER

S	M	T	W	T	F	S
				1	2	3	4
5	6	7	8	9	10	11
12	13	14	15	16	17	18
19	20	21	22	23	24	25
26	27	28	29	30		

OCTOBER

S	M	T	W	T	F	S
						1	2
3	4	5	6	7	8	9
10	11	12	13	14	15	16
17	18	19	20	21	22	23
24	25	26	27	28	29	30
31						

NOVEMBER

S	M	T	W	T	F	S
	1	2	3	4	5	6
7	8	9	10	11	12	13
14	15	16	17	18	19	20
21	22	23	24	25	26	27
28	29	30				

DECEMBER

S	M	T	W	T	F	S
			1	2	3	4
5	6	7	8	9	10	11
12	13	14	15	16	17	18
19	20	21	22	23	24	25
26	27	28	29	30	31	

Calendar 7

JANUARY
S	M	T	W	T	F	S
						1
2	3	4	5	6	7	8
9	10	11	12	13	14	15
16	17	18	19	20	21	22
23	24	25	26	27	28	29
30	31					

FEBRUARY
S	M	T	W	T	F	S
	1	2	3	4	5	
6	7	8	9	10	11	12
13	14	15	16	17	18	19
20	21	22	23	24	25	26
27	28					

MARCH
S	M	T	W	T	F	S
	1	2	3	4	5	
6	7	8	9	10	11	12
13	14	15	16	17	18	19
20	21	22	23	24	25	26
27	28	29	30	31		

APRIL
S	M	T	W	T	F	S
					1	2
3	4	5	6	7	8	9
10	11	12	13	14	15	16
17	18	19	20	21	22	23
24	25	26	27	28	29	30

MAY
S	M	T	W	T	F	S
1	2	3	4	5	6	7
8	9	10	11	12	13	14
15	16	17	18	19	20	21
22	23	24	25	26	27	28
29	30	31				

JUNE
S	M	T	W	T	F	S
			1	2	3	4
5	6	7	8	9	10	11
12	13	14	15	16	17	18
19	20	21	22	23	24	25
26	27	28	29	30		

JULY
S	M	T	W	T	F	S
					1	2
3	4	5	6	7	8	9
10	11	12	13	14	15	16
17	18	19	20	21	22	23
24	25	26	27	28	29	30
31						

AUGUST
S	M	T	W	T	F	S
	1	2	3	4	5	6
7	8	9	10	11	12	13
14	15	16	17	18	19	20
21	22	23	24	25	26	27
28	29	30	31			

SEPTEMBER
S	M	T	W	T	F	S
				1	2	3
4	5	6	7	8	9	10
11	12	13	14	15	16	17
18	19	20	21	22	23	24
25	26	27	28	29	30	

OCTOBER
S	M	T	W	T	F	S
						1
2	3	4	5	6	7	8
9	10	11	12	13	14	15
16	17	18	19	20	21	22
23	24	25	26	27	28	29
30	31					

NOVEMBER
S	M	T	W	T	F	S
	1	2	3	4	5	
6	7	8	9	10	11	12
13	14	15	16	17	18	19
20	21	22	23	24	25	26
27	28	29	30			

DECEMBER
S	M	T	W	T	F	S
				1	2	3
4	5	6	7	8	9	10
11	12	13	14	15	16	17
18	19	20	21	22	23	24
25	26	27	28	29	30	31

Calendar 8

JANUARY
S	M	T	W	T	F	S
1	2	3	4	5	6	7
8	9	10	11	12	13	14
15	16	17	18	19	20	21
22	23	24	25	26	27	28
29	30	31				

FEBRUARY
S	M	T	W	T	F	S
			1	2	3	4
5	6	7	8	9	10	11
12	13	14	15	16	17	18
19	20	21	22	23	24	25
26	27	28	29			

MARCH
S	M	T	W	T	F	S
				1	2	3
4	5	6	7	8	9	10
11	12	13	14	15	16	17
18	19	20	21	22	23	24
25	26	27	28	29	30	31

APRIL
S	M	T	W	T	F	S
1	2	3	4	5	6	7
8	9	10	11	12	13	14
15	16	17	18	19	20	21
22	23	24	25	26	27	28
29	30					

MAY
S	M	T	W	T	F	S
	1	2	3	4	5	
6	7	8	9	10	11	12
13	14	15	16	17	18	19
20	21	22	23	24	25	26
27	28	29	30	31		

JUNE
S	M	T	W	T	F	S
					1	2
3	4	5	6	7	8	9
10	11	12	13	14	15	16
17	18	19	20	21	22	23
24	25	26	27	28	29	30

JULY
S	M	T	W	T	F	S
1	2	3	4	5	6	7
8	9	10	11	12	13	14
15	16	17	18	19	20	21
22	23	24	25	26	27	28
29	30	31				

AUGUST
S	M	T	W	T	F	S
			1	2	3	4
5	6	7	8	9	10	11
12	13	14	15	16	17	18
19	20	21	22	23	24	25
26	27	28	29	30	31	

SEPTEMBER
S	M	T	W	T	F	S
						1
2	3	4	5	6	7	8
9	10	11	12	13	14	15
16	17	18	19	20	21	22
23	24	25	26	27	28	29
30						

OCTOBER
S	M	T	W	T	F	S
1	2	3	4	5	6	
7	8	9	10	11	12	13
14	15	16	17	18	19	20
21	22	23	24	25	26	27
28	29	30	31			

NOVEMBER
S	M	T	W	T	F	S
				1	2	3
4	5	6	7	8	9	10
11	12	13	14	15	16	17
18	19	20	21	22	23	24
25	26	27	28	29	30	

DECEMBER
S	M	T	W	T	F	S
						1
2	3	4	5	6	7	8
9	10	11	12	13	14	15
16	17	18	19	20	21	22
23	24	25	26	27	28	29
30	31					

Calendar 9

JANUARY
S	M	T	W	T	F	S
		1	2	3	4	5
6	7	8	9	10	11	12
13	14	15	16	17	18	19
20	21	22	23	24	25	26
27	28	29	30	31		

FEBRUARY
S	M	T	W	T	F	S
					1	2
3	4	5	6	7	8	9
10	11	12	13	14	15	16
17	18	19	20	21	22	23
24	25	26	27	28	29	

MARCH
S	M	T	W	T	F	S
					1	2
3	4	5	6	7	8	9
10	11	12	13	14	15	16
17	18	19	20	21	22	23
24	25	26	27	28	29	30
31						

APRIL
S	M	T	W	T	F	S
	1	2	3	4	5	6
7	8	9	10	11	12	13
14	15	16	17	18	19	20
21	22	23	24	25	26	27
28	29	30				

MAY
S	M	T	W	T	F	S
		1	2	3	4	
5	6	7	8	9	10	11
12	13	14	15	16	17	18
19	20	21	22	23	24	25
26	27	28	29	30	31	

JUNE
S	M	T	W	T	F	S
						1
2	3	4	5	6	7	8
9	10	11	12	13	14	15
16	17	18	19	20	21	22
23	24	25	26	27	28	29
30						

JULY
S	M	T	W	T	F	S
	1	2	3	4	5	6
7	8	9	10	11	12	13
14	15	16	17	18	19	20
21	22	23	24	25	26	27
28	29	30	31			

AUGUST
S	M	T	W	T	F	S
				1	2	3
4	5	6	7	8	9	10
11	12	13	14	15	16	17
18	19	20	21	22	23	24
25	26	27	28	29	30	31

SEPTEMBER
S	M	T	W	T	F	S
1	2	3	4	5	6	7
8	9	10	11	12	13	14
15	16	17	18	19	20	21
22	23	24	25	26	27	28
29	30					

OCTOBER
S	M	T	W	T	F	S
		1	2	3	4	5
6	7	8	9	10	11	12
13	14	15	16	17	18	19
20	21	22	23	24	25	26
27	28	29	30	31		

NOVEMBER
S	M	T	W	T	F	S
					1	2
3	4	5	6	7	8	9
10	11	12	13	14	15	16
17	18	19	20	21	22	23
24	25	26	27	28	29	30

DECEMBER
S	M	T	W	T	F	S
1	2	3	4	5	6	7
8	9	10	11	12	13	14
15	16	17	18	19	20	21
22	23	24	25	26	27	28
29	30	31				

Calendar 10

JANUARY
S	M	T	W	T	F	S
				1	2	3
4	5	6	7	8	9	10
11	12	13	14	15	16	17
18	19	20	21	22	23	24
25	26	27	28	29	30	31

FEBRUARY
S	M	T	W	T	F	S
1	2	3	4	5	6	7
8	9	10	11	12	13	14
15	16	17	18	19	20	21
22	23	24	25	26	27	28
29						

MARCH
S	M	T	W	T	F	S
	1	2	3	4	5	6
7	8	9	10	11	12	13
14	15	16	17	18	19	20
21	22	23	24	25	26	27
28	29	30	31			

APRIL
S	M	T	W	T	F	S
				1	2	3
4	5	6	7	8	9	10
11	12	13	14	15	16	17
18	19	20	21	22	23	24
25	26	27	28	29	30	

MAY
S	M	T	W	T	F	S
						1
2	3	4	5	6	7	8
9	10	11	12	13	14	15
16	17	18	19	20	21	22
23	24	25	26	27	28	29
30	31					

JUNE
S	M	T	W	T	F	S
	1	2	3	4	5	
6	7	8	9	10	11	12
13	14	15	16	17	18	19
20	21	22	23	24	25	26
27	28	29	30			

JULY
S	M	T	W	T	F	S
				1	2	3
4	5	6	7	8	9	10
11	12	13	14	15	16	17
18	19	20	21	22	23	24
25	26	27	28	29	30	31

AUGUST
S	M	T	W	T	F	S
1	2	3	4	5	6	7
8	9	10	11	12	13	14
15	16	17	18	19	20	21
22	23	24	25	26	27	28
29	30	31				

SEPTEMBER
S	M	T	W	T	F	S
			1	2	3	4
5	6	7	8	9	10	11
12	13	14	15	16	17	18
19	20	21	22	23	24	25
26	27	28	29	30		

OCTOBER
S	M	T	W	T	F	S
					1	2
3	4	5	6	7	8	9
10	11	12	13	14	15	16
17	18	19	20	21	22	23
24	25	26	27	28	29	30
31						

NOVEMBER
S	M	T	W	T	F	S
1	2	3	4	5	6	
7	8	9	10	11	12	13
14	15	16	17	18	19	20
21	22	23	24	25	26	27
28	29	30				

DECEMBER
S	M	T	W	T	F	S
			1	2	3	4
5	6	7	8	9	10	11
12	13	14	15	16	17	18
19	20	21	22	23	24	25
26	27	28	29	30	31	

Calendar 11

JANUARY
S	M	T	W	T	F	S
			1	2	3	4
5	6	7	8	9	10	11
12	13	14	15	16	17	18
19	20	21	22	23	24	25
26	27	28	29	30	31	

FEBRUARY
S	M	T	W	T	F	S
						1
2	3	4	5	6	7	8
9	10	11	12	13	14	15
16	17	18	19	20	21	22
23	24	25	26	27	28	29

MARCH
S	M	T	W	T	F	S
1	2	3	4	5	6	7
8	9	10	11	12	13	14
15	16	17	18	19	20	21
22	23	24	25	26	27	28
29	30	31				

APRIL
S	M	T	W	T	F	S
			1	2	3	4
5	6	7	8	9	10	11
12	13	14	15	16	17	18
19	20	21	22	23	24	25
26	27	28	29	30		

MAY
S	M	T	W	T	F	S
					1	2
3	4	5	6	7	8	9
10	11	12	13	14	15	16
17	18	19	20	21	22	23
24	25	26	27	28	29	30
31						

JUNE
S	M	T	W	T	F	S
1	2	3	4	5	6	
7	8	9	10	11	12	13
14	15	16	17	18	19	20
21	22	23	24	25	26	27
28	29	30				

JULY
S	M	T	W	T	F	S
			1	2	3	4
5	6	7	8	9	10	11
12	13	14	15	16	17	18
19	20	21	22	23	24	25
26	27	28	29	30	31	

AUGUST
S	M	T	W	T	F	S
						1
2	3	4	5	6	7	8
9	10	11	12	13	14	15
16	17	18	19	20	21	22
23	24	25	26	27	28	29
30	31					

SEPTEMBER
S	M	T	W	T	F	S
	1	2	3	4	5	
6	7	8	9	10	11	12
13	14	15	16	17	18	19
20	21	22	23	24	25	26
27	28	29	30			

OCTOBER
S	M	T	W	T	F	S
				1	2	3
4	5	6	7	8	9	10
11	12	13	14	15	16	17
18	19	20	21	22	23	24
25	26	27	28	29	30	31

NOVEMBER
S	M	T	W	T	F	S
1	2	3	4	5	6	7
8	9	10	11	12	13	14
15	16	17	18	19	20	21
22	23	24	25	26	27	28
29	30					

DECEMBER
S	M	T	W	T	F	S
		1	2	3	4	5
6	7	8	9	10	11	12
13	14	15	16	17	18	19
20	21	22	23	24	25	26
27	28	29	30	31		

Calendar 12

JANUARY
S	M	T	W	T	F	S
				1	2	3
4	5	6	7	8	9	10
11	12	13	14	15	16	17
18	19	20	21	22	23	24
25	26	27	28	29	30	31

FEBRUARY
S	M	T	W	T	F	S
1	2	3	4	5	6	7
8	9	10	11	12	13	14
15	16	17	18	19	20	21
22	23	24	25	26	27	28
29						

MARCH
S	M	T	W	T	F	S
1	2	3	4	5	6	
7	8	9	10	11	12	13
14	15	16	17	18	19	20
21	22	23	24	25	26	27
28	29	30	31			

APRIL
S	M	T	W	T	F	S
				1	2	3
4	5	6	7	8	9	10
11	12	13	14	15	16	17
18	19	20	21	22	23	24
25	26	27	28	29	30	

MAY
S	M	T	W	T	F	S
						1
2	3	4	5	6	7	8
9	10	11	12	13	14	15
16	17	18	19	20	21	22
23	24	25	26	27	28	29
30	31					

JUNE
S	M	T	W	T	F	S
	1	2	3	4	5	
6	7	8	9	10	11	12
13	14	15	16	17	18	19
20	21	22	23	24	25	26
27	28	29	30			

JULY
S	M	T	W	T	F	S
				1	2	3
4	5	6	7	8	9	10
11	12	13	14	15	16	17
18	19	20	21	22	23	24
25	26	27	28	29	30	31

AUGUST
S	M	T	W	T	F	S
1	2	3	4	5	6	7
8	9	10	11	12	13	14
15	16	17	18	19	20	21
22	23	24	25	26	27	28
29	30	31				

SEPTEMBER
S	M	T	W	T	F	S
		1	2	3	4	
5	6	7	8	9	10	11
12	13	14	15	16	17	18
19	20	21	22	23	24	25
26	27	28	29	30		

OCTOBER
S	M	T	W	T	F	S
					1	2
3	4	5	6	7	8	9
10	11	12	13	14	15	16
17	18	19	20	21	22	23
24	25	26	27	28	29	30
31						

NOVEMBER
S	M	T	W	T	F	S
1	2	3	4	5	6	
7	8	9	10	11	12	13
14	15	16	17	18	19	20
21	22	23	24	25	26	27
28	29	30				

DECEMBER
S	M	T	W	T	F	S
			1	2	3	4
5	6	7	8	9	10	11
12	13	14	15	16	17	18
19	20	21	22	23	24	25
26	27	28	29	30	31	

Calendar 13

JANUARY
S	M	T	W	T	F	S
					1	2
3	4	5	6	7	8	9
10	11	12	13	14	15	16
17	18	19	20	21	22	23
24	25	26	27	28	29	30
31						

FEBRUARY
S	M	T	W	T	F	S
	1	2	3	4	5	6
7	8	9	10	11	12	13
14	15	16	17	18	19	20
21	22	23	24	25	26	27
28	29					

MARCH
S	M	T	W	T	F	S
	1	2	3	4	5	
6	7	8	9	10	11	12
13	14	15	16	17	18	19
20	21	22	23	24	25	26
27	28	29	30	31		

APRIL
S	M	T	W	T	F	S
					1	2
3	4	5	6	7	8	9
10	11	12	13	14	15	16
17	18	19	20	21	22	23
24	25	26	27	28	29	30

MAY
S	M	T	W	T	F	S
1	2	3	4	5	6	7
8	9	10	11	12	13	14
15	16	17	18	19	20	21
22	23	24	25	26	27	28
29	30	31				

JUNE
S	M	T	W	T	F	S
			1	2	3	4
5	6	7	8	9	10	11
12	13	14	15	16	17	18
19	20	21	22	23	24	25
26	27	28	29	30		

JULY
S	M	T	W	T	F	S
					1	2
3	4	5	6	7	8	9
10	11	12	13	14	15	16
17	18	19	20	21	22	23
24	25	26	27	28	29	30
31						

AUGUST
S	M	T	W	T	F	S
	1	2	3	4	5	6
7	8	9	10	11	12	13
14	15	16	17	18	19	20
21	22	23	24	25	26	27
28	29	30	31			

SEPTEMBER
S	M	T	W	T	F	S
				1	2	3
4	5	6	7	8	9	10
11	12	13	14	15	16	17
18	19	20	21	22	23	24
25	26	27	28	29	30	

OCTOBER
S	M	T	W	T	F	S
						1
2	3	4	5	6	7	8
9	10	11	12	13	14	15
16	17	18	19	20	21	22
23	24	25	26	27	28	29
30	31					

NOVEMBER
S	M	T	W	T	F	S
		1	2	3	4	5
6	7	8	9	10	11	12
13	14	15	16	17	18	19
20	21	22	23	24	25	26
27	28	29	30			

DECEMBER
S	M	T	W	T	F	S
				1	2	3
4	5	6	7	8	9	10
11	12	13	14	15	16	17
18	19	20	21	22	23	24
25	26	27	28	29	30	31

Calendar 14

JANUARY
S	M	T	W	T	F	S
						1
2	3	4	5	6	7	8
9	10	11	12	13	14	15
16	17	18	19	20	21	22
23	24	25	26	27	28	29
30	31					

FEBRUARY
S	M	T	W	T	F	S
		1	2	3	4	5
6	7	8	9	10	11	12
13	14	15	16	17	18	19
20	21	22	23	24	25	26
27	28	29				

MARCH
S	M	T	W	T	F	S
		1	2	3	4	
5	6	7	8	9	10	11
12	13	14	15	16	17	18
19	20	21	22	23	24	25
26	27	28	29	30	31	

APRIL
S	M	T	W	T	F	S
						1
2	3	4	5	6	7	8
9	10	11	12	13	14	15
16	17	18	19	20	21	22
23	24	25	26	27	28	29
30						

MAY
S	M	T	W	T	F	S
	1	2	3	4	5	6
7	8	9	10	11	12	13
14	15	16	17	18	19	20
21	22	23	24	25	26	27
28	29	30	31			

JUNE
S	M	T	W	T	F	S
				1	2	3
4	5	6	7	8	9	10
11	12	13	14	15	16	17
18	19	20	21	22	23	24
25	26	27	28	29	30	

JULY
S	M	T	W	T	F	S
						1
2	3	4	5	6	7	8
9	10	11	12	13	14	15
16	17	18	19	20	21	22
23	24	25	26	27	28	29
30	31					

AUGUST
S	M	T	W	T	F	S
		1	2	3	4	5
6	7	8	9	10	11	12
13	14	15	16	17	18	19
20	21	22	23	24	25	26
27	28	29	30	31		

SEPTEMBER
S	M	T	W	T	F	S
					1	2
3	4	5	6	7	8	9
10	11	12	13	14	15	16
17	18	19	20	21	22	23
24	25	26	27	28	29	30

OCTOBER
S	M	T	W	T	F	S
1	2	3	4	5	6	7
8	9	10	11	12	13	14
15	16	17	18	19	20	21
22	23	24	25	26	27	28
29	30	31				

NOVEMBER
S	M	T	W	T	F	S
			1	2	3	4
5	6	7	8	9	10	11
12	13	14	15	16	17	18
19	20	21	22	23	24	25
26	27	28	29	30		

DECEMBER
S	M	T	W	T	F	S
					1	2
3	4	5	6	7	8	9
10	11	12	13	14	15	16
17	18	19	20	21	22	23
24	25	26	27	28	29	30
31						

WORDS DESCRIBING PERIODS OF TIME

annually	yearly; occurring once every 12 months
biannually	occurring twice a year (at unequally spaced intervals)
bicentennial	relating to a period of 200 years
biennial	relating to a period of 2 years
bimonthly	occurring once every 2 months
biweekly	occurring once every 2 weeks
centennial	relating to a period of 100 years (1 century)
daily	occurring once every 24 hours
decennial	relating to a period of 10 years (1 decade)
diurnal	daily; of a day
duodecennial	relating to a period of 12 years
fortnightly	occurring once every 2 weeks
millennial	relating to a period of 1,000 years (1 millenium)
monthly	occurring once every 30 days (approximately)
novennial	relating to a period of 9 years
octennial	relating to a period of 8 years
perennial	occurring year after year
quadrennial	relating to a period of 4 years (1 olympiad)
quadricentennial	relating to a period of 400 years
quincentennial	relating to a period of 500 years
quindecennial	relating to a period of 15 years
quinquennial	relating to a period of 5 years
semiannually	occurring once every 6 months (at equally spaced intervals)
semicentennial	relating to a period of 50 years
semidiurnal	occurring twice a day
semimonthly	occurring twice a month
semiweekly	occurring twice a week
septennial	relating to a period of 7 years
sesquicentennial	relating to a period of 150 years
sexennial	relating to a period of 6 years
thrice weekly	occurring three times a week
triennial	relating to a period of 3 years
trimonthly	occurring once every 3 months
triweekly	occurring once every 3 weeks
undecennial	relating to a period of 11 years
vicennial	relating to a period of 20 years
weekly	occurring once every 7 days

A "jiffy" is an actual unit of time. It is $1/100$ of a second.

MAJOR HOLIDAYS

AMERICAN

Dates marked with an asterisk (*) are the officially designated national holidays.

*January 1	New Year's Day
January 15	Martin Luther King Jr.'s Birthday
Third Monday in January	Martin Luther King Jr.'s Birthday (observed)
January 19	Robert E. Lee's Birthday (Southern states)
January 20	Inauguration Day
February 2	Groundhog Day
February 12	Lincoln's Birthday
February 14	Valentine's Day
February 22	Washington's Birthday
Third Monday in February	Washington's Birthday (observed as Presidents' Day)
March 17	St. Patrick's Day
March or April	Easter Sunday
April 1	April Fools' Day
April 14	Pan American Day
May 1	May Day
Second Sunday in May	Mother's Day
Third Saturday in May	Armed Forces Day
May 30	Memorial Day
*Last Monday in May	Memorial Day (observed)
June 3	Jefferson Davis's Birthday (Southern states)
June 14	Flag Day
Third Sunday in June	Father's Day
*July 4	Independence Day
*First Monday in September	Labor Day
September 17	Citizenship Day
Fourth Friday in September	Native American Day
October 12	Columbus Day
*Second Monday in October	Columbus Day (observed)
October 24	United Nations Day
October 31	Halloween
First Tuesday after the first Monday in November	Election Day
*November 11	Veterans' Day
*Fourth Thursday in November	Thanksgiving Day
*December 25	Christmas Day

CANADIAN

January 1	New Year's Day
March or April	Good Friday
	Easter Monday
Last Monday before May 25	Victoria Day
July 1	Canada Day
First Monday in September	Labour Day
Second Monday in October	Thanksgiving Day
November 11	Remembrance Day
December 25	Christmas Day
December 26	Boxing Day

OTHER

January	Australia Day on the last Monday in Australia
January 1	New Year's Day throughout the Western world and in India, Indonesia, Japan, Korea, the Philippines, Singapore, Taiwan, and Thailand; founding of Republic of China (Taiwan)
January 2	Berchtoldstag in Switzerland
January 3	Genshi-Sai (First Beginning) in Japan
January 5	Twelfth Night (Wassail Eve or Eve of Epiphany) in England
January 6	Epiphany, observed by Catholics throughout Europe and Latin America
mid-January	Martin Luther King Jr.'s birthday on the third Monday in the U.S. Virgin Islands
January 15	Adults' Day in Japan
January 20	St. Agnes' Eve in Great Britain
January 26	Republic Day in India
January–February	Chinese New Year and Vietnamese New Year (Tet)
February	Hamstrom on the first Sunday in Switzerland
February 3	Setsubun (Bean-throwing Festival) in Japan
February 5	Promulgation of the Constitution Day in Mexico
February 6	New Zealand Day in New Zealand
February 11	National Foundation Day in Japan
February 27	Independence Day in the Dominican Republic
March 1	Independence Movement Day in Korea; Constitution Day in Panama

March 8	International Women's Day in UN member nations
March 17	St. Patrick's Day in Ireland and Northern Ireland
March 19	St. Joseph's Day in Colombia, Costa Rica, Italy, and Spain
March 21	Benito Juarez's Birthday in Mexico
March 22	Arab League Day in Arab League countries
March 23	Pakistan Day in Pakistan
March 25	Independence Day in Greece; Lady Day (Quarter Day) in Great Britain
March 26	Fiesta del Arbol (Arbor Day) in Spain
March 29	Youth and Martyrs' Day in Taiwan
March 30	Muslim New Year in Indonesia
March–April	Carnival/Lent/Easter: The pre-Lenten celebration of Carnival (Mardi Gras) and the post-Lenten celebration of Easter are movable feasts widely observed in Christian countries.
April 1	Victory Day in Spain; April Fools' Day (All Fools' Day) in Great Britain
April 5	Arbor Day in Korea
April 6	Van Riebeeck Day in South Africa
April 7	World Health Day in UN member nations
April 8	Buddha's Birthday in Korea and Japan; Hana Matsuri (Flower Festival) in Japan
April 14	Pan American Day in the Americas
April 19	Declaration of Independence Day in Venezuela
April 22	Queen Isabella Day in Spain
April 23	St. George's Day in England
April 25	Liberation Day in Italy; ANZAC Day in Australia and New Zealand
April 26	Union Day in Tanzania
April 29	Emperor's Birthday in Japan
April 30	Queen's Birthday in The Netherlands; Walpurgis Night in Germany and Scandinavia
April–May	Independence Day in Israel
May	Constitution Day on first Monday in Japan

continues

Other Holidays, continued

May 1	May Day–Labor Day in the Commonwealth of Independent States and most of Europe and Latin America
May 5	Children's Day in Japan and Korea; Victory of General Zaragosa Day in Mexico; Liberation Day in The Netherlands
May 8	V-E Day in Europe
May 9	Victory over Fascism Day in the Commonwealth of Independent States
May 14	Independence Day in Paraguay
May 31	Republic Day in South Africa
June 2	Founding of the Republic Day in Italy
June 5	Constitution Day in Denmark; World Environment Day in UN member nations
June 6	Memorial Day in Korea; Flag Day in Sweden
June 8	Muhammad's Birthday in Indonesia
June 10	Portugal Day in Portugal
June 12	Republic Day in the Commonwealth of Independent States; Independence Day in the Philippines
mid-June	Queen's Official Birthday on second Saturday in Great Britain; Midsummer Celebrations in Sweden
June 16	Soweto Day in U.N. member nations
June 20	Flag Day in Argentina
June 29	Feast of Saints Peter and Paul in Chile, Colombia, Costa Rica, Italy, Peru, Spain, Vatican City, and Venezuela
July 1	Half-year Holiday in Hong Kong; Bank Holiday in Taiwan; Dominion Day in Canada
July 5	Independence Day in Venezuela
July 9	Independence Day in Argentina
July 10	Bon (Feast of Fortune) in Japan
July 12	Orangemen's Day in Northern Ireland
July 14	Bastille Day in France
mid-July	Feria de San Fermin during second week in Spain
July 17	Constitution Day in Korea

July 18	National Day in Spain
July 20	Independence Day in Colombia
July 21–22	National Holiday in Belgium
July 22	National Liberation Day in Poland
July 24	Simon Bolivar's Birthday in Ecuador and Venezuela
July 25	St. James' Day in Spain
July 28–29	Independence Day in Peru
August	Bank Holiday on first Monday in Fiji, Grenada, Guyana, Hong Kong, Ireland, and Malawi; Discovery Day on first Monday in Trinidad and Tobago; Independence Day on first Tuesday in Jamaica
August 1	Lammas Day in England; National Day in Switzerland
August 9	National Day in Singapore
August 10	Independence Day in Ecuador
August 14	Independence Day in Pakistan
August 15	Independence Day in India and Korea; Assumption Day in Catholic countries
August 16	National Restoration Day in the Dominican Republic
August 17	Independence Day in Indonesia
August 31	Independence Day in Trinidad and Tobago
September	Rose of Tralee Festival in Ireland
September 7	Independence Day in Brazil
September 9	Choxo-no-Sekku (Chrysanthemum Day) in Japan
September 14	Battle of San Jacinto Day in Nicaragua
mid-September	Sherry Wine Harvest in Spain
September 15	Independence Day in Costa Rica, Guatemala, and Nicaragua; Respect for the Aged Day in Japan
September 16	Independence Day in Mexico and Papua New Guinea
September 18–19	Independence Day in Chile
September 28	Confucius' Birthday in Taiwan
October	Thanksgiving Day in Canada on second Monday; Kruger Day in South Africa during second week
October 1	National Day in People's Republic of China; Armed Forces Day in Korea; National Holiday in Nigeria
October 2	Mahatma Gandhi's Birthday in India

October 3	National Day in the Federal Republic of Germany; National Foundation Day in Korea
October 5	Republic Day in Portugal
October 9	Korean Alphabet Day in Korea
October 10	Founding of Republic of China in Taiwan
October 12	Columbus Day in Spain and widely throughout Latin America
October 19	Ascension of Muhammad Day in Indonesia
October 20	Revolution Day in Guatemala; Kenyatta Day in Kenya
October 24	United Nations Day in UN member nations
October 26	National Holiday in Australia
October 28	Greek National Day in Greece
November 1	All Saints' Day, observed by Catholics in most countries
November 2	All Souls' Day in Ecuador, El Salvador, Luxembourg, Macao, Mexico, San Marino, Uruguay, and Vatican City
November 3	Culture Day in Japan
November 4	National Unity Day in Italy
November 5	Guy Fawkes' Day in Great Britain
November 11	Armistice Day in Belgium, French Guiana, and Tahiti; Veterans' Day in France; Remembrance Day in Canada and Bermuda
November 12	Sun Yat-sen's Birthday in Taiwan
November 15	Proclamation of the Republic Day in Brazil
November 19	National Holiday in Monaco
November 20	Anniversary of the Revolution in Mexico
November 23	Kinro-Kansha-No-Hi (Labor/ Thanksgiving Day) in Japan
November 30	National Heroes' Day in the Philippines
December 5	Discovery by Columbus Day in Haiti
December 6	Independence Day in Finland
December 8	Feast of the Immaculate Conception, widely observed in Catholic countries
December 10	Constitution Day in Thailand; Human Rights Day in UN member nations
mid-December	Nine Days of Posada during third week in Mexico
December 25	Christmas Day, widely observed in all Christian countries
December 26	St. Stephen's Day in Austria, Ireland, Italy, Liechtenstein, San Marino, and Switzerland; Boxing Day in Great Britain and Northern Ireland
December 28	National Day in Nepal
December 31	New Year's Eve throughout the world; Omisoka (Grand Last Day) in Japan; Hogmanay Day in Scotland

ADDITIONAL SOURCES OF INFORMATION

Chase, William D., and Helen M. Chase. *Chase's Annual Events.* Contemporary Books, annual.

Fitzpatrick, Gary L. *International Time Tables.* Scarecrow Press, 1990.

Landes, David S. *Revolution in Time: Clocks and the Making of the Modern World.* Harvard University Press, 1983.

Macey, Samuel L. *Encyclopedia of Time.* Garland, 1994.

———. *Time: A Bibliographic Guide.* Garland, 1991.

Mossman, Jennifer, ed. *Holidays and Anniversaries of the World.* Gale Research, 1990.

Thompson, Sue Ellen, and Barbara W. Carlson. *Holidays, Festivals and Celebrations of the World Dictionary.* Omnigraphics, 1994.

Westrheim, Margo. *Calendars of the World.* Oneworld, 1993.

2

WEIGHTS AND MEASURES

U.S. CUSTOMARY SYSTEM OF WEIGHTS AND MEASURES	23
METRIC SYSTEM OF MEASUREMENT	26
COMMON CONVERSION FACTORS	28
TEMPERATURE CONVERSIONS	29
SPECIAL WEIGHTS AND MEASURES	30
ADDITIONAL SOURCES OF INFORMATION	32

U.S. CUSTOMARY SYSTEM OF WEIGHTS AND MEASURES

The units of weights and measures commonly used today in the United States were derived during the colonial period from units used in Great Britain for many centuries.

LENGTH

1 nail (cloth)	=	2.25 inches		
1 palm	=	3 inches		
1 hand	=	4 inches		
1 span	=	6 inches		
1 quarter (cloth)	=	9 inches		
1 foot	=	12 inches		
1 pace	=	30 inches	=	2.5 feet
1 yard	=	36 inches	=	3 feet
1 fathom	=	6 feet	=	2 yards
1 rod	=	16.5 feet	=	5.5 yards
1 furlong	=	660 feet	=	220 yards
1 mile	=	5,280 feet	=	1,760 yards
1 nautical mile	=	6,076.1155 feet		

AREA

1 square foot	=	144 square inches		
1 square yard	=	9 square feet		
1 rood	=	10,890 square feet	=	40 square rods
1 acre	=	43,560 square feet	=	4 roods
1 square mile	=	640 acres		

VOLUME

1 cubic foot	=	1,728 cubic inches
1 cubic yard	=	27 cubic feet

CAPACITY (DRY MEASURE)

1 pint	=	33.6003125 cubic inches		
1 quart	=	67.200625 cubic inches	=	2 pints
1 gallon	=	268.8025 cubic inches	=	4 quarts
1 peck	=	537.605 cubic inches	=	2 gallons
1 bushel	=	2,150.42 cubic inches	=	4 pecks
1 cranberry barrel	=	5,876 cubic inches		
1 barrel	=	7,056 cubic inches		
1 cord-foot (wood)	=	16 cubic feet		
1 cord (wood)	=	128 cubic feet	=	8 cord-feet
1 freight ton	=	40 cubic feet		
1 register ton	=	100 cubic feet		

Go to "Chemistry," "Mathematics," and "Physics" in chapter 4; "Standard Sizes Chart" in chapter 19

Six Quick Ways to Measure When You Don't Have a Ruler

A Closer Look

1. Most credit cards are $3^3/_8$ inches by $2^1/_8$ inches.
2. Standard business cards are printed $3^1/_2$ inches wide by 2 inches long.
3. Floor tiles are usually manufactured in 12-inch by 12-inch squares.
4. U.S. paper currency is $6^1/_8$ inches wide by $2^5/_8$ inches long.
5. The diameter of a quarter is approximately 1 inch, and the diameter of a penny is approximately $3/_4$ inch.
6. A standard sheet of paper is $8^1/_2$ inches wide by 11 inches long.

CAPACITY (LIQUID MEASURE)

1 fluid dram	=	60 minims	
1 teaspoon	=	80 minims	
1 tablespoon	=	240 minims	=	3 teaspoons
1 fluid ounce	=	480 minims	=	2 tablespoons
1 gill	=	4 fluid ounces	
1 cup	=	8 fluid ounces	=	2 gills
1 pint	=	16 fluid ounces	=	2 cups
1 quart	=	32 fluid ounces	=	2 pints
1 gallon	=	128 fluid ounces	=	4 quarts
1 barrel	=	31.5 gallons	=	7,276.5 cubic inches
1 petroleum barrel	=	42 gallons	=	9,702 cubic inches

MASS (AVOIRDUPOIS)

1 dram	=	27.34375 grains	
1 ounce	=	16 drams	
1 pound	=	16 ounces	
1 hundredweight	=	100 pounds	
1 ton	=	2,000 pounds	=	20 hundredweights

MASS (TROY AND APOTHECARY)

1 scruple	=	20 grains	
1 pennyweight	=	24 grains	
1 dram	=	60 grains	= 3 scruples
1 ounce	=	480 grains	= 8 drams
1 pound	=	12 ounces	

ANGLE

1 minute	=	60 seconds
1 degree	=	60 minutes
1 sign	=	30 degrees
1 octant	=	45 degrees
1 sextant	=	60 degrees
1 quadrant	=	90 degrees
1 semicircle	=	180 degrees
1 circle	=	360 degrees

METRIC SYSTEM OF MEASUREMENT

The metric system is a system of weights and measures, based on decimals or units of ten, that was developed in the 1790s in revolutionary France and revised and refined several times since that period. In 1960, an international conference gave it the official name *Système International d'Unités* (International System of Units or SI). Today, virtually all countries except the United States are totally committed to adopting this system.

On December 23, 1975, President Gerald R. Ford signed the U.S. Metric Conversion Act, declaring a national policy of encouraging voluntary conversion to the metric system. Federal agencies have made a transition to the metric system, but adoption elsewhere in the country has been more gradual than anticipated in 1975.

BASIC UNITS

The metric system is often considered a simpler form of measurement in that it includes only seven basic units for different types of measurement.

The basic unit of length is the *meter (m)*, currently defined as the path traveled by light in a vacuum in 1/299,792.458 of a second.

The basic unit of mass is the *kilogram (kg)*, currently defined as the mass of a platinum-iridium cylinder preserved in a vault at Sèvres, near Paris, by the International Bureau of Weights and Measures.

The basic unit of time is the *second (sec)*, currently defined as the duration of 9,192,631,770 cycles of radiation given off by the element cesium 133 under certain conditions.

The basic unit of temperature is the *Kelvin (K)*, which is the same size as a Celsius degree. The Kelvin is based on the fact that the lowest temperature possible in theory (absolute zero) is 273.16 degrees below zero Celsius. Thus, 0 K = −273.16°C. This unit is named after the British physicist Lord Kelvin (William Thomson; 1824–1907).

The basic unit of electric current is the *ampere (A)*, defined as the current that, if maintained in two straight parallel wires of infinite length and negligible cross section, and placed in a vacuum, will produce between the wires a force of 0.0000002 newton (defined in the following section) per meter of length. This unit is named after the French physicist André M. Ampère (1775–1836).

The basic unit of luminosity intensity is the *candela (cd)*, currently defined as the light given off by 1/600,000 square meters of a black body (a perfect radiator) at the freezing point of platinum under a pressure of 101,325 newtons per square meter.

The basic unit of substance is the *mole (mol)*, defined as the amount of substance equal to the molecular weight of that substance.

DERIVED UNITS

All other metric units are derived from the seven basic units defined in the preceding section.

One *newton (N)* is the force that imparts to a mass of one kilogram an acceleration of one meter per second. One *pascal (Pa)*, the unit of pressure, is one newton per square meter. One *joule (J)*, the unit of energy, is the work done by a force of one newton acting through a distance of one meter. These units are named after, respectively, the English mathematician and natural philosopher Sir Isaac Newton (1642–1727); the French mathematician, physicist, and philosopher Blaise Pascal (1623–62); and the English physicist James P. Joule (1818–89).

In electricity, one *coulomb (C)* is the electric charge transported through a conductor by a current of one ampere flowing for one second. One *volt (V)* is the electromotive force or difference in potential between two points in an electric field that requires one joule of work to move a positive charge of one coulomb from the point of lower potential to the point of higher potential. One *ohm* is the electrical resistance of a circuit in which an electromotive force of one volt maintains a current of one ampere. One *watt (W)*, equal to one joule per second, is the electrical power developed in a circuit by a current of one ampere flowing through a potential difference of one volt. These units are named after, respectively, the French physicist Charles A. Coulomb (1736–1806), the Italian physicist Count Alessandro Volta (1745–1827), the German physicist Georg Simon Ohm (1787–1854), and the Scottish engineer and inventor James Watt (1736–1819).

METRIC PREFIXES

The metric or SI system is based on the decimal system and follows a consistent name scheme using the prefixes listed below. Multiples and submultiples always related to the power of 10 are combined with the basic metric units to provide the multiples and submultiples in the metric or SI system. For example, centi + meter = centimeter, meaning one one-hundredth of a meter.

Prefix	Symbol	Multiples	Equivalent	Prefix	Symbol	Multiples	Equivalent
exa	E	10^{18}	quintillionfold	deci	d	10^{-1}	tenth part
peta	P	10^{15}	quadrillionfold	centi	c	10^{-2}	hundredth part
tera	T	10^{12}	trillionfold	milli	m	10^{-3}	thousandth part
giga	G	10^{9}	billionfold	micro	μ	10^{-6}	millionth part
mega	M	10^{6}	millionfold	nano	n	10^{-9}	billionth part
kilo	k	10^{3}	thousandfold	pico	p	10^{-12}	trillionth part
hecto	h	10^{2}	hundredfold	femto	f	10^{-15}	quadrillionth part
deka	da	10	tenfold	atto	a	10^{-18}	quintillionth part

TABLES OF METRIC WEIGHTS AND MEASURES

LENGTH

10 millimeters (mm) = 1 centimeter (cm)
10 centimeters = 1 decimeter (dm)
10 decimeters = 1 meter (m)
10 meters = 1 dekameter (dam)
10 dekameters = 1 hectometer (hm)
10 hectometers = 1 kilometer (km)

The highest temperature ever recorded on Earth was 136°F on September 13, 1992, in Azizia, Libya

AREA

100 sq. millimeters (mm²) = 1 sq. centimeter (cm²)
10,000 sq. centimeters = 1 sq. meter (m²)
100 sq. meters = 1 are (a)
100 ares = 1 hectare (ha)
100 hectares = 1 sq. kilometer (km²)

VOLUME

1,000 cu. millimeters (mm³) =
    1 cu. centimeter (cm³)
1,000 cu. centimeters = 1 cu. decimeter (dm³)
1,000 cu. decimeters = 1 cu. meter (m³)

CAPACITY (DRY AND LIQUID)

10 milliliters (ml) = 1 centiliter (cl)
10 centiliters = 1 deciliter (dl)
10 deciliters = 1 liter (l)
10 liters = 1 dekaliter (dal)
10 dekaliters = 1 hectoliter (hl)
10 hectoliters = 1 kiloliter (kl)

MASS

10 milligrams (mg) = 1 centigram (cg)
10 centigrams = 1 decigram (dg)
10 decigrams = 1 gram (g)
10 grams = 1 dekagram (dag)
10 dekagrams = 1 hectogram (hg)
10 hectograms = 1 kilogram (kg)
1,000 kilograms = 1 metric ton (t)

Go to "Cooking Equivalents and Substitutions" and "Champagne Bottle Sizes" in chapter 19

COMMON CONVERSION FACTORS

To Convert From	To	Multiply By
Acres	Hectares	0.40468586
Acres	Kilometers, square	0.004046856
Acres	Meters, square	4046.856
Centimeters	Meters	0.01
Centimeters, square	Meters, square	0.0001
Feet	Centimeters	30.48
Feet	Meters	0.3048
Feet	Kilometers	0.0003048
Feet, cubic	Liters	28.316847
Feet, cubic	Meters, cubic	0.028316847
Feet, square	Centimeters, square	929.0304
Feet, square	Meters, square	0.09290304
Gallons, U.S. liquid	Liters	3.785412
Gallons, U.S. liquid	Meters, cubic	0.003785412
Grams	Ounces, troy	0.032151
Grams	Pounds, troy	0.002679
Hectares	Kilometers, square	0.01
Hectares	Meters, square	10,000
Inches	Centimeters	2.54
Inches	Meters	0.0254
Inches, cubic	Milliliters	16.387064
Inches, cubic	Liters	0.016387064
Inches, cubic	Meters, cubic	0.000016387064
Inches, square	Centimeters, square	6.4516
Inches, square	Meters, square	0.00064516
Kilograms	Ounces, troy	32.15075
Kilograms	Pounds, troy	2.679229
Kilograms	Tons, metric	0.001
Kilometers, square	Hectares	100
Kilometers, square	Miles, square	0.3861
Liters	Milliliters	1000
Liters	Meters, cubic	0.001
Meters	Millimeters	1000
Meters	Centimeters	100
Meters	Kilometers	0.001
Meters, cubic	Liters	1000
Meters, cubic	Tons, register	0.353147
Miles, nautical	Kilometers	1.852

To Convert From	To	Multiply By
Miles, square	Hectares	258.99881
Miles, square	Kilometers, square	2.5899881
Miles, statute	Centimeters	160934.4
Miles, statute	Meters	1609.344
Miles, statute	Kilometers	1.609344
Ounces, avoirdupois	Grams	28.349523
Ounces, avoirdupois	Kilograms	0.028349523
Ounces, troy	Pounds, troy	0.083333
Ounces, troy	Grams	31.10348
Pints, U.S. liquid	Millimeters	473.176473
Pints, U.S. liquid	Liters	0.473176473
Pounds, avoirdupois	Grams	453.59237
Pounds, avoirdupois	Kilograms	0.45359237
Pounds, avoirdupois	Quintals	0.0045359237
Pounds, avoirdupois	Tons, metric	0.00045359237
Pounds, troy	Ounces, troy	12
Pounds, troy	Grams	373.2417216
Quarts, dry	Liters	1.101221
Quarts, dry	Dekaliters	0.1101221
Quarts, liquid	Milliliters	946.352946
Quarts, liquid	Liters	0.946352946
Quintals	Tons, metric	0.1
Ton-miles, long	Ton-kilometers, metric	1.635169
Ton-miles, short	Ton-kilometers, metric	1.4359972
Tons, long	Kilograms	1016.047
Tons, long	Tons, metric	1.016047
Tons, metric	Quintals	10
Tons, register	Meters, cubic	2.831685
Tons, short	Kilograms	907.185
Tons, short	Tons, metric	0.907185
Yards	Centimeters	91.44
Yards	Meters	0.9144
Yards, cubic	Liters	764.5549
Yards, cubic	Meters, cubic	0.7645549
Yards, square	Meters, square	0.836127

Mile/Kilometer Conversions			
Miles to Kilometers		**Kilometers to Miles**	
1	1.6	1	0.6
2	3.2	2	1.2
3	4.8	3	1.9
4	6.4	4	2.5
5	8.0	5	3.1
6	9.7	6	3.7
7	11.3	7	4.3
8	12.9	8	5.0
9	14.5	9	5.6
10	16.1	10	6.2
20	32.2	20	12.4
30	48.3	30	18.6
40	64.4	40	24.9
50	80.5	50	31.1
60	96.6	60	37.3
70	112.7	70	43.5
80	128.7	80	49.7
90	144.8	90	55.9
100	160.9	100	62.1
1,000	1,609.3	1,000	621.4

A Closer Look

Weights/Measures

TEMPERATURE CONVERSIONS

The following can be used as general guidelines to tell the weather in both Celsius and Fahrenheit.

0°C	Freezing point of water (32°F)
10°C	A warm winter day (50°F)
20°C	A mild spring day (68°F)
30°C	Quite warm—almost hot (86°F)
37°C	Normal body temperature (98.6°F)
40°C	Heat wave conditions (104°F)
100°C	Boiling point of water (212°F)

To convert degrees Fahrenheit to degrees Celsius, subtract 32 from the Fahrenheit temperature, multiply the difference by 5, and then divide the product by 9. To convert degrees Celsius to degrees Fahrenheit, multiply the Celsius temperature by 1.8 and add 32.

Absolute zero, the theoretically lowest temperature possible, is equal to −273°C and −459.4°F.

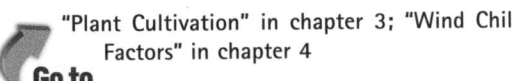

Go to "Plant Cultivation" in chapter 3; "Wind Chill Factors" in chapter 4

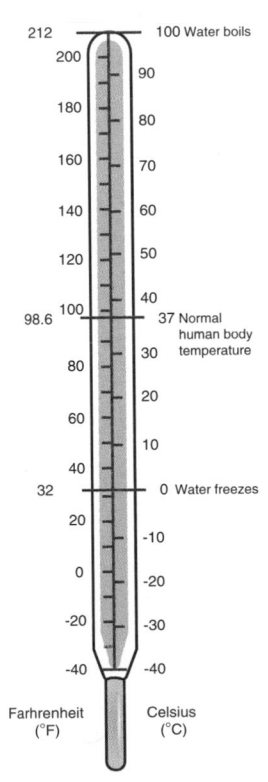

Weights/Measures

SPECIAL WEIGHTS AND MEASURES

astronomical unit (AU)   The unit of length used in astronomy equal to the mean distance of Earth from the Sun, or about 93 million miles.

bale   A large bundle of goods. In the United States, the approximate weight of a bale of cotton is 500 pounds.

board foot (fbm)   A measurement used in lumber: 144 cubic inches (12 inches by 12 inches by 1 inch).

bolt   Used in measuring cloth: 40 yards.

British thermal unit (Btu)   A unit of heat energy measured as the amount of heat required to raise the temperature of 1 pound of water from 60° to 61°F at a constant pressure of 1 standard atmosphere (the weight of the atmosphere at mean sea level). One Btu is equal to 1054.5 joules in the meter-kilogram-second system of measurements.

bundle   Two reams of paper.

caliber   The diameter of a bore of a gun, usually expressed in modern U.S. and British usage in hundredths or thousandths of an inch and typically written as a decimal fraction.

Without using precision instruments, Eratosthenes measured the radius of the Earth in the 3rd century B.C. *and came within 1% of the value determined by today's technology.*

carat   Originally the weight of a seed of the carob tree in the Mediterranean region, today it has two separate meanings: (1) 200 milligrams, or 3.086 grains troy, used for measuring the weight of gemstones; and (2) a measure of the amount of gold per 24 parts of gold alloy; in this sense, it also spelled *karat*. Thus, 24-carat gold is pure, and 18-carat gold is $^3/_4$ gold and $^1/_4$ other metal.

case   Four bundles of paper.

chain (ch)   A unit of length equal to 66 feet and usually divided into 100 links. Used in surveying.

decibel   A unit of relative loudness. The smallest amount of change that can be detected by the human ear is 1 decibel. A 20-decibel sound is 10 times as loud as a 10-decibel sound; a 30-decibel sound is 100 times as loud.

10 decibels	A light whisper
20 decibels	Quiet conversation
30 decibels	Normal conversation
40 decibels	Light traffic
50 decibels	A typewriter; loud conversation
60 decibels	A noisy office
70 decibels	Normal traffic; a quiet train
80 decibels	Raucous music; the subway
90 decibels	Heavy traffic; thunder
100 decibels	A plane at takeoff

The speed of sound is usually placed at 1,088 feet per second at 32° F at sea level.

ell (English) $1^1/_4$ yards or $^1/_{32}$ bolt. Used for measuring cloth.

em   A printer's measure designating the square width of any given type size. The em of 10-point type is 10 points. An en is one-half of an em.

freight ton (measurement ton)   40 cubic feet of merchandise. Used for cargo freight.

gauge   A measure of shotgun bore diameter. Gauge numbers originally referred to the number per pound of round lead balls of a diameter equal to that of the bore. Today, an international agreement assigns millimeter measures to each gauge.

Gauge	Bore Diameter in mm
6	23.34
10	19.67
12	18.52
14	17.60
16	16.81
20	15.90

A Closer Look

Historic Weights and Measures

	Units	Location	Customary	Metric
Volume	amphora	Greece	10.3 gal.	38.8 l
		Rome	6.84 gal.	26 l
	bath	Israel	2.250 cu. in.	37 l
	ephah	Israel	1.1 bu.	40 l
	gallon, beer	England	282 cu. in.	4.62 l
	hekat	Israel	291 cu. in.	4.77 l
	tun	England	252 gal.	954 l
Weight	denarius	Rome	0.17 oz.	4.6 g
	dinar	Arabia	0.15 oz.	4.2 g
	drachma	Greece	0.154 oz.	4.36 g
	livre	France	1.08 lb.	490 g
	livre (demikilo)	France	1.10 lb.	500 g
	mite	England	0.05 grain	3.24 mg
	obol	Greece	11.2 grains	0.73 g
	pfund	Germany	1.1 lb.	500 g
	pound, tower:	England		
	12 oz.		5,400 grains	350 g
	15 oz.		6,750 grains	437 g
	16 oz.		7,200 grains	467 g
	shekel	Israel	0.5 oz.	14.1 g
	shekel, trade	Babylonia	0.3 oz.	8.37 g
Length	cubit	Greece	18.3 in.	46.5 cm
		Israel	21.8 in.	38.2 cm
		Rome	17.5 in.	44.4 cm
	hand	England U.S.	4 in.	10.2 cm
	stadion	Greece	622 ft.	190 m
	stadium	Rome	606 ft.	185 m

great gross 12 gross, or 1,728.

gross 12 dozen, or 144.

hand A unit of measure equal to 4 inches. Used especially to measure the height of horses.

hertz A unit of electromagnetic wave frequency equal to one cycle per second.

hogshead (hhd) Two liquid barrels.

horsepower The power needed to lift 33,000 pounds a distance of 1 foot in 1 minute (about $1\frac{1}{2}$ times the power an average horse can exert) or to lift 550 pounds 1 foot in 1 second. Used to measure the power of steam engines, gasoline engines, etc.

Go to "Words Describing Periods of Time" in chapter 1; "Food Weights and Measures" in chapter 19

knot A unit for measuring the speed of ships. One knot is 1 nautical mile per hour, 10 knots is 10 nautical miles per hour, and so on.

league Any of various units of distance from about 2.4 to 4.6 statute miles.

The length of the Mayflower was measured in score-feet (1 score-foot is equal to 20 feet). After outliving its usefulness, the Mayflower was dismantled and rebuilt as a barn.

light-year A unit of length in interstellar astronomy equal to the distance that light travels in 1 year in a vacuum, or about 5,878,000,000,000 miles.

magnum A large bottle of wine holding about $\frac{2}{5}$ gallon.

parsec   The unit of measure for interstellar space equal to a distance having a heliocentric parallax of 1 second, or to 206,265 times the radius of Earth's orbit, or to 3.26 light-years, or to 19.2 trillion miles.

pica   One-sixth inch, or 12 points. Used to measure typographical material.

pipe   Two hogsheads. Used to measure wine and other liquids.

point   0.013836 (approximately $^1/_{72}$) inch or $^1/_{12}$ pica. Used in printing to measure type size.

quintal   100,000 grams, or 220.46 pounds avoirdupois.

quire   24 or 25 sheets of paper.

ream   480 or 500 sheets of paper, or 20 quires.

Early systems of measurement used body parts to calculate length. A cubit ran from elbow to middle fingertip. The distance from fingertip to fingertip of outstretched arms was a fathom.

ADDITIONAL SOURCES OF INFORMATION

ORGANIZATIONS AND SERVICES

National Institute of Standards and Technology
(formerly National Bureau of Standards)
Gaithersburg, MD, 20899
http://www.nist.gov

BOOKS

American Society for Testing and Materials. *Standard Practice for Use of International System of Units (SI): The Modernized Metric System.* ASTM, 1991.

Blocksma, Mary. *Reading the Numbers: A Survival Guide to the Measurements, Numbers, and Sizes Encountered in Daily Life.* Penguin, 1989.

Cook, James L. *Conversion Factors.* Oxford, 1991.

Darton, Mike, and John Clark. *The Macmillan Dictionary of Measurement.* Macmillan, 1994.

The Economist. Desk Companion: How to Measure, Convert, Calculate and Define Practically Anything. Henry Holt, 1994.

Johnstone, William D. *For Good Measure.* NTC Publishing Group, 1996.

Sutcliffe, Andrea, ed. *Numbers: How Many, How Far, How Long, How Much.* Harper Perennial, 1996.

3

THE BIOLOGICAL WORLD

ANATOMICAL DRAWINGS OF THE HUMAN BODY   34

THE SCIENCE OF TAXONOMY   36

THE ANIMAL KINGDOM   37

PETS   42

ANIMAL FIRST AID   45

THE PLANT KINGDOM   49

PLANT CULTIVATION   58

COMMON BIOLOGICAL TERMS   62

ADDITIONAL SOURCES OF INFORMATION   65

ANATOMICAL DRAWINGS OF THE HUMAN BODY
THE SKELETAL SYSTEM
FRONT VIEW

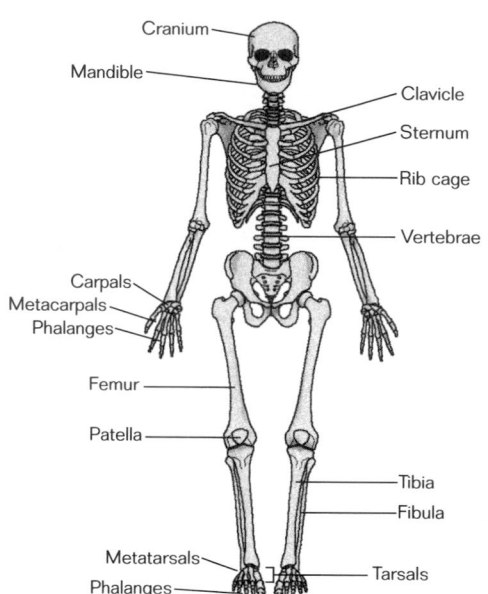

REAR VIEW

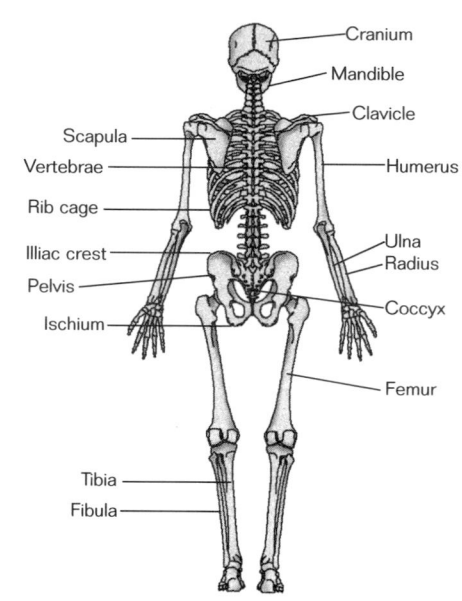

SKULL BONES

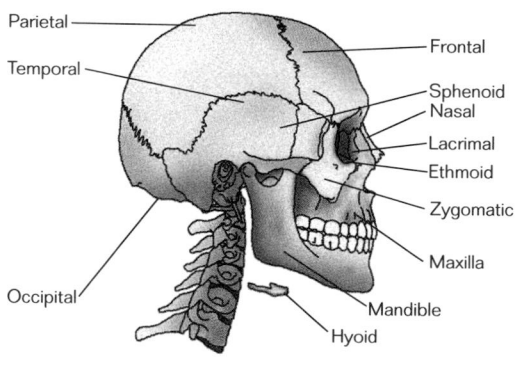

THE EYE

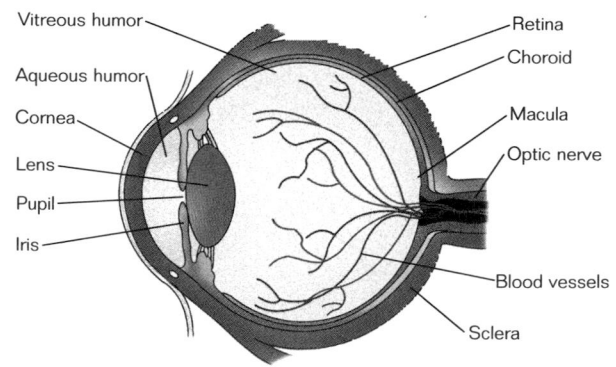

THE EAR

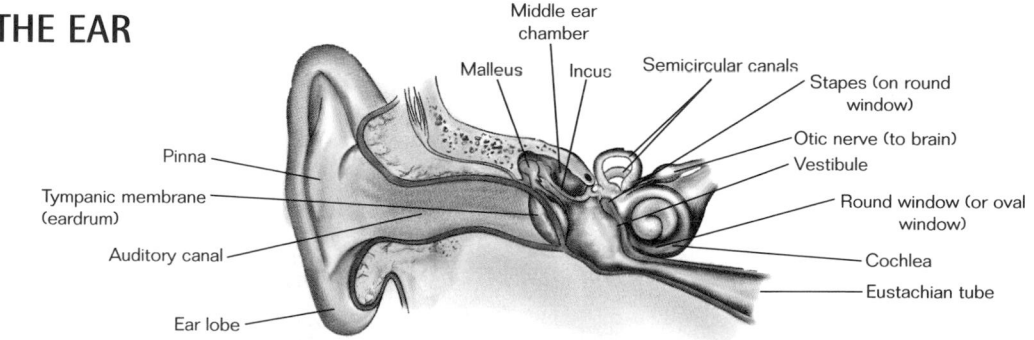

THE BRAIN
PARTS

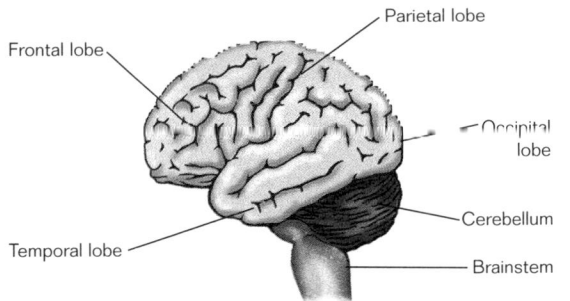

- Frontal lobe
- Parietal lobe
- Occipital lobe
- Temporal lobe
- Cerebellum
- Brainstem

FUNCTIONS

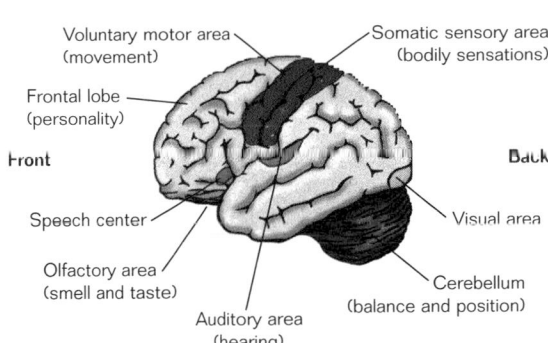

- Voluntary motor area (movement)
- Frontal lobe (personality)
- Front
- Speech center
- Olfactory area (smell and taste)
- Auditory area (hearing)
- Somatic sensory area (bodily sensations)
- Back
- Visual area
- Cerebellum (balance and position)

THE MUSCLE SYSTEM
FRONT VIEW

Superficial layer

- Frontalis
- Temporalis
- Zygomaticus
- Platysma
- Deltoid
- Pectoralis major
- Serratus anterior
- Biceps
- Brachialis
- Rectus abdominis
- Brachio radialis
- Obliquus externus
- Gracilis
- Sartorius
- Rectus femoris
- Vastus medialis
- Vastus lateralis
- Gastrocnemius
- Tibialis anterior
- Soleus

Deep layer

- Orbicularis oculi
- Masseter
- Sternocleidomastoid
- Trapezius
- Pectoralis minor
- Biceps
- Intercostalis
- Iliacus
- Psoas major
- Extensor digitorum communis
- Adductor brevis
- Adductor longus
- Adductor magnus
- Peroneus longus
- Extensor digitorum longus

REAR VIEW

Deep layer

- Splenius capitis
- Levator scapulae
- Rhomboideus
- Teres minor
- Teres major
- Semispinalis
- Erector spinae
- Gluteus minimus
- Obturator internus
- Vastus lateralis
- Gracilis
- Biceps femoris
- Popliteus
- Soleus
- Tibialis posterior
- Flexor digitorum longus
- Peroneus longus

Superficial layer

- Sternocleidomastoid
- Trapezius
- Infraspinatus
- Deltoid
- Triceps
- Latissimus dorsi
- Brachioradialis
- Flexor carpi ulnaris
- Extensor carpi ulnaris
- Gluteus medius
- Gluteus maximus
- Iliotibial tract
- Biceps femoris
- Semitendinosus
- Semimembranosus
- Gastrocnemius
- Soleus
- Achilles tendon

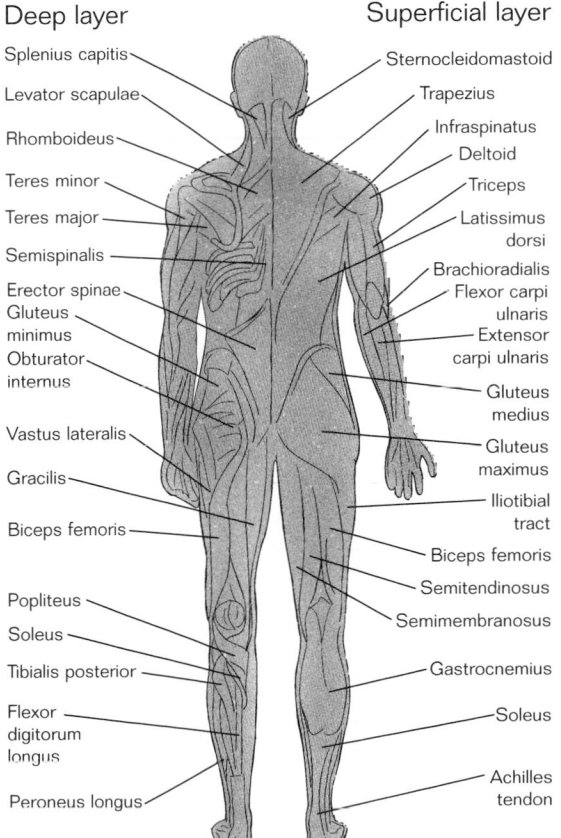

THE DIGESTIVE SYSTEM

THE RESPIRATORY SYSTEM

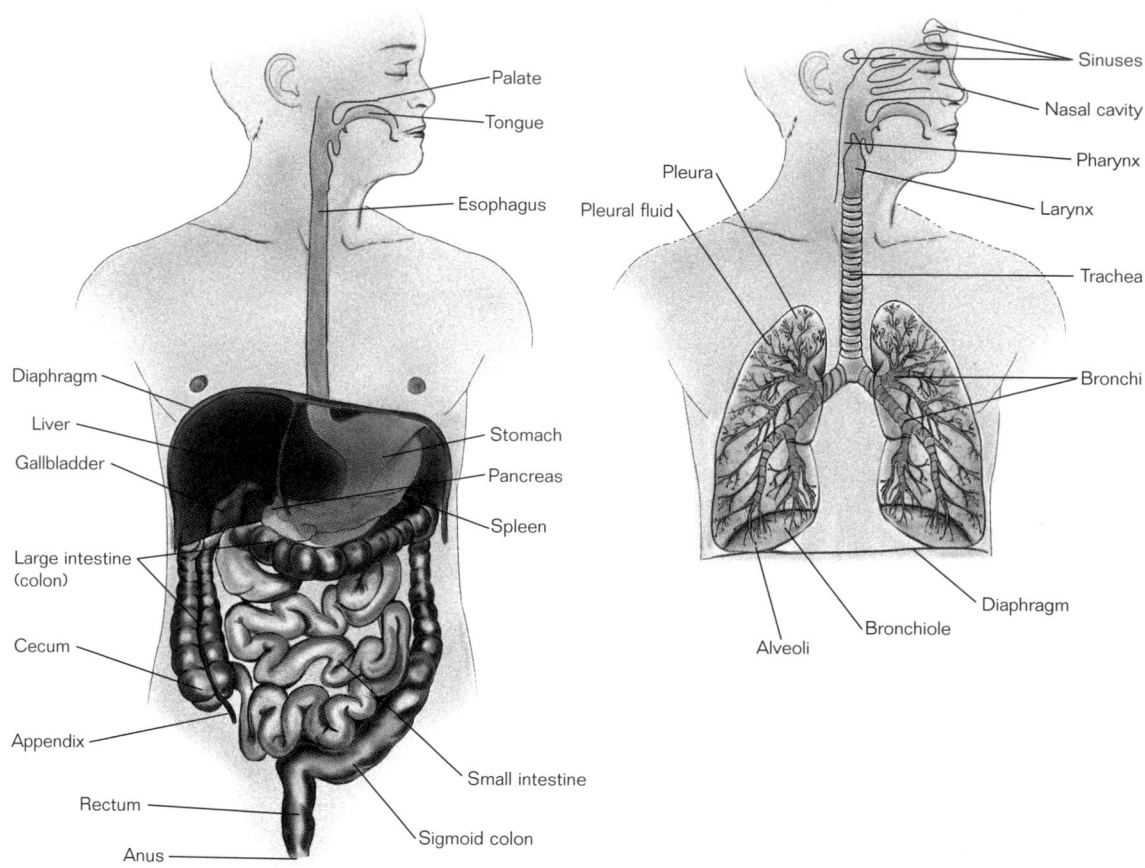

THE SCIENCE OF TAXONOMY

Taxonomy, more recently known as systematics, is the science of naming living organisms in a way that reflects their natural relationships. Although taxonomy dates back to the days of Aristotle, modern taxonomy was developed in the 1700s by Carolus Linnaeus, whose system of binomial nomenclature assigned

Taxonomic Level	Name	Distinguishing Feature
Kingdom	Animalia	Animal
Phylum	Chordata	Spinal cord
Subphylum	Vertebrata	Segmented backbone
Superclass	Tetrapoda	Four limbs
Class	Mammalia	Suckle young
Subclass	Theria	Live birth
Infraclass	Eutheria	Placenta
Order	Primates	Most highly developed
Superfamily	Hominoidea	Humanlike
Family	Hominidae	Two-legged
Genus	Homo	Human
Species	Sapiens	Modern human

to each organism a two-word Latin name designating its genus and species.

Biologists now classify life on Earth into a hierarchy of groups of related organisms. These groups are called *taxa* (singular, *taxon*). From most inclusive to least inclusive, the taxa are called *kingdom, phylum* (plural, *phyla*), *class, order, family, genus* (plural, *genera*), and *species*. Intermediate taxonomic levels are occasionally created at any level by using the prefixes *super-, sub-,* and *infra-*. The table on page 36 shows the taxonomy of modern humans.

THE ANIMAL KINGDOM

The kingdoms of living organisms are divided into several phyla, classes, orders, and families. The examples below discuss vertebrates in terms of orders. Invertebrates are then discussed according to phyla.

THE ORDERS OF MAMMALS

More than one million different species of animals exist in the world. All animals with backbones, including humans, are chordates. That is, in the language of taxonomy, they belong to the phylum Chordata. Their subphylum is Vertebrata, meaning that their backbones are segmented. Mammals, members of the class Mammalia of vertebrate animals that includes humans, are the most highly advanced organisms on Earth. Warm-blooded and hairy, they have four-chambered hearts and relatively large brains. All but two species suckle their young.

The approximately 4,000 species of mammals are divided into 26 orders. Ten of these live in North America. Some orders include a wide range of animals; for example, shrews, lemurs, marmosets, monkeys, apes, and humans are all primates, one order of the class of mammals. Other orders are made up of only one sort of creature; order Chiroptera, for example, consists of 18 families of bats.

The Latin names of the orders of mammals given here are followed by their common names and the families that make up each order. Examples of the various types of animals included in each family also are given.

SUBCLASS PROTOTHERIA (MONOTREMES, OR EGG-LAYING ANIMALS)

Order Monotremata (egg-laying mammals)

These more primitive mammals make up the families *Tachyglossidae* (echidnas, also called spiny anteaters) and *Ornithorhynchidae* (platypuses).

SUBCLASS THERIA (ALL OTHER ORDERS OF LIVING MAMMALS)

INFRACLASS METATHERIA (MARSUPIALS)

Order Dasyuromorphia

This order has three families, two represented by a single living species. The Tasmanian tiger (family *Thylacinidae),* a larger carnivorous, wolflike animal, may in fact now be extinct. The numbat, or banded anteater (family *Myrmecobiidae)* feeds on ants and termites and has no pouch for carrying its young. The third family *(Dasyuridae)* are insectivorous and carnivorous marsupials, and include the marsupiak mice and the Tasmanian devil.

Order Didelphimorphia

This order includes the earliest marsupials known, dating back about 90 million years ago. Most are omnivorous (although some are fruit- or insect-eating) and most do not have pouches for carrying their young. Living forms include the Virginia opossum.

Order Diprotodontia

The families *Phascolarctidae* (koalas), *Vombatidae* (wombats), *Phalangeridae* (possums and cuscuses), *Petauridae* (gliders), and *Macropodidae* (kangaroo-like marsupials) are mainly herbivorous. The pygmy possums (family *Burramyidae)* and some gliders, on the other hand, are insectivorous. The honey possums (family *Tarsipedidae*), as their name implies, feed on pollen and nectar.

Biological World

Order Microbiotheria (monito del monte)

This order has only one living species (family *Microbiotheridae*), a small pouched and insectivorous marsupial that constructs nests in thickets of bamboo in the beech forests of southern Chile and Argentina.

Order Notoryctemorphia (marsupial mole)

This order has only one living species (family *Notoryctidae*). Resembling the true moles and having large foreclaws and a tough leathery shield on its nose, it literally swims through Australian sand dunes.

Order Paucituberculata (shrew opossums)

There is only one family (*Caenolestidae*) of these small pouchless mammals, which are ground-dwelling and strongly insectivorous.

Koalas and humans are the only animals with unique prints. Koala prints cannot be distinguished from human fingerprints.

Order Peramelemorphia

This order includes the only marsupials—bandicoots (family *Peramelidae*) and the bilbies (family *Thylacomyidae*)—to have an advanced chorioallantoic placenta like those of the placental mammals. Small- to medium-sized, they use their elongate muzzles to feed chiefly on insects and other small animals.

INFRACLASS EUTHERIA (PLACENTALS)

Order Artiodactyla (even-toed hoofed animals)

Hoofed animals with an even number of toes include those that ruminate, or digest their food in four-chamber stomachs and chew cuds, and those that do not ruminate. Those that ruminate are the families *Girrafidae* (giraffes), *Cervidae* (deer, moose, reindeer, elk), *Antilocapridae* (pronghorn antelope), and *Bovidae* (cattle, bison, yaks, waterbucks, wildebeest, gazelles, springboks, sheep, musk oxen, goats). *Nonruminators* include the families Suidae (pigs), *Tayassuidae* (peccaries), *Hippopotamidae* (hippopotamuses), and *Camelidae* (camels, llamas).

Order Carnivora (meat eaters)

There are two suborders of these toe-footed creatures. They include the *Canidae* (wolves, dogs, jackals, foxes), *Ursidae* (bears, giant pandas), *Procyonidae* (coatis, raccoons, lesser pandas), and *Mustelidae* (martens, weasels, skunks, otters), which are all part of one superfamily characterized by long snouts and unretractable claws; and *Felidae* (cats, lions, cheetahs, leopards), *Hyaenidae* (hyenas), and *Viverridae* (mongooses, civets), all of which have retractable claws.

Order Cetacea (whales and porpoises)

Two suborders of order Cetacea are the toothed whales, which have regular conical teeth, and the baleen, or whalebone, whales, which have irregular whalebone surfaces instead of teeth. Toothed whales include the families *Physeteridae* (sperm whales), *Monodontidae* (narwhals, belugas), *Phocoenidae* (porpoises), and *Delphinidae* (dolphins, killer whales). Baleens are in the family *Eschrichtiidae* (gray whales), *Balaenidae* (right whales), or *Balaenoptridae* (fin-backed whales, humpback whales).

Order Chiroptera (bats)

There are two suborders of bats, the only mammals that can fly. Suborder *Megachiroptera* contains one family, the *Pteropodidae* (flying foxes, Old World fruit bats). Suborder *Microchiroptera* contains 17 families, including *Rhinopomatidae* (mouse-tailed bats), *Emballonuridae* (sheath-tailed bats), *Craseonycteridae* (hog-nosed or butterfly bats), *Noctilionidae* (bulldog or fisherman bats), *Nycteridae* (slit-faced bats), *Megadermatidae* (false vampire bats), and *Rhinolophidae* (horseshoe bats).

Order Dermoptera (colugos or flying lemurs)

These gliding tree mammals from Asia do not fly and are not lemurs, but they are known as flying lemurs, or family *Cynocephalidae*.

Order Hyracoidae (hyraxes, dassies)

Order Hyracoidae is one of three orders that has only one modern family remaining. *Procavia capensis* (the African rock hyrax) is one of nine living species in the family *Procaviidae.*

Order Insectivora (insect eaters)

The three members are the families *Talpidae* (moles), *Soricidae* (shrews), and *Erinaceidae* (hedgehogs).

Order Lagomorpha (pikas, hares, and rabbits)

Two families make up this order: *Ochotonidae* (pikas) and *Leporidae* (hares and rabbits of all sorts).

Order Macroscelidea (elephant shrews)

This order, represented by the family *Macroscelididae,* was once considered part of the order Insectivora. The elephant shrew has well-developed eyes and ears and a narrow, flexible, and elongate (but not retractable) trunklike snout that it uses to locate insect prey.

Order Perissodactyla (odd-toed hoofed animals)

The two suborders, Hippomorpha and Ceratomorpha, include creatures that have an odd number of toes. Families in this order are the *Equidae* (horses, donkeys, zebras), the *Tapiridae* (tapirs), and the *Rhinocerotidae* (rhinoceroses).

Order Pholidata (pangolins)

Family *Manidae* (pangolins) is the sole family in this order.

Order Pinnipedia (seals and walruses)

In the fin-footed order, there are *Otariidae* (eared seals, sea lions), *Odobenidae* (walruses), and *Phocidae* (earless seals).

Order Primates (primates)

The order to which people belong is divided into two suborders: the Prosimii, who have longer snouts than their relatives; and the Anthropoidae. The first group includes the families *Tupaiidae* (tree shrew), *Lemuridae* (lemurs), *Daubentonliidae* (aye-ayes), *Lorisidae* (lorises, pottos), and *Tarsiidae* (tarsiers). The anthropoids include the families *Callitrichidae* (marmosets), *Cebidae* (New World monkeys), *Cercopithecidae* (baboons, Old World monkeys), *Hylobatidae* (gibbons), *Pongidae* (gorillas, chimpanzees, orangutans), and *Hominidae* (human beings).

Order Proboscidea (elephants)

Large enough to have an order all to itself is family *Elephantidae.*

Order Rodentia (gnawing mammals)

Order Rodentia, containing the most prolific mammals, includes three suborders. It takes in the families *Aplodontidae* (mountain beavers), *Sciuridae* (chipmunks, squirrels, marmots), *Cricetidae* (field mice, lemmings, muskrats, hamsters, gerbils), *Muridae* (Old World mice, rats), *Heteromyidae* (New World mice), *Geomyidae* (gophers), and *Dipodidae* (jerboas).

Order Scandentia (tree shrews)

This order, represented by the single family *Tupaiidae,* was once considered part of the order Insectivora. The squirrel-like tree shrew has a long snout and feeds mainly on insects and fruit.

Order Sirenia (dugongs and manatees)

The families *Trichechidae* (manatees) and *Dugongidae* (dugongs and other sea cows) make up the order Sirenia.

Order Tubulidentata (aardvarks)

Another mammal in an order by itself is family *Orycteropodidae.*

Order Xenarthra Edentata (toothless mammals)

Three families of mammals get by without teeth: *Dasypodidae* (armadillos), *Bradypodidae* (sloths), and *Myrmecophagidae* (hairy anteaters).

THE PHYLA OF INVERTEBRATES

Invertebrates are members of the animal kingdom with no spinal column, or backbone. They make up about 95 percent of all animal species. There are 20 phyla of invertebrates, the 2 largest being Arthropoda and Mollusca. Following are some of the phyla of invertebrates and descriptions of their members.

Phylum Annelida (segmented worms)

Also called annelid worms, this phylum includes earthworms, leeches, and marine worms. Annelid worms have soft bodies, are symmetrical, and can be anywhere from $1/32$ of an inch (half a millimeter) to 10 feet (3 meters) in length.

Phylum Arthropoda (arthropods)

This is the largest phylum of invertebrates, as well as the one with the most creatures; almost 80 percent of all animal species are arthropods. Arthropods have segmented bodies covered by external skeletons, called *exoskeletons,* which are molted from time to time to allow for growth. Their appendages ("arms" and "legs") are paired. Among the animals in this phylum are spiders, horseshoe crabs, crustaceans, insects, and centipedes.

Phylum Coelenterata (coelenterates)

Mostly marine invertebrates, coelenterates have three-layered body walls, tentacles, primitive nervous systems, and special stinger cells to protect themselves. Animals in this phylum include jellyfish, sea anemones, and corals.

Phylum Echinodermata (echinoderms)

Another marine invertebrate, the echinoderm, lives on the floor of the sea. Echinoderms are headless and have tube feet and external skeletons just below the surface of the skin. They can regenerate virtually any part of their bodies. Starfish, sea urchins, sand dollars, and sea cucumbers are some of the members of this phylum.

Go to "Major Zoos and Aquariums" in chapter 11; "Animal Highlights of the Most Popular National Wildlife Refuges" in chapter 24

Phylum Platyhelminthes (flatworms)

As their name implies, these organisms are basically flat, soft-bodied, and symmetrical. These very primitive creatures come in two varieties: an aquatic group that includes planarians and a parasitic one that counts flukes and tapeworms among its members.

Phylum Mollusca (mollusks)

Most mollusks live inside shells and reside in the water. They have soft, unsegmented bodies and a powerful foot that enables them to move around. Clams, oysters, scallops, bivalves, octopuses, and squid are mollusks.

Phylum Nematoda (roundworms)

These wormlike animals have an outer coat made of noncellular material and a fluid-filled chamber that separates their body walls from their insides. They live both in water and on land. Among their number are rotifers, nematodes, and horsehair worms.

Phylum Porifera (sponges)

Porifera is the most primitive multicellular phylum. Sponges live mostly in colonies in the water, attached to rocks. They are basically sacs taking in water through small holes; their skeletons are formed from hard substances that become stuck in their body walls.

EXTINCT ANIMALS

Extinction has happened to species and subspecies throughout the time creatures have lived on this planet. The most well known cases involved the "great dying" of the dinosaurs some 50 to 75 million years ago.

If creatures great and small have in fact been dying off throughout the ages, why is there suddenly concern about animals becoming extinct? Isn't extinction part of the natural order of things?

The answer is no, at least not on the scale it has occurred in recent times. Over most of the last 300 years, the rate of extinction of species was about one per year. At present, the rate of species extinction is at least a thousand times as great as that. This biodepletion is most rapid in tropical forests, which, though they cover only 6 percent of the Earth's land surface, shelter at least 50 percent of all species.

The two hemispheres of a dolphin's brain operate independently. For 8 hours, the entire brain is awake. The left side then sleeps for eight hours. When it wakes up, the right side sleeps for 8 hours. Thus the dolphin gets 8 hours sleep without ever having to stop physically.

The cause of this rapid acceleration in the rate of extinctions is human activity. With some species, like the dodo, the extinction was unintentional: people introduced predators to the dodo's island home where previously there had been none. Other creatures, such as the Eastern buffalo, were purposefully killed off by human beings who wanted to "make room" for themselves.

In the late 20th century, extinctions are more likely to be a result of human activity. Rural landfills take in urban garbage, open land is blacktopped, factories produce toxins as by-products, and engineers alter waterways. These activities all have a direct impact on the ecosystems that support animal life.

A major cause of the extinction of species in tropical forests is the number of impoverished farmers who are moving into and clearing the forests. Species also suffer from climatic change—the planetary warming from the buildup of carbon dioxide and other greenhouse gases in the global atmosphere.

Increased awareness of the fragile links of interdependence among all of Earth's creatures, and of the impact that human activities can have on those creatures, have led some to hope that the latest era of "great dying" may soon stop. It remains to be seen, however, if the forces already in motion can be stopped in time to save the hundreds of species that teeter on the brink of extinction.

Listed here are the number of different animals thought to be extinct as of the mid-1990s and the popular names of those animals. Exact figures are difficult to determine because endangered species often make the transition to extinction quickly and without notice. Occasionally populations of animals thought to be extinct are discovered to be extant (in existence). In these lists, the number of varieties is in parentheses.

BIRDS

Akioloa (4)
Alauwahio (2)
Amazon (3)
Bonin night heron
Caracara
Chatham Island bellbird
Chatham Island fernbird
Conure (2)
Courser
Delalande's coucal
Dodo (2)
Duck (2)
Elephant bird
Emu (2)
Eskimo curlew
Finch (5)

Flycatcher (2)
Gadwall
Great amakihi
Great auk
Grosbeak (2)
Guadalupe flicker
Guadeloupe rufous-sided towhee
Heath hen
Huia
Ivory-billed woodpecker
Jamaican pauraqué
Kioea
Kusaie crake
Laysan apapane
Laysan millerbird
Lord Howe Island blackbird
Lord Howe Island fantail

Macaw (4)
Mamo (2)
Merganser
Moas (15)
New Caledonian lorikeet
Norfolk Island kaka
Nukupuu (3)
O-O (3)
Oahu akepa
Omao (3)
Ostrich, Arabian
Owl (10)
Painted vulture
Parakeet (8)
Parrot (3)
Petrel
Pigeon (7)

continues

Quail (2)
Quelili
Rail (17)
Réunion fody
Ryukyu kingfisher
Saint Kitts Puerto Rican
    bullfinch
Sandpiper (2)
São Tomé grosbeak
Serpent eagle
Shelduck
Solitaire (2)
Sparrow (3)
Spectacled cormorant
Starling (6)
Tanna dove
Thrush (2)
Towhee
Ula-ai-hawane
White eye (2)
White gallinule
Wren (6)

FISH

Alvord cutthroat
Cisco (2)
Chub (2)
Clear Lake splittail
Killifish (2)
Lake Ontario kiyi
Lake Titicaca orestias
Miller Lake lamprey
Minnow (2)
New Zealand grayling
Pupfish (2)
Shiner (3)
Spinedace (2)

Sucker (4)
Trout (2)
Utah Lake sculpin

MAMMALS

Agouti (2)
Arizona jaguar
Atlantic gray whale
Aurochs
Badlands bighorn sheep
Bali tiger
Bandicoot (4)
Bat (6)
Bear (3)
Blue buck
Buffalo (2)
Burchell's zebra
Caribbean monk seal
Caucasian wisent
Christmas Island musk shrew
Dawson's caribou
Elk (2)
Gopher (3)
Greenland tundra reindeer
Hartebeest (2)
Hispaniolan hexolobodon
Hutia (5)
Ibex (2)
Isolobodon (2)
Lion (2)
Mouse (2)
Nesophont (6)
Penasco chipmunk
Potoroo (3)
Puerto Rican caviomorph
Puerto Rican ground sloth

Puerto Rican hutia
Puerto Rican paca
Quagga
Queen Charlotte caribou
Quemi (2)
Rat (12)
Rufous gazelle
Schomburgk's deer
Sea mink
Shamanu
Southern California kit fox
Steller's sea cow
Syrian onager
Tarpan
Vole (2)
Wallaby (2)
Warrah
Wisconsin cougar
Wolf (10)

REPTILES

Ameiva (2)
Galliwasp
Gecko (2)
Iguana (2)
Lizard (4)
Racer snake (2)
Round Island boa
Skink (3)
Tortoise (11)
Tree snake (2)

AMPHIBIANS

Coqui (2)
Leopard frog (2)
Palestinian painted frog

PETS

Though a wide variety of animals are kept as pets, the overwhelming majority are dogs and cats. Veterinarians and other animal-care experts suggest a number of basic rules to be considered by everyone contemplating pet ownership.

CHOOSING A PET

Do research on the kind of animal you want to get. Make sure you have the ability and finances to house and feed the animal (especially relevant with large dogs) and to pay for its medical care. Don't buy animals as gifts. If the recipient is not willing and able to care for the animal, it will be a disaster for all concerned.

When choosing a dog, don't base your choice on looks without considering the purpose for which it was bred (e.g., don't turn a hunting dog into a house dog). Make sure you have enough time to spend with a puppy. Puppies shouldn't be left alone for more than 3 or 4 hours. Make sure the puppy is bright and alert, though not hyperactive. Check for any signs of ill health and have the puppy examined by a veterinarian before accepting it. Don't separate a puppy from its mother and littermates before it is 6 weeks old.

Go to
"Traveling with Pets" in chapter 24

When choosing a kitten, try to meet its parents and observe their temperament. A kitten should respond to attention and not mind being held. It should have a healthy-looking coat and pink gums, and there should be no evidence of any discharge from its eyes or ears. Obtain a certificate of vaccinations and have the kitten examined by a veterinarian.

TRAINING

Never hit your dog or yell at it—such an action will only make the dog afraid or resentful. Because the dog craves affection and approval, a firm "No!" or "Bad dog!" is more than enough. A quick tug on your dog's leash or collar, however, is permissible to discourage unwanted behavior, especially with larger dogs. Using your leg to push your dog off balance is an acceptable way of teaching it not to jump on people.

Issue reprimands immediately so that your dog associates your displeasure with a specific offense. Dragging your dog to the scene after the fact does no good.

When toilet training your dog, don't put pieces of newspaper down indoors, which will only make the dog think it's all right to eliminate in the house. Take your dog out first thing in the morning, 15 minutes after each meal, after vigorous play, and just before bedtime. Praise your dog for eliminating outside. Don't allow your dog access to the entire house until it is properly trained.

All dogs should be obedience-trained so that they respond to five basic commands: heel, sit, down, stay, and come. This is especially important with large aggressive breeds such as Dobermans, Rottweilers, and German shepherds. Dogs should be praised when they respond properly, and training should be incorporated into your dog's daily routine so that it remains effective. If you can't handle the job yourself, seek professional help. Options include group obedience lessons, a private trainer, and board and training kennels.

When disciplining a kitten, say "No!" in a deep voice. Shaking your kitten gently by the scruff of the neck as its mother would do, is permissible. Squirting your cat with water can be effective in discouraging unwanted behavior, but it must be done while the offense is being committed.

When a snail hatches from an egg, it is a miniature adult, shell and all. The shell grows with the snail, and the snail never leaves its shell.

Cats instinctively bury their stools; thus, getting your cat to use a litter box should not be hard. If your kitten eliminates outside the box, putting the stool in there will usually convey the message. Use absorbent clay litters and remove the stools every day with a slotted spoon. Replace the litter every third day and wash the pan with hot water, soap, and chlorine bleach. Keep on using the same type of litter once your cat is used to it.

SPAYING AND NEUTERING

Experts advise pet owners against breeding their animals at home because of the medical expenses involved (immunizations for the litter and possible health problems on the mother's part during or after pregnancy) and because of the possibility of not finding homes for the offspring. More than 15 million dogs and cats are put down every year because of overpopulation.

Neutering does not change a male dog's personality or his instinct to protect his home and those he loves. It simply makes him less aggressive toward other male dogs and stops him from marking his territory with urine.

Female cats will go into heat every 2 to 3 weeks if they are not mated. If they are going to be spayed, it should be done before the first onset of heat. The procedure should not be performed, however, before the cat is 5 or 6 months old.

Neutering of male cats will prevent roaming, spraying, and fighting. The operation can be performed either before or after sexual maturity.

Biological World

PETS AND CHILDREN

Cats generally mix well with children and will tolerate treatment from a child that they would not accept from an adult. Experts recommend, however, that kittens not be introduced into a household where there are very young children who may frighten the cat with loud noise or rough handling. Parents should wait until the child is old enough to understand the animal's needs and play an active role in caring for it.

Relations between dogs and children should be carefully considered. For pet owners with young children, experts recommend a choice of breeds known for their gentle disposition and patience. These breeds include the basenji, bassett hound, beagle, boxer, bulldog, collie, Dalmatian, springer spaniel, German shepherd, golden retriever, Great Dane, Irish setter, Labrador retriever, and standard poodle. Less desirable breeds include the Afghan hound, Chow Chow, dachshund, Doberman, miniature schnauzer, Rottweiler, Weimaraner, and most varieties of terrier.

When a new baby is introduced into a household that already has a dog, a number of steps can be taken to prepare the pet for this dramatic change:

1. As the birth of your child approaches, prepare your dog gradually for the reduced attention that he or she is bound to receive by gradually modifying the amount of time you spend with the dog.
2. Bring home an article of your baby's clothing from the hospital and let your dog get used to the scent.
3. Praise your dog when the baby is around, so it associates good things with the baby.
4. Closely supervise your baby when it begins to crawl and interact with your dog. The dog will not necessarily recognize the baby as a human and may feel threatened.

NUTRITION

Allergies, gastrointestinal disorders, kidney disease, cancer, and other pet ailments can be linked to junk in pet foods. (Some dog foods, for example, contain grain hulls and peanut shells.) The best bet is to buy premium brands with meat-based protein sources.

Don't mix brands of pet food together, because each brand has its own balance of proteins, vitamins, and minerals.

Avoid low-quality foods, many of which contain materials that pets will be unable to digest. These undigestible materials will pass right through the system without providing any nutritional benefit.

Avoid soft, moist, processed diets wrapped in cellophane. They have little nutritional value and cause a disease of the red blood cells in cats.

Don't overfeed pets. Veterinarians estimate that three of five dogs are overweight. Dogs should not be more than 20 percent over the ideal weight for their particular breed. High-quality, low-calorie food can help in this area.

PET STAINS

In addition to removing the stain itself, remove any lingering odor so that your pet is not drawn back to the spot and prompted to urinate there again. To do this, it is necessary to use an enzyme odor remover, which breaks down urine molecules into carbon dioxide and water. Ordinary household cleaners will often leave enough traces of odor for your pet's sensitive olfactory organs to detect.

See also "Stain Removal: Urine" in chapter 19.

IMMUNIZATION
DOGS

5–8 weeks	Canine distemper-measles, CPI (parinfluenza)
8–16 weeks	DHLPP (distemper, hepatitis, leptospirosis, parainfluenza, parvovirus)
14–16 weeks	Rabies
12 months and then annually	DHLPP
12 months and then every three months	Rabies

Each locality may have specific requirements for immunizations and frequency of booster shots, and dog owners should check with their veterinarians. In some areas, for example, vaccination against Lyme disease, coronavirus, and kennel cough may also be necessary. In general, keep your dog away from strange dogs before the vaccination series is complete.

CATS

Any age	Upper respiratory infections (2–3 vaccinations 2–4 weeks apart)
8–12 weeks	Distemper (2–3 vaccinations 2–4 weeks apart)
	Rabies (2 vaccinations 2–4 weeks apart)
	Feline leukemia (2 vaccinations 2–4 weeks apart; 1 vaccination 2–4 months later)
12 weeks or older	Distemper (1 vaccination, then a yearly booster shot)
	Rabies (1 vaccination, then a yearly booster)
	Feline leukemia (1 vaccination, then a yearly booster shot)
	Upper respiratory infections (1 vaccination, then a yearly booster shot)

A stool sample should be checked whenever shots are given.

ANIMAL FIRST AID

Animals, like people, suffer medical problems. Emergency and nonemergency ailments and traumas require quick attention to prevent serious situations from turning into life-threatening ones.

The meow of a cat is actually two distinctive sounds. The "me" is a friendly greeting, but the "ow" means "I'm willing to defend myself." Although cats often meow at humans, they rarely meow at other cats.

Some problems—bleeding that cannot be stopped or convulsions, for instance—require the immediate attention of an expert in veterinary medicine. Many other problems, however, can be treated by the animal's owner.

The following are some common animal ailments and injuries. The symptoms and treatments for each are described. As with any medical condition, if the symptoms persist or the animal's owner is unsure about the nature of the problem, professional assistance should be sought.

BROKEN BONES

Symptoms   Some bone breaks show obvious symptoms: twisted or distorted limbs; or, in the case of a compound fracture, bone fragments sticking through the skin. Less apparent breaks cause great pain and discomfort. The animal will cry or bite when the affected area is touched; will lie around, often on the affected area; and will usually not walk, although in some cases it will walk despite the break, notably when the pelvis is broken. The fracture will not bear weight. Swelling of the affected area within 24 hours can be expected from any sort of fracture.

Treatment   Treatment of compound fractures by a veterinarian should be sought as soon as possible. Other breaks should be treated by a veterinarian within 24 hours. Apply an ice pack or cold wet compress to the affected area; change regularly. Protect the animal from further injury by confining it to a small room. Apply a temporary splint to broken limbs to avoid further dislocation.

See also "Treatment for Health Emergencies: Fractures, Dislocations, and Sprains" in chapter 17.

BURNS

Symptoms   All burns are painful to the touch. *Electrical burns* are the most serious and can cause heart attacks and death. The burned area will show seared flesh, reddened skin, lesions, and blisters. The animal may suffer respiratory distress; paleness or blueness, especially in lips, gums, and eyelid linings; rigidity in limbs; glassy stare; collapse; and shock. *Thermal burns* cause a singed or charred area; the exposed skin is reddened or inflamed, and the wound is warm or hot to the touch. *Friction burns* are similar in appearance to thermal burns, but the skin is chafed or scraped and has bare spots; bare skin is rubbed raw, is reddish in color, and is irritated or inflamed. The trauma causing the friction burn may leave cuts, lacerations, or embedded foreign matter.

Treatment   Depending on the type and extent of the burn, it can often be treated at home. Electrical burns can stop an animal's heart and must be treated immediately by a veterinarian; if shock occurs, keep the animal warm with heating pads or hot water bottles and a blanket or heavy coat and seek veterinary treatment immediately. Thermal burns can be treated topically by applying the jelly-like substance from an aloe plant, a solution made from Domeboro® (available at most pharmacies), or vitamin E oil. Friction burns can be treated in the same way as thermal burns; however, if foreign matter is embedded, or the burn does not respond to treatment, the animal should be taken to a veterinarian.

See also "Treatment for Health Emergencies: Burns" and "Electric Shock" in chapter 17 and "Home Remedies: Burns—First Degree" in chapter 18.

CAT DISEASES

Symptoms   Four major diseases affect the well-being of cats. *Cat distemper* induces high fever, lethargy, vomiting, and diarrhea; young kittens can develop distemper very quickly and will often die of it without exhibiting symptoms. *Rhinotracheitis* causes fever, sneezing, loss of appetite, and dehydration; additional symptoms can include discharge from eyes and nose, congestion, and swelling of membranes in the respiratory tract. *Calici virus* is characterized by sneezing and discharge from the eyes and nose; it may cause fever, lethargy, loss of appetite, dehydration, and ulcers on the tongue. *Pneumonitis* usually causes labored breathing, sneezing, coughing, snorting, wheezing,

and listlessness; it may induce a loss of body fluids and very high temperatures.

Treatment   Three of these diseases—cat distemper, rhinotracheitis, and calici virus—can be prevented by annual vaccinations. All four must be treated as quickly as possible by a veterinarian if symptoms are present. Professional treatment will, in most cases, effect a cure.

CONSTIPATION

Symptoms   The animal struggles or strains during a bowel movement without passing a stool, avoids food, and becomes nervous or irritated.

Treatment   Feed the animal brans, cereal foods, vegetables (peas, carrots, corn), or kibble; use infant-size glycerine suppositories or soap suppositories; give an enema if the animal will allow it; add a small amount of stool softener, such as Metamucil®, to food; give mineral oil or milk of magnesia, but dosages should depend on size and type of animal (consult a veterinarian).

See also "Home Remedies: Constipation" in chapter 18.

DENTAL DISORDERS

Symptoms   Tartar, a brown crust, appears on teeth, starting at the gum line; tooth enamel erodes, especially in cats; bone fragments, foreign matter, food particles, or hair accumulate on teeth; bad breath is present. *Throat* or *mouth infections* cause coughing and discharges from mouth or nose. *Gingivitis* develops when tartar or dirty teeth are untreated. *Uremia* can cause blackish tartar, bad breath, and extraordinary thirst.

Treatment   Clean the animal's teeth monthly with a mixture of one teaspoon salt or hydrogen peroxide to half a cup of water; apply to teeth with a cotton swab or soft toothbrush. Include hard food, such as kibble, in the animal's diet; provide hard things for the animal to chew on. Infections, gingivitis, or uremia should be treated by a veterinarian.

DIARRHEA

Symptoms   The animal passes liquid stool during bowel movement; there may be abnormal coloration of stool.

Treatment   Remove grease, oils, and milk from the animal's diet; avoid high-fiber foods, kibble, and dry catmeal; feed the animal a mix of 1 part cooked hamburger, drained of grease, and 1 part rice. If diarrhea results from ingestion of foreign matter (from teething or eating plants, soap, or other household materials), treat it with small doses of Pepto-Bismol® or Kaopectate®. If symptoms persist for more than 24 hours, or if blood is present in stool, consult a veterinarian.

DOG DISEASES

Symptoms   A number of conditions affect only dogs. *Canine distemper* causes severe diarrhea and may cause high fever, discharge from eyes and nose, thickening of foot pads, coughing, muscle contractions, convulsions, and pneumonia. *Infectious canine hepatitis* usually results in fever, lethargy, and congestion of the mucous membranes; it also can cause loss of appetite and insatiable thirst. *Leptospirosis* is characterized by high fever, lethargy, loss of appetite, congestion in the whites of the eyes, and possibly pain in walking, jaundice, vomiting, and diarrhea. *Infectious canine tracheobronchitis (kennel cough)* causes high fever and severe dry coughing spasms.

Treatment   All four of these diseases can be prevented by annual vaccinations. If a dog is not vaccinated, early diagnosis of the symptoms of each disease is imperative. None of these diseases can be treated at home; take the dog to a veterinarian as soon as possible.

PARASITES, EXTERNAL

Symptoms   Fleas, ticks, lice, maggots, and mites are common external parasites that prey on animals. All cause animals to scratch excessively, which can lead to hair loss. *Fleas* are tiny brown insects that move through the animal's coat. *Ticks* are small, round, dark-colored insects with hard shells that attach themselves to an animal's skin. *Lice* are small, dark-gray insects that remain in one place on an animal's body. *Maggots* look like small worms. *Mites,* which are invisible to the unaided eye, characteristically cause skin and ear irritation.

Treatment   External parasites can be readily eliminated and controlled with commercially available powders, baths, sprays, and dips. Check the labels of such treatments carefully to be sure they are appropriate for use on your animal and that they will control the parasite in question. Fleas can be controlled with flea collars, sprays, powders, baths, or dips; treat animal and surrounding furniture and carpets to eliminate infestations. Ticks can be pulled off by hand; the animal should then be treated with spray, powder, or bath to eliminate unseen ticks; treat surrounding furniture and carpets to eliminate infestations. Lyme disease, which is spread by ticks, can be prevented by vaccination. Lice can be treated with the same potions that work on fleas and ticks. Maggots are an increasingly rare parasite that, if present, should be treated by a veterinarian. Mites can cause recurring mange in dogs, or other recurring skin conditions in other animals; any recurring condition should be treated by a veterinarian.

See also "Treatment for Health Emergencies: Insect Bites" in chapter 17.

PARASITES, INTERNAL

Symptoms   All internal parasites drain an animal's natural defenses, leaving it susceptible to infections and diseases. All are likely to cause loss of appetite and lethargy. *Tapeworms* leave visible, light-colored segments (that look like rice kernels in stools), around sleeping areas, under the animal's tail, or near its anus. *Roundworms* look like spaghetti; they are light yellow, 2 to 4 inches long, have slightly pointed ends, and can be seen in stools or vomit. *Hookworms* are almost invisible to the naked eye, but can cause diarrhea (often with blood present), cramps, pale gums and lips, a dry coat, a slight cough, and noticeable weight loss. *Whip-worms* cause symptoms similar to those caused by hookworms, as well as possible inflammation of the colon. *Heartworms* block an animal's arteries, causing tiredness, listlessness, a poor coat, weight loss, and constant panting and coughing. *Coccidia* (one-celled protozoa) cause diarrhea, emaciation, and discharges from the animal's eyes and nose. *Toxoplasmosis* is a parasite that afflicts mostly cats; it frequently presents no symptoms at all.

Treatment   An infestation of internal parasites is a debilitating condition that should be dealt with by a veterinarian. Preventive medications for heartworm are available.

RABIES

Symptoms   Rabies—whose symptoms include fever, loss of appetite, and an inability to swallow that results in drooling—can cause encephalitis, convulsions, or paralysis. One type of rabies causes animals to attack anything that moves (cars, animals, people); another type causes only the other symptoms.

Treatment   Prevention of rabies is possible through regular vaccinations. Once contracted, however, there is no effective treatment for rabies, and the animal will have to be destroyed.

See also "Treatment for Health Emergencies: Animal Bites" in chapter 17.

RESPIRATORY INFECTIONS

Symptoms   Sneezing, coughing, runny eyes, swollen glands, difficulty swallowing, labored breathing, fever.

Treatment   If symptoms such as sneezing, coughing, and runny eyes are present but the animal remains active and eats normally, the condition is probably not serious, and no treatment is needed. A veterinarian should examine the animal if symptoms continue for a while, if the animal becomes lethargic and loses appetite, if there are discharges of pus from its nose, if congestion becomes heavy or labored breathing is continued, or if fever of more than 102°F is present.

SHOCK

Symptoms   Weakness, collapse, pale or muddy-colored gums, fast heartbeat, difficulty breathing, no breathing, dilated pupils, low body temperature.

Treatment   Keep the animal warm by applying heating pads or hot water bottles and wrapping the animal in heavy blankets or coats. Take the animal to a veterinarian at once.

SKIN PROBLEMS

Symptoms   Localized skin conditions cause inflammation or irritation and may cause bald spots of red, raw, or discolored skin. More serious disorders such as moist eczema, wet dermatitis, or acute pruritis cause raw, oozing bald spots that may be damp to the touch or oozing pus. A lump on the animal's skin that does not go away within a few days may be a tumor. Other skin problems can cause dry, flaky skin; an oily coat; and constant biting, licking, or scratching. Symmetrical skin disorders affect both sides of an animal's body equally; a generalized condition affects the animal's whole body.

Treatment   Bald patches of red or raw skin and damp, oozing hot areas should be treated by a veterinarian. Localized inflammation can be treated with soothing topical sprays and lotions. Dry skin or coat can be soaked several times a day with water or a solution made from Domeboro® tablets (available at most pharmacies); small quantities of oil added to the animal's food also will help. Itchiness can be corrected with a solution of 1 part Alpha-Keri® (available from most pharmacies) to 20 or 30 parts water applied with a spray bottle; repeat as needed. A well-balanced diet, with appropriate levels of vitamins, can maintain healthy skin. Any skin condition that does not go away, or that reappears after treatment, should be treated by a veterinarian.

SPRAINS

Symptoms   Sprains usually occur in the joints of an animal's limbs, causing rapid swelling. The affected area will be hot to the touch. The animal will not walk normally, if it walks at all.

Treatment   Apply cold compresses or ice packs gently to the swollen area; keep the area cool for a day or two, changing the compress or ice when necessary. Wrap the affected area snugly with cloth, gauze, or athletic bandages; secure the wrapping to be sure the animal does not scratch or bite it off. Keep the animal quiet, discourage activity, and avoid stairs. For sprains that heal and recur, apply hot towels or compresses; keep the injured area moist and warm for several days. If a sprain does not heal, or pain and swelling continue or are severe, see a veterinarian.

See also "Treatment for Health Emergencies: Fractures, Dislocations, and Sprains" in chapter 17 and "Home Remedies: Sprains and Strains" in chapter 18.

WOUNDS

Symptoms   *Cuts* can be recognized by the presence of smoothly separated tissue and possible bleeding. *Lacerations* result in jaggedly torn skin, bleeding, swelling, irritation, and black or blue discoloration of the skin. *Abrasions* rub or scrape away the outer layers of skin, causing pain, swelling, redness, and heat. *Bruises* or *contusions* leave black-and-blue tissue and swelling.

Treatment   Any serious wound should be treated by a veterinarian if the bleeding will not stop, if blood is gushing out, or if shock is present. For cuts that are bleeding, apply a pressure bandage (clean gauze or cloth wrapped around some padding) pressed firmly but gently against the wound; an ice bag, pressed firmly but gently on the area; or a tourniquet. After the bleeding has been controlled, clean the wound with hydrogen peroxide or Bactine®, and then dry it. Keep skin from wrinkling or bunching, and then apply an antiseptic or antibiotic to a gauze square and wrap snugly in place.

Change the dressing daily and keep the animal from removing it. Lacerations can be treated in the same way as cuts, but an ice bag must be used to reduce swelling and prevent further inflammation. Abrasions require the application of a soothing cream, ointment, or lotion (Solarcaine®, Nupercainal®, Unguentine® ointment, or calamine lotion); a bandage is not needed, but the animal must be kept from licking the treated area. Bruises and contusions are best treated with cold compresses or ice packs.

See also "Treatment for Health Emergencies: Abrasions" and "Black Eyes and Bruises" in chapter 17.

THE PLANT KINGDOM

ORDERS OF PLANTS

There are more than 130 orders of plants. The following list includes some of the most common or important plant orders. The Latin names of the orders of plants given here are followed by their common names. Examples of the various types of plants included in each order are also given.

ORDER ASTERALES

The members of this order belong to a single large family consisting of some 15,000 to 20,000 species. Asterales includes many popular garden ornamentals, including asters, mums, dahlias, daisies, marigolds, sunflowers, and zinnias. Other members are common weeds, such as dandelions, ragweeds, and thistles. Lettuce and safflower are among the economically important members of Asterales. Distribution is worldwide.

ORDER BEGONIALES (BEGONIAS)

This order of flowering plants consists of organisms ranging from small plants to relatively large shrubs. They are distributed mainly in the tropics around the world, but are popular cultivated plants in subtropical and temperate climates as well. There are about 1,000 species of the familiar begonia.

ORDER BETULALES (BIRCHES)

This order of flowering trees and shrubs are dominant in northern temperate and Arctic regions. Many of these plants are economically important. Birches are major sources of cabinet woods, and alders are important soil-builders. Other members of this order include ironwoods, hornbeams, and hazelnuts.

ORDER CACTALES (CACTI)

Cacti are often spiny, fleshy stemmed plants characteristically found in arid and semiarid regions. They are native to the Americas, but are cultivated worldwide for their unusual shapes and striking blossoms.

Some species are useful economically, especially in Mexico and Central and South America. Familiar members of the order include prickly pears, barrel cacti, saguaro, cereus, and opuntia.

ORDER CORNALES (DOGWOODS)

The more than 3,700 members of this order display considerable variety in form. Most of its 10 families are woody flowering plants, mainly shrubs, but several species, such as the ivy, are climbers. Other notable members of the order include dogwoods, sour gums, ginsengs, and parsleys. They are distributed worldwide, but are chiefly found in northern temperate zones.

The oldest living thing in the world is a creosote bush in California's Mojave Desert, whose age is estimated at nearly 12,000 years.

ORDER FABALES

This order is second only to the grasses (Poales) in economic importance. It includes a variety of food products, including beans, peanuts, and peas. Other members, such as alfalfa and clover, provide grazing for animals. More than 20,000 species comprise this order, which can be found worldwide, especially in temperate regions.

ORDER FAGALES (BEECHES)

This order consists exclusively of deciduous or evergreen shrubs and trees, which often form forests that cover wide areas. They are mainly distributed over the Northern Hemisphere. Common members of this order include beeches, oaks, and chestnuts.

ORDER GERANIALES (GERANIUMS)

About 4,000 species comprise this order of flowering plants, which are chiefly tropical in distribution. The order displays considerable variety in size and shape, from small annual plants to trees of the tropical rainforest. Although the order has some value as ornamental plants, it is generally not an economically important plant group. The major exception is flax, the source of a fiber that has been used by humans since prehistoric times.

ORDER JUGLANDES (WALNUTS)

The members of this order are generally large forest trees, found primarily in temperate areas but also in subtropical zones. They are distributed throughout eastern North America, Central America, western South America, and eastern Asia. Walnuts, hickories, and pecans are useful not only for their edible nuts, but for their valuable wood.

ORDER LAURALES (LAURELS)

Members of this order can be found worldwide, with the greatest concentration in the tropics. They are woody, with a simple, alternating leaf structure. Several members of this order are economically useful, such as the avocado, cinnamon, and sassafras trees.

ORDER MAGNOLIALES (MAGNOLIAS)

All members of this order are woody; most are small flowering trees, although the tulip tree can reach a height of 150 feet (46 meters). They are mainly distributed throughout wet, tropical regions, but some species survive in temperate climates. Besides the tulip tree, other common members of this order include magnolias and nutmegs.

ORDER NYMPHAEALES (WATER LILIES)

Not surprisingly, the members of this order are aquatic plants. They are cultivated worldwide for their beauty, but their natural habitats are temperate and tropical regions. Most are perennials.

ORDER OLEALES (OLIVES)

The members of this important order of small, woody flowering plants can be found throughout the world, except in the polar regions. Several families—especially the lilacs, jasmines, privets, and forsythia—are popular ornamental plants. Ashes are a notable source of hardwood timber, while the olive is widely cultivated as a source of olives and olive oil.

ORDER PRIMULALES (PRIMROSES)

This order contains nearly 2,000 species of flowering plants. Two of its three families are entirely composed of trees and shrubs; some of these are climbers or epiphytes (plants that grow on other plants, and are not rooted in soil). The order is important because of its ornamental value. Representative members include cyclamen, primrose, and loosestrife.

ORDER ROSALES (ROSES)

Members of this order are among the most frequently encountered plants in temperate zones around the world. They are especially cultivated for their beauty and hardiness. Some of its members are valuable food plants, including apples, pears, peaches, apricots, and plums. Roses, flowering cherries, spirea, mountain ash, firethorn, and hawthorn are other familiar members of this order.

Go to "Major Botannical Gardens and Arboretums" in chapter 11

BOTANICAL NAMES OF PLANTS

The abbreviation "sp." following a genus indicates that the common name refers to all species of that genus.

Common Name	Botanical Name	Common Name	Botanical Name
Acacia, giraffe	*Acacia giraffae*	Asparagus, garden	*Asparagus officinalis*
Adder's-tongue	*Erythronium sibiricum*	Aspen, European	*Populus tremula*
	Ophioglossum vulgatum islandicum	quaking	*P. tremuloides*
		Aster	*Aster* sp.
Alder, European	*Alnus glutinosa*	Attalea	*Attalea funifera*
hazel	*A. rugosa*	Avocado, American	*Persea americana*
red	*A. ruba*	Balloon vine	*Cardiospermum halicacabum*
Alfalfa	*Medicago sativa*	Balsam, garden	*Impatiens balsamina*
Almond	*Prunus amygdalus*	Barley	*Hordeum vulgare*
Aloe	*Aloe* sp.	Bean, broad	*Vicia faba*
Amaryllis	*Amaryllis* sp.	kidney	*Phaseolus vulgaris*
Angelica	*Angelica polyclada*	sieva	*P. lunatus*
garden	*A. archangelica*	Beech, American	*Fagus grandifolia*
Apple	*Malus pumila*	European	*F. sylvatica*
	M. sylvestris	Beet, common	*Beta vulgaris*
Apricot	*Prunus armeniaca*	Birch, European white	*Betula pendula*
Arborvitae, eastern	*Thuja occidentalis*	paper	*B. papyrifera*
giant	*T. plicata*	sweet	*B. lenta*
Arum, East Asian	*Pinellia ternata*	white	*B. populifolia*
Ash, European	*Fraxinus excelsior*	yellow	*B. lutea*
green	*F. pennsylvanica*	Blackberry	*Rubus* sp.
white	*F. americana*	Bladderpod	*Lesquerella densipila*

continues

Continued

Common Name	Botanical Name	Common Name	Botanical Name
Blood-lily, Katharine	*Haemanthus katharinae*	Cocklebur, oriental	*Xanthium orientale*
Blueberry, highbush	*Vaccinium corymbosum*	Coconut	*Cocos nucifera*
Brake, sword	*Pteris ensiformis*	Coffee, Arabian	*Coffea arabica*
Bryony, white	*Bryonia alba*	Coneflower, pinewoods	*Rudbeckia bicolor*
Buckwheat	*Fagopyrum sagittatum*	Coreopsis, goldenwave	*Coreopsis drummondii*
Buttercup, creeping	*Ranunculus repens*	lance	*C. lanceolata*
Cabbage	*Brassica oleracea*	plains	*C. tinctoria*
	B. oleracea capitata	Corn	*Zea mays*
Kerguelen	*Pringlea antiscorbutica*	Cornflower	*Centaurea cyanus*
Cacao	*Theobroma cacao*	Coronilla, crownvetch	*Coronilla varia*
Calotrope, fantan	*Calotropis procera*	Cosmos	*Cosmos* sp.
Capeberry, South African	*Myrica cordifolia*	Cotton, Levant	*Gossypium herbaceum*
Carpotroche	*Carpotroche brasiliensis*	Sea Island	*G. barbadense*
Carrot	*Daucus carota*	upland	*G. hirsutum*
Cashew	*Anacardium occidentale*	Coventry bells	*Campanula trachelium*
Castor bean	*Ricinus communis*	Cowpea	*Vigna glabra*
Catalpa, Chinese	*Catalpa ovata*	yard-long	*V. sesquipedalis*
northern	*C. speciosa*	common	*V. sinensis*
Cedar	*Cedrus* sp.	Crotalaria	*Crotalaria vitellina*
California incense	*Libocedrus decurrens*	Croton, purging	*Croton tiglium*
Celery, garden	*Apium graveolens dulce*	Cucumber	*Cucumis sativus*
wild	*A. graveolens*	Currant, European black	*Ribes nigrum*
Chaulmoogra tree	*Gynocardia odorata*	red	*R. sativum*
common	*Hydnocarpus anthelmintica*	Cypress, Arizona	*Cupressus arizonica*
wight	*H. wightiana*	bald	*Taxodium distichum*
Cherry, black	*Prunus serotina*	Dahlia	*Dahlia* sp.
mazzard	*P. avium*	Dandelion	*Taraxacum officinale*
pin	*P. pennsylvanica*	Daphne	*Daphne* sp.
Chestnut, Chinese	*Castanea mollissima*	Date	*Phoenix dactylifera*
common horse-	*Aesculus hippocastanum*	Davallia, Fiji	*Davallia fejeensis*
Chickpea, gram	*Cicer arietinum*	Desert willow	*Chilopsis linearis*
Chinaberry	*Melia azedarach*	Dock, curly	*Rumex crispus*
Chrysanthemum, corn	*Chrysanthemum segetum*	Dogbane	*Apocynum* sp.
Pyrenees	*C. maximum*	Dogwood, cornelian cherry	*Cornus mas*
Cinchona, ledgerbark	*Cinchona ledgeriana*	flowering	*C. florida*
Clarkia, rose	*Clarkia elegans*	Dollar plant	*Lunaria annua*
Clover, alsike	*Trifolium hybridum*	Douglas fir	*Pseudotsuga menziesii*
burdock	*T. lappaceum*	common	*P. taxifolia*
crimson	*T. incarnatum*	Eggplant	*Solanum melongena*
Egyptian	*T. alexandrinum*	garden	*S. melongena esculentum*
Persian	*T. resupinatum*	Elm, American	*Ulmus americana*
red	*T. pratense*	Endive	*Cichorium endivia*
strawberry	*T. fragiferum*	Erysimum, plains	*Erysimum asperum*
subterranean	*T. subterraneum*	Eucalyptus	*Eucalyptus* sp.
uckling	*T. dubium*	Euphorbia, snow-on-	*Euphorbia marginata*
yellow sweet	*Melilotus officinalis*	the-mountain	
white	*Trifolium repens*	False-cypress, Lawson's	*Chamaecyparis lawsoniana*
white sweet	*Melilotus alba*	nootka	*C. nootkatensis*
Clubmoss, common	*Lycopodium clavatum*		

Common Name	Botanical Name	Common Name	Botanical Name
Fern, common staghorn	*Platycerium bifurcatum*	reed canary	*Phalaris arundinacea*
common sword	*Nephrolepis exaltata*	Sudan	*Sorghum vulgare sudanense*
filmy	*Hymenophyllum atrovirens*	Hackberry, common	*Celtis occidentalis*
grape	*Botrychium virginianum*	Hart's-tongue	*Phyllitis scolopendrium*
holly	*Crytomium falcatum*	Hemlock, eastern	*Tsuga canadensis*
lady	*Athyrium filix-femina*	western	*T. heterophylla*
maidenhair	*Adiantum pedatum*	Hemp	*Cannabis sativa*
pine	*Anemia adiantifolia*	Hibiscus, kenaf	*Hibiscus cannabinus*
royal	*Osmunda regalis*	Hickory, shagbark	*Carya ovata*
tropical	*Gleichenia flabellata*	Holly, American	*Ilex opaca*
water	*Azolla pinnata*	English	*I. aquifolium*
wood	*Thelypteris normalis*	Hollyhock	*Althaea rosea*
Fescue, alta	*Festuca elatior arundinacea*	Horsetail, common	*Equisetum arvense*
meadow	*F. elatior*	Hyssop, hedge	*Gratiola* sp.
red	*F. rubra*	Indigo	*Indigofera* sp.
Fig	*Ficus carica*	Iris, blue flag	*Iris versicolor*
Filbert	*Corylus* sp.	German	*I. germanica*
Fir, cascades	*Abies amabilis*	grass	*I. graminea*
grand	*A. grandis*	Ironweed, kinka oil	*Vernonia anthelmintica*
noble	*A. procera*	Jacaranda	*Jacaranda* sp.
red	*A. magnifica*	Jimsonweed	*Datura stramonium*
white	*A. concolor*	Juniper, Savin	*Juniperus sabina*
Flax, common	*Linum usitatissimum*	Kale	*Brassica oleracea acephala*
Forget-me-not	*Myosotis* sp.	Kamala tree	*Mallotus philippinensis*
Foxglove, common	*Digitalis purpurea*	Knotweed, prostrate	*Polygonum aviculare*
Grecian	*D. lanata*	Lamb's quarter	*Chenopodium album*
Frenchweed	*Thlaspi arvense*	Larch, western	*Larix occidentalis*
Ginkgo	*Ginkgo biloba*	Larkspur, rocket	*Delphinium ajacis*
Gladiolus, common	*Gladiolus hortulanus*	Lemon	*Citrus limon*
horticultural		Lentil	*Lens culinaris*
Gooseberry, Chinese	*Actinidia chinensis*	Lespedeza, common	*Lespedeza striata*
Gourd, snake	*Trichosanthes* sp.	Korean	*L. stipulacea*
Grape, European	*Vitis vinifera*	wand	*L. intermedia*
fox	*V. labrusca*	Lettuce	*Lactuca sativa*
roundleaf	*Ribes rotundifolium*	Licania	*Licania rigida*
Grass, Bermuda	*Cynodon dactylon*	Lilac, common	*Syringa vulgaris*
buffalo	*Buchloe dactyloides*	Lily, regal	*Lilium regale*
Canada blue	*Pao compressa*	Linden, American	*Tilia americana*
canary	*Phalaris canariensis*	Litsea	*Litsea* sp.
cocksfoot orchard	*Dactylis glomerata*	Locust, black	*Robinia pseudoacacia*
colonial bent-	*Argostis tenuis*	Lotus, East Indian	*Nelumbo nucifea*
common carpet-	*Axonopus affinis*	Lupine	*Lupinus arcticus*
crested wheat-	*Asgropyron cristatum*	tree	*L. angustifolius*
dallis	*Paspalum dilatatum*	Macadamia,	*Macadamia ternifolia*
desert wheat-	*Agropyron desertorum*	Queenslandnut	
Italian rye-	*Lolium multiflorum*	Magnolia, great-leaved	*Magnolia macrophylla*
Johnson	*Sorghum halepense*	southern	*M. grandiflora*
Kentucky, blue-	*Poa pratensis*	Malope	*Malope trifida*
perennial rye-	*Lolium perenne*	Mango, common	*Mangifera indica*
quack	*Agropyron repens*		

continues

Continued

Common Name	Botanical Name	Common Name	Botanical Name
Maple, red	*Acer rubrum*	Petunia	*Petunia* sp.
silver	*A. saccharinum*	Phlox, Drummond	*Phlox drummondii*
sugar	*A. saccharum*	Pine, Austrian	*Pinus nigra*
Marattia	*Marattia salicina*	eastern white	*P. strobus*
Marbleseed, western	*Onosmodium occidentale*	jack	*P. banksiana*
Marigold	*Tagetes* sp.	loblolly	*P. taeda*
winter cape	*Dimorphoteca aurantiaca*	longleaf	*P. palustris*
Meadowrue, Sierra	*Thalictrum polycarpum*	ponderosa	*P. ponderosa*
Milkweed, common	*Asclepias syriaca*	shore	*P. contorta*
Millet, pearl	*Pennisetum glaucum*	shortleaf	*P. echinata*
Morning glory, common	*Ipomoea purpurea*	slash	*P. caribea*
orizaba	*I. orizabensis*	sugar	*P. lambertiana*
Muskmelon	*Cucumis melo*	western white	*P. monticola*
Mustard, black	*Brassica nigra*	Pineapple	*Ananas comosus*
white	*B. hirta*	Pink, clove	*Dianthus caryophyllus*
Nasturtium	*Tropaeolum* sp.	Pistachio	*Pistacia* sp.
Niger seed	*Guizotia abyssinica*	Plum, garden	*Prunus domestica*
Oak, black	*Quercus velutina*	Japanese	*P. salicina*
English	*Q. robur*	Podocarpus	*Podocarpus* sp.
scarlet	*Q. coccinea*	Polypody, rock	*Polypodium virginianum*
southern red	*Q. falcata*	Pomegranate, common	*Punica granatum*
white	*Q. alba*	Poplar, eastern	*Populus deltoides*
Oat, common	*Avena sativa*	Mongolian	*P. suaveolens*
Okra	*Hibiscus esculentus*	yellow, or tulip tree	*Liriodendron tulipfera*
Olive	*Olea europaea sativa*	Poppy, corn	*Papaver rhoeas*
common	*O. europaea*	opium	*P. somniferum*
Oncoba, gorli	*Oncoba echinata*	oriental	*P. orientale*
Onion, garden	*Allium cepa*	Portulaca, common	*Portulaca grandiflora*
Orange, sweet	*Citrus sinensis*	Potato	*Solanum tuberosum*
trifoliate	*Poncirus trifoliata*	Primrose, evening	*Oenothera biennis*
Palm, African oil	*Elaeis guineensis*	Lemarck	*O. lamarckiana*
Pansy, wild	*viola tricolor*	Pumpkin	*Cucurbita pepo*
Parinarium	*Parinarium* sp.	Purslane, common	*Portulaca oleracea*
Parsley	*Petroselinum crispum*	Pycnanthus, akomu	*Pycnanthus kambo*
common curly	*P. latifolium*	Quillwort	*Isoetes braunii*
Parsnip	*Pastinaca sativa*	Radish, garden	*Raphanus sativus*
Pea, field	*Pisum sativum arvense*	Rape, bird	*Brassica campestris*
garden	*P. sativum*	winter	*B. napus*
sweet	*Lathyrus odoratus*	Red cedar, eastern	*Juniperus virginiana*
Peach	*Prunus persica*	Redtop	*Agrostis alba*
Peanut	*Arachis hypogaea*	Redwood	*Sequoia sempervirens*
Pear	*Pyrun communis*	Rhododendron, catawba	*Rhododendron catawbiense*
Peavine, flat	*Lathyrus sylvestris*	Rhubarb, garden	*Rheum rhaponticum*
Pecan	*Carya illinoensis*	medicinal	*R. officinale*
Peony, fernleaf	*Paeonia tenuifolia*	sorrel	*R. palmatum*
Pepper, bush red	*Capsicum frutescens*	Rice	*Oryza sativa*
Pepperwort	*Marsilea minuta*	Rose, cabbage	*Rosa centifolia*
Perilla, common	*Pefrilla frutescens*	Rubber, pará	*Hevea brasiliensis*
Persimmon, common	*Diospyros virginiana*	Rutabaga	*Brassica napobrassica*

Common Name	Botanical Name	Common Name	Botanical Name
Rye	*Secale cereale*	Tallow wood	*Ximenia americana*
Safflower	*Carthamus tinctorius*		*X. caffra*
Sage, garden	*Salvia officinalis*	Tara vine	*Taraktogenos kurzii*
scarlet	*S. splendens*	Tetradenia, Asian	*Tetradenia glauca*
Salsify, vegetable-oyster	*Tragopogon porrifolius*	Timothy	*Phleum pratense*
Scammony, glorybind	*Convolvulus scammonia*	Tobacco	*Nicotiana glutinosa*
Scarlet runner	*Phaseolus coccineus*	common	*N. tabacum*
Sequoia, giant	*Sequoiadendron giganteum*	Tomato, common	*Lycopersicon esculentum*
	Sequoia gigantea	Trefoil, bird's foot	*Lotus corniculatus*
Sesame, oriental	*Sesamum indicum*	Tulip	*Tulipa* sp.
Snapdragon, common	*Antirrhinum majus*	Tung oil tree	*Aleurites fordii*
Sorghum	*Sorghum bicolor*	Tupelo, water	*Nyssa acquatica*
Soybean	*Glycine max*	Turnip	*Brassica rapa*
Spicebush, Japanese	*Lindera obtusiloba*	Vetch, common	*Vicia sativa*
Spiderwort	*Tradescantia paludosa*	hairy	*V. villosa*
Virginia	*T. virginiana*	Hungarian	*V. pannonica*
Spikemoss	*Selaginella selaginoides*	narrow leaf	*V. angustifolia*
Spinach	*Spinacia oleracea*	one-flower	*V. articulata*
Spruce, Norway	*Picea abies*	Vetch, common, *cont.*	
red	*P. rubens*	purple	*V. benghalensis*
Sitka	*P. sitchensis*	tiny	*V. hirsuta*
white	*P. glauca*	wooly pod	*V. dasycarpa*
Spurge, South American	*Sebastiania fruticosa*	Violet, field	*Viola arvensis*
Spurry, corn	*Spergula avensis*	Walnut, eastern black	*Juglans nigra*
Sterculia, hazel	*Sterculia foetida*	Waterlily	*Nymphaea alba*
Stillingia	*Stillingia* sp.	Watermelon	*Citrullus vulgaris*
Stock, common	*Matthiola incana*	Waterweed, Canadian	*Elodea canadensis*
Strawberry, chiloe	*Fragaria chiloensis*	Wheat	*Triticum aestivum*
pine	*F. ananassa*	Willow, basket	*Salix viminalis*
Strophanthus	*Strophanthus glaber*	big catkin	*S. gracilistyla*
arrow poison	*S. sarmentosus*	black	*S. nigra*
Sugarcane	*Saccharum officinarum*	pussy	*S. discolor*
Sumac	*Rhus* sp.	white	*S. alba*
Sunflower, common	*Helianthus annuus*	Yellow trumpet, Florida	*Stenolobium stans*
Sweetcane	*Saccharum spontaneum*	Yew, English	*Taxus baccata*
Sweetgum, American	*Liquidambar styraciflua*	Pacific	*T. brevifolia*
Sweet potato	*Ipomoea batatas*	Yucca	*Yucca* sp.
Sweet William	*Dianthus barbatus*	Zinnia, oblong leaf	*Zinnia angustifolia*

Biological World

GROUND COVERS

Common Name	Botanical Name
Sunlit Areas	
Pussytoes	*Antennaria neodioica* (1, 6)
Bearberry	*Arctostaphylas uva-ursi* (1, 2, 3, 6)
Cranberry cotoneaster	*Cotoneaster apiculata* (1)
Bearberry cotoneaster	*Cotoneaster dammeri* and *cultivars* (1)
Purpleleaf wintercreeper	*Euonymus colorata* (3, 4, 6)
Creeping juniper	*Juniperus horizontalis* and *cultivars* (6)
Japanese juniper	*Juniperus procumbens nana* (4, 6)
Hall's honeysuckle	*Lonicera japonica halliana* (3, 4, 6)
Pachistima	*Pachistima canbyi* (1, 2, 6)
Wineleaf cinquefoil	*Potentilla tridentata* (1, 2, 6)
Cinquefoil	*Potentilla verna nana* (1, 5)
Stonecrop	*Sedum species* (5, 6)
Barren strawberry	*Waldsteinia ternata* (1, 3, 6)
Shade	
Carpet bugle	*Ajuga reptans* and *cultivars* (3, 4)
Lily of the valley	*Convallaria majalis* (4, 5)
Wintercreeper	*Euonymus fortunei* varieties (3, 4, 6)
English ivy	*Hedera helix* and *cultivars* (4, 6)
Plantain lily	*Hosta species* (5)
Lily turn	*Liriope spicata* (6)
Japanese spurge	*Pachysandra terminalis* (2, 6)
Periwinkle or myrtle	*Vinca minor* and *cultivars* (3, 6)

1. Requires well-drained soil
2. Requires acid soil
3. Good in sunlit areas or shade
4. Confine; may grow out of bounds
5. Herbaceous
6. Foliage retention in winter

VINES FOR SPECIAL USES

Common Name	Botanical Name
Five-leaf akebia	*Akebia quinata* (1, 2, 3, 4)
Virgin's-bower	*Clematis species* and *hybrids* (1, 2, 3, 4)
Wintercreeper	*Euonymus fortunei* (2, 3)
English ivy	*Hedera helix* and *cultivars* (2)
Climbing hydrangea	*Hydrangea petiolaris* (1, 2)
Boston ivy	*Parthenocissus tricuspidata* (2)
Japanese wisteria	*Wisteria floribunda* (1, 2, 3, 4)

1. Flowering
2. Wall cover
3. Screening
4. Trellis

Go to "Treatment for Health Emergencies: Poisoning: Plant Poisons" and "Poison Control Centers" in chapter 17

POISONOUS CULTIVATED AND WILD PLANTS

The following chart lists 50 poisonous plants. It tells which portions, or areas, of the plant are toxic, describes symptoms of the illnesses they cause, and indicates which plants are or may be fatal.

Plants	Toxic Portions	Symptoms of Illness; Degree of Toxicity
Autumn crocus	Bulbs	Nausea, vomiting, diarrhea; may be fatal.
Azalea	All parts	Nausea, vomiting, depression, breathing difficulty, prostration, coma; fatal.
Belladonna	Young plants, seeds	Nausea, twitching muscles, paralysis; fatal.
Bittersweet	Leaves, seeds, roots	Vomiting, diarrhea, chills, convulsions, coma.
Bleeding heart (Dutchman's-breeches)	Foliage, roots	Nervous symptoms, convulsions.
Buttercups	All parts	Digestive system injury.
Caladium	All parts	Intense burning and irritation of the tongue and mouth; can be fatal if the base of the tongue swells, blocking air passage of the throat.
Castorbean	Seeds, foliage	Burning in mouth, convulsions; fatal.
Cherry	Twigs, foliage	Gasping, excitement, prostration.
Daffodil	Bulbs	Nausea, vomiting, diarrhea; may be fatal.
Daphne	Berries (red or yellow)	Severe burns to mouth and digestive tract followed by coma; fatal.
Delphinium	Young plants, seeds	Nausea, twitching muscles, paralysis; fatal.
Dumbcane (Dieffenbachia)	All parts	Intense burning and irritation of the tongue and mouth; fatal if the base of the tongue swells, blocking air passage of the throat.
Elderberry	Roots	Nausea and digestive upset.
Elephant ear	All parts	Intense burning and irritation of the tongue and mouth; fatal if the base of the tongue swells, blocking air passage of the throat.
English holly	Berries	Severe gastroenteritis.
English ivy	Leaves, berries	Stomach pains, labored breathing, possible coma.
Foxglove	Leaves, seeds, flowers	Irregular heartbeat and pulse, usually accompanied by digestive upset and mental confusion; may be fatal.
Goldenchain	All parts, especially seeds	Excitement, staggering convulsions, coma; may be fatal.
Horse chestnut	All parts	Nausea, twitching muscles, sometimes paralysis.
Hyacinth	Bulbs	Nausea, vomiting, diarrhea; may be fatal.
Hydrangea	Buds, leaves, branches	Severe digestive upset, gasping, convulsions; may be fatal.
Iris	Freshly underground portions	Severe but not usually serious digestive upset.
Jack-in-the-pulpit	All parts, especially roots	Intense irritation and burning of the tongue and mouth.
Jimson weed (thorn apple; datura)	All parts	Abnormal thirst, distortion of vision, delirium, incoherence, coma; may be fatal.
Larkspur	Young plants, seeds	Nausea, twitching muscles, paralysis; fatal.
Laurel	All parts	Nausea, vomiting, depression, breathing difficulty, prostration, coma; fatal.
Lily of the valley	Leaves, flowers	Irregular heartbeat and pulse usually accompanied by digestive upset and mental confusion; may be fatal.
Mayapple	Unripe apples, leaves, and roots	Diarrhea, severe digestive upset.
Mistletoe	All parts, especially berries	Fatal
Monkshood	All parts, especially roots	Digestive upset and nervous excitement; juice in plant parts is fatal.

continues

Continued

Plants	Toxic Portions	Symptoms of Illness; Degree of Toxicity
Morning glory	Seeds	Large amounts cause severe mental disturbances; fatal.
Mushrooms, wild	All parts of many varieties	Fatal.
Narcissus	Bulbs	Nausea, vomiting, diarrhea; may be fatal.
Nightshade	All parts, especially unripe berries	Intense digestive disturbances and nervous symptoms; often fatal.
Oak	Foliage, acorns	Gradual kidney failure.
Oleander	All parts	Severe digestive upset, heart trouble, contact dermatitis; fatal.
Philodendron	All parts	Intense burning and irritation of the tongue and mouth; fatal if the base of the tongue swells, blocking air passage of the throat.
Poinsettia	All parts	Severe digestive upset; fatal.
Poison hemlock	All parts	Stomach pains, vomiting, paralysis of the central nervous system; may be fatal.
Poison ivy and oak	All parts	Intense itching, watery blisters, red rash.
Poppy	Foliage, roots	Nervous symptoms, convulsions.
Potato	Foliage, green parts of vegetable	Intense digestive disturbances, nervous symptoms.
Privet	Berries, leaves	Mild to severe digestive disturbances; may be fatal.
Rhododendron	All parts	Nausea, vomiting, depression, breathing difficulty, prostration, coma; fatal.
Rhubarb	Leaf blade	Kidney disorder, convulsions, coma; fatal.
Rosary pea	Seeds, foliage	Burning in mouth, convulsions; fatal.
Snowdrop	Bulbs	Vomiting, nervous excitement.
Tomato	Vines	Digestive upset, nervous disorders.
Wisteria	Seeds, pods	Mild to severe digestive disturbances.

PLANT CULTIVATION

WHEN TO PLANT

Seeds, seedlings, and young plants should be planted outdoors according to the instructions specific to their variety. Here are general guidelines on when to plant what.

Plant Type	Variety	Warmer Zones	Cooler Zones
Vegetables	tender	spring, summer	late spring
	hardy	fall, winter	spring, summer
Flowers	perennials	fall, winter, spring	spring, late summer
	annuals	year-round	spring, summer
	bulbs, tender	spring	spring
	bulbs, hardy	fall	fall
Woody Plants	shrubs	fall, winter, spring	spring, fall
	trees	fall, winter, spring	spring, fall

USDA HARDINESS ZONES

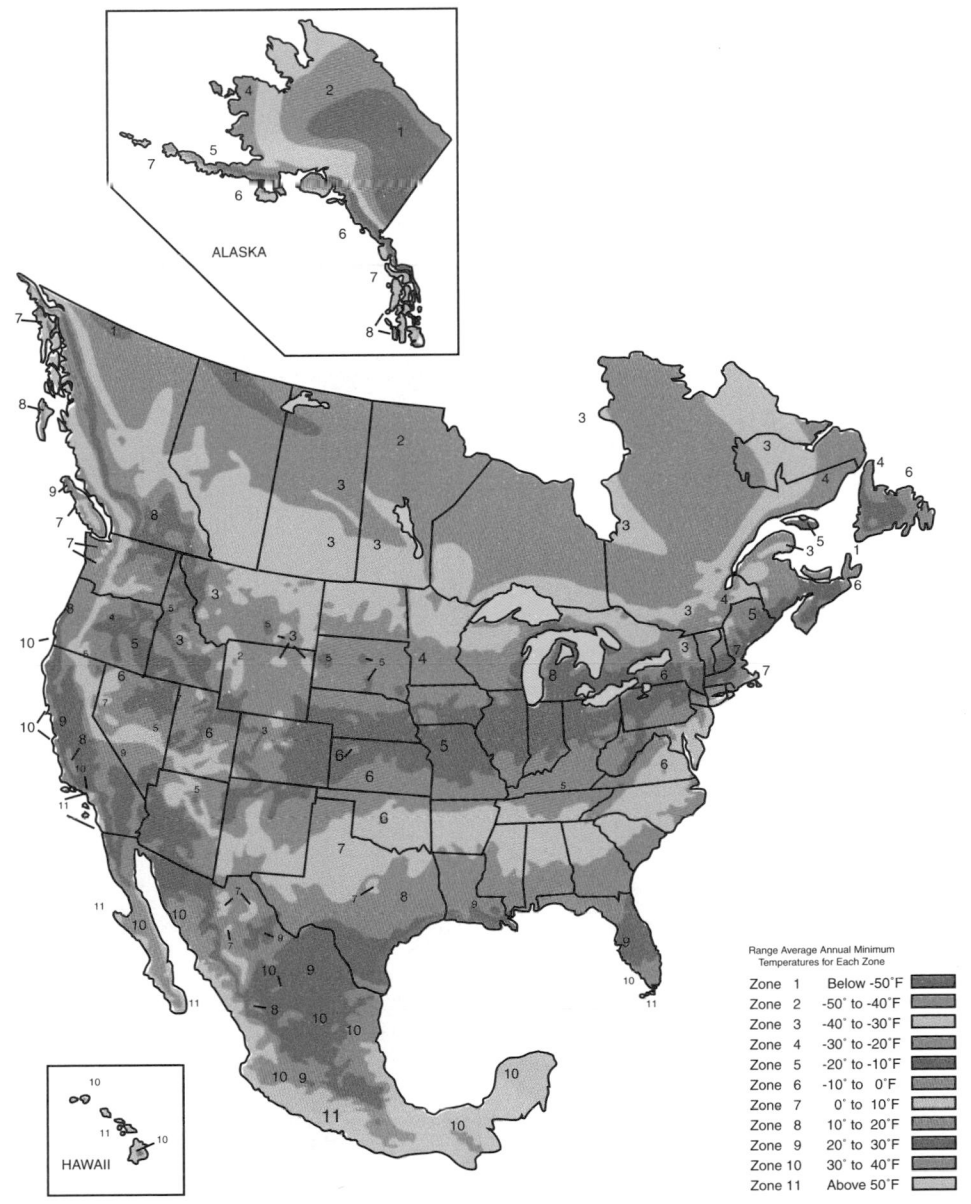

ALASKA

HAWAII

Range Average Annual Minimum
Temperatures for Each Zone

Zone 1	Below -50˚F
Zone 2	-50˚ to -40˚F
Zone 3	-40˚ to -30˚F
Zone 4	-30˚ to -20˚F
Zone 5	-20˚ to -10˚F
Zone 6	-10˚ to 0˚F
Zone 7	0˚ to 10˚F
Zone 8	10˚ to 20˚F
Zone 9	20˚ to 30˚F
Zone 10	30˚ to 40˚F
Zone 11	Above 50˚F

Biological World

FROST DATES

SPRING

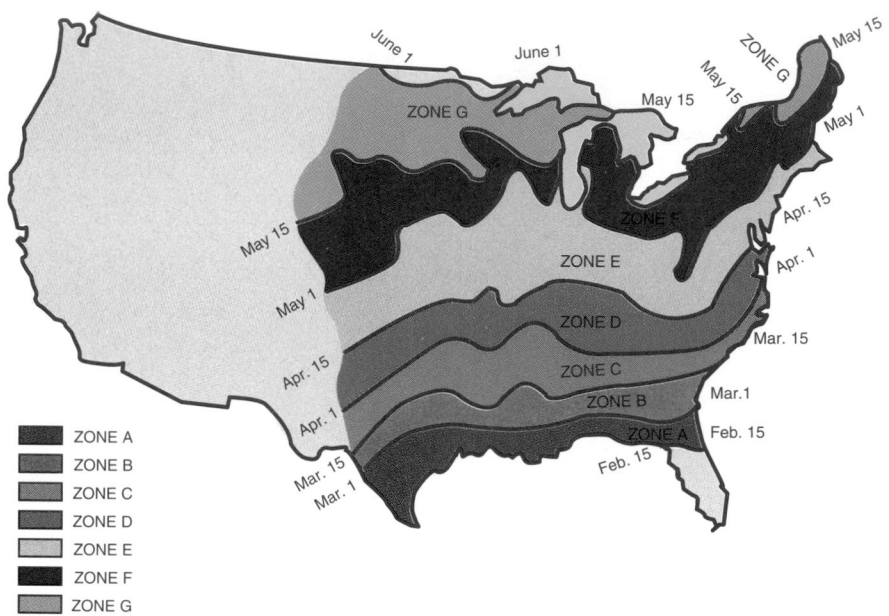

A zone map of the United States based on the average dates of the latest killing frost in spring east of the Rocky Mountains. Source: United States Department of Agriculture.

AUTUMN

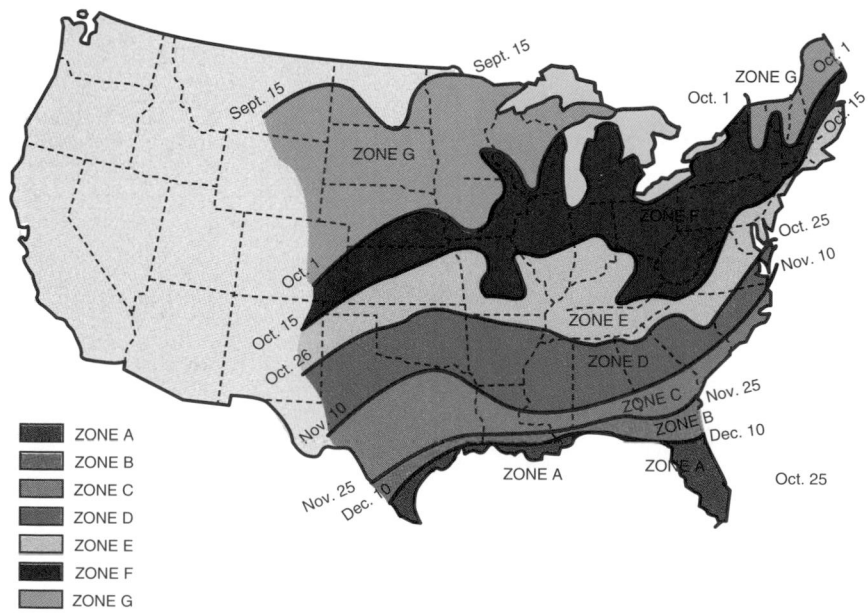

A zone map of the central and eastern part of the United States based on the average dates of the first killing frost in autumn. Source: United States Department of Agriculture.

GERMINATION TABLES
ANNUAL FLOWERS

Flower	Approximate Number of Days until Germination	Flower	Approximate Number of Days until Germination
Acrolinium	8–10	Gaillardia	12–15
Ageratum	7–11	Gomphrena	20–25
Alyssum, sweet	10–13	Helichrysum	5–10
Browallia	18–20	Larkspur	15–20
Cacalia	8–12	Lupine	25–30
Calendula	10–12	Marigold	5–8
California poppy	5–10	Nicotiana	20–25
Candytuft	6–9	Petunia	18–20
Canterbury bell	12–15	Phlox Drummondi	20–25
Celosia (coxcomb)	20–25	Pinks	5–8
Centaurea (ragged robin)	5–20	Portulaca	18–20
Chrysanthemum	6–8	Scabiosa	18–20
Cosmos	5–15	Snapdragon	20–25
Cynoglossum	11–15	Sweetpea	15–20
Flax	13–16	Verbena	8–10
Four-o'clock	12–15	Zinnia	5–8

VEGETABLE GARDEN PLANTS

Vegetable	Approximate Number of Days until Germination	Vegetable	Approximate Number of Days until Germination
Asparagus	21–28	Kohlrabi	6–8
Beans, bush	6–10	Lettuce	6–10
Beans, bush lima	6–10	Muskmelon	6–10
Beans, pole	6–10	Mustard	4–5
Beans, pole lima	7–12	Okra	15–20
Beets	7–10	Onion	8–12
Broccoli	6–10	Parsley	18–24
Brussels sprouts	6–10	Parsnip	12–18
Cabbage	6–10	Peas	6–10
Cabbage, Chinese	6–10	Pepper	10–14
Carrots	10–15	Pumpkin	6–10
Cauliflower	6–10	Radish	4–6
Celery	12–20	Rhubarb	12–14
Chard, Swiss	7–10	Rutabaga	4–7
Collards	6–10	Spinach	6–12
Corn, sweet	7–12	Squash, bush	6–10
Cress, garden	4–5	Squash, vine	6–10
Cucumber	6–8	Tomato	6–10
Eggplant	10–15	Turnip	4–7
Endive	8–12	Watermelon	8–12

Biological World

COMMON BIOLOGICAL TERMS

abaxial   Facing away from the stem or central axis of a plant or animal.

abiogenesis   A theory that living things can develop from nonliving material, as in spontaneous generation.

adaptation   The modification of an organism or part of an organism to adjust to new conditions or a new environment, as in adjustment of the eyes to bright light.

adenosine triphosphate (ATP)   A chemical compound present in all living cells that provides energy derived from food or sunlight for processes that require activity, such as contraction of a muscle or conduction of a nerve impulse.

The largest dinosaur egg ever discovered came from the Hypselosaurus. Measuring 1 foot by 10 inches, it had a liquid capacity of almost 6 pints.

appendage   A structure attached to a larger structure or part of an organism. Arms, legs, and other projections of body areas are examples of appendages.

ATP   *See* **adenosine triphosphate.**

bacteria   Tiny, one-celled plant organisms that are generally parasitic and lacking in chlorophyll. They are commonly involved in processes of fermentation and decay, and many species are the cause of diseases in humans and animals.

bladder   A saclike organ with a membranous wall that serves to collect or hold a fluid or gas. An example is the urinary bladder or the air bladder of marine animals.

blastula   A stage in the development of an embryo after the early phase of cell division when the cells form a hollow ball. The wall of the sphere is a single layer of cells, the blastoderm. The various organs, such as the gut, nervous system, and appendages, eventually evolve from cells of the blastula.

bud   An undeveloped appendage of an organism. A plant bud may develop into flowers or leaves while the bud of an animal embryo may become an arm, leg, or wing. Some bacteria and yeast cells reproduce by issuing buds, each of which becomes a new organism.

bug   Any of a large number of creeping or flying insects, mainly of the order Hemiptera. Examples of "true bugs" include bed bugs, cinch bugs, squash bugs, and giant water bugs.

calyx   A cuplike portion of a plant or animal organ. Examples include the sepals, or outermost parts of a flower, and the funnel-shaped part of a kidney that collects urine as it drains toward the bladder.

carnivore   Any meat-eating animal, particularly a member of the order Carnivora, which includes wolves, coyotes, bears, dogs, and cats.

cell   The basic structural unit of living things. It usually consists of a membranous wall containing protoplasm, a souplike mixture of proteins, enzymes, and other organic chemicals needed for survival and reproduction. Most cells also contain a nucleus that in turn holds the DNA molecules, or genetic material, that control the various cell functions.

chlorophyll   Any of nearly a dozen kinds of green pigments present in most plant cells. Chlorophylls are able to convert the energy from sunlight into carbohydrates, which plants form from carbon dioxide and water present in the environment. The carbohydrates in turn become a source of energy for animals and humans after the plant material is eaten.

chromosome   A rod-shaped unit of DNA present in the nucleus of a cell that is capable of reproducing itself. It contains a portion of the genetic or hereditary traits of the species it represents. The number of chromosomes and their shapes and sizes vary among different species and sexes within a species. Human males, for example, possess a Y-shaped chromosome that is not normally present in female cells and that governs masculine physical traits.

deoxyribonucleic acid (DNA) A large molecule of nucleic acid found in the nuclei, usually in the chromosomes, of living cells. DNA controls such functions as the production of protein molecules in the cell and carries the template for reproduction of all the inherited characteristics of its particular species.

DNA *See* **deoxyribonucleic acid.**

embryo The young of a species at a very early stage of development, such as the rudimentary plant that bursts forth from a seed when it germinates, or the bird that has not yet hatched from its egg. In mammals, the embryo stage occurs after the cells of the blastula begin to specialize for the development of the fetus.

endogenous Pertaining to factors influencing an organism that originate within that organism, as distinguished from *exogenous* factors, such as environmental influences, that originate on the outside.

evolution The process by which a species of plants or animals gradually develops over a period of many generations from a simpler to a more complex form of organism. The traits of the simpler organism are often continued into the more complex form of the same organism, as can be observed in the brain and other structures of the human body.

exogenous *See* **endogenous.**

fauna The animal life of a region or period of history.

female The sex of an animal that produces ova and bears offspring.

fermentation A process whereby complex carbohydrates or other organic substances are converted to other chemicals by the action of enzymes

produced by molds, yeasts, or bacteria. An example is the conversion of sugars to alcohol.

fertilization The union of a male and a female reproductive cell resulting in the formation of a new organism. The term is also used to describe the process or enrichment of the soil for growing crops.

flora The plant life of a region or period of history.

genitalia The reproductive sex organs of a male or female of the species, particularly structures on the outside of the body.

genotype *See* **phenotype.**

genus A subdivision of a biological family. It is composed of a group of related species, such as the genus *Canis,* which includes various species of dogs.

gonads The male and female reproductive organs.

haploid Half the number of chromosomes ordinarily present in the nucleus of a cell. During reproduction, the offspring receives a haploid number of chromosomes from each parent, making a full, or diploid, set.

herbaceous Herblike, usually used to describe a plant in which persistent woody tissue does not develop.

herbivore An animal that feeds entirely or mainly on plant materials.

hormone A chemical secretion of a gland or other tissue that triggers an action in another gland or tissue in a different part of the body.

immunity A quality of being able to resist an infectious disease.

inbreeding The mating of closely related individuals, as in self-pollinating plants or animals that are brothers and sisters.

joint An area between two parts or segments of an organism, such as the junction of two separate bones of an animal or the node of a plant.

karyotype   The general appearance of a set of chromosomes of an individual. Karyotype may be used to determine sex, genetic defects, and other chromosome-related factors.

kernel   The entire grain or seed of a cereal plant.

larva   The young, immature form of an organism that undergoes a change in structure to become an adult. The caterpillar and the maggot are examples of larvae.

leaf   An outgrowth of a stem of a plant, usually green, in which many living functions, such as photosynthesis, respiration, and food and water storage, take place.

lipid   Any of a group of fatty substances, including oils and waxes, produced by plant or animal tissues. Lipids generally are insoluble in water, but they can be dissolved in alcohol, benzene, or similar organic solvents.

male   The sex of an animal that produces spermatozoa or of a plant that produces pollen.

mammal   A warm-blooded, air-breathing vertebrate of the class Mammalia, possessing hair and mammary glands.

Mendel's laws   A series of natural principles of heredity discovered by Gregor Mendel. They govern such factors as dominant and recessive traits resulting from the interaction of genes that are inherited in pairs.

metabolism   The chemical and energy changes associated with the consumption of food and oxygen, the production of heat, and the calories used in physical activity.

natural selection   A principle proposed by Charles Darwin to explain the ability of various species to adapt to changes in the environment. Called "survival of the fittest," the theory offered an explanation for the survival of some species and extinction of others.

neuron   The structural and functional unit of a nerve, including the cell body and its axon and dendrite fibers.

nucleus   A structure present in most plant and animal cells. It contains the chromosomes and ribonucleic acid (RNA) molecules that direct the cell's life functions.

osmosis   The diffusion of water through a semi-permeable membrane from the side with a greater concentration of a solution to the side with a lesser concentration.

osseous   Pertaining to bones, as something composed of bone or resembling bone.

phenotype   The physical features or appearance of an individual, as distinguished from the genotype, or genetic composition of his or her cells. Two or more people with the same physical appearance may belong to the same phenotype.

pistil   The female sex structure of a plant, usually containing the ovary.

Protozoa   A phylum, or large group, of one-celled animals.

receptor   Any cell or group of cells that is the target of a stimulus, such as the retina of the eye.

regeneration   The ability of some plants and animals to restore or replace lost tissues or structures, such as a claw or feather.

stamen   The pollen-producing structure of a plant. It usually consists of an anther, the actual pollen producer, on the tip of a flower filament.

stimulus   An environmental influence, such as a chemical or physical irritant, that induces or brings about a response in a cell or organism.

symbiosis   A relationship in which two organisms live together for the mutual benefit of each.

terrestrial   Pertaining to plant or animal life on land rather than in water.

"Biology Symbols" in chapter 12

Go to

tissue A group of cells with similar structures and functions.

tropism The involuntary response of an organism to a stimulus, such as the response of a plant to gravity or sunlight.

vacuole Any of the spaces scattered about the protoplasm of a cell, usually containing fluid.

zygote The fertilized egg cell of a plant or animal.

ADDITIONAL SOURCES OF INFORMATION

ORGANIZATIONS AND SERVICES

American Horticultural Society
7931 E. Boulevard Dr.
Alexandria, VA 22308

American Society for the Prevention of Cruelty to Animals
424 E. 92nd St.
New York, NY 10028

Garden Club of America
598 Madison Ave.
New York, NY 10022

Men's Garden Clubs of America
5560 Merle Hay Rd.
Des Moines, IA 50323

National Wildlife Federation
1412 16th St., NW
Washington, DC 20036

BOOKS

American Kennel Club Staff. *The Complete Dog Book.* 18th ed. Howell, 1992.

Animal Medical Center Staff and William J. Kay. *Complete Book of Cat Health.* Macmillan, 1985.

Animal Medical Center Staff, et al. *The Complete Book of Dog Health.* Howell, 1990.

Bondwell, Sally. *The American Animal Hospital Association of Dog Health and Care.* Quill, 1996.

Day, David. *The Doomsday Book of Animals: A Natural History of Vanished Species.* Viking Penguin, 1983.

Ehrlich, Paul R., David S. Dobkin, and Darryl Wheye. *Birds in Jeopardy: The Imperiled and Extinct Birds of the United States and Canada, Including Hawaii and Puerto Rico.* Stanford University Press, 1992.

Gerstenfeld, Sheldon L. *The Cat Care Book.* Addison-Wesley, 1989.

Grzimek, Bernhard, ed. *Encyclopedia of Animals.* 15 vols. McGraw-Hill, 1990.

Harrison, Marina, and Lucy D. Rosenfeld. *Gardenwalks.* Michael Kesend Publishing, 1997.

Humphries, Jim. *Dr. Jim's Animal Clinic for Dogs.* Howell, 1994.

Macdonald, David, ed. *The Encyclopedia of Mammals.* Facts On File, 1984.

Mackey, Betty, et al. *The Gardener's Home Companion.* Macmillan, 1991.

Margulis, Lynn, and Karlene V. Schwartz. *Five Kingdoms: An Illustrated Guide to the Phyla of Life on Earth.* 2nd ed. Freeman, 1988.

The New International Wildlife Encyclopedia. 21 vols. Purnell Reference Books, 1980.

Perrins, Christopher M., and Alex L. A. Middleton, eds. *The Encyclopedia of Birds.* Facts On File, 1985.

Peterson, Roger T. *Peterson's First Guide to Birds.* Houghton Mifflin, 1986.

Peterson, Roger T. *Peterson's First Guide to Wildflowers.* Houghton Mifflin, 1986.

Riley, Laura, and William Riley. *Guide to the National Wildlife Refuges.* Macmillan, 1992.

Sussman, Les. *The American Animal Hospital Association Encyclopedia of Cat Health and Care.* Quill, 1996.

Biological World

Taylor, Norman. *Taylor's Master Guide to Gardening.* Houghton Mifflin, 1994.

West, Geoffrey, ed. *Black's Veterinary Dictionary.* 15th ed. B and N Imports, 1985.

Whitfield, Philip. *Macmillan Illustrated Animal Encyclopedia.* Macmillan, 1984.

4

THE PHYSICAL SCIENCES, MATH, AND TECHNOLOGY

ASTRONOMY	68
CHEMISTRY	80
GEOLOGY AND GEOPHYSICS	84
METEOROLOGY	95
PHYSICS	99
MATHEMATICS	102
COMPUTERS	107
SPACE EXPLORATION	115
COMMON ENGINEERING TERMS	117
ADDITIONAL SOURCES OF INFORMATION	119

ASTRONOMY

PHASES OF THE MOON

The Moon is the closest natural body to the Earth. Eight phases of the Moon are visible because the Moon has no light of its own. Its daylight side reflects the light of the Sun. As pictured below at the new moon, the dark side of the Moon is turned toward the Earth, and the Moon cannot be seen. The second phase is a waxing crescent moon, followed by a half moon, or first quarter. A waxing gibbous moon is then succeeded by a full moon. The Moon then begins to wane, through a waning gibbous moon, a third or last quarter moon, a waning crescent moon, and back to a new moon again. The cycle takes 27.3 days to complete.

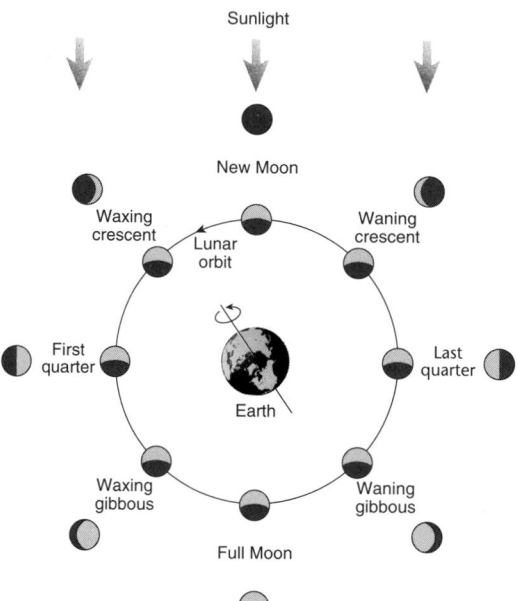

Sunlight

New Moon

Waxing crescent   Lunar orbit   Waning crescent

First quarter   Earth   Last quarter

Waxing gibbous   Waning gibbous

Full Moon

LUNAR AND SOLAR ECLIPSES

An eclipse occurs when a celestial body, such as the Earth or Moon, casts a shadow so that another celestial body seems to disappear. As each of the celestial bodies is in constant motion with respect to the others, and the alignment of the bodies is not always perfect, an eclipse seldom lasts more than a few minutes, and it may be either total or partial.

An eclipse of the Moon (lunar eclipse) occurs when the Sun, Earth, and Moon are in a straight line so that the Moon is in the shadow of Earth. It is visible from any point on the Earth facing the Moon at the time of the eclipse.

A total solar eclipse takes place when the Earth, Moon, and Sun are in alignment in such a way that the umbra of the shadow of the Moon reaches the Earth. (The *umbra* is the dark central part of the cone-shaped shadow projecting from the Moon to Earth during this phenomenon.) All the light of the Sun is blocked or eclipsed because of the Moon's position. The *penumbra* (the lighter shadow) shows a partial solar eclipse.

In an annular solar eclipse, the alignment is just the same as in a total solar eclipse, but the Moon is too far away from the Earth at the time for the umbra of the shadow to reach Earth. The circle of the Moon is not large enough to block our seeing the Sun, so a ring of light from the corona, or outer fringe, of the Sun can be seen surrounding the moon's circle.

The shadow of the Moon during a solar eclipse is visible only along an arc-shaped path on a portion of the Earth, and the shadow moves at a speed between 1,060 and 2,100 miles per hour, depending on the latitude of the shadow, the rotation of the Earth, and the speed of the Moon through its own orbit.

Because the Sun, Earth, and Moon travel in relatively predictable orbits, astronomers since the days of ancient Babylonia (700 B.C.) have been able to calculate the future dates on which the Sun, Earth, and Moon will once again be in alignment. Therefore, astronomers can forecast the time and place of eclipses many years in advance. For example, at regular intervals of 18 years, 9 to 11 days (depending on leap years), and 8 hours (a period of one saros), the Sun and Moon will return to the same orbital node relative to Earth. During one saros, there are usually 41 total or partial solar eclipses and 29 lunar eclipses, or an average of

Total Lunar Eclipse

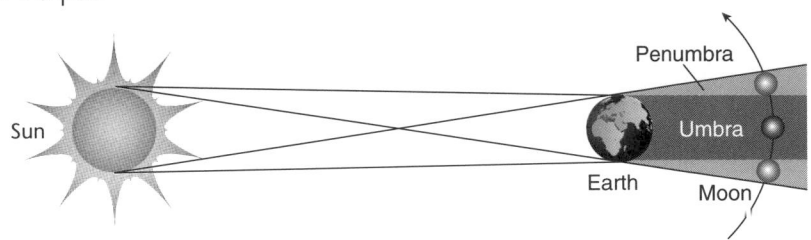

Annular Solar Eclipse

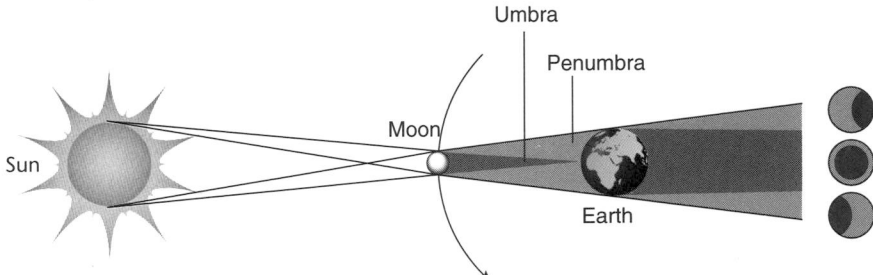

Total Solar Eclipse

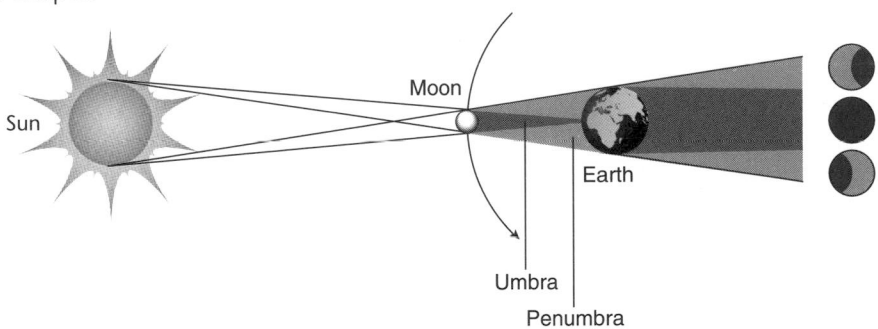

about 4 eclipses a year. But each successive solar eclipse is observed about 120 degrees to the west of the previous phenomenon and can be expected to recur at the same longitude on Earth after a period equivalent to three times the length of one saros. Each solar eclipse may affect an area only about 100 miles wide, and any given place on Earth can expect a total eclipse about once every 400 years.

Go to "Reckoning Days and Hours" and "Calendars: The Seasons" in chapter 1

On rare occasions, sunlight can appear to be green. Known as a "green flash," this phenomenon occurs briefly when the Sun sets or rises on an extremely clear horizon. It is produced by the greater bending of green and blue rays as sunlight is refracted in the Earth's atmosphere.

Sciences

TOTAL ECLIPSES OF THE SUN, 1900–2010

Date	Approximate Duration (min:sec)	Maximum Width (miles)	Course of Central Line
1900 May 28	2:10	58	Mexico, United States, Spain, North Africa
1901 May 18	6:17	149	Indian Ocean, Sumatra, Borneo, New Guinea
1903 September 21	2:02	157	Antarctica
1904 September 9	6:19	146	Pacific Ocean
1905 August 30	3:46	123	Canada, Spain, North Africa, Arabia
1907 January 14	2:24	119	Soviet Union, China
1908 January 3	4:20	93	Pacific Ocean
1908 December 23	0:12	6	South America, Atlantic Ocean, Indian Ocean
1909 June 17	0:24	32	Greenland, Russia
1910 May 9	4:14	371	Antarctica
1911 April 28	4:58	120	Pacific Ocean
1912 April 17	0:02	1	Atlantic Ocean, Europe, Russia
1912 October 10	2:02	54	Brazil, South Atlantic Ocean
1914 August 21	2:15	113	Greenland, Europe, Middle East
1916 February 3	2:36	69	Pacific Ocean, South America, Atlantic Ocean
1918 June 8	2:23	70	Pacific Ocean, United States
1919 May 29	6:50	153	South America, Atlantic Ocean, Africa
1921 October 1	1:52	189	Antarctica
1922 September 21	5:59	142	Indian Ocean, Australia
1923 September 10	3:37	106	Pacific Ocean, Central America
1925 January 24	2:32	130	Northeast United States, Atlantic Ocean
1926 January 14	4:11	92	Africa, Indian Ocean, Borneo
1927 June 29	0:50	48	England, Scandinavia, Arctic Ocean, Soviet Union
1928 May 19	—	—	(Umbra barely touched Antarctica)
1929 May 9	5:07	122	Indian Ocean, Malaya, Philippines
1930 April 28	0:01	1	Pacific Ocean, United States, Canada
1930 October 21	1:55	54	South Pacific Ocean
1932 August 31	1:45	104	Arctic Ocean, East Canada
1934 February 14	2:53	79	Borneo, Pacific Ocean
1936 June 19	2:31	83	Greece, Turkey, Soviet Union, Pacific Ocean
1937 June 8	7:04	156	Pacific Ocean, Peru
1938 May 29	4:04	420	South Atlantic Ocean
1939 October 12	1:32	276	Antarctica
1940 October 1	5:35	137	South America, Atlantic Ocean, Africa
1941 September 21	3:22	91	Soviet Union, China, Pacific Ocean
1943 February 4	2:39	146	Japan, Pacific Ocean, Alaska
1944 January 25	4:09	91	South America, Atlantic Ocean, Africa
1945 July 9	1:15	57	Canada, Greenland, Scandinavia, Soviet Union
1947 May 20	5:14	124	Argentina, Brazil, Central Africa
1948 November 1	1:56	53	Africa, Indian Ocean
1950 September 12	1:13	90	Arctic Ocean, Soviet Union, Pacific Ocean
1952 February 25	3:05	89	Africa, Arabia, Iran, Soviet Union
1954 June 30	2:35	96	United States, Canada, Scandinavia, Soviet Union
1955 June 20	7:08	159	Indian Ocean, Thailand, Pacific Ocean

Date	Approximate Duration (min:sec)	Maximum Width (miles)	Course of Central Line
1956 June 8	4:44	269	South Pacific Ocean
1957 October 23	—	—	(Umbra touched Antarctica)
1958 October 12	5:11	131	Pacific Ocean, Argentina
1959 October 2	3:01	76	Atlantic Ocean, Africa
1961 February 15	2:44	164	Europe, Soviet Union
1962 February 5	4:08	92	Borneo, New Guinea, Pacific Ocean
1963 July 20	1:40	63	Pacific Ocean, Alaska, Canada
1965 May 30	5:16	124	New Zealand, Pacific Ocean
1966 November 12	1:57	53	South America, Atlantic Ocean
1967 November 2	—	—	(Umbra touched Antarctica)
1968 September 22	0:40	68	Soviet Union
1970 March 7	3:28	99	Pacific Ocean, Mexico, Eastern United States
1972 July 10	2:36	111	Soviet Union, North Canada
1973 June 30	7:04	160	Atlantic Ocean, Central Africa, Indian Ocean
1974 June 20	5:08	216	Indian Ocean, Australia
1976 October 23	4:46	125	Africa, Indian Ocean, Australia
1977 October 12	2:37	63	Pacific Ocean, Colombia, Venezuela
1979 February 26	2:52	195	Northwest United States, Canada, Greenland
1980 February 16	4:08	93	Africa, Indian Ocean, India, China
1981 July 31	2:03	68	Soviet Union, Pacific Ocean
1983 June 11	5:11	125	Indian Ocean, New Guinea
1984 November 22	1:59	53	New Guinea, South Pacific Ocean
1985 November 12	1:59	431	Antarctica
1986 October 3	0:01	1	North Atlantic Ocean
1987 March 29	0:08	3	South Atlantic Ocean, Central Africa
1988 March 18	3:46	109	Sumatra, Borneo, Philippines
1990 July 22	2:33	130	Soviet Union, Pacific Ocean
1991 July 11	6:54	161	Hawaii, Mexico, South America
1992 June 30	5:20	186	South Atlantic Ocean
1994 November 3	4:15	119	Bolivia, Brazil, South Atlantic Ocean
1995 October 24	2:10	49	India, Southeast Asia, Indonesia
1997 March 9	2:50	231	Arctic Ocean, Russia
1998 February 26	4:08	95	Pacific Ocean, Venezuela, Atlantic Ocean
1999 August 11	2:23	70	Central Europe, Middle East, India
2001 June 21	4:57	124	South Atlantic Ocean, Africa, Madagascar
2002 December 4	2:04	54	Southern Africa, Indian Ocean
2003 November 23	1:57	308	Antarctica
2005 April 8	0:42	17	South Pacific Ocean, Colombia, Venezuela
2006 March 29	4:07	114	Africa, Turkey, Georgia, Russia, Kazakhstan
2008 August 1	2:27	147	China, Russia, Kazakhstan
2009 July 22	6:39	161	India, China, Pacific Ocean
2010 July 11	5:20	161	Pacific Ocean, Chile

Sciences

THE PLANETS

Planet	Mean Distance from Sun (millions of miles)	(millions of kilometers)	Sidereal Period of Revolution (years)	(days)	Diameter (miles)	(kilometers)	Period of Rotation (days)
Mercury	36	57.9	0.241	87.97	3,100	4,878	58.7
Venus	67	108.2	0.615	224.70	7,700	12,104	−243.0
Earth	93	149.6	1.000	365.26	7,920	12,756	0.997
Mars	141	227.9	1.881	686.98	4,200	6,794	1.026
Jupiter	483	778.3	11.862		88,640	142,796	0.413
Saturn	886	1,427.0	29.46		74,500	120,000	0.443
Uranus	1,782	2,869.6	84.01		32,000	52,400	−0.65
Neptune	2,793	4,496.6	164.79		31,000	50,450	0.72
Pluto	3,670	5,913	247.7		1,500	2,400	6.387

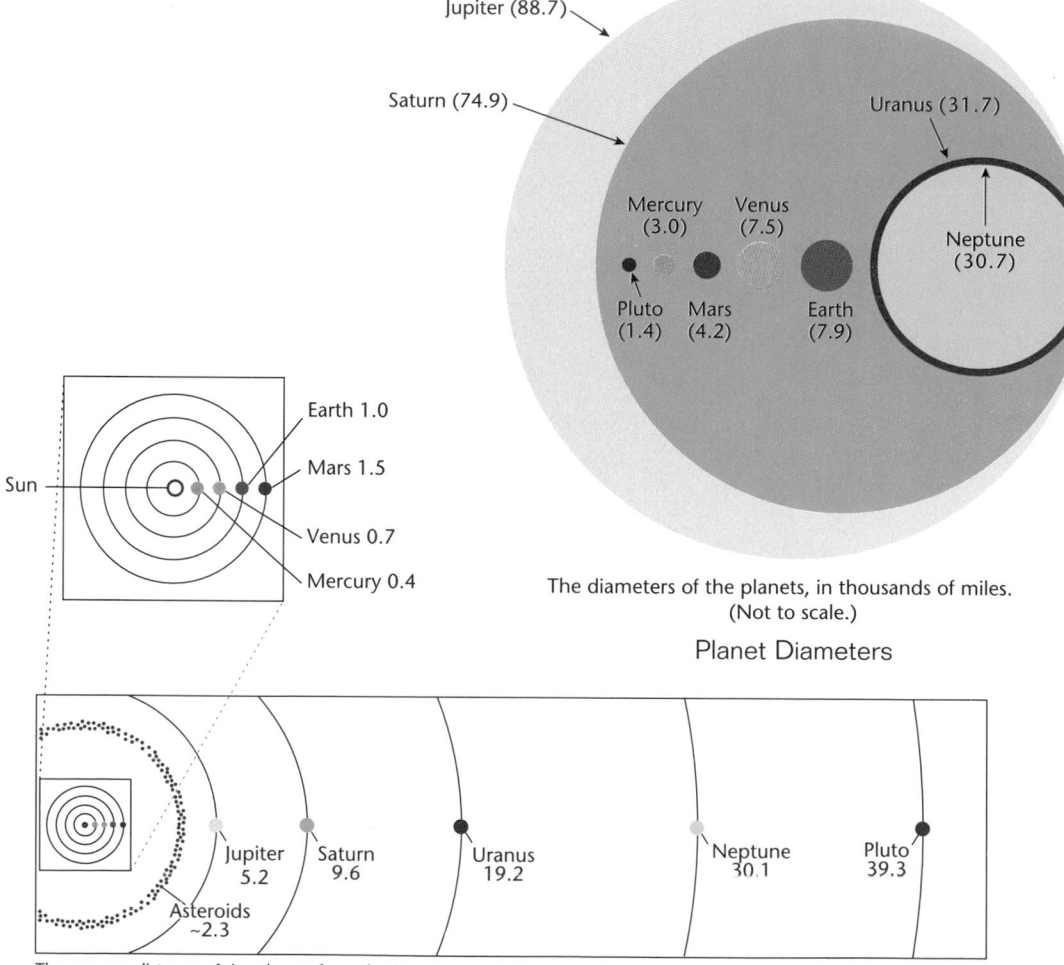

The diameters of the planets, in thousands of miles.
(Not to scale.)

Planet Diameters

The average distance of the planets from the Sun. The numbers in the diagram are astronomical units (A.U.), that is, the average distance between the Earth and the Sun. One A.U. is 9.3×10^7 miles, or 1.50×10^8 kilometers. (Not to scale.)

Distance of Planets from the Sun

THE LIFE OF A STAR

A star begins its life by condensing out of the gases and dust that make up a nebula. Gravity causes the resulting globule to contract, thus heating up its center. When the temperature rises to a critical level, the mass starts to glow, becoming a protostar. The protostars with sufficient mass begin to convert hydrogen gas to helium by a nuclear reaction called fusion; those with insufficient mass become "failed stars," often called brown dwarf stars. If the star is successful at creating fusion, it enters its mature stages, in which it spends most of its life.

As the star ages, the core temperature rises enough so that the star becomes unstable. The core begins to deteriorate, while the outer layers swell out and cool, forming a red giant. At this stage, the typical star begins to shed its outer layers, creating a planetary nebula. When the outer layers have completely dissipated, only the tightly packed core, known as a white dwarf, remains.

If the star has a greater initial mass than an average star, however, the accelerated rate of core deterioration results in the star's sudden collapse, followed by a catastrophic explosion known as a supernova. Hypothetically, the superdense material forming at its core may not explode at all; instead, it could go on shrinking to form a black hole.

The Hertzsprung-Russell diagram, which charts stellar luminosity against temperature, traces the evolutionary stages and characteristics of a star's life cycle.

Hertzsprung-Russell Diagram

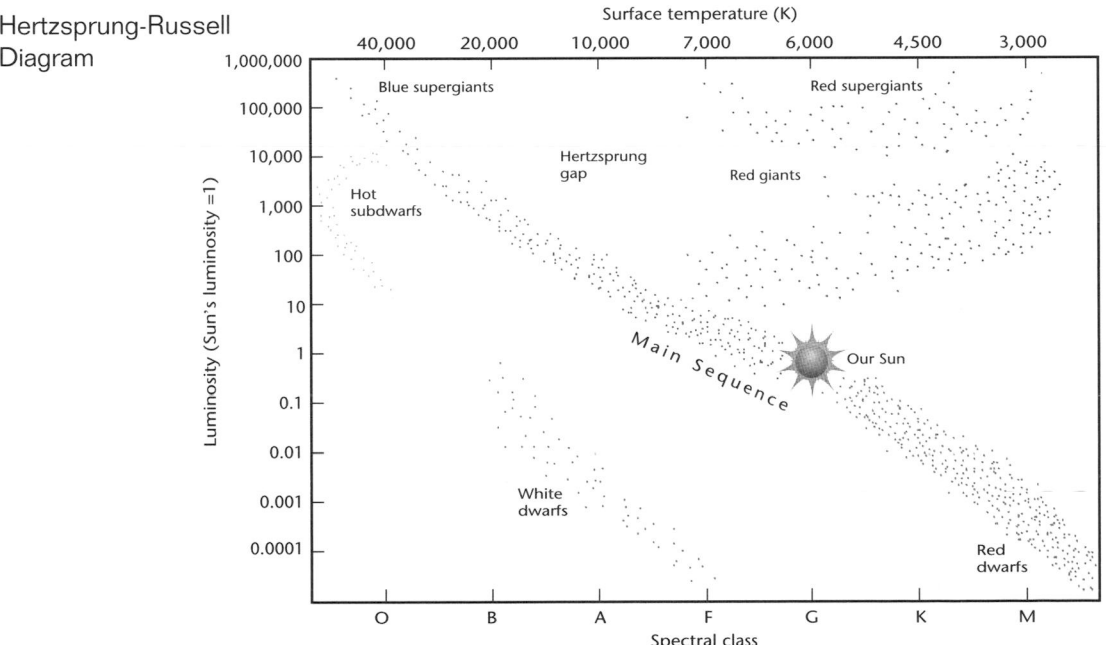

TYPES OF STARS

Not all stars are similar to our Sun. The differences are based on ages, size, formation, and structure of each star. The following is a brief list of the major stellar types.

black dwarfs Stars in the latest stage of stellar life. After a star about the size of our Sun becomes a white dwarf, its energy is dissipated into space, and it is no longer luminous. Theoretically, the universe is not old enough to have formed any black dwarfs.

black holes Theoretical regions of space that form when a massive star collapses. Because their gravitational field is so strong, light (photons) cannot escape—thus black holes can never really be seen. Black holes are inferred to exist by their gravitational effects on material falling into them. The binary star system Cygnus X-1 and the

Sciences

A Closer Look

Understanding the Invisible

A black hole is a theoretical region of space in which the gravitational field is so strong that photon (light) particles cannot escape. To imitate a black hole's density, the Earth would have to be crushed to the size of a marble. Black holes are thought to be massive stars at the ends of their stellar lives. The problem with detecting a black hole is obvious. Because they don't produce or reflect light, seeing them in the inky, black nighttime sky is impossible. Astronomers infer the presence of a black hole by the gravitational effects on the material falling into it.

J. Robert Oppenheimer and Hartland Snyder conceived the idea of a "black hole" in 1939 on the basis of Einstein's theory of general relativity. The idea was ignored, however, for several decades. One of the first possible black holes was found in the binary system Cygnus X-1, an X-ray source in the constellation of Cygnus. In 1994, astronomers using the Hubble Space Telescope noted that the region around the elliptical galaxy M87 in the Virgo Cluster was a possible black hole. In 1997, astronomers collected dramatic evidence for a supermassive black hole in NGC 4486B, a small elliptical satellite galaxy of M87. Even more amazing, many astronomers speculate that the core of our own Milky Way galaxy is a black hole. All this evidence is circumstantial; but if the effects in these regions are not caused by black holes, no alternative hypothesis is available.

center of our own galaxy are thought to harbor black holes.

blue supergiants   The hottest, bluest, and most luminous stars. They are rare, and have large masses and low densities. Rigel in the constellation of Orion is a blue supergiant star.

hot subdwarfs   Stars with extremely high densities; they are also found at the center of most planetary nebulas, such as at the center of the Ring Nebula in the constellation Lyra.

neutron stars   The remains of a star with a mass between 1.4 and 3 solar masses. These stars collapse so violently that protons and electrons are rammed together to form neutrons. The mass of a neutron star is greater than the Sun, but a neutron star's size is only about 5 miles across *See also* **pulsars.**

novae   Usually associated with binary star systems, in which one of the stars is a white dwarf. As the mass from the companion star hits the white dwarf star, a fusion reaction occurs, and the star responds with a burst of brightness. Unlike the rare supernovae, novae appear once every few years.

pulsars   Thought to be rotating neutron stars. Their rotational speeds vary, from 642 times per second to once every 4 seconds. First discovered in 1967, pulsars send out radio waves in specific directions, much like a lighthouse beam of light sweeping around the sky.

red giants   Stars in the late stages of stellar life. They have low density and are brighter and larger than our Sun. Arcturus, in the constellation Boötes, is a red giant; it is predicted that our Sun will become a red giant at the end of its life, about 5 to 6 billion years from now.

red supergiants   The largest and brightest of stars, with a large mass and low density. Betelgeuse, in the constellation of Orion, is a red supergiant.

supernovae   Massive stars that undergo a gravitational collapse, then a gigantic explosion, blasting away the outer layers into space. The resulting gases spread out into space, with the core collapsing into a neutron star, or possibly a black hole. Seeing a supernova from Earth is rare. A supernova observed in the constellation of Taurus in 1054 produced the Crab Nebula. In 1987, one was viewed in the Large Magellanic Cloud, a neighboring galaxy.

variable stars   Stars that change in brightness over time. There are numerous reasons for variability in stars: two stars eclipsing each other, explosions on the star, or a natural pulsation caused by an imbalance between the star's outer layer and core. Depending on the type of variable star, brightness can vary over the course of a day, a year, or several years.

white dwarfs   Stars at the end of stellar life. They form when a star depletes its thermonuclear energy, ceasing fusion. As the star collapses under its own weight, it becomes very dense. The gravitational energy is converted to heat, and the star continues to shine. The companion star of Sirius, in the constellation of Canis Major, is a white dwarf.

white holes   Theoretical stars that have properties opposite from black holes. Instead of pulling matter into them, white holes are regions in which matter spontaneously appears.

CONSTELLATIONS

THE 12 ZODIACAL CONSTELLATIONS

Aquarius, the Water-Bearer
Aries, the Ram
Cancer, the Crab
Capricornus, the Goat
Gemini, the Twins
Leo, the Lion
Libra, the Balance or Scales
Pisces, the Fish
Sagittarius, the Archer
Scorpius, the Scorpion
Taurus, the Bull
Virgo, the Virgin

THE 28 CONSTELLATIONS NORTH OF THE ZODIAC

Andromeda, the Chained Lady
Aquila, the Eagle
Auriga, the Charioteer
Boötes, the Herdsman
Camelopardalis, the Giraffe
Canes Venatici, the Hunting Dogs
Cassiopeia, the Lady in the Chair
Cepheus, the King
Coma Berenices, Berenice's Hair
Corona Borealis, the Northern Crown
Cygnus, the Swan
Delphinus, the Dolphin
Draco, the Dragon
Equuleus, the Colt
Hercules (Kneeling)
Lacerta, the Lizard
Leo Minor, the Lesser Lion
Lynx, the Lynx
Lyra, the Lyre
Ophiuchus, the Serpent Holder
Pegasus, the Winged Horse
Perseus, the Hero
Sagitta, the Arrow
Serpens, the Serpent

Triangulum, the Triangle
Ursa Major, the Greater Bear
Ursa Minor, the Lesser Bear
Vulpecula, the Fox

THE 48 CONSTELLATIONS SOUTH OF THE ZODIAC

Antlia, the Air Pump
Apus, the Bird of Paradise
Ara, the Altar
Caelum, the Engraver's Chisel
Canis Major, the Greater Dog
Canis Minor, the Lesser Dog
Carina, the Keel
Centaurus, the Centaur
Cetus, the Whale
Chamaeleon, the Chameleon
Circinus, the Pair of Compasses
Columba, (Noah's) Dove
Corona Australis, the Southern Crown
Corvus, the Crow
Crater, the Bowl
Crux, the (Southern) Cross
Dorado, the Gilthead or Swordfish
Eridanus, the River
Fornax, the Furnace
Grus, the Crane
Horologium, the Clock
Hydra, the Water-Serpent or Hydra (fem.)
Hydrus, the Water-Snake or Sea-Serpent (masc.)
Indus, the Indian
Lepus, the Hare
Lupus, the Wolf
Mensa, the Table Mountain
Microscopium, the Microscope
Monoceros, the Unicorn
Musca, the Fly
Norma, the Square or Rule
Octans, the Octant
Orion, the Hunter
Pavo, the Peacock
Phoenix, the Fabulous Bird
Pictor, the Painter's Easel
Piscis Austrinus, the Southern Fish
Puppis, the Stern
Pyxis, the (Ship's) Compass
Reticulum, the Net
Sculptor, the Sculptor's Shop
Scutum, the Shield
Sextans, the Sextant
Telescopium, the Telescope
Triangulum Australe, the Southern Triangle
Tucana, the Toucan
Vela, the Sails
Volans, the Flying Fish

Sciences

THE 25 NEAREST STAR SYSTEMS

Components in the following table are referred to as A, B, or C in the case of multiple-star systems.

A *light-year* is the distance light travels in a year, equal to 5.88 trillion miles (9.46 trillion kilometers).

Rank	Name	Components	Constellation	Distance from Sun (light–years)
1a	Proxima Cantauri		Centauras	4.23
1b	Rigil Kentaurus	A & B	Centaurus	4.35
2	Barnard's Star		Ophiuchus	5.98
3	Wolf 359		Leo	7.80
4	Lalande 21185		Ursa Major	8.23
5	L 726-8	A & B	Cetus	8.57
6	Sirius	A & B	Canis Major	8.57
7	Ross 154		Sagittarius	9.56
8	Ross 248		Andromeda	10.33
9	Epsilon Eridani		Eridanus	10.67
10	Ross 128		Virgo	10.83
11	L 789-6	A, B, & C	Aquarius	11.08
12	Groomsbridge 34	A & B	Andromeda	11.27
13	Epsilon Indi		Indus	11.29
14	61 Cygni	A & B	Cygnus	11.30
15	BD +59° 1915	A & B	Draco	11.40
16	Tau Ceti		Cetus	11.40
17	Procyon	A & B	Canis Minor	11.41
18	Lacaille 9352		Piscis Austrinus	11.47
19	GJ 111		Cancer	11.83
20	GJ 1061		Horologium	12.06
21	L 725-32		Cetus	12.20
22	BD +05° 1668		Canis Minor	12.34
23	Lacaille 8760		Microscopium	12.61
24	Kapteyn's Star		Pictor	12.63
25	Krüger 60	A & B	Cepheus	12.95

COMMON ASTRONOMY TERMS

Additional terms are defined in the preceding astronomy sections.

aberration   The apparent displacement of a star owing to the orbital motion of Earth and the bending of light rays from the star. As the Earth travels around the Sun, the aberration causes the star to appear to trace an ellipse about its true position.

absorption nebula   A nebula seen in silhouette because it is absorbing or blocking light from behind. It is also called a dark nebula.

accretion   The process where small particles coalesce by collisions or mutual gravitational pull, creating larger bodies. Accretion is suspected as a major process in the formation of the planets and satellites in any solar system.

albedo   The proportion of light reflected from a celestial body. The Moon reflects only about 7 percent of the sunlight falling on it, whereas the albedo of Venus is more than 70 percent owing to its heavy cloud cover, which reflects a greater proportion of light.

altitude   Number of degrees above the horizon of an object on the celestial plane.

aphelion   The point in an object's orbit that is farthest from the Sun. *See also* **perihelion.**

apogee   The point in the Moon's orbit (or any other orbiting body, such as an artificial satellite) when it is farthest from the Earth. *See also* **perigee.**

asterism   A pattern of stars that does not constitute one of the 88 official constellations. For example, the Big Dipper in the constellation of Ursa Major is an asterism.

asteroid   A small, rocky object or minor planet that orbits the Sun. Most asteroids have orbits in the asteroid belt, located between the orbits of Mars and Jupiter. More than 5,000 of these objects have been identified, and it is likely that thousands more exist undetected in the solar system. Asteroids may be the debris from collisions between larger celestial bodies or the remnants of extinct comets.

astrometry   The measure of the positions and apparent motions of celestial objects and the attempt to understand the factors that influence such movements.

astronomical unit   An astronomical distance, equal to the average distance from the Earth to the Sun, or about 93,000,000 miles (150,000,000 kilometers).

big bang model   A theory that describes the beginning of our universe as a titanic explosion. This explosion did not occur at a particular point in space, according to the theory, but rather was a transition from enormous density and temperature throughout all space to conditions of even lower density and lower temperature as space itself expanded. After the hypothetical explosion, the universe was swamped with energy in the form of radiant energy and various atomic particles. This phase was followed by a cooling and thinning out of the universe. It is believed that the universe is still expanding at this time.

binary star   Two stars that are gravitationally attracted to each other. *See also* **double star.**

celestial sphere   An imaginary sphere used to locate the positions and track the motions of all astronomical objects.

comet   A small object composed of rock, ice, and gases moving about the Sun in an elliptical orbit. A comet has three distinct components: the *nucleus,* made up of rock and ice; the *coma,* consisting of gases and dust; and the *tail,* formed when gases and dust spread out from the nucleus or coma. Short-period comets complete their orbits in less than 200 years; long-period comets make take thousands of years to revolve around the Sun, or may never return at all (parabolic orbit). Some astronomers believe that comets originate in the Oort cloud, a hypothetical region or space that lies outside the solar system.

corona   The outer envelope, or "atmosphere," of gas surrounding the Sun, possibly extending to the orbit of Earth. During an eclipse of the Sun, the corona may be visible around the edges of the moon. It has a density that is about one-millionth that of the atmosphere of Earth.

The light that leaves the Sun takes 8 minutes to reach the earth.

cosmogony   The study of how the universe was formed.

cosmology   The study of the universe at large, of the distribution and behavior of the matter and energy in it, of the laws governing these factors, and of its origin and evolution.

dark matter   Matter that is thought to exist in the universe but has not yet been observed. It is based on measurements of unexplained gravitational effects on visible matter.

declination   On the celestial sphere, the coordinate analogous to latitude on the Earth. Declination is measured in degrees, minutes, and seconds of arc north (positive above the celestial equator) or south (negative below the celestial equator).

Doppler effect   The phenomenon in which, as a source of waves (i.e., sound or light) and the observer move relative to each other, the emitted wavelength appears to change. In astronomy, Doppler shifts are used to determine the velocity and direction of distant objects. For example, light from a galaxy shifts to the red on the electromagnetic spectrum if the galaxy is moving away from the observer (red shift) and to the blue if the galaxy is moving toward the observer (blue shift).

double star   Two stars that appear close together along a line of sight. Double stars may be an optical double, which are stars that just appear to be close as seen from Earth but are physically quite distant from one another; or true binaries, stars that are gravitationally bound to one another.

ecliptic   The apparent path of the Sun in the sky as seen from Earth.

fireball   A bright meteor, with an apparent magnitude ranging from about –5 to –20 (to compare, the Sun has an apparent magnitude of –26.7). Fireballs are sometimes seen during the day.

galaxy   A large system of stars, usually containing between 1 million and 1 trillion stars, along with clouds of gas and dust. Galaxies are sometimes classified according to their shapes as spiral, elliptical, or irregular.

globular cluster   A nearly spherical, dense cluster of hundreds of thousands to millions of stars.

The Milky Way galaxy contains several hundred billion stars and is about 100,000 light years across. Our solar system orbits the Milky Way once every 250 million years.

gravitational collapse   The contraction of a star when the pressure of thermonuclear reactions can no longer sustain the force of self-gravitation. Collapse occurs at the end of a star's life when its fuel of hydrogen and other elements is depleted. Depending on its original mass, the star may evolve into a white dwarf, a neutron star, or a black hole, or it may explode as a supernova.

inferior conjuction   The passage of Mercury or Venus between the Earth and the Sun.

libration   The effect that allows an observer on Earth to see about 59 percent of the Moon's surface, slightly more than would otherwise be visible. Because the Moon's rotation and orbital period are equal (on average), the Moon always keeps the same face to the Earth. Libration occurs because the Moon's elliptical orbit speed is not constant and its orbit is slightly tilted.

meteor   A meteoroid that produces a streak of light as it enters the Earth's atmosphere and is vaporized by the resulting friction. This phenomenon is quite common when the Earth passes through swarms of meteoroids. The resulting meteor showers are usually associated with a specific constellation and time of year. Meteors are commonly called shooting or falling stars.

meteorite   A meteor that passes through the outer layers of the Earth's atmosphere and strikes the planet's surface. The resulting explosive impact buries or disperses the meteorite, leaving a crater behind. Meteorites are classified as *siderites* (containing only metals, chiefly nickel and iron), *aerolites* (stony objects consisting of a variety of mineral elements), and *siderolites* (meteorites composed of both metal and stone).

meteoroid   A small, solid particle of rock or other material that orbits the Sun, often along the same path as comets. Meteoroids form when a comet breaks up or leaves debris in its wake. Thousands of meteoroids traveling in closely grouped packs are called a swarm.

Milky Way   The spiral galaxy in which our solar system is located. It contains about 150 billion stars, has a diameter of 500,000 light-years, and is about 12 billion years old.

nadir   The point directly below the observer, or 90 degrees below the horizon. *See also* **zenith.**

nebula   A concentration of gas and dust in the galaxy.

oblate The shape of a planet or natural satellite that is not completely spherical but bulges in the center and is flattened at the poles. The shape is usually caused by rapid spinning or the gravitational pull from an accompanying moon. For example, rapidly rotating Jupiter is an oblate spheroid.

occulation The crossing of one body in front of another, such as the Moon in front of a star, relative to an observer.

opposition The point in a planet's orbit when it is 180 degrees from the Sun, usually as observed from Earth.

orbit The path of an object around a central body; gravitational attraction keeps the bodies in orbit.

parallax The change in the relative position of an object when viewed from different places; in astronomy, the closer the object, the greater the parallax.

perigee The point where the Moon (or any other orbiting body, such as an artificial satellite) is closer in its orbit to the Earth. *See also* **apogee.**

perihelion The point in the orbit of an object when it is closest to the Sun. *See also* **aphelion.**

perturbation A local gravitational disturbance in the uniform motion of a body because of the gravitational influence of another object. For example, a comet orbiting the Sun can be perturbed by a close encounter with Jupiter, the solar system's largest planet, which influences the orbit of the comet.

planetoid A mostly obsolete term, usually used to describe the larger remnants of rocks left over from the formation of the solar system.

plasma Matter in the form of electrically charged particles; the state in which most of the universe exists.

proper motion The apparent angular motion of an object across the sky, determined as change in position with respect to the background star; caused by the star's true motion and the relative motion of the solar system.

quasar A contraction of the word *quasi-stellar,* used to describe celestial objects with a starlike appearance. Quasars are the most distant objects known. They have large red shifts indicating great recessional velocities and emit energy that is more than a thousand times that of an average galaxy.

About half of the stars we can see are actually two stars that orbit each other.

red shift The shift of a spectrum of light toward long, red wavelengths owing to the Doppler effect of recession of a star. The faster an object recedes from Earth, the greater the shift of its light toward the red end of the spectrum.

revolution The movement of an object around a central body.

right ascension The angle of an object eastward from the vernal equinox, along the celestial equator; right ascension is measured in hours, minutes, and seconds.

rotation The movement of a body as it turns on its axis.

sidereal time Time that is measured by the rotation of Earth with respect to the stars, as distinguished from solar time, which is based on the rotation of Earth with respect to the Sun.

solar wind A stream of particles, primarily proton and electrons, that constantly flows outward from the Sun.

space-time A four-dimensional way of describing events and locations with three units of distance and one of time. Under the influence of gravity, space-time can actually warp and bend.

"Astronomers" in chapter 5; "Astronomy Symbols" in chapter 12
Go to

Sciences

spectrum   Radiation (usually visible light) broken into its component wavelengths.

spectroscope   An instrument used to determine the spectrum or wavelength of a ray of light emanating from an object. A spectroscope is often used in astronomy.

star   A spherical celestial body consisting of a large mass of hot gas held together by its own gravity. It is self-luminating because of extensive internal nuclear reactions. Our Sun is a typical star.

superior conjunction   For a planet (Mercury or Venus) inside the Earth's orbit, the condition when the planet is behind the Sun, relative to the Earth.

syzygy   The condition when three celestial bodies are arranged in a straight line. Syzygy occurs during solar and lunar eclipses, when the Sun, Moon, and Earth are aligned.

terminator   The line separating sunlight and darkness on a planet or moon.

transit   The movement of a smaller object across the lighted face of a larger object, such as the movement of Mercury across the face of the Sun, or the moon Io across the face of the planet Jupiter.

universe   The entirety of all that is known to exist. The size of the observable universe is limited to the distance light has traveled since the Big Bang.

zenith   The point directly overhead from the observer, or 90 degrees above the horizon. *See also* **nadir.**

zodiacal light   A faint cone of light seen along the ecliptic at sunset, usually around the time of the equinox. It is caused by sunlight scattering small dust particles that possibly have an interplanetary origin.

CHEMISTRY

ELEMENTS AND THEIR SYMBOLS

Atomic Number	Symbol	Element	Atomic Number	Symbol	Element	Atomic Number	Symbol	Element
1	H	Hydrogen	22	Ti	Titanium	43	Tc	Technetium
2	He	Helium	23	V	Vanadium	44	Ru	Ruthenium
3	Li	Lithium	24	Cr	Chromium	45	Rh	Rhodium
4	Be	Beryllium	25	Mn	Manganese	46	Pd	Palladium
5	B	Boron	26	Fe	Iron	47	Ag	Silver
6	C	Carbon	27	Co	Cobalt	48	Cd	Cadmium
7	N	Nitrogen	28	Ni	Nickel	49	In	Indium
8	O	Oxygen	29	Cu	Copper	50	Sn	Tin
9	F	Fluorine	30	Zn	Zinc	51	Sb	Antimony
10	Ne	Neon	31	Ga	Gallium	52	Te	Tellurium
11	Na	Sodium	32	Ge	Germanium	53	I	Iodine
12	Mg	Magnesium	33	As	Arsenic	54	Xe	Xenon
13	Al	Aluminum	34	Se	Selenium	55	Cs	Cesium
14	Si	Silicon	35	Br	Bromine	56	Ba	Barium
15	P	Phosphorus	36	Kr	Krypton	57	La	Lanthanum
16	S	Sulfur	37	Rb	Rubidium	58	Ce	Cerium
17	Cl	Chlorine	38	Sr	Strontium	59	Pr	Praseodymium
18	Ar	Argon	39	Y	Yttrium	60	Nd	Neodymium
19	K	Potassium	40	Zr	Zirconium	61	Pm	Promethium
20	Ca	Calcium	41	Nb	Niobium	62	Sm	Samarium
21	Sc	Scandium	42	Mo	Molybdenum	63	Eu	Europium

Sciences

Atomic Number	Symbol	Element	Atomic Number	Symbol	Element	Atomic Number	Symbol	Element
64	Gd	Gadolinium	80	Hg	Mercury	96	Cm	Curium
65	Tb	Terbium	81	Tl	Thallium	97	Bk	Berkelium
66	Dy	Dysprosium	82	Pb	Lead	98	Cf	Californium
67	Ho	Holmium	83	Bi	Bismuth	99	Es	Einsteinium
68	Er	Erbium	84	Po	Polonium	100	Fm	Ferium
69	Tm	Thulium	85	At	Astatine	101	Md	Mendelevium
70	Yb	Ytterbium	86	Rn	Radon	102	No	Nobelium
71	Lu	Lutetium	87	Fr	Francium	103	Lw	Lawrencium
72	Hf	Hafnium	88	Ra	Radium	104	Rf	Rutherfordium
73	Ta	Tantalum	89	Ac	Actinium	105	Db	Dubnium
74	W	Tungsten	90	Th	Thorium	106	Sg	Seaborgium
75	Re	Rhenium	91	Pa	Protactinium	107	Bh	Bohrium
76	Os	Osmium	92	U	Uranium	108	Hs	Hassium
77	Ir	Iridium	93	Np	Neptunium	109	Mt	Meitnerium
78	Pt	Platinum	94	Pu	Plutonium			
79	Au	Gold	95	Am	Americium			

The names of six recently created chemical elements, 104 through 109, are subject to confirmation by the International Union of Pure and Applied Chemistry in August 1998.

THE PERIODIC TABLE OF THE ELEMENTS

The Periodic Table of the Elements is a listing of the chemical symbols (and often many of their physical characteristics) of 109 elements. The first 92 elements occur in nature, with a few exceptions: astatine (atomic number 85), technetium (atomic number 43), and some other elements are artificial although their artificiality is debated. The remaining elements have been artificially created in laboratory particle accelerators. The chemical elements exist in a free state or combined with another element.

In the Periodic Table, the elements are arranged in order of increasing atomic number from left to right and from top to bottom. The horizontal rows of elements are called *periods;* the vertical columns of related elements are called *groups.* Across the table, there is a general trend from metallic to non-metallic elements; down a group, there is an increase in atomic size and in eletropositive behavior. The members of a group have similar behavior because of similarities in their electron configurations.

The first three periods are the short periods, containing elements with only *s* and *p* level electrons (the lowest energy levels) and having only up to 2 and 8 electrons, respectively. Period 1 consists of hydrogen (H) and helium (He) only, the two most abundant elements in the universe. Period 2 elements begin filling the second energy level, and the period ends with neon (Ne, atomic number 10). In Period 3, the third level is filled, ending with argon (Ar, atomic number 18).

Periods 4 and 5 are longer, each with 18 elements. Period 4 begins with potassium (K) followed by calcium (Ca). But after that, higher energy electrons (the *d* orbitals) begin to fill, giving the next elements in the center of the table characteristics unlike any of the previous elements. These elements, with their incomplete *d* subshell, are known as *transition* elements. This pattern repeats for Period 5 elements. Periods 6 and 7 contain 32 elements each. The Period 6 elements that follow lanthanum (La, atomic number 57) are called *lanthanoids.* This is also called the *rare earth series* and includes cerium (Ce) through lutetium (Lu).

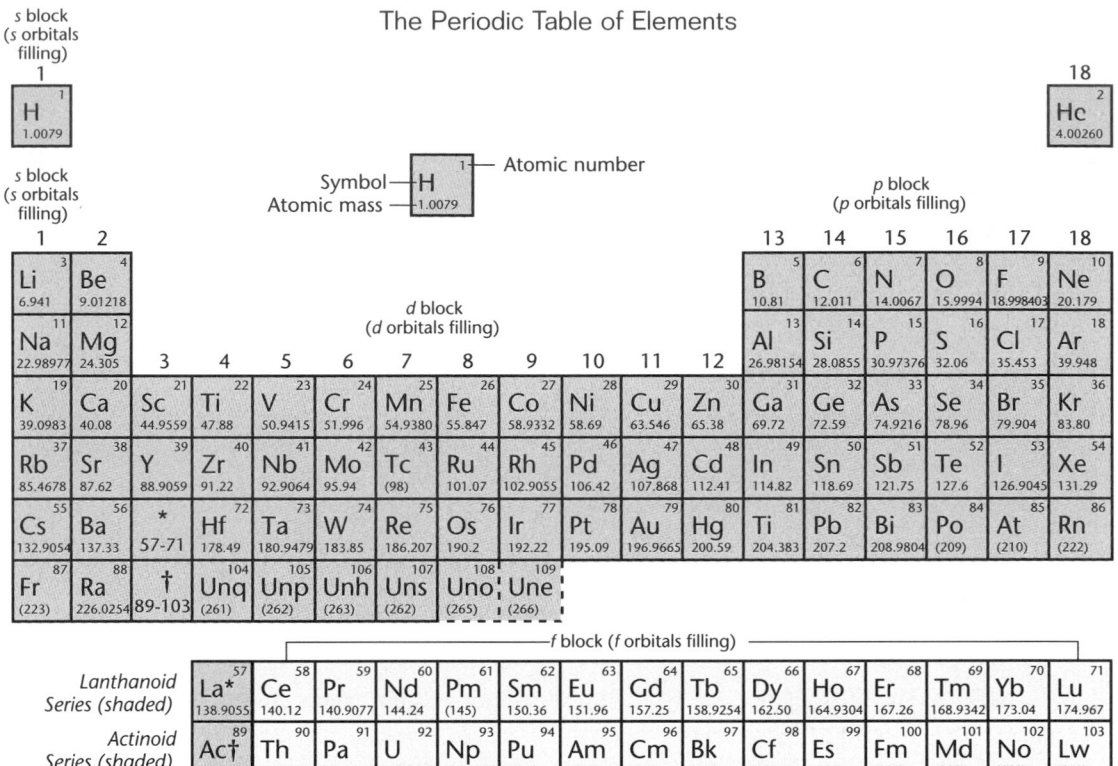

The Periodic Table of Elements

Period 7's transitional elements follow actinium (Ac, atomic number 89) and are called *actinoids*. This group includes thorium (Th) through lawrencium (Lw). Both of these groups are filling the *f* sublevel orbitals.

The Periodic Table can be divided into three basic groups: metals, nonmetals, and semimetals. In general, when you view the table, the metals are on the left, the nonmetals are on the extreme right, and the semimetals are in the center.

Metals make up the majority of the groups of elements. Most metals such as sodium (Na) are solid at room temperature, with mercury (Hg) being the only liquid metal. Metals have higher melting and boiling points because the atoms in the crystals are tightly packed together. In addition, their densities are high because the heavy nuclei are also tightly packed together. Metals have only a few (usually no more than four) valence electrons in the outermost shells. These are electrons that are often given up in

a reaction, forming metallic, positive ions. Metals (such as gold and copper) are generally good conductors of electricity. Elements of Group 1, including lithium, sodium, and potassium (but excluding hydrogen), are known as alkali metals; Group 2 metals, including magnesium and calcium, are the alkaline earth metals.

Nonmetals are usually dull in appearance, brittle, and not good electrical conductors. Many of the chemically active nonmetals are the halogens (Group 7), the group of elements that includes chlorine, bromine, and iodine. This group is highly reactive and electronegative and contains fluorine, the most highly electronegative element.

COMMON CHEMISTRY TERMS

Additional terms are defined in "Common Physics Terms" in this chapter.

acid   A substance that, in liquid form, will turn blue litmus paper red, react with alkalis (bases) to form salts, and dissolve metals to form salts. On the pH scale of 0 to 14, acids register in numbers less than 7.

alcohol   Any of a group of organic compounds that contains a hydroxyl (OH) group. A common example is ethyl alcohol (C_2H_5OH).

alkali   Any compound that has chemical qualities of a base, such as reacting with acids to form salts. On the pH scale, alkalis register in numbers larger than 7.

anion   An ion with a negative electrical charge.

base   An alkaline substance, either in molecular or ionic form, that will accept or receive a proton from another chemical unit. An example is a hydroxyl ion.

benzene ring   A common organic molecule structure consisting of a ring of six carbon atoms with an equal number of attached hydrogen atoms (C_6H_6). Many organic chemicals occur in a benzene ring format with various atoms or radicals substituted for one or more hydrogen atoms, as in toluene and xylene as variations of benzene.

bond   A strong electrical force that holds atoms together in molecules, crystals, and other combinations. A molecular bond may depend on the attractive force of an electron whose orbit spans the outer shells of two or more component atoms. In double bonds, two pairs of electrons may be shared equally by adjacent atoms.

catalyst   A substance that accelerates a chemical reaction without becoming a part of the end product of the reaction. A catalyst can generally be recovered in its original form following the reaction.

compound   A substance formed by the combination of two or more chemical elements that cannot be separated from the combination by physical means. The constituent atoms, however, can usually be separated by means of chemical reactions.

Go to "Chemists" in chapter 5; "Chemistry Symbols" in chapter 12; "Chemical Additives" in chapter 19

electrolyte   Any chemical, such as a mineral, that when melted or dissolved in water will show an electrical attraction or conduct an electric current.

electron   A negatively charged particle that moves in an orbit about the nucleus of an atom.

element   A substance composed of atoms with the same atomic number or the same number of protons in their nuclei. Examples include oxygen, hydrogen, carbon, and gold.

hydrocarbon   Any of a large group of chemical compounds consisting primarily of carbon and hydrogen atoms, usually associated with current or past life processes.

hydroxyl   Pertaining to the negatively charged OH (oxygen + hydrogen) radical in an organic compound.

inorganic chemistry   A branch of chemical science that deals primarily with elements and compounds that do not include hydrocarbons.

isotope   One of two or more atoms having the same atomic number but a different mass number due to the different number of neutrons in their nuclei. An example is zinc, which has isotopes with five different mass numbers ranging from 64 to 70. However, all of the isotopes have equal nuclear charges, orbital electrons, and chemical properties.

mass number   The atomic weight of an isotope, calculated from the numbers of protons and neutrons in the nucleus.

matter   Anything that has weight or fills space, such as a solid, liquid, or gas.

organic chemistry   A branch of chemistry that specializes in the composition, properties, and reactions of hydrocarbon compounds.

oxidation   Any chemical reaction that increases the number of oxygen atoms in a compound, or in which the positive valence is increased by a loss of electrons.

Sciences

pH   A symbol for hydrogen ion activity of a substance as an expression of the negative logarithm of the concentration of hydrogen ions in moles per liter. Values of pH range from 0 to 14, with a pH of 7 representing acid-base neutrality. The degree of acidity increases as the number progresses toward zero, while alkalinity increases as the pH number approaches 14.

polymer   A huge molecule composed of repeating units of the same molecule. An example is polyethylene, formed by linking ethylene molecules into a giant chain.

reduction   A chemical reaction in which a substance gains electrons or loses part of its positive valence. Reduction generally occurs in a reaction that also involves oxidation.

solute   A substance that is dissolved in a solution.

solvent   The substance that represents the greatest proportion of parts of a solution when two or more substances, such as a solid and liquid, are mixed.

valence   A number that represents the combining power of an element, ion, or radical. The valence of hydrogen is +1, while the valence of oxygen is −2.

GEOLOGY AND GEOPHYSICS
LAYERS OF THE EARTH

Because the Earth's interior is inaccessible to observation, geologists have discerned its many layers by indirect methods. Earthquakes reveal the Earth's interior structure because certain seismic waves travel at varying speeds through materials of different densities. Other properties of the planet's interior can be inferred from magnetic, thermal, and gravitational characteristics.

CRUST

The Earth's outer solid *crust* surrounds the mantle. The crust makes up about 0.6 percent of the Earth's volume and 0.4 percent of its mass. Its overall thickness varies widely: beneath the oceans, the crust (mainly composed of basalt) ranges between 3 and 6.8 miles (5 to 11 kilometers) thick; beneath the continents, the crust (mostly light rocks such as granite) ranges between 12 and 40 miles (19 and 64 kilometers) thick.

The upper layer of the Earth is called the *lithosphere.* It includes the oceanic and continental crusts and part of the cooler, solid upper mantle.

MANTLE

The *mantle* makes up 84 percent of the Earth by volume and 67 percent by mass. It is about 1,802 miles (2,900 kilometers) thick and consists of silica, plus iron-, magnesium-, and other metal-rich minerals. The *Gutenberg discontinuity* separates the Earth's mantle from the outer core; the *Mohoovičić discontinuity* separates the uppermost portion of the mantle from the crust.

If the 4.6 billion years of Earth's existence were only a single day, the 40,000 years of human existence would cover only the last 2 seconds.

The hot plastic *asthenosphere,* part upper mantle and lower crust, separates the more brittle crust-mantle lithosphere above from the mesosphere below. Thought to be responsible for the movement of the lithospheric plates (crustal plates) that slowly "carry" the continents around the planet, the asthenosphere is about 186 miles (300 kilometers) thick. The more solid *mesosphere,* located below the asthenosphere, includes part of the upper mantle and all of the lower mantle.

CORE

The inner and outer *core* make up about 15 percent of the Earth by volume and 32 percent by mass. The *inner core* is about 800 miles (1,287 kilometers) thick; the *outer core* is about 1,400 miles (2,253 kilometers) thick. The inner core, thought to be solid, extends from the center of the Earth to the lower border of the outer core. The outer core, which appears to have characteristics of a liquid, extends to the Gutenberg discontinuity, the border

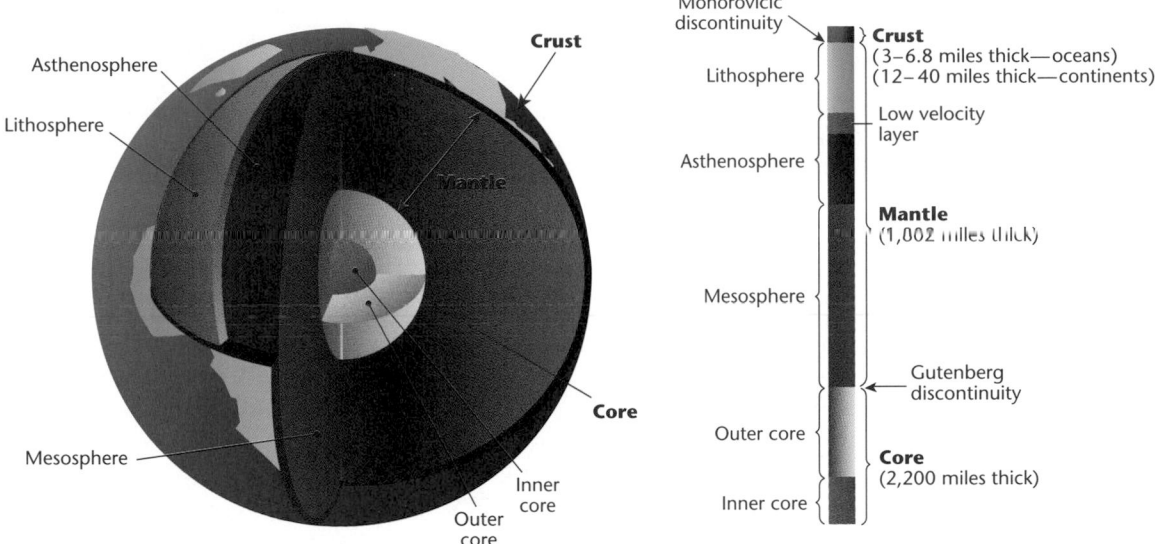

between the mantle and outer core. Because of its extreme density, the entire core seems to be composed of mostly iron, with smaller amounts of other dense elements such as nickel. The pressure within the solid inner core reaches about 3 million atmospheres (1 atmosphere equals the atmosphere pressure at sea level); temperatures measure between 7,200 and 9,000°F (4,000 to 5,000°C)—nearly as hot as the Sun's surface. The heat is from the natural radioactive decay of uranium; it is also from dissipated heat from the Earth as it cooled after formation.

GEOLOGICAL TIME CHART

Age in Millions of Years	Era	Period or Epoch		Important Physical Events	Animal Life
.01 ▶		Quaternary	Holocene	Repeated extensions of ice caps in arctic and north temperate areas	Modern human beings
			Pleistocene	Continents generally elevated, mountains high, deserts widespread	Primitive man
±.5 ▶	CENOZOIC		Pliocene	Mountain building in northwestern North America	Gorillas
				Deformation of Tethys geosyncline; Alps and Himalayas rise	
13 ±1 ▶		Tertiary	Miocene	Extensive erosion surfaces cut on Appalachians and Rockies	Whales, sabertooths
				Cool, dry climates over much of world	
25 ±1 ▶			Oligocene	Initiation of mountain building in Tethys geosyncline	Apes, bats
				River and floodplain deposits begin on Great Plains	

(left axis label: MILLIONS OF YEARS BEFORE THE PRESENT)

continues

(side tab: Sciences)

Continued

Age in Millions of Years	Era	Period or Epoch		Important Physical Events	Animal Life
36±2 ▶	CENOZOIC	Tertiary	Eocene	Climates warm and uniform; widespread jungles and forests	Alligators
58±2 ▶			Paleocene	Basins develop between ranges along Pacific Coast and Rockies	Kangaroos, birds, horses, camels, monkeys, elephants
65 ±2 ▶	MESOZOIC	Cretaceous		Mountain building in Rockies; seas invade much of western North America and cover Atlantic and Gulf coastal plains	Ancient birds, snakes, modern fish
135 ±5 ▶		Jurassic		Widespread mild, uniform climates Mountain building along Pacific Coast of North America Extensive marine invasions of southern and central Europe	Flying reptiles
180 ± ▶		Triassic		Fault basins in eastern North America Extensive deserts and dead seas develop in North America and Eurasia	Ichthyosaurs, tyrannosaurs
230 ±10 ▶	PALEOZOIC	Permian		Continents generally elevated Appalachian and Ural mountains complete their development Tethys geosyncline from Spain to India	Ammonites, finbacked reptiles
280 ±10 ▶		Carboniferous		Mountain building in southern North America and central Europe Extensive seas over much of interior North America	Amphibians, clams, lung fish
310 ±10 ▶		Devonian		Catskill delta built from New England mountains into New York and Pennsylvania Mountain building in northeastern North America Extensive submergence of geosynclines and interior of North America	Starfish
405 ±10 ▶		Silurian		Formation of Caledonian mountains in northwestern Europe Dead seas in Michigan, New York, Ohio, southeastern Canada Deltas and gravel beaches along eastern edge of Appalachian geosyncline	Sea scorpions, corals, sharks
425 ±10 ▶		Ordovician		Mountain building in northeastern North America Over 60 percent of North American continent covered by seas	Snails, jawless fish, echinoids
500 ±10 ▶		Cambrian		Climates generally mild and uniform Seas invade North American continent Geosynclines develop around edge of North America	Protozoans, trilobites

MILLIONS OF YEARS BEFORE THE PRESENT

Sciences

Age in Millions of Years	Era	Period or Epoch	Important Physical Events	Animal Life
c. 600 ▶			Fault basins in Lake Superior region	Jellyfish, flagellates, amoebas, worms, sponges
1,000 ▶	PRECAMBRIAN		Deformation and mountain building through central North America	
2,000 ▶			Geosynclines develop throughout central North America	
3,000 ▶			Extensive mountain building in Lake Superior region	
			Oldest dated rocks	
4,000 ▶			Probable origin of Earth from solar dust cloud	

PLATE TECTONICS

About six large plates and more than a dozen small crustal (lithospheric or tectonic) plates make up the Earth's crust, all moving around the planet in different directions and at various speeds (fractions of an inch per year). Most plates lie beneath a combination of ocean and continent; several lie only beneath ocean.

The theory of *plate tectonics* states that the lithosphere is divided into plates, or tabular blocks, that interact with each other over time. The crust and part of the solid upper mantle make up each crustal plate. The true mechanism for the movement of the crustal plates is still unknown. Scientists theorize that convection in the upper mantle–lower crust, or asthenosphere, slowly "carries" the lithospheric plates around the planet; another theory states that convection at a depth of about 375 to 435 miles (603 to 700 kilometers) in the part of the mantle (mesosphere) is transferred to the asthenoshere and moves the plates.

Crustal plates are created, are destroyed, and move past each other in a variety of ways.

Go to "The Animal Kingdom" and "The Plant Kingdom" in chapter 3; "Major Zoos and Aquariums" and "Major Botanical Gardens and Arboretums" in chapter 11

Plate movement in ocean basins includes *sea-floor spreading,* or diverging plates. A rift in the ocean floor constantly forms new crustal material—usually from volcanic action—and the ocean floor literally spreads apart. For example, the Mid-Atlantic Ridge is an area of sea-floor spreading that splits the Atlantic Ocean; the plates move laterally about 1 inch (2.54 centimeters) per year. Shallow, substantial earthquakes are associated with diverging plates.

When one plate sinks under another, it is called *subduction,* with the subducting plate gradually breaking apart. The destructive plate margins where this occurs are called *subduction zones.* The surface expression of this activity takes the form of volcanic island areas associated with oceanic trenches, or a volcanic mountain region on an adjacent landmass. For example, the Japan Trench off the island of Honshu is the line where the Pacific plate subducts under the Eurasian plate. Some of the largest and deepest earthquakes are associated with subducting plates.

When two plates ram into one another, it is called *colliding plate boundaries,* causing the crust to buckle from intense pressure. For example, the Himalayas were formed by the collision of the Indo-Australian plate and the Eurasian plate. Deep, substantial earthquakes are associated with

Sciences

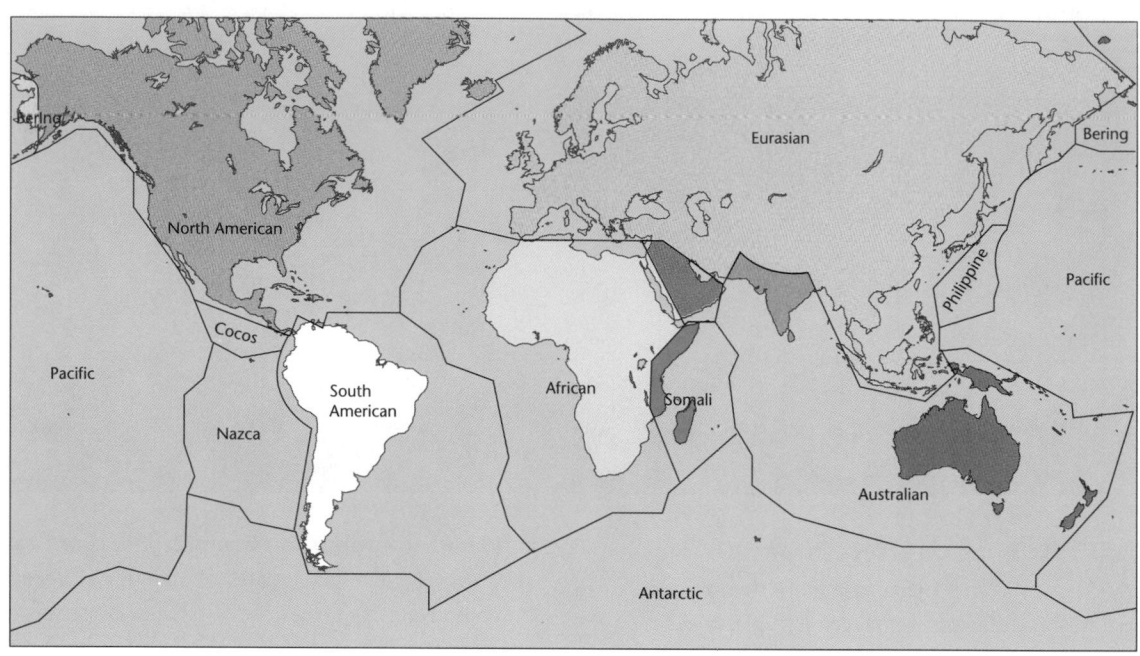

Crustal Plates Around the World (locations of crustal plates are approximate)

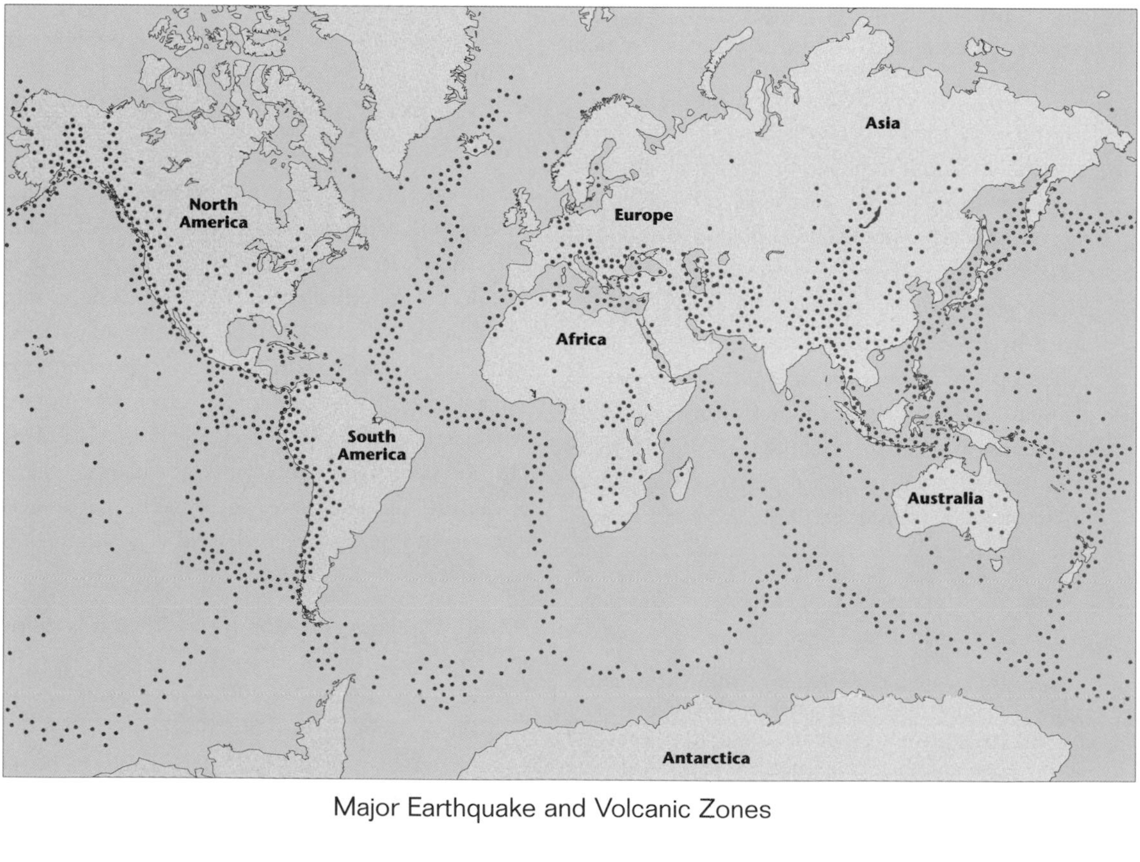

Major Earthquake and Volcanic Zones

Sciences

colliding plates. Even today, the Himalayas are still rising because of this collision—about $^1/_5$ inch (5 millimeters) per year.

When plates slide by each other, and no plate is created or destroyed, it is called a *transform boundary plate*. For example, along the San Andreas Fault in California, the Pacific plate slides northwest past the North American plate. (Contrary to popular belief, part of California will not "fall" into the ocean; rather part of the state is simply a section of the Pacific plate moving northwest at about 0.5 inch [1.3 centimeters] per year.) Shallow, substan-

tial earthquakes are associated with transform boundary plates.

Crustal plates have moved across the planet for at least the past 600 million years—and probably for billions of years before. Scientists believed that a supercontinent called *Pangaea* existed about 250 million years ago. (Pangaea was first proposed by Alfred Wegener in 1915.) By 180 million years ago, the supercontinent had broken up into *Gondwanaland,* or Gondwana (a hypothetical continent formed by the union of South America, Africa, Australia, India, and Antarctica), and

---

A Closer Look

Measuring an Earthquake

The *Mercalli earthquake intensity scale,* developed by Italian seismologist Giuseppe Mercalli in 1902, is a measure of an earthquake's destructiveness. The scale was modified by American seismologists in the 1930s (called the modified Mercalli scale). Modern technology has made the Mercalli scale obsolete, although the method is often used to fill in "seismic blanks" when there is an insufficient number of seismographs.

Level	Characteristic Effects in Populated Areas
I	Generally not felt; detectable by seismographs.
II	Felt by few people; objects may swing if suspended.
III	Felt by few people; mostly indoors; vibrations like a passing truck.
IV	Felt by many people indoors but few outdoors; windows, dishes, and doors rattle.
V	Felt by nearly everyone; sleepers awaken; small unstable objects may fall and break; doors move.
VI	Felt by everyone; some heavy furniture moves; people walk unsteadily; windows and dishes break; books fall from shelf; bushes and trees visibly shake.
VII	Difficult to stand; moderate to heavy damage to poorly constructed buildings; plaster, loose bricks, tiles, and stones fall; small landslides along slopes; water becomes turbid.
VIII	Difficult to steer cars; damage to good unbraced masonry; chimneys, monuments, towers, and elevated tanks fall; tree branches break; steep slopes crack.
IX	Extensive building damage; good masonry damaged seriously; foundations crack; serious damage to reservoirs; underground pipes break.
X	Most masonry, frame structures, and foundations destroyed; numerous large landslides; water thrown on banks of rivers and lakes; railroad tracks bend slightly.
XI	Few masonry buildings stand; railroad tracks bend severely; many bridges destroyed; underground pipelines completely inoperative.
XII	Nearly total destruction; large rock masses displaced; objects thrown into the air.

The *Richter scale,* used to measure earthquake intensity, was developed in 1935, by Charles Richter. The scale is logarithmic, which means that each successive whole number represents a 10-fold increase in power. (Although seismologists no longer use the Richter scale, the popular press often continues to refer to the scale, as so many readers are familiar with it.)

Each magnitude number represents the maximum amplitude of a seismic wave at a distance of 100 miles (161 kilometers). The difference in time between the first and second (primary and secondary) waves is measured, and an empirical factor is added (which takes into account the fact that the waves become weaker as they travel away from the focus) to determine the magnitude of the quake.

The most intense earthquake ever recorded, in Japan in 1933, measured 8.9 on the Richter scale. The 1989 earthquake in northern California measured 7.1 on this scale.

Sciences

Laurasia (composed of North America and Eurasia). About 65 million years ago—at approximately the time of extinction of the dinosaurs—the two continents began to separate, slowing forming the familiar outlines of today's continents. Scientists estimate that in 50 million years, the west coast of North America will tear itself free from the mainland, Australia will move northward and collide with Indonesia, and Africa and Asia will split apart at the Red Sea.

See also "Earth's Layers" and "Earthquakes" in this chapter.

EARTHQUAKES

Earthquakes are considered one of the most deadly natural catastrophes that can affect human life. Most often, a quake occurs in earthquake-prone zones where two tectonic plates meet, split, or slip by one another (*see* "Plate Tectonics," earlier in this chapter); the type of plate contact determines whether the earthquake will be shallow or deep. During the movement of these plates, intense forces overcome the friction between the plates. If the plates become "locked together," forces build up and eventually must give away—with the plates lurching into new positions and creating an earthquake. Other earthquakes form in association with volcanic regions, where the buildup of heat and pressure often triggers smaller tremors and localized quakes.

The *focus* is the point under the Earth's surface where the earthquake energy is released. The point on the surface just above the focus is called the *epicenter.* Most earthquake foci occur no more than 62 miles (100 kilometers) below the surface.

SOME IMPORTANT MINERALS AND THEIR USES

Mineral	Chemical Composition	Occurrence/ Important Producers	Uses
Arsenic	As	Chile, China, France, Sweden, Mexico, U.S.	Glassmaking, insecticides, preservatives
Beryl	$Be_3A_{12}Si_6O_{18}$	Brazil, South Africa, U.S.	Beryllium ore, gemstones
Borax	$Na_2B_4O_7 10H_2O$	Tibet, U.S.	Antiseptic, disinfectant, flux, soap, water softener
Calcite	$CaCO_3$	Worldwide*	Building stones, portland cement, quicklime, soil conditioner
Chromite	$FeCr_2O_4$	Brazil, Philippines, South Africa, Turkey, former USSR	Chemicals, chromium ore, refractories
Chrysotile (serpentine)	$Mg_3Si_2O_5(OH)_4$	Canada, Russia, U.S.	Asbestos
Copper	Cu	Canada, Chile, Russia, U.S.	Chemicals, electronics, metal alloys, wire
Corundum	Al_2O_3	Greece, India, Myanmar, Sri Lanka, Thailand, U.S.	Abrasives, bearings, gemstones
Diamond	C	Australia, Brazil, South Africa, U.S.	Drills, gemstones, industrial abrasives, jewelry, tools and dies
Dolomite	$CaMg(CO_3)_2$	Worldwide†	Building stones, cement productions, magnesium source, refractories
Emerald	$Be_3Al_2Si_6O_{18}$	Australia, Columbia, Rhodesia, U.S., former USSR	Gemstones
Fluorite	CaF_2	Germany, Mexico, U.S.	Chemicals, metallurgy, optics
Gold	Au	Australia, Canada, South Africa, U.S.	Coins, dentistry, electronics, jewelry
Graphite	C	Madagascar, Mexico, Sri Lanka, U.S.	Brake linings, electronics, lubricants, pencils

* Usually mined as limestone or marble.   † Usually mined as the rock dolomite.

Mineral	Chemical Composition	Occurrence/ Important Producers	Uses
Gypsum	$CaSO_4 \cdot 2H_2O$	Canada, France, Great Britain, Mexico, U.S.	Building materials, flux, plaster of paris, retardant (in cement)
Halite	NaCl	Worldwide	Chemical, rock salt
Hematite	Fe_2O_3	Brazil, Canada, U.S., Venezuela	Iron ore, pigment, polishing agent
Kaolinite	$Al_4Si_4O_{10}(OH)_2$	Worldwide/esp. England	Ceramics (esp. porcelain), paper (as coating)
Limonite	$Fe_2O_3 \cdot 3H_2O$	Worldwide/esp. U.S.	Iron ore, pigment
Magnesite	$MgCO_3$	Austria, China, U.S.	Cement production, chemicals, magnesium ore, refractories
Mercury	Hg	Mexico, Spain, U.S.	Barometers and thermometers, dentistry, electronics, lamps, medicines
Olivine	$(Mg,Fe)_2SiO_4$	Myanmar, U.S.	Gemstones, ornamental stone, refractories
Opal	SiO_2H_2O	Australia, Honduras, Mexico, U.S.	Gemstones
Platinum	Pt	Canada, South Africa, former USSR	Jewelry, catalytic converters, oil refining
Quartz	SiO	Worldwide	Building materials, electronics, gems, glass manufacture, jewelry, optics
Ruby	Al_2O_3	Myanmar, Sri Lanka, Thailand	Bearings, lasers, gemstones
Sapphire	Al_2O_3	Australia, Myanmar, Sri Lanka, Thailand, U.S.	Bearings, dies, gauges, gemstones
Siderite	$FeCO_3$	Germany, Great Britain	Iron ore
Silver	Ag	Canada, Mexico, Peru, U.S.	Coins, electronics, electroplating, jewelry, photography, silverware
Spinel	$MgAl_2O_4$	Myanmar, Sri Lanka, Thailand, U.S.	Gemstones
Sulfur	S	Worldwide/esp. Mexico, U.S.	Chemicals, explosives, fertilizers, sulfa drugs, sulfuric acid
Talc	$Mg_3Si_4O_{10}(OH)$	Brazil, France, Japan, U.S.	Ceramics, face powder, lubricants, paints, paper (as filler), sinks and countertops, talcum powder
Topaz	$Al_2SiO_4(F,OH)_2$	Brazil, Russia, U.S.	Gemstones
Uraninite	UO_2	Canada, South Africa, U.S.	Uranium ore (pitchblende)
Wolframite	$(Fe,Mn)WO_4$	Australia, England, Malay Peninsula, Myanmar, Portugal	Tungsten ore
Wollastonite	$CaSiO_3$	Finland, Italy, Romania, U.S.	Ceramics, paints (as filler)
Zircon	$ZrSiO_4$	Australia, Brazil, India, Sri Lanka, U.S.	Gemstones, zirconium ore

Sciences

IGNEOUS, SEDIMENTARY, AND METAMORPHIC ROCKS

Igneous rocks form by cooling and subsequent hardening of molten material. Intrusive igneous rocks are produced when magma hardens slowly underground. Extrusive igneous rocks result when lava, molten material that flows on the surface, solidifies quickly.

Sedimentary rocks form from the accumulation of eroded material that is transported and deposited by water, wind, or glaciers. Detrital sediments result when preexisting rock erodes; chemical sediments occur through precipitation in shallow marine environments.

Metamorphic rocks form when preexisting igneous or sedimentary rocks are transformed by external forces. Regional metamorphism alters rocks through heat and pressure, usually deep underground. Contact metamorphism occurs when a magma intrusion heats the surrounding country rock. Dynamic metamorphism is the product of tectonic forces, usually along thrust faults.

IGNEOUS, SEDIMENTARY, AND METAMORPHIC ROCKS

Name	Type	Texture	Mineral Composition
Igneous			
Andesite	Extrusive	Coarse grains/crystalline	Feldspar, pyroxene, mica
Anorthosite	Intrusive	Coarse grains/crystalline	Feldspar; traces of iron oxides, pyroxene, olivine
Basalt	Extrusive	Fine grains/crystalline	Feldspar, pyroxene, usu. magnetite
Gabbro	Intrusive	Coarse grains/crystalline	Feldspar, pyroxene, olivine, magnetite
Granite	Intrusive	Coarse grains/crystalline	Quartz, feldspar; mica, hornblende, muscovite often present
Obsidian	Extrusive	Glassy/crystalline	Silicate minerals, often quartz and feldspar
Pegmatite	Intrusive	Coarse grains/crystalline	Quartz, feldspar; mica or pyroxene often present
Porphyry	Intrusive	Medium grains/crystalline	Feldspar, quartz, olivine, or pyroxene embedded in dark-colored groundmass
Pumice	Extrusive	Fine grains/crystalline	Quartz, feldspar
Rhyolite	Extrusive	Fine grains/often glassy/crystalline	Quarty, alkali feldspars, light-colored
Sedimentary			
Breccia	Detrital	Coarse, angular grains	Cemented rock fragments; calcite or silica
Chalk	Chemical	Fine, rounded grains	Calcite
Chert	Chemical	Fine grains/crystalline	Silica
Clay	Detrital	Fine, angular grains	Clay minerals, quartz, feldspar, mica
Coal	Chemical	Fine-medium grains	Organic matter (high carbon content)
Conglomerate	Detrital	Coarse, rounded grains	Cemented rock fragments; silica, iron oxides, or calcite
Dolomite	Chemical	Fine-coarse grains/crystalline	Dolomite
Flint	Chemical	Fine grains/crystalline	Silica
Gypsum	Chemical	Crystalline	Gypsum
Limestone	Chemical	Fine-coarse, angular, or rounded grains	Calcite; lesser amounts of quartz, organic matter, or fossils often present
Sandstone	Detrital	Medium, angular or rounded grains	Quartz; lesser amounts of calcite, silica, iron oxides, feldspar, or mica
Shale	Detrital	Fine, angular grains	Clay minerals, mica, usu. organic matter or fossils
Siltstone	Detrital	Fine, angular grains	Quartz, calcite
Metamorphic			
Gneiss	Regional	Coarse grains/foliated, crystalline	Quartz, feldspar; garnet, hornblende, mica may be present
Marble	Contact	Coarse-fine grains/crystalline	Calcite or dolomite
Quartzite	Contact	Coarse grains/nonfoliated	Quartz
Schist	Regional	Medium grains/foliated	Quartz, feldspar, mica
Slate	Regional	Fine grains/foliated	Quartz, feldspar, mica, clay minerals

COMMON GEOLOGY AND CARTOGRAPHY TERMS

Additional terms are defined in the preceding geology and geophysics sections.

abyssal zone   A region of greatest ocean depth, generally greater than 1,000 meters, including the deep-sea trenches. Biological activity is rare in the abyssal zone; light does not penetrate the water, as the depth and pressure are tremendous. The region represents about 250 million square kilometers of Earth's surface.

age An interval of geological time that indicates when a body of rock was formed in the surface of Earth. A group of ages forms an epoch.

alluvium The sediment carried by rivers, including deposits from estuaries, lakes, and other freshwater bodies draining into a river. The particles of sediment are generally smaller than 0.02 millimeter, depending on such factors as valleyside slopes in the watershed, the distance carried downstream, and progressive wear on the particles as they move downstream.

barrier beach An accumulation of sand, rock, and other material lying parallel to the coast but separated from it by a channel; a barrier beach measures from a few meters to a few kilometers in width. Large barrier beaches may be identified as barrier islands. They are formed by the action of waves but are usually vulnerable to overwashing or breaching during severe storms.

bathyal zone A zone of ocean water ranging from about 200 meters to 1,000 meters in depth, generally located along continental slopes. Unlike the abyssal zone, light reaches the upper layer of the bathyal zone, and there is abundant biological activity in the water. The bathyal zone of the world covers a total of about 40 million square kilometers.

bed The smallest division of stratified sedimentary rock, usually occurring as a relatively thin sheet of sedimentary material separating distinctively different layers above and below it. A bed often marks a particular event in geologic history, such as a volcanic eruption, and it may contain fossils that help identify its age.

Cambrian The earliest period of the Paleozoic era, about 600 million years ago. Rocks formed at this period contain the earliest fossil remains of invertebrate animals.

continental drift The shifting of continental landmasses from one location to another on the face of Earth, owing to seafloor spreading.

Coriolis effect A force produced on objects moving on a north-south line on the surface of Earth because of the angular velocity of Earth as it rotates from west to east. Thus, a projectile fired directly southward from the North Pole would be deviated to the west. The Coriolis force affects mainly the flow of air in the atmosphere.

creep The slow movement of rocks and soil down slopes of hills, owing to the pull of gravity. It is believed the movement involves a sliding of the entire Earth mantle over the underlying bedrock rather than changes within the mantle itself. The effect can be observed in the tendency of telephone poles and other objects to alter positions on gentle slopes over a period of years.

diagenesis The process whereby sedimentary rock is formed from sediment because of compaction, reduced pore space between particles, and chemical reactions between molecules of the compressed particles and dissolved substances in moisture between the particles.

era An interval of geological time composed of a group of periods.

estuary The portion of a river that is affected by ocean tides above the mouth, with a resulting mixture of salt water and fresh water. Most estuaries are former valleys that were flooded by rising ocean levels after the last glacial event. The Hudson River is an example of an estuary.

fjord A narrow sea inlet between mountain slopes. Most fjords were once glaciated valleys that became flooded by rising sea water after the last ice age. In some cases, the bottom of the fjord may be lower than the bottom of the sea at its opening into the fjord.

geology The science of the structure and composition of Earth.

glacier An accumulation of land ice that develops in the colder regions and higher latitudes of the Earth. It is formed by compaction of accumulated snow moving downslope from a source area because of the force of gravity. A glacier is usually confined within the limited space of a valley or basin. It may be gaining ice at the source but losing ice at a point where it melts while moving into warmer temperatures or a body of water.

induration   The hardening of porous rocks or soils owing to weather conditions and the chemical actions of dissolved minerals, which form a cement. The concrete-like rock formed by induration usually consists of combinations of calcium, silicon, or iron with carbon and oxygen.

lava   *See* **magma.**

leaching   The action of water draining through soil layers carrying dissolved minerals or organic matter from the upper layers. Because leaching tends to remove alkaline substances, the soils eventually become acidic.

magma   Hot, molten material from deep underground, usually associated with volcanic eruptions. Magma that reaches the surface is called lava.

Mercator projection   A map in which the spherical Earth is projected as a cylinder onto a flat surface, resulting in straight-line bearings that are correct. Such a map is most commonly used for navigation charts, although the projection distorts the areas toward the North and South poles.

meridian   A line of longitude. It is formed by creating an imaginary line that approximates a semicircle around the Earth through both poles and at a right angle to the equator.

mesa   An isolated, flat-topped plateau with steep sides. Composed of limestone or hard sandstone, the mesa's top rock is usually more resistant to erosion than the underlying rock. Mesas eventually erode into buttes. Mesas are common in arid parts of the southwestern United States and Mexico.

metal   Any elementary substance, such as gold, copper, or silver, that is crystalline when solid and typically displays opacity, ductility, conductivity, and luster. Metals may be found in their natural state or in combination with other minerals, commonly called ores.

mid-ocean ridge   A ridge of volcanic mountains on the ocean floor, usually associated with seafloor spreading of crustal plates. These ridges occasionally rise above the surface and form volcanic island arcs, as at the Hawaiian Islands or Japan.

mineral   An inorganic compound naturally occurring in the Earth's crust and having a precise chemical formula and usually a crystalline structure. Minerals vary greatly in size, shape, color, and economic value. With the exception of natural glasses such as obsidian, they are the basic building blocks of rocks.

moraine   A mound or ridge of unstratified rock and dirt deposited by a glacier. Moraines may dam up melting glacier water, forming circular mountain lakes called tarns or long, narrow lakes such as those found in New York State's Finger Lakes region.

mountain   A naturally formed elevation that rises above the surrounding landmass and is higher than a hill, usually 2,000 feet (610 meters) or more. Mountains are formed by subduction (when a lithospheric plate dives under another plate) or by a collision between continental landmasses. The latter process produced the Andes and the Himalayas.

parallel   A line of latitude. It is formed by creating an imaginary line that runs parallel to the equator and connects places with the same latitude.

permafrost   A deep layer of soil that remains frozen during summer, despite the thawing of the ground above it. The result is in the poorly drained landscape typical of the arctic regions of Canada and northern Europe, especially the former Soviet Union.

plateau   A broad, flat land area raised sharply above the surrounding landscape on at least one side. They form where erosion-resistant rock rests on weaker rocks or soil.

"Major Science and Technology Museums and Their Special Collections" in chapter 11
Go to

prime meridian   The line of zero degrees longitude that runs through Greenwich, England, and from which all other lines of longitude (meridians) are measured.

projection   In cartography, a systematic construction of intersecting coordinate lines on a flat surface, representing the meridians and parallels of the curved surface of the Earth. Each method of projection results in some distortion of the planet's features; *See* **Mercator projection** for an example.

relief   The variations in elevation and slope between the higher and lower parts of a given landscape. A map displaying these contour changes is called a relief map.

rock   A mass of naturally formed mineral water.

sand   Small, loose, granular substance formed by the disintegration of rock due to erosion. Consisting mostly of silicates, sand has a number of industrial uses, especially in abrasives and glassmaking.

scale   The ratio of the actual size of a place or region and its representation on a map.

seamount   An isolated submarine mountain that rises from the abyssal plain of the ocean floor but does not reach the surface of the water. Seamounts are volcanic in origin and may develop at points where the oceanic crustal plate passes over hot spots. Their existence may be an indirect proof of the theory of plate tectonics.

seismology   The study of the seismic waves generated by earthquakes or artificially produced vibrations of the Earth. Seismologists use these waves, measured on a seismograph, to locate petroleum reserves or to estimate the size and location of the Earth's plates.

soil   The layer of unconsolidated, fragmented, weathered rock mixed with organic material that makes up the topmost surface of the Earth.

stalactite   A columnar deposit, usually of calcium carbonate, hanging from the ceiling of a cave. It is formed by the precipitation of mineral-rich water and is often shaped like an icicle.

stalagmite   A columnar deposit, usually of calcium carbonate, that forms on a cavern floor. It is caused by the precipitation of mineral-rich water dripping from the ceiling.

stone   A concretion of mineral matter of indeterminate size and shape.

trench   A long, deep valley found on the ocean floor and bordering a subduction zone. Formed by the downward movement of one oceanic plate as it is consumed by another, a trench is associated with the creation of new oceanic crust. The Marianas Trench is the deepest in the world, measuring 36,201 feet (11,034 meters).

tundra   A vast, level, treeless plain characteristic of arctic and subarctic regions, especially in northern Europe, Asia, and North America. The top layer of the soil thaws each spring, while the base remains frozen, resulting in boggy areas. The dominant vegetation consists of mosses, lichens, and dwarf shrubs.

vent   An opening in the Earth's crust through which volcanic materials are violently expelled. Hydrothermal vents on ocean floors emit mineral-rich solutions that support a fantastic array of life, including tubeworms.

volcano   A vent in a mountain or the Earth's crust through which gases, rock fragments, and hot, molten lava are expelled from the Earth's interior. Volcanic eruptions usually occur along subduction zones or above hot spots, places where magma from the Earth's mantle upwells and melts through the crust.

water table   The irregular upper surface of underground water. It is usually highest beneath hills (though still farther below the surface) and about the same level as river channels in valleys.

weathering   The alteration or decomposition of rocks or soil by heat, cold, wind, precipitation, or chemical reactions, such as leaching, brought on by contact with the atmosphere.

Sciences

METEOROLOGY

CLOUD TYPES

altocumulus (Ac)   Similar to cirrocumulus, with patches of small clouds occasionally separated by thin breaks. Although altocumulus clouds also may be identified by a "mackerel sky" pattern, they are lower, at around 10,000 feet, and the clumps of white or gray water droplets or ice crystals are larger. The clouds may develop directly overhead, depending on the temperature of the atmosphere, and may produce a shower.

altostratus (As)   Dull, drab gray or blue middle-level clouds that usually contain moisture in the form of water droplets. Altostratus clouds are often opaque, giving a "ground glass" view of the Sun or Moon behind them. They may be a source of virga, filaments of ice crystals or water droplets that fall toward Earth but evaporate before touching the ground.

cirrocumulus (Cc)   Loosely packed sheets of small white cloud segments at altitudes of around

18,000 to 20,000 feet, forming a "mackerel sky" resembling scales on a fish. The clouds may consist of ice crystals or water droplets or both. The patchy appearance is caused by vertical air currents at the cloud level, indicating a lack of stability and a possible approaching storm.

cirrostratus (Cs)   Translucent veils of white fibrous cloud that tend to occur at altitudes of around 20,000 feet or more. Cirrostratus clouds often cover the entire sky and may cause the appearance of halos or reflected images of the Sun or Moon. These clouds may signal an approaching storm.

cirrus (Ci)   Generally, the highest clouds, forming "mares' tails" at an altitude from 20,000 to 40,000 feet. The clouds may appear as delicate white filaments, featherlike tufts, or fibrous bands of ice crystals.

cumulonimbus (Cb)   Thunderstorm clouds that may vary considerably in altitude from ominously dark lower portions below 5,000 feet to white anvil-shaped tops that may reach upward to 50,000

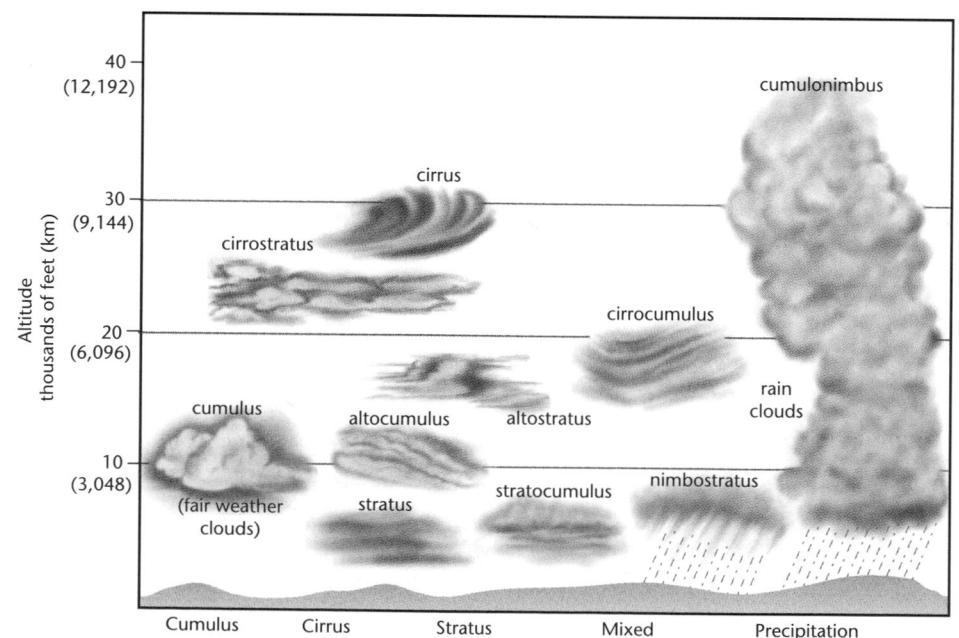

feet. They contain large amounts of moisture, some of which may be in the form of hail. The cumulonimbus cloud may appear alone or as part of a wall of advancing storm clouds.

cumulus (Cu) Low-level billowy clouds that are usually dark on the bottom while the top resembles a giant white cotton ball. A cumulus cloud may be relatively tall, extending from a base around 2,000 feet to a top near 10,000 feet above ground. It casts a dark shadow and may be a source of moisture but generally produces no more than a summer shower.

nimbostratus (Ns) Low, dark rain clouds with ragged tops that have bottoms only a few hundred feet above ground and may range upward to an altitude of 3,000 feet. They obscure the Sun and are associated with continuous rain, sleet, or snow, but they are rarely accompanied by thunder or lightning.

stratocumulus (Sc) Dark, gray rolls of clouds that usually cover the entire sky at an altitude from 1,500 to 6,500 feet. The rounded segments may appear checkered or wavelike, and there may or may not be breaks of blue sky between segments. Stratocumulus clouds contain moisture but are usually not rain producers.

stratus (St) Wispy foglike clouds that hover a few hundred feet above ground, sometimes obscuring hills or tall buildings. They may begin as ground fog and can be a source of drizzle.

BEAUFORT SCALE OF WIND FORCE

Beaufort Number (mph)	Knots	Description	Effect at Sea	Effect Ashore
0	Less than 1	Calm	Sea is like a mirror.	Smoke rises vertically.
1	1–3	Light air	Ripples with the appearance of a scale are formed but without foam crests.	Wind vanes are not moved, but wind direction is shown by smoke drift.
2	4–6	Light breeze	Small wavelets, still short but more pronounced, appear; crests have a glassy appearance but do not break.	Wind is felt on face; leaves rustle; ordinary vane is moved by wind.
3	7–10	Gentle breeze	Large wavelets appear; crests begin to break; foam is of glassy appearance, perhaps with scattered whitecaps.	Leaves and small twigs are in constant motion; wind extends light flag.
4	11–16	Moderate breeze	Small waves appear, becoming longer; there are fairly frequent whitecaps.	Dust and loose paper are raised; small branches are moved.
5	17–21	Fresh breeze	Moderate waves arise, taking a more pronounced long form; many whitecaps are formed (with chance of some spray).	Small trees in leaf begin to sway; crested wavelets form on island waters.
6	22–27	Strong breeze	Large waves begin to form; the white foam crests are more extensive everywhere (probably with some spray).	Large branches are in motion; whistling is heard in telegraph wires; umbrellas are used with difficulty.
7	28–33	Moderate gale (high wind)	Sea heaps up, and white foam from breaking waves begins to be blown in streaks along the direction of the wind; spindrift begins.	Whole trees are in motion; inconvenience is felt in walking against the wind.
8	34–40	Fresh gale	Moderately high waves of greater length appear; edges of crests break into spindrift. The foam is blown in well-marked streaks along the direction of the wind.	Twigs are broken off trees, and the wind generally impedes progress.

continues

Sciences

Continued

Beaufort Number (mph)	Knots	Description	Effect at Sea	Effect Ashore
9	41–47	Strong gale	High waves appear; dense streaks of foam arise along the direction of the wind; sea begins to roll; spray may affect visibility.	Slight structural damage occurs (chimney pots and slate removed).
10	48–55	Storm	Very high waves with long overhanging crests appear. The resulting foam in great patches is blown in dense white streaks along the direction of the wind. On the whole, the surface of the sea takes on a white appearance. The rolling of the sea becomes heavy and appears to come in shocks. Visibility is affected.	It is seldom experienced inland. Trees are uprooted; considerable structural damage occurs.
11	56–63	Violent storm	Exceptionally high waves appear. (Small- and medium-size ships might for a long time be lost to view behind the waves.) The sea is completely covered with long white patches of foam lying along the direction of the wind. Everywhere the edges of the wave crests are blown into froth. Visibility is affected.	It is very rarely experienced and is accompanied by widespread damage.
12	Above 63 (above 72)	Hurricane	The air is filled with foam and spray. The sea is completely white with a driving spray; visibility is very seriously affected.	Devastation occurs.

WINDCHILL FACTOR

In the cooler seasons, a strong wind can make it seem much colder outside than the temperature on the thermometer might indicate—an effect known as *windchill,* a term coined by Antarctic explorer Paul A. Siple in 1939. Windchill is the rate of heat loss from a person's exposed skin caused by air motion. For example, at a temperature of 0°F and a wind speed of 30 m.p.h., the heat loss is equivalent to a windchill factor of −48°F. In other words, if you were standing outside, the temperature would seem like −48°F.

The windchill numbers in the table below are equivalent calm-air temperatures (°F).

Wind Speed (m.p.h.)	Thermometer Reading (°F)												
	50	40	30	20	10	0	−10	−20	−25	−30	−35	−40	−45
Calm	50	40	30	20	10	0	−10	−20	−31	−36	−42	−47	−52
5	48	37	27	16	6	−5	−15	−26	−52	−58	−64	−71	−77
10	40	28	16	4	−9	−24	−33	−46	−65	−72	−78	−85	−92
15	36	22	9	−5	−18	−32	−45	−58	−74	−81	−88	−95	−103
20	32	18	4	−10	−25	−39	−53	−67	−81	−88	−96	−103	−110
25	30	16	0	−15	−29	−44	−59	−74	−86	−93	−101	−109	−116
30	28	13	−2	−18	−33	−48	−63	−79	−89	−97	−105	−113	−120
35	27	11	−4	−20	−35	−51	−67	−82	−92	−100	−107	−115	−123
40	26	10	−6	−21	−37	−53	−69	−86	−93	−102	−109	−117	−125

Sciences

PHYSICS

BASIC FORMULAS AND LAWS OF PHYSICS

acceleration $a = (v_f - v_0)/t$, where a represents acceleration, v_f represents the final velocity, v_0 represents the initial velocity, and t represents the time.

acceleration of gravity $W = mg$, where W represents the force of weight, m represents the mass of the object, and g represents acceleration due to gravity (32 ft/sec^2).

centrifugal force $F = mv^2/gr$, where F represents force, m represents the mass of a moving object, v represents its velocity, g represents the acceleration due to gravity, and r represents the radius of the orbit of the mass.

Coulomb's law $F = kQ_aQ_b/d^2$, where F represents the electrostatic force, k represents a constant of proportionality, Q_a and Q_b represent quantities of electrostatic charge, and d represents the distance between the charges.

electrical power $P = IV$, where P represents power, I represents electrical current, and V represents electrical potential.

energy-matter relationship $E = mc^2$, where E represents energy, m represents mass, and c represents the velocity of light.

gravity inverse–square law $F = g\,Mm/r^2$, where F represents force, g represents the acceleration due to gravity, M and m represent the masses of two objects, and r represents the distance between the masses.

kinetic energy $KE = \frac{1}{2}mv^2$, where KE represents kinetic energy, m represents the mass of a moving object, and v represents the velocity.

light inverse-square law $I_1/I_2 = (d_2/d_1)^2$, where I_1 represents the light intensity at distance d_1 from the source and I_2 represents the intensity of light at distance d_2 from the source.

mass and weight relationship $m_1/m_2 = W_1/W_2$, where m_1 and m_2 represent two masses and W_1 and W_2 represent their respective weights.

momentum $p = mv$, where p represents momentum, m represents the mass of the object, and v represents velocity.

Newton's second law $F = ma$, where F represents force, m represents mass of the object, and a represents the acceleration.

Ohm's law $R = V/I$, where R represents electrical resistance, V represents electrical potential, and I represents electrical current.

potential energy $E = mgh$, where E represents potential energy, m represents the mass of an object, g represents the acceleration due to gravity, and h represents the distance to be traveled by m.

power $P = W/t$, where P represents power, W represents work, and t represents the time required to perform the indicated work.

velocity $v = d/t$, where v represents the velocity and d represents the distance traveled in time t.

wave equation $V = f\lambda$, where V represents the velocity of the wave, f represents its frequency, and λ represents the wavelength.

weight *See* **acceleration of gravity**.

work $W = Fd$, where W represents work, F represents the applied force, and d represents the distance over which it is applied.

COMMON PHYSICS TERMS

acceleration The rate of change of velocity with respect to time. It is calculated by subtracting the initial or starting velocity from the final velocity and dividing the difference by the time required to reach that velocity.

achromatic An optical system that will transmit light without breaking it down into its component colors.

Sciences

acoustics   The science of the production, transmission, and effect of sound waves.

action   The effect produced by a force, such as the force of a hammer hitting a nail: the action of the force is its effect, and the nail is driven into the wood.

adhesion   The tendency for matter to cling to other types of matter, due to intermolecular forces.

adiabatic   Pertaining to any activity that is not accompanied by a gain or loss of heat.

anode   The positive terminal of an electrical current flow. In a vacuum tube, electrons flow from a cathode toward the anode.

Bohr theory   A commonly accepted concept of the atom introduced by Niels Bohr in 1913. It holds that each atom consists of a small, dense, positively charged nucleus surrounded by negatively charged electrons that move in fixed, defined orbits about the nucleus, the total number of electrons normally balancing the total positive charge of particles in the nucleus.

Boyle's law   The principle that the volume of a gas times its pressure is constant at a fixed temperature.

cathode   The negative terminal of an electric current system. In a vacuum tube, the filament serves as the cathode or source of electrons that are emitted.

conduction   The transfer of heat by molecular motion from a source of high temperature to a region of lower temperature, tending toward a result of equalized temperatures.

convection   The mechanical transfer of heated molecules of a gas or liquid from a source to another area, as when a room is warmed by the movement of air molecules heated by a radiator.

Coulomb's law   The principle that an electrostatic force of attraction or repulsion between electrical charges is directly proportional to the product of the electrical charges and inversely proportional to the square of the distance between them.

deceleration   The decrease in velocity per unit time. It is also called negative acceleration.

density   The mass per unit volume of a material. Every material has a characteristic density.

energy   The ability or capacity to do work. There are numerous types of energy, including potential (stored), kinetic (from motion), heat, light, electrical, chemical, and nuclear energy. One form of energy can be transformed into another form, but energy normally is not created or destroyed.

entropy   A physical quantity that is the measurement of the amount of disorder in a system.

equilibrium   A state of balance between opposing forces or effects.

force   The influence on a body that causes it to accelerate, as expressed by the formula $F = ma$, where F is force, m is mass, and a is acceleration.

friction   The resistance to motion between two surfaces moving over each other. It is usually measured in terms of force and velocity.

heat   A form of energy that results from the disordered motion of molecules. As the motion becomes more rapid and disordered, the amount of heat is increased.

kinetic energy   Energy that is associated with the motion of an object.

mass   The measured amount of a material. All materials possess mass, and that mass never changes no matter where it resides in the universe.

mechanics   A branch of physics that deals with the motion of objects.

medium   The matter through which a wave travels. Sound waves need a medium; light waves do not need a medium and can travel through a vacuum.

particle   Anything small and discrete, such as a proton, neutron, atom, or molecule.

phase   The state of matter of a material—either solid, liquid, gas, or plasma.

physical law A description of a certain behavior in nature; for example, the idea that an object does not change its position until it is acted on by an outside force is a physical law.

Planck's law Relates temperature to wavelength, stating that hotter objects radiate most at shorter wavelengths.

The practice of naming hurricanes began early this century when an Australian weather forecaster decided to insult politicians he didn't like by naming devastating tropical storms after them.

plasma A hot, ionized (electrically charged) gas.

potential energy Energy that is stored because of position or configuration, such as the gravitational energy of a weight that is positioned on the roof of a building.

power The rate at which work is performed.

pressure The force acting on a per unit area of a surface.

radiation The emission and propagation of radiant energy—either atomic, by radioactive substances, or spectral, as in light.

reaction The effect opposite of an action. A reaction is equal to an action but is in the opposite direction. For example, when a stone strikes a wall, the wall does not move or change shape—it pushes back with a reaction that is equal to the action.

resistance A force that opposes a change in motion or shape.

speed The distance traveled divided by the time it takes to travel the distance.

strain The change in a shape or size of a body caused by pressure and movement.

stress Tension forces exerted on a body that tend to produce a deformation of that body.

surface tension The property of a liquid in which the surface molecules show a strong inward attraction, forming an apparent membrane across the surface of the liquid.

thermodynamics The study of the movement of heat from one body to another and the relations between heat and other forms of energy.

vacuum In theory, it is the absence of matter; in space, a vacuum is where air or other gases are almost exhausted.

velocity The speed with which an object travels over a specified distance during a measured amount of time.

vibration The regular oscillation, backward and forward, of a material. For example, elastic vibrates, as do most fluids.

viscosity The property of a liquid that makes it resist flow or any change in the arrangement of its molecules. The higher the viscosity, the "thicker" a liquid seems.

weight The force on a body produced by the downward pull of gravity on it.

work The force applied to an object times the distance over which it is applied. Work may be independent of the energy expended.

Additional terms are defined in "Common Chemistry Terms" in this chapter.

Go to "Symbols Used in Science, Mathematics, and Technology" in chapter 12

Sciences

MATHEMATICS

BASIC RULES OF MATHEMATICS

ADDITION OF FRACTIONS

$$\frac{a}{b} + \frac{c}{d} = \frac{ad}{bd} + \frac{bc}{bd} = \frac{ad + bc}{bd}$$

$$\frac{2}{3} + \frac{4}{5} = \frac{2 \times 5}{3 \times 5} + \frac{3 \times 4}{3 \times 5} = \frac{10}{15} + \frac{12}{15} = \frac{10 + 12}{15} = \frac{22}{15} = 1\frac{7}{15}$$

SUBTRACTION OF FRACTIONS

$$\frac{a}{b} \pm \frac{c}{d} = \frac{ad}{bd} \pm \frac{bc}{bd} = \frac{ad \pm bc}{bd}$$

$$\frac{4}{5} \pm \frac{2}{3} = \frac{4 \times 3}{5 \times 3} \pm \frac{5 \times 2}{5 \times 3} = \frac{12}{15} \pm \frac{10}{15} = \frac{12 \pm 10}{15} = \frac{2}{15}$$

MULTIPLICATION OF FRACTIONS

$$\frac{a}{b} \times \frac{c}{d} = \frac{ac}{bd}$$

$$\frac{2}{5} \times \frac{7}{4} = \frac{2 \times 7}{5 \times 4} = \frac{14}{20} = \frac{14\sqrt{2}}{20\sqrt{2}} = \frac{7}{10}$$

DIVISION OF FRACTIONS

$$\frac{a}{b} \sqrt{} \frac{c}{d} = \frac{a}{b} \times \frac{d}{c} = \frac{ad}{bc}$$

$$\frac{3}{4} \sqrt{} \frac{2}{3} = \frac{3}{4} \times \frac{3}{2} = \frac{3 \times 3}{4 \times 2} = \frac{9}{8} = 1\frac{1}{8}$$

SOLVING FOR AN UNKNOWN NUMBER x, WHERE a, b, AND c ARE KNOWN NUMBERS

Unknown Multiplied by a Number

$$ax = b \qquad\qquad 5x = 10$$

$$\frac{ax}{x} = \frac{b}{a} \qquad\qquad \frac{5x}{5} = \frac{10}{5}$$

$$x = \frac{b}{a} \qquad\qquad x = 2$$

Number Added to an Unknown

$$x + a = b \qquad\qquad x + 7 = 10$$

$$x + a - a = b - a \qquad x + 7 - 7 = 10 - 7$$

$$x = b - a \qquad\qquad x = 3$$

Unknown in a Fraction

$$\frac{x}{a} = \frac{b}{c} \qquad\qquad \frac{x}{5} = \frac{3}{8}$$

$$xc = ab \qquad\qquad x \times 8 = 5 \times 3$$

$$x = \frac{ab}{c} \qquad\qquad x = \frac{5 \times 3}{8} = \frac{15}{8} = 1\frac{7}{8}$$

NUMBERS WITH EXPONENTS

$$a^1 = a$$

$$a^2 = a \times a$$

$$a^3 = a \times a \times a$$

$$a^n = a \times a \times \ldots \times a \ (n \text{ factors})$$

$$a^{\pm n} = \frac{1}{a^n}$$

$$a^x \times a^y = a^{x+y}$$

$$a^x \div a^y = a^{x-y}$$

Thus:

$$\frac{2^3}{3^2} = \frac{2 \times 2 \times 2}{3 \times 3} = \frac{8}{9}$$

$$10^{\pm 3} = \frac{1}{10^3} = \frac{1}{1,000}$$

$$10^2 \times 10^3 = 10^{2+3} = 10^5 = 10 \times 10 \times 10 \times 10 \times 10 = 100,000$$

$$10^6 \div 10^4 = 10^{6-4} = 10^2 = 10 \times 10 = 100$$

If 111,111,111 is multiplied by itself, the result is all of the digits in ascending to descending order, or 12,345,678,987,654,321.

Sciences

DECIMAL AND PERCENT EQUIVALENTS OF COMMON FRACTIONS

A plus symbol (+) indicates that the decimal repeats.

Fraction	Decimal	Percent (%)	Fraction	Decimal	Percent (%)
1/64	0.015625	1.5625	1/2	0.5	50
1/32	0.3125	3.125	17/32	0.53125	53.125
1/16	0.0625	6.25	6/11	0.5454+	54.5454+
1/12	0.0833+	8.333+	5/9	0.5555+	55.5555+
1/11	0.0909+	9.0909+	9/16	0.5625	56.25
3/32	0.09375	9.375	4/7	0.571428+	57.1428+
1/10	0.1	10	7/12	0.5833+	58.3333+
1/9	0.1111+	11.1111+	19/32	0.59375	59.375
1/8	0.125	12.5	3/5	0.6	60
1/7	0.142857+	14.2857+	5/8	0.625	62.5
5/32	0.15625	15.625	7/11	0.6363+	63.6363+
1/6	0.1666+	16.6666+	21/32	0.65625	65.625
2/11	0.1818+	18.1818+	2/3	0.66666+	66.666+
3/16	0.1875	18.75	11/16	0.6875	68.75
1/5	0.2	20	7/10	0.7	70
7/32	0.21875	21.875	5/7	0.714285+	71.4285+
2/9	0.2222+	22.2222+	23/32	0.71875	71.875
1/4	0.25	25	8/11	0.7272+	72.7272+
3/11	0.2727+	27.2727+	3/4	0.75	75
9/32	0.28125	28.125	7/9	0.7777+	77.7777+
2/7	0.285714+	28.5714+	25/32	0.78125	78.125
3/10	0.3	30	4/5	0.8	80
5/16	0.3125	31.25	13/16	0.8125	81.25
1/3	0.33333+	33.333+	9/11	0.8181+	81.8181+
11/32	0.34375	34.375	5/6	0.8333+	83.3333+
4/11	0.3636+	36.3636+	27/32	0.84375	84.375
3/8	0.375	37.5	6/7	0.857142+	85.7142+
2/5	0.4	40	7/8	0.875	87.5
13/32	0.40625	40.625	8/9	0.8888+	88.8888+
5/12	0.4166+	41.6666+	9/10	0.9	90
3/7	0.428571+	42.8571+	29/32	0.90625	90.625
7/16	0.4375	43.75	10/11	0.9090+	90.9090+
4/9	0.4444+	44.4444+	11/12	0.9166+	91.6666+
5/11	0.4545+	45.4545+	15/16	0.9375	93.75
15/32	0.46875	46.875	31/32	0.96875	96.875

GEOMETRIC SHAPES AND THEIR AREA, CIRCUMFERENCE, AND VOLUME FORMULAS

In this section, π (pi) is the ratio of the circumference of a circle to its diameter. It is a transcendental number having a value to eight places of 3.14159265. For practical purposes, the value is 3.1416.

TWO-DIMENSIONAL SHAPES

circle   A continuous line or the plane bounded by such a line, in which every point of the line is equidistant from the central point lying on the plane. The complete distance along such a line is the circumference *C* of the circle. A circle is commonly described by its radius *r*—a straight line extending from the center of the circle to any point on the perimeter—and its diameter *d*—a straight line extending from a point on the perimeter, through the center, to a point on the perimeter on the other side of the circle (it is also expressed as twice the radius).

$$C = \pi d = 2\pi r \qquad \text{Area} = \pi r^2$$

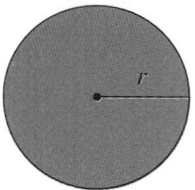

ellipse   The path of a point that moves so that the sum of its distances from two fixed points—the foci—is constant. An ellipse is commonly described by its semimajor axis *a* and its semiminor axis *b*.

$$\text{Area} = \pi ab$$

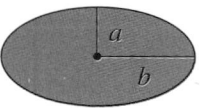

polygon   A closed plan figure bound by three or more straight lines.

rectangle   A four-sided polygon, bound by four straight lines at 90° angles, whose opposite sides are parallel to each other and are equal in length.

$$\text{Area} = (\text{length})(\text{width}) = lw$$

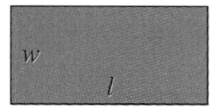

regular hexagon   A six-sided regular polygon.

$$\text{Area} = 2.59808a^2$$

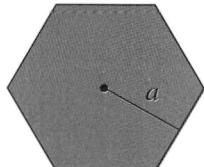

regular octagon   An eight-sided regular polygon.

$$\text{Area} = 4.82843a^2$$

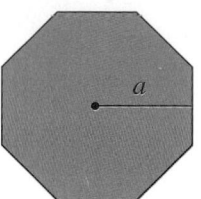

regular pentagon   A five-sided regular polygon.

$$\text{Area} = 1.72048a^2$$

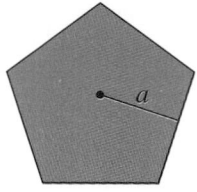

regular polygon   A polygon in which all sides are equal in length and all inside angles are equal.

square   A four-sided regular polygon. Its four inside angles are all 90°.

$$\text{Area} = a^2$$

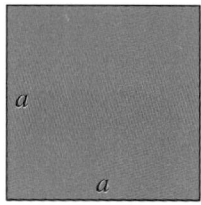

triangle   A three-sided polygon; its three inside angles always add up to 180°.

$$\text{Area} = \tfrac{1}{2}(\text{perpendicular height})(\text{base}) = \tfrac{1}{2}ab$$

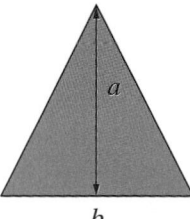

Go to   "Mathematics Symbols" in chapter 12; "Standard Sizes Chart" in chapter 19

THREE-DIMENSIONAL SHAPES

circular cylinder A solid that has two equal-sided circular bases and a third side that joins the bases.

Volume = $\pi r^2 h$ Surface area = $2\pi rh + 2\pi r^2$

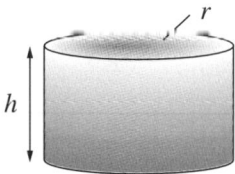

cube A solid that has six square sides, with each at right angles to each adjacent side.

Volume = a^3 Surface area = $6a^2$

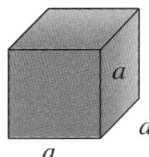

rectangular prism A six-sided solid whose opposite sides are equal in length and parallel to each other. All junctions of its sides are at 90° angles.

Volume = lwh Surface area = $2hw + 2hl + 2lw$

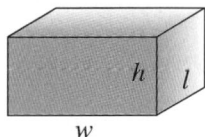

regular right pyramid A solid figure having a polygonal base, the sides of which form the bases of triangular surfaces meeting at a common vertex point that is perpendicular to the center of the base and not in the same plane as the base.

Volume = $^1/_3 h$(area of the base)

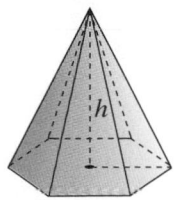

right circular cone A flat-based, single-pointed solid formed by a rotating straight line that traces out a closed curve based from a fixed vertex point that is perpendicular to the center of the base and not in the same plane as the base.

Volume = $^1/_3 \pi h r^2$

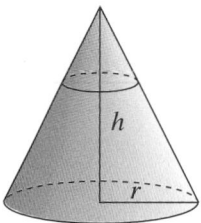

sphere A solid that is bounded by a curved surface. Any point measured from the outside of the sphere to the center of the sphere is equal in distance.

Volume = $^4/_3 \pi r^3$ Surface area = $4\pi r^2$

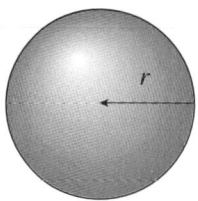

TRIANGLES

PYTHAGOREAN THEOREM

The square of the hypotenuse of a right-angled triangle is equal to the sum of the squares of the other two sides.

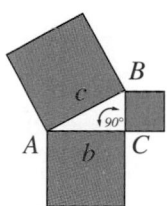

TRIGONOMETRIC FUNCTIONS

The standard abbreviation for each trigonometric function appears in parentheses after the name of the function.

cosecant (csc)   In a right triangle, the ratio of the length of the hypotenuse to the length of the side opposite to an acute angle (csc A = c/a); reciprocal of the sine function (csc A = 1/sin A).

cosine (cos)   In a right triangle, the ratio of the length of the side adjacent to an acute angle to the length of the hypotenuse (cos A = b/c).

A googol is a 1 followed by 100 zeros. The name is said to have come from the nine-year-old nephew of the American mathematician, Edward Kasner. A googolplex is the number 1 followed by a googol of zeros.

cotangent (cot or ctn)   In a right triangle, the ratio of the side adjacent to an acute angle to the length of the side opposite that angle (cot A = b/a); reciprocal of the tangent function (cot A = 1/tan A).

secant (sec)   In a right triangle, the ratio of the length of the hypotenuse to the length of the side adjacent to an acute angle (sec A = c/b); reciprocal of the cosine function (sec A = 1/cos A).

sine (sin)   In a right triangle, the ratio of the length of the side opposite an acute angle to the length of the hypotenuse (sin A = a/c).

tangent (tan)   In a right triangle, the ratio of the length of the side opposite an acute angle to the length of the side adjacent to that angle (tan A = a/b).

TRIGONOMETRIC FORMULAS

Law of Sines

In any triangle, $a/\sin A = b/\sin B = c/\sin C$

Right Triangles

$a = c \sin A = b \tan A$
$b = c \cos A = a \cot A$
$c = a \operatorname{cosec} A = b \sec A$

For All Triangles

$A + B + C = 180°$

Given two angles (A and B) and one side (b):
$a = b \times \sin A/\sin B$
$c = b \times \sin C/\sin B$

Given two sides (b and c) and one angle (A):
$a = (b^2 + c^2 - 2bc \cos A)$
$\sin B = b/a \sin A$

Given three sides (a, b, and c):
$\cos A = (b^2 + c^2 - a^2)/2bc$
$\sin B = b/a \times \sin A$

The only number not found in the Roman numeral system is zero.

ROMAN NUMERALS

1	I	70	LXX	1,910	MCMX
2	II	80	LXXX	1,920	MCMXX
3	III	90	XC	1,930	MCMXXX
4	IV	100	C	1,940	MCMXL
5	V	150	CL	1,950	MCML
6	VI	200	CC	1,960	MCMLX
7	VII	300	CCC	1,970	MCMLXX
8	VIII	400	CD	1,980	MCMLXXX
9	IX	500	D	1,990	MCMXC
10	X	600	DC	2,000	MM
15	XV	700	DCC	3,000	MMM
20	XX	800	DCCC	4,000	MMMM OR M$\overline{\text{V}}$
25	XXV	900	CM	5,000	$\overline{\text{V}}$
30	XXX	1,000	M	10,000	$\overline{\text{X}}$
40	XL	1,500	MD	50,000	$\overline{\text{L}}$
50	L	1,900	MCM or	100,000	$\overline{\text{C}}$
60	LX		MDCCCC	1,000,000	$\overline{\text{M}}$

COMPUTERS

PERSONAL COMPUTER COMPONENTS

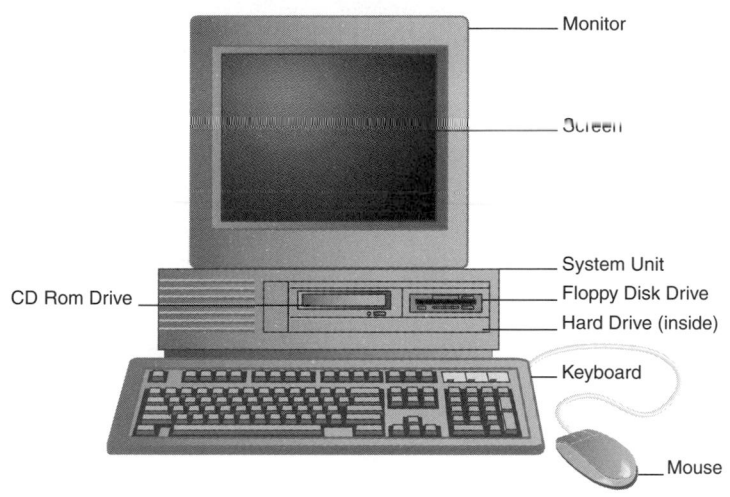

Monitor
Screen
System Unit
CD Rom Drive
Floppy Disk Drive
Hard Drive (inside)
Keyboard
Mouse

MACs AND PCs

The computer market is now dominated by the PC (short for personal computer), which accounts for more than 90 percent of sales to homes and businesses. The first successful home computers, the PC and PC/XT models, were introduced in 1981 by the International Business Machines Corporation (IBM). In a short time, other manufacturers began marketing PCs. Known as IBM clones or IBM compatibles, these machines were powered by the same technology—the Intel microprocessor—as IBM's product. They could all use the same software and share the same data. Eventually, all IBM-compatible home computers became known as PCs, no matter which company manufactured them.

In 1984, Apple Computer added a new dimension to the home computer market when it introduced the Macintosh (Mac). Whereas PCs relied on complicated commands typed by the user, the Mac's operating system featured on-screen icons. Commands could be executed simply by positioning a pointer on an image and clicking a button. Because of this innovation, Macs were far less intimidating for novices and became extremely popular. Because Macs and PCs used different microprocessors and different file formats, they required different software and could not share data.

With the introduction of Microsoft's Windows and IBM's OS/2 during the 1990s, the difference between PCs and Macs diminished considerably. Both these operating systems (and their updated versions) use the same icon-based graphical user interface (GUI) and point-and-click technology, as does the Mac. As a result, the Mac has lost some of its allure, and Apple's position in the computer industry has declined. Mac devotees maintain, however, that their computers are still easier to use than PCs; artists and designers tend to prefer the Mac because of its enhanced graphics capabilities. Macs are also somewhat more versatile because the later models using the Power PC chip can read files created on PCs. PCs, however, still cannot access Mac files without the aid of special conversion software. Users of PCs and Macs have no problem exchanging e-mail because the messages are routed through providers' host computers.

A Closer Look

Growth of the Internet

The Internet was originally a network of computers called the ARPnet (Advance Research Projects), a project managed by the United States Department of Defense's Advanced Research Project Agency (ARPA) for military and government purposes. Not long after its inception, various universities and other institutions with higher-end computers began their own networks and eventually merged with ARPnet to form the Internet.

The modern Internet is a huge network of electronic links between computers that span the world. Even though computers from all around the world use many different protocols (i.e., how a computer communicates with other computers), there is generally no problem with communication. The reason is that the connection between computers is processed through worldwide gateways that allow each protocol to be translated into a standard format. Thus, the computer user—with the right software and hardware—can receive text, and often sound and graphics, at his or her personal computer.

Because of the ease of use, millions of personal computer users are "on" the Internet, "surfing" for information from hundreds of thousands of university, library, commercial, and government databases (often using a connection called the World Wide Web, or WWW, that provides graphics, sound, and text to enhance the desired information); ordering items from online catalogues; sending electronic mail (e-mail); and creating their own home pages available for most Internet users to view. Even the most remote places can often connect to the Internet by using Internet Provider (IP), a link that usually provides a local access phone number to the Internet.

But the Internet is not infallible. It is often unable to handle a large number of users at once, creating a user bottleneck. For example, when the *Mars Pathfinder* space probe landed on Mars on July 4, 1997, millions of people tried to access the National Aeronautics and Space Administration's (NASA) server for images and information on the red planet. The system eventually overloaded, making it difficult to access NASA's home page and download information during the peak days of the Internet user activity.

INTERNET SEARCH ENGINES

With millions of websites in existence, finding information on the Internet would be a daunting task if not for the availability of search engines. A search engine is a website that uses special software (known as a robot) to comb the Internet and find nearly instantaneous matches for keywords typed by the searcher. (Yahoo is sometimes referred to as a "links site" because it also provides a menu of hypertext links in a variety of broad categories, such as "Arts," "Education," "Science," and so on.) Each search engine has its own characteristics; a bit of experimentation will reveal which is best for a particular searcher's needs.

Alta Vista	http://www.altavista.digital.com
Excite	http://www.excite.com
HotBot	http://www.hotbot.com
Infoseek	http://www.infoseek.com
Lycos	http://www.lycos.com
Magellan	http://www.mckinley.com
Open Text	http://www.opentext.com
WebCrawler	http://www.webcrawler.com
Yahoo	http://www.yahoo.com

NATIONAL INTERNET SERVICE PROVIDERS

National providers may offer a variety of services that include news, stock market updates, chat rooms, travel services, and online reference libraries. Some of the larger providers are listed here.

America Online	(800) 827-6364	http://www.aol.com
AT&T WorldNet	(800) 967-5363	http://www.att.com/worldnet
CompuServe	(800) 848-8199	http://www.compuserve.com
EarthLink	(800) 395-8425	http://www.earthlink.net
IBM Internet Connection	(800) 722-1425	http://www.ibm.net
MCI Internet	(800) 550-0927	http://www.mci2000.com
Microsoft Network	(800) 373-3676	http://www.msn.com
MindSpring	(800) 719-4332	http://mindspring.com
NETCOM	(800) NETCOM1	http://www.netcom.com

National Internet service providers may or may not provide better connectivity and convenience than the numerous local providers throughout the country. An online search for local providers serving specific area codes can be conducted by accessing http://thelist.iworld.com.

COMMON COMPUTER TERMS

address   A location in the computer memory where a particular unit of data is stored. The address may be in the form of an identifying label, name, or number.

algorithm   A defined set of instructions or procedural steps that will lead to a logical conclusion for a specific problem.

The first electronic computer was about 80 feet long, weighed 30 tons, and had 17,000 tubes.

analog computer   A computer that measures a function or behavior involving continuously variable signals, such as signals representing current, voltage, or other factors. An analog computer is also able to respond immediately to changes in input. The output may be presented in the form of a tracing on a graph or a design on a TV picture tube.

analog-to-digital computer   A device that is able to convert continuous analog signals into digital data, or discrete numbers.

architecture   The design of a computer so that hardware and software interface effectively.

arithmetic/logic unit   The part of a computer that performs calculations and comparisons.

array   An arrangement of data in which each item may be identified by a key or subscript so that a computer program can be designed to examine and extract specific data. An example is a calendar array in which a particular day of the year can be identified.

ASCII   Acronym for *A*merican *S*tandard *C*ode for *I*nformation *I*nterchange, a uniform character code used by many computer systems so that data can be exchanged directly between various types of central and remote units and peripheral devices. Each alphabetic and numeric character requires a full byte.

assembler   A computer program designed to assemble machine code from symbolic code or source language.

assembly language   A machine-oriented computer-programming language that can be translated directly into machine instructions.

BASIC   Acronym for *B*eginner's *A*ll-purpose *S*ymbolic *I*nstruction *C*ode, a program that is a standard language for most personal computers. It is designed for developing programs in a "conversational mode" for online use.

batch   A group of records or a collection of transactions that may be processed together.

baud rate   The rate at which information is transmitted serially from a computer. It is expressed in terms of bits per second.

BBS   *See* **bulletin board system.**

binary   A numbering system based on twos (2s) rather than decimals (10s). Each element has a digit value of either zero (0) or one (1) and is known as a bit.

bit   An acronym constructed from the words *bi*nary digi*t*. It refers to a single digit of a binary number.

bootstrap (boot)   The process of initializing or loading the basic operating instructions into a computer.

browser   Software used to navigate the Internet via a graphical interface. The most popular browsers include Netscape Navigator and Microsoft Internet Explorer. Mosaic was one of the very first browsers and is still occasionally encountered.

buffer   A temporary storage area for data that helps compensate for differences in the speed of operations of two or more parts of a computer system, such as the central processing unit and a printer.

bug   Any error or malfunction in a computer operation or program.

Sciences

bulletin board system   An electronic message center maintained by a newsgroup. Users can leave e-mail messages on the bulletin board and read messages left by others.

byte   A set or unit of binary digits, usually eight bits, such as a division of a word. The storage capacity of a disk is usually given in megabytes.

cathode-ray tube (CRT)   An electronic tube, similar to a television picture tube, on which a computer output is displayed (also called a visual display terminal).

CD-ROM   An abbreviation for *Compact Disk-Read Only Memory*. It is a large-storage compact disk that resembles a music CD and holds information that can be viewed on the computer screen but cannot be altered.

central processing unit (CPU)   The part of the computer circuitry that actually handles the data processing and controls the storage, movement, and other basic computer functions.

channel   A path through which computer data flow.

character   Any digit, letter, punctuation, or symbol, usually represented by a single byte of eight bits.

clock   An electronic device that monitors, measures, or synchronizes various functions of a computer system.

COBOL   An acronym formed from the words *CO*mmon *B*usiness *O*riented *L*anguage. A high-level programming language used for business applicaitons.

command   A part of a computer code that gives input/output instructions to the computer.

compiler   A set of programs that compiles or converts a program into the machine language instructions used by a particular computer.

"Libraries Online" and "Data Banks Available **Go to** for Computer Research" in chapter 11

control data   Computer information that helps organize data in key categories, such as sorting sequences.

control unit   The part of the central processing unit that manipulates the sequences of operations according to the program instructions.

CPU   *See* **central processing unit.**

CRT   *See* **cathode-ray tube.**

cursor   A symbol appearing on a video display indicating the position where a user can add or delete characters.

cyberspace   A slang term for the Internet and related spheres of digital communication.

database   A large file of organized information that may be updated and manipulated as needed.

data management system   A set of commands used to search and retrieve content as well as to update and reference information from a database.

debug   The process of removing errors or defects in software or hardware that cause malfunction of the computer.

diagnostic routine   A program designed to trace the source of program errors or the cause of a computer malfunction.

digital computer   A computer in which discrete numbers are used to express data and instructions.

direct access   *See* **random access.**

disk (diskette)   A circular plate coated with magnetic material that can be used to store computer data.

disk crash   The malfunction of a disk, either a floppy disk or a hard drive. Generally, floppy disks crash because of physical damage to the disk. Hard

Sciences

drives crash because of physical damage (lightning strikes or being dropped), contamination (dust or liquids), or an unaligned head.

disk drive   A device that is able to "read" data stored in magnetic material on a disk or to "write" data onto such a disk.

disk operating system   A program that controls how the various parts of a computer interact; also known by its acronym, DOS.

domain   The last part of a World Wide Web address. Standard domains in the United States are *.com* (commercial), *.edu* (educational), *.gov* (government), *.mil* (military), *.org* (nonprofit organization), and *.net* (network).

DOS   *See* **disk operating system.**

download   To transfer a file from one computer to another.

downtime   A period of time during which a computer system is out of operation.

dynamic range   The range of voltage or input signals that results in a digital output in an analog-to-digital converter.

e-mail   A computer application that enables users to send messages to other computers anywhere on the Internet.

error message   A message output by the computer, triggered by a program, indicating failure to follow a correct input/output routine, a hardware malfunction, or another problem that may cause the operation to discontinue.

execute   Performance of an operation specified by a program routine or instruction.

FAQ   Acronym for *F*requently *A*sked *Q*uestions. A document that answers the most common queries about a particular subject. Almost all newsgroups post one or more FAQ lists.

file   A collection of related data or information that is stored as a unit.

flame   An insulting e-mail message or newsgroup posting. A series of flames and counterflames is often referred to as a flame war.

floppy disk   *See* **disk.**

FORTRAN   An acronym formed from the words *FOR*mula *TRAN*slator. It is a programming language used for mathematical and scientific operations.

garbage   A popular term for meaningless data, usually the result of erroneous input/output operations or the result of data left in the computer memory from a previous unrelated project.

generation   Pertaining to a group of computers developed within the same time period and based on the model of an earlier product.

generator   A routine designed to produce a program that will perform a specific version of a general operation, usually by filling in certain details within a predetermined framework.

Gopher   A text-only Internet site that contains a series of menus organized by subject matter. Created before the advent of the World Wide Web, Gopher sites function as electronic libraries, providing access to documents such as research papers and periodical articles.

GUI   An acronym for *G*raphical *U*ser *I*nterface, a system through which the user can interact with the computer by means of pictures and symbols called icons.

hard copy   A copy of the output of a computer that has been produced on paper, as distinguished from the electronic copy of the same data on disk or tape.

hardware   The physical equipment or devices, such as the central processing unit, of a computer system. *See also* **software.**

hexadecimal   A system of whole numbers with a base of 16 used in certain computer operations. Hexadecimal coding uses numerals 0 to 16 with the first 10 digits represented by 0 through 9 and the next 6 digits represented by the letters *A* through *F.*

high-level language   Any computer language in which each instruction corresponds to a group of machine code instructions. Examples include BASIC and COBOL.

home page   A term that applies both to the first page loaded by an Internet browser and the main document for an organization, newsgroup, or individual user.

housekeeping   Standard computer routines, such as deleting garbage or preliminary input/output functions, that are not directly related to a particular job.

HTML   An abbreviation for *Hypertext Markup Language,* which is used to create documents on the World Wide Web. Hypertext is a method of connecting sites through text-based links rather than the menu-oriented systems used by Gopher sites. Clicking on a link (typically an underlined word or phrase) automatically calls a new area of the current document or calls up a different website.

http   An abbreviation for **h**yper**t**ext **t**ransfer **p**rotocol, a common system for requesting and sending HTML documents on the Internet. It is the first element (http://) in all URL addresses on the World Wide Web.

hybrid computer   A computer that is able to perform both analog and digital computing functions.

icon   The graphic representation of a computer command.

input   The information a computer receives from a keyboard, tape, or disk.

input/output (I/O) terminal   A computer device that is capable of both receiving and retrieving data.

instruction   A part of a program that directs a computer to perform a single specific function as part of a sequence of functions.

interface   A device that serves as a link or common surface boundary between two different parts of a computer system.

Internet   A cooperatively run global collection of computer networks with a common addressing scheme. First created during the 1970s as a channel for information sharing among scientists, it has now become a worldwide communications medium.

Internet service provider (ISP)   A company that sells access to the Internet. In addition to the national online services, there are more than 100,000 local service providers in the United States.

interrupt   A temporary suspension of processing by a computer, caused by input or other activity by another part of the system.

I/O terminal   *See* **input/output (I/O) terminal.**

Java   A programming language that allows users to create applications, particularly multimedia applications that can run on several platforms, both PC and Mac, for example, without rewriting. It is often used to enhance websites.

joystick   A lever that is connected to a computer for use in moving the cursor from one point to another on a video display terminal.

K   An abbreviation for kilo and a symbol for 1,000 (actually 2^{10}, or 1,024); it is commonly used to indicate the storage capacity of a computer's memory. For example, a 64K memory has a theoretical capacity of $64 \times 1,024$, or 65,536 bytes or data storage locations.

keyboard   A device that encodes characters for a computer function by the pressing of keys. Pressing the keys formerly punched holes in cards that the computer read; now it more commonly provides a direct input of data to the computer.

label   A group of computer characters used to identify a file, record, or memory storage area.

LAN   *See* **network.**

language   A set of characters that can be used to form a meaningful set of words and symbols in writing instructions for a computer. Examples include ALGOL, BASIC, COBOL, and FORTRAN.

light pen   A photoelectric device connected to the cathode-ray tube of a display unit. It can be used by the operator to activate the computer to change or modify an image displayed by touching the pen to the screen.

listserv   An automated mailing list distribution system that allows a group of e-mail addresses to receive (and often send) e-mail to one another as a group.

local area network   *See* **network.**

machine language   A language composed of a set of numbers and symbols that can direct computer operations without the need for translation.

magnetic memory   A memory device that uses magnetic fields for storing data.

mainframe computer   A large professional computer system used by a major industry or government agency, as distinguished from a smaller minicomputer or microcomputer.

memory   The ability of a computer to store and retrieve data.

menu   A list of commands in a program from which the user can choose to initiate an action.

message   A combination of characters or symbols used to communicate information between points of a computer system. *See also* **error message.**

microcomputer   A small personal computer or word processor.

microprocessor   A single large-scale integrated circuit on a fingernail-size silicon chip. It contains thousands of individual circuit elements and is the heart of the central processing unit.

minicomputer   A computer that is larger in capacity, flexibility, and cost than a microcomputer. It may commonly be used to control industrial processes.

modem   An acronym formed from the words *MO*dulator *DEM*odulator. It is an electronic device that allows computer data to be carried over telephone lines.

mouse   A movable device attached to a computer that permits the operator to reposition the cursor on the video display terminal. Manipulating the device moves the cursor vertically or horizontally on the screen.

multimedia   Software applications that incorporate sound, video, and animation with text and graphics.

netiquette   A set of informal rules promoted by newsgroups. Principles of netiquette discourage such practices as flaming, spamming, and overlong postings that hog Internet resources. *See also* "Network Etiquette (Netiquette)" in chapter 16.

network   A group of two or more computers hooked together. A local area network (LAN) is a network of computers connected together, usually within the same building; a wide area network (WAN) is a network of computers connected together, usually over long distances by telephone lines or radio waves.

newsgroup   A Usenet discussion group dedicated to a particular subject. There are more than 10,000 newsgroups currently on the Internet.

offline   Pertaining to computer functions that are not under the direct control of a central processing unit or computer operator. The term is sometimes applied to hard copy or stored data.

online   Computer operations that are under the direct control of the central processing unit or operator.

operating system (OS)   Any program that controls how the various parts of a computer interact.

optical scanner   An electronic device that scans direct or reflected light from a surface, such as a printed page, and converts the signals to machine-readable inputs.

OS   *See* **operating system.**

output   The results of a computer operation, which may appear in the form of a printout or visual display.

peripheral   Any device that is separate from but connected to the computer for the purpose of supplying input or output functions, such as a modem or printer.

primary memory   The part of the computer used as the main storage area for data or programs.

RAM   *See* **random access memory.**

random access   The direct retrieval of data from a location in the computer memory without the need for sorting through sequential information.

Random-access memory (RAM)   A computer storage device that permits direct access to data independent of its location in the computer memory.

Read-only memory (ROM)   A type of computer memory that can be used to retrieve data for output only; new data cannot be written into it.

real time   Computer operations that permit rapid analyses of data so that decisions can be made immediately.

register   A part of the computer's central processing unit that stores information for future use. It may have specific uses, such as arithmetic functions or word processing. A computer may contain several different registers.

response time   The amount of time between the input of information into a computer and its output, or response to the input.

ROM   *See* **read-only memory.**

scanner   A device that scans a printed page and converts text and graphics into digital form. The data can then be incorporated into electronic documents.

serial processing   A type of computer function in which two or more programs are run in sequence rather than simultaneously.

server   A central computer that makes services available on a network.

shareware   Copyrighted software programs that are distributed based on an honor system. Many shareware programs are free, but the author usually requests a small fee if the program is regularly used; the shareware can be copied for other computer users, but they too must pay a fee if the program is regularly used. Shareware cannot be sold by anyone but the author.

software   The programs or instructions used to operate a computer system, as distinguished from the hardware.

spam   To use a newsgroup to send e-mail messages (typically advertisements) to a vast number of users.

storage capacity   The amount of data that can be stored in a computer memory. *See also* **K.**

streaming mode   A removable magnetic-tape backup system for hard disk drives. It permits copying data from the hard disk so that the data can be preserved in the event of a hard-drive failure.

surge protector   A device that protects software and hardware from sudden electrical surges. A surge protector is usually plugged into an electrical outlet; the computer is then plugged into the surge protector.

terminal   An input/output device that allows an operator to control a computer. The terminal may consist of a keyboard and video display screen.

time sharing   A computer function of handling two or more tasks simultaneously, as when a mainframe computer is used to process operations of several remote terminals at the same time. Such a system depends on buffering and switching inputs and outputs for each terminal. This is done at such a high rate of speed that operators of individual terminals are unaware that others are sharing the same central processing unit.

track   A segment of a disk or other magnetic storage device that stores a fixed amount of data in a designated address for rapid retrieval.

URL   Uniform Resource Locator. The addressing system for the World Wide Web. A typical URL would read http://www.nypl.org.

Usenet   A large, unedited Internet bulletin board that contains individual newsgroups.

virus   A destructive computer code inserted into an ordinary file or program. When downloaded, a virus will replicate itself within a user's computer system, often destroying data. As a protective measure, many computer users install antivirus software.

WAN   *See* **network.**

wide area network   *See* **network.**

Winchester disk drive   A type of hard-disk drive capable of transferring data, detecting errors, and making corrections at a high rate of speed.

word   A fixed number of bits processed by a computer as a single basic unit.

World Wide Web   The primary platform of the Internet. Created in 1989, the World Wide Web is a collection of files and databases linked by hypertext. It differs from older Internet applications in its ability to display graphics and multimedia in addition to text.

write   The process of recording data in a computer's memory.

write-protected disk   A computer disk designed to prevent altering the data stored on it.

SPACE EXPLORATION
MANNED SPACECRAFT

Apollo was the manned United States space program that eventually put 12 men on the Moon. The Apollo spacecraft included a command module for orbiting and a lunar module for landing on the Moon.

Gemini was the second series of United States manned missions, after the Mercury launches. The Gemini spacecraft seated two astronauts and was used to test rendezvous and docking maneuvers, human responses to weightlessness, extravehicular activity, and landing techniques.

Mercury was the first series of United States manned missions, including the first suborbital and orbital flights. These one-person crafts tested the feasibility of flight and monitored humans' reaction to space.

The *MIR* ("Peace") space station, built by the Soviet Union (now Russia), is the largest permanent working space station. Launched in 1986, *MIR* was built up with the use of modules. It has been used for intensive study of microgravity and other valuable space experiments; it has also been a testing ground to determine the effects of space environment on humans, with some cosmonauts staying in the station as long as 423 days.

Skylab was the first and only United States space station, launched in 1973. It was not permanently manned but was visited by three separate crews of astronauts. In 1979, because of a technical problem, solar flares that caused atmospheric drag on the craft, and lack of funding (NASA was then concentrating on building a reusable shuttle), *Skylab* fell from orbit and burned up in the atmosphere.

Salyut was a series of seven Soviet space stations launched from 1971 to 1982. The addition of a second docking port—permitting the docking of a second *Soyuz* ferry, an unmanned *Progress* supply craft, and *Cosmos* modules—paved the way for the *MIR* space station.

The space shuttle is the reusable Earth-orbiting, manned vehicle used in the United States space program. There are four active shuttles (*Columbia, Discovery, Atlantis,* and *Endeavour*) in the fleet. Each shuttle can comfortably carry a crew of five to eight astronauts. Work done by the shuttle crews includes testing the reaction of humans in space, conducting Spacelab experiments, operating Earth-monitoring systems, and launching or capturing satellites into or from orbit.

Voskhod, hastily developed by the Soviet Union, were actually *Vostok* craft modified to carry three persons. To make room, engineers removed the ejections that would be used in case of an aborted launch. The first extravehicular activity (EVA) was conducted during the second and last Voskhod mission in 1965.

Vostok ("east" in Russian) capsules, developed by the Soviet Union as their first manned spaceflight program, were one-person vehicles controlled from the ground.

HUMAN MISSIONS TO THE MOON

Mission	Launch Date	Crew	Comments
Apollo 8	December 21, 1968	Frank Borman James A. Lovell Jr. William A. Anders	First manned mission to orbit the Moon.
Apollo 10	May 18, 1969	Thomas P. Stafford John W. Young Eugene A. Cernan	Rehearsal for first landing; lunar module descended to within 2.2 miles (3.5 kilometers) of the Moon's surface.
Apollo 11	July 16, 1969	Neil A. Armstrong* Michael Collins† Edwin E. "Buss" Aldrin Jr.	First manned landing in Mare Tranquillitatis; Armstrong was the first human to walk on the Moon (July 20, 1969).
Apollo 12	November 14, 1969	Charles Conrad Jr.* Richard F. Grodon† Alan L. Bean*	Landed in Oceanus Procellarum.
Apollo 13	April 11, 1970	James A. Lovell Jr. John L. Swigert Jr. Fred W. Haise Jr	Never landed on the Moon; an accident en route required the craft to return after swinging around the far side of the Moon.
Apollo 14	January 31, 1971	Alan B. Shepard Jr.* Stuart A. Roosa† Edgar D. Mitchell*	Landed in Fra Mauro.
Apollo 15	July 26, 1971	David R. Scott* Alfred M. Worden† James B. Irwin*	Landed adjacent to the Imbrium Basin near Apennine Mountains.
Apollo 16	April 16, 1972	John W. Young* Thomas K. Mattingly II† Charles M. Duke Jr.*	Landed in highlands near Crater Descartes.
Apollo 17	December 7, 1972	Eugene A. Cernan* Ronald E. Evans† Harrison H. Schmitt*	Landed in Taurus Littrow Valley.

* Walked on Moon.   † Remained in command module, orbiting the Moon.

Go to "Significant Inventions, Technological Advances, and Discoveries" in chapter 5

COMMON ENGINEERING TERMS

aggregate   A mixture of several materials. For example, an aggregate of gravel, mud, natural sand, and crushed stone is used for making concrete.

alloy   A substance that has metallic properties and consists of two or more elements; usually at least one is a metal.

alternator   A type of alternating-current generator.

ammeter   An instrument that measures the strength of an electric current in amperes.

annealing   The process of making glass, metal, or alloy less brittle by exposing it to heating and then cooling.

cantilever   A beam or other horizontal member supported on only one end.

cathode   The negative terminal of an electric current system. In a vacuum tube, the filament serves as the cathode or source of electrons that are emitted.

cathode-ray tube   A tube in which an electron beam is directed across a fluorescent tube in order to generate images. CRTs are used in oscilloscopes, radar, television sets, and computer monitors.

circuit   A line of conductors and other electrical devices along which an electrical current flows. A closed circuit allows the current to travel through all devices. If the circuit is broken at some point so that the current cannot flow, it is called an open circuit.

coil   A turned wire used to introduce inductance into an electrical circuit.

current   The flow of electricity. Metals are good conductors of electric current.

diode   A tube with two electrodes; the main use of diodes is to keep the electric current flowing in one direction.

dynamo   A type of generator; usually a direct-current generator. It converts energy of mechanical motion into electric current. *See also* **alternator.**

elasticity   The ability of an object or material to return to its original size and shape, after being pushed or pulled by an outside force. For example, rubber is elastic.

electrode   A rod, plate, or wire that is used to conduct electric current out of or into any device.

electromagnet   A coil with a soft iron core that acts as a magnet when an electric current is passed through it.

electromotive force   The force that moves an electric current around a circuit. For example, a generator produces an electromotive force.

engine   A machine that applies power to do work. It converts various forms of energy into mechanical force and motion.

expansion joint   A space left in structures or roads that allows for the expansion and contraction of the material, caused by heating and cooling of the surrounding environment.

filament   A metallic wire that is heated in an incandescent lamp in order to produce light.

fuse   A safety device that protects a circuit from receiving too much current. The fuse's wire melts in response to too much electric current passing through it, thus breaking the circuit.

galvanometer   An instrument that detects, measures, and determines the direction of a small electric current.

gasket   A deformable material, usually a ring of plastic or metal, that is used to make a pressure-tight joint between two (usually stationary) parts.

generator   A machine that converts mechanical energy into electrical energy.

"Major Scientists and Engineers" in chapter 5
Go to

Sciences

girder   A large beam of wood, metal, or concrete, usually found in skyscrapers and other large buildings. It is used for structural support.

insulator   A device with high resistance to heat, electricity, or sound; for example, an electrical insulator prevents electricity from sending current to other objects.

lubricant   A substance applied to a surface to reduce friction.

machine   A device that helps to do work. Most machines either overcome a force or change the direction of the applied force.

microphone   A device that acts as a transformer and amplifier of sound waves into electric currents.

motor   A machine that converts electrical energy into mechanical energy.

oscilliscope   An instrument that produces an image of varying electrical voltages on a cathode-ray tube.

polymer   Large molecules made up of a series of molecular units, similar to beads on a string. Natural polymers include rubber, wool, and cotton; synthetic polymers include nylon and polythene. Polymers are often called giant molecules.

pulley   A wheel over which a rope, chain, or wire passes. Pulleys are used to ease the pulling of objects or lifting of heavy weights.

pulley system   An arrangement of two or more pulleys that form a machine.

radar (*radio detection and ranging*)   An instrument in which a cathode-ray tube receives reflected radio waves to detect distant objects.

radio   A system of transmitting sound signals (as electric impulses) through the air using electromagnetic waves.

receiver   A device that transforms radio waves and translates them mainly into sounds or pictures.

relay   A device that controls a large electrical current along another circuit by switching on or off. The relay uses a small electric current to control the larger current.

resistor   A device that resists an electric current.

rheostat   *See* **variable resistor.**

stator   A stationary machine part about which a rotor turns.

switch   A device that is used to switch parts of a circuit on or off. When the switch is on, the electric current is flowing through; when the switch is off, the electric current is cut off.

television   A system for transmitting video and audio signals using electromagnetic waves. A television uses a cathode-ray tube to produce images built from 625 constantly changing lines, each of which contains 400 small dots of light.

thermocouple   Shortened term for thermoelectric couple.

thermoelectricity   The production of an electric current directly from heat, or the reverse.

transformer   A device that changes the voltage of an alternating current. Transformers are used to modify the high voltage received from power lines so that it can be used by homes that require lower voltage for electrical devices.

tube (or valve)   An electrical device that allows electric current to flow only in one direction. Such devices are also referred to as diodes, triodes, etc., depending on the number of electrodes present.

variable resistor (or rheostat)   A device that variably resists an electrical current. The resistance can be changed by varying the contacts, allowing the resistor to slide around a length of wire.

voltmeter   An instrument that measures electromotive force or potential difference between two points, usually in volts.

ADDITIONAL SOURCES OF INFORMATION

ORGANIZATIONS AND SERVICES

American Association for the Advancement of Science
1333 H St., NW
Washington, DC 20005

American Astronomical Society
200 Florida Ave., NW
Washington, DC 20009

American Chemical Society
1155 16th St., NW
Washington, DC 20036

American Geophysical Union
2000 Florida Ave., NW
Washington, DC 20009-1277

American Institute of Physics
1 Physics Ellipse
College Park, MD 20740

National Academy of Sciences
2101 Constitution Ave., NW
Washington, DC 20418

National Aeronautics and Space Administration
300 E St., SW
Washington, DC 20546

National Oceanic and Atmospheric Administration
Department of Commerce
Washington, DC 20230

National Science Foundation
4201 Wilson Blvd.
Arlington, VA 22230

National Technical Information Service
Department of Commerce
5285 Port Royal Rd.
Springfield, VA 22161

National Weather Service Public Affairs
8060 13th St.
Silver Spring, MD 20910

New York Academy of Sciences
2 E. 63rd St.
New York, NY 10021

Smithsonian Institution
1000 Jefferson Dr., SW
Washington, DC 20560

MAGAZINES

Air & Space/Smithsonian
P.O. Box 420113
Palm Coast, FL 32142-0113
http://www.smithsonianmag.si.edu

Astronomy
21027 Crossroads Circle
P.O. Box 1612
Waukesha, WI 53187
http://www.astronomy.com

Discover Magazine
114 Fifth Ave.
New York, NY 10011
http://stage.enews.com/magazines/discover

Earth
21027 Crossroads Circle
P. O. Box 1612
Waukesha, WI 53187
http://www.earthmag.com

Physics Today
500 Sunnyside Blvd.
Woodbury, NY 11797-2999
http://www.aip.org/pt/

Popular Mechanics
224 W. 57th St.
New York, NY 10019
http://popularmechanics.com

Popular Science
2 Park Ave.
New York, NY 10016
http://www.popsci.com

Scientific American
415 Madison Ave.
New York, NY 10017
http://www.sciam.com

Sky & Telescope
P. O. Box 9111
Cambridge, MA 02178-9111
http://www.skypub.com/s_t/s_tshtml

Smithsonian Magazine
P. O. Box 420113
Palm Coast, FL 32142-0113
http://www.smithsonianmag.si.edu

BOOKS

Abell, George O., David Morrison and Sidney C. Wolff. *Exploration of the Universe.* 6th ed. Saunders College, 1991.

Sciences

Beatty, J. Kelly and Andrew Chaikin. *The New Solar System.* 3rd ed. Sky Publishing, 1990.

Blackburn, David and Geoffrey Holister, eds. *G. K. Hall Encyclopedia of Modern Technology.* G. K. Hall, 1987.

Clapham, Christopher. *The Concise Oxford Dictionary of Mathematics.* Oxford University Press, 1996.

Clarke, Donald and Mark Dartford, eds. *The New Illustrated Science and Invention Encyclopedia: How It Works.* Marshall Cavendish, 1994.

Considine, Douglas and Glenn D. Considine, eds. *Van Nostrand's Scientific Encyclopedia.* 8th ed., 2 vols. Van Nostrand Reinhold, 1997.

Curtis, Anthony R. *Space Almanac.* 2nd ed. Gulf, 1992.

Daintith, John, ed. *A Dictionary of Chemistry.* 3rd ed. Oxford University Press, 1996.

Day, John A. and John A. Day. *A Field Guide to the Atmosphere.* Houghton Mifflin, 1983.

Dean, John A. *Lange's Handbook of Chemistry.* 14th ed. McGraw-Hill, 1996.

Hallam, Anthony. *Encyclopedia of the Planet Earth.* Bookthrift, 1986.

Hawking, Stephen. *A Brief History of Time: From the Big Bang to Black Holes.* Bantam, 1990.

Lambert, David and the Diagram Group. *The Field Guide to Geology.* Facts on File, 1997.

Lide, David R., ed. *CRC Handbook of Chemistry and Physics: A Ready-Reference Book of Chemical and Physical Data.* 78th ed. CRC Press, 1997.

Ludlum, David., et al. *Clouds and Storms* (National Audubon Society Pocket Guide). Knopf, 1995.

Macaulay, David. *The Way Things Work.* Houghton-Mifflin, 1988.

Moore, Patrick. *Atlas of the Universe.* Rand McNally, 1994.

The New York Public Library Science Desk Reference. Macmillan, 1995.

Parker, Sybil P., ed. *McGraw-Hill Dictionary of Scientific and Technical Terms.* 5th ed. McGraw-Hill, 1994.

Parker, Sybil P., ed. *McGraw-Hill Encyclopedia of Science and Technology.* 8th ed. McGraw-Hill, 1997.

Pellant, Chris, *Rocks and Minerals.* Dorling Kindersley, 1992.

Pough, Frederick H. and Roger Tory Peterson. *Peterson's First Guide to Rocks and Minerals.* Houghton-Mifflin, 1991.

Ralston, Anthony and Edwin D. Reilly, eds. *Encyclopedia of Computer Science.* 3rd ed. International Thompson, 1993.

Smith, Peter J., ed. *The Earth.* Prentice Hall, 1986.

Williams, Jack. *The Weather Book.* 2nd ed. Vintage, 1997.

5

INVENTIONS AND
SCIENTIFIC DISCOVERIES

SIGNIFICANT INVENTIONS, 122
TECHNOLOGICAL ADVANCES, AND
SCIENTIFIC DISCOVERIES

MAJOR SCIENTISTS AND ENGINEERS 141

ADDITIONAL SOURCES OF INFORMATION 153

SIGNIFICANT INVENTIONS, TECHNOLOGICAL ADVANCES, AND SCIENTIFIC DISCOVERIES

Date	Invention/Advance/Discovery	Inventor/Origin
B.C.		
c. 12,000	Fire	Unknown
c. 5000	Woven cloth	Mesopotamia, Egypt
	Copper working	Rudna Glava, Yugoslavia
c. 3500	Wheeled vehicles	Sumeria, Syria
	Potter's wheel	Middle East
	Gold mining	Mesopotamia, Africa
	Sundial	Middle East
c. 3150	Irrigation	China, Egypt
c. 3000	Ox-drawn plow	Egypt
c. 2780	First step pyramid	Imhotep
c. 2700	Great Pyramid of Cheops	Cheops
c. 2640	Silk production	Si-ling Chi
c. 2500	Kite	China
	Cotton production	China, India
c. 1350	22-letter alphabet	Phoenicians
c. 1300	Musical notation	Ugarit, Syria
c. 700	First aqueduct	Sennacherib
570	Geographical and star charts	Anaximander of Miletus
430	Concept of atomic structure	Democritus
c. 400	Profession of medicine	Hippocrates
300	Deductive system of mathematics	Euclid
	Abacus	Asia, Middle East
c. 260	Theory that sun is the center of the solar system	Aristarchus
c. 250	Principles of the lever and other simple machines	Archimedes
c. 221	Beginning of the Great Wall of China	Shih Hwang-ti
c. 190	Ellipse and hyperbola	Appollonius
c. 140	Trigonometry	Hipparchus
	Wheel bearings	On a wagon found at Dejbjerg, Jutland
c. 85	Seed-planting machine	China
c. 40	Rotary winnowing machine	China

The Kite

A Closer Look

The kite is not only the earliest form of flying machine, but also one of the few ancient technological objects to be used continuously into modern times. There is evidence that kites were known in China as early as 2500 B.C., and they eventually came to be used for recreational, religious, and military purposes throughout Asia and the Pacific islands. Kites served a ceremonial function, for example, in Polynesian myth, in which gods were personified in kite form.

One of the first references to kites in Europe is found in the 1300s: A German book contains an illustration of soldiers using a kite to drop a bomb over the walls of an enemy castle. By the 1600s, kites had lost their military overtones, growing popular as toys for children. In 1752, Benjamin Franklin used a kite to show the electrical nature of lightning. During the nineteenth century, kites saved lives—shipwrecked boats would use them to carry lines to potential rescuers onshore.

Also in the 1800s, kites were important in early studies of aeronautics. Lawrence Hargrave of Australia was one of the first to try to make the kite into a flying machine, a forerunner of our modern glider.

Inventions

Leonardo da Vinci

Modern science has its roots in the Italian Renaissance, and perhaps the most striking example of "the Renaissance Man" is Leonardo da Vinci (1452–1519). Although he is best known for his work as an artist, Leonardo's scientific contributions may rival his renowned *Mona Lisa*. In 1493, Leonardo sketched a design for a hovering machine that he called a "helix pteron," an early version of our modern helicopter. He designed and built the first swinging miter lock gates for canals. And he sketched the separation of traffic on two levels—a forerunner of modern road systems. In his scientific contributions, Leonardo was a precursor of two other Renaissance greats, Copernicus and Galileo.

Date	Invention/Advance/Discovery	Inventor/Origin
A.D.		
c. 80	Magnetism	China
c. 100	Paper making	China
c. 170	Function of the arteries	Galen
c. 180	Rotary fan	China
c. 230	Wheelbarrow	China
c. 500	Algebra	India
	Decimal system	India, Mesopotamia
c. 550	Water mill	Greece
580	Iron-chain suspension bridge	China
c. 600	Zero	India
640	Windmill	Persia
c. 700	Porcelain	T'ang dynasty
886	24-hour-day measurement system	Alfred the Great
c. 900	Moldboard plow	China
980	Canal locks	Ciao Wei-Yo
c. 1100	Rocket	China
1150	Paper mill	Spain
c. 1150	Gunpowder	China
1250	Magnifying glass	Roger Bacon
1260	Gun/cannon	Konstantin Anklitzen
1269	360° compass	Petrus Peregrinus de Maricourt
1280	Belt-driven spinning wheel	Hans Speyer
1285	Eyeglasses	Alessandro de Spina
1287	Nitric acid	Raymond Lully
1326	Metal cannon	Rinaldo di Villamagna
1335	Public striking clock	Palace Chapel of the Visconti, Milan, Italy
1360	Mechanical clock	Henri de Vick of Wurttemburg for King Charles V of France
1410	Wire	Rodolph of Nuremberg
1450	Printing press with movable type	Johann Gutenberg
1455	Cast-iron pipe	Castle of Dillenburgh, Germany
1474	Lunar nautical navigation	Regiomontanus
1489	Addition (+) and subtraction (−) signs in mathematics	Johann Widman
1493	Drawing of a flying machine	Leonardo da Vinci
1500	Portable clock	Peter Henlein
1520	Spirally grooved rifle barrel	August Kotter
1525	Portable shotgun (harquebus)	Marquis of Pescara

Inventions

continues

Continued

Date	Invention/Advance/Discovery	Inventor/Origin
c. 1535	Heliocentric planetary model	Copernicus
1538	Optic nerve	Constanzo Varolio
1540	Artificial limbs	Ambroise Parase
	Pistol	Camillo Vettelli
1550	Screwdriver	Gunsmiths and armorers (location unknown)
	Wrench	Unknown
	Ligature to stop bleeding during surgery	Ambroise Paré
1557	Enamel	Bernard Palissy
	Platinum	Julius Caesar Scaliger
1561	Dredger	Pieter Breughel
1565	Graphite pencil	Konrad Gesner
1569	Screw-cutting machine and ornamental turning lathe	Jacques Besson
1581	Pendulum motion	Galileo Galilei
1582	Modern calendar	Pope Gregory XIII and Christoph Clavius
1585	Time bomb	Dutch siege of Antwerp
1589	Hosiery-knitting machine	Rev. William Lee
1590	Compound microscope	Zacharias Jannsen
	Law of falling bodies	Galileo Galilei
1592	Wind-powered sawmill	Cornelius Corneliszoon
	Thermoscope (primitive thermometer)	Galileo Galilei
1597	Proportional compass (sector)	Galileo Galilei
1599	Silk-knitting machine	Rev. William Lee
1600	Wind-driven land vehicle	Simon Stevin
1603	Pantograph	Christoph Scheiner
1606	Surveying chain	Edmund Gunter
1609	Astronomical telescope	Galileo Galilei
	Laws of planetary motion	Johannes Kepler
1611	Coke (for iron)	Simon Sturtevant
	Rainbow theory	Johannes Kepler
1611	Double convex microscope	Johannes Kepler
1614	Logarithms	John Napier
1615	Solar-powered motor	Salomon de Caux
	Surveying by triangulation	Willebrord Snell von Roigen
1616	Function of the heart and complete circulation of the blood	William Harvey
	Medical thermometer	Santorio Santorii (Sanctorius)
1621	Rectilinear slide rule	William Oughtred
1630	Circular slide rule	Richard Delamain
1631	Multiplication (×) sign	William Oughtred
	Vernier scale	Pierre Vernier
1637	Analytic geometry	René Descartes
1638	Micrometer	William Gascoigne
1642	Calculating machine	Blaise Pascal
1643	Barometer (Torricellian tube)	Evangelista Torricelli and Vincenzo Viviani
1647	Map of moon and star catalog	Helvius (Johannes Hewelcke)
1648	Hydrochloric acid	Johann Rudolph Glauber
	Concept of air pressure in barometers	Blaise Pascal
1650	Lymph glands	Olof Rudbeck

Date	Invention/Advance/Discovery	Inventor/Origin
1654	Air vacuum pump	Otto von Guericke
	Basic laws of probability	Blaise Pascal and Pierre de Fermat
1656	Pendulum clock	Christiaan Huygens
1658	Clock balance spring	Robert Hooke
	Red blood cells	Jan Swammerdam
1661	Wood (methyl) alcohol	Robert Boyle
1662	Boyle's law/gas pressure laws	Robert Boyle
	Statistical mathematics	Sir William Petty
1664	Hygrometer	Francesco Folli
1666	Principles of integral calculus	Isaac Newton
1667	Blood transfusion (lamb to boy)	Jean-Baptiste Denis
	Wind gauge	Christian Forner
1668	Reflecting telescope	Isaac Newton
1669	Phosphorus	Hennig Brand
1671	Silk-spinning machine	Edmund Blood
	Binary number system	Gottfried Wilhelm Leibnitz
1674	Tourniquet	Morel, France
1675	Calibrated foot ruler	Unknown
	Speed of light	Ole Römer
1676	Artificial water filtration	William Woolcott
1679	Pressure cooker	Denis Papin
1682	Halley's comet	Edmond Halley
1683	Bacteria	Anton van Leeuwenhoek
	Spermatozoa	Anton van Leeuwenhoek
1684	Theory of gravity	Isaac Newton
	Foundations of integral and differential calculus	Gottfried Leibniz
1694	Plant pollen	Rudolph Jakob Camerarius
1695	Epsom salts	Nehemiah Grew
	Periodicity of comet orbit	Edmond Halley
1699	Portable fire pump	Dumaurier Duperrier
1701	Machine seed drill	Jethro Tull
1702	Tidal pump	George Sorocold
	Boron/borax	Guillaume Homberg
1709	Coke smelting (iron)	Abraham Derby
	Anemometer	Wolfius
	Alcohol thermometer	Gabriel Fahrenheit
1711	Tuning fork	John Shore
1712	Steam engine	Thomas Newcomen
1716	True porcelain (Meissen)	Johann Friedrich Bottger
1717	Fahrenheit temperature scale	Gabriel Fahrenheit
1718	Mercury thermometer	Gabriel Fahrenheit
1719	Color printing	Jakob Christof Le Blon
1729	Aberration of light	Rev. James Bradley
1731	Octant (Hadley's quadrant)	John Hadley
1732	Copper-zinc alloy	Christopher Pinchbeck
	Threshing machine	Michael Menzies
1733	Arsenic	George Brandt
	Flint-glass lens	Chester Moor Hall
	Fly shuttle (weaving)	John Kay
1735	Plant classification system	Carl Linnaeus

continues

Inventions

Continued

Date	Invention/Advance/Discovery	Inventor/Origin
1736	Scarlet fever	William Douglass
1740	Curare (drug)	Charles Marie de Lacondamine
1742	Crucible steel production	Benjamin Huntsman
	Celsius temperature scale	Anders Celsius
1743	Wool carding machine	David Bourne
	Compound lever	John Wyatt
1746	Leyden jar (prototype of electrical condenser)	Pieter van Musschenbroeck and E. G. von Kleist
1747	Scurvy cure	James Lind
1748	Sea quadrant	B. Cole
1750	Dyanometer	Gaspard de Prony
1751	Nickel	Axel Frederik Cronstedt
1752	Lightning conductor	Benjamin Franklin
1755	Iron-girder bridge	M. Garvin
1756	Carbon dioxide	Joseph Black
1757	Sextant	John Campbell
1758	Achromatic lens (for eyeglasses)	John Dolland
	Refracting telescope	John Dolland
1760	Screw manufacturing machine	Job and William Wyatt
	Cast-iron cog wheel	Carron Iron Works, Scotland
1761	Mass production of steel scissors	Robert Hinchliffe
	Medical percussion method (diagnostic technique)	Joseph Leopold Avenbrugger
1762	Fire extinguisher	Ambrose Godfrey
1764	Spinning jenny	James Hargreaves
1766	Hydrogen	Henry Cavendish
1768	Aerometer	Antoine Baumé
1769	Steam automobile	Joseph Cugnot
	Steam tractor	Joseph Cugnot
	Hydraulic spinning machine	Richard Arkwright
1770	Sulfur dioxide	Joseph Priestley
	Electric battery	John Cuthbertson
1772	Nitrogen	Daniel Rutherford
1774	Oxygen	Karl Wilhelm Scheele, Joseph Priestley, and Antoine-Laurent Lavoisier
	Ammonia	Joseph Priestley
	Barium	Karl Wilhelm Scheele
	Chlorine	Karl Wilhelm Scheele
	Manganese	Karl Wilhelm Scheele
1775	Chain-driven machine	Crane (England)
	Digitalis (as drug)	William Withering
1776	One-person submarine	David Bushnell
1777	Circular saw	Samuel Miller
	Iron boat	Yorkshire, England
1778	Mortise tumbler (lock)	Robert Barron
	Flush toilet	Joseph Bramah
	Molybdenum	Karl Wilhelm Scheele
1779	Glycerine	Karl Wilhelm Scheele
1780	Artificial insemination	Lazzaro Spallanzani
1781	Uranus	William Herschel

Date	Invention/Advance/Discovery	Inventor/Origin
1782	Tellurium	Franz Joseph Müller
	Hot-air balloon	Joseph-Michel and Jacques-Étienne Montgolfier
1783	Hydrogen balloon	Jacques Alexandre Charles and the Robert brothers
	Tungsten	Don Fausto d'Elhuyar and Juan José d'Elhuyar
1784	Bifocal lenses	Benjamin Franklin
	Model helicopter	Launoy (France)
	Rope-spinning machine	Robert March
	Shrapnel shell	Henry Shrapnel
1785	Automatic gristmill	Oliver Evans
	Methane and ethylene	Claude Louis Berthollet
	Rule of electrical forces	Charles Coulomb
1786	Steamboat	John Fitch
1787	Roller bearings	John Garnett
	Power loom	Edmund Cartwright
1789	Uranium	Martin Heinrich Klaproth
	Zirconium	Martin Heinrich Klaproth
	Table of 31 chemical elements	Antoine Lavoisier
1790	Semaphore (visual telegraph)	Claude Chappé
	Cotton spinning and weaving machine (first U.S. patent)	William Pollard
1793	Cotton gin	Eli Whitney
	Astigmatism	Thomas Young
	Strontium	Thomas Charles Hope
	Daltonism (color blindness)	John Dalton
1794	Ball bearings	Philip Vaughan
1795	Hydraulic press	Joseph Bramah
1796	Lithography	Aloys Senefelder
	Smallpox vaccine	Edward Jenner
1797	Chromium	Louis Nicolas Vaquelin
	First parachute jump	André Jacques Garnerin
1798	Process of mass production	Eli Whitney
1799	Metric system	French Academy of Sciences
1800	Infrared light	William Herschel
	Method for storing electricity	Alessandro Volta
	Submarine (metal clad)	Robert Fulton
1801	Asteroid	Giuseppe Piazzi
	Niobium	Charles Hatchett
	Wave theory of light	Thomas Young
	Ultraviolet light	Johann Wilhelm Ritter (and William Hyde Wollaston)
1803	Modern atomic theory	John Dalton
	Iridium	Smithson Tennant
	Palladium and rhodium	William Hyde Wollaston
	Spray gun (aerosol medication)	Alan de Vilbiss
1804	Fishnet-making machine	Joseph Marie Charles Jacquard
	Food canning process	Nicolas Appert
1805	Mechanical silk loom	Joseph Marie Charles Jacquard
	Amphibious vehicle	Oliver Evans
	Morphine	Friedrich Wilhelm Adam Serturner

Inventions

continues

Continued

Date	Invention/Advance/Discovery	Inventor/Origin
1806	Beaufort wind scale	Francis Beaufort
	Carbon paper	Ralph Wedgwood
1807	Patent for gas-driven automobile	Isaac de Rivez
	Long-distance steamboat	Robert Fulton
	Potassium	Humphrey Davy
	Sodium	Humphrey Davy
	Sensory-motor nerve system	Charles Bell
1810	Homeopathy	Samuel Hahnemann
	Ammonia-soda reaction	Augustin Jean Fresnel
	Metronome	Dietrich Nikolaus Winkel
	Mowing machine	Peter Gaillard
1811	Avogadro's law	Amedeo Avogadro
	Iodine	Bernard Courteois
1813	Gun cartridge	Samuel Pauly
	Gas meter	Samuel Clegg
	Mine safety lamp	Humphrey Davy and George Stephenson
1814	Steam locomotive	George Stephenson
1816	Stethoscope	René Théophile and Hyacinthe Laënnec
	Phosphorus match	François Derosne
1817	Parkinson's disease	James Parkinson
	Lithium	John August Arfwedson
	Dental plate	Anthony A. Plantson
1818	Cadmium	Friedrich Strohmeyer
	Selenium	Johan Jakob Berzelius
	Hydrogen peroxide	Baron Louis-Jacques Thénard
	Strychnine	Pierre-Joseph Pelletier and Joseph-Bienaimé Caventou
	Geothermal energy experiment	F. de Larderel
1819	Dental amalgam	Charles Bell
	Dioptric system (for lighthouses)	Augustin Jean Fresnel
1820	Diphtheria	Pierre Fidèle Bretonneau
	Quinine	Pierre-Joseph Pelletier and Joseph-Bienaimé Caventou
	Electromagnetism	Hans Christian Oersted
1821	Caffeine	Pierre Joseph Pelletier
	Electric motor principle	Michael Faraday
	Heliotrope	Carl Friedrich Gauss
1822	Thermocouple	Thomas Johann Seebeck
1823	Electromagnet	William Sturgeon
1824	Galvanometer	André-Marie Ampère
	Magnetic pull	Dominique François Jean Arago
1825	Binocular telescope	J. P. Lemière
1826	Gas stove	James Sharp
1827	Aluminum	Friedrich Wohler
	Electrical resistance	George Simon Ohm
	Astigmatic lens	George Biddell Airy
	Microphone	Charles Wheatstone
	Trifocal lens	John Isaac Hawkins
	Water turbine	Benoît Fourneyron

Date	Invention/Advance/Discovery	Inventor/Origin
1828	Differential gear	Onésiphore Pecqueur
	Stethoscope with earpiece	Pierre Adolphe Poirry
	Cocoa	Conrad van Houten
	Beryllium	Friedrich Wohler
	Thorium	Johan Jakob Berzelius
1830	Vanadium	Nils Gabriel Sefstrom
	Thermostat	André Ure
	Friction match	Charles Sauria
	Lawn mower	Edwin Beard Budding
	Paraffin	Karl, Baron von Reichenbach
1831	Electric bell	Joseph Henry
	Reaping machine	Cyrus McCormick
	Electromagnetic induction	Michael Faraday
	Electromagnetic balance	Antoine César Becquerel
	Magnetic north pole	James Clark Ross
	Chloroform	Samuel Guthrie
1833	Differential calculating machine	Charles Babbage
	Creosote	Karl, Baron von Reichenbach
	Nervous reflex	Marshall Hall
1834	Galvanic cells (continuous electric light)	James Bowman Lindsay
1835	Automatic revolver	Samuel Colt
1836	Steam shovel	William Smith Otis
	Stroboscope	Joseph Antoine Ferdinand Plateau
	Combine harvester	H. Hoare and J. Hascall
	Acetylene	Edmund Davy
1837	Braille reading system	Louis Braille
	Daguerreotype	Louis Jacques Mandé Daguerre
	Electric telegraph	William Fothergill Cooke and Charles Wheatstone
	Electric motor	Thomas Davenport
	Morse code	Samuel F. B. Morse
1838	Plant cells	Matthias Jakob Schleiden
	Stereoscope	Charles Wheatstone
1839	Animal cells	Theodore Schwann
	Protoplasm	Jan Evangelista Purkinje
	Vulcanization of rubber	Charles Goodyear
	First fuel cell	William Robert Grove
1840	Ozone	Christian Friedrich Schonbein
	Chronoscope	Charles Wheatstone
	Electroplating	John Wright
1841	Incandescent lamp	Frederick de Moleyne
1842	Carbon electrode battery	Robert Wilhelm Eberhard von Bunsen
	Underwater telegraph cable	Samuel F. B. Morse
	Ether anesthesia	Crawford Williamson Long
1844	Nitrous oxide anesthesia	Horace Wells and Gardner Q. Colton
1845	Rotary printing press	Richard M. Hoe
	Giant telescope	William Parsons
1846	Sewing machine	Elias Howe
	Use of anesthetic gases in surgery	William Morton
	Neptune	Johann Gottfield Galle and Heinrich Ludwig d'Arrest

continues

Inventions

Continued

Date	Invention/Advance/Discovery	Inventor/Origin
1847	Nitroglycerine	Ascanio Sobrero
	Chloroform anesthesia	Jacob Bell and James Young Simpson
1850	Foucault's pendulum (proving Earth's rotation)	Jean Bernard Léon Foucault
1851	Doppler principle	Christian Doppler
	Absolute zero	Lord Kelvin (William Thompson)
	Odometer	William Grayson
	Ophthalmoscope	Herman von Helmholtz
	Flash photography	Henry F. Talbot
1852	Steam-powered airship	Henri Giffard
	Piloted glider	George Cayley
	Microfilm	John Benjamin Dancer
	Fluorescence	George Gabriel Stokes
1853	Hypodermic syringe	Charles Gabriel Pravaz and Alexander Wood
1854	Paleozoic fossils	Adam Sedgwick
1855	Spinal anesthesia	J. L. Corning (U.S.)
	Bunsen burner	Robert Wilhelm Eberhard von Bunsen
	Stopwatch	Edward Daniel Johnson
	Safety match	Johan Edvard Lundstrom
	Battlefield nursing care	Florence Nightingale
1857	Passenger elevator	Elisha G. Otis
1858	Cell replication theory	Rudolf Virchow
	Mobius band	August Mobius
	Atomic and molecular weights	Stanislao Cannizzaro
1859	Cathode rays	Julius Plucker
	Theory of evolution through natural selection	Charles Darwin
	Internal combustion engine (coal gas)	Joseph-Etienne Lenoir
	Technique for drilling oil wells	Edwin Drake
	Ironclad ship	France (*La Gloire*)
1860	Linoleum	Frederick Walton
	Snap button	John Newnham
	Cesium	Robert Wilhelm Eberhard von Bunsen and Gustav Robert Kirchoff
1861	Pneumatic drill	Germain Sommelier
	Speech center of brain	Pierre Paul Broca
1862	Machine gun	Richard Jordan Gatling
1863	Phonograph (machine that wrote down what was played on a piano)	Fenby (U.S.)
	TNT	J. Wilbrand
	Sodium carbonate process	Ernest Solvay
1864	Electromagnetic wave transmission	Mahlon Loomis
	Pasteurization	Louis Pasteur
	Refutation of spontaneous generation	Louis Pasteur
	Nitroglycerine and dynamite explosives	Alfred Nobel
	Railroad sleeping car	George Pullman
1865	Electric arc welding	Henry Wilde
	Reinforced concrete	W. B. Wilkinson
	Yale cylinder lock	Linus Yale, Jr.
	Offset printing (web press)	William Bullock
	Genetics	Gregor Johann Mendel

Date	Invention/Advance/Discovery	Inventor/Origin
1866	Transatlantic cable	Cyrus West Field, Samuel Canning, and Daniel Gooch
	Lip reading	Alexander Melville Bell
1867	Formaldehyde	August Wilhelm von Hofmann
	Barbed wire	Lucien B. Smith
	Introduction of antiseptic practices in hospitals	Joseph Lister
	Bicycle	Ernest Michaux
	Typewriter	Christopher Latham Sholes
1868	Margarine	Hippolyte Megé-Mouries
	Stapler	Charles Henry Gould
	Plywood	John K. Mayo
	Helium (in Sun's chromosphere)	Edward Frankland and Joseph Normal Lockyer
1869	Periodic law	Dmitri Ivanovitch Mendeleyev
	Color photography	Charles Cros and Louis Ducos du Hauron
	Celluloid	John Wesley Hyatt and Isaiah Smith Hyatt
1871	Wind tunnel	Francis Herbert Wenham
1872	Hydroplane	Rev. Charles Meade Ramus
	Solar water distillation	Charles Wilson
1873	Direct current electric motor	Zénobe Théophile Gramme
	Electromagnetic radiation	James Clerk-Maxwell
1875	Mimeograph	Thomas Alva Edison
1876	Articulating telephone	Alexander Graham Bell
	Dewey decimal system	Melvil Dewey
	Carburetor (surface type)	Gottlieb Daimler
	Refrigerator	Karl Paul Gottfried von Linde
1877	Differential gear	James Starley
	Switchboard	Edwin T. Holmes
	Four-cycle internal combustion engine	Nikolaus August Otto
	Phonograph	Thomas Alva Edison
	Liquid oxygen	Louis-Paul Cailletet and Raoul Pictet
1878	Cathode ray tube	William Crookes
	Milking machine	L. O. Colvin
	Electric alternator	Zénobe Théophile Gramme and Hippolyte Fontaine
	Carbon filament	Joseph Wilson Swann
1879	Arc lighting system	Edwin James Houston and Elihu Thomson
	Cash register	James J. Ritty
	Saccharin	Constantin Fahlberg and Ira Remsen
	Incandescent bulb patent	Thomas Alva Edison
1880	Hearing aid	R. G. Rhodes
	First successful roll film	George Eastman
	Inoculation	Louis Pasteur
1881	Interferometer	Albert A. Michelson
	Rechargeable battery	Camille Fauré
	Telephotography	Shelford Bidwell
1882	Induction coil	Lucien Gaulard and John Gibbs
	Commercial electric fan	Schuyler Skaats Wheeler
	Skyscraper	William Le Baron Jenny
	Three-wire system for transporting electrical power	Thomas Alva Edison

continues

Inventions

Continued

Date	Invention/Advance/Discovery	Inventor/Origin
1882 *(cont'd)*	Fountain pen	Lewis Edson Waterman
	Carburetor (float-feed spray)	Edward Butler
	Tuberculosis and cholera germs	Robert Koch
1883	Long-span suspension bridge (Brooklyn Bridge)	John Augustus Roebling
1884	Steam turbine	Charles Parsons
	Local anesthesia (cocaine)	K. Koller
	Gram bacteria test	Hans Christian Joachim Gram
1885	Ammonium picrate (explosive)	Eugène Turpin
	Gas-engine automobile	Gottlieb Daimler, Wilhelm Maybach, and Karl Friedrich Benz
1886	Aluminum electrolysis process	Paul Louis Toussaint Héroult and Charles Martin Hall
	Railway car brake	George Westinghouse
	Comptometer	Dorr Eugene Felt
	Linotype machine	Ottmar Mergenthaler
1887	Mach supersonic scale	Ernst Mach
	Contact lens	Eugen A. Frick
	Electrocardiogram	Augustus Desire Walker
1888	Alternating current motor	Nikola Tesla
	Cellulose photographic film	John Carbutt
	Monorail	Charles Lartigue
	Monotype	Tolbert Lanston
	Hand camera	George Eastman
	Gas-engine farm tractor	Charter Engine Co. (U.S.)
	Cotton picker	Angus Campbell
	Data-processing computer	Herman Hollerith
1889	Active molecules	Svante August Arrhenius
	Cordite	James Dewar and Frederick Augustus Abel
	Lysine (amino acid)	Edmund Drechsel
1890	Motion pictures	William Friese-Greene
	Electric subway train	London, England
1891	Electric motor car	William Morrison
	Silicon carbide	Eduard Goodrich Acheson
	Flashlight	Bristol Electric Lamp Co. (England)
	Aluminum boat	Escher Wyss & Co. (Switzerland)
	Zipper	Whitcomb L. Judson
	Diphtheria antitoxin	Emil Adolf von Behring and Shibasaburo Kitasato
1892	Cholera vaccine	Waldemar Mordecai Wolff Haffkine
	Phagocytes	Illya Mechnikov
	Vacuum flask (early thermos)	Sir James Dewar
	Viruses	Dmitri Iosifovich Ivanovsky
	Viscose rayon	C. F. Cross and E. J. Bevan
1893	Photoelectric cell	Julius Elster and Hans F. Geitel
	Electric toaster	Crompton & Co. (England)
	Diesel engine	Rudolf Diesel
1894	Argon gas	John William Strutt and William Ramsay
	Helium	William Ramsay
	Escalator	Jesse W. Reno

Inventions

Date	Invention/Advance/Discovery	Inventor/Origin
1895	X-rays	Wilhelm Konrad von Roentgen
	Electric hand drill	Wilhelm Fein
	Photographic typesetting	William Friese-Greene
	First public motion picture showing with on-screen projection	Louis Lumière and Auguste Lumière
	Wireless telegraph	Guglielmo Marconi
	Gas-engine motorcycle	Count Albert de Dion and Georges Bouton
1896	Electron	Joseph John Thomas
	Histidine (amino acid)	Albrecht Kossel and Sven A. Hedin
	Science of radioactivity	Henri Becquerel
1897	Conditioned reflexes	Ivan Petrovic Pavlov
	Cause of malaria (mosquito)	Ronald Ross
	Digestion physiology	Ivan Petrovic Pavlov
	Plasticine	William Harbutt
	Worm gear	Frederick W. Lanchester
1898	Antineuritic vitamin B	Christiaan Eijkman
	Krypton	William Ramsay and Morris William Travers
	Neon	William Ramsay and Morris William Travers
	Xenon	William Ramsay and Morris William Travers
	Vitamin-deficiency diseases	Christiaan Eijkman
	Loudspeaker	Horace Short
1899	Aspirin	Felix Hoffman
1900	Radon	Friedrich Ernst Dorn
	Tryptophan (amino acid)	Frederick Gowland Hopkins
	Paper clip	Johann Vaaler
	Alkaline battery	Thomas Alva Edison
	Tractor	Benjamin Holt
1901	Blood groups	Karl Landsteiner
	Valine and proline (amino acids)	Emil Hermann Fischer
	Electric typewriter	Thaddeus Cahill
	Vacuum cleaner	H. Cecil Booth
	Quantum theory	Max Karl Ernst Planck
1902	Hormones	William Maddock Bayliss and Ernest H. Starling
	Ionosphere	Arthur Edwin Kennelly and Oliver Heaviside
	Radium	Pierre Curie and Marie Curie
	Air conditioning	Willis H. Carrier
	Disc brakes	Frederick W. Lanchester
1903	First successful airplane flight	Orville Wright and Wilbur Wright
	Barbiturates	Emil Herman Fischer and Emil Adolf von Bering
1904	Diode vacuum tube	John Ambrose Fleming
1905	Theory of relativity	Albert Einstein
	Silicones	Frederic S. Kipping
	Chemical foam fire extinguisher	Alexander Laurent
	Hydraulic centrifugal clutch	Hermann Fottinger
1906	Crystal radio apparatus	H. H. C. Dunwoody
	Animated cartoon film	James S. Blackton and Walter Booth
	Motion-picture sound	Eugen Augustin Lauste
	Wasserman test (for syphilis)	August von Wasserman

Inventions

continues

Continued

Date	Invention/Advance/Discovery	Inventor/Origin
1907	Detergents (household)	Henkel et Cié (Germany)
	Upright vacuum cleaner (attached dust bag)	J. Murray Spangler
	Modern color photography	Louis Lumière
1908	Bakelite	Leo Henrik Baekeland
	Cellophane	Jacques E. Brandenberger
1909	Synthetic ammonia	Fritz Haber
	Typhus fever body louse	Charles Jules Henri Nicolle
	IUD (intrauterine device)	R. Richter
1910	Tumor virus	Francis Peyton Rous
	Gene theory of heredity	Thomas Morgan
	Neon lighting	Georges Claude
1911	Cosmic rays	Victor Franz Hess
	Theory of atomic structure	Ernest Rutherford and Niels Bohr
	Superconductivity	Heike Kamerlingh Onnes
	Binet intelligence test	Alfred Binet
	Calculating machine (full automatic multiplication and division)	Jay R. Monroe
	Monoplane	Léon Levasseur
1912	Diffraction of X rays	Max Theodor Felix von Laue
	Thiamine (vitamin B$_1$)	Casimir Funk
	Diesel locomotive	North British Locomotive Co. (England)
	Cabin biplane (airliner forerunner)	Igor Sikorsky
1913	Stainless steel	Harry Brearley
	Vitamin A	Thomas B. Osborne, Lafayette B. Mendel, Elmer V. McCollum, and M. Davis
	Isotope labeling	Georg von Hevesy and Friedrich A. Paneth
	Moving assembly line for mass production	Henry Ford
1914	Brassiere	Mary Phelps Jacob
	Leica 35mm camera	Oskar Barnack
	Tear gas	Dr. von Tappen
1915	Amplitude modulation (AM) radio	Hendrick Johannes van der Bijl and Raymond A. Heising
	British army tank	Walter Wilson and William Tritton
1917	VHF electromagnetic waves	Guglielmo Marconi
	SONAR detection system	Paul Langevin and Robert Boyle
1918	Vitamin D	Edward Mellanby
	Electric food mixer	Universal Co. (U.S.)
	Domestic refrigerator	Nathaniel Wales and E. J. Copeland
1920	Commercial radio broadcasts	Station KDKA, Pittsburgh, PA (U.S.)
1921	Insulin	Frederick G. Banting and Charles H. Best
	Hydraulic four-wheel brakes	Duesenberg Motor Co. (U.S.)
	Lie detector	John Larsen
	Wirephoto	Western Union Cables (U.S.)
1922	Vitamin E	Herbert McLean Evans
	Three-dimensional movies	Perfect Pictures (U.S.)
1924	Spin dryer	Savage Arms Corp.(U.S.)

Inventions

Date	Invention/Advance/Discovery	Inventor/Origin
1925	Quantum mechanics	Max Born and Werner Karl Heisenberg
	Technetium and rhenium	Ida Eva Noddack, Walter Karl, and Friedrich Noddack
	Wave mechanics	Erwin Schrödinger
	Hi-fi radio loudspeaker	C. W. Rice and E. W. Kellogg
1926	Aerosol can	Erik Rotheim
	Synthetic rubber	I. G. Farben (Germany)
	Liquid-fueled rocket	Robert H. Goddard
	Television	John Logie Baird, C. F. Jenkins, and D. Mihaly
1927	Iron lung	Philip Drinker and Louis Shaw
	Pop-up toaster	Charles Strite
	First solo, nonstop transatlantic flight	Charles Lindbergh
	Uncertainty principle in physics	Werner Heisenberg
	Sex hormones	Bernhard Zondek and Selmar Ascheim
1928	Penicillin	Alexander Fleming
	Vitamin C	Albert von Nagyrapolt Szent-Györgyi
	Particles in visible light	Chandrasekhara Raman
	Geiger counter	Hans Geiger
	Teletype	Edward Ernst Kleinschmidt
	PVC (polyvinylchloride)	Carbide Corp., Carbon Chemical Corp., and Du Pont (U.S.)
	Tomography	Andre Bocage
1929	Electron microscope	Max Knoll and Ernst Ruska
	Coaxial cable	Bell Telephone Laboratories (U.S.)
	Brain-wave electroencephalograph	Hans Berger
	Frozen food	Clarence Birdseye
	First color television image transmission	Bell Telephone Laboratories (U.S.)
1930	Pluto	Clyde Tombaugh
	Pepsin	John Howard Northrop
	Cyclotron	Ernest O. Lawrence and N. E. Edlesfsen
	Polystyrene	I. G. Farben (Germany)
	TV electronic scanning suitable for the home	Philo T. Pharnsworth
1931	Neutrino	Wolfgang Pauli
	Radio astronomy	Karl Jansky
	Photographic exposure meter	J. Thomas Rhamstine
	Fiberglass	Owens Illinois Glass Co. (U.S.)
	Blood bank	Sergei Sergeivitch
	TWX (teletypewriter exchange)	Bell Telephone & Telegraph (U.S.)
	Electric razor	Jacob Schick
	Cathode-ray tube for television transmission	Vladimir Zworykin
1932	Neutron	James Chadwick
	Proton bombardment (lithium disintegration)	John Douglas Cockcroft and Ernest Thomas Sinton Walton
	Positron	Carl David Anderson and Patrick M. Stuart Blackett
	Deuterium (heavy hydrogen)	Harold Urey
	Defibrillator	William Bennett Kouwenhoven
	Nylon and neoprene	Wallace Carothers and Arnold Collins

Inventions

continues

Continued

Date	Invention/Advance/Discovery	Inventor/Origin
1933	Riboflavin (vitamin B_2)	Richard Kuhn
	Pantothenic acid	Roger J. Williams
	Frequency modulation (FM)	Edwin H. Armstrong
	Polyethylene	Reginald Gibson and E. W. Fawcett
1934	Cerenkov effect	Pavel Alekseevich Cerenkov
	Vitamin K	Carl Peter Henrik Dam and Edward Adelbert Doisy
	Progesterone	Adolf Friedrich Johann Butenandt
	Vitamin B_6	Albert von Nagyrapolt Szent-Györgyi
1935	Meson	Hideki Yakawa
	Electronic hearing aid	Edwin A. Steven
	Richter earthquake scale	Charles Francis Richter
1936	Jet engine	Frank Whittle and Hans von Ohain
	Helicopter (contra-rotating rotors)	Henrich Focke
	Plexiglas	I. G. Farben (Germany)
1937	Citric acid cycle	Hans Adolf Krebs
	Niacin	Conrad A. Elvehjem
	Radio telescope	Grote Reber
1938	Cortisone	Edward C. Kendall, Philip S. Hench, and Tadeus Reichstein
	Folic acid	P. L. Day
	Teflon	Roy Plunkett
	LSD	Albert Hofman and Arthur Stoll
	Pressurized airplane cabin	Transcontinental Airways, Boeing 307 Stratoliner
	Ballpoint pen	Lázló J. Biro and Georg Biro
	Fluorescent lighting	Arthur H. Compton and George Inman
	Photocopy machine	Chester Carlson
	First clear plastic contact lens	T. Obrig and F. Muller
1939	Jet aircraft	Hans von Ohain
	Binary calculator	John Atanasoff and George R. Stibitz
	DDT	Paul Hermann Müller
	Microfilm camera	Elgin G. Fassel
	Betatron	Donald W. Kerst
	Concept of black hole	J. Robert Oppenheimer and Hartland S. Snyder
1940	Plutonium	Glenn Theodore Seaborg and Edwin Mattison McMillan
	Radar	Robert M. Page (word coined by S. M. Tucker)
	Automatic transmission	General Motors (U.S.)
	Cavity magnetron (radar tube)	John Randall
1941	Microwave radar	U.S. Radiation Laboratory
	Dacron	John R. Whinfield
	First color television system	Peter Goldmark
1942	First sustained and controlled release of nuclear energy	Enrico Fermi and team
	Vitamin H (biotin)	Vincent du Vigneaud
1943	Streptomycin	Selman A. Waksman
	Electronic computer	Max Newman and T. H. Flowers

Date	Invention/Advance/Discovery	Inventor/Origin
1944	Americium	Glenn T. Seaborg and Albert Ghiorso
	Curium	Glenn T. Seaborg and Albert Ghiorso
	Sequence-controlled calculator	Howard Aiken
1945	Artificial kidney	Willem J. Kolff
	Atomic bomb	J. Robert Oppenheimer and Manhattan Project team
	Tupperware	Earl W. Tupper
	Vinyl floor covering	Du Pont (U.S.)
1946	Electronic vacuum tube computer (ENIAC)	John W. Mauchly and J. Presper Eckert
1947	Coenzyme A	Fritz A. Lipman
	Vitamin B_{12} as cure for pernicious anemia	Karl A. Folkers
	Radiocarbon dating	Willard Frank Libby
	Holography	Dennis Gabor
	Supersonic aircraft	Bell XS-1 (U.S.)
	First supersonic flight	Chuck Yeager
1948	Transistor	William Shockley, John Bardeen, and Walter H. Brattain
	Atomic clock	William F. Libby
	Cybernetics	Norbert Wiener
	Long-playing phonographic record (microgroove record)	Peter Goldmark
	Solid electric guitar	Leo (Clarence) Fender, "Doc" Kauffman, and George Fullerton
	Velcro	Georges de Mestral
	Corneal contact lenses	Kevin Tuohy
1949	Berkelium	Glenn T. Seaborg and Stanley G. Thompson
	Jet airliner	R. E. Bishop and team
1950	Chlorpromazine (tranquilizer)	Paul Charpentier
	Radioimmunoassay	Rosalyn Sussman Yalow
	Xerographic copying machine	Haloid Co. (U.S.)
1951	Oral contraceptive pill	Gregory Goodwin Pincus, Min Chuch Chang, John Rock, and Carl Djerassi
1952	Artificial heart valve	Charles A. Hufnagel
	Hydrogen bomb	Edward Teller and team
	Experimental videotape	John Mullin and Wayne Johnson
	Transistor radio	Sony (Japan)
1953	DNA (deoxyribonucleic acid)	Francis H. Compton Crick and James D. Watson
	Fermium	Albert Ghiorso and Stanley G. Thompson
	Measles vaccine	John F. Enders and Thomas Peebles
	Reperine (antidepressant drug)	Nathan S. Kline
	Reserpine (antihypertensive)	Nathan S. Kline
	Heart-lung machine	John H. Gibbon
1954	Regular broadcast of color television	National Broadcasting Co. (U.S.)
1955	Fiber optics	Narinder S. Kapany
	Mendelevium	Albert Ghiorso
	RNA synthesis	Severo Ochoa
	Ultrasound (to observe heart)	Leskell (U.S.)
	Polio vaccine (killed-virus)	Jonas Salk
	Felt-tip pen	Esterbrook (England)
	Stereo tape recording	EMI Stereosonic Tapes
	Hovercraft	Christopher S. Cockerell

Inventions

continues

Continued

Date	Invention/Advance/Discovery	Inventor/Origin
1956	Amniocentesis	St. Mary's Hospital (England)
	Human growth hormone	Choh Hao Li
	DNA synthesis with enzymes, nucleotides	Arthur Kornberg
	Plastic contact lens	Norman Bier
1957	BCS theory (superconductivity)	John Bardeen, Leon N. Cooper, and J. Robert Schrieffer
	Interferon (protein)	Alick Isascs and Jean Lindeman
	Mossbauer effect (gamma radiation)	Rudolph Ludwig Mossbauer
	Polio vaccine (live virus)	Albert S. Sabin
	Artificial satellite	*Sputnik* (USSR)
	FORTRAN (computer language)	John Backus and team for IBM (U.S.)
	Intercontinental ballistic missile	USSR
	Laser theory	Gordon Gould
	Artificial-heart pacemaker	Clarence Lillehie
1958	Laser	Charles A. Townes and Arthur L. Schawlow
	Communications satellite	*SCORE* (U.S.)
	ALGOL computer language	Switzerland
	Nobelium	Albert Ghiorso
	Van Allen radiation belts	James A. Van Allen
	Integrated circuit	Jack S. Kilby, Texas Instruments (U.S.)
1959	Tunnel diode	Sony, Japan, based on work by Leo Esaki
	Microwave radio system	Pacific Great Eastern Railway between Vancouver and Dawson Creek–Fort St. John, British Columbia, Canada
	COBOL computer language	Grace Murray Hopper
	Ion engine	Alvin T. Forrester
1960	Argon ion laser	D. R. Herriott, A. Javan, and W. R. Bennett at Bell Laboratories (U.S.)
	Vertical takeoff and landing aircraft	Frank Taylor and team at Short Brothers & Harland (Northern Ireland)
	Weather satellite	*TIROS* (U.S.)
	Muonium	Vernon W. Hughes and coworkers
1961	Manned space flight	*Vostok 1* (U.S.S.R.)
	Stereophonic radio broadcast	Zenith and General Electric Companies (U.S.)
	Valium	Hoffman-LaRoche Laboratories (Switzerland)
	Kenyapithecus wickeri (hominid)	Louis S. B. Leakey
1962	Minicomputer	Digital Corp. (U.S.)
	Robotics	Rand Corp. and IBM (U.S.)
	X-ray astronomical sources	Riccardo Giacconi
	Muon neutrino	Leon Max Lederman, Melvin Schwartz, and Jack Steinberger
1963	Cassette tapes	Philips Co. (The Netherlands)
	Quarks	Murray Gell-Mann and George Zweig
	Quasars	Marten Schmidt
1964	BASIC computer language	Thomas E. Kurtz and John G. Kemeny
	Carbon fiber	RAF Farnborough (England)
	Home-use transistor videotape recorder	Sony (Japan)
	Laser eye surgery	H. Vernon Ingram

Inventions

Quarks

A Closer Look

Murray Gell-Mann and George Zweig formulated the concept of quarks in 1963 to explain the large variety of new elementary particles, called hadrons, that were being discovered. (Protons and neutrons are two types of hadrons.) Quarks are hypothetical particles presumed to be the basic constituents of hadrons. Quarks come in various "flavors," such as up, down, strange, and charmed.

But Gell-Mann and Zweig's theory left unanswered the question of why no one had ever observed isolated quarks. One theory stated that hadrons are composed of strings of quarks that are bound together so tightly that an infinite amount of energy would be required to break the bonds.

The search for quarks continued, and in 1969 strong evidence of their existence was discovered at the Stanford Linear Accelerator Center (SLAC). Richard E. Taylor of SLAC, Henry W. Kendall of MIT, and Jerome I. Friedman of MIT shared the 1990 Nobel prize for this work.

Date	Invention/Advance/Discovery	Inventor/Origin
1965	Word processor	IBM (U.S.)
	Rubella vaccine	Paul D. Parkman and Harry M. Meyer, Jr.
1966	Integrated radio circuit	Sony (Japan)
	Noise reduction system for audiotapes	Ray M. Dolby
1967	Bubble memory prototype (computers)	A. H. Bobeck and team at Bell Telephone Laboratories (U.S.)
	Pulsars	Jocelyn Bell Burnell
1968	Holographic storage technique	Bell Telephone Laboratories (U.S.)
	Hemoglobin molecule structure (complete)	Max Ferdinand Perutz
1969	Manned moon landing	*Apollo 11* (U.S.)
	PASCAL computer language	Niklaus Wirth
	Videotape cassette	Sony (Japan)
	Jumbo jet airliner	Joe Sutherland and team at Boeing (U.S.)
	Antibody chemical and molecular structure	Rodney Robert Porter
1970	Bar code system	Monarch Marking (U.S.) and Plessey Telecommunications (England)
	Computer floppy disk	IBM (U.S.)
	Remote-controlled lunar vehicle	*Lunokhod 1* (USSR)
1971	Earth-orbiting space station	*Salyut 1* (USSR)
	Liquid crystal display (LCD)	Hofmann-LaRoche Laboratories (Switzerland)
	Quartz digital watch	George Theiss and Willy Crabtree
1972	Video disk	Philips Co. (The Netherlands)
	Video game	Noland Bushnel
	Artificial hip	John Charnley
	Enkephalin (brain chemical)	John Hughes
	Antimatter particles	Yuri Dmitriyevich Prokoshkin and coworkers
	Black holes	Robert L. F. Boyd
1973	Computerized axial tomography (CAT scan)	Allan Macleod Cormac and Godfrey N. Hounsfield
	Microcomputer	Trong Truong
	Recombinant DNA	Paul Berg
1974	Nonimpact printing	Honeywell (U.S.)
	J/psi atomic particle	Burton Richter and Samuel Chao Chung Ting
1975	Hybrid cells	Jack Lucy and Ted Cocking
	Monoclonal antibodies	César Milstein
	Betamax videotaping system	Sony (Japan)
	Video home system (VHS)	Matsushita/JVC (Japan)

Inventions

continues

Continued

Date	Invention/Advance/Discovery	Inventor/Origin
1976	Charm subatomic particle	Stanford Linear Accelerator Center (U.S.)
	Mars space probe landings	*Viking I* and *Viking II* (U.S.)
1977	Upsilon particle	Leon Lederman
	Neutron bomb	U.S. military
	Space shuttle	NASA (U.S.)
	Alkyd paint	Winsor & Newton Ltd. (England)
1978	Cyclosporin A	Tony Allison and Roy Calne
	Human insulin	Genentech (U.S.)
	Charon (Pluto's moon)	James Walter Christy and Robert S. Harrington
	Test-tube baby	Patrick C. Steptoe and Robert G. Edwards
1979	Single-cell protein process	ICI Agricultural Division (England)
1980	Solar-powered aircraft	Paul Macready
1981	Anti-interferon	Medical Research Council's Molecular Biology Laboratory (England)
	First official recognition of AIDS	Centers for Disease Control (U.S.)
	Silicon 32-bit chip	Hewlett-Packard, U.S.
	Nuclear magnetic resonance (NMR) scanner	Thorn-EMI Research Laboratories and Nottingham University (England)
1982	Abnormal cancer-causing genes	Robert Weinberg and Mariano Barbacid
	Artificial heart	Robert Jarvik
	Airborne observatory	NASA (U.S.)
1983	W and Z particles	Carlo Rubbia and Simon van der Meer
	Biopol (biodegradable plastic)	ICI Agricultural Division (England)
	Biosensors	Cambridge Life Sciences (England)
	Carbon-fiber aircraft wing	Great Britain
	512K dynamic access memory chip	IBM (U.S.)
1984	Gene cloning	National Institutes of Health (U.S.); Transgene (France); and Otago University (New Zealand)
	Genetically engineered blood-clotting factor	Genentech (U.S.)
	Compact disk player	Sony and Fujitsu Companies (Japan) and Philips Co. (The Netherlands)
	Megabit computer chip	IBM (U.S.)
	Isolation of virus believed to cause AIDS	Robert C. Gallo (U.S. National Cancer Institute); Luc Montagnier (Pasteur Institute, France); and Myron Essex (Harvard School of Public Health, U.S.)
1985	Cloned leprosy genes (for vaccines)	Ron Davis and coworkers
	Anxiety chemical (human brain)	Alessandro Guidotti and Erminio Costa
	CD-ROM (compact disc read-only memory)	Hitachi (Japan)
	Image digitizer	Optronics (England)
	Polymer electric conductor	Terje Skotheim and team at Brookhaven National Laboratory (U.S.)
	Soft bifocal contact lens	Sofsite Contact Lens Laboratory (U.S.)
	Positron emission tomography	Michael Phelps
	Publication of the first image from a positron transmission microscope	James Van House and Arthur Rich
	First baby born from frozen embryo	Australia

Inventions

Date	Invention/Advance/Discovery	Inventor/Origin
1986	DNA fingerprinting	Alec Jeffreys
	Diminished ozone shield	Susan Solomon at National Oceanic and Atmospheric Administration (U.S.)
	High-temperature superconductivity	Georg Bednorz and Karl Alex Müller
	Synthetic skin	G. Gregory Gallico, III
1987	Higher-temperature superconductivity	C. W. Chu, M. K. Wu, and coworkers
	Alzheimer's disease gene	National Institutes of Health (U.S.); University of Cologne (Germany)
	Gene-altered bacteria	Advanced Genetic Sciences (U.S.)
1988	Galaxy 12 billion light-years away	Simon J. Lilly
	Patented animal life	Philip Leder and Timothy Stewart
1989	Introduction of foreign gene into human patient	Steven A. Rosenberg and coworkers at National Institutes of Health (U.S.)
1991	Controlled nuclear fusion	Joint European Torus (Oxfordshire, England)
	X-ray research showing first photographs of the human brain recalling a word	Dr. Marcus Raichle and coworkers
1992	Fluctuations in cosmic background radiation	George Smoot
1994	Proof of Fermat's last theorem	Andrew John Wiles
1995	Decipherment of entire DNA sequence of living organism	Craig J. Venter and Hamilton Smith
1997	Cloning of adult animal	Ian Wilmut
	Atom laser	Wolfgang Ketterle

MAJOR SCIENTISTS AND ENGINEERS

AEROSPACE ENGINEERS

Goddard, Robert Hutchings (1882–1945). American physicist who launched the first liquid-propellant rocket.

Tsiolkovsky, Konstantin Eduardovich (1857–1935). Russian rocket pioneer and research scientist in aeronautics and astronautics who was one of the first to publish scientific papers about space flight.

ASTRONOMERS

Aristotle (384–322 B.C.). Greek philosopher who developed many of the astronomical beliefs of his time, including the idea that the Earth was the center of the universe, into a cosmological system that dominated astronomy for nearly 1,800 years. He believed that everything in the universe was composed of four "basic elements"—earth, water, air, and fire.

Brahe, Tycho (1546–1601). Danish astronomer and one of the greatest astronomical observers before the advent of the telescope. His accurate measurements of planetary positions were the foundation for Johannes Kepler's formulation of the laws of planetary motion.

The Wright Brothers' historic flight covered a distance less than the length of today's space shuttle.

Cassini, Giovanni Domenico (1625–1712). Italian-born French astronomer who discovered several moons around Saturn and the dark division in Saturn's rings. He was the first of four generations of astronomers.

Copernicus, Nicolaus (1473–1543). Polish astronomer who revolutionized astronomy by proposing that the Sun, not the Earth, is the center of the solar system.

Eratosthenes of Cyrene (c. 276–c. 194 B.C.). Hellenic librarian and astronomer who was the first

Inventions

to estimate fairly accurately the circumference of the Earth.

Galileo Galilei (1564–1642). Italian astronomer and physicist who was the first to use a telescope for astronomical observations, discovering the moons around Jupiter and the phases of Venus.

U.S. Army Lt. Thomas E. Selfridge was the first person to be killed in an airplane accident. The pilot of the flight was Orville Wright.

Hale, George Ellery (1868–1938). American astrophysicist who discovered magnetic fields in sunspots and who secured funding for several large telescopes, including the 200-inch reflector on Palomar Mountain in California.

Halley, Edmond (1656–1742). British astronomer and physicist who determined the periodicity of the comet that bears his name.

Hawking, Stephen William (1942–   ). British theoretical physicist who is especially known for his theories on black holes and the origin and evolution of the universe.

Herschel, Sir John Frederick William (1792–1871). British astronomer, son of William Herschel, who made the first exhaustive study of the southern sky and made significant contributions to the development of photography.

Herschel, Sir William (1738–1822). German-born British astronomer who discovered the planet Uranus. He also founded modern stellar astronomy, discovered nearly 1,000 double stars, determined the general shape and size of the Milky Way, and published numerous catalogs of nebulae and clusters.

Hewish, Anthony (1924–   ). British radio astronomer whose work in radio scintillation led to the discovery of pulsars.

"Astronomy," "Meterology," and "Space Exploration" in chapter 4; "Astronomy Symbols" **Go to** and Weather Symbols" in chapter 12

Hipparchus (c. 170–c. 120 B.C.). Greek astronomer and geographer who worked out the epicycle theory of the solar system, with the Earth at the center. He also discovered the precession of the equinox, calculated the length of a year within 6.5 minutes, and devised the first known star map.

Hoyle, Sir Fred (1915–   ). British astrophysicist who developed the steady-state hypothesis of the universe.

Hubble, Edwin Powell (1889–1953). American astronomer and cosmologist whose work demonstrated that the universe was expanding. He also formulated the Hubble constant, which measures the rate of expansion of the universe and is used to determine the age of the universe.

Jansky, Karl Guthe (1905–50). American radio engineer who, by discovering radio emissions from the Milky Way galaxy, founded the field of radio astronomy.

Jeans, Sir James Hopwood (1877–1946). British mathematician, astronomer, and physicist who was the first to propose that matter is continuously created throughout the universe. He also wrote numerous popular astronomy books.

Kepler, Johannes (1571–1630). German astronomer who formulated the three principal laws governing the motion and elliptical orbits of planetary bodies, thus eliminating the epicycle models that had governed astronomy for close to 2,000 years.

Kuiper, Gerard Peter (1905–73). Dutch-born American astronomer who studied lunar and planetary surface features. He discovered Mirända, a satellite at Uranus, and Nereid, a satellite of Neptune.

Laplace, Marquis Pierre Simon de (1749–1827). French mathematician, astronomer, and physicist who contributed extensively to celestial mechanics. Among other things, he established that the solar system has long-term stability. His

Inventions

nebular hypothesis postulated that the planets resulted from a primitive nebula that rotated around the sun.

Lowell, Percival (1855–1916). American astronomer who developed theories of life on Mars and predicted the existence of a ninth planet (Pluto, which would not be discovered until 1930).

Oort, Jan Hendrik (1900–92). Dutch astronomer who detected the rotation of the Milky Way galaxy and who postulated that a sphere of incipient cometary material, now called the Oort Cloud, surrounds the solar system far outside the orbit of Pluto.

Piazzi, Giuseppe (1746–1826). Italian astronomer who discovered Ceres, the first asteroid (minor planet).

Ptolemy (Claudius Ptolemaeus) (c. A.D. 2nd century). Egyptian astronomer and encyclopedist who made extensive use of epicycles and other devices to achieve a fairly accurate match of observations with the idea that the Earth was the center of the universe. His achievement enabled the geocentric hypothesis to dominate astronomy for over a thousand years.

Sagan, Carl Edward (1934–96). American astronomer and exobiologist who increased public awareness and support of science through his popular writings and television presentations.

Schiaparelli, Giovanni Viginio (1835–1910). Italian astronomer who studied the planets and is known mostly for his report of *canali* (channels) on the planet Mars.

Shagley, Harlow (1885–1972). American astronomer who established the size and structure of our Milky Way galaxy.

Shoemaker, Eugene (1928–97). American astrogeologist who established the meteoric nature of Meteor Crater in Arizona, helped map the Moon for the Apollo missions, and searched for asteroids that crossed the orbit of Earth.

Tombaugh, Clyde William (1906–97). American astronomer who discovered the planet Pluto in 1930.

Whipple, Fred Lawrence (1906–). American astronomer whose "dirty snowball" model of comet composition postulated that a cometary nuclei consists of a frozen mixture of water, carbon dioxide, ammonia, methane, and particles of dust, silicates, and other materials.

BIOLOGISTS

Audubon, John James (1785–1851). French-American ornithologist and naturalist who is known for his bird drawings and paintings.

Bateson, William (1861–1926). British biologist who coined the term *genetics* (the causes and effects of heritable characteristics). He was a strong proponent of Gregor Mendel's work on heredity.

Borlaug, Norman Ernest (1914–). American agronomist and plant breeder who was one of the creators of the green revolution in agriculture. He won the Nobel prize for peace in 1970 for his work on breeding "miracle" wheat for India and Mexico.

Burbank, Luther (1849–1926). American plant breeder who developed new varieties of many plants, including the Burbank potato, berries, and plums.

Cohen, Stanley H. (1922–). American biochemist who determined that DNA molecules could be cut, separated, and joined, thus paving the way for genetic engineering. He also worked on the mechanisms responsible for cell and organ growth.

Cuvier, Baron, Georges Léopold Chrétien Frédéric Dagobert (1769–1832). French comparative anatomist, paleontologist, and taxonomist who developed the first method of classifying mammals and founded the science of comparative anatomy. He was the first to propose that catastrophes were responsible for the extinction of species.

Inventions

Darwin, Charles Robert (1809–82). British naturalist who revolutionized biology with his theory of evolution through the process of natural selection. He also provided geological evidence for evolution and made detailed observations of volcanoes and earthquakes.

de Vries, Hugo Marie (1848–1935). Dutch plant physiologist and geneticist who promoted the works of Gregor Mendel, which had been ignored for four decades. He also determined that mutations occur in organisms.

Lamarck, Jean Baptiste Pierre Antoine de Monet, Chevalier de (1744–1829). French naturalist who proposed an early theory of evolution. He was the first to distinguish between invertebrates and vertebrates, and he developed a classification system for invertebrates.

Leeuwenhoek, Anton van (1632–1723). Dutch microscopist who discovered numerous organisms, including protists, sperm (which he correctly assumed as the source of reproduction), and bacteria.

Linnaeus, Carolus (Carl von Linné) (1707–78). Swedish naturalist who introduced certain classifications of organisms that are still in use today.

Mendel, Gregor Johann (1822–84). Austrian monk and botanist who discovered the basic laws of heredity, based on his studies of pea plants.

Miller, Stanley Lloyd (1930–   ). American chemist who created a primitive atmosphere that demonstrated how amino acids might have been generated in the oceans of a primitive Earth.

Sachs, Julius von (1832–97). German botanist who greatly developed the field of plant physiology. He was the first to demonstrate that photosynthesis occurs in chloroplasts.

Theophrastus (c. 372–c. 287 B.C.). Greek botanist and philosopher who described some 500 species of plants.

"Major Zoos and Aquariums" and "Major Botanical Gardens and Arboretums" in **Go to** chapter 11

Tull, Jethro (1674–1741). British agriculturist, writer, and inventor who invented a machine for planting seeds. He is best known for his suggestions on plant cultivation, such as the use of manure and hoeing around crops to remove weeds.

Wallace, Alfred Russel (1823–1913). British naturalist who formulated a theory of evolution by natural selection independently of Charles Darwin.

CHEMISTS

Arrhenius, Svante August (1859–1927). Swedish physical chemist whose work established the basis for modern electrochemistry. He also developed the theory of panspermia, in which bacterial spores were thought to travel from space to Earth. He won the Nobel prize for chemistry in 1903.

Avogadro, Lorenzo Romano Amedeo Carlo, count of Quaregna and Cerreto (1776–1856). Italian physicist and chemist who expanded on Gay-Lussac's law of combining volumes and determined the formula for water. He differentiated molecules from atoms and was the first to use the word *molecule*. He developed Avogadro's constant and is considered one of the founders of modern physical chemistry.

Boyle, Robert (1627–91). Irish-born chemist and physicist who explored the characteristics of gases and developed Boyle's law, which states that pressure and volume are inversely proportional for a fixed mass of gas at constant temperatures.

Cannizzaro, Stanislao (1826–1910). Italian chemist who established the use of atomic weights in chemical formulas and calculations.

Cavendish, Henry (1731–1810). English chemist and physicist who discovered hydrogen and determined the mass of the Earth.

Crookes, Sir William (1832–1919). British chemist and physicist who discovered the element thallium (using the then-new method of spectroscopy), invented the radiometer, and investigated radioactivity.

Curie, Marie Sklodowska (1867–1934). Polish-born French chemist who isolated the radioactive elements radium (with her husband Pierre Curie and Gustav Bemont) and polonium (with Pierre Curie) and was the first person to win two Nobel prizes (for physics in 1903 and for chemistry in 1911).

Curie, Pierre (1859–1906). French physicist who codiscovered radium and polonium and shared the Nobel prize for physics in 1903. He also discovered the piezoelectric effect, in which certain substances produce a current as the result of pressure.

Dalton, John (1766–1844). British chemist and physicist who determined the law of partial pressures and formulated an atomic theory of matter.

Davy, Sir Humphry (1778–1829). British chemist who established the important connection between electrochemistry and the elements, discovered the elements sodium and potassium, and invented a safety lamp for miners.

Hodgkin, Dorothy Crowfoot (1910–   ). British chemist who determined the structure of vitamin B_{12} and analyzed the structure of penicillin. She won the Nobel prize for chemistry in 1964.

Langmuir, Irving (1881–1957). American chemist who studied chemical reactions at high temperatures and low pressures, leading to the development of the gas-filled tungsten lamp. He also worked on thermal effects on gases, which led to using atomic hydrogen in welding torches. He won the Nobel prize for chemistry in 1932.

Lavoisier, Antoine Laurent (1743–94). French chemist who was one of the first to quantify methods in chemistry. He determined the nature of combustion, noted the composition of the atmosphere, articulated the law of conservation of matter, and wrote the first modern chemistry book.

"The Animal Kingdom" and "The Plant Kingdom" in chapter 3;
Go to

Mendeleev, Dmitri Ivanovich. (1834–1907). Russian chemist who published the first periodic table of the elements in 1869.

Newlands, John Alexander Reina (1837–98). British chemist who was one of the first to determine periodicity in the properties of chemical elements.

An 11-year-old California boy mixed soda water powder with water, then accidentally left it on the back porch with the stirring stick still in it. The mixture froze during the night. His discovery later became known as the "popsicle."

Nobel, Alfred Bernhard (1833–96). Swedish chemist, engineer, and inventor of dynamite and several other explosives. His fortune endowed the Nobel prizes.

Pauling, Linus Carl (1901–94). American chemist who applied quantum theory to molecular structures, establishing modern theoretical organic chemistry. He also determined the role of electrons in the formation of molecules and developed theories on ionic and covalent bonding, for which he won the Nobel prize for chemistry in 1954. He was also awarded the Nobel prize for peace in 1962 for his efforts to stop nuclear weapons testing.

Priestley, Joseph (1733–1804). British chemist and Presbyterian minister who first reported the discovery of oxygen. (Although Carl Scheele discovered the element earlier, he published his results after Priestley.)

Proust, Joseph Louis (1754–1826). French chemist who worked to measure the mass of each component of a compound. He formulated the law of constant proportions, which states that compounds always contain certain elements in the same proportion, regardless of the method of preparation.

Inventions

Soddy, Frederick (1877–1966). English chemist who proposed the isotope theory of the elements and determined how radioactive elements break down. He won the Nobel prize for chemistry in 1921.

Urey, Harold Clayton (1893–1981). American physical chemist whose pioneering isotope-separation methods enabled him to discover heavy water and deuterium (the heavy isotope of hydrogen). He also extensively studied the origin of the Earth and the other planets.

COMPUTER SCIENTISTS

Babbage, Charles (1792–1871). British mathematician and inventor who developed one of the first early calculating machines, called the difference engine.

Hollerith, Herman (1860–1929). American inventor who developed the first electrically driven computer; it used punch cards to count the census.

Hopper, Grace Murray (1906–92). American computer programmer who helped invent COBOL, the computer language for business use.

Jacquard, Joseph Marie (1752–1834). French inventor who created the Jacquard loom; with this device, he programmed complicated carpet patterns onto punched cards.

Pascal, Blaise (1623–62). French mathematician, physicist, and religious philosopher who invented the first mechanical calculating machine and founded the modern theory of probabilities.

Turing, Alan Mathison (1912–54). British mathematician who developed the idea of a universal computer called the Turing machine, which could solve any type of mathematical problem by reducing it to coding in a given set of commands. (Bell Laboratories put his ideas into practice in 1939, by developing the first relay computer.)

Go to   "Computers" in chapter 4; "Data Banks Available for Computer Research" in chapter 11

Von Neumann, John (1903–57). Hungarian-born American mathematician who developed principles of design for digital computers and supervised the construction of the first stored-program computer.

EARTH SCIENTISTS AND ENVIRONMENTALISTS

Agassiz, Jean Louis Rodolphe (1807–73). Swiss-born American geologist and biologist who introduced the idea of the Ice Age, a period when ice sheets covered most of the Northern Hemisphere.

Agricola, Georgius (Georg Bauer) (1494–1555). German mineralogist who coined the word *fossil* but did not differentiate fossils from other types of rock.

Brongniart, Alexandre (1770–1847). French geologist and paleontologist who pioneered the idea of using fossils to identify ages and layers of sedimentary rock.

Buys Ballot, Christoph Hendrik Diederik (1817–90). Dutch meteorologist who formulated the law for determining areas of low pressure based on observing the wind's direction.

Carson, Rachel Louise (1907–64). American ecologist and author of several scientific and popular publications concerning ecology and the environment, many of which inspired environmental protection policies.

Today a desktop computer can store a million times more information than the first computer and is 50,000 times faster.

Conybeare, William Daniel (1787–1857). British geologist and minister who synthesized the ideas of catastrophism (that geologic changes occur in brief bursts separated by long quiet periods) and progressivism (the biological theory that a series of creations yields organisms that are increasingly more complex).

Inventions

Coriolis, Gustave-Gaspard   (1792–1843). French physicist who, in 1835, first described the curving deflection of winds caused by the Earth's rotation, now called the Coriolis effect.

Cousteau, Jacques-Yves   (1910–97). French oceanographer who developed the aqualung, underwater photography techniques, and the bathyscaph. He was also an author and filmmaker who increased public awareness of the diversity of ocean life and environmental problems of the oceans and the Earth.

Dana, James Dwight   (1813–95). American geologist and mineralogist who wrote the first standard reference books in geology and mineralogy.

Drake, Edwin Laurentine   (1819–80). American investor who drilled the world's first oil well in Titusville, Pennsylvania, in 1859. His work greatly advanced geological studies in the search for more oil.

Ewing, William Maurice   (1913–74). American oceanographer who made detailed maps of the sea bottom using refraction of waves caused by explosions (similar to sonar). He helped describe the Mid-Atlantic Ridge, an area of sea-floor spreading that cuts through the Atlantic Ocean.

Gilbert, Grove Karl   (1843–1918). American geologist and geomorphologist who developed the foundations of 20th-century earth science. He contributed detailed descriptions of river and other geologic processes that became standards for his time.

Hadley, George   (1685–1768). English lawyer and climatologist who suggested that the Earth's rotation from west to east caused the trade winds to blow from the northeast in the Northern Hemisphere and from the southeast in the Southern Hemisphere.

Hall, Sir James   (1761–1832). British chemist and geologist who was one of the first scientists to use laboratory experiments to test geologic theories.

He also showed that crystals form from melted rock.

Humboldt, (Friedrich Wilhelm Heinrich) Alexander, Baron von   (1769–1859). Prussian scientific explorer who made detailed investigations of the Earth's magnetism, identified the Jurassic Period of geologic time, and explored the cold current running north along the Pacific coast of South America.

Hutton, James   (1726–97). Scottish natural philosopher who was the founder of modern geology and geomorphology. He was the first to propose the idea of uniformitarianism—that is, that all geologic features can be explained by rocks from the past.

Leakey, Louis Seymour Bazett   (1903–72) and **Leakey, Mary Nichol**   (1913–96). British anthropologists and husband-and-wife team who found some of the oldest humanoid fossils in the Olduvai Gorge, Africa, including members of the Australopithecines. Mary later found a 3.75 million-year-old humanoid fossil at Laetoli, Africa.

Leakey, Richard Erskine Frere   (1944–   ). Kenyan paleontologist, son of Louis and Mary Leakey. He found some of the oldest known humanoid fossils in Kenya, including a nearly complete fossil of a large *Homo erectus* (found with colleagues) in Kenya.

Leopold, Aldo   (1886–1948). American naturalist who was one of the first scientists to arouse public interest in wilderness conservation. He wrote *A Sand County Almanac* (1949).

Lyell, Sir Charles   (1797–1875). Scottish geologist whose *Principles of Geology* was one of the most influential works on geology. He shared James Hutton's belief that the present is the key to the past and held that fossils were the best guides to describing geologic rock layers. He was also one of the first to postulate that the Earth was millions of years old.

Inventions

Maury, Matthew Fontaine (1806–73). American hydrologist and oceanographer who wrote the first text of modern oceanography, detailing the trade winds and ocean currents.

Mohs, Friedrich (1773–1839). German mineralogist who was the first to classify minerals based on hardness.

Muir, John (1838–1914). British-born American naturalist who is noted for his work to gain popular and federal support of forest conservation.

Playfair, John (1748–1819). Scottish mathematician, geologist, and philosopher who expanded on the work of his friend James Hutton. Playfair's law states that river tributaries are as deep as the surrounding major valley; he used this information to distinguish river valleys from glacial hanging valleys.

Pytheas (fl. 350 B.C.). Greek geographer and explorer who observed the strong Atlantic tides and correctly theorized that they were caused by the Moon.

Richter, Charles Francis (1900–85). American seismologist who developed a scale (the Richter scale) for measuring the intensity, or magnitude, of earthquakes.

Torricelli, Evangelista (1608–47). Italian mathematician and physicist who is considered the father of hydrodynamics. He proposed an experiment (later performed by his colleague Vincenzo Viviani) that demonstrated that atmospheric pressure determines the height a fluid will rise in a tube when it is inverted over a saucer of the same liquid. This idea led to the development of the barometer.

Wegener, Alfred Lothar (1880–1930). German geologist and meteorologist who suggested the idea of continental drift in 1912, noting that the coastlines of several continents fit roughly together into a supercontinent that he named Pangaea. His ideas were not accepted until the 1960s, when geomagnetic and oceanographic evidence established the theory of plate tectonics.

Werner, Abraham Gottlob (1750–1817). German mineralogist and geologist who developed the first systematic classification of minerals.

White, Gilbert (1720–93). British naturalist whose *Natural History and Antiquities of Selborne* was one of the first known works on ecology.

MATHEMATICIANS

Archimedes (c. 287–212 B.C.). Greek mathematician who is considered to be the greatest mathematician and engineer of ancient times. He derived the theory of the lever, discovered the principle of buoyancy, and developed methods for determining the volumes of geometric solids.

The mother of Mike Nesmith (formerly of the rock group The Monkees) invented Liquid Paper.

Bernoulli, Daniel (1700–82). Netherlands-born Swiss mathematician who is known for his pioneering work on hydrodynamics.

Cauchy, Baron Augustin Louis (1789–1857). French mathematician whose work concentrated on complex analysis. With the concepts of limit and continuity, he introduced rigor into the development of calculus.

Euclid (c. 330–c. 260 B.C.). Greek mathematician whose systematic proof of theorems in his *Elements of Geometry* formed the basis of most mathematical thought for the next 2,000 years.

Euler, Leonhard (1707–83). Swiss mathematician and physicist who was one of the founders of pure mathematics. The most prolific mathematician in history, he contributed to calculus, geometry, mechanics, and number theory.

Fermat, Pierre de (1601–65). French mathematician who helped lay the foundation for analytical geometry. He was also the founder of the modern theory of numbers.

Go to "Geology and Geophysics" and "Mathematics" in chapter 4; "Symbols Used in Science, Mathematics, and Technology" in chapter 12

Inventions

Gauss, Karl Friedrich (1777–1855). German mathematician who worked on electricity and magnetism and on planetary orbits.

Hero of Alexandria (fl. 1st century A.D.). Greek mathematician and inventor who was best known for his formulation for the area of a triangle. He was also the inventor of the first known steam-powered engine.

Hypatia (c. 370–415). Egyptian mathematician and philosopher who was the first notable female mathematician.

Möbius, August Ferdinand (1790–1868). German mathematician who discovered the Möbius strip, a figure that has only one side and one edge. He also made major contributions to analytical geometry and topology.

Omar Khayya'm (1048–?). Best known for his *Rubaiyat* (a collection of poetical quatrains), he was a Persian mathematician and astronomer who was the first to demonstrate that a cubic equation might have two roots. His work was a step toward the unification of algebra and geometry.

Pappus of Alexandria (fl. 320 A.D.). Greek mathematician who wrote a compendium of eight books covering mathematical knowledge of his time.

Pythagoras (c. 580–c. 500 B.C.). Greek mathematician and philosopher who is credited with the theorem on right-angled triangles named after him and founding the science of acoustics.

Russell, Bertrand Arthur William, Earl (1872–1970). British philosopher and mathematician who had great influence in mathematical logic through the three-volume *Principia Mathematica* (1910, 1912, 1913) that he cowrote with Alfred North Whitehead.

Tartaglia (Niccolò Fontana) (1500–57). Italian mathematician, topographer, and military scientist who provided an algebraic solution to cubic equations and produced that first translation of Euclid's *Elements* into a modern language (Italian).

MEDICAL SCIENTISTS

Avicenna (980–1037). Persian physician whose encyclopedic *Canon of Medicine* was the authoritative treatise on medicine until the 17th century.

Bernard, Claude (1813–78). French physiologist who introduced the concepts that the functions of the various organs within the body are closely interrelated and that the body maintains a constant internal environment despite external changes.

Blackwell, Elizabeth (1821–1910). The first female physician in the United States. Her small practice in New York expanded into the New York Infirmary for Women and Children, which had an all-female staff.

Bowman, Sir William (1816–92). British physician who founded histological anatomy and ophthalmic surgery. Working with a microscope, he made detailed descriptions of nerves, skin, and muscles. He also did major work on eye diseases.

Broca, Pierre Paul (1824–80). French physician, anthropologist, and surgeon who was the first to identify the speech center in the brain.

Crick, Francis Harry Compton (1916–). British molecular biologist who with James Watson discovered the double-helix structure of DNA, for which they shared the Nobel prize for physiology or medicine in 1962.

Darwin, Erasmus (1731–1802). British physician who developed ideas on animal causation and classification of disease. He also worked out a theory of biological evolution somewhat similar to the one his grandson, Charles Darwin, developed years later.

Ehrlich, Paul (1854–1915). German physician, bacteriologist, and chemist who discovered numerous bacterial toxins and antitoxins; he was also the first to use chemotherapy in medicine. He shared the 1908 Nobel prize for physiology or medicine with Ilja Mecnikov for their immunity studies.

Erasistratus of Chios (c. 276–c. 194 B.C.). Greek anatomist and physician whose work was the most respected of his time. Studies by Herophilus of Chalcedon and Erasistratus laid the foundation for anatomy and physiology. He also was one of the first to discover that the brain was the center of intelligence.

Fleming, Sir Alexander (1881–1955). British bacteriologist who discovered how the human body defends itself against bacterial infection. He also worked on eradicating syphilis. He shared the Nobel prize for physiology or medicine in 1945 with Sir Howard Florey and Ernst Chain for the discovery of penicillin.

Flourens, Jean Pierre Marie (1794–1867). French physician and anatomist who studied the physiology of the nervous system and the formation and growth of bones. He also discovered chloroform's anesthetic properties.

Franklin, Rosalind (1920–58). British crystallographer whose X-ray diffraction studies of DNA suggested a helical structure.

Freud, Sigmund (1856–1939). Austrian psychiatrist who laid the foundation for modern psychoanalysis. He introduced the concepts of ego, superego, and id and is known for his work on the interpretation of dreams.

Galen (c. 130–c. 200). Turkish-born physician who became one of the most famous and influential doctors of Rome. He developed a physiological model of the human body that was held as the standard for anatomy for centuries.

Harvey, William (1578–1657). British physician who discovered that heart pulsations caused blood to circulate around the body.

Herophilus of Chalcedon (c. 335–c. 280 B.C.). Greek doctor whose studies, together with those of Erasistratus, laid the foundations for anatomy and physiology.

Hippocrates of Cos (c. 460–c. 370 B.C.). Greek physician who developed ideas that led to the Hippocratic oath. He started a school of medicine at Cos, where he encouraged the separation of medicine and religion.

Jenner, Edward (1749–1823). British physician who discovered the smallpox vaccine. He was also the founder of immunology and the pioneer of modern virology.

Jung, Carl Gustav (1875–1961). Swiss psychologist and psychiatrist who founded analytic psychology. His work contradicted many of the ideas of Sigmund Freud.

Pasteur, Louis (1822–95). French chemist and microbiologist who developed the germ theory of disease. He also developed the first vaccine against rabies and was the founder of microbiology.

Pavlov, Ivan Petrovich (1849–1936). Soviet physiologist who worked on blood circulation, digestion, and the physiology of the brain and nervous system. He is best known for his demonstration of the phenomenon of the conditioned reflex.

Sabin, Albert Bruce (1906–93). Polish-born American microbiologist who invented the first oral polio vaccine.

Salk, Jonas Edward (1914–95). American microbiologist who formulated the first successful polio vaccine, which was administrated by injection.

Stokes, William (1804–78). Irish physician who advanced the fields of cardiac and pulmonary disease.

Sydenham, Thomas (1624–89). English physician who was one of the founders of epidemiology. He was instrumental in describing numerous diseases, including measles and scarlet fever.

In 1809, Meslitta Bentz invented the world's first drip coffeemaker by making a filter out of her son's notebook paper.

Watson, James Dewey (1928–   ). American biochemist who, with Francis Crick, discovered the double-helix structure of DNA for which they shared the Nobel prize for physiology or medicine in 1962.

Wilkins, Maurice (Hugh Frederick) (1916–   ). New Zealand–born British biophysicist who, with James Watson, Francis Crick, and Rosalind Franklin, discovered the structure of DNA. He shared the 1962 Nobel prize with Watson and Crick (Franklin died before the award was presented).

PHYSICISTS

Alvarez, Luis Walter (1911–88). American physicist who won the Nobel prize for physics in 1968 for his work in advancing the field of high-energy particle physics. He developed the practical linear accelerator. Alvarez and his son Walter, along with several others, first proposed the theory that massive extinctions around the time of the boundary between the Cretaceous and Tertiary periods were caused by the impact of a large meteorite or asteroid.

Ampere, Andre Marie (1775–1836). French physicist and mathematician who laid the foundation of the science of electrodynamics and determined that electric currents produce magnetic fields.

Becquerel, Antoine Henri (1852–1908). French physicist who discovered the natural radioactivity produced by uranium.

Bohr, Niels Hendrik David (1885–1962). Danish physicist who was the first to apply quantum theory to atomic structure and to note the connection between spectral lines and the energy levels of electrons. For his work with atoms, he was awarded the Nobel prize for physics in 1922.

Celsius, Anders (1701–44). Swedish astronomer who was the developer of the temperature scale that was named after him.

"Physics" in chapter 4; "Major Science and Technology Museums and Their Special Collections" in chapter 11   **Go to**

Chadwick, Sir James (1891–1974). British physicist who discovered the neutron, for which he was awarded the Nobel prize for physics in 1932.

Coriolis, Gaspard Gustave de (1792–1843). French physicist who was first to coin the term *kinetic energy.* He was also the first to describe the effect (named after him) that deals with the apparent force on a moving object when observed from a rotating system. This Coriolis force governs the movement of atmospheric winds.

de Broglie, Prince Louis Victor Pierre Raymond (1892–1987). French physicist who discovered the wave nature of electrons and other particles. For this work, he won the Nobel prize for physics in 1929.

Doppler, Christian Johann (1803–53). Austrian physicist who discovered that a wave frequency changes when the source and observer are in motion relative to each other (called the Doppler effect).

Einstein, Albert (1879–1955). German-born theoretical physicist who helped establish quantum theory (first put forth by Max Planck) by using it to describe photoelectric effects, work for which he was awarded the Nobel prize for physics in 1921. He also developed the theories of special and general relativity.

Fahrenheit, Daniel Gabriel (1686–1736). Polish-born Dutch physicist who developed the temperature scale that was named after him. He invented a mercury thermometer.

Faraday, Michael (1791–1867). British physicist and chemist who proposed the idea of magnetic "lines of force," developed the first electric generator, and pioneered the study of low temperatures. He also discovered benzene.

Inventions

A Closer Look

Schrodinger's Cat Paradox

The theory of quantum mechanics states that for a specific event, there is not one but numerous possible states that may exist simultaneously at a microscopic level. When we observe the event—that is, make a measurement—one of the states becomes "real" on our (macroscopic) level.

In 1935, Erwin Schrodinger published an essay dealing with paradoxes that were occurring in the then-new field of quantum mechanics. He sought to explain the influence of measurement on an event by using his now famous Schrodinger's Cat paradox. In this imaginary setting, a cat is placed in a sealed box with a flask of poisonous gas. The decay of a radioactive atom "triggers" a mechanism that shatters the flask and kills the cat. In the course of an hour, the atom may decay, triggering the gas, but also, with equal probability, it may not.

We open the box after an hour and observe the radioactive atom. Until that measurement is made, the cat exists in our sealed box in two probable states, dead or alive, based on the equal probability of whether or not the atom has decayed. This question is resolved by our observation; that is, one of the states becomes "real," and the cat is either ready for some milk or needs to be buried.

Although this is a thought experiment, in the late 1990s physicists at the National Institute of Standards and Technology (NIST) in Boulder, Colorado, succeeded in creating a "Schrodinger-cat-like state of matter" in a single beryllium atom. The researchers trapped the atom with nonuniform electric fields and cooled it to near standstill. Then laser pulses were used to vibrate the atom's electrons, creating a dual presence, as if two atoms existed in distinct locations at the same time. The two states were separated by a distance larger than the normal area of the atom. For a brief period, the atom appeared to exist in two places, or states, similar to Schrodinger's cat.

Fermi, Enrico (1901–54). Italian-American physicist who produced the first controlled chain reaction in a nuclear reactor. He produced several new radioactive isotopes by neutron bombardment, work for which he won the Nobel prize for physics in 1938.

Feynman, Richard Phillips (1918–88). American theoretical physicist known for his work on the basic principles of quantum electrodynamics, for which he shared the Nobel prize for physics in 1965.

Foucault, Jean Bernard Leon (1819–68). French physicist who invented the gyroscope, developed a method for demonstrating the rotation of the Earth (using what is now called a Foucault pendulum), and was the first to accurately determine the velocity of light.

Franklin, Benjamin (1706–90). American statesman and scientist who experimented with electricity and introduced the terms *positive* and *negative* to describe electric charge.

Grimaldi, Francesco Maria (1618–63). Italian physicist who discovered optical diffraction and accepted the idea of waves of light. He also made one of the first lunar maps and started the tradition of naming the Moon's features after famous scientists.

Hertz, Heinrich Rudolf (1857–94). German physicist who discovered radio waves.

Joliot-Curie, Frédéric (1900–58) and **Irène** (1897–1956). French physicists who developed the first artificial radioactive substance, an isotope of phosphorus; for this work, they were awarded the Nobel prize for chemistry in 1935. Irène was the daughter of chemists Marie and Pierre Curie.

Joule, James Prescott (1818–89). British physicist who measured the amount of heat produced by an electric current. He also determined that if a gas expands without performing work, its temperature falls.

Kelvin, Lord William Thomson (1824–1907). British theoretical and experimental physicist who proposed the absolute scale of temperature and the idea that mechanical energy tends to dissipate as heat, which Rudolf Clausius later developed into the concept of entropy.

Mach, Ernst (1838–1916). Austrian physicist who discovered that airflow becomes disturbed at the speed of sound. Mach numbers (which represent how fast a craft is traveling beyond the speed of sound) were named after him.

Maxwell, James Clerk (1831–79). British physicist who developed equations that served as a basis for the understanding of electromagnetism. He also determined that light is electromagnetic radiation, developed the kinetic theory of gases, and proved the particle nature of Saturn's rings.

Newton, Sir Isaac (1642–1727). English physicist and mathematician who invented calculus, determined the nature of white light, constructed the first reflecting telescope, and formulated the laws of motion and the theory of universal gravitation.

Ohm, Georg Simon (1789–1854). German physicist who determined the law (named after him) that states that electrical current is equal to the ratio of the voltage to the resistance.

Planck, Max Karl Ernst Ludwig (1858–1947). German physicist who developed the quantum theory to explain the nature of black-body radiation. For this work, he won the Nobel prize for physics in 1918.

Roentgen, Wilhelm Conrad (1845–1923). German physicist who discovered X rays, for which he was awarded the Nobel prize for physics in 1901.

Rutherford, Ernest, Lord (1871–1937). New Zealand–born British physicist who established the basic structure of the atom. He was also the first to change one element to another by an artificial nuclear reaction, for which he won the Nobel prize for chemistry in 1908.

Schrödinger, Erwin (1887–1961). Austrian physicist who founded wave mechanics to describe the behavior of electrons in atoms. For this work, he shared the Nobel prize for physics in 1933.

Thomson, William. *See* **Kelvin, Lord William Thomson.**

Torricelli, Evangelista (1608–47). Italian physicist who used Galileo Galilei's ideas on the laws of motion to describe the motion of fluids.

Volta, Count Alessandro Giuseppe Antonio Anastasio (1745–1827). Italian physicist who built the first chemical battery and was the first to produce electric current without using animal tissues.

Wilson, Charles Thomson Rees (1869–1959). British physicist who invented the Wilson Cloud Chamber, which revolutionized the study of particle physics by allowing the tracks of subatomic particles to be easily viewed.

ADDITIONAL SOURCES OF INFORMATION

Biographical Dictionary of Mathematicians. Charles Scribner's Sons, 1991.

Biographical Dictionary of Scientists. Charles Scribner's Sons, 1981.

Boyer, Carl. *History of Mathematics.* John Wiley & Sons, Inc., 1991.

Concise Biographical Dictionary of Scientists. Charles Scribner's Sons, 1981.

Hall, A. R., E. J. Holyard, Charles Singer, and Trevor Williams. *A History of Technology.* Oxford University Press, 1984.

Macaulay, David. *The Way Things Work.* Houghton-Mifflin, 1988.

McNeil, Ian. *Encyclopedia of the History of Technology.* Routledge, 1990.

Inventions

Newman, James. *World of Mathematics.* Simon and Schuster, 1956.

Pacey, Arnold. *Technology in World Civilization: A Thousand-Year History.* The M.I.T. Press, 1990.

Strandh, Sigvard. *The History of the Machine.* A&W Publishers Inc., 1979.

Williams, Trevor. *Science: A Short History of Discovery in the Twentieth Century.* Oxford University Press, 1990.

II

THE WORLD OF IDEAS

CHAPTER SIX   157
PERFORMANCE AND ENTERTAINMENT ARTS

CHAPTER SEVEN   217
THE VISUAL ARTS

CHAPTER EIGHT   247
LITERATURE

CHAPTER NINE   281
RELIGIONS

CHAPTER TEN   309
PHILOSOPHY

CHAPTER ELEVEN   335
LIBRARIES AND MUSEUMS

6

PERFORMANCE AND ENTERTAINMENT ARTS

ILLUSTRATED LIST OF MUSICAL INSTRUMENTS	158
MAJOR COMPOSERS OF CLASSICAL MUSIC	164
MAJOR JAZZ COMPOSERS AND PERFORMERS	175
COMMON MUSIC TERMS	178
BASIC POSITIONS FOR BALLET	188
MAJOR DANCERS AND CHOREOGRAPHERS	190
COMMON DANCE TERMS	195
MAJOR PLAYWRIGHTS	198
MAJOR FILM DIRECTORS	204
THE ACADEMY AWARDS	209
ADDITIONAL SOURCES OF INFORMATION	216

ILLUSTRATED LIST OF MUSICAL INSTRUMENTS

STRINGED INSTRUMENTS

Stringed instruments are divided into three classifications: plucked, hammered, and bowed.

PLUCKED

guitar family   The guitar is a flat-backed stringed instrument of Spanish origin. It has a long, fretted neck and usually six strings, which are strummed or plucked with the fingers or a plectrum, or pick. Members of the guitar family include the banjo, which is strung with at least four but usually five strings and is generally played with the fingers, and the four-stringed ukulele, originally from Portugal but introduced into the Hawaiian Islands about 1879.

harp   Originating in Mesopotamia and Egypt, the harp is an instrument with strings stretched vertically in an open triangular frame and played by plucking with the fingers. The modern harp usually has 46 strings and seven foot pedals that permit the playing of halftones.

harpsichord family   The harpsichord is a stringed instrument with one or more keyboards, also called manuals. The instrument has two or more strings for each note and produces tones when the strings are plucked with quills or leather points.

Guitar

Harp

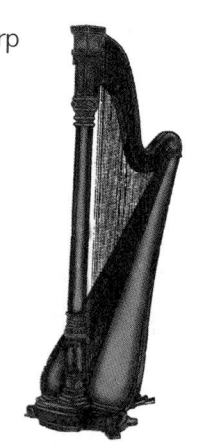

lute family   The lute is an ancient stringed instrument related to the guitar, with a large pear-shaped body, a fretted finger board, and a head with tuning pegs, which is often angled backward from the neck. The strings can be played with either a plectrum or the fingers.

Lute

lyre   Resembling a small harp, the lyre was used by the ancient Greeks to accompany singers and reciters.

vihuela   This medieval and Renaissance Spanish instrument is strung like a lute but has a guitar-shaped body.

zither   The zither is a flat-backed instrument usually having 30 to 40 strings stretched over a shallow horizontal soundboard. The instrument is played on a table or resting on the knees. It can be plucked with the fingers or played with a plectrum.

HAMMERED

clavichord   The clavichord, predecessor of the piano, is a stringed musical instrument with a rectangular keyboard. The strings are struck at various points from below by metal wedges, or tangents, attached directly to the key ends, producing a vibrato effect.

piano   This large keyboard instrument was introduced in Italy around 1700. Its steel wire strings sound when struck by covered hammers operated from the keyboard. In upright pianos, the strings are vertical; in wingshaped pianos, they are horizontal.

BOWED

hurdy-gurdy This instrument of the Middle Ages is shaped like a lute or viol but played by turning a crank attached to a rosined wheel that causes the strings to vibrate. The hurdy-gurdy is most often associated with traveling musicians of the 17th century.

viol family Viols are stringed instruments played with a curved bow, characterized generally by six strings, frets, a flat back, and C-shaped sound holes. These instruments, used chiefly in the 16th and 17th century, vary in size from the treble viol to the bass viol.

violin family These instruments were developed in the 17th century but became popular around 1700. They are played with a bow, are characterized by four strings tuned in fifths, and have fretless fingerboards. The violin is the highest pitched of the family. The viola, slightly larger than the violin, is tuned a fifth lower. The larger violoncello, or more commonly called the cello, is a rich-toned bass instrument. The largest and deepest-toned of all the violins is the double bass.

Violin   Viola

Violoncello

Double Bass

WIND INSTRUMENTS

Wind instruments are divided into three classifications: open mouthpiece, reed type, and brass type.

OPEN MOUTHPIECE

flute family The flute is a high-pitched wind instrument consisting of a long slender tube, played by blowing across a hole near one end. The player can produce various tones by fingering the holes and keys along its length. Variations include the smaller piccolo and the larger alto flute and bass flute.

Flute

Piccolo

panpipes Primitive and varied in form, the panpipe is made of a row or rows of reeds or tubes of gradual length and bound together. The player blows across the open upper ends to produce sound.

pipe organ The pipe organ is a large wind instrument consisting of various sets of pipes. A keyboard controls the flow of air into the pipes, where sound is produced. Simple organs were widely used in religious services in 10th-century Europe. By the

Middle Ages, portable and indoor tabletop organs were introduced.

recorder family   Unlike flutes, which are blown from the side, recorders are end blown. They have eight finger holes and a reedless mouthpiece. This instrument was popular from the Renaissance through the 18th century. Other members of the recorder family include the six-holed flagolet as well as the double and triple flagolets.

REED TYPE

bagpipe family   The bagpipe is a shrill-toned instrument with one double-reed pipe operated by finger stops and one or more drone pipes. The pipes are sounded by air forced with the arm from a leather bag, which is kept filled by the breath. The bagpipe is an ancient instrument, with Asian predecessors dating from the first millennium B.C.

bassoon family   This double-reed bass woodwind instrument dates from the Baroque musical period (1600–1750). It has a long, curved stem attached to the mouthpiece and is built in four joints: the wing, butt, long joint, and bell. The normal bassoon's range is two octaves lower than the oboe, and the contrabassoon sounds an octave further down.

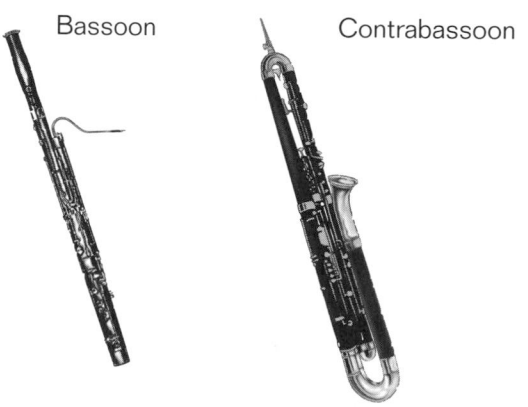

Bassoon   Contrabassoon

clarinet family   Clarinets are single-reed woodwind instruments with a long wooden or metal tube ending in a slightly flared bell. Orchestral types of clarinets have a variety of pitches, notably B-flat and A. The bass clarinet's tones are an octave lower than B-flat, and the E-flat clarinet is the sopranino.

A Clarinet   B-flat Clarinet

Bass Clarinet

oboe family   Oboes are double-reed orchestral instruments with a range of nearly three octaves and a high, penetrating, melancholy tone. The modern oboe has a flared bell while other members of the oboe family have hollow ends shaped like bulbs.

Oboe   Baritone/Bass Oboe

Performance Arts

reed-organ family The reed organ differs from the pipe organ in that it produces the tones with a set of free metal reeds. Other members of the reed-organ family include the harmonica and the accordion.

saxophone family The saxophone is a single-reed, keyed woodwind instrument with a conical bore and metal body. The two principal categories of saxophone are orchestral and band. The band, or military, saxophones are the type most commonly seen, particularly the alto and tenor.

Soprano Saxophone

Alto Saxophone

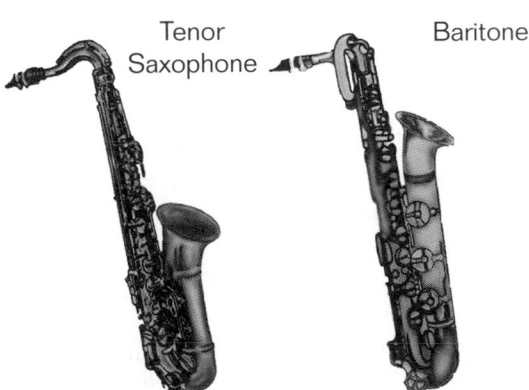

Tenor Saxophone

Baritone

BRASS TYPE

horn family The term *horn* commonly designates an orchestral valved instrument with a flared end. The French horn is a circular instrument with three valves and a funnel-shaped mouthpiece.

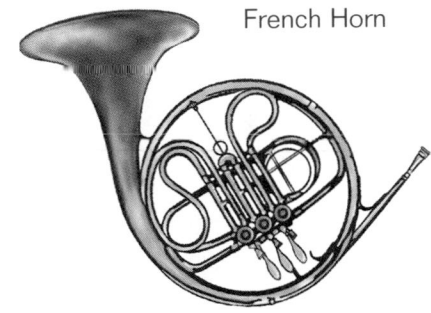

French Horn

saxhorn family These valved brass-band instruments have a full, even tone and range in pitch from soprano to contrabass. Members of the saxhorn family include the alto horn, baritone, and euphonium.

trombone family The trombone is a large brass wind instrument consisting of a long tube bent parallel to itself twice and ending in a bell mouth. The two types of trombones are the slide and the valve. The slide trombone produces different tones when the slide is moved in or out. The valve trombone is played, like the trumpet, with valves.

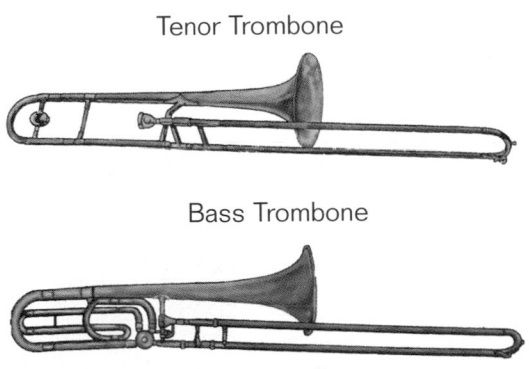

Tenor Trombone

Bass Trombone

Performance Arts

Modern nanotechnology has allowed scientists to produce a guitar no bigger than a blood cell. The guitar is 10 micrometers long with 6 strings.

trumpet family The trumpet consists of a tube in an oblong loop or loops, with a flared bell and, in today's version, three valves for producing changes in key. Other members of the trombone family include the cornet and the bugle.

Cornet

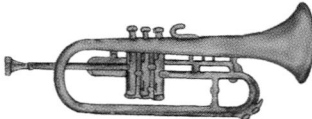

Trumpet

Bugle

tuba family This largest-valved brass instrument has a bass pitch. The tuba consists of a conical bore and three to five valves. Various types of tubas include the sousaphone, double B-flat, double C, E-flat, and F.

Sousaphone   Tuba

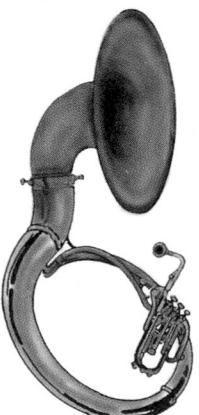
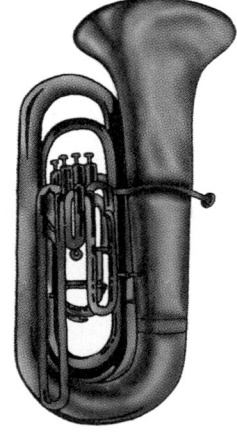

PERCUSSION INSTRUMENTS

Percussion instruments are divided into two classifications: definite pitch and indefinite pitch.

DEFINITE PITCH

glockenspiel The glockenspiel consists of chromatically tuned, flat metal bars set in a frame. It is played with small hammers and produces bell-like tones.

kettledrum Kettledrums consist of hollow hemispheres of copper or brass with a parchment head stretched across the top. The head can be tightened or loosened to change the pitch.

Kettledrum

tubular bells An 18th-century invention, tubular bells are metal tubes of varying lengths hung vertically in a frame. They are struck with mallets and produce bell-like tones.

xylophone family The xylophone consists of a series of wooden bars or other material graduated in length so that they sound the notes of the scale when struck with mallets.

INDEFINITE PITCH

bass drum The bass drum is the largest and lowest-toned of the double-headed drums and lends itself to both marching bands and symphony orchestras.

castanets These small, hollowed pieces of hard wood or ivory are held in the hand by a connecting cord and clicked together with the fingers to beat time to music.

cymbals Either handheld or mounted and struck with a stick, cymbals are circular, slightly concave brass plates that produce a variety of metallic sounds. Specific types of drum cymbals include the ride cymbal, hi-hats, and crash cymbals.

gong The gong is a slightly convex metallic disk that gives a loud resonant tone when struck with sticks or mallets. Flat gongs lack a definite pitch, but a knob, or boss, located at the gong's center lends it a specific pitch.

side drum or snare drum This instrument consists of a wooden or metal cylinder with two heads and wires, known as snares, strung across the bottom head for added vibration. The player strikes the upper head with sticks or wire brushes, which causes the snares to reverberate.

tambourine This instrument is a shallow, single-headed drum with jingling metal disks on the rim. The player shakes or hits the tambourine with the hand or sticks.

tenor drum This 19th-century invention is slightly deeper than the side drum and lacks snares. The tenor drum is a marching instrument usually played with felt-headed sticks.

triangle The triangle consists of a steel rod bent into a triangle shape, left open at one angle. It produces a high-pitched tinkling sound when struck with another steel rod.

ELECTRONIC INSTRUMENTS AND DEVICES

electric guitar The electric guitar's sounds are amplified by means of an electronic pickup that converts string vibrations into electric impulses. In the 1920s the body was hollow, but in the 1940s a solid body replaced the sound box with wood or fiberglass.

electronic organ The electronic organ consists of rotating tone wheels and fixed-pitch oscillators or vibrating reeds to generate sound like that of an acoustic organ.

Musical Instrument Digital Interface (MIDI) At its most basic form, the MIDI allows musicians to play multiple digital instruments from one mechanism. It transmits the information in a series of digital codes. The MIDI can be used for more complicated arrangements as well, such as connecting a variety of instruments to a master computer.

signal processor Electrified instruments transmit signal sounds to a number of devices (such as equalizers, pitch transposers, compressors, and limiters). These devices alter pitch, tone, and other components of the instrument, even making one musical instrument sound like another.

synthesizer This machine, equipped with a keyboard, contains filters, oscillators, and voltage-control amplifiers that are used to generate sounds

---

The Makeup of a Symphony Orchestra

A Closer Look

Strings	12 to 14 first violins, 10 to 12 second violins, 8 to 10 violas, 6 to 8 cellos, 4 to 6 double basses.
Woodwinds	2 flutes, 2 oboes, 2 clarinets, 2 bassoons.
Brass	2 trumpets, 2 or 4 horns, 2 or 3 trombones, 1 tuba.
Percussion	2 or 3 kettledrums and various instruments of definite pitch (glockenspiel, bells, xylophone) and indefinite pitch (snare drum, bass drum, cymbals, triangle).
Harps	1 or 2 (2 are called for more often than 1).

A larger orchestra would have this typical composition:

Strings	16 first violins, 14 second violins, 12 violas, 10 cellos, 8 double basses.
Woodwinds	2 flutes and piccolo, 2 oboes and English horn, 2 clarinets and bass clarinet, 2 bassoons and contrabassoon.
Brass	3 trumpets, 4 horns, 3 trombones, 1 tuba.
Percussion	As above.
Harps	As above.

Performance Arts

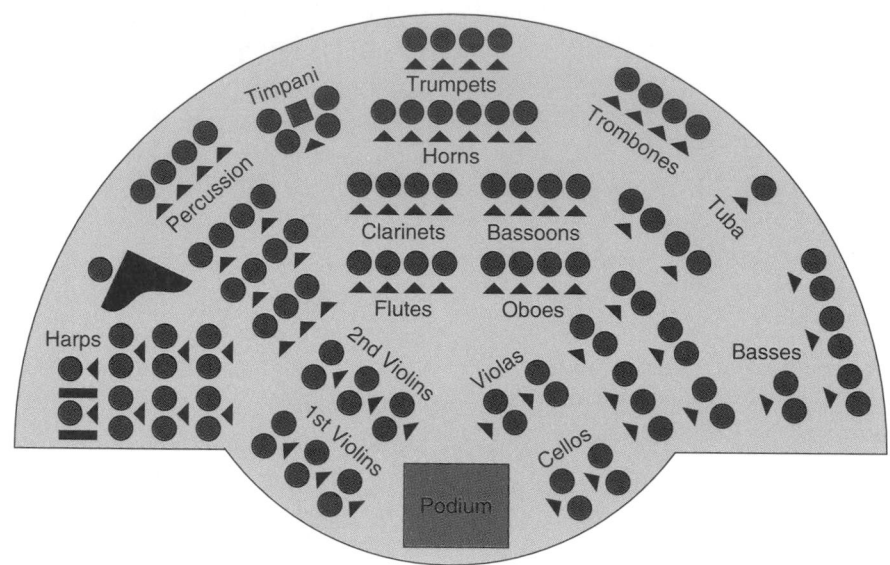

Instrument Positions in the Classic Orchestra

unobtainable from ordinary instruments or to imitate instruments and voices.

MAJOR COMPOSERS OF CLASSICAL MUSIC

AMERICAN

Amram, David (1930–), b. Pennsylvania. Composer and musical director of the New York Shakespeare Festival (1956–68) and the Lincoln Center Repertory Theater (1963–65). He has composed incidental music for plays, orchestra, opera, choral works, and jazz concerts.

Barber, Samuel (1910–81), b. Pennsylvania. Winner, two Pulitzer prizes, for the opera *Vanessa* (1958) and for *Piano Concerto No. 1* (1963). Known for their romantic style, his works also include two symphonies, the overture to *The School for Scandal* (1932), and the popular *Adagio for Strings* (1938).

Beach, Amy Marcy (1867–1944), b. New Hampshire. Composer whose symphonies, Mass, and concerto were widely performed in the United States and abroad, particularly between 1893 and 1914. She was one of the first women composers in the United States to achieve wide respect and

popularity. Her works include *Gaelic Symphony in E Minor, op. 32* (1896), *Piano Concerto in C Sharp Minor* (1899), and *Scottish Legend, op. 54* (1903).

Bernstein, Leonard (1918–90), b. Massachusetts. Conductor and music director of the New York Philharmonic (1958–69). He composed symphonies, songs, and ballets and is best known for his musicals, including *West Side Story* (1957). His world renown also stemmed from his ability to discuss music vividly and in a way intelligible to the musically uneducated person.

Blitzstein, Marc (1905–64), b. Pennsylvania. Pianist, composer, librettist. He was a student of Schoenberg. Among his most important works are orchestral variations; a piano concerto; operas, including the choral opera *The Cradle Will Rock* (1937); ballets; and film music.

Bloch, Ernest (1880–1959), b. Switzerland. Director of the Cleveland Institute of Music (1920–25) and the San Francisco Conservatory (1925–30). Influenced by his Jewish heritage, his works include symphonies, such as *Hivers-Printemps* (1905), *Israel* (1912–17), *America* (1926), *Voice in the Wilderness,* and *Evocations;* opera; chamber music; choral works; a piano sonata; songs; and *Avodath Hakodesh* (1933), a sacred service for Reformed Judaism.

Cage, John (1912–92), b. California. Originator of controversial and experimental theories, performances, and compositions. He is best known for his experiments with random-chance music and for introducing performances with prepared piano. His works include the *Music of Changes* for piano (1951), derived from the ideas of *I Ching; Imaginary Landscape No. 4* for 12 radios tuned randomly (1951); and *4'33"* (1952), in which no sound is called for. Cage collaborated with dancer Merce Cunningham, artist Marcel Duchamp, and others.

All popular songs can be accompanied on a guitar using only three chords. Typical chords are G, C, and D7.

Copland, Aaron (1900–90), b. New York. Composer of three symphonies, a piano concerto, other orchestral works, chamber music, and ballets, including *Billy the Kid* (1938) and *Rodeo* (1942). The creator of a distinctly American music, Copland received the Pulitzer prize in 1945 for *Appalachian Spring* (1944).

Corigliano, John (1938–), b. New York. Composer whose lyrical and rhythmical expression is in the tradition of Bartók and Prokofiev. His works include *Kaleidoscope* (1959) for two pianos, *Violin Sonata* (1963), and the score for the film *Altered States* (1981).

Cowell, Henry Dixon (1897–1965), b. California. Pianist and composer of symphonies, an opera, and the piano concerto *Tales of Our Countryside* (1939). Cowell founded the New Musical Society (1927); he invented (with Leon Theremin) an electronic instrument called the "rhythmicon" and a method of playing the piano with forearm, elbow, and fist. His books on music include *New Musical Resources* (1930) and *Charles Ives and His Music* (1955).

Dello Joio, Norman (1913–), b. New York. Concert pianist, organist, and award-winning composer whose style reflects the influence of American jazz, Italian opera, and the neoclassicism of the early 1900s. His works include piano sonatas, chamber music, orchestral and choral pieces, and

ballets. He won the 1957 Pulitzer prize in music for his *Meditations on Ecclesiastes* for orchestra.

Gershwin, George (1898–1937), b. New York. Composer of music in a distinct blend of classical, popular, and jazz styles. Gershwin's works include numerous popular songs and musical comedies and more ambitious concert pieces: *Rhapsody in Blue* (1924), *An American in Paris* (1928), and the jazz opera *Porgy and Bess* (1935).

Hanson, Howard (1896–1981), b. Nebraska. Conductor and composer of romantic works, including symphonies, piano music, and the opera *Merry Mount* (1934). He served as director of the Eastman School of Music (1924–64) in Rochester, New York, and received the 1944 Pulitzer prize in music for his *Symphony No. 3, The Requiem* (1943).

Ives, Charles (1874–1954), b. Connecticut. Composer of advanced and innovative works and winner of the Pulitzer prize in 1947 for his *Symphony No. 3*. His compositions—including four symphonies, chamber and choral music, songs, and piano works—stressed American folk and popular music, jazz, military marches, patriotic songs, and revival hymns.

MacDowell, Edward (1860–1908), b. New York. Best known as a composer of piano works, MacDowell also wrote orchestral works, symphonic poems, and a suite that appropriates melodies of northern Native Americans. He was the first head of the department of music at Columbia University (1896–1904).

Menotti, Gian Carlo (1911–), b. Italy. Composer of ballets, a piano concerto, and some of the most popular operas of the mid–20th century. He won the 1950 Pulitzer prize for *The Consul* and the 1955 Pulitzer prize for *The Saint of Bleecker Street*. He founded the Festival of Two Worlds in Spoleto, Italy.

Moore, Douglas (1893–1969), b. New York. Composer of works noted for their use of the American vernacular, including the operas *The Devil and Daniel Webster* (1939) and *The Ballad of Baby Doe* (1956). He was the author of *Listening to Music* (1931) and *From Madrigal to Modern Music* (1942) and won the 1951 Pulitzer prize for *Giants of the Earth* (1951).

Piston, Walter (1894–1976), b. Maine. Professor at Harvard and neoclassical composer of orchestral works, string quartets, sonatas, chamber music, and the ballet *The Incredible Flautist* (1938). Piston wrote studies of harmony and counterpoint. He won the Pulitzer prize in 1948 for his *Symphony No. 3* and in 1961 for his *Symphony No. 7*.

Schoenberg, Arnold (1874–1951), b. Austria. Originator of the revolutionary 12-tone system. The theory is exemplified in his works of 1921–33, including *Five Pieces* (1923) for piano and *Serenade* (1923) for seven instruments and bass baritone.

Schuman, William (1910–92), b. New York. President of the Juilliard School of Music (1945–61) and Lincoln Center (1962–69). Schuman composed ballets and concertos as well as chamber, orchestral, and choral works that featured energetic melodies, lively rhythms, and brilliant orchestrations. He was the winner of the first Pulitzer prize for music in 1943 for *A Free Song*.

Sessions, Roger (1896–1985), b. New York. Composer of intense, intellectual works, including eight symphonies, a violin concerto, piano works, organ pieces, and songs. His books include *Questions About Music* (1970). Sessions's most popular work is the orchestral suite *The Black Maskers* (1923), and he won the 1982 Pulitzer prize for *Concerto for Orchestra*.

Thomson, Virgil (1896–1989), b. Missouri. Music critic and composer. Based on early American hymns and folk songs, his works include two operas (with librettos by Gertrude Stein), a ballet, choral and chamber music, pieces for theater and film (among them *The River*, 1937), keyboard music, and songs. He wrote several books, including *The State of Music* (1939) and *Music, Right and Left* (1951). Thomson won the 1949 Pulitzer prize for the documentary *Louisiana Story*.

Varèse, Edgar (1883–1965), b. France. Founder and conductor of the New Symphony Orchestra, New York (1919), and founder of the International Composers Guild (1921). Varèse was a leading experimental composer of the early 1920s and wrote nontraditional works for orchestra with electronic music. His *Poème Electronique* (1958) is considered a major work in this field.

Zwilich, Ellen Taafe (1939–   ), b. Florida. Composer and first woman to receive the Pulitzer prize in music composition, in 1983, for her *Symphony No. 1*. Her works have been characterized as romantic with a lush Straussian flavor. Among her other works is *Trio for Piano, Violin, and Cello* (1987).

AUSTRIAN

Berg, Alban (1885–1935). Composer in Arnold Schoenberg's 12-tone system. Principal works are the opera *Wozzeck* (1925), the unfinished opera *Lulu* (1937), orchestral pieces, concertos, string quartets, *Lyric Suite* (1926–28), and a piano sonata.

Bruckner, Anton (1824–96). Organist and composer of romantic music. Much revised by his friends, his original compositions were published in 1929. Principal works include nine symphonies, choral works, and chamber music for string quintet.

The setting for the musical Sound of Music is Salzburg, Austria, which is also Mozart's birthplace.

Czerny, Karl (1791–1857). Virtuoso pianist and composer of many works for piano. Best known for his technical studies, Czerny was a pupil of Beethoven and a teacher of Liszt.

Haydn, Franz Joseph (1732–1809). Consummate artist of the classical style in music, who has been called the "father of the symphony." Among his works are more than 100 symphonies, numerous concertos, 20 operas (five are lost), marionette operas, church music, string quartets, piano trios, keyboard sonatas and variations, songs, and 377 arrangements of Scottish and Welsh airs. His most famous works include *The Bird* quartet (1781), the oratorios *The Creation* (1798) and *The Seasons* (1801), and the *Surprise Symphony* (1791).

Haydn, Johann Michael (1737–1806). Brother of Franz Joseph Haydn and composer of oratorios and church music, symphonies, concertos, divertimenti, quintets, and other instrumental works.

Mahler, Gustav (1860–1911). Conductor of the Hamburg and Vienna operas and the Metropolitan Opera in New York. He composed nine symphonies, as well as songs, in a late Romantic style, including *Resurrection Symphony* (1894) and *Symphony of a Thousand* (1907).

Mozart, Wolfgang Amadeus (1756–91). Master of the classical style in all its forms of his time. Mozart began to compose and perform at age 6; at age 11 he had composed three symphonies and 30 other works and arranged some piano concertos of Johann Sebastian Bach. His principal works include the operas *The Marriage of Figaro* (1786), *Don Giovanni* (1787), and *The Magic Flute* (1791); chamber music; piano sonatas and fantasias; 50 symphonies; and church music, including the *Requiem* (1791). One of his most popular compositions is *A Little Night Music* (1787). Mozart's works are noted for their lyrical charm.

Schubert, Franz Seraph Peter (1797–1828). Composer of numerous symphonies, masses, quartets, and sonatas, but most notably of songs in the spirit of early romantic poetry. His works after 1823 consummate his lyrical, melodic style, as in the *No. 9 C Major Symphony* ("The Great") (1828); 22 piano sonatas, including the *Wanderer Fantasie* (1822); and the *Piano Trio in B-flat major* (1827) and *Piano Trio in E-flat major* (1827).

Strauss. Family of Viennese musicians. **Johann I** (1804–49) was the composer of waltzes famous throughout Europe. He was the father of **Johann II** (1825–99), who became his rival and who composed more than 400 waltzes, including *The Blue Danube* (1866) and *Tales from the Vienna Woods* (1868), as well as operettas. Johann II's brothers, **Josef** (1827–70) and **Eduard I** (1835–1916), were also successful composers and conductors.

Webern, Anton von (1883–1945). Editor, conductor, and composer in the 12-tone system of Arnold Schoenberg. Webern wrote a symphony for small orchestra, three cantatas, a string quartet, a concerto for nine instruments, songs, and other works. His major choral works include *Das Augenlicht* (1935), *First Cantata* (1939), and *Second Cantata* (1943).

BRITISH

Britten, (Edward) Benjamin (1913–76). Major 20th-century composer famous for his vocal music and operas. The latter include *Peter Grimes* (1945), *The Rape of Lucretia* (1946), *Billy Budd* (1951), *The Turn of the Screw* (1954), and *A Midsummer Night's Dream* (1960). Among his most popular works are *A Ceremony of Carols* (1942), *A Young Person's Guide to the Orchestra* (1945), and the *War Requiem* (1962).

Byrd, William (1543–1623). Organist and composer. A master of 16th-century polyphony, Byrd excelled in the composition of church music, including *Gradualia* (1605–07).

Delius, Frederick (1862–1934). Composer of orchestral works, including *Paris* (1899), *Appalachia* (1896), and *Brigg Fair* (1907); choral works, including *Sea Drift;* and the operas *A Village Romeo and Juliet* (1901) and *Fennimore and Gerda* (1910).

Dowland, John (c. 1563–1626). Lutenist and composer of the most important English collection of songs for the lute. His most famous work is *Lachrymae* (1605), a collection of dance pieces.

Elgar, Sir Edward (1857–1934). Composer best known for *Pomp and Circumstance,* a set of five marches; an adaptation of *Pomp and Circumstance* (1902) for the coronation of King Edward VII; *The Dream of Gerontius* (1900); *The Enigma Variations* (1899) for orchestra; and *Introduction and Allegro for Strings* (1905).

Gibbons, Orlando (1583–1625). Organist and composer of anthems, madrigals, chamber music, and keyboard pieces.

Holst, Gustav (1874–1934). Composer who combined an interest in folk music with a knowledge of Hindu scales and Sanskrit literature. His later music experimented with harmony and polytonality. Principal works include the operas *Savitri* (1908) and *The Perfect Fool* (1923); for orchestra, *The Planets* (1914–16) and *Egdon Heath* (1927); and for chorus, *Hymns from the Rig-Veda* (1910) and *Hymn for Jesus* (1917).

Morley, Thomas   (1557–1602). Composer, theorist, and organist at St. Paul's Cathedral. Morley was granted a monopoly on music printing (1598) and wrote the first comprehensive treatise on composition in English (1597). He became known for his light songs, including canzonets, airs, and madrigals.

Purcell, Henry   (c. 1659–95). Organist at Westminster Abbey and composer of music for more than 40 plays, including the first important English opera, *Dido and Aeneas* (1689), and *The Fairy Queen* (1692), a masque. He also wrote odes, songs, cantatas, church music, chamber music, and keyboard works.

Sullivan, Sir Arthur   (1842–1900). Conductor, organist, and composer. His works include the grand opera *Ivanhoe* (1891); ballads; oratorios; cantatas, including *The Golden Legend;* church music; a symphony; songs; and works for piano. He is best known for light operas to librettos by W. S. Gilbert.

Tallis, Thomas   (c. 1505–85). Organist and composer. He was granted a monopoly in music printing with William Byrd (1575). Tallis's works include church music and secular pieces for vocals and keyboard.

Vaughan Williams, Ralph   (1872–1958). Composer noted for his adaptations of English folk music and Tudor church music. Principal compositions include *A London Symphony* (1913), *Norfolk Rhapsodies* (1906), and *The Lark Ascending* (1914), all for orchestra; *A Sea Symphony* (1910) and *Five Mystical Songs* (1911) for chorus; the operas *Hugh the Drover* (1914), *Riders to the Sea* (1937), and *The Pilgrim's Progress* (1951); and works for stage, chamber music, and songs.

FRENCH

Berlioz, Hector   (1803–69). Conductor and composer of romantic works. Berlioz is best known for his genius with orchestration and his way of relating musical works to story ideas, as in the *Symphonie Fantastique* (1830). He also wrote the symphonic work *Harold in Italy* (1834), the opera *Damnation of Faust* (1846), and the oratorio *Childhood of Christ* (1850–54).

Bizet, Georges   (1838–75). Composer best known for the operas *Carmen* (1875), *The Pearlfishers* (1863), *The Young Maid of Perth* (1867), and *Djmileh* (1872). His *Symphony in C Major* (1868) is highly regarded. His music is melodic and tightly organized, with uncomplicated orchestral accompaniment.

Boulanger, Lili   (1893–1918). Composer in an impressionist style. She composed over 50 works in the genres of secular and sacred music, chorus with and without orchestra, cantatas, chamber music, songs, and an uncompleted opera. Boulanger is best known for her cantata *Faust et Hélène* (1913), for which she was awarded the Prix de Rome.

Boulez, Pierre   (1925–   ). Composer of experimental works using the serial technique, including *Pli selon pli* (1962) and *Memoriales* (1975). Many of his compositions contain unusual rhythms with separate sounds, reflecting his interest in Asian music. He served as music director of the New York Philharmonic (1971–77).

Couperin, François   (1668–1733). Member of a family of distinguished organists. Organist to the king at Versailles, he composed music for organ and harpsichord, instrumental ensembles, secular songs, and church music. He wrote a well-known textbook, *The Art of Playing the Harpsichord.*

Debussy, Claude   (1862–1918). Composer noted for his impressionist style. Orchestral works include *La Mer* (1903–05) and *Nocturnes* (1893–99); piano works include *Clair de lune* (1890), preludes, études, arabesques, and *The Children's Corner* (1906–08). Debussy also wrote choral works, an opera, and the well-known tone poem *Prelude to the Afternoon of a Faun* (1894).

Delibes, (Clément Philibert) Léo   (1836–91). Composer of operas, including *Le Roi l'a dit* (1873) and *Lakmé* (1883), and ballets, including *Coppélia* (1870) and *Sylvia* (1876).

Dukas, Paul   (1865–1935). Composer best known for the orchestral scherzo *Sorcerer's Apprentice* (1897), the opera *Ariane et barbe-Bleue* (1907), and the ballet *La Peri* (1912).

Fauré, Gabriel   (1845–1924). Organist and composer who excelled in songwriting and an adventurous use of harmony. He wrote the operas *Prométhée* (1900) and *Pénélope* (1913), orchestral music, chamber works, and piano and church music. Fauré was the teacher of Maurice Ravel.

Franck, César (1822–90). A teacher who influenced an entire generation of composers. Distinctive compositions include *Symphony in D Minor* (1888), the *Symphonic Variations* (1885) for piano and orchestra, *Prelude, Chorale, and Fugue* (1884), and the opera *Hulda* (1894).

Gounod, Charles (1818–93). Composer of the operas *Faust* (1859) and *Romeo and Juliet* (1867). Gounod also wrote church music, symphonies, and cantatas. His music includes elements of seriousness, melodrama, and sentimentality.

Honegger, Arthur (1892–1955). Founding member of the Parisian group "The Six" in 1916 with Erik Satie, Darius Milhaud, and Jean Cocteau. Rejecting romanticism and impressionism, Honegger is best known for the oratorio *King David* (1921) and for *Pacific 231* (1923) and *Joan of Arc at the Stake* (1935), both for orchestra.

Ibert, Jacques François Antoine (1890–1962). Ibert's colorful works include a suite for orchestra, *Escales* (1922); *Divertissement* (1930); music for theater and film; chamber music; and works for piano and organ. He served as director of the Académie de France in Rome (1937) and the Paris Opera (1955).

Lully, Jean-Baptiste (orig. Lulli, Giambattista) (1632–87). Lully composed for the comedy ballets of Molière and was the founder of the French opera *(tragédie lyrique)*. He also composed court ballets, divertissements, church music, and two instrumental suites. His best-known works include *Cadmus and Hermione* (1673), *Amadis de Gaule* (1684), and *Roland* (1685).

Massenet, Jules Emile Frédéric (1842–1912). Best known for his pop operas *Le Roi de Lahore* (1877), *Manon* (1884), *Werther* (1892), and *Le Jongleur de Notre-Dame* (1902). Massenet also wrote oratorios, orchestral works, concertos, and songs.

Messiaen, Olivier Eugène Prosper Charles (1908–92). Organist and composer of symphonic

poems and works for piano, organ, and vocals. He became known for using birdcalls, electronic sounds, religious songs, and Oriental themes in his compositions. Messiaen helped form the group "Jeune France" in 1936 and wrote a treatise on composition. His works include the 10-movement symphony *Turangalila* (1949).

Milhaud, Darius (1892–1974). A member of the Parisian group "The Six," Milhaud composed works that combine jazz, polytonality, and Brazilian elements. He is well known for the opera *Christophe Colomb* (1930) and for ballets, including *Creation of the World* (1923).

Offenbach, Jacques (1819–80). Composer of 90 operettas, including the popular *Orpheus in the Underworld* (1858), *La Belle Hélène* (1864), and *La Vie Parisienne* (1866). His best work is thought to be *The Tales of Hoffmann,* which was unfinished at his death and later completed by Ernest Guiraud.

Poulenc, Francis (1899–1963). Member of the Parisian circle "The Six," Poulenc composed ballets, including *Les Biches* (1924); chamber music; a concerto for two pianos; songs; choral works; a cantata; and operas, among them *Dialogues of the Carmelites* (1957). He was noted for his vocal music featuring beautiful melodies and sensitive lyrics.

Rameau, Jean-Philippe (1683–1764). Theorist and important composer of French opera. His works include the operas *Castor et Pollux* (1737) and *Dardanus* (1739), the opera-ballet *Les Indes galantes* (1735), and the ballet-bouffon *Platée* (1745). His *Treatise of Harmony* (1722) laid the foundation for the modern theory of harmony.

Ravel, Maurice (1875–1937). Leading exponent of impressionism, who relied on the strong melodies and rich textures of 19th-century classical music. Ravel's principal works include *Rapsodie espagnole* (1908), *Daphnis and Chloe* (1912), and *Bolero* (1928), all for orchestra; and *Valses nobles et sentimentales* (1911) and *Gaspard de la nuit* (1908), both for piano.

Saint-Saëns, Charles Camille (1835–1921). Pianist and composer. Saint-Saëns began performing at age 10 and later composed symphonic poems under the influence of Franz Liszt; operas, including *Samson et Dalila* (1877); and concertos.

Performance Arts

Satie, Erik (1866–1925). Composer noted for his ironic, humorous style and ranked as a leader in the development of modern music. Satie composed three ballets, including *Parade* (1917); operettas; a symphonic drama, *Socrates;* songs; and piano pieces.

GERMAN

Bach, Johann Sebastian (1685–1750). Baroque organist and composer; one of the greatest creators of Western music. Among his religious works are more than 200 cantatas, the *Mass in B Minor* (1733–49), and the *St. Matthew Passion* (1727). His other works include *The Well-Tempered Clavier* (1722), a collection of preludes and fugues; the Brandenburg concertos (1721); and many sonatas and suites. He had 20 children, 10 of whom survived, including **Wilhelm Friedemann** (1710–84), organist and composer; **Carl Philipp Emanuel** (1714–88), composer of religious music, symphonies, concertos, sonatas, and chamber music; **Johann Christoph Friedrich** (1732–95), composer; and **Johann Christian** (1735–82), composer of operas, chamber music, and church music.

Beethoven, Ludwig van (1770–1827). Considered one of the greatest composers of instrumental works, particularly symphonies, he is regarded as one of the founding fathers of musical romanticism. Beethoven was a student of Haydn, whose influence permeates his early works. By 1824 he had lost his hearing, but he continued to compose under the sponsorship of aristocratic patrons. His works include *Fidelio* (1805), an opera; a violin concerto and five piano concertos; the *Egmont* overture (1810); 32 piano sonatas, including the *Appassionata* (1804–05); 16 string quartets; the *Mass in D (Missa Solemnis)* (1818–23); and nine symphonies, the best known of which are the *Third (Eroica)* (1804), the *Fifth (Victory)* (1805), the *Sixth (Pastoral)* (1809), and the *Ninth (Choral)*. The *Ninth,* completed in 1823, is considered the greatest of his works.

Brahms, Johannes (1833–97). Developer of a romantic style that was both lyrical and classical. His principal works include four symphonies, two overtures, and two serenades for orchestra; two piano concertos, one violin concerto, and one concerto for violin and cello; *A German Requiem* (1857–68), his best-known choral work; piano solos, including variations on themes by Paganini, Handel, and Schumann; chamber music; rhapsodies; ballades; piano duets; waltzes; Hungarian dances; songs; folk song arrangements; and 11 choral preludes for organ.

Bruch, Max (1838–1920). Famous for his setting of the melody to the Jewish prayer *Kol Nidre* (1880) for cello and orchestra. His works also include three symphonies, three operas, an operetta, choral works, and chamber music.

Gluck, Christoph Willibald von (1714–87). Composer of more than 100 operas, among them *Orfeo ed Euridice* (1762) and *Alceste* (1767), which established a new style of Italian opera; 11 symphonies; instrumental trios; seven odes by Friedrich Klopstock for solo voice and keyboard; and a flute concerto.

Handel, George Frideric (1685–1759). Baroque composer most famous for the oratorio *Messiah* (1742). Trained in law and music in Germany, Handel produced his operas in Italy and London, incorporating German, Italian, and English styles. Among his works are many operas, including *Almira* (1705), *Ottone* (1723), and *Orlando* (1733); *Music for the Royal Fireworks* (1749) and *Water Music* (1717); suites for harpsichord; chamber music; and many Italian cantatas.

Hindemith, Paul (1895–1963). Composer, teacher, theorist, performer, and conductor who brought a neoclassical element to contemporary music. Early works, such as the opera *Murder, Hope of Women* (1921), reflect the expressionism of the period. Later works, including *Ludus Tonalis* (1942), exemplify his new theory of tonality expounded in *The Craft of Musical Composition* (1941, 1945). Hindemith was banned by the Nazis for his modernity. His best-known work is a symphony from his opera *Mathis the Painter* (1938).

Humperdinck, Engelbert (1854–1921). Composer of six operas, including the popular *Hansel and Gretel* (1893); incidental music; vocal works; and songs.

Mendelssohn, Felix (1809–47). Pianist, conductor, and composer of orchestral works, including five symphonies and the overture to *A Midsummer Night's Dream* (1826); choral works, including the oratorios *St. Paul* (1836) and *Elija* (1846); operas; incidental music; several collections of piano works; *Songs Without Words* (1832); and songs. His music contains smooth progressions in harmony accompanying melodies that are easy to sing.

Meyerbeer, Giacomo (1791–1864). Composer of operas in a spectacular style that influenced Richard Wagner. His works include *Robert le Diable* (1831), *Les Huguenots* (1836), and *Le Prophète* (1849).

Orff, Carl (1895–1982). Composer of stage works that combined instrumental singing, gestures, and dance, including the cantata *Carmina Burana* (1937); the opera *Der Mond* (1939); and musical plays. Orff developed a widely used system for teaching music to children.

Schumann, Clara Josephine Wieck (1819–96). Pianist and composer of piano works and songs. She was a renowned interpreter of music, particularly the works of her husband, Robert Schumann.

Schumann, Robert (1810–56). Composer of piano music, including sonatas and impromptus, and of orchestral works. His compositions include *Symphonic Études* (1834), *Fantasia in C Major* (1836), *Album for the Young* (1848), and *Piano Concerto in A Minor* (1845). The *Rhenish Symphony* (1850) combined classical and romantic elements.

Frederic Handel was known to have a fiery temper. During an argument with an opera singer, he picked her up by the waist and dangled her out of a two-story window.

Strauss, Richard (1864–1949). Composer of numerous operas, many with librettos by Hugo von Hoffmansthal, including the famous *Der Rosenkavalier* (1911); two ballets; tone poems for orchestra, including *Also sprach Zarathustra* (1896); concertos; *Metamorphosen* (1945) for 23 solo strings; chamber music; songs; and piano works.

Wagner, Richard (1813–83). Composer of operas and architect of a theory of the "total" work of art, in which drama, spectacle, and music are fused. Principal works include *Der Ring des Nibelungen* (1853–74), which was made up of four operas: *Das Rheingold* (1854), *Die Walküre* (1856), *Siegfried* (1857–69), and *Götterdämmerung* (1874); *Tristan und Isolde* (1859), and *Parsifal* (1882). Exiled for his role in the revolution of 1848, Wagner resettled in Bavaria in 1864, where he constructed his theater at Bayreuth.

Weber, Carl Maria von (1786–1826). Composer, conductor, pianist, critic, and virtual creator of romantic German opera. Principal works include the operas *Der Freischütz* (1821) and *Oberon* (1826), choral and orchestral pieces, piano sonatas, concertos, dances, and songs.

ITALIAN

Bellini, Vincenzo (1801–35). Composer of emotional and technically challenging operas, including *La Straniera* (1829), *La Sonnambula* (1831), *Norma* (1831), and *I Puritani* (1835).

Boccherini, Luigi (1743–1805). Cellist and composer. His principal compositions are for chamber music; he also wrote symphonies, concertos, and vocal music. His most popular works are his *Concerto in B-flat* (1770) for cello, and the minuet from his *String Quartet No. 3* (1771).

Boito, Arrigo (1842–1918). Poet and composer of operas, including *Mefistofele* (1868) and *Nerone* (1918). Boito is known chiefly for his librettos, notably for *Otello* (1887) and *Falstaff* (1893) by Giuseppe Verdi.

Cherubini, Maria Luigi (1760–1842). Composer of about 30 operas, among them the classic "rescue" opera *The Water Carrier* (1800); church music; string quartets; and piano sonatas. He served as director of the Paris Conservatory (1822).

Clementi, Muzio (1752–1832). Pianist and composer of symphonies, piano sonatas, and piano studies, including *Gradus ad Parnassum* (1817).

Corelli, Arcangelo (1653–1713). Violinist and composer. His trio sonatas, solo violin sonatas, and concerti grossi established a style of composition for the violin.

Dallapiccola, Luigi (1904–75). Composer of 12-tone atonal music characterized by delicate counterpoint, lyrical line and textures, and subtle tone colors. He is most noted for his operas *The Prisoner* (1944) and *Odysseus* (1968), the oratorio *Job* (1950), and the *Christmas Concerto* (1956).

Donizetti, Gaetano (1797–1848). Prolific composer of operas. His best-known works included *Lucrezia Borgia* (1833), *La Favorite* (1840), and the comic operas *L'Elisir d'amore* (1832) and *Don Pasquale* (1843).

Leoncavallo, Ruggiero (1858–1919). Composer of operas. His most successful was *Pagliacci* (1892). He wrote his own librettos, a ballet, and a symphonic poem.

Mascagni, Pietro (1863–1945). Opera composer and conductor. His most famous work is *Cavalleria Rusticana* (1890).

Monteverdi, Claudio (1567–1643). Ordained priest and composer of church music, including masses, vespers, and madrigals. He also wrote secular vocal music, at least 12 operas, and ballets. His works helped change the strict style of Renaissance music to the emotional style of the baroque movement. His *Orfeo* (1607) is called the first modern opera.

Palestrina, Giovanni Pierluigi da (Johannes Praenestinus) (c. 1525–94). Organist, choirmaster, and composer of church music, including masses, motets, and lamentations. He also wrote both sacred and secular madrigals.

Pergolesi, Giovanni Battista (1710–36). Composer of operas and comic intermezzos that became the prototype of the *opera buffa;* church music, including his renowned *Stabat Mater* (1736); and sonatas, which contributed to the development of the form.

Puccini, Giacomo (1858–1924). Composer of many operas with highly emotional melodies and orchestral brilliance. Best known are *La Bohème* (1896), *Tosca* (1900), and *Madame Butterfly*

(1904). *Turandot* was completed after his death by Franco Alfano.

Respighi, Ottorino (1879–1936). Composer of operas, tone poems, and other orchestral works, chamber music, concertos, and songs. Among his most popular works are *The Fountains of Rome* (1917) and *The Pines of Rome* (1924), both symphonic poems.

Rossini, Gioacchino (1792–1868). Composer of operas. The best known are *William Tell* (1829) and *The Barber of Seville* (1816). Rossini also wrote cantatas, songs, piano pieces, and woodwind quintets.

Scarlatti, Alessandro (1660–1725). Conductor and the most prolific composer of Italian operas of his time. Besides composing about 80 operas, he wrote 20 oratorios, some 600 cantatas, 10 masses, a passion, motets, and other church music, chamber pieces, concertos, and works for harpsichord.

Scarlatti, (Giuseppe) Domenico (1685–1757). Son of Alessandro Scarlatti, and greatest Italian composer for harpsichord of his time. He wrote 550 pieces, now called sonatas, as well as concertos, operas, cantatas, masses, a *Stabat Mater,* and two *Salve Reginas.*

Tartini, Giuseppe (1692–1770). Violinist, teacher, composer, and theorist. He composed over 100 violin concertos and symphonies, solo sonatas, trio sonatas, and church music; published treatises on violin playing and acoustics; and established a violin school in Padua (1728).

Verdi, Giuseppe (1813–1901). Foremost composer of operas. His works are performed more often today than those of any other opera composer. They include *Rigoletto* (1851), *La Traviata* (1853), and the supreme *Otello* (1887) and *Falstaff* (1893). Verdi also composed church music, including the *Requiem* (1874), *Ave Maria* (1880), *Stabat Mater* (1898), and *Te Deum* (1898).

Vivaldi, Antonio (1678–1741). Violinist, composer, and ordained priest. Master of the Italian baroque, Vivaldi is best known for his instrumental music and the concertos *The Four Seasons* (1725). He also wrote church music, an oratorio, and nearly 50 operas.

RUSSIAN

Borodin, Aleksandr (1833–87). Composer and scientist. His works include three symphonies; *In the Steppes of Central Asia* (1880) for orchestra; string quartets; and the opera *Prince Igor* (1887), completed after his death by Nicolai Rimsky-Korsakov and Aleksandr Glazunov (1890).

Glinka, Mikhail (1804–57). Composer of two operas and other works. *A Life for the Czar* (1836) and *Ruslan and Ludmilla* (1842) established a Russian style against the conventions of Italian opera. Glinka introduced folk song into instrumental composition in the orchestral fantasia *Kamarinskaya.*

The Russian composer Alexander Borodin not only wrote the opera Prince Igor *but was also a professional chemist and the author of "On the Analogy of Arsenical with Phosphoric Acid."*

Khachaturian, Aram (1903–78). Armenian composer whose works are distinguished for their incorporation of oriental folk elements. He is best known for the ballet *Gayane* (1942) and its popular "Sabre Dance" theme.

Mussorgsky, Modest (1839–81). Composer of operas and orchestral works. Mussorgsky is best known for his operas *Boris Godunov* (1868, 1874) and *Khovanschina* (1886), as well as for *Pictures at an Exhibition* (1874) for piano and *Night on Bald Mountain* (1860–66) for orchestra.

Prokofiev, Sergei (1891–1953). Composer, pianist, and conductor. His principal compositions are the operas *Love for Three Oranges* (1921) and *War and Peace* (1942); *Peter and the Wolf* (1936) and *Classical Symphony* (1918), both for orchestra and narrator; and seven symphonies, piano concertos, ballets, and piano sonatas.

Rachmaninoff, Sergei (1873–1943). Composer, pianist, and conductor whose works are filled with passion, power, and a feeling of melancholy. Rachmaninoff emigrated to the United States at age 17. His compositions include three operas;

orchestral works, including the tone poem *Isle of the Dead* (1909); four concertos, including the *Second Piano Concerto* (1901); choral works; chamber music; and songs.

Rimsky-Korsakov, Nicolai (1844–1908). Composer of operas and orchestral works, including the popular symphonic suite *Scheherazade* (1888). His greatest works are the operas *Mlada* (1892), *Christmas Eve* (1895), *Sadko* (1898), and *The Golden Cockerel* (1907). His orchestration influenced the work of Igor Stravinsky and others.

Rubinstein, Anton (1829–94). Pianist and composer; founder of the Conservatory in St. Petersburg (1862). A representative of traditional Western ideas against the current of nationalism, he composed *Musical Portraits (Faust, Ivan the Terrible, Don Quixote)* for orchestra, 19 operas, 6 symphonies (including *The Ocean*), chamber music, 5 piano concertos, and other works.

Scriabin, Aleksandr (1872–1915). Composer and pianist. Scriabin experimented with esoteric harmonies related to theosophical ideas in *The Divine Poem* (1905) and *Poem of Ecstasy,* both for orchestra. He wrote sonatas, preludes, and *Prometheus* (1909–10), which includes the use of a "color organ" for slide projection.

Shostakovich, Dmitri (1906–75). Composer of chamber and symphonic works characterized by a bold, expressive modern style. Shostakovich alternated between political and satirical composition, later trying to bring his work closer to official prescriptions. His works include 15 symphonies, among them *May the First* (1930) and the outstanding *Ninth Symphony* (1940); operas; ballets, including *Lady Macbeth of Mtsensk* (1934) and revised in 1962 as *Katerina Ismailova;* piano works; sonatas; and 15 string quartets.

Stravinsky, Igor (1882–1971). Composer of the epochal ballets *The Firebird* (1910), *Petrouchka* (1911), and *Rite of Spring* (1913). Later works, such as *The Soldier's Tale* (1918), for narrator and instruments, and the ballet suite *Apollon Musagète* (1928) are more austere and neoclassical. Stravinsky settled in the United States in 1941, where he experimented with 12-tone composition, as in *Requiem Canticles* (1966).

Performance Arts

Tchaikovsky, Peter Ilyich (1840–93). One of the most important Russian composers. His music is characterized by masterful orchestration and spirited yet often melancholy melodies. Tchaikovsky is best known for his ballet music, including *Swan Lake* (1876), *The Sleeping Beauty* (1889), and *The Nutcracker* (1892); and for his operas *Eugene Onegin* (1878) and *Queen of Spades* (1890). He also wrote symphonies, including the popular *Symphony No. 5* (1888), chamber music, and choral works; and he published books on harmony, autobiographical essays, and translations.

OTHER

Albéniz, Isaac (1860–1909). Spanish composer and pianist. Albéniz is known for his later piano works, notably *Iberia* (1906–09); he also wrote operas, including *The Magic Opal* (1893).

Bartók, Béla (1881–1945). Hungarian pianist and composer who studied and collected Hungarian folk music and developed a musical style that emphasized energetic rhythm, folk song scales, dissonance, and highly personal forms. His principal works include orchestral pieces; the opera *Duke Bluebeard's Castle* (1918); the ballet *The Wooden Prince* (1914–16); the pantomime *The Miraculous Mandarin* (1919, 1924, 1935); chamber music; piano works, including the *Mikrokosmos* (1926–37); and arrangements of folk songs. He emigrated to the United States in 1940.

Chávez, Carlos (1899–1978). Mexican composer of works using the idioms of Indian folk music, including *Xochipilli Macuilxochitl* (1940). Well-known works are the symphonic ode *Clio* (1969) and *Discovery* (1969).

Chopin, Frédéric François (1810–49). Polish composer and pianist. Called "the poet of the piano," he composed hundreds of pieces for that instrument, most notably two piano concertos, and other pieces including *Fantaisie-Impromptu* (1834).

Dvořák, Antonín (1841–1904). Czech composer of symphonies, operas, dances, and choral works in a nationalistic spirit and neoromantic style. His works include the *Symphonic Variations, Slavonic Rhapsodies,* and the opera *The Peasant Rogue* (1877). His best-known work, the *Symphony from the New World* (1893), contains elements of both Czech and American music.

Falla, Manuel de (1876–1946). Spanish composer and pianist. He published little but was the outstanding Spanish composer of his time. Principal works are the operas *La Vida Breve* (1905) and *El Retablo de Maese Pedro* (1923); the ballets *El Amor Brujo* (1915) and *The Three-Cornered Hat* (1919); and the *Fantasia Béticu* (1919) for piano.

Grainger, Percy Aldridge (1882–1961). Australian pianist and composer who settled in the United States in 1914. Head of the music department at New York University, he was known for his arrangements of traditional tunes from a variety of sources and for his interpretation of Edvard Grieg's piano music. His choral works include *Marching Song of Democracy* (1917) and *Tribute to Foster* (1930).

Granados, Enrique (1867–1916). Spanish pianist and composer, born in Cuba. Granados founded and directed the Academía Granados (1901) and composed seven operas, orchestral works, chamber music, a collection of *Tonadillas,* and *Goyescas* (1916), based on the paintings of Goya.

Grieg, Edvard (1843–1907). Norwegian composer, conductor, and pianist. Principal works include the overture *I Host* (1866), two suites from *Peer Gynt* (1876, 1888, 1891), *At a Southern Convent Gate* (1871) for chorus, and the 10-volume *Lyric Pieces* for piano.

Janáček, Leoš (1854–1928). Czech composer. Janáček wrote 10 operas, including *Jenufa* (1904); orchestral, choral, and piano works; chamber music; and songs. He published collections of Moravian folk music and a treatise on harmony.

Kodály, Zoltán (1882–1967). Hungarian composer and music educator whose works are distinguished by the influence of native folk music. His best-known works are the suites from *Háry János* (1927) and *Psalmus Hungaricus* (1923). Kodály developed a widely used method of teaching music.

Lasso, Orlando di (Roland de Lassus) (1532–94). Belgian composer. Among his many works are masses, motets, magnificats, and other church music. The complete edition of his nearly 2,000 works consists of 60 volumes.

Liszt, Franz (1811–86). Hungarian composer who spent time in Paris and Rome and is credited with developing the rhapsody as a form of serious music and employing the term *symphonic poem* for a composition. He was an unsurpassed virtuoso pianist and a composer of symphonies, including *Faust* (1857); piano concertos, études, and 19 *Hungarian Rhapsodies* (1839–85); choral pieces; fantasia and fugues for organ; and songs.

Nielsen, Carl (1865–1931). Danish composer of operas, symphonies, string quartets, piano pieces, and songs, including *Hymns amoris* (1896). Nielsen served as director of the Copenhagen Conservatory (1915–27).

Paderewski, Ignace (1860–1941). Polish pianist and composer. One of the most renowned pianists of modern times, in 1919 Paderewski was prime minister of Poland. He composed many piano works, the opera *Manru* (1901), a symphony, a concerto, and songs.

Sibelius, Jean (1865–1957). Finnish composer. Sibelius attempted a national music, as in *En Saga* (1892) and *Lemminkäinen's Homecoming* (1895), based on the Finnish epic *The Kalevala.* Notable works include *The Swan of Tuonela* (1893), *Finlandia* (1900), and *The Oceanides* (1914).

Smetana, Bedřich (1824–84). Czech composer whose nationalist music was based on folk songs and dances, as in the opera *The Bartered Bride* (1866). Smetana wrote his best instrumental works despite deafness, especially *The Moldau,* which is part of *My Country* (1879), and the string quartets *From My Life* (1876).

Villa-Lobos, Heitor (1887–1959). Brazilian composer and educator. His works show the influence of Indian music and Brazilian folk songs; they include five operas, six symphonies, symphonic poems, serenades, choral music, piano solos, and songs.

Wieniawski, Henri (1835–80). Polish violinist and composer. Among Wieniawski's compositions are two concertos and popular pieces, including *Légende.*

MAJOR JAZZ COMPOSERS AND PERFORMERS

Armstrong, Louis "Satchmo" (c. 1890–1971), b. Louisiana. Trumpeter and singer; first internationally known jazz soloist. He introduced the music of New Orleans to the world, inaugurated the style of improvisation, and was the first to record scat singing. His most influential recording may be "West End Blues" (1939), but his most famous is "Hello, Dolly" (1969).

Basie, William "Count" (1904–84), b. New Jersey. Pianist and bandleader. His brand of Kansas City jazz became the classic swing-band style, featuring spare keyboard playing with a precise four-beat rhythm section. He started The Barons of Rhythm in Kansas City, Missouri, in 1935 and then moved to New York in 1936. His hits include "Jumpin' at the Woodside" (1938) and "Stay Cool" (1946).

Beiderbecke, Bix (1903–31), b. Iowa. Cornetist, pianist, and composer. Famous for his solos, he was known as the first great white jazz musician. He advanced simple jazz into a more complex form built around improvisation and extended chords. His improvisations on "Singin' the Blues" (1927) were much admired and imitated.

Carter, Betty (1930–   ), b. Michigan. Vocalist noted for her scat singing, humming, moaning, and extraordinary technique. She performed with the bands of Max Roach, Charlie Parker, Miles Davis, and others from the late 1940s through the late 1950s.

Christian, Charlie (c. 1916–42), b. Texas. A major contributor to the bebop movement, he was also among the first to capitalize on the sound of the electric guitar. He was admired for his innovative use of harmonic inversions, dissonance, and long strings of uninflected eighth notes. Major works include "Seven Come Eleven" (1939), "Gone With What Wind" (1940), and "Breakfast Feud" (1941).

Coleman, Ornette (1930–   ), b. Texas. Saxophonist and composer. He was a major influence on the avant-garde or "free-jazz" movement of the late 1950s and early 1960s, with a revolutionary style of breaking the restrictions of chords, ordinary harmony, bar lines, and tempered scales. Major recordings include "Something Else" (1958), "Congeniality" (1959), and "A Dedication to Poets and Writers" (1962).

Coltrane, John (1926–67), b. North Carolina. Tenor/soprano saxophonist, composer, and bandleader. His explosive style and angular melodic lines have influenced jazz musicians. He is credited with developing polytonality in modern jazz, and his quartet, which performed from 1960 to 1965, ranks among the best. His masterworks include "Giant Steps" (1959) and "A Love Supreme" (1964).

Davis, Miles (1926–91), b. Illinois. Trumpeter, composer, and bandleader. His lyrical and inventive playing made him a trendsetter for more than four decades. A major contributor to the bebop and cool forms of jazz, he pioneered the jazz-rock movement in the 1960s. His influential recordings include "Steamin'" (1956), "Kind of Blue" (1959), and "Bitches Brew" (1969).

Ellington, Edward Kennedy "Duke" (1899–1974), b. Washington, D.C. Pianist, composer, and bandleader. Nominated for a Pulitzer prize, he is considered the most important composer of big-band music. He wrote and arranged many jazz classics, popular songs, and blues or "mood" pieces. "Mood Indigo" (1930), "It Don't Mean a Thing (If It Ain't Got That Swing)" (1932), "Sophisticated Lady" (1933), and "In a Sentimental Mood" (1935) are among his many great recordings.

Evans, Bill (1929–80), b. New Jersey. Pianist, arranger, and composer whose soft harmonies, intricate voicing, and melodic improvising changed the sound of the piano in jazz. He earned national recognition for his playing in "Kind of Blue" (1959) with the Miles Davis Sextet.

Fitzgerald, Ella (1918–96), b. Virginia. Vocalist acclaimed for her pure tone, voice control, improvisation, and interpretation of ballads. Her first hit was "A Tisket, A Tasket" (1938), and she became world famous in 1946 when she sang with the *Jazz at the Philharmonic* concert series.

Gillespie, John Birks "Dizzy" (1917–93), b. South Carolina. Trumpeter and bandleader who pioneered the bebop movement in 1945 along with Charlie Parker. His Latin-influenced sound and virtuosity in upper-register playing are evident in his compositions "Salt Peanuts" (1945) and "A Night in Tunisia" (1946).

Goodman, Benny (1909–86), b. Illinois. Clarinetist and bandleader known as the "Pied Piper of Swing." He played with symphony orchestras and pioneered interracial bands. His best-known recordings include "After You've Gone" (1935) and "Moonglow" (1936).

Hancock, Herbie (1940–   ), b. Illinois. Pianist and composer whose highly individual keyboard style blends blues and bebop. He joined the Miles Davis Quintet in 1963 and helped expand the traditional jazz concept of the rhythm section and its relationship to the soloist. He contributed to the rock-jazz movement of the late 1960s and 1970s with his composition "Maiden Voyage" (1965).

Hawkins, Coleman (1904–69), b. Missouri. His powerful, original style and rich tone made him the dominant tenor saxophonist during the late 1930s and early 1940s. He played with Fletcher Henderson's orchestra (1923–43). His most celebrated recording is "Body and Soul" (1939).

Henderson, Fletcher (c. 1897–1952), b. Georgia. Bandleader, arranger, and trumpeter who pioneered the concept of the big band in the swing era. His best works include "Down South Camp Meeting" (1934), "Wrappin' It Up" (1934), and "King Porter Stomp" (1935).

Hines, Earl "Fatha" (c. 1903–83), b. Pennsylvania. Pianist and bandleader. He is known for his innovative "trumpet-style" single-note solos coupled with powerful rhythm and bass patterns. His best recordings include "A Monday Date" (1928) and "Skip the Gutter" (1928) with Louis Armstrong.

Holiday, Billie "Lady Day" (1915–59), b. Maryland. Vocalist famous for her melancholy improvisations of ballads and popular songs. She was discovered by record producer and critic John Hammond in 1933 and sang with Benny

Goodman, Lester Young, Count Basie, and other great jazz musicians. She developed a large public following with her recordings of "Strange Fruit" (1939) and "Lover Man" (1944).

Joplin, Scott   (1868–1917), b. Texas. Composer and pianist who popularized the early jazz form of ragtime. His composition "The Maple Leaf Rag" (c. 1899) became an instant hit. His works include 33 rags, about two dozen songs, and a ragtime opera.

Lewis, John A.   (1920–   ), b. Illinois. Pianist and composer known for applying classical forms to jazz based on improvisation and carefully worked-out changes of tempo, key, meter, and instrumentation. He was one of the pioneers of cool jazz and founded the Modern Jazz Quartet. His noted works include "Bluesology" (1956) and "Between the Devil and the Deep Blue Sea" (1957).

Miller, Glenn   (1904–44), b. Iowa. Trombonist, arranger, and star bandleader during the big-band swing era. His distinctive sound combined a clarinet and four saxophones. "In the Mood" (1939) and "String of Pearls" (1941) were among his many hit songs.

Mingus, Charlie   (1922–79), b. Arizona. Double bassist, pianist, composer, arranger, and bandleader. He combined gospel and jazz forms to create a funky sound. He was the dominant bassist of the late 1950s and early 1960s. Best compositions include "Goodbye Pork Pie Hat" (1959) and "Better Git It in Your Soul" (1959).

Monk, Thelonious   (1917–82), b. North Carolina. Pianist and composer noted for his spare style, slow tempo, and distinctive phrasing. Monk was a major contributor to bebop. "'Round About Midnight" (1947) and "Criss Cross" (1951) are among his many important compositions.

Morton, Ferdinand "Jelly Roll"   (c. 1890–1941), b. Louisiana. Pianist, composer, and preeminent soloist who recorded about 175 sides and piano rolls between 1923 and 1929. Combining blues, rags, and marches, he is considered the first important jazz composer. His influential works included "The Pearls" (1919), "Wolverine Blues" (1923), "Grandpa's Spells" (1923), and "Smokehouse Blues" (1926).

Parker, Charlie "Bird"   (1920–55), b. Kansas. Alto saxophonist and composer whose virtuosity and inventive melodic lines made him a major influence in bebop. "Groovin' High" (1945) and "Out of Nowhere" (1948) are among his most innovative solos.

Reinhardt, Django   (1910–53), b. Belgium. Considered the most important jazz guitarist. His swing style of playing was characterized by a full sound, strong rhythms, salvos of sixteenth notes, vibrato, and surprising melodic lines. Notable works include "Tiger Rag" (1934) and "Stardust" (1935).

Smith, Bessie   (1894–1937), b. Tennessee. Vocalist considered the greatest of all the classic blues singers. She achieved the height of her fame in the 1920s pioneering jazz-oriented blues. Her best recordings include "Down-hearted Blues" (1923) and "Cold in Hand Blues" (1925).

Tatum, Art   (1910–56), b. Ohio. Pianist known for his dazzling high-speed arpeggios and elaborate runs stretching the length of the keyboard. Tatum was the premier pianist of New York's Swing Street clubs from the 1930s through the 1950s. "Tea for Two" (1923), "Tiger Rag" (1933), and "Stompin' at the Savoy" (1953) are among his many great recordings.

Beethoven dedicated his third symphony, the Eroica, *to Napoleon but later tore it up when Napoleon crowned himself Emperor of France.*

Vaughan, Sarah "Sassy"   (1924–90), b. New Jersey. Vocalist renowned for her operatic power, elegant phrasing, and extraordinarily wide range. She became popular while singing with Billy Eckstine's band in the mid-1940s. "Lover Man" (1945), recorded with Charlie Parker and Dizzy Gillespie, established her reputation.

Waller, Thomas "Fats"   (1904–43), b. New York. Pianist, songwriter, and entertainer. Waller's jazz ragtime style of playing in the 1920s and 1930s made many of his songs jazz standards. His notable works, "Honeysuckle Rose" (1929) and "Ain't

Performance Arts

Misbehavin'" (1929), brought him fame as a satirical songwriter and entertainer.

Williams, Mary Lou (1910–81), b. Georgia. Pianist, arranger, and composer. Known as "the first great female instrumentalist in jazz," she created harmonically innovative arrangements ranging from swing to avant-garde. She arranged scores for the bands of Earl Hines, Benny Goodman, and Duke Ellington. Her most famous composition is "Zodiac Suite" (1945).

Young, Lester "Prez" (1909–59), b. Mississippi. Tenor saxophonist and premier soloist credited with transforming the "hot" jazz of the 1930s into the "cool" jazz of the 1940s and 1950s. His influential recordings include "Shoe Shine Boy" (1936), "Lady Be Good" (1936), and "Lester Leaps In" (1939).

COMMON MUSIC TERMS

a cappella Choral music without accompaniment (literally, "in the church style").

accelerando A direction to gradually increase the tempo.

accent The emphasis given to one tone over another.

accidental A sign used to indicate chromatic alteration; a sharp, double sharp, flat, double flat, or natural prefixed to single notes.

accompaniment Secondary instrument or background vocal added to the principal instrument or soloist.

acoustics The science of sound, which deals with intensity, quality, resonance, pitch, tone, and other qualities of sound.

adagietto A direction to play slightly faster than adagio.

adagio A direction to play slowly; between andante and largo.

adagissimo A direction to play very slowly.

Go to "Music" under "Reference Works for General Information" in chapter 11; "Music Symbols" in chapter 12

ad libitum A direction to interpret, improvise, or omit, according to the player's preference.

affetuoso A direction to play affectionately, with warmth.

agitato A direction to play in an agitated, restless, hurried manner.

air A tune or melody; the French 18th-century term for song; also, an instrumental piece whose melodic style is similar to that of a solo song.

alla breve A direction to play twice as fast as the notation signifies; $^2/_2$ instead of $^4/_4$.

allargando A direction to play slower, louder.

allegretto A direction to play with moderately quick movement; between andante and allegro.

allegro A direction to play quickly, briskly.

allemande A moderately slow dance of German origin.

allentando A direction to slow down.

alto The highest adult male voice, or lowest female voice; also, a tenor violin or viola.

andante A direction to play in moderate tempo; "walking" speed; between allegretto and adagio.

andantino A direction to play in tempo slightly quicker than andante.

animato A direction to play with animation.

answer In a fugue, the second or fourth statement of the subject.

anthem A choral piece for use in church services.

appassionato A direction to play passionately.

appoggiatura An inharmonious note preceding a principal note, marked with a diagonal line through it, of short or long duration.

arabesque A lyrical piece in a fanciful style; a term used first by Schumann and later by Debussy.

aria An extended vocal solo in an opera or oratorio.

arioso A piece of recitative song, but more song-like.

arpeggio   The technique of playing the notes of a chord successively rather than simultaneously.

ascending   Moving upward on a musical scale.

assai   A direction to play very quickly.

a tempo   A direction to play in time, following a deviation from the regular tempo.

atonal   Having no recognized tonal center or key.

aubade   Morning music, in contrast to *serenade,* or evening music.

augmentation   Presentation of a theme in notes of doubled value; the opposite of *diminution.*

auxiliary note   Usually, a grace note one degree above or below a principal note.

ballad   A narrative song, originally accompanied by dancing; also, an instrumental piece in ballad style.

bar line   A line drawn vertically across the staff to divide into measures.

baritone   The male voice between bass and tenor; also, any musical instrument intermediary between bass and tenor.

baroque   A term signifying the music composed between 1600 and 1750, characterized by homophonic texture with the uppermost part carrying the melody over the bass line; a search for affective expression; the development of new styles for various functions and new techniques, such as dissonance and tonality.

bass   The lowest male voice, or lowest part in a musical composition; also, short for the double bass or bass tuba.

beat   A unit of rhythm or time in a composition as indicated by the conductor's gesture; each unit of a measure with respect to accent.

bebop (bop)   One of the principal styles of jazz developed in the early 1940s, characterized by complicated melody lines and chord patterns played at exceptional speed.

bel canto   The Italian vocal techniques of the 18th century with an emphasis on beauty of sound and brilliance of performance rather than dramatic expression or romantic emotion.

berceuse   A cradle song.

binary   Musical form in which both main sections are repeated and where the first section characteristically is tonally not self-contained but demands a resolution in the second part (AB).

bolero   A Spanish dance accompanied by castanets.

bowing   A method of using the bow on stringed instruments as indicated by signs for down bow (∏) or up bow (V).

brace   A vertical line used to join two or more staves.

If handled carefully, a compact disk may last around 150 years.

buffa   In the comic style.

buffo   The singer of a comic part.

cadence   A progression of chords that seems to move to a harmonic close or point of rest.

cadenza   An ornamental passage near the end of a composition.

canon   A contrapuntal composition in which the same melody is imitated by one or more voices overlapping in time in the same or related key.

cantata   A vocal form from the baroque period that consists of arias, recitatives, duets, and choruses. The term now refers to secular or sacred choral works accompanied by orchestra, similar to the oratorio but shorter.

canticle   Religious song or chant.

canzona   A form of Italian lyric poetry corresponding to the ode, set to music in a style similar to a madrigal, though simpler; also, an instrumental piece in the style of a song.

canzonet   A vocal piece in a light vein, somewhat like a dance song, usually with instrumental accompaniment; a short instrumental piece.

capriccio   A short composition in free form.

castrato   A male singer castrated as a boy to maintain a soprano or alto voice range.

catch   A humorous round for three or more voices.

chaconne   A musical form based on a reiterated harmonic pattern.

chamber music   Instrumental compositions performed by a small ensemble, with one player for each part.

chanson   A song for solo voice or vocal ensemble; also, an instrumental piece of vocal character.

chant   A sacred song, usually monophonic and in free rhythm and used in accordance with prescribed ritual. The chant is the oldest form of choral music.

chorale   A psalm or hymn tune sung in church; also, a harmonization of a chorale melody.

chord   The combination of three or more tones played at once. A *diatonic chord* uses only notes proper to the key. A *triad* is a chord of three notes in which the lowest is combined with the third and fifth above it. A *common chord* is a triad in root position. A *dominant chord* is founded on the dominant of the key. An *inverted chord* uses a tone other than the root as its lowest tone.

chromatic scale   Consecutive series of notes that employ only a progression of semitones.

classical   Term for the period and style of music from about 1700 to about 1830, characterized by regular, short, clearly articulated phrases combined with symmetrical patterns and textures. Haydn, Mozart, and Beethoven are its chief representatives.

clef   A character that indicates the pitch of a particular line on a staff.

coda   A passage that brings a piece or movement to a conclusion.

comma   The small difference in pitch that occurs in the same note when obtained through different combinations of octaves, perfect fifths, and pure thirds.

common time   Four-four (⁴/₄) time—that is, four quarter notes to a measure.

compound interval   An interval that extends beyond an octave.

compound time   Time in which each beat of the bar is divisible into three, in contrast to *simple time,* in which each is divisible into two.

concertmaster   The leader of the first violins, next in rank to the conductor.

concerto   A composition for solo instrument, usually with orchestral accompaniment.

concerto grosso   A style of composition developed during the Baroque period (1600–1750) in which two groups of musicians, one large and one small, alternate in an echo effect.

concert pitch   Pitch at which the piano and other nontransposing instruments play.

console   The part of the organ from which the player controls the instrument—the keyboard, pedals, and so on—as distinguished from the pipes.

consonance   Combination of pitches that produce little tension and are generally considered pleasing; opposite of dissonance.

consort   A chamber ensemble; also, music written for such a group.

con spirito   A direction to play in a lively manner.

continuo   The bass, or lowest, line of a composition.

contralto   The range of a low female voice; alto.

cool   Style of modern jazz pioneered in the 1950s and 1960s, characterized by understated and emotionally subdued arrangements played by small ensembles.

counterpoint   Music consisting of two or more melodic lines played simultaneously.

countersubject   The contrasting motif to the subject of a fugue.

countertenor   The male alto voice.

couplet   Two lines having the same meter.

courante   A lively dance in triple time; also, the second part of a suite.

crescendo   A direction to increase the volume.

cut time   Another term for $^2/_2$ meter.

da capo   A direction to repeat from the beginning.

decrescendo   A direction to decrease the volume.

descant   A different melody sung in a higher pitch and simultaneously with the main melodic line. It is the earliest form of polyphony, with contrasting motions between the parts.

The first composer to have one of his works performed in space was Dmitri Shostakovich.

descending   Moving downward on a musical scale.

development   The extension of a theme through contrapuntal elaboration, modulation, rhythmical variation, etc.

diatonic   Referring to minor and major scales that employ a particular combination of whole tones and half tones; the harmony and melodies that use only the pitches of a particular diatonic scale.

diminished chord   A chord in which the highest and lowest tones form a diminished interval.

diminished interval   A perfect or minor interval reduced by a semitone.

diminuendo   Diminishing; getting softer.

diminution   The breaking up of the notes in a melody into quick figures, as is done in variations.

dissonance   A combination of tones that are unresolved, jarring.

divertimento   An 18th-century form of instrumental chamber music having several short movements.

divertissement   A fantasia on well-known tunes.

divisi   In orchestral music, an indication that a group of players who play the same parts are to play two or more separate parts.

do   The first tone of a diatonic scale.

dolce   A direction to play softly, sweetly.

dolente, doloroso   Sorrowful.

dominant   The fifth tone of the major or minor diatonic scale.

dominant chord   A chord with the fifth pitch of a scale as its root.

doppio movimento   Twice as fast.

Dorian mode   A church mode represented on the white keys of a keyboard instrument by an ascending scale from D to D.

dot   Written after a note, an indication of the prolongation of its length by one-half; the double dot indicates by three-fourths. Above or below the note, the dot indicates staccato.

double stop   A chord of two notes played on a bowed string instrument, obtaining a two-part harmony.

doxology   In Christian worship, a hymn of praise to God.

duet   A composition for two players or two voices, with or without accompaniment.

duple   Two units to the measure, such as $^2/_2$, $^2/_4$, or $^2/_8$.

duration   The length of a tone.

dynamics   Varying and contrasting degrees of intensitiy or loudness.

eighth   A note whose value is one-eighth of a whole note.

enharmonic   Tones that have the same pitch when played on tempered instruments but that are different in notation, such as C (♯) and D (♭).

episode   The section of a fugue in which the main melody is not heard.

estinto   So soft that it can hardly be heard.

étude   A study; an exercise in technique.

exposition   The statement of the musical material on which a movement is based.

expression marks   Marks used to help the interpretation of a work; they are concerned with dynamics, tempo, and mood, and indicate forte, allegro, con spirito, etc.

fa   The fourth note of a diatonic scale.

falsetto   The false voice; an adult male voice in the alto and treble range.

fantasia   A piece in which the composition follows the fancy rather than any conventional form; of an improvisational character.

fermata   A symbol ($\frown$) placed over the note to show that it is to be played longer than its normal duration.

fifth   The interval between the tonic and the fifth tone above it. In the key of C major, C to G is a fifth.

figuration   The extended use of a particular melodic or harmonic figure; the ornamental treatment of a passage.

finale   The last movement of a work of several movements—for example, the conclusion of a concerto or the last act of an opera.

flat   A sign ($\flat$) indicating that the pitch is to be lowered by one semitone.

form   The pattern of design of a work; its basic elements are repetition, variation, and contrast in the areas of harmony, rhythm, and tone.

forte   A direction to play loudly.

fortissimo   A direction to play very loudly.

forza   A direction to play with force.

forzando   Strongly accenting.

fourth   The interval between the tonic and the fourth diatonic tone above it; in the key of C major, C to F is a fourth.

fugue   A composition in which three or more voices enter at different times and imitate the main melody in different ways according to a set pattern.

fundamental   Also called the tonic; the lowest tone of a chord when the chord is founded on that tone; also, the lowest note in the harmonic series.

funk (funky)   Style of African American music popular in the mid-1960s that combines soul and jazz. It is characterized by complex interlocking syncopated rhythm patterns in duple meter.

galop   A quick dance in $^2/_4$ time popular in the 19th century.

giocoso   Jocose; merry.

glee   A simple part song, generally for male voices.

glissando   The execution of rapid scales by sliding the finger rapidly across keys or strings.

grace note   An ornamental note not essential to the melody and not counted as part of the measure.

grandezza   Grandeur.

grave   A direction to play slowly, solemnly.

grazioso   A direction to play gracefully.

Gregorian chant   A style of church music for unaccompanied voices, without definite rhythm, in one of the eight church modes.

half note   A note having half the time value of a whole note and twice that of a quarter note.

harmonic   A tone whose frequency is an integral multiple of a single frequency known as the fundamental tone.

harmony   The simultaneously sounded pitches, as in chords.

homophonic   Single-voiced; music in which one melody or part is supported by chords; the opposite of *polyphonic.*

imitation   The use of the same or similar melodic material in different voices successively.

impresario   The conductor or manager of an opera or concert company.

impromptu   An improvised composition without fixed form.

incidental music   Music for performance during the action of a play or film.

interlude   A short piece played between the acts of a drama; the verses of a song, parts of a church service, or sections of a cantata.

intermezzo   A play with music performed between the acts of an opera or drama that gave rise to opera buffa; an interlude; a short movement in a symphony.

interval   The distance in pitch between two notes, harmonic if they are played together, melodic if they are played in succession. *Perfect interval:* the prime, fourth, fifth, and octave. *Major interval:* the second, third, sixth, and seventh of the major scale. *Minor interval:* a chromatic half step smaller than a major interval. *Augmented interval:* a chromatic half step larger than perfect and major. *Diminished interval:* A chromatic half step smaller than perfect and minor.

intonation   The degree of accuracy with which pitches are produced.

inversion   The transposition of the lower and upper notes of an interval. In an inverted chord, the lowest tone is not its root; an inverted melody is one in which its intervals are inverted.

Ionian mode   A mode of church music represented on the white keys of a keyboard by an ascending scale from C to C.

key   The main pitch or tonal center to which all of the composition's pitches are related.

key signature   Sharps or flats placed at the beginning of a composition to indicate its key.

la   The sixth tone of a diatonic scale.

largo   A direction to play broadly, more slowly than adagio but not as slowly as grave.

leading tone   The seventh degree or tone of the scale; a semitone below the tonic.

legato   A direction to play smoothly and continuously.

lento   A direction to play slowly, but not as slowly as largo.

libretto   The text of an opera or oratorio.

litany   A song of invocation to God.

madrigal   An unaccompanied song for three or more voices using counterpoint and imitation.

maestoso   A direction to play in a majestic, stately manner.

magnificat   Canticle of the Virgin Mary sung as part of the evening service in Reformed churches and at vespers in the Catholic church.

major   Applied to chords, intervals, scales, and keys; a standard in contrast to diminished, augmented, or minor.

major scale   A diatonic scale in which the half steps occur between the third and fourth and the seventh and eighth tones.

march   A composition usually in duple meter and in simple, strongly marked rhythms and regular phrases for a procession or parade.

mass   A musical setting of the liturgy of the Eucharist.

mazurka   A polkalike Polish folk dance in triple time with strong accents on the normally weak second and third beats.

measure   A unit of rhythm or musical time, indicated by bar lines.

Mozart's full name was Johannes Chrysostomus Wolfangus Thiophilus Mozart, but he is often known as "Amadeus" which means "beloved of God."

mediant   The third tone of a diatonic scale.

melody   A rhythmically organized succession of single tones that form a musical idea.

mensural music   A medieval term for music with definite note values, as distinguished from plainsong.

meter   A scheme of accents; a grouping of beats into units of measure.

mezzo   Medium, half; moderate.

mezzo-forte   A direction to play moderately loudly.

mezzo-soprano   The female voice between soprano and alto.

Performance Arts

mi   The third tone in the diatonic scale.

middle C   The pitch represented by the first ledger line below the treble clef or the first above the bass clef.

minor   Intervals, scales, keys, and chords having intervals a semitone less than major.

minor scale   A diatonic scale having a minor third between the first and third tones and having several forms with different intervals above the fifth.

minuet   A slow, graceful dance of French origin in triple time; a composition in this rhythm.

mode   A selection of tones arranged in a scale that forms the basic tonal substance of a composition.

modulation   The change from one key to another through a succession of chords.

molto   Very.

monophony   Music consisting of a single melodic line without additional parts or accompaniment, as in plainsong or folk song.

mordent   An ornament played by quickly alternating a note with the note below it.

morendo   A fading away.

motet   An unaccompanied vocal composition with sacred lyrics from the 13th century.

motif   A short, significant melodic and/or rhythmic figure that recurs throughout a composition or section as a unifying element.

motion   The pattern of changing pitch levels in a melody.

natural   A musical symbol indicating the removal of a sharp or flat from a particular pitch.

nocturne   A musical composition in the romantic style, usually for piano, with an expressive melody over a broken-chord accompaniment.

note   A symbol used to express the relative time value of tones.

obbligato   An added melody, usually played by a solo instrument to enhance a vocal line.

octave   The distance between two pitches having the same name and located 12 half steps apart.

octet   A composition of eight parts or voices; also, the group of its performers.

opera   A drama set to music, in which words are sung in the form of recitatives, arias, and ensembles, usually accompanied by orchestra and generally performed with sets and costumes.

operetta   A light opera, usually humorous, with spoken dialogue, dances, and, almost unfailingly, a happy ending.

opus   A numbered musical work or composition.

oratorio   A musical setting of scriptural text set without costumes, scenery, or action.

orchestra   A large group of musicians who play together on various musical instruments, including strings, woodwinds, brass, and percussion.

overture   An introduction to a large composition such as an opera or oratorio; however, it can be independent or the predecessor of a symphonic poem.

parallel motion   The relative changes of pitches in two or more simultaneous voice-parts when the intervals separating them remain the same.

part   In orchestral or chamber music, the music or melodic line for a particular series of notes for voice or instrument.

partita   A set of related instrumental pieces; a series of variations or a suite.

part song   A 19th-century choral composition in the homophonic style in which the top part is the only carrier of the melody.

passion music   A musical setting for the story of the suffering and death of Christ.

pasticcio   An operatic medley of the 18th century made up of contributions of two or more composers.

pastorale   A musical composition suggestive of rural life.

pentatonic scale   A five-toned scale without semitones; the diatonic scale with fourth and seventh tones omitted.

phrase   A complete musical idea.

pianissimo   A direction to play very softly.

piano   A direction to play softly.

piano quartet   A term usually applied to quartets for piano, violin, viola, and cello.

piano quintet   A combination of piano with string quartet.

pitch   The perceived highness or lowness of a sound.

pizzicato   For violins and other bowed instruments, a direction that the string is to be picked with the finger.

plainsong   A nonmetrical chant in one of the church modes.

poco   Little.

polka   A lively dance in ²/₄ time that originated in Bohemia c. 1830.

polonaise   A Polish dance in ³/₄ time adopted as a musical form by Chopin.

polyphony   Contrapuntal music; a style in which two or more melodies are interwoven; the opposite of *homophony.*

prelude   An introductory movement complete in itself, as opposed to an introduction, which leads directly into the principal section; a short piano piece in one movement.

Roger Miller was inspired to write the classic song "King of the Road" when he saw a sign just west of Chicago that said, "Trailers for Sale or Rent."

program music   Music intended to depict a story or image.

progression   *Melodic:* the passage from tone to tone; *harmonic:* the passage from chord to chord.

quartet   A composition of four parts or voices; also, the performers of a four-part composition.

quintet   A composition of five voices or instruments; also, the performers of a five-part composition.

ragtime   Style of American music popular from about 1890 to the beginning of World War I, characterized by syncopated melodies set against a rhythmically strong bass.

re   The second tone of a diatonic scale.

recitative   A style of singing resembling dramatic speech.

refrain   Repeated lines that occur at the end of each stanza of a song or poem.

register   The range of a voice or instrument; a portion of the range of an instrument, as in upper register or lower register.

requiem   A mass for the dead; also, a musical setting for such a mass.

resolution   The progression from a dissonant tone or harmony to one that is consonant.

rest   A symbol indicating pause or silence.

rinforzando   A sudden accent on a single note or chord.

ritardando   A direction to slow the tempo gradually.

ritenuto   Immediate reduction in tempo.

romance   A short vocal or instrumental composition of a romantic character without fixed form.

rondo   A form of instrumental composition with a refrain that occurs at least three times in its original key between contrasting couplets.

root   The tonic of a triad or chord; the lowest tone, unless the chord is inverted.

round   A canon for three or more voices; the common name for a circle canon in which each singer returns from the conclusion of the melody to its beginning, repeating it.

scale   A series of tones arranged according to rising pitches.

Performance Arts

scat A technique of jazz singing that uses nonsense syllables for improvising vocal solos.

scherzo A playful, humorous instrumental composition, usually in a rapid ³/₄ meter.

second The interval between the tonic and the second tone of a diatonic scale; in the key of C major, C to D is a second.

semitone One-half of a whole tone.

septet A composition for seven voices or instruments.

sequence Repetition of a short musical phrase at a different pitch.

serenade An impromptu or unsolicited vocal or instrumental performance, often outdoors; an instrumental composition in several movements for a small group, between the symphony and the suite.

seventh The interval between the tonic and the seventh tone of a diatonic scale; in the key of C major, C to B is a seventh.

sharp A sign (♯) indicating that the pitch is to be raised by a half step.

si (or **ti**) The seventh tone in a diatonic scale.

signature A symbol placed on the staff at the beginning of a piece that shows the key and the meter.

sixth The interval between the tonic and the sixth tone of a diatonic scale; in the key of C major, C to A is a sixth.

slur A curved line over a series of notes that are to be played smoothly and continuously.

sol The fifth tone of a diatonic scale.

solo A piece performed either alone or with accompaniment.

sonata An instrumental composition of three or four independent movements varying in mood, character, and tempo.

sonatina A short, simple sonata.

soprano The highest female or boy's voice; the treble.

sostenuto Sustaining the tone to or beyond the nominal value.

sotto voce In a low voice.

staccato Direction to play notes in a distinct, detached manner.

staff The five horizontal lines on and between which notes are written.

stretto Compressed; in a fugue, the overlapping of subject and answer.

subdominant The dominant below; the fourth tone of the diatonic scale, in the same relation to the key note from below as the dominant is from above.

subito Suddenly.

subject A melody or melody fragment that, because of its character, design, position, or treatment, is used in the basic musical form of a composition.

submediant The sixth tone of a diatonic scale.

subtonic The seventh tone of a diatonic scale; leading tone.

suite An instrumental composition consisting of a series of movements or distinct compositions; originally, a cycle of dance tunes.

supertonic The second tone of a diatonic scale.

symphonic poem Originated by Franz Liszt, a large narrative orchestral work in one movement based on a nonmusical idea, either poetic or realistic.

symphony A sonata for orchestra, usually in four contrasting movements.

syncopation A rhythmic pattern that places emphasis on beats that are not normally accented, thus creating a catchy, lilting sound.

tempo The speed at which a composition is played.

tenor The highest natural adult male voice; also, the instrument of corresponding range.

ternary form The form of a composition in three parts with repetition following one contrast (ABA).

texture The way in which melody and harmony are combined to create layers of sound.

theme and variation A musical form in which the theme is repeated and varied.

third The interval between the tonic and the third tone of a diatonic scale; in the key of C major, C to E is a third.

ti (or **si**) The seventh tone in a diatonic scale.

tie A curved line that combines the duration of two notes of the same pitch.

time Used synonymously with measure or rhythm.

time signature The meter of a composition, shown by two numbers, one above the other; the lower tells the kind of note that represents one beat; the upper tells the number of these notes that make up a measure.

toccata A composition popular in the 16th century, for organ or harpsichord, and resembling the capriccio.

tonal center The tonic pitch around which a composition or scale is centered.

tone A sound of definite duration and pitch; a note.

tone cluster A group of notes played simultaneously with forearm, elbow, and fist in a method introduced by Henry Cowell.

tonic The first tone of a diatonic scale; also called fundamental. In the key of C major, C is the tonic.

transposition The rewriting or playing of a composition in a key other than the original one.

treble clef G clef; indicates that the pitch G is located on the second line above middle C.

tremolo Rapid repetition of a note to resemble trembling.

triad A chord composed of a fundamental tone and the third and fifth above it.

trio A composition for three parts or voices; the second part of a minuet or march.

triplet A group of three notes played in the time value of two.

triple time Time in which there are three beats to a measure.

Houseflies and car horns have something in common. Most American car horns beep in the key of F. The housefly buzzes in the key of F.

turn An embellishment consisting of a group of four or five notes that turn around the principal note.

tutti Indications for passages for the whole orchestra as distinguished from those of the soloist.

twelve-tone music A method of composition based on a chromatic scale of 12, rather than 8, tones, developed by Arnold Schoenberg.

unison Equal pitch; performance of the same part by all voices.

variation Development of a theme through a variety of forms; differences in rhythm, key, harmony, etc.

vivace A direction to play in a lively manner.

voice Vocal or instrumental part of a composition.

waltz A dance in triple time performed by couples, which reached its peak of popularity during the 19th century; also, music in this rhythm.

whole note The longest note in common use.

whole tone An interval of a major second; the interval of two semitones.

Performance Arts

BASIC POSITIONS FOR BALLET

FEET

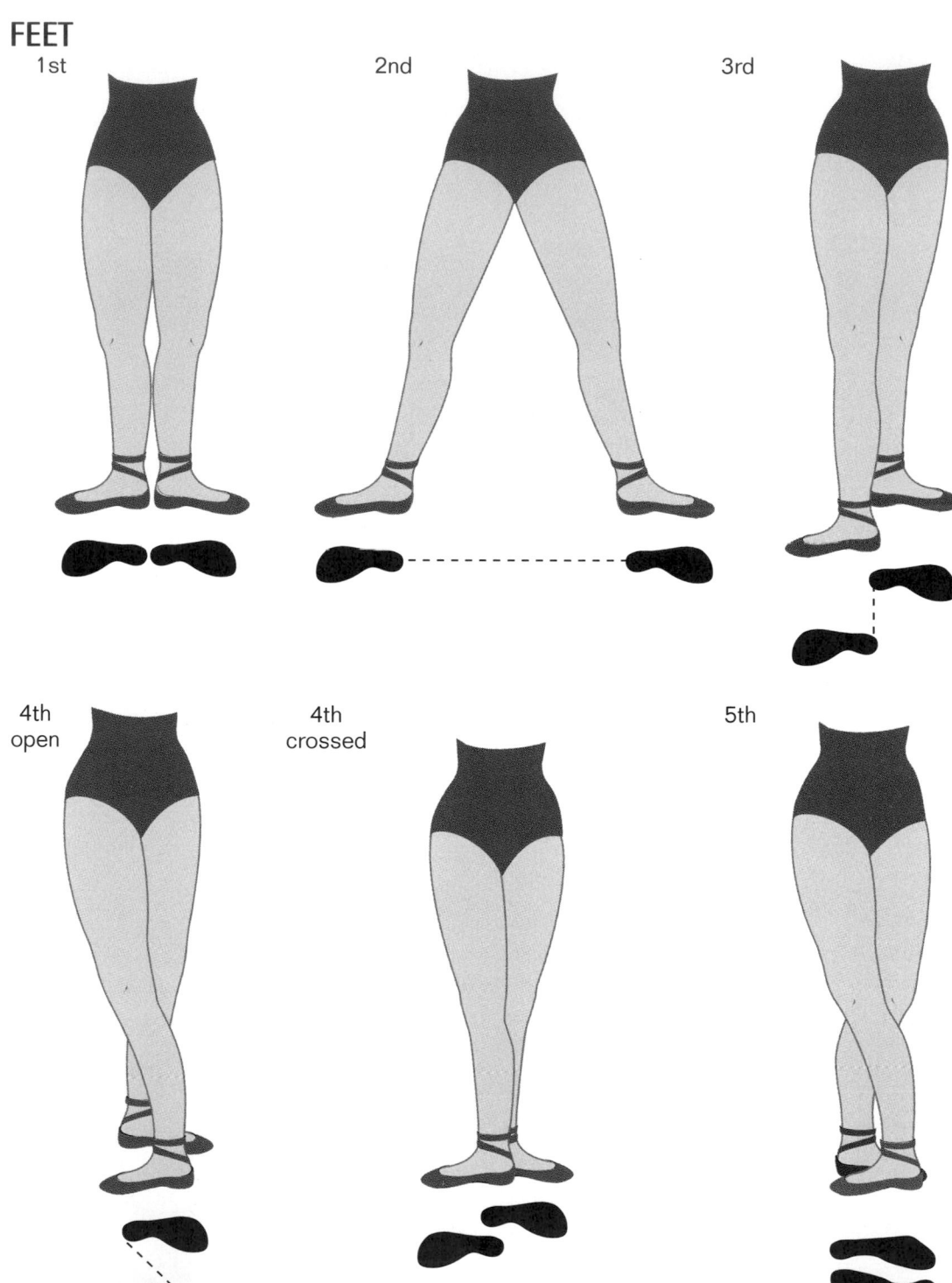

1st

2nd

3rd

4th open

4th crossed

5th

ARMS

1st

2nd

2nd demi-seconde
(half-second)

3rd

4th en haur
(above)

4th en avant
(in front)

5th
en hour
(above)

5th
en avant
(in front)

5th
en bas
(low)

MAJOR DANCERS AND CHOREOGRAPHERS

AMERICAN

Ailey, Alvin (1931–89). Choreographer noted for blending African, modern, and jazz elements, as seen in works such as *Revelations* (1960) and *Cry* (1971). His Alvin Ailey American Dance Theater was formed in 1958.

Arpino, Gerald (1928–   ). Choreographer. Principal choreographer of the Joffrey Ballet, he became its artistic director in 1988. His sometimes trendy, energetic works include *Viva Vivaldi!* (1965) and *Trinity* (1970).

Astaire, Fred (1899–1987). Actor and dancer in musical comedies on Broadway, such as *The Band Wagon,* and films, including *Top Hat* (1935) and *Shall We Dance?* (1937). Having started in vaudeville with his sister, Adele, Astaire later costarred with Judy Garland, Rita Hayworth, and Ginger Rogers. He was distinguished by his original and graceful tap dancing.

Balanchine, George (1904–83). Russian-born American choreographer. Balanchine worked with Diaghilev's Ballets Russes (1924–29) and then came to America, founding the School of American Ballet in 1934. The New York City Ballet was created in 1948, with Balanchine as artistic director. He was an avatar of neoclassicism and the plotless ballet. Some of his major works, such as *Apollo* (1928) and *Agon* (1957), use the music of Stravinsky; other important works include *Serenade* (1934) and *Jewels* (1967).

Bujones, Fernando (1955–   ). One of the few American dancers to base his career primarily on classical ballets, Bujones starred with the American Ballet Theater from 1975 to 1985 and then embarked on a career as a guest artist and choreographer. He is best known for his performances in *Don Quixote, La Bayadère, Swan Lake, Giselle,* and *La Sylphide.*

Castle, Vernon (1887–1918) and **Irene** (1893–1969). Exhibition ballroom dancers whose elegance and style contributed to the spread of ballroom dancing before World War I. They created the Castle Walk and popularized the tango and other dances.

Cunningham, Merce (1919–   ). Choreographer. He danced with Martha Graham's company, forming his own troupe in 1953, collaborating often with John Cage. His avant-garde and abstract works use isolated movements and the random ordering of dance movements. His works include *Summerspace* (1958) and the consecutively numbered *Events* (begun in 1964).

d'Amboise, Jacques (1934–   ). Dancer and leading interpreter of the works of Balanchine during his years with the New York City Ballet (1949–84). He founded the National Dance Institute, which brings dance to New York City schoolchildren.

de Mille, Agnes (1909–93). Choreographer. De Mille created ballets rooted in American folklore, such as *Rodeo* (1942) and *Fall River Legend* (1948). She also choreographed musicals for Broadway, including *Oklahoma!* (1943), and wrote *Dance to the Piper* (1952) and other books on dance.

Duncan, Isadora (1877–1927). Dancer; one of the first figures in modern dance. Turning to ancient Greece for inspiration, she rejected the rigid system of ballet and created an expressive form of dance, which she performed dressed in a flowing tunic. Her works include *Marseillaise* (1915) and *Marche Slave* (1917).

Dunham, Katherine (1912–   ). Choreographer and teacher. Through such works as the *Tropical Revues,* she was one of the first to bring African and Caribbean dance to the American stage. She also choreographed *Cabin in the Sky* (1940) for Broadway.

Farrell, Suzanne (1945–   ). Dancer with the New York City Ballet (1961–69, 1975–89) and Ballets of the 20th Century (1970–75). One of the leading interpreters of the works of Balanchine, Farrell created important roles in such ballets as *Don Quixote* (1965).

Feld, Eliot (1943–   ). Choreographer. He joined the American Ballet Theater in 1963, choreographing his first works, *Harbinger* and *At Midnight* (both 1967), there. In 1968, he formed the American Ballet company; and in 1974, the Feld Ballet.

Graham, Martha (1894–1991). Choreographer. A leader of modern dance, she created a rigorous technique, which includes the contraction, a dramatic percussive movement based on the body's movement during intake and release of breath. Her works such as *Appalachian Spring* (1944) explore American roots; others, such as *Night Journey* (1947) and *Clytemnestra* (1958), draw on Greek mythology, exploring the psychology and passions of their protagonists.

Gregory, Cynthia (1946–). Dancer. Noted for her virtuoso technique and majestic presence, she joined the San Francisco Ballet in 1961 and American Ballet Theater in 1965, where she was a principal dancer until 1991.

Holm, Hanya (1898–1992). German-born choreographer and teacher. A protégée of Mary Wigman, she started choreographing her own modern dance works in America, including *Trend* (1937). She also choreographed *Kiss Me Kate* (1948) and *My Fair Lady* (1956) for Broadway.

Horton, Lester (1906–53). Dancer, choreographer, and teacher. A leader in modern dance and influenced by Native American dance, he formed the Lester Horton Dancers in 1934. Among his notable students was Alvin Ailey.

Humphrey, Doris (1895–1958). A dancer with Denishawn, she left in 1927 to start a company with Charles Weidman. Her choreography is based on the principle of fall and recovery, which caters to the range of movement from balance to unbalance. Her works include *The Shakers* (1930) and *With My Red Fires* (1936).

Jamison, Judith (1944–). Jamison's career has been identified with the Alvin Ailey American Dance Theater, which she joined in 1965. She has starred in numerous Ailey ballets, including *Cry, Maskela Language, Choral Dances,* and *Revelations.*

Joffrey, Robert (1930–88). Choreographer. He formed his first company in 1954, and in 1956 he founded what became the Robert Joffrey Ballet. Joffrey's works include *Pas de Déesses* (1954) and *Astarte* (1967).

Jones, Bill T. (1952–). The recipient of a MacArthur Fellowship in 1993, Jones is a postmodernist who performs only in his own works and those of his collaborators. These include *Negroes for Sale* (1972), *Stories, Steps, and Stomps* (1978), and *War Between the States* (1993).

Kelly, Gene (1912–96). Actor, dancer, choreographer. In films such as *An American in Paris* (1952) and *Invitation to the Dance* (1956), he tried to make the choreography integral to the story and explored cinematic techniques for filming dance.

Kirkland, Gelsey (1953–). Kirkland achieved stardom as a principal dancer with both the New York City Ballet and the American Ballet Theater. She is best known for partnering Mikhail Baryshnikov in *Hamlet Connotations, Awakening,* and *Theme and Variations.*

Kirstein, Lincoln (1907–96). A promoter of American ballet, he brought George Balanchine to America and cofounded with him the School of American Ballet. He was general director of the New York City Ballet (1948–89) and wrote *Dance: A Short History of Classic Theatrical Dancing* (1935) and other books.

Limón, Jose (1908–72). Born in Mexico, Limón is regarded as the most electrifying performer in modern dance history. He performed with the Humphrey/Weidman Group from 1930 until 1945, when he founded the Jose Limón Dance Company.

Martins, Peter (1946–). Born in Denmark, he first danced with the Royal Danish Ballet (1965–1969). Martins then joined the New York City Ballet in 1970, becoming co–ballet master in chief in 1983 and ballet master in chief in 1990. Among his works, which follow in George Balanchine's neoclassical tradition, are *Calcium Night Light* (1977), *Eight Easy Pieces* (1979), *Ecstatic Orange* (1987), and *Jazz* (1993).

Mitchell, Arthur (1934–). Dancer with the New York City Ballet from 1955. In 1968, he founded the Dance Theater of Harlem, the first black classical dance company.

Nikolais, Alwin (1912–1993). Choreographer and founder of the Nikolais Dance Theater. His

Performance Arts

works, such as *Kaleidoscope* (1956), are theatrical productions in which dance, lighting, and sound play equal roles, forming abstract yet evocative patterns.

Robbins, Jerome (1918–   ). Dancer and choreographer for the Ballet Theater (1941–44), where he choreographed *Fancy Free* (1944), and the New York City Ballet, where he was associate artistic director (1949–56) and later codirector (1983–90). His ballets combine the classical idiom with influences from jazz, modern, and social dance. Among his important works are *Goldberg Variations* (1971) and *Dances at a Gathering* (1969). His choreography for Broadway includes *West Side Story* (1957) and *Fiddler on the Roof* (1964).

Robinson, Bill (Bojangles) (1878–1949). Tap dancer who brought a new lightness to tap. Gaining renown with his appearance in the revue *Blackbirds* in 1928, he appeared in movies, including *The Little Colonel* with Shirley Temple.

St. Denis, Ruth (1879–1968). Dancer. Inspired by the Orient, her dances, such as *Radha* (1904) and *The Cobras* (1906), were both exotic and spiritual. In 1915, St. Denis founded Denishawn—the first school of modern dance—with her husband, Ted Shawn.

Shawn, Ted (1891–1972). Founder of Denishawn with Ruth St. Denis. In the 1930s, he started Men Dancers; with works such as *The Kinetic Molpai* (1935), he focused attention on male dancing. Shawn also founded the Jacob's Pillow Dance Festival.

Tallchief, Maria (1925–   ). Dancer with the Ballet Russe de Monte Carlo (1942–47) and the New York City Ballet (1948–1965). She founded the Chicago City Ballet and later was artistic director of the Lyric Opera of Chicago Ballet.

Taylor, Paul (1930–   ). Choreographer. He formed his own company in 1954, and his imaginative modern dance works are often characterized by their humor. His works include *Arden Court* (1981) and *Company B* (1991).

Tetley, Glen (1926–   ). At various times in his career, Tetley has danced and choreographed for Martha Graham, Jerome Robbins, and the American Ballet Theater. Among his best-known works are *Pierrot Lunaire* (1962), *Embrace Tiger and Return to Mountain* (1968), and *Sphinx* (1977).

Tharp, Twyla (1942–   ). Choreographer of idiosyncratic works that use ballet idiom to novel effect. She had her own modern dance company (1965–88) and then served as artistic associate with the American Ballet Theater (1988–91). Her works include *Deuce Coupe* (1973) and *Push Comes to Shove* (1976). She also choreographed the films *Hair* (1979) and *Amadeus* (1984) and directed *Singing in the Rain* (1985) on Broadway.

Villella, Edward (1936–   ). Dancer. As a member of the New York City Ballet (1957–79), he was noted for his virile dancing. He has been artistic director of the Miami City Ballet since 1985.

Weidman, Charles (1901–75). Dancer and choreographer. After dancing with Denishawn, he founded a company with Doris Humphrey in 1927 and later began his own company. His works, known for their humor, include *Flickers* and *And Daddy Was a Fireman*.

BRITISH

Ashton, Sir Frederick (1904–88). A pioneer of British ballet, he was chief choreographer of the Sadler's Wells (now Royal) Ballet from 1935, and its director from 1963 to 1970. His works, noted for their lyrical classicism, include *Symphonic Variations* (1946), *Les Patineurs* (1937), and *Ondine* (1958).

Dolin, Anton (1904–83). English dancer with Diaghilev's Ballets Russes (1924–29) and Ballet Theater. One of Britain's first danseurs nobles, in 1949 he founded the London Festival Ballet with Alicia Markova and served as artistic director.

Fonteyn, Dame Margot (1919–91). English dancer and prima ballerina assoluta of the Royal Ballet, which she joined in 1934 when it was the Vic Wells Ballet. Known for her musicality and refinement, she was the partner of Rudolf Nureyev after 1962; her major roles include Aurora in *Sleeping Beauty* and Juliet in *Romeo and Juliet.*

MacMillan, Kenneth (1929–92). The creator of more than 60 ballets, MacMillan was a bold innovator who expanded the dramatic and intellectual horizons of the dance, often grappling with social, psychological, and political themes. His masterworks include *The Burrow* (1958), *The Invitation* (1960), *Requiem* (1976), *Isadora* (1981), and *Valley of Shadows* (1983).

Markova, Dame Alicia (1910–   ). English dancer with the Ballets Russes (1925–29), Ballet Theater (1941–45), and other companies. Markova was one of the leading interpreters of *Giselle* and the first British ballerina of international renown.

Rambert, Dame Marie (1888–1982). Polish-born dancer, teacher, and ballet director. She advised Nijinsky on rhythm when he was choreographing *Le Sacre du printemps* and later became one of the pioneers of modern British ballet, founding her Ballet Rambert in 1935.

Tudor, Antony (1908–87). English choreographer of ballets of psychological drama. He was associated with the American Ballet Theater (1939–49), then known as Ballet Theater, and later served as associate artistic director (1974–80). Among the ballets that exemplify his use of gesture to express character are *Lilac Garden* (1936) and *Pillar of Fire* (1942).

Valois, Dame Ninette de (1898–   ). A founder of modern British ballet. After dancing with the Ballets Russes (1923–26), she founded a school in London; and in 1931, a company, the Vic Wells Ballet, which became the Sadler's Wells Ballet and then the Royal Ballet. Her works include *The Rake's Progress* (1935) and *The Haunted Ballroom* (1934).

FRENCH

Béjart, Maurice (1927–   ). Choreographer. He founded the Ballet de l'Etoile in 1953, and later the Ballets of the 20th Century. In 1988, his troupe moved to Lausanne, Switzerland. Béjart's controversial works are highly theatrical and sometimes mystical; they include *Symphony for a Lonely Man* (1955) and *Ring Around the Ring* to Wagner (1991).

Camargo, Marie (1710–70). Dancer at the Paris Opera and rival of Marie Sallé, Camargo shortened the dancer's skirt to show her brilliant entrechats and other beats and eliminated the heels from her shoes for greater freedom of movement.

Noverre, Jean Georges (1727–1810). Choreographer and ballet reformer who tried with the *ballet d'action* to highlight the expressiveness of the ballet and integrate dance with drama. He wrote down his ideas in his *Letters sur la danse et sur les ballets*.

Perrot, Jules (1810–92). Dancer and ballet master of the Imperial Theater in St. Petersburg (1851–58). A leading dancer and choreographer of the Romantic era, he choreographed *La Esmeralda* and parts of *Giselle* (1841).

Petit, Roland (1924–   ). Founder of the Ballets de Paris de Roland Petit (1948) and director of the Ballet National de Marseilles since 1972. His story ballets combine high and popular art; his works include *Le Jeune homme et la mort* (1946) and *Le Loup* (1953).

Sallé, Marie (1707–56). Dancer with the Paris Opera (1727–40) and rival of Camargo. An advocate of the use of pantomime in ballet, Sallé was noted for her expressiveness and intelligence.

Vestris, Auguste (1760–1842). Dancer and teacher and illegitimate son of Gaetano. As premier danseur of the Paris Opera, he was noted for his exceptional elevation and virtuosity.

Vestris, Gaetano (1728–1808). Italian-born dancer and choreographer. Known as "the god of the dance," he became premier danseur of the Paris Opera in 1751 and cochoreographer in 1761. He was the first to discard the mask worn by dancers in performance.

RUSSIAN

Baryshnikov, Mikhail (1948–   ). A principal with the Kirov Ballet (1968–74), the Russian dancer defected to the West in 1974, joining the American Ballet Theater and serving as its director (1980–89). He then formed the White Oak Dance Project. His virtuosity and purity of classical style make him one of the leading male dancers of the period.

Danilova, Alexandra (1904–). Russian-born dancer. Noted for her charm and elegance, she was a ballerina with the Ballets Russes (1927–29) and prima ballerina with the Ballet Russe de Monte Carlo (1938–52). She taught at the School of American Ballet (1964–89) and appeared in the film *The Turning Point* (1977).

Diaghilev, Sergei Pavlovich (1872–1929). Russian impresario and founder of the Ballets Russes (1909). He brought together leading choreographers, composers, and artists, from Fokine and Balanchine to Stravinsky and Picasso, whose collaborations revolutionized the ballet.

Eglevsky, Andre (1917–77). Russian-born dancer. A leading dancer with the Ballet Russe de Monte Carlo (1939–42), Ballet Theater (1942–43), and New York City Ballet (1951–58). He founded the Eglevsky Ballet Company in 1961.

Fokine, Michel (1880–1942). Russian-born choreographer for the Ballets Russes (1909–12, 1914–15). His emphasis on dramatic coherence and on the unity of the style of dance and decor with the subject matter revolutionized the ballet. His important works include *The Firebird* (1910) and *Petrouchka* (1911).

Ivanov, Lev (1834–1901). Russian choreographer. His most important ballets were *The Nutcracker* (1892) and the second and fourth acts of *Swan Lake* (1894).

Karsavina, Tamara (1885–1978). Russian dancer with the Ballets Russes and partner of Nijinsky. She created important roles in *The Firebird* and *Petrouchka* and wrote her autobiography, *Theatre Street.*

Lifar, Serge (1905–86). Russian dancer with the Ballets Russes (1923–29), where he created the title role in Balanchine's *Prodigal Son.* As director of the Paris Opera Ballet (1929–45, 1947–58), he reinvigorated French ballet, choreographing many works including *Icare* (1935) and *Suite en blanc* (1943).

Makarova, Natalia (1940–). Russian dancer. A leading member of the Kirov Ballet (1959–70), she defected to the West, where she danced with the American Ballet Theater, the Royal Ballet, and

other companies. She won a Tony for her performance in the musical *On Your Toes.*

Massine, Léonide (1895–1979). Russian-born dancer and choreographer with the Ballets Russes (1914–21, 1925–28) and the Ballet Russe de Monte Carlo (1932–42). His works include *Parade* (1917) and *Gaîté, Parisienne* (1938).

Nijinska, Bronislava (1891–1972). The sister of Vaslav Nijinsky, she also worked with the Ballets Russes as a dancer and innovative choreographer, incorporating sport and satire into ballet. Among her important ballets are *Les Noces* (1923) and *Les Biches* (1924).

Nijinsky, Vaslav (1889–1950). Polish-Russian dancer and choreographer with the Ballets Russes, creating important roles in Fokine's ballets, such as *Petrouchka.* Considered by many to be the greatest dancer of the 20th century, he also choreographed works such as *L'Après-midi d'un faune* (1912) and *Le Sacre du printemps* (1913), which were radical breaks with ballet tradition.

Nureyev, Rudolf (1938–93). Russian dancer with the Kirov Ballet, he defected to the West in 1961, where he often partnered Dame Margot Fonteyn with the Royal Ballet. A leading dancer of his time, he was noted for his virtuosity and animal sensuality. He was director of the Paris Opera from 1983 to 1989.

Pavlova, Anna Matveyevna (1881–1931). Russian ballerina. She danced briefly with the Ballets Russes and then toured with her own company, introducing ballet to people all over the world. An outstanding ballerina, she was known for her grace and lightness and the spiritual quality of her dancing.

Petipa, Marius (1818–1910). French-born dancer who became first ballet master of the Imperial Theater of St. Petersburg in 1862. Russian ballet reached its apogee under his direction. He was one of the leading choreographers in ballet history, and his works include *La Bayadère* (1877) and *The Sleeping Beauty* (1890).

Plisetskaya, Maya (1925–). Leading Russian ballerina with the Bolshoi Ballet, which she joined in 1945. She is noted for her virtuosity and dramatic presence and for the pliancy of her arms.

Ulanova, Galina Sergeyevna (1910–). Russian dancer and teacher noted for her dramatic projection and lyricism. After joining the Kirov Ballet in 1928, she left to dance with the Bolshoi Ballet (1944–61), becoming the prima ballerina of Soviet ballet.

Youskevitch, Igor (1912–94). Russian-born dancer with the Ballet Russe de Monte Carlo (1938–44) and the Ballet Theater (1946–55). He was admired for his nobility and elegance and for his partnership with Alicia Alonso.

OTHER

Alonso, Alicia (1921–). Cuban dancer known for the purity of her classical style, particularly in the role of Giselle. After dancing with the American Ballet Theater and other companies, she founded the National Ballet of Cuba in 1959.

Bournonville, Auguste (1805–79). Danish choreographer. His Romantic works, such as *Napoli* (1842), form the core of the repertory of the Royal Danish Ballet.

Bruhn, Erik (1928–86). Danish-born dancer noted for his immaculate technique and nobility of style. After dancing with the American Ballet Theater and other companies, he was artistic director of the National Ballet of Canada (1983–86).

Cerrito, Fanny (1817–1909). Italian dancer, one of the leading ballerinas of the Romantic era. Noted for her strength and sensuous appeal, she created the leading role in *Ondine* (1843).

Elssler, Fanny (1810–84). Austrian daughter of an assistant to Franz Joseph Haydn, Elssler was one of the great ballerinas of the Romantic era, noted for her dramatic projection and earthiness. Her most famous dance was the Cachucha in *Le Diable boiteux* (1836).

Grisi, Carlotta (1819–99). Italian dancer with the Paris Opera. One of the great Romantic ballerinas, she created the title role in *Giselle*, whose libretto was written for her by Théophile Gautier.

Jooss, Kurt (1901–79). German choreographer whose theatrical works combined classical and modern modes of dance. His important works include *The Green Table,* a scathing indictment of war, and *Big City* (1932).

Taglioni, Marie (1804–84). Italian ballerina, the incarnation of the spiritual and lyrical ideal of the Romantic era. In the title role of *La Sylphide* (1832), she brought toe dancing to a new artistic level.

Wigman, Mary (1886–1973). German dancer and choreographer. The first major European modern dancer, Wigman choreographed somber works in an expressionist mode. Her works include *Totenmal* (1930).

COMMON DANCE TERMS

abstract dance   A plotless work composed of pure dance movements, although the composition may suggest a mood or subject.

adagio   Any dance to slow music; also, part of the classical pas de deux in ballet.

air, en l'   In ballet, a step done off the ground—for instance, tour en l'air, rond de jambe en l'air. It is the opposite of par terre.

allegro   A dance with a fast or moderate tempo.

allongé   In ballet, an elongated line; in particular, the horizontal line of an arabesque with one arm stretched front and the other back.

arabesque   In ballet, the extension of one leg straight in back at 90 degrees, with shoulders square; the position of the arms may vary.

assemblé   In ballet, a jump from one to both feet, usually landing in fifth position.

attitude   In ballet, a pose in which one leg is raised in back or in front with knee bent, usually with one arm raised.

balancé   A step that rocks from one foot to the other, usually in ³/₄ time.

ballet   From the Italian *balletto,* diminutive of *ballo,* "dance." Classical theatrical dancing based on the *danse d'école,* the rules and vocabulary that were codified around 1700 in France.

ballet blanc   A ballet in which the women wear white tutus, such as the second and fourth acts of *Swan Lake.*

ballet d'action   A ballet with a plot, usually tragic, advocated by reformer Jean Georges Noverre, ballet master of the Paris Opera, to bring dramatic coherence to the performance of ballet.

ballet de cour, le (court ballet)   Spectacles for entertainment, usually with allegorical or mythological themes, performed by the aristocracy in the 16th and 17th centuries, combining music, recitatives, and mime.

ballo   Standard Italian dances and their music of the 15th and 16th centuries.

ballon   In ballet, the ability of a dancer to remain suspended in air during a jump; elasticity in jumping.

ballroom dances   Social dances usually performed by couples, including the fox-trot, waltz, tango, rumba, and cha cha.

bas, en   In ballet, low, as in placement of arms.

basic movement   In ballroom dance, a characteristic figure that remains constant.

basse danse   A solemn court dance usually in duple time, popular in the 15th and 16th centuries.

battement   A beating movement of the legs.

bourrée, pas de   A series of small, fast steps executed with the feet very close together.

brisé   In ballet, a jump off one foot that is "broken" by a beating of the legs in the air.

cabriole   In ballet, a leap in which the lower leg beats against the upper one at an angle, before the dancer lands again on the lower leg.

cachucha   A Spanish dance in $^3/_4$ or $^3/_8$ time with castanets.

cakewalk   An African American dance in which couples strut and compete with high kicks and fast steps.

cambré   In ballet, a bend from the waist to the side or to the back.

cancan   Originating around 1830 as a social dance, by 1844 it had become a raucous dance performed in French music halls.

chassé   A sliding step in which one foot "chases" and displaces the other.

chat, pas de   Catlike leap in which one foot follows the other into the air, knees bent; the landing is in the fifth position.

ciseaux   A jump in which the legs open in second position in the air, resembling a scissors.

coda   In ballet, the third and final part of the classical pas de deux.

contraction   A basic movement in the technique of Martha Graham, based on breath inhalation and exhalation.

contredanse   Popular social dance during the 18th century; done in rows or circles, it may have derived from English country dancing.

corps de ballet   The members of a ballet company who do not perform solo.

country dance   Traditional English dance in which dancers form two facing lines.

croisée   In ballet, a position with the body at an oblique angle and the working leg crossing the line of the body.

danseur noble   A male dancer who performs the "princely" roles of the classical ballet, such as the Prince in *Swan Lake.*

dégagé   In ballet, shifting weight from one foot to the other.

développé   In ballet, an unfolding of the leg in the air.

écarté   In ballet, a position with one leg extended at an oblique angle while the body is also at an oblique angle.

effacé   In ballet, a position of the body at an oblique angle and partly hidden.

entrechat   A ballet movement in which the dancer repeatedly crosses his or her legs in the air.

épaulement   In ballet, the position of the torso from the waist up.

fandango   A lively Spanish dance in triple time performed with castanets or tambourines.

fermé   In ballet, a closed position of the feet.

five positions   In ballet, the basic positions of the feet. *First position:* feet in a straight line, heels touching. *Second position:* feet in a straight line, heels apart. *Third position:* one foot in front of the other, parallel to it, with heel of front foot in hollow instep of back foot. *Fourth position:* one foot in front of the other, parallel, but apart. *Fifth position:* one foot in front of the other, parallel, with heel in front foot touching toe of back foot. See illustrations on page 188.

flamenco   A Sevillian gypsy dance, possibly originating in India, also with Moorish and Arabian influences, originally accompanied by songs and clapping and later by the guitar, and characterized by its heelwork (*taconeo*).

fondu   In ballet, a lowering of the body by bending the knee.

fouetté en tournant   A spectacular movement in which the dancer propels himself or herself around a supporting leg with rapid circular movements of the other leg while remaining in a fixed spot.

fox-trot   A social dance of American origin in duple time.

glissade   In ballet, a gliding step that usually connects two steps.

haut, en   In ballet, a position of the arms above the head.

jeté   In ballet, a leap from one leg to the other in which one leg is thrown to the side, front, or back. *Grand jeté:* a large leap forward.

jitterbug   A lively social dance popular during the 1930s; it originated at the Savoy Ballroom in Harlem in 1928, where it was known as the Lindy.

kabuki   A Japanese dance drama featuring stylized narrative choreographic movements.

mazurka   A Polish national dance in triple time with an accent on the second beat, characterized by

proud bearing; clicking of heels; and *holubria,* a special turning step.

minuet   A slow and graceful dance, the most popular dance of the 18th century, characterized by symmetrical figures and elaborate curtsies and bows.

morris dance   An English folk dance that appeared in the 15th century, in which dancers wore bells on their legs and characters included a fool, a boy on a hobby horse, and a man in blackface.

ouvert   In ballet, an open position of the feet.

par terre   In ballet, steps performed on the floor. It is the opposite of en l'air.

pas de deux   A dance for two, usually a woman and a man. In its traditional form, it begins with an entrée and adagio, followed by solo variations for each dancer, and a coda.

pavane   A grave, processional court dance popular in the 16th and 17th centuries.

penché   In ballet, leaning forward.

piqué   In ballet, stepping directly onto the point of a foot.

pirouette   A turn on one leg, with the toe of the other leg touching the knee of the turning leg.

plié   A bending of the knees in any of the five positions. *Demi plié:* a half bending of the knees, with heels on the floor. *Grand plié:* a full bending of the knees.

point   A position on the tip of the toes. *Demi-point:* a position on the balls of the feet.

polka   A Bohemian folk dance in duple time with a hop on the fourth beat. It became a popular ballroom dance in the mid-19th century.

port de bras   In ballet, the positions of the arms.

premier danseur   Principal male dancer.

promenade   In ballet, a slow turn of the body on the whole foot.

quadrille   A social dance popular in the 19th century. It was a square dance in five sections, each in a different time.

reel   Popular in Britain, Ireland, and Scotland, it is a lively dance for two or more couples; also, the second part of the Virginia reel. The Highland fling is a variant.

relevé   In ballet, a rising with a spring movement to point or demi-point.

révérence   A ballet bow or curtsy in which one foot is pointed in front and the body leans forward.

spotting   A fixing of the eyes on one spot as long as possible during turns to avoid dizziness and to keep one's orientation.

square dance   An American folk dance with an even number of couples forming a square, two lines, or a circle. The dance consists of figures announced by a caller.

tango   A social dance in $^2/_4$ time, which, after originating in Spain, developed in Argentina, where it was influenced by black dance style and rhythm.

tour en l'air   In ballet, a turn while jumping straight up in the air.

variation   Any solo performance in a ballet.

waltz   A social dance in $^3/_4$ time that became widely popular in the 19th century. It developed from the Landler, a German-Austrian turning dance.

MAJOR PLAYWRIGHTS

AMERICAN

Albee, Edward   (1928–   ). Playwright, producer, director. His masterpiece, *Who's Afraid of Virginia Woolf?* (1962), concerns the illusions with which we try to fill our lives. Other works include *The Zoo Story* (1959) and *A Delicate Balance* (1966).

Barry, Philip   (1896–1949). His most successful plays are witty and elegant comedies about the social elite. They deal with the true nature of love and marriage and with a quest for personal fulfillment. His works include *Holiday* (1929), *The Animal Kingdom* (1932), and *The Philadelphia Story* (1939).

Chayefsky, Paddy (Sidney)   (1923–81). Playwright and television writer and screenwriter. His

most notable television plays, such as *Marty* (1953), and stage plays, such as *The Tenth Man* (1959), are about the search for love as a source of spiritual redemption. His screenplays include *Network* (1976).

Guare, John   (1938–   ). Playwright known for satires and black comedies that explore American society, often within the context of family relationships. In addition to writing stage works such as *The House of Blue Leaves* (1971) and *Six Degrees of Separation* (1990), he also wrote the screenplay for *Atlantic City* (1980).

Hellman, Lillian   (1905–84). Dramatist. Her tightly constructed plays skillfully depict human perversity and evil. Among her best are *The Children's Hour* (1934), *The Little Foxes* (1939), and *Watch on the Rhine* (1941).

Henley, Beth   (1952–   ). Her dark, comedic plays contain elements of the Southern Gothic tradition. She is best known for *Crimes of the Heart* (1981), which won the Pulitzer prize.

Inge, William   (1913–1973). Playwright. His tightly constructed realistic dramas deal with small-town life in the American Midwest, giving form to the yearnings and the guilt of simple people. Among his best plays are *Come Back, Little Sheba* (1950), *Picnic* (1953), *Bus Stop* (1955), and *Dark at the Top of the Stairs* (1957).

Mamet, David   (1947–   ). Dramatist best known for *American Buffalo* (1975), which depicts the sinister forces pervading American business.

Miller, Arthur   (1915–   ). Outstanding contemporary dramatist. His concern with the moral problems of American society led him to probe the psychological causes of behavior. His classic *Death of a Salesman* (1949) won the Pulitzer prize; other plays include *The Crucible* (1953) and *A View from the Bridge* (1955).

Odets, Clifford   (1906–63). Leading playwright of the Group Theatre and the most important of the American social dramatists of the 1930s. His plays of social and political protest include *Waiting for Lefty* (1935) and *Awake and Sing* (1935). Among his other works are *Golden Boy* (1937), *The Big Knife* (1949), and *The Country Girl* (1951).

"Important Authors" in chapter 8 **Go to**

O'Neill, Eugene (1888–1953). Probably the greatest American dramatist; also one of the bleakest and most pessimistic. He essayed almost every modern dramatic form. His later, naturalistic plays deal with the inevitability of fate: *The Iceman Cometh* (1939), *Long Day's Journey into Night* (1941), and *A Moon for the Misbegotten* (1943). Other significant works include *Anna Christie* (1920), *Desire Under the Elms* (1924), and *Ah, Wilderness!* (1933). He won the Pulitzer prize four times and, in 1936, the Nobel prize for literature.

Rabe, David (1940–   ). Dramatist known for his harsh view of American society, particularly U.S. conduct during the Vietnam War. His best-known plays are *The Basic Training of Pavlo Hummel* (1973) and *Streamers* (1976).

Saroyan, William (1908–81). Playwright and novelist. His essential theme is the triumph of childlike goodness over the corruption of a materialistic society. He won the Pulitzer prize for his classic *The Time of Your Life* (1939) but refused the award.

Shepard, Sam (1943–   ). Playwright and actor. Myth and reality clash in his plays, which explore the disintegration of American values and the chaos beneath. His works include *Operation Sidewinder* (1970); *Buried Child* (1978), which won a Pulitzer prize; and *Fool for Love* (1984).

Sherwood, Robert (1896–1955). Dramatist and biographer. His plays deal with the conflict between man's civilized values and his frequent descent into savagery. Among his best works are *The Petrified Forest* (1935), *Idiot's Delight* (1936), and *There Shall Be No Night* (1940).

Simon, Neil (1927–   ). Playwright and screenwriter. He has had more Broadway comedy hits than any other playwright. Among his well-known plays and musicals are *Barefoot in the Park* (1963); *The Odd Couple* (1965); *Sweet Charity* (1966); *The Sunshine Boys* (1972); *Brighton Beach Memoirs* (1983); and *Lost in Yonkers* (1991), which won the Pulitzer prize and Tony award.

Wasserstein, Wendy (1950–   ). Awarded the Pulitzer prize in 1989 for *The Heidi Chronicles,* Wasserstein focuses on the lives of modern women, their search for identity, and their attitude to the traditional roles projected for them.

Wilder, Thornton (1897–1975). Playwright, novelist, and essayist. His work is a celebration of human existence; he sees man and the universe as intimately related. His major plays are *Our Town* (1938), *The Skin of Our Teeth* (1942), which both won Pulitzer prizes, and *The Matchmaker* (1953).

Williams, Tennessee (1911–83). Probably the greatest American dramatist since Eugene O'Neill. His essential theme is the vulnerability of beauty to time and to a society dominated by violence. Among his most significant plays are *The Glass Menagerie* (1945); *A Streetcar Named Desire* (1947), which won a Pulitzer prize; *Summer and Smoke* (1948), *Cat on a Hot Tin Roof* (1955), which also won a Pulitzer; and *Night of the Iguana* (1961).

Wilson, August (1945–   ). One of the most acclaimed American dramatists, Wilson has chronicled the African American experience through each decade of the 20th century. He has won the Pulitzer prize twice, for *Fences* in 1987 and *The Piano Lesson* in 1990.

Wilson, Lanford (1937–   ). Dramatist and screenwriter whose works explore the conflict between traditional values and modern life. Among his best plays are *The Hot l Baltimore* (1973) and *Talley's Folly*, which won the Pulitzer prize in 1980.

BRITISH

Beaumont, Francis (c. 1584–1616). Jacobean dramatist, best known for his collaborations with John Fletcher. They developed a new form called "tragicomedy," which allowed for the treatment of serious themes without a tragic resolution. Their works include *Philaster* (1610) and *The Maid's Tragedy* (c. 1611). Beaumont alone wrote *The Knight of the Burning Pestle* (c. 1607), a burlesque of the historical romances of the time.

Churchill, Caryl (1938–   ). Playwright. Known for using experimental techniques, she examines contemporary society from a feminist and socialist point of view. Among her works are *Light Shining in Buckinghamshire* (1976), *Cloud Nine* (1981), and *Serious Money* (1982).

Performance Arts

Coward, Noël (1899–1973). Playwright, actor, composer, and director. His comedies present witty, stylish people acting in accordance with their unconventional morality and in league against more banal types. His best plays are *Private Lives* (1930), *Design for Living* (1930), and *Blithe Spirit* (1933).

Dekker, Thomas (c. 1572–1632). Dramatist and pamphleteer. He centered his plays on contemporary life and merged Elizabethan romance with everyday realism, exhibiting sympathy for society's outcasts. His best plays are *The Shoemaker's Holiday* (1600), *The Honest Whore, Part I* (with Thomas Middleton, 1604; *Part II,* 1630), *Westward Ho!* (with John Webster, 1604), *The Roaring Girl* (with Middleton, 1607–08), and *The Witch of Edmonton* (with William Rowley and John Ford, 1621).

Eliot, Thomas Stearns (T. S.) (1888–1965). Poet, critic, and playwright, born in America. He spearheaded a new interest in formal verse drama. His most admired play, *Murder in the Cathedral* (1935), derived its form from Greek tragedy, medieval morality plays, and church ritual. Other plays include *The Cocktail Party* (1949).

Fletcher, John (1579–1625). Prolific and immensely popular playwright who collaborated with Francis Beaumont and many others, apparently including Shakespeare (*The Two Noble Kinsmen* [1613] and *Henry VIII* [1613]). Alone, Fletcher wrote two early tragedies, *Valentinian* (1610–14) and *Bonduca* (1609–14), and the comedies *Wit Without Money* (c. 1614) and *Rule a Wife and Have a Wife* (1624). He helped to lay the basis for the Restoration "comedy of manners."

Goldsmith, Oliver (c. 1728–74). Irish-born essayist, poet, novelist, and comic playwright. He ridiculed the sentimental comedy of the time and promoted what he called "laughing comedy," designed to make us smile at our own follies. His comic masterpiece is *She Stoops to Conquer* (1773).

Hare, David (1947–   ). Dramatist and screenwriter who often probes the political and moral condition of England and the world at large. In addition to writing plays such as *Slag* (1970), *Plenty* (1978), and *Pravda* (1985), he created the

screenplay for *Strapless* (1990) and wrote *Licking Hitler* (1978) for British television.

Jonson, Ben (1572–1637). Dramatist, poet, and literary critic. He developed the "comedy of humours," which featured characters dominated by one overruling passion. His masterpieces are *Volpone* (1605–06), *Epicoene* (1610), *The Alchemist* (1610), and *Bartholomew Fair* (1614).

Kyd, Thomas (1558–94). Author of *The Spanish Tragedy* (1592), which introduced the theme of vengeance into Elizabethan drama; the "tragedy of revenge" became popular throughout the period. Kyd drew his inspiration from the Roman tragedies of Seneca.

Marlowe, Christopher (1564–93). Poet and playwright who ushered in the great age of Elizabethan drama. His distinctive blank verse—called "Marlowe's mighty line"—established this verse style as a basic tool of Elizabethan playwrights. His masterpieces are *Tamburlaine the Great: Part I* (c. 1586–87; *Part II,* 1587), *Dr. Faustus* (c. 1588), *The Jew of Malta* (c. 1589), and *Edward II* (1591). Marlowe, often in trouble with the law, was murdered in 1593.

Middleton, Thomas (c. 1570–1627). Jacobean dramatist with a dark and pessimistic vision of human corruption. In his comedies, the manners of the age are held up to scathing ridicule; his tragedies are remarkable for their penetrating psychological realism. His plays include *A Trick to Catch the Old One* (c. 1607), *A Chaste Maid in Cheapside* (1611), *The Changeling* (with William Rowley, 1622), and *Women Beware Women* (c. 1625).

Osborne, John (1929–94). His work was fueled by a disgust for the quality of life in contemporary Britain. In the opening of his most famous play, *Look Back in Anger* (1956), his protagonist, Jimmy Porter, a working-class intellectual rebel, opens fire on the establishment. Among Osborne's other works are *The Entertainer* (1957), *Luther* (1961), and *Inadmissible Evidence* (1964).

Pinter, Harold (1930–   ). Dramatist and actor. The motivation for the action in his plays is typically omitted; the characters evade real communication. The central motif is often two people in a room, involved in a seemingly commonplace situation that is gradually invested with menace, dread, and mystery. Pinter's language reproduces the inflections and rambling irrelevancy of everyday speech. His best plays include *The Birthday Party* (1958), *The Dumb Waiter* (1959), *The Homecoming* (1965), and *Betrayal* (1978).

Shakespeare, William (1564–1616). Elizabethan poet and dramatist. The most influential writer in English literature and perhaps the greatest dramatist of all time. His plays resonate with the full range of human emotion and experience. In his dramatic poetry, the English language reached perfection. As Ben Jonson wrote in his great tribute, "He was not of an age, but for all time!" Shakespeare wrote tragedies, comedies, and histories. His tragedies are *Titus Andronicus* (1594), *Romeo and Juliet* (c. 1595–96), *Julius Caesar* (1599), *Hamlet* (1602), *Othello* (1602–03), *Timon of Athens* (1604–05), *King Lear* (1605–06), *Macbeth* (1605–06), *Antony and Cleopatra* (1606–07), and *Coriolanus* (1607–10). His comedies are *The Comedy of Errors* (1591–94), *The Taming of the Shrew* (1593–94), *The Two Gentlemen of Verona* (1594–95), *Love's Labour's Lost* (1593–95), *A Midsummer Night's Dream* (1595–96), *The Merchant of Venice* (1596–97), *Much Ado About Nothing* (1598–99), *The Merry Wives of Windsor* (1598–99), *As You Like It* (1599–1600), *Twelfth Night* (1599–1600), *Troilus and Cressida* (1601–02), *All's Well That Ends Well* (1602–03), *Measure for Measure* (1603–04), *Pericles* (1606–08), *Cymbeline* (1609–10), *The Winter's Tale* (1610–11), and *The Tempest* (1611). The histories are *Henry VI: Part I* (1589–91), *Henry VI: Part II* (1590–91), *Henry VI: Part III* (1590–91), *Richard III* (1593), *Richard II* (1595), *King John* (1596–97), *Henry IV: Part I* (1597–98), *Henry IV: Part II* (1597–98), *Henry V* (1598–99), and *Henry VIII* (1613).

Shaw, George Bernard (1856–1950). Irish-born dramatist, journalist, critic, and Fabian socialist. His plays combine brilliant, incisive wit with a moral purpose: to expose the follies of the contemporary social order. He created a "drama of ideas," in which philosophical discussion becomes a theatrical event. Among his best-known works are *Arms and the Man* (1894), *Man and Superman*

(1905), *Major Barbara* (1905), *Pygmalion* (1912), *Heartbreak House* (1913–19), and *Saint Joan* (1923).

Sheridan, Richard Brinsley (1751–1816). Irish-born comic playwright, theatrical manager, and politician. Sheridan sought to restore a comedy of wit to the post-Restoration theater, which had been engulfed by middle-class moralizing. His masterpieces are *The Rivals* (1775) and *The School for Scandal* (1777).

Stoppard, Tom (1937–   ). Playwright, born in Czechoslovakia. Heavily influenced by Beckett and the Theatre of the Absurd, he is best known for *Rosencrantz and Guildenstern Are Dead* (1967) and *The Real Inspector Hound* (1968).

Tourneur, Cyril (1575–1626). Jacobean dramatist, author of two famous tragedies of revenge, both based on Senecan drama: *The Revenger's Tragedy* (1606–07: the authorship of this play is in dispute but is generally ascribed to Tourneur) and *The Atheist's Tragedy* (1607–11).

Webster, John (c. 1580–1634). Jacobean dramatist and creator of two outstanding tragedies, *The White Devil* (1609–12) and *The Duchess of Malfi* (1613–14). His vision was one of dark, brooding pessimism.

Wilde, Oscar (1854–1900). Irish-born playwright, novelist, poet, and aesthete. Famous for his epigrammatic wit and for his eccentricity in dress and lifestyle, Wilde used his satirical gifts to expose the shallowness and hypocrisy of Victorian society. His comic masterpiece is *The Importance of Being Earnest* (1895).

FRENCH

Anouilh, Jean (1910–87). Dramatist and screenwriter. His plays, which are laced with humor, deal with the impossibility of purity surviving in a world dominated by compromise. Among his best-known works are *Thieves' Carnival* (1932), *Antigone* (1944), *The Waltz of the Toreadors* (1952), and *The Lark* (1953).

Beckett, Samuel (1906–   ). Playwright and novelist, born in Ireland. One of the originators of the Theatre of the Absurd, he mixes comedy with existential anguish to express the dilemma of 20th-century man, beset by an undefined sense of guilt and a loss of purpose. His major works include *Waiting for Godot* (1952) and *Endgame* (1957).

Corneille, Pierre (1606–84). The first of the great French neoclassic dramatists. His early masterpiece, *Le Cid* (1637), was harshly criticized by the French Academy because it did not adhere to the "classical unities." All his later tragedies followed the rules. Other works include *Horace* (1640), *Cinna* (1640–41), and *Polyeuctes* (1641–42).

Genet, Jean (1919–86). Novelist and preeminent dramatist of the Theatre of the Absurd. In the face of the void, his deeply alienated characters assume inauthentic roles, which become ritualized. Genet's best plays include *The Maids* (1947), *The Balcony* (1956), and *The Blacks* (1959).

Giraudoux, Jean (1882–1944). Novelist and dramatist. Many of his plays are reinterpretations of Greek myth. Among his best works are *Tiger at the Gates* (1935) and *The Madwoman of Chaillot* (1946).

Hugo, Victor Marie (1802–85). Poet, novelist, playwright, and politician; he was the acknowledged leader of French Romanticism. The famous "battle" that disrupted the premiere of his tragedy *Hernani* (1830) marked a watershed in the history of the Romantic movement. Other plays include *The King Amuses Himself* (1832—the source for Verdi's *Rigoletto*), *Ruy Blas* (1838), and *The Burgraves* (1843).

Ionesco, Eugene (1912–94). Dramatist, born in Romania. One of the leading exponents of the Theatre of the Absurd. At the core of his work is the idea that human existence, language, and effort are essentially meaningless. His most famous plays are *The Bald Soprano* (1950), *The Lesson* (1951), and *Rhinoceros* (1959).

Molière (Jean Baptiste Poquelin) (1622–73). Actor, director, and theater manager. He took the stylized comic archetypes of the commedia dell'arte and made them human, while retaining the "flaw" that always led them to folly. The result was a new genre, "character comedy." His satires caused great controversy. His greatest plays are *The School for Wives* (1662), *Tartuffe* (1664), *The Misanthrope* (1666), *The Miser* (1668), and *The Bourgeois Gentleman* (1670).

Racine, Jean (1639–99). Exemplar of French classicism and master of the Alexandrine line. The classical unities of time, place, and action provided an ideal framework for the concise action of his tragedies. His protagonists are usually driven by a single, dominant passion. His greatest works are *Andromache* (1667), *Bérénice* (1670), *Phèdre* (1676), and *Athalie* (1691).

Rostand, Edmund (1868–1918). Poet and dramatist, responsible for the brief revival of the romantic spirit in the era of naturalism. His one masterpiece, *Cyrano de Bergerac* (1897), is a tour de force of dramatic poetry.

Sartre, Jean-Paul (1905–80). Philosopher, novelist, essayist, and playwright. His dramas expound his existential philosophy: that man is essentially free, in a universe without God; and that he is defined by his own acts and is obliged to choose responsibly. Among his best-known works are *No Exit* (1944) and *Dirty Hands* (1948). Sartre won the Nobel prize for literature in 1964.

GERMAN

Brecht, Bertolt (1895–1956). Playwright, poet, stage director, and theorist. He created "epic theater," the purpose of which was to make people first *think,* and only later feel, about what they were seeing. The technique he used was alienation—the creation of emotional distance between the spectator and the event. Paradoxically, his ironic dramas are deeply moving. Among his greatest plays are *In the Jungle of Cities* (1923), *The Threepenny Opera* (1928), *Galileo* (1938–39), *Mother Courage and Her Children* (1941), and *The Good Woman of Setzuan* (1943).

Buchner, Georg (1813–37). Three plays established Buchner as a seminal figure. His themes were distinctly modern: man's loneliness, his helplessness before the events of history and the conditions of society, and the absurdity of a world without God. Works by Buchner include *Danton's Death* (1835) and *Woyzeck* (1836).

GREEK

Aeschylus (525–456 B.C.). The originator of Greek tragedy as we know it. He added a second actor to the drama (thus making true stage dialogue possible), and he raised tragic diction to the level of grandeur. He explored themes of cosmic justice and the transmission of evil from generation to generation. He probably wrote some 90 plays, of which 7 survive complete, including *Prometheus Bound* (466–459 B.C.) and the trilogy *The Oresteia* (458 B.C.).

Aristophanes (c. 445–385 B.C.). The only surviving (and probably greatest) writer of Attic (ancient Athenian) old comedy. His freewheeling and joyous plays blend political satire, personal lampoon, portraits of domestic life, dance, music, and fantasy. Only 11 of his more than 40 plays survive, including *The Acharnians* (425 B.C.), *The Clouds* (423 B.C.), *The Wasps* (422 B.C.), *Peace* (422 B.C.), *The Birds* (414 B.C.), *Lysistrata* (411 B.C.), and *The Frogs* (405 B.C.).

Euripides (480–406 B.C.). Last of the great Greek tragedians. Influenced by the rationalism of the sophists, Euripides was distinctively modern. The depth of his characterization was new to the Attic stage, prefiguring psychological realism. His hatred of war was the mainspring of some of his best dramas. He wrote 92 plays, of which 19 survive, including *Alcestis* (438), *Medea* (431), *The Trojan Women* (415), *Electra* (413), *Iphegenia in Tauris* (412), *Orestes* (408), and *The Bacchae* (405).

Sophocles (c. 496–406 B.C.). The second of the great Greek tragedians. He introduced a third speaking actor, thus making possible more complex dramatic interactions. By creating self-contained works rather than the customary trilogies, he narrowed the focus to one solitary individual at the critical moment of his life, refusing to yield to time or circumstance. He wrote approximately 123 plays, of which 7 survive, including *Antigone* (c. 442–441 B.C.), *Oedipus Rex* (c. 430–426 B.C.), *Electra* (c. 409 B.C.), and *Oedipus at Colonus* (c. 404–401 B.C.).

IRISH

O'Casey, Sean (1880–1964). His plays present an antiheroic view of life, alternately tragic and comic. He mocked sentimental patriotism by looking at the brutality of war through the eyes of working-class Irish women. Among his best works are *The Shadow of a Gunman* (1923), *Juno and the Paycock* (1924), and *The Plough and the Stars* (1926).

Synge, John Millington (1871–1909). Poet and dramatist. His Irish peasant characters aspire to a wild life of freedom and fantasy, which they achieve in imagination as expressed through their powerful and poetic Irish idiom. Among his works are *In the Shadow of the Glen* (1903), *Riders to the Sea* (1904), and *The Playboy of the Western World* (1907). Synge was cofounder of the Abbey Theatre in Dublin, with William Butler Yeats and Lady Gregory.

ROMAN

Plautus (c. 251–184 B.C.). Popular comic playwright. His plays were based on Greek comedy and performed in Greek dress. A typical plot presents a young lover kept from his beloved by a stubborn father, a greedy pimp, or lack of money. A clever slave contrives an elaborate intrigue to unite the lovers, and the play follows the ups and downs of the scheme. Among his surviving works are *Pseudolus* (191 B.C.) and *The Menaechmi* (date unknown).

Seneca (4 B.C.–A.D. 65). Tragic playwright, stoic philosopher, and statesman. The form of his plays follows the conventions of Greek tragedy; but the content reflects his concern with the stoic absolutes of passion and reason. His plays deal with the triumph of evil in a single human soul and its devastating impact on the outer world. Nine of his plays survive, including *Agamemnon*, *Medea*, and *Phaedra* (dates unknown).

RUSSIAN

Chekhov, Anton Pavlovich (1860–1904). Great modern dramatist and short-story writer. He depicts the provincial aristocracy before the revolution, trapped in a stultifying environment and paralyzed by a lack of will. Stanislavsky's productions at the Moscow Art Theatre of Chekhov's greatest plays—*The Seagull* (1896), *Uncle Vanya* (1899), *The Three Sisters* (1901), and *The Cherry Orchard* (1904)—made the Russian theater famous throughout the world.

Gorky, Maxim (Alexei Maximovich Peshkov) (1868–1936). Russian novelist, short-story writer, and playwright. Writing out of his own experience of poverty, he won international fame for his drama of the slums, *The Lower Depths* (1902).

SPANISH

Calderón de la Barca, Pedro (1600–81). Poet and last great playwright of the Spanish Golden Age. He wrote more than 200 full-length plays, as well as more than 70 one-act sacramental dramas, called "autos." In a time when the Spanish Empire was crumbling, his essential themes were faith and honor. Among his best-known plays are *The Phantom Lady* (1629), *Life Is a Dream* (1631–32), *Devotion to the Cross* (1633), *Secret Vengeance for Secret Insult* (1635), and *The Mayor of Zalamea* (1640–44).

García Lorca, Federico (1899–1936). Spanish poet and playwright, executed by Franco's soldiers soon after the outbreak of the Spanish Civil War. His poetic tragedies deal with the conflict between the individual and society—a conflict particularly bitter in Spain, where life was tightly regulated by an unyielding conservative moral code. His most famous plays are *Blood Wedding* (1933), *Yerma* (1934), and *The House of Bernarda Alba* (1936).

Molina, Tirso de (Gabriel Tellez) (c. 1571–1648). A disciple of Lope de Vega and the second great dramatist of the Spanish Golden Age. His most famous play is *The Trickster of Seville* (c. 1625), in which he created the great modern myth of Don Juan.

Vega Carpio, Lope de (1562–1635). Member of the Spanish Armada and the first great dramatist of the Spanish Golden Age. He established the *commedia* (new comedy) as the principal dramatic form in the Spain of his time. His works include *The Peasant in his Nook* (1611–15), *Fuenteovejuna* (1612), *The King's the Best Magistrate* (1620–23), and *The Knight from Olmedo* (1620–25).

OTHER

Ibsen, Henrik (1828–1906). Norwegian playwright. Generally credited with being the "father of modern drama," he demonstrated the power of psychological realism. His plays often present individuals in bitter conflict with the norms of society. His masterpieces include *Peer Gynt* (1867), *A Doll's House* (1879), *Ghosts* (1881), *An Enemy of the People* (1883), *The Wild Duck* (1884), and *Hedda Gabler* (1891).

Pirandello, Luigi (1867–1936). Italian dramatist and novelist, winner of the 1934 Nobel prize for literature. The playwright par excellence of the conflict between illusion and reality, he depicts with eloquence the isolation of the individual from society and from himself. Among his best-known plays are *Right You Are—If You Think You Are* (1917), *Six Characters in Search of an Author* (1921), and *The Man with the Flower in His Mouth* (1923).

Strindberg, Johan August (1849–1912). Swedish playwright and seminal modern dramatist, best known for his intensely psychological plays about tormented male-female relationships. His later plays prefigure expressionism. Among his best-known works are *The Father* (1887), *Miss Julie* (1889), *The Dance of Death* (*Part I* and *Part II*—1900), and *A Dream Play* (1902).

MAJOR FILM DIRECTORS

AMERICAN

Capra, Frank (1897–1991), b. Sicily. A pioneer of screwball comedy with the Academy Award–winning *It Happened One Night* (1934), he is best known for fast-paced populist comedy-dramas such as *Mr. Deeds Goes to Town* (1936) and *Mr. Smith Goes to Washington* (1939) that show the triumph of the individual against the system. His Christmas fable *It's a Wonderful Life* (1946) is a television staple.

Coppola, Francis Ford (1939–), b. Michigan. In signature works *The Godfather* (1972) and *The Godfather Part II* (1974), he fused his strengths—epic scale, operatic staging, and understanding of family conflict—into modern film tragedy. Other films, such as *Apocalypse Now* (1979), *Peggy Sue Got Married* (1986), and *The Godfather Part III* (1990), have varied in subject matter but share Coppola's ambitiousness.

Performance Arts

A Brief History of Film

A Closer Look

Experiments in motion pictures began in the United States and Europe during the late 19th century. American inventor Thomas Alva Edison patented the first movie machine, the Kinetoscope, in 1891. Four years later, French inventors Louis and Auguste Lumière demonstrated the camera-projector called the *cinématographe.* American filmmaker Edwin S. Porter's eight-minute *The Great Train Robbery* (1903) launched the movies as mass entertainment.

American filmmakers soon became preeminent. Major studios were situated in New York, with D. W. Griffith the medium's most influential director. In dozens of films, he developed a grammar of shots and lighting effects to evoke audience emotion. His highly successful *The Birth of a Nation* (1915) pioneered the idea of film as art.

Between 1910 and 1920, American filmmaking shifted to Hollywood. Leading directors such as Cecil B. De Mille (*The Ten Commandments,* 1923), Ernst Lubitsch (*The Marriage Circle,* 1924), and John Ford (*The Iron Horse,* 1924) offered a variety of genres—epics, romantic comedies, and westerns. Mack Sennett pioneered film slapstick with the Keystone Cops and introduced English comic Charlie Chaplin. Portraying the forlorn "Tramp" in *The Kid* (1921), *The Gold Rush* (1925), and others, Chaplin became one of the first international movie stars.

Several other countries established themselves as filmmaking centers. Germany was the birthplace of the expressionist movement, embodied in Robert Weine's *The Cabinet of Dr. Caligari* (1919). In Russia, Sergei Eisenstein's *Potemkin* (1925) epitomized the idea of *montage.* France became a rich film source, with such humanistic directors as René Clair and Abel Gance.

The 1927 U.S. film *The Jazz Singer* introduced sound to movies, revolutionizing the industry worldwide. Genres requiring witty or action-oriented dialogue, such as gangster movies and screwball comedies, gained primacy, as did extravagant musicals. The American studios, including Metro-Goldwyn-Mayer, Paramount, and Warner Bros., honed a "studio system" that produced a steady stream of films and stars for Depression-era audiences seeking escape. American stars of the period included James Cagney, Bette Davis, Clark Gable, Cary Grant, and Katharine Hepburn. The system reached its apex in 1939, with dozens of now-classic films, including the Civil War epic *Gone With the Wind* (1939).

High artistic achievements marked European cinema during the years before WW II. Notable films included Jean Renoir's antiwar classic *Grand Illusion* (1937) and Leni Riefenstahl's Nazi paean *Triumph of the Will* (1935).

WW II and its aftermath also brought heightened realism to international filmmaking. Italian directors Roberto Rossellini and Vittorio De Sica ushered in neorealism with, respectively, *Open City* (1949) and *The Bicycle Thief* (1945). Countering the trend toward realism were such stylized, idiosyncratic filmmakers as Italy's Federico Fellini (*La Dolce Vita,* 1960) and Swedish psychological master Ingmar Bergman (*The Seventh Seal,* 1956).

In the 1950s and 1960s, a group of French directors (many of them film critics), initiated the *nouvelle vague* (new wave). This movement of quirky, original films included François Truffaut's *The Four Hundred Blows* (1959) and Jean-Luc Godard's *Breathless* (1960). German cinema reinvented itself after WW II with the varied social critiques of directors Werner Herzog, Wim Wenders, and Rainer Werner Fassbinder (*The Marriage of Maria Braun,* 1979).

Nonwestern cinema gained an international following after World War II through the works of Japanese directors Akira Kurosawa (*Rashomon,* 1950) and Yasujiro Ozu (*Tokyo Story,* 1953) and Indian filmmaker Satyajit Ray (*Pather Panchali,* 1955). National cinemas that have come to prominence since the 1970s include those of Australia and New Zealand, the former offering such filmmakers as Peter Weir and the latter, Jane Campion.

Changing tastes, decreased film attendance, and corporate takeovers effectively destroyed the American studio system by the end of the 1960s. In its wake came increased experimentation and independence through filmmakers such as Stanley Kubrick, Robert Altman, Francis Ford Coppola (*The Godfather,* 1972) and Martin Scorsese (*Raging Bull,* 1980). In recent years, independent studios have grown in stature, becoming known for supporting high-quality original filmmaking such as Quentin Tarantino's *Pulp Fiction* (1994).

American films since the 1970s have been distinguished by the big-budget blockbuster. Primarily special-effects-laden fare for an increasingly younger target audience, the blockbuster has been dominated by two directors: George Lucas and Steven Spielberg. Lucas's *Star Wars* (1977) and its sequels made hundreds of millions of dollars and reinvented the outer-space film. With *Jaws* (1975) and *E.T.* (1982), Spielberg became the leading director of big-budget, high-tech films. However, director James Cameron's *Titanic* (1997) eclipsed all previous records for gross revenues and garnered 11 Academy Awards as well.

Performance Arts

De Mille, Cecil B. (1881–1959), b. Massachusetts. Specializing at first in spicy modern narratives, he became known as the master of religious and historical epics such as *The Ten Commandments* (1923; remade 1956). He is credited with helping to establish Hollywood as a film capital. His sweeping entertainments include *The Sign of the Cross* (1932), *Samson and Delilah* (1949), and *The Greatest Show on Earth* (1952).

Ford, John (1895–1973), b. Maine. The most celebrated and enduring American director, he combined strong storytelling and visual poetry in classic meditations on the country's conflict between frontier and civilization. Though successful in silents (*The Iron Horse*, 1924), he left his legacy in sound films. He won the Academy Award for best director for three films: *The Grapes of Wrath* (1940), *How Green Was My Valley* (1941), and *The Quiet Man* (1952). Other influential works include *Stagecoach* (1939), *My Darling Clementine* (1946), and *The Searchers* (1956).

Griffith, D. W. (1875–1948), b. Kentucky. A pioneer in shaping the medium, and American cinema's standard bearer, he infused cinematic power into basic techniques of camera use, editing, and lighting. His Civil War epic *Birth of a Nation* (1915) is a hallmark in the development of film as art. Other major films from his hundreds of works include *Intolerance* (1916), *Broken Blossoms* (1919) and *Orphans of the Storm* (1922). His career ended soon after the advent of sound film.

Hawks, Howard (1896–1977), b. Indiana. Prized for his storytelling ability and stylistic economy, he directed definitive works in several genres: gangster dramas (*Scarface*, 1932), screwball comedy (*Bringing Up Baby*, 1938; *His Girl Friday*, 1940), action films (*Only Angels Have Wings*, 1939), and westerns (*Red River*, 1948). He introduced actress Lauren Bacall in *To Have and Have Not* (1944), with Humphrey Bogart; insolent and fearless, the two actors embody the ideal Hawksian man and woman. He won an honorary Academy Award (1974).

Kubrick, Stanley (1928–   ), b. New York. He left a career as a still photographer to become a cool, meticulous maker of visually stunning films.

His sardonic, often pessimistic works include *Paths of Glory* (1957), *Dr. Strangelove* (1964), *2001: A Space Odyssey* (1968), *A Clockwork Orange* (1971), and *Full Metal Jacket* (1987). He has resided in Britain since the 1960s.

Lang, Fritz (1890–1976), b. Austria. In Germany, expressionist films *Dr. Mabuse* (1922), *Metropolis* (1927), and *M* (1931) conveyed tension and inexorable fate. He left Germany in 1933 after his film *The Testament of Dr. Mabuse* (1933) was banned by Nazis. He directed several films in Hollywood, many concerning injustice or corruption, including *Fury* (1936), *Hangmen Also Die* (1943), and *The Big Heat* (1953).

Lubitsch, Ernst (1892–1947), b. Germany. With the wit, visual brevity, and sexual polish known as "the Lubitsch Touch," he directed scores of sophisticated comedies, musicals, and dramas in Germany and America. Many remain classics: *The Marriage Circle* (1924), *The Love Parade* (1929), *Monte Carlo* (1930), *Trouble in Paradise* (1932), *Ninotchka* (1939). He received an honorary Academy Award in 1937.

Scorsese, Martin (1942–   ), b. New York. Over decades of rough urban dramas, he has defined New York City as an underworld where denizens find resolution and redemption through violence. Notable New York films include *Mean Streets* (1973), *Taxi Driver* (1976), *Goodfellas* (1990), and *Raging Bull* (1980), hailed by some as the finest American film of the decade. Other films include *The Color of Money* (1986) and *The Age of Innocence* (1993). He is active in film preservation.

George Lucas was riding in a car with a friend when the car went over a bump. His friend said, "Oops, I just ran over a wookie back there." Thus was created the word that George later used in the Star Wars film.

Spielberg, Steven (1947–   ), b. Ohio. One of the most commercially successful directors in film history, he specializes in big-budget adventure or science-fiction films that include *Jaws* (1975), *Close*

Encounters of the Third Kind (1977), *Raiders of the Lost Ark* (1981), *E.T.* (1982), and *Jurassic Park* (1993). He gained respect as a serious filmmaker with the Holocaust drama *Schindler's List* (1993), which won an Academy Award for best picture.

Welles, Orson (1915–85), b. Wisconsin. His stunning first film *Citizen Kane* (1941) influenced generations of filmmakers in its structure, composition, and cinematography—and the audacity of its maker, who became a lifelong boy wonder. Although later films were often compromised by studio intervention or self-indulgence, many are exceptional: *The Magnificent Ambersons* (1942), *The Lady From Shanghai* (1948), and *Touch of Evil* (1958).

Wilder, Billy (1906–), b. Austria. Blending masterful timing, wit, and worldliness, he created some of Hollywood's smartest comedies and most cynical dramas. Notable works include *Double Indemnity* (1944), *Sunset Boulevard* (1950), *Stalag 17* (1953), *Sabrina* (1954), and *Some Like It Hot* (1959). *The Lost Weekend* (1945) and *The Apartment* (1960) won Academy Awards for best picture and director.

ASIAN

Chen Kaige (1952–), b. China. A major presence in post–Cultural Revolution filmmaking, he is known for his mix of high drama and emotional subtlety in such films as *Yellow Earth* (1984), *King of Children* (1987), and *Farewell My Concubine* (1993). His early cinematographer, Zhang Yimou, also became a noted director.

Kurosawa, Akira (1910–), b. Japan. The humanistic filmmaker's ability to convey universal messages in works like *Drunken Angel* (1948) and *Rashomon* (1950) has bridged cultures and brought decades of worldwide appeal. His samurai films have been influential: *The Seven Samurai* (1954) inspired *The Magnificent Seven* (1960); *Hidden Fortress* (1958) informed the *Star Wars* trilogy. Other notable films include *Yojimbo* (1961) and pioneering Shakespeare adaptations, *Throne of Blood* (1957) and *Ran* (1985).

Ozu, Yasujiro (1903–63), b. Japan. With films like *The Flavor of Green Tea Over Rice* (1952) and *Tokyo Story* (1953), he is renowned for his simply filmed, delicate dramas of middle-class family life. He is also praised in his country for capturing Japan's national sensibility. Other representative films include *Early Spring* (1956) and *Late Autumn* (1961).

Ray, Satyajit (1921–92), b. Calcutta. Acclaimed for his humanity and subtle cinematic style, he gained early success with *Pather Panchali* (1955), the first entry in his "Apu Trilogy," about a Bengali child. Other parts are *The Unvanquished* (1957) and *The World of Apu* (1958). Later, more thematically and cinematically daring films include *The Lonely Wife* (1964) and *Distant Thunder* (1973). He won an honorary Academy Award (1992).

BRITISH

Chaplin, Charles (1889–1977), b. England. The preeminent director and star of silent film immortalized his "Tramp" character in films including *The Tramp* (1915) and *The Kid* (1921). Cofounding the studio United Artists, he directed some of his finest works for it: *The Gold Rush* (1925), *City Lights* (1931), and *Modern Times* (1936). His increasingly serious sound films include *The Great Dictator* (1940), *Monsieur Verdoux* (1947), and *Limelight* (1952). Accused of Communist affiliations, he was denied reentry to the United States in 1952 and did not return for 20 years. He won special Academy Awards in 1927–1928 and 1972. He was knighted in 1975.

Hitchcock, Alfred (1899–1980), b. England. Cinema's unmatched master of suspense built his international reputation in the 1930s with British thrillers *The Man Who Knew Too Much* (1934, remade 1956), *The 39 Steps* (1935), and *The Lady Vanishes* (1938). In Hollywood, his works became more lavish and cinematically refined, with top stars and crew. Some classic works include *Notorious* (1946), *Rear Window* (1954), *Vertigo* (1958), *North by Northwest* (1959), and *Psycho* (1960).

Lean, David (1908–91), b. England. He gained early notice with his literary adaptations *Brief Encounter* (1945) and *Great Expectations* (1946) but is most respected for his grand, ironic epics, notably *The Bridge on the River Kwai* (1957) and

Performance Arts

Lawrence of Arabia (1962). Blending human drama and 20th-century history, each won the Academy Award for best picture. Later films include *Doctor Zhivago* (1965) and *A Passage to India* (1984). He was knighted in 1984.

Powell, Michael (1905–90), b. England, and **Emeric Pressburger** (1902–88), b. Hungary. Successful filmmakers alone, they are renowned for their literate, visually stunning collaborations in the 1940s and 1950s. Among them are *The Life and Death of Colonel Blimp* (1943), *I Know Where I'm Going* (1945), *Black Narcissus* (1947), and the quintessential ballet film *The Red Shoes* (1948). Powell faced severe criticism following his study of a psychopath, *Peeping Tom* (1960).

FRENCH

Godard, Jean-Luc (1930–   ), b. France. Beginning with *Breathless* (1960), the former film critic influenced French New Wave and avant-garde filmmaking with his visually surprising, improvisational works. Acclaimed works of the period also include *The Little Soldier* (1960) and *Alphaville* (1965). By the late 1960s, he became more formless and didactic in works such as *Masculine Feminine* (1966) and *Weekend* (1968). After a hiatus, he turned to more humanistic filmmaking, with *First Name: Carmen* (1983) and others.

Renoir, Jean (1894–1979), b. France. Son of impressionist painter Auguste Renoir, he is unsurpassed at conveying the human condition through poetic, fluid filmmaking. The antiwar classic *Grand Illusion* (1937) and social meditation *The Rules of the Game* (1939) are considered his masterpieces. Other works include *Boudu Saved from Drowning* (1932), *Toni* (1935), and *The Crime of Monsieur Lange* (1936).

Truffaut, François (1932–84), b. France. Beginning with *The 400 Blows* (1959), he established himself as the central force of French New Wave. Tender and exuberant, his films are also renowned for their insight into human emotions. Among other major works are *Shoot the Piano Player* (1960), *Jules and Jim* (1961), and *The Wild Child* (1970). Notable books include *Hitchcock/Truffaut* (1983).

GERMAN

Fassbinder, Rainer Werner (1946–82), b. Germany. His spirited, iconoclastic dramas about modern German society made him a major force in rebuilding German cinema after World War II. A feverish worker, he made up to four films per year until his death at 36. Representative works include *Effi Briest* (1974), *Despair* (1978), *The Marriage of Maria Braun* (1979), and *Veronika Voss* (1982).

Murnau, F. W. (1888–1931), b. Germany. With *Nosferatu the Vampire* (1922) and *The Last Laugh* (1924), he refined a visually expressive style that influenced generations of filmmakers. His first U.S. work, *Sunrise* (1927), is considered one of the most beautiful works in film history. Other U.S. films include *Our Daily Bread* (1930) and *Tabu* (1931), codirected with Robert Flaherty.

Ophüls, Max (1902–57), b. Germany. Prizing *mise-en-scène* above plot, he was a master of fluid camera work and lush decor with an otherworldly, baroque quality that suited his often romantic tales. Among his most acclaimed works are *Letter From an Unknown Woman* (1948), *La Ronde* (1950), *The Earrings of Madame De* (1953), and *Lola Montez* (1955). His son is filmmaker Marcel Ophüls.

ITALIAN

Antonioni, Michelangelo (1912–   ), b. Italy. A major force in postwar Italian cinema, he is noted for conveying the emotional void of modern existence in such works as *The Red Desert* (1964), *L'Avventura* (1960), *Blow-Up* (1966), and *The Passenger* (1975). He is expert in using the physical world to communicate metaphysical and psychological states.

De Sica, Vittorio (1902–74), b. Italy. With *Shoeshine* (1946) and *The Bicycle Thief* (1948), he made two pivotal (and Academy Award–winning) works of Italian neorealism. Other of his humane, varied works include *Umberto D* (1952); *The Condemned of Altona* (1962); *Yesterday Today and Tomorrow* (1963); and *The Garden of the Finzi-Continis* (1971); the latter two winning foreign-film Academy Awards.

Fellini, Federico (1920–93), b. Italy. Humanistic, sharply observed, and sensual, he is Italy's most beloved and acclaimed filmmaker. He gained international fame with the autobiographical *I Vitelloni* (1953) and followed with *La Strada* (1954), which won the Academy Award for best foreign film. Other milestone films include *The Nights of Cabiria* (1957) and *8½* (1963), also Academy Award winners for best foreign film; *La Dolce Vita* (1960), the psychological study *Juliet of the Spirits* (1965); and the playful *Amarcord* (1973).

OTHER

Bergman, Ingmar (1918–), b. Sweden. Early films *Smiles of a Summer Night* (1955) and *The Seventh Seal* (1957) won prizes at the Cannes Film Festival and established his ability to portray human relationships and explore religious and philosophical concerns, often crises of faith and personal detachment. Other works include *Wild Strawberries* (1957), *Persona* (1966), *Cries and Whispers* (1972), and *Fanny and Alexander* (1983).

Buñuel, Luis (1900–83), b. Spain. A critical and cult favorite, he first demonstrated his outrageous visual style with the Surrealist classic *Un Chien andalou* (1928, with Salvador Dali). Later works

incorporated fearless criticism of the Catholic church and other social institutions; among them are *L'Age d'or* (1930), *Los Olvidados* (1950), *Viridiana* (1961), and *That Obscure Object of Desire* (1977).

Eisenstein, Sergei (1898–1948), b. Latvia. A seminal voice in formulating film language, he developed the practice of *montage* in works including *The Battleship Potemkin* (1925), *October/Ten Days That Shook the World* (1928), and *The General Line* (1929). Later works, such as *Alexander Nevsky* (1938), further refined its use. A noted film theorist, he wrote such books as *Film Sense* (1942) and *Film Form* (1949).

Sembène, Ousmane (1923–), b. Senegal. The foremost filmmaker in sub-Saharan Africa, he established the region as a rich cinematic source from his first release, *Black Girl* (1966). It and other works, including *The Money Order* (1968), *The People* (1977), and *Camp de Thiaroye* (1988), explore conflicts between African and western cultures. From the 1960s, he has been a respected novelist and short story writer (*The Last of the Empire*, 1981).

THE ACADEMY AWARDS

The Academy Awards began in 1927. The awards for Best Supporting Actor and Best Supporting Actress were not included until 1936. The award for Best Foreign Film was added in 1956.

1927–28
Best Actor: Emil Jannings *(The Way of All Flesh)*
Best Actress: Janet Gaynor *(Seventh Heaven)*
Best Director: Frank Borzage *(Seventh Heaven);* Lewis Milestone *(Two Arabian Knights)*
Best Picture: *Wings*

1928–29
Best Actor: Warner Baxter *(In Old Arizona)*
Best Actress: Mary Pickford *(Coquette)*
Best Director: Frank Lloyd *(The Divine Lady)*
Best Picture: *Broadway Melody*

1929–30
Best Actor: George Arliss *(Disraeli)*
Best Actress: Norma Shearer *(The Divorcee)*
Best Director: Lewis Milestone *(All Quiet on the Western Front)*
Best Picture: *All Quiet on the Western Front*

1930–31
Best Actor: Lionel Barrymore *(A Free Soul)*
Best Actress: Marie Dressler *(Min and Bill)*
Best Director: Norma Taurog *(Skippy)*
Best Picture: *Cimarron*

1931–32
Best Actor: Frederic March *(Dr. Jekyll and Mr. Hyde);* Wallace Berry *(The Champ)*
Best Actress: Helen Hayes *(The Sin of Madelon Claudet)*
Best Director: Frank Borzage *(Bad Girl)*
Best Picture: *Grand Hotel*

1932–33
Best Actor: Charles Laughton *(The Private Life of Henry VIII)*
Best Actress: Katharine Hepburn *(Morning Glory)*
Best Director: Frank Lloyd *(Cavalcade)*
Best Picture: *Cavalcade*

Performance Arts

1934

Best Actor: Clark Gable *(It Happened One Night)*

Best Actress: Claudette Colbert *(It Happened One Night)*

Best Director: Frank Capra *(It Happened One Night)*

Best Picture: *It Happened One Night*

1935

Best Actor: Victor McLaglen *(The Informer)*

Best Actress: Bette Davis *(Dangerous)*

Best Director: John Ford *(The Informer)*

Best Picture: *Mutiny on the Bounty*

1936

Best Actor: Paul Muni *(The Story of Louis Pasteur)*

Best Actress: Luise Rainer *(The Great Ziegfeld)*

Best Supporting Actor: Walter Brennan *(Come and Get It)*

Best Supporting Actress: Gale Sondergard *(Anthony Adverse)*

Best Director: Frank Capra *(Mr. Deeds Goes to Town)*

Best Picture: *The Great Ziegfeld*

1937

Best Actor: Spencer Tracy *(Captains Courageous)*

Best Actress: Luise Rainer *(The Good Earth)*

Best Supporting Actor: Joseph Schildkraut *(The Life of Emile Zola)*

Best Supporting Actress: Alice Brady *(In Old Chicago)*

Best Director: Leo McCarey *(The Awful Truth)*

Best Picture: *The Life of Emile Zola*

1938

Best Actor: Spencer Tracy *(Boys Town)*

Best Actress: Bette Davis *(Jezebel)*

Best Supporting Actor: Walter Brennan *(Kentucky)*

Best Supporting Actress: Fay Bainter *(Jezebel)*

Best Director: Frank Capra *(You Can't Take It with You)*

Best Picture: *You Can't Take It with You*

1939

Best Actor: Robert Donat *(Goodbye Mr. Chips)*

Best Actress: Vivien Leigh *(Gone with the Wind)*

Best Supporting Actor: Thomas Mitchell *(Stagecoach)*

Best Supporting Actress: Hattie McDaniel *(Gone with the Wind)*

Best Director: Victor Fleming *(Gone with the Wind)*

Best Picture: *Gone with the Wind*

1940

Best Actor: James Stewart *(The Philadelphia Story)*

Best Actress: Ginger Rogers *(Kitty Foyle)*

Best Supporting Actor: Walter Brennan *(The Westerner)*

Best Supporting Actress: Jane Darwell *(The Grapes of Wrath)*

Best Director: John Ford *(The Grapes of Wrath)*

Best Picture: *Rebecca*

1941

Best Actor: Gary Cooper *(Sergeant York)*

Best Actress: Joan Fontaine *(Suspicion)*

Best Supporting Actor: Donald Crisp *(How Green Was My Valley)*

Best Supporting Actress: Mary Astor *(The Great Lie)*

Best Director: John Ford *(How Green Was My Valley)*

Best Picture: *How Green Was My Valley*

1942

Best Actor: James Cagney *(Yankee Doodle Dandy)*

Best Actress: Greer Garson *(Mrs. Miniver)*

Best Supporting Actor: Van Heflin *(Johnny Eager)*

Best Supporting Actress: Teresa Wright *(Mrs. Miniver)*

Best Director: William Wyler *(Mrs. Miniver)*

Best Picture: *Mrs. Miniver*

1943

Best Actor: Paul Lukas *(Watch on the Rhine)*

Best Actress: Jennifer Jones *(The Song of Bernadette)*

Best Supporting Actor: Charles Coburn *(The More the Merrier)*

Best Supporting Actress: Katina Paxinou *(For Whom the Bell Tolls)*

Best Director: Michael Curtiz *(Casablanca)*

Best Picture: *Casablanca*

1944

Best Actor: Bing Crosby *(Going My Way)*

Best Actress: Ingrid Bergman *(Gaslight)*

Best Supporting Actor: Barry Fitzgerald *(Going My Way)*

Best Supporting Actress: Ethel Barrymore *(None But the Lonely Heart)*

Best Director: Leo McCarey *(Going My Way)*

Best Picture: *Going My Way*

1945

Best Actor: Ray Milland *(The Lost Weekend)*

Best Actress: Joan Crawford *(Mildred Pierce)*

Best Supporting Actor: James Dunn *(A Tree Grows in Brooklyn)*

Best Supporting Actress: Anne Revere *(National Velvet)*

Best Director: Billy Wilder *(The Lost Weekend)*

Best Picture: *The Lost Weekend*

1946

Best Actor: Frederic March *(The Best Years of Our Lives)*

Best Actress: Olivia de Havilland *(To Each His Own)*

Best Supporting Actor: Harold Russell *(The Best Years of Our Lives)*

Best Supporting Actress: Anne Baxter *(The Razor's Edge)*

Best Director: William Wyler *(The Best Years of Our Lives)*

Best Picture: *The Best Years of Our Lives*

1947

Best Actor: Ronald Coleman *(A Double Life)*

Best Actress: Loretta Young *(The Farmer's Daughter)*

Best Supporting Actor: Edmund Gwenn *(Miracle on 34th Street)*

Best Supporting Actress: Celeste Holm *(Gentleman's Agreement)*

Best Director: Elia Kazan *(Gentleman's Agreement)*

Best Picture: *Gentleman's Agreement*

1948

Best Actor: Laurence Olivier *(Hamlet)*

Best Actress: Jane Wyman *(Johnny Belinda)*

Best Supporting Actor: Walter Huston *(Treasure of Sierra Madre)*

Best Supporting Actress: Claire Trevor *(Key Largo)*

Best Director: John Huston *(The Treasure of the Sierra Madre)*

Best Picture: *Hamlet*

1949

Best Actor: Broderick Crawford *(All the King's Men)*

Best Actress: Olivia de Havilland *(The Heiress)*

Best Supporting Actor: Dean Jagger *(Twelve O'Clock High)*

Best Supporting Actress: Mercedes McCambridge *(All the King's Men)*

Best Director: Joseph L. Mankiewicz *(A Letter to Three Wives)*

Best Picture: *All the King's Men*

1950

Best Actor: Jose Ferrer *(Cyrano de Bergerac)*

Best Actress: Judy Holliday *(Born Yesterday)*

Best Supporting Actor: George Sanders *(All About Eve)*

Best Supporting Actress: Josephine Hull *(Harvey)*

Best Director: Joseph L. Mankiewicz *(All About Eve)*

Best Picture: *All About Eve*

1951

Best Actor: Humphrey Bogart *(The African Queen)*

Best Actress: Vivien Leigh *(A Streetcar Named Desire)*

Best Supporting Actor: Karl Malden *(A Streetcar Named Desire)*

Best Supporting Actress: Kim Hunter *(A Streetcar Named Desire)*

Best Director: George Stevens *(A Place in the Sun)*

Best Picture: *An American in Paris*

1952

Best Actor: Gary Cooper *(High Noon)*

Best Actress: Shirley Booth *(Come Back, Little Sheba)*

Best Supporting Actor: Anthony Quinn *(Viva Zapata!)*

Best Supporting Actress: Gloria Grahame *(The Bad and the Beautiful)*

Best Director: John Ford *(The Quiet Man)*

Best Picture: *The Greatest Show on Earth*

1953

Best Actor: William Holden *(Stalag 17)*

Best Actress: Audrey Hepburn *(Roman Holiday)*

Best Supporting Actor: Frank Sinatra *(From Here to Eternity)*

Best Supporting Actress: Donna Reed *(From Here to Eternity)*

Best Director: Fred Zinnemann *(From Here to Eternity)*

Best Picture: *From Here to Eternity*

1954

Best Actor: Marlon Brando *(On the Waterfront)*

Best Actress: Grace Kelly *(The Country Girl)*

Best Supporting Actor: Edmond O'Brien *(The Barefoot Contessa)*

Best Supporting Actress: Eva Marie Saint *(On the Waterfront)*

Best Director: Elia Kazan *(On the Waterfront)*

Best Picture: *On the Waterfront*

1955

Best Actor: Ernest Borgnine *(Marty)*

Best Actress: Anna Magnani *(The Rose Tattoo)*

Best Supporting Actor: Jack Lemmon *(Mister Roberts)*

Best Supporting Actress: Jo Van Fleet *(East of Eden)*

Best Director: Delbert Mann *(Marty)*

Best Picture: *Marty*

1956

Best Actor: Yul Brynner *(The King and I)*

Best Actress: Ingrid Bergman *(Anastasia)*

Best Supporting Actor: Anthony Quinn *(Lust for Life)*

Best Supporting Actress: Dorothy Malone *(Written on the Wind)*

Best Director: George Stevens *(Giant)*

Best Picture: *Around the World in Eighty Days*

Best Foreign Film: *La Strada*

1957

Best Actor: Alec Guinness *(The Bridge on the River Kwai)*

Best Actress: Joanne Woodward *(The Three Faces of Eve)*

Best Supporting Actor: Red Buttons *(Sayonara)*
Best Supporting Actress: Miyoshi Umeki *(Sayonara)*
Best Director: David Lean *(The Bridge on the River Kwai)*
Best Picture: *The Bridge on the River Kwai*
Best Foreign Film: *The Nights of Cabiria*

1958

Best Actor: David Niven *(Separate Tables)*
Best Actress: Susan Hayward *(I Want to Live)*
Best Supporting Actor: Burl Ives *(The Big Country)*
Best Supporting Actress: Wendy Hiller *(Separate Tables)*
Best Director: Vincente Minnelli *(Gigi)*
Best Picture: *Gigi*
Best Foreign Film: *My Uncle*

1959

Best Actor: Charlton Heston *(Ben-Hur)*
Best Actress: Simone Signoret *(Room at the Top)*
Best Supporting Actor: Hugh Griffith *(Ben-Hur)*
Best Supporting Actress: Shelley Winters *(The Diary of Anne Frank)*
Best Director: William Wyler *(Ben-Hur)*
Best Picture: *Ben-Hur*
Best Foreign Film: *Black Orpheus*

1960

Best Actor: Burt Lancaster *(Elmer Gantry)*
Best Actress: Elizabeth Taylor *(Butterfield 8)*
Best Supporting Actor: Peter Ustinov *(Spartacus)*
Best Supporting Actress: Shirley Jones *(Elmer Gantry)*
Best Director: Billy Wilder *(The Apartment)*
Best Picture: *The Apartment*
Best Foreign Film: *The Virgin Spring*

1961

Best Actor: Maximillian Schell *(Judgment at Nuremberg)*
Best Actress: Sophia Loren *(Two Women)*
Best Supporting Actor: George Chakiris *(West Side Story)*
Best Supporting Actress: Rita Moreno *(West Side Story)*
Best Director: Jerome Robbins, Robert Wise *(West Side Story)*
Best Picture: *West Side Story*
Best Foreign Film: *Through a Glass Darkly*

1962

Best Actor: Gregory Peck *(To Kill a Mockingbird)*
Best Actress: Anne Bancroft *(The Miracle Worker)*
Best Supporting Actor: Ed Begley *(Sweet Bird of Youth)*
Best Supporting Actress: Patty Duke *(The Miracle Worker)*

Best Director: David Lean *(Lawrence of Arabia)*
Best Picture: *Lawrence of Arabia*
Best Foreign Film: *Sundays and Cybele*

1963

Best Actor: Sidney Poitier *(Lilies of the Field)*
Best Actress: Patricia Neal *(Hud)*
Best Supporting Actor: Melvyn Douglas *(Hud)*
Best Supporting Actress: Margaret Rutherford *(The V.I.P.s)*
Best Director: Tony Richardson *(Tom Jones)*
Best Picture: *Tom Jones*
Best Foreign Film: *8¹/²*

1964

Best Actor: Rex Harrison *(My Fair Lady)*
Best Actress: Julie Andrews *(Mary Poppins)*
Best Supporting Actor: Peter Ustinov *(Topkapi)*
Best Supporting Actress: Lila Kedrova *(Zorba the Greek)*
Best Director: George Cukor *(My Fair Lady)*
Best Picture: *My Fair Lady*
Best Foreign Film: *Yesterday, Today and Tomorrow*

1965

Best Actor: Lee Marvin *(Cat Ballou)*
Best Actress: Julie Christie *(Darling)*
Best Supporting Actor: Martin Balsam *(A Thousand Clowns)*
Best Supporting Actress: Shelley Winters *(A Patch of Blue)*
Best Director: Robert Wise *(The Sound of Music)*
Best Picture: *The Sound of Music*
Best Foreign Film: *The Shop on Main Street*

1966

Best Actor: Paul Scofield *(A Man for All Seasons)*
Best Actress: Elizabeth Taylor *(Who's Afraid of Virginia Woolf?)*
Best Supporting Actor: Walter Matthau *(The Fortune Cookie)*
Best Supporting Actress: Sandy Dennis *(Who's Afraid of Virginia Woolf?)*
Best Director: Fred Zinnemann *(A Man for All Seasons)*
Best Picture: *A Man for All Seasons*
Best Foreign Film: *A Man and a Woman*

1967

Best Actor: Rod Steiger *(In the Heat of the Night)*
Best Actress: Katharine Hepburn *(Guess Who's Coming to Dinner)*
Best Supporting Actor: George Kennedy *(Cool Hand Luke)*
Best Supporting Actress: Estelle Parsons *(Bonnie and Clyde)*

Best Director: Mike Nichols *(The Graduate)*
Best Picture: *In the Heat of the Night*
Best Foreign Film: *Closely Watched Trains*

1968

Best Actor: Cliff Robertson *(Charly)*
Best Actress: Katharine Hepburn *(The Lion in Winter)*; Barbra Streisand *(Funny Girl)*
Best Supporting Actor: Jack Albertson *(The Subject Was Roses)*
Best Supporting Actress: Ruth Gordon *(Rosemary's Baby)*
Best Director: Sir Carol Reed *(Oliver!)*
Best Picture: *Oliver!*
Best Foreign Film: *War and Peace*

1969

Best Actor: John Wayne *(True Grit)*
Best Actress: Maggie Smith *(The Prime of Miss Jean Brodie)*
Best Supporting Actor: Gig Young *(They Shoot Horses Don't They?)*
Best Supporting Actress: Goldie Hawn *(Cactus Flower)*
Best Director: John Schlesinger *(Midnight Cowboy)*
Best Picture: *Midnight Cowboy*
Best Foreign Film: *Z*

1970

Best Actor: George C. Scott *(Patton; refused)*
Best Actress: Glenda Jackson *(Women in Love)*
Best Supporting Actor: John Mills *(Ryan's Daughter)*
Best Supporting Actress: Helen Hayes *(Airport)*
Best Director: Franklin Schaffner, Frank McCarthy *(Patton)*
Best Picture: *Patton*
Best Foreign Film: *Investigation of a Citizen Above Suspicion*

1971

Best Actor: Gene Hackman *(The French Connection)*
Best Actress: Jane Fonda *(Klute)*
Best Supporting Actor: Ben Johnson *(The Last Picture Show)*
Best Supporting Actress: Cloris Leachman *(The Last Picture Show)*
Best Director: William Friedkin *(The French Connection)*
Best Picture: *The French Connection*
Best Foreign Film: *The Garden of the Finzi-Continis*

1972

Best Actor: Marlon Brando *(The Godfather; refused)*
Best Actress: Liza Minnelli *(Cabaret)*
Best Supporting Actor: Joel Grey *(Cabaret)*
Best Supporting Actress: Eileen Heckart *(Butterflies Are Free)*

Best Director: Bob Fosse *(Cabaret)*
Best Picture: *The Godfather*
Best Foreign Film: *The Discreet Charm of the Bourgeoisie*

1973

Best Actor: Jack Lemmon *(Save the Tiger)*
Best Actress: Glenda Jackson *(A Touch of Class)*
Best Supporting Actor: John Houseman *(The Paper Chase)*
Best Supporting Actress: Tatum O'Neal *(Paper Moon)*
Best Director: George Roy Hill *(The Sting)*
Best Picture: *The Sting*
Best Foreign Film: *Day for Night*

1974

Best Actor: Art Carney *(Harry and Tonto)*
Best Actress: Ellen Burstyn *(Alice Doesn't Live Here Anymore)*
Best Supporting Actor: Robert DeNiro *(The Godfather, Part II)*
Best Supporting Actress: Ingrid Bergman *(Murder on the Orient Express)*
Best Director: Francis Ford Coppola *(The Godfather, Part II)*
Best Picture: *The Godfather, Part II*
Best Foreign Film: *Amarcord*

1975

Best Actor: Jack Nicholson *(One Flew over the Cuckoo's Nest)*
Best Actress: Louise Fletcher *(One Flew over the Cuckoo's Nest)*
Best Supporting Actor: George Burns *(The Sunshine Boys)*
Best Supporting Actress: Lee Grant *(Shampoo)*
Best Director: Milos Forman *(One Flew over the Cuckoo's Nest)*
Best Picture: *One Flew over the Cuckoo's Nest*
Best Foreign Film: *Dersu Uzala*

1976

Best Actor: Peter Finch *(Network)*
Best Actress: Faye Dunaway *(Network)*
Best Supporting Actor: Jason Robards *(All the President's Men)*
Best Supporting Actress: Beatrice Straight *(Network)*
Best Director: John G. Avildsen *(Rocky)*
Best Picture: *Rocky*
Best Foreign Film: *Black and White in Color*

1977

Best Actor: Richard Dreyfuss *(The Goodbye Girl)*
Best Actress: Diane Keaton *(Annie Hall)*
Best Supporting Actor: Jason Robards *(Julia)*

Best Supporting Actress: Vanessa Redgrave *(Julia)*
Best Director: Woody Allen *(Annie Hall)*
Best Picture: *Annie Hall*
Best Foreign Film: *Madame Rosa*

1978

Best Actor: Jon Voight *(Coming Home)*
Best Actress: Jane Fonda *(Coming Home)*
Best Supporting Actor: Christopher Walken *(The Deer Hunter)*
Best Supporting Actress: Maggie Smith *(California Suite)*
Best Director: Michael Cimino *(The Deer Hunter)*
Best Picture: *The Deer Hunter*
Best Foreign Film: *Get Out Your Handkerchiefs*

1979

Best Actor: Dustin Hoffman *(Kramer vs. Kramer)*
Best Actress: Sally Field *(Norma Rae)*
Best Supporting Actor: Melvyn Douglas *(Being There)*
Best Supporting Actress: Meryl Streep *(Kramer vs. Kramer)*
Best Director: Robert Benton *(Kramer vs. Kramer)*
Best Picture: Kramer vs. Kramer
Best Foreign Film: *The Tin Drum*

1980

Best Actor: Robert De Niro *(Raging Bull)*
Best Actress: Sissy Spacek *(Coal Miner's Daughter)*
Best Supporting Actor: Timothy Hutton *(Ordinary People)*
Best Supporting Actress: Mary Steenburgen *(Melvin and Howard)*
Best Director: Robert Redford *(Ordinary People)*
Best Picture: *Ordinary People*
Best Foreign Film: *Moscow Does Not Believe in Tears*

1981

Best Actor: Henry Fonda *(On Golden Pond)*
Best Actress: Katharine Hepburn *(On Golden Pond)*
Best Supporting Actor: John Gielgud *(Arthur)*
Best Supporting Actress: Maureen Stapleton *(Reds)*
Best Director: Warren Beatty *(Reds)*
Best Picture: *Chariots of Fire*
Best Foreign Film: *Memphisto*

1982

Best Actor: Ben Kingsley *(Gandhi)*
Best Actress: Meryl Streep *(Sophie's Choice)*
Best Supporting Actor: Louis Gossett, Jr. *(An Officer and a Gentleman)*
Best Supporting Actress: Jessica Lange *(Tootsie)*
Best Director: Richard Attenborough *(Gandhi)*
Best Picture: *Gandhi*
Best Foreign Film: *To Begin Again*

1983

Best Actor: Robert Duvall *(Tender Mercies)*
Best Actress: Shirley MacLaine *(Terms of Endearment)*
Best Supporting Actor: Jack Nicholson *(Terms of Endearment)*
Best Supporting Actress: Linda Hunt *(The Year of Living Dangerously)*
Best Director: James L. Brooks *(Terms of Endearment)*
Best Picture: Terms of Endearment
Best Foreign Film: *Fanny and Alexander*

1984

Best Actor: F. Murray Abraham *(Amadeus)*
Best Actress: Sally Field *(Places in the Heart)*
Best Supporting Actor: Haing S. Ngor *(The Killing Fields)*
Best Supporting Actress: Dame Peggy Ashcroft *(A Passage to India)*
Best Director: Milos Forman *(Amadeus)*
Best Picture: *Amadeus*
Best Foreign Film: *Dangerous Moves*

1985

Best Actor: William Hurt *(Kiss of the Spider Woman)*
Best Actress: Geraldine Page *(The Trip to Bountiful)*
Best Supporting Actor: Don Ameche *(Cocoon)*
Best Supporting Actress: Angelica Houston *(Prizzi's Honor)*
Best Director: Sydney Pollack *(Out of Africa)*
Best Picture: *Out of Africa*
Best Foreign Film: *The Official Story*

1986

Best Actor: Paul Newman *(The Color of Money)*
Best Actress: Marlee Matlin *(Children of a Lesser God)*
Best Supporting Actor: Michael Caine *(Hannah and Her Sisters)*
Best Supporting Actress: Dianc Wicst *(Hannah and Her Sisters)*
Best Director: Oliver Stone *(Platoon)*
Best Picture: *Platoon*
Best Foreign Film: *The Assault*

1987

Best Actor: Michacl Douglas *(Wall Street)*
Best Actress: Cher *(Moonstruck)*
Best Supporting Actor: Sean Connery *(The Untouchables)*
Best Supporting Actress: Olympia Dukakis *(Moonstruck)*
Best Director: Bernardo Bertolucci *(The Last Emperor)*
Best Picture: *The Last Emperor*
Best Foreign Film: *Babette's Feast*

Performance Arts

1988

Best Actor: Dustin Hoffman *(Rain Man)*
Best Actress: Jody Foster *(The Accused)*
Best Supporting Actor: Kevin Kline *(A Fish Called Wanda)*
Best Supporting Actress: Geena Davis *(The Accidental Tourist)*
Best Director: Barry Levinson *(Rain Man)*
Best Picture: *Rain Man*
Best Foreign Film: *Pelle the Conquerer*

1989

Best Actor: Daniel Day-Lewis *(My Left Foot)*
Best Actress: Jessica Tandy *(Driving Miss Daisy)*
Best Supporting Actor: Denzel Washington *(Glory)*
Best Supporting Actress: Brenda Fricker *(My Left Foot)*
Best Director: Oliver Stone *(Born on the Fourth of July)*
Best Picture: *Driving Miss Daisy*
Best Foreign Film: *Cinema Paradiso*

1990

Best Actor: Jeremy Irons *(Reversal of Fortune)*
Best Actress: Kathy Bates *(Misery)*
Best Supporting Actor: Joe Pesci *(Goodfellas)*
Best Supporting Actress: Whoopi Goldberg *(Ghost)*
Best Director: Kevin Costner *(Dances with Wolves)*
Best Picture: *Dances with Wolves*
Best Foreign Film: *Journey of Hope*

1991

Best Actor: Anthony Hopkins *(The Silence of the Lambs)*
Best Actress: Jodie Foster *(The Silence of the Lambs)*
Best Supporting Actor: Jack Palance *(City Slickers)*
Best Supporting Actress: Mercedes Ruehl *(The Fisher King)*
Best Director: Jonathan Demme *(The Silence of the Lambs)*
Best Picture: *The Silence of the Lambs*
Best Foreign Film: *Mediterraneo*

1992

Best Actor: Al Pacino *(Scent of a Women)*
Best Actress: Emma Thompson *(Howard's End)*
Best Supporting Actor: Gene Hackman *(Unforgiven)*
Best Supporting Actress: Marisa Tomei *(My Cousin Vinny)*
Best Director: Clint Eastwood *(Unforgiven)*
Best Picture: *Unforgiven*
Best Foreign Film: *Indochine*

1993

Best Actor: Tom Hanks *(Philadelphia)*
Best Actress: Holly Hunter *(The Piano)*
Best Supporting Actor: Tommy Lee Jones *(The Fugitive)*
Best Supporting Actress: Anna Paquin *(The Piano)*
Best Director: Steven Spielberg *(Schindler's List)*
Best Picture: *Schindler's List*
Best Foreign Film: *Belle Epoque*

1994

Best Actor: Tom Hanks *(Forrest Gump)*
Best Actress: Jessica Lange *(Blue Sky)*
Best Supporting Actor: Martin Landau *(Ed Wood)*
Best Supporting Actress: Diane Wiest *(Bullets over Broadway)*
Best Director: Robert Zemeckis *(Forrest Gump)*
Best Picture: *Forrest Gump*
Best Foreign Film: *Burnt by the Sun*

1995

Best Actor: Nicolas Cage *(Leaving Las Vegas)*
Best Actress: Susan Sarandon *(Dead Man Walking)*
Best Supporting Actor: Kevin Spacey *(The Usual Suspects)*
Best Supporting Actress: Mira Sorvino *(Mighty Aphrodite)*
Best Director: Mel Gibson *(Braveheart)*
Best Picture: *Braveheart*
Best Foreign Film: *Antonia's Line*

1996

Best Actor: Geoffrey Rush *(Shine)*
Best Actress: Frances McDormand *(Fargo)*
Best Supporting Actor: Cuba Gooding, Jr. *(Jerry Maguire)*
Best Supporting Actress: Juliette Binoche *(The English Patient)*
Best Director: Anthony Minghella *(The English Patient)*
Best Picture: *The English Patient*
Best Foreign Film: *Kolya*

1997

Best Actor: Jack Nicholson
Best Actress: Helen Hunt
Best Supporting Actor: Robin Williams
Best Supporting Actress: Kim Basinger
Best Director:
Best Picture: *Titanic*
Best Foreign Film: *Character*

Go to "Book Awards and Their Recipients" in chapter 8

Performance Arts

ADDITIONAL SOURCES OF INFORMATION

MAGAZINES

Back Stage
1515 Broadway
New York, NY 10036
http://www.backstagecasting.com

Entertainment Weekly
1271 Avenue of the Americas
New York, NY 10020
http://www.pathfinder.com

People Magazine
1271 Avenue of the Americas
New York, NY 10020
http://www.pathfinder.com

Popular Photography
1633 Broadway
New York, NY 10019

Premiere
215 Lexington Ave.
New York, NY 10016
http://www.premieremag.com

TV Guide Magazine
200 Madison Ave.
New York, NY 10016
http://www.tvguide.com

BOOKS

MUSIC

Arnold, Denis, ed. *The New Oxford Companion to Music.* 2 vols. Oxford University Press, 1988.

Atkins, Ronald, ed. *All that Jazz: The Illustrated Story of Jazz Music.* Smithmark, 1996.

Jezic, Diane Peacock. *Women Composers: The Lost Tradition Found.* 2nd ed. Feminist Press, 1996.

Kennedy, Michael. *The Oxford Dictionary of Music.* 2nd ed. Oxford University Press, 1995.

Kerfeld, Barry. *The New Grove Dictionary of Jazz.* St. Martin's Press, 1994.

Kobbe, Gustave. *The Definitive Kobbe's Opera Book.* Rev. ed. Putnam, 1987.

Randel, Don Michael, ed. *The Harvard Biographical Dictionary of Music.* Belknap Press, 1996.

Randel, Don Michael, ed. *The New Harvard Dictionary of Music.* Belknap Press, 1986.

Sadie, Stanley, ed. *The New Grove Dictionary of Music and Musicians.* 20 vols. Groves Dictionaries of Music, 1995.

Sadie, Stanley, ed. *The New Grove Dictionary of Opera.* 4 vols. Groves Dictionaries of Music, 1995.

DANCE

Brenser, Martha, ed. *International Dictionary of Ballet.* St. James Press, 1993.

Cohen, Selma Jeanne, ed. *International Encyclopedia of Dance.* 6 vols. Oxford University Press, 1998.

Kirstein, Lincoln. *Dance: A Short History of Classic Theatrical Dancing.* Princeton Book Co., 1994.

Koegler, Horst. *The Concise Oxford Dictionary of Ballet.* Oxford University Press, 1982.

McDonagh, Don. *The Rise and Fall and Rise of Modern Dance.* Chicago Review, 1990.

McQuade. *The Schirmer Biographical Dictionary of Dance.* Macmillan, 1998.

Stephenson, Richard M., and Joseph Iaccarino. *The Complete Book of Ballroom Dancing.* Doubleday, 1992.

STAGE AND FILM

Banham, Martin, and Sarah Stanton, eds. *Cambridge Paperback Guide to the Theatre.* Cambridge University Press, 1996.

Berney, K. A., ed. *Contemporary Dramatists.* 5th ed. St. James Press, 1993.

Corey, Melinda, and George Ochoa, comps. *A Cast of Thousands: A Compendium of Who Played What in Film.* Facts on Filc, 1992.

Hartnoll, Phyllis, and Peter Found, eds. *The Concise Oxford Companion to the Theatre.* 2nd ed. Oxford University Press, 1992.

Hochman, Stanley. *McGraw-Hill Encyclopedia of World Drama.* 2nd ed. 5 vols. McGraw-Hill, 1984.

Shipley, Joseph T. *The Crown Guide to the World's Great Plays.* Crown, 1984.

7

THE VISUAL ARTS

MAJOR PAINTERS AND SCULPTORS   218

ART MOVEMENTS AND STYLES   230

COMMON ART TERMS   232

MAJOR ARCHITECTS   235

ARCHITECTURAL MOVEMENTS AND STYLES   240

ILLUSTRATIONS OF ARCHITECTURAL ELEMENTS   242

COMMON ARCHITECTURAL TERMS   244

ADDITIONAL SOURCES OF INFORMATION   246

MAJOR PAINTERS AND SCULPTORS

AMERICAN

Albers, Josef (1888–1976), b. Germany. Painter and designer, teacher at the Bauhaus, and director of the Yale School of Art. He is best known for his *Homage to the Square* series (begun 1949) and for his widely studied color theories.

Calder, Alexander (1898–1976), b. Pennsylvania. Sculptor best known for his mobiles and playful wire constructions of circuses, begun in 1926. Much of his later work is large, heavy sculpture, often for public areas.

Cassatt, Mary (1845–1926), b. Pennsylvania. Artist who spent much of her life in Paris, where she was allied with the Impressionists. She is best known for paintings of women with children, such as *The Bath* (1892), and for etchings, such as *The Letter* (1891).

Cornell, Joseph (1903–72), b. New York. His surrealist-influenced constructions are boxes filled with found objects and collaged images, arranged in privately symbolic ways. Some of the best-known examples are *Medici Slot Machine* (1942) and *Hôtel du Nord* (1953).

Davies, Arthur Bowen (1862–1928), b. New York. Member of The Eight and an organizer of the historic 1913 Armory Show. His symbolic, idyllic paintings include landscapes such as *Unicorns* (1906).

Davis, Stuart (1894–1964), b. Pennsylvania. Davis developed a distinctly American interpretation of cubism in his brightly colored paintings, such as *Hot Still-Scape for Six Colors* (1940) and *Colonial Cubism* (1954).

de Kooning, Willem (1904–97), b. The Netherlands. A leader of abstract expressionism in the United States, de Kooning is best known for his monumental, violently painted *Woman* series, begun in the early 1950s.

Demuth, Charles (1883–1935), b. Pennsylvania. One of the first to incorporate geometric shapes of modern technology into painting. His best-known work is *I Saw the Figure 5 in Gold* (1928).

Dove, Arthur Garfield (1880–1946), b. New York. In his paintings of abstracted natural forms, such as *Waterfall* (1925) and *Rise of the Full Moon* (1937), Dove was a forerunner of abstract expressionism.

Eakins, Thomas (1844–1916), b. Pennsylvania. An important portraitist, Eakins was criticized for innovations such as working from live nude models. His best-known works include *The Gross Clinic* (1875), which shows an operation in progress, and *Max Schmitt in a Single Scull* (1871).

Feininger, Lyonel (1871–1956), b. New York. Feininger, who taught at the Bauhaus (1919–32), developed a style of delicate architectural forms fractured by rays of light, as in *Church at Gelmeroda* (1936).

Frankenthaler, Helen (1928–), b. New York. Frankenthaler developed a technique of staining canvases with paint, creating sensuous abstract works such as *Mountains and Sea* (1952), a seminal work in this style, and *Arden* (1961).

Gorky, Arshile (1904–48), b. Armenia. An influence on abstract expressionism, Gorky painted abstract but often biomorphic forms in brilliant, glowing colors, as in *The Liver Is the Cock's Comb* (1944).

Henri, Robert (1865–1929), b. Ohio. Painter and influential teacher. As a member of The Eight, he was a leader in the rebellion against academic art. Henri is best known for his dramatic portraits, such as *Woman in Manteau* (1898), *Himself* (1913), and *Herself* (1913).

Hofmann, Hans (1880–1966), b. Germany. Founder of two U.S. art schools important in the development of abstract expressionism. Hofmann boldly manipulated violent, clashing colors, as in *Effervescence* (1944) and *The Gate* (1959).

Homer, Winslow (1836–1910), b. Massachusetts. One of the most prominent 19th-century American painters, Homer is best known for his dramatic seascapes, such as *West Point, Prout's Neck, Maine,* and *On a Lee Shore* (both 1900).

Hopper, Edward (1882–1967), b. New York. Hopper painted lonely street scenes, buildings, and interiors, giving careful attention to light and shade, as in *Nighthawks* (1942) and *Early Sunday Morning* (1930).

Indiana, Robert (1928–   ), b. Indiana. Pop artist best known for his bold and vivid signlike paintings and sculpture, such as the *Love* series (begun 1966).

Johns, Jasper (1930–   ), b. Georgia. A founder of pop art, Johns uses everyday signs, symbols, and objects—such as flags, targets, and beer cans—in his paintings and sculptures. An example is the painting *Three Flags* (1958).

Kline, Franz (1910–62), b. Pennsylvania. He painted large canvases with dynamic black and white brush strokes, as in *White Forms* (1955) and *Mahoning* (1956). His work exemplifies abstract expressionism.

Lichtenstein, Roy (1923–97), b. New York. Pop artist known for his paintings based on comic strips. Examples are *Masterpiece* (1962) and *Good Morning, Darling* (1964).

Louis, Morris (1912–62), b. Maryland. He used a technique of soaking poured paint through canvases, so that the canvas essentially became dyed by the paint. His work includes the *Veil* series (1954, 1958) and the *Unfurled* series (1960–61).

Moses, Grandma (Anna Mary Robertson Moses) (1860–1961), b. New York. A farmer's wife who began painting in her seventies. Her primitive, colorful works of farm life, such as *Sugaring-Off* (1943), achieved wide popularity.

Motherwell, Robert (1915–91), b. Washington. Painter, writer, and important theoretician of abstract expressionism. His works are characterized by amorphous shapes in austere colors; best known is the series *Elegy for the Spanish Republic,* begun in 1949.

Nevelson, Louise (1900–88), b. Russia. Sculptor known for her large works of painted wood, metal, and found objects. Examples are *Sky Cathedral* (1958) and *World* (1966).

If a statue of a horse has both front legs in the air, the rider died in battle. If the horse has one front leg in the air, the rider died as a result of battle. If the horse has all four legs on the ground, the rider died of natural causes.

Newman, Barnett (1905–71), b. New York. Painter whose works bridged abstract expressionism and the color field movement. His canvases are typically large planes of flat color with thin vertical stripes, such as *Onement I* (1948) and *Concord* (1949). He also produced sculpture.

Noguchi, Isamu (1904–88), b. California. Sculptor well known for his abstract works designed for architectural spaces, such as the sculpture garden for the UNESCO building in Paris (1958) and the entrance for the Museum of Modern Art in Tokyo (1969).

O'Keeffe, Georgia (1887–1986), b. Wisconsin. Painter whose most characteristic images are sculptural, organic forms such as bones and flowers. She lived in New Mexico and often used elements of the southwestern landscape, as in *Cow's Skull: Red, White, and Blue* (1931).

Oldenburg, Claes (1929–   ), b. Sweden. Leader of the pop-art movement, known for his giant sculptures of common objects, such as *Dual Hamburger* (1962) and *Lipstick* (1969).

Parrish, Maxfield (1870–1966), b. Pennsylvania. Creator of posters, magazine covers, and book illustrations in a distinctive, decorative style.

Pollock, Jackson (1912–56), b. Wyoming. A pioneer of abstract expressionism, Pollock developed a method called action painting. His canvases are typically large, with paint dripped, poured, and thrown in complex, dense rhythms, as in *Number 1* (1948), *Number 32* (1950), and *Blue Poles* (1953).

Prendergast, Maurice Brazil (1859–1924), b. Canada. Member of The Eight. He painted landscapes and figures in a colorful, decorative style influenced by the Nabis, as in *The Promenade* (1913).

Rauschenberg, Robert (1925–), b. Texas. His collagelike "combine paintings" appropriating everyday images and objects represent a transition between abstract expressionism and pop art. His work includes *Bed* (1955) and *Monogram* (1959).

Reinhardt, Ad (Adolph) (1913–67), b. New York. Associated with minimalism, Reinhardt began painting monochrome canvases by 1953. He is best known for his *Black Paintings,* begun in 1960.

Remington, Frederic (1861–1909), b. New York. Painter, sculptor, illustrator, and writer whose subject was life on the western plains. His works include the sculpture *Bronco Buster* (1895) and the painting *Evening on a Canadian Lake* (1905).

Rivers, Larry (1923–), b. New York. In his use of popular images from sources such as artworks and advertising, Rivers was a forerunner of pop art. His paintings include *Washington Crossing the Delaware* (1953) and the *Dutch Masters* series (1963). He has also done sculpture.

Rockwell, Norman (1894–1978), b. New York. Illustrator best known for his *Saturday Evening Post* covers (1916–63). His realistically drawn, popular works portray anecdotal scenes of small-town America. *The Four Freedoms* (1943) are among his most famous paintings.

Rothko, Mark (1903–70), b. Russia. Important figure in abstract expressionism. His canvases contain soft-edged, luminously colored rectangular forms. His work includes *No. 10* (1950) and a series of murals for an ecumenical chapel in Houston (1967–69).

Sargent, John Singer (1856–1925), b. Italy. Painter known for his vivid portraits of high society, such as *The Daughters of Edward D. Boit* (1882) and *Madame X* (1884). He also produced impressionistic watercolor landscapes.

Segal, George (1924–), b. New York. Sculptor known for his life-size plaster human figures in everyday environments, such as *Woman in Restaurant Booth* (1961) and *Cinema* (1963). Segal is associated with pop art.

Shahn, Ben (1898–1969), b. Lithuania. Versatile artist of social-realistic work that often tells a story without preaching. In the early 1930s, he did a series of 23 paintings based on the Sacco-Vanzetti trial.

Sheeler, Charles (1883–1965), b. Pennsylvania. Photographer and painter known for his depictions of industrial forms reduced to cool, formal simplification. His works include the paintings *Ballardvale Revisited* (1949) and *Steel-Croton* (1953).

Smith, David (1906–65), b. Indiana. Renowned abstract sculptor of welded metal forms. He worked on his large *Cubi* series from the late 1950s until his death.

Stella, Frank (1936–), b. Massachusetts. Abstract painter of large, colorful works on irregularly shaped canvases. Works such as *Empress of India* (1965) use series of angular stripes; later works such as *Guadalupe Island* (1979) exhibit sweeping arched forms and wildly exuberant colors.

Sully, Thomas (1783–1872), b. England. A leading portraitist, especially of national figures. His most famous work is the historical painting *Washington's Passage of the Delaware* (1819).

Warhol, Andy (1930–87), b. Pennsylvania. Leader of the pop art movement. His works are notable for the repetition of everyday images, such as Campbell's soup cans, and for figures from popular culture, such as Marilyn Monroe (both series begun 1962).

West, Benjamin (1738–1820), b. Pennsylvania. Working in both Neoclassical and Romantic styles, he produced paintings such as *The Death of General Wolfe* (1770) and *Death on a Pale Horse* (1802). West worked mainly in England and was a founder and president of the Royal Academy of Arts there.

Whistler, James Abbott McNeill (1834–1903), b. Massachusetts. Painter and graphic artist whose works show a brilliant sense of color and design. His paintings include *The White Girl: Symphony in White No. 1* (1862) and *The Artist's Mother: Arrangement in Gray and Black* (1871). His series of *Nocturnes* foreshadowed abstract art.

Wood, Grant (1891–1942), b. Iowa. Painter best known for his stern figures and stylized landscapes of the rural Midwest. *American Gothic* (1930) is a quintessential American work.

Wyeth, Andrew (1917–   ), b. Pennsylvania. Popular painter of rural landscapes and portraits in a meticulous, naturalistic style. His best-known work is *Christina's World* (1948). In 1986, Wyeth astonished the public with the appearance of a previously secret series, the *Helga* paintings.

BELGIAN/FLEMISH

Bruegel, Pieter, the Elder (c. 1525–69). Flemish painter of peasants at work and play, genre scenes, landscapes, and illustrations of proverbs. His paintings include *The Corn Harvest* (1565) and *The Peasant Wedding* (c. 1567).

Ensor, James (Baron) (1860–1949). Belgian painter and etcher. Ensor created innovative and grotesque compositions, such as *The Temptation of St. Anthony* (1887) and *The Entry of Christ into Brussels* (1888), opening the way for the surrealist movement.

Limbourg, Herman, Jean, and **Pol** (active 1380–1416). Flemish brothers who worked in France for the Duke of Berry. Their *Les Très Riches Heures du Duc de Berry* (1413–16) is an exquisite, colorful, illuminated manuscript, showing activities of daily life.

Magritte, René (1898–1967). A leading Belgian surrealist painter. His works, such as *The Key of Dreams* (1930) and *The Human Condition* (1934), are odd fantasies based on everyday situations, or plays on relationships between pictures and words.

Rubens, Peter Paul (1577–1640). The foremost Flemish artist and a major baroque figure. Working with great freedom and vitality, Rubens produced dynamic, monumental paintings. His works include *The Raising of the Cross* (1610–11), a series of allegorical paintings on the life of Marie de Médici (1622–25), and *The Judgment of Paris* (1638–39).

Van der Weyden, Rogier (c. 1400–64). Flemish painter. His religious works, such as *The Descent from the Cross* (1435) and *The Last Judgment* (c. 1450), combine monumentality with a profound sense of emotion. His penetrating portraits include *Francesco d'Este* (c. 1455).

Van Dyck, Sir Anthony (1599–1641). A major Flemish baroque artist. Van Dyck's many portraits of the aristocracy include a number of Charles I of England (his royal patron from 1632 on) such as *Portrait of Charles I Hunting* (c. 1635). Van Dyck also painted religious works, such as *The Lamentation* (1634).

Van Eyck, Jan (c. 1390–1441). A master of Flemish painting. In works such as the church altarpiece in Ghent (1426–32) and the *Arnolfini Wedding Portrait* (1434), Van Eyck achieved an unprecedented luminosity, intensity of color, and detail.

BRITISH

Bacon, Francis (1909–92), b. Ireland. Painter of disturbing, hallucinatory images, as in *Three Studies at the Base of a Crucifixion* (1944) and his series based on Velázquez's *Pope Innocent X* portrait, begun in the 1950s.

Blake, William (1757–1827). Painter, engraver, and poet. Blake, a mystic and visionary, created paintings and engravings for John Linnell's editions of the *Book of Job* (1821–26) and Dante's *Divine Comedy* (1824–27), and for his own poetic works in an unearthly, highly personal style.

Constable, John (1776–1837). Leading English landscape painter. In works such as *The White Horse* (1819), *The Hay Wain* (1821), and *Salisbury Cathedral* (1827), he carefully observed natural phenomena and changes.

Gainsborough, Thomas (1727–88). Portraitist and landscape painter. His well-known works include *Mr. and Mrs. Robert Andrews* (1748), *Mrs. Siddons* (1785), and his most famous painting, *The Blue Boy* (1770).

Hogarth, William (1697–1764). Painter and engraver of satirical works, often on moral themes and told in a series of scenes, such as *The Rake's Progress* (1733–35) and *Marriage à la Mode* (1743–45).

Moore, Henry (1898–1986). Sculptor whose abstract and figurative works are characterized by smooth organic shapes and hollows. His many public commissions include works for the Time-Life building in London (1952–53) and for Lincoln Center for the Performing Arts in New York City (1962–65).

Reynolds, Sir Joshua (1723–92). Reynolds, first president of the Royal Academy of Arts, painted portraits of nearly every important figure of his day with great versatility. His works include *Commodore Keppel* (1753) and *Mrs. Siddons as the Tragic Muse* (1784).

Rossetti, Dante Gabriel (1828–82). Painter and poet; one of the founders of the Pre-Raphaelite Brotherhood in 1848. His sensual and symbolic works include *The Annunciation* (1850) and *Beata Beatrix* (1864).

Turner, Joseph Mallord William (1775–1851). The foremost English landscape painter. Turner depicted atmospheric effects with a style of shimmering light and luminous colors, as in *Calais Pier* (1803) and *The Grand Canal* (1835).

DUTCH

Bosch, Hieronymus (Jerom Bos) (c. 1450–1516). Painter of bizarre and colorful religious allegories, filled with grotesque figures and animals and obscure symbolism. His works include *The Garden of Earthly Delights* (c. 1505–10) and *The Temptation of St. Anthony* (c. 1500).

The Dutch painter Rembrandt, often called the master of light and shade, painted almost 100 self-portraits.

Hals, Frans (c. 1580–1666). He painted lively and naturalistic portraits and genre scenes in vivid, sparkling colors. His works include *The Banquet of the Officers of the St. George Militia* (1616) and *The Laughing Cavalier* (1624).

Mondrian, Piet (1872–1944). A founder of the Stijl group and the magazine *Die Stijl*. Mondrian developed a geometric style known as "neoplasticism." Typical works consist of primary-color squares bounded by black outlines, as in *Composition in Yellow and Blue* (1929) and *Red, Yellow, and Blue Composition* (1930).

Rembrandt Harmenszoon van Rijn (1606–69). A master of the Dutch school, he produced some 600 paintings distinguished by their profound humanity, including *The Anatomy Lesson of Dr. Tulp* (1632), *The Blinding of Samson* (1636), and *The Night Watch* (1642). Rembrandt also painted nearly 100 self-portraits, dating from the 1620s to his last years.

Van Gogh, Vincent (1853–90). One of the most influential 19th-century artists. Many of Van Gogh's vibrant, expressive paintings were produced in a 29-month period preceding his suicide. Among his most famous works are *The Potato Eaters* (1885), *The Night Café* (1888), *Starry Night* (1889), and a number of self-portraits.

Vermeer, Jan (Johannes) (1632–75). Vermeer mainly painted intimate interiors, often with solitary figures, depicting them with clarity and luminous, subtle colors. His work includes *Head of a Girl* (c. 1665), *Woman Weighing Pearls* (c. 1665), and *The Letter* (1666).

FLEMISH

See "Belgian/Flemish" above.

FRENCH

Arp, Jean (Hans) (1887–1966). Creator of abstract paintings, sculptures, and collages using organic forms, such as *Squares Arranged According to the Laws of Chance* (1916–17) and *Navel, Shirt, and Head* (1926). Arp was associated with dadaism and surrealism.

Bonnard, Pierre (1867–1947). A founder of the Nabis, Bonnard was a painter, lithographer, and illustrator. He excelled at domestic interiors with subtle lighting effects. His work includes *Bowl of Fruit* (1933).

Braque, Georges (1882–1963). A figure in fauvism and, with Picasso, a founder of cubism. Braque's works include the monumental *Nude* (1907–08) and *Woman with a Mandolin* (1937).

Cézanne, Paul (1839–1906). Postimpressionist painter. His works include *The Card Players* (1890–92), *Bathers* (1898–1905), and a series of increasingly abstracted, geometric landscapes of Mont Sainte-Victoire. Cézanne had a profound influence on modern art, especially cubism.

Chardin, Jean-Baptiste-Siméon (1699–1779). Painter of genre scenes and still lifes in a subtle, delicate, unsentimental style. His works include *Return from Market* (1739) and *Saying Grace* (c. 1740).

Corot, Jean-Baptiste Camille (1796–1875). Influential landscape painter whose delicately lit, carefully observed works include *View of the Forest of Fontainebleau* (1831) and *View of Avray* (c. 1840).

Courbet, Gustave (1819–77). The initiator of realism, Courbet was a revolutionary at odds with political authority and visual idealization. His paintings include *The Stone Breakers* (1849) and *The Artist's Studio* (1854–55).

Daumier, Honoré (1808–79). Painter, lithographer, and sculptor. A great social satirist, Daumier produced some 4,000 lithographs, such as *Rue Transnonain, 15 Avril, 1834* (1834) and *The Legislative Body* (1834).

David, Jacques-Louis (1748–1825). The leading neoclassical painter. David's work reflects his passion for the ideas of the French Revolution and for classical art. His paintings include *The Oath of the Horatii* (1784) and *The Death of Marat* (1793).

Degas, Edgar (1834–1917). Painter and sculptor. He exhibited with the impressionists, although his approach differed from theirs. His paintings, such as *The Bellini Family* (1858–59) and *The Glass of Absinthe* (1876), often use daring spatial innovations.

Delacroix, Eugène (1798–1863). The foremost French romantic painter. His exuberant, freely painted, and richly colored works include *The Death of Sardanapalus* (1827) and *Liberty Leading the People* (1830).

Dubuffet, Jean (1901–85). Painter and sculptor of semiabstract, primitive works. He often used mixed media such as asphalt, pebbles, and glass to enrich his paintings' surface. His works include the *Topographies* and *Texturologies* series (1957–59).

Duchamp, Marcel (1887–1968). Painter and sculptor. He created cubist works and also cofounded dadaism. His "ready-mades" are everyday objects exhibited as art. His works include the painting *Nude Descending a Staircase* (1912), the ready-made *Fountain* (1917), and the construction *The Bride Stripped Bare by Her Bachelors, Even* (1915–23).

Dufy, Raoul (1877–1953). Painter, illustrator, and decorator known for his fauvist landscapes, seascapes, and portraits of society, including *Riders in the Wood* (1931) and *Cowes Regatta* (1934).

Fragonard, Jean-Honoré (1732–1806). Rococo painter of playful, erotic scenes, done in delicate colors and free brushwork. His works include *The Swing* (1769) and four *Progress of Love* paintings (1771–73).

Gauguin, Paul (1848–1903). Postimpressionist painter. At age 35, he left his career and family to devote himself to painting; he developed a style called synthetism. His best-known works, using flat planes, solid figures, and bright colors, were done in Tahiti and include *Nevermore* (1897) and *Where Do We Come From? What Are We? Where Are We Going?* (1897).

Géricault, Théodore (Jean Louis André Théodore) (1791–1824). A founder of romanticism. His works, based on contemporary events, were done in a powerful, spontaneous style. They include *A Cavalry Officer* (1812) and *The Raft of the Medusa* (1819).

Ingres, Jean-Auguste-Dominique (1780–1867). A leading neoclassic painter, Ingres was also deeply influenced by Raphael. His works, including *La Grande Odalisque* (1814), *La Comtesse d'Haussonville* (1845), and *The Turkish Bath* (1859–62), are both rigidly academic and richly sensual.

Léger, Fernand (1881–1955). He created a distinctive style, characterized by flat planes of color and simplified forms based on the surfaces of machines. His paintings include *The City* (1919) and *Le Grand Déjeuner* (1921).

Lorrain, Claude (Claude Gellée, called Claude) (1600–82). In his influential landscape paintings, such as *The Embarkation of the Queen of Sheba* (1648) and *The Expulsion of Hagar* (1668), he depicted atmospheric and lighting variations in a lyrical, sensitive style.

Maillol, Aristide (1861–1944). Sculptor, painter, and woodcut artist. His best-known works

are his calm, monumental female nudes, such as *The Mediterranean* (c. 1901).

Manet, Édouard (1832–83). He introduced extraordinary thematic and technical innovations. His *Luncheon on the Grass* and *Olympia* (both 1863), both paintings of contemporary women, nude and unidealized, shocked viewers of the time. His works also include *A Bar at the Folies-Bergères* (1881).

Matisse, Henri (1869–1954). Painter, sculptor, and lithographer. Matisse, a leader of the Fauves, was a master of vivid color and line used in decorative, sensual patterns. His paintings include *La Joie de Vivre* (1905–06) and *The Dance* (1910).

Millet, Jean-François (1814–75). Realist painter associated with the Barbizon School. His unidealized scenes of peasant life include *The Sower* (1850) and *The Angelus* (1855–57).

Monet, Claude (1840–1926). A founder of impressionism and a major landscape painter. His works include many series of the same subject seen under different atmospheric and lighting conditions, such as haystacks (1891), the Rouen Cathedral (1892–94), and water lilies (1899–1926).

Morisot, Berthe (1841–95). The first woman to join the Impressionists. Morisot's paintings have a delicate, luminous style and smooth brushwork. Her works include *The Cradle* (1873) and *Young Woman at the Dance* (1880).

Pissarro, Camille (1830–1903), b. Virgin Islands. Impressionist painter who was also influenced by pointillism. His works include *Red Roofs* (1877) and *The Boulevard Montmartre at Night* (1897).

Poussin, Nicolas (1594–1665). Painter who developed the standard for French classical art, though he spent most of his life in Italy. His contemplative, precise works include *The Rape of the Sabine Women* (1636–37) and *The Holy Family on the Steps* (1648).

Renoir, Pierre Auguste (1841–1919). Impressionist painter of sensuous, joyous, light-filled works, such as *Moulin de la Galette* (1876), *The Bathers* (1884–87), and *Luncheon of the Boating Party* (1881).

Rodin, Auguste (1840–1917). Sculptor of unusual power and expression. Many of his most famous works, such as *The Thinker* (1879–1900) and *The Kiss* (1886–98), are enlarged figures from his great unfinished *Gates of Hell* (begun 1880). Other well-known works include *The Burghers of Calais* (1884–86) and *Balzac* (1892–97).

Rouault, Georges (1871–1958). Expressionist; also associated with the Fauves. His subjects, in paintings such as *Little Olympia* (1906), *Three Judges* (1913), and *Christ Mocked* (1932), were prostitutes, corrupt judges, and Christ.

Rousseau, Henri (1844–1910). Self-taught painter of naive, stylized, colorful works, often of jungle scenes, including *Sleeping Gypsy* (1897) and *The Dream* (1910).

Rousseau, Théodore (1812–67). A leading figure of the Barbizon School. His landscapes, such as *Descent of the Cattle* (1835), are full of gravity and intensity.

Seurat, Georges (1859–91). Painter who developed the pointillist or neoimpressionist technique of using small dots of pure color. His works include *Bathing at Asnières* (1883–84) and *A Sunday Afternoon on the Island of La Grande Jatte* (1885–86).

Toulouse-Lautrec, Henri de (1864–1901). Painter and lithographer. He depicted music halls, cabarets, and brothels in an unidealized, vivid way, as in *At the Moulin de la Galette* (1892) and *In the Parlor at the Rue des Moulins* (1894).

Vuillard, Édouard (1868–1940). Painter, lithographer, and member of the Nabis, known for his intimate interiors and interest in flat patterns, as in *Mother and Sister of the Artist* (c. 1893) and *Sitting Room with Three Lamps* (1899).

Watteau, Jean-Antoine (1684–1721). Rococo painter. In works such as *A Pilgrimage to Cythera* (1717) and *La Toilette* (1720), he depicted delicate, sensuous scenes in an exquisitely colored, lyrical manner.

GERMAN

Beckmann, Max (1884–1950). Expressionist painter. His highly personal style reflected the misery of contemporary events in Germany. His works include *The Night* (1918–19) and a series of nine triptychs, including *Departure* (1932–35).

Dürer, Albrecht (1471–1528). Painter, engraver, and most influential artist of the German school. Dürer is known for his technical mastery and his adoption of the principles of the Italian Renaissance. His works include the *Apocalypse* woodcuts (1498), the engraving *St. Jerome in his Study* (1514), and the painting *Four Apostles* (1526).

Ernst, Max (1891–1976). A founder of dadaism and surrealism. His grotesque, sometimes whimsical paintings include *Two Children Are Threatened by a Nightingale* (1924) and *The Temptation of St. Anthony* (1945).

Grosz, George (1893–1959). Painter known for his savage caricatures of post–World War I bourgeois society, such as *The Suicide* (1916) and *Eclipse of the Sun* (1926). He left Germany for the United States in 1933.

Grünewald, Mathias (Mathis Gothardt Neithardt) (c. 1475–1528). Religious painter of unusually expressive works, most frequently of the crucifixion of Christ. His masterpiece is the Isenheim altarpiece (1515).

Holbein, Hans, the Younger (c. 1497–1543). Outstanding portrait and religious painter of the Northern Renaissance. His works include *Sir Thomas More* (1527) and the *Madonna of the Burgomeister Meyer* (c. 1528).

Kollwitz, Käthe Schmidt (1867–1945). Graphic artist and sculptor whose works reflect her socialist and pacifist views. They include the etching series *Peasants' War* (1902–08) and the lithography series *The War* (1923) and *Death* (1934–35).

ITALIAN

Angelico, Fra (Guido or **Guidolino di Pietro,** also known as **Giovanni da Fiesole)** (c. 1400–55). Religious painter of great expressiveness; a master of graceful line and color. Among his works are the frescoes for San Marco in Florence, including *The Annunciation* (c. 1447), and scenes from the lives of saints Stephen and Lawrence in the Vatican (c. 1447–49).

Bellini, family of Renaissance painters. **Jacopo** (c. 1400–70) ran a workshop in Venice with his sons **Gentile** (1429–1507) and **Giovanni** (c. 1430–1516). Jacopo's work includes *The Madonna and Child with Lionello d'Este* (c. 1441). Gentile excelled at depicting contemporary Venetian ceremonies, as in *The Procession in the Piazza San Marco* (1496). Giovanni, probably the most talented, produced expressive works such as *St. Francis in Ecstasy* (c. 1475) and the San Zaccaria altarpiece (1505).

The most looked-at painting in the Louvre is Leonardo da Vinci's Mona Lisa.

Bernini, Giovanni Lorenzo (Gianlorenzo) (1598–1680). Sculptor, architect, painter, and leading baroque artist. His dramatic, masterful sculptures include *David* (1623) and *The Ecstasy of St. Theresa* (1645–52). Among his paintings is *Saints Andrew and Thomas* (1627).

Boccioni, Umberto (1882–1916). Painter, sculptor, and major figure of futurist art. His works include the painting *The City Rises* (1910) and the sculpture *Unique Forms of Continuity in Space* (1913).

Botticelli, Sandro (Alessandro di Mariano Filipepi) (c. 1444–1510). A favorite of the Medici, this Renaissance painter was a supreme colorist and master of the rhythmic line. He is known for his mythological scenes, such as *Primavera* (c. 1478) and *The Birth of Venus* (c. 1482). His religious works include *Madonna of the Magnificat* (c. 1485).

Canova, Antonio (1757–1822). Neoclassical sculptor. His graceful, polished works include the tomb of Pope Clement XIV (1783–87) and *Pauline Borghese as Venus* (1805–07).

Caravaggio, Michelangelo Merisi da (c. 1573–1610). An influential painter whose bold works are masterpieces of dramatic light and shadow, featuring figures with strong physical presence. They include *The Calling of St. Matthew* (c. 1598) and *The Conversion of St. Paul* (1600–01).

Carracci, family of painters. The brothers **Annibale** (1560–1609) and **Agostino** (1557–1602) and their cousin **Ludovico** (1555–1619) established an important academy of painting in Bologna. Annibale, the most talented, and Agostino painted richly sculptural, decorative frescoes for the Farnese Palace in Rome (1597–1600). Annibale also did landscape paintings, such as *Landscape with the Flight into Egypt* (1604).

Cellini, Benvenuto (1500–71). Sculptor, metalsmith, and author. His works include the gold and enamel saltcellar of Francis I (1540) and his masterpiece, the Mannerist *Perseus with the Head of Medusa* (1545–54).

Chirico, Giorgio de (1888–1978), b. Greece. Forerunner of surrealism. His best-known paintings are characterized by deep perspective, solitary figures, and objects used out of context. They include *Mystery and Melancholy of a Street* (1914) and *Disquieting Muses* (1916–17).

Correggio (Antonio Allegri) (c. 1494–1534). He painted graceful, delicately lit works, especially on mythological themes, such as *Jupiter and Io* (c. 1530), and illusionistic ceiling frescoes, such as *The Assumption of the Virgin* for the cathedral in Parma (1526–30).

da Vinci, Leonardo. *See* **Leonardo da Vinci.**

della Robbia, Florentine family of sculptors and ceramicists known for their enameled terra-cotta. **Luca** (c. 1400–82) founded a workshop; his works include *The Resurrection* and *The Ascension* (both late 1440s), for the Florence Cathedral. His nephew **Andrea** (1435–1525), best known for his medallions for the Foundling Hospital in Florence, continued the workshop with his sons, **Luca II, Giovanni,** and **Girolamo.**

Donatello (Donato di Niccolo di Betto Bardi) (c. 1386–1466). An innovative Renaissance artist, he developed a technique of shallow relief, *schiacciato.* Donatello's powerful and expressive sculptures include *David* (c. 1408), *St. George* (c. 1415), and *Mary Magdelene* (c. 1456).

Ghiberti, Lorenzo (1378–1455). Major early Renaissance sculptor. His two pairs of bronze doors for the Florence Baptistery, with their finely modeled scenes, are his masterpieces (1403–24 and 1425–52). His life-size bronzes include *St. John the Baptist* (1412–16) and *St. Matthew* (1419).

Giorgione (Giorgione da Castelfranco) (c. 1476–1510). His poetic and warmly colored works had a major influence on Venetian painting. They include *The Tempest* (c. 1500–10), *The Three Philosophers* (c. 1505–10), and *Sleeping Venus,* which was completed by Titian (c. 1510).

Giotto (Giotto di Bondone) (c. 1266–1337). Most important early Italian painter. His monumental figures and realistic treatment of pictorial space were major innovations. His works include the *Ognissanti Madonna* (c. 1310); frescoes in the Arena Chapel, Padua (finished 1313); and frescoes in the Bardi and Peruzzi chapels, Santa Croce, Florence (1320s).

Leonardo da Vinci (1425–1519). Painter, sculptor, architect, engineer, and scientist. His balanced, beautifully painted designs embody the High Renaissance; his studies of perspective and anatomy were also highly influential. His paintings include *The Virgin of the Rocks* (1483–85), *The Last Supper* (1495–98), and the *Mona Lisa* (1503–06).

Lippi. Family of Florentine painters. **Fra Filippo** (c. 1406–69) was an important early Renaissance artist whose works include *The Coronation of the Virgin* (1441) and the frescoes for the Prato cathedral (1452–65). His son, **Filippino** (c. 1457–1504), painted a fresco cycle for the Strozzi Chapel, Santa Maria Novella, Florence (1495–1502).

When Michelangelo painted the scene of the last judgment in the Sistine Chapel, he put in hell those people he didn't like, including Pope Julius II, the man who forced him to paint the chapel.

Mantegna, Andrea (1431–1506). Early Renaissance painter and engraver. His works show monumental forms and an interest in perspective. They include frescoes for the Ovetari Chapel in the Church of the Eremitani in Padua (1448–57), and the S. Zeno Altarpiece (1456–59).

Michelangelo Buonarroti (1475–1564). Sculptor, painter, architect, poet. The influence of this foremost Renaissance figure on Western art was supreme. His works, all in a heroic style, include the sculptures *Pietà* (1499), *David* (1501–04), *Moses* (1513–16), and the tombs of Lorenzo and Giuliano de Medici (1519–34). Also among his monumental works are the *Book of Genesis* frescoes (1508–12) on the Sistine Chapel's ceiling and the *Last Judgment* fresco (1534–41) on its altar wall.

Modigliani, Amedeo (1884–1920). Painter and sculptor. His style is characterized by an elongated, smooth line. Most of his works are portraits and female nudes, such as the paintings *Jeanne Hébuterne* (1919) and *Reclining Nude* (1919).

Piero della Francesca (c. 1420–92). Major Renaissance painter. His works are characterized by strong symmetricality and angularity and an interest in precise ratios of perspective. They include frescoes of *The Legend of the True Cross* in the Church of San Francesco, Arezzo (1452–64), and *The Flagellation of Christ* (c. 1456).

Pisano, family of sculptors. **Nicola** (c. 1220–84) worked in an elaborate, architectural style; his works include pulpits for the Pisa Baptistery (finished 1260) and Siena Cathedral (1265–68). His son, **Giovanni** (c. 1250–1314), created the decorative facade, Siena Cathedral (1284–96), and the pulpit, Pisa Cathedral (1302–10).

Raphael (Santi or **Sanzio)** (1483–1520). His exquisitely balanced paintings epitomize the High Renaissance. They include frescoes for the Vatican's Stanza della Segnatura, including *The School of Athens* (finished 1511); *Galatea* (c. 1512); and *The Sistine Madonna* (1512).

Tintoretto (Jacopo Robusti) (1518–94). A great Venetian mannerist who employed dramatic lighting, coloring, and foreshortening. Among his paintings are a cycle in the Scuola di San Rocco in Venice, including an enormous *Crucifixion* (1564–87), and *The Last Supper* (1592–94).

Titian (Tiziano Vecellio) (c. 1490–1576). High Renaissance painter whose innovations, especially his expressive use of color, were influential. His works include *The Assumption of the Virgin* (1516–18), *Pope Paul III and His Grandsons* (1546), and the *Pietà* (1576).

Uccello, Paolo (c. 1396–1475). Florentine painter; early master of perspective. His colorful, decorative works, including three panels of *The Battle of San Romano* (c. 1455) and a cycle of frescoes for Santa Maria Novella, Florence (c. 1445), are notable for their foreshortening.

Veronese, Paolo (Paolo Caliari) (1528–88). Venetian painter whose large works depicting scenes of sumptuous ceremonies are distinguished by opulent colors. They include *The Marriage at Cana* (1562), *The Feast in the House of Levi* (1573), and decorative paintings for the Ducal Palace, Venice (1577–82).

Verrocchio, Andrea del (Andrea di Michele di Francesco di Cioni) (1435–88). Leading early Renaissance sculptor and painter. His sculptures include *The Doubting of Thomas* (1465); among his

paintings is *The Baptism of Christ* (1472), in which he was assisted by his pupil, Leonardo da Vinci.

MEXICAN

Kahlo, Frida (1907–54). Painter of vivid works, especially self-portraits, conveying intense psychic and physical pain. They include *Frida and Diego Rivera* (1931) and *The Love Embrace of the Universe, the Earth (Mexico), Diego, Me and Señor Xolotl* (1949).

Orozco, José Clemente (1883–1949). Muralist whose monumental scenes contain humanitarian symbolism. His murals are in the New School for Social Research, New York City (1931), and Dartmouth College, New Hampshire (1932–34).

Rivera, Diego (1886–1957). A founder of the Mexican mural renaissance. His works pay homage to Mexico's history and workers. They include *The History of Mexico,* National Palace of Mexico City (1929–36), and a series at the Detroit Institute of Arts (1933).

Siqueiros, David Alfaro (1896–1974). One of the three great Mexican muralists. His dynamic brushwork reflects revolutionary themes. Siqueiros's murals include a series at the Plaza Art Center, Los Angeles (1932), and *The Liberation of Chile* at the Mexican School, Chillán, Chile (1942).

Tamayo, Rufino (1899–1991). A leading Mexican painter. His decorative works are influenced by cubism, fauvism, and themes from Mexican folklore. They include *Sleeping Musicians* (1950) and a series of murals at Smith College, Massachusetts (1943).

RUSSIAN

Chagall, Marc (1887–1985). Russian painter who lived mainly in France. His poetic, colorful, and symbolic works are often based on Jewish folklore. They include *I and the Village* (1911), *Self-Portrait with Seven Fingers* (1911), and murals for the Metropolitan Opera House, New York City (installed 1966).

Gabo, Naum (Naum Neemia Pevsner) (1890–1977). Russian-born American constructivist sculptor and theorist. His works include *Column* (1923) and *Kinetic Construction* (1920), a sculpture with a motor. In his *Realist Manifesto,* he proposed that concepts of time and space be included in art.

Kandinsky, Wassily (1866–1944). Russian painter, a founder of the avant-garde *Blaue Reiter* group, and a teacher at the Bauhaus. His series of *Compositions, Improvisations,* and *Impressions,* beginning in 1910, are often seen as the first purely abstract works.

Malevich, Kasimir Severinovich (1878–1935). Russian painter and founder of suprematism. He is known for his sparse geometric paintings, including *Black Square* (1915) and the *White on White* series (c. 1918). He described his theories in the book *The Non-Objective World* (1915).

Tatlin, Vladimir Evgrafovich (1885–1953). Russian artist and a founder of constructivism. His works include the *Relief Constructions* series (begun 1913) and the *Corner Reliefs* (begun 1915).

SPANISH

Dalí, Salvador (1904–89). Surrealist painter who worked in a precise style. His hallucinatory images can be seen in *The Persistence of Memory* (1931), *Crucifixion* (1951), and *The Last Supper* (1955).

El Greco. *See* **Greco, El.**

Goya y Lucientes, Francisco Jose de (1746–1828). Highly original painter and graphic artist. His expressive works are often telling social satires. They include the paintings *Nude Maja* and *Clothed Maja* (both c. 1804) and *Charles IV and His Family* (1800); and etching series, such as *Los Caprichos* (1799) and *Disasters of War* (1810–14).

Greco, El (Domenikos Theotokopoulos) (1541–1614), b. Crete. Painter of dynamic scenes, often of religious ecstasy. His works, distinguished by elongated figures and vivid highlights, include *The Disrobing of Christ* (1577–79), *The Burial of Count Orgaz* (1586), and *View of Toledo* (1600).

Gris, Juan (José Victoriano González) (1887–1927). A developer of synthetic cubism, he used simple forms and a rhythmic style in his paintings and collages. His works include *Homage to Picasso* (1911–12), *The Violin* (1916), and *Violin and Fruit Dish* (1924).

Miró, Joan (1893–1983). Surrealist painter. He worked in a playful, lyrical style, with colorful, amoebic shapes. His works include *Harlequin's Carnival* (1924–25), *Dog Barking at the Moon* (1926), and ceramic murals for the UNESCO building, Paris (1955–58).

Murillo, Bartolemé Estéban (1618–82). Religious and portrait painter. Among his important works are a series for the Charity Hospital in Seville (1671–73), portraits, and many depictions of the Immaculate Conception.

Picasso, Pablo (Pablo Ruiz y Picasso) (1881–1973). Painter, sculptor, graphic artist, ceramicist. He was an enormously versatile, original, and prolific artist. His *Les Desmoiselles d'Avignon* (1907) is a seminal cubist work. Other important paintings include *The Three Musicians* (1921) and *Guernica* (1937).

Ribera, Jusepe de (1591–1652). Baroque painter, mainly of religious scenes. His naturalistic yet mystical works include *The Martyrdom of St. Bartholomew* (c. 1630) and *The Mystic Marriage of St. Catherine* (1648).

Velázquez, Diego Rodríguez de Silva y (1599–1660). One of the greatest of Spanish painters. He was a master of shimmering tones and brilliant colors. His expressive works include *The Surrender of Breda* (1634–35), *Pope Innocent X* (1650), and *The Maids of Honor* (1656).

Zurbarán, Francisco de (1598–1664). Baroque painter. His works, mostly religious, combine severity with spiritual intensity. They include *The Apotheosis of St. Thomas Aquinas* (1631) and *St. Serapion* (1628).

OTHER EUROPEAN

Brancusi, Constantin   (1876–1957). Romanian sculptor whose economical, simple style was radically innovative. His works include *Bird in Space* (1919) and the immense *Endless Column,* erected in a park near his birthplace (1937).

Giacometti, Alberto   (1901–66). Swiss sculptor and painter, known especially for his sculptures of elongated figures, such as *The Forest* (1950) and *Walking Man* (1960).

Klee, Paul   (1879–1940). Swiss painter whose works, such as *Twittering Machine* (1922) and *Park Near L(ucerne)* (1938), combine theories of abstraction with playful childlike inventiveness. Klee was associated with the *Blaue Reiter* group.

Klimt, Gustav   (1862–1918). Austrian painter; a founder of the Vienna Secession group and a figure of the art nouveau movement. His exotic, erotic, symbolic works include *Judith* (1909) and *The Kiss* (1907–08).

Kokoschka, Oskar   (1886–1980). Austrian expressionist painter. He produced many portraits and landscapes, such as *Le Marquis de Montesquiou* (1909–10) and *Jerusalem* (1929–30), as well as a series of self-portraits.

Munch, Edvard   (1863–1944). Leading Norwegian painter and graphic artist. He foreshadowed expressionism with his charged images of terror, despair, and isolation, as in the paintings *The Scream* (1893) and *Vampire* (1895).

Phidias (Pheidias)   (c. 500–432 B.C.). One of the greatest of ancient Greek sculptors, although none of his original works survive. He sculpted the enormous *Athena Parthenos,* Athens (c. 447–439 B.C.); and the *Zeus,* Olympia, one of the Seven Wonders of the Ancient World (c. 435 B.C.).

Praxiteles   (c. 370–330 B.C.). He was considered the greatest Greek sculptor of his time. His *Hermes with the Infant Dionysus* (c. 350–330 B.C.) is the only existing original work by an ancient master.

He also sculpted the *Aphrodite of Cnidus* (c. 350–330 B.C.).

Schiele, Egon   (1890–1918). Austrian expressionist painter and graphic artist who developed an angular, linear style. Many of his works are nudes, often in disturbing, erotic poses. His paintings include *The Embrace* (1917) and *Paris von Gütersloh* (1918).

ART MOVEMENTS AND STYLES

abstract expressionism   Movement in painting, originating in New York City in the 1940s. It emphasized spontaneous personal expression, freedom from accepted artistic values, surface qualities of paint, and the act of painting itself. Jackson Pollock, Willem de Kooning, Robert Motherwell, and Franz Kline are important abstract expressionists.

art deco   A design style prevalent during the 1920s and 1930s, characterized by a sleek use of straight lines and slender forms.

art nouveau   A decorative art movement that emerged in the late 19th century. Characterized by dense asymmetrical ornamentation in sinuous forms, it is often symbolic and of an erotic nature. Gustav Klimt worked in an art-nouveau style.

Ash Can School   Group of American artists active from 1908 to 1918. It included members of The Eight, such as Robert Henri and Arthur Davies; Edward Hopper was also part of the Ash Can group. Their work featured scenes of urban realism.

Barbizon School   An association of French landscape painters, c. 1840–70, who lived in the village of Barbizon and who painted directly from nature. Théodore Rousseau was a leader; Jean-Baptiste Corot and Jean-François Millet were also associated with the group.

"Major Art Museums and Their Special Collections" in chapter 11
Go to

baroque A movement in European painting in the 17th and early 18th centuries, characterized by violent movement, strong emotion, and dramatic lighting and coloring. Giovanni Bernini, Michelangelo Caravaggio, and Peter Paul Rubens were among important baroque artists.

Byzantine A style of the Byzantine Empire and its provinces, c. 330–1450. Appearing mostly in religious mosaics, manuscript illuminations, and panel paintings, it is characterized by rigid, monumental, stylized forms with gold backgrounds.

classicism Refers to the principles of Greek and Roman art of antiquity with its emphasis on harmony, proportion, balance, and simplicity. In a general sense, classicism refers to art based on accepted standards of beauty.

color field painting A technique in abstract painting developed in the 1950s. It focuses on the lyrical effects of large areas of color, often poured or stained onto the canvas. Barnett Newman, Mark Rothko, and Helen Frankenthaler painted in this manner.

conceptual art A movement of the 1960s and 1970s that emphasized the artistic idea over the art object. It attempted to free art from the confines of the gallery and the pedestal.

constructivism A Russian abstract movement founded by Vladimir Tatlin, Naum Gabo, and Antoine Pevsner, c. 1915. It focused on art for the industrial age. Tatlin believed in art with a utilitarian purpose.

cubism A revolutionary movement begun by Pablo Picasso and Georges Braque in the early 20th century. It employs an analytic vision based on fragmentation and multiple viewpoints.

dadaism A movement, c. 1915–23, that rejected accepted aesthetic standards. It aimed to create antiart and nonart, often employing a sense of the absurd.

"Literary Movements, Periods, and Styles" in chapter 8
Go to

The Eight A group of American painters who united out of opposition to academic standards in the early 20th century. Members of the group were Robert Henri, Arthur Davies, Maurice Prendergast, William James Glackens (1870–1938), Ernest Lawson (1873–1939), Everett Shinn (1876–1953), John Sloan (1871–1951), and George Luks (1867–1933).

expressionism Refers to art that uses emphasis and distortion to communicate emotion. More specifically, it refers to early-20th-century northern European art, especially in Germany, c. 1905–25. Artists such as Georges Rouault, Oskar Kokoschka, and Egon Schiele painted in this manner.

fauvism From the French word *fauve,* meaning "wild beast." A style adopted by artists associated with Henri Matisse, c. 1905–08. They painted in a spontaneous manner, using bold colors.

folk art Works of a culturally homogeneous people without formal training, generally according to regional traditions and involving crafts.

futurism An Italian movement, c. 1909–19, that attempted to integrate the dynamism of the machine age into art. Umberto Boccioni was a futurist artist.

Gothic A European movement beginning in France. Gothic sculpture emerged c. 1200; Gothic painting appeared later in the 13th century. The artworks are characterized by a linear, graceful, elegant style more naturalistic than that which had existed previously in Europe.

impressionism A late-19th-century French school of painting. It focused on transitory visual impressions, often painted directly from nature, with an emphasis on the changing effects of light and color. Claude Monet, Pierre Renoir, and Camille Pissarro were important Impressionists.

mannerism A style, c. 1520–1600, that arose in reaction to the harmony and proportion of the High Renaissance. Mannerism featured elongated and contorted poses, crowded canvases, and harsh lighting and coloring.

The Visual Arts

minimalism   A movement in American painting and sculpture that originated in the late 1950s. It emphasized pure, reduced forms and strict, systematic compositions.

Al Capp, the creator of Lil Abner, once said, "Abstract art is a product of the untalented, sold by the unprincipled to the utterly bewildered."

Nabis   From the Hebrew word for "prophet." A group of French painters active in the 1890s who worked in a subjective, sometimes mystical style, stressing flat areas of color and pattern. Pierre Bonnard and Édouard Vuillard were members.

naive art   Artwork, usually paintings, characterized by a simplified style, nonscientific perspective, and bold colors. The artists are generally not professionally trained. Henri Rousseau and Grandma Moses worked in this style.

neoclassicism   A European style of the late 18th and early 19th centuries. Its elegant, balanced works revived the order and harmony of ancient Greek and Roman art. Jacques-Louis David and Antonio Canova are examples of neoclassicists.

op art   An abstract movement in Europe and the United States, begun in the mid-1950s, based on the effects of optical patterns. Josef Albers worked in this style.

photorealism   A figurative movement that emerged in the United States and Britain in the late 1960s and 1970s. The subject matter, usually everyday scenes, is portrayed in an extremely detailed, exacting style. It is also called superrealism, especially when referring to sculpture.

pointillism   A method of painting developed by Georges Seurat and Paul Signac (1863–1935) in the 1880s. It used dabs of pure color that were intended to mix in the eyes of viewers rather than on the canvas. It is also called divisionism or neoimpressionism.

pop art   A movement that began in Britain and the United States in the 1950s. It used the images and techniques of mass media, advertising, and popular culture, often in an ironic way. Works of Andy Warhol, Roy Lichtenstein, and Claes Oldenburg exemplify this style.

postimpressionism   A term coined by British art critic Roger Fry to refer to a group of 19th-century painters, including Paul Cézanne, Paul Gauguin, and Vincent Van Gogh, who were dissatisfied with the limitations of impressionism. The term has since been used to refer to various reactions against impressionism, such as fauvism and expressionism.

Pre-Raphaelite Brotherhood   A group of English painters formed in 1848. These artists attempted to recapture the style of painting preceding the Italian artist Raphael. They rejected industrialized England and focused on painting from nature, producing detailed, colorful works. Dante Rossetti was a founding member.

realism   In a general sense, refers to objective representation. More specifically, a 19th-century movement, especially in France, that rejected idealized academic styles in favor of everyday subjects. Honoré Daumier, Jean-François Millet, and Gustave Courbet were realists.

Renaissance   Meaning "rebirth" in French. Refers to Europe, c. 1400–1600. Renaissance art, which began in Italy, stressed the forms of classical antiquity, a realistic representation of space based on scientific perspective, and secular subjects. The works of Leonardo da Vinci, Michelangelo, and Raphael exemplify the balance and harmony of the High Renaissance (c. 1495–1520).

rococo   An 18th-century European style, originating in France. In reaction to the grandeur and massiveness of the baroque, rococo employed refined, elegant, highly decorative forms. Jean-Honoré Fragonard worked in this style.

Romanesque   A European style developed in France in the late 11th century. Its sculpture is ornamental, stylized, and complex. Some

Romanesque frescoes survive, painted in a monumental, active manner.

romanticism   A European movement of the late 18th to mid–19th century. In reaction to neoclassicism, it focused on emotion over reason and on spontaneous expression. The subject matter was invested with drama and usually painted energetically in brilliant colors. Eugène Delacroix, Théodore Géricault, Joseph Turner, and William Blake were Romantic artists.

suprematism   A Russian abstract movement originated by Kasimir Malevich, c. 1913. It was characterized by flat geometric shapes on plain backgrounds and emphasized the spiritual qualities of pure form.

surrealism   A movement of the 1920s and 1930s that began in France. It explored the unconscious, often using images from dreams. It used spontaneous techniques and featured unexpected juxtapositions of objects. René Magritte, Salvador Dali, Joan Miró, and Max Ernst painted surrealist works.

symbolism   A painting movement that flourished in France in the 1880s and 1890s in which subject matter was suggested rather than directly presented. It featured decorative, stylized, and evocative images.

COMMON ART TERMS

acrylic   Water-soluble paint made from pigments and a plastic binder.

aquatint   An etching technique in which a solution of asphalt or resin is used on the plate. Aquatint produces prints with rich, gray tones.

caricature   An artwork humorously exaggerating the qualities, defects, or peculiarities of a person or idea.

cartoon   A humorous sketch or drawing usually telling a story or caricaturing some person or action. In fine arts, a preparatory sketch or design for a picture or ornamental motif to be transferred to a fresco or tapestry.

carving   In sculpture, the cutting of a form from a solid, hard material such as stone or wood, in contrast to the technique of modeling.

casting   In sculpture, a technique of reproducing a work by pouring into a mold a substance such as plaster or molten metal, which then hardens.

chiaroscuro   The rendering of light and shade in painting; the subtle gradations and marked variations of light and shade for dramatic effect.

collage   A composition made of cut and pasted pieces of materials, sometimes with images added by the artist.

colors, complementary   Two colors at opposite points on the color scale—for example, orange and blue, green and red.

colors, primary   Red, yellow, and blue, the mixture of which will yield all other colors in the spectrum but which themselves cannot be produced through a mixture of other colors.

colors, secondary   Orange, green, and purple—colors produced by mixing two primary colors.

composition   The organization of forms and colors within an artwork.

drypoint   A technique of engraving, using a sharp-pointed needle, that produces a furrowed edge resulting in a print with soft, velvety lines.

encaustic   A painting technique using pigments dissolved in hot wax.

engraving   The art of producing printed designs through various methods of incising on wood or metal blocks, which are then inked and printed.

etching   The technique of producing printed designs through incising on a coated metal plate, which is then bathed in corrosive acid, inked, and printed.

figure   A representation of a human or an animal form.

"Common Music Terms" and "Common Dance Terms" in chapter 6
Go to

The Visual Arts

foreshortening   Reducing or distorting in order to represent three-dimensional space as perceived by the eye, according to the rules of perspective.

fresco   Meaning "fresh" in Italian. The technique of painting on moist lime plaster with colors ground in water.

frieze   A band of painted or sculpted decoration, often at the top of a wall.

genre painting   A realistic style of painting in which everyday life forms the subject matter, as distinguished from religious or historical painting.

gesso   Ground chalk or plaster mixed with glue, used as a base coat for tempera and oil painting.

gouache   A method of watercolor painting, but prepared with a more gluey base, producing a less transparent effect.

highlight   On a represented form, a point of most intense light.

impasto   Paint applied very thickly. It often projects from the picture surface.

landscape   Painting in which natural scenery is the subject.

lithography   A printing process in which ink impressions are taken from a flat stone or metal plate prepared with a greasy substance, such as an oily crayon.

modeling   In sculpture, the building up of form using a soft medium such as clay or wax, as distinguished from carving. In painting and drawing, using color and lighting variations to produce a three-dimensional effect.

monochrome   A painting or drawing executed in a single color.

monotype   A single print made from a metal or glass plate on which an image has been represented in paint, ink, etc.

mural   A large painting or decoration done on a wall.

oil   A method of painting with pigments mixed with oil, producing a vast range of light and color effects.

palette   A flat board used by a painter to mix and hold colors, traditionally oblong, with a hole for the thumb; also, a range of colors used by a particular painter.

pastel   A soft, subdued color; also, a drawing stick made of ground pigments, chalk, and gum water.

perspective   A method of representing three-dimensional volumes and spatial relationships on a flat surface to produce an effect similar to what is seen by the eye.

polychrome   Of many or various colors.

polyptych   In painting, a work made of several panels or scenes joined together. A diptych has two panels; a triptych, three.

primary colors   *See* **colors, primary.**

relief   In sculpture, the projection of an image or form from its background. Sculpture formed in this manner is described as high relief or low relief (bas-relief), depending on the degree of projection. In painting or drawing, the apparent projection of parts conveying the illusion of three dimensions.

secondary colors   *See* **colors, secondary.**

stenciling   A method of producing images or letters from sheets of cardboard, metal, or other materials from which forms have been cut away.

still life   The representation of inanimate objects in painting, drawing, or photography.

tempera   A painting technique using pigments mixed with egg yolk and water. Tempera produces clear, pure colors.

texture   The visual and tactile quality of a work of art based on the particular way the materials are handled; also, the distribution of tones or shades of a single color.

The Visual Arts

tone The effect of the harmony of color and values in a work.

trompe l'oeil Meaning "fool the eye" in French. In painting, the fine, detailed rendering of objects to convey the illusion that the painted forms are real and three-dimensional.

value In painting, the degree of lightness or darkness in a color.

wash In painting, a thin layer of translucent color.

watercolor Painting in pigments suspended in water. It can produce brilliant colors and transparent effects.

woodcut A print made by carving on a wood block, which is then inked and printed.

MAJOR ARCHITECTS

AMERICAN

Bulfinch, Charles (1763–1844), b. Massachusetts. He designed the first theater in New England, the Federal Street Theater (1794); the Massachusetts State House (1795–97); and the Massachusetts General Hospital (1818–23), all in Boston. In his completion of the design of the Capitol building, Washington, D.C. (1818–30), he achieved a model for state capitols throughout the country.

Burnham, Daniel Hudson (1846–1912), b. New York. Architect and city planner. With his partner, John Root, he designed the first major skeleton skyscraper, the Masonic Temple Building, Chicago (1892). Alone, Burnham designed the Flatiron Building, New York City (1903), and Union Station, Washington, D.C. (1903–07).

Fuller, (Richard) Buckminster (1895–1983), b. Massachusetts. Architect and engineer. His revolutionary designs, such as the geodesic dome, aimed at achieving the maximum effect with a minimal investment of materials.

Graves, Michael (1934–   ), b. Indiana. Postmodern architect. His influences range from classical Greece and Rome to the work of Le Corbusier. Graves's designs are known for their use of color and mix of delicacy and strength. They include the Fargo-Moorhead Cultural Center Bridge, Fargo, North Dakota, and Moorhead, Minnesota (1977); and the Public Services Building, Portland, Oregon (1980–82).

Gropius, Walter (1883–1969), b. Germany. A great modern functionalist. In 1919, he reorganized the Weimar School of Art into the Bauhaus. He designed the glass Fagus Factory, Alfeld (1911–12), and the Bauhaus buildings, Dessau (1925–26). His U.S. work includes the Pan American Building, New York City (1957). In 1946, he and young associates formed The Architects Collaborative (TAC), working together on buildings such as the United States Embassy, Athens (1956).

Hunt, Richard Morris (1827–95), b. Vermont. Architect. His work, which closely follows historical styles, exemplifies 19th-century eclecticism. He designed the Lenox Library (1870–77) and the Tribune Building (1873–76), both in New York City; and various mansions, such as those for the Vanderbilts in New York City and Newport, Rhode Island.

Jefferson, Thomas (1743–1826), b. Virginia. President, statesman, architect, and scientist. Jefferson, a self-taught architect, designed Monticello, his house near Charlottesville, Virginia (1768–82); the Virginia State Capitol in Richmond (1785–99); and the University of Virginia, Charlottesville (1817–26).

Jenney, William Le Baron (1832–1907), b. Massachusetts. Architect and engineer. His 10-story-high Home Insurance Building in Chicago (1884–85) is often considered to have been the first skyscraper. It was the first steel-framed office building.

Johnson, Philip Cortelyou (1906–   ), b. Ohio. He is noted for his glass-walled house in New Canaan, Connecticut (1949), and for the New York State Theater at Lincoln Center (1964), his collaboration with Mies van der Rohe on the Seagram Building (1958), and the American Telephone and Telegraph Building (1978–84), all in New York City. Johnson's writings include *The International Style* (1932), which he coauthored.

Kahn, Louis Isadore (1901–74), b. Estonia. Kahn designed the Yale University Art Gallery, New Haven (1951–53); the Kimbell Art Museum, Fort Worth (1966–72); and many housing projects, such as Carver Court Housing, Coatesville, Pennsylvania (1941–43). The Richards Medical Research Building, University of Pennsylvania (1957–64), has been admired for its integration of form and function.

Latrobe, Benjamin Henry (1764–1820), b. England. Considered the first professional architect in the United States, Latrobe produced some of the best monumental architecture of his time in classic revival style. His works include the Bank of Pennsylvania, Philadelphia (1799); and the Roman Catholic Cathedral, Baltimore, the first cathedral built in the United States (1805–18). He also worked on the Capitol, Washington, D.C. (1803–17).

Mies van der Rohe, Ludwig (1886–1969), b. Germany. A director of the Bauhaus (1930–33) and a founder of modern architecture. His U.S. buildings, mainly unornamented skyscrapers, include Chicago's Lake Shore Drive Apartments (1948–51); the Chicago Federal Center (1959–73); and, with Philip Johnson, the Seagram Building, New York City (1958).

Pei, I(eoh) M(ing) (1917–   ), b. China. He carefully integrates his expressive works with their surrounding environment. His buildings include the Mile High Center, Denver (1955); the John Hancock Tower, Boston (1973); the East Wing of the National Gallery of Art, Washington, D.C.

(1978); and a pyramidal addition to the Louvre Museum, Paris (1989).

Richardson, Henry Hobson (1838–86), b. Louisiana. His monumental building, Trinity Church, Boston (1872–77), exemplifies the "Richardson romanesque" style. His work also includes the Marshall Field store, Chicago (1885–87).

Mills, Robert (1781–1855), b. South Carolina. Mills, a classic revivalist, was appointed architect of public buildings in Washington, D.C. There, he built the Patent Office (1836–40), the Treasury (1836–42), and the Post Office (1839–42). In 1833, he designed the Washington Monument (built 1848–84).

Saarinen, Eero (1910–61), b. Finland. Son of Eliel. His works, especially his domed constructions, are innovative. His projects include the Kresge Auditorium, Massachusetts Institute of Technology, Cambridge (1953–56); Dulles International Airport, Chantilly, Virginia (1958–62); and the Gateway Arch, St. Louis (1959–64). He also designed furniture, especially chairs.

Saarinen, (Gottlieb) Eliel (1873–1950), b. Finland. Architect and city planner. He designed the National Museum (1902–04) in Helsinki, Finland. His work in the United States includes several buildings at the Cranbrook Foundation, where he was president of the Academy of Art; and, with his son, Eero, performance halls at the Berkshire Music Center in Tanglewood, Massachusetts (late 1930s–early 1940s). Saarinen's writings include *The City: Its Growth, Its Decay, Its Future* (1943).

Strickland, William (1788–1854), b. New Jersey. Classic revivalist architect. His most original work is the Merchants' Exchange, Philadelphia (1832–34). Also in Philadelphia, he built the Second Bank of the United States (1818–24) and the U.S. Mint (1829–33). He was a founder and first president of the American Institution of Architects.

Sullivan, Louis Henry (1856–1924), b. Massachusetts. Prominent in the development of modern architecture, Sullivan propounded the theory that form should follow function. He designed the Wainwright Building, St. Louis (1890–91); the Transportation Building at the World's Columbian Exposition, Chicago (1893); and the Stock Exchange in Chicago (1893–94).

Venturi, Robert (1925–   ), b. Pennsylvania. Venturi uses architectural elements from popular culture in his work, which includes Guild House, Philadelphia (1962–66); the Humanities and Social Sciences Building, State University of New York, Purchase (1968–70); and the new building for the Seattle Art Museum (1991). His writings include *Complexity and Contradiction in Architecture* (1966).

Walter, Thomas Ustick (1804–87), b. Pennsylvania. As government architect in Washington, D.C., from 1851 to 1865, he added the Senate and House wings to the Capitol, built its central dome, and designed the interior of the Library of Congress. Walter was a founder and president of the American Institute of Architects.

White, Stanford (1853–1906), b. New York. Architect. He worked in partnership with Charles Follen McKim and William Rutherford Mead. White's accomplishments include the first Madison Square Garden (1887–91), the Washington Memorial Arch (1889–92), and the New York Herald Building (1890–95), all in New York City. White's buildings reflect his passion for graceful, decorative elements and rich ornamentation.

Wright, Frank Lloyd (1867–1959), b. Wisconsin. Architect. His innovative approach integrated modern technology into architectural aesthetics. He is especially known for his dramatic interior spaces. His buildings include the Larkin Building, Buffalo, New York (1904); the Imperial Hotel, Tokyo (1915–22); the Kaufmann house, "Falling Water," Bear Run, Pennsylvania (1936–39); a Unitarian church, Madison, Wisconsin (1947); and the Guggenheim Museum, New York City (1959).

BRITISH

Adam, Robert (1728–92). Scottish architect. He designed, with his brother James, numerous public and private buildings in England and Scotland in a distinctive and decorative style that combines Palladian, Renaissance, and classical elements. Notable examples are Osterley Park (1761–80) and Syon House (1762–69), both in Middlesex, England.

Chambers, Sir William (1723–96), b. Sweden. His *Treatise on the Decorative Part of Civil Architecture* (1759) was a classic design text. He is known for Somerset House, London (begun 1776); and for decorative architecture in Kew Gardens, Surrey, England, especially the Chinese Pagoda (1763).

Jones, Inigo (1573–1652). One of the first great English architects. He broke from the Jacobean style, thus beginning the Renaissance and the Georgian periods in English architecture. His works include the Queen's House, Greenwich Palace, Kent (1616–35); and the royal banqueting hall, Whitehall Palace, London (1619–22). Both employ Palladian principles.

Lutyens, Sir Edwin Landseer (1869–1944). The leading English architect of his time, Lutyens combined romantic and classical styles. His outstanding achievement is the plan of New Delhi, India, centering on the Viceroy's House (1912–31). Other works include war memorials, such as the Cenotaph in London (1919–20), and the British Embassy in Washington, D.C. (1927–28).

Mackintosh, Charles Rennie (1868–1928). Scottish architect, artist, and furniture designer. His interiors, such as those for four Glasgow tearooms (1896–1919), display a sumptuous art nouveau style. His buildings, such as the Glasgow School of Art (1896–99), are subtly proportioned.

Paxton, Sir Joseph (1803–65). Architect and horticulturist. His Great Conservatory, a greenhouse in Chatsworth, England (1836–40), served as a model for the glass Crystal Palace, which he

The Visual Arts

built for the Great Exhibition of 1851 in London. Paxton's use of glass and iron in this building was a great technological innovation.

Pugin, Augustus Welby Northmore (1812–52). Architect, designer, and author. Pugin, a Gothic revivalist, worked on the interior and ornamentation of the Houses of Parliament (1844–52) and designed more than 65 churches, including Saint George's, London (1840–48). His writings, however, were more influential than his buildings.

Nash, John (1752–1835). Architect and city planner. Nash, a leader in the neoclassic Regency style, planned the layout of Regent Street and Regent's Park in London (built c. 1818), remodeled Buckingham Palace (1824–30), and worked on the "Indian"-style Royal Pavilion in Brighton (1815–21).

Smirke, Sir Robert (1781–1867). Classic revivalist architect. His best-known work is the main facade of the British Museum, London (1823–47). Other achievements include the Royal College of Physicians (1822–25) and the General Post Office (1823–29), also in London. Upon his retirement, his brother Sydney Smirke (1798–1877) continued work on the British Museum (1854–57).

Soane, Sir John (1753–1837). Soane, a classic revivalist, developed a complicated and highly personal style. His works in London include the Bank of England (begun 1788), the Dulwich College Art Gallery (1811–14), and his own eccentric house at Lincoln's Inn Fields (1812–13), now a museum.

Vanbrugh, Sir John (1664–1726). Architect and dramatist. His buildings include Blenheim Palace, Oxfordshire (1705–16), which epitomizes the English baroque; and the Queen's Theatre in the Haymarket, London (1704–05). He designed theatrical, picturesque country houses, such as Seaton Delaval, Northumberland (begun 1720).

Wren, Sir Christopher (1632–1723). Astronomer, architect, and mathematician. His elegant and dignified designs were highly influential. He designed St. Paul's Cathedral, London (1675–1710), and 52 other London churches, including St. Mary-le-Bow (1671–80). Other works include the Sheldonian Theatre, Oxford (1664–69), and Trinity College Library, Cambridge (1679–84).

FRENCH

Garnier, Jean Louis Charles (1825–98). His principal work is the ornate Opéra in Paris, with its grand staircase (1861–75). He also designed the Casino at Monte Carlo (1878–81) and Bischofsheim's Observatory, Nice (1880–88).

Hardouin Mansart, Jules (1646–1708). Baroque architect. In 1699, he became chief architect of the royal buildings. Some of his major works are at the Palace of Versailles, including the Galerie des Glaces and the Grand Trianon (both 1678–89). In Paris, he designed the Church of the Invalides (1679–91) and the Place Vendôme (1698).

Labrouste, Henri (Pierre François Henri) (1801–75). He was one of the first to successfully use metal construction in architecture, as he did in the reading room of the Bibliothèque Sainte-Geneviève, Paris (1843–50). He also worked extensively on the Bibliothèque Nationale (1854–75).

Le Corbusier (Charles-Édouard Jeanneret) (1887–1965). b. Switzerland. His innovative buildings and writings express a revolutionary approach toward aesthetic and technological architectural problems. His works, reflecting industrial as well as sculptural influences, include the Villa Savoye, Poissy, France (1928–31); collaboration on the United Nations buildings, New York City (1947–53); and buildings for the new capital of the Punjab, Chandigarh, India (1951–65).

Ledoux, Claude Nicolas (1736–1806). This imaginative neoclassicist's buildings include the Pavilion de Louveciennes and the theater at Besançon in France (both 1771–73). He is known for his architectural treatise of 1804 and for his plans for Chaux, an ideal city for the workers of the salt mines of Arc-et-Senans, France.

ITALIAN

Alberti, Leone Battista (1404–72). Architect and painter. His treatise, *De Re Aedificatoria* (c. 1450), established architecture as an intellectual field. His works include the exteriors of the churches of San Francesco in Rimini (c. 1450–61) and Sant'Andrea in Mantua (c. 1470–72).

Bernini, Giovanni Lorenzo (Gian Lorenzo) (1598–1680). Major Italian baroque architect and sculptor. As architect of St. Peter's in Rome, he designed the ornate baldachin (canopy) under the dome (1624–33) and the monument for St. Peter's chair (1657–66). From 1656 to 1667, he worked on the piazza and colonnade in front of St. Peter's. His Cornaro Chapel, in the church of Santa Maria della Vittoria, Rome (1647–51), is a dynamic melding of sculpture and architecture.

Borromini, Francesco (1599–1667). Italian baroque architect. His influential designs for churches and palaces were complex and extravagant. His works include the churches of San Carlo alle Quattro Fontane (1634–41) and Sant'Ivo alla Sapienza (1642–60) and the completion of the church of Sant'Agnese, Piazza Navona (1653–57), all in Rome.

Bramante (Donato di Angelo di Antonio) (1444–1514). Leading Italian High Renaissance architect. He designed much of the church of Santa Maria presso San Satiro (c. 1480) and the east end of Santa Maria delle Grazie (c. 1492), both in Milan. His plans for St. Peter's, Rome (1505–06), though not fully carried out, were influential.

Brunelleschi, Filippo (1377–1446). The first great architect of the Italian Renaissance. His masterpiece is the celebrated ribbed octagonal dome for the Florence Cathedral (1420–36). His other works include the Foundling Hospital (1419) and the churches of San Lorenzo (begun c. 1420) and Santo Spirito (begun 1436), all in Florence.

da Vinci, Leonardo.   *See* **Leonardo da Vinci.**

Giotto (Giotto di Bondone) (c. 1266–1337). Florentine architect and painter. In 1334, he was appointed architect of the Florence Cathedral. His main accomplishment is the multicolored bell tower called Giotto's Tower (begun 1334).

Leonardo da Vinci (1452–1519). Painter, sculptor, architect, engineer, and scientist. Around 1488, Leonardo did architectural work for the Milan Cathedral; he later worked on the reconstructions of cathedrals in Pavia and Piacenza. Beginning in 1506, he served as architect and engineer in Milan for Louis XII. In Rome, from 1513 to about 1515, he worked on several projects for the Vatican. Although most of Leonardo's designs were not executed, his architectural studies are of great historic importance.

Michelangelo Buonarroti (1475–1564). Italian Renaissance sculptor, painter, architect, and poet. Michelangelo's designs include the Medici Chapel (1520–34), where he powerfully combined architecture and sculpture, and the Laurentian Library (begun 1524), both at San Lorenzo, Florence. His work includes designs for St. Peter's (1546–64); its monumental dome, completed after Michelangelo's death, is based largely on his ideas.

Palladio, Andrea (1508–80). Italian Renaissance architect; a leading figure in Western architecture. Classical models were of extreme importance to him. He published a famous treatise in 1570. His works include rebuilding the Basilica at Vicenza, Italy (1549–80); many houses, including the Villa Barbaro, Maser, Italy (1554–58); and the Villa Rotunda, Vicenza (1567–70). In Venice, he built the churches of San Giorgio Maggiore (1560–80) and Il Redentore (1576–80).

Piranesi, Giovanni Battista (1720–1778). Architect and designer. Although he constructed few buildings—among them, Santa Maria del Priorato (1764) in Rome—his imaginative designs and theoretical writings were a major influence on European neoclassicism. His *Antichità Romane* (1756) and *Parere su l'Architettura* presented classical Rome as the creative foundation for a contemporary architecture.

The Visual Arts

OTHER

Aalto, Alvar (1898–1976). Finnish architect and furniture designer. The works of this leading 20th-century architect combine Finnish building traditions with modern techniques. They include the Municipal Library, Viipuri, Finland (1933–35); the Finnish Pavilion for the World's Fair, New York City (1939); and the undulating Baker House, Massachusetts Institute of Technology, Cambridge, Massachusetts (1946–49).

Behrens, Peter (1868–1940). German architect and industrial designer. His factory buildings, such as the A. E. G. Turbine Factory, Berlin (1908–09), show a simple, utilitarian approach. He is also known for the German Embassy, Leningrad (1911–12). Le Corbusier, Ludwig Mies van der Rohe, and Walter Gropius were his students.

Berlage, Hendrik Petrus (1856–1934). Pioneering modern Dutch architect. He is known for the redbrick Stock Exchange (1897–1903) and the Diamond Workers' Union Building (1899–1901), both in Amsterdam. He was also active in urban planning and furniture design.

Gaudí y Cornet, Antonio (1852–1926). Spanish architect whose colorful, sculptural, undulating style has similarities to art nouveau as well as surrealism. His masterpiece is the unfinished Expiatory Church of the Holy Family, Barcelona (begun 1883; work still in progress). Other examples of his work are Parc Güell (1900–14) and Casa Battló (1904–06) in Barcelona.

Hoffmann, Josef Franz Maria (1870–1956). Austrian architect and decorator; a leader of the early-20th-century Viennese style. He is known for his use of rectilinear forms with delicate ornamentation, as in the Palais Stoclet, Brussels (1905–11).

Loos, Adolf (1870–1933). Austrian architect. His purity of form influenced the development of the modern functional style. His best-known works include the office and store building on Michaelerplatz and the Steiner House, both in Vienna (both 1910).

Mendelsohn, Erich (1887–1953). German architect. In Germany, he built the Herman and Co. hat factory, Luckenwalde (1921–23), and the sculptural Einstein Tower Observatory, Potsdam (1919–24). He designed several buildings in Israel, including the Hebrew University on Mount Scopus, Jerusalem (1937–39), and four synagogues in the United States.

Niemeyer, Oscar (1907–   ). Brazilian architect. Influenced by Le Corbusier, Niemeyer is a daring and original designer. He collaborated on the United Nations buildings, New York City (1947–53); directed the building of Brazil's new capital, Brasília (1950–60); and designed the Mondadori Headquarters in Milan (1968–75).

Wagner, Otto (1841–1918). Austrian architect. The most significant work by this pioneer of modern architecture is the Postal Savings Bank Office, Vienna (1904–12). He also designed stations for the Vienna Municipal Railway (1894–1901) and the church at Steinhof (1905–07). His writings, including *Modern Architecture* (1895), were influential.

ARCHITECTURAL MOVEMENTS AND STYLES

baroque   A style that flourished in the 17th and early 18th centuries, characterized by exuberant decoration, curvaceous forms, and a grand scale generating a sense of movement; later developments within the movement show more restraint.

Bauhaus   The style of the Bauhaus School, founded in Germany by Walter Gropius in 1919, emphasizing simplicity, functionalism, and craftsmanship.

Byzantine   A style of the Byzantine Empire, dating from the 5th century. Its churches are characterized by masonry construction around a central plan, with domes, foliage patterns on stone capitals, and interiors decorated with mosaics and frescoes.

"Seven Wonders of the Ancient World" in chapter 26
Go to

classical revival   A movement in England and the United States in the late 18th and 19th centuries that looked to the traditions of Greek and Roman antiquity. Robert Mills, William Strickland, Sir Robert Smirke, and Sir John Soane participated in this movement.

classicism   The architecture of Greek and Roman antiquity, distinguished by the qualities of simplicity, harmony, and balance; also, a later style that emphasizes these values.

Georgian   The prevailing style of English architecture during the reigns of George I, II, and III (1714–1820), based on the principles of the Italian Renaissance architect Andrea Palladio.

Gothic   A style employed in Europe during the 13th, 14th, and 15th centuries. It is characterized by the use of pointed arches and ribbed vaults, piers, and buttresses in the support of its stone construction. The style is exemplified in France by the Cathedral of Notre Dame in Paris and the cathedrals in Amiens and Chartres.

A Hindu temple represents a mountaintop or the abode of the gods, while the inner part of the temple is the "womb" chamber, representing birth.

Gothic revival   A movement in the United States and Britain in the late 18th and 19th centuries that returned to building styles of the Gothic period.

international style   A movement that developed in the 1920s, characterized by a regularized surface, a lightening of mass, and, often, large expanses of glass. Walter Gropius, Mies van der Rohe, and Le Corbusier worked in this style.

Norman   A building style created by the Normans (1066–c. 1200) based on the Italian romanesque and characterized by sparsely decorated masonry and the use of the round arch. The style was used principally in castles, churches, and abbeys of massive proportions.

postmodernism   A style that emerged in the 1970s characterized by references to and evocations of past architectural styles, particularly the classical tradition. It is frequently colorful and wittily ornamentative. Michael Graves works in this style.

Renaissance   A European style of the 15th and 16th centuries, beginning in Italy. Ancient Roman elements were adapted to contemporary uses, with attention to the principles of the architect Vitruvius and to existing ruins. Symmetry, simplicity, and exact mathematical relationships were emphasized.

rococo   A style originating in France, c. 1720, developed out of baroque types and characterized by elegant, delicate ornamentation and refined use of different materials, such as stucco, metal, or wood, for an ethereal effect.

Romanesque   A style developed in Europe, c. 1050, characterized by heavy masonry and the use of the round arch, barrel and groin vaults, narrow openings, the vaulting rib, the vaulting shaft, and central and western towers.

Tudor   A style of English architecture prevalent during the reigns of the Tudors (1485–1558), transitional between Gothic and Palladian, with emphasis on country manors.

ILLUSTRATIONS OF ARCHITECTURAL ELEMENTS

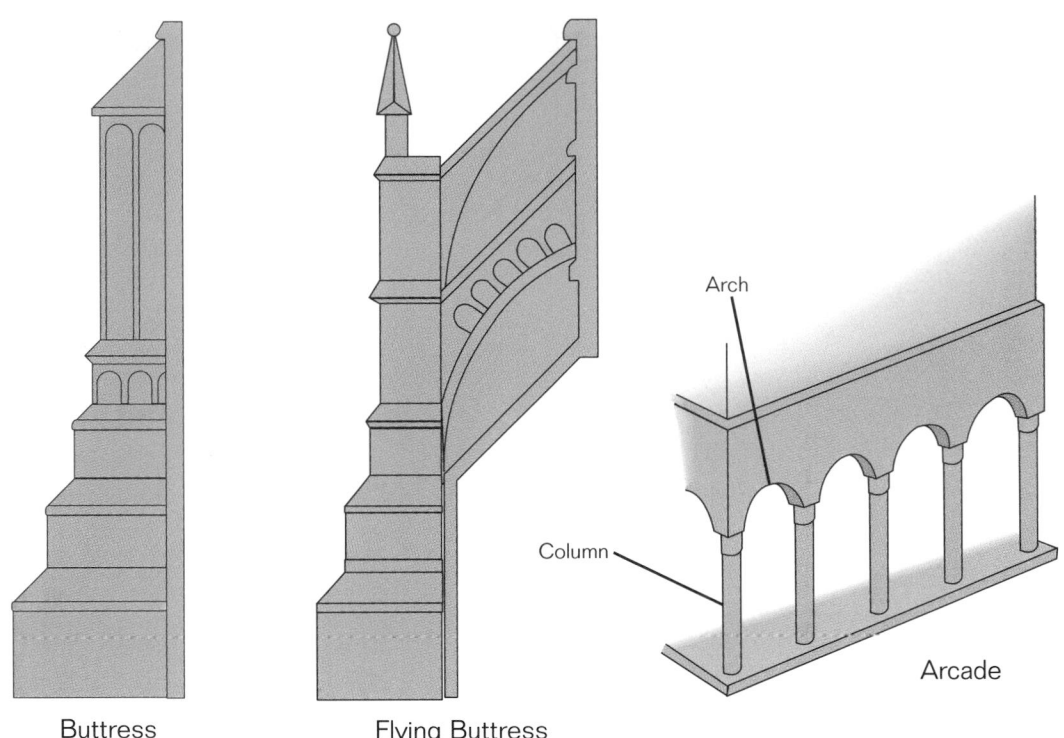

Buttress

Flying Buttress

Arch

Column

Arcade

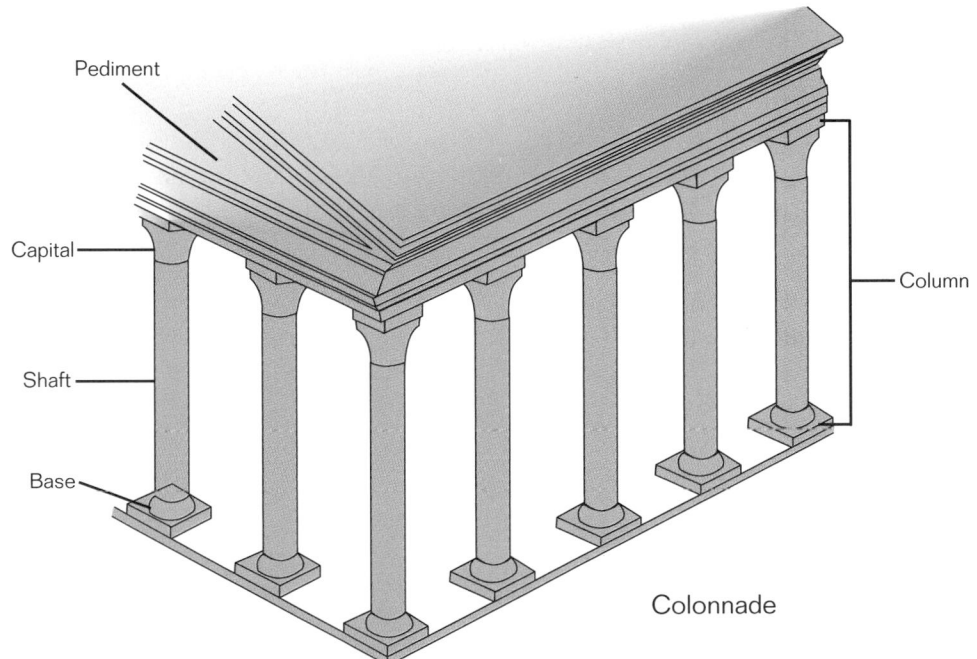

Pediment

Capital

Shaft

Base

Column

Colonnade

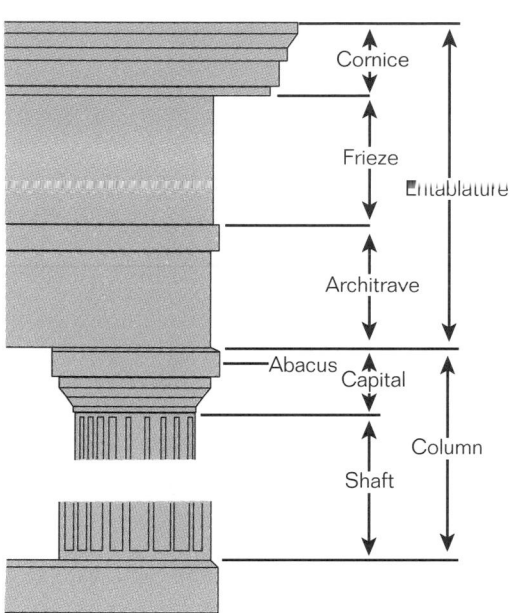

Column and Entablature

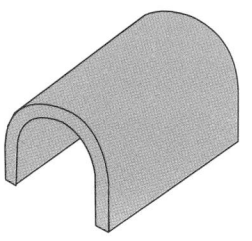

Barrel Vault

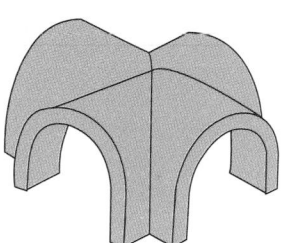

Groined Vault

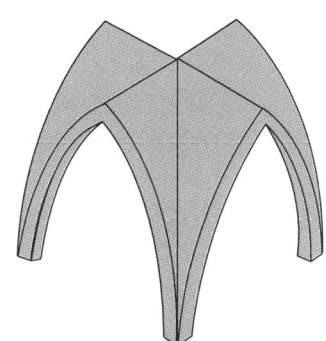

Ribbed Vault

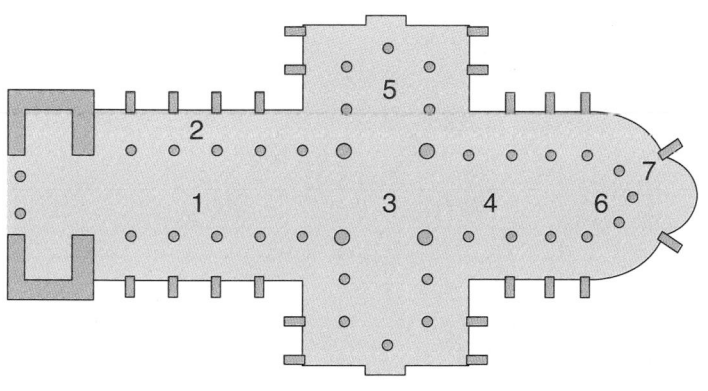

Church Interior

1. Nave   5. Transept
2. Aisle   6. Apse
3. Crossing   7. Ambulatory
4. Choir

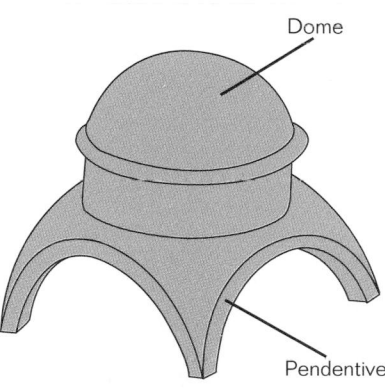

Vaulted Roof

The Visual Arts

COMMON ARCHITECTURAL TERMS

abacus   A stone slab at the top of a classical column aiding the support of the architrave.

acropolis   The elevated stronghold in ancient Greek cities.

adobe   Sun-dried brick used in places with warm, dry climates, such as Egypt and Mexico; also, the structures built out of adobe bricks.

aisle   A passageway of a Christian church or a Roman basilica running parallel to the nave, separated from it by an arcade or colonnade.

ambulatory   A continuous aisle in a building, especially around the apse in a church.

apse   A semicircular area at the end of a church; in most churches it contains the altar.

arcade   A series of arches supported by columns or piers, or a passageway formed by these arches.

arch   A curved structure used to span an opening.

architrave   The lowest part of an entablature resting on the capital of a column.

ashlar   Stones hewn, squared, and smoothed for use in building, as distinguished from rough building stones.

atrium   In an ancient Roman house, a central room open to the sky, usually having a pool for the collection of rainwater. In churches, a front courtyard.

attic   The story above the cornice of a building.

baldachin   An ornamented canopy over an altar, tomb, or throne.

baptistery   A part of a church or a separate building, often octagonal or round, in which baptisms take place.

basilica   In ancient Roman architecture, a large oblong building, generally with double columns and a semicircular apse at one end. In Christian architecture, a church with a nave, apse, and aisles.

beam   A long piece of heavy wood, steel, etc., used as a horizontal support in construction.

buttress   A projecting support built into or against the external wall of a building, typically used in Gothic buildings. A flying buttress is an arch that transfers the thrust of a vault to a lower support.

campanile   A bell tower, especially one that stands apart from any other building.

cantilever   A horizontal projection, such as a balcony or beam, supported at one end only.

choir   A square or rectangular area in a church between the apse and the crossing.

clerestory   A row of windows in the upper part of a wall, especially in a church, to admit light below.

cloister   In religious institutions, a courtyard with covered walks.

colonnade   A row of columns, usually equidistant, supporting a beam or entablature.

column   A cylindrical vertical support usually consisting of a base, shaft, and capital.

Composite Order   A Roman order; its capital combines the Corinthian acanthus leaf decoration with volutes from the Ionic Order.

Corinthian Order   The latest of the three Greek orders, similar to the Ionic, but with the capital decorated with carvings of the acanthus leaf.

cornice   The upper part of an entablature, extending beyond the frieze; also, ornamental molding projecting along the top of a building or wall.

crossing   In a church, the area where the transept and the nave intersect, usually emphasized by a dome or tower.

dome   A vaulted roof of circular or polygonal shape.

Doric Order   The first and simplest of the three Greek orders and the only one that normally has no base.

entablature The upper horizontal part of a classical order, between a capital and the roof; it consists of the architrave, frieze, and cornice.

facade Any important face of a building, usually the principal front with the main entrance.

forum The main public square of an ancient Roman city.

frieze The middle part of an entablature, often decorated with sculpture.

gargoyle A spout placed on the roof gutter of a Gothic building to carry away rainwater; usually carved in the shapes of fanciful animals and grotesque beasts.

Ionic Order Second of the three Greek orders. Its capital is decorated with spiral scrolls (volutes).

lantern A small structure on top of a dome, tower, or roof, often open to admit light below.

lintel *See* **post and lintel.**

loggia A roofed gallery with an open arcade or colonnade on at least one side.

minaret A slender, lofty tower with balconies, attached to a Muslim mosque.

module The measurement by which parts of a building are related to one another. An example is the diameter of a column.

narthex The transverse entrance hall of a church.

nave In a Roman basilica, the central aisle. In a church, the main section extending from the entrance to the crossing.

obelisk A tall, tapering, four-sided stone shaft with a pyramidal top.

ogive The pointed arch used in Gothic architecture.

order A term applied to the three styles of Greek columns and entablatures (Doric, Ionic, and Corinthian) and to the Roman Composite and Tuscan orders, developed from the original three orders.

pagoda A multistoried building, typically Asian, forming a tower with upward curving roofs over the individual stories.

pediment In a classical building, the triangular gable between the horizontal entablature and the sloping roof; in general, an architectural feature over a door or window.

pendentive A curved triangle at the corners of a square or polygonal room, used at the opening of a dome.

pier An upright masonry support.

pilaster A flattened, shallow column or pier projecting from a wall. It usually has a base, shaft, and capital but is decorative rather than structural.

portico A structure usually attached to a building, such as a porch, consisting of a roof supported by piers or columns.

post and lintel A method of construction in which vertical beams (posts) are used to support a horizontal beam (lintel).

pyramid A quadrilateral masonry mass with steeply sloping sides meeting at an apex; in ancient Egypt, pyramids were used as royal tombs.

relief Moldings and ornamentation projecting from the surface of a wall.

spandrel The triangular area between the sides of two adjacent arches.

spire A tall, tapering, pointed roof on a tower, as in the top of a steeple.

tracery Ornament of ribs, bars, etc., in panels or screens, as in the upper part of a Gothic window.

transept A structure that forms the arms of a cross-shaped church.

turret A small tower, usually starting at some distance from the ground, attached to a building such as a castle or fortress.

Tuscan Order A Roman order resembling the Doric, but with a base and an unfluted shaft.

vault   An arched brick or stone ceiling or roof. The simplest form is the **barrel vault,** a single continuous arch; the **groined vault** consists of two barrel vaults joined at right angles; a **ribbed vault** has a web of ribs added to the groins.

volute   A spiral scroll used on Ionic and Corinthian capitals.

westwork   In German Romanesque, a monumental entrance to a church consisting of towers, with a chapel above.

ziggurat   In ancient Assyria and Babylonia, a tower in the shape of a stepped pyramid. It formed the base of a temple.

ADDITIONAL SOURCES OF INFORMATION

Boorstin, Daniel J. *The Creators: A History of Heroes of the Imagination.* Random House, 1992.

Fleming, John et al. *Penguin Dictionary of Architecture.* 4th ed. Viking Penguin, 1991.

Hunt, William D., Jr. *Encyclopedia of American Architects.* McGraw-Hill, 1980.

Janson, Horst W. *History of Art.* 4th ed. Abrams, 1991.

Kostof, Spiro. *A History of Architecture: Settings and Rituals.* 2nd ed. Oxford University Press, 1995.

Marks, Claude. *World Artists, 1950–1980.* H. W. Wilson Co., 1984.

————. *World Artists, 1980–1990.* H. W. Wilson Co., 1991.

Musgrove, John, ed. *A History of Architecture: Sir Banister-Fletcher's.* 19th ed. Butterworth, 1987.

Phaidon Encyclopedia of Art and Artists. Phaidon Press Ltd., 1978.

Random House Library of Painting and Sculpture. Random House, 1981.

8

LITERATURE

IMPORTANT AUTHORS	248
LITERARY MOVEMENTS, PERIODS, AND STYLES	261
PSEUDONYMS OF FAMOUS AUTHORS	264
POET LAUREATES	266
BOOK AWARDS AND THEIR RECIPIENTS	267
THE GREAT BOOKS: A READING LIST	271
THE NEW YORK PUBLIC LIBRARY'S BOOKS OF THE CENTURY	272
COMMON LITERARY TERMS	276
ADDITIONAL SOURCES OF INFORMATION	279

IMPORTANT AUTHORS

Any list of "important" authors is subject to debate. The following list is not all-inclusive but does include most of the authors who have made a substantial contribution to the literature of their country, their continent, and the world at large.

The titles and years of first publication of each author's major works are given. In those instances where an author is known by a pseudonym, he or she is listed by that pseudonym with the real name in brackets.

A dagger (†) indicates that the author was awarded a Nobel prize in literature. For American authors, an asterisk (*) designates a book that was awarded a Pulitzer prize in literature, and a plus sign (+) indicates that the work was awarded a National Book Award.

The shortest complete sentence in the English language is "I am."

AMERICAN

Agee, James (1909–55): *Let Us Now Praise Famous Men* (1941), **A Death in the Family* (1957), *Agee on Film* (1958)

Aiken, Conrad (1889–1973): *The House of Dust: A Symphony* (1920), **Selected Poems* (1929), *Conversation; or, Pilgrim's Progress* (1940), *The Soldier* (1944), *The Kid* (1947), *Ushant: An Essay* (1952)

Alcott, Louisa May (1832–88): *Little Women* (1868–69), *Little Men* (1871), *Silver Pitchers and Independence* (1876), *Spinning-Wheel Stories* (1884)

Algren, Nelson (1909–81): *The Man with the Golden Arm* (1949), *A Walk on the Wild Side* (1956)

Anderson, Sherwood (1876–1941): *Winesburg, Ohio* (1919), *The Triumph of the Egg* (1921), *A Story Teller's Story* (1924), *Dark Laughter* (1925), *Beyond Desire* (1932)

Asimov, Isaac (1920–92): *I, Robot* (1950), *Foundation* series (1951, 1952, 1953, 1982, 1986, 1988, 1993), *The Gods Themselves* (1972)

Auchincloss, Louis [Stanton] (1917–): *Portrait in Brownstone* (1962), *The Winthrop Covenant* (1976), *Life, Law and Letters* (1979), *Diary of a Yuppie* (1987)

Auden, W(ystan) H(ugh) (1907–73): *Spain* (1937), *For the Time Being* (1945), **The Age of Anxiety: A Baroque Eclogue* (1948), *Collected Shorter Poems, 1930–44* (1950), *Making, Knowing and Judging* (1956), *The Dyer's Hand* (1962), *Collected Poems* (1976)

Audubon, John James (1785–1851): *The Birds of America* (1827–38)

Austin, Mary (1868–1934): *Isidro* (1905), *A Woman of Genius* (1912), *The Ford* (1917), *Earth Horizon* (1932)

Baldwin, James (1924–87): *Go Tell It on the Mountain* (1953), *Notes of a Native Son* (1955), *Nobody Knows My Name* (1961), *Another Country* (1962), *Just Above My Head* (1979)

Baraka, Imamu Amiri (formerly LeRoi Jones, 1934–): *Dutchman* (1964), *The Slave* (1964), *The Toilet* (1964), *Black Music* (1967), *Black Magic . . .* (1969), *Selected Plays and Prose* (1979), *Selected Poetry* (1979)

Barth, John [Simmons] (1930–): *The Sot-Weed Factor* (1960), *Giles Goat-Boy* (1966), +*Chimera* (1972), *The Last Voyage of Somebody the Sailor* (1991)

Barthelme, Donald (1931–89): *Come Back, Dr. Caligari* (1964), *Snow White* (1967), *City Life* (1970), *Sixty Stories* (1982)

Bartlett, John (1820–1905): *Familiar Quotations* (1855)

Go to "Pseudonyms of Famous Authors" and "Book Awards and Their Recipients" in this chapter

Baum, Lyman Frank (1856–1919): *The Wonderful Wizard of Oz* (1900)

Beattie, Ann (1947–): *Distortions* (1976), *Chilly Scenes of Winter* (1976), *Where You'll Find Me* (1986), *Picturing Will* (1990)

Bellow, Saul† (1915–): *Dangling Man* (1944), +*The Adventures of Augie March* (1953), *Henderson the Rain King* (1959), +*Herzog* (1964), +*Mr. Sammler's Planet* (1971), **Humboldt's Gift* (1975), *The Dean's December* (1982), *More Die of Heartbreak* (1987)

Benchley, Robert (1889–1945): *Love Conquers All* (1922), *My Ten Years in a Quandary* (1936), *Benchley Beside Himself* (1943)

Benét, Stephen Vincent (1898–1943): **John Brown's Body* (1928), *Ballads and Poems, 1915–30* (1931), *Thirteen O'Clock* (1937), **Western Star* (1943)

Benét, William Rose (1886–1950): *Oxford Anthology of American Literature* (editor, 1938), **The Dust Which Is God* (1941)

Bierce, Ambrose (c. 1842–1914): *Tales of Soldiers and Civilians* (1891), *Can Such Things Be?* (1893), *The Devil's Dictionary* (1911)

Bontemps, Arna (1902–73): *God Sends Sunday* (1931), *Drums at Dusk* (1939), *Sam Patch* (1951), *One Hundred Years of Negro Freedom* (1961)

Boyle, Kay (1903–92): *Wedding Day* (1930), *Plagued by the Nightingale* (1931), *Death of a Man* (1936), *Thirty Stories* (1946), *The Underground Woman* (1975), *Fifty Stories* (1980)

Bradbury, Ray (1920–): *The Martian Chronicles* (1950), *The Illustrated Man* (1951), *Fahrenheit 451* (1953), *Something Wicked This Way Comes* (1962), *I Sing the Body Electric* (1969)

Bradstreet, Anne (c. 1612–72): *The Tenth Muse Lately Sprung Up in America* (1650)

Brooks, Gwendolyn (1917–): **Annie Allen* (1949), *In the Mecca* (1968), *Family Pictures* (1970)

Buck, Pearl† (1892–1973): **The Good Earth* (1931), *My Several Worlds* (1954), *Imperial Woman* (1956), *Command the Morning* (1959), *A Bridge for Passing* (1962)

Burroughs, Edgar Rice (1875–1950): *Tarzan of the Apes* (1914)

Burroughs, William S. (1914–97): *The Naked Lunch* (1959), *Nova Express* (1964), *Cities of the Red Night* (1981)

Capote, Truman (1924–84): *Other Voices, Other Rooms* (1948), *The Grass Harp* (1951), *Breakfast at Tiffany's* (1958), *In Cold Blood* (1966)

Cather, Willa (1873–1947): *O Pioneers!* (1913), *The Song of the Lark* (1915), *My Antonía* (1918), **One of Ours* (1922), *Shadows on the Rock* (1931)

Chandler, Raymond (1888–1959): *The Big Sleep* (1939), *Farewell, My Lovely* (1940), *The Long Goodbye* (1954)

Cheever, John (1912–82): +*The Wapshot Chronicle* (1957), *The Wapshot Scandal* (1964), *Falconer* (1977), **The Stories of John Cheever* (1978)

Chopin, Kate (1851–1904): *Bayou Folk* (1894), *The Awakening* (1899)

Cooper, James Fenimore (1789–1851): *The Spy* (1821), *The Pioneers* (1823), *The Pilot* (1823), *The Last of the Mohicans* (1826), *The Prairie* (1827), *The American Democrat* (1838), *The Pathfinder* (1840), *The Deerslayer* (1841)

Crane, Stephen (1871–1900): *Maggie: A Girl of the Streets* (1893), *The Red Badge of Courage* (1895), *The Black Riders* (1895), *The Open Boat* (1898), *The Monster* (1899)

cummings, e.e. [Edward Estlin] (1894–1962): *The Enormous Room* (1922), *&* (1925), *Is 5* (1926), *50 Poems* (1940), *I x I* (1944), *95 Poems* (1958), +*Poems 1923–1954* (1955)

Dickinson, Emily (1830–86): *Poems* (1890), *Poems: Second Series* (1891), *Poems: Third Series* (1896), *The Single Hound* (1914)

Didion, Joan (1934–   ): *Slouching Towards Bethlehem* (1968), *The White Album* (1979), *Play It As It Lays* (1970), *Democracy* (1984)

Dillard, Annie (1945–   ): **Pilgrim at Tinker Creek* (1974), *Teaching a Stone To Talk* (1982), *The Living* (1992)

Doctorow, E(dgar) L(awrence) (1931–   ): *The Book of Daniel* (1971), *Ragtime* (1975), *Loon Lake* (1980), *+World's Fair* (1986), *Billy Bathgate* (1989)

Dos Passos, John (1896–1970): *Manhattan Transfer* (1925), *The 42nd Parallel* (1930), *1919* (1932), *The Big Money* (1936)

Dreiser, Theodore (1871–1945): *Sister Carrie* (1900), *The Financier* (1912), *The Titan* (1914), *The Genius* (1915), *An American Tragedy* (1925)

Edel, Leon (1907–   ): **+Henry James: A Life* (5 vols., 1953–1972), *Bloomsbury, A House of Lions* (1979), *Stuff of Sleep and Dreams* (1982)

Eliot, T(homas) S(tearns)† (1888–1965): *Prufrock and Other Observations* (1917), *The Waste Land* (1922), *Murder in the Cathedral* (1935), *Four Quartets* (1943)

Ellison, Ralph (1914–94): *+Invisible Man* (1952)

Emerson, Ralph Waldo (1803–82): *Nature* (1836), "The American Scholar" (1837), *Essays: First Series* (1841), *Essays: Second Series* (1844), *Conduct of Life* (1860), *Society and Solitude* (1870)

Faulkner, William† (1897–1962): *Soldier's Pay* (1926), *Sartoris* (1929), *The Sound and the Fury* (1929), *As I Lay Dying* (1930), *Absalom, Absalom!* (1936), *The Hamlet* (1940), *Collected Stories* (1951), **+A Fable* (1954), **The Reivers* (1962)

Fitzgerald, F. Scott (1896–1940): *Tales of the Jazz Age* (1922), *The Great Gatsby* (1925), *Tender Is the Night* (1934), *The Last Tycoon* (1941)

Franklin, Benjamin (1706–90): *Poor Richard's Almanack* (1733–58), *Autobiography* (1771–88)

Frost, Robert (1874–1963): *North of Boston* (1914), *Mountain Interval* (1916), **New Hampshire* (1923), **Collected Poems* (1930), **A Further Range* (1936), **A Witness Tree* (1942), *In the Clearing* (1962)

Gardner, John (1933–82): *Grendel* (1971), *October Light* (1976), *Freddy's Book* (1980)

Ginsberg, Allen (1926–97): *Howl and Other Poems* (1956), *Kaddish and Other Poems* (1961), **The Fall of America: Poems of These States* (1973)

Hammett, Dashiell (1894–1961): *The Maltese Falcon* (1930), *The Thin Man* (1932)

Hawkes, John Clendennin Burne, Jr. (1925–   ): *The Lime Twig* (1961), *The Blood Oranges* (1971), *Death, Sleep and the Traveler* (1974)

Hawthorne, Nathaniel (1804–64): *Twice-Told Tales* (1837; enlarged 1842), *The Scarlet Letter* (1850), *The House of the Seven Gables* (1851)

Heinlein, Robert A. (1907–88): *Stranger in a Strange Land* (1961), *Time Enough for Love* (1973)

Heller, Joseph (1923–   ): *Catch-22* (1961), *Something Happened* (1974), *Good as Gold* (1979)

Hellman, Lillian (1905–84): *An Unfinished Woman* (1969), *Pentimento* (1973), *Scoundrel Time* (1976)

Hemingway, Ernest† (1899–1961): *The Sun Also Rises* (1926), *A Farewell to Arms* (1929), *To Have and Have Not* (1937), *For Whom the Bell Tolls* (1940), **The Old Man and the Sea* (1952), *A Moveable Feast* (1964)

Henry, O. [William Sydney Porter] (1862–1910): *Cabbages and Kings* (1904), *The Four Million* (1906), *The Trimmed Lamp* (1907), *The Voice of the City* (1908), *Whirligigs* (1910), *Strictly Business* (1910), *Sixes and Sevens* (1911), *Rolling Stones* (1913), *Postscripts* (1923)

Hersey, John [Richard] (1914–93): **A Bell for Adano* (1944), *Hiroshima* (1946), *The Wall* (1950)

Howells, William Dean (1837–1920): *The Rise of Silas Lapham* (1885), *A Traveler from Altruria* (1894)

Hughes, Langston (1902–67): *The Weary Blues* (1926), *The Ways of White Folks* (1934), *Shakespeare in Harlem* (1941), *Ask Your Mama* (1961)

Hurston, Zora Neale (1891–1960): *Mules and Men* (1935), *Their Eyes Were Watching God* (1937), *Dust Tracks on a Road* (1942)

Irving, Washington (1783–1859): *History of New York* (1809), *The Sketch Book* (1819–20), *The Crayon Miscellany* (3 vols., 1835)

Jackson, Shirley (1919–65): *The Lottery* (1949), *The Bird's Nest* (1954), *The Haunting of Hill House* (1959), *We Have Always Lived in the Castle* (1962)

James, Henry (1843–1916): *The American* (1877), *The Europeans* (1878), *Daisy Miller* (1879), *The Portrait of a Lady* (1881), *The Bostonians* (1886), *Embarrassments* (1896), *The Two Magics* (1898), *The Awkward Age* (1899), *The Ambassadors* (1903), *The Golden Bowl* (1904)

Jarrell, Randall (1914–65): *Selected Poems* (1955), +*The Woman at the Washington Zoo* (1960)

Jong, Erica (1942–   ): *Fear of Flying* (1973), *Fanny* (1980)

Kerouac, Jack (1922–69): *On the Road* (1957), *The Dharma Bums* (1958), *Desolation Angels* (1965)

Kosinski, Jerzy (1933–91): *The Painted Bird* (1965), +*Steps* (1968), *Being There* (1971), *Cockpit* (1975), *Passion Play* (1979), *Pinball* (1982), *The Hermit of 69th Street* (1988)

Lardner, Ring (1885–1933): *You Know Me, Al: A Busher's Letters* (1916), *How to Write Short Stories* (1924), *The Love Nest and Other Stories* (1926)

Lewis, Sinclair† (1885–1951): *Main Street* (1920), *Babbitt* (1922), *Arrowsmith* (1925), *Dodsworth* (1929)

London, Jack (1876–1916): *The Call of the Wild* (1903), *The Sea-Wolf* (1904), *White Fang* (1906), *The Iron Heel* (1908), *Martin Eden* (1909)

Longfellow, Henry Wadsworth (1807–82): *Voices of the Night* (1839), *Ballads and Other Poems* (1841), *Hiawatha* (1855), *The Courtship of Miles Standish* (1858), *The Tales of a Wayside Inn* (1863)

Lowell, James Russell (1819–91): *A Fable for Critics* (1848), *The Vision of Sir Launfal* (1848), *The Cathedral* (1869)

Lowell, Robert (1917–77): *Land of Unlikeness* (1944), *Lord Weary's Castle* (1946), *The Mill of the Kavanaughs* (1951), *Old Glory* (1964), *Dolphin* (1973)

Lowry, Malcolm (1909–57): *Ultramarine* (1933), *Under the Volcano* (1947), *Hear Us O Lord from Heaven Thy Dwelling Place* (1961)

Mailer, Norman (1923–   ): *The Naked and the Dead* (1948), *An American Dream* (1965), *The Armies of the Night* (1968), *The Executioner's Song* (1979), *Ancient Evenings* (1983), *Tough Guys Don't Dance* (1987), *Harlot's Ghost* (1990)

Malamud, Bernard (1914–86): +*The Magic Barrel* (1958), *+The Fixer* (1967), *The Tenants* (1971), *God's Grace* (1982)

McCarthy, Mary (1912–89): *The Groves of Academe* (1952), *Memories of a Catholic Girlhood* (1957), *The Group* (1963), *Cannibals and Missionaries* (1979), *Intellectual Memoirs: New York, 1936–1938* (1992)

McCullers, Carson (1917–67): *The Heart Is a Lonely Hunter* (1940), *Member of the Wedding* (1946), *Clock Without Hands* (1961)

Melville, Herman (1819–91): *Typee* (1846), *Omoo* (1847), *White-Jacket* (1850), *Moby-Dick* (1851)

Mencken, H(enry) L(ouis) (1880–1956): *The American Language* (1919, rev. 1921, 1923, 1936; suppl. 1945, 1948)

Michener, James (1907–97): *Tales of the South Pacific* (1947), *Hawaii* (1959), *The Source* (1965), *The Drifters* (1971), *Chesapeake* (1978), *Caribbean* (1979), *Texas* (1985), *Alaska* (1988), *Mexico* (1992)

Miller, Henry (1891–1980): *Tropic of Cancer* (1934), *Tropic of Capricorn* (1939)

Mitchell, Margaret (1900–49): **Gone with the Wind* (1936)

Morrison, Toni [Chloe Anthony Wofford]† (1931–   ): *The Bluest Eye* (1970), *Sula* (1973), *+Song of Solomon* (1977), *Tar Baby* (1981), **Beloved* (1987), *Jazz* (1992)

Oates, Joyce Carol (1938–   ): *A Garden of Earthly Delights* (1967), *Expensive People* (1968), *+Them* (1969), *Bellefleur* (1980), *On Boxing* (1987), *You Must Remember This* (1988), *American Appetites* (1989), *Black Water* (1992)

Paine, Thomas (1737–1809): *Common Sense* (1776), *The Age of Reason* (1794–95)

Parker, Dorothy (1893–1967): *Men I'm Not Married To* (1922), *Women I'm Not Married To* (1922), *Laments for the Living* (1930), *After Such Pleasures* (1933), *Here Lies* (1942), *Collected Poems: Not So Deep as a Well* (1937)

Percy, Walker (1916–90): *+The Moviegoer* (1961), *The Last Gentleman* (1966), *Love in the Ruins* (1971), *The Thanatos Syndrome* (1987)

Plath, Sylvia (1932–63): *The Colossus* (1960), *The Bell Jar* (1963), *Ariel* (1965), **Collected Poems* (1981)

Poe, Edgar Allan (1809–49): *Poems by Edgar A. Poe* (1831), *Tales of the Grotesque and Arabesque* (1840), *Tales* (1845), *The Raven and Other Poems* (1845)

Porter, Katherine Anne (1890–1980): *Flowering Judas* (1930), *Pale Horse, Pale Rider* (1939), *The Leaning Tower* (1944), *Ship of Fools* (1962), **+Collected Stories* (1965)

Pound, Ezra (1885–1972): *Cantos* (1970)

Pynchon, Thomas (1937–   ): *V.* (1963), *The Crying of Lot 49* (1966), *+Gravity's Rainbow* (1973), *Vineland* (1990), *Mason & Dixon* (1997)

Rand, Ayn (1905–82): *The Fountainhead* (1943), *Atlas Shrugged* (1957)

Roth, Philip (1933–   ): *+Goodbye, Columbus* (1959), *Letting Go* (1962), *Portnoy's Complaint* (1969), *The Great American Novel* (1973), *The Ghost Writer* (1979), *The Counterlife* (1986), *The Facts: A Novelist's Autobiography* (1988), *Deception* (1990), *Patrimony: A True Story* (1991), *+Sabbath's Theater* (1995)

Salinger, J. D. (1919–   ): *The Catcher in the Rye* (1951), *Franny and Zooey* (1961)

Sandburg, Carl (1878–1967): *Chicago Poems* (1916), **Cornhuskers* (1918), **Complete Poems* (1950)

Saroyan, William (1908–81): *The Daring Young Man on the Flying Trapeze* (1934), *The Human Comedy* (1943), *One Day in the Afternoon of the World* (1964)

Sexton, Anne (1928–74): **Live or Die* (1966), *Love Poems* (1969)

Singer, Isaac Bashevis (1904–91)†: *Satan in Goray* (1935), *The Family Moskat* (1950), *Gimpel the Fool* (1957), *The Spinoza of Market Street* (1961), *A Crown of Feathers and Other Stories* (1973), *Old Love* (1979), *The King of the Fields* (1988)

Stein, Gertrude (1874–1946): *Three Lives* (1909), *The Autobiography of Alice B. Toklas* (1933), *Yes Is for a Very Young Man* (1946)

Steinbeck, John† (1902–68): *Tortilla Flat* (1935), *Of Mice and Men* (1937), *The Long Valley* (1938), **The Grapes of Wrath* (1939), *East of Eden* (1952)

Stowe, Harriet Beecher (1811–96): *Uncle Tom's Cabin* (1852)

Styron, William (1925–   ): *Lie Down in Darkness* (1951), **The Confessions of Nat Turner* (1967), *+Sophie's Choice* (1979)

Thoreau, Henry David (1817–62): *Civil Disobedience* (1849), *Walden* (1854), *The Maine Woods* (1864)

Twain, Mark [Samuel Langhorne Clemens] (1835–1910): *The Innocents Abroad* (1869), *Roughing It* (1872), *The Adventures of Tom Sawyer* (1876), *The Adventures of Huckleberry Finn* (1884), *Following the Equator* (1897)

Tyler, Anne (1941–): *A Slipping-Down Life* (1970), *Searching for Caleb* (1976), *Morgan's Passing* (1980), *Dinner at the Homesick Restaurant* (1982), *The Accidental Tourist* (1985), *Breathing Lessons* (1988), *Saint Maybe* (1991)

Updike, John (1932–): *Rabbit, Run* (1960), *The Centaur* (1964), *Couples* (1968), *+Rabbit Is Rich* (1981), *The Witches of Eastwick* (1984), *Rabbit at Rest* (1990)

Vonnegut, Kurt Jr. (1922–): *Cat's Cradle* (1963), *Slaughterhouse-Five; or The Children's Crusade* (1969), *Breakfast of Champions* (1973), *Bluebeard* (1987)

Walker, Alice (1944–): *Meridian* (1976), *+The Color Purple* (1982), *The Temple of My Familiar* (1988)

Warren, Robert Penn (1905–89): *All the King's Men* (1946), *Promises* (1957), *The Cave* (1959)

Webster, Noah (1758–1843): *An American Dictionary of the English Language* (2 vols., 1828)

Welty, Eudora (1909–): *The Bride of the Innisfallen* (1955), *Thirteen Stories* (1965), *The Optimist's Daughter* (1970), *The Collected Stories of Eudora Welty* (1980), *One Writer's Beginnings* (1984)

Wharton, Edith (1862–1937): *Ethan Frome* (1911), *Xingu and Other Stories* (1916), *The Age of Innocence* (1920)

White, E. B. (1899–1985): *One Man's Meat* (1942), *Here Is New York* (1949), *Charlotte's Web* (1952), *The Elements of Style* (1959)

Whitman, Walt (1819–92): *Leaves of Grass* (1855), *Drum-Taps* (1865), *Passage to India* (1871), *Two Rivulets* (1876), *November Boughs* (1888)

Wilson, Edmund (1895–1972): *Axel's Castle* (1931), *The Wound and the Bow* (1941), *Patriotic Gore* (1962)

Wolfe, Thomas (1900–38): *Look Homeward, Angel* (1929), *Of Time and the River* (1935), *The Web and the Rock* (1939)

Wolfe, Tom [Thomas Kennerly Wolfe, Jr.] (1931–): *The Pump House Gang* (1968), *The Electric Kool-Aid Acid Test* (1968), *+The Right Stuff* (1975), *The Bonfire of the Vanities* (1988)

Wouk, Herman (1915–): *The Caine Mutiny* (1951), *Marjorie Morningstar* (1955), *The Winds of War* (1971), *War and Remembrance* (1978)

Wright, Richard (1908–60): *Native Son* (1940), *Black Boy* (1945), *The Outsider* (1953)

AFRICAN

Armah, Ayi Kweh (Ghanaian, 1939–): *The Beautiful Ones Are Not Yet Born* (1968), *Why Are We So Blest?* (1972)

Beti, Mongo [Alexandre Biyidi] (Cameroonian, 1932–): *Le pauvre Christ de Bomba* (1956), *Mission terminée* (1957), *Le roi miraculé* (1958)

Cavafy, C. P. (Egyptian, 1863–1933): *Poems* (1935)

Gordimer, Nadine† (South African, 1923–): *Occasion for Loving* (1963), *A Guest of Honor* (1970), *Burgher's Daughter* (1979), *Something Out There* (1984), *My Son's Story* (1991)

Laye, Camara (Guinean, 1928–80): *The African Child* (1953), *The Radiance of the King* (1954), *The Guardian of the Word* (1978)

Mahfouz, Naguib† (Egyptian, c. 1911–): *New Cairo* (1946), *Midaq Alley* (1947), *Between the Two Palaces* (1956), *The Palace of Desire* (1957), *The Sugar Bowl* (1957), *Miramar* (1967), *Respected Sir* (1987), *Wedding Song* (1987)

Paton, Alan Stewart (South African, 1903–88): *Cry the Beloved Country* (1948)

Sembene, Ousmane (Senegalese, 1923–): *The Black Docker* (1956), *The Storm* (1964), *The Money Order* (1965)

Senghor, Léopold Sédar (Senegalese, 1906–): *Shadow Songs* (1945), *Nocturnes* (1961), *Negritude and Humanism* (1964)

Soyinka, Wole† (Nigerian 1934–): *Three Plays* (1963), *The Road* (1965), *The Forest of a Thousand Daemons* (1968), *Aké* (1981)

ASIAN

Bashō [Matsuo Munefusa] (Japanese, 1644–94): *The Narrow Road to the Deep North* (1689)

Chatterje, Bankim-Chandra (Indian, 1838–94): *The Chieftain's Daughter* (1880), *Kopal-Kundala: A Tale of Bengali Life* (1885), *Krishna Kante's Will* (1895)

Confucius (Chinese, c. 551–479 B.C.): *The Analects of Confucius*

Kawabata, Yasunari† (Japanese, 1899–1972): *Snow Country* (1948), *Thousand Cranes* (1952), *Beauty and Sadness* (1965)

Lao-tzu (Chinese, c. 6th century B.C.): *Tao-te-ching*

Li Po (Chinese, 701–762): *Complete Works*

Mishima, Yukio (Japanese, 1925–70): *Confession of a Mask* (1949), *Forbidden Colors* (2 vols., 1951–53), *The Sailor Who Fell from Grace with the Sea* (1963), *The Sea of Fertility* (4 vols., 1969–71)

Murasaki, Shikibu (Japanese, c. 978–1015): *The Tale of the Genji* (c. 1010)

Natsume Sōseki Kinosuke (Japanese, 1867–1916): *I Am a Cat* (1905–07), *The Three-Cornered World* (1907), *And Then* (1910)

Omar Khayyam (Persian, 1048–1131): *Rubaiyat* (1859)

Rushdie, Salman (Indian, 1947–): *Grimus* (1975), *Midnight's Children* (1981), *Shame* (1983), *The Satanic Verses* (1989), *Haroun and the Sea of Stories* (1991)

Tagore, Rabindranath† (Indian, 1861–1941): *Gitanjali: Song Offering* (1912), *King of the Dark Chamber* (1914), *Gora* (1924)

Tanizaki Junichirō (Japanese, 1886–1965): *Tattoo* (1911), *The Secret History of the Lord Musashi* (1935), *The Key* (1956), *Seven Japanese Tales* (1963)

Ts'ao Hsüeh-ch'in [Tsao Chan] (Chinese, c. 1715–63): *Dream the of Red Chamber* (c. 1763)

AUSTRALIAN

Clavell, James [du Maresq] (1924–94): *King Rat* (1962), *Tai-Pan* (1966), *Shogun* (1975), *Noble House* (1981), *Gai-Jin* (1993)

Franklin, Miles [Stella Maria Sarah Miles] (1879–1954): *My Brilliant Career* (1901), *Some Everyday Folk and Dawn* (1909), *All That Swagger* (1936)

Greer, Germaine (1939–): *The Female Eunuch* (1970), *Sex and Destiny: The Politics of Human Fertility* (1984), *The Madwoman's Underclothes: Essays and Occasional Writings* (1986), *Daddy, We Hardly Knew You* (1989)

Hospital, Janette Turner (1942–): *The Ivory Swing* (1982), *Borderline* (1985), *Isobars* (1990)

Keneally, Thomas (Michael) (1935–): *The Chant of Jimmie Blacksmith* (1972), *Season in Purgatory* (1976), *Confederates* (1979), *Schindler's List* (1982), *Woman of the Inner Sea* (1992), *A River Town* (1995)

Malouf, (George Joseph) David (1934–): *Johnno* (1975), *An Imaginary Life* (1978), *Harland's Half Acre* (1984), *Remembering Babylon* (1993), *Conversations at Curlow Creek* (1996)

McCullough, Colleen (1937–): *Tim* (1974), *The Thorn Birds* (1977), *An Indecent Obsession* (1981), *The Ladies of Missalonghi* (1987), *The First Man in Rome* (1990), *Caesar's Women* (1996)

Moorehead, Alan [McCrae] (1910–83): *Gallipoli* (1956), *The White Nile* (1960), *The Blue Nile* (1962), *Cooper's Creek* (1963)

Richardson, Henry Handel [Ethel Florence Lindesay Richardson Robertson] (1870–1946): *Maurice Guest* (1908), *The Getting of Wisdom* (1910), *The Fortunes of Richard Mahoney* (trilogy; 1917–1929)

Shute, Nevil [Nevil Shute Norway] (1899–1960): *Lonely Road* (1932), *No Highway* (1940), *A Town Like Alice* (1950), *On the Beach* (1957), *Trustee from the Toolroom* (1960)

West, Morris L(anglo) (1916–   ): *The Devil's Advocate* (1959), *The Shoes of the Fisherman* (1963), *The Tower of Babel* (1967), *Harlequin* (1974), *The Clowns of God* (1981), *Lazarus* (1990), *The Lovers* (1993)

BRITISH

Amis, Kingsley (English, 1922–95): *Lucky Jim* (1954), *One Fat Englishman* (1963), *Jake's Thing* (1978), *Stanley and the Women* (1984), *Old Devils* (1986), *Difficulties with Girls* (1988)

Austen, Jane (English, 1775–1817): *Sense and Sensibility* (1811), *Pride and Prejudice* (1813), *Emma* (1816), *Persuasion* (1818)

Belloc, Joseph Hilaire Peter (English, 1870–1953): *The Bad Child's Book of Beasts* (1896), *On Nothing* (1908), *Cautionary Tales for Children* (1908), *On Everything* (1909), *On Anything* (1910)

Blake, William (English, 1757–1827): *Poetical Sketches* (1783), *Songs of Innocence* (1789), *The Marriage of Heaven and Hell* (1793), *The Visions of the Daughters of Albion* (1793), *Songs of Experience* (1794), *Milton* (1804)

Boswell, James (English, 1740–95): *The Life of Samuel Johnson* (1791)

Brontë, Charlotte (English, 1816–55): *Jane Eyre* (1847)

Brontë, Emily (English, 1818–48): *Wuthering Heights* (1847)

Browning, Elizabeth Barrett (English, 1806–61): *The Seraphim and Other Poems* (1838), *Sonnets from the Portuguese* (1850), *Aurora Leigh* (1857), *Last Poems* (1862)

Browning, Robert (English, 1812–89): *Bells and Pomegranates* (1841–46), *Dramatic Lyrics* (1842), *Dramatic Romances and Lyrics* (1845), *Christmas Eve and Easter Day* (1850), *Men and Women* (1855), *Dramatis Personae* (1864)

Burgess, Anthony (English, 1917–93): *A Clockwork Orange* (1962), *Napoleon Symphony: A Novel in Four Movements* (1974), *Earthly Powers* (1980), *Enderby's Dark Lady* (1984)

Burns, Robert (Scottish, 1759–96): *Poems, Chiefly in the Scottish Dialect* (1786), *The Scots Musical Museum* (1787–96)

Byron, Lord [George Gordon] (English, 1788–1824): *Childe Harold's Pilgrimage*, Cantos I and II (1812), *Childe Harold*, Cantos III and IV (1816, 1817), *The Prisoner of Chillon* (1816), *Manfred* (1817), *Don Juan* (1819–24)

Carroll, Lewis [Charles Lutwidge Dodgson] (English, 1832–98): *Alice's Adventures in Wonderland* (1865), *Through the Looking Glass* (1871)

Chaucer, Geoffrey (English, c. 1340–1400): *The Canterbury Tales* (after 1387)

Isaac Asimov was not only a highly prolific author, he was also extremely versatile. He wrote over 400 books and is the only author to have a book in every major Dewey-decimal category.

Christie, Agatha (English, 1891–1976): *The Murder of Roger Ackroyd* (1926), *Murder on the Orient Express* (1934), *Death on the Nile* (1937), *And Then There Were None* (1940), *The Pale Horse* (1961)

Clarke, Arthur C(harles) (English, 1917–   ): *Childhood's End* (1953), *2001: A Space Odyssey* (1968), *Rendezvous with Rama* (1973), *The*

Fountains of Paradise (1979), *3001: The Final Odyssey* (1997)

Coleridge, Samuel Taylor   (English, 1772–1834): *Lyrical Ballads* (1798), *Sybilline Leaves* (1817), *Biographia Literaria* (1817), *The Poetical Works* (1834)

Conrad, Joseph   (English, 1857–1924): *The Nigger of the "Narcissus"* (1897), *Lord Jim* (1900), *Typhoon* (1902), *Nostromo* (1904), *Chance* (1914), *Victory* (1915)

Defoe, Daniel   (English, 1660–1731): *Robinson Crusoe* (1719), *Moll Flanders* (1722), *Roxanna* (1724)

Dickens, Charles   (English, 1812–70): *Oliver Twist* (1838), *Nicholas Nickleby* (1839), *A Christmas Carol* (1843), *David Copperfield* (1850), *Bleak House* (1853), *A Tale of Two Cities* (1859), *Great Expectations* (1861), *Edwin Drood* (1870)

Donne, John   (English, 1572–1631): *The Anniversaries* (1611, 1612), *Songs and Sonnets* (1633)

Doyle, Sir Arthur Conan   (English, 1859–1930): *Study in Scarlet* (1887), *The Sign of the Four* (1890), *The Adventures of Sherlock Holmes* (1892), *The Valley of Fear* (1915), *The Case Book of Sherlock Holmes* (1927)

Dryden, John   (English, 1631–1700): *All for Love* (1678), *Absalom and Achitophel* (1681), *The Medal* (1682), *MacFlecknoe* (1682)

Durrell, Lawrence   (English, 1912–90): *The Alexandria Quartet* (1957–60)

Eliot, George [Mary Ann Evans]   (English, 1819–80): *Silas Marner* (1861), *Middlemarch* (1871–72)

Fielding, Henry   (English, 1707–54): *The Tragedy of Tragedies; or, The Life and Death of Tom Thumb the Great* (1731), *Joseph Andrews* (1742), *Tom Jones* (1749)

Forster, E. M.   (English, 1879–1970): *A Room with a View* (1908), *Howard's End* (1910), *A Passage to India* (1924)

Golding, William†   (English, 1911–93): *Lord of the Flies* (1954), *Free Fall* (1959), *Rites of Passage* (1980)

Hardy, Thomas   (English, 1840–1928): *Far from the Madding Crowd* (1874), *The Return of the Native* (1878), *Tess of the D'Urbervilles* (1891), *Jude the Obscure* (1896)

Hopkins, Gerard Manley   (English, 1844–89): *Poems* (1918)

Johnson, Samuel   (English, 1709–84): *A Dictionary of the English Language* (1755)

Keats, John   (English, 1795–1821): *The Poems of John Keats* (1817), *Endymion* (1818), *Lamia, Isabella, and The Eve of St. Agnes and Other Poems* (1820)

Kipling, Rudyard†   (English, 1865–1936): *Plain Tales from the Hills* (1888), *The Phantom Rickshaw* (1889), *Barrack-Room Ballads* (1892), *The Jungle Book* (1894), *The Second Jungle Book* (1895), *Captains Courageous* (1897), *Kim* (1901), *Just So Stories* (1902)

Lawrence, D(avid) H(erbert)   (English, 1885–1930): *Sons and Lovers* (1913), *Women in Love* (1920), *Lady Chatterley's Lover* (1928)

Lessing, Doris   (English, 1919–   ): *The Grass Is Singing* (1950), *Martha Quest* (1952), *The Golden Notebook* (1962), *Briefing for a Descent into Hell* (1971), *Shikasta* (1979), *The Good Terrorist* (1985), *The Fifth Child* (1988)

Malory, Sir Thomas   (English, ?–1471): *Le Morte d'Arthur* (1485)

Marvell, Andrew   (English, 1621–78): *Miscellaneous Poems* (1681)

Maugham, William Somerset   (English, 1874–1965): *Of Human Bondage* (1915), *Cakes and Ale* (1930), *The Summing Up* (1938), *The Razor's Edge* (1944)

Literature

Milton, John (English, 1608–74): *Paradise Lost* (1667), *Paradise Regained* (1671)

Orwell, George [Eric Blair] (English, 1903–50): *Animal Farm* (1945), *1984* (1949)

Pope, Alexander (English, 1688–1744): *An Essay on Criticism* (1711), *The Rape of the Lock* (1714)

Scott, Sir Walter (Scottish, 1771–1832): *The Heart of Midlothian* (1818), *The Bride of Lammermoor* (1819), *Ivanhoe* (1819), *Kenilworth* (1821)

Mark Twain's Tom Sawyer (1876) *was the first novel ever written on a typewriter.*

Shelley, Mary Wollstonecraft (English, 1797–1851): *Frankenstein, or the Modern Prometheus* (1818)

Shelley, Percy Bysshe (English, 1792–1822): *Prometheus Unbound* (1820), *Adonais* (1821)

Spenser, Edmund (English, c. 1552–99): *The Faerie Queene* (1590)

Stevenson, Robert Louis (Scottish, 1850–94): *Treasure Island* (1883), *The Strange Case of Dr. Jekyll and Mr. Hyde* (1886)

Swinburne, Algernon Charles (English, 1837–1909): *Atalanta in Calydon* (1865), *Poems and Ballads: First Series* (1866), *Poems and Ballads: Second Series* (1878), *Astrophel* (1894), *A Tale of Balen* (1896)

Tennyson, Alfred (Lord) (English, 1809–92): *Poems, Chiefly Lyrical* (1830), *Poems* (1832), *Poems* (1842), *Locksley Hall* (1842), *In Memoriam* (1833–50), *Maud, and Other Poems* (1855), *Idylls of the King* (1859–85)

Thackeray, William Makepeace (English, 1811–63): *Barry Lyndon* (1844), *Vanity Fair* (1847–48)

Thomas, Dylan Marlais (English-Welsh, 1914–53): *Eighteen Poems* (1934), *Twenty-Five Poems* (1936), *A Child's Christmas in Wales* (1952), *Under Milk Wood* (1954), *Adventures in the Skin Trade* (1955)

Trollope, Anthony (English, 1815–82): *The Warden* (1855), *Barchester Towers* (1857)

Wells, H(erbert) G(eorge) (English, 1866–1946): *The Time Machine* (1895), *The Island of Dr. Moreau* (1896), *The Invisible Man* (1897), *The War of the Worlds* (1898), *The First Man in the Moon* (1901), *Kipps* (1905), *Tono-Bungay* (1909)

Woolf, Virginia (English, 1882–1941): *Mrs. Dalloway* (1925), *To the Lighthouse* (1927), *A Room of One's Own* (1929)

Wordsworth, William (English, 1770–1850): *Lyrical Ballads* (1798), *Poems Chiefly of Early and Late Years* (1842)

CANADIAN

Atwood, Margaret (1939–   ): *The Circle Game* (1966), *Surfacing* (1972), *Selected Poems* (1976), *Dancing Girls* (1977), *Life Before Man* (1979), *Bodily Harm* (1981), *The Handmaid's Tale* (1985), *Cat's Eye* (1988)

Connor, Ralph [Charles William Gordon] (1860–1937): *Black Rock: A Tale of the Selkirks* (1898), *The Sky Pilot: A Tale of the Foothills* (1899), *The Men from Glengarry: A Tale of the Ottawa* (1901), *Glengarry School Days: A Story of Early Days in Glengarry* (1902), *The Foreigner: A Tale of Saskatchewan* (1909), *The Sky Pilot in No Man's Land* (1919)

Davies, Robertson (1913–95): *A Mixture of Frailties* (1958), *Fifth Business* (1970), *The Rebel Angels* (1981), *What's Bred in the Bone* (1985), *The Lyre of Orpheus* (1990)

Leacock, Stephen (1869–1944): *Literary Lapses* (1910), *Nonsense Novels* (1911), *Sunshine Sketches of a Little Town* (1912), *Arcadian Adventures with the Idle Rich* (1914), *My Discovery of the West* (1937)

Montgomery, Lucy Maude (1874–1942): *Anne of Green Gables* (1908), *Emily of New Moon* (1923), *The Blue Castle* (1926), *A Tangled Web* (1931), *Jane of Lantern Hill* (1937)

Munro, Alice (1931–): *Dance of the Happy Shades* (1968), *Lives of the Girls and Women* (1971), *Who Do You Think You Are?* (1978), *The Progress of Love* (1986)

Pratt, E. J. (1882–1964): *The Witches' Brew* (1925), *Titans: Two Poems* (1926), *The Fable of the Goats and Other Poems* (1932), *The Titanic* (1935), *Brebeuf and His Brethren* (1940), *Towards the Last Spike* (1952), *The Collected Poems of E. J. Pratt* (1958)

Richler, Mordecai (1931–): *A Choice of Enemies* (1957), *The Apprenticeship of Duddy Kravitz* (1959), *Cocksure* (1968), *St. Urbain's Horseman* (1971), *Solomon Gursky Was Here* (1989)

Roberts, Sir Charles G. D. (1860–1943): *Orion, and Other Poems* (1880), *In Divers Tones* (1887), *Songs of the Common Day* (1893), *Earth's Enigmas* (1896), *The Vagrant of Time* (1927), *The Iceberg, and Other Poems* (1934), *Further Animal Stories* (1936)

Ross, Sinclair (1908–): *As for Me and My House* (1941), *The Well* (1958), *The Lamp at Noon and Other Stories* (1968), *Whir of Gold* (1970), *Sawbones Memorial* (1974)

FRENCH

Balzac, Honoré de (1799–1850): *Droll Tales* (1832–37), *The Human Comedy* (1842–53)

Baudelaire, Charles Pierre (1821–67): *Les fleurs du mal* (1857), *Les paradis artificiels* (1860), *Les épaves* (1861), *Nouvelles fleurs du mal* (1866), *Petits poèmes en prose* (1869)

Breton, André (1896–1966): *Le Surréalisme et la peinture* (1928), *Nadja* (1928), *Les Vases communicants* (1932), *L'Amour fou* (1937), *Arcane 17* (1945)

Camus, Albert† (1913–60): *The Stranger* (1942, rev. 1953), *The Myth of Sisyphus and Other Essays* (1942), *Caligula* (1944), *The Plague* (1947), *The Rebel* (1951), *The Fall* (1956), *Exile and the Kingdom* (1957)

Colette [Sidonie-Gabrielle Colette] (1873–1954): *Claudine* (1900–03), *The Vagrant* (1910), *Mitsou* (1918), *Chéri* (1920), *A Lesson in Love* (1928), *Gigi* (1944)

Dumas, Alexandre, père (1802–70): *The Count of Monte Cristo* (1844–45), *The Three Musketeers* (1844), *The Corsican Brothers* (1844)

Flaubert, Gustave (1821–80): *Madame Bovary* (1857), *Sentimental Education* (1869)

Gide, André† (1869–1951): *The Immoralist* (1902), *Straight Is the Gate* (1909), *The Pastoral Symphony* (1919), *The Counterfeiters* (1926)

Hugo, Victor Marie (1802–85): *The Hunchback of Notre-Dame* (1831), *Lucretia Borgia* (1833), *Les Misérables* (1862)

Malraux, André (1901–76): *Man's Fate* (1933), *Man's Hope* (1937)

Maupassant, Henri René Albert Guy de (1850–93): *Boule de suif* (1880), *La Maison Tellier* (1881), *Bel-Ami* (1885), *Pierre et Jean* (1888), *Yvette* (1885)

Mauriac, François Charles† (1885–1970): *Genetrix* (1923), *Thérèse* (1927), *The Desert of Love* (1929), *A Woman of the Pharisees* (1941)

Montaigne, Michel de (1533–92): *Essais* (1580)

Proust, Marcel (1871–1922): *Remembrance of Things Past* (7 vols., 1913–27)

Rabelais, François (c. 1494–1553): *Gargantua and Pantagruel* (1532–64)

Rimbaud, Arthur (1854–91): *A Season in Hell* (1873), *Illuminations* (1886)

Rostand, Edmond (1868–1918): *The Princess Faraway* (1895), *Cyrano de Bergerac* (1897)

Sand, George [Amandine Aurore Lucie Dupin] (1804–76): *Indiana* (1832), *Lelia* (1833), *The*

Companion of the Tour of France (1841), *Consuelo* (1842–43), *He and She* (1859), *The Marquis of Villemer* (1860–61)

Sartre, Jean-Paul† (1905–80): *Nausea* (1938), *The Flies* (1943), *Being and Nothingness* (1943), *No Exit* (1944), *The Condemned of Altona* (1959)

Stendhal [Marie-Henri Beyle] (1788–1842): *The Red and the Black* (1830), *The Charterhouse of Parma* (1839)

Tocqueville, Alexis de (1805–59): *Democracy in America* (2 vols., 1835; 2 supplementary vols., 1840), *The Old Regime and the Revolution* (1856)

Valéry, Paul (1871–1945): *Charmes* (1922)

Verne, Jules (1828–1905): *A Voyage to the Center of the Earth* (1864), *Twenty Thousand Leagues Under the Sea* (1870), *Around the World in Eighty Days* (1873)

Voltaire [François-Marie Arouet] (1694–1778): *Candide* (1759)

Zola, Émile (1840–1902): *Thérèse Raquin* (1867), *Nana* (1880), *Germinal* (1885)

GERMAN

Böll, Heinrich† (1917–85): *Traveler, If You Come to Spa* (1950), *Adam, Where Art Thou?* (1951), *Billiards at Half-past Nine* (1959), *The Clown* (1963), *Group Portrait with Lady* (1971), *The Lost Honor of Katharina Blum* (1974), *The Safety Net* (1982)

Canetti, Elias† (1905–94): *Auto-da-Fé* (1936), *Crowds and Power* (1960)

Goethe, Johann Wolfgang von (1749–1832): *Wilhelm Meister's Apprenticeship* (1795–96), *Faust,* Part I (1808) and Part II (1827–33)

Grass, Günter (1927–): *The Tin Drum* (1959), *The Flounder* (1977), *The Rat* (1986)

Grimm, Wilhelm (1786–1859) and **Grimm, Jakob** (1785–1863): *Grimm's Fairy Tales* (1812–15)

Hesse, Hermann† (1877–1962): *Demian* (1919), *Siddhartha* (1922), *Steppenwolf* (1927)

Kafka, Franz (1883–1924): *Metamorphosis* (1915), *The Judgment* (1916), *In the Penal Colony* (1919), *The Trial* (1925), *The Castle* (1926), *Amerika* (1927)

Mann, Thomas† (1875–1955): *Buddenbrooks* (1900), *Death in Venice* (1912), *The Magic Mountain* (1924)

Rilke, Rainer Maria (1875–1926): *Poems from the Book of Hours* (1905), *New Poems* (2 vols., 1907–08), *Duino Elegies* (1923), *Sonnets to Orpheus* (1923)

ITALIAN

Boccaccio, Giovanni (1313–75): *Decameron* (1351–53)

Calvino, Italo (1923–85): *The Path of the Nest of Spiders* (1947), *The Watcher and Other Stories* (1958), *Cosmicomics* (1965), *T Zero* (1967), *Invisible Cities* (1972), *If on a Winter's Night a Traveler* (1979), *Mr. Palomar* (1985)

Dante Alighieri (1265–1321): *Divine Comedy* (c. 1310–20)

Manzoni, Alessandro (1785–1873): *The Betrothed* (1827)

Petrarch (1304–74): *Collected Works* (1544)

LATIN AMERICAN

Borges, Jorge Luis (Argentinian, 1899–1986): *A Universal History of Infamy* (1935), *Six Problems for Don Isidro Parodi* (1942), *Ficciones* (1944), *The Aleph and Other Stories* (1949), *Labyrinthe* (1960), *The Book of Sand* (1975)

Cesaire, Aimé (West Indian, 1913–): *Return to My Native Land* (1939), *State of the Union* (1946), *The Tragedy of King Christophe* (1963)

Fuentes, Carlos (Mexican, 1928–): *The Death of Artemio Cruz* (1962), *Distant Relations* (1981), *The Old Gringo* (1986), *Christopher Unborn* (1989), *The Campaigo* (1990)

García Márquez, Gabriel† (Colombian, 1928–): *One Hundred Years of Solitude* (1967), *The Autumn of the Patriarch* (1975), *Love in the Time of Cholera* (1988), *The General in His Labyrinth* (1989)

Guzmán, Martín Luis (Mexican, 1887–1976): *The Eagle and the Serpent* (1928), *Memorias de Pancho Villa* (4 vols., 1938–40)

Machado de Assis, Joaquim Maria (Brazilian, 1839–1908): *The Posthumous Memoirs of Braz Cubas* (1881), *Philosopher or Dog?* (1891), *Dom Casmurro* (1899)

Márquez, Gabriel García. *See* **García Márquez, Gabriel.**

Naipaul, V. S. (Trinidadian, 1932–): *The Mystic Masseur* (1957), *A House for Mr. Biswas* (1961), *The Middle Passage* (1962), *In a Free State* (1971)

Neruda, Pablo [Neftalí Ricardo Reyes Basoalto]† (Chilean, 1904–73): *Twenty Love Poems and a Story of Despair* (1924), *Canto General* (1950), *Elementary Odes* (3 vols., 1954–57), *We Are Many* (1967), *End of the World* (1969)

Paz, Octavio† (Mexican, 1914–1998): *The Labyrinth of Solitude* (1950), *Sun-Stone* (1957), *Salamandra 1958–1961* (1962), *Ladera este (1962–1968)* (1969), *Vuelta* (1976)

Vargas Llosa, Mario (Peruvian, 1936–): *The Green House* (1966), *Conversations in the Cathedral* (1969), *The War of the End of the World* (1984), *The Real Life of Alejandro Mayta* (1986)

RUSSIAN

Blok, Alexander Alexandrovich (1880–1921): *Verses About the Beautiful Lady* (1904), *The Puppet Show* (1906), *A Frightful World* (c. 1910), *Dances of Death* (c. 1910), *Black Blood* (c. 1910), *The Twelve* (1918)

Bulgakov, Mikhail (1891–1940): *The Master and Margarita* (1967), *The Heart of a Dog* (1968)

Chekhov, Anton Pavlovich (1860–1904): *Motley Tales* (1886), *The Duel* (1892), *Uncle Vanya* (1899), *The Seagull* (1896), *Three Sisters* (1900), *The Cherry Orchard* (1904)

The Yongle Dadian (thesaurus of the Chinese Yongle reign) is the longest book ever written, containing 22,937 chapters in 11,095 volumes. More than 2,000 Chinese scholars worked for five years to complete the book.

Dostoyevsky, Fyodor Mikhaylovich (1821–81): *Notes from the Underground* (1864), *Crime and Punishment* (1866), *The Idiot* (1869), *The Possessed* (1871–72), *The Brothers Karamazov* (1880)

Gogol, Nikolai (1809–52): *Arabesques* (1835), *Mirgorod* (1835), *The Inspector General* (1836), *Dead Souls* (1842), *Collected Works* (1842)

Gorky, Maxim (1868–1936): *Foma Gordeyev* (1899), *Twenty-Six Men and a Girl and Other Stories* (1902), *The Lower Depths* (1902), *Mother* (1906)

Mandelstam, Osip Emilevich (1891–1938): *Kamen* (1913), *Tristia* (1922), *Journey to Armenia* (1933)

Nabokov, Vladimir Vladimirovich (1889–1977): *Lolita* (1955), *Invitation to a Beheading* (1959), *Pale Fire* (1962), *Speak, Memory* (1967)

Pasternak, Boris Leonidovich† (1890–1960): *My Sister—Life* (1922), *Doctor Zhivago* (1957)

Pushkin, Alexander Sergeevich (1789–1837): *Eugene Onegin* (1831)

Solzhenitsyn, Aleksandr I.† (1918–): *One Day in the Life of Ivan Denisovich* (1962), *The Cancer Ward* (1968), *The Gulag Archipelago* (1973–76)

Tolstoy, Leo [Count Lev Nikolayevich] (1828–1910): *War and Peace* (1863–69), *Anna Karenina* (1875–77)

Turgenev, Ivan (1818–83): *A Month in the Country* (1855), *A Sportsman's Sketches* (1852), *A Nest of Gentlefolk* (1859), *On the Eve* (1860), *Fathers and Sons* (1862), *Smoke* (1867)

OTHER EUROPEAN

Andersen, Hans Christian (Danish, 1805–75): *Fairy Tales for Children* (1835–42), *Tales and Stories* (1839), *New Fairy Tales* (1843–47), *New Tales and Stories* (1858–67)

Blasco Ibañez, Vicente (Spanish, 1867–1928): *The Fruit of the Vine* (1896), *Blood and Sand* (1898), *The Mayflower* (1902), *The Cabin* (1905), *Reeds and Mud* (1908)

Capek, Karel (Czech, 1890–1938): *R.U.R.* (1921), *Tales from One Pocket* (1929), *Tales from the Other Pocket* (1929), *Hordubal* (1933), *Meteor* (1934), *An Ordinary Life* (1934)

Catullus (Roman, c. 84 B.C.–54 B.C.): verse

Cervantes Saavedra, Miguel de (Spanish, 1547–1616): *Don Quixote* (1605–15), *Exemplary Novels* (1613)

Dinesen, Isak [Karen Christence Dinesen, Baroness Blixen-Finecke] (Danish, 1885–1962): *Seven Gothic Tales* (1934), *Out of Africa* (1937), *Winter's Tales* (1942), *Last Tales* (1957)

García Lorca, Federico (Spanish, 1898–1936): *Canciones* (1927), *Ode to Walt Whitman* (1933), *Lament for the Death of Ignacio Sanchez Mejias* (1935), *Poet in New York* (1940)

Gombrowicz, Witold (Polish, 1904–69): *Memoir from Adolescence* (1933), *Ferdydurke* (1937), *Pornografia* (1960)

Hamsun, Knut† (Norwegian, 1859–1952): *Hunger* (1890), *Mysteries* (1892), *The Growth of the Soil* (1917)

Hasek, Jaroslav (Czech, 1883–1923): *The Good Soldier Svejk and Other Strange Stories* (1912), *The Good Soldier Svejk and His Fortunes in the World War* (4 vols., 1921–23)

Homer (Greek, c. 700 B.C.): *The Iliad*, *The Odyssey*

Joyce, James (Irish, 1882–1941): *Dubliners* (1914), *Portrait of the Artist as a Young Man* (1916), *Ulysses* (1922), *Finnegan's Wake* (1939)

Ovid (Roman, 43 B.C.–A.D. 17): *Amores* (c. 16 B.C.), *Heroines*, *Metamorphoses*

Petronius (Roman, ?–66): *Satyricon* (c. 50)

Plutarch (Greek, c. 46–120): *Moralia*, *Parallel Lives*

Sappho (Greek, c. 612 B.C.–?): verse

Swift, Jonathan (Irish, 1667–1745): *Gulliver's Travels* (1726)

Undset, Sigrid† (Norwegian, 1882–1949): *Kristin Lavransdatter* (1920–22), *Olaf Andunsson* (1925–27)

Virgil [Publius Vergilius Maro] (Roman, 70–19 B.C.): *Georgics* (37–30 B.C.), *Bucolics* (37 B.C.), *Aeneid* (30–19 B.C.)

Wilde, Oscar (Irish, 1854–1900): *The Portrait of Dorian Gray* (1891), *Salome* (1893), *The Importance of Being Earnest* (1899)

Yeats, William Butler† (Irish, 1865–1939): *The Wind Among the Reeds* (1899), *The Wild Swans at Coole* (1919), *The Winding Stair* (1929), *Collected Poems* (1933)

LITERARY MOVEMENTS, PERIODS, AND STYLES

aestheticism A 19th-century European movement emphasizing aesthetic values over social or moral themes. Advocating "art for art's sake," leading aesthetes imbued their work with a flamboyant, nearly hedonistic quality. Charles Baudelaire and Oscar Wilde were among the movement's most notable figures.

Angry Young Men A group of English writers, chiefly from the working or middle classes, who became prominent in the 1950s. Their work, characterized by a bitter disillusionment with traditional English society, produced the figure of the antihero, one who rebels against the Establishment. The group's leaders included Kingsley Amis and John Osborne.

baroque   Grandiose, ornate artistic style prevalent from the late 16th to the early 18th century. Initially associated with architectural forms, the term was later applied to the fine arts. In literature, the baroque style employed dramatic motifs and strong emotions in an attempt to expand the artistic vision.

The saying, "The female of the species is more deadly than the male," comes from Rudyard Kipling's 1911 poem, "The Female of the Species."

Beat Generation   A group of American writers whose work expressed their alienation from middle-class society during the 1950s and 1960s. Led by Jack Kerouac and Allen Ginsberg, they disdained conventional values, focusing instead on self-discovery through drugs, sexual experience, and exotic travel.

Bloomsbury Group   A group of writers, artists, and intellectuals who held informal discussions in Bloomsbury, a section of London, throughout the early 20th century. Although individual members such as John Maynard Keynes (1883–1946), Lytton Strachey (1880–1932), and Virginia Woolf (1882–1941) were influential figures, the group produced no uniform moral or aesthetic principles.

classical   The period in which Greek and Roman literature flourished. The works of Aeschylus, Dante, Homer, Ovid, and other classical writers generally displayed clarity, harmony, restraint, and rationality over ambiguity, extravagance, and a free play of the imagination.

classicism   In a general sense, any literary style or movement that adheres to the principles of classical

literature. In English literature, the term refers to the reaction of 18th- and 19th-century writers to romanticism. *See also* **neoclassicism.**

dadaism   A European movement founded during World War I and devoted to the negation of traditional artistic values. Dadaists embraced nihilism, irrationality, and the absurd, often shocking their audiences. The movement's leaders included André Breton (1896–1966) and Tristan Tzara (1896–1963). Breton later broke with Tzara and founded *surrealism.*

decadence   A movement originating in 19th-century France that emphasized the autonomy of art, the rejection of middle-class society, a sophisticated despair, and unconventional, often morbid experiences. Charles Baudelaire and Arthur Rimbaud were among the leading *décadents.*

Elizabethan   Pertaining to the drama and literature produced during the reign of Elizabeth I of England (1558–1603). The Elizabethan age saw the flowering of English literature, with its classical humanism and dazzling achievements in drama and verse forms. William Shakespeare, Christopher Marlowe, and Edmund Spenser were notable Elizabethans.

The Enlightenment   An intellectual movement in the late 17th and 18th centuries that sought the perfection of human society through applied reason. Rejecting conventional religious authority, its members postulated instead a rational unity of God, man, and nature. Jean-Jacques Rousseau and Voltaire were among its most influential thinkers.

expressionism   An early-20th-century movement stressing individual expression and subjective truth as opposed to conventional forms and objective reality. Its followers used distorted imagery and narrative compression to depict violent emotions and the workings of the subconscious mind.

futurism   A European movement (c. 1908–1920) advocating the abandonment of conventional syntax and the uninhibited use of images drawn from the age of technology. Futurists exalted at the speed of modern life and anticipated *dadaism* by embracing the bizarre and the experimental.

Gothic   In literature, the term applies to a specific form of the novel, popular in the late 18th and early 19th centuries, that featured supernatural horrors and violent events, often with a medieval setting.

Graveyard School   A preromantic movement of 18th-century English poets. Its members adopted a melancholy tone in their verses, which were usually set in graveyards or other gloomy locations.

imagism   A movement in American and English poetry beginning about 1910. Borrowing freely from foreign verse techniques such as the *haiku* and *free verse,* it demanded precision in the use of imagery. Ezra Pound was influential within this movement.

impressionism   In modern literature, the term refers especially to poems and novels that focus on the author's or character's inner life and subjective impressions. James Joyce, Thomas Mann, Marcel Proust, and Virginia Woolf employed impressionistic techniques, such as the stream of consciousness.

Irish Renaissance   A period of intense creative energy, beginning in the 19th century, aimed at the revival of Ireland's native culture. At the height of the movement, from 1900 to 1920, writers such as John Millington Synge and William Butler Yeats turned to traditional Irish folklore and themes for inspiration. The movement's influence continues to the present.

Jacobean   Pertaining to the literature produced during the reign of James I of England (1603–1625). The period was one of great social upheaval. Reflecting the times, English literature rejected Elizabethan optimism for a darker, more cynical view of human affairs. William Shakespeare's greatest works were written in this period.

Go to "Art Movements and Styles" and "Architecture Styles and Movements" in chapter 7; "Philosophical Movements and Schools of Thought" in chapter 10

Lost Generation   A term coined by Gertrude Stein to describe a group of expatriate American writers who came into prominence after World War I (1914–1918). Their work was characterized by disillusionment with postwar society. F. Scott Fitzgerald and Ernest Hemingway were among the group's notable figures.

modernism   A 20th-century (c. 1910–1945) movement emphasizing a self-conscious break with past literary forms and the development of experimental techniques and fresh motifs. The Irish author James Joyce's use of interior monologue and myth as narrative structures typify modernism's concern with untried forms of expression.

naturalism   A late-19th-century and early-20th-century movement that rejected sentimentality, subjectivity, and preconceived notions of morality in art. Naturalist writers often chose their subjects from the lower depths of society, viewing their characters' sordid lives or tragic fates with scientific detachment. Thomas Hardy, Émile Zola, and Theodore Dreiser were among the leading naturalists.

neoclassicism   In European literature, the term refers to the emphasis placed on balance, restraint, clarity, and proportion in the works of late-17th-century and 18th-century writers such as Alexander Page, Jean Racine, Jonathan Swift, and Voltaire.

Parnassians   Late-19th-century school of French poets. Reacting against the emotionalism and subjectivity of romanticism, they attempted to replicate the precision of plastic arts such as sculpture in their work. The objective poetry thus created was a precursor of the realistic novel and drama.

Pre-Raphaelite Brotherhood   A group of poets and artists established in London in 1848. They asserted the superiority of nature in their work, rejecting formal or academic techniques in favor of sensual imagery and religious symbolism. Algernon Swinburne was one of its leaders.

realism   Movement originating in the early 19th century that portrayed the details of everyday life in factual, objective language and without idealization. The author sought to let the story tell itself, devoid of sentiment and thematic manipulation. Honoré de Balzac, Gustave Flaubert, and Henrik Ibsen wrote in this manner.

Renaissance   From the French word for "rebirth." It pertains to the literature produced in Europe from the mid-14th to the end of the 16th century. Marked by a revival in classical values and learning, the period witnessed an outburst of creative activity unmatched in the history of western culture. Miguel de Cervantes, François Rabelais, and William Shakespeare were among the leading figures of the period.

romanticism   Movement originating in 18th-century Europe as a reaction to neoclassicism. Romantic works typically emphasized intense emotions, sensual imagery, and individualism and often featured lurid themes and sensational plots. Samuel Taylor Coleridge, Johann Goethe, and Jean-Jacques Rousseau are usually associated with this movement.

socialist realism   A state-mandated literary style that writers were obligated to follow in the former Soviet Union (c. 1932–1990). Under this doctrine, all literary works were to display the steady progress of Soviet society toward achieving the goals of socialism. In practice, it was a tool by which the state could control freedom of expression.

Sturm und Drang   German phrase meaning "storm and stress." Nationalistic, 18th-century German movement emphasizing dramatic story lines, turbulent emotions, and the individual's revolt against society. Johann Goethe's early work was written in this fashion.

surrealism   A movement founded in France in the 1920s. It attempted to express the workings of the subconscious mind through automatic writing and irrational, often juxtaposed imagery. André Breton was the movement's principal architect.

symbolism   A European movement originating with French poetry in the late 19th century. It sacrificed objective representation and realistic narrative techniques in favor of a pattern of images or symbols that conveyed the author's meaning. Joseph Conrad, Arthur Rimbaud, and Virginia Woolf employed symbolism in their writing.

Transcendentalism   A 19th-century American movement centered in New England. It advocated a reliance on personal conscience over the dictates of external authority or moral conventions. Ralph Waldo Emerson and Henry David Thoreau were among its leaders.

Victorian   Pertaining to the drama and literature produced during the reign of Queen Victoria of England (1837–1901). Although associated with strict codes of moral conduct and social stagnation, the age witnessed a crisis in religious faith and growing social unrest. Joseph Conrad, Charles Dickens, George Eliot, George Bernard Shaw, and Oscar Wilde produced much of their greatest work during this period.

PSEUDONYMS OF FAMOUS AUTHORS

Real Name	Pseudonym or Pen Name
Brian W. Aldiss	Jael Cracken, Arch Mendicant, Peter Pica, John Runciman, C. C. Shackelton
Kingsley Amis	Robert Markham
Hans Christian Andersen	Villiam Christian Walter
Poul Anderson	A. A. Craig, Michael Karageorge, Winston P. Sanders
François-Marie Arouet	Voltaire
Isaac Asimov	Dr. A., Paul French, Dale E. George
Louis Auchincloss	Andrew Lee
Neftali Ricardo Reyes Basoalto	Pablo Neruda

Real Name	Pseudonym or Pen Name
L. Frank Baum	Edith Van Dyne
Robert Benchley	Guy Fawkes
Marie-Henri Beyle	Stendhal
Ambrose Bierce	Dod Grile
Eric Arthur Blair	George Orwell
Anne Brontë	Acton Bell, Lady Geralda, Olivia Vernon, Alexandria Zenobia
Charlotte Brontë	C. B., Currer Bell, Marquis of Douro, Genius, Lord Charles Wellesley
Emily Jane Brontë	R. Alcon, Ellis Bell
William S. Burroughs	William Lee
Barbara Cartland	Barbara Hamilton McCorquodale
Agatha Christie	Agatha Christie Mallowen, Mary Westmacott
Arthur C. Clarke	E. G. O'Brien, Charles Willis
Samuel Langhorne Clemens	Mark Twain
Michael Crichton	Jeffrey Hudson, John Lange
Karen Christence Dinesen,	Isak Dinesen
	Baroness Blixen-Finecke
Charles Lutwidge Dodgson	Lewis Carroll
Amandine Aurore Lucie Dupin	George Sand
Edward Estlin Cummings	e. e. cummings
Mary Ann Evans	George Eliot
Howard Fast	E. V. Cunningham, Walter Ericson
Erle Stanley Gardner	A. A. Fair, Charles M. Green, Carleton Kendrake, Charles J. Kenny
Theodor Seuss Geisel	Theo Lesieg, Dr. Seuss
Edward St. John Gorey	Eduard Blutig, Mrs. Regera Dowdy, Redway Grode, O. Mude, Hyacinthe Phypps, Ogdred Weary, Dreary Wodge
Dashiell Hammett	Peter Collinson
Robert A. Heinlein	Anson MacDonald, Lyle Monroe, John Riverside, Caleb Saunders, Simon York
Eleanor Alice Burford Hibbert	Eleanor Burford, Philippa Carr, Elbur Ford, Victoria Holt, Kathleen Kellow, Jean Plaidy, Ellalice Tate
L. Ron Hubbard	Elron, Tom Esterbrook, Rene La Fayette, Capt. B. A. Northrop, Kurt von Rachen
Ford Madox Hueffer	Ford Madox Ford
E. Howard Hunt	John Baxter, Gordon Davis, Robert Dietrich, David St. John
LeRoi Jones	Imamu Amiri Baraka
Dean Koontz	David Axton, Brian Coffey, Deanna Dwyer, K. R. Dwyer, John Hill, Leigh Nichols, Andrew North, Richard Paige, Owen West, Aaron Wolfe
Teodor Jozef Konrad Korzeniowski	Joseph Conrad
Louis LaMoore	Louis L'Amour, Tex Burns
T. E. Lawrence	J. H. Ross, T. E. Shaw
Manfred Lee and Frederic Dannay	Ellery Queen, Barnaby Ross
Salvatore A. Lombino	Hunt Collins, Evan Hunter, Richard Marsten, Ed McBain
Robert Ludlum	Jonathon Ryder, Michael Shepherd
James du Maresq	James Clavell
Alan McCrae	Alan Moorehead
Kenneth Millar	John Ross Macdonald, Ross Macdonald
Edna St. Vincent Millay	Nancy Boyd
Mystery Writers of America, California chapter	Theo Durrant
Nevil Shute Norway	Nevil Shute
Conor Cruise O'Brien	Donat O'Donnell
Dorothy Parker	Constant Reader

continues

Literature

Pseudonyms of Famous Authors *continued*

Real Name	Pseudonym or Pen Name
Eric Partridge	Vigilans
William Sydney Porter	O. Henry
William Saroyan	Sirak Goryan
John Simmons	John Barth
Terry Southern	Maxwell Kenton
Irving Stone	Irving Tannenbaum
Gore Vidal	Edgar Box
Nathan Wallenstein Weinstein	Nathanael West
J. A. Wight	James Herriot
John Burgess Wilson	Anthony Burgess, Joseph Kell
Chloe Anthony Wofford	Toni Morrison
Willard Huntington Wright	S. S. Van Dine

POET LAUREATES

ENGLISH

In 1616, Ben Jonson was named England's first poet laureate; however, the title did not become an official royal office until 1668, when John Dryden assumed the honored post. Since that time, the office has been awarded for life. The poet laureate is responsible for composing poems for court and national occasions. At the time of each laureate's death, it is the duty of the prime minister to nominate successors from which the reigning sovereign will choose. It is the Lord Chamberlain who appoints the poet laureate by issuing a warrant to the laureate-elect. The life appointment is always announced in the *London Gazette*.

Laureateship	Poet	Birth and Death Dates
1668–88	John Dryden	1631–1700
1689–92	Thomas Shadwell	1643?–92
1692–1715	Nahum Tate	1652–1715
1715–18	Nicholas Rowe	1674–1718
1718–30	Laurence Eusden	1688–1730
1730–57	Colley Cibber	1671–1757
*1757–85	William Whitehead	1715–85
1785–90	Thomas Warton	1728–90
1790–1813	Henry James Pye	1745–1813
1813–43	Robert Southey	1774–1843
1843–50	William Wordsworth	1770–1850
†1850–92	Alfred, Lord Tennyson	1809–92
1896–1913	Alfred Austin	1835–1913
1913–30	Robert Bridges	1844–1930
1930–67	John Masefield	1878–1967
1968–72	Cecil Day-Lewis	1904–72
1972–84	Sir John Betjeman	1906–84
1984–	Ted Hughes	1930–

* The 1757 appointment was declined by Thomas Gray.   † The 1850 appointment was declined by Samuel Rogers.

AMERICAN

Laureateship	Poet	Birth and Death Dates
1986–87	Robert Penn Warren	1905–89
1987–88	Richard Wilbur	1921–
1988–89	Howard Nemerov	1920–91
1990–91	Mark Strand	1934–
1991–92	Joseph Brodsky	1940–96
1992–93	Mona Van Duyn	1921–
1993–95	Rita Dove	1952–
1995–1997	Robert Haas	1941–
1997–	Robert Pinsky	1940–

BOOK AWARDS AND THEIR RECIPIENTS

NOBEL PRIZE IN LITERATURE

1901 René F. A. Sully-Prudhomme, France
1902 Theodor Mommsen, Germany
1903 Bjørnstjerne Bjørnson, Norway
1904 Frederic Mistral, France
     José Echegaray, Spain
1905 Henryk Sienkiewicz, Poland
1906 Giosue Carducci, Italy
1907 Rudyard Kipling, Great Britain
1908 Rudolph C. Eueken, Germany
1909 Selma Lagerlöf, Sweden
1910 Paul J. L. von Heyse, Germany
1911 Maurice Maeterlinck, Belgium
1912 Gerhart Hauptmann, Germany
1913 Rabindranath Tagore, India
1914 No award
1915 Romain Rolland, France
1916 Verner von Heidenstamm, Sweden
1917 Karl A. Gjellerup, Denmark
     Henrik Pontoppidan, Denmark
1918 No award
1919 Carl F. G. Spitteler, Switzerland
1920 Knut Hamsun, Norway
1921 Anatole France, France
1922 Jacinto Benavente y Martinez, Spain
1923 William Butler Yeats, Ireland
1924 Wladyslaw S. Reymont, Poland
1925 George Bernard Shaw, Great Britain
1926 Grazia Deledda, Italy
1927 Henri Bergson, France
1928 Sigrid Undset, Norway
1929 Thomas Mann, Germany
1930 Sinclair Lewis, U.S.
1931 Erik A. Karlfeldt, Sweden
1932 John Galsworthy, Great Britain
1933 Ivan A. Bunin, Russia

1934 Luigi Pirandello, Italy
1935 No award
1936 Eugene O'Neill, U.S.
1937 Roger Martin du Gard, France
1938 Pearl S. Buck, U.S.
1939 Frans E. Sillanpää, Finland
1940 No award
1941 No award
1942 No award
1943 No award
1944 Johannes V. Jensen, Denmark
1945 Gabriela Mistral, Chile
1946 Hermann Hesse, Switzerland
1947 André Gide, France
1948 T. S. Eliot, Great Britain
1949 William Faulkner, U.S.
1950 Bertrand Russell, Great Britain
1951 Pär F. Lagerkvist, Sweden
1952 François Mauriac, France
1953 Sir Winston Churchill, Great Britain
1954 Ernest Hemingway, U.S.
1955 Halldor K. Laxness, Iceland
1956 Juan Ramón Jiménez, Puerto Rico
1957 Albert Camus, France
1958 Boris L. Pasternak, U.S.S.R. (prize declined)
1959 Salvatore Quasimodo, Italy
1960 Saint-John Perse, France
1961 Ivo Andric, Yugoslavia
1962 John Steinbeck, U.S.
1963 Giorgos Scferis, Grcece
1964 Jean-Paul Sartre, France (prize declined)
1965 Mikhail Sholokhov, U.S.S.R.
1966 Samuel Joseph Agnon, Israel
     Nelly Sachs, Sweden
1967 Miguel Angel Asturias, Guatemala

continues

Literature

Nobel Prize in Literature *continued*

1968	Yasunari Kawabata, Japan	1982	Gabriel García Márquez, Colombia-Mexico
1969	Samuel Beckett, Ireland	1983	William Golding, Great Britain
1970	Aleksandr I. Solzhenitsyn, U.S.S.R.	1984	Jaroslav Siefert, Czechoslovakia
1971	Pablo Neruda, Chile	1985	Claude Simon, France
1972	Henrich Böll, Federal Republic of Germany	1986	Wole Soyinka, Nigeria
		1987	Joseph Brodsky, U.S.
1973	Patrick White, Australia	1988	Naguib Mahfouz, Egypt
1974	Eyvind Johnson, Sweden	1989	Camilo José Cela, Spain
	Harry Edmund Martinson, Sweden	1990	Octavio Paz, Mexico
1975	Eugenio Montale, Italy	1991	Nadine Gordimer, South Africa
1976	Saul Bellow, U.S.	1992	Derek Walcott, Trinidad-U.S.
1977	Vicente Aleixandre, Spain	1993	Toni Morrison, U.S.
1978	Isaac Bashevis Singer, U.S.	1994	Kenzaburo Oe, Japan
1979	Odysseus Elytis, Greece	1995	Seamus Heaney, Ireland
1980	Czeslaw Milosz, Poland-U.S.	1996	Wislawa Szymborska, Poland
1981	Elias Canetti, Bulgaria-Great Britain	1997	Dario Fo, Italy

PULITZER PRIZE IN LETTERS

FICTION

1918	Ernest Poole, *His Family*	1949	James Gould Cozzens, *Guard of Honor*
1919	Booth Tarkington, *The Magnificent Ambersons*	1950	A. B. Guthrie, Jr., *The Way West*
		1951	Conrad Richter, *The Town*
1920	No award	1952	Herman Wouk, *The Caine Mutiny*
1921	Edith Wharton, *The Age of Innocence*	1953	Ernest Hemingway, *The Old Man and the Sea*
1922	Booth Tarkington, *Alice Adams*	1954	No award
1923	Willa Cather, *One of Ours*	1955	William Faulkner, *A Fable*
1924	Margaret Wilson, *The Able McLaughlins*	1956	MacKinlay Kantor, *Andersonville*
1925	Edna Ferber, *So Big*	1957	No award
1926	Sinclair Lewis, *Arrowsmith* (prize declined)	1958	James Agee, *A Death in the Family*
1927	Louis Bromfield, *Early Autumn*	1959	Robert Lewis Taylor, *The Travels of Jaimie McPheeters*
1928	Thornton Wilder, *The Bridge of San Luis Rey*		
1929	Julia M. Peterkin, *Scarlet Sister Mary*	1960	Allen Drury, *Advise and Consent*
1930	Oliver LaFarge, *Laughing Boy*	1961	Harper Lee, *To Kill a Mockingbird*
1931	Margaret Ayer Barnes, *Years of Grace*	1962	Edwin O'Connor, *The Edge of Sadness*
1932	Pearl S. Buck, *The Good Earth*	1963	William Faulkner, *The Reivers*
1933	T. S. Stribling, *The Store*	1964	No award
1934	Caroline Miller, *Lamb in His Bosom*	1965	Shirley Ann Grau, *The Keepers of the House*
1935	Josephine W. Johnson, *Now in November*	1966	Katherine Anne Porter, *The Collected Stories of Katherine Anne Porter*
1936	Harold L. Davis, *Honey in the Horn*		
1937	Margaret Mitchell, *Gone W0ith the Wind*	1967	Bernard Malamud, *The Fixer*
1938	John P. Marquand, *The Late George Apley*	1968	William Styron, *The Confessions of Nat Turner*
1939	Marjorie Kinnan Rawlings, *The Yearling*	1969	N. Scott Momaday, *House Made of Dawn*
1940	John Steinbeck, *The Grapes of Wrath*	1970	Jean Stafford, *Collected Stories*
1941	No award	1971	No award
1942	Ellen Glasgow, *In This Our Life*	1972	Wallace Stegner, *Angle of Repose*
1943	Upton Sinclair, *Dragon's Teeth*	1973	Eudora Welty, *The Optimist's Daughter*
1944	Martin Flavin, *Journey in the Dark*	1974	No award
1945	John Hersey, *A Bell for Adano*	1975	Michael Shaara, *The Killer Angels*
1946	No award	1976	Saul Bellow, *Humboldt's Gift*
1947	Robert Penn Warren, *All the King's Men*	1977	No award
1948	James A. Michener, *Tales of the South Pacific*	1978	James Alan McPherson, *Elbow Room*

1979	John Cheever, *The Stories of John Cheever*	1990	Oscar Hijuelos, *The Mambo Kings Play Songs of Love*
1980	Norman Mailer, *The Executioner's Song*		
1981	John Kennedy Toole, *A Confederacy of Dunces*	1991	John Updike, *Rabbit at Rest*
		1992	Jane Smiley, *A Thousand Acres*
1982	John Updike, *Rabbit Is Rich*	1993	Robert Olen Butler, *A Good Scent from a Strange Mountain*
1983	Alice Walker, *The Color Purple*		
1984	William Kennedy, *Ironweed*	1994	E. Annie Proulx, *The Shipping News*
1985	Alison Lurie, *Foreign Affairs*	1995	Carol Shields, *The Stone Diaries*
1986	Larry McMurtry, *Lonesome Dove*	1996	Richard Ford, *Independence Day*
1987	Peter Taylor, *A Summons to Memphis*	1997	Steven Milhauser, *Martin Dressler: The Tale of an American Dreamer*
1988	Toni Morrison, *Beloved*		
1989	Anne Tyler, *Breathing Lessons*		

GENERAL NONFICTION

1962	Theodore White, *The Making of the President 1960*	1978	Carl Sagan, *The Dragons of Eden*
		1979	Edward O. Wilson, *On Human Nature*
1963	Barbara W. Tuchman, *The Guns of August*	1980	Douglas R. Hofstadter, *Gödel, Escher, Bach: An Eternal Golden Braid*
1964	Richard Hofstadter, *Anti-Intellectualism in American Life*		
		1981	Carl E. Schorske, *Fin-de-Siecle Vienna: Politics and Culture*
1965	Howard Mumford Jones, *O Strange New World*		
		1982	Tracy Kidder, *The Soul of a New Machine*
1966	Edwin Way Teale, *Wandering Through Winter*	1983	Susan Sheehan, *Is There No Place on Earth for Me?*
1967	David Brion Davis, *The Problem of Slavery in Western Culture*		
		1984	Paul Starr, *Social Transformation of American Medicine*
1968	Will and Ariel Durant, *Rousseau and Revolution*		
		1985	Studs Terkel, *The Good War*
1969	Norman Mailer, *The Armies of the Night*	1986	Joseph Lelyveld, *Move Your Shadow*
	René, Jules Dubois, *So Human an Animal: How We Are Shaped by Surroundings and Events*		J. Anthony Lukas, *Common Ground*
		1987	David K. Shipler, *Arab and Jew*
		1988	Richard Rhodes, *The Making of the Atomic Bomb*
1970	Eric H. Erikson, *Gandhi's Truth*		
1971	John Toland, *The Rising Sun*	1989	Neal Sheehan, *A Bright Shining Lie: John Paul Vann and America in Vietnam*
1972	Barbara W. Tuchman, *Stilwell and the American Experience in China, 1911–1945*		
		1990	Dale Maharidge and Michael Williamson, *And Their Children After Them*
1973	Frances FitzGerald, *Fire in the Lake*		
	Robert Coles, *Children of Crisis* (vols. 2 and 3)	1991	Bert Holldobler and Edward O. Wilson, *The Ants*
1974	Ernest Becker, *The Denial of Death*	1992	Daniel Yergin, *The Prize*
1975	Annie Dillard, *Pilgrim at Tinker Creek*	1993	Garry Wills, *Lincoln at Gettysburg*
1976	Robert N. Butler, *Why Survive? Being Old in America*	1994	David Remick, *Lenin's Tomb*
		1995	Jonathon Weiner, *The Beak of the Finch*
1977	William W. Warner, *Beautiful Swimmers*	1996	Tina Rosenberg, *The Haunted Land*
		1997	Richard Kluger, *Ashes to Ashes*

NATIONAL BOOK AWARD

The National Book Award was known as the American Book Award from 1980 to 1986. The award reverted to its original name in 1987.

FICTION

1950	Nelson Algren, *The Man with the Golden Arm*	1953	Ralph Ellison, *Invisible Man*
		1954	Saul Bellow, *The Adventures of Augie March*
1951	William Faulkner, *Collected Stories*	1955	William Faulkner, *A Fable*
1952	James Jones, *From Here to Eternity*	1956	John O'Hara, *Ten North Frederick*

continues

National Book Award; Fiction *continued*

1957	Wright Morris, *The Field of Vision*	1976	William Gaddis, Jr., *JR*
1958	John Cheever, *The Wapshot Chronicle*	1977	Wallace Stegner, *The Spectator Bird*
1959	Bernard Malamud, *The Magic Barrel*	1978	Mary Lee Settle, *Blood Ties*
1960	Philip Roth, *Goodbye, Columbus*	1979	Tim O'Brien, *Going After Cacciato*
1961	Conrad Richter, *The Waters of Kronos*	1980	William Styron, *Sophie's Choice*
1962	Walker Percy, *The Moviegoer*	1981	Wright Morris, *Plains Song*
1963	J. F. Powers, *Morte D'Urban*	1982	John Updike, *Rabbit Is Rich*
1964	John Updike, *The Centaur*	1983	Alice Walker, *The Color Purple*
1965	Saul Bellow, *Herzog*	1984	Ellen Gilchrist, *Victory over Japan: A Book of Stories*
1966	Katherine Anne Porter, *The Collected Stories of Katherine Anne Porter*	1985	Don DeLillo, *White Noise*
1967	Bernard Malamud, *The Fixer*	1986	E. L. Doctorow, *World's Fair*
1968	Thornton Wilder, *The Eighth Day*	1987	Larry Heinemann, *Paco's Story*
1969	Jerzy Kosinski, *Steps*	1988	Pete Dexter, *Paris Trout*
1970	Joyce Carol Oates, *Them*	1989	John Casey, *Spartina*
1971	Saul Bellow, *Mr. Sammler's Planet*	1990	Charles Johnson, *Middle Passage*
1972	Flannery O'Connor, *The Complete Stories of Flannery O'Connor*	1991	Norman Rush, *Mating*
1973	John Barth, *Chimera*	1992	Cormac McCarthy, *All the Pretty Horses*
	John Williams, *Augustus*	1993	E. Annie Proulx, *The Shipping News*
1974	Thomas Pynchon, *Gravity's Rainbow*	1994	William Gaddis, *A Frolic of His Own*
	Isaac Bashevis Singer, *A Crown of Feathers and Other Stories*	1995	Philip Roth, *Sabbath's Theater*
1975	Robert Stone, *Dog Soldiers*	1996	Andrea Barrett, *Ship Fever and Other Stories*
	Thomas Williams, *The Hair of Harold Roux*	1997	Charles Frazier, *Cold Mountain*

NONFICTION

From 1964 to 1979, the category of general nonfiction was eliminated. Prizes were given instead in specialized categories, such as history, contemporary affairs, and biography.

1950	Ralph L. Rusk, *Ralph Waldo Emerson*	1980	Tom Wolfe, *The Right Stuff*
1951	Newton Arvin, *Herman Melville*	1981	Maxine Hong Kingston, *China Men*
1952	Rachel Carson, *The Sea Around Us*	1982	Tracy Kidder, *The Soul of a New Machine*
1953	Bernard A. DeVoto, *The Course of an Empire*	1983	Fox Butterfield, *China: Alive in the Bitter Sea*
1954	Bruce Catton, *A Stillness at Appomattox*	1984	Robert V. Remini, *Andrew Jackson and the Course of American Democracy, 1833–1845*
1955	Joseph Wood Krutch, *The Measure of Man*	1985	J. Anthony Lukas, *Common Ground: A Turbulent Decade in the Lives of Three American Families*
1956	Herbert Kubly, *An American in Italy*		
1957	George F. Kennan, *Russia Leaves the War*	1986	Barry Lopez, *Arctic Dreams*
1958	Catherine Drinker Bowen, *The Lion and the Throne*	1987	Richard Rhodes, *The Making of the Atom Bomb*
1959	J. Christopher Herold, *Mistress to an Age: A Life of Madame de Stael*	1988	Neil Sheehan, *A Bright Shining Lie: John Paul Vann and America in Vietnam*
1960	Richard Ellmann, *James Joyce*	1989	Thomas L. Friedman, *From Beirut to Jerusalem*
1961	William L. Shirer, *The Rise and Fall of the Third Reich*	1990	Ron Chernow, *The House of Morgan: An American Banking Dynasty and the Rise of Modern Finance*
1962	Lewis Mumford, *The City in History: Its Origins, Its Transformations and Its Prospects*		
		1991	Orlando Patterson, *Freedom*
1963	Leon Edel, *Henry James, Vol. II: The Conquest of London; Henry James, Vol. III: The Middle Years*	1992	Paul Monette, *Becoming a Man: Half a Life Story*
		1993	Gore Vidal, *United States: Essays 1952–1992*

| 1994 | Sherwin B. Nuland, *How We Die: Reflections on Life's Final Chapter* | 1996 | James Carroll, *An American Requiem: God, My Father, and the War That Came Between Us* |
| 1995 | Tina Rosenberg, *The Haunted Land: Facing Europe's Ghosts after Communism* | 1997 | Joseph Ellis, *American Sphinx: The Character of Thomas Jefferson* |

THE GREAT BOOKS: A READING LIST

These books and writings about our civilization are recommended reading by The Great Books Foundation. They are listed in alphabetical order by author.

Adams, Henry	*The Education of Henry Adams* (1907)
Aeschylus	*Agamemnon* (458 B.C.)
Aristotle (4th century B.C.)	*Politics*
	"On Happiness" (excerpt from *Nicomachean Ethics*)
	"On Tragedy"
Augustine, St.	*The City of God* (413–26)
Bible	*Genesis*
	Exodus
	Job
	Ecclesiastes
	The Gospel of Mark
Burke, Edmund	*Reflections on the Revolution in France* (1790)
Chaucer, Geoffrey	*The Canterbury Tales* (after 1387)
Chekhov, Anton Pavlovich	*Rothschild's Fiddle* (1894)
	Uncle Vanya (1896)
Clausewitz, Karl von	"What is War?" [excerpt from *On War* (1833)]
Conrad, Joseph	"Heart of Darkness" [story in *Typhoon and Youth* (1902)]
Dante, Alighieri	"The Inferno" [canticle in *Divine Comedy* (c. 1310–20)]
Darwin, Charles	"The Moral Sense of Man and the Lower Animals" [excerpts from *On the Origin of Species* (1859) and *The Descent of Man* (1871)]
Dewey, John	"The Virtues" [excerpt from *Ethics* (1908)]
	"Habits and Will" [excerpt from *Human Nature and Conduct* (1922)]
Diderot, Denis	*Rameau's Nephew* (posthumously published in 1805)
Dostoevsky, Fyodor Mikhailovich	*Notes from the Underground* (1864)
Euripides (5th century B.C.)	*Medea*
	Iphigeneia at Aulis
Flaubert, Gustave	"A Simple Heart" (short story, c. 1850)
Freud, Sigmund	"On Dreams" [excerpt from *The Interpretation of Dreams* (1900)]
Gibbon, Edward	*The History of the Decline and Fall of the Roman Empire* (1776, 1781, 1787–88)
Goethe, Johann Wolfgang von	*Faust,* Part I (1808)
Gogol, Nikolai	"The Overcoat" (First part of novel *Dead Souls*)
Hamilton, Alexander; Jay, John; Madison, James	The Federalist (1787–88)
Herodotus (5th century B.C.)	"The Persian Wars" (excerpt from his *History*)
Hobbes, Thomas	*Origin of Government*
Homer (8th or 7th) century B.C.	*The Iliad*
Hume, David	"Of Personal Identity" [excerpt from *A Treatise on Human Nature* (1739–40)]
	"Of Justice and Injustice" [excerpt from *Essays, Moral and Political* (1741–42)]
James, Henry	*The Beast in the Jungle* (1903)
Kafka, Franz	*The Metamorphosis* (1915)
Kant, Immanuel	*Conscience*
	"First Principles of Morals" [excerpt from *Fundamental Principles of the Metaphysic of Ethics* (1785)]

continues

The Great Books: A Reading List *continued*

Kierkegaard, Søren Aabye	"The Knight of Faith" [excerpt from *Fear and Trembling* (1843)]
Locke, John	"Of Civil Government" [excerpt from the second of his *Two Treatises of Government* (1690)]
Machiavelli, Niccolò	*The Prince* (1513)
Maimonides (12th century)	"On Evil" [excerpt from *Guide for the Perplexed*]
Marx, Karl	"Alienated Labour" [excerpt from *Das Kapital* (1867)]
Melville, Herman	*Billy Budd, Sailor* (1924)
Mill, John Stuart	*On Liberty* (1859)
	Utilitarianism (1863)
Molière	*The Misanthrope* (1666)
Montaigne, Michel Eyquem de	"Of Experience" [Book III, Chapter 13 (1578) of his *Essays*]
Montesquieu, Baron de	"Principles of Government" [excerpt from *The Spirit of the Laws* (1748)]
Nietzsche, Friedrich	*Thus Spoke Zarathustra* (1883–92)
Plato (4th century B.C.)	*The Republic*
	Symposium
	The Crito
	The Apology
Rousseau, Jean-Jacques	*The Social Contract* (1762)
Schopenhauer, Arthur	"The Indestructibility of Our Inner Nature" [excerpt from *The World as Will and Representation* (1818)]
Shakespeare, William	*Hamlet* (1600–01)
	Othello (1604)
	King Lear (1606)
	Anthony and Cleopatra (1607–08)
	The Tempest (1611)
Shaw, George Bernard	*Caesar and Cleopatra* (1899)
Simmel, Georg	"Individual Freedom" [excerpt from *The Philosophy of Money* (1900)]
Smith, Adam	*Inquiry into the Nature and Causes of the Wealth of Nations* (1776)
Sophocles (5th century B.C.)	*Antigone*
	Oedipus the King
Swift, Jonathon	*Gulliver's Travels* (1726)
Thoreau, Henry David	*Civil Disobedience* (1849)
Thucydides (5th century B.C.)	*History of the Peloponnesian War*
Tocqueville, Alexis de	"The Power of the Majority" [excerpt from *Democracy in America* (1835, 1840)]
Tolstoy, Count Leo Nikolayevich	*The Death of Ivan Ilych* (1886)
Weber, Max	*The Protestant Ethic and the Spirit of Capitalism* (1920)

THE NEW YORK PUBLIC LIBRARY'S BOOKS OF THE CENTURY

LANDMARKS OF MODERN LITERATURE

Anton Chekhov	*Tri sestry [The Three Sisters]* (1901)
Marcel Proust	*A la recherche du temps perdu [Remembrance of Things Past]* (3 vols., 1913–27)
Gertrude Stein	*Tender Buttons: Objects Food Rooms* (1914)
Franz Kafka	*Die Verwandlung [The Metamorphosis]* (1915)
Edna St. Vincent Millay	*Renascence and Other Poems* (1917)
William Butler Yeats	*The Wild Swans at Coole* (1917)
Luigi Pirandello	*Sei personaggi in cerca d'autore [Six Characters in Search of an Author]* (1921)
T. S. Eliot	*The Waste Land* (1922)
James Joyce	*Ulysses* (1922)
Thomas Mann	*Der Zauberberg [The Magic Mountain]* (1924)
F. Scott Fitzgerald	*The Great Gatsby* (1925)
Virginia Woolf	*To the Lighthouse* (1927)

Federico García Lorca   *Primer romancero gitano [Gypsy Ballads]* (1928)
Richard Wright   *Native Son* (1940)
William Faulkner   *The Portable Faulkner* (1946)
W. H. Auden   *The Age of Anxiety: A Baroque Eclogue* (1947)
Samuel Beckett   *En attendant Godot [Waiting for Godot; A Tragicomedy in Two Acts]* (1952)
Ralph Ellison   *Invisible Man* (1952)
Vladimir Nabokov   *Lolita* (1955)
Jorge Luis Borges   *Ficciones [Fictions]* (1944; 2nd augmented edition, 1956)
Jack Kerouac   *On the Road* (1957)
Gabriel García Márquez   *Cien años de soledad [One Hundred Years of Solitude]* (1967)
Philip Roth   *Portnoy's Complaint* (1969)
Toni Morrison   *Song of Solomon* (1977)

NATURE'S REALM

Maurice Maeterlinck   *La vie des abeilles [The Life of the Bee]* (1901)
Marie Sklodowska Curie   *Traité de radioactivité [Treatise on Radioactivity]* (1910)
Albert Einstein   *The Meaning of Relativity* (1922)
Roger Tory Peterson   *A Field Guide to the Birds* (1934)
Aldo Leopold   *A Sand County Almanac* (1949)
Konrad Z. Lorenz   *Er redete mit dem Vieh, den Vögeln und den Fischen: [King Solomon's Ring: New Light on Animal Ways]* (1949)
Rachel Carson   *Silent Spring* (1962)
    Smoking and Health [known as *The Surgeon General's Report*] (1964)
James Watson   *The Double Helix: A Personal Account of the Discovery of the Structure of DNA* (1968)
Edward O. Wilson   *The Diversity of Life* (1992)

PROTEST AND PROGRESS

Jacob Riis   *The Battle with the Slum* (1902)
W. E. B. Du Bois   *The Souls of Black Folk* (1903)
Upton Sinclair   *The Jungle* (1906)
Jane Addams   *Twenty Years at Hull-House* (1910)
Lillian Wald   *The House on Henry Street* (1915)
Lincoln Steffens   *The Autobiography of Lincoln Steffens* (1931)
John Dos Passos   *U.S.A.* (1937)
John Steinbeck   *The Grapes of Wrath* (1939)
James Agee and Walker Evans   *Let Us Now Praise Famous Men* (1941)
Lillian Smith   *Strange Fruit* (1944)
Paul Goodman   *Growing Up Absurd* (1960)
James Baldwin   *The Fire Next Time* (1963)
Malcolm X   *The Autobiography of Malcolm X* (1965)
Randy Shilts   *And the Band Played On* (1987)
Alex Kotlowitz   *There Are No Children Here* (1991)

COLONIALISM AND ITS AFTERMATH

Joseph Conrad   *Lord Jim* (1900)
Rudyard Kipling   *Kim* (1901)
Mohandas K. Gandhi   *Satyagraha [Non-Violent Resistance]* (1921–40)
E. M. Forster   *A Passage to India* (1924)
Albert Camus   *L'étranger [The Stranger]* (1942)
    United Nations Charter (1945)
Alan Paton   *Cry, the Beloved Country* (1948)
Edward Steichen   *The Family of Man: The Photographic Exhibition Created by Edward Steichen for the Museum of Modern Art* (1955)

continues

Literature

Colonialism and Its Aftermath *continued*

Chinua Achebe	*Things Fall Apart* (1958)
Frantz Fanon	*Les damnés de la terre [The Wretched of the Earth]* (1961)
Jean Rhys	*Wide Sargasso Sea* (1966)
Tayeb el-Salih	*Mawsim al-Hijra ila al-Shamal [Season of Migration to the North]* (1969)
V. S. Naipaul	*Guerrillas* (1975)
Buchi Emecheta	*The Bride Price* (1976)
Ryszard Kapuscinski	*Cesarz [The Emperor]* (1978)
Rigoberta Menchú	*Me llamo Rigoberta Menchú y así me nació conciencia [I, Rigoberta Menchú]* (1983)
Marguerite Duras	*L'amant [The Lover]* (1984)

MIND AND SPIRIT

Emile Durkheim	*Le suicide: étude de sociologie [Suicide: A Study in Sociology]* (1897)
Sigmund Freud	*Die Traumdeutung [The Interpretation of Dreams]* (1900)
Havelock Ellis	*Studies in the Psychology of Sex* (1901–28)
William James	*The Varieties of Religious Experience: A Study in Human Nature* (1902)
Kahlil Gibran	*The Prophet* (1923)
Bertrand Russell	*Why I Am Not a Christian* (1927)
Margaret Mead	*Coming of Age in Samoa* (1928)
Jean-Paul Sartre	*L'être et le néant [Being and Nothingness]* (1943)
Benjamin Spock	*The Common Sense Book of Baby and Child Care* (1946)
The Holy Bible	*Revised Standard Version* (1952)
Paul Tillich	*The Courage to Be* (1952)
Ken Kesey	*One Flew Over the Cuckoo's Nest* (1962)
Timothy Leary	*The Politics of Ecstasy* (1968)
Elisabeth Kübler-Ross	*On Death and Dying* (1969)
Bruno Bettelheim	*The Uses of Enchantment* (1976)

POPULAR CULTURE AND MASS ENTERTAINMENT

Bram Stoker	*Dracula* (1897)
Henry James	*The Turn of the Screw* (1898)
Arthur Conan Doyle	*The Hound of the Baskervilles* (1902)
Edgar Rice Burroughs	*Tarzan of the Apes* (1912)
Zane Grey	*Riders of the Purple Sage* (1912)
Agatha Christie	*The Mysterious Affair at Styles* (1920)
Dale Carnegie	*How to Win Friends and Influence People* (1936)
Margaret Mitchell	*Gone With the Wind* (1936)
Raymond Chandler	*The Big Sleep* (1939)
Nathanael West	*The Day of the Locust* (1939)
Grace Metalious	*Peyton Place* (1956)
Dr. Seuss	*The Cat in the Hat* (1957)
Robert A. Heinlein	*Stranger in a Strange Land* (1961)
Joseph Heller	*Catch-22* (1961)
Truman Capote	*In Cold Blood: A True Account of a Multiple Murder and Its Consequences* (1965)
Jim Bouton	*Ball Four: My Life and Hard Times Throwing the Knuckleball in the Big Leagues* (1970)
Stephen King	*Carrie* (1974)
Tom Wolfe	*The Bonfire of the Vanities* (1987)

WOMEN RISE

Edith Wharton	*The Age of Innocence* (1920)
Carrie Chapman Catt and Nettie Rogers Shuler	*Woman Suffrage and Politics: The Inner Story of the Suffrage Movement* (1923)

Margaret Sanger	*My Fight for Birth Control* (1931)
Zora Neale Hurston	*Dust Tracks on a Road* (1942)
Simone de Beauvoir	*Le deuxième sexe [The Second Sex]* (1949)
Doris Lessing	*The Golden Notebook* (1962)
Betty Friedan	*The Feminine Mystique* (1963)
Maya Angelou	*I Know Why the Caged Bird Sings* (1969)
Robin Morgan, editor	*Sisterhood Is Powerful: An Anthology of Writings from the Women's Liberation Movement* (1970)
Susan Brownmiller	*Against Our Will: Men, Women and Rape* (1975)
Alice Walker	*The Color Purple* (1982)

ECONOMICS AND TECHNOLOGY

Thorstein Veblen	*The Theory of the Leisure Class: An Economic Study of Institutions* (1899)
Max Weber	*Die protestantische Ethik und der Geist des Kapitalismus [The Protestant Ethic and the Spirit of Capitalism]* (1904)
Henry Adams	*The Education of Henry Adams* (1907)
John Maynard Keynes	*The General Theory of Employment, Interest and Money* (1936)
Friedrich A. von Hayek	*The Road to Serfdom* (1944)
Milton Friedman	*A Theory of the Consumption Function* (1957)
John Kenneth Galbraith	*The Affluent Society* (1958)
Jane Jacobs	*The Death and Life of Great American Cities* (1961)
Helen Leavitt	*Superhighway—Superhoax* (1970)
E. F. Schumacher	*Small Is Beautiful: A Study of Economics as if People Mattered* (1973)
Ed Krol	*The Whole Internet: User's Guide & Catalog* (1992)

UTOPIAS AND DYSTOPIAS

H. G. Wells	*The Time Machine* (1895)
Theodor Herzl	*Der Judenstaat [The Jewish State]* (1896)
L. Frank Baum	*The Wonderful Wizard of Oz* (1900)
J. M. Barrie	*Peter Pan in Kensington Gardens* (1906)
Charlotte Perkins Gilman	*Herland* (1915)
Aldous Huxley	*Brave New World* (1932)
James Hilton	*Lost Horizon* (1933)
B. F. Skinner	*Walden Two* (1948)
George Orwell	*Nineteen Eighty-four* (1949)
Ray Bradbury	*Fahrenheit 451* (1953)
Ayn Rand	*Atlas Shrugged* (1957)
Anthony Burgess	*A Clockwork Orange* (1962)
Margaret Atwood	*The Handmaid's Tale* (1985)

WAR, HOLOCAUST, TOTALITARIANISM

Arnold Toynbee	*Armenian Atrocities: The Murder of a Nation* (1915)
John Reed	*Ten Days That Shook the World* (1919)
Siegfried Sassoon	*The War Poems* (1919)
Jaroslav Hasek	*Osudy dobrého vojáka Svejka za svetové války [The Good Soldier Schweik]* (1920–23)
Adolf Hitler	*Mein Kampf* (1925–26)
Erich Maria Remarque	*Im Westen nichts Neues [All Quiet on the Western Front]* (1928)
Anna Akhmatova	*Rekviem [Requiem]* (1935-40)
Ernest Hemingway	*For Whom the Bell Tolls* (1940)
Arthur Koestler	*Darkness at Noon* (1941)
John Hersey	*Hiroshima* (1946)
Anne Frank	*Her Achterhuis [The Diary of a Young Girl]* (1947)
Winston Churchill	*The Gathering Storm* (1948)

continues

War, Holocaust, Totalitarianism *continued*

Elie Wiesel	*La nuit [Night]* (1958)
Mao Zedong	*Quotations from Chairman Mao* (1966)
Dee Alexander Brown	*Bury My Heart at Wounded Knee: An Indian History of the American West* (1970)
Aleksandr I. Solzhenitsyn	*Arkhipelag Gulag, 1918–1956 [The Gulag Archipelago, 1918–1956: An Experiment in Literary Investigation]* (1973–75)
Michael Herr	*Dispatches* (1977)
Art Spiegelman	*Maus: A Survivor's Tale* (2 vols., 1986–91)

OPTIMISM, JOY, GENTILITY

Sarah Orne Jewett	*The Country of the Pointed Firs* (1896)
Helen Keller	*The Story of My Life* (1903)
G. K. Chesterton	*The Innocence of Father Brown* (1911)
Juan Ramón Jiménez	*Platero y yo [Platero and I; An Andalusian Elegy]* (1914)
George Bernard Shaw	*Pygmalion* (1914)
Emily Post	*Etiquette in Society, in Business, in Politics, and at Home* (1922)
P. G. Wodehouse	*The Inimitable Jeeves* (1923)
A. A. Milne	*Winnie-the-Pooh* (1926)
Willa Cather	*Shadows on the Rock* (1931)
Irma S. Rombauer	*The Joy of Cooking: A Compilation of Reliable Recipes with a Casual Culinary Chat* (1931)
J. R. R. Tolkien	*The Hobbit* (1937)
Margaret Wise Brown	*Goodnight Moon* (1947)
Harper Lee	*To Kill a Mockingbird* (1960)
Langston Hughes	*The Best of Simple* (1961)
Elizabeth Bishop	*The Complete Poems, 1927–1979* (1983)

FAVORITES OF CHILDHOOD AND YOUTH

Beatrix Potter	*The Tale of Peter Rabbit* (1901)
Betty Smith	*A Tree Grows in Brooklyn* (1943)
C. S. Lewis	*The Lion, the Witch and the Wardrobe* (1950)
J. D. Salinger	*The Catcher in the Rye* (1951)
E. B. White	*Charlotte's Web* (1952)
Ezra Jack Keats	*The Snowy Day* (1962)
Maurice Sendak	*Where the Wild Things Are* (1963)
Patricia MacLachlan	*Sarah, Plain and Tall* (1985)

COMMON LITERARY TERMS

allegory   A story with an underlying meaning symbolized by the characters and action.

alliteration   The repetition of the same sounds—usually initial consonants of words or of stressed syllables—in any sequence of neighboring words.

allusion   A reference to a familiar person or event, often from literature.

anachronism   A chronological error in literature that places a person, event, or object in an impossible historical context.

anagram   A word or phrase created by transposing the letters of another word.

analogy   The relation of one thing to something familiar.

antagonist   The major character opposing a hero or a protagonist.

anthropomorphism   The assigning of human characteristics and feelings to animals and nonhuman things.

anticlimax   Something that works against a climax, such as humor; a sudden descent from the lofty to the trivial.

antihero   A protagonist lacking in heroic qualities like courage, idealism, and honesty.

antithesis   A rhetorical figure in which sharply opposing ideas are expressed within a balanced grammatical structure.

assonance   The close repetition of similar vowel sounds.

autobiography   The story of one's life as written by oneself.

ballad   A poem, often meant to be sung, that tells a story.

bathos   A sudden descent from the lofty to the ordinary or ridiculous.

belles-lettres   Literature. Currently, lighter writings or appreciative essays on the beauties of literature.

bibliography   A list of books on a similar subject or by a given author or authors.

biography   The story of someone's life as written by another.

blank verse   Unrhymed poetry, especially poetry written in iambic pentameter.

cacophony   Discordant sounds, sometimes used in poetry for effect.

cadence   The natural rhythm of language determined by its inherent alternation of stressed or unstressed syllables.

caesura   A pause or break in a line of verse.

climax   The point of high emotional intensity at which a story or play reaches its peak.

conceit   A fanciful image, especially an elaborate or startling analogy.

couplet   Two successive lines of poetry, usually rhymed.

denouement   Literally, the "unknotting": the final unraveling of the plot following the climax.

diction   The choice and arrangement of words in a literary work.

doggerel   Crudely written poetry.

elegy   A poetic lament.

epic   An extended narrative poem, exalted in style and heroic in theme.

epistolary novel   A novel written in the form of correspondence.

essay   A short written work of nonfiction, usually on one topic.

euphony   Harmonious sounds, often used in poetry for effect.

fable   A prose or poetic story that illustrates a moral.

fiction   Narrative writing drawn from the imagination of the author rather than from history or fact.

foot   A group of syllables forming a metrical unit.

free verse   A poem without regular meter or line length.

genre   A literary type or class.

haiku   An unrhymed poem form, originated by the Japanese, consisting of three lines of five, seven, and five syllables that record the essence of a moment.

hero   A character, often the protagonist, who exhibits qualities such as courage, idealism, and honesty.

high comedy   Comedy that is characterized by intellect or wit.

historical novel   A narrative that places fictional characters or events in historically accurate surroundings.

hyperbole   A deliberate overstatement.

iamb   A metrical foot that contains one short or unstressed syllable preceding one long or stressed syllable.

iambic pentameter   Poetry consisting of five parts per line, each part having one short or unstressed syllable and one long or stressed syllable.

imagery   Figurative language used to evoke particular mental pictures.

irony   An expression of a meaning that contradicts the literal meaning.

literature   Novels, stories, poems, and plays of high standards that entertain, inform, stimulate, or provide aesthetic pleasure.

low comedy   Humorous material that employs physical actions or jokes of questionable taste.

malapropism   A mistaken substitution of one word for another that sounds similar, generally with humorous effect.

metaphor   A figure of speech in which two unlikely objects are compared by identification or by the substitution of one for the other.

meter   The pattern of stressed and unstressed syllables in poetry.

motif   A theme, character, or verbal pattern that recurs in literature or folklore.

myth   A legend, usually made up in part of historical events, that helps define the beliefs of a people and that often has evolved as an explanation for rituals and natural phenomena.

nonfiction   A historically accurate narrative.

novel   A long work of fictional prose.

novella   A short novel; also, the early tales or short stories of French and Italian writers.

ode   A lyric poem marked by strong feelings and an involved style.

onomatopoeia   Formation of a word by imitating the natural sound associated with the object or action involved; the use of words that are so named.

oxymoron   A figure of speech that employs two contradictory terms. For examples, *see* "Oxymoron: Pairings of Contradictory or Incongruous Words" in chapter 13.

palindrome   A word, a sentence, or a group of sentences (sometimes in verse) that reads the same backward and forward. For examples, *see* "Palindromes" in chapter 13.

parable   A short story that illustrates a moral.

paradox   An apparently contradictory statement that contains a truth that reconciles the contradiction.

parody   A humorous, often exaggerated, imitation of a serious literary work.

pathetic fallacy   The assigning of human attributes to nature.

pathos   An element that evokes feelings of pity, tenderness, and sympathy.

personification   The assigning of human attributes to abstractions, objects, and other nonhuman things.

plot   The organization of individual incidents in a narrative or play.

poem   A rhythmic expression of feelings or ideas, often using metaphor, meter, and rhyme.

poetic license   The practice of violating rules, expectations, or conventions to achieve a desired effect.

prologue   An introductory speech or monologue, given by an actor or actress before a play, which helps to set the stage for what is to come.

prose   Literary expression not marked by rhyme or metrical regularity.

protagonist   The main character of a play, novel, or story, usually the hero.

pun A humorous and often clever play on words in which one word evokes another with a similar sound but a different meaning.

refrain A phrase or verse that is repeated throughout a poem or song.

rhetorical question A question put forth to achieve an effect or make a point, to which an answer is not expected.

rhyme The repetition of similar or identical sounds at the ends of lines of verse.

rhythm The pattern of stressed and unstressed syllables in a line of poetry or prose.

satire Ridicule of a subject; the work in which it is contained.

short story A brief work of narrative prose.

simile A comparison of two unlike things that usually employs *like* or *as*.

soliloquy A dramatic monologue meant to convey the thoughts of a character in a play.

sonnet A poem consisting of fourteen iambic pentameter lines with a rigidly prescribed rhyming scheme.

spondee A type of metrical foot with two stressed syllables.

spoonerism The transposition of the initial sounds of two or more words, often with humorous results. Named for a Professor Spooner of Oxford, who was famous for such transpositions.

style An author's individual method and tone.

subplot A secondary plot in a story.

symbol In literature, something that stands for, or means, something else.

theme The central idea or thesis of a work.

trochee A metrical foot that contains one long or stressed syllable preceding one short or unstressed syllable.

verse Lines of writing arranged in metrical patterns, or a single such line.

ADDITIONAL SOURCES OF INFORMATION

Atkinson, Frank. *Dictionary of Literary Pseudonyms.* 4th ed. American Library Association, 1986.

Baldick, Chris. *The Concise Oxford Dictionary of Literary Terms.* Oxford University Press, 1991.

Baldwin, Neil, and Diane Osen, eds. *The Writing Life: National Book Award Authors.* Random House, 1995.

Bauer, Andrew. *The Hawthorn Dictionary of Pseudonyms.* Hawthorn Books, 1971.

Beckson, Karl, and Arthur Ganz. *Literary Terms: A Dictionary.* Farrar, Straus & Giroux, 1989.

Bede, Jean-Albert, and William B. Edgerton, eds. *Columbia Dictionary of Modern European Literature.* Columbia University Press, 1980.

Colby, Vineta, ed. *World Authors, 1975–1980.* H. W. Wilson, 1985.

Colby, Vineta, ed. *World Authors, 1980–1985.* H. W. Wilson, 1991.

Contemporary Authors. 156 vols. Gale Research, 1962–1997.

Contemporary Authors: New Revision Series. 58 vols. Gale Research, 1962–1997.

Contemporary Literary Criticism. 100 vols. Gale Research, 1973–1997.

Cuddon, J. A. *Dictionary of Literary Terms.* Doubleday, 1977.

Drabble, Margaret, ed. *The Oxford Companion to English Literature.* rev. 5th ed., Oxford University Press, 1995.

Foster, David, and Virginia R. Foster. *Modern Latin American Literature.* 2 vols. Frederick Ungar, 1975.

Literature

Frye, Northrop, Sheridan Baker, and George Perkins. *The Harper Handbook to Literature.* Harper & Row, 1985.

Hart, James D. *The Oxford Companion to American Literature.* 6th ed. Oxford University Press, 1995.

Herdeck, Donald E. *African Authors: A Companion to Black African Writing.* Black Orpheus Press, 1973.

Holman, Clarence Hugh. *A Handbook to Literature.* 5th ed. Macmillan, 1986.

Murphy, Bruce, ed. *Benet's Readers Encyclopedia of American Literature.* 4th ed. HarperCollins, 1996.

National Book Foundation. *The National Book Awards: Forty-one Years of Literary Excellence: Winners and Finalists, 1950–1991.* National Book Foundation, 1991.

Ousby, Ian. *The Cambridge Guide to Literature in English.* Cambridge University Press, 1993.

Toye, William, ed. *The Oxford Companion to Canadian Literature.* Oxford University Press, 1983.

Twentieth-Century Literary Criticism. 65 vols. Gale Research, 1978–1996.

Wakeman, John, ed. *World Authors, 1950–1970.* H. W. Wilson, 1975.

Wakeman, John, ed. *World Authors, 1970–1975.* H. W. Wilson, 1980.

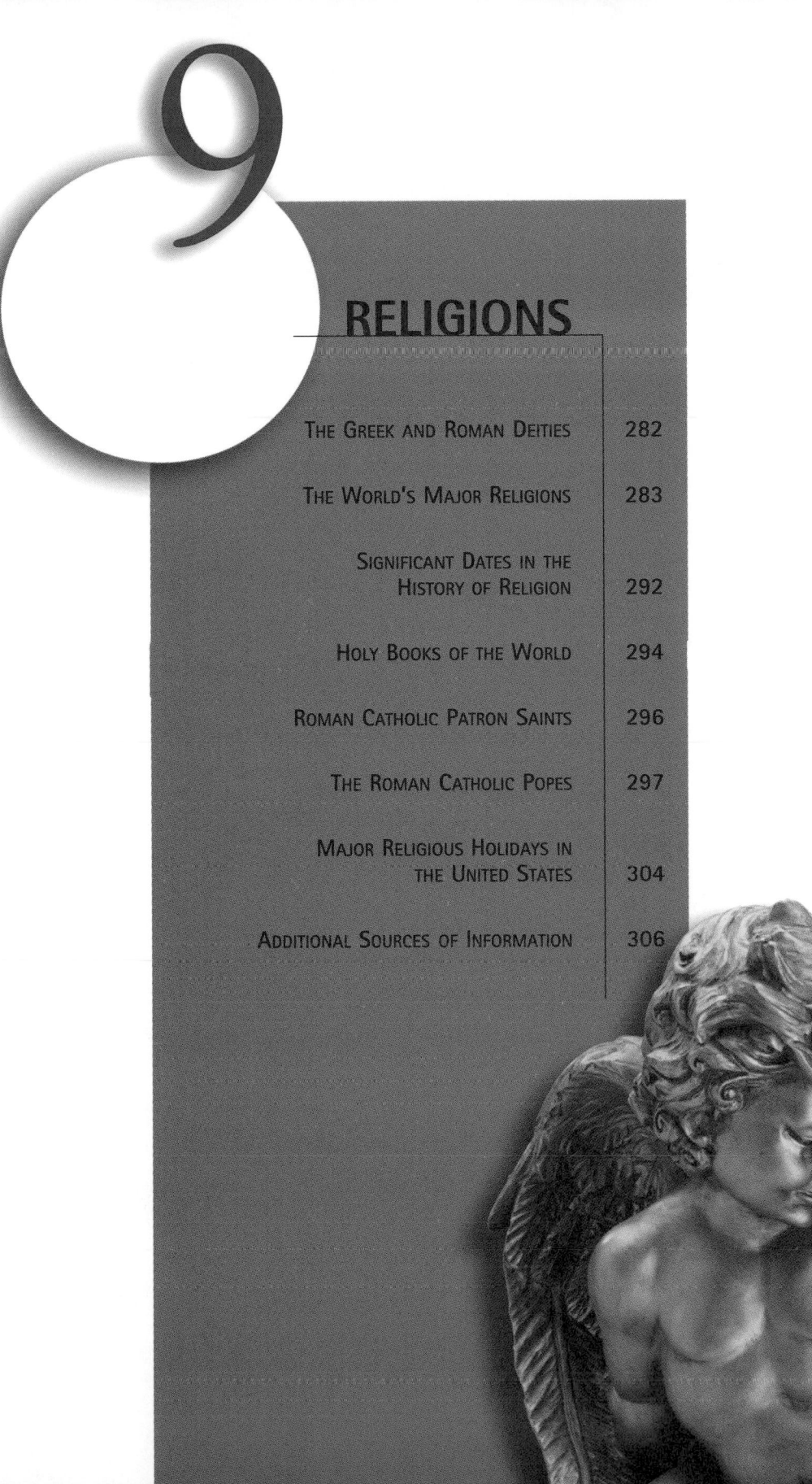

9 RELIGIONS

THE GREEK AND ROMAN DEITIES	282
THE WORLD'S MAJOR RELIGIONS	283
SIGNIFICANT DATES IN THE HISTORY OF RELIGION	292
HOLY BOOKS OF THE WORLD	294
ROMAN CATHOLIC PATRON SAINTS	296
THE ROMAN CATHOLIC POPES	297
MAJOR RELIGIOUS HOLIDAYS IN THE UNITED STATES	304
ADDITIONAL SOURCES OF INFORMATION	306

THE GREEK AND ROMAN DEITIES

Images of the gods and goddesses of ancient Greece and Rome have had a lasting impact on Western religious thought. They have also played an important part in the development of the arts, philosophy, and psychology. The following lists give the names of these ancient deities as well as the spheres of influence ascribed to them.

Greek	Roman	Sphere of Influence
Adonis	———	Symbolizes the death of nature each autumn and its rebirth in the spring
Aelous	———	God of the winds
Aphrodite	Venus	Goddess of love and beauty
Apollo	———	God of beauty, youth, poetry, music, prophecy, and archery
Ares	Mars	God of war
Artemis	Diana	Goddess of the hunt, moon, and nature
Asclepius	Aesculapius	God of medicine
Athena	Minerva	Goddess of wisdom
Chaos	———	God of the shapeless void that preceded creation of the Earth
Cronus	Saturn	Leader of the Titans who ruled the heavens after overthrowing his father, Uranus
Demeter	Ceres	Goddess of the earth, grain, and harvests
Dionysus	Bacchus (Liber)	God of wine
Dis (Hades)	Pluto	God of the underworld
Eos	Aurora	Goddess of dawn
Eris	Discordia	Goddess of strife and discord
Eros	Cupid (Amor)	God of love
Fates	Fates	Three sisters—Clotho, Lachesis, and Atropis (called Nona, Decuma, and Morta by the Romans)—who spun the thread of human destiny and cut it with their shears when they pleased
Flora	———	Goddess of flowers
Furies	Furies	Three goddesses, their heads (Eumenides) topped by serpents, who punished those who escaped human justice
Gorgons	———	Three winged sisters—Euryale, Medusa, and Stheno—the sight of whom turned mortals to stone
Graces	Graces	Three sisters—Agaia, Euphrosyne, and Thalis—who were goddesses of banquets, dances, social enjoyments, and the arts
Hebe	Juventas	Goddess of youth
Hephaestus	Vulcan	God of fire
Hera	Juno	Sister and wife of Zeus; queen of the goddesses
Herakles	Hercules	Son of Zeus; greatest of Greek heroes, who performed 12 labors and was eventually granted immortality
Hermaphroditus	———	Son of Hermes and Aphrodite who was joined forever to the nymph of the fountain of Salmacis, creating one body with the sexual characteristics of both males and females
Hermes	Mercury	Messenger of the gods; patron of thieves
Hestia	Vesta	Goddess of the hearth
Hygeia	———	Goddess of health
Hymen	———	God of marriage
Hypnus	Somnus	God of sleep
———	Janus	Porter of heaven, who opens the year; also god of gates and doors, with two opposing faces
———	Lares	Spirits of ancestors who watch over homes and cities
———	Lemures	Spirits of the dead, both good and bad

Greek	Roman	Sphere of Influence
Metis	Prudence	First wife of Zeus, who helped him become king of gods; personification of prudence
Morpheus	——	God of dreams
Muses	Camenae	Nine sisters, daughters of Zeus, who are goddesses of the arts and sciences: Clio (history), Euterpe (lyric poetry), Thalia (comedy), Melpomene (tragedy), Terpsichore (dance), Erato (erotic poetry), Polyhymnia (sacred poetry), Urania (astronomy), and Calliope (epic poetry; chief of the Muses)
Nemesis	——	Goddess of vengeance
Nike	Victoria	Goddess of victory
Nymphs	——	Nature spirits who oversee water, trees, mountains, valleys, and particular locations
Nyx	Nox	Goddess of night
Pan	Faunus	God of flocks and shepherds
Persepshone	Proserpine	Goddess of the underworld; symbol of the death of nature each autumn and its rebirth each spring
Plutus	——	God of wealth
——	Pomona	Goddess of fruit and gardens
Poseidon	Neptune	God of the oceans
Priapus	——	God of fertility
Psyche	Psyche	Goddess of the soul, who was united with Eros, or Cupid
Rhea	Ops	Wife of Cronus; mother of the Olympian gods and goddesses Demeter, Hades, Hera, Hestia, Poseidon, and Zeus
——	Romulus	Founder of the city of Rome; raised by a wolf with his twin brother, Remus
Satyrs	Satyrs	Field and forest gods with goats' feet and horns who represent nature's bounty and lust
Selene	Luna	Goddess of the moon
Sirens	——	Sea nymphs whose singing enchanted those who heard it
Thanatos	Mors	God of death
Titans	Titans	Sons and daughters of Uranus, who took power when Cronus overthrew their father: Atlas, Coeus, Crius, Dione, Epimetheus, Hyperion, Iapetus, Leto, Maia, Mnemosyne, Oceanus, Ophion, Pallas, Phoebe, Prometheus, Rhea, Tethys, Themis, and Thia
Tyche	Fortuna	Goddess of fortune or fate
Uranus	——	God of heaven; father of the Titans
Zeus	Jupiter (Jove)	Chief god of Olympus; ruler of heaven, who wielded thunder and lightning.

—— indicates no corresponding deity in this culture.

THE WORLD'S MAJOR RELIGIONS

Religious beliefs of one sort or another are an intrinsic aspect of virtually every society that has ever existed on this planet. Many of these beliefs are organized and codified, often based on the teachings and writings of one or more founders. Other belief systems are less rigid in their external structures and may be transmitted orally from one generation to the next, whether by family members or by religious leaders within the community.

While all religious beliefs are of vital importance to those who hold them, the less formalistic belief systems—variously referred to as animist or tribal religions, and adhered to by peoples all over the world—have proven somewhat enigmatic to Western minds. This section, therefore, deals only with those religions that are recognizable as such to

Westerners, ones that employ certain readily identifiable tenets, beliefs, and doctrines.

BAHA'I

Baha'i has more than 6 million followers worldwide and 300,000 followers in the United States. It was founded by Mirza Husayn 'Ali Nuri, who took the name Bahá'u'lláh (Glory of God) while in exile in Baghdad. Bahá'u'lláh's coming had been foretold by Mirza Ali Muhammad, known as al-Bab, who founded Babism in 1844, from which the Baha'i faith grew. The central tenets of the Baha'i faith are the oneness of God, the oneness of humanity, and the common foundation of all religion. Baha'ists also believe in the equality of men and women, universal education, world peace, and the creation of a world federal system of government.

BUDDHISM

Buddhism has 323 million followers worldwide and 780,000 followers in the United States. It was founded by Siddhartha Gautama, known as the Buddha (Enlightened One), in southern Nepal in the 6th and 5th centuries B.C. The Buddha achieved enlightenment through meditation and gathered a community of monks to carry on his teachings. Buddhism teaches that meditation and the practice of good religious and moral behavior can lead to Nirvana, the state of enlightenment, although before achieving Nirvana, one is subject to repeated lifetimes that are good or bad depending on one's actions *(karma)*. The doctrines of the Buddha describe temporal life as featuring "four noble truths": Existence is a realm of suffering; desire, along with the belief in the importance of one's self, causes suffering; achievement of Nirvana ends suffering; and Nirvana is attained only by meditation and by following the path of righteousness in action, thought, and attitude.

CONFUCIANISM

A faith with 6 million followers worldwide (the number of followers in the United States is uncertain), Confucianism was founded by Confucius, a Chinese philosopher, in the 6th and 5th centuries B.C. Confucius's sayings and dialogues, known collectively as the *Analects,* were written down by his followers. Confucianism, which grew out of a strife-ridden time in Chinese history, stresses the relationship between individuals, their families, and society, based on *li* (proper behavior) and *jen* (sympathetic attitude). Its practical, socially oriented philosophy was challenged by the more mystical precepts of Taoism and Buddhism, which were partially incorporated to create neo-Confucianism during the Sung dynasty (A.D. 960–1279). The overthrow of the Chinese monarchy and the Communist revolution during the 20th century have severely lessened the influence of Confucianism on modern Chinese culture.

HINDUISM

A religion with 780 million followers worldwide and 910,000 followers in the United States, Hinduism developed from indigenous religions of India in combination with Aryan religions brought to India c. 1500 B.C. and codified in the Veda and the Upanishads, the sacred scriptures of Hinduism. Hinduism is a term used broadly to describe a vast array of sects to which most Indians belong. Although many Hindus reject the caste system—in which people are born into a particular subgroup that determines their religious, social, and work-related duties—it is widely accepted and classifies society at large into four groups: the Brahmins or priests, the rulers and warriors, the farmers and merchants, and the peasants and laborers. The goals of Hinduism are release from repeated reincarnation through the practice of yoga, adherence to Vedic scriptures, and devotion to a personal guru. Various deities are worshiped at shrines; the divine trinity, representing the cyclical nature of the universe, is made up of Brahma the creator, Vishnu the preserver, and Shiva the destroyer.

ISLAM

Islam has 1.1 billion followers worldwide and 5.1 million followers in the United States. It was founded by the prophet Muhammad, who received the holy scriptures of Islam, the Koran, from Allah

(God) c. A.D. 610. Islam (Arabic for "submission to God") maintains that Muhammad is the last in a long line of holy prophets, preceded by Adam, Abraham, Moses, and Jesus. In addition to being devoted to the Koran, followers of Islam (Muslims) are devoted to the worship of Allah through the Five Pillars: the statement "There is no god but God, and Muhammad is his prophet"; prayer, conducted five times a day while facing Mecca, the birthplace of Muhammad and the holy city of the Islamic world (Mecca is the capital of the Hejaz region of Saudi Arabia); the giving of alms; the keeping of the fast of Ramadan during the ninth month of the Muslim year; and the making of a pilgrimage to Mecca at least once, if possible. The two main divisions of Islam are the Sunni and the Shiite. The Wahabis are the most important Sunni sect; the Shiite sects include the Assassins, the Druses, and the Fatimids, among countless others.

JUDAISM

Stemming from the descendants of Judah in Judea, Judaism was founded c. 2000 B.C. by Abraham, Isaac, and Jacob and has 14 million followers worldwide and 4.3 million followers in the United States. Judaism espouses belief in a monotheistic God, who is creator of the universe and who leads His people, the Jews, by speaking through prophets. His word is revealed in the Hebrew Bible (or Old Testament), especially in that part known as the Torah. The Torah also contains, according to rabbinic tradition, a total of 613 biblical commandments, including the Ten Commandments, which are explicated in the Talmud. Jews believe that the human condition can be improved, that the letter and the spirit of the Torah must be followed, and that a Messiah will eventually bring the world to a state of paradise. Judaism promotes community among all people of Jewish faith, dedication to a synagogue or temple (the basic social unit of a group of Jews, led by a rabbi), and the importance of family life. Religious observance takes place both at home and in the temple. Judaism is divided into three main groups who vary in their interpretation

of those parts of the Torah that deal with personal, communal, international, and religious activities: the Orthodox community, which views the Torah as derived from God and therefore absolutely binding; the Reform movement, which follows primarily its ethical content; and the Conservative Jews, who follow most of the observances set out in the Torah but allow for change in the face of modern life. A fourth group, Reconstructionist Jews, rejects the concept of the Jews as God's chosen people, yet maintains rituals as part of the Judaic cultural heritage.

ORTHODOX CHURCH

With 218 million followers worldwide and over 5 million followers in the United States, the Orthodox Church is the third-largest Christian community in the world. It began its split from the Roman Catholic Church in the 5th century; the break was finalized in 1054. The followers of the Orthodox Church are in fact members of many different denominations, including the Church of Greece, the Church of Cyprus, and the Russian Orthodox Church. Orthodox religion holds biblical Scripture and tradition, guided by the Holy Spirit as expressed in the consciousness of the entire Orthodox community, to be the source of Christian truth. It rejects doctrine developed by the Western churches. Doctrine was established by seven ecumenical councils held between 325 and 787 and amended by other councils in the late Byzantine period. Relations between the Orthodox churches and Roman Catholicism have improved since Vatican Council II (1962–65).

PROTESTANTISM

Protestantism is a form of Christian faith. It includes any member of the various Christian churches established as a result of the Reformation, the 16th-century religious movement that aimed at reforming the Roman Catholic Church. The following is a list of major Protestant denominations and their beliefs.

"Holy Books of the World" in this chapter and "Religion Symbols" in chapter 12 **Go to**

Religions

MAJOR PROTESTANT DENOMINATIONS IN THE UNITED STATES

Denomination	Founder	Followers	Tenets
Amish Mennonites	Founded in Switzerland in the 1500s after secession from the Zurich state church; the followers of Jacob Ammann broke from the other Mennonites in Switzerland and Alsace in 1693; most Amish Mennonites emigrated to Pennsylvania in the 18th century when others rejoined the main Mennonite group.	80,000 Amish Mennonites; 200,000 Mennonites primarily located in the United States.	The Bible is the sole rule of faith; beliefs are outlined in the *Dordrecht Confession of Faith* (1632); Mennonites shun worldly ways and modern innovation (education and technology); the sacraments are adult baptism and communion.
Baptists	Founded by John Smyth in England in 1609 and Roger Williams in Rhode Island in 1638.	36 million in the United States; 38 million worldwide.	No creed; authority stems from the Bible; most Baptists oppose the use of alcohol and tobacco; baptism is by total immersion.
Church of Christ	Organized by Presbyterians in Kentucky in 1804 and in Pennsylvania in 1809.	1.6 million in the United States; 3 million worldwide.	The New Testament is believed in, and what is written in the Bible is followed without elaboration; rites are not ornate; baptism is of adults.
Church of England	King Henry VIII of England broke with the Roman Catholic Church; he issued the Act of Supremacy in 1534, which declared the king of England to be the head of the Church of England.	300,000 in the Anglican Orthodox Church in North America; 27 million worldwide.	Supremacy of the Bible is the test of doctrine; emphasis is on the most essential Christian doctrines and creeds; the *Book of Common Prayer* is used; the Church of England is part of the Anglican community, which is represented in the United States mainly by the Episcopal Church.
Disciples of Christ	Founded on the American frontier at the beginning of the 19th century as a means of cutting through doctrinal disputes to achieve Christian unity.	937,000, mostly in the United States.	Rigorous adherence to the New Testament as the basis of Christian faith; literal interpretation of the Bible; rejection of ecclesiastical institutions except for the congregation.

Denomination	Founder	Followers	Tenets
Episcopal Church	U.S. offshoot of the Church of England; it installed Samuel Seabury as its first bishop in 1784 and held its first General Convention in 1789; the Church of England, headed by King Henry VIII, had broken with the Roman Catholic Church in 1534.	2.5 million in the United States; 70 million worldwide.	Worship is based on the *Book of Common Prayer* and interpretation of the Bible; services range from spartan to ornate, from liberal to conservative; baptism is of infants.
Lutheran Church	Based on the writings of Martin Luther, who broke (1517–21) with the Roman Catholic Church and led the Protestant Reformation; the first Lutheran congregation in North America was founded in 1638 in Wilmington, Delaware; the first North American regional synod was founded in 1748 by Heinrich Melchior Mühlenberg.	9 million in the United States; 63 million worldwide.	Faith is based on the Bible and the Augsburg Confession (written in 1530); salvation comes through faith alone; services include the Lord's Supper communion; Lutherans are mostly conservative in religious and social ethics; infants are baptized; the church is organized in synods; the two largest synods in the United States are the Evangelical Lutheran Church in America and the Lutheran Church Missouri Synod.
Mennonites	*See* Amish Mennonites.		
Methodist Church	Reverend John Wesley began evangelistic preaching within the Church of England in 1738; a separate Wesleyan Methodist Church was established in 1791; the Methodist Episcopal Church was founded in the United States in 1784.	13.5 million in the United States; 26 million worldwide.	The name derives from the founders' desire to study religion "by rule and method" and follow the Bible interpreted by tradition and reason; worship varies by denomination within Methodism (the United Methodist Church is the largest congregation); the church is perfectionist in social dealings; communion and the baptism of infants and adults are practiced.

continues

Continued

Denomination	Founder	Followers	Tenets
Pentecostal churches	The churches grew out of the "holiness movement" that developed among Methodists and other Protestants in the first decade of the 20th century.	10.6 million in the United States; 200 million worldwide.	Baptism in the Holy Spirit, speaking in tongues, faith healing, and the second coming of Jesus are believed in; of the various Pentecostal churches, the Assemblies of God is the largest; a perfectionist attitude toward secular affairs is common; services feature enthusiastic sermons and hymns; adult baptism and communion are practiced.
Presbyterian Church	Grew out of Calvinist churches of Switzerland and France; John Knox founded the first Presbyterian church in Scotland in 1557; the first presbytery in North America was established by Irish missionary Francis Makemie in 1706.	3.7 million in the United States; 50 million worldwide.	Faith is in the Bible; the sacraments are infant baptism and communion; the church is organized as a system of courts in which clergy and lay members (presbyters) participate at local, regional, and national levels; services are simple, with emphasis on the sermon.
Reformed churches	The churches trace their origin to the Swiss Reformation in the 16th century. The first Reformed church in the United States was founded by Alexander Whitaker in Virginia in 1611.	2 million in United States; number of followers worldwide is uncertain.	Confirmation of the Trinity and the humanity and divinity of Christ; belief in the justification of grace through faith.
Seventh-Day Adventist Church	Grew out of the teachings of William Miller in the 1840s; formally founded in North America in 1863.	775,000 in the United States; 8 million worldwide.	The Bible is the only creed; the second coming of Jesus is emphasized; members abstain from alcoholic beverages and tobacco; baptism and communion are practiced.
United Church of Christ	Formed in 1957 by the union of the General Council of Congregational Christian Churches with the Evangelical and Reformed Churches.	1.5 million, mostly in the United States.	Belief in the Bible is guided by the *Statement of Faith* (written in 1959); the church is organized by congregations, which are represented at a general synod that set policy; services are simple, with emphasis on the sermon; infant baptism and communion are practiced.

OTHER CHRISTIAN–BASED RELIGIONS AND ORGANIZATIONS

Religion/Org.	Founder	Followers	Tenets
The Church of Jesus Christ of Latter-Day Saints (Mormons)	Joseph Smith, in the 1820s, found golden tablets with *The Book of Mormon* inscribed on them; church headquarters were established in upstate New York in 1830, then in Ohio in 1831; after two more attempts to establish a permanent home for the church (the second resulting in Smith's death at the hands of a mob), Salt Lake City, Utah, was founded in 1847 under the leadership of Brigham Young.	4.7 million in the United States; 7.7 million worldwide.	Faith is based on the Bible, *The Book of Mormon, The Doctrine and Covenants,* and *The Pearl of Great Price,* all of which are considered scripture; stress is placed on revelation through the connection of spiritual and physical worlds and through proselytizing; members abstain from alcohol and tobacco and believe in community self-reliance; public services are conservative; there is baptism, laying on of hands, and communion; a secret temple holds other cermonies, including baptism for the dead.
Jehovah's Witnesses	Founded by Charles T. Russell in the United States in the late 19th century.	945,000 in the United States; 4 million worldwide.	Belief is in the imminent second coming of Christ and the potential salvation of mortal souls during the millennium; all members are ministers who proselytize their faith with door-to-door missionary work; members refuse service in the armed forces, will not salute national flags or participate in politics, will not accept blood transfusion, (but will accept all other forms of medical treatment), and discourage smoking, drunkenness, and gambling.

continues

Continued

Religion/Org.	Founder	Followers	Tenets
Religious Society of Friends (Quakers)	George Fox in England in the 17th century began preaching against organized churches, professing a doctrine of the Inner Light.	100,000 in the United States; 300,000 worldwide.	Reliance is on the Inner Light, the voice of God's Holy Spirit experienced within each person; meetings are characterized by quiet meditation without ritual or sermon; Quakers are active in peace, education, and social welfare movements; they refuse to bear arms or take oaths; earlier schisms are still reflected in three main affiliations of Friends.
Unitarian Universalist Association	The denomination resulted from the merger in 1961 of the Universalist Church of America (organized in 1779) and the American Unitarian Association (founded in 1825).	200,000 in the United States; 330,000 worldwide.	Members profess no creed; strong social, ethical, and humanitarian concerns are manifest in the search for religious truth through freedom of belief; theists, humanists, and agnostics are accepted in religious fellowship; efforts are aimed at the creation of a worldwide interfaith religious community; many members come from other denominations and religions.

ROMAN CATHOLICISM

The Roman Catholic Church, with 900 million followers worldwide and 60 million followers in the United States, is the largest Christian church in the world. It claims direct historical descent from the church founded by the apostle Peter. The pope in Rome is the spiritual leader of all Roman Catholics. He administers church affairs through bishops and priests. Members accept the gospel of Jesus Christ and the teachings of the Bible, as well as the church's interpretations of these. God's grace is conveyed through the seven sacraments, especially the Eucharist or communion that is celebrated at mass, the regular service of worship. The other six sacraments are baptism, confirmation, penance, holy orders, matrimony, and anointing of the sick. Redemption through Jesus Christ is professed as the sole method of obtaining salvation, which is necessary to ensure a place in heaven after life on earth.

New York's Cathedral of St. John the Divine, begun in 1892, is only now nearing completion. Taking more than 100 years to construct, it will be the largest cathedral in the world when finished.

"Roman Catholic Patron Saints" and "The **Go to** Roman Catholic Popes" in this chapter

ROSICRUCIANISM

Rosicrucianism, a modern movement begun in 1868 by R. W. Little, claims ties to an older Society of the Rose and Cross that was founded in Germany in 1413 by Christian Rosencreuz. The number of its followers is uncertain. The Ancient Mystical Order Rosae Crusis (AMORC) was founded in San Jose, California, in 1915 by H. Spencer Lewis. The Rosicrucian Brotherhood was established in Quakertown, Pennsylvania, by Reuben Swinburne Clymer in 1902. Both sects could be classified as either fraternal or religious organizations, although they claim to empower members with cosmic forces by unveiling secret wisdom regarding the laws of nature.

SHINTO

Shinto, with 2.8 million followers worldwide (the number of followers in the United States is uncertain), is the ancient native religion of Japan, established long before the introduction of writing to Japan in the 5th century A.D. The origins of its beliefs and rituals are unknown. Shinto stresses belief in a great many spiritual beings and gods, known as *kami,* who are paid tribute at shrines and honored by festivals, and reverence for ancestors. Although Shinto has no overall dogma, adherents are expected to remember and celebrate the *kami,* support the societies of which the *kami* are patrons, remain pure and sincere, and enjoy life.

TAOISM

Both a philosophy and a religion, Taoism was founded in China by Lao-tzu, who is traditionally said to have been born in 604 B.C. Its number of followers is uncertain. It derives primarily from the *Tao-te-ching,* which claims that an ever-changing universe follows the Tao, or path. The Tao can be known only by emulating its quietude and effortless simplicity; Taoism prescribes that people live simply, spontaneously, and in close touch with nature and that they meditate to achieve contact with the Tao. Temples and monasteries, maintained by Taoist priests, are important in some Taoist sects. Since the Communist revolution, Taoism has been actively discouraged in the People's Republic of China, although it continues to flourish in Taiwan.

Madalyn Murray O'Hair, the renowned atheist who opposed prayer in schools, mysteriously disappeared on September 28, 1995, along with her son Jon Garth and adopted family member Robin Murray. Theories range from flight to avoid the IRS to foul play.

ZOROASTRIANISM

An ancient religion that influenced both Judaism and Christianity, Zoroastrianism arose in Persia (modern-day Iran) at least as early as the 6th century B.C. Based mainly on a Persian text known as the *Avesta,* Zoroastrianism rejected the worship of multiple gods, adhering to belief only in Ahura Mazda, the "Wise Lord." With the advent of the Sasanid dynasty in the 3rd century A.D., Zoroastrianism became Persia's state religion, but it declined dramatically after the Islamic conquest of the 8th century. The remnant of Zoroastrian believers eventually made their way to western India, where they are now known as Farsis, or Parsees. Numbering about 185,000 worldwide and 20,000 in the United States, they still adhere to their ancient religion. Among other beliefs, they revere the forces of nature, particularly fire, as expressions of Ahura Mazda's divine power.

Religions

SIGNIFICANT DATES IN THE HISTORY OF RELIGION

B.C.

c. 2000	Abraham, founder of Judaism, is alive.
c. 13th century	Moses, Hebrew lawgiver, is alive.
c. 1100–c. 500	The Vedas, sacred texts of the Hindus, are compiled.
604	Traditional birth date of Lao-tzu, founder of Taoism.
588	Traditional date of Zoroaster's revelation.
c. 563–c. 483	Buddha, founder of Buddhism, is alive.
551–479	Confucius, founder of Confucianism, is alive.
c. 200	The *Bhagavad Gita,* important Hindu text, is written.
6 or 4	Jesus of Nazareth, founder of Christianity, is born.

A.D.

33?	The Crucifixion and death of Jesus Christ.
64?	Peter, disciple of Jesus and, according to tradition, first bishop of Rome, dies.
c. 70–c. 100	First four books of the New Testament—Matthew, Mark, Luke, and John—are written.
5th century	Two Buddhist sects—Zen and Pure Land (or Amidism)—are established.
c. 570–632	Muhammad the prophet—whose teachings, recorded in the Koran, form the basis of Islam—is alive.
622	Muhammad flees persecution in Mecca and settles in Yathrib (later Medina); the first day of the lunar year in which this event, known as the Hegira, takes place marks the start of the Muslim era.

936	Traditional date of the arrival from Iran of the first Parsis (followers of Zoroastrianism) in India.
1054	Catholic Pope Leo IX condemns the patriarch of Constantinople, finalizing the split between the Orthodox Church and the Roman Catholic Church.
c. 1224–74	Saint Thomas Aquinas, Italian philosopher and Roman Catholic theologian, is alive.
1309–77	The Roman Catholic papacy is seated in Avignon, France.
1483–1546	Martin Luther, leader of the Protestant Reformation in Germany and author of "95 Theses" (1517) is alive.
1491–1556	Ignatius Loyola, founder of the Jesuit Order of Roman Catholic priests, is alive.
1509–64	John Calvin, leader of the Protestant Reformation in France, is alive.
1549	The first Christian mission in Japan is established.
1582	Jesuit Matteo Ricci is the first missionary to be sent to China.
1620	Plymouth Colony in North America is founded in December by 102 English Puritan separatists, known as Pilgrims.

One of the Dead Sea scrolls, the "Copper" scroll, lists 64 underground hiding places in Israel that supposedly contain gold, silver, aromatics, and manuscripts. These are believed to be treasures from the Temple at Jerusalem that were hidden for safekeeping.

1624–91	George Fox, English founder of the Protestant Society of Friends (the Quakers), is alive.
1703–91	John Wesley, English founder of the Protestant movement that later became the Methodist Church, is alive.
1869–70	The first Roman Catholic Vatican Council, at which the dogma of papal infallibility is promulgated, is convened by Pope Piux IX.
1869–1948	Mohandas K. Gandhi, Indian spiritual and political leader who helped his country achieve independence from Britain and sought rapprochement between Hindus and Muslims, is alive.
1933–45	The systematic persecution and attempted extermination of European Jews by Adolf Hitler's Nazi party, known as the Holocaust, takes place.
1948	The independent Jewish state of Israel is declared.
1962–65	The second Roman Catholic Vatican Council, at which changes were made in the liturgy and greater participation in services by lay church members was encouraged, is convened by Pope John XXIII and concluded by Pope Paul VI.

The Ten Commandments

During their exodus from the land of Egypt, Moses led the people of Israel to Mount Sinai, where God issued to Moses the Ten Commandments. These commandments form the foundation of both Jewish and Christian morality. The following is from Exodus, chapter 20; the bold numbers indicate the verse number (the Ten Commandments also appear, with slightly different wording, in Deuteronomy 5:6–21).

1. **2** I am the Lord thy God, which have brought thee out of the land of Egypt, out of the house of bondage,

2. **3** Thou shalt have no other gods before me.

   4 Thou shalt not make unto thee any graven image, or any likeness of any thing that is in heaven above, or that is in the earth beneath, or that is in the water under the earth.

   5 Thou shalt not bow down thyself to them, nor serve them; for I the Lord thy God am a jealous God, visiting the iniquity of the fathers upon the Children unto the third and fourth generation of them that hate me; **6** And showing mercy unto thousands of them that love me, and keep my commandments.

3. **7** Thou shalt not take the name of the Lord thy God in vain; for the Lord will not hold him guiltless that taketh his name in vain.

4. **8** Remember the sabbath day, to keep it holy, **9** Six days shalt thou labour, and do all thy work; **10** But the seventh day is the sabbath of the Lord thy God; in it thou shalt not do any work, thou, nor thy son, nor thy daughter, thy manservant, nor thy maidservant, nor thy cattle, nor thy stranger that is within thy gates; **11** For in six days the Lord made heaven and earth, the sea, and all that in them is, and rested the seventh day; wherefore the Lord blessed the sabbath day, and hallowed it.

5. **12** Honour thy father and thy mother; that thy days may be long upon the land which the Lord thy God giveth thee.

6. **13** Thou shalt not kill.

7. **14** Thou shalt not commit adultery.

8. **15** Thou shalt not steal.

9. **16** Thou shalt not bear false witness against thy neighbour.

10. **17** Thou shalt not covet they neighbour's house, thou shalt not covet thy neighbor's wife, nor his manservant, nor his maidservant, nor his ox, nor his ass, nor anything that is thy neighbor's.

HOLY BOOKS OF THE WORLD

The Analects   A collection of Confucius's teachings thought to have been recorded by his students. They are considered the only sayings that can safely be attributed to him.

Bhagavad Gita   A Sanskrit poem that is part of the Indian epic known as the *Mahabharata*. It describes, in a dialogue between Lord Krishna and Prince Arjuna, the Hindu path to spiritual wisdom and the unity with God that can be achieved through *karma* (action), *bhakti* (devotion), and *jnana* (knowledge). The *Bhagavad-Gita* was probably written sometime between 200 B.C. and A.D. 200.

Five Classics   Five works traditionally attributed to Confucius that form the basic texts of Confucianism. They are the *Spring and Autumn Annals,* a history of Confucius's native district; the *I Ching* (or *Book of Changes*), a system of divining the future; the *Book of Rites,* which outlines ceremonies and describes the ideal government; the *Book of History;* and the *Book of Songs,* a collection of poetry. Together they promulgate a system of ethics for managing society based on sympathy for others, etiquette, and ritual. Although the dates of these books are uncertain, they were probably written before the 3rd century B.C.

Koran   (Arabic, **al-Qur'ân**)   The primary holy book of Islam. It is made up of 114 *suras,* or chapters, which contain impassioned appeals for belief in God, encouragement to lead a moral life, portrayals of damnation and beatitude, stories of Islamic prophets, and rules governing the social and religious life of Muslims. Believers maintain that

The Seven Canonical Hours

A Closer Look

Psalms 118:164 states: "Seven times a day I praise you." These hours were designated as matins and lauds, prime, tierce, sext, nones, vespers, and compline.

the Koran contains the verbatim word of God, revealed to the prophet Muhammad through the angel Gabriel. Some of the *suras* were written during Muhammad's lifetime, but an authoritative text was not produced until c. A.D. 650.

The shortest verse in the Bible is "Jesus wept" (John 11:35).

New Testament   The second portion of the Christian Bible, which contains 27 books that form the basis of Christian belief. These books include the sayings of Jesus; the story of his life and work; the death and resurrection of Jesus now celebrated as Easter; the teachings and writings of the apostles; and instruction for converting nonbelievers and for performing baptisms, blessings, and other rituals. The New Testament is believed to have been written c. A.D. 100, some 70 to 90 years after the death of Jesus.

Old Testament   The Christian name for the Hebrew Bible. It is the sacred scripture of Judaism and the first portion of the Christian Bible. According to Jewish teachings, it is made up of three parts: *the Law* (also known as the Torah or Pentateuch), consisting of the first five books (Genesis, Exodus, Leviticus, Numbers, and

The Four Horsemen of the Apocalypse

A Closer Look

The Book of Revelation, attributed to John the Apostle, refers to four horsemen who will ride forth to the detriment of humankind.

Pestilence	Rides a white horse, carrying a bow and a crown
War	Rides a red horse and swings a great sword
Famine	Rides a black horse and carries scales
Death	Rides a pale horse and has Hades close behind

Religions

THE BOOKS OF THE BIBLE

The Old Testament

Genesis	Nahu
Exodus	Habakkuk
Leviticus	Zephaniah
Numbers	Haggai
Deuteronomy	Zachariah
Joshua	Malachi
Judges	Psalms
I Samuel	Proverbs
II Samuel	Job
I Kings	The Song of Songs
II Kings	Ruth
Isaiah	Lamentations
Jeremiah	Ecclesiastes
Ezekiel	Esther
Hosea	Daniel
Joel	Ezra
Amos	Nehemiah
Obadiah	I Chronicles
Jonah	II Chronicles
Micah	

The New Testament

Matthew	I Peter
Mark	II Peter
Luke	I John
John	II John
Acts	III John
Romans	Jude
I Corinthians	Revelation
II Corinthians	
Galatians	
Ephesians	
Philippians	
Colossians	
I Thessalonians	
II Thessalonians	
I Timothy	
II Timothy	
Titus	
Philemon	
Hebrew	
James	

Deuteronomy), which describes the origins of the world, the covenant between the Lord and Israel, the exodus and entry into the promised land, and the various rules governing social and religious behavior; *the Prophets*, including the former prophets (Joshua, Judges, I and II Samuel, I and II Kings) and the latter prophets (Isaiah, Jeremiah, Ezekiel, and the 12 minor prophets), which describes the history of the Israelites, the stories of heroes, kings, judges, and wars, and the choosing of David as leader of the Israelites; and *the Writings* (including Psalms, Job, Song of Solomon, and Ruth, among others), which describes the reactions of the people to the laws and covenants, as well as prayers and praises of the covenant. Some books of the Old Testament regarded as sacred by the Jews are not accepted as such by Christians; among Christians there are differences between Roman Catholics and Protestants about the inclusion of some books, the order of the books, and the original sources used in translating them. Scholars generally agree that the Old Testament was compiled from c. 1000 B.C. to c. 100 B.C.

Talmud   A compilation of Jewish oral law and rabbinical teachings that is separate from the scriptures of the Hebrew Bible, or Old Testament. The Talmud is made up of two parts: the *Mishna*, which is the oral law itself, and the *Gemara*, which is a commentary on the *Mishna*. The Talmud contains both a legal section (the *Halakah*) and a portion devoted to legends and stories (the *Aggada*). The authoritative Babylonian Talmud was compiled in the 6th century.

Tao-te-ching (The Way and Its Power)   The basic text of the Chinese philosophy and religion known as Taoism. It is made up of 81 short chapters or poems that describe a way of life marked by quiet effortlessness and freedom from desire. This state is thought to be achieved by following the creative, spontaneous life force of the universe, called the Tao. The book is attributed to Lao-tzu, but it was probably a compilation by a number of writers over a long period of time.

Upanishads   The basis of Hindu religion and philosophy that form the final portion of the *Veda*.

The 112 Upanishads describe the relationship of the *Brahman,* or universal soul, to the *atman,* or individual soul; they also provide information about Vedic sacrifice and yoga. The original texts of the Upanishads come from various sources and were written beginning c. 900 B.C.

Veda   The sacred scripture of Hinduism. Four Vedas make up the *Samhita,* a collection of prayers and hymns that are considered to be revelations of eternal truth written by seer-poets inspired by the gods. The *Rig-Veda,* the *Sama-Veda,* and the *Yajur-Veda* are books of hymns; the *Atharva-Veda* compiles magic spells. These writings maintain that the *Brahman,* or Absolute Self,

underlies all reality and can be known by invoking gods through the use of hymns or mantras. The Vedic texts were compiled between c. 1000 B.C. and c. 500 B.C., making them the oldest known group of religious writings.

A Closer Look

The Twelve Apostles

The twelve men who were chosen to be the missionaries of Christ's word were Peter, Andrew, James (the Greater), John, Thomas, James (the Less), Jude (or Thaddaeus), Philip, Bartholomew, Matthew, Simon, and Judas Iscariot (who was replaced by Mathias). St. Paul is also considered an apostle.

ROMAN CATHOLIC PATRON SAINTS

Protector of	Saint(s)	Protector of	Saint(s)
Accountants	Matthew	Cripples	Giles
Actors	Genesius	Dancers	Vitus
Air travelers	Joseph of Cupertino	Deaf	Francis de Sales
Altar boys	John Berchmans	Dentists	Apollonia
Architects	Barbara	Desperate situations	Jude
Art	Catherine of Bologna	Domestic animals	Antony
Artists	Luke	Dying	Joseph
Astronomers	Dominic	Ecologists	Francis of Assisi
Athletes	Sebastian	Editors	John Bosco
Authors	Francis de Sales	Emigrants	Frances Xavier Cabrini
Bakers	Elizabeth of Hungary	Eyes	Lucy and Odilia
Bankers	Matthew	Falsely accused	Raymund Nonnatus
Barren women	Antony of Padua	Farmers	Isidore the Farmer
Beggars	Alexius	Fathers	Joseph
	Giles	Finders of lost objects	Anthony
Blind	Raphael	Firefighters	Florian
Bookbinders	Peter Celestine	Fire prevention	Catherine of Siena
Bookkeepers	Matthew	Fishermen	Andrew
Booksellers	John of God		Peter
Bowels	Erasmus	Foundlings	Holy Innocents
Boy Scouts	George	France	Denis
Bricklayers	Stephen	Funeral directors	Joseph of Arimathea
Brides	Nicholas of Myra	Gardeners	Adelard
Broadcasters	Archangel Gabriel	Girls	Agnes
Builders	Vincent Ferrer	Glassworkers	Luke
Cab drivers	Fiacre	Gravediggers	Antony the Abbot
Cancer victims	Peregrine Laziosi	Grocers	Michael
Carpenters	Joseph	Hairdressers	Martin de Porres
Charitable societies	Vincent de Paul	Heart patients	John of God
Childbirth	Gerard Majella	Hopeless cases	Jude
Children	Nicholas of Myra	Hospitals	Camillus de Lellis
Church	Joseph		John of God
Comedians	Vitus	Hotel keepers	Amand
Cooks	Martha	Hungary	Stephen

Protector of	Saint(s)	Protector of	Saint(s)
Invalids	Roch	Printers	Augustine
Ireland	Patrick		Genesius
Jewelers	Eligius		John of God
Journalists	Francis de Sales	Prisoners	Dismas
Laborers	Isidore	Radio workers	Gabriel
Lawyers	Thomas More	Rheumatism	James the Greater
	Yves	Sailors	Brendan
Learning	Ambrose		Erasmus
Librarians	Jerome	Scholars	Brigid
Lost articles	Antony of Padua	Scientists	Albert the Great
Lovers	Valentine	Sculptors	Claude
Mariners	Nicholas of Tolentine	Secretaries	Genesius
Married women	Monica	Servants	Martha
Mentally ill	Dympna	Sick	John of God
Messengers	Gabriel		Camillus de Lellis
Midwives	Raymund Nonnatus	Skaters	Lidwina
Missions	Francis Xavier	Skiers	Bernard
	Thérèse of Lisieux	Social justice	Joseph
	Leonard of Port Maurice	Social workers	Louise de Marillac
Mothers	Monica	Soldiers	George
Musicians	Cecelia		Martin of Tours
	Gregory		Michael the Archangel
Nurses	Agatha	Students	Catherine of Alexandria
	Camillus de Lellis		Thomas Aquinas
	John of God	Surgeons	Cosmas and Damian
Orators	John Chrysostom		Luke
Orphans	Jerome Emiliani	Tax collectors	Matthew
Painters	Luke	Teachers	Gregory
Pawnbrokers	Nicholas of Myra		John Baptist de la Salle
Philosophers	Catherine of Alexandria	Television	Clare of Assisi
	Justin	Theologians	Alphonsus Liguori
Physicians	Cosmas and Damian		Augustine
	Luke	Throat	Blaise
Plasterers	Bartholomew	Travelers	Christopher
Poets	David	Vintners	Amand
Police officers	Michael		Urban
Poor	Antony of Padua		Vincent
Postal workers	Gabriel	Vocations	Alphonsus
Preachers	Catherine of Alexandria	Widows	Paula
		Women in labor	Anne
	John Chrysostom	Writers	Francis de Sales
Pregnant women	Gerard Majella	Youth	Aloysius Gonzaga
Priests	John Vianney		

THE ROMAN CATHOLIC POPES

The religious head of the Roman Catholic Church is known as the pope or the bishop of Rome. He is elected by the College of Cardinals, who as a group rank next to the pope in ecclesiastical authority. New popes are elected upon the death or retirement of a current pope. To be elected, a new pope must be named on two-thirds of the ballots cast, and each member of the College of Cardinals must vote. Once elected, a pope must be asked by the dean of cardinals if he accepts the post. If he does, he is then asked to choose a name. The custom of a pope changing his name upon election originated shortly before the year 1000.

The following table includes all the popes of the Roman Catholic Church, beginning with St. Peter the Apostle, who is traditionally considered to be the first pope because of his appointment by Jesus and his role in organizing the church. Also included are the so-called antipopes, those who were elected or claimed to be pope at various times during church history but whose positions were later invalidated; their names appear in brackets. The table gives the names of the popes, the years of their papacies, and the original names of those who changed their names upon election. Alternative spellings of names are given in parentheses.

ROMAN CATHOLIC POPES

Pope	Reign	Original Name
St. Peter the Apostle	died c. 64	Symeon (Simon)
St. Linus	c. 66–c. 78	
St. Anacletus (Cletus)	c. 79–c. 91	
St. Clement I	c. 91–c. 100	
St. Evaristus	c. 100–c. 109	
St. Alexander I	c. 109–c. 116	
St. Sixtus I	c. 116–c. 125	
St. Telesphorus	c. 125–c. 136	
St. Hyginus	c. 136–c. 142	
St. Pius I	c. 142–c. 155	
St. Anicetus	c. 155–c. 166	
St. Soter	c. 166–c. 174	
St. Eleutherius (Eleutherus)	c. 174–189	
St. Victor I	189–198	
St. Zephyrinus	198–217	
St. Callistus I (Calixtus)	217–222	
[St. Hippolytus]	217–235	
St. Urban I	222–230	
St. Pontianus (Pontian)	July 21, 230–September 29, 235	
St. Anterus	November 21, 235–January 3, 236	
St. Fabian	January 10, 236–January 20, 250	
St. Cornelius	March 251–June 253	
[Novatian]	March 251–c. 258	
St. Lucius I	June 25, 253–March 5, 254	
St. Stephen I	May 12, 254–August 2, 257	
St. Sixtus II	August 30, 257–August 6, 258	
St. Dionysius	July 22, 260–December 26, 268	
St. Felix I	January 3, 269–December 30, 274	
St. Eutychian	January 4, 275–December 7, 283	
St. Gaius (Caius)	December 17, 283–April 22, 296	
St. Marcellinus	June 30, 296–c. 304	
St. Marcellus I	November/December 306–January 16, 308	
St. Eusebius	April 18, 310–October 21, 310	
St. Miltiades (Melchiades)	July 2, 311–January 11, 314	
St. Silvester I	January 31, 314–December 31, 335	
St. Mark	January 18, 336–October 7, 336	
St. Julius I	February 6, 337–April 12, 352	
Liberius	May 17, 352–September 24, 366	
[Felix II]	c. 355–November 22, 365	
St. Damasus I	October 1, 366–December 11, 384	

Pope	Reign	Original Name
[Ursinus]	September 366–November 367	
St. Siricius	December 384–November 26, 399	
St. Anastasius I	November 27, 399–December 19, 401	
St. Innocent I	December 22, 401–March 12, 417	
St. Zosimus	March 18, 417–December 26, 418	
St. Boniface I	December 28, 418–September 4, 422	
[Eulalius]	December 27, 418–April 3, 419	
St. Celestine I	September 10, 422–July 27, 432	
St. Sixtus III	July 31, 432–August 19, 440	
St. Leo I	August/September 440–November 10, 461	
St. Hilary (Hilarus)	November 19, 461–February 29, 468	
St. Simplicius	March 3, 468–March 10, 483	
St. Felix III (II)	March 13, 483–March 1, 492	
St. Gelasius I	March 1, 492–November 21, 496	
Anastasius II	November 24, 496–November 19, 498	
St. Symmachus	November 22, 498–July 19, 514	
[Lawrence]	November 22, 498–February 499; 501–506	
St. Hormisdas	July 20, 514–August 6, 523	
St. John I	August 13, 523–May 18, 526	
St. Felix IV (III)	July 12, 526–September 22, 530	
Boniface II	September 22, 530–October 17, 532	
[Dioscorus]	September 22, 530–October 14, 530	
John II	January 2, 533–May 8, 535	Mercury
St. Agapitus I	May 13, 535–April 22, 536	
St. Silverius	June 8, 536–November 11, 537	
Vigilius	c. 538–June 7, 555	
Pelagius I	April 16, 556–March 3, 561	
John III	July 17, 561–July 13, 574	Catelinus
Benedict I	June 2, 575–July 30, 579	
Pelagius II	November 26, 579–February 7, 590	
St. Gregory I	September 3, 590–March 12, 604	
Sabinian	September 13, 604–February 22, 606	
Boniface III	February 19, 607–November 12, 607	
St. Boniface IV	September 15, 608–May 8, 615	
St. Deusdedit I	October 19, 615–November 8, 618	
Boniface V	December 23, 619–October 25, 625	
Honorius I	October 27, 625–October 12, 638	
Severinus	May 28, 640–August 2, 640	
John IV	December 24, 640–October 12, 642	
Theodore I	November 24, 642–May 14, 649	
St. Martin I	July 5, 649–June 17, 653	
St. Eugene I	August 10, 654–June 2, 657	
St. Vitalian	July 30, 657–January 27, 672	
Deusdedit III (Adeodatus II)	April 11, 672–June 17, 676	
Donus	November 2, 676–April 11, 678	
St. Agatho	June 27, 678–January 10, 681	
St. Leo II	August 17, 682–July 3, 683	
St. Benedict II	June 26, 684–May 8, 685	
John V	July 23, 685–August 2, 686	

Religions

continues

Continued

Pope	Reign	Original Name
Conon	October 21, 686–September 21, 687	
[Theodore]	687	
[Paschal]	687	
St. Sergius I	December 15, 687–September 9, 701	
John VI	October 30, 701–January 11, 705	
John VII	March 1, 705–October 18, 707	
Sisinnius	January 15, 708–February 4, 708	
Constantine	March 25, 708–April 9, 715	
St. Gregory II	May 19, 715–February 11, 731	
St. Gregory III	March 18, 731–November 28, 741	
St. Zachary (St. Zacharius)	December 3, 741–March 15, 752	
Stephen	March 22 or 23, 752–March 25 or 26, 752	
Stephen II (III)	March 26, 752–April 26, 757	
St. Paul I	May 29, 757–June 28, 767	
[Constantine]	July 5, 767–August 6, 768	
[Philip]	July 31, 768	
Stephen III (IV)	August 7, 768–January 24, 772	
Adrian I (Hadrian I)	February 1, 772–December 25, 795	
St. Leo III	December 26, 795–June 12, 816	
Stephen IV (V)	June 22, 816–January 24, 817	
St. Paschal I	January 24, 817–February 11, 824	
Eugene II	February 824–August 827	
Valentine	August 827–September 827	
Gregory IV	September 827–January 25, 844	
[John]	January 844	
Sergius II	January 844–January 27, 847	
St. Leo IV	April 10, 847–July 17, 855	
Benedict III	September 29, 855–April 17, 858	
[Anastasius (Bibliothecarius)]	August 855–September 855	
St. Nicholas I	April 24, 858–November 13, 867	
Adrian II (Hadrian II)	December 14, 867–November or December 872	
John VIII	December 14, 872–December 16, 882	
Marinus I	December 16, 882–May 15, 884	
St. Adrian III (St. Hadrian III)	May 17, 884–September 885	
Stephen V (VI)	September 885–September 14, 891	
Formosus	October 6, 891–April 4, 896	
Boniface VI	April 896	
Stephen VI (VII)	May 896–August 897	
Romanus	August 897–November 897	
Theodore II	November 897	
John IX	January 898–January 900	
Benedict IV	May/June 900–August 903	
Leo V	August 903–September 903	
[Christopher]	September 903–January 904	
Sergius III	January 29, 904–April 14, 911	
Anastasius III	c. June 911–c. August 913	
Lando	c. August 913–c. March 914	
John X	March 914–May 928	

Pope	Reign	Original Name
Leo VI	May 928–December 928	
Stephen VII (VIII)	December 928–February 931	
John XI	February or March 931–December 935 or January 936	
Leo VII	January 3, 936–July 13, 939	
Stephen VIII (IX)	July 14, 939–October 942	
Marinus II	October 30, 942–May 946	
Agapetus (Agapitus) II	May 10, 946–December 955	
John XII	December 16, 955–May 14, 964	Octavian
Leo VIII	December 4, 963–March 1, 965	
Benedict V	May 22, 964–June 23, 964	
John XIII	October 1, 965–September 6, 972	
Benedict VI	January 19, 973–July 974	
[Boniface VII]	June 974–July 974	Franco
	August 984–July 20, 985	
Benedict VII	October 974–July 10, 983	
John XIV	December 983–August 20, 984	Peter Canepanova
John XV	August 985–March 996	
Gregory V	May 3, 996–February 18, 999	Bruno
[John XVI]	February 997–May 998	John Philagathos
Silvester II	April 2, 999–May 12, 1003	Gerbert
John XVII	May 16, 1003–November 6, 1003	John Sicco
John XVIII	December 25, 1003–July 1009	John Fasanus
Sergius IV	July 31, 1009–May 12, 1012	Peter
Benedict VIII	May 17, 1012–April 9, 1024	Theophylact
[Gregory]	1012	
John XIX	April 19, 1024–October 20, 1032	Romanus
Benedict IX	October 21, 1032–September 1044	Theophylact
	March 10, 1045–May 1, 1045	
	November 8, 1047–July 16, 1048	
Silvester III	January 20, 1045–March 10, 1045	John of Sabina
Gregory VI	May 1, 1045–December 20, 1046	John Gratian
Clement II	December 24, 1046–October 9, 1047	Suidger
Damasus II	July 17, 1048–August 9, 1048	Poppo
St. Leo IX	February 12, 1049–April 19, 1054	Bruno
Victor II	April 13, 1055–July 28, 1057	Gebhard
Stephen IX (X)	August 2, 1057–March 29, 1058	Frederick of Lorraine
[Benedict X]	April 5, 1058–January 24, 1059	John Mincius
Nicholas II	December 6, 1058–July 19 or 26, 1061	Gerard
Alexander II	September 30, 1061–April 21, 1073	Anselm
[Honorius II]	October 28, 1061–May 31, 1064	Peter Cadalus
St. Gregory VII	April 22, 1073–May 25, 1085	Hildebrand
[Clement III]	June 25, 1080	Guibert
	March 24, 1084–September 8, 1100	
Victor III	May 24, 1086	Daufer (Daufari)
	May 9, 1087–September 16, 1087	
Urban II	March 12, 1088–July 29, 1099	Odo (Eudes)
Paschal II	August 13, 1099–January 21, 1118	Rainerius
[Theodoric]	September 1100–January 1101	
[Albert (Adalbert)]	1101	

Continued

Pope	Reign	Original Name
[Silvester IV]	November 18, 1105–April 12, 1111	Maginulf
Gelasius II	January 24, 1118–January 29, 1119	John of Gaeta
[Gregory VIII]	March 8, 1118–April 1121	Maurice Burdinus
Calistus II	February 2, 1119–December 14, 1124	Guido
Honorius II	December 21, 1124–February 13, 1130	Lamberto of Ostia
[Celestine II]	December 15–16, 1124	Teobaldo Boccapecci
Innocent II	February 14, 1130–September 24, 1143	Gregorio Papareschi
[Anacletus II]	February 14, 1130–January 25, 1138	Pietro Pierleoni
[Victor IV]	March 1138–May 29, 1138	Gregorio Conti
Celestine II	September 26, 1143–May 8, 1144	Guido of Citta di Castello
Lucius II	March 12, 1144–February 15, 1145	Gherardo Caccianemicic
Eugene III	February 15, 1145–July 8, 1153	Bernardo Pignatelli
Anastasius IV	July 8, 1153–December 3, 1154	Corrado
Adrian IV (Hadrian IV)	December 4, 1154–September 1, 1159	Nicholas Breakspear
Alexander III	September 7, 1159–August 30, 1181	Orlando (Roland) Bandinelli
[Victor IV]	September 7, 1159–April 20, 1164	Ottaviano
[Paschal III]	April 22, 1164–September 20, 1168	Guido of Crema
[Calistus III]	September 1168–August 29, 1178	Giovanni
[Innocent III]	September 29, 1179–January 1180	Lando
Luicius III	September 1, 1181–November 25, 1185	Ubaldo Allucingoli
Urban III	October 25, 1185–October 20, 1187	Umberto Crivelli
Gregory VIII	October 21, 1187–December 17, 1187	Alberto de Morra
Clement III	December 19, 1187–March 1191	Paolo Scolari
Celestine III	March/April 1191–January 8, 1198	Giacinto Bobo
Innocent III	January 8, 1198–July 16, 1216	Lotario
Honorius III	July 18, 1216–March 18, 1227	Cencio Savelli
Gregory IX	March 19, 1227–August 22, 1241	Ugo (Ugolino)
Celestine IV	October 25, 1241–November 10, 1241	Goffredo da Castiglione
Innocent IV	June 25, 1243–December 7, 1254	Sinibaldo Fieschi
Alexander IV	December 12, 1254–May 25, 1261	Rinaldo, Count of Segni
Urban IV	August 29, 1261–October 2, 1264	Jacques Pantaléon
Clement IV	February 5, 1265–November 29, 1268	Guy Foulques
Gregory X	September 1, 1271–January 10, 1276	Tedaldo Visconti
Innocent V	January 21, 1276–June 22, 1276	Pierre of Tarentaise
Adrian V (Hadrian V)	July 11, 1276–August 18, 1276	Ottobono Fieschi
John XXI	September 8, 1276–May 20, 1277	Pedro Juliñao (Peter of Spain)
Nicholas III	November 25, 1277–August 22, 1280	Giovanni Gaetano
Martin IV	February 22, 1281–March 28, 1285	Simon de Brie (Brion)
Honorius IV	April 2, 1285–April 3, 1287	Giacomo Savelli
Nicholas IV	February 22, 1288–April 4, 1292	Girolamo Masci
St. Celestine V	July 5, 1294–December 13, 1294	Pietro del Morrone
Boniface VIII	December 24, 1294–October 11, 1303	Benedetto Caetani
Benedict XI	October 22, 1303–July 7, 1304	Niccolò Boccasino
Clement V	June 5, 1305–April 20, 1314	Bertrand de Got
John XXII	August 7, 1316–December 4, 1334	Jacques Duèse
[Nicholas V]	May 12, 1328–July 25, 1330	Pietro Rainalducci
Benedict XII	December 20, 1334–April 25, 1342	Jacques Fournier
Clement VI	May 7, 1342–December 6, 1352	Pierre of Rosier d'Engleton

Pope	Reign	Original Name
Innocent VI	December 18, 1352–September 12, 1362	Étienne Aubert
Urban V	September 28, 1362–December 19, 1370f	Guillaume de Grimoard
Gregory XI	December 30, 1370–March 27, 1378	Pierre Roger de Beaufort
Urban VI	April 8, 1378–October 15, 1389	Bartolomeo Prignano
[Clement VII]	September 20, 1378–September 16, 1394	Robert of Cambrai
Boniface IX	November 2, 1389–October 1, 1404	Pietro Tomacelli
[Benedict XIII]	September 28, 1394–July 26, 1417	Pedro de Luna
Innocent VII	October 17, 1404–November 6, 1406	Cosimo Gentile de'Migliorati
Gregory XII	November 30, 1406–July 4, 1415	Angelo Correr
[Alexander V]	June 26, 1409–May 3, 1410	Pietro Philarghi (Peter of Candia)
[John XXIII]	May 17, 1410–May 29, 1415	Baldassare Cossa
Martin V	November 11, 1417–February 20, 1431	Oddo Colonna
[Clement VIII]	June 10, 1423–July 26, 1429	Gil Sanchez, Muñoz
[Benedict XIV]	November 12, 1425–?	Bernard Garnier
Eugene IV	March 3, 1431–February 23, 1447	Gabriele Condulmaro
[Felix V]	November 5, 1439–April 7, 1449	Amadeus VIII, Duke of Savoy
Nicholas V	March 6, 1447–March 24, 1455	Tommaso Parentucelli
Callistus III	April 8, 1455–August 6, 1458	Alfonso de Boria (Borgia)
Pius II	August 19, 1458–August 15, 1464	Enea Silvo
Piccolomini (Paul II)	August 30, 1464–July 26, 1471	Pietro Barbo
Sixtus IV	August 9, 1471–August 12, 1484	Francesco della Roverre
Innocent VIII	August 29, 1484–July 25, 1492	Giovanni Battista Cibò
Alexander VI	August 11, 1492–August 18, 1503	Rodrigo de Borja y Borja (Borgia)
Pius III	September 22, 1503–October 18, 1503	Francesco Todeschini
Julius II	November 1, 1503–February 21, 1513	Giuliano dell Rovere
Leo X	March 11, 1513–December 1, 1521	Giovanni de' Medici
Adrian VI (Hadrian VI)	January 9, 1522–September 14, 1523	Adrian Florensz Dedal
Clement VII	November 19, 1523–September 25, 1534	Giulio de' Medici
Paul III	October 13, 1534–November 10, 1549	Alessandro Farnese
Julius III	February 8, 1550–March 23, 1555	Giovanni Maria Ciocchi del Monte
Marcellus II	April 9, 1555–May 1, 1555	Marcello Cervini
Paul IV	May 23, 1555–August 18, 1559	Giampietro Carafa
Pius IV	December 25, 1559–December 9, 1565	Giovanni Angelo edici
St. Pius V	January 7, 1566–May 1, 1572	Michele Ghislieri
Gregory XIII	May 14, 1572–April 10, 1585	Ugo Boncompagni
Sixtus V	April 24, 1585–August 27, 1590	Felice Peretti
Urban VII	September 15, 1590–September 27, 1590	Giambattista Castagna
Gregory XIV	December 5, 1590–October 16, 1591	Niccolò Sfondrati
Innocent IX	October 29, 1591–December 30, 1591	Giovanni Antonio Achinetti
Clement VIII	January 30, 1592–March 5, 1605	Ippolito Aldobrandini
Leo XI	April 1, 1605–April 27, 1605	Alessandro Ottaviano de' Medici
Paul V	May 16, 1605–January 28, 1621	Camillo Borghese
Gregory XV	February 9, 1621–July 8, 1623	Alessandro Ludovisi
Urban VIII	August 6, 1623–July 29, 1644	Mafeo Barberini
Innocent X	September 15, 1644–January 1, 1655	Giambattista Pamfili
Alexander VII	April 7, 1655–May 22, 1667	Fabio Chigi
Clement IX	June 20, 1667–December 9, 1669	Giulio Rospigliosi
Clement X	April 29, 1670–July 22, 1676	Emilio Altieri
Innocent XI	September 21, 1676–August 12, 1689	Benedetto Odescalchi

Religions

continues

Continued

Pope	Reign	Original Name
Alexander VIII	October 6, 1689–February 1, 1691	Pietro Ottoboni
Innocent XII	July 12, 1691–September 27, 1700	Antonio Pignatelli
Clement XI	November 23, 1700–March 19, 1721	Giovanni Francesco Albani
Innocent XIII	May 8, 1721–March 7, 1724	Michelangelo dei Conti
Benedict XIII	May 27, 1724–February 21, 1730	Pietro Francesco Orsini
Clement XII	July 12, 1730–February 6, 1740	Lorenzo Corsini
Benedict XIV	August 17, 1740–May 3, 1758	Prospero Lorenzo Lambertini
Clement XIII	July 6, 1758–February 2, 1769	Carlo della Torre Rezzonico
Clement XIV	May 18, 1769–September 22, 1774	Lorenzo Ganganelli
Pius VI	February 15, 1775–August 29, 1799	Giovanni Angelo Brachi
Pius VII	March 14, 1800–July 20, 1823	Luigi Barnab à Chiaramonte
Leo XII	September 28, 1823–February 10, 1829	Annibale Sermattei della Genga
Pius VIII	March 31, 1829–November 30, 1830	Francesco Saverio Castiglione
Gregory XVI	February 2, 1831–June 1, 1846	Bartolomeo Albert Cappellari
Pius IX	June 16, 1846–February 7, 1878	Giovanni Maria Mastai-Ferretti
Leo XIII	February 20, 1878–July 20, 1903	Gioacchino Vincenzo Pecci
St. Pius X	August 4, 1903–August 20, 1914	Giuseppe Melchiorre Sarto
Benedict XV	September 3, 1914–January 22, 1922	Giacomo Della Chiesa
Pius XI	February 6, 1922–February 10, 1939	Ambrogio Damiano Archille Ratti
Pius XII	March 2, 1939–October 9, 1958	Eugenio Maria Giuseppe
John XXIII	October 28, 1958–June 3, 1963	Angelo Giuseppe Roncalli
Paul VI	June 21, 1963–August 6, 1978	Giovanni Battista Montini
John Paul I	August 26, 1978–September 28, 1978	Albino Luciani
John Paul II	October 16, 1978–	Karol Wojtyla

MAJOR RELIGIOUS HOLIDAYS IN THE UNITED STATES

January 6	*Feast of the Epiphany* (Christian) marks the arrival of the Three Wise Men who sought the newborn baby Jesus and the Twelfth Night, or end, of the Christmas season.
February 2	*Candlemas* (Christian) celebrates the presentation of the Christ child in the temple and the purification of the Blessed Virgin Mary 40 days after she gave birth to Jesus; mostly observed in Roman Catholic, Orthodox, and Anglican churches.
February or March	*Purim* (Jewish), the Feast of Lots, memorializes Queen Esther's prevention of the annihilation of the Persian Jews; it is a celebratory festival of food, entertainment, and costumes held on the 14th day of the lunar month of Adar or Adar II.
	Shrove Tuesday (Christian), or Mardi Gras, is the last day before Lent; it is celebrated by eating rich foods forbidden during Lent and by carnivals in such cities as New Orleans, Rio de Janeiro, and Nice.
February, March, or April	*Lent* (Christian) is a 40-day period of fasting and penitence in preparation for Easter. It begins on Ash Wednesday in Western churches and on the Monday 41 days before Easter in the Orthodox Church.

March or April	*Passover* (Jewish), or Pesach, commemorates the time when Moses led the Jews out of Egypt; it is celebrated for seven days by Reform and Israeli Jews and for eight days by Orthodox and Conservative Jews, starting on the 14th day of the lunar month Nisan with a meal of remembrance called a seder.

Palm Sunday (Christian) celebrates Jesus' triumphal ride into Jerusalem and the start of Holy Week; it is observed the Sunday before Easter.

Maundy Thursday (Christian), the Thursday before Easter, marks the Last Supper, the Agony in the Garden, and the arrest of Jesus.

Good Friday (Christian), the Friday before Easter, commemorates Jesus' Crucifixion.

Holy Saturday (Christian), the Saturday before Easter, is observed primarily in Roman Catholic, Orthodox Eastern, and Anglican churches.

Easter Sunday (Christian) celebrates the day Jesus Christ rose from the dead.

May or June

Ascension Day (Christian) celebrates Christ's ascent to heaven; it is held 40 days after Easter.

Shavuot (Jewish) celebrates the harvest of grain while also observing the receipt of the Ten Commandments by Israel; it is held for one day by Reform and Israeli Jews or for two days by Orthodox and Conservative Jews, starting the sixth day of the lunar month of Sivan.

Pentecost (Christian), or Whitsunday, marks the descent of the Holy Spirit on the Apostles; it is held 50 days after Easter.

August 15

The Assumption of the Blessed Virgin Mary (Roman Catholic and Orthodox) is the principal feast day in honor of Mary, celebrating her assumption, body and soul, into heaven after her death.

September or October

Rosh Hashanah (Jewish) marks the start of the new year with solemn prayer and the blowing of the shofar, a ram's horn; it is observed for one day by Reform and Israeli Jews or for two days by Orthodox and Conservative Jews, starting the first day of the lunar month of Tishri.

Yom Kippur (Jewish), the Day of Atonement, is a day of fasting and repentance for the previous year's sins; it concludes the 10 days of penitence that began on Rosh Hashanah; it is observed on the 10th day of the lunar month of Tishri.

Sukkoth (Jewish), the Feast of the Tabernacles, is an autumn harvest festival that recalls the wandering of the Jews in the wilderness; it is celebrated for eight days (seven in Israel) starting on the 15th day of the lunar month of Tishri.

Sunday nearest October 31

Reformation Sunday (Protestant) celebrates the day Martin Luther nailed his "95 Theses" to a church door, heralding the start of the Protestant Reformation.

Go to "Major Foreign Holidays" in chapter 1; "Seven Wonders of the Ancient World" in chapter 26

continues

Major Religious Holidays, continued

November 1	*All Saints' Day* (Christian) is the feast day honoring all martyrs and the Virgin Mary; it is celebrated by Roman Catholic, Orthodox, and Anglican churches; it is also known as All Hallow's Day and is preceded by Halloween on October 31.
Sunday nearest November 30	*Advent* (Christian) is the period of repentance through Christmas Eve preparation for the anniversary of the birth of Christ.
December	*Hanukkah* (Jewish), the Festival of Lights, is marked by the lighting of eight candles in a menorah; it commemorates the restoration of traditional worship and the rededication of the temple in Jerusalem after the victory of the Jews over the troops of the Syrian emperor Antiochus; it is held for eight days beginning on the 25th day of the lunar month of Kislev.
December 8	*Feast of the Immaculate Conception* (Roman Catholic) honors the Virgin Mary's state of freedom from original sin from the time of her conception.
December 9	*Feast of the Conception of St. Anne* (Orthodox) celebrates the conception of the Virgin Mary.
December 25	*Christmas Day* (Christian) celebrates the birth of Jesus Christ; in many Western countries, it has become a nonsectarian winter holiday.
_____*	*Eid-al-Fitr* (Islamic) is one of the two main festivals of Islam; this holiday concludes the month of Ramadan and is a day of thanksgiving for the blessings of Ramadan. Large early morning worship services are followed by small private celebrations. It is held on the first day of Shawwal, the tenth month.
_____*	*Eid-al Adha* (Islamic), the Feast of Sacrifice, is the second of the two main festivals of Islam; it follows the day of pilgramage, or Haj; it is traditionally celebrated with a large prayer services and commemorates Abraham's willingness to sacrifice his son Ismael to Allah. Because an animal was substituted for Ismael, animals are sometimes sacrificed and their meat given to the needy. It is held on the tenth day of the twelfth month, Thw al-Hijjah.
_____*	First day of Muharram, the first month, (Islamic) celebrates the hegira of Muhammad to Medina. The beginning of the Islamic year.
_____*	*Ramadan* (Islamic) is a month of fasting to celebrate the revelation of the Koran. It is the ninth month of the Islamic calendar.

* The Islamic calendar works on a lunar cycle; annual holidays thus advance about 10 days a year on the solar calendar. It takes Ramadan, for example, 36 years to move around the entire solar year.

ADDITIONAL SOURCES OF INFORMATION

Cavendish, Richard, ed. *Man, Myth and Magic: The Illustrated Encyclopedia of Mythology, Religion and the Unknown.* Rev. 94 ed. Marshall Cavendish, 1994.

Glasse, Cyril. *The Concise Encyclopedia of Islam.* Harper & Row, 1991.

Holy Days in the United States, History, Theology, Celebration. U.S. Catholic Conference, 1984.

Kelly, J. N. D. *The Oxford Dictionary of Popes.* Oxford University Press, 1989.

Kolatch, Alfred J. *The Jewish Book of Why/the Second Jewish Book of Why.* Jonathan David Publications, 1989.

Martin, Richard P., ed. *Bulfinch's Mythology: The Age of Fable, the Age of Chivalry, Legends of Charlemagne.* HarperCollins, 1991.

Meagher, Paul Kevin, Thomas C. O'Brien, and Sister Consuelo Maria Aherne, eds. *Encyclopedic Dictionary of Religion.* 3 vols. Catholic University Press, 1984.

Marthaler, Beard, ed. *New Catholic Encyclopedia.* 19 vols. Publishers Guild (vols. 1–18) and Jack Heraty and Association (vol. 19), 1967–95. McGraw-Hill, 1967.

Parrinder, Geoffrey. *The Wisdom of the Early Buddhists.* New Directions, 1977.

Parrinder, Geoffrey, ed. *World Religions: From Ancient History to the Present.* Facts On File, 1988.

Powers, Mala. *Follow the Year: A Family Celebration of Christian Holidays.* Harper & Row, 1988.

Suzuki, Shunryu. *Zen Mind, Beginner's Mind.* John Weatherhill, 1986.

Las Vegas, known as "the gambling capital of the country," is also the "city of religion," having more churches, synagogues, and temples per capita than any other U.S. city.

Telushkin, Joseph. *Jewish Literacy: The Most Important Things to Know About the Jewish Religion, Its People, Its History.* William Morrow, 1991.

Walsh, Michael. ed. *Butler's Lives of the Saints.* Concise ed. HarperCollins, 1991.

Religions

Religions

10

PHILOSOPHY

MAJOR WORLD PHILOSOPHERS	310
HOW TO ARGUE LOGICALLY	313
PHILOSOPHICAL MOVEMENTS AND SCHOOLS OF THOUGHT	317
FAMOUS PHILOSOPHICAL QUOTES	319
COMMON PHILOSOPHICAL TERMS	322
MORE THAN JUST PHILOSOPHERS	324
GOD'S EXISTENCE: PROOFS FOR	328
GOD'S EXISTENCE: ARGUMENTS AGAINST	329
ADDITIONAL SOURCES OF INFORMATION	333

MAJOR WORLD PHILOSOPHERS

Abelard, Peter (1079–1142). French philosopher. One of the most influential medieval logicians and theologians. Around 1113, while teaching theology in Paris, Abelard fell in love with his student Heloise, whom he secretly married; he was condemned for heresy a few years later because of his nominalist views. He wrote *Sic et Non.*

Anaxagoras (c. 500–428 B.C.). Greek preSocratic philosopher who is said to have made Athens the center of philosophy and to have been Socrates's teacher; he rejected the four-elements theory of Empedocles and posited instead an infinite number of unique particles of which all objects are composed.

Anaximander (c. 611–547 B.C.). Greek preSocratic thinker who believed the universal substance to be "the boundless" or "the indefinite," rather than something resembling familiar objects. Unlike Thales (his teacher) and Anaximenes, he did not believe that a single element underlies all things.

Anaximenes (6th century B.C.). One of the preSocratics and an associate of Anaximander. He agreed with Thales that one type of substance underlies the diversity of observable things. Anaximenes believed that air was that universal substance and that all things are made of air in different degrees of density.

Anselm, St. (1033–1109). Italian monk and Scholastic theologian who became archbishop of Canterbury. St. Anselm founded Scholasticism, integrated Aristotelian logic into theology, and believed that reason and revelation are compatible. He is most famous for his influential ontological argument for God's existence.

Aquinas, St. Thomas (1225–74). The greatest thinker of the Scholastic School. His ideas, in 1879, were made the official Catholic philosophy. He incorporated Greek ideas into Christianity by showing Aristotle's thought to be compatible with church doctrine. In Aquinas's system, reason and faith (revelation) form two separate but harmonious realms whose truths complement rather than oppose one another. He presented influential philosophical proofs for the existence of God. His works include *Summa Theologica* (1267–1273) and *On Being and Essence.*

Aristotle (384–322 B.C.). Greek philosopher, scientist, logician, and student of many disciplines. Aristotle studied under Plato and became the tutor of Alexander the Great. In 335, Aristotle opened the Lyceum, a major philosophical and scientific school in Athens. He emphasized the observation of nature and analyzed all things in terms of "the four causes." In ethics, he stressed that virtue is a mean between extremes and that a person's highest goal should be the use of his or her intellect. Most of Aristotle's works were lost to Christian civilization from the 5th through the 12th centuries. Among his writings are *Metaphysics, Politics,* and *Rhetoric.*

Augustine of Hippo, St. (354–430). The greatest of the Latin church fathers and possibly the most influential Christian thinker after St. Paul. St. Augustine emphasized a person's need for grace. His *Confessions* and *The City of God* were highly influential.

Averroes (1126–98). Spanish-born Arabian philosopher, lawyer, and physician whose detailed commentaries on Aristotle were influential for over 300 years. He emphasized the compatibility of faith and reason but believed philosophical knowledge to be derived from reason. The church condemned his views.

Avicenna (980–1037). Islamic medieval philosopher born in Persia. His Neoplatonist interpretation of Aristotle greatly influenced medieval philosophers, including St. Thomas Aquinas. Avicenna was also a physician; his writings on medicine were important for nearly 500 years.

Ayer, Alfred Jules (1910–89). British proponent of logical positivism. Maintaining that philosophical arguments have no validity unless they can be verified by empirical means, Ayer proposed linguistic analysis as the essential method of philosophic investigation. His most influential work is *Language, Truth, and Logic* (1936).

Bacon, Sir Francis   (1561–1626). English statesman, essayist, and philosopher. He was one of the great precursors of the tradition of British empiricism and of belief in the importance of scientific method. He emphasized the use of inductive reasoning in the pursuit of knowledge.

Bentham, Jeremy   (1748–1832). English philosopher and lawyer and one of the founders of utilitarianism. Bentham was a highly influential reformer of the British legal, judicial, and prison systems. He is the author of *Introduction to the Principles of Morals and Legislation* (1789).

Berkeley, George   (1685–1753). Irish philosopher and an Anglican bishop; one of the British empiricists. Berkeley held to a "subjective idealism." He believed that everything that exists is dependent on being perceived by a mind. According to this view, material objects are simply collections of sensations or "ideas" in the mind of a person or of God. His works include *Essay Toward a New Theory of Vision* (1709) and *A Treatise Concerning the Principles of Human Knowledge* (1710).

Boethius   (c. 475–535). Roman statesman, philosopher, and translator of Aristotle, whose *Consolation of Philosophy* (written in prison) was widely read throughout the Middle Ages; it showed reason's role in the face of misfortune and was the link between the ancient philosophers and the Scholastics.

Buber, Martin   (1878–1965). German-Israeli philosopher influenced by Jewish mysticism and existentialism, a major force in 20th-century Jewish thought and philosophy of religion. His *I and Thou* (1923) held that God and man can have a direct and mutual "dialogue."

Comte, Auguste   (1798–1857). French founder of positivism and social reformer. Comte put forth a "religion of humanity" that replaced the notion of God with the notion of humankind as a whole. He invented the term *sociology.*

Democritus   (c. 460–370 B.C.). Greek philosopher who proposed a mechanistic theory of the world that required no supernatural forces, only the constant motion of the indestructible atoms of which everything is composed. He held that perception is an unreliable source of knowledge and that knowledge can be obtained through reason only.

Derrida, Jacques   (1930–   ). French philosopher and founder of deconstructionism, which challenges traditional Western concepts of meaning. In the view of deconstructionists, language refers only to language, and all written works may have innumerable meanings independent of the author's intention.

Descartes, René   (1596–1650). French philosopher and scientist, considered the father of modern philosophical inquiry. Descartes tried to extend mathematical method to all knowledge in his search for certainty. Discarding the medieval appeal to authority, he began with "universal doubt," finding that the only thing that could not be doubted was his own thinking. The result was his famous "*Cogito, ergo sum,*" or "I think, therefore I am." His major works are the *Discourse on Method* (1637) and *Meditations on First Philosophy* (1641).

Dewey, John   (1859–1952). Leading American philosopher, psychologist, and educational theorist. Dewey developed the views of Charles S. Peirce (1839–1914) and William James into his own version of pragmatism. He emphasized the importance of inquiry in gaining knowledge and attacked the view that knowledge is passive.

Diderot, Denis   (1713–84). Materialist thinker of the French Enlightenment and originator of the *Encyclopédie* (1751–72).

Diogenes   (c. 400–325 B.C.). Greek founder of cynicism who rejected social conventions and supposedly lived in a tub in defiance of conventional comforts.

Empedocles (c. 495–435 B.C.). Greek pre-Socratic philosopher who believed the universe to consist of four elements: air, fire, water, and earth. Empedocles held that the interaction between love and hate causes the mixing of the elements.

Engels, Friedrich (1820–95). German socialist thinker and historian and the cofounder of Marxism. He was Marx's lifelong collaborator and coauthor of the *Communist Manifesto* (1848) and an originator of the philosophy of dialectical materialism.

Epictetus (c. 50–138). Stoic moral philosopher who established a school of philosophy after being freed as a slave. His *Manual* teaches that only by detaching ourselves from what is not in our power can we attain inward freedom.

Epicurus (341–270 B.C.). Founder of the Epicurean philosophy and a follower of Democritus, the greatest ancient philosopher of atomism. Virtually all of Epicurus's writings are lost.

Foucault, Michel (1926–84). French philosopher and historian of ideas whose major works analyze the origin and growth of social institutions. In *Madness and Civilization* (1961), Foucault explores society's response to mental illness; *Discipline and Punish* (1975) examines the treatment of criminals.

Hegel, Georg Wilhelm Friedrich (1770–1831). German philosopher whose idealistic system of metaphysics was highly influential. It was based on a concept of the world as a single organism developing by its own inner logic through trios of stages called "thesis, antithesis, and synthesis" and gradually coming to embody reason. Hegel held the monarchy to be the highest development of the state. His works include *The Science of Logic* (1812, 1813, 1816) and *Phenomenology of Mind* (1807).

Heidegger, Martin (1889–1976). German philosopher who studied with Husserl. Heidegger's own philosophy, which was influenced by Kierkegaard, emphasized the need to understand "being," especially the unique ways that humans act

in and relate to the world. He wrote *Being and Time* (1927).

Heraclitus (c. 535–475 B.C.). Pre-Socratic philosopher opposed to the idea of a single ultimate reality. Heraclitus believed that all things are in a constant state of change.

Hobbes, Thomas (1588–1679). English materialist and empiricist; one of the founders of modern political philosophy. In *Leviathan* (1651), Hobbes argued that because men are selfish by nature, a powerful absolute ruler is necessary. In a "social contract," men agree to give up many personal liberties and accept such rule.

Hume, David (1711–76). British empiricist whose arguments against the proofs for God's existence are still influential. In his *Treatise of Human Nature* (1739–40), Hume held that moral beliefs have no basis in reason, but are based solely on custom.

Husserl, Edmund (1859–1938). German philosopher who founded the phenomenology movement. He aimed at a completely accurate description of consciousness and conscious experience. His works include *Logical Investigations* (1900–01) and *Ideas Pertaining to a Pure Phenomenology and Phenomenological Philosophy* (1913).

James, William (1842–1910). American philosopher and psychologist, one of the founders of pragmatism, and one of the most influential thinkers of his era. James viewed consciousness as actively shaping reality, defined truth as "the expedient" way of thinking, and held that ideas are tools for guiding our future actions rather than reproductions of our past experiences. His writings include *The Will to Believe* (1897) and *Pragmatism* (1907).

Kant, Immanuel (1724–1804). German philosopher, possibly the most influential of modern times. He synthesized Leibniz's rationalism and Hume's skepticism into his "critical philosophy": in *The Critique of Pure Reason* (1781), Kant wrote that

How to Argue Logically

We like to think that we speak logically all the time, but we are aware that we sometimes use illogical means to persuade others of our point of view. In the heat of an impassioned argument, or when we are afraid our disputant has a stronger case, or when we don't quite have all the facts we'd like to have, we are prone to engage in faulty processes of reasoning, using arguments we hope will appear sound.

Such defective arguments are called *fallacies* by philosophers who, starting with Aristotle, have catalogued and classified these fallacious arguments. There are now over 125 separate fallacies, most with their own impressive-sounding names, many of them in Latin.

Some arguments have easily recognizable defects. For instance, in the *argument ad hominem,* a person's views are criticized because of a logically irrelevant personal defect: "You can't take Smith's advice on the stock market; he's a known philanderer." In the *genetic fallacy,* something is mistakenly reduced to its origins: "We know that emotions are nothing more than physiology; after all, medical research has shown emotions involve the secretion of hormones." Another illogical argument is named for the erroneous thinking a wagering person may fall prey to, the *gambler's fallacy* (also called the *Monte Carlo fallacy*): "I'm betting on heads; it's got to come up since we've just had nine straight tails."

Some fallacies may not be recognized as erroneous reasoning because they are such commonly used forms of argument. For instance, if we say, "I'm sure my cold is due to the weather; I started sneezing right after it went from 60 degrees to 31 degrees in three hours," we are committing the fallacy with the Latin name of *post hoc ergo propter hoc* ("after this, therefore because of this"). Many a political argument exemplifies the fallacy of *arguing in a circle:* "Only wealthy men are capable of leading the country; after all, leadership can be learned only if you have had money to exercise power." Many prejudicial or stereotypical arguments commit the *fallacy of division,* or of applying to the part what may be true of the whole: "North Dakota has wide-open spaces; because Jack's farm is there, it must be quite large." The converse of this is the *fallacy of composition,* where properties of the parts are erroneously attributed to the whole: "Every apple on this tree is rotten; therefore, the tree itself is hopelessly diseased."

It may be a surprise to realize that some widely accepted forms of argument are just as fallacious as the most logically defective reasoning. When we appeal to the beliefs or behavior of the majority to prove the truth of something, we are committing the *fallacy of consensus gentium:* "Imbibing alcohol cannot be bad for people, because all cultures studied have used alcohol." Or consider the person who argues that "Tragedy is the highest form of literature; after all, didn't Aristotle consider it such?" This is a form of the *fallacy of arguing from authority.* There is also the *fallacy of ignoratio elenchus,* which has nothing to do with ignorance; its name means that the point made is irrelevant to the issue at hand, as in the untenable view of a lawyer who says, "Ladies and gentlemen of the jury, you cannot convict my client of manslaughter while driving under the influence; after all, advertisements for alcohol exist everywhere in our culture."

ideas do not conform to the external world, but rather the world can be known only insofar as it conforms to the mind's own structure. In *The Critique of Practical Reason* (1788), Kant claimed that morality requires a belief in God, freedom, and immortality, although these can be proved neither scientifically nor by metaphysics. Finally, in his *Foundations of the Metaphysic of Morals* (1785), he presented the concept of the categorical imperative.

Kierkegaard, Søren (1813–55). Danish philosopher, religious thinker, and extraordinarily influential founder of existentialism. Kierkegaard held that "truth is subjectivity," that religion is an individual matter, and that man's relationship to God requires suffering. He wrote *Either/Or* (1843) and *Fear and Trembling* (1843).

Leibniz, Gottfried Wilhelm (1646–1716). German philosopher, diplomat, and mathematician; one of the great minds of all time. Leibniz was an inventor (with Sir Isaac Newton) of calculus and a forefather of modern mathematical logic. He held that the entire universe is one large system expressing God's plan. His writings include *New Essays on Human Understanding* (1703–04).

Locke, John (1632–1704). Highly influential founder of British empiricism. In his *Essay Concerning Human Understanding* (1690), Locke wrote that all ideas come to mind from experience and that none are innate. He also held that authority derives solely from the consent of the governed, a view that deeply influenced the American Revolution and the writing of the U.S. Constitution. His *Two Treatises on Government* (1690) express his political thought.

Lucretius (c. 99–55 B.C.). Roman Epicurean philosopher and poet. In *De Rerum Natura* (On the Nature of Things), Lucretius depicted the entire world, including the soul, as composed of atoms.

Machiavelli, Niccolò (1469–1527). Italian Renaissance statesman and political writer. In *The Prince* (1513), one of the most influential political books of modern times, Machiavelli argues that any act of a ruler designed to gain and hold power is permissible. The term *Machiavellian* is used to refer to any political tactics that are cunning and power-oriented.

Maimonides (Moses ben Maimon) (1135–1204). Spanish-born medieval Jewish philosopher and thinker. Maimonides tried to synthesize Aristotelian and Judaic thought. His works, such as *Guide for the Perplexed,* had enormous influence on Jewish and Christian thought.

Marcus Aurelius (121–180). Roman emperor from A.D. 161 and a proponent of the Stoic philosophy. His *Meditations* held that death is as natural as birth and that the world is rational and orderly. Although a great humanitarian, Marcus Aurelius persecuted the Christians of his time.

Marx, Karl (1818–83). German revolutionary thinker, social philosopher, and economist. His ideas, formulated with Friedrich Engels, laid the foundation for 19th-century socialism and 20th-century communism. Although Marx was initially influenced by Georg Hegel, he soon rejected Hegel's idealism in favor of materialism. His *Communist Manifesto* (1848) and *Das Kapital*

(1867) are among the most important writings of the last 200 years.

Mill, John Stuart (1806–73). English empiricist philosopher, logician, economist, and social reformer. His *System of Logic* (1843) described the basic rules for all scientific reasoning. As a student of Jeremy Bentham, he elaborated on utilitarian ethics; in *On Liberty* (1859), he presented a plea for the sanctity of individual rights against the power of any government.

Montesquieu, Baron de (Charles-Louis de Secondat) (1689–1755). French political philosopher, influenced by John Locke. In *Spirit of the Laws* (1748), Montesquieu put forth the theory of separation of powers that strongly influenced the writing of the U.S. Constitution.

Moore, G. E. (George Edward) (1873–1958). British philosopher who emphasized the "common sense" view of the reality of material objects. In ethics, Moore held that goodness is a quality known directly by moral intuition and that it is a fallacy to try to define it in terms of anything else.

More, Sir Thomas (1478–1535). A leading Renaissance humanist and statesman; Lord Chancellor of England. More was beheaded for refusing to accept the king as head of the church. Influenced by Greek thinking, he believed in social reform and drew a picture of an ideal peaceful state in his *Utopia* (1516).

Nietzsche, Friedrich Wilhelm (1844–1900). German philosopher, philologist, and poet. As a moralist, he rejected Christian values and championed a "Superman" who would create a new, life-affirming, heroic ethic by his "will to power." His works include *Thus Spake Zarathustra* (1883–85) and *Beyond Good and Evil* (1886).

Parmenides (fl. c. 500 B.C.). The founder of Western metaphysics. This pre-Socratic thinker held that "being" is the basic substance and ultimate reality of which all things are composed and that motion, change, time, difference, and reality are illusions of the senses.

The Greek philosopher Epicurus believed that the only evil in the world was pain.

Pascal, Blaise (1623–62). French philosopher, mathematician, scientist, and theologian. His posthumous *"Pensées"* ("Thoughts") argues that reason is by itself inadequate for man's spiritual needs and cannot bring man to God, who can be known only through mystic understanding.

Plato (c. 428–348 B.C.). Athenian father of Western philosophy and student of Socrates, after whose death he traveled widely. Upon returning to Athens, Plato founded an academy, where he taught until he died. His writings are in the form of dialogues between Socrates and other Athenians. Many of Plato's views are set forth in *The Republic* (c. 370 B.C.), where an ideal state postulates philosopher kings, specially trained at the highest levels of moral and mathematical knowledge. Plato's other works analyzed moral virtues, the nature of knowledge, and the immortality of the soul. His views on cosmology strongly influenced the next 2,000 years of scientific thinking.

Plotinus (205–270). Egyptian-born founder of Neoplatonism, who synthesized the ideas of Plato and other Greek philosophers. Plotinus believed all reality is caused by a series of outpourings (called emanations) from the divine source. Although not himself a Christian, he was a major influence on Christianity.

Pythagoras (c. 582–507 B.C.). Greek philosopher, mathematician, and mystic; founder of a religious brotherhood that believed in the immortality and the transmigration of the soul. Pythagoras may have been the first thinker to assert that numbers constitute the true nature of all things; he also may have coined the term *philosophy.*

Quine, Willard Van Orman (1908–   ). A leading American linguistic philosopher, Quine has explored the connections between language and logic and made important contributions to set theory. Among his best-known works are *Word and Object* (1960) and *Theories and Things* (1981).

Rawls, John (1921–   ). American philosopher whose major work, *A Theory of Justice* (1971), revived interest in political theory. Rawls has attempted to provide a modern philosophical foundation for the idea of the social contract, first developed by John Locke and Jean Jacques Rousseau.

Rousseau, Jean-Jacques (1712–78). Swiss-French thinker, born in Geneva. Rousseau has been enormously influential in political philosophy, educational theory, and the romantic movement. In *The Social Contract* (1762), he viewed governments as being expressions of the people's "general will," or rational people's choice for the common good. Rousseau emphasized a person's natural goodness.

Russell, Bertrand (1872–1970). English philosopher and logician influential as an agnostic and a pacifist. Early work with Alfred North Whitehead gave birth to modern logic; they coauthored *Principia Mathematica* (3 vols., 1910–13). Russell changed his views numerous times but always sought to establish philosophy, especially epistemology, as a science.

Ryle, Gilbert (1900–76). British philosopher who was a leader in linguistic analysis. Ryle's work related grammar and word usage to the principles of logic. His main work, *The Concept of Mind* (1949), challenged Descartes's distinction between mind and body, arguing that the mind is a set of capacities belonging to the body.

Santayana, George (1863–1952). Spanish-born American philosopher and poet; a student of William James. Santayana attempted to reconcile Platonism and materialism, studied how reason works, and found "animal faith," or impulse, to be the basis of reason and belief. Among his works are *The Sense of Beauty* (1896) and *The Life of Reason* (5 vols., 1905–06).

Sartre, Jean-Paul (1905–80). French philosopher, novelist, and dramatist; one of the founders of existentialism. Sartre was a Marxist through much of his life. He held that man is "condemned to be free" and to bear the responsibility of making free choices. His primary philosophical work was *Being and Nothingness* (1943).

Schopenhauer, Arthur   (1788–1860). German post-Kantian philosopher who held that although irrational will is the driving force in human affairs, it is doomed not to be satisfied. He believed that only art and contemplation could offer escape from determinism and pessimism. Schopenhauer strongly influenced Friedrich Nietzsche, Sigmund Freud, Leo Tolstoy, Marcel Proust, and Thomas Mann. He wrote *The World as Will and Representation* (1818).

Scotus, John Duns   (c. 1266–1308). Scottish-born Scholastic philosopher who tried to integrate Aristotelian ideas into Christian theology. Scotus emphasized that all things depend not just on God's intellect but on divine will as well. He wrote *On the First Principle.*

Smith, Adam   (1723–90). Scottish philosopher and economist. The author of *An Inquiry into the Nature and Causes of the Wealth of Nations* (1776), he believed that if government left the marketplace to its own devices, an "invisible hand" would guarantee that the results would benefit the populace. Smith has had enormous influence on economists into the present day.

Socrates   (c. 470–399 B.C.). Athenian philosopher who allegedly wrote down none of his views, supposedly from his belief that writing distorts ideas. His chief student, Plato, is the major source of knowledge about his life. Socrates questioned Athenians about their moral, political, and religious beliefs, as depicted in Plato's dialogues; his questioning technique, called dialectic, has greatly influenced Western philosophy. In 399 B.C., he was brought to trial on charges of corrupting the youth and religious heresy. Sentenced to die, he drank poison.

Spinoza, Benedict (Baruch)   (1623–77). Dutch-born philosopher expelled from the Amsterdam Jewish community for heresy in 1656; he was attacked by Christian theologians 14 years later. In *Ethics Demonstrated in Geometrical Order* (1677), Spinoza presents his views in a mathematical system of deductive reasoning. A proponent of monism, he held—in contrast to Descartes—that mind and body are aspects of a single substance, which he called God or nature.

Thales of Miletus   (c. 636–546 B.C.). Regarded as the first Western philosopher, this pre-Socratic monist thinker is said to have believed that the fundamental principle of all things, or universal substance, is water. All of his writings are lost.

Unamuno, Miguel de   (1864–1936). The major Spanish philosopher of his time. Unamuno criticized philosophic abstractions such as "man" for ignoring concrete men. He held that reason by itself is virtually useless and cannot reveal the basic fact of human immortality. He wrote *The Tragic Sense of Life in Men and Nations* (1913).

Voltaire (François Marie Arouet)   (1694–1778). French philosopher, essayist, and historian; one of the major thinkers of the Enlightenment. A Deist who was anti-Christian, Voltaire widely advocated tolerance of liberal ideas and called for positive social action. His novel *Candide* (1759) is a parody of the optimism of Gottfried Leibniz.

Whitehead, Alfred North   (1861–1947). British philosopher and mathematician who worked with Bertrand Russell. Whitehead tried to integrate 20th-century physics into a metaphysics of nature.

William of Ockham (Occam)   (c. 1285–1349). Franciscan monk and important English theologian and philosopher. In his nominalism, he opposed much of the thought of St. Thomas Aquinas and of medieval Aristotelianism; he also rejected the pope's power in the secular realm.

Wittgenstein, Ludwig   (1889–1951). Austrian-born philosopher who spent the last 20 years of his life in England. Wittgenstein was one of the most influential philosophers of the 20th century, primarily through his emphasis on the importance of the study of language. His *Tractatus Logico-Philosophicus*

(1921) influenced analytic philosophy. His later views emphasized that philosophic problems are often caused by linguistic confusions.

Zeno of Elea (c. 490–430 B.C.). Pre-Socratic philosopher and disciple of Parmenides. Zeno argued that motion, change, and plurality are logical absurdities and that only an unchanging being is real. His four arguments against motion (Zeno's paradoxes) attempted to demonstrate logically that the notions of time and motion are erroneous.

Zeno (of Citium) the Stoic (c. 334–262 B.C.). Greek philosopher born in Cyprus; the founder of Stoicism.

PHILOSOPHICAL MOVEMENTS AND SCHOOLS OF THOUGHT

analytical philosophy An influential 20th-century movement whose major proponents include Bertrand Russell, Ludwig Wittgenstein, and such logical positivists as Rudolph Carnap (1891–1970) and Willard Van Orman Quine. This school of thought emphasizes restating philosophical problems in highly structured terms based on modern logic.

anthroposophy The philosophy of Rudolf Steiner (1861–1925), an Austrian-born thinker who held that cultivating man's spiritual development is humanity's most important task. His followers founded a large number of schools worldwide based on his philosophy.

Aristotelianism A system of thought originating with the teachings of Aristotle (4th century B.C.), who held that knowledge originates in experience and observation, from which comes an understanding of the universal. His teachings and writings were influential in the Western world until the fall of Rome, when all but his writings on logic were lost to Christian civilization in Europe. His empiricism was embraced by medieval thinkers, especially St. Thomas Aquinas. Aristotle's works were preserved in Syrian and Arabic cultures and were revived in the West at the end of the 12th century.

British empiricism The empiricism of John Locke, George Berkeley, and David Hume in the 17th and 18th centuries. They shared the axiom that our knowledge of the world derives from experience or sensation rather than from reason. This view was opposed to rationalism, as well as to the Platonic notion of Forms as the source of knowledge.

British idealism (neo-Hegelianism) The philosophy of Georg Hegel as followed in England and Scotland in the mid–19th century. The most prominent members of this school were Thomas Hill Green (1836–82), Bernard Bosanquet (1848–1923), and Francis Herbert Bradley (1846–1924). They were united in their opposition to empiricism and utilitarianism and in their emphasis on mind and spirit as primary.

Cambridge Platonists A group of 17th-century English philosophers and theologians who tried to provide Christian theology with a philosophical defense based on Platonic and Neoplatonic theories. Ralph Cudworth (1617–88) was the most prominent member.

Cartesianism The views of René Descartes as interpreted by 17th-century rationalistic, dualistic, and theistic philosophers. They held that the search for knowledge and certainty can be based on logical analysis and mathematical principles. Nicolas Malebranche (1638–1715) was the most prominent of Descartes's followers.

Cynics A school of Greek philosophers founded in the 4th century B.C. by Diogenes. According to legend, Diogenes walked around night and day with a lighted lantern seeking an honest man but could not find one. The Cynics held that virtue was the only good and that happiness was to be attained only by living in a simple state of nature with as few desires and needs as possible. They advocated moderation, self-discipline, and training of the mind as well as the body.

Cyrenaics A school of philosophy of the 4th century B.C. in Athens, founded by Cyrene, a disciple of Socrates. Cyrenaics believed that only momentary feelings of pleasure or pain can be known; they held that the good life is one that maximizes pleasure derived from satisfying one's bodily desires. Unlike the Epicureans, the Cyrenaics focused on physical sensation and the primacy of personal experience. *See also* **hedonism.**

deism A philosophical viewpoint appearing in England in the 17th and 18th centuries and in France in the 18th century. Deists held that although God created the universe and its laws, He then removed Himself from any ongoing interaction with the material world.

dialectical materialism The philosophy of Karl Marx and many of his followers. It holds that matter is the primary reality and that it obeys the dynamic laws of change. The most fundamental of these laws is that progress occurs through conflict and struggle between opposing forces (thesis and antithesis), such as between different classes and between capitalism and communism. Essentially deterministic, this philosophy maintains that individuals have no influence over the course of history. *See also* **Marxism.**

Eleatics A school of pre-Socratic philosophers (5th century B.C.) from Elea in southern Italy, of whom Parmenides and Zeno of Elea are the best known. The Eleatics denied the reality of what is known to the senses, holding that the ultimate reality is an undifferentiated and unchanging "being."

Encyclopedists A group of 18th-century French writers who combined to produce an encyclopedia of philosophy, art, and science (1751–65), edited by Denis Diderot and Jean d'Alembert (1717–83). The work was skeptical about religion and advocated liberal, democratic political views. At the time, it was the largest compendium of human knowledge that had ever been produced.

Enlightenment (Age of Reason) A mainly 18th-century European philosophical movement. Its thinkers strove to make reason the ruler of human life; they believed that all people could

gain knowledge and liberation. They sought the perfection of human society through applied reason. Rejecting conventional religious and secular authority, this movement substituted tolerance, humanism, and positive social action by the state. Major Enlightenment figures include Voltaire, Jean-Jacques Rousseau, Denis Diderot, and Baron de Montesquieu in France; David Hume in England; and Gotthold Ephraim Lessing (1729–81) and Johann Gottfried von Herder (1744–1803) in Germany. *See also* **philosophes.**

Epicureanism An ethical doctrine established in Greece in the 3rd century B.C. Based on the teachings of Epicurus, it maintained that pleasure is the highest good and that pleasure can only be attained through a life of virtuous conduct. Epicureans sought mental pleasures over bodily ones.

existentialism A philosophy of the 19th and 20th centuries. The dogma holds that because there are no universal values, a person's essence is not predetermined but is based only on free choice; a person is in a state of anxiety because of his or her realization of free will; and there is no objective truth. Major existentialists were Søren Kierkegaard, Friedrich Nietzsche, Jean-Paul Sartre, Martin Heidegger, Karl Jaspers (1883–1969), and the religious existentialists Martin Buber and Gabriel Marcel (1889–1973).

hedonism The ethical doctrine holding that pleasure is the highest or the only good in life, and that a person should strive for pleasure and the avoidance of pain. In ancient Greece, the Cyrenaics emphasized physical sensation, while the Epicureans stressed the importance of simple living and virtuous moral conduct. The utilitarians in the 19th century were also proponents of hedonism.

Hegelianism (neo-Hegelianism) A school of thought associated with Georg Hegel in the 19th and early 20th centuries, especially in England, America, France, and Italy. Francis Herbert Bradley (1846–1924), Josiah Royce (1855–1916), and Benedetto Croce (1866–1952) were prominent

Famous Philosophical Quotes

A Closer Look

Aristotle	"Man is by nature a political animal."
Sir Francis Bacon	"Knowledge is power."
Jeremy Bentham	"The greatest happiness of the greatest number is the foundation of morals and legislation."
Confucius	"Hold faithfulness and sincerity as first principles."
René Descartes	*"Cogito, ergo sum"* (Latin for "I think, therefore I am").
Ralph Waldo Emerson	"Nature is a mutual cloud, which is always and never the same."
Friedrich Engels	"The state is not 'abolished,' it withers away."
Georg Hegel	"What experience and history teach us is this—that people and governments have never learned anything from history, or acted on principles deduced from it."
Thomas Hobbes	"The life of man [in a state of nature is], solitary, poor, nasty, brutish, and short."
Immanuel Kant	"Happiness is not an ideal of reason but of imagination."
John Locke	"No man's knowledge here can go beyond his experience."
Niccolò Machiavelli	"God is not willing to do everything, and thus take away our free will and that share of glory which belongs to us."
Karl Marx	"The proletarians have nothing to lose [in this revolution] but their chains. They have a world to win. Workers of the world, unite!"
	"Religion is the opium of the people."
	"The class struggle necessarily leads to the dictatorship of the proletariat."
John Stuart Mill	"Liberty consists in doing what one desires."
Friedrich Nietzsche	"I teach you the Superman. Man is something to be surpassed."
Thomas Paine	"Suspicion is the companion of mean souls, and the bane of all good society."
Plato	"The life which is unexamined is not worth living."
Jean-Jacques Rousseau	"Man was born free, and everywhere he is in chains."
Bertrand Russell	"It is undesirable to believe a proposition when there is no ground whatever for supposing it true."
Seneca	"Even while they teach, men learn."
Socrates	"There is only one good, knowledge, and one evil, ignorance."
Voltaire	"If God did not exist, it would be necessary to invent Him."

Philosophy

members; they emphasized the importance of spirit and the belief that ideas and moral ideals are fundamental.

intuitionism   Any philosophy holding that intuition is the basis of knowledge or of philosophy. French philosopher Henri Bergson (1859–1941) was a prominent advocate. In particular, intuitionism refers to a British school of thought that maintains that all ethical knowledge rests on moral intuition.

linguistic philosophy (linguistic analysis)   The 20th-century school of thought whose key tenet is that philosophical problems are best approached by asking questions about the use of words and by

analyzing how language works in specific social contexts.

logical positivism   A 20th-century school founded in the 1920s in Europe that was extremely influential for American and English philosophers. It attempted to introduce mathematical and scientific methodology into philosophy. It rejected metaphysical speculation in favor of a vigorous analysis of experience and language, without which understanding is not possible. The school advocated the principle of verifiability, according to which all statements that could not be validated empirically were meaningless. Logical positivism held that this principle showed that all of metaphysics, religion, and ethics was incapable of being proved either true or false. *See also* **Vienna Circle.**

Manichaeanism A religious-philosophical doctrine that originated in Persia in the 3rd century A.D. and reappeared throughout the next 1,300 years. It holds that the entire universe, especially human life, is a struggle between the opposing forces of good and evil (light and darkness).

Bertrand Russell said, "The point of philosophy is to start with something so simple as not to seem worth stating, and to end with something so paradoxical that no one will believe it."

Marxism The political, economic, and philosophical theories developed by Karl Marx and Friedrich Engels in the second half of the 19th century. The philosophical side of Marxism is called dialectical materialism; it emphasizes economic determinism. *See also* **dialectical materialism.**

Miletian School The pre-Socratics from Miletus in Greece—Thales and his two best-known pupils, Anaximander and Anaximenes.

Neoplatonism A school of philosophy that flourished from the 2nd to the 5th centuries A.D. It was founded by Plotinus and was influential for the next thousand years.

nihilism An extremist movement in 19th-century Russia. *Ethical nihilism* is the theory that morality cannot be justified in any way and that all moral values are, therefore, meaningless and irrational. *Political nihilism* is the social philosophy that society and its social, political, and economic popularized institutions are so corrupt that their complete destruction is desirable. Nihilists may, therefore, advocate violence and even terrorism in the name of overthrowing what they believe to be a corrupt social order. The term *nihilism* was first popularized in *Fathers and Sons* (1862) by the Russian novelist Turgenev.

Ordinary Language Philosophy The 20th-century school advocating that we can best understand and resolve philosophic problems by analyzing how people other than philosophers ordinarily use language and the presuppositions underlying such use; the school holds that everyday language is adequate for philosophy. Ludwig Wittgenstein, Gilbert Ryle, and John L. Austin (1911–60) were the most influential members of this school.

personalism A term applied to any philosophy that makes personality (whether of people, God, or spirit) the supreme value or the source of reality. Personalism as a movement flourished in England and America in the 19th and 20th centuries. Personalists are usually idealists.

phenomenology A 20th-century school founded by Edmund Husserl and an important influence on existentialism. This school developed its own philosophical "method" of using intuition for describing consciousness and experience. Phenomenologists claim that this method can be used to study the inherent qualities of phenomena as they appear to the mind. They attempt to classify and describe all phenomena without resorting to universal concepts or preconceived notions of reality. The focus is on the phenomena, not on how it is perceived.

philosophes Term applied to 18th-century French Enlightenment thinkers such as Jean-Jacques Rousseau, Denis Diderot, and Voltaire.

Platonism Thoughts and writings developed in the 4th century B.C. in Athens by Plato, the greatest student of Socrates. Platonism's chief tenet is that the ultimate reality consists of unchanging, absolute, eternal entities called Ideas or Forms; all earthly physical objects are not truly real but merely partake in the Forms.

pragmatism An American philosophy developed in the 19th century by Charles Sanders Peirce (1839–1914) and William James and elaborated on in the 20th century by John Dewey. Its central precepts are that thinking is primarily a guide to action and that the truth of a concept or idea could be determined only by testing it against experimental results and practical consequences.

Pre-Socratics Name given to all Greek "theorists of nature" or philosophers who lived before Socrates. Major pre-Socratics include Anaximander, Pythagoras, and Thales.

Pythagoreans Followers of Pythagoras. The group flourished until about 400 B.C. and were influential in philosophy, religion, mathematics, and science. They strongly influenced the thinking of Plato and Neoplatonists.

Scholasticism A movement (c. 9th century–17th century), especially at the medieval universities, that attempted to reconcile Christian dogma with the empiricism of Aristotle. Its adherents used highly analytical logical and linguistic methods of argumentation, especially with respect to the problem of universals. Aquinas, the movement's greatest thinker, demonstrated that faith and reason were separate but compatible ideas; his teachings were accepted by the Catholic church.

17th-century rationalists A broad term referring to the rationalism shared by René Descartes, Gottfried Leibniz, and Benedict Spinoza. It held that reason and deduction could provide knowledge of the world independent of experience.

Sophists Wandering teachers in the 4th and 5th centuries B.C. in ancient Greece who taught any subjects that their paying students wished to learn, from grammar to public speaking. They were strongly ridiculed by Plato, who held that they were less interested in truth than in pleasing their students for a fee.

Stoicism A Greek school founded by Zeno in the 3rd century B.C. Stoics held that people should submit to natural law and that a person's chief duty is to conform to his destiny. They also believed the soul to be another form of matter, and thus not immortal. Stoics rejected material comfort and advocated freedom from earthly passions and desires. They viewed reality as materialistic and

defined the organizing principle of the universe as force, or God.

Thomism The philosophical and theological system developed by St. Thomas Aquinas in the 13th century. Specifically, it refers to Aquinas's synthesis of philosophy and theology, in which reason seeks knowledge through experiment and observation, while faith seeks understanding through divine revelation. The two are thus never in conflict; rather, both come from God. Thomism is accepted as a vital doctrine in the Roman Catholic Church.

transcendentalism A 19th-century movement developed in New England and expounded by Ralph Waldo Emerson (1803–82) and Henry David Thoreau (1817–62). It maintains that beyond our material world of experience is an ideal spiritual reality that can be grasped intuitively. It advocates a reliance on personal conscience, based on perception and experience, over the dictates of external authority or moral conventions.

utilitarianism A theory of morality formulated in the 19th century and holding that all actions should be judged for rightness or wrongness in terms of their consequences; thus, the amount of pleasure people derive from those consequences becomes the measure of moral goodness. Jeremy Bentham believed that happiness was the sole consequence by which actions should be judged. John Stuart Mill equated morality with the attainment of the maximum good for the greatest number of people. *See also* **principle of utility** under "Common Philosophical Terms."

Vienna Circle A major school of logical positivism founded by Moritz Schlick (1882–1936) in the 1920s. It was known for its hostility to metaphysics and theology and for its belief that physics is the model for all knowledge of the world. Other leading members of the school were Rudolph Carnap (1891–1970) and Otto Neurath (1882–1945).

"Major World Philosophers" and "Common Philosophical Terms" in this chapter
Go to

Young Hegelians   A group of thinkers in Germany in the first half of the 19th century whose views strongly influenced Karl Marx. They were followers of Georg Hegel who believed that the political conditions under which they lived were irrational. They held that the goal of philosophy should be to promote a revolution of ideas and critical thinking about the world. Ludwig Feuerbach (1804–72) was the most important of the Young Hegelians.

COMMON PHILOSOPHICAL TERMS

Entries in this glossary include basic terms and concepts used by philosophers, branches of philosophy, and "isms" that describe various philosophical attitudes, beliefs, doctrines, positions, precepts, theories, and viewpoints.

absolutism   The doctrine that there is one explanation of all reality—the absolute—that is unchanging and objectively true. Absolutists (such as G. W. F. Hegel) hold that this absolute, such as God or mind, is eternal and that in it all seeming differences are reconciled.

aesthetics (esthetics)   The philosophical study of art, or of beauty in general. It attempts to systematically answer such questions as, What is beauty? How do we evaluate works of art? Are aesthetic judgments objective or subjective? How does art embody truth and convey knowledge? How does beauty in art relate to beauty in nature?

agnosticism   The belief that it is impossible to know whether God exists, or to have any other theological knowledge. Thomas H. Huxley (1825–95) and Bertrand Russell were influential agnostics.

altruism   The ethical theory that morality consists of concern for and the active promotion of the interests of others. Altruists strongly disagree with the doctrine of egoism, which states that individuals act only in their own self-interest.

analytic statement   A statement true by definition, such as "All triangles have three sides."

anarchism   A political philosophy that advocates the abolition of an organized state as the ruling government. Its advocates believe that individuals should be free to organize themselves in the ways that best enable them to fulfill their needs and ideals. The Russian thinker Mikhail Bakunin (1814–76) was an influential anarchist.

angst   A German word meaning anxiety, anguish, or dread. The term was used by Martin Heidegger and other adherents of existentialism to express their belief that anxiety characterizes the human condition and that dread arises from our realization that we are totally responsible for all of our choices.

a posteriori knowledge   Knowledge based on or derived from sensory experience.

a priori knowledge   Knowledge acquired by the mind or reasoning alone, without any specific basis in experience—for instance, 2 + 2 = 4.

argument   An attempt to relate one set of statements, called the premises or the starting point, to another set, called the conclusion or the end point, by valid means. Arguments are either inductive or deductive. *See also* **syllogism.**

asceticism   The view that attention to the body's needs is evil, an obstacle to moral and spiritual development, and displeasing to God. According to this view, humans are urged to withdraw into an inner spiritual world to reach the good life.

associationism   A philosophical theory of the mind that holds that all mental states can be analyzed as separate component items and that all mental activity can be explained by the combining and recombining of these items, often called ideas. David Hume and John Stuart Mill were prominent advocates of this view. *See also* **association of ideas.**

association of ideas (laws of association)   The principles by which the mind connects ideas. Aristotle included similarity, contrast, and closeness; David Hume held the basic laws to be resemblance, closeness in time or place, and causality. Hume and John Stuart Mill are the two most prominent philosophers who emphasized association as the basic principle of the mind. *See also* **associationism.**

Followers of conservative Franciscan philosopher Duns Scotus were called Dunsmen or Duncemen. Resisting more progressive forms of learning, they became regarded as dull or stupid. Hence, the term dunce.

atheism   The rejection of the belief in God. Some atheists have held that there is nothing in the world that requires a God in order to be explained. Atheism is not the same as agnosticism, which holds that we can have knowledge neither of the existence nor of the nonexistence of God.

atomism   The theory that reality is composed of simple and indivisible units (atoms) that are completely separate from and independent of one another. Philosophers have differed as to the nature of atoms; for instance, the Greek thinkers Leucippus and Democritus (5th century B.C.) held that the atoms are different-shaped bits of matter.

bad faith   Term used by Jean-Paul Sartre for self-deception and the deception of others caused by denying one's freedom of choice and one's responsibility for making decisions.

becoming   That which changes from one form to another, or, in Plato, that which is known only by experience and exists only temporarily. *See also* **being.**

being   Frequently used in metaphysics to contrast with appearance or nonexistence; often synonymous with unchanging substance, ultimate reality, God, infinity, or all that exists. Aristotle held that being is the subject matter of metaphysics. *See also* **becoming.**

Go to "Philosophical Movements and Schools of Thought" and "Major World Philosophers" in this chapter

bioethics   A branch of philosophy that studies ethical issues that arise from conflicts between human rights and medical and biological research and the technology they use. Areas of concern are genetic manipulation, euthanasia, and brain control.

Buridan's ass   A story, falsely attributed to the 14th-century thinker John Buridan, in which an ass, faced with two equally desirable bales of hay, starves to death because he cannot find a good reason for preferring one bale to the other.

categorical imperative   Immanuel Kant's term for the binding moral law, which dictates that one should act only according to a maxim that could serve as a universal law—for instance, to treat humanity as an end and never only as a means.

cause   Whatever is responsible for change, action, or motion. Historically, Aristotle's analysis of cause falls into four types: material cause, the substance a thing is made of; formal cause, the design of the thing; efficient cause, the maker of the thing; and final cause, its purpose or function. David Hume argued that all knowledge of cause comes from our actual experience of observed regularities.

certainty   According to René Descartes, a condition of knowing that anything is true; various types of statements—for example, $1 + 1 = 2$, or all widows are female—have certainty.

chain of being   An idea, originating with Plato and very influential in Western thought into the Renaissance, that all possible things are realized in the world in an ordered chain of diminishing complexity and richness, from God down to the tiniest, humblest bit of matter. The view captures the concept of the universe as an ordered hierarchy.

conceptualism   The doctrine, intermediate between nominalism and realism, that general ideas, such as the idea of man or of redness, exist explicitly in the human mind as concepts and implicitly in the minds of all people. These concepts are not arbitrary ideas, but reflect the similarities between particular things.

cosmogony A theory or story about the origin of the universe, either scientific or mythological. Cosmogonies are also called creation myths.

cosmology The systematic study of the origin and structure of the universe as a whole. In such philosophers as Plato, Aristotle, and Immanuel Kant, cosmology was based on metaphysical speculation; today cosmology is a branch of the physical sciences.

counterexample A specific fact that refutes or negates a generalization; for instance, a black swan is a counterexample to the statement "All swans are white."

deductive reasoning Reasoning from a general statement to a particular or specific example; for example, "All cats are mortal; William is a cat; therefore, William is mortal." *See also* **syllogism.**

deontology The ethical philosophy that makes duty the basis of all morality. According to deontological theorists, such as Immanuel Kant, some acts—such as keeping a promise or telling the truth—are moral obligations regardless of their consequences.

determinism The view that every event has a cause and that everything in the universe is absolutely dependent on and governed by causal laws. Because determinists believe that all events, including human actions, are predetermined, determinism is typically thought to be incompatible with free will.

dialectic A term with different meanings for different philosophers. It derives from the Greek word meaning "to converse" and is used to describe Socrates's method of teaching by question-and-answer technique. Plato used the word to mean the

More Than Just Philosophers

A Closer Look

Before knowledge was as specialized as it is today, many of the greatest philosophers followed their other interests while creating or studying philosophical systems. They did groundbreaking work in areas as far afield from philosophy proper as geometry, zoology, literary criticism, and calculus.

Perhaps Aristotle was the model for some of these thinkers, because he was regarded not only in his own time but also throughout most of the Middle Ages as a universal genius whose knowledge on any subject he had written on could hardly be questioned. His nonphilosophical writings were astonishingly broad; even a partial list of his subjects, which include physics, zoology, botany, sociology, political theory, and economics, is testimony to one of the greatest minds of all time.

Even medicine and the law were not too far afield for some of the great philosophers. Avicenna, Averroes, and John Locke were trained in medicine; Avicenna's *Canon of Medicine* was the most influential medieval medical treatise. And Jeremy Bentham, a founder of utilitarianism, was one of the most influential jurists and lawyers of the 19th century; his work deeply influenced reform of the British penal, judicial, and parliamentary systems.

History, too, is a philosopher's domain. *History of England*, not his philosophy books, brought David Hume success and renown in mid-18th-century England.

Both mathematics and logic were fruitfully developed by philosophers when they were not writing philosophical works. Gottfried Leibniz is the coinventor of calculus, along with Sir Isaac Newton; Blaise Pascal is one of the founders of the modern theory of probability; and Descartes invented analytical geometry almost single-handedly.

Logic, although now a separate discipline, was a part of philosophy until the late 19th century. Aristotle was the founder of logic, but many other philosophers have invented or organized entire sections of the field. John Stuart Mill formulated the "rules" of scientific experimentation that are now called Mill's methods; and Bertrand Russell and Alfred North Whitehead wrote *Principia Mathematica*, probably the most important work in modern logic.

The list of philosophers engaged in other fields is seemingly endless. Examples include Friedrich Nietzsche, whose *On the Birth of Tragedy* is a classic in Greek studies and literary criticism; William James, whose *Principles of Psychology* deeply influenced decades of thinking in that field; and John Dewey, the father of the American progressive education movement.

study of the Forms. To Immanuel Kant, it meant a method of criticizing claims of knowledge going beyond experience. Georg Hegel means by it the necessary pattern of thinking.

doubt   According to René Descartes, the argument that nothing can be considered true unless it can never be doubted under any conditions. Descartes doubted everything "systematically" to find out if anything is indubitable; his "*Cogito, ergo sum*" ("I think, therefore I am") survived his test.

dualism   Any philosophical theory holding that the universe consists of, or can only be explained by, two independent and separate forces, such as matter and spirit, the forces of good and evil, or the supernatural and natural. *See also* **mind-body problem.**

duty   According to many ethical theories, the basis of the virtuous life. The Stoics held that man has a duty to live virtuously and according to reason; and Immanuel Kant held that his categorical imperative is the highest law of duty, no matter what the consequences.

egocentric predicament   The belief that each of us is limited to, and by, our unique pattern of perceptions. Any knowledge of the world outside our minds would thus be colored by our perceptions. *See also* **solipsism.**

egoism   The ethical theory that each person should forward his or her own self-interest. Egoists sometimes argue that this is not selfishness, but that self-interest is compatible with helping others as well. Some egoists also argue that, psychologically speaking, human beings always in fact seek their own well-being.

élan vital   *See* **vitalism.**

empirical   Based on experience, observation, or facts—in short, describing any knowledge derived from or validated by sensory experience.

empiricism   The view that all knowledge of the world derives solely from sensory experience, using observation and experimentation if needed; empiricism also holds that reason on its own can never provide knowledge of reality unless it also utilizes experience. Empiricism suggests that any concept of the physical world is nothing more than a generalization derived from particular circumstances.

epistemology   The branch of philosophy that studies how knowledge is gained, how much we can know, and what justification there is for what is known.

eschatology   In theology, the study of "final things," such as death, resurrection, immortality, the second coming of Christ, and the day of judgment.

essence   That which makes a specific thing what it is and not something else; its nature. While the Greek philosophers viewed essence and substance as basically the same, St. Thomas Aquinas and the philosophy of Scholasticism held that even nonexistent things have natures or essences distinguishable from the fact of their existence.

esthetics   *See* **aesthetics.**

euthanasia   The act of allowing a terminally ill person to freely choose when and how he or she will die; mercy killing.

fatalism   The belief that "what will be will be," because all past, present, and future events have already been predetermined by God or another all-powerful force. In religion, this view may be called predestination; it holds that whether our souls go to heaven or hell is determined before we are born and is independent of our good deeds.

Forms   According to Plato, the eternal, unchanging, immaterial, and perfect archetypes of which all existing things are merely imperfect copies; also called Ideas.

four elements   According to many early Greek philosophers, the four basic constituents of the physical world: earth, air, fire, and water.

free will   The theory that human beings have freedom of choice or self-determination; that is, that given a situation, a person could have done other than what he did. Philosophers have argued that free will is incompatible with determinism. *See also* **indeterminism.**

golden mean   The ethical doctrine, originating with Aristotle, that virtuous actions fall exactly between too much of some quality, such as impulsive behavior, and too little of it, such as timidity. It is associated with ethics calling for moderation.

Peanuts creator Charles M. Schulz once quipped, "There's a difference between a philosophy and a bumper sticker."

golden rule   The fundamental moral rule of most religions, especially Christianity, that states, "Do unto others as you would have others do unto you."

greatest happiness principle   *See* **principle of utility; utilitarianism** under "Philosophical Movements and Schools of Thought."

Hobson's choice   A choice offered without any real alternative—therefore, not really a choice at all.

humanism   Any philosophic view that holds that humankind's well-being and happiness in this lifetime are primary and that the good of all humanity is the highest ethical goal. Twentieth-century humanists tend to reject all beliefs in the supernatural, relying instead on scientific methods and reason. The term is also used to refer to Renaissance thinkers, especially in 15th-century Italy, who emphasized the revival of classical studies, or the humanities, and knowledge and learning not based on religious sources.

idealism   A term applied to any philosophy holding that mind or spiritual values, rather than material things or matter, are primary in the universe.

immortality   The view that the individual soul is eternal, and thus survives the death of the body it resides in. *See also* **transmigration of souls.**

indeterminism   The view that there are events that do not have any cause; many proponents of

free will believe that acts of choice are capable of not being determined by any physiological or psychological cause.

inductive reasoning   Any process of reasoning from something particular to something general, or from a part to a whole. Inductive reasoning can be valid or invalid.

innate ideas   Ideas that are inborn and part of the mind at birth, rather than based on specific experiences. René Descartes believed there are "clear and distinct" ideas that are innate and that form the basis of all knowledge. Plato believed that knowledge of the Forms derives from innate ideas.

instrumentalism   A theory that holds that ideas and concepts should be regarded as tools or instruments to be used in specific situations. As such, they cannot be described as true or false, but only as effective or ineffective. This theory was first put forth by John Dewey.

justice   According to most philosophers, starting with Plato, the harmonious balance between the rights of the various members of a society. Justice is usually understood as including such social virtues as fairness, equality, and correct and impartial treatment.

language, philosophy of   *See* **philosophy of language.**

language game   A concept introduced by Ludwig Wittgenstein, who drew an analogy between how we use language and how we play games: Both have rules and moves that make sense only in the context of a particular game. Wittgenstein and his followers used this concept to point out that philosophers frequently try to make moves in one context that make sense only in another, as when they try to verify religious statements as if they were a part of science.

logic   The study of the rules and the nature of reasoning and of valid or sound patterns of thought. Aristotle classified many of the rules of reasoning. In the late 19th and early 20th centuries, logic was advanced into a branch of mathematics. Currently, mathematical logic is a growing field independent of philosophy. *See also* **syllogism.**

materialism   The theory that holds that the nature of the world is dependent on matter, or that matter is the only fundamental substance; thus, spirit and mind either do not exist or are manifestations of matter. Prevalent throughout the history of western civilization, this theory appeared as early as the 4th century B.C. in the teachings of Democritus, and it formed the basis for dialectical materialism, the philosophical doctrine underlying communism.

mathematical logic   *See* **logic.**

mathematics, philosophy of   *See* **philosophy of mathematics.**

mechanism   The philosophical theory that states that living organisms, including humans, are complex machines, because they are composed of matter.

metaethics   A branch of philosophy that analyzes ethics. It is concerned with such issues as, How are moral decisions justified? What is the foundation of any ethical view? What language is used to state moral beliefs?

metaphysics   The branch of philosophy concerned with the ultimate nature of reality and existence as a whole. Metaphysics also includes the study of cosmology and philosophical theology. Aristotle produced the first "system" of metaphysics.

metempsychosis   *See* **transmigration of souls.**

mind   *See* **philosophy of mind.**

mind-body problem   A central problem of modern philosophy that originated with René Descartes. It asks how the mind and the body are related.

monad   According to Leibniz, the ultimate and indivisible units of all existence. Monads are not material, like atoms; each monad is self-activating, a unique center of force. All monads are in a "preestablished harmony" with each other and with God, the supreme monad.

monism   A term introduced in the 18th century to describe any theory that explains all phenomena by a single unifying principle or that reduces everything in the universe to one fundamental substance, energy, or force. In Georg Hegel, this concept can be seen in his vision of the world as a single organism, developing through a dialectical process. Benedict Spinoza held that mind and spirit are aspects of single entity, which he called God or nature.

mysticism   Any philosophy whose roots are in mystical experiences, intuitions, or direct experiences of the divine. In such experiences, the mystic believes that his or her soul has temporarily achieved union with God. Mystics believe reality can be known only in this manner, not through reasoning or everyday experience.

myth of Er   A parable at the end of Plato's *Republic* about the fate of souls after bodily death; according to Plato, the soul must choose wisdom in the afterlife to guarantee a good life in its next cycle of incarnation.

natural law   The theory that there is a higher law than the humanmade laws put forth by specific governments. This law is universal, unchanging, and a fundamental part of human nature. Advocates of this view believe that natural law can be discovered by reason alone. The theory originated with the Stoics and was elaborated on by St. Thomas Aquinas, among others.

natural rights   Certain freedoms or privileges that are held to be an innate part of the nature of being a human being and that cannot be denied by society. These are different from civil rights, which are granted by a specific nation or government. Philosophers have differed on which rights are natural, but usually included are life, liberty, equality, equal treatment under the law, the pursuit of happiness, and equality of opportunity. John

---

A Closer Look

God's Existence—Proofs For

While theology may take God's existence as absolutely necessary on the basis of authority, faith, or revelation, many philosophers—and some theologians—have thought it possible to demonstrate by reason that there must be a God.

St. Thomas Aquinas, in the 13th century, formulated the famous "five ways" by which God's existence can be demonstrated philosophically:

1. *The "unmoved mover" argument.* We know that there is motion in the world; whatever is in motion is moved by another thing; this other thing also must be moved by something; to avoid an infinite regression, we must posit a "first mover," which is God.
2. *The "nothing is caused by itself" argument.* For example, a table is brought into being by a carpenter, who is caused by his parents. Again, we cannot go on to infinity, so there must be a first cause, which is God.
3. *The cosmological argument.* All physical things—even mountains, boulders, and rivers—come into being and go out of existence, no matter how long they last. Therefore, because time is infinite, there must be some time at which none of these things existed. But if there were nothing at that point in time, how could there be anything at all now, because nothing cannot cause anything? Thus, there must always have been at least one necessary thing that is eternal, which is God.
4. *Objects in the world have differing degrees of qualities such as goodness.* But speaking of more or less goodness makes sense only by comparison with what is the maximum goodness, which is God.
5. *The teleological argument (argument from design).* Things in the world move toward goals, just as the arrow does not move toward its goal except by the archer's directing it. Thus, there must be an intelligent designer who directs all things to their goals, and this is God.

Two other historically important "proofs" are the ontological argument and the moral argument. The former, made famous by St. Anselm in the 11th century and defended in another form by René Descartes, holds that it would be logically contradictory to deny God's existence. St. Anselm began by defining God as "that [being] than which nothing greater can be conceived." If God existed only in the mind, He then would not be the greatest conceivable being, for we could imagine another being that is greater because it would exist both in the mind and in reality, and that being would then be God. Therefore, to imagine God as existing only in the mind but not in reality leads to a logical contradiction; this proves the existence of God both in the mind and in reality.

Immanuel Kant rejected not only the ontological argument but the teleological and cosmological arguments as well, based on his theory that reason is too limited to know anything beyond human experience. He did argue, however, that religion could be established as presupposed by the workings of morality in the human mind ("practical reason"). God's existence is a necessary presupposition of there being any moral judgments that are objective, that go beyond mere relativistic moral preferences; such judgments require standards external to any human mind—that is, they presume God's mind.

Locke's influential views on natural rights inspired the writers of the U.S. Constitution.

naturalism A philosophic view stating that all there is in reality is what the physical and human sciences (for example, physics or psychology) study and that there is no need to posit any supernatural forces or being, such as God, mind, or spirit.

naturalistic fallacy A belief of many 20th-century philosophers in England and the United States that it is invalid to infer any statements of morality (for example, "Men ought to act kindly") from factual statements (for example, "Kindness is a natural quality"). The notion tries to derive *ought* from *is* and was first described by David Hume.

necessary and contingent truth Terms used by philosophers to contrast two types of statements, such as "All widowers are male," which is necessarily true, and "All widowers are over 20 years old," which may be true but is not necessarily true.

nominalism A doctrine, prevalent in the Middle Ages, that maintained that ideas and objects exist only in the particular instance, not as abstract concepts or forms. In opposition to realism, it held that

God's Existence—Arguments Against

Arguments against God's existence have been given by philosophers, atheists, and agnostics. Some of these arguments find God's existence incompatible with observed facts; some are arguments that God does not exist because the concept of God is incoherent or confused. Others are criticisms of the proofs offered *for* God's existence.

One of the most influential and powerful "proofs" that there is no God proceeds from "The Problem from Evil." This argument claims that the following three statements cannot *all* be true: (a) evil exists; (b) God is omnipotent; and (c) God is all-loving. The argument is as follows:

- If God can prevent evil, but *doesn't,* then He isn't all-loving.
- If God intends to prevent evil, but *cannot,* then He isn't omnipotent.
- If God *both* intends to prevent evil and is capable of doing so, then how can evil exist?

Another argument claims that the existence of an all-knowing God is incompatible with the fact of free will—that humans do make choices. If God is omniscient, He must know beforehand exactly what a person will do in a given situation. In that case, a person is not in fact free to do the alternative to what God knows he or she will do, and free will must be an illusion. To take this one step further, if one chooses to commit a sin, how can it then be said that one sinned freely?

David Hume provided powerful critiques of the main arguments for God's existence. Against the cosmological argument (Aquinas's third argument), Hume argued that the idea of a necessarily existing being is absurd. He stated, "Whatever we can conceive as existent, we can also conceive as nonexistent." Hume also asked why the ultimate source of the universe could not be the entire universe itself, eternal and uncaused, without a God?

Hume also criticized the argument from design (Aquinas's fifth argument). In particular, he emphasized that there is no legitimate way we can infer the properties of God as the creator of the world from the qualities of His creation. For instance, Hume questioned how we can be sure that the world was not created by a team; or that this is not one of many attempts at creations, the first few having been botched; or, on the other hand, that our world is not a poor first attempt "of an infant deity who afterwards abandoned it, ashamed of his lame performance."

Philosophy

all universals are merely names and have no existence of their own.

non sequitur   A Latin phrase meaning "it does not follow"; any argument where the conclusion drawn has not even the slightest connection to the premises offered.

objectivism   The view that there are moral truths that are valid universally and that it is wrong to knowingly gain pleasure from causing another pain.

obligation   In ethics, a moral necessity to do a specific deed. Some ethicists, following Immanuel Kant, hold that moral obligations are absolute. *See also* **categorical imperative.**

Ockham's razor   A principle attributed to the 14th-century English philosopher William of Ockham. It states that entities should not be multiplied beyond necessity, or that one should choose the simplest explanation, the one requiring the fewest assumptions and principles.

ontology   A branch of metaphysics that studies the nature of existence or reality, as such, as opposed to specific types of existing entities.

operationalism (operationism)   A philosophy of science according to which any scientific concept must be definable in terms of concrete, observable activities or the operations to which it refers.

optimism   The philosophic attitude that this is the best of all possible worlds, that hope and joy are justified, and that all things are ordered for the best. According to optimists, such as Gottfried Leibniz, evil either is an illusion or will be compensated for by an even greater good.

pantheism   The belief that God and the universe are identical; among modern philosophers, Benedict Spinoza is considered to be a pantheist.

particulars   *See* **universals.**

Pascal's wager   An argument made by Blaise Pascal for believing in God. Pascal said that either the tenets of Roman Catholicism are true or they are not. If they are true, and we wager that they are true, then we have won an eternity of bliss; if they are false, and death is final, what has the bettor lost? On the other hand, if one wagers against God's existence and turns out to be wrong, there is eternal damnation.

pessimism   The philosophic attitude holding that hope is unreasonable, that a person is born to sorrow, and that this is the worst of all possible worlds. Arthur Schopenhauer's philosophy is an example of extreme pessimism.

phenomenalism   The doctrine that the only knowledge we can ever have is of appearances, and thus that we can never know the nature of ultimate reality. Major adherents of the philosophy were John Stuart Mill and some members of the Vienna Circle.

philosopher king   In Plato's *Republic,* a philosopher trained by formal study in disciplines including mathematics and philosophy. Plato emphasized that philosopher kings' leadership would be shown by their ability to see the Forms, or universal ideals. *See also* **Forms.**

philosophy of language   The area of philosophic study whose subject matter is the nature and workings of language. Detailed discussions of such topics as meaning, reference, grammar, and symbols infuse this branch of philosophy.

philosophy of mathematics   A branch of philosophy that studies such questions as, What are mathematical statements about? Why is mathematics true? How do we come to have mathematical knowledge? Why is mathematics so useful in studying reality?

philosophy of mind   The area of philosophy that studies the mind, consciousness, and mental functions such as thinking, intention, imagination, and emotion. It is not one specific branch of philosophy, but rather an aspect of most traditional branches, such as metaphysics, epistemology, and aesthetics.

philosophy of religion   A branch of philosophy concerned with such questions as, What is religion? What is God? Can God's existence be proved? Is there immortality? What is the relationship between faith, reason, and revelation? Is there a divine purpose in the world?

philosophy of science   The branch of philosophy that studies the nature of science. It is particularly concerned with the methods, concepts, and assumptions of science, as well as with analyzing scientific concepts such as space, time, cause, scientific law, and verification.

physicalism   A theory about knowledge that originated within the Vienna Circle. It holds that all factual statements can be reduced to observations of physical objects and events. *See also* **operationalism.**

Plato's cave   An analogy in Plato's *Republic* between reality and illusion. The main image is of people who see on the walls of a cave only the shadows of the real objects moving around outside the cave. When these people leave the cave and see the real objects, they cannot, upon returning to the cave, convince those who have never left of the reality of the objects.

pluralism   The view that there are more than two kinds of fundamental, irreducible realities in the universe, or that there are many separate and independent levels of reality.

political philosophy   The branch of philosophy that studies a person as a political animal. It is concerned with such questions as, What obligations do I have to my government? How is political power justified? Under what conditions is war justified? It also studies the nature of property, justice, freedom, liberty, and political rights.

positivism   A theory originated by French philosopher Auguste Comte. It holds that all knowledge is defined by the limits of scientific investigation; thus, philosophy must abandon any quest for knowledge of an ultimate reality or any knowledge beyond that offered by science.

predestination   *See* **fatalism.**

premises   *See* **argument.**

principle (or law) of noncontradiction   Dating back to Aristotle, this universally accepted "law of thought" has two parts: A statement cannot be both true and false; nothing can both have a quality, like red, and not have it, at the same time.

The long sought-after philosopher's stone was believed by alchemists to have the power to change base metals into silver or gold.

principle of sufficient reason   The philosophical doctrine of Leibniz that asserts that for every fact there is a reason for its being the way it is rather than another way, even though we may not know that reason.

principle of utility (greatest happiness principle)   The basic tenet of utilitarianism. It states that the highest ethical good provides the greatest happiness for the greatest number of people.

psychologism   A view of philosophy holding that all philosophic concepts and problems are explainable based on psychological principles and that they should be treated by some form of psychological analysis. Advocates of this view may disagree on the type of psychological approach that is appropriate.

QED   Latin for *quod erat demonstrandum* ("that which was to be demonstrated"). This abbreviation is often used right before or after stating a conclusion, as a synonym for *therefore, thus,* or *as was to be shown.*

rationalism   A doctrine holding that reason or thinking alone, without recourse to observation or experience, can apprehend basic truths. The notion of innate, universal concepts is naturally associated with this theory. René Descartes, Gottfried Leibniz, Benedict Spinoza, and Georg Hegel were all essentially rationalists in their approach to the foundations of knowledge.

realism   The major medieval and modern view, other than nominalism, on the problem of universals. *Extreme realism,* which is close to Plato's theory of Forms, holds that universals exist independently of both particular things and the human mind; *moderate realism,* put forth by St. Thomas Aquinas, holds that universals exist as ideas in God's mind, through which He creates things.

reincarnation   *See* **transmigration of souls.**

relativism   The precept that people's ideas of right and wrong vary considerably from place to place and time to time; therefore, there are no universally valid ethical standards.

religion, philosophy of   *See* **philosophy of religion.**

science, philosophy of   *See* **philosophy of science.**

sensationalism   An empiricist theory of knowledge that holds that sensations are both the source of all knowledge and the ultimate verification of any statements. Thomas Hobbes originated the view; Étienne Condillac (1715–1880) and Ernst Mach (1838–1916) developed it.

sense data   The sensory qualities or feelings we experience directly, such as shapes, colors, and smells, without any interpretation of the material objects that may be causing them. Some empiricists and sensationalist philosophers make sense data the foundation of all factual knowledge.

skepticism   The philosophic theory that no certain knowledge can be attained by humans. Broadly speaking, skepticism states that all knowledge should be questioned and tested—for instance, by the scientific method.

social contract   That concept of an agreement between people, or between people and government or ruler, in which it is agreed that some personal liberties will be given up in exchange for the security of stable political rule. The term is used in the political philosophy of Thomas Hobbes, John Locke, and Jean-Jacques Rousseau to justify a form of political authority.

solipsism   The theory that one cannot know anything other than his or her own thoughts, feelings, or perceptions; therefore, other people and the real world must be projections of one's own mind with no existence in and of themselves. *See also* **egocentric predicament.**

spiritism   A term referring to the belief that spirits of the dead communicate with the living—for instance, at seances or through a medium.

spiritualism   The view that the ultimate reality in the universe is the spirit. Advocates of this view may disagree about the nature of the spirit.

state of nature   A term used by 17th- and 18th-century social philosophers such as Thomas Hobbes, John Locke, and Jean-Jacques Rousseau. It referred to the condition of humans without political organization, or before government.

subjectivism   The theory that all moral values are completely dependent on the personal tastes, feelings, or inclinations of the individual and have no source of validity outside such human subjective states of mind.

substance   A changeless, self-subsistent entity, not dependent on anything else, that underlies being in all its forms. It has been identified with God, mind, matter, and self-contained ultimate realities. *See also* **monad.**

supernaturalism   The belief that there are forces, energies, or beings beyond the material world—such as God, spirit, or occult forces—that affect events in our world.

syllogism   A kind of deductive reasoning or argument. As defined by Aristotle, it was considered the basis of reasoning for over two thousand years. In every syllogism, there are two statements (premises) from which a conclusion follows necessarily. Syllogisms are of three basic logical types, as illustrated by the following examples. *See also* **argument.**

1. If a broom is new, it sweeps clean; the broom is new; therefore, it sweeps clean.
2. Either the horse is male or female; the horse is not female; therefore, it is male.
3. All philosophers are men; all men are mortal; therefore, all philosophers are mortal.

synthetic statement   A factual statement describing a state of affairs, such as "Triangles are used in architectural studios."

tabula rasa   A Latin phrase meaning "blank slate," used by John Locke to describe the state of the human mind at birth. Locke believed there are no innate ideas and that the mind gets all of its ideas from experience.

tautology   Any statement that is necessarily true merely because of its meaning, such as "Bachelors are unmarried males" or "Every green object is colored." *See also* **necessary and contingent truth.**

teleological ethics   In contrast with deontological ethics, this moral theory holds that whether an action is morally right depends solely on its expected consequences.

transcendent   Beyond the realm of sense experience. In many religious views, God is held to be transcendent.

transmigration of souls (mctcmpsychosis; reincarnation)   The belief that the same soul can, in different lifetimes (incarnations), reside in different bodies, human or animal. While typically a part of most Eastern religions, the doctrine came into Western philosophy from Pythagoras and his contemporaries in the 6th century B.C. and especially through Plato.

universals The properties, or the abstract or general words, that apply to many individual things, called particulars. Redness, for instance, is a universal that applies to all red things.

utopianism The belief in the possibility or desirability of not just a better but a perfect society. The term derives from Sir Thomas More's *Utopia* (1516), which depicts an ideal state. Utopian states also appear in the writings of Plato and Sir Francis Bacon.

vitalism The theory that living organisms are inherently different from inanimate bodies; thus, life cannot be explained fully by materialistic theories as it is based on a vital force that is unlike other physical forces. Aristotle, Hans Driesch (1867–1941), and Henri Bergson (1859–1941) were prominent vitalists. In Bergson's view, the élan vital is the evolutionary force in organisms that propels life to achieve higher levels of structure.

will to believe A phrase made famous by William James. He held that in the absence of decisive evidence, the mind may create belief in order to act, often resulting in discovery. He also maintained that believing in such situations is a human right that should not be backed away from.

will to power The view, expounded by Friedrich Nietzsche, that power is the chief motivating force in human nature. The view was influential in 20th-century psychology and social science.

ADDITIONAL SOURCES OF INFORMATION

ORGANIZATIONS AND SERVICES

The Philosophy Documentation Center (Bowling Green State University, Bowling Green, OH 43403) is a key source of information. Its publications include U.S. and international directories of philosophers and *The Philosopher's Index,* a bibliographic journal and a series of cumulative bibliographies dating to 1940, arranged by author and subject. In conjunction with the InteLex Corporation, the PDC is also developing an online service that will provide subscription-based access to philosophy journals. The PDC and InteLex currently operate Past Masters®, an online database containing the complete works of more than 20 philosophers ranging from Aristotle to Wittgenstein. The PDC home page can be accessed at http://www.bgsu.edu/offices/phildoc.

BOOKS

Brown, Stuart, Diané Collinson, and Robert Wilkinson, eds. *Biographical Dictionary of 20th-Century Philosophers.* Routledge, 1996.

Copleston, Frederick C. *History of Philosophy.* 9 vols. Doubleday, 1985.

deGeorge, Richard T. *The Philospher's Guide to Sources, Research Tools, Professional Life, and Related Fields.* Regents Press of Kansas, 1980.

Durant, Will. *The Story of Philosophy.* Pocket Books, 1983.

Edwards, Paul, ed. *The Encyclopedia of Philosophy.* 4 vols. Free Press, 1973.

Ferm, Vergilius. *A History of Philosophical Systems.* Philosophical Library, 1950.

Lacey, A. R. *A Dictionary of Philosophy.* 3rd ed. Routledge, 1996.

Magill, Frank N., ed. *Masterpieces of World Philosophy.* HarperCollins, 1990.

O'Connor, D. J. *A Critical History of Western Philosophy.* Free Press, 1985.

Reese, William L., ed. *Dictionary of Philosophy and Religion: Eastern and Western Thought.* 2nd ed. Humanities Press, 1996.

Runes, Dagobert D., ed. *Dictionary of Philosophy.* Rowman & Allanhead, 1984.

Russell, Bertrand. *A History of Western Philosophy.* Simon & Schuster, 1984.

Urmson, James O. *A Concise Encyclopedia of Western Philosophy and Philosophers.* 3rd ed. Hyman, 1990.

Weiner, Philip P., ed. *Dictionary of the History of Ideas: Studies of Selected Pivotal Ideas.* 5 vols. Scribners, 1985.

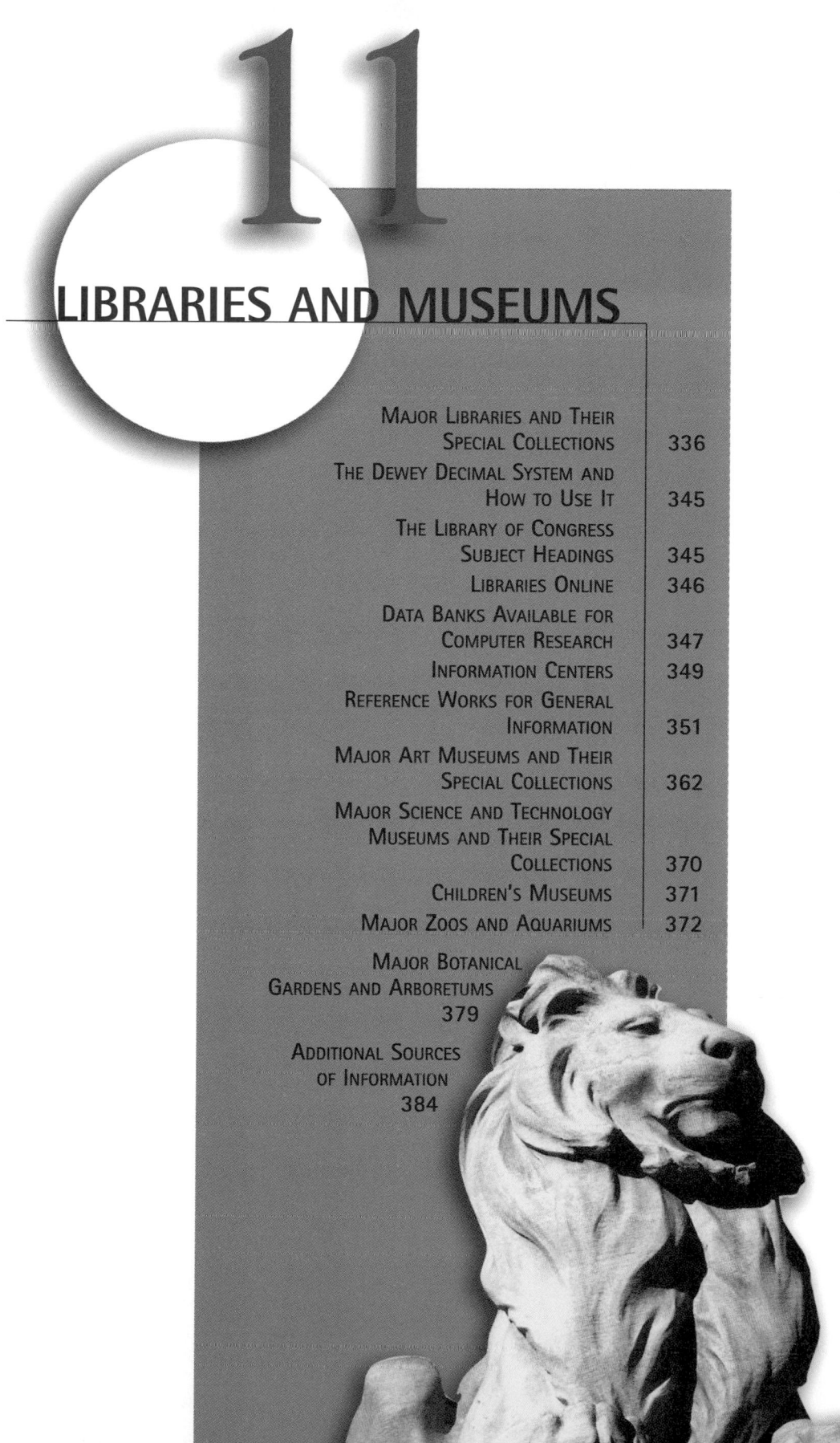

11

LIBRARIES AND MUSEUMS

MAJOR LIBRARIES AND THEIR
SPECIAL COLLECTIONS   336

THE DEWEY DECIMAL SYSTEM AND
HOW TO USE IT   345

THE LIBRARY OF CONGRESS
SUBJECT HEADINGS   345

LIBRARIES ONLINE   346

DATA BANKS AVAILABLE FOR
COMPUTER RESEARCH   347

INFORMATION CENTERS   349

REFERENCE WORKS FOR GENERAL
INFORMATION   351

MAJOR ART MUSEUMS AND THEIR
SPECIAL COLLECTIONS   362

MAJOR SCIENCE AND TECHNOLOGY
MUSEUMS AND THEIR SPECIAL
COLLECTIONS   370

CHILDREN'S MUSEUMS   371

MAJOR ZOOS AND AQUARIUMS   372

MAJOR BOTANICAL
GARDENS AND ARBORETUMS
379

ADDITIONAL SOURCES
OF INFORMATION
384

MAJOR LIBRARIES AND THEIR SPECIAL COLLECTIONS

UNITED STATES

Arizona

University of Arizona Library
Tucson, AZ 85721
520-621-2101
http://dizzy.library.arizona.edu/

Established in 1891, the University of Arizona has more than 3.7 million volumes, with special collections on photography as an art form, fine arts, drama, private presses, Southwestern Americana, Arizona, science history, science fiction, and Mexican colonial history.

American libraries are used by two-thirds of the population but are financed with less than 1% of tax dollars.

California

County of Los Angeles Public Library
South State Cooperative Library System
7400 E. Imperial Hwy.
Downey, CA 90241
310-940-8465
http://www.colapublib.org/support/

Founded in 1912, this library system contains more than 5.5 million volumes, with special collections on Afro-American studies, Asian-Pacific studies, California, multimedia, mountaineering, Hispanic-Americans, Native Americans, and poetry. The collection is dispersed among 114 community, mobile, and institutional libraries.

Los Angeles Public Library System
630 W. Fifth St.
Los Angeles, CA 90071
213-228-7515
http://www.lapl.org/

Founded in 1872, this public library system has 62 branches with more than 6.1 million volumes. Its special collections are on California studies, children's literature, cooking, genealogy, Native American studies, modern languages, orchestral scores, U.S. patents, and standards and specifications.

Stanford University Libraries
Stanford, CA 94305
415-723-5553
http://www.sul.stanford.edu/

Founded in 1892, Stanford's libraries contain 5.4 million volumes. Its special collections cover transportation, music, science, California, Irish literature, engineering mechanics, children's literature, Chicano studies, theater, and Hebraica and Judaica.

University of California, Berkeley
245 Doe Library
Berkeley, CA 94720
510-642-3773
http://www.lib.berkeley.edu/

Founded in 1871, this library contains more than 8.1 million volumes. Special collections include the letters, literary manuscripts, and scrapbooks of Samuel Clemens (Mark Twain Collection) and Recollections of Persons Who Have Contributed to the Development of the West (Regional Oral History Office).

University of California Los Angeles Library
11334 University Research Library
P.O. Box 951575
Los Angeles, CA 90095
310-825-1201
http://www.library.ucla.edu/

Founded in 1919, the University of California Los Angeles Library has holdings of more than 6.4 million books. It has special collections on British Commonwealth history, contemporary Western writers, early English children's books, folklore, Latin American studies, Mazarinades, mountaineering, and Western Americana.

University of Southern California
Edward L. Doheny Memorial Library
University Park
Los Angeles, CA 90089
213-740-2543
http://www.usc.edu/library/DML/

Founded in 1880, the University of Southern California has more than 2.7 million volumes, with a number of independent departmental libraries whose subject matter ranges from architecture and fine arts to gerontology. Its special collections include Native American ethnopharmacology, American literature, cinema, dentistry, international relations, Latin American studies, and philosophy.

Colorado

University of Colorado, Boulder
University Libraries Campus Box 184
Boulder, CA 80309
303-492-7511
http://www.colorado.edu/search.html

Founded in 1876, the University of Colorado maintains holdings of more than 2 million volumes, with special collections on juvenile literature, the history of silver, mountaineering, and Western U.S. history.

Connecticut

Yale University Library
120 High St.
P.O. Box 208240
New Haven, CT 06520
203-432-2798
http://www.library.yale.edu/un/unhome.htm

The second largest university library in the United States, Yale has 10.5 million volumes in its collection. Its rare books total more than 500,000. Yale's special collections are numerous; they include works by James Boswell, the Aaron Burr family, Daniel Defoe, John Dryden, James Joyce, D. H. Lawrence, the Lindbergh family, Marcus Aurelius, H. L. Mencken, Napoleon, Mark Twain, and Edith Wharton. Founded in 1701, the Yale Library has more than 50 subjects of special strength, including Babylonian tablets, futurism, legal thought, playing cards, sporting books, urban and regional planning, and Western Americana.

District of Columbia

Folger Shakespeare Library
201 E. Capitol St., SE
Washington, DC 20003-1094
202-544-4600
http://www.folger.edu/

Opened in 1932, the Folger Shakespeare Library houses the world's largest collection of Shakespeare's printed works. The collection includes approximately 280,000 books and manuscripts; 27,000 paintings, drawings, engravings and prints; and musical instruments, costumes, and films.

The Library of Congress
Washington, DC 20540
202-707-5000
http://lcweb.loc.gov/global/ncp/ncp.html

The nation's largest single library, the Library of Congress, established in 1800, contains over 80 million items, including about 20 million books and pamphlets. Its collections include over 1 million volumes on Hispanic and Portuguese culture and the largest collection of Russian literature outside Russia. Special collections include books for the blind and physically handicapped, cartography, folk music, law books, manuscripts, microforms, motion pictures, music, the Orient, prints and photographs, and more than half a million rare books. The library's first priority is service to the Congress of the United States. It also registers creative work for copyright and provides services to both the public and libraries throughout the country.

Florida

University of Florida Libraries
204 Library West
Gainesville, FL 32611
352-392-0342
http://www.fcla.edu.susstuff/suslibs.html

Founded in 1905, this system contains more than 3 million volumes, with special collections on Florida history, Latin America, Judaica, aerial photographs, coastal engineering, New England literature, Brazilian law, and Florida newspapers.

Georgia

University of Georgia Libraries
Athens, GA 30602
706-542-0621
http://www.chem.ucla.edu/chempointers.html

Founded in 1800, this library system contains more than 3.3 million volumes, with special collections on music, theater, Georgia, Confederate imprints, Georgia authors, 19th- and 20th-century politics, and Georgia newspapers.

Hawaii

Hawaii State Library System
Office of the State Librarian
465 S. King St.
Honolulu, HI 96813
808-586-3704
http://www.hcc.hawaii.edu/hspls/hslov.html

Founded in 1852, Hawaii's libraries contain more than 3.4 million volumes, with a special collection devoted to Hawaiian history.

Illinois

Chicago Public Library
400 S. State St.
Chicago, IL 60605
312-747-4999
http://cpl.lib.uic.edu/CPL.html

Libraries

Founded in 1872, Chicago's libraries offer more than 11.5 million volumes with special collections of national, U.S., foreign, and trade bibliographies; Chicago information; foreign-language encyclopedias; Abraham Lincoln papers; miniature books; early American newspapers; and World War I and II posters.

Northwestern University Library
1935 Sheridan Rd.
Evanston, IL 60208
847-491-7658
http://www.library.nwu.edu/

Founded in 1856, Northwestern holds more than 3 million volumes and bound periodicals, with special collections on Africa, architecture, contemporary music scores, feminism, German classics, Italian futurism, manuscripts, and printing.

University of Chicago Libraries
1100 E. 57th St.
Chicago, IL 60637
312-702-8740
http://www.lib.uchicago.edu/

The University of Chicago, founded in 1891, contains more than 5.8 million volumes. It maintains special collections of English Bibles, Lincolniana, modern poetry, anatomical illustrations, and Kentucky and Ohio River Valley history; children's books; early theology and Bible criticism; German fiction, 1790–1850; and books on ophthalmology.

University of Illinois Library at Urbana–Champaign
1408 W. Gregory Dr.
Urbana, IL 61801
217-333-0790
http://www.uiuc.edu/

This library's collection includes more than 8.1 million volumes, with special collections on American humor and folklore, freedom of expression, 16th- and 17th-century Italian drama, 19th-century publishing, Carl Sandburg, and H. G. Wells. Founded in 1868.

Indiana

Indiana University at Bloomington
Tenth Street and Jordan Avenue
Bloomington, IN 47405
812-855-3403
http://www.indiana.edu/~libweb/index.html

Founded in 1824, Indiana University has amassed a collection of more than 5.7 million volumes, with special collections of English and American literature, 19th-century British plays, English history, scientific and medical history, the works of Aristotle, and 19th-century French opera.

Iowa

University of Iowa Libraries
Iowa City, IA 52242
319-353-5867
http://www.lib/uiowa.edu/

Established in 1855, Iowa's libraries contain more than 3.6 million volumes, with special collections on Leigh Hunt and his friends, Abraham Lincoln, American Indians, Iowa authors, typography, the Union Pacific Railroad, editorial cartoons, the French Revolution, and the history of medicine.

Kansas

University of Kansas Libraries
Watson Library
Lawrence, KS 66045
913-864-3956
http://falcon.cc.ukans.edu/~cpierard/tour/tourwel.htm

Established in 1866, the University of Kansas libraries contain in excess of 2.9 million volumes, with special collections on Anglo-Saxons, botany, children's books, Chinese classics, Colombia, the Continental Renaissance, economics, historical cartography, Irish history and literature, Kansas history, poetry, opera, ornithology, sound recordings, travel, and women.

Maryland

Enoch Pratt Free Library
400 Cathedral St.
Baltimore, MD 21201
301-396-5430
http://www.pratt.lib.md.us/

Founded in 1886, Enoch Pratt's collection of 2.3 million volumes has a special H. L. Mencken section and a Maryland history collection.

Johns Hopkins University
Milton S. Eisenhower Library
3400 N. Charles St.
Baltimore, MD 21218
410-516-8325
http://milton.mse.jhu.edu:8001/milton.html

Established in 1876, Johns Hopkins has more than 2.4 million volumes, with special collections on economics, Lord Byron, French drama, modern German drama, German literature, sheet music, slavery, and trade unions.

Massachusetts

Boston Public Library
666 Boylston St.
Boston, MA 02117
617-536-5400
http://www.bpl.org/

Founded in 1852, the Boston library system is believed to be the oldest free municipal library system supported by taxation anywhere in the world. It has 6.3 million volumes, with the following special collections: the library of John Quincy Adams; military science, history, and the Civil War; astronomy, mathematics, and navigation; Robert and Elizabeth Browning; Daniel Defoe; drama; genealogy; government documents; heraldry; music; patents; Christian Science; the Sacco-Vanzetti papers; Walt Whitman; and World War I.

Harvard University Library
Wadsworth House
Cambridge, MA 02138
617-495-3650
http://hul.harvard.edu/libinfo/index.html

With more than 13 million volumes, the Harvard Library, founded in 1638, is the largest university library in the United States. Its special collections are numerous. They include the Trotsky archive; the Theodore Roosevelt Collection; and works by such authors as Dante, T. S. Eliot, Faulkner, Goethe, Kipling, Longfellow, Milton, Petrarch, Rousseau, Shakespeare, Steinbeck, and Thomas Wolfe. Some of its branches are located outside Massachusetts, such as the Harvard Library in New York and the Dumbarton Oaks Research Library and Collection in Washington, D.C. Others specialize in topics ranging from music to divinity and include Harvard's famed law library and the fine arts library at the Fogg Art Museum.

Massachusetts Institute of Technology (MIT) Libraries
Room 14S-216
Cambridge, MA 02139
617-253-5651
http://libraries.mit.edu

Founded in 1862, MIT's library holdings total approximately 2.4 million volumes, with special collections devoted to the early history of aeronautics, architecture and planning, civil engineering, 19th-century U.S. glass manufacturers, early works in mathematics and physics, shipbuilding and naval history, and spectroscopy.

University of Massachusetts at Amherst
W. E. B. DuBois Library
Amherst, MA 01003
413-545-0284
http://www.library.umass.edu/web.html

Founded in 1865, this university system maintains holdings in excess of 2.6 million volumes, with special collections on slavery and antislavery pamphlets; county atlases of New England, New York, and New Jersey; and the French Revolution.

Michigan

Detroit Public Library
5201 Woodward Ave.
Detroit, MI 48202
313-833-1000
http://www.detroit.lib.mi.us/

Founded in 1865, Detroit's library contains more than 2.7 million volumes, with special collections on automotive history, labor history, and black music, dance, and drama.

In the 10th century, the Grand Vizier of Persia took his entire library with him wherever he went. The 117,000-volume library was carried by camels trained to walk in alphabetical order.

Michigan State University Library
East Lansing, MI 48824
517-355-8700
http://www.lib.msu.edu

Established in 1855, Michigan State has holdings of more than 3.9 million volumes, with special collections on American popular culture, American radical history, apiculture, cookery, criminology, fencing, illuminated manuscripts in facsimile, natural science, and veterinary history.

University of Michigan Libraries
Ann Arbor, MI 48109
313-764-9356
http://www.lib.umich.edu/

Founded in 1817, the University of Michigan's libraries contain nearly 6 million volumes, the fifth-largest collection in the country. The system consists of 18 collections located around campus. Major facilities include a medical and a fine-arts library.

Libraries

Separately administered are a library of Americana, a law library, a business-administration library, and the Gerald R. Ford Presidential Library.

Wayne State University Libraries
Detroit, MI 48202
313-577-4023
http://www.lib.wayne.edu/index.html

Wayne State has more than 2.9 million volumes, with special collections on 19th-century Spanish history, social studies, women and the law, law, and children and young people.

Minnesota

University of Minnesota Libraries–Twin Cities
499 O. Meredith Wilson Library
309 19th Ave. South
Minneapolis, MN 55455
612-624-4520
http://www.lib.umn.edu/

Founded in 1851, this university system contains more than 5.2 million volumes, with special collections on American and English literature, the history of quantum physics, ballooning, dime novels, information processing, Sherlock Holmes, children's literature, performing arts, private presses, August Strindberg, and the history of biology and medicine.

Missouri

Kansas City Public Library
311 E. 12th St.
Kansas City, MO 64106
816-221-2685
http://www.kcpl.lib.mo.us/

Founded in 1873, this library's collection numbers more than 2 million volumes, with special collections on black history and Missouri Valley history and genealogy.

Linda Hall Library of Science, Engineering and Technology
5109 Cherry St.
Kansas City, MO 64110-2498
816-363-4600
http://www.lhl.lib.mo.us/

Founded in 1946, the Linda Hall Library's holdings include more than 1 million volumes, with special collections in scientific journals; research monographs; conference and symposium proceedings; engineering standards and specifications; patent specifications and trademarks; unclassified NASA,

Department of Energy, and government contractor reports; and geological maps.

St. Louis University Libraries
St. Louis University
St. Louis, MO 63103
314-977-3100
http://www.slu.edu/libraries/

Founded in 1818, this system contains more than 1.2 million bound volumes and government documents. Libraries on campus include a divinity library, a library of the School of Social Service, a law library, and a medical library.

University of Missouri–Columbia
Elmer Ellis Library
Columbia, MO 65201
314-882-4701

Established in 1839, this library holds more than 2.7 million volumes, with special collections devoted to American best-sellers, criminal law, philosophy, World War I and II posters, cartoons, and Fourth of July orations.

Washington University Libraries
One Brookings Dr.
St. Louis, MO 63130
314-935-5400

Founded in 1853, this system maintains more than 3 million volumes, with special collections on German language and literature, Romance languages and literature, classical archeology and numismatics, architecture, musicology, history of the Russian Revolution and the Soviet Union, American and New York Stock Exchange reports, printing, and early history of communications-semantics.

New Jersey

Princeton University Library
Princeton, NJ 08544
609-258-3180

This university was founded as the College of New Jersey, Elizabeth, in 1746. The principal building in its library system is the Harvey S. Firestone Memorial Library, constructed in 1948. Princeton has approximately 4.7 million volumes, with special collections devoted to the Brontës, Disraeli, aeronautics, American historical manuscripts, chess, civil rights, coins, Emily Dickinson, emblem books, fishing and angling, graphic arts, Mormon history, mountaineering, papyrus manuscripts, publishing, sports, women, and famous individuals.

Rutgers, The State University of New Jersey
University Libraries
169 College Ave.
New Brunswick, NJ 08903
908-932-7505

Established in 1766, this venerable library contains more than 2.9 million volumes. It has a special collection of New Jersey public-sector collective-bargaining contracts.

New York

Brooklyn Public Library System
Grand Army Plaza
Brooklyn, NY 11238
718-230-2100

Founded in 1896 and consolidated with the Brooklyn Library in 1902, the library system now has 58 branches with a total of more than 4.1 million books. Special collections cover Brooklyn history, chess and checkers, the Civil War, costumes, fire protection, and Walt Whitman.

Columbia University
University Libraries
535 W. 114th St.
New York, NY 10027
212-854-2247

Founded in 1761, Columbia offers more than 6.9 million volumes, with special collections on anatomy, architecture, cancer research, fine arts, physiology, and plastic surgery.

Cornell University Libraries
Ithaca, NY 14853
607-255-4144

With approximately 5.8 million volumes, the Cornell libraries include special collections on Southeast Asia, civil engineering, medical dissertations, field recordings, early-16th-century music, beekeeping, food and beverages, and labor history.

New York Public Library
Astor, Lenox & Tilden Foundations
Fifth Avenue at 42nd Street
New York, NY 10018
212-930-0800

Established in 1895 by the consolidation of the Astor and Lenox libraries and the Tilden Trust, the New York Public Library, encompassing 85 neighborhood branches and 4 research centers with noncirculatory collections, contains more than 50 million cataloged items: books, manuscripts, microfilm, prints, maps, recordings, photographs, and sheet music. Among its special collections are ones on black history and culture; performing arts; English and American literature; bindings and illustrated books; Japanese prints; tobacco; early Bibles including the Gutenberg; maps, photographs and prints; Jewish, Oriental, Slavonic cultures, and U.S. history and genealogy.

New York State Library
State Education Department, Cultural Education
  Center
Empire State Plaza
Albany, NY 12230
518-474-5930
http://www.nysl.nysed.gov/

Founded in 1818, New York State's library contains more than 2.3 million volumes, with special collections on Dutch colonial records, New York State political and social history, and the Shakers.

New York University
Elmer Holmes Bobst Library
70 Washington Sq. South
New York, NY 10012
212-998-2505
http://www.nyu.edu/library/bobst

Established in 1831, New York University's holdings total approximately 4 million volumes, with special collections on Lewis Carroll, Robert Frost, rare Judaica and Hebraica, mathematics, and the history of dentistry.

Queens Borough Public Library System
89-11 Merrick Blvd.
Jamaica, NY 11432
718-990-0700
http://www.queens.lib.ny.us/

Organized in 1896, this library system contains more than 7.2 million books and has 62 branches. It maintains special collections of Long Island history and genealogy and a collection of over 1.5 million pictures.

State University of New York at Buffalo
University Libraries
432 Capen Hall
Buffalo, NY 14260
716-645-2967
http://ublib.buffalo.edu/libraries/

Founded in 1922, the State University libraries hold more than 2.3 million volumes, with special collections of poetry, the works of J. Frank Dobie, New York State governors' autographs, and books on science and engineering and the history of medicine.

Syracuse University Libraries
E. S. Bird Library
222 Waverly Ave.
Syracuse, NY 13244
315-443-2573
http://libwww.syr.edu/

Established in 1871, Syracuse University has holdings of more than 2.6 million volumes, with special collections on Stephen Crane, Loyalists in the American Revolution, economic history, Margaret Bourke-White, Rudyard Kipling, and cartoonists; science-fiction books and manuscripts; and the papers of Averell Harriman, Dorothy Thompson, and Benjamin Spock.

University of Rochester
Rush Rhees Library
Rochester, NY 14627
716-275-4461
http://www.lib.rochester.edu/

Founded in 1850, the Rochester library's holdings include more than 2.3 million volumes, with special collections on 19th- and 20th-century public affairs, 19th-century botany and horticulture, American literature, regional history, and Leonardo da Vinci.

North Carolina

Duke University
William R. Perkins Library
Durham, NC 27708
919-660-5800
http://www.lib.duke.edu/reference/index.htm

Founded in 1838, Duke's library contains more than 4.5 million volumes, with special collections on American almanacs, architecture, city directories, Samuel Taylor Coleridge, Confederate imprints, Ralpho Waldo Emerson, Latin American history, manuscripts, the Methodist Church, newspapers, the Philippines, utopias, and Wesleyana.

University of North Carolina at Chapel Hill
Walter Royal Davis Library
Chapel Hill, NC 27514
919-962-1301
http://www.lib.unc.edu/davis.html

Founded in 1795, North Carolina's library contains more than 4.2 million volumes, with special collections on North Carolina and Southern history.

Ohio

Cleveland Public Library
325 Superior Ave.
Cleveland, OH 44114

216-623-2800
http://www.cpl.org/

Founded in 1869, the Cleveland Public Library contains 2.5 million volumes. Its special collections are devoted to folklore, the Orient, and chess.

Ohio State University Libraries
William Oxley Thompson Memorial Library
1858 Neil Avenue Mall
Columbus, OH 43210
614-292-6151
http://www.lib.ohio-state.edu

Established in 1873, Ohio State offers approximately 4 million volumes and bound periodicals. Special collections include those on the American Association of Editorial Cartoonists, American fiction to 1925, American sheet music, Australia, daguerreotypes and ambrotypes, dance notation, Reformation history, and science-fiction magazines.

Public Library of Cincinnati and Hamilton County
800 Vine St.
Library Square
Cincinnati, OH 45202
513-369-6900
http://www.einet.net/hytelnet/us767.html

Founded in 1853, Cincinnati's library has more than 3.5 million volumes, with 139,337 maps and special collections on local history, genealogy, theology, art, music, theater, and oral history.

Oklahoma

University of Oklahoma
University Libraries
410 W. Brooks
Norman, OK 73019
405-325-2611
http://www.ou.edu/www/ou_info/ou_library.html

Founded in 1895, the University of Oklahoma's library holds more than 2.2 million volumes, with special collections devoted to early science, Western history, Native American papers, political speeches, theater, film, and dance.

Pennsylvania

Carnegie Library of Pittsburgh
4400 Forbes Ave.
Pittsburgh, PA 15213
412-622-3100
http://www.clpgh.org/clp/

Founded in 1895, the Carnegie Library collection contains more than 2.4 million volumes, with approximately 69,000 in foreign languages. It maintains special collections on architecture and design, the Atomic Energy Commission, cartoons, local history, U.S. patents, World War I, and 19th-century American and German music journals.

Free Library of Philadelphia
1901 Vine St.
Philadelphia, PA 19103
215-686-5322
http://www.libertynet.org/flp/

Founded in 1891, the Free Library contains 6.7 million volumes and bound periodicals, with special collections on orchestral music, common law, automobile history, Americana, cuneiform tablets, Charles Dickens, Edgar Allan Poe, Beatrix Potter, Arthur Rackham, theater, and maps (including over 130,000 single-sheet maps, atlases, and geographies).

Pennsylvania State University
Fred Lewis Pattee Library
University Park, PA 16802
814-865-0401
http://www.libraries.psu.edu/

Established in 1857, Penn State's library has approximately 2 million volumes, with special collections on American sociology, anthropology, art, architecture, Australia, Bibles, black literature, the Columbus family papers, English literature, photography, Pennsylvania, science fiction, surrealism, and the United Steelworkers of America.

University of Pennsylvania Libraries
Van Pelt Library
3420 Walnut St.
Philadelphia, PA 19104
215-898-7091
http://www.library.upenn.edu/vanpelt/

Founded in 1749, the University of Pennsylvania's libraries hold more than 4.2 million volumes, with special collections on church history, the Spanish Inquisition, canon law, witchcraft, Shakespeare, alchemy and chemistry, Aristotle, Bibles, Jonathan Swift, Sanskrit manuscripts, Theodore Dreiser, Washington Irving, and the Spanish Golden Age of literature, as well as Benjamin Franklin imprints.

University of Pittsburgh
University Libraries
Pittsburgh, PA 15260
412-648-7710
http://www.pitt.edu/NewPittInfo/libraries.html

Founded in 1873, the University of Pittsburgh has holdings of more than 3.3 million volumes, with special collections on ballet, 19th- and 20th-century

American and English theater, popular culture, early history and travel, children's literature, "Mr. Rogers' Neighborhood" videos, and ethnic organizations.

South Carolina

University of South Carolina
Thomas Cooper Library
Columbia, SC 29208
803-777-3142
http://www.sc.edu/library/

Founded in 1801, South Carolina's system contains more than 2.3 million volumes, with special collections on archeology, ornithology, aerial photography, and rare medical books.

Texas

Dallas Public Library
1515 Young St.
Dallas, TX 75201
214-670-1400
http://www.lib.ci.dallas.tx.us

Founded in 1901, Dallas's library contains over 3 million volumes. Special collections cover business histories; children's literature; classical literature; classical recordings; Dallas black history; and diaries and manuscripts on dance, fashion, genealogy, grants, printing, and Texas.

Houston Public Library
500 McKinney Ave.
Houston, TX 77002
713-247-2700
http://www.hpl.lib.tx.us/hpl/index.html

Founded in 1901, the Houston Public Library has more than 4.1 million volumes, with special collections of Bibles; books on the Civil War, genealogy, Texas, and petroleum; Salvation Army posters; early Houston photographs; early printing and illuminated manuscripts; juvenile literature; and sheet music.

University of Texas Libraries
Perry-Castaneda Library
Austin, TX 78713
512-495-4350
http://www.lib.utexas.edu/Libs/PCL/

Founded in 1883, this university library system serves a student body of more than 46,000. With more than 7 million books and bound periodicals, its holdings are divided among individual libraries devoted to Asia; film; the Middle East; Latin America; public affairs; architecture and planning; chemistry; classics; engineering; fine arts; geology; physics, mathematics, and astronomy; science; business research;

humanities; population research; and law. Its special collections cover Southern history, Canada, British Commonwealth literature, the U.S. Volleyball Association, and oral histories.

Utah

University of Utah
Marriott Library
Salt Lake City, UT 84199
801-581-8558
http://www.lib.utah.edu/

Founded in 1850, Utah's library contains in excess of 2 million volumes, with special collections on the Middle East, Western Americana, and the history of medicine.

Virginia

University of Virginia
University Library
Charlottesville, VA 22903
804-924-3026
http://www.lib.virginia.edu/

Established in 1819, Virginia's library holds more than 4.1 million books and bound periodicals, with special collections devoted to American literature, the American Revolution, Americana, the Civil War and Reconstruction, political cartoons, Ceylon, classical studies, Stephen Crane, Oliver Cromwell, John Dos Passos, evolution, William Faulkner, finance, Robert Frost, Gothic novels, Bret Harte, Nathaniel Hawthorne, international law, Washington Irving, Thomas Jefferson, modern art, Mark Twain, typography and printing, Virginia, voyages and travels, and Walt Whitman.

Washington

University of Washington Libraries
Allen Library, Room 482
Seattle, WA 98195
206-543-1760
http://www.lib.washington.edu/

Founded in 1862, this university's holdings exceed 5.3 million volumes, with special collections devoted to East Asia, fisheries, forest resources, oceanography, and the Pacific Northwest.

Wisconsin

Milwaukee Public Library
814 W. Wisconsin Ave.
Milwaukee, WI 53233
414-286-3000
http://www.mpl.org/

Founded in 1878, the Milwaukee Public Library has more than 2.3 million volumes, with special collections on the Great Lakes, H. G. Wells, British and American authors, genealogy, and cookbooks.

University of Wisconsin–Madison
General Library System and Memorial Library
728 State St.
Madison, WI 53706
608-262-3193
http://www.library.wisc.edu/

The University of Wisconsin has amassed a collection of more than 4.5 million volumes since its founding in 1850. Special collections include those on alchemy, American gifts, bookplates, Brazilian positivism, Buddhism, children's literature, C. S. Lewis's letters, Calvinist theology and Dutch history, chess, Early American women authors, history of chemistry, medieval history, Mexican pamphlets, Polish literature and history, Tibetan studies, Mark Twain, and Welsh theology.

CANADA

Alberta

University of Alberta
University Library
Edmonton, Alberta T6G 2J8
403-492-3790
http://libits.library.ualberta.ca/library.html

Established in 1909, Alberta's university system contains more than 3.7 million volumes, with special collections on literature, Native Americans, Victorian book arts, western Canada, and theology and canon law.

Ontario

University of Toronto Library System
Toronto, Ontario M5S 1A5
416-978-2282
http://library.utoronto.ca/

Founded in 1827, the University of Toronto has holdings of more than 8 million volumes, with extensive sections of sheet music, films, slides, maps, and photographs. Its special collections include those on Shakespeare, the history of science, Darwin, Victorian natural history, ornithology, medical and related sciences, Italian plays, juvenile drama, Canada, and Canadian authors.

British Columbia

University of British Columbia Library
1956 Main Mall
Vancouver, British Columbia V6T 1Z1
604-822-3310
http://www.library.ubc.ca/

Established in 1915, British Columbia's library holds more than 3.5 million volumes, with special collections on Pacific Northwest history, Canada, the Orient, the history of science, English literature, and Canadian and Japanese maps.

Quebec

McGill University Libraries
3459 McTavish St.
Montreal, Quebec H3A 1Y1
514-398-4744
http://www.library.mcgill.ca/

Founded in 1821, this university system serves an enrollment of about 24,000 students and has holdings of 1.6 million volumes. Its special collections cover architecture, William Blake, Canada, entomology, early geology, the history of science and medicine, natural history and ornithology, printing, Shakespeare, and 16th- and 17th-century tracts.

THE DEWEY DECIMAL SYSTEM AND HOW TO USE IT

Melvil Dewey (1851–1931) believed in organization. Even as a child, he was busy devising a way to arrange his family's pantry to make it more efficient. Before his system of classifying library books was adopted, many libraries relied on systems that filed books by size or color—cumbersome and not very useful methods at best. While working as a librarian at Amherst College, Dewey developed a system that is used by most school and small public libraries today. Published anonymously in 1876, his classifications divide nonfiction books into 10 broad categories:

000–099	General works (encyclopedias and similar works)
100–199	Philosophy (how people think and what they believe)
200–299	Religion (including mythology and religions of the world)
300–399	Social sciences (folklore and legends, government, manners and customs, vocations)

400–499	Language (dictionaries, grammars)
500–599	Pure science (mathematics, astronomy, chemistry, nature study)
600–699	Technology (applied sciences—aviation, building, engineering, homemaking)
700–799	Arts (photography, drawing, painting, music, sports)
800–899	Literature (plays, poetry)
900–999	History (ancient and modern, geography, travel)

Each of these sections is further divided for accuracy in classification. For example, the numbers 500–599 cover the pure sciences, such as astronomy, chemistry, mathematics, paleontology, and physics. Each of these areas has its own division and section number. All books on mathematics are assigned numbers in the 510 to 519 range; mathematics is then broken down into types, such as algebra, arithmetic, and geometry. Geometry's specific number is 513, which can be subdivided through the use of decimal points to provide 10 basic categories. Additional digits can be added, creating an ever more precise categorization system.

Books are arranged alphabetically within each classification by the first letters of the author's last name. Therefore, a library that has several books on American history of the colonial period will assign the same basic number (973.2) to all the books and shelve them alphabetically.

Dewey's aim was to create a system that would be simple enough for even casual users to understand, but complex enough to meet a library's expanding needs. His system was developed to meet the needs of many libraries. A second popular system was created to fit the requirements of a specific library, the Library of Congress. This system, now in wide use, is even more detailed and has the advantage of being able to accommodate growth of knowledge in unexpected areas.

THE LIBRARY OF CONGRESS SUBJECT HEADINGS

The Library of Congress Classification System is used in most large public and university libraries today. A Library of Congress (LC) number contains

A Closer Look

Cataloging in Publication Data

On the copyright page of most books, under the heading "Cataloging in Publication Data," are numbers and abbreviations that help librarians index new acquisitions for the card catalog. These data can be helpful to readers as well. A typical entry is shown below with an explanation of each part of the entry:

Library of Congress Cataloging in Publication Data

[Author] McLanathan, Richard B. K.

[Title] World art in American museums.

[Possible subject card headings, in order of importance] 1. Art—United States—Guidebooks. 2. Art museums—United States—Guidebooks. 3. Museums—United States—Guidebooks. 4. Art—Canada—Guidebooks. 5. Art—museums—Guidebooks. 6. Museums—Canada—Guidebooks.

1. Title.

[Library of Congress No.] N510.M34 1983 708.13 *[Dewey Decimal No.]*

ISBN 0-385-18515-4 *[International Standard Book Number: country number; publisher number; title number; and check digit. The ISBN was started by the British in 1967 and adopted in the United States a year later.]*

three lines: a letter at the top, a number in the middle, and a letter/number combination at the bottom.

The Library of Congress went through several systems before devising its own method. Because the Library of Congress contains almost every book ever published in the United States, as well as valuable tapes and research materials, it needs a highly flexible system. The Library of Congress Classification System contains 21 classes:

A General works
B Philosophy, psychology, and religion
C Auxiliary sciences of history
D History: general and outside the Americas
E History: America (general) and United States (general)
F History: United States (local), Canada, Central and South America, Caribbean
G Geography, anthropology, recreation
H Social sciences
J Political science
K Law
L Education
M Music
N Fine arts
P Language and literature
Q Science
R Medicine
S Agriculture
T Technology
U Military science
V Naval science
Z Bibliography and library science

Each of these classes can be divided into a subclass with the addition of a second letter. With the addition of numbers, the category becomes even more specific. The flexibility of the system becomes apparent when one sees that the alphabet permits 26 subdivisions of any one class. Each of the subdivisions can be broken down further by using the numbers 1 to 9999.

Librarians recommend that researchers turn to *Subject Headings Used in the Dictionary Catalog of the Library of Congress* for assistance. Because the LC system groups related topics together, a researcher may discover unexpected, related avenues to pursue.

Cataloging in Publication Data might also include information on a book's illustrator, whether a book has an index or bibliography, and number of pages.

LIBRARIES ONLINE

Internet links to more than 2,000 libraries (as well as various information services) in more than 70 countries can be found on the Lib Web SunSITE (http://sunsite.berkeley.edu/Libweb). Especially noteworthy among library home pages is the Library of Congress site (http://www.loc.gov). The site provides access to the Library of Congress catalog and catalogs of other libraries, allows users to call up information on a wide variety of subjects, and contains links to other Internet sites. It also offers access to the American Memory collection, which contains both multimedia presentations and documents; THOMAS, a survey of all the legislation pending before Congress; and text and graphics from current and recent Library of Congress exhibitions.

In addition to the various libraries' home pages, the Internet also offers a number of virtual libraries—collections of electronic documents and hypertext links—that exist solely in cyberspace:

Internet Public Library
http://www.ipl.org

Carrie: A Full-Text Electronic Library
http://www.ukans.edu/carrie/carrie_main.html

CyberStacks
http://www.public.iastate.edu/
~CYBERSTACKS

Library Gazebo Kiosk
http://www.netins.net/showcase/gazebo/
kiosk.html

Public Libraries with Internet Services
http://sjcpl.lib.in.us

WebCATS: Library Catalogues on the Web
http://www.lights.com/webcats

The Virtual Library
http://thorplus.lib.purdue.edu/vlibrar/
index.html

DATA BANKS AVAILABLE FOR COMPUTER RESEARCH

CompuServe, Inc.
Information Services
P.O. Box 20212
5000 Arlington Centre Blvd.
Columbus, OH 43220

800-848-9000
614-457-0802 in Ohio or Canada
http://www.compuserve.com

This fee-based online system offers forums for users of various computers, with electronic editions of newspapers and computer magazines, an international newswire, conferences, and message boards. CompuServe provides remote computing services, a videotex information service, and a value-added network service, as well as games, entertainment, and personal finance services.

DIALOG Information Services, Inc.
3460 Hillview Ave.
Palo Alto, CA 94304
800-334-2564
415-858-2700
http://www.krinfo.com

This fee-based online system provides access to approximately 280 databases, making it possible to search through thousands of newspapers, general-interest and trade magazines, and other publications in seconds. It includes databases compiled by Dun & Bradstreet, Moody's Investor's Service, and Standard & Poor's.

Dow Jones News/Retrieval
P.O. Box 300
Princeton, NJ 08534
609-520-4000
http://www.bis.dowjones.com

This fee-based online computer service offers an interactive information service with up-to-the-minute news and information to the business and financial community. Stories from the *Wall Street Journal, Barron's,* and the *Dow Jones News Service* appear as quickly as 90 seconds after filing and go back as far as 90 days. Dow Jones also offers online stock trading and portfolio management services.

Lexis-Nexis
P.O. Box 933
Dayton, OH 45401
800-227-4908
800-843-6476 (LEXIS-NEXIS EXPRESS)
http://www.lexis-nexis.com

This legal, news, and business information service provides online access to more than 73,000 databases containing more than 1 billion separate documents. Areas covered include statutes, legal cases, and online law libraries; national and international news summaries from leading U.S. newspapers and magazines

Libraries

A Closer Look

Getting Started in Genealogy

The search for a greater understanding of our ancestors has boomed in the United States since the American Bicentennial celebration and the publication of Alex Haley's immensely popular *Roots*. Genealogists lament that too many of us live in historical vacuums, unable to name more than a generation or two of our closest relatives. To help you join this search for a history that extends beyond the last few generations, experts offer several tips:

1. Begin with your closest family members, recording basic information that is already known to you and working backward. This part of the investigation can be quite far-reaching if you contact distant relatives and check sources that they suggest. You may be fortunate enough to have access to family Bibles, letters, and diaries. Vital records such as birth and death certificates can yield a wealth of information at this stage.

2. Consult popular references for research techniques. Some of the best follow.
   - Andereck, Paul A., and Richard A. Pence. *Computer Genealogy: A Guide to Research Through High Technology.* Ancestry Publishing, 1991.
   - Beard Field, Timothy. *How to Find Your Family Roots.* McGraw-Hill, 1977.
   - Cerny, Johni, and Wendy Elliot. *The Library: A Guide to the LDS Family History Library.* Ancestry Publishing, 1988. The book is an explanatory guide to the largest single collection of genealogical works, run by the Church of Jesus Christ of Latter Day Saints.
   - Doane, Gilbert Harry, and James B. Bell. *Searching for Your Ancestors: The How and Why of Genealogy.* 6th ed. University of Minnesota Press, 1992. This introductory guide to genealogical research covers techniques and sources for locating genealogical data.
   - Eakle, Arlene, and Johni Cierny. *The Source: A Guidebook of American Genealogy.* Ancestry Publishing, 1984. The book is a compilation of resources, research techniques, and record sources.
   - Kurzweil, Arthur. *From Generation to Generation.* Schocken Books, 1982. This volume addresses genealogical techniques and subjects particular to Jewish family history, from locating information on European shtetls to Sephardic research.

3. Check out the libraries. Extensive genealogical collections exist at the Library of Congress, the New York Public Library, the Los Angeles Public Library, the Newberry Library in Chicago, and the Allen County Public Library in Fort Wayne, Indiana. Specialized libraries, such as the famed Genealogical Library of the Church of Jesus Christ of Latter-Day Saints in Salt Lake City, Utah, can be extremely helpful. This particular library offers more than 1.3 million reels of microfilm of all types of documents useful to genealogists. Also visit or contact local libraries in areas where your ancestors are known to have lived.

4. Consider contacting the following organizations, which have extensive genealogical records:

American Family Records Association
P.O. Box 15505
Kansas City, MO 64106
816-373-6570

Ellis Island
http://www.ellisisland.org

Genealogical Libraries on the WWW
http://genealogy.org

Federation of Genealogical Societies
http://www.fgs.org

Jewish Genealogical Society
P.O. Box 6398
New York, NY 10128
212-330-8257

Library of Congress
Local History and Genealogy Reading Room
1st Street and Independence Avenue
Washington, DC 20540
202-707-5000
http://leweb.loc.gov

National Archives and Records Administration
Consultant's Office
7th Street and Pennsylvania Avenue, NW
Washington, DC 20408
202-501-5402
http://www.nara.gov

National Genealogical Society
4527 17th St., N
Arlington, VA 22207
703-525-0050
http://www.genealogy.org/~ngs/

Libraries

A Closer Look

Major Genealogical Libraries

Burton Collection, Detroit Public Library, 5201 Woodward Ave., Detroit, MI 48202

Dallas Public Library, 1515 Young St., Dallas, TX 75201

Daughters of the American Revolution Library, 1776 D St., NW, Washington, DC 20006 (to be used with the Library of Congress and National Genealogical Society Library, 4527 17th St. N, Arlington, VA 22207)

Genealogical Society Library, 50 E. N. Temple St., Salt Lake City, UT 84150

Los Angeles Public Library, 630 W. 5th St., Los Angeles, CA 90071

Newberry Library, 60 W. Walton St., Chicago, IL 60610

New England Genealogical Society, 101 Newbury St., Boston, MA 02116

New York Historic Genealogical and Biographical Society, 122–6 E. 58th St., New York, NY 10022

New York Public Library, 5th Avenue and 42nd Street, New York, NY 10018

Allen County Public Library, 301 W. Wayne St., Fort Wayne, IN 46802

State Historical Society of Wisconsin, 816 State St., Madison, WI 53706

Western Reserve Historical Society, 10825 East Blvd., Cleveland, OH 44106

---

and worldwide wire services; company records and analysts' reports; and access to corporate financial data from the EDGAR system of the U.S. Securities and Exchange commission. Nonsubscribers can use LEXIS-NEXIS EXPRESS to conduct specific searches for a onetime fee.

Ovid Technologies
333 Seventh Ave.
New York, NY 10001
800-950-2035
212-563-3006
http://www.ovid.com

Ovid provides online access to bibliographic and full-text databases for academic, biomedical, and scientific research. Its clients represent Canada, Latin America, Europe, the Middle East, and Africa, as well as the United States.

Questel-Orbit
800 Westpark Dr.
McLean, VA 22102
800-456-7248
703-442-0900
http://www.questel.orbit.com

This international online information company specializes in patent, trademark, scientific, chemical, and business information covering the United States and the world.

WILSONLINE
The H. W. Wilson Company
950 University Ave.
Bronx, NY 10452
800-367-6770
212-588-8400
http://www.hwwilson.com

WILSONLINE provides online access to *The Readers' Guide to Periodical Literature*, the *Business Periodicals Index*, the *Index to Legal Periodicals*, the *Education Index*, and numerous other periodical resources. It is used widely by corporations, government agencies, libraries, schools, and universities. Its database covers more than 3,000 periodicals and 500,000 books.

INFORMATION CENTERS

American Crafts Council Library
72 Spring St.
New York, NY 10012
212-274-0630

Questions about the history of crafts or about learning how to pursue a particular craft, such as weaving or pottery, are answered. Calls may be made Tuesday through Friday between 10 A.M. and 5 P.M., EST.

American Museum of Natural History Library
79th Street and Central Park West
New York, NY 10024
212-769-5400
http://amnh.org

Founded in 1869, this special library has 400,000 volumes devoted to subjects ranging from anthropology to travel and expedition, with sections on biology, ethnology, entomology, geology, herpetology, history of science, ichthyology, living and fossil invertebrates, mammalogy, mineralogy, museology, ornithology, and paleontology. Its special collections are devoted to astronomical instruments, rare books and manuscripts, rare films, and many other areas. The museum's librarians offer assistance in all areas.

Libraries

Consumer Information Center

Pueblo, CO 81009
719-948-4000
http://www.pueblo.gsa.gov/

This federal government agency provides a wide selection of free publications such as its monthly *National Consumer Buying Alert* and guides to solar energy, tire buying, nutrition, budgeting, housing, and gardening. Write for a free catalog or specify your area of interest.

Educational Resources Information Center (ERIC)

1200 19th St. NW
Washington, DC 20208
800-LET-ERIC
202-219-2289
http://www/aspensys.com/eric/index.html

The National Institute of Education within the U.S. Department of Education sponsors ERIC, the educational information system, to provide literature pertaining to various aspects of education. General questions about education are also answered. If a computer search is necessary, a charge will be imposed; otherwise, the information is free. ERIC also provides referrals to other organizations, including its own clearinghouses on adult, career, and vocational education; counseling and personnel services; educational management; elementary and early childhood education; handicapped and gifted children; higher education; information resources; junior colleges; languages and linguistics; reading and communications skills; rural education and small schools; science, mathematics, and environmental education; social studies/social science education; teacher education; tests, measurements, and evaluation; and urban education. Calls are accepted between 8 A.M. and 5:30 P.M., EST, weekdays.

Museum of Television and Radio

25 W. 52nd St.
New York, NY 10019
212-621-6800
http://www.mtr.org
and
465 N. Beverly Dr.
Beverly Hills, CA 90210
310-786-1025

Founded in 1976, this museum has collected more than 10,000 radio and 8,000 TV tapes from the 1920s to the present and 2,400 radio scripts, with 1,600 available on microfiche. Its staff is knowledgeable about all aspects of broadcasting and has access to a thousand-volume library of books and magazines.

The National Archives

Central Reference Service Division
Washington, DC 20408
202-501-5402
http://www.nara.gov

This federal government agency is responsible for keeping the permanent records of the U.S. government. Its holdings include maps, photographs, films, U.S. Census records, and all types of correspondence generated and received by government officials. The archives also contain ship passenger records dating as far back as 1820 and military records from the Revolutionary War. Some of its holdings occasionally overlap those of the Library of Congress. Call between 8:45 A.M. and 5:15 P.M., EST, weekdays.

Nutrition Information Center

The New York Hospital–Cornell Medical Center
Memorial Sloan-Kettering Cancer Center
515 E. 71st St., Room 904
New York, NY 10021
212-746-5454

Advice is provided on clinical nutrition, nutrition research, and general nutrition. The staff will also furnish educational materials, make referrals, and assist in program planning. Calls may be made weekdays between 9 A.M. and 5 P.M., EST.

The Performing Arts Library

Roof Terrace Level
John F. Kennedy Center for the Performing Arts
Washington, DC 20566
202-416-8780

Both the public and professional artists may call the library for information and reference assistance on broadcasting, dance, film, music, theater, and related areas. The library is a joint project of the Kennedy Center and the Library of Congress.

United Nations

2 United Nations Plaza, DC2-853
New York, NY 10017
800-253-9646
http://www.un.org

This international organization's publications cover a wide range of topics, including human rights, public finance, atomic energy, treaties, and international statistics. The UN makes materials available in hardbound and paperback books, pamphlets, bulletins, periodicals, and official records—all in English, and frequently also in Spanish, French, and Russian. Write for a catalog and details of current offerings.

Go to
"Federal Information Centers" in chapter 22

United States Military Academy Library
West Point, NY 10996
914-938-3833
http://www.usma.edu

> Founded in 1802, the academy's library contains 400,000 volumes pertaining to the history of the military as well as government documents.

REFERENCE WORKS FOR GENERAL INFORMATION

The following lists are not meant to be comprehensive but are intended to serve as wide-ranging sources for the subjects. A library will provide further reference materials and works on each of the subjects.

GENERAL REFERENCE WORKS

American Reference Books Annual. Libraries Unlimited, 1970–.

> This annual volume covers 1,300 to 1,800 new titles each year, reviewing about 300 categories of reference books. The most recent works in many disciplines are listed.

Bartlett's Familiar Quotations: A Collection of Passages, Phrases and Proverbs Traced to Their Sources in Ancient and Modern Literature. 16th ed. Little Brown, 1992.

> This work lists more than 22,500 familiar and world-famous quotations along with a 600-page keyword subject index.

Books in Print. Bowker, 1947–.

> This annual listing of books now in print or slated for publication by January 31 of the following year currently contains well over 700,000 titles.

Carruth, Gorton, ed. *The Volume Library.* The Southwestern Company, 1917–.

> This two-volume, 2.5-million-word family encyclopedia is revised annually. It covers subjects of interest to students and their families and is illustrated and thoroughly indexed.

Encyclopaedia Britannica. 15th ed. Encyclopaedia Britannica, 1987.

> A major comprehensive reference tool for any library.

Encyclopedia Britannica CD 98. Encyclopedia Britannica, 1998.

> An easily accessed CD reference with extensive cross-referencing and yearly updates.

Ethridge, James M., ed. *The Directory of Directories: An Annotated Guide to Business and Industrial Directories, Professional and Scientific Rosters, and Other Lists and Guides of All Kinds.* 2nd ed. Information Enterprises, 1982.

> The work lists 5,200 directories with categories such as business, education, and leisure, providing full details on each publication.

Guinagh, Kevin, ed. *Dictionary of Foreign Phrases and Abbreviations.* 3rd ed. H. W. Wilson, 1982.

> This helpful dictionary defines more than 5,000 French, German, Greek, Italian, Latin, and Spanish abbreviations, phrases, proverbs, and quotations.

Guinness Book of Records. Bantam, 1955–; Facts On File, 1991–.

> An annual guide to "the biggest, largest, longest, most" all-time records.

Information Industry Market Place: An International Directory of Information Products and Services. Bowker, 1978.

> This international directory describes information collection centers, database and abstract publishers, information brokers, support services and suppliers, conferences, associations, periodicals, and reference books.

Parry, Melanie, ed. *Chambers' Biographical Dictionary.* 6th ed. Larousse, 1997.

> Introduced in 1897, *Chambers'* currently lists more than 17,500 biographies spanning the history of the world.

Libraries

Readers' Guide to Periodical Literature. H. W. Wilson, 1900–.

> *The Readers' Guide* provides a quick overview of current events through indexing of 174 general-interest U.S. magazines in a range of subject areas.

Sheehy, Eugene P., ed. *Guide to Reference Books.* American Library Association, 1986.

> Found on nearly every reference librarian's basic bookshelf, Sheehy's *Guide* is grouped into five main categories: general reference works; humanities; social and behavioral sciences; history and area studies; and science, technology, and medicine.

Who's Who in America. Marquis Who's Who, 1899–.

> The individuals listed in *Who's Who* provide the data to be included, so entries vary in completeness and accuracy. The work includes biographical details on approximately 72,000 Americans and others prominently linked to America.

World Almanac and Book of Facts. Newspaper Enterprise Association, 1868–.

> A handy and easy-to-use reference, the *World Almanac* is updated annually. It provides statistics and factual data on economic, educational, industrial, political, religious, and social issues.

World Book Encyclopedia. World Book-Childcraft International, 1992.

> Easy to use, the *World Book* is targeted at elementary through high school students, providing general reference information.

ANTHROPOLOGY AND ETHNOLOGY

Allen, James Paul, and Eugene James Turner. *We the People: An Atlas of America's Ethnic Diversity.* Macmillan, 1988.

> An atlas devoted to ethnic settlement in the United States. Maps show the distribution of ethnic groups in America; the text discusses the immigration history in the United States and migrations of ethnic populations.

Glazer, Nathan, and Daniel P. Moynihan, eds. *Ethnicity: Theory and Experience.* Harvard University Press, 1975.

> A classic collection of articles dealing with sociological theory as well as ethnic experience in the United States.

Hunter, David E., and Philip Whitten, eds. *Encyclopedia of Anthropology.* Harper & Row, 1976.

> The first English-language encyclopedia in anthropological studies, this volume is compact, comprehensive, and accessible. It includes some 1,400 articles on pertinent topics, supplemented by generous illustrations, maps, diagrams, and photographs.

Thernstrom, Stephan, Ann Orlov, and Oscar Handlin, eds. *Harvard Encyclopedia of American Ethnic Groups.* Belknap Press at Harvard University Press, 1980.

> Defining *ethnic* in the widest possible way, this book contains substantial articles on American ethnic groups. Origins, migration and settlement, history in America, socioeconomic structure, religion and politics, and many other topics are addressed.

APPLIED ARTS

Boger, Louise A. *The Dictionary of Antiques and Decorative Arts.* Rev. ed. Scribner, 1979.

> This volume is international in scope, with short articles and illustrations covering furniture, glass, ceramics, styles, terms, and biographies.

Kovel, Ralph, and Terry Kovel. *Kovel's Antiques and Collectibles Price List.* Crown, annual.

> This book includes prices for more than 50,000 antiques and collectible items.

Kovel, Ralph, and Terry Kovel. *Kovel's Know Your Antiques.* Crown, 1990.

> This guide offers tips on how to recognize and evaluate any antique, large or small, like an

expert. It covers pottery, porcelain, silver, pewter, furniture, pressed and cut glass, prints, bottles, ironware, tinware, letters, sheet music, autographs, books, magazines, and more. This volume also provides advice about caring for antiques and recognizing frauds as well as bibliographies for each specialty.

Kovel, Ralph, and Terry Kovel. *Kovel's Know Your Collectibles.* Crown, 1981.

> This guide advises on what collectible objects are likely to increase in value and how to preserve, protect, and sell them. It covers ceramics, pottery, furniture, glass, toys, print advertisements, and many other items, with bibliographies for each major specialty.

Liman, Ellen. *The Collecting Book.* Penguin, 1980.

> This book thoroughly describes individual collecting areas such as advertising memorabilia, comic books, tobacco items, clothing, boxes and tins, pottery, glass, and toys. It includes chapters on buying, preserving, and displaying collectibles, as well as numerous black-and-white photographs and extensive references to related publications and organizations.

ART AND ARCHITECTURE

American Art Directory. Bowker, 1898–.

> A biennial guide to the thousands of art councils, museums, art libraries, and art schools in the United States, Canada, and abroad.

Artist's Market. Writer's Digest, 1974–.

> This annual publication details names, addresses, contacts, payments, and other data for 4,000 purchasers of cartoons, illustrations, and photographs. It is considered a standard in its field.

Bell, Doris L. *Contemporary Art Trends: A Guide to Sources, 1960–1980.* Scarecrow Press, 1981.

> This work identifies 41 contemporary art trends with listings of appropriate books and museum catalogs. It also contains a listing of 200 contemporary art journals and a bibliography.

Hamlin, Talbot. *Architecture Through the Ages.* Putnam, 1953.

> This excellent college text offers a survey history from the social point of view. Indexed and illustrated.

Mayer, Ralph. *The HarperCollins Dictionary of Art Terms and Techniques.* HarperCollins, 1992.

> This book defines more than 3,200 terms used in the fields of ceramics, drawing, painting, printmaking, and sculpture.

Libraries in the U.S. issue more cards than VISA, have more children enrolled in summer programs than Little League, and have more visitors each week than all museums and zoos combined.

Musgrove, John, ed. *Sir Bannister Fletcher's A History of Architecture.* 19th ed. Butterworth, 1987.

> This comprehensive view of architectural history has been revised and expanded to include worldwide coverage. It is extensively illustrated, with glossary, index, and bibliographies appended to each chapter.

Phaidon Dictionary of Twentieth-Century Art. 2nd ed. Dutton, 1977.

> This concise and thorough survey covers international art movements and artists in depth from 1900.

Placzek, Adolph K., ed. *Macmillan Encyclopedia of Architects.* 4 vols. Free Press, 1982.

> This volume offers a social and historical view of architecture through the ages, from ancient to modern times, in Europe, the Middle East, and North America.

Wilkes, Joseph A., and Robert T. Packard. *Encyclopedia of Architecture: Design, Engineering and Construction.* Wiley, 1990.

> This five-volume work addresses the history of Western architecture over the past 200 years and

Libraries

covers 500 different topics, with 3,000 photographs. Each article was prepared by experts in the field.

ASTRONOMY

Eicher, David J. *The Universe from Your Backyard: A Guide to Deep Sky Objects from Astronomy Magazine.* Cambridge University Press, 1988.

A useful guide for all amateur astronomers.

Moore, Patrick, ed. *The International Encyclopedia of Astronomy.* Orion, 1987.

This popular reference work condenses difficult concepts into readable prose. No prior knowledge of astronomy is assumed. More than 2,500 entries include several major essays by experts in various fields as well as shorter articles. Illustrated in full color.

Muirden, James. *The Amateur Astronomer's Handbook.* 3rd ed. Harper, 1982.

This is an excellent guide for beginners who want to select equipment and set up their own observatories. It includes celestial charts and tables of eclipses and planetary positions.

Pasachoff, Jay M. *Contemporary Astronomy.* 4th ed. CBS College Publishing, 1989.

This textbook is perfect for beginners who have no background in mathematics or physics, presenting astronomical concepts in clear, colloquial English.

BUSINESS

Brownstone, David M., and Gorton Carruth. *Where to Find Business Information: A World Guide for Everyone Who Needs the Answers to Business Questions* (A Hudson Group Book). 2nd ed. Wiley, 1982.

More than 5,000 English-language publications from around the world are listed and briefly described, with concentration on current periodical publications and services, especially magazines, newsletters, computerized databases, printouts, and microforms. The compendium deals with all subjects of interest to business.

Business Periodicals Index: A Cumulative Subject Index to Periodicals in the Fields of Accounting, Advertising, Banking and Finance, General Business, Insurance, Labor and Management, Marketing and Purchasing, Office Management, Public Administration, Taxation, Specific Businesses, Industries, and Trades. H. W. Wilson, 1958–.

This monthly index provides data on approximately 250 periodicals and certain U.S. government documents.

Consumers Index to Product Evaluations and Information Sources. Pierian Press, 1973–. Quarterly; annual cumulation.

A quarterly guide to consumer magazine articles in 14 subject areas.

Consumer Reports Buying Guide. Consumers Union, 1936–.

Issued annually as the December issue of *Consumer Reports,* this guide is a starting point for a comparative analysis of all types of products. It contains test results, brand and model ratings and rankings, and general buying advice on products as diverse as stereos and orange juice. It also provides a subject index to evaluations from the previous five years of *Consumer Reports.*

Dow Jones Irwin Business Almanac. Dow Jones-Irwin, 1977–.

This annual almanac provides business, financial, and tax statistics. It includes a short business directory and a review of the previous year's significant business news.

Dun and Bradstreet Million Dollar Directory. Dun and Bradstreet, 1959–.

This annual directory offers alphabetical listings of industries and businesses with a net worth of at least $1 million. It includes the name, address, corporate officers, Standard Industrial Classification (SIC) number, approximate sales, and number of employees for approximately 39,000 U.S. companies.

Dun and Bradstreet's Guide to Your Investments. Crowell, 1973–.

> An introductory guide for amateur stock-market investors, this annual explains basic concepts for all types of investments: common and preferred stocks, bonds, real estate, stock options, small business investment companies, and formula investing.

Fortune World Business Directory. Time, Inc., 1957–.

> Taken from the annual listing in the May issue of *Fortune* magazine ranking the 500 largest U.S. industrial corporations, this directory includes the "Fortune 500" plus the 50 largest banks.

Franchise Opportunities Handbook. U.S. Bureau of Industrial Economics and Minority Business Development Agency, 1972–.

> One of the best publications on franchising, this annual guide provides details on equity capital needed to buy specific franchises, available training, and support services.

Help: (Washington): The Useful Almanac. Everest House, 1977–.

> This annual almanac offers up-to-date information for consumers. It is arranged topically, with material on health, real estate, nutrition, energy, education, insurance, and numerous other subjects.

Moody's Handbook of Common Stocks. Moody's Investors Service, 1965–.

> Described as a quick-reference tool, Moody's quarterly publishes data on approximately 1,000 stocks, outlining capitalization, earnings, and the projected outlook for each.

Standard and Poor's Register of Corporations, Directors and Executives. Standard and Poor's, 1928–.

> A standard in the field, Standard and Poor's *Register* offers three volumes each year with current information on about 46,000 U.S. and Canadian companies. The volumes include biographies of executives as well as separate listings of newly added individuals and companies, obituaries for the previous year, and complete data on each company.

Standard Directory of Advertisers. National Register Publishing, 1907–.

> This annual directory lists over 17,000 companies that advertise nationally through various media. The directory provides details on officers and sales personnel, product lines, advertising agencies, and media.

Thomas Register of American Manufacturers and Thomas Register Catalog File. Thomas Publications, 1905–.

> This annual authoritative listing of manufacturers is grouped by more than 70,000 product classifications. Its 17 volumes contain lists of products and services; company names, addresses, and phone numbers; names of executives; and ratings. Also included are a brand-name index and company catalogs.

U.S. Master Tax Guide. Commerce Clearing House, 1917–.

> Using information on the Internal Revenue Code regulations and court and tax court decisions, this annual handbook covers all aspects of preparing federal income taxes for corporations, estates and trusts, individuals, and partnerships. It is considered a standard in its field.

COMMUNICATIONS

Barnouw, Eric, ed. *International Encyclopedia of Communications.* 4 vols. Oxford University Press, 1989.

> This comprehensive, illustrated four-volume encyclopedia covers the entire spectrum of communications studies. Most articles are followed by brief bibliographies, and the work is extensively cross-referenced.

Brown, Les. *Les Brown's Encyclopedia of Television.* Zoetrope, 1982.

> This reference work covers television terminology, notable television programs, and profiles of

Libraries

important television personalities, including actors, directors, producers, and writers.

Representative American Speeches Series. H. W. Wilson, 1967–.

This annual publication includes selected major speeches with biographical notes on the speaker.

Writers Market: Where to Sell What You Write. Writer's Digest, 1929–.

An essential annual reference for freelance writers that gives the pertinent data on more than 4,500 publishers of books, periodicals, audiovisual materials, greeting cards, plays, and other materials. It includes basics of copyright law and authors' rights.

EDUCATION

American Council on Education. *American Universities and Colleges.* 14th ed. Walter de Gruyter, 1992.

This comprehensive directory provides information about the structure of higher education in the United States, as well as complete details on each of the more than 1,700 institutions granting baccalaureate or higher degrees.

Durnin, Richard G. *American Education: A Guide to Information Sources.* Gale, 1982.

This bibliography covers books relating to American education, with 107 topical chapters listing works on childhood through higher education. Most works included are recent publications, but classic works also are described.

Good, Carter V. *Dictionary of Education.* 3rd ed. McGraw-Hill, 1973.

This volume offers definitions of technical and professional terms and concepts in all areas of education.

The World of Learning. Europa Publications, 1947–.

This annual directory of international institutions includes educational and scientific institutions and organizations listed by country.

ETHNIC STUDIES
See **Anthropology and Ethnology.**

FILM

Halliwell, Leslie, and John Walker, eds. *Halliwell's Film and Video Guide, 1998.* HarperCollins, 1997 (published annually).

This regularly revised comprehensive work covers a wide range of popular film lore.

Katz, Ephraim. *The Film Encyclopedia.* 2nd ed. Harper, 1994.

This volume covers directors, producers, actors, composers, and screenwriters, as well as major studios and film centers; it does not list individual movies.

GEOGRAPHY AND TRAVEL GUIDES

Rand McNally Comprehensive World Atlas. 2nd ed. Rand McNally, 1991.

This atlas includes 350 color maps and map inserts, with individual maps of each U.S. state and Canadian province. It also provides a list of 1980 census totals for about 20,000 U.S. political subdivisions. The main index contains 82,000 entries.

Rand McNally Road Atlas, latest edition. United States, Canada, and Mexico. Rand McNally.

This annual publication offers maps of all 50 states, each Canadian province, Central America, Mexico, and Puerto Rico, plus a 23,000-item place-name index. It also includes information on population, national park areas, mileage, recreational and historical sites, area codes, time zones, and how to compute miles per gallon.

Webster's New Geographical Dictionary. Rev. ed. Merriam-Webster, 1995.

This work presents basic geographic, demographic, economic, and historical notes on world countries, regions, cities, and natural features, with maps.

Libraries

HISTORY

Barraclough, Geoffrey, ed. *The Times Concise Atlas of World History*. 4th ed. Hammond, 1995.

> Seven sections detail the history of the world, beginning with "The World of Early Man" and concluding with "The Age of Global Civilizations." This work contains approximately 600 maps and illustrations depicting the rise and fall of major civilizations, as well as significant religious and historical events.

Barzun, Jacques, and Henry G. Graff. *The Modern Researcher*. 5th ed. Harcourt Brace Jovanovich, 1992.

> This essential reference stresses historical research and provides methodologies useful to those in the humanities and social sciences.

Carruth, Gorton. *The Encyclopedia of American Facts & Dates*. 9th ed. HarperCollins, 1993.

> This chronologically arranged encyclopedia of American history has become a standard reference book for students and others seeking basic information. It covers explorations, treaties, battles, politics, literature, and science, among other topics.

LAW

Black, Henry Campbell et al. *Black's Law Dictionary: Definitions of the Terms and Phrases of American and English Jurisprudence, Ancient and Modern*. 6th ed. West, 1990.

> A standard reference in the field, *Black's* gives detailed definitions in all aspects of law, including criminal procedure, estate planning, accounting, taxes, and commercial transactions.

Cohen, Morris L., and Robert C. Berring. *How to Find the Law*. 9th ed. West, 1989.

> A basic text for law students, as well as a helpful tool for the layman investigating resources and methodologies of legal research.

LINGUISTICS

Guinagh, Kevin, ed. *Dictionary of Foreign Phrases and Abbreviations*. 3rd ed. H. W. Wilson, 1982.

> This dictionary contains definitions for more than 5,000 French, German, Greek, Italian, Latin, and Spanish abbreviations, phrases, quotations, and proverbs that appear in the English language. Similar expressions are cross-referenced.

Merriam-Webster's Collegiate Dictionary. 10th ed. Merriam-Webster, 1993.

> Almost 160,000 entries are offered, with pronunciations, functional labels, inflected forms, word histories, usage, and word divisions. Also included is the first known date of use for each word. The dictionary contains sections with biographical and geographical entries, foreign words and phrases, degree-granting colleges and universities, signs and symbols, and a style manual.

Roget's International Thesaurus. 5th ed. HarperCollins, 1992.

> Topical listings of more than 250,000 words are provided, with an alphabetical index for easy use.

Strunk, William, Jr., and E. B. White. *The Elements of Style*. 3rd ed. Macmillan, 1979.

> A classic book noted for its simplicity and directness, *Elements* consists of only five chapters: "Elementary Rules of Usage," "Elementary Principles of Composition," "A Few Matters of Form," "Words and Expressions Commonly Misused," and "An Approach to Style."

Webster's New World Dictionary. 3rd College ed. Simon & Schuster, 1988.

> This authoritative dictionary provides over 150,000 entries, with in-depth etymologies, pronunciations, foreign expressions, a syllabification system, and over 11,000 Americanisms.

LITERATURE

Drabble, Margaret, ed. *The Oxford Companion to English Literature*. 5th ed. Oxford University Press, 1995.

> Entries on English fiction, authors, and literary schools and movements are presented.

Libraries

Garland, Henry, and Mary Garland. *The Oxford Companion to German Literature.* 2nd ed. Oxford University Press, 1986.

German writers and their works, with cultural and historical background, are provided.

Gassner, John, and Edward Quinn, eds. *The Reader's Encyclopedia of World Drama.* Crowell, 1969.

The book has entries on playwrights, critics, national dramatic literatures, and histories. Emphasis is on drama as literature.

Granger, Edith. *Granger's Index to Poetry.* Columbia University, 1986.

This standard work is indexed by title, first line, author, and subject.

Hart, James D. *Oxford Companion to American Literature.* 6th ed. Oxford University Press, 1995.

This volume has entries on American fiction, authors, and literary schools and movements.

Harvey, Paul, and J. E. Heseltine. *The Oxford Companion to French Literature.* Oxford University Press, 1969.

This volume covers authors and their works, with survey articles, terms, and movements from the Middle Ages to 1939.

Howatson, M. C. *The Oxford Companion to Classical Literature.* 2nd ed. Oxford University Press, 1989.

This comprehensive guide has entries on authors, characters, plots, literary forms, and cultural and historical background. A chronological table and maps are included.

MLA International Bibliography of Books and Articles on the Modern Languages and Literatures. Modern Language Association of America, 1921–. Annual.

This useful reference covers articles and books in English, French, German, Spanish, Italian, Portuguese, Rumanian, and other languages.

Reader's Adviser. 6 vols. Bowker, 1988.

This basic guide to literature covers the best in English and American fiction, poetry, essays, biographies, and other areas in the fields of reference, history, philosophy, and science.

MEDICAL SCIENCE

American Medical Association Encyclopedia of Medicine. Charles B. Clayman, M.D., ed. Random House, 1989.

This clear, systematic account of current medical knowledge and terminology covers a wide range of diseases, their causes, and symptoms.

American Medical Association Family Medical Guide. 3rd ed. Charles R. Clayman, ed. 1994.

This layperson's handbook features articles on diseases and disorders, diagnostic charts, and an index of drugs and medications.

American Medical Association Home Medical Advisor. Charles R. Clayman, Jeffrey R. M. Kinz, and Harriet S. Meyer, eds. Random House, 1988.

This is a self-help guide to symptoms, disorders, diseases, and medical emergencies, illustrated with charts.

Physicians' Desk Reference to Pharmaceutical Specialties and Biologicals. Medical Economics, 1947–.

This compendium, commonly referred to as the PDR, is a standard reference work for physicians and other health professionals. It offers details on dosage, contraindications, side effects, precautions, and undesirable interactions of pharmaceutical products.

The Wellness Encyclopedia. Staff of the University of California, Berkeley, Wellness Letter, eds. Houghton Mifflin, 1991.

This comprehensive guide focuses on preventive health through good eating, exercise, and risk reduction for disease.

MUSIC

Abraham, Gerald. *The Concise Oxford History of Music.* Oxford University Press, 1985.

This scholarly survey of Western music from ancient to modern times is presented chronologically. It describes the musical styles of each period and region, with extensive bibliographies.

Grout, Donald J. *A History of Western Music.* 5th ed. Norton, 1996.

This standard one-volume history of music is used in thousands of colleges and graduate schools. This illustrated volume contains a bibliography, chronology, and glossary.

Havlice, Patricia Pate. *Popular Song Index.* Scarecrow Press, 1975. Supplement, 1978. Second Supplement, 1984.

More than 300 songbooks from the period 1940 to 1972, including children's songs, folk songs, hymns, and popular music, are anthologized. The supplement includes another 72 anthologies from the period 1970 to 1975.

Randel, Don Michael. *New Harvard Dictionary of Music.* Harvard University Press, 1986.

This comprehensive dictionary includes definitions and brief articles on music history, aesthetics, and theory.

Sadie, Stanley, ed. *The New Grove Dictionary of Music and Musicians.* Reprint ed. 20 vols. Grove's Dictionaries of Music, 1995.

This comprehensive dictionary includes entries and articles on composers, performers, theorists, music publishers, scholars, terminology, genres, and orchestras, with exhaustive bibliographies.

MYTHOLOGY, FOLKLORE, AND POPULAR CUSTOMS

Martin, Richard P., ed. *Bulfinch's Mythology: The Age of Fable, the Age of Chivalry, the Legends of Charlemagne.* HarperCollins, 1991.

The classic work on mythology, *Bulfinch's* summarizes Greek, Roman, Norse, Arthurian, and other myths, with notes on the *Iliad,* the *Odyssey,* and the *Aeneid.*

Mercatante, Anthony. *The Facts On File Encyclopedia of World Mythology and Legend.* Facts On File, 1988.

This comprehensive reference covers world mythologies in thematic, biographical, and narrative essays.

Thompson, Stith. *The Folktale.* University of California Press, 1977.

Considered a standard in the field, this work discusses the form and development of folk stories, with summaries of the most popular folktales of Europe, western Asia, and the Native North Americans. It also covers various methods of researching and studying folktales and folklore.

PHILOSOPHY

Edwards, Paul. *Encyclopedia of Philosophy.* Free Press, 1973.

An excellent scholarly reference, this four-volume encyclopedia contains hundreds of articles relevant to political science as well as biographies of scores of key figures such as Aristotle, Darwin, Hobbes, Jefferson, Locke, Machiavelli, Malthus, Marx, Mill, Plato, and Rousseau.

Magill, Frank N., ed. *Masterpieces of World Philosophy: More Than 100 Classics of the World's Greatest Philosophers Analyzed and Explained.* HarperCollins, 1990.

This book contains more than 100 synopses and commentaries on key figures in Eastern and Western philosophy, including analyses of important influences on their development.

POLITICAL SCIENCE

Congressional Quarterly's Guide to Congress. Latest ed. Congressional Quarterly.

This accurate, nonpartisan guide to the history, power, structure, and workings of Congress includes the texts of the Articles of Confederation, Constitution, Declaration of

Independence, and important preconstitutional documents.

Greenstein, F. I., and N. W. Polsby. *The Handbook of Political Science.* Addison-Wesley, 1975.

> This is an extremely useful encyclopedic survey of the entire field, including administration, civil rights, civil liberties, elections, and federalism.

Lesko, Mathew. *Information U.S.A.* Viking Penguin, 1986.

> This book bills itself as "the ultimate guide to the largest source of information on earth," the U.S. government. It includes names, addresses, and phone numbers to locate information about hundreds of subjects, including consumer products, child care, medical services, educational opportunities, grants and loans, databases, marketing surveys, and government services.

Robert, Henry M. *Robert's Rules of Order.* 11th ed., rev. HarperCollins, 1991.

> This completely revised edition provides the authoritative guide to parliamentary procedure.

Washington Information Directory. Congressional Quarterly, 1975–.

> This annual publication describes 5,000 congressional, executive, and nongovernmental agencies, committees, and organizations. It is considered an indispensable guide to both official and unofficial Washington.

RECREATION AND SPORTS

Guinness Book of Sports Records 1995–96. Facts On File, 1996.

> A handy reference to record-setting facts and figures for men's and women's sports.

Webster's Sports Dictionary. G. & C. Merriam, 1976.

> This authoritative sports reference book defines terms for all popular spectator sports (baseball, basketball, football), international games (cricket, soccer), and recreational pursuits (hunting,

mountain climbing). Diagrams and drawings further illuminate the subject.

RELIGION

Adams, Charles J., ed. *A Reader's Guide to the Great Religions.* 2nd ed. The Free Press, 1977.

> Through bibliographic essays, this work covers major religions as well as ancient beliefs, religions of Mexico and Central and South America, the Sikh religion, and the Jains. It includes a subject index and an index of authors, compilers, translators, and editors for the serious researcher.

Attwater, Donald. *The Penguin Dictionary of Saints.* Rev. ed. Penguin, 1984.

> This book provides brief biographical sketches of 750 of the best-known saints. The selections are worldwide but emphasize those in Great Britain.

Brandon, S. G. F., ed. *Dictionary of Comparative Religions.* Macmillan, 1978.

> Thorough and concise, this volume defines anthropology, iconography, philosophy, and the psychology of primitive, ancient, Asian, and Western religions. Articles describe practices and philosophies of specific religions, with terminology for each and pertinent bibliographies.

The Illustrated Bible Dictionary. 3 vols. Tyndale House, 1980.

> Comprehensive and well organized, this dictionary is based on the revised standard version. It offers definitions from all aspects of books of the Bible; major works and doctrines; and history, geography, customs, and cultures of biblical times. Extensive photographs, charts, diagrams, cross-references, and a useful index are included.

Morrison, Clinton. *An Analytical Concordance to the Revised Standard Version of the New Testament.* Westminster Press, 1979.

> This massive work contains both a concordance and an index-lexicon. Entries give the English word followed by a subtitle line with three

Libraries

elements: definition, Greek word, and an English transliteration of the Greek word. Included are complete listings of each passage in which the subject word appears, with an explanation of its use in context.

SCIENCE AND TECHNOLOGY

Chambers Science and Technology Dictionary. W. R. Chambers Ltd. and Cambridge University Press, 1988.

> A revision and expansion of a classic work, the *Chambers Dictionary* provides 45,000 understandable, alphabetical definitions of terms used in a variety of scientific disciplines.

Chen, Ching-Chih. *Scientific and Technical Information Sources.* 2nd ed. MIT, 1986.

> Although the book is primarily a guide for science and technology librarians, it is a useful guide to relevant sources for the layperson.

McGraw-Hill Encyclopedia of Science and Technology. 7th ed. McGraw-Hill, 1996.

> This 20-volume compendium continues to be the basic reference source covering important topics from earliest times to the present. Annual updates are available.

SOCIAL SCIENCE

Sills, David L., ed. *International Encyclopedia of the Social Sciences.* Macmillan, 1977. Biographical supplement, 1979.

> This scholarly summary of the social sciences offers articles on specific topics, as well as some 600 biographies.

UNESCO Dictionary of the Social Sciences. Julius Gould and William L. Kolb, eds. The Free Press, 1964.

> This excellent reference includes about 2,000 signed articles defining terminology in anthropology, economics, political science, sociology, and other social-science specialties.

See also **Anthropology and Ethnology; Political Science;** and **Sociology.**

SOCIOLOGY

Barnes, Harry Elmer, and Howard Becker. *Social Thought from Lore to Science.* 3rd ed. Peter Smith, 1982.

> This is a three-volume encyclopedic inventory of the history of sociology

Directory of Counseling Services. International Association of Counseling Services, 1969–.

> This annual publication lists members of the American Personnel and Guidance Association who offer public and private counseling dealing with education, family, marriage, personal problems, rehabilitation, and vocational guidance.

STATISTICS AND DEMOGRAPHY

Bureau of the Census Catalog. U.S. Bureau of the Census, 1946–.

> This catalog provides listings of all published and unpublished material (tape, cards, or microform) created by the Census Bureau during the period covered.

Kotz, Samuel, and Normal L. Johnson, eds. *Encyclopedia of Statistical Sciences,* 9 vols. Wiley, 1982–1988; updates 1997-8.

> Information on many topics in statistical history and application of statistical methods is presented in this nine-volume work, intended primarily for readers who seek more information than general references can offer.

United Nations Statistical Yearbook. United Nations, 1949–.

> This annual publication is considered the best source for international statistics. It offers data on such topics as agriculture, balance of payments, communications, construction, energy, population, transport, and wages and prices in 150 countries and territories.

THEATER AND PERFORMING ARTS

Hatnoll, Phyllis, ed. *The Oxford Companion Guide to World Theatre.* 4th ed. Oxford University Press, 1983.

Libraries

Articles on all aspects of theater are included, from history to theater architecture, technical theater, terminology, and experimental theater. Also included are articles on national dramatic literature, plays, actors, playwrights, and teachers.

Hughes, Catherine. *American Theater Annual.* Gale Research, 1976–.

All plays opening on and off Broadway during the year are listed, with details of cast members, opening and closing dates, plot summaries, and review excerpts.

Koegler, Horst. *The Concise Oxford Dictionary of Ballet.* 2nd ed. Oxford University Press, 1982.

This book contains more than 5,000 alphabetically arranged entries covering all areas of ballet: choreographers, composers, dancers, history, schools and companies, and basic definitions.

Notable Names in the American Theater. James T. White, 1976.

This major work is divided into nine sections: "New York Productions"; "Premieres in America"; "Premieres of American Plays Abroad"; "Theater Group Biographies"; "Theater Building Biographies"; "Awards"; "Bibliographical Biography"; "Necrology"; and, most valuable, "Notable Names in the American Theater." The sections cover administrators, agents, archivists, authors, casting directors, composers, conductors, critics, designers, directors, educators, historians, lyricists, performers, playwrights, producers, and teachers.

Theatre World. Crown, annual.

This theater yearbook gives a complete pictorial and statistical record of each Broadway season from 1944–45 to the present.

MAJOR ART MUSEUMS AND THEIR SPECIAL COLLECTIONS

Internet links to numerous museums can be found on the Virtual Library Museums Pages, supported by the International Council of Museums. The organization's home page can be accessed at http://icom.org/vlmp.

UNITED STATES

Arizona

University Art Museum
Arizona State University Art Collections
Nelson Fine Arts Center and Matthews Center
Arizona State University
Tempe, AZ 85287
602-965-ARTS

Founded in 1950, Arizona State's collection includes American paintings of the 18th and 19th centuries; a fine print collection with Rembrandts, Whistlers, and Dürers; fine Americana and decorative arts, particularly pottery; European painting and sculpture; Latin American arts; and crafts.

A researcher at the Smithsonian Museum removed a lens from the compound eye of a half-billion-year-old trilobite (a marine invertebrate animal), attached it to a microscope, and took a photograph of a building.

California

The Fine Arts Museums of San Francisco
California Palace of the Legion of Honor
100 34th Ave.
San Francisco, CA 94121
415-750-3662

M. H. deYoung Museum
75 Tea Garden Dr.
Golden Gate Park
San Francisco, CA 94118
415-750-3600

These museums are run by a joint administration, although they are not located near each other. Founded in 1924 and 1895, respectively, each museum has extensive collections. The deYoung includes the Hearst collection of Flemish Gothic tapestries; fine primitive pre-Columbian artifacts; Northwest Coast Native American, African, and Oceanic arts collections; and Renaissance and Baroque art. The California Palace is noted for its 18th-century French furniture and decorative arts; its French paintings, including those of Monet, Renoir, Fragonard, Boucher, Manet, and Corot; Rodin sculptures; and an extraordinary collection of prints and drawings of all periods.

J. Paul Getty Museum
17985 Pacific Coast Hwy.
Malibu, CA 90265
310-459-7611

The world's best-endowed museum, the Getty was created in 1953. This popular museum is housed in a re-creation of the 1st century B.C. Villa dei Paryri at Herculaneum, complete with elaborate gardens. The Getty has acquired extraordinary classical collections, including illuminated manuscripts and French decorative arts.

Huntington Library, Art Collections, and Botanical Garden
1151 Oxford Rd.
San Marino, CA 91108
818-405-2100

In the Huntington complex, established in 1919, a beautiful garden setting enhances the extraordinary collections of 18th-century British paintings, including Gainsborough's *Blue Boy* and Lawrence's *Pinkie;* Renaissance bronzes and 18th-century marbles; early editions of Shakespeare and Chaucer in the extensive library; and prints and drawings. The setting includes a Japanese garden and 16th-century samurai's house.

Los Angeles County Museum of Art
5905 Wilshire Blvd.
Los Angeles, CA 90036
213-857-6111

Established in 1910, this museum houses a general collection in three pavilions surrounded by a sculpture garden with works from Rodin's time to the present. Its acquisitions include early Near and Middle Eastern antiquities; Roman, Greek, Western, and modern art; Far Eastern collections; textiles; costumes; Indian arts; pottery; Italian mosaics; pre-Columbian, African, and Oceanic arts; and 19th- and 20th-century American and European paintings.

Norton Simon Museum
411 W. Colorado Blvd.
Pasadena, CA 91105
818-449-6840

Established in 1924 as the Pasadena Museum of Modern Art, this museum has developed worldwide prominence through the loans of collector Norton Simon. His collections include European art from the Renaissance to recent times, with Old Masters of the highest quality.

Colorado
The Denver Art Museum
100 W. 14th Avenue Pkwy.
Denver, CO 80204
303-640-2295

The Denver Art Museum is noted for its collection of primitive African, Oceanic, American Native American, and Northwest Indian arts; its Peruvian art; its collection of the arts of China, Japan, Korea, India, Southeast Asia, Tibet, and the Middle and Near East; period rooms; Impressionist, post-Impressionist, and modern paintings; prints, drawings, and photographs; and the Neusteter Institute of Fashion, Costume, and Textiles.

Connecticut
The New Britain Museum of American Art
56 Lexington St.
New Britain, CT 06052
203-229-0257

The New Britain Collection, established in 1903, focuses on outstanding American paintings from colonial times to the present. It includes Hudson River School painters and the Low memorial collection of American illustration, with N. C. Wyeth classics.

Yale Center for British Art
1080 Chapel St.
P.O. Box 208280
New Haven, CT 06520
203-432-2800

This collection of British watercolors, drawings, paintings, books, and prints is the largest of its kind outside Great Britain. Established in 1977, the center was the gift of Paul Mellon, a lifelong collector of British art.

Yale University Art Gallery
1111 Chapel St.
New Haven, CT 06520
203-432-0600

This outstanding world art collection has been built up since the gallery's founding in 1832. It includes the Jarves collection of early Italian paintings; collections of American silver, painting, and decorative arts; modern art; Greek and Roman vases; manuscripts; prints and drawings; and primitive arts.

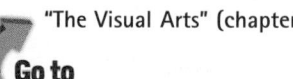
"The Visual Arts" (chapter 7)

Libraries

Delaware
Delaware Art Museum
2301 Kentmere Pkwy.
Wilmington, DE 19806
302-571-9590

The Delaware Art Museum, founded in 1912, specializes in American paintings, with examples by Hudson River School painters such as John Sloan, Howard Pyle, and the Wyeth family. There is an extensive collection of English pre-Raphaelites, a research library on American arts, and prints and drawings.

Henry Francis Du Pont Winterthur Museum
Route 52
Winterthur, DE 19735
302-888-4600

Founded in 1930, Winterthur has an outstanding collection of American furniture, furnishings, and decorative arts from the colonial period to the mid–19th century. Period rooms display extensive collections of ceramics, glass, Chinese porcelain, fabrics, lighting fixtures, and carpets.

District of Columbia
Arthur M. Sackler Gallery, Smithsonian Institution
1050 Independence Ave., SW
Washington, DC 20560
202-357-4880

This gallery contains a permanent collection of Asian art, including ancient works from China, the Indian subcontinent, and Southeast Asia as well as scrolls and other work by notable 20th-century painters.

Freer Gallery of Art, Smithsonian Institution
12th Street at Jefferson Drive, SW
Washington, DC 20560
202-357-4880

Established in 1906, the Freer has one of the world's best collections of Oriental art and a comprehensive collection of Whistler paintings (his close friend Charles Freer gathered the collection and donated it).

Hirshhorn Museum and Sculpture Garden, Smithsonian Institution
Independence Avenue at 7th Street, SW
Washington, DC 20560
202-357-3091

Created in 1966 to specialize in modern art, the Hirshhorn's collection is so vast that only a small portion can be displayed at any time.

National Gallery of Art
Constitution Avenue and 4th Street, NW
Washington, DC 20565
202-737-4215

The National Gallery was endowed by Andrew Mellon in 1937 and continues to benefit from his children's donations. It includes paintings and sculptures of all schools of Western art, decorative arts, and drawings and prints, with all the classic masters represented.

National Museum of American Art, The Smithsonian Institution
8th and G sts., NW
Washington, DC 20560
202-357-2247

Housed in the historic Greek Revival Old Patent Office, the museum has a definitive collection of American arts, including graphic and decorative arts, from colonial times to the present.

The J. Paul Getty museum is the richest in the world. It paid $22 million for Fra Bartolommeo's The Rest on the Flight Into Egypt with Saint John the Baptist.

Hawaii
Honolulu Academy of Arts
900 S. Beretania St.
Honolulu, HI 96814
808-538-8700

The academy, founded in 1927, has a general collection representing everything from ancient Near Eastern and Mediterranean arts to European and American arts. Medieval art, the Michener Collection of Japanese prints, Monet's *Water Lilies,* and the arts of Africa, Oceania, and the Americas are also included.

Illinois
The Art Institute of Chicago
Michigan Avenue at Adams Street
Chicago, IL 60603
312-443-3600

Founded in 1879, the Art Institute of Chicago has excellent collections in all areas of art. It is noted for the works of Old Masters, Impressionists, and American and Far Eastern artists; graphics; and Thorne miniature rooms. Famed works include Seurat's *Sunday Afternoon on the Island of la Grande*

Jatte, Rembrandt's *Young Girl at an Open Half-Door,* and Mary Cassatt's *The Bath.*

Oriental Institute Museum
University of Chicago
1155 E. 58th St.
Chicago, IL 60637
312-962-9520

Founded in 1919, the Oriental Institute houses a top collection of archeology and art of the ancient Near East, Babylonia, Egypt, early Christian cultures, and Islamic civilization.

Indiana

Indiana University Art Museum
Fine Arts Building
Bloomington, IN 47405
812-855-5445

This fine general collection, founded in 1941, includes everything from ancient to contemporary art, with Egyptian, Greek, and Roman sculpture; coins and glass; Western fine and decorative arts from the 14th to the 20th centuries; and Far Eastern arts.

Indianapolis Museum of Art
1200 W. 38th St.
Indianapolis, IN 46208
317-923-1331

Noted for its Chinese, primitive, and American art, this museum, founded in 1883, has an outstanding general collection of Old Masters, Turner watercolors, and European and American decorative arts.

Kansas

Wichita Art Museum
619 Stackman Dr.
Wichita, KS 67203
316-268-4921

Established in 1935, this museum's outstanding collection ranges from art of the Old West by Charles M. Russell to Eakins's *Starting Out After Rail.* It is noted for its American paintings, sculptures, prints, and drawings.

Kentucky

J. B. Speed Art Museum
2035 S. Third St.
Louisville, KY 40208
502-636-2893

This extensive collection, founded in 1925, includes European painting, sculpture, and decorative arts from the Middle Ages to the present; French and Flemish tapestries; and Kentuckiana.

Maryland

The Baltimore Museum of Art
Art Museum Dr.
Baltimore, MD 21218
410-396-6300

Best known for its classic modern collections, this outstanding museum, established in 1914, displays contemporary drawings, period rooms illustrating stylistic development in Maryland, Old Masters paintings, and Far Eastern art.

Walters Art Gallery
600 N. Charles St.
Baltimore, MD 21201
410-547-9000

Assembled by father and son, the Walters Art Gallery opened in 1931 with exquisite medieval treasures and Byzantine and Islamic art; early Christian liturgical vessels, Renaissance enamels, and jewelry; paintings from various periods; and Greek, Roman, and Etruscan art.

Massachusetts

Fogg Art Museum
32 Quincy St.
Harvard University
Cambridge, MA 02138
617-495-9400

With the largest and most extensive art collection of any university in the United States, the Fogg, opened in 1895, is particularly noted for its drawings and prints of all periods. It also has a fine collection of Chinese sculptures, stones and bronzes, jades, and ceramics.

Isabella Stewart Gardner Museum
280 The Fenway
Boston, MA 02115
617-566-1401

This personal collection, founded in 1900, covers a wide range of world art, with masterpieces such as Titian's *The Rape of Europa,* Giotto's *Presentation of the Child Jesus in the Temple,* and Botticelli's *Madonna of the Eucharist.*

Museum of Fine Arts
465 Huntington Ave.
Boston, MA 02115
617-267-9300

This collection, founded in 1870, includes masterpieces from around the world. It is noted for its Far Eastern, ancient, Egyptian, Greek, and Roman collections; its Old Masters, Impressionist, and

Libraries

post-Impressionist works; and its American paintings and decorative arts. It also has American silver, prints and drawings, ancient musical instruments, and ship models. Famed works include Paul Revere's Liberty Bowl, Renoir's *Le Bal...Bougival,* and a Greek marble *Head of Aphrodite.*

Old Sturbridge Village
2 Old Sturbridge Village Rd.
Sturbridge, MA 01566
508-347-3362

Set up in 1938 as a living history museum, Old Sturbridge has a considerable collection of tools, crafts, arts and artifacts, decorative arts, and more than 100 period buildings of the 18th and 19th centuries.

Michigan
The Detroit Institute of Arts
5200 Woodward Ave.
Detroit, MI 48202
313-833-7900

Founded in 1885, this institute is renowned for its comprehensive collection of world arts, especially its Old Master paintings of northern Europe, French 18th-century decorative arts, art of the ancient world, period rooms, prints and drawings, and American arts since colonial times.

Henry Ford Museum and Greenfield Village
20900 Oakwood Blvd.
Dearborn, MI 48121
313-271-1620

Described as a "Disneyland of Americana," the indoor/outdoor facilities, established in 1929, of the museum and village offer demonstrations of crafts and manufacturing techniques that complement its extensive collections of arts, crafts, artifacts, and technology. Activities include everything from antique car rallies to country fairs on its 14 acres.

Minnesota
The Minneapolis Institute of Arts
2400 Third Ave. S.
South Minneapolis, MN 55404
612-870-3000

This outstanding general collection is strongest in European paintings from Old Masters to the present. Founded in 1912, the institute also houses the Pillsbury Collection of Chinese bronzes, Japanese prints and paintings, textiles, and photographs.

Walker Art Center
Vineland Pl.
Minneapolis, MN 55403
612-375-7600

Founded in 1879, this museum contains contemporary art, including paintings, sculpture, drawings, and prints. Its renowned Minneapolis Sculpture Garden is a 7$\frac{1}{2}$-acre urban garden featuring 40 sculptures and a conservatory with horticultural displays.

Missouri
Nelson-Atkins Museum of Art
4525 Oak St.
Kansas City, MO 64111
816-561-4000

This museum contains prestigious collections of European and American art. Its renowned Oriental Collection consists of the Chinese Temple Room, galleries displaying furniture and porcelain, a specially humidified gallery of delicate scroll paintings, a sculpture gallery, and a display of glazed T'ang dynasty tomb figures.

The St. Louis Art Museum
Forest Park
St. Louis, MO 63110
314-721-0067

Founded in 1881, the St. Louis Art Museum contains a comprehensive collection of art from all eras of civilization. Among its more than 35,000 works are important pre-Columbian and German Expressionist collections.

New Jersey
The Art Museum
Princeton University
Princeton, NJ 08544
609-258-3788

Opened in 1882, this comprehensive collection contains a wide spectrum of world art, including Chinese paintings and bronzes, classical antiquities, and French paintings and sculptures.

New Mexico
The University of New Mexico Art Museum
Fine Arts Center
Albuquerque, NM 87131
505-277-7315

Established in 1963, the museum has important collections of 19th- and 20th-century prints and photographs and American paintings of the 20th century, with emphasis on artists who worked in New Mexico.

New York

Albany Institute of History and Art
125 Washington Ave.
Albany, NY 12210
518-463-4478

Founded in 1791, the institute's collection focuses on the fine and decorative arts of Albany and Hudson River artists, with portraits, silver, furniture, and period rooms.

The Brooklyn Museum of Art
200 Eastern Pkwy.
Brooklyn, NY 11238
718-638-5000

The Brooklyn Museum was founded in 1823 and has amassed comprehensive collections of Egyptian and classical arts; American arts; European and American graphics; and pre-Columbian, African, Native American, and other primitive arts.

The Cloisters
Fort Tryon Park, NY 10040
212-923-3700

A branch of the Metropolitan Museum devoted exclusively to medieval art, the Cloisters was built on a 4$^1/_2$-acre site overlooking the Hudson. It was opened in 1938 and incorporates four medieval cloisters, an arcade, a chapel, and exhibition rooms. The museum features 12th- and 13th-century Byzantine and Romanesque art from France and Spain.

Cooper-Hewitt National Museum of Design, The Smithsonian Institution
2 E. 91st St.
New York, NY 10128
212-860-6868

Established in 1897, the Cooper-Hewitt is housed in the Carnegie mansion. Its excellent collection of decorative arts includes furniture, fabrics, wallpaper, ceramics, drawings, prints, architecture and design publications, and metalwork. It boasts the world's largest collection of Winslow Homer drawings and sketches by other late-19th-century artists.

The Frick Collection
1 E. 70th St.
New York, NY 10021
212-288-0700

The former home of Henry Clay Frick, built in 1914 as an 18th-century model, still has most of its original furnishings intact, including excellent European paintings from the 14th through the 18th centuries.

Guggenheim Museum
See **Solomon R. Guggenheim Museum.**

The Jewish Museum
1109 Fifth Ave.
New York, NY 10128
212-423-3200

This preeminent U.S. collection numbers over 23,000 objects spanning 4 millennia, ranging from ancient Eastern Mediterranean archeological artifacts to contemporary art and including paintings, sculpture, ceramics, textiles, wood, metalwork, photography, drawings, prints, coins, medals, and broadcast materials. A permanent exhibit, The Jewish Experience, spans 4,000 years of history and culture.

The Metropolitan Museum of Art
Fifth Avenue at 82nd St.
New York, NY 10028
212-879-5500

One of the world's major museums, founded in 1870, the Metropolitan houses definitive collections covering about 5,000 years of art. A few of the highlights include medieval armor collections, Tiffany stained-glass windows, the complete Temple of Dendur (an early Christian structure from Egypt), extensive painting collections, sculpture, decorative arts, and a re-creation of a classic Ming dynasty Chinese garden court.

Museum of American Folk Art
2 Lincoln Sq.
New York, NY 10023
212-977-7170

This museum, established in 1961, elevates the crafts of the past to fine-art status. It includes collections of quilts, weathervanes, folk paintings, sculptures, weavings, and needlework from the colonial period to the early 20th century.

The Museum of Modern Art
11 W. 53rd St.
New York, NY 10019
212-708-9480

Begun in 1929, this exceptional collection traces the evolution of art from the Impressionist period forward. It represents a variety of disciplines, including drawings and prints, industrial design, architecture, paintings, sculpture, and decorative arts.

Libraries

The Solomon R. Guggenheim Museum
1071 Fifth Ave.
New York, NY 10128
212-423-3500

Founded in 1937, this excellent collection of modern drawings, prints, paintings, and sculpture emphasizes abstract and nonobjective subjects. It is housed in a stunning Frank Lloyd Wright building.

Whitney Museum of American Art
945 Madison Ave.
New York, NY 10021
212-570-3600

Opened in 1966, the Whitney houses New York's largest collection of 20th-century art, with changing exhibitions of drawings, paintings, sculpture, and architecture. It shows contemporary avant-garde film and video and holds the Biennial of Contemporary American Art, a major showcase of the best recent work.

Ohio

Cincinnati Art Museum
Eden Park
Cincinnati, OH 45202
513-721-5204

Founded in 1886, this major museum has an excellent, comprehensive general collection noted for its Near Eastern and American arts, Old Masters, medieval art, musical instruments, and drawings and prints. It includes works by Corot, Titian, Grant Wood, Gainsborough, Goya, and Velazquez.

Cleveland Museum of Art
11150 East Blvd.
Cleveland, OH 44106
216-421-7340

This excellent museum, founded in 1913, has a wide-ranging collection representing the artistic accomplishments of cultures throughout the world. It is recognized for one of the best Far Eastern collections and for its medieval art, Old Masters, classical antiquities, and American arts from the colonial time forward.

The Toledo Museum of Art
2445 Monroe St. at Scottwood Avenue
P.O. Box 1013
Toledo, OH 43697
419-255-8000

This museum is a renowned cultural center for art and music, featuring extensive collections of glass, European and American paintings, sculpture, and decorative arts. Collections range from ancient Egypt, Greece, and Rome through the Middle Ages and the Renaissance to contemporary Europe and America.

Oklahoma

Gilcrease Museum
1400 Gilcrease Museum Rd.
Tulsa, OK 74127
918-596-2700

This exceptional art collection, founded in 1942, captures the saga of America from prehistoric to modern times; the Gilcrease's art of the Old West is rivaled only by that of the Smithsonian. The institute also has maps, books, documents, artifacts, and manuscripts.

Oregon

Portland Art Museum
1219 SW Park Ave.
Portland, OR 97205
503-226-2811

The Portland, founded in 1892, focuses on Native American arts of the Northwest. It also includes a unique collection of Cameroon art, pre-Columbian arts, Renaissance painting and sculpture, Ethiopian crosses, and European and American painting and sculpture.

Pennsylvania

The Carnegie Museum of Art
4400 Forbes Ave.
Pittsburgh, PA 15213
412-622-3131

This museum, founded in 1896, displays art from around the world, including American art since the colonial period; ancient and classical art; African, pre-Columbian, and Native American art; and European painting, sculpture, and decorative arts from the Renaissance forward. Works by Van Gogh, Cézanne, and Monet are included.

Pennsylvania Academy of the Fine Arts
118 N. Broad St.
Philadelphia, PA 19102
215-972-7600

Founded in 1805, the Pennsylvania Academy offers an excellent collection of American art from the 18th century to the present, with major works by Thomas Eakins, Charles Willson Peale, and William Rush.

Philadelphia Museum of Art
26th St. and Benjamin Franklin Pkwy.
Philadelphia, PA 19101
215-763-8100

This museum, established in 1876, is noted for its masterpieces from the 12th to the 19th centuries; Barberini tapestries designed by Rubens; arms and armor; glass; European and American period rooms; folk, decorative, and primitive art; and the Stieglitz Center collection of photographs.

The University Museum of Archaeology and Anthropology, University of Pennsylvania
33rd and Spruce sts.
Philadelphia, PA 19104
215-898-4000

Founded in 1887, the museum is renowned for its worldwide acquisitions of ancient and primitive art, its collection of Native American gold, and the largest grouping of West African art in the Americas. It has sponsored more than 275 expeditions to gather outstanding artifacts from the ancient Near, Middle, and Far East; Southeast Asia; the Mediterranean; the Pacific; Europe; Africa; and the Americas.

Texas

Amon Carter Museum
3501 Camp Bowie Blvd.
Fort Worth, TX 76107
817-738-1933

Housed since its founding in 1961 in an impressive building designed by Philip Johnson, this museum concentrates on American paintings and sculptures from the 19th century forward, specializing in the works of the Old West. It also has a fine print collection and excellent Remingtons and Russells.

Kimbell Art Museum
3333 Camp Bowie Blvd.
P.O. Box 9440
Fort Worth, TX 76107
817-332-8451

Noted for its masterpieces from around the world, this collection, founded in 1972, ranges from 12th-century panel paintings to J. M. W. Turner landscapes, Gainsboroughs, and Goyas.

The Museum of Fine Arts
1001 Bissonet
P.O. Box 6826
Houston, TX 77015
713-639-7300

This wide-ranging collection of world art, established in 1900, is especially strong in contemporary art; pre-Columbian and Native American art; Old Masters; and later European and American paintings and sculptures.

Virginia

Colonial Williamsburg
134 N. Henry St.
Williamsburg, VA 23185
804-229-1000

This village-style museum, founded in 1926, showcases American arts from colonial times forward. Colonial Williamsburg has 88 preserved and restored buildings dating from 1693 to 1837 and 50 reconstructed 18th-century buildings surrounded by gardens.

Virginia Museum of Fine Arts
2800 Grove Ave.
Richmond, VA 23221
804-367-0844

This museum, which opened its doors in 1936, features important collections of British sporting art and French Impressionist and post-Impressionist art, American paintings since World War II, and art nouveau and art deco objects; a collection of Russian imperial Easter eggs by Fabergé; and one of the nation's leading collections of art from India, Nepal, and Tibet. Among its holdings are works by Goya and Monet.

Wisconsin

Elvehjem Museum of Art, University of Wisconsin
800 University Ave.
Madison, WI 53706
608-263-2246

Established in 1962, this is one of the three largest university museums in the United States. Its wide-ranging collection of world art dates back to ancient times, with fine examples of classical coins and marbles; American painting, sculpture, and decorative arts from the 18th century forward; Indian miniatures; and Socialist Realist (propagandist) paintings from Russia.

CANADA

Alberta

The Glenbow Museum
130 9th Ave., SE
Calgary, Alberta T26 OP3
403-268-4100

This museum features exhibits on military history, mineralogy, and western Canadian history. These include artifacts from Indian and Inuit peoples as well as the Hudson Bay Company and the Canadian Pacific Railroad, which was built during the 19th century. The art gallery features works by historical and contemporary western Canadian artists, including Francis N. Hopkins, Emily Carr, John Hall, Ron Moppett, and Chris Cran.

BRITISH COLUMBIA

**The Royal British Columbia Museum
of Anthropology**
675 Belleville St.
Victoria, British Columbia V8V 1X4
604-387-3701

The Royal British Columbia Museum displays a range of exhibitions depicting the accomplishments of native peoples, the achievements of early explorers and settlers, and British Columbia's natural heritage and archeological past. It includes a 14-foot-high woolly mammoth roaming a barren hilltop 10,000 years ago and a native Indian penitentiary.

Ontario

Art Gallery of Hamilton
123 King St. West
Hamilton, Ontario L8P 4S8
416-527-6610

A major North American museum, this gallery was established in 1914. It is noted for its collection of Canadian art; 20th-century British and American painting, sculpture, drawings, and prints; and French Impressionist works.

Museum of Civilization
Victoria Memorial Museum Building
Metcalfe and McLeod sts.
Ottawa, Ontario K1A 0M8
613-992-3497

Opened in 1845, this museum specializes in history and folk culture, with excellent collections of the arts and crafts of Native Americans, particularly Eskimos and Northwest Coast Indians.

National Gallery of Canada
380 Sussex Dr.
Ottawa, Ontario K1N 9N4
613-990-1985

With more than 40,000 works, this museum contains the largest collection of Canadian art in the world and includes painting, sculpture, prints, drawings, photographs, video, film, and Inuit art.

Royal Ontario Museum
100 Queens Park
Toronto, Ontario M5S 2C6
416-586-5549

From suits of armor to suits by Chanel, from totem poles to monstrous dinosaurs, the ROM is the largest museum in Canada. It is one of the world's few multidisciplinary museums combining art, archeology, and science. The museum features a planetarium, as well as a prominent display of historical and contemporary ceramic art.

MAJOR SCIENCE AND TECHNOLOGY MUSEUMS AND THEIR SPECIAL COLLECTIONS

American Museum of Natural History
Central Park West at 79th St.
New York, NY 10024
212-769-5000

One of the world's largest natural history museums, opened in 1869, it has exceptional collections on Native Americans, Eskimos, dinosaurs, wildlife, minerals, and fossil specimens.

The Field Museum of Natural History
Roosevelt Rd. at Lake Shore Dr.
Chicago, IL 60605
312-922-9410

Founded in 1893, the Field Museum contains definitive collections on anatomy, anthropology, costumes, ethnology, geology, Native American artifacts, science, textiles, and zoology. Among its highlights are a full-scale replica of a Pawnee Earth Lodge and an herbarium.

Franklin Institute Science Museum and Planetarium
20th and the Benjamin Franklin Pkwy.
Philadelphia, PA 19103
215-448-1200

Founded in 1824, this comprehensive museum offers collections featuring science, history, industry, technology, aeronautics, astronomy, space exploration, and stamps and coins.

Museum of Science
Science Park
Boston, MA 02114
617-589-0100

Founded in 1830, this science and technology museum includes collections of mineral and plant specimens, mounted animals, and exhibits on human physiology. Interactive exhibits demonstrate the principles of electricity as well as the inner workings of computers. The planetarium features rotating shows relating to space.

"The Physical Sciences, Mathematics, **Go to**
and Technology" (chapter 4)

National Air and Space Museum, Smithsonian Institution
Sixth St. and Independence Ave., SW
Washington, DC 20560
203-357-2700

Founded in 1946, this museum houses a definitive collection of aeronautical and astronautical items; aircraft and spacecraft; and instruments, equipment, art, uniforms, and personal memorabilia related to air and space.

The Royal Tyrrell Museum
P.O. Box 7500
Drumheller, Alberta T0J 0Y0
Canada
403-823-7707

Canada's only museum devoted to paleontology features hands-on displays and computer simulations covering 4.5 billion years of Earth's history. Forty full dinosaur skeletons make up the world's largest exhibit of complete dinosaurs.

CHILDREN'S MUSEUMS

There are more than 90 museums located throughout the United States devoted to children. Although most museums offer at least a few special programs for children, those listed here focus almost exclusively on young visitors. A representative group is described in detail. For additional information, see the listing "Children's and Junior Museums" in *The Official Museum Directory*, published annually by the American Association of Museums.

Brooklyn Children's Museum
145 Brooklyn Ave.
Brooklyn, NY 11213
718-735-4400

Founded in 1899, this was the world's first children's museum. Its teaching collection includes more than 50,000 items, with exhibits on cultural history, natural history, and technology. It houses a greenhouse, a steam engine, and a gristmill. Children may attend workshops in school classes or groups. A portable loan collection and children's resource library is also available.

Capital Children's Museum
800 Third St., NE
Washington, DC 20002
202-675-4120

Founded in 1974, Capital Children's International Hall has a hands-on exhibit on Mexico where children learn to make their own tortillas, weave, and do other Mexican arts and crafts. Additional facilities include a living room, metric exhibit, simple machines display, computer classroom, communications exhibit, and futuristic center.

Children's Museum
Museum Wharf
300 Congress St.
Boston, MA 02210
617-426-6500

Located on Boston's picturesque waterfront, Children's Museum was founded in 1913. It offers special collections of Native American and Japanese art; Americana; games, toys, dolls, and dollhouses; and bird, insect, shell, and mineral specimens. The Exhibit Center presents participatory and cased exhibitions on child development, natural history, science and technology, careers, handicaps, and cross-cultural understanding. Its Resource Center makes available over 10,000 books, games, and other items to teachers, parents, students, and visitors.

The Children's Museum of Manhattan
212 W. 83rd St.
New York, NY 10024
212-721-1223

Founded in 1979, this museum features hands-on, participatory exhibits related to science, nature, and art. A center for media and performing arts includes a television production and editing studio where children create their own television programs. Other activities include making paper, painting and drawing in an art studio, and creating postage stamps. Children contribute their art, toys, and found objects to the museum's rotating exhibits.

Eugene Field House and Toy Museum
634 S. Broadway
St. Louis, MO 63102
314-421-4689

Founded in 1936, this museum is housed in the birthplace of Eugene Field. It contains a collection of antique toys and dolls, along with a library on the works of Field.

Libraries

The Exploratorium
3601 Lyon St.
San Francisco, CA 94123
415-563-7337

Housed in the Palace of Fine Arts, this science museum offers 500 participatory exhibits and artworks illustrating the physical nature of the world and the sensory mechanisms through which we perceive it. Founded in 1969, it hosts field trips, concerts, lectures, and school groups.

Kidspace—A Participatory Museum
390 S. El Molino
Pasadena, CA 91101
213-449-9144

Kidspace offers creative learning experiences for children, as in a mock television studio that children operate, a radio booth for broadcasting, and a medical clinic. There is even a robot who talks to visitors. Parents may host birthday parties in the museum.

Los Angeles Children's Museum
310 N. Main St.
Los Angeles, CA 90012
213-687-8801

Children participate in a variety of activities at this museum in such places as Sticky City, with giant foam blocks for construction fun; City Streets, with city vehicles and street signs; TV Studios, where children create their own news broadcasts; and Workshop Place, which fosters creativity in arts and crafts.

Please Touch Museum
210 N. 21st St.
Philadelphia, PA 19103
215-963-0667

Founded in 1976, the Please Touch Museum issues a children's newspaper and offers special exhibits on cultural artifacts of daily life, folk art and sculpture, natural science, technology, musical instruments, games, registered toys, costumes, masks, foot gear, and hats.

MAJOR ZOOS AND AQUARIUMS

Zoos, or zoological gardens, are private or public parks where animals of all sorts are exhibited and studied. Zoos have existed in one form or another for thousands of years, dating back to ancient China, Egypt, and Rome.

Most major cities throughout the world have zoos. Zoos vary widely in scale and type, from petting zoos that allow contact between children and animals to primate research centers to amusement parks that put on shows with trained animals.

Aquariums are facilities with tanks (usually with glass sides) for a pool/bowl for keeping live water animals and plants.

The following list of major zoos and aquariums in the United States and Canada is arranged by state and province. The name, address, and phone number of each zoo and aquarium are given, as well as the number of species and specimens and, where available, the facility's specialty.

Links to Web sites for many other U.S. zoos and aquariums are provided at

http://www.mindspring.com/~zoonet/states.htm

UNITED STATES

Alabama
Birmingham Zoo
2630 Cahaba Rd.
Birmingham, AL 35223
205-879-0409
http://www.birminghamzoo.com/
223 species, 793 specimens

Arizona
Arizona-Sonora Desert Museum
2021 N. Kinney Rd.
Tucson, AZ 85743
520-883-1380
http://www.desert.net/museum/index.htmlx
289 species, 4,792 specimens
Specialty: natural history of the Arizona-Sonora desert

Phoenix Zoo
455 N. Gavlin Pkwy.
Phoenix, AZ 85008
602-273-1341
http://aztec.asu.edu/phxzoo/homepage.html
342 species, 1,264 specimens

Arkansas

Little Rock Zoo
1 Jonesboro Dr.
Little Rock, AR 72205
501-666-2406
http://www.littlerockzoo.com/index.html
170 species, 600 specimens

California

Chaffee Zoological Gardens (formerly **Fresno Zoo**)
894 W. Belmont Ave.
Fresno, CA 93728
209-498-2671
http://www.chaffeezoo.org
203 species, 616 specimens

The Los Angeles Zoo
5333 Zoo Dr.
Los Angeles, CA 90027-1498
213-666-4650
http://www.lazoo.org/
530 species, 1,857 specimens

Marine World Africa USA
2001 Marine World Pkwy.
Vallejo, CA 94589
707-643-ORCA
324 species, 2,361 specimens

Oakland Zoo
9777 Golf Links Rd.
Oakland, CA 94605
510-632-9525
http://www.oaklandzoo.org/
50 species, 330 specimens
Specialty: baby animals

San Diego Zoo
P.O. Box 551
San Diego, CA 92112
619-234-3153
http://www.sandiegozoo.org/Zoo/zoo.html
845 species, 3,888 specimens
Specialties: lemurs, tortoises, marsupials

San Francisco Zoo
1 Zoo Rd.
San Francisco, CA 94132-1098
415-753-7080
http://www.sfzoo.com/html/home.html
351 species, 6,867 specimens
Specialties: apes, cats

Santa Ana Zoo
1801 E. Chestnut Ave.
Santa Ana, CA 92701
714-835-7484
http://santaanazoo.org/
96 species, 267 specimens
Specialty: primates

Sea World of California
1720 S. Shores Rd.
San Diego, CA 92109
619-222-3901
572 species, 18,367 specimens
Specialties: trained marine mammals, waterfowl, fish

Steinhart Aquarium at California Academy of Sciences
Golden Gate Park
San Francisco, CA 94118
415-750-7145

T. Wayland Vaughan Aquarium-Museum
Scripps Institute of Oceanography
University of California
La Jolla, CA 92093
619-452-4086
203 species, 1,402 specimens
Specialties: marine fish and invertebrates of southern California

Colorado

Cheyenne Mountain Zoological Park
4250 Cheyenne Mountain Zoo Rd.
Colorado Springs, CO 80906
719-475-9555
132 species, 502 specimens
Specialties: primates, large felids, hoofed mammals

Denver Zoo
2300 Steele St.
Denver, CO 80205
303-376-4800
http://www.denverzoo.org/
548 species, 4,448 specimens
Specialties: waterfowl, North American hoofed mammals

Connecticut

Beardsley Zoological Gardens
1875 Noble Ave.
Bridgeport, CT 06610
203-576-8126
101 species, 301 specimens
Specialty: fauna of North and South America

Libraries

Mystic Marinelife Aquarium
55 Coogan Blvd.
Mystic, CT 06355-1997
203-536-9631

District of Columbia

National Zoological Park
3001 Connecticut Ave., NW
Washington, DC 20008
202-673-4717
http://www.si.edu/natzoo/
491 species, 4,746 specimens

Florida

Busch Gardens
P.O. Box 9158
Tampa, FL 33674
813-988-5555
369 species, 3,381 specimens
Specialties: African hoofed mammals, parrots

Dreher Park Zoo
1301 Summit Blvd.
West Palm Beach, FL 33405-2494
407-533-0887
100 species, 400 specimens
Specialties: South American and South Floridian
    animals

Jacksonville Zoological Park
8605 Zoo Rd.
Jacksonville, FL 32218
904-757-4463
210 species, 703 specimens

Marineland of Florida
RFD 1, P.O. Box 122
St. Augustine, FL 32086
904-471-1111
106 species, 613 specimens
Specialties: marine mammals, marine theme displays

Miami Metrozoo
12400 SW 152nd St.
Miami, FL 33177-1499
305-251-0401
http://members.aol.com/miamizoo/index.html
270 species, 3,148 specimens

Georgia

Zoo Atlanta
800 Cherokee Ave., SE
Atlanta, GA 30315
404-624-5600
278 species, 998 specimens
Specialties: amphibians, reptiles, giant apes

Hawaii

Honolulu Zoo
151 Kapahulu Ave.
Honolulu, HI 96815-4096
808-971-7175
207 species, 766 specimens
Specialty: Galapagos tortoise

Waikiki Aquarium
University of Hawaii
2777 Kalakaua Ave.
Honolulu, HI 96815
808-923-9741
326 species, 2,300 specimens
Specialty: aquatic life of Hawaii and the tropical Pacific

Illinois

**Chicago Zoological Park
(Brookfield Zoo)**
3300 Golf Rd.
Brookfield, IL 60513
708-485-2200
http://www.nwu.edu/ev-chi/parks/brookfield/
411 species, 2,176 specimens
Specialties: Tropic World, Seven Seas

John G. Shedd Aquarium
1200 S. Lake Shore Dr.
Chicago, IL 60605
312-939-2438
772 species, 6,662 specimens

Lincoln Park Zoological Gardens
2200 N. Cannon Dr.
Chicago, IL 60614
312-742-2000
http://www.lpzoo.com/
423 species, 1,758 specimens
Specialties: primates, South American mammals

Indiana

Fort Wayne Children's Zoo
3411 Sherman Blvd.
Fort Wayne, IN 46808
219-427-6800
http://www.kidszoo.com/home.html
199 species, 812 specimens

Indianapolis Zoo
1200 W. Washington St.
Indianapolis, IN 46222
371 species, 2,408 specimens

Mesker Park Zoo
2421 Bement Ave.
Evansville, IN 47712
812-428-0715
http://www.evansville.net/~mpzoo
203 species, 644 specimens
Specialty: large geographic exhibits

Kansas

Topeka Zoological Park
635 SW Gage Blvd.
Topeka, KS 66606-2066
913-272-5821
126 species, 367 specimens

Kentucky

Louisville Zoological Garden
1100 Trevilian Way
P.O. Box 37250
Louisville, KY 40213
502-451-0440
http://www.lglou.com/louzoo/
412 species, 2,156 specimens

Louisiana

Aquarium of the Americas
Woldenberg Riverfront Park
New Orleans, LA 70130
504-861-2537
http://www.audoboninstitute.org/html/
aa_aquariumain.html
500 species, 10,000 specimens

Audubon Park & Zoological Garden
6500 Magazine St.
New Orleans, LA 70178
504-861-2537
http://www.audoboninstitute.org/html/aa_zoomain.
html
401 species, 1,535 specimens

Greater Baton Rouge Zoo
Greenwood Park, Highway 19
Baker, LA 70704
504-775-3877
212 species, 993 specimens

Maryland

Baltimore Zoo
Druid Hill Park
Mansion House
Baltimore, MD 21217
301-396-7102

241 species, 1,086 specimens
Specialty: black-footed penguins

National Aquarium in Baltimore
Pier 3, 501 E. Pratt St.
Baltimore, MD 21202
410-576-3823
588 species, 8,561 specimens

Massachusetts

Franklin Park Zoo
1 Franklin Park Rd.
Boston, MA 02121
617-442-2002
http://ftp.std.com/homepages/std/museums/fpzoo.info.
html
252 species, 1,576 specimens

New England Aquarium
Central Wharf
Boston, MA 02110
617-973-5220

http://www.neaq.org/
412 species, 7,606 specimens
Specialties: marine fish, invertebrates of the world

Michigan

Detroit Zoological Park
8450 W. 10 Mile Rd.
P.O. Box 39
Royal Oak, MI 48068
313-398-0900
http://www.detroitzoo.org/
282 species, 1,287 specimens
Specialties: polar bears, penguins

Potter Park Zoological Gardens
1301 S. Pennsylvania Ave.
Lansing, MI 48912
517-483-4221
124 species, 342 specimens

Saginaw Children's Zoo
1435 S. Washington Ave.
Saginaw, MI 48601
517-776-1657
28 species, 120 specimens

Minnesota

Lake Superior Zoological Gardens
7210 Fremont St.
Duluth, MN 55807
125 species, 491 specimens

Minnesota Zoological Garden
13000 Zoo Blvd.
Apple Valley, MN 55124
612-432-9200
http://www.mnzoo.com/
311 species, 1,818 specimens

St. Paul's Como Zoo
Midway Pkwy. and Kaufman Dr.
St. Paul, MN 55103
612-488-4041
103 species, 335 specimens
Specialties: large mammals

Mississippi

Jackson Zoological Park
2918 W. Capitol St.
Jackson, MS 39209
601-352-2585
http://techlink.net/jacksonzoo/
140 species, 426 specimens

Missouri

Kansas City Zoological Gardens
6700 Zoo Dr.
Kansas City, MO 64132
816-871-5700
http://www.kansascity.com/zoo/
162 species, 586 specimens

St. Louis Zoological Park
1 Government Dr.
St. Louis, MO 63110
314-781-0900
http://www.stlzoo.org/
720 species, 4,364 specimens

Nebraska

Folsom Children's Zoo
2800 A St.
Lincoln, NE 86502
402-475-6741
50 species, 173 specimens

Omaha's Henry Doorly Zoo
3701 S. 10th St.
Omaha, NE 68107-2200
402-773-8401
http://www.omaha.org/zoo.htm
475 species, 9,338 specimens
Specialties: largest cat complex in North America

New Jersey

Turtle Back Zoo
560 Northfield Ave.
South Mountain Reservation, NJ 07052
201-731-5800
171 species, 647 specimens
Specialty: turtles

New Mexico

Rio Grande Zoological Park
903 10th St., SW
Albuquerque, NM 87102
505-843-7413
292 species, 1,204 specimens
Specialty: hoofed mammals

New York

Buffalo Zoological Gardens
Delaware Park
Buffalo, NY 14214
716-837-3900
237 species, 1,424 specimens

Central Park Wildlife Conservation Center (formerly Central Park Zoo)
830 Fifth Avenue
New York, NY 10021
212-861-6030
108 species, 10,717 specimens

Aquarium for Wildlife Conservation (formerly New York Aquarium)
West 8th St. and Surf Ave.
Brooklyn, NY 11224
718-265-FISH
287 species, 23,107 specimens

International Wildlife Conservation Park (formerly Bronx Zoo)
185th St. and Southern Blvd.
Bronx, NY 10460
718-367-1010
681 species, 4,756 specimens

Staten Island Zoo
614 Broadway
Staten Island, NY 10310
718-442-3100
http://www.earthcom.net~sizoo/
187 species, 422 specimens
Specialty: reptiles

Libraries

North Carolina

North Carolina Zoological Park
NC Highway 159
Asheboro, NC 27203
800-488-0444
910-879-7000
http://www.nczoo.org/
Specialty: African wildlife

North Dakota

Dakota Zoo
Dakota Zoological Society
P.O. Box 711
Bismarck, ND 58502
701-223-7543
142 species, 657 specimens
Specialty: North American fauna

Ohio

Cincinnati Zoo & Botanical Garden
3400 Vine St.
Cincinnati, OH 45220
513-281-4701
http://www.cincyzoo.org/
702 species, 427,547 specimens
   (425,000 invertebrates)
Specialties: insects, amphibians, great apes, cats

Cleveland Aquarium
Gordon Park
601 E. 72nd St.
Cleveland, OH 44103

Cleveland Metroparks Zoo
3900 Brookside Park Dr.
Cleveland, OH 44109
216-661-6500
http://clemetzoo.com/
506 species, 3,279 specimens
Specialties: Geoffroy's tamarin, white stork

Columbus Zoological Gardens
9990 Riverside Dr.
Powell, OH 43065
http://www.colszoo.org/
680 species, 8,260 specimens
Specialties: gorillas, reptiles, cichlids

Toledo Zoo
2700 Broadway
P.O. Box 4010
Toledo, OH 43609-4010
419-385-5721
http://www.toledozoo.org/
433 species, 2,364 specimens

Oklahoma

Oklahoma City Zoological Park
2101 NE 50th St.
Oklahoma City, OK 73112
405-424-3344
http://www.cpb.uokhsc.edu/okc/okczoo/zoomap.html
520 species, 1,879 specimens

Tulsa Zoological Park
5701 E. 36th St. North
Tulsa, OK 74115
918-596-2401
267 species, 1,148 specimens
Specialties: North American animals, plants, earth
   sciences

Oregon

Metro Washington Park Zoo
4001 SW Canyon Rd.
Portland, OR 97231
503-226-1561
http://www.zooregon.org/
192 species, 1,643 specimens
Specialties: elephants, chimpanzees

Pennsylvania

Philadelphia Zoological Garden
3400 W. Girard Ave.
Philadelphia, PA 19104-1196
215-243-1100
http://www.phillyzoo.org/
497 species, 1,824 specimens
Specialties: waterfowl, great apes, reptiles

Pittsburgh Zoo
Hill Rd.
Pittsburgh, PA 15206
412-665-3640
http://zoo.pgh.pa.us
369 species, 3,945 specimens

Rhode Island

Roger Williams Park Zoo
1000 Elmwood Ave.
Providence, RI 02907-3600
410-785-3510
http://users.ids.net/~rwpz/index.htm
143 species, 464 specimens

South Carolina

Riverbanks Zoological Park and Botanical Gardens
500 Wildlife Pkwy.
Columbia, SC 29202
803-779-8717
http://www.riverbanks.org/
439 species, 2,117 specimens

South Dakota

Great Plains Zoo and Museum
805 S. Kiwanis Ave.
Sioux Falls, SD 57104
605-339-7059
69 species, 271 specimens
Specialty: animals of the North American Great Plains

Tennessee

Knoxville Zoological Gardens
P.O. Box 6040
Knoxville, TN 37914
423-637-5331
http://www.knoxville-zoo.org/
241 species, 879 specimens
Specialties: large cats, African elephants, red pandas,
    Southern white rhinoceros

Memphis Zoological Garden and Aquarium
2000 Galloway Ave.
Memphis, TN 38112
901-726-4787
http://www.memphiszoo.org/
403 species, 2,847 specimens
Specialties: aquatic animals, rare ruminants

Texas

Abilene Zoological Gardens
Hwy. 36 at Loop 322
Abilene, TX 79604
915-676-6085
http://www.abilene.com/visitors/zoo.html
153 species, 498 specimens

Caldwell Zoo
2203 Martin Luther King Blvd.
Tyler, TX 75710
903-593-0121
221 species, 1,020 specimens

Dallas Aquarium
P.O. Box 26113
Dallas, TX 75226
214-670-8453
375 species, 2,875 specimens

Dallas Zoo
621 E. Clarendon Dr.
Dallas, TX 75203
214-670-6825
330 species, 1,454 specimens

Forth Worth Zoo
1989 Colonial Pkwy.
Fort Worth, TX 76110
817-871-7050
http://www.rwnet.com/FWZoo/
758 species, 4,408 specimens

Gladys Porter Zoo
500 Ringgold St.
Brownsville, TX 78520
956-546-7187
http://www.gpz.org/
381 species, 1,765 specimens

Houston Zoological Gardens
1513 N. MacGregor
Houston, TX 77030
713-525-3300
724 species, 3,159 specimens

San Antonio Zoological Garden and Aquarium
3903 N. St. Mary's St.
San Antonio, TX 78212-3173
210-734-7184
http://www.sazoo-aq.org/
738 species, 3,401 specimens
Specialties: antelope, waterfowl, whooping cranes

Utah

Utah's Hogle Zoo
2600 E. Sunnyside Ave.
Salt Lake City, UT 84108
801-582-1631
http://www.xmission.com/~hoglezoo/
311 species, 1,164 specimens

Virginia

Virginia Zoological Park
3500 Granby St.
Norfolk, VA 23504
804-441-2374
http://sites.communitylink.org/vazoo/index.html
110 species, 331 specimens

Washington

Seattle Aquarium
Pier 59, Waterfront Park
Seattle, WA 98010
206-386-4320
393 species, 21,050 specimens

Woodland Park Zoological Gardens
5500 Phinney Ave. North
Seattle, WA 98103-5897
206-684-4880
http://www.zoo.org/
258 species, 2,411 specimens

Wisconsin

Henry Vilas Zoo
500 S. Randall Ave.
Madison, WI 53715
608-266-4732
http://www.vilaszoo.org/
182 species, 618 specimens

Milwaukee County Zoological Gardens
10001 W. Blue Mound Rd.
Milwaukee, WI 53226
414-771-5500
http://www.except.com/Milwaukee_Zoo/
321 species, 3,054 specimens

Racine Zoological Garden
2131 N. Main St.
Racine, WI 53402
414-636-9189
101 species, 281 specimens

CANADA

Alberta

Calgary Zoo, Botanical Garden & Prehistoric Park
P.O. Box 3036, Station B
Calgary, Alberta T2M 4R8
403-232-9300
http://www.calgaryzoo.ab.ca/www.mbnet.mb.ca/city/
    parks/envserv/zoo/zoo.html
307 species, 1,295 specimens
Specialty: northern fauna

British Columbia

Stanley Park Zoological Gardens
Stanley Park
Vancouver, British Columbia V6G 1Z4
604-683-1040
94 species, 298 specimens
Specialties: North American mammals and birds

Vancouver Public Aquarium
Stanley Park
P.O. Box 3232
Vancouver 3, British Columbia V6B 3X8
604-685-3364
638 species, 9,499 specimens
Specialties: marine mammals, fishes and invertebrates
    of the Northeast Pacific

Manitoba

Assiniboine Park Zoo
2355 Corydon Ave.
Winnipeg, Manitoba R3P 1R5
204-986-6921
http://www.mbnet.mb.ca/city/parks/envserv/zoo/
    zoo.html
296 species, 1,156 specimens
Specialty: Nearctic animals

Ontario

Toronto Zoo
361A Old Finch Ave.
Scarborough, Ontario M1B 5K7
416-392-5900
http://www.torontozoo.com/
517 species, 3,489 specimens

Quebec

Aquarium de Quebec
Ministre du Loisir, de la Chasse et de la Pêche
1675 avenue des Hôtels
Sainte Foy, Quebec G1W 4S3
418-659-5264
250 species, 3,500 specimens

Jardin Zoologique de Quebec
8191 avenue du Zoo
Charlesbourg, Quebec G1G 4G4
418-622-0313
233 species, 794 specimens
Specialty: North American fauna

Montreal Aquarium
La Ronde
St. Helen's Island
Montreal, Quebec H3C 1A9
514-872-4656
319 species, 2,088 specimens

Société Zoologique de Granby
347 rue Bourget
Case Postale 514
Granby, Quebec J2G 1E8
514-372-9113
201 species, 720 specimens

MAJOR BOTANICAL GARDENS AND ARBORETUMS

Botanical gardens are places where collections of plants and trees are kept for exhibition and scientific study. Arboretums are places where many kinds of trees and shrubs are grown for exhibition or study.

The following list of major botanical gardens and arboretums in the United States is arranged by state.

Addresses, phone numbers, and Web sites of numerous other botanical gardens and arboreta that are members of the American Association of Botanical Gardens and Arboreta are listed at http://www.mobot.org/AAGBA/member-list.html.

Alabama

Birmingham Botanical Gardens
2612 Lane Park Rd.
Birmingham, AL 35523
205-879-1227
http://www.bbgardens.org/

Arizona

Desert Botanical Garden
1201 N. Galvin Pkwy.
Papago Park
Phoenix, AZ 85008
602-941-1225
http://www.mobot.org/AABGA/member.pages/
  desert.html

California

Balboa Park
Laurel St. and 6th Ave.
San Diego, CA 92101
619-239-0512

Huntington Library, Art Collections, and Botanical Gardens
1151 Oxford St.
San Marino, CA 91108
626-405-2100
http://www.huntington.org/

J. Paul Getty Museum and Gardens
17985 Pacific Coast Hwy.
Malibu, CA 90265
213-454-6541

Strybing Arboretum and Botanical Gardens
9th Ave. at Lincoln Way
Golden Gate Park
San Francisco, CA 94122
415-661-1316
http://www.mobot.org/AABGA/member.pages/strybing/

Villa Montalvo Arboretum
15400 Montalvo Rd.
Saratoga, CA 95070
408-867-3421

Colorado

Denver Botanic Garden
909 York St.
Denver, CO 80206
303-331-4000
http://www.botanicgardens.org/

Connecticut

Caprilands Herb Farm
534 Silver St.
Coventry, CT 06238
860-742-7244

Gertrude Jekyll Garden
Hollow Rd.
Woodbury, CT 06798
203-263-2855

Harkness Memorial State Park
275 Great Neck Rd.
Waterford, CT 06385
860-443-5725

Delaware

Nemours Mansion and Gardens
P.O. Box 109
Wilmington, DE 19899
302-651-6912

Henry Francis du Pont Winterthur Museum
Rte. 52
Winterthur, DE 19735
800-448-3883

District of Columbia

Dumbarton Oaks
1703 32nd St., NW
Washington, DC 20007
202-339-6410

Gardens of the Washington National Cathedral
Massachusetts and Wisconsin aves.
Washington, DC 20016-5098
202-537-6200

"Domestic Travel: National Wildlife Refuges" in chapter 24
Go to

United States Botanical Garden
245 First St., SW
Washington, DC 20024
202-226-4082
http://www.aoc.gov
(closed for about 3 years beginning September 1, 1997,
  for renovation and reconstruction)

United States National Arboretum
3501 New York Ave., NE
Washington, DC 20002
202-245-4523
http://www.ars-grin.gov/ars/Beltsville/na/

Florida

Edison and Ford Winter Estates
2350 McGregor Blvd.
Ft. Myers, FL 33901
941-334-3614

Fairchild Tropical Garden
10901 Old Cutler Rd.
Miami, FL 33156-4299
305-667-1651
http://www.ftg.org

Cypress Gardens
5651 Cypress Gardens Rd.
Winter Haven, FL 33884
941-324-2111
http://www.florida.com/cypressgardens/index.html

Alfred B. Maclay State Gardens
3540 Thomasville Rd.
Tallahassee, FL 32308
904-487-4115

Georgia

Atlanta Botanical Garden
1345 Piedmont Ave.
Atlanta, GA 30309
404-876-5859

Callaway Gardens
U.S. Highway 27
P.O. Box 2000
Pine Mountain, GA 31822-2000
800-241-0910

The State Botanical Garden of Georgia
2450 S. Milledge Ave.
Athens, GA 30605-1624
706-542-1244

Hawaii

Foster Botanic Garden
180 N. Vineyard Blvd.
Honolulu, HI 96817
808-538-7258

Idaho

Ann Morrison Memorial Park
South Capitol Blvd.
Boise, ID 83702
208-368-7844

Illinois

Chicago Botanic Garden
P.O. Box 400
Glencoe, IL 60022
847-835-5440
http://www.chicago-botanic.org/

Garfield Park Conservatory
300 N. Central Park Blvd.
Chicago, IL 60624
312-746-5100

Lincoln Park Conservatory
2400 N. Stockton Dr.
Chicago, IL 60614
312-742-7736

Indiana

Indianapolis Museum of Art
Eli Lilly Botanical Garden
1200 W. 38th St.
Indianapolis, IN 46208
317-923-1331
http://cissus.mobot.org/AABGA/Member.pages/
  Indianapolis.mus.art.html

Iowa

Des Moines Botanical Center
909 E. River Dr.
Des Moines, IA 50316
515-242-2734

Kansas

Reinisch Rose Garden
635 SW Gage Blvd.
Topeka, KS 66606-2066
913-272-5821

Louisiana

Around the World Tropical Gardens
U.S. Route 167 South and Ridge Rd.
Lafayette, LA 70506
504-831-2002

Maine

Asticou Azalea Garden
Asticou Way
Mount Desert Island
Northeast Harbor, ME 04662
207-276-5456

Maryland

Hampton National Historic Site
535 Hampton Lane
Towson, MD 21286
410-962-0688

Massachusetts

Arnold Arboretum
125 Arborway
Jamaica Plain, MA 02130-3500
617-524-1718
http://www.arboretum.harvard.edu

Berkshire Botanical Garden
Routes 102 and 183
Stockbridge, MA 01262
413-298-3926

Botanic Garden of Smith College
Lyman Plant House
College Lane
Northhampton, MA 01063
413-585-2748
http://www.smith.edu/garden/

Stanley Park
400 Western Ave.
Westfield, MA 01086
413-568-9312
http://www.stanleypark.org

Michigan

Anna Scripps Whitcomb Conservatory
Belle Island Park
Detroit, MI 48207
313-267-7133

Matthaei Botanical Garden
University of Michigan
1800 Dixboro Rd.
Ann Arbor, MI 48105-9741
313-998-7061

Missouri

Missouri Botanical Garden
P.O. Box 299
St. Louis, MO 63166-0299
314-577-5100
http://www.mobot.org/welcome.html

New Hampshire

Aspet
Saint-Gaudens National Historic Site
R.R. 3, P.O. Box 73
Cornish, NH 03745
603-675-2175

New Jersey

Deep Cut Park Horticultural Center
352 Red Hill Rd.
Middletown, NJ 07748
908-671-6050

Frelinhuysen Arboretum
53 E. Hanover Ave.
P.O. Box 1295
Morristown, NJ 07962-1295
201-326-7600

Rutgers University Research and Display Gardens
P.O. Box 231
122 Ryders Lane
New Brunswick, NJ 08903
908-932-8010

New Jersey State Botanical Garden at Skylands
Morris Rd.
Ringwood, NJ 07458
201-962-9534

New Mexico

Living Desert Zoo and Gardens
P.O. Box 100
Carlsbad, NM 88220
505-887-5516

New York

Brooklyn Botanic Garden
1000 Washington Ave.
Brooklyn, NY 11225-1099
718-622-4433
http://www.bbg.org/

New York Botanical Garden
200th St. and Southern Blvd.
Bronx, NY 10458-5126
718-817-8700
http://www.pathfinder.com/vg/Gardens/NYBG/
    index.html

Vanderbilt Mansion National Historic Site
519 Albany Post Rd.
Hyde Park, NY 12538
914-229-9115

North Carolina
Botanical Gardens at Asheville
151 W. T. Weaver Blvd.
Asheville, NC 28804
704-252-5190

Sarah P. Duke Memorial Gardens
Duke University
P.O. Box 90341
Durham, NC 27708-0341
919-684-3698

North Carolina Botanical Garden
CB 3375 Totten Center
University of North Carolina
Chapel Hill, NC 27599-3375
919-962-0522
http://www.ils.unc.edu/botanical/gardens.html

North Dakota
International Peace Garden
R.R. 1, Box 116
Dunseith, ND 58329
701-263-4390

Ohio
Dawes Arboretum
7770 Jacksontown Rd., SE
Newark, OH 43056-9380
800-44DAWES
614-323-2355

Cleveland Botanical Garden
11030 East Blvd.
Cleveland, OH 44106
216-721-1600
http://cbgarden.org/

Holden Arboretum
9500 Sperry Rd.
Kirtland, OH 44094-5172
216-256-1110
http://www.holdenarb.org

Oklahoma
Garden Exhibition Building & Horticultural Gardens
3400 NW 36th St.
Oklahoma City, OK 73112
405-943-0827

Oregon
Berry Botanic Garden
11505 SW Summerville Ave.
Portland, OR 97219-8309
503-636-4112
http://www.berrybot.org/

Pennsylvania
Horticulture Center
P.O. Box 21601
Philadelphia, PA 19131-0901
215-879-4062

Zooamerica North America Wildlife Park
Route 743
Hershey, PA 17033
717-534-3860

John Bartram's Historic Garden
54th Street and Lindbergh Boulevard
Philadelphia, PA 19143
215-729-5281

Longwood Gardens
P.O. Box 501
Kennet Square, PA 19348-0501
610-388-1000
http://www.longwoodgardens.org/

Morris Arboretum of the University of Pennsylvania
9414 Meadowbrooke Ave.
Philadelphia, PA 19118
215-247-5777
http://www.mobot.org/AABGA/Member.pages/Morris/morris.html

Tyler Arboretum
515 Painter Rd.
Media, PA 19063-4424
610-566-5431

Rhode Island
Hammersmith Farm
Bellevue Ave.
Newport, RI 02840
401-846-7346

South Carolina
Brookgreen Gardens
1931 Brookgreen Dr.
Murrells Inlet, SC 29576
803-237-4218

Magnolia Plantation and Gardens
Rte. 4
Charleston, SC 29414
803-571-1266

Libraries

Middletown Place
4300 Ashley River Rd.
Charleston, SC 29414
803-556-6020

Tennessee

Goldsmith Civic Garden Center
Memphis Botanical Garden
750 Cherry Rd.
Memphis, TN 38117-4619
901-685-1566
http://www.mobot.org/AABGA/Member.pages/
memphis.bot.gnd.html

Rock City Gardens
1400 Patten Rd.
Lookout Mountain, GA 30750
706-820-2531
http://www.seerockcity.com/

Texas

Dallas Arboretum and Botanical Garden
8617 Garland Rd.
Dallas, TX 75218
214-327-8263

Fort Worth Botanic Garden
3220 Botanic Garden Blvd.
Fort Worth, TX 76107
817-871-7686

National Wildflower Research Center
4801 La Crosse Ave.
Austin, TX 78739
512-292-4200

Samuel Grand Park Garden
6200 E. Grand Ave.
Dallas, TX 75223
214-670-1383

Virginia

Colonial Gardens
Colonial Williamsburg
134 N. Henry St.
Williamsburg, VA 23185
804-229-1000

Monticello
Home of Thomas Jefferson
P.O. Box 316
Charlottesville, VA 22902

804-984-9888
804-293-2158
http://www.monticello.org/

Mount Vernon
George Washington Parkway
Mount Vernon, VA 22121
703-780-2000
http://www.mountvernon.org/

Pavillion Gardens
University of Virginia
Charlottesville, VA 22903
804-924-7969
http://www.virginia.edu

Washington

Washington Park Arboretum
University of Washington
P.O. Box 358010
Seattle, WA 98195-8010
206-543-8800
http://weber.u.washington.edu/~wpa/

Wisconsin

Mitchell Park Horticultural Conservatory
524 S. Layton Blvd.
Milwaukee, WI 53215
414-649-9830
http://www.uwm.edu/Dept/Biology/domes/

Olbrich Botanical Gardens
3330 Atwood Ave.
Madison, WI 53704
608-246-4551

ADDITIONAL SOURCES OF INFORMATION

American Library Directory 1997–98. 50th ed. 2 vols. R. R. Bowker, 1997.

The Official Museum Directory 1997. 27th ed. 2 vols. R. R. Bowker, 1996.

The World of Learning 1998. 48th ed. Europa, 1998.

Libraries

III

THE WAY WE COMMUNICATE

CHAPTER TWELVE   387
SYMBOLS AND SIGNS

CHAPTER THIRTEEN   403
ALPHABETS AND WORDS

CHAPTER FOURTEEN   435
GRAMMAR AND PUNCTUATION

CHAPTER FIFTEEN   445
LETTERS AND FORMS OF ADDRESS

12

SYMBOLS AND SIGNS

SYMBOLS USED IN SCIENCE, MATHEMATICS, AND TECHNOLOGY	388
CULTURAL SYMBOLS	393
SYMBOLS TO GUIDE THE TRAVELER	396
SYMBOLIC ALPHABETS	399
BUSINESS AND MONETARY SYMBOLS	401
PROOFREADERS' MARKS	401
SMILEYS	402
ADDITIONAL SOURCES OF INFORMATION	402

SYMBOLS USED IN SCIENCE, MATHEMATICS, AND TECHNOLOGY

ASTRONOMY SYMBOLS

SOLAR SYSTEM OBJECTS

☉	the Sun
☾, ☽	the Moon
☿	Mercury
♀	Venus
⊕	Earth
♂	Mars
♃	Jupiter
♄	Saturn
♅, ♅	Uranus
♆	Neptune
♇	Pluto
☄	comet
①, ②, ③, etc.	asteroids in the order of their discovery

PHASES OF THE MOON

●	new moon
☽, ☽	first quarter
○	full moon
☾, ☾	last quarter

STELLAR OBJECTS

*	fixed star
α, β, γ, etc.	stars (of a constellation) in the order of their brightness: the Greek letter is followed by the Latin genitive of the name of the constellation

ASPECTS AND NODES

☌	conjunction: with reference to bodies having the same longitude, or right ascension
□	quadrature: being 90° apart in longitude, or right ascension
☍	opposition: being 180° apart in longitude, or right ascension
☊	ascending node
☋	descending node

PHYSICAL CHARACTERS

A	albedo
D	diameter
M	mass
R	radius

"Astronomy" in chapter 4

Go to

UNITS OF MEASUREMENT

A.U.	astronomical unit
l.y.	light year
pc	parsec
h, ^{h}	hours [5h or 5^h]
m, ^{m}	minutes of time [5m or 5^m]
s, ^{s}	seconds of time [16s or 16^s]
°	degrees of arc
'	minutes of arc
"	seconds of arc

DIRECTIONS

+	toward the zenith; toward the north celestial, ecliptic, or galactic pole
−	toward the nadir; toward the south celestial, ecliptic, or galactic pole
γ	vernal equinox

ORBITAL ELEMENTS

a	mean distance, semimajor axis
e	eccentricity of orbit
i	inclination to the ecliptic
P	sidereal period of revolution or rotation
Ω	longitude of ascending node
ω	argument of perihelion

COORDINATES

h	altitude
A	azimuth
δ	declination
α, R.A.	right ascension
β	celestial latitude
λ	celestial longitude
b	galactic latitude
l	galactic longitude

OTHER SYMBOLS

Δ	distance from earth
π	parallax
ø	geographical or astronomical latitude

Although the @ has no name in the United States (it's just called the "at symbol"), other countries call it "monkey's tail," "little snail," "cat's tail," or "spider monkey."

BIOLOGY SYMBOLS

♃	perennial herb
♂, ♂	male organism or cell; staminate plant or flower
♀	female organism or cell; pistillate plant or flower
☿	perfect, or hermaphroditic, plant, or flower
∪	individual, especially female, organism
□	individual, especially male, organism
×	crossed with; hybrid
+	wild type
P	parental generation
F	filial generation; offspring
F_1, F_2, F_3, etc.	offspring of the first, second, third, etc., filial generation

Go to
"The Biological World" (chapter 3)

CHEMISTRY SYMBOLS

+	"and," "plus," or "together with," used between the symbols of reacting substances in chemical equations; when placed above a symbol or to its right as a superscript, the plus sign indicates a unit charge of positive electricity; the sign also indicates dextrorotation
—	single bond, used between the symbols of elements or groups that form a compound; when placed above a symbol or to its right as a superscript, the dash indicates a unit charge of negative electricity; it also signifies levorotation or the removal of a part from a compound
•	separates parts of a compound considered loosely joined (free radical)
⬡	benzene ring
=	"forms" or "results in," used between the symbols of reacting substances in chemical equations; a double bond; two unit charges of negative electricity when placed above a symbol or to its right as a superscript
≡	triple bond or triple negative charge
:	unshared pair of electrons; sometimes a double bond
⦙	triple bond
( )	groups or radicals within a compound
[ ]	with parentheses, shows certain radicals; in coordination formulas, shows relationship to the central atom
⌒ or ⌣	unites attached atoms or groups in structural formulas for cyclic compounds
→	gives, passes over to, or leads to; reaction direction
⇄	is in equilibrium with; forms and is formed from; reversible reaction
↓	precipitation of a substance
↑	gas expelled
≡, ⇌	is equivalent to; used in equations to show how much of one substance will react with a given amount of another so that no excess of either remains
<	bivalent element
>	bivalent radical

Go to
"Chemistry" (chapter 4)

ELECTRONICS SYMBOLS

BATTERIES

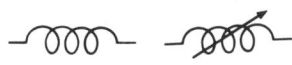

Single Cell   Multicell

CAPACITORS

Fixed

Variable

HEADSETS

Single   Double

INDUCTORS

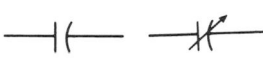

Fixed   Variable

INSTRUMENTS

Ammeter

Ohmeter

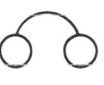

Voltmeter   Wattmeter

Symbols/Signs

LAMPS

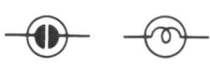

Neon   Filament

RECTIFIERS

Half Wave   Full Wave

RESISTORS

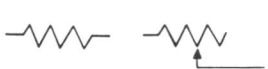

Fixed   Variable

TRANSFORMERS

VACUUM-TUBE TRIODES

WIRES

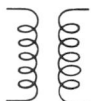      

Air Core   Iron Core   Directly Heated Cathode   Indirectly Heated Cathode   Connected   Not Connected

OTHER SYMBOLS

   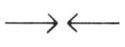

Alternating Current Source   Antenna   Ground   Spark Gap   Single Throw Switch

MATHEMATICS SYMBOLS

"Heating and Electrical Units of Measurement" in chapter 2 **Go to**

OPERATION

+	plus; positive
−	minus; negative
~	difference
×	multiplied by
÷	divided by
±	plus or minus
∓	minus or plus
!	factorial
Σ	summation of
∏	product
√	square root
∛	cube root
∜	fourth root
$\sqrt[n]{}$	nth root
$|b|$	absolute value of b, magnitude of b

RELATION

=	equal to
≠	not equal to
≡	identical with; congruent to (in number theory)
≈	nearly equal to
>	greater than
>>	much greater than
<	less than
<<	much less than
≧ *or* ≥	greater than or equal to
≦ *or* ≤	less than or equal to
≯	not greater than
≮	not less than
∝	varies directly as; is proportional to
:	is to; the ratio of
::	proportion
∺	geometrical proportion

FUNCTIONS

f(x)	function
log	logarithm
ln	natural logarithm

GROUPING

( )	parentheses	
[ ]	brackets	indicate that the quantities enclosed by them are to be taken together
{ }	braces	

CONSTANTS

e	base (2.718) of natural logarithms
π	pi (3.1416)
∞	infinity
i	imaginary unit ($\frac{x}{=}$)

GEOMETRY

$\angle$	angle
$\llcorner$	right angle
$\perp$	perpendicular
$\parallel$	parallel
$\bigcirc$ *or* $\odot$	circle
$\frown$	arc of a circle
$\bigcirc$	ellipse
$\varnothing$	diameter
$\triangle$	triangle
$\square$	square
$\square$	rectangle
$\boxplus$	cube
$\square$	rhomboid
$\circ$	degree
$'$	minute
$''$	second
$\simeq$	congruent to (in geometry)
m	slope
r	radius
d	diameter

SET THEORY AND LOGIC

$\cup$	union
$\cap$	intersection
Λ *or* ϕ	empty set; null set
$\in$	is an element of
$\notin$	is not an element of
$\therefore$	therefore
$\because$	since
$\vdash$	is deducible from

CALCULUS

d	differential of
∂	partial differential
$\int$	integral
$\oint$	contour integral
lim	limit

Fractions and Decimals

%	percent

"Mathematics" in chapter 4; "First Aid" **Go to** (chapter 17); "Heath and Nutrition" (chapter 18)

MEDICINE AND PHARMACOLOGY SYMBOLS

Å	angstrom unit		in d.	daily
Ā,ĀĀ, āā, āa	of each		lot.	a lotion
a.c.	before meals		ⓜ	heart murmur
ad	up to; so as to make		ℳ, ℳ	minim
add.	let there be added; add		μ	micron
ad lib.	at pleasure; as needed or desired		μμ	micromicron
agit.	shake		mod. praesc.	in the manner prescribed
aq.	water		O., o.	a pint
b. (i.) d.	twice daily		ol.	oil
c̄	with		oz.	ounce
cap.	take; capsule		p.c.	after meals
coch.	a spoonful		pil.	pill(s)
d.	give		p.r.n.	as circumstances may require
dil.	dilute *or* dissolve		pulv.	powder
Dx	diagnosis		Px	past history
fldxt.	fluid extract		q. (i.) d.	four times daily
ft.	make		q.l.	as much as you please
ft. mist.	let a mixture be made		q.s.	as much as will suffice
ft. pulv.	let a powder be made		q.v.	as much as you like
gr.	a grain		℞	take: used at the beginning of a prescription
gtt.	drops		rep.	let it be repeated
H.	hour		Rh+	positive blood factor
haust.	a draft		RH-	negative blood factor
Hx	history		δ	$^1/_{1000}$ of a second

continues

s̄	without		t. (i.) d.	three times daily
S, Sig.	write: used in prescriptions to indicate the directions to be placed on the label of the medicine		ut dict.	as directed
			w/v	weight in volume
			ʒ	ounce
sol.	solution		f ʒ	fluidounce
s.o.s.	if necessary		ʒ	dram
s̄s̄	one half		f ʒ	fluidram
tab.	tablet		Э	scruple

PHYSICS SYMBOLS

α	alpha particle		*e*	electronic charge of electron
Å	angstrom unit		*E*	electric field
β	beta ray		*G*	conductance; weight
γ	gamma radiation		*h*	Planck's constant
ε	electromotive force		*H*	enthalpy
η	efficiency		*L*	inductance
Λ	equivalent conductivity; permeance		*n*	index of refraction
λ	wavelength		*P*	momentum of a particle
μ	magnetic moment		*R*	universal gas constant
v	frequency		*S*	entropy
ρ	density; specific resistance		*T*	absolute temperature; period
σ	conductivity		*V*	electrical potential; frequency
φ	luminous flux; magnetic flux		*W*	energy
φ	fluidity		*X*	magnification; reactance
Ω	ohm		*Y*	admittance
B	magnetic induction; magnetic field		*Z*	impedance
c	speed of light			

Go to
"Physics" and "Meteorology" in chapter 4

WEATHER SYMBOLS
FRONTS

Warm	Cold	Occluded	Stationary

GROUND VISIBILITY

Fog (Light)	Fog (Heavy)	Haze	Visibility Reduced by Smoke

PRECIPITATION

Drizzle	Rain Showers	Hail Showers	Sleet	Snow	Snow (Drifting, Slight to Moderate)

SKY CONDITIONS

Clear Sky   Cloudy (Partly)   Cloudy (Completely Overcast)

STORMS

Lightning   Thunderstorm   Tornado   Tropical Storm   Hurricane   Sandstorm or Dust Storm

WIND SPEEDS

Calm   Approx. 1 mph (1 knot)   Approx. 6 mph (5 knots)   Approx. 12 mph (10 knots)   Approx. 58 mph (50 knots)

CULTURAL SYMBOLS

MUSIC SYMBOLS

𝅝	whole note	𝄾	eighth rest	¢	[2/2] time
𝅗𝅥	half note	𝄿	sixteenth rest	𝄴	[6/8] time
𝅗𝅥.	dotted half note	𝅀	thirty-second rest	𝄞	treble, or G, clef
𝅘𝅥	quarter note	𝅁	sixty-fourth rest	𝄢	bass, or F, clef
𝅘𝅥𝅮	eighth note	♯	sharp	𝄡	alto, or C, clef
𝅘𝅥𝅯	sixteenth note	X	double sharp		measure
𝅘𝅥𝅰	thirty-second note	♭	flat		final bar
𝅘𝅥𝅱	sixty-fourth note	♭♭	double flat		repeat
	whole rest	♮	natural		repeat measure
	half rest	¾	³/₄ time		
𝄽	quarter rest	C	⁴/₄ time	D.C.	repeat from the beginning

Symbols/Signs

p	piano (soft)	*ff*	fortissimo (very loud)		tie
pp	pianissimo (very soft)	<	crescendo		trill
f	forte (loud)	>	decrescendo		

Common Music Terms" in chapter 6; "Major World Religions" in chapter 9 **Go to**

RELIGION SYMBOLS

BUDDHISM

Buddha

Lotus

The Wheel

CHRISTIANITY

Celtic Cross

Latin Cross

Orthodox Cross

Agnus Dei

Chi Rho

Descending Dove; Holy Spirit

HINDUISM

Mandala

Om

Shiva

ISLAM

Star and Crescent

JUDAISM

Menorah

Star of David

Ten Commandments

SHINTO

Torii

TAOISM

Water: Life-Giving Source

Yin-Yang

Symbols/Signs

ZODIAC SIGNS

Symbols		Signs	Planet	Element	Personality Traits
		Aries The Ram Mar. 21–Apr. 19	Mars	fire	bold, impulsive, confident, independent
		Taurus The Bull Apr. 20–May 20	Venus	earth	patient, determined, stubborn, devoted
		Gemini The Twins May 21–June 21	Mercury	air	ambitious, alert, intelligent, temperamental
		Cancer The Crab June 22–July 22	Moon	water	moody, sensitive, impressionable, sympathetic
		Leo The Lion July 23–Aug. 22	Sun	fire	noble, generous, enthusiastic, temperamental
		Virgo The Virgin Aug. 23–Sept. 22	Mercury	earth	intellectual, methodical, placid, tactless
		Libra The Scales Sept. 23–Oct. 23	Venus	air	just, sympathetic, orderly, persuasive, sociable
		Scorpio The Scorpion Oct. 24–Nov. 21	Mars	water	loyal, philosophical, willful, domineering
		Sagittarius The Archer Nov. 22–Dec. 21	Jupiter	fire	practical, imaginative, mature, just
		Capricorn The Goat Dec. 22–Jan. 19	Saturn	earth	ambitious, blunt, loyal, persistent
		Aquarius The Water Carrier Jan. 20–Feb. 18	Uranus	air	unselfish, generous, idealistic, original
		Pisces The Fishes Feb. 19–Mar. 20	Neptune	water	sympathetic, sensitive, timid, methodical

Symbols/Signs

The swastika predates Hinduism and is considered an auspicious sign in India. It is the symbol painted on each toe in drawings of Buddha's footprint. It was also used by Native Americans.

"Astronomy: Constellations" in chapter 4

Go to

BIRTHSTONES AND FLOWERS

Month	Birthstone	Flower
January	garnet	snowdrop
February	amethyst	primrose
March	aquamarine or bloodstone	violet
April	diamond	daisy
May	emerald	hawthorn
June	pearl, alexandrite, or moonstone	rose
July	ruby	water lily
August	sardonyx or peridot	poppy
September	sapphire	morning glory
October	opal or tourmaline	hops
November	topaz	chrysanthemum
December	turquoise or lapis lazuli	holly

"Botantical Names of Plants" in chapter 3; "Some Important Minerals and Their Uses" in chapter 4   **Go to**

SYMBOLS TO GUIDE THE TRAVELER

MAP AND CHART SYMBOLS
BOUNDARIES

International	Provincial or State	County	Township	Incorporated Village

CITIES AND TOWNS

Capital City   Urban Area   Town or Village

CULTURAL, HISTORICAL, AND RECREATIONAL SYMBOLS

Points of Interest   Campsites   Winter Sports Area   State Monuments, Memorials, and Historical Sites   Ruins   National Wildlife Refuge   Ranger Station

Symbols/Signs

HYDROGRAPHIC FEATURES

Intermittent
River

Intermittent
Lake

Freshwater
Lake: Reservoir

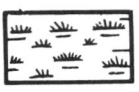

Marsh: Swamp

Dams

Falls

NATURAL FEATURES

Glaciers and Ice Shelves

Passes

Elevation Above Sea Level

ROADS AND RAILROADS

Superhighway

Superhighway
Under Construction

Dual Highway

Main Road

Secondary Road

Bridge and
Road

Drawbridge
and Road

Tunnel and
Road

Railroad Track,
Single

Railroad Tracks,
Two or More

Railroad
Station

DISTRESS SIGNALS

The symbols below, used for ground-to-air communication, may be made of strips of fabric or parachutes, pieces of wood, tree branches, stones, or any other material.

I
Need
Doctor

II
Need
Medicine

X
Cannot
Proceed

F
Need Food
and Water

Need
Weapons

K
Indicate
Direction

Going
This Way

D
Aircraft
Damaged

Attempting
Take Off

Safe to
Land

LL
All Well

L
Need Fuel
and Oil

N
No

Y
Yes

Don't
Understand

W
Need
Engineer

Need Compass
and Map

Need Signal
Lamp

ROAD SIGNS

Curve   Intersection   Opening Bridge   Road Works   Tunnel   Pedestrian Crossing

Watch Out for Children   Animals Crossing   Road Narrows   Slippery Road   Danger

No Entry   Road Closed   Closed to Motor Vehicles   Closed to Motorcycles   Closed to Pedestrians

No Left Turns   No U Turns   Overtaking Prohibited   Speed Limit   End of All Restrictions

Yield   Stop   Direction to Follow   Traffic Circle

Parking   Hospital   Mechanical Help   Telephone

Filling Station   Camping Site   Caravan Site   Youth Hostel

SYMBOLIC ALPHABETS
SEMAPHORE CODE

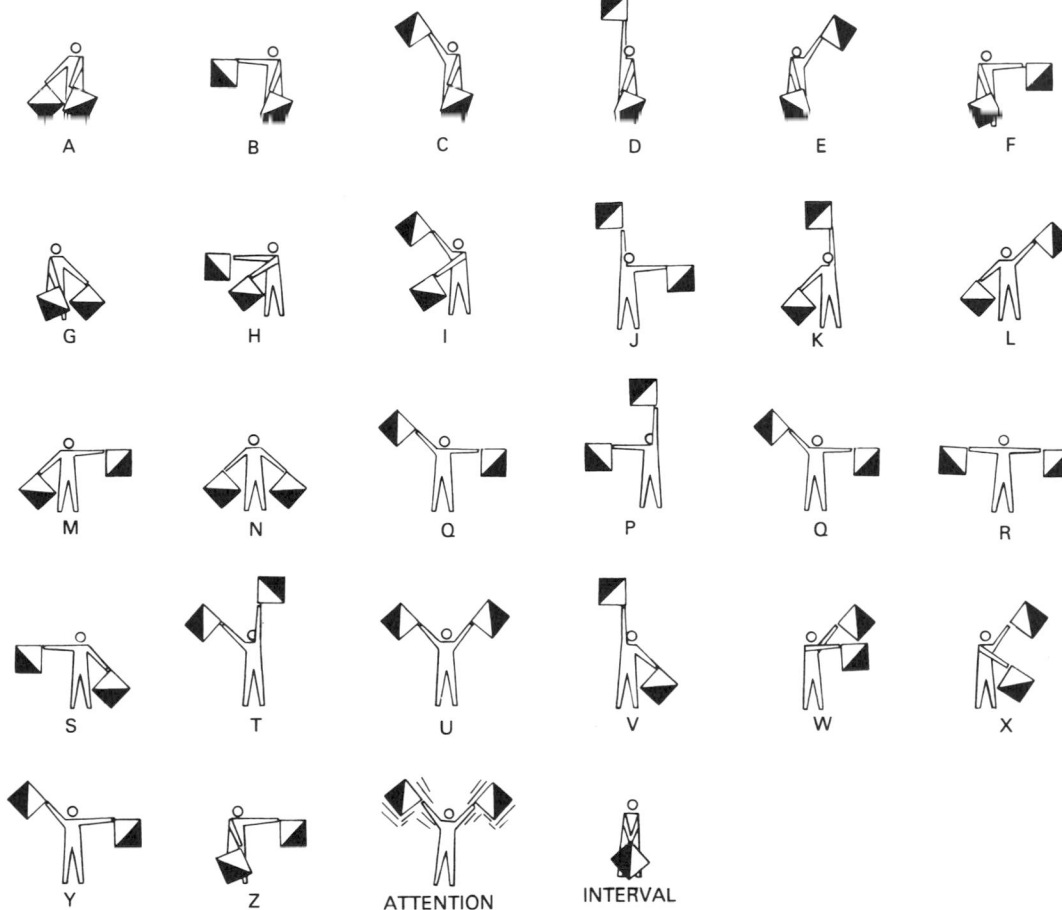

INTERNATIONAL RADIO ALPHABET AND MORSE CODE

A	Alpha	· —	**P**	Papa	· — — ·	**4**	four	· · · · —
B	Bravo	— · · ·	**Q**	Quebec	— — · —	**5**	five	· · · ·
C	Charlie	— · — ·		(kaybec)		**6**	six	— · · · ·
D	Delta	— · ·	**R**	Romeo	· — ·	**7**	seven	— — · · ·
E	Echo	·	**S**	Sierra	· · ·	**8**	eight	— — — · ·
F	Foxtrot	· · — ·	**T**	Tango	—	**9**	nine	— — — — ·
G	Golf	— — ·	**U**	Uniform	· · —	**10**	ten	— — — — —
H	Hotel	· · · ·	**V**	Victor	· · · —	**.**	period	· — · — · —
I	India	· ·	**W**	Whiskey	· — —	**,**	comma	— — · · — —
J	Juliet	· — — —	**X**	X-ray	— · · —	**?**	question	· · — — · ·
K	Kilo	— · —	**Y**	Yankee	— · — —		mark	
L	Lima	· — · ·	**Z**	Zulu	— — · ·	**;**	semicolon	— · — · — ·
	(leema)		**1**	one	· — — — —	**:**	colon	— — — · · ·
M	Mike	— —	**2**	two	· · — — —	**-**	hyphen	— · · · · —
N	November	— ·	**3**	three	· · · — —	**'**	apostrophe	· — — — — ·
O	Oscar	— — —						

SIGN LANGUAGE

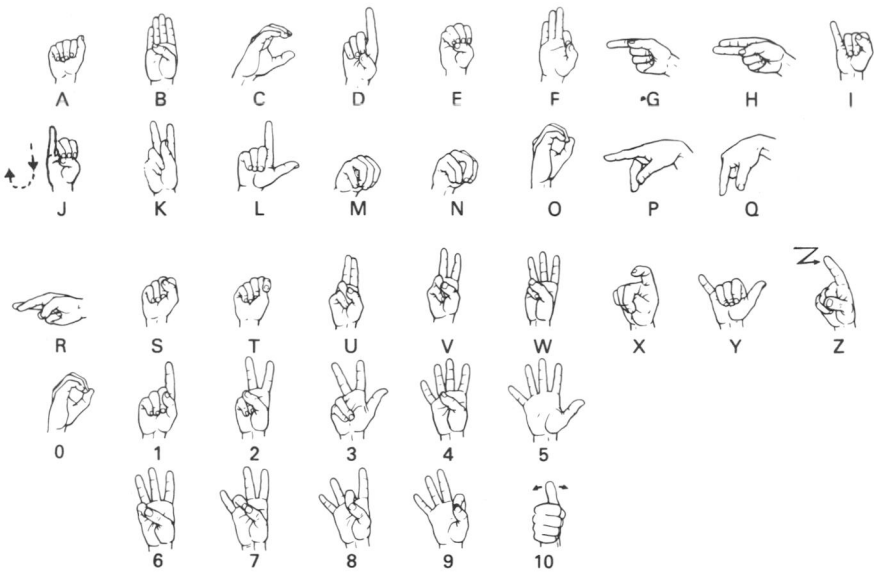

BRAILLE ALPHABET, NUMBERS, AND PUNCTUATION

Between 1826 and 1837, Louis Braille, a blind Frenchman, developed a system of printing and writing for the blind that uses raised dots representing letters, numbers, and punctuation.

The six dots of the Braille cell are arranged and numbered:

```
1 •   • 4
2 •   • 5
3 •   • 6
```

The capital sign, dot 6,

```
1 •   • 4
2 •   • 5
3 •   ● 6
```

placed before a letter makes a capital letter.

The number sign, dots 3, 4, 5, 6,

```
1 •   ● 4
2 •   ● 5
3 ●   ● 6
```

placed before the characters a–j, makes the numbers 1 through 0. For example: <u>a</u> preceded by the number sign is 1, <u>b</u> is 2, etc.

George Washington was a Freemason and adopted the pyramid (a symbol of knowledge and wisdom) and the all-seeing eye of God as national emblems. They are still found on dollar bills.

The system illustrated on the next page is Standard English Braille - Grade 1 (letters, numerals, and punctuation). Grade 2 Braille additionally makes use of approximately 300 contractions (combinations of cells to shorten the lengths of a word). Grade 3 Braille, rarely used, employs additional contractions.

Go to "Telecommunications Device for the Deaf (TDD)" and "Books for Blind and Physically Handicapped Persons" in chapter 22

a	b	c	d	e	f	g	h	i	j
1	2	3	4	5	6	7	8	9	10

k	l	m	n	o	p	q	r	s	t

u	v	w	x	y	z

comma	colon	semicolon	period	exclamation point	parenthesis
,	:	;	.	!	( )

question mark	hyphen	apostrophe	left quotation mark	right quotation mark
?	–	'	"	"

BUSINESS AND MONETARY SYMBOLS

A/C, a/c	account; account current		P/A	power of attorney
A/O, a/o	account of		P/C, p/c	prices current; petty cash
B/D	bank draft		P/N	promissory note
B/E	bill of exchange		w/	with
B/L	bill of lading		W/B	waybill
B/P	bills payable		w/o	without
B/R	bills receivable		@	at/per/priced at
B/V	book value		#	number, pounds
C/D	carried down; certificate of deposit		%	percent/per hundred
C/N	circular note; credit note		¢	cent
C/O	care of; carried over; cash order		$	dollar
d/d	delivered		DM	deutsche mark
D/O	delivery order		F	franc
G/A	general average		L	lira
L/C, l/c	letter of credit		£	pound
M/D, m/d	month's date		R	ruble
N/S, n/s	not sufficient funds		R	rupee
o/c	overcharge		Y, ¥	yen
O/S	out of stock			

Symbols/Signs

PROOFREADERS' MARKS

∧	Insert material as indicated in margin
⅋	Delete
stet	Restore deleted material; let it stand (in text, use dots to indicate what is to be restored)
⌒	Close up; print as one word
⌒̃	Delete and close up
tr	Transpose (in text, indicate by or to change order of)
sp	Spell out
#	Insert space
eq #	Space evenly
hr #	Insert hair space
⎕	Insert or indent one em space
⊓	Move up
⊔	Move down
⌋	Move to the right
⌐	Move to the left
⌋⌐	Center
‖	Align vertically
=	Align horizontally; straighten type
9	Turn over inverted letter
wf	Wrong font
×	Broken type; reset
¶	Begin a new paragraph
no ¶	Do not begin a new paragraph; run paragraphs together
(/)	Insert parentheses
[/]	Insert brackets
̭	Insert comma
;/	Insert semicolon
:/	Insert colon
⊙	Insert period
?	Insert question mark
⋅/⋅/⋅/⋅	Insert ellipses
∛	Insert apostrophe (or single quotation mark)
∜ ∜	Insert quotation marks
|=|	Insert hyphen
⊥ₘ	Insert em dash
⊥ₙ	Insert en dash
∨	Insert superscript or superior
∧	Insert subscript or inferior
cap	Capitalize lowercase letter
lc	Lowercase capital letter
s.c.	Set in SMALL CAPITALS (in text, indicated by double underline)
rom	Set in roman type
bf	Set in **boldface** type
ital	Set in *italic* type

"Diacritical Marks" in chapter 13; **Go to** "Grammar and Punctuation" (chapter 14); and "Network Etiquette (Netiquette)" in chapter 16

SMILEYS

Smileys, also known as emoticons, or emotional icons) are faces viewed sideways that are added to online messages in order to convey feelings.

:-)	Happy
:-(	Sad
;-)	Winking
:-t	Cross
:-o	Surprised
8-|	In suspense
|-|	Asleep (indicates boredom)
:-&	Tongue-tied
:-#	Lips are sealed
:-\	Undecided

ADDITIONAL SOURCES OF INFORMATION

Adkins, Jan. *Symbols: A Silent Language.* Walker and Company, 1984.

Campbell, Joseph, and M. J. Abadie. *The Mythic Image.* Princeton University Press, 1981.

Cirlot, J. E. *A Dictionary of Symbols.* Philosophy Library, 1972.

Cooper, J. C. *An Illustrated Encyclopaedia of Traditional Symbols.* Thames and Hudson, 1987.

Dreyfuss, Henry, ed. *Symbol Sourcebook: An Authoritative Guide to International Graphic Symbols.* Van Nostrand Reinhold, 1984.

Modley, Rudolf, and William R. Meyers. *Handbook of Pictorial Symbols.* Dover, 1976.

13

ALPHABETS AND WORDS

ALPHABETIZATION	404
ACRONYMS	404
COMMON ABBREVIATIONS	407
COMMONLY MISUSED WORDS	412
SPELLING GUIDELINES	413
COMMONLY MISSPELLED WORDS	413
PHONETIC SYMBOLS	415
AMERICAN ENGLISH AND BRITISH ENGLISH: SPELLING AND NAME DIFFERENCES	415
DIACRITICAL MARKS	415
THE INDO-EUROPEAN FAMILY OF LANGUAGES	416
FREQUENTLY USED FOREIGN WORDS AND PHRASES	417

GREEK PREFIXES AND SUFFIXES
422

LATIN PREFIXES AND SUFFIXES
424

COMMON CROSSWORD-PUZZLE WORDS
425

FOREIGN ALPHABETS
432

ADDITIONAL SOURCES OF INFORMATION
433

ALPHABETIZATION

There are two ways of alphabetizing a list of words, terms, or names. In both cases, the compiler of the list compares the first letters of the entries, then the second letter, and so forth. In a word-by-word list, the first word of each entry is considered, then the second, and third if necessary; hyphens are ignored. A letter-by-letter list is considered without regard for whether the entry consists of one word or more than one; spaces and hyphens are ignored.

The following list is arranged according to the word-by-word system:

> sea
> Sea Side Heights
> seafood
> seagull
> seal
> seaside
> season ticket
> seasoning
> second best
> second name
> secondary

Here is the same list compiled under the letter-by-letter system:

> sea
> seafood
> seagull
> seal
> seaside
> Sea Side Heights
> seasoning
> season ticket
> secondary
> second best
> second name

Either method of alphabetization is acceptable, as long as it is scrupulously adhered to. Although some lists may be better served by one approach or the other, neither is considered more correct.

ACRONYMS

Acronyms are pronounceable formations made by combining the initial letters or syllables of a string of words. Some abbreviations look like acronyms but are listed as abbreviations because they are not pronounced as words; for example, CIA (usually pronounced "C-I-A") and DAR (usually pronounced "D-A-R"). A few acronyms may be pronounced either as words ("REM") or as abbreviations ("R-E-M"). Acronyms marked with an asterisk (*) have been generally accepted and used as common words.

Acronym	Stands for
ABEND	**ab**normal **end**
ACE	**A**merican **C**ouncil on **E**ducation
ACTION	**A**merican **C**ouncil **to** **I**mprove **O**ur **N**eighborhoods
AID	**A**gency for **I**nternational **D**evelopment
AID	**A**merican **I**nstitute of **D**ecorators
AID	**A**rmy **I**ntelligence **D**epartment
AIDS	**a**cquired **i**mmune **d**eficiency **s**yndrome
AIIM	**A**ssociation for **I**nformation and **I**mage **M**anagement
ALCOA	**Al**uminum **Co**mpany of **A**merica
ALGOL	**alg**orithmic **o**riented **l**anguage
ALIBI	**a**daptive **l**ocation of **i**nternetworked **b**ases of **i**nformation
ALINK	**a**ctive **link**
AMEX	**Am**erican **Ex**press Company
AMEX	**Am**erican Stock **Ex**change
AMVETS	**Am**erican **Vet**erans of World War II
ANSI	**A**merican **N**ational **S**tandards **I**nstitute
ARC	**A**IDS-**r**elated **c**omplex
ARCO	**A**tlantic **R**ichfield **Co**mpany
ASCAP	**A**merican **S**ociety of **C**omposers, **A**uthors, and **P**ublishers
ASCII	**A**merican **S**tandard **C**ode for **I**nformation **I**nterchange
AWACS	**a**irborne **w**arning **a**nd **c**ontrol **s**ystem
AWOL, awol*	**a**bsent **with**out **l**eave
BAM	**B**rooklyn **A**cademy of **M**usic
BAM	**b**asic **a**ccess **m**ethod
BART	**B**ay **A**rea **R**apid **T**ransit
BASIC	**B**eginner's **A**ll-purpose **S**ymbolic **I**nstruction **C**ode (computer language)
BASS	**B**ass **A**nglers **S**portsman **S**ociety
BIB	**B**ureau of **I**nternational **B**roadcasting
BIOS	**b**asic **i**nput/**o**utput **s**ystem
bit*	**bi**nary dig**it**
BIZNET	American **Bu**siness **Net**work (database)
BOLD	**b**ibliographic **o**n-**l**ine **d**isplay (document retrieval system)
CAB	**C**ivil **A**eronautics **B**oard
CAD	**c**omputer-**a**ided **d**esign
CALM	**C**itizens **A**gainst **L**egalized **M**urder
CARE	**C**ooperative for **A**merican **R**elief **E**verywhere

Acronym	Stands for
CAT (scan)	computerized axial tomography
CD-ROM	compact disk–read only memory
CLASSMATE	Computer Language to Aid and Stimulate Scientific, Mathematical and Technical Education
CODEC	coder/decoder
COMSAT	Communications Satellite Corporation
CONOCO	Continental Oil Company
CONUS	Continental United States
CORE	Congress of Racial Equality
COSMIC	Computer Software Management and Information Center
CURE	Citizens United for Racial Equality
DAM	Dayton Art Museum
DAM	Denver Art Museum
DELCO	Dayton Engineering Laboratory Company
DEW	distant early warning
DISCO	Defense Industrial Security Clearing Office
DOS	disk operating system
EARS	Electronic Airborne Reaction System
EARS	Electronically Agile Radar System
EARS	Emergency Airborne Reaction System
ELECTRA	Electrical, Electronics and Communications Trade Association
ENDEX	Environmental Data Index
EPCOT®	Experimental Prototype Community of Tomorrow
EXIMBANK	Export-Import Bank of the United States
FAQ	frequently asked questions
FEDLINK	Federal Library Information Network
FEW	Federally Employed Women
FICA	Federal Insurance Contributions Act (Social Security)
FLIP	Flexible Loan Insurance Program
FLIP	floating instrument platform
GAAP	generally accepted accounting principles
GAG	Graphic Arts Guild
GARB	Garment and Allied Industries Requirements Board
GATT	General Agreement on Tariffs and Trade
GENIE	General Electric Network for Information Exchange
GEO	Geostationary Earth Orbit
GEOS	graphic environment operating system
GILS	Government Information Locator Service
GIPSY	general information processing system

Acronym	Stands for
GLAD	Gay and Lesbian Advocates and Defenders
GOES	Geostationary Operational Environmental Satellite
GRAD	graduate resume accumulation and distribution
GUPCO	Gulf Petroleum Corporation
HALF	Human Animal Liberation Front
HART	Honolulu Area Rapid Transit
HEAL	Health Education Assistance Loans
HUD	(Department of) Housing and Urban Development
IMAX®	Maximum Image
INLAW	infantry laser weapon
INTELSAT	International Telecommunications Satellite Consortium
INTERMARC	International Machine-Readable Catalog
INTERPOL	International Criminal Police Organization
INTERTELL	International Intelligence Legion
JAG	judge advocate general
JOBS	Job Opportunities in the Business Sector
JUMPS	Joint Uniform Military Pay System
LAN	local area network
laser*	light amplification by stimulated emission of radiation
LEAP	Loan and Educational Aid Program
LEM	lunar excursion module
LILCO	Long Island Lighting Company
LORAN	Long-range Navigation
MACOM	major army command
MAD	mutually assured destruction
MADD	Mothers Against Drunk Driving
MARC	machine-readable cataloging
maser*	microwave amplification stimulated emission of radiation
MASH	mobile army surgical hospital
MOMA	Museum of Modern Art (New York)
NAFTA	North American Free Trade Agreement
NAM	network access machine
NAM	National Association of Manufacturers
NAPA	National Automotive Parts Association

A Closer Look

Recurrent Letters of the Alphabet

The letters of the alphabet in the order of their normal recurrence from most frequent to least frequent: E, T, A, O, I, N, S, H, R, D, L, U, C, M, P, F, Y, W, G, B, V, K, J, X, Z, Q.

Acronym	Stands for
NAPA	National Police Officers' Association of America
NARAD	Navy Research and Development
NARCO	United National Narcotics Commission
NASA	National Aeronautics and Space Administration
NASCAR	National Association of Stock Car Auto Racing
NASDAQ	National Association of Securities Dealers Automatic Quotation
NATO	North Atlantic Treaty Organization
NECCO	New England Confectionery Company
NOAA	National Oceanographic and Atmospheric Administration
NOMAD	navy oceanographic and meteorological device
NORAD	North American Defense Command
NOW	National Organization for Women
NOW	negotiable order of withdrawal (a NOW account is a savings account on which checks can be drawn)
OASIS	Overseas Access Service for Information Systems
ODECO	Ocean Drilling and Exploration Company
ODESY	On-Line Data Entry System
OPEC	Organization of Petroleum Exporting Countries
OSHA	Occupational Safety and Health Administration
OXFAM	Oxford Famine Relief
PAC	Pacific Air Command
PAC	political action committee
PATCO	Port Authority Transit Corporation
PATH	Port Authority Trans-Hudson
PEN	Poets, Playwrights, Editors, Essayists, and Novelists
PEST	People for Environmentally Sustainable Transport
PET	parent effectiveness training
PET	positron emission tomography
PIN	personal identification number
PIN	Police Information Network
PIM	personal information manager
PIRG	public interest research group
POSIX	Portable Operating System Interface for Computer Environments
PUSH	People United to Serve Humanity
radar*	radio detecting and ranging
RAM	random access memory
READ	real-time electronic access and display

Acronym	Stands for
RIF	Reading Is Fundamental
ROM	read-only memory
SAC	Strategic Air Command
SADD	Students Against Drunk Driving
SAFE	system for automated flight efficiency
SAG	Screen Actors Guild
SALT	Strategic Arms Limitation Talks
SAM	surface-to-air missile
SAP	system access protocol
SARA	Superfund Amendments and Reauthorization Act (1986)
SCOPE	Scientific Committee on Problems of the Environment
SCOR	Scientific Committee on Oceanic Research
SCOSTEP	Scientific Committee on Solar-Terrestrial Physics
scuba*	self-contained underwater breathing apparatus
SEATO	Southeast Asia Treaty Organization
SEP	simplified employee pension
snafu*	situation normal—all fouled up
sonar*	sound navigation ranging
START	Strategic Arms Reduction Talks
SUNOCO	Sun Oil Company
SWAK	sealed with a kiss
SWAT	Special Weapons and Tactics
TAC	Tactical Air Command
TIROS	Television and Infra-Red Observation Satellite
UNESCO	United Nations Educational, Social, and Cultural Organization
UNICEF	United Nations International Children's Emergency Fund
VISTA	Volunteers in Service to America
WAC	Women's Army Corps
WAIS	wide area information server
WAN	wide area network
WARMER	World Action for Recycled Material and Energy from Rubbish
WASP	white Anglo-Saxon Protestant
WATS	Wide Area Telecommunications Service
WAVES	Women Accepted for Volunteer Emergency Service (navy)
WHO	World Health Organization
WISE	World Information Systems Exchange
WORM	write once–read many
WUDO	Western European Defense Organization
yuppie*	young urban professional
zip*	zone improvement plan (code)

Alphabets

COMMON ABBREVIATIONS

An abbreviation is a shortened form of a word or phrase. Some abbreviations, such as Mr. and Mrs., always substitute for the longer form. Abbreviations are not limited to, but frequently are used for, titles, academic degrees, organizations, measurements, and scientific words. An asterisk (*) indicates a frequently used abbreviation that is incorrect according to the scientific metric notation system.

Abbr.	Stands for
1GL	first-generation language
2DR	two-door
2GL	second-generation language
2WD	two-wheel drive
3GL	third-generation language
4DR	four-door
4GL	fourth-generation language
4WD	four-wheel drive
a	acre
AAA	American Automobile Association
ABC	American Broadcasting Company
ABM	antiballistic missile
AC	alternating current
ACLU	American Civil Liberties Union
ACT	American College Test
AD, A.D.	*anno domini* (Latin, in the year of our Lord)
A/D	analog to digital
ADA	American Dental Association
addn.	addition
addnl.	additional
adm.	administration, administrative
AEC	Atomic Energy Commission
AEF	American Expeditionary Force (World War I)
aet.	*aetatis* (Latin, of age, aged)
AF	air force
AFB	air force base
AFC	American Football Conference
AFDC	Aid to Families with Dependent Children
AFL	American Football League
AFL-CIO	American Federation of Labor and Congress of Industrial Organizations
Afr.	Africa, African
AFT	American Federation of Teachers
AFT	automatic fine tuning
AFTP	Anonymous File Transfer Protocol
agcy.	agency
agt.	agent
AH, A.H.	*anno Hegirae/anno Hebraico* (Latin, in the year of the Hegira/Latin, in the Hebrew year)

Abbr.	Stands for
AHL	American Hockey League
AI	artificial intelligence
AIA	American Institute of Architects
aka, a.k.a.	also known as
AKC	American Kennel Club
AL	American League
AM	amplitude modulation
A.M.	*anno mundi* (Latin, in the year of the world)
A.M., AM, a.m.	*ante meridiem* (Latin, before noon)
AMA	American Medical Association
AMU	atomic mass unit
anon.	anonymous
AP	Associated Press
A/P	accounts payable
APA	American Psychological Association
APB	all points bulletin
APO	army post office (overseas)
appl.	applied
approx.	approximately
appt.	appointment
Apr.	April
APR	annual percentage rate
apt.	apartment
A/R	accounts receivable
ARV	American Revised Version
ASAP	as soon as possible (pronounced "A-S-A-P" or "A-SAP")
assn.	association
asoc.	associate
asst.	assistant
AST	Alaska Standard Time
AT&T	American Telephone and Telegraph Company
ATM	automated/automatic teller machine
ATTN, attn.	attention
atty.	attorney
ATV	all-terrain vehicle
Aug.	August
AV	audiovisual
AV	Authorized Version
AVR	automatic voice recognition
b.	born
B and B, B&B	bed and breakfast
B and E	breaking and entering
BBB	Better Business Bureau

Go to "Weights and Measures" in chapter 2; "Symbols and Signs" in chapter 12; "Abbreviated Titles That Follow Names" in chapter 15

Alphabets

Abbr.	Stands for
BBC	British Broadcasting Corporation
bbl.	barrel(s)
BC, B.C.	before Christ
BC, B.C.E.	before the Christian era
bef.	before
bf, b.f.	boldface
BLT	bacon, lettuce, and tomato
BMOC	big man on campus
BP	blood pressure
B.P.O.E.	Benevolent and Protective Order of Elks
BR	bedroom
BSA	Boy Scouts of America
bu.	bushel
BV, BVM	Blessed Virgin, Blessed Virgin Mary
b/w	black and white
BX	base exchange (commissary)
BYOB	bring your own beer/ booze/bottle
C	centigrade, Celsius
c., ca.	*circa* (Latin, about)
calc.	calculate, calculated
cam	camera
Cantab.	*Cantabrigiensis* (Latin, of Cambridge)
caps	capital letters
CATV	community antenna television, *now called* cable television
CBS	Columbia Broadcasting System
cc	cubic centimeter
cc, CC	carbon copy
CCC	Civilian Conservation Corps
CCU	cardiac/coronary/critical care unit
CD	certificate of deposit
CDC	Centers for Disease Control
CDT	Central Daylight Time
CEO	chief executive officer
cf.	*confer* (Latin, compare)
CIA	Central Intelligence Agency
cm	centimeter
c/o	in care of
C.O.D., COD	cash on delivery
COO	chief operating officer
CP	Communist party
cpi	characters per inch
CPI	consumer price index
CPR	cardiopulmonary resuscitation
CPU	central processing unit
CSA	Confederate States of America
CST	Central Standard Time
cu.	cubic
DAR	Daughters of the American Revolution
dB	decibel
DB	database
d/b/a	doing business as

Abbr.	Stands for
DC	District of Columbia or district current
Dec.	December
dept.	department
dist.	district
div.	division
DMV	Department (Division) of Motor Vehicles
DMZ	demilitarized zone
DNA	deoxyribonucleic acid
DOA	dead on arrival
DOB	date of birth
doz.	dozen
Dr.	Doctor
D.S.M.	Distinguished Service Medal
D.S.O.	Distinguished Service Order
DST	Daylight Savings Time
DTs	*delerium tremens* (Latin, trembling delirium)
DUI	driving under the influence
DWI	driving while intoxicated
ED	emotional disability, emotionally disabled
EDS	Electronic Data Systems
EEO	equal employment opportunity
e.g.	*exempli gratia* (Latin, for example)
eng.	engineering
Eng.	English
engr.	engineer
engr.	engraved
EPA	Environmental Protection Agency
ERA	earned run average
esp.	especially
EST	Eastern Standard Time
et al.	*et alii, et aliae, et alia* (Latin, and others)
etc.	*et cetera* (Latin, and others of the same kind; and so forth)
ex.	example
exch.	exchange
exec.	executive
ext.	extension
f., F	female, feminine
f., ff.	and following
F	Fahrenheit
FAA	Federal Aviation Administration
fax	facsimile
FBI	Federal Bureau of Investigation
FCC	Federal Communications Commission
FDA	Food and Drug Administration
FDIC	Federal Deposit Insurance Corporation
Feb.	February

Go to "Cooking Measurement Abbreviations" in chapter 19; "Airline Codes, Toll-Free Numbers, and Web Sites" and "Airport Codes" in chapter 24

Alphabets

Abbr.	Stands for
fed.	federal
FHA	Federal Housing Administration
fig.	figure
FM	frequency modulation
f.o.b., FOB	free on board
fr.	from
Fr.	French
Fri.	Friday
FRM	fixed rate mortgage
FRS	Federal Reserve System
ft.	foot
f/t	full time
FTC	Federal Trade Commission
f/x	special effects
FWD	front-wheel drive
FYI	for your information
G	giga (metric prefix meaning 1,000,000,000)
GAO	General Accounting Office
G.A.R.	Grand Army of the Republic
GED	General Educational Development (tests)
GED	general equivalency diploma
Gk.	Greek
GMAT	Graduate Management Admission Test (pronounced "G-MAT")
GMT	Greenwich Mean Time
GNP	gross national product
GOP	Grand Old Party (Republican party)
gov., govt.	government
G.P.	general practitioner
GPA	grade point average
GPO	Government Printing Office
GRE	Graduate Record Examination
GSA	General Services Administration
GSA	Girl Scouts of America
GSO	general staff officer
GUI	graphical user interface
HEW	(Department of) Health, Education, and Welfare
H.M.S.	His/Her Majesty's Ship
hp	horsepower
HQ	headquarters
hr.	hour
HR	home run
H.R.	House of Representatives
H.R.H.	His/Her Royal Highness
HS	high school
ht., hgt.	height
HTML, html	hypertext markup language
HVAC	heating, ventilating, and air conditioning
ibid.	*ibidem* (Latin, in the same place)

Abbr.	Stands for
I.B.M.	International Business Machines Corporation
ICBM	intercontinental ballistic missile
ICC	Interstate Commerce Commission
ICF	intermediate care facility
ICU	intensive care unit
i.e.	*id est* (Latin, that is)
IGY	International Geophysical Year
IHS	Jesus (Greek contraction)
ILGWU	International Ladies' Garment Workers' Union
in.	inch
INRI	*Iesus Nazarenus Rex Iudaeorum* (Latin, Jesus of Nazareth, King of the Jews)
INS	Immigration and Naturalization Service
I.O.U.	I owe you
I.Q.	intelligence quotient
IRA	individual retirement account
IRA	Irish Republican Army
IRS	Internal Revenue Service
ISBN	international standard book number
ISO	International Organization for Standardization
Jan.	January
Jr.	Junior
k	karat
k	kilo (metric prefix meaning 1,000)
K	Kelvin
kb (K*, KB*)	kilobyte
kbps (KBps*)	kilobytes per second
kg	kilogram
KGB	*Komitet Gosudarstvennoi Bezopasnosti* (Russian, State Security Committee)
kHz	kilohertz
KJV	King James Version
km	kilometer
kW (kw*)	kilowatt
kWh (kwh*)	kilowatt-hour
l	liter
lat.	latitude
Lat.	Latin
lb.	pound
lc, l.c.	lowercase
L.C.	Library of Congress
LCD	liquid crystal display
LD	learning disability, learning disabled
LDS	Latter-Day Saints
LED	light-emitting diode
LMT	Local Mean Time
long.	longitude
LSAT	Law School Admission Test

Alphabets

Abbr.	Stands for
ltr.	letter
m	meter
m.	married
m., M	male, masculine
M	mega (metric prefix meaning 1,000,000)
Mac	Macintosh computer
Mar.	March
max.	maximum
MB	megabyte (1,024 kilobytes)
MBps	megabytes per second
MC, emcee	Master of Ceremonies
mg	milligram
mgr.	manager
MHz	megahertz
mi.	mile
min.	minimum, minute
ml	milliliter
mm	millimeter
mo.	month
M.O.	money order
M.O.	*modus operandi* (Latin, mode of operation)
Mon.	Monday
MP, M.P.	Military Police
mph	miles per hour
ms., mss.	manuscript, manuscripts
MSG	monosodium glutamate
MVP	most valuable player
MYOB	mind your own business
N/A	not applicable
NAACP	National Association for the Advancement of Colored People
N.B.	*nota bene* (Latin, note well)
NBA	National Basketball Association
NBC	National Broadcasting Company
NCAA	National Collegiate Athletic Association
NCO	noncommissioned officer
NEA	National Education Association
NEA	National Endowment for the Arts
NFL	National Football League
NHL	National Hockey League
NIH	National Institutes of Health
NL	National League
NLRB	National Labor Relations Board
NMHA	National Mental Health Association
non seq.	*non sequitur* (Latin, it does not follow, meaning an illogical response that does not follow from the information preceding)
NOS	not otherwise specified

Abbr.	Stands for
Nov.	November
NR	not rated
NRA	National Recovery Administration
NRA	National Rifle Association
NRC	National Research Council
NRC	Nuclear Regulatory Commission
N.S.	New Style
NSA	National Security Agency
NSC	National Security Council
NSF	National Science Foundation
NSF	not sufficient funds
NTSB	National Transportation Safety Board
Oct.	October
OCR	optical character recognition
op. cit.	*opere citato* (Latin, in the work cited)
O.S.	Old Style
OT	occupational therapy
OT, o/t	overtime
OTC	over-the-counter (non-prescription)
Oxon.	*Oxoniensis* (Latin, of Oxford)
oz.	ounce
PA (system)	public address (system)
p and h	postage and handling
P&I	principal and interest
P&L	profit and loss
PB&J	peanut butter and jelly
PBS	Public Broadcasting Service
PC	personal computer
PCB	polychlorinated biphenyl
PDA	public display of affection
PDR	*Physicians Desk Reference*
PDT	Pacific Daylight Time
PE	physical education
perp.	perpetrator
pk.	peck
P.M., PM, p.m.	*post meridiem* (Latin, after noon)
P.M.	prime minister
PMS	premenstrual syndrome
pmt.	payment
POE	place of employment
POV	point of view
POW, PW	prisoner of war
ppb	parts per billion
ppm	parts per million
ppt	parts per thousand
prep., prep	preparatory
Pres.	President
prev.	previous
PRN	*pro re nata* (Latin, for an occasion that has written—as needed)
pro tem.	*pro tempore* (Latin, for the time being)
P.S., PS	postscript

Go to "Two-Letter State and Territory Abbreviations," "Geographic Directional Abbreviations," and "Street Designators (Street Suffixes)" in chapter 25

Abbr.	Stands for
PSA	public service announcement
psi	pounds per square inch
PST	Pacific Standard Time
psych	psychology
pt.	pint
p/t	part-time
PTA	Parent-Teacher Association
PX	post exchange (commissary)
QA	quality assurance
Q.E.D.	*quod erat demonstrandum* (Latin, which was to be demonstrated)
QMHP	qualified mental health professional
QMRP	qualified mental retardation professional
qt.	quart
qty.	quantity
q.v.	*quod vide* (Latin, which see)
R&B	rhythm and blues
R&D	research and development
RBC	red blood cells, red blood cell count
rbi	runs batted in
RDA	recommended daily allowance
REM	rapid eye movement (pronounced "R-E-M" or "REM")
RFD	rural free delivery
RIP, R.I.P.	*requiescat in pace* (Latin, rest in peace)
RNA	ribonucleic acid
ROTC	Reserve Officers' Training Corps (pronounced "R-O-T-C" or "ROTC")
rpm	revolutions per minute
RR	railroad
R and R	rest and relaxation
RSV	Revised Standard Version
R.S.V.P., RSVP	*repondez s'il vous plait* (French, respond if you please)
rtw	ready to wear
Rx	prescription
S&H	shipping and handling
S-M, S and M	sadism and masochism
SASE	self-addressed stamped envelope
Sat.	Saturday
SBA	Small Business Administration
SBS	sick building syndrome
sc, s.c.	small capitals
SCLC	Southern Christian Leadership Conference
SDI	Strategic Defense Initiative
SDS	Students for a Democratic Society
sec.	seconds
SEC	Securities and Exchange Commission
Sen.	Senate
Sept.	September
seq.	*sequentes* (Latin, the following)
SNF	skilled nursing facility

Abbr.	Stands for
SOS	international Morse code distress signal (dot dot dot dash dash dash dot dot dot), often wrongly thought to stand for "Save Our Ship"; however, the letters "SOS" spelled by the signal actually do not stand for words
SPCA	Society for the Prevention of Cruelty to Animals
SPQR	*senatus populusque romanus* (Latin, the Senate and the Roman people)
sq.	square
Sr.	Senior
SRO	standing room only
SSA	Social Security Administration
SSN	Social Security number
Sun.	Sunday
T	ton
TA	teaching assistant
TA	transactional analysis
TB	tuberculosis
TBA, tba	to be announced
TD	touchdown
TDD	telecommunications device for the deaf
temp.	temporary
TF	task force
TGIF	thank God it's Friday
Thurs.	Thursday
TIA	transient ischemic attack
TLC	tender loving care
TM	trademark
TM	transcendental meditation
TMJ	temporomandibular joint
TNT	trinitrotoluene
TOEFL	Test of English as a Foreign Language
TSS	toxic shock syndrome
TTY	teletypewriter
Tues.	Tuesday
TVA	Tennessee Valley Authority
uc, u.c.	uppercase
UFO	unidentified flying object
UHF	ultra high frequency
UK	United Kingdom
UN	United Nations
UPI	United Press International
US, USA	United States, United States of America
USA	United States Army
USAF	United States Air Force
USCG	United States Coast Guard
USDA	United States Department of Agriculture
USIA	United States Information Agency
USMC	United States Marine Corps
USN	United States Navy
USO	United Service Organization

Abbr.	Stands for
USS	United States Ship
USSR	Union of Soviet Socialist Republics
v., vs.	versus
VA	Veterans Administration
VD	venereal disease
VDT	video display terminal
VFW	Veterans of Foreign Wars
VHF	very high frequency
VIP	very important person
viz.	*videlicet* (Latin, namely)
VP	Vice President
W	watt
WB	World Bank
WBC	white blood cells/white blood cell count
WC	water closet (toilet)
WCTU	Women's Christian Temperance Union
Wed.	Wednesday
wk.	week
WP	word processing
WPA	Works Progress Administration
WTO	World Trade Organization
WWW	World Wide Web
WYSIWYG	what you see is what you get
Xmas	Christmas
XO	executive officer
yd.	yard
YTD	year to date
YMCA	Young Men's Christian Association
YMHA	Young Men's Hebrew Association
YWCA	Young Women's Christian Association
YWHA	Young Women's Hebrew Association
yr.	year

COMMONLY MISUSED WORDS

accept	to receive; to answer affirmatively
except	to leave out (verb); with the exclusion of (preposition)
affect	to influence; to pretend
effect	a result, an influence, an impression (noun); to bring about (verb)
antagonist	an adversary
protagonist	the leading character
anxious	worried, uneasy
eager	impatiently desirous
bathos	triteness, sentimentality
pathos	sympathy
brake	to reduce speed
break	to separate; to collapse; to destroy

capital	a city that is a seat of government; money; an uppercase letter
capitol	the building in which a legislature meets
compare	to examine differences and similarities
contrast	to examine differences
diagnosis	the identification of a disease or situation
prognosis	a prediction of the likely course of a disease or situation
dinner	the main meal of the day, at noontime or in the evening
supper	the evening meal
dyeing	coloring with dye
dying	ceasing to live
emigrate	to leave a country to live elsewhere
immigrate	to enter a country to live there
flair	skill, talent
flare	a bright light; an outburst
gorilla	an ape
guerrilla	a member of an irregular military force
hole	a space, a void
whole	complete, intact
illegible	cannot be read because of bad printing or handwriting
unreadable	uninteresting, not worth reading
ingenious	brilliant, clever
ingenuous	simple, naive
its	belonging to it
it's	it is
lay	to put; to set down
lie	to rest in a horizontal position; to make an untrue statement
liable	responsible; likely
libel	a defamatory statement
majority	more than half
plurality	more votes than any other candidate; the margin of victory
notable	worthy, impressive
notorious	widely known and ill-regarded
peace	harmony; the absence of war
piece	part of a whole
personal	intimate; having to do with a specific person
personnel	the employees of a company or organization

pray	to address a deity; to implore
prey	a victim
principal	main (adjective); the person in charge (noun)
principle	a moral rule; a law
put (someone) down	to criticize or disparage someone
put (someone) on	to mislead someone, especially in a joking way
recollect	to remember
re-collect	to collect again
sail	fabric that catches the wind to propel a boat (noun); to ride in a boat, especially one that is wind-powered (verb)
sale	a discounted offering; the act of selling
stationary	not moving
stationery	writing materials
talk to	to address others
talk with	to converse together
viral	having to do with a virus
virile	manly
whose	of which; of who
who's	who is
your	belonging to you
you're	you are

SPELLING GUIDELINES

Many words in American English are spelled just as they sound. That is, a long *a* sound is often spelled with an *a*. Aside from the old saw "*i* before *e* except after *c*, unless sounded as *a* as in *neighbor* and *weigh*," there are few easy ways of remembering the intricacies of correct spelling. The following table shows the ways in which various sounds common in English words can be spelled.

Sound	Spellings
a	sat, meringue, salmon, laugh
ah	father, aunt, calm, sergeant, Afrikaans
aw	saw, caught, order, ought, walk
ay	fade, aerobic, plain, cay, break, neigh, whey, regime
ch	cello, chip, question, nature
e	any, guess, leopard, friend, bread
ee	me, see, lea, ski, either, Aesop, very, believe, phoenix
er	earth, jerk, stir, turn, author, martyr
f	fall, telephone, rough
ih	hit, English, women, busy, cabbage, build, carriage, sieve
i	ice, sly, geyser, high, buy, die, papaya, eye
j	jam, ledge, tragedy
k	kelp, character, slack, acre, aqua, account
n	nap, know, pneumonia, gnaw
oh	bone, oat, soul, oh, folk, brooch, crow, though, bureau, load
oo	do, loo, blew, sue, you, cruise
ow	cow, bough, sauerkraut, found
sh	push, ocean, chauffeur, special, fascist, tissue, compulsion, nation, vicious, noxious, nauseous, sure
uh	up, oven, trouble, was, does
v	love, of
z	xylophone, zebra, visible
zh	regime, division, brazier

COMMONLY MISSPELLED WORDS

abscess
accept/except
accessory
accidentally
accommodate
accompany
accrue
acknowledgment
acquaintance
acquire
address
affect/effect
aisle/isle
allege

all right
already
amateur
analogous
antarctic
antecedent
apparent
appearance
arctic
argument
arithmetic
asparagus
asthma
athletic

attendance
attorney
auxiliary

banana
baptize
bargain
battalion
bazaar
beginning
believe
benign
biscuit
bizarre
bookkeeper

buoyant
bureau
burglar

calendar
cantaloupe
capital/capitol
cashmere
caterpillar
ceiling
cellar
cemetery
cereal/serial
chamois
chandelier

changeable
chaperon(e)
chauffeur
chief
cinnamon
circuit
circumference
cocoa
colonel/kernel
commitment
committee
compliment/
    complement
comptroller

concede
conceive
conscientious
conscious
consensus
consignment
convenient
coquette
corduroy
correspondent
cough
counterfeit
crucifixion

debt
definite
dependent
design
desirable
desperately
dessert/desert
devise
diaphragm
diarrhea
dictionary
diphtheria
disappear
disappoint
dispel
dissatisfied

effect/affect
eighth
embarrass
embezzle
environment
equipped
erroneous
especially
etiquette
exaggerate
exceed
excel
existence
expense

familiar
fascinate

fatigue
February
fiancé
fiancée
financier
foreclosure
forehead
foreign
foreword/forward
formerly/formally
forth/fourth
forty
fragile
freight

gauge
gingham
glacier
government
grammar
grease
guarantee
guess
guest

handkerchief
harass
height
heir
hemorrhage
hygiene
hypocrisy

idol/idle
incite/insight
independence
indict
indispensable
infinitesimal
irresistible
isthmus
its/it's

judgment

khaki

laboratory
larynx

laugh
league
library
license
licorice
literature
lose/loose
lying

mackerel
maintenance
malign
maneuver
manual
mathematics
mattress
medicine
minuscule
mischief
missionary
misspell
misstate
molasses
mortgage
mosquitoes

necessary
neighbor
niece
noticeable
nuisance

obedience
occasion
occur
occurred
occurrence
o'clock
offense
omitted

parallel
parliament
perseverance
phenomenon
physician
plaid
pneumonia

politically
porcelain
possess
potatoes
prairie
precede/proceed
preferred
principle/principal
privilege
probably
protégé
protégée
pseudonym
psychology
ptomaine

quiet/quite

rarefy
raspberry
receipt
receive
recess
recognize
recommend
reference
remittance
rendezvous
repellent
repentance
reservoir
résumé
reverence
rhythm
ridiculous

sacrilege
sacrilegious
sandwich
satire/satyr
scissors
secretary
seize
separately
siege
sieve
similar
sincerely

soliloquy
special
squirrel
stationary/
   stationery
straight/strait
strengthen
succeed
success
suit/suite
superintendent
supersede
susceptible
synagogue
syringe

tariff
temperance
tenement
than/then
their/there/they're
threshold
to/too/two
tobacco
tomatoes
tragedy
transferred
truly
Tuesday

usually

vaccinate
vacuum
villain
vinegar

warrant
Wednesday
weird
wholly
whose/who's
withhold

yolk
your/you're

zephyr

No other words in the English language rhyme with the words month, orange, silver, or purple.

Go to "American English and British English: Punctuation Differences" in chapter 14

PHONETIC SYMBOLS
VOWELS

iy	beat	ʌ	but	
ɪ	bit	ə	banana, sister	
ɛ	bet	aɪ	by	
æ	bat	aʊ	bound	
ɑ	box, car	ɔɪ	boy	
ɔ	bought, horse	ɝ	burn	
oʷ	bone	ɪɚ	beer	
ʊ	book	ɛɚ	bare	
uʷ	boot	ʊɚ	tour	

CONSONANTS

ŋ	velar nasal—si**ng**
θ	dental fricative—**th**ing
ð	dental fricative—**th**is
ʃ	postalveolar fricative—**sh**ort
ʒ	postalveolar fricative—mea**s**ure
tʃ	palatal fricative—i**tch**
dʒ	palatal fricative—**j**ust
ɹ	dental/alveolar/postalveolar approximant—bi**rd**
ɾ	retroflex tap (or flap)—wri**t**er
ʔ	glottal plosive—pause between vowels in **cooperate**

AMERICAN ENGLISH AND BRITISH ENGLISH: SPELLING AND NAME DIFFERENCES

It has been said that the United States and Great Britain are two nations divided by a single language. This is true in a number of ways. In the first place, spellings of the same words can be decidedly different. The following list shows some common examples of the variances between American and British spellings.

American	British
center	centre
check (money)	cheque
color	colour
curb	kerb
defense	defence
gray	grey
honor	honour
inquire	enquire
jail	gaol
jewelry	jewellery
labor	labour
organization	organisation
pajamas	pyjamas
peddler	pedlar

American	British
pretense	pretence
program	programme
realize	realise
recognize	recognise
theater	theatre

The two versions of the English language also diverge when it comes to the names for many everyday objects and events. It is easy for a visitor from across the Atlantic to provoke amusement from the natives by calling a cloth used to wipe one's mouth a *napkin* in England, or by asking an American waiter for the *W.C.* The following is a list of some common American terms and their counterparts in the United Kingdom.

American	British
apartment	flat
bathroom	toilet, W.C., or loo
Big Dipper	the Plough
candy	sweets
checkers	draughts
closet	cupboard
corn	maize
cracker	biscuit
diaper	nappy
drugstore	chemist's
elevator	lift
faucet	tap
gas, gasoline	petrol
hood (of car)	bonnet
line	queue
napkin	serviette
oven	cooker
round-trip ticket	return ticket
suspenders	braces
truck	lorry
trunk (of car)	boot
underpass	subway
undershirt	vest
vacation	holiday

DIACRITICAL MARKS

´	acute accent (as in *café*)
˘	breve (pronunciation symbol that indicates a short vowel)
̧	cedilla (as in (*François*)
^	circumflex (as in *château*)
¨	diaeresis or umlaut (as in *Köln*)
`	grave accent (as in *à la carte*)
–	macron (pronunciation symbol that indicates a long vowel)
~	tilde (as in *São Tomé*)

THE INDO–EUROPEAN FAMILY OF LANGUAGES

"CENTRUM" LANGUAGES

"SATEM" LANGUAGES

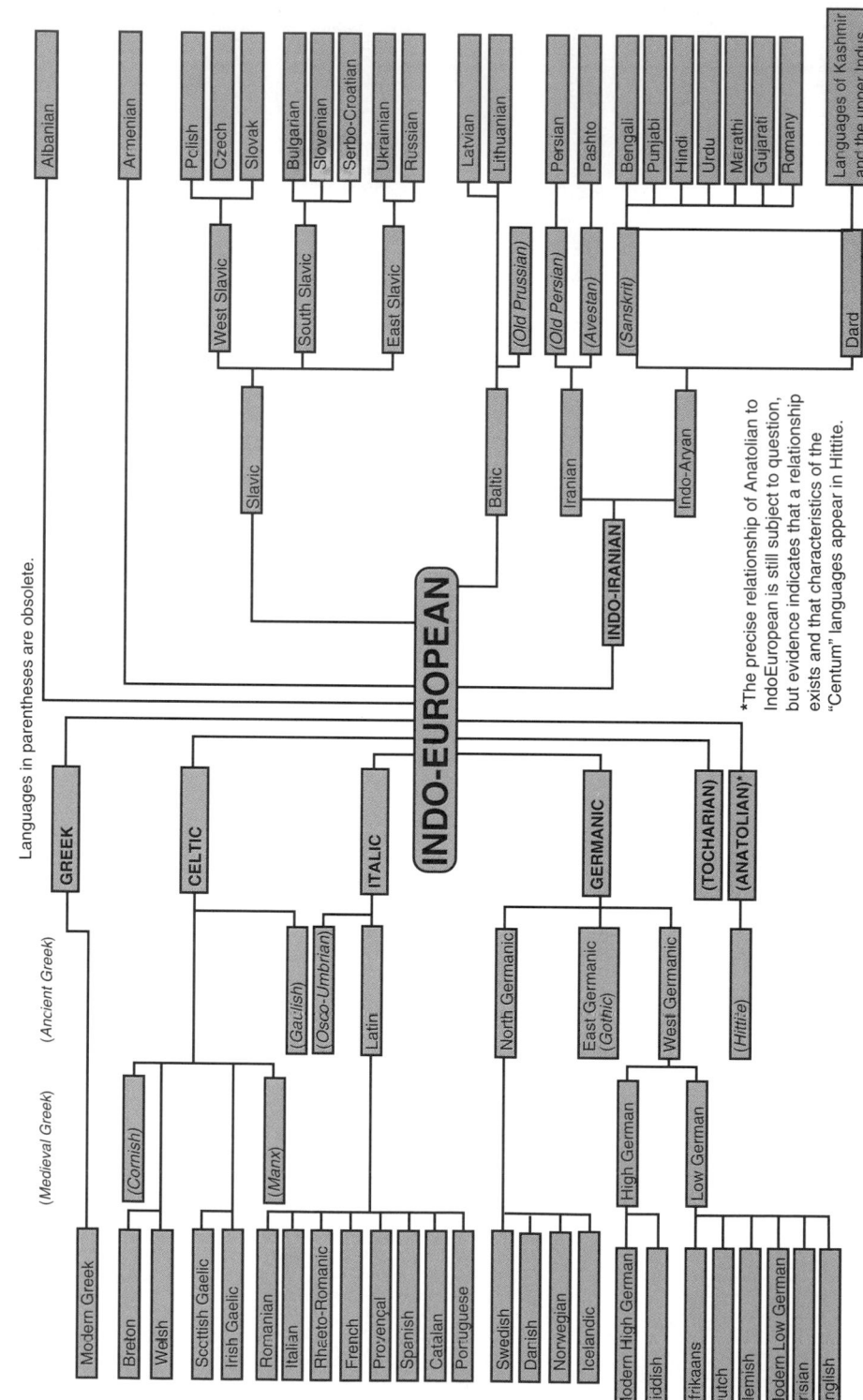

Languages in parentheses are obsolete.

*The precise relationship of Anatolian to IndoEuropean is still subject to question, but evidence indicates that a relationship exists and that characteristics of the "Centum" languages appear in Hittite.

FREQUENTLY USED FOREIGN WORDS AND PHRASES

KEY TO ABBREVIATIONS

A	Arabic	Gr	German	It	Italian	Sp	Spanish
Fr	French	H	Hebrew	L	Latin	R	Russian
Gk	Greek	Hw	Hawaiian	lit.	literally	Y	Yiddish

Word/Phrase	Meaning
à bas (F)	down with
ab initio (L)	from the beginning
ab ovo usque ad mala (L)	from soup to nuts (lit., "from the egg to the apples")
ab urbe condita (L)	from the founding of the city (Rome, 753 B.C.)
a cappella (It)	in the church style (vocally)
adagio (It)	slowly
ad astra per aspera (L)	to the stars through difficulties
ad eundum (L)	to the same degree
ad hoc (L)	for a particular purpose (lit., "to this")
ad infinitum (L)	without end
ad libitum (L)	ad lib, freely (lit., "to pleasure")
ad nauseam (L)	to the point of disgust
aere perennius (L)	more durable than bronze
aficionado (Sp)	enthusiast, fan
alea jacta est (L)	the die is cast
alfresco (It)	in the open air
alma mater (L)	old school (lit., "fostering mother")
aloha (Hw)	greeting or farewell
amor con amor se paga (Sp)	one good turn deserves another (lit., "love is repaid with love")
amor vincit omnia (L)	love conquers all
ancien régime (Fr)	the old regime (pre–French revolution)
anno domini; A.D. (L)	in the year of the Lord
annus mirabilis (L)	wonderful year
a posteriori (L)	inductive (lit. "from what comes after")
après moi, le déluge (Fr)	after me, the deluge
a priori (L)	deductive (lit., "from what comes before")
arma virumque cano (L)	I sing of arms and the man (Virgil)
ars gratia artis (L)	art for art's sake
ars longa, vita brevis (L)	art is long, life is short
au contraire (Fr)	on the contrary
au courant (Fr)	up to date, contemporary
au naturel (Fr)	nude, plain
aurea mediocritas (L)	golden mean
autre temps, autre mœhurs (Fr)	other times, other customs
avant-garde (Fr)	forward, advanced; vanguard
ave atque vale (L)	hail and farewell
beau geste (Fr)	noble gesture
beau idéal (Fr)	highest ideal
bête noire (Fr)	someone or something strongly detested (lit., "black beast")
biensénce (Fr)	decorum, mannerliness
billet doux (Fr)	love letter
Blitzkreig (Gr)	lightning war
bon marché (Fr)	inexpensive (lit., "good market")
bon mot (Fr)	clever turn of phrase
bonne chance (Fr)	good luck

Alphabets

Word/Phrase	Meaning
bon vivant (Fr)	partygoer; one who enjoys life
bon voyage (Fr)	good journey
campesino (Sp)	peasant, farmer
canard (Fr)	insult, hoax (lit., "duck")
carpe diem (L)	seize the day
carte blanche (Fr)	free hand, no restrictions (lit., "white card")
cause célèbre (Fr)	scandal; notorious incident
caveat emptor (L)	let the buyer beware
c'est la vie (Fr)	that's life
ceteris paribus (L)	other things being equal
chacun á son gout (Fr)	each to his own taste
chef d'œhuvre (Fr)	masterpiece
cherchez la femme (Fr)	look for the woman
chutzpah (Y)	gall, daring
ciao (It)	good-bye, so long
circa (c., ca.)	about, approximately
cogito ergo sum (L)	I think, therefore I am
cognoscenti (It)	intellectuals; those in the know
comédie de mœhurs (Fr)	comedy of manners
comme il faut (Fr)	proper, appropriate
con mucho gusto (Sp)	with pleasure
corpus delicti (L)	evidence (lit., "body of the crime")
coup de grâce (Fr)	final blow
coup d'état (F)	overthrow of government
credo quia absurdum (L)	I believe because it is absurd
cui bono? (L)	to whose benefit?
cul de sac (Fr)	dead end (lit., "end of the bag")
cum grano salis (L)	with a grain of salt
de capo (It)	from the top
déclassé (Fr)	fallen in social standing
décolletage (Fr)	low-cut style
de facto (L)	in fact
de gustibus non est disputandum (L)	there is no arguing about taste
de jure (L)	in law
demi-monde (Fr)	underworld; other side of the tracks
de mortuis nil nisi bonum (L)	of the dead [say nothing] but good
Deo gratias (L)	thanks be to God
Deo volente (L)	God willing
dernier cri (Fr)	the last word
déshabillé (Fr)	carelessly or scantily dressed
deus ex machina (L)	desperate or contrived solution (lit., "god from the machine")
Ding an sich (Gr)	the thing in itself
dolce far niente (It)	sweet idleness
Doppelgänger (Gr)	phantom double
Drang nach Osten (Gr)	drive toward the east
dum spiro spero (L)	while there's life, there's hope
embarras de richesses (Fr)	embarrassment of riches
enfant terrible (Fr)	prodigy
en passant (Fr)	in passing; by the way
entre nous (Fr)	privately, between us
épater le bourgeois (Fr)	shock the middle class
e pluribus unum (L)	from many, one
ersatz (Gr)	fake, imitation
et cetera (etc.) (L)	and others

Word/Phrase	Meaning
Eureka! (Gk)	I've found it!
ex cathedra (L)	with high authority (lit., "from the chair")
exempli gratia (e.g.) (L)	by way of example
ex post facto (L)	after the fact
fait accompli (Fr)	accomplished fact
faute de mieux (Fr)	for want of something better
faux pas (Fr)	social error (lit., "false step")
f̶i̶ ̶ ̶ ̶ ̶ ̶ ̶ ̶f̶ ̶ ̶ ̶ ̶ ̶ ̶ ̶ (Fr)	̶ ̶
fin de siècle (Fr)	end of century; decadent
flagrante delicto (L)	caught in the act (lit., "with the crime blazing")
gaudeamus igitur (L)	let us therefore rejoice
glasnost (R)	openness
gnothi seauton (Gk)	know yourself
gonif (Y)	thief
goy (Y)	gentile
habeas corpus (L)	writ requiring a court appearance (lit., "[that] you have the body")
haut monde (Fr)	high society
hoi polloi (Gk)	common people, mob
homo lupus homini (L)	man is a wolf to man
honi soi qui mal y pense (Fr)	shame to him who thinks evil of it
hubris (Gk)	overweening pride, arrogance
idée fixe (Fr)	fixed idea, obsession
id est (i.e.) (L)	that is
infra dignitatem (infra dig.) (L)	beneath one's dignity
in loco parentis (L)	in the place of parents
in medias res (L)	in the middle of things
in vino veritas (L)	in wine, truth
ipso facto (L)	by the fact itself
joie de vivre (Fr)	good spirits, exuberance (lit., "joy of living")
jus gentium (L)	law of nations
kamikaze (J)	suicide pilot (lit., "divine wind")
klutz (Y)	clumsy person
kvetch (Y)	complain, carp
la belle dame sans merci (Fr)	the beautiful woman without mercy
laissez-faire (Fr)	noninterference (lit., "let [people] do [as they wish]")
lapsus linguae (L)	slip of the tongue
Lebensraum (Gr)	living room; elbow room
lèse majesté (Fr)	treason
l'état, c'est moi (Fr)	I am the state
lingua franca (L)	common language (lit., "French tongue")
macher (Y)	big shot
magnum opus (L)	major work
mañana (Sp)	tomorrow
manqué (Fr)	failed
maven (Y)	expert, authority
mazel tov (Y)	congratulations
mea culpa (L)	my fault
memento mori (L)	reminder of death
mens sana in corpore sano (L)	a sound mind in a sound body
meshuggah (Y)	crazy
mirabile dictu (L)	amazingly (lit., "remarkable to say")
modus operandi (M.O.) (L)	method of operation
morituri te salutamus (L)	we who are about to die salute you
mutatis mutandis (L)	with the needed changes made

Word/Phrase	Meaning
ne plus ultra (L)	the best
n'est-ce pas? (Fr)	isn't that true?
noblesse oblige (Fr)	the responsibility of noble birth
nom de plume (Fr)	pen name
non sequitur (L)	something that does not follow
nosh (Y)	nibble, eat
nota bene (N.B.) (L)	note well
nunc aut nunquam (L)	now or never
obiter dictum (L)	something said in passing; a peripheral comment
o tempora, o mores! (L)	o the times, o the customs!
panem et circenses (L)	bread and circuses
par excellence (Fr)	above all, preeminently
par exemple (Fr)	for example
pari passu (L)	at an equal pace
parvenu (Fr)	newcomer, upstart; noveau riche
passim (L)	here and there
per diem (L)	by the day
per favore (It)	please
persona non grata (L)	unwanted person
pièce de résistance (Fr)	showpiece item
pied à terre (Fr)	in-town apartment; temporary lodging
plus ça change, plus c'est la même chose (Fr)	the more things change, the more they are the same
pons asinorum (L)	insoluble problem (lit., "bridge of asses")
por favor (Sp)	please
prego (It)	please; you're welcome
prima facie (L)	on the face of it; at first sight
primus inter pares (L)	first among equals
prix fixe (Fr)	fixed price
pro bono publico (L)	for the public good
quid pro quo (L)	fair exchange; tit for tat
quién sabe? (Sp)	who knows?
quod erat demonstrandum (Q.E.D.) (L)	as has been demonstrated
quod vide (q.v.) (L)	which see (used as cross-reference)
raison d'être (Fr)	reason for being
rara avis (L)	rarity (lit., "rare bird")
reductio ad absurdum (L)	reduction to absurdity (in logical argument)
répondez s'il vous plaît (R.S.V.P.) (Fr)	respond if you please
requiescat in pace (R.I.P.) (L)	rest in peace
salaam aleicham (A)	peace
sancta sanctorum (L)	holy of holies
sangfroid (Fr)	aplomb; composure
savoir faire (Fr)	social savvy (lit., "to know what to do")
schadenfreude	pleasure taken in problems of others
schlemiel (Y)	unlucky person, loser
schmaltz (Y)	excessive sentimentality
schtick (Y)	gimmick; a performer's idiosyncracy
semper fidelis (L)	always faithful
shalom (H)	greeting or farewell (lit., "peace")
sic (L)	thus
sic semper tyrannis (L)	thus always to tyrants
sic transit gloria mundi (L)	thus passes the glory of the world
sine qua non (L)	something indispensable (lit., "without which not")

Alphabets

Word/Phrase	Meaning
sotto voce (It)	softly (lit., "in a soft voice")
status quo (L)	current state of affairs
Sturm und Drang (Gr)	storm and stress
sui generis (L)	one of a kind, unique
tabula rasa (L)	clean slate (lit., "erased tablet")
tant mieux (Fr)	all the better
tant pis (Fr)	all the worse
tempus fugit (L)	time flies
terra firma (L)	solid ground
terra incognita (L)	unknown territory
tête-à-tête (Fr)	intimate conversation (lit., "head to head")
tout de suite (Fr)	immediately
tout le monde (Fr)	everyone
tovarish (R)	comrade
trompe l'œhil (Fr)	illusionary art or decor (lit., "fool the eye")
vade mecum (L)	handbook, guide (lit., "go with me")
vaya con Dios (Sp)	go with God
veni, vedi, vici (L)	I came, I saw, I conquered
verboten (Gr)	forbidden
verbum sapienti sat (L)	a word to the wise is enough
volte-face (Fr)	about-face, reversal
vox clamantis in deserto (L)	a voice crying in the desert
vox populi, vox Dei (L)	the voice of the people is the voice of God
Wanderjahre (Gr)	year of travel
Wanderlust (Gr)	desire to travel
Weltanschauung (Gr)	philosophy, outlook
Weltschmerz (Gr)	world-weariness (lit., "world pain")
Wunderkind (Gr)	prodigy
yenta (Y)	gossip or busybody
Zeitgeist (Gr)	spirit of the times

A Closer Look

Common Phrases in Major World Languages

English	French	German	Italian	Spanish	Chinese	Japanese
Hello/ good day	Bonjour	Guten Tag	Buon giorno	Hola/ Buenos días	Ni hao	Kon-nichiwa
Please	S'il vous plaît	Bitte	Per favore	Con su permiso/ por favor	Qíng	Douzo
Thank you	Merci	Danke	Grazie	Gracias	Xìe xìe	Arigatou
Excuse me/ pardon me	Excusez-moi/ pardon	Entschuldigen Sie	Mi scusi	Discúlpeme	Qíng ràng	Gomennasai/ shitsurei shimasu
Yes	Oui	Ja	Sì	Sí	Shì	Hai
No	Non	Nein	No	No	Bú shì	Iie
Good-bye/ so long	Au revoir/ à bientôt	Auf Wiedersehen	Arrivederci	Adiós/ hasta la vista	Zài jiàn	Sayounara

Alphabets

GREEK PREFIXES AND SUFFIXES

PREFIXES

Prefix	Meaning in English	Prefix	Meaning in English	Prefix	Meaning in English
a	not	chole, cholo	bile	ergo	work
acantho	spiny, thorny	chondro	cartilage	erythro	red
acous	hearing	choreo	dance	ethno	race, nation
acro	top, tip	choro	country	eu	good
adeno	gland	chrom(at)o	color	ex	out
aero	air, gas	chrono	time	exo	outside, external
allo	other	chryso	gold	galacto	milk
amphi	both, around	cleisto	closed	gam(o)	copulation, together
amylo	starch	clino	slope	gastro	stomach
an	not	cocci	berry-shaped	geo	earth, land
ana	again, thorough, thoroughly	coela	stomach	geronto	old age
		conio	dust	glosso	tongue
andro	man	copro	excrement	gluc, glyc	sweet
anem(o)	wind	cosmo	universe	glypto,	carving
anthropo	man	cranio	skull	glyph	
anti	against	cryo	cold	gnath(o)	jaw
apo	away	crypto	hidden	gon(o)	reproduction (sexual)
arch(i)	chief	cteno	comb, rake		
arche(o), archae(o)	old, ancient	cymo	wave	grapho	writing
		cysto	bladder	gymno	nude, naked
arthro	joint	cyto	cell	gynec(o), gynaec(o)	woman
aster, astro	star	dactylo	finger		
atmo	vapor	deca	ten	haemato	blood
auto	self	dendro	tree	hagio	holy
azo	nitrogen	dermo, dermato	skin	halo	salt, sea
baro	weight			haplo	simple
batho, bathy	deep	deutero	second	hecto	hundred
		di(s)	apart	helico	spiral
biblio	book	dia	through	helio	sun
bio	life	dino	terrible	hema	blood
blepharo	eyelid	diplo	double	hemi	half
bracchio	arm	dodeca	twelve	hepato	liver
brachy	short	dyna, dynamo	force, power	hepta	seven
branchio	gills			hetero	different
broncho	throat	dys	evil, difficult	hexa	six
caco	evil	echino	spiny	histo	tissue
cardio	heart	ecto	outside, external	hodo	path, way
carpo	fruit	ef	out	holo	whole, complete
cath, cato	down, thorough, thoroughly	ele, em, en	in, into	homeo	similar, like
		encephalo	brain	homo	same
ceno	common	ennea	nine	hydro	water
cephalo	head	entero	gut	hyeto	rain
cero	wax	ento	inside, interior	hygro	wet
chilo	lip	entomo	insect	hylo	matter
chiro	hand	eo	dawn, early	hymeno	membrane
chloro	green	eph, epi	on	hyper	above

Prefix	Meaning in English	Prefix	Meaning in English	Prefix	Meaning in English
hypno	sleep	onto	being	pyo	pus
hypo	under	oo	egg	pyro	fire
hypso	high	ophio	snake	rheo	flow
hystero	womb	opthalm(o)	eye	rhino	nose
iatro	medicine	ornitho	bird	rhizo	root
ichthyo	fish	oro	mouth	sacchro	sugar
iso	equal	ortho	straight	sapro	decompose
kerato	horn	osteo	bone	sarco	flesh
kinesi,	movement	oto	ear	scato	excrement
kineto		oxy	sharp	schisto,	split
lepto	slender	pachy	thick	schizo	
leuko	white	paleo,	ancient, old	sclero	hard
litho	stone	palaeo		seleno	moon
logo	word, oral	pan	all	sidero	iron
lyo, lysi	dissolving	para	close, beside	somato	body
macro	large	patho	suffering, disease	speleo	cave
malaco	soft	pedo	child	spermato	seed
mega,	great	penta	five	sphygmo	pulse
megalo		peri	around, very	splanchno	guts
melano	black	petro	stone	stato	position
mero	part	phago	eating	stauro	cross
meso	middle	phlebo	vein	steno	short, narrow
meta	beyond, after,	phono	sound	stereo	solid
	changed	photo	light	stomato	mouth
metro	measure	phreno	brain	stylo	pillar
micro	small	phyco	seaweed	sy, syl,	with
miso	hatred	phyllo	leaf	sym, syn	
mono	one, single	phylo	species	tachy	rapid
morpho	shape	physio	nature	tauto	same
myelo	spinal cord	phyto	plant	tele	distant
mylo	fungus	picro	bitter	teleo	final
myo	muscle	piezo	pressure	telo	distant, final
necro	dead body	pleuro	side (of body)	thalasso	sea
neo	new	pluto	riches	thanato	death
nepho	cloud	pneumato	breath, spirit	theo	god
nephro	kidney	pneumo	lung	thermo	heat
neuro	nerve	polio	gray matter	thio	sulfur
noso	sickness	poly	many	toco	child, birth
noto	back (of body)	pro	before, forward	topo	place
nycto	night	proto	first	toxico	poison
octa, octo	eight	pseudo	false	trachy	rough
odonto	tooth	psycho	mind, spirit, soul	xeno	foreign
oligo	few	psychro	cold	zoo	living
ombro	rain	ptero	wing	zygo	double
oneiro	dream				

The Hawaiian alphabet has only 12 letters: the five vowels and the consonants H, K, L, M, N, P, and W.

SUFFIXES

Suffix	Meaning in English	Suffix	Meaning in English	Suffix	Meaning in English
algia	pain	iasis	disease	phany	manifestation
androus	man	iatrics, iatry	medical treatment	phobe, phobia	fear
archy	rule, government	itis	inflammation		
biosis	life	kinesis	movement	phone, phony	sound
blast	bud	lepsy	seizure, fit		
branch	gills	lith	stone	phyllous	leaf
carpous	fruit	logy	science of, list	phyte	plant
cele	hollow	lysise, lyte	dissolving	plasia, plasis	growth
cephalic, cephalous	head	machy	battle, fight		
		mancy, mantic	foretelling	plasm	matter
chrome	color			plast	cell
coccous	berry-shaped	mania(c)	craving	plegia	paralysis
cracy, crat	rule, government	mere, merous	part	plerous	wing
dendron	tree			rrhagia, rrhagic, rrhea	flow
derm	skin	meter, metry	measure		
drome, dromous	run (race)	morphic, morphous	shape	saur	lizard
emia	blood	mycete	fungus	scope, scopy	observation
gamy	marriage	nomy	science of, law of	sect, section	cutting
gen(ous), geny, gony	giving birth to, bearing	odont	tooth	soma, some	body
		odynia	pain	sophy	wisdom
gnathous	jaw	oid	like, similar	sperm, spermous	seed
gnomy, gnosis	knowledge	oma	tumor	stichous	row
gon	angle	opia	eye, sight	stome, stomous	mouth
gonium	seed	opsia	sight		
gram, graph(y)	writing	opsis	appearance	taxis, taxy	order
		pathy	suffering, disease	tomy	cutting
hedral, hedron	side, sided	phage, phagous	eating	trophy	feed
				tropous, tropy	turned

LATIN PREFIXES AND SUFFIXES

PREFIXES

Prefix	Meaning in English	Prefix	Meaning in English	Prefix	Meaning in English
a, abs	from	calci	lime	de	not, down
ac, ad, af, ag, al, an, ap, as, at	to, toward	centi	hundred	deci	tenth
		cerebro	brain	demi	half
		cervico	neck	denti	tooth
alti, alto	high	circum	around	di(s)	apart
ambi	both	cirro	curl	digit(i)	finger
ante	before	cis	near, on the near side of	dorsi, dorso	back (of body)
api	bee	co, col, com, con, cor	with, thorough, thoroughly	e, ec, ef	out
aqui	water			equi	equal
arbori	tree			ex	out
audio	hearing	contra	against	extra	outside, external
avi	bird	costo	rib	febri	fever
bacci	berry	cruci	cross	ferri, ferro	iron
brevi	short	cupro	copper, bronze	fissi	split

Prefix	Meaning in English	Prefix	Meaning in English	Prefix	Meaning in English
fluvio	river	oculo	eye	recti	straight
gemmi	bud	of, op	against	reni	kidney
igni	fire	oleo	oil	retro	backward
il, im, in	not, against, in, into, on	omni	all	sacro	dedicated
		oro	mouth	sangui	blood
inguino	groin	ossi	bone	se	apart
inter	between	ovi, ovo	egg	sebi, sebo	fatty
intra, intro	inside, interior	pari	equal	septi	seven
ir	not, against, in, into, on	per	through, very	sidero	star
		pinni	fin, web	somni	sleep
juxta	close, near, beside	pisci	fish	spiro	breath
labio	lip	plano	flat	stelli	star
lacto	milk	plumbo	lead (metal)	sub, suc, suf, sum, sup	under
ligni	wood	pluvio	rain		
luni	moon	post	after		
magni	great	pre	before	super, supra	above
mal(e)	bad, evil	preter	beyond	terri	land, earth
multi	many	primi	first	trans	through, on the far side of
naso	nose	pro	for, forward		
nati	birth	pulmo	lung	ultra	beyond
nocti	night	quadri	four	uni	one, single
ob, oc	against	quinque	five	vari(o)	different
octa, octo	eight	re	again		

SUFFIXES

Suffix	Meaning in English	Suffix	Meaning in English	Suffix	Meaning in English
cidal, cide	kill	fugal, fuge	run away from	pennale	wing
fid	split	grade	walking	vorous	eating

COMMON CROSSWORD-PUZZLE WORDS

Certain words frequently appear in crossword puzzles. Following is a list of such words, particularly ones not used regularly in everyday speech. Many of these words will be recognized by avid crossword-puzzle solvers. People new to crosswords will find familiarity with the list helpful in checking and building a crossword vocabulary.

Word	Meaning	Word	Meaning	Word	Meaning
aalii	tree; wood	adit	mine entrance	Aire	French river
Aare	Swiss river	adze	shaping tool	ait	river island
abbé	monk; cleric	Aeolus	Greek god of wind	alae	winglike part
abele	white poplar	aga	Muslim chief	alar	winged
abet	aid; assist	agar	moss; culture medium	alef	Hebrew letter
abou	father (Arabic)	agee	awry; askew	alen	Danish length
acer	maple genus	agha	Muslim leader	Aleut	Alaskan Indian
Acre	Israeli city	agora	assembly	Alma	Crimean river
acta	deeds	Agra	site of Taj Mahal	aloe	bitter herb; lily
Adah	wife of Lamech	aile	winged (heraldry)	alop	askew
Adak	Alaskan island	Aino, Ainu	Japanese aborigine	ama	cup; candlenut
Adar	Jewish month			amah	Oriental nurse

continues

Common Crossword Puzzle Words, Continued

Word	Meaning	Word	Meaning	Word	Meaning
ameer	Arab chieftain	axil	leaf angle	cava	pepper shrub; vein
amir	Arab chieftain	axon	nerve-cell process	Cayuga	Iroquoian tribe
Amos	biblical prophet	Baal	god; idol	cere	wax; wrap
ana	collection; anthology	baft	astern	Ceres	grain goddess
anas	duck genus	Bahia	Brazilian state; bay	Clare	Irish county
ani	blackbird; cuckoo	baht	Siamese coin	Clio	muse of history
anil	indigo shrub	Baku	Caspian harbor	Comus	god of mirth
anile	old-womanish; feeble	Bali	Indonesian island	Coos	Oregon tribe
anion	ion; particle	Balt	Lett; Lithuanian	copa	Spanish measure
anise	fragrant seed	banc	judge's bench	cor	heart; brightest star
anoa	wild Celebes ox	bane	evil; scourge	corium	dermis; layer
ans	Belgian commune	bani	Romanian money	cos	lettuce
ansa	loop; handle	Bann	Irish river	Cree	Indian tribe
ante	poker stake; before	Barre	Vermont city	Crimea	Russian peninsula
anti	opposed	Baya	Bantu tribe	cuir	leather (French)
A one	first-rate; tops	Beda	Arabian city	cull	choose; assort
apa	wallaba tree	beka	biblical money;	cuya	Cuban timber tree
apis	bee; Egyptian sacred		Hebrew weight	dace	carplike fish
	bull	Belem	Brazilian city	Dade	Florida county
apod	footless	Benares	Indian city	dado	groove
Apollo	sun god	Bera	Arabian city	Dail	Irish parliament
Aral	Soviet sea	berm	bank; lodge	daler	Dutch money
Aran	Irish island	Berne	Swiss city	Davos	Swiss resort
Ares	Greek god of war	bes	ancient Roman weight	Dee	English river
aria	opera solo	besa	Abyssinian money	dhai	midwife
aril	seed covering	besant	old French money	dhak	East Indian dye tree
artel	union; cooperative	bezant	circle (heraldry)	dhal	lentil
arum	cuckoopint; flowerin	bhar	Indian weight	dhan	cattle; property
	plant	bilk	cheat	dhow	Oriental sailing ship
Asgard	abode of Norse gods	binh	Annam weight	dinar	Bulgarian or Yugoslav
Astarte	Phoenician love goddess	bisse	snake (heraldry)		money
atap	palm; nipa	Blanc	peak in Alps	dop	diamond holder
ates	sweetsop	boa	feathered scarf; con-	dopp	dip
Atka	Aleutian tribe		strictor	Duma	Russian council
atle	Tamarisk salt tree	bole	friable clay	durn	gatepost
Atli	Norse king	bolo	knife; machete	dyad	pair
Aton	Egyptian solar deity	Bonn	West German city	Dyak	Borneo tribe
atri	Italian commune	brae	Scottish hillside	dyne	unit of force
Attica	Greek district; New	brut	dry wine	ebon	black
	York State prison	cabal	secret group; junta	Edda	Icelandic saga; Norse
Attu	Alaskan island	Caen	French city		prose
Aude	French river	Caddo	Indian tribe	ede	Dutch commune
Auk	diving bird	cadi	Muslim judge	Eder	German river
aune	French length	Cain	Abel's brother	Edo	Tokyo
aux	French commune	calp	limestone	Eger	German river
avav	pepper shrub; hum-	cam	gear	Ela	highest note; Guido's
	mingbird	Carib	South American		note
avocet	bird; plover		Indian	Elam	biblical kingdom
awn	beard on grain	carr	pool	élan	dash; ardor

Oxymoron: A Pairing of Contradictory or Incongruous Words

A Closer Look

bittersweet	home office	passively aggressive
clearly confused	jumbo shrimp	randomly organized
cruel kindness	linear curve	same difference
definite maybe	liquid gas	sweet sorrow
eloquent silence	nonalcoholic beer	taped live
idiot savant	nondairy creamer	war games
genuine imitation	old news	working vacation
good grief	open secret	

Word	Meaning	Word	Meaning	Word	Meaning
Elbe	German river	Faroe	Danish islands	grao	Portuguese weight
Elia	Lamb pen name; Kazan	fass	Austrian measure	gulden	Dutch money
Elul	Jewish month	faun	satyr; Roman half goat	Hades	Greek underworld
emir	Muslim chieftain	Faunus	rural deity	hadj	pilgrimage
emu	ostrichlike bird	fels	Indian money	haft	handle
Enna	Sicilian city	fete	festival	ha ha	laugh; sunken fence
Enns	Austrian river	fiat	command; decree	haka	dance
Enos	Seth's son	fief	feudal estate	Hamar	city in Norway
ente	grafted (heraldry)	fils	son (French)	Hamite	biblical tribe
ento	inner (prefix)	flak	antiaircraft bursts	Han	river in China
Enyo	Ares' mother	flan	custard	hart	stag
Eolus	Colorado mountain	flay	skin	hemo	blood (prefix)
epee	fencing blade	fosse	moat; pit	Hera	queen goddess
ephah	Hebrew measure	Frey	Norse god	Herat	Afghanistan city
epi	finial; spire	Frigg	Odin's wife	Hermes	Greek god
Erda	Norse earth goddess	gad	rove	Herod	biblical ruler
eri	silkworm	Gael	Celt	Herr	Mister (German)
Eris	goddess of discord	gam	mouth; leg	Hesse	German state
Erlau	Hungarian commune	gaol	prison	Hilo	Hawaiian city
ern	sea eagle	gar	needle fish	hin	Hebrew measure
erne	sea eagle; Irish river	gard	French department	Hiram	biblical ruler
Erse	Gaelic	gare	railway station (French)	hiro	Japanese length
esker	glacial ridge	Gaspé	Canadian peninsula	Hler	Norse god
esne	serf	gata	shark	hoar	frost
esse	existence; abstract being	Gaza	biblical city	hod	brick tray; coal scuttle
Este	Italian commune	Gerd	Frey's wife	Hood	Oregon mountain
Estes	Colorado park	Geri	Odin's wolf	hora	Israeli dance
estop	prevent by law	ghat	range; pass	Horeb	biblical mountain
et al.	and others (Latin abbreviation)	gila	lizard	Hosea	biblical prophet
etui	vanity case; needle case	Gilead	biblical mountain	Hoth	Norse god
evoe	bacchanals' cry	gnu	antelope; wildebeest	huk	Philippine guerrilla
ewer	pitcher	Goa	former Portuguese colony	hula	Hawaiian dance
exe	English river	Golo	Bantu tribe	Hun	barbarian; vandal
fane	temple	Goshen	biblical land of plenty	Hydra	nine-headed monster
fanon	cape; orale	gowl	monster	iamb	verse foot
faro	card game	gradus	ancient Roman length	ibex	wild goat
		graf	German count	ibid.	same place (abbreviation)
				ibis	wading bird

Alphabets

continues

Palindromes

A Closer Look

A palindrome can be a single word, a verse, a sentence, a series of sentences, or a number that reads the same forward and backward. People have been creating palindromes in all languages since at least as early as the third century B.C. Palindromic sentences often become jokes when meanings are ascribed to them and when punctuation is added. For example, the two best-known English palindromes are "Able was I ere I saw Elba," which was not written by but could have been uttered by Napoleon, and "Madam, I'm Adam," which is fun to think of as the first introduction. Note that "madam" alone is a palindromic word, but sentences are more amusing:

Enid and Edna dine.
A man, a plan, a canal, Panama!
Draw, O Caesar, erase a coward.

Al lets Dell call Ed Stella.
Dennis sinned.
Ma is a nun, as I am.

Naomi, did I moan?
Niagara, O roar again!
He lived as a devil, eh?

And here is a palindromic conversation between two owls:

"Too hot to hoot!"
"Too hot to woo!"
"Too wot?"
"Too hot to hoot!"
"To woo!"
"Too wot?"
"To hoot! Too hot to hoot!"

Common Crossword Puzzle Words, Continued

Word	Meaning	Word	Meaning	Word	Meaning
Ibo	West African tribe	itea	Virginia willow	Kano	Nigerian walled city
ici	here (French)	ixia	iris	kaph	Hebrew letter
icon	religious image	jako	parrot	Kara	Arabian sea
Ida	Asia Minor range;	jama	tunic	kava	Polynesian beverage
	Crete mountain	jami	mosque	kawa	Pepper shrub
Idas	killer of Castor	jann	genie	kela	Arabian weight
ideo	idea (prefix)	jara	palm	keno	lotto; bingolike game
ides	Roman date	Jebu	West African tribe	Kent	English county
iglu	Eskimo hut	Jehu	biblical ruler	kepi	military cap
ilex	holly	Jena	German city	kerf	notch
ilia	hipbones	jeté	ballet jump	khat	Turkish length
imam	caliph	jhow	Tamarisk shrub	Kiel	German canal
immi	Swiss measure	jib	triangular sail	Kiev	Russian city
Indus	Indian river	jilt	cheat; reject	kil	monk's cell; Irish
inee	arrow poison	jinn	demon		church; kilometer
Inez	Don Juan's mother	Joad	English philosopher		(abbreviation)
Inga	shrub genus	Joshua	biblical ruler	kiln	oven
Iole	Hercules' captive	Jove	chief Roman god	Kiowa	Indian tribe
Iona	Scottish isle	juba	African dance	kipe	basket
Ionia	Asia Minor district	Jung	psychiatrist	kiri	Kaffir war club
iota	Greek letter; bit	Juno	Roman queen of gods	kiwi	flightless bird
Irra	Babylonian god	junu	charm	Kobe	Honshu port
Isar	Bavarian river	jura	French department	Koko	Lord High Executioner
Iser	Czech river	kabul	Indian river	kola	nut
Isere	French river	kadi	judge	kopek	Russian money
Isis	Egyptian goddess; sister	Kafir	Bantu tribe	koss	Indian length
	and wife of Osiris	kana	Japanese writing	kraal	enclosure

Alphabets

Word	Meaning	Word	Meaning	Word	Meaning
kris	dagger	mano	hand grinding stone	nimb	halo
Krishna	Hindu god	marl	clayey soil	nipa	drink; East Indian
krona	Icelandic money	Maui	Hawaiian island		palm
Kronos	Titan	Mayo	Irish county;	oast	kiln; oven
kudu	African antelope		mayonnaise	obi	Oriental sash
Kurd	Turkish tribe	Mede	ancient Persian	obit	death notice
kvas	Russian sour beer	Medusa	Gorgon	oca	edible tuber
lac	resin	mega	great (prefix)	octo	eight (prefix)
lact	milk (prefix)	meld	declare, in cards	oda	harem room
Lagos	capital of Nigeria	Melos	Aegean island	odea	music hall
lait	milk (French)	merl	blackbird	Order	Baltic river
		Metz	French city	oeuf	egg (French)
lama	Buddhist monk;	mil	wire measure	ogee	arch; molding
	Tibetan priest	Milo	Greek Island	Okie	migratory worker
Lamech	biblical patriarch	Minos	Greek king	okra	gumbo
lar	gibbon	moa	flightless bird; ostrich	ola	palm leaf
lath	strip of wood	Moab	biblical tribe	olay	palm leaf
lave	bathe	moho	honey-eating bird	olio	medley
lea	meadow	mohr	gazelle	olla	jar; meat dish
Leda	Castor's mother; swan	mojo	voodoo charm	Olor	swan genus
lees	dregs	moki	New Zealand raft	Omei	China mountains
Lena	Asian river	Moro	Philippine Muslim	omni	all (prefix); Atlanta
Lenape	Indian tribe	Mors	Roman god of death		arena
Leto	Apollo's mother	Morta	goddess of fate	Omsk	Russian city
Levi	Jacob's son; Hebrew	Muir	Alaska glacier	oner	individual; corker
	tribe	mumm	disguise	onus	burden
Leyte	Pacific island	nacre	mother-of-pearl	opah	colorful fish
libra	Mexican weight	nae	no (Scottish)	ope	unlock (poetic)
Lido	Adriatic resort	Nahor	biblical patriarch	orca	killer whale
limn	portray	naif	lustrous	Orel	Russian port
limu	edible seaweed	Namur	Belgian commune	orle	heraldic bearing
Linz	Austrian city	nard	anoint; spice	Orly	French airport
liss	fleur-de-lis	neap	tide	orne	French department
lobo	timber wolf	neb	beak; nose	ort	morsel; leftover
loch	Scottish lake	Nebo	biblical mountain	osier	willow tree
Loki	Norse god	née	born (French)	Ossa	Greek mountain
loup	half-mask (French)	Nene	English river;	otic	pertaining to the ear
luff	sail into wind		Hawaiian bird	Otoe	Oklahoma tribe
Luna	moon goddess	nep	catnip	oyez	attention; court cry
Lys	Belgian river	Nereid	sea nymph	paal	Javanese length
Maas	Dutch river	ness	promontory	pac	boot, moccasin
mage	magician	Nestor	Greek king	paca	rodent
Maia	Hermes' mother	neve	glacier; snow	padre	priest; cleric
Main	German river	newt	eft	pala	Indian weight
mani	peanut	nez	nose (French)	palp	tentacle; feeler

continues

The word **posh** *is supposedly an acronym for "port outward, starboard home." The term was coined to describe how rich people, traveling by sea to the Indies, avoided getting the morning sun on their side of the ship.*

Alphabets

Common Crossword Puzzle Words, Continued

Word	Meaning	Word	Meaning	Word	Meaning
Panay	Philippine island	sans	without (French)	Taos	New Mexico town
pard	leopard	sari	Indian dress	tapa	bark cloth
parr	young fish	sego	edible bulb	Tara	Irish capital; plantation in *Gone With the Wind*
pas	dance step	sera	antitoxins; evening (Italian)		
pavis	shield; cover			tare	biblical weed; allowance
Pelée	Martinique volcano	serac	glacial ridge; white cheese	tarn	lake; pool
pelu	hardwood tree			taro	edible root
peri	fairy	sere	dry; parched	tat	make lace; crochet
phon	loudness	serif	part of printer's letter	tec	detective
phot	light unit	seta	bristle	tela	membrane; tissue
pica	type measure	Seth	biblical patriarch; Adam's son	tele	from a distance (prefix)
Pico	Azores volcano			tern	gull
rale	rattle; breathing noise	shay	carriage	Terra	earth goddess
Rama	incarnation of Vishnu	Shem	biblical patriarch	Thalia	one of the Graces
rame	branch	shiv	knife	Thetis	Achilles' mother
rana	Indian prince	Sikh	Hindu soldier	tia	aunt (Spanish)
rani	Indian queen	sine	trigonometry function	tic	spasm
rati	Indian weight	sire	lord; father; beget	tio	uncle (Spanish)
Remi	ancient people of Gaul	Siva	Hindu god	Tioga	New York county
rena	rockfish	skag	part of a ship's keel	toga	Roman cloak
ret	soak flax	skew	twist	tole	lacquered metalware
rete	network	Skye	Hebrides island	Toltec	Mexican tribe
Rhea	Titan; Cronus's wife	sloe	plum; blackthorn	tome	large volume
Rhus	sumac genus	Smee	Captain Hook's assistant; pintail duck	tong	Chinese secret society
ria	narrow inlet; estuary			tor	craggy hill; pea
rial	Iranian coin	snee	dirk; knife	tort	civil wrong
rien	nothing (French)	soir	evening (French)	torte	rich cake
Riga	Baltic city	Sol	sun god	tret	waste allowance
rime	frost	sora	marsh bird	Triton	Greek god of sea
ripa	riverbank	Spad	biplane; nail	Truk	Island in Carolines
rom	gypsy husband	Spes	Roman goddess of hope	tsar	Russian despot
rood	crucifix			tsun	Chinese length
Rosa	shrub genus	Sri	Hindu goddess	tun	vat; cask
Ross	Antarctic sea	SRO	box-office sign	tutu	New Zealand shrub, ballet skirt
roti	roasted (French)	stere	dry measure		
rotl	Muslim weight	stet	let it stand	tyro	novice
Ruhr	German river; industrial area	stile	wall step; set of steps	über	over (German)
		stoa	portico	uca	crab
rune	mysterious sign; old alphabet character	suet	hard fat	uke	ukulele
		Suva	Fiji capital	ule	rubber tree
rupee	Indian money	Taal	Afrikaans	ulex	spine shrub
Saar	European river	Tabor	biblical mountain	Ulm	German city
Sac	Algonquin Indian; pouch	tabu	forbidden	ulna	elbow bone
		tace	body armor	unde	wavy; lined (heraldry)
sago	starch; pudding	tael	Oriental weight	ungula	hoof; claw
samp	cereal; maize; pudding	tamp	pack; ram	Ural	Russian river; range

The word dude *was coined by Oscar Wilde and his friends. It is a combination of the words* duds *and* attitude.

Word	Meaning	Word	Meaning	Word	Meaning
Urd	Norse goddess of destiny	vivo	lively (music)	yaba	cabbage tree
urde	key-shaped (heraldry)	viz	namely	yak	ox
Uri	Swiss commune	voce	voice (Italian)	Yalu	Korean river
Uria	Bathsheba's husband	vole	rodent	yamp	tuber
ursa	bear	WAC	female GI	yapa	palm-leaf mat
urus	ox; aurochs	Waco	Texas city	yegg	burglar
Ute	Colorado Indian	wadd	black ocher	Yemen	Arabian state
Utu	Babylonian god	wadi	dry riverbed	yen	Japanese money; urge
uvea	iris layer	wale	cloth ridge	yin	Chinese weight
uvic	grapelike	wang	Dutch East Indies weight	Ymir	Norse giant
Vaal	South African river	weft	web; yarn	Yser	Belgian river
vair	heraldic tincture	weir	fish trap	zak	Dutch measure
vale	valley; glen; farewell	wen	cyst; old English letter	zany	nutty; crazy
vari	diverse (prefix)	woad	dyestuff	Zara	Italian province
vasa	ducts	Wodan	Norse god	zee	final letter; zed
Veda	Hindu bible	Woden	Norse god	Zen	Buddhist sect
vega	meadow	Wotan	Norse god	zero	nothing; cipher
veld	South African grassland	xema	Arctic gull	zeta	Greek letter
Venus	Roman goddess of love	Xenia	Ohio city	Zeus	chief Olympian god
vert	green	xeno	foreign (prefix)	Zion	hill; heaven
Vesta	goddess of hearth	xeres	wine; sherry	Zulu	Bantu tribe
Vishnu	Hindu god	Xosa	Kaffir tribe	Zuni	Pueblo Indian
vita	life (Latin)	Xtian	Christian	zwei	two (German)
vite	quick (French)				

There are nine different ways to pronounce the letters ough. *All are contained in the sentence, "A rough-coated, dough-faced, thoughtful ploughman strode through the streets of Scarborough; after falling into a slough, he coughed and hiccoughed."*

Go to
"94 Acceptable Two–Letter Scrabble® Words" in chapter 23

Alphabets

FOREIGN ALPHABETS

GREEK			ARABIC			HEBREW			CYRILLIC	
Forms	**Name**	**Latin†**	**Form**	**Name**	**Latin†**	**Forms**	**Name**	**Latin†**	**Forms**	**Latin†**
Α α	alpha	a (ā)	ا	alif		א	aleph		А а	a
Β β	beta	b	ب	bā	b	ב	beth	b	Б б	b
									В в	v
Γ γ	gamma	g, n	ت	tā	t	ג	gimel	g	Г г	g
Δ δ	delta	d	ث	thā	th	ד	daleth	d	Д д	d
Ε ε	epsilon	e	ج	jīm	j	ה	he	h	Е е	(y) e
Ζ ζ	zeta	zd, z	ح	ḥā	ḥ	ו	vav	v	Ж ж	zh
Η η	eta	ē	خ	khā	kh	ז	zayin	z	З з	z
Θ θ	theta	th*	د	dāl	d	ח	het	ch (H)	И и Й й	j (i, ĭ)
Ι ι	iota	i	ذ	dhāl	dh	ט	teth	ṭ	К к	k
Κ κ	kappa	k	ر	rā	r	י	yod	y	Л л	l
Λ λ	lambda	l	ز	zāy	z	כ ך	kaf	k, ch	М м	m
Μ μ	mu	m	س	sīn	s	ל	lamed	l	Н н	n
Ν ν	nu	n	ش	shīn	sh	מ ם	mem	m	О о	o
Ξ ξ	xi	x	ص	sād	ṣ	נ ן	nun	n	П п	p
Ο ο	omicron	o	ض	dād	ḍ	ס	samekh	s	Р р	r
Π π	pi	p	ط	tā	ṭ	ע	ayin	'	С с	s
Ρ ρ	rho	r, hr	ظ	zā	z	פ ף	pe	p, f	Т т	t
Σ σ ς	sigma	s	ع	'ayn	'	צ ץ	sadhe	ts	У у	u
Τ τ	tau	t	غ	ghayn	gh	ק	koph	q	Ф ф	f
Υ υ	upsilon	u (u, ü)	ف	fā	f	ר	resh	r	Х х	kh
Φ φ	phi	ph*	ق	qāf	q	שׂ	sin	ś	Ц ц	ts
Χ χ	chi	ch*	ك	kāf	k	שׁ	shin	sh	Ч ч	ch
Ψ ψ	psi	ps	ل	lām	l	ת	tav	t	Ш ш	sh
Ω ω	omega	ō	م	mīm	m				Щ щ	shch
			ن	nūn	n				Ъ ъ	"
			ه	hā	h				Ы ы	y
			و	wāw	w				Ь ь	'
			ي	yā	y				Э э	e
									Ю ю	yu
									Я я	ya

Gamma is transliterated as *n* when it precedes *kappa, xi, chi,* or another *gamma; upsilon* is transliterated as *u* when it is the final element in a diphthong. The *sigma* form **ς** is used only in final position.

*The letters *th, ph,* and *ch* represent strongly aspirated stops, *t, p,* and *k,* respectively.

The forms shown are of the letters in isolation. They may vary when used in words. The letter *alif* does not have a sound.

Pronunciation of vowels in letter names: *ā = a* in *father, ī = i* in *machine, ū = u* in *rule.*

The second form (and the second transliteration) of a letter when shown is used at the end of a word only. Vowels are shown by a system of subscript and superscript dots; the symbols shown are consonants. The letter *aleph* does not have a sound.

The Cyrillic alphabet is used for writing various Slavic languages, including Russian.

† The columns headed "Latin" show the letters used when these alphabets are transliterated into the Latin alphabet. The sounds represented by these letters are similar to the standard sounds in English. Diacritics indicate that the sound is somewhat different from the English sound represented by the letter shown; for any great difference the sound is shown in parentheses after the letter, using the pronunciation symbols of this dictionary.

Alphabets

ADDITIONAL SOURCES OF INFORMATION

WEB SITES

The CMU Pronouncing Dictionary
Maintained by Kevin Lonzo, Robotics Institute, Carnegie Mellon University.
http://www.speech.cs.cmu.edu/cgi-bin/cmudict

The King's English
Online edition (copyright 1996 by the Trustees of Columbia University) of the 2nd edition of the book by Henry Watson Fowler and Francis George Fowler (copyright 1908 by the Clarendon Press).
http://www.columbia.edu/acis/bartleby/fowler/

Merriam-Webster Online
Includes a searchable dictionary and thesaurus and other helpful language information links (copyright 1997 Merriam-Webster).
http://www.m-w.com/

The World Wide Web Acronym and Abbreviation Server
A searchable database of acronyms and abbreviations.
http://www.ucc.ie/info/net/acronyms/acro.html

Yahoo!—Reference: Dictionaries: Language
List of links to online dictionaries in many languages (copyright 1994–98 by Yahoo! Inc.).
http://www.yahoo.com/Reference/Dictionaries/Language/

BOOKS

The American Heritage Book of English Usage. Houghton Mifflin, 1996.

Axtell, Roger E. *Do's and Taboos of Using English Around the World.* Wiley, 1995.

Chapman, Robert L., ed. *New Dictionary of American Slang.* HarperCollins, 1987.

Chapman, Robert L., ed. *Roget's International Thesaurus.* 5th ed. HarperCollins, 1992.

The Chicago Manual of Style. 14th ed. University of Chicago Press, 1993.

Chisholm, William S., Jr. *Webster's New World Guide to Pronunciation.* Simon & Schuster, 1984.

Ciardi, John. *The Complete Browser's Dictionary.* HarperCollins, 1991.

Donadio, Stephen, et al., eds. *The New York Public Library Book of 20th Century American Quotations.* The Stonesong Press/Warner Books, 1992.

Ehrlich, Eugene. *The Highly Selective Dictionary for the Extraordinarily Literate.* HarperCollins, 1997.

Ehrlich, Eugene. *Veni Vidi Vici: Conquer Your Enemies, Impress Your Friends with Everyday Latin.* HarperPerennial, 1995.

Funk, Charles Earle. *A Hog on Ice and Other Curious Expressions.* HarperCollins, 1985.

The word facetiously has all the vowels, including y, in order.

Heifetz, Josefa. *The Word Lover's Dictionary: Unusual, Obscure, and Preposterous Words.* Carol Publishing, 1995.

Jones, Daniel. *English Pronouncing Dictionary.* Cambridge University Press, 1997.

Kemp, Peter, consultant ed. *The Oxford Dictionary of Literary Quotations.* Oxford University Press, 1997.

Knowles, Elizabeth M., ed. *The Oxford Dictionary of Phrase, Proverb, and Quotation.* Oxford University Press, 1997.

Laird, Charlton, and the editors of Webster's New World dictionaries. *Webster's New World Thesaurus.* Macmillan, 1997.

Preston, Charles, and Barbara Ann Kipfer. *The USA Today Crossword Puzzle Dictionary.* Stonesong Press/Hyperion, 1996.

Pulliam, Tom, and Clare Grundman. *The New York Times Crossword Puzzle Dictionary.* Times Books, 1995.

Safire, William. *I Stand Corrected: More on Language.* Times Books, 1986

Safire, William. *Watching My Language.* Random House, 1996.

Alphabets

Strunk, William, Jr., and E. B. White. *The Elements of Style*. 3rd ed. Macmillan, 1979.

Sutcliffe, Andrea, ed. *The New York Public Library Writer's Guide to Style and Usage*. The Stonesong Press/HarperCollins, 1994.

Webster's New World College Dictionary. 3rd ed. Simon & Schuster, 1997.

Zinsser, William. *On Writing Well: An Informal Guide to Writing Nonfiction*. 5th rev. ed. HarperCollins, 1994.

Alphabets

14

GRAMMAR AND PUNCTUATION

THE PARTS OF SPEECH	436
MODIFIERS	437
SENTENCE STRUCTURE	437
PUNCTUATION	441
AMERICAN ENGLISH AND BRITISH ENGLISH: PUNCTUATION DIFFERENCES	441
ADDITIONAL SOURCES OF INFORMATION	444

The purpose of language is to communicate thoughts and ideas from one person to another. To do this effectively, all those using a given language must do so in the same way, putting words and sentences together in similar fashion so that they are readily understood by anyone familiar with that language.

This is not to say that everyone must write the same sentence to communicate the same concept. On the contrary, American English is so varied that it is possible to express the same basic idea in any number of ways. And each of those ways can be equally correct.

A very difficult sentence to punctuate is: "That that is is that that is not is not." The correct punctuation is: "That that is, is; that that is not, is not."

What makes a variety of different sentences equally valid is grammar. Grammar is a set of rules that defines the ways words can and cannot be used. These rules are not arbitrarily imposed on the language by English teachers or grammarians; they have, instead, grown out of the language itself and can be observed in action in the everyday speech and writing of those who grew up speaking and writing it.

Much of grammar is intuitive and can be understood by anyone who has spoken American English for any length of time, even without a knowledge of the rules. For instance, the sentence *You be not home go yet* is readily recognized as incorrect even without knowledge of the rules of word order.

But because American English is a complex and difficult language, it is sometimes helpful to have the rules at hand in case logic and intuition fail. What follows, then, are the basics of grammar, spelling, punctuation, and alphabetization for American English. The information presented here is by no means exhaustive, and, because language is a constantly changing thing, there can never be a "final word" as to what is correct and what is incorrect. Still, this guide should help provide a start in understanding grammar, usage, and punctuation.

THE PARTS OF SPEECH

The parts of speech define the ways words can be used in various contexts. Every word in the English language functions as at least one part of speech; many words can serve, at different times, as two or more parts of speech, depending on the context.

adjective   A word or combination of words that modifies a noun *(blue-green, central, half-baked, temporary)*.

adverb   A word that modifies a verb, an adjective, or another adverb *(slowly, obstinately, much)*.

article   Any of three words used to signal the presence of a noun. *A* and *an* are known as indefinite articles; *the* is the definite article.

conjunction   A word that connects other words, phrases, or sentences *(and, but, or, because)*.

interjection   A word, phrase, or sound used as an exclamation and capable of standing by itself *(oh, Lord, damn, my goodness)*.

noun   A word or phrase that names a person, place, thing, quality, or act *(Fred, New York, table, beauty, execution)*. A noun may be used as the subject of a verb, the object of a verb, an identifying noun, the object of a preposition, or an appositive (an explanatory phrase coupled with a subject or object).

preposition   A word or phrase that shows the relationship of a noun to another noun *(at, by, in, to, from, with)*.

pronoun   A word that substitutes for a noun and refers to a person, place, thing, idea, or act that was mentioned previously or that can be inferred from the context of the sentence *(he, she, it, that)*.

verb   A word or phrase that expresses action, existence, or occurrence *(throw, be, happen)*. Verbs can be transitive, requiring an object *(her* in *I met her),* or intransitive, requiring only a subject *(The sun rises).* Some verbs, like *feel,* are both transitive *(Feel the fabric)* and intransitive *(I feel cold,* in which *cold* is an adjective and not an object).

MODIFIERS

There are two basic types of modifiers: single-word modifiers, which are generally adverbs or adjectives; and phrases, which are usually introduced by prepositions. Modifiers should be placed as close as possible to the words they modify to ensure clarity.

Adjectives, which modify nouns, often precede the nouns they modify. They serve to restrict, characterize, or further define the nouns immediately following. Thus, *great* in the sentence *You did a great job* is an adjective modifying the noun *job.*

Nouns can also be used to modify nouns. They, too, appear immediately before the noun being modified, and only their position in the sentence indicates that they are acting as modifiers rather than nouns. The noun *telephone* works as a modifier of the noun *booth* when it appears in the phrase *a telephone booth.*

When two or more adjectives each modify the noun independently, they are separated by commas *(a silly, cheerful mood).* When the first adjective modifies an idea expressed by the combination of the second adjective and the noun, no comma is used *(a pretty oil painting).* In some cases, two or more adjectives are combined, often with a hyphen, so that they function as a single adjective. In these compound adjectives, the first term modifies the second, which modifies the noun *(a high-flying airplane).*

Adverbs modify verbs, adjectives, or other adverbs or phrases. They can often be recognized by their characteristic *-ly* ending. When modifying verbs, adverbs generally appear immediately after the verbs *(quickly* in the sentence *He walked quickly through the room).* When used to modify an adjective, the adverb will immediately precede the adjective *(a swiftly moving deer);* such compounds are not hyphenated.

In ancient Rome, authors did not punctuate their writing. It was up to the reader to insert the punctuation he felt was proper.

Phrases that modify nouns are often introduced by prepositions and immediately follow the nouns they modify. An example of a modifying phrase is *in the corner* in the sentence *The dog in the corner wagged her tail.* While useful in defining the nouns to which they are attached, modifying phrases are not as important to the sentence in the way a subject, verb, and object are. Such phrases can be essential or nonessential. In the sentence *The dog in the corner wagged her tail,* the phrase *in the corner* is essential because it identifies *which* dog wagged her tail. Clauses that modify nouns or pronouns contain a subject and a verb and can be either essential or nonessential. When they are introduced by relative pronouns (such as *who, what, that, which,* and *whose),* they are known as relative clauses. An example is *who wants to know* in the sentence *Anyone who wants to know can get the information.* Relative clauses are also known as dependent clauses because they cannot stand alone.

SENTENCE STRUCTURE

Individual words, even once their parts of speech are identified, do not communicate very much by themselves. They must be combined in such a way that they can convey meaning. This is done by forming sentences that combine words that have meaning in and of themselves (nouns, verbs, adjectives, adverbs, and pronouns) with those that are solely functional (conjunctions, prepositions, interjections, and articles).

Three main types of sentences can be constructed from these parts. Statements are sentences that tell of a fact, an occurrence, or an opinion; they provide information *(My daughter is almost three years old)*. Questions are sentences that seek out information *(How old is your daughter?)*. Commands are sentences that make a demand *(Tell your daughter to keep her hands off the cookies)*. In addition, there are exclamations *(You're a fool!)*, answers to questions *(Fine, thank you)*, sounds or cries *(Yipes!)*, and calls to others *(Yoo-hoo, Buzzy!)*.

SIMPLE SENTENCES

Every sentence includes two basic components, the subject and the predicate. The subject is what the sentence is about, and the predicate is what the sentence says about the subject:

The car (subject)	*has a flat tire.* (predicate)

Often, the subject performs an action upon the predicate *(Herb kicked the ball)*. A sentence may have a compound subject (***Ducks and geese*** *fly south for the winter)*, a compound predicate *(We* ***had dinner and went dancing***), or both.

The predicate contains at least one verb and sometimes one or more objects; the verb expresses the action of the sentence, and the object is the recipient of the action. Two types of sentences, however, do not contain objects. In sentences that have linking verbs (whose sole function is to connect subject and predicate), the predicate describes the subject with a predicate (identifying) noun or a predicate adjective *(My favorite food is* ***spinach***; *I feel* ***happy***). When the verb is intransitive (it does not act upon anything), it takes no object, and the predicate consists solely of action *(The coyotes* ***howled***).

Transitive verbs, however, take one of two types of objects. Direct objects are the recipients of the verb's action *(Mary scrambled* ***eggs***), and indirect objects describe to or for whom the action occurs *(I loaned* ***Jackie*** *my sweater)*. Indirect objects always precede direct objects in a sentence.

COMPOUND, COMPLEX, AND COMPOUND-COMPLEX SENTENCES

These three types of sentences are made up of two or more clauses, each of which contains a subject and a predicate. An independent or main clause can stand on its own as a complete sentence, but a dependent or subordinate clause cannot. A compound sentence consists of two or more independent clauses *(Jane enjoyed scuba diving, but her husband preferred golf)*. A complex sentence has one independent clause and one or more dependent clauses:

When I arrived at the office, (dependent)	*I found the memo on my desk.* (independent)

Compound-complex sentences combine the two:

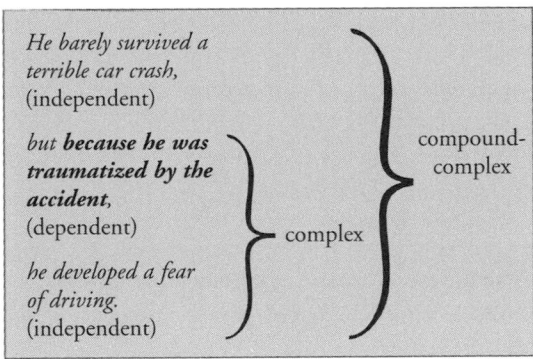

Dependent clauses may function as adjectives *(The woman* ***who gave the speech*** *was a famous athlete)*, as adverbs *(We walked along the beach* ***as the sun was setting***), or as nouns *(She was disappointed* ***that she could not attend the party***). Dependent clauses that are essential to the meaning of a sentence are called restrictive clauses *(The tree* ***that grew in the courtyard*** *was planted a century ago)*. Those that are not essential are called nonrestrictive clauses *(His mother,* ***who recently had a facelift,*** *is quite vain)*.

Sentences may also use prepositional phrases in the role of adjectives *(The machine* ***in the factory*** *ran day and night)* or adverbs (***After several years*** *abroad, Chris was ready to come home).* A prepositional phrase is made up of a preposition *(over, at, with, during)* and its object *(Meet me in St. Louis).*

See also "Modifiers" earlier in this chapter.

SUBJECT-VERB AGREEMENT

The verb generally follows the subject in statements *(We are happy).* It is often the first word in commands *(Come over here,* in which the subject *You* is understood, though not written). The verb precedes the subject in questions *(Am I blue?).* The verb and the subject must agree in number if the verb is one that can show number. Verbs that show number are the conjugations of *to be* and the third-person singular present tense form of verbs, which usually end in *-s* (*he shops,* but *they shop* for plural form). Both the subject and verb must be either singular *(I am)* or plural *(we are).*

A few subjects pose particularly tricky problems of subject-verb agreement. *Either* and *neither* are frequently misconstrued as plural subjects, although they should always be paired with singular verbs *(Neither of us is ready).* Other subjects, such as *none* and *pair,* can be used in singular or plural constructions, depending on their meaning. For instance, when *none* means "not one," it is singular *(None of the guests is here);* when it means "not any," it is plural *(None are more beautiful than a rose).*

Compound subjects can also pose agreement difficulties. Most of the time a compound subject is plural *(Paul and Carol are ready for vacation).* But when a compound subject expresses a thought or concept that is definitely singular, it should be followed by a singular verb *(Hitting a ball and driving it over the outfield wall is a skill few can master).*

TENSE, VOICE, AND MOOD

Verbs not only define the action of a sentence but also describe the nature of that action through tense, voice, and mood.

Verbs have six tenses that characterize the timing of the action. The present tense indicates an action as now taking place *(I see; She goes)* or a state or condition as now existing *(The plums are ripe);* an action that is habitual *(He speaks with an accent);* or an action that is always the same *(The clock strikes twelve at noon).* The past tense indicates an action completed or in progress in the past but not continuing into the present *(I saw; She went; He spoke)* or a state or condition in existence at a former time *(The plums were ripe).* The future tense, always formed with *shall* or *will,* indicates an action that will occur in the future *(I shall see; She will go; He will speak)* or a state that will exist in the future *(The plums will be ripe).*

The present perfect tense, always formed with *have* or *has,* indicates an action or state as completed at the time of speaking but not at any definite time in the past *(I have seen him many times; She has gone to the conference; He has spoken often before)* or an action or state that occurred in the past and continues in the present *(The plums have been ripe for days).* The past perfect, always formed with *had,* indicates an action or state as completed before a specified or implied time in the past *(I had seen the movie before it was reviewed; She had gone home before the announcement was made; He had spoken before the bell rang; The plums had been ripe long before they were picked).* The future perfect tense, always formed with *shall have* or *will have,* indicates an action as completed or a state as having ended in relation to a specified time in the future *(I shall have seen the video before it must be returned; She will have gone before her brother arrives; He will have spoken before the break for lunch; By the time they are picked, the plums will have been ripe for several days).* Each tense has a progressive form, formed by combining with verb *to be* and adding the *-ing* suffix, which is used to indicate that the action or state expressed by the verb is continuing *(I have been walking for hours).*

Most verbs are made into past tense by adding the *-ed* suffix, regardless of whether the verb's action is performed by the subject *(I walked to the store)* or on the subject *(My dog was walked).* But as the examples in the preceding paragraph indicate, a number of verbs are made into other tense forms in ways that follow no general rule at all. The only rule that can be applied is the age-old maxim "When in doubt, consult a dictionary."

In every tense, verbs take one of two voices—active or passive—that indicate whether the subject of a sentence is the doer or receiver of the action. The active voice makes the subject the doer *(The children saw everything in the museum)*; the passive voice makes the subject the recipient of the action *(The children will be seen by a doctor).*

F. Scott Fitzgerald once said, "Cut out all those exclamation marks. An exclamation mark is like laughing at your own jokes."

Likewise, in every tense, verbs also have one of three moods. A verb's indicative mood is used to make a statement or ask a question *(I see every one of his movies; Did you see his latest film?).* The imperative mood makes a request or command *(See if you*

can fix this; See here!).* In the subjunctive mood, a verb expresses a thought that is not fact at the time the sentence is spoken or written *(If they could see me now, they'd be amazed; It remains to be seen if the business will be a success).*

VERBALS

In the form of verbals, verbs function not only as words of action but also as adjectives, nouns, or adverbs. Verbals cannot serve as the verb in the predicate of a sentence because they are incomplete forms of the verb. They can, however, be modified by adverbs just as verbs are. There are three types of verbals: participles, gerunds, and infinitives.

Participles combine the work of a verb and an adjective and end with the *-ing* or *-ed* suffix. Present participles, which express present or continuing action or state of being, end with *-ing* and take the active voice *(The boy is **growing**; It turned into an **exciting** game).* Past participles, which express completed action or a time or state gone by, end with *-ed* and take the passive voice *(He was **thrilled**

Four Common Grammatical Problems

A Closer Look

Double Negative   Do not use two negative words to express a single negative statement.

WRONG: I **don't** owe Amy **no** money.
RIGHT: I **don't** owe Amy any money.
RIGHT: I owe Amy **no** money.

Dangling Participial Phrase   A participial phrase modifies the first noun or pronoun following the comma that ends the participial phrase.

WRONG: Sitting in the living room, a loud **knock** on the door was heard by Ellen.
RIGHT: Sitting in the living room, **Ellen** heard a loud knock on the door.

Split Infinitive   Do not place an adverb between the parts of an infinitive.

WRONG: I try **to** often **visit** Laura.
RIGHT: I try **to visit** Laura often.

Parallel Structure   When parts of a sentence are parallel in meaning, place them in parallel or similar constructions.

WRONG: Her morning consisted of a leisurely breakfast and strolling downtown.
RIGHT: Her morning consisted of **a** leisurely breakfast and **a** stroll downtown.

Or:

WRONG: We are responsible for choosing the costumes and that they should all be the correct size.
RIGHT: We are responsible for **choosing** the costumes and **making sure** that they are all the correct size.

*to be there; She admired the **polished** brass).* The perfect participle links the present participle with the word *having* and takes the active voice (***Having worn out their welcome,** our houseguests finally left).*

Gerunds function as nouns and end with *-ing.* They may be used and modified just like ordinary nouns in simple and complex grammatical structures (***Eating** all those nachos was not a good idea; The dog's **barking** kept me awake all night; She loved nothing more than **throwing** a party).*

Almost always accompanied by the word *to,* the infinitive may be used as a noun, an adjective, or an adverb. In its noun form, the infinitive resembles the gerund (*Mark liked **to work** alone).* As an adjective, it modifies a noun (*It was her dream **to visit** Borneo);* and as an adverb, it modifies a verb (*The engine struggled **to turn** over).* For the sake of style, the *to* is sometimes dropped from the infinitive (*I feel the earth [to] **move** under my feet).*

PUNCTUATION

Punctuation helps to make sense of the various parts constituting a sentence. It shows where to pause or stop, defines possession and contraction, sets off nonessential modifiers and asides, indicates excitement or interrogation, clarifies incompletion or continuation, and denotes dialogue and special terms.

TERMINATING PUNCTUATION

Four punctuation marks that can signal the end of a sentence are the period (.), the question mark (?), the exclamation point (!), and the ellipsis (. . .).

The **period** is used at the end of any sentence that is not a question or an exclamation. It shows that a sentence is finished and is followed by a space and a capital letter beginning the next sentence.

The **question mark** is used to terminate a sentence that is a question (*How much do you think this is worth?),* to terminate a question within quoted dialogue (*"Do you like my haircut?" he asked),* or to terminate a question within a sentence (*Will the Orioles lose every game this year? is the question on the minds of fans everywhere).* The question mark is not used to set off indirect questions (*Everyone wants to know whether the Orioles will continue losing).*

The **exclamation point** terminates sentences that convey excitement (*What a finish that play has!)* or are emphatic (*Leave me alone!).* It can also be used to terminate individual words used as interjections (*You'll get here today? Terrific!),* even when an interjection is within a sentence (*Take four parts gin, add one part vermouth, and, behold! you have a martini).*

Ancient Greek texts had no punctuation and no spaces between words.

The **ellipsis** indicates that one or more words are missing. When used at the end of a complete sentence, an ellipsis is made up of four dots (*I had hoped to go. . . .).* Four dots indicate that although what's there makes a complete sentence, one or more words have been omitted from the end of the sentence. A four-dot ellipsis can also indicate the omission of one or more sentences. When the middle portion of a sentence has been omitted, a three-dot ellipsis is used.

PAUSE PUNCTUATION

The punctuation marks that can indicate a pause are the comma (,), the semicolon (;), the colon (:), the dash (—), and the ellipsis (. . .).

Commas are used to separate two main clauses set apart by a conjunction, such as *and, but,* or *or* (*I'd hoped to be done this afternoon, but I'm not sure that's possible).* Commas can separate shorter clauses that do not have a conjunction between them (*I work, I sleep, I work some more).* They are also used to set off all manner of words and phrases, such as adverbial clauses (*When he was finished, he set down his knife);* transitional expressions (*Her remarks, on the other hand, were uncalled for);* conjunctions (*We are often late; however, we must be back by five o'clock);* illustrative expressions (*They were confused; that is, they* *felt bewildered and afraid);* and nonrestrictive clauses *(Your writing, although it is quite good, is not what we're looking for).*

In addition, commas are used to separate a series of words or phrases *(Hope, charity, and faith were not enough to sustain her);* to set off direct address *(You know, son, that's a good idea);* to set a direct quotation apart from the speaker *("Don't quote me," he said);* and to set off a question being asked about the previous part of the sentence *(It was fun, wasn't it?).*

Finally, commas indicate the inference of a word not stated, especially one used earlier in the sentence *(For us it's money; for them, food);* set off the parts of an address, place name, or date *(They went to London, England, to conduct research; She arrived on Monday 25, 1998);* and separate a name from a title following it *(Paul Fargis, President).*

The **semicolon** signals a more complete stop than is indicated by the comma. It is used to separate parts of a sentence that contain commas *(Our organization runs on the dedication, concern, and compassion of its staff; the generosity, moral support, and wisdom of its directors; and the gratitude, hope, and joy expressed by those it serves).* A semicolon can also join clauses that are not connected by a coordinating conjunction *(They left for London yesterday; I am leaving today)* as well as those joined by conjunctive adverbs *(It's easy to lie; however, lying is a bad habit to get into).*

The **colon** represents the closest thing to the full stop indicated by a period. It can mark the separation of an enumerated list or extract from the rest of a text *(The Ten Commandments:)* or can introduce an appositive *(She wanted only one thing: sleep)* or series *(It's easy to list the things money won't buy: love, health, happiness, and peace).* The colon also precedes an illustrative or explanatory phrase; many style guides recommend beginning such phrases with capital letters if they can function as sentences in and of themselves *(His Excellency demands satisfaction: He will expect you on the dueling field at dawn).*

Colons are frequently used in contexts other than sentences. They can separate book titles from their subtitles *(Curious Customs: The Stories Behind 296 Popular American Rituals);* set off the salutation in business correspondence *(Dear Mr. President:)* and the labels in memoranda *(To:);* and separate the elements of time *(8:45),* ratios *(3:5 mix of boys to girls),* and biblical references *(Deuteronomy 1:5).*

Watch out for spell checkers! If you ran the following sentence through your computer's spell checker, it would tell you that nothing was wrong: "I have bin trying too improve my spelling for sum time now cents my secretary always says that it isn't two grate."

The **dash,** known as the em dash to compositors and editors, represents an abrupt shift within a sentence. It separates a clause or phrase from the rest of the sentence, whether for emphasis *(You want—my god, you need—an expert)* or to introduce a parenthetical remark *(He hopes to turn a profit—something I can't see happening anytime soon—within six months).* Dashes also are used to separate quoted material from its author *("I still find the Strunkian wisdom a comfort"—E. B. White).*

The **ellipsis** is used in dialogue to indicate faltering speech *("We want . . . that is . . . ").*

BRACKETS AND PARENTHESES

Brackets [ ] are specialized tools for setting off material from the rest of the text. They can be used with editorial comments: The *main point [emphasis mine] has been missed;* or as parentheses within parentheses: *It is hoped (some might say prayed [even atheists pray sometimes]) that she will pull through.* Brackets should not be used when simple parentheses will do.

Parentheses ( ) are used to set off explanatory words and phrases that demand more of a break than is shown by commas and less than that indicated by dashes: *We can't bear it (or so we believe);* to surround numbers when enumerating points in a sentence: *He hopes (1) to be employed and (2) to make lots of money;* to give abbreviations: *American Telephone & Telegraph (AT&T);* and to indicate potential plurals or other alternatives: *Please tell us which course(s) of action you wish to take.*

APOSTROPHES, SINGLE QUOTATION MARKS, AND DOUBLE QUOTATION MARKS

Apostrophes are used to indicate a contraction *(didn't)* or a possessive by adding *'s* to most words *(Mr. Marx's humor);* an apostrophe alone is added to form the possessive of plurals *(the kittens' tails).* Apostrophes also appear in shortened forms of the year *(the '80s)* and for plurals of numbers, letters, and terms *(She received two A's and three B's).*

Single quotation marks are used for quotes within quotes *("'I'm not sure,' is what I think he said," she responded)* and for titles and special terms mentioned in dialogue *("She said she doesn't read the 'His' column anymore," he told his buddy).*

Charlotte Brontë and William Wordsworth asked their publishers to correct the punctuation in their manuscripts.

Double quotation marks are used for direct quotations and dialogue *("What was she up to?" he asked);* to set off special terms *(soldiers are sometimes called "grunts");* and to indicate the titles of stories, articles, songs, book chapters, TV and radio shows, poems, and lectures.

Punctuating a sentence that contains quotation marks can be tricky. Commas used to set off quoted material from the speaker are placed within the quotation marks *("I hope it's finished," she said).* A period is also placed within the quotation marks *("We're done.").* A question mark or exclamation point ending a sentence that ends in a quotation mark is placed within the quotation marks too *("Will you marry me?").* However, when quoted material is used in a question, but is not itself a question, the question mark is placed outside *(Do you think he really meant "till death do us part"?).*

AMERICAN ENGLISH AND BRITISH ENGLISH: PUNCTUATION DIFFERENCES

As if confusion about spelling and word choice were not enough, (see "American English and British English: Spelling and Name Differences" in Chapter 13), there are also punctuation differences between American and British English. Although American English always uses double quotation marks to indicate speech, British English, especially in older texts, usually uses single quotation marks. A few more recent British publications use double quotation marks.

In both American and British English, periods and commas at the end of a quote come before the closing quotation marks when the quote is a full sentence (or a full sentence broken up by a connecting phrase such as *he said*):

> *"When you come to meet me," she explained hastily, "please bring the blue folders."*

In American English, the placement of periods and commas remains the same even when the quote is a sentence fragment. But in British English, periods and commas punctuating sentence fragments are placed outside quotation marks.

AMERICAN ENGLISH: *She described the party as "a sumptuous affair," and said that she arrived home "long after midnight."*

BRITISH ENGLISH: *She described the party as "a sumptuous affair", and said that she arrived home "long after midnight".*

Grammar

ADDITIONAL SOURCES OF INFORMATION

The American Heritage Book of English Usage. Houghton Mifflin, 1996.

Blamires, Harry. *The Queen's English.* Bloomsbury, 1994.

The Chicago Manual of Style. 14th ed. University of Chicago Press, 1993.

Fowler, H. W. *Dictionary of Modern English Usage.* 3rd ed. Rev. by R. W Burchfeld. Oxford University Press, 1996.

Greenbaum, Sidney. *The Oxford English Grammar.* Oxford University Press, 1996.

Kramer, Melinda G., et al. *Prentice-Hall Handbook for Writers.* Prentice-Hall, 1995.

Maggio, Rosalie. *The Bias-Free Word-Finder.* Beacon Press, 1992.

Martin, Phyllis. *Word Watcher's Handbook: A Deletionary of the Most Abused and Misused Words.* St. Martin's Press, 1991.

MLA Handbook for Writers of Research Papers. 4th ed. Modern Language Association, 1995.

The New York Public Library Writer's Guide to Style and Usage. HarperCollins, 1994.

Strunk, W., Jr. and E. B. White. *The Elements of Style.* 3rd ed. Macmillan, 1979.

Words into Type. 3rd ed. Prentice-Hall, 1986.

Zinsser, William. *On Writing Well: An Informal Guide to Writing Nonfiction.* Rev. ed. Harper & Row, 1985.

15

LETTERS AND
FORMS OF ADDRESS

PERSONAL LETTERS   446

BUSINESS PROTOCOL AND FORMS OF ADDRESS   446

ADDITIONAL SOURCES OF INFORMATION   455

PERSONAL LETTERS

The demise of personal letter writing is considered by many to be a sad comment on the overall lack of civility in our society. Many people arrange their lives in such a way that they never need to write a letter except for business reasons. There are, however, several situations in which a note or letter is expected. And there are many other circumstances in which written communication will delight the recipient.

Thank-you notes should always be sent to the host and hostess of an overnight guest, for wedding presents, and for presents of any sort that the giver has not been thanked for personally. Thank-you notes to the host or hostess of a party or to someone who has done a favor are not required, but they will make the writer's gratitude clear and warm the heart of the person who gets them.

Other occasions demand notes or letters as well. The death of someone in a friend's family is one such event, especially if you cannot express your condolences personally at a wake or during *shiva*. A letter of condolence need not be long and involved, but it should be a personal, handwritten note, not just a printed sympathy card.

Every time you lick a stamp, you consume $^1/_{10}$ calorie.

Formal invitations require a written response. Wedding invitations are the most common kind of formal invitation that people receive. While response cards are frequently included with wedding invitations, a personal response in addition to or in place of the response card will be greatly appreciated.

When a friend or family member has something important to celebrate—a promotion or graduation, or receipt of an award or other honor—a congratulatory note will make the celebration even happier. Even the briefest of notes adds a warmth that cannot be conveyed by a phone call.

Personal letter writing can also be done for no good reason at all. Or rather, you may write letters to friends and family simply to keep in touch with them and to let them know that you are thinking of them. These are perhaps the most enjoyable letters to receive.

The U.S. Postal Service handles 40% of the world's mail volume. Japan, the second-largest carrier of cards and letters, handles only 8%.

Personal letters, while not requiring a strict format, do have a few guidelines. The date should be written at the top, either in the center or the right-hand corner. The salutation, which may be a bit warmer than it would for a business letter ("My dearest Jeanne,"), should be followed by a comma instead of a colon.

The body or text of a personal letter is, of course, a highly personal matter. It should be written with less of an eye to what would be stylistically or grammatically correct and more of an eye to expressing feelings and thoughts. A personal letter should sound like you, and techniques that would be out of place in a business letter, such as using dashes, ellipses, and sentence fragments, can be employed in personal correspondence.

Closings for personal letters are also a matter of choice. "Love," is appropriate for those you do love; "Fondly," or "All my best," or "Affectionately," might be right for friends. As with the rest of the letter, the closing should express your own feelings.

BUSINESS PROTOCOL AND FORMS OF ADDRESS

BUSINESS LETTERS

Like business phone calls, business letters should be brief and to the point. The first line below the letterhead should include the date, with the name, company, and address of the recipient appearing two lines below it at the left margin. Two lines below the address, the salutation is given.

Go to

"Business Etiquette" in chapter 16; "U.S. Postal Service" in chapter 25

If the recipient is known personally, he or she can be greeted by first name ("Dear Fred:"). If the recipient is known casually or not at all, use Mr. or Ms. ("Dear Mr. Burrows:" or "Dear Ms. Johnston:") When the addressee is unknown, "Dear Sir or Madam:" or something like "Dear Sales Manager:" can be used.

The first paragraph of a business letter should clearly explain the purpose of writing. It should be straightforward and concise. If the letter is being written at the suggestion of someone else, this should be stated in the first paragraph along with the reason for writing.

The length of a business letter is determined by what needs to be said. If a reply is desired, the last paragraph should simply state, "I look forward to hearing from you at your earliest convenience." A response by a specific date should not be demanded unless there is a good reason for doing so.

Appropriate closings for a business letter include "Best wishes," "Sincerely," "Sincerely yours," or "Yours truly." Informal closings like "Yours," or "Cheers," should not be used. The signature can be either your full name ("Henry Wiggins") or, if the writer and the recipient are well acquainted, a first name alone ("Henry"). The writer's full name and company title should be typed below the signature unless they appear at the top of the letterhead.

HOW TO PREPARE A RÉSUMÉ

A résumé is a tool that can be used to obtain a job interview. Along with a cover letter, a résumé is the first impression a prospective employee makes on a potential employer. Therefore, it is important that the résumé provide as much relevant information as possible about the person being described in it: you. It is also important that the résumé be kept brief—no more than one full side of a sheet of 8½-by-11-inch paper.

A résumé must be neatly typed, with at least a ¾-inch margin on both sides, top, and bottom. Single-space all information in the résumé, leaving one line of space between blocks of information. Use underlining, capital letters, small capitals, bold and italic type, and bullets or asterisks to highlight important information.

Begin a résumé with your name, address, and home and business telephone numbers. They can be laid out on the page in any way you find visually pleasing, so far as space allows. Do not include your age, marital status, or other personal facts.

Many résumés then list a career goal, such as "Career goal: Systems engineer responsible for monitoring, maintaining, and improving plant facilities" or "Objective: Position as illustrator/designer with opportunity to create book jackets from concept through mechanicals." Including a career goal is a good tactic if you are looking for a specific type of job; however, job hunters who would consider any of several possible careers are better off omitting any specific career goal.

The glue on Israeli postage stamps is certified kosher.

Most résumés then present a chronological outline of work experience, starting with one's current or most recent job and working backward. For each job listed, the important duties and skills involved should be outlined or described. Depending on how much "real world" experience you have, relevant high school or college employment, internships, and part-time work can be included. Such a portion of a typical résumé might look like the one on page 448.

This section is followed by one outlining your educational background, again from your most recent experience backward. List the date, school or course attended, and certificate or diploma obtained. Depending on the extent of your work experience, you may want to give a more detailed description of your higher education. If you are a college student,

Work Experience	
1996–present	Vice President, Marketing, *Techno Corp.*
	Responsible for developing, implementing, and overseeing marketing of all services provided by this computer firm.
	—Created company's first five-year marketing plan —Developed continuing training program for sales force —Increased client billings by 25 percent
1993–1996	Marketing Director, *Numbercrunch, Inc.*

you may want to list your high school and any pertinent coursework or special achievements.

In the last part of your résumé, list any work you have done with civic or charitable organizations and any awards or certificates of recognition you have received. Place these under an appropriate heading, such as "COMMUNITY SERVICE." If you have no such background, leave this section out of your résumé.

Finally, it is unnecessary to write "References available upon request" at the bottom of a résumé. Anyone looking at it will assume you can provide references and will ask for them if and when they are needed.

At one time in England, a physician was called Doctor, but a surgeon was called Mister.

SPOKEN AND WRITTEN FORMS OF ADDRESS

This section gives the correct forms of address for U.S. government officials, diplomats, UN officers, religious leaders, royalty, the British peerage, and military personnel. For each personage, the table on pages 449–453 gives the appropriate form or forms to be used in letter addresses, in letter salutations,

in direct conversation, and in more formal introductions.

In Elizabethan England, a person of higher social standing was addressed as Goodman or Goodwife. A lower member of a clerical order was called Sir Priest.

In diplomatic and other public circles, "Sir" is generally considered an acceptable alternative to the formal address in both written and spoken greetings; this greeting does not apply to religious or titled persons. The use of "Madam" or "Ma'am" for a female addressee is less customary but still acceptable, especially for high officeholders ("Madam Governor"). This rule also holds for high officials of foreign countries.

For greetings in which "Mr." is used, the feminine equivalent may be "Madam" or, less formally, "Mrs.," "Miss," or "Ms." Although there is no formal rule for the use of "Ms.," the preference of the addressee should be respected.

Go to "American English and British English: Spelling and Name Differences" in chapter 13; "American English and British English: Punctuation Differences" in chapter 14

continues

Forms of Address

Person	Letter Address	Letter Greeting	Spoken Greeting	Formal Introduction
Government Officials—Federal				
President of the United States	The President The White House Washington, DC 20500	Dear Mr. (*or* Madam) President	Mr. (*or* Madam) President	The president *or* the president of the United States *or* President Jones
Former President	The Honorable John J. Jones Address	Dear Mr. (*or* Mrs., Ms.) Jones	Mr. (*or* Mrs., Mrs.) Jones	Former president John J. Jones
Vice President	The Vice President Executive Office Building Washington, DC 20501	Dear Mr. (*or* Madam) Vice President	Mr. (*or* Madam) vice president	The vice president *or* the vice president of the United States *or* Vice President Jones
Cabinet members	The Honorable John (*or* Jane) Jones The Secretary of _____	Dear Mr. (*or* Madam) Secretary	Mr. (*or* Madam) secretary	The Secretary of _____, John (*or* Jane) J. Jones
Attorney General	The Honorable John (*or* Jane) Jones The Attorney General Washington, D.C.	Dear Mr. (*or* Madam) Attorney General	Mr. (*or* Madam) attorney general	The attorney general, John (*or* Jane) J. Jones
Chief Justice	The Chief Justice The Supreme Court Washington, DC 20543	Dear Mr. (*or* Madam) Justice *or* Dear Mr. (*or* Madam) Chief Justice	Mr. (*or* Madam) chief justice	The chief justice *or* Chief Justice Jones
Associate Justice	Mr. Justice Jones *or* Madam Justice Jones The Supreme Court Washington, DC 20543	Dear Mr. (*or* Madam) Justice	Mr. (*or* Madam)	Mr. (*or* Madam) Justice Jones *or* Justice Jones
Senator	The Honorable John (*or* Jane) Jones United States Senate Washington, DC 20510	Dear Senator Jones	Senator Jones	Senator Jones from Montana
Speaker of the House	The Honorable John (*or* Jane) Jones Speaker of the House of Representatives United States House of Representatives Washington, DC 20515	Dear Mr. (*or* Madam) Speaker	Mr. (*or* Madam) speaker	The speaker of the House of Representatives

Continued

Person	Letter Address	Letter Greeting	Spoken Greeting	Formal Introduction
Representative	The Honorable John (*or* Jane) Jones United States House of Representatives Washington, DC 20515	Dear Mr. (*or* Mrs., Ms.) Jones	Mr. (*or* Mrs., Ms.) Jones	Representative Jones from New Jersey
Diplomats and Consuls				
U.S. Ambassador	The Honorable John (*or* Jane) Jones Ambassador of the United States American Embassy Address	Dear Mr. (*or* Madam) Ambassador	Mr. (*or* Madam) ambassador	The American ambassador *or* The ambassador of the United States of America
Consul	John (*or* Jane) Jones, Esq. American Consul Address	Dear Mr. (*or* Mrs., Ms.) Jones	Mr. (*or* Mrs., Ms.) Jones	Mr. (*or* Mrs., Ms.) Jones
Foreign Ambassador	His (*or* Her) Excellency John (*or* Jane) Johnson Ambassador of _____ Address	Excellency *or* Dear Mr. (*or* Madam) Ambassador	Mr. (*or* Madam) ambassador	The Ambassador of _____
United Nations Officials				
Secretary-General of the United Nations	His Excellency Milo Jones Secretary-General of the United Nations United Nations Plaza New York, NY 10017	Excellency *or* Dear Mr. Secretary-General	Mr. Jones *or* the secretary-general	The secretary-general of the United Nations
U.S. Representative to the United Nations	The Honorable John (*or* Jane) Jones United States Permanent Representative to the United Nations United Nations Plaza New York, NY 10017	Dear Mr. (*or* Madam) Ambassador	Mr. (*or* Madam) ambassador	The United States representative to the United Nations
Foreign Heads of State				
Premier	His (*or* Her) Excellency John (*or* Amelia) Smith Premier of _____	Excellency *or* Dear Mr. (*or* Madam) Premier	Your excellency	The premier of _____

Person	Letter Address	Letter Greeting	Spoken Greeting	Formal Introduction
President of a republic	His (*or* Her) Excellency John (*or* Amelia) Smith President of _____	Excellency *or* Dear Mr. (*or* Madam) President	Your Excellency	President Smith
Prime minister	His (*or* Her) Excellency John (*or* Amelia) Smith	Excellency *or* Dear Mr. (*or* Madam) Prime Minister	Mr. (*or* Madame) prime minister	The Prime minister of _____
Government Officials—State and Local				
Governor	The Honorable John (*or* Jane) Jones Governor of _____ State Capitol Address	Dear Governor Jones	Governor *or* Governor Jones	Governor Jones *or* The governor of _____ (only used outside his or her state)
State representative (includes assembly person, delegate)	The Honorable John (*or* Jane) Jones Address	Dear Mr. (*or* Mrs., Ms.) Jones	Mr. (*or* Mrs., Ms.) Jones	Mr. (*or* Mrs., Ms.) Jones
State senator	The Honorable John (*or* Jane) Jones Address	Dear Senator Jones	Senator Jones	Senator Jones
Justice of State Supreme Court	The Honorable John (*or* Jane) Jones Justice Division Supreme Court of the State of _____ Address	Dear Justice Jones	Mr. *or* Madam Justice Jones *or* Justice Jones	Mr. (*or* Madam) Justice Jones *or* Justice Jones
Mayor	The Honorable John (*or* Jane) Jones His (*or* Her) Honor the Mayor City Hall Address	Dear Mayor Jones	Mayor Jones *or* Mr. (*or* Madam) Mayor *or* Your Honor	Mayor Jones *or* The Mayor
Religious Officials*				
The Pope	His Holiness the Pope *or* His Holiness Pope John XII Vatican City Rome, Italy	Your Holiness *or* Most Holy Father	Your Holiness *or* Most Holy Father	His Holiness the Holy Father *or* the Pope *or* the Pontiff
Cardinal	His Eminence John Cardinal Jones, Archbishop of _____ Address	Your Eminence *or* Dear Cardinal Jones	Your Eminence *or* Cardinal Jones	His Eminence Cardinal Jones

continues

* If the cleric holds a doctorate in divinity, it is customary to add the designation D.D. after his or her name in the letter address.

Continued

Person	Letter Address	Letter Greeting	Spoken Greeting	Formal Introduction
Bishop (Catholic)	The Most Reverend John Jones, Bishop (or Archbishop) of ___ Address	Your Excellency or Dear Bishop (Archbishop) Jones	Your Excellency or Bishop (Archbishop) Jones	Bishop (Archbishop) Jones
Monsignor	The Reverend Monsignor James Harding Address	Right Reverend and dear Monsignor or Dear Monsignor Harding	Monsignor Harding or Monsignor	Monsignor Harding
Priest	The Reverend John Jones Address	Reverend Father or Dear Father Jones	Father or Father Jones	Father Jones
Brother	Brother John or Brother John Jones Address	Dear Brother John or Dear Brother	Brother or Brother John	Brother John
Sister	Sister Mary Luke Address	Dear Sister Mary Luke or Dear Sister	Sister Mary Luke or Sister	Sister Mary Luke
Protestant Clergy	The Reverend John (or Jane) Jones	Dear Reverend Jones	Reverend Jones	The Reverend John Jones
Bishop (Episcopal)	The Right Reverend John Jones Bishop of ___ Address	Dear Bishop Jones	Bishop Jones	The Right Reverend John Jones, Bishop of Detroit
Rabbi	Rabbi Arthur (or Anne) Milgrom Address	Dear Rabbi Milgrom	Rabbi Milgrom or Rabbi	Rabbi Arthur Milgrom
Foreign Royalty and Nobility				
King or Queen	His (Her) Majesty King (Queen) ___ Address (letters traditionally are sent to reigning monarchs not directly but via the private secretary)	Your Majesty	Your Majesty or Sir or Madam	Varies depending on titles, holdings, etc.
Other royalty	His (Her) Royal Highness, the Prince (Princess) of ___ Address	Your Royal Highness or	Your Royal Highness or Sir or Madam	His (Her) Royal Highness, the Duke (Duchess) of Gloucester
Duke/Duchess	His/Her Grace, the Duke/Duchess of ___	My Lord Duke/Madam or Dear Duke/Duchess of ___	Your Grace or Duke/Duchess	His/Her Grace, the Duke/Duchess of Bridgeport
Marquess/ Marchioness	The Most Honorable the Marquess/Marchioness of Bridgeport	My Lord/Madam or Dear Lord/Lady Bridgeport	Lord/Lady Bridgeport	Lord/Lady Bridgeport
Earl	The Right Honorable the Earl of Franklin	My Lord or Dear Lord Franklin	Lord Franklin	Lord Franklin

Person	Letter Address	Letter Greeting	Spoken Greeting	Formal Introduction
Countess (wife of an earl)	The Right Honorable the Countess of Franklin	Madam or Dear Lady Franklin	Lady Franklin	Lady Franklin
Viscount/ Viscountess	The Right Honorable the Viscount/Viscountess Tyburn	My Lord/Lady or Dear Lord/Lady Tyburn	Lord/Lady Tyburn	Lord/Lady Tyburn
Baron/Baroness	The Right Honorable Lord/ Lady Austin	My Lord/Madam or Dear Lord/Lady Austin	Lord/Lady Austin	Lord/Lady Austin
Baronet	Sir John Jones, Bt.	Dear Sir or Dear Sir John	Sir John	Sir John Jones
Wife of Baronet	Lady Jones	Dear Madam or Dear Lady Jones	Lady Jones	Lady Jones
Knight	Sir John Jones	Dear Sir or Dear Sir John	Sir John	Sir John Jones
Wife of knight	Dear Madam or Dear Lady Jones	Dear Lady Jones	Lady Jones	Lady Jones

Military Personnel

For commissioned officers in the U.S. armed services, the full rank is used as a title only in addressing letters and in formal introductions: one writes to Major General Ann Jones, U.S. Army, and introduces her as Major General Jones. In greetings, the full rank is shortened to General: "Dear General Jones." Similar acceptable shortened greetings follow.

For enlisted personnel, a similar principle applies. Sergeants—whether staff sergeants, gunnery sergeants, or first sergeants—are greeted simply as "Sergeant"; privates first class are referred to as "Private"; and, in the navy and Coast Guard, chief petty officers are referred to as "Chief." Other non-commissioned officers are greeted by their ranks although, informally, lower grades may be referred to generically as "Soldier" or "Sailor."

The universal terms of respect that lower ranks must use when addressing senior officers are "Sir" and "Madam." These terms are not applied to non-commissioned officers, however; the appropriate affirmative response to a sergeant, for example, is "Yes, Sergeant."

Service	Full Rank	Greetings
Army, Air Force, Marines	General of the army	General
	Lieutenant General	General
	Brigadier General	General
	Lieutenant Colonel	Colonel
	First Lieutenant	Lieutenant
	Second Lieutenant	Lieutenant
Navy, Coast Guard	Fleet Admiral	Admiral
	Vice Admiral	Admiral
	Rear Admiral	Admiral
	Lieutenant Commander	Commander
	Lieutenant, Junior Grade	Lieutenant

GRADES AND RANKS FOR U.S. MILITARY PERSONNEL
COMMISSIONED OFFICERS

Grade	Air Force, Army, and Marine Corps	Navy and Coast Guard
O–10	General	Admiral
O–9	Lieutenant general	Vice admiral
O–8	Major general	Rear admiral (upper half)
O–7	Brigadier general	Rear admiral (lower half)
O–6	Colonel	Captain
O–5	Lieutenant colonel	Commander
O–4	Major	Lieutenant commander
O–3	Captain	Lieutenant
O–2	First lieutenant	Lieutenant (junior grade)
O–1	Second lieutenant	Ensign
Special grades[1]	General of the air force General of the army	Fleet admiral

[1] Five-star commissioned officers. The marine corps does not have a special grade for commissioned officers. No five-star generals are living at this time.

WARRANT OFFICERS

Grade	All Services
W-5	Chief warrant officer
W-4	Chief warrant officer
W-3	Chief warrant officer
W-2	Chief warrant officer
W-1	Warrant officer

Roman Catholic cardinals place the word "Cardinal" between their first and last names to show humility; for example, Timothy Cardinal Manning.

ENLISTED PERSONNEL

Grade	Air Force	Army	Marine Corps	Navy and Coast Guard
E-9	Chief master sergeant	Sergeant major	Sergeant major Master gunnery sergeant	Master chief petty officer
E-8	Senior master sergeant	First sergeant Master sergeant	First sergeant Master sergeant	Senior chief petty officer
E-7	Master sergeant	Sergeant first class	Gunnery sergeant	Chief petty officer
E-6	Technical sergeant	Staff sergeant	Staff sergeant	Petty officer first class
E-5	Staff sergeant	Sergeant	Sergeant	Petty officer second class
E-4	Sergeant	Corporal	Corporal	Petty officer third class
E-3	Airman first class	Private first class	Lance corporal	Seaman
E-2	Airman	Private	Private first class	Seaman apprentice
E-1	Airman basic	Private	Private	Seaman recruit
Special grades[1]	Chief master sergeant of the air force	Sergeant major of the army	Sergeant major of the marine corps	Master chief petty officer of the navy

[1] Senior enlisted advisers. Each branch of service has only one adviser.

ABBREVIATED TITLES THAT FOLLOW NAMES

An abbreviated title can tell more about a person than his or her name. It identifies a rank or position, membership in a monastic or secular order, academic degree, or military or civil honor. The following list includes some familiar as well as some obscure abbreviated titles.

Abbreviation Title

A.B.	*Artium Baccalaureus* (Latin, Bachelor of Arts)
A.M.	*Artium Magister* (Latin, Master of Arts)
A.R.A.	Associate of the Royal Academy
A.S.	Associate of Science
B.A.	Bachelor of Arts
Bart., Bt.	Baronet
B.C.S.W.	Board-Certified Social Worker
B.D.	Bachelor of Divinity
B.S.	Bachelor of Science
B.S.S.	Bachelor of Social Science
C.P.A.	Certified Public Accountant
C.S.W.	Certified Social Worker
D.A.	District Attorney
D.B.	*Divinitatis Baccalaureus* (Latin, Bachelor of Divinity)
D.C.	Doctor of Chiropractic
D.D.	*Divinitatis Doctor* (Latin, Doctor of Divinity)
D.D.S.	Doctor of Dental Surgery
D.O.	Doctor of Osteopathy
D.S.O.	Distinguished Service Order
D.V.M.	Doctor of Veterinary Medicine
Esq.	Esquire
F.R.S.	Fellow of the Royal Society
J.D.	*Juris Doctor* (Latin, Doctor of Law, Doctor of Jurisprudence), *Jurum Doctor* (Latin, Doctor of Laws)
J.P.	Justice of the Peace
Kt.	Knight
L.H.D.	*Litterarum Humaniorum Doctor* (Latin, Doctor of Humanities)
Litt.D.	*Litterarum Doctor* (Latin, Doctor of Letters)
LL.B.	*Legum Baccalaureus* (Latin, Bachelor of Laws)
LL.D.	*Legum Doctor* (Latin, Doctor of Laws)

Go to "Acronyms" and "Common Abbreviations" in chapter 13

L.P.N.	Licensed Practical Nurse
M.A.	Master of Arts
M.B.A.	Master of Business Administration
M.D.	*Medicinae Doctor* (Latin, Doctor of Medicine)
M.Div.	Master of Divinity
M.Ed.	Master of Education
M.P.	Member of Parliament
M.S.	Master of Science
M.S.W.	Master of Social Work
N.P.	Notary Public
Ph.B.	*Philosophiae Baccalaureus* (Latin, Bachelor of Philosophy)
Ph.D.	*Philosophiae Doctor* (Latin, Doctor of Philosophy)
Ph.G.	Graduate in Pharmacy
Psy.D.	Doctor of Psychology
R.	*Rex, Regina* (Latin, King, Queen)
R.N.	Registered Nurse
R.Ph.	Registered Pharmacist
S.B.	Bachelor of Science
S.J.	Society of Jesus
S.M.	Master of Science
S.T.B.	*Sacrae Theologiae Baccalaureus* (Latin, Bachelor of Sacred Theology)

ADDITIONAL SOURCES OF INFORMATION

Blumenthal, Lassor A. *The Art of Letter Writing.* Putnam, 1986.

De Vries, Mary A. *The Elements of Correspondence.* Macmillan, 1994.

Holberg, Andrea, ed. *Forms of Address: A Guide for Business and Social Use.* Rice University Press, 1994.

Mark, Lisbeth. *The Book of Hierarchies: A Compendium of Steps, Ranks, Orders, Levels, Classes, Grades, Tiers, Arrays, Degrees, Lines, Divisions, Categories, Precedents, Priorities & Other Distinctions.* William Morrow, 1984.

McCaffree, Maryjane, and Pauline Innis. *Protocol: The Complete Handbook of Diplomatic, Official and Social Usage,* rev. ed. Devon, 1989.

Swartz, Oretha D. *Service Etiquette,* 4th ed. Naval Institute Press, 1988.

IV

DAILY LIFE

CHAPTER SIXTEEN   459
ETIQUETTE

CHAPTER SEVENTEEN   473
FIRST AID

CHAPTER EIGHTEEN   495
HEALTH AND NUTRITION

CHAPTER NINETEEN   535
HOUSEHOLD TIPS

CHAPTER TWENTY   573
PERSONAL FINANCES

CHAPTER TWENTY-ONE   597
LEGAL INFORMATION

CHAPTER TWENTY-TWO   637
USEFUL ADDRESSES AND PHONE NUMBERS

16

ETIQUETTE

WEDDING ETIQUETTE   460

BUSINESS ETIQUETTE   466

NETWORK ETIQUETTE (NETIQUETTE)   468

PARTIES   468

DEATHS AND FUNERALS   471

ADDITIONAL SOURCES OF INFORMATION   472

For most people, etiquette in everyday life has little to do with white gloves and raised pinkies, although this is a common image of what etiquette is all about. In fact, etiquette involves the use of good manners, consideration for others, and adherence to unspoken rules of behavior that are expected to be followed in certain situations.

When knights in armor rode past their king, they raised their visors to identify themselves. This custom eventually became the military salute.

This chapter explains the basic rules of conduct expected of late-20th-century Americans when they engage in a number of common business and social activities. It is hardly exhaustive—a great many books have been written on planning and organizing a wedding, for instance—and it docs not cover the moral, psychological, or social implications of etiquette. But the chapter does describe what can be expected to occur when one participates in certain activities and what is expected of those who participate.

WEDDING ETIQUETTE

Because weddings vary greatly in their level of formality and style, each component of a wedding—from the invitations to the reception—is flexible. The rule of thumb is that the various elements that make up a wedding should be compatible. That is, if a formal, evening church wedding is held, it should be preceded by formal, engraved invitations and followed by a formal, sit-down dinner; likewise, a wedding held in an open field in the countryside would call for an informal dining arrangement, perhaps a buffet.

INVITATIONS AND ANNOUNCEMENTS

Wedding invitations, like weddings themselves, come in two basic varieties: formal and informal. A formal, traditional invitation is engraved or printed in black ink on high-quality white or ivory paper.

The size of the paper is either 5-by-7 inches, folded in half before being put in an envelope, or 4-by-5 inches, inserted into an envelope without folding.

The wording of a formal wedding invitation is written in the third person, and the date and time are written out in full. A typical example might read:

> Mr. and Mrs. Henry Appleton
> request the honor of your presence
> at the marriage of their daughter
> Carol June
> to
> Mr. Alan Hart
> Saturday, the fourth of February
> at eleven o'clock
> St. Albert's Church
> Bayonne, New Jersey

The invitation to the wedding ceremony itself can also invite the recipient to a reception afterward. If all those receiving invitations to the reception are not invited to the ceremony, or vice versa, a separate invitation to the reception is printed and, for those invited to both events, included with the wedding invitation. The reception invitation or the combined invitation should include the instructions "R.S.V.P."

Traditionally, the invitation is covered with a piece of tissue paper and enclosed with the reception invitation (and a response card and its envelope, if desired) in an inner envelope. The names of those invited, including a couple's children if they are also invited, are written out in full on the inner envelope. This inner envelope is then enclosed in an outer envelope that bears the handwritten names of all invited and their address, without abbreviations. Modern custom allows the bride's parents to forgo using an inner envelope altogether when sending out invitations.

Other enclosures that may be sent with the wedding invitation include cards designating reserved pews, "At-Home" cards that announce when the bride and groom will return from their honeymoon and where they will reside, and maps or other travel information.

Nontraditional, informal invitations can be designed and printed or handwritten in whatever style or form the bride and groom desire. They should, however, be in good taste—avoiding garish colors and bad poetry—and in harmony with the style of the wedding itself.

Wedding announcements usually are sent to people who would like to know about the wedding but who would not be expected to attend. They use the same paper and printing as the invitations. The wording is also similar, although the parents of both the bride and the groom are often mentioned and the words *announce the marriage of* replace *request the honor of your presence at the marriage of.* Wedding announcements are sent out the day of, or shortly after, the wedding.

Response to a wedding invitation is dictated by the type of invitation. A formal invitation traditionally is answered with a third-person, handwritten note that might read:

Mr. and Mrs. Harold Sloane
accept with pleasure (or regret they will be
unable to attend)
Mr. and Mrs. Appleton's
kind invitation for
Saturday, the fourth of February.

Of course, if a response card is enclosed, it may simply be filled out and returned. If the invitation is less formal, a handwritten response in more standard, informal English is correct.

SHOWERS

Bridal or wedding showers can be given by any close friend of the bride. They should not be given by a member of the bride's immediate family.

There is no set rule for the number of showers that can be held before a wedding, although only members of the wedding party are invited to more than one shower. Nor is there a hard-and-fast rule for the types of parties they should be; serving anything from coffee and cake to cocktails to a light supper is appropriate.

Unless it is a surprise shower, the guest list is drawn up by the bride (or the bride and groom if both are

to be present). The host for the party should set the limit on the number of guests. Guests invited to the shower should also be invited to the wedding, unless the wedding is to be very small.

Much of today's formal etiquette originated in the French royal court in the 1600s. Because nobles did not work, they developed elaborate social customs to avoid boredom.

Everyone attending a shower is expected to bring a present, which is opened at the party. The host or another friend of the bride should keep a list of who gave what, so that thank-you notes can be sent later on.

BACHELOR DINNER

Several days before the wedding, a bachelor dinner can be given for the groom. It is usually held in a private room of a restaurant and hosted by the best man or the ushers, although a groom may give his own bachelor dinner.

Generally, the men drink and eat a great deal. At some point in the evening, the groom toasts his bride-to-be. It is rarely appropriate to break the glasses after such a toast, although this was once the custom. The only important rule regarding bachelor dinners is that they should not be held the night before the wedding, so that there is adequate time for the groom to recover from the festivities.

REHEARSAL DINNER

The wedding rehearsal takes place the day before the wedding and is usually followed by a dinner party, or "rehearsal dinner." Customarily, the groom's parents host this dinner party, but it can be given by the bride's family or a close friend of the couple. Those invited include the members of the bridal party, immediate family, out-of-town family members who have been invited to the wedding, and the person performing the ceremony. Seating for rehearsal dinners may be arranged at one long table or, to fit more guests, at a U-shaped table. (See illustrations on next page.)

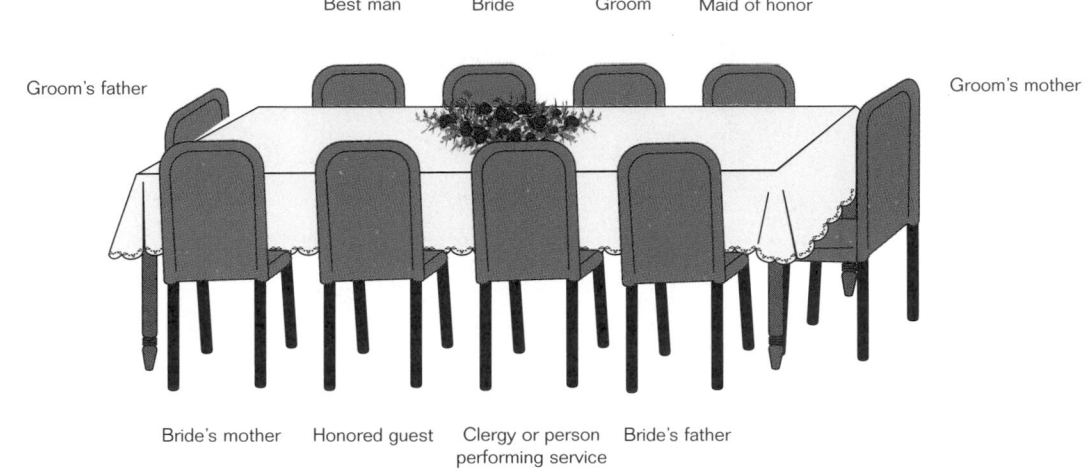

Rehearsal Dinner—Seating Arrangement at One Long Table

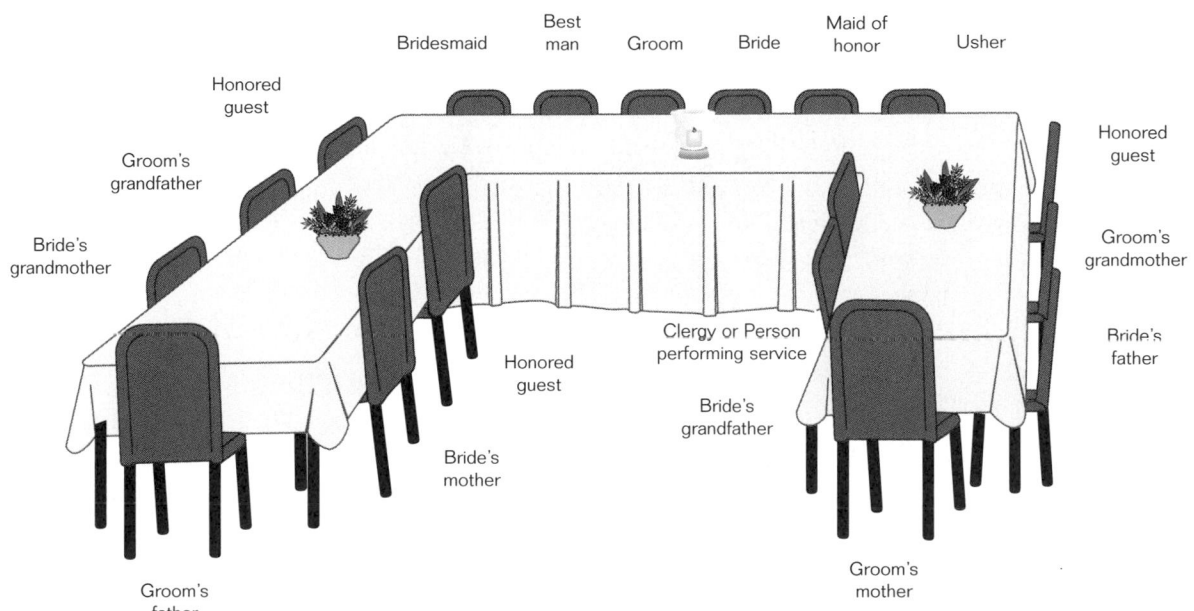

Rehearsal Dinner—Seating Arrangement at a U-shaped Table

CEREMONY

The wedding ceremony itself can be as formal or informal as the bride and groom wish it to be. Weddings are held in city halls, open fields, private homes, reception halls, restaurants, and churches and synagogues. For most weddings to which guests are invited, and especially church and synagogue weddings, a prescribed series of events will take place.

First comes the processional. In Christian and Reform Jewish weddings, the ushers come down the aisle first, arranged in height order, followed by any junior ushers. They are followed by junior bridesmaids, then bridesmaids, in height order, with the shortest first. Then comes the maid or matron of honor, the flower girls, the ring bearer, and, finally, the bride, holding the right arm of her father. The groom and the best man wait at the front of the room with the clergy.

Orthodox and Conservative Jewish processionals are led by the ushers, who are followed by the bridesmaids. Next come the rabbi and cantor followed by the best man and then the groom, accompanied by his mother and father. The maid of honor is next; she is followed by the bride, who walks between her mother and father.

The guests stand during the processional and remain standing until the clergy has asked them to sit, usually after opening remarks or a prayer. Once at the front of the room, the bride's father (or parents) steps back or to one side, and the groom steps forward to meet his bride. Bride and groom stand next to each other holding hands or with her hand on his arm, if they wish.

In Protestant ceremonies, the father of the bride gives her away before sitting down in the first pew. In Roman Catholic ceremonies, the father of the bride sits with his wife as soon as the bride is delivered to the groom. Orthodox and Conservative Jewish ceremonies require that the parents of the bride and groom remain at the front of the room; if there is space, they stand under the marriage canopy, known as a *chuppah*.

The actual events of the wedding ceremony differ widely among various denominations. Most Christian services include a blessing of the ring or rings. (If the bride is wearing an engagement ring, she should put it on her right hand for the service and then place it outside the wedding band afterward.) Orthodox Jewish services are mostly in Hebrew, and two glasses of wine are shared by the couple before the groom breaks the goblet at the end of the ceremony.

The recessional for Christian and Reform Jewish weddings is led by the bride and groom. They are followed by the flower girl, the best man and maid or matron of honor, and the ushers and bridesmaids; a line of bridesmaids follows the bride and a line of ushers follows the groom. Orthodox and Conservative Jewish recessionals are led by the bride and groom, followed by the bride's parents, the groom's parents, the maid of honor with the best man, the flower girl, and the rabbi and cantor. Bridesmaids and ushers bring up the rear. In Orthodox ceremonies, all the men are on one side, and all the women on the other.

RECEPTION

The style of the reception will follow the style of the rest of the wedding. Ordinarily, photographs are taken immediately after the ceremony; they are ordered and paid for by the bride's family.

A receiving line greets guests as they come into the room. The line consists of the mothers of the bride and groom, the wedded couple, the maid of honor, and, at the discretion of those involved, the fathers of the couple, the bridesmaids, the best man, and the ushers.

Formal receptions have assigned tables for those attending. The bridal party will generally be at the head table, and a parents' table will be nearby. Other guests should be assigned to tables with people whose company they will enjoy.

Almost all receptions include a toast to the bride and groom, which is proposed by the best man. The groom should reply with thanks after the toast

Etiquette

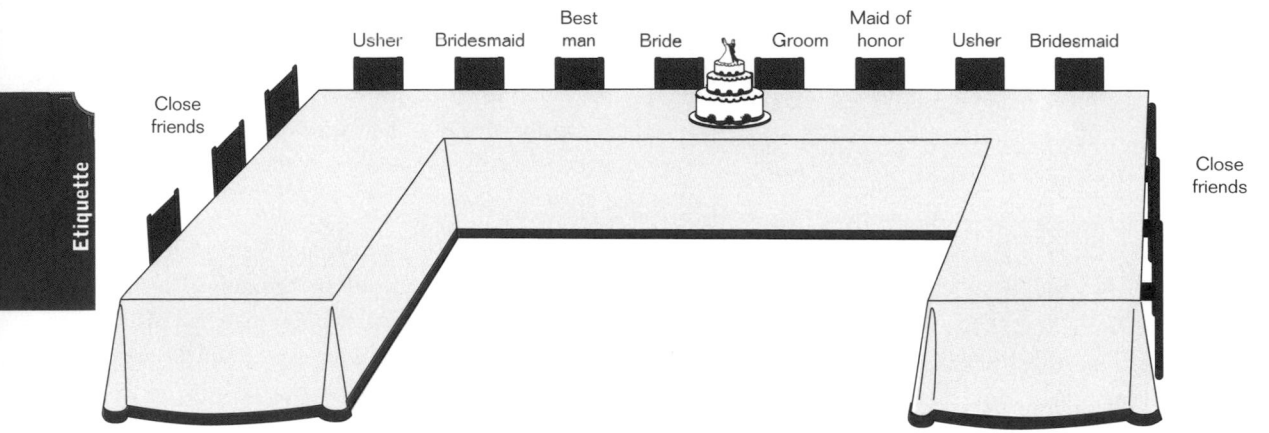

Reception—Seating Arrangement at Head Table

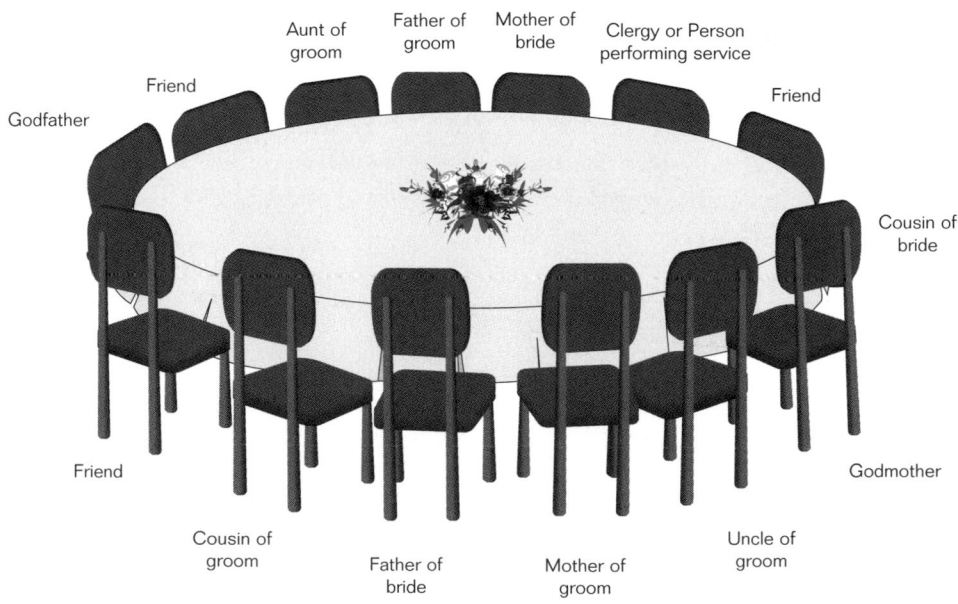

Reception—Seating Arrangement at Parents' Table

has been drunk and offer a toast to his bride; other toasts may be offered as well. The toasts can be followed by dancing or a meal, if one is to be served. The wedding cake is cut just before dessert, or shortly before the bride and groom leave the reception if it is not a formal dinner. The bride cuts the first slice, with the help of her new husband, from the bottom tier of the cake, and the couple offer each other a bite. The top layer of the cake, with its decorations, is removed and saved for the bride and groom, while the remainder is cut up and served to the guests.

At the reception's end, the bride usually will toss her bouquet from stairs or a landing, turning her back and throwing it over her shoulder to her bridesmaids or other female friends; the one who catches it is supposed to marry next. Then the newlyweds change clothes, say good-bye to their families, and, led by the best man, leave in a shower of paper rose petals, rice, or birdseed.

GIFTS AND THANK-YOU NOTES

Gifts can be sent to the address on the At-Home card, if one is enclosed with the invitation, or to the home of the bride's mother. They also can be brought to the reception. Custom dictates that a wedding gift can be given to the bride and groom within the first year of their marriage. A note should be included explaining why the gift was

---

Division of Wedding Expenses

A Closer Look

Today, the groom and his family often offer to share some of the wedding expenses that tradition-ally have been borne by the bride's family. This is a significant change of custom, as the costs of tra-ditional weddings have become too prohibitive for many families to absorb. If the groom's family does not offer to share expenses, however, the bride's family should plan a wedding in accordance with their means.

The traditional division of expenses is listed below. In addition to the change noted above, it should be kept in mind that there are numerous exceptions and variations depending on religion, ethnicity, or local custom. Many items may be omitted without diminishing the ceremony in any way.

Expenses Paid by Bride's Family
Bridal consultant, if needed
Invitations and announcements
Flowers for the church and receptions, bouquets for
    the bridesmaids, bouquet for bride (sometimes given
    by groom)
Music for the ceremony, including organist or choir fee
Transportation of bridal party to church or synagogue
    and reception
Bride's presents to her bridesmaids
Bride's present to groom (optional)
Groom's wedding ring
Sexton's fee (church fee)
Accommodations for out-of-town bridesmaids
All expenses of reception, including music

Expenses Paid by Bridesmaids
Dress and accessories
Transportation to and from town of wedding
Gift to the couple and contribution to a gift from all
    bridesmaids to the bride

Expenses Paid by Groom's Family
Bride's rings, both engagement and wedding
Groom's present to bride (optional)
Groom's presents to ushers and best man
Groom's boutonniere and boutonnieres for ushers
Ties and gloves for the ushers
Clergy member's fee; tips to altar boys
Corsages for immediate members of both families and
    bride's going-away corsage
Accommodations for out-of-town ushers
Bachelor dinner (optional, and often given by ushers)
Rehearsal dinner (optional, but becoming more
    standard)
Honeymoon

Expenses Paid by Ushers
Transportation to and from town of wedding
Rental of wedding attire
Gift to the couple and contribution to a gift from all
    ushers to the groom
Bachelor dinner (optional, and often given by groom)

Expenses Paid by Out-of-Town Guests
Transportation and accommodations
Gift to the couple

delayed. Among some people, money is an appropriate wedding gift; it is usually presented to the bride in an envelope, which she will place in a special purse or in a box or basket put out for this purpose. Envelopes, and usually gifts as well, are not opened until after the reception.

Thank-you notes should be handwritten and should mention the gift that was given. They should be sent shortly after the couple's honeymoon is over.

ANNIVERSARY GIFTS

Etiquette authorities differ on the appropriate gifts to be presented on the occasion of individual wedding anniversaries. The following list represents a modern consensus, with the eight oldest and most traditional gifts indicated in *italic*.

1	*Paper* or plastic
2	Cotton or calico
3	Leather
4	Linen, silk, or synthetics (rayon, nylon)
5	*Wood*
6	Iron
7	Copper, wool, or brass
8	Bronze or electrical appliances
9	Pottery
10	*Tin* or aluminum
11	Steel
12	Silk or linen
13	Lace
14	Ivory
15	*Crystal* or glass
20	*China*
25	*Silver*
30	Pearls
35	Coral or jade
40	Rubies or garnets
45	Sapphires or tourmalines
50	*Gold*
55	Emeralds or turquoise
60	*Diamonds* or gold
75	Diamonds or gold

BUSINESS ETIQUETTE

The business world is extraordinarily demanding and extremely competitive. In it, there are really only a few criteria on which members will be judged: competence, initiative, leadership, and how well one gets along with others. In this last area, manners play a crucial role, for individuals must be able to present themselves well and deal well with others if they wish to succeed in business.

APPOINTMENTS

Business life requires that people meet each other face-to-face to conduct transactions or exchange information. To do so, they schedule appointments. The first rule regarding business appointments is that they should be kept if at all possible; failing to show up for an appointment will be taken as a sign of uninterest, carelessness, and lack of professionalism. If an appointment cannot be kept, it should be canceled as far in advance as possible. If an individual is unavoidably delayed, he or she should telephone the host or have someone else make the call.

When the Chinese greet someone they never look directly into the person's eyes, but lower their eyes slightly as a sign of deference and respect.

When guests are shown into the office where the appointment will take place, the host should rise from his or her desk, shake hands, and greet them; if the host and guests have not met before, they should introduce themselves. The guests should be offered seats, and the host should either sit back down at the desk or sit with the visitors. Coffee or tea may be offered by the host but should not be requested by the guests.

Any business meeting should get to the business at hand as quickly as possible. It is just as important to listen as it is to talk, not simply to be polite but to get the most out of the meeting. It is also important not to interrupt others during meetings. Taking notes during a business meeting is acceptable.

The host usually will conclude a business meeting, either by making remarks that sum up the discussion or by suggesting outright that everything pertinent has now been discussed. It is important for guests to pick up on such cues, gather their belongings, thank the host, shake hands, and leave. A follow-up letter, thanking the host for the meeting and outlining whatever was agreed upon at the meeting, should be sent by the next business day.

ENTERTAINMENT

Business entertaining generally takes place in an office; over breakfast, lunch, or dinner at a restaurant; or over drinks after work. The purpose of business entertaining is to conduct business in a congenial setting that is less formal than an office.

The person initiating business entertainment acts as the host. That person is responsible for deciding on the setting, making reservations, and paying the bill. The site chosen for entertaining a client or colleague should be appropriate to the person being invited and the nature of the business relationship; a prestigious restaurant would be right for entertaining a major client, while drinks at a clubby bar might be a good choice for entertaining a vendor who regularly sells supplies to the company.

Regardless of the setting, it should be kept in mind that business is the main purpose of the get-together. The host should endeavor to bring up the business at hand before the guest becomes impatient. However, business discussions should not interfere with the pleasure of enjoying the meal.

In 1907, President Theodore Roosevelt set a world record for handshaking by shaking hands with 8,513 people at a New Year's Day White House presentation.

The host should pick up the check when it is brought to the table, look it over, and pay it. Because business entertaining should give both parties more or less equal status, it makes no difference whether the host is a man or a woman. There is no reason for a guest even to show a pretense of wanting to pick up the check; the guest can express his or her thanks to the host as she or he is leaving.

GIFTS

Gift giving is not at all unusual among people who work together. Bosses often give gifts to employees for birthdays, Christmas, or Secretaries' Day; staff members may give the boss a present for holidays or birthdays; office colleagues sometimes give each other gifts; and executives can give presents to clients or vendors.

Such gifts are generally not lavish, although the type of gift is dictated by the nature of the relationship. Bosses tend to give larger presents to their employees than staff members give to the boss. Gifts to colleagues reflect the degree of friendship between them. Clients or vendors give and receive gifts appropriate to the amount of business transacted and the longevity of the relationship.

Business gifts should be less personal than gifts for a friend. A date book or similar office accessory, costume jewelry, a tie, or a bottle of wine makes a good, inexpensive business gift. More lavish presents, like theater tickets, food baskets, or a case of wine, can be given to long-standing clients or employees.

THE TELEPHONE

For many companies, the telephone is an essential tool for conducting business. Proper telephone manners can make it an effective tool.

Many people think that having a secretary or assistant place calls will enhance the image of an executive. In fact, having others place calls for oneself is an inconvenience, both for the secretary or assistant who must place the call and for the person receiving the call, who must wait for the executive to get on the line. People in business should place their own phone calls.

When the call goes through, the caller should identify himself or herself by name and company; if the nature of the call is not readily apparent, the caller should volunteer this information. With some companies, this process will have to be repeated two or three times—with the switchboard operator, a secretary, and the person being called.

Go to

"Business Letters" in chapter 15

A caller should not take offense if asked to identify the reason for the call, although this type of questioning is often a thinly disguised way of keeping a boss insulated from people he or she does not want to receive calls from. Screening phone calls is acceptable, but not if the caller is then asked to hold the line and finally is told that the person being called is not available. As with placing calls, the most convenient and polite way of dealing with incoming calls is to answer them yourself; if you are too busy to answer the phone yourself, a secretary should keep the interrogation of a caller to a minimum.

People answering business phones should identify themselves and ask if they can help the caller. They should be attentive, organized, and unhurried. If answering someone else's phone, they should be ready to take a message.

Business phones should not be used for personal calls. If a personal call must be made, or if one is received, it should be kept as brief as possible. Similarly, business calls should be kept brief and to the point. Chattiness and rudeness are always to be avoided in business telephone calls.

NETWORK ETIQUETTE (NETIQUETTE)

Just as social and business etiquette involves the use of good manners and consideration for others, network etiquette, or "netiquette," follows conventions on how people should conduct themselves when using a computer network or the Internet. Here are a few tips to keep in mind once you're online and surfing the Internet.

- When composing electronic mail, you must choose words carefully. Sending e-mail is not a secure procedure; because there is no control over where e-mail goes after it's sent, anyone could be reading your message.
- Unlike face-to-face or telephone conversations, computer communications make facial

expressions or verbal emphasis difficult to convey. In addition, type styles are not transmitted well—if at all. If used for emphasis, they will sometimes produce an unreadable garbled message on the recipient's end. Instead of using italic or boldface to add emphasis, you can use *asterisks* or write in UPPERCASE. Avoid using uppercase too often in messages you send on the Internet because it is the equivalent of shouting. "Smileys" or "emoticons" are faces viewed sideways that are added to online messages to convey feelings: :) stands for a smile, :(stands for a frown, and ;) stands for a wink. "Smileys" are discussed in Chapter 12.

- While surfing the Net, a person cannot be judged by his age, weight, sex, or color, but a person can and will be judged by the quality of his or her writing. Correct spelling and grammar count.
- You may never see or meet the people you communicate with, so it's easy to be rude. Remember that you are interacting with other people, not simply with a computer screen.

PARTIES

GENERAL ASPECTS

Parties come in all shapes and sizes. They can be held for holidays, anniversaries, housewarmings, birthdays, weddings, or farewells, or just to have some friends over. Parties range from sit-down dinners in banquet halls to tea and cookies in living rooms. But whatever the size or style of the party, certain aspects need to be tended to make it a success.

INVITATIONS

Invitations can be given in writing, in person, or by telephone, depending on the sort of party they are for. Engraved invitations are sent for formal parties, such as weddings and anniversary parties. Less formal events require less formal invitations; handwritten notes on personal stationery or printed invitation cards with blanks that can be filled in can be used. Invitations to small informal parties can be issued by telephone. Invitations should be sent out about three weeks before a party.

R.S.V.P.s

Your invitation should include a request that guests respond if you want to know in advance who will be coming. A formal invitation can include a response card or just "R.S.V.P." Informal invitations can include a statement like "Unless we hear otherwise, we'll expect you on the third" or "Please let us know if you can make it." Telephone invitations will usually get immediate responses; however, if you are invited by telephone and do not know whether you can attend, it is acceptable to put off a response. In any case, it is important to respond to an invitation as quickly as possible so that the hosts can plan accordingly.

ATTIRE

Formal events call for certain types of attire, especially for men. *White tie* is the most formal evening attire and includes a white tie, wing collar, and tailcoat. *Black tie* is the more common evening wear and includes a tuxedo, a bow tie, and a white, soft shirt. When the occasion calls for *semiformal* attire, that usually means a sport coat, shirt, tie, and nice slacks for men, and a dress or pantsuit for women.

In Polynesia, people greet one another by rubbing noses.

FORMAL DINNER PARTIES

SEATING ARRANGEMENTS

The host and hostess, as well as any guests of honor, are the people around whom seating arrangements are set at more formal dinner parties. The host and hostess will usually sit at either end of the table; a male guest of honor sits at the hostess's right and a female guest of honor at the host's right. Other guests are told where to sit by the host and hostess,

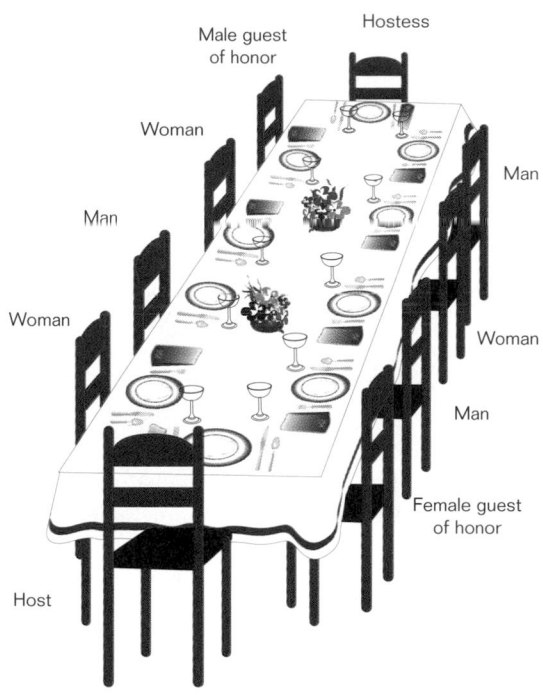

Formal Dinner Party—Seating Arrangement

either personally or by using place cards. Although it is customary to alternate men and women at a sit-down dinner, this practice can be ignored if there are more members of one sex than of the other. Husbands and wives can be seated together or separated. Obviously, buffet dinner parties, cocktail parties, and other informal get-togethers do not require any sort of specific seating arrangement; guests can be expected to fend for themselves.

TABLEWARE

A place setting at a formal dinner party can be somewhat intimidating to guests unfamiliar with such events. The arrangement of plates, glasses, and utensils is fairly standard, however, and fairly easy to deal with, as illustrated on the next page.

The basic setting should be in place when the guests sit down. A service plate is in the center, usually with the napkin on top of it. Flanking the plate will be the flatware: a dessert or salad fork to the

Etiquette

a Oyster or shellfish fork
b Soup spoon
c Fork and knife for fish
d Fork and knife for meat

e Fork and knife for salad and cheese
f Sherry glass (with soup)
g White wineglass (with fish)
h Red wineglass (with meat)

i Water goblet
j Champagne glass (with dessert)
k Butter plate and knife

Formal Dinner Party—Place Setting

a Water goblet
b Wine glass
c Coffee cup and saucer
d Coffee spoon

e Soup spoon
f Dessert spoon
g Knife
h Dessert or salad fork

i Dinner fork
j Salad plate
k Butter plate and knife

Informal Dinner Party—Place Setting

immediate left of the plate; a dinner fork to the left of it; and a fish fork, if needed, on the outside. To the right of the plate are, from closest to farthest, the salad knife; the meat knife; the fish knife; a soup or fruit spoon (or both); and, if shellfish is being served, a shellfish fork. Utensils are used in order from the outside in.

Glasses are placed above the knives to the right of the plate. There will be a water goblet and, extending to the right from there, a champagne glass, one or two wineglasses, and a sherry glass.

In addition to the service plate, a butter plate is placed above the forks, to the left of the service plate. The butter knife is set across the butter plate.

Formal etiquette dictates that a soup bowl must always be tipped away from, never toward, the diner.

SERVING

Food at a formal dinner party is usually served by hired help. Guests are served from the left, and plates are cleared from the right. The female guest of honor is served first; if there is no guest of honor, women are served before men or, if this is hard to manage, a woman is served the first plate with the other guests served in order. The hostess is served last. Warmed dinner plates are usually brought out just before the entree is served. A clean service plate should be brought out for each of the other courses.

INFORMAL DINNER PARTIES

If the dinner party is less formal and fewer courses are served, the basic place setting is arranged with fewer utensils. (See illustration on preceeding page.)

DEATHS AND FUNERALS

Plans for death should be discussed with family and loved ones before such plans are likely to be needed. A person's desires regarding the sort of funeral held, disposal of the body by burial or cremation, and donation of organs need to be known. Practical matters—where to find insurance papers, the will, bills, bank accounts, safety deposit boxes, or investment holdings—also should be dealt with in advance.

FUNERAL ARRANGEMENTS

Funeral directors provide a variety of services and handle the details of funeral arrangements, such as placement of a death notice in the newspaper; selection of a coffin; and travel to church, synagogue, and graveyard. Many of these arrangements can be made in advance or at the time of death. The death notice includes the deceased's name and date of death, the names of immediate family members who survive, and the place and time of the wake and funeral if the funeral is not private.

WAKES

Traditionally, wakes were held at the dead person's home, but today wakes are usually held at a funeral home. They are strictly a Christian phenomenon; Jews sit *shiva* during a seven-day period of mourning and remembrance immediately after burial. Anyone may attend a wake, unless it is kept private. The hours and days are set and usually appear in the death notice in the newspaper. Nonfamily members should sign the guest book provided at the funeral home, stay just long enough to express sympathy to the bereaved family, and then leave. Expressions of sympathy are best if they come from the heart; when at a loss for what to say, a simple "I'm sorry" is enough. Standing, kneeling, or praying at the coffin is optional.

FLOWERS

Sending flowers is a customary way of expressing sympathy, especially if attendance at the wake or funeral is not possible. They can be sent to the funeral home or the church along with a card. Flowers are not appropriate for Jewish funerals or if the death notice requests donations to charity instead.

FUNERAL SERVICES

Unless specified as private in the death notice, funeral services can be attended by anyone. They should be viewed not as an obligation but as an opportunity to publicly bid farewell to the person who died and to show concern for the survivors. Religious affiliation is unimportant; one may attend a funeral service regardless of faith. It is important to speak to the bereaved family at the funeral service; if sympathy has already been expressed at the wake, a positive comment about the service, the eulogy, or the church or synagogue would be appropriate.

BURIAL

For Jews, burial takes place within 24 hours, or as quickly as possible. Christians are buried two or more days after death. Close friends and family members are generally the only people expected to attend the actual interment.

A reception generally is held after the burial. The funeral director or a family member will invite those present to attend. It can be held at the home of a relative or at a catering hall or restaurant. Food and drink are provided by the bereaved family or arranged for by them.

LETTERS OR CALLS OF CONDOLENCE

Letters or calls of condolence are appropriate in lieu of attendance at a wake or funeral service. They should be brief and should focus on memories of the dead person, sympathy for the survivors, and offers of help to the survivors. Avoid pity in such communications or visits, and make clear that a response is not expected soon.

AFTER BURIAL

It is important to be available to the grieving family after all ceremonies are over. If the family is Jewish, they will sit *shiva* for seven days; it is appropriate to drop by and bring food but not flowers.

If the family is Christian, stop by a few days later to listen and talk. Whatever the religious affiliation, friends who are willing to listen and talk to bereaved family members are highly valued at this time.

ADDITIONAL SOURCES OF INFORMATION

Baldrige, Letitia. *Letitia Baldrige's Complete Guide to the New Manners for the 90s.* Simon & Schuster, 1990.

Baldrige, Letitia. *Letitia Baldrige's New Complete Guide to Executive Manners.* Rev. ed. Rawson Associates (Macmillan), 1993.

Martin, Judith. *Miss Manners' Guide to Excruciatingly Correct Behavior.* Budget Book Service, 1997.

Martin, Judith. *Miss Manners' Guide to Rearing Perfect Children.* Atheneum, 1997.

Post, Elizabeth. *Emily Post on Entertaining: Answers to the Most Often Asked Questions About Entertaining at Home and in Business.* Rev. ed. HarperCollins, 1994.

Post, Elizabeth. *Emily Post's Complete Book of Wedding Etiquette including Planner.* Rev. ed. HarperCollins, 1991.

Post, Elizabeth. *Emily Post's Etiquette.* 16th ed. HarperCollins, 1997.

Rees, Nigel. *Best Behaviour: A Complete Guide to Manners in the 1990s.* Bloomsbury, 1992.

Shea, Virginia. *Netiquette.* Albion, 1994.

Tuckerman, Nancy, and Nancy Dunnan. *The Amy Vanderbilt Complete Book of Etiquette.* 1st ed. Doubleday, 1995.

Woodard, Chiquita. *Great Ideas for Great Gifts: More Than 1000 Suggestions for Every Person and Every Occasion.* Hyperion, 1998.

Etiquette

17

FIRST AID

Lifesaving Procedures	474
Treatment for Health Emergencies	480
Directory of Poison Control Centers	488
Additional Sources of Information	493

LIFESAVING PROCEDURES

The American Medical Association recommends that when a person is injured or becomes suddenly ill one should ***immediately call for medical help.*** After help is summoned, priority should be given to these objectives:

1. Maintain breathing and circulation
2. Prevent loss of blood
3. Prevent further injury
4. Prevent shock

MAINTAINING BREATHING AND CIRCULATION

When breathing stops, the victim has enough oxygen in the blood and other tissues to sustain life for only a few minutes. Any delay in restoring the flow of oxygen to the brain and other body organs can result in death or permanent damage. Start artificial respiration and manual external cardiac massage immediately if the person is not breathing. Basic cardiopulmonary resuscitation (CPR)—mouth-to-mouth breathing and external cardiac massage—does not require equipment. It can be done by only one or two rescuers, but having more rescuers increases the chances for success.

If you are not directly involved in the rescue effort, you can help by calling a doctor, an emergency medical service (EMS), or the police or fire department. But rescuers should not wait for professional support to arrive. Seconds count. Rescue may involve three related actions: opening an airway

---

Methods of Cardiopulmonary Resuscitation (CPR)

A Closer Look

Mouth-to-Mouth Breathing

Step 1: If there are no signs of breathing or there is no significant pulse, place one hand under the victim's neck and gently lift. At the same time, push with the other hand on the victim's forehead. This will move the tongue away from the back of the throat to open the airway. If available, a plastic "stoma," or oropharyngeal airway device, should be inserted now.

Step 2: While maintaining the backward head tilt position, place your cheek and ear close to the victim's mouth and nose. Look for the chest to rise and fall while you listen and feel for breathing. Check for about 5 seconds.

Step 3: Next, while maintaining the backward head tilt, pinch the victim's nose with the hand that is on the victim's forehead to prevent leakage of air, open your mouth wide, take a deep breath, seal your mouth around the victim's mouth, and blow into the victim's mouth with four quick but full breaths. For an infant, give gentle puffs and blow through the mouth *and* nose and do not tilt the head back as far as for an adult.

If you do not get an air exchange when you blow, it may help to reposition the head and try again.

If there is still no breathing, give one breath every 5 seconds for an adult and one gentle puff every 3 seconds for an infant until breathing resumes.

If the victim's chest fails to expand, the problem may be an airway obstruction. Mouth-to-mouth respiration should be interrupted briefly to apply first aid for choking.

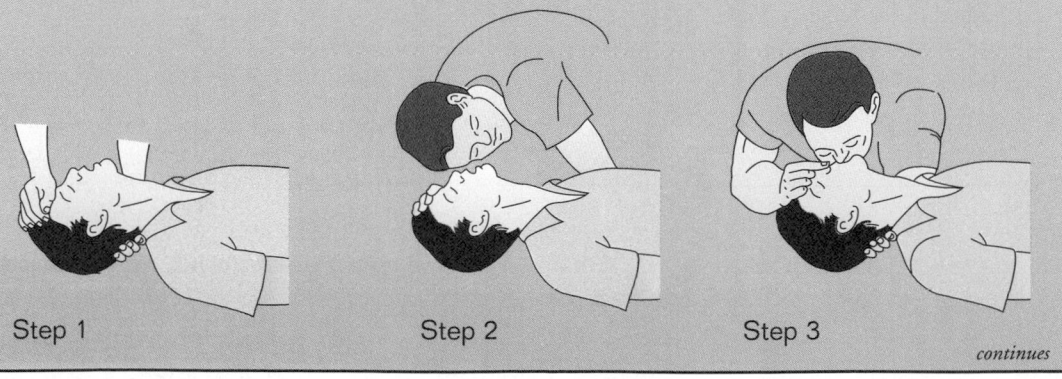

Step 1   Step 2   Step 3

continues

Methods of Cardiopulmonary Resuscitation (CPR), continued

Cardiac Massage

Check the carotid artery pulse. If there is no pulse, begin external cardiac massage by squeezing the heart between the sternum (breastbone) and the spinal column. To begin external cardiac massage, take a position facing the victim and uncover his or her chest. Find the bottom (xiphoid process) of the breastbone and place your index and middle fingers next to it to mark the location. Next, place the heel of your other hand on the sternum, just above the xiphoid process. Remove your first hand and place it on the second, interlocking the fingers. Holding your arms straight, rock back and forth from the hips and press downward so the sternum is depressed between one and two inches. Do not press on the xiphoid process and do not exert enough pressure to cause internal injuries to the liver or other organs in the area.

If possible, mouth-to-mouth breathing and external cardiac massage should be combined at a rate of 12 breath cycles and 60 chest compressions per minute. If at least two rescuers are available, one should perform mouth-to-mouth breathing while the other does chest compressions.

Check frequently for signs of a carotid artery pulse, a return of normal skin coloring, or signs of spontaneous breathing. Even if normal breathing returns, remain ready to resume CPR if necessary and until a doctor or other professional medical help arrives.

Mouth-to-Nose Breathing

When mouth-to-mouth breathing is not feasible, mouth-to-nose breathing can be performed in a similar manner by placing your mouth over the victim's nose and holding his or her lips closed between the thumb and forefinger.

For Small Children

If the victim is a small child, your mouth can be placed over both the nose and mouth. Be careful about extending the neck of an infant because soft tissues in the neck may obstruct the upper airway if the head is tilted too far.

External cardiac massage for a small child should be done with the pressure of two thumbs or two fingers, and compression should be limited to a depth of only one-half to one inch, depending on the size of the child.

For Drowning Victims

If drowning is the cause, do not wait until the victim can be transported to shore or placed on a flat surface to begin CPR. Mouth-to-mouth artificial respiration can be started while the victim is in a boat or is floating in the water. See the "Choking" and "Drowning" subsections in "Treatment for Health Emergencies" later in this chapter.

to the lungs, restoring breathing, and restoring circulation.

First, place the victim on his or her back on a hard, flat surface, such as the floor. If breathing has stopped because of poisonous gas or lack of oxygen, move the victim quickly to fresh air before beginning CPR.

Second, examine the victim closely for possible injuries or other obstacles that would interfere with CPR action. Check for a pulse in the carotid artery, on either side of the neck beneath the chin. Try to get the attention of the victim by talking, pinching, or tapping. If there is no response, assume that the person is unconscious. Look, listen, and feel for any signs of air moving in or out of the victim's lungs.

PREVENTING LOSS OF BLOOD

Heavy bleeding, or hemorrhaging, is a life-threatening emergency. Bleeding from a large artery can result in death in less than five minutes. As with maintaining breathing and circulation, immediate action is needed. Notify a doctor, an emergency medical service (EMS), the police, or the fire department. If the victim can be moved safely and quickly, take him or her to a nearby hospital emergency room.

COVERING THE WOUND

Unless there are injuries or other conditions that might interfere, keep the victim lying down with the bleeding part of the body raised higher than the rest of the body. If the bleeding is external, as from an open wound, place a clean cloth, handkerchief, pad, or similar object directly over the wound and press firmly, with both hands if necessary.

If blood soaks through the cloth, add more cloth and keep pressing, but do not take off the original pad or cloth until the bleeding is under control. Ice placed directly over the wound may help reduce the blood flow by causing constriction of the blood vessel that is the source of blood loss.

There are four basic blood types: A, B, O, and AB. The most common is type O, present in 40% to 60% of the population.

Apply firm pressure to the pressure point (see **Pressure Points** below) to control blood flow to the wound. If possible, apply pressure to the pressure point with one hand while your other hand presses a pad over the wound. Do not apply a

Pressure Points

Fingers usually can be applied without worsening a victim's condition to control bleeding at a pressure point. There are a half-dozen pressure points where bleeding from an artery can be stopped or reduced by pressing the artery against a bone located next to it.

Neck, Mouth, or Throat

To stop bleeding from the neck, mouth, or throat area, apply pressure at a point near the base of the neck where an artery passes alongside the trachea, or windpipe. Place the thumb of the hand against the back of the victim's neck and the fingers on the neck just below the larynx, or Adam's apple. Then push the fingers against the artery.

Lower Arm

An artery supplying the lower arm passes close to the bone of the upper arm about halfway along the length of the upper arm. By applying pressure at that point, pressing the artery against the arm bone, bleeding from nearly any point beyond can be stopped.

Upper Arm

A pressure point for controlling the loss of blood in the area of the upper arm, shoulder, or armpit should be found where an artery passes over the outer surface of the top rib. Place the thumb in the position shown (the top rib is indicated in the drawing) and the fingers over the shoulder so that they press against the area behind the collarbone. Apply pressure to the artery crossing the top rib.

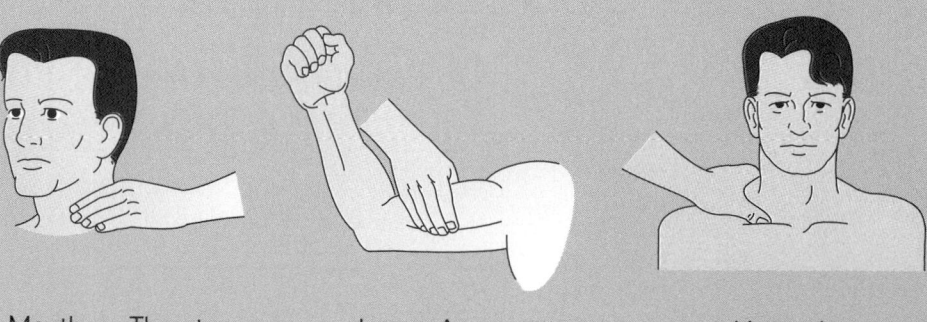

Neck, Mouth, or Throat   Lower Arm   Upper Arm

continues

Pressure Points, continued

Head Below Eye and Above Jawbone

Bleeding from an artery supplying the area of the face below the level of the eye usually can be controlled by finding the pressure point on the artery that crosses the edge of the jawbone.

Head Above Eye Level

For bleeding above the level of the eye, the rescuer should be able to find a pressure point where an artery passes over one of the skull bones in front of the upper portion of the ear, as shown in the drawing.

Leg or Foot

To stop bleeding from a leg or foot, apply pressure at a point in the area of the groin where the femoral artery passes over one of the bones of the pelvis, as shown in the drawing. If the blood flow slackens or stops, you can assume you have found the pressure point.

If at first you do not find the exact pressure point location, try again. The locations may vary somewhat with different body builds. You will know when you find the correct place, because bleeding will diminish or stop. As when a tourniquet is used, remember to release pressure at intervals to allow some blood to flow to deprived tissues. Do not continue compressing an artery if bleeding stops.

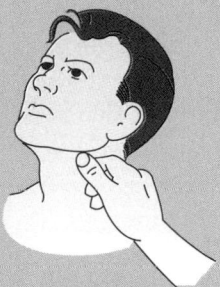

Head Below Eye and
Above Jawbone

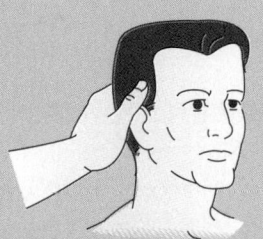

Head Above Eye Level

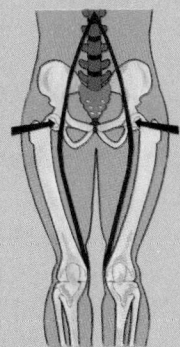

Leg or Foot

---

tourniquet unless there is no other way to stop the loss of blood. A tourniquet can result in the death of tissues in an arm, leg, hand, or foot and may lead to amputation.

GENERAL CARE OF THE VICTIM

Heavy bleeding leads to symptoms of shock: thirst, cold and clammy skin, dizziness, and falling blood pressure. Keep the victim flat and covered with a blanket or coat. Also, maintain body temperature by making sure the victim is not lying on a cold or damp surface.

Go to "Anatomical Drawings of the Human Body" in chapter 3; "Medicine and Pharmacology Symbols" in chapter 12

Unless the victim is unconscious or suffering from an abdominal wound, allow him or her to drink water or other beverages as needed; blood loss requires replacement of fluids. Do not give a wounded person alcoholic beverages, which would have the effect of increasing fluid depletion.

If the victim has suffered an open abdominal or chest wound and professional medical help is not immediately available, cover any protruding organs with a clean damp cloth held in place with a bandage or by hand pressure.

An open chest wound may result in a lung collapse unless the wound can be covered quickly with a gauze or cloth pad held in place by a firm bandage to prevent air from moving in or out of the lung. If a gauze pad is not available, make a pad from plastic sheeting, aluminum foil, or other clean material to form an airtight seal. If a bandage is not available, use a belt to hold the pad in place. Do not touch an open wound except as necessary to apply pressure or a pad or other dressing. Never try to explore a wound to locate fragments of metal, glass, or other debris that may have caused the injury.

An ice-cream headache is triggered when cold food or drink hits the roof of the mouth. The pain peaks in about 25 to 60 seconds, and skin temperature on the forehead falls almost 2 degrees Fahrenheit.

ADVISING DOCTORS AND EMS PERSONNEL

If a tourniquet is applied to stop the loss of blood from an arm or leg so seriously damaged that it may have to be amputated, be sure to advise the doctor or emergency medical service (EMS) personnel who will eventually take charge. Better yet, attach a note or write a message with lipstick on the victim's forehead that a tourniquet has been used. Do not assume that a hospital emergency-room doctor or intern many miles away will be aware that a tourniquet or any other special first-aid measures may have been applied at the scene of the accident.

PREVENTING FURTHER INJURY

First aid in an emergency should be limited to no more than is necessary to save a life or prevent further injury. In most cases, do not move an injured person from an accident site before a doctor, emergency personnel, or police or fire personnel arrive. An exception is a situation, such as a building fire or potential explosion, in which the lives of the rescuers as well as the victims could be in danger. If there is an injury to the neck or spine, a victim should not be moved until a stretcher or other carrying device that provides firm support is available. Improper movement of the victim could cause a

broken or dislocated bone that may damage an internal organ or pinch or sever a vital nerve trunk and result in death or permanent disability.

If the victim appears to have a head injury, movement should be delayed until a doctor has examined the person. Even then, any movement should be supervised by a physician. Do not move the head, or other body parts, if there is bleeding from the nose, mouth, or ears. If the victim is unconscious, you must assume that he or she has a head injury.

Never assume that an unconscious, disoriented, or apparently incoherent person is drunk. The victim may have suffered a head injury in a fall, a physical assault, or an accident. There are numerous causes of impaired consciousness, including brain hemorrhage, concussion, carbon-monoxide poisoning, epilepsy, encephalitis, diabetic coma, hypoglycemia, heart trouble, psychiatric disorders, and barbiturates or other medications. Never give alcoholic beverages to an accident victim, and never offer fluids of any kind to a person who is unconscious or semiconscious or who has internal injuries.

PREVENTING SHOCK

Shock can be expected at any accident scene. It is a common, natural reaction to any severe physical or psychological injury. Generally, shock results from an automatic change in a person's blood circulation, as nature suddenly diverts blood to the vital organs in an effort to ensure the victim's survival. This natural reaction, however, can lead to death through circulatory collapse.

Shock prevention is next in priority to maintaining respiration and control of bleeding. Watch for—but do not wait for—the common shock signs: (1) a weak, rapid pulse, (2) skin that is cold and moist with "cold sweat," (3) dilated pupils or eyes that appear "vacant," (4) restless or abnormally anxious behavior, (5) nausea or thirst, (6) faintness and weakness. If the person becomes quiet and slips into unconsciousness, shock has already progressed beyond the first stages.

First-Aid Kits

A Closer Look

Many people are confused about the meanings of terms, such as bandages and dressings, used by health professionals. Dressings are held in place by bandages. A *dressing* can be anything placed over an open wound to control bleeding, absorb blood or secretions, and prevent infectious agents from entering the body through the wound. The best kind of dressing is a piece of sterile gauze, but in an emergency, any clean material may become a dressing—even a sheet, a piece of plastic, or a newspaper. Fluffy materials, such as cotton wool, however, should not be used because the loose fibers will stick to body tissues.

A *bandage* is a strip of muslin, gauze, or other material used to hold a compress or dressing in place. A *roller bandage* is a long strip of cloth that can be used as a dressing or compress as well as a bandage. A *triangular bandage* is one cut from a square of cloth along a diagonal line. A *compress* is a square of fabric, generally of flannel or wool, used to apply heat, cold, or medications to the skin.

An ideal family first aid kit should contain the following:

12	4-by-4-inch sterile dressings in sealed envelopes
12	2-by-2-inch sterile dressings in sealed envelopes
2	15-foot-long roller bandages, 1 inch wide
2	15-foot-long roller bandages, 2 inches wide
1	roll of adhesive tape
4	triangular bandages with safety pins
1	clean bedsheet
2	small bath towels
2	large bath towels
1	pair of blunt-nose scissors
1	pair of tweezers

1	pair of needle-nose pliers
1	eyedropper
1	set of measuring spoons
12	wooden tongue blades (for finger splints)
12	wood splints, 12–18 inches long
1	bar of antiseptic soap
1	package of salt
1	package of baking soda
1	package of aspirin tablets
1	package of antihistamine tablets
1	package of anti-motion-sickness tablets
1	large package of adhesive bandages, assorted sizes
1	package of paper cups

A usual first-aid measure for shock is to position the victim so that the head is lower than the rest of the body, thus allowing gravity to pull blood toward the brain. An exception may be necessary if the victim has a head injury and cannot be moved.

Keep the victim warm and protected from the weather. Providing too much warmth, however, can lead to sweating with loss of vital body fluids and redirection of the blood flow from the vital organs to the surface of the body. Fluids may be given to a shock victim under certain circumstances—if the person is conscious, does not have internal injuries, and can swallow. Fluids can be vital for the survival of a victim who has suffered burns. It is better to give fluids in the early stages of shock, because fluids may not be absorbed from the digestive system later. If the accident site is some distance from the nearest hospital or doctor's office, small amounts of warm water or tea may be offered. But do not offer fluids if emergency service personnel or other professional help are nearby and the victim is likely to be anesthetized for surgery. If a physician is available, by telephone or otherwise, let the doctor make the final decision about fluids for accident victims.

Some persons at an accident scene may suffer only minor cuts and bruises but experience psychological shock. The signs and symptoms are the same as for victims with serious physical injuries. Time and personnel permitting, psychological shock cases should receive the same care for their shock symptoms as the severely injured. If those with psychological shock are allowed to slip into unconsciousness with possible circulatory failure, their condition will obviously complicate the overall rescue effort.

TREATMENT FOR HEALTH EMERGENCIES

ABRASIONS

A minor break in the skin, such as one caused by scraping or rubbing against a rough surface, should be washed with soap and water and treated with mild antiseptic, such as hydrogen peroxide. Then cover the abrasion with a sterile gauze dressing held in place with a bandage. If signs of infection appear, consult a doctor.

ANIMAL BITES

Animal bites, whether from a pet or a wild animal, can cause a puncture wound, a laceration, or an avulsion, in which part of the flesh is torn away. First aid should be directed toward control of bleeding and protecting the wound from infection until it can be examined by a doctor. Unless the wound is extremely painful or bleeding profusely, clean it with soap and water and cover it with a sterile dressing before taking the victim to a doctor's office or hospital emergency room.

Many animal bites require a tetanus shot and, if the animal is identified as being rabid, additional protection against rabies. In most communities, local health authorities require notification of any serious animal bite.

BLACK EYES AND BRUISES

Black eyes and bruises are actually a type of closed wound in which blood from a damaged vessel in the soft tissues has leaked into a space beneath the skin. Apply ice or a cold compress to reduce the swelling and control the further loss of blood under the skin. In most cases, the pool of blood will be reabsorbed and the skin color will return to normal.

BOILS AND BLISTERS

A *boil* is a tender, often painful, pus-filled swelling of the skin. A boil is also known as a *furuncle*, and a group of furuncles is a *carbuncle*. Boils should be treated quickly and carefully to prevent the spread of a more serious infection and the formation of a scar. A boil around the nose or face can be particularly serious and should be treated with antibiotics by a doctor. Most other boils should be treated with moist heat to cause spontaneous rupture and drainage. The pus contains staphylococcus bacteria and should not be allowed to spread the infection.

Blisters are fluid-filled skin eruptions that may be caused by allergy, injury, sunburn, insect bites, infection, friction, irritation, or drug reaction. Correcting the cause is important if the cause is an infection, allergy, or drug reaction. Most ordinary blisters can be treated with a mild antiseptic and a protective dressing. Do not puncture a blister. If the blister is accidentally broken, treat it as a wound.

BURNS

Burns can be caused by contact with heat, chemicals, electricity, or radiation. One of the effects is "burn shock," in which body fluid is diverted from normal blood flow to the brain, heart, and other vital organs to the burned area of the body. Burn shock is the same as physical or psychological shock and can even follow severe sunburn. Small thermal burns, as those caused from fire, steam, or touching a hot object, usually result in pain, a reddened skin area, and blisters. In many cases, the burn can be treated with ice or cold water. Do not try to open a blister. It can be protected by a pad held in place with a loose bandage.

Never apply ointments or grease, including butter or margarine, baking soda, or other household substances, to a burned skin area.

In addition to all of the riches found in King Tut's tomb, archaeologists also found a personal first-aid kit that included bandages and a finger sling.

A severe or extensive thermal burn requires professional care in a hospital. A doctor and/or emergency personnel should be summoned. While waiting for professional medical care, the victim should be made to lie down with the head and chest lower than the legs (shock position). Cover the burned area with a clean cloth to exclude air. Infection is a common complication if the skin is broken. If the victim is conscious and can swallow, provide adequate nonalcoholic liquids to drink. Because of burn shock, body tissues require fluid replacement. See "Lifesaving Procedures; Preventing Shock" earlier in this chapter.

FIRST- AND SECOND-DEGREE BURNS

First-degree burns are marked by redness or other skin discoloration, pain, and swelling. An ordinary sunburn is typical of a first-degree burn. These burns generally are treated as small thermal burns and usually will heal with the application of cold water followed by a dry dressing.

Second-degree burns are often the result of exposure to flame, scalding liquids, or a very severe sunburn. The skin is usually reddish, mottled, and damaged, with signs of body fluid loss. These burns are treated as extensive thermal burns, requiring professional medical care.

THIRD-DEGREE BURNS

Third-degree burns are marked by damage to tissues beneath the skin. The area may resemble a second-degree burn at first, but it quickly progresses to a whitish or charred coloration. Third-degree burns often result from contact with high-voltage electricity, steam, or boiling water, or from an accident in which the person is trapped in burning clothing. A third-degree burn is a true medical emergency. While ice or cold water may be used as a first-aid measure for first- or second-degree burns, nothing should be applied to a third-degree burn. Do not even remove clothing from burn areas. Burn areas can be covered temporarily, however, with sterile dressings, clean sheets, or even plastic garment bags. Do not put plastic materials over facial burns.

If the third-degree burn victim is conscious and not vomiting, small amounts of fluid should be offered. The recommended beverage is lukewarm water containing a teaspoon of salt and one-half teaspoon of baking soda per quart of liquid, to be sipped at a rate of one ounce every four or five minutes while waiting for professional medical help.

The first known dentists were the Etruscans, who in 700 B.C. carved false teeth from mammals' teeth and created partial bridges that could be used to eat.

CHEMICAL BURNS

Chemical burns, either acid or alkali, are generally corrosive reactions that tend to affect the skin, eyes, and digestive tract. They usually result from spills, leaks, and splashes. A strong acid or alkali can cause permanent tissue damage. An alkali burn may be more serious than an acid burn because an acid usually is neutralized by contact with body tissues, whereas an alkali can continue causing damage until it is neutralized by another substance or washed away with copious amounts of water.

As a result, all chemical burns should be flooded—not merely rinsed—with water. It is usually important to remove contaminated clothing, which tends to absorb the chemical and hold it next to the skin, exacerbating the damage. Water flooding should continue while clothing is being removed. If possible, insert a hose under the clothing to inject water between the skin and the contaminated fabric.

CHOKING

Obstruction of the airways leading to the lungs can be caused by food, candy, chewing gum, or other objects accidentally inhaled. If air is unable to reach the lungs, the body's oxygen supply can become exhausted in a few minutes, resulting in death.

Note: A person whose windpipe (trachea) is blocked cannot talk but must make those around aware that he or she is choking, using sign language or any other means so that first aid can be given immediately.

There are two accepted ways of giving first aid to a choking person.

1. The Heimlich maneuver, which consists of a series of thrusts to the upper abdomen. Stand behind the victim and put your arms around his or her upper abdomen so that your hands can be clasped in a fist at the bottom of the victim's breastbone. Then quickly push your fist upward into the victim's chest, putting pressure on the lungs so that any air in them will be squeezed backward up into the windpipe, pushing the obstruction into the mouth. The Heimlich maneuver may have to be repeated six or more times to dislodge a foreign body in the throat. If the victim is pregnant or very obese, the rescue pressure should be directed through the chest rather than the abdomen.

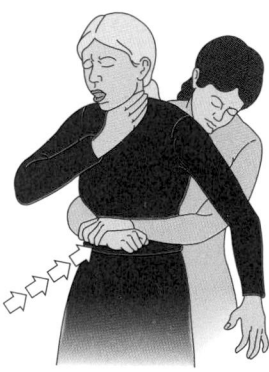

2. Firm blows over the spinal column between the shoulder blades. Stand behind the choking person and help him or her lean over, using one hand on the victim's chest to lend support. Then hit high on the back with the heel of your hand. Four or more back blows may be needed to dislodge the object in the windpipe.

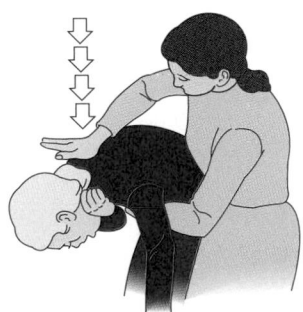

CONCUSSIONS

A concussion can result from a head injury and may be accompanied by a brief or longer period of unconsciousness. The victim may experience headache, blurred vision, or other signs of nervous system damage and may lapse into a coma. The victim, even if conscious, should be treated as an unconscious person. Keep the person quiet and warm, watch for signs of shock, and help maintain breathing if necessary while awaiting arrival of a doctor or emergency medical service (EMS) personnel.

CONVULSIONS

A convulsion, or seizure, involves a disturbance of the nervous system that affects the muscles of movement. The person experiencing a convulsion may have uncontrollable twitching of the muscles, or the muscles may become rigidly contracted. There are many possible causes and types of such seizures. In general, however, first aid should be aimed at protecting the victim from self-injury. Place a firm but soft object, such as a folded handkerchief, in the mouth to protect the tongue. Do not try to protect the tongue with a hard object that may damage the teeth, and do not insert your fingers between the jaws of the victim. Clothing about the neck should be loosened. Place pillows, cushions, or rolled blankets about the head and body. Meanwhile, summon a doctor or EMS personnel.

DROWNING

Drowning is a form of asphyxiation due to an inability of the victim to get oxygen into the lungs. It may also be complicated by inhalation of fluid into the lungs. First aid for a drowning victim requires CPR procedures to maintain breathing and circulation. Do not waste time trying to squeeze water out of the lungs, particularly if the accident occurred in freshwater. If the victim has been in seawater, try to keep the body positioned with the head and chest lower than the abdomen and legs to assist fluid drainage from the lungs. See the "Methods of Cardiopulmonary Resuscitation (CPR)" sidebar earlier in this chapter.

First Aid

ELECTRIC SHOCK

Severe electric shock can be caused by contact with ordinary electric lines in a home, office, or factory, as well as by high-voltage lines or a lightning bolt. An electric charge can have a number of effects on the body, including muscular contractions or seizures, paralysis of the lungs, abnormal heart function, bone fractures, thermal burns, and changes in blood chemistry.

Saving a person from further injury or death by electrocution should be done carefully so that the rescuer does not also become a victim. The electric shock victim first must be safely separated from contact with the electricity by turning the electricity off or by removing a wire or electric appliance with an insulated tool, such as a dry stick. In some cases, it may be easier to throw a loop of rope or cloth about the victim's arm or leg and drag him or her away from the source of electricity. If the victim is alive but unconscious, summon a doctor or EMS personnel. If breathing has stopped or there is no pulse, begin CPR immediately while awaiting the arrival of medical professionals.

FRACTURES, DISLOCATIONS, AND SPRAINS

Fractures, dislocations, and sprains generally will require the use of splints and, for arm injuries, slings to prevent movement. Splints can be made with wood, pillows, or rolled-up newspaper, if necessary. See illustrations on page 484.

A *fracture* is a broken bone. If medical help is not available, these emergency treatment methods should be followed:

- Call an ambulance.
- While waiting for professional medical help, prevent movement by splinting the injury in the position in which you found it. No attempt should be made to try to reset a broken bone.
- If the broken bone punctures the skin, control the bleeding with direct pressure. Cover the wound with sterile dressing and secure it in place.
- Keep the person warm and watch closely for signs of shock.

A *dislocation* is an injury in which a bone is displaced from its proper position at a joint. Suspect a dislocation if the injured part is swollen or visibly out of shape, or if the person is in intense pain and cannot put weight on the injured part. If medical help is not available, these emergency methods should be followed:

- Without an X ray, it is difficult to tell whether a bone is dislocated or fractured, so treat the injury as if a fracture has occurred. To prevent movement, splint the joint in the position in which you found it. Do not try to correct the dislocation yourself.
- Take the person to an emergency room for an X ray and examination.

"Health and Nutrition" (chapter 18)

Go to

Leg Splint

Arm Splint

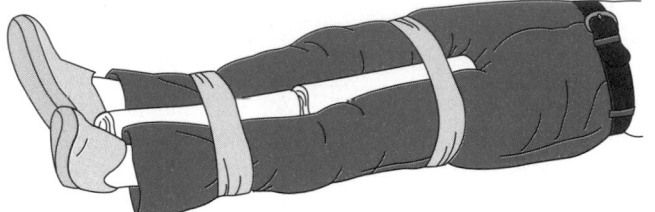

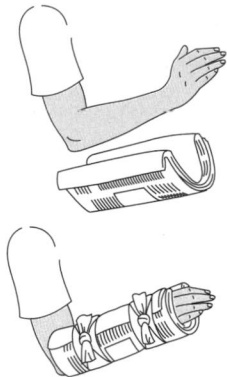

Splint and Sling Combinations

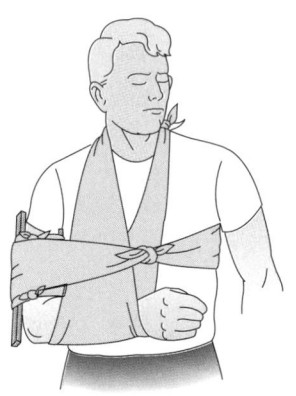

Sprain Treatment

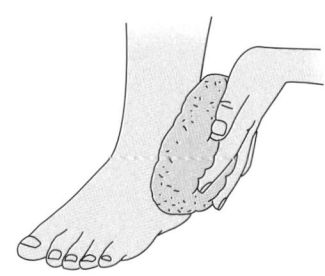
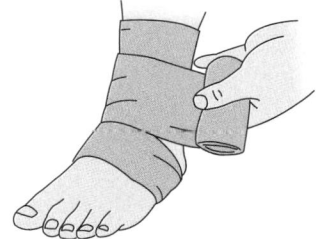

TREATMENT OF SPRAINS

A *sprain* is an injury to the ligaments. It occurs when a ligament or muscle is wrenched or twisted outside its normal range of movement and ligaments are torn. For a serious sprain, which may be indistinguishable from a fracture, treat the injury as if a fracture has occurred. For less severe, less painful sprains, follow these emergency methods:

- Do not let the person stand on or use the injured body part.
- Apply ice and compress the injury to decrease swelling.
- Support and immobilize the sprain with an elastic bandage.
- Keep the sprain elevated with either a pillow or sling.

First Aid

FROSTBITE

The most common cold-weather injury is frostbite. Severe cold can constrict the blood vessels, thereby reducing the normal flow of warm blood to the exposed tissues. The symptoms usually include a very cold feeling in the exposed skin area followed by a loss of feeling. The skin may appear flushed or red at first, but later it becomes white or a grayish yellow. Because of the loss of feeling, the victim is often unaware of the danger of frostbite.

The victim should be taken into a warm environment, and all tight or wet clothing in the affected body area should be removed. The frostbitten area should be immersed in warm—but not extremely hot—water (experts recommend a water temperature of around 105°F).

You can offer the victim hot coffee, tea, cocoa, or soup, but smoking should be avoided because it has an effect similar to that of cold, causing constriction of blood vessels. Do not rub the frostbitten tissues. If bleeding, swelling from fluid accumulation, or other complications develop after the exposed areas have thawed, notify a doctor immediately.

HEAT CRAMPS, HEAT EXHAUSTION, HEATSTROKE

Prolonged exposure to high temperatures can lead to several life-threatening health problems. The most serious effects are heat exhaustion and heatstroke. *Heat cramps* are usually in the form of painful muscle spasms caused by excessive sweating and loss of body salt. The skin may be hot and dry or cool and clammy. In most cases, heat cramps can be treated with food and liquid containing sodium chloride (ordinary table salt).

Heat exhaustion, or heat prostration, is due to loss of body fluid. It is marked by nausea, weakness, excessive sweating, and faintness. The skin is pale and clammy, the pulse is weak, and the victim may show signs of shock. The loss of body fluid results in loss of blood volume and, in turn, a deficiency of oxygenated blood reaching the brain. Have the victim lie flat with the head down and give him or her small sips of cool, slightly salted liquids every few minutes. Do not give the victim too much fluid too rapidly.

Heatstroke, or sunstroke, is the most serious type of heat injury. It may begin suddenly with headache, dizziness, and fatigue. The skin is hot, dry, and flushed, and the pulse is extremely rapid. The victim can develop a very high fever of around 105°F, experience convulsions, or become unconscious. Unless first aid is given immediately, the person may suffer circulatory collapse and die. Cool the body by wrapping the victim in wet clothing or bedding. Use snow or ice, if available, or immerse the person in cool water while awaiting the arrival of an emergency medical service (EMS) crew or a physician. Check the victim's temperature every 10 minutes to make sure the body temperature does not fall too rapidly. Hypothermia, or excessively cold body temperature, could complicate the condition.

INSECT BITES

Bites or stings of ants, bees, hornets, wasps, yellow jackets, mosquitoes, and other insects usually result in the injection of substances under the skin of the person attacked. The body's reaction may vary from mild itching to a severe form of shock, depending on the venom or other foreign protein injected and the sensitivity of the person to the substance. Some hypersensitive persons can experience an extreme allergic reaction, known as *anaphylactic shock*, marked by breathing difficulty or circulatory failure within a few minutes after a bite or sting. Such individuals require special prescription drugs that should be carried when they expect to be near stinging or biting insects.

For most people who experience insect bites and stings, first aid may require only the application of ice or a cold compress to slow the rate of venom absorption. If the insect leaves its stinger in the skin, remove it with care, as the venom sac usually is still attached and should not be squeezed.

First Aid

Ticks and other insects that may cling to the skin may require application of a petroleum product or similar irritant in order to remove them. In addition to causing local pain, swelling, and irritation, bites of ticks and other insects can result in serious infections requiring hospitalization.

NOSEBLEEDS

Nosebleeds are usually caused by rupture of the numerous capillaries in the soft tissues near the tip of the nose. A nosebleed may be started by an injury, high blood pressure, physical activity, or sudden change in atmospheric pressure, as may occur in traveling from sea level to a mountaintop. First aid requires keeping the victim quiet and in a seated position with the head leaning forward. Apply pressure to the outside of the bleeding nostril, or insert gauze pads in one or both nostrils and squeeze the outside of the nose toward the midline. Also, apply ice or a cold compress to the nose and surrounding areas of the face. If the nose continues to bleed, notify a doctor.

POISONING

A poison is anything that may be injurious to health or dangerous to life if it is swallowed, inhaled, or touched by the skin. Common sources of poisons include contaminated foods, carbon-monoxide gas, cleaning products and solvents, certain household plants, pesticides, and medicines.

In any case of a swallowed poison, the container of food or other substance should be saved, with the label and any remaining contents, so that doctors or poison control center personnel can recommend the most rapid and effective treatment.

First aid for most cases of swallowed poisons depends on the type of substance involved and the condition of the victim. Do not try to induce vomiting in any poisoning victim if he or she is unconscious or having convulsions.

Go to "Directory of Poison Control Centers" in this chapter; "Poisonous Cultivated and Wild Plants" in chapter 3; "Disposal of Hazardous Household Chemicals" in chapter 19

CORROSIVE POISONS

Do not induce vomiting if the victim may have swallowed a corrosive substance, such as an acid or alkali, or has a burning pain in the mouth or throat. Examples of corrosive substances are toilet-bowl cleaners, drain cleaners, lye, washing soda, and chlorine bleach.

- Do not attempt to "neutralize" swallowed acids or alkalis.
- Do not use activated charcoal for swallowed corrosive poisons.
- Do give the victim adequate amounts of milk or water.
- Do begin CPR if breathing stops.

FOOD POISONING

Food poisoning may be caused by enterotoxins, or poisons produced by bacteria that may or may not still be in the food. Symptoms usually include nausea and vomiting, cramps, diarrhea, fever, and headache, which may begin minutes to hours after the food has been eaten.

First aid in most cases includes bed rest, preferably close to a bathroom, and avoidance of any food or beverage until vomiting has stopped. When vomiting has ended, the victim should be offered sweetened tea or soft drinks and strained broth or bouillon with a little salt added. It is important to replace the body fluids and electrolytes (minerals) lost in vomiting or diarrhea.

In addition to vomiting, cramps, or diarrhea, symptoms of poisoning may include loss of consciousness, confusion or disorientation, an unusual odor on the breath, pain or a burning sensation in the mouth or throat, and stains or discoloration in or about the mouth from the leaves or berries of poisonous plants.

If the symptoms are severe, with signs of shock or the presence of blood or mucus in the diarrhea, a doctor should be notified.

A potentially fatal form of food poisoning that does not always cause vomiting or diarrhea is botulism.

It is caused by a bacteria-produced poison, usually found in home-canned or processed foods. Botulism attacks the nervous system. The victim may feel no symptoms for a day or two and then experience visual problems, dry mouth and swallowing difficulty, and constipation as the poison gradually paralyzes various organ systems. Immediate hospitalization is needed to prevent the spread of the paralyzing effects to the respiratory system.

INHALED POISONS

A common type of inhaled poison is carbon-monoxide gas, as produced by a car or truck engine in a confined area or by a faulty furnace or fireplace. The first symptoms are usually headache, yawning, breathing difficulty, dilated pupils, dizziness, faintness, ringing in the ears (tinnitus), nausea, and heart palpitations, followed by loss of consciousness. A distinctive sign is a cherry-red coloring of the mucous membranes. Persons with a light complexion may show a similar bright red coloring of the skin.

In the 16th century, people believed that a piece of red coral would stop bleeding, cure madness, and protect against curses.

First aid requires fresh air and oxygen. Give mouth-to-mouth resuscitation until an emergency medical service (EMS) unit can arrive to provide 100-percent oxygen by mask. Do not give any stimulants, but keep the victim warm and as quiet as possible.

In rescuing a person from an inhaled poison, such as smoke or carbon monoxide, protect yourself against becoming a victim of the same dangerous situation. Be sure that oxygen is available by opening doors or windows of an enclosed space. If possible, carry an independent air supply if you must enter a confined or overheated area to rescue a victim of inhaled poisons. When a second rescuer is present, tie a rope around your waist and give the other end to the second rescuer, who can pull you to safety if you also are overcome by poisonous fumes.

NONCORROSIVE POISONS

Most medicines, such as aspirin, may be noncorrosive poisons. Generally, the doctor may recommend that you try to induce vomiting if the person has swallowed a noncorrosive poison that is not a petroleum distillate product. If you do not know whether the swallowed substance is corrosive or noncorrosive—or even if it is actually poisonous—call a poison control center.

To induce vomiting, use syrup of ipecac (1 tablespoon for a child; 2 tablespoons for an adult) when it is available. The syrup of ipecac should be followed with one or more 8-ounce glasses of water.

If the person does not vomit within 15 minutes after one dose of syrup of ipecac, repeat the dose.

If syrup of ipecac is not available, use soapy water or a handwashing liquid detergent dissolved in water, or place the handle of a spoon or your finger at the back of the victim's throat. If the victim is a child, hold the child with the head lower than the hips while you induce vomiting. This position will reduce the chance of vomit entering the lungs.

Save a sample of the vomit so that it can be analyzed in a medical laboratory.

PETROLEUM DISTILLATES

For swallowed petroleum distillates, such as gasoline, kerosene, lighter fluid, paint thinner, or furniture polish, call the nearest poison control center or hospital emergency room immediately for specific instructions. The exact type and amount of the poison may determine the treatment. Some products contain more than one kind of poison.

Symptoms may include coughing, choking, cyanosis (blue skin), breath holding, a burning sensation in the stomach, lethargy, coma, convulsions, and spontaneous vomiting.

First Aid

- Do not induce vomiting. There is a great risk that some of the vomited poison may enter the lungs; some hydrocarbon products are more than a hundred times as poisonous in the lungs as in the digestive tract.
- Do, if recommended by a doctor, give the person a glass of milk to dilute the poison and reduce stomach irritation.

PLANT POISONS

The major contact poison plants in North America are poison ivy, poison oak, and poison sumac. They are usually identified by their clusters of three shiny leaflets. Signs and symptoms of contact with these plants include itching skin and blisters. These are effects of a poisonous resin in the leaves. Some first-aid relief can be had by diluting and washing away the resin with a strong laundry soap and water. Follow-up treatments can include moistened dressings, starch baths, or oatmeal baths to relieve the itching. Do not break the blisters. If the blisters are oozing and crusting, exposing them to dry air may give some relief. More serious adverse effects can result from chewing the leaves of poison ivy or inhaling the smoke of plants being burned. Swallowing or inhaling the resin causes painful swelling of the lining of the throat, accompanied by fever and weakness. The symptoms may require professional medical treatment.

A study of American coins and currency revealed the presence of bacteria, including staphylococcus, E. coli, and klebsiella, on 18% of the coins and 7% of the bills.

SNAKEBITES

Most snakebites should be treated like those of any wild animal. If the bite is from a poisonous snake, the symptoms may vary according to the type of snake and its venom. But most poisonous snake bites will be followed immediately by an intense pain and a feeling of numbness in the bite area. The bite of a pit viper, such as a rattlesnake, cottonmouth, or copperhead, is often identified by fang punctures about one-half inch apart. Such a bite may also produce swelling. Other snakebites may or may not leave fang marks. A wound from the bite of a coral snake may show a chewing action of the snake's jaws.

In general, a snakebite victim should remain still. Any body movement will tend to increase the spread of venom. If the bite is in an arm or leg, the limb should be immobilized and kept lower than the level of the heart. If a hospital or other medical facility is less than 30 to 40 minutes away, the victim should be delivered there for professional care as quickly as possible. Other first-aid measures are suggested only for cases in which a doctor or hospital is not easily available.

A constriction band should be tied around the arm or leg a few inches above the bite and between the bite and the heart. The bite may be washed with soap and water and covered with a sterile dressing. Ice or a cold compress can be applied, but not directly over the bite. As in any other serious injury, the victim should be monitored closely for signs of shock. In some cases, an incision can be made in the bite area for removal of some of the venom by suction. Incision and suction, however, should be performed only if a doctor is not available and immediately after the bite has been inflicted. The person making the incision should be aware that when cutting into an arm or leg, there is a high risk of causing permanent damage to nerves, blood vessels, muscles, or other tissue.

DIRECTORY OF POISON CONTROL CENTERS

Following is a list of poison control centers and state offices that can refer you to local poison control centers. Also, check your local phone directory for nearby centers.

UNITED STATES

Alabama

Alabama Poison Center
205-345-0600
800-462-0800 (Alabama only)

Regional Poison Control Center
The Children's Hospital of Alabama
205-939-9201
205-933-4050
800-292-6678 (Alabama only)

Alaska

Anchorage Poison Center
Providence Hospital Pharmacy
907-261-3193
800-478-3193 (Alaska only)

Arizona

Arizona Poison and Drug Information Center
Arizona Health Sciences Center
520-626-6016
800-362-0101 (Arizona only)

Samaritan Regional Poison Center
Good Samaritan Regional Medical Center
602-253-3334
800-362-0101 (Arizona only)

Arkansas

Arkansas Poison and Drug Information Center
University of Arkansas for Medical Sciences
501-686-5540
800-376-4766 (Arkansas only)

California

California Poison Control System
800-876-4766 (800-8-POISON) (California only)

Colorado

Rocky Mountain Poison and Drug Center
303-629-1123

Connecticut

University of Connecticut Health Center
203-674-3056
800-343-2722 (Connecticut only)

Delaware

The Poison Control Center
215-386-2100

District of Columbia

National Capital Poison Center
202-625-3333

Florida

The Florida Poison Information Center
Tampa General Hospital
813-256-4444
800-282-3171 (Florida only)

Georgia

Georgia Poison Center
Hughes Spalding Children's Hospital
404-616-9000
800-282-5846 (Georgia only)

Hawaii

Hawaii Poison Center
808-941-4411

Idaho

Idaho Poison Center
208-334-4570
800-632-8000 (Idaho only)

Illinois

BroMenn Poison Control Center
BroMenn Regional Medical Center
309-454-6666

Regional Poison Control Center
Rush-Presbyterian-St. Luke's Medical Center
312-942-5969
800-942-5969

Indiana

Indiana Poison Center
317-929-2323
800-382-9097 (Indiana only)

Iowa

Poison Information Center
515-241-6254
800-362-2327 (Iowa only)

Kansas

Mid-American Poison Control Center
University of Kansas Medical Center
913-588-6633
800-332-6633 (Kansas only)

Kentucky

Kentucky Regional Poison Center
Kosair Children's Hospital
502-589-8222
800-722-5725 (Kentucky only)

Louisiana

Louisiana Drug and Poison Information Center
Northeast Louisiana University
318-362-5393
800-256-9822 (Louisiana only)

Maine

Maine Poison Control Center
207-871-2950
800-442-6305 (Maine only)

Maryland

Maryland Poison Center
410-528-7701
800-492-2414 (Maryland only)
    For DC suburbs, see **District of Columbia**

Massachusetts

Massachusetts Poison Control System
617-232-2120
800-682-9211

Michigan

Blodgett Regional Poison Center
800-632-2727 (Michigan only)

Poison Control Center
Children's Hospital of Michigan
313-745-5711
800-764-7661

Minnesota

Hennepin Regional Poison Center
Hennepin County Medical Center
612-347-3141
Pet line: 612-337-7387

Minnesota Regional Poison Center
St. Paul-Ramsey Medical Center
612-221-2113

Mississippi

Mississippi Regional Poison Control Center
University of Mississippi Medical Center
601-354-7660

Missouri

Regional Poison Center
Cardinal Glennon Children's Hospital
314-772-5200
800-366-8888

Montana

Rocky Mountain Poison and Drug Center
303-629-1123

Nebraska

The Poison Center
402-390-5555
800-955-9119 (Nebraska and Wyoming only)

Nevada

Rocky Mountain Poison and Drug Center
303-629-1123 (Southern Nevada)

Washoe Medical Center
702-328-4129 (Northern Nevada)

New Hampshire

New Hampshire Poison Information Center
Dartmouth Hitchcock Medical Center
603-650-8000
800-562-8236 (New Hampshire only)

New Jersey

**New Jersey Poison Information and Education
    System**
800-764-7661

New Mexico

New Mexico Poison and Drug Information Center
University of New Mexico
505-843-2551
800-432-6866 (New Mexico only)

New York

Central New York Poison Control Center
SUNY Health Science Center
315-476-4766
800-252-5655

Finger Lakes Regional Poison Center
University of Rochester Medical Center
716-275-5151
800-333-0542

Hudson Valley Poison Center
Phelps Memorial Hospital Center
914-336-3030
800-336-6997

New York City Poison Control Center
N.Y.C. Department of Health
212-340-4494

Western New York Regional Poison Control Center
Children's Hospital of Buffalo
716-878-7654, 7655, 7856, 7857

North Carolina

Carolinas Poison Center
704-355-4000
800-848-6946

Duke Poison Control Center
North Carolina Regional Center
919-684-8111
800-672-1697 (North Carolina only)

North Dakota

North Dakota Poison Information Center
701-234-5575
800-732-2200 (North Dakota, Minnesota and South
 Dakota only)

Ohio

Central Ohio Poison Center
614-228-1323
800-682-7625

Cincinnati Drug & Poison Information Center
 and Regional Poison Control System
513-558-5111
800-872-5111 (Ohio only)

Oklahoma

Oklahoma Poison Control Center
405-271-5454
800-522-4611 (Oklahoma only)

Oregon

Oregon Poison Center
Oregon Health Sciences University
503-494-8968
800-452-7165 (Oregon only)

A Closer Look

The Signs and Signals of Heart Attacks and Strokes

Heart-Attack Warning Signs

- Uncomfortable pressure, fullness, squeezing, or pain in the center of the chest lasting two minutes or more
- Spreading of pain to shoulders, neck, or arms
- Severe pain, dizziness, fainting, sweating, nausea, or shortness of breath

Not all of these signals are always present. Don't wait! Get help immediately.

Stroke Warning Signs

- Sudden, temporary weakness or numbness of the face, arm, and leg on one side of the body
- Temporary loss of speech, or trouble speaking or understanding speech
- Temporary dimness or loss of vision, particularly in one eye
- Unexplained dizziness, unsteadiness, or sudden falls

Many major strokes are preceded by "little strokes," warning signals, like the above, experienced days, weeks, or months before the more severe event.

In Case of Emergency

- If you are having chest discomfort that lasts for two minutes or more, call the emergency medical service (EMS) in your area.
- If you can get to a hospital faster by car, have someone drive you.

Before an Emergency

- Find out which hospitals in your area offer 24-hour emergency cardiac care.
- Select in advance the facility nearest your home and office, and tell your family and friends so that they will know what to do.
- Keep a list of emergency rescue service numbers next to your telephone and in a prominent place in your pocket, wallet, or purse.

Pennsylvania

Central Pennsylvania Poison Center
University Hospital
717-531-6111
800-521-6110

Pittsburgh Poison Center
412-681-6669

The Poison Control Center (greater Philadelphia
metropolitan area)
215-386-2100
800-722-7112

Rhode Island

Rhode Island Poison Center
401-444-5727

South Carolina

Palmetto Poison Center
College of Pharmacy
University of South Carolina
803-765-7359
800-922-1117 (South Carolina only)

South Dakota

McKennan Poison Control
605-336-3894
800-952-0123 (South Dakota only)

Tennessee

Middle Tennessee Regional Poison Center
Vanderbilt University Medical Center
615-936-2034
800-288-9999

Texas

North Texas Poison Center
800-746-7661

Texas Poison Control Network at Galveston
The University of Texas Medical Branch
409-765-1420 (Galveston)
713-654-1701 (Houston)
800-764-7661 (Texas only)

Utah

Utah Poison Control Center
801-581-2151
800-456-7707 (Utah only)

Vermont

Vermont Poison Center
802-658-3456

Virginia

Blue Ridge Poison Center
University of Virginia
804-924-5543
800-451-1428

Georgetown University Hospital
202-625-3333

Virginia Poison Center
Virginia Commonwealth University
804-828-9123
800-552-6337 (Virginia only)

Washington

Washington Poison Center
Children's Hospital and Medical Center
206-526-2121
800-732-6985 (Washington only)

West Virginia

West Virginia Poison Center
304-348-4211
800-642-3625 (West Virginia only)

Wisconsin

Poison Center
University Hospital
608-262-3702
800-815-8855

Wyoming

The Poison Center
402-390-5555
800 955-9119 (Wyoming and Nebraska only)

CANADA

British Columbia

B. C. Drug and Poison Information Centre
604-682-5050
800-567-8911

First Aid

Ontario
Ontario Regional Poison Control Centre
The Hospital for Sick Children
416-813-5900
800-268-9017 (Ontario only)

Nova Scotia and Prince Edward Island
Poison Information Centre
902-420-0161 (Nova Scotia)
800-565-8161 (Prince Edward Island)

Quebec
Quebec Poison Control Center
418-656-8090

ADDITIONAL SOURCES OF INFORMATION

ORGANIZATIONS AND SERVICES
American College of Emergency Physicians
P.O. Box 619911
Dallas, TX 75261-9911
800-798-1822
http://www.acep.org

American Medical Association
515 N. State St.
Chicago, IL 60610
312-464-5000
http://www.ama-assn.org

American National Red Cross
17th and D sts., NW
Washington, DC 20006
703-206-6000
http://www.redcross.org/index.html

National Association of Emergency Medical Technicians
102 W. Leake St.
Clinton, MS 39056-4252
800-346-2368
http://www.nacmt.org

BOOKS
Brown, Andrew J. *First Aid: Principles and Practices.* Macmillan, 1987.

Clayman, Charles. *The American Medical Association Family Medical Guide.* 3rd ed. Random House, 1994.

Handal, Kathleen. *The American Red Cross First Aid and Safety Handbook.* Little Brown & Co., 1992.

Zydio, Stanley, and James A. Hill. *The American Medical Association Handbook of First Aid and Emergency Care.* Random House, 1990.

First Aid

First Aid

18

HEALTH AND NUTRITION

QUESTIONS TO ASK YOUR DOCTOR	496
THE PATIENT'S BILL OF RIGHTS	498
APPROXIMATE DATES OF CHILDBIRTH	500
PRECAUTIONS DURING PREGNANCY	500
IMMUNIZATION SCHEDULE	502
EXPECTED NUMBER OF DEATHS	503
LIFE EXPECTANCY IN 1995	504
RECOMMENDED WEIGHTS	504
HOME REMEDIES	506
LOOKING FOR SIGNS OF BREAST CANCER	511
INFECTIOUS DISEASES AND HOW THEY ARE SPREAD	513
DENTAL CARE	514
LIVING WILLS	515
DEATHS AND DEATH RATES 1970 TO 1996	516
COMBINING FORMS OF MEDICAL TERMS	519

RECOMMENDED DAILY ALLOWANCES
520

VITAMIN/MINERAL FOOD CHART
522

ACTIVITIES AND THE CALORIES
THEY CONSUME
530

SAFE ALCOHOL CONSUMPTION
531

ADDITIONAL SOURCES OF INFORMATION
532

QUESTIONS TO ASK YOUR DOCTOR

"I wish I'd asked the doctor about that" is a common lament after routine checkups and more serious consultations as well. Hidden symptoms of illness (such as pain, emotional stability, or changes in eating or sleeping habits) must be reported. Your physician may need to be reminded of important facts about your family history, previous health problems, and other factors that can affect diagnosis and treatment. Many professionals suggest making a list of health-related questions/concerns before seeing the doctor. Consider the following for inclusion in your list.

At routine checkups—individual concerns related to problems experienced since the last visit:

- I have been experiencing _____ [headaches, back pain, unexplained drowsiness, trouble sleeping, dizziness, etc.]. What could that mean? What do you recommend?
- I have a family history of _____ [heart disease, diabetes, high blood pressure, breast cancer, etc.]. Could my symptoms indicate that I am developing a problem?

Other general areas of concern:

- What are my cholesterol levels? What should they be? What do my numbers mean?
- What is my blood pressure? What should it be? What do my numbers mean?
- Do I need medication? How long will I need to take it?
- Do I need to make any major lifestyle changes [stop smoking, modify activities, stop/start/ change exercise program, change diet, etc.]?

When X rays, blood tests, or other types of tests are recommended:

- Why do I need to have this test? What will the results tell you?
- Are there any risks involved in having this test performed?

- When will I get the results? Depending on the results, what treatment or other tests may be recommended?
- Will the test be painful? How long will it take?
- How should I prepare for the test? Can it be scheduled early in the morning [if overnight fasting is required]? What about other medications I am taking? Should I take them while fasting for the test? Can I drink water to swallow my pills? [If you are diabetic or take any medication that must be taken with food or liquid, remind the doctor of your situation and get specific instructions, especially when consulting a specialist who is not your regular physician.]
- How much will the test cost?

When immunization or nonsurgical treatment is recommended:

- What are the benefits of this treatment?
- Are there any risks involved with this treatment? What physical or emotional side effects can I expect?
- Are there other treatments with fewer side effects or risks that I should consider?
- What will this treatment cost?
- How can I tell if the treatment is working?

About medication:

- What are the risks/benefits associated with this medication?
- How will this medication interact with prescriptions I am already taking? Should I avoid alcohol or certain foods?
- Please explain exactly how this medication is to be taken. In the morning or night? With food or milk, or on an empty stomach? What if I forget to take it?
- Is this medication expensive? Would a generic prescription be as effective?
- How will I know if the medication is working? What problems should I call you about?

Go to   "Anatomical Drawings of the Human Body" in chapter 3; "Health Insurance" in Chapter 20; and "Medicare" in chapter 25

Shelf Life of Medicine

A Closer Look

Pharmacists generally do not mark containers with expiration dates, although the containers usually show the dates of the original prescriptions. If a prescription drug is more than one year old but is not in its original container clearly showing the expiration date, it should be replaced. First-aid creams in tubes usually have expiration dates marked on the tubes, but the dates are generally hard to see. After the components separate, the creams should not be used. Vitamins and minerals will keep for a long time if protected from heat, moisture, and light. A good rule of thumb about the shelf life of drugs is "When in doubt, throw it out." Following is a list of the shelf life of some common drugs.

Cold tablets	1–2 years
Laxatives	2–3 years
Minerals	6 years or more
Nonprescription painkiller tablets	1–4 years
Prescription antibiotics	2–3 years
Prescription antihypertension tablets	2–4 years
Travel sickness tablets	2 years
Vitamins	6 years or more

If surgery is recommended:

- What procedure are you recommending? [Ask for details about the procedure.]
- Why do I need this operation?
- Are there other types of treatment available? If so, what are they?
- What are the benefits of having the procedure?
- What are the risks involved in this procedure?
- What is the prognosis if I choose not to have surgery?
- Who will perform the operation? What experience do you (does she/he) have with this type of procedure?
- I'd like to get a second opinion. Is there someone you'd recommend that I see?
- What type of anesthesia will be used? What are the risks involved? Are there alternatives?
- Will this be performed as inpatient or outpatient surgery? [If what seems to be a major procedure will be performed on an outpatient basis, ask further questions.] How long will I be in the hospital?
- Where will the procedure be performed? Is there a good success rate for this operation at that hospital? [A hospital may have high success rates with a procedure performed there frequently, whereas another medical center nearby has less success because that type of surgery is not often scheduled.]

- How much will the surgery cost? What is your fee? [Also check with your insurance company to see how much of the cost will be covered and how much your own cost will be.]
- How should I prepare for the surgery? Can it be scheduled early in the morning [if overnight fasting is required]?
- What about regular medications I am taking? Should I take them before surgery? Can I drink water to swallow my pills? What about after surgery? Will I take my regular medications as usual? Should I bring my prescriptions to the hospital with me? [If you take medication for chronic conditions such as diabetes or mental/emotional illness, be sure to discuss these issues with both the surgeon and your regular physician. If new orders for your regular medications are to be written in the hospital and you will be there for an extended stay, take a list of your prescriptions with you. Once there, ask what you are being given. If the amounts or medications are unfamiliar, check with your doctor.]
- How much pain can I expect after the operation? How long will it last? Will I need medication for pain during the recovery period?
- How long will my recovery period be? Will I need special care at home after I leave the hospital?

Health/Nutrition

- Should I expect to have an emotional reaction following my surgery? What support groups or coping methods do you recommend?
- After I leave the hospital, what symptoms should I call to report? When will a follow-up visit be scheduled?
- Will there be any restrictions on my activities [driving, climbing stairs, lifting, bending, sexual intercourse, etc.]? How long will it be before I can return to work?
- What should I tell my family about the surgery?

THE PATIENT'S BILL OF RIGHTS

The provision of a written statement of patient rights has become standard practice in many health-care institutions in recent years. Such documents typically emphasize the health provider's intention to treat each patient with respect, to acknowledge the patient's right to refuse treatment/make decisions concerning treatment, to provide the best available treatment regardless of an individual's ability to pay for care, and to keep each patient's medical information confidential. The issues of a person's right to self-determination (decisions concerning treatment and the right to refuse treatment) and the protection of confidential medical records are usually central. A list of the patient's responsibilities concerning care usually follows the enumeration of rights.

An example of a typical patient's bill of rights is the following document that is now law in Florida.

Go to "First Aid" in chapter 17; "Insurance" in chapter 20; "Forms and Contracts" in chapter 21; "Disabilities" in chapter 22

The Patient's Bill of Rights

Each health-care facility or provider shall observe the following standards:

Individual Dignity

1. The individual dignity of a patient must be respected at all times and upon all occasions.
2. Every patient who is provided health-care services retains certain rights to privacy, which must be respected without regard to the patient's economic status or source of payment for his care. This patient's rights to privacy must be respected to the extent consistent with providing adequate medical care to the patient and with the efficient administration of the health-care facility or provider's office. However, this subparagraph does not preclude necessary and discreet discussion of a patient's case of examination by appropriate medical personnel.
3. A patient has the right to a prompt and reasonable response to a question or request. A health-care facility shall respond in a reasonable manner to the request of a patient's health-care provider for medical services to the patient. The health-care facility shall also respond in a reasonable manner to the patient's request for other services customarily rendered by the health-care facility to the extent such services do not require the approval of the patient's health-care provider or are not inconsistent with the patient's treatment.
4. A patient in a health-care facility has the right to retain and use personal clothing or possessions as space permits, unless for him to do so would infringe upon the right of another patient or is medically or programmatically contraindicated for documented medical, safety, or programmatic reasons.

Information

1. A patient has the right to know the name, function, and qualifications of each health-care provider who is providing medical services to the patient. A patient may request such information from his responsible provider or the health-care facility in which he is receiving medical services.

2. A patient in a health-care facility has the right to know what patient support services are available in the facility.

3. A patient has the right to be given by his health-care provider information concerning diagnosis, planned course of treatment, alternatives, risks, and prognosis, unless it is medically inadvisable or impossible to give this information to the patient, in which case the information must be given to the patient's guardian or a person designated as the patient's representative. A patient has the right to refuse this information.

4. A patient has the right to refuse any treatment based on information required by this paragraph, except as otherwise provided by law. The responsible provider shall document any such refusal.

5. A patient in a health-care facility has the right to know what facility rules and regulations apply to patient conduct.

6. A patient has the right to express grievances to a health-care provider, a health-care facility, or the appropriate state licensing agency regarding alleged violations of patients' rights. A patient has the right to know the health-care provider's or health-care facility's procedures for expressing a grievance.

7. A patient in a health-care facility who does not speak English has the right to be provided an interpreter when receiving medical services if the facility has a person readily available who can interpret on behalf of the patient.

Financial Information and Disclosure

1. A patient has the right to be given, upon request, by the responsible provider, his designee, or a representative of the health-care facility full information and necessary counseling on the availability of known financial resources for the patient's health care.

2. A health-care provider or a health-care facility shall, upon request, disclose to each patient who is eligible for Medicare, in advance of treatment, whether the health-care provider or the health-care facility in which the patient is receiving medical services accepts assignment under Medicare reimbursement as payment in full for medical services and treatment rendered in the health-care provider's office or health-care facility.

3. A health-care provider or a health-care facility shall, upon request, furnish a patient, prior to provision of medical services, a reasonable estimate of charges for such services. Such reasonable estimate shall not preclude the health-care provider or health-care facility from exceeding the estimate or making additional charges based upon changes in the patient's condition or treatment needs.

4. A patient has the right to receive a copy of an itemized bill upon request. A patient has a right to be given an explanation of charges upon request.

Access to Health Care

1. A patient has the right to impartial access to medical treatment or accommodations, regardless of race, national origin, religion, physical handicap, or source of payment.

2. A patient has the right to treatment for any emergency medical condition that will deteriorate from failure to provide such treatment.

continues

Patient's Bill of Rights, Continued

Experimental Research

In addition to the provisions of s. 766.103, a patient has the right to know if medical treatment is for purposes of experimental research and to consent prior to participation in such experimental research. For any patient, regardless of ability to pay or source of payment for his care, participation must be a voluntary matter; and a patient has the right to refuse to participate. The patient's consent or refusal must be documented in the patient's care record. [Florida statutes chapter 381 (026).]

APPROXIMATE DATES OF CHILDBIRTH

Find the date of the last menstrual period in the top line (lightface type) of the pair of lines. The dark number (boldface type) in the line below will be the expected day of delivery.

Jan	1	2	3	4	5	6	7	8	9	10	11	12	13	14	15	16	17	18	19	20	21	22	23	24	25	26	27	28	29	30	31		
Oct	**8**	**9**	**10**	**11**	**12**	**13**	**14**	**15**	**16**	**17**	**18**	**19**	**20**	**21**	**22**	**23**	**24**	**25**	**26**	**27**	**28**	**29**	**30**	**31**	**[1**	**2**	**3**	**4**	**5**	**6**	**7**	**Nov**	
Feb	1	2	3	4	5	6	7	8	9	10	11	12	13	14	15	16	17	18	19	20	21	22	23	24	25	26	27	28					
Nov	**8**	**9**	**10**	**11**	**12**	**13**	**14**	**15**	**16**	**17**	**18**	**19**	**20**	**21**	**22**	**23**	**24**	**25**	**26**	**27**	**28**	**29**	**30**	**[1**	**2**	**3**	**4**	**5**	**Dec**				
Mar	1	2	3	4	5	6	7	8	9	10	11	12	13	14	15	16	17	18	19	20	21	22	23	24	25	26	27	28	29	30	31		
Dec	**6**	**7**	**8**	**9**	**10**	**11**	**12**	**13**	**14**	**15**	**16**	**17**	**18**	**19**	**20**	**21**	**22**	**23**	**24**	**25**	**26**	**27**	**28**	**29**	**30**	**31**	**[1**	**2**	**3**	**4**	**5**	**Jan**	
Apr	1	2	3	4	5	6	7	8	9	10	11	12	13	14	15	16	17	18	19	20	21	22	23	24	25	26	27	28	29	30			
Jan	**6**	**7**	**8**	**9**	**10**	**11**	**12**	**13**	**14**	**15**	**16**	**17**	**18**	**19**	**20**	**21**	**22**	**23**	**24**	**25**	**26**	**27**	**28**	**29**	**30**	**31**	**[1**	**2**	**3**	**4**	**Feb**		
May	1	2	3	4	5	6	7	8	9	10	11	12	13	14	15	16	17	18	19	20	21	22	23	24	25	26	27	28	29	30	31		
Feb	**5**	**6**	**7**	**8**	**9**	**10**	**11**	**12**	**13**	**14**	**15**	**16**	**17**	**18**	**19**	**20**	**21**	**22**	**23**	**24**	**25**	**26**	**27**	**28**	**[1**	**2**	**3**	**4**	**5**	**6**	**7**	**Mar**	
June	1	2	3	4	5	6	7	8	9	10	11	12	13	14	15	16	17	18	19	20	21	22	23	24	25	26	27	28	29	30			
Mar	**8**	**9**	**10**	**11**	**12**	**13**	**14**	**15**	**16**	**17**	**18**	**19**	**20**	**21**	**22**	**23**	**24**	**25**	**26**	**27**	**28**	**29**	**30**	**31**	**[1**	**2**	**3**	**4**	**5**	**6**	**Apr**		
July	1	2	3	4	5	6	7	8	9	10	11	12	13	14	15	16	17	18	19	20	21	22	23	24	25	26	27	28	29	30	31		
Apr	**7**	**8**	**9**	**10**	**11**	**12**	**13**	**14**	**15**	**16**	**17**	**18**	**19**	**20**	**21**	**22**	**23**	**24**	**25**	**26**	**27**	**28**	**29**	**30**	**[1**	**2**	**3**	**4**	**5**	**6**	**7**	**May**	
Aug	1	2	3	4	5	6	7	8	9	10	11	12	13	14	15	16	17	18	19	20	21	22	23	24	25	26	27	28	29	30	31		
May	**8**	**9**	**10**	**11**	**12**	**13**	**14**	**15**	**16**	**17**	**18**	**19**	**20**	**21**	**22**	**23**	**24**	**25**	**26**	**27**	**28**	**29**	**30**	**31**	**[1**	**2**	**3**	**4**	**5**	**6**	**7**	**June**	
Sept	1	2	3	4	5	6	7	8	9	10	11	12	13	14	15	16	17	18	19	20	21	22	23	24	25	26	27	28	29	30			
June	**8**	**9**	**10**	**11**	**12**	**13**	**14**	**15**	**16**	**17**	**18**	**19**	**20**	**21**	**22**	**23**	**24**	**25**	**26**	**27**	**28**	**29**	**30**	**[1**	**2**	**3**	**4**	**5**	**6**	**7**	**July**		
Oct	1	2	3	4	5	6	7	8	9	10	11	12	13	14	15	16	17	18	19	20	21	22	23	24	25	26	27	28	29	30	31		
July	**8**	**9**	**10**	**11**	**12**	**13**	**14**	**15**	**16**	**17**	**18**	**19**	**20**	**21**	**22**	**23**	**24**	**25**	**26**	**27**	**28**	**29**	**30**	**31**	**[1**	**2**	**3**	**4**	**5**	**6**	**7**	**Aug**	
Nov	1	2	3	4	5	6	7	8	9	10	11	12	13	14	15	16	17	18	19	20	21	22	23	24	25	26	27	28	29	30			
Aug	**8**	**9**	**10**	**11**	**12**	**13**	**14**	**15**	**16**	**17**	**18**	**19**	**20**	**21**	**22**	**23**	**24**	**25**	**26**	**27**	**28**	**29**	**30**	**31**	**[1**	**2**	**3**	**4**	**5**	**6**	**Sept**		
Dec	1	2	3	4	5	6	7	8	9	10	11	12	13	14	15	16	17	18	19	20	21	22	23	24	25	26	27	28	29	30	31		
Sept	**7**	**8**	**9**	**10**	**11**	**12**	**13**	**14**	**15**	**16**	**17**	**18**	**19**	**20**	**21**	**22**	**23**	**24**	**25**	**26**	**27**	**28**	**29**	**30**	**[1**	**2**	**3**	**4**	**5**	**6**	**7**	**Oct**	

PRECAUTIONS DURING PREGNANCY

Good nutrition and prenatal medical care are essentials for maternal well-being and delivery of a healthy baby. It is also important to be aware of lifestyle habits, environmental hazards, and communicable diseases that may adversely affect the developing child. The following is a list of known risk factors for pregnancy. Consult your doctor for specifics if you are pregnant and have been exposed to one of these hazards.

ALCOHOL

Research has shown that heavy drinking during pregnancy leads to greatly increased chances of a child with fetal alcohol syndrome or some other congenital birth defect. It is not known whether

Health/Nutrition

occasional social drinking is harmful to a developing fetus, so most doctors recommend against any alcohol consumption during pregnancy.

CAFFEINE

Excessive use during pregnancy may cause your baby's birth weight to be a little lower than average. Low birth weight is associated with increased vulnerability to infection and disease. Caffeine is found in tea, coffee, chocolate, some cola drinks, and some over-the-counter medications.

CHEMICALS

Prolonged exposure to lead, arsenic, formaldehyde, mercury, benzene, or ethylene oxide (or inhalation of their fumes) may increase the chances of having a miscarriage.

CHICKEN POX (VARICELLA)

When a pregnant mother develops chicken pox, the fetus has a 25 percent chance of also becoming infected. A small number of infants affected develop birth defects, including scars, eye problems, poor growth, an underdeveloped limb, small head size, delayed development, and/or mental retardation. The fetus is most at risk if the mother develops chicken pox between the eighth and twentieth weeks of pregnancy. Infection shortly before delivery can cause serious problems for the newborn, but the baby can be treated with a vaccine to prevent/lessen chicken pox's effects. The vaccine is not recommended during pregnancy, however, as its effects on the developing fetus are not yet clear.

DRUGS AND MEDICATIONS

Drug use during pregnancy can result in addicted infants who experience painful, life-threatening withdrawal symptoms after birth. In addition, some drugs and prescription and nonprescription medications may cause birth defects or can cause complications during pregnancy and childbirth. Always consult your physician regarding pregnancy and medication usage.

Go to "Disposal of Hazardous Household Chemicals" in chapter 19; "Average Cost of Raising a Child" in chapter 20; and "Family Planning in chapter 22

FIFTH DISEASE (ERYTHEMA INFECTIOSUM)

Fifth disease is caused by a virus and occurs most often in children from ages 4 to 14. Symptoms include a mild fever, sore throat, flulike aches or pains, a bright red rash on the face, and a bumpy rash on other parts of the body. Adults often have no noticeable symptoms and children may not show symptoms until several weeks after infection. Contracting fifth disease in pregnancy (especially during the first half) can cause miscarriage, stillbirth, or heart problems if the fetus is also infected.

HOT TUBS, SAUNAS, AND STEAM BATHS

Research indicates that an increase in the mother's core body temperature may cause developmental abnormalities in the fetus, premature labor, or both. Hot showers or baths at home are okay, but saunas, steam baths, and immersion above the hips in hot tubs should be avoided.

MEASLES

Pregnant women who contract red measles (rubella) may have an increased risk of miscarriage or delivering an infant with low birth weight. Infection with German measles during pregnancy is known to put the fetus at risk for development of birth defects.

RADIATION

Avoid X rays of the abdomen whenever possible during pregnancy. X rays of the head, mouth, and extremities are permissible if medical staff are aware of your condition and take proper precautions. Also avoid environmental areas where excess radiation may be present, as prenatal exposure to radiation can cause birth defects.

Health/Nutrition

Vaccines

Vaccines are disease-specific immunizations. Here are the periods of effectiveness for common vaccines:

A Closer Look

Vaccine	Immunization Period
Combination (diphtheria, tetanus toxoids, and whooping cough)	Unknown
Diphtheria (antitoxin)	2–3 months
Diphtheria (toxoid)	Unknown
Measles (attenuated virus)	Over 10 years
Measles (immune blood serum, gamma globulin, or placental extract)	A few weeks
Mumps (attenuated virus)	Probably life
Poliomyelitis (dead or attenuated virus)	Unknown
Rabies (attenuated virus)	Unknown
Rubella (attenuated virus)	Unknown
Tetanus (antitoxin)	A few weeks
Tetanus (toxoid)	Unknown
Typhoid (dead germs)	2–3 years
Whooping cough (dead germs)	2–5 years

SMOKING

Research has shown that heavy smoking (more than a pack of cigarettes per day) results in smaller babies with increased vulnerability to infection and illness. Smoking during pregnancy also increases the risk of miscarriage or stillbirth. As with the use of alcohol, it is not known whether any level of smoking is completely safe for the developing fetus, so it is best to stop smoking completely before becoming pregnant.

TOXOPLASMOSIS

Toxoplasmosis is a parasitic infection usually contracted by eating undercooked infected meat, raw eggs, or unpasturized milk; handling infected soil; or handling cat litter from an outdoor cat that is infected. About 40 percent of women who become infected during pregnancy will pass the infection on to their unborn infants. Fetal infections may interfere with development of the brain, eyes, heart, kidneys, blood, liver, or spleen.

IMMUNIZATION SCHEDULE FOR INFANTS, CHILDREN, AND ADULTS

The following information is based on U.S. Preventive Services Task Force Recommendations.

Children Under 10 Years Old

Immunizations	Frequency
DTaP or DTP (Diptheria/ tetanus/pertussis[1])	5 immunizations: at 2, 4, and 6 mos., between 15–18 mos.; and once between 4–6 yrs.
Polio	4 immunizations: at 2, 4, between 6–18 mos., 4–6 yrs.
MMR (Measles, mumps, rubella)	2 immunizations: between 12–15 mos. and 4–6 yrs. If missed, give by ages 11–12.
H. influenzae[2] type B (hib)	3 or 4 immunizations, depending on the vaccine: at 2, 4, and 6 mos. and between 12–15 mos.
Hepatitis B	3 immunizations: at birth, 1 mo., and 6 mos.; or between 0–2 mos., 1–2 mos. later, and between 6–18 mos.
Varicella[3]	1 immunization: between 12–18 mos., or anytime for older children with no previous immunization and no history of chicken pox

Ages 11 to 24

Immunizations	Frequency
Tetanus-diphtheria (Td)	1 booster between 11–16 yrs. and then periodically[4]
Hepatitis B	If not previously immunized, 3 immunizations: at current (next) visit, 1 mo. later, and 6 mos. later
MMR	1 immunization: between 11–12 yrs. if second dose was not received at 4–6 yrs.
Varicella	1 immunization: between 11–12 yrs. if susceptible to chicken pox
Rubella	1 immunization: after 12 yrs. for females who are not pregnant

Ages 25 to 64

Rubella serology or vaccination history	1 immunization: recommended for all females of childbearing age
Tetanus-diphtheria (Td)	1 booster every 10 yrs., or as recommended[4]

Ages 65 and Older

Tetanus-diphtheria (Td)	1 booster every 10 yrs., or as recommended[4]
Pneumonia	1 immunization: administered one time to all people whose immune systems have not been compromised[4]
Influenza	1 immunization: annually

[1] Whooping cough   [2] Influenza (the flu)   [3] Chicken pox   [4] Discuss with your physician

For more information, call the Centers for Disease Control's National Immunization Information Hot Line at 800-232-2522 (English) or 800-232-0233 (Spanish), or visit the Web site at http://www.cdc.gov/nip.

EXPECTED NUMBER OF DEATHS AT GIVEN PERIODS OF LIFE PER 100,000 INFANTS BORN ALIVE IN 1995

Period of Life (Birthday to Birthday)	Number of Deaths During Interval	Number of Persons Remaining (Alive) at End of Interval
At birth	N/A	100,000
Birth to age 1	757	99,243
1 to 5	159	99,084
5 to 10	98	98,986
10 to 15	125	98,861
15 to 20	410	98,451
20 to 25	527	97,924
25 to 30	583	97,341
30 to 35	779	96,562
35 to 40	1,013	95,549
40 to 45	1,315	94,234
45 to 50	1,755	92,479
50 to 55	2,586	89,893
55 to 60	3,844	86,049
60 to 65	5,770	80,279
65 to 70	7,888	72,391
70 to 75	10,573	1,818
75 to 80	13,140	48,678
80 to 85	15,520	33,158
85 and above	33,158	0

Source: U.S. National Center for Health Statistics, *Monthly Vital Statistics Report* (Vol. 45, No. 11, Sec. 2, June 12, 1997).

Health/Nutrition

LIFE EXPECTANCY IN 1995 BY RACE, SEX, AND AGE

EXPECTATION OF LIFE IN YEARS					
Exact Age in Years at Birth	Total Population	White		All Other Races	
		Males	Females	Males	Females
1	75.8	73.4	79.6	67.9	75.7
5	75.4	72.9	79.0	67.8	75.6
10	71.5	69.1	75.1	64.0	71.7
15	66.6	64.1	70.2	59.1	66.8
20	61.6	59.2	65.2	54.2	61.9
25	56.9	54.5	60.4	49.6	57.0
30	52.2	49.9	55.5	45.2	52.3
35	47.5	45.2	50.6	40.8	47.5
40	42.8	40.7	45.8	36.6	42.9
45	38.3	36.1	41.0	32.4	38.3
50	33.8	31.7	36.3	28.5	33.9
55	29.3	27.3	31.7	24.6	29.6
60	25.1	23.2	27.3	21.0	25.4
65	21.1	19.3	23.0	17.6	21.5
70	17.4	15.7	19.1	14.5	17.9
75	14.1	12.5	15.4	11.7	14.5
80	11.0	9.7	12.0	9.3	11.5
85	8.3	7.2	8.9	7.0	8.7
90	6.0	5.2	6.3	5.2	6.3

Sources: U.S. National Center for Health Statistics, *Vital Statistics of the United States* (annual) and *Monthly Vital Statistics Report* (Vol. 45, No. 11, Sec. 2, June 12, 1997).

RECOMMENDED WEIGHTS

FOR ADULTS ONLY: CALCULATING THE BODY MASS INDEX

Nutritionists and fitness experts have moved away from using desirable weight and height charts to determine whether adult clients should gain or lose weight for optimum health. (Height/weight charts are still used for children because their bodies change so rapidly.) The current measure of fatness or leanness is the Body Mass Index (BMI). To calculate your BMI, use this formula:

$$\frac{[\textit{your weight in pounds}] \times 703}{[\textit{your height in inches}] \times [\textit{your height in inches}]} = \text{BMI}$$

For example, if you weigh 150 pounds and are 5 feet 6 inches tall, your BMI would be as follows:

$$\frac{125 \times 703}{66 \times 66} = \frac{105,450}{4,356} = 24.2$$

If the result is less than 25, you are not overweight. If the result is more than 25, you are considered overweight according to the federal health guidelines released in June 1998. However, some individuals, such as weightlifters and professional athletes, may have a high BMI without being overweight, while others may have a near-normal BMI but have too much weight concentrated around their waistline. Seek a doctor's advice if your BMI is 25 or more or if you're unsure of your status.

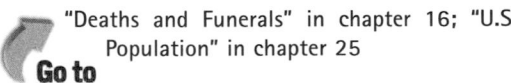 "Deaths and Funerals" in chapter 16; "U.S. Population" in chapter 25
Go to

HEIGHT AND WEIGHT CHARTS FOR CHILDREN

DESIRABLE WEIGHTS IN POUNDS FOR BOYS 5 TO 18 YEARS OLD

Height (in inches)	Age (in years)													
	5	6	7	8	9	10	11	12	13	14	15	16	17	18
38	34	34												
39	35	35												
40	36	36												
41	38	38	38											
42	39	39	39	39										
43	41	41	41	41										
44	44	44	44	44										
45	46	46	46	46	46									
46	47	48	48	48	48									
47	49	50	50	50	50	50								
48		52	53	53	53	53								
49		55	55	55	55	55	55							
50		57	58	58	58	58	58	58						
51			61	61	61	61	61	61	61					
52			63	64	64	64	64	64	64					
53			66	67	67	67	67	68	68					
54				70	70	70	70	71	71	72				
55				72	72	73	73	74	74	74				
56				75	76	77	77	77	78	78	80			
57					79	80	81	81	82	83	83			
58					83	84	84	85	85	86	87			
59						87	88	89	89	90	90	90		
60						91	92	92	93	94	95	96		
61							95	96	97	99	100	103	106	
62							100	101	102	103	104	107	111	116
63							105	106	107	108	110	113	118	123
64								109	111	113	115	117	121	126
65								114	117	118	120	122	127	131
66									119	122	125	128	132	136
67									124	128	130	134	136	139
68										134	134	137	141	143
69										137	139	143	146	149
70										143	144	145	148	151
71										148	150	151	152	154
72											153	155	156	158
73											157	160	162	164
74											160	164	168	170

Health/Nutrition

Go to "Children" in chapter 22; "Parenting" in chapter 22

DESIRABLE WEIGHTS IN POUNDS FOR GIRLS 5 TO 18 YEARS OLD

Height (in inches)	Age (in years)													
	5	6	7	8	9	10	11	12	13	14	15	16	17	18
38	33	33												
39	34	34												
40	36	36	36											
41	37	37	37											
42	39	39	39											
43	41	41	41	41										
44	42	42	42	42										
45	45	45	45	45	45									
46	47	47	47	48	48									
47	49	50	50	50	50	50								
48		52	52	52	52	53	53							
49			54	55	55	56	56							
50			56	57	58	59	61	62						
51			59	60	61	61	63	65						
52			63	64	64	64	65	67						
53			66	67	67	68	68	69	71					
54				69	70	70	71	71	73					
55				72	74	74	74	75	77	78				
56					76	78	78	79	81	83				
57					80	82	82	82	84	88	92			
58						84	86	86	88	93	96	101		
59						87	90	90	92	96	100	103	104	
60						91	95	95	97	101	105	108	109	111
61							99	100	101	105	108	112	113	116
62							104	105	106	109	113	115	117	118
63								110	110	112	116	117	119	120
64								114	115	117	119	120	122	123
65								118	120	121	122	123	125	126
66									124	124	125	128	129	130
67									128	130	131	133	133	135
68									131	133	135	136	138	138
69										135	137	138	140	142
70										136	138	140	142	144
71										138	140	142	144	145

HOME REMEDIES

The following should not be considered medical advice and is prepared for informational purposes only. Always consult a professional health-care practitioner for medical problems. Do not give aspirin to children under the age of 15 unless directed by a physician.

Go to "Treatment for Health Emergencies" and "Directory of Poison Control Centers" in chapter 17

ALLERGIES, SEASONAL

Symptoms   Watery eyes, stuffy nose, coughing. *Asthma* symptoms include a wheezing/hacking cough that may get worse at night, causes a tight feeling in the chest, and is often accompanied by panicky feelings of being unable to breathe. See your doctor if you experience these symptoms.

Remedies   Drink plenty of fluids to flush your system of allergens. Avoid strenuous exercise, especially if it causes asthmatic wheezing (see your doctor). Sleep with your head/chest elevated to facilitate breathing. Don't smoke or wear cologne, and avoid others who do. Keep your home and office dust-free (vacuum with a special filter, if necessary). Stay away from known irritants, such as smoke, perfumes, animals, and outdoor activities. Over-the-counter antihistamines and analgesics usually provide some relief, but remember that antihistamines cause drowsiness, and follow package directions carefully. Decongestants can provide temporary relief, but nasal congestion may return when use is discontinued. Horseradish and red/cayenne pepper can also be used as decongestants, either by adding them to food or by placing a small pinch under the nostrils or on the tongue. Get plenty of rest, and see your doctor if symptoms persist.

BACK PAIN FROM MUSCLE STRAIN

Symptoms Pain that occurs when you move the affected portion of your back, which may ache and be sore to the touch; swelling and bruising may be present in severe cases. (Always call your doctor about sudden, unexpected back pain that occurs for no reason or about pain that moves from one body part to another, is severe, lasts more than 2 to 3 days, or is accompanied by fever or vomiting.)

Remedies Rest in bed to take pressure off the back and allow it to heal. Take analgesics, such as aspirin, ibuprofen, naproxen sodium, or acetaminophen. If there is swelling or bruising, apply a cold pack (ice in a plastic bag wrapped in a towel) for 20 minutes and then remove the pack for 20 minutes, repeating this process for 2 to 3 hours.

BURNS, FIRST-DEGREE

Symptoms A feeling of heat with pain and reddening but no blistering. If signs of infection (fever, chills, swelling, increased redness, or pus in the burned area) develop, seek medical attention. (Always see a doctor for more serious burns or any that cover a large area of the body.)

Remedies Hold the burned area under cold tap water for 5 to 10 minutes to stop the burn process and reduce the amount of skin damage. (Don't apply ice or ice water, which can further damage the skin.) Leave the burn uncovered and keep it elevated, if possible. Use a dry, sterile dressing if necessary. Do not rub butter or salve onto the burn, as this can cause more damage. Analgesics may be taken orally to relieve pain, but experts advise against using local anesthetic sprays or ointments, as these can slow the healing process and may cause allergic reactions. *See also* "Treatment for Health Emergencies: Burns" in chapter 17.

COLDS, SORE THROATS, AND COUGHS DUE TO COLDS

Symptoms Sneezing, runny nose, slight fever (101°F or less). Call a doctor if any of the following symptoms develop: a bright red sore throat; difficulty breathing or wheezing; irritability; lethargy; confusion/delirium; earache; visible pus deposits in the throat; enlarged/tender neck glands; persistent dry cough; cough that produces thick yellow-green or gray phlegm; a bad odor from the throat, nose, or ears; or a fever of over 103°F (104°F in a child under 12, 100.5°F in an infant less than two months old, or 102°F in an adult over 60).

Remedies Bed rest if feverish; plenty of fluids; analgesics for aches and pains; chicken soup; foods and drinks rich in vitamin C.

Influenza was so named by 15th-century Italians because they thought the disease was caused by the influence of the stars and planets.

CONSTIPATION

Symptoms Hard, small, dry bowel movements (usually fewer than three times a week); pain and difficulty having bowel movements; feeling bloated and uncomfortable; an urge to defecate but inability to do so.

Remedies   Drink plenty of water (8 to 10 glasses per day) and exercise regularly. Eat foods containing plenty of fiber, such as beans, whole grain and bran cereals, fresh fruits, and vegetables (such as asparagus, brussels sprouts, cabbage, and carrots). Respond immediately to the urge to have a bowel movement—putting it off is one of the major causes of constipation, especially in busy, stressed people. Adults and children may become constipated from a reluctance to defecate in public bathrooms (at school or work) because of lack of privacy or time constraints. If this is a problem, try eating fruit or cereal an hour before bedtime and setting the alarm to rise 30 minutes earlier than usual. Eat a high-fiber breakfast soon after getting out of bed. Then shower, dress, and prepare for the day. The extra fiber, early breakfast, and morning time to spare will facilitate the occurrence of bowel movements before leaving home for the day. Keep in mind that bowel movements are a very individual matter; some people normally have more than one a day, but for others, three or four times a week is the norm. Laxatives, stool softeners, and enemas should be used rarely and with great caution, as they are habit-forming. If you become dependent on such products, gradually reduce the amount used while making healthy lifestyle changes; abrupt withdrawal can cause serious problems. Extreme constipation can result in intestinal blockage— a very serious matter—so it is important to check with your doctor if constipation is a long-standing problem or causes major discomfort.

FLU (INFLUENZA)

Symptoms   Headache, general aches and pains, fatigue, chills, fever up to 104°F, burning sensation in the eyes, dry cough. Symptoms may resemble a cold but are more severe and develop faster; the person seems to get sick very quickly. People over age 65 and those with chronic illnesses should receive annual influenza immunizations, as complications from the flu can be severe.

Remedies   Bed rest, analgesics for aches and pains, and warm fluids. Use over-the-counter

medications to reduce symptoms if desired, but be sure to follow directions carefully. Decongestants can provide temporary relief, but nasal congestion may return when use is discontinued. Horseradish and red/cayenne pepper can also be used as decongestants, either by adding them to food or placing a small pinch under the nostrils or on the tongue.

HEADACHES

Symptoms   Generalized pain in the head or neck area. (Seek medical attention for pain that is localized on one side of the face or head; sudden, severe headaches of any type; persistent pain accompanied by nausea, high fever, or other symptoms; pain resulting from an injury or blow to the head or face; or pain accompanied by disorientation, drowsiness, or confusion.)

Remedies   Relax in a quiet area. Eat a nutritional meal if your stomach is empty. Take analgesics to relieve pain. Apply heat to relax tense muscles in the neck and shoulders. Use ice packs on the head itself. Wipe the brow and neck with vinegar. Some headaches respond well to aspirin and hot coffee; others are made worse by caffeine. If headaches are frequent, try to identify their cause (stress, hunger, menstrual cycle, certain foods) and work to remove it.

HICCUPS

Symptoms   Quick, jerky inhalations accompanied by a peculiar noise, caused by a spasmodic jerking of the diaphragm muscle. Hiccups usually stop within a few minutes but can continue for hours, days, or weeks. Sometimes the condition even requires hospitalization because they disturb sleep and preclude normal respiration. Call your health-care provider if hiccups continue more than 1 day.

Remedies   Regular, rhythmic breathing. The diaphragm muscle is not under voluntary control, but forcing yourself to breathe in a very regular pattern should get it back into a normal rhythm. Take deep enough breaths so that the diaphragm area (center of the lower rib cage down to the waist) moves in and out; quick shallow breaths that move only the upper chest will not solve the problem. (Avoid very deep, too-slow breaths, as these may cause hyperventilation.) If the hiccups do not respond within a minute or two, wait 5 minutes and try again. If you still have no success, try holding your breath. Breathe out until you have emptied your lungs as much as possible and then hold it as long as you can without becoming really uncomfortable. Then take a deep breath and hold it (again, only until you begin to feel uncomfortable). Breathe normally for a few minutes to see if the hiccups subside; then repeat.

HYPERVENTILATION

Symptoms   Dizziness, shortness of breath, chest pain or tightness, numbness/tingling of the extremities or around the mouth. In most cases, there is no obvious breathing irregularity—that is, one cannot tell that the hyperventilating person is breathing too deeply or too fast.

Remedies   Until medical attention is available, hold a paper bag over the mouth and nose, crumpling the edges so that little air can escape. Exhale into the bag and then inhale while still holding it over the mouth and nose. Repeat this procedure until symptoms subside (sometimes it takes several minutes).

Note: The symptoms of hyperventilation are also symptoms of some life-threatening medical conditions. Also, frequent/chronic hyperventilation can cause serious complications. Therefore, it is recommended that you seek medical attention immediately if any of the symptoms described here are present, even if hyperventilation is suspected.)

INDIGESTION

Symptoms   Mild abdominal discomfort soon after eating; feeling "too full" after a heavy meal.

Remedies   Drink $1/2$ cup of tepid water mixed with 1 tablespoon of vinegar, 1 tablespoon of lemon juice, or the juice of one freshly squeezed lime.

INSECT BITES

Symptoms   Localized pain, itching, swelling. (If allergic symptoms such as all-over itching, a rash, or breathing difficulties occur, seek emergency medical attention immediately.)

Remedies   For bee stings, a drop of ammonia applied directly to the wound will often stop the pain and prevent swelling; alternatively, use an antihistamine gel or ointment. If bites are numerous, you may want to take an over-the-counter antihistamine orally to reduce discomfort, but remember that such products usually make you drowsy. *See also* "Treatment for Health Emergencies: Insect Bites" in chapter 17.

On his first voyage to the South Pacific, Captain Cook lost almost half of his crew to scurvy (caused by lack of vitamin C). Once the cause of scurvy was discovered, lemon juice was issued on all British navy ships.

INSOMNIA

Symptoms   Inability to fall or stay asleep at night despite feeling tired and in need of rest, resulting in daytime drowsiness and fatigue. Symptoms may include feelings of anxiety, obsessive thinking or planning, or excessive worrying when trying to fall asleep.

Remedies   Get plenty of exercise in the late afternoon or early evening, but avoid strenuous workouts just before bedtime. Don't take naps during the day. Set a regular bedtime and stick to it (at least until difficulties are resolved), and also set a regular time to wake up. A light snack before bedtime may be helpful, but don't overdo it. Try wheat germ, brown rice, celery, milk, turkey, bananas, figs, yogurt, or tuna snacks because they are rich in tryptophan, an amino acid that promotes sleep. Avoid potatoes, cheese, chocolate, tomatoes, and spinach, all of which contain tryamine, a stimulant.

If you smoke, try to cut down—nicotine is a powerful stimulant. Work to reduce other chemical/nutritional stimulants, too, such as iced tea, colas, and coffee. Decrease alcohol consumption and review all medications (prescription and over-the-counter) for their side effects. If you have been taking any form of sleep aid, your body needs time to adjust to falling asleep on its own. If anxiety or stress is keeping you awake, spend time relaxing before going to bed. Soak in a warm bath, gaze into the fireplace, or listen to music by candlelight (gazing at a lighted candle can actually make you sleepy). Once in bed, try not to dwell on your problems. Take some deep, slow breaths, and think soothing thoughts. If you do not fall asleep within 15 or 20 minutes, get out of bed and go into another room. Engage in a relaxing activity until you feel sleepy, and then go back to bed and try again.

PREMENSTRUAL SYNDROME (PMS)

Symptoms   Feeling bloated, out of sorts, irritable, and/or depressed.

Remedies   Make a calendar charting menstrual periods and PMS symptoms over several months and use it to predict the next episode. Cut down on salty foods, chocolate, and caffeine for a day or two prior to anticipated onset. Try to reschedule stressful events that occur during periods of PMS; avoid highly emotional situations and postpone major decisions until hormone levels return to normal. Get plenty of rest, exercise, and good nutrition. When PMS symptoms occur, drink plenty of water to reduce water retention and flush impurities from the system. Take diuretics only on the advice of a physician, as overuse can cause serious medical problems.

RASHES, PLANT–ALLERGY

Symptoms   Redness and/or small bumps accompanied by itching, usually after contact with plants such as poison oak or poison ivy.

Remedies   Calamine lotion may provide some relief, but an over-the-counter antihistamine gel or ointment will work better. Taking oral antihistamines may be necessary, especially at bedtime, to avoid scratching and infecting the area. Rashes due to contact with such plants may persist for weeks, are easily spread and infected by scratching, and are difficult to cure at home. If symptoms are still present in 2 to 3 days, see your doctor. *See also* "Poisonous Cultivated and Wild Plants" in chapter 3; "Treatment for Health Emergencies: Poisoning: Plant Poisons" in chapter 17.

RASHES, HEAT

Symptoms   Redness and a burning sensation when skin is touched.

Remedies   Take a cool (not cold) bath; apply cool compresses wet with a solution of baking soda and water, or apply calamine lotion. Leave the area open to the air if possible to avoid irritation, and stay out of the heat. If rash persists, see your doctor.

(*Note:* Some rashes are symptoms of illnesses such as infection or food allergies. If you do not know what may have caused a rash, see your doctor, especially if symptoms persist.)

If you burn your mouth when eating spicy foods, instead of reaching for water, eat something sweet.

SPRAINS AND STRAINS OF THE ANKLE, FOOT, HAND, WRIST, OR ELBOW

Symptoms   Pain and swelling of the injured limb (full range of motion still present; limb still capable of bearing weight). Seek medical attention if the skin is broken, the limb cannot move normally in all directions, numbness/blue discoloration occurs, or bones seem out of place and are painful when pressed.

Remedies   Elevate the injured limb to reduce swelling. Apply an ice pack to the injured area for

20 minutes; then remove the pack for 20 minutes. Repeat this cycle until swelling stops or improves. Rest the limb as much as possible to prevent further injury, and keep it elevated. After the first few days, applying heat to the area will promote healing, but do not apply heat initially as this can make swelling worse. You may wrap the injured limb loosely in a stretch bandage for support and comfort. Analgesics may be taken for the pain. See your doctor if symptoms are still present after 5 days. *See also* "Treatment for Health Emergencies: Fractures, Dislocations, and Sprains" in chapter 17.

STREP THROAT

Symptoms   Redness and pain or burning sensation when swallowing. If neck glands are swollen or tender, see your doctor. Strep throat symptoms include white pus areas in the back of the throat; fever; sometimes headaches, stomach pain, or a rash on the body. (However, these symptoms do not always indicate strep throat, and one may have strep throat without experiencing these symptoms.) Consult your physician if symptoms of strep throat appear, if pain is severe, or if a sore throat persists more than 2 to 3 days.

Remedies   Cut down on smoking, rest your voice, and use a humidifier or vaporizer to moisten the air. (Smoking, excessive vocalizing, and too-low humidity can cause or aggravate coughs and sore throats.) Throat soothers include gargling with salt water several times a day ($^1/_2$ to 1 teaspoon of salt in a cup of warm water), hot tea with lemon and honey, and medicated throat lozenges. (Plain lemon drops work well, too; the sourness stimulates the production of saliva to moisten your throat.) Analgesics may be taken to relieve pain.

LOOKING FOR SIGNS OF BREAST CANCER

It is important for you to know the signs of breast cancer, because most breast cancers are discovered by women themselves, not their doctors. If you discover any of the signs of breast cancer, see your doctor immediately. It is a frightening experience to find a lump or another possible cancer sign, but you should know that 8 of 10 lumps are *not* cancerous. Many women have naturally lumpy breasts. But your doctor should determine whether a lump or other sign is actually cancer or a harmless condition.

To find out how many calories it takes to maintain your current weight, multiply your weight by 15.

ASK FOR A BREAST EXAM

Don't be embarrassed. Asking your doctor or nurse for a breast examination as part of an office visit is one good way to learn what is normal for your breasts. But examination by a doctor is not enough—you, too, should examine your breasts monthly. Ask your doctor or nurse to teach you breast self-examination (BSE) to be sure you are practicing it correctly.

PRACTICE BREAST SELF-EXAMINATION (BSE)

Breast self-examination (BSE) is an important key to early diagnosis. Along with regular examination by your physician, monthly BSE can give you peace of mind because it helps you know how your breasts normally feel.

Knowing the normal feel of your breasts makes it easier to notice any changes early, when treatment is most effective. To examine your breasts correctly, you should follow the six steps described page 512.

WHEN TO EXAMINE YOUR BREASTS

Every month! If you menstruate, the best time to practice breast self-examination (BSE) is 2 or 3 days after the end of your period, when your breasts are least likely to be tender or swollen. If you no longer menstruate, choose a day such as your birth date to practice BSE. That way, you will remember to do it every month.

HOW TO PERFORM A BREAST SELF-EXAMINATION

1. Stand before a mirror. Inspect both breasts for anything unusual, such as any discharge from the nipples or puckering, dimpling, or scaling of the skin.

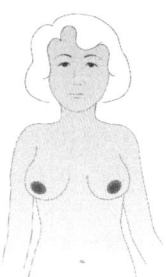

2. Watching closely in the mirror, clasp hands behind your head and press hands forward. This step and step 3 are designed to emphasize any changes in the shape or contour of your breasts. As you do them, you should be able to feel your chest muscles tighten.

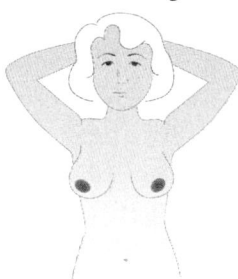

3. Press hands firmly on hips and bow slightly toward the mirror as you pull your shoulders and elbows forward.

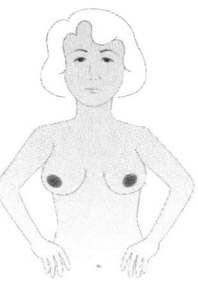

Note: Some women do the next part of the exam in the shower: Fingers glide over soapy skin, making it easy to concentrate on the texture underneath.

4. Raise your left arm. Use three or four fingers of your right hand to explore your left breast firmly, carefully, and thoroughly. Beginning at the outer edge, press the flat part of your fingers in small circles, moving the circles slowly around the breast. Gradually work toward the nipple. Be sure to cover the entire breast. Pay special attention to the area between the breast and the armpit, including the armpit itself. Feel for any unusual lump or mass under the skin.

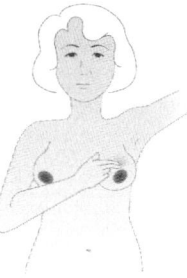

5. Gently squeeze the nipple and look for a discharge. Repeat the exam on your right breast.

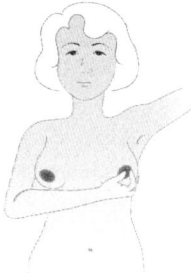

6. Repeat steps 4 and 5 lying down. Lie flat on your back with your left arm over your head and a pillow or folded towel under your left shoulder. This position flattens the breast and makes it easier to examine. Use the same circular motion described earlier. Repeat on your right breast.

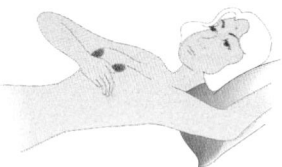

WHEN TO GET A MAMMOGRAM

The National Cancer Institute, the American College of Radiology, and the American Cancer Society recommend regular mammograms for women over 40, either annually, or once every 2 years, depending on a woman's age and medical history. Detection through mammography screening can lead to early treatment, adding years to the lives of women receiving such treatment.

Unfortunately, only a little more than a third of American women follow these guidelines. Of the 34 million women who do not get mammograms as recommended, about 4 million are expected to contract breast cancer at some point.

The ventriloquist Paul Winchell was not only the voice of Tigger in the Winnie the Pooh *films, he also invented the artificial heart. He donated the patent for his life-saving device to the University of Utah.*

Consult your physician for more information about whether it is time for you to get a mammogram.

INFECTIOUS DISEASES AND HOW THEY ARE SPREAD

Disease	Agent	Transmission
AIDS (acquired immune deficiency syndrome)	Virus	Contact of body fluid (semen, blood, vaginal secretions) with that of an infected person. Sexual contact and sharing of unclean paraphernalia for intravenous drugs are the most common means of transmission.
Blastomycosis	Fungus	Inhaling contaminated dust
Botulism	Bacteria	Consuming contaminated food
Chicken pox	Virus	Direct or indirect contact with infected person
Common cold	Virus	Direct or indirect contact with infected person
Diphtheria	Bacteria	Direct contact with infected person
Encephalitis	Virus	Mosquito bite
Gonorrhea	Bacteria	Sexual contact
Hepatitis	Virus	Direct or indirect contact with infected person
Herpes simplex	Virus	Direct contact with infected person
Histoplasmosis	Fungus	Inhaling contaminated dust
Hookworm	Nematode	Contact with contaminated soil
Infectious mononucleosis	Virus	Direct or indirect contact with infected person
Influenza	Virus	Direct or indirect contact with infected person
Lyme disease	Bacteria	Deer tick bite
Malaria	Protozoa	Mosquito bite
Measles	Virus	Direct or indirect contact with infected person
Mumps	Virus	Direct or indirect contact with infected person
Pertussis (whooping cough)	Bacteria	Direct or indirect contact with infected person
Poliomyelitis	Virus	Direct contact with infected person
Rubella (German measles)	Virus	Direct or indirect contact with infected person
Scarlet fever	Bacteria	Direct or indirect contact with infected person
Spotted fever	Rickettsia	Tick bite
Syphilis	Bacteria	Sexual contact
Tapeworm	Nematode	Consuming infected meat or fish
Toxoplasmosis	Protozoa	Consuming raw meat; contact with contaminated soil
Trichomoniasis	Protozoa	Sexual contact
Typhus	Rickettsia	Lice, flea, tick bite
Yellow fever	Virus	Mosquito bite

DENTAL CARE

Dental-care professionals offer the following advice to maintain healthy teeth that will last a lifetime:

1. Have regular dental checkups.
2. Limit the amount of sugary foods you eat, and brush teeth immediately after eating sweets.
3. Brush teeth at least twice daily with a fluoride toothpaste.
4. Use a toothbrush with rounded bristles and be sure it is not too hard. Look for one that has American Dental Association (ADA) approval. And get a new toothbrush every 3 to 4 months—worn-down bristles do not clean your teeth well.
5. Floss regularly—at least once per day.
6. Drink fluoridated water (available in about half of the cities and towns in the United States). For added protection, especially if fluoridated water is not available, your dentist may prescribe a fluoridated gel, rinse, or tablet. Fluoride drops can be used for infants.
7. Follow other recommendations from your dentist concerning tooth and gum care.

Osteopathy

Osteopathic physicians (D.O.s) are licensed to perform surgery, prescribe medication, and specialize in all areas of medicine from neurosurgery to psychiatry. Their approach to treatment emphasizes the importance of body mechanics and manipulative methods to detect and correct faulty structure and function. Noninvasive therapies are used whenever possible, with the goal of restoring the body to health by freeing it to heal itself. Osteopaths are specially trained in manual treatment of musculoskeletal disorders. They can specialize in sports medicine as well as pediatrics, general practice, or obstetrics/gynecology. They utilize generally accepted physical, pharmacological, and surgical methods of diagnosis.

For more information, contact the American Osteopathic Association's Public Relations Department, 142 E. Ontario St., Chicago, IL 60611 (telephone: 800-621-1773 or 312-280-5800), or see its Web site at http://www.am-osteo-assn.org/.

Chiropractic

Chiropractic is based on the philosophy that the structure of the human body, particularly the spinal column, has a profound effect on the functioning of all systems and organs of the body. Manipulation of the spine is perhaps the best-known type of chiropractic treatment. Its purpose is to align misplaced vertebrae to relieve unhealthy pressure on the nerves connecting the brain and body, thus restoring all functions to health. Doctors of Chiropractic (D.C.s) base their diagnoses on information collected via physical examination, patient history, X rays, magnetic resonance imagings (MRIs), laboratory tests, and other traditional diagnostic tools. Their whole-person approach may include physiological therapeutics—such as heat or massage, acupuncture, trigger point therapy, and counseling on stress management and lifestyle issues—as well as spinal and extravertebral manipulations. Treatment does not include pharmaceutical or surgical interventions, but nutritional counseling is often provided, as chiropractic doctors receive intensive education in all aspects of healthy nutrition.

For more information, contact the American Chiropractic Association, 1701 Clarendon Blvd., Arlington, VA 22209 (telephone: 703-276-8800; fax: 703-243-2593), or stop by the Chiropractic Online service at Web site http://www.amerchiro.org/.

Fluoride is a mineral that is present in most water to some extent. The water-fluoridation process used in the United States since 1945 is a means of ensuring that everyone receives the benefits of enough fluoride to prevent the tooth decay that seemed inevitable before its implementation. Fluoride is important to oral health for several reasons:

- It helps to deactivate the bacteria that cause tooth decay.
- It is an essential part of the repair process as tooth enamel rebuilds small areas of decay before large cavities form.
- It makes tooth enamel more resistant to the acid formed by bacteria.

Fluoride is most effective on the smooth surfaces of the teeth and least effective on the chewing surfaces on the back teeth (molars). Regular brushing

---

A Closer Look

Homeopathy

The homeopathic approach to health care treats the whole person—body, mind, and spirit. One of its basic principles is the Law of Similars, which advocates stimulation of the body's own defense system by ingesting minute amounts of a substance that produces the same symptoms as the illness. (Homeopathic physicians point out that this approach is similar to the process of immunization used in conventional medicine.) The second basic principle is the use of minimum dosage to produce effective results. This concept is based on many practitioners' experience that use of an extreme dilution of the required substance (reducing the amount of substance to 1 part in 10,000 or even 100,000) produces better results than a stronger dosage. In addition to these foundations for treatment, homeopathic practitioners believe that symptoms of illness are often the body's own defense at work, and that treatment based on suppressing symptoms may interfere with the body's own healing process.

Health-care providers who practice homeopathy may be identified by one or more of these sets of initials:

RSHom (NA)	Member of the Registered Society of Homeopaths in North America
DHANP	Diplomate of the Homeopathic Association of Naturopathic Physicians
DHt	Diplomate of Homeotheraputics
CCH	Certified in Classical Homeopathy

For more information, contact The National Center for Homeopathy, 801 N. Fairfax St., Ste. 306, Alexandria, VA 22314 (telephone: 703-548-7790; fax: 703-548-7792; e-mail: nchinfo@igc.apc.org), or visit the center's Web site at http://www.healthy.net/pan/pa/homeopathic/natcenhom/whishome.htm.

---

and flossing also help to prevent tooth decay by removing bacteria-containing plaque (an invisible sticky coating on teeth) that produces cavity-causing acid.

To protect teeth further against decay, plastic sealants are now widely used and recommended. The application is a simple one: the teeth are cleaned and wiped completely dry, and the substance is painted onto the tooth surface. The resulting coating (which may be clear or tinted) can last as long as 10 years, protecting teeth from the bacteria that cause decay. Many dentists now recommend that a sealant be applied to children's teeth immediately after the adult teeth appear, before any decay begins to occur.

For detailed information on preventive dental care and specific problems, see your dentist. Or contact the American Dental Association, 211 E. Chicago Ave., Chicago, IL 60611 (telephone: 312-440-2500; fax: 312-440-2800), or visit the ADA's Web site at http://www.ada.org/.

Go to "Living Will" in chapter 20; "Aging" in chapter 22; "Social Security" in chapter 25

LIVING WILLS

One of the most controversial issues in society today is a person's right to decide whether to live or die. With the enormous advances in medical care during recent decades, many more families are being asked to make difficult choices about life-sustaining measures for loved ones who are critically ill and unable to make their own decisions. Senior citizens, nursing-home patients, those who are seriously ill, and members of the public at large are now encouraged to record their thoughts by executing living wills. When properly prepared and executed, a living will can speak for someone who no longer has the ability to speak for herself.

Many states have legislation in place regarding the right of terminally ill persons or family members to decide to withhold life-sustaining measures, and the law in your state may not be as conservative or liberal as you would prefer. But laws are changing constantly in this field. Experts in the field suggest executing a living will that not only conforms to state legislative guidelines, but also includes information that may be of value in the future if state laws change.

Health/Nutrition

There are numerous resources available for anyone desiring to create a living will. Check the reference section of your public library for handbooks containing sample living wills for every state with current legislation, and generic forms for states without such laws. Or contact one of the organizations listed below for information on creating living wills and related legal issues.

Choice in Dying
200 Varick St.
New York, NY
212-366-5540
Fax: 212-366-5337
http://www.echonyc.com/~choice/

Death with Dignity Education Center
520 El Camino Real, Ste. 710
San Mateo, CA 94402-1720
415-344-6489
Fax: 415-344-8100
E-mail: ddec@aol.com

Euthanasia Research & Guidance Organization (ERGO!)
24829 Norris Lane
Junction City, OR 97448-9559
541-998-3285
Fax: 541-998-1873
http://www.efn.org/~ergo

DEATHS AND DEATH RATES FROM SELECTED CAUSES, 1970 TO 1996

Causes of death are ranked according to 1996 mortality rates. Beginning with 1980, deaths are classified according to the ninth revision of *International Classification of Diseases;* for 1970, they are classified according to the revision in use at that time.

Go to "Statistics and Demography" under "Reference Works for General Information" in chapter 11

Rank/Cause of Death	Deaths per 1,000 People							Crude Death Rate per 100,000 People[1]						
	1970	1980	1990	1993	1994	1995	1996[2]	1970	1980	1990	1993	1994	1995	1996[2]
All causes	1,921.0	1,989.8	2,148.5	2,268.6	2,286.0	2,312.1	2,322.4	945.3	878.3	863.8	880.0	876.9	880.0	875.4
1. Major cardiovascular diseases	1,008.0	988.5	916.0	948.1	945.2	951.4	951.3	496.0	436.4	368.3	367.8	362.6	362.1	358.6
Percent of total	52.4	49.7	42.6	41.8	41.3	41.1	41.0	52.5	50.0	42.6	41.8	41.4	41.1	41.0
Diseases of heart	735.5	761.1	720.1	743.5	734.1	737.6	733.8	362.0	336.0	289.5	288.4	281.6	280.7	276.6
Percent of total	38.3	38.3	33.5	32.8	32.1	31.9	31.6	38.3	38.3	33.5	32.8	32.1	31.9	31.6
Rheumatic fever and rheumatic heart disease	14.9	7.8	6.0	5.7	5.5	5.1	5.0	7.3	3.5	2.4	2.2	2.1	2.0	1.9
Hypertensive heart disease (with or without renal disease)[3]	15.0	24.8	23.4	23.0	23.8			7.4	10.9	9.5	8.9	9.1		
Hypertensive heart disease[3]						25.0	25.9						9.5	9.8
Hypertensive heart disease and renal disease[3]						2.5	2.5						0.9	0.9
Ischemic heart disease	666.7	565.8	489.2	490.1	487.5	481.3	476.8	328.1	249.7	196.7	190.1	187.0	183.2	179.7
Other diseases of endocardium	6.7	7.2	13.0	15.2	14.5	16.2	17.3	3.3	3.2	5.2	5.9	5.6	6.2	6.5

Rank/Cause of Death	Deaths per 1,000 People							Crude Death Rate per 100,000 People[1]						
	1970	1980	1990	1993	1994	1995	1996[2]	1970	1980	1990	1993	1994	1995	1996[2]
All other forms of heart disease	32.3	155.5	188.4	207.0	200.1	207.4	206.3	15.9	68.7	75.8	80.3	76.8	78.9	77.8
Hypertension (with or without renal disease)	8.3	7.8	9.2	11.2	11.7	12.5	12.9	4.1	3.5	3.7	4.4	4.5	4.8	4.9
Cerebrovascular diseases	207.2	170.2	144.1	150.1	154.4	158.0	160.4	101.9	75.1	57.9	58.2	59.2	60.1	60.5
Arteriosclerosis	31.7	29.4	18.0	17.3	18.0	16.7	18.8	15.6	13.0	7.3	6.7	6.9	6.4	6.3
Other diseases of arteries, arterioles, and capillaries	25.3	20.0	24.6	26.0	27.1	26.6	27.3	12.5	8.8	9.9	10.1	10.4	10.1	10.3
2. Malignancies[4]	330.7	416.5	505.3	529.9	536.9	538.5	544.3	162.8	183.9	203.2	205.6	206.0	204.9	205.2
Percent of total	*17.2*	*20.9*	*23.5*	*34.4*	*23.5*	*23.3*	*23.4*	*17.2*	*20.9*	*23.5*	*23.4*	*23.5*	*23.3*	*23.4*
Of respiratory and intrathorasic organs	69.5	108.5	146.4	154.2	154.3	156.4	158.6	34.2	47.9	58.9	59.8	59.2	59.5	59.8
Of digestive organs and peritoneum	94.7	110.6	120.8	124.5	127.2	126.6	127.7	46.6	48.8	48.6	48.3	48.8	48.2	48.1
Of genital organs	41.2	46.4	57.5	60.4	62.1	60.5	60.4	20.3	20.5	23.1	23.4	23.8	23.0	22.8
Of breast	29.9	35.9	43.7	43.9	43.3	44.2	44.1	14.7	15.8	17.6	17.0	16.6	16.8	16.6
Of urinary organs	15.5	17.8	20.7	21.8	22.0	22.6	23.2	7.6	7.9	8.3	8.4	8.4	8.6	8.7
Leukemia	14.5	16.5	18.6	19.5	20.1	20.1	20.5	7.1	7.3	7.5	7.6	7.7	7.7	7.7
3. Chronic obstructive pulmonary diseases and allied conditions[5]	30.9	56.1	86.7	101.1	101.9	102.9	106.1	15.2	24.7	34.9	39.2	39.1	39.2	40.0
Percent of total	*1.6*	*2.8*	*4.0*	*4.5*	*4.5*	*4.5*	*4.6*	*1.6*	*2.8*	*4.0*	*4.5*	*4.5*	*4.5*	*4.6*
Bronchitis, chronic and unspecified	5.8	3.7	3.6	3.8	3.6	3.3	3.2	2.9	1.6	1.6	1.5	1.4	1.3	1.2
Emphysema	22.7	13.9	15.7	17.6	17.3	16.9	17.4	11.2	6.1	6.3	6.8	6.6	6.4	6.5
Asthma	2.3	2.9	4.8	5.2	5.7	5.6	5.6	1.1	1.3	1.9	2.0	2.2	2.1	2.1
Other[5]	([5])	35.6	62.6	74.5	75.3	77.0	80.0	([5])	15.7	25.2	28.9	28.9	29.3	30.1
4. Accidents and adverse effects	114.6	105.7	92.0	90.5	90.1	93.3	93.9	56.4	46.7	37.0	35.1	34.6	35.5	35.4
Motor vehicle	54.6	53.2	46.8	41.9	42.2	43.4	43.4	26.9	23.5	18.8	16.3	16.2	16.5	16.4
All other	60.0	52.5	45.2	48.6	48.0	50.0	50.4	29.5	23.3	18.2	18.9	18.4	19.0	19.0
5. Pneumonia and influenza	62.7	54.6	79.5	82.8	82.1	82.9	82.6	30.9	24.1	32.0	32.1	31.5	31.6	31.1
Pneumonia	59.0	51.9	77.4	81.8	80.8	82.3	82.0	29.0	22.9	31.1	31.7	31.0	31.3	30.9
Influenza	3.7	2.7	2.1	1.0	1.3	0.6	0.6	1.8	1.2	0.8	0.4	0.5	0.2	0.2
6. Diabetes mellitus	38.3	34.9	47.7	53.9	55.4	59.3	61.6	18.9	15.4	19.2	20.9	21.2	22.6	23.2
7. Other infectious and parasitic disease[7]	6.9	5.1	32.2	44.4	48.5	50.3	39.7	3.4	2.2	13.0	17.2	18.6	19.1	15.0
8. Suicide	23.5	26.9	30.9	31.1	32.4	31.3	30.9	11.6	11.9	12.4	12.1	12.4	11.9	11.6
9. Symptoms, signs, and ill-defined conditions	25.8	28.8	24.1	26.5	26.6	27.3	30.4	12.7	12.7	9.7	10.3	10.2	10.4	11.4

continues

Health/Nutrition

Continued

Health/Nutrition

Rank/Cause of Death	Deaths per 1,000 People							Crude Death Rate per 100,000 People[1]						
	1970	1980	1990	1993	1994	1995	1996[2]	1970	1980	1990	1993	1994	1995	1996[2]
10. Chronic liver diseases and cirrhosis	31.4	30.6	25.8	25.2	25.7	25.2	25.1	15.5	13.5	10.4	9.8	9.9	9.6	9.5
11. Nephritis, nephrotic syndrome, and nephrosis	8.9	16.8	20.8	23.3	23.6	23.7	24.4	4.4	7.4	8.3	9.0	9.1	9.0	9.2
12. Septicemia	3.5	9.4	19.2	20.6	19.9	21.0	21.4	1.7	4.2	7.7	8.0	7.6	8.0	8.1
13. Homicide and legal intervention	16.8	24.3	24.9	26.0	23.7	22.9	20.7	8.3	10.7	10.0	10.1	9.1	8.7	7.8
14. Certain conditions originating in the perinatal period	43.2	22.9	17.7	15.1	14.1	13.5	12.8	21.3	10.1	7.1	5.9	5.4	5.1	4.8
15. Congenital anomalies	16.8	13.9	13.1	12.4	11.9	11.9	11.9	8.3	6.2	5.3	4.8	4.6	4.5	4.5
16. Benign neoplasms[6]	4.8	6.2	6.8	7.4	7.0	7.8	7.8	2.4	2.7	2.7	2.9	2.7	3.0	2.9
17. Hernia of abdominal cavity and intestinal obstruction without mention of hernia	7.2	5.4	5.8	5.9	6.0	6.2	6.5	3.6	2.4	2.3	2.3	2.3	2.4	2.5
18. Ulcer of stomach and duodenum	8.6	6.1	6.2	5.9	6.0	5.5	5.1	4.2	0.0	2.5	2.3	2.3	2.1	1.9
19. Anemias	3.4	3.2	4.1	4.3	4.2	4.6	4.4	1.7	1.4	1.6	1.7	1.6	1.7	1.6
20. Viral hepatitis	1.0	0.8	1.6	2.5	2.8	3.4	3.8	0.5	0.4	0.6	1.0	1.1	1.3	1.4
21. Nutritional deficiencies	2.5	2.4	3.0	3.5	3.2	3.6	3.7	1.2	1.0	1.2	1.3	1.2	1.4	1.4
22. Cholelithiasis and other disorders of gall bladder	4.0	3.3	3.0	2.8	2.6	2.8	2.8	2.0	1.5	1.2	1.1	1.0	1.0	1.1
23. Tuberculosis	5.2	2.0	1.8	1.6	1.6	1.3	1.2	2.6	0.9	0.7	0.6	0.6	0.5	0.5
24. Infections of kidney	8.2	2.7	1.3	1.0	1.0	0.9	0.9	4.0	1.2	0.5	0.4	0.4	0.3	0.3
25. Meningitis	1.7	1.4	1.0	0.8	0.9	0.8	0.8	0.8	0.6	0.4	0.3	0.4	0.3	0.3
26. Acute bronchitis and bronchiolitis	1.3	0.6	0.6	0.7	0.5	0.5	0.5	0.6	0.3	0.3	0.3	0.2	0.3	0.3
27. Hyperplasia of prostate	2.2	0.8	0.5	0.4	0.5	0.4	0.5	1.1	0.3	0.2	0.2	0.2	0.2	0.2
N/A All other causes	108.8	120.0	172.9	195.6	206.1	217.4	225.6	53.5	53.0	69.5	75.9	79.1	82.8	85.0

Sources: U.S. National Center for Health Statistics, *Vital Statistics of the United States* (annual) and *Monthly Vital Statistics Report.*

[1] Figures for 1970, 1980, and 1990 (census years) are based on the resident population of the United States enumerated as of April 1. Figures for 1993 to 1996 are based on resident popular estimates as of July 1 and include nonresidents.

[2] Figures for 1996 are preliminary.

[3] Data are grouped differently for 1995–1996.

[4] Also includes other types of malignancies not listed.

[5] Data for 1970 includes only bronchitis, emphysema, and asthma (no listing for "other"); data that is included in "other" category for later years was included in "all other causes" category in 1970.

[6] Includes neoplasms of unspecified nature; beginning with 1980, also includes carcinoma in situ.

[7] Includes human immunodeficiency virus (HIV).

COMBINING FORMS OF MEDICAL TERMS

Prefix	Meaning of Prefix	Example	Prefix	Meaning of Prefix	Example
a-, ab-, an-	away, lack of, without	astigmatism	galact-	milk	galactose
acro-	extremity, end	acroparesthesia	gastro-	stomach	gastroenteric
adeno-	gland	adenous	gloss-	tongue	glossitis
adreno-	adrenal gland	adrenocortex	hemi-	half	hemiplegic
aero-	gas, air	aerophagia	hepato-	liver	hepatocolic
allo-	different, another	allorhythmia	hydro-	water	hydrocephalic
ambi-	both, both sides	ambidextrous	hyper-	above, beyond	hyperacidity
antero-	before, in front of	anterograde	hypo-	below, less	hypoglycemia
anti-	against	antiseptic	ileo-	end of small intestine	ileocolic
arterio-	artery	arteriospasm	ilio-	flank, upper hip bone	iliopelvic
arthro-, arthr-	joint	arthritis	infra-	below, inferior	infraorbital
bacterio-	bacteria	bacteriological	inter-	between	interdigital
blephari-	eyelash, eyelid	blepharitis	intra-	within	intrauterine
brady-	slow	bradycardia	kerat-	cornea, hard tissue	keratoid
broncho-	windpipe	bronchospasm	laryngo-, laryging-	voice box	laryngitis
cardio-	heart, heart region	cardiovascular			
cephalo-	head	cephalometry	leuko-, leuk-	white	leukocyte
cerebro-	brain	cerebrovascular	mega-	abnormally large	megacolon
cervico-	neck	cervicobrachial	mela-	black	melanin
chole-	bile	cholecystis	myelo-, myel-	marrow, nerve sheath	myelination
chondro-	cartilage	chondroblastoma	myo-	muscle	myospasm
chromo-	color	chromogen	neo-	new	neoplasm
chylo-	lymph	chylomicron	nephro-, nephr-	kidney	nephritis
contra-	against, opposite	contraindication	neuro-, neuri-, neur-	nerve	neuritis
costo-	rib	costochondral			
cyst-	bladder, sac	cystitis	osteo-	bone	osteoarthritis
dacryo-	tears	dacryocystitis	peri-, pneumo-	around or about the lungs or air	pericardial pneumonia
derma-	skin	dermatitis			
dextro-	right side	dextromanual	sacro-	sacrum (triangular bone above tailbone)	sacroiliac
dys-	abnormal, bad, painful	dysentery			
encephalo-, encephal-	brain	encephalitis	sero-	serum, blood	serofibrous
			tachy-	rapid	tachycardia
endo-	inside	endocardium	thrombo-	blood clot	thrombosis
entero-	intestines	enterospasm	tracheo-	windpipe	tracheotomy
ep-, epi-	at, over, upon	epiglottis	utero-	uterus, womb	uterotomy
ex-, exo-	out, outside	excrement	vaso-	blood vessel	vasodilator
fibrino-	threadlike	fibrinogen	ventro-	belly, abdominal	ventroptosia
fibro-	fiber, fibrous	fibrocystic	zymo-	enzyme, fermentation	zymocide

> "Common Biological Terms" in chapter 3; "Medical Science" under "Reference Works for General Information" in chapter 11; "Medicine and Pharmacology Symbols" in chapter 12
>
> **Go to**

Health/Nutrition

RECOMMENDED DAILY (OR DIETARY) ALLOWANCES

In the following tables, heights and weights are medians of the U.S. population and are not meant to suggest ideal height-to-weight ratios.

PROTEINS

	Age (years)	Weight (pounds)	Heights (inches)	Protein (grams)
Males	11–14	99	62	45
	15–18	145	69	59
	19–24	160	70	58
	25–50	174	70	63
	51+	170	68	63
Females	11–14	101	62	46
	15–18	120	64	44
	19–24	128	65	46
	25–50	138	64	50
	51+	143	63	50
Pregnant				65
Nursing				62–65

FAT-SOLUBLE VITAMINS

	Age (years)	Weight (pounds)	Height (inches)	Vitamin A (IUs)*	Vitamin D (IUs)	Vitamin E (IUs)
Males	11–14	99	62	1,000	10	10
	15–18	145	69	1,000	10	10
	19–24	160	70	1,000	10	10
	25–50	174	70	1,000	5	10
	51+	170	68	1,000	5	10
Females	11–14	101	62	800	10	8
	15–18	120	64	800	10	8
	19–24	128	65	800	10	8
	25–50	138	64	800	5	8
	51+	143	63	800	5	8
Pregnant				800	10	10
Nursing				1,200–1,300	10	11–12

*IUs = International Units

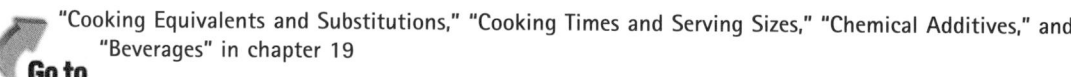 "Cooking Equivalents and Substitutions," "Cooking Times and Serving Sizes," "Chemical Additives," and "Beverages" in chapter 19

Go to

WATER-SOLUBLE VITAMINS

	Age (years)	Weight (pounds)	Height (inches)	Vitamin C (mg*)	Foliate (mg)	Niacin (mg)	Riboflavin (mg)	Thiamin (mg)	Vitamin B_6 (mg)	Vitamin B_{12} (mg)
Males	11–14	99	62	50	150	17	1.5	1.3	1.7	2.0
	15–18	145	69	60	200	20	1.8	1.5	2.0	2.0
	19–24	160	70	60	200	19	1.7	1.5	2.0	2.0
	25–50	174	70	60	200	19	1.7	1.5	2.0	2.0
	51+	170	78	60	200	15	1.4	1.2	2.0	2.0
Females	11–14	101	62	50	150	15	1.3	1.1	1.4	2.0
	15–18	120	64	60	180	15	1.3	1.1	1.5	2.0
	19–24	128	65	60	180	15	1.3	1.1	1.6	2.0
	25–50	138	64	60	180	15	1.3	1.1	1.6	2.0
	51+	143	63	60	180	13	1.2	1.0	1.6	2.0
Pregnant				70	400	17	1.6	1.5	2.2	2.2
Nursing				90–95	260–280	20	1.7–1.8	1.6	2.1	2.6

*mg = milligrams

MINERALS

	Age (years)	Weight (pounds)	Height (inches)	Calcium (mg)	Phosphorus (mg)	Iodine (mg)	Iron (mg)	Magnesium (mg)	Zinc (mg)
Males	11–14	99	62	1,200	1,200	150	12	270	15
	15–18	145	69	1,200	1,200	150	12	400	15
	19–24	160	70	1,200	1,200	150	10	350	15
	25–50	174	70	800	800	150	10	350	15
	51+	170	68	800	800	150	10	350	15
Females	11–14	101	62	1,200	1,200	150	15	280	12
	15–18	120	64	1,200	1,200	150	15	300	12
	19–24	128	65	1,200	1,200	150	15	280	12
	25–50	138	64	800	800	150	15	280	12
	51+	143	63	800	800	150	10	280	12
Pregnant				1,200	1,200	175	30*	320	15
				1,200	1,200	200	15	355	16–19

*A pregnant woman often requires iron supplement tablets because of the difficulty of providing an adequate iron intake in an otherwise balanced diet.

Health/Nutrition

VITAMIN/MINERAL FOOD CHART (BEST FOOD SOURCES FOR EACH VITAMIN AND MINERAL)

Consult your physician before taking vitamin or mineral dietary supplements or giving them to children. Follow medical advice and label directions carefully, and keep both prescription and nonprescription supplements out of the reach of children. Overdoses can be harmful or fatal.

VITAMINS

Vitamin	Chief Functions	Results of Deficiency	Characteristics
Vitamin A Provitamin, carotene	Essential for maintaining the integrity of epithelial membranes; helps maintain resistance to infections; necessary for the formation of rhodopsin and prevention of night blindness	**Mild:** Retarded growth; increased susceptibility to infection; abnormal function of gastro intestinal, genitourinary, and res-- piratory tracts due to altered epi- thelial membranes; dry, shriveled, thickened skin, sometimes pustule formation; night blindness **Severe:** Xerophthalmia, a charac- teristic eye disease, and other local infections	Fat-soluble; not destroyed by ordinary cooking temperatures; destroyed by high temperatures when oxygen is present; marked capacity for storage in liver *Note:* Excessive intake of carotene, from which vitamin A is formed, may produce yellow discoloration of the skin (carotenemia).
Thiamin **Vitamin B$_1$**	Important role in carbohydrate metabolism; essential for maintenance of normal digestion and appetite; essential for normal functioning of nervous tissue	**Mild:** Loss of appetite; impaired digestion of starches and sugars; colitis, constipation, or diarrhea; emaciation **Severe:** Nervous disorders of various types; loss of coordinating power of muscles; beriberi; paralysis	Water-soluble; not readily destroyed by ordinary cooking temperature; destroyed by exposure to heat, alkali, or sulfites; not stored in body
Riboflavin **Vitamin B$_2$**	Important in formation of certain enzymes and in cellular oxidation; normal growth; prevention of cheilosis and glossitis	Impaired growth; lassitude and weakness; cheilosis; glossitis, atrophy of skin; anemia; photophobia; cataracts	Water-soluble; alcohol-soluble; not destroyed by heat in cooking unless with alkali; unstable in light, especially in presence of alkali
Niacin Nicotinic acid Nicotinamide Antipellagra vitamin	As the component of two impor- tant enzymes, it is important in glycolysis, tissue respiration, and fat synthesis; nicotinic acid but not nicotinamide causes vasodilation and flushing; prevents pellagra	Pellagra; gastrointestinal disturbances; mental disturbances	Soluble in hot water and alcohol; not destroyed by heat, light, air, or alkali; not destroyed in ordinary cooking
Vitamin B$_{12}$ Cyanoco- balamin	Produces remission in pernicious anemia; essential for normal development of red blood cells	Pernicious anemia	Soluble in water or alcohol; unstable in hot alkaline or acid solutions

Good Sources	Recommended Daily Allowances	
Natural: Animal fats (butter, cheese, cream, egg yolk, whole milk); fish liver oil; liver; vegetables (green leafy, especially escarole, kale, and parsley; and yellow, especially carrots) **Artificial:** Concentrates in several forms; irradiated fish oils	Males 11 yrs. and older	1,000mg retinol equivalents
	Females 11 yrs. and older	800mg retinol equivalents
	Pregnant females	1,000mg retinol equivalents
	Lactating females	1,200mg retinol equivalents
	Children	400–700mg retinol equivalents
	Infants	400mg retinol equivalents
Natural: Widely distributed in plant and animal tissues but seldom occurs in high concentration, except in brewer's yeast; other good sources are whole-grain cereals, peas, beans, peanuts, oranges, heart, liver, kidney, many vegetables and fruits, and nuts **Artificial:** Concentrates from yeast; rice polishings; wheat germ	Males 11 yrs. and older	1.2–1.5mg
	Females 11 yrs. and older	1.0–1.1mg
	Pregnant females	1.4–1.6mg
	Lactating females	1.5–1.7mg
	Children	0.7–1.2mg
	Infants	0.3–0.5mg
Eggs, green vegetables, liver, kidney, lean meat, milk, wheat germ, dried yeast, enriched foods	Males 11 yrs. and older	1.4–1.8mg
	Females 11 yrs. and older	1.2–1.3mg
	Pregnant females	1.6mg
	Lactating females	1.7–1.8mg
	Children	0.8–1.2mg
	Infants	0.4–0.5mg
Yeast, lean meat, fish, legumes, whole-grain cereals and peanuts, enriched foods	Males 11 yrs. and older	16–19 mg
	Females 11 yrs. and older	13–15 mg
	Pregnant females	17 mg
	Lactating females	20 mg
	Children	9–16 mg
	Infants	6–8 mg
Liver, kidney, dairy products; most of vitamin required by humans is synthesized by intestinal bacteria	Males 11 yrs. and older	3 mcg
	Females 11 yrs. and older	3 mcg
	Pregnant females	4 mcg
	Lactating females	5 mcg
	Children	2–5mcg
	Infants	1–2mcg

Health/Nutrition

continues

Continued

Vitamin	Chief Functions	Results of Deficiency	Characteristics
Vitamin C Ascorbic acid	Essential to formation of intracellular cement substances in a variety of tissues including skin, dentin, cartilage, and bone matrix; important in healing of wounds and fractures of bones; prevents scurvy; facilitates absorption of iron	**Mild:** Lowered resistance to infections; joint tenderness; susceptibility to dental caries, pyorrhea, and bleeding gums **Severe:** Hemorrhage; anemia; scurvy	Soluble in water; easily destroyed by oxidation, and heat hastens the process; lost in cooking, particularly if water in which food was cooked is discarded; loss is greater if cooked in iron or copper utensils; quick-frozen foods lose little; stored in the body to a limited extent
Vitamin D	Regulates absorption of calcium and phosphorus from the intestinal tract; antirachitic	**Mild:** Interferes with utilization of calcium and phosphorus in bone and teeth formation; irritability; weakness **Severe:** Rickets may be common in young children; osteomalacia in adults	Soluble in fats and organic solvents; relatively stable under refrigeration; stored in liver; often associated with vitamin A
Vitamin E Alpha tocopherol	Normal reproduction in rats; prevention of muscular dystrophy in rabbits and sheep	Red blood cell resistance to rupture is decreased	Fat soluble; stable to heat in absence of oxygen
Vitamin B$_6$ Pyridoxine	Essential for metabolism of tryptophan; needed for utilization of certain other amino acids	Dermatitis around eyes and mouth; neuritis; anorexia; nausea and vomiting	Soluble in water and alcohol; rapidly inactivated in presence of heat, sunlight, or air
Folacin (Folic acid)	Essential for normal functioning of hematopoietic system	Anemia	Slightly soluble in water; easily destroyed by heat in presence of acid; decreases when food is stored at room temperature *Note:* A large dose may prevent the appearance of anemia in a case of pernicious anemia but still permits neurological symptoms to develop.

* IUs = International Units

Health/Nutrition

Good Sources	Recommended Daily Allowances	
Natural: Abundant in most fresh fruits and vegetables, especially citrus fruit and juices and tomatoes **Artificial:** Ascorbic acid; cevitamic acid	Males 11 yrs. and older	50–60mg
	Females 11 yrs. and older	50–60mg
	Pregnant females	80 mg
	Lactating females	100mg
	Children	45mg
	Infants	35mg
	The infant diet is likely to be deficient in vitamin C unless orange or tomato juice or another form is added.	
Butter, egg yolks, fish liver oils, fish having fat distributed through the flesh, (such as salmon, tuna fish, herring) sardines, liver, oysters, yeast, and foods irradiated with ultraviolet light; formed in the skin by exposure to sunlight; artificially prepared forms exist	Males 11 yrs. and older	200–400 IU*
	Females 11 yrs. and older	200–400 IU*; after age 22, none except during pregnancy or lactation
	Pregnant females	400–600 IU*
	Lactating females	400–600 IU*
	Children	400 IU*
	Infants	400 IU*
Lettuce and other green, leafy vegetables, wheat germ oil, margarine, rice	Males 11 yrs. and older	8–10mg
	Females 11 yrs. and older	8mg
	Pregnant females	10mg
	Lactating females	11mg
	Children	10–15 IU*
	Infants	5 IU*
Blackstrap molasses, meat, cereal grains, wheat germ	Males 11 yrs. and older	1.8–2.2mg
	Females 11 yrs. and older	1.8–2.2mg
	Pregnant females	2.6mg
	Lactating females	2.5mg
	Children	0.9–1.6mg
	Infants	0.3–0.6mg
Glandular meats; yeast; green, leafy vegetables	Males 11 yrs. and older	0.4mg
	Females 11 yrs. and older	0.4mg
	Pregnant females	800mg
	Lactating females	500mg
	Children	100–300mg
	Infants	30–45mg

Health/Nutrition

continues

MINERALS

Mineral	Chief Functions	Results of Deficiency
Calcium (Ca++)	Necessary for formation of bones and teeth; functioning of nerves and muscles; blood clotting; activation of enzymes that convert food to energy	Rickets (soft, deformed bones) and poor growth in children; osteoporosis in adults; muscle cramps
Iodine (I-)	Necessary for normal thyroid function; regulates oxidation in cells	Disturbance in thyroid function (hypothyroidism); in infants, stunting and mental retardation (cretinism)
Iron* (Fe++)	Necessary for production of hemoglobin and myoglobin (structures that enable oxygen to be carried in blood and stored in muscles)	Fatigue; weakness; headaches; shortness of breath; iron-deficiency anemia
Phosphorus (PO$_4$)	Necessary for formation of bones and teeth; activation of enzymes that convert food to energy; maintenance of body's proper chemical balance; nerve/muscle function	Weakness; pain in bones (deficiency is rare)
Magnesium (Mg++)	Essential to bone growth and production of cells and genetic material; cofactor in enzymatic release of energy; regulates neuromuscular sensitivity	Muscle cramps and weakness; twitching; confusion; (deficiency most often seen in alcoholics and people taking diuretics or dehydrated from prolonged diarrhea)

*At least 110,000 cases of accidental overdose of iron pills in children under 6 have been reported. Some were hospitalized and at least 35 died. From 1988 to 1982, children's deaths due to iron poisoning accounted for almost $1/6$ of all children's poisoning deaths reported to poison control centers. (The number/percentage is increasing, probably due to the increased use of iron supplements

Good Sources	Recommended Daily Allowances		
Milk and milk products; dark-green, leafy vegetables; broccoli; oysters; tofu; bone meal	Males and females	11–24 yrs.	1,200mg
		21 yrs. and older	800mg
	Pregnant/Lactating females		1,200mg
	Children	1–10 yrs.	800mg
	Infants	birth–6 mos.	400mg
		7 mos.–1 yr.	600mg
Seafood, iodized salt (in micrograms)	Males and females	11 yrs. and older	150mcg
	Pregnant females		25mcg
	Lactating females		50mcg
	Children	1–3 yrs.	70mcg
		4–6 yrs.	90mcg
		7–10 yrs.	120mcg
	Infants	birth–6 mos.	40mcg
		7 mos.–1 yr.	50mcg
Red meat and liver; egg yolks; green leafy vegetables; dried apricots; acidic foods prepared in cast-iron pots; whole-grain breads and cereals	Males	11–18 yrs.	12mg
		19 yrs. and older	10mg
	Females	11–50 yrs.	15mg
		51+ yrs.	10mg
	Pregnant females		30mg
	Lactating females		15mg
	Children	1–10 yrs.*	10mg
	Infants	birth–6 mos.*	6mg
		7 mos.–1 yrs.*	10mg
Milk and milk products; egg yolks; meat, poultry, and fish; whole-grain breads and cereals; beans; nuts	Males and females	11–24 yrs.	1,200mg
		25–51+ yrs.	800mg
	Pregnant/lactating females		1,200mg
	Children	1–10 yrs.	800mg
	Infants	birth–60 mos.	300mg
		7 mos.–1 yr.	500mg
Green, leafy vegetables; nuts; beans; whole-grain breads and cereals; oysters; scallops	Males	11–14 yrs.	270mg
		15–18 yrs.	400mg
		19 yrs. and older	350mg
	Females	11–14 yrs.	280mg
		15–18 yrs.	300mg
		19 yrs. and older	280mg
	Pregnant females	320 mg	
	Lactating females	1–6 mos.	355mg
		7 mos.–1 yr.	340mg
	Children	1–3 yrs.	80mg
		4–6 yrs.	120mg
		7–10 yrs.	170mg
	Infants	birth–6 mos.	40mg
		7 mos.–1 yr.	60mg

among adults.) New federal labeling/packaging regulations went into effect in July 1997 to address the issue; however, parents must be aware of this danger. Ingestion of as few as five tablets/200mg has caused death in children; immediate medical attention is required for any incident of known or possible overdose. Iron poisoning can also be harmful to adults.

continues

Continued

Mineral	Chief Functions	Results of Deficiency
Potassium (K+)	Essential to regulation of fluid balance; aids in natural impulse transmission and muscle contraction	Muscle weakness; cardiac arrest; kidney damage (deficiency most often seen in people taking diuretics or dehydrated from prolonged diarrhea)
Selenium (Se)	Necessary for prevention of fat and body chemical breakdown	Deficiency almost unknown in humans, can cause cardiomyopathy
Sodium (Na+)	Necessary to maintenance of fluid balance	Deficiency rare in U.S.; sodium loss due to extremely heavy perspiration (usually in athletes) can cause muscle cramps, weakness, headache
Zinc (Zn++)	Essential element in enzymes necessary for digestion	Wounds slow to heal; loss of taste/appetite; stunted growth and sexual development in children

Health/Nutrition

Good Sources	Recommended Daily Allowances		
Bananas, citrus fruits, dried fruits; deep yellow vegetables; potatoes; beans; milk; whole grain breads and cereals	Males and females (including pregnant or lactating)	19–51+ yrs.	2,000mg
	Children	1 yr.	1,000mg
		2–5 yrs.	1,400mg
		6–9 yrs.	1,000mg
		10–18 yrs.	2,000mg
	Infants	birth–6 mos.	500mg
		7 mos.–1 yr.	700mg
Chicken; egg yolks; seafood; whole-grain breads and cereals; mushrooms, onions, and garlic	Males	11–14 yrs.	40 mcg
		15–18 yrs.	50 mcg
		19–51+ yrs.	70 mcg
	Females	11–14 yrs.	45 mcg
		15–18 yrs.	50 mcg
		19–51+ yrs.	65 mcg
	Pregnant females		65 mcg
	Lactating females		75 mcg
	Children	1–6 yrs.	20 mcg
		7–10 yrs.	30 mcg
	Infants	birth–6 mos.	10 mcg
		7 mos.–1 yr.	15 mcg
Table salt; processed foods; milk; drinking water (some locations)	Males and females	19–51+ yrs.	500mg
	Children	1 yr.	225mg
		2–5 yrs.	300mg
		6–9 yrs.	400mg
		10–18 yrs.	500mg
	Infants	birth–6 mos.	120mg
		7 mos.–1 yr.	200mg
Beef, liver; oysters/shellfish; yogurt; wheat germ; beans; fortified cereals	Males	11 yrs. and older	15mg
	Females	11 yrs. and older	12mg
	Pregnant females		30mg
	Lactating females		15mg
	Children 1–10 yrs.		10mg
	Infants birth–1 yr.		5mg

Health/Nutrition

ACTIVITIES AND THE CALORIES THEY CONSUME

Activity		Calories Expended per Hour* Person weighing:				
		100 lbs.	125 lbs.	150 lbs.**	175 lbs.	200 lbs.
Rest and light activity	Lying down or sleeping	53	67	80	93	107
	Sitting	67	83	100	117	133
	Typing	73	92	110	128	147
	Driving	80	100	120	140	160
	Standing	93	117	140	163	187
	Housework	120	150	180	210	240
	Shining shoes	123	154	185	216	247
Moderate activity	Bicycling (5^1/$_2$ mph)	140	175	210	245	280
	Walking (2^1/$_2$ mph)	140	175	210	245	280
	Gardening	147	183	220	257	293
	Canoeing (2^1/$_2$ mph)	153	192	230	268	307
	Golf (foursome)	167	208	250	292	333
	Lawn mowing (power mower)	167	208	250	292	333
	Fencing	200	250	300	350	400
	Rowing a boat (2^1/$_2$ mph)	200	250	300	350	400
	Swimming (^{1}/$_4$ mph)	200	250	300	350	400
	Calisthenics	200	250	300	350	400
	Walking (3^1/$_4$ mph)	200	250	300	350	400
	Badminton	200	250	350	350	400
	Horseback riding (trotting)	200	250	350	350	400
	Square dancing	200	250	350	350	400
	Volleyball	233	250	350	350	400
	Roller skating	233	292	350	408	467
	Stacking heavy objects (boxes, logs)	233	292	350	408	467
Vigorous activity	Baseball pitching	240	300	360	420	480
	Ditch digging (hand shovel)	267	333	400	467	533
	Ice-skating (10 mph)	267	333	400	467	533
	Chopping or sawing wood	267	333	400	467	533
	Bowling (continuous)	267	333	400	467	533
	Tennis	280	350	420	490	560
	Aerobic dancing	300	375	450	525	600
	Waterskiing	320	400	480	560	640
	Hill climbing (100 feet per hour)	327	408	490	572	653
	Basketball	333	417	500	583	667
	Football	333	417	500	583	667
	Jogging (5 mph)	367	458	550	642	733
	Skiing (10 mph)	400	500	600	700	800
	Squash and handball	400	500	600	700	800
	Bicycling (13 mph)	440	550	660	770	880
	Rowing (machine)	480	600	720	840	960
	Scull rowing (race)	560	700	840	980	1,120
	Running (10 mph)	600	750	900	1,050	1,200

* All figures are approximate, as individual differences in metabolism and how activities are performed affect energy expenditure.

** To approximate your own caloric usage, divide the figure under the "Person weighing 150 pounds" column by 150 to get the approximate caloric expenditure per pound, and then multiply the result by your own body weight.

SAFE ALCOHOL CONSUMPTION

The effects of drinking alcoholic beverages depend in part on the amount of actual ethyl alcohol consumed and one's body weight. The level of alcohol in the blood is calculated in terms of milligrams (1 milligram = $^1/_{28,350}$ of an ounce) of pure alcohol per deciliter (1 deciliter = 3.5 fluid ounces) of blood. This is usually expressed as mg/dl. Twelve ounces of beer, 4 ounces of wine, or a 1.5-ounce shot of 80-proof whiskey, gin, or vodka contain approximately the same amount of ethyl alcohol: 8 grams, or 8,000 mg.

Blood alcohol concentrations often are expressed as a percentage of blood, as 0.05 percent for 50 milligrams of alcohol per deciliters of blood. It is recommended that drinkers keep their blood alcohol concentration (BAC) below 0.04 percent.

Depending on body weight and other factors, it takes the average adult nearly 1 hour for his or her liver to metabolize (break down) 8 grams of alcohol. Alcohol tends to accumulate in the blood because it is absorbed faster than it is metabolized.

Alcohol is absorbed through the membranes of the mouth and esophagus, from the stomach, and from the intestines. The rate of absorption is affected by proteins, fats, and carbohydrates in the digestive tract, which can slow absorption; by carbonation in drink mixers, which increases absorption; by the amount of water added to dilute the alcoholic beverage or the water or soft drinks consumed between alcoholic beverages; and by the presence of congeners (chemicals such as methyl alcohol, tannins, and histamines) present in the type of alcoholic beverage being consumed. The health of the drinker is also important, as a healthy liver metabolizes alcohol more efficiently.

> **Go to** "Precautions During Pregnancy: Alcohol" in this chapter; "Beverages" in chapter 19

A blood level of 20 to 30 mg/dl (the equivalent of 0.02 to 0.03 percent, or one or two drinks for an average adult) causes central nervous system changes in behavior, coordination, and ability to think clearly. Because alcohol is an anesthetic, the drinker may not notice the changes in his or her own behavior.

At a blood level of 50 mg/dl (0.05 percent), the drinker may experience sedation or a tranquilized feeling. Between 50 and 150 mg/dl (0.05 to 0.15 percent), there is a definite loss of coordination.

A concentration of 80 to 100 mg/dl (0.08 to 0.10 percent) is considered evidence of "legal intoxication" in many states, even though the alcohol level may be estimated by a breath test rather than actual blood analysis.

At blood levels between 150 and 200 mg/dl (0.15 and 0.20 percent), a person is obviously intoxicated and may show signs of delirium.

At levels between 300 and 400 mg/dl (0.30 and 0.40 percent), the drinker usually loses consciousness.

At levels above 500 mg/dl (0.50 percent), the heart and respiration become so depressed that they cease to function, and death follows.

DRINKING AND DRIVING

It is unsafe to drink and drive; in addition, many states have very strict driving-while-intoxicated (DWI) laws. The table on the next page is intended as a general guideline of how long to wait after imbibing before driving a motor vehicle. The time varies, however, from person to person, and the best rule is "Don't drink and drive."

In the table, one drink equals $1^1/_2$ ounces of liquor (86 proof), or 4 ounces of wine or champagne, or 12 ounces of beer.

WAITING PERIOD BEFORE DRIVING AFTER DRINKING

Body Weight	1 Drink	2 Drinks	3 Drinks	4 Drinks	5 Drinks	6 Drinks
100–119 pounds	0 hours	3 hours	6 hours	10 hours	13 hours	16 hours
120–139 pounds	0 hours	2 hours	5 hours	8 hours	10 hours	12 hours
140–159 pounds	0 hours	2 hours	4 hours	6 hours	8 hours	10 hours
160–179 pounds	0 hours	1 hour	3 hours	5 hours	7 hours	9 hours
180–199 pounds	0 hours	0 hours	2 hours	4 hours	6 hours	7 hours
200–219 pounds	0 hours	0 hours	2 hours	3 hours	5 hours	6 hours
Over 219 pounds	0 hours	0 hours	1 hour	3 hours	4 hours	6 hours

ADDITIONAL SOURCES OF INFORMATION

ORGANIZATIONS AND SERVICES

Alcoholics Anonymous
World Services Office
P.O. Box 459 Grand Central Station
New York, NY 10163
212-870-3400
http://www.alcoholics-anonymous.org/

Alzheimer's Association
919 N. Michigan Ave., Ste. 1000
Chicago, IL 60611-1676
800-272-3900 (24-hour line) or 312-335-8700
http://www.alz.org/

The American Academy of Allergy, Asthma, & Immunology
611 E. Wells St.
Milwaukee, WI 53202
800-822-2762 (24-hour referral line)
http://www.aaaai.org/

American Academy of Neurology
1080 Montreal Ave.
St. Paul, MN 55116
612-695-1940
http://www.aan.com/

American Academy of Ophthalmology
P.O. Box 7424
San Francisco, CA 94120-7424
415-561-8200
http://www.eyenet.org/

American Cancer Society
1599 Clifton Rd., NE
Atlanta, GA 30329-4251
800-227-2345
http://www.cancer.org/

American Chronic Pain Association
P.O. Box 850
Rocklin, CA 95677
916-632-0922
Fax: 916-632-3208

American Diabetes Association
1660 Duke St.
Alexandria, VA 22314
800-232-3472 (English and Spanish)
Fax: 703-549-6995
http://www.diabetes.org/

American Heart Association
Nation's Capital Affiliate
5335 Wisconsin Ave., NW, Ste. 940
Washington, DC 20015-2030
202-686-6888
Fax: 202-686-6162
http://americanheart.org/affilli/DC/

American Lung Association
1740 Broadway
New York, NY 10019-4374
http://www.lungusa.org/

American Medical Association
515 N. State St.
Chicago, IL 60610
312-464-5000
http://www.ama-assn.org/

American Optometric Association
243 N. Lindbergh Blvd.
St. Louis, MO 63141
314-991-4100
http://www.aoanet.org/

American Speech-Language-Hearing Association
10801 Rockville Pike
Rockville, MD 20852
800-498-2071
TTY: 301-897-5700
Fax: 301-571-0457
http://www.asha.org/

Health/Nutrition

Hot Lines and Information Services

AIDS Hot Line	800-342-AIDS
Alzheimer's Disease and Related Disorders Association	800-621-0379
Cancer Hot Line	800-4-CANCER
Depression Hot Line	800-551-0008
Dial-a-hearing screening test	800-222-EARS
Dial-a-hearing screening test (in PA)	800-345-EARS
Insurance Information Institute	800-221-4954
Medicare Hot Line	800-638-6833
Shriner's Hospital free children's hospital care referral line	800-237-5055

Arthritis Foundation
1330 Peachtree St.
Atlanta, GA 30309
800-283-7800 (24-hour recording) or 404-872-7100
http://www.arthritis.org/

The Center for Nutrition Policy and Promotion
U.S. Department of Agriculture
1120 20th St., NW, Ste. 200, North Lobby
Washington, DC 20036
202-418-2312
Fax: 202-208-2321
http://www.usda.gov/fsc/cnpp.htm

Center for Science in the Public Interest
Nutrition Action Healthletter
1875 Connecticut, NW, Ste. 300
Washington, DC 20009
202-332-9110
Fax: 202-265-4954
http://www.cspinet.org/index2.html

Centers for Disease Control and Prevention (CDC)
1600 Clifton Rd., NE
Atlanta, GA 30333
404-639-3311
http://www.cdc.gov/

CDC National AIDS Clearinghouse
P.O. Box 6003
Rockville, MD 20849-6003
800-342-2437 (English)
800-344-7432 (Spanish)
TTY: 800-243-7889
http://www.cdcnac.org/index.html

National Association for People With AIDS
(NAPWA)
1413 K St., NW
Washington, DC 20005
202-898-0414
Fax: 202-898-0435
http://www.thecure.org/

National Cancer Institute
9000 Rockville Pike
Bethesda, MD 20205
http://www.nci.nih.gov/
http://www.cancernet.nci.nih.gov/

National Council on Alcoholism and Drug
Dependence
12 W. 21th St.
New York, NY 10010
800-622-2255 (24-hour HOPE line) or 212-206-6770
Fax: 212-645-1690
http://www.mcadd.org/

National Institute of Child Health and Human
Development
Public Information and Communications Branch
Bldg. 31, Room 2A-32
31 Center Dr., MSC 2425
Bethesda, MD 20892-2425
301-496-5133
http://www.nih.gov/nichd/home2_home.html

National Institutes of Health
9000 Rockville Pike
Bethesda, MD 20205
http://www.nih.gov/

National Library of Medicine
8600 Rockville Pike
Bethesda, MD 20894
888-346-3656 or 301-594-5983
DOCLINE Service Desk: 800-633-5666
http://www.nlm.nih.gov/

National Women's Health Network
514 10th St., NW, Ste. 400
Washington, DC 20004
202-347-1140

Health/Nutrition

The President's Council on Physical Fitness and Sports
Attention: Director of Information
701 Pennsylvania Ave., NW, Ste. 250
Washington, DC 20004
202-272-3430

SMOKENDERS, Inc.
725 Independence Ave.
Washington, DC 20003
800-828-4357
http://www.smokenders.com/

MAGAZINES

Natural Health
Box 1200
Brookline Village, MA 02147
http://www.naturalhealth.com

Prevention
33 E. Minor St.
Emmaus, PA 18098
http://www.healthyideas.com

Self
350 Madison Ave.
New York, NY 10017
http://www.phys.com

Weight Watchers Magazine
360 Lexington Ave.
New York, NY 10017
http://www.weight-watchers.com

BOOKS

Alcoholics Anonymous: The Story of How Many Thousands of Men and Women Have Recovered from Alcoholism. Alcoholics Anonymous World Services, 1994.

Cancer Research Institute HelpBook: What to Do When Cancer Strikes. (To order, send $2 postage and handling to Cancer Research Institute HelpBook, P.O. Box 5199, FDR Station, New York, NY 10150-5199, or call 800-992-2623.)

The Complete Food Count Guide. Editors of *Consumer Guide* with the Nutrient Analysis Center, Chicago Center for Clinical Research. Publications International, 1996.

Cottrell, Randall R. *Wellness: Weight Control.* Dushkin, 1991.

Dunford, Randall Earl. *Your Health and the Indoor Environment: A Complete Guide to Better Health Through Control of the Indoor Atmosphere.* NuDawn Publishing, 1994.

Dupont, Robert L., and John P. McGovern. *A Bridge to Recovery: An Introduction to 12-Step Programs.* American Psychiatric Press, 1994.

Fries, James F., M.D. *Arthritis: A Comprehensive Guide to Understanding Your Arthritis.* 3rd ed. Addison-Wesley, 1990.

Garrison, Robert H., Jr., and Elizabeth Somer. *The Nutrition Desk Reference.* 2nd ed. Keats, 1990.

Greif, Judith, and Beth Ann Golden. *AIDS Care at Home: A Guide for Caregivers, Loved Ones, and People with AIDS.* Wiley, 1994.

Herbert, Victor, and Genell J. Subak-Sharpe, eds. *The Mount Sinai School of Medicine Complete Book of Nutrition.* St. Martin's Press, 1990.

Klesges, Robert C., and Margaret DeBon. *How Women Can Finally Stop Smoking.* Hunter House, 1994.

Larson, David E., ed. *The Mayo Clinic Family Health Book.* 2nd ed. William Morrow, 1996.

Morgentaler, Abraham. *The Male Body: A Physician's Guide to What Every Man Should Know About His Sexual Health.* Fireside, 1993.

Northrup, Christine. *Women's Bodies, Women's Wisdom: Creating Physical and Emotional Health and Healing.* Bantam Books, 1994.

Wexler, Nancy. *Mama Can't Remember Anymore: How to Manage the Care of Aging Parents.* Wein & Wein, 1992.

Yudofsky, Stuart C., Robert E. Hales, and Tom Ferguson. *What You Need to Know About Psychiatric Drugs.* American Psychiatric Association, 1991.

19

HOUSEHOLD TIPS

Food	536
Chemical Additives	547
Beverages	553
Clothing	557
Standard Sizes of Materials and Tools	566
Disposal of Hazardous Household Chemicals	568
Recycling	567
Composting	567
How to Build a Fire	567
Baby-Sitter Checklist	570
Car-Maintenance Checklist	570
Additional Sources of Information	570

FOOD

Properly preparing, storing, and cooking food is vital to a healthy, well-run household. The tips below provide information commonly needed in the kitchen.

COOKING EQUIVALENTS AND SUBSTITUTIONS

COMMON KITCHEN MEASURES

pinch (a few grains) = less than ¹/₈ teaspoon
3 teaspoons = 1 tablespoon
2 tablespoons = 1 fluid ounce
4 tablespoons = ¹/₄ cup
5 tablespoons + 1 teaspoon = ¹/₃ cup
16 tablespoons = 1 cup
1 cup = ¹/₂ pint or 8 fluid ounces
2 cups = 1 pint
2 pints = 1 quart
4 quarts = 1 gallon
2 dry pints = 1 dry quart
8 dry quarts = 1 peck
4 pecks = 1 bushel

COOKING MEASUREMENT ABBREVIATIONS

Measure	Abbreviation
degrees Celsius	°C
degrees Fahrenheit	°F
fluid ounce	fl. oz.
gram	g
kilogram	kg
liter	l
milligram	mg
milliliter	ml
ounce	oz.
pint	pt.
pound	lb.
quart	qt.
tablespoon	tbsp.
teaspoon	tsp.

Go to "Recommended Daily (or Dietary) Allowances" and "Activities and the Calories They Consume" in chapter 18

METRIC COOKING MEASURE EQUIVALENTS

Customary	Metric
1 teaspoon	4.9 milliliters
1 tablespoon	14.8 milliliters
1 ounce (dry)	28.35 grams
1 fluid ounce	29.57 milliliters
1 cup	236.6 milliliters
1 pint	473.2 milliliters
1 quart	946.4 milliliters
0.9 quart (dry)	1 liter
1.06 quarts (liquid)	1 liter
1 pound	454 grams
2.2 pounds	1 kilogram
32° Fahrenheit (freezing point)	0° Celsius
212° Fahrenheit (boiling point)	100° Celsius

FOOD WEIGHTS AND MEASURES

Bread

1-pound loaf	12 to 16 slices
1 slice	¹/₂ cup soft or ¹/₄ cup dry bread crumbs

Dairy

1 pound cheese	4 to 5 cups, shredded
1 pound cottage cheese	2 cups
3 ounces cream cheese	6 tablespoons
8 ounces cream cheese	1 cup
1 pound butter	2 cups (4 sticks)
1 quart milk	4 cups
1 pound instant nonfat dry milk	5 quarts liquid skim milk
13-ounce can evaporated milk	1²/₃ cups
¹/₂ pint cream	1 cup
1 cup heavy cream	2 cups, whipped

Eggs

3 to 4	1 cup
8 to 10 whites	1 cup
12 to 14 yolks	1 cup
1 yolk	2 tablespoons

Flour

1 pound all-purpose flour	4 cups, sifted
1 pound cake flour	4³/₄ to 5 cups, sifted
1 pound whole-wheat flour	3¹/₂ to 3³/₄ cups, unsifted
1 pound cornmeal	3 cups

Go to
"U.S. Customary System of Weights and Measures" and "Metric System of Measurements" in chapter 2

Fruit

juice of 1 medium lemon	2 to 3 tablespoons
juice of 1 medium orange	1/3 to 1/4 cup
granted rind of medium orange	1 tablespoon
1 apple	1 cup, sliced
1 pound apples	3 cups, pared and sliced
3 to 4 bananas (1 pound)	1 3/4 cups, mashed
1 pound cherries	2 cups, pitted
1 pound cranberries	2 cups
1 pound grapes	2 1/2 cups, seeded
1 pound raisins	2 1/2 cups
1 pound cut candied fruit	3 cups
1 pound finely cut dates	1 1/2 cups

Meat and Poultry

1 pound ground cooked meat	5 cups
1 pound diced cooked meat	5 cups
3 1/2-pound chicken	3 cups diced, cooked

Nuts

1 pound almonds in shell	1 1/4 cups, shelled
1 pound pecans in shell	2 cups, chopped
1 pound walnuts in shell	1 1/2 to 1 3/4 cups, chopped
1/4 pound chopped nuts	about 1 cup

Sweeteners and Flavorings

1 pound confectioners' sugar	3 1/2 cups
1 pound brown sugar	2 1/4 to 2 1/2 cups, firmly packed
1 pound granulated sugar	2 cups
1 pound honey, molasses, or syrup	1 1/3 cups or syrup
1 pound cocoa	4 cups
1 ounce unsweetened chocolate	1 square
6-ounce package chocolate chips	1 cup

Vegetables

1 whole bay leaf	1/4 teaspoon, crushed
1 pound split peas	2 1/2 cups
1 large green pepper	1 cup, diced
1/4 pound sliced mushrooms (1 1/4 cups)	1/4 to 1/2 cup, cooked
1 medium onion	1/2 cup, chopped
1 pound potatoes (3 medium)	2 1/2 cups, sliced
1 pound green beans (3 cups)	2 1/2 cups, cooked
1 pound cabbage	2 1/2 cups, cooked
1 pound carrots	2 1/2 cups, diced, or 2 cups, cooked
1 medium bunch celery	4 1/2 cups, chopped
1 pound tomatoes (3 medium)	1 1/2 cups, cooked

FOOD SUBSTITUTIONS

Ingredient	Substitution
Baking powder (1 teaspoon)	1/4 teaspoon baking soda + 1/2 teaspoon cream of tartar
Baking powder (1 1/4 teaspoons)	1/2 teaspoon baking soda + 2 tablespoons vinegar
Black pepper	White pepper or paprika
Bouillon (1 cup)	1 bouillon cube dissolved in 1 cup hot water
Bread crumbs (1 cup)	3/4 cup cracker crumbs
Butter (1 cup)	1 cup margarine or 1 cup vegetable shortening or 7/8 cup lard
Buttermilk or sour milk (1 cup)	1 cup yogurt or 1 cup whole milk + 1 tablespoon lemon juice or 1 tablespoon vinegar or 1 3/4 teaspoons cream of tartar
Carrots	Parsnips or baby white turnips
Chocolate Semisweet (1 2/3 ounces)	1 ounce unsweetened chocolate + 4 teaspoons sugar
Unsweetened (1 ounce—1 square)	3 tablespoons cocoa powder + 1 tablespoon shortening
Cream, heavy (1 cup)	7/8 cup buttermilk or yogurt + 3 tablespoons butter
Croutons	Cubes of crustless white bread sautéed in butter
Curry powder	Turmeric plus cardamom, ginger powder, and cumin
Dry mustard	Prepared mustard
Egg, for thickening or baking	2 egg yolks

continues

Household Tips

Ingredient	Substitution
Flour	
All-purpose, for thickening	1¹/₂ teaspoons cornstarch *or* 1¹/₂ teaspoons arrowroot *or* 1 tablespoon quick-cooking tapioca
All-purpose, for bread baking	Up to ¹/₂ cup bran, whole-wheat flour, *or* cornmeal + enough all-purpose flour to fill cup
Cake (1 cup sifted)	1 cup minus 2 tablespoons all-purpose flour
Fresh herbs (1 tablespoon)	¹/₃ to ¹/₂ teaspoon dried herbs
Honey (1 cup)	1¹/₄ cups sugar + ¹/₄ cup liquid
Lemon juice	Vinegar *or* lime juice *or* white wine
Mayonnaise, homemade (¹/₂ cup)	¹/₂ cup commercial mayonnaise + ¹/₂ teaspoon lemon juice + ¹/₂ teaspoon prepared mustard
Olive oil	Vegetable oil
Onion, chopped (1 cup)	1 tablespoon instant minced onion, reconstituted
Parsley	Chervil
Scallions	Green or white onions, *or* onion powder to taste
Shallots	2 parts onion + 1 part garlic
Sugar, granulated (1 tablespoon) (1 cup)	1 tablespoon maple sugar 1³/₄ cups confectioners' sugar *or* 1 cup molasses + ¹/₂ teaspoon baking soda
Tomato sauce (2 cups)	³/₄ cup tomato paste + 1 cup water
Wine vinegar	Cider vinegar with a little red wine or white distilled vinegar with a little white wine
Yeast, active dry	1³/₅-ounce cake yeast (1 tablespoon—1 package)

KOSHER SUBSTITUTIONS

According to Jewish dietary laws, certain food items, such as pork products, shellfish, and some cuts of beef, are not allowed to be eaten. Also, meat and dairy products are not to be eaten at the same time. Below is a list of ingredients that may be problematic in preparing a kosher dish. On the right are acceptable replacements for these items.

Ingredient	Substitution
Butter	In pastry: all-vegetable margarine or vegetable shortening
	To sauté vegetables: all-vegetable margarine
	To fry meat or poultry: equal parts rendered chicken fat and oil; oil; equal parts oil and all-vegetable margarine
Ham or bacon	Used as flavoring: an equal quantity of anchovies, mushrooms, or pungent vegetables
Milk or cream	In chicken stew, soup, or sauce: for each ¹/₂ cup, ¹/₂ cup chicken stock mixed with 1 egg yolk and 1 teaspoon cornstarch
	In pancakes: an equal quantity of water, 1 tablespoon oil for each cup of flour, and twice as many eggs
Shellfish	An equal amount of firm fish that has both fins and scales

LOW-FAT SUBSTITUTIONS

Without changing your diet, you can significantly reduce your intake of fat by making the following substitutions for basic ingredients:

Ingredient	Substitution
Baker's chocolate, unsweetened	For each ounce, ¹/₄ cup cocoa powder + 2 tsp. margarine
Butter	On vegetables and popcorn: butter substitute such as Butter Buds
	For sautéing onions and garlic: nonstick cooking spray and broth in a nonstick pan
	To prevent burning: chicken broth
Crème fraiche	Plain low-fat yogurt

Household Tips

Ingredient	Substitution
Eggs	For scrambled eggs and omelettes: egg substitute such as Egg Beaters
	For baking: 2 egg whites for 1 egg; 3 egg whites *or* 1 egg and 1 white for 2 eggs
Heavy cream	For whipped cream: substitute Cool Whip *or* low fat whipped cream in a spray can
	For cooking: replace 1/2 cup cream with 1 tbsp. Butter Buds combined with 1/3 cup skim milk
Roux	Use cornstarch, arrowroot, or pureed vegetables, *or* make the roux with 1 tbsp. Butter Buds and 1/3 cup skim milk instead of the butter
Sour cream	Plain low-fat yogurt *or* 1 cup low-fat cottage cheese combined with 2 tbsp. skim milk and 1 tbsp. lemon juice in the blender
Whole milk	Skim *or* low-fat milk

On Thanksgiving Day, 1997, Americans consumed 45 million turkeys.

COOKING TIMES AND SERVING SIZES

When cooking meat, poultry, fish, and shellfish, the oven temperatures and cooking time used depends on the size of the serving.

OVEN TEMPERATURE SETTINGS

175° to 225°F	Warm
250° to 275°F	Very slow
300° to 325°F	Slow
350° to 375°F	Moderate
400° to 425°F	Hot
450° to 475°F	Very hot

ROASTING MEAT AND POULTRY

Recommended oven temperatures are given in parentheses. Use a meat thermometer to monitor internal temperatures.

To Roast Chicken (375°F)

Chickens weighing between 2 and 4 pounds can be roasted for 30 minutes per pound. Add 15 minutes to the total roasting time if the chicken is stuffed. When the chicken is done, a meat thermometer inserted in the thickest part of the thigh will read 190°F; a thermometer inserted in the stuffing will read 165°F. Estimate 1/2 pound per serving.

To Roast Beef (325°F)

Cut	Weight in Pounds	Minutes per Pound	Internal Temperature (°F)
Standing rib	4–8		
rare		20–25	140
medium		25–30	160
well-done		30–35	170
Rolled rib	5–7		
rare		30–35	140
medium		35–40	160
well-done		40–45	170
Rib eye	4–6		
rare		20	140
medium		22	160
well-done		24	170
Sirloin tip	3 1/2–4	35–40	160
Tenderloin (roast at 425°F)			
whole	4–6	10	140
half	2–3	20	140

Household Tips

To Roast Lamb (325°F)

Cut	Weight in Pounds	Minutes per Pound	Internal Temperature (°F)
Leg	5–8	30–35	175–180
Shoulder	4–6	30–35	175–180
Cushion shoulder	3–5	30–35	175–180
Rib (rack)	4–5	40–45	175–180
Rolled shoulder	3–5	40–45	175–180
Crown roast	4–6	40–45	175–180

To Roast Pork (350°F)

To prevent trichinosis, pork must always be cooked to an internal temperature of 150° to 160°F.

Cut	Weight in Pounds	Minutes per Pound	Internal Temperature (°F)
Loin, center	3–5	20–22	150–160
Loin, half	5–7	22–25	150–160
Loin, rolled	3–5	25–30	150–160
Sirloin	3–4	25–30	150–160
Crown	4–6	20–22	150–160
Picnic shoulder	5–8	20–22	150–160
Rolled shoulder	3–5	22–25	150–160
Fresh ham (leg)			
whole	10–14	20–22	150–160
half	5–7	22–25	150–160
Spareribs	3	30	150–160

To Roast Ham and Other Cured Pork (325°F)

Cut	Weight in Pounds	Minutes per Pound	Internal Temperature (°F)
Whole ham	10–14		
uncooked		20	160
fully cooked		10	130
Half ham	5–7		
uncooked		25	160
fully cooked		15	130
Picnic shoulder	5–8	30	170
Rolled shoulder	2–4	40	170

To Roast Veal (325°F)

Cut	Weight in Pounds	Minutes per Pound	Internal Temperature (°F)
Leg	5–8	25–30	170
Loin	4–6	30–35	170
Rib (rack)	3–5	35–40	170
Rolled rump	3–5	40–45	170
Rolled shoulder	4–6	40–45	170

To Roast Duck or Goose (325°F)

Roast duck or goose about 30 minutes per pound. Estimate 1 pound per serving.

To Roast Turkey (325°F)

Turkey is done when a meat thermometer inserted in the thickest part of the thigh reads 185°F, or when a thermometer inserted in the stuffing reads 165°F. Plan on ½ pound per serving.

Ready-to-Cook Weight in Pounds	Total Number of Hours
4–8	3–4
8–12	4–4½
12–16	4½–5
16–20	6–7½
20–24	7½–9

BROILING MEAT AND POULTRY

To Broil Steak (place 2 inches from preheated oven broiler)

For a 1-inch-thick sirloin, porterhouse, T-bone, or ribeye:

Rare	5 minutes each side
Medium	7 minutes each side
Well-done	10 minutes each side

For a 1½-inch-thick sirloin, porterhouse, T-bone, or ribeye:

Rare	6 minutes each side
Medium	8 minutes each side
Well-done	12 minutes each side

For filet mignon, decrease the cooking time by 1 minute on each side. When grilling steak over hot charcoals, have the grill 3 inches from the fire and cook the meat 1 minute less on each side.

To Broil Lamb (place 2 inches from preheated oven broiler)

1-inch chops or patties	about 6 minutes on each side
1½-inch chops	9 minutes on each side
2-inch chops	11 minutes on each side

To Broil Pork (place 2 inches from preheated oven broiler)

Chops (¾ to 1 inch thick), shoulder steaks (½ to ¾ inch thick), and patties (1 inch thick) should be broiled about 11 minutes on each side.

For all boneless meat, allow ⅓ to ½ pound per serving; if the meat contains bone, estimate ½ to ¾ pound per serving.

A Closer Look

Carving a Turkey

Before carving a turkey or other whole bird, allow it to rest breast side up on a platter outside the oven for 10 to 20 minutes, depending on size. This allows the juices to settle into the meat. While the bird is resting, make sure your carving knife (not serrated) is very sharp, and assemble a second large platter and a long two-tined carving fork.

1. Pierce the knee joint with the fork and bend the leg away from the body. Slice between the thigh and body to expose the hip joint, and then work the knife between the ball and socket to cut the leg from the body. Separate the thigh from the drumstick, slice the meat from each, and arrange on the serving platter. Repeat for the other leg.
2. Pierce the meaty part of the wing with the fork and pull the wing away from the body. Cut between the body and the wing, then through the wing joint to remove the wing from the body. Cut the wing in half at the joint and add the pieces to the serving platter, or remove the meat from the wing and arrange for serving.
3. Starting near the neck, slice the breast lengthwise across the grain of the meat. Continue removing slices until you reach the breastbone, and then turn the bird around and repeat for the second breast. Place the slices on the serving platter and enjoy.

Household Tips

COOKING FISH AND SHELLFISH

To Cook Fish

Fish can be cooked at either a very high temperature for a short time or a low temperature for a longer period. Following are general guidelines:

Baked	10 minutes at 500°F
Broiled	15 minutes
Deep-fried	2 minutes at 370°F
Pan-fried	10 minutes
Poached or steamed	10 minutes per pound

Allow ³/₄ to 1 pound of whole fish per serving, ¹/₂ pound per serving of dressed fish, fillets, and steaks.

To Cook Shellfish

There are many ways to cook shellfish. Here are just a few.

Starting with boiling water, drop in seafood and let it simmer as follows:

Shrimp	5 minutes
Crab	20 minutes
Lobster	20 to 40 minutes

Clams can be steamed until their shells just open.

Shrimp, scallops, clams, and oysters can be deep-fried at 370°F for about 3 minutes.

Allow the following quantities per serving:

1 quart unshelled soft-shell clams
1 to 2 crabs
1 small lobster or 1 pound unshelled lobster
6 to 8 oysters
²/₃ cup or ¹/₃ pound shelled scallops
¹/₄ pound unshelled shrimp

COOKING TIMES FOR FRESH VEGETABLES

Vegetable	Amount per Serving	Cooking Time (in minutes)*
Artichoke	1 whole	30–40
Asparagus	5–7 stalks	10–15
Beans (green and wax)	¹/₃ pound	5–10
Beans (lima)	³/₄ pound	20–25
Beets	¹/₃ pound	35–45, whole
Broccoli	¹/₂ pound	10–15
Brussels sprouts	¹/₃ pound	5–10
Cabbage	¹/₃ pound	5
Carrots	¹/₃ pound	10–15
Cauliflower	¹/₃ pound	20–25, whole; 10–15, flowerets
Corn	1–2 ears	5
Eggplant	¹/₄ medium, sliced, broiled, or sautéed	5–10
Mushrooms	¹/₄ pound, caps or sliced and sautéed	5
Onions	¹/₃ pound	20–30, whole
Peas	¹/₂ pound	5–10
Peppers (green)	1 medium, sliced sautéed	3–5
Potatoes	1 medium	20–25, sliced; 90, baked, 350°F
	3 small new	20–25, whole
Potatoes (sweet) or yams	1 medium, sliced	30–35
Spinach	¹/₂ pound	5
Squash (summer) or zucchini	¹/₂ pound, sliced, boiled, or sautéed	5–10
Tomatoes	¹/₂ pound, sliced	5–10 (without water)
Turnips	¹/₃ pound, cubed	25–30

* Boiled or steamed unless otherwise noted.

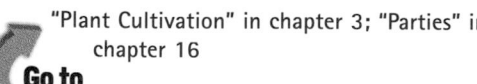 "Plant Cultivation" in chapter 3; "Parties" in chapter 16

Go to

COOKING FRESH FRUIT

To cook any of the fruits below, prepare the fruit according to the directions and add to the proper amount of boiling water. Add sugar and cook for the appropriate time.

Fruit	Amount[1]	How to Prepare	Amount of Boiling Water (cups)	Amount of Sugar (cups)	Cooking Time After Adding Fruit (in minutes)
Apples	8 medium	Pare and slice	$1/2$	$1/4$	8 to 10 (slices)
					12 to 15 (sauce)
Apricots	15	Halve; pit and peel if desired	$1/2$	$3/4$	5
Cherries	1 quart	Remove pits	1	$2/3$	5
Cranberries	1 pound	Sort	1 or 2, as desired[2]	2	5
Peaches	6 medium	Pare, pit, and halve or slice	$3/4$	$3/4$	5
Pears	6 medium	Pare, core, and halve or slice	$2/3$	$1/3$	10 (soft varieties); 20 to 25 (firm varieties)
Plums	8 large	Halve, pit	$1/2$	$2/3$	5
Rhubarb	$1 1/2$ pounds	Slice	$3/4$	$2/3$	2 to 5

[1] Makes 6 servings, about $1/2$ cup each. [2] Cranberries make 6 servings with 1 cup water; 8 servings with 2 cups water.

SERVING LARGER GROUPS

Here's how much to buy when you need to feed a crowd.

Type	8 Servings	12 Servings	16 Servings
Meat/Poultry/Fish			
Boneless	2–3 lbs.	3–4 lbs.	5–6 lbs.
Chops, roasts	3–5 lbs.	5–7 lbs.	7–9 lbs.
Ribs	6–8 lbs.	9–12 lbs.	12–15 lbs.
Whole birds	8–10 lbs.	12–14 lbs.	16–20 lbs.
Greens			
Lettuce	1–2 heads	2–3 heads	4–5 heads
Cooked leafy greens, peas	4 lbs.	6 lbs.	8 lbs.
Other vegetables	2 lbs.	3 lbs.	4 lbs.
Frozen, in 1-lb. bags	2 bags	3 bags	4 bags
Starches			
Potatoes	2–3 lbs.	4–5 lbs.	6–7 lbs.
Rice (uncooked)	2 cups	4 cups	6 cups
Pasta (uncooked)	1 lb.	2 lbs.	3 lbs.
Potato or pasta salad	1 quart	2 quarts	3 quarts
Dessert			
Cakes	1	1	2
Pies	1	2	3
Ice cream	2 pints	4 pints	6 pints
Drinks			
Iced drinks	2 liters	4 liters	6 liters
Coffee (ground)	$1/4$ lb.	$1/2$ lb.	1 lb.

Household Tips

Refrigeration Food Storage Times

Food	Maximum Recommended	Food	Maximum Recommended
Beef	3–5 days	Frankfurters	1 week
Butter	2 weeks	Ground meat	1–2 days
Canned goods	1 year	Milk	1 week
Cereal	2–3 months	Pasta	2 years
Cheese	1–3 weeks	Poultry	1–2 days
Eggs	1–2 weeks	Rice	2 years
Fish	1 day		

A Closer Look

Temperature of Food for Control of Bacteria

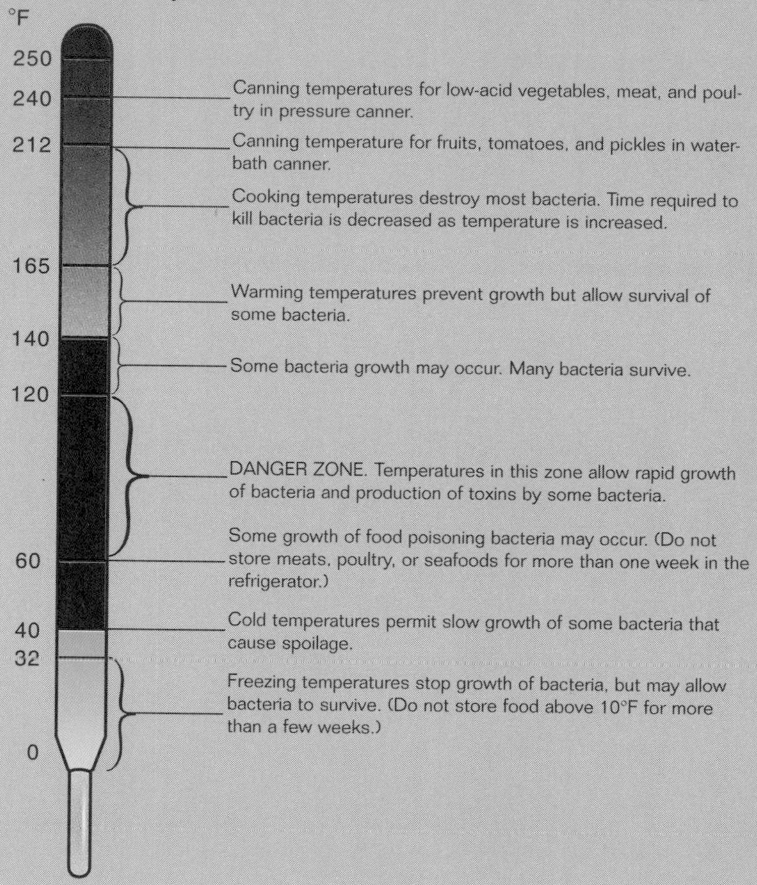

A Closer Look

°F

- 250
- 240 — Canning temperatures for low-acid vegetables, meat, and poultry in pressure canner.
- 212 — Canning temperature for fruits, tomatoes, and pickles in water-bath canner.
- Cooking temperatures destroy most bacteria. Time required to kill bacteria is decreased as temperature is increased.
- 165 — Warming temperatures prevent growth but allow survival of some bacteria.
- 140 — Some bacteria growth may occur. Many bacteria survive.
- 120
- DANGER ZONE. Temperatures in this zone allow rapid growth of bacteria and production of toxins by some bacteria.
- Some growth of food poisoning bacteria may occur. (Do not store meats, poultry, or seafoods for more than one week in the refrigerator.)
- 60
- 40 — Cold temperatures permit slow growth of some bacteria that cause spoilage.
- 32 — Freezing temperatures stop growth of bacteria, but may allow bacteria to survive. (Do not store food above 10°F for more than a few weeks.)
- 0

Household Tips

"Temperature Conversions" in chapter 12

Go to

FOOD HOT LINES

To provide consumers with information on cooking, health, and nutrition, several organizations have established toll-free telephone services.

Nutrition Hot Line
American Institute for Cancer Research
800-843-8114

American Seafood Institute
800-328-3474

Turkey Talk-Line
Butterball
800-323-4848 (November–December only)

Meat and Poultry Hot Line
Department of Agriculture
800-535-4555

Holiday Bake-Line
Land-O-Lakes
800-782-9606 (November–December only)

Consumer Nutrition Hot Line
National Center for Nutrition and Dietetics
800-366-1655

Cholesterol Information Center
National Heart, Lung and Blood Institute
301-251-1222

PANTRY BASICS

Certain ingredients are used so frequently by the typical home cook that they should always be ready. Keep the following basics on hand at all times to simplify weekly and daily shopping and cooking.

Canned goods   fruit juice, soft drinks, tomato sauce, soups, canned beans, peanut butter, tuna fish

Condiments   ketchup, prepared mustard, mayonnaise, maple syrup, Tabasco® sauce, soy sauce, Worcestershire sauce, horseradish, salad dressing, tahini

Dry goods   coffee, tea, breakfast cereal, rice, pasta, dried beans, flour, bread crumbs, baking soda, baking powder, yeast, cornstarch, cream of tartar

Fats and oils   butter, olive oil, vegetable oil

Fresh foods   bread, milk, eggs, cheese, yogurt, celery, carrots, potatoes, garlic, onions, lemons, limes

Seasonings   sugar, salt, black pepper, paprika, oregano, basil, bay leaves, cayenne pepper, dry mustard, curry powder, chili powder, cumin, coriander, thyme, sage, rosemary, dill, tarragon, ginger, cinnamon, nutmeg, cloves, cocoa, vanilla extract, honey, wine vinegar, balsamic vinegar

HERBS AND SPICES

Herbs can provide creative, flavorful alternatives to salt for seasoning foods. Through the skillful use of herbs and spices, you can create imaginative flavors and turn simple foods into gourmet delights.

Employees at the Ivory Soap company overmixed a batch of soap, causing it to be filled with excess bubbles. As a result, the soap floated. Customers loved it, and Ivory soap has been floating ever since.

Herbs and spices differ only in that herbs grow in temperate areas while spices grow in tropical regions. Many people like to grow their own herbs in order to have a fresh supply throughout the growing season. Professional cooks also prefer fresh herbs. But fresh herbs are less concentrated, and two to three times as much of them should be used if a recipe calls for dried herbs.

Here are some tips for cooking with herbs and spices.

- In general, the weaker the flavor of the main staple item, the lower the level of added seasoning required to achieve a satisfactory balance of flavor in the end product.
- Dried herbs are stronger than fresh, and powdered herbs are stronger than crumbled. A useful formula is $1/4$ teaspoon powdered herb = $3/4$ to 1 teaspoon crumbled = 2 teaspoons fresh.

- Leaves should be finely chopped because the more cut surface exposed, the more flavor will be absorbed.
- A mortar and pestle can be kept in the kitchen to powder-dry herbs when necessary.
- Scissors are often the best utensil for cutting fresh herbs.
- Be conservative with amounts until you are familiar with the strength of an herb. The aromatic oils can be too strong if a great deal is used.
- The flavoring of herbs is lost by extended cooking. Add herbs to soups or stews about 45 minutes before completing the cooking. For cold foods such as dips, cheeses, vegetables, and dressings, herbs should be added several hours, or even overnight, before using.
- For casseroles and hot sauces, add finely chopped fresh or dried herbs directly to the mixture.
- To become familiar with the specific flavor of an herb, try mixing it with butter and/or cream cheese, letting it set for at least an hour, and then spreading it on a plain cracker.
- Dried herbs should be stored in plastic bags, boxes, or tins rather than cardboard containers. They should be out of direct sunlight and away from the stove.

As a world commodity, coffee is second only to crude oil.

SELECTING HERBS AND SPICES TO GO WITH FOODS

Food	Herbs and Spices
Beef	Bay leaf, chives, cloves, cumin, garlic, hot pepper, marjoram, rosemary, savory
Bread	Allspice, caraway, cardamom, curry powder, marjoram, oregano, poppy seed, rosemary, thyme
Cakes	Allspice, cardamom, ginger
Cheese	Anise, basil, chervil, chives, curry, dill, fennel, garlic, marjoram, oregano, parsley, sage, thyme
Fish	Sweet basil, chervil, dill, fennel, French tarragon, garlic, parsley, thyme
Fruit	Anise, cinnamon, coriander, cloves, ginger, lemon verbena, mint, rose geranium, sweet cicely
Lamb	Garlic, marjoram, oregano, rosemary, thyme
Pork	Coriander, cumin, garlic, ginger, hot pepper, pepper sage, savory, thyme
Poultry	Garlic, oregano, rosemary, sage, savory
Salads	Anise, basil, chives, dill, French tarragon, garlic chives, marjoram, mint, oregano, parsley, savory, sorrel, tarragon (many are best used fresh or added to salad dressing; otherwise, use herb vinegars for extra flavor)
Sauces	Allspice, basil, cardamom, chili powder, chives, cumin, curry, fennel, ginger, marjoram, oregano, parsley, rosemary
Soups	Bay leaf, chervil, French tarragon, marjoram, parsley, savory, rosemary
Stews	Allspice, basil, cardamom, chili powder, curry, dill, ginger, parsley, sage
Vegetables	Basil, chervil, chives, dill, French tarragon, marjoram, mint, parsley, pepper, thyme

Herbal Salt Substitutes

These can be placed in shakers and used instead of salt.

Basic salt substitute   Use 2 teaspoons garlic powder and 1 teaspoon each of basil, oregano, and powdered lemon rind (or dehydrated lemon juice). Put ingredients into a blender and mix well. Store in a glass container and add rice to prevent caking.

Tangy salt substitute   Mix well 3 teaspoons basil; 2 teaspoons each of savory (summer is best), celery seed, ground cumin seed, sage, and marjoram; and 1 teaspoon lemon thyme. Powder with a mortar and pestle.

Spicy seasoning   Mix in a blender 1 teaspoon each of cloves, pepper, and coriander seed (crushed); 2 teaspoons paprika; and 1 tablespoon rosemary. Store in an airtight container.

Household Tips

CHEMICAL ADDITIVES

Additives are substances not naturally found in foods that are introduced during processing to improve flavor, appearance, or consistency or to preserve freshness.

COMMON ADDITIVE TERMS

Antioxidants   retard the oxidation of unsaturated fats and oils, colorings, and flavorings. Oxidation leads to rancidity, flavor changes, and loss of color. Most of these effects are caused by the reaction of oxygen in the air with fats.

Chelating agents   trap trace amounts of metal atoms that would otherwise cause food to discolor or go rancid.

Emulsifiers   keep oil and water mixed together.

Flavor enhancers   contribute little or no flavor of their own, but accentuate the natural flavor of foods. They are most often used when very little of a natural ingredient is present.

Thickening agents   are natural or chemically modified carbohydrates that absorb some of the water present in food, thereby making the food thicker. Thickening agents "stabilize" factory-made foods by keeping the complex mixtures of oils, water, acids, and solids well mixed.

TYPES OF ADDITIVES

The information on the following pages comes from the Center for Science in the Public Interest and is available from the organization as a color chart entitled "Chemical Cuisine." The address is 1875 Connecticut Ave., NW, Suite 300, Washington, DC 20009-5728.

Following each entry is a letter that corresponds to one these three categories:

(A) *Avoid.* The additive is unsafe in the amounts normally consumed or is poorly tested.
(C) *Caution.* The additive may be unsafe, is poorly tested, or is used in foods that people tend to eat too much of.
(S) *Safe.* The additive appears to be safe.

CHEMICAL ADDITIVES

ALGINATE; PROPYLENE GLYCOL ALGINATE Thickening agent, foam stabilizer *Ice cream, cheese, candy, yogurt*	Alginate, an apparently safe derivative of seaweed (kelp), maintains the desired texture in dairy products, canned frosting, and other factory-made foods. Propylene glycol alginate, a chemically modified algin, thickens acidic foods (soda pop, salad dressing) and stabilizes the foam in beer. (S)
ALPHA TOCOPHEROL (vitamin E) Antioxidant, nutrient *Vegetable oil*	Vitamin E is abundant in whole wheat, rice germ, and vegetable oils. It is destroyed by the refining and bleaching of flour. Vitamin E prevents oils from turning rancid. (S)
ARTIFICIAL COLORINGS	Most artificial colorings are synthetic chemicals that do not occur in nature. Though some are safer than others, colorings are not listed by name on labels. Colorings are used almost solely in foods of low nutritional value (candy, soda pop, gelatin desserts, etc.). Several dyes have caused allergic reactions (Yellow No. 5) or promoted cancer, and there is evidence that colorings may cause hyperactivity in some sensitive children. The use of coloring usually indicates that fruit or other natural ingredients have not been used. (A)
ARTIFICIAL FLAVORINGS *Soft drinks, candy, breakfast cereals, gelatin desserts, other food items.*	Hundreds of chemicals are used to create flavors; many may be used in a single flavoring, as in cherry soda pop. Most flavoring chemicals also occur in nature and are probably safe, but they may cause hyperactivity in some children. (A)

continues

Chemical Additives Continued

ASCORBIC ACID (vitamin C); ERYTHORBIC ACID Antioxidant, nutrient, color stabilizer *Oily foods, cereals, soft drinks, cured meats*	Ascorbic acid helps maintain the red color of cured meats and prevents the formation of nitrosamines (see also SODIUM NITRITE). It helps prevent loss of color and flavor by reacting with unwanted oxygen. It is used as a nutrient additive in drinks and breakfast cereals. Sodium ascorbate is a more soluble form of ascorbic acid. Erythorbic acid (sodium erythorbate) serves the same functions as ascorbic acid but has no value as a vitamin. (S)
ASPARTAME Artificial sweetener *Drink mixes, gelatin, desserts, other foods*	Aspartame, made up of two amino acids, was thought to be the perfect artificial sweetener, but questions have arisen about the quality of the cancer tests done on it. In addition, some individuals have reported severe behavioral effects after drinking diet soda. People with PKU should avoid it. (C)
BETA CAROTENE Coloring, nutrient *Margarine, shortening, non-dairy whiteners, butter*	Beta carotene is used as an artificial coloring and a nutrient supplement. The body converts it to vitamin A, which is part of the light-detection mechanism of the eye. (S)
BROMINATED VEGETABLE OIL (BVO) Emulsifier, clouding agent *Soft drinks*	BVO keeps flavor oils in suspension and gives a cloudy appearance to citrus-flavored soft drinks. The residues of BVO found in body fat are cause for concern. Safer substitutes are available. (A)
BUTYLATED HYDROXYANISOLE (BHA) Antioxidant *Cereals, chewing gum, potato chips, vegetable oil*	BHA retards rancidity in fats, oils, and oil-containing foods. While most studies indicate it is safe, a 1982 Japanese study demonstrated that it causes cancer in rats. This synthetic chemical often can be replaced by safer chemicals. (A)
BUTYLATED HYDROXYTOLUENE (BHT) Antioxidant *Cereals, chewing gum, potato chips, oils, other edibles*	BHT retards rancidity in oils. It both increased and decreased the risk of cancer in various animal studies. Residues of BHT occur in human fat. BHT is unnecessary or is easily replaced by safe substitutes. (A)
CAFFEINE Stimulant *Coffee, tea, cocoa (natural), soft drinks (additive)*	Caffeine may cause miscarriages or defects and should be avoided by pregnant women. It also keeps many people from sleeping. New evidence indicates that caffeine may cause fibrocystic breast disease in some women. (A)
CALCIUM (OR SODIUM) PROPIONATE Preservative *Bread, rolls, pies, cakes*	Calcium propionate prevents mold on bread and rolls. The calcium is a beneficial mineral; the propionate is safe. Sodium propionate is used in pies and cakes because calcium alters the action of chemical leavening agents. (S)
CALCIUM (OR SODIUM) STEAROLYL LACTYLATE Dough conditioner, whipping agent *Bread dough, cake fillings, artificial whipped cream, processed egg white*	This additive strengthens bread dough so that it can be used in bread-making machinery for more uniform grain and volume. It acts as a whipping agent in dried, liquid, or frozen egg white and artificial whipped cream. Sodium stearoyl fumerate serves the same purpose. (S)
CARRAGEENAN Thickening and stabilizing agent *Ice cream, jelly, chocolate milk, infant formula*	Carrageenan is obtained from seaweed. Large amounts of carrageenan have harmed test animals' colons; the small amounts in food are probably safe. Better tests are needed. (C)

Go to "Vitamin/Mineral Food Chart" in chapter 18

Household Tips

CASEIN; SODIUM CASEINATE Thickening and whitening agent *Ice cream, ice milk, sherbet, coffee creamers*	Casein, the principal protein in milk, is a nutritious protein that contains adequate amounts of all the essential amino acids. (S)
CITRIC ACID; SODIUM CITRATE Acid flavoring, chelating agent *Ice cream, sherbet, fruit drinks, candy, carbonated beverages, instant potatoes*	Citric acid is versatile, widely used, cheap, and safe. It is an important metabolite in virtually all living organisms and is especially abundant in citrus fruits and berries. It is used as a strong acid, a tart flavoring, and an antioxidant. Sodium citrate, also safe, is a buffer that controls the acidity of gelatin desserts, jam, ice cream, candy, and other foods. (S)
CORN SYRUP Sweetener, thickener *Candy, toppings, syrups, snack foods, imitation dairy foods*	Corn syrup is a sweet, thick liquid made by treating cornstarch with acids or enzymes. It may be dried and used as corn syrup solids in coffee whiteners and other dry products. Corn syrup contains no nutritional value other than calories, promotes tooth decay, and is used mainly in low-nutrition foods. (C)
DEXTROSE (GLUCOSE, CORN SUGAR) Sweetener, coloring agent *Bread, caramel, soda pop, cookies, other foods*	Dextrose is an important chemical in every living organism. A sugar, it is a source of sweetness in fruits and honey. Added to foods as a sweetener, it represents empty calories and contributes to tooth decay. Dextrose turns brown when heated and contributes to the color of bread crust and toast. (C)
DIGLYCERIDES	*See* MONOGLYCERIDES and DIGLYCERIDES.
ETHYLENEDIAMINE TETRA-ACETIC ACID (EDTA) Chelating agent *Salad dressing, margarine, sandwich spreads, mayonnaise, processed fruits and vegetables, canned shellfish, soft drinks*	Modern food-manufacturing technology, which involves metal rollers, blenders, and containers, results in trace amounts of metal contamination in food. EDTA traps metal impurities, which would otherwise promote rancidity and the breakdown of artificial colors. (S)
FERROUS GLUCONATE Coloring, nutrient *Black olives, vitamin pills*	Used by the olive industry to generate a uniform jet-black color and in pills as a source of iron, this substance is safe. (S)
FUMARIC ACID Tartness agent *Powdered drinks, pudding, pie, fillings, gelatin desserts*	A solid at room temperature, inexpensive, and highly acidic, fumaric acid is the ideal source of tartness and acidity in dry food products. However, it dissolves slowly in cold water, a drawback cured by adding dioctyl sodium sulfosuccinate (DSS), a poorly tested, detergentlike additive. (S)
GELATIN Thickening and gelling agent *Powdered dessert mix, yogurt, ice cream, cheese spreads, beverages*	Gelatin is a protein obtained from animal bones, hooves, and other parts. It has little nutritional value because it contains little or none of several essential amino acids. (S)
GLYCERIN (GLYCEROL) Maintainer of water content *Marshmallows, candy, fudge, baked goods*	Glycerin forms the backbone of fat and oil molecules and is quite safe. The body uses it as a source of energy or as a starting material in making more complex molecules. (S)
GUMS (ARABIC, FURCELLERAN, GHATTI, GUAR, KARAYA, LOCUST BEAN, TRAGACANTH) Thickening agents, stabilizers *Beverages, ice cream, frozen puddings, salad dressings, dough, cottage cheese, candy, drink mixes*	Gums derive from natural sources (bushes, trees, or seaweed) and are poorly tested. They are used to thicken foods, prevent sugar crystals from forming in candy, stabilize beer foam (arabic), form gel in pudding (furcelleran), encapsulate flavor oils in powdered drink mixes, and keep oil and water mixed in salad dressings. Tragacanth sometimes causes severe allergic reactions. (S)

Household Tips

continues

Chemical Additives Continued

HEPTYL PARABEN Preservative *Beer, noncarbonated soft drinks*	Heptyl paraben—short for the heptyl ester of parahydroxybenzoic acid—is a preservative. Studies suggest that this chemical is safe, but, like other additives in alcoholic beverages, it has never been tested in the presence of alcohol. (C)
HYDROGENATED VEGETABLE OIL Source of oil or fat *Margarine, processed foods*	Vegetable oil, usually a liquid, can be made into a semisolid by treating it with hydrogen. Hydrogenation reduces levels of polyunsaturated oils. Many people eat too much oil and fat of all kinds, natural and hydrogenated. High-fat diets promote obesity, heart disease, and possibly cancer. (C)
HYDROLYZED VEGETABLE PROTEIN (HVP) Flavor enhancer *Instant soups, frankfurters, sauce mixes, beef stew*	HVP consists of vegetable (usually soybean) protein that has been chemically broken down into the amino acids of which it is composed. HVP is used to bring out the natural flavor of food. (S)
INVERT SUGAR Sweetener *Candy, soft drinks, many other foods*	Invert sugar, an even mixture of dextrose and fructose (two sugars), is sweeter and more soluble than sucrose (table sugar). Invert sugar forms when sucrose is split in two by an enzyme or acid. It contributes to tooth decay. (C)
LACTIC ACID Acidity regulator *Spanish olives, cheese, frozen desserts, carbonated beverages*	This safe acid occurs in almost all living organisms. It inhibits spoilage in Spanish-type olives, balances the acidity in cheese making, and adds tartness to frozen desserts, carbonated fruit-flavored drinks, and other goods. (S)
LACTOSE Sweetener *Whipped topping mix, breakfast pastry*	Lactose is a carbohydrate found only in milk. One-sixth as sweet as table sugar, it is added to food as a slightly sweet source of carbohydrate. Milk turns sour when bacteria convert lactose to lactic acid. Many non-Caucasians have difficulty digesting lactose. (S)
LECITHIN Emulsifier, antioxidant *Baked goods, margarine, chocolate, ice cream*	A common constituent of animal and tissues, lecithin is a source of the nutrient choline. It keeps oil and water from separating, retards rancidity, reduces spattering in a frying pan, and leads to fluffier cakes. Major sources are egg yolks and soybeans. (S)
MANNITOL Sweetener, other uses *Chewing gum, low-calorie foods*	Not quite as sweet as sugar and poorly absorbed by the body, mannitol contributes only half as many calories as sugar. Used as the "dust" on chewing gum, it prevents gum from absorbing moisture and becoming sticky. (S)
MONOGLYCERIDES and DIGLYCERIDES Emulsifiers *Baked goods, margarine, candy, peanut butter*	These substances make bread softer, improve the stability of margarine, and make caramel less sticky. They prevent staleness and keep the oil in peanut butter from separating. Monoglycerides and diglycerides are safe, though most foods they are used in are high in refined flour, sugar, or fat. (S)
MONOSODIUM GLUTAMATE (MSG) Flavor enhancer *Soup, seafood, poultry, cheese, sauces, stews, other foods*	This amino acid brings out the flavor of protein-containing foods. Large amounts of MSG fed to infant mice destroyed nerve cells in the brain. Public pressure forced baby food companies to stop using MSG. MSG causes "Chinese restaurant syndrome," a burning sensation in the back of the neck and forearms, tightness of the chest, and headaches in some people. (C)
PHOSPHORIC ACID; PHOSPHATES Acidulant, chelating agent, buffer, emulsifier, nutrient, discoloration inhibitor *Baked goods, cheese, powdered foods, cured meats, soft drinks, cereals, dehydrated potatoes*	Phosphoric acid acidifies and flavors cola beverages. Phosphate salts are in hundreds of processed foods for many purposes. Calcium and iron phosphates act as mineral supplements. Sodium aluminum phosphate is a leavening agent. Calcium and ammonium phosphates serve as food for yeast in bread. Sodium acid pyrophosphate prevents discoloration. Phosphates are not toxic, but their widespread use has led to dietary imbalances that may contribute to osteoporosis. (C)

POLYSORBATE 60 Emulsifier *Baked goods, frozen desserts,* *imitation dairy products*	Polysorbate 60 is short for polyoxyethylene-(20)-sorbitan monostearate. Along with its close relatives, polysorbate 65 and 80, it works the same way that and diglycerides do, but smaller amounts are needed. They keep baked goods from going stale, keep dill oil dissolved in bottled dill pickles, help coffee whiteners dissolve in coffee, and prevent oil from separating out of artificial whipped cream. (S)
PROPYL GALLATE Antioxidant *Vegetable oils, meat products,* *potato sticks, chicken soup* *base, chewing gum*	This substance retards the spoilage of fats and oils and is often used with BHA and BHT because of the synergistic effect these additives have. The best long-term feeding study on this additive was peppered with suggestions but not proof of cancer. (A)
QUININE Flavoring *Tonic water, quinine water,* *bitter lemon*	This drug can cure malaria and is used as a bitter flavoring in a few soft drinks. There is a slight chance that quinine may cause birth defects, so pregnant women should avoid quinine-containing beverages and drugs. It has been very poorly tested. (A)
SACCHARIN Synthetic sweetener *Diet products*	Saccharin is 350 times sweeter than sugar. Studies have not shown that saccharin helps people lose weight. In 1977, the FDA proposed that saccharin be banned because of repeated evidence that it causes cancer. It is gradually being replaced by aspartame. (A)
SALT (SODIUM CHLORIDE) Flavoring *Most processed foods*	Salt is used liberally in many processed foods. Other additives contribute additional sodium. A diet high in sodium may cause high blood pressure, which increases the risk of heart attack and stroke. (A)
SODIUM BENZOATE Preservative *Fruit juices, carbonated drinks,* *pickles, preserves*	Manufacturers have used sodium for over 70 years to prevent the growth of microorganisms in acidic foods. (S)
SODIUM CARBOXY- **METHYL-CELLULOSE** **(CMC)** Thickening and stabilizing agent *Ice cream, beer, pie fillings, icings,* *diet foods, candy*	CMC is made by reacting cellulose with derivative of acetic acid. Studies indicate that CMC is safe. (S)
SODIUM NITRITE; **SODIUM NITRATE** Preservative, coloring, flavoring *Bacon, ham, frankfurters,* *luncheon meats, smoked fish,* *corned beef*	Nitrite can lead to the formation of small amounts of potent cancer-causing chemicals (nitrosamines), particularly in fried bacon. Nitrite is tolerated in foods because it can prevent the growth of bacteria that cause botulism poisoning. Nitrite also stabilizes the red color in cured meats and gives a characteristic flavor. Companies should find safer methods of preventing botulism. Sodium nitrate is used in dry-cured meats because it slowly breaks down into nitrite. (A)
SORBIC ACID; **POTASSIUM SORBATE** Prevents growth of mold *Cheese, syrup, jelly, cakes,* *wines, dry fruits*	These additives occur naturally in many plants and are safe under normal circumstances. (S)
SORBITAN **MONOSTEARATE** Emulsifier *Cakes, candy, frozen desserts,* *puddings, icings*	Like monoglycerides, diglycerides, and polysorbates, this additive keeps oil and water mixed. In chocolate candy, it prevents the discoloration that occurs when the candy is warmed up then cooled down. (S)

Household Tips

continues

Chemical Additives Continued

SORBITOL Sweetener, thickening agent, maintainer of moisture *Dietetic drinks and foods, candy, shredded coconut, chewing gum*	Sorbitol occurs naturally in fruits and berries and is a close relative of the sugars; however, it is half as sweet as sugar. It is used in noncariogenic chewing gum because oral bacteria do not metabolize it well. Large amounts of sorbitol (2 ounces for adults) have a laxative effect, but otherwise it is safe. Diabetics use sorbitol because it is absorbed slowly and does not cause blood sugar to increase rapidly. (S)
STARCH; MODIFIED STARCH Thickening agent *Soups, gravies, baby foods*	Starch, the major component of flour, potatoes, and corn, is used as a thickening agent. It does not, however, dissolve in cold water. Chemists have solved this problem by reacting starch with various chemicals. These modified starches are added to some foods to improve their consistencies and to keep the solids suspended. Starch and modified starches make foods look thicker and richer than they really are. (S)
SUGAR (SUCROSE) Sweetener *Table sugar, sweetened foods*	Sucrose, ordinary table sugar, occurs naturally in fruit, sugar cane, and sugar beets. Americans each consume about 65 pounds of refined sugar per year. Sugar, corn syrup, and other refined sweeteners make up about one-eighth of the average diet, but they contain no vitamins, minerals, or protein. (A)
SULFUR DIOXIDE; SODIUM BISULFITE Preservative, bleach *Dried fruits, wines, processed potatoes*	Sulfiting agents prevent discoloration (in dried fruits, some "fresh" shrimp, and some dried, fried, and frozen potatoes) and bacterial growth (in wines). They also destroy vitamin B_1 and can cause severe reactions in asthmatics. This additive has caused at least seven deaths. (A)
VANILLIN; ETHYL VANILLIN Substitute for vanilla *Ice cream, baked goods, beverages, chocolate, candy, gelatin desserts*	Vanilla flavoring is derived from a bean, but vanillin, the major flavor component of vanilla, is cheaper to produce in a factory. A derivative, ethyl vanillin, comes closer to matching the taste of real vanilla. Both chemicals are safe. (S)

OUTLAWED ADDITIVES

Name	Year Outlawed	Use
Cobalt sulfate	1966	Beer foam stabilizer
Cyclamate	1970	Artificial sweetener
Dulcin	1950	Artificial sweetener
Green No. 1	1966	Coloring agent
Orange B	1978	Coloring agent
Red No. 2	1976	Coloring agent
Safrole	1960	Root beer flavoring
Violet No. 1	1973	Coloring agent

Go to "Consumer Information and Protection" in chapter 22; "Treatment for Health Emergencies" in chapter 17; "Home Remedies" in chapter 18

BEVERAGES

Selecting and serving beverages, especially alcoholic beverages, can often be confusing. The information below is intended to aid hosts and hostesses serve their guests responsibly and pleasurably.

AMOUNT OF LIQUOR NEEDED FOR NUMBER OF DRINKS SERVED

Liquor is commonly sold in 750-milliliter and 1-liter bottles. A 750-milliliter bottle is equivalent to 25.4 fluid ounces. One liter is equivalent to 33.8 fluid ounces.

A Closer Look

Champagne Bottle Sizes

Name	Capacity	Bottles
Bottle	0.75 liter	1
Magnum	1.5 liters	2
Jeroboam	3 liters	4
Rehoboam	4.5 liters	6
Methuselah	6 liters	8
Salmanazar	9 liters	12
Balthazar	12 liters	16
Nebuchadnezzar	15 liters	20

Number of People	Number of Drinks	Amount Needed
For cocktails		
4	10 to 16	one 750-ml bottle
6	15 to 22	two 750-ml bottles
8	18 to 24	two 750-ml bottles
12	20 to 40	three 750-ml bottles
20	40 to 65	three 1-liter bottles
For buffet or dinner		
4	8 cocktails	one 750-ml bottle
	8 glasses of wine	two 1-liter bottles
	4 liqueurs	one 750-ml bottle
	10 highballs	one 750-ml bottle
6	12 cocktails	one 750-ml bottle
	12 glasses of wine	three 1-liter bottles
	8 liqueurs	one 750-ml bottle
	16 highballs	two 750-ml bottles
8	16 cocktails	one 750-ml bottle
	16 glasses of wine	three 1-liter bottles
	16 liqueurs	one 750-ml bottle
	18 highballs	two 750-ml bottles
20	40 cocktails	three 750-ml bottles
	40 glasses of wine	seven 1-liter bottles
	25 liqueurs	two 750-ml bottles
	50 highballs	three 1-liter bottles
For after-dinner party		
4	12 to 16	one 750-ml bottle
6	18 to 26	two 750-ml bottles
8	20 to 34	two 750-ml bottles
12	25 to 45	three 750-ml bottles
20	45 to 75	three 1-liter bottles plus one 750-ml bottle

Household Tips

MIXING DRINKS

Always be sure of your ingredients and measure them accurately. A jigger is 1¹/₂ ounces; a pony, ³/₄ ounce; a bar spoon, ¹/₂ teaspoon; and a dash, 7 to 10 drops.

Ice should always be the first ingredient that goes into the glass. Use new ice for every drink and do not let drinks stand too long before serving. The best bartenders chill cocktail glasses in the refrigerator before serving.

Drinks containing fruit juices, eggs, or other dissimilar ingredients should always be shaken fast and vigorously. The ingredients will mix more readily and completely in a shaker or an electric blender. Never shake drinks mixed with carbonated water or ginger ale. Stir them smoothly and not too vigorously for about half a minute. This will keep the drink sparkling and prevent a flat taste. It also will chill the drink properly and thoroughly.

When a drink calls for fruit juice, use fresh juice if possible. The juice is put into the mixing glass with the proper amount of sugar or other sweetener before the liquor.

Fine granulated sugar can be used for sweetening in most cases. Many people prefer simple syrup, which can easily be made by dissolving ¹/₂ pound of fine granulated sugar in ³/₄ cup of boiling water. One teaspoon of simple syrup is equivalent to one teaspoon of sugar.

For drinks requiring a twist of lemon, orange, or lime, use a piece of peel about 1¹/₂ inches long and ¹/₄ inch wide. Twist this over the drink to extract a bit of oil, and then drop in the peel.

ALCOHOLIC DRINK RECIPES

Except where otherwise indicated, *shake* means to shake with cracked ice and then strain into a glass; *stir* means to stir over ice in the glass; and *straight up* means served without ice.

"Safe Alcohol Consumption" and "Precautions During Pregnancy" in chapter 18
Go to

Alexander   Shake 1 oz. brandy, 1 oz. crème de cacao, and 1 oz. cream.

Bacardi Cocktail   Shake 1¹/₂ oz. Bacardi® rum, the juice of ¹/₂ lime, and ¹/₂ teaspoon grenadine.

B & B   Stir ¹/₂ oz. benedictine and ¹/₂ oz. brandy (or cognac); B & B may also be served straight up.

Black Russian   Stir 1¹/₂ oz. vodka and ³/₄ oz. Kahlua®.

Black Velvet   Pour equal parts Guinness® stout and champagne over ice in a tall glass.

Bloody Mary   Shake or stir 1¹/₂ oz. vodka, 3 oz. tomato juice, the juice of ¹/₂ lemon, a dash each of Worcestershire® and Tabasco® sauce, and a pinch each of salt, pepper, and celery salt.

Bronx Cocktail   Shake 1 oz. gin, ¹/₂ oz. dry vermouth, ¹/₂ oz. sweet vermouth, and ¹/₂ oz. orange juice.

Bullshot   Substitute consommé for tomato juice and follow the directions for Bloody Mary.

Champagne Cocktail   Mix 1 lump sugar, 2 dashes angostura bitters, and 1 oz. brandy; top with chilled champagne.

Cuba Libre (Rum and Coke®)   Over ice in a tall glass, pour 1 oz. light rum and the juice of ¹/₂ lime; top with cola.

Daiquiri   Shake 1¹/₂ oz. light rum, the juice of 1 lime, and 1 teaspoon powdered sugar (often served with the addition of crushed fruit or fruit juice as strawberry daiquiri, peach daiquiri, etc.; blended with crushed ice, it becomes a frozen daiquiri).

Gibson   A martini with the addition of a pearl onion instead of the traditional olive.

Gimlet   Shake 1 oz. gin and 1 oz. Rose's® lime juice or the juice of 1 lime.

Gin and Tonic   Pour 2 oz. gin over ice in a tall glass; top with tonic water.

Gin Fizz Shake 2 oz. gin, the juice of $\frac{1}{2}$ lemon, and 1 teaspoon powdered sugar; top with soda water in a tall glass.

Grasshopper Shake $\frac{1}{2}$ oz. crème de menthe, $\frac{1}{2}$ oz. white crème de cacao, and $\frac{1}{2}$ oz. cream.

Harvey Wallbanger Add 1 oz. Galliano® to a Screwdriver.

Jack Rose Shake $1\frac{1}{2}$ oz. apple brandy, the juice of $\frac{1}{2}$ lime, and 1 teaspoon grenadine.

Kir To a glass of chilled white wine, add 1 teaspoon crème de cassis.

Mai Tai Shake 2 oz. rum, 1 oz. curaçao, the juice of $\frac{1}{2}$ lime, $\frac{1}{2}$ oz. grenadine, $\frac{1}{2}$ oz. almond-flavored syrup, and $\frac{1}{2}$ teaspoon powdered sugar; serve over crushed ice.

Manhattan Stir with cracked ice $1\frac{1}{2}$ oz. whiskey, $\frac{3}{4}$ oz. sweet vermouth, and a dash of angostura bitters; serve over ice or straight up with a maraschino cherry.

Margarita Shake $1\frac{1}{2}$ oz. tequila, $\frac{1}{2}$ oz. Cointreau® or triple sec, and the juice of $\frac{1}{2}$ lime; serve in a chilled, salt-rimmed glass.

Martini Stir gin and dry vermouth; strain into a chilled glass. The original ratio of gin to vermouth was 2:1, but contemporary tastes tend toward "drier" ratios of 3:1, 5:1, and even 7:1. Serve straight up with an olive or, less traditionally, over ice or with a lemon twist. Made with a pearl onion, it is called a Gibson; with vodka, a vodka martini or Vodkatini.

Mint Julep Mix in a tall glass 1 lump sugar, 1 tablespoon water, and 4 sprigs of mint; fill the glass with crushed ice; add 2 oz. bourbon, and serve with straws, without stirring.

Old-Fashioned Mix in a short glass $\frac{1}{2}$ lump sugar, 2 dashes angostura bitters, and 1 dash water; stir in ice cubes and 2 oz. whiskey.

Orange Blossom Shake 1 oz. gin and 1 oz. orange juice.

Pimm's Cup Over ice in a tall glass, pour 1 oz. Pimm's No. 1 Cup®; top with lemonade, 7-Up®, or ginger ale.

Piña Colada Over crushed ice in a tall glass, pour $\frac{1}{2}$ oz. light rum; $\frac{1}{2}$ oz. dark rum; 1 oz. each of orange, lime, and pineapple juice; and 1 dash of grenadine. Top with coconut milk.

Before refrigerators, ice was cut from frozen lakes in the winter, put aboard ships, and transported around the world.

Pink Gin Add 1 dash angostura bitters to 2 oz. gin. Pink Gin may be served straight up or with water or soda and ice.

Planter's Punch Over crushed ice in a tall glass, pour 2 oz. soda water, the juice of 2 limes, and 2 teaspoons powdered sugar; stir to frost glass; add 2 dashes angostura bitters and 2 oz. rum.

Rickey Over cracked ice, pour 2 oz. gin and the juice of $\frac{1}{2}$ lime; top with soda water. This traditional gin rickey is often modified by substituting other spirits—hence, Scotch rickey, Irish rickey, etc.

Rob Roy Using Scotch whiskey, follow the directions for a Manhattan.

Rusty Nail Stir 2 oz. Scotch whiskey with 1 oz. Drambuie®.

Salty Dog Stir 2 oz. gin, 2 oz. grapefruit juice, and $\frac{1}{4}$ teaspoon salt.

Sangre A Bloody Mary made with tequila instead of vodka.

Screwdriver Over ice in a tall glass, pour 2 oz. vodka; top with orange juice.

7 & 7 Over ice, pour $1\frac{1}{2}$ oz. Seagram's® whiskey; top with 7-Up.®

Sidecar Shake 1 oz. brandy, $\frac{1}{2}$ oz. Cointreau® or triple sec, and the juice of $\frac{1}{2}$ lemon.

Household Tips

Singapore Sling   Shake 2 oz. gin, $\frac{1}{2}$ oz. cherry brandy, the juice of $\frac{1}{2}$ lemon, and 1 teaspoon powdered sugar; pour over ice cubes in a tall glass and top with soda water.

Stinger   Shake or stir 1 oz. brandy and 1 oz. white crème de menthe.

Tequila Sunrise   Shake or stir in a tall glass $1\frac{1}{2}$ oz. tequila and 3 oz. orange juice; add 1 oz. grenadine; do not stir.

Toddy   Dissolve 1 lump sugar in a little water in a short glass; add 2 oz. spirits (brandy, gin, rum, or whiskey) and top with water (with boiling water, the drink is a hot toddy).

Tom Collins   Shake 2 oz. gin, the juice of $\frac{1}{2}$ lemon, and 1 teaspoon powdered sugar; pour over ice cubes in a tall glass and top with soda water (made with vodka in place of gin, this is a Vodka Collins).

Whiskey Sour   Shake 2 oz. whiskey, the juice of $\frac{1}{2}$ lemon, and $\frac{1}{2}$ teaspoon powdered sugar.

White Lady   Shake $1\frac{1}{2}$ oz. gin, 1 teaspoon powdered sugar, 1 teaspoon cream, and 1 egg white.

Zombie   Blend with cracked ice 3 oz. rum, $\frac{1}{2}$ oz. apricot brandy, 1 oz. pineapple juice, the juice of 1 lime and 1 orange, and 1 teaspoon powdered sugar. Strain into a tall frosted glass; float $\frac{1}{2}$ oz. rum (151 proof) on top before serving with straws.

WINES AND THEIR SERVICE

Red table wines should be served cool or at room temperature. Room temperature means about 65 to 68°F, so some cooling may be necessary. Red wines go well with all foods with the possible exception of seafood. White table wines, rosé wines, and all sparkling wines—both red and white—should be served well chilled. Dry wines should not be served with sweet dishes.

So that corks stay moist and tight, store wines on their sides. If the cork is removed an hour or two before serving, red wines will expand a bit and give off a delightful scent. Smell the cork to see if it is sour-smelling; if so, the wine has started to turn to vinegar and should not be served; it can, however, be kept for cooking.

Many good wines will contain a small amount of sediment. This is harmless and will settle on the bottom of the bottle if it is stood upright for about two hours before serving. When serving champagne, hold the bottle at a slight angle for a few seconds after the cork is removed. This reduces the amount of frothing and maintains a maximum amount of sparkle.

Wineglasses should be placed to the right of the water goblet; they are arranged according to their use, the first wineglass being closest to the water goblet. If more than one wine is served, the glasses used first are removed when the course is through.

The person serving should fill his or her own glass one-quarter full and then taste the wine to check the quality and flavor. Then the other glasses should be filled half to three-quarters full but never to the very top. Wine is poured as soon as a course is served. The person pouring should not lift the glasses from the table.

When more than one wine is served, remember that light wine comes before heavy or full wine, dry white wine precedes sweet red wine, and dry red wine is served before white sweet wine. The "correct" wine is always the one you like best; however, certain wines complement certain foods. The following wine and food list is a guide to what people generally like. One's own taste should be the final judge.

SELECTING WINES TO GO WITH FOODS

After Dinner   Brandy, Cointreau, benedictine, créme de menthe.

Canapés, Crackers, Olives, Cheese Dips, Other Hors d'Oeurves   Sherry, vermouth, or champagne.

Cheese or Nuts   Port, sherry, red Burgundy, muscatel, zinfandel, Barbera.

A Closer Look

How to Store Coffee		
Bean form	Room temperature	4–5 weeks
	Freeze	5–6 months (grind amount needed only)
	Refrigerator	Avoid
Ground	Room temperature	7–10 days
	Freezer	5–6 weeks
	Refrigerator	Up to 3 weeks

Desserts   Sweet sauterne, champagne, port, muscatel, Tokay.

Fowl   Rhine wine, dry sauterne, champagne, Bordeaux, white or red Burgundy (with game).

Meats   Claret, red Burgundy, rosé, (with cold cuts).

Seafood   Chablis, Rhine wine, Moselle, dry sauterne, white Burgundy.

Soups   Sherry or Madeira.

PRIME WINE VINTAGES BY REGION/VARIETY

The years of prime wine vintages are given in descending order of quality.

Australia

Coonawara Cabernet: 1990, 1993, 1991, 1988
Hunter Valley Chardonnay: 1991, 1995, 1994, 1989
Chile: 1996, 1995, 1992, 1988

California

Cabernet Sauvignon: 1991, 1987, 1990, 1993
Chardonnay: 1991, 1990, 1987, 1995
Pinot Noir: 1994, 1991, 1990, 1985
Zinfandel: 1994, 1990, 1995, 1993

France

Alsace: 1990, 1989, 1988, 1992
Bordeaux, red: 1990, 1989, 1995, 1988
Bordeaux, white: 1990, 1989, 1988, 1995
Burgundy, red: 1990, 1995, 1989, 1993
Burgundy, white: 1990, 1995, 1989, 1992
Loire: 1990, 1995, 1989, 1994
Rhone: 1990, 1989, 1988, 1995

Germany

Mosel Reisling: 1990, 1995, 1994, 1993
Rheingau Reisling: 1990, 1992, 1995, 1993

Italy

Barolo: 1990, 1984, 1995, 1988
Chianti: 1990, 1995, 1988, 1994
Vino Nobile: 1990, 1995, 1988, 1994

Spain

Ribera del Duero: 1995, 1990, 1989, 1994
Rioja: 1995, 1994, 1989, 1991

CLOTHING

The following section contains instructions about properly washing clothing, removing stains, and choosing the right size.

WASHING INSTRUCTIONS FOR DIFFERENT FABRIC TYPES

Cottons and Linens   Separate whites and colors. Pretreat and soak heavily soiled articles. Load washer about 3 pounds lighter than manufacturer's recommendation. Wash whites and colorfast items in very hot water with all-purpose detergent for a full washer cycle. Extremely dirty articles should be washed separately. Use cool water for colors that are likely to bleed, with a shorter cycle for lightly soiled loads. For lightweight and sheer cottons, wash whites in warm water and colors in cool water with an all-purpose detergent for a shortened washing cycle.

Synthetics   Wash white nylon separately from other synthetics, as they pick up color easily. A 3- or 4-pound load of easy-care fabrics washes and dries with fewer wrinkles than a capacity load. Wash in

Household Tips

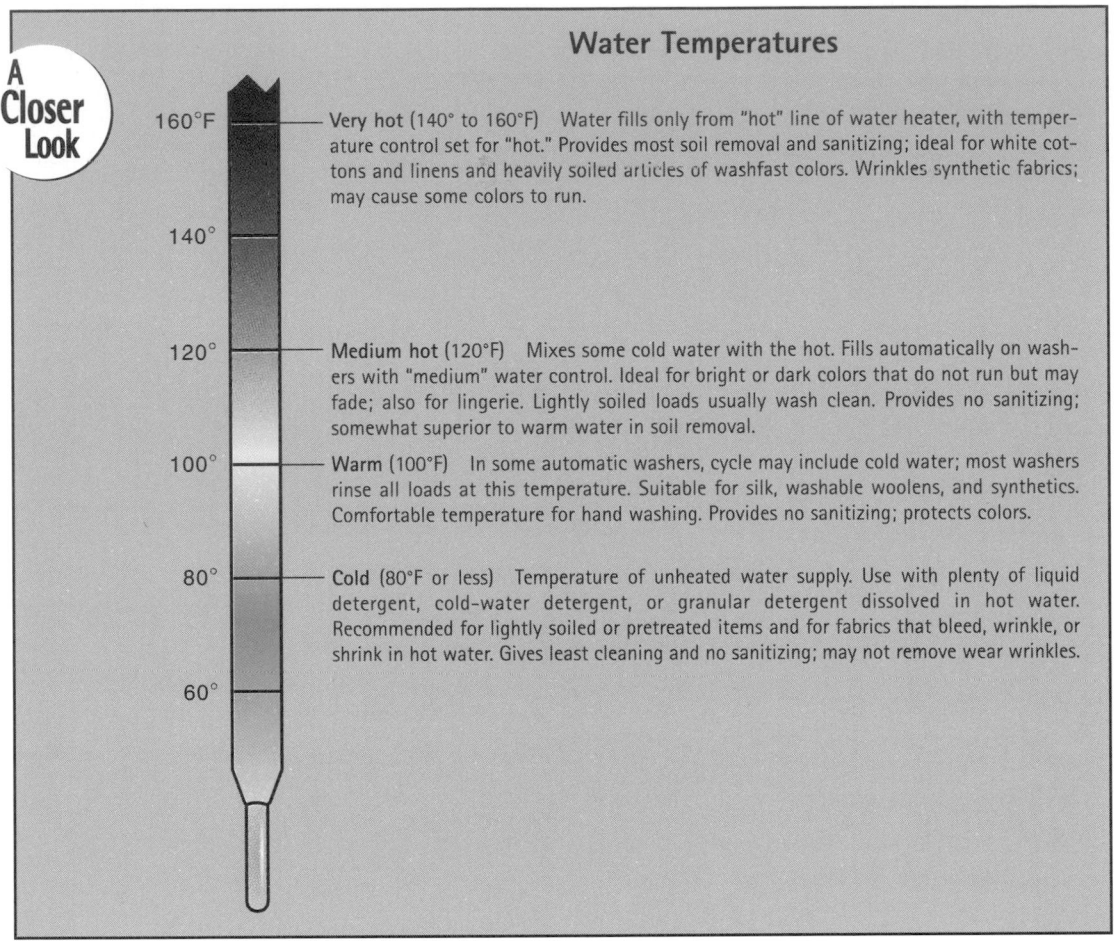

Water Temperatures

160°F — **Very hot (140° to 160°F)** Water fills only from "hot" line of water heater, with temperature control set for "hot." Provides most soil removal and sanitizing; ideal for white cottons and linens and heavily soiled articles of washfast colors. Wrinkles synthetic fabrics; may cause some colors to run.

140°

120° — **Medium hot (120°F)** Mixes some cold water with the hot. Fills automatically on washers with "medium" water control. Ideal for bright or dark colors that do not run but may fade; also for lingerie. Lightly soiled loads usually wash clean. Provides no sanitizing; somewhat superior to warm water in soil removal.

100° — **Warm (100°F)** In some automatic washers, cycle may include cold water; most washers rinse all loads at this temperature. Suitable for silk, washable woolens, and synthetics. Comfortable temperature for hand washing. Provides no sanitizing; protects colors.

80° — **Cold (80°F or less)** Temperature of unheated water supply. Use with plenty of liquid detergent, cold-water detergent, or granular detergent dissolved in hot water. Recommended for lightly soiled or pretreated items and for fabrics that bleed, wrinkle, or shrink in hot water. Gives least cleaning and no sanitizing; may not remove wear wrinkles.

60°

warm or cool water with an all-purpose detergent and a shortened washing cycle. Use hot water for badly soiled articles.

Woolens and Delicates Hand wash in cold water with Woolite® or a similar detergent and rinse thoroughly. Roll woolens tightly in a towel to remove excess water (do not wring) and dry flat on a drying rack. Allow delicates to drip-dry. Follow manufacturer's instructions when "dry clean only" appears on the care label.

TECHNIQUES FOR WASHING FABRICS

Soaking To help loosen stains and dirt, soak heavily soiled articles, dusty curtains and draperies, and certain stained fabrics before washing. Agitate the items for a few minutes in the washer with

warm water and detergent, using about half the detergent needed for washing. Extract the water before washing as usual. If you have to soak only a few items, use a small container such as a bucket. Submerge the fabric in a warm detergent solution for 15 minutes or until stains diminish. Agitate with your hands and extract excess water before washing as usual.

Loading A washer load made up of two large sheets or tablecloths with a variety of smaller articles washes more effectively than one made up of all large articles. Bulky pieces such as blankets, bedspreads, and throw rugs should be washed individually.

Rinsing To maximize effective rinsing, do not overload your washer or add more detergent than recommended by the manufacturer. If the machine does not extract water efficiently, have its spinning mechanism checked.

To reach out-of-the-way places with your vacuum cleaner, use an empty wrapping paper tube as an extension. Flatten the end of the tube to reach into tight crevices.

Using Fabric Softener   Fabric softeners make textiles softer and fluffier while minimizing wrinkles and deep creases. Softeners also reduce the static electricity that builds up on some fabrics when they rub against each other. Add fabric softener to the final rinse water in proportion to the weight of the clothes rather than the volume of water. Some softeners come in sheets that you can add to the dryer. To keep fabrics soft, use a softener each time you wash, as washing removes any softener added to previous loads.

STAIN REMOVAL

Many common stains fall into one of three categories: greasy, nongreasy, and combination. These stains can be removed by following the appropriate method for each given below. When necessary, separate directions are given for washable and nonwashable articles. Directions for nonwashables are for articles made of fabrics that are not damaged by the application of small amounts of water.

GREASY STAINS

Washable Articles   Regular washing, either by hand or by machine, removes some greasy stains. Some stains can be removed by rubbing soap or detergent into the stain and then rinsing with warm water. On some wash-and-wear or permanent-press fabrics, it may be necessary to rub soap or detergent thoroughly into the stain and allow it to stand for several hours, or overnight, before rinsing. Often, however, a grease solvent is necessary; this is effective even after an article has been washed. Sponge the stain thoroughly with the grease solvent and dry. Repeat if necessary. It often takes extra time to remove greasy stains from a fabric with a special finish.

A yellow stain may remain after a solvent treatment if the stain has been set by age or heat. To remove a yellow stain, use a chlorine or peroxygen bleach. If it is safe for the fabric, a strong sodium perborate treatment is usually the most effective.

Nonwashable Articles   Sponge stains well with grease solvent and dry. Repeat if necessary. It may take extra time to remove greasy stains from fabrics with a special finish.

A yellow stain may remain after a solvent treatment if the stain has been set by age or heat. To remove a yellow stain, use a chlorine or peroxygen bleach. If safe for the fabric, a strong sodium perborate treatment is usually the most effective.

NONGREASY STAINS

Many fresh stains can be removed by simple treatments. Stains set by heat or age may be difficult or impossible to remove.

Washable Articles   Sometimes, regular laundry methods will remove nongreasy stains; in other cases, laundering will actually set the stains. Sponge the stain with cool water or soak it in cool water for 30 minutes or longer; some stains require an overnight soak. If the stain persists after sponging or soaking, work a soap or detergent into it and then rinse. If the stain remains after detergent treatment, use a chlorine or peroxygen bleach.

Nonwashable Articles   Sponge the stain with cool water. If it remains, rub soap or detergent on the stain and work it into the fabric. Rinse. A final sponging with alcohol helps to remove the soap or detergent and to dry the fabric more quickly. Test alcohol on the fabric first to be sure it does not affect the dye. Dilute the alcohol with 2 parts of water before using it on acetate. If the stain remains after rinsing, use a chlorine or peroxygen bleach.

COMBINATION STAINS

Combination stains are caused by materials that contain both greasy and nongreasy substances.

Washable Articles   Sponge the stain with cool water or soak in cool water for 30 minutes or longer. If the stain persists, work soap or detergent into it and then rinse thoroughly. Allow the article to dry. If a greasy stain remains, sponge with a grease solvent. Allow the article to dry. Repeat if necessary. If a colored stain remains after the fabric dries, use a chlorine or peroxygen bleach.

Nonwashable Articles   Sponge the stain with cool water. If it remains, rub soap or detergent on the stain and work it into the fabric. Rinse the spot well with water. Allow the article to dry. If a greasy stain remains, sponge with a grease solvent. Allow to dry. Repeat if necessary. If a colored stain remains after the fabric dries, use a chlorine or peroxygen bleach.

SPECIFIC STAINS

Adhesive Tape   Scrape gummy matter from stains carefully with a dull table knife; avoid damaging fabric. Sponge with a grease solvent.

Early mattresses were filled with straw and held up with a rope stretched across the bed frame. If the rope was tight, sleep was comfortable. Hence the phrase, "sleep tight."

Alcoholic Beverages   Follow directions for nongreasy stains. An alternative method, if alcohol does not affect the color of the fabric, is to sponge the stain with rubbing alcohol. Dilute alcohol with 2 parts of water before using on acetate. If a stain remains, use a chlorine or peroxygen bleach.

The alcohol in alcoholic beverages will cause bleeding of some dyes, which results in loss of color or formation of a dye ring around the edge of the stain. When either change occurs, the original appearance of the fabric cannot be restored.

Antiperspirants and Deodorants   Wash or sponge the stain thoroughly with soap or detergent and warm water. Rinse. If the stain is not removed, use a chlorine or peroxygen bleach. Antiperspirants that contain such substances as aluminum chloride are acid; they may cause fabric damage and change the color of some dyes. Fabric color may be restored by sponging with ammonia. Dilute ammonia with an equal volume of water for use on wool or silk. Rinse.

Blood   Follow directions for nongreasy stains, with one variation. If the stain is not removed by soap or detergent, put a few drops of ammonia on it and repeat the treatment with detergent. Rinse. Follow with a bleach treatment if necessary. Bloodstains that have been set by heat will be difficult to remove.

Candy and Syrup   For chocolate candy and syrup, follow directions for combination stains. For other candy and syrup, follow directions for nongreasy stains.

Carbon Paper   Work soap or detergent into the stain; rinse well. If the stain is not removed, put a few drops of ammonia on it and repeat the treatment; rinse well. Repeat again if necessary.

Chewing Gum   Scrape gum off without damaging fabric. The gum can be scraped off more easily if it is first hardened by rubbing it with ice. If a stain remains, sponge thoroughly with a grease solvent.

Chlorine Bleach   Use one of the following treatments to remove yellow chlorine bleach stains from fabrics with resin finishes, or to prevent such stains from appearing. Always treat the fabric before ironing it. On some fabrics, the yellow stains form before ironing; on others, after ironing. In either case, ironing before the chlorine is removed weakens the fibers.

Yellow stains caused by the use of chlorine bleach on wool and silk cannot be removed. White or faded spots caused by use of chlorine bleach on colored fabrics cannot be restored to the original color.

Treatment for any fabric: Rinse fabric thoroughly with water. Then soak for 30 minutes or longer in a solution containing 1 teaspoon of sodium thiosulfate to each quart of warm water. Rinse thoroughly. To strengthen the treatment, make the sodium thiosulfate solution as hot as is safe for the fabric.

Treatment for white or colorfast fabrics: Rinse the fabric thoroughly with water. Then use a color remover, following the directions given on the package for removing stains.

Coffee and Tea *With cream:* Follow directions for combination stains.

Without cream: Follow directions for nongreasy stains.

Alternatively, for both types of stains, and if safe for the fabric, pour boiling water through the spot from a height of 1 to 3 feet.

Correction Fluid Sponge the stain with acetone or amyl acetate. Use amyl acetate on acetate, Arnel®, Dynel®, and Verel®; use acetone on other fabrics.

Cosmetics and Crayon *Washable articles:* Apply undiluted liquid detergent to the stain, or dampen the stain and rub in soap or detergent until thick suds are formed. Work in until the outline of the stain is gone; then rinse well. Repeat if necessary. It may help to dry the fabric between treatments.

Nonwashable articles: Sponge with a grease solvent until no more color is removed. If the stain is not removed, use the method given for washable articles.

Dyes Follow directions for nongreasy stains; if bleach is needed, use chlorine bleach or color remover. A long soak in sudsy water often is effective on fresh dye stains.

Fish Slime, Mucus, Vomit Follow directions for nongreasy stains or treat the stain with a lukewarm solution of salt and water—1/4 cup salt to each quart of water. Sponge the stain with the solution or soak the stain in it. Rinse well.

Fruit, Fruit Juices Follow directions for nongreasy stains or, if it is safe for the fabric, pour boiling water through the spot from a height of 1 to 3 feet. When any fruit juice is spilled on a fabric, it is a good idea to sponge the spot immediately with cool water. Some fruit juices, citrus among them, are invisible on the fabric after they dry but turn yellow on aging or heating. This yellow stain may be difficult to remove.

Furniture Polish Follow directions for greasy stains or, if the polish contains wood stain, follow directions given for paint.

Glue and Mucilage *Airplane glue, household cement:* Follow directions for correction fluid.

Casein glue: Follow directions for nongreasy stains.

Plastic glue: Wash the stain with soap or detergent and water before the glue hardens; some types of glues cannot be removed after they have hardened.

To remove some dried plastic glue stains, immerse the stain in a hot 10-percent acetic acid solution or hot vinegar. Keep acid or vinegar at or near the boiling point until the stain is removed. This may take 15 minutes or longer. Rinse with water.

Other types of glues and mucilage: Follow directions for nongreasy stains, but soak the stain in hot water instead of cool.

Grass, Flowers, Foliage *Washable articles:* Work soap or detergent into the stain; then rinse. If it is safe for the dye, sponge the stain with alcohol. Dilute the alcohol with 2 parts of water for use on acetate. If the stain remains, use a chlorine or peroxygen bleach.

Nonwashable articles: Use the methods for washable articles, but try alcohol first if it is safe for the dye.

Ink, Ballpoint Sponge the stain repeatedly with acetone or amyl acetate, or spray it with hair spray. This will remove fresh stains. Old stains may also require bleaching. Washing removes some types of ballpoint ink stains but sets other types. To see whether the stain will wash out, mark a scrap of similar material with the ink and wash it.

Household Tips

Ink, Black (India ink) Treat the stain as soon as possible. These stains are very hard to remove if dry.

Washable articles: Force water through the stain until all loose pigment is removed; otherwise, the stain will spread when treated. Wash with soap or detergent, several times if necessary. Then soak the stain in warm suds containing 1 to 4 tablespoons of ammonia to a quart of water. Dried stains may need to be soaked overnight. An alternative method is to force water through the stain until all loose pigment is removed, wet the spot with ammonia, and then work soap or detergent into it. Rinse. Repeat if necessary.

The first vacuum cleaner was so large it had to be drawn by horses and required a team of men to use it.

Nonwashable articles: Force water through the stain until all loose pigment is removed; otherwise, the stain will spread when you treat it. Sponge stain with a solution of water and ammonia (1 tablespoon of ammonia per 1 cup of water). Rinse with water. If stain remains, moisten it with ammonia and then work soap or detergent into it. Rinse. Repeat if necessary. If ammonia changes the color of the fabric, sponge first with water and then moisten with vinegar. Rinse well.

Ink, Drawing (colors other than black) Follow directions for nongreasy stains. If bleach is needed, use a color remover if it is safe for the dye. If a color remover is not safe, try other bleaches.

Ink, Writing *Washable articles.* Follow directions for nongreasy stains. Because writing inks vary greatly in composition, it may be necessary to try more than one kind of bleach. Try a chlorine bleach on all fabrics for which it is safe. For other fabrics, try peroxygen bleach. A few types of inks require treatment with color removers. A strong bleach treatment may be needed. A strong bleach, however, may leave a faded spot on some colored fabrics. If a yellow stain remains after bleaching, treat it as a rust stain.

Nonwashable articles: If possible, use a blotter (for small stains) or absorbent powder to remove excess ink before it soaks into the fabric. Then follow directions for washable articles.

Iodine *Washable articles:* Three methods for removing iodine stains are given below. If the method you try first does not remove the stain, try another.

Water: Soak in cool water until the stain is removed; some stains require soaking overnight. If the stain remains, rub it with soap or detergent and wash it in warm suds. If the stain is not removed, soak the fabric in a solution containing 1 tablespoon of sodium thiosulfate to each pint of warm water, or sprinkle the crystals on the dampened stain. Rinse well as soon as the stain is removed.

Steam: Moisten the stain with water; then hold it in the steam from a boiling teakettle.

Alcohol: If alcohol is safe for the dye, cover the stain with a pad of cotton soaked in it. If necessary, keep the pad wet for several hours. Dilute with 2 parts water for use on acetate.

Nonwashable articles: Try the steam or alcohol methods given above.

Mildew *Washable articles:* Treat mildew spots while they are fresh, before the mold growth has a chance to weaken the fabric. Wash the mildewed article thoroughly and dry it in the sun. If the stain remains, treat it with a chlorine or peroxygen bleach.

Nonwashable articles: Send the article to a dry cleaner promptly.

Mud Let the stain dry; then brush well. If the stain remains, follow directions for nongreasy stains. Stains from iron-rich clays not removed by this method should be treated as rust stains.

Mustard *Washable articles:* Rub soap or detergent into the dampened stain; rinse. If the stain is not removed, soak the article in a hot detergent solution for several hours, or overnight if necessary. If the stain remains, use a bleach.

Nonwashable articles: If alcohol is safe for the dye, sponge the stain with it. Dilute the alcohol with 2 parts of water for use on acetate. If alcohol cannot be used, or if it does not remove the stain completely, follow the treatment for washable articles but omit the soaking.

Nail Polish Follow directions for correction fluid. Nail polish removers also can be used to remove stains. Before using nail polish remover on acetate, Arnel®, Dynel®, or Verel®, test it on a scrap of material to make sure it will not damage the fabric.

To improve the fuel efficiency of your car, keep the car windows closed. Wind resistance due to open windows can eat up 5 miles a gallon.

Paint, Varnish Treat stains promptly, as they are always harder—and sometimes impossible—to remove after they have dried on fabric. Because there are so many different kinds of paints and varnishes, no one method will remove all stains. Read the label on the container; if a certain solvent is recommended as a thinner, it may be more effective in removing stains than the other solvents recommended.

Washable articles: To remove fresh stains, rub soap or detergent into the stain and wash. If the stain has dried or is only partially removed by washing, sponge it with turpentine until no more paint or varnish is removed (for aluminum paint stains, dry cleaning may be more effective than turpentine). While the stain is still wet with the solvent, work soap or detergent into it, put the article in hot water, and soak it overnight. Thorough washing will remove most types of paint stains. If the stain remains, repeat the treatment.

Nonwashable articles: Sponge fresh stains with turpentine until no more paint is removed (for aluminum paint stains, dry cleaning may be more effective than turpentine). If the stain remains, put a drop of liquid detergent on it and work it into the

fabric with the edge of the bowl or a spoon. Alternatively, sponge the stain with turpentine and treat with detergent as many times as necessary. If alcohol is safe for the dye, sponge the stain with it to remove turpentine and detergent. Dilute the alcohol with 2 parts of water for use on acetate. If alcohol is not safe for the dye, sponge the stain first with warm soap or detergent solution, then with water.

Pencil A soft eraser will remove pencil marks from some fabrics. If the marks cannot be erased, follow directions for carbon paper.

Perfume Follow directions for alcoholic beverages.

Perspiration Wash or sponge the stain thoroughly with soap or detergent and warm water. Work carefully because some fabrics are weakened by perspiration; silk is the fiber most easily damaged. If perspiration has changed the color of the fabric, try to restore it by treating it with ammonia or vinegar. Apply ammonia to fresh stains and apply vinegar to old stains; rinse with water.

If an oily stain remains, follow directions for greasy stains. Remove any yellow discoloration with a chlorine or peroxygen bleach. If it is safe for the fabric, the strong sodium perborate treatment recommended for greasy-stain removal is often the most effective for these stains.

Rust *Oxalic-acid method:* PRECAUTION: OXALIC ACID IS POISONOUS IF SWALLOWED. Moisten the stain with oxalic-acid solution (1 tablespoon of oxalic-acid crystals in 1 cup warm water). If the stain is not removed by a single treatment, heat the solution and repeat. If the stain is stubborn, place oxalic-acid crystals directly on it. Moisten the stain with water as hot as is safe for the fabric; allow it to stand a few minutes, or dip it in hot water. Repeat if necessary. Do not use this method on nylon. Rinse the article thoroughly. If it is allowed to dry in the fabric, oxalic acid will cause damage.

Household Tips

Cream-of-tartar method: If the treatment is safe for the fabric, boil the stained article in a solution containing 4 teaspoons of cream of tartar to each pint of water. Boil until the stain is removed. Rinse thoroughly.

Lemon-juice method: Spread the stained portion over a pan of boiling water and squeeze lemon juice on it; or sprinkle salt on the stain, squeeze lemon juice on it, and spread the fabric in the sun to dry. Rinse thoroughly. Repeat if necessary.

Color removers can be used to remove rust stains from white fabrics.

Scorch Stains   If the article is washable, follow the directions for nongreasy stains. To remove light scorch stains from an article that is nonwashable, apply hydrogen peroxide. The strong treatment may be needed to remove the stains. Repeat if necessary. Severe scorch stains cannot be removed, however, because the fabric already has been damaged.

Shellac   Using alcohol, sponge or soak the stain. Dilute the alcohol with 2 parts water for use on acetate. If alcohol bleeds the dye, try turpentine.

Shoe Polish   Because there are many different kinds of shoe polish, no one method will remove all stains. It may be necessary to try more than one of the methods given below.

1. Follow directions for cosmetics.
2. Sponge the stain with alcohol if it is safe for the dye in the fabric. Dilute the alcohol with 2 parts water for use on acetate.
3. Sponge the stain with grease solvent or turpentine. If turpentine is used, remove it by sponging with a warm soap or detergent solution or with alcohol.

If the stain is not removed by any of these methods, use a chlorine or peroxygen bleach. If safe for the fabric, the strong sodium perborate treatment recommended for greasy-stain removal is often the most effective.

Soft Drinks   Follow directions for nongreasy stains. When any soft drink is spilled on a fabric, sponge the spot immediately with cool water. Some soft drinks are invisible after they dry but turn yellow on aging or heating. The yellow stain may be difficult to remove.

A dirty car air filter can increase fuel consumption by as much as 10%.

Soot, Smoke   Follow directions for cosmetics.

Tar   Follow directions for greasy stains. If the stain is not removed by this method, sponge it with turpentine.

Urine   To remove stains caused by normal urine, follow directions for nongreasy stains. If the color of the fabric has been changed, sponge the stain with ammonia. If this treatment does not restore the color, sponging with acetic acid or vinegar may help. If the stain is not removed by one or both of these methods, see directions for medicines and yellowing.

Yellowing, Brown Stains   To remove storage stains—or unknown yellow or yellow-brown stains—from fabrics, use as many of the following treatments as necessary, if safe for the fabric, in the order given.

1. Wash.
2. Use a mild treatment of a chlorine or peroxygen bleach.
3. Use the oxalic-acid method for treating rust stains.
4. Use a strong treatment of a chlorine or peroxygen bleach.

CLOTHING SIZE CONVERSION TABLES

WOMEN

Blouses and sweaters

U.S.	32	34	36	38	40	42	44
British	34	36	38	40	42	44	46
Continental	40	42	44	46	48	50	52

Coats and dresses

U.S.	8	10	12	14	16	18	20
British	30	32	34	36	38	40	42
Continental	36	38	40	42	44	46	48

Shoes

U.S.	$5-5^{1}/_{2}$	$6-6^{1}/_{2}$	$7-7^{1}/_{2}$	$8-8^{1}/_{2}$	9
British	$3^{1}/_{2}-4$	$4^{1}/_{2}-5$	$5^{1}/_{2}-6$	$6^{1}/_{2}-7$	$7^{1}/_{2}$
Continental	36	37	38	39	40

Stockings

U.S. and British	8	$8^{1}/_{2}$	9	$9^{1}/_{2}$	10	$10^{1}/_{2}$
Continental	0	1	2	3	4	5

MEN

Hats

U.S.	$6^{5}/_{8}$	$6^{3}/_{4}$	$6^{7}/_{8}$	7	$7^{1}/_{8}$	$7^{1}/_{4}$	$7^{3}/_{8}$	$7^{1}/_{2}$
British	$6^{1}/_{2}$	$6^{5}/_{8}$	$6^{3}/_{4}$	$6^{7}/_{8}$	7	$7^{1}/_{8}$	$7^{1}/_{4}$	$7^{3}/_{8}$
Continental	53	54	55	56	57	58	59	60

Shirts

U.S. and British	14	$14^{1}/_{2}$	15	$15^{1}/_{2}$	16	$16^{1}/_{2}$	17
Continental	36	37	38	39	41	42	43

Shoes

U.S.	7	$7^{1}/_{2}$	8	$8^{1}/_{2}$	9	$9^{1}/_{2}$	10	$10^{1}/_{2}$	11
British	$6^{1}/_{2}$	7	$7^{1}/_{2}$	8	$8^{1}/_{2}$	9	$9^{1}/_{2}$	10	$10^{1}/_{2}$
Continental	39	40	41	42	43	43	44	44	45

Socks

U.S. and British	$9^{1}/_{2}$	10	$10^{1}/_{2}$	11	$11^{1}/_{2}$	12	$12^{1}/_{2}$
Continental	39	40	41	42	43	44	45

Suits and coats

U.S. and British	34	36	38	40	42	44	46
Continental	44	46	48	50	52	54	56

Household Tips

STANDARD SIZES OF MATERIALS AND TOOLS

Most materials and tools used in household repairs and improvements are sold in standardized sizes. The charts below list sizes commonly encountered in hardware and home supply stores.

INTERIOR MATERIALS

WALLS

Type	Thicknesses	Lengths	Widths
Decorative hardboard (embossed surface)	$1/4$"	4' to 16'	4'
Fiberboard (burlap or cork-surfaced)	$15/32$"	8', 10', 12', 14'	4'
Gypsum board (plain or vinyl-surfaced)	$1/4$", $3/8$", $1/2$"	6' to 16'	2', 4'
Hardboard (tempered or untempered)	$3/8$", $3/16$", $1/4$", $5/16$"	6' to 16'	4'
Hardwood plywood (prefinished)	$5/32$", $3/16$", $1/4$", $7/16$"	7', 8'	4'
Hardwood plywood (veneered paneling)	$1/8$" to $3/4$"	7', 8', 9', 10'	4'
Particle-core plywood	$3/4$", $7/16$"	7', 8', 9', 10'	4'
Plastic-surfaced hardboard	$1/8$", $3/16$", $1/4$"	6', 7', 8', 10'	16", 4'
Prefinished hardboard	$1/8$", $3/16$", $1/4$"	6' to 16'	16", 4'
Textured plywood (rough-sawn, brushed, grooved)	$3/8$", $5/8$"	8', 9', 10'	4'
Unfinished plywood	$3/4$" to $1 7/8$"	8', 9', 10'	4'
Vinyl-surfaced plywood	$3/16$", $1/4$", $5/16$"	7', 8'	4'
Wood-grained hardboard	$3/16$", $1/4$"	7', 8', 9', 10'	4'

CEILINGS

Type	Thicknesses	Lengths	Widths
Acoustical panels	$1/2$", $3/4$", 1"	2', 8', 10', 12', 14'	2', 4'
Acoustical tiles	$1/2$"	12"	12"
Decorative acoustical tile (embossed, textured, etc.)	$1/2$"	12", 2', 4'	12", 2'
Fiberglass acoustical panels	2"	8', $10 1/2$', $12 1/2$', 14', 16'	4'
Plastic-surfaced hardboard blocks	$1/4$"	16"	16"
Wood-grained planks	$1/2$"	4'	$5 3/16$", $6 3/8$", $8 3/16$"

FLOORS

Type	Thicknesses	Lengths	Widths
Asphalt (or asphalt-asbestos) tile	$1/8$", $3/16$"	9"	9"
Ceramic-tile sheets	$1/8$", $1/4$"	12"	12"
Indoor-outdoor carpet	N/A	As desired	3', 6', 9', 12', 15'
Indoor-outdoor carpet tile	N/A	9", 12"	9", 12"
Sheet vinyl	N/A	As desired	6', 9', 12'
Vinyl and vinyl-asbestos tile	$1/2$" to $1/8$"	9", 12", 18", 36"	4", 9", 12", 18", 36"
Wood parquet blocks	$5/16$", $7/16$"	9", 10"	9", 10"
Wood strips	$3/8$"	2"	1' to 8'

BATHROOM FIXTURES

Types	Lengths	Depths	Heights
Bathtubs	4'6", 5', 5'6"	2', 2'6", 2'7", 2'8"	1'2", 1'3", 1'4"
Compact corner tubs	3'2", 3'6", 4'	3'3", 3'10", 4'1^1/$_2$"	12"
One-piece fiberglass recessed shower units	3', 4', 5'	3'	6'1^1/$_2$"
One-piece fiberglass tub/shower units	5'	2'8^7/$_8$"	6'1^1/$_2$"
Shower stalls	2'6" to 3'6"	2'6" to 3'6"	6'3" to 6'5"
Sinks	19" to 30"	16" to 20"	2'7" (counter height)
Toilets (tank size)	18" to 23^1/$_2$"	25" to 30"	18^1/$_2$" to 40"

KITCHEN EQUIPMENT

Type	Widths	Depths	Heights
Built-in ovens (set in cabinet)	23^3/$_4$" to 36"	23^1/$_2$"	29^3/$_4$"
Built-in ranges (set in countertop)	12" to 42"	19" to 22"	34" to 36"
Dishwashers	24"	24^1/$_4$" to 30"	34" to 36"
Double sinks (set in counters)	32"	20"	2'7"
Drop-in ranges and ovens (recessed into base cabinets)	30"	24" to 27^1/$_4$"	34" to 36"
Freestanding ranges and ovens	20" to 42"	24^3/$_4$" to 26^5/$_8$"	35" to 36"
Freezers (chest)	46^1/$_2$" to 72"	29", 32"	36", 37"
Freezers (upright)	24" to 32"	26" to 32"	57" to 71"
Ranges and eye-level ovens	30"	27^1/$_8$" to 28^3/$_4$"	59^1/$_8$", 64^1/$_8$"
Refrigerators	28" to 35"	25" to 30"	61" to 36"
Single sinks (set in counters)	24", 30"	21"	2'7"
Slide-in ranges and ovens (set between base cabinets)	20" to 36"	24" to 26^7/$_8$"	34" to 36"
Triple sinks (set in counters)	42", 45"	21", 22"	2'7"

EXTERIOR MATERIALS

SIDING

Type	Thicknesses	Lengths	Widths
Aluminum (horizontal)	N/A	9'4^1/$_2$", 10', 12'6", 16'	8", 10"
Hardboard lap (horizontal)	^{3}/$_8$", ^{7}/$_{16}$"	12', 16'	6", 8", 9", 10", 12"
Hardboard panels (vertical)	^{1}/$_4$", ^{5}/$_{16}$", ^{3}/$_8$", ^{7}/$_{16}$"	6', 7', 8', 9', 10', 16'	4'
Plywood panels (vertical—roughsawn, brushed, grooved)	^{3}/$_8$", ^{1}/$_2$", ^{5}/$_8$"	8', 9', 10', 12'	4'
Prefinished steel (horizontal)	N/A	12'6"	8", 9^1/$_2$"
Vinyl lap (horizontal)	N/A	12^1/$_2$"	8", 12"
Vinyl V-grooved (vertical)	N/A	10'	10"
Wood lap (horizontal)	^{1}/$_2$", ^{5}/$_8$", ^{3}/$_4$"	3' to 20'	6", 8", 10", 12"

continues

Household Tips

Continued

DOORS AND WINDOWS

Type	Thicknesses	Heights	Widths
Bifold, 2-door units	1$\frac{1}{8}$", 1$\frac{3}{8}$".	6'8"	2', 2'8", 3'
Bifold, 4-door units	1$\frac{1}{8}$", 1$\frac{3}{8}$"	6'8"	3', 4', 5', 6'
Flush (hollow, solid)	1$\frac{3}{8}$", 1$\frac{3}{4}$", 2$\frac{1}{4}$"	6'8", 7'	6"
Louvered	1$\frac{1}{8}$", 1$\frac{3}{8}$"	6'6", 6'8", 7'	1'3" to 3'
Panel	1$\frac{3}{8}$", 1$\frac{3}{4}$"	6'8", 7'	1'2" to 3'4"
Sash (with one or more glass panels)	1$\frac{3}{8}$", 1$\frac{3}{4}$"	6'8", 7'	2' to 3'6"
Sliding glass, 2-panel units	N/A	6'8"	5', 6', 6'2$\frac{1}{4}$", 8'8$\frac{1}{4}$"
Sliding glass, 3-panel units	N/A	6'8"	9', 9'3$\frac{3}{4}$", 12', 12'2$\frac{3}{4}$"
Steel entry (single, double, sidelight)	1$\frac{3}{4}$"	6'8"	2'8", 3'

DISPOSAL OF HAZARDOUS HOUSEHOLD CHEMICALS

Many of the ordinary household cleaners and other materials we use every day must be disposed of properly to avoid endangering ourselves, our pets, and our environment. Never throw containers of flammable, reactive, or corrosive liquids such as paint, solvents, or automotive fluid in the trash, where they might leak or evaporate dangerously. Read the label for disposal information and adhere to community regulations regarding the disposal of these substances. The following methods are recommended for the safe disposal of toxic household waste.

Method A   For small amounts, dilute with lots of water and pour down the drain. For large amounts, use method D.

Method B   In a well-ventilated place away from pets and people, allow to evaporate, or combine it with an absorbent material such as cat litter and allow to solidify. Wrap thoroughly in plastic and discard in trash.

Material	Method A	Method B	Method C	Method D
Antifreeze	■			
Brake fluid			■	■
Car batteries			■	■
Contact cement		■		
Degreasers				
Diesel fuel			■	■
Furniture polish				■
Kerosene			■	
Motor oil			■	■
Paint—latex		■		
Paint—oil base				■
Paint stripper	■			
Paint thinner				■
Paintbrush cleaner—phosphate	■			
Paintbrush cleaner—solvent				■
Power-steering fluid			■	■
Rust remover	■			
Solvent-based glue, adhesive, sealant				■
Transmission fluid			■	■
Water-based glue, adhesive, sealant		■		
Wood finish				■
Wood preservative				■

Method C Recycle at a local center set up for this purpose, or use method D.

Method D Save for special collection by local authorities or call your local health department, cooperative extension service, or environmental protection agency for instructions.

RECYCLING

You can help protect the environment by taking three steps to limit the amount of garbage sent to landfills and incinerators:

1. Reduce the amount of disposable material you use in the form of shopping bags, paper towels, product packaging, and so on.
2. Reuse as many items as possible (such as coffee cans to hold nails, newspaper as packing material, old sheets as drop cloths).
3. Recycle as much of the rest as possible.

Many organic materials, such as food and yard waste, can go into a compost pile (see next section), and a growing number of other items are now recycled through community programs. Follow your city's recycling laws and make the most of voluntary recycling centers that take up the slack. To make recycling easier, post a list of recyclables in your kitchen or garage and set up separate containers to sort them according to local regulations. Rinse out containers before discarding and, where applicable, return deposit cans and bottles. Most municipalities have facilities to recycle the following items.

Paper	Newspaper, magazines, catalogs, corrugated cardboard, smooth (gray) cardboard, egg and produce cartons, beverage cartons, paper bags, wrapping paper, office paper, junk mail, paperback books, telephone books
Plastic	Bottles and jugs
Glass	Bottles and jars
Metal	Cans, aluminum foil and trays, utensils, pots and pans, appliances, furniture, machine parts, tools, nuts and bolts

COMPOSTING

Composting is a great way to recycle certain biodegradable materials to the benefit of your yard and garden. In a compost heap, you may dispose of fruit and vegetable peels, stems, leaves and cores, pulp from your juicing machine, crushed eggshells, coffee grinds, cut flowers, woodstove ashes, sawdust, chicken and rabbit droppings, grass clippings, hedge trimmings, small wood chips, leaves, pine needles, sod, and dirt. Finished compost can be worked into yard and garden soil to enrich it and make your plantings thrive. Here's how to make compost:

1. Collect equal parts wet or green material and dried or brown material, making sure both have been reduced to fairly small pieces.
2. Using alternating layers of green and brown, build a pile roughly 3' x 3' x 3'. This pile can be freestanding, or you can use one of the many compost containers on the market. Dampen the pile as you build, and sprinkle in some fresh soil or compost starter (available at garden stores) as a catalyst.
3. For the first month, turn the pile once a week to aerate and to blend decomposed material with fresh material. Use a pitchfork for this job and wet the compost if necessary.
4. After the first month, insert a compost thermometer into the pile to monitor its temperature. Decomposing compost will heat up to the 120° to 160°F range; turn the pile whenever it cools below this temperature. The compost is ready to use when it no longer heats up.

HOW TO BUILD A FIRE

Before starting a fire in your fireplace, make sure you have a screen to keep sparks and coals inside. For best results, use a rack to elevate the fire and allow air to flow underneath. Keep fireplace tools handy for tending the fire as it burns.

1. Remove most of the soot and ashes from previous fires, leaving larger coals and charred logs.
2. Crumple or loosely roll several sheets of newspaper and arrange on top of the coals.
3. Lay short, dry kindling over the newspaper in a crisscross or side-by-side pattern. If the logs or wood pieces you will use are damp or green, place fire-starters beneath the kindling.
4. Put a few small to medium logs atop the kindling. Larger pieces can be added after the fire has established itself.
5. Open the flue. Use long fireplace matches to light the fire in several places, from below.

BABY-SITTER CHECKLIST

Whenever you leave your children with a baby-sitter, it is important to provide the sitter with the basic information he or she will need to care for your children and to handle any emergencies. Show the sitter around your home, explaining door locks, alarm systems, and fire extinguishers; point out first-aid supplies and telephones; and indicate the location of your children's toys, clothing, and food. In addition, leave the following list of phone numbers and vital data by the telephone.

Your home address and phone number(s)
Children's names, ages, heights, and weights
Mother's name, location, and phone number(s)
Father's name, location, and phone number(s)
Fire department/paramedics phone number(s)
Police department phone number(s)
Poison-control center phone number(s)
Children's doctor's name, address, and phone number
Nearest hospital/emergency room, address, and phone number
Taxi or car service name and phone number(s)
Nearest reliable neighbor's name, address, and phone number
Reliable friends/relatives' names, addresses, and phone numbers
Children's school name(s) and phone number(s):
Children's health-insurance-plan number and insurer's phone number(s)
Children's health problems (allergies, asthma, etc.)
Mealtimes and bedtimes
Children's duties
Children's food and play preferences
Baby-sitter's duties

CAR-MAINTENANCE CHECKLIST

You can keep your car running longer and better by following a few simple maintenance routines. Your owner's manual indicates how often you should change fluids, tune the engine, rotate the tires, etc. Follow the manufacturer's recommendations, increasing the frequency of maintenance for cars that see heavy use or lots of stop-and-go driving. If you or your car's monitoring systems detect problems, maintenance should be performed as needed. Your maintenance schedule should include a number of basic procedures.

Fluids

Change motor oil and filter
Replace antifreeze/coolant
Replace automatic-transmission fluid and filter
Refill windshield-washer fluid and change blades

Engine

Change spark plugs
Check alternator and starter
Clean battery and terminals
Clean/replace air filter
Check timing
Check intake manifold
Check/replace PCV (positive crankcase ventilation)
Check/replace belts

Tires

Check air pressure
Check treads, replace tire if less than $1/16$"
Rotate tires
Check brakes/pads
Check wheel alignment

ADDITIONAL SOURCES OF INFORMATION

ORGANIZATIONS AND SERVICES

Auto Safety Hot Line
U.S. Department of Transportation
400 7th St., SW, Room 5326
Washington, DC 20580
800-424-9393

This hot line provides information on air bags, seat belts, child seats, auto recalls, and other safety issues. Open 9 A.M. to 5 P.M. EST.

Energy Conservation Center
Public Service Electric and Gas Company
P.O. Box 1258
Newark, NY 07101
000-054-4444

Specialists can provide information on specific energy needs such as weatherization, appliance efficiency and rebates, and home energy audit publications. The center receives calls weekdays between 9 A.M. and 5 P.M., EST.

Genova Plumbers Hot Line
7034 E. Court St.
Davison, MI 48423
800-521-7488

The staff can suggest solutions to plumbing problems involving gutters and plastic fittings as well as more technical problems. The hotline operates weekdays between 8 A.M. and 5 P.M., EST.

Major Appliance Consumer Action Panel
  (MACAP)
20 N. Wacker Dr.
Chicago, IL 60606
800-621-0477
312-984-5858 (in Illinois, Alaska, and Hawaii)

MACAP responds to written inquiries about problems with major appliances. Call for further instructions. It is open weekdays from 8:30 A.M. to 5 P.M., CST.

Shopsmith, Inc.
6530 Poe Ave.
Dayton, OH 45414
800-543-7586

Shopsmith answers questions related to woodworking. If they cannot answer your question, they will research the information and call back. Call weekdays between 9 A.M. and midnight and Saturdays between 9 A.M. and 6 P.M., EST.

Soap and Detergent Association
475 Park Ave. South
New York, NY 10016
212-725-1262

This association answers questions on all aspects of soaps and detergents. They also have free publications. Call Monday through Friday from 9 A.M. to 4:45 P.M., EST.

MAGAZINES
COOKING AND DINING

Bon Appetit
6300 Wilshire Blvd.
Los Angeles, CA 90048
www.bonappetit.com

Food and Wine
1120 Avenue of the Americas
New York, NY 10036
www.chefnet.com

Gourmet
560 Lexington Ave.
New York, NY 10022
www.gourmet.com

HOME AND GARDENING

Architectural Digest
6300 Wilshire Blvd.
Los Angeles, CA 90048
www.epicurious.com

Better Homes and Gardens
1716 Locust St.
Des Moines, IA 50309
www.bhglive.com

Country Living
5400 S. 60th St.
Box 643
Greendale, WI 53129
www.countryliving.com

The Family Handyman
7900 International Dr.
Minneapolis, MN 55425
www.readersdigest.com

Horticulture
98 N. Washington St.
Boston, MA 02114

House Beautiful
224 W. 57th St.
New York, NY 10019
http://homearts.com

Metropolitan Home
1633 Broadway
New York, NY 10029

Southern Living
2100 Lakeshore Dr.
Birmingham, AL 35209
www.pathfinder.com

BOOKS

Bernstein, Peter, and Christopher Ma. *The Practical Guide to Practically Everything*. Random House, 1997.

Brody, Jane. *Jane Brody's Good Food Book*. Bantam, 1987.

Bykofsky, Sheree, and Paul Fargis. *The Big Book of Life's Instructions*. The Stonesong Press/Harper-Collins, 1995.

Cunningham, Marion, ed. *Fannie Farmer Cookbook*. Knopf, 1990.

Dadd, Barbara Lynn. *Home Safe Home*. Tarcher/Putnam, 1997.

Family Circle Magazine. The Family Circle Good Cook's Book. Simon & Schuster, 1993.

Green, Mark. *The Consumer Bible*. Workman, 1995.

Heloise. *All-New Hints from Heloise*. Perigee, 1989.

Johnson, Hugh. *Wine*. Fireside/Simon & Schuster, 1987.

Kaplan, Leon. *Keep This Book in Your Glove Compartment*. Berkley Books, 1997.

Mr. Boston Official Bartender's Guide. Warner, 1987.

Reader's Digest Association. *The Family Handyman Helpful Hints*. Reader's Digest Association, 1995.

Rombauer, Irma S., Ethan Becker and Marion Rombauer Becker. *The Joy of Cooking*. Rev. ed. Simon & Schuster, 1997.

Rosso, Julee, and Sheila Lukins. *The New Basics Cookbook*. Workman, 1989.

The Stanley Complete Step-by-Step Book of Home Repair and Improvement. Simon & Schuster, 1993.

20

PERSONAL FINANCES

TABLES OF COMMON INTEREST	574
MAKING A BUDGET	575
HOW MUCH CAN YOU SPEND ON HOUSING?	576
AVERAGE COST OF RAISING A CHILD	576
CALCULATING YOUR NET WORTH	576
INSURANCE	578
CREDIT AND LOANS	582
REAL ESTATE AND MORTGAGES	583
INVESTMENTS AND RETIREMENT	586
TIPPING	595
ADDITIONAL SOURCES OF INFORMATION	596

Personal finances are often a mystifying subject. The objective of making more from your income than just enough to live on is shared by many. But faced with a huge assortment of possible investments, insurance plans, real-estate ventures, and retirement plans, how can you, as an individual, decide on the best course of action?

This chapter provides a starting point. It contains information on making a budget, the types of insurance available, loans, real estate, and mortgages. Social Security and retirement planning are covered, and glossaries of financial and real-estate terms are included. You should consult books and periodicals devoted to financial planning, or professional financial planners, however, before you create a master plan for your personal finances.

In America, 10% of the population controls 90% of the wealth.

TABLES OF COMMON INTEREST

SIMPLE INTEREST

Simple interest is computed on the amount of the principal (total amount borrowed) of a loan. That principal is multiplied by the rate of interest; the resulting figure then is multiplied by the time over which the loan will be repaid.

SIMPLE INTEREST ON A $100 LOAN

Time	Annual Rate							
	5%	6%	7%	8%	9%	10%	15%	20%
1 month	.4167	.5000	.5833	.6667	.7500	.8333	1.2500	1.6667
6 months	2.5000	3.0000	3.5000	4.0000	4.5000	5.0000	7.5000	10.0000
12 months	5.0000	6.0000	7.0000	8.0000	9.0000	10.0000	15.0000	20.0000
24 months	10.0000	12.0000	14.0000	16.0000	18.0000	20.0000	30.0000	40.0000
36 months	15.0000	18.0000	21.0000	24.0000	27.0000	30.0000	45.0000	60.0000

COMPOUND INTEREST

Compound interest is computed by multiplying the sum of the principal and the accrued interest by the rate of interest. This calculation must be performed each time the principal is compounded. To determine the approximate number of years it will take for the principal to double, divide the interest rate percent into 72.

COMPOUND INTEREST ON $100 PRINCIPAL, COMPOUNDED ANNUALLY

Time	Annual Rate					
	5%	6%	7%	8%	9%	10%
6 months	2.50	3.00	3.50	4.00	4.50	5.00
1 year	5.00	6.00	7.00	8.00	9.00	10.00
2 years	10.25	12.36	14.49	16.64	18.81	21.00
3 years	15.76	19.10	22.50	25.97	29.50	33.10
4 years	21.55	26.25	31.08	36.05	41.16	46.41
5 years	27.63	33.82	40.26	46.93	53.86	61.05

MORTGAGE AMORTIZATION FACTORS

Monthly mortgage payments include a percentage of the principal plus interest on the principal. The size of the monthly payment reflects the amount of the loan, the term of the loan, and the interest rate that applies—whether fixed or variable.

MONTHLY PRINCIPAL + INTEREST PAYMENT ON A $100,000 LOAN

Term	Interest rate							
	4%	5%	6%	7%	8%	9%	10%	15%
5 years	1841.65	1887.12	1933.28	1980.12	2027.64	2075.84	2124.71	2379.00
10 years	1012.45	1060.66	1110.21	1161.08	1213.28	1266.76	1321.51	1613.35
15 years	739.69	790.79	843.86	898.83	955.65	1014.27	1074.61	1399.59
20 years	605.98	659.96	716.43	775.30	836.44	899.72	965.03	1316.79
25 years	527.84	584.59	644.30	706.80	771.82	839.20	908.71	1280.84
30 years	477.42	536.82	599.55	665.30	733.76	804.62	877.58	1264.45
35 years	442.77	504.69	570.19	638.86	710.26	783.99	859.67	1256.81
40 years	417.94	482.20	550.21	621.43	695.31	771.36	849.16	1253.22

MAKING A BUDGET

The first step in personal financial planning is to get a clear picture of where you currently stand. An inventory of expected income and expenses projected on both a monthly and an annual basis will allow individuals and families to create a budget. A budget helps to keep expenses within the boundaries of income while also showing what amount, if any, is available for investments.

Following are outlines of income and expense categories that you should include in any personal budget. Note that expenses include fixed obligations and flexible or discretionary outlays, which you can change as circumstances and objectives change.

Income

 Salaries (total in household) _____

 Bonuses, tips _____

 Investments (interest, dividends, capital gains, real-estate income) _____

  TOTAL INCOME _____

Expenses

 Housing (rent or mortgage payments) _____

 Utilities (gas, electric, water, telephone) _____

 Taxes (federal, state, and local income; local real estate; Social Security) _____

 Interest payments (car, bank loan, credit card, other loans) _____

 Principal payments (amount of borrowed principal repaid) _____

 Insurance (health, life, property) _____

 Education (tuition, supplies, room and board) _____

 Personal expenses _____

 Contributions _____

 Food _____

 Transportation _____

  TOTAL FIXED OUTLAYS _____

Personal Finances

Clothing   _____
Entertainment   _____
Vacations and recreation   _____
Furniture, appliances, and home improvements   _____
Health and beauty   _____
Savings (general or specific for future purchases or objectives)   _____
Miscellaneous   _____
    TOTAL VARIABLE OUTLAYS   _____

TOTAL EXPENSES   _____

    AMOUNT AVAILABLE FOR INVESTING   _____
    (total income minus total expenses)

Budgets are useful only when the amounts specified in each category are not regularly exceeded. If you have trouble keeping a budget, you should make sure that your spending targets reflect your actual expenses and that the members of your household understand the ultimate benefits of budgeting income and expenses.

HOW MUCH CAN YOU SPEND ON HOUSING?

To figure out how much you can afford in monthly rent or mortgage payments, first calculate your total monthly income. If you rent, the total of your rent plus other debt outlays (for credit cards, school loans, etc.) should not exceed 35 percent of your income. If you own your home, the total of your mortgage principal, mortgage interest, real-estate taxes, and homeowner's insurance should not exceed 28 percent of your income. *See also* "Real Estate and Mortgages," later in this chapter.

AVERAGE COST OF RAISING A CHILD

The Agricultural Research Service of the U.S. Department of Agriculture calculates that it costs a two-parent, two-child family $97,710–$192,780 to raise a child to the age of 18. The cost per child increases by a factor of 1.26 for a family with only one child, while it decreases by a factor of 0.78 for a family with three children.

TOTAL SPENDING IN DOLLARS FOR CHILD REARING OVER 18 YEARS

Yearly Income	Yearly Expense (age 0–3)	Total Housing	Total Food	Total Transport	Total Clothes	Total Health Care	Total Education & Child Care	Total Books, Toys, etc.	Total Expenditures
32,000 or less	4,960	30,540	19,650	16,530	9,330	6,840	5,790	9,030	97,710
32,000–54,100	6,870	43,020	23,700	23,070	10,860	8,460	9,840	13,710	132,660
54,000 or more	10,210	69,780	30,270	27,750	14,370	10,050	16,590	23,970	192,780

CALCULATING YOUR NET WORTH

Use the following chart to calculate your current net worth. Be sure to include amounts held individually and jointly to evaluate your family's net worth.

Personal Finances

Assets

Cash on hand and liquid assets

    Checking and savings accounts   _____

    Cash value of life insurance   _____

    U.S. savings bonds   _____

    Equity in pension funds   _____

    Money-market funds   _____

    Brokerage funds   _____

    Trusts   _____

    Debts owed you   _____

    Other   _____

    TOTAL   _____

Personal Holdings

    Car(s) (current value)   _____

    Home(s)   _____

    Boat(s)   _____

    Major appliances   _____

    Furs and jewelry   _____

    Antiques and collectibles   _____

    Art   _____

    Other   _____

    TOTAL   _____

Investments

    Common stocks   _____

    Preferred stocks   _____

    Corporate and municipal bonds   _____

    Mutual funds   _____

    Certificates of deposit   _____

    Business investments   _____

    Real-estate investments   _____

    IRAs   _____

    Other   _____

    TOTAL   _____

  TOTAL ASSETS   _____

Liabilities

    Bills due   _____

    Revolving charge and bank-card debts   _____

    Taxes due   _____

    Outstanding mortgage   _____

    Outstanding loans (bank, insurance, etc.)   _____

    Stock margin accounts payable   _____

    Other debts   _____

  TOTAL LIABILITIES   _____

  NET WORTH (Assets minus liabilities)   _____

INSURANCE

Life is full of risks. One way you can minimize the effects of these risks is to obtain insurance. By insuring your health, your life, your property, and your car, as well as getting coverage for loss of income in the event of a disability, you can ensure that you and your family remain financially stable even if catastrophe strikes. Additionally, you can use some types of insurance to further your personal financial goals.

HEALTH INSURANCE

Health insurance covers the costs of medical care. It is available to individuals and families through private insurers, Blue Cross/Blue Shield organizations, health maintenance organizations (HMOs), and preferred provider organizations (PPOs). Although many Americans are covered by one of these plans (paid for by or organized through employers, unions, or other groups), you can buy individual policies to provide additional coverage or to replace the group benefits. For the self-employed, individual policies are often the only choice available.

PRIVATE INSURANCE

Health insurance obtained from a private company can cover a wide variety of services and may pay for these services directly or through reimbursements to the insured individual. Patients are free to select their own doctors under these plans.

basic coverage   Usually includes hospital expenses (such as room and board), surgeon's fees, diagnostic charges, anesthesia, operating- or delivery-room fees, medicines, and medical equipment. Also included in some basic policies are reasonable medical expenses for outpatient care, emergency-room treatment, nursing care, and even prescription drugs and eyeglasses. The typical basic plan includes an annual deductible, generally around $200 for an individual, which must be spent before coverage begins. The plan then pays a set percentage, usually 80 percent, of covered costs for specified illnesses and conditions. Such plans frequently pay according to a predetermined fee schedule. Any amounts in excess of the scheduled fee are considered to be beyond the limits of "reasonable" expenses and will not be reimbursed or paid out. Basic plans without any supplemental insurance are considered insufficient, because they often exclude common medical conditions. In addition, the limits of coverage are often too low to provide adequate protection.

major-medical coverage   Pays only for major medical expenses beyond those covered by basic insurance plans. There is a deductible, a coinsurance provision that requires the insured individuals to pay a set percentage of medical costs up to a set amount, and a high ceiling on liability. There are generally few excluded conditions or fee schedules. Important provisions to look for in major-medical policies include guaranteed renewability to age 65, a reasonable cutoff for the coinsurance provision, and full coverage for acute-care facilities.

comprehensive medical coverage   Combines basic and major-medical coverage into one package. It provides a set amount of basic coverage after a deductible and then coverage for charges beyond that amount and for other major medical expenses. A coinsurance provision comes into effect at some point.

The manual for IRS employees includes provisions for collecting taxes after a nuclear war.

BLUE CROSS/BLUE SHIELD

The basic difference between Blue Cross/Blue Shield plans and those offered by private companies is the way payments for covered expenses are handled. Blue Cross usually pays hospital costs directly to the care provider instead of reimbursing the insured individual. Blue Shield plans come in three varieties: **full-service coverage** that pays health-care providers directly for all covered conditions, **indemnity coverage** that reimburses the insured individual, and **partial service benefits** that provide full coverage for those with incomes below a certain level and indemnity coverage for those with incomes above that level.

HEALTH MAINTENANCE ORGANIZATIONS (HMOs)

HMOs provide medical care to those who pay a quarterly fee. HMOs are oriented toward preventive health care, and people who pay the premium are entitled to medical, surgical, and hospital care. Some plans also cover the costs of some prescription medicines and provide partial coverage of dental services. Some HMOs provide the services of several doctors at a single location connected with a hospital. Others allow subscribers to receive care from doctors in their individual offices; the doctors then are reimbursed by the HMO on a fee-for-service basis. Important aspects of an HMO that you should scrutinize are the patient-to-physician ratio, the services for which deductibles or additional fees are charged, the availability of maternity benefits, and the relationship of the HMO or participating doctor to a hospital.

PREFERRED PROVIDER ORGANIZATIONS (PPOs)

PPOs resemble HMOs in most respects, cutting the cost of health care by negotiating lower rates with selected providers. But you have more freedom of choice with a PPO, because it covers care not only by selected providers but by professionals outside the network. Some plans, however, require that you apply for preapproval of treatment by nonnetwork providers. Even when treatment is pre-approved, a lower percentage of your costs is reimbursed than for care by preferred providers. You generally must pay out-of-network providers up front and submit a claim to the PPO to get your money back.

LIFE INSURANCE

The purpose of life insurance is to provide future financial security for your family. Life insurance provides an immediate estate that will enable your family to maintain the household after you die. You also can use life insurance to build up cash reserves for future expenses, such as retirement or college tuition.

By purchasing a life-insurance policy, you are buying into a risk-sharing group. Although no one can predict with any reliability when any individual is going to die, it is possible to predict with great accuracy the number of nonsmoking 32-year-old women who exercise regularly and are not overweight who will die at any given point over the next 40 years. The costs of premiums for people of different ages in various risk categories then can be calculated on the basis of how much the insurance company will pay in benefits to each group's beneficiaries.

You have six types of life insurance to choose from, all but one of which (term insurance) fall into the category of cash-value insurance. Term insurance works the same way automobile or homeowner's insurance works—the insured item being your life. Cash-value plans add investment to the picture, crediting a portion of your premiums to an interest-bearing account. You can borrow against the account while you are alive, and the cash value is paid out tax-free to your beneficiaries upon your death.

term insurance   Provides a death benefit to beneficiaries for a specified period of time. It can be renewable or convertible to whole life and features a low initial premium that rises with each new term. Term life typically has no cash value.

whole life insurance   Offers protection for life at a fixed premium. It provides a fixed death benefit and a cash value that can be borrowed against and increases over the years.

universal life insurance   Offers permanent protection, flexible premiums and death benefits, and a cash value based on premiums paid to date and current interest rates.

"Life Expectancy in 1995 by Race, Sex, and Age" in chapter 18; "Government Benefits" **Go to** in chapter 25

Personal Finances

excess interest whole life insurance Provides permanent protection, a fixed premium that the insurer may adjust after the policy is issued, a fixed death benefit, a cash value that grows depending on market conditions, and the possibility that premiums may be reduced or dispensed with for one or more years if investments are sufficiently profitable.

variable life insurance Offers permanent protection; fixed or flexible premiums; policyholder control over the investment of the policy's cash value; and variable death benefits and cash values, depending on the performance of the investments account.

adjustable life insurance Gives permanent protection that can be reduced to a shorter term if desired, a death benefit that can be raised or lowered, and premiums that can be increased or decreased.

The American Council of Life Insurance recommends that you evaluate your life-insurance needs, buy from a company licensed in your state, select a trustworthy insurance agent, compare costs of similar policies, ask about lower premium rates for nonsmokers, and read your policies and understand them. After selecting coverage that is right for you, inform your beneficiaries about the kind and amount of life insurance you own, keep your policy in a safe place at home, keep the company's name and policy number in a safe deposit box, and check your coverage periodically to be sure it meets your current needs.

DISABILITY INSURANCE

Disability insurance provides coverage for loss of income when an illness or injury prevents you from working. Compulsory temporary disability insurance is provided in California, Hawaii, New Jersey, New York, Rhode Island, and Puerto Rico. Social Security also provides disability coverage at varying levels, depending on family size and the recipient's age.

In addition, three types of disability insurance are available through private companies:

noncancelable Policies that protect your income as long as you continue to make premium payments. Coverage may be increased as income increases.

guaranteed renewable Policies that are less expensive than noncancellable ones, because insurers can increase premium rates.

optionally renewable Policies that can be renewed or not renewed each year, with variable premium rates. They are the least expensive private option.

PROPERTY AND LIABILITY INSURANCE

The purchase of a home is the largest investment most individuals will make in their lifetimes. The home also represents the largest portion of their total financial worth. It therefore makes sense to insure against its possible damage or loss. Even renters stand to lose a substantial amount of money if the uninsured contents of their apartments or houses are destroyed.

A wide array of homeowner's insurance policies is available, including coverage for renters and apartment dwellers. The type of coverage most appropriate for you depends on the sort of risks your property is exposed to and the value of the property. Some policies cover only specific causes of damage or loss, while others provide "all-risk" coverage that pays for any loss or damage except that specifically excluded by the policy. Available homeowner's policies follow:

homeowner's 1 Covers damage caused by fire, lightning, extended perils (such as windstorms, hail, smoke damage, explosions, riots, and vehicular and aircraft damage), vandalism, malicious mischief, theft, and personal liability. This very limited policy is seldom sold or purchased.

homeowner's 2 Adds extended coverage for a variety of other potential problems—such as broken water pipes, freezing of plumbing fixtures, and building collapse—to the coverage offered in homeowner's 1.

homeowner's 3 An "all risks" policy for buildings that is more extensive than either 1 or 2. It also can cover personal property to a limited extent.

homeowner's 4 Covers personal property only. The extent of coverage is generally the same as in 2, but the policy is designed for renters.

homeowner's 5 Provides the most comprehensive "all risks" coverage for homes and personal property.

homeowner's 6 Designed for condominium owners. It covers loss of personal property and loss of use of the dwelling.

homeowner's 8 More limited than homeowner's 1. Homeowner's 8 is a named-perils policy designed for owners of older homes where the cost of reconstructing the home in the event of a catastrophic loss exceeds the market value of the home.

Homeowner's policies cover more than just a home and its contents. Most types include the main dwelling, any other structures on the property, personal belongings that are kept in the dwelling or elsewhere, costs of additional living expenses, and comprehensive personal liability—including medical payments and damage to others' property.

Comprehensive personal liability insurance protects against the loss of your home or property in the event that someone is injured accidentally, whether the injury occurs at the home or elsewhere (such as on a golf course or during a softball game). This type of insurance pays up to a set amount for each occurrence of personal liability (injury and property damage) and up to set amounts for medical payments to others and damage to others' property. Excluded from the comprehensive personal liability insurance provisions of most homeowner's policies are losses resulting from business or professional activities; use of boats, ships, and planes; intentional injury or damage; acts of war or nuclear accidents; and liabilities covered by other insurance policies, such as workers' compensation. Additional liability insurance is available for some of these situations.

AUTOMOBILE INSURANCE

When you are evaluating the risks to which you are regularly exposed, driving a car is one risk you must consider. The possibility of an accident involving your car is so great that most states have made at least limited automobile insurance mandatory.

Automobile insurance covers three broad risk categories:

liability insurance Covers personal injuries and property damage resulting from ownership, maintenance, or use of a vehicle. Separate limits for payments apply to each person involved in an accident and to the property damage incurred.

medical insurance Covers the medical costs incurred in an accident up to a set amount per person per accident.

collision insurance Pays the costs of having a car repaired after it has been damaged in an accident.

Additional automobile insurance, such as comprehensive insurance, also is available to pay for damages resulting from fire or theft. Insurance also is available for damages resulting from an uninsured driver, towing and labor, and transportation needed while a damaged car is repaired. Many states mandate the inclusion of no-fault personal injury insurance in any automobile insurance policy; this provides benefits for those injured in an accident, regardless of who was responsible for the accident.

The types of coverage and the monetary limits of the policy, the driver's age, the frequency of use of the vehicle, the driver's accident history, and the place where the vehicle is kept are considered in determining the cost of liability insurance. Costs for coverage of damage to a vehicle are calculated on the purchase price of the vehicle and its age. When evaluating insurance policies, it is important to compare what is *not* covered by a given policy— its exclusions—as well as what *is* covered and how much it will cost. Comparative shopping and a trustworthy insurance agent can help you choose wisely when buying insurance for your vehicles.

Personal Finances

CREDIT AND LOANS

One key to enhancing personal finances is credit. With loans, credit cards, revolving-charge plans at department stores, and other methods of delaying payment, people obtain goods and services for which they otherwise would have to wait. Of course, use of credit results in debts and interest charges that must be paid to maintain a good credit rating and ensure the availability of more credit.

Getting credit is a fairly straightforward procedure. You can apply to a bank for a loan or a bank credit card—such as VISA® or MasterCard®—or to a department store or gasoline company for a revolving charge account by filling out an application form. These companies will ask about your income, employment history, length and type of residence, credit history, and major assets (car, home, etc.) to determine your creditworthiness.

The average American carries 8 credit cards. The average credit card holder pays approximately $300 in interest per year.

A positive credit history—meaning that you have received credit and made payments on time—is one of the strongest recommendations for further credit. If you have never had credit before, a good first step is to obtain a department-store or gasoline-company credit card (these types of cards are often easier to get than bank credit cards) or to take out a small loan at a bank where you keep a savings and/or checking account. Having a reasonably large amount of money in the bank also can help persuade issuers to provide you with credit.

When you want to obtain credit, especially once you have established creditworthiness, comparison shopping is very important. Different states have different limits on the amount of interest that can be charged on consumer loans and bank cards. Interest rates on loans can range from less than 2 percent per month to 36 percent per year or more.

Credit-card rates range from less than 11 percent to 22 percent or more per year. You do not need to be a resident of a state to get credit from lending institutions headquartered there, and you can apply by mail.

The amount of indebtedness you should assume is not easy to calculate. Credit-granting institutions base their decisions on your gross income and expenses. Your own decision about how much credit you should use is harder to come by. Calculating the amount of money you have available from your income after deducting monthly expenses will give you some idea of what you can afford, although other factors—such as ever-decreasing balances in your checking and savings accounts, use of overdrafts or credit to cover regular expenses, and difficulty making payments on credit lines you already have—may suggest that additional credit is not a good idea.

Problems that can arise from credit, such as billing errors or unfair denial of credit, can be remedied under federal regulations. The Fair Credit Billing Act requires that, if you notify a creditor in writing about an error on a bill, your complaint must be acknowledged within 30 days and resolved within 90 days. The Equal Credit Opportunity Act requires creditors to give you a reason if you are denied credit and prohibits discrimination based on race, gender, age, marital status, religion, national origin, or receipt of public assistance.

If you are denied credit on the basis of a negative report from a credit bureau, you can obtain the information that agency supplied to the creditor free of charge if you request it within 30 days of being turned down, or for a small fee at any time. You can challenge the accuracy of any item in your credit file; this forces the credit bureau to investigate the item and remove it if it cannot be substantiated. Any item in your file also can be amended at your request to include a 100-word explanation that will be added to your file.

Hundreds of credit bureaus exist throughout the United States, but three companies predominate nationally. Contact one of the following for information on your credit rating:

Equifax Credit Information Systems
P.O. Box 105873
Atlanta, GA 30348
800-548-4548 for residents of GA, VT, or MA
800-233-7654 for residents of MD
000-605-1111
http://www.equifax.com

Trans Union Corporation
Consumer Disclosure Center
P.O. Box 390
Springfield, PA 19064-0390
714-680-7292
800-682-7654
800-916-8800
http://www.tuc.com

Experian (Formerly TRW)
P.O. Box 949
Allen, TX 75013-0949
800-682-7654
800-643-3334
800-392-1122
http://www.experian.com

REAL ESTATE AND MORTGAGES

American society is geared toward home ownership. The desire to own a home, and the labyrinthine process of purchasing one, can have a tremendous impact on an individual's or a family's finances. A home represents the single largest financial commitment most people will make in their lifetimes. It therefore requires a careful, reasoned decision based on a thorough examination of the steps involved in the purchase. What follows are some of the basics involved in buying a home and obtaining a mortgage. Potential home buyers are cautioned to seek out as much additional information as is practical from specialized books, real-estate professionals, and friends who have made similar purchases.

THE DECISION TO BUY A HOME

Owning their own home is something most people believe to be desirable regardless of their financial circumstances. They think that owning a home is a perfect investment and that renting is akin to throwing money away. This is not always the case. Home ownership often includes a great many hidden expenses, while renters take care of the basic need for shelter at a set monthly cost without having to deal with headaches such as various taxes, sewage disposal, or sidewalk repairs.

You need to consider a number of factors when deciding whether to buy your own home. First among these should be the way you lead your life. Home ownership can provide greater space, a chance to set down roots, the option to make any alterations you choose, the possibility of providing yard space and better schools for your children, and the pride of having a home of your own. Renters have greater flexibility about when they can move, generally pay less of their income for shelter, avoid the ancillary costs and added work of maintaining a residence, and can use any excess funds for investments that offer a guaranteed rate of return.

Also of great importance in the decision to buy a home is your current financial situation. Home ownership requires enough money to make a down payment (generally at least 10 percent of the purchase price, and often 20 or 25 percent) to obtain a mortgage and to make payments on that mortgage for many years to come. Renters need to have enough money to make some sort of security deposit and to pay the rent each month.

AFFORDABILITY

It is best to shop for a mortgage before you shop for a home so that you know how much money is available to you. A long-standing rule of thumb is that the annual cost of a home should not exceed 25 percent of your gross annual income. If you can manage monthly payments that do not exceed 25 percent of your income, you will probably have little trouble obtaining a mortgage or making the payments.

But even if mortgage payments come to 25 percent of your income, the cost of a home will be substantially more. You will need funds to cover utilities, water and sewage costs, various taxes, repairs, improvements, and even garbage cans and yard equipment. Additional costs may include commuting expenses. It is wise to set aside an additional 10 percent of the basic annual costs for unseen expenses.

A penny minted in 1727 was the first U.S. coin to have the words "United States of America." It also bore the motto, "Mind Your Own Business."

A careful evaluation of present and projected income and expenses—including money spent on nonessential interests, hobbies, and pastimes—will give you some idea of what you can afford to pay for a home on a monthly basis. From there, you can look at mortgage-payment schedules to find out how much of a mortgage you can afford.

One thing to keep in mind when deciding what you can afford is that many experts advise against buying the most expensive house in a given neighborhood. A lower-priced home in a higher-priced neighborhood offers greater security and a better likelihood of seeing the property value increase.

See also "How Much Can You Spend on Housing?", earlier in this chapter.

AN OLD HOME OR A NEW ONE?

If you have a choice between buying a new home or one that has been occupied, you must weigh the pluses and minuses of each. The value of similar new and used homes in similar neighborhoods will go up about equally, but other aspects of each type of home may make you choose one over the other.

New homes have more modern amenities, are often less likely to suffer system breakdowns (that is, plumbing, heating, and water supply), should not require much upkeep or many repairs, and often can be mortgaged for a greater percentage of the price over a longer term. Older homes frequently are less expensive, have larger rooms, are better

built, have finished landscaping, and are closer to the center of town. The individual merits of the actual houses you look at will guide you in making a final choice.

THE DOWN PAYMENT

Among the many decisions to be made in the home-buying process is whether to make a large or small down payment.

While a higher down payment can reduce your monthly payments or the term of the mortgage, there are a number of advantages in making as small a down payment as possible: You retain access to your money; the money you pay in later years will be less valuable, because of inflation, than money spent now; and the interest included in your mortgage payments is tax deductible, so the more you borrow, the more you can deduct.

THE MORTGAGE

At one time, the only mortgages widely available in the United States were fixed-rate mortgages that required fixed monthly payments for a specific period, usually 25 or 30 years. Recently, however, a wide variety of mortgage options has become available.

graduated payment mortgage (GPM) Has a fixed rate of interest but varying payments. Payments begin at a low amount and are increased at a fixed rate each year, rising to a level higher than on a fixed-rate mortgage. Initial payments may be lower than the cost of interest, in which case the unpaid interest is added to the principal. This type of mortgage is good for first-time buyers who expect their incomes to rise during the course of the mortgage.

pledged-account mortgage (PAM) A variation of the GPM based on the difference between payments and the accrued interest from a savings account pledged to that purpose by the borrower.

adjustable-rate mortgage (ARM) Has a flexible interest rate that varies according to a selected interest-rate index. The rate may go up when the index goes up, and most rates go down when the index goes down. This type of mortgage may contain limitations on the maximum and minimum rates. The changing rate can affect the monthly payment, the term, or the outstanding principal. Some plans change the rate more frequently than they change the payments. This can result in underpayments on interest that then are added to the outstanding balance.

graduated-payment adjustable-rate mortgage (GPARM) Combines features of GPMs and ARMs. Some plans defer interest in the early years, others set rising payments during the first several years, and still others fix low payments early on. Countless variations are possible.

wraparound mortgage Allows the buyer to assume the balance of a lower-rate mortgage from the seller, making payments to amortize both that original mortgage and the additional amount being borrowed at prevailing rates. This mortgage reduces the overall interest rate on the total amount.

shared-appreciation mortgage (SAM) In return for a reduced interest rate for the borrower, the lender receives a set portion of the amount by which the home has appreciated when it is sold or the loan is paid. Because the final value of the home cannot be determined in advance, additional interest can be due if the value has not appreciated sufficiently.

reverse mortgage Really not a mortgage at all, but a way of getting monthly payments in return for some of the equity in a house. It is advantageous for people over the age of 75 with significant equity and insufficient cash.

points Charged by many lenders in addition to the mortgage payments themselves. These additional amounts—each point is equal to 1 percent of the loan—are paid by the buyer at the time the mortgage goes into effect (at the closing).

See also "Mortgage Amortization Factors," earlier in this chapter.

GOING TO CONTRACT

Anything and everything can and possibly will go wrong when it comes time to draw up a contract and close the deal to buy a home. No list of potential pitfalls could be considered all-inclusive. The best advice is to obtain a lawyer who is familiar with the kind of property purchase you are making and to read every word in every document presented to you with your lawyer.

COMMON REAL-ESTATE TERMS

amortization A gradual paying off of a mortgage by periodic installments.

appraisal An estimation of a property's value, often made by lenders before deciding the amount of a mortgage.

assessed valuation A value placed on a property as a basis for taxation.

assumable mortgage A mortgage taken over from the seller of a property by the buyer.

balloon payment The final payment on a loan or mortgage, usually larger than the previous payments.

binder An agreement by the buyer to cover the down payment on the purchase of real estate before a final contract is drawn up.

broker Usually a licensed agent who acts on behalf of the seller of a property, making arrangements for the sale.

closing The meeting of a buyer, a seller, a banker, and attorneys for all parties at which a real-estate sale is completed with the writing of checks. It usually takes place 30 to 60 days after the signing of the contract.

commission The amount paid to a real-estate broker for services rendered.

condominium A multiple-unit dwelling, townhouse, or detached house; the owner buys a title to a single unit and an undivided interest in common areas (the land, roof, elevator, etc.).

contract   A binding agreement between parties to transact real estate under agreed-upon terms.

cooperative apartment   A multiple-unit dwelling; buyers purchase individual shares in a cooperative corporation that owns the building. Each share entitles the holder to a proprietary lease on an apartment in the building.

deed   A written document that conveys ownership of real property.

equity   The value of an owner's real property after deducting mortgages and liens.

escrow   A written agreement or something of value placed in the care of someone else and, once conditions are met, delivered to a designated party. Often used for payment of taxes along with mortgage payments.

Fannie Mae   The Federal National Mortgage Association—the largest secondary mortgage agency.

Federal Housing Administration (FHA)   A division of the federal government's Department of Housing and Urban Development that insures mortgages.

Freddie Mac   The Federal Home Loan Mortgage Corporation, which buys mortgages from lenders, allowing the lenders to make new mortgages.

Ginnie Mae   The Government National Mortgage Association (GNMA), which buys FHA insured loans from lenders.

indexing   A means of adjusting the interest rate on a loan or mortgage according to an agreed-upon index or indicator.

interest   Money paid to a lender for use of borrowed principal.

lien   A claim on the property of another granted as security for the payment of a loan or mortgage.

mortgage   A written instrument that creates a lien on a given property in return for a loan.

point   An amount equal to 1 percent of a loan, charged to the borrower by the lender.

prepayment penalty   An additional fee charged for paying off a mortgage before it is due.

principal   The amount of money borrowed from a lender for a mortgage, upon which interest is computed.

title   A written document that gives evidence of property ownership.

INVESTMENTS AND RETIREMENT

If you are like most people, your main source of income for the greater part of your life is the salary or fees you earn from working. This income may or may not be adequate to support the lifestyle you want to maintain. If you would like to increase your income, you might consider making investments. Even if your earned income is enough for the present, you might want to invest now to plan for a secure retirement.

SETTING GOALS

There is little point in considering investments without developing the goals you hope to reach by making those investments. Investing is a means to an end. That end generally can be described as financial security—having enough income to live on after you retire. But a more specific set of goals is essential.

You must develop short-term and long-term strategies. Calculate the amounts you have available to invest now and those you can make available in the future. Then figure the rate of return you require from your investments, taking into account the amount of income you will need those investments to produce in the future after factoring in inflation. You also need to evaluate your need for access to the principal or profit on short notice, along with whether you are willing to take greater risks for a potentially higher return or will accept lower profits in return for greater security.

Personal Finances

Other aspects you should consider when creating short- and long-term goals are diversification of your investments to reduce risks, the tax status of the income your investments will produce, and the availability of loans using your investments as collateral.

Setting goals is a continual process. Your current goals should be based on how you envision your future.

CHOOSING YOUR INVESTMENTS

Once you have decided on your investment goals, you must answer the most difficult question of all: What should you invest in? The possibilities are almost limitless.

It is unwise to select an investment without close scrutiny. Selecting a stock because someone—even a stockbroker—tells you "it's a good bet" is not a good way to handle your money. You can select the types of investments you believe will be most effective in helping you reach your short- and long-term goals. But you then should seek professional assistance from an appropriate source: bankers for information about money-market accounts, individual retirement accounts (IRAs), or certificates of deposit (CDs); or stockbrokers for information about stocks and bonds.

Be aware, however, that these investment professionals stand to profit from the advice they give. The less ethical may try to steer you toward investments that are not ideal for you.

France had the first supermarket in the world. It was started by relatives of the people who started the Texas Big Bear supermarket chain.

The first and best investment you can make, one that guarantees a return and does not put your money at risk, is to pay off your debts. Investing $2,000 in a mutual fund that pays 10 percent does not make sense if you are paying 18 percent interest on a $2,000 credit-card balance. Using the money to pay off the debt will put you 8 percent ahead of the game.

Here are the most widely used investment vehicles.

bank accounts These investments involve virtually no risk (they are insured by the federal government) and are very liquid (they allow for easy access to your money), but they offer low returns. Checking and savings accounts require no minimum investment, although many checking accounts require a minimum balance if you want to avoid transaction fees. Keep enough money in your checking account to avoid fees, and if the account does not pay interest, put the remainder of your ready cash in a savings account. Bank accounts are good short-term investments for money that you need to keep on hand.

life insurance Cash-value life-insurance policies invest a portion of your premiums in an account that bears interest at a moderate rate and grows over time. While low-risk, this investment is relatively expensive when you consider the unspectacular rate of return. You can borrow against the value of your policy while you are alive, but you cannot withdraw funds or the interest you earn. Cash-value life insurance does pay a tax-free death benefit to your heirs when you die, but that savings is minimal unless you are in a high tax bracket. A better choice for low-risk investing would be bonds, and for long-term investing, stocks.

annuities Offered by insurance companies, annuities resemble a combination of cash-value life insurance and individual retirement accounts (IRAs). You contribute to the plan during the accumulation phase, it grows and compounds without taxation, and you receive distributions after age $59^1/_2$. Penalties apply for early withdrawal, and if you die before the pay-out phase begins, your beneficiaries receive a sum equal to your investment. Although they are tax-deferred, annuities include high fees to make up for high operating expenses, sapping your returns. (See "Planning for

Retirement," later in this chapter, for more viable investments.)

bonds When you purchase a bond, you lend money to the issuer of the bond. Bonds are safe investments—you get back your investment plus interest when the bond matures—but lose value relative to other investments when interest rates rise. Depending on the type of bond, this investment can tie up your money for one week to 30 years. Bonds offer a moderate return on your investment, which in some cases will be tax-free. The different types of bonds are issued by banks (certificates of deposit), state governments (municipal bonds), the federal government (treasuries), mortgage holders (Ginnie Maes), and corporations (corporate bonds). Bank CDs generally require a minimum $500 investment and mature in one week to five years, penalizing early withdrawal of your money. Municipal bonds and treasuries may require as little as $25 to invest and mature in an average of 10 years. Treasury bills, one type of U.S. bond, are six-month instruments in $10,000 denominations. These bills offer market interest rates with high security, can easily be sold, and are not subject to state and local income taxes. A minimum investment of $500 or more is required by various Ginnie Maes, which mature after a period of up to 30 years. Corporate bonds involve a minimum deposit of $1,000 and mature in one to 30 years, but they can be cashed in easily before they mature. Bonds represent a stable vehicle for the short- to long-term investment of money that you will not need in the interim. You can purchase bonds individually or through diversified bond funds (see "Mutual Funds," later in this chapter).

stocks A share of stock is a small piece of a publicly held company, so its performance as an investment depends on the fortunes of that company. Stocks pay dividends that reflect the company's profitability, and they grow or decline in capital value according to the financial health of the company. As a result, stocks may fluctuate greatly in value and yield unreliable dividends, making them a poor short-term investment choice. And because companies may fail at any time, the funds you invest in stocks may disappear completely. Thus, you should not invest in stocks unless you can afford to lose the money you put into them, you have the stomach to ride out the company's hard times, and you can stand to put your money at risk. In return for your patience and intestinal fortitude, however, stocks can offer phenomenal returns over the long run, making them an excellent way to build wealth for the future. Investing in individual stocks requires time-consuming research into companies, detailed reporting to the IRS, and the payment of transaction fees to a broker. To avoid these drawbacks, as well as to minimize risk through diversification, invest in a stock fund that consists of a portfolio of various stocks and is managed by an investment professional (see "Mutual Funds," later in this chapter). Stocks are a good way to invest disposable income for the long term.

real estate In terms of risk and return, real estate is comparable to stock as an investment. The value of real estate goes up and down with the local economy, and the capital investment is substantial, but in the long term, owning real estate is a superb way to build wealth. If you own your home, you build equity as you pay off your mortgage, which increases your net worth (you also may borrow against your equity if necessary). You will pay real-estate taxes and the various expenses of home ownership, but you also will receive tax breaks to offset that expense. You can achieve the same results and bring in rent money by investing in real estate other than your home, but being a landlord brings many headaches. Only the very wealthy can afford to hold nonrental property other than their primary residence, because they pay taxes on it, tie up large sums of capital, and do not see a penny of profit until they sell (and profit is not guaranteed). Real-estate oddities such as limited partnerships and time shares most often offer high risk without high returns while they tie up your money. But owning your home is a very worthwhile long-term investment if you buy wisely.

small business   Given the rate at which small businesses fail, investing in a small business is not for the faint of heart. The returns, however, can be staggering if careful research and management combine with good luck. You can minimize your risk by starting your own business instead of buying out someone or investing in an ongoing enterprise. That way, you have complete control over your investment, even if you do have to put in long hours to make it pay off. As with stock, you should be prepared to lose your money, and as with real estate, you should view a small business as a long-term investment.

miscellaneous   Precious metal received a lot of attention as an investment in the 1970s and 1980s, but the rapid growth in value of precious metals at that time is uncharacteristic. More typically, precious metals represent a hedge against inflation, but they do not outpace inflation as an investment. Collectibles such as coins, stamps, antiques, or wine are not good investments. The risk is very high, and the potential returns are disproportionately mediocre; it is also quite difficult to turn these investments into cash.

WORTH THE RISK?

All investments involve risk. As you plan your investment strategy, you must decide what kinds of risks you are willing to take. The rule of thumb is that lower-risk investments yield lower returns and higher-risk investments yield higher returns, but this oversimplifies the picture. In addition to weighing the historical performance of a potential investment, you must consider your investment goals and timeline.

If you want to make long-term investments to finance your retirement, for instance, you will do better putting money into a volatile vehicle like stocks than into a stable but low-yielding one like a money-market account. When all is said and done, your investment probably will grow more over the years—despite the risks. Nevertheless, it is unwise to put your entire nest egg into one volatile basket.

Always keep a portion of your investments in lower-risk vehicles such as bonds, and diversify your high-risk investments across several different vehicles. That way, if one investment collapses, you won't go broke.

You can put about $50 in pennies in a half-gallon milk container.

For shorter-term goals like saving up for a new car, you are better off with lower-risk investments that are unlikely to lose value in the near future. Emergency money or money you will need within the next five years should not go into risky investments.

Who you are should come into play as well. If you like to play it safe with your money, accept that your investment results will be solid but not spectacular. If you are attracted by the prospect of big money, accept that you will have to take some risks. Older investors, those with limited funds to invest, or people with greater financial and family commitments should take fewer risks; while younger, wealthier, and unmarried investors can afford to venture into the unknown.

MUTUAL FUNDS

Mutual funds are professionally managed portfolios of investment vehicles like stocks and bonds. When you invest in a mutual fund, your money goes into a large pool with that of many other investors. With that large pool of cash, money managers can invest in a portfolio geared to meet specific goals, such as stability or growth. Many investors find mutual funds an attractive way to go, because the legwork is done by a professional, they can achieve diversification even with a small investment, and their transaction costs are reduced.

When choosing a mutual fund, consider the individual fund's historical performance as well as the performance of other, similar funds managed by the same firm. You should choose a fund that fits in with your financial picture and investment goals and consider the possible tax impact of its dividends and capital-gains distributions. And don't forget to figure in the cost of the fund—both the up-front load, or commission, charged by the broker (many no-load funds are available) and the ongoing operating fees charged by the fund. Operating fees can take a significant bite out of your returns.

Mutual funds fall into several categories based on the types of investments you make:

money-market funds   The safest type of fund, money-market accounts are virtually identical to bank savings accounts from the investor's standpoint, except they require a minimum deposit to open ($1,000–$25,000) and they offer check-writing privileges. Money-market funds also pay higher interest, yet they keep your money as safe as money in savings accounts by investing it in conservative vehicles such as short-term bank certificates of deposit (CDs), U.S. Treasury bonds, and corporate bonds. The interest on some funds is tax-free. Money-market funds are good short-term investments for funds that you need to keep liquid.

bond funds   The manager of a bond fund assembles a portfolio of bonds that mature at about the same rate. Short-term funds feature bonds with a maturity cycle of 2 to 3 years, intermediate-term funds focus on bonds that mature in 7 to 10 years, and long-term funds include 20-year instruments. As the bonds come due, managers reinvest in similar bonds. Bond funds emphasize dividends, or income, over capital growth and are reasonably safe.

stock funds   Specializing in small, medium, or large companies, stock funds may focus on capital growth or value. **Value-oriented funds** are portfolios of stocks that are well priced in relation to the size and profitability of the company. **Growth-oriented funds** feature companies whose revenues and profits are growing quickly. Growth and small-company orientation translate into higher risk and return, while value and large-company orientation

make a fund safer relative to other stock investments. Stock funds may specialize in overseas companies, in certain industries, or in socially responsible or environmentally conscious companies. **Index funds** select a portfolio meant to mirror the performance of a stock-market index, such as the *Standard and Poor's 500* (an index of the stocks of America's 500 largest corporations). Index funds often outperform the market, because they cost less to manage, using computers rather than people to select stocks.

hybrid funds   These mutual funds combine investment in a variety of vehicles, usually stocks and bonds. They are safer and slower growing than stock funds, but riskier and higher yielding than bond funds. If your investment strategy is middle-of-the-road, but you don't have enough money to invest in separate stock funds and bond funds, a hybrid fund offers a good alternative.

funds of funds   Investment companies sell mutual-fund packages that consist of funds that invest in other funds. This can simplify your investment strategy even further than conventional mutual funds, allowing you to buy into a diversified portfolio that includes both stock funds and bond funds. It is essential to shop carefully to find a high-quality fund of funds, or the benefits of simplicity may be canceled out by poor performance.

MAJOR MUTUAL FUND COMPANIES

American Century Services
800-345-7475
http://www.americancentury.com

Charles Schwab & Company
800-526-8600
http://www.schwab.com

Dreyfus Service Corp.
800-443-9792
http://www.dreyfus.com

Fidelity Investments
800-544-6666
http://www.fidelity.com

Personal Finances

Franklin Templeton Group
800-342-FUND

Jack White & Company
800-431-3500
http://www.jackwhiteco.com

Janus
888-223-0351
http://www.janus.com

Scudder Investor Services
800-SCUDDER
http://funds.scudder.com

Strong Funds
800-368-1480
http://www.strong-funds.com

T. Rowe Price
http://www.troweprice.com

Transamerica Securities
800-89-ASK-US
http://funds.transamerica.com

Vanguard Group
800-662-7447
http://www.vanguard.com

PLANNING FOR RETIREMENT

Although few working people require income from their investments to meet routine expenses, most people will require income from outside sources in order to retire in security and comfort. There are three potential providers of retirement income: pension plans funded by an employer, government retirement funds, and an individual's own retirement fund. The best way to ensure your financial security after retirement is to arrange for retirement income from at least two or even all three of these sources.

employer-funded retirement plans   Can be pension plans, profit-sharing plans, or a combination of the two. Most pension plans define the benefits due and eligibility qualifications required of each employee in advance. They are designed to provide employees with a guaranteed income after they reach a certain age, generally 65, and retire. Some plans allow for early retirement at reduced benefits. In addition to providing income after retirement, many plans also provide vested benefits for employees who stop working for the company before they reach the minimum retirement age, death benefits, medical benefits, and a pension for surviving spouses.

employer-sponsored plans   Include 401(k) plans, in which you contribute a percentage of your paycheck before taxes and reduce your taxable income (and sometimes the employer matches your contribution), and 403(b) plans, which are like 401(k)s but are available to employees of not-for-profit and public-sector organizations.

profit-sharing plans   Differ from pension plans in that an employer's contributions to the fund are dependent on company profits. Profit-sharing plans also may have provisions for vesting at an earlier age and withdrawal and loan privileges.

If you are self-employed or own a small business with fewer than 20 employees, you have two options for setting up a retirement plan for your business. **Simplified employee pension individual retirement accounts** (SEP-IRAs) let you save up to 13 percent of pretax income, up to $22,500 a year. **Keogh plans** allow for the contribution of up to 20 percent of pretax income, to a maximum of $30,000 annually. Under a Keogh, you can establish a vesting schedule that requires employees to remain with the company a certain number of years before they are entitled to their entire savings.

Social Security   The basic retirement plan provided by the government. More than 90 percent of the workers in the United States are earning benefits under Social Security through contributions they and their employers make in the form of Social Security taxes. Social Security provides monthly payments to qualified workers who retire at age 62 or older; health insurance for the elderly under Medicare; and monthly payments to disabled workers and to spouses and children of workers who retire, become disabled, or die. The dollar amount of benefits is dependent on the rate set by the government as well as on other sources of income the retiree has available. People qualify for Social Security benefits on the basis of "quarters of coverage." Workers earn one credit toward coverage for a set amount of income they earn, up to four credits each calendar year. A worker is eligible for retirement benefits if he or she has earned as many credits as the number of calendar years between age 21 (or since 1950) and retirement.

individual retirement plans   Can be created according to needs and financial resources using many of the investments outlined above. The most popular individual plan, the **individual retirement account** (IRA), allows some individuals to deduct contributions of up to $2,000 a year from their income taxes. Married couples who file taxes jointly can take the full deduction if their adjusted gross income (AGI) is less than $40,000 or if one or both spouses are not covered by an employer-sponsored retirement plan. A single taxpayer with an income of less than $25,000 also is eligible for the full deduction. Single taxpayers earning between $25,000 and $35,000 and married joint-filers earning between $40,000 and $50,000 can take a partial deduction, depending on their income. If you are investing for the long term, it may make sense to maintain an IRA even if you cannot deduct your contributions. Many IRAs are simply mutual funds tailored to the needs of retirement-minded investors, so they can be used in much the same way and may better meet your retirement investing goals than other funds. In addition, conventional IRAs are tax-free until they pay out in your retirement years. A type of IRA called the Roth IRA was instituted in 1998. This IRA involves different tax options and is best explored with the aid of an IRA consultant at a bank or other financial institution.

COMMON INVESTMENT TERMS

accrued interest   Interest earned by a bond since the last payment was made.

AMEX   The American Stock Exchange.

appreciation   The increase in value of an investment.

asset   Something you own or that is owed to you.

bear market   A declining stock market.

bid and asked price   The highest price offered for a security at a given time *(bid)* and the lowest price accepted for that security at that time *(asked)*.

Big Board   The New York Stock Exchange.

blue chip   The stock of a top-rated company known for the quality of its products and the security and return on investment of its stock; also the company itself.

bond   A corporation's note acknowledging indebtedness for a certain amount and promising to pay interest at a given rate on that amount as well as to pay back the principal on a certain date. *See also* **junk bond; Treasury bond.**

book value   The theoretical worth of a share of stock as shown on a company's balance sheet. This has little relationship to the stock's market value.

bull market   A rising stock market.

capital gain or capital loss   The gain or loss resulting from the sale of an asset.

capital stock   All shares of stock in a company, both common and preferred.

capitalization   All securities issued by a company, including bonds, common and preferred stock, and debentures.

collateral   Property or securities used by a borrower to secure a loan.

convertible securities   Securities that can be exchanged by the holder for common stock or another security.

coupon bond   A bond with coupons attached that are clipped by the holder and presented for payment of interest due.

current assets   The total amount of cash, securities, inventory, and receivables expected during the normal business cycle of a company, usually one year.

current liabilities The total amount of debt and other payments that will be due during the normal business cycle of a company, usually one year.

debenture An unsecured promissory note backed by a company's general credit.

discount The amount of money below the issuing price of a stock or bond at which it sells.

discretionary account A securities account that leaves some or all decisions about purchases and sales to the discretion of a broker.

dividend A payment by a company equally divided among its stockholders. *See also* **stock dividend.**

Dow Jones average The average price of selected stocks, used as an indicator of the stock market's performance.

equity The interest stockholders have in a company, or the amount of property a property holder actually has paid for as opposed to the portion held by a mortgage.

ex-dividend A stock that does not pay a recently declared dividend to its new purchaser.

Federal Deposit Insurance Corporation (FDIC) The federal agency that insures amounts of up to $100,000 deposited in qualified banks.

fiduciary Someone who acts on behalf of another in financial matters.

gilt-edged security A high-grade preferred stock or bond issued by a company with a strong performance record.

income fund A mutual fund designed to provide current income.

individual retirement account (IRA) A tax-sheltered and sometimes tax-deductible retirement plan.

interest The money paid by a borrower to a lender for the use of the borrowed money.

investment The use of money to make more money.

junk bond A high-risk, high-yielding corporate bond.

Keogh plan A tax-sheltered retirement plan for self-employed people with no pension plans.

liabilities All claims against and amounts owed by a person or company.

listed stock Stock traded on a securities exchange.

margin The portion of a stock's price paid by the buyer when the broker arranges for the remainder to be purchased on credit.

market order An order to buy or sell at the current market price of a security.

maturity The date on which a bond or loan is to be paid off.

money-market fund A mutual fund that invests in short-term financial securities.

municipal bond A bond issued by a local government.

mutual fund An investment company that continually offers new stock and redeems outstanding shares on demand.

odd lot An amount of stock bought or sold in units other than 10 shares or 100 shares.

offer The price at which someone is willing to sell.

over-the-counter market The arena in which stocks not listed on exchanges are bought and sold.

par The issuing value of a share of common stock.

preferred stock Stock that must receive its share of earnings before payment is made on common stock.

premium The amount over par value by which a preferred stock is sold.

puts and calls   Options that give the right to sell or buy a specified number of shares of stock at a specified price within a specified time.

red herring   A preliminary prospectus issued to gauge interest in a new stock issue.

Securities and Exchange Commission (SEC) The federal agency that oversees securities trading.

stock   Ownership shares in a company.

stock dividend   Shares distributed to current shareholders in a company in proportion to those they hold.

stock split   The division of currently outstanding shares into a larger number of shares.

tax shelter   A way in which taxes on income may be legally decreased, eliminated, or deferred.

tender offer   An offer by one company to purchase shares of stock in another company directly from its stockholders.

Treasury bill   A short-term U.S. government security sold at a discount in competitive bidding.

Treasury bond   A long-term U.S. government bond issued in $1,000 denominations.

yield   The amount of dividend or interest expressed as a percentage of the selling price.

zero-coupon bonds   Bonds that are sold at a discount from their face value but do not pay interest.

TIPPING

The following list suggests what are generally considered to be adequate amounts to tip various people for services rendered. Keep in mind that tips are a way of expressing satisfaction. Larger tips should be given to those who provide extraordinarily good service; smaller tips or no tip at all should be given when service is poor.

Location	Person	Amount
Airport	Skycap	$1–$2 per bag
	In-flight personnel	None
Barbershop	Haircutter	15% of the cost, generally a minimum of $1
Beauty shop	One operator	15% of bill
	Several operators	10% of bill to person who sets hair; 10% divided among others
	Manicurist	$1–$2 or more, depending on cost
Cruise ship	Staff	Allow 15% of the total fare for tips. Divide one half between cabin and dining stewards
	Cabin steward	4% of total fare
	Dining-room steward	4% of total fare
	Deck Steward and others	Divide the remaining 7% of total fare among the rest of the service staff
	Bar steward	15% of bar bill when served
	Wine steward	15% of wine bill when served
Hotel	Housekeeping	No tip for one-night stays; $1–$2 a night or $5–$10 a week for longer stays
	Room-service waiter	15% of bill
	Bellhop	$1 per bag for bringing you to your room with luggage; 50 cents for opening and showing the room
	Lobby attendant	None for opening door or calling taxi from stand; $1 or more for help with luggage or finding a taxi on the street
	Desk clerk	None unless special service is given during long stay; then, $5
Restaurant	Waiter	15% of bill, more for better-than-average service
	Headwaiter/maitre d'	None, unless special services are provided; then, about $5
	Wine steward	15% of wine bill
	Bartender	10–15% of bar bill
	Busperson	None
	Server at counter	15% of bill
	Coat-check attendant	$1 for one or two coats
	Rest-room attendant	50 cents if provided with a handtowel only. $1 or more if special services are provided
	Car-park attendant	$1-$2 given when car is brought to you
Sports arena	Usher	$1 per party if shown to your seat
Taxi	Driver	15% of fare, no less than 50¢
Train	Dining-car waiter	15% of bill
	Steward/bar-car waiter	15% of bar bill
	Redcap or porter	Posted rate plus 50¢

Go to   "Domestic Travel" and "Foreign Travel" in chapter 24

Personal Finances

ADDITIONAL SOURCES OF INFORMATION

ORGANIZATIONS AND SERVICES

Consult the following organization for referrals to reputable financial planners:

Institute of Certified Financial Planners
7600 E. Eastman Ave.
Suite 301
Denver, CO 80231-4397
303-759-4900
800-282-PLAN (national referral line)
http://www.icfp.org

MAGAZINES AND NEWSPAPERS

The following publications offer substantial coverage of events and trends that affect personal finances. Addresses and phone numbers are for subscriptions.

Barron's National Business Weekly
200 Burnett Rd.
Chicopee, MA 01020
800-544-0422

Business Week
1221 Avenue of the Americas
New York, NY 10020
800-635-1200
http://www.businessweek.com

Entrepreneur
P.O. Box 57050
Irvine, CA 92619
800-274-6229
http://www.entrepreneurmag.com

Forbes
60 Fifth Ave.
New York, NY 10011
800-888-9896
http://www.forbes.com

Fortune
1271 Avenue of the Americas
New York, NY 10020
800-621-8000
http://www.pathfinder.com

Kiplinger's Personal Finance Magazine
The Kiplinger Washington Editors, Inc.
1729 H St., NW
Washington, DC 20006
800-544-0155
http://kiplinger.com

Money (monthly)
P.O. Box 54429
Boulder, CO 80322
800-541-1000
http://www.pathfinder.com

The Wall Street Journal
420 Lexington Ave.
New York, NY 10017
800-568-7625
http://www.info.wsj.com

BOOKS

Clifford, Denis, and Cora Johnson. *Plan Your Estate,* 3rd ed. Nolo Press, 1996.

Dunnan, Nancy. *Dun and Bradstreet Guide to Your Investments 1997.* HarperPerennial, 1997.

Eisenberg, Richard. *The Money Book of Personal Finance.* Warner, 1996.

Feinberg, Andrew. *Downsize Your Debt.* Penguin, 1993.

Garner, Robert J., et al. *Ernst & Young's Personal Financial Planning Guide.* Wiley, 1996.

Kiplinger's Buying & Selling a Home. The Kiplinger Washington Editors, 1996.

Loeb, Marshall. *Marshall Loeb's Money Guide.* Little Brown, annual.

Rowland, Mary. *A Commonsense Guide to Mutual Funds.* Bloomberg Press, 1996.

Tyson, Eric. *Personal Finances for Dummies,* 2nd ed. IDG Books, 1996.

Personal Finances

21

LEGAL INFORMATION

FORMS AND CONTRACTS	598
STATUTE OF LIMITATIONS	619
COPYRIGHTS	619
PATENTS	621
THE DEATH PENALTY	620
FEDERAL JUDICIAL SYSTEM	623
SUPREME COURT JUSTICES	623
SUPREME COURT DECISIONS	624
COMMON LEGAL TERMS	626
ADDITIONAL SOURCES OF INFORMATION	634

FORMS AND CONTRACTS

The documents in the following sections are fairly standard versions of simple agreements, requests, or statements. They are meant to demonstrate the basic content of similar documents. Because laws vary from state to state (and because agreements can have their own special circumstances, terms, or other complexities), it is always a good idea to consult with a lawyer before drawing up or signing a contract.

BILL OF SALE

Bill of Sale

of

_____

STATE OF   )
)   ss:
COUNTY OF   )

KNOW YE ALL MEN BY THESE PRESENTS,

That I, _____ , of

_____ ,

Street Address   *City*   *State*   *Zip*

for and in consideration of payment of the sum of $ _____ , the receipt of which is hereby acknowledged, do hereby grant, bargain, sell, and convey to:

_____ , of

_____ ,

Street Address   *City*   *State*   *Zip*

and his/her heirs, executors, administrators, successors, and assigns the following property:

_____

_____

_____

_____

I hereby warrant that I am the lawful owner of said property and that I have full legal right, power, and authority to sell said property. I further warrant said property to be free of all encumbrances and that I will warrant and defend said property hereby sold against any and all persons whomsoever.

IN WITNESS WHEREOF, I, the seller, have hereto set my hand and seal this _____ day of _____ , 19_____ .

(Signed) _____
                                          Seller

CERTIFICATE OF NOTARY

A certificate of notary often accompanies agreements or statements; it may be required in some localities. A certificate of notary might be useful with the following documents in this section:

- Bill of Sale
- Declaration of Gift
- Living Will
- Power of Attorney
- Privacy Act/Freedom of Information Act Request
- Request for Reason for Adverse Credit Action

Certificate of Notary

STATE OF   )
)   ss:
COUNTY OF   )

On this _____ day of _____ , 19___ , before me personally came and appeared _____ , known, and known to me, to be the individual described in and who executed the foregoing instrument, and who duly acknowledged to me that he/she executed same for the purpose therein contained.

IN WITNESS WHEREOF, I hereunto set my hand and official seal.

_____
Notary Public

My commission expires:_____

CONTRACT

Agreement Between Owner and Contractor

THIS AGREEMENT is hereby entered into this _____ day of _____ , 19_____ ,
between _____ , of

_____

| *Street Address* | *City* | *Street* | *Zip* | *Phone* |

hereinafter called Owner, and _____ , of

_____

| *Street Address* | *City* | *Street* | *Zip* | *Phone* |

hereinafter called the Contractor.

The said parties, for the considerations hereinafter mentioned, hereby agree to the following:

Description of the Work

1. The Contractor shall provide all materials and labor required to perform all of the work for:

as shown on the drawing(s), and set forth in the specifications and/or description(s) prepared by
_____ , which drawing(s) and specifications and/or description(s) are identi-
fied by the signatures of the parties to this agreement, and which form a part of this agreement and are
incorporated by reference herein for all purposes.

Payment

2. Under the terms of this agreement, the Owner agrees to pay the Contractor, for materials to be furnished and work to be done, the sum of _____ ($ _____), subject to any addi-
tions or deductions as hereinafter provided for in this agreement, and to make the following payments:

_____

_____

_____

and that the final payment shall be made subject to the hereinafter stated conditions of this agreement.

It is agreed that no payment made under this agreement shall be considered conclusive evidence of
full performance of this contract, either wholly or in part by the Contractor, and that acceptance of payment shall not be considered by the Contractor to be acceptance by the Owner of any defective materials or workmanship.

Liens

3. Final payment shall not be due until such time as the Contractor has provided the Owner with a
release of any liens arising from this agreement; or receipts for payment in full for all materials and labor

for which a lien could be filed; or a bond satisfactory to the Owner indemnifying the Owner against any lien.

Timely Completion of the Work

4. The Contractor agrees that the various portions of the work shall be completed on or before the following dates:

_____

_____

_____

and the entire work shall be completed on or before the _____ day of _____ , 19_____.

In the event the work is not completed by the aforementioned date, the Owner shall be entitled to receive as damages from the Contractor, the sum of _____ ($ _____) per _____ , it being agreed that the aforementioned sum is reasonable, taking into account the difficulty in determining the exact amount of damages the Owner would sustain in the event of said delay, and that the agreed sum shall be considered as liquidated damages.

If the Contractor is delayed in the completion of the work by any changes ordered in the work, by acts of God, fire, flood, or any other unavoidable casualties; or by labor strikes, late delivery of materials; or by neglect of the Owner, his agents or representatives; or by any subcontractor employed by the Contractor; the time for completion of the work shall be extended for the same period as the delay occasioned by any of the aforementioned causes.

Surveys and Easements

5. The Owner shall provide and pay for all surveys. All easements for access across the property of another, and for permanent changes, and for the construction or erection of structures shall also be obtained and paid for by the Owner.

Licenses, Permits, and Building Codes

6. The Contractor shall obtain and pay for all permits and licenses required for the prosecution and timely completion of the work. The Contractor shall comply with all appropriate regulations relating to the conduct of the work and shall advise the Owner of any specifications or drawings which are at variance therewith.

Materials and Equipment

7. The Contractor shall provide and pay for all materials, tools, and equipment required for the prosecution and timely completion of the work. Unless otherwise specified in writing, all materials shall be new and of good quality.

Samples

8. Whenever the Owner may require, the Contractor will furnish for approval all samples as directed, and the work shall be in accordance with approved samples.

Labor and Supervision

9. In the prosecution of the work the Contractor shall at all times keep a competent foreman and a sufficient number of workers skilled in their trades to suitably perform the work.

continues

Agreement Between Owner and Contractor, Continued

The foreman shall represent the Contractor and, in the absence of the Contractor, all instructions given by the Owner to the foreman shall be binding upon the Contractor as though given to the Contractor. Upon request of the foreman, instructions shall be in writing.

Alterations and Changes

10. All changes and deviations in the work ordered by the Owner must be in writing, the contract sum being increased or decreased accordingly by the Contractor. Any claims for increases in the cost of the work must be presented by the Contractor to the Owner in writing, and written approval of the Owner shall be obtained by the Contractor before proceeding with the ordered change or revision.

In the event that additional work, not shown on the drawings and/or not described in the specifications, is required to comply with laws, regulations, or building codes, such additional work shall be considered as done under the terms of this agreement.

Correction of Deficiencies

11. The Contractor agrees to reexecute any work that does not conform to the drawings and specifications, warrants the work performed, and further agrees that he shall remedy any defects resulting from faulty materials or workmanship that shall become evident during a period of one year after completion of the work. This provision shall apply with equal force to all work performed by subcontractors as to work that is performed by direct employees of the Contractor.

Protection of the Work

12. It shall be the responsibility of the Contractor to reasonably protect the work, the property of the Owner, and adjacent property and the public; and the Contractor shall be responsible for any damage, injury, or death resulting from his negligence or from any intentional act of the Contractor or the Contractor's employees, agents, or subcontractors.

Cleaning Up

13. The Contractor shall keep the premises free from the accumulation of waste and, upon completion of the work, shall remove all waste, equipment, and other materials and leave the premises in broom-clean condition.

Contractor's Liability Insurance

14. The Contractor shall obtain insurance to protect himself against claims for property damage arising out of his or any subcontractor's performance of this contract; and to protect himself against claims under provisions of Workman's Compensation and any similar employee benefit acts, and from claims for bodily injury, including death, due to performance of this contract by the Contractor or any subcontractor employed for the performance of this contract.

Owner's Liability Insurance

15. It shall be the responsibility of the Owner, at the Owner's option, to obtain insurance to protect himself from the contingent liability of claims for property damage and bodily injury, including death, that may arise from the performance of this contract.

Fire Insurance with Extended Coverage

16. The Owner shall obtain fire insurance with extended coverage at 100 percent of the value of the entire structure, including materials and labor related to the work described in this agreement. Certificates of insurance shall be filed with the Contractor if he so requests. The aforesaid fire insurance

need not include tools, equipment, scaffolding, or forms owned or rented by the Contractor, any subcontractor, or their respective employees.

Owner's Right to Terminate the Agreement

17. In the event the Contractor shall fail to meet the provisions of this agreement, the Owner shall, after seven (7) days' written notice to the Contractor and his surety, have the right to take possession of the premises in order to complete the work as specified in the agreement. The Owner may deduct the cost thereof from any payment then and thereafter due to the Contractor or may, at his option, terminate the agreement, take possession of any materials, and complete the work as he deems appropriate. If the unpaid balance of the contracted sum exceeds the Owner's expenses of completing the work, such excess shall be paid to the Contractor. If such expense shall exceed the unpaid balance, the Contractor shall pay the difference to the Owner.

Contractor's Right to Terminate the Agreement

18. In the event the Owner shall fail to pay the Contractor within seven (7) days after the date upon which payment shall become due, the Contractor shall have the right, after seven (7) days' written notice to the Owner, to stop work and may, at his option, terminate the agreement and recover from the Owner payment for all work executed, plus any loss sustained, plus a reasonable profit, plus damages.

In the event the work is stopped by any court or other public authority for a period of thirty (30) days through no fault of the Contractor, the Contractor shall have the right to stop work and may, at his option, terminate the agreement and recover from the Owner payment for all work executed, plus any loss sustained, plus a reasonable profit, plus damages.

Assignment of Rights

19. Neither the Owner nor Contractor shall have the right to assign any rights or interest occurring under this agreement without the written consent of the other; nor shall the Contractor assign any sums due, or to become due, to him under the provisions of this agreement.

Access and Inspection

20. The Owner, Owner's representative, and public authorities shall at all times have access to the work.

An appropriately licensed representative of the Owner, whose authority shall be set forth in writing by the Owner, shall have the authority to direct the removal of any materials and the taking down of any portions of the work failing to meet drawings, specifications, laws, regulations, or building codes; the reexecution of said work deemed as being done under the provisions of Article 11 of this agreement.

Any other removal of materials or taking down of any portions of the work as directed by the Owner's representative shall be in writing and at the sole expense of the Owner.

Attorney Fees

21. Attorney fees and court costs shall be paid by the defendant in the event that judgment must be obtained, and is, to enforce this agreement or any breach thereof.

IN WITNESS WHEREOF, the parties hereto set their hands and seals the day and year written above.

_____   _____
Witness as to Owner   *Owner*

_____   _____
Witness as to Contractor   *Contractor*

DECLARATION OF GIFT

Declaration of Gift

TO ALL TO WHOM THESE PRESENTS SHALL COME OR MAY CONCERN, KNOW
THAT on this _____ day of _____ , 19___ ,
I, _____ , of
_____ ,

| Street | City | State | Zip |

being of sound and disposing mind and memory, do hereby irrevocably give, bestow, and deliver up
to _____ ,
of _____ ,

| Street | City | State | Zip |

all of my right, title, and interest in the following described property valued at _____
_____ ($ _____):

_____

_____

_____

_____

_____

_____

_____

_____

_____

IN WITNESS WHEREOF, I hereunto set my hand and seal on the date above mentioned.

_____

LEASES

"Open" Rental Agreement

THIS AGREEMENT is made this _____ day of _____ , 19_____ ,
between _____ , of

_____

| Street Address | City | State | Zip |

hereinafter called "Owner," and _____ , of

_____

| Street Address | City | State | Zip |

hereinafter called "Renter."

Property

_____

_____

_____

_____

| Year | Make | Model/Type |

_____

| Capacity | Horsepower | Serial No. |

    The Owner warrants that to the best of his/her knowledge and belief, the aforesaid property is free of any known faults or deficiencies which would affect its safe and dependable operation under normal and prudent usage.

Rental Period

The Owner agrees to rent the above-described property to the Renter for a period of _____
beginning _____ and ending _____ .

Use of Property

_____

_____

_____

_____

_____

The Renter further agrees that the rented property (A) shall not be used beyond any rated capacity; (B) shall not be used for any illegal purpose; (C) shall not be used in any manner for which it was not designed, built, or designated by the manufacturer; (D) will not be used in a negligent manner; (E) will

continues

not be operated by any other person without the written permission of the Owner; and (F) will not be removed from the designated area of use or operation.

Area of Use or Operation

The Renter agrees to operate/use the above-described property only at the following location or within the following described area(s):

_____

_____

_____

Insurance

The Renter hereby agrees that he/she shall fully indemnify the Owner for any and all damage to or loss of the rented property and any accessories or related equipment during the term of this Agreement whether caused by fire, theft, flood, vandalism, or any other cause, except that which shall be determined to have been caused by a fault or deficiency of the rented property, accessories, or equipment.

Rental Rate

The Renter hereby agrees to pay the Owner at the rate of $ _____ per _____ for the use of said property and any accessories/equipment. Any fuel used shall be paid for by the Renter.

Deposit

The Renter further agrees to make a deposit of $ _____ with the Owner, said deposit to be used, in the event of loss of or damage to the rented property and any accessories/equipment during the term of this Agreement, to defray fully or partially the cost of necessary repairs or replacement. In the absence of any damage or loss, said deposit shall be credited toward payment of the rental fee, and any excess shall be returned to the Renter.

Return of Property to Owner

The Renter hereby agrees to return the rented property and any accessories/equipment to the Owner at _____ no later than _____ .

Termination of Agreement

It is mutually agreed that the Renter shall have the right to terminate this Agreement at any time by payment of one full day's rental for each 24-hour period or any part thereof, during which the Renter has retained possession of the property and any accessories/equipment during the term of this Agreement.

IN WITNESS WHEREOF, the parties hereto hereby execute this Agreement.

(Signed) _____

Renter

(Signed) _____

Owner

Legal Information

Seasonal Lease Agreement—Furnished Country/Seashore House

Landlord_____

Address   *Phone*

Managing Agent _____

Address   *Phone*

Premises _____

_____

Tenant _____

_____

Address   *Phone*

Tenant _____

_____

Address   *Phone*

1. The LANDLORD hereby leases to _____ (and) _____ , hereinafter termed TENANT, the premises described above for a term of _____ beginning _____ and ending _____ , at a monthly rate of $_____ , making a total rental amount payable under this lease of $_____ .

2. The tenant agrees to pay the rent in the following manner:_____ (Landlord specify if payments are to be made by mail, and if so, to what address. If payments are to be made to the landlord or his agent in person, state the place where, and the person to whom, payments should be made.)

3. The tenant, in addition to rent, agrees to pay all charges for water, gas, fuel oil, and electricity used during the term of the lease, such charges to be paid monthly in addition to rent.

4. Upon receipt of any payment for rent or utilities in cash, the landlord agrees to issue a receipt stating the tenant's name, a description of the premises, the amount paid, the date paid, and the period for which rent or utilities is paid.

5. The tenant agrees to place a security deposit of $ _____ , to be used by the landlord at the termination of this lease for the cost of replacing or repairing damage, if any, to the premises or furnishings caused by the intentional or negligent acts of the tenant.

6. The landlord agrees to return said security deposit to the tenant upon the tenant's vacating the premises subject to the terms and conditions herein.

7. The tenant agrees to take good care of the premises and of the furnishings therein, and at the end of the term of this lease to deliver up to the landlord the premises and furnishings in good order, normal wear and tear excepted.

8. The landlord covenants that the leased premises are, to the best of his or her knowledge, clean, safe, sound, and healthful and that there exists no violation of any applicable housing code, law, or

continues

Seasonal Lease Agreement, Continued

regulation of which he or she is aware, and that no such violation will be permitted to exist during the term of this lease or any extension thereof.

9. The tenant shall promptly comply with all laws, orders, ordinances, and regulations pertaining to his or her use of the premises, and the tenant shall not keep therein any article or thing of a dangerous, flammable, or explosive nature that might be pronounced "hazardous" or "extra hazardous" by any responsible insurance company.

10. The tenant shall, in case of fire, give immediate notice to the proper authorities and to the landlord, who will cause the damage to be promptly repaired; but if the premises be so damaged that the landlord shall decide to terminate this lease, then upon 10 days' personal or written notice to the tenant, this lease shall terminate and the accrued rent shall be paid up to the time of the fire.

11. The tenant shall do no cooking in any room used for sleeping purposes, but shall have the right to use jointly with any other tenants a room set aside by the landlord for that purpose.

12. The tenant shall, at reasonable times, give access to the landlord or his agents for any reasonable and lawful purpose. Except in situations of compelling emergency, the landlord shall give the tenant at least 24 hours' notice of intention to seek access, the date and time at which access will be sought, and the reason therefor.

13. In the event of default by the tenant, the tenant shall remain liable for all rent due or to become due during the term of this lease. The landlord shall have the obligation to relet the premises in the landlord's name for the balance of the term, or longer, and will apply proceeds of such reletting toward the reduction of the tenant's obligations enumerated herein.

14. The tenant shall permit the landlord or his agents to show the premises at reasonable hours, to persons desiring to rent or purchase same, 30 days prior to the expiration of this lease, and will permit the notice "To Let" or "For Sale" to be placed on said premises and remain thereon without hindrance or molestation after said date.

15. The tenant shall not assign this lease, nor underlet or underlease the premises, or any part thereof, nor make any alterations to the premises, nor permit same to be used at any time during the term of this lease for any other purpose than a private residence.

16. This lease, and any attached List of Furnishings signed by both parties and dated, and incorporated herein by reference for all purposes, constitutes the entire agreement between the parties hereto. No changes shall be made herein except by writing, signed by each party and dated.

17. In the event legal action is required to enforce any provision of this agreement, the prevailing party shall be entitled to recover reasonable attorney's fees and costs.

18. This lease, when filled out and signed, is a binding legal obligation.

IN WITNESS WHEREOF, the parties hereto have executed this agreement.

_____	_____
Witness as to landlord	*Landlord*
	By _____
_____	_____
Witness as to landlord	*Landlord*
	_____
	Tenant
_____	Dated this _____ day of _____ , 19_____ .
Witness as to landlord	

Lease Agreement—Unfurnished Apartment

Landlord _____

_____
                        Address   *Phone*

Managing Agent _____

_____
                        Address   *Phone*

Premises _____
                        Address   *Apt. No.*

Tenant _____

Tenant _____

1. The LANDLORD hereby leases to _____ (and) _____ , hereinafter termed TENANT, the premises described above for a term of beginning and ending _____ , at a monthly rate of $ _____ , making a total rental amount payable under this lease of $ _____ .

2. The tenant agrees to pay the rent herein provided subject to the terms and conditions set forth herein.

3. Rent shall be payable in equal monthly installments to be paid in advance on the _____ day of each month.

4. Rent shall be payable in the following manner:
(Specify above if payments are to be made by mail, and if so, to what address. If payments are to be made to the landlord or the landlord's agent in person, state the place where, and the person to whom, payments are to be made.)

5. Upon receiving any payment of rent in cash, the landlord agrees to issue a receipt stating the tenant's name, a description of the premises, the amount of rent paid, the date paid, and the period for which rent is paid.

6. The landlord covenants that the leased premises are, to the best of his or her knowledge, clean, safe, sound, and healthful and that there exists no violation of any applicable housing code, law, or regulation of which he or she is aware.

7. The tenant agrees to comply with all sanitary laws, ordinances, and rules, and all orders of the Board of Health or other authorities affecting the cleanliness, occupancy, and preservation of the premises during the term of this lease.

8. The tenant shall use the leased premises exclusively as a private residence for no more than _____ persons, and the tenant will not make alterations therein without the written consent of the landlord.

9. The tenant shall keep fixtures in said apartment in good order and repair, and the tenant shall cause to be made, at the tenant's expense, all required repairs to heating and air-conditioning apparatus, refrigerator, range, electric and gas fixtures, and plumbing work whenever such damage shall have resulted from misuse, waste, or neglect, it being understood that the landlord is to have same in good order and repair when giving possession.

continues

Legal Information

Lease Agreement—Unfurnished Apartment, Continued

10. The tenant shall not keep or have in the leased premises any article or thing of a dangerous, flammable, or explosive nature that might be pronounced "hazardous" or "extra hazardous" by any responsible insurance company.

11. The tenant shall give prompt notice to the landlord of any dangerous, defective, unsafe, or emergency condition in the leased premises, said notice being given by any suitable means. The landlord shall repair and correct said conditions promptly upon receiving notice thereof from the tenant.

12. The landlord covenants that all essential services are now provided and shall be provided at all times during the term of this lease and any extension, renewal, or continuation thereof, except where any interruption of essential services shall be for maintenance or for cause beyond control of the landlord such as strike, storm, civil insurrection, fire, or acts of God. "Essential services" hereunder are defined as heat, hot and cold running water, a properly functioning toilet, light in public areas, and suitable building security.

13. The _____ shall pay for gas and electricity except to the extent otherwise set forth herein.

14. The landlord covenants that consumption of electricity for the public halls and other common areas and use and consumption of gas for heat or hot water in public areas are recorded on separate meters, and that said electricity and gas are and will at all times be billed to and paid by the landlord.

15. The tenant covenants that during the last 30 days of this lease, or any renewal thereof, the landlord or his agents, with reasonable notice, and at reasonable hours, have the privilege of showing the premises to prospective buyers or tenants.

16. The tenant shall, at reasonable times, give access to the landlord or his agents for any reasonable and lawful purpose. Except in situations of compelling emergency, or to show the premises for rental or sale, the landlord agrees to give the tenant 24 hours' notice, stating the time and date when access will be sought, and the reason therefor.

17. The landlord covenants that the tenant and the tenant's family shall have, hold, and enjoy the leased premises for the term of this lease, subject to the provisions and conditions set forth herein.

18. The tenant covenants that he shall not commit nor permit a nuisance in or upon the premises, that he shall not maliciously or by reason of gross negligence damage the premises, and that he shall not engage in conduct so as to interfere substantially with the comfort and safety of occupants of adjacent apartments or buildings.

19. The tenant agrees to place a security deposit with the landlord in the amount of $ _____ , to be used by the landlord for the cost of replacing and/or repairing damage, if any, to the premises caused by the intentional or negligent acts of the tenant.

20. The landlord agrees, within 10 days of receiving said security deposit, to deposit same in an interest-bearing account in a banking organization, in which said deposit shall earn interest at a rate which shall be the prevailing rate earned by other such deposits made with banking organizations in such circumstances.

21. The landlord agrees, within 10 days of making such deposit, to notify the tenant, in writing, of the name and address of the banking organization in which the deposit of security money has been made.

22. The landlord shall be entitled to receive, as administrative expenses, an amount equal to 1 percent per annum upon the security payment so deposited, which shall be in lieu of all other administrative and custodial expenses. The balance of the interest paid by the banking organization shall be the money

of the tenant and shall be paid to the tenant on each anniversary of this lease or any extension or renewal thereof.

23. The landlord agrees to return said security deposit to the tenant within 10 days of the tenant's vacating the leased premises subject to the terms and conditions set forth herein.

24. In the event of any breach by the tenant of any of the tenant's covenants or agreements herein, the landlord may give the tenant five days' notice to cure said breach, setting forth in writing which covenants or agreements have been breached. If any breach is not cured within said five day period, or reasonable steps to effectuate said cure are not commenced and diligently pursued within said five-day period and thereafter until said breach has been cured, the landlord may terminate this lease upon five days' additional notice to the tenant, with said notice being in lieu of a Notice to Quit, which tenant hereby waives. The tenant shall then become liable for the cost of landlord's normal redecorating and cleaning expenses related to preparation of the premises for rental to a succeeding tenant.

Said termination shall be ineffective if the tenant cures said breach or commences and diligently pursues reasonable steps to effectuate such cure at any time prior to the expiration of said five-day termination. Upon terminating this lease as provided herein, the landlord or his agent may commence proceedings against the tenant for his removal as provided for by law.

25. In the event of any breach by the landlord of any of the landlord's covenants or agreements herein, the tenant may give the landlord 10 days' notice to cure said breach, setting forth in writing the manner in which said covenants and agreements have been breached. If said breach is not cured within said 10-day period, or reasonable steps to effectuate said cure are not commenced and diligently pursued within said 10-day period and thereafter until said breach has been cured, rent hereunder shall be fully abated from the time at which said 10 days' notice expired until such time as the landlord has fully cured the breach set forth in the notice provided for in this paragraph.

26. In no case shall any abatement of rent hereunder be effected where the condition set forth in the notice provided for herein was created by the intentional or negligent act of the tenant, but the landlord shall have the burden of proving that rent abatement may not be effected for the foregoing reason.

27. The landlord agrees to deliver possession of the leased premises at the beginning of the term provided for herein. In the event of the landlord's failure to deliver possession at the beginning of said term, the tenant shall have the right to rescind this lease and to recover any consideration paid under terms of this agreement.

28. The tenant agrees that this lease shall be subject to and subordinate to any mortgage or mortgages now on said premises or which any owner of said premises may hereafter at any time elect to place on said premises.

29. Unless otherwise provided for elsewhere in this lease, any notice required or authorized herein shall be given in writing, one copy of said notice mailed via U.S. certified mail, return receipt requested, and one copy of said notice mailed via U.S. first-class mail.

Notice to the tenant shall be mailed to him at the leased premises. Notice to the landlord shall be mailed to him, or to the managing agent, at their respective addresses as set forth herein, or at such new address as to which the tenant has been duly notified.

30. This lease constitutes the entire agreement between the parties hereto. No changes shall be made herein except by writing, signed by each party and dated. The failure to enforce any right or remedy

continues

Legal Information

Lease Agreement—Unfurnished Apartment, Continued

hereunder, and the payment and acceptance of rent hereunder, shall not be deemed a waiver by either party of such right or remedy in the absence of a writing as provided for herein.

31. In the event legal action is required to enforce any provision of this agreement, the prevailing party shall be entitled to recover reasonable attorney's fees and costs.

32. The landlord and tenant agree that this apartment lease, when filled out and signed, is a binding legal obligation.

IN WITNESS WHEREOF, the parties hereto have executed this agreement.

_____
Landlord

By _____

_____
Witness as to landlord

_____
Witness as to landlord

_____
Tenant

_____
Witness as to tenant

_____
Witness as to tenant

_____
Tenant

_____
Witness as to tenant

_____
Witness as to tenant

Dated this _____ day of _____ , 19___ .

LIVING WILL

Living Will

Directive to Physicians:

I, _____ , of

_____ ,

    Street Address   *Apt. No.*   *City*   *State*   *Zip*

being of sound mind, do hereby willfully and voluntarily make known my desire that my life not be prolonged under any of the following conditions, and do hereby further declare:

1. If I should, at any time, have an incurable condition caused by any disease or illness, or by any accident or injury, and be determined by any two or more physicians to be in a terminal condition whereby the use of "heroic measures" or the application of life-sustaining procedures would only serve to delay the moment of my death, and where my attending physician has determined that my death is imminent whether or not such "heroic measures" or life-sustaining measures are employed, I direct that such measures and procedures be withheld or withdrawn and that I be permitted to die naturally.

2. In the event of my inability to give directions regarding the application of life-sustaining procedures or the use of "heroic measures," it is my intention that this directive shall be honored by my family and physicians as my final expression of my right to refuse medical and surgical treatment, and my acceptance of the consequences of such refusal.

3. I am mentally, emotionally, and legally competent to make this directive and I fully understand its import.

4. I reserve the right to revoke this directive at any time.

5. This directive shall remain in force until revoked.

    IN WITNESS WHEREOF, I have hereunto set my hand and seal this _____ day of _____ , 19_____ .

(Signed) _____

Declaration of Witness:

The declarant is personally known to me and I believe him/her to be of sound mind and emotionally and legally competent to make the herein-contained **Directive to Physicians**. I am not related to the declarant by blood or marriage, nor would I be entitled to any portion of the declarant's estate upon his/her decease, nor am I an attending physician of the declarant, nor an employee of the attending physician, nor an employee of a health-care facility in which the declarant is a patient, nor a patient in a health-care facility in which the declarant is a patient, nor am I a person who has any claim against any portion of the estate of the declarant upon his/her decease.

(Signed) _____   (Signed) _____

        Witness   *Witness*

_____   _____

        Address   *Address*

POWER OF ATTORNEY

Power of Attorney

STATE OF   )

)   ss:

COUNTY OF   )

KNOW YE ALL MEN BY THESE PRESENTS,

That I, _____ , of

_____ ,

    Street Address   *Apt. No.*   *City*   *State*   *Zip*

do hereby make, constitute, and appoint _____ , of

_____ ,

    Street Address   *Apt. No.*   *City*   *State*   *Zip*

as my true and lawful Attorney-in-Fact, for me and in my name, place, and stead to:

_____

_____

_____

_____

_____

    I further give and grant to my said Attorney-in-Fact full power and authority to do and perform every act necessary and proper to be done in the exercise of any of the foregoing powers as fully as I might or could do if personally present, with full power of substitution and revocation, hereby ratifying and confirming all that my said Attorney-in-Fact shall lawfully do, or cause to be done by virtue hereof.

    This instrument may not be changed orally.

    IN WITNESS WHEREOF, I have hereunto set my hand and seal this day of _____ , 19__ .

                             (Signed) _____

PRIVACY ACT/FREEDOM OF INFORMATION ACT REQUEST

Attn: _____

    This is a request under provisions of Title 5 USC, Sec. 552, the Freedom of Information Act, and Title 5 USC, Sec. 552a, the Privacy Act.

    Please furnish me with copies of all records on me retrievable by the use of an individual identifier and by the use of any combination of identifiers (e.g., name + date of birth + Social Security number, etc.) that are contained in the following systems of records:

_____

_____

_____

_____

    In order to identify myself and to facilitate your search of records systems, I provide the following information:

Last Name	*First*	*Middle*

Street	*City*	*State*	*Zip*

Date of Birth	*Place of Birth*	*Sex*	*Social Security Number*

    In the event that any part or all of my records are withheld, I request a complete list of all records being withheld and the specific exemption being claimed for the withholding of each.

    In the event that search and copying fees are estimated to exceed $ _____ , I request an opportunity to review such records, or to have a duly authorized representative review such records, in order to select those to be copied.

    If you have any questions regarding this request, please telephone me at _____ weekdays between _____ and _____ or write to me at the above address.

    As provided for by Sec. 552(a)(6)(i) of the Freedom of Information Act, I shall expect to receive a reply within ten (10) business days.

Sincerely,

_____

PROMISSORY NOTE

Promissory Note

$ _____

Date _____

_____ after the above date I promise to pay to the order of _____
(*number of days*)

the sum of _____ ($ _____),
together with interest at _____ percent per annum, payable at
_____.

The maker and endorser of this note further agree to waive demand, notice of nonpayment and protest, and in case suit shall be brought for the collection hereof, or the same has to be collected upon demand of an attorney, to pay reasonable attorney's fees for making such collection. Deferred interest payments to bear interest from maturity at _____ percent per annum, payable semiannually.

(Signed) _____
Maker

(Signed) _____
Endorser

Due _____

REQUEST FOR REASON FOR ADVERSE CREDIT ACTION

Request for Reason for Adverse Credit Action

Date: _____

Dear _____

On _____ , I was notified that my application for credit dated _____ was denied based upon information received by you from a source other than a consumer credit reporting agency.

Pursuant to my right under the Fair Credit Reporting Act, Title 15 USC, Sec. 1681m(b), I hereby request that the nature of the information received by you be disclosed to me.

Please forward such information to me at the above address.

Thank you for your prompt attention to this matter.

Sincerely,

_____

SECURITY AGREEMENT

Security Agreement

STATE OF _____)

_____)   ss:

COUNTY OF _____)

KNOW YE ALL MEN BY THESE PRESENTS,

That I, _____ , of

_____ ,

    Street Address   *Apt. No.*   *City*   *State*   *Zip*

hereinafter called "Debtor," hereby grant to _____ , of

_____ ,

    Street Address   *Apt. No.*   *City*   *State*   *Zip*

hereinafter called the "Secured Party," a security interest in the following described property as collateral to secure payment of the obligation described herein.

Collateral

_____

_____

_____

_____

Obligation

_____

_____

_____

_____

    Default in the payment of all or any part of the obligation described is a default under this Agreement. Upon such default, the Secured Party may declare all of the above-described obligation(s) immediately due and payable and shall have the remedies of a secured party under provisions of the Uniform Commercial Code. In the event legal action is required to enforce any provision of this Agreement, the prevailing party shall be entitled to recover reasonable attorney's fees and costs.

    The Debtor hereby agrees to exercise reasonable caution and care in use of the herein-described collateral; to adequately insure or keep insured the described collateral; not to attempt to sell, assign, or dispose of said collateral or his/her interest therein; not to encumber nor to permit any encumbrance against same; and not to remove said collateral from the county where the Debtor resides without written permission of the Secured Party.

Legal Information

continues

Security Agreement, Continued

> EXECUTED this _____ day of _____ , 19___ .
>
> (Signed) _____
>
> *Debtor*
>
> (Signed) _____
>
> *Secured Party*

STATUTE OF LIMITATIONS

A statute of limitations defines the time span after an alleged offense during which legal action may be brought. After that time has elapsed, legal proceedings cannot be initiated, regardless of a case's merits.

If you angrily shake your fist at someone, it's legally considered "assault." If you follow up your actions by punching the person in the nose, the offense is "assault and battery."

FEDERAL STATUTE OF LIMITATIONS

CAPITAL OFFENSES

There is no limitation on prosecution in cases punishable by death and in the crime of murder, even when the death penalty is not prescribed.

NONCAPITAL OFFENSES

The limitation on noncapital offenses is five years, although Congress may make specific exceptions.

STATE STATUTE OF LIMITATIONS

This varies by crime and by state. On the World Wide Web, check http://www.findlaw.com/11stategov/index.html for links to Web pages for all 50 states. Each state Web page has extensive links to legal resources within that state, including legislative information, state constitution, statutes, and court opinions.

COPYRIGHTS

The copyright law protects works of authorship, published or unpublished, in any tangible medium of expression. Under this law, creators of—among other things—books, theatrical works, computer programs, videotapes, movies, music, lyrics, choreography, pantomimes, and recordings can secure exclusive rights to perform, display, or reproduce their works. These individuals have a property right for their work and may license it for reproduction or other use.

However, anyone may make "fair use" of copyrighted material. The definition of this term depends on who is using the material, how much is used, the percentage of the entire work that the excerpt used constitutes, the purpose of the use, and the effect such use may have on the ability of the copyright holder to derive income from his or her creation. For example, a teacher may be able to photocopy a few pages of a book for use in a classroom, but an advertising firm may be entitled to quote no more than a few lines from the same book in an ad without obtaining permission from the copyright holder. And while it may be lawful to quote 200 words from a novel without asking permission, the same would not be true in the case of a poem if the 200 words constituted the whole poem.

The most recent version of the copyright law took effect in 1978. Works created before 1978 are protected for 28 years from the time they are first published. The copyright may be renewed for an additional 47 years. Works created since the beginning of 1978 may be copyrighted for the life of the author plus 50 years after his or her death. For

The Death Penalty

A Closer Look

States That Have Capital Punishment			States and Districts That Do Not Have Capital Punishment
Alabama	Kentucky	Ohio	Alaska
Arizona	Louisiana	Oklahoma	District of Columbia
Arkansas	Maryland	Oregon	Hawaii
California	Mississippi	Pennsylvania	Iowa
Colorado	Missouri	South Carolina	Maine
Connecticut	Montana	South Dakota	Massachusetts
Delaware	Nebraska	Tennessee	Michigan
Florida	Nevada	Texas	Minnesota
Georgia	New Hampshire	Utah	North Dakota
Idaho	New Jersey	Virginia	Rhode Island
Illinois	New Mexico	Washington	Vermont
Indiana	New York	Wyoming	West Virginia
Kansas	North Carolina		Wisconsin

works made for hire, and for anonymous and pseudonymous works (unless the author's identity is revealed in Copyright Office records), the term is 100 years from creation or 75 years from first publication, whichever period is shorter.

On March 1, 1989, the United States joined the Berne Convention for the Protection of Literary and Artistic Works, an international copyright treaty. Under this convention, works are copyrighted from the moment they are fixed, or notated in some tangible form, such as in writing or on audiotape.

Works published as of March 1, 1989, need not display a copyright notice, but it is still recommended. Works created but not published before 1978 and works registered with the Copyright Office as unpublished works before 1978 also are under no obligation to display a copyright notice. Works published or registered before March 1, 1989, are subject to pre-Berne requirements regarding the display of a copyright notice.

This notice includes the word "Copyright" or the abbreviation "Copr." the year the work was first published, and the name of the owner of the copyright. The copyright symbol, a "C" in a circle (except for recordings, which use a circled "P"), also must be displayed.

Displaying the notice of copyright is sufficient to establish exclusive rights to an original work. In many cases, however, formal registration of a copyright claim is a prerequisite for filing suit for infringement for works whose country of origin is the United States. In addition, subject to certain exceptions, the remedies of statutory damages and attorneys' fees are not available for those infringements occurring before registration.

In 1992, Congress passed legislation that applies the same principles of fair use governing published works to unpublished works created between 1964 and 1977 (inclusive). The legislation also prescribes more stringent criminal sanctions for copyright infringement, designating certain violations as felonies.

A copy of any work registered for copyright must be deposited with the Library of Congress. Works that are not registered for copyright also may need to be deposited there.

In addition to the Berne Convention, the United States is a member of the Universal Copyright Convention, another multilateral agreement. Most countries of the world belong to one or both of these conventions, offering international copyright protection to all authors' registered works. The

Legal Information

basic feature of this protection is "national treatment," under which the alien author is treated by a country in the same manner that it treats its own authors.

As of 1995, the international implementation of *General Agreement on Tariffs and Trade* (GATT) restored copyright protection to certain foreign works that had entered the public domain in the U.S. GATT also criminalized the production and distribution of pirated sound recordings and music videos.

The rapid expansion of digital media such as CD-ROMs and online databases has prompted confusion and debate over the limits of copyright. In the late 1990s, Congress was formulating legislation meant to govern the vast new territory of electronic rights where existing copyright law seemed insufficient. Until updated legislation is signed, the creators of proprietary material must rely on the old law to provide protection in the new media.

Currently, filing for copyright registration costs $20. For more information and application forms, write to

Register of Copyrights
The Library of Congress
Washington, DC 20559
http://lcweb.loc.gov/copyright

PATENTS

Congressional grants of patents and copyrights are based on Article I, Section 8 of the Constitution, which states that "Congress shall have power . . . to promote the progress of science and useful arts, by securing for limited times to authors and inventors the exclusive rights to their respective writings and discoveries."

A patent is the grant of a property right to an inventor, excluding others from making, using, or selling his or her invention. The invention may consist of "any new and useful process, machine, manufacture, or composition of matter, or any new and useful improvements thereof . . ." This patent law also covers ornamental designs, plants, and new forms of animal life. But no one can patent printed matter or a way of doing business.

In addition to being useful, the invention must be new. If the inventor describes the invention in a printed publication, uses the invention publicly, or places it on sale, he or she must apply for a patent before one year goes by; otherwise, any right to a patent is lost.

The Patent and Trademark Office currently receives more than 150,000 applications for patents each year, and it has granted more than 5 million patents since 1790. The agency grants new patents only after a diligent search of the records to make sure that the patent is original. Inventors may use the agency's Search Room (patent-research library) in Washington or any of the many patent-depository libraries throughout the United States to conduct their own searches before filing.

Although inventors can handle their own applications, the agency advises that the process is complex enough to require a patent attorney—a lawyer who also has a degree in engineering or physical science.

Only the inventor may apply for a patent. If the inventor is dead or incapacitated, a legal representative or guardian may apply. If two or more persons shared the ideas for the invention, they may apply jointly. But if one person had the idea and the other financed its development, only the person with the original idea may apply.

The application consists of a written description of the invention, with "claims" relating its distinguishing features—ways in which it does things in an entirely novel manner or improves significantly on previous inventions. If applicable, pen-and-ink or color drawings must accompany the description. Models usually are unnecessary. The Patent Office keeps all documents submitted in application for a patent strictly confidential while the application process runs it course.

It is not uncommon for some or all of the claims to be rejected on the first action by the patent examiner; relatively few applications are allowed as filed. The applicant responds to the examiner's objections with clarification and explanation. If the Patent Office finally rejects the application, the inventor can take the case to the Board of Patent Appeals and Interferences. If the board turns down the application, the inventor has recourse through the Court of Appeals for the Federal Circuit or a civil suit in U.S. District Court in Washington, D.C.

About 1 percent of all patent applications encounter a problem because two or more applications are filed by different inventors claiming substantially the same patentable invention. Only one of the inventors can receive a patent, and the procedure to determine that one is called an *interference*. Each party to such a proceeding must submit evidence proving when the invention was made. As in the case of the rejection of any other patent, the decision of the examiners can be appealed.

If a patent applied for before June 8, 1995, is granted, it is good for 17 years. Under the terms of the GATT international treaty, most patents applied for after that date have a term of 20 years if granted (patents on ornamental designs have a term of 14 years).

Small entities—individual inventors, small businesses, and not-for-profit organizations—pay a filing fee of $375 for most patents and an additional fee of $625 if the patent is issued. For ornamental designs, the fees are $155 (filing fee) and $215 (upon issue of patent), and for plant varieties, the fees are $255 and $315. Large entities such as corporations pay twice these amounts. Inventors also must pay maintenance fees after $3^1/_2$, $7^1/_2$, and $11^1/_2$ years. Currently, these fees for small entities are $450, $905, and $1,365. For large entities, fees are $900, $1,810, and $2,730.

"Significant Inventions, Technological **Go to** Advances, and Scientific Discoveries" in chapter 5

Once a patent is granted, all documents relating to it become available for public inspection. The Patent Office can keep such information secret, however, if its commissioner decides that such information is vital to the national security.

As with any other property, patents may be sold or assigned in whole or in part to someone else. The patent holder also may license others to use the process or produce the product under specific conditions. The Patent Office cautions that a part owner of a patent—no matter how small his or her interest—may make, use, and sell the invention for his or her own profit without regard to the other owner. He or she also may sell the interest (or any part of it) or license others to use or make it. Therefore, inventors should be very careful when agreeing to sell a part interest in their patent.

Patented articles must be marked with the word "Patent" and the number of the patent. Some people use "Patent Pending" or "Patent Applied For" to inform others of the status of a patent claim, but such words have no legal effect. To combat infringement of a patent, the person holding the patent may bring a civil suit.

Patents granted by the Patent and Trademark Office protect inventions in the United States only. However, the United States is a signatory of several treaties that facilitate applications for patent protection in other countries. For further information, write to

Commissioner of Patents and Trademarks
Washington, DC 20231
800-786-9199
http://www.uspto.gov

FEDERAL JUDICIAL SYSTEM

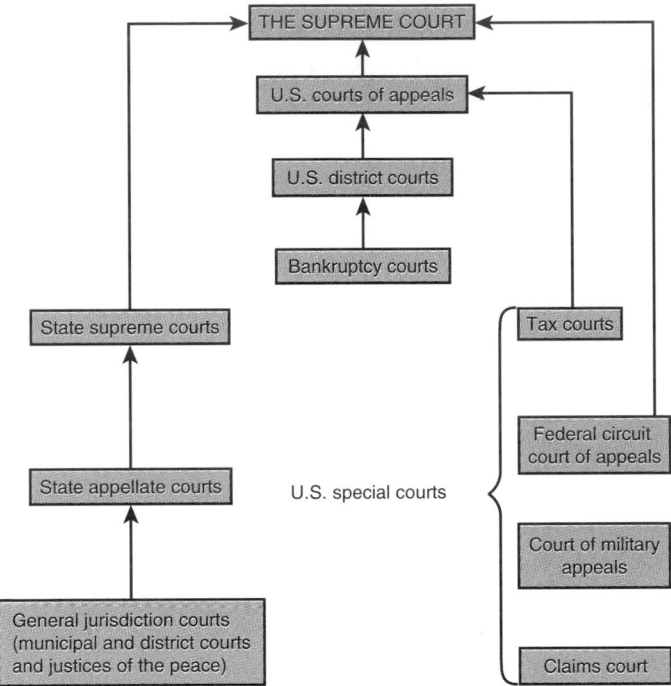

SUPREME COURT JUSTICES

This section lists all the Supreme Court justices in U.S. history. The first date for each justice is the year when the justice took the oath of office. The second date is the last year the person served as a Supreme Court justice. Some justices were appointed in the preceding year but actually assumed office during the first year listed.

Justice	Term	Justice	Term	Justice	Term
John Jay*	1789–95	Alfred Moore	1800–04	James M. Wayne	1835 67
James Wilson	1789–98	John Marshall*	1801–35	Roger B. Taney*	1836–64
John Blair, Jr.	1790–96	William Johnson	1804–34	Philip P. Barbour	1836–41
William Cushing	1790–1810	Henry Brockholst	1807–23	John Catron	1837–65
John Rutledge	1790–91	Livingston		John McKinley	1838–52
James Iredell	1790–99	Thomas Todd	1807–26	Peter V. Daniel	1842–60
Thomas Johnson	1792–93	Gabriel Duval	1811–35	Samuel Nelson	1845–72
William Paterson	1793–1806	Joseph Story	1812–45	Levi Woodbury	1845–51
John Rutledge*	†1795	Smith Thompson	1823–43	Robert C. Grier	1846–70
Oliver Ellsworth*	1796–1800	Robert Trimble	1826–28	Benjamin R. Curtis	1851–57
Samuel Chase	1796–1811	John McLean	1830–61	John A. Campbell	1853–61
Bushrod Washington	1798–1829	Henry Baldwin	1830–44	Nathan Clifford	1858–81

*   Chief Justice
†   John Rutledge took the oath of office as Chief Justice in 1795 as a recess appointee. However, the Senate rejected his appointment later that year.

Justice	Term	Justice	Term	Justice	Term
David Davis	1862–77	Charles E. Hughes	1910–16	Fred M. Vinson*	1946–53
Samuel F. Miller	1862–90	Horace H. Lurton	1910–14	Thomas C. Clark	1949–67
Noah H. Swayne	1862–81	Joseph R. Lamar	1911–16	Sherman Minton	1949–56
Stephen J. Field	1863–97	Willis Van Devanter	1911–37	Earl Warren*	1953–69
*Salmon P. Chase	1864–73	Mahlon Pitney	1912–22	John Marshall	1955–71
Joseph P. Bradley	1870–92	James C. McReynolds	1914–41	Harlan II	
William Strong	1870–80	Louis D. Brandeis	1916–39	William J. Brennan, Jr.	1956–90
Ward Hunt	1873–82	John H. Clarke	1916–22	Charles E. Whittaker	1957–62
Morrison R. Waite*	1874–88	William H. Taft*	1921–30	Potter Stewart	1958–81
John M. Harlan	1877–1911	George Sutherland	1922–38	Byron R. White	1962–93
William B. Woods	1881–87	Pierce Butler	1923–39	Arthur J. Goldberg	1962–65
Stanley Matthews	1881–89	Edward T. Sanford	1923–30	Abe Fortas	1965–69
Samuel Blatchford	1882–93	Harlan F. Stone	1925–41	Thurgood Marshall	1967–91
Horace Gray	1882–1902	Charles E. Hughes*	1930–41	Warren E. Burger*	1969–86
Melville W. Fuller*	1888–1910	Owen J. Roberts	1930–45	Harry A. Blackmun	1970–94
Lucius Q. C. Lamar	1888–93	Benjamin N. Cardozo	1932–38	Lewis F. Powell, Jr.	1972–87
David J. Brewer	1890–1910	Hugo L. Black	1937–71	William H. Rehnquist	1972–86
Henry B. Brown	1891–1906	Stanley F. Reed	1938–57	John Paul Stevens	1975–
George Shiras, Jr.	1892–1903	Felix Frankfurter	1939–62	Sandra Day O'Connor	1981–
Howell E. Jackson	1893–95	William O. Douglas	1939–75	William H. Rehnquist*	1986–
Edward D. White	1894–1910	Frank Murphy	1940–49	Antonin Scalia	1986–
Rufus W. Peckham	1896–1909	Harlan F. Stone*	1941–46	Anthony M. Kennedy	1988–
Joseph McKenna	1898–1925	James F. Byrnes	1941–42	David H. Souter	1990–
Oliver W. Holmes	1902–32	Robert H. Jackson	1941–54	Clarence Thomas	1991–
William R. Day	1903–22	Wiley B. Rutledge	1943–49	Ruth Bader Ginsburg	1993–
William H. Moody	1906–10	Harold H. Burton	1945–58	Stephen Gerald Breyer	1994–
Edward D. White*	1910–21				

*Chief Justice

SUPREME COURT DECISIONS

The following Supreme Court decisions are among the most significant in the 19th and 20th centuries.

1803 *Marbury v. Madison.* For the first time, the Court ruled an act of Congress unconstitutional, establishing the principle of judicial review.

1819 *McCullock v. Maryland.* The Court's ruling upheld the constitutionality of the creation of the Bank of the United States and denied to the states the power to tax such an institution because, as Justice John Marshall put it, "the power to tax is the power to destroy."

1819 *Trustees of Dartmouth College v. Woodward.* The Court ruled that a state could not arbitrarily alter the terms of a contract.

Although this case applied to a college, its implications widened in later years when the same principle was used to limit the ability of states to interfere with business contracts.

1857 *Dred Scott v. Sanford.* The Missouri Compromise was declared unconstitutional because it deprived a person (a slave) of his property without due process of law. This was only the second time the Court had asserted the power of judicial review. The decision also stated that slaves are not citizens of any state or of the United States.

1877 *Munn v. Illinois.* States were allowed to regulate businesses when "a public interest" was involved. This principle was weakened by rulings in other cases in the late 19th century.

Legal Information

1895 ***U.S. v. E. C. Knight Co.***   In stating that manufacturing and commerce are not connected, and that the Sherman Act (an antitrust act) could not be applied to manufacturers, the Court seriously impaired the government's ability to regulate monopolies.

1896 ***Plessy v. Ferguson.***   The Court ruled that state laws enforcing segregation by race are constitutional if accommodations are equal as well as separate. This ruling was overturned by the Court's 1954 *Brown v. Board of Education of Topeka* decision.

1904 ***Northern Securities Co. v. U.S.***   The Court backed government action against big businesses that restrained trade, in effect putting teeth in the Sherman Act.

1908 ***Muller v. Oregon.***   The Court ruled that a state could legislate maximum working hours based on evidence compiled by future Supreme Court Justice Louis D. Brandeis.

1911 ***Standard Oil Co. of New Jersey et al. v. U.S.***   The Court dissolved the Standard Oil Trust—not because of its size, but because of its unreasonable restraint of trade. The principle involved is called "the rule of reason."

1919 ***Schenck v. U.S.***   The Court upheld the World War I Espionage Act. In a landmark decision dealing with free speech, Justice Oliver W. Holmes said that a person who encourages draft resistance during a war is a "clear and present danger."

1935 ***Schechter v. U.S.***   Invalidating the National Industrial Recovery Act of the New Deal, the Court declared that Congress could not delegate its powers to the president.

1951 ***Dennis et al. v. U.S.***   The Court ruled the 1946 Smith Act constitutional. The act made it a crime to advocate the overthrow of the government by force. In its 1957 *Yates v. U.S.* decision, the Court tempered this ruling by permitting such advocacy in the abstract if it is not connected to action to achieve the goal.

1954 ***Brown v. Board of Education of Topeka.*** In an example of sociological jurisprudence, the Court held that laws enforcing segregated schools were unconstitutional. It called for desegregation of schools "with all deliberate speed."

1957 ***Roth v. U.S.***   This ruling based obscenity decisions on whether a publication appeals to "prurient interests." The Court also said that obscene material is that which lacks any "redeeming social importance."

1961 ***Mapp v. Ohio.***   The Court extended the federal exclusionary rule to the states. This rule prevented prosecutors from using illegally obtained evidence in a criminal trial.

1962 ***Baker v. Carr.***   The Court held that state legislatures must be apportioned to provide equal protection under the law (14th Amendment). A follow-up decision applied the same principle to the size of congressional districts, insisting that they be approximately equal in population.

1966 ***Miranda v. Arizona.***   The Court declared that before questioning suspects, police must inform them of their right to remain silent; that any statements they make can be used against them; and that they have the right to remain silent until they have an attorney, which the state will provide if they cannot afford one.

1972 ***Furman v. Georgia.***   The Court found unconstitutional all death-penalty statutes then in force in the states. However, it held out the possibility that if these statutes were rewritten to be less subjective and randomly imposed, they might be constitutional (as the Court has subsequently held in many instances).

1973 ***Roe v. Wade.***   The Court ruled state laws prohibiting abortion unconstitutional, except as they apply to the last trimester of pregnancy, on the basis that the 14th Amendment provides for a woman's freedom to make a private decision about her reproductive practices.

1978 *University of California v. Bakke.* The ruling allowed a university to admit students on the basis of race if the school's goal is to combat discrimination. Subsequent decisions of the Court have filled in the details of how government and business may use quotas to make up for racism in the past.

1986 *Bowers v. Hardwick.* In a case involving the enforcement of Georgia's law against sodomy, the Court ruled that states have the power to regulate sexual relations in private between consenting adults.

Upset with colleagues who did not properly study bills, a Texas congressman introduced a bill commending Mr. Albert DiSalvo for his outstanding work in population control. The bill passed unanimously. At the time, Mr. DiSalvo was on trial for a series of murders. He was better known as "The Boston Strangler."

1989 *Webster v. Reproductive Health Services.* The Court upheld a Missouri law forbidding public employees to perform most abortions, prohibiting the use of public buildings for abortions, and requiring a fetal-viability test prior to abortions after the 20th week of pregnancy. This case set a precedent allowing other states to restrict access to abortions.

1993 *Harris v. Forklift Systems, Inc.* In a suit brought by a Tennessee woman against her former employer, the Court found that workers may claim sexual harassment even when severe economic or emotional damage does not result. The decision broadened Title VII civil-rights protections against sexual discrimination in the workplace and enlarged the legal definition of sexual harassment.

1996 *Romer v. Evans* The Court struck down an amendment to Colorado's state constitution that barred homosexuals from seeking civil-rights protection against discrimination.

COMMON LEGAL TERMS

accessory An accessory *before* the fact helps another person commit or try to commit a crime but is not present at the commission of the crime. An accessory *during* the fact witnesses a crime but does not do what he or she could do to prevent it. An accessory *after* the fact helps another avoid arrest for the commission of a crime.

accomplice An individual who joins with another to commit a crime. The accomplice bears equal responsibility under the law.

actus reus A wrongful act, as opposed to *mens rea*—thoughts and intentions behind the act. For example, in a murder, *homicide* is the *actus reus,* and *malice aforethought* is the *mens rea.*

adjudication A final judgment in a legal proceeding.

affidavit A written statement sworn or affirmed to be true before a person legally authorized to administer an oath.

age of consent The minimum age for marrying without parental consent; also, the minimum age for consensual sexual relations. Sexual intercourse with someone below the age of consent can result in a charge of assault or statutory rape, even if both people participate willingly.

alibi An assertion or fact placing the defendant at the time of the crime in another location than the scene of that crime.

amicus curiae Latin for "friend of the court." A person or organization not party to a case who submits information useful to the court in that proceeding. Amicus curiae briefs generally are submitted when the suit involves matters of wide public interest.

amnesty An act of government forgiving members of a group, such as unregistered gun owners or illegal aliens, who normally would be subject to prosecution.

appeal   A request to a superior court to reverse the decision of a lower court or government agency or to grant a new trial.

appellate court   A court whose jurisdiction is confined to reviewing decisions of lower courts or agencies.

arraignment   A court procedure in which formal charges are brought against a defendant, who is advised of his or her constitutional rights and may have the opportunity to offer a plea.

assault   A threatened or attempted physical attack in which the attacker appears to have the ability to bring about bodily harm if not stopped. *Aggravated assault* involves an attack perpetrated with recklessness and intent to injure seriously or an assault with a deadly weapon. *Battery* is an assault in which the assailant makes physical contact with the victim.

attachment   A court writ authorizing legal authorities to seize property that may be needed for the payment of a judgment in a judicial proceeding. *See also* **writ.**

bail   Security provided to ensure the presence of a defendant in court during the course of a case. Defendants raising this security are said to "make bail"; those fleeing and forfeiting the security have "jumped bail." The actual document securing the defendant's release is the "bail bond."

bar   A collective term for all lawyers practicing in a particular court system.

battery   *See* **assault.**

bench warrant   A court order authorizing a public official to arrest a person and bring that individual to court.

bequest   Personal property bequeathed (given as a gift) in a will. *Devise* is the term for handing down real property (land and what is built upon it or affixed to it) through a will.

beyond a reasonable doubt   The degree to which jurors must be convinced before they may convict a person of a crime. The jurors must find the prosecution's case proven beyond the point at which a reasonable, average, prudent person would be convinced before returning a verdict of guilty.

bill of particulars   The specific events to be dealt with in a criminal trial, presented to the defendant so that he or she may effectively prepare a defense.

binding over   The action of a lower court shifting a case to a grand jury or superior court when the inferior court believes that a crime has been committed. Also, a court order to jail a defendant during the course of a proceeding.

boilerplate   Language uniformly found in certain types of documents—for instance, the "small print" in a contract that people often neglect to read.

breach of contract   Failure to do something required in a contract. *See also* **contract.**

breaking and entering   The illegal entrance into premises with criminal intent. Simply pushing a door open and walking in may constitute breaking and entering.

brief   A document in which a lawyer makes his or her client's case by raising legal points and citing authorities.

burden of proof   In a civil case, the requirement that a plaintiff or defendant must show that the majority of evidence is on his or her side in order to win a suit. In a criminal case, the prosecutor's burden of proof is to prove every fact involved in a charge.

burglary   Unlawful presence in a building with the intent of committing a felony or taking something of value. *See also* **robbery.**

capacity   The ability to understand the facts and significance of one's behavior. A defendant cannot be convicted of a crime in which he or she did not have the legal capacity to comprehend it.

cease and desist order   A legal order preventing a person or organization from continuing a specific activity. A *mandatory injunction,* on the other hand, orders the performance of a specified act.

certiorari   A writ in which a superior court commands an inferior court to deliver the records of a proceeding to the superior body so that it may decide whether there is basis for appeal.

At last count there were more than 5 million federal laws. Ignorance of the law is still no excuse.

character witness   *See* **witness.**

chattel   Personal, rather than real, property. A *chattel mortgage,* for example, is a loan to buy an expensive item, such as a car, in which the item, or *chattel,* is security for the debt.

circumstantial evidence   Evidence based not on direct observation or knowledge but implied from things already known.

civil contempt   *See* **contempt of court.**

class action   A lawsuit brought by a group of people with a shared purpose.

clemency   A reduction of criminal punishment, often granted to prevent the execution of a prisoner.

codicil   An addition to a will altering it.

common-law marriage   A relationship in which two people live together as husband and wife without formally getting married.

community property   Property owned by a husband and wife jointly.

competency hearing   A procedure to determine legal capacity (for example, of a defendant in a criminal case), understand the charges, and cooperate with a lawyer in preparing a defense. *Compos mentis* is a finding of competence to stand trial; *non compos mentis* is the finding of a lack of competence to go to trial.

complaint   The first statement of facts (in a civil proceeding) or accusation (in a criminal case).

compos mentis   *See* **competency hearing.**

consent decree   An agreement between two parties sanctioned by the court—for example, between a company and the government, involving allegations of violations of antitrust laws. In the consent decree, the company would agree to cease such practices without formally admitting guilt.

conspiracy   The plotting by two or more people to break the law.

contempt of court   Anything done to hinder the work of the court. *Civil contempt* involves failure to follow a court order benefiting another party in a case, as in the failure to pay court-ordered damages; *criminal contempt* consists of the obstruction of justice.

contract   A commitment between two or more parties, enforceable by law.

corpus delicti   The object upon which a crime has been committed. The term does not necessarily refer to a body, although a corpse with a knife in its back would be an example in a homicide.

corroborating evidence   Additional evidence of a different character to the same point that backs up proof already offered in a proceeding.

criminal contempt   *See* **contempt of court.**

criminal negligence   *See* **negligence.**

cross-examination   The interrogation of a witness to discredit or show in a new light testimony that was offered by that person during direct examination.

custody   In a divorce case, the right to house, care for, and discipline a child.

damages   A court-ordered monetary award to someone who has suffered loss or injury by another.

de facto   Actually exercising power though not legally or officially established. A practice sanctioned by custom, as opposed to *de jure,* a practice formally backed by law.

de jure   *See* **de facto.**

decree   A court's decision in a case; its judgment.

defamation   The damaging of another person's reputation through writing (*libel*) or speech (*slander*).

default judgment   A court determination made against a defendant who fails to show up in court or fails to take some other court-required action.

defendant   A person or institution being sued or accused in a legal proceeding.

deposition   A pretrial interrogation of a witness, usually in a lawyer's office.

devise   *See* **bequest.**

directed verdict   A verdict declared by the court in a civil trial before the jury gets the case. Judges render this verdict when the facts and the law in a case point to a definite conclusion. There cannot be a directed verdict of guilty in a criminal trial, since that would violate a defendant's right to trial by jury.

discovery   A pretrial process that enables one side in a litigation to elicit information from the other side relating to the facts in the case.

disorderly conduct   A broad spectrum of offenses, such as drunkenness or fighting, that disturb the public peace.

district attorney   *See* **prosecutor.**

docket   A list of cases to be tried by a court—its calendar. Also, a summary of a court's activities.

double jeopardy   The condition of being tried a second time for a crime after the first case has been decided. Double jeopardy is prohibited by the 5th Amendment of the U.S. Constitution.

due process   The general doctrine that legislation must promote the legitimate aims of government (*substantive due process*) and that nobody can be deprived of liberty or property through unfair procedures (*procedural due process*).

easement   The right to use another person's land.

emancipation   The parental yielding of authority over, control over, and responsibility for a minor.

eminent domain   The right of the state to convert private property to public property.

entrapment   A defense by which a defendant seeks to show that he or she would not have committed an unlawful act if not tricked into doing it by law-enforcement officials.

equal protection   The 14th-Amendment requirement that all groups of people be treated equally by the legal system.

estate   Everything an individual owns.

eviction   The dispossessing of a tenant from land or premises he or she has occupied.

evidence   Testimony, documents, and objects used to prove matters of fact at a trial.

exclusionary rule   A rule preventing introduction at a criminal trial of evidence obtained in violation of the 4th Amendment's prohibition against unreasonable searches and seizures, even if that evidence otherwise would be admissible. *See also* **search and seizure.**

executor/executrix   A man or woman, respectively, appointed to administer the provisions of a will.

eyewitness   A person who can testify as to what happened because he or she was there when it happened and saw it. Technically, a person who offers testimony of something overheard is an *earwitness.*

fair hearing   A special administrative procedure set up to ensure that a person will not be harmed or denied his or her rights without due process of law before a court can intervene. Examples of extraordinary circumstances calling for a fair hearing include loss of welfare benefits and deportation.

fair use The conditions under which a person can use material copyrighted by another.

false imprisonment *See* **kidnapping.**

false pretenses The means used to take another's property through trickery. This crime involves the intent to secure the title to the property through some seemingly legal transaction. *See also* **larceny.**

fee An interest in which land is or may become possessory; *freehold* is land held in fee.

felony A serious crime, as opposed to a *misdemeanor*. The distinction often is made in terms of the applicable punishment; felonies are punishable by a certain minimum prison term—under federal law, one year.

felony murder A homicide committed in the course of another crime, such as a burglary.

fiduciary A person in a position of trust who acts for the benefit of another person. Examples are executors, corporate directors, and infant guardians.

finding The basis in fact or law for a judgment. *See also* **judgment.**

fraud The injury of a person or group of persons through deceit.

freehold *See* **fee.**

frisk *See* **stop and frisk.**

garnishment The legal impoundment of funds by which a creditor sends notices through the court to the debtor's employer, thus seizing the debtor's salary to pay off the debt owed to the creditor.

grand jury A jury of from 12 to 23 people empowered to look into possible criminal activity in an area, report on it, and indict individuals when it finds evidence that they have committed a crime.

grand larceny *See* **larceny.**

grandfather clause A provision in some laws allowing people who had legally engaged in an activity prior to its restriction by law to continue to engage in that activity.

guardian A person entrusted to look out for the interests of a minor or an incompetent person. The specific fiduciary relationship is defined by law and court orders.

habeas corpus The order by a judge to have a prisoner brought to court to determine the legality of the imprisonment.

hearsay evidence Statements made outside of court attesting to some fact; therefore the person making the statements may not be cross-examined or otherwise scrutinized. For example, if A testifies in court that he heard B say something, in most cases, B's statement will not be admissible as evidence.

homicide An act in which one person causes the death of another. *See also* **manslaughter; murder.**

hung jury A jury that is unable to reach a verdict.

immunity from prosecution The exemption of a witness from prosecution to thwart a refusal to testify based on constitutional rights. The witness cannot be prosecuted on the basis of anything he or she says while testifying under such immunity.

impanel To select a jury.

in camera A judicial proceeding from which the public is excluded. Although the term literally means "in chambers," the proceeding can be held anywhere outside of open court.

in loco parentis A person or institution acting toward a minor "in place of parents" without a formal adoption procedure—for example, the relationship between a school and a student.

in rem A proceeding involving property without reference to the claims of people on that property.

indictment A document delivered to a grand jury in which a public prosecutor accuses one or more persons of committing a crime. If the grand jury thinks the evidence submitted is sufficient to warrant a trial, it endorses the indictment as a true bill.

infant   A person who has not reached the age of majority (usually 18), at which he or she enjoys the full rights of citizenship and is legally responsible for his or her acts.

information   A prosecuting attorney's written accusation of criminal activity, similar to an indictment but not presented to a grand jury. Information may be used to initiate proceedings against defendants in state, but not federal, courts.

infringement   A violation of a law or right.

injunction   A court order preventing someone from doing a specific act.

injury   The violation of a person's rights to the point where he or she suffers any kind of damage, including financial.

inquest   A coroner's investigation into the cause of death.

insanity   A mental state in which a person lacks legal responsibility.

intestate   Without a will.

judgment   A court's final decision in a case. *See also* **verdict.**

jury   A representative group of people who determine issues of fact at a trial. The Constitution guarantees the right to trial by jury for all crimes punishable by imprisonment for more than six months. In civil trials, juries range in number from 6 to 12 people. State trial juries do not need a unanimous vote to convict (with the exception of six-person juries), but federal juries do.

kidnapping   The illegal seizure and removal of a person without his or her consent. *False imprisonment* involves illegally confining a person against his or her will without moving that person and may be committed by police officers who fail to make arrests properly.

larceny   The act of gaining the use or possession of property through an overtly illegal act, as in stealing a car. *Grand larceny* involves the theft of an object worth more than a specified amount. *See also* **robbery.**

leading question   A lawyer's question to a witness that predetermines the answer, thus putting words in the witness's mouth. Such questions are legitimate during cross-examination but not during direct examination.

libel   *See* **defamation.**

magistrate   An official, such as a justice of the peace, who performs low-level judicial functions.

majority, age of   *See* **infant.**

malfeasance   Wrongful conduct by a public official. *Misfeasance* is the misperforming of a proper act. *Nonfeasance* is the nonperformance of an act that a person has agreed to or is duty-bound to do.

malice aforethought   An antisocial state of mind, often at issue in a murder trial, marked by cruelty and recklessness for which there is no justification. *See also* **manslaughter.**

malpractice   Wrongful conduct by a professional, either through negligence or lack of ethics.

mandamus   A writ commanding someone, often a public official, to perform some act. Mandamus frequently is issued when time is of the essence. *See also* **writ.**

mandatory injunction   *See* **cease and desist order.**

manslaughter   Homicide without malice aforethought. *Voluntary manslaughter* is homicide with mitigating circumstances—for example, a fight in which one person kills another. *Involuntary manslaughter* is killing through criminal negligence, as in drunk driving.

material witness   *See* **witness.**

mens rea   *See* **actus reus.**

Miranda rule   The obligation of the police, when interrogating someone after an arrest, to read to that person his or her constitutional rights. These rights include the right to a lawyer, to remain silent until advised by counsel, and to know that anything he or she say may be used as evidence.

misdemeanor   *See* **felony.**

misfeasance   *See* **malfeasance.**

mistrial   The ending of a trial before the rendering of a verdict. Possible causes include a hung jury or the incapacity of the judge, jurors, or attorneys.

mitigating circumstances   Conditions under which a crime was committed that tend to reduce the punishment in a case—for example, the circumstances leading to a crime of passion.

moral turpitude   Baseness, depravity, vileness, or extreme antisocial behavior. A person's moral turpitude is sometimes taken into account by a judge when sentencing.

murder   Homicide with malice aforethought. Murder in the second degree generally involves less premeditation than the same crime in the first degree. *See also* **malice aforethought; premeditation.**

negligence   Carelessness, acting without reasonable caution, putting another person at risk of injury, or not performing an act that one is obliged to do, with the same consequences. In *criminal negligence,* there is the added element of recklessness.

next of kin   Closest blood relatives or, lacking them, the next closest relations, even if they are related only by marriage.

nolo contendere   A defendant's statement that the charges in a case will not be contested.

non compos mentis   *See* **competency hearing.**

nonfeasance   *See* **malfeasance.**

notary public   A person with the authority to administer oaths, witness documents, and accept depositions.

on the merits   A court judgment resting on the facts in the case rather than on a legal technicality.

open court   Judicial proceedings fully accessible to the public.

pardon   An act by which a governor or the president can excuse a person from punishment and restore his or her civil rights; however, a pardon usually does not wipe out a conviction.

parole   The release of a person from prison under controlled conditions. The parolee must fulfill certain requirements, such as reporting regularly to a parole officer.

perjury   The act of lying while under oath.

plaintiff   The person who initiates a lawsuit.

plea   A defendant's answer to a complaint.

plea bargain   A deal between the prosecutor and the accused, in which the accused pleads guilty in return for lesser punishment than might be received at the end of a trial.

polling the jury   A proceeding in which the judge asks each juror, after the verdict has been rendered, to restate his or her decision in the case.

power of attorney   A document in which one person authorizes another to act as an agent on his or her behalf.

preliminary hearing   A proceeding held after an arrest but before an indictment to see whether there is sufficient evidence to continue holding the prisoner and proceed with a case. *See also* **indictment.**

premeditation   The degree of planning and forethought sufficient to show intent to commit an act—often a factor in determining the degree of guilt in a murder case.

In Atlanta, Georgia, it is illegal to tie a giraffe to a telephone pole or street lamp.

preponderance of evidence   The standard of proof used to settle civil lawsuits—determining which side's evidence has greater weight.

presentment A grand jury's accusation, based not on material presented to it by a prosecutor, but on its own investigation.

preventive detention The holding of a prisoner without bail; also accomplished by setting bail so high that the prisoner cannot meet it.

In Memphis, Tennessee, it's against the law to sell teddy bears or yo-yos on Sunday.

pro bono Meaning "for the good"—the taking of a case by an attorney without a fee. Pro bono cases often are defended on behalf of groups backing important causes.

probable cause The rule under which police need to have a reasonable belief that someone has committed a crime before making an arrest, or that the object for which they are searching in connection with a crime is at a specific location before they search for and seize it. *See also* **search and seizure.**

probate The process by which the legitimacy of a will is established.

probation The suspension of a person's sentence, leaving that individual at liberty but under court supervision.

process A writ requiring that a person appear in court.

prosecutor The person responsible for bringing the accused to justice. Depending on the level on which he or she functions, the prosecutor usually is called a *district attorney, county prosecutor, federal prosecutor,* or, if appointed by a legislature to conduct an investigation, a *special prosecutor.*

protective custody The imprisonment of an individual for his or her own protection.

public defender A lawyer provided by the state to an accused person who cannot afford or refuses counsel.

real property Land and what is built on it, growing upon it, and affixed to it.

reasonable doubt *See* **beyond a reasonable doubt.**

release on one's own recognizance To free the accused on a promise to appear in court rather than on bail.

restraining order A temporary order granted to prevent some action until a hearing can be held on that action.

robbery The use of violence or intimidation to seize another person's property. *See also* **burglary.**

search and seizure A law-enforcement procedure involving the search of a person or premises when police have probable cause to suspect they will find and be able to seize criminal evidence. *See also* **probable cause; search warrant.**

search warrant A court order authorizing law-enforcement officials to look for objects or people involved in the commission of a crime and to produce them in court. The order stipulates the places that the officials may search.

self-defense A plea by which a person may justify the use of force to ward off an attack if the attack was unprovoked, retreat was impossible, and the threat of harm seemed imminent.

self-incrimination An act in a legal proceeding by which a person says something that causes him or her to appear guilty of some type of crime. Under the 5th Amendment, a person cannot be forced to make such a statement.

sequester To prevent a jury from having outside contacts until a trial is finished.

show cause order A court order, issued at the request of one party, requiring a second party to convince the court, usually within a matter of days, that a specific act should not be carried out or allowed.

slander *See* **defamation.**

statute of limitations The period of time during which a person may initiate a legal action. See "Statute of Limitations," earlier in this chapter.

statutory rape   A criminal offense involving sex with a boy or girl under the age of consent; the age differs in various states.

stay   A court order preventing some act or proceeding until a specific condition is met or the stay is lifted.

stop and frisk   A procedure in which police who believe a suspect may be carrying a weapon with the intent to use it can stop that person and search the suspect's outer layer of clothing for a weapon.

subpoena   A court writ requiring a person to appear to testify at a judicial proceeding at a specific time and place under penalty of law.

The Speaker of the House in Great Britain is not allowed to speak.

summary judgment   A procedure by which a party in a civil dispute, if it believes that the other side's argument is without merit, can move to have a case resolved before going to trial.

summons   A notice to appear in court as a defendant in a suit.

testament   *See* **will.**

tort   A violation of legal duty, not involving a contract, that results in harm to another person or another person's property—for example, an act of libel that damages a person's reputation.

true bill   *See* **indictment.**

verdict   A judge or jury's finding of fact. The *judgment*, not the verdict, is the final determination in a case. For example, a judge can declare a jury's verdict *false*—that is, invalid—because it is not based on the evidence.

voir dire   A term usually applied to the interrogation of people to determine their competency as jurors. The term, which is French for "speak the truth," also describes a trial hearing without the

jury present to determine a matter of fact or law, such as the validity of a confession.

waiver   The conscious forgoing of a legal right.

warrant   A court writ directing a public employee to do something—for example, to make an arrest.

will   A document specifying the disposition of a person's property after his or her death. Most states require two or three people to witness a will. Although *will* generally means the same thing as *testament*, the latter applies only to the distribution of personal property, as opposed to real property.

witness   A person who testifies in court under oath. A *material witness* is one whose testimony is central to a case; a *character witness* testifies to the character of an individual.

writ   A written order from a judicial body commanding a law-enforcement officer to do something specified.

wrongful death statute   A law that enables survivors or the person administering an estate to sue for monetary compensation for a death caused by some person or persons. The law is based on the fact that the death deprives survivors or the estate of the services or income of the deceased.

youthful offender   One who, at a judge's discretion, may be sentenced with special consideration given to his or her age. The category applies to defendants older than juveniles (no longer minors) but not yet, in the opinion of the judge, adults. Offender is usually between the ages of 18 and 25.

ADDITIONAL SOURCES OF INFORMATION

ORGANIZATIONS AND SERVICES
American Bar Association (ABA)
750 N. Lakeshore Dr.
Chicago, IL 60611
312-988-5522
http://www.abanet.org

The ABA publishes the *Directory of Lawyer Referral Services*, which lists services located throughout the United States and covers a range of general and special-interest needs. The office is open from 9 A.M. to 5 P.M., CST.

American Civil Liberties Union (ACLU)
125 Broad St.
New York, NY 10004
212-549-2500
http://www.aclu.org

The ACLU monitors civil-rights issues and incidents across the country and files lawsuits against parties whose actions violate the U.S. Constitution. Through a variety of publications and activities, its educational arm seeks to raise the public's awareness of constitutional topics. The office is open weekdays from 9 A.M. to 5:30 P.M., EST.

NAACP Legal Defense and Education Fund
99 Hudson St.
16th Floor
New York, NY 10013
212-219-1900

The staff at the NAACP Legal Defense Fund will put individuals or groups who feel that they have been discriminated against in touch with an attorney who can help. The office is open weekdays from 9:30 A.M. to 5 P.M., EST.

National Center for Youth Law
114 Sansome St.
Suite 900
San Francisco, CA 94104
415-543-3307
info@youthlaw.org

This organization provides counseling and referrals related to legal matters affecting young people, including juvenile justice and child welfare. The office is open from 9 A.M. to 5 P.M., PST.

National Legal Aid & Defender Association
1625 K St., NW
8th Floor
Washington, DC 20006
202-452-0620
http://www.nlada.org/

This association acts as a clearinghouse of organizations providing legal services for those without the means to pay. The office is open from 9 A.M. to 5:30 P.M., EST.

NOW Legal Defense and Education Fund
99 Hudson St.
Suite 1201
New York, NY 10013
212-925-6635
http://www.nowldef.org

This organization provides referrals for legal issues related to women's rights, such as economic inequality, pregnancy discrimination, and problems with changing one's surname. The office is open weekdays from 9:30 A.M. to 5:30 P.M., EST.

BOOKS

American Bar Association. *The American Bar Association Family Legal Guide.* Times Books/ Random House, 1994.

American Bar Association. *The American Lawyer: How and When to Choose One.* ABA, 1986.

Belli, Melvin, and Allen P. Wilkinson. *Everybody's Guide to the Law.* Harper Perennial, 1987.

Black, Henry C. *Black's Law Dictionary,* 6th ed. West, 1990.

Bove, Alexander A., Jr. *The Complete Book of Wills and Estates.* Henry Holt, 1989.

Coughlin, George Gordon, Jr. *Your Handbook of Everyday Law.* HarperCollins, 1993.

Elias, Stephen, and Susan Levinkind. *Legal Research: How to Find and Understand the Law.* Nolo Press, 1995.

Gifis, Steven H. *Law Dictionary.* Barron's, 1996.

Hall, Kermit L., ed. *The Oxford Companion to the Supreme Court.* Oxford, 1992.

Kubey, Craig. *You Don't Always Need a Lawyer.* Consumer Reports Books, 1991.

Pressman, David. *Patent It Yourself.* Nolo Press, 1995.

Rosenbaum, David G. *The Layman's Law Guide to Patents, Trademarks, and Copyrights.* Career Press, 1995.

Ventura, John. *Law for Dummies.* IDG Books, 1996.

Wilson, Lee. *The Copyright Guide.* Allworth Press, 1996.

Legal Information

22

USEFUL ADDRESSES
AND PHONE NUMBERS

Aging	638
Alcoholism and Drug Abuse	643
Children	644
Consumer Information and Protection	645
Disabilities	668
Domestic Violence Resources	668
Family Planning	671
Federal Government Agencies and Bureaus	671
Federal Information Centers	673
Parenting	674
Radio and Television Networks	674
Hot Lnes and Information Services	675
United States Service Academies	677
Additional Sources of Information	678

AGING

PRIVATE ORGANIZATIONS

American Association of Retired Persons
National Gerontology Resource Center
1909 K St., NW
Washington, DC 20049
202-872-4700
http://www.aarp.org

American Association of Retired Persons
Widowed Persons Service
1909 K St., NW
Washington, DC 20049
202-872-4700
http://www.aarp.org

American Society on Aging
833 Market St., Suite 511
San Francisco, CA 94103
415-882-2910
http://www.asaging.org

Andrus Gerontology Center
University of Southern California
Los Angeles, CA 90089
213-740-8241
http://www.usc.edu/dept/gero

Associacion Nacional por Personas Mayores
Library Resource Center
2727 W. 6th St., Suite 270
Los Angeles, CA 90057
213-487-1922

National Senior Citizens Law Center
1101 14th St., NW, Suite 400
Washington, DC 20005
202-289-6976
http://www.nsclc.org

Self-Help for the Elderly
445 Grant Ave.
San Francisco, CA 94108
415-982-9171

STATE COMMISSIONS AND OFFICES

State commissions and offices on aging are responsible for coordinating services for older Americans. They can provide information on programs, services, and opportunities for the aging.

Alabama

Commission on Aging
RSA Plaza, Suite 470
770 Washington Ave.
Montgomery, AL 36130
205-242-5743
800-243-5463 (Alabama only)
http://webserver.dsmd.state.al.us/coa

Alaska

Commission on Aging
Division of Senior Services
Department of Administration
3601 C St., #380
Anchorage, AK 99503
907-563-5654
http://www.state.ak.us/local/akpages/ADMIN/dss/
   homess.html

Arizona

Aging and Adult Administration
Department of Economic Security
1789 W. Jefferson, 950A
Phoenix, AZ 85007
602-542-4446
http://www.azleg.state.az/us/ars/ars.htm

Arkansas

Division of Aging and Adult Services
Department of Human Services
P.O. Box 1437
Little Rock, AR 72203-1437
501-682-2441
800-482-8049 (Arkansas only)
http://www.state.ar/us/dhs/index2.html

California

Department of Aging
1600 K St.
Sacramento, CA 95814
916-322-3887
916-323-8913 (TDD)
800-231-4024 (California only)
http://www.aging.state.ca.us/

Go to "Investments and Retirement" in chapter 20

Colorado

Division of Aging and Adult Services
Colorado Department of Social Services
110 16th St., 2nd Floor
Denver, CO 80203-1714
303-620-4147
http://www.state.co.us/gov_dir/human_services_dir/
AAS/index.htm

Connecticut

Elderly Services Division
Department of Social Services
25 Sigourney St., 10th Floor
Hartford, CT 06106
203-424-5281
800-443-9946 (voice/TDD in CT)
http://www.dss.state.ct.us/svcs/elderly.htm

Delaware

Division of Aging
Department of Health and Social Services
1901 N. DuPont Highway
New Castle, DE 19720
302-577-4791
800-223-9074 (Delaware only)
http://www.state.de.us/govern/agencies/dhss/
irm/dsaapd/doahome.htm

District of Columbia

D.C. Office on Aging
One Judiciary Sq.
441 4th St., NW, Suite 900 South
Washington, DC 20001
202-724-5622
http://www.ci.washington.dc.us

Florida

Department of Elder Affairs
Bldg. B, Suite 152
4040 Esplanade Way
Tallahassee, FL 32399
904-414-2000
http://fcn.state.fl.us/doea/doea.htm

Georgia

Office of Aging
2 Peachtree St., NE, 18th Floor
Atlanta, GA 30303
404-657-5258
http://www.state.ga.us/Departments/DHR/aging.html

Hawaii

Executive Office on Aging
335 Merchant St., Room 241
Honolulu, HI 96813
808-586-0100
800-468-4644 (Hawaii only)
http://www.state.hi.us

Idaho

Idaho Office on Aging
Statehouse, Room 108
Boise, ID 83720
208-334-3833
http://www.state.id.us/icoa

Illinois

Department on Aging
421 E. Capitol Ave.
Springfield, IL 62701
217-785-2870
800-252-8966 (voice/TDD)
http://www.state.il.us/aging

Indiana

Aging/In-Home Care Services Division
Department of Human Services
P.O. Box 7083
Indianapolis, IN 46207-7083
317-232-7020
800-622-4972 (toll free in IN)
http://www.state.in.us

Iowa

Department of Elder Affairs
914 Grand Ave., Suite 236
Des Moines, IA 50319
515-281-5187
800-532-3213 (Iowa only)
http://www.state.ia.us

Kansas

Department on Aging
Docking State Office Bldg.
Room 122 South
915 Southwest Harrison St.
Topeka, KS 66612-1500
913-296-4986
800-432-3535 (Kansas only)
http://www.k4s.org/kdoa/default.htm

Kentucky

Division for Aging Services
Department for Social Services
275 E. Main St., 6th Floor West
Frankfort, KY 40621
502-564-6930
502-564-5497 (TDD)
800-372-2991 (Kentucky only)
800-372-2973 (TDD Kentucky only)
http://cfc-chs.chr.state.ky.us/cfachome.htm

Louisiana

Governors Office of Elder Affairs
P.O. Box 80374
Baton Rouge, LA 70898
504-925-1700
http://www.state.la.us

Maine

Bureau of Elder and Adult Services
35 Anthony Ave.
Statehouse, Station 11
Augusta, ME 04333-0011
207-626-5335
http://www.state.me.us/beas/dhs_beas.htm

Maryland

Office on Aging
301 W. Preston St., 10th Floor
Baltimore, MD 21201
410-225-1100
410-383-7555 (TDD)
800-243-3425 (Maryland only)
http://www.inform.umd.edu/UMS+STATE/
  MD_Resources/OOA/index.html

Massachusetts

Executive Office of Elder Affairs
1 Ashburton Pl., 5th Floor
Boston, MA 02111
617-727-7750
800-882-2003 (Massachusetts only)
800-872-0166 (TDD Massachusetts only)
800-922-2275 (TDD in Massachusetts—Elder Abuse
  Hotline)
http://www.state.ma.us/massgov.htm

Michigan

Office of Services to the Aging
P.O. Box 30026
Lansing, MI 48909
517-373-8230
http://www.state.mi.us/mdch/index.htm

Minnesota

Minnesota Board on Aging
444 Lafayette Rd.
St. Paul, MN 55155-3843
612-296-2544
800-652-9747 (Minnesota only)
http://www.dhs.state.mn.us/aging/default.htm

Mississippi

Council on Aging
Division of Aging and Adult Services
750 N. State St.
Jackson, MS 39203
601-359-4929
800-345-6347 (Mississippi only)
http://www.mdhs.state.ms.us/aas.html

Missouri

Division of Aging
P.O. Box 1337
Jefferson City, MO 65102
314-751-8535
800-392-0210 (Missouri only)
http://www.state.mo.us/dss/da/da.htm

Montana

Coordinator of Aging Services
Governor's Office
State Capitol
Helena, MT 59620
406-444-4204
800-332-2272 (Montana only)
http://www.dphhs.mt.gov/whowhat/sltc.htm

Nebraska

Nebraska Department on Aging
State Office Bldg.
P.O. Box 95044
Lincoln, NE 68509
402-471-2306
http://www.hhs.state.ne.us/ags/agsindex.htm

Nevada

Division for Aging Services
Department of Human Resources
340 N. 11th St.
Las Vegas, NV 89158
702-486-3545
http://www.state.nv.us

New Hampshire

Division of Elderly and Adult Services
State Office Park South
115 Pleasant St., Annex Bldg. #1
Concord, NH 03301
603-271-4680
800-351-1888 (New Hampshire only)
http://www.state.nh.us/dhhs/ofs/ofscstlc.htm

New Jersey

Division of Senior Affairs
Department of Health and Senior Services
101 S. Broad St., CN 807
Trenton, NJ 08625-0807
609-292-3766
800-792-8820 (New Jersey only)
http://www.state.nj.us/health/senior/sraffair.htm

New Mexico

State Agency on Aging
224 E. Palace Ave., 4th Floor
Santa Fe, NM 87501
505-827-7640 (voice/TDD)
800-432-2080 (New Mexico only)
http://www.state.nm.us

New York

New York State Office for the Aging
Agency Bldg. 2, ESP
Albany, NY 12223
518-474-5731
800-342-9871 (New York only)
http://aging.state.ny.us/nysofa

North Carolina

Division of Aging
Department of Human Resources
693 Palmer Dr.
Caller Box No. 2953
Raleigh, NC 27626-0531
919-733-3983
800-662-7030 (voice/TDD in North Carolina only)
http://www.state.nc.us

North Dakota

Aging Services
Department of Human Service
P.O. Box 7070, Northbrook Shopping Center
N. Washington St., 600 East Blvd.
Bismarck, ND 58507-7070
701-328-2577
800-472-2622
http://www.state.nd.us/hms/dhs.htm

Ohio

Ohio Department of Aging
50 W. Broad St., 9th Floor
Columbus, OH 43266-0501
614-466-5500
614-466-6191 (TDD)
800-282-1206 (Ohio only—nursing home information)
http://www.state.oh.us

Oklahoma

Special Unit on Aging
P.O. Box 25352
Oklahoma City, OK 73125
405-521-2281
405-521-2827 (TDD)
http://www.state.ok.us

Oregon

Senior and Disabled Services Division
Department of Human Resources
500 Summer St., NE, 2nd Floor
Salem, OR 97310-0105
503-945-5811
800-232-3020 (voice/TDD in Oregon)
http://www.sdsd.hr.state.or.us

Pennsylvania

Department of Aging
Rachel Carson State Office Bldg.
400 Market St., 7th Floor
Harrisburg, PA 17101
717-783-1549
http://www.state.pa.us/PA_Exec/Aging/overview.html

Rhode Island

Department of Elderly Affairs
160 Pine St.
Providence, RI 02903
401-277-2880 (voice/TDD)
800-322-2880 (Rhode Island only)
http://www.state.ri.us/stdept/sd23.htm

South Carolina

Division on Aging
Office of the Governor
202 Arbor Lake Dr., #301
Columbia, SC 29223
803-737-7500
800-868-9095
http://www.leginfo.state.sc.us/man97/stategov/
  state5.html

South Dakota

Office of Adult Services and Aging
700 Governors Dr.
Pierre, SD 57501
605-773-3656
http://www.state.sd.us

Tennessee

Commission on Aging
Andrew Jackson Bldg.
500 Deaderick Bldg., 9th Floor
Nashville, TN 37243-0860
615-741-2056
http://www.state.tn.us

Texas

Texas Department on Aging
P.O. Box 12786, Capitol Station
Austin, TX 78711
512-424-6840
http://www.state.tx.us/agency/340.html

Utah

Division of Aging and Adult Services
P.O. Box 45500
Salt Lake City, UT 84145-0500
801-538-3910
http://www.dhs.state.ut.us/welcome.htm

Vermont

Department of Aging and Disabilities
103 S. Main St.
Waterbury, VT 05671-2301
802-241-2400 (voice/TDD)
http://www.state.vt.us/dad/index.htm

Virginia

Department for the Aging
700 E. Franklin St., 10th Floor
Richmond, VA 23219
804-225-2271 (voice/TDD)
800-552-4464 (Virginia only)
800-552-3402 (Virginia only—Ombudsman Hotline)
http://www.aging.state.va.us

Washington

Aging and Adult Services Administration
P.O. Box 45050
Olympia, WA 98504-5050
360-586-3768
800-422-3263 (WA only)
http://www.state.wa.us

West Virginia

Commission on Aging
State Capitol
Charleston, WV 25305
304-348-3317
http://www.state.wv.us

Wisconsin

Bureau on Aging
217 S. Hamilton St., Suite 300
Madison, WI 53707
608-266-2536
http://www.dhfs.state.wi.us/aging/ageindex.htm

Wyoming

Division on Aging
139 Hathaway Bldg.
Cheyenne, WY 82002-0480
307-777-7986
800-442-2766 (Wyoming only)
http://wdhfs.state.wy.us/wdh/default.htm

American Samoa

Territorial Administration on Aging
Government of American Samoa
Pago Pago, AS 96799
011-684-633-1251
http://www.samoanet.com/asg

Guam

Office of Aging
Government of Guam
P.O. Box 2816
Agana, GU 96910
011-671-734-2942
http://168.123.2.104/pubhealth/index.html

Puerto Rico

Office of Elder Affairs
Ponce de Leon Ave., #1603
Corbain Plaza Stop 23
U.M. Office C
San Ture, PR 00908
809-721-5710
http://fortaleza.govpr.org

Virgin Islands

Virgin Islands: Senior Citizens Affairs
Department of Human Services
19 Estate Diamond Fredericksted
St. Croix, VI 00840
809-772-4950 ext. 46
http://www.gov.vi/human

ALCOHOLISM AND DRUG ABUSE

Al-Anon Family Group Headquarters
1600 Corporate Landing Parkway
Virginia Beach, VA 23454-5617
800-344-2666
http://www.al-anon.alateen.org

**Alcohol and Drug Problems Association
of North America**
1555 Wilson Blvd., Suite 300
Arlington, VA 22209
703-875-8684

**Alcohol, Drug Abuse and Mental Health
Administration**
U.S. Department of Health and Human Services
Parklawn Bldg.
5600 Fishers Lane
Rockville, MD 20857
303-443-3783
http://www.os.dhhs.gov

Alcoholics Anonymous World Services
475 Riverside Dr.
New York, NY 10163
212-870-3400
http://www.alcoholics-anonymous.org

American Council on Alcoholism
8501 La Salle Rd.
Towson, MD 21204
800-527-5344
http://www.aca-usa.org

American Council on Alcohol Problems
3426 Bridgeland Dr.
Bridgton, MO 65044
314-739-5944
http://www.netmin.org/acap

**Association of Halfway House Alcoholism Programs
of North America**
680 Stewart Ave.
St. Paul, MN 55102-4117
612-227-7818

BACCHUS and GAMMA
Peer Education Network
P.O. Box 10430
Denver, CO 80210
303-871-3068
http://www.bacchusgamma.org

"Safe Alcohol Consumption" in chapter 18

Go to

Do It Now Foundation
P.O. Box 27568
Tempe, AZ 85285
602-491-0393

Families Anonymous
P.O. Box 3475
Culver City, CA 90231
800 736 9805

Narcotics Anonymous
P.O. Box 9999
Van Nuys, CA 94109
818-780-3951
http://www.wsoinc.com

National Association for Children of Alcoholics
11426 Rockville Pike, Suite 100
Rockville, MD 20852
301-468-0985
888-554-COAS (888-554-2627)
http://www.health.org/nacoa

**National Association of Alcoholism and Drug Abuse
Counselors**
3717 Columbia Pike
Arlington, VA 22204
703-920-4644
http://www.naadac.org

National Association on Drug Abuse Problems
355 Lexington Ave.
New York, NY 10017
212-986-1170

National Cocaine Hotline
800-262-2476

**National Council on Alcoholism and Drug
Dependence**
12 W. 21st St.
New York, NY 10010
800-NCA-CALL (800-622-2255)
http://www.ncadd.org

National Families in Action
Drug Information Center
2296 Henderson Mill Rd.
Atlanta, GA 30345
770-934-6364
http://www.emory/nfia

National Federation of Parents for Drug-Free Youth
1423 N. Jefferson
Springfield, MO 65802
417-836-3709

National Parents Resource Institute for Drug Education
3610 Dekalb Technology Pkwy, Suite 105
Atlanta, GA 30340
800-279-6361
http://www.prideusa.org

Odyssey Institute Corporation
5 Headley Farms Rd.
Westport, CT 06880
203-255-4198

Women in Need, Inc.
115 W. 31st St.
New York, NY 10001
212-695-7330

CHILDREN

CHILD ABUSE

American Association for Protecting Children
c/o American Humane Association
63 Inverness Dr. East
Englewood, CO 80112
800-227-4645
http://www.amer.humane.org

Clearinghouse on Child Abuse and Neglect Information
Department of Health and Human Services
P.O. Box 1182
Washington, DC 20013
202-251-5157
http://www.calib.com/nccanch

National Committee to Prevent Child Abuse
332 S. Michigan Ave.
Chicago, IL 60604
312-663-3520
800-CHILDREN (800-244-5373)
http://www.childabuse.org

National Network of Youth Advisory Boards
P.O. Box 402036
Ocean View Bridge
Miami Beach, FL 33140
305-532-2607

Parents Anonymous
675 W. Foothill Blvd., Suite 220
Claremont, CA 91711
909-621-6184
http://www.parentsanonymous-natl.org

"Traveling Tips for the Disabled" in chapter 24

Go to

DISABLED CHILDREN

Association for Children with Retarded Mental Development
345 Hudson St.
New York, NY 10014
212-741-0100
http://www.acrmd.com

Clearinghouse on Handicapped and Gifted Children
Department of Education
1920 Association Dr.
Reston, VA 22091
800-328-0272
http://www.cec.sped.org/ericec.htm

National Center for Learning Disabilities
381 Park Ave. South, Suite 1420
New York, NY 10016
212-545-7510
888-575-7373
http://www.ncld.org

National Information Center for Children and Youth with Handicaps
P.O. Box 1492
Washington, DC 20013
202-884-8200
800-695-0285
http://www.nichcy.org

RUNAWAYS

American Youth Work Center
1200 17th St., NW
Washington, DC 20036
202-785-0764
800-599-2455
http://www.youthtoday

Contact Center
P.O. Box 81826
Lincoln, NE 68501
402-464-0602

National Runaway Switchboard
3080 N. Lincoln Ave.
Chicago, IL 60657
800-621-4000
http://www.nrscrisisline.org

National Network for Youth
1319 F St., NW, Suite 401
Washington, DC 20004
202-783-7949
http://www.nn4youth.org

CONSUMER INFORMATION AND PROTECTION

BETTER BUSINESS BUREAUS

Some locations are serviced by local bureaus in adjoining states. To locate the bureau nearest you, use the zip code search or state directory at http://www.bbb.org/bureaus/index.html.

UNITED STATES—NATIONAL HEADQUARTERS

Council of Better Business Bureaus
4200 Wilson Blvd., Suite 800
Arlington, VA 22203
703-276-0100
http://www.bbb.org

STATE, COUNTY, AND CITY GOVERNMENT CONSUMER PROTECTION OFFICES

Listed below are consumer protection offices that are part of state, county, and city governments. Some are located in governors' offices, state attorney generals' offices, or mayors' offices. Check in your state to see which office can help resolve complaints, furnish information or helpful publications, or provide other services. As a general rule, the first place to go for help with a consumer problem is the local office nearest your home. If you are having a problem with a business outside your state, however, contact the consumer office in the state in which you made the purchase. Because most offices require that complaints be in writing, you might save time by writing, rather than calling, with your initial complaint.

Alabama—State Office

Director
Consumer Protection Division
Office of the Attorney General
11 S. Union St.
Montgomery, AL 36130
205-242-7334
800-392-5658 (Alabama only)

Alaska

The Consumer Protection Section in the Office of the Attorney General has been closed. Consumers with complaints are being referred to the Better Business Bureaus in Anchorage and Fairbanks, small claims court, and private attorneys.

Arizona—State Offices

Chief Counsel
Consumer Protection Office of the Attorney General
1275 W. Washington St., Room 259
Phoenix, AZ 85007
602-542-3702
602-542-5763
800-352-8431 (Arizona only)

Assistant Attorney General
Consumer Protection Office of the Attorney General
402 W. Congress St., Suite 315
Tucson, AZ 85701
602-628-6504

Arizona—County Offices

County Attorney
Apache County Attorney's Office
P.O. Box 637
St. Johns, AZ 85936
602-337-4364, ext. 240

County Attorney
Cochise County Attorney's Office
P.O. Drawer CA
Bisbee, AZ 85603
602-432-9377

County Attorney
Coconino County Attorney's Office
Coconino County Courthouse
100 E. Birch
Flagstaff, AZ 86001
602-779-6518

County Attorney
Gila County Attorney's Office
1400 E. Ash St.
Globe, AZ 85501
602-425-3231

County Attorney
Graham County Attorney's Office
Graham County Courthouse
800 W. Main
Safford, AZ 85546
602-428-3620

County Attorney
Greenlee County Attorney's Office
P.O. Box 1387
Clifton, AZ 85533
602-865-3842

County Attorney
La Paz County Attorney's Office
1200 Arizona Ave.
P.O. Box 709
Parker, AZ 85344
602-669-6118

County Attorney
Mohave County Attorney's Office
315 N. 4th St.
Kingman, AZ 86401
602-753-0719

County Attorney
Navajo County Attorney's Office
Governmental Complex
Holbrook, AZ 86025
602-524-6161

County Attorney
Pima County Attorney's Office
1400 Great American Tower
32 N. Stone
Tucson, AZ 85701
602-740-5733

County Attorney
Pinal County Attorney's Office
P.O. Box 887
Florence, AZ 85232
602-868-5801

County Attorney
Santa Cruz County Attorney's Office
2100 N. Congress Dr., Suite 201
Nogales, AZ 85621
602-281-4966

County Attorney
Yavapai County Attorney's Office
Yavapai County Courthouse
Prescott, AZ 86301
602-771-3344

County Attorney
Yuma County Attorney's Office
168 S. Second Ave.
Yuma, AZ 85364
602-329-2270

Arizona—City Office

Supervising Attorney
Consumer Affairs Division
Tucson City Attorney's Office
110 E. Pennington St., 2nd Floor
P.O. Box 27210
Tucson, AZ 85726-7210
602-791-4886

Arkansas—State Office

Director
Consumer Protection Division
Office of Attorney General
200 Tower Bldg.
323 Center St.
Little Rock, AR 72201
501-682-2341 (voice/TDD)
800-482-8982 (voice/TDD in Arkansas)

California—State Offices

Director
California Department of Consumer Affairs
400 R St., Suite 1040
Sacramento, CA 95814
916-445-1254 (consumer information)
916-522-1700 (TDD)

Office of the Attorney General
Public Inquiry Unit
P.O. Box 944255
Sacramento, CA 94244-2550
916-322-3360

Bureau of Automotive Repair
California Department of Consumer Affairs
10240 Systems Parkway
Sacramento, CA 95827
916-366-5100

California—County Offices

Coordinator
Alameda County Consumer Affairs Commission
4400 MacArthur Blvd.
Oakland, CA 94619
415-530-8682

District Attorney
Contra Costa County District Attorney's Office
725 Court St., 4th Floor
P.O. Box 670
Martinez, CA 94553
415-646-4500

Senior Deputy District Attorney
Business Affairs
Fresno County District Attorney's Office
2220 Tulare St., Suite 1000
Fresno, CA 93721
209-488-3156

District Attorney
Consumer and Major Business Fraud Section
Kern County District Attorney's Office
1215 Truxtun Ave.
Bakersfield, CA 93301
805-861-2421

Director
Los Angeles County Department of Consumer
  Affairs
500 W. Temple St., Room B-96
Los Angeles, CA 90012
213-974-1452

Director
Citizens Service Office
Marin County Mediation Services
Marin County Civic Center, Room 412
San Rafael, CA 94903
415-499-6190

Deputy District Attorney
Consumer Protection Division
Marin County District Attorney's Office
Hall of Justice, Room 183
San Rafael, CA 94903
415-499-6450

District Attorney
Mendocino County District
Attorney's Office
P.O. Box 1000
Uklah, CA 95482
707-463-4211

Coordinator
Monterey County Office of Consumer Affairs
P.O. Box 1369
Salinas, CA 93902
408-755-5073

Deputy District Attorney
Consumer Affairs Division
Napa County District Attorney's Office
931 Parkway Mall
P.O. Box 720
Napa, CA 94559
707-253-4059

Deputy District Attorney in Charge
Major Fraud Unit
Orange County District Attorney's Office
801 Civic Center Dr. West, Suite 120
Santa Ana, CA 92701
714-541-7600

If you want to send a letter to the North Pole, the correct address is North Pole, AK 99705.

Deputy District Attorney in Charge
Consumer and Environmental Protection Unit
Orange County District Attorney's Office
801 Civic Center Dr. West, Suite 120
Santa Ana, CA 92702-0808
714-541-7600

Deputy District Attorney
Economic Crime Division
Riverside County District Attorney's Office
4075 Main St.
Riverside, CA 92501
714-275-5400

Supervising Deputy District Attorney
Consumer and Environmental Protection Division
Sacramento County District Attorney's Office
P.O. Box 749
Sacramento, CA 95812-0749
916-440-6174

Director
Consumer Fraud Division
San Diego County District Attorney's Office
P.O. Box X-1011
San Diego, CA 92112
619-531-3507 (fraud complaint line)

Attorney
Consumer and Environmental Protection Unit
San Francisco County District Attorney's Office
732 Brannan St.
San Francisco, CA 94103
415-552-6400 (public inquiries)
415-553-1814 (complaints)

Deputy District Attorney
Consumer and Business Affairs Division
San Joaquin County District Attorney's Office
222 E. Weber, Room 202
P.O. Box 990
Stockton, CA 95202
209-468-2419

Director, Economic Crime Unit
Consumer Fraud Department
San Luis Obispo County District Attorney's Office
County Government Center
1050 Monterey St., Room 235
San Luis Obispo, CA 93408
805-549-5800

Deputy in Charge
Consumer Fraud and Environmental Protection Unit
San Mateo County District Attorney's Office
401 Marshall St.
Hall of Justice and Records
Redwood City, CA 94063
415-363-4656

Deputy District Attorney
Consumer Protection Unit
Santa Barbara County District Attorney's Office
1105 Santa Barbara St.
Santa Barbara, CA 93101
805-568-2300

Deputy District Attorney
Consumer Fraud Unit
Santa Clara County District Attorney's Office
70 W. Hedding St., West Wing
San Jose, CA 95110
408-299-7400

Director
Santa Clara County Department of Consumer Affairs
2175 The Alameda
San Jose, CA 95126
408-299-4211

Coordinator
Division of Consumer Affairs
Santa Cruz County District Attorney's Office
701 Ocean St., Room 200
Santa Cruz, CA 95060
408-425-2054

Deputy District Attorney
Consumer Affairs Unit
Solano County District Attorney's Office
600 Union Ave.
Fairfield, CA 94533
707-421-6860

Deputy District Attorney
Consumer Fraud Unit
Stanislaus County District Attorney's Office
P.O. Box 442
Modesto, CA 95353
209-571-5550

Deputy District Attorney
Consumer and Environmental Protection Division
Ventura County District Attorney's Office
800 S. Victoria Ave.
Ventura, CA 93009
805-654-3110

Supervising Deputy District Attorney
Special Services Unit—Consumer/Environmental
Yolo County District Attorney's Office
P.O. Box 245
Woodland, CA 95695
916-666-8424

California—City Offices

Supervising Deputy City Attorney
Consumer Protection Division
Los Angeles City Attorney's Office
200 N. Main St.
1600 City Hall East
Los Angeles, CA 90012
213-485-4515

Consumer Affairs Specialist
Consumer Division
Santa Monica City Attorney's Office
1685 Main St., Room 310
Santa Monica, CA 90401
213-458-8336

Colorado—State Offices

Consumer Protection Unit
Office of the Attorney General
1625 Broadway
Denver, CO 80202
303-620-4500

Consumer and Food Specialist
Department of Agriculture
700 Kipling St., Suite 4000
Lakewood, CO 80215-5894
303-239-4114

Colorado—County Offices

District Attorney
Archuleta, LaPlata, and San Juan Counties District Attorney's Office
P.O. Drawer 3455
Durango, CO 81302
303-247-8850

District Attorney
Boulder County District Attorney's Office
P.O. Box 471
Boulder, CO 80306
303-441-3700

Executive Director
Denver County District Attorney's Consumer Fraud
  Office
303 W. Colfax Ave., Suite 1300
Denver, CO 80204
303-640-3555 (inquiries)
303-640-3557 (complaints)

Chief Deputy District Attorney
Economic Crime Division
El Paso and Teller Counties District Attorney's
  Office
326 S. Tejon
Colorado Springs, CO 80903-2083
719-520-6002

District Attorney
Pueblo County District Attorney's Office
Courthouse
215 W. 10th St.
Pueblo, CO 81003
719-546-6030

Consumer Fraud Investigator
Weld County District Attorney's Consumer Office
P.O. Box 1167
Greeley, CO 80632
303-356-4000 ext. 4735

Connecticut—State Offices

Commissioner
Department of Consumer Protection
State Office Bldg.
165 Capitol Ave.
Hartford, CT 06106
203-566-4999
800-538-2277 (Connecticut only)

Assistant Attorney General
Antitrust/Consumer Protection
Office of Attorney General
110 Sherman St.
Hartford, CT 06105
203-566-5374
800-538-2277 (Connecticut only)

Connecticut—City Office

Director
Middletown Office of Consumer Protection
City Hall
Middletown, CT 06457
203-344-3492

Delaware—State Offices

Director
Division of Consumer Affairs
Department of Community Affairs
820 N. French St., 4th Floor
Wilmington, DE 19801
302-571-4080
800-443-2179

Deputy Attorney General for Economic Crime
  and Consumer Protection
Office of Attorney General
820 N. French St.
Wilmington, DE 19801
800-736-4000

District of Columbia

Director
Department of Consumer and Regulatory Affairs
614 H St., NW
Washington, DC 20001
202-727-7000

Florida—State Offices

Assistant Director
Department of Agriculture and Consumer Services
Division of Consumer Services
218 Mayo Bldg.
Tallahassee, FL 32399
904-488-2226
800-342-2176 (TDD, Florida only)
800-327-3382 (information and education,
  Florida only)

Chief
Consumer Litigation Section
The Capitol
Tallahassee, FL 32399-1050
904-488-9105

Chief
Consumer Division
Office of the Attorney General
4000 Hollywood Blvd., Suite 505 South
Hollywood, FL 33021
305-985-4780

Florida—County Offices

Director
Broward County Consumer Affairs Division
115 S. Andrews Ave., Room 119
Fort Lauderdale, FL 33301
305-357-6030

Consumer Advocate
Metropolitan Dade County Consumer Protection Division
140 W. Flagler St., Suite 902
Miami, FL 33130
305-375-4222

Chief
Dade County Economic Crime Unit
Office of the State Attorney
1469 Northwest 13th Terrace, Room 600
Miami, FL 33125
305-324-3030

Manager
Hillsborough County Department of Consumer Affairs
412 E. Madison St., Room 1001
Tampa, FL 33602
813-272-6750

Chief
Orange County Consumer Fraud Unit
250 N. Orange Ave.
P.O. Box 1673
Orlando, FL 32802
407-836-2490

Citizens Intake
Palm Beach County Office of State Attorney
P.O. Drawer 2905
West Palm Beach, FL 33402
407-355-3560

Director
Palm Beach County Department of Consumer Affairs
3111 S. Dixie Highway, Suite 128
West Palm Beach, FL 33405
407-355-2670

Administrator
Pasco County Consumer Affairs Division
7530 Little Rd.
New Port Richey, FL 34654
813-847-8110

Director
Pinellas County Office of Consumer Affairs
P.O. Box 17268
Clearwater, FL 34622-0268
813-530-6200

Coordinator
Seminole Economic Crime Unit
Office of State Attorney
100 E. First St.
Sanford, FL 32771
407-322-7534

State Attorney
Consumer Fraud Unit
700 S. Park Ave.
Titusville, FL 32780
407-264-5230

Florida—City Offices

Chief of Consumer Affairs
City of Jacksonville Division of Consumer Affairs
421 W. Church St., Suite 404
Jacksonville, FL 32202
904-630-3667

Chairman
Lauderhill Consumer Protection Board
1176 NW 42nd Way
Lauderhill, FL 33313
305-321-2450

Chairman
Tamarac Board of Consumer Affairs
7525 NW 88th Ave.
Tamarac, FL 33321
305-722-5900 (ext. 389 10 A.M.–noon, Tues., Wed., Thurs.)

Georgia—State Office

Administrator
Governors Office of Consumer Affairs
2 Martin Luther King, Jr. Dr., SE
Plaza Level—East Tower
Atlanta, GA 30334
404-651-8600
404-656-3790
800-869-1123 (Georgia only)

Hawaii—State Offices

Director
Office of Consumer Protection
Department of Commerce and Consumer Affairs
828 Fort St. Mall, Suite 600B
P.O. Box 3767
Honolulu, HI 96812-3767
808-586-2630

Investigator
Office of Consumer Protection
Department of Commerce and Consumer Affairs
75 Aupuni St.
Hilo, HI 96720
808-933-4433

Investigator
Office of Consumer Protection
Department of Commerce and Consumer Affairs
3060 Eiwa St.
Lihue, HI 96766
808-241-3365

Investigator
Office of Consumer Protection
Department of Commerce and Consumer Affairs
54 High St.
P.O. Box 3767
Honolulu, HI 96812
808-586-2630

Idaho—State Office

Deputy Attorney General
Office of the Attorney General
Consumer Protection Unit
Statehouse, Room 113A
Boise, ID 83720-1000
208-334-2424
800-432-3545 (Idaho only)

Illinois—State Offices

Director
Governors Office of Citizens Assistance
222 S. College
Springfield, IL 62706
217-782-0244
800-252-8666 (Illinois only)

Chief
Consumer Protection Division
Office of the Attorney General
100 W. Randolph, 12th Floor
Chicago, IL 60601
312-814-3580
312-793-2852 (TDD)

Assistant Attorney General and Chief
Consumer Protection Division
Office of the Attorney General
500 S. Second St.
Springfield, IL 62706
217-782-9011
800-252-8666 (Illinois only)

Director
Department of Citizen Rights
100 W. Randolph, 13th Floor
Chicago, IL 60601
312-814-3289
312-814-7123 (TDD)

Illinois—Regional Offices

Assistant Attorney General
Carbondale Regional Office
Office of the Attorney General
626A E. Walnut St.
Carbondale, IL 62901
618-457-3505
618-457-4421 (TDD)

Assistant Attorney General
Champaign Regional Office
Office of the Attorney General
34 E. Main St.
Champaign, IL 61820
217-333-7691 (voice/TDD)

Assistant Attorney General
East St. Louis Regional Office
Office of the Attorney General
8712 State St.
East St. Louis, IL 62203
618-398-1006
618-398-1009 (TDD)

Assistant Attorney General
Granite City Regional Office
Office of the Attorney General
1314 Niedringhaus
Granite City, IL 62040
618-877-0404

Assistant Attorney General
Kankakee Regional Office
Office of the Attorney General
1012 N. 5th Ave.
Kankakee, IL 60901
815-935-8500

Assistant Attorney General
LaSalle Regional Office
Office of the Attorney General
1222 Shooting Park Rd., Suite 106
Peru, IL 61354
815-224-4861
815-224-4864 (TDD)

Assistant Attorney General
Mount Vernon Regional Office
Office of the Attorney General
3405 Broadway
Mt. Vernon, IL 62864
618-242-8200 (voice/TDD)

Assistant Attorney General
Peoria Regional Office
Office of the Attorney General
323 Main St.
Peoria, IL 61602
309-671-3191
309-671-3089 (TDD)

You can have a birthday greeting sent from the President of the United States to anyone 80-years-old or older. Send your request a few months in advance to your local congressman or senator.

Assistant Attorney General
Quincy Regional Office
Office of the Attorney General
523 Main St.
Quincy, IL 62301
217-223-2221 (voice/TDD)

Assistant Attorney General
Rockford Regional Office
Office of the Attorney General
119 N. Church St.
Rockford, IL 61101
815-987-7580
815-987-7579 (TDD)

Assistant Attorney General
Rock Island Regional Office
Office of the Attorney General
1614 Second Ave.
Rock Island, IL 61201
309-793-0950
309-793-0956 (TDD)

Assistant Attorney General
Waukegan Regional Office
Office of the Attorney General
12 S. County St.
Waukegan, IL 60085
708-336-2207
708-336-2374 (TDD)

Assistant Attorney General
West Frankfort Regional Office
Office of the Attorney General
222 E. Main St.
West Frankfort, IL 62896
618-937-6453

Assistant Attorney General
West Chicago Regional Office
Office of the Attorney General
122A County Farm Rd.
Wheaton, IL 60187
708-653-5060 (voice/TDD)

Illinois—County Offices

Consumer Fraud Division
Cook County Office of the State's Attorney
303 Daley Center
Chicago, IL 60602
312-443-4600

State's Attorney
Madison County Office of the State's Attorney
325 E. Vandalia
Edwardsville, IL 62025
618-692-6280

Director
Consumer Protection Division
Rock Island County Office of the State's Attorney
County Courthouse
Rock Island, IL 61201
309-786-4451, ext. 229

Illinois—City Offices

Consumer Fraud
Wheeling Township
1616 N. Arlington Heights Rd.
Arlington Heights, IL 60004
708-259-7730 (Wed. only)

Commissioner
Chicago Department of Consumer Services
121 N. LaSalle St., Room 808
Chicago, IL 60602
312-744-4090
312-744-9385 (TDD)

Administrator
Des Plaines Consumer Protection Commission
1420 Miner St.
Des Plaines, IL 60016
708-391-5363

Indiana—State Office

Chief Counsel and Director
Consumer Protection Division
Office of the Attorney General
219 State House
Indianapolis, IN 46204
317-232-6330
800-382-5516 (Indiana only)

Indiana—County Offices

Director
Consumer Protection Division
Lake County Prosecutor's Office
2293 N. Main St.
Crown Point, IN 46307
219-755-3720

Marion County Prosecuting Attorney
560 City-County Bldg.
200 E. Washington St.
Indianapolis, IN 46204-3363
317-236-3522

Vanderburgh County Prosecuting Attorney
108 Administration Bldg.
Civic Center Complex
Evansville, IN 47708
812-426-5150

Indiana—City Office

Director
Gary Office of Consumer Affairs
Annex East
1100 Massachusetts St.
Gary, IN 46407
219-886-0145

Iowa—State Office

Assistant Attorney General
Consumer Protection Division
Office of the Attorney General
1300 E. Walnut St., 2nd Floor
Des Moines, IA 50319
515-281-5926

Kansas—State Office

Deputy Attorney General
Consumer Protection Division
Office of the Attorney General
301 W. 10th
Kansas Judicial Center
Topeka, KS 66612-1597
913-296-3751
800-432-2310 (Kansas only)

Kansas—County Offices

Head
Consumer Fraud Division
Johnson County District Attorney's Office
Johnson County Courthouse
P.O. Box 728
Olathe, KS 66061
913-782-5000

Chief Attorney
Consumer Fraud and Economic Crime Division
Sedgwick County District Attorney's Office
Sedgwick County Courthouse
Wichita, KS 67203
316-268-7921

Assistant District Attorney
Shawnee County District Attorney's Office
Shawnee County Courthouse, Room 212
Topeka, KS 66603-3922
913-291-4330

Kansas—City Office

Assistant City Attorney
Topeka Consumer Protection Division
City Attorney's Office
215 E. 7th St.
Topeka, KS 66603
913-295-3883

Kentucky—State Offices

Director
Consumer Protection Division
Office of the Attorney General
209 Saint Clair St.
Frankfort, KY 40601-1875
502-564-2200
800-432-9257 (Kentucky only)

Administrator
Consumer Protection Division
Office of the Attorney General
107 S. 4th St.
Louisville, KY 40202
502-588-3262
800-432-9257 (Kentucky only)

Louisiana—State Office

Chief
Consumer Protection Section
Office of the Attorney General
State Capitol Bldg.
P.O. Box 94005
Baton Rouge, LA 70804-9005
504-342-7373

Louisiana—County Office

Chief
Consumer Protection Division
Jefferson Parish District Attorney's Office
200 Huey P. Long Ave.
Gretna, LA 70053
504-364-3644

Maine—State Offices

Superintendent
Bureau of Consumer Credit Protection
State House Station No. 35
Augusta, ME 04333-0035
207-582-8718
800-332-8529

Chief
Consumer and Antitrust Division
Office of the Attorney General
State House Station No. 6
Augusta, ME 04333
207-289-3716 (9 A.M.–1 P.M.)

Number 10 Downing Street in London still has the 23 chairs used by Gladstone and Disraeli during Queen Victoria's reign. Only one of the chairs has arms.

Maryland—State Offices

Chief
Consumer Protection Division
Office of the Attorney General
200 St. Paul Pl.
Baltimore, MD 21202-2021
301-528-8662 (9 A.M.–3 P.M.)
301-576-6372 (TDD in Baltimore area)
301-565-0451 (TDD in DC metro area)
800-969-5766

Director
Licensing & Consumer Services
Motor Vehicle Administration
6601 Ritchie Highway, NE
Glen Burnie, MD 21062
301-768-7420

Consumer Affairs Specialist
Eastern Shore Branch Office
Consumer Protection Division
Office of the Attorney General
Salisbury District Court/Multiservice Center
201 Baptist St., Suite 30
Salisbury, MD 21801-4976
301-543-6620

Director
Western Maryland Branch Office
Consumer Protection Division
Office of the Attorney General
138 E. Antietam St., Suite 210
Hagerstown, MD 21740-5684
301-791-4780

Maryland—County Offices

Administrator
Howard County Office of Consumer Affairs
9250 Rumsey Rd.
Columbia, MD 21045
301-313-7220
301-313-7201/2323 (TDD)

Executive Director
Montgomery County Office of Consumer Affairs
100 Maryland Ave., 3rd Floor
Rockville, MD 20850
301-217-7373

Executive Director
Prince George's County Consumer Protection Commission
9201 Basil Ct.
Landover, MD 20785
301-925-5100
301-925-5167 (TDD)

Massachusetts—State Offices

Chief
Consumer Protection Division
Department of the Attorney General
200 Portland St.
Boston, MA 02114
617-727-8400 (information and referral)

Secretary
Executive Office of Consumer Affairs and Business Regulation
One Ashburton Pl., Room 1411
Boston, MA 02108
617-727-7780 (information and referral)

Managing Attorney
Western Massachusetts Consumer Protection Division
Department of the Attorney General
436 Dwight St.
Springfield, MA 01103
413-784-1240

Massachusetts—County Offices

Complaint Supervisor
Consumer Fraud Prevention
Franklin County District Attorney's Office
238 Main St.
Greenfield, MA 01301
413-774-5102

Director
Consumer Fraud Prevention
Hampshire County District Attorney's Office
1 Court Square
Northhampton, MA 01060
413-586-9225

Project Coordinator
Worcester County Consumer Rights Project
340 Main St., Room 370
Worcester, MA 01608
508-754-7420 (9:30 A.M.–4 P.M.)

City Offices
Commissioner
Mayor's Office of Consumer Affairs and Licensing
Boston City Hall, Room 613
Boston, MA 02201
617-725-3320

Director
Consumer Information Center
Springfield Action Commission
P.O. Box 1449 Main Office
Springfield, MA 01101
413-737-4376 (Hampton and Hampshire counties)

Michigan—State Offices

Assistant in Charge
Consumer Protection Division
Office of the Attorney General
P.O. Box 30213
Lansing, MI 48909
517-373-1140

Executive Director
Michigan Consumers Council
414 Hollister Bldg.
106 W. Allegan St.
Lansing, MI 48933
517-373-0947
517-373-0701 (TDD)

Director
Bureau of Automotive Regulation
Michigan Department of State
P.O. Box 30046
Lansing, MI 48918-1200
517-373-7858
800-292-4204 (Michigan only)

Michigan—County Offices

Prosecuting Attorney
Bay County Consumer Protection Unit
Bay County Bldg.
Bay City, MI 48708-5994
517-893-3594

Director
Consumer Protection Department
Macomb County Office of the Prosecuting Attorney
Macomb Court Bldg., 6th Floor
Mt. Clemens, MI 48043
313-469-5350

Director
Washtenaw County Consumer Services
4133 Washtenaw St.
P.O. Box 8645
Ann Arbor, MI 48107-8645
313-971-6054

Michigan—City Office

Director
City of Detroit
Department of Consumer Affairs
1600 Cadillac Tower
Detroit, MI 48226
313-224-3508

Minnesota—State Offices

Director
Office of Consumer Services
Office of the Attorney General
117 University Ave.
St. Paul, MN 55155
612-296-2331

Consumer Services Division
Office of the Attorney General
320 W. 2nd St.
Duluth, MN 55802
218-723-4891

Minnesota—County Office

Citizen Protection Unit
Hennepin County Attorney's Office
C2000 County Government Center
Minneapolis, MN 55487
612-348-4528

Minnesota—City Office

Director
Consumer Affairs Division
Minneapolis Department of Licenses & Consumer Services
One City Hall
Minneapolis, MN 55415
612-348-2080

Mississippi—State Offices

Special Assistant Attorney General and Chief
Consumer Protection Division
Office of the Attorney General
P.O. Box 22947
Jackson, MS 39225-2947
601-354-6018

Director
Regulatory Services
Department of Agriculture and Commerce
500 Greymont Ave.
P.O. Box 1609
Jackson, MS 39215
601-354-7063

Consumer Counselor
Gulf Coast Regional Office of the Attorney General
P.O. Box 1411
Biloxi, MS 39533
601-436-6000

Missouri—State Offices

Office of the Attorney General
Consumer Complaints or Problems
P.O. Box 899
Jefferson City, MO 65102
314-751-3321
800-392-8222 (Missouri only)

Chief Counsel
Trade Offense Division
Office of the Attorney General
P.O. Box 899
Jefferson City, MO 65102
314-751-3321
800-392-8222 (Missouri only)

Montana—State Office

Consumer Affairs Unit
Department of Commerce
P.O. Box 20051
Helena, MT 59620
406-444-4312
800-332-2272

Nebraska—State Office

Assistant Attorney General
Consumer Protection Division
Department of Justice
2115 State Capitol
P.O. Box 98920
Lincoln, NE 68509
402-471-2682

Nebraska—County Office

Douglas County Attorney
County Attorney's Office
428 Hall of Justice
17th and Farnam
Omaha, NE 68183
402-444-7040

Nevada—State Offices

Commissioner of Consumer Affairs
Department of Commerce
State Mail Room Complex
Las Vegas, NV 89158
702-486-7355
800-992-0900 (Nevada only)

Consumer Services Officer
Consumer Affairs Division
Department of Commerce
4600 Kietzke Lane, M-245
Reno, NV 89502
702-688-1800
800-992-0900 (Nevada only)

Nevada—County Office

Investigator
Consumer Fraud Division
Washoe County District Attorney's Office
P.O. Box 11130
Reno, NV 89520
702-328-3456

New Hampshire—State Office

Chief Consumer Protection and Antitrust Bureau
Office of the Attorney General
33 Capital St.
State House Annex
Concord, NH 03301
603-271-3641

New Jersey—State Offices

Director
Division of Consumer Affairs
Department of Law and Public Safety
P.O. Box 45027
Newark, NJ 07101
932-648-4010
800-242-5846

Commissioner
Department of the Public Advocate
CN 850, Justice Complex
Trenton, NJ 08625
609-292-7087
800-792-8600 (New Jersey only)

Deputy Attorney General
New Jersey Division of Law
1207 Raymond Blvd.
P.O. Box 45029
Newark, NJ 07101
973-648-7579
800-242-5846

New Jersey—County Offices

Director
Atlantic County Consumer Affairs
1333 Atlantic Ave., 8th Floor
Atlantic City, NJ 08401
609-345-6700

Director
Bergen County Office of Consumer Protection
21 Main St., Room 101-E
Hackensack, NJ 07601-7000
201-646-2650

Director
Burlington County Office of Consumer Affairs
49 Rancocas Rd.
Mount Holly, NJ 08060
609-265-5054

Director
Camden County Office of Consumer Affairs
1800 Pavilion West
2101 Ferry Ave., Suite 609
Camden, NJ 08104
609-757-8397

Director
Cape May County Department of Consumer Affairs
DN-310, Central Mail Room
Cape May Court House
Cape May, NJ 08210
609-463-6475

Director
Cumberland County Department of Consumer Affairs and Weights and Measures
788 E. Commerce St.
Bridgeton, NJ 08302
609-453-2202

Director
Essex County Division of Consumer Services
15 S. Munn Ave., 2nd Floor
East Orange, NJ 07018
973-678-8071/8928

Director
Gloucester County Department of Consumer Protection/Weights and Measures
152 N. Broad St.
Woodbury, NJ 08096
609-853-3349
609-848-6616 (TDD)

Director
Hudson County Division of Consumer Affairs
595 Newark Ave.
Jersey City, NJ 07306
201-795-6295

Director
Hunterdon County Division of Consumer Affairs
P.O. Box 283
Lebanon, NJ 08833
908-236-2249

Director
Mercer County Division of Consumer Affairs
640 S. Broad St., Room 229
Trenton, NJ 08650-0068
609-989-6671

Director
Middlesex County Division of Consumer Affairs
149 Kearny Ave.
Perth Amboy, NJ 08861
732-324-4600

Director
Monmouth County Division of Consumer Affairs
1 E. Main St.
P.O. Box 1255
Freehold, NJ 07728-1255
732-431-7900

Director
Morris County Division of Consumer Affairs
P.O. Box 900
Morristown, NJ 07963-0900
973-285-6070
973-584-9189 (TDD)

Director
Ocean County Division of Consumer Affairs
P.O. Box 2191
County Administration Bldg., Room 130-1
Toms River, NJ 08754-2191
732-929-2105

Director
Passaic County Division of Consumer Affairs
County Administration Bldg.
309 Pennsylvania Ave.
Paterson, NJ 07503
973-881-4547

Director
Somerset County Division of Consumer Affairs
County Administration Bldg.
P.O. Box 3000
Somerville, NJ 08876
908-231-7000, ext. 7400

Office Manager
Union County Division of Consumer Affairs
300 North Avenue East
P.O. Box 186
Westfield, NJ 07091
908-654-9840

Director
Warren County Division of Consumer Affairs
Dumont Administration Bldg.
Route 519
Belvedere, NJ 07823
908-475-6500

New Jersey—City Offices

Director
Brick Division of Consumer Affairs
Municipal Bldg.
401 Chambers Bridge Rd.
Brick, NJ 08723
732-477-3000, ext. 296

Director
Cinnaminson Division of Consumer Affairs
Municipal Bldg.
1621 Riverton Rd.
Cinnaminson, NJ 08077
609-829-6000

Director
Clark Division of Consumer Affairs
430 Westfield Ave.
Clark, NJ 07066
732-388-3600

Director
Elizabeth Division of Consumer Affairs
City Hall
60 W. Scott Plaza
Elizabeth, NJ 07203
908-820-4183

Director
Fort Lee Consumer Protection Board
Bourough Hall
309 Main St.
Fort Lee, NJ 07024
201-592-3579

Director
Glen Rock Division of Consumer Affairs
Municipal Bldg., Harding Plaza
Glen Rock, NJ 07452-2100
201-670-3956

Consumer Advocate
City Hall
94 Washington St.
Hoboken, NJ 07030
201-420-2038

Director
Livingston Division of Consumer Affairs
357 S. Livingston Ave.
Livingston, NJ 07039
973-535-7976

Director
Middlesex Borough Division of Consumer Affairs
1200 Mountain Ave.
Middlesex, NJ 08846
732-356-8090

Director
Mountainside Division of Consumer Affairs
1455 Coles Ave.
Mountainside, NJ 07092
908-232-6600

Director
North Bergen Consumer Affairs
Municipal Bldg.
4233 Kennedy Blvd.
North Bergen, NJ 07047
201-330-7292

Director
Nutley Division of Consumer Affairs
City Hall
228 Chestnut St.
Nutley, NJ 07110
973-284-4936

Director
Parsippany Division of Consumer Affairs
Municipal Bldg., Room 101
1001 Parsippany Blvd.
Parsippany, NJ 07054
973-263-7011

Director
Perth Amboy Division of Consumer Affairs
City Hall
260 High St.
Perth Amboy, NJ 08861
732-826-0290, ext. 61, 62

Director
Plainfield Action Services
510 Watchung Ave.
Plainfield, NJ 07060
908-753-3519

Director
Secaucus Department of Consumer Affairs
Municipal Government Center
Secaucus, NJ 07094
201-330-2019

Director
Union Township Division of Consumer Affairs
Municipal Bldg.
1976 Morris Ave.
Union, NJ 07083
908-688-6763

Director
Wayne Township Division of Consumer Affairs
475 Valley Rd.
Wayne, NJ 07470
973-694-1800, ext. 290

Director
Weehawken Division of Consumer Affairs
400 Park Ave.
Weehawken, NJ 07087
201-319-6005

Director
West New York Division of Consumer Affairs
428 60th St.
West New York, NJ 07093
201-861-2522

New Mexico—State Office

Consumer Protection Division
Office of the Attorney General
P.O. Drawer 1508
Santa Fe, NM 87504
505-827-6000
800-432-2070 (New Mexico only)

New York—State Offices

Chairperson and Executive Director
New York State Consumer Protection Board
99 Washington Ave.
Albany, NY 12210-2891
518-474-8583

Assistant Attorney General
Bureau of Consumer Frauds and Protection
Office of the Attorney General
State Capitol
Albany, NY 12224
518-474-5481

Chairperson and Executive Director
New York State Consumer Protection Board
250 Broadway, 17th Floor
New York, NY 10007-2593
212-417-4908 (complaints)
212-417-4482 (main office)

Assistant Attorney General
Bureau of Consumer Frauds and Protection
Office of the Attorney General
120 Broadway
New York, NY 10271
212-341-2345

New York—Regional Offices

Assistant Attorney General in Charge
Binghamton Regional Office
Office of the Attorney General
59–61 Court St., 7th Floor
Binghamton, NY 13901
607-773-7877

Assistant Attorney General in Charge
Buffalo Regional Office
Office of the Attorney General
65 Court St.
Buffalo, NY 14202
716-847-7184

Assistant Attorney General in Charge
Plattsburgh Regional Office
Office of the Attorney General
70 Clinton St.
Plattsburgh, NY 12901
518-563-8012

Assistant Attorney General in Charge
Poughkeepsie Regional Office
Office of the Attorney General
235 Main St.
Poughkeepsie, NY 12601
914-485-3920

Assistant Attorney General in Charge
Rochester Regional Office
Office of the Attorney General
144 Exchange Blvd.
Rochester, NY 14614
716-546-7430

Assistant Attorney General in Charge
Suffolk Regional Office
Office of the Attorney General
300 Motor Parkway
Hauppauge, NY 11788
516-231-2400

Office Wagon Number 123 was the address for the Ringling Brothers and Barnum and Bailey Circus main office and ticket wagon.

Assistant Attorney General in Charge
Syracuse Regional Office
Office of the Attorney General
615 Erie Blvd. West
Syracuse, NY 13204-2465
315-448-4848

Assistant Attorney General in Charge
Utica Regional Office
Office of the Attorney General
207 Genesee St.
Utica, NY 13501
315-793-2225

New York—County Offices

Deputy Director of General Services
Broome County Bureau of Consumer Affairs
Governmental Plaza
P.O. Box 1766
Binghamton, NY 13902
607-778-2168

Director
Dutchess County Department of Consumer Affairs
38-A Dutchess Turnpike
Poughkeepsie, NY 12603
914-471-6322

Assistant District Attorney
Consumer Fraud Bureau
Erie County District Attorney's Office
25 Delaware Ave.
Buffalo, NY 14202
716-858-2424

Commissioner
Nassau County Office of Consumer Affairs
160 Old Country Rd.
Mineola, NY 11501
516-535-2600

Commissioner
Orange County Department of Consumer Affairs
and Weights and Measures
99 Main St.
Goshen, NY 10924
914-294-5151, ext. 1762

District Attorney
Orange County District Attorney's Office
County Government Center
255 Main St.
Goshen, NY 10924
914-294-5471

Director
Putnam County Department of Consumer Affairs
Myrtle Ave.
Mahopac Falls, NY 10542-0368
914-621-2317

Director/Coordinator
Rockland County Office of Consumer Protection
County Office Bldg.
18 New Hempstead Rd.
New City, NY 10956
914-638-5282

Director
Steuben County Department of Weights,
Measures, and Consumer Affairs
3 E. Pulteney Square
Bath, NY 14810
607-776-9631
607-776-9631, ext. 2101 (voice/TDD)

Commissioner
Suffolk County Department of Consumer Affairs
Suffolk County Center
Hauppauge, NY 11788
516-360-4600

Director
Ulster County Consumer Fraud Bureau
285 Wall St.
Kingston, NY 12401
914-339-5680, ext. 240

Chief
Frauds Bureau
Westchester County District Attorney's Office
111 Grove St.
White Plains, NY 10601
914-285-3303

Director
Westchester County Department of Consumer Affairs
Michaelian Office Bldg., Room 104
White Plains, NY 10601
914-285-2155

New York—City Offices

Director
Babylon Consumer Protection Board
Town Hall Office Annex
281 Phelps Lane
North Babylon, NY 11703
516-422-7636

Town of Colonie Consumer Protection Board
Memorial Town Hall
Newtonville, NY 12128
518-783-2790

Commissioner
Mt. Vernon Office of Consumer Affairs
City Hall
Mt. Vernon, NY 10550
914-665-2433

Commissioner
New York City Department of Consumer Affairs
42 Broadway
New York, NY 10004
212-487-4444

Director
Bronx Neighborhood Office
New York City Department of Consumer Affairs
1932 Arthur Ave., Room 104-A
Bronx, NY 10457
718-579-6766

Director
Brooklyn Neighborhood Office
New York City Department of Consumer Affairs
1360 Fulton St., Room 320
Brooklyn, NY 11216
718-636-7092

Director
Queens Neighborhood Office
New York City Department of Consumer Affairs
120-55 Queens Blvd., Room 301A
Kew Gardens, NY 11424
718-261-2922

Director
Staten Island Neighborhood Office
New York City Department of Consumer Affairs
Staten Island Borough Hall, Room 422
Staten Island, NY 10301
718-390-5154

Director
City of Oswego Office of Consumer Affairs
City Hall
West Oneida St.
Oswego, NY 13126
315-342-8150

Chairperson
Ramapo Consumer Protection Board
Ramapo Town Hall
237 Route 59
Suffern, NY 10901-5399
914-357-5100

Schenectady Bureau of Consumer Protection
City Hall
Jay St., Room 22
Schenectady, NY 12305
518-382-5061

Director
White Plains Department of Weights and Measures
77 S. Lexington Ave.
White Plains, NY 10601-2512
914-422-6359

Director
Yonkers Office of Consumer Protection, Weights and Measures
201 Palisade Ave.
Yonkers, NY 10703
914-377-6807

North Carolina—State Office

Special Deputy Attorney General
Consumer Protection Section
Office of the Attorney General
Raney Bldg.
P.O. Box 629
Raleigh, NC 27602
919-733-7741

North Dakota—State Offices

Office of the Attorney General
State Capitol Bldg.
Bismarck, ND 58505
701-328-2210
800-472-2600 (North Dakota only)

North Dakota—County Office

Executive Director
Quad County Community Action Agency
27$^1/_2$ S. 3rd St.
Grand Forks, ND 58201
701-746-5431

Ohio—State Offices

Consumer Frauds and Crimes Section
Office of the Attorney General
30 E. Broad St.
State Office Tower, 25th Floor
Columbus, OH 43266-0410
614-466-4986 (complaints)
614-466-1393 (TDD)
800-282-0515 (Ohio only)

Office of Consumers' Counsel
77 S. High St., 15th Floor
Columbus, OH 43266-0550
614-466-9605 (voice/TDD)
800-282-9448 (Ohio only)

Ohio—County Offices

Director
Economic Crime Division
Franklin County Office of the Prosecuting Attorney
369 S. High St.
Columbus, OH 43215
614-462-3555

County Prosecutor
Consumer Protection Division
Lake County Office of the Prosecuting Attorney
Lake County Courthouse
Painesville, OH 44077
216-357-2683
800-899-5253 (Ohio only)

Assistant Prosecuting Attorney
Montgomery County Fraud Section
Dayton Montgomery County Courts Bldg.
301 W. 3rd St.
Dayton, OH 45402
513-225-5757

Prosecuting Attorney
Portage County Office of the Prosecuting Attorney
466 S. Chestnut St.
Ravenna, OH 44266-0671
216-296-4593

Prosecuting Attorney
Summit County Office of the Prosecuting Attorney
53 University Ave.
Akron, OH 44308-1680
216-379-2800

Ohio—City Offices

Chief
Cincinnati Office of Consumer Services
Division of Human Services
City Hall, Room 126
Cincinnati, OH 45202
513-352-3971

Director
Youngstown Office of Consumer Affairs and
    Weights and Measures
City Hall
26 S. Phelps St.
Youngstown, OH 44503-1318
216-742-8884

Oklahoma—State Offices

Assistant Attorney General
Office of the Attorney General
4545 N. Lincoln Blvd., Suite 260
Oklahoma City, OK 73105
405-521-4274

Administrator
Department of Consumer Credit
4545 Lincoln Blvd., Suite 104
Oklahoma City, OK 73105-3408
405-521-3653

Oregon—State Office

Attorney in Charge
Financial Fraud Section
Department of Justice
Justice Bldg.
Salem, OR 97310
503-378-4320

Pennsylvania—State Offices

Director
Bureau of Consumer Protection
Office of the Attorney General
Strawberry Square, 14th Floor
Harrisburg, PA 17120
717-787-9707
800-441-2555 (Pennsylvania only)

Consumer Advocate
Office of Consumer Advocate—Utilities
Office of the Attorney General
1425 Strawberry Square
Harrisburg, PA 17120
717-783-5048 (utilities only)

Director
Bureau of Consumer Services
Pennsylvania Public Utility Commission
203 North Office Bldg.
Harrisburg, PA 17120
717-787-4970
800-782-1110 (Pennsylvania only)

Pennsylvania—Branch Offices

Deputy Attorney General
Bureau of Consumer Protection
Office of the Attorney General
27 N. 7th St.
Allentown, PA 18101
215-821-6690

Deputy Attorney General
Bureau of Consumer Protection
Office of the Attorney General
919 State St., Room 203
Erie, PA 16501
814-871-4371

Attorney in Charge
Bureau of Consumer Protection
Office of the Attorney General
132 Kline Village
Harrisburg, PA 17104
717-787-7109
800-441-2555 (Pennsylvania only)

Deputy Attorney General
Bureau of Consumer Protection
Office of the Attorney General
IGA Bldg.
Route 219 North
P.O. Box 716
Ebensburg, PA 15931
814-949-7900

Deputy Attorney General
Bureau of Consumer Protection
Office of the Attorney General
21 S. 12th St., 2nd Floor
Philadelphia, PA 19107
215-560-2414
800-441-2555 (Pennsylvania only)

Deputy Attorney General
Bureau of Consumer Protection
Office of the Attorney General
Manor Complex, 5th Floor
564 Forbes Ave.
Pittsburgh, PA 15219
412-565-5394

Deputy Attorney General
Bureau of Consumer Protection
Office of the Attorney General
State Office Bldg.
Room 358
100 Lackawanna Ave.
Scranton, PA 18503
717-963-4913

Pennsylvania—County Offices

Director
Beaver County Alliance for Consumer Protection
699 5th St.
Beaver, PA 15009-1997
412-728-7267

Director/Chief Sealer
Bucks County Bureau of Consumer Protection,
  Weights and Measures
50 N. Main St.
Doylestown, PA 18901
215-348-7442

Director
Chester County Bureau of Consumer Protection,
  Weights and Measures
Courthouse, 5th Floor, North Wing
High and Market Sts.
West Chester, PA 19380
215-344-6150

Consumer Mediator
Cumberland County Bureau of Consumer Affairs
One Courthouse Square
Carlisle, PA 17013-3387
717-240-6180

Director
Delaware County Office of Consumer Affairs,
  Weights and Measures
Government Center Bldg.
Second and Olive Sts.
Media, PA 19063
215-891-4865

Director
Montgomery County Consumer Affairs Department
County Courthouse
Norristown, PA 19404
215-278-3565

City Office
Chief Economic Crime Unit
Philadelphia District Attorney's Office
1421 Arch St.
Philadelphia, PA 19102
215-686-8750

Rhode Island—State Offices

Director
Consumer Protection Division
Department of the Attorney General
72 Pine St.
Providence, RI 02903
401-277-2104
401-274-4400, ext. 354 (voice/TDD)
800-852-7776 (Rhode Island only)

Executive Director
Rhode Island Consumers' Council
365 Broadway
Providence, RI 02909
401-277-2764

South Carolina—State Offices

Administrator, Consumer Affairs
Consumer Protection Office
Office of the Attorney General
P.O. Box 5757
Columbia, SC 29250-5757
803-734-9452
803-734-9455 (TDD)
800-922-1594 (South Carolina only)

State Ombudsman
Office of Executive Policy and Program
1205 Pendleton St., Room 308
Columbia, SC 29201
803-734-0457
803-734-1147 (TDD)

South Dakota—State Office

Assistant Attorney General
Division of Consumer Affairs
Office of the Attorney General
State Capitol Bldg.
500 E. Capitol
Pierre, SD 57501-5070
605-773-4400

Tennessee—State Offices

Deputy Attorney General
Antitrust and Consumer Protection Division
Office of the Attorney General
450 James Robertson Parkway
Nashville, TN 37243-0485
615-741-2672

Director
Division of Consumer Affairs
Department of Commerce and Insurance
500 James Robertson Pkwy., 5th Floor
Nashville, TN 37243-0600
615-741-4737
800-342-8385 (Tennessee only)
800-422-CLUB (health club hotline, Tennessee only)

Texas—State Offices

Assistant Attorney General
Consumer Protection Division
Office of the Attorney General
714 Jackson St., Suite 700
Dallas, TX 75202-4506
214-742-8944

Assistant Attorney General
Consumer Protection Division
Office of the Attorney General
6090 Surety Dr., Room 260
El Paso, TX 79905
915-772-9476

25 Main St. in Cooperstown, New York is the site of the famous Baseball Hall of Fame.

Assistant Attorney General
Consumer Protection Division
Office of the Attorney General
1019 Congress St., Suite 1550
Houston, TX 77002-1702
713-223-5886

Assistant Attorney General
Consumer Protection Division
Office of the Attorney General
1208 14th St., Suite 900
Lubbock, TX 79401-3997
806-747-5238

Assistant Attorney General
Consumer Protection Division
Office of the Attorney General
3600 N. 23rd St., Suite 305
McAllen, TX 78501-1685
512-682-4547

Assistant Attorney General
Consumer Protection Division
Office of the Attorney General
115 E. Travis St., Suite 925
San Antonio, TX 78205-1607
512-225-4191

Office of Consumer Protection
State Board of Insurance
816 Congress Ave., Suite 1400
Austin, TX 78701-2430
512-322-4143

Texas—County Offices

Assistant District Attorney and Chief
Specialized Crime Division
Dallas County District Attorney's Office
133 N. Industrial Blvd., LB 19
Dallas, TX 75207-4313
214-653-3820

Assistant District Attorney and Chief
Consumer Fraud Division
Harris County District Attorney's Office
201 Fannin, Suite 200
Houston, TX 77002-1901
713-221-5836

Texas—City Office

Director
Department of Environmental and Health Services
City Hall
1500 Marilla, Room 7A-North
Dallas, TX 75201
214-670-5216

Utah—State Offices

Director
Division of Consumer Protection
Department of Commerce
160 E. 300 South
P.O. Box 45802
Salt Lake City, UT 84145-0802
801-530-6601

Assistant Attorney General for Consumer Affairs
Office of the Attorney General
115 State Capitol
Salt Lake City, UT 84114
801-538-1331

Vermont—State Offices

Assistant Attorney General and Chief
Public Protection Division
Office of the Attorney General
109 State St.
Montpelier, VT 05609-1001
802-828-3171

Supervisor
Consumer Assurance Section
Department of Agriculture, Food and Market
120 State St.
Montpelier, VT 05620-2901
802-828-2436

Virginia—State Offices

Antitrust and Consumer Litigation Section
Office of the Attorney General
900 E. Main St.
Richmond, VA 23219

Director
Office of Consumer Affairs
Department of Agriculture and Consumer Services
Washington Bldg., Suite 100
P.O. Box 1163
Richmond, VA 23219
804-786-2042
804-371-6344 (TDD)
800-552-9963 (Virginia only)

Investigator
Northern Virginia Branch
Office of Consumer Affairs
Department of Agriculture and Consumer Services
100 N. Washington St., Suite 412
Falls Church, VA 22046
703-532-1613

Virginia—County Offices

Section Chief
Arlington County Office of Citizen and Consumer
Affairs
#1 Courthouse Plaza, Suite 314
2100 Clarendon Blvd.
Arlington, VA 22201
703-358-3260

Director
Fairfax County Department of Consumer Affairs
3959 Pender Dr., Suite 200
Fairfax, VA 22030-6093
703-246-5949
703-591-3260 (TDD)

Administrator
Prince William County Office of Consumer Affairs
4370 Ridgewood Center Dr.
Prince William, VA 22192-9201
703-792-7370

Virginia—City Offices

Director
Alexandria Office of Citizens Assistance
City Hall
P.O. Box 178
Alexandria, VA 22313
703-838-4350
703-838-5056 (TDD)

Coordinator
Division of Consumer Affairs
City Hall
Norfolk, VA 23501
804-441-2821
804-441-2000 (TDD)

Assistant to the City Manager
Roanoke Consumer Protection Division
364 Municipal Bldg.
215 Church Ave., SW
Roanoke, VA 24011
703-981-2583

Director
Consumer Affairs Division
Office of the Commonwealth's Attorney
Judicial Center, Bldg. 10B
2305 Judicial Blvd.
Virginia Beach, VA 23456-9050
757-426-5836

Washington—State Offices

Director of Consumer Services
Consumer and Business Fair Practices Division
Office of the Attorney General
900 Fourth Ave., Suite 2000
Seattle, WA 98164
206-464-6431
800-551-4636 (Washington only)

Chief
Consumer and Business Fair Practices Division
Office of the Attorney General
W. 1116 Riverside Ave.
Spokane, WA 99201
509-456-3123

Contact Person
Consumer and Business Fair Practices Division
Office of the Attorney General
1019 Pacific Ave., 3rd Floor
Tacoma, WA 98402-4411
206-593-2904

Washington—City Offices

Director
Department of Weights and Measures
3200 Cedar St.
Everett, WA 98201
206-259-8810

Chief Deputy Prosecuting Attorney
Fraud Division
900 4th Ave., #1002
Seattle, WA 98164
206-296-9010

Director
Seattle Department of Licenses and Consumer Affairs
102 Municipal Bldg.
600 4th Ave.
Seattle, WA 98104-1893
206-684-8484

West Virginia—State Offices

Director
Consumer Protection Division
Office of the Attorney General
812 Quarrier St., 6th Floor
Charleston, WV 25301
304-348-8986
800-368-8808 (West Virginia only)

Director
Division of Weights and Measures
Department of Labor
1800 Washington St. East
Bldg. 3, Room 319
Charleston, WV 25305
304-348-7890

West Virginia—City Office

Director
Department of Consumer Protection
P.O. Box 2749
Charleston, WV 25330
304-348-8172

Wisconsin—State Offices

Administrator
Division of Trade and Consumer Protection
Department of Agriculture, Trade, and
  Consumer Protection
801 W. Badger Rd.
P.O. Box 8911
Madison, WI 53708
608-266-9836
800-422-7128 (Wisconsin only)

Regional Supervisor
Division of Trade and Consumer Protection
Department of Agriculture, Trade, and
  Consumer Protection
927 Loring St.
Altoona, WI 54720
715-839-3848
800-422-7128 (Wisconsin only)

Regional Supervisor
Division of Trade and Consumer Protection
Department of Agriculture, Trade, and
  Consumer Protection
200 N. Jefferson St., Suite 146A
Green Bay, WI 54301
414-448-5111
800-422-7128 (Wisconsin only)

Regional Supervisor
Consumer Protection Regional Office
Department of Agriculture, Trade, and
  Consumer Protection
3333 N. Mayfair Rd., Suite 114
Milwaukee, WI 53222-3288
414-257-8956

Assistant Attorney General
Office of Consumer Protection and Citizen
  Advocacy
Department of Justice
P.O. Box 7856
Madison, WI 53707-7856
608-266-1852
800-362-8189

Assistant Attorney General
Office of Consumer Protection and Citizen
  Advocacy
Department of Justice
Milwaukee State Office Bldg.
819 N. 6th St., Room 520
Milwaukee, WI 53203-1678
414-227-4948
800-362-8189

Wisconsin—County Offices

District Attorney
Marathon County District Attorney's Office
Marathon County Courthouse
Wausau, WI 54401
715-847-5555

Assistant District Attorney
Consumer Fraud Unit
Milwaukee County District Attorney's Office
821 W. State St., Room 412
Milwaukee, WI 53233-1485
414-278-4792

Consumer Fraud Investigator
Racine County Sheriff's Department
717 Wisconsin Ave.
Racine, WI 53403
414-636-3125

Wyoming—State Office

Assistant Attorney General
Office of Attorney General
123 State Capitol Bldg.
Cheyenne, WY 82002
307-777-7874

American Samoa

Assistant Attorney General
Consumer Protection Bureau
P.O. Box 7
Pago Pago, AS 96799
011-684-633-4163/64

Puerto Rico

Secretary
Department of Consumer Affairs (DOCA)
Minillas Station
P.O. Box 41059
Santurce, PR 00940
809-721-0940

Secretary
Department of Justice
P.O. Box 192
San Juan, PR 00902
809-721-2900

Virgin Islands

Commissioner
Department of Licensing and Consumer Affairs
Property and Procurement Bldg.
Subbase #1, Room 205
St. Thomas, VI 00802
809-774-3130

DISABILITIES

TELECOMMUNICATIONS DEVICE FOR THE DEAF

Hearing- and speech-impaired people who use a telecommunications device for the deaf (known as TDD or TTY) can get help with calls made from a TDD to a TDD by using the following service:

TDD/TTY Operator Services
800-855-1155

The TDD operator can help you if you have telecommunications devices for the deaf to make:

- Credit card calls (if you have a telephone credit card)
- Collect calls (calls paid for by the person you are calling)
- Third-number telephone calls (calls billed to a number other than the one you are calling to or from)
- Person-to-person calls (calls to a specific person)
- Calls from a hotel or motel
- Calls from a coin phone (credit card, collect, or bill to third-number calls only)

The TDD operator can also help you:

- Get the number if you have a problem with a call
- Get assistance for problems with calls
- Get telephone numbers that you cannot find in the telephone book
- Report problems with your telephone

The TDD operator cannot interpret voice to TDD or TDD to voice.

Remember, most calls made with the help of an operator are more expensive, so dial calls yourself when you can to save money.

Go to "Sign Language" and "Braille Alphabet, Numbers, and Punctuation" in chapter 12

BOOKS FOR BLIND AND PHYSICALLY HANDICAPPED PERSONS

The **Library of Congress** has a free reading program for blind and physically handicapped individuals and offers publications in Braille and recorded books and magazines to persons who cannot hold a book or see well enough to read regular print. Special playback equipment is available on a loan basis from the Library of Congress, and cassettes and recordings on discs can be ordered from about 158 cooperating libraries. Anyone who is medically certified as unable to hold a book or read ordinary print because of a visual handicap can borrow these materials postage-free and return them in the same manner. For more information, contact:

National Library Service for the Blind and Physically Handicapped
The Library of Congress
Washington, DC 20542
202-707-5100
800-424-9100

Recording for the Blind and Dyslexic (RFB) is a national nonprofit service organization that provides free cassettes of educational textbooks and other resources to medically certified individuals. Eligibility extends to visually, physically, and perceptually handicapped individuals. One of RFB's special services is a collection of cassettes of a wide variety of consumer publications from the federal government. There is a one-time registration fee. For more information and an application, contact:

Recording for the Blind and Dyslexic
20 Roszel Rd.
Princeton, NJ 08540
609-452-0606
800-221-4792 (toll free outside New Jersey)
http://www.rfbd.org

DOMESTIC VIOLENCE RESOURCES

Below is a partial listing of domestic violence resources in the United States. Where possible, a statewide, toll-free hot line is listed; for states that do not have one, there is an organization that can refer you to legal assistance, crisis counseling, and shelters in your area.

National

Domestic Violence Resource Center
National Criminal Justice Resource Center
Box 6000-AIQ
Rockville, MD 20850
301-251-5063
800-627-6872
http://www.ncjrs.org

National Coalition Against Domestic Violence
P.O. Box 18749
Denver, CO 80218
303-839-1852

National Domestic Violence Hot Line
800-799-7233

Alabama

Alabama Coalition Against Domestic Violence
205-832-4842 (8 A.M.–5 P.M. weekdays)

Alaska

Alaska Network on Domestic Violence and Sexual Assault
907-586-3650

Arkansas

Arkansas Coalition Against Violence to Women and Children
800-332-4443 (state hotline, 24 hours)

California

Central California Coalition on Domestic Violence
800-925-3993 (call for referrals)

Northern California Coalition for Battered Women and their Children
415-457-2464 (9 A.M.–5 P.M. weekdays)

Colorado

Colorado Coalition Against Domestic Violence
303-573-9018 (call collect, 9 A.M.–5 P.M.)

Connecticut

Connecticut Coalition Against Domestic Violence
203-524-5890 (call collect, 8:30 A.M.–4:30 P.M. weekdays)

Delaware

Family Violence Program
Battered Women's Hot Line
302-762-6110 (24 hours)

District of Columbia

DC Coalition Against Domestic Violence
Emergency Domestic Relations Project
202-662-9640 (9 A.M.–5:30 P.M.)

Florida

Florida Coalition Against Domestic Violence
407-628-3885 (call collect, 9 A.M.–5 P.M. After business hours, an answering machine gives out a toll-free hot line number.)

Georgia

Georgia Advocates for Battered Women and Children
404-524-3847 (9 A.M.–5 P.M.)

Idaho

Idaho Council on Domestic Violence
208-334-5580 (call collect, 8 A.M.–5 P.M. weekdays)

Illinois

Illinois Coalition Against Domestic Violence
217-789-2830 (9 A.M.–5 P.M.)

Indiana

Indiana Coalition Against Domestic Violence
812-882-7900
800-332-7385 (state hot line, 24 hours)

Kansas

Kansas Coalition Against Sexual and Domestic Violence
316-232-2757
316-231-8251 (call collect, 9 A.M.–5 P.M., hours may vary)

Kentucky

Lincoln Trail Domestic Violence Program (Elizabethtown)
800-767-5838

YWCA Spouse Abuse Center (Lexington)
800-544-2022

Louisiana

Project S.A.V.E.
504-523-3755 (9 A.M.–5 P.M.)

Maine

Caring Unlimited
207-324-1957 (call collect, 24-hour hot line)

Maryland

Maryland Network Against Domestic Violence
410-268-4393 (8 A.M.–5 P.M.; no collect calls accepted, but will call victims back if requested)

Massachusetts

Massachusetts Coalition of Battered Women's Services
617-426-8492 (call collect, 9 A.M.–5 P.M.)

Minnesota

Minnesota Coalition for Battered Women
612-646-6177 (call collect, 9 A.M.–5 P.M. weekdays)
612-646-0994 (emergency hot line, call collect 24 hours)

Mississippi

Mississippi Coalition Against Domestic Violence
601-435-1968 (8 A.M.–5 P.M.)

Montana

Montana Coalition Against Domestic Violence
406-586-0263 (eastern Montana, 24 hours)

Violence Free Crisis Line
406-752-7273 (northwestern Montana, 24 hours)

Womensplace
800-543-7606 (western Montana, 24 hours)

Nebraska

Nebraska Domestic Violence and Sexual Assault Coalition
402-476-6256 (8 A.M.–5 P.M. weekdays)

Nevada

Nevada Network Against Domestic Violence
800-992-5757 (state hot line, 24 hours)

New Hampshire

Helpline
800-852-3311 (multi-issue state hot line, 24 hours)

New Jersey

New Jersey Coalition for Battered Women
800-572-7233 (state hot line, 24 hours; bilingual, TTY accessible for the deaf)

New Mexico

New Mexico State Coalition Against Domestic Violence
800-773-3645 (state hot line)

Women's Community Association
505-247-4219 (24 hours)

New York

New York State Coalition Against Domestic Violence
800-942-6906 (English, 24 hours)

Poder
800-942-6908 (Spanish, 7 A.M.–11 P.M.)

North Carolina

North Carolina Coalition Against Domestic Violence
919-490-1467 (9 A.M.–5 P.M. weekdays)

North Dakota

North Dakota Council on Abused Women's Services
800-472-2911 (state hot line, 24 hours)

Ohio

Turning Point
800-232-6505 (state hot line, 24 hours)

Oklahoma

Oklahoma Coalition on Domestic Violence and Sexual Assault
800-522-SAFE (state hot line, 24 hours)

Oregon

Oregon Coalition Against Domestic and Sexual Violence
503-239-4486/87 (9 A.M.–5 P.M.)

Pennsylvania

Pennsylvania Coalition Against Domestic Violence
800-932-4632 (8 A.M.–5 P.M.)

Rhode Island

Rhode Island Council on Domestic Violence
401-723-3051 (call collect, 8:30 A.M.–4:30 P.M.)

South Dakota

South Dakota Coalition Against Domestic Violence and Sexual Assault
605-698-3947
605-226-1212 (hours may vary)

Texas

Women's Advocacy Project
800-777-3247 (legal hot line, daytime)
800-374-4673 (family violence hot line, daytime)

Vermont

Vermont Network Against Domestic Violence and Sexual Assault
802-223-1302 (weekdays, daytime)

Virginia

Virginians Against Domestic Violence
804-780-3505 (call collect, 9 A.M.–3 P.M.)

Washington

Washington State Domestic Violence Hot Line
800-562-6025 (24 hours)

West Virginia

Department of Health and Human Resources
800-352-6513 (state multi-issue hot line)

Wisconsin

Wisconsin Coalition Against Domestic Violence
608-255-0539 (9 A.M.–5 P.M. weekdays)

Wyoming

Wyoming Family Violence and Sexual Assault Statewide Referral
800-442-8337 (24 hours)

FAMILY PLANNING

Family Planning Council
260 S. Broad St., Suite 1000
Philadelphia, PA 19102
215-985-2600
http://www.familyplanning.org

International Planned Parenthood Foundation
120 Wall St.
New York, NY 10005
212-248-6400
http://www.ippf.org/

National Family Planning and Reproductive Health Association
122 C St., NW
Washington, DC 20001
202-628-3535
http://www.nfprha.org

"Precautions During Pregnancy" in chapter 18; "Average Cost of Raising a Child" in chapter 20
Go to

Planned Parenthood Federation of America
810 Seventh Ave.
New York, NY 10019
212-541-7800
http://www.ppfa.org/ppfa

Population Institute
107 2nd St., NE
Washington, DC 20002
202-544-3300
http://www.populationinstitute.org

Resolve
1310 Broadway
Somerville, MA 02144-1779
617-643-2424
http://www.resolve.org

FEDERAL GOVERNMENT AGENCIES AND BUREAUS

Here is a selection of federal agencies that offer a wide range of information, enforcement, and/or complaint-handling services for products and services used by the general public. Many offices also have telecommunications devices for the deaf (TDDs). Voice users can call 800-877-8339 for the help of a relay operator from the Federal Information Relay Service.

Agriculture Department
Office of the Consumer Adviser
Washington, DC 20250
202-382-9681
http://www.usda.gov

Civil Rights Commission
Congressional and Community Relations
1121 Vermont Ave., NW
Washington, DC 20425
202-376-8312
202-376-8116 (voice/TDD)
http://www.usccr.gov

Commerce Department
Consumer Affairs
14th St. and Constitution Ave., NW
Washington, DC 20230
202-377-5001
http://www.doc.gov

Commodity Futures Trading Commission
Office of Governmental Affairs
2033 K St., NW
Washington, DC 20581
202-254-3067 (complaints)
202-254-8630 (information)
http://www.cftc.gov

Consumer Information Center
Pueblo, CO 81009
719-948-4000
http://www.pueblo.gsa.gov

Consumer Product Safety Commission
Product Safety Hot Line
Washington, DC 20207
800-638-CPSC (hot line)
800-638-8270 (TDD hot line)
http://www.cpsc.gov

Education Department
Consumer Affairs Staff
Room 3061
Washington, DC 20202
202-401-3679
http://www.ed.gov

Energy Department
Office of Consumer and Public Liaison
Washington, DC 20585
202-586-5373
http://www.doe.gov

Environmental Protection Agency
Public Information Center
Washington, DC 20460
202-382-2080
202-382-4565 (voice/TDD)
800-426-4791 (safe drinking water hot line)
http://www.epa.gov

Federal Communications Commission
Consumer Assistance and Small Business Office
1919 M St. NW
Washington, DC 20554
202-632-7000
202-632-6999 (TDD)
http://www.fcc.gov

Federal Deposit Insurance Corporation
Office of Consumer Affairs
550 17th St., NW
Washington, DC 20429
202-898-3536
202-898-3535 (voice/TDD)
800-424-5488
800-442-5488 (TDD)
http://www.fdic.gov

Federal Home Loan Mortgage Corporation
8200 Jones Branch Dr.
McLean, VA 22102
703-903-2039

Federal Maritime Commission
Office of Informal Inquiries and Complaints
1100 L St., NW
Washington, DC 20573
202-523-5807
http://www.fmc.gov

Federal Reserve System
Board of Governors
Division of Consumer and Community Affairs
Washington, DC 20551
202-452-3946
202-452-3544 (TDD)
http://www.bog.frb.fed.us

Federal Trade Commission
Public Reference Section
6th St. and Pennsylvania Ave., NW
Washington, DC 20580
202-326-2222 (publications)
http://www.ftc.gov

Health and Human Services Department
Food and Drug Administration
Consumer Affairs and Information Staff
5600 Fishers Lane
Rockville, MD 20857
301-827-4420
http://www.os.dhhs.gov

Inspector General's Hot Line
800-368-5779

Housing and Urban Development Department
Washington, DC 20410
800-347-3735 (HUD fraud hot line)
http://www.hud.gov

Interior Department
Consumer Affairs Administrator
Office of the Secretary
Washington, DC 20240
202-208-5521
http://www.doi.gov

Interstate Commerce Commission
Office of Compliance and Consumer Assistance
Washington, DC 20423
202-358-7110
http://www.dot.gov

"Federal Judicial System" in chapter 21;
"Federal Government" in chapter 25
Go to

Labor Department
Coordinator of Consumer Affairs
Washington, DC 20210
202-523-6060
http://www.dol.gov

National Credit Union Administration
1776 G St., NW
Washington, DC 20456
202-682-9640
http://www.ncua.gov

Every year, thousands of people visit 12305 Fifth Helena Dr. in Brentwood, California. It's the first house that Marilyn Monroe owned and the house where she died.

National Health Information Center
Health and Human Services Department
P.O. Box 1133
Washington, DC 20013-1133
800-336-4797
http://nhic-nt.health.org

National Institute of Standards and Technology
Office of Weights and Measures
Washington, DC 20234
301-975-4004
http://www.nist.gov

National Labor Relations Board
1717 Pennsylvania Ave., NW
Washington, DC 20570
202-632-4950
http://www.nlrb.gov

Nuclear Regulatory Commission
Office of Governmental and Public Affairs
Washington, DC 20555
301-492-0240
301-492-4626 (voice/TDD)
http://www.nrc.gov

Peace Corps
Recruitment
1990 K St., NW
Washington, DC 20526
800-424-8580
http://www.peacecorps.gov

Postal Rate Commission
Office of the Consumer Advocate
1333 H St., NW
Washington, DC 20268
202-789-6830
http://www.prc.gov

Securities and Exchange Commission
Office of Filings, Information, and
  Consumer Services
450 5th St., NW
Washington, DC 20549
202-272-7440 (investor complaints)
202-272-5624 (SEC information line)
202-272-2552 (voice/TDD)
http://www.sec.gov

Small Business Administration
Office of Consumer Affairs
409 3rd St., SW
Washington, DC 20416
202-205-6948 (complaints)
800-U-ASK-SBA (information)
202-205-7333 (TDD)
http://www.sba.gov

Transportation Department
400 7th St.
Washington, DC 20590
800-FAA-SURE (air safety)
202-366-2220 (airline service complaints)
800-424-9393 (auto safety hot line outside D.C.)
800-424-9153 (auto safety hot line TDD outside D.C.)
202-267-0972 (boating safety classes)
800-368-5647 (boating safety hot line)
800-368-5647 (railway safety)
http://www.dot.gov

United States Postal Service
Consumer Advocate
United States Postal Service
Washington, DC 20260-6720
202-268-2284
202-268-2310 (voice/TDD)
http://www.usps.gov

Veterans Affairs Department
810 Vermont Ave., NW
Washington, DC 20420
202-233-2411
http://www.va.gov

FEDERAL INFORMATION CENTERS

The Federal Information Center (FIC) offers information about federal government services, programs, and regulations. The FIC can also tell you which federal agency to contact for help with specific problems.

Their toll-free number is 800-688-9889 (800-326-2996 for TDD users). The FIC is open for public inquiries from 9:00 A.M. to 8:00 P.M., Eastern time, Monday through Friday, except federal holidays. They can also be reached on the World Wide Web at http://fic.info.gov/.

PARENTING

ADOPTION

Adoptive Families of America
3333 Highway 100 West
Minneapolis, MN 55422
612-535-4829
http://www.adoptivefam.org

National Adoption Center
1500 Walnut St., Suite 701
Philadelphia, PA 19102
215-735-9988
800-TO-ADOPT
http://www.adopt.org

National Adoption Information Clearinghouse
P.O. Box 1182
Washington, DC 20013-1182
703-352-3488
http://www.calib.com/naic

North American Council on Adoptable Children
970 Raymond Ave., Suite 106
St. Paul, MN 55114
612-644-3036

Orphan Voyage
2141 Road 2300
Cedaredge, CO 81413
303-856-3937

SINGLE-PARENT FAMILIES

America's Society of Separated and Divorced Men
575 Keep St.
Elgin, IL 60120
847-695-2200

Big Brothers/Big Sisters of America
230 N. 13th St.
Philadelphia, PA 19107
215-567-7000
http://www.bbbsa.org

Parents Without Partners
401 N. Michigan Ave.
Chicago, IL 60611
800-637-7974
http://www.parentsplace.com/readroom/pwp

Single Mothers By Choice
P.O. Box 1642
Gracie Square Station
New York, NY 10028
212-988-0993

RADIO AND TELEVISION NETWORKS

ABC, Inc.
77 W. 66th St.
New York, NY 10023
http://www.abc.com
    ABC Entertainment
    ABC News
    ABC Sports
    ABC Productions
    ABC Radio Networks
    ABC Television Network Group
    ABC Broadcast Group
    ABC Publishing Group

American Movie Classics (AMC)
150 Crossways Park West
Woodbury, NY 11797
http://www.amctv.com

Arts & Entertainment Television Network (A&E)
235 E. 45th St.
New York, NY 10017
http://www.aetv.com

Associated Press Broadcast Services
1825 K St., NW
Washington, DC 20006-1202
http://wire.ap.org
    AP News Service
    Associated Press Broadcasters, Inc.
    Radio Division

Black Entertainment Television (BET)
1900 W. Place, NE
Washington, DC 20018
http://www.betnetworks.com

Bravo
150 Crossways Park West
Woodbury, NY 11797
http://www.bravotv.com

Cable News Network (CNN)
One CNN Center
Box 105366
Atlanta, GA 30348-5366
http://www.cnn.com

Hot Lines and Information Services

A Closer Look

Air safety hot line	800-FAA-SURE (800-322-7873)
Auto safety hot line	800-424-9393
Child abuse hot line	800-4-A-CHILD (800-422-4453)
Domestic violence hot line	800-799-SAFE (800-799-7233)
Drug hot line	800-662-HELP (800-662-4357)
Gay/lesbian youth hot line	800-347-TEEN (800-347-8336)
National Center for Missing and Exploited Children	800-843-LOST (800-843-5678)
National Organization for Victim Assistance (NOVA)	800-879-NOVA (800-879-6682)
National Runaway Switchboard	800-621-4000
Parents who have kidnapped their children hot line	800-A-WAY-OUT (800-292-9688)
Product safety hot line	800-638-2772

Cable News Network Financial News (CNNFN)
New York Cable News Network
5 Penn Plaza, 20th Floor
New York, NY 10001
http://www.cnnfn.com

Cable Satellite Public Affairs Network (C-Span)
400 N. Capitol St., NW, Suite 650
Washington, DC 20001
http://www.c-span.org

Cartoon Network
1010 Techwood Dr., NW
Atlanta, GA 30318
http://filmzine.com/SpaceGhost/cartoonnet.html

CBS Corporation
51 W. 52nd St.
New York, NY 10019-6188
http://www.cbs.com
    CBS Affiliate Relations Division
    CBS Entertainment Division
    CBS Marketing Division
    CBS News Division
    CBS Operations and Administration
    CBS Radio Division
    CBS Sports Division
    CBS Television Network Division

Cinemax
1100 Avenue of the Americas
New York, NY 10036
http://www.cinemax.com

Classic Sports Network, Inc.
300 Park Ave. South
New York, NY 10010
http://www.classicsports.com

Go to "Newspapers" in chapter 25

Comedy Central
1775 Broadway
New York, NY 10019
http://www.comcentral.com

Consumer News and Business Channel (CNBC)
2200 Fletcher Ave.
Fort Lee, NJ 07024
http://www.cnbc.com

Court TV
600 Third Ave.
New York, NY 10016
http://www.courtv.com

The Discovery Channel
7700 Wisconsin Ave.
Bethesda, MD 20814-3522
http://www.discovery.com

The Disney Channel
3800 W. Alameda Ave.
Burbank, CA 91505
http://www.disney.com/DisneyChannel/

E! Entertainment Television, Inc.
11 W. 42nd St., 19th Floor
New York, NY 10036
and
5670 Wilshire Blvd.
Los Angeles, CA 90036
http://www.eonline.com

Entertainment and Sports Programming Network (ESPN)
ESPN Plaza
Bristol, CT 06010
http://espnet.sportszone.com

The Family Channel
2877 Guardian Lane
Virginia Beach, VA 23452
http://www.familychannel.com

Fox Broadcasting Company
10201 W. Pico Blvd.
Los Angeles, CA 90035
http://www.foxnetwork.com

fX Network
212 Fifth Ave.
New York, NY 10010
http://www.fxnetworks.com

Game Show Network
550 Madison Ave.
New York, NY 10022
http://www.spe.sony.com/Pictures/gsn/index.html

The Golf Channel
90 Park Ave.
New York, NY 10016
http://www.golf.com/golfchannel

Home Box Office, Inc. (HBO)
1100 Avenue of the Americas
New York, NY 10036
http://www.hbo.com

Home and Garden TV
1180 Avenue of the Americas
New York, NY 10036
http://www.hgtv.com

Home Shopping Networks
Box 9090
Clearwater, FL 33758-9090

Independent Film Channel
150 Crossways Park West
Woodbury, NY 11797
http://www.ifctv.com

The Learning Channel
7700 Wisconsin Ave.
Bethesda, MD 20814-3522
http://www.discovery.com

Lifetime Television
309 W. 49th St.
New York, NY 10019
http://www.lifetimetv.com

Madison Square Garden Network (MSG)
Two Pennsylvania Plaza
New York, NY 10121
http://www.msgnetwork.com

MSNBC
1 MSNBC Plaza
Secaucus, NJ 07094
http://www.msnbc.com

MTV Networks, Inc.
1515 Broadway
New York, NY 10036
http://www.mtv.com

The Nashville Network
2806 Opryland Dr.
Nashville, TN 37214

National Public Radio (NPR)
635 Massachusetts Ave., NW
Washington, DC 20036
http://www.npr.com

NBC, Inc.
30 Rockefeller Plaza
New York, NY 10112
http://www.nbc.com
   NBC Entertainment
   NBC News
   NBC Sports Division
   NBC Television Network
   NBC Television Stations

Nickelodeon
1515 Broadway
New York, NY 10036
http://nick-at-nite.com

Odyssey Channel
74 Trinity Place
New York, NY 10006

Ovation, The Arts Network
201 N. Union St., Suite 210
Alexandria, VA 22314
http://www.ovationtv.com

The Playboy Channel
608 N. Lake Shore Dr.
Chicago, IL 60611
http://www.playboy.com/playboy/guide/cgi/
  playboy-guide.cgi

Public Broadcasting Service (PBS)
Headquarters
1320 Braddock Place
Alexandria, VA 22314-1698
http://www.pbs.org

   National Press Relations/CA
   4401 Sunset Blvd.
   Los Angeles, CA 90027

   National Press Relations/NY
   1790 Broadway
   New York, NY 10019-1412

QVC
1365 Enterprise Dr.
West Chester, PA 19380
http://www.qvc.com

Reuters Information Services, Inc.
1700 Broadway
New York, NY 10019
http://www.reuters.com

The SciFi Channel
1230 Avenue of the Americas
New York, NY 10020
http://www.scifi.com

Sheridan Broadcasting Networks
655 Third Ave., 24th Floor
New York, NY 10017

Showtime
1633 Broadway, 15th Floor
New York, NY 10019
http://www.showtimeonline.com

The Travel Channel
2690 Cumberland Parkway
Atlanta, GA 30339
http://www.travelchannel.com

Turner Classic Movies
1050 Techwood Dr., NW
Atlanta, GA 30318
http://www.turner.com

Turner Network Television (TNT)
1050 Techwood Dr., NW
Atlanta, GA 30348
http://www.tnt-tv.com

TV Food Network
1177 Avenue of the Americas
New York, NY 10036
http://www.foodtv.com/index.html

United Paramount Network
11800 Wilshire Blvd.
Los Angeles, CA 90025
http://www.upn.com

United Press International (UPI)
1510 H St., NW
Washington, DC 20005
http://www.upi.com
    UPI National Broadcast
    UPI Radio Network

USA Network
1230 Avenue of the Americas
New York, NY 10020
http://www.usanetwork.com

VH1
1515 Broadway
New York, NY 10036
http://www.vh1.com

Viewer's Choice
909 Third Ave.
New York, NY 10022
http://www.ppv.com

Warner Bros. Network
4000 Warner Blvd., Bldg. 34R
Burbank, CA 91522

The Weather Channel
300 Interstate North Parkway
Atlanta, GA 30339
http://www.weather.com

Westwood One, Inc.
9540 Washington Blvd.
Culver City, CA 90232

    Mutual Broadcasting System, Inc.
    25060 W. Avenue Stanford
    Valencia, CA 91355

    NBC Radio Network
    25060 W. Avenue Stanford
    Valencia, CA 91355

UNITED STATES SERVICE ACADEMIES

United States Air Force Academy
United States Air Force Academy, CO 80840-5025
719-333-3812
http://www.usafa.af.mil

United States Coast Guard Academy
New London, CT 06320
800-444-8501
800-883-8724
http://www.cga.edu

United States Merchant Marine Academy
Kings Point, NY 11024-1699
516-773-5391
800-732-6267 (outside New York)
http://www.usmma.edu

United States Military Academy
West Point, NY 10996-1788
914-938-2006
http://www.usma.edu

United States Naval Academy
Annapolis, MD 21402-5018
410-293-1000
800-638-9156
http://www.nadn.navy.mil

ADDITIONAL SOURCES OF INFORMATION

MAGAZINES

AGING

Modern Maturity
American Association of Retired Persons
3200 E. Carson St.
Lakewood, CA 90712
http://www.aarp.org

CONSUMER INFORMATION AND PROTECTION

Accent on Living
P.O. Box 700
Gilum Rd. and High Dr.
Bloomington, IL 61702
http://www.blvd.com

Consumer Reports
Consumers Union of the U.S., Inc.
101 Truman Ave.
Yonkers, NY 10703
http://www.consumerreports.org

Consumers Digest
5705 N. Lincoln Ave.
Chicago, IL 60659
http://www.consumersdigest.com

GENERAL INTEREST

The Atlantic Monthly
77 N. Washington St.
Boston, MA 02117
http://www.theatlantic.com

Ebony
820 S. Michigan Ave.
Chicago, IL 60605
http://ebonymag.com

Harpers
666 Broadway
New York, NY 10012
http://www.harpers.org

Life
1271 Avenue of the Americas
New York, NY 10020
http://www.pathfinder.com

National Geographic
17th and M Sts., NW
Washington, DC 20036
http://www.nationalgeographic.com

The New Yorker
20 W. 43rd St.
New York, NY 10036

People
1271 Avenue of the Americas
New York, NY 10020
http://www.pathfinder.com

Psychology Today
49 E. 21st St.
New York, NY 10010

Reader's Digest
Reader's Digest Rd.
Pleasantville, NY 10570
http://www.readersdigest.com

Saturday Evening Post
1100 Waterway Blvd.
Indianapolis, IN 46202
http://www.satevepost.org

Smithsonian
900 Jefferson Dr.
Washington, DC 20560
http://www.smithsonianmag.si.edu

Utne Reader
1624 Harmon Place
Minneapolis, MN 55403
http://www.utne.com

Vanity Fair
350 Madison Ave.
New York, NY 10017
http://www.condenast.co.uk

MEN'S INTERESTS

Details
632 Broadway
New York, NY 10012
http://www.swoon.com

Esquire
224 W. 57th St.
New York, NY 10019
http://www.esquire2b.com

GQ
350 Madison Ave.
New York, NY 10017
http://www.swoon.com

Playboy
680 N. Lake Shore Dr.
Chicago, IL 60611
http://www.playboy.com

PARENTING

American Baby
245 W. 17th St.
New York, NY 10011

Child Magazine
375 Lexington Ave.
New York, NY 10017

Expecting
375 Lexington Ave.
New York, NY 10017

Parents Magazine
375 Lexington Ave.
New York, NY 10017

WOMEN'S INTERESTS

Bride's
350 Madison Ave.
New York, NY 10017
http://www.condenast.co.uk

Cosmopolitan
224 W. 57th St.
New York, NY 10019
http://www.cosmomag.com

Elle
1633 Broadway
New York, NY 10019
http://www.ellemag.com

Essence
1500 Broadway
New York, NY 10036
http://www.essence.com

Family Circle
375 Lexington Ave.
New York, NY 10017

Glamour
350 Madison Ave.
New York, NY 10017
http://www.swoon.com

Good Housekeeping
224 W. 57th St.
New York, NY 10019
http://www.goodhousekeeping.com

Harpers Bazaar
224 W. 57th St.
New York, NY 10019
http://www.hearstcorp.com/mag6.html

Ladies' Home Journal
100 Park Ave.
New York, NY 10017
http://www.lhj.com

Mademoiselle
350 Madison Ave.
New York, NY 10017
http://www.swoon.com

McCall's
375 Lexington Ave.
New York, NY 10011

Modern Bride
249 W. 17th St.
New York, NY 10011
http://www.modernbride.com

Ms.
230 Park Ave.
New York, NY 10169
http://www.womweb.com

New Woman
215 Lexington Ave.
New York, NY 10016
http://www.erack.com/nwoman/main.htm

Redbook
224 W. 57th St.
New York, NY 10019
http://homearts.com

Vogue
350 Madison Ave.
New York, NY 10017
http://www.condenast.co.uk

Woman's Day
1633 Broadway
New York, NY 10019

Working Woman
230 Park Ave.
New York, NY 10169
http://www.womweb.com

BOOKS

AGING

Beers, Mark & Steven Urice. *Aging in Good Health: A Complete Essential Medical Guide for Men and Women over Fifty and their Families.* Pocket Books, 1992.

Binstock, Robert H. and Linda K. George, eds. *Handbook of Aging and the Social Sciences,* 4th ed. Academic Press, 1995.

Vierck, Elizabeth. *Factbook on Aging.* ABC-Clio, 1990.

ALCOHOLISM AND DRUG ABUSE

Bratter, Thomas E. *Alcoholism and Substance Abuse: Strategies for Clinical Intervention.* Free Press, 1985.

Evans, Glen, et al. *The Encyclopedia of Alcoholism.* 2nd ed. Facts on File, 1991.

National Directory of Drug Abuse and Alcoholism Treatment and Prevention Programs. Gordon Press, 1991.

Sabroe, Knud-Erik. *Alcohol and Society: Patterns and Attitudes.* Coronet Books, 1994.

CONSUMER INFORMATION AND PROTECTION

Consumer Guide Buying Guide. Consumer Guide, annual.

Consumer Reports Buying Guide. Consumer Reports, annual.

Consumer Resource Handbook. U.S. Office of Consumer Affairs, annual.

Consumer Sourcebook. Gale Research, biannual.

DISABILITIES

Bondo, Bruce E. *Tax Options & Strategies: A State by State Guide for Persons with Disabilities, Senior Citizens, Veterans and their Families.* Demos Vermande, 1995.

Doyle, Brian. *Disability, Discrimination and Equal Opportunities: A Comparative Study of the Employment Rights of Disabled Persons.* Mansell, 1995.

Witt, Melanie A. *Job Strategies for People with Disabilities: Enable Yourself for Today's Job Market.* Peterson's Guides, 1992.

DOMESTIC VIOLENCE

Berry, Dawn Bradley. *Domestic Violence Sourcebook: Everything You Need to Know.* Lowell House, 1996.

FAMILY PLANNING

Freeman, Sarah and Vern Bullough. *The Complete Guide to Fertility and Family Planning.* Prometheus Books, 1992.

Pocket Guide for Family Planning Service Providers. J. H. Piego, 1995.

PARENTING

Anton-Johnson, Susan. *Free Child Care in your Community: How to Find It.* Arts & Images, 1990.

Casey, Eileen. *Maternity Leave: The Working Woman's Guide to Combining Pregnancy, Motherhood and Career.* Avon, 1995.

Starer, Dan. *Who to Call: The Parent's Sourcebook.* Quill, 1992.

GENERAL

Berkman, Robert L. *Find It Fast.* HarperPerennial, 1997.

Information Please Almanac 1997, 50th ed. Houghton Mifflin, 1996.

Jaszczak, Sandra, ed. *Encyclopedia of Associations,* 32nd ed. Gale Research, 1997.

Lesko, Matthew. *Lesko's Info-Power III.* Visible Ink, 1996.

Levine, Michael. *The Address Book,* 8th ed. Perigee, 1997.

The World Almanac and Book of Facts. World Almanac Books, annual.

V

RECREATION

Chapter Twenty-three 683
Sports and Games

Chapter Twenty-four 733
Travel

23

SPORTS AND GAMES

AUTO RACING	684
BASEBALL	686
BASKETBALL	690
BICYCLE RACING	693
BOWLING	694
FOOTBALL	694
GOLF	699
HORSE RACING	700
ICE HOCKEY	702
SOCCER	705
TENNIS	707
VOLLEYBALL	709
OLYMPIC GAMES	710
MAJOR SPORTS FIGURES	712

BOARD GAMES	719
CARD GAMES	724
ADDITIONAL SOURCES OF INFORMATION	727

AUTO RACING

Track races are held on oval asphalt tracks that are rectangular in shape with straightaways and banked (curved and sloped upward) corners. Road races are held on courses that include straight sections, hills, and various types of turns, such as hairpins and doglegs. Drag races are held on a drag strip, a straight paved track usually about 440 yards long.

Stock cars are late-model American-made production sedans (with front-mounted engines, doors, fenders, and a windshield) that have been modified to increase their power and speed. They typically race 200 to 600 miles on oval tracks.

Formula 1 cars are custom-built according to specifications that govern such elements as body design and engine size. The basic vehicle has a smooth contour to decrease air resistance, a low driver's seat in an open cockpit, no fenders, a spoiler near the back to hold the car to the road, and a rear-mounted engine. Formula 1 cars are used in Grand Prix races that are held on road courses up to 200 miles long.

When Barney Oldfield became the first man to drive a car 60 mph, most doctors claimed that such speed would cause deafness.

Indy cars are similar to Formula 1 cars but have different engine sizes, chassis (frame) formats, and transmission configurations. Such cars race on oval tracks for 150 miles or longer.

Drag-racing vehicles include *pro stock* (modified production cars) and *dragsters* (long, narrow-framed single seaters with large rear wheels).

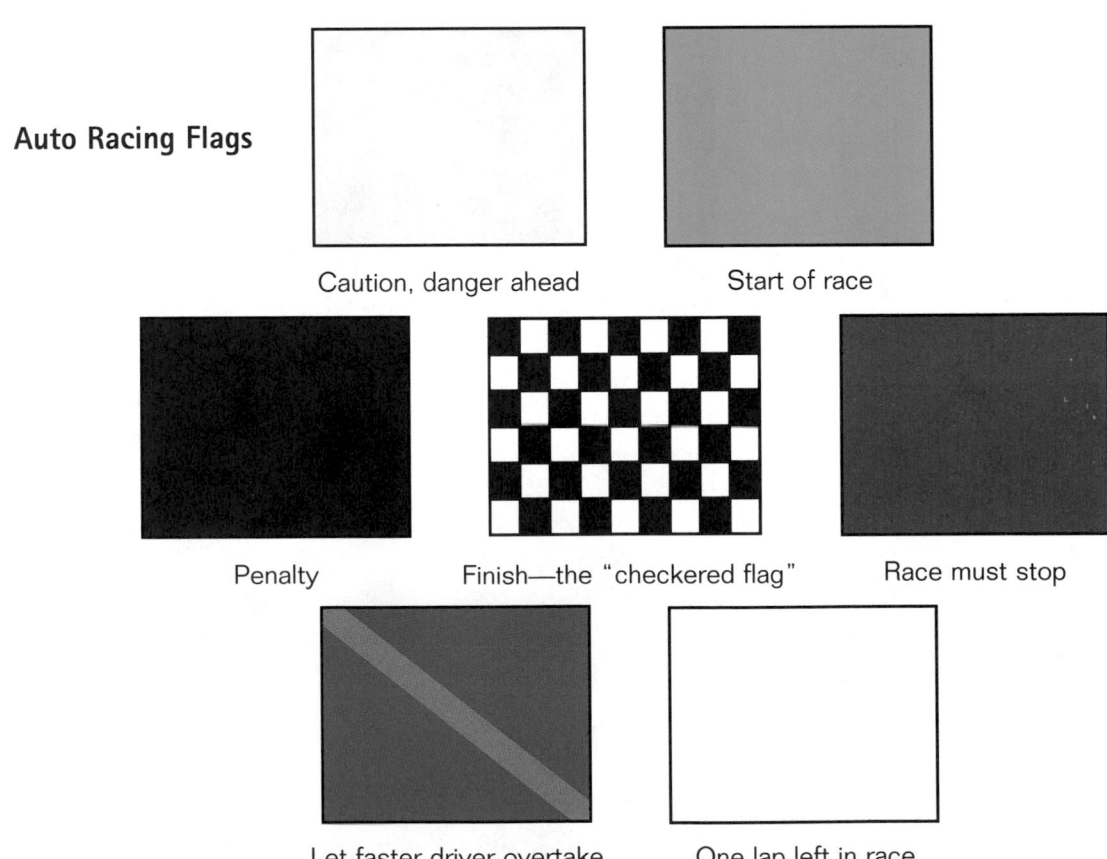

Auto Racing Flags

Caution, danger ahead

Start of race

Penalty

Finish—the "checkered flag"

Race must stop

Let faster driver overtake

One lap left in race

INDIANAPOLIS 500

A major auto race in the United States for many years has been the Indianapolis 500, which consists of 250 laps around the 2½-mile-long oval track at the Indianapolis Motor Speedway in Indiana. The winners since 1911 follow.

Date	Driver	Car	Average m.p.h.
1911	Ray Harroun	Marmon	74.602
1912	Joe Dawson	National	78.719
1913	Jules Goux	Peugeot	75.933
1914	Rene Thomas	Delage	82.474
1915	Ralph DePalma	Mercedes	89.840
1916	Dario Resta	Peugeot	84.001[1]
1917	No race held		
1918	No race held		
1919	Howard Wilcox	Peugeot	85.050
1920	Gaston Chevrolet	Monroe	88.618
1921	Tommy Milton	Frontenac	89.621
1922	Jimmy Murphy	Murphy Special	94.484
1923	Tommy Milton	H.C.S. Special	90.954
1924	L. L. Corum–Joe Boyer	Duesenberg Special	98.234
1925	Peter DePaolo	Duesenberg Special	101.127
1926	Frank Lockhart	Miller Special	95.904[2]
1927	George Souders	Duesenberg Special	97.545
1928	Louis Meyer	Miller Special	99.482
1929	Ray Keech	Simplex Piston Ring Special	97.585
1930	Billy Arnold	Harry Hartz Special	100.448
1931	Louis Schneider	Bowes Seal Fast Special	96.629
1932	Fred Frame	Miller-Hartz Special	104.144
1933	Louis Meyer	Tydol Special	104.162
1934	William Cummings	Boyle Products Special	104.863
1935	Kelly Petillo	Gilmore Speedway Special	106.240
1936	Louis Meyer	Ring Free Special	109.069
1937	Wilbur Shaw	Shaw-Gilmore Special	113.580
1938	Floyd Roberts	Burd Piston Ring Special	117.200
1939	Wilbur Shaw	Bolye Special	115.035
1940	Wilbur Shaw	Bolye Special	114.277
1941	Floyd Davis–Mauri Rose	Noc-Out Hose Clamp Special	115.117
1942	No race held		
1943	No race held		
1944	No race held		
1945	No race held		
1946	George Robson	Thorne Engineering Special	114.820
1947	Mauri Rose	Blue Crown Spark Plug Special	116.338
1948	Mauri Rose	Blue Crown Spark Plug Special	119.814
1949	Bill Holland	Blue Crown Spark Plug Special	121.327
1950	Johnny Parsons	Kurriss-Kraft Wynns Special	124.001[3]
1951	Lee Wallard	Belanger Special	126.244
1952	Troy Ruttman	Agajanian Special	128.922
1953	William Vukovich	Fuel Injection Special	128.740
1954	William Vukovich	Fuel Injection Special	130.840
1955	Robert Sweikert	Zink Special	128.209
1956	Pat Flaherty	Zink Special	128.490

[1] 300 miles   [2] 400 miles   [3] 345 miles

continues

Indianapolis 500 Winners Continued

Date	Driver	Car	Average m.p.h.
1957	Sam Hanks	Belond Exhaust Special	135.601
1958	Jimmy Bryan	Belond Special	133.791
1959	Rodger Ward	Leader CARD Special	135.856
1960	Jim Rathmann	Ken-Paul Special	138.767
1961	A. J. Foyt	Bowes Special	139.130
1962	Rodger Ward	Leader Card Special	140.292
1963	Parnelli Jones	Agajanian Special	143.137
1964	A. J. Foyt	Sheraton-Thompson Special	147.350
1965	Jim Clark	Lotus-Ford	150.686
1966	Graham Hill	Lola-Ford	144.317
1967	A. J. Foyt	Coyote Ford	151.207
1968	Bobby Unser	Offenhauser-Eagle	152.882
1969	Mario Andretti	Hawk-Ford	156.867
1970	Al Unser	P. J. Colt-Ford	155.749
1971	Al Unser	Johnny Lightning Special	157.735
1972	Mark Donohue	Sunoco McLaren-Offy	162.962
1973	Gordon Johncock	Eagle-Offenhauser	159.036[4]
1974	Johnny Rutherford	McLaren-Offenhauser	158.589
1975	Bobby Unser	Eagle-Offenhauser	149.213[5]
1976	Johnny Rutherford	McLaren-Offenhauser	148.725[6]
1977	A. J. Foyt	Coyote-Foyt	161.331
1978	Al Unser	Lola-Cosworth	161.363
1979	Rick Mears	Penske-Cosworth	158.899
1980	Johnny Rutherford	Chaparral	142.862
1981	Bobby Unser	Penske-Cosworth	138.085
1982	Gordon Johncock	Wildcat-Cosworth	162.026
1983	Tom Sneva	March-Cosworth	162.117
1984	Rick Mears	March-Cosworth	163.612
1985	Danny Sullivan	March-Cosworth	152.982
1986	Bobby Rahal	March-Cosworth	170.722
1987	Al Unser	March-Cosworth	162.175
1988	Rick Mears	Penske-Chevrolet	149.809
1989	Emerson Fittipaldi	Penske-Chevrolet	167.581
1990	Arie Luyendyk	Lola-Chevrolet	185.981
1991	Rick Mears	Penske-Chevrolet	176.460
1992	Al Unser, Jr.	Galmer-Chevrolet	134.479
1993	Emerson Fittipaldi	Penske-Chevrolet	157.207
1994	Al Unser, Jr.	Penske-Ilmor Mercedes	160.872
1995	Jacques Villeneuve	Reynard-Ford Cosworth	153.616
1996	Buddy Lazier	Reynard-Ford Cosworth	147.956
1997	Arie Luyendyk	Aurora G-Force	145.827
1998	Eddie Cheever Jr.	Dallara-Aurora	145.155

[4] 332.5 miles   [5] 435 miles   [6] 255 miles

BASEBALL

Baseball, named for the three bases and home plate that are parts of the playing field, has 9 or 10 players on each side. The offensive team sends to home plate one batter at a time, who uses a wooden or metal bat to try to hit a small cowhide-covered ball thrown from the pitcher to the catcher, two members of the defensive team. The defensive team also consists of four infielders and three outfielders. If the batter hits the ball on the ground, he must run toward first base; he is out if a defensive player throws the ball to a teammate standing on first base

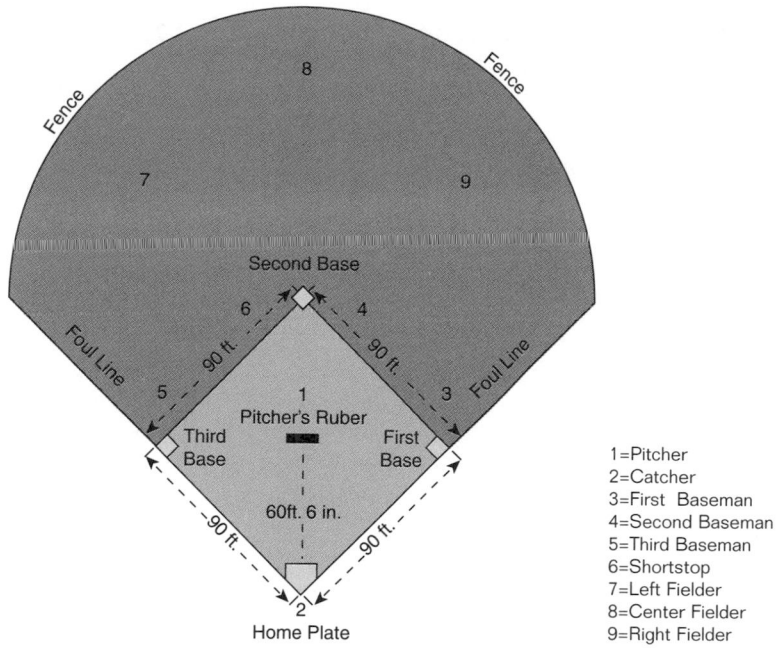

1=Pitcher
2=Catcher
3=First Baseman
4=Second Baseman
5=Third Baseman
6=Shortstop
7=Left Fielder
8=Center Fielder
9=Right Fielder

Baseball Field

before the runner reaches the base. The batter is also out if the ball he hits is caught by a defensive player before it hits the ground. A strike is called if the batter in a swing fails to strike the pitched ball, fails to swing at a pitch determined by the umpire to be a strike, or hits the ball into foul territory. Three strikes put the batter out (a strikeout). Outs may also be made when a defensive player who has the ball tags a base runner when the runner is between bases, or when a defensive player who has the ball steps on second base, third base, or home plate if the runner is forced to move to that base because the batter or another base runner is moving to occupy the preceding base.

The offensive team attempts to score runs by causing offensive base runners to go around all four bases and cross home plate safely. The offensive team scores runs by accumulating hits, which are balls hit between the two foul lines that go uncaught, allowing a batter to safely reach first base (a single), second base (a double), or third base (a triple), thus driving runners ahead of him to circle the bases. Batters can also reach base and move the runners ahead a base by obtaining a walk, four pitches that the batter does not swing at and that are determined by the umpire not to be strikes. Runs also can be scored with a home run, whereby a batter hits the ball over the outfield fence or far enough that he can circle the bases. The game is divided into nine innings, with three outs for each team in each inning. The batting, or offensive, team takes the field (defensive positions) after making three outs, when the opponents become batters. At the end of nine innings, the team that has accumulated the most runs is the winner. If both teams have scored the same number of runs at the end of nine innings, extra innings are played until the tie is broken.

Cleveland Indians star Lou Boudreau blew his nose and blew a game. He forgot that putting a towel to his face was the "steal" sign.

Sports/Games

U.S. AND CANADIAN MAJOR LEAGUE BASEBALL TEAMS

AMERICAN LEAGUE (AL)

Eastern Division	Central Division	Western Division
Baltimore Orioles	Chicago White Sox	Anaheim Angels
Boston Red Sox	Cleveland Indians	Oakland Athletics
New York Yankees	Detroit Tigers	Seattle Mariners
Tampa Bay Devil Rays	Kansas City Royals	Texas Rangers
Toronto Blue Jays	Minnesota Twins	

NATIONAL LEAGUE (NL)

Eastern Division	Central Division	Western Division
Atlanta Braves	Chicago Cubs	Arizona Diamondbacks
Florida Marlins	Cincinnati Reds	Colorado Rockies
Montreal Expos	Houston Astros	Los Angeles Dodgers
New York Mets	Milwaukee Brewers	San Diego Padres
Philadelphia Phillies	Pittsburgh Pirates	San Francisco Giants
	St. Louis Cardinals	

WORLD SERIES

After each major league team plays a regular-season schedule of 162 games, the three division winners in each league plus a wild-card team (the second-place division team with the best won-lost record) meet in a series of play-offs to determine the league pennant winner. The American League pennant winner then meets the National League pennant winner in October in a best-of-seven-games World Series for the major league championship that has been played since 1903 (except for the years 1904 and 1994). A best-of-nine-games World Series was played in 1903, 1919, 1920, and 1921. Tied games were played in 1907 and 1912. Winners and losers of the World Series follow.

Year	Winner	League	Loser	League	Games
1903	Boston Red Sox	AL	Pittsburgh Pirates	NL	5–3
1904	No series				
1905	New York Giants	NL	Philadelphia Athletics	AL	4–1
1906	Chicago White Sox	AL	Chicago Cubs	NL	4–2
1907	Chicago Cubs	NL	Detroit Tigers	AL	4–0–1
1908	Chicago Cubs	NL	Detroit Tigers	AL	4–1
1909	Pittsburgh Pirates	NL	Detroit Tigers	AL	4–3
1910	Philadelphia Athletics	AL	Chicago Cubs	NL	4–1
1911	Philadelphia Athletics	AL	New York Giants	NL	4–2
1912	Boston Red Sox	AL	New York Giants	NL	4–3–1
1913	Philadelphia Athletics	AL	New York Giants	NL	4–1
1914	Boston Braves	NL	Philadelphia Athletics	AL	4–0
1915	Boston Red Sox	AL	Philadelphia Phillies	NL	4–1
1916	Boston Red Sox	AL	Brooklyn Dodgers	NL	4–1
1917	Chicago White Sox	AL	New York Giants	NL	4–2

Year	Winner	League	Loser	League	Games
1918	Boston Red Sox	AL	Chicago Cubs	NL	4–2
1919	Cincinnati Reds	NL	Chicago White Sox	AL	5–3
1920	Cleveland Indians	AL	Brooklyn Dodgers	NL	5–2
1921	New York Giants	NL	New York Yankees	AL	5–3
1922	New York Giants	NL	New York Yankees	AL	4–0
1923	New York Yankees	AL	New York Giants	NL	4–2
1924	Washington Senators	AL	New York Giants	NL	4–3
1925	Pittsburgh Pirates	NL	Washington Senators	AL	4–3
1926	St. Louis Cardinals	NL	New York Yankees	AL	4–3
1927	New York Yankees	AL	Pittsburgh Pirates	NL	4–0
1928	New York Yankees	AL	St. Louis Cardinals	NL	4–0
1929	Philadelphia Athletics	AL	Chicago Cubs	NL	4–1
1930	Philadelphia Athletics	AL	St. Louis Cardinals	NL	4–2
1931	St. Louis Cardinals	NL	Philadelphia Athletics	AL	4–3
1932	New York Yankees	AL	Chicago Cubs	NL	4–0
1933	New York Giants	NL	Washington Senators	AL	4–1
1934	St. Louis Cardinals	NL	Detroit Tigers	AL	4–3
1935	Detroit Tigers	AL	Chicago Cubs	NL	4–2
1936	New York Yankees	AL	New York Giants	NL	4–2
1937	New York Yankees	AL	New York Giants	NL	4–1
1938	New York Yankees	AL	Chicago Cubs	NL	4–0
1939	New York Yankees	AL	Cincinnati Reds	NL	4–0
1940	Cincinnati Reds	NL	Detroit Tigers	AL	4–3
1941	New York Yankees	AL	Brooklyn Dodgers	NL	4–1
1942	St. Louis Cardinals	NL	New York Yankees	AL	4–1
1943	New York Yankees	AL	St. Louis Cardinals	NL	4–1
1944	St. Louis Cardinals	NL	St. Louis Browns	AL	4–2
1945	Detroit Tigers	AL	Chicago Cubs	NL	4–3
1946	St. Louis Cardinals	NL	Boston Red Sox	AL	4–3
1947	New York Yankees	AL	Brooklyn Dodgers	NL	4–3
1948	Cleveland Indians	AL	Boston Braves	NL	4–2
1949	New York Yankees	AL	Brooklyn Dodgers	NL	4–1
1950	New York Yankees	AL	Philadelphia Phillies	NL	4–0
1951	New York Yankees	AL	New York Giants	NL	4–2
1952	New York Yankees	AL	Brooklyn Dodgers	NL	4–3
1953	New York Yankees	AL	Brooklyn Dodgers	NL	4–2
1954	New York Giants	NL	Cleveland Indians	AL	4–0
1955	Brooklyn Dodgers	NL	New York Yankees	AL	4–3
1956	New York Yankees	AL	Brooklyn Dodgers	NL	4–3
1957	Milwaukee Braves	NL	New York Yankees	AL	4–3
1958	New York Yankees	AL	Milwaukee Braves	NL	4–3
1959	Los Angeles Dodgers	NL	Chicago White Sox	AL	4–2
1960	Pittsburgh Pirates	NL	New York Yankees	AL	4–3
1961	New York Yankees	AL	Cincinnati Reds	NL	4–1
1962	New York Yankees	AL	San Francisco Giants	NL	4–3
1963	Los Angeles Dodgers	NL	New York Yankees	AL	4–0
1964	St. Louis Cardinals	NL	New York Yankees	AL	4–3
1965	Los Angeles Dodgers	NL	Minnesota Twins	AL	4–3
1966	Baltimore Orioles	AL	Los Angeles Dodgers	NL	4–0
1967	St. Louis Cardinals	NL	Boston Red Sox	AL	4–3
1968	Detroit Tigers	AL	St. Louis Cardinals	NL	4–3

Sports/Games

continues

World Series Winners Continued

Year	Winner	League	Loser	League	Games
1969	New York Mets	NL	Baltimore Orioles	AL	4–1
1970	Baltimore Orioles	AL	Cincinnati Reds	NL	4–1
1971	Pittsburgh Pirates	NL	Baltimore Orioles	AL	4–3
1972	Oakland Athletics	AL	Cincinnati Reds	NL	4–3
1973	Oakland Athletics	AL	New York Mets	NL	4–3
1974	Oakland Athletics	AL	Los Angeles Dodgers	NL	4–1
1975	Cincinnati Reds	NL	Boston Red Sox	AL	4–3
1976	Cincinnati Reds	NL	New York Yankees	AL	4–0
1977	New York Yankees	AL	Los Angeles Dodgers	NL	4–2
1978	New York Yankees	AL	Los Angeles Dodgers	NL	4–2
1979	Pittsburgh Pirates	NL	Baltimore Orioles	AL	4–3
1980	Philadelphia Phillies	NL	Kansas City Royals	AL	4–2
1981	Los Angeles Dodgers	NL	New York Yankees	AL	4–2
1982	St. Louis Cardinals	NL	Milwaukee Brewers	AL	4–3
1983	Baltimore Orioles	AL	Philadelphia Phillies	NL	4–1
1984	Detroit Tigers	AL	San Diego Padres	NL	4–1
1985	Kansas City Royals	AL	St. Louis Cardinals	NL	4–3
1986	New York Mets	NL	Boston Red Sox	AL	4–3
1987	Minnesota Twins	AL	St. Louis Cardinals	NL	4–3
1988	Los Angeles Dodgers	NL	Oakland Athletics	AL	4–1
1989	Oakland Athletics	AL	San Francisco Giants	NL	4–0
1990	Cincinnati Reds	NL	Oakland Athletics	AL	4–1
1991	Minnesota Twins	AL	Atlanta Braves	NL	4–3
1992	Toronto Blue Jays	AL	Atlanta Braves	NL	4–3
1993	Toronto Blue Jays	AL	Philadelphia Phillies	NL	4–2
1994	No series				
1995	Atlanta Braves	NL	Cleveland Indians	AL	4–2
1996	New York Yankees	AL	Atlanta Braves	NL	4–2
1997	Florida Marlins	NL	Cleveland Indians	AL	4–3

BASKETBALL

Basketball usually is played indoors on a rectangular wooden court by two teams, each with five players. At both ends of the court are suspended two goals, or baskets (18 inches in diameter), consisting of a circular metal rim 10 feet above the floor attached to a square backboard made of wood, plastic, or fiberglass. A cord net is hung below the rim. The object is to shoot the ball so that it goes through the basket from above and to prevent your opponents from doing the same. Basketball uses a large rubber ball covered with leather.

Play begins with a jump ball. The official throws the ball upward at the center circle between two opposing players. The two players try to tip or slap the ball to a teammate and thus gain possession of the ball. Each team defends one goal. There are offensive and defensive halves of the court for each team, divided by the midcourt line. A player advances the ball down the court by passing to a teammate, dribbling (bouncing the ball while walking or running), or shooting the ball at the basket. Running or walking while holding the ball is not permitted. If a shot goes in the basket, two points are awarded to the shooting team. If a shot is missed (usually hitting the rim or backboard), a defensive player may rebound the ball (catch it as it bounces away from the basket). He then may begin to advance the ball to the other end of the court in preparation for a shot by his team. An offensive player may also rebound a missed shot and shoot again. A shot made from beyond the three-point line (22 feet from the center of the basket on NBA courts) scores three points instead of the usual two.

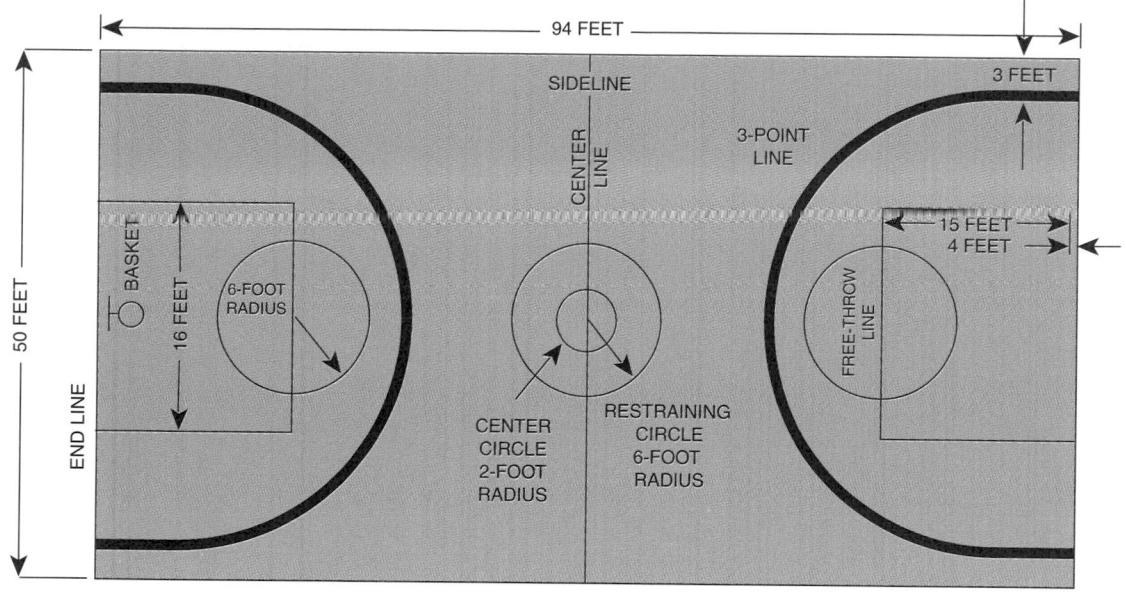

Basketball Court

Holding, pushing, grabbing, and similar types of body contact are not permitted; these are called fouls. They may result in a foul shot or free throw, an unimpeded shot taken by the offended player from a line on the court 15 feet from the basket. A successful free throw scores one point.

Professional basketball games are divided into four 12-minute quarters; the team with more points at the end of that time wins the game.

NATIONAL BASKETBALL ASSOCIATION (NBA) TEAMS

EASTERN CONFERENCE

Atlantic Division	Central Division
Boston Celtics	Atlanta Hawks
Miami Heat	Charlotte Hornets
New Jersey Nets	Chicago Bulls
New York Knicks	Cleveland Cavaliers
Orlando Magic	Detroit Pistons
Philadelphia 76ers	Indiana Pacers
Washington Wizards	Milwaukee Bucks
	Toronto Raptors

WESTERN CONFERENCE

Midwest Division	Pacific Division
Dallas Mavericks	Golden State Warriors
Denver Nuggets	Los Angeles Clippers
Houston Rockets	Los Angeles Lakers
Minnesota Timberwolves	Phoenix Suns
San Antonio Spurs	Portland Trail Blazers
Utah Jazz	Sacramento Kings
Vancouver Grizzlies	Seattle SuperSonics

NATIONAL BASKETBALL ASSOCIATION CHAMPIONS

After each National Basketball Association (NBA) team plays a regular-season schedule of 82 games, the eight teams in each conference with the best won-lost records meet in a series of play-offs to determine the conference champion. The Eastern Conference champion then meets the Western Conference champion in the spring in a best-of-seven-games series for the NBA championship. Winners and losers of the NBA championship series are listed on the next page.

Year	NBA Winners	Conference	Losers	Conference	Games
1947	Philadelphia Warriors	E	Chicago Stags	W	4–1
1948	Baltimore Bullets	W	Philadelphia Warriors	E	4–2
1949	Minneapolis Lakers	W	Washington Capitols	E	4–2
1950	Minneapolis Lakers	W	Syracuse Nationals	E	4–2
1951	Rochester Royals	W	New York Knickerbockers	E	4–3
1952	Minneapolis Lakers	W	New York Knickerbockers	E	4–3
1953	Minneapolis Lakers	W	New York Knickerbockers	E	4–1
1954	Minneapolis Lakers	W	Syracuse Nationals	E	4–3
1955	Syracuse Nationals	E	Fort Wayne Pistons	W	4–3
1956	Philadelphia Warriors	E	Fort Wayne Pistons	W	4–1
1957	Boston Celtics	E	St. Louis Hawks	W	4–3
1958	St. Louis Hawks	W	Boston Celtics	E	4–2
1959	Boston Celtics	E	Minneapolis Lakers	W	4–0
1960	Boston Celtics	E	St. Louis Hawks	W	4–3
1961	Boston Celtics	E	St. Louis Hawks	W	4–1
1962	Boston Celtics	E	Los Angeles Lakers	W	4–3
1963	Boston Celtics	E	Los Angeles Lakers	W	4–2
1964	Boston Celtics	E	San Francisco Warriors	W	4–1
1965	Boston Celtics	E	Los Angeles Lakers	W	4–1
1966	Boston Celtics	E	Los Angeles Lakers	W	4–3
1967	Philadelphia 76ers	E	San Francisco Warriors	W	4–2
1968	Boston Celtics	E	Los Angeles Lakers	W	4–2
1969	Boston Celtics	E	Los Angeles Lakers	W	4–3
1970	New York Knickerbockers	E	Los Angeles Lakers	W	4–3
1971	Milwaukee Bucks	W	Baltimore Bullets	E	4–0
1972	Los Angeles Lakers	W	New York Knickerbockers	E	4–1
1973	New York Knickerbockers	E	Los Angeles Lakers	W	4–1
1974	Boston Celtics	E	Milwaukee Bucks	W	4–3
1975	Golden State Warriors	W	Washington Bullets	E	4–0
1976	Boston Celtics	E	Phoenix Suns	W	4–2
1977	Portland Trail Blazers	W	Philadelphia 76ers	E	4–2
1978	Washington Bullets	E	Seattle Supersonics	W	4–3
1979	Seattle Supersonics	W	Washington Bullets	E	4–1
1980	Los Angeles Lakers	W	Philadelphia 76ers	E	4–2
1981	Boston Celtics	E	Houston Rockets	W	4–2
1982	Los Angeles Lakers	W	Philadelphia 76ers	E	4–2
1983	Philadelphia 76ers	E	Los Angeles Lakers	W	4–0
1984	Boston Celtics	E	Los Angeles Lakers	W	4–3
1985	Los Angeles Lakers	W	Boston Celtics	E	4–2
1986	Boston Celtics	E	Houston Rockets	W	4–2
1987	Los Angeles Lakers	W	Boston Celtics	E	4–2
1988	Los Angeles Lakers	W	Detroit Pistons	E	4–3
1989	Detroit Pistons	E	Los Angeles Lakers	W	4–0
1990	Detroit Pistons	E	Portland Trail Blazers	W	4–1
1991	Chicago Bulls	E	Los Angeles Lakers	W	4–1
1992	Chicago Bulls	E	Portland Trail Blazers	W	4–2
1993	Chicago Bulls	E	Phoenix Suns	W	4–2
1994	Houston Rockets	W	New York Knickerbockers	E	4–3
1995	Houston Rockets	W	Orlando Magic	W	4–0
1996	Chicago Bulls	E	Seattle Supersonics	W	4–2
1997 & '98	Chicago Bulls	E	Utah Jazz	W	4–2 & 4–2

BICYCLE RACING

Road-racing bicycles have a free front wheel, multiple gears on the rear wheel, and a brake for each wheel. Track-racing bicycles have a single fixed gear on the rear wheel and no brakes. Cyclo-cross bicycles have typical road gears but have stronger rims and fatter tires.

The basic types of road races are (1) *time trials,* in which cyclists start at intervals and race either over a fixed distance (generally between 10 and 100 miles) to achieve the fastest time, or for a fixed time (generally 12 or 24 hours) to achieve the longest distance; (2) *criteriums,* in which cyclists ride a predetermined number of laps (covering a total distance ranging from 10 to 60 miles) on a closed circuit of 1 to 3 miles; (3) *road races,* in which cyclists ride from point to point, around several long circuits, or complete a combination of the two over a course that features long, steep climbs; and (4) *multiday stage races,* lasting from three days to three weeks, that include a combination of time trials, criteriums, and road races and whose winner is the cyclist with the lowest accumulated time for all stages.

Track races are held on steeply banked tracks either outdoors or inside buildings called *velodromes.* The basic types of track races are (1) *sprints,* in which two or more cyclists compete over a short distance (generally 1,000 meters for men and 500 meters for women); (2) *handicaps,* a massed-start event where the order in which each cyclist starts is determined by past proven speed; and (3) *pursuits,* in which two cyclists or teams start directly opposite from each other and then try to catch up to one another (over a distance of 4 to 5 kilometers) before reaching the finish.

In cyclo-cross races (generally 1 to 15 kilometers long), cyclists race off-road and encounter such obstacles as fences, streams, mud, sand, forests, ditches, fallen trees, gates, creek beds, and artificial hurdles, forcing them to dismount occasionally and carry their bicycles.

TOUR DE FRANCE

The most famous stage race is the Tour de France, a three-week event held annually in France and portions of other European countries in late June and early July and ranging in length from 2,500 to 3,000 miles. The course is changed each year and includes steep mountain climbs. Winners of the Tour de France follow.

Year	Cyclist	Home Country	Year	Cyclist	Home Country
1903	Maurice Garin	France	1921	Leon Scieur	Belgium
1904	Henri Cornet	France	1922	Firmin Lambot	Belgium
1905	Louis Trousselier	France	1923	Henri Pelissier	France
1906	Rene Pottier	France	1924	Ottavio Bottecchia	Italy
1907	Lucien Petit-Breton	France	1925	Ottavio Bottecchia	Italy
1908	Lucien Petit-Breton	France	1926	Lucien Buysse	Belgium
1909	Francois Faber	France	1927	Nicolas Frantz	Luxembourg
1910	Octave Lapize	France	1928	Nicolas Frantz	Luxembourg
1911	Gustave Garrigou	France	1929	Maurice Dewaele	Belgium
1912	Odile Defraye	Belgium	1930	Andre Leducq	France
1913	Phillippe Thys	Belgium	1931	Antonin Magne	Italy
1914	Phillippe Thys	Belgium	1932	Andre Leducq	France
1915	*Race not held*		1933	Georges Speicher	France
1916	*Race not held*		1934	Antonin Magne	Italy
1917	*Race not held*		1935	Romain Maes	Belgium
1918	*Race not held*		1936	Sylvere Maes	Belgium
1919	Firmin Lambot	Belgium	1937	Roger Lapebie	France
1920	Phillippe Thys	Belgium	1938	Gino Bartali	Italy

continues

Tour de France Winners Continued

Year	Cyclist	Home Country
1939	Sylvere Maes	Belgium
1940	*Race not held*	
1941	*Race not held*	
1942	*Race not held*	
1943	*Race not held*	
1944	*Race not held*	
1945	*Race not held*	
1946	*Race not held*	
1947	Jean Robic	France
1948	Gino Bartali	Italy
1949	Fausto Coppi	Italy
1950	Fredi Kubler	Switzerland
1951	Hugo Koblet	Switzerland
1952	Fausto Coppi	Italy
1953	Louison Bobet	France
1954	Louison Bobet	France
1955	Louison Bobet	France
1956	Roger Walkowiak	France
1957	Jacques Anquetil	France
1958	Charly Gaul	Luxembourg
1959	Fredrico Bahamontes	Spain
1960	Gastone Nencimi	Italy
1961	Jacques Anquetil	France
1962	Jacques Anquetil	France
1963	Jacques Anquetil	France
1964	Jacques Anquetil	France
1965	Felice Gimondi	Italy
1966	Lucien Aimar	France
1967	Roger Pingeon	France
1968	Jan Janssen	Holland

Year	Cyclist	Home Country
1969	Eddy Merckx	Belgium
1970	Eddy Merckx	Belgium
1971	Eddy Merckx	Belgium
1972	Eddy Merckx	Belgium
1973	Luis Ocana	Spain
1974	Eddy Merckx	Belgium
1975	Bernard Thevenet	France
1976	Lucien Van Impe	Belgium
1977	Baernard Thevenet	France
1978	Bernard Hinault	France
1979	Bernard Hinault	France
1980	Joop Zoetemelk	Holland
1981	Bernard Hinault	France
1982	Bernard Hinault	France
1983	Laurent Fignon	France
1984	Laurent Fignon	France
1985	Bernard Hinault	France
1986	Greg LeMond	United States
1987	Stephen Roche	Ireland
1988	Pedro Delgado	Spain
1989	Greg LeMond	United States
1990	Greg LeMond	United States
1991	Miguel Indurain	Spain
1992	Miguel Indurain	Spain
1993	Miguel Indurain	Spain
1994	Miguel Indurain	Spain
1995	Miguel Indurain	Spain
1996	Bjarne Riis	Denmark
1997	Jan Ullrich	Germany

BOWLING

Bowling, or tenpins, is an indoor sport in which a player attempts to knock down 10 wooden pins that are arranged in a triangular formation. The player accomplishes this by rolling a ball down a wooden lane, or alley. The ball, which weighs at most about 16 pounds, is fitted with three holes for thumb and finger grips. Each game is divided into 10 frames, and the bowler is allowed a maximum of two rolls per frame, except for the last frame, where he is allowed three. If a player knocks down all 10 pins with one roll, it is called a strike; the second roll of the frame is not used, except for the 10th frame, where three strikes are possible. If a player knocks down all 10 pins using both rolls of the frame, it is called a spare. The number of pins knocked down by the end of the game determines the score, with spares scoring 10 plus the number of pins knocked down on the next roll, and strikes scoring 10 plus the number of pins knocked down on the next two rolls. A perfect game of 12 consecutive strikes scores 300.

FOOTBALL

American football has 11 players on each team and is played on a large rectangular field. At each end of the field is an end zone, where the goalposts are placed. The object is to gain possession of an inflated leather or pigskin ball and move it across the opponents' goal line by running or passing, thus scoring a touchdown, which is worth six points. Passing the ball is usually done by the

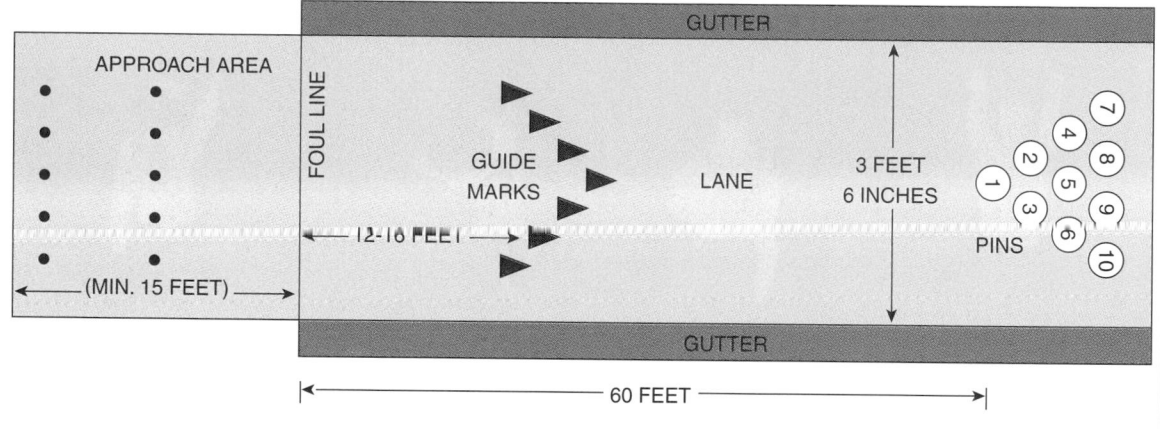

Bowling Alley

quarterback. Players also score points by kicking the ball through the goalposts. This opportunity is given automatically after a touchdown; the point is called a point after touchdown, or extra point. A field goal scores three points. The defensive team can score by downing an offensive player in his own end zone. This is called a safety and scores two points.

The term "down" in football has been used since the late 19th cen-tury. When a ball carrier was tackled, he would yell "down" to keep opponents from piling on top of him.

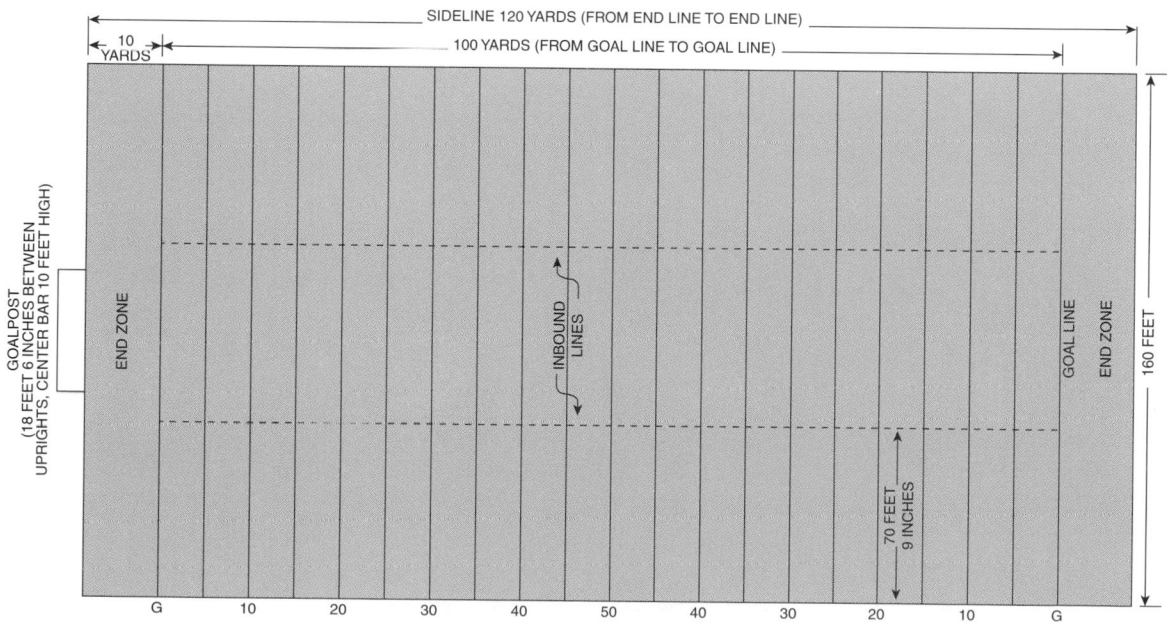

Football Field

Sports/Games

Official Football Signals

TOUCHDOWN,
FIELD GOAL, or
SUCCESSFUL TRY

ILLEGAL FORWARD PASS
If followed by raised hand
flung downward:
INTENTIONAL GROUNDING
OF PASS.

FIRST DOWN

DEAD BALL or NEUTRAL
ZONE ESTABLISHED
With raised fist closed: FOURTH DOWN.

LOSS OF DOWN

ILLEGAL CHUCKING

NO TIME-OUT or
TIME-IN WITH WHISTLE

DELAY OF GAME or
EXCESS TIME-OUT
If followed by forearms rotated
over and over in front of body:
ILLEGAL FORMATION.

PERSONAL FOUL

HOLDING

ILLEGAL USE OF HANDS

PENALTY REFUSED,
INCOMPLETE PASS, PLAY
OVER, or MISSED GOAL

Sports/Games

DOUBLE TOUCH

PASS JUGGLED
INBOUNDS AND CAUGHT
OUT OF BOUNDS

SAFETY

INTERFERENCE WITH
FORWARD PASS or
FAIR CATCH

INVALID FAIR
CATCH SIGNAL

INELIGIBLE RECEIVER, or
INELIGIBLE MEMBER OF
KICKING TEAM DOWNFIELD

TIME-OUT
If followed by placing one hand on
top of cap: REFEREE'S TIME-
OUT; if followed by arm swung at
side: TOUCHBACK.

OFFSIDE, ENCROACHING,
or FREE KICK VIOLATION

ILLEGAL MOTION AT SNAP

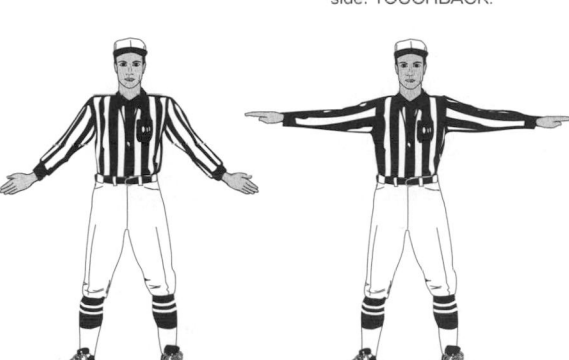

CRAWLING, PUSHING, or
HELPING RUNNER

UNSPORTSMANLIKE
CONDUCT

ILLEGAL CUT

The offensive team must gain 10 yards in four tries, called downs, or give up possession of the ball. If 10 or more yards are gained, the offense has four more downs to advance the ball. If on the fourth down (or, rarely, before) it seems unlikely that the 10-yard minimum will be reached, the offense has the option of kicking the ball to the opponents. This is called a punt, and the defensive team, after catching the ball, goes on offense. The defensive team may also gain possession of the ball, and thus become the offense, by catching a ball passed by the quarterback that was intended for a teammate (interception), or by recovering the ball after it has been dropped by an offensive player (fumble). The defense hinders the attempts of the offense to gain yardage by tackling the ball carrier and pulling him to the ground. Because blocking and tackling can be very rough, football players wear protective helmets and substantial padding.

In 1950 the Los Angeles Rams were the first professional football team to put an insignia on their helmets. They painted yellow horns on their blue leather helmets.

The game is divided into four 15-minute periods; the team with the most points after the end of that time is the winner.

NATIONAL FOOTBALL LEAGUE (NFL) TEAMS

NATIONAL FOOTBALL CONFERENCE (NFC)

Eastern Division	Central Division	Western Division
Arizona Cardinals	Chicago Bears	Atlanta Falcons
Dallas Cowboys	Detroit Lions	Carolina Panthers
New York Giants	Green Bay Packers	New Orleans Saints
Philadelphia Eagles	Minnesota Vikings	San Francisco 49ers
Washington Redskins	Tampa Bay Buccaneers	St. Louis Rams

AMERICAN FOOTBALL CONFERENCE (AFC)

Eastern Division	Central Division	Western Division
Buffalo Bills	Baltimore Ravens	Denver Broncos
Indianapolis Colts	Cincinnati Bengals	Kansas City Chiefs
Miami Dolphins	Jacksonville Jaguars	Oakland Raiders
New England Patriots	Pittsburgh Steelers	San Diego Chargers
New York Jets	Tennessee Oilers	Seattle Seahawks

THE SUPER BOWL

After each National Football League (NFL) team plays a regular-season schedule of 16 games, the three division winners in each conference plus wild-card teams (the three teams with the best won-lost records in the rest of the conference) meet in a series of play-off games to determine the conference champion. The National Football Conference (NFC) champion then meets the American Football Conference (AFC) champion in January in the Super Bowl game for the NFL championship. The first four Super Bowls were played between the champions of the National Football League and the American Football League (AFL); the leagues then merged. Winners and losers of the Super Bowl are listed on the next page.

SUPER BOWL WINNERS

Bowl	Year	Winner	Conference	Loser	Conference	Score
I	1967	Green Bay Packers	NFL	Kansas City Chiefs	AFL	35–10
II	1968	Green Bay Packers	NFL	Oakland Raiders	AFL	33–14
III	1969	New York Jets	AFL	Baltimore Colts	NFL	16–7
IV	1970	Kansas City Chiefs	AFL	Minnesota Vikings	NFL	23–7
V	1971	Baltimore Colts	AFC	Dallas Cowboys	NFC	16–13
VI	1972	Dallas Cowboys	NFC	Miami Dolphins	AFC	24–3
VII	1973	Miami Dolphins	AFC	Washington Redskins	NFC	14–7
VIII	1974	Miami Dolphins	AFC	Minnesota Vikings	NFC	24–7
IX	1975	Pittsburgh Steelers	AFC	Minnesota Vikings	NFC	16–6
X	1976	Pittsburgh Steelers	AFC	Dallas Cowboys	NFC	21–17
XI	1977	Oakland Raiders	AFC	Minnesota Vikings	NFC	32–14
XII	1978	Dallas Cowboys	NFC	Denver Broncos	AFC	27–10
XIII	1979	Pittsburgh Steelers	AFC	Dallas Cowboys	NFC	35–31
XIV	1980	Pittsburgh Steelers	AFC	Los Angeles Rams	NFC	31–19
XV	1981	Oakland Raiders	AFC	Philadelphia Eagles	NFC	27–10
XVI	1982	San Francisco 49ers	NFC	Cincinnati Bengals	AFC	26–21
XVII	1983	Washington Redskins	NFC	Miami Dolphins	AFC	27–17
XVIII	1984	Los Angeles Raiders	AFC	Washington Redskins	NFC	38–9
XIX	1985	San Francisco 49ers	NFC	Miami Dolphins	AFC	38–16
XX	1986	Chicago Bears	NFC	New England Patriots	AFC	46–10
XXI	1987	New York Giants	NFC	Denver Broncos	AFC	39–20
XXII	1988	Washington Redskins	NFC	Denver Broncos	AFC	42–10
XXIII	1989	San Francisco 49ers	NFC	Cincinnati Bengals	AFC	20–16
XXIV	1990	San Francisco 49ers	NFC	Denver Broncos	AFC	55–10
XXV	1991	New York Giants	NFC	Buffalo Bills	AFC	20–19
XXVI	1992	Washington Redskins	NFC	Buffalo Bills	AFC	37–24
XXVII	1993	Dallas Cowboys	NFC	Buffalo Bills	AFC	52–17
XXVIII	1994	Dallas Cowboys	NFC	Buffalo Bills	AFC	30–13
XXIX	1995	San Francisco 49ers	NFC	San Diego Chargers	AFC	49–26
XXX	1996	Dallas Cowboys	NFC	Pittsburgh Steelers	AFC	27–17
XXXI	1997	Green Bay Packers	NFC	New England Patriots	AFC	35–21
XXXII	1998	Denver Broncos	AFC	Green Bay Packers	NFC	31–24

GOLF

Golf is an outdoor game in which players hit a small hard ball with specially designed clubs that consist of a metal shaft and a wooden or metal club head. The object is to strike the ball with the club so that the ball goes into a cup that is sunk in the ground and marked with a flag. A standard golf course is divided into 18 holes, each with a tee, where the initial stroke is made; a grass fairway; and a green, a smooth grass surface where the cup is located. Each player attempts to reach the green and hit the ball into the cup using as few strokes as possible. Obstacles—such as water, tall grass called rough, or traps filled with sand—may be found near the green or fairway. As many as 14 different types of clubs may be used depending on the length of shot required or the terrain. The distance from tee to cup varies greatly, but generally the distance is from 100 to 600 yards. The length and difficulty of the hole determine the par, the number of strokes that a good golfer would need to put the ball into the cup. After 18 holes, the player with the lowest number of strokes is the winner of that round. Golf tournaments are typically won by the player with the best (lowest) cumulative score after four rounds.

THE MASTERS

Four major golf tournaments carry the most important titles in professional golf. They are the Masters, the Professional Golfer's Associatio0n (PGA) Tournament, the U.S. Open, and the British Open. The Masters, played at the Augusta National Golf Club in Augusta, Georgia, is the title most sought in professional golf. The winners of the Masters Tournament follow.

Year	Winner	Score	Year	Winner	Score
1934	Horton Smith	284	1967	Gay Brewer	280
1935	Gene Sarazen*	282	1968	Bob Goalby	277
1936	Horton Smith	285	1969	George Archer	281
1937	Byron Nelson	283	1970	Billy Casper*	279
1938	Henry Picard	285	1971	Charles Coody	279
1939	Ralph Guldahl	279	1972	Jack Nicklaus	286
1940	Jimmy Demaret	280	1973	Tommy Aaron	283
1941	Craig Wood	280	1974	Gary Player	278
1942	Byron Nelson*	280	1975	Jack Nicklaus	276
1943	No tournament held		1976	Ray Floyd	271
1944	No tournament held		1977	Tom Watson	276
1945	No tournament held		1978	Gary Player	277
1946	Herman Keiser	282	1979	Fuzzy Zoeller*	280
1947	Jimmy Demaret	281	1980	Severiano Ballesteros	275
1948	Claude Harmon	279	1981	Tom Watson	280
1949	Sam Snead	282	1982	Craig Stadler*	284
1950	Jimmy Demaret	283	1983	Severiano Ballesteros	280
1951	Ben Hogan	280	1984	Ben Crenshaw	277
1952	Sam Snead	286	1985	Bernhard Langer	282
1953	Ben Hogan	274	1986	Jack Nicklaus	279
1954	Sam Snead*	289	1987	Larry Mize*	285
1955	Cary Middlecoff	279	1988	Sandy Lyle	281
1956	Jack Burke	289	1989	Nick Faldo	283
1957	Doug Ford	283	1990	Nick Faldo	278
1958	Arnold Palmer	284	1991	Ian Woosnam	277
1959	Art Wall, Jr.	284	1992	Fred Couples	275
1960	Arnold Palmer	282	1993	Bernhard Langer	277
1961	Gary Player	280	1994	Jose Maria Olazabal	279
1962	Arnold Palmer*	280	1995	Ben Crenshaw	274
1963	Jack Nicklaus	286	1996	Nick Faldo	276
1964	Arnold Palmer	276	1997	Tiger Woods	270
1965	Jack Nicklaus	271	1998	Mark O'Meara	279
1966	Jack Nicklaus*	288			

*Won in a playoff.

HORSE RACING

Horses are raced either under saddle (by a jockey) or in harness (with a driver). Saddle racing occurs either on flat courses or involves jumping over artificial obstructions such as ditches, hedges, and walls (steeplechases) or framelike barriers (hurdles). In harness races, a horse trained as a trotter or pacer is driven from a small two-wheeled vehicle called a sulky.

Thoroughbred saddle racing, run on flat courses, involves purebred (pedigreed) horses bred especially for racing. Thoroughbred horses originated from a cross between Arabian stallions and English mares. Competitions differ according to distance, horse age, weight to be carried, and other considerations. In *sweepstakes,* owners pay a stake (fee) for their horses to be eligible. In *handicaps,* horses are given different weights, based on their past performance, to equalize their chances to win. Top weights are assigned to better horses; lesser weights are assigned to those horses considered inferior.

A horse's age is established by January 1st in the year in which it is born. Horses must be at least two years old to run in flats, three years old to run in steeplechases, and four years old to run in hurdles.

Flat races are run counterclockwise on oval tracks; thus the horses turn left. Distances are measured in furlongs (1 furlong = $\frac{1}{8}$ mile = 220 yards).

THE TRIPLE CROWN

The best-known horse races in the United States are the Kentucky Derby ($1\frac{1}{4}$ miles; at Churchill Downs in Louisville, KY), the Preakness Stakes ($1\frac{13}{16}$ miles; at Pimlico Race Course in Baltimore, MD), and the Belmont Stakes ($1\frac{1}{2}$ miles; at Belmont Park in Elmont, NY). These three races for three-year-olds make up horse racing's Triple Crown. Eleven horses have won all three events.

Year	Horse	Year	Horse
1919	Sir Barton	1946	Assault
1930	Gallant Fox	1948	Citation
1935	Omaha	1973	Secretariat
1937	War Admiral	1977	Seattle Slew
1941	Whirlaway	1978	Affirmed
1943	Count Fleet		

WINNING HORSES IN THE KENTUCKY DERBY

Year	Horse	Year	Horse	Year	Horse
1875	Aristides	1901	His Eminence	1927	Whiskery
1876	Vagrant	1902	Alan-a-Dale	1928	Reigh Count
1877	Baden Baden	1903	Judge Himes	1929	Clyde Van Dusen
1878	Day Star	1904	Elwood	1930	Gallant Fox
1879	Lord Murphy	1905	Agile	1931	Twenty Grand
1880	Fonso	1906	Sir Huon	1932	Burgoo King
1881	Hindoo	1907	Pink Star	1933	Brokers Tip
1882	Apollo	1908	Stone Street	1934	Cavalcade
1883	Leonatus	1909	Wintergreen	1935	Omaha
1884	Buchanan	1910	Donau	1936	Bold Venture
1885	Joe Cotton	1911	Meridian	1937	War Admiral
1886	Ben Ali	1912	Worth	1938	Lawrin
1887	Montrose	1913	Donerail	1939	Johnstown
1888	Macbeth II	1914	Old Rosebud	1940	Gallahadion
1889	Spokane	1915	Regret	1941	Whirlaway
1890	Riley	1916	George Smith	1942	Shut Out
1891	Kingman	1917	Omar Khayyam	1943	Count Fleet
1892	Azra	1918	Exterminator	1944	Pensive
1893	Lookout	1919	Sir Barton	1945	Hoop Jr.
1894	Chant	1920	Paul Jones	1946	Assault
1895	Halma	1921	Behave Yourself	1947	Jet Pilot
1896	Ben Brush	1922	Morvich	1948	Citation
1897	Typhoon II	1923	Zev	1949	Ponder
1898	Plaudit	1924	Black Gold	1950	Middleground
1899	Manuel	1925	Flying Ebony	1951	Count Turf
1900	Lieutenant Gibson	1926	Bubbling Over	1952	Hill Gail

continues

Winning Horses in the Kentucky Derby Continued

Year	Horse
1953	Dark Star
1954	Determine
1955	Swaps
1956	Needles
1957	Iron Liege
1958	Tim Tam
1959	Tomy Lee
1960	Venetian Way
1961	Carry Back
1962	Decidedly
1963	Chateaugay
1964	Northern Dancer
1965	Lucky Debonair
1966	Kauai King
1967	Proud Clarion
1968	Forward Pass*

Year	Horse
1969	Majestic Prince
1970	Dust Commander
1971	Canonero II
1972	Riva Ridge
1973	Secretariat
1974	Cannonade
1975	Foolish Pleasure
1976	Bold Forbes
1977	Seattle Slew
1978	Affirmed
1979	Spectacular Bid
1980	Genuine Risk
1981	Pleasant Colony
1982	Gato del Sol
1983	Sunny's Halo

Year	Horse
1984	Swale
1985	Spend a Buck
1986	Ferdinand
1987	Alysheba
1988	Winning Colors
1989	Sunday Silence
1990	Unbridled
1991	Strike the Gold
1992	Lil E. Tee
1993	Sea Hero
1994	Go for Gin
1995	Thunder Gulch
1996	Grindstone
1997	Silver Charm
1998	Real Quiet

*In 1968, Dancer's Image finished first but was disqualified.

ICE HOCKEY

Ice hockey is played on a rectangular rink that is surrounded by a wooden wall. At each end of the ice is placed a netted goal. Six skaters make up each team, including the goalie, whose job it is to protect the goal. By using wooden sticks, the players attempt to propel a rubber disc, called the puck, across the ice and into the opponents' goal. This scores a point.

The game begins with a faceoff in the center of the ice. The official drops the puck between two players, one from each team. Both teams try to gain control of the puck and to advance it toward the opponent's goal by skating with the puck, passing it to a teammate, or shooting it directly toward the goal. The defense tries to hinder this advance by deflecting or intercepting a pass or shot or by body-checking an opposing player. This is physically blocking an opponent with a hip or shoulder.

There is a wide range of penalties for which an offending player may be removed from the ice for a stated number of minutes. During this time, the penalized team plays with one fewer player than its opponents, giving a power play to the fully manned team. Penalty times range from two minutes for minor violations to ejection from the game for the most serious fouls. Holding on to the puck or to an opponent, checking from behind, tripping, using the stick illegally, and fighting all normally result in penalties. The offensive player in control of the puck must cross his own blue line before any of his teammates. In moving down the ice and attacking the opponent's end, if an attacking player without the puck crosses that line first, he is offside. This is a violation, leading to a resetting of the puck and a new faceoff.

There are only 2 days in the entire year without games played in one of the 4 major professional sports (football, hockey, basketball, and baseball)—the day before and the day after the Major League All-Star game.

Hockey is a rough sport and players wear hip pads, shoulder pads, padded gloves, and helmets. The game consists of three 20-minute periods with rest periods in between. The team with more goals at the end of that time wins the game.

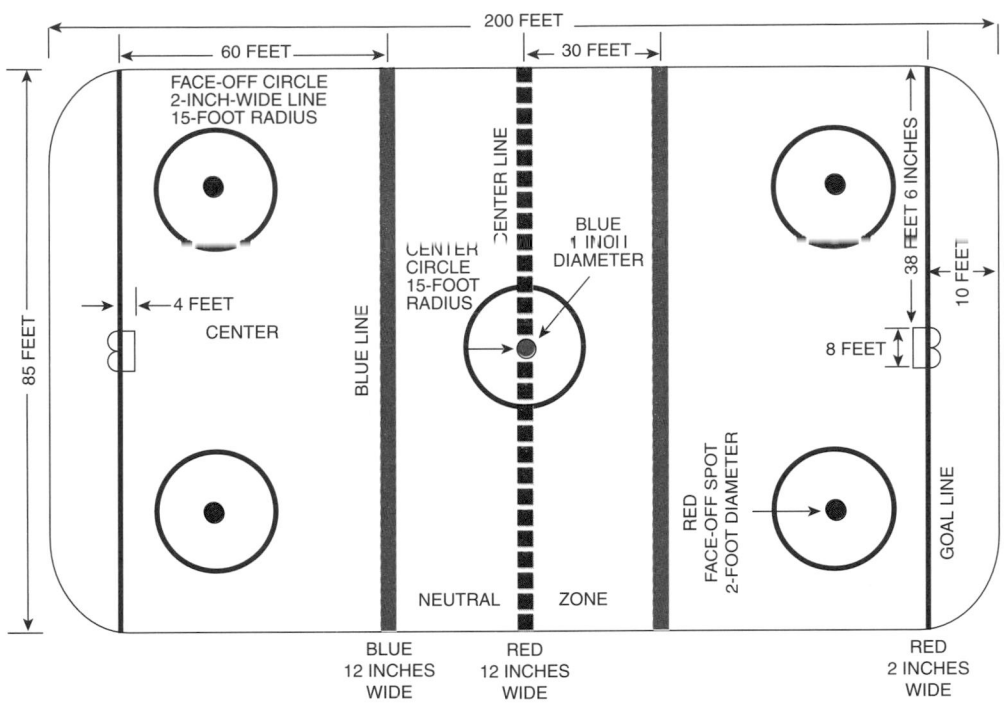

Ice Hockey Rink

NATIONAL HOCKEY LEAGUE (NHL) TEAMS

WESTERN CONFERENCE

Pacific Division	Central Division
Anaheim Mighty Ducks	Chicago Blackhawks
Calgary Flames	Dallas Stars
Colorado Avalanche	Detroit Red Wings
Edmonton Oilers	Phoenix Coyotes
Los Angeles Kings	St. Louis Blues
San Jose Sharks	Toronto Maple Leafs
Vancouver Canucks	

EASTERN CONFERENCE

Northeast Division	Atlantic Division
Boston Bruins	New Jersey Devils
Buffalo Sabres	New York Islanders
Carolina Hurricanes	New York Rangers
Montreal Canadiens	Philadelphia Flyers
Ottawa Senators	Florida Panthers
Pittsburgh Penguins	Tampa Bay Lightning
	Washington Capitals

THE STANLEY CUP

In 1893 the governor-general of Canada, Lord Stanley of Preston, presented a cup (then called the Dominion Challenge Trophy) to be awarded annually to the country amateur hockey champion. After two professional leagues, the National Hockey Association (NHA) and the Pacific Coast Hockey Association (PCHA), began a playoff in 1911, the winner was awarded the cup. In 1917 the NHA disbanded, and the NHL was formed. From 1923 to 1926 the West Coast Hockey League (WCHL) champion also participated in the Stanley Cup playoffs. After 1926 the Stanley Cup has been awarded exclusively to the NHL champion.

Under the present system each National Hockey League (NHL) team plays a regular-season schedule of 82 games. The eight teams in each conference with the highest point total (two points are awarded for each win, and one point for each tie) then meet in a series of playoffs to determine the conference champion. The Western Conference champion then meets with the Eastern Conference champion in the spring in a best-of-seven-games series for the NHL championship. The winners of the Stanley Cup follow.

THE STANLEY CUP WINNERS

Season	Winner	Loser	Games
1926–27	Ottawa Senators	Boston Bruins	2–0
1927–28	New York Rangers	Montreal Maroons	3–2
1928–29	Boston Bruins	New York Rangers	2–0
1929–30	Montreal Canadiens	Boston Bruins	2–0
1930–31	Montreal Canadiens	Chicago Black Hawks	3–2
1931–32	Toronto Maple Leafs	New York Rangers	3–0
1932–33	New York Rangers	Toronto Maple Leafs	3–1
1933–34	Chicago Black Hawks	Detroit Red Wings	3–1
1934–35	Montreal Maroons	Toronto Maple Leafs	3–0
1935–36	Detroit Red Wings	Toronto Maple Leafs	3–1
1936–37	Detroit Red Wings	New York Rangers	3–2
1937–38	Chicago Black Hawks	Toronto Maple Leafs	3–1
1938–39	Boston Bruins	Toronto Maple Leafs	4–1
1939–40	New York Rangers	Toronto Maple Leafs	4–2
1940–41	Boston Bruins	Detroit Red Wings	4–0
1941–42	Toronto Maple Leafs	Detroit Red Wings	4–3
1942–43	Detroit Red Wings	Boston Bruins	4–0
1943–44	Montreal Canadiens	Chicago Black Hawks	4–0
1944–45	Toronto Maple Leafs	Detroit Red Wings	4–3
1945–46	Montreal Canadiens	Boston Bruins	4–1
1946–47	Toronto Maple Leafs	Montreal Canadiens	4–2
1947–48	Toronto Maple Leafs	Detroit Red Wings	4–0
1948–49	Toronto Maple Leafs	Detroit Red Wings	4–0
1949–50	Detroit Red Wings	New York Rangers	4–3
1950–51	Toronto Maple Leafs	Montreal Canadiens	4–1
1951–52	Detroit Red Wings	Montreal Canadiens	4–0
1952–53	Montreal Canadiens	Boston Bruins	4–1
1953–54	Detroit Red Wings	Montreal Canadiens	4–3
1954–55	Detroit Red Wings	Montreal Canadiens	4–3
1955–56	Montreal Canadiens	Detroit Red Wings	4–1
1956–57	Montreal Canadiens	Boston Bruins	4–1
1957–58	Montreal Canadiens	Boston Bruins	4–2
1958–59	Montreal Canadiens	Toronto Maple Leafs	4–1
1959–60	Montreal Canadiens	Toronto Maple Leafs	4–0
1960–61	Chicago Black Hawks	Detroit Red Wings	4–2
1961–62	Toronto Maple Leafs	Chicago Black Hawks	4–2
1962–63	Toronto Maple Leafs	Detroit Red Wings	4–1
1963–64	Toronto Maple Leafs	Detroit Red Wings	4–3
1964–65	Montreal Canadiens	Chicago Black Hawks	4–3
1965–66	Montreal Canadiens	Detroit Red Wings	4–2
1966–67	Toronto Maple Leafs	Montreal Canadiens	4–2
1967–68	Montreal Canadiens	St. Louis Blues	4–0
1968–69	Montreal Canadiens	St. Louis Blues	4–0
1969–70	Boston Bruins	St. Louis Blues	4–0

Season	Winner	Loser	Games
1970–71	Montreal Canadiens	Chicago Black Hawks	4–3
1971–72	Boston Bruins	New York Rangers	4–2
1972–73	Montreal Canadiens	Chicago Black Hawks	4–2
1973–74	Philadelphia Flyers	Boston Bruins	4–2
1974–75	Philadelphia Flyers	Buffalo Sabres	4–2
1975–76	Montreal Canadiens	Philadelphia Flyers	4–0
1976–77	Montreal Canadiens	Boston Bruins	4–0
1977–78	Montreal Canadiens	Boston Bruins	4–2
1978–79	Montreal Canadiens	New York Rangers	4–1
1979–80	New York Islanders	Philadelphia Flyers	4–2
1980–81	New York Islanders	Minnesota North Stars	4–1
1981–82	New York Islanders	Vancouver Canucks	4–0
1982–83	New York Islanders	Edmonton Oilers	4–0
1983–84	Edmonton Oilers	New York Islanders	4–1
1984–85	Edmonton Oilers	Philadelphia Flyers	4–1
1985–86	Montreal Canadiens	Calgary Flames	4–1
1986–87	Edmonton Oilers	Philadelphia Flyers	4–3
1987–88	Edmonton Oilers	Boston Bruins	4–0
1988–89	Calgary Flames	Montreal Canadiens	4–2
1989–90	Edmonton Oilers	Boston Bruins	4–1
1990–91	Pittsburgh Penguins	Minnesota North Stars	4–2
1991–92	Pittsburgh Penguins	Chicago Black Hawks	4–0
1992–93	Montreal Canadiens	Los Angeles Kings	4–1
1993–94	New York Rangers	Vancouver Canucks	4–3
1994–95	New Jersey Devils	Detroit Red Wings	4–0
1995–96	Colorado Avalanche	Florida Panthers	4–0
1996–97	Detroit Red Wings	Philadelphia Flyers	4–0
1997–98	Detroit Red Wings	Washington Capitals	4–1

SOCCER

Soccer, often referred to as "football" outside the United States, is played by two opposing teams of 11 players each on a rectangular field. At either end of the field is a goal, constructed of a pair of upright 8-foot-high posts with a 24-foot-long crossbar. The object of the game is for one set of players to force the ball into the goal defended by the opposing team.

At the beginning of a game, the choice of field ends and the opportunity to kick off are decided by a coin toss. Once play has started, players may not touch the ball with their hands with two exceptions: Goalkeepers within their areas may touch the ball with their hands, and when the ball goes out of bounds by crossing the touch lines, it is thrown back by hand. The team in possession of the ball is the offensive team. By kicking the ball or using their heads, members of the offensive team try to move the ball down the field until one of its members is in a position to shoot the ball into the goal of the opposing team.

The defending team may gain possession of the ball by intercepting passes or by tackling opposing players. A tackle can be either a use of the feet or a charge against an opponent's shoulder. The penalty for a violent or dangerous tackle is a direct free kick at the ball by the opposing side.

When the ball goes out of play by passing over the goal line beyond the goalposts, it is restarted by the opposing team. The defending team kicks the ball back into play from within that half of the goal area nearest to where the ball crossed the line; the offensive team kicks it back from the corner circle at the

Sports/Games

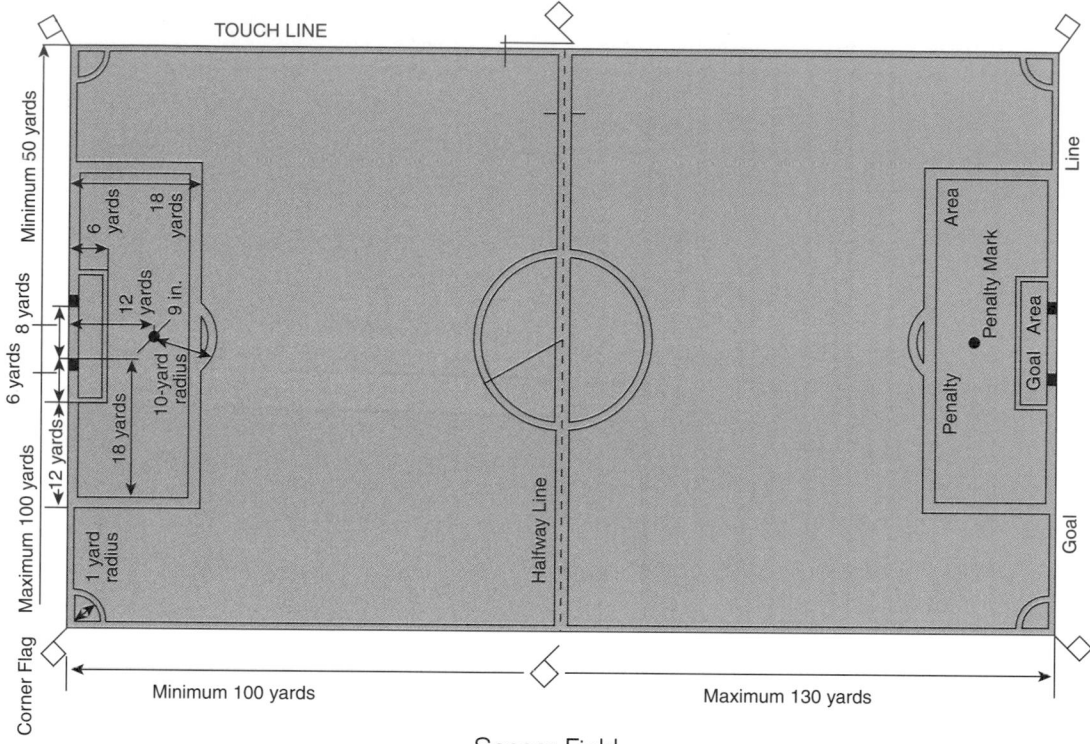

Soccer Field

nearest corner flag. As with free kicks, generally, the ball may not be touched again by the kicker until it has been touched by another player. A goal may be scored from a direct corner kick.

When a goal is scored, the game is restarted with a kickoff by the team conceding the goal. A match consists of two 45-minute periods. At the end of the match, the team scoring the greater number of goals is the winner. If no goals are scored, or an equal number of goals is scored by both teams, the game is considered a draw.

THE WORLD CUP

The World Cup championship, the contest for international soccer supremacy, is played every four years at different locations throughout the world. The results since 1930 are listed in the following table.

WORLD CUP WINNERS		
Year	Winner	Loser
1930	Uruguay	Argentina
1934	Italy	Czechoslovakia
1938	Italy	Hungary
1942	No competition	
1946	No competition	
1950	Uruguay	Brazil
1954	West Germany	Hungary
1958	Brazil	Sweden
1962	Brazil	Czechoslovakia
1966	England	West Germany
1970	Brazil	Italy
1974	West Germany	Netherlands
1978	Argentina	Netherlands
1982	Italy	West Germany
1986	Argentina	West Germany
1990	West Germany	Argentina
1994	Brazil	Italy
1998	France	Brazil

TENNIS

Tennis is played either indoors or outdoors on a rectangular court, which may be grass, clay, or synthetic. A small felt-covered rubber ball is hit back and forth over a net with wooden or metal rackets, which are fitted with strings made of lamb's gut, nylon, or synthetic material. The net, which is 3 feet above the court's surface at its midpoint, is stretched across the court. Tennis may be played either as singles, with one player on each side, or as doubles, with two players on each side. In doubles, the court is 9 feet wider than in singles, because of the addition of two doubles alleys.

To initiate play, the server stands behind the baseline and to the right of the center mark and hits the ball with the racket so that the ball lands in the diagonally opposite service court of the opponent. If this first serve does not land in this service area because it is hit too long or too wide, or hits the net, the server may try again with a second serve. If this second serve is not a legal serve, the receiver scores a point. At each point, the serve alternates left to right, with the server always serving from behind the baseline to the diagonally opposite service court. The receiver attempts to return a legal serve by hitting the ball anywhere into the opponent's court, which includes the alleys in doubles. Play continues until one player (or one team, in doubles) fails to make a legal return. A point is then scored by the opponent.

Four points, designated as 15, 30, 40, and game, constitute a game; a player must win each game by at least two points. Thus, if after six points in any game, each player has scored three, the score is 40–40 (this is called deuce). One player must then score two consecutive points to win the game; this player has the advantage after winning the first of these two points. Having the advantage, if the player wins the second consecutive point, he or she wins the game; but if the opponent wins that point, the score goes back to 40–40, or deuce. Play then continues until one player wins the game by scoring two consecutive points.

Each player (or team, in doubles) alternates by serving one game and receiving the next. The first to win six games wins a set, provided the margin of victory is two games or more. Thus, if the score reaches six games to four, the set is over, but at six to five, play continues. If the score reaches six to six, a tiebreaker is usually employed. A match consists of the best two out of three sets in women's play and usually the best three out of five in men's play.

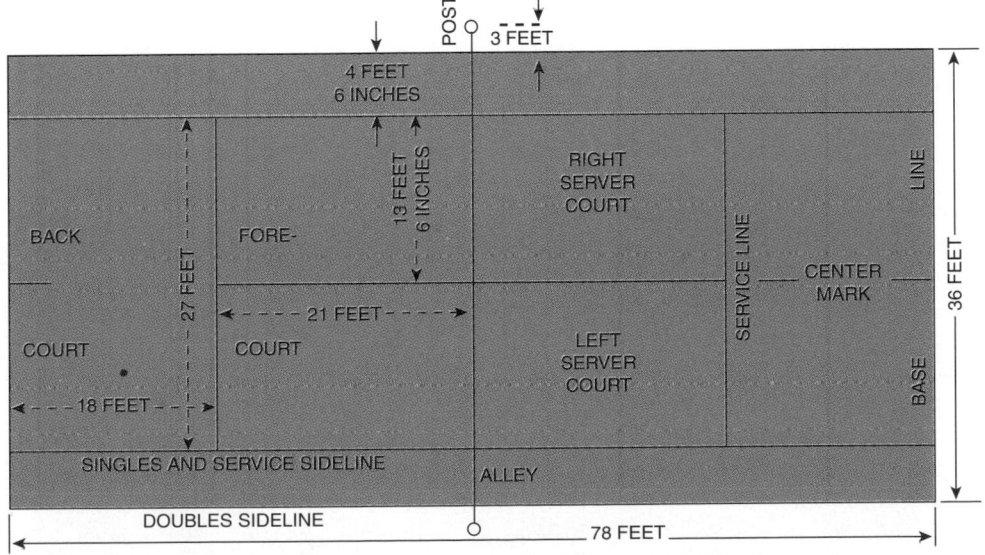

Tennis Court

WIMBLEDON

There are four major championships in professional tennis that make up the Grand Slam: the French Open; the Australian Open; the U.S. Open; and the All-England Lawn Tennis Championships, better known as Wimbledon. Wimbledon is the oldest and most prestigious tournament of the four. The winners since 1877 follow.

MEN'S SINGLES CHAMPIONS

1877	Spencer W. Gore	1918	No tournament held	1959	Alex Olmedo
1878	P. F. Hadow	1919	Gerald Patterson	1960	Neale Fraser
1879	J. T. Hartley	1920	Bill Tilden	1961	Rod Laver
1880	J. T. Hartley	1921	Bill Tilden	1962	Rod Laver
1881	William Renshaw	1922	Gerald Patterson	1963	Chuck McKinley
1882	William Renshaw	1923	William Johnston	1964	Roy Emerson
1883	William Renshaw	1924	Jean Borotra	1965	Roy Emerson
1884	William Renshaw	1925	Jean Rene Lacoste	1966	Manuel Santana
1885	William Renshaw	1926	Jean Borotra	1967	John Newcombe
1886	William Renshaw	1927	Henri Cochet	1968	Rod Laver
1887	Herbert Lawford	1928	Jean Rene Lacoste	1969	Rod Laver
1888	Ernest Renshaw	1929	Henri Cochet	1970	John Newcombe
1889	William Renshaw	1930	Bill Tilden	1971	John Newcombe
1890	Willoughby Hamilton	1931	Sidney Wood	1972	Stan Smith
1891	Wilfred Baddeley	1932	Ellsworth Vines	1973	Jan Kodes
1892	Wilfred Baddeley	1933	Jack Crawford	1974	Jimmy Connors
1893	Joshua Pim	1934	Fred Perry	1975	Arthur Ashe
1894	Joshua Pim	1935	Fred Perry	1976	Bjorn Borg
1895	Wilfred Baddeley	1936	Fred Perry	1977	Bjorn Borg
1896	Harold Mahoney	1937	Donald Budge	1978	Bjorn Borg
1897	Reginald Doherty	1938	Donald Budge	1979	Bjorn Borg
1898	Reginald Doherty	1939	Bobby Riggs	1980	Bjorn Borg
1899	Reginald Doherty	1940	No tournament held	1981	John McEnroe
1900	Reginald Doherty	1941	No tournament held	1982	Jimmy Connors
1901	Arthur Gore	1942	No tournament held	1983	John McEnroe
1902	H. Laurence Doherty	1943	No tournament held	1984	John McEnroe
1903	H. Laurence Doherty	1944	No tournament held	1985	Boris Becker
1904	H. Laurence Doherty	1945	No tournament held	1986	Boris Becker
1905	H. Laurence Doherty	1946	Yvon Petra	1987	Pat Cash
1906	H. Laurence Doherty	1947	Jack Kramer	1988	Stefan Edberg
1907	Norman Brookes	1948	Bob Falkenburg	1989	Boris Becker
1908	Arthur Gore	1949	Ted Schroeder	1990	Stefan Edberg
1909	Arthur Gore	1950	Budge Patty	1991	Michael Stich
1910	Anthony F. Wilding	1951	Dick Savitt	1992	Andre Agassi
1911	Anthony F. Wilding	1952	Frank Sedgman	1993	Pete Sampras
1912	Anthony F. Wilding	1953	Vic Seixas	1994	Pete Sampras
1913	Anthony F. Wilding	1954	Jaroslav Drobny	1995	Pete Sampras
1914	Norman Brookes	1955	Tony Trabert	1996	Richard Krajicek
1915	No tournament held	1956	Lew Hoad	1997	Pete Sampras
1916	No tournament held	1957	Lew Hoad	1998	Pete Sampras
1917	No tournament held	1958	Ashley Cooper		

WOMEN'S SINGLES CHAMPIONS

1884	Maud Watson	1920	Suzanne Lenglen	1960	Maria Bueno
1885	Maud Watson	1921	Suzanne Lenglen	1961	Angela Mortimer
1886	Blanche Bingley	1922	Suzanne Lenglen	1962	Karen Susman
1887	Lottie Dod	1923	Suzanne Lenglen	1963	Margaret Smith
1888	Lottie Dod	1924	Kitty McKane	1964	Maria Bueno
1889	Blanche Bingley Hillyard	1925	Suzanne Lenglen	1965	Margaret Smith
1890	L. Rice	1926	Kitty McKane Godfree	1966	Billie Jean King
1891	Lottie Dod	1927	Helen Wills	1967	Billie Jean King
1892	Lottie Dod	1928	Helen Wills	1968	Billie Jean King
1893	Lottie Dod	1929	Helen Wills	1969	Ann Jones
1894	Blanche Bingley Hillyard	1930	Helen Wills Moody	1970	Margaret Smith Court
1895	Charlotte Cooper	1931	Cilly Aussem	1971	Evonne Goolagong
1896	Charlotte Cooper	1932	Helen Wills Moody	1972	Billie Jean King
1897	Blanche Bingley Hillyard	1933	Helen Wills Moody	1973	Billie Jean King
1898	Charlotte Cooper	1934	Dorothy Round	1974	Chris Evert
1899	Blanche Bingley Hillyard	1935	Helen Wills Moody	1975	Billie Jean King
1900	Blanche Bingley Hillyard	1936	Helen Jacobs	1976	Chris Evert
1901	Charlotte Cooper Sterry	1937	Dorothy Round	1977	Virginia Wade
1902	Muriel Robb	1938	Helen Wills Moody	1978	Martina Navratilova
1903	Dorothea Douglass	1939	Alice Marble	1979	Martina Navratilova
1904	Dorothea Douglass	1940	No tournament held	1980	Evonne Goolagong
1905	May Sutton	1941	No tournament held	1981	Chris Evert Lloyd
1906	Dorothea Douglass	1942	No tournament held	1982	Martina Navratilova
1907	May Sutton	1943	No tournament held	1983	Martina Navratilova
1908	Charlotte Cooper Sterry	1944	No tournament held	1984	Martina Navratilova
1909	Dora Boothby	1945	No tournament held	1985	Martina Navratilova
1910	Dorothea Douglass Chambers	1946	Pauline Betz	1986	Martina Navratilova
1911	Dorothea Douglass Chambers	1947	Margaret Osborne	1987	Martina Navratilova
1912	Ethel Larcombe	1948	A. Louise Brough	1988	Steffi Graf
1913	Dorothea Douglass Chambers	1949	A. Louise Brough	1989	Steffi Graf
1914	Dorothea Douglass Chambers	1950	A. Louise Brough	1990	Martina Navratilova
1915	No tournament held	1951	Doris Hart	1991	Steffi Graf
1916	No tournament held	1952	Maureen Connolly	1992	Steffi Graf
1917	No tournament held	1953	Maureen Connolly	1993	Steffi Graf
1918	No tournament held	1954	Maureen Connolly	1994	Conchita Martinez
1919	Suzanne Lenglen	1955	A. Louise Brough	1995	Steffi Graf
		1956	Shirley Fry	1996	Steffi Graf
		1957	Althea Gibson	1997	Martina Hingis
		1958	Althea Gibson	1998	Jana Novotna
		1959	Maria Bueno		

VOLLEYBALL

Volleyball is played either outdoors or indoors on a rectangular court, with six players to a side. An inflated ball is hit back and forth over a net; the players try to prevent the ball from hitting the court on their own side. The net's top is 8 feet above the floor ($7^1/_2$ feet in women's play). To initiate play, a player serves the ball by hitting it with the hand or fist and thereby sending it over the net toward the opponent's court. After the serve, the ball may be hit with any part of the body. The ball may be hit a maximum of three times by each team, the final hit sending the ball over the net. Catching or holding the ball is not permitted.

If the receiving team allows the ball to hit the floor on its side, or hits the ball out of bounds, the serving team scores a point and serves again. If the serving team allows the ball to hit the floor, hits it out of bounds, or fails to make a legal serve, the serve is transferred to the opponents, but no point is scored. The first team to reach 15 points wins the game, provided the margin of victory is at least two points. In championship play, a match is won by winning three out of five games.

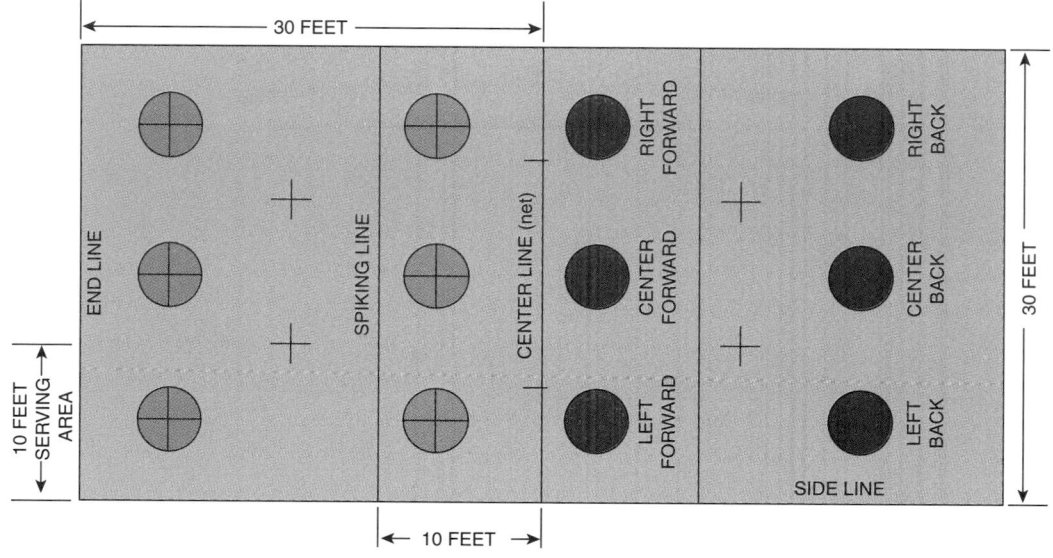

Volleyball Court

OLYMPIC GAMES

The modern Olympic Games began in Athens in 1896, to promote greater international understanding through athletics. The games originated in ancient Greece sometime prior to 776 B.C., but were discontinued after 392 A.D. The Olympic Games competition is held every four years at different locations throughout the world. Since 1994 winter and summer games have been played in alternating four-year cycles. Winter games occurred in 1994, 1998, and so on; summer games occurred in 1996, 2000, and so on.

LOCATIONS

SUMMER GAMES

1896	Athens, Greece	1932	Los Angeles, California
1900	Paris, France	1936	Berlin, Germany
1904	St. Louis, Missouri	1940	No games held
1908	London, England	1944	No games held
1912	Stockholm, Sweden	1948	London, England
1920	Antwerp, Belgium	1952	Helsinki, Finland
1924	Paris, France	1956	Melbourne, Australia
1928	Amsterdam, The Netherlands	1960	Rome, Italy

1964	Tokyo, Japan	1984	Los Angeles, California
1968	Mexico City, Mexico	1988	Seoul, South Korea
1972	Munich, West Germany	1992	Barcelona, Spain
1976	Montreal, Canada	1996	Atlanta, Georgia
1980	Moscow, USSR	2000	Sydney, Australia

WINTER GAMES

1924	Chamonix, France	1964	Innsbruck, Austria
1928	St. Moritz, Switzerland	1968	Grenoble, France
1932	Lake Placid, New York	1972	Sapporo, Japan
1936	Garmisch-Partenkirchen, Germany	1976	Innsbruck, Austria
1940	No games held	1980	Lake Placid, New York
1944	No games held	1984	Sarajevo, Yugoslavia
1948	St. Moritz, Switzerland	1988	Calgary, Canada
1952	Oslo, Norway	1992	Albertville, France
1956	Cortina, Italy	1994	Lillehammer, Norway
1960	Squaw Valley, California	1998	Nagano, Japan
		2002	Salt Lake City, Utah

1996 SUMMER OLYMPIC EVENTS

Men and Women		Men	Women
Archery	Gymnastics	Baseball (team)	Rhythmic gymnastics
Badminton	Handball (team)	Boxing	Softball (team)
Basketball (team)	Judo	Modern pentathlon	Synchronized swimming (team)
Beach volleyball	Rowing	Water polo (team)	
Canoeing/Kayaking	Shooting	Weight lifting	
Cycling	Soccer (team)	Wrestling—Freestyle	
Diving	Table tennis	Wrestling—Greco-Roman	
Equestrian*	Tennis		
Fencing	Volleyball		
Field hockey (team)	Yachting		

Men's Swimming	Women's Swimming
50m, 100m, 200m, 400m, 1,500m freestyle	50 m, 100m, 200m, 400m, 800m freestyle
100m, 200m backstroke	100m, 200m backstroke
100m, 200m breaststroke	100m, 200m breaststroke
100m, 200m butterfly	100m, 200m butterfly
200m, 400m individual medley	200m, 400m individual medley
400m, 800m freestyle relay	400m, 800m freestyle relay
400m medley relay	400m medley relay

continues

Continued

Men's Track and Field	Women's Track and Field
100m, 200m, 400m dash	100m, 200m, 400m dash
800m, 1,500m, 5,000m, 10,000m run	800m, 1,500m, 5,000m, 10,000m run
110m, 400m hurdles	100m, 400m hurdles
400m relay (4 × 100)	400m relay (4 × 100)
1,600m relay (4 × 400)	1,600m relay (4 × 400)
3,000m steeplechase	10km walk
20km, 50km walk	Marathon
Marathon	High jump
High jump	Long jump
Long jump	Triple jump
Triple jump	Discus
Discus	Javelin
Hammer throw	Pole vault
Javelin	Shot put
Pole vault	Heptathlon
Shot put	
Decathlon	

* In equestrian events, men and women competed against one another; in shooting, they competed separately, as well as against one another.

1998 WINTER OLYMPIC GAMES

Except for bobsledding, all winter sports at the 1998 Olympic games were divided into two classes, one for men and the other for women. Only men competed in bobsledding events. In pairs figure skating and ice dancing, men and women performed together.

Alpine skiing	Downhill
	Slalom
	Giant slalom
	Super giant slalom
	Combined
Biathlon	*Men:* 20km individual, 10km sprint, 30km relay (4 × 7.5)
	Women: 15km individual, 7.5km sprint, 30km relay (4 × 7.5)
Bobsledding	4-man
	2-man
Cross-country skiing	*Men:* 10km and 30km classical, 15km free with pursuit start, 50m free, 40km relay (4 × 10)
	Women: 5km and 15km classical, 10km free with pursuit start, 30km free, 20km relay (4 × 5)
Curling	
Figure skating	Men's singles
	Women's singles
	Pairs
	Ice dancing

Freestyle skiing	Moguls
	Aerials
Ice hockey (team)	
Luge	
Nordic combined	Individual
	Team
Ski jumping	90m, 120m (individual)
	90m (team)
Snowboarding	Giant slalom
	Halfpipe
Short track speed skating	*Men:* 500m, 1,000m, 5,000m relay
	Women: 500m, 1,000m, 3,000m relay
Speed Skating	*Men:* 500m, 1,000m, 1,500m, 5,000m, 10,000m
	Women: 500m, 1,000m, 1,500m, 3,000m, 5,000m

Sports/Games

MAJOR SPORTS FIGURES

The following list of leading sports personalities is not meant to be comprehensive. The athletes selected have made notable contributions to their respective sports or the world of sports at large. Many are popular contemporary figures whose current accomplishments only hint at their long-term potential, or who have achieved a measure of notoriety through their individual style. Every effort has been made to include American and international athletes, men and women, and figures from as wide a variety of sports as possible.

Each figure is an American unless otherwise noted. All are listed by the name under which they are best known; bracketed names indicate that the athlete began his or her career under that name. If an individual was or is involved in a team sport, the team or teams with which that person is most closely associated are included as well.

Aaron, Henry (Hank) (1934–). Baseball player (outfielder); Milwaukee-Atlanta Braves, Milwaukee Brewers. He holds numerous major league records, including career home runs (755) and runs batted in (2,297).

Abdul-Jabbar, Kareem [Lew Alcindor] (1947–). Basketball player (center); Milwaukee Bucks, Los Angeles Lakers. The NBA's all-time leading scorer (38,387 points), he won most valuable player honors six times.

Ali, Muhammed [Cassius Clay] (1942–). Boxer, noted for his wit. Ali won the heavyweight championship three times. During the Vietnam War, he refused induction into the military and was suspended and stripped of his title.

Ashe, Arthur (1943–93). Tennis player. He won the U.S. Open (1968) and Wimbledon (1975) singles championships. After contracting AIDS, he became a leading spokesperson in the fight against that disease.

Bannister, Roger (1929–). British middle-distance runner. He was the first person to run a mile in under 4 minutes (May 6, 1954).

Becker, Boris (1967–). German tennis player. At 17, he became the youngest male ever to win the Wimbledon singles championship (1985). He has also won the U.S. Open (1989) and two other Wimbledon titles.

Biondi, Matt (1965–). Swimmer. He won seven medals, including five gold, at the 1988 Olympics. His career total of 11 medals in Olympic competition tied him with Mark Spitz for the most medals won by an American.

Blair, Bonnie (1964–). Speed skater. She won gold medals in three consecutive Olympics (1988, 1992, 1994) and was the recipient of the 1992 Sullivan Award.

The University of Alabama football team was originally called the Red Elephants. After they won the 1920 Rose Bowl, a sportswriter said, "they washed over their opponents like a crimson tide." The team has been known as the Crimson Tide ever since.

Bird, Larry (1956–). Basketball player (forward); Boston Celtics. A three-time NBA most valuable player (1984–86), he is credited (with Magic Johnson) for the sharp increase in the sport's popularity in the mid-1980s.

Borg, Bjorn (1956–). Swedish tennis player. A five-time Wimbledon singles champion, he led Sweden to its first Davis Cup title (1975). He was noted for his strong base-line play and dazzling shots.

Brown, Jim (1936–). Football player (fullback); Cleveland Browns. During his career, he gained 12,312 yards and was named the NFL's most valuable player three times. He retired after the 1965 season to become an actor.

Bryant, Paul ("Bear") (1913–83). College football coach; various universities. He led Alabama to 25 winning seasons and 6 national championships.

His career total of 323 victories is second on the all-time list.

Bubka, Sergei (1963–   ). Ukrainian pole vaulter. The first to clear the 20-foot barrier (both indoors and outdoors), he holds the world record in this event. He won a gold medal at the 1988 Olympics.

Butkus, Dick (1942–   ). Football player (linebacker); Chicago Bears. An eight-time NFL Pro Bowl selection, he was noted for his aggressive, relentless style of play and bruising tackles.

Button, Dick (1929–   ). Figure skater. Twice an Olympic gold medalist (1948, 1952), he won the world championship five consecutive years (1948–52). He later became famous for his commentary during televised skating events.

Chamberlain, Wilt (1936–   ). Basketball player (center); Philadelphia–San Francisco Warriors, Philadelphia 76ers, Los Angeles Lakers. He led the NBA in scoring seven times, setting a single-game record with 100 points (1962).

Cobb, Ty (1886–1961). Baseball player (outfielder); Detroit Tigers. Cobb won 12 batting titles during his 24-year career, and his lifetime batting average of .367 is the highest in major league history.

Comaneci, Nadia (1961–   ). Romanian gymnast. She achieved seven perfect scores while winning gold medals in the all-around, balance-beam, and uneven-bar competitions at the 1976 Olympics.

Connors, Jimmy (1952–   ). Tennis player. Noted for his on-court tantrums and powerful service, he is the all-time leader among men, with 109 tournament titles, including five U.S. Open and two Wimbledon championships.

Corbett, James J. ("Gentleman Jim") (1866–1933). Boxer. Considered to have been the first "scientific" fighter, Corbett was heavyweight champion from 1892 to 1897. His 1891 bout with Peter Jackson went 61 rounds, ending in a draw.

Devers, Gail (1966–   ). Sprinter. She overcame Graves' disease to win two Olympic gold medals in the 100-meter dash (1992, 1996).

DiMaggio, Joe (1914–   ). Baseball player (outfielder); New York Yankees. He hit safely in a major league record 56 consecutive games (1941). Known as the "Yankee Clipper" for his graceful style, he won the American League most valuable player award three times.

Ederle, Gertrude (1906–   ). Swimmer. In 1926, she became the first woman to swim the English Channel, breaking the existing men's record for the crossing.

Evans, Janet (1971–   ). Swimmer. She won three gold medals at the 1988 Olympics and added another gold and a silver at the 1992 Games.

Evert, Chris (1954–   ). Tennis player. Second among women in all-time tournament victories with 157, she captured six U.S. Open championships and three Wimbledon titles. She was noted for her cool, unflappable on-court demeanor.

Faldo, Nick (1957–   ). British golfer. Winner of the Masters tournament in 1989, 1990, and 1996, he also won three British Open titles (1987, 1990, 1992) and led the European team to victory in the 1995 Ryder Cup.

Fleming, Peggy (1948–   ). Figure skater. She was U.S. champion for five consecutive years (1964–68) and also captured three straight world titles (1966–68). After winning a gold medal in the 1968 Winter Olympics, she starred with the Ice Follies and Holiday on Ice.

Foreman, George (1948–   ). Boxer. He twice held a heavyweight title (1973–74, 1994–95). At 45, he was the oldest fighter ever to win a championship bout.

Fosbury, Dick (1947–   ). High jumper. A gold medalist in the 1968 Olympics, he invented the technique known as the "Fosbury flop."

Foyt, A. J. (1935–   ). Race car driver. A four-time winner of the Indianapolis 500, he also captured seven U.S. Auto Club championships. His 67 lifetime victories in Indy car racing are a record.

Gehrig, Lou (1903–41). Baseball player (first baseman); New York Yankees. He set the major league record for consecutive games played (2,130; broken, 1995) and career grand-slam home runs (23), and he still holds the American League single-season record for runs batted in (184; set 1931). His career was prematurely ended by amyotrophic lateral sclerosis (ALS), now widely known as Lou Gehrig's disease.

Gibson, Althea (1927–). Tennis player. She won both the U.S. Open and Wimbledon singles championships in consecutive years (1957–58). She was the first African American to compete in either event and the first to be named Associated Press female athlete of the year.

Girardelli, Marc (1963–). Luxembourg skier. He won an unprecedented fifth overall World Cup Alpine championship in 1993. Despite this accomplishment, he never took the gold medal in an Olympic Alpine race.

Graf, Steffi (1969–). German tennis player. In 1988, at the age of 19, she won the coveted Grand Slam of tennis (Australian, French, U.S. Open, Wimbledon). She has captured five U.S. Open and seven Wimbledon championships.

Gretzky, Wayne (1961–). Canadian hockey player (center); Edmonton Oilers, other teams. The leading scorer in NHL history, he received the Hart Trophy as the league's most valuable player nine times (1980–87, 1989). His smooth, dominant ice style earned him the nickname "The Great One."

Griffey, Ken, Jr. (1969–). Baseball player (outfielder); Seattle Mariners. Noted for his charismatic personality and acrobatic fielding, Griffey twice led the American League in home runs (1994, 1997).

Halas, George ("Papa Bear") (1895–1983). Football executive and coach. He founded the Chicago Bears in 1920 and led the team to five

NFL championships during his 40 years as its head coach. His 324 career victories are second on the all-time list.

Hamilton, Scott (1958–). Figure skater. He reigned as U.S. and world champion four consecutive years (1981–84) and won an Olympic gold medal in 1984.

Heiden, Eric (1958–). Speed skater. He won all five gold medals in men's events at the 1980 Olympics and was world champion three consecutive years (1977–79). He was the 1980 Sullivan Award winner.

Henderson, Rickey (1958–). Baseball player (outfielder); Oakland A's, New York Yankees, other teams. He holds the major league single-season record for stolen bases (130), set in 1982, and is the all-time career stolen-base leader (still active).

Henie, Sonja (1912–69). Norwegian figure skater. She won 10 consecutive world championships (1927–36) and earned 3 Olympic gold medals (1928, 1932, 1936). Henie transformed the sport by introducing ballet movements into her routines.

Hogan, Ben (1912–97). Golfer. He won four U.S. Open titles and captured both the PGA and the Masters championships twice. He survived serious injuries sustained in a 1949 car crash and returned to win the 1950 U.S. Open.

Jackson, Reggie (1946–). Baseball player (outfielder); Oakland A's, New York Yankees, other teams. Noted for his flamboyant style, he led the American League in home runs four times, and hit five round-trippers (including three in the final game) in the 1977 World Series. His many World Series heroics earned him the nickname "Mr. October."

Johnson, Earvin ("Magic") (1959–). Basketball player (guard); Los Angeles Lakers. With Larry Bird, he helped bring the sport to a new level of popularity in the mid-1980s. He won NBA most valuable player honors three times and ranks second in career assists. He retired after announcing that he had contracted the HIV virus but returned to lead the "Dream Team" to a gold medal in the 1992 Olympics.

Johnson, Randy (1963–). Baseball player (pitcher); Seattle Mariners. He led the American League in strikeouts four consecutive seasons (1992–95). At 6'10", his imposing mound presence has earned him the nickname "Big Unit."

Jordan, Michael (1963–). Basketball player (guard); Chicago Bulls. A nine-time NBA leading scorer (1987–93, 1996–97) and four-time winner of the league's most-valuable-player award, Jordan has led the Bulls to five championships in seven seasons (1991–93, 1996–97). He is regarded by many as the greatest player in the history of the game for his dazzling moves and clutch performances.

Joyner-Kersee, Jackie (1962–). Track and field performer. Twice an Olympic gold-medal winner in the heptathlon (1988, 1992), she is widely considered to be one of world's greatest female athletes.

Killy, Jean Claude (1943–). French skier. He won three gold medals in Alpine events (downhill, slalom, giant slalom) in the 1968 Olympics and twice took the World Cup overall championship (1967, 1968).

King, Billie Jean (1943–). Tennis player. King won the U.S. Open singles championship 4 times and captured 6 Wimbledon titles. Her 39 Grand Slam titles (including doubles and mixed-doubles play) is third on the all-time list. In 1973 she defeated Bobby Riggs in the "Battle of the Sexes" tennis exhibition.

Laver, Rod (1938–). Australian tennis player. He twice won tennis's Grand Slam (1962, 1969) and earned four Wimbledon titles (1961–62, 1968–69).

Lemieux, Mario (1965–). Canadian hockey player; Pittsburgh Penguins. He led the NHL in scoring five times (1988–89, 1992–93, 1996) and

earned the league's most valuable player award three times (1988, 1993, 1996). Despite recuperating from Hodgkin's disease, he was the NHL's scoring champ in 1993.

Leonard, Sugar Ray (1956–). Boxer. He held titles in five different weight classes (welterweight, junior middleweight, middleweight, light heavyweight, super middleweight) over his 14-year career.

Lewis, Carl (1961–). Track and field performer. He won nine gold medals in running events (4 x 100m relay; 100m and 200m dashes) and the long jump in the 1988 and 1992 Olympics.

Lombardi, Vince (1913–70). Football coach; Green Bay Packers, Washington Redskins. He led the Packers to five NFL championships and victories in Super Bowls I and II. The trophy awarded to the Super Bowl champion is named in his honor.

Louganis, Greg (1960–). Diver. He twice won Olympic gold medals in springboard and platform diving (1984, 1988). He remained competitive despite having contracted the HIV virus.

Louis, Joe (1914–81). Boxer. Nicknamed the "Brown Bomber," he held the world heavyweight championship from 1937 to 1949.

Mantle, Mickey (1931–95). Baseball player (outfielder); New York Yankees. He won the American League triple crown in 1956 and hit a record 18 World Series home runs. He was named the AL's most-valuable-player three times.

Marciano, Rocky (1923–69). Boxer. The world heavyweight champion from 1952 to 1956, he retired undefeated with 49 victories (43 by knockouts).

Marino, Dan (1961–). Football player (quarterback); Miami Dolphins. Among the NFL's all-time leading quarterbacks, he is third in passing efficiency and first in both touchdown passes and passing yardage. He is considered one of the greatest passers in league history, despite never having won a Super Bowl.

Maris, Roger (1934–85). Baseball player (outfielder); New York Yankees, St. Louis Cardinals, other teams. In 1961, he set a major league record for homers in a season with 61. Maris was twice named the AL's most valuable player (1960, 1961).

Mays, Willie (1931–). Baseball player (outfielder); New York San Francisco Giants, New York Mets. Third on the all-time career home-run list (660), his enthusiastic play and effervescent personality led to his nickname "Say Hey Kid."

McEnroe, John (1959–). Tennis player. Third on the all-time tournament victory list with 77, he won four U.S. Open singles championships (1979–81, 1984) and three Wimbledon singles titles (1981, 1983–84). He was noted for his short temper on court.

Messier, Mark (1961–). Canadian hockey player (center); Edmonton Oilers, New York Rangers. Twice chosen the NHL's most valuable player (1990, 1992), he led the Rangers to the team's first Stanley Cup championship in 54 years (1994).

Montana, Joe (1956–). Football player (quarterback); San Francisco 49ers, Kansas City Chiefs. Montana ranks in the top five in career passing percentage, yardage, completions, and touchdowns. He is the only player to win the Super Bowl MVP award three times (1982, 1985, 1990).

Morceli, Noureddine (1970–). Algerian middle-distance runner. He holds world records in four events (1,500 meter, mile, 2,000 meter, and 3,000 meter).

Moser-Proll, Annemarie (1953–). Austrian skier. She won six World Cup Alpine overall championships (1971–75, 1979) and took the gold medal in the women's downhill at the 1980 Olympics.

Namath, Joe (1943–). Football player (quarterback); New York Jets. He led the Jets to victory over the heavily favored Baltimore Colts in Super Bowl III after guaranteeing a win, putting the upstart AFL on an equal footing with the older, established NFL. His flamboyant off-field personality led to his nickname "Broadway Joe."

Navratilova, Martina (1956–). Tennis player (born Czechoslovakia). She won nine Wimbledon championships and four U.S. Open titles (1983–84, 1986, 87) on her way to 56 career Grand Slam titles (singles and doubles) and a record 161 victories in all.

Nicklaus, Jack ("Golden Bear") (1940–). Golfer. The leading money winner on the PGA tour eight times, he captured six Masters tournaments among his 70 career wins, second on the all-time list.

Nurmi, Paavo (1897–1973). Finnish distance runner. He won six Olympic gold medals (1920, 1924, 1928) and broke numerous world records in the 1,500m, 5,000m, and cross-country events.

Owens, Jesse (1913–80). Track and field competitor. He broke four world records in one afternoon of competition (May 25, 1935) and won four gold medals in the 1936 Olympics.

Palmer, Arnold (1929–). Golfer. In 1968 he became the first to earn $1 million on the PGA tour. He captured four Masters (1958, 1960, 1962, 1964) and two British Opens (1961–62) on his way to over 70 career tournament wins.

Payton, Walter (1954–). Football player (running back); Chicago Bears. The NFL's career rushing leader (16,726 yards), he led the league five consecutive seasons (1976–80).

Pelé [Edson Arantes do Nascimento] (1940–). Brazilian soccer player. He scored 1,281 goals during his 22-year career, and led Brazil to three World Cup championships (1958, 1962, 1970). His speed and acrobatic skills earned him an international following.

Petty, Richard (1937–). Race car driver. The winner of seven NASCAR national championships, Petty achieved seven Daytona 500 victories and a record 200 career wins.

Plante, Jacques (1929–86). Canadian hockey player (goalie); Montreal Canadiens. He won the Vezina Trophy (awarded to the NHL's top goalie) seven times. He was the first goalie to wear a protective mask in a game (1959).

Rice, Jerry (1962–   ). Football player (receiver); San Francisco 49ers. He holds NFL records for career touchdowns (156) and receptions (942). Rice was the most valuable player in Super Bowl XXIII (1989).

Richard, Maurice ("Rocket") (1921–   ). Canadian hockey player (right wing); Montreal Canadiens. He scored 544 regular-season and 82 playoff goals and starred on eight Stanley Cup champions.

Rickey, Branch (1881–1965). Baseball executive; St. Louis Cardinals, Brooklyn Dodgers, Pittsburgh Pirates. Known for his innovative ideas, he signed Jackie Robinson to a major league contract with the Dodgers, thus breaking baseball's so-called color barrier (1947). He also established the sport's first farm system (Cardinals, 1919).

Ripken, Cal, Jr. (1960–   ). Baseball player (infielder); Baltimore Orioles. Twice the American League's most valuable player (1983, 1991), he broke Lou Gehrig's record for consecutive games played in 1995.

Robinson, Jackie (1919–72). Baseball player (infielder); Brooklyn Dodgers. The first African American to play in the major leagues (1947), he was selected the National League's most valuable player in 1949.

Rockne, Knute (1888–1931). Football coach; Notre Dame (college). Rockne helped to modernize the game by introducing the platoon system and stressing the forward pass. He built Notre Dame into a perennial college-football powerhouse.

Rodman, Dennis (1961–   ). Basketball player (forward); various teams. Noted for his eccentric personal style and aggressive play, he led the NBA in rebounding six consecutive seasons (1991–96).

Ruth, Babe [George Herman] (1895–1948). Baseball player (outfielder, pitcher); Boston Red Sox, New York Yankees. Ruth set major league records for home runs in a season (60, in 1927) and career (714); both were later eclipsed.

Ryan, Nolan (1947–   ). Baseball player (pitcher); various teams. He holds numerous major league records, including strikeouts in a season (383, in 1973), career strikeouts (5,714), and career no-hit games (7).

Rudolph, Wilma (1940–94). Sprinter. She took three gold medals in the 1960 Olympics (100m and 200m dashes, 4 x 10m relay). She was the Sullivan Award winner in 1961.

Sampras, Pete (1971–   ). Tennis player. He won the U.S. Open four times and captured three Wimbledon titles. Through the 1997 season, he was the top-ranked male player in the world.

Seles, Monica (1973–   ). Tennis player. Twice the U.S. Open champion (1991, 1992), her career was sidetracked after she was attacked by a knife-wielding fan during a match in Germany (1993).

Shoemaker, Willie (1931–   ). Jockey. He rode three Kentucky Derby and five Belmont Stakes champions and retired as horse racing's leading career money winner.

Shula, Don (1930–   ). Football coach; Baltimore Colts, Miami Dolphins. He led six teams to the Super Bowl, winning twice (with the Dolphins). His 1972 Miami team went 14–0. He retired as the NFL's all-time leader in victories (347).

Simpson, O(renthal) J(ames) (1947–   ). Football player (running back); Buffalo Bills. Simpson set the NFL single-season rushing record with 2,003 yards (1974; broken 1984) and led the league in rushing four times. In his 1995 criminal trial, Simpson was found not guilty of the murders of his ex-wife, Nicole Brown Simpson and her friend, Ronald Goldman. In 1997 he was found liable for the murders in a subsequent civil trial.

Smith, Dean (1931–). Basketball coach; North Carolina (college). He led his teams to 25 NCAA tournament appearances and won national championships in 1982 and 1993. He is college basketball's all-time "winningest" coach.

Spitz, Mark (1950–). Swimmer. Spitz won seven gold medals in the 1972 Olympics, setting world records in each event. His 11 career medals (9 gold, 1 silver, 1 bronze) in two Olympic appearances (1968, 1972) are the most by an American (tied with Biondi).

Stengel, Casey [Charles Dillon] (1890–1975). Baseball manager; various teams. He led the New York Yankees to 10 American League pennants (1949–53, 1955–58, 1960) and 7 World Series titles (1949–53, 1956, 1958) and was the first manager of the expansion New York Mets (1962). He was famous for his eccentric use of language, termed "Stengelese."

Thorpe, Jim (1888–1953). Multisport athlete. He won both the pentathlon and the decathlon in the 1912 Olympics but was later disqualified for a prior loss of his amateur status. His medals were restored in 1982. He also played professional baseball (1913–19) and football (1919–26). Thorpe is considered the greatest Native American athlete of all time.

Tyson, Mike (1966–). Boxer. At 19, he became the youngest fighter to win a heavyweight championship (1986). The undisputed champion from 1987 to 1990, he was stripped of his crown after a felony rape conviction (1992). He regained the title in 1996 but lost it to Evander Holyfield in 1997.

Weissmuller, Johnny (1904–84). Swimmer. He won 52 national championships and 5 Olympic gold medals and set 67 world records. After retiring, he earned fame as the lead actor in a series of Tarzan films.

Witt, Katarina (1965–). German figure skater. She twice won Olympic gold medals (1984,

1988) and captured four world championships (1984–85, 1987–88).

Wooden, John (1910–). Basketball coach; UCLA (college). He won a record 10 national championships (1964–65, 1967–73, 1975). His UCLA team set an NCAA record with 88 consecutive wins (1971–74).

Woods, Tiger (1975–). Golfer. He was the first player to win three consecutive U.S. Amateur titles (1994–96) and the youngest golfer to win the Masters (1997, with a record low score of 270 and a record margin of 12 strokes). His early professional successes and enthusiastic followers have created a popular phenomenon known as "Tigermania."

Young, Cy (1867–1955). Baseball player (pitcher); various teams. He holds the major league records for career wins (511) and losses (316). The annual award given to the best pitcher in each league is named in his honor.

Zaharias, Babe Didrikson (1914–56). Multisport athlete. She captured two gold medals in the 1932 Olympics (80m hurdles, javelin), earned All-America honors in basketball (1930–32), and won numerous amateur and professional golf tournaments (in the 1940s and 1950s). She is considered one of the greatest female athletes of all time.

BOARD GAMES
BACKGAMMON

Backgammon is a board game played by two players, each with 15 markers, or stones, which at the beginning of the game are placed in a standard initial configuration (see diagram) on the board. The board is divided into two tables, each with 12 triangular spaces, or points. Each player rolls two dice to determine the number of points moved by the stones, with black moving around the board in one direction and white moving in the opposite direction. The numbers on each die can be combined to move one stone the total amount indicated, or each

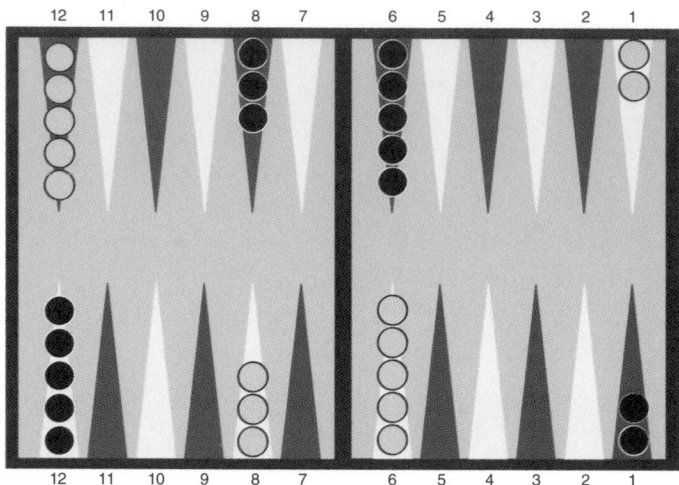

Backgammon Starting Position

die's value can be applied separately to single stones. If "doubles" are thrown (such as two 6s), the player can move twice as many points as are shown on the dice—in this case, four stones can move 6 spaces each, one can move 6 spaces and one 18 spaces, two can move 12 spaces each, or one stone can move 24 spaces. The object of the game is to be the first person to move his or her stones around the board and then off, called bearing off. A player may begin bearing off only when all of his or her stones are on the table opposite his or her beginning table. Each number on the die must correspond exactly with the number of the point a stone is on in order to bear the stone off. However, when all the stones are off the six point, a roll of 6 may bear off a stone on the five point; when all stones are off the six and five points, a roll of 6 or 5 may bear off a stone on the four point, and so on.

A university study found that people spend more on refreshments at tractor pulls than they do at football games.

Any number of stones of the same color may stay on one point, but stones of the opposite color may not occupy the same point. A point occupied by two or more stones of the same color is said to be closed; it prevents the opponent from landing there. A point occupied by one marker (or none) is open. A single stone on any point is called a blot, and the opponent may land there with a hit. The opponent then places the blot on the bar, thereby sending it back to the owner's beginning table. The blot can reenter the game only when the owner rolls a number on one of the dice corresponding to an open point or one occupied by stones of the owner's color on his or her beginning table. All blots on the bar must reenter the table before the owner makes another move.

Backgammon depends on the roll of the dice and is therefore partially a game of chance, but it can also involve complex strategy and tactics. The game may make use of the doubling cube, which is a die with a number on each face (2, 4, 8, 16, 32, 64). Using this cube, either player can at any point in the game double the stakes, whether they be points, as in tournament play, or money, as in the gambling version.

CHECKERS

Checkers is played by two players on a board with 64 squares alternating light and dark. Only the dark squares of the board are used. The board is eight squares wide and eight squares long. Each player uses 12 wooden discs called checkers, usually red for one player and black for the other. The

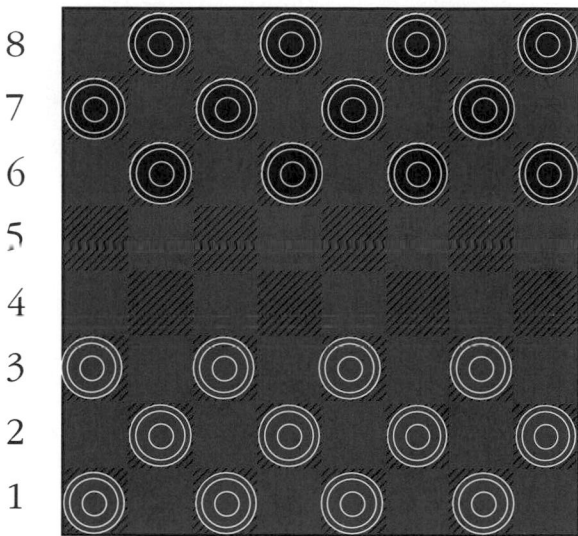

Checkers Starting Position

pieces are set up on the dark squares of the first three ranks, four in each rank. Black moves first, and the players alternate turns by moving one checker forward diagonally toward the opposing player's checkers. The object is to jump over the opponent's pieces, which are then removed from play. A player wins when all the opponent's pieces have been removed. If a player manages to advance a piece to the last rank on the opposite end of the board, that piece becomes a king and thereby acquires the capability of moving backward as well as forward.

CHESS

Chess is a game for two players, one directing the white pieces and one directing the black pieces. It is played on a board with 64 squares of alternating colors, black and white. The board is eight squares wide and eight long. Squares on the board are normally referred to by coordinates, using numbered ranks and lettered files. Each player has 16 pieces: eight pawns, two rooks, two knights, two bishops, a queen, and a king. To start the game, the pieces are set up using the 32 spaces of ranks 1 and 2 (for one color) and 7 and 8 (for the other color). Rooks occupy the outermost files (a and h), with knights

placed next to them (b and g); next to them are the bishops (c and f). Toward the center of the board (d and e) the king and queen are placed, with the white queen on a white square and the black queen on a black square. The pawns are placed in front of these pieces, using ranks 2 and 7.

The object of the game is to capture the opponent's king by placing him in checkmate. In this position, the king is under attack by an opposing piece (check), and wherever the king moves, it remains under attack by that or another opposing piece. The attacking side thus wins the game. If a player feels that checkmate is unavoidable, he or she may give up, or resign. If neither white nor black is able to checkmate the opponent or force resignation, a draw may be agreed upon. If the king is not in check and if a player can make no moves, or if all otherwise legal moves would expose his king to check, the game ends in a stalemate.

Any piece may capture, or take, an opponent's piece by landing on the square occupied by that piece. The king, however, cannot be captured and is instead put into check when attacked. If a piece is captured, it is removed from the board. If a pawn reaches the last rank (1 or 8), it is immediately

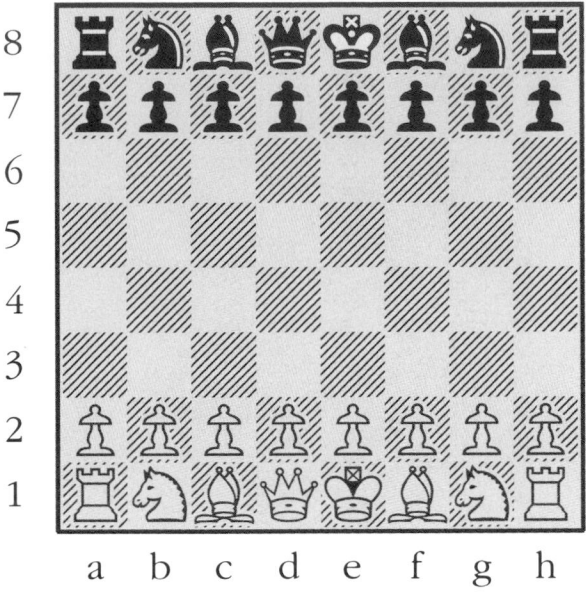

Chess Starting Position

"promoted" to a queen, rook, bishop, or knight at its owner's wish, without regard to the number of them the owner already has.

Each type of piece moves in a prescribed way. A rook moves forward or back, left or right as many squares in one direction as is desired. Knights move two squares in one direction (forward, back, left, or right) and one square at right angles to the first direction—or one square in one direction and two squares at right angles to the first move—resulting in an L-shaped move. The knight is the only piece that may jump over another piece. Bishops move diagonally any number of spaces in one direction. The queen moves forward, back, left, right, or diagonally any number of spaces in one direction. The king moves as the queen does, but one space at a time. Pawns move forward only, one space at a time, except for the first move, which may be two spaces. Pawns capture pieces by moving diagonally. There are only two instances in which pieces may move in other than these prescribed ways:

1. *Castling* is a two-part move involving the king and a rook. If neither of these pieces has moved previously, if there are no pieces between them, and if the king is neither in check nor would move through or to a guarded square, the king may move two spaces toward the rook, and the rook may move to the square on the other side of the king.

2. If, by moving ahead two squares on its first move, a black pawn lands next to a white pawn on the same rank, the white pawn may capture the black pawn by moving diagonally to the square immediately behind the black pawn. This is called taking *en passant,* or capturing in passing. Of course, a black pawn may capture a white pawn in the same way.

MONOPOLY®

Monopoly® uses a board with 40 spaces around the perimeter. Players, starting with a fixed amount of money, roll two dice and, in turn, advance their tokens around the board the number of spaces indicated by the dice. If a player lands on any of 22 properties, that player may buy it at a stated price. This money goes into the bank. The player then receives a deed for that property, which states the rent that an opposing player must pay the owner if the player lands on it. The object of the game is to

A
Closer
Look

The Most Landed-On Spaces on the Monopoly® Game Board

According to Irvin R. Hertzel of Iowa State University, there are 10 spaces on the Monopoly® game board you can count on landing on more than the others. Using a computer, Hertzel, a mathematician, was able to figure out the overall probability of landing on each square. The following are the 10 most landed-on spaces.

1. Illinois Avenue
2. Go
3. B. & O. Railroad
4. Free Parking
5. Tennessee Avenue
6. New York Avenue
7. Reading Railroad
8. St. James Place
9. Water Works
10. Pennsylvania Railroad

In addition to the color-coded properties, which are given street names, there are also four railroads and two utility companies that may be purchased. These also carry rents, but they may not be developed. If a player lands on any of six spaces, three called "Chance" and three "Community Chest," that player must pick up a card from two piles placed in the center of the board and follow its instructions. These involve monetary transactions either beneficial or harmful to the player. There is a neutral space called "Free Parking," a "Jail" space, two tax spaces, and a space called "Go." Play begins on the Go space, and the players collect $200 each time they circle the board and pass it.

In informal play, Monopoly® may involve considerable negotiation and trading among players. The game ends when all but one player has gone bankrupt; the remaining player is the winner.

SCRABBLE®

Scrabble® is a word game for two, three, or four players. The game uses a Scrabble® board with 225 spaces, 100 lettered tiles, 2 blank tiles, and a tile rack for each player. Each player, starting with seven letters, attempts to form words on the board using letters from his or her own hand and from words on the board. Words may read from left to

accumulate the properties and, by charging rent when an opponent lands there, to drive opposing players into bankruptcy. Properties are grouped by colors, with two or three to a group. If a player acquires all the properties within a single color, that player may develop those properties by purchasing houses and hotels. These dramatically increase the rent.

A
Closer
Look

94 Acceptable Two-Letter Scrabble® Words

aa	be	fa	lo	om	ti
ad	bi	go	ma	on	to
ae	bo	ha	me	op	uh
ag	by	he	mi	or	um
ah	da	hi	mm	os	un
ai	de	hm	mo	ow	up
al	do	ho	mu	ox	us
am	ef	id	my	oy	ut
an	eh	if	na	pa	we
ar	el	in	ne	pe	wo
as	em	is	no	pi	xi
at	en	it	nu	re	xu
aw	er	jo	od	sh	ya
ax	es	ka	oe	si	ye
ay	et	la	of	so	
ba	ex	li	oh	ta	

right or from top to bottom. Usually a new word uses one letter from a word already on the board, with which it interlocks at right angles, as in a crossword. Letters may be added to an existing word to form a new one.

Each player, after using some or all of his or her tiles to form a word on the board, replenishes the playing hand from the pool of remaining tiles, which are facedown. Thus, each player always has seven tiles with which to form words, except toward the end of the game, when the pool runs out.

Each letter has a numerical value associated with it; this number is marked on the tile. Players score for each word formed, based on the value of each letter in the word. Scores are recorded with pencil and paper. Players may augment scores by using certain premium spaces on the board. These special spaces result in doubling or tripling the values of single letters or complete words. When no player is able to form additional words, each player's score is tallied. Values of unplayed letters for each player are subtracted. The highest score wins the game.

CARD GAMES

BLACKJACK

Blackjack is a gambling game that uses a standard 52-card deck. Ace counts as 1 or 11 points; king, queen, jack, and 10 count as 10 each; all other cards count as their face number. The object is to hold two or more cards totaling 21 or as close to 21 as possible without going over. Cards are dealt one at a time, clockwise, starting with the player at the dealer's left. Each player receives one card facedown and one card faceup. After this initial deal, each player may stand and refuse more cards or take additional cards faceup. For example, having been dealt a king down and a 6 up (totaling 16), if the player chooses to take an additional card and receives another 6, that player is out with 22. An ace and a picture card or a 10 is called blackjack; it totals 21 and beats all other hands.

Various betting methods are used, but usually bets are made before and after the initial deal and after each subsequent deal. All players play against the dealer, and bets are settled depending on which hands are closest to but not over 21; if the dealer has the same count as a given player, the hand is considered a standoff.

BRIDGE

Contract bridge uses a standard 52-card deck and is a game for four players, in partnerships of two. The teams are designated North–South and East–West. Cards in each suit rank ace (high), king, queen, jack, 10, 9, . . . 2 (low); and suits rank spades (high), hearts, diamonds, and clubs (low). Each player receives cards, dealt one at a time clockwise, starting at the dealer's left.

Each player in turn gets a chance to make a bid, which is a statement of the intention to win more than six tricks. At the same time, the player either declares a high-ranking suit (trump) or declares no trump. If a player chooses not to bid, he or she may pass. Bids go around the table in clockwise rotation, with each bid being higher than any preceding bid. A bid may be doubled by an opponent or redoubled by a partner. These double the scoring value of a bid if it is played. This bidding segment of the game is called the auction, and the highest bid becomes the contract. One member of the contracting team declares the trump and becomes the declarer. That person's partner spreads his or her hand faceup on the table and becomes the dummy.

The object of the game is to win tricks in order to fulfill the contract or to defeat the opponent's attempt to fulfill it. The player to the declarer's left leads, and all players must follow suit if possible. A trick is won by the highest card of the suit led if no trump is played, or by the highest trump played.

When all 13 tricks have been taken, the result is scored. There is a complicated scoring system depending primarily on whether the contract was made and by how much. The two members of a partnership score their combined tricks as a single unit. Extra points may be scored in several ways. A bonus is scored if a doubled or redoubled bid is made. One of two types of slams is scored if the contracting team wins 12 tricks or all 13. Honor points are scored when a player receives certain cards in the deal (ace, king, queen, jack, 10 of trump, or the four aces if no trump has been declared).

When a side accumulates 100 or more points in trick scores, the game is over. The side that first wins two out of three games wins a rubber. After each rubber, partnerships may change and play may begin again.

PINOCHLE

Pinochle is played by two to four players and uses a 48-card deck, which includes two of each rank from 9 to ace in all four suits. The rank of cards in each suit is ace (high), 10, king, queen, jack, 9. Cards are dealt three at a time, clockwise, starting to the dealer's left. In two-hand pinochle, both players receive 12 cards; in three-hand (auction pinochle), each receives 15; and in four-hand (partnership pinochle), each receives 12 cards. The remaining cards, if any, form the stock. After an ad hoc high-ranking suit, called trump, has been determined, the player to the left of the dealer leads by placing a card in the middle, followed by each player in rotation. Tricks are won by the high trump or by the higher card of the suit led if no trump is played. The winner of the trick leads for the next trick. Except in two-hand pinochle, a player must always follow the suit that is led, if possible.

Cards taken in tricks determine the scoring, with each ace counting 11, each ten 10, each king 4, each queen 3, and each jack 2. Nines do not score. A player can also score points by winning the last trick. In addition, certain combinations of cards, called melds, have scoring value. These include the flush (ace, 10, king, queen, jack in the same suit); the marriage (king and queen in the same suit); groups of cards of the same rank (four aces, four

kings, etc.); and two special melds, the nine of trump and the pinochle (queen of spades and jack of diamonds).

Points taken in tricks are added to those accumulated by melding. Usually the player or team that first reaches 1,000 points wins the game.

POKER

Poker is a popular card game that uses a standard 52-card deck, with cards ranking ace (high), king, queen, jack, 10, 9, … 2 (low). The ace can also rank low if used as part of ace-2-3-4-5. Jokers are sometimes used as wild cards, which can stand for any card the holder chooses. There are hundreds of forms of poker, but invariably the cards are dealt clockwise, one at a time, starting with the player to the dealer's left. Usually each player receives five cards facedown, but depending on the type of poker, more cards may be dealt, or some may be dealt faceup.

Poker is a gambling game that uses chips of different monetary value. Bets by players go into a pile of chips called the pot. The object is to win the pot, either by showing the best hand or by making a bet that no one is willing to match. The rank of poker hands without wild cards is as follows. The top six hands are illustrated on the next page.

1. *Royal flush:* a sequence of ace, king, queen, jack, 10 of the same suit
2. *Straight flush:* five cards in sequence in the same suit
3. *Four of a kind:* four cards of the same rank
4. *Full house:* three of a kind and a pair
5. *Flush:* five cards of the same suit
6. *Straight:* five cards in sequence, regardless of suit
7. *Three of a kind:* three cards of the same rank
8. *Two pair:* two cards of the same rank and two others of a different rank
9. *One pair:* two cards of the same rank
10. *High card:* five unmatched cards, one with the highest rank of the five

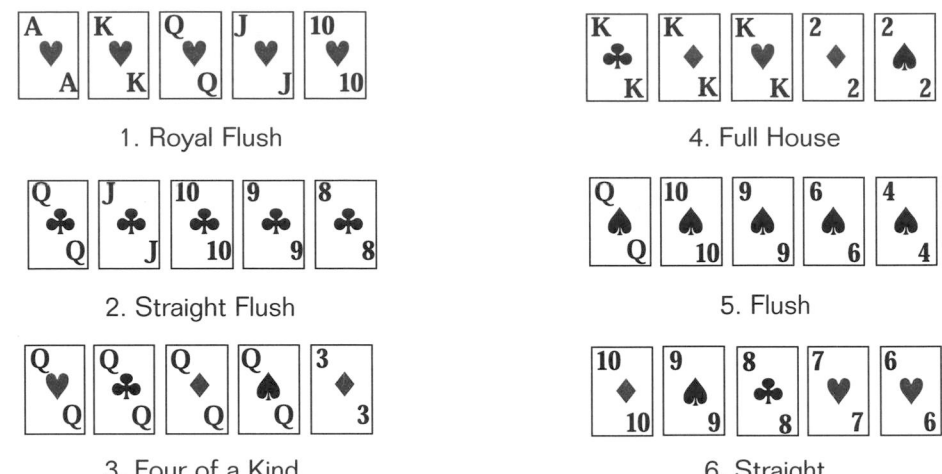

1. Royal Flush   4. Full House

2. Straight Flush   5. Flush

3. Four of a Kind   6. Straight

Top Six Winning Poker Hands

RUMMY

Rummy uses a regular deck of 52 cards. The cards rank king (high), queen, jack, 10, . . . 2, ace (low). Cards are dealt one at a time, clockwise, starting at the dealer's left. The number of cards dealt to each player depends on the number of players in the game: with two players, 10 cards each; with three or four players, 7 cards each; with five or six players, 6 cards each. The undealt remainder of the deck is placed facedown, forming the stock. Its top card is turned up next to the stock, forming the discard pile. The object is to form groups (three or more cards of the same rank) or sequences (three or more cards of the same suit in sequence of rank). Forming groups or sequences is called melding.

One at a time and proceeding clockwise, players draw one card from the top of the stack or the top of the discard pile. If melding is possible, groups or sequences are placed faceup in front of the player. A player may also lay off, or add to his or her own or an opponent's melds. A player's turn ends by his placing one card faceup on the discard pile. When one player melds all the cards remaining in a hand, that player goes out, thus ending that deal, which is then scored. The player going out scores his or her own melds plus the points left in the opponents' hands. The other players score just their own melds. Aces count as 1; all picture cards count as 10; and

the rest of the cards count as their face number. High score wins.

Except when going out, a player must discard one card after each play, whether or not that player has melded or laid off.

SOLITAIRE

Solitaire, or Patience, refers to a group of card games played by one person. The most popular and best known of these games is Klondike. Using a standard 52-card deck, the player deals a tableau or layout, consisting of seven piles of cards. The first pile on the far left has one card, the second pile two, and so on to the far right pile, which has seven cards. These cards are dealt facedown except for the top card in each pile. On these piles, descending sequences are built in alternating colors. For example, a red 9 may be placed on a black 10. Entire sequences or individual cards may be moved from pile to pile, provided correct colors and sequences are maintained. If a down card in a pile is revealed, it is turned faceup and may then become part of a sequence. When a pile is exhausted, a king may replace it.

When they become available, aces are placed above the original layout. The object is to build sequences in suit from the four aces (the foundations) up to the four kings, thus using all cards of the original layout as well as the remaining cards, which form the stock. From the stock, the player turns up one card at a time, forming a waste pile. The top card of the waste pile is available for play on the layout or foundations. The player goes through the stock only once and wins the game if he or she successfully places the entire deck on the foundations. Many players employ alternative, more liberal methods of dealing the stock.

ADDITIONAL SOURCES OF INFORMATION

ORGANIZATIONS AND SERVICES

GENERAL

Amateur Athletic Union of the U.S.
c/o The Walt Disney World Resort
P.O. Box 10000
Lake Buena Vista, FL 32830-1000
407-934-7200
http://aausports.org

National Collegiate Athletic Association (NCAA)
6201 College Blvd.
Overland Park, KS 66211-2422
913-339-1906
http://www.ncaa.org

AUTO RACING

American Hot Rod Association (AHRA)
N. 111 Hayford Rd.
Spokane, WA 99204
509-244-2372

Championship Auto Racing Teams (CART)
755 W. Big Beaver, Ste. 00
Bloomfield Hills, MI 48084
248-362-8800

National Association for Stock Car Racing
http://www.nascar.com/index.html

National Hot Rod Association (NHRA)
2035 Financial Way
Glendora, CA 91740
818-914-4761

BASEBALL

American League (AL)
350 Park Ave.
New York, NY 10022
212-339-7600
http://www.majorleaguebaseball.com/al/

Baseball Hall of Fame
P.O. Box 590
Cooperstown, NY 13326
607-547-7200
http://www.baseballhalloffame.org

Major League Baseball Commissioner's Office
350 Park Ave.
New York, NY 10022
212-339-7800
http://www.majorleaguebaseball.com

National Association of Professional Baseball Leagues
(minor league clubs)
P.O. Box A
St. Petersburg, FL 33731
813-822-6937
http://www.minorleaguebaseball.com

National League (NL)
350 Park Ave.
New York, NY 10022
212-339-7700
http://www.majorleaguebaseball.com/nl/

BASKETBALL

Basketball Hall of Fame
P.O. Box 179
1150 West Columbus Ave.
Springfield, MA 01101-0179
413-781-6500
http://www.hoophall.com

National Basketball Association (NBA)
645 Fifth Ave.
New York, NY 10022
212-826-7000
http://www.nba.com

BICYCLE RACING

United States Cycling Federation (USCF)
(amateur)
c/o USOC
1 Olympic Plaza
Colorado Springs, CO 80909
719-578-4581

BOWLING

National Bowling Association
377 Park Ave. South
7th Floor
New York, NY 10016
212-689-8308
http://www.inlink.com/~tnbainc/

Professional Bowler's Association of America (PBA)
1720 Merriman Rd.
P.O. Box 5118
Akron, OH 44334-0118
330-836-5568
http://www.pba.org

FOOTBALL

National Football Foundation and Hall of Fame
22 Maple Ave.
Morristown, NJ 07960
973-829-1933

National Football League (NFL)
280 Park Ave.
New York, NY 10017
212-450-2000
http://www.nfl.com

Pro Football Hall of Fame
2121 George Halas Dr., NW
Canton, OH 44708
330-456-8207
http://www.profootballhof.com

GOLF

Ladies Professional Golf Association (LPGA)
100 International Golf Dr.
Daytona Beach, FL 32124-1092
904-274-6200
http://www.lpga.com

Professional Golfer's Association of America (PGA)
100 Avenue of the Champions
P.O. Box 109601
Palm Beach Gardens, FL 33410-9601
561-624-8400
http://www.pga.com/index.html

U.S. Golf Association (USGA)
Liberty Corner Rd.
P.O. Box 708
Far Hills, NJ 07931-0708
908-234-2300
http://www.usga.org

U.S. Golf Association Hall of Fame
Golf House
Far Hills, NJ 07931-0708
908-234-2300

HORSE RACING

National Museum of Racing and Hall of Fame
191 Union Ave.
Saratoga Springs, NY 12866
518-584-0400
http://www.imh.org/imh/nmr/

U.S. Trotting Association
750 Michigan Ave.
Columbus, OH 43215-1191
614-224-2291
http://www.ustrotting.com

ICE HOCKEY

American Hockey League (AHL)
425 Union St.
West Springfield, MA 01089-4108
413-781-2030
http://www.canoe.ca/AHL/home.html

Hockey Hall of Fame
BCE Place
30 Yonge St.
Toronto, Ontario MSE 1X8
Canada
416-360-7735
http://www.hhof.com

National Hockey League (NHL)
1800 McGill College Ave., Ste. 2600
Montreal, Quebec H3A 3J6
Canada
514-288-9220
http://www.nhl.com

SOCCER

U.S. Soccer Federation
1801-11 South Prairie Ave.
Chicago, IL 60616
312-808-1300
http://www.US-Soccer.com/

TENNIS

International Tennis Hall of Fame and Museum
Newport Casino
194 Bellevue Ave.
Newport, RI 02840
401-849-3990
800-457-1144
http://www.tennisfame.org

U.S. Tennis Association (USTA)
70 West Red Oak Ln.
White Plains, NY 10604
914-696-7000
http://www.usta.com

TRACK AND FIELD

Intercollegiate Association of Amateur Athletes of America (IC4A)
P.O. Box 3
Centerville, MA 02632
508-771-5060

International Amateur Athletics Federation
17 rue Princesse Florestine
BP 359
MC 98007 Monaco Cedex
(011) 33 377 93 10 88 88
http://www.iaaf.org

USA Track and Field
P.O. Box 120
Indianapolis, IN 46206-0120
317-261-0500
http://www.usatf.org/index.htm

U.S. Track and Field Hall of Fame
P.O. Box 120
Indianapolis, IN 46206-0120
317-261-0483
http://www.usatf.org/athletes/hof/index.shtml

VOLLEYBALL

United States Volleyball Association (USVBA)
3595 E. Fountain Blvd., Ste. I-2
Colorado Springs, CO 80910-1740
719-637-8300

OLYMPIC GAMES

United States Olympic Committee (USOC)
Olympic Plaza
Colorado Springs, CO 80909-5760
719-632-5551
http://www.olympic_vsa.org

BOARD AND CARD GAMES

American Contract Bridge League (ACBL)
2990 Airways Blvd.
Memphis, TN 38116-3847
901-332-5586
http://www. acbl.org

National Scrabble Association (NSA)
c/o Williams & Co.
P.O. Box 700
Greenport, NY 11944
516-477-0033

United States Chess Federation (US Chess)
5054 NYS
New Windsor, NY 12553
914-562-8350

MAGAZINES

Sports Illustrated
1271 Avenue of the Americas
New York, NY 10020
www.pathfinder.com

BOOKS

GENERAL

Diagram Group. *Rules of the Game: The Complete Illustrated Encyclopedia of All the Sports of the World.* Rev ed. St. Martin's, 1995.

Donavan, Michael Leo. *The Name Game: Football, Baseball, Hockey & Basketball——How Your Favorite Sports Teams Were Named.* Warwick, 1997.

Kent, Michael, ed. *The Oxford Dictionary of Sports Science and Medicine.* Oxford University Press, 1995.

Palmatier, Robert S., and Harold L. Ray. *Dictionary of Sports Idioms.* NTC, 1993.

Porter, David L., ed. *Biographical Dictionary of American Sports.* 4 vols. Greenwood, 1987–89.

AUTO RACING

Golenbock, Peter, and Greg Fielden. *The Stock Car Racing Encyclopedia.* Macmillan General Reference, 1997.

Gunnell, John A., ed. *Race Car Flashback: A Celebration of America's Affair with Auto Racing from 1900 to the 1980s.* Motorbooks International, 1994.

Taylor, Rich. *Indy: 75 Years of Auto Racing's Greatest Spectacle.* St. Martin's, 1991.

BASEBALL

The Baseball Encyclopedia: The Complete and Definitive Record of Major League Baseball. 10th ed. Macmillan General Reference, 1996.

Bjarkman, Peter C., ed. *Encyclopedia of Major League Baseball: American League Team Histories.* Carroll & Graf, 1993.

Bjarkman, Peter C., ed. *Encyclopedia of Major League Baseball: National League Team Histories.* Carroll & Graf, 1993.

Dewey, Donald, et al. *Encyclopedia of Major League Baseball Teams.* HarperCollins, 1993.

Dickson, Paul. *The Dickson Baseball Dictionary.* Harcourt Brace, 1998.

Neft, David S., Richard M. Cohen, and Michael L. Neft. *The Sports Encyclopedia: Baseball.* 18th ed. St. Martin's, 1998.

Nemec, David. *The Great Encyclopedia of 19th Century Major League Baseball.* Donald I. Fine, 1996.

Pietrusza, David. *Major Leagues: The Formation, Sometimes Absorption and Mostly Inevitable Demise of 18 Professional Baseball Organizations, 1871 to Present.* McFarland, 1991.

Riley, James A. *The Biographical Encyclopedia of the Negro Baseball Leagues.* Carroll & Graf, 1994.

Solomon, Burt. *The Baseball Timeline: The Day-By-Day History of Baseball from Valley Forge to the Present Day.* Avon Books, 1997.

Thorn, John, et al., eds. *Total Baseball: The Official Encyclopedia of Major League Baseball.* 5th ed. Viking, 1997.

Ward, Geoffrey C., and Ken Burns. *Baseball: An Illustrated History.* Knopf, 1994.

BASKETBALL

Douchant, Mike. *Encyclopedia of College Basketball.* Gale Research, 1994.

Hollander, Zander. *The Complete Handbook of Pro Basketball.* Signet, annual.

Neft, David S., and Richard M. Cohen. *The Sports Encyclopedia: Pro Basketball.* St. Martin's, 1992.

Sachare, Alex, ed. *The Official NBA Basketball Encyclopedia.* 2nd ed. Villard, 1994.

Savage, Jim. *Encyclopedia of the NCAA Basketball Tournament: The Complete Independent Guide to College Basketball's Championship Event.* Dell, 1990.

Vancil, Mark. *The NBA at Fifty.* Park Lane, 1996.

BICYCLE RACING

Abt, Samuel. *Pedaling for Glory: Victory and Drama in Professional Bicycle Racing.* Motorbooks International, 1997.

Nye, Peter. *Heart of Lions: The History of American Bicycle Racing.* W. W. Norton, 1989.

Ritchie, Andrew. *Bicycle Racing Record Book.* Motorbooks International, 1998.

Sutherland, Sandra W. *No Brakes!: Bicycle Track Racing in the United States.* Iris, 1996.

BOWLING

Allen, George, and Dick Ritger. *Complete Guide to Bowling Principles: The Encyclopedia.* Technical Education, 1994.

FOOTBALL

Carroll, Bob, et al., eds. *Total Football: The Official Encyclopedia of the National Football League.* HarperCollins, 1997.

Maher, Tod, and Bob Gill, eds. *The Pro Football Encyclopedia: The Complete and Definitive Record of Professional Football.* Macmillan General Reference, 1997.

Neft, David S., Richard M. Cohen, and Rich Korch. *The Sports Encyclopedia: Pro Football.* 15th ed. St. Martin's, 1997.

Ours, Robert. *College Football Encyclopedia: The Authoritative Guide to 124 Years of College Football.* Prima, 1993.

GOLF

Campbell, Malcolm. *Random House International Encyclopedia of Golf: The Definitive Guide to the Game.* Random House, 1991.

Glenn, Rhonda. *The Illustrated History of Women's Golf.* Taylor, 1991.

Green, Robert. *The Illustrated Encyclopedia of Golf.* HarperCollins, 1994.

Peper, George. *Golf Magazine's Encyclopedia of Golf: The Complete Reference.* HarperCollins, 1993.

HORSE RACING

Ainslie, Tom. *Ainslie's Complete Guide to Thoroughbred Racing.* Fireside, 1988.

Bowen, Edward L. *The Jockey Club's Illustrated History of Thoroughbred Racing in America.* Bullfinch, 1994.

Stout, Nancy. *Great American Thoroughbred Racetracks.* Rizzoli International, 1991.

ICE HOCKEY

Fischler, Stan. *Fischler's Illustrated History of Hockey.* Warwick, 1993.

Hollander, Zander. *The Complete Encyclopedia of Hockey.* 4th ed., rev. Gale Research, 1992.

SOCCER

Duarte, Orlando. *The Encyclopedia of World Cup Soccer.* McGraw-Hill, 1994.

Glanville, Brian. *The Story of the World's Cup.* Faber & Faber, 1993.

Lablanc, Michael L., and Richard Henshaw. *The World Encyclopedia of Soccer.* Gale Research, 1993.

Murray, Bill. *The World's Game: A History of Soccer.* University of Illinois Press, 1998.

TENNIS

Collins, Bud, and Zander Hollander, eds. *Bud Collins's Tennis Encyclopedia.* 3rd ed. Visible Ink Press, 1997.

Gillmeister, Heiner. *Tennis: A Cultural History.* Cassell Academic, 1997.

Savage. Jim. *The Grand Slam Tennis Encyclopedia: The Definitive Record of Wimbledon, the Australian Open, the French Open, and the U.S. Open.* Macmillan General Reference, 1996.

TRACK AND FIELD

Lawson, Gerald. *World Record Breakers in Track & Field Athletics.* Human Kinetics, 1997.

VOLLEYBALL

Kessel, John. *Volleyball Encyclopedia.* Sports Support Syndicate, 1996.

Shewman, Byron. *Volleyball Centennial: The First 100 Years.* Masters, 1996.

OLYMPIC GAMES

Wise, Michael T., et al., eds. *Chronicle of the Olympics, 1896–1996.* Dorling-Kindersley, 1996.

Young, David C. *The Modern Olympics: A Struggle for Revival.* Johns Hopkins University Press, 1996.

BOARD AND CARD GAMES

Mohn, Merilyn Simonds. *The New Games Treasury: More Than 500 Indoor and Outdoor Favorites with Strategies, Rules and Traditions.* Houghton Mifflin, 1997.

TRAVEL

BASIC INFORMATION	734
DOMESTIC TRAVEL	747
INTERNATIONAL TRAVEL	780
INTERNATIONAL CURRENCIES	788
ADDITIONAL SOURCES OF INFORMATION	818

BASIC INFORMATION

Whether you're planning a weekend getaway nearby or an extended stay on another continent, careful preparation is essential to a safe and successful trip.

TRAVELERS' CHECKLIST

Things to Do

✓ Arrange for the post office to hold your mail, or have someone collect it daily.

✓ Stop all deliveries to your home.

✓ Arrange for the care of animals, plants, and lawn.

✓ Put your valuables in a safety-deposit box.

✓ Notify your neighbors and the police of absence and let them know how you can be reached.

✓ Leave a key with a neighbor.

✓ Arrange for travelers' insurance coverage, if needed.

✓ Notify your travel agent of any special needs you might have, such as the use of an airport wheelchair.

✓ Reconfirm your airline ticket and other reservations.

✓ Tag your luggage with brightly colored stickers or ribbons for easy identification.

✓ Set timers or leave a light on.

✓ Empty the refrigerator and turn it on low.

✓ Turn off the hot water.

✓ Lock all doors and windows.

Things to Bring

✓ Airline or other tickets and travel documents.

✓ Auto registration, if driving.

✓ Passport, visas, and health certificates.

✓ Medical information and doctor's name and telephone number.

✓ Special prescriptions or prescription medications.

✓ Insurance papers.

✓ Credit cards.

✓ Travelers' checks and personal checks.

✓ Cash, including some in the currency of the country to which you are traveling.

A Closer Look

Travelers' First-Aid Kit

Antiseptic lotion or ointment
Aspirin or acetaminophen
Cold and cough remedies
Gauze bandages and adhesive tape, elastic bandages
Heating pad
Ice pack
Identification bracelet
Insect repellent and insect-bite medication
Medical information regarding condition, allergies, medications, blood type, and special needs
Milk of magnesia and diarrhea medication
Moleskin for blisters and calluses
Physician's name, address, and telephone number
Prescription medications and refills
Sunscreen and sunburn relief lotion
Telephone numbers of emergency contacts
Thermometer
Throat lozenges
Vitamins

✓ Names and addresses of people to contact in an emergency.

✓ Names, addresses, phone numbers, reservation numbers, and dates for places where you will be staying.

✓ Lightweight fold-up tote bag for purchases.

✓ Addresses of friends and family to whom to send mail.

✓ Extra pair of eyeglasses (or contacts) and your eyeglass (or contact) prescription.

TIPS FOR TRAVELERS WITH DISABILITIES

Determination and good planning are the keys to enjoyable travel for people with disabilities. If you have a disability, check with your health-insurance agent about vacation coverage. In addition, engage a travel agent who specializes in handling travelers with disabilities. Here are some further tips.

AIR TRAVEL

Telephone the airline ahead of time about boarding and seating arrangements and possible extra charges. Virtually all major airports have some barrier-free facilities, and special arrangements can be made for passengers with disabilities.

Traveling with Pets

A Closer Look

Although most travelers leave home without them, vacationing with pets is possible; if you plan carefully, taking your pet along can save on guilt, worry, and even money. It's easier to leave the goldfish in the care of friends, but the family dog can go with you almost anywhere. Information and suggestions to make this easier appear below.

Travel Checklist

- ✓ Proper identification (name and address tag)
- ✓ Thermos of water
- ✓ Plastic bowls
- ✓ Proof of up-to-date immunizations
- ✓ Pet carrier
- ✓ First-aid kit, including bandages, antiseptic, and medications (including tranquilizers) prescribed by your veterinarian
- ✓ Food (and can opener, if needed)
- ✓ Certificate of good health signed by your veterinarian
- ✓ Leash and muzzle
- ✓ Flea powder or flea collar
- ✓ Blanket
- ✓ Pet toys
- ✓ Grooming tools

Pretravel Suggestions

Introduce your pet to car travel with trial runs.

Allow your pet to become familiar with the pet carrier before your trip.

Do not feed your pet for several hours before the trip.

Exercise your pet right before leaving.

Travel Restrictions

Automobile   No restrictions.

Bus   Except for seeing-eye dogs, pets are prohibited on buses in interstate travel.

Train   Pets may be taken only in private compartments or in the baggage car.

Airplane   Pets can come on board in pet carriers or can remain in the baggage compartment. Restrictions vary, so inquire of individual airlines in advance.

National park   Pets are allowed on leashes except in bathing areas.

State and private park   Restrictions vary, so check with the individual facility.

Hotel, motel, and campground   Most do accept pets; notify the owner ahead of time.

International Travel (Including Hawaii)

Most countries require a recent certificate of good health and proof of immunizations. In addition, the following places may require a quarantine (at the owner's expense) for the number of days indicated. The number of days in quarantine may vary according to the type of pet and its state of health. Check with individual embassies or consulates for specific requirements.

Hawaii	180	Norway	120
Hong Kong	180	Panama	180
Jamaica	180	Singapore	30
Jordan	42	Sweden	120
Korea	21	Trinidad and Tobago	180
Malta	180	United Kingdom	180
Mauritius	180		

Returning Home

Upon your return, a quarantine officer at customs will check documents and inspect your animal. The official may require confinement of any animal that you have purchased abroad; typically confinement is in your own home rather than in official quarantine. Pets purchased abroad also will require proof of immunization, certificates of good health, and payment of an import duty.

Travel

BUSES

Because of space limitations, bus lines generally are less accommodating than other carriers for travelers with disabilities. Many, however, do have special seating and reduced rates.

RAILROADS

Trains normally have seating arrangements and toilet facilities for travelers with disabilities. Call ahead to arrange for seating and assistance.

SEA TRAVEL

Travel by ship is possible, but it can be difficult, because oceangoing vessels are not designed for travelers with disabilities. Generally they are not barrier-free.

PARKS/CAMPING

Many domestic and international campsites provide accommodations for travelers with disabilities, and some European sites are even designated as "Handi-Camps." Information on facilities for travelers with disabilities may be obtained from local chapters of the Easter Seal Society, and a national-park guide for travelers with disabilities is available from the National Park Service, U.S. Department of the Interior, Washington, DC 20240.

HOTELS/MOTELS

Many hotel and motel chains have special facilities for travelers with disabilities, as do some nonchain hotels and motels. Check with your travel agent.

FURTHER INFORMATION

Access-Able Travel Source
http://www.access-able.com/

Mobility International
541-343-1284
Fax 541-343-6812

National Park Service
(for information on U.S. highway rest areas)
202-208-6843

Society for the Advancement of Travel for the Handicapped (SATH)
212-447-7284
Fax 212-725-8253

CAR-RENTAL AGENCY TOLL-FREE NUMBERS AND WEB SITES

Alamo
(U.S. and international)
800-462-5266
800-522-9292 TDD
http://www.goalamo.com

AutoEurope
(U.S. and Europe)
800-223-5555
http://www.auto-europe.com/

Avis
(U.S. and international)
800-331-1212 domestic
800-331-1084 international
800-331-2323 TDD
http://www.avis.com/

Budget
(U.S. and international)
800-527-0700 domestic
800-472-3325 international
800-826-5510 TDD
http://www.budgetrentacar.com/

Dollar/EuroDollar
(U.S. and international)
800-800-4000 domestic
800-800-6000 international
800-232-3301 TDD
http://www.dollarcar.com/

Enterprise
(U.S. and Canada)
800-736-8227
http://www.pickenterprise.com/

Europe by Car
(Europe)
800-223-1516
http://www.europebycar.com/

Hertz
(U.S. and international)
800-654-3131 domestic
800-654-3001 international
800-654-2280 TDD
http://www.hertz.com/

Kemwel Holiday Autos
(U.S. and international)
800-678-0678
http://www.kemwel.com/

National
(U.S. and international)
800-227-7368 domestic
800-227-3876 international
800-328-6323 TDD
http://www.nationalcar.com/

Many businesses provide TDD lines, which are telecommunication devices for the deaf.

Payless
(U.S. and international)
800-729-5377
http://www.paylesscar.com/

Rent-a-Wreck
(U.S. and international)
800-535-1391
http://rentawreck.com/raw/

Thrifty
(U.S. and international)
800-367-2277
800-358-5856 TDD
http://www.thrifty.com/

Ugly Duckling
(U.S.)
800-843-3825
http://www.uglyduckling.com/

Value
(U.S.)
800-327-2501
http://www.go-value.com/

HOTEL/MOTEL CHAIN TOLL-FREE NUMBERS AND WEB SITES

Bed & Breakfast Reservation Services Worldwide
(U.S. and international)
800-364-7242
http://www.bandworldwide.org/

Best Western
(U.S. and international)
800-780-7234
800-528-2222 TDD
http://www.bestwestern.com/

Clarion
(U.S. and international)
800-252-7466
800-228-3323 TDD
http://www.clarioninn.com/

Comfort Inn
(U.S. and international)
800-228-5150
800-228-3323 TDD
http://www.comfortinn.com/

Days Inn
(U.S. and international)
800-329-7466
800-228-3323 TDD
http://www.daysinn.com/

Delta
(U.S. and international)
800-268-1133
http://www.deltahotels.com/

Doubletree/Red Lion
(U.S. and Mexico)
800-222-8733
800-528-9898 TDD
http://doubletreehotels.com/

EconoLodge
(U.S. and Canada)
800-424-6423
800-228-3323 TDD
http://www.hotelchoice.com/

Embassy Suites
(U.S. and international)
800-362-2779
http://www.embassy-suites.com/

Hampton Inn
(U.S. and international)
800-726-7866
800-451-4833 TDD
http://www.hampton-inn.com/

Hilton
(U.S. and international)
800-445-8667
800-368-1133 TDD
http://www.hilton.com/

Holiday Inn
(U.S. and international)
800-465-4329
http://www.holiday-inn.com/

Howard Johnson
(U.S. and international)
800-446-4656
800-654-8442 TDD
http://hojo.com/

"Symbols to Guide the Traveler" in chapter 12 **Go to**

Hyatt
(U.S. and international)
800-233-1234
http://www.hyatt.com/

LaQuinta
(U.S.)
800-531-5900
800-426-3101 TDD
http://www.laquinta.com/

Marriott
(U.S. and international)
800-228-9290
http://www.marriott.com/

Quality Inn
(U.S. and international)
800-228-5151
800-228-3323 TDD
http://www.hotelchoice.com/

Radisson
(U.S. and international)
800-333-3333
800-906-2200 TDD
http://www.radisson.com/

Ramada Inn
(U.S. and Canada)
800-272-6232
800-228-3232 TDD
http://www.ramada.com/

Red Lion/Doubletree
(U.S. and Mexico)
800-222-8733
800-528-9898 TDD
http://www.doubletreehotels.com/

Rodeway Inn
(U.S. and international)
800-228-2000
800-228-3323 TDD
http://www.hotelchoice.com

Sheraton
(U.S. and international)
800-325-3535
800-325-1717 TDD
http://www.sheraton.com/

Sleep Inn
(U.S. and international)
800-753-3746
http://www.hotelchoice.com

Summit International
(U.S. and international)
800-457-4000
http://www.summithotels.com/

Westin
(U.S. and international)
800-228-3000
800-221-8818 TDD
http://www.westin.com/

AIRLINE CODES, TOLL-FREE NUMBERS, AND WEB SITES

Airline (Home Country)	Code	Toll-Free Number(s)	Web Site
ACES (Colombia)	VX	800-846-2237	http://www.aces.colombia.com/default2.html
Aer Lingus (Ireland)	EI	800-223-6537	http://www.aerlingus.ie/
Aero Costa Rica (Costa Rica)	ML	800-237-6274	http://www.centralamerica.com/cr/tran/aero.htm
Aeroflot Russian International Airlines (Russia)	SU	800-995-5555	http://www.aeroflot.org/
Aerolineas Argentinas (Argentina)	AR	800-333-0276	http://www.aerolineas.com.ar/english/html/serv.htm
Aeromar (Dominican Republic)	VM	800-950-0747	http://www.dominicana.com/aeromar/
Aeromexico (Mexico)	AM	800-237-6639	http://www.wotw.com/aeromexico/
Aeroperu (Peru)	PL	800-777-7717	http://www.travelx.com/aeroperu.html
Air Afrique (Côte d'Ivoire)	RK	800-456-9192	http://www.sinergia.it/airafrique.htm
Air Aruba (Aruba)	FQ	800-882-7822	http://www.interknowledge.com/air-aruba/
Air Caledonie/Air Calin (New Caledonia)	SB	800-677-4277	http://www.pacificislands.com/airlines/caledonie.html
Air Canada (Canada)	AC	800-776-3000 800-361-8071 TDD	http://www.aircanada.ca/
Air China (China)	CA	800-986-1985	http://www.sunflower.singnet.com.sg/singapor/airchina.html

Airline (Home Country)	Code	Toll–Free Number(s)	Web Site
Air Fiji (Fiji Islands)	PC	800-677-4277	http://www.pacificislands.com/airlines/fiji.html
Air France/Air Inter Europe (France)	AF	800-237-2747	http://www.airfrance.fr/
Air India (India)	AI	800-223-2250	http://www.allindia.com/airindia/
Air Jamaica (Jamaica)	JM	800-523-5585	http://www.montego-bay-jamaica.com/ airjamaica/
Air Madagascar (Madagascar)	MD	800-821-3388	http://www.zip.com.au/~lemurweb/ Madagascar/md.html
Air Mauritius (Mauritius)	MK	800-537-1182	http://www.cyber.be/air-mauritius
Air Nauru (Nauru)	ON	800-677-4277	http://www.pacificislands.com/airlines/ nauru.html
Air Nevada (U.S.)	LW	800-634-6377	http://www.pcap.com/airnev.html
Air New Zealand (New Zealand)	NZ	800-926-7255	http://www.airnz.com/
Air Outer Mer/AOM Airlines (France)	IW	800-892-9136	http://www.aom.ch/
Air Seychelles (Seychelles)	HM	800-677-4277	http://www.network.it/airsey.htm
Air South (U.S.)	WV	800-247-7688	http://www.airsouth.com/
Air UK (United Kingdom)	UK	800-249-2478	http://www.airuk.co.uk/
Air Ukraine (Ukraine)	6U	800-857-2463	None
Air Vanatu (Micronesia)	NF	800-677-4277	http://www.pacificislands.com/airlines/ vanuatu.html
Air Zimbabwe (Zimbabwe)	UM	800-742-3006	None
Air Tran Airlines (U.S.)	J7	800-825-8538	http://www.airtran.com/
Alaska Airlines (U.S.)	AS	800-252-7522	http://www.alaska-air.com/
Alitalia (Italy)	AZ	800-223-5730	http://www.alitalia.it/english/index.html
All Nippon Airways/ANA (Japan)	NH	800-235-9262	http://www.metrotel.co.uk/travlog/ana.html
Aloha Airlines (U.S.)	AQ	800-367-5250 800-554-4833 TDD	http://www.alohaair.com/
American Airlines (U.S.)	AA	800-433-7300 800-543-1586 TDD	http://www.americanair.com/
American Trans Air/ATA (U.S.)	TZ	800-225-2995 800-293-6194 TDD	http://www.halcyon.com/integra/ata.html
American West Airlines (U.S.)	HP	800-235-9292 800-526-8077 TDD	http://www.america.west.com/
Ansett Australia (Australia)	AN	800-366-1300	http://www.ansett.com.au/
Asiana Airlines (South Korea)	OZ	800-227-4262	http://www.asiana.co.kr/
Austrian Airlines (Austria)	OS	800-843-0002	http://www.aua.com/
Avianca Colombia (Colombia)	AV	800-284-2622	http://www.avianca.com/
Aviateca (Guatemala)	GU	800-327-9832	http://www.flylatinamerica.com/ acc_aviateca.html
Bahamasair (Bahamas)	UP	800-222-4262	http://www.successfx.com/bahamasair/
Balkan Bulgarian Airlines (Bulgaria)	LZ	800-852-0944	http://www.balkanair.com/
British Airways (United Kingdom)	BA	800-247-9297	http://www.us.british-airways.com/
British Midland (United Kingdom)	BD	800-788-0555	http://www.iflybritishmidland.com/
BWIA International (Trinidad and Tobago)	BW	800-538-2942	http://www.bwiacaribbean.com/
Canadian Airlines (Canada)	CP	800-426-7000	http://www.cdnair.ca/
Carnival Airlines (U.S.)	KW	800-824-7386	http://www.carnivalair.com/homepage.htm
Cathay Pacific Airways (Hong Kong)	CX	800-233-2742	http://www.cathay-usa.com/
Cayman Airlines (Cayman Islands)	KX	800-441-3003	http://www.caymanis.com/cayair.htm
China Airlines (Taiwan)	CI	800-227-5118	http://www.china-airlines.com/

continues

Continued

Airline (Home Country)	Code	Toll–Free Number(s)	Web Site
China Eastern Airlines (China)	MU	800-200-5118	http://www.206.170.104.72/
Comair—a subsidiary of Delta Airlines (U.S.)	DL	800-354-9822	http://www.fly-comair.com/
Continental Airlines (U.S.)	CO	800-525-0280 (domestic) 800-231-0856 (international)	http://www.flycontinental.com/
Copa (Panama)	CM	800-892-2672	http://www.copaair.com/
Croatia Airlines (Croatia)	OU	800-247-5353	None
Cyprus Airways (Cyprus)	CY	800-333-2977	http://www.world-travel-net.co.uk/guide/airline/p009.htm
Czech Airlines/CSA (Czech Republic)	OK	800-223-2365	http://www.csa.cz/
Delta Airlines (U.S.)	DL	800-221-1212	http://www.delta-air.com/
Eastwind Airlines (U.S.)	W9	800-644-3592	http://www.pages.prodigy.com/X/S/A/XSNN68A/Eastwind.htm
Egypt Air (Egypt)	MS	800-334-6787	None
El Al Israel Airlines (Israel)	LY	800-223-6700	http://www.elal.co.it/
Emirates Air (United Arab Emirates)	EK	800-777-3999	http://www.ekgroup.com/
Ethiopian Airlines (Ethiopia)	ET	800-445-2733 (Eastern U.S.) 800-433-9677 (Midwestern and Western U.S.)	http://www.africanet.com/africanet/homepage/eth-air/default.htm
EVA Airways (Taiwan)	BR	800-695-1188	http://www.evaair.com.tw/
Finnair (Finland)	AY	800-950-5000	http://www.finnair.fi/
Frontier Airlines (U.S.)	S9	800-432-1359	http://www.flyfrontier.com/
Garuda Indonesia (Indonesia)	GA	800-342-7832	http://www.inn.bppt.go.id/commercial/check-in.html
Gulf Air (Persian Gulf)	GF	888-359-4853	http://www.gulfairco.com/
Guyana Airways (Guyana)	GY	800-242-4210	http://www.turq.com/guyanair.html
Hawaiian Airlines (U.S.)	HA	800-367-5320	http://www.hawaiianair.com/
Horizon Air—a subsidiary of Alaska Airlines (U.S.)	AS	800-547-9308	http://www.horizonair.com/
Iberia Airlines (Spain)	IB	800-772-4642	http://www.iberia.com/ingles/home.htm
Icelandair (Iceland)	FI	800-223-5500	http://www.centrum.is/icelandair/
Japan Airlines/JAL (Japan)	JL	800-525-3663	http://www.jal.co.jp/index.html
Kenya Airways (Kenya)	KQ	800-343-2506	http://www.150.252.23.102/Webtest/Uganda/Kenya.htm
Kiwi International (U.S.)	KP	800-538-5494	http://www.members.aol.com/chnaclppr/airline/kiwi.htm
KLM Royal Dutch Airlines (The Netherlands)	KL	800-374-7747	http://www.klm.nl/
Korean Air (South Korea)	KE	800-438-5000	http://www.mabuhay.com/Korean_Air
Kuwait Airways (Kuwait)	KU	800-424-1128	http://www.travelfirst.com/sub/kuwaitair.html
LACSA Airlines (Costa Rica)	LR	800-225-2272	http://www.flylatinamerica.com/acc_lacsa.html
Laker Airways (U.S.)	6F	888-525-3724	http://www.lakerair.com/
Lan Chile (Chile)	LA	800-735-5526	http://www.lanchile.com/

Airline (Home Country)	Code	Toll–Free Number(s)	Web Site
Lauda Airlines (Austria)	NG	800-645-3880	http://www.laudaair.com/engl/indexe.htm
LOT Polish Airlines (Poland)	LO	800-223-0593	http://www.pan.net/lot/
LTU International Airways (Germany)	LT	800-888-0200	http://www.ltu.de/
Lufthansa Airlines (Germany)	LH	800-645-3880	http://www.lufthansa.com/
Malaysian Airlines/MAS (Malaysia)	MH	800-552-9264	http://www.malaysiairlines.com.my/
MALEV Hungarian Airlines (Hungary)	MA	800-223-6884	http://www.malev-airlines.com/
Martinair Holland (The Netherlands)	MP	800-627-8462	http://www.travelx.com/martinairholland.html
Mesa Airlines (U.S.)	YV	800-637-2247	http://www.mesa_air.com/
Mexicana Airlines (Mexico)	MX	800-531-7921	http://www.mexicana.com/
Midway Airlines (U.S.)	JI	800-446-4392 or 888-226-4392	http://www.geocities.com/CapeCanaveral/ Lab/5441/
Midwest Express Airlines (U.S.)	YX	800-452-2022	http://www.midwestexpress.com/
New England Airlines (U.S.)	EJ	800-243-2460	http://www.ids.net/flybi/nea/
Nica Airlines (Nicaragua)	6Y	800-831-6422	http://www.flylatinamerica.com/acc_nica.html
Northwest Airlines (U.S.)	NW	800-225-2525 (domestic) 800-447-4747 (international)	http://www.nwa.com/
Olympic Airways (Greece)	OA	800-223-1226	http://agnhol.gr/info/olympic1.html
Pacific Coastal Airlines (U.S.)	8P	800-663-2872	http://www.pacific-coastal.com/
Pan American World Airways/ Pan Am (U.S.)	PA	800-359-7262	http://www.panam.com/
Peninsula Airways/Penair (U.S.)	KS	800-448-4226	http://www.penair.com/
Philippine Airlines (The Philippines)	PR	800-435-9725	http://www.sequel.net/PAL
Polynesian Airlines (Western Samoa)	PH	800-677-4277	http://www.pacificislands.com/airlines/ polynesian.html
Qantas Airways (Australia)	QF	800-227-4500	http://www.anzac.com/qantas/qantas.htm
Reno Air (U.S.)	QQ	800-736-6247	http://www.renoair.com/
Royal Air Maroc (Morocco)	AT	800-344-6726	http://www.xbrcom.qc.ca/ RAM/RAM_home.html
Royal Jordanian Airlines (Jordan)	RJ	800-223-0470	http://www.rja.com.jo/
Royal Nepal Airlines (Nepal)	RA	800-266-3725	http://www.asian-trekking.com/mac.htm
Royal Tonga Airline (Tonga)	WR	800-486-6426	None
Sabena Belgian World Airlines (Belgium)	SN	800-950-1000	http://www.sabena.com/
Saudi Arabian Airlines (Saudi Arabia)	SV	800-472-8342	http://ec.upi.edu/~zakharia/ saudi-communications.html
Scandinavian Airlines/SAS (Scandinavia)	SK	800-221-2350	http://www.sas.se/
Singapore Airlines (Singapore)	SQ	800-742-3333	http://www.singaporeair.com/
Solomon Airlines (Solomon Islands)	IE	800-677-4277	http://www.pacificislands.com/ airlines/solomon.html
South African Airways/SAA (South Africa)	SA	800-722-9675	http://www.saa.co.za/saa/
Southwest Airlines (U.S.)	WN	800-435-9792	http://www.iflyswa.com/
Sunflower Airlines (Fiji Islands)	PI	800-707-3454	http://www.fijiguide.com/Sunflower/ sunad.html
Swissair (Switzerland)	SR	800-221-4750	http://www.swissair.com/

Travel

continues

Continued

Airline (Home Country)	Code	Toll–Free Number(s)	Web Site
TACA International Airlines (El Salvador)	TA	800-535-8780	http://www.flylatinamerica.com/ acc_taca.html
Taesa Airlines (Mexico)	JV	800-328-2372	http://www.wotw.com/wow/mexico/ city/taesa.html
TAP Air Portugal (Portugal)	TP	800-221-7370	http://actionsites.com/tap/index.html
Thai Airways International (Thailand)	TG	800-221-2500	http://metroel.co.uk/travlog/thaiair.html
Transbrasil Airlines (Brazil)	TR	800-872-3153	http://www.transbrasil.com.br/
Travel Air (Costa Rica)	8T	800-924-2727	http://www.centralamerica.com/cr/tran/ travlair.htm
Turkish Airlines/THY/Turk Hava Yollari (Turkey)	TK	800-874-8875	http://www.turkishairlines.com/
Trans World Airlines/TWA (U.S.)	TW	800-221-2000 (domestic) 800-892-4141 (international)	http://www.twa.com/
United Airlines (U.S.)	UA	800-241-6522	http://www.ual.com/
Ukraine International Airlines (Ukraine)	PS	800-876-0114	http://www.iminet.com/SMS/ukraine/ index.html
USAirways/USAir (U.S.)	US	800-428-4322	http://www.usairways.com/
Varig Brazilian Airlines (Brazil)	RG	800-468-2744 or 800-262-1706	http://www.freesun.be/varig/ varigwelcome.html
VASP Brazilian Airlines (Brazil)	VP	800-732-8277	http://www.vasp.com/br/
Virgin Atlantic Airways (U.K.)	VS	800-862-8621	http://www.fly.virgin.com/atlantic
Western Pacific Airlines (U.S.)	W7	800-930-3030	http://www.westpac.com/
WestJet Airlines (Canada)	WJ	800-538-5696	http://www.westjet.com/
World Airways (U.S.)	WO	800-967-5350	http://www.worldair.com/

AIRPORT CODES, NAMES, AND LOCATIONS
UNITED STATES AIRPORTS

Code	U.S. Airport	Location
ACY	Atlantic City International Airport	Atlantic City, NJ
ATL	Hartsfield International Airport	Atlanta, GA
AUS	Robert Mueller/Bergstrom International Airport	Austin, TX
BDL	Bradley International Airport	Hartford, CT
BHM	Birmingham International Airport	Birmingham, AL
BNA	Nashville International Airport	Nashville, TN
BOS	Logan International Airport	Boston, MA
BRO	Brownsville/South Padre Island International Airport	Brownsville, TX
BUR	Burbank/Pasadena/Glendale Airport	Burbank, CA
BWI	Baltimore/Washington International Airport	Baltimore, MD
CAE	Columbia Metropolitan Airport	Columbia, SC
CHS	Charleston International Airport	Charleston, SC
CLE	Hopkins International Airport	Cleveland, OH
CLT	Charlotte/Douglas International Airport	Charlotte, NC

Code	U.S. Airport	Location
CMH	Port Columbus International Airport	Columbus, OH
CVG	Cincinnati/Northern Kentucky International Airport	Covington, KY/Cincinnati, OH
DCA	Ronald Reagan Washington National Airport	Washington, DC
DEN	Denver International Airport	Denver, CO
DFW	Dallas/Ft. Worth International Airport	Dallas, TX
DTW	Detroit Metropolitan Airport	Detroit, MI
EWR	Newark International Airport	Newark, NJ
FLL	Ft. Lauderdale/Hollywood International Airport	Ft. Lauderdale, FL
GPT	Gulfport/Biloxi Regional Airport	Biloxi, MS
HNL	Honolulu International Airport	Honolulu, HI
HOU	William P. Hobby Airport	Houston, TX
HSV	Huntsville International Airport	Huntsville, AL
IAD	Dulles International Airport	Washington, DC
IAH	Houston Intercontinental Airport	Houston, TX
JAN	Jackson International Airport	Jackson, MS
JAX	Jacksonville International Airport	Jacksonville, FL
JFK	John F. Kennedy International Airport	New York, NY
LAS	McCarran International Airport	Las Vegas, NV
LAX	Los Angeles International Airport	Los Angeles, CA
LGA	La Guardia Airport	New York, NY
MCI	Kansas City International Airport	Kansas City, MO
MCO	Orlando International Airport	Orlando, FL
MEM	Memphis International Airport	Memphis, TN
MIA	Miami International Airport	Miami, FL
MKE	General Mitchell International Airport	Milwaukee, WI
MOB	Mobile Regional Airport	Mobile, AL
MSP	Minneapolis/St. Paul International Airport	Minneapolis, MN
MSY	New Orleans International Airport	New Orleans, LA
MYR	Myrtle Beach International Airport	Myrtle Beach, SC
OAK	Metropolitan Oakland International Airport	Oakland, CA
OKC	Will Rogers World Airport	Oklahoma City, OK
ORD	O'Hare International Airport	Chicago, IL
PDX	Portland International Airport	Portland, OR
PHL	Philadelphia International Airport	Philadelphia, PA
PHX	Sky Harbor International Airport	Phoenix, AR
PIT	Pittsburgh International Airport	Pittsburgh, PA
RIC	Richmond International Airport	Richmond, VA
RNO	Reno/Tahoe International Airport	Reno, NV
SAN	San Diego International Airport	San Diego, CA
SAT	San Antonio International Airport	San Antonio, TX
SAV	Savannah International Airport	Savannah, GA
SDF	Standiford Field	Louisville, KY
SEA	Seattle/Tacoma International Airport	Seattle, WA
SFO	San Francisco International Airport	San Francisco, CA
SJC	San Jose International Airport	San Jose, CA
SLC	Salt Lake City International Airport	Salt Lake City, UT
SMF	Sacramento Metropolitan Airport	Sacramento, CA
SRQ	Sarasota/Bradenton International Airport	Sarasota, FL
STL	Lambert–St. Louis International Airport	St. Louis, MO
TPA	Tampa International Airport	Tampa, FL
TUL	Tulsa International Airport	Tulsa, OK

INTERNATIONAL AIRPORTS

Code	International Airport	Location
ACA	General Juan N. Alvarez Airport	Acapulco, Mexico
AEP	Jorge Newbery Airpark	Buenos Aires, Argentina
ALA	Almaty International Airport	Almaty, Kazakhstan
AMS	Schiphol International Airport	Amsterdam, The Netherlands
ANR	Deurne Airport	Antwerp, Belgium
ANU	V. C. Bird/Coolidge International Airport	Antigua Island, Antigua
ARN	Arlanda International Airport	Stockholm, Sweden
ASB	Ashgabat Saparmurat International Airport	Ashgabat, Turkmenistan
ASU	President Stroessner Airport	Asuncion, Paraguay
ATH	Hellinikon International Airport	Athens, Greece
AUA	Queen Beatrix International Airport	Oranjestad, Aruba
AUH	Nadia International Airport	Abu Dhabi, United Arab Emirates
ALK	Auckland International Airport	Auckland, New Zealand
BAH	Muharraq International Airport	Bahrain, Bahrain
BAK	Baku Bina International Airport	Baku Bina, Azerbaijan
BBQ	Codrington Airport	Barbuda Island, Barbuda
BBU	Bucharest Airport	Bucharest, Romania
BCN	Barcelona Transoceanic Airport	Barcelona, Spain
BDA	Kindley Field	Bermuda
BEY	Beirut International Airport	Beirut, Lebanon
BFN	Bloemfonein Airport	Bloemfontein, South Africa
BFS	Belfast International Airport	Belfast (Northern Ireland), United Kingdom
BGI	Grantley Adams International Airport	Bridgetown, Barbados
BIM	South Bimini International Airport	Bimini, Bahamas
BJS	Beijing (Peking) Airport	Beijing (Peking), China
BJX	Leon International Airport	Leon, Mexico
BKK	Don Muang International Airport	Bangkok, Thailand
BNE	Brisbane International Airport	Brisbane (Queensland), Australia
BOG	Bogotá Airport	Bogotá, Colombia
BOM	Sahar International Airport	Bombay, India
BRU	Brussels Airport	Brussels, Belgium
BSL	Basel/Mulhouse EuroAirport	Basel, Switzerland
BUD	Budapest Ferihegyi Airport	Budapest, Hungary
BZE	Philip Goldson International Airport	Belize City, Belize
CAI	Cairo International Airport	Cairo, Egypt
CAN	Guangzhou Airport	Canton, China
CAS	Casablanca Airport	Casablanca, Morocco
CCS	Caracas International Airport	Caracas, Venezuela
CCU	Dum Dum International Airport	Calcutta, India
CDG	Charles de Gaulle Airport	Paris (Roissy), France
CGH	São Paulo Congonhas Airport	São Paulo, Brazil
CGN	Cologne/Bonn Airport	Cologne, Germany
CHC	Christchurch International Airport	Christchurch, New Zealand
CJU	Cheju International Airport	Cheju, South Korea
CPH	Kastrup International Airport	Copenhagen, Denmark
CRL	Charleroi Brussels South Airport	Brussels, Belgium
CUN	Cancun International Airport	Cancun, Mexico
CUR	Hato Airport	Curacao, Netherlands Antilles

Code	International Airport	Location
DBV	Dubrovnik Airport	Dubrovnik, Croatia
DEL	Indira Gandhi International Airport	New Delhi, India
DOH	Doha Airport	Doha, Qatar
DUB	Dublin Airport	Dublin, Ireland
DUR	Durban International Airport	Durban, South Africa
DUS	Dusseldorf Airport	Dusseldorf, Germany
EBB	Entebbe International Airport	Entebbe, Uganda
EZE	Ezeiza International Airport	Buenos Aires, Argentina
FCO	Fiumicino (Leonardo da Vinci) Airport	Rome, Italy
FDO	San Fernando International Airport	San Fernando, Argentina
FLR	Peretola Airport	Florence, Italy
FPO	Freeport International Airport	Freeport, Bahamas
FRA	Frankfurt International Airport	Frankfurt, Germany
FRU	Bishkek/Frunze Manas International Airport	Bishkek (Chuy), Kyrgyzstan
GCJ	Johannesburg/Grand Central International Airport	Johannesburg, South Africa
GCM	Owen Roberts Airport	Grand Cayman, Cayman Islands
GDL	Miguel Hidalgo y Costilla Airport	Guadalajara, Mexico
GEN	Gardermoen Airport	Oslo, Norway
GIG	Rio de Janeiro/Galeao International Airport	Rio de Janeiro, Brazil
GLA	Glasgow Airport	Glasgow (Scotland), United Kingdom
GND	Grenville Airport	Grenville, Grenada
GVA	Geneva International Airport	Geneva, Switzerland
GYE	Simon Bolivar Airport	Guayaquil, Ecuador
HAM	Hamburg International Airport	Hamburg, Germany
HEL	Helsinki-Vantaa International Airport	Helsinki, Finland
HIJ	Hiroshima Airport	Hiroshima, Japan
HKG	Kai Tek (Chek Lap Kok) International Airport	Hong Kong, China
HND	Haneda International Airport	Tokyo, Japan
JCN	Inchon International Airport	Inchon, South Korea
INN	Kranebitten Airport	Innsbruck, Austria
IST	Ataturk/Yesilkov International Airport	Istanbul, Turkey
JAV	Ilulissat Airport	Jakobshavn, Greenland
JRS	Atarot Airport	Jerusalem, Israel
KBL	Kabul Airport	Kabul, Afghanistan
KDL	Kärdla Airport	Kärdla, Estonia
KHI	Quaid-e-Azam International Airport	Karachi, Pakistan
KIN	Norman Manley Airport	Kingston, Jamaica
KIX	Kansai International Airport	Osaka, Japan
KTP	Tinson Airport	Kingston, Jamaica
KUL	Sultan Abdul Aziz Shah, Subang International Airport	Kuala Lumpur, Malaysia
KWI	Kuwait Airport	Kuwait
LED	St. Petersburg (Leningrad) International Airport	St. Petersburg (Leningrad), Russia
LGW	Gatwick Airport	London (England), United Kingdom
LHR	Heathrow International Airport	London (England), United Kingdom
LIM	Jorge Chavez International Airport	Lima, Peru
LIS	Lisbon Airport	Lisbon, Portugal
LPA	Las Palmas/Gran Canaria Airport	Las Palmas/Gran Canaria (Canary Islands), Spain

continues

Continued

Code	International Airport	Location
LPB	J. F. Kennedy/El Alto Airport	La Paz, Bolivia
LUX	Luxembourg Airport	Luxembourg
MAD	Madrid Barajas Airport	Madrid, Spain
MAN	Ringway International Airport	Manchester (England), United Kingdom
MBJ	Sangster Airport	Montego Bay, Jamaica
MCT	Muscat Airport	Muscat, Oman
MEL	Tullamarine International Airport	Melbourne (Victoria), Australia
MEX	Benito Juarez International Airport	Mexico City, Mexico
MFM	Macau International Airport	Macau, Macao
MGA	A. C. Sandino Airport	Managua, Nicaragua
MLA	Malta International Airport	Malta
MLE	Hulele International Airport	Malé, Maldives
MRX	Caribe Santiago Mariño International Airport	Margarita Island, Venezuela
MUC	Strauss International Airport	Munich, Germany
MVD	Carrasco Airport	Montevideo, Uruguay
NAP	Naples International Airport	Naples, Italy
NAS	Nassau International Airport	Nassau, Bahamas
NEV	Nevis Airport	Charlestown, Nevis
NRT	Narita International Airport	Tokyo, Japan
OHD	Ohrid Airport	Ohrid, Republic of Macedonia
ORY	Orly Airport	Paris (Orly), France
PAP	Port-au-Prince Airport	Port-au-Prince, Haiti
PEK	Beijing (Peking) Capital Airport	Beijing (Peking), China
PER	Perth International Airport	Perth (Western Australia), Australia
PMI	Palma de Mallorca Airport	Balearic Islands, Spain
POP	Puerto Plata Airport	Puerto Plata, Dominican Republic
POS	Piarco International Airport	Port of Spain (Trinidad Island), Trinidad
PTP	Le Raizet Airport	Pointe-a-Pitre, Guadeloupe
PTY	General Omar Torrijos Herrara Airport	Panama City, Panama
PVR	Ordaz International Airport	Puerto Vallarta, Mexico
QCA	Makkah Airport	Mecca (Makkah), Morocco
RAD	Beef Island Airport	Tortola, British Virgin Islands
REK	Reykjavik Airport	Reykjavik, Iceland
RIX	Riga International Airport	Riga, Latvia
RUH	King Khalid Airport	Riyadh, Saudi Arabia
SAL	San Salvador International Airport	San Salvador, El Salvador
SCL	Comodoro Arturo Merino Benite Airport	Santiago, Chile
SDA	Saddam International Airport	Baghdad, Iraq
SDQ	Airport of the Americas	Santo Domingo, Dominican Republic
SEL	Kimpo International Airport	Seoul, South Korea
SHA	Hongqiao Airport	Shanghai, China
SHJ	Sharjah International Airport	Sharjah, United Arab Emirates
SIN	Changi International Airport	Singapore
SIP	Simferopol International Airport	Adygea, Ukraine
SJO	Juan Santamaria International Airport	San Jose, Costa Rica
SJU	Marin International Airport	San Juan, Puerto Rico
SLL	Salalah International Airport	Salalah, Oman
SLU	Vigie Airport	Castries, St. Lucia

Code	International Airport	Location
SKB	St. Kitts Airport	Basseterre, St. Kitts
STT	Cyril E. King Airport	Charlotte Amalie (St. Thomas), U.S. Virgin Islands
STX	Alexander Hamilton Airport	Christensted (St. Croix), U.S. Virgin Islands
SVO	Sheremetyevo International Airport	Moscow, Russia
SXF	Schönefeld Airport	Berlin, Germany
SXM	Princess Juliana Airport	Philipsburg (St. Martin), Netherlands Antilles
SYD	Kingsford-Smith International Airport	Sydney (New South Wales), Australia
TAS	Tashkent International Airport	Tashkent, Uzbekistan
TLV	Ben Gurion Airport	Tel Aviv, Israel
TPE	Chiang Kai Shek Airport	Taipei, Taiwan
TRN	Turin International Airport	Turin, Italy
TXL	Tegel Airport	Berlin, Germany
UIO	Quito Airport	Quito, Ecuador
ULN	Ulan Bator Airport	Ulan Bator, Mongolia
VIE	Vienna International Airport	Vienna, Austria
VNO	Vilnius International Airport	Vilnius, Lithuania
VVI	Viru Viru International Airport	Santa Cruz, Bolivia
WAW	Okęcie Airport	Warsaw, Poland
XPL	Comayagua Airport	Comayagua, Honduras
YAP	Yap International Airport	Yap Island, Micronesia
YEG	Edmonton International Airport	Edmonton (Alberta), Canada
YOW	Macdonald-Cartier International Airport	Ottawa (Ontario), Canada
WQX	Gander International Airport	Gander (Newfoundland), Canada
YUL	Dorval International Airport	Montreal (Quebec), Canada
YVR	Vancouver International Airport	Vancouver (British Columbia), Canada
YWG	Winnipeg International Airport	Winnipeg (Monitoba), Canada
YXU	Greater London International Airport	London (Ontario), Canada
YYC	Calgary International Airport	Calgary (Alberta), Canada
YYJ	Victoria International Airport	Victoria (British Columbia), Canada
YYZ	Pearson International Airport	Toronto (Ontario), Canada
ZAG	Zagreb Airport	Zagreb, Croatia
ZAZ	Zaragoza International Airport	Zaragoza, Spain
ZRH	Zurich-Kloten Airport	Zurich, Switzerland

DOMESTIC TRAVEL

STATE TOURISM OFFICES

Alabama Bureau of Tourism and Travel
P.O. Box 4927
Montgomery, AL 36103-4927
800-252-2262, 334-242-4169, 334-242-4717 (TDD)
Fax: 334-242-4554
http://www.touralabama.org/
E-mail: alabamat@mont.mindspring.com

Alaska Division of Tourism
P.O. Box 110801
Juneau, AK 99811
907-465-2010
Fax: 907-465-2287
http://www.stateak.us/tourism/
E-mail: GoNorth@commerce.state.ak.us

Arizona Office of Tourism
2702 N. 3rd St., Suite 4015
Phoenix, AZ 85009
800-842-8257
Fax: 602-277-9289
http://www.arizonaguide.com/

Arkansas Department of Parks and Tourism
One Capitol Mall
Little Rock, AR 72201
800-NATURAL or 501-682-7777
Fax: 501-682-1364
http://1800natural.com/

California Office of Tourism
P.O. Box 1499
Sacramento, CA 95812
800-462-2543
http://gocalif.ca.gov/

The Boston University Bridge is the only place in the world where it is possible for a boat to sail under a train running under a car driving under an airplane.

Colorado Travel and Tourism Authority
Tourism Board
P.O. Box 3524
Englewood, CO 80155
800-265-6723
http://colorado.com/vacation1.htm

Connecticut Department of Economic and Community Development
Office of Tourism
505 Hudson St.
Hartford, CT 06106
800-282-6863 or 860-270-8080
http://www.state.ct.us/tourism.htm

D.C. Convention and Visitors Association
1212 New York Ave. NW
Washington, DC 20005
800-422-8644 or 202-789-7000
Fax: 202-789-7037
http://www.washington.org/

Delaware Tourism Office
99 Kings Hwy., Box 1401
Dover, DE 19903
800-441-8846 or 800-282-8667 in Delaware
Fax: 302-739-5749
http://www.state.de.us/tourism/intro.htm

Florida Division of Tourism
126 W. Van Buren St.
Tallahassee, FL 32399
904-487-1462
Fax: 904-921-9158
http://www.state.fl.us/commerce/

Georgia Department of Industry, Trade and Tourism
P.O. Box 1776
Atlanta, GA 30301
800-847-4842 or 404-656-3590
http://www.georgia-on-my-mind.org/

Hawaii Visitors Bureau
2270 Kalakaua Ave., Suite 801
Honolulu, HI 96815
800-353-5846 or 808-923-1811
Fax: 808-922-8991
http://www.visit.hawaii.org/

Idaho Travel Council
Idaho Department of Commerce
P.O. Box 83720
Boise, ID 83720-0093
800-635-7820 or 208-334-2470
Fax: 208-334-2631
http://www.idoc.state.id.us/

Illinois Bureau of Tourism
100 W. Randolph St., Suite 3-400
Chicago, IL 60601
800-226-6632 or 217-785-6334
http://www.enjoyillinois.com

Indiana Department of Commerce
Tourist Development Division
One N. Capitol Ave., Suite 700
Indianapolis, IN 46204-2288
800-291-8844 or 317-232-8860
Fax: 317-233-6887
http://www.state.in.us/tourism/index.html

Iowa Division of Tourist
200 E. Grand Ave.
Des Moines, IA 50309
800-345-4692 or 515-242-4705
http://www.state.ia.us/tourism/

Kansas Department of Commerce and Housing
Division of Travel and Tourism
700 SW Harrison St., Suite 1200
Topeka, KS 66601-3712
800-252-6727, 913-296-7091, or 913-296-3487 (TDD)
Fax: 913-296-6988
http://kicin.cecase.ukans.edu/kdoch/html/tour1.html

Kentucky Department of Travel Development
500 Mero St., Suite 2200
Frankfort, KY 40601
800-225-8747 (TDD-equipped) or 502-564-4930
Fax: 502-564-5695
http://www.state.ky.us/tour/tour.htm
E-mail: travel@exch.tour.state.ky.us

Travel

Louisiana Department of Culture, Recreation, and Tourism
Office of Tourism
P.O. Box 94291
Baton Rouge, LA 70804-9291
800-334-8626 or 504-342-8119
Fax: 504-342-8390
http://www.louisianatravel.com/

Maine Publicity Bureau
Office of Tourism
P.O. Box 2300
Hallowell, ME 04347-2300
800-533-9595 or 207-623-0363
Fax: 207-623-0388
http://www.visitmaine.com/

Maryland Office of Tourist Development
217 E. Redwood St., 9th Floor
Baltimore, MD 21202
800-543-1036 or 800-634-7386
http://www.mdisfun.org

Massachusetts Office of Travel and Tourism
100 Cambridge St., 13th Floor
Boston, MA 02202
800-447-6277 or 617-727-3201
http://www.mass-vacation.com/

Michigan Department of Commerce
Travel Bureau
P.O. Box 30226
Lansing, MI 48909
888-784-7328, 800-543-2937, or 800-722-8191 (TDD)
http://www.michigan.org/

Minnesota Office of Tourism
500 Metro Square
121 Seventh Place
East St. Paul, MN 55101-2112
800-657-3700 or 612-296-5029
http://www.exploreminnesota.com/

Mississippi Department of Economic and Community Development
Division of Tourism
P.O. Box 849
Jackson, MS 39205
800-927-6378 or 601-359-3297
Fax: 601-359-5757
http://www.mississippi.org/

Missouri Division of Tourism
P.O. Box 1055
Jefferson City, MO 65102
800-877-1234 or 314-751-4133
http://www.ecodev.state.mo.us/tourism

Travel Montana
Department of Commerce
1424 9th Ave.
Helena, MT 59620-0533
800-847-4868 or 406-444-2654
Fax: 406-444-1800
http://travel.mt.gov/

Nebraska Tourism Office
P.O. Box 94666
Lincoln, NE 68509-4666
800-228-4307, ext. 754
http://www.ded.state.ne.us/tourism/index.htm
E-mail: tourism@ded2.ded.state.ne.us

Nevada State Board on Tourism
Capitol Complex
Carson City, NV 89710
800-638-2328 or 702-687-4322
Fax: 702-687-6779
http://www.travelnevada.com/

New Hampshire Office of Travel and Tourism Development
P.O. Box 1856
Concord, NH 03302-1856
800-386-4664
http://www.visitnh.gov/
E-mail: request@visitnh.gov

New Jersey Department of Commerce and Economic Development
Division of Travel and Tourism
P.O. Box 826
Trenton, NJ 08625-0826
800-537-7397 or 609-633-2623
Fax: 609-633-7418
http://www.state.nj.us/travel/

New Mexico Department of Tourism
491 Old Santa Fe Trail
Santa Fe, NM 87503
800-733-6396 or 505-827-7336
http://www.newmexico.org/
E-mail: enchantment@newmexico.org

New York—I ♥ NY
Empire State Development Travel Information Center
One Commerce Plaza
Albany, NY 12245
800-225-5697 or 518-474-4116
Fax: 518-486-6416
http://www.iloveny.state.ny.us/

Go to "States and Territories" in chapter 25; "United States" in the atlas

**North Carolina Department of Commerce
Travel and Tourism Division**
301 N. Wilmington St.
Raleigh, NC 27601-2825
800-847-4862 or 919-733-4171
http://www.commerce.state.nc.us/commerce/press/
  travelgu.html

North Dakota Tourism
Liberty Memorial Bldg.
604 East Blvd.
Bismarck, ND 58505-0825
800-435-5663 or 701-328-2525
Fax: 701-328-4878
http://www.ndtourism.com/
E-mail: msmail.tharris@ranch.state.ND.US

Ohio Division of Travel and Tourism
P.O. Box 1001
Columbus, OH 43216-0101
800-282-5393 or 614-466-8844
http://www.ohiotourism.com/

Oklahoma Tourism and Recreation Department
15 N. Robinson, Room 801
P.O. Box 52002
Oklahoma City, OK 73152-2002
800-652-6552 or 405-521-2409
Fax: 405-521-3992
http://www.otrd.state.ok.us/

Oregon Tourism Commission
775 Summer St., NE
Salem, OR 97310
800-547-7842 or 800-543-8838
http://www.traveloregon.com/

**Pennsylvania Office of Travel, Tourism, and Film
  Production**
Room 400, Forum Building
Harrisburg, PA 17120
800-847-4874 or 717-232-8880
http://www.state.pa.us/visit/

**Rhode Island Economic Development
  Corporation
Tourism Division**
One W. Exchange St.
Providence, RI 02903
800-845-2000, 800-556-2484, or 401-277-2601
Fax: 401-273-8270
http://visitrhodeisland.com/

**South Carolina Department of Parks, Recreation,
  and Tourism**
1205 Pendleton St.
Columbia, SC 29201-0071
800-868-2492 or 803-734-0122
Fax: 803-734-1163
http://www.travelsc.com/

**South Dakota Department of Tourism
  and Economic Development**
Capitol Lake Plaza
711 E. Wells Ave.
c/o 500 E. Capitol Ave.
Pierre, SD 57501-5070
800-732-5682 or 605-773-3301
Fax: 605-773-3256
http://www.state.sd.us/state/executive/tourism/
  tourism.html
E-mail: SDINFO@goed.state.sd.us

Tennessee Department of Tourism Development
Rachel Jackson Bldg., 5th Floor
320 6th Ave. N.
Nashville, TN 37202-3170
800-836-6200 or 615-741-2159
http://www.state.tn.us/tourdev/
E-mail: tourdev@www.state.tn.us

Texas Department of Tourism
P.O. Box 12728
Austin, TX 78711
800-888-8839 or 512-462-9191
http://www.traveltex.com/

Utah Travel Council
Council Hall
Salt Lake City, UT 84114
800-200-1160 or 801-538-1030
Fax: 801-538-1399
http://www.utah.com/

Vermont Department of Tourism and Marketing
134 State St.
P.O. Box 1471
Montpelier, VT 05601-1471
800-837-6668 or 802-828-3237
Fax: 802-828-3233
http://www.travel-vermont.com/

"Time Adjustments: Daylight Savings Time in
the United States" in chapter 1
Go to

Virginia Tourism Office
901 E. Byrd St.
Richmond, VA 23219
800-847-4882
Fax: 804-786-1919
http://www.virginia.org/

Washington State Tourism Division
P.O. Box 42500
Olympia, WA 98504
800-544-1800 or 360-586-2012
http://www.tourism.wa.gov/

West Virginia Division of Tourism and Parks
2101 Washington St. E.
Charleston, WV 25305
800-225-5982 or 304-558-5766
http://www.state.wv.us/tourism/default.htm

Wisconsin Department of Tourism
201 W. Washington, 2nd Floor
P.O. Box 7976
Madison, WI 53707-7976
800-432-8747, 608-266-7621,
   or 608-267-0756 (TDD)
Fax: 608-266-3404
http://badger.state.wi.us/agencies/tourism

Wyoming Division of Tourism
Interstate 25 at College Drive
Cheyenne, WY 82002
800-225-5996 or 307-777-7777
Fax: 307-777-6904
http://www.state.wy.us/state/tourism/tourism.html

WEATHER CHARTS

AVERAGE PRECIPITATION FOR SELECTED STATES AND CITIES (IN INCHES)

State	City	Jan/Feb	Mar/Apr	May/Jun	Jul/Aug	Sep/Oct	Nov/Dec
Alabama	Mobile	5.1	5.4	5.4	6.9	4.4	4.7
Alaska	Juneau	4.1	3.0	3.3	4.7	7.3	4.7
Arizona	Phoenix	0.7	0.6	0.1	0.9	0.8	0.8
California	Los Angeles	2.5	1.4	0.1	0.1	0.3	1.7
	San Francisco	3.8	2.2	0.1	0.04	0.7	3.0
Colorado	Denver	0.6	1.5	2.1	1.7	1.1	0.8
Connecticut	Hartford	3.3	3.7	3.9	3.4	3.7	4.0
Delaware	Wilmington	3.0	3.4	3.7	3.8	3.2	3.4
District of Columbia	Washington	2.7	2.9	3.5	3.9	3.2	3.1
Florida	Jacksonville	3.6	3.2	4.6	6.8	5.0	2.5
	Miami	2.0	2.6	7.7	6.6	6.6	2.2
Georgia	Atlanta	4.8	5.0	3.9	4.3	3.2	4.1
Hawaii	Honolulu	2.9	1.9	0.8	0.5	1.5	3.4
Idaho	Boise	1.3	1.3	0.9	0.4	0.8	1.4
Illinois	Chicago	1.4	3.2	3.6	3.9	3.1	2.7
Indiana	Indianapolis	2.4	3.4	3.7	4.0	2.8	3.3
Iowa	Des Moines	1.0	2.8	4.1	4.0	3.1	1.6
Kansas	Dodge City	0.5	1.7	3.2	2.8	1.6	0.7
Kentucky	Louisville	3.1	4.4	4.0	4.0	2.9	3.7
Louisiana	New Orleans	5.5	4.7	5.2	6.1	4.3	5.1
Maine	Portland	3.4	3.9	3.5	3.0	3.5	4.7
Massachusetts	Boston	3.6	3.6	3.2	3.0	3.2	4.1
Michigan	Detroit	1.8	2.8	3.3	3.3	2.5	2.7
Minnesota	Duluth	1.0	2.1	3.4	3.8	3.2	1.5
	Minneapolis	0.9	2.2	3.7	3.6	2.5	1.3
Mississippi	Jackson	5.0	5.7	4.1	4.1	3.4	5.4

continues

Continued

AVERAGE PRECIPITATION FOR SELECTED STATES AND CITIES (IN INCHES)

State	City	Jan/Feb	Mar/Apr	May/Jun	Jul/Aug	Sep/Oct	Nov/Dec
Missouri	Kansas City	1.1	2.8	4.9	4.2	4.1	1.8
	St. Louis	2.0	3.5	3.8	3.4	2.9	3.2
Montana	Helena	0.6	0.9	1.9	1.1	0.8	0.6
Nebraska	Omaha	0.8	2.4	4.2	3.4	3.0	1.3
Nevada	Reno	1.0	0.5	0.6	0.3	0.4	0.9
New Jersey	Atlantic City	3.3	3.6	3.0	4.0	2.9	3.5
New Mexico	Albuquerque	0.5	0.5	0.6	1.5	0.9	0.5
New York	Albany	2.3	3.0	3.5	3.3	2.9	3.1
	Buffalo	2.5	2.8	3.3	3.6	3.3	3.8
	New York	3.3	4.0	4.0	4.2	3.7	4.2
North Carolina	Raleigh	3.6	3.2	3.8	4.0	3.0	3.1
North Dakota	Bismarck	0.4	1.2	2.5	1.9	1.2	0.5
Ohio	Cleveland	2.1	3.0	3.6	3.5	3.0	3.1
	Columbus	2.2	3.2	4.0	4.0	2.6	3.0
Oklahoma	Oklahoma City	1.3	2.7	4.8	2.6	3.5	1.7
Oregon	Portland	4.6	3.0	1.8	0.9	2.2	5.7
Pennsylvania	Philadelphia	3.0	3.5	3.7	4.0	3.0	3.4
	Pittsburgh	2.5	3.3	3.7	3.5	2.7	2.9
Rhode Island	Providence	3.7	4.1	3.5	3.4	3.6	4.4
South Carolina	Charleston	3.4	3.5	5.5	6.9	3.9	2.7
South Dakota	Huron	0.6	1.6	3.0	2.2	1.4	0.6
Tennessee	Memphis	4.0	5.4	4.3	3.6	3.3	5.4
	Nashville	3.7	4.6	4.2	3.7	3.0	4.4
Texas	Dallas–Ft. Worth	2.0	3.1	3.9	2.3	3.5	2.1
	Houston	3.1	3.1	5.1	3.5	4.6	3.6
Utah	Salt Lake City	1.2	2.0	1.4	0.8	1.4	1.3
Vermont	Burlington	1.7	2.5	3.3	3.9	3.1	2.8
Virginia	Norfolk	3.6	3.4	3.8	4.0	3.5	3.0
	Richmond	3.2	3.3	3.7	4.7	3.4	3.2
Washington	Seattle-Tacoma	4.7	2.9	1.6	1.0	2.6	5.9
Wisconsin	Milwaukee	1.5	3.1	3.0	3.5	2.9	2.4
Wyoming	Lander	0.6	1.4	2.1	0.6	1.1	0.7

The interstate highway system requires that 1 mile in every 5 must be straight. These sections can be used as airstrips in time of war or other emergencies.

Go to "Meteorology" in chapter 4; "Weather Symbols" in chapter 12

NORMAL DAILY MEAN TEMPERATURE——SELECTED CITIES (IN °F)

Airport data except as noted. Based on standard 30-year period, 1961 through 1990.

State	Station	Jan	Feb	Mar	Apr	May	June	July	Aug	Sep	Oct	Nov	Dec	Annual Avg
Alabama	Mobile	49.9	53.2	60.5	67.8	74.5	80.4	82.3	81.8	77.9	68.4	59.8	53.0	**67.5**
Alaska	Juneau	24.2	28.4	32.7	39.7	47.0	53.0	56.0	55.0	49.4	42.2	32.0	27.1	**40.6**
Arizona	Phoenix	53.6	57.7	62.2	69.9	78.8	88.2	93.5	91.5	85.6	74.5	61.9	54.1	**72.6**
Arkansas	Little Rock	39.1	43.6	53.1	62.1	70.2	78.4	81.9	80.6	74.1	63.0	52.1	42.8	**61.8**
California	Los Angeles	56.8	57.6	58.0	60.1	62.7	65.7	69.1	70.5	69.9	66.8	61.6	56.9	**63.0**
	Sacramento	45.2	50.7	53.6	58.3	65.3	71.6	75.7	75.1	71.5	64.2	53.3	45.3	**60.8**
	San Diego	57.4	58.6	59.6	62.0	64.1	66.8	71.0	72.6	71.4	67.7	62.0	57.4	**64.2**
	San Francisco	48.7	52.2	53.3	55.6	58.1	61.5	62.7	63.7	64.5	61.0	54.8	49.4	**57.1**
Colorado	Denver	29.7	33.4	39.0	48.2	57.2	66.9	73.5	71.4	62.3	51.4	39.0	31.0	**50.3**
Connecticut	Hartford	24.6	27.5	37.5	48.7	59.8	68.5	73.7	71.6	63.3	52.2	41.9	29.5	**49.9**
Delaware	Wilmington	30.6	33.4	42.7	52.2	62.5	71.5	76.4	75.0	68.0	56.2	46.3	35.8	**54.2**
District of Columbia	Washington	34.6	37.5	47.2	56.5	66.4	75.6	80.0	78.5	71.3	59.7	49.8	39.4	**58.0**
Florida	Jacksonville	52.4	55.2	61.1	67.0	73.4	79.1	81.6	81.2	78.1	69.8	61.9	55.1	**68.0**
	Miami	67.2	68.5	71.7	75.2	78.7	81.4	82.6	82.8	81.9	78.3	73.6	69.1	**75.9**
Georgia	Atlanta	41.0	44.8	53.5	61.5	69.2	76.0	78.8	78.1	72.7	62.3	53.1	44.5	**61.3**
Hawaii	Honolulu	72.9	73.0	74.4	75.8	77.5	79.4	80.5	81.4	81.0	79.6	77.2	74.1	**77.2**
Idaho	Boise	29.0	35.9	42.4	49.1	57.5	66.5	74.0	72.5	62.6	51.8	39.9	30.1	**50.9**
Illinois	Chicago	21.0	25.4	37.2	48.6	58.9	68.6	73.2	71.7	64.4	52.8	40.0	26.6	**49.0**
	Peoria	21.6	26.3	39.0	51.4	61.9	71.5	75.5	73.1	66.1	54.0	41.2	27.0	**50.7**
Indiana	Indianapolis	25.5	29.6	41.4	52.4	62.8	71.9	75.4	73.2	66.6	54.7	43.0	30.9	**52.3**
Iowa	Des Moines	19.4	24.7	37.3	50.9	62.3	71.8	76.6	73.9	65.1	53.5	39.0	24.4	**49.9**
Kansas	Wichita	29.5	34.8	45.4	56.4	65.6	75.7	81.4	79.3	70.3	58.6	44.7	33.0	**56.2**
Kentucky	Louisville	31.7	35.7	46.3	56.3	65.3	73.2	77.2	75.8	69.5	57.6	47.1	36.9	**56.1**
Louisiana	New Orleans	51.3	54.3	61.6	68.5	74.8	80.0	81.9	81.5	78.1	69.1	61.1	54.5	**68.1**
Maine	Portland	20.8	23.3	33.0	43.3	53.3	62.4	68.6	67.3	59.1	48.5	38.7	26.5	**45.4**
Maryland	Baltimore	31.8	34.8	44.1	53.4	63.4	72.5	77.0	75.6	68.5	56.6	46.8	36.7	**55.1**
Massachusetts	Boston	28.6	30.3	38.6	48.1	68.2	67.7	73.5	71.9	64.8	54.8	45.3	33.6	**51.3**
Michigan	Detroit	22.9	25.4	35.7	47.3	58.4	67.6	72.3	70.5	63.2	51.2	40.2	28.3	**48.6**
	Sault Ste. Marie	12.9	14.0	24.0	38.2	50.5	58.0	63.8	62.6	55.1	45.3	33.0	19.0	**39.7**
Minnesota	Duluth	7.0	12.3	24.4	38.6	50.8	59.8	66.1	63.7	54.2	43.7	28.4	12.8	**38.5**
	Minneapolis– St. Paul	11.8	17.9	31.0	46.4	58.5	68.2	73.6	70.5	60.5	48.8	33.2	17.9	**44.9**
Mississippi	Jackson	44.1	47.9	56.7	64.6	72.0	78.8	81.5	80.9	75.9	64.7	55.8	47.8	**64.2**
Missouri	Kansas City	25.7	31.2	42.7	54.5	64.1	73.2	78.5	76.1	67.5	56.6	43.1	30.4	**53.6**
	St. Louis	29.3	33.9	45.1	56.7	66.1	75.4	79.8	77.6	70.2	58.4	46.2	33.9	**56.1**
Montana	Great Falls	21.2	27.4	33.3	43.6	53.1	61.6	68.2	66.9	56.6	47.5	33.9	23.9	**44.8**
Nebraska	Omaha	21.1	26.9	38.6	51.9	62.4	72.1	76.9	74.1	65.1	53.4	39.0	25.1	**50.6**
Nevada	Reno	32.9	38.0	42.8	48.6	56.5	65.1	71.6	69.6	60.4	50.8	40.3	32.7	**50.8**
New Hampshire	Concord	18.6	21.8	32.4	43.9	55.2	64.2	69.5	67.3	58.8	47.8	37.1	24.3	**45.1**
New Jersey	Atlantic City	30.9	33.0	41.5	50.0	60.4	69.4	74.7	73.4	66.1	54.9	45.8	35.8	**53.0**
New Mexico	Albuquerque	34.2	40.0	46.9	55.2	64.2	74.2	78.5	75.9	68.6	57.0	44.3	35.3	**56.2**

continues

Continued

NORMAL DAILY MEAN TEMPERATURE––SELECTED CITIES (IN °F)

State	Station	Jan	Feb	Mar	Apr	May	June	July	Aug	Sep	Oct	Nov	Dec	Annual Avg
New York	Albany	20.6	23.5	34.3	46.4	57.6	66.9	71.8	69.6	61.3	50.2	39.7	26.5	**47.4**
	Buffalo	23.6	24.5	33.8	45.2	56.6	65.9	71.1	69.0	61.9	51.1	40.5	29.1	**47.7**
	New York[1]	31.5	33.6	42.4	52.5	62.7	71.6	76.8	75.5	68.2	57.5	47.6	36.6	**54.7**
North Carolina	Charlotte	39.3	42.5	50.9	59.4	67.4	75.7	79.3	78.3	72.4	61.3	52.1	42.6	**60.1**
	Raleigh	38.9	42.0	50.4	59.0	67.0	74.3	78.1	77.1	71.1	60.1	51.2	42.6	**59.3**
North Dakota	Bismarck	9.2	15.7	28.2	43.0	55.0	64.4	70.4	68.3	57.0	45.7	28.6	14.0	**41.6**
Ohio	Cincinnati	28.1	31.8	43.0	53.2	62.9	71.0	75.1	73.5	67.3	55.1	44.3	33.5	**53.2**
	Cleveland	24.8	27.2	37.3	47.6	58.0	67.6	71.9	70.4	63.9	52.8	42.6	30.9	**49.6**
	Columbus	26.4	29.6	40.9	51.0	61.2	69.2	73.2	71.5	65.5	53.7	42.9	31.9	**51.4**
Oklahoma	Oklahoma City	35.9	40.9	50.3	60.4	68.4	76.7	82.0	81.1	73.0	62.0	49.6	39.3	**60.0**
Oregon	Portland	39.6	43.6	47.3	51.0	57.1	63.5	68.2	68.6	63.3	54.5	46.1	40.2	**53.6**
Pennsylvania	Philadelphia	30.4	33.0	42.4	52.4	62.9	71.8	76.7	75.5	68.2	56.4	46.4	35.8	**54.3**
	Pittsburgh	26.1	28.7	39.4	49.6	59.5	67.9	72.1	70.5	63.9	52.4	42.3	31.5	**50.3**
Rhode Island	Providence	27.9	29.7	37.4	47.4	57.3	66.9	72.7	71.3	64.1	53.6	44.0	32.8	**50.4**
South Carolina	Columbia	43.8	46.8	55.2	63.0	70.9	77.4	80.8	79.7	74.2	63.3	54.6	46.9	**63.1**
South Dakota	Sioux Falls	13.8	19.7	32.5	46.9	58.4	68.3	74.3	71.4	60.9	48.6	33.0	18.3	**45.5**
Tennessee	Memphis	39.7	44.2	53.1	62.9	71.2	79.1	82.6	81.0	74.2	63.1	52.5	43.7	**62.3**
	Nashville	36.2	40.4	50.2	59.2	67.7	75.6	79.3	78.1	71.8	60.4	50.0	40.5	**59.1**
Texas	Dallas–Fort Worth	43.4	47.9	56.7	65.5	72.8	81.0	85.3	84.9	77.4	67.2	56.2	46.9	**65.4**
	El Paso	42.8	48.1	55.1	63.4	71.8	80.4	82.3	80.1	74.4	64.0	52.4	44.1	**63.2**
	Houston	50.4	53.9	60.6	68.3	74.5	80.4	82.6	82.3	78.2	69.6	61.0	53.5	**67.9**
Utah	Salt Lake City	27.9	34.1	41.8	49.7	58.8	69.1	77.9	75.6	65.2	53.2	40.8	29.7	**52.0**
Vermont	Burlington	16.3	18.2	30.7	43.9	56.3	65.2	70.5	67.9	58.9	47.8	36.8	23.0	**44.6**
Virginia	Norfolk	39.1	41.0	48.6	57.0	66.1	74.1	78.2	77.2	71.9	61.2	52.5	43.8	**59.2**
	Richmond	35.7	38.7	48.0	57.3	66.0	73.9	78.0	76.8	70.0	58.6	49.6	40.1	**57.7**
Washington	Seattle-Tacoma	40.1	43.5	45.6	49.2	55.1	60.9	65.2	65.6	60.6	52.8	45.3	40.5	**52.0**
	Spokane	27.1	33.3	38.7	45.9	53.9	62.0	68.8	68.4	58.9	47.3	35.1	27.8	**47.3**
West Virginia	Charleston	32.1	35.5	45.9	54.8	63.5	71.4	75.1	73.9	67.7	56.2	46.8	37.0	**55.0**
Wisconsin	Milwaukee	18.9	23.0	33.3	44.4	54.6	65.0	70.9	69.3	61.7	50.3	37.7	24.4	**46.1**
Wyoming	Cheyenne	26.5	29.3	33.6	42.5	52.0	61.3	68.4	66.4	57.4	47.0	35.2	27.8	**45.6**

[1] City office data.

SUNSHINE, AVERAGE WIND SPEED, MEAN NUMBER OF DAYS MINIMUM TEMPERATURE BELOW 32°F, AND AVERAGE RELATIVE HUMIDITY—SELECTED CITIES

Airport data, except as noted. For period of record through 1990, except as noted.

State	Station	Average Percentage of Possible Sunshine — Length of Record (yr.)	Annual	Average Wind Speed (m.p.h.) — Length of Record (yr.)	Annual	Jan	July	Minimum Temperature 32°F or Less — Length of Record (yr.)	Mean Number (days)	Average Relative Humidity (percent) — Length of Record (yr.)	Annual A.M.	Annual P.M.	Jan A.M.	Jan P.M.	July A.M.	July P.M.
Alabama	Mobile	40[1]	59[1]	42	9.0	10.4	7.0	28	23	28	86	57	81	61	89	60
Alaska	Juneau	33	30	45	8.3	8.3	7.5	46	142	24	84	73	80	77	83	70
Arizona	Phoenix	95	86	45	6.3	5.3	7.2	30	8	30	51	23	66	32	45	20
Arkansas	Little Rock	32	62	48	7.8	8.6	6.7	30	60	30	84	57	80	61	88	56
California	Los Angeles	32	73	42	7.5	6.7	7.8	31	(Z)	31	79	64	69	59	86	68
	Sacramento	42	78	41	7.9	7.2	9.0	40	17	30	82	46	90	70	76	28
	San Diego	50	68	50	6.9	5.9	7.4	30	(Z)	30	76	62	70	56	82	66
	San Francisco	38	66	63	10.6	7.2	13.6	31	2	31	84	61	86	66	86	59
Colorado	Denver	41	70	42	8.7	8.7	8.3	30	157	30	67	40	63	49	68	34
Connecticut	Hartford	36	57	36	8.5	9.0	7.5	31	135	31	76	52	71	56	78	51
Delaware	Wilmington	(NA)	(NA)	42	9.1	9.8	7.8	43	100	43	78	55	75	60	79	54
District of Columbia	Washington	42	56	42	9.4	10.0	8.2	30	71	30	74	53	69	55	76	53
Florida	Jacksonville	39	63	41	8.0	8.2	7.1	49	15	54	88	56	87	57	88	58
	Miami	14	73	41	9.3	9.5	7.9	26	(Z)	26	84	61	84	59	84	63
Georgia	Atlanta	55	61	52	9.1	10.5	7.6	30	54	30	82	56	78	59	88	60
Hawaii	Honolulu	38	69	41	11.4	9.7	13.3	21	—	21	72	56	75	62	67	51
Idaho	Boise	48	64	51	8.8	8.0	8.4	51	124	51	69	43	70	67	54	22
Illinois	Chicago	10	55	32	10.3	11.6	8.2	32	133	32	80	60	76	67	82	57
	Peoria	47	57	47	10.0	11.2	7.8	31	129	31	83	61	79	68	86	59
Indiana	Indianapolis	46	55	42	9.6	10.9	7.4	31	118	31	83	62	80	70	87	60
Iowa	Des Moines	40	59	41	10.9	11.7	9.0	29	135	29	79	60	75	67	82	57
Kansas	Wichita	37	65	37	12.3	12.2	11.3	37	111	37	80	55	79	62	78	48
Kentucky	Louisville	43	56	43	8.4	9.7	6.7	30	89	30	81	58	76	64	85	58
Louisiana	New Orleans	17	60	42	8.2	9.4	6.1	44	13	42	87	63	85	66	91	66
Maine	Portland	50	57	50	8.8	9.2	7.6	50	157	50	79	59	76	61	80	59
Maryland	Baltimore	40	57	40	9.2	9.7	8.0	40	97	37	77	54	71	57	81	53

continues

Travel

Continued

State	Station	Average Percentage of Possible Sunshine Length of Record (yr.)	Annual	Average Wind Speed (m.p.h.) Length of Record (yr.)	Annual	Jan	July	Minimum Temperature 32°F or Less Length of Record (yr.)	Mean Number (days)	Average Relative Humidity (percent) Length of Record (yr.)	Annual A.M.	Annual P.M.	Jan A.M.	Jan P.M.	July A.M.	July P.M.
Massachusetts	Boston	55	58	33	12.5	13.9	11.0	26	98	26	72	58	67	57	74	57
Michigan	Detroit	25	53	32	10.4	12.0	8.5	32	136	32	81	60	80	69	82	53
	Sault Ste. Marie	49	47	49	9.3	9.8	7.8	49	181	49	85	67	81	75	89	61
Minnesota	Duluth	40	52	41	11.1	11.6	9.4	29	185	29	81	63	76	70	85	59
	Minneapolis–St. Paul	52	58	52	10.6	10.5	9.4	31	156	31	78	59	74	67	80	54
Mississippi	Jackson	26	60	27	7.4	8.6	5.9	27	50	27	91	58	87	64	93	59
Missouri	Kansas City	18	62	18	10.8	11.5	9.4	18	110	18	81	60	76	63	84	57
	St. Louis	31	57	41	9.7	10.6	8.0	30	100	30	83	59	81	65	85	56
Montana	Great Falls	46	61	49	12.8	15.3	10.1	29	157	29	66	45	66	60	65	29
Nebraska	Omaha	54	60	54	10.6	10.9	8.9	25	141	26	81	59	78	65	84	57
Nevada	Reno	42	79	48	6.6	5.6	7.0	27	174	27	70	32	79	51	63	18
New Hampshire	Concord	49	54	48	6.7	7.2	5.7	25	173	25	81	54	75	58	84	52
New Jersey	Atlantic City	30	56	32	10.1	11.0	8.5	26	110	26	81	56	77	58	83	57
New Mexico	Albuquerque	51	76	3	11.8	11.7	10.6	30	119	30	60	29	70	40	60	27
New York	Albany	52	52	52	8.9	9.8	7.4	25	149	25	80	57	77	63	81	55
	Buffalo	47	49	51	12.0	14.3	10.3	30	133	30	80	63	79	72	78	55
	New York	104	58	58	9.4	10.7	7.6	77	80	61	72	56	68	60	75	55
North Carolina	Charlotte	40	63	41	7.5	7.9	6.6	30	67	30	83	54	78	55	87	57
	Raleigh	36	59	41	7.8	8.5	6.7	26	78	26	85	54	78	55	89	58
North Dakota	Bismarck	51	59	51	10.2	10.0	9.2	31	186	31	80	56	74	68	83	47
Ohio	Cincinnati	7	52	43	9.1	10.7	7.1	28	108	28	81	59	78	67	85	57
	Cleveland	47	49	49	10.6	12.3	8.6	30	124	30	79	62	77	69	81	57
	Columbus	39	49	41	8.5	10.1	6.6	31	119	31	80	59	76	67	84	56
Oklahoma	Oklahoma City	36	68	42	12.4	12.8	10.9	25	77	25	79	54	77	59	80	49
Oregon	Portland	41	48	42	7.9	9.9	7.6	50	43	50	86	60	86	76	82	45
Pennsylvania	Philadelphia	48	56	50	9.5	10.3	8.1	31	97	31	76	55	73	59	79	54
	Pittsburgh	38	46	38	9.1	10.7	7.2	31	123	30	78	57	75	65	93	54
Rhode Island	Providence	37	58	37	10.6	11.2	9.5	27	119	27	75	55	70	56	77	56

State	Station	Average Percentage of Possible Sunshine		Average Wind Speed (m.p.h.)				Minimum Temperature 32°F or Less		Average Relative Humidity (percent)						
		Length of Record (yr.)	Annual	Length of Record (yr.)	Annual	Jan	July	Length of Record (yr.)	Mean Number (days)	Length of Record (yr.)	Annual A.M.	Annual P.M.	Jan A.M.	Jan P.M.	July A.M.	July P.M.
South Carolina	Columbia	37	64	42	6.9	7.2	6.3	24	61	24	87	51	82	54	89	54
South Dakota	Sioux Falls	48[3]	63[3]	42	11.1	11.1	9.8	27	168	27	81	60	76	67	82	53
Tennessee	Memphis	35	64	42	8.9	10.1	7.5	49	57	51	81	57	78	63	84	57
	Nashville	48	56	49	8.0	9.2	6.5	25	76	25	84	57	79	63	89	57
Texas	Dallas–Ft. Worth	12	64	37	10.8	11.2	9.6	27	40	27	82	56	79	59	80	48
	El Paso	48	83	48	8.9	8.4	8.3	30	65	30	57	27	65	34	62	29
	Houston	21	56	21	7.9	8.3	7.0	21	21	21	90	59	85	63	92	58
Utah	Salt Lake City	52	66	61	8.9	7.7	9.6	31	125	31	67	43	79	69	52	22
Vermont	Burlington	47	49	47	8.9	9.7	7.9	26	156	25	77	59	71	63	78	53
Virginia	Norfolk	26	61	42	10.7	11.5	9.0	42	54	42	78	57	74	58	82	59
	Richmond	40	62	42	7.7	8.1	6.8	61	85	56	83	53	80	57	85	56
Washington	Seattle–Tacoma	24	46	42	9.0	9.8	8.3	31	31	31	83	62	81	74	82	49
	Spokane	42	54	43	8.9	8.8	8.6	31	139	31	77	52	85	78	64	27
West Virginia	Charleston	47[4]	40[4]	43	6.3	7.5	5.0	43	100	43	83	56	77	62	90	60
Wisconsin	Milwaukee	50	54	50	11.6	12.7	9.7	30	141	30	81	64	76	68	82	61
Wyoming	Cheyenne	51	65	33	13.0	15.4	10.3	31	171	31	65	44	57	50	70	38

— Represents zero.

(NA) Not available

Z (/) Represents less than one-half day.

[1] Recording site is in Montgomery, AL.

[2] City office data.

[3] Recording site is in Rapid City, SD.

[4] Recording site is in Elkins, WV.

AIR MILEAGE FROM NEW YORK CITY—DOMESTIC

Albuquerque	1,810
Atlanta	747
Baltimore	170
Boston	188
Chicago	711
Denver	1,628
Detroit	483
Kansas City, Mo.	1,097
Los Angeles	2,446
Memphis	953
Miami	1,095
Nashville	758
New Orleans	1,173
Omaha	1,144
Philadelphia	83
Phoenix	2,142
Portland	2,455
St. Louis	873
Salt Lake City	1,972
San Francisco	2,568
Seattle	2,419
Washington, D.C.	204

NATIONAL PARK DIRECTORY

For detailed information on the National Parks, write to the Superintendent of Documents at the Government Printing Office in Washington, DC 20402, or call 202-512-1800. The GPO's *The National Parks: Index* describes the facilities at each park.

Acadia National Park, Bar Harbor, Maine
Area: 41,888 acres
Open: Year-round
Major attractions: Mountains (highest point on Atlantic Coast) showing marine erosion and glaciation; lakes; forests; marine life.
Activities: Camping, fishing, hiking, horseback riding, nature walks, picnicking, swimming, sea cruises.

Arches National Park, Moab, Utah
Area: 73,379 acres
Open: Year-round
Major attractions: Huge rock formations caused by erosion; mountains; Colorado River gorge.
Activities: Camping, fishing, canoeing, white-water boating.

Badlands National Park, Interior, South Dakota
Area: 242,755 acres
Open: Year-round
Major attractions: Multicolored peaks and spires caused by erosion; fossil sites; wildlife; Pine Ridge Indian Reservation near site of Wounded Knee battleground.
Activities: Camping, fishing, hiking, picnicking.

Big Bend National Park, Big Bend National Park, Texas
Area: 801,163 acres
Open: Year-round
Major attractions: Mountains, canyons, desert, U.S. and Mexican flowers, trees, wildlife.
Activities: Camping, boating, fishing, hiking, horseback riding, picnicking, pack trips.

Biscayne National Park, Homestead, Florida
Area: 173,467 acres
Open: Year-round
Major attractions: Underwater coral reefs, marine life.
Activities: Boating, snorkeling, scuba diving.

Bryce Canyon National Park, Bryce Canyon, Utah
Area: 35,836 acres
Open: Year-round
Major attractions: Multicolored rock erosions.
Activities: Camping, fishing, hiking, boating, picnicking, museum tours.

Canyonlands National Park, Moab, Utah
Area: 337,570 acres
Open: Year-round
Major attractions: Rock formations, ancient cliff dwellings, Green River and Colorado River canyons.
Activities: Boating, white-water trips, hiking, camping, fishing, horseback riding, picnicking.

Capitol Reef National Park, Torrey, Utah
Area: 241,905 acres
Open: Year-round
Major attractions: Colorful rock formations, desert plants and wildlife, pioneer exhibits.
Activities: Camping, hiking, fishing, four-wheel-drive trails.

Carlsbad Caverns National Park, Carlsbad, New Mexico
Area: 46,775 acres
Open: Year-round
Major attractions: Possibly world's largest cavern with spectacular underground formations; above-ground desert plants; rock formations.
Activities: Cavern tours, hiking, nature walks, picnicking.

Channel Islands National Park, Ventura,
California
Area: 249,355 acres
Open: Year-round
Major attractions: Marine life, sea birds.
Activities: Hiking, boating, fishing, picnicking, scuba
diving, snorkeling.

Crater Lake National Park, Crater Lake, Oregon
Area: 183,224 acres
Open: Year-round
Major attractions: Deepest lake in the United States
(2,000 feet) in crater of extinct volcano; multicol-
ored rocks; forests; mountain flowers; wildlife.
Activities: Camping, hiking, fishing, boating, cross-
country skiing.

Denali National Park and Preserve, Denali, Alaska
Area: 4,716,726 acres
Open: Year-round
Major attractions: Peaks of Alaska Range, including
Mount McKinley (20,320 feet—highest point in
North America); rare wildlife and subarctic plant
life; huge Denali fault; break in earth's crust.
Activities: Camping, dog-sledding, hiking, fishing.

Everglades National Park, Homestead, Florida
Area: 1,506,499 acres
Open: Year-round
Major attractions: Immense subtropical wilderness,
mangrove swamps, wild animals, rare birds.
Activities: Boating, camping, fishing, guided tours,
hiking, nature walks, picnicking.

Gates of the Arctic National Park and Preserve,
Fairbanks, Alaska
Area: 7,523,888 acres
Open: Year-round
Major attractions: Snow-covered peaks of Brooks
Range north of Arctic Circle; tundra wilderness;
wildlife.
Activities: Hunting, fishing, camping, mountain
climbing.

Glacier Bay National Park, Gustavus, Alaska
Area: 3,226,000 acres
Open: Year-round (Visitor center open only during
the summer months.)
Major attractions: Great Mendenhall Glacier; iceberg
formations from glaciers; dense coastal rain
forests; wildlife; nearby, Mount Logan, highest
point in Canada (19,850 feet).
Activities: Camping, hiking, hunting, fishing.

Glacier National Park, West Glacier, Montana
Area: 1,056,000 acres
Open: Year-round (Most park services and facilities
are available from late May through September. In

late fall, winter, and spring there are very limited
services available in the park.)
Major attractions: Rugged mountain peaks of
Continental Divide; glaciers; numerous alpine
lakes and streams; rare wildflowers; wildlife;
ancient Blackfoot hunting grounds.
Activities: Hiking on old hunting and exploration
trails, nature walks, horseback riding, camping,
fishing.

Grand Canyon National Park, Grand Canyon,
Arizona
Area: 1,218,376 acres
Open: Year-round
Major attractions: Mile-deep, 1.5-billion-year-old
canyon of Colorado River, showing geologic fea-
tures with fossil plants and animals; multicolored
rocks; wide range of wild plants and animals;
Havasupai Indian reservation.
Activities: Camping, hiking, horseback riding, boat-
ing, white-water trips, nature walks, picnicking.

Grand Teton National Park, Moose, Wyoming
Area: 309,993 acres
Open: Year-round
Major attractions: Mountains; trails of famous early
explorers; perennial snow fields; wild plants, ani-
mals, and birds.
Activities: Camping, hiking, fishing, boating, horse-
back riding.

Great Basin National Park, Baker, Nevada
Area: 77,100 acres
Open: Year-round
Major attractions: The South Snake Range (example
of a desert mountain island), Wheeler Peak
(13,063 feet), Lehman Caves, alpine lakes, ancient
bristlecone-pine groves.
Activities: Hiking, biking, camping, limestone cave
tours, guided walks, campfire programs.

Great Smoky Mountains National Park,
Gatlinburg, Tennessee
Area: 520,269 acres
Open: Year-round
Major attractions: Highest mountains in the eastern
United States (6,500 feet), wide range of plants,
wildlife.
Activities: Camping, fishing, hiking, nature walks,
museums, horseback riding, picnicking.

Guadalupe Mountains National Park, Salt Flat,
Texas
Area: 86,415 acres
Open: Year-round
Major attractions: Desert wilderness, limestone fossil
reef, wildlife, highest point in Texas (8,749 feet).
Activities: Camping, hiking.

Travel

Haleakala National Park, Makawao, Maui, Hawaii
Area: 28,655 acres
Open: Year-round
Major attractions: Haleakala crater, scenic pools, rare wildlife, semitropical vegetation.
Activities: Hiking, nature walks, picnicking.

Hawaii Volcanoes National Park, Hawaii National Park, Hawaii
Area: 229,178 acres
Open: Year-round
Major attractions: Volcano activity, semitropical plants, birds.
Activities: Hiking, nature walks, camping.

Hot Springs National Park, Hot Springs, Arkansas
Area: 5,839 acres
Open: Year-round
Major attractions: Ancient hot springs for bathing with reputed therapeutic benefits.
Activities: Bathing, museum tours, hiking, nature trails, picnicking, camping.

Isle Royale National Park, Houghton, Michigan
Area: 571,790 acres
Open: April through October 31
Major attractions: Historic fisheries, hardwood and evergreen forests, pre-Columbian copper mines, wildlife.
Activities: Camping, hiking, fishing, kayaking, boating (no cars permitted on island).

Katmai National Park and Preserve, King Salmon, Alaska
Area: 3,700,000 acres
Open: May through September
Major attractions: Varied subarctic environment, Alagnak Wild River, Valley of 10,000 Smokes, wildlife.
Activities: Fishing, wildlife-watching, kayaking.

Kenai Fjords National Park, Seward, Alaska
Area: 670,000 acres
Open: May through September
Major attractions: Mountains, ice fields, fjord system, varied marine life.
Activities: Fishing, boating, mountain climbing, camping, hiking, bird-watching (150 species).

Kings Canyon National Park, Three Rivers, California
Area: 460,331 acres
Open: May through October
Major attractions: High Sierra peaks, giant sequoia trees, mile-deep canyon, alpine lakes, glaciers and snowfields, wildlife.
Activities: Camping, hiking, horseback riding, fishing, cross-country skiing.

Kobuk Valley National Park, Kotzebue, Alaska
Area: 1,750,000 acres
Open: Year-round
Major attractions: Baird Mountain peaks, forests, tundra, great sand dunes, prehistoric archeological sites, arctic wildlife.
Activities: Hiking, boating, mountain climbing, fishing.

Lake Clark National Park and Preserve, Anchorage, Alaska
Area: 2,636,839 acres
Open: Year-round
Major attractions: Aleutian Range peaks, Cook Inlet, live volcanoes, fossils, forests, wildlife.
Activities: Camping, fishing, boating, hiking, bird-watching, hunting.

Lassen Volcanic National Park, Mineral, California
Area: 106,372 acres
Open: Year-round (Access is difficult in winter and spring.)
Major attractions: Live volcano (intermittent eruptions from 1914 to 1921), hot springs.
Activities: Camping, hiking (150 miles of trails), boating, winter sports.

Mammoth Cave National Park, Mammoth Cave, Kentucky
Area: 52,419 acres
Open: Year-round
Major attractions: Large cavern (330 miles of passageways), underground river.
Activities: Boating, camping, fishing, hiking, nature walks, picnicking.

Mesa Verde National Park, Mesa Verde National Park, Colorado
Area: 51,333 acres
Open: May through October
Major attractions: Pre-Columbian cliff dwellings; lookout showing six mountain ranges in four states.
Activities: Camping, picnicking, hiking, cliff-dwelling tours.

Mount Rainier National Park, Ashford, Washington
Area: 235,613 acres
Open: Year-round
Major attractions: Mountain terrain featuring glaciers, forests, and subalpine meadows.
Activities: Hiking, winter sports, camping, guided climbs to summit (14,410 feet) for experienced mountaineers.

Travel

North Cascades National Park, Sedro Woolley, Washington
Area: 504,781 acres
Open: Year-round
Major attractions: Alpine wilderness area featuring mountains, lakes, forests, glaciers, wildlife.
Activities: Camping, fishing, hiking, boating, horseback riding.

Olympic National Park, Port Angeles, Washington
Area: 922,654 acres
Open: Year-round
Major attractions: Rain forests of giant evergreens; mountains; glaciers; wildlife; rocky beaches on peninsula between Pacific Ocean and Puget Sound.
Activities: Camping, fishing, hiking, bird-watching, horseback riding, boating.

Petrified Forest National Park, Petrified Forest National Park, Arizona
Area: 93,530 acres
Open: Year-round
Major attractions: World's largest display of petrified coniferous trees in six groups of logs now in the form of jasper and agate; prehistoric Indian rock carvings; painted desert of eroded layers of red and yellow sediment.
Activities: Hiking, nature walks, picnicking, camping.

Redwood National Park, Crescent City, California
Area: 110,132 acres
Open: Year-round
Major attractions: Redwood forests, including tallest known tree in the world; Pacific Ocean coastline.
Activities: Camping, hiking, fishing, white-water trips nearby.

Rocky Mountain National Park, Estes Park, Colorado
Area: 265,198 acres
Open: Year-round
Major attractions: Mountains, lakes, streams, forests, wildflower meadows, wild animals.
Activities: Camping, hiking, fishing, horseback riding, mountaineering classes, winter skiing.

Sequoia National Park, Three Rivers, California
Area: 402,482 acres
Open: Year-round
Major attractions: High Sierra peaks, including Mount Whitney (14,494 feet); sequoia forests; wildlife.
Activities: Camping, hiking, fishing, horseback riding, photographic trips.

Shenandoah National Park, Luray, Virginia
Area: 196,039 acres
Open: Year-round
Major attraction: Blue Ridge Mountains, hardwood forests, wildflowers.
Activities: Camping, hiking, horseback riding, nature walks, picnicking.

Theodore Roosevelt Memorial National Park, Medora, North Dakota
Area: 70,446 acres
Open: Year-round
Major attractions: Little Missouri River badlands; site of former President Theodore Roosevelt's ranch; wildlife.
Activities: Hiking, camping, picnicking, float trips, bird-watching.

Virgin Islands National Park, St. John, U.S. Virgin Islands
Area: 14,689 acres
Open: Year-round
Major attractions: Tropical plant and animal life, marine life, sandy beaches, colonial plantations, early Carib relics.
Activities: Camping, fishing, hiking, nature walks, picnicking, swimming, diving.

Voyageurs National Park, International Falls, Minnesota
Area: 219,400 acres
Open: Year-round
Major attractions: Evergreen forests, ancient rock outcroppings, bogs, glacial lakes, wildlife.
Activities: Boating (access to interior is mainly by boat), camping, fishing, hiking, canoeing.

Wind Cave National Park, Hot Springs, South Dakota
Area: 28,060 acres
Open: Year-round
Major attractions: Limestone caverns, bison herds, wildlife.
Activities: Camping, hiking, nature walks, picnicking.

Wrangell–St. Elias National Park and Preserve, Glennallen, Alaska
Area: 8,945,000 acres
Open: Year-round
Major attractions: Largest U.S. national park; greatest concentration of peaks over 14,000 feet in North America; rugged coastline; boreal forests; alpine tundra; wildlife.
Activities: Mountain climbing, hunting, fishing, camping, boating.

Yellowstone National Park, Yellowstone National Park, Wyoming

Area: 2,219,791 acres

Open: Year-round

Major attractions: Oldest national park; spectacular wilderness; Old Faithful geyser; hot springs; lakes, streams, and waterfalls; wildlife; the Grand Canyon of the Yellowstone.

Activities: Camping, hiking, fishing, photography, horseback riding, boating, picnicking, winter ski touring.

Yosemite National Park, Yosemite National Park, California

Area: 761,170 acres

Open: Year-round

Major attractions: Mountain peaks over 10,000 feet, spectacular granite domes and monoliths, highest waterfall in the United States, sequoia groves, wildlife.

Activities: Camping, hiking, rock climbing; mountaineering, horseback riding, fishing, downhill and cross-country skiing in winter.

Zion National Park, Springdale, Utah

Area: 146,597 acres

Open: Year-round (Visitor center open from Memorial Day through Labor Day.)

Major attractions: Huge canyons and gorges carved by mountain rivers, colorful rock cliffs, wildlife.

Activities: Camping, hiking, horseback riding, boating.

NATIONAL WILDLIFE REFUGES LOCATIONS AND FACILITIES

This is not a listing of the entire Refuge System, but of only those refuges that offer visitor opportunities. The address given is that of the office that administers the refuge; it does not necessarily reflect the location of the refuge.

Refuge conditions, regulations, and activities are varied and subject to change. Please check with the refuge manager regarding conditions, regulations, and facilities for persons with disabilities before taking a trip to a refuge.

Go to "The Animal Kingdom" and "The Plant Kingdom" in chapter 3

ACTIVITIES	Bon Secour, P.O. Box 1650, Gulf Shores, AL 36542	Choctaw, Box 808, Jackson, AL 36545
Food/lodging nearby	■	■
Species list	■	
Refuge leaflet		■
Swimming		
Picnicking		
Camping		
Fishing	■	■
Hunting		■
Backcountry use		
Environmental study area		■
Boating—motorized		
Boating—nonmotorized		
Bicycling		
Auto tour		
Foot trails		
Visitor Ctr., Contact Station		
RECOMMENDED BEST WILDLIFE VIEWING — Winter		■
Fall	■	■
Summer		
Spring		■

Alabama

Eufaula, Route 2, Box 97-B, Eufaula, AL 36027 (Alabama and Georgia)

Wheeler, Box 1643, Decatur, AL 35602

Alaska

Alaska Maritime (Headquarters), 202 W. Pioneer Ave., Homer, AK 99603

  Alaska Peninsula Unit

  Aleutian Islands Unit, Box 5251, FPO Seattle, WA 98791

  Bering Sea Unit

  Chukchi Sea Unit

  Gulf of Alaska Unit

Alaska Peninsula, P.O. Box 277, King Salmon, AK 99613

  Becharof

Arctic, 101 12th Ave., Box 20, Fairbanks, AK 99701

Innoko, P.O. Box 69, McGrath, AK 99627

Izembek, Box 127, Cold Bay, AK 99571

Kanuti, 101 12th Ave., Box 20, Fairbanks, AK 99701

Kenai, P.O. Box 2139, Soldorna, AK 99669

Kodiak, 1390 Buskin River Rd., Kodiak, AK 99615

Koyukuk, Box 287, Galena, AK 99741

Nowitna, Box 287, Galena, AK 99741

Selawik, Box 270, Kotzebue, AK 99752

Tetlin, Box 155, Tok, AK 99780

Togiak, P.O. Box 270, Dillingham, AK 99576

Yukon Delta, P.O. Box 346, Bethel, AK 99559

Yukon Flats, 101 12th Ave., Box 20, Fairbanks, AK 99701

Arizona

Buenos Aires, P.O. Box 106, Sasabe, AZ 85633

Cabeza Prieta, Box 418, Ajo, AZ 85321

Cibola, Box AP, Blythe, CA 92225 (Arizona and California)

Havasu, Box A, Needles, CA 92363 (Arizona and California)

Imperial, Box 72217, Martinez Lake, AZ 85364 (Arizona and California)

Kofa, Box 6290, Yuma, AZ 85607

San Bernardino, RR #1, Box 228R, Douglas, AZ 85607

continues

Travel

Continued

	Food/lodging nearby	Species list	Refuge leaflet	Swimming	Picnicking	Camping	Fishing	Hunting	Backcountry use	Environmental study area	Boating—motorized	Boating—nonmotorized	Bicycling	Auto tour	Foot trails	Visitor Ctr., Contact Station	Winter	Fall	Summer	Spring
																	RECOMMENDED BEST WILDLIFE VIEWING			
Arkansas																				
Felsenthal, P.O. Box 67, Manila, AR 72442	■		■				■			■	■	■			■		■	■		■
Holla Bend, Box 1043, Russellville, AR 72801	■	■	■				■			■				■			■	■	■	■
Wapanocca, Box 279, Turrell, AR 72384	■	■	■				■	■		■	■			■		■	■	■	■	■
Big Lake, Box 67, Manila, AR 72442	■	■	■				■						■							
Cache River																				
White River, Box 308, 321 W. 7th St., De Witt, AR 72042	■	■	■				■				■				■	■	■	■	■	■
California																				
Cibola (*See Arizona*)																				
Havasu (*See Arizona*)																				
Imperial (*See Arizona*)																				
Kern, Box 670, Delano, CA 93216	■	■	■							■				■	■	■	■	■		
Klamath Basin Refuges, Route 1, Box 74, Tulelake, CA 96134		■	■					■												
Clear Lake								■					■					■	■	
Lower Klamath (Oregon and California)		■						■				■	■				■		■	■
Tule Lake	■	■	■				■	■			■	■						■	■	■
Modoc, Box 1610, Alturas, CA 96101																				
Sacramento Valley Refuges, Route 1, Box 311, Willows, CA 95988	■	■	■				■	■						■	■	■	■	■		
Colusa		■	■				■	■								■	■			
Delevan	■	■	■				■	■								■	■	■		
Sacramento	■	■	■				■	■								■	■			
Sutter																				

continues

Salton Sea, P.O. Box 120, Calipatria, CA 92223

Coachella Valley

Tijuana Slough

San Francisco Bay, Box 524, Newark, CA 94560-0524

Antioch Dunes

Humboldt Bay

Salinas River

San Pablo Bay

San Luis, Box 2176, Los Banos, CA 93635

Kesterson

Merced

Colorado

Alamosa, Box 1148, Alamosa, CO 81101

Monte Vista

Arapaho, Box 457, Walden, CO 80480

Brown's Park, 1318 Highway 318, Maybell, CO 81640

Connecticut

Salt Meadow, Box 307, Charlestown, RI 02813

Stewart B. McKinney, 910 Lafayette Blvd., Bridgeport, CT 06604

Delaware

Bombay Hook, Route 1, Box 147, Smyrna, DE 19977

Prime Hook, Route 1, Box 195, Milton, DE 19968

Florida

Arthur R. Marshall Loxahatchee, 10216 Lee Rd., Boynton Beach, FL 33437

Hobe Sound

Chassahowitzka, P.O. Box 4139, Homosassa, FL 32647

Cedar Keys

Crystal River

Egmont Key

Lower Suwannee

Passage Key

Pinellas

Travel

Travel

Continued

ACTIVITIES

Refuge	Food/lodging nearby	Species list	Refuge leaflet	Swimming	Picnicking	Camping	Fishing	Hunting	Backcountry use	Environmental study area	Boating—motorized	Boating—nonmotorized	Bicycling	Auto tour	Foot trails	Visitor Ctr., Contact Station	Winter	Fall	Summer	Spring
Florida, cont.																				
J. N. "Ding" Darling, 1 Wildlife Dr., Sanibel, FL 33957	■	■	■				■			■	■	■		■		■		■	■	■
Caloosahatchee	■						■			■								■		■
Island Bay	■									■								■		■
Matlacha Pass	■									■										■
Pine Island	■									■								■		■
Lake Woodruff, Box 488, DeLeon Springs, FL 32028	■		■							■		■			■			■	■	■
Merritt Island, Box 6504, Titusville, FL 32780	■	■	■							■	■	■		■	■	■		■		■
Pelican Island	■	■	■									■						■		■
National Key Deer, Box 510, Big Pine Key, FL 33043	■	■	■				■	■		■			■			■		■		■
Crocodile Lake																			■	
Great White Heron	■	■					■	■		■				■				■	■	■
Key West	■	■																	■	■
St. Marks, Box 68, St. Marks, FL 32355	■	■	■				■	■	■	■	■		■	■	■	■		■		■
St. Vincent, Box 447, Apalachicola, FL 32320							■											■		■
Georgia																				
Eufaula (*See Alabama*)																				
Okefenokee, Rt. 2, Box 338, Folkston, GA 31537	■	■	■				■			■			■	■	■	■		■		■
Piedmont, Round Oak, GA 31038	■	■	■				■		■					■		■		■		■
Savannah Coastal Refuges, Box 8487, Savannah, GA 31402			■							■										
Blackbeard Island	■		■				■	■		■					■			■		■
Harris Neck	■		■				■			■	■		■	■				■		■

RECOMMENDED BEST WILDLIFE VIEWING: Winter · Fall · Summer · Spring

continues

Savannah (Georgia and South Carolina)

Tybee

Wassaw

Wolf Island

Hawaii

Hawaiian and Pacific Islands Refuges, P.O. Box 50167, Honolulu, HI 96850

Hawaiian Islands

James C. Campbell

Kakahaia

Kilauea Point, Box 87, Kilauea, Kauai; HI 96754

Hanalei

Idaho

Deer Flat, Box 448, Nampa, ID 83653-0448

Snake River Islands

Kootenai, HCR 60, Box 283, Bonners Ferry, ID 83805

Southeast Idaho Refuges, 250 S. Fourth Ave., Pocatello, ID 83201

Bear Lake, 370 Webster, P.O. Box 9, Montpelier, ID 83254

Camas, HC 69, Box 1700, Hamer, ID 83425

Grays Lake, HC 70, Box 4090, Wayan, ID 83285

Minidoka, Route 4, P.O. Box 290, Rupert, ID 83350

Illinois

Chautauqua, Route 2, Havana, IL 62644

Crab Orchard, Box J, Carterville, IL 62918

Mark Twain, 311 N. 5th St., Suite 100, Quincy, IL 62301

Batchtown Dvision, Box 142, Brussels, IL 63013

Calhoun Division, Box 142, Brussels, IL 62013

Gardner Division, P.O. Box 88, Annada, MO 63330

Gilbert Lake Division, Box 142, Brussels, IL 62013

Keithsburg Division, Route 1, Wapello, IA 52653

Upper Mississippi River Wildlife and Fish Refuge (*See* Minnesota)

Savanna District, Post Office Blg., Savanna, IL 61074

Travel

Travel

Continued

	Winter	Fall	Summer	Spring

ACTIVITIES (columns) / **Refuges** (rows). Marks (■) indicate available activities and recommended best wildlife viewing seasons.

Refuge	Food/lodging nearby	Species list	Refuge leaflet	Swimming	Picnicking	Camping	Fishing	Hunting	Backcountry use	Environmental study area	Boating—motorized	Boating—nonmotorized	Bicycling	Auto tour	Foot trails	Visitor Ctr., Contact Station	Winter	Fall	Summer	Spring
Indiana																				
Muscatatuck, Box 189 A, Route 7, Seymour, IN 47274	■	■	■				■	■		■		■	■	■	■	■	■	■		■
Iowa																				
De Soto, Route 1, Box 114, Missouri Valley, IA 51555 (Iowa and Nebraska)	■	■	■		■		■	■		■	■	■	■	■	■	■	■	■		■
Mark Twain (See Illinois)																				
Big Timber Division, Route 1, Wapello, IA 52653	■	■	■				■	■			■	■			■	■				■
Louisa Division, Route 1, Wapello, IA 52653	■						■	■		■	■	■		■					■	■
Union Slough, Route 1, Box 52, Titonka, IA 50480	■						■	■		■				■					■	■
Upper Mississippi River Wildlife and Fish Refuge (See Minnesota)																				
McGregor District, P.O. Box 460, McGregor, IA 52157	■	■	■		■	■	■	■	■	■	■	■				■	■	■	■	■
Kansas																				
Flint Hills, Box 128, Hartford, KS 66854	■	■	■				■	■		■		■			■	■	■			■
Kirwin, Route 1, Box 103, Kirwin, KS 67644	■	■	■		■	■	■	■			■			■	■	■	■	■		■
Quivira, Route 3, Box 48A, Stafford, KS 67578	■				■	■	■	■		■				■		■	■	■		■
Louisiana																				
Bogue Chitto, 1010 Gause Blvd., Blg. 936, Slidell, LA 70458	■	■	■				■	■			■	■		■				■		■
Catahoula, P.O. Drawer LL, Jena, LA 71342	■	■	■			■	■	■			■			■				■	■	■
D'Arbonne, Box 3065, Monroe, LA 71201	■						■	■	■	■	■							■	■	■
Upper Ouachita							■	■	■		■							■	■	■
Delta-Breton, Venice, LA 70091	■	■	■				■	■		■	■							■	■	■
Lacassine, Route 1, Box 186, Lake Arthur, LA 70549	■	■	■				■	■		■	■	■						■	■	■

Sabine, MRH 107, Hackberry, LA 70645

Tensas River, Route 2, Box 295, Tallulah, LA 71282

Maine

Moosehorn, Box X, Calais, ME 04619

   Cross Island

   Franklin Island

Petit Manan, P.O. Box 279, Milbridge, ME 04658

Rachel Carson, Route 2, Box 751, Wells, ME 04090

Maryland

Blackwater, Route 1, Box 121, Cambridge, MD 21613

Eastern Neck, Route 2, Box 225, Rock Hall, MD 21661

Massachusetts

Great Meadows, Weir Hill Rd., Sudbury, MA 01776

   Oxbow

Parker River, Northern Boulevard, Plum Island, Newburyport, MA 01950

   Monomoy

   Nantucket

Michigan

Seney, Seney, MI 49883

Shiawassee, 6975 Mower Rd., Route 1, Saginaw, MI 48601

Minnesota

Agassiz, Middle River, MN 56737

Big Stone, 25 NW 2nd St., Ortonville, MN 56278

Minnesota Valley, 4101 E. 80th St., Bloomington, MN 55420

Minnesota Wetlands Complex, Route 1, Box 76, Fergus Falls, MN 56537

Detroit Lakes Wetland Management District, Route 3,
   Box 47D, Detroit Lakes, MN 56501

Fergus Falls, Wetland Management District, Route 1,
   Box 76, Fergus Falls, MN 56537

Litchfield Wetland Management District,
   305 N. Sibley, Litchfield, MN 55353

Morris Wetland Management District, Route 1,
   Box 208, Morris, MN 56267

Rice Lake, Route 2, Box 67, McGregor, MN 55760

continues

Travel

Travel

Continued

ACTIVITIES / Wildlife Viewing →	Food/lodging nearby	Species list	Refuge leaflet	Swimming	Picnicking	Camping	Fishing	Hunting	Backcountry use	Environmental study area	Boating—motorized	Boating—nonmotorized	Bicycling	Auto tour	Foot trails	Visitor Ctr., Contact Station	Winter	Fall	Summer	Spring
Minnesota, cont.																				
Sherburne, Route 2, Zimmerman, MN 55398	■	■	■					■		■		■		■	■				■	■
Tamarac, Rural Route, Rochert, MN 56578	■	■	■		■		■	■		■		■		■	■					■
Upper Mississippi River Wildlife and Fish Refuge (Headquarters) 51 E. 4th St., Winona, MN 55987 (Illinois, Iowa, Minnesota, Wisconsin)																				
Winona District	■	■	■	■		■	■			■		■			■	■			■	■
Mississippi																				
Mississippi Sandhill Crane Complex, Box 6?9, Gautier, MS 39553	■	■	■							■					■	■			■	■
Noxubee, Route 1, Box 142, Brooksville, MS 39739	■	■	■				■	■		■					■	■		■	■	■
Yazoo, Route 1, Box 286, Hollandale, MS 38748		■					■	■									■	■		■
Hillside														■						
Morgan Brake	■	■	■				■	■	■	■		■						■	■	■
Panther Swamp	■	■	■				■	■	■	■		■						■	■	■
Missouri																				
Mark Twain (*See* Illinois)																				
Clarence Cannon, Box 88, Annada, MO 63330	■	■	■							■				■	■	■		■		■
Mingo, Route 1, Box 103, Puxico, MO 63960	■	■	■		■		■			■		■		■	■	■		■		■
Squaw Creek, Box 101, Mound City, MO 64470	■	■			■		■					■	■	■				■		■
Swan Lake, Box 68, Sumner, MO 64681	■	■					■						■					■		■
Montana																				
Benton Lake, Box 450, Black Eagle, MT 59414	■	■	■							■		■		■	■	■		■		■
Bowdoin, Box J, Malta, MT 59538	■	■	■					■						■				■		■

Charles M. Russell, Box 110, Lewistown, MT 59457

Lee Metcalf, Box 257, Stevensville, MT 59870

Medicine Lake, HC 51, Box 2, Medicine Lake, MT 59247

National Bison Range, Moiese, MT 59824

Red Rock Lakes, Monida Star Route, Box 15, Lima, MT 59739

Nebraska

Crescent Lake, HC 68, Box 21, Ellsworth, NE 69340

Fort Niobrara, Hidden Timber Route, HC 41, Box 67, Valentine, NE 69201

Valentine

Rainwater Basin Wetland Management District, Box 1786, Kearney, NE 68847

Nevada

Desert National Wildlife Range, 1500 N. Decatur Blvd., Las Vegas, NV 89108

Ash Meadows

Pahranagat

Ruby Lake, Ruby Valley, NV 89833

Sheldon, P.O. Box 111, Room 308, U.S. Post Office Blg., Lakeview, OR 97630

Stillwater, Box 1236, 1510 Rio Vista Rd., Fallon, NV 89408

Fallon

New Hampshire

Wapack, Weir Hill Rd., Sudbury, MA 01776

New Jersey

Edwin B. Forsythe, Box 72, Oceanville, NJ 08231

Barnegat, Box 544, Barnegat, NJ 08005

Brigantine

Great Swamp, Pleasant Plains Rd., RD 1, Box 152, Basking Ridge, NJ 07920

New Mexico

Bitter Lake, Box 7, Roswell, NM 88201

Bosque del Apache, Box 1246, Socorro, NM 87801

Sevilleta, General Delivery, San Acacia, NM 87831

continues

Travel

Continued

ACTIVITIES

Location	Food/lodging nearby	Species list	Refuge leaflet	Swimming	Picnicking	Camping	Fishing	Hunting	Backcountry use	Environmental study area	Boating—motorized	Boating—nonmotorized	Bicycling	Auto tour	Foot trails	Visitor Ctr., Contact Station	Winter	Fall	Summer	Spring
New Mexico, cont.																				
Las Vegas, Route 1, Box 399, Las Vegas, NM 87701	■	■	■					■						■	■	■		■		■
Maxwell, Box 276, Maxwell, NM 87728	■	■	■		■	■	■				■	■				■	■	■		
New York																				
Iroquois, P.O. Box 517, Alabama, NY 14003	■	■	■				■	■		■		■	■		■	■		■		■
Montezuma, 3395 Route 5/20 East, Seneca Falls, NY 13148	■	■	■				■	■		■								■		■
Wertheim, P.O. Box 21, Shirley, NY 11967	■	■	■							■		■		■				■		■
Morton	■									■								■		■
Target Rock	■	■	■							■								■		■
North Carolina																				
Alligator River, P.O. Box 1969, Manteo, NC 27954							■	■		■					■		■	■	■	■
Currituck																	■	■	■	■
Pea Island	■	■	■							■					■	■	■	■	■	■
Mackay Island, P.O. Box 31, Knotts Island, NC 27950 (North Carolina and Virginia)	■	■	■				■			■						■		■		■
Mattamuskeet, Route 1, Box N-2, Swanquarter, NC 27885	■						■							■				■		■
Cedar Island	■	■	■				■			■							■	■	■	■
Pungo	■	■	■				■			■							■	■	■	■
Swanquarter	■	■	■				■			■							■	■	■	■
Pee Dee, Box 780, Wadesboro, NC 28170	■	■	■				■			■				■			■	■	■	■

RECOMMENDED BEST WILDLIFE VIEWING

Travel

North Dakota

Arrowwood, Rural Route 1, Pingree, ND 58476

Long Lake, Moffit, ND 58560

Valley City Wetland Management District, Rural Route 1, Valley City, ND 58072

Audubon, Rural Route 1, Coleharbor, ND 58531

Lake Ilo, Dunn Center, ND 58626

Des Lacs, Box 578, Kenmare, ND 58746

Crosby Wetland Management District, Box 148, Crosby, ND 58730

Lostwood, Rural Route 2, Kenmare, ND 58746

Devils Lake Wetland Management District, Box 908, Devils Lake, ND 58301

Lake Alice

Sullys Hill National Game Preserve, Ft. Totten, ND 58335

J. Clark Salyer, P.O. Box 66. Upham, ND 58789

Kulm Wetland Management District, Box E, Kulm, ND 58456

Tewaukon, Rural Route 1, Box 75, Cayuga, ND 58013

Upper Souris, Rural Route 1, Foxholm, ND 58738

Ohio

Ottawa, 14000 W. State, Route 2, Oak Harbor, OH 43449

Oklahoma

Little River, General Delivery, Broken Box, OK 74962

Salt Plains, Route 1, Box 76, Jet, OK 73749

Sequoyah, Route 1, Box 18A, Vian, OK 74962

Tishomingo, Route 1, Box 151, Tishomingo, OK 73460

Washita, Route 1, Box 68, Butler, OK 73625

Optima

Wichita Mountains, Route 1, Box 448, Indiahoma, OK 73552

Oregon

Hart Mountain National Antelope Refuge, U.S. Post Office Bldg., Lakeview, OR 97630

Klamath Basin Refuges, Route 1, Box 74, Tulelake, CA 96134

Bear Valley

continues

Travel

Continued

Travel

Refuge	Spring	Summer	Fall	Winter	Visitor Ctr., Contact Station	Foot trails	Auto tour	Bicycling	Boating—nonmotorized	Boating—motorized	Environmental study area	Backcountry use	Hunting	Fishing	Camping	Picnicking	Swimming	Refuge leaflet	Species list	Food/lodging nearby
Oregon, cont.																				
Klamath Forest	■	■	■										■	■				■	■	■
Lower Klamath (Oregon and California)	■	■	■			■	■	■					■					■	■	■
Upper Klamath	■	■	■						■					■				■	■	■
Malheur, Box 245, Princeton, OR 97720	■		■		■		■		■	■	■			■				■	■	■
Umatilla, P.O. Box 239, Umatilla, OR 97882 (Oregon and Washington)	■		■						■									■		
Cold Springs			■						■	■			■							
McKay Creek	■		■						■	■			■	■				■		■
Western Oregon Refuges, 26208 Finley Refuge Rd., Corvallis, OR 97333	■		■										■					■		■
Ankeny	■		■		■													■	■	■
Bandon Marsh		■																		■
Baskett Slough	■				■	■												■	■	■
Cape Meares	■	■		■																■
William L. Finley	■		■			■													■	■
Willapa (*See* Washington)																				
Columbian White-tailed Deer	■			■	■	■	■		■	■				■				■	■	■
Lewis and Clark						■								■						
Pennsylvania																				
Erie, RD 1, Wood Duck Lane, Guy Mills, PA 16327	■	■	■	■	■	■					■			■					■	■
Tinicum National Environmental Center, Suite 104, Scott Plaza 2, Philadelphia, PA 19113	■	■	■	■		■		■			■			■				■	■	■

continues

Travel

Puerto Rico and Virgin Islands

Caribbean Islands, Box 510, Carr. 301, KM 5.4, Boqueron, PR 00622

Buck Island (Virgin Islands)

Cabo Rojo (Puerto Rico)

Culebra (Puerto Rico)

Desecheo (Puerto Rico)

Green Cay (Virgin Islands)

Sandy Point (Virgin Islands)

Rhode Island

Ninigret, Shoreline Plaza, Route 1A, Box 307, Charlestown, RI 02813

Block Island

Sachuest Point

Trustom Pond

South Carolina

Cape Romain, 390 Bulls Island Rd., Awendaw, SC 29429

Carolina Sandhills, Route 2, Box 330, McBee, SC 29101

Pinckney Island

Santee, Route 2, Box 66, Summerton, SC 29148

South Dakota

Lacreek, HWC 3, Box 14, Martin, SC 57551

Lake Andes, Route 1, Box 77, Lake Andes, SD 57356

Karl E. Mundt

Madison Wetland Management District, Box 48, Madison, SD 57042

Sand Lake, Rural Route 1, Box 25, Columbia, SD 57433

Waubay, Rural Route 1, Box 79, Waubay, SD 57273

Tennessee

Cross Creeks, Route 1, Box 229, Dover, TN 37058

Hatchie, Box 187, Brownsville, TN 38012

Chickasaw

Lower Hatchie

Reelfoot, Route 2, Highway 157, Union City, TN 38261

Lake Isom

Tennessee, Box 849, Paris, TN 38242

Travel

Continued

	Food/lodging nearby	Species list	Refuge leaflet	Swimming	Picnicking	Camping	Fishing	Hunting	Backcountry use	Environmental study area	Boating—motorized	Boating—nonmotorized	Bicycling	Auto tour	Foot trails	Visitor Ctr., Contact Station	Winter	Fall	Summer	Spring
Texas																				
Anahuac, Box 278, Anahuac, TX 77514	■	■	■				■	■		■		■				■	■			■
McFaddin	■		■			■		■			■	■					■			■
Texas Point	■		■					■			■	■					■			■
Aransas, Box 100, Austwell, TX 77950		■	■		■		■			■			■	■	■	■		■		■
Attwater Prairie Chicken, Box 518, Eagle Lake, TX 77434	■		■											■	■	■		■		■
Brazoria, Box 1088, Angleton, TX 77515			■				■	■			■	■					■	■		■
Big Boggy								■			■	■								
San Bernard							■	■			■	■						■		■
Buffalo Lake, Box 228, Umbarger, TX 79091	■	■	■		■									■	■	■		■		
Grulla (New Mexico and Texas)	■													■						
Muleshoe, Box 549, Muleshoe, TX 79347		■	■		■					■				■		■	■	■		■
Hagerman, Route 3, Box 123, Sherman, TX 75090	■	■	■		■		■				■			■	■	■		■		■
Laguna Atascosa, Box 450, Rio Hondo, TX 78583		■	■		■		■				■			■			■	■		■
Santa Ana, Route 1, Box 202A, Alamo, TX 78516	■																■			
Rio Grande Valley																				
Utah																				
Bear River Migratory Bird Refuge, Box 459, Brigham City, UT 84302 (temp. closed)								■												
Fish Springs, P.O. Box 568, Dugway, UT 84022		■	■		■									■				■		■
Ouray, 1680 W. Highway 40, Rm. 1220, Vernal, UT 84078		■	■				■	■						■				■		■
Vermont																				
Missisquoi, Route 2, Swanton, VT 05488	■	■					■	■							■			■		

Travel

Virgin Islands (*See Puerto Rico and Virgin Islands*)

Virginia

Back Bay, 4005 Sandpiper Rd., P.O. Box 6286, Virginia Beach, VA 23462

Chincoteague, Box 62, Chincoteague, VA 23336

Eastern Shore of Virginia, RFD 1, Box 122B, Cape Charles, VA 23310

Great Dismal Swamp, P.O. Box 349, Suffolk, VA 23434 (North Carolina and Virginia)

Mason Neck, 14416 Jefferson Davis Hwy., Ste. 20-A, Lorton, VA 22191

Presquile, Box 620, Hopewell, VA 23860

Washington

Columbia, 44 S. 8th Ave., P.O. Drawer F, Othello, WA 99344

Nisqually, 100 Brown Farm Rd., Olympia, WA 98506

Dungeness, P.O. Box 698, Sequin, WA 98380

San Juan Islands, 100 Brown Farm Rd., Olympia, WA 98506

Ridgefield, 301 N. Third, P.O. Box 457, Ridgefield, WA 98642

Conboy Lake, P.O. Box 5, Glenwood, WA 98619

Turnbull, Route 3, Box 385, Cheney, WA 99004

Umatilla, P.O. Box 239, Umatilla, OR 97882 (Oregon and Washington)

McNary, Box 308, Burbank, WA 99323

Toppenish, Route 1, Box 1300, Toppenish, WA 98948

Willapa, HC 101, Box 910, Ilwaco, WA 98624

Columbian White-tailed Deer (Oregon and Washington)

Lewis and Clark (*See Oregon*)

Wisconsin

Horicon, West 4279 Headquarters Rd., Mayville, WI 53050

Necedah, Star Route W., Box 386, Necedah, WI 54646

Upper Mississippi River Wildlife and Fish Refuge (*See Minnesota*)

La Crosse District, P.O. Box 415, La Crosse, WI 54601

Trempealeau, Route 1, Trempealeau, WI 54661

Wyoming

National Elk, Box C, Jackson, WY 83001

Seedskadee, P.O. Box 67, Green River, WY 82935

ANIMAL HIGHLIGHTS OF THE MOST POPULAR NATIONAL WILDLIFE REFUGES

State	Refuge	Wildlife
Alabama	Wheeler	22 species of geese and ducks
Alaska	Kenai	Moose, mountain goat, wolf, coyote, loon, bald eagle
Arizona	Imperial	Bighorn sheep, mule deer, blue heron
Arkansas	Felsenthal	Deer, beaver, waterfowl, wild turkey, red-cockaded woodpecker
California	San Francisco Bay	Waterfowl, avocet, black-necked stilt
Colorado	Brown's Park	Antelope, mule deer, elk, mountain lion, black bear, eagle, sage grouse, waterfowl
Florida	St. Mark's	Alligator, otter, spadefoot toad, jaguarundi, black bear, eagles, many bird species
Georgia	Okefenokee	Alligator, bobcat, egret, heron, woodpecker
Idaho	Bear Lake	White-faced ibis, blue- and black-crowned night heron, snowy egret, Franklin and California gulls
Illinois	Crab Orchard	Beaver, deer, bald eagle, wild turkey, Canadian geese
Iowa	DeSoto	Snow geese, eagle, redheaded woodpecker, red-tailed hawk, many duck species
Kansas	Kirwin	Deer, eagle, pheasant, quail, sandhill crane, wild turkey, Canadian geese
Louisiana	Tensas River	Black bear, otter, bobcat, barred owl, wild turkey, waterfowl, songbirds
Maine	Moosehorn	Black bear, beaver, porcupine, warbler, woodcock
Maryland	Blackwater	Sika deer, southern bald eagle, waterfowl
Massachusetts	Monomoy	Shorebird and waterfowl species
Michigan	Seney	Black bear, white-tailed deer, eagle, sandhill crane, loon
Minnesota	Tamarac	Deer, beaver, coyote, white pelican, trumpeter swan, bald eagle
Mississippi	Noxubee	White-tailed deer, red-cockaded woodpecker, wild turkey, waterfowl
Missouri	Mingo	Deer, otter, eagle, wild turkey, waterfowl
Montana	Charles M. Russell	Pronghorn antelope, bighorn sheep, sage and sharp-tailed grouse
Nebraska	Fort Niobrara	Bison, elk, Texas longhorn, white-tailed and mule deer, coyote, porcupine, prairie dog
Nevada	Stillwater	Long-billed dowitcher, canvasback duck

Best Vacation Bets

 **A Closer Look**

Sylvia McNair's book *Vacation Places Rated* assesses over 100 U.S. vacation areas, rating them on such features as urban activities, climate, access to recreational areas, population density, and "special attractions" such as amusement parks and professional sports events. These are McNair's top 10 choices:

1. Seattle area, including Mount Rainier and the North Cascades, Washington
2. Los Angeles
3. Hawaii
4. Miami, the Gold Coast, and the Keys, Florida
5. San Francisco
6. Boston
7. Chicago
8. Denver and Rocky Mountain National Park, Colorado
9. New York City
10. Tampa Bay area and the southwest coast, Florida

Go to "Major Zoos and Aquariums" and "Major Botanical Gardens and Arboretums" in chapter 11

State	Refuge	Wildlife
New Jersey	Forsythe (Brigantine Division)	Otter, red fox, many species of waterfowl, shorebird, wading bird, raptor, warbler
New Mexico	Bosque del Apache	Porcupine, scarlet-crowned greater sandhill crane, snow geese, wild turkey
New York	Iroquois	Blue heron, hooded merganser, wood duck
North Carolina	Alligator River	Red wolf
North Dakota	Des Lacs	Snow geese, grouse, white pelican, ruddy duck, Sprague's pipit, LeConte's and Baird's sparrow
Oklahoma	Wichita Mountains	Bison, elk, Texas longhorn, prairie dog, reptile species, bird species
Oregon	Malheur	Deer, white pelican, bald and golden eagle, greater sandhill crane
Pennsylvania	Erie	Beaver, deer, fox
Rhode Island	Ninigret	Otter, muskrat, coyote, gray and red fox, 300 species of birds
South Carolina	Cape Romain	Alligator, otter, deer, wild turkey, oyster catcher, royal tern, black skimmer
South Dakota	Lacreek	Mule and white-tailed deer, trumpeter swan, white pelican, American bittern
Tennessee	Reelfoot	Bald eagle, waterfowl, songbird species
Texas	Hagerman	Road runner, scissor-tailed flycatcher, white pelican, sparrow species, waterfowl
Utah	Fish Springs	Deer, coyote, swan, ibis
Vermont	Missisquoi	Beaver, waterfowl
Virginia	Chincoteague	Wild pony, sika and white-tailed deer, Delmarva fox squirrel, 300 bird species
Washington	Columbia	Coyote, mule deer, sandhill crane, swan, duck, geese
Wisconsin	Horicon	Mink, raccoon, coyote, red fox, white-tailed deer, heron, egret, Canadian geese, duck
Wyoming	National Elk	Elk, coyote, bald eagle, trumpeter swan

A Closer Look

Best Theme Parks

Although the traditional American tourist attractions—from Mount Rushmore to the Grand Canyon to the Statue of Liberty to the Golden Gate Bridge—are still high on many travelers' itineraries, since the 1950s the greatest volume of visitors has been seen at "theme" amusement parks modeled on the pioneering, enormously successful Disneyland. U.S. amusement parks entertain over 170 million visitors a year. These are the top 10 according to *Amusement Business Magazine.*

1. **Disneyland, Anaheim, California**
   http://www.disney.com/Disneyland
2. **Magic Kingdom, Walt Disney World, Buena Vista, Florida**
   http://www.disney.com/DisneyWorld/ThemeParks/par41.htm
3. **Epcot Center, Walt Disney World, Buena Vista, Florida**
   http://www.disney.com/DisneyWorld/ThemeParks/par42.htm
4. **Disney MGM Studios, Walt Disney World, Buena Vista, Florida**
   http://www.disney.com/DisneyWorld/ThemeParks/par43.htm
5. **Universal Studios, Orlando, Florida**
   http://www.usf.com/
6. **Universal Studios—Hollywood, Universal City, California**
   http://www.mca.com/unicity
7. **Sea World, Orlando, Florida**
   http://www.4adventure.com/seaworld/sw_florida/frame.html
8. **Busch Gardens, Tampa Bay, Florida**
   http://www.4adventure.com/buschgardens/bg_tampa/bottombar.html
9. **Six Flags Great Adventure, Jackson, New Jersey**
   http://www.sixflags.com/newjersey/
10. **Sea World, San Diego, California**
    http://www.4adventure.com/seaworld/sw_california/frame.html

INTERNATIONAL TRAVEL

GOVERNMENT TOURIST INFORMATION CENTERS

The following list includes the U.S. locations (and/or English-language Web sites when available) for official tourist information centers of other nations. Tourist information also may be obtained by contacting the appropriate embassy (*see* "Requirements Before Proceeding Abroad: Individual Country Requirements," later in this chapter, for embassy addresses, telephone numbers, and Web sites). Additional information for certain countries may be obtained from the following regional associations:

European Travel Commission
(Members: Austria, Belgium, Bulgaria, Cyprus, Czech Republic, Denmark, Finland, France, Germany, Great Britain, Greece, Hungary, Iceland, Ireland, Italy, Luxembourg, Malta, Monaco, Netherlands, Norway, Poland, Portugal, Slovenia, Spain, Sweden, Switzerland, and Turkey)
One Rockefeller Plaza
New York, NY 10020
212-218-1200
http://www.visiteurope.com/

Scandinavian National Tourist Offices
(Members: Denmark, Finland, Iceland, Norway, Sweden)
655 Third Ave.
New York, NY 10017
800-346-4636 or 212-949-2333
Fax: 212-983-5260
http://www.travelfile.com/get?SCANDINAVIA

The following list includes national tourist offices and associated Web sites.

Anguilla Tourist Information Office
c/o Medhurst & Associates, Inc.
The Huntington Atrium
775 Park Ave., Suite 105
Huntington, NY 11743
800-553-4939, 516-271-2600
Fax: 516-425-0903
http://www.turq.com/anguilla.html

Antigua and Barbuda Department of Tourism and Trade
610 Fifth Ave., Suite 311
New York, NY 10020
212-541-4117
Fax: 212-757-1607
http://www.antigua-barbuda.org/

Argentina National Tourist Council
12 W. 56th St.
New York, NY 10019
212-603-0443
Fax: 212-315-5545
http://emb-eeuu.mrecic.gov.ar/tourism.htm

Aruba Tourism Authority
1000 Harbor Blvd.
Weehawken, NJ 07087
800-862-7822 or 201-330-0800
Fax: 201-330-8757
http://www.interknowledge.com/aruba/index.html

Australian Tourist Commission
100 Park Ave., 25th Floor
New York, NY 10017
800-333-0199 or 212-687-6300
Fax: 212-661-3340
http://tourism.gov.au/

Austrian National Tourist Office
P. O. Box 1142
New York, NY 10108-1142
212-944-6880
Fax: 212-730-4568
http://www.anto.com/

Bahamas Tourist Office
150 E. 52nd St., 28th Floor North
New York, NY 10022
800-327-7678 or 212-758-2777
Fax: 212-753-6531
http://www.interknowledge.com/bahamas/

Consulate General of Bangladesh
211 E. 43rd St., Suite 502
New York, NY 10017
212-599-6767
Fax: 212-682-9211

Barbados Tourism Authority
800 Second Ave., Second Floor
New York, NY 10017
800-221-9831 or 212-986-6516
Fax: 212-573-9850
http://www.barbados.org/

Belgian National Tourist Office
780 Third Ave., Suite 1501
New York, NY 10017
212-758-8130
Fax: 212-355-7675
http://www.visitbelgium.com/

If you walked the entire length of China's Great Wall, you would be walking farther than the distance between New York City and Miami, Florida.

Belize Tourist Board
415 Seventh Ave., 18th Floor
New York, NY 10001
800-624-0686 or 212-563-6011
Fax: 212-563-6033
http://www.turq.com/belize.html

Bermuda Department of Tourism
310 Madison Ave., Suite 201
New York, NY 10017
800-223-6106 or 212-818-9800
Fax: 212-983-5289
http://www.bermudatourism.com/

Bhutan Travel Inc.
120 E. 56th St., Suite 1130
New York, NY 10022
800-950-9908 or 212-838-6382
Fax: 212-750-1269

Tourism Corporation of Bonaire
10 Rockefeller Plaza, Suite 900
New York, NY 10020
800-826-6247 or 212-956-5911
Fax: 212-956-5913
http://www.interknowledge.com/bonaire/index.html

Brazilian Tourism Center
16 W. 46th St.
New York, NY 10036
212-730-0515
http://www.brasil.emb.nw.dc.us/ecotour/ecotour.htm

British Virgin Islands Tourist Board
370 Lexington Ave., Suite 1605
New York, NY 10017
800-835-8530 or 212-696-0400
Fax: 212-949-8254

"The Atlas" on pages 985–994

Go to

Bulgarian Tourist Information Center
41 E. 42nd St., Suite 508
New York, NY 10017
212-573-5530
http://www.bulgaria.com/

Canadian Tourism Commission
http://info.ic.gc.ca/Tourism/

Cayman Islands Department of Tourism
420 Lexington Ave., Suite 2733
New York, NY 10170
212-682-5582
Fax: 212-986-5123
http://www.caymans.com/

Chilean National Tourism Board
9700 S. Dixie Hwy., 10th Floor
Miami, FL 33156
800-995-4888
http://www.prochile.cl/index.en.html

Chinese National Tourist Office
350 Fifth Ave., Suite 6413
New York, NY 10118
212-760-9700
Fax: 212-760-8809
http://www.travelfile.com/get?chinanto

Costa Rican National Tourist Board
800-343-6332

Curaçao Tourist Board
475 Park Ave. South, Suite 2000
New York, NY 10016
800-270-3350 or 212-683-7660
Fax: 212-683-9337
http://www.interknowledge.com/curacao/

Cyprus Tourism Organization
13 E. 40th St.
New York, NY 10016
212-683-5280
Fax: 212-683-5282
http://www.cyprustourism.org/

Czech Tourist Authority
1109–1111 Madison Ave.
New York, NY 10028
212-288-0830
Fax: 212-288-0971
http://www.czech.cz/new_york/

Danish Tourist Board
655 Third Ave.
New York, NY 10017
212-885-9700
Fax: 212-885-9710
http://www.deninfo.com/

Dominica Tourist Office
10 E. 21st St., Suite 600
New York, NY 10010
212-475-7542
Fax: 212-475-4728
http://www.dominica.dm/tourism.htm

Dominican Republic Tourist Office
1501 Broadway, Suite 410
New York, NY 10036
888-374-6361 or 212-575-4966
Fax: 212-575-5448
http://www.erols.com/peralta/embassy/
    infodr.htm#Tourism

Egyptian Tourist Authority
630 Fifth Ave., Suite 1706
New York, NY 10111
212-332-2570
Fax: 212-956-6439
http://touregypt.net/

Fiji Visitors Bureau
5777 W. Century Blvd., Suite 220
Los Angeles, CA 90045
800-932-3454 or 310-568-1616
Fax: 310-670-2318
http://www.fijifvb.gov.fj/

Finnish Tourist Board
655 Third Ave.
New York, NY 10017
800-346-4636, 212-949-2333, or 212-885-9700
Fax: 212-983-5260
http://www.vn.fi/vn/um/index.html (home page of
    the Finnish Ministry for Foreign Affairs)

French Government Tourist Office
444 Madison Ave.
New York, NY 10022
212-838-7800
Fax: 212-838-7855
http://www.francetourism.com/

**French Polynesia
Tahiti Tourist Promotion Board**
300 Continental Blvd., Suite 180
El Segundo, CA 90245
310-414-8484
Fax: 310-414-8490

German National Tourist Office
122 E. 42nd St., 52nd Floor
New York, NY 10168-0072
212-661-7200
Fax: 212-661-7174
http://www.germany-tourism.de/

Greek National Tourist Office
645 Fifth Ave., Olympic Tower
New York, NY 10022
212-421-5777
Fax: 212-826-6940
http://www.vacation.forthnet.gr/gnto.html

Grenada Board of Tourism
820 Second Ave., Suite 900D
New York, NY 10017
800-927-9554 or 212-687-9554
Fax: 212-573-9731
http://www.interknowledge.com/grenada/

Guam Visitors Bureau
1150 Marina Village Pkwy., Suite 104
Alameda, CA 94501
800-873-4826 or 510-865-0366
Fax: 510-865-5165

Guatemalan Tourist Commission
299 Alhambra Circle, Suite 510
Miami, FL 33134
800-742-4529 or 305-442-0651
Fax: 305-442-1013

Honduras Tourism Institute
299 Alhambra Circle
Coral Gables, FL 33114
305-461-0600
http://www.turq.com/honduras.html

Hong Kong Tourist Association
590 Fifth Ave., 5th Floor
New York, NY 10036
212-869-5008
Fax: 212-730-2605
http://www.hkta.org/usa/index.html

Hungarian Tourist Board
Embassy of the Republic of Hungary
150 E. 58th St., 33rd Floor
New York, NY 10155-3398
212-355-0240
Fax: 212-207-4103
http://www.hungaryemb.org/HunNatTourOff.htm

Icelandic Tourist Board
655 Third Ave.
New York, NY 10017
212-949-2333
Fax: 212-983-5260
http://www.arctic.is/touristb/

Travel

Government of India Tourist Office
1270 Avenue of the Americas, Suite 1808
New York, NY 10020
212-586-4901
Fax: 212-586-3274
http://www.tourindia.com/

Tourism Indonesia
http://www.tourismindonesia.com/index2.htm

Irish Tourist Board
345 Park Ave., 17th Floor
New York, NY 10154
800-223-6470 or 212-418-0800
Fax: 212-371-9052
http://www.ireland.travel.ie/

Israel Ministry of Tourism Information Center
800 Second Ave., 16th Floor
New York, NY 10017
888-774-7723 or 212-499-5600
Fax: 212-499-5665
http://www.goisrael.com/

Italian Government Tourist Board
630 Fifth Ave.
New York, NY 10111
212-245-4822
Fax: 212-586-9249
http://www.italyemb.nw.dc.us/italy/tourinfo.htm

Jamaica Tourist Board
801 Second Ave., 20th Floor
New York, NY 10017
800-526-2422 or 212-856-9727
Fax: 212-856-9730
http://www.jamaicatravel.com/

Japanese National Tourist Organization
One Rockefeller Plaza, Suite 1250
New York, NY 10020
212-757-5640
Fax: 212-307-6754
http://www.jnto.go.jp/

Kenya Tourist Office
9150 Wilshire Blvd., Suite 160
Beverly Hills, CA 90212
310-274-6635
Fax: 310-859-7010
http://www.africanvacation.com/kenya/

Korea, Republic of (South Korea)
Korea National Tourism Office
Two Executive Dr., 7th Floor
Fort Lee, NJ 07024
800-868-7567 or 201-585-0909
Fax: 201-585-9041
http://www.travelfile.com/get/KNTO.html

Luxembourg National Tourist Office
17 Beekman Pl.
New York, NY 10022
212-935-8888
Fax: 212-935-5896
http://195.218.0.11/ont/default.htm

Macau Government Tourist Office
Asia Pacific Travel Ltd.
P.O. Box 350
Kenilworth, Illinois 60043-0350
800-331-7150 or 847-251-6400
Fax: 847-256-5601
http://macau.tourism.gov.mo/

Malaysia Tourism Promotion Board
595 Madison Ave., Suite 1800
New York, NY 10022
800-558-6787 or 212-754-1113
Fax: 212-754-1116
http://tourism.gov.my/

Malta National Tourist Office
350 Fifth Ave., Suite 4412
New York, NY 10118
212-695-9520
Fax: 212-695-8229
http://visitmalta.com/

Mauritius Tourist Promotion Authority
8 Haven Ave., Suite 227
Port Washington, NY 11050
516-944-3763
http://www.mauritius.net

Mexican Government Tourist Office
1911 Pennsylvania Ave.
Washington, DC 20006
000-446-3942 or 202-728-1750
Fax: 202-728-1758
http://mexico-travel.com/

Monaco Government Tourist and Convention Bureau
565 Fifth Ave.
New York, NY 10017
800-753-9696 or 212-286-3330
Fax: 212-286-9890
http://www.monaco.mc/usa/

Moroccan National Tourist Office
20 E. 46th St., Suite 503
New York, NY 10017
212-557-2520
Fax: 212-949-8148

Nepal Tourist Information
820 Second Ave., Suite 202
New York, NY 10017
212-370-4188
Fax: 212-953-2038

The Netherlands Board of Tourism
225 N. Michigan Ave., Suite 1854
Chicago, IL 60601
888-464-6552 or 312-819-1740
http://www.nbt.nl/holland

New Zealand Tourism Board
501 Santa Monica Blvd., Suite 300
Santa Monica, CA 90401
800-388-5494 or 310-395-7480
Fax: 310-395-5453
http://www.nztb.org.nz/

Northern Ireland Tourist Board
212-922-0101
Fax: 212-922-0099
http://www.northern-ireland.com/
See also **United Kingdom–British Tourist
  Authority.**

**Norwegian Information Service in the United
  States**
825 Third Ave., 17th Floor
New York, NY 10022
212-421-7333
Fax: 212-754-0583
http://www.norway.org/tourism.htm

**Papua New Guinea Tourist Information Center
  at Air Niugini**
5000 Birch St., Suite 3000
Newport Beach, CA 92660
714-752-5440
Fax: 714-476-3741

Philippines Department of Tourism
556 Fifth Ave.
New York, NY 10036
212-575-7915
Fax: 212-302-6759

Polish National Tourist Office
275 Madison Ave., Suite 1711
New York, NY 10016
212-338-9412
Fax: 212-338-9283
http://www.polandtour.org/

"Foreign Dialing Codes" in chapter 26

Go to

Portuguese National Tourist Office
590 Fifth Ave., 4th Floor
New York, NY 10036-4704
800-767-8842 or 212-354-4403
Fax: 212-764-6137
http://www.portugal.org/tourism/tourism.html

Puerto Rico Tourism Company
575 Fifth Ave., 23rd Floor
New York, NY 10017
800-223-6530 or 212-599-6262
Fax: 212-818-1866

Romania National Tourist Office
342 Madison Ave., Suite 210
New York, NY 10173
212-697-6971
Fax: 212-697-6972
http://www.rezq.com/ont/main.htm

Russian National Tourist Office
800 Third Ave., Suite 3101
New York, NY 10022
212-758-1162
Fax: 212-758-0933
http://www.russia-travel.com/

Saba and St. Eustatius Tourist Office
P.O. Box 6322
Boca Raton, FL 33427-6322
800-722-2394 or 561-394-8580
Fax: 561-488-4294
http://www.turq.com/saba/
http://www.turq.com/statia/

St. Kitts and Nevis Tourist Office
414 E. 75th St., 5th Floor
New York, NY 10021
800-582-6208 or 212-535-1234
Fax: 212-734-6511
http://www.interknowledge.com/stkitts-nevis/

St. Lucia Tourist Board
820 Second Ave.
New York, NY 10017
800-456-3984 or 212-867-2950
Fax: 212-867-2795
http://www.interknowledge.com/st-lucia/index.html

St. Maarten Tourism Office
675 Third Ave., Suite 1806
New York, NY 10017
800-786-2278 or 212-953-2084
Fax: 212-953-2145
http://www.interknowledge.com/
  st-maarten/index.html

Travel

St. Martin Office of Tourism (*See also* **France**.)
http://www.interknowledge.com/
    st-martin/index.html

St. Vincent and the Grenadines Tourist Office
801 Second Ave., 21st Floor
New York, NY 10017
800-729-1726 or 212-687-4981
Fax: 212 949 5946
http://www.turq.com/stvincent/

Scottish Tourist Board (*See also* **United
    Kingdom–British Tourist Authority**.)
http://www.holiday.scotland.net/

Seychelles Tourist Office
235 E. 40th St., Suite 24A
New York NY 10016
212-687-9766
Fax: 212-922-9177

Singapore Tourist Promotion Board
590 Fifth Ave., 12th Floor
New York, NY 10036
212-302-4861
Fax: 212-302-4801
http://www.asia-online.com.sg/sog/

Slovakia Travel Service
10 E. 40th St., Suite 3604
New York, NY 10016
212-725-0948
Fax: 212-213-4461
http://members.aol.com/viktvl/slovakia/page01.htm

Slovenian Tourist Office
345 E. 12th St.
New York, NY 10003
212-358-9024
Fax: 212-358-9025
http://www.sloveniatravel.com/

South African Tourism Board
500 Fifth Ave.
New York, NY 10110
800-822-5368 or 212-730-2929
Fax: 212-764-1980

**Tourist Office of Spain in the United States
    of America**
666 Fifth Ave., 35th Floor
New York, NY 10103
212-265-8822
Fax: 212-265-8864
http://www.okspain.org/

Sri Lanka Tourist Board
609 Fifth Ave., Suite 308
New York, NY 10017
212-935-0369

Swedish Travel and Tourism Council
655 Third Ave.
P.O. Box 4649, Grand Central Station
New York, NY 10163-4649
212-885-9700
Fax: 212-885-9710
http://www.gosweden.org/

Switzerland Tourism
608 Fifth Ave.
New York, NY 10020
212-757-5944
Fax: 212-262-6116
http://www.switzerlandtourism.ch/

Taiwan Visitors Association
One World Trade Center, Suite 7953
New York, NY 10018
212-466-0691
Fax: 212-432-6436

Thailand Tourist Authority
Five World Trade Center, Suite 3443
New York, NY 10048
212-432-0433
Fax: 212-912-0920
http://www.tat.or.th/

Tonga Consulate General
360 Post St., Suite 604
San Francisco, CA 94108
415-781-0365
Fax: 415-781-3964

**Trinidad and Tobago Tourism Development
    Authority**
7000 Boulevard East
Guttenberg, NJ 07093
800-748-4224 or 888-595-4868
Fax: 201-869-7628
http://www.tidco.co.tt/tourism/index.html

Tunisia National Tourist Office
http://www.tourismtunisia.com

Turkish Tourism and Information Office
821 United Nations Plaza
New York, NY 10017
212-687-2194
Fax: 212-599-7568
http://www.turkey.org/turkey/tourism.htm

Travel

Turks and Caicos Islands Tourist Office
331 Madison Ave.
New York, NY 10017
800-241-0824 or 212-888-4110

United Kingdom–British Tourist Authority
551 Fifth Ave., Suite 701
New York, NY 10176
800-462-2748 or 212-986-2200
Fax: 212-986-1188
http://www.visitbritain.com/

Uruguay Ministry of Tourism
http://www.turismo.gub.uy/index-e.html

**U.S. Virgin Islands Division of Tourism
(St. Croix, St. John, St. Thomas)**
1270 Avenue of the Americas, Suite 2108
New York, NY 10020
212-332-2222
Fax: 212-332-2223
http://www.usvi.net

Venezuelan Tourism Association
P.O. Box 3010
Sausalito, CA 94966
800-331-0100 or 415-331-0100
http://www.venezuela1.com/frame2E.htm

Wales Tourist Board (*See also* **United Kingdom–
British Tourist Authority.**)
http://www.tourism.wales.gov.uk/

Zambia National Tourist Board
800 Second Ave., 9th Floor
New York, NY 10017
212-972-7200
Fax: 212-758-1319
http://www.zamnet.zm/zamnet/zntb/zntb.html

Zimbabwe Tourist Office
1270 Avenue of the Americas, Suite 412
New York, NY 10020
800-421-2381 or 212-332-1090
Fax: 212-332-1093

INTERNATIONAL AUTO REGISTRATION MARKS

Afghanistan	AFG	Costa Rica	CR	Iraq	IRQ		
Albania	AL	Cuba	C	Ireland	IRL		
Alderney	GBA	Cyprus	CY	Isle of Man	GBM		
(Channel Islands)		Czech Republic	CZ	Israel	IL		
Algeria	DZ	Denmark	DK	Italy	I		
Andorra	AND	Ecuador	EC	Ivory Coast	CI		
Argentina	RA	Egypt	ET	Jamaica	JA		
Australia	AUS	El Salvador	ES	Japan	J		
Austria	A	Ethiopia	ETH	Jersey	GBJ		
Bahamas	BS	Faroe Islands	FR	Jordan	JOR		
Bahrain	BRN	Fiji	FJI	Kenya	EAK		
Bangladesh	BD	Finland	SF	Kuwait	KWT		
Barbados	BDS	France	F	Laos	LAO		
Belgium	B	Gambia	WAG	Lebanon	RL		
Belize	BH	Germany, Federal	D	Lesotho	LS		
Benin	DY	Republic of		Liberia	LB		
Botswana	RB	Ghana	GH	Libya	LAR		
Brazil	BR	Gibraltar	GBZ	Liechtenstein	FL		
Brunei	BRU	Great Britain	GB	Luxembourg	L		
Bulgaria	BG	Greece	GR	Madagascar	RM		
Burundi	RU	Grenada	WG	Malawi	MW		
Cambodia	K	Guatemala	GCA	Malaysia	MAL		
Canada	CDN	Guernsey	GBG	Mali	RMM		
Central African	RCA	Guyana	GUY	Malta	M		
Republic		Haiti	RH	Mauritania	RIM		
Chile	RCH	Hong Kong	HK	Mauritius	MS		
Colombia	CO	Hungary	H	Mexico	MEX		
Congo, Republic	RCB	Iceland	IS	Monaco	MC		
of the		India	IND	Morocco	MA		
Congo, Democratic	ZRE	Indonesia	RI	Myanmar	BUR		
Republic of		Iran	IR	Netherlands	NL		

Netherlands Antilles	NA	St. Vincent	WV	Switzerland	CH		
New Zealand	NZ	Samoa	WS	Syria	SYR		
Nicaragua	NIC	San Marino	RSM	Taiwan	RC		
Niger	RN	Senegal	SN	Tanzania	EAT		
Nigeria	WAN	Seychelles	SY	Thailand	T		
Norway	N	Sierre Leone	WAL	Togo	TG		
Pakistan	PAK	Singapore	SGP	Trinidad and Tobago	TT		
Panama	PA	Slovakia	Q	Tunisia	TN		
Papua New Guinea	PNG	Somalia	SP	Turkey	TR		
Paraguay	PY	South Africa	ZA	Uganda	EAU		
Peru	PE	South Korea	ROK	United States	USA		
Philippines	RP	South Yemen	AND	Uruguay	ROU		
Poland	PL	Spain	E	Vatican City	SCV		
Portugal	P	Sri Lanka	CL	Venezuela	YV		
Romania	RO	Suriname	SME	Vietnam	VN		
Rwanda	RWA	Swaziland	SD	Zambia	Z		
St. Lucia	WL	Sweden	S	Zimbabwe	ZW		

AVERAGE TEMPERATURES (°F) FOR INTERNATIONAL CITIES

The averages below are compiled by the National Weather Service.

Location	Jan–Mar (Avg high/low)	Apr–Jun (Avg high/low)	Jul–Sep (Avg high/low)	Oct–Dec (Avg high/low)
Acapulco	88/72	90/77	90/75	90/72
Athens	60/44	86/52	92/67	75/47
Bangkok	93/68	95/76	90/76	88/68
Berlin	46/26	72/39	75/50	56/29
Bermuda	68/57	81/59	85/72	79/60
Bogotá	68/48	67/51	66/49	66/49
Buenos Aires	85/60	72/41	64/42	82/50
Cairo	75/47	95/57	96/68	86/50
Calcutta	93/55	97/75	90/78	89/55
Caracas	79/56	81/60	80/61	79/58
Dublin	51/34	65/39	67/48	57/37
Hong Kong	67/55	85/67	87/77	81/59
Java	86/74	87/74	88/73	87/74
Jerusalem	65/41	85/50	87/62	81/45
Istanbul	51/37	77/45	82/61	68/41
Kathmandu	77/35	86/53	84/66	80/37
Lima	83/66	80/58	68/56	78/58
Lisbon	63/46	77/53	82/62	72/47
London	50/36	69/42	71/52	58/38
Madrid	59/35	80/45	87/57	65/36
Manila	91/69	93/73	88/75	88/70
Mexico City	75/42	78/51	74/53	70/43
Montevideo	83/59	71/43	63/43	79/49
Munich	48/23	70/38	74/48	56/26
Nairobi	79/54	75/53	75/51	76/55
Nassau	79/64	87/69	89/75	85/67
Panama	90/71	87/74	87/74	87/73
Paris	54/34	73/43	76/53	60/36

continues

Average Temperatures for International Cities Continued

Location	Jan–Mar (Avg high/low)	Apr–Jun (Avg high/low)	Jul–Sep (Avg high/low)	Oct–Dec (Avg high/low)
Port-au-Prince	89/68	92/71	94/73	90/69
Quito	72/46	71/45	73/44	72/45
Rio de Janeiro	85/72	80/64	76/63	82/66
Rome	59/40	82/50	87/62	71/44
St. Lucia	84/69	88/71	88/73	87/70
San Juan	80/70	85/72	86/75	85/72
Santiago	85/49	74/37	66/37	83/45
Santo Domingo	89/68	92/71	94/73	90/69
Seoul	47/15	80/41	87/59	67/20
Singapore	88/73	89/75	88/75	87/74
Taipei	70/53	89/63	92/73	81/57
Tokyo	54/29	76/46	86/66	69/33
Toronto	37/15	73/34	79/51	56/21
Vancouver	50/32	69/40	74/49	57/35

AIR MILEAGE FROM NEW YORK CITY—INTERNATIONAL

Acapulco	2,260
Amsterdam	3,639
Antigua	1,783
Aruba	1,963
Athens	4,927
Barbados	2,100
Beijing	6,844
Bermuda	771
Bogotá	2,487
Bombay	7,808
Brussels	3,662
Buenos Aires	5,302
Caracas	2,123
Copenhagen	3,849
Curaçao	1,993
Frankfurt	3,851
Geneva	3,859
Glasgow	3,211
Hamburg	3,806
Hong Kong	8,095
Johannesburg	7,964
Kingston	1,583
Kuwait City	6,366
Lima	3,651
Lisbon	3,366
London	3,456
Madrid	3,588
Manchester	3,336
Mexico City	2,086
Milan	4,004
Moscow	4,680
Nassau	1,101
Oslo	3,671
Paris	3,628
Reykjavík	2,600
Rio de Janeiro	4,816
Rome	4,280
St. Croix	1,680
San Juan	1,609
Santo Domingo	1,560
Sydney	9,932
Tel Aviv	5,672
Tokyo	6,755
Zurich	3,926

INTERNATIONAL CURRENCIES

The table on the opposite page lists the official names for selected currencies around the world. Colonial legacies have made certain names—dollar, peso, franc, and pound, for example—widespread. The traveler should not assume equivalency in value, or transferability, among units sharing a name; that is, one cannot spend Central African *francs* in France or Turkish *lira* in Rome.

The column titled "Smaller Monetary Unit" lists the anglicized form of the plural—e.g., Czech 100 halers—followed by the native language plural in parentheses (haleru). When no smaller unit is given, the traveler may assume none exists. Where more than one term is used locally for the same unit, both names are given, separated by *or*. Units of measurement with the word *new* preceding them are the current international exchange unit. There may be an older unit of currency still in circulation that is not to be confused with the new unit.

The abbreviations used are as follows:

CFA   Communauté financieére africaine (African Financial Community)

CFP   Communauté financieére pacific (Pacific Financial Community)

INTERNATIONAL CURRENCIES

Location	Currency	Smaller Monetary Unit
Afghanistan	afghani	100 puls
Albania	lek	100 qintars (qindarka)
Algeria	dinar	100 centimes
American Samoa	U.S. dollar	100 cents
Andorra	peseta (= 1 Spanish peseta)	——
	franc (= 1 French franc)	——
Angola	(new) kwanza (kwanza reajustado)	100 lwei
Anguilla	East Caribbean dollar	100 cents
Antigua and Barbuda	East Caribbean dollar	100 cents
Argentina	peso	100 centavos
Armenia	dram	100 luma
Aruba	florin	100 cents
Australia	dollar	100 cents
Austria	schilling	100 groschen
Azerbaijan	manat	100 gopik
Bahamas	dollar	100 cents
Bahrain	dinar	1,000 fils
Bangladesh	taka	100 paisa or poisha
Barbados	dollar	100 cents
Belarus	ruble	100 kopeks (rarely used)
Belgium	franc	100 centimes
Belize	dollar	100 cents
Benin	franc CFA	100 centimes
Bermuda	dollar	100 cents
Bhutan	ngultrum	100 chetrum
Bolivia	boliviano	100 centavos
Bosnia and Herzegovina	dinar	100 para
Botswana	pula	100 thebe
Brazil	real	100 centavos
British Virgin Islands	U.S. dollar	100 cents
Brunei	ringitt or dollar	100 sen or cents
Bulgaria	lev	100 stotinki
Burkina Faso	franc CFA	100 centimes
Burundi	franc	100 centimes
Cambodia	(new) riel	100 sen
Cameroon	franc CFA	100 centimes
Canada	dollar	100 cents
Cape Verde	escuda	100 centavos
Cayman Islands	dollar	100 cents
Central Africa Republic	franc CFA	100 centimes
Chad	franc CFA	100 centimes

Travel

continues

International Currencies Continued

Location	Currency	Smaller Monetary Unit
Chile	(new) peso	100 centavos
China	yuan or renminbi	10 jiao = 100 fen
Cocos Islands	Australian dollar	100 cents
Colombia	peso	100 centavos
Comoros	franc	100 centimes
Congo	franc CFA	100 centimes
Congo, Democratic Republic of (formerly Zaire)	(new Congolese) franc	100 centimes
Cook Islands	New Zealand dollar	100 cents
Costa Rica	colon	100 centimos
Côte d'Ivoire	franc CFA	100 centimes
Croatia	kuna	100 lipas
Cuba	peso	100 centavos
Cyprus	pound	100 cents
Czech Republic	koruna	100 halers (haleru)
Denmark	krone	100 öre
Djibouti	franc	100 centimes
Dominica	East Caribbean dollar	100 cents
Dominican Republic	peso	100 centavos
Ecuador	sucre	100 centavos
Egypt	pound	100 piastres = 10 milliemes
El Salvador	colon	100 centavos
Equatorial Guinea	ekwele (CFA franc)	100 centimos
Eritrea	birr	100 cents
Estonia	kroon	100 senti
Ethiopia	birr	100 cents
Falkland Islands	pound	100 pence
Faroe Islands	Denmark krone	100 öre
Fiji	dollar	100 cents
Finland	markka or finmark	100 pennia
France	franc	100 centimes
French Guiana	French franc	100 centimes
French Polynesia	franc CFP	100 centimes
Gabon	franc CFA	100 centimes
Gambia	dalasi	100 bututs
Georgia	lari	100 tetri
Germany	mark	100 pfennigs (pfennige)
Ghana	(new) cedi	100 pesewas
Greece	drachma	100 lepta
Greenland	Denmark krone	100 öre
Grenada	East Caribbean dollar	100 cents
Guadeloupe	French franc	100 centimes
Guam	U.S. dollar	100 cents
Guatemala	quetzal	100 centavos
Guernsey	U.K. pound	100 pence
Guinea	syli	10 francs = 100 centimes
Guinea-Bissau	franc CFA	100 centimes
Guyana	dollar	100 cents
Haiti	gourde	100 centimes

Location	Currency	Smaller Monetary Unit
Honduras	lempira	100 centavos
Hong Kong	dollar	100 cents
Hungary	forint	100 filler
Iceland	krona	100 aurar
India	rupee	100 paise
Indonesia	rupiah	100 sen (no longer used)
Iran	rial (10 rials = 1 roman)	100 dinars (1,000 dinars = 1 roman)
Iraq	dinar	1,000 fils
Ireland	punt or pound	100 pingin or pence
Israel	(new) shekel	100 (new) agorot
Italy	lira	100 centesimi
Ivory Coast (*see* Còte d'Ivoire)		
Jamaica	dollar	100 cents
Japan	yen	100 sen (no longer used)
Jordan	dinar	1,000 fils
Kazakhstan	tenge	100 tiyn
Kenya	shilling	100 cents
Korea, Democratic People's Republic of (North Korea)	won	100 chon
Korea, Republic of (South Korea)	won	100 chon
Kuwait	dinar	1,000 fils
Kyrgyzstan	som	100 tiyin
Laos	(new) kip	100 at
Latvia	lat	100 santims
Lebanon	pound or livre	100 piastres
Lesotho	loti (plural is "maloti")	100 lisente
Liberia	dollar	100 cents
Libya	dinar	1,000 dirhams
Liechtenstein	Swiss franc	100 centimes
Lithuania	litas	100 centu
Luxembourg	franc	100 centimes
Macau	pataca	100 avos
Macedonia	denar	———
Madagascar	franc 95 (francs = 1 aviary)	100 centimes
Malawi	kwacha	100 tambala
Malaysia	ringgit	100 sen
Maldives	rufiyaa	100 lari
Mali	franc CFA	100 centimes
Malta	lira or pound	100 cents
Martinique	French franc	100 centimes
Mauritania	ouguiya	5 khoums
Mauritius	rupee	100 cents
Mexico	(new) peso	100 centavos
Micronesia	U.S. dollar	100 cents
Moldova	leu	———
Monaco	French franc	100 centimes
Mongolia	tugrik	100 mongos
Montserrat	East Caribbean dollar	100 cents
Morocco	dirham	100 centimes

continues

International Currencies Continued

Location	Currency	Smaller Monetary Unit
Mozambique	metical	100 centavos
Myanmar	kyat	100 pyas
Namibia	South African rand	100 cents
Nauru	Australian dollar	100 cents
Nepal	rupee	100 paise
Netherland Antilles	guilder	100 cents
Netherlands	guilder or florin	100 cents
New Caledonia	franc CFP	100 centimes
New Zealand	dollar	100 cents
Nicaragua	gold cordoba	100 centavos
Niger	franc CFA	100 centimes
Nigeria	naira	100 kobo
Norway	krone	100 øre
Oman	rial	1,000 baizas
Pakistan	rupee	100 paisa
Palau	U.S. dollar	100 cents
Panama	balboa	100 centesimos
Papua New Guinea	kina	100 toeas
Paraguay	guarani	100 centimos
Peru	(new) sol	100 centimos
Philippines	peso	100 centavos
Poland	(new) zloty	100 groszy
Portugal	escudo	100 centavos
Puerto Rico	U.S. dollar	100 cents
Qatar	riyal	100 dirhams
Romania	leu	100 bani
Russia	rouble	100 kopecks
Rwanda	franc	100 centimes
St. Helena	pound	100 (new) pence
St. Kitts and Nevis	East Caribbean dollar	100 cents
St. Lucia	East Caribbean dollar	100 cents
St. Vincent and the Grenadines	East Caribbean dollar	100 cents
San Marino	Italian lira	100 centesimi
São Tom and Principé	dobra	100 centimos
Saudi Arabia	riyal	100 halalas (halalah)
Senegal	franc CFA	100 centimes
Serbia and Montenegro	(new) dinar	100 paras
Seychelles	rupee	100 cents
Sierra Leone	leone	100 cents
Singapore	dollar	100 cents
Slovakia	koruna	100 haliers (halierov)
Slovenia	tolar	100 stotins (stotinov)
Solomon Islands	dollar	100 cents
Somalia	shilling	100 cents
South Africa	rand	100 cents
South Korea	won	100 chon
Spain	peseta	100 centimos
Sri Lanka	rupee	100 cents

Location	Currency	Smaller Monetary Unit
Sudan	pound	100 piastres
Suriname	guilder	100 cents
Swaziland	lilangeni (plural is "emalangeni")	100 cents
Sweden	krona	100 öre
Switzerland	franc	100 centimes
Syria	pound	100 piastres
Tahiti (*see* French Polynesia)		
Taiwan	(new) dollar	100 cents
Tajikistan	rubl	——
Tanzania	shilling	100 cents
Thailand	baht	100 sastangs
Togo	franc	100 centimes
Tonga	pa'anga	100 seniti
Trinidad and Tobago	dollar	100 cents
Tunisia	dinar	1,000 millimes
Turkey	lira	100 kurus
Turks and Caicos Islands	U.S. dollar	100 cents
Uganda	shilling	100 cents
Ukraine	hryunia	100 kopiykas
United Arab Emirates	dirham	100 fils
United Kingdom	pound	100 pence
United States	dollar	100 cents
Uruguay	peso uruguayo	100 centésimos
U.S. Virgin Islands	U.S. dollar	100 cents
Uzbekistan	som	100 tiyin
Vanuatu	vatu	100 centimes
Vatican	Italian lira	100 centesimi
Venezuela	bolivar	100 centimos
Vietnam	(new) dong	10 hao = 100 xu
Western Samoa	tala	100 sene
Yemen	rial	100 fils
Zambia	kwacha	100 ngwee
Zimbabwe	dollar	100 cents

REQUIREMENTS BEFORE PROCEEDING ABROAD

This listing is prepared solely for the information of U.S. citizens traveling as tourists and does not apply to persons planning to immigrate to foreign countries. A visa is generally an endorsement or stamp placed by officials of a foreign country on a U.S. passport that allows the bearer to visit that country.

PASSPORTS

Persons who travel to a country where a U.S. passport is not required should have documentary

IMPORTANT

Travelers should check passport and visa requirements with the consular officials of the countries to be visited well in advance of their departure dates, because such information is subject to change.

evidence of their U.S. citizenship and identity to facilitate reentry into the United States. Countries that do not require a passport to enter or depart frequently require this evidence. Documentary evidence of U.S. citizenship may be an expired passport, a certified birth certificate, certificate of naturalization, certificate of citizenship, or report of birth abroad of a citizen of the United States. Documentary evidence of identity may be a valid driver's license or government identification provided they identify you by physical description or photograph.

Some Arab and African countries will not issue visas or allow entry if your passport gives evidence of travel to Israel. If this applies to you, consult the nearest U.S. passport agency for guidance.

In addition to the passport agencies listed below, passport applications and information are available at approximately 3,500 post offices and courthouses in the United States.

Boston Passport Agency
Thomas P. O'Neill Federal Bldg.
10 Causeway St., Suite 247
Boston, MA 02222-1094
Services provided to Maine, Massachusetts, New Hampshire, Rhode Island, upstate New York, and Vermont

Chicago Passport Agency
Kluczynski Federal Bldg.
230 S. Dearborn St., Suite 380
Chicago, IL 60604-1564
Services provided to Illinois, Indiana, Michigan, and Wisconsin

Honolulu Passport Agency
First Hawaiian Tower
1132 Bishop St., Suite 500
Honolulu, HI 96813-2809
Services provided to American Samoa, the Federated States of Micronesia, Guam, Hawaii, and the Northern Mariana Islands

Houston Passport Agency
Mickey Leland Federal Bldg.
1919 Smith St., Suite 1100
Houston, TX 77002-8049
Services provided to Kansas, Oklahoma, New Mexico, and Texas

Los Angeles Passport Agency
Federal Bldg.
11000 Wilshire Blvd., Suite 1000
Los Angeles, CA 90024-3615
Services provided to California (all counties south of and including San Luis Obispo, Kern, and San Bernardino) and Nevada (Clark County only)

Miami Passport Agency
Claude Pepper Federal Office Bldg.
51 SW First Ave., 3rd Floor
Miami, FL 33120-1680
Services provided to Florida, Georgia, Puerto Rico, South Carolina, and the U.S. Virgin Islands

National Passport Center
31 Rochester Ave.
Portsmouth, NH 03801-2900
Services provided: Passport by Mail (Form DSP-82) applications accepted

New Orleans Passport Agency
Postal Services Bldg.
701 Loyola Ave., Suite T-12005
New Orleans, LA 70113-1931
Services provided to Alabama, Arkansas, Iowa, Kentucky, Louisiana, Mississippi, Missouri, North Carolina, Ohio, Tennessee, and Virginia (except District of Columbia suburbs)

New York Passport Agency
376 Hudson St.
New York, NY 10014
Services provided to New York City and Long Island
(Call 212-206-3500 only regarding an emergency application for someone leaving within two weeks.)

Philadelphia Passport Agency
U.S. Custom House
200 Chestnut St., Room 103
Philadelphia, PA 19106-2970
Services provided to Delaware, New Jersey, Pennsylvania, and West Virginia

San Francisco Passport Agency
95 Hawthorne St., 5th Floor
San Francisco, CA 94105-3901
Services provided to Arizona, California (all counties north of and including Monterey, Kings, Oulare, and Inyo), Nevada (except Clark County), and Utah

Seattle Passport Agency
Henry Jackson Federal Bldg.
915 Second Ave., Suite 992
Seattle, WA 98174-1091
Services provided to Alaska, Colorado, Idaho, Minnesota, Montana, Nebraska, North Dakota, Oregon, South Dakota, Washington, and Wyoming

 "Countries of the World" in chapter 26

Go to

Stamford Passport Agency
One Landmark Square
Broad and Atlantic sts.
Stamford, CT 06901-2667
Services provided to Connecticut and New York
(Westchester County)

Washington Passport Agency
1111 19th St. NW, Room 300
Washington, DC 20524
Services provided to Maryland, Northern Virginia
(including Alexandria, Arlington County, and
Fairfax County), and the District of Columbia

Special Issuance Agency
1111 19th St. NW, Room 300
Washington, DC 20524
Services provided: Applications accepted for
diplomatic, official, and no-fee passports

Call the National Passport Information Center's passport information number, 900-225-5674 (TDD 900-225-7778), to obtain more information, to request a passport application, or to check on the status of a passport application. Automated information is available 24 hours a day, 7 days a week. Operators can be reached Monday through Friday (excluding federal holidays) from 8:00 A.M. to 8:00 P.M. Eastern Standard time. Services are provided in English and Spanish.

Visit the U.S. State Department Passport Services at their Web site: http://travel.state.gov/passport_services.html.

VISAS

IMPORTANT

It is the responsibility of the traveler to obtain visas, where required, from the appropriate embassy or nearest consulate of the country to be visited before proceeding abroad.

Allow sufficient time for processing your visa application, especially if you apply by mail. Most foreign consular representatives are located in principal cities, particularly Chicago, New Orleans, New York, San Francisco, and Washington, D.C. In many instances, a traveler may be required to obtain visas from the consular office in the area of his or her residence. You can obtain addresses of foreign consular offices in the United States by consulting the *Congressional Directory* (available in most libraries), by accessing the U.S. State Department's online list of foreign consular offices in the U.S. (http://www.state.gov/www/travel/consular_offices/fco_index.html), or by visiting the Web sites listed below and in the "Government Tourist Information Centers" and "Additional Sources of Information" sections of this chapter.

For further assistance, you can also contact travel agents and visa information services such as World Wide Visas (800-527-1861), International Visa Service (800-627-1112), World Travel Guide Online Service (http://www.wtgonline.com/), and Travel Document Systems (800-874-5100; Washington, DC, local number 202-638-3800; fax 202-638-4674; Web site http://www.traveldocs.com/). In addition, the U.S. State Department's Bureau of Consular Affairs (http://travel.state.gov/) offers a wealth of information for travelers including health and safety advisories.

IMMUNIZATIONS

Under the International Health Regulations adopted by the World Health Organization, a country may require certificates of immunization against yellow fever. A few countries still require a cholera immunization as well. Check with healthcare providers or your records to ensure other immunizations (for example, tetanus and polio) are up to date. Prophylactic medication for malaria and certain other preventive measures are advisable for some travelers. No immunizations are required to return to the United States. Pertinent information is included in *Health Information for International Travel,* available from the U.S. Government Printing Office, Washington, DC 20402, for $5, or you can obtain it from your local health department or physician, or by contacting the Centers for Disease Control at 404-639-2572 or their Web site at http://www.cdc.gov/.

An increasing number of countries have established regulations regarding AIDS testing, particularly for long-term visitors. Check with the embassy or consulate of the country you plan to visit for the latest information on whether this is a requirement for entry.

CONTACT INFORMATION FOR INDIVIDUAL COUNTRIES—ONLINE SOURCES

Country	Supplemental Web Site
Afghanistan, Islamic State of	http://frankenstein.worldweb.net/afghan/#gov
Albania, Republic of	http://www.albanian.com/main/countries/albania/index.html
Algeria, Democratic and Popular Republic of	http://www.undp.org/missions/algeria/p135.htm
Andorra	http://www.andorra.ad/cniauk.html
Angola, Republic of	http://www.angola.org/
Anguilla	http://city.net/countries/anguilla/
Antigua and Barbuda	http://www.undp.org/missions/antigua_barbuda/
Argentina	http://emb-eeuu.mrecic.gov.ar/
Armenia, Republic of	http://www.armeniaemb.org/
Aruba	http://city.net/countries/aruba/
Australia	http://www.aust.emb.nw.dc.us/
Austria	http://www.austria.org/govoff.htm#embassy
Azerbaijan, Republic of	http://ourworld.compuserve.com/homepages/Azerbaijan/
Bahamas, Commonwealth of	http://www.interknowledge.com/bahamas/
Bahrain, State of	http://www.bpmb.com/entry.htm
Bangladesh, People's Republic of	http://www.undp.org/missions/bangladesh/
Barbados	http://www.caribnet.net/caribnet/countries/barb.html
Belarus	http://www.undp.org/missions/belarus/
Belgium	http://www.belgium-emb.org/usa/
Belize	http://www.belize.com/
Benin, Republic of	http://www.sas.upenn.edu/African_Studies/Country_Specific/Benin.html
Bermuda	http://www.bermudatourism.com/
Bhutan	http://city.net/countries/bhutan/
Bolivia	http://www.boliviaweb.com/
Bosnia and Herzegovina, Republic of	http://www.bosnianembassy.org/
Botswana, Republic of	http://cy.co.za/atg/stbrob.html
Brazil	http://www.brasil.emb.nw.dc.us/
British Virgin Islands[1]	http://www.britishvirginislands.com/index.htm
Brunei Darussalam, State of	http://sunsite.nus.sg/SEAlinks/brunei-info.html
Bulgaria, Republic of	http://www.bulgaria.com/embassy/wdc/
Burkina Faso	http://city.net/countries/burkina_faso/
Burundi, Republic of	http://198.76.84.1/HORN/burundi/burundi.html
Cambodia, Kingdom of	http://embassy.org/cambodia/main.htm
Cameroon, Republic of	http://www.compufix.demon.co.uk/camweb/Main.html
Canada	http://www.cdn-emb.washdc.org/
Cape Verde, Republic of	http://www.capeverdeusembassy.org/
Cayman Islands	http://caribbean-on-line.com/earlettd/cy/cy.html
Central African Republic	http://www.wtgonline.com/country/cf/gen.html
Chad, Republic of	http://city.net/countries/chad/
Chile	http://www.rree.cl/index.en.html

[1] Includes Anegarda, Jost van Dyke, Tortola, and Virgin Gorda

Country	Supplemental Web Site
China, People's Republic of	http://www.china-embassy.org/
Colombia	http://www.colombiaemb.org/
Comoros Islands (Federal Islamic Republic of the Comoros)	http://www.ksu.edu/sasw/comoros/comoros.html
Congo, Democratic Republic of (formerly Zaire)	http://city.net/countries/zaire/
Congo, Republic of the	http://city.net/countries/congo/
Cook Islands	http://www.microstate.net/cgi-win/mstatead.exe/showmicro,115/
Costa Rica	http://www.wtgonline.com/country/cr/gen.html
Côte d'Ivoire, Republic of (Ivory Coast)	http://city.net/countries/cote_divoire/
Croatia	http://idt.net/~croatia/
Cuba	http://www.lonelyplanet.com/dest/cam/cub.htm
Curaçao	http://www.interknowledge.com/curacao/anxex.htm
Cyprus, Republic of the	http://kypros.org/Embassy/
Czech Republic	http://www.czech.cz/washington/
Denmark, Kingdom of (including Greenland and the Faroe Islands)	http://www.denmarkemb.org/
Djibouti, Republic of	http://www.arab.net/djibouti/djibouti_contents.html
Dominica, Commonwealth of	http://www.dominica.dm/
Dominican Republic	http://www.erols.com/peralta/embassy/embassy.htm
Ecuador (including the Galapagos Islands)	http://www.ecuador.org/ecuador/
Egypt, Arab Republic of	http://www-ceg.ceg.uiuc.edu/~haggag/consulate2.html (Chicago Consulate)
El Salvador	http://www.latinworld.com/countries/elsalvador/
Equatorial Guinea, Republic of	http://city.net/countries/equatorial_guinea/
Eritrea	http://www.cs.indiana.edu/hyplan/dmulholl/eritrea/eritrea.html
Estonia	http://www.estemb.org/
Ethiopia, Federal Democratic Republic of	http://www.cs.indiana.edu/hyplan/dmulholl/ethiopia/ethiopia.html
European Union[2]	http://www.eurunion.org/
Fiji	http://www.fijifvb.gov/content1.htm
Finland	http://www.finland.org/
Former Yugoslav Republic of Macedonia (FYROM)	http://www.vmacedonia.com/
France[3]	http://www.info-france.usa-org/
French Guiana	http://www.lonelyplanet.com.au/dest/sam/fgu.htm
French Polynesia[4]	http://www.polynesia.com/
French West Indies[5]	http://expedia.msn.com/wg/places/Guadeloupe/HSBD.htm
Gabonese Republic (Gabon)	http://city.net/countries/gabon/
Gambia	http://www.gambia.com/
Georgia, Republic of	http://www.parliament.ge/

[2] includes Belgium, Denmark, Finland, France, Germany, Greece, Ireland, Italy, Luxembourg, the Netherlands, Portugal, Spain, Sweden, and the United Kingdom   [3] including French Guiana, French Polynesia, and French West Indies   [4] including the Society Islands, French Southern and Antarctic Lands, Tuamotu, Gambier, French Austral, Marquesas, Kerguelen, Crozet, New Caledonia, Tahiti, Wallis, and Futuna Islands   [5] including Guadeloupe, Isles des Saintes, La Desirade, Marie Galante, Martinique, St. Barthelemy, and St. Martin

continues

Contact Information Continued

Country	Supplemental Web Site
Germany, Federal Republic of	http://www.germany-info.org/
Ghana	http://www.ghana-embassy.org/ or http://www.undp.org/missions/ghana/
Gibraltar	http://www.gibraltar.gi/
Greece	http://www.greekembassy.org/
Greenland	http://www.greenland-guide.dk/
Grenada	http://www.turq.com/grenada.html
Guatemala	http://www.lonelyplanet.com.au/dest/cam/gua.htm
Guinea, Republic of	http://city.net/countries/guinea/
Guinea-Bissau, Republic of	http://www.sas.upenn.edu/African_Studies/Country_Specific/G_Bissau.html
Guyana, Co-operative Republic of	http://www.turq.com/guyana.html
Haiti	http://city.net/countries/haiti/
Holy See, Apostolic Nunciature of the (the Vatican)	http://www.vatican.va/index.html
Honduras	http://www.latinworld.com/countries/honduras/
Hong Kong (Special Administrative Region of the People's Republic of China)	http://www.hkta.org/
Hungary, Republic of	http://www.hungaryemb.org/
Iceland	http://www.iceland.org/
India	http://www.indiagov.org/
Indonesia, Republic of	http://www.kjri-la.com/
Iran	http://www.salamiran.org/
Iraq	http://www.undp.org/missions/iraq/
Ireland	http://www.ireland.travel.ie/
Israel and the Occupied Territories[6]	http://www.israelemb.org/
Italy	http://www.italyemb.nw.dc.us/italy/index.htm
Jamaica	http://www.emlyn-hall.com/jamaica/embassy/washdc/
Japan	http://www.embjapan.org/
Jordan, Hashemite Kingdom of	http://www.iiconsulting.com/jordan/
Kazakhstan	http://www.traveldocs.com/kz/kzicarp.htm
Kenya	http://www.sas.upenn.edu/African_Studies/Country_Specific/Kenya.html
Kiribati, Republic of (formerly Gilbert Islands)	http://www.earth.tohoku.ab.jp/kiribati/kiribati.html
Korea, Democratic People's Republic of (North Korea)	http://darkwing.oregon.edu/~fclsing/kstuff/nkshelf.html
Korea, Republic of (South Korea)	http://korea.emb.washington.dc.us/
Kuwait, State of	http://www.undp.org/missions/kuwait/
Kyrgyz Republic (Kyrgyzstan)	http://www.kyrgyzstan.org/
Laos (Lao People's Democratic Republic)	http://www.laoembassy.com/
Latvia	http://www.seas.gwu.edu/guest/latvia/
Lebanon	http://www.erols.com/lebanon/
Lesotho, Kingdom of	http://www.microstate.com/cgi-win/mstatead.exe/showmicro,192/
Liberia, Republic of	http://city.net/countries/liberia/
Libya	http://www.arab.net/libya/libya_contents.html
Liechtenstein	http://www.newsnet.li/tourist/fl/fleninh.htm
Lithuania	http://www.ltembassyus.org/
Luxembourg, Grand Duchy of	http://www.luxembourg.lu/

[6] Jerusalem, Gaza, Golan Heights, and the West Bank

Country	Supplemental Web Site
Macau	http://www.macau.gov.mo/indexe.shtml
Madagascar, Democratic Republic of	http://www.embassy.org/madagascar/
Malawi	http://www.microstate.com/cgi-win/mstatead.exe/showmicro,195/
Malaysia (and the Borneo States, Sarawak, and Sabah)	http://www.interknowledge.com/malaysia/index.html
Maldives	http://city.net/countries/maldives/
Mali, Republic of	http://www.traveldocs.com/ml/
Malta	http://visitmalta.com/
Marshall Islands, Republic of the	http://www.clark.net/pub/miemb/
Mauritania, Republic of	http://www.embassy.org/mauritania/
Mauritius	http://www.mauritius.net/
Mexico	http://quicklink.com/mexico/
Micronesia, Federated States of (Kosrae, Yap, Panape, and Truk)	http://www.fsmgov.org/fsmun/
Moldova, Republic of	http://www.moldova.org/
Monaco, Principality of	http://www.monaco.mc/usa/
Mongolia	http://www.soros.org/mongolia.html
Morocco	http://www.maghreb.net/countries/morocco/
Mozambique, Republic of	http://www.wtgonline.com/country/mz/gen.html
Myanmar, Union of	http://triton.ori.u-tokyo.ac.jp/~moe/myanmar.html
Namibia	http://www.republicofnamibia.com/
Nauru, Republic of	http://www.traveldocs.com/nr/
Nepal, Kingdom of	http://www.undp.org/missions/nepal/
Netherlands	http://www.netherlands-embassy.org/
Netherlands Antilles[7]	http://city.net/countries/netherlands_antilles/
New Zealand	http://www.emb.com/nzemb/
Nicaragua	http://www.latinworld.com/countries/nicaragua/
Niger, Republic of	http://www.txdirect.net/~jmayer/fon.html#LiNiger
Nigeria, Republic of	http://www.traveldocs.com/ng/
Niue	http://www.microstate.com/cgi-win/mstatead.exe/showmicro,154/
Norfolk Island	http://www.ozemail.com.au/~jbp/pds/contents.html
Northern Mariana Islands, Commonwealth of the	http://www.microstate.net/cgi-win/mstatead.exe/showmicro,186/
Norway, Kingdom of	http://www.norway.org/embassy/index.html
Oman, Sultanate of	http://www.omanet.com/back.htm
Pakistan	http://www.imran.com/Pakistan/Pakistan_Embassy.html
Palau, Republic of	http://www.microstate.com/cgi-win/mstatead.exe/showmicro,187/
Panama	http://city.net/countries/panama/
Papua New Guinea	http://www.lonelyplanet.com.au/dest/aust/png.htm
Paraguay	http://www.latinworld.com/countries/paraguay/
Peru	http://www.wtgonline.com/country/pe/gen.html
Philippines	http://www.sino.net/asean/philippn.html
Poland, Republic of	http://www.polishworld.com/polemb/
Portugal[8]	http://www.portugal.org/
Qatar, State of	http://www.liii.com/~hajeri/qatar.html
Romania	http://www.embassy.org/romania/
Russia	http://www.russianembassy.org/

Travel

[7] including Bonaire, Curaçao, Saba, St. Maarten, and Statia [St. Eustatius]
[8] including Azores and the Madeira Islands

continues

Contact Information Continued

Country	Supplemental Web Site
Rwanda, Republic of	http://city.net/countries/rwanda/
St. Kitts and Nevis	http://expedia.msn.com/wg/places/StKittsandNevis/HSBD.htm
St. Lucia	http://www.turq.com/stlucia.html
St. Vincent and the Grenadines	http://www.turq.com/stvincent/
San Marino, Republic of	http://www.omniway.sm/about_e.htm
São Tome and Principé	http://www.traveldocs.com/st/
Saudi Arabia, Kingdom of	http://www.saudi.net/
Senegal, Republic of	http://www.sas.upenn.edu/African_Studies/Country_Specific/Senegal.html
Serbia and Montenegro ("Federal Republic of Yugoslavia")	http://ourworld.compuserve.com/homepages/yuembassy/
Seychelles	http://city.net/countries/seychelles/
Sierra Leone	http://www.Sierra-Leone.org/
Singapore	http://metroscope.com/sing.html
Slovak Republic	http://savba.savba.sk/logos/list-e.html
Slovenia, Republic of	http://www.ntz-nta.si/
Solomon Islands	http://www.microstate.net/cgi-win/mstatead.exe/showmicro,188/
Somali Democratic Republic (Somalia)	http://city.net/countries/somalia/
South Africa	http://www.southafrica.net/
Spain	http://www.spaintour.com/
Sri Lanka	http://piano.symgrp.com/srilanka/
Sudan, Republic of	http://webzone1.co.uk/www/sudan/
Suriname, Republic of	http://www.surinam.net/surinam.html
Swaziland, Kingdom of	http://www.realnet.co.sz/
Sweden	http://www.swedenemb.org/
Switzerland	http://www.swissemb.org/
Syrian Arab Republic (Syria)	http://www.arab.net/syria/syria_contents.html
Taiwan, Republic of China on	http://www.taipei.org/
Tajikistan	http://www.soros.org/tajikstan.html
Tanzania, United Republic of (Zanzibar)	http://www.traveldocs.com/tz/index.htm
Thailand, Kingdom of	http://www.thaiembdc.org/
Togo, Republic of	http://www.republicoftogo.com/english/home.html
Tonga	http://www.netstorage.com/kami/tonga/index.html
Trinidad and Tobago	http://www.tidco.co/tt/
Tunisia	http://tunisia-online.com/
Turkey, Republic of	http://www.turkey.org/turkey/
Turkmenistan	http://www.infi.net/~embassy/
Tuvalu Island	http://www.microstate.net/cgi-win/mstatead.exe/showmicro,178/
Uganda, Republic of	http://city.net/countries/uganda/
Ukraine	http://www.undp.org/missions/ukraine/
United Arab Emirates (UAE)[9]	http://www.uae.org.ae/
United Kingdom (UK)[10]	http://www.britain-info.org/
Uruguay	http://www.embassy.org/uruguay/
Uzbekistan, Republic of	http://ourworld.compuserve.com/homepages/Uzbeks/
Vanuatu	http://city.net/countries/vanuatu/

[9] Abu Dabi, Dubai, Sharjah, Ras Al Khaimah, Fujairah, Ajman, and Umm Al Quwain
[10] England, Northern Ireland, Scotland, and Wales

Country	Supplemental Web Site
Venezuela	http://venezuela.mit.edu/embassy/
Vietnam	http://www.vietnamembassy-usa.org/
Western Samoa	http://www.interwebinc.com/samoa/missions.html
Yemen, Republic of	http://yemen-online.com/
Zambia, Republic of	http://www.http://www.zamnet.zm/
Zimbabwe	http://www.zimweb.com/Embassy/Zimbabwe/

CONTACT INFORMATION FOR INDIVIDUAL COUNTRIES

Afghanistan, Islamic State of No tourist or business visas are being issued at this time. Operations at the Afghanistan embassy in Washington were temporarily suspended by the U.S. State Department effective August 21, 1997. Embassy address: Embassy of the Islamic State of Afghanistan, 2341 Wyoming Ave. NW, Washington, DC 20008 (202-234-3770, fax 202-328-3516).

IMPORTANT

International travelers should always visit the U.S. State Department Web site at http://travel.state.gov for up-to-date travel warnings and advisories for U.S. citizens and residents. A number of countries listed on the following pages are on the State Department's list of countries where unnecessary travel is discouraged or where all travel is advised against. As political situations can be volatile, always check with the State Deparment before traveling abroad.

Albania, Republic of Embassy address: Embassy of the Republic of Albania at 1150 18th St. NW, Washington, DC 20005 (202-223-4942, fax 202-628-7342).

Algeria, Democratic and Popular Republic of Embassy address: Embassy of the Democratic and Popular Republic of Algeria at 2118 Kalorama Road NW, Washington, DC 20008 (202-265-2800, fax 202-667-2174).

Andorra Embassy address: Andorran Mission to the United Nations, Two United Nations Plaza, 25th Floor, New York, NY 10018 (212-750-8064, fax 212-750-6630). *See also* **Spain.**

Angola, Republic of Embassy address: Consular Section of the Embassy of the Republic of Angola, 1050 Connecticut Ave. NW, Suite 760, Washington, DC 20036 (202-785-1156, fax 202-822-9049).

Anguilla. *See* **British West Indies**.

Antigua and Barbuda Embassy address: Embassy of Antigua and Barbuda, 3216 New Mexico Ave. NW, Washington, DC 20016 (202-362-5122, fax 202-362-5225).

Argentina Contact the Consular Section of the Argentine Embassy at 1718 Connecticut Ave. NW, Suite 200, Washington, DC 20009 (202-797-8826, fax 202-319-1771); or the nearest consulate: Atlanta (404-880-0805), Chicago (312-819-2610), Houston (713-871-8935), Los Angeles (213-954-9155), Miami (305-373-7794), or New York (212-603-0400).

Armenia, Republic of Embassy address: Embassy of the Republic of Armenia at 2225 R St. NW, Washington, DC 20008 (202-319-1976, fax 202-319-2982); or the consulate general in Los Angeles (310-657-6102). Or contact Intourist Ltd. (212-757-5902), which offers comprehensive visa services for all member countries, including Armenia, of the Commonwealth of Independent States (CIS).

Aruba Embassy address: Embassy of the Netherlands, 4200 Linnean Ave. NW, Washington, DC 20008 (202-244-5300, fax 202-362-3430); or the nearest consulate general: Chicago (312-856-0110), Houston (713-622-8000), Los Angeles (310-268-1598), or New York (212-246-1429). *See also* **Netherlands.**

Australia   Embassy address: Embassy of Australia, 1601 Massachusetts Ave. NW, Washington, DC 20036 (800-242-2878 or 202-797-3000, fax 202-797-3168); or the nearest consulate general: Atlanta (404-880-1700), Honolulu (808-524-5050), Houston (713-629-9131), Los Angeles (310-229-4800), New York (212-408-8400), or San Francisco (415-362-6160).

Austria   Embassy address: Consular Section of the Embassy of Austria, 3524 International Ct. NW, Washington, DC 20008 (202-895-6767, fax 202-895-6773); or the nearest consulate general: Chicago (312-222-1515), Los Angeles (310-444-9310), or New York (212-737-6400).

Azerbaijan, Republic of   Embassy address: Embassy of the Republic of Azerbaijan, 927 15th St. NW, Suite 700, Washington, DC 20005 (202-842-0001, fax 202-842-0004). Or contact Intourist Ltd. (212-757-5902), which offers comprehensive visa services for all member countries, including Azerbaijan, of the Commonwealth of Independent States (CIS).

Azores. *See* **Portugal.**

Bahamas, Commonwealth of   Embassy address: Embassy of the Commonwealth of the Bahamas, 2220 Massachusetts Ave. NW, Washington, DC 20008 (202-319-2660); or the nearest consulate: Miami (305-373-6295) or New York (212-421-6420).

Bahrain, State of   Embassy address: Embassy of the State of Bahrain, 3502 International Dr. NW, Washington, DC 20008 (202-342-0741, fax 202-362-2192), or the Permanent Mission to the United Nations, Two United Nations Plaza, E. 44th St., New York, NY 10017 (212-223-6200).

Bangladesh, People's Republic of   Embassy address: Embassy of the People's Republic of Bangladesh, 2201 Wisconsin Ave. NW, Washington, DC 20007 (202-342-8373, fax 202-333-4971).

Barbados   Embassy address: Embassy of Barbados, 2144 Wyoming Ave. NW, Washington, DC 20008 (202-939-9200, fax 202-332-7467), or the consulate general in New York (212-867-8435).

Belarus   Embassy address: Embassy of Belarus, 1619 New Hampshire Ave. NW, Washington, DC 20009 (202-986-1606, fax 202-986-1805), or the consulate general in New York (212-682-5392). Or contact Intourist Ltd. (212-757-5902), which offers comprehensive visa services for all member countries, including Belarus, of the Commonwealth of Independent States (CIS).

Belgium   Embassy address: Embassy of Belgium, 3330 Garfield St. NW, Washington, DC 20008 (202-333-6900, fax 202-333-3079); or the nearest consulate general: Atlanta (404-659-2150), Chicago (312-263-6624), Los Angeles (213-857-1244), or New York (212-586-5110).

Belize   Embassy address: Embassy of Belize, 2535 Massachusetts Ave. NW, Washington, DC 20008 (202-332-9636, fax 202-332-6888), or the Belize Mission in New York (212-599-0233).

Benin, Republic of   Embassy address: Embassy of the Republic of Benin, 2737 Cathedral Ave. NW, Washington, DC 20008 (202-232-6656, fax 202-265-1996).

Bermuda   *See* **United Kingdom.**

Bhutan   Consulate Address: consulate general of Bhutan, Two United Nations Plaza, 27th Floor, New York, NY 10017 (212-826-1919, fax 212-826-2998).

Bolivia   Embassy address: Consular Section of the Embassy of Bolivia, 3014 Massachusetts Ave. NW, Washington, DC 20008 (202-483-4410, fax 202-328-3712); or the nearest consulate general: Miami (305-358-3450), Houston (713-780-8001), New York (212-687-0530) or San Francisco (415-495-5173).

Bonaire. *See* **Netherlands Antilles.**

Bosnia and Herzegovina, Republic of Embassy address: consulate general of Bosnia and Herzegovina, 866 United Nations Plaza, Suite 580, New York, NY 10017 (212-751-9015, fax 212-751-9019).

Botswana, Republic of Embassy address: Embassy of the Republic of Botswana, Suite 7M, 3400 International Dr. NW, Washington, DC 20008 (202-244-4990, fax 202-244-4164); or the nearest honorary consulate: Houston (713-622-1900) or Los Angeles (213-626-8484).

Brazil Embassy address: Consular Section of the Embassy of Brazil, 3009 Whitehaven St. NW, Washington, DC 20008-3613 (202-238-2828, fax 202-238-2818); or the nearest consulate: Atlanta (404-521-0061), Boston (617-542-4000), Chicago (312-464-0244), Houston (713-961-3063), Los Angeles (213-651-2664), Miami (305-285-6200), New York (212-757-3080), or San Francisco (415-981-8170).

British Virgin Islands (including **Anegarda, Jost van Dyke, Tortola,** and **Virgin Gorda**) *See* **United Kingdom.**

British West Indies (including **Anguilla, Cayman Islands, Montserrat,** and **Turks and Caicos Islands**) *See* **United Kingdom.**

Brunei Darussalam, State of Embassy address: Embassy of the State of Brunei Darussalam, 2600 Virginia Ave. NW, Suite 300, Washington, DC 20037 (202-342-0159, fax 202-342-0158), or the Brunei Permanent Mission to the United Nations, 866 United Nations Plaza, Room 248, New York, NY 10017 (212-838-1600).

Bulgaria, Republic of Embassy address: the Consular Section of the Embassy of the Republic of Bulgaria, 1621 22nd St. NW, Washington, DC 20008 (202-387-7969, fax 202-234-7973).

Burkina Faso Embassy address: Embassy of Burkina Faso, 2340 Massachusetts Ave. NW, Washington, DC 20008 (202-332-5577, fax 202-265-6972); or the nearest honorary consulate: Atlanta (404-378-7278), Los Angeles (213-824-5100), or New Orleans (504-945-3152).

Burundi, Republic of Embassy address: Embassy of the Republic of Burundi, 2233 Wisconsin Ave. NW, Suite 212, Washington, DC 20007 (202-342-2574), or the Permanent Mission of Burundi to the United Nations (212-687-1180).

Cambodia, Kingdom of Embassy address: Royal Embassy of Cambodia, 4500 16th St. NW, Washington, DC 20011 (202-726-7742, fax 202-726-8381), or the Permanent Mission of Cambodia to the United Nations, 866 United Nations Plaza, Room 420, New York, NY 10017 (212-421-7626).

Cameroon, Republic of Embassy address: Embassy of the Republic of Cameroon, 2349 Massachusetts Ave. NW, Washington, DC 20008 (202-265-8790, fax 202-387-3826).

Canada Embassy address: Canadian Embassy, 501 Pennsylvania Ave. NW, Washington, DC 20001 (202-682-1740) or the nearest consulate general: Atlanta (404-532-2000), Boston (617-262-3760), Buffalo (716-858-9500), Chicago (312-616-1860), Dallas (214-922-9806), Detroit (313-567-2340), Los Angeles (213-346-2700), Minneapolis (612-332-7486), New York (212-596-1628), or Seattle (206-443-1377).

Cape Verde, Republic of Embassy address: Embassy of the Republic of Cape Verde, 3415 Massachusetts Ave. NW, Washington, DC 20007 (202-965-6820, fax 202-965-1207) or the consulate general, 535 Boylston St., 2nd Floor, Boston, MA 02116 (617-353-0014).

Cayman Islands. *See* **British West Indies.**

Central African Republic Embassy address: Embassy of the Central African Republic, 1618 22nd St. NW, Washington, DC 20008 (202-483-7800, fax 202-332-9893).

Chad, Republic of Embassy address: Embassy of the Republic of Chad, 2002 R St. NW, Washington, DC 20009 (202-462-4009, fax 202-265-1937).

Chile   Embassy address: Embassy of Chile, 1732 Massachusetts Ave. NW, Washington, DC 20036 (202-785-1746, fax 202-887-5579); or the nearest consulate general: Chicago (312-654-8780), Houston (713-621-5853), Los Angeles (310-785-0113), Miami (305-373-8623), New York (212-980-3366), Philadelphia (215-829-9520), San Francisco (415-982-7662), or San Juan, PR (787-725-6365).

China, People's Republic of   Embassy address: Embassy of the People's Republic of China, 2300 Connecticut Ave. NW, Washington, DC 20008 (202-328-2500, fax 202-588-0032); or the nearest consulate general: Chicago (312-346-0287), Houston (713-524-4311), Los Angeles (213-380-2506), New York (212-330-7409) or San Francisco (415-563-4857).

China, Republic of. *See* **Taiwan.**

Colombia   Embassy address: Embassy of Colombia, 2118 Leroy Place NW, Washington, DC 20008 (202-387-8338, fax 202-232-8643); or the nearest consulate general: Atlanta (404-237-1045), Boston (617-536-6222), Chicago (312-923-1196), Houston (713-527-8919), Los Angeles (213-653-4299 or 213-653-9863), Miami (305-448-5558 or 305-441-0437), Minneapolis (612-933-2408), New Orleans (504-525-5580), New York (212-949-9898), St. Louis (314-991-3636), San Francisco (415-495-7195), San Juan, PR (787-754-6885), or Washington, DC (202-332-7476 or 202-332-7573).

Comoros Islands (Federal Islamic Republic of the Comoros)   Embassy address: Mission and Embassy of the Federal and Islamic Republic of Comoros, 336 E. 45th St., 2nd Floor, New York, NY 10017 (212-972-8010, fax 212-983-4712).

Congo, Democratic Republic of (formerly **Zaire**)   The U.S. State Department advises against travel to this country. Embassy address: Zairian Embassy, 1800 New Hampshire Ave. NW, Washington, DC 20009 (202-234-7690), or the Permanent Mission to the United Nations, 2 Henry Ave., North Caldwell, New Jersey 07006 (201-812-1636).

Congo, Republic of the   Embassy address: Embassy of the Republic of the Congo, 4891 Colorado Ave. NW, Washington, DC 20011 (202-726-0825, fax 202-726-1860), or the Permanent Mission of the Congo to the United Nations, 14 E. 65th St., New York, NY 10021 (212-744-7840).

Cook Islands   Consulate address: Consulate for the Cook Islands, Kamehameha Schools, #16, Kapalama Heights, Honolulu, HI 96817 (808-847-6377). *See also* **New Zealand.**

Costa Rica   Embassy address: Consular Section of the Embassy of Costa Rica, 2112 S St. NW, Washington, DC 20008 (202-328-6628); or the nearest consulate general: Atlanta (404-951-7025), Chicago (312-263-2772), Houston (713-266-1527), Miami (305-371-7485), New Orleans (504-887-8131), New York (212-425-2620), or San Francisco (415-392-8488).

Côte d'Ivoire, Republic of (Ivory Coast)   Embassy address: Embassy of the Republic of Côte d'Ivoire, 2424 Massachusetts Ave. NW, Washington, DC 20008 (202-797-0300), or the honorary consulate in San Francisco (415-391-0176).

Croatia   Embassy address: Embassy of Croatia, 2343 Massachusetts Ave. NE, Washington, DC 20002 (202-588-5899, fax 202-588-8936), or the consulate general in New York (212-599-3066).

Cuba   Travel to Cuba is restricted by U.S. Department of Treasury regulations requiring that citizens obtain a license to visit Cuba. Contact the Licensing Division, Office of Foreign Assets Control, U.S. Department of the Treasury, 1500 Pennsylvania Ave. NW, Treasury Annex, Washington, DC 20220 (202-622-2480, fax 202-622-1657, info-by-fax service 202-622-0077). As the U.S. does not maintain diplomatic relations with Cuba, there is no Cuban embassy in the United States. For more information about entry requirements and visas, contact the Cuban Interests Section, 2639 16th St. NW, Washington, DC 20009 (202-797-8518).

Curaçao. *See* **Netherlands Antilles.**

Cyprus, Republic of the Embassy address: Embassy of the Republic of Cyprus, 2211 R St. NW, Washington, DC 20008 (202-462-5772); the consulate general in New York (212-686-6016); or the nearest honorary consulate: Atlanta (404-941-3764), Boston (617-497-0219), Detroit (513-582-1411), Houston (713-928-2264), Los Angeles (310-397-0771), New Orleans (504-388-8701), Philadelphia (215-928-4290), or Seattle (206-827-1700).

Czech Republic Embassy address: Embassy of the Czech Republic, 3900 Spring of Freedom St. NW, Washington, DC 20008 (202-274-9123, fax 202-966-8540); or the consulate general in Los Angeles (310-473-0889) or New York (212-717-5643, fax 212-717-5064).

Denmark, Kingdom of (including **Greenland** and the **Faroe Islands**) Embassy address: Royal Danish Embassy, 3200 Whitehaven St. NW, Washington, DC 20008 (202-234-4300, fax 202-328-1470); or the nearest consulate: Chicago (312-787-8780), Los Angeles (310-443-2090), or New York (212-223-4545).

Djibouti, Republic of Embassy address: Embassy of the Republic of Djibouti, 1156 15th St. NW, Suite 515, Washington, DC 20005 (202-331-0270), or the Djibouti Mission to the United Nations, 866 United Nations Plaza, Suite 4011, New York, NY 10017 (212-753-3163).

Dominica, Commonwealth of Consulate address: Consulate of the Commonwealth of Dominica, 820 2nd Ave., Suite 900, New York, NY 10017 (212-599-8478).

Dominican Republic Embassy address: Embassy of the Dominican Republic, 1715 22nd St. NW, Washington, DC 20008 (202-332-6280); or the nearest consulate general: Boston (617-482-8121), Chicago (312-486-8400), Houston (713-266-0165), Miami (305-358-3220), New Orleans (504-522-1843), New York (212-768-2480),

Philadelphia (215-923-3006), San Francisco (415-982-5144), or San Juan, PR (787-833-4756).

Ecuador (including the **Galapagos Islands**) Embassy address: Embassy of Ecuador, 2535 15th St. NW, Washington, DC 20009 (202-234-7166); or the nearest consulate general: Boston (617-523-2700), Chicago (312-329-0266), Houston (713-622-1787), Los Angeles (213-628-3014), Miami (305-539-8214), Newark (201-642-0208), New Orleans (504-523-3229), New York (212-808-0170), Philadelphia (215-925-9060), San Francisco (415-957-5921), or San Juan, PR (787-723-6572).

Egypt, Arab Republic of Embassy address: Embassy of the Arab Republic of Egypt, 3521 International Ct. NW, Washington, DC 20008 (202-895-5400 Embassy; 202-966-6342 Consulate); or the nearest consulate general: Chicago (312-828-9162), Houston (713-961-4915), New York (212-759-7120), or San Francisco (415-346-9700).

El Salvador Consulate address: consulate general of El Salvador, 1010 16th St. NW, 3rd Floor, Washington, DC 20036 (202-331-4032); or the nearest consulate: Boston (617-577-9111), Chicago (312-322-1393), Houston (713-270-6239 or 214-637-1018), Los Angeles (213-383-5776), Miami (305-371-8850), New Orleans (504-522-4266), New York (212-889-3608), or San Francisco (415-781-7924).

England. *See* **United Kingdom.**

Equatorial Guinea, Republic of Embassy address: Embassy of the Republic of Equatorial Guinea, 1511 K St. NW, Suite 405, Washington, DC 20005 (202-393-0348).

Eritrea Embassy address: Embassy of Eritrea, 910 17th St. NW, Suite 400, Washington, DC 20006 (202-319-1991, fax 202-319-1304).

Estonia Embassy address: Estonian Embassy, 2131 Massachusetts Ave. NW, Washington, DC 20008 (202-588-0101), or the consulate general of

Estonia, 630 Fifth Ave., Suite 2415, New York, NY 10111 (212-247-7634 or 212-247-1450).

Ethiopia, Federal Democratic Republic of Embassy address: Embassy of Ethiopia, 2134 Kalorama Rd. NW, Washington, DC 20008 (202-234-2281, fax 202-483-2407).

European Union (Belgium, Denmark, Finland, France, Germany, Greece, Ireland, Italy, Luxembourg, the Netherlands, Portugal, Spain, Sweden, and the **United Kingdom)** Established to promote cooperation between the United States and the member states of the Union, the European Union's Delegation of the European Commission to the United States offers helpful information on trade agreements, international policies, justice matters, and many other topics of interest to prospective travelers in Europe. For more information, contact the European Union, Delegation of the European Commission to the United States, 2300 M St. NW, Washington, DC 20007 (202-862-9500, fax 202-429-1766).

Faroe Islands. *See* **Denmark.**

"Federal Republic of Yugoslavia." *See* **Serbia and Montenegro.**

Fiji Embassy address: Embassy of Fiji, 2233 Wisconsin Ave. NW, Suite 240, Washington, DC 20007 (202-337-8320, fax 202-337-1996), or Fiji's Mission to the United Nations, One United Nations Plaza, 630 Third Ave., 7th Floor, New York, NY 10017 (212-687-4130).

Finland Embassy address: Embassy of Finland, 3301 Massachusetts Ave. NW, Washington, DC 20008 (202-298-5800, fax 202-298-6030); or the nearest consulate general: Los Angeles (310-203-9903) or New York (212-750-4400).

Former Yugoslav Republic of Macedonia (FYROM) Embassy address: Embassy of the Former Yugoslav Republic of Macedonia, 3050 K St. NW, Suite 210, Washington, DC 20007 (202-337-3063, fax 202-337-3093), or the consulate general, 866 United Nations Plaza, Suite 4018, New York, NY 10017 (212-317-1727).

France (including **French Guiana, French Polynesia,** and **French West Indies**) Embassy address: Consular Section of the Embassy of France, 4101 Reservoir Rd. NW, Washington, DC 20007 (202-944-6200); or the nearest consulate: Atlanta (404-522-4226), Boston (617-542-7374), Chicago (312-787-5359), Honolulu (808-599-4458), Houston (713-528-2181), Los Angeles (310-235-3200), Miami (305-372-9798), New Orleans (504-523-5772), New York (212-606-3644), or San Francisco (415-397-4330).

French Guiana. *See* **France.**

French Polynesia (including the **Society Islands, French Southern** and **Antarctic Lands, Tuamotu, Gambier, French Austral, Marquesas, Kerguelen, Crozet, New Caledonia, Tahiti,** and **Wallis** and **Futuna Islands**). *See* **France.**

French West Indies (including **Guadeloupe, Isles des Saintes, La Desirade, Marie Galante, Martinique, St. Barthelemy,** and **St. Martin**). *See* **France.**

Gabonese Republic (Gabon) Embassy address: Embassy of the Gabonese Republic, 2034 20th St. NW, Washington, DC 20009 (202-797-1000, fax 202-332-0668), or the Permanent Mission of the Gabonese Republic to the United Nations, 18 E. 41st St., 6th Floor, New York, NY 10017 (212-686-9720).

Galapagos Islands. *See* **Ecuador.**

Gambia Embassy address: Embassy of the Gambia, 1155 15th St. NW, Washington, DC 20005 (202-785-1399, fax 202-785-1430), or the Permanent Mission of the Gambia to the United Nations, 820 2nd Ave., 9th Floor, New York, NY 10017 (212-949-6640).

Georgia, Republic of Embassy address: Embassy of the Republic of Georgia, 1511 K St. NW, Suite 424, Washington, DC 20005 (202-393-6060). Or contact Intourist Ltd. (212-757-5902), which offers comprehensive visa services for all member countries, including Georgia, of the Commonwealth of Independent States (CIS).

Germany, Federal Republic of Embassy address: Embassy of the Federal Republic of Germany, 4645 Reservoir Rd. NW, Washington, DC 20007 (202-298-4000, fax 202-298-4249); or the nearest consulate general: Atlanta (404-659-4760), Boston (617-536-4414), Chicago (312-580-1199), Detroit (313-962-6526), Houston (713-627-7770), Los Angeles (213-930-2703), Miami (305-358-0290), New York (212-308-8700), San Francisco (415-775-1061), or Seattle (206-682-4312).

Ghana Embassy address: Embassy of Ghana, 3512 International Dr. NW, Washington, DC 20008 (202-686-4520), or the consulate general, 19 E. 47th St., New York, NY 10017 (212-832-1300).

Gibraltar. *See* **United Kingdom.**

Great Britain. *See* **United Kingdom.**

Greece Embassy address: Consular Section of the Embassy of Greece, 2211 Massachusetts Ave. NW, Washington, DC 20008 (202-939-5818); or the nearest consulate: Atlanta (404-261-3313), Boston (617-542-3240), Chicago (312-372-5356), Houston (713-840-7522), Los Angeles (213-385-1447), New Orleans (504-523-1167), New York (212-988-5500), or San Francisco (415-775-2102).

Greenland. *See* **Denmark.**

Grenada Embassy address: Embassy of Grenada, 1701 New Hampshire Ave. NW, Washington, DC 20009 (202-265-2561), or the Permanent Mission of Grenada to the United Nations (212-599-0301).

Guadeloupe (French West Indies). *See* **France.**

Guatemala Embassy address: Embassy of Guatemala, 2220 R St. NW, Washington, DC 20008-4081 (202-745-4952); or the nearest consulate: Chicago (312-332-3170), Houston (713-953-9531), Los Angeles (213-365-9251), Miami (305-443-4828), New York (212-686-3837), or San Francisco (415-788-5651).

Guinea, Republic of Embassy address: Embassy of the Republic of Guinea, 2112 Leroy Pl. NW, Washington, DC 20008 (202-483-9420, fax 202-483-8688).

Guinea-Bissau, Republic of Embassy address: Embassy of the Republic of Guinea-Bissau, 918 16th St. NW, Mezzanine Suite, Washington, DC 20006 (202-872-4222).

Guyana, Cooperative Republic of Embassy address: Embassy of Guyana, 2490 Tracy Pl. NW, Washington, DC 20008 (202-265-6900, fax 202-232-1297), or the consulate general, 866 United Nations Plaza, 3rd Floor, New York, NY 10017 (212-527-3215, fax 212-527-3229).

Haiti Embassy address: Embassy of Haiti, 2311 Massachusetts Ave. NW, Washington, DC 20008 (202-332-4090); or the nearest consulate: Chicago (312-922-4004), Miami (305-859-2003), New York (212-697-9767), or San Juan, PR (787-764-1392).

Holy See, Apostolic Nunciature of the (the Vatican) Contact Apostolic Nunciature of the Holy See, 3339 Massachusetts Ave. NW, Washington, DC 20008 (202-333-7121). *See also* **Italy.**

Honduras Embassy address: Embassy of Honduras, 3007 Tilden St. NW, Washington, DC 20008 (202-966-7702, fax 202-966-9751); or the nearest consulate: Chicago (312-951-6382), Houston (713-622-4572), Los Angeles (213-383-9244), Miami (305-447-8927), New Orleans (504-522-3118), New York (212-269-3611), or San Francisco (415-392-0076).

Hong Kong (Special Administrative Region of the People's Republic of China). *See* **China, People's Republic of.**

Hungary, Republic of Embassy address: Embassy of the Republic of Hungary, 3910 Shoemaker St. NW, Washington, DC 20008 (202-362-6730); or the nearest consulate general: Los Angeles (310-473-9344) or New York (212-752-0661).

Iceland Embassy address: Embassy of Iceland, 1156 15th St. NW, Suite 1200, Washington, DC 20005 (202-265-6653), or the consulate general in New York (212-686-4100).

India Embassy address: Embassy of India, 2536 Massachusetts Ave. NW, Washington, DC 20008 (202-939-9839/9849); or the nearest consulate general: Chicago (312-718-6280), New York (212-879-7805), or San Francisco (415-668-0683).

Indonesia, Republic of Embassy address: Embassy of the Republic of Indonesia, 2020 Massachusetts Ave. NW, Washington, DC 20036 (202-775-5200); or the nearest consulate: Chicago (312-938-0101), Houston (713-785-1691), Los Angeles (213-383-5126), New York (212-879-0600), or San Francisco (415-474-9571).

Point Roberts, Washington, is cut off from the rest of the state by British Columbia, Canada. To travel between Point Roberts and the rest of the state, you must pass through both Canadian and U.S. customs.

Iran The United States does not maintain diplomatic or consular relations with Iran. Embassy address: Embassy of Pakistan, Iranian Interests Section, 2209 Wisconsin Ave. NW, Washington, DC 20007 (202-965-4990).

Iraq The United States suspended diplomatic and consular operations in Iraq in 1990. Since February 1991, U.S. passports are not valid for travel in, to, or through Iraq without authorization from the Department of State. Application for exemptions to this restriction should be submitted in writing to Passport Services, Attention: CA/PPT/PAS, U.S. Department of State, 1111 19th St. NW, Washington, DC 20524. U.S. citizens need a Treasury Department license in order to engage in any transactions related to travel to and within Iraq. Before planning any travel to Iraq,

U.S. citizens should contact the Licensing Division, Office of Foreign Assets Control, Department of the Treasury, 1331 G St. NW, Washington, DC 20220 (202-622-2480). Passport, visa, and AIDS test required. For more visa information, contact the Iraqi Interest Section, 1801 P St. NW, Washington, DC 20036 (202-483-7500).

Ireland Embassy address: Embassy of Ireland, 2234 Massachusetts Ave. NW, Washington, DC 20008 (202-462-3939); or the nearest consulate general: Boston (617-267-9330), Chicago (312-337-1868), New York (212-319-2555), or San Francisco (415-392-4214).

Israel and the **Occupied Territories (Jerusalem, Gaza, Golan Heights**, and the **West Bank**) Embassy address: Embassy of Israel, 3514 International Dr. NW, Washington, DC 20008 (202-364-5500); or the nearest consulate general: Atlanta (404-875-7851), Boston (617-542-0041), Chicago (312-565-3300), Houston (713-627-3780), Los Angeles (213-852-5500), Miami (305-358-8111), New York (212-499-5300), Philadelphia (215-546-5556), or San Francisco (415-398-8885).

Italy Embassy address: Embassy of Italy, 1601 Fuller St. NW, Washington, DC 20009 (202-328-5500); or the nearest consulate general: Boston (617-542-0483), Chicago (312-467-1550), Detroit (313-963-8560), Houston (713-850-7520), Los Angeles (310-820-0622), Miami (305-374-6322), Newark (201-643-1448), New Orleans (504-524-2272), New York (212-737-9100), Philadelphia (215-592-7329) or San Francisco (415-931-4924).

Ivory Coast. *See* **Côte d'Ivoire.**

Jamaica Embassy address: Embassy of Jamaica, 1520 New Hampshire Ave. NW, Washington, DC 20036 (202-452-0660, fax 202-452-0081); or the nearest consulate: Boston (617-266-8604), Chicago (312-663-0023), Los Angeles (310-559-3822), Miami (305-374-8431), New York (212-935-9000), or Seattle (206-872-8950).

Japan Embassy address: Embassy of Japan, 2520 Massachusetts Ave. NW, Washington, DC 20008 (202-939-6800); or the nearest consulate: Anchorage (907-279-8428), Atlanta (404-892-2700), Boston (617-973-9772), Chicago (312-280-0400), Detroit (313-567-0120), Guam (671-646-1290), Honolulu (808-536-2226), Houston (713-652-2977), Los Angeles (213-617-6700), Miami (305-530-9090), New Orleans (504-529-2101), New York (212-371-8222), San Francisco (415-777-3533), or Seattle (206-682-9107).

Jordan, Hashemite Kingdom of Embassy address: Embassy of the Hashemite Kingdom of Jordan, 3504 International Dr. NW, Washington, DC 20008 (202-966-2664).

Kazakhstan Travelers with a valid visa for another country in the Commonwealth of Independent States (CIS) are permitted to transit Kazakhstan for up to three days, but may be asked for proof of onward travel arrangements. The embassy does not issue letters of invitation to citizens interested in private travel to Kazakhstan. Requirements for business travel include company letter, confirmation from host organization, and registration with the Ministry of Foreign Affairs of Kazakhstan by host organization. Embassy address: Embassy of Kazakhstan, 3421 Massachusetts Ave. NW, Washington, DC 20008 (202-333-4504, fax 202-333-4509). Or contact Intourist Ltd. (212-757-5902), which offers comprehensive visa services for all CIS countries, including Kazakhstan.

Kenya Embassy address: Embassy of Kenya, 2249 R St. NW, Washington, DC 20008 (202-387-6101, fax 202-462-3829); or the nearest consulate general: Los Angeles (310-274-6635) or New York (212-486-1300).

Kiribati, Republic of (formerly **Gilbert Islands**) Embassy address: Consular Section of the British Embassy, 19 Observatory Cir. NW, Washington, DC 20008 (202-588-7800, fax 202-588-7850).

Korea, Democratic People's Republic of (North Korea) The United States currently does not maintain diplomatic or consular relations with North Korea. The Swedish Embassy, in Cambodia, is acting as the consular protecting power for the U.S. government there. A U.S. Treasury Department license must be obtained for any U.S. citizen to engage in any travel-related transaction, whether travel will be to or within North Korea. Before planning any travel to North Korea, contact the Licensing Division, Office of Foreign Assets Control, Department of the Treasury, 1331 G St. NW, Washington, DC 20220 (202-622-2480). (Visa information must be obtained from a consulate in a country that maintains diplomatic relations with North Korea, such as France.)

Korea, Republic of (South Korea) Embassy address: Embassy of the Republic of Korea (Consular Division), 2320 Massachusetts Ave. NW, Washington, DC 20008 (202-939-5663); or the nearest consulate general: Atlanta (404-522-1611), Boston (617-348-3660), Chicago (312-822-9485), Guam (671-472-6109), Honolulu (808-595-6109), Houston (713-961-0186), Los Angeles (213-385-9300), Miami (305-372-1555), New York (212-752-1700), San Francisco (415-921-2251), or Seattle (206-441-1011).

Kuwait, State of Embassy address: Embassy of the State of Kuwait, 2940 Tilden St. NW, Washington, DC 20008 (202-966-0702), or its consulate, 321 E. 44th St., New York, NY 10017 (212-973-4300).

Kyrgyz Republic (Kyrgyzstan) Visas from CIS member states, except Georgia and Tajikistan, allow for temporary stays in the Kyrgyz Republic for up to three days if the traveler is in transit. Embassy address: Embassy of the Kyrgyz Republic, 1732 Wisconsin Ave. NW, Washington, DC 20007 (202-338-5141, fax 202-338-5139). Or contact Intourist Ltd. (212-757-5902), which offers comprehensive visa services for all member countries, including Kyrgyzstan, of the Commonwealth of Independent States (CIS).

Laos (Lao People's Democratic Republic) Embassy address: Consular Section of the Embassy of the Lao People's Democratic Republic, 2222 S St. NW, Washington, DC 20008 (202-332-6416, fax 202-332-4923).

Latvia Embassy address: Embassy of Latvia, 4325 17th St. NW, Washington, DC 20011 (202-726-8213, fax 202-726-6785).

Lebanon Embassy address: Embassy of Lebanon, 2560 28th St. NW, Washington, DC 20008 (202-939-6300, fax 202-939-6324); or the nearest consulate general: Detroit (313-567-0233), Los Angeles (213-467-1253), or New York (212-744-7905).

Lesotho, Kingdom of Embassy address: Embassy of the Kingdom of Lesotho, 2511 Massachusetts Ave. NW, Washington, DC 20008 (202-797-5533).

Liberia, Republic of Embassy address: Embassy of the Republic of Liberia, 5303 Colorado Ave. NW, Washington, DC 20011 (202-723-0437); or the nearest consulate: Atlanta (404-753-4754), Chicago (312-643-8635), Detroit (313-342-3900), Los Angeles (213-277-7692), New Orleans (504-523-7784), or New York (212-687-1025).

Libya Since December 1981, U.S. passports are not valid for travel in, to, or through Libya without authorization from the Department of State. Application for exemption to this restriction should be submitted in writing to Passport Services, U.S. Department of State, 1111 19th St. NW, Washington, DC 20524, Attention: CA/PPT/PAS. In addition, U.S. citizens need a Treasury Department license in order to engage in any transactions related to travel to and within Libya. Before planning any travel to Libya, U.S. citizens should contact the Licensing Division, Office of Foreign Assets Control, Department of the Treasury, 1331 G St. NW, Washington, DC 20220 (202-622-2480). Application and inquiries for visas must be made through a country that maintains diplomatic relations with Libya.

Liechtenstein Embassy address: Embassy of Switzerland, 2900 Cathedral Ave. NW, Washington, DC 20008 (202-745-7900, fax 202-387-2564); or the nearest consulate general: Atlanta (404-870-2000), Chicago (312-915-0061), Houston (713-650-0000), Los Angeles (310-575-1145), New York (212-758-2560), or San Francisco (415-788-2272).

Lithuania Embassy address: Embassy of Lithuania, 2622 16th St. NW, Washington, DC 20009 (202-234-5860, fax 202-328-0466), or the consulate general of Lithuania in New York, 420 Fifth Ave., New York, NY 10018 (212-354-7849).

Luxembourg, Grand Duchy of Embassy address: Embassy of Luxembourg, 2200 Massachusetts Ave. NW, Washington, DC 20008 (202-265-4171), or the nearest consulate in New York (212-888-6664) or San Francisco (415-788-0816).

Macau (Macau is a Chinese territory administered by Portugal. China will regain sovereignty over Macau on December 20, 1999.) Embassy address: Embassy of Portugal at 2125 Kalorama Rd. NW, Washington DC 20008 (202-328-8610, fax 202-462-3726); the nearest Portuguese consulate in Boston (617-536-8740), Newark (201-622-7300), New Bedford (508-997-6151), New York (212-246-4580), Providence (401-272-2003), San Francisco (415-346-3400), or Washington, DC (202-332-3007); or the American consulate general in Hong Kong (852-2523-9011).

Macedonia. *See* **Former Yugoslav Republic of Macedonia (FYROM).**

Madagascar, Democratic Republic of Embassy address: Embassy of the Democratic Republic of Madagascar, 2374 Massachusetts Ave. NW, Washington, DC 20008 (202-265-5525, fax 202-483-7603); or the nearest consulate: New York (212-986-9491), Berkeley (800-856-2721), or Philadelphia (215-893-3067).

Malawi Embassy address: Embassy of Malawi, 2408 Massachusetts Ave. NW, Washington, DC 20008 (202-797-1007), or the Malawi Mission to the United Nations, 600 Third Ave., New York, NY 10016 (212-949-0180).

Malaysia (and the **Borneo States, Sarawak,** and **Sabah**)   Embassy address: Embassy of Malaysia, 2401 Massachusetts Ave. NW, Washington, DC 20008 (202-328-2700); or the nearest consulate: Los Angeles (213-892-1238) or New York (212-490-2722).

Maldives   Contact the Maldives Mission to the United Nations in New York (212-599-6195).

Mali, Republic of   Embassy address: Embassy of the Republic of Mali, 2130 R St. NW, Washington, DC 20008 (202-332-2249).

Malta   Embassy address: Embassy of Malta, 2017 Connecticut Ave. NW, Washington, DC 20008 (202-462-3611). Or contact the nearest consulate: Detroit (313-525-9777); Houston (713-497-2100 or 713-999-1812); Independence, MO (816-833-0033); Los Angeles (213-939-5011); Minneapolis (612-228-0935); New York (212-725-2345); or San Francisco (415-468-4321).

Mariana Islands. *See* **Northern Mariana Islands.**

Marshall Islands, Republic of the   Embassy address: Embassy of Marshall Islands, 2433 Massachusetts Ave. NW, Washington, DC 20008 (202-234-5414); the Permanent Mission to the United Nations, 220 E. 42nd St., New York, NY 10017 (211-983-3040); or the nearest consulate general: Honolulu (808-942-4422) or Santa Ana, CA (714-474-0331).

Martinique (French West Indies). *See* **France.**

Mauritania, Republic of   Embassy address: Embassy of the Republic of Mauritania, 2129 Leroy Place NW, Washington, DC 20008 (202-232-5700, fax 202-232-5701), or the Permanent Mission to the United Nations, 211 E. 43rd St., Suite 2000, New York, NY 10017 (212-986-7963).

Mauritius   Embassy address: Embassy of Mauritius, Suite 441, 4301 Connecticut Ave. NW, Washington, DC 20008 (202-244-1491); or the

nearest honorary consulates: Atlanta (404-239-6471 or 404-264-7100) or Los Angeles (818-788-3720).

Mayotte Island. *See* **France.**

Mexico   Embassy address: Embassy of Mexico's Consular Section, 2827 16th St. NW, Washington, DC 20009-4260 (202-736-1000); or the nearest consulate general: Atlanta (404-266-1913), Chicago (312-855-1380), Denver (303-331-1110), Houston (210-227-1085, 214-630-7341, 713-542-2300, 512-478-9031 and 915-533-4082), Miami (305-716-4977), Los Angeles (213-351-6800), New Orleans (504-522-3596), New York (212-689-0460), Phoenix (602-242-7398), San Diego (619-231-8414), San Francisco (415-392-5554), or San Juan, PR (787-764-0258).

Micronesia, Federated States of (Kosrae, Yap, Panape, and **Truk**)   Embassy address: Embassy of the Federated States of Micronesia, 1725 N St. NW, Washington, DC 20036 (202-223-4383), or the nearest consulate in Guam (671-646-9154) or Honolulu (808-836-4775).

Miquelon Island. *See* **France.**

Moldova, Republic of   Embassy address: Embassy of the Republic of Moldova, 1533 K St. NW, Suite 333, Washington, DC 20005, (202-667-1130). Or contact Intourist Ltd. (212-757-5902), which offers comprehensive visa services for all member countries, including Moldova, of the Commonwealth of Independent States (CIS).

Monaco, Principality of   Consulate address: consulate general of Monaco at 565 Fifth Ave., New York, NY 10017 (212-759-5227); or the nearest honorary consulate of the Principality of Monaco: Chicago (312-642-1242), Los Angeles (213-655-8970), New Orleans (504-522-5700), New York (212-759-5227), San Francisco (415-362-5050), or San Juan, PR (787-721-4215).

Mongolia   All foreigners are required to be registered with the Civil Registration Information Center Police Department in Mongolia upon arrival, regardless of duration of stay, and are warned to do so in order to avoid being denied exit and/or fined upon departure. Embassy address: Embassy of Mongolia, 2833 M St. NW, Washington, DC 20007 (202-333-7117), or the United Nations Mission of Mongolia, Six E. 77th St., New York, NY 10021 (212-861-9460).

Montenegro. *See* **Serbia and Montenegro.**

Montserrat. *See* **British West Indies.**

Morocco   Embassy address: Embassy of Morocco, 1601 21st St. NW, Washington, DC 20009 (202-462-7979), or its consulate general in New York (212-213-9644).

Mozambique, Republic of   Embassy address: Embassy of the Republic of Mozambique, Suite 570, 1990 M St. NW, Washington, DC 20036 (202-293-7146).

Myanmar, Union of   Embassy address: Embassy of the Union of Myanmar, 2300 S St. NW, Washington, DC 20008 (202-332-9044), or the Permanent Mission of Myanmar to the United Nations, 10 E. 77th St., New York, NY 10021 (212-535-1310).

Namibia   Embassy address: Embassy of Namibia at 1605 New Hampshire Ave. NW, Washington, DC 20009 (202-986-0540), or the Permanent Mission of Namibia to the United Nations, 135 W. 36th St., New York, NY 10016 (212-685-2003, fax 212-685-1561).

Nauru, Republic of   Embassy address: Consulate of the Republic of Nauru in Guam, Ada Professional Bldg., Marine Dr., 1st Floor, Agana, GU 96910 (671-649-7106/7107).

Nepal, Kingdom of   Embassy address: Royal Nepalese Embassy, 2131 Leroy Pl. NW, Washington, DC 20008 (202-667-4550), or the consulate general in New York (212-370-4188).

Netherlands, The   Embassy address: Embassy of the Netherlands, 4200 Linnean Ave. NW, Washington, DC 20008 (202-244-5300, fax

202-362-3430); or the nearest consulate general: Chicago (312-856-0110), Houston (713-622-8000), Los Angeles (310-268-1598), or New York (212-246-1429).

Netherlands Antilles (including **Bonaire, Curaçao, Saba, St. Maarten,** and **Statia [St. Eustatius]**)   Embassy address: Embassy of the Netherlands, 4200 Linnean Ave. NW, Washington, DC 20008 (202-244-5300, fax 202-362-3430); or the nearest consulate general: Chicago (312-856-0110), Houston (713-622-8000), Los Angeles (310-268-1598), or New York (212-246-1429).

New Caledonia (French Polynesia). *See* **France.**

New Zealand   Embassy address: Embassy of New Zealand, 37 Observatory Cir. NW, Washington, DC 20008 (202-328-4800), or the consulate general in Los Angeles (310-207-1605).

Nicaragua   Consulate address: Consulate of Nicaragua, 1627 New Hampshire Ave. NW, Washington, DC 20009 (202-939-6531); or the nearest consulate: Houston (713-272-9628), Los Angeles (213-252-1170), Miami (305-220-6900), New Orleans (504-523-1507), New York (212-983-1981), or San Francisco (415-765-6821).

Niger, Republic of   Embassy address: Embassy of the Republic of Niger, 2204 R St. NW, Washington, DC 20008 (202-483-4224).

Nigeria, Republic of   The U.S. State Department has issued the following entry-requirement-related information for this country: "A visa is required and must be obtained in advance; airport visas are not available. Promises of entry into Nigeria without a visa are credible indicators of a fraudulent commercial scheme in which the perpetrators seek to exploit the foreign traveler's illegal presence in Nigeria with threats of extortion or bodily harm. U.S. citizens cannot legally depart Nigeria unless they can prove, by presenting their entry visas, that they entered Nigeria legally." Embassy address: Embassy of the Republic of Nigeria, 2201 M St. NW, Washington, DC 20037

(202-822-1500 or 1522), or the consulate general in New York (212-715-7200).

Niue. *See* **New Zealand.**

Norfolk Island. *See* **Australia.**

Northern Ireland. *See* **United Kingdom.**

Northern Mariana Islands, Commonwealth of the   Self-governing commonwealth in political union with the U.S.; no restrictions on entry/travel for U.S. citizens.

North Korea. *See* **Korea, Democratic People's Republic of.**

Norway, Kingdom of   Embassy address: Royal Norwegian Embassy, 2720 34th St. NW, Washington, DC 20008 (202-333-6000, fax 202-337-0870); or the nearest consulate general: Houston (713-521-2900), Miami (305-358-4386), Minneapolis (612-332-3338), New York (212-421-7333), or San Francisco (415-986-0766).

Oman, Sultanate of   Embassy address: Embassy of the Sultanate of Oman, 2535 Belmont Rd. NW, Washington, DC 20008 (202-387-1980).

Pakistan   Embassy address: Consular Section of the Embassy of Pakistan, 2315 Massachusetts Ave. NW, Washington, DC 20008 (202-939-6295); or the nearest consulate: Los Angeles (310-441-5114) or New York (212-879-5800).

Palau, Republic of   Embassy address: Embassy of the Republic of Palau, 2000 L St. NW, Suite 407, Washington, DC 20036 (202-452-6814, fax 202-452-6281).

Panama   Embassy address: Embassy of Panama, 2862 McGill Ter. NW, Washington, DC 20008 (202-483-1407); or the nearest consulate: Houston (713-622-4451), New Orleans (504-525-3458), New York (212-840-2450), or San Francisco (415-391-4268).

Papua New Guinea   Embassy address: Embassy of Papua New Guinea, Suite 300, 1615 New Hampshire Ave. NW, Washington, DC 20009 (202-745-3680).

Paraguay   Embassy address: Embassy of Paraguay, 2400 Massachusetts Ave. NW, Washington, DC 20008 (202-483-6960).

Peru   Embassy address: Embassy of Peru, 1700 Massachusetts Ave. NW, Washington, DC 20036 (202-833-9860); or the nearest consulate: Chicago (312-853-6173), Houston (713-781-5000), Los Angeles (213-383-9896), Miami (305-374-1407), New York (212-644-2850), San Francisco (415-362-5185), or San Juan, PR (787-763-0679).

Philippines   Embassy address: Embassy of the Philippines, 1600 Massachusetts Ave. NW, Washington, DC 20036 (202-467-9300); or the nearest consulate general: Chicago (312-332-6458), Guam (671-646-4620), Honolulu (808-595-6316), Los Angeles (213-387-5321), New York (212-764-1330), or San Francisco (415-433-6666).

Poland, Republic of   Embassy address: Consular Division of the Embassy of the Republic of Poland, 2224 Wyoming Ave. NW, Washington, DC 20008 (202-232-4517); or the nearest consulate general: Boston (617-357-1980), Chicago (312-337-8166), Los Angeles (310-442-8500), New York (212-889-8360), or San Juan, PR (809-721-0495).

Portugal (including **Azores** and the **Madeira Islands**)   Embassy address: Embassy of Portugal at 2125 Kalorama Rd. NW, Washington DC 20008 (202-328-8610, fax 202-462-3726); or the nearest consulate: Boston (617-536-8740), Newark (201-622-7300), New Bedford (508-997-6151), New York (212-246-4580), Providence (401-272-2003), San Francisco (415-346-3400), or Washington, DC (202-332-3007).

Qatar, State of   Embassy address: Embassy of the State of Qatar, Suite 200, 4200 Wisconsin Ave. NW, Washington, DC 20016 (202-274-1600).

Reunion Island. *See* **France.**

Romania   Embassy address: Embassy of Romania, 1607 23rd St. NW, Washington, DC

20008 (202-232-4747, fax 202-232-4748); or the nearest consulate general: Los Angeles (310-444-0043) or New York (212-682-9120).

Russia   Embassy address: Consular Section of the Embassy of Russia, 1825 Phelps Pl. NW, Washington, DC 20008 (202-939-8907, fax 202-298-5749); or the nearest consulate general: New York (212-348-0926), San Francisco (415-928-6878), or Seattle (206-728-1910). Or contact Intourist Ltd. (212-757-5902), which offers comprehensive visa services for all member countries, including Russia, of the Commonwealth of Independent States (CIS).

Santa Fe, New Mexico, founded in 1607, is the oldest continuously occupied state capital. It has no regularly scheduled airline service and no passenger train service.

Rwanda, Republic of   Embassy address: Embassy of the Republic of Rwanda, 1714 New Hampshire Ave. NW, Washington, DC 20009 (202-232-2882, fax 202-232-2882); the Permanent Mission of Rwanda to the United Nations, 124 E. 39th St., New York, NY 10016 (212-696-0644); or the nearest consulate general: Chicago (708-205-1188) or Denver (303-321-2400).

Saba. *See* **Netherlands Antilles.**

St. Barthelemy (French West Indies). *See* **France.**

St. Eustatius (Statia). *See* **Netherlands Antilles.**

St. Kitts and Nevis   Embassy address: Embassy of St. Kitts and Nevis, OECS Bldg., 3216 New Mexico Ave. NW, Washington, DC 20016 (202-686-2636), or the Permanent Mission to the United Nations, 414 E. 75th St., 5th Floor, New York, NY 10021 (212-535-1234).

St. Lucia   Embassy address: Embassy of St. Lucia, 3216 New Mexico Ave., Washington, DC 20016 (202-364-6792), or the Permanent Mission to the United Nations, 820 Second Ave., Suite 900E, New York, NY 10017 (212-697-9360).

St. Maarten. *See* **Netherlands Antilles.**

St. Martin (French West Indies). *See* **France.**

St. Pierre. *See* **France.**

St. Vincent and the Grenadines   Embassy address: Embassy of St. Vincent and the Grenadines, 3216 New Mexico Ave., Washington, DC 20016 (202-342-6730), or its consulate, 801 Second Ave., 21st Floor, New York, NY 10017 (212-687-4490).

San Marino, Republic of   Consulate address: Consulate of the Republic of San Marino, 1899 L St. NW, Suite 500, Washington, DC 20036 (202-223-3517), or the nearest honorary consulate: Detroit (313-528-1190) or New York (516-242-2212).

São Tome and Príncipé   Contact the Permanent Mission of São Tome and Príncipé to the United Nations, 122 E. 42nd St., Suite 1604, New York, NY 10168 (212-697-4211).

Saudi Arabia, Kingdom of   Embassy address: Royal Embassy of Saudi Arabia, 601 New Hampshire Ave. NW, Washington, DC 20037 (202-944-3126); or the nearest consulate general: Houston (713-785-5577), Los Angeles (213-208-6566), or New York (212-752-2740).

Scotland. *See* **United Kingdom.**

Senegal, Republic of   Embassy address: Embassy of the Republic of Senegal, 2112 Wyoming Ave. NW, Washington, DC 20008 (202-234-0540).

Serbia and Montenegro ("Federal Republic of Yugoslavia")   Embassy address: Embassy of the "Federal Republic of Yugoslavia" (Serbia and Montenegro), 2410 California St. NW, Washington, DC 20008 (202-462-6566, fax 202-797-9663).

Seychelles   Contact the Permanent Mission of Seychelles to the United Nations, 820 Second Ave., Suite 900F, New York, NY 10017 (212-687-9766).

Sierra Leone Embassy address: Embassy of Sierra Leone, 1701 19th St. NW, Washington, DC 20009 (202-939-9261).

Singapore Embassy address: Embassy of Singapore, 3501 International Pl. NW, Washington, DC 20008 (202-537-3100).

Slovak Republic Embassy address: Embassy of the Slovak Republic, 2201 Wisconsin Ave. NW, Suite 250, Washington, DC 20007 (202-965-5164).

Slovenia, Republic of Embassy address: Embassy of the Republic of Slovenia, 1525 New Hampshire Ave. NW, Washington, DC 20036 (202-667-5363), or the consulate general of Slovenia in New York (212-370-3006).

Solomon Islands Contact the Solomon Islands Mission to the United Nations at 820 Second Ave., Suite 800A, New York, NY 10017 (212-599-6192).

Somali Democratic Republic (Somalia) Contact the consulate of the Somali Democratic Republic in New York (212-688-9410).

South Africa Consulate address: Consular Office of the Embassy of South Africa, 3201 New Mexico Ave. NW, Washington, DC 20016 (202-966-1650); or the nearest consulate: Chicago (312-939-7929), Los Angeles (310-657-9200), or New York (212-213-4880).

South Korea. *See* **Korea, Republic of.**

Spain Embassy address: Embassy of Spain, 2375 Pennsylvania Ave. NW, Washington, DC 20037 (202-728-2330); or the nearest consulate general: Boston (617-536-2506), Chicago (312-782-4588), Houston (713-783-6200), Los Angeles (213-938-0158), Miami (305-446-5511), New Orleans (504-525-4951), New York (212-355-4080), San Juan, PR (787-758-6090), or San Francisco (415-922-2995).

Sri Lanka Embassy address: Embassy of Sri Lanka, 2148 Wyoming Ave. NW, Washington, DC 20008 (202-483-4025); or the nearest consulate general: Honolulu (808-373-2040), Newark (201-627-7855), New Orleans (504-362-3232), New York (212-986-7040), or Oxnard, CA (805-323-8975).

Statia (St. Eustatius). *See* **Netherlands Antilles.**

Sudan, Republic of the Embassy address: Embassy of the Republic of the Sudan, 2210 Massachusetts Ave. NW, Washington, DC 20008 (202-338-8565), or its consulate general, 655 Third Ave., 5th Floor, New York, NY 10017 (212-573-6033).

Suriname, Republic of Embassy address: Embassy of the Republic of Suriname, Suite 108, 4301 Connecticut Ave. NW, Washington, DC 20008 (202-244-7488 and 7490), or the consulate in Miami (305-593-2163).

Swaziland, Kingdom of Embassy address: Embassy of the Kingdom of Swaziland, 3400 International Dr. NW, Suite 3M, Washington, DC (202-362-6683).

Sweden Embassy address: Embassy of Sweden, 1501 M St. NW, Washington, DC 20005 (202-467-2600, fax 202-467-2656); or the nearest consulate general: Chicago (312-781-6262), Houston (713-953-1417), Los Angeles (310-445-4008), Minneapolis (612-332-6897), New York (212-751-5900), or San Francisco (415-788-2631).

Switzerland Embassy address: Embassy of Switzerland, 2900 Cathedral Ave. NW, Washington, DC 20008 (202-745-7900, fax 202-387-2564); or the nearest consulate general: Atlanta (404-870-2000), Chicago (312-915-0061), Houston (713-650-0000), Los Angeles (310-575-1145), New York (212-758-2560), or San Francisco (415-788-2272).

Syrian Arab Republic (Syria) The U.S. State Department cautions travelers that "Entry to Syria is not granted to persons with passports bearing an Israeli visa or entry/exit stamps, or to persons born in the Gaza region or of Gazan descent. Foreigners who wish to stay 15 days or more in Syria must register with Syrian Immigration by their fifteenth day in Syria. Americans between the ages of 18 and 45 who are of Syrian birth or recent descent are subject to the Syrian compulsory military service requirement, unless they receive an exemption from the Syrian Embassy in the United States prior to their entry into Syria. Embassy address: Embassy of the Syrian Arab Republic, 2215 Wyoming Ave. NW, Washington, DC 20008 (202-232-6313).

Tahiti (French Polynesia). *See* **France.**

Taiwan, Republic of China on Contact the Taipei Economic and Cultural Representative Office (TECRO), 4201 Wisconsin Ave. NW, Washington, DC 20016 (202-895-1800); or the nearest TECRO location: Atlanta (404-872-0123), Boston (617-737-2050), Chicago (312-616-0100), Guam (671-472-5865), Honolulu (808-595-6347), Houston (713-626-7445), Kansas City (816-531-1298), Los Angeles (213-389-1215), Miami (305-443-8917), New York (212-486-0088), San Francisco (415-362-7680), or Seattle (206-441-4586).

Tajikistan Embassy address: Consular Section of the Embassy of Russia, 1825 Phelps Pl. NW, Washington, DC 20008 (202-939-8907); or the nearest consulate general: New York (212-348-0926, 0955, 0626), San Francisco (415-928-6878), or Seattle (206-728-1910). Or contact Intourist Ltd. (212-757-5902), which offers comprehensive visa services for all member countries, including Tajikistan, of the Commonwealth of Independent States (CIS).

Charles Lindbergh was not the first person to fly the Atlantic. Eight years before Lindbergh's flight, two men copiloted a twin-engine plane from Newfoundland to Ireland. Lindbergh's achievement was doing it alone.

Tanzania, United Republic of (Zanzibar) Embassy address: Embassy of the United Republic of Tanzania, 2139 R St. NW, Washington, DC 20008 (202-939-6125), or the Tanzanian Permanent Mission to the United Nations, 205 E. 42nd St., 13th Floor, New York, NY 10017 (212-972-9160).

Thailand, Kingdom of Embassy address: Royal Thai Embassy, 1024 Wisconsin Ave. NW, Washington, DC 20007 (202-944-3608); or the nearest consulate general: Chicago (312-236-2447), Los Angeles (213-937-1894), or New York (212-754-1770).

Togo, Republic of Embassy address: Embassy of the Republic of Togo, 2208 Massachusetts Ave. NW, Washington, DC 20008 (202-234-4212).

Tonga Consulate address: consulate general of Tonga, 360 Post St., Suite 604, San Francisco, CA 94108 (415-781-0365).

Trinidad and Tobago Embassy address: Embassy of Trinidad and Tobago, 1708 Massachusetts Ave. NW, Washington, DC 20036 (202-467-6490), or the consulate in New York (212-682-7272).

Tunisia The U.S. State Department cautions travelers that "Americans born in the Middle East or with Arabic names have experienced delays in clearing Immigration at airports upon arrival. American citizens of Tunisian origin are expected to enter Tunisia as Tunisians, on their Tunisian passports. If the Tunisian/American succeeds in entering on an American passport, there is a high probability that a Tunisian passport will be required before exiting the country." Embassy address: Embassy of Tunisia, 1515 Massachusetts Ave. NW, Washington, DC 20005 (202-862-1850); or the nearest consulate: New York (212-272-6962) or San Francisco (415-922-9222).

Turkey, Republic of Embassy address: Embassy of the Republic of Turkey, 1714 Massachusetts Ave. NW, Washington, DC 20036 (202-659-8200, fax 202-659-0744); or the nearest consulate: Chicago

(312-263-0644), Houston (713-622-5849), Los Angeles (213-937-0118), or New York (212-949-0160).

Japan's New Tokyo International Airport is only 40 miles from Tokyo; however, due to traffic, it typically takes 4 hours or more to catch a flight.

Turkmenistan Embassy address: Embassy of Turkmenistan, 2207 Massachusetts Ave. NW, Washington, DC 20008 (202-588-1500). Or contact Intourist Ltd. (212-757-5902), which offers comprehensive visa services for all member countries, including Turkmenistan, of the Commonwealth of Independent States (CIS).

Turks and Caicos Islands. *See* **British West Indies.**

Tuvalu Island Embassy address: British Embassy, 19 Observatory Cir. NW, Washington, DC 20008 (202-588-7800, fax 202-588-7850), or the Embassy of Tuvalu, 16 Gorrie St., Suva, Fiji (679-301-355).

Uganda, Republic of Embassy address: Embassy of the Republic of Uganda, 5909 16th St. NW, Washington, DC 20011 (202-726-7100), or the Permanent Mission to the United Nations (212-949-0110).

Ukraine Embassy address: Embassy of Ukraine, 3350 M St. NW, Washington, DC 20007 (202-333-7507); or the nearest consulate: Chicago (312-642-4388) or New York (212-371-5690). Or contact Intourist Ltd. (212-757-5902), which offers comprehensive visa services for all member countries, including Ukraine, of the Commonwealth of Independent States (CIS).

United Arab Emirates (UAE) (Abu Dabi, Dubai, Sharjah, Ras Al Khaimah, Fujairah, Ajman, and **Umm Al Quwain)** Embassy address: Embassy of the United Arab Emirates, 3000 K St. NW, Washington, DC 20007 (202-338-6500).

United Kingdom (UK) (England, Northern Ireland, Scotland, and Wales) Embassy address: Consular Section of the British Embassy, 19 Observatory Cir. NW, Washington, DC 20008 (202-588-7800, fax 202-588-7850); or the nearest consulate general: Los Angeles (310-477-3322), Atlanta (404-524-3836), Chicago (312-346-1810), Boston (617-248-9555), New York (212-745-0200), Cleveland (216-621-7674) or San Francisco (415-981-3030).

Uruguay Embassy address: Consular Office of the Embassy of Uruguay, 2715 M St., 3rd Floor NW, Washington, DC 20007 (202-331-4219, fax 202-331-8142); or the nearest consulate: Miami (305-443-9764), New Orleans (504-525-8354), New York (212-753-8191), San Francisco (415-986-5222), or Santa Monica (310-394-5777).

Uzbekistan, Republic of Embassy address: Embassy of the Republic of Uzbekistan, 1511 K St. NW, Suite 623, Washington, DC 20005 (202-638-4266, fax 202-638-4268), or the Uzbekistan Consulate, 866 United Nations Plaza, Suite 327A, New York, NY 10017 (212-754-6178 or 7403). Or contact Intourist Ltd. (212-757-5902), which offers comprehensive visa services for all member countries, including Uzbekistan, of the Commonwealth of Independent States (CIS).

Vanuatu Contact the Vanuatu Mission to the United Nations, 865 United Nations Plaza, 4th Floor, Room 41, First Ave. and 48th St., New York, NY 10017 (212-593-0144, fax 212-593-0219), or the Consular Section of the British Embassy, 19 Observatory Cir. NW, Washington, DC 20008 (202-588-7800, fax 202-588-7850).

Vatican. *See* **Holy See, Apostolic Nunciature of the.**

Venezuela Embassy address: Consular Section of the Embassy of Venezuela, 1099 30th St. NW, Washington, DC 20007 (202-342-2214); or the nearest consulate: Boston (617-266-9355), Chicago (312-236-9655), Houston (713-961-5141), Miami (305-577-0302), New Orleans

Travel

(504-522-3284), New York (212-826-1660), San Francisco (415-512-8340), or San Juan, PR (787-766-4250).

Vietnam   Contact the Embassy of Vietnam, 1233 20th St. NW, Suite 501, Washington, DC 20036 (general information and tourist visas: 202-861-2293 or 202-861-0694, fax 202-861-1297; business visas: 202-861-2291, fax 202-861-0917).

Wales. *See* **United Kingdom.**

Western Samoa   Contact the Western Samoan Mission to the United Nations, 820 Second Ave., Suite 800, New York, NY (212-599-6196), or the honorary consulate in Honolulu (808-677-7197).

Yemen, Republic of   Embassy address: Embassy of the Republic of Yemen, Suite 705, 2600 Virginia Ave. NW, Washington, DC 20037 (202-965-4760), or Yemen's Mission to the United Nations, 866 United Nations Plaza, Room 435, New York, NY 10017 (212-355-1730).

Zaire. *See* **Congo, Democratic Republic of.**

Zambia, Republic of   Embassy address: Embassy of the Republic of Zambia, 2419 Massachusetts Ave. NW, Washington, DC 20008 (202-265-9717).

Zanzibar. *See* **Tanzania.**

Zimbabwe   Embassy   address: Embassy   of Zimbabwe, 1608 New Hampshire Ave. NW, Washington, DC 20009 (202-332-7100).

CUSTOMS INFORMATION

At reentry into the United States, you must declare all articles in your possession that you have acquired abroad, stating their actual purchase price or, if they were not purchased, their market value in the country where you acquired them. You must fill out a declaration form before reaching customs to show to U.S. customs inspectors.

If you were out of the country for 48 hours or more, you will be exempt from paying duty and federal tax on the first $400 worth of goods. Generally, values above that amount are subject to

duty at a straight 10%. For example, if you bring in $600 worth of goods, you will pay about $20 in duty. If you are traveling with your family, remember that each family member is allowed the same $400 exemption.

The items brought into the United States must be for your own use or for personal gifts. You may not resell them for profit.

If you leave the United States with foreign-made goods already in your possession, be sure to register them, using their serial numbers, with the customs office *before* leaving; or bring proof (sales slips, for example) with you that you bought them in the United States. If you lack proof of domestic purchase or registration, you may be charged duty upon reentry.

There are customs restrictions on bringing in certain plants, animals, medications, and foods; and children may not bring in alcohol. You can get a list of restricted items from the U.S. Department of Agriculture, Washington, DC 20205.

For further information, contact the local office of the Treasury Department or the U.S. Customs Service, P.O. Box 7407, Washington, DC 20004, 202-566-8195, http://www.customs.ustreas.gov/travel/index.html (a comprehensive Web site that may answer all of your questions).

ADDITIONAL SOURCES OF INFORMATION

WEB SITES

Access-Able Travel
http://www.access-able.com/
Especially for travelers with disabilities, contains links to many other helpful sites.

All of the Embassies of Washington D.C.
TeleDiplomacy, Inc.
http://www.embassy.org/embassies/index.html
Contact information for foreign government offices in the United States.

All the Hotels on the Web
Internet Marketing Services, Ltd.
http://www.all-hotels.com/

Breezenet's Guide to Airport Rental Cars
http://www.bnm.com/rcar.htm

The Centers for Disease Control
Home Travel Information Page
http://www.cdc.gov/travel/travel.html

How Far Is It?
Bali Online
http://www.indo.com/distance/
Mileage Calculator

Microsoft Expedia Worldwide Links
Microsoft Corporation
http://links.expedia.msn.com/wg/

National Park Service
http://www.nps.gov/nps

Travel Document Systems
http://www.traveldocs.com/
Country-by-country information plus downloadable
    passport and visa applications and services online

U.S.-based Embassies and Consulates
infoCatch
http://www.embassyweb.com
Links to foreign embassies on-line

The U.S. State Department's Travel Warnings Site
http://206.161.109.6/travel_warnings.html

**Washington Post's International Information
    Online**
The Washington Post Company
http://www.washingtonpost.com/
    wp-srv/inatl/front.htm

World Travel Guide Online Service
Columbus Group
http://www.wtgonline.com/

MAGAZINES

Condé Nast Traveler
350 Madison Ave.
New York, NY 10017
http://www.condenast.co.uk

Travel & Leisure
1120 Avenue of the Americas
New York, NY 10036
http://www.traveleisure.com

BOOKS

Axtell, Roger E. *Do's and Taboos of Using English
Around the World*. Wiley, 1995.

Berlitz Pocket Guides. Berlitz Travel Guide, 1989–.

Birnbaum, Stephen. *Birnbaum's Travel Guides* series. Published through 1995 by Houghton Mifflin.

Bredesen, Eric. *Moto Europa: The Complete Guide to European Motoring*. Seren Publishing, 1995.

The Business Travel Adviser for the European Union & Selected European Countries. International Media Communications, 1996.

Colwell, Stephen D., and Ann R. Shulman. *Trouble-free Travel: And What to Do When Things Go Wrong*. Robin Leonard and Marcia Stewart, eds. Nolo Press, 1996.

Fodor's Guides. Fodor's Travel Publications, 1980–.

Frome, Michael. *Frommer's National Park Guide*, 29th ed. Macmillan Travel, 1995.

Frommer's Guides. Prentice-Hall, 1977–.

Graber, Eden, and Paula M. Siegel. *Fielding's Traveler's Medical Companion*. Fielding Travel Books, 1990.

Hostelling International guidebook series. International Youth Hostel Federation, 1994–.

Hostelling North America: The Official Guide to Hostels in Canada and the United States of America. Hostelling International–American Youth Hostels/ Hostelling International–Canada, 1996.

Jones, John Oliver. *U.S. Outdoor Atlas & Recreation Guide*. 2nd ed. Houghton Mifflin, 1994.

Lange, W. Robert. *The Doctor's Guide to Protecting Your Health Before, During, and After International Travel*. Pilot Books, 1997.

Lefkon, Wendy, ed. *Birnbaum's Walt Disney World for Kids by Kids*. Hyperion and Hearst, 1994.

Martin, Don W., and Betty Woo Martin, comps. *The Toll-Free Traveler: The Complete (800) and (888) Directory for Pleasure and Business Travel in the U.S. and Canada*. Pine Cone Press, 1997.

Mobil Travel Guide: Major Cities. Fodor's Travel Publications, 1997–.

Nwanna, Gladson I., Ph.D. *Americans Traveling Abroad: What You Should Know Before You Go.* World Travel Institute Press, 1994.

Rand McNally Atlas of the World. Rand McNally, 1994.

Reader's Digest Travel Guide USA. Reader's Digest Association, 1994.

Riley, Laura and William. *Guide to the National Wildlife Refuges.* Macmillan, 1992.

Simony, Maggy, ed. *The Traveler's Reading Guide: Ready-Made Reading Lists for the Armchair Traveler.* Facts on File, 1993.

Wade, Betsy. *The New York Times Practical Traveler Handbook: An A–Z Guide to Getting There and Back.* Times Books, 1994.

Travel

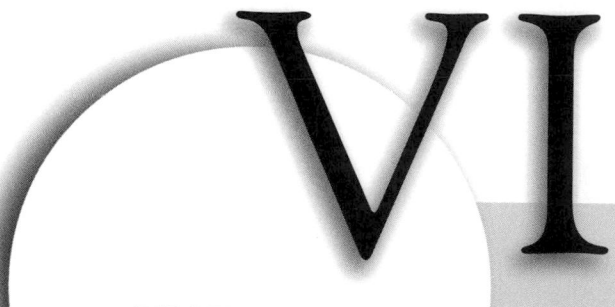

VI

THE POLITICAL WORLD

CHAPTER TWENTY–FIVE   823
THE UNITED STATES

CHAPTER TWENTY–SIX   921
THE WORLD

25

THE UNITED STATES

CULTURE AND HISTORY	824
FEDERAL GOVERNMENT	859
STATES AND TERRITORIES	875
STATISTICS	881
U.S. POSTAL SERVICE	898
NEWSPAPERS	906
ADDITIONAL SOURCES OF INFORMATION	911

CULTURE AND HISTORY

IMPORTANT DATES IN AMERICAN HISTORY

1492	Columbus sails to Caribbean Islands.
1497	John Cabot explores North America from Canada to Delaware.
1513	Juan Ponce de Leon explores Florida.
1524	Giovanni da Verrazano leads French expedition along the coast from Carolina to Nova Scotia, entering New York harbor.
1565	St. Augustine, Florida, is founded.
1579	Francis Drake claims California for Britain.
1586	St. Augustine is destroyed by Francis Drake.
1587	Virginia Dare is the first baby born in America to English parents.
1607	The first European settlement in America is established at Jamestown, Virginia.
1609	Henry Hudson explores New York harbor and the Hudson River to Albany; Samuel de Champlain explores Lake Champlain in upstate New York; Spaniards settle Santa Fe, New Mexico.
1619	The first black slaves land at Jamestown, Virginia; the House of Burgesses, the first representative assembly in America, is established in Virginia.
1620	Pilgrims land in Plymouth, Massachusetts; the Mayflower Compact is drafted and signed.
1623	The Dutch found New Netherlands (later New York).
1626	Peter Minuit buys Manhattan Island from Native Americans.
1630	The Massachusetts Bay Colony is founded.
1631	Roger Williams, pioneer of religious tolerance, arrives in America.
1634	Maryland is founded as a Catholic colony.
1635	New Hampshire is founded by Captain John Mason; the first public school, the Boston Latin School, is established.
1636	Harvard, the first college in America, is founded; Roger Williams founds Providence, Rhode Island.
1639	The first constitution in America is written, the Fundamental Orders of Connecticut.
1647	Margaret Brent is the first woman to claim the right to vote.
1648	The first labor organization in the United States is authorized in the Massachusetts Bay Colony.
1652	Rhode Island enacts first American law declaring slavery illegal.
1654	The first Jews arrive in New Amsterdam.
1663	The Colony of New Jersey is founded by Sir William Berkeley and Sir George Carteret; the Carolinas are founded.
1664	The English capture New Netherlands.
1682	William Penn founds Pennsylvania.
1688	The first formal protest against slavery is made, by Pennsylvania Quakers.
1692	Nineteen persons (mostly women) are executed for "witchcraft" in Salem, Massachusetts.
1712	A slave revolt in New York leads to the execution of 21 blacks; 6 commit suicide.
1731	The first circulating library is founded in Philadelphia.
1732	Georgia is founded by James Oglethorpe and others; Benjamin Franklin publishes the first *Poor Richard's Almanac*.
1741	The second slave uprising takes place in New York; 13 are hanged, 13 burned, and 71 deported.
1749	Black slavery is legalized in Georgia.
1754	The French and Indian War begins (called the Seven Years' War in Europe).
1758	The first Indian reservation is established.

A Closer Look		

Admission of 13 Original States

State	Date of Admission	State	Date of Admission
1. Delaware	December 7, 1787	8. South Carolina	May 23, 1788
2. Pennsylvania	December 12, 1787	9. New Hampshire	June 21, 1788
3. New Jersey	December 18, 1787	10. Virginia	June 25, 1788
4. Georgia	January 2, 1788	11. New York	July 26, 1788
5. Connecticut	January 9, 1788	12. North Carolina	November 21, 1789
6. Massachusetts	February 6, 1788	13. Rhode Island	May 29, 1790
7. Maryland	April 28, 1788		

1763   The French and Indian War ends.

1764   The Sugar Act places duties on lumber, foodstuffs, molasses, and rum in the colonies.

1765   Passage of the Stamp Act by Britain leads to the Declaration of Rights, signed by nine colonies opposed to taxation without representation.

1766   Britain repeals the Stamp Act.

1767   The Townshend Acts levy taxes on glass, painter's lead, paper, and tea.

1770   Five colonists are killed in the Boston Massacre.

1773   The Boston Tea Party takes place.

1774   The Intolerable Acts passed by Parliament curtail Massachusetts's self-rule and bar the use of Boston Harbor until tea is paid for; the first Continental Congress, an advisory council, is organized in response to this legislation.

1775   The American Revolution begins with the battles of Lexington and Concord.

1776   France and Spain each donate 1 million livres in arms to Americans; the Declaration of Independence is drafted and signed; Nathan Hale is executed by the British as a spy; the first fraternity, Phi Beta Kappa, is founded at the College of William and Mary; the Journeymen Printers' Strike is the first in the United States.

1777   The Continental Congress adopts a flag with stars and stripes; Washington defeats Lord Cornwallis at the battle of Princeton; Major General John Burgoyne captures Fort Ticonderoga, but Americans defeat him at Saratoga; the *Federalist Papers,* arguing for the ratification of the Constitution, begin publication.

1778   France agrees to assist the United States and sends a fleet; the British evacuate Philadelphia.

1779   George Washington orders a military campaign against the Iroquois.

1780   Benedict Arnold is discovered to be a traitor and escapes to Great Britian.

1781   Colonial and French armies defeat the British at Yorktown, the last major battle of the Revolutionary War; the Articles of Confederation, the first written U.S. constitution, is ratified.

1783   The Revolutionary War ends with a treaty.

1784   The first daily newspaper, *Pennsylvania Packet and General Advertiser,* is published in Philadelphia.

1787   The Constitutional Convention begins in Philadelphia; Delaware ratifies the Constitution, thus becoming the first state admitted to the Union.

1788   New Hampshire is the ninth state to ratify the Constitution, thereby putting it into effect.

1789   George Washington is chosen the first president; John Adams, vice president, Thomas Jefferson, secretary of state; and Alexander Hamilton, secretary of the treasury.

1790   Congress meets in Philadelphia, the temporary capital, and votes to found a new capital on the Potomac River; the United States signs the first treaty with the Iroquois.

1791   The Bill of Rights goes into effect; Vermont is the first state to enter the Union after the original 13 colonies.

United States

1793   The invention of the cotton gin by Eli Whitney revives slavery in the South; the First Fugitive Slave Act is passed, making it a crime to harbor an escaped slave or to interfere with a slave's arrest.

1794   Suppression by the U.S. militia of the Whiskey Rebellion, in which farmers protest the liquor tax of 1791, establish the authority of the new federal government.

1800   The seat of government moves from Philadelphia to Washington, D.C.; Congress passes a land act encouraging the purchase of property at low prices.

1801   Tripoli declares war on the United States.

1803   The Supreme Court declares an act of Congress unconstitutional in *Marbury v. Madison;* the United States buys the Louisiana Territory from Napoleon, doubling its land holdings.

1804   President Jefferson orders the Lewis and Clark expedition to explore the northwest; Vice President Aaron Burr and Alexander Hamilton duel; Hamilton dies the next day.

1805   Conflict with Tripoli ends.

1807   Robert Fulton makes the first steamboat trip.

1808   The importation of slaves is outlawed (about 250,000 slaves are illegally imported between 1808 and 1860).

1811   While Shawnee Chief Tecumseh is away making alliances with other tribal leaders, Indiana Governor William Henry Harrison and 1,000 men destroy his settlement in the Battle of Tippecanoe, thwarting plans for an Indian confederacy.

1812   The War of 1812 begins.

1814   The War of 1812 ends with the Treaty of Ghent.

1816   The first savings bank is established, the Provident Institute for Savings, in Boston.

1817   The First Seminole War begins in the Spanish territory of Florida, with raids by U.S. troops on Seminole Indians reputedly harboring runaway slaves.

1818   The Connecticut state legislature is the first in the United States to eliminate the property requirement for voting.

1819   Florida is ceded to the United States by Spain.

1820   The Missouri Compromise dictates that Missouri be admitted to the Union as a slave state and Maine as a free state, and prohibits slavery in parts of the Louisiana Purchase.

1821   Troy Female Seminary, the first women's college in the United States, is founded by Emma Willard.

1823   President James Monroe, in the Monroe Doctrine, declares to Congress that the Western Hemisphere is to be off-limits to European colonization.

1825   The Erie Canal is opened, cutting travel time from New York City to Buffalo and the Great Lakes by one-third.

1827   *Freedom's Journal,* the first black U.S. newspaper, is published.

1828   The first U.S. passenger railroad, Baltimore & Ohio, begins service; the first Native American newspaper, *Cherokee Phoenix,* begins publication.

1829   The first school for the blind is incorporated in the United States.

1830   President Jackson signs the Indian Removal Act.

1831   Nat Turner leads a slave rebellion in Virginia.

1832   The first meeting of the New England Anti-Slavery Society is held; Oberlin College, Ohio, becomes the first college to establish coeducation.

1836   Texans are besieged at the Alamo in San Antonio; Texas declares independence from Mexico.

1837   The panic of 1837 begins a seven-year depression.

1838   Cherokees begin the Trail of Tears, their 1,200-mile forced march to Oklahoma.

1841   Oberlin College, Ohio, becomes the first college to confer degrees on women; the first wagon train leaves from Independence, Missouri, for California.

United States

Secession of American States

A Closer Look

	State	Date of Secession		State	Date of Secession
1.	South Carolina	December 20, 1860	7.	Texas	February 1, 1861
2.	Mississippi	January 9, 1861	8.	Virginia	April 17, 1861
3.	Florida	January 10, 1861	9.	Arkansas	May 6, 1861
4.	Alabama	January 11, 1861	10.	North Carolina	May 20, 1861
5.	Georgia	January 19, 1861	11.	Tennessee	June 8, 1861
6.	Louisiana	January 26, 1861			

1843   Sojourner Truth, former slave, begins an abolitionist lecture tour.

1844   The first telegraph message is sent from Washington to Baltimore by Samuel F. B. Morse; Margaret Fuller becomes the first female journalist to work for a major U.S. newspaper, the *New York Tribune.*

1846   The United States declares war on Mexico; as a result, the United States obtains Texas, California, Arizona, New Mexico, Nevada, Utah, and part of Colorado; a treaty with Great Britain gives the United States the Oregon Territory to the 49th parallel; Henry David Thoreau is jailed for tax resistance.

1847   The first U.S. postage stamp is issued; Michigan becomes the first state to abolish capital punishment; Frederick Douglass founds the abolitionist newspaper *North Star.*

1848   The United States signs the Treaty of Guadeloupe Hidalgo with Mexico, ending the Mexican War and increasing U.S. territory; the first women's rights convention is held in Seneca Falls, New York; gold is discovered in California.

1849   Eighty thousand gold prospectors flood California.

1850   Senator Henry Clay's Compromise of 1850 admits California to the Union as a nonslave state, while Utah and New Mexico enter with no decision on slavery.

1852   *Uncle Tom's Cabin,* by Harriet Beecher Stowe, is published.

1853   The American Labor Union is founded.

1854   The Republican party is formed in opposition to the Kansas-Nebraska Act, which left the issue of slavery to a vote by settlers.

1857   The Dred Scott decision by the Supreme Court upholds slavery.

1858   The Lincoln-Douglas debates are held in Illinois.

1859   John Brown, abolitionist, captures the U.S. arsenal at Harper's Ferry, West Virginia; Brown is hanged for treason.

1860   A nationwide shoemakers' strike wins workers higher wages; the National Labor Union is founded.

1861   The American Miners Association, the first national coal miners' union, is founded; the Civil War begins when Confederates fire on Fort Sumter, South Carolina; the first transcontinental telegraph line is completed.

1862   Slavery is abolished in Washington, D.C.; the Homestead Act grants land to settlers.

1863   Harriet Tubman frees 750 slaves in a raid; President Lincoln issues the Emancipation Proclamation and delivers the Gettysburg Address; draft riots in New York City kill approximately a thousand.

1864   Black prisoners of war are massacred by Confederate soldiers at Fort Pillow, Tennessee; General Sherman marches through Georgia, capturing Atlanta; the *New Orleans Tribune,* a black-run daily newspaper, begins publication; 133 Cheyenne and Arapahoe are killed by Colorado cavalry volunteers at Sand Creek.

United States

Readmission of American States

A Closer Look

State	Date of Readmission		State	Date of Readmission
1. Tennessee	July 24, 1866		7. North Carolina	June 25, 1868
2. Arkansas	June 22, 1868		8. South Carolina	June 25, 1868
3. Alabama	June 25, 1868		9. Virginia	January 26, 1870
4. Florida	June 25, 1868		10. Mississippi	February 23, 1870
5. Georgia	June 25, 1868*		11. Texas	March 30, 1870
6. Louisiana	June 25, 1868			

* Readmitted a second time on July 15, 1870

Year	Event
1865	The Confederacy surrenders at Appomattox, Virginia, ending the Civil War; the first state civil rights law is passed in Massachusetts; the Thirteenth Amendment abolishes slavery; the Ku Klux Klan is formed in Pulaski, Tennessee; President Lincoln is assassinated.
1868	Impeachment proceedings begin against President Andrew Johnson; the Fourteenth Amendment is ratified, guaranteeing due process to all but Native Americans; a U.S.-Sioux treaty is signed at Fort Laramie, Wyoming.
1869	The first national black labor group, the Colored National Labor Convention, meets in Washington, D.C.; the Central Pacific and Union Pacific railroads are linked at Promontory, Utah, forming the first transcontinental railroad; Elizabeth Cady Stanton and Susan B. Anthony establish the National Women's Suffrage Association to press for women's voting rights; Wyoming territory is the first to grant suffrage to women.
1870	The first woman candidate for U.S. president, Victoria Claflin Woodhull, announces she will run; the first sorority, Kappa Alpha Theta, is established at De Pauw University.
1871	The Great Chicago Fire takes place.
1872	Susan B. Anthony is arrested for voting; the Amnesty Act restores rights to Southern citizens except for 500 Confederate leaders; Yellowstone, the first U.S. national park, opens in Wyoming.
1873	The first illustrated daily newspaper, *New York Daily Graphic,* is established.
1875	The Civil Rights Act gives equal rights to blacks in public accommodations and jury duty.
1876	General Custer is defeated at the battle of Little Bighorn.
1877	The United States violates its treaty with the Dakota Sioux by seizing the Black Hills; Chief Joseph surrenders with a starving remnant of the Nez Perce people.
1879	F. W. Woolworth opens his first 5 & 10 store.
1881	Sitting Bull surrenders; President Garfield is shot and killed; Booker T. Washington founds Tuskegee Institute for blacks; Spelman College opens in Atlanta to educate black women.
1881	The Supreme Court rules that Native Americans are aliens; the Civil Rights Act of 1875 is invalidated by the Supreme Court; the Brooklyn Bridge opens.
1885	The first skyscraper is built in Chicago.
1886	The Haymarket Square massacre takes place in Chicago as a bomb explodes and protesters demanding an eight-hour day are arrested; Geronimo surrenders to Arizona Territory leaders; the American Federation of Labor (AFL) is founded.
1887	Crazy Horse is assassinated while in custody.
1888	The Great Blizzard in the East causes 400 deaths.
1889	Jane Addams founds Hull-House, an immigrant settlement house and center for social reform, in Chicago.

1890   The United Mine Workers is formed; Sitting Bull is killed by police at Standing Rock Reservation, South Dakota; 200 Sioux are massacred by troops at Wounded Knee, South Dakota; the Sherman Antitrust Act is passed by Congress to fight business monopolies; William Kemmler is the first criminal to be executed by electrocution, at Auburn Prison, New York; Ellis Island becomes a port of entry for immigrants. *How the Other Half Lives,* by social reformer Jacob Riis, is published.

1893   Financial panic lasting for four years begins.

1894   Led by Eugene V. Debs, members of the American Railway Union hold a massive strike against the Pullman Palace Car Company.

1896   The Supreme Court's *Plessy v. Ferguson* decision upholds the "separate but equal" doctrine.

1898   The United States declares war on Spain; U.S. troops invade Puerto Rico to liberate it from Spain; Admiral Dewey captures Manila; feminist theorist Charlotte Perkins Gilman's *Women and Economics* is published.

1899   Philippine insurrection against U.S. rule begins; *The Awakening,* an early feminist novel by Kate Chopin, is published; the Open Door Policy makes China an international market and preserves its integrity as a nation.

1900   The International Ladies Garment Workers Union is founded; prohibitionist Carry Nation leads the first bottle-smashing raid, in Wichita, Kansas.

1901   President William McKinley is assassinated by anarchist Leon Czolgosz; J. P. Morgan incorporates the U.S. Steel Corporation, the first billion-dollar company.

1902   The last Philippine resistance to U.S. intervention ends.

1903   Panama declares its independence from Colombia, with U.S. support, and signs the Panama Canal Treaty; Orville and Wilbur Wright make the first flights in a mechanically propelled plane; Mary Harris "Mother" Jones leads a week-long march of child mill workers from Pennsylvania to President Theodore Roosevelt's New York City home.

1904   Civil rights leader Mary McLeod Bethune founds Daytona Literary and Industrial School for Training Negro Girls in Florida.

1905   The Niagara Movement, later to become the NAACP, is founded.

1906   The San Francisco earthquake and fire occurs.

1907   Charles Curtis of Kansas becomes the first Native American U.S. senator.

1908   The United States bars Japanese immigration; women demonstrate in New York City, demanding an end to sweatshops and child labor; the Federal Bureau of Investigation (FBI) is established; the first Ford Model T is sold.

1909   The National Association for the Advancement of Colored People (NAACP) is founded; Native American leader Geronimo dies.

1911   The Triangle Shirt Waist Company fire in New York City kills 146 sweatshop workers, mostly women, and leads to demands for better working conditions.

1912   The "Bread and Roses" strike by 10,000 textile workers begins in Lawrence.

1913   Ratification of the Sixteenth Amendment authorizes income tax; the Federal Reserve System is adopted; the Seventeenth Amendment is ratified, providing for popular election of the U.S. Senate; the first important U.S. exhibition of modern art is held at the New York City Armory.

1914   The Colorado National Guard burns a striking miner's camp and kills 13 children and 7 adults in the Ludlow Massacre.

1915   The Women's International League for Peace and Freedom is founded; 25,000 women march in New York City demanding suffrage; Haiti becomes a U.S. protectorate after U.S. troops land there.

1916   The National Women's Party is founded; the first public birth control clinic opens in Brooklyn, New York; Jeannette Rankin of Montana becomes the first woman elected to the House of

Representatives; Margaret Sanger is arrested for operating a birth control clinic; the United States buys the Virgin Islands from Denmark; a military government is established in the Dominican Republic as the country is occupied by U.S. Marines.

1917   Women picket the White House for the right to vote; Puerto Rico becomes a U.S. territory; the United States declares war on Germany, entering World War I; a wartime draft is enacted; Emma Goldman is sentenced to two years for aiding draft resisters.

1918   The Sedition Act becomes law; World War I ends.

1919   The Supreme Court holds that freedom of speech does not apply to draft resistance; the Communist Party of America is founded; Congress overrides President Wilson's veto of Prohibition legislation.

1920   Five thousand alleged subversives are arrested nationwide in "Palmer raids"; the sale of alcoholic beverages is banned under the Eighteenth Amendment; women win the right to vote with ratification of the Nineteenth Amendment; the League of Women Voters is founded; the first transcontinental airmail route is established between New York City and San Francisco.

1921   Immigration is curtailed by quotas set by Congress; the Ku Klux Klan begins a revival of violence against blacks in the North, South, and Midwest; major powers meet at the Limitation of Armaments Conference to reduce naval construction, outlaw poison gas, restrict submarine attacks on merchantmen, and discuss the integrity of China; Margaret Sanger establishes the American Birth Control League, the predecessor to Planned Parenthood.

1922   Rebecca L. Felton, from Georgia, is appointed the first woman U.S. senator.

1923   Under presidential pressure, U.S. Steel institutes the eight-hour day, setting a landmark precedent.

1924   The Supreme Court upholds the involuntary sterilization of mentally retarded persons; Native Americans are declared citizens by Congress; the first U.S. gay rights organization, the Society for Human Rights, is founded in Chicago.

1925   Nellie Taylor Ross, the first woman governor in the United States, is sworn in, in Wyoming; John T. Scopes is convicted of teaching the theory of evolution; Tennessee bans the teaching of evolution.

1927   Charles Lindbergh makes the first solo, nonstop, transatlantic flight; *The Jazz Singer,* the first sound film, is released.

1928   Amelia Earhart is the first woman to fly across the Atlantic.

1929   The stock market crashes, beginning the Great Depression.

1931   The Scottsboro Boys trial begins in Alabama; the Empire State Building opens in New York City.

1932   Hattie Caraway, of Arkansas, is the first woman elected to the U.S. Senate.

1933   President Franklin Roosevelt closes all U.S. banks; during the "100 days," a special session of Congress, important New Deal legislation is passed, including the establishment of the National Recovery Administration and the Tennessee Valley Authority (TVA); Frances Perkins, Secretary of Labor, becomes the first woman Cabinet member; the Twenty-first Amendment, ending Prohibition, is passed.

1935   The Works Projects Administration (WPA) is established; the National Labor Relations Act, recognizing workers' right to organize and bargain collectively, passes; President Roosevelt signs the Social Security Act.

1936   Black track star Jesse Owens wins four gold medals at the Berlin Olympics, embarrassing Hitler.

1937   Amelia Earhart and her copilot disappear over the Pacific.

1938   The national minimum wage is enacted; the "War of the Worlds" broadcast by Orson Welles causes nationwide fear that Martians have invaded Earth.

1939   Sit-down strikes are outlawed by the Supreme Court; World War II begins with the German invasion of Poland.

1940   The Alien Registration Act (Smith Act) is passed; Congress approves the first peacetime draft.

1941   The Ford Motor Company signs its first contract with the United Auto Workers; the Japanese attack Pearl Harbor, bringing the United States into World War II.

1942   President Roosevelt issues an executive order to intern 120,000 Japanese Americans on the West Coast; the Manhattan Project begins developing the atomic bomb; 492 die in a fire at Boston's Coconut Grove nightclub.

1943   President Roosevelt bars all war contractors from racial discrimination; a race riot in Detroit leaves 34 dead.

1944   Allies stage the D-Day invasion of Normandy; Congress passes the G.I. Bill of Rights, providing veterans' benefits.

1945   The Yalta conference, attended by Roosevelt, Churchill, and Stalin, brings Russia into World War II against Japan; Roosevelt dies; Truman becomes President; Nazi Germany is defeated, ending World War II in Europe; U.S. troops liberate the concentration camp at Dachau; the first atomic bomb is exploded at Alamogordo, New Mexico; the United States drops atomic bombs on Hiroshima and Nagasaki; Japan surrenders, ending World War II in the Pacific; Congress passes the Communist Control Act; the United Nations Charter is adopted.

1946   The Atomic Energy Commission is formed; the Philippines is given independence.

1947   The cold war begins; aid is given to Greece and Turkey under the Truman Doctrine; Jackie Robinson, the first black major league baseball player, appears in his first game with the Brooklyn Dodgers; the Marshall Plan for European recovery is announced; the Department of Defense is created; the Central Intelligence Agency (CIA) and the National Security Council are established under the National Security Act; the House of Representatives cites the Hollywood Ten, accused of subversion, for contempt of Congress.

1948   Twelve Communist party leaders are indicted by the United States on grounds that they advocated the overthrow of the government; Alger Hiss, denying that he transmitted confidential government documents to spies, is indicted for perjury.

1949   The North Atlantic Treaty Organization (NATO) is formed by the United States, Canada, and 10 European nations.

1950   The United States recalls all consular personnel from the People's Republic of China; Truman orders the development of the hydrogen bomb; Senator Joseph McCarthy accuses State Department employees of Communist party affiliation; two of the Hollywood Ten are imprisoned for refusing to cooperate with the House Un-American Activities Committee; the Korean conflict begins; the United States sends 35 military advisers and agrees to give military and economic aid to South Vietnam.

1951   Julius and Ethel Rosenberg and Morton Sobel are convicted of espionage conspiracy; the Mattachine Society, an early gay rights organization, is formed in California; atomic energy is first used to generate electricity in the United States; Korean cease-fire talks begin.

1952   The United States explodes the world's first hydrogen bomb; the Immigration and Naturalization Act is passed, lifting the last racial and ethnic barriers to naturalization.

1953   President Truman announces development of the hydrogen bomb; Julius and Ethel Rosenberg are executed; Vice President Richard Nixon gives his "Checkers" speech; the Korean conflict ends.

1954   Seven thousand square miles of the Pacific are irradiated by a Bikini Island hydrogen bomb test, which contaminates Japanese fishermen; the U.S. Air Force begins flying French reinforcements to Indochina; the *Brown v. Board of Education* ruling by the Supreme Court outlaws segregation in public schools; the Senate censures Joseph McCarthy; the Southeast Asia Treaty Organization

(SEATO) is formed, consisting of the United States, Great Britain, France, Australia, New Zealand, the Philippines, Pakistan, and Thailand.

1955   Rosa Parks refuses to give up her bus seat to a white person and begins the Montgomery, Alabama, bus boycott; the AFL and CIO merge, electing George Meany the first president; the United States agrees to help train the South Vietnamese army.

1956   Passage of the Federal Aid Highway Act inaugurates the first interstate highway system.

1957   Elizabeth Eckford is blocked from becoming the first black student at Little Rock Central High School; nine black students enroll at Little Rock High School with the help of federal troops; Congress approves the first bill protecting blacks' right to vote since the Reconstruction era.

1958   The United States launches its first satellite into orbit.

1959   Alaska and Hawaii become the forty-ninth and fiftieth states, respectively.

1960   More than 70,000 black and white students participate in sit-ins to protest a Greensboro, North Carolina, incident in which four blacks were denied service at a lunch counter.

1961   The United States breaks diplomatic ties with Cuba; the Bay of Pigs invasion of Cuba is thwarted; "freedom riders" test segregation laws in the Deep South; the Student Non-Violent Coordinating Committee (SNCC) voter registration drive begins in the South; the FBI launches its Socialist Worker Disruption Program; Alan B. Shepard, Jr. travels on the first U.S. manned space flight.

1962   The United States announces resumption of atmospheric nuclear testing after test-ban negotiations fail; James Meredith becomes the first black to enroll at the University of Mississippi; President Kennedy orders a blockade of Cuba, which begins the Cuban Missile Crisis; John H. Glenn, Jr., becomes the first American to orbit in space; *Silent Spring,* by Rachel Carson, is published, launching the environmental movement.

1963   The Supreme Court rules that states must provide free legal counsel for indigents; the Supreme Court bars mandatory Bible readings in public schools; Martin Luther King, Jr., leads a civil rights march on Washington, D.C.; a White House–Kremlin "hot line" is installed; the War Resisters League organizes its first demonstration against U.S. involvement in Vietnam; President Kennedy is assassinated; Congress passes the first Clean Air Act.

1964   The Twenty-fourth Amendment eliminates the poll tax in federal elections; a Civil Rights Act is passed by Congress; Congress passes the Gulf of Tonkin Resolution, giving President Lyndon Johnson power to wage war in Indochina; Martin Luther King, Jr., receives the Nobel prize for peace; Panama suspends relations with the United States, which offers to negotiate a new Canal treaty; students at the University of California, Berkeley, protest limitations on their rights of free speech and assembly; Malcolm X disassociates himself from the separatist Nation of Islam and founds the Organization of Afro-American Unity.

1965   Malcolm X, black leader, is assassinated; 49 people are arrested during protests at Chase Manhattan Bank against loans to South Africa; Martin Luther King, Jr., leads a march on Selma, Alabama; a massive electric power failure blacks out most of the Northeast for the night of November 9–10; the Supreme Court holds that the "right of privacy" covers the use of contraceptives.

1966   Federal courts outlaw the last poll tax; the National Organization for Women (NOW) is founded; Medicare begins to pay the health-care expenses of U.S. citizens age 65 and older.

1967   Two hundred thousand people march against the Vietnam War in New York City; Thurgood Marshall becomes the first black Supreme Court justice; six days of racial rioting in Newark, New Jersey, leave 23 dead; week-long racial rioting in Detroit leaves 43 dead; J. Edgar Hoover, director of the FBI, authorizes activities against black nationalist groups.

1968   Four black student demonstrators are killed by police in Orangeburg, South Carolina; 500 unarmed Vietnamese are killed by U.S. troops in the My Lai massacre; Martin Luther King, Jr., is assassinated; Robert F. Kennedy is assassinated hours after his California primary victory; the

American Indian Movement is founded; a coalition of women's groups interrupts the Miss America Pageant in the first mass demonstration of the modern women's movement; the United States ends the bombing of North Vietnam; Representative Shirley Chisholm, from New York, becomes the first black woman elected to Congress.

1969   The Stonewall rebellion, at a bar in New York City, starts the modern gay rights movement; the Woodstock festival in upstate New York draws 300,000 for "three days of peace and music"; the Chicago Seven conspiracy trial begins, in which seven defendants are accused of inciting a riot at the 1968 Democratic National Convention; 2 million people nationwide demonstrate against U.S. involvement in Vietnam; 78 Native Americans seize Alcatraz Island, demanding it be made into a cultural center; Black Panthers Fred Hampton and Mark Clark are murdered by Chicago police; the United States begins peace talks with Vietnam, as troop withdrawal starts; Neil Armstrong becomes the first person to walk on the moon.

1970   Chicano activists gather in Crystal City, Texas, to found La Raza Unida Party; U.S. postal workers hold their first strike; the Ohio National Guard kills four students in a Vietnam War protest at Kent State University; Mississippi police kill two black students at Jackson State University; the United Farm Workers begins a lettuce boycott; the Environmental Protection Agency (EPA) is established; Congress passes the Occupational Safety and Health Act; the Chicago Seven are found not guilty, although five are convicted of crossing state lines with intent to incite riots; the first two U.S. women generals are named by President Nixon; the first Earth Day celebration takes place.

1971   Five hundred thousand people demonstrate in Washington, D.C., against the Vietnam War, and 14,000 are arrested; Native Americans leave Alcatraz Island after holding it for 19 months; the Twenty-sixth Amendment is ratified, lowering the national voting age from 21 to 18; 43 are killed in an uprising at Attica state prison in New York.

1972   The Watergate break-in, which leads to the resignation of President Nixon, takes place; Nixon makes an unprecedented visit to China; the Senate approves a constitutional amendment barring discrimination against women because of their sex and sends the measure to the states to ratify; the Supreme Court rules the death penalty unconstitutional, and, in a unanimous decision, upholds the use of busing for school integration.

1973   A peace treaty is signed with Vietnam in Paris; President Nixon signs the Endangered Species Act; Oglala Sioux occupy Wounded Knee, South Dakota, and declare an independent Oglala Sioux nation; Spiro T. Agnew resigns as vice president, and Gerald Ford becomes the first appointed vice president; Nixon fires Archibald Cox, special prosecutor in the Watergate case, and William Ruckelshaus in the "Saturday Night Massacre"; Attorney General Elliot Richardson resigns; five of seven defendants in the Watergate trial plead guilty, and two are convicted; in the *Roe v. Wade* decision, the Supreme Court rules that a state may not prevent a woman from having an abortion during the first six months of pregnancy; Congress overrides Nixon's veto of the War Powers Act, which curbs a president's power to commit armed forces to hostilities abroad without congressional approval.

1974   The Organization of Petroleum Exporting Countries (OPEC) lifts the oil embargo; the House Judiciary Committee votes Articles of Impeachment against President Nixon, and Nixon resigns; President Ford pardons Nixon.

1975   North Vietnamese troops enter Saigon; the Mohawk tribe reclaims part of its homeland in New York State; former Attorney General John N. Mitchell and ex-presidential advisers H. R. Haldeman and John D. Ehrlichman are found guilty in the Watergate trial; Congress votes $405 million in aid for South Vietnamese refugees; Vice President Rockefeller's blue-ribbon panel uncovers illegal CIA operations, including records on 300,000 persons and groups and infiltration by agents into black, antiwar, and political movements.

1976   The death penalty is ruled by the Supreme Court to be a constitutionally acceptable form of punishment; the nation celebrates its Bicentennial.

1977   President Carter pardons 10,000 Vietnam draft resisters; the Department of Energy is established; the National Women's Conference convenes in Houston.

1978   The "longest walk," by 300 Native Americans, begins, to protect treaty rights; gay activist and city council member Harvey Milk and Mayor George Moscone are assassinated in San Francisco; the Senate votes to give the Panama Canal to Panama. The Middle East "Framework for Peace" is signed by Egypt and Israel after a Camp David conference led by President Carter.

1979   The Three Mile Island nuclear power plant has a near meltdown; 110,000 demonstrate in Washington, D.C., against nuclear power; Iranian students seize the U.S. embassy in Teheran.

1980   President Carter announces an embargo on the sale of grain and high technology to the Soviet Union because of its invasion of Afghanistan; the U.S. Olympic Committee votes not to participate in the Olympic Games in Moscow.

1981   Iran releases 52 American hostages held 444 days; John Hinckley, Jr., shoots President Reagan and three others; 100,000 protest U.S. intervention in El Salvador; Sandra Day O'Connor is appointed the first woman Supreme Court justice; 11,500 air traffic controllers strike and are fired by President Reagan; the first reusable spacecraft, the space shuttle *Columbia*, completes its two-day mission.

1982   The ERA lapses without ratification; the Vietnam War Memorial is dedicated in Washington, D.C.; Anne M. Gorsuch becomes the first Cabinet-level administrator to be cited for contempt of Congress, for refusing to turn over documents from the Environmental Protection Agency.

1983   Five thousand U.S. Marines and Army Rangers invade the island of Grenada; Congress applies the War Powers Act, demanding that troops leave Grenada; Federal District Judge Jack Tanner orders Washington State to pay female employees according to "comparable worth"; Dr. Sally K. Ride becomes the first American woman astronaut to travel in space; the Supreme Court holds that the Internal Revenue Service can deny tax exemptions to private schools that practice racial discrimination.

1984   Dr. Kathryn D. Sullivan becomes the first woman astronaut to walk in space; Geraldine A. Ferraro is the first woman candidate on a major party ticket to run for vice president; the CIA acknowledges that it mined Nicaraguan harbors, touching off a controversy in Congress; veterans of the Vietnam War reach an out-of-court settlement with seven chemical companies in their class-action suit relating to the use of Agent Orange; a Salt Lake City federal judge rules that the United States had been negligent in its aboveground testing of nuclear weapons in Nevada from 1951 to 1962; the Senate votes to impose economic sanctions on South Africa in protest against apartheid; Palestinian Liberation Organization (PLO) hijackers seize an Italian cruise ship with Americans aboard, killing one; the United States and the Soviet Union meet at their first summit conference in six years; Congress passes the Gramm-Rudman Act in an attempt to curb the federal deficit.

1985   The United States and the Soviet Union agree to resume negotiations on reducing nuclear arms and the space weapons race. Soviet leader Chernenko dies and is succeeded by Mikhail Gorbachev; the Supreme Court bars public school teachers from positions in parochial schools; a summit-meeting agreement is reached by Reagan and Gorbachev on stepping up arms control talks and cultural ties.

1986   The first official observance of the birthday of Martin Luther King, Jr. takes place; the space shuttle *Challenger* explodes moments after liftoff, killing all crew members, including a civilian, Christa McAuliffe; the United States bombs Tripoli and Benghazi, Libya, in retaliation against terrorist attacks; the antiviral drug azidothymidine (AZT) is found to improve the health of some AIDS patients; U.S. officials announce that AIDS cases and deaths will increase tenfold in the next five years; Congress passes antidrug legislation; the United States imposes more economic sanctions against South Africa; President Reagan walks out on arms talks with Soviet leader Mikhail Gorbachev in Iceland because of a disagreement over the development of the U.S. "Star Wars" program.

1987   The Iran-Contra affair dominates public attention when it is revealed that arms were traded for hostages and money was funneled to Swiss bank accounts and used to finance the contras in Nicaragua; insider trading is revealed on Wall Street during the bull market; the United States violates the SALT II treaty with the Soviet Union; President Reagan appoints a commission to study the AIDS crisis and backs AIDS education; a clean-water act is passed over a presidential veto; the United States imposes duties on Japanese imports to curb the trade deficit; in a landmark case, surrogate mother Mary Beth Whitehead is denied custody of "Baby M"; the drug AZT is approved for fighting AIDS; animal forms are granted patent rights; U.S. ships are involved in a conflict in the Persian Gulf; Robert Bork is nominated by President Reagan to the Supreme Court but withdraws in the face of strong opposition; the Federal Communications Commission (FCC) drops the Fairness Doctrine, which allowed equal time on radio and television for controversial issues; "Black Monday" marks the end of the bull market, when Wall Street experiences its three biggest one-day point losses ever.

1988   Panamanian General Noriega is indicted on drug bribery charges, disrupting U.S.-Panama relations; Supreme Court Justice Anthony Kennedy is confirmed; the U.S.-Canada Trade Agreement approves lower barriers to trade; the space shuttle *Discovery* is launched successfully after delays caused by the 1986 tragedy; the United States agrees after a 13-year hiatus to meet with the Palestine Liberation Organization.

1989   In the largest spill in U.S. history, the Exxon *Valdez* strikes a reef in Prince William Sound, dumping 11 million gallons of oil on the Alaska shoreline; the federal Resolution Trust Corporation is created to liquidate the assets of failed savings and loan associations; Ronald Brown is elected chair of the Democratic National Committee, becoming the first black to lead a major political party; Oliver North is convicted by a jury for his involvement in the Iran-Contra affair; the Supreme Court upholds the right to burn the U.S. flag and hands down the Webster decision, upholding a Missouri law prohibiting public employees from performing most abortions; President Bush declares the "war on drugs"; an earthquake in northern California leaves 60 dead and several thousand injured.

1990   Iraq annexes Kuwait, prompting the United States to send a large military force to the Persian Gulf; Washington, D.C., mayor Marion Barry is arrested and convicted on drug charges; Cincinnati museum director Dennis Barrie is indicted on obscenity charges for exhibiting photographs by Robert Mapplethorpe; Congress approves the Americans with Disabilities Act, prohibiting discrimination against people with physical or mental disabilities; Charles Keating, owner of a failed savings and loan, is indicted on 42 counts of criminal fraud; 87 die in a fire at the Happy Land social club in New York City.

1991   The United States attacks Iraq in a monthlong air assault culminating in a 100-hour ground war, causing about 100,000 Iraqi casualties and forcing Iraq to retreat from Kuwait; Clarence Thomas is appointed to the Supreme Court despite allegations of his sexual harassment of a colleague; the "October Surprise" theory, purporting that the 1980 Reagan campaign made a secret deal with Iran to keep the U.S. embassy hostages in captivity until after the election, gains wide exposure; basketball star Magic Johnson announces he has tested positive for the AIDS virus.

1992   The United States denies political asylum to thousands of Haitian refugees; Robert Alton Harris is put to death in California's first execution in 25 years, becoming the focus of a national debate over the death penalty; a California jury acquits four white Los Angeles police officers in the beating of black motorist Rodney King, after the beating was videotaped and broadcast around the world; that verdict provokes rioting in Los Angeles and other U.S. cities; the House of Representatives is engulfed in scandal regarding overdrafts of accounts at the House bank; President Bush draws international criticism at the UN Conference on Environment and Development (known as the "Earth Summit") for refusing to support a treaty intended to protect endangered species; President Bush and Russian President Boris Yeltsin hold the first U.S.-Russia Summit and agree on new strategic arms reductions goals; the Supreme Court upholds the underlying principle of *Roe v. Wade* while also permitting states to enact some restrictions on a woman's right to obtain an abortion, as long as they do not pose an "undue burden"; Panamanian General Noriega is convicted on racketeering, drug trafficking, and money-laundering charges; the United States, Mexico, and Canada conclude negotiations on the North American Free Trade Agreement; Hurricane Andrew causes devastation in Florida and Louisiana; the United States sends forces into Somalia to guarantee the delivery of humanitarian aid to the famine-ridden country.

1993   Janet Reno is sworn in as first female Attorney General; cult leader David Koresh and many followers die in a Texas compound fire; President Clinton touches off controversy with his attempt to end the ban on homosexuals in the military; a Federal trial finds two Los Angeles police officers guilty of violating the civil rights of black motorist Rodney King; Sheik Omar Abdel Rahman and 14 others are indicted in a bombing that killed six at the World Trade Center in New York City; the Supreme Court rules that redrawing congressional districts along racial lines is unconstitutional; floods ravage the Midwest throughout the summer, causing $12 billion in damage and leaving tens of thousand homeless; Congress passes a deficit reduction bill, levying $241 billion in new taxes; President Clinton introduces legislation aimed at reform of the nation's health-care system; Ruth Bader Ginsburg becomes the second woman to serve on the Supreme Court, filling the seat vacated by Justice Byron White; Boeing, IBM, and other leading corporations announce major layoffs in the name of "downsizing"; Clinton signs the Brady Bill, imposing a five-day waiting period for all gun purchases.

1994   A major earthquake strikes Los Angeles, causing 60 deaths and billions in property damage; former CIA agent Aldrich Ames receives life sentence for selling information to Soviet agents; President Clinton and First Lady Hillary Rodham Clinton come under scrutiny for previous financial dealings in the Whitewater affair; former football star O. J. Simpson is charged with the murder of his ex-wife, Nicole Brown Simpson, and her friend Ronald Goldman; administration's health-care proposals fail to win congressional approval; Stephen G. Breyer replaces Justice Harry Blackmun on the Supreme Court; Republicans score heavy victories in midterm elections, winning control of both the House and Senate; apparent attacks on the White House, including gunshots and the crash of a small plane, lead to an increase in security measures, including the closing of Pennsylvania Avenue.

1995   104th Congress convenes, with Republicans controlling both houses for the first time since 1953; Republicans vow to pass legislation outlined in their Contract with America, aiming to cut federal spending and reduce the size of government; the Simpson trial begins in Los Angeles; an independent prosecutor brings indictments in Whitewater case; the stock market continues to boom as the Dow Jones industrial average reaches new highs; 169 die in a bomb explosion at federal office building in Oklahoma City; Timothy McVeigh and Terry Nichols, members of a right-wing group, are arrested as suspects in the Oklahoma City bombing; a midsummer heat wave causes 800 deaths in the Midwest and Northeast; Robert Packwood resigns from the Senate following charges of sexual misconduct and obstruction of justice; Congress pursues the Whitewater investigations; O. J. Simpson is acquitted by a mostly black jury, and the verdict appears to divide the country along racial lines; 800,000 African-American men convene in Washington for the Million Man March; federal government operations shut down as Congress refuses to release funds in budget dispute with the White House.

1996   Government shutdown ends with a budget compromise; a record-breaking blizzard blankets the Northeast; Commerce Secretary Ron Brown dies in a plane crash in Croatia; the Whitewater probe continues; FBI arrests Theodore Kaczynski in the Unabomber case; an arson campaign continues against black churches in the South, with the toll reaching 30 attacks in 18 months; Congress approves a raise of the minimum wage; TWA Flight 800 crashes in the ocean off Long Island, touching off massive investigation and renewed concerns about terrorism; President Clinton signs a welfare reform bill, ending a 60-year policy of open-ended benefits and shifting responsibility to the states; Texaco settles an antibias suit for $176 million; Clinton wins reelection by a landslide, defeating challenger Bob Dole, but Republicans maintain control of Congress.

1997   The White House and Congress agree on a plan to balance the federal budget by 2002; Congress begins a probe into Democratic fund-raising practices; Speaker Newt Gingrich is reprimanded by the House of Representatives for ethics violations and ordered to pay a $300,000 fine; spring flooding does extensive damage in the Upper Midwest; more stringent federal immigration rules take effect; a civil jury holds O. J. Simpson liable for the death of Nicole Brown Simpson and Ronald Goldman; Madeleine K. Albright becomes the first woman secretary of state; Timothy McVeigh is convicted of murder in the Oklahoma City bombing case; tobacco companies and state attorneys general reach accord on proposed new tobacco regulations and payments to states for smoking-related health costs.

1998   President Clinton fights allegations that he had sexual relations with White House intern Monica Lewinsky and then encouraged her to lie about the affair under oath; Ramzi Yousef, the mastermind behind the 1993 World Trade Center bombing, is sentenced to a 240-year sentence, with no chance of parol; severe weather conditions wreak havoc on communities across the United States, including ice storms, flooding, mudslides, tornadoes, fires, and hurricanes; a string of school shootings in Oregon, Arkansas, and Pennsylvania raise concerns about juvenille crime; British au pair Louise Woodward is convicted of manslaughter in the death of 8-month-old Matthew Eappen; the sexual harrassment suit filed by former Arkansas state employee Paula Jones is dismissed by the presiding judge; unemployment rate falls to a 28-year low and the U.S. economy has its strongest growth in 2 years; Unabomber Theodore Kaczynski is sentenced to life in prison; the Justice Department files an antitrust case against Microsoft, alleging they exert their market power to prevent competition; Terry Nichols is sentenced to life in prison for the 1995 Oklahoma City bombing case; striking General Motor workers virtually halt GM's American production.

United States

HISTORIC DOCUMENTS AND PRONOUNCEMENTS
THE DECLARATION OF INDEPENDENCE

IN CONGRESS, JULY 4, 1776

The unanimous Declaration of the thirteen united States of America

When in the Course of human events, it becomes necessary for one people to dissolve the political bands which have connected them with another, and to assume among the powers of the earth, the separate and equal station to which the Laws of Nature and of Nature's God entitle them, a decent respect to the opinions of mankind requires that they should declare the causes which impel them to the separation.

We hold these truths to be self-evident, that all men are created equal, that they are endowed by their Creator with certain unalienable rights, that among these are life, liberty and the pursuit of happiness. That to secure these rights, governments are instituted among men, deriving their just powers from the consent of the governed,—That whenever any form of government becomes destructive of these ends, it is such principles and organizing its powers in such form, as to them shall seem most likely to effect their safety and happiness. Prudence, indeed, will dictate that governments long established should not be changed for light and transient causes; and accordingly all experience hath shown, that mankind are more disposed to suffer, while evils are sufferable, than to right themselves by abolishing the forms to which they are accustomed. But when a long train of abuses and usurpations, pursuing invariably the same object evinces a design to reduce them under absolute despotism, it is their right, it is their duty, to throw off such government, and to provide new guards for their future security.—Such has been the patient sufferance of government. The history of the present King of Great Britain is a history of repeated injuries and usurpations, all having in direct object the establishment of an absolute tyranny over these States. To prove this, let facts be submitted to a candid world.

He has refused his assent to laws, the most wholesome and necessary for the public good.

He has forbidden his Governors to pass laws of immediate and pressing importance, unless suspended in their operation till his assent should be obtained; and when so suspended, he has utterly neglected to attend to them.

He has refused to pass other laws for the accommodation of large districts of people, unless those people would relinquish the right representation in the legislature, a right inestimable to them and formidable to tyrants only.

He has called together legislative bodies at places unusual, uncomfortable, and distant from the depository of their public records, for the sole purpose of fatiguing them into compliance with his measures.

He has dissolved Representative Houses repeatedly, for opposing with manly firmness his invasions on the rights of the people.

He has refused for a long time, after such dissolutions, to cause others to be elected; whereby the legislative powers, incapable of annihilation, have returned to the people at large for their exercise; the State remaining in the mean time exposed to all the dangers of invasion from without, and convulsions within.

United States

He has endeavoured to prevent the population of these States; for that purpose obstructing the laws for naturalization of foreigners; refusing to pass others to encourage their migrations hither, and raising the conditions of new appropriations of lands.

He has obstructed the administration of justice, by refusing his assent to laws for establishing judiciary powers.

He has made Judges dependent on his will alone, for the tenure of their offices, and the amount and payment of their salaries.

He has erected a multitude of new offices, and sent hither swarms of officers to harass our people, and eat out their substance.

He has kept among us, in times of peace, standing armies without the consent of our legislatures.

He has affected to render the military independent of and superior to the civil power.

He has combined with others to subject us to a jurisdiction foreign to our constitution, and unacknowledged by our laws; giving his assent to their acts of pretended legislation:

For quartering large bodies of armed troops among us:

For protecting them, by a mock trial, from punishment for any murders which they should commit on the inhabitants of these States:

For cutting off our trade with all parts of the world:

For imposing taxes on us without our consent:

For depriving us in many cases, of the benefits of trial by jury:

For transporting us beyond seas to be tried for pretended offenses:

For abolishing the free system of English laws in a neighbouring province, establishing therein an arbitrary government, and enlarging its boundaries so as to render it at once an example and fit instrument for introducing the same absolute rule into these colonies:

For taking away our charters, abolishing our most valuable laws, and altering fundamentally the forms of our governments:

For suspending our own legislatures, and declaring themselves invested with power to legislate for us in all cases whatsoever.

He has abdicated government here, by declaring us out of his protection and waging war against us.

He has plundered our seas, ravaged our coasts, burnt our towns, and destroyed the lives of our people.

He is at this time transporting large armies of foreign mercenaries to complete the works of death, desolation and tyranny, already begun with circumstances of cruelty and perfidy scarcely paralleled in the most barbarous ages, and totally unworthy of the head of a civilized nation.

He has constrained our fellow citizens taken captive on the high seas to bear arms against their country, to become the executioners of their friends and brethren, or to fall themselves by their hands.

United States

continues

THE DECLARATION OF INDEPENDENCE, Continued

He has excited domestic insurrections amongst us, and has endeavoured to bring on the inhabitants of our frontiers, the merciless Indian savages, whose known rule of warfare is an undistinguished destruction of all ages, sexes and conditions.

In every stage of these oppressions we have petitioned for redress in the most humble terms: Our repeated petitions have been answered only by repeated injury. A prince, whose character is thus marked by every act which may define a tyrant, is unfit to be the ruler of a free people.

Nor have we been wanting in attentions to our British brethren. We have warned them from time to time of attempts by their legislature to extend an unwarrantable jurisdiction over us. We have reminded them of the circumstances of our emigration and settlement here. We have appealed to their native justice and magnanimity, and we have conjured them by the ties of our common kindred to disavow these usurpations, which, would inevitably interrupt our connections and correspondence. They too have been deaf to the voice of justice and of consanguinity. We must, therefore, acquiesce in the necessity which denounces our separation, and hold them, as we hold the rest of mankind, enemies in war, in peace friends.

WE, THEREFORE, the Representatives of the United States of America, in General Congress, Assembled, appealing to the Supreme Judge of the world for the rectitude of our intentions, do, in the name, and by authority of the good people of these Colonies, solemnly publish and declare, That these United Colonies of the British Crown, and that all political connection between them and the State of Great Britain, is and ought to be totally dissolved; and that as free and independent States, they have full power to levy war, conclude peace, contract alliances, establish commerce, and to do all other acts and things which independent States may of right do. And for the support of this Declaration, with a firm reliance on the protection of Divine Providence, we mutually pledge to each other our lives, our fortunes and our sacred honor.

Georgia

BUTTON GWINNETT   GEO. WALTON
LYMAN HALL

North Carolina

WM. HOOPER   JOHN PENN
JOSEPH HEWES

South Carolina

EDWARD RUTLEDGE   THOMAS LYNCH JUNR.
THOS. HEYWARD JUNR.   ARTHUR MIDDLETON

Maryland

SAMUEL CHASE   CHARLES CARROLL
WM. PACA   OF CARROLLTON
THOS. STONE

Virginia

GEORGE WYTHE	THOS. NELSON JR.
RICHARD HENRY LEE	FRANCIS LIGHTFOOT LEE
TH. JEFFERSON	CARTER BRAXTON
BENJA. HARRISON	

Pennsylvania

ROBT. MORRIS	JAS. SMITH
BENJAMIN RUSH	GEO. TAYLOR
BENJA. FRANKLIN	JAMES WILSON
JOHN MORTON	GEO. ROSS
GEO. CLYMER	

Delaware

CAESAR RODNEY	THO. M'KEAN
GEO. READ	

New York

WM. FLOYD	FRANS. LEWIS
PHIL. LIVINGSTON	LEWIS MORRIS

New Jersey

RICHD. STOCKTON	JOHN HART
JNO. WITHERSPOON	ABRA CLARK
FRAS. HOPKINSON	

New Hampshire

JOSIAH BARTLETT	MATTHEW THORNTON
WM. WHIPPLE	

Massachusetts Bay

JOHN HANCOCK	ROBT. TREAT PAINE
SAML. ADAMS	ELBRIDGE GERRY
JOHN ADAMS	

Rhode Island

STEP. HOPKINS	WILLIAM ELLERY

Connecticut

ROGER SHERMAN	WM. WILLIAMS
SAML. HUNTINGTON	OLIVER WOLCOTT

United States

THE CONSTITUTION OF THE UNITED STATES OF AMERICA

PREAMBLE

WE THE PEOPLE of the United States, in order to form a more perfect Union, establish justice, insure domestic tranquility, provide for the common defense, promote the general welfare, and secure the blessings of liberty to ourselves and our posterity, do ordain and establish this Constitution for the United States of America.

ARTICLE I

SECTION 1. All legislative powers herein granted shall be vested in a Congress of the United States, which shall consist of a Senate and House of Representatives.

SECTION 2. The House of Representatives shall be composed of members chosen every second year by the people of the several States, and the electors in each State shall have the qualifications requisite for electors of the most numerous branch of the State Legislature.

No person shall be a Representative who shall not have attained to the age of twenty-five years, and been seven years a citizen of the United States, and who shall not, when elected, be an inhabitant of that State in which he shall be chosen.

Representatives and direct taxes shall be apportioned among the several States which may be included within this Union, according to their respective numbers, which shall be determined by adding to the whole number of free persons, including those bound to service for a term of years, and excluding Indians not taxed, three-fifths of all other persons. The actual enumeration shall be made within three years after the first meeting of the Congress of the United States, and within every subsequent term of ten years, in such manner as they shall by law direct. The number of representatives shall not exceed one for every thirty thousand, but each State shall have at least one Representative; and until such enumeration shall be made, the State of New Hampshire shall be entitled to choose three, Massachusetts eight, Rhode Island and Providence Plantations one, Connecticut five, New York six, New Jersey four, Pennsylvania eight, Delaware one, Maryland six, Virginia ten, North Carolina five, South Carolina five, and Georgia three.

When vacancies happen in the representation from any State, the executive authority thereof shall issue writs of election to fill such vacancies.

The House of Representatives shall choose their Speaker and other officers; and shall have the sole power of impeachment.

SECTION 3. The Senate of the United States shall be composed of two Senators from each State, chosen by the legislature thereof, for six years and each Senator shall have one vote.

Immediately after they shall be assembled in consequence of the first election, they shall be divided as equally as may be into three classes. The seats of the Senators of the first class shall be vacated at the expiration of the second year, of the second class at the expiration of the fourth year, and of the third class at the expiration of the sixth year, so that one-third may be chosen every second year; and if vacancies happen by resignation, or otherwise, during the recess of the legislature of any State, the executive thereof may make temporary appointments until the next meeting of the legislature, which shall then fill such vacancies.

No person shall be a Senator who shall not have attained to the age of thirty years, and been nine years a citizen of the United States, and who shall not, when elected, be an inhabitant of that State for which he shall be chosen.

The Vice President of the United States shall be President of the Senate, but shall have no vote, unless they be equally divided.

The Senate shall choose their other officers, and also a President pro tempore, in the absence of the Vice President, or when he shall exercise the office of President of the United States.

The Senate shall have the sole power to try all impeachments. When sitting for that purpose, they shall be on oath or affirmation. When the President of the United States is tried, the Chief Justice shall preside: and no person shall be convicted without the concurrence of two thirds of the members present.

Judgment in cases of impeachment shall not extend further than to removal from office, and disqualification to hold and enjoy any office of honor, trust or profit under the United States: but the party convicted shall nevertheless be liable and subject to indictment, trial, judgment and punishment, according to law.

SECTION 4. The times, places and manner of holding elections for Senators and Representatives, shall be prescribed in each State by the legislature thereof; but the Congress may at any time by law make or alter such regulations, except as to the places of choosing Senators.

The Congress shall assemble at least once in every year, and such meeting shall be on the first Monday in December, unless they shall by law appoint a different day.

SECTION 5. Each House shall be the judge of the elections, returns and qualifications of its own members, and a majority of each shall constitute a quorum to do business; but a smaller number may adjourn from day to day, and may be authorized to compel the attendance of absent members, in such manner, and under such penalties as each House may provide.

Each House may determine the rules of its proceedings, punish its members for disorderly behavior, and, with the concurrence of two-thirds, expel a member.

Each House shall keep a journal of its proceedings, and from time to time publish the same, excepting such parts as may in their judgment require secrecy; and the yeas and the nays of the members of either house on any question shall, at the

desire of one-fifth of those present, be entered on the journal.

Neither House, during the session of Congress, shall, without the consent of the other, adjourn for more than three days, nor to any other place than that in which the two Houses shall be sitting.

SECTION 6. The Senators and Representatives shall receive a compensation for their services, to be ascertained by law, and paid out of the Treasury of the United States. They shall in all cases, except treason, felony and breach of the peace, be privileged from arrest during their attendance at the session of their respective Houses, and in going to and returning from the same; and for any speech or debate in either House, they shall not be questioned in any other place.

No Senator or Representative shall, during the time for which he was elected, be appointed to any civil office under the authority of the United States, which shall have been created, or the emoluments whereof shall have been increased during such time; and no person holding any office under the United States, shall be a member of either House during his continuance in office.

SECTION 7. All bills for raising revenue shall originate in the House of Representatives; but the Senate may propose or concur with amendments as on other bills.

Every bill which shall have passed the House of Representatives and the Senate, shall, before it becomes a law, be presented to the President of the United States; if he approves he shall sign it, but if not he shall return it, with his objections to that House in which it shall have originated, who shall enter the objections at large on their journal, and proceed to reconsider it. If after such reconsideration two thirds of that House shall agree to pass the bill, it shall be sent, together with the objections, to the other House, by which it shall likewise be reconsidered, and if approved by two thirds of that House, it shall become a law. But in all such cases the votes of both Houses shall be determined by yeas and nays, and the names of the persons voting for and against the bill shall be entered on the journal of each House respectively. If any bill shall not be returned by the President within ten days (Sundays excepted) after it shall have been presented to him, the same shall be a law, in like manner as if he had signed it, unless the Congress by their adjournment prevent its return, in which case it shall not be a law.

Every order, resolution, or vote to which the concurrence of the Senate and House of Representatives may be necessary (except on a question of adjournment) shall be presented to the President of the United States; and before the same shall take effect, shall be approved by him, or being disapproved by him, shall be repassed by two thirds of the Senate and House of Representatives, according to the rules and limitations prescribed in the case of a bill.

SECTION 8. The Congress shall have power to lay and collect taxes, duties, imposts and excises, to pay the debts and provide for the common defense and general welfare of the United States; but all duties, imposts and excises shall be uniform throughout the United States;

To borrow money on the credit of the United States;

To regulate commerce with foreign nations, and among the several States, and with the Indian tribes;

To establish a uniform rule of naturalization, and uniform laws on the subject of bankruptcies throughout the United States;

To coin money, regulate the value thereof, and of foreign coin, and fix the standard of weights and measures;

To provide for the punishment of counterfeiting the securities and current coin of the United States;

To establish post offices and post roads;

To promote the progress of science and useful arts, by securing for limited times to authors and inventors the exclusive right to their respective writings and discoveries;

To constitute tribunals inferior to the Supreme Court;

To define and punish piracies and felonies committed on the high seas, and offenses against the law of nations;

To declare war, grant letters of marque and reprisal, and make rules concerning captures on land and water;

To raise and support armies, but no appropriation of money to that use shall be for a longer term than two years;

To provide and maintain a navy;

To make rules for the government and regulation of the land and naval forces;

To provide for calling forth the militia to execute the laws of the Union, suppress insurrections and repel invasions;

To provide for organizing, arming, and disciplining the militia, and for governing such part of them as may be employed in the service of the United States, reserving to the States respectively, the appointment of the officers, and the authority of training the militia according to the discipline prescribed by Congress;

To exercise exclusive legislation in all cases whatsoever, over such district (not exceeding ten miles square) as may, by cession of particular States, and the acceptance of Congress, become the seat of the Government of the United States, and to exercise like authority over all places purchased by the consent of the legislature of the State in which the same shall be, for the erection of forts, magazines, arsenals, dock-yards, and other needful buildings;— And

To make all laws which shall be necessary and proper for carrying into execution the foregoing powers, and all other powers vested by this Constitution in the Government of the United States, or in any department or officer thereof.

SECTION 9. The migration or importation of such persons as any of the States now existing shall think proper to admit, shall not be prohibited by the Congress prior to the year one thousand eight hundred and eight, but a tax or duty may be imposed on such importation, not exceeding ten dollars for each person.

The privilege of the writ of habeas corpus shall not be suspended, unless when in cases of rebellion or invasion the public safety may require it.

No bill of attainder or ex post facto law shall be passed.

No capitation, or other direct, tax shall be laid, unless in proportion to the census or enumeration herein before directed to be taken.

No tax or duty shall be laid on articles exported from any State.

No preference shall be given by any regulation of commerce or revenue to the ports of one State over those of another: nor shall vessels bound to, or from, one State, be obliged to enter, clear, or pay duties in another.

No money shall be drawn from the Treasury, but in consequence of appropriations made by law; and a regular statement and account of the receipts and expenditures of all public money shall be published from time to time.

No title of nobility shall be granted by the United States: And no person holding any office of profit or trust under them, shall, without the consent of the Congress, accept of any present, emolument, office, or title, of any kind whatever, from any King, Prince, or foreign State.

SECTION 10. No State shall enter into any treaty, alliance, or confederation; grant letters of marque and reprisal; coin money; emit bills of credit; make any thing but gold and silver coin a tender in payment of debts; pass any bill of attainder, ex post facto law, or law impairing the obligation of contracts, or grant any title of nobility.

No State shall, without the consent of the Congress, lay any imposts or duties on imports or exports, except what may be absolutely necessary for executing its inspection laws: and the net produce of all duties and imposts, laid by any state on imports or exports, shall be for the use of the Treasury of the United States; and all such laws shall be subject to the revision and control of the Congress.

No State shall, without the consent of Congress, lay any duty of tonnage, keep troops, or ships of war in time of peace, enter into any agreement or compact with another State, or with a foreign power, or engage in war, unless actually invaded, or in such imminent danger as will not admit of delay.

ARTICLE II

SECTION 1. The executive power shall be vested in a President of the United States of America. He shall hold his office during the term of four years, and together with the Vice President, chosen for the same term, be elected, as follows:

Each State, shall appoint, in such manner as the legislature thereof may direct, a number of electors, equal to the whole number of Senators and Representatives to which the State may be entitled in the Congress; but no Senator or Representative, or person holding an office of trust or profit under the United States, shall be appointed an elector.

The electors shall meet in their respective States, and vote by ballot for two persons, of whom one at least shall not be an inhabitant of the same State with themselves. And they shall make a list of all the persons voted for, and of the number of votes for each; which list they shall sign and certify, and transmit sealed to the seat of the Government of the United States, directed to the President of the Senate. The President of the Senate shall, in the presence of the Senate and House of

United States

Representatives, open all the certificates, and the votes shall then be counted. The person having the greatest number of votes shall be the President, if such number be a majority of the whole number of electors appointed; and if there be more than one who have such majority, and have an equal number of votes, then the House of Representatives shall immediately choose by ballot one of them for President; and if no persons have a majority, then from the five highest on the list the said House shall in like manner choose the President. But in choosing the President, the votes shall be taken by States, the representation from each State having one vote; a quorum for this purpose shall consist of a member or members from two-thirds of the States, and a majority of all the States shall be necessary to a choice. In every case, after the choice of the President, the person having the greatest number of votes of the electors shall be the Vice President. But if there should remain two or more who have equal votes, the Senate shall choose from them by ballot the Vice President.

The Congress may determine the time of choosing the electors, and the day on which they shall give their votes; which day shall be the same throughout the United States.

No person except a natural born citizen, or a citizen of the United States, at the time of the adoption of this Constitution, shall be eligible to the office of President; neither shall any person be eligible to that office who shall not have attained to the age of thirty-five years, and been fourteen years a resident within the United States.

In case of the removal of the President from office, or of his death, resignation, or inability to discharge the powers and duties of the said office, the same shall devolve on the Vice President, and the Congress may by law provide for the case of removal, death, resignation, or inability, both of the President and Vice President, declaring what officer shall then act as President, and such officer shall act accordingly, until the disability be removed, or a President be elected.

The President shall, at stated times, receive for his services, a compensation, which shall neither be increased nor diminished during the period for which he shall have been elected, and he shall not receive within that period any other emolument from the United States, or any of them.

Before he enter on the execution of his office, he shall take the following oath or affirmation:—"I do solemnly swear (or affirm) that I will faithfully execute the office of President of the United States, and will to the best of my ability, preserve, protect and defend the Constitution of the United States."

SECTION 2. The President shall be Commander in Chief of the Army and Navy of the United States, and of the militia of the several States, when called into the actual service of the United States; he may require the opinion, in writing, of the principal officer in each of the executive departments, upon any subject relating to the duties of their respective offices, and he shall have power to grant reprieves and pardons for offenses against the United States, except in cases of impeachment.

He shall have power, by and with the advice and consent of the Senate, to make treaties, provided two-thirds of the Senators present concur; and he shall nominate, and by and with the advice and consent of the Senate, shall appoint ambassadors, other public ministers and consuls, Judges of the Supreme Court, and all other officers of the United States, whose appointments are not herein otherwise provided for, and which shall be established by law: but the Congress may by law vest the appointment of such inferior officers, as they think proper, in the President alone, in the courts of law, or in the heads of departments.

The President shall have power to fill up all vacancies that may happen during the recess of the Senate, by granting commissions which shall expire at the end of their next session.

SECTION 3. He shall from time to time give to the Congress information of the State of the Union, and recommend to their consideration such measures as he shall judge necessary and expedient; he may, on extraordinary occasions, convene both Houses, or either of them, and in case of disagreement between them, with respect to the time of adjournment, he may adjourn them to such time as he shall think proper; he shall receive ambassadors and other public ministers; he shall take care that the laws be faithfully executed, and shall commission all the officers of the United States.

SECTION 4. The President, Vice President and all civil officers of the United States, shall be removed from office on impeachment for, and conviction of, treason, bribery, or other high crimes and misdemeanors.

ARTICLE III

SECTION 1. The judicial power of the United States, shall be vested in one Supreme Court, and in such inferior courts as the Congress may from time to time ordain and establish. The judges, both of the Supreme and inferior Courts, shall hold their offices during good behavior, and shall, at stated times, receive for their services, a compensation, which shall not be diminished during their continuance in office.

SECTION 2. The judicial power shall extend to all cases, in law and equity, arising under this Constitution, the laws of the United States, and treaties made, or which shall be made, under their authority;—to all cases affecting ambassadors, other public ministers and consuls;—to all cases of admiralty and maritime jurisdiction;—to controversies to which the United States shall be a party;—to controversies between two or more States;—between a State and citizens of another State;—between citizens of different States,—between citizens of the same State claiming lands under grants of different States, and between a State, or the citizens thereof, and foreign States, citizens or subjects.

In all cases affecting ambassadors, other public ministers and consuls, and those in which a State shall be a party, the Supreme Court shall have original jurisdiction. In all the other cases before mentioned, the Supreme Court shall have appellate jurisdiction, both as to law and fact, with such exceptions, and under such regulations as the Congress shall make.

The trial of all crimes, except in cases of impeachment, shall be by jury; and such trial shall be held in the State where the said crimes shall have been committed; but when not committed within any State, the trial shall be at such place or places as the Congress may by law have directed.

SECTION 3. Treason against the United States, shall consist only in levying war against them, or in adhering to their enemies, giving them aid and comfort. No person shall be convicted of treason unless on the testimony of two witnesses to the same overt act, or on confession in open court.

The Congress shall have power to declare the punishment of treason, but no attainder of treason shall work corruption of blood, or forfeiture except during the life of the person attainted.

ARTICLE IV

SECTION 1. Full faith and credit shall be given in each State to the public acts, records, and judicial proceedings of every other State. And the Congress may by general laws prescribe the manner in which such acts, records, and proceedings shall be proved, and the effect thereof.

SECTION 2. The citizens of each State shall be entitled to all privileges and immunities of citizens in the several States.

A person charged in any State with treason, felony, or other crime, who shall flee from justice, and be found in another State, shall on demand of the executive authority of the State from which he fled, be delivered up, to be removed to the State having jurisdiction of the crime.

No person held to service or labor in one State, under the laws thereof, escaping into another, shall,

United States

in consequence of any law or regulation therein, be discharged from such service or labor, but shall be delivered up on claim of the party to whom such service or labor may be due.

SECTION 3. New States may be admitted by the Congress into this Union; but no new State shall be formed or erected within the jurisdiction of any other State; nor any State be formed by the junction of two or more States, or parts of States, without the consent of the legislatures of the States concerned as well as of the Congress.

The Congress shall have power to dispose of and make all needful rules and regulations respecting the Territory or other property belonging to the United States; and nothing in this Constitution shall be so construed as to prejudice any claims of the United States, or of any particular State.

SECTION 4. The United States shall guarantee to every State in this Union a republican form of Government, and shall protect each of them against invasion; and on application of the legislature, or of the executive (when the legislature cannot be convened) against domestic violence.

ARTICLE V

The Congress, whenever two thirds of both Houses shall deem it necessary, shall propose amendments to this Constitution, or on the application of the legislatures of two thirds of the several States, shall call a convention for proposing amendments, which, in either case, shall be valid to all intents and purposes, as part of this Constitution, when ratified by the legislatures of three fourths of the several States, or by conventions in three fourths thereof, as the one or the other mode of ratification may be proposed by the Congress; provided that no amendment which may be made prior to the year one thousand eight hundred and eight shall in any manner affect the first and fourth clauses in the Ninth Section of the First Article; and that no State, without its consent, shall be deprived of its equal suffrage in the Senate.

ARTICLE VI

All debts contracted and engagements entered into, before the adoption of this Constitution, shall be as valid against the United States under this Constitution, as under the Confederation.

This Constitution, and the laws of the United States which shall be made in pursuance thereof; and all treaties made, or which shall be made, under the authority of the United States, shall be the supreme law of the land; and the judges in every State shall be bound thereby, any thing in the Constitution or laws of any State to the contrary notwithstanding.

The Senators and Representatives before mentioned, and the members of the several State legislatures, and all executive and judicial officers, both of the United States and of the several States, shall be bound by oath or affirmation, to support this Constitution; but no religious test shall ever be required as a qualification to any office or public trust under the United States.

ARTICLE VII

The ratification of the conventions of nine States shall be sufficient for the establishment of this Constitution between the States so ratifying the same.

Done in convention by the unanimous consent of the States present the seventeenth day of September in the year of our Lord one thousand seven hundred and eighty seven and of the independence of the United States of America the twelfth. In witness whereof we have hereunto subscribed our names,

GO. WASHINGTON—*President* and deputy from Virginia

Attest WILLIAM JACKSON *Secretary*

New Hampshire
JOHN LANGDON   NICHOLAS GILMAN

Massachusetts
NATHANIEL GORHAM   RUFUS KING

Connecticut
WM. SAML. JOHNSON   ROGER SHERMAN

New York
ALEXANDER HAMILTON

New Jersey
WIL. LIVINGSTON   WM. PATERSON
DAVID BREARLEY   JONA: DAYTON

Pennsylvania
B. FRANKLIN   THOS. FITZSIMONS
THOMAS MIFFLIN   JARED INGERSOLL
ROBT MORRIS   JAMES WILSON
GEO. CLYMER   GOUV. MORRIS

Delaware
GEO. READ   RICHARD BASSETT
GUNNING BEDFORDJUN   JACO. BROOM
JOHN DICKINSON

Maryland
JAMES MCHENRY   DANL. CARROLL
DAN OF ST. THOS. JENIFER

Virginia
JOHN BLAIR   JAMES MADISON JR.

North Carolina
WM. BLOUNT   HU. WILLIAMSON
RICHD. DOBBS SPAIGHT

South Carolina
J. RUTLEDGE   CHARLES PINCKNEY
CHARLES COTESWORTH   PIERCE BUTLER
  PINCKNEY

Georgia
WILLIAM FEW   ABR. BALDWIN

George Washington was not the first president of the United States. He was the ninth. In 1781 John Hanson of Maryland was named the first "president of the United States in Congress assembled."

Amendments

[The first ten amendments to the Constitution are called the *Bill of Rights* and were adopted in 1791.]

ARTICLE I

Congress shall make no law respecting an establishment of religion, or prohibiting the free exercise thereof; or abridging the freedom of speech, or of the press; or the right of the people peaceably to assemble, and to petition the Government for a redress of grievances.

ARTICLE II

A well regulated militia, being necessary to the security of a free State, the right of the people to keep and bear arms, shall not be infringed.

ARTICLE III

No soldier shall, in time of peace be quartered in any house, without the consent of the owner, nor in time of war, but in a manner to be prescribed by law.

ARTICLE IV

The right of the people to be secure in their persons, houses, papers, and effects, against unreasonable searches and seizures, shall not be violated, and no warrants shall issue, but upon probable cause, supported by oath or affirmation, and particularly describing the place to be searched, and the persons or things to be seized.

ARTICLE V

No person shall be held to answer for a capital, or otherwise infamous crime, unless on a presentment or indictment of a Grand Jury, except in cases arising in the land or naval forces, or in the militia, when in actual service in time of war or public danger; nor shall any person be subject for the same offense to be twice put in jeopardy of life or limb; nor shall be compelled in any criminal case to be a witness against himself, nor be deprived of life, liberty, or property, without due process of law; nor

United States

shall private property be taken for public use, without just compensation.

Article VI

In all criminal prosecutions, the accused shall enjoy the right to a speedy and public trial, by an impartial jury of the State and district wherein the crime shall have been committed, which district shall have been previously ascertained by law, and to be informed of the nature and cause of the accusation; to be confronted with the witnesses against him; to have compulsory process for obtaining witnesses in his favor, and to have the assistance of counsel for his defense.

Article VII

In suits at common law, where the value in controversy shall exceed twenty dollars, the right of trial by jury shall be preserved, and no fact tried by a jury, shall be otherwise reexamined in any Court of the United States, than according to the rules of the common law.

Article VIII

Excessive bail shall not be required, nor excessive fines imposed, nor cruel and unusual punishments inflicted.

Article IX

The enumeration in the Constitution, of certain rights, shall not be construed to deny or disparage others retained by the people.

Article X

The powers not delegated to the United States by the Constitution, nor prohibited by it to the States, are reserved to the States respectively, or to the people.

Article XI

The judicial power of the United States shall not be construed to extend to any suit in law or equity, commenced or prosecuted against one of the United States by citizens of another State, or by citizens or subjects of any foreign State.

Article XII

The electors shall meet in their respective States, and vote by ballot for President and Vice President, one of whom, at least, shall not be an inhabitant of the same State with themselves; they shall name in their ballots the person voted for as President, and in distinct ballots the person voted for as Vice President, and they shall make distinct lists of all persons voted for as President, and of all persons voted for as Vice President, and of the number of votes for each, which lists they shall sign and certify, and transmit sealed to the seat of the government of the United States, directed to the President of the Senate;—The President of the Senate shall, in the presence of the Senate and House of Representatives, open all the certificates and the votes shall then be counted;—The person having the greatest number of votes for President, shall be the President, if such number be a majority of the whole number of electors appointed; and if no person have such majority, then from the persons having the highest numbers not exceeding three on the list of those voted for as President, the House of Representatives shall choose immediately, by ballot, the President. But in choosing the President, the votes shall be taken by States, the representation from each State having one vote; a quorum for this purpose shall consist of a member or members from two-thirds of the States, and a majority of all the States shall be necessary to a choice. And if the House of Representatives shall not choose a President whenever the right of choice shall devolve upon them, before the fourth day of March next following, then the Vice President shall act as President, as in the case of the death or other constitutional disability of the President.—The person having the greatest number of votes as Vice President, shall be the Vice President, if such number be a majority of the whole number of electors appointed, and if no person have a majority, then from the two highest numbers on the list, the Senate shall choose the Vice President; a quorum for the purpose shall consist of two-thirds of the whole number of Senators, and a majority of the whole number shall be necessary to a choice. But no person constitutionally ineligible to the office of President shall be eligible to that of Vice President of the United States.

Article XIII

Section 1. Neither slavery nor involuntary servitude, except as a punishment for crime whereof the party shall have been duly convicted, shall exist within the United States, or any place subject to their jurisdiction.

Section 2. Congress shall have power to enforce this article by appropriate legislation.

Article XIV

Section 1. All persons born or naturalized in the United States, and subject to the jurisdiction thereof, are citizens of the United States and of the State wherein they reside. No State shall make or enforce any law which shall abridge the privileges or immunities of citizens of the United States; nor shall any State deprive any person of life, liberty, or property, without due process of law; nor deny to any person within its jurisdiction the equal protection of the laws.

Section 2. Representatives shall be apportioned among the several States according to their respective numbers, counting the whole number of persons in each State, excluding Indians not taxed. But when the right to vote at any election for the choice of electors for President and Vice President of the United States, Representatives in Congress, the executive and judicial officers of a State, or the members of the legislature thereof, is denied to any of the male inhabitants of such State, being twenty-one years of age, and citizens of the United States, or in any way abridged, except for participation in rebellion, or other crime, the basis of representation therein shall be reduced in the proportion which

the number of such male citizens shall bear to the whole number of male citizens twenty-one years of age in such State.

Section 3. No person shall be a Senator or Representative in Congress, or elector of President and Vice President, or hold any office, civil or military, under the United States, or under any State, who, having previously taken an oath, as a member of Congress, or as an officer of the United States, or as a member of any State legislature, or as an executive or judicial officer of any State, to support the Constitution of the United States, shall have engaged in insurrection or rebellion against the same, or given aid or comfort to the enemies thereof. But Congress may by a vote of two-thirds of each house, remove such disability.

Section 4. The validity of the public debt of the United States, authorized by law, including debts incurred for payment of pensions and bounties for services in suppressing insurrection or rebellion, shall not be questioned. But neither the United States nor any State shall assume or pay any debt or obligation incurred in aid of insurrection or rebellion against the United States, or any claim for the loss or emancipation of any slave; but all such debts, obligations and claims shall be held illegal and void.

Section 5. The Congress shall have power to enforce, by appropriate legislation, the provisions of this article.

Article XV

Section 1. The right of citizens of the United States to vote shall not be denied or abridged by the United States or by any State on account of race, color, or previous condition of servitude.

Section 2. The Congress shall have power to enforce this article by appropriate legislation.

Article XVI

The Congress shall have power to lay and collect taxes on incomes, from whatever source derived,

United States

without apportionment among the several States, and without regard to any census or enumeration.

ARTICLE XVII

SECTION 1. The Senate of the United States shall be composed of two Senators from each State, elected by the people thereof, for six years; and each Senator shall have one vote. The electors in each State shall have the qualifications requisite for electors of the most numerous branch of the State legislatures.

SECTION 2. When vacancies happen in the representation of any State in the Senate, the executive authority of such State shall issue writs of election to fill such vacancies: *Provided,* that the legislature of any State may empower the executive thereof to make temporary appointments until the people fill the vacancies by election as the legislature may direct.

SECTION 3. This amendment shall not be so construed as to affect the election or term of any Senator chosen before it becomes valid as part of the Constitution.

ARTICLE XVIII

SECTION 1. After one year from the ratification of this article the manufacture, sale, or transportation of intoxicating liquors within, the importation thereof into, or the exportation thereof from the United States and all territory subject to the jurisdiction thereof for beverage purposes is hereby prohibited.

SECTION 2. The Congress and the several States shall have concurrent power to enforce this article by appropriate legislation.

SECTION 3. This article shall be inoperative unless it shall have been ratified as an amendment to the Constitution by the legislatures of the several States, as provided in the Constitution, within seven years from the date of the submission hereof to the States by the Congress.

ARTICLE XIX

SECTION 1. The right of citizens of the United States to vote shall not be denied or abridged by the United States or by any State on account of sex.

SECTION 2. Congress shall have power to enforce this article by appropriate legislation.

ARTICLE XX

SECTION 1. The terms of the President and Vice President shall end at noon on the 20th day of January, and the terms of Senators and Representatives at noon on the 3d day of January, of the years in which such terms would have ended if this article had not been ratified; and the terms of their successors shall then begin.

SECTION 2. The Congress shall assemble at least once in every year, and such meeting shall begin at noon on the 3d day of January, unless they shall by law appoint a different day.

SECTION 3. If, at the time fixed for the beginning of the term of the President, the President elect shall have died, the Vice President elect shall become President. If a President shall not have been chosen before the time fixed for the beginning of his term, or if the President elect shall have failed to qualify, then the Vice President elect shall act as President until a President shall have qualified; and the Congress may by law provide for the case wherein neither a President elect nor a Vice President elect shall have qualified, declaring who shall then act as President, or the manner in which one who is to act shall be selected, and such person shall act accordingly until a President or Vice President shall have qualified.

SECTION 4. The Congress may by law provide for the case of the death of any of the persons from whom the House of Representatives may choose a President whenever the right of choice shall have devolved upon them, and for the case of the death of any of the persons from whom the Senate may choose a Vice President whenever the right of choice shall have devolved upon them.

United States

SECTION 5. Sections 1 and 2 shall take effect on the 15th day of October following the ratification of this article.

SECTION 6. This article shall be inoperative unless it shall have been ratified as an amendment to the Constitution by the legislatures of three-fourths of the several States within seven years from the date of its submission.

ARTICLE XXI

SECTION 1. The eighteenth article of amendment to the Constitution of the United States is hereby repealed.

SECTION 2. The transportation or importation into any State, Territory, or possession of the United States for delivery or use therein of intoxicating liquors, in violation of the laws thereof, is hereby prohibited.

SECTION 3. This article shall be inoperative unless it shall have been ratified as an amendment to the Constitution by conventions in the several States, as provided in the Constitution, within seven years from the date of the submission hereof to the States by the Congress.

ARTICLE XXII

SECTION 1. No person shall be elected to the office of the President more than twice, and no person who has held the office of President, or acted as President, for more than two years of a term to which some other person was elected President shall be elected to the office of the President more than once. But this article shall not apply to any person holding the office of President when this article was proposed by the Congress, and shall not prevent any person who may be holding the office of President, or acting as President, during the term within which this article becomes operative from holding the office of President or acting as President during the remainder of such term.

SECTION 2. This article shall be inoperative unless it shall have been ratified as an amendment to the Constitution by the legislatures of three-fourths of the several States within seven years from the date of its submission to the States by the Congress.

ARTICLE XXIII

SECTION 1. The District constituting the seat of Government of the United States shall appoint in such manner as the Congress may direct:

A number of electors of President and Vice President equal to the whole number of Senators and Representatives in Congress to which the District would be entitled if it were a State, but in no event more than the least populous State; they shall be in addition to those appointed by the States, but they shall be considered, for the purposes of the election of President and Vice President, to be electors appointed by a State; and they shall meet in the District and perform such duties as provided by the twelfth article of amendment.

SECTION 2. The Congress shall have power to enforce this article by appropriate legislation.

Article XXIV

SECTION 1. The right of citizens of the United States to vote in any primary or other election for President or Vice President, for electors for President or Vice President, or for Senator or Representative in Congress, shall not be denied or abridged by the United States or any State by reason of failure to pay any poll tax or other tax.

SECTION 2. The Congress shall have power to enforce this article by appropriate legislation.

ARTICLE XXV

SECTION 1. In case of the removal of the President from office or of his death or resignation, the Vice President shall become President.

SECTION 2. Whenever there is a vacancy in the office of the Vice President, the President shall nominate a Vice President who shall take office upon confirmation by a majority vote of both Houses of Congress.

SECTION 3. Whenever the President transmits to the President pro tempore of the Senate and the Speaker of the House of Representatives his written declaration that he is unable to discharge the powers and duties of his office, and until he transmits to them a written declaration to the contrary, such powers and duties shall be discharged by the Vice President as Acting President.

SECTION 4. Whenever the Vice President and a majority of either the principal officers of the executive departments or of such other body as Congress may by law provide, transmit to the President pro tempore of the Senate and the Speaker of the House of Representatives their written declaration that the President is unable to discharge the powers and duties of his office, the Vice President shall immediately assume the powers and duties of the office as Acting President.

Thereafter, when the President transmits to the President pro tempore of the Senate and the Speaker of the House of Representatives his written declaration that no inability exists, he shall resume the powers and duties of his office unless the Vice President and a majority of either the principal officers of the executive department or of such other body as Congress may by law provide, transmit within four days to the President pro tempore of the Senate and the Speaker of the House of Representatives their written declaration that the President is unable to discharge the powers and duties of his office. Thereupon Congress shall decide the issue, assembling within forty-eight hours for that purpose if not in session. If the Congress, within twenty-one days after receipt of the latter written declaration, or, if Congress is not in session, within twenty-one days after Congress is required to assemble, determines by two-thirds vote of both Houses that the President is unable to discharge the powers and duties of his office, the Vice President shall continue to discharge the same as Acting President; otherwise, the President shall resume the powers and duties of his office.

ARTICLE XXVI

SECTION 1. The right of citizens of the United States who are eighteen years of age or older, to vote shall not be denied or abridged by the United States or by any State on account of age.

SECTION 2. The Congress shall have power to enforce this article by appropriate legislation.

THE MONROE DOCTRINE

In his message to Congress on December 2, 1823, President James Monroe established what has come to be known as the Monroe Doctrine, a statement of U.S. foreign policy that expresses opposition to the extension of European control or influence in the Western Hemisphere. Following is part of Monroe's message:

"In the discussions to which this interest has given rise, and in the arrangements by which they may terminate, the occasion has been deemed proper for asserting as a principle in which rights and interest of the United States are involved, that the American continents, by the free and independent condition which they have assumed and maintain, are henceforth not to be considered as subjects for future colonization by any European power. . . . We owe it, therefore, to candor and to the amicable relations existing between the United States and those powers to declare that we should consider any attempt on their part to extend their system to any portion of this hemisphere as dangerous to our peace and safety. With the existing colonies or dependencies of any European power we have not interfered and shall not interfere. But with the governments who have declared their independence and maintain it, and whose independence we have, on great consideration and on just principles, acknowledged, we could not view any interposition for the purpose of oppressing them or controlling in any other manner their destiny by any European power in any other light than as the manifestation of an unfriendly disposition toward the United States."

THE EMANCIPATION PROCLAMATION

President Abraham Lincoln first issued the Emancipation Proclamation, freeing the slaves, on September 22, 1862. The final proclamation was issued on January 1, 1863, as follows:

United States

By the President of the United
States of America:

A Proclamation.

Whereas on the 22d day of September, A.D. 1862, a proclamation was issued by the President of the United States, containing, among other things, the following, to wit:

"That on the 1st day of January, A.D. 1863, all persons held as slaves within any State or designated part of a State the people whereof shall then be in rebellion against the United States shall be then, thenceforward, and forever free; and the executive government of the United States, including the military and naval authority thereof, will recognize and maintain the freedom of such persons and will do no act or acts to repress such persons, or any of them, in any efforts they may make for their actual freedom.

"That the executive will on the 1st day of January aforesaid, by proclamation, designate the States and parts of States, if any, in which the people thereof, respectively, shall then be in rebellion against the United States; and the fact that any State or the people thereof shall on that day be in good faith represented in the Congress of the United States by members chosen thereto at elections wherein a majority of the qualified voters of such States shall have participated shall, in the absence of strong countervailing testimony, be deemed conclusive evidence that such State and the people thereof are not then in rebellion against the United States."

Now, therefore, I, Abraham Lincoln, President of the United States, by virtue of the power in me vested as Commander-in-Chief of the Army and Navy of the United States in time of actual armed rebellion against the authority and government of the United States, and as a fit and necessary war measure for suppressing said rebellion, do, on this 1st day of January, A.D. 1863, and in accordance with my purpose so to do, publicly proclaimed for the full period of one hundred days from the first day above mentioned, order and designate as the States and parts of States wherein the people thereof, respectively, are this day in rebellion against the United States the following, to wit:

Arkansas, Texas, Louisiana (except the parishes of St. Bernard, Plaquemines, Jefferson, St. John, St. Charles, St. James, Ascension, Assumption, Terrebonne, Lafourche, St. Mary, St. Martin, and Orleans, including the city of New Orleans), Mississippi, Alabama, Florida, Georgia, South Carolina, North Carolina, and Virginia (except the forty-eight counties designated as West Virginia, and also the counties of Berkeley, Accomac, Northampton, Elizabeth City, York, Princess Anne, and Norfolk, including the cities of Norfolk and Portsmouth), and which excepted parts are for the present left precisely as if this proclamation were not issued.

And by virtue of the power and for the purpose aforesaid, I do order and declare that all persons held as slaves within said designated States and parts of States are, and henceforward shall be, free; and that the Executive Government of the United States, including the military and naval authorities thereof, will recognize and maintain the freedom of said persons.

And I hereby enjoin upon the people so declared to be free to abstain from all violence, unless in necessary self-defense; and I recommend to them that, in all cases when allowed, they labor faithfully for reasonable wages.

And I further declare and make known that such persons of suitable condition will be received into the armed service of the United States to garrison forts, positions, stations, and other places, and to man vessels of all sorts in said service.

And upon this act, sincerely believe to be an act of justice, warranted by the Constitution upon military necessity, I invoke the considerate judgment of mankind and the gracious favor of Almighty God.

THE GETTYSBURG ADDRESS

On November 19, 1863, President Abraham Lincoln gave a speech at the ceremonies dedicating the battlefield of Gettysburg (in Pennsylvania) as a national cemetery for the soldiers who were killed in that Civil War battle. By then, he viewed the war as a fight not only to save the Union, but also to establish freedom and equality for all under the law. Attracting little attention at the time, the speech later came to be considered as one of the most memorable statements in democracy. The wording of the Nicolay draft (at the Library of Congress), thought to be the earliest copy of the speech that has survived, is as follows:

Four score and seven years ago our fathers brought forth, upon this continent, a new nation, conceived in liberty, and dedicated to the proposition that "all men are created equal"

Now we are engaged in a great civil war, testing whether that nation, or any nation so conceived, and so dedicated, can long endure. We are met on a great battle field of that war. We come to dedicate a portion of it, as a final resting place for those who died here, that the nation might live. This we may, in all propriety do. But, in a larger sense, we can not dedicate—we can not consecrate—we can not hallow, this ground—The brave men, living and dead, who struggled here, have hallowed it, far above our poor power to add or detract. The world will little note, nor long remember what we say here; while it can never forget what they did here.

It is rather for us, the living, we here be dedicated to the great task remaining before us—that, from these honored dead we take increased devotion to that cause for which they here, gave the last full measure of devotion—that we here highly resolve these dead shall not have died in vain; that the nation, shall have a new birth of freedom, and that government of the people for the people, shall not perish from the earth.

THE U.S. FLAG

Americans feel strongly about the U.S. flag. To many, it is the preeminent symbol of the freedom of the United States of America.

HISTORY

The "Stars and Stripes" as we know it today, with its blue field of 50 white stars and 13 red and white stripes representing the original 13 colonies, underwent several transformations.

The first flag raised in the United States was hoisted by John Cabot in 1497; it flew the banners of England and St. Mark. As settlers populated the colonies, each territory adopted its own flag. By 1707, each colony had its own flag, the forerunners of the individual state flags today. The first colonial flag representing all the colonies, however, was believed to have been raised on Prospect Hill in Boston at the Battle of Bunker Hill in 1775. The "Continental Colors" bore the cross of the British flag in the upper left corner with 13 alternating red and white stripes extending horizontally. In 1777, the first Continental Congress "Resolved, that the Flag of the United States be thirteen stripes alternate red and white, that the Union be thirteen stars white on a blue field, representing a constellation."

As the new Union grew, Congress voted in 1794 to add two stripes and two stars to represent the two new states of Vermont and Kentucky. This flag was flown at Fort McHenry, Maryland, during the War of 1812 and was the inspiration of Francis Scott Key's "Star-Spangled Banner." By 1818, five more states had joined, and on April 4, Congress voted to keep the number of stripes at 13 and to add a star to the field for every new state, the stars for the new states being added on July 4 after each state's admission to the Union.

The table on page 857 shows the order in which states joined the Union and the number of revisions the flag went through before arriving at its current design. *See also* "Admission of the 13 Original States" in this chapter.

THE PLEDGE OF ALLEGIANCE

"I pledge allegiance to the flag of the United States of America, and to the Republic for which it stands, one nation under God, indivisible, with liberty and justice for all."

THE U.S. FLAG: 1777–1960

Date Used	Number of Stars	Design Number	New States
June 14, 1777	13	1	Original 13 colonies
May 1, 1795	15	2	Vermont, Kentucky
July 4, 1818	20	3	Tennessee, Ohio, Louisiana, Indiana, Mississippi
July 4, 1819	21	4	Illinois
July 4, 1820	23	5	Alabama, Maine
July 4, 1822	24	6	Missouri
July 4, 1836	25	7	Arkansas
July 4, 1837	26	8	Michigan
July 4, 1845	27	9	Florida
July 4, 1846	28	10	Texas
July 4, 1847	29	11	Iowa
July 4, 1848	30	12	Wisconsin
July 4, 1851	31	13	California
July 4, 1858	32	14	Minnesota
July 4, 1859	33	15	Oregon
July 4, 1861	34	16	Kansas
July 4, 1863	35	17	West Virginia
July 4, 1865	36	18	Nevada
July 4, 1867	37	19	Nebraska
July 4, 1877	38	20	Colorado
July 4, 1890	43	21	North Dakota, South Dakota, Montana, Washington, Idaho
July 4, 1891	44	22	Wyoming
July 4, 1896	45	23	Utah
July 4, 1908	46	24	Oklahoma
July 4, 1912	48	25	New Mexico, Arizona
July 4, 1959	49	26	Alaska
July 4, 1960	50	27	Hawaii

The phrase "under God" was added to the pledge by an Act of Congress in 1954. The original pledge, written in 1892 by Francis Bellamy, contained the phrase "my flag."

CARE AND USE

Wherever and whenever it is displayed, the first requirement for flying the U.S. flag is that it be flown with respect. To show respect and honor to the symbol of the United States, fly it only in good weather, on all holidays and special occasions, and on official buildings such as schools when they are in session, post offices, courthouses, and the like. The flag generally is flown only from sunrise to sunset and at full staff. If it is displayed at night, it should be lit. Fly the flag at half-staff to commemorate the death of an official and until noon on Memorial Day.

When handling the flag, never let it touch the ground. Hoist the flag quickly and lower it ceremoniously to the tempo of "Taps." When it flies with other flags, it should appear prominently above them. The flag should be to its own right (to the left, viewed face-on) with its staff in front of the staff of the other flag when placed against a wall with another flag. In a group of flags, the U.S. flag should be at the center. (The flag of the United Nations and a navy chaplain's church pennant may be flown above the U.S. flag.)

If the flag is hung on a pole extending from a building, the union (the field of stars) should be away from the building; when the flag is hung over the center of a street, the union should be to the north in an east-west street and to the east in a north-south street.

On a platform, the flag may be hung flat against the wall behind and above the speaker with the field of stars to the audience's left. In a church or public auditorium, the flag on its staff should be to the Speaker's right as he or she faces the audience and all other flags to the speaker's left. If the flag is flown anywhere else in the chancel or on a platform, it should be to the right of the audience as they face the platform.

Salute when the flag passes in a parade or review, is being raised or lowered, is present at the playing of the national anthem, or is present at the saying of the Pledge of Allegiance.

Civilians should salute the flag by standing at attention and placing their right hands over their hearts. Men should remove their hats and hold them over their left shoulders with their right hand. Military personnel in uniform should give the military salute. Noncitizens should stand at attention.

The flag at the White House is flown only when the president is in residence and only from sunrise to sunset. At the Capitol building, the flag flies over the appropriate wing when the House or Senate is in session. The flag is flown all night long and is lit by lights from the Capitol dome. Other special national monuments also fly the flag at night, notably Fort McHenry National Monument in Baltimore, Maryland, where Francis Scott Key was inspired to write "The Star-Spangled Banner."

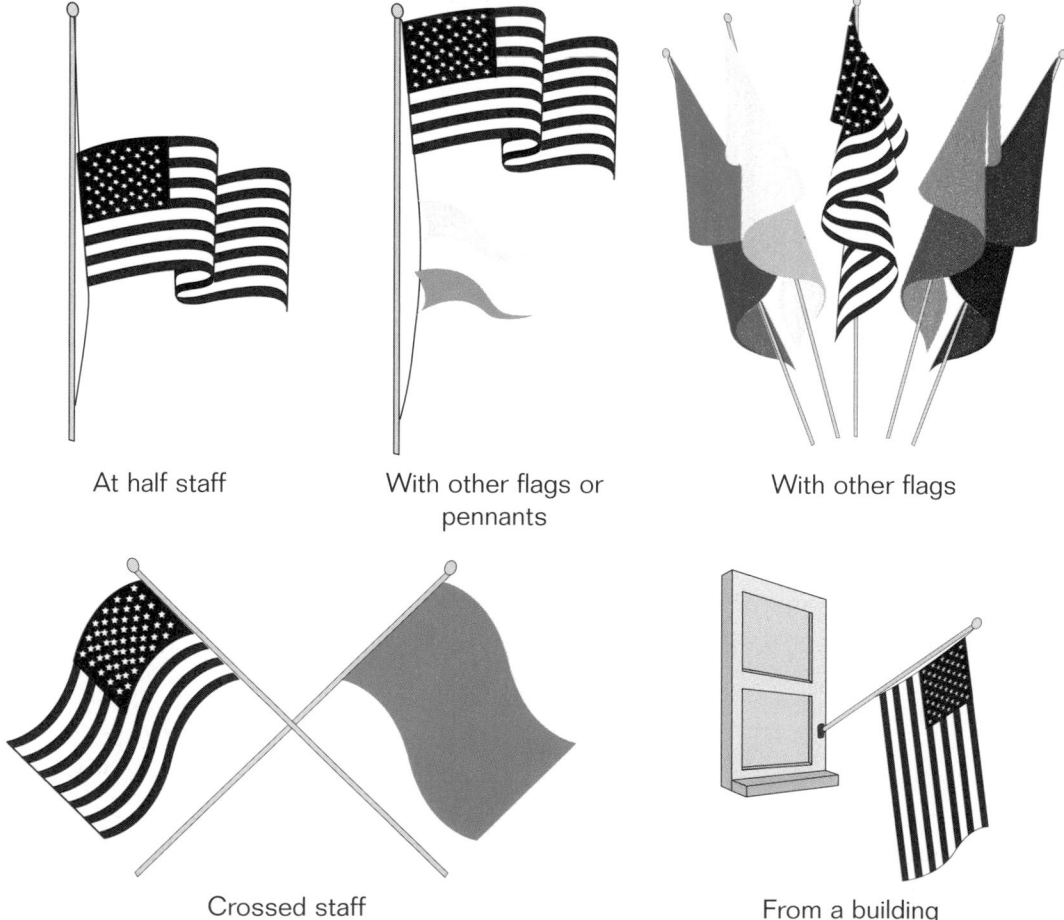

At half staff

With other flags or pennants

With other flags

Crossed staff

From a building

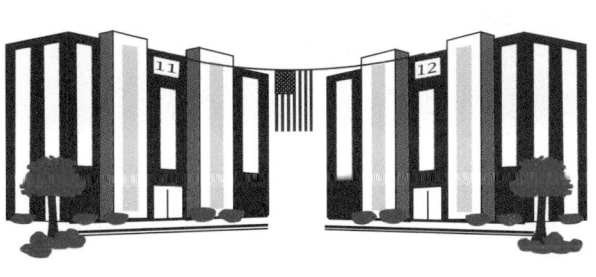

Over a street

On a platform

Against a wall

FEDERAL GOVERNMENT

The federal government has grown from tiny to tremendous over the past 220+ years. Its scope and responsibilities bring it into touch with every American's life.

FEDERAL GOVERNMENT STRUCTURE

The chart on page 860 shows the structure of the U.S. government and its departments and agencies as of October 15, 1996. As the chart shows, the Constitution set forth the organization of the government, which operates on a system of checks and balances. The three branches of government—legislative, executive, and judicial—each have the power to check the others. The legislative branch, the Congress, has the power to propose and make laws; the executive branch contains the office of the president, who has the ultimate power to enforce the law and oversee the government; and the judicial branch explains the law by ruling on the constitutionality of laws and trying cases.

Croatia was the first country to recognize the United States as an independent country in 1776.

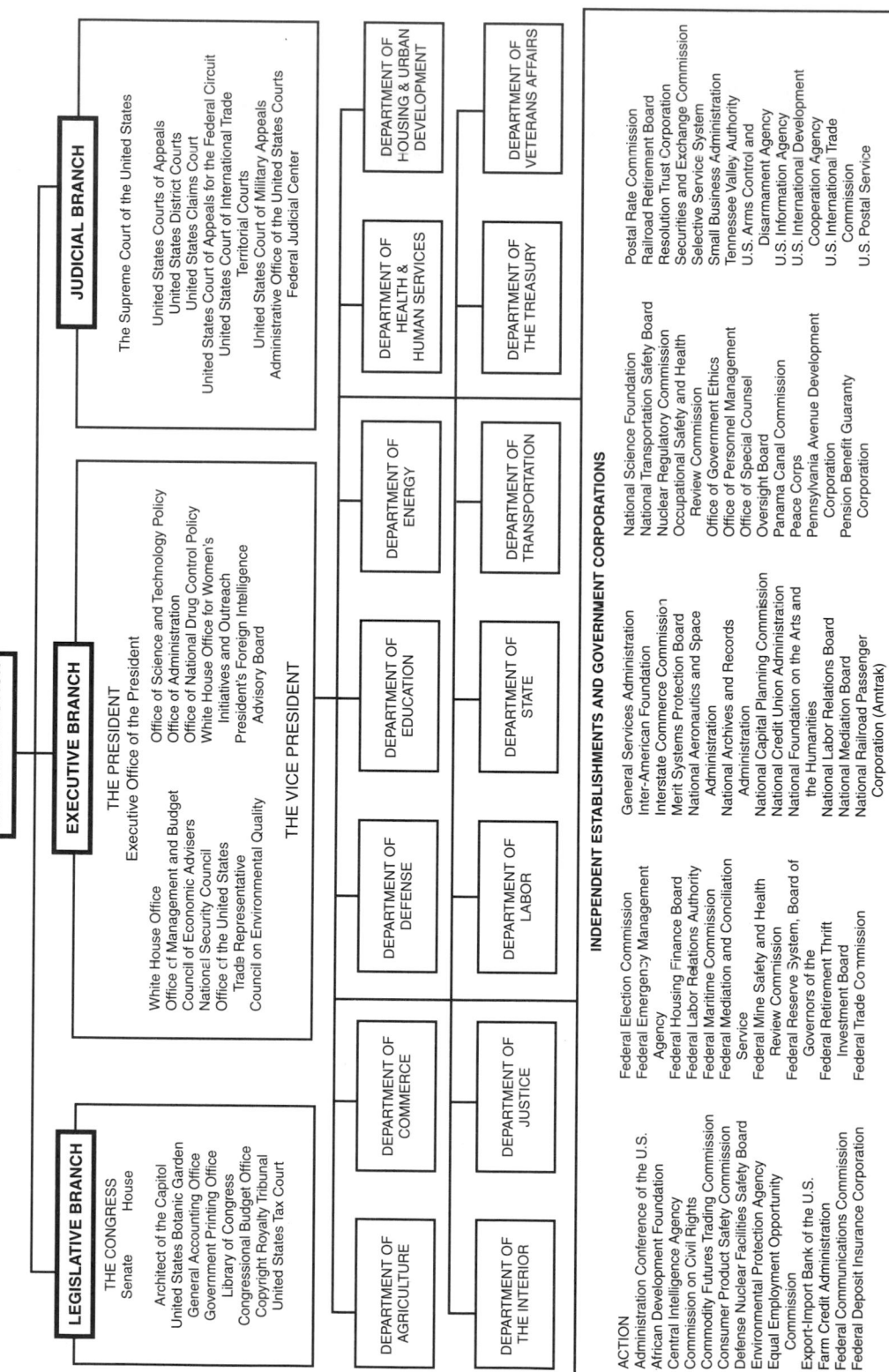

Federal Government Structure

PRESIDENTS AND VICE PRESIDENTS OF THE UNITED STATES

President	Term	Year of Birth–Death	Party	Vice President	Year of Birth–Death	Congresses
1. George Washington	4/30/1789–3/3/1797	1732–1799	F	John Adams	1735–1826	1, 2, 3, 4
2. John Adams	3/4/1797–3/3/1801	1735–1826	F	Thomas Jefferson	1743–1826	5, 6
3. Thomas Jefferson	3/4/1801–3/3/1805	1743–1826	D-R	Aaron Burr	1756–1836	7, 8
	3/4/1805–3/3/1809			George Clinton	1739–1812	9, 10
4. James Madison	3/4/1809–3/3/1813	1751–1836	D-R	George Clinton	1739–1812	11, 12
	3/4/1813–3/3/1817			Elbridge Gerry	1744–1814	13, 14
5. James Monroe	3/4/1817–3/3/1825	1758–1835	D-R	Daniel D. Tompkins	1774–1825	15, 16, 17, 18
6. John Quincy Adams	3/4/1825–3/3/1829	1767–1848	D-R	John C. Calhoun	1782–1850	19, 20
7. Andrew Jackson	3/4/1829–3/3/1833	1767–1845	D	John C. Calhoun	1782–1850	21, 22
	3/4/1833–3/3/1837			Martin Van Buren	1782–1862	23, 24
8. Martin Van Buren	3/4/1837–3/3/1841	1782–1862	D	Richard M. Johnson	1780–1850	25, 26
9. William Henry Harrison	3/4/1841–4/4/1841	1773–1841	W	John Tyler	1790–1862	27
10. John Tyler	4/6/1841–3/3/1845	1790–1862	W	—	—	27, 28
11. James K. Polk	3/4/1845–3/3/1849	1795–1849	D	George M. Dallas	1792–1864	29, 30
12. Zachary Taylor	3/4/1849–7/9/1850	1784–1850	W	Millard Fillmore	1800–1874	31
13. Millard Fillmore	7/10/1850–3/3/1853	1800–1874	W	—	—	31, 32
14. Franklin Pierce	3/4/1853–3/3/1857	1804–1869	D	William R. King	1786–1853	33, 34
15. James Buchanan	3/4/1857–3/3/1861	1791–1868	D	John C. Breckinridge	1821–1875	35, 36
16. Abraham Lincoln	3/4/1861–3/3/1865	1809–1865	R	Hannibal Hamlin	1809–1891	37, 38
	3/4/1865–4/15/1865			Andrew Johnson	1808–1875	39
17. Andrew Johnson	4/15/1865–3/3/1869	1808–1875	NU	—	—	39, 40
18. Ulysses S. Grant	3/4/1869–3/3/1873	1822–1885	R	Schuyler Colfax	1823–1885	41, 42
	3/4/1873–3/3/1877			Henry Wilson	1812–1875	43, 44
19. Rutherford B. Hayes	3/4/1877–3/3/1881	1822–1893	R	William A. Wheeler	1819–1887	45, 46
20. James Garfield	3/4/1881–9/19/1881	1831–1881	R	Chester A. Arthur	1829–1886	47
21. Chester A. Arthur	9/20/1881–3/3/1885	1829–1886	R	—	—	47, 48
22. Grover Cleveland	3/4/1885–3/3/1889	1837–1908	D	Thomas A. Hendricks	1819–1885	49, 50
23. Benjamin Harrison	3/4/1889–3/3/1893	1833–1901	R	Levi P. Morton	1824–1920	51, 52
24. Grover Cleveland	3/4/1893–3/3/1897	1837–1908	D	Adlai E. Stevenson	1835–1914	53, 54
25. William McKinley	3/4/1897–3/3/1901	1843–1901	R	Garret A. Hobart	1844–1899	55, 56
	3/4/1901–9/14/1901			Theodore Roosevelt	1858–1919	57
26. Theodore Roosevelt	9/14/1901–3/3/1905	1858–1919	R	—	—	57, 58
	3/4/1905–3/3/1909			Charles W. Fairbanks	1852–1918	59, 60
27. William H. Taft	3/4/1909–3/3/1913	1857–1930	R	James S. Sherman	1855–1912	61, 62
28. Woodrow Wilson	3/4/1913–3/3/1921	1856–1924	D	Thomas R. Marshall	1854–1925	63, 64, 65, 66
29. Warren G. Harding	3/4/1921–8/2/1923	1865–1923	R	Calvin Coolidge	1872–1933	67, 68
30. Calvin Coolidge	8/3/1923–3/3/1925	1872–1933	R	—	—	68
	3/4/1925–3/3/1929			Charles G. Dawes	1865–1951	69, 70
31. Herbert C. Hoover	3/4/1929–3/3/1933	1874–1964	R	Charles Curtis	1860–1936	71, 72
32. Franklin D. Roosevelt	3/4/1933–1/20/1941	1882–1945	D	John N. Garner	1868–1967	73, 74, 75, 76
	1/20/1941–1/20/1945			Henry A. Wallace	1888–1965	77, 78
	1/20/1945–4/12/1945			Harry S Truman	1884–1972	79
33. Harry S Truman	4/12/1945–1/20/1949	1884–1972	D	—	—	79, 80
	1/20/1949–1/20/1953			Alben W. Barkley	1877–1956	81, 82
34. Dwight D. Eisenhower	1/20/1953–1/20/1961	1890–1969	R	Richard M. Nixon	1913–1994	83, 84, 85, 86
35. John F. Kennedy	1/20/1961–11/22/1963	1917–1963	D	Lyndon B. Johnson	1908–1973	87, 88

F = Federalist; D-R = Democratic-Republican; D = Democrat; W = Whig; R = Republican; NU = National Union Party, a coalition of Republicans and War Democrats (Andrew Johnson was a Democrat).

United States

Presidents and Vice Presidents, Continued

President	Term	Year of Birth–Death	Party	Vice President	Year of Birth–Death	Congresses
36. Lyndon B. Johnson	11/22/1963–1/20/1965	1908–1973	D	—	—	88
	1/20/1965–1/20/1969			Hubert H. Humphrey	1911–1978	89, 90
37. Richard M. Nixon	1/20/1969–1/20/1973	1913–1994	R	Spiro T. Agnew	1918–1996	91, 92
	1/20/1973–8/9/1974			Spiro T. Agnew*	1913–	93
				Gerald R. Ford		
38. Gerald R. Ford	8/9/1974–1/20/1977	1913–	R	Nelson A. Rockefeller	1908–1979	93, 94
39. James (Jimmy) Carter	1/20/1977–1/20/1981	1924–	D	Walter F. Mondale	1928–	95, 96
40. Ronald Reagan	1/20/1981–1/20/1989	1911–	R	George Bush	1924–	97, 98, 99, 100
41. George Bush	1/20/1989–1/20/1993	1924–	R	J. Danforth Quayle	1947–	101, 102
42. William Clinton	1/20/1993–	1946–	D	Albert A. Gore, Jr.	1948–	103, 104, 105

* Spiro T. Agnew resigned on October 10, 1973. Gerald R. Ford was inaugurated December 6, 1973.

A Closer Look

The Sequence of Presidential Succession

1. Vice President
2. Speaker of the House
3. President Pro Tempore of the Senate
4. Secretary of State
5. Secretary of the Treasury
6. Secretary of Defense
7. Attorney General
8. Secretary of the Interior
9. Secretary of Agriculture
10. Secretary of Commerce
11. Secretary of Labor
12. Secretary of Health and Human Services
13. Secretary of Housing and Urban Development
14. Secretary of Transportation
15. Secretary of Energy
16. Secretary of Education

Any successor to the presidency must meet the requirements for the office as established in the Constitution.

WHERE TO WRITE YOUR SENATORS AND REPRESENTATIVES

Constituents can write to their senators and representatives at the following addresses:

Senator's name
United States Senate
Washington, DC 20510

Representative's name
United States House of Representatives
Washington, DC 20515

Listings of specific addresses of members of Congress are in the more current edition of *The Congressional Staff Directory* or *Congressional Quarterly's Washington Directory,* both of which are available in local libraries. These books also list the home offices of members of Congress. Local telephone directories may also be consulted.

Both the Senate and House have offices in the Capitol Building, but additional offices are housed at the following buildings:

SENATE OFFICES

Dirksen Senate Office Building
Constitution Avenue between 1st and 2nd sts., NE

Hart Senate Office Building
2nd Street and Constitution Avenue, NE

Russell Senate Office Building
Constitution Avenue between Delaware Avenue and 1st Street, NE

HOUSE OFFICES

Cannon House Office Building
Independence Avenue between C and 1st sts., SE

Longworth House Office Building
Independence Avenue between C and South Capitol sts., SE

Rayburn House Office Building
Independence Avenue between South Capitol and 1st sts., SE

Go to "Business Protocols and Forms of Address" in chapter 15

The Electoral College

A Closer Look

The president and vice president of the United States are elected not by popular vote, but by the Electoral College, as stipulated in Article II, Section 1, of the U.S. Constitution. On Election Day, each state selects a number of electors equal to that of its U.S. senators and representatives; these electors are all affiliated with the party that has received the highest popular vote in the state. Including the District of Columbia's three electoral votes, the total is 538, with a majority of 270 votes needed to win. The votes are counted in a joint session of Congress on January 6. If no candidate for president has won a majority, the House selects one of the three leading candidates, with all members from a state voting in a bloc; if no vice presidential candidate has a majority, the Senate, voting as individuals, choose one from the top two candidates.

In three presidential elections, the winners of the largest number of popular votes failed to win the presidency:

1824 None of the four candidates—William Crawford, Andrew Jackson, John Quincy Adams, and Henry Clay—received a majority of the electoral votes. The House of Representatives chose John Quincy Adams to be president. John C. Calhoun was chosen vice president by the Electoral College.

1876 Democratic presidential nominee Samuel Tilden and vice presidential nominee Thomas A. Hendricks led their Republican counterparts Rutherford B. Hayes and William A. Wheeler in popular votes (4,284,020 to 4,036,572) and electoral votes (184 to 165). But a controversy raged over 20 unassigned electoral votes. To resolve contradictions between two sets of election returns, one each from the Democrats and the Republicans, Congress established a commission of five senators, five congressmen, and five Supreme Court justices, whose verdict could be overturned only if both the House and Senate disputed it. The commission, which consisted of eight Republicans and seven Democrats, gave the Republicans all of the disputed votes; while the House voted against the decision, the Senate upheld it, bringing Hayes and Wheeler into office.

1888 The Democratic nominees were Grover Cleveland and Allen G. Thurman; the Republican candidates were Benjamin Harrison and Levi P. Morton. While Cleveland led Harrison 5,540,050 to 5,444,337 in popular votes, Harrison was ahead in electoral votes, 233 to 168, and won the election.

COMMON LEGISLATIVE TERMS

Many terms below are defined in the context of the U.S. Congress. Some of the terms may be applicable as well, with some variation, to state legislatures.

act A bill that has been approved by both the Senate and the House of Representatives and has been signed by the president or passed over his veto, thus becoming law. Acts are sometimes reviewed by the Supreme Court to determine their constitutionality.

amendment A change or revision in the wording of a pending bill or other measure by striking out existing language, by inserting new language, or both.

appropriate act A legislative act authorizing the expenditure of federal funds for a specific purpose or purposes.

bill A measure proposing legislation to create a new act or to amend or repeal existing law.

budget A statement of future federal government expenses and revenues initially formulated by the president and the executive branch. Congress considers the proposed budget in a series of appropriation acts initially introduced in the House of Representatives.

caucus An informal group of legislators that exists to promote issues of common interest (based, for example, on regional, political, ideological, ethnic, or economic concerns) and that possibly shares research staff.

cloture A parliamentary maneuver in the Senate to force the end of a filibuster, thus permitting a measure, amendment, or motion to come to a vote. Cloture, which limits consideration of a pending matter to an additional 30 hours, can be invoked only by an affirmative vote of three-fifths (normally 60 members) of the full Senate.

coalition   A combination of individuals or parties, usually needed to gain a majority vote.

committee of the whole   The legislative forum in which the entire membership of the House of Representatives meets under special rules of procedure (most notably limiting individual debate to five minutes instead of the usual hour) in order to expedite their deliberations on certain categories of legislation.

committee   A legislative group in either house of Congress that considers bills, resolutions, and other legislative matters over which the committee has jurisdiction. Committees are fact-finding bodies that hold hearings and listen to witnesses as well as investigate and debate issues, and then prepare a piece of legislation or a bill to present to the whole body for debate. *See also* **conference committee; joint committee; standing committee.**

conference committee   A temporary group of members of both houses of Congress assigned to reconcile differing versions of the same bill passed in the House and Senate. *See also* **joint committee.**

Only two people signed the Declaration of Independence on July 4: John Hancock and Charles Thomson. Most of the rest signed on August 2. The last signature was added five years later.

Congressional Record   A substantially verbatim account of the daily proceedings of Congress, kept since 1873.

deficit   The amount by which expenditures (outlays) exceed revenues (receipts) in a given fiscal period. Deficit spending occurs when the government borrows money to cover the difference between income and spending. *See also* **surplus.**

filibuster   A procedural strategy by which a Senator controls the floor and debates a bill at length in order to block or delay Senate action on it. *See also* **cloture.**

impeachment   The formal presentation of charges against a public official accused of misconduct in order to bring about his or her trial and removal from office, if convicted. The House of Representatives can vote for impeachment of federal officials; the Senate is responsible for trying them.

initiative   The procedure by which voters petition a state legislature for a new law. Typically, the legislature rejects the initiative and puts it out to a referendum by the voters. *See also* **referendum.**

joint committee   A committee that includes members of both the Senate and the House and that can publish studies and background reports within its specified jurisdictions, but normally lacks authority to report legislation.

line-item veto   The power of a chief executive to veto particular parts of a bill rather than reject the bill as a whole.

lobbyist   A person representing a special interest who seeks to influence lawmakers or a regulatory agency by pressing the views of a group, organization, or industry on issues under consideration.

majority leader   The leader of the party holding the majority of members in the House or Senate. The majority leader plans strategy, guides debate, maintains party discipline, and speaks for the party either in support of or criticism of the president. The Senate majority leader also leads the Senate as a whole and must negotiate the agenda with the minority party.

majority party   The party holding the majority of the seats in a legislative body.

mandate   A vote of confidence from the people, often used loosely to indicate broad support for a party's policy initiative.

minority leader   The leader of the party holding a minority of seats in a legislative body, who serves as the party's principal spokesperson and strategist.

minority party   The party holding a minority of seats in a legislative body.

override   Congress's negation of a president's vote by voting for a bill with a two-thirds majority.

pocket veto   The indirect veto of a bill by the president. A pocket veto occurs when the president has not signed a bill within 10 days of its presentation to him and Congress has adjourned within those 10 days.

political action committee (PAC)   A group formed outside of political parties in order to raise money for donation to lawmakers who support the group's policies and aims.

president pro tempore   The constitutionally recognized officer of the Senate who presides over the chamber when the vice president of the United States, who also functions as president of the Senate, is absent. Normally, however, the president pro tempore appoints a succession of other senators to serve as the presiding officer.

quorum   A predetermined minimum number of members of a legislative assembly who must be present in order for the assembly to conduct business.

reapportionment   A change or adjustment in the size or boundaries of legislative districts based on population increases or decreases.

recall   A special popular vote held in order to consider removing an elected official before he or she has completed his or her term of office.

referendum   A legislative issue on which voters can vote directly, usually at the time of an election. *See also* **initiative.**

representative   Any elected official who represents voters in a legislative body; the term most often refers to a member of the House of Representatives, the lower house of Congress. States elect differing numbers of representatives to Congress, depending on their population as determined by the federal census. Representatives serve two-year terms.

rider   An attempt to secure passage of a controversial proposal by attaching it as an amendment to a nonrelated bill whose passage is otherwise considered essential.

senator   A member of the Senate, the upper house of Congress. Each state elects two senators, who serve overlapping terms of six years.

Speaker of the House   The presiding officer in the House, elected by the consensus of the majority party.

standing committee   A permanent committee in either the House or the Senate that is assigned jurisdiction over particular issues.

surplus   The amount by which revenues (receipts) exceed expenditures (outlays) in a given fiscal period. *See also* **deficit.**

veto   The power given to the president under the Constitution to refuse to sign a bill and so prevent it from becoming law. The president may return it to the Congress with notes on his objections. *See also* **line-item veto; override; pocket veto.**

whip   An elected representative who serves as an assistant to the majority or minority leader and who is responsible for gathering members of his or her party and making sure they are present when a crucial partisan vote occurs.

HOW A BILL BECOMES LAW
FIRST READING

To become law, a bill is introduced by a senator or representative in the Senate or Congress and is assigned a number or title by the clerk of the House. The bill is then assigned to the committee of the Senate or House that is responsible for the particular area the bill relates to (for example, a bill providing aid to farmers would go to the Committee on Agriculture). The committee debates the bill, listens to the opinions of interested people and members of the Congress, and sometimes offers amendments to the bill. The bill is then voted on by the committee and, if passed, is sent back to the clerk of the House. If the bill is unacceptable to the committee when they receive it, they may table it, killing consideration of the bill. This process is called the first reading of the bill.

SECOND AND THIRD READINGS

In the second reading, the clerk of the House reads the bill to the House, which then debates it and suggests amendments. At the third reading, after the bill is debated, a vote is called for and the title of the bill is read before the vote.

Only three women have appeared on U.S. currency: Martha Washington, Pocahontas, and Susan B. Anthony.

PASSAGE

If the bill passes, it is sent to the other house, where it is again debated, amendments are added, and a vote is taken. If it passes with amendments, a joint congressional committee (composed of members of both the House and the Senate) tries to reach a compromise between the two versions of the bill. If not passed by the second house, the bill dies.

PRESIDENTIAL ACTION

When the bill is passed, it is sent to the president. If he signs it, it becomes law. If he holds the bill for 10 days (not including Sundays), it automatically becomes law without his signature, unless Congress has adjourned during that time, in which case the bill is automatically killed in a process known as a *pocket veto*. If the president disapproves of the bill, he vetoes it, sending it back to the house that originally produced it, along with his objections.

Once back in the house, the bill is debated again in light of the president's comments and a roll-call vote is taken. To remain an active bill, it must receive at least a two-thirds vote from that house. If it does not, it is defeated. If the bill does get the support of two-thirds of that house, it is sent to the other house, where it again must receive a vote of two-thirds to override a presidential veto.

FINANCES

FEDERAL RECEIPTS, BY SOURCE: FISCAL YEARS 1980–1996

Figures are given in millions of dollars.

SOURCE	1980	1990	1992	1993	1994	1995	1996, est.
Total Receipts	517,112	1,031,321	1,090,453	1,153,535	1,257,737	1,355,213	1,426,775
Individual income taxes	244,069	466,884	475,964	509,680	543,055	590,244	630,873
Corporation income taxes	64,600	93,507	100,270	117,520	140,385	157,004	167,108
Social insurance	157,803	380,047	413,689	428,300	461,475	484,473	507,535
Employment taxes and contributions	138,748	353,891	385,491	396,939	428,810	451,045	473,186
Old-age and survivors insurance	96,581	255,031	273,137	281,735	302,607	284,091	311,713
Disability insurance	16,628	26,625	29,289	30,199	32,419	66,988	55,728
Hospital insurance	23,217	68,556	79,108	81,224	90,062	96,024	101,848
Railroad retirement/pension fund	2,323	2,292	2,449	2,367	2,323	2,424	2,399
Railroad social security equivalent account	—	1,387	1,508	1,414	1,399	1,518	1,498
Unemployment insurance	15,336	21,635	23,410	26,556	28,004	28,878	29,810
Other retirement contributions	3,719	4,522	4,788	4,805	4,661	4,550	4,539
Excise taxes[1]	24,329	35,345	45,569	48,057	55,225	57,484	53,886
Federal funds	15,563	15,591	21,836	24,522	31,226	26,941	25,412
Alcohol	5,601	5,695	8,011	7,583	7,539	7,216	7,189
Tobacco	2,443	4,081	5,049	5,875	5,691	5,878	5,872
Ozone depletion	—	360	637	854	761	616	205

United States

SOURCE	1980	1990	1992	1993	1994	1995	1996, est.
Excise taxes[1], *cont.*							
Trust funds	8,766	19,754	23,733	23,535	23,999	30,543	28,474
Highways	6,620	13,867	16,733	18,039	16,668	22,611	24,554
Airport and airway	1,874	3,700	4,645	3,262	5,189	5,534	2,281
Black lung disability	272	665	626	634	567	608	620
Hazardous substance response	—	818	818	826	807	867	363
Aquatic resources	—	218	271	276	301	306	320
Leaking underground storage	—	122	157	153	152	165	54
Vaccine injury compensations	—	159	118	38	179	138	123
Oil spill liability	—	143	295	229	48	211	34
Estate and gift taxes	6,389	11,500	11,143	12,557	15,225	14,763	15,924
Customs duties	7,174	16,707	17,359	18,802	20,099	19,301	19,313
Federal Reserve deposits	11,767	24,319	22,920	14,908	18,023	23,378	23,752

— Represents or rounds to zero. [1] Totals reflect interfund and intragovernmental transactions and/or other functions, not shown separately.

FEDERAL OUTLAYS, BY BRANCH AND DETAILED FUNCTION: FISCAL YEARS 1990–1996

Figures are given in millions of dollars; outlays stated in terms of checks issued or cash payments.

Branch and Function	1990	1992	1993	1994	1995	1996, est.
Total Outlays	1,252,515	1,380,856	1,408,675	1,460,841	1,519,133	1,572,411
Legislative branch	2,241	2,677	2,406	2,552	2,625	2,695
The Judiciary	1,646	2,308	2,628	2,677	2,910	3,297
Funds appropriated to President[1]	10,087	11,113	11,526	10,511	11,161	10,445
Departments:						
Agriculture	46,012	56,437	63,144	60,753	56,665	54,840
Commerce	3,734	2,567	2,798	2,915	3,401	3,789
Defense—Military	289,755	286,632	278,574	268,646	259,556	254,325
Defense—Civil	24,975	28,270	29,266	30,407	31,669	32,255
Education	23,109	26,047	30,290	24,699	31,332	30,404
Energy	12,084	15,523	16,972	17,839	17,617	14,678
Health and Human Services	175,531	231,560	253,835	278,901	303,081	327,429
Housing and Urban Development	20,167	24,470	25,181	25,845	29,044	26,432
Interior	5,790	6,539	6,784	6,900	7,405	6,939
Justice	6,507	9,802	10,170	10,005	10,788	12,964
Labor[2]	25,215	47,078	44,651	37,047	32,090	34,404
State	3,979	5,007	5,384	5,718	5,344	5,500
Transportation	28,650	32,491	34,457	37,228	38,777	38,994
Treasury	255,172	292,987	298,804	307,577	348,579	364,956
Veterans Affairs	28,998	33,897	35,487	37,401	37,771	37,606
Independent agencies:						
Environmental Protection Agency	5,108	5,950	5,930	5,855	6,351	6,329
General Services Administration	−123	469	743	334	707	469
NASA[3]	12,429	13,961	14,305	13,695	13,378	14,190
Office of Personnel Management	31,949	35,596	36,794	38,596	41,276	42,374
Small Business Administration	692	546	785	779	677	957
Other independent agencies	72,808	18,007	−11,428	10,281	4,199	9,503
Undistributed offsetting receipts	−98,930	−117,111	−119,711	−123,469	−137,628	−139,866

[1] Represents international affair funds mainly. [2] Includes Pension Benefit Guaranty Corporation.
[3] National Aeronautics and Space Administration.

continues

United States

Federal Outlays Continued

Branch and Function	1990	1992	1993	1994	1995	1996, est.
Outlays, by Function	1,252,515	1,380,856	1,408,675	1,460,841	1,519,133	1,572,411
National defense	299,331	298,350	291,086	281,642	272,066	265,556
Dept. of Defense—Military	289,755	286,892	278,561	268,622	259,442	254,258
Military personnel	75,622	81,171	75,904	73,137	70,809	67,449
Operation and maintenance	88,340	91,984	94,094	87,880	90,881	91,690
Procurement	80,972	74,881	69,936	61,769	54,982	48,131
R and D, test, and evaluation	37,458	34,632	36,968	34,762	34,594	34,434
Military construction	5,080	4,262	4,831	4,979	6,823	6,524
Family housing	3,501	3,271	3,255	3,316	3,571	4,028
Other	−1,218	−3,308	−6,428	2,779	−2,218	2,002
Atomic energy defense activities	8,988	10,619	11,017	11,892	11,777	10,245
Defense related activities	587	839	1,508	1,128	847	1,053
International affairs	13,764	16,107	17,248	17,083	16,434	14,830
International development and humanitarian assistance	5,498	6,133	5,827	7,049	7,599	6,895
Conduct of foreign affairs	3,050	3,894	4,325	4,557	4,192	4,138
Other	72,808	18,007	−11,428	10,281	4,199	9,503
Income security	147,022	196,948	207,250	214,031	220,449	228,342
General retirement and disability insurance	5,148	5,483	4,347	5,720	5,106	4,943
Federal employee retirement and disability	51,983	57,572	60,047	62,487	65,834	67,936
Housing assistance	15,891	18,904	21,542	23,884	27,524	26,573
Food and nutrition assistance	23,964	32,622	35,148	36,773	37,594	39,034
Other income security	31,146	42,901	48,366	56,439	60,753	63,840
Unemployment compensation	18,889	39,466	37,802	28,729	23,638	25,986
Health	57,716	89,497	99,415	107,122	115,418	121,211
Health-care services	47,642	77,719	86,860	94,259	101,931	107,686
Health research	8,611	10,021	10,794	11,000	11,569	11,533
Consumer and occupational health and safety	1,462	1,757	1,762	1,863	1,918	1,992
Medicare	98,102	119,024	130,552	144,747	159,855	177,586
Social Security	248,623	287,585	304,585	319,565	335,846	350,924
Veterans benefits and services	29,112	34,138	35,720	37,642	37,938	37,748
Income security for veterans	15,241	17,296	17,758	19,613	18,966	18,121
Educ., training, and rehab.	278	783	826	1,115	1,124	1,117
Hospital and medical care	12,134	14,091	14,812	15,678	16,428	17,081
Housing for veterans	517	901	1,299	197	329	284
Other	943	1,067	1,025	1,039	1,091	1,145
Education, training, employment, and social services	38,755	45,248	50,012	46,307	54,263	54,131
Elementary, secondary, and vocational education	9,918	12,402	13,481	14,258	14,694	16,002
Higher education	11,107	11,268	14,483	7,876	14,172	11,440
Research and general educ. aids	1,577	1,996	2,040	2,086	2,120	2,269
Training and employment	5,619	6,479	6,700	7,097	7,430	7,617
Other labor services	810	884	948	958	965	962
Social services	9,723	12,219	12,360	14,031	14,882	15,841

Branch and Function	1990	1992	1993	1994	1995	1996, est.
Commerce and housing credit	66,952	10,093	−22,719	−5,118	−14,441	−10,744
Mortgage credit	3,845	4,320	1,554	−501	−1,038	−3,999
Postal service	2,116	1,169	1,602	1,233	−1,839	−189
Deposit insurance	57,891	2,518	−27,957	−7,570	−17,827	−13,465
Other commerce	3,100	2,085	2,083	1,719	6,263	6,909
Transportation	29,485	33,333	35,004	38,066	39,350	39,769
Ground transportation	18,954	20,347	21,251	23,940	25,297	26,124
Air transportation	7,234	9,313	10,049	10,146	10,020	9,865
Water transportation	3,151	3,430	3,423	3,648	3,732	3,471
Other transportation	146	244	281	333	301	309
Natural resources and environment	17,080	20,025	20,239	21,064	22,105	21,550
Water resources	4,401	4,559	4,258	4,528	4,791	4,729
Conservation and land management	3,553	4,581	4,777	5,161	5,318	4,876
Recreational resources	1,876	2,378	2,620	2,619	2,828	2,568
Pollution control and abatement	5,170	6,075	6,061	6,050	6,512	6,517
Other natural resources	2,080	2,432	2,522	2,706	2,656	2,860
Energy	3,341	4,500	4,319	5,219	4,936	3,217
Supply	1,976	3,226	3,286	3,899	3,584	2,009
Conservation	365	468	521	582	671	681
Emergency preparedness	442	319	336	275	223	171
Information, policy, and regs	559	486	176	462	458	356
Community/regional develop	8,498	6,838	9,052	10,454	10,641	12,878
Community development	3,530	3,643	3,681	4,133	4,744	5,519
Area and regional development	2,868	2,315	2,443	2,166	2,615	2,689
Disaster relief and insurance	2,100	881	2,928	4,156	3,282	4,670
Agriculture	11,958	15,205	20,490	15,046	9,773	7,718
Farm income stabilization	9,761	12,666	17,847	12,350	7,015	4,987
Research and services	2,197	2,539	2,643	2,695	2,758	2,731
Net interest	184,221	199,421	198,811	202,957	232,173	241,059
On-budget	*200,212*	*223,059*	*225,599*	*232,160*	*265,478*	*277,499*
Off-budget	*−15,991*	*−23,637*	*−26,788*	*−29,203*	*−33,305*	*−36,440*
Interest on the public debt	264,724	292,323	292,502	296,278	332,414	344,628
Interest received by on-budget trust funds	−46,321	−54,193	−55,537	−56,494	−59,867	−61,158
Interest received by off-budget trust funds	−15,991	−23,637	−26,788	−29,203	−33,305	−36,440
Other interest	−18,191	−15,071	−11,367	−7,623	−7,069	−5,971
General science/space/technology	14,444	16,409	17,030	16,227	16,724	16,877
Gen. science and basic research	2,835	3,571	3,938	3,863	4,131	3,978
General government	10,734	12,990	13,009	11,303	13,835	13,590
Legislative functions	1,763	2,124	2,124	2,042	1,995	2,066
Exec. direction and management	160	188	197	244	248	295
Central fiscal operations	6,004	6,612	6,976	7,417	7,936	7,576
General property and records management	31	692	1,005	590	920	661
General-purpose fiscal assistance	2,161	1,865	1,935	1,899	2,057	2,096
Other general government	792	1,775	1,321	987	1,630	1,600
Deductions, offsetting receipts	−361	−480	−739	−2,087	−1,077	−854

continues

Federal Outlays Continued

Branch and Function	1990	1992	1993	1994	1995	1996, est.
Administration of justice	9,993	14,426	14,955	15,256	16,23	18,764
Federal law enforcement	4,648	6,462	6,674	6,624	6,384	7,475
Federal litigative and judicial	3,577	5,054	5,336	5,470	6,123	6,368
Federal correctional activities	1,291	2,114	2,124	2,315	2,749	3,013
Criminal justice assistance	477	795	822	847	967	11,908
Undistributed offsetting receipts	*−36,615*	*−39,280*	*−37,386*	*−37,772*	*−44,455*	*−42,268*

FEDERAL CIVILIAN EMPLOYMENT

FEDERAL CIVILIAN EMPLOYMENT, BY BRANCH AND AGENCY: 1990–1995

Agency	1990	1993	1994	1995	Percent change 1990–95	Percent change 1994–95
Total, all agencies	3,128,267	3,013,508	2,971,584	2,918,674	−6.7	−1.8
Legislative Branch, total[1]	37,495	38,258	35,357	33,367	−11.0	−5.6
Judicial Branch	23,605	28,120	28,035	28,993	22.8	3.4
Executive Branch, total	3,067,167	2,947,130	2,908,192	2,856,314	−6.9	−1.8
Executive Departments	2,065,542	1,972,569	1,907,895	1,781,220[2]	−13.8	−6.6
State	25,288	26,077	25,596	24,859	−1.7	−2.9
Treasury	158,655	156,073	156,373	155,951	−1.7	−0.3
Defense	1,034,152	921,179	879,878	830,738	−19.7	−5.6
Justice	83,932	97,898	97,910	103,262	23.0	5.5
Interior	77,679	84,864	80,704	76,439	−1.6	−5.3
Agriculture	122,594	124,199	119,558	113,321	−7.6	−5.2
Commerce	69,920	38,680	37,642	36,803	−47.4	−2.2
Labor	17,727	17,407	16,732	16,204	−8.6	−3.2
Health & Human Services	123,959	130,216	128,244	59,788[4]	−51.8	−53.4
Housing & Urban Development	13,596	13,459	13,218	11,822	−13.0	−10.6
Transportation	67,364	69,144	64,896	63,552	−5.7	−2.1
Energy	17,731	20,336	19,899	19,589	10.5	−1.6
Education	4,771	5,002	4,813	4,988	4.5	3.6
Veterans Affairs[3]	248,174	268,035	262,432	263,904	6.3	0.6
Independent agencies[1]	999,894	972,930	998,729	1,073,521[2]	7.4	7.5
American Battle Monuments Comm	396	394	380	374	5.6	−1.6
Armed Forces Retirement Home	966	875	1,056	960	−0.6	−9.1
Arms Control & Disarmament Agency	216	216	233	266	23.1	14.2
Board of Gov. Fed. Reserve System	1,525	1,678	1,669	1,715	12.5	2.8
Commodity Futures Trading Comm.	542	551	551	544	0.4	−1.3
Consumer Product Safety Comm.	520	532	484	486	−6.5	0.4
Corp. Natl. & Community Service	(X)	33	607	574	(X)	−5.4
Defense Nuclear Facilities Safety Bd.	25	92	102	106	324.0	3.9
Environmental Protection Agency	17,123	18,415	18,092	17,910	4.6	−1.0
Equal Employment Opportunity Comm.	2,880	2,868	2,914	2,796	−2.9	−4.0
Export-Import Bank of U.S.	343	467	462	443	29.2	−4.1
Farm Credit Administration	515	436	412	380	−26.2	−7.8

(X) Not applicable.   [1] Includes branches, or agencies, not shown separately.   [2] Sizable changes due to the Social Security Administration, which was separated from the Department of Health and Human Services to become an independent agency effective April 1995.   [3] Formerly Veterans Administration.   [4] Formerly Federal Home Loan Bank Board.

Agency	1990	1993	1994	1995	Percent change 1990–95	Percent change 1994–95
Independent agencies, *cont.*						
Federal Communications Commission	1,778	1,807	2,015	2,116	19.0	5.0
Federal Deposit Insurance Corporation	17,641	21,701	18,775	14,765	–16.3	–21.4
Federal Election Commission	250	277	316	327	30.8	3.5
Fed. Emergency Mgmt. Agency	3,137	5,099	5,221	5,256	67.5	0.7
Federal Housing Finance Board[4]	65	114	104	113	73.8	8.7
Federal Labor Relations Authority	251	250	229	221	–12.0	–3.5
Federal Maritime Commission	230	201	200	169	–26.5	–15.5
Federal Med. & Council Service	316	308	309	297	–6.0	–3.9
Fed. Reg. Thrift Invest Board	93	102	105	110	18.3	4.8
Federal Trade Commission	988	971	969	996	0.8	2.8
General Services Administration	20,277	20,502	19,257	16,500	–18.6	–14.3
Holocaust Memorial Council	26	185	188	207	696.2	10.1
Int. Boun. & Wat. Comm. (U.S. & Mex.)	260	258	248	236	–9.2	–4.8
International Trade Commission	491	455	464	442	–10.1	–4.7
Interstate Commerce Comm.	656	644	553	397	–39.5	–28.2
Merit Sys. Protection Board	310	316	296	271	–12.6	–8.4
National Archives & Recds. Admin.	3,120	3,082	3,073	2,833	–9.2	–7.8
National Aeronautics & Space Admin.	24,872	24,826	23,338	21,635	–13.0	–7.3
Natl. Credit Union Administration	900	962	921	912	1.3	–1.0
Natl. Fnd Arts & Humanities	547	561	564	493	–9.9	–12.6
Natl. Labor Relations Board	2,263	2,108	2,077	2,050	–9.4	–1.3
Natl. Science Foundation	1,318	1,223	1,252	1,292	–2.0	3.2
Natl. Trans. Safety Board	366	365	358	368	0.5	2.8
Nuclear Regulatory Commission	3,353	3,476	3,336	3,212	–4.2	–3.7
Office of Personnel Management	6,636	6,776	5,340	4,354	–34.4	–18.5
Panama Canal Commission	8,240	8,568	8,562	9,060	10.0	5.8
Peace Corps	1,178	1,235	1,223	1,179	0.1	–3.6
Pension Benefit Guarantee Corp.	574	727	697	716	24.7	2.7
Railroad Retirement Board	1,772	1,782	1,683	1,544	–12.9	–8.3
Securities & Exchange Commission	2,302	2,717	2,689	2,852	23.9	6.1
Selective Service System	288	267	230	218	–24.3	–5.2
Small Business Administration	5,128	5,526	6,824	5,085	–0.8	–25.5
Smithsonian Institution, Summary	5,092	5,497	5,527	5,444	6.9	–1.5
Social Security Administration	(X)	(X)	(X)	66,850[2]	(X)	(X)
Tennessee Valley Authority	28,392	18,986	18,846	16,545	–41.7	–12.2
U.S. Information Agency	8,555	8,283	7,888	7,480	–12.6	–5.2
U.S. International Development Cooperation Agency	4,698	4,273	4,059	3,755	–20.1	–7.5
U.S. Postal Service	816,886	790,286	822,699	845,393	3.5	2.8

GOVERNMENT BENEFITS

The federal government provides financial assistance to U.S. citizens through a number of its agencies. You will find most government offices listed in the phone book under "U.S. Government." To name just a few of the agencies that offer aid to U.S. citizens, the Department of Education oversees student financial assistance, the Department of Health and Human Services provides for Medicare/Medicaid, the Department of Housing and Urban Development offers federal funds for low-income housing, and the Small Business Administration offers loans to small businesses. In this section, the benefits most Americans can receive from Social Security and Medicare hospital and medical insurance are outlined. Up-to-the-minute information on regulations and benefit amounts is provided online by the Social Security Administration's Web site (http://www.ssa.gov).

SOCIAL SECURITY

Under the Old-Age, Survivors, and Disability Insurance program, commonly known as Social Security, working Americans who retire after age 62 or become disabled are entitled to receive cash benefits. Spouses and dependents are also eligible for limited benefits. Employees have an amount deducted from their wages each payday based on their average indexed monthly earnings (AIME); in 1996, the rate was 7.65 percent on earnings up to $65,100. Workers retiring at 65 receive full benefits as calculated from their AIME, while those retiring at ages 62 to 64 can collect immediately but are subject to reduced payment rates. Increases in Social Security benefit amounts are based on the Consumer Price Index. In January 1996, monthly payments for retired workers averaged $886, while the average disabled worker received $709.

To be fully insured and receive *retirement benefits,* a worker must have earned as many credits of coverage as the number of calendar years between age 21 (or since 1950) and retirement. In 1996, for every $640 in wages, a worker earned one credit of coverage, for up to four credits annually. Workers who have earned credit during at least 20 of the last 40 calendar quarters are eligible for *disability benefits.* (Disabled workers under age 31 must have worked during one-half the quarters after age 21, and a minimum of six quarters, to be eligible for benefits.) Blind persons qualify simply by being fully insured—that is, by having earned a number of credits equal to the number of years they have worked. *Survivor benefits,* payable to the spouse and dependents of deceased workers, are available if the worker earned six quarters of coverage during the last 13 calendar quarters.

Retirement Benefits

At age 62, retiring workers become eligible to collect Social Security payments. Those who begin collecting at this age, however, are permanently eligible for only 80 percent of the maximum possible payment, called the primary insurance amount (PIA); in general, workers retiring before age 65 have their benefits reduced by five-ninths of 1 percent for each month they receive benefits before reaching that age.

The Indian chief Tecumseh put a curse on U.S. presidents elected in years ending in 0. Seven such presidents in a row died in office. Ronald Reagan, elected in 1980, survived an assassination attempt, breaking Tecumseh's curse.

Spouses of workers who receive Social Security retirement or disability benefits may get a spouse's insurance benefit of half of the worker's PIA when the spouse reaches 65. As with the worker's benefits, spouses may begin getting reduced payments at age 62. Payments are also available for divorced spouses provided they were married to the worker for at least 10 years.

Disability Benefits

If a worker is unable to work because he or she is severely disabled, Social Security offers a monthly disability payment. The worker receives the payments until he or she is able to work again. If the worker is still disabled by age 65, the payments become those for a retired worker.

If a fully insured worker retires or is disabled, his or her spouse and children under 18 are entitled to half of the unreduced benefit. Benefits usually stop after children reach 18, although payments can continue until age 19 provided the child is enrolled in an elementary or secondary school full-time.

Survivor Benefits

Benefits are available to spouses of deceased, fully insured workers under one or more of the following conditions:

1. If the spouse is age 65 or over, he or she receives the full amount of the deceased's PIA; at age 60, he or she can start receiving payments at a reduced rate. (Widowed spouses of workers who had retired before age 65 are eligible for the reduced rate the worker would have received.)

If a spouse of a deceased worker becomes disabled before or within seven years after the worker's death, the last month in which he or she received mother's or father's insurance benefits (payments for dependent children), or the last month he or she previously received surviving spouse's benefits, the widow or widower is eligible for benefits of 71.5 percent of the worker's PIA.

MONTHLY SOCIAL SECURITY BENEFITS FOR SELECTED FAMILIES

	Earnings		
	Career Level/Average	Low[1]	Maximum
Beneficiary Family	($247,815.00 in 1996)	($11,617.00)	($62,700.00)
Primary insurance amount (PIA) (worker retiring at 65)	$886.00	$537.00	$1,248.00
Maximum family benefit (worker retiring at 65)	1,615.20	805.50	2,184.00
Disability maximum family benefit (worker disabled at 55; in 1991)*	1,331.50	757.30	1,946.70
Disabled worker: (worker disabled at 55)			
Worker alone	887.00	538.00	1,297.00
Worker, spouse, and 1 child	1,331.00	756.00	1,945.00
Retired worker, claiming benefits at age 62:			
Worker alone[2]	709.00	430.00	999.00
Worker with spouse claiming benefits at—			
Age 65 or over	1,152.00	698.00	1,623.00
Age 60	1,041.00	631.00	1,467.00
Widow or widower claiming benefits at—			
Age 65 or over[3]	886.00	537.00	1,248.00
Age 60	633.00	384.00	892.00
Disabled widow or widower claiming benefits at age 50–59[4]	633.00	384.00	892.00
1 surviving child	664.00	402.00	936.00
Widow or widower age 65 or over and 1 child[5]	1,550.00	804.00	2,184.00
Widowed mother or father and 1 child[5]	1,328.00	804.00	1,872.00
Widowed mother or father and 2 children[5]	1,614.00	804.00	2,181.00

* Assumes work beginning at age 22.   [1] Estimate.   [2] Assumes maximum reduction.   [3] A widow(er)'s benefit amount is limited to the amount the spouse would have been receiving if still living but not less than 82.5 percent of the PIA.   [4] Effective January 1984, disabled widow(er)s claiming benefit at ages 50–59 will receive benefit equal to 71.5 percent of the PIA (based on the 1983 Social Security Amendment provision).   [5] Based on worker dying at age 65.

2. As with children of disabled or retired workers, surviving children receive benefits until they are 18 or 19 if they are enrolled in school full-time. Benefits for such children are three-quarters of the amount the worker would have received had he or she lived to collect full benefits.

3. The spouse of a deceased worker receives an additional 75 percent of the PIA—in what is called a "mother's or father's benefit"—if he or she cares for a child of the worker under age 16; these payments stop when the child reaches that age. Unless the spouse remarries, payments resume when he or she reaches age 60, as described above.

4. Dependent parents age 62 or over may receive benefits if they relied on the deceased worker for at least one-half of their support. Each parent receives 75 percent of the deceased's PIA; if only one parent survives, he or she gets 82.5 percent of the PIA.

5. A cash payment of $255 is made to a spouse who lived with the deceased worker or to a spouse or child eligible for immediate monthly survivor benefits.

Self-Employed and Household Workers

Self-employed persons are eligible for the same Social Security benefits and earn credits at the same rate as other workers. However, they must pay into the program at a higher rate (15.3 percent in 1996) and file taxes quarterly.

Household workers—maids, cooks, laundry workers, nursemaids, baby-sitters, chauffeurs, etc.—also are covered provided they are paid $1,000 or more in cash in a calendar year by at least one employer. Carfare can be applied if it is paid in cash, but room and board cannot be claimed. Whether the job is regular, full-time, or part-time, household workers can receive this benefit by showing their Social Security cards to their employers. The employer deducts the Social Security tax from the worker's pay and sends the total amount to the federal government.

Farm Owners and Workers

Self-employed farmers pay contributions to Social Security at the same rate as other self-employed persons. They can report two-thirds of their gross earnings if their earnings are $2,400 or less. Those whose gross income is $2,400 or more, and whose net income is $1,600 or less, can report $1,600. Cash or crop shares from a tenant or share farmer can be counted only if the farmer participated materially in the production or management.

Tennessee and Missouri are bordered by more states than any other. They are each bordered by 8 states.

A worker's earnings from farm work count toward benefits if the employer pays him or her at least $150 in cash in a given year, or if the employer spends $2,500 or more a year for agricultural labor.

MEDICARE

Medicare provides hospital and medical insurance for Social Security and Railroad Retirement beneficiaries 65 and over. Its hospital insurance program paid out about $113 billion in 1990, and its medical insurance program gave $63 billion in benefits. It also provides for those persons who are entitled to receive Social Security disability benefits for two years and to those with end-stage renal disease. Persons age 65 and over not otherwise eligible for hospital benefits may receive them by paying a special monthly premium on a voluntary basis. All persons over age 65 may receive supplemental medical insurance by paying a monthly premium.

Hospital Insurance

Those eligible for hospital insurance are covered for the following:

1. All necessary inpatient hospital care for the first 60 days of each benefit period, except for a deductible ($736 in 1996). For days 61–90, Medicare pays for services over and above a coinsurance amount ($184 per day in 1996).

After 90 days, the beneficiary has 60 reserve days for which Medicare helps pay. The coinsurance amount for reserve days was $386 in 1996.

2. Up to 100 days' care in a skilled nursing facility in each benefit period. Hospital insurance pays for all covered services for the first 20 days; for the 21st to 100th day, the beneficiary pays coinsurance ($92 a day in 1996).

3. Visits by nurses or other health workers (not doctors) from a home health agency.

4. Hospice care for terminally ill individuals.

Medical Insurance

Medical insurance is available to anyone over age 65 who agrees to pay a monthly premium ($72.50 in 1996), which is subsidized by a government contribution. The premium is usually deducted from Social Security payments. People may enroll in the program in a seven-month period beginning three months before their 65th birthday; those enrolling later must pay higher premiums.

Except for doctors' charges for X-ray or clinical laboratory services for hospital-bed patients, which are paid in full by individuals, members of this program pay 20 percent (after the first $100) of the total amount required for the following services:

1. Hospital, office, or home physicians' and surgeons' fees.

2. Diagnostic tests, surgical dressings, and splints; rental or purchase of medical equipment; the services of a physical therapist at home or in the office; outpatient physical therapy received from a hospital or an extended-care facility for those who have used up their hospital insurance coverage.

3. Physical therapy furnished under the supervision of a practicing hospital, clinic, skilled-nursing facility, or agency.

4. Certain services by podiatrists.

5. All outpatient services of a participating hospital (including diagnostic tests).

6. Services of licensed chiropractors who meet government standards, but only for manual manipulation treatment of the spine and treatment of subluxation of the spine proven by X ray.

7. Supplies related to colostomies.

Home health services are covered 100 percent when medically necessary.

STATES AND TERRITORIES

The states and territories of the United States each have idiosyncrasies ranging from the exact form of their state government to their state symbols. The following section covers information particular to the individual states and territories.

GOVERNMENT

STATES

All states (except Nebraska) have a lawmaking body, in most cases called a *legislature* or *general assembly,* that is divided into two houses. (Nebraska's state government is unicameral, or single-chambered, and all its officials are called senators.) In most states, the upper house is called the Senate, and the lower house is called the House of Representatives. State senators usually are elected every four years, and representatives or assembly members are elected every two years. State legislatures generally meet biennially, though a few meet annually.

Twenty-seven of the United States have some territory north of some portion of Canada.

The table on page 876 lists the name of each of the 50 states along with the year it became a state, the official abbreviation used by the United States Postal Service, the capital, and the name of the lawmaking body.

See also "Admission of the 13 Original States," "Secession of American States," and "Readmission of American States" earlier in this chapter.

THE 50 STATES OF THE UNITED STATES

State	Date Entered Union	Capital	Name of Lawmaking Body
Alabama	1819	Montgomery	Legislature
Alaska	1959	Juneau	Legislature
Arizona	1912	Phoenix	Legislature
Arkansas	1836	Little Rock	General Assembly
California	1850	Sacramento	Legislature (Assembly*)
Colorado	1876	Denver	General Assembly
Connecticut	1788	Hartford	General Assembly
Delaware	1787	Dover	General Assembly
Florida	1845	Tallahassee	Legislature
Georgia	1788	Atlanta	General Assembly
Hawaii	1959	Honolulu	Legislature
Idaho	1890	Boise	Legislature
Illinois	1818	Springfield	General Assembly
Indiana	1816	Indianapolis	General Assembly
Iowa	1846	Des Moines	General Assembly
Kansas	1861	Topeka	Legislature
Kentucky	1792	Frankfort	General Assembly
Louisiana	1812	Baton Rouge	Legislature
Maine	1820	Augusta	Legislature
Maryland	1788	Annapolis	General Assembly (House of Delegates*)
Massachusetts	1788	Boston	General Court
Michigan	1837	Lansing	Legislature
Minnesota	1858	St. Paul	Legislature
Mississippi	1817	Jackson	Legislature
Missouri	1821	Jefferson City	General Assembly
Montana	1889	Helena	Legislative Assembly
Nebraska	1867	Lincoln	Legislature
Nevada	1864	Carson City	Legislature (Assembly*)
New Hampshire	1788	Concord	General Court
New Jersey	1787	Trenton	Legislature (General Assembly*)
New Mexico	1912	Santa Fe	Legislature
New York	1788	Albany	Legislature (Assembly*)
North Carolina	1789	Raleigh	General Assembly
North Dakota	1889	Bismarck	Legislative Assembly
Ohio	1803	Columbus	General Assembly
Oklahoma	1907	Oklahoma City	Legislature
Oregon	1859	Salem	Legislative Assembly
Pennsylvania	1787	Harrisburg	General Assembly
Rhode Island	1790	Providence	General Assembly
South Carolina	1788	Columbia	General Assembly
South Dakota	1889	Pierre	Legislature
Tennessee	1796	Nashville	General Assembly
Texas	1845	Austin	Legislature
Utah	1896	Salt Lake City	Legislature
Vermont	1791	Montpelier	General Assembly
Virginia	1788	Richmond	General Assembly (House of Delegates*)
Washington	1889	Olympia	Legislature
Wisconsin	1848	Madison	Legislature (Assembly*)

* The name of the lower house.

United States

TERRITORIES

TERRITORIES OF THE UNITED STATES

State	Date Acquired	Capital	Legislature
American Samoa	1899	Pago Pago	Legislature
Federated States of Micronesia	1947	Pohnpei	Legislature
Guam	1950	Agana	Legislature*
Marshall Islands	1947	Majuro	Parliament and Council of Local Chiefs
Midway Islands	1867		Administered by the U.S. Navy
Northern Mariana Islands	1947	Saipan	Legislature
Palau	1947	Koror	Legislature
Puerto Rico	1898	San Juan	Legislative Assembly
Virgin Islands	1927	Charlotte Amalie	Legislature*

* Legislatures are unicameral.

FLOWERS, BIRDS, MOTTOES, AND NICKNAMES

STATES

State	Flower	Bird	Motto	Nickname
Alabama	Camellia	Yellowhammer	We dare defend our rights	Heart of Dixie; Camellia State
Alaska	Forget-me-not	Willow ptarmigan	North to the future	The Last Frontier
Arizona	Saguaro	Cactus wren	*Diat Deus* (God enriches)	Grand Canyon State
Arkansas	Apple blossom	Mockingbird	*Regnat populus* (The people rule)	Land of Opportunity
California	Golden poppy	California valley quail	*Eureka* (I have found it)	Golden State
Colorado	Blue columbine	Lark bunting	*Nil sine numine* (Nothing without providence)	Centennial State
Connecticut	Mountain laurel	American robin	*Qui transtulit sustinet* (He who transplanted still sustains)	Constitution State; Nutmeg State
Delaware	Peach blossom	Blue hen chicken	Liberty and independence	First State; Diamond State
District of Columbia	American Beauty rose	Wood thrush	*Justitia Omnibus* (Justice for all)	Capital City
Florida	Orange blossom	Mockingbird	In God we trust	Sunshine State
Georgia	Cherokee rose	Brown thrasher	Wisdom, justice, and moderation	Empire State of the South; Peach State
Hawaii	Hibiscus	Nene goose	The life of the land is perpetuated in righteousness	Aloha State
Idaho	Syringa	Mountain bluebird	*Esto perpetua* (It is perpetual)	Gem State
Illinois	Native violet	Cardinal	State sovereignty—national union	Prairie State; Land of Lincoln
Indiana	Peony	Cardinal	Crossroads of America	Hoosier State
Iowa	Wild rose	Goldfinch	Our liberties we prize and our rights we will maintain	Hawkeye State
Kansas	Sunflower	Western meadowlark	*Ad astra per aspera* (To the stars through difficulties)	Sunflower State
Kentucky	Goldenrod	Kentucky cardinal	United we stand, divided we fall	Bluegrass State
Louisiana	Magnolia	Eastern brown pelican	Union, justice, and confidence	Pelican State

continues

Continued

State	Flower	Bird	Motto	Nickname
Maine	Pine cone and tassel	Chickadee	*Dirigo* (I direct)	Pine Tree State
Maryland	Black-eyed Susan	Baltimore oriole	...*Fatti maschii, parole femine* (Manly deeds, womanly words)	Old Line State; Free State
Massachusetts	Mayflower	Chickadee	*Ense petit placidam sub libertate quietem* (By the sword we seek peace, but peace only under liberty)	Bay State; Colony State
Michigan	Apple blossom	Robin	*Si quaeris peninsulam amoenam circumspice* (If you seek a pleasant peninsula, look about you)	Great Lake State; Wolverine State
Minnesota	Showy lady slipper	Common loon	*L'Etoile du nord* (Star of the north)	North Star State; Gopher State
Mississippi	Magnolia	Mockingbird	*Virtute et armis* (By valor and arms)	Magnolia State
Missouri	Hawthorn	Bluebird	*Salus populi suprema lex esto* (The welfare of the people shall be the supreme law)	Show-Me State
Montana	Bitterroot	Western meadowlark	*Oro y plata* (Gold and silver)	Treasure State
Nebraska	Goldenrod	Meadowlark	Equality before the law	Cornhusker State
Nevada	Sagebrush	Mountain bluebird	All for our country	Sagebrush State; Battle-Born State
New Hampshire	Purple lilac	Purple finch	Live free or die	Granite State
New Jersey	Purple violet	Eastern goldfinch	Liberty and prosperity	Garden State
New Mexico	Yucca	Roadrunner	*Crescit eundo* (It grows as it goes)	Land of Enchantment
New York	Rose (any color)	Bluebird	*Excelsior* (Ever upward)	Empire State
North Carolina	Dogwood	Cardinal	*Esse quam videri* (To be rather than to seem)	Tar Heel State; Old North State
North Dakota	Wild prairie rose	Western meadowlark	Liberty and union, now and forever, one and inseparable	Peace Garden State
Ohio	Scarlet carnation	Cardinal	With God, all things are possible	Buckeye State
Oklahoma	Mistletoe	Scissor-tailed flycatcher	*Labor omnia vincit* (Labor conquers all things)	Sooner State
Oregon	Oregon grape	Western meadowlark	The union	Beaver State
Pennsylvania	Mountain laurel	Ruffed grouse	Virtue, liberty, and independence	Keystone State
Rhode Island	Violet	Rhode Island hen	Hope	Little Rhody; Ocean State
South Carolina	Carolina jessamine	Carolina wren	*Dum spiro spero* (While I breathe, I hope)	Palmetto State
South Dakota	Pasqueflower	Pheasant	Under God, the people rule	Coyote State; Sunshine State
Tennessee	Iris	Mockingbird	Agriculture and commerce	Volunteer State
Texas	Bluebonnet	Mockingbird	Friendship	Lone Star State
Utah	Sego Lily	Seagull	Industry	Beehive State
Vermont	Red clover	Thrush	Freedom and unity	Green Mountain State
Virginia	Flowering dogwood	Cardinal	*Sic semper tyrannis* (Thus always to tyrants)	Old Dominion
Washington	Rhododendron	Willow goldfinch	*Alki* (By and by)	Evergreen State
West Virginia	Big rhododendron	Cardinal	*Montani semper liberi* (Mountaineers are always free)	Mountain State
Wisconsin	Wood violet	Robin	Forward	Badger State
Wyoming	Indian paintbrush	Meadowlark	Equal rights	Equality State

TERRITORIES

Territory	Flower	Bird	Motto
American Samoa	Paogo (Ula-fala)	None	*Samoa Muamua le Atua* (In Samoa, God is first)
Guam	Puti tai nobio (buogainvillea)	Toto (fruit dove)	Where America's day begins
Puerto Rico	Maga	Reinita	*Joannes est nomen eius* (John is his name)
Virgin Islands	Yellow elder or yellow trumpet	Yellow breast	None

NAME ORIGINS

Alabama   Originally the name for "tribal town," the territory of Alabama was later the home of the Alabama, or Alibamon, Indians of the Creek confederacy.

Alaska   The Russians adopted the word, meaning "great lands" or "land that is not an island," from the Aleutian word *alakshak.*

Arizona   The Spanish coined the name either from the Pima Indian word meaning "little spring place" or from the Aztec *arizuma,* which means "silver-bearing."

Arkansas   Once the territory of the Siouan Quapaw (downstream people), *Arkansas* is the French derivative of this Indian name.

California   The name of a fictitious earthly paradise in *Las Serged de Esplandian,* a 16th-century Spanish romance. It is believed that Spanish conquistadors named this state.

Colorado   A Spanish word for "red." The name *Colorado* first referred to the Colorado River.

Connecticut   The Algonquin and Mohican Indian word for "long river place."

Delaware   This version of the name of Lord De La Warr, a governor of Virginia, was first used to name the Delaware River and later adopted by the Europeans to rename the local Indians, originally called the Lenni-Lenape.

District of Columbia   Named for Christopher Columbus in 1791.

"North America" and "United States" in the atlas
Go to

Florida   In his search for the "Fountain of Youth," Ponce de Leon named this region "flowery Easter" or "feast of flowers" on Easter Sunday, 1513.

Georgia   Named for King George II of England, who granted James Oglethorpe a charter to found the colony of Georgia in 1732.

Hawaii   Commonly believed to be an English adaptation of the native word for "homeland," *hawaiki* or *owhyhee.*

Idaho   A name coined by the state meaning "gem of the mountains" or "light on the mountains." Originally the name *Idaho* was to be used for the Pike's Peak mining territory in Colorado, and later for the mining territory of the Pacific Northwest. Others believe the name derives from the Kiowa Apache word for the Comanche.

Illinois   From *Illini,* the French version of the Algonquin word meaning "men" or "soldiers."

Indiana   English-speaking settlers named the territory to mean "land of the Indians."

Iowa   From the Siouan *Ouaouia,* meaning "one who puts to sleep."

Kansas   Derived from the Siouan *Kansa* or *Kaw,* meaning "people of the south wind," who lived south of the settlements of the northern Great Plains.

Kentucky   Originally the term for the Kentucky Plains in Clark County, *Kentucky* is believed to derive from the Indian word meaning "dark and bloody ground," "meadowland," or "land of tomorrow."

United States

Louisiana Present-day Louisiana is just a fraction of the territory that was named for the French king Louis XIV by Sieur de La Salle.

Maine Originally a French territory, *Maine* was the ancient French word for "province." It is also believed that it refers to the mainland, as distinct from the many islands off the state's coast.

Maryland Named for Queen Henrietta Maria, wife of Charles I of England.

Massachusetts The name of the Indian tribe that lived near Milton, Massachusetts, meaning "large hill place."

Michigan Believed to be from the Chippewa word *micigama,* meaning "great water," after Lake Michigan, although Alouet defined it in 1672 as designating a clearing.

Minnesota Named from the Sioux description of the Minnesota River, "sky-tinted water" or "muddy water."

Mississippi Most likely derived from the Chippewa words *mici* (great) and *zibi* (river), it was first written as "Michi Sepe" by La Salle's lieutenant Henri de Tonti.

Missouri The Siouan word meaning "muddy water."

Montana Derived from the Latin word meaning "mountainous."

Nebraska From the Omaha or Oto word for "flat water" or "spreading water," describing the Platte and Nebraska rivers.

Nevada Spanish word meaning "snow-clad."

New Hampshire Captain John Mason named this colony for his home county in England in 1629.

New Jersey Named after the Isle of Jersey in England by John Berkeley and Sir George Carteret.

New Mexico Named by the Spanish for the territory north and west of the Rio Grande.

New York Originally named New Netherland, New York was later named after the Duke of York and Albany, who received a patent to the region from his brother Charles II of England and captured it from the Dutch in 1644.

North Carolina From the Latin name *Carolus,* meaning "Charles." The colony was originally given to Sir Robert Heath by Charles I and was to be called Province of Carolana. Carolana was divided into North and South Carolina in 1710.

The United States consumes approximately 24% of the world's energy.

North Dakota From the Sioux word meaning "friend" or "ally."

Ohio From an Iroquois Indian word variously meaning "great," "fine," or "good river."

Oklahoma The Choctaw Indian word meaning "red man," which was coined by the Reverend Allen Wright, a Choctaw-speaking Indian.

Oregon Though its exact origin is unclear, one theory maintains that it may have been a variation on the name of the Wisconsin River, which was called *Ouaricon-sint* on a French map dated 1715. Later, the English explorer Major Robert Rogers named a river "called by the Indians Ouragon" in his request to seek a Northwest Passage from the Great Lakes. Another theory derives the word from the Algonquin *wauregan,* meaning "beautiful water."

Pennsylvania Named after Admiral Sir William Penn, the father of the colony's founder, the Quaker William Penn. The literal translation is "Penn's woods."

Rhode Island Possibly named by Giovanni de Verrazano, who charted an island about the size of an island of the same name in the Mediterranean. Another theory suggests Rhode Island was named

Roode Eylandt by Dutch explorer Adrian Block because of its red clay.

South Carolina   *See* **North Carolina.**

South Dakota   *See* **North Dakota.**

Tennessee   The state of Franklin, or Frankland, from 1784 to 1788, it was finally named after the Cherokee villages called *tanasi* on the Little Tennessee River.

Texas   Also written *texias, tejas,* and *teysas, Texas* is a variation on the Caddo Indian word for "friend" or "ally."

Utah   Meaning "upper" or "higher," *Utah* is derived from a name used by the Navajos (Utes) to designate a Shoshone tribe.

Vermont   It is believed Samuel de Champlain coined the name from the French words *vert* (green) and *mont* (mountain). Later, Dr. Thomas Young proposed this name when the state was formed in 1777.

Virginia   Named for the Virgin Queen of England, Queen Elizabeth I, by Sir Walter Raleigh, who first visited its shores in 1584.

Washington   Originally named the Territory of Columbia, it was changed to *Washington* in honor of the first U.S. president because of the already existing District of Columbia.

West Virginia   Named when this area of Virginia refused to secede from the Union in 1861.

Wisconsin   A Chippewa word that was spelled *Ouisconsin* and *Mesconsing* by early explorers. Wisconsin was formally named by Congress when it became a state.

There have been two Liberty Bells. The first was made in England in 1752 for the Pennsylvania State House, which became Independence Hall. The second was made in Philadelphia and cracked on July 8, 1835, as it rang out the death of Chief Justice John Marshall.

Wyoming   The Algonquin word meaning "large prairie place," the name was adopted from Wyoming Valley, Pennsylvania, the site of an Indian massacre. It was widely known from Thomas Campbell's poem "Gertrude of Wyoming."

STATISTICS

U.S. POPULATION

The United States boasts a heterogenous population, which, according to the 1995 figures, has risen 5.6 percent, from 248.7 million to 262.7 million, since the 1990 census. The tables in this section were drawn primarily from the Bureau of the Census in the Department of Commerce and reflect the most accurate profiles available of the population by race, sex, age, and region.

United States

United States

U.S. POPULATION BY AGE, RACE, AND HISPANIC ORIGIN: 1995

Sex	Total	Age (in years)														
	All Years	Under 5	5–9	10–14	15–19	20–24	25–29	30–34	35–39	40–44	45–49	50–54	55–59	60–64	65–74	75
	Population (in thousands)															
All races[1]	262,755	19,591	19,220	18,915	18,065	17,882	19,005	21,868	22,249	20,219	17,449	13,630	11,085	10,146	18,259	14,773
Male	128,314	10,025	9,848	9,685	9,265	9,087	9,530	10,902	11,071	9,990	8,560	6,622	5,317	4,727	8,342	5,347
Female	134,441	9,566	9,377	9,229	8,799	8,795	9,476	10,966	11,178	10,228	8,889	7,008	5,767	5,320	10,714	9,426
White	218,085	15,451	15,237	15,040	14,362	14,317	15,403	17,984	18,458	16,930	14,858	11,725	9,541	8,724	16,664	13,411
Male	106,994	7,924	7,818	7,721	7,390	7,324	7,796	9,062	9,282	8,461	7,370	5,754	4,626	4,152	7,455	4,859
Female	111,092	7,527	7,418	7,319	6,972	6,993	7,607	8,922	9,176	8,469	7,488	5,971	4,915	4,571	9,189	8,553
Black	33,141	3,100	3,025	2,877	2,282	2,638	2,594	2,825	2,788	2,399	1,855	1,381	1,138	988	1,617	1,102
Male	15,721	1,570	1,535	1,460	1,430	1,299	1,240	1,325	1,307	1,109	846	620	500	425	674	381
Female	17,420	1,530	1,491	1,417	1,392	1,338	1,355	1,500	1,481	1,282	1,008	761	638	563	943	721
Native American, Eskimo, Aleut	2,242	207	228	234	201	185	180	186	177	156	125	93	72	58	58	56
Male	1,110	105	116	118	101	95	93	93	87	75	61	45	34	27	38	22
Female	1,132	103	111	115	100	90	87	93	90	80	64	49	38	31	46	35
Asian, Pacific Islander	9,287	823	731	764	680	743	828	872	825	743	611	430	334	276	414	203
Male	4,489	426	374	387	343	369	401	422	395	346	282	203	158	122	176	86
Female	4,797	407	356	377	336	373	427	450	431	398	329	227	176	154	238	118
Hispanic origin	26,994	3,312	2,661	2,428	2,278	2,334	2,500	2,533	2,156	1,725	1,311	961	762	634	946	554
Male	13,676	1,664	1,361	1,239	1,168	1,229	1,341	1,333	1,110	867	644	461	359	293	419	207
Female	13,318	1,568	1,300	1,189	1,110	1,104	1,159	1,200	1,045	858	667	500	402	341	528	347
	Population (in thousands)															
All races[1]	100.0	7.5	7.3	7.2	6.9	6.8	7.2	8.3	8.5	7.7	6.6	5.2	4.2	3.8	7.1	5.6
White	100.0	7.1	7.0	7.2	6.9	6.8	7.2	8.3	8.5	7.8	6.8	5.4	4.4	4.0	7.6	6.1
Black	100.0	7.1	7.0	6.9	6.6	6.6	7.1	8.2	8.4	7.2	5.6	4.2	3.4	3.0	4.9	3.3
Native American, Eskimo, Aleut	100.0	9.3	10.1	10.4	9.0	8.2	8.0	8.3	7.9	6.9	5.6	4.2	3.2	2.6	3.8	2.5
Asian, Pacific Islander	100.0	9.0	7.9	8.2	7.3	8.0	8.9	9.4	8.9	8.0	6.6	4.6	3.6	3.0	4.5	2.2

[1] Includes other races, not shown separately.

U.S. POPULATION BY STATE: 1996

State	Population (in thousands)	Rank	State	Population (in thousands)	Rank
Alabama	4,253	22	Montana	870	44
Alaska	604	48	Nebraska	1,637	37
Arizona	4,218	23	Nevada	1,530	38
Arkansas	2,404	33	New Hampshire	1,148	42
California	31,589	1	New Jersey	7,945	9
Colorado	3,747	25	New Mexico	1,685	36
Connecticut	3,275	28	New York	18,136	3
Delaware	717	46	North Carolina	7,195	11
District of Columbia	554	(X)	North Dakota	641	47
Florida	14,166	4	Ohio	11,151	7
Georgia	7,201	10	Oklahoma	3,278	27
Hawaii	1,187	40	Oregon	3,141	29
Idaho	1,163	41	Pennsylvania	12,072	5
Illinois	11,830	6	Rhode Island	990	43
Indiana	5,803	14	South Carolina	3,673	26
Iowa	2,842	30	South Dakota	729	45
Kansas	2,565	32	Tennessee	5,256	17
Kentucky	3,860	24	Texas	18,724	2
Louisiana	4,342	21	Utah	1,951	34
Maine	1,241	39	Vermont	585	49
Maryland	5,042	19	Virginia	6,618	12
Massachusetts	6,074	13	Washington	5,431	15
Michigan	9,549	8	West Virginia	1,828	35
Minnesota	4,610	20	Wisconsin	5,123	18
Mississippi	2,697	31	Wyoming	480	50
Missouri	5,324	16			

(X) Not applicable

United States

IMMIGRANT ADMISSIONS TO THE UNITED STATES

BY DECADE AND YEAR: 1820–1994

Immigration admissions are given in thousands for fiscal years ending in year shown, except as noted.

Period	Total Number	Rate[1]	Period	Total Number	Rate[1]
1820 to 1990	56,994	3.4	1981 to 1990	7,338	3.1
1820 to 1830[2]	152	1.2	1970	373	1.8
1831 to 1840[3]	599	3.9	1980	531	2.3
1841 to 1850[4]	1,713	8.4	1981	597	2.6
1851 to 1860[5]	2,598	9.3	1982	594	2.6
1861 to 1870[6]	2,315	6.4	1983	560	2.4
1871 to 1880	2,812	6.2	1984	544	2.3
1881 to 1890	5,247	9.2	1985	570	2.4
1891 to 1900	3,688	5.3	1986	602	2.5
1901 to 1910	8,795	10.4	1987	602	2.5
1911 to 1920	5,736	5.7	1988	643	2.6
1921 to 1930	4,107	3.5	1989[6]	1,091	4.4
1931 to 1940	528	0.4	1990	1,536	6.1
1941 to 1950	1,035	0.7	1991[6]	1,827	7.2
1951 to 1960	2,515	1.5	1992[6]	974	3.8
1961 to 1970	3,322	1.7	1993[6]	904	3.5
1971 to 1980	4,493	2.1	1994[6]	804	3.1

[1] Annual rate per 1,000 U.S. population. Rate computed by dividing sum of annual immigration totals by sum of annual U.S. population totals for same number of years.   [2] Oct. 1, 1819, to Sept. 30, 1830.   [3] Oct. 1, 1830, to Dec. 31, 1840.   [4] Calendar years.   [5] Jan. 1, 1861, to June 30, 1870.   [6] Includes persons who were granted permanent residence under the legalization program of the Immigration Reform and Control Act of 1986.

BY COUNTRY OF BIRTH: FISCAL YEARS 1971 TO 1994

Immigrant admissions are given in thousands.

Country of Birth	1971–1980	1981–1990	1991–1993	1994
All countries	4,493.3	7,338.1	3,705.4	804.4
Europe[1]	**801.3**	**705.6**	**438.9**	**160.9**
France	17.8	23.1	8.6	2.7
Germany	66.0	70.1	23.7	7.0
Greece	93.7	29.1	5.8	1.4
Ireland	14.1	32.8	30.6	17.3
Italy	130.1	32.9	7.7	2.3
Poland	43.6	97.4	72.5	28.0
Portugal	104.5	40.0	9.4	2.2
Romania	17.5	38.9	20.2	3.4
Soviet Union, former[2]	43.2	84.0	159.2	63.4
Armenia	(NA)	(NA)	(NA)	4.0
Azerbaijan	(NA)	(NA)	(NA)	3.8
Belarus	(NA)	(NA)	(NA)	5.4
Moldova	(NA)	(NA)	(NA)	2.3
Russia	(NA)	(NA)	(NA)	15.2

(NA) Not Available.   [1] Includes countries not shown separately.   [2] Includes other republics and unknown republics, not shown separately.   [3] Data for Taiwan included with China.   [4] Includes Australia, New Zealand, and unknown countries.

Country of Birth	1971–1980	1981–1990	1991–1993	1994
Europe, Soviet Union, former, *cont.*				
Ukraine	(NA)	(NA)	(NA)	21.0
Uzbekistan	(NA)	(NA)	(NA)	3.4
Spain	30.0	15.8	4.9	1.4
United Kingdom	123.5	142.1	32.7	16.3
Yugoslavia	42.1	19.2	8.1	3.4
Asia[1]	**1,633.8**	**2,817.4**	**1,073.5**	**292.6**
Bangladesh	(NA)	15.2	17.7	3.4
Cambodia	8.4	116.6	7.5	1.4
China[3]	202.5	388.8	137.5	54.0
Hong Kong	47.5	63.0	30.0	7.7
India	176.8	261.9	121.9	34.9
Iran	46.2	154.8	47.6	11.4
Iraq	23.4	19.6	9.7	6.0
Israel	26.6	36.3	13.8	3.4
Japan	47.9	43.2	23.0	6.1
Jordan	29.6	32.6	13.0	4.0
Korea	272.0	338.8	63.9	16.0
Laos	22.6	145.6	25.9	5.1
Lebanon	33.8	41.6	17.3	4.3
Pakistan	31.2	61.3	39.5	8.7
Philippines	360.2	495.3	188.1	53.5
Syria	13.3	20.6	8.7	2.4
Taiwan	(3)	(3)	43.9	10.0
Thailand	44.1	64.4	21.1	5.5
Turkey	18.6	20.9	7.2	1.8
Vietnam	179.7	401.4	192.7	41.3
North America[1]	**1,645.0**	**3,125.0**	**1,896.4**	**272.2**
Canada	114.8	119.2	45.9	16.1
Mexico	637.2	1,653.3	1,286.5	111.4
Caribbean[1]	759.8	892.7	337.0	104.8
Barbados	20.9	17.4	3.7	0.9
Cuba	276.8	159.2	35.8	14.7
Dominican Republic	148.0	251.8	128.8	51.2
Haiti	58.7	140.2	68.6	13.3
Jamaica	142.0	213.8	60.0	14.3
Trinidad and Tobago	61.8	39.5	22.0	6.3
Central America[1]	132.4	458.7	226.8	39.9
El Salvador	34.4	214.6	100.4	17.6
Guatemala	25.6	87.9	47.9	7.4
Honduras	17.2	49.5	25.3	5.3
Nicaragua	13.0	44.1	33.9	5.3
Panama	22.7	29.0	9.7	2.4
South America[1]	**284.4**	**455.9**	**189.2**	**47.4**
Argentina	25.1	25.7	10.6	2.3
Brazil	13.7	23.7	17.5	4.5
Chile	17.6	23.4	6.6	1.6
Colombia	77.6	124.4	45.7	10.8

United States

continues

Continued

BY COUNTRY OF BIRTH: FISCAL YEARS 1971 TO 1994			
Country of Birth	1971–1980	1981–1990	1991–1993	1994
South America, *cont.*				
Ecuador	50.2	56.0	24.6	5.9
Guyana	47.5	95.4	29.1	7.7
Peru	29.1	64.4	36.6	9.2
Africa[1]	**91.5**	**192.3**	**91.0**	**26.7**
Egypt	25.5	31.4	12.7	3.4
Ethiopia	(NA)	27.2	15.0	3.9
Ghana	(NA)	14.9	6.8	1.5
Nigeria	8.8	35.3	16.9	4.0
Other countries[4]	**37.3**	**41.9**	**16.4**	**4.6**

(NA) Not Available.   [1] Includes countries not shown separately.   [2] Includes other republics and unknown republics, not shown separately.   [3] Data for Taiwan included with China.   [4] Includes Australia, New Zealand, and unknown countries.

The following table covers immigrants who were allowed to enter the United States under the 1953 Refugee Relief Act and later acts; Hungarian parolees under the July 1958 Act; refugee-escapee parolees under the July 1960 Act; conditional entries by refugees under the October 1965 Act; Cuban parolees under the November 1966 Act; beginning 1978, Indochina refugees under the Act of October 1977; beginning 1980, refugee-parolees under the Act of October 1978, and asylees under the Act of March 1980; and beginning 1981 refugees under the Act of March 1980.

BY COUNTRY OF BIRTH (AS PERMANENT RESIDENTS UNDER REFUGEE ACTS): FISCAL YEARS 1971–1994			
Country of Birth	1971–1980	1981–1990	1991–1993	1994
Total	539,447	1,013,620	383,459	121,434
Europe[1]	**71,858**	**155,512**	**158,862**	**54,978**
Albania	395	353	1,812	733
Bulgaria	1,238	1,197	1,176	138
Czechoslovakia	3,646	8,204	1,097	41
Greece	478	1,408	194	65
Hungary	4,358	4,942	1,126	37
Poland	5,882	33,889	6,448	334
Romania	6,812	29,798	12,901	1,119
Soviet Union, former[2]	31,309	72,306	130,955	50,756
Azerbaijan	(NA)	(NA)	(NA)	2,668
Belarus	(NA)	(NA)	(NA)	5,156
Moldova	(NA)	(NA)	(NA)	2,154
Russia	(NA)	(NA)	(NA)	10,359
Ukraine	(NA)	(NA)	(NA)	19,366
Uzbekistan	(NA)	(NA)	(NA)	3,211
Spain	5,317	736	183	55
Yugoslavia	11,297	324	201	506

Country of Birth	1971–1980	1981–1990	1991–1993	1994
Asia[1]	**210,683**	**712,092**	**154,967**	**45,768**
Afghanistan	542	22,946	6,415	1,665
Cambodia	7,739	114,064	5,053	557
China[3]	13,760	7,928	2,673	774
Hong Kong	3,468	1,916	350	02
Iran	364	46,773	15,483	2,186
Iraq	6,851	7,540	2,414	4,400
Laos	21,690	142,964	23,700	4,482
Philippines	216	3,403	592	103
Syria	1,336	2,145	463	34
Thailand	1,241	30,259	11,375	3,076
Turkey	1,193	1,896	204	156
Vietnam	150,266	324,453	83,947	27,318
North America[1]	**252,633**	**121,840**	**53,205**	**14,204**
Cuba	251,514	113,367	29,475	11,998
El Salvador	45	1,383	2,803	275
Nicaragua	36	5,590	18,793	6
South America[1]	**1,244**	**1,976**	**1,223**	**383**
Africa[1]	**2,991**	**22,149**	**15,155**	**6,078**
Egypt	1,473	426	105	37
Ethiopia	1,307	18,542	10,532	2,530
Other	**38**	**51**	**47**	**23**

(NA) Not available.   [1] Includes other countries, not shown separately.   [2] Includes other republics and unknown republics, not shown separately.   [3] Includes Taiwan.

U.S. ECONOMY

PERSONAL INCOME PER CAPITA, BY REGION AND STATE: 1980–1995

Region, Division, and State	Current Dollars					Constant (1992) Dollars					Income Rank	
	1980	1990	1993	1994	1995	1980	1990	1993	1994	1995	1980	1995
United States	**9,940**	**18,666**	**20,809**	**21,699**	**22,788**	**16,991**	**20,090**	**20,274**	**20,648**	**21,188**	**(X)**	**(X)**
Northeast	**10,699**	**21,699**	**24,141**	**25,073**	**26,209**	**18,289**	**23,355**	**23,520**	**23,859**	**24,369**	**(X)**	**(X)**
New England	**10,582**	**21,934**	**24,148**	**25,203**	**26,506**	**18,089**	**23,608**	**23,527**	**23,982**	**24,645**	**(X)**	**(X)**
Maine	8,218	17,039	18,687	19,481	20,527	14,048	18,339	18,206	18,537	19,086	38	34
New Hampshire	9,803	20,227	22,312	23,679	25,151	16,757	21,771	21,738	22,532	23,385	23	6
Vermont	8,546	17,442	19,394	20,100	20,927	14,609	18,773	18,895	19,126	19,458	35	31
Massachusetts	10,659	22,247	24,410	25,608	26,994	18,221	23,945	23,782	24,368	25,099	12	3
Rhode Island	9,576	19,032	21,231	21,948	23,310	16,369	20,484	20,685	20,885	21,674	26	17
Connecticut	12,170	25,427	28,087	29,044	30,303	20,803	27,367	27,365	27,637	28,176	2	1
Middle Atlantic	**10,738**	**21,617**	**24,139**	**25,028**	**26,106**	**18,356**	**23,267**	**23,518**	**23,816**	**24,273**	**(X)**	**(X)**
New York	10,906	22,321	24,844	25,726	26,782	18,643	24,024	24,205	24,480	24,902	7	4
New Jersey	11,648	24,182	26,834	27,741	28,858	19,911	26,027	26,144	26,397	26,832	4	2
Pennsylvania	9,923	18,883	21,314	22,195	23,279	16,962	20,324	20,766	21,120	21,645	17	18
Midwest	**9,872**	**18,067**	**20,328**	**21,542**	**22,617**	**16,875**	**19,446**	**19,805**	**20,499**	**21,029**	**(X)**	**(X)**
East North Central	**10,077**	**18,297**	**20,627**	**21,825**	**22,982**	**17,226**	**19,693**	**20,096**	**20,768**	**21,369**	**(X)**	**(X)**
Ohio	9,738	17,548	19,730	20,882	22,021	16,646	18,887	19,223	19,871	20,475	25	21
Indiana	9,215	16,816	19,219	20,261	21,273	15,752	18,099	18,725	19,280	19,780	31	29
Illinois	10,875	20,159	22,533	23,607	24,763	18,590	21,697	21,953	22,464	23,025	8	8
Michigan	10,154	18,237	20,599	22,173	23,551	17,357	19,629	20,069	21,098	21,898	15	15
Wisconsin	9,772	17,398	19,824	20,887	21,839	16,704	18,726	19,314	19,875	20,306	24	22
West North Central	**9,374**	**17,520**	**19,619**	**20,870**	**21,753**	**16,024**	**18,857**	**19,114**	**19,859**	**20,226**	**(X)**	**(X)**
Minnesota	9,982	18,779	20,911	22,257	23,118	17,063	20,212	20,373	21,179	21,495	16	19
Iowa	9,346	16,684	18,412	20,176	21,012	15,976	17,957	17,938	19,199	19,537	27	30
Missouri	9,256	17,409	19,501	20,562	21,627	15,822	18,737	18,999	19,566	20,109	30	26
North Dakota	7,641	15,321	17,212	18,610	18,663	13,062	16,490	16,769	17,709	17,353	47	42
South Dakota	7,701	15,630	18,122	19,562	19,506	13,164	16,823	17,656	18,615	18,137	45	37
Nebraska	8,988	17,379	19,693	20,819	21,703	15,364	18,705	19,186	19,811	20,179	32	25
Kansas	9,829	17,642	19,880	20,762	21,825	16,802	18,988	19,369	19,756	20,293	22	23
South	**8,958**	**16,895**	**19,085**	**19,936**	**20,945**	**15,313**	**18,184**	**18,594**	**18,970**	**19,475**	**(X)**	**(X)**
South Atlantic	**9,204**	**18,230**	**20,341**	**21,222**	**22,342**	**15,733**	**19,621**	**19,818**	**20,194**	**20,774**	**(X)**	**(X)**
Delaware	10,356	19,719	22,015	22,919	24,124	17,703	21,224	21,449	21,809	22,430	14	11
Maryland	10,824	22,090	23,937	24,869	25,927	18,503	23,776	23,321	23,664	24,107	9	5
District of Columbia	12,508	24,648	29,346	30,721	32,274	21,381	26,529	28,591	29,233	30,008	(X)	(X)
Virginia	9,857	19,537	21,650	22,503	23,597	16,850	21,028	21,093	21,413	21,940	19	14
West Virginia	7,972	13,967	16,230	17,089	17,915	13,627	15,033	15,813	16,261	16,657	43	48
North Carolina	8,000	16,275	18,719	19,579	20,604	13,675	17,517	18,238	18,631	19,158	42	33
South Carolina	7,558	15,106	16,877	17,713	18,788	12,920	16,259	16,443	16,855	17,469	48	40
Georgia	8,353	17,123	19,244	20,198	21,278	14,279	18,430	18,749	19,220	19,784	37	28
Florida	9,835	18,788	20,795	21,654	22,916	16,812	20,222	20,260	20,605	21,307	21	20
East South Central	**7,730**	**14,792**	**17,089**	**18,020**	**18,884**	**13,214**	**15,921**	**16,649**	**17,147**	**17,558**	**(X)**	**(X)**
Kentucky	8,051	14,747	16,887	17,752	18,612	13,762	15,872	16,453	16,892	17,305	40	43
Tennessee	8,010	15,905	18,458	19,446	20,376	13,692	17,119	17,983	18,504	18,946	41	36
Alabama	7,656	14,903	17,104	17,925	18,781	13,087	16,040	16,664	17,057	17,463	46	41
Mississippi	6,868	12,571	14,713	15,791	16,531	11,740	13,530	14,335	15,026	15,371	50	50

Region, Division, and State	Current Dollars					Constant (1992) Dollars					Income Rank	
	1980	1990	1993	1994	1995	1980	1990	1993	1994	1995	1980	1995
South, *cont.*												
West South Central	9,329	15,908	18,151	18,906	19,816	15,947	17,122	17,684	17,990	18,425	(X)	(X)
Arkansas	7,371	13,784	15,980	16,818	17,429	12,600	14,736	15,569	16,003	16,205	49	49
Louisiana	8,672	14,281	16,555	17,615	18,827	14,824	15,371	16,129	16,762	17,505	34	39
Oklahoma	9,308	15,119	17,041	17,602	18,152	15,911	16,273	16,603	16,749	16,878	28	46
Texas	9,840	16,749	19,023	19,719	20,654	16,821	18,027	18,534	18,764	19,204	20	32
West	10,889	19,296	21,036	21,629	22,852	18,614	20,768	20,495	20,581	21,248	(X)	(X)
Mountain	9,455	16,589	18,975	19,789	20,900	16,162	17,855	18,487	18,831	19,433	(X)	(X)
Montana	8,728	14,741	17,624	17,824	18,482	14,920	15,866	17,171	16,961	17,185	33	44
Idaho	8,433	15,301	17,717	18,406	19,264	14,415	16,469	17,261	17,515	17,912	36	38
Wyoming	11,356	16,902	19,850	20,377	21,321	19,412	18,192	19,339	19,390	19,824	6	27
Colorado	10,616	18,814	21,560	22,320	23,449	18,147	20,250	21,005	21,239	21,803	13	16
New Mexico	8,147	14,213	16,295	17,025	18,055	13,926	15,298	15,876	16,200	16,788	39	47
Arizona	9,272	16,265	18,194	19,153	20,421	15,850	17,506	17,726	18,225	18,987	29	35
Utah	7,942	14,060	16,354	17,171	18,223	13,576	15,133	15,933	16,339	16,944	44	45
Nevada	11,559	20,254	22,727	23,817	25,013	19,759	21,800	22,142	22,663	23,257	5	7
Pacific	11,403	20,240	21,774	22,301	23,581	19,492	21,785	21,214	21,221	21,926	(X)	(X)
Washington	10,716	19,265	21,838	22,542	23,639	18,318	20,735	21,276	21,450	21,980	11	13
Oregon	9,863	17,199	19,534	20,467	21,736	16,860	18,511	19,032	19,476	20,210	18	24
California	11,681	20,654	21,893	22,353	23,699	19,968	22,230	21,330	21,270	22,035	3	12
Alaska	13,692	20,881	22,887	23,431	24,182	23,405	22,474	22,298	22,296	22,484	1	10
Hawaii	10,774	20,906	23,566	24,043	24,738	18,417	22,501	22,960	22,878	23,001	10	9

(X) Not applicable.

HOUSEHOLD MEDIAN INCOME, BY RACE AND HOUSEHOLD TYPE: 1994

ITEM	All Households	FAMILY HOUSEHOLDS				NONFAMILY HOUSEHOLDS		
		Total	Married Couple	Male Householder Wife Absent	Female Householder Husband Absent	Total	Single-Person Household	
							Male Householder	Female Householder
Median Income (dollars)								
All households	32,264	39,390	45,041	30,472	19,872	18,947	21,216	13,431
White	34,028	41,334	45,555	32,227	22,605	19,783	22,153	13,912
Black	21,027	25,475	40,432	23,073	14,650	13,320	15,223	9,621
Hispanic[2]	23,421	25,210	29,915	25,596	13,200	15,789	17,474	8,382
Number (1,000)								
All households	98,990	69,305	53,858	3,226	12,220	29,686	10,140	14,592
Under $5,000	4,044	1,947	648	102	1,197	2,097	665	1,327
$5,000 to $9,999	9,368	3,687	1,458	244	1,984	5,682	1,489	4,006
$10,000 to $14,999	9,025	4,646	2,732	288	1,626	4,380	1,408	2,679
$15,000 to $19,999	8,346	5,036	3,362	342	1,333	3,310	1,208	1,693
$20,000 to $24,999	8,142	5,278	3,834	301	1,143	2,864	1,075	1,345
$25,000 to $34,999	14,032	10,016	7,630	548	1,838	4,016	1,617	1,619
$35,000 to $49,999	16,138	12,627	10,341	614	1,671	3,512	1,349	1,134
$50,000 to $74,999	16,373	16,989	12,487	508	993	2,384	831	550

[1] Includes other nonfamily households not shown separately. [2] Persons of Hispanic origin may be of any race.

United States

HOUSEHOLD INCOME—PERCENT DISTRIBUTION, BY INCOME LEVEL AND SELECTED CHARACTERISTICS: 1994

Characteristic	Number of Households (1,000)	Percent Distribution							Median Income (Dollars)
		Under $10,000	$10,000–$14,000	$15,000–$24,999	$25,000–$34,999	$35,000–$49,999	$50,000–$74,999	$75,000 and over	
TOTAL[1]	**98,990**	**13.5**	**9.1**	**16.7**	**14.2**	**16.3**	**16.5**	**13.7**	**32,264**
Age of householder									
15 to 24 years	5,444	23.2	14.6	25.7	17.7	11.2	5.7	1.9	19,340
25 to 34 years	19,453	11.2	7.6	17.2	16.7	20.5	17.8	9.0	33,151
35 to 44 years	22,914	8.6	5.4	12.3	14.2	19.2	22.4	17.8	41,667
45 to 54 years	17,590	7.6	4.9	11.0	11.7	17.5	22.3	25.0	47,261
55 to 64 years	12,224	13.6	7.0	15.2	13.9	16.3	17.1	16.9	35,232
65 years and over	21,365	23.4	17.7	24.0	13.2	9.6	6.7	5.2	18,095
White	83,737	11.7	8.7	16.4	14.4	16.7	17.3	14.6	34,028
Black	11,655	26.3	11.5	18.9	12.8	13.3	10.8	6.3	21,027
Hispanic[2]	7,735	20.5	12.2	20.4	14.9	14.4	10.9	6.7	23,421
Northeast	19,593	13.9	8.4	14.8	12.9	15.8	17.1	17.0	34,926
Midwest	23,683	12.9	8.7	17.4	14.7	17.3	16.7	12.4	32,505
South	34,766	14.8	9.9	17.4	14.9	15.9	15.4	11.6	30,021
West	20,948	11.8	8.9	16.4	13.5	16.3	17.7	15.3	34,452
Size of household									
1 person	24,732	30.3	16.5	21.5	13.1	10.0	5.6	3.0	16,222
2 persons	31,834	8.1	8.4	18.7	16.2	17.8	17.1	13.6	33,955
3 persons	16,827	8.7	5.7	13.9	14.2	18.6	21.3	17.7	41,043
4 persons	15,321	7.1	4.5	10.3	12.3	19.4	24.7	21.7	46,757
5 persons	6,616	7.6	5.7	11.8	13.1	18.2	22.4	21.4	44,135
6 persons	2,279	7.2	6.0	12.7	12.9	19.7	20.0	21.5	42,683
7 or more persons	1,382	9.9	8.2	15.8	14.3	16.7	17.9	17.1	36,622
Family households	69,305	8.1	6.7	14.9	14.5	18.2	20.2	17.4	39,390
Married couple	53,858	3.9	5.1	13.4	14.2	19.2	23.2	21.1	45,041
Male householder, wife absent	3,226	10.7	8.9	19.9	17.0	19.0	15.8	8.6	30,472
Female householder, husband absent	12,220	26.0	13.3	20.3	15.0	13.7	8.1	3.6	19,872
Nonfamily householder	29,686	26.2	14.8	20.8	13.5	11.8	8.0	4.9	18,947
Male householder	13,190	17.7	11.8	21.3	15.8	15.1	11.1	7.2	24,593
Female householder	16,496	33.0	17.1	20.4	11.7	9.2	5.6	3.0	14,948
Educational attainment of householder[3]									
Total	93,546	13.0	8.8	16.1	14.0	16.6	17.2	14.3	33,486
Less than 9th grade	8,242	34.0	18.3	22.6	11.3	7.8	4.2	1.9	14,275
9th to 12th grade (no diploma)	9,644	27.5	15.6	21.1	14.0	11.4	7.2	3.1	17,543
High school graduate	29,647	13.3	10.0	18.4	16.4	18.5	15.6	8.0	30,071
Some college, no degree	16,786	9.1	7.2	16.8	15.4	19.8	19.8	11.8	35,879
Associate degree	6,403	6.9	5.7	14.4	14.6	20.0	22.6	15.8	40,258
Bachelor's degree or more	22,824	3.5	3.0	8.7	10.55	16.2	24.6	33.4	57,440
Bachelor's degree	14,380	3.9	3.5	9.9	12.1	17.1	25.4	28.2	52,370
Master's degree	5,506	2.6	2.2	7.2	9.1	17.1	25.3	36.6	61,045
Professional degree	1,710	2.6	2.1	6.7	6.6	11.1	18.2	52.2	18,002
Doctorate degree	1,227	2.9	2.4	5.3	4.6	9.9	21.5	53.5	78,157
Tenure									
Owner occupied	64,045	8.2	7.2	14.2	13.6	17.8	20.6	18.5	40,299
Renter occupied	33,159	23.0	12.6	21.2	15.3	13.8	9.3	4.8	21,534
Occupier paid no cash rent	1,787	29.2	13.2	22.2	13.2	11.1	7.7	3.5	18,462

[1] Includes other races not shown separately.   [2] Persons of Hispanic origin may be of any race.   [3] 25 years old and over.

United States

CRIME IN THE UNITED STATES

CRIME BY TYPE: 1984–1994
Data refer to offenses known to the police. Minus sign (-) indicates decrease.

ITEM AND YEAR	VIOLENT CRIME						PROPERTY CRIME			
	Total	Total	Murder[1]	Forcible Rape	Robbery	Aggravated Assault	Total	Burglary	Larceny —Theft	Motor Vehicle Theft
Number of offenses (1,000)										
1984	11,882	1,273	18.7	84.2	485	685	10,609	2,984	6,592	1,032
1985	12,431	1,329	19.0	88.7	498	723	11,103	3,073	6,926	1,103
1986	13,212	1,489	20.6	91.5	543	834	11,723	3,241	7,257	1,224
1987	13,509	1,484	20.1	91.1	518	855	12,025	3,236	7,500	1,289
1988	13,923	1,566	20.7	92.5	543	910	12,357	3,218	7,706	1,433
1989	14,251	1,646	21.5	94.5	578	952	12,605	3,168	7,872	1,565
1990	14,476	1,820	23.4	102.6	639	1,055	12,656	3,074	7,946	1,636
1991	14,873	1,912	24.7	106.6	688	1,093	12,961	3,157	8,142	1,662
1992	14,438	1,932	23.8	109.1	672	1,127	12,506	2,980	7,915	1,611
1993	14,145	1,926	24.5	106.0	660	1,136	12,219	2,835	7,821	1,563
1994	13,992	1,864	23.3	102.1	619	1,120	12,128	2,712	7,876	1,539
Percent change, number of offenses										
1984 to 1994	17.8	46.4	24.6	21.3	27.6	63.5	14.3	−9.1	19.5	49.1
1991 to 1992	−3.1	1.0	−3.8	2.3	−2.4	3.0	−3.6	−5.9	−2.9	−3.2
1992 to 1993	−2.1	−0.3	2.9	−2.9	−1.8	0.8	−2.3	−5.1	−1.2	−3.1
1993 to 1994	−1.1	−3.3	−5.2	−3.8	−6.6	−1.4	−0.8	−4.5	0.7	−1.6
Rate per 100,000 population										
1984	5,031	539	7.9	35.7	205	290	4,492	1,264	2,791	437
1985	5,207	557	7.9	37.1	209	303	4,651	1,287	2,901	462
1986	5,480	618	8.6	37.9	225	346	4,863	1,345	3,010	508
1987	5,550	610	8.3	37.4	213	351	4,940	1,330	3,081	529
1988	5,664	637	8.4	37.6	221	370	5,027	1,309	3,135	583
1989	5,741	663	8.7	38.1	233	383	5,078	1,276	3,171	630
1990	5,820	732	9.4	41.2	257	424	5,089	1,236	3,195	658
1991	5,898	758	9.8	42.3	273	433	5,140	1,252	3,229	659
1992	5,660	758	9.3	42.8	264	442	4,903	1,168	3,103	631
1993	5,484	747	9.5	41.1	256	440	4,738	1,099	3,032	606
1994	5,374	716	9.0	39.2	238	430	4,658	1,042	3,025	591
Percent change, rate per 100,000 population										
1984 to 1994	6.8	32.8	13.9	9.8	16.1	48.3	3.7	−17.6	8.4	35.2
1991 to 1992	−4.2	0.0	−5.4	1.2	−3.3	2.0	−4.8	−7.2	−4.1	−4.4
1992 to 1993	−3.2	−1.5	2.1	−4.1	−3.1	−0.5	−3.5	−6.3	−2.3	−4.1
1993 to 1994	−2.0	−4.3	−5.6	−4.8	−7.6	−2.3	−1.7	−5.5	−0.2	−2.5

− indicates decrease.   [1] Includes nonnegligent manslaughter.

CRIME RATES BY STATE (1992–1994) AND BY TYPE (1994)

Rates are offenses known to the police per 100,000 population.

REGION, DIVISION, AND STATE	1992 Total	1993 Total	1994 Total	1994 Violent Crime Total	1994 Violent Crime Murder[1]
United States	**5,660**	**5,483**	**5,374**	**716**	**9.0**
Northeast	**4,837**	**4,613**	**4,345**	**662**	**7.1**
New England	**4,614**	**4,431**	**4,136**	**489**	**3.9**
Maine	3,524	3,154	3,273	130	2.3
New Hampshire	3,081	2,905	2,741	117	1.4
Vermont	3,410	3,972	3,250	97	1.0
Massachusetts	5,003	4,894	4,441	708	3.5
Rhode Island	4,578	4,499	4,119	376	4.1
Connecticut	5,053	4,560	4,548	456	6.6
Middle Atlantic	**4,914**	**4,676**	**4,417**	**722**	**8.2**
New York	5,858	5,551	5,071	966	11.1
New Jersey	5,064	4,801	4,661	614	5.0
Pennsylvania	3,393	3,271	3,272	427	5.9
Midwest	**4,975**	**4,806**	**4,816**	**601**	**7.5**
East North Central	**5,136**	**4,953**	**4,951**	**657**	**8.4**
Ohio	4,666	4,485	4,461	486	6.0
Indiana	4,687	4,465	4,593	525	7.9
Illinois[1]	5,765	5,618	5,626	961	11.7
Michigan	5,611	5,453	5,445	766	9.8
Wisconsin	4,319	4,054	3,944	271	4.5
West North Central	**4,594**	**4,454**	**4,496**	**468**	**5.3**
Minnesota	4,591	4,386	4,341	359	3.2
Iowa	3,957	3,846	3,655	315	1.7
Missouri	5,097	5,095	5,308	744	10.5
North Dakota	2,903	2,820	2,736	82	0.2
South Dakota	2,999	2,958	3,102	228	1.4
Nebraska	4,324	4,117	4,440	390	3.1
Kansas	5,320	4,975	4,894	479	5.8
South	**6,155**	**5,983**	**5,848**	**769**	**10.7**
South Atlantic	**6,428**	**6,334**	**6,257**	**830**	**10.1**
Delaware	4,848	4,872	4,148	561	4.7
Maryland	6,225	6,107	6,123	948	11.6
District of Columbia[3]	11,407	11,761	11,085	2,663	70.0
Virginia	4,299	4,116	4,048	358	8.7
West Virginia	2,610	2,533	2,528	216	5.4
North Carolina	5,802	5,652	5,625	655	10.9
South Carolina	5,893	5,903	6,001	1,031	9.6
Georgia	6,405	6,193	6,010	668	10.0
Florida	8,358	8,351	8,250	1,147	8.3
East South Central	**4,589**	**4,528**	**4,624**	**654**	**10.3**
Kentucky	3,324	3,260	3,499	605	6.4
Tennessee	5,136	5,240	5,120	748	9.3
Alabama	5,268	4,879	4,903	684	11.9
Mississippi	4,282	4,418	4,837	494	15.3

[1] Includes nonnegligent manslaughter.   [2] Forcible rape figures for 1992 and 1994 were estimated using the national rate of forcible rapes when grouped by like agencies, as figures submitted were not in accordance with national Uniform Crime Reporting program guidelines.

	1994					
Violent Crime			Property Crime			
Forcible Rape[2]	Robbery	Aggravated Assault	Total	Burglary	Larceny —Theft	Motor Vehicle Theft
39.2	238	430	4,658	1,042	3,025	591
26.3	291	337	3,682	804	2,280	599
28.6	134	322	3,647	829	2,271	547
25.6	22	80	3,143	721	2,279	143
35.8	27	53	2,624	464	1,958	203
27.6	12	56	3,153	737	2,268	149
30.2	168	506	3,733	881	2,151	701
27.4	87	257	3,744	913	2,311	520
24.6	188	237	4,093	890	2,587	616
25.7	346	343	3,695	795	2,283	617
25.9	477	452	4,105	906	2,490	709
24.9	288	296	4,047	912	2,475	660
26.1	187	208	2,845	552	1,844	449
42.9	200	350	4,215	886	2,869	460
44.2	231	373	4,295	898	2,889	508
47.1	188	245	3,976	866	2,682	427
35.6	130	352	4,068	851	2,782	435
33.3	373	543	4,665	1,005	3,096	564
70.8	229	457	4,679	967	3,056	656
23.5	113	130	3,674	646	2,667	361
39.8	128	295	4,027	858	2,822	347
59.7	118	179	3,982	792	2,876	314
23.5	47	243	3,340	667	2,492	180
37.0	231	465	4,564	1,053	2,999	512
23.4	11	47	2,654	325	2,179	151
42.0	19	166	2,875	546	2,208	121
30.8	75	280	4,051	676	2,991	384
37.1	120	3116	4,415	1,121	2,955	339
43.4	221	494	5,080	1,206	3,329	545
41.2	254	524	5,427	1,271	3,570	585
75.6	126	355	3,587	790	2,446	350
40.7	403	493	5,175	1,043	3,368	763
43.7	1,107	1,442	8,423	1,761	5,213	1,449
28.5	133	188	3,690	639	2,772	279
20.3	42	148	2,313	586	1,547	180
33.0	181	430	4,970	1,473	3,196	302
54.3	186	780	4,970	1,274	3,337	360
34.7	223	400	5,343	1,154	3,632	557
52.3	329	757	7,103	1,701	4,491	912
41.5	163	439	3,971	1,047	2,531	393
35.3	94	470	2,893	750	1,919	224
49.2	207	482	4,372	1,142	2,670	560
35.2	171	465	4,219	1,044	2,843	332
45.4	163	271	4,434	1,292	2,646	405

continues

United States

Crime Rates by State Continued

REGION, DIVISION, AND STATE	1992, Total	1993, Total	1994 Total	1994 Violent Crime Total	1994 Violent Crime Murder[1]
West South Central	**6,589**	**6,228**	**5,866**	**732**	**12.0**
Arkansas	4,762	4,811	4,799	595	12.0
Louisiana	6,546	6,847	6,671	982	19.8
Oklahoma	5,432	5,294	5,570	652	6.9
Texas	7,058	6,439	5,872	707	11.0
West	**6,388**	**6,220**	**6,152**	**805**	**9.4**
Mountain	**6,012**	**5,929**	**6,097**	**581**	**7.3**
Montana	4,596	4,790	5,019	177	3.3
Idaho	3,996	3,845	4,077	286	3.5
Wyoming	4,575	4,163	4,290	273	3.4
Colorado	5,959	5,527	5,318	510	5.4
New Mexico	6,434	6,266	6,188	889	10.7
Arizona	7,029	7,432	7,925	703	10.5
Utah	5,659	5,237	5,301	305	2.9
Nevada	6,204	6,180	6,677	1,002	11.7
Pacific	**6,521**	**6,324**	**6,172**	**887**	**10.2**
Washington	6,173	5,952	6,028	511	5.5
Oregon	5,821	5,766	6,296	521	4.9
California	6,679	6,457	6,174	1,013	11.8
Alaska	5,570	5,568	5,708	766	6.3
Hawaii	6,112	6,277	6,681	262	4.2

CRIME RATES BY TYPE AND LARGEST CITIES: 1994

Rates are offenses known to the police per 100,000 population.

CITY RANKED BY POPULATION SIZE, 1994[1]	Crime Index Total	Violent Crime Total	Violent Crime Murder[1]	Violent Crime Forcible Rape
New York, NY	7,226.1	1,860.9	21.3	36.3
Los Angeles, CA	7,840.0	2,059.0	23.8	43.8
Chicago, IL	(2)	(2)	33.1	(2)
Houston, TX	7,285.4	1,307.5	21.3	53.0
Philadelphia, PA	6,434.6	1,322.5	25.9	46.2
San Diego, CA	6,564.5	1,087.0	9.7	34.5
Phoenix, AZ	10,048.3	1,080.5	21.5	40.7
Dallas, TX	9,476.7	1,589.0	27.8	90.1
Detroit, MI	11,917.2	2,687.2	52.9	109.2
San Antonio, TX	8,768.8	647.2	19.4	56.5
Honolulu, HI	6,906.5	287.0	4.0	30.2
San Jose, CA	4,484.5	725.6	4.0	46.0
Las Vegas, NV	7,728.2	1,251.4	14.0	76.3
San Francisco, CA	8,341.8	1,461.4	12.3	39.4
Baltimore, MD	12,552.2	2,834.4	43.4	86.2
Jacksonville, FL	9,623.7	1,519.9	15.5	94.5
Columbus, OH	8,696.8	1,043.6	15.4	104.8
Milwaukee, WI	8,149.8	1,043.7	22.1	68.2
Memphis, TN	9,770.1	1,568.3	25.3	110.6
Washington, DC	11,077.9	2,662.6	70.0	43.7

1994						
Violent Crime			Property Crime			
Forcible Rape[2]	Robbery	Aggravated Assault	Total	Burglary	Larceny—Theft	Motor Vehicle Theft
48.1	**199**	**473**	**5,134**	**1,188**	**3,382**	564
41.9	129	413	4,204	1,097	2,792	315
41.6	267	650	5,609	1,079	3,803	608
49.6	128	467	4,919	1,251	3,193	475
49.5	205	441	5,166	1,168	3,395	603
40.0	**256**	**500**	**5,346**	**1,163**	**3,384**	800
42.2	**130**	**402**	**5,516**	**1,105**	**3,830**	581
27.2	33	114	4,842	722	3,834	286
27.9	18	236	3,791	719	2,877	195
33.6	17	219	4,017	651	3,205	162
43.2	107	354	4,809	926	3,490	393
52.4	141	685	5,299	1,327	3,467	505
36.0	162	495	7,221	1,476	4,679	1,067
42.2	64	196	4,996	791	3,907	298
68.7	352	569	5,676	1,355	3,562	759
39.2	**303**	**535**	**5,284**	**1,184**	**3,221**	880
60.5	140	306	5,516	1,044	3,972	501
43.2	138	334	5,776	1,101	3,970	705
34.9	357	609	5,161	1,223	2,958	981
69.0	146	545	4,942	800	3,601	540
30.4	104	124	6,418	1,190	4,687	541

Violent Crime		Property Crime			
Robbery	Aggravated Assault	Total	Burglary	Larceny—Theft	Motor Vehicle Theft
988.8	814.5	5,365.2	1,204.6	2,859.9	1,300.7
868.0	1,123.4	5,781.0	1,226.2	3,120.5	1,434.3
1,210.5	1,440.9	7,314.9	1,563.6	4,323.4	1,427.9
567.7	665.5	5,977.9	1,451.5	3,239.2	1,287.2
814.2	436.2	5,112.2	903.9	2,588.3	1,620.0
329.0	704.8	5,486.6	1,102.8	3,012.0	1,371.8
320.7	697.6	8,967.9	1,983.7	5,063.9	1,920.3
666.0	805.2	7,887.7	1,680.7	4,542.1	1,664.9
1,249.4	1,275.8	9,229.9	2,167.3	4,170.2	2,829.4
278.1	293.1	8,121.6	1,642.4	5,491.5	987.7
120.1	132.7	6,619.5	1,137.5	4,831.7	650.3
136.0	539.5	3,758.9	714.3	2,490.1	554.6
505.6	655.6	6,476.8	1,548.9	3,900.1	1,027.8
893.2	516.5	6,880.4	1,086.2	4,547.0	1,247.2
1,525.3	1,179.4	9,717.8	2,150.6	5,736.4	1,830.8
499.7	910.2	8,103.8	2,089.2	5,023.9	990.7
555.5	367.8	7,653.2	2,019.9	4,596.1	1,037.3
638.9	314.4	7,106.2	1,345.7	4,060.8	1,699.6
793.8	638.6	8,201.8	2,503.4	3,834.7	1,863.7
1,107.2	1,441.8	8,415.3	1,760.9	5,205.8	1,448.6

continues

Crime Rates by Type and Largest Cities Continued

CITY RANKED BY POPULATION SIZE, 1994[1]	Crime Index, Total	Violent Crime		
		Total	Murder[1]	Forcible Rape
El Paso, TX	7,159.6	950.0	7.8	41.2
Boston, MA	9,534.0	1,915.5	15.3	81.4
Seattle, WA	10,717.8	1,210.1	12.8	58.9
Charlotte, NC	9,686.0	1,726.7	16.5	66.4
Nashville-Davidson, TN	10,065.0	1,798.4	14.0	97.4
Austin, TX	7,941.0	635.0	7.2	48.7
Denver, CO	6,933.1	920.8	15.8	71.6
Cleveland, OH	7,456.1	1,529.7	26.1	148.0
New Orleans, LA	10,089.7	1,886.9	85.8	88.3
Fort Worth, TX	9,189.3	1,277.8	27.9	87.4
Portland, OR	11,815.7	1,902.1	10.8	86.4
Oklahoma City, OK	12,004.7	1,402.9	14.1	118.4
Long Beach, CA	7,530.3	1,416.7	17.9	37.4
Tucson, AZ	12,254.8	1,106.0	8.4	65.5
Kansas City, MO	12,551.4	2,435.3	32.3	111.6
Virginia Beach, VA	4,966.0	270.9	7.7	33.9
Atlanta, GA	16,118.5	3,571.0	46.4	102.6
St. Louis, MO	16,350.7	3,750.7	63.5	77.9
Sacramento, CA	10,326.7	1,206.3	15.9	44.7
Fresno, CA	12,041.1	1,620.0	22.0	50.2
Tulsa, OK	7,400.7	1,215.5	11.0	77.6
Miami, FL	17,177.0	3,413.6	30.5	58.2
Minneapolis, MN	11,167.0	1,907.6	16.7	155.9
Pittsburgh, PA	7,148.8	1,113.7	17.4	70.8
Cincinnati, OH	8,012.7	1,323.1	10.4	104.1
Toledo, OH	9,130.5	1,104.5	12.1	107.3
Buffalo, NY	9,552.2	2,124.2	27.7	86.3
Wichita, KS	9,208.3	742.2	13.3	70.7
Mesa, AZ	8,295.9	749.4	5.4	38.0
Colorado Springs, CO	6,667.6	481.5	4.5	73.0
Tampa, FL	17,481.0	3,482.6	21.0	101.1
Santa Ana, CA	6,023.1	1,050.8	25.3	27.3
Arlington, TX	7,253.1	852.0	6.3	50.2
Anaheim, CA	6,554.6	947.9	8.6	32.3
Corpus Christi, TX	9,817.6	856.3	4.7	64.3
Louisville, KY	6,430.5	1,004.7	18.8	51.4
St. Paul, MN	7,101.1	995.6	10.6	98.1
Newark, NJ	13,827.1	3,840.6	35.4	76.4
Birmingham, AL	12,191.8	2,444.8	49.8	100.7
Norfolk, VA	7,635.0	916.0	23.5	60.4
Anchorage, AK	7,356.9	976.9	8.7	78.1
Aurora, CO	7,813.9	1,448.0	5.9	58.1
St. Petersburg, FL	9,844.9	2,254.5	9.4	87.5
Riverside, CA	9,203.3	1,626.8	15.2	55.2
Lexington-Fayette, KY	6,799.7	980.4	9.7	48.9
Rochester, NY	9,613.2	1,154.3	26.4	61.7
Jersey City, NJ	8,119.4	1,865.1	16.0	32.0
Raleigh, NC	7,243.6	951.4	13.2	39.0
Baton Rouge, LA	14,052.4	2,449.7	28.2	79.4
Akron, OH	7,102.8	960.7	10.2	86.6
Stockton, CA	10,499.9	1,613.5	19.7	54.2

Violent Crime		Property Crime			
Robbery	Aggravated Assault	Total	Burglary	Larceny —Theft	Motor Vehicle Theft
192.2	708.8	6,209.7	756.7	4,762.2	690.7
762.5	1,056.4	7,618.5	1,221.3	4,378.3	2,019.0
469.4	669.1	9,507.7	1,515.2	6,803.7	1,188.9
514.7	1,129.2	7,959.3	1,958.9	5,400.8	599.5
508.7	1,178.2	8,266.6	1,600.2	5,520.6	1,145.8
301.4	277.7	7,306.0	1,377.2	5,160.1	768.7
335.4	498.0	6,012.3	1,518.1	3,272.1	1,222.1
775.1	580.6	5,926.4	1,581.7	2,554.4	1,790.3
976.1	736.7	8,202.8	2,037.3	4,431.3	1,734.2
503.7	658.7	7,911.5	1,756.3	5,020.7	1,134.5
506.2	1,298.7	9,913.6	1,727.8	6,125.0	2,060.8
379.0	891.4	10,601.8	2,233.2	7,308.3	1,060.3
767.3	594.1	6,113.6	1,453.0	3,057.0	1,603.6
229.3	802.9	11,148.8	1,632.3	7,976.6	1,539.9
848.8	1,442.5	10,116.2	2,723.4	5,718.4	1,674.4
142.5	86.8	4,695.1	759.8	3,713.9	221.3
1,299.4	2,122.5	12,547.5	2,951.3	7,511.6	2,084.6
1,543.1	2,066.1	12,600.0	3,207.2	7,105.9	2,286.9
588.5	557.2	9,120.4	2,073.7	4,775.4	2,271.4
734.3	813.5	10,421.1	2,001.5	4,871.2	3,548.4
280.6	846.3	6,185.1	1,715.8	3,289.0	1,180.4
1,537.2	1,787.7	13,763.4	2,967.8	8,064.9	2,730.7
928.7	806.3	9,259.4	2,387.6	5,738.1	1,133.7
669.8	355.7	6,035.1	1,176.1	3,409.7	1,449.3
580.7	627.9	6,689.7	1,640.5	4,577.2	472.0
523.0	462.1	8,026.1	1,985.6	4,849.5	1,191.0
1,007.8	1,002.3	7,428.0	2,247.2	3,774.6	1,406.2
334.8	323.4	8,466.1	2,053.2	5,328.9	1,083.9
129.0	576.9	7,546.5	1,582.8	4,863.4	1,100.3
128.5	275.5	6,186.0	971.7	4,865.1	349.2
1,146.4	2,214.1	13,998.4	2,964.1	7,297.5	3,736.8
604.4	393.8	4,972.3	836.8	2,864.0	1,271.6
228.1	567.4	6,401.1	1,210.1	4,325.1	865.9
406.2	500.9	5,606.7	1,175.6	3,201.7	1,229.4
177.7	609.7	8,961.3	1,534.2	6,939.8	487.2
473.0	461.4	5,425.8	1,593.5	2,945.3	887.1
318.0	568.9	6,105.5	1,485.7	3,881.0	738.8
2,130.8	1,598.0	9,986.5	2,375.4	4,118.8	3,492.3
730.7	1,563.6	9,746.9	2,392.4	6,009.7	1,344.8
460.3	371.9	6,719.0	1,199.8	4,823.1	696.1
287.4	602.8	6,380.0	897.2	4,619.0	863.7
246.4	1,137.5	6,365.9	1,193.7	4,667.9	504.3
619.7	1,537.9	7,590.3	1,931.8	5,067.2	591.4
502.6	1,053.8	7,576.4	2,068.9	3,894.3	1,613.2
294.4	627.5	5,819.3	1,300.9	4,235.8	282.6
710.0	356.3	8,458.8	2,272.5	5,292.9	913.4
969.6	847.5	6,254.2	1,854.8	2,803.6	1,595.9
361.7	537.5	6,292.3	1,554.6	4,292.6	445.0
648.7	1,693.3	11,602.6	2,362.8	7,256.8	1,985.0
360.5	503.4	6,142.2	1,350.4	3,879.9	911.8
641.4	898.3	8,886.4	2,041.3	4,991.3	1,853.8

CRIME RATES BY TYPE AND AREA: 1994

Number of crimes given in thousands. Rate is per 100,000 population. Estimated totals based on reports from city and rural law enforcement agencies representing 96 percent of the national population.

Type of Crime	United States		Metropolitan Areas		Other Cities		Rural Areas	
	Total	Rate	Total	Rate	Total	Rate	Total	Rate
TOTAL	13,992	5,374	12,209	5,894	1,134	5,318	648	2,034
Violent crime	**1,864**	**716**	**1,682**	**812**	**107**	**500**	**75**	**237**
Murder and nonnegligent manslaughter	23	9	21	10	1	5	2	5
Forcible rape	102	39	85	41	8	39	8	26
Robbery	619	238	598	288	16	75	5	17
Aggravated assault	1,120	430	978	472	81	382	60	189
Property crime	**12,128**	**4,658**	**10,527**	**5,082**	**1,028**	**4,818**	**573**	**1,797**
Burglary	2,712	1,042	2,305	1,113	206	965	202	632
Larceny—theft	7,786	3,025	6,770	3,268	773	3,623	333	1,046
Motor vehicle theft	1,539	591	1,452	901	49	230	38	119

U.S. POSTAL SERVICE

ZIP CODES

Five-digit ZIP (Zone Improvement Plan) codes were introduced in 1964 to identify each postal delivery area in the United States. In some areas, two cities may share a ZIP code; in others, such as New York City, one geographic area may have many ZIP codes, including separate ZIP codes for each major office building. In this book, the Zip codes are representative rather than specific for the larger cities. In New York City, for example, the indicated ZIP code is 10199, which is technically the ZIP code for the Manhattan borough postmaster. In 1983, the USPS introduced the ZIP +4 code, an expanded version of ZIP codes. Use of the four-digit add-on is voluntary, and it is primarily intended for the use of businesses and bulk mailers. For the ZIP code for a specific address in any area served by the U.S. Postal Service, the reader should consult a copy of the *U.S. Postal Service National Five-Digit ZIP Code & Post Office Directory*, available at any local post office and revised yearly, or use the U.S. Postal Service online ZIP code service at http://www.usps.gov/ncsc.

Aberdeen, SD	57401	Anaheim, CA	92803	Aspen, CO	81611
Abilene, TX	79604	Anchorage, AK	99501	Athens, GA	30601
Addison, IL	60101	Anderson, IN	46011	Atlanta, GA	30304
Akron, OH	44309	Anderson, SC	29621	Atlantic City, NJ	08401
Alameda, CA	94501	Annapolis, MD	21401	Attleboro, MA	02703
Albany, GA	31706	Ann Arbor, MI	48106	Auburn, AL	36830
Albuquerque, NM	87101	Anniston, AL	36201	Auburn, NY	13021
Alexandria, LA	71301	Antioch, CA	94509	Auburn, WA	98002
Alexandria, VA	22313	Appleton, WI	54911	Augusta, GA	30901
Alhambra, CA	91802	Arcadia, CA	91006	Aurora, GA	80010
Allen Park, MI	48101	Arlington, TX	76010	Aurora, IL	60504
Allentown, PA	18101	Arlington Heights, IL	60004	Austin, TX	78710
Alton, IL	62002	Artesia, CA	90701	Azusa, CA	91702
Altoona, PA	16601	Arvada, CO	80004	Bakersfield, CA	93302
Amarillo, TX	79120	Asheville, NC	28810	Baldwin Park, CA	91706
Ames, IA	50010	Ashland, KY	41101	Baltimore, MD	21233

Bangor, ME	04401	Bremerton, WA	98310	Chicopee, MA	01020
Barberton, OH	44203	Bridgeport, CT	06602	Chula Vista, CA	91910
Bartlesville, OK	74003	Bristol, CT	06010	Cicero, IL	60650
Baton Rouge, LA	70821	Brockton, MA	02401	Cincinnati, OH	45234
Battle Creek, MI	49016	Broken Arrow, OK	74012	Claremont, CA	91711
Bay City, MI	48706	Brookfield, WI	53045	Clarksville, TN	37040
Bayonne, NJ	07002	Brookline, MA	02146	Clearwater, FL	34618
Baytown, TX	77520	Brooklyn Center, MN	55429	Cleveland, OH	44101
Beaumont, TX	77707	Brooklyn Park, MN	55443	Cleveland, TN	37311
Beavercreek, OH	45434	Brook Park, OH	44142	Cleveland	44118
Beaverton, OR	97005	Brownsville, TX	78520	Heights, OH	
Bell, CA	90201	Brunswick, OH	44212	Clifton, NJ	07015
Belleville, IL	62220	Bryan, TX	77801	Clifton, IA	52732
Belleville, NJ	07109	Buena Park, CA	90622	Clovis, CA	93612
Bellevue, WA	98009	Buffalo, NY	14240	Clovis, NM	88101
Bellflower, CA	90706	Burbank, CA	91505	Coconut Grove, FL	33233
Bell Gardens, CA	90201	Burlingame, CA	94010	College Station, TX	77840
Bellingham, WA	98225	Burlington, IA	52601	Colorado	80901
Beloit, WI	53511	Burlington, NC	27215	Springs, CO	
Bergenfield, NJ	07621	Burlington, VT	05401	Columbia, MO	65201
Berkeley, CA	94704	Burnsville, MN	55337	Columbia, SC	29292
Berwyn, IL	60402	Burton, MI	48509	Columbia, TN	38401
Bessemer, AL	35020	Butte, MT	59701	Columbus, GA	31908
Bethel Park, PA	15102	Calumet City, IL	60409	Columbus, IN	47201
Bethesda, MD	20814	Camarillo, CA	93010	Columbus, MS	39701
Bethlehem, PA	18016	Cambridge, MA	02140	Columbus, OH	43216
Bettendorf, IA	52722	Camden, NJ	08101	Compton, CA	90220
Beverly, MA	01915	Campbell, CA	95008	Concord, CA	94520
Beverly Hills, CA	90210	Canton, OH	44711	Concord, NH	03301
Billings, MT	59101	Cape Coral, FL	33910	Coon Rapids, MN	55433
Biloxi, MS	39530	Cape Girardeau, MO	63701	Coral Gables, FL	33114
Binghamton, NY	13902	Carbondale, IL	62901	Coral Springs, FL	33065
Birmingham, AL	35203	Carlsbad, CA	92008	Corona, CA	91720
Bismarck, ND	58501	Carlsbad, NM	88220	Corpus Christi, TX	78469
Blacksburg, VA	24060	Carrollton, TX	75006	Corvallis, OR	97333
Blaine, MN	55434	Carson, CA	90745	Costa Mesa, CA	92626
Bloomfield, NJ	07003	Carson City, NV	89701	Council Bluffs, IA	51501
Bloomington, IL	61701	Casper, WY	82601	Covina, CA	91722
Bloomington, IN	47401	Cedar Falls, IA	50613	Covington, KY	41011
Bloomington, MN	55420	Cedar Rapids, IA	52401	Cranston, RI	02910
Blue Springs, MO	64015	Champaign, IL	61820	Crystal, MN	55428
Boca Raton, FL	33432	Chandler, AZ	85224	Culver City, CA	90230
Boise, ID	83708	Chapel Hill, NC	27514	Cumberland, MD	21502
Bolingbrook, IL	60439	Charleston, SC	29423	Cupertino, CA	95014
Bossier City, LA	71111	Charleston, WV	25301	Cuyahoga Falls, OH	44222
Boston, MA	02205	Charlotte, NC	28228	Cypress, CA	90630
Boulder, CO	80302	Charlottesville, VA	22906	Dallas, TX	75260
Bountiful, UT	84010	Chattanooga, TN	37421	Daly City, CA	94015
Bowie, MD	20715	Chelsea, MA	02150	Danbury, CT	06810
Bowling Green, KY	42101	Chesapeake, VA	23320	Danville, IL	61832
Bowling Green, OH	43402	Chester, PA	19013	Danville, VA	24541
Boynton Beach, FL	33435	Cheyenne, WY	82001	Davenport, IA	52802
Bradenton, FL	34206	Chicago, IL	60607	Davis, CA	95616
Brattleboro, VT	05301	Chicago Heights, IL	60411	Dayton, OH	45401
Brea, CA	92621	Chico, CA	95926	Daytona Beach, FL	32114

United States

Dearborn, MI	48120	Fairborn, OH	45324	Goldsboro, NC	27530
Dearborn Heights, MI	48127	Fairfield, CA	94533	Grand Forks, ND	58201
Decatur, AL	35602	Fairfield, OH	45014	Grand Island, NE	68802
Decatur, IL	62521	Fair Lawn, NJ	07410	Grand Junction, CO	81501
Deerfield Beach, FL	33441	Fall River, MA	02720	Grand Prairie, TX	75051
De Kalb, IL	60115	Fargo, ND	58102	Grand Rapids, MI	49501
Delray Beach, FL	33444	Farmington, NM	87401	Granite City, IL	62040
Del Rio, TX	78840	Fayetteville, AR	72701	Great Falls, MT	59401
Denton, TX	76201	Fayetteville, NC	28302	Greeley, CO	80631
Denver, CO	80201	Ferndale, MI	48220	Green Bay, WI	54303
Des Moines, IA	50318	Findlay, OH	45839	Greenfield, WI	53220
Des Plaines, IL	60018	Fitchburg, MA	01420	Greensboro, NC	27420
Detroit, MI	48233	Flagstaff, AZ	86001	Greenville, MS	38701
Dothan, AL	36303	Flint, MI	48502	Greenville, NC	27834
Downers Grove, IL	60515	Florence, AL	35631	Greenville, SC	29602
Downey, CA	90241	Florence, SC	29501	Gresham, OR	97030
Dubuque, IA	52001	Florissant, MO	63033	Grosse Pointe, MI	48230
Duluth, MN	55806	Fond du Lac, WI	54935	Gulfport, MS	39503
Duncanville, TX	75138	Fontana, CA	92335	Hackensack, NJ	07602
Dunedin, FL	32132	Fort Collins, CO	80521	Hagerstown, MD	21740
Durham, NC	27701	Fort Dodge, IA	50501	Hallandale, FL	33009
East Chicago, IN	46312	Fort Lauderdale, FL	33110	Haltom City, TX	76117
East Cleveland, OH	44112	Fort Lee, NJ	07024	Hamilton, OH	45011
East Detroit, MI	48021	Fort Myers, FL	33906	Hammond, IN	46320
East Lansing, MI	48823	Fort Pierce, FL	34981	Hampton, VA	23670
Easton, PA	18042	Fort Smith, AR	72901	Hanover Park, IL	60103
East Orange, NJ	07019	Fort Wayne, IN	46802	Harlingen, TX	78550
East Providence, RI	02914	Fort Worth, TX	76161	Harrisburg, PA	17107
East St. Louis, IL	62201	Frankfort, KY	40601	Hartford, CT	06101
Eau Claire, WI	54703	Frederick, MD	21701	Harvey, IL	60426
Edina, MN	55424	Fredericksburg, VA	22404	Hattiesburg, MS	39402
Edmond, OK	73034	Freeport, IL	61032	Haverhill, MA	01831
Edmonds, WA	98020	Freeport, NY	11520	Hawthorne, CA	90250
El Cajon, CA	92020	Fremont, CA	94538	Hayward, CA	94544
El Dorado, AR	71730	Fresno, CA	93706	Hazelton, PA	18201
Elgin, IL	60120	Fridley, MN	55432	Hempstead, NY	11551
Elizabeth, NJ	07207	Fullerton, CA	92634	Hialeah, FL	33010
Elk Grove, IL	60007	Gadsden, AL	35901	Highland, IN	46322
Elkhart, IN	46515	Gainesville, FL	32608	Highland Park, IL	60035
Elmhurst, IL	60126	Gaithersburg, MD	20877	Highland Park, MI	48203
Elmira, NY	14901	Galesburg, IL	61401	High Point, NC	27260
El Monte, CA	91731	Galveston, TX	77550	Hillsboro, OR	97123
El Paso, TX	79910	Gardena, CA	90247	Hilo, HI	96720
Elyria, OH	44035	Garden City, MI	48135	Hobbs, NM	88240
Emporia, KS	66801	Garden Grove, CA	92642	Hoboken, NJ	07030
Englewood, CO	80110	Garfield, NJ	07026	Hoffman Estates, IL	60195
Enid, OK	73701	Garfield Heights, OH	44125	Holland, MI	49423
Erie, PA	16515	Garland, TX	75040	Hollywood, FL	33022
Escondido, CA	92025	Gary, IN	46401	Holyoke, MA	01040
Euclid, OH	44112	Gastonia, NC	28052	Honolulu, HI	96820
Eugene, OR	97401	Glendale, AZ	85301	Hopkinsville, KY	42240
Evanston, IL	60201	Glendale, CA	91209	Hot Springs, AR	71901
Evansville, IN	47708	Glendora, CA	91740	Houma, LA	70360
Everett, MA	02149	Glenview, IL	60025	Houston, TX	77201
Everett, WA	98203	Gloucester, MA	01930	Huber Heights, OH	45424

Huntington, WV	25704	Lakewood, OH	44107	Lynwood, CA	90262
Huntington Beach, CA	92647	Lake Worth, FL	33461	Macon, GA	31213
		La Mesa, CA	91941	Madison, WI	53714
Huntington Park, CA	90255	La Mirada, CA	90638	Madison Heights, MI	48071
Huntsville, AL	35813	Lancaster, CA	93534	Malden, MA	02148
Hurst, TX	76053	Lancaster, OH	43130	Manchester, NH	03103
Hutchinson, KS	67501	Lancaster, PA	17604	Manhattan, KS	66502
Idaho Falls, ID	83401	Lansing, IL	60438	Manhattan Beach, CA	90266
Independence, MO	64050	Lansing, MI	48924	Manitowoc, WI	54220
Indianapolis, IN	46206	La Puente, CA	91747	Mankato, MN	56001
Inglewood, CA	90311	Laredo, TX	78041	Mansfield, OH	44901
Inkster, MI	48141	Largo, FL	34640	Maple Heights, OH	44137
Iowa City, IA	52240	Las Cruces, NM	88001	Maplewood, MN	55109
Irvine, CA	92713	Las Vegas, NV	89199	Marietta, GA	30060
Irving, TX	75015	Lawrence, IN	46226	Marion, IN	46952
Irvington, NJ	07111	Lawrence, KS	66044	Marion, OH	43302
Ithaca, NY	14850	Lawrence, MA	04842	Marlborough, MA	01752
Jackson, MI	49201	Lawton, OK	73501	Marshalltown, IA	50158
Jackson, MS	39205	Leavenworth, KS	66048	Mason City, IA	50401
Jackson, TN	38301	Lebanon, PA	17042	Massillon, OH	44646
Jacksonville, FL	32203	Lee's Summit, MO	64063	Maywood, IL	60153
Jamestown, NY	14701	Leominster, MA	01453	McAllen, TX	78501
Janesville, WI	53545	Lewiston, ID	83501	McKeesport, PA	15134
Jefferson City, MO	65101	Lewiston, ME	04240	Medford, MA	02155
Jersey City, NJ	07303	Lexington, KY	40511	Medford, OR	97501
Johnson City, TN	37601	Lima, OH	45802	Melbourne, FL	32901
Johnstown, PA	15901	Lincoln, NE	68501	Melrose, MA	02176
Joliet, IL	60436	Lincoln Park, MI	48146	Memphis, TN	38101
Jonesboro, AR	72401	Linden, NJ	07036	Menlo Park, CA	94025
Joplin, MO	64801	Lindenhurst, NY	11757	Menomonee Falls, WI	53051
Kalamazoo, MI	49001	Little Rock, AR	72231	Mentor, OH	44060
Kankakee, IL	60901	Littleton, CO	70220	Merced, CA	95340
Kansas City, KS	66106	Livermore, CA	94550	Meriden, CT	06450
Kansas City, MO	64108	Livonia, MI	48150	Meridian, MS	39301
Kearny, NJ	07032	Lodi, CA	95240	Merrillville, IN	46410
Kenner, LA	70062	Logan, UT	84321	Mesa, AZ	85201
Kennewick, WA	99336	Lombard, IL	60148	Mesquite, TX	75149
Kenosha, WI	53140	Lompoc, CA	93436	Miami, FL	33152
Kent, OH	44240	Long Beach, CA	90809	Miami Beach, FL	33139
Kettering, OH	45429	Long Beach, NY	11561	Middletown, CT	06457
Killeen, TX	76541	Long Branch, NJ	07740	Middletown, OH	45042
Kingsport, TN	37660	Longmont, CO	80501	Midland, MI	48640
Kingston, NC	38501	Longview, TX	75602	Midland, TX	79711
Kingsville, TX	78363	Longview, WA	98632	Midwest City, OK	73130
Kirkwood, MO	63122	Lorain, OH	44052	Milford, CT	06460
Knoxville, TN	37950	Los Altos, CA	94022	Milpitas, CA	95035
Kokomo, IN	46902	Los Angeles, CA	90052	Milwaukee, WI	53203
La Crosse, WI	54601	Los Gatos, CA	95030	Minneapolis, MN	55401
Lafayette, IN	47901	Louisville, KY	40231	Minnetonka, MN	55345
Lafayette, LA	70501	Loveland, CO	80538	Minot, ND	58701
La Habra, CA	90631	Lowell, MA	01853	Mishawaka, IN	46544
Lake Charles, LA	70601	Lubbock, TX	79402	Missoula, MT	59801
Lakeland, FL	33805	Lufkin, TX	75901	Mobile, AL	36601
Lakewood, CA	90714	Lynchburg, VA	24506	Modesto, CA	95350
Lakewood, CO	80215	Lynn, MA	01901	Moline, IL	61265

United States

Monroe, LA	71203	North Charleston, SC	29406	Pascagoula, MS	39567
Monroeville, PA	15146	North Chicago, IL	60064	Passaic, NJ	07055
Monrovia, CA	91016	North Las Vegas, NV	89030	Paterson, NJ	07510
Montclair, NJ	07042	North Little Rock, AR	72114	Pawtucket, RI	02860
Montebello, CA	90640	North Miami, FL	33261	Peabody, MA	01960
Monterey, CA	93940	North Miami	33160	Pembroke Pines, FL	33024
Monterey Park, CA	91754	Beach, FL		Pensacola, FL	32501
Montgomery, AL	36119	North Olmsted, OH	44070	Peoria, IL	61601
Moore, OK	73160	North Richland	76180	Perth Amboy, NJ	08861
Moorhead, MN	56560	Hills, TX		Petaluma, CA	94952
Morgantown, WV	26505	North Tonawanda, NY	14120	Petersburg, VA	23804
Mountainview, CA	94042	Norwalk, CA	90650	Phenix City, AL	36867
Mount Prospect, IL	60056	Norwalk, CT	06856	Philadelphia, PA	19104
Mount Vernon, NY	10551	Norwich, CT	06360	Phoenix, AZ	85027
Muncie, IN	47302	Norwood, OH	45212	Pico Rivera, CA	90660
Murfreesboro, TN	37130	Novato, CA	94947	Pine Bluff, AR	71601
Murray, UT	84107	Nutley, NJ	07110	Pinellas Park, FL	34665
Muskegon, MI	49440	Oak Forest, IL	60452	Pittsburg, CA	94565
Muskogee, OK	74401	Oaklando, CA	94615	Pittsburg, PA	15290
Nacogdoches, TX	75961	Oak Lawn, IL	60455	Pittsfield, MA	01201
Nampa, ID	83651	Oak Park, IL	60301	Placentia, CA	92670
Napa, CA	94558	Oak Park, MI	48237	Plainfield, NJ	07061
Naperville, IL	60540	Oak Ridge, TN	37830	Plano, TX	75074
Nashua, NH	03060	Ocala, FL	32678	Plantation, FL	33318
Nashville, TN	37229	Oceanside, CA	92054	Pleasant Hill, CA	94523
National City, CA	91950	Odessa, TX	79761	Pleasanton, CA	94566
Naugatuck, CT	06770	Ogden, UT	84401	Plum, PA	15239
New Albany, IN	47150	Oklahoma City, OK	73125	Plymouth, MN	55447
Newark, CA	94560	Olathe, KS	66061	Pocatello, ID	83201
Newark, DE	19711	Olympia, WA	98501	Pomona, CA	91766
Newark, NJ	07102	Omaha, NE	68108	Pompano Beach, FL	33060
Newark, OH	43055	Ontario, CA	91761	Ponca City, OK	74601
New Bedford, MA	02740	Orange, CA	92613	Pontiac, MI	48343
New Berlin, WI	53151	Orange, NJ	07051	Portage, IN	46368
New Britain, CT	06050	Orem, UT	84057	Port Arthur, TX	77640
New Brunswick, NJ	08901	Orlando, FL	32802	Port Huron, MI	48060
New Castle, PA	16108	Oshkosh, WI	54901	Portland, ME	04101
New Haven, CT	06511	Ottumwa, IA	52501	Portland, OR	97208
New Iberia, LA	70560	Overland Park, KS	66204	Portsmouth, NH	03801
New London, CT	06320	Owensboro, KY	43201	Portsmouth, OH	45662
New Orleans, LA	70113	Oxnard, CA	93030	Portsmouth, VA	23707
Newport, RI	02840	Pacifica, CA	94044	Poughkeepsie, NY	12601
Newport Beach, CA	92660	Paducah, KY	42001	Providence, RI	02904
Newport News, VA	23607	Palatine, IL	66067	Provo, UT	84601
New Rochelle, NY	10802	Palm Springs, CA	92263	Pueblo, CO	81003
Newton, MA	02158	Palo Alto, CA	94303	Quincy, IL	62301
New York, NY	10199	Panama City, FL	32401	Quincy, MA	02269
Niagara Falls, NY	14302	Paramount, CA	90723	Racine, WI	53403
Niles, IL	60648	Paramus, NJ	07652	Rahway, NJ	07065
Norfolk, VA	23501	Paris, TX	75460	Raleigh, NC	27611
Normal, IL	61761	Parkersburg, WV	26101	Rancho Cucamonga,	91730
Norman, OK	73069	Park Ridge, IL	60068	CA	
Norristown, PA	19401	Parma, OH	44129	Rancho Palos	90274
Northampton, MA	01060	Pasadena, CA	91109	Verdes, CA	
Northbrook, IL	60062	Pasadena, TX	77501	Rapid City, SD	57701

Raytown, MO	64133	San Buenaventura	93001	Sparks, NV	89431
Reading, PA	19612	(Ventura), CA		Spartanburg, SC	29301
Redding, CA	96001	San Clemente, CA	92672	Spokane, WA	99210
Redlands, CA	92373	San Diego, CA	92199	Springfield, IL	62703
Redondo Beach, CA	90277	Sandusky, OH	44870	Springfield, MA	01101
Redwood City, CA	94064	Sandy, UT	84070	Springfield, MO	65801
Reno, NV	89510	San Francisco, CA	94188	Springfield, OH	45501
Renton, WA	98058	San Gabriel, CA	91776	Springfield, OR	97477
Revere, MA	02151	San Jose, CA	95101	Stamford, CT	06904
Rialto, CA	92376	San Leandro, CA	94577	State College, PA	16801
Richardson, TX	75080	San Luis Obispo, CA	93401	Sterling Heights, MI	48311
Richfield, MN	55423	San Mateo, CA	94402	Steubenville, OH	43952
Richland, WA	99352	San Rafael, CA	94901	Stillwater, OK	74074
Richmond, CA	94802	Santa Ana, CA	92799	Stockton, CA	95208
Richmond, IN	47374	Santa Barbara, CA	93102	Stow, OH	44224
Richmond, VA	23232	Santa Clara, CA	95051	Strongsville, OH	44136
Ridgewood, NJ	07450	Santa Cruz, CA	95060	Suffolk, VA	23434
Riverside, CA	92507	Santa Fe, NM	87501	Sunnyvale, CA	94086
Riviera Beach, FL	33404	Santa Maria, CA	93454	Sunrise, FL	33345
Roanoke, VA	24022	Santa Monica, CA	90406	Superior, WI	54880
Rochester, MI	48308	Santa Rosa, CA	95402	Syracuse, NY	13220
Rochester, MN	55901	Sarasota, FL	34230	Tacoma, WA	98413
Rochester, NY	14692	Saratoga, CA	95070	Tallahassee, FL	32301
Rockford, IL	61125	Savannah, GA	31402	Tamarac, FL	33320
Rock Hill, SC	29730	Sayreville, NJ	08872	Tampa, FL	33630
Rock Island, IL	61201	Schaumburg, IL	60194	Taunton, MA	02780
Rockville, MD	20850	Schenectady, NY	12305	Taylor, MI	48180
Rockville Center, NY	11570	Scottsdale, AZ	85251	Tempe, AZ	85282
Rocky Mount, NC	27801	Scranton, PA	18505	Temple, TX	76501
Rome, GA	30161	Seal Beach, CA	90740	Terre Haute, IN	47808
Rome, NY	13440	Seaside, CA	93955	Texarkana, TX	75501
Rosemead, CA	91770	Seattle, WA	98109	Texas City, TX	75590
Roseville, MI	48066	Selma, AL	36701	Thornton, CO	80229
Roseville, MN	55113	Shaker Heights, OH	44120	Thousand Oaks, CA	91360
Roswell, NM	88201	Shawnee Mission, KS	66202	Tinley Park, IL	60477
Royal Oak, MI	48068	Shawnee, OK	74801	Titusville, FL	32780
Sacramento, CA	95813	Sheboygan, WI	53081	Toledo, OH	43601
Saginaw, MI	48065	Shelton, CT	06484	Topeka, KS	66603
St. Charles, MO	63301	Sherman, TX	75090	Torrance, CA	90510
St. Clair Shores, MI	48080	Shreveport, LA	71102	Torrington, CT	06790
St. Cloud, MN	56301	Silver Springs, MD	20907	Trenton, NJ	08650
St. Joseph, MO	64501	Simi Valley, CA	93065	Troy, MI	48099
St. Louis, MO	63155	Sioux City, IA	51101	Troy, NY	12180
St. Louis Park, MN	55426	Sioux Falls, SD	57101	Tucson, AZ	85726
St. Paul, MN	55101	Skokie, IL	60076	Tulsa, OK	74103
St. Petersburg, FL	33730	Slidell, LA	70458	Turlock, CA	95380
Salem, MA	01970	Somerville, MA	02143	Tuscaloosa, AL	35401
Salem, OR	97301	Somerville, NJ	08876	Tustin, CA	92680
Salina, KS	67401	South Bend, IN	46624	Twin Falls, ID	83301
Salinas, CA	93907	South Euclid, OH	44121	Tyler, TX	75712
Salt Lake City, UT	84199	Southfield, MI	48037	Union City, CA	94587
San Angelo, TX	76902	South Gate, CA	90280	Union City, NJ	07087
San Antonio, TX	78284	Southgate, MI	48195	University City, MO	63130
San Bernardino, CA	92403	South San Francisco,	94080	Upland, CA	91786
San Bruno, CA	94066	CA		Upper Arlington, OH	43221

Urbana, IL	61801	Waukegan, IL	60085	Wichita, KS	67276
Utica, NY	13504	Waukesha, WI	53186	Wichita Falls, TX	76307
Vacablle, CA	95688	Wausau, WI	54401	Wilkes-Barre, PA	18701
Valdosta, GA	31601	Wauwatosa, WI	53213	Williamsport, LA	17701
Vallejo, CA	94590	Weirton, WV	26062	Wilmette, IL	60091
Valley Stream, NY	11580	West Allis, WI	53214	Wilmington, DE	19850
Vancouver, WA	98661	West Covina, CA	91793	Wilmington, NC	28402
Vicksburg, MS	39180	Westfield, MA	01085	Wilson, NC	27893
Victoria, TX	77901	Westfield, NJ	07090	Winona, MN	55987
Vineland, NJ	08360	West Haven, CT	06516	Winston-Salem, NC	27102
Virginia Beach, VA	23450	West Jordan, UT	84084	Woburn, MA	01801
Visalia, CA	93277	Westland, MI	48185	Woodland, CA	95695
Vista, CA	92083	West Lafayette, IN	47906	Woonsocket, RI	02895
Waco, TX	76702	West Memphis, AR	72301	Worcester, MA	01613
Walla Walla, WA	99362	West Mifflin, PA	15122	Wyandotte, MI	48192
Walnut Creek, CA	94596	Westminster, CA	92683	Wyoming, MI	49509
Waltham, MA	02154	Westminster, CO	80030	Yakima, WA	98903
Warner Robins, GA	31093	West New York, NJ	07093	Yonkers, NY	10702
Warren, MI	48090	West Orange, NJ	07052	Yorba Linda, CA	92686
Warren, OH	44481	West Palm Beach, FL	33406	York, PA	17405
Warwick, RI	02886	Wheaton, IL	60187	Youngstown, OH	44501
Washington, DC	20013	Wheat Ridge, CO	80033	Ypsilanti, MI	48197
Waterbury, CT	06701	Wheeling, WV	26003	Yuma, AZ	85364
Waterloo, IA	50701	White Plains, NY	10602	Zanesville, OH	43701
Watertown, NY	13601	Whittier, CA	90605		

TWO-LETTER STATE AND TERRITORY ABBREVIATIONS

Alabama	AL	Kentucky	KY	Islands	
Alaska	AK	Louisiana	LA	Ohio	OH
American Samoa	AS	Maine	ME	Oklahoma	OK
Arizona	AZ	Marshall Islands	MH	Oregon	OR
Arkansas	AR	Maryland	MD	Palau	PW
California	CA	Massachusetts	MA	Pennsylvania	PA
Colorado	CO	Michigan	MI	Puerto Rico	PR
Connecticut	CT	Minnesota	MN	Rhode Island	RI
Delaware	DE	Mississippi	MS	South Carolina	SC
District of Columbia	DC	Missouri	MO	South Dakota	SD
Federated States of	FM	Montana	MT	Tennessee	TN
Micronesia		Nebraska	NE	Texas	TX
Florida	FL	Nevada	NV	Utah	UT
Georgia	GA	New Hampshire	NH	Vermont	VT
Guam	GU	New Jersey	NJ	Virginia	VA
Hawaii	HI	New Mexico	NM	Virgin Islands	VI
Idaho	ID	New York	NY	Washington	WA
Illinois	IL	North Carolina	NC	West Virginia	WV
Indiana	IN	North Dakota	ND	Wisconsin	WI
Iowa	IA	Northern Mariana	MP	Wyoming	WY
Kansas	KS				

GEOGRAPHIC DIRECTIONAL ABBREVIATIONS

North	N	West	W	Southwest	SW
East	E	Northeast	NE	Northwest	NW
South	S	Southeast	SE		

STREET DESIGNATORS (STREET SUFFIXES)

Alley	ALY	Forge	FRG	Path	PATH
Annex	ANX	Fork	FRK	Pike	PIKE
Arcade	ARC	Forks	FRKS	Pines	PNES
Avenue	AVE	Fort	FT	Place	PL
Bayou	BYU	Freeway	FWY	Plains	PLNS
Beach	BCH	Gardens	GDNS	Plaza	PLZ
Bend	BND	Gateway	GTWY	Point	PT
Bluff	BLF	Glen	GLN	Port	PRT
Bottom	BTM	Green	GRN	Prairie	PR
Boulevard	BLVD	Grove	GRV	Radial	RADL
Branch	BR	Harbor	HBR	Ranch	RNCH
Bridge	BRG	Haven	HVN	Rapids	RPDS
Brook	BRK	Heights	HTS	Rest	RST
Burg	BG	Highway	HWY	Ridge	RDG
Bypass	BYP	Hill	HL	River	RIV
Camp	CP	Hills	HLS	Road	RD
Canyon	CYN	Hollow	HOLW	Row	ROW
Cape	CPE	Inlet	INLT	Run	RUN
Causeway	CSWY	Island	IS	Shoal	SHL
Center	CTR	Islands	ISS	Shoals	SHLS
Circle	CIR	Isle	ISLE	Shore	SHR
Cliffs	CLFS	Junction	JCT	Shores	SHRS
Club	CLB	Key	KY	Spring	SPG
Corner	COR	Knolls	KNLS	Springs	SPGS
Corners	CORS	Lake	LK	Spur	SPUR
Course	CRSE	Lakes	LKS	Square	SQ
Court	CT	Landing	LNDG	Station	STA
Courts	CTS	Lane	LN	Stream	STRM
Cove	CV	Light	LGT	Street	ST
Creek	CRK	Loaf	LF	Summit	SMT
Crescent	CRES	Locks	LCKS	Terrace	TER
Crossing	XING	Lodge	LDG	Trace	TRCE
Dale	DL	Loop	LOOP	Track	TRAK
Dam	DM	Mall	MALL	Trail	TRL
Divide	DV	Manor	MNR	Trailer	TRLR
Drive	DR	Meadows	MDWS	Tunnel	TUNL
Estates	EST	Mill	ML	Turnpike	TPKE
Expressway	EXPY	Mills	MLS	Union	UN
Extension	EXT	Mission	MSN	Valley	VLY
Fall	FL	Mount	MT	Viaduct	VIA
Falls	FLS	Mountain	MTN	View	VW
Ferry	FRY	Neck	NCK	Village	VLG
Field	FLD	Orchard	ORCH	Ville	VL
Fields	FLDS	Oval	OVAL	Vista	VIS
Flats	FLT	Park	PARK	Walk	WALK
Ford	FRD	Parkway	PKY	Way	WAY
Forest	FRST	Pass	PASS	Wells	WLS

United States

MAJOR DAILY NEWSPAPERS

NATIONAL

Christian Science Monitor
One Norway St.
Boston, MA 02115-3195
http://www.csmonitor.com

USA Today
1000 Wilson Blvd.
Arlington, VA 22209
http://www.usatoday.com

Wall Street Journal
200 Liberty St.
New York, NY 10281
http://www.wsj.com

LOCAL (BY STATE)

Alabama

Birmingham News
2200 4th Ave. N.
Birmingham, AL 35203

Birmingham Post-Herald
P.O. Box 2553
Birmingham, AL 35202-2553

Montgomery Advertiser
P.O. Box 1000
Montgomery, AL 36101-1000

Alaska

Anchorage Daily News
P.O. Box 149001
Anchorage, AK 99514-9001

Arizona

Arizona Republic
P.O. Box 1950
Phoenix, AZ 85001-1950

Arizona Daily Star
P.O. Box 26807
Tucson, AZ 85726-6807

Phoenix Gazette
P.O. Box 1950
Phoenix, AZ 85001-1950

Arkansas

Arkansas Democrat-Gazette
Capitol Avenue and Scott
P.O. Box 2221
Little Rock, AR 72203

California

Fresno Bee
3425 N. 1st St.
Fresno, CA 93726-6819

Los Angeles Times
Times Mirror Square
Los Angeles, CA 90012

Sacramento Bee
2100 Q St.
P.O. Box 15779
Sacramento, CA 95852

San Diego Union-Tribune
350 Camino de la Reina
San Diego, CA 92108

San Francisco Chronicle
901 Mission St.
San Francisco, CA 94103

San Francisco Examiner
110 Fifth St.
San Francisco, CA 94103

Colorado

Denver Post
1560 Broadway
Denver, CO 80202

Rocky Mountain News
400 West Colfax Ave.
Denver, CO 80201

Connecticut

Hartford Courant
285 Broad St.
Hartford, CT 06115-2510

New Haven Register
40 Sargent Dr.
New Haven, CT 06511

Delaware

News-Journal
P.O. Box 19850
Wilmington, DE 19850

District of Columbia

Washington Post
1150 15th St., NW
Washington, DC 20071

Florida

Florida Times Union
One Riverside Ave.
Jacksonville, FL 32202-4924

Fort Lauderdale Sun-Sentinel
200 E. Las Olas Blvd.
Ft. Lauderdale, FL 33301-2293

Miami Herald
One Herald Plaza
Miami, FL 33132-1693

Orlando Sentinel
633 N. Orange Ave.
Orlando, FL 32801

St. Petersburg Times
P.O. Box 1121
St. Petersburg, FL 33701

Georgia

Atlanta Journal and Constitution
72 Marietta St., NW
Atlanta, GA 30303

Hawaii

Honolulu Advertiser
605 Kapiolani Blvd.
Honolulu, HI 96813

Honolulu Star Bulletin
P.O. Box 3080
Honolulu, HI 96802

Idaho

Idaho Statesman
1200 N. Curtis Rd.
Boise, ID 83707

Illinois

Chicago Sun-Times
401 N. Wabash Ave.
Chicago, IL 60611

Chicago Tribune
435 N. Michigan Ave.
Chicago, IL 60611

Indiana

Indianapolis Star News
307 N. Pennsylvania St.
Indianapolis, IN 46204-1811

Post-Tribune
1065 Broadway St.
Gary, IN 46402-2998

South Bend Tribune
225 W. Colfax Ave.
South Bend, IN 46626-0001

Iowa

Des Moines Register
P.O. Box 957
Des Moines, IA 50304

Kansas

Topeka Capital-Journal
616 Jefferson St.
Topeka, KS 66607-1197

Wichita Eagle
825 E. Douglas St.
Wichita, KS 67201

Kentucky

Courier-Journal
525 W. Broadway
Louisville, KY 40202-2137

Herald-Leader
100 Midland Ave.
Lexington, KY 40508

Louisiana

The Advocate
525 Lafayette St.
Baton Rouge, LA 70821

Times-Picayune
3800 Howard Ave.
New Orleans, LA 0140

Maine

Daily News
491 Main St.
Bangor, ME 04402

Portland Press Herald
P.O. Box 1460
390 Congress St.
Portland, ME 04101

Maryland

The Baltimore Sun
501 N. Calvert St.
Baltimore, MD 21278-0001

Massachusetts

Boston Globe
135 Morrissey Blvd.
Boston, MA 02107

Boston Herald
1 Herald Square
Boston, MA 02106

Michigan

Detroit Free Press
321 W. Lafayette Blvd.
Detroit, MI 48226

Detroit News
615 W. Lafayette Blvd.
Detroit, MI 48226

Teddy Roosevelt was the youngest president ever to serve, taking office after the assassination of William McKinley.

Minnesota

St. Paul Pioneer Press
345 Cedar St.
St. Paul, MN 55101-1057

Star Tribune
425 Portland Ave.
Minneapolis, MN 55488-0001

Mississippi

Clarion Ledger
311 E. Pearl St.
Jackson, MS 39205

Missouri

Kansas City Star
1729 Grand Ave.
Kansas City, MO 64108

Post-Dispatch
900 N. Tucker Blvd.
St. Louis, MO 63101

Montana

Billings Gazette
401 N. Broadway
Billings, MT 59101-1243

Great Falls Tribune
P.O. Box 5468
Great Falls, MT 59403

Nebraska

Lincoln Journal
926 P St.
Lincoln, NE 68501

Lincoln Star
926 P St.
Lincoln, NE 68508

World-Herald
World-Herald Square
Omaha, NE 68102

Nevada

Las Vegas Review-Journal
1111 W. Bonanza
Las Vegas, NV 89125

Las Vegas Sun
800 S. Valley View
Box 4275
Las Vegas, NV 89127

Reno Gazette Journal
P.O. Box 22000
Reno, NV 89520-2000

New Hampshire

Union-Leader
P.O. Box 9555
Manchester, NH 03108

New Jersey

Asbury Park Press
3601 Hwy. 66
Neptune, NJ 07754

Record
150 River St.
Hackensack, NJ 07601

Star-Ledger
Star-Ledger Plaza
Newark, NJ 07102-1200

New Mexico

Albuquerque Journal
7777 Jefferson NE
Albuquerque, NM 87109

Albuquerque Tribune
7777 Jefferson NE
Albuquerque, NM 87109

New York

Buffalo News
One News Plaza
P.O. Box 100
Buffalo, NY 14240

Newsday
235 Pinelawn Rd.
Melville, NY 11747-4250

New York Daily News
450 W. 33rd St.
New York, NY 10001

John F. Kennedy was the youngest president elected to the office.

New York Post
1211 Sixth Ave.
New York, NY 10036

New York Times
229 W. 43rd St.
New York, NY 10036-3913

North Carolina
Observer
P.O. Box 32188-28232
Charlotte, NC 28232

News & Observer
215 S. McDowell St.
Raleigh, NC 27602

North Dakota
Bismark Tribune
P.O. Box 1498
707 E. Front Ave.
Bismark, ND 58502-1498

Ohio
Akron Beacon Journal
44 E. Exchange St.
Akron, OH 44328-0001

Blade
541 Superior St.
Toledo, OH 43660-0001

Cincinnati Enquirer
312 Elm St.
Cincinnati, OH 45202-2410

Cincinnati Post
125 E. Court St.
Cincinnati, OH 45202-1211

Cleveland Plain Dealer
1801 Superior Ave.
Cleveland, OH 44114-2198

Columbus Dispatch
34 S. Third St.
Columbus, OH 43215

Daily News
Fourth and Ludlow sts.
Dayton, OH 45401

Oklahoma
Oklahoman
9000 N. Broadway
Oklahoma City, OK 73114

Tulsa World
P.O. Box 1770
Tulsa, OK 74102

Oregon
The Oregonian
1320 SW Broadway
Portland, OR 97201-3469

Pennsylvania
Philadelphia Daily News
400 N. Broad St.
Philadelphia, PA 19101

Philadelphia Inquirer
400 N. Broad St.
Philadelphia, PA 19101

Pittsburgh Post-Gazette
P.O. Box 957
50 Boulevard of Allies
Pittsburgh, PA 15222

Pittsburgh Press
34 Boulevard of Allies
Pittsburgh, PA 15230

Rhode Island
Journal-Bulletin
75 Fountain St.
Providence, RI 02902

South Carolina
Post & Courier
134 Columbus St.
Charleston, SC 29403-4800

The State
P.O. Box 1333
Columbia, SC 29202

United States

South Dakota

Argus Leader
P.O. Box 5034
Sioux Falls, SD 57117-5034

Tennessee

Commercial Appeal
495 Union Ave.
Memphis, TN 38103-3221

Nashville Banner
1100 Broadway
Nashville, TN 37203-3116

About 4 million slaves were freed after the American Civil War.

News-Sentinel
204 W. Church Ave.
Knoxville, TN 37902-1612

Tennessean
1100 Broadway
Nashville, TN 37203-3116

Texas

Austin American-Statesman
P.O. Box 670
Austin, TX 78767

Dallas Morning News
Communications Center
Dallas, TX 75265

Express-News
P.O. Box 2171
San Antonio, TX 78297

Fort Worth Star-Telegram
400 W. 7th St.
Fort Worth, TX 76102

Houston Chronicle
801 Texas Ave.
Houston, TX 7700

Houston Post
4747 Southwest Fwy.
Houston, TX 77027

Utah

Deseret News
30 E. First St.
Salt Lake City, UT 84110

Salt Lake Tribune
143 S. Main St.
Salt Lake City, UT 84111

Vermont

Free Press
191 College St.
Burlington, VT 05401

Virginia

Virginian-Pilot
150 W. Brambleton Ave.
Norfolk, VA 23510

Richmond Times-Dispatch
P.O. Box 85333
Richmond, VA 23293-1000

Washington

Seattle Post-Intelligencer
101 Elliott Ave., W
Seattle, WA 98119

Seattle Times
P.O. Box 70
Seattle, WA 98111-1070

West Virginia

Herald Dispatch
P.O. Box 2017
946 Fifth Ave.
Huntington, WV 25720

News-Register
1500 Main St.
Wheeling, WV 26003

Wisconsin

Milwaukee Journal Sentinel
333 W. State St.
Milwaukee, WI 53203-1305

State Journal
P.O. Box 8058
Madison, WI 53708

Wyoming

Wyoming Tribune-Eagle
702 W. Lincolnway
Cheyenne, WY 82001

ADDITIONAL SOURCES OF INFORMATION

MAGAZINES

NEWSMAGAZINES

Newsweek
251 W. 57th St.
New York, NY 10019
http://www.newsweek.com

Time
1271 Avenue of the Americas
New York, NY 10020
http://www.pathfinder.com

U.S. News & World Report
2400 N St., NW
Washington, DC 20037
http://www.usnews.com

PUBLIC, SOCIAL, AND POLITICAL AFFAIRS

Mother Jones
731 Mission St.
San Francisco, CA 94103
http://www.motherjones.com

The Nation
72 Fifth Ave.
New York, NY 10011
http://www.thenation.com

The New Republic
1220 19th St., NW
Washington, DC 20036
http://www.enews.com/magazines/tnr

BOOKS

Andriot, Jay, ed. *Guide to U.S. Government Statistics.* Documents Index, 1997.

Barone, Michael, Grant Ujifusa, and Richard E. Cohen. *The Almanac of American Politics 1998.* Times Books, 1997.

Baydo, Gerald. *U.S.A.: A Synoptic History of America.* John Wiley & Sons, 1981.

Congress and the Nation. Congressional Quarterly, published every four years.

Congressional Quarterly Almanac. Congressional Quarterly, annual.

Congressional Quarterly Weekly. Congressional Quarterly, weekly.

Consumer's Resource Handbook. U.S. Office of Consumer Affairs, latest edition.

Cordasco, Francesco. *Dictionary of American Immigration History.* Scarecrow Press, 1990.

Flags of America. 2nd ed. National Flag Foundation, 1994.

Foner, Eric, and John A. Garraty, eds. *The Reader's Companion to American History.* Houghton Mifflin, 1991.

Garwood, Alfred N. *Almanac of the Fifty States.* Information Publication, 1987.

Hatch, Jane M. *The American Book of Days.* 3rd ed. H. W. Wilson, 1978.

Hornsby, Alton. *Chronology of Afro American History.* 2nd ed. Gale Research, Inc., 1997.

Kane, Joseph Nathan. *Nicknames and Sobriquets of U.S. Cities, States, and Countries.* 3rd ed. Scarecrow Press, 1979.

Lesko, Matthew. *Information U.S.A.* Viking, 1986.

Ornstein, Norman J., Thomas E. Mann, and Michael J. Malbin. *Vital Statistics on Congress 1997–1998.* Congressional Quarterly, 1997.

Schlesinger, Arthur M., Jr., ed. *The Almanac of American History.* Putnam, 1984.

Shearer, Benjamin F., and Barbara S. Shearer. *State Names, Seals, Flags and Symbols: A Historical Guide.* Greenwood, 1994.

Statistical Abstract of the United States. U.S. Bureau of the Census, annual.

Urdang, Laurence, ed. *The Timetables of American History.* Touchstone, 1996.

United States

United States

26

THE WORLD

COUNTRIES OF THE WORLD	914
GREAT EVENTS IN WORLD HISTORY	931
MAJOR WARS, BATTLES, AND OTHER ARMED CONFLICTS	940
WORLD EXPLORATION AND DISCOVERY	947
POPULATION OF MAJOR WORLD CITIES	954
THE UNITED NATIONS	958
INTERNATIONAL ORGANIZATIONS	961
SEVEN WONDERS OF THE ANCIENT WORLD	962
ROYAL RULERS OF EUROPE AND ASIA	963
GENEALOGY CHARTS OF THE BRITISH MONARCHY	966
CONNECTIONS BETWEEN ROYAL FAMILIES	969
PRIME MINISTERS	970
FOREIGN DIALING CODES	972
ADDITIONAL SOURCES OF INFORMATION	974

COUNTRIES OF THE WORLD

Afghanistan
Area: 647,500 km² (249,999 mi²)
Capital: Kabul
Government: In transition
Population: 22,664,136
Languages: Pushtu, Afghan Persian, Turkic
Religions: Sunni Muslim, Shi'a Muslim

Albania
Area: 28,750 km² (11,100 mi²)
Capital: Tirana
Government: In transition
Population: 3,249,136
Languages: Albanian, Greek
Religions: Muslim, Greek Orthodox, Roman Catholic

Algeria
Area: 2,381,740 km² (919,590 mi²)
Capital: Algiers
Government: Republic
Population: 29,183,032
Languages: Arabic, French, Berber dialects
Religion: Sunni Muslim

Andorra
Area: 450 km² (174 mi²)
Capital: Andorra la Vella
Government: Coprincipality of France and Spain
Population: 67,509
Languages: Catalan, French, Castilian
Religion: Roman Catholic

Angola
Area: 1,246,700 km² (481,351 mi²)
Capital: Luanda
Government: In transition
Population: 10,342,899
Languages: Portuguese, Bantu dialects
Religions: Indigenous beliefs, Roman Catholic,
    Protestant

Anguilla
Area: 91 km² (35 mi²)
Capital: The Valley
Government: Dependent territory of United Kingdom
Population: 7,147
Language: English
Religions: Anglican, Methodist

Antarctica
Area: 14,000,000 km² (8,750,000 mi²)
Capital: None
Government: Various nations—including Argentina,
    Australia, Chile, France, New Zealand, Norway, and
    United Kingdom—claim areas of the continent;

Antarctic Treaty of 1959, signed by 42 nations, places
    these claims in abeyance and stipulates peaceful uses
    of Antarctica.
Population: No indigenous inhabitants; seasonal popu-
    lation of researchers averages about 4,000 in summer
    and 1,000 in winter.

Antigua and Barbuda
Area: 440 km² (170 mi²)
Capital: Saint John's
Government: Parliamentary democracy affiliated with
    United Kingdom
Population: 65,647
Languages: English, local dialects
Religions: Anglican, Methodist, Roman Catholic

Argentina
Area: 2,766,890 km² (1,068,296 mi²)
Capital: Buenos Aires
Government: Republic
Population: 36,672,997
Languages: Spanish, English, Italian, German, French
Religions: Roman Catholic, Protestant, Jewish

Armenia
Area: 29,283 km² (11,306 mi²)
Capital: Yerevan
Government: Presidential republic
Population: 3,463,574
Languages: Armenian, Russian
Religion: Armenian Apolistic

Aruba
Area: 193 km² (75 mi²)
Capital: Oranjestad
Government: Independent territory of The Netherlands
Population: 66,404
Languages: Dutch, Papiamento, Spanish, English
Religions: Roman Catholic, Protestant

Australia
Area: 7,686,850 km² (2,967,893 mi²)
Capital: Canberra
Government: Federal parliamentary state affiliated with
    Great Britain
Population: 18,260,863
Languages: English, native languages
Religions: Anglican, Roman Catholic, other Protestant
    faiths

Austria
Area: 83,850 km² (32,374 mi²)
Capital: Vienna
Government: Federal republic
Population: 8,013,614
Language: German
Religions: Roman Catholic, Protestant

Azerbaijan
Area: 86,506 km² (33,400 mi²)
Capital: Baku
Government: Parliamentary republic
Population: 7,676,953
Languages: Azeri, Russian
Religions: Muslim

If there were only 100 people in the world, half would live in just 5 countries: 21 in China, 15 in India, 5 in the former Soviet Union, 5 in the United States, and 4 in Indonesia.

Bahamas
Area: 13,940 km² (5,382 mi²)
Capital: Nassau
Government: Independent commonwealth affiliated with United Kingdom
Population: 259,367
Languages: English, Creole
Religions: Baptist, Anglican, Roman Catholic, other Protestant

Bahrain
Area: 620 km² (239 mi²)
Capital: Manama
Government: Monarchy
Population: 590,042
Languages: Arabic, English, Farsi, Urdu
Religions: Shi'a Muslim, Sunni Muslim

Bangladesh
Area: 144,000 km² (55,598 mi²)
Capital: Dhaka
Government: Republic
Population: 123,062,800
Languages: Bangla, English
Religions: Muslim, Hindu

Barbados
Area: 460 km² (166 mi²)
Capital: Bridgetown
Government: Parliamentary democracy affiliated with United Kingdom
Population: 257,030
Language: English
Religions: Anglican, Pentecostal, Methodist, Roman Catholic

Barbuda
See **Antigua and Barbuda.**

Belarus
Area: 207,718 km² (80,200 mi²)
Capital: Minsk
Government: Constitutional republic
Population: 10,415,973
Languages: Byelorussian, Russian
Religions: Russian Orthodox, Baptist

Belgium
Area: 30,520 km² (11,784 mi²)
Capital: Brussels
Government: Constitutional monarchy
Population: 10,131,863
Languages: Flemish, French
Religions: Roman Catholic, Protestant

Belize
Area: 22,960 km² (8,865 mi²)
Capital: Belmopan
Government: Parliamentary democracy affiliated with United Kingdom
Population: 219,296
Languages: English, Spanish, Maya, Garifuna
Religions: Roman Catholic, Anglican, Methodist

Benin
Area: 112,620 km² (43,483 mi²)
Capital: Porto-Novo
Government: Multiparty democracy
Population: 5,709,529
Languages: French, Fon, Yoruba, tribal dialects
Religions: Indigenous beliefs, Muslim, Christian

Bermuda
Area: 50 km² (19 mi²)
Capital: Hamilton
Government: Dependent territory of United Kingdom
Population: 62,099
Language: English
Religions: Anglican, Roman Catholic, African Methodist

Bhutan
Area: 47,000 km² (18,147 mi²)
Capital: Thimphu
Government: Monarchy
Population: 1,822,625
Languages: Dzongkha, other Tibetan dialects, Nepalese dialects
Religions: Lamaistic Buddhist, Hindu

Bolivia
Area: 1,098,580 km² (424,162 mi²)
Capitals: La Paz and Sucre
Government: Republic
Population: 7,165,257
Languages: Spanish, Quechua, Aymara
Religions: Roman Catholic, Protestant

Bosnia and Herzegovina
Area: 51,129 km² (19,741 mi²)
Capital: Sarajevo
Government: Republic
Population: 2,656,240
Languages: Serbian, Croatian
Religions: Muslim, Serbian Orthodox, Roman Catholic

Botswana
Area: 600,370 km² (231,803 mi²)
Capital: Gaborone
Government: Parliamentary republic
Population: 1,477,630
Languages: English, Setswana
Religions: Indigenous beliefs, Christian

Brazil
Area: 8,511,970 km² (3,286,472 mi²)
Capital: Brasília
Government: Federal republic
Population: 162,661,214
Languages: Portuguese, Spanish, English, French
Religion: Roman Catholic

British Virgin Islands
Area: 150 km² (58 mi²)
Capital: Road Town
Government: Dependent territory of United Kingdom
Population: 13,195
Language: English
Religions: Methodist, Anglican, other Protestant faiths,
    Roman Catholic

Brunei
Area: 5,770 km² (2,228 mi²)
Capital: Bandar Seri Begawan
Government: Constitutional sultanate
Population: 299,939
Languages: Malay, English, Chinese
Religions: Muslim, Buddhist, Christian, indigenous
    beliefs

Bulgaria
Area: 110,910 km² (42,822 mi²)
Capital: Sofia
Government: Emerging democracy
Population: 8,612,757
Language: Bulgarian
Religions: Bulgarian Orthodox, Muslim, Jewish, Roman
    Catholic

Burkina Faso
Area: 274,200 km² (105,869 mi²)
Capital: Ouagadougou
Government: Parliamentary
Population: 10,623,323

Languages: French, Sudanic tribal dialects
Religions: Indigenous beliefs, Muslim, Christian

Burma
See **Myanmar.**

Burundi
Area: 27,830 km² (10,745 mi²)
Capital: Bujumbura
Government: Republic
Population: 5,943,057
Languages: Kirundi, French, Swahili
Religions: Roman Catholic, indigenous beliefs,
    Protestant, Muslim

Cambodia
Area: 181,040 km² (69,900 mi²)
Capital: Phnom Penh
Government: Constitutional monarchy
Population: 10,861,218
Languages: Khmer, French
Religions: Theravada Buddhist

Cameroon
Area: 475,440 km² (183,567 mi²)
Capital: Yaoundé
Government: Unitary republic
Population: 14,261,557
Languages: English, French, African languages
Religions: Indigenous beliefs, Christian, Muslim

Canada
Area: 9,976,140 km² (3,851,788 mi²)
Capital: Ottawa
Government: Confederation affiliated with United
    Kingdom
Population: 29,857,369
Languages: English, French
Religions: Roman Catholic, United Church, Anglican

Cape Verde
Area: 4,030 km² (1,556 mi²)
Capital: Praia
Government: Republic
Population: 449,066
Languages: Portuguese, Crioulo
Religions: Roman Catholic and indigenous beliefs

Cayman Islands
Area: 260 km² (100 mi²)
Capital: George Town
Government: Dependent territory of United Kingdom
Population: 36,646
Language: English
Religions: United Church, Anglican, Baptist, Roman
    Catholic

Central African Republic
Area: 622,980 km² (240,533 mi²)
Capital: Bangui
Government: Military republic
Population: 3,274,426
Languages: French, Sangho, Arabic, Hunsa, Swahili
Religions: Christian (with animist beliefs), indigenous
    beliefs, Muslim

Chad
Area: 1,284,000 km² (495,752 mi²)
Capital: N'Djamena
Government: Republic
Population: 6,976,845
Languages: French, Arabic, Sara, Sango
Religions: Muslim, Christian, indigenous beliefs/
    animism

Chile
Area: 756,950 km² (292,258 mi²)
Capital: Santiago
Government: Republic
Population: 14,333,258
Language: Spanish
Religions: Roman Catholic, Protestant, Jewish

China
Area: 9,596,960 km² (3,705,386 mi²)
Capital: Beijing
Government: Communist
Population: 1,210,604,956
Languages: Mandarin, Yue, Wu, Minbei, Minnan,
    Xiang, Gan, Hakka dialects, minority languages
Religions: Officially atheist; Confucianist, Taoist,
    Buddhist, Muslim, Christian

Christmas Island
Area: 135 km² (52 mi²)
Capital: The Settlement
Government: Territory of Australia
Population: 889
Language: English
Religions: Buddhist, Muslim, Christian

Colombia
Area: 1,138,910 km² (439,733 mi²)
Capital: Bogotá
Government: Republic
Population: 38,813,161
Language: Spanish
Religion: Roman Catholic

Comoros
Area: 2,170 km² (838 mi²)
Capital: Moroni
Government: Independent republic

Population: 569,273
Languages: Arabic, French
Religions: Sunni Muslim, Roman Catholic

Congo, Democratic Republic of (formerly Zaire)
Area: 2,345,410 km² (905,563 mi²)
Capital: Kinshasa
Government: Republic
Population: 46,498,539
Languages: French, Lingala, Swahili, Kingwana,
    Kikongo, Tshiluba
Religions: Roman Catholic, Protestant, Kimbanguist,
    Muslim, indigenous beliefs

Congo, Republic of the
Area: 342,000 km² (132,046 mi²)
Capital: Brazzaville
Government: Republic
Population: 2,527,841
Languages: French, Lingala, Kikongo
Religions: Christian, animist, Muslim

Cook Islands
Area: 240 km² (93 mi²)
Capital: Avarua
Government: Self-governing in association with New
    Zealand
Population: 19,561
Language: English
Religion: Cook Islands Christian Church

Costa Rica
Area: 51,100 km² (19,730 mi²)
Capital: San José,
Government: Democratic republic
Population: 3,463,083
Languages: Spanish, English
Religion: Roman Catholic

Croatia
Area: 56,524 km² (21,824 mi²)
Capital: Zagreb
Government: Republic
Population: 5,004,112
Language: Croatian
Religion: Roman Catholic

Cuba
Area: 110,860 km² (42,803 mi²)
Capital: Havana
Government: Communist
Population: 11,007,446
Language: Spanish
Religion: Roman Catholic

Cyprus
Area: 9,250 km² (3,571 mi²)
Capital: Nicosia

Government: Republic; northern part administered
   by Turkey
Population: 736,636
Languages: Greek, Turkish, English
Religions: Greek Orthodox, Muslim, Armenian,
   Maronite

The Czech Republic
Area: 78,864 km² (30,342 mi²)
Capital: Prague
Government: Parliamentary democracy
Population: 10,321,120
Language: Czech
Religions: Roman Catholic, Czech Brethren

Denmark
Area: 43,070 km² (16,629 mi²)
Capital: Copenhagen
Government: Constitutional monarchy
Population: 5,210,833
Languages: Danish, Faroese, Greenlandic, German
Religions: Evangelical Lutheran, other Protestant faiths,
   Roman Catholic

Djibouti
Area: 22,000 km² (8,494 mi²)
Capital: Djibouti
Government: Republic
Population: 427,642
Languages: French, Arabic, Somali, Afar
Religions: Muslim, Christian

Dominica
Area: 750 km² (290 mi²)
Capital: Roseau
Government: Parliamentary democracy
Population: 82,926
Languages: English, French patois
Religions: Roman Catholic, Methodist, Pentecostal,
   Seventh-Day Adventist, Baptist

Dominican Republic
Area: 48,730 km² (18,815 mi²)
Capital: Santo Domingo
Government: Republic
Population: 8,088,881
Language: Spanish
Religion: Roman Catholic

Ecuador
Area: 283,560 km² (109,483 mi²)
Capital: Quito
Government: Republic
Population: 11,466,291
Languages: Spanish, Indian languages (especially
   Quechua)
Religion: Roman Catholic

Egypt
Area: 1,001,450 km² (386,660 mi²)
Capital: Cairo
Government: Republic
Population: 62,575,107
Languages: Arabic, English, French
Religions: Muslim, Coptic Christian

El Salvador
Area: 21,040 km² (8,124 mi²)
Capital: San Salvador
Government: Republic
Population: 5,828,987
Languages: Spanish, Nahua
Religions: Roman Catholic, Protestant Evangelical

Equatorial Guinea
Area: 28,050 km² (10,830 mi²)
Capital: Malabo
Government: Republic
Population: 431,282
Languages: Spanish, Pigdin English, Fang, Bubi, Ibo
Religions: Christian, pagan

Eritrea
Area: 123,300 km² (45,754 mi²)
Capital: Asmara
Government: In transition
Population: 3,909,628
Languages: Afar, Bilen, Kunama, Nara, Arabic,
   Tobedawi, Saho, Tigre, Tigrinya
Religions: Muslim, Eritrean Orthodox Christian

Estonia
Area: 45,100 km² (17,413 mi²)
Capital: Tallinn
Government: Republic
Population: 1,459,428
Language: Estonian
Religion: Lutheran

Ethiopia
Area: 1,221,900 km² (471,776 mi²)
Capital: Addis Ababa
Government: Constitutional republic
Population: 57,171,662
Languages: Amharic, Tigrinya, Orominga, Guaraginga,
   Somali, Arabic, English
Religions: Muslim, Ethiopian Orthodox, animist

Falkland Islands
Area: 12,170 km² (4,699 mi²)
Capital: Stanley
Government: Dependent territory of United Kingdom
Population: 2,317
Language: English
Religions: Anglican, Roman Catholic

Faroe Islands
Area: 1,400 km² (541 mi²)
Capital: Tórshavn
Government: Self-governing overseas administrative
   division of Denmark
Population: 49,349
Languages: Faroese, Danish
Religion: Evangelical Lutheran

Fiji
Area: 18,270 km² (7,054 mi²)
Capital: Suva
Government: Military republic
Population: 782,381
Languages: English, Fijian, Hindustani
Religions: Christian, Hindu, Muslim

Finland
Area: 337,030 km² (130,127 mi²)
Capital: Helsinki
Government: Republic
Population: 5,100,213
Languages: Finnish, Swedish, Lapp, Russian
Religions: Evangelical Lutheran, Greek Orthodox

France
Area: 547,030 km² (211,208 mi²)
Capital: Paris
Government: Republic
Population: 59,317,450
Languages: French, regional dialects
Religions: Roman Catholic, Protestant, Jewish, Muslim

French Guiana
Area: 91,000 km² (35,135 mi²)
Capital: Cayenne
Government: Overseas department of France
Population: 151,187
Language: French
Religion: Roman Catholic

French Polynesia
Area: 4,000 km² (1,544 mi²)
Capital: Papeete
Government: Overseas territory of France
Population: 224,911
Languages: French, Tahitian
Religions: Protestant, Roman Catholic

Gabon
Area: 267,670 km² (103,347 mi²)
Capital: Libreville
Government: Republic
Population: 1,172,798
Languages: French, Fang, Myene, Bateke,
   Bapounou/Eschira, Bandjabi
Religions: Christian, animist, Muslim

The Gambia
Area: 11,300 km² (4,363 mi²)
Capital: Banjul
Government: Republic
Population: 1,020,178
Languages: English, Mandinka, Wolof, Fula, local
   dialects
Religions: Muslim, Christian, indigenous beliefs

Georgia
Area: 69,699 km² (26,911 mi²)
Capital: Tbilisi
Government: Republic
Population: 5,219,810
Languages: Georgian, Russian
Religions: Georgian Orthodox

Germany
Area: 356,910 km² (137,803 mi²)
Capital: Berlin
Government: Federal republic
Population: 83,536,115
Language: German
Religions: Protestant, Roman Catholic

Ghana
Area: 238,540 km² (92,100 mi²)
Capital: Accra
Government: Republic
Population: 17,698,271
Languages: English, Akan, Moshi-Dagomba, Ewe,
   Ga-Adangbe
Religions: Indigenous beliefs, Muslim, Christian

Gibraltar
Area: 6.5 km² (2.5 mi²)
Capital: Gibraltar
Government: Dependent territory of United Kingdom
Population: 32,067
Languages: English, Spanish, Italian, Portuguese,
   Russian
Religions: Roman Catholic, Anglican, Muslim, Jewish

Greece
Area: 131,940 km² (50,942 mi²)
Capital: Athens
Government: Presidential parliamentary
Population: 10,718,518
Language: Greek
Religions: Greek Orthodox, Muslim

Greenland
Area: 2,175,600 km² (839,999 mi²)
Capital: Nuuk (Godthåb)
Government: Self-governing overseas administrative
   division of Denmark
Population: 58,203

Languages: Eskimo dialects, Danish
Religion: Evangelical Lutheran

Grenada
Area: 340 km² (131 mi²)
Capital: St. George's
Government: Parliamentary democracy affiliated with
    United Kingdom
Population: 94,961
Languages: English, French patois
Religions: Roman Catholic, Anglican, other Protestant
    faiths

Guadeloupe
Area: 1,780 km² (687 mi²)
Capital: Basse-Terre
Government: Overseas department of France
Population: 407,768
Languages: French, Creole
Religions: Roman Catholic, Hindu, pagan African

Guatemala
Area: 108,890 km² (42,042 mi²)
Capital: Guatemala City
Government: Republic
Population: 11,277,614
Languages: Spanish, Quiche, Cakchiquel, Kekchi, other
    Indian dialects
Religions: Roman Catholic, Protestant, traditional
    Mayan

Guernsey
Area: 194 km² (75 mi²)
Capital: St. Peter Port
Government: British crown dependency
Population: 64,975
Languages: English, French, Norman-French
Religions: Anglican, Roman Catholic, other Protestant
    faiths

Guinea
Area: 245,860 km² (94,927 mi²)
Capital: Conakry
Government: Republic
Population: 7,411,981
Languages: French, tribal languages
Religions: Muslim, Christian, indigenous beliefs

Guinea-Bissau
Area: 36,120 km² (13,948 mi²)
Capital: Bissau
Government: Republic
Population: 1,151,330
Languages: Portuguese, Criolo, African languages
Religions: Indigenous beliefs, Muslim, Christian

Guyana
Area: 214,970 km² (83,000 mi²)
Capital: Georgetown

Government: Republic
Population: 712,091
Languages: English, Amerindian dialects
Religions: Christian, Hindu, Muslim

Haiti
Area: 27,750 km² (10,714 mi²)
Capital: Port-au-Prince
Government: Republic
Population: 6,731,539
Languages: French, Creole
Religions: Roman Catholic/voodoo, Protestant

Honduras
Area: 112,090 km² (43,278 mi²)
Capital: Tegucigalpa
Government: Republic
Population: 5,605,193
Languages: Spanish, Amerindian dialects
Religions: Roman Catholic, Protestant

Hong Kong
Area: 1,040 km² (402 mi²)
Capital: None
Government: Special administrative region of China
Population: 6,305,413
Languages: Cantonese, English
Religions: Local religions, Christian

Hungary
Area: 93,030 km² (35,919 mi²)
Capital: Budapest
Government: Republic
Population: 10,002,541
Language: Hungarian (Magyar)
Religions: Calvinist, Lutheran

Iceland
Area: 103,000 km² (39,768 mi²)
Capital: Reykjavík
Government: Republic
Population: 268,369
Languages: Icelandic
Religions: Evangelical Lutheran, other Protestant faiths,
    Roman Catholic

India
Area: 3,287,590 km² (1,269,338 mi²)
Capital: New Delhi
Government: Federal republic
Population: 952,107,694
Languages: Hindi, English, Bengali, Telugu, Marathi,
    Tamil, Urdu, Gujarati, Malayalan, Kannada, Oriya,
    Punjabi, Assamese, Kashmiri, Sindhi, Sanskrit,
    Hindustani
Religions: Hindu, Muslim, Christian, Sikh, Buddhist,
    Jains

Indonesia
Area: 1,904,570 km² (735,272 mi²)
Capital: Jakarta
Government: Republic
Population: 206,611,600
Languages: Bahasa Indonesian, Javanese, English, Dutch
Religions: Muslim, Protestant, Roman Catholic, Hindu, Buddhist

Iran
Area: 1,648,000 km² (636,293 mi²)
Capital: Teheran
Government: Theocratic republic
Population: 66,094,264
Languages: Farsi, Turk, Kurdish, Arabic, Luri, Baloch
Religions: Shi'a Muslim, Sunni Muslim, Zoroastrian, Jewish, Christian, Baha'i

Iraq
Area: 434,920 km² (167,923 mi²)
Capital: Baghdad
Government: Republic
Population: 21,422,292
Languages: Arabic, Kurdish, Assyrian, Armenian
Religions: Shi'a Muslim, Sunni Muslim, Christian

Ireland
Area: 70,280 km² (27,135 mi²)
Capital: Dublin
Government: Republic
Population: 3,562,902
Languages: Irish (Gaelic), English
Religions: Roman Catholic, Anglican

Israel
Area: (excluding occupied territories) 20,770 km² (8,019 mi²)
Capital: Jerusalem
Government: Parliamentary democracy
Population: 5,215,022 (excluding occupied territories)
Languages: Hebrew, Arabic
Religions: Jewish, Muslim, Christian, Druze
See also **West Bank and Gaza Strip.**

Italy
Area: 301,230 km² (116,305 mi²)
Capital: Rome
Government: Republic
Population: 57,460,274
Languages: Italian, German, French, Slovene
Religion: Roman Catholic

Ivory Coast
Area: 322,460 km² (124,502 mi²)
Capital: Abidjan (also Yamoussoukro)
Government: Republic
Population: 14,762,445

Languages: French, Dioula, tribal languages
Religions: Indigenous beliefs, Muslim, Christian

Jamaica
Area: 10,990 km² (4,243 mi²)
Capital: Kingston
Government: Parliamentary democracy affiliated with United Kingdom
Population: 2,593,918
Languages: English, Creole
Religions: Protestant, Roman Catholic, spiritualist cults

Japan
Area: 377,835 km² (145,882 mi²)
Capital: Tokyo
Government: Constitutional monarchy
Population: 125,568,504
Language: Japanese
Religions: Shinto, Buddhist, Christian

Jersey
Area: 117 km² (45 mi²)
Capital: Saint Helier
Government: British crown dependency
Population: 87,250
Languages: English, French, Norman-French
Religions: Anglican, other Protestant faiths, Roman Catholic

Jordan
Area: 91,880 km² (35,475 mi²) (excluding West Bank)
Capital: Amman
Government: Constitutional monarchy
Population: 4,212,152 (excluding West Bank)
Languages: Arabic, English
Religions: Sunni Muslim, Christian

Kazakhstan
Area: 2,717,428 km² (1,049,200 mi²)
Capital: Alma Alta
Government: Constitutional republic
Population: 16,916,463
Languages: Kazakh, Russian
Religion: Muslim

Kenya
Area: 582,650 km² (224,961 mi²)
Capital: Nairobi
Government: Republic
Population: 28,176,686
Languages: English, Swahili, local languages
Religions: Protestant, Roman Catholic, indigenous beliefs, Muslim

Kiribati
Area: 710 km² (274 mi²)
Capital: Tarawa
Government: Republic

Population: 80,919
Languages: English, Gilbertese
Religions: Roman Catholic, Protestant, Seventh-Day
  Adventist, Baha'i

There are two independent nations smaller than New York City's Central Park: Vatican City and Monaco. Each is less than one square mile.

Korea, Democratic People's Republic of (North Korea)
Area: 120,540 km² (46,540 mi²)
Capital: Pyongyang
Government: Communist
Population: 23,904,424
Language: Korean
Religions: Buddhist, Confucianist

Korea, Republic of (South Korea)
Area: 98,480 km² (38,023 mi²)
Capital: Seoul
Government: Republic
Population: 45,482,291
Language: Korean
Religions: Confucianist, Christian, Buddhist,
  Shamanist, Chondokyo

Kuwait
Area: 17,820 km² (6,880 mi²)
Capital: Kuwait
Government: Nominal constitutional monarchy
Population: 1,950,047
Languages: Arabic, English
Religions: Sunni Muslim, Shi'a Muslim, Christian,
  Hindu, Parsi

Kyrgyzstan
Area: 198,509 km² (76,642 mi²)
Capital: Frunze
Government: Constitutional republic
Population: 4,529,648
Languages: Kirghiz, Russian
Religions: Muslim

Laos
Area: 236,800 km² (91,428 mi²)
Capital: Vientiane
Government: Communist
Population: 4,975,772
Languages: Lao, French, English
Religions: Buddhist, animist

Latvia
Area: 63,701 km² (24,595 mi²)
Capital: Riga
Government: Republic
Population: 2,468,982
Languages: Latvian
Religions: Lutheran, Russian Orthodox, Catholic

Lebanon
Area: 10,400 km² (4,015 mi²)
Capital: Beirut
Government: Republic
Population: 3,776,317
Languages: Arabic, French, Armenian, English
Religions: Muslim and Christian, each divided into
  sects (17 in all)

Lesotho
Area: 30,350 km² (11,718 mi²)
Capital: Maseru
Government: Modified constitutional monarchy
Population: 1,970,781
Languages: Sesotho, English, Zulu, Xhosa
Religions: Christian, indigenous beliefs

Liberia
Area: 111,370 km² (43,000 mi²)
Capital: Monrovia
Government: Republic
Population: 2,109,789
Languages: English, Niger-Congo languages
Religions: Indigenous beliefs, Christian, Muslim

Libya
Area: 1,759,540 km² (679,358 mi²)
Capital: Tripoli
Government: Military dictatorship
Population: 5,445,436
Languages: Arabic, Italian, English
Religion: Sunni Muslim

Liechtenstein
Area: 160 km² (62 mi²)
Capital: Vaduz
Government: Constitutional monarchy
Population: 31,011
Languages: German, Alemannic
Religions: Roman Catholic, Protestant

Lithuania
Area: 65,190 km² (25,170 mi²)
Capital: Vilnius
Government: Republic
Population: 3,718,000
Languages: Lithuanian
Religions: Roman Catholic

Luxembourg
Area: 2,586 km² (998 mi²)
Capital: Luxembourg
Government: Constitutional monarchy
Population: 406,901
Languages: Luxembourgish, German, French, English
Religions: Roman Catholic, Protestant, English

Macau
Area: 16 km² (6 mi²)
Capital: Macau
Government: Overseas territory of Portugal until 1999
Population: 496,837
Languages: Portuguese, Cantonese
Religions: Buddhist, Roman Catholic

Macedonia
Area: 25,713 km² (9,928 mi²)
Capital: Skopje
Government: Republic
Population: 2,104,035
Language: Macedonian
Religions: Eastern Orthodox, Muslim

Madagascar
Area: 587,040 km² (226,656 mi²)
Capital: Antananarivo
Government: Republic
Population: 13,670,507
Languages: French, Malagasy
Religions: Indigenous beliefs, Christian, Muslim

Malawi
Area: 118,480 km² (45,745 mi²)
Capital: Lilongwe
Government: Constitutional republic
Population: 9,452,844
Languages: English, Chichewa, Tombuka
Religions: Protestant, Roman Catholic, Muslim, indigenous beliefs

Malaysia
Area: 329,750 km² (127,316 mi²)
Capital: Kuala Lumpur
Government: Constitutional monarchy with hereditary rulers in peninsular states
Population: 19,962,893
Languages: Malay, English, Chinese dialects, Tamil, Hakka dialects, tribal languages
Religions: Muslim, Buddhist, Hindu, Confucianist, Christian

Maldives
Area: 300 km² (116 mi²)
Capital: Male
Government: Republic
Population: 270,758
Languages: Divehi, English
Religion: Sunni Muslim

Mali
Area: 1,240,000 km² (478,764 mi²)
Capital: Bamako
Government: Republic
Population: 9,653,261
Languages: French, Bambara
Religions: Muslim, indigenous beliefs, Christian

Malta
Area: 320 km² (124 mi²)
Capital: Valletta
Government: Parliamentary democracy
Population: 372,314
Languages: Maltese, English
Religion: Roman Catholic

Man, Isle of
Area: 588 km² (227 mi²)
Capital: Douglas
Government: British crown dependency
Population: 73,459
Languages: English, Manx Gaelic
Religions: Anglican, other Protestant faiths, Roman Catholic

Martinique
Area: 1,100 km² (425 mi²)
Capital: Fort-de-France
Government: Overseas department of France
Population: 399,151
Languages: French, Creole patois
Religions: Roman Catholic, Hindu, pagan African

Mauritania
Area: 1,030,700 km² (397,953 mi²)
Capital: Nouakchott
Government: Republic
Population: 2,336,048
Languages: Hasaniya Arabic, French, Toucouleur, Fula, Sarakole, Wolof
Religion: Muslim

Mauritius
Area: 1,860 km² (718 mi²)
Capital: Port Louis
Government: Parliamentary democracy affiliated with United Kingdom
Population: 1,139,047
Languages: English, Creole, French, Hindi, Urdu, Hakka, Bojpoori
Religions: Hindu, Roman Catholic, Anglican, Muslim

Mayotte
Area: 375 km² (145 mi²)
Capital: Dzaoudzi
Government: Territorial collectivity of France
Population: 100,838
Languages: Mahorian, French
Religions: Muslim, Christian

Mexico
Area: 1,972,550 km² (761,602 mi²)
Capital: Mexico City
Government: Federal republic
Population: 95,772,462
Language: Spanish
Religions: Roman Catholic, Protestant

Moldova
Area: 33,701 km² (13,012 mi²)
Capital: Kishinev
Government: Republic
Population: 4,463,847
Language: Romanian
Religions: Russian Orthodox, Seventh-Day Adventist

Monaco
Area: 1.9 km² (.7 mi²)
Capital: Monaco
Government: Constitutional monarchy
Population: 31,719
Languages: French, English, Italian, Monegasque
Religion: Roman Catholic

Mongolia
Area: 1,565,000 km² (604,247 mi²)
Capital: Ulaanbaatar
Government: Republic
Population: 2,496,617
Languages: Khalkha Mongol, Turkic, Russian, Chinese
Religions: Tibetan Buddhist, Muslim

Montserrat
Area: 100 km² (39 mi²)
Capital: Plymouth
Government: Dependent territory of United Kingdom
Population: 12,771
Language: English
Religions: Anglican, other Protestant faiths, Roman Catholic

Morocco
Area: 446,550 km² (172,413 mi²)
Capital: Rabat
Government: Constitutional monarchy
Population: 29,779,156
Languages: Arabic, French, Berber dialects
Religions: Muslim, Christian, Jewish

Mozambique
Area: 801,950 km² (309,633 mi²)
Capital: Maputo
Government: Republic
Population: 17,877,927
Languages: Portuguese, indigenous languages
Religions: Indigenous beliefs, Christian, Muslim

Myanmar (formerly Burma)
Area: 676,550 km² (261,216 mi²)
Capital: Yangon
Government: Military
Population: 49,975,625
Languages: Burmese, ethnic languages
Religions: Buddhist, Christian, Muslim, animist beliefs

Namibia
Area: 824,290 km² (318,258 mi²)
Capital: Windhoek
Government: Republic
Population: 1,677,243
Languages: Afrikaans, German, English, indigenous languages
Religions: Christian, indigenous beliefs

Nauru
Area: 20 km² (8 mi²)
Capital: Yaren
Government: Republic
Population: 10,273
Languages: Nauruan, English
Religions: Protestant, Roman Catholic

Nepal
Area: 140,800 km² (54,363 mi²)
Capital: Kathmandu
Government: Constitutional monarchy
Population: 22,094,033
Languages: Nepali, local languages
Religions: Hindu, Buddhist, Muslim

The Netherlands
Area: 37,310 km² (14,405 mi²)
Capital: Amsterdam and The Hague
Government: Constitutional monarchy
Population: 15,531,940
Language: Dutch
Religions: Roman Catholic, Protestant

Netherlands Antilles
Area: 960 km² (371 mi²)
Capital: Willemstad (on Curacao)
Government: Autonomous territory of The Netherlands
Population: 208,968
Languages: Dutch, Papiamento, English, Spanish
Religions: Roman Catholic, Protestant, Jewish, Seventh-Day Adventist

The World

New Caledonia
Area: 19,060 km² (7,359 mi²)
Capital: Nouméa
Government: Overseas territory of France
Population: 187,784
Languages: French, Melanesian-Polynesian dialects
Religions: Roman Catholic, Protestant

New Zealand
Area: 268,680 km² (103,737 mi²)
Capital: Wellington
Government: Parliamentary democracy affiliated with United Kingdom
Population: 3,547,983
Languages: English, Maori
Religions: Anglican, Presbyterian, Roman Catholic

Nicaragua
Area: 129,494 km² (49,998 mi²)
Capital: Managua
Government: Republic
Population: 4,272,352
Languages: Spanish, English, Amerindian dialects
Religion: Roman Catholic

Niger
Area: 1,267,000 km² (489,189 mi²)
Capital: Niamey
Government: Republic (under military control)
Population: 9,113,001
Languages: French, Hausa, Djerma
Religions: Muslim, indigenous beliefs, Christian

Nigeria
Area: 923,770 km² (356,668 mi²)
Capital: Lagos
Government: Military
Population: 103,912,489
Languages: English, Hausa, Yoruba, Ibo, Fulani
Religions: Muslim, Christian, indigenous beliefs

Niue
Area: 260 km² (100 mi²)
Capital: Alofi
Government: Self-governing territory affiliated with New Zealand
Population: 1,837
Languages: Polynesian (Tongan-Samoan dialect), English
Religions: Ekalesia Nieu, Mormon

Norfolk Island
Area: 40 km² (15.4 mi²)
Capital: Kingston
Government: Territory of Australia
Population: 2,756

Languages: English, Norfolk
Religions: Anglican, other Protestant faiths, Roman Catholic, Seventh-Day Adventist

Norway
Area: 324,220 km² (125,181 mi²)
Capital: Oslo
Government: Constitutional monarchy
Population: 4,315,941
Languages: Norwegian, Lapp, Finnish
Religions: Evangelical Lutheran, other Protestant faiths, Roman Catholic

Oman
Area: 212,460 km² (82,031 mi²)
Capital: Muscat
Government: Absolute monarchy
Population: 2,186,548
Languages: Arabic, English, Baluchi, Urdu
Religions: Ibadhi Muslim, Sunni Muslim, Shi'a Muslim, Hindu

Pakistan
Area: 803,940 km² (310,401 mi²)
Capital: Islamabad
Government: Federal republic
Population: 129,275,660
Languages: Urdu, English, Punjabi, Sindhi, Pushtu, Baluchi
Religions: Muslim, Christian, Hindu

Palau
Area: 458 km² (177 mi²)
Capital: Koror
Population: 16,952
Government: Parliamentary republic
Languages: Palauan, English
Religions: Christian, Modekngei

Panama
Area: 78,200 km² (30,193 mi²)
Capital: Panama
Government: Centralized republic
Population: 2,655,094
Languages: Spanish, English
Religions: Roman Catholic, Protestant

Papua New Guinea
Area: 461,690 km² (178,259 mi²)
Capital: Port Moresby
Government: Parliamentary democracy affiliated with United Kingdom
Population: 4,394,537
Languages: Motu, local dialects, English
Religions: Roman Catholic, Protestant

Paraguay
Area: 406,750 km² (157,046 mi²)
Capital: Asunción
Government: Republic
Population: 5,504,146
Languages: Spanish, Guarani
Religions: Roman Catholic, Mennonite, other
    Protestant faiths

Peru
Area: 1,285,220 km² (496,223 mi²)
Capital: Lima
Government: Republic
Population: 24,523,408
Languages: Spanish, Quechua, Aymara
Religion: Roman Catholic

Philippines
Area: 300,000 km² (115,830 mi²)
Capital: Manila
Government: Republic
Population: 74,480,848
Languages: Philipino (Tagalog), English
Religions: Roman Catholic, Muslim, Buddhist

Poland
Area: 312,680 km² (120,727 mi²)
Capital: Warsaw
Government: Democratic state
Population: 38,642,565
Language: Polish
Religions: Roman Catholic, Russian Orthodox,
    Catholic

Portugal
Area: 92,080 km² (35,552 mi²)
Capital: Lisbon
Government: Republic
Population: 9,865,114
Language: Portuguese
Religions: Roman Catholic, Protestant

Qatar
Area: 11,000 km² (4,247 mi²)
Capital: Doha
Government: Traditional monarchy
Population: 547,761
Languages: Arabic, English
Religion: Muslim

Réunion
Area: 2,510 km² (969 mi²)
Capital: Saint-Denis
Government: Overseas department of France
Population: 679,198
Languages: French, Creole
Religion: Roman Catholic

Romania
Area: 237,500 km² (91,699 mi²)
Capital: Bucharest
Government: Republic
Population: 21,657,162
Languages: Romanian, Hungarian, German
Religions: Romanian Orthodox, Roman Catholic,
    Protestant, Greek Catholic

Russia
Area: 17,075,352 km² (6,592,800 mi²)
Capital: Moscow
Government: Constitutional republic
Population: 148,190,419
Language: Russian
Religions: Russian Orthodox, Baptist, Jewish

Rwanda
Area: 26,340 km² (10,170 mi²)
Capital: Kigali
Government: Republic (under military control)
Population: 6,853,359
Languages: Kinyarwanda, French, Kiswahili
Religions: Roman Catholic, Protestant, indigenous
    beliefs, Muslim

St. Helena
Area: 410 km² (158 mi²)
Capital: Jamestown
Government: Dependent territory of the United
    Kingdom
Population: 6,782
Language: English
Religions: Anglican, other Protestant faiths, Roman
    Catholic

St. Kitts and Nevis
Area: 269 km² (104 mi²)
Capital: Basseterre
Government: Constitutional monarchy affiliated with
    United Kingdom
Population: 41,369
Language: English
Religions: Anglican, other Protestant faiths, Roman
    Catholic

St. Lucia
Area: 620 km² (239 mi²)
Capital: Castries
Government: Parliamentary democracy affiliated with
    United Kingdom
Population: 157,862
Languages: English, French patois
Religions: Roman Catholic, Protestant, Anglican

St. Pierre and Miquelon
Area: 242 km² (93 mi²)
Capital: Saint-Pierre

Government: Territorial collectivity of France
Population: 6,809
Language: French
Religion: Roman Catholic

St. Vincent and the Grenadines
Area: 340 km² (131 mi²)
Capital: Kingstown
Government: Constitutional monarchy affiliated with
    United Kingdom
Population: 118,344
Languages: English, French patois
Religions: Anglican, other Protestant faiths, Roman
    Catholic, Seventh-Day Adventist

San Marino
Area: 60 km² (23 mi²)
Capital: San Marino
Government: Republic
Population: 24,521
Language: Italian
Religion: Roman Catholic

São Tomé and Principe
Area: 960 km² (371 mi²)
Capital: São Tomé and Principe
Government: Republic
Population: 144,128
Language: Portuguese
Religions: Roman Catholic, Evangelical Protestant,
    Seventh-Day Adventist

Saudi Arabia
Area: 2,149,690 km² (829,995 mi²)
Capital: Riyadh
Government: Monarchy
Population: 19,409,058
Language: Arabic
Religion: Muslim

Senegal
Area: 196,190 km² (75,748 mi²)
Capital: Dakar
Government: Republic
Population: 9,092,749
Languages: French, Wolof, Pulaar, Diola, Mandingo
Religions: Muslim, indigenous beliefs, Christian

Seychelles
Area: 455 km² (176 mi²)
Capital: Victoria
Government: Republic
Population: 77,575
Languages: English, French, Creole
Religions: Roman Catholic, Anglican

Sierra Leone
Area: 71,740 km² (27,699 mi²)
Capital: Freetown

Government: Republic
Population: 4,793,121
Languages: English, Mende, Krio, Temne
Religions: Muslim, indigenous beliefs, Christian

Singapore
Area: 633 km² (244 mi²)
Capital: Singapore
Government: Republic
Population: 3,396,924
Languages: Chinese, Tamil, Malay, English
Religions: Buddhist, Muslim, Christian, Hindu, Sikh,
    Taoist Confucianist

Slovakia
Area: 49,035 km² (18,928 mi²)
Capital: Bratislava
Government: Parliamentary democracy
Population: 5,374,362
Language: Slovak
Religions: Roman Catholic, Greek Catholic, Protestant,
    Jewish, Orthodox

Slovenia
Area: 20,246 km² (7,817 mi²)
Capital: Ljubljana
Government: Republic
Population: 1,951,433
Language: Slovene
Religions: Roman Catholic, Protestant

Solomon Islands
Area: 28,450 km² (10,985 mi²)
Capital: Honiara
Government: Independent parliamentary state within
    British Commonwealth
Population: 412,902
Languages: Melanesian pigdin, English, local dialects
Religions: Anglican, Roman Catholic, other Protestant
    faiths

Somalia
Area: 637,660 km² (246,201 mi²)
Capital: Mogadishu
Government: In transition
Population: 9,639,151
Languages: Somali, Arabic, Italian, English
Religion: Sunni Muslim

South Africa
Area: 1,221,040 km² (471,444 mi²)
Capital: Pretoria, Cape Town
Government: Republic
Population: 41,743,459
Languages: Afrikaans, English, Zulu, Xhosa, Tswana
Religions: Christian, Hindu, Muslim

The World

Spain
Area: 504,750 km² (194,884 mi²)
Capital: Madrid
Government: Parliamentary monarchy
Population: 38,853,397
Languages: Castilian Spanish, Catalan, Galician, Basque
Religion: Roman Catholic

Sri Lanka
Area: 65,610 km² (25,332 mi²)
Capital: Colombo
Government: Republic
Population: 18,553,074
Languages: Sinhala, Tamil, English
Religions: Buddhist, Hindu, Christian, Muslim

Sudan
Area: 2,505,810 km² (967,493 mi²)
Capital: Khartoum
Government: Military
Population: 31,065,229
Languages: Arabic, Nubian, Ta Bedawie, Nilotic and Nilo-Hamitic dialects, Sudanic dialects, English
Religions: Sunni Muslim, indigenous beliefs, Christian

Suriname
Area: 163,270 km² (63,039 mi²)
Capital: Paramaribo
Government: Republic
Population: 436,418
Languages: Dutch, English, Sranan Tongo, Javanese
Religions: Hindu, Muslim, Roman Catholic, Protestant

Svalbard
Area: 62,049 km² (23,597 mi²)
Capital: Longyearbyen
Government: Territory of Norway
Population: 2,914
Languages: Russian, Norwegian
Religion: Evangelical Lutheran

Swaziland
Area: 17,360 km² (6,703 mi²)
Capital: Mbabane
Government: Independent monarchy within British commonwealth
Population: 998,730
Languages: English, siSwati
Religions: Christian, indigenous beliefs

Sweden
Area: 449,960 km² (173,729 mi²)
Capital: Stockholm
Government: Constitutional monarchy
Population: 8,861,270
Languages: Swedish, Lapp, Finnish
Religions: Evangelical Lutheran, Roman Catholic

Switzerland
Area: 41,290 km² (15,942 mi²)
Capital: Bern
Government: Federal republic
Population: 7,124,745
Languages: German, French, Italian, Romansch
Religions: Roman Catholic, Protestant, Jewish

Syria
Area: 185,180 km² (71,498 mi²)
Capital: Damascus
Government: Military republic
Population: 15,608,648
Languages: Arabic, Kurdish, Armenian, Aramaic, Circassian, French
Religions: Sunni Muslim, Alawite, Druze, other Muslim sects, Christian

Taiwan
Area: 35,980 km² (13,892 mi²)
Capital: Taipei
Government: Republic
Population: 21,304,000
Languages: Mandarin Chinese, Taiwanese and Hakka dialects
Religions: Buddhist, Confucianist, Taoist, Christian

Tajikistan
Area: 139,909 km² (54,019 mi²)
Capital: Dushanbe
Government: Republic
Population: 5,916,373
Languages: Tadzhik, Russian
Religion: Muslim

Tanzania
Area: 945,090 km² (364,899 mi²)
Capital: Dar es Salaam
Government: Republic
Population: 29,058,470
Languages: Swahili, English
Religions: Christian, Muslim, indigenous beliefs

Thailand
Area: 514,000 km² (198,455 mi²)
Capital: Bangkok
Government: Constitutional monarchy under martial law
Population: 58,851,357
Languages: Thai, English, local dialects
Religions: Buddhist, Muslim

Togo
Area: 56,790 km² (21,927 mi²)
Capital: Lomé
Government: One-party republic
Population: 4,570,530

Languages: French, Ewe, Mina, Dagomba, Kabyè
Religions: Indigenous beliefs, Christian, Muslim

Tokelau
Area: 10 km² (4 mi²)
Capital: None (various local government agencies)
Government: Territory of New Zealand
Population: 1,503
Languages: Tokelauan, English
Religions: Congregational Christian Church, Roman
 Catholic

Tonga
Area: 748 km² (289 mi²)
Capital: Nuku'alofa
Government: Constitutional monarchy
Population: 106,466
Languages: Tongan, English
Religion: Christian

Trinidad and Tobago
Area: 5,130 km² (1,981 mi²)
Capital: Port-of-Spain
Government: Parliamentary democracy
Population: 1,272,385
Languages: English, Hindi, French, Spanish
Religions: Roman Catholic, Hindu, Protestant, Muslim

Tunisia
Area: 163,610 km² (63,170 mi²)
Capital: Tunis
Government: Republic
Population: 9,019,687
Languages: Arabic, French
Religions: Muslim, Christian, Jewish

Turkey
Area: 780,580 km² (301,382 mi²)
Capital: Ankara
Government: Republican parliamentary democracy
Population: 62,484,478
Languages: Turkish, Kurdish, Arabic
Religions: Muslim (mostly Sunni), Christian, Jewish

Turkmenistan
Area: 488,000 km² (188,417 mi²)
Capital: Ashkhabad
Government: Republic
Population: 4,149,283
Languages: Turkmen, Russian
Religion: Sunni Muslim

Turks and Caicos Islands
Area: 430 km² (166 mi²)
Capital: Grand Turk (Cockburn Town)
Government: Dependent territory of United Kingdom
Population: 14,302

Language: English
Religions: Baptist, Methodist, Anglican, Seventh-Day
 Adventist

Tuvalu
Area: 26 km² (10 mi²)
Capital: Funafuti
Government: Democracy affiliated with United
 Kingdom
Population: 10,146
Languages: Tuvaluan, English
Religion: Protestant

Uganda
Area: 236,040 km² (91,135 mi²)
Capital: Kampala
Government: One-party republic
Population: 20,158,176
Languages: English, Luganda, Swahili, Bantu and
 Nilotic languages
Religions: Roman Catholic, Protestant, Muslim,
 indigenous beliefs

Ukraine
Area: 603,729 km² (233,100 mi²)
Capital: Kiev
Government: Republic
Population: 50,864,009
Languages: Ukrainian, Russian
Religions: Russian Orthodox, Baptist, Roman Catholic,
 Jewish

United Arab Emirates
Area: 83,600 km² (32,278 mi²)
Capital: Abu Dhabi
Government: Federation of seven emirates
Population: 3,057,337
Languages: Arabic, Farsi, English, Hindi, Urdu
Religions: Muslim, Christian, Hindu

United Kingdom
Area: 244,820 km² (94,525 mi²)
Capital: London
Government: Constitutional monarchy
Population: 58,489,975
Languages: English, Welsh, Scottish Gaelic
Religions: Anglican, other Protestant faiths, Roman
 Catholic, Jewish

United States
Area: 9,372,610 km² (3,618,765 mi²)
Capital: Washington, D.C.
Government: Federal republic
Population: 262,755,000
Languages: English, Spanish
Religions: Protestant, Roman Catholic, Jewish

The World

Uruguay
Area: 176,220 km² (68,039 mi²)
Capital: Montevideo
Government: Republic
Population: 3,238,952
Language: Spanish
Religions: Roman Catholic, Protestant, Jewish

Uzbekistan
Area: 447,293 km² (172,700 mi²)
Capital: Tashkent
Government: Republic
Population: 23,418,381
Languages: Uzbek, Russian
Religion: Muslim

Vanuatu
Area: 14,760 km² (5,699 mi²)
Capital: Port-Vila
Government: Republic
Population: 177,504
Languages: English, French, Bislama
Religion: Christian

Vatican City
Area: 0.438 km² (108.7 acres)
Capital: Vatican City
Government: Independent papal state
Population: 830
Languages: Italian, Latin
Religion: Roman Catholic

Venezuela
Area: 912,050 km² (352,143 mi²)
Capital: Caracas
Government: Republic
Population: 21,983,188
Languages: Spanish, Amerindian dialects
Religion: Roman Catholic

Vietnam
Area: 329,560 km² (127,243 mi²)
Capital: Hanoi
Government: Communist
Population: 73,976,973
Languages: Vietnamese, French, Chinese, English, Khmer, tribal dialects
Religions: Buddhist, Confucianist, Taoist, Roman Catholic, indigenous beliefs, Muslim, Protestant

Wallis and Futuna
Area: 274 km² (106 mi²)
Capital: Mata-Utu
Government: Overseas territory of France
Population: 14,659
Languages: French, Wallisian
Religion: Roman Catholic

West Bank and Gaza Strip
Area: 6,240 km² (2,410 mi²)
Capital: None
Government: Israeli military rule
Population: 1,427,741 (excluding Israeli settlers)
Languages: Arabic, Hebrew, English
Religions: Muslim, Jewish, Christian

Western Sahara
Area: 2,860 km² (1,097 mi²)
Capital: None
Government: Moroccan administrative protectorate
Population: 222,631
Languages: Hassaniya Arabic, Moroccan Arabic
Religion: Muslim

Western Samoa
Area: 2,860 km² (1,104 mi²)
Capital: Apia
Government: Constitutional monarchy
Population: 214,384
Languages: Samoan, English
Religions: Congregational, Roman Catholic, other Protestant faiths

Yemen
Area: 527,970 km² (203,849 mi²)
Capital: Sanaa
Government: Republic
Population: 13,483,178
Language: Arabic
Religions: Muslim, Christian, Hindu

Yugoslavia, Federal Republic of
(Consists of Serbia, the largest republic of preindependence Yugoslavia, and Montenegro, the smallest republic) This country has not been recognized by the United States.
Area: 134,563 km² (51,955 mi²)
Capital: Belgrade
Government: Federal republic
Population: 10,611,558
Languages: Serbian, Hungarian (Vojvodina), Albanian (Kosovo), Montenegrin
Religions: Serbian Orthodox, Muslim, Roman Catholic

Zambia
Area: 752,610 km² (290,583 mi²)
Capital: Lusaka
Government: Multiparty state
Population: 9,159,072
Languages: English, local languages and dialects
Religions: Christian, Muslim, Hindu, indigenous beliefs

Go to "The World's Major Religions" in chapter 9; "Frequently Used Foreign Words and Phrases" in chapter 13

The World

Zimbabwe
Area: 390,580 km² (150,803 mi²)
Capital: Harare
Government: Parliamentary democracy
Population: 11,271,314
Languages: English, Shona, Sindebele
Religions: Indigenous/Christian beliefs, Christian, indigenous beliefs, Muslim

GREAT EVENTS IN WORLD HISTORY

Throughout prehistory, antiquity, and the early Middle Ages, it is often difficult to place exact dates. Therefore, most of the dates in this timeline up to the year A.D. 1000 should be considered approximate.

1,600,000 B.C.	Earliest humanlike ancestors.
250,000 B.C.	Earliest *Homo sapiens.*
70,000 B.C.	Neanderthals use stone tools and fire.
40,000 B.C.	Ice Age ends; Cro-Magnons migrate into Europe.
30,000 B.C.	Neanderthals disappear.
28,000 B.C.	Asians cross land bridge between Asia and America.
20,000 B.C.	European cave art exists.
12,000 B.C.	Dog domesticated from Asian wolf.
8000 B.C.	Agriculture develops in Near East.
7000 B.C.	Jericho settled and soon walled to protect from attack.
6500 B.C.	Wheel invented by Sumerians.
6000 B.C.	First true pottery made.
5000 B.C.	Copper, first shapable metal, smelted in Persia.
4236 B.C.	Earliest date on Egyptian calendar.
3760 B.C.	Earliest date on Jewish calendar.
3600 B.C.	Bronze made in southwestern Asia.
3100 B.C.	Egypt united under first dynasty.
3000 B.C.	Phoenicians migrate to eastern Mediterranean.
2780 B.C.	First Egyptian pyramid built.
2700 B.C.	Cheops builds Great Pyramid at Giza.
2697 B.C.	Huang-ti becomes "Yellow Emperor" of China.

2640 B.C.	Legendary Empress Si Ling-chi introduces silk production in China.
2340 B.C.	Sargon establishes Semitic and Sumerian civilizations.
2150 B.C.	Aryans invade Indus Valley.
2000 B.C.	Bronze Age begins in Europe.
1760 B.C.	Shang dynasty is founded in China.
1750 B.C.	Hammurabi, Babylonian king, issues code of laws.
1400 B.C.	Iron Age begins in Asia.
1250 B.C.	Exodus of Israelites from Egypt.
1193 B.C.	Greeks destroy city of Troy.
1100 B.C.	Pa-out-She, Chinese scholar, compiles first dictionary.
1050 B.C.	Dorian tribes invade Peloponnesus.
1000 B.C.	Hebrews establish Jerusalem as capital of Israel.
994 B.C.	Teutons migrate to Rhine River area.
815 B.C.	Carthage is founded by Phoenicians.
776 B.C.	First Olympic Games are held in Greece.
753 B.C.	Rome is founded.
580 B.C.	King Nebuchadnezzar builds Hanging Gardens of Babylon.
563 B.C.	Buddha is born.
559 B.C.	Cyrus establishes Persian Empire.
551 B.C.	Confucius is born.
460 B.C.	Pericles establishes democracy in Athens.
450 B.C.	Herodotus becomes known as father of history.
336 B.C.	Alexander III, king of Macedonia, begins world conquest.
300 B.C.	Meng-Tse spreads philosophy of Confucius in Orient.
236 B.C.	Asoka, emperor of India, becomes Buddhist missionary.
218 B.C.	Hannibal leads army from Spain over Alps to Italy.
215 B.C.	Great Wall of China is built.
63 B.C.	Cicero, orator, compiles record of Roman life.
55 B.C.	Julius Caesar conquers Gaul, invades Britain.
27 B.C.	Caesar Augustus becomes first Roman emperor.
5 B.C.	Jesus Christ is born.

A.D. 30   Jesus is executed.

A.D. 32   Saul of Tarsus (Paul) begins early Christian missionary work.

A.D. 64   Rome under Nero is partly destroyed by fire.

A.D. 79   Eruption of Vesuvius destroys Pompeii.

A.D. 132 Bar-Kokhba leads revolt against Rome and makes Israel independent.

A.D. 250 Mani founds Manichaeism, religion popular in Middle Ages.

A.D. 268 Goths invade Greece.

A.D. 312 Constantine becomes first Christian emperor of Rome.

A.D. 370 Asian Huns invade Europe.

A.D. 391 Augustine begins work as founder of Christian theology.

A.D. 406 Vandals invade Gaul; Romans leave Britain.

A.D. 410 Goths sack Rome.

A.D. 425 Angles, Saxons, and Jutes invade Britain.

A.D. 433 Attila the Hun begins reign.

A.D. 476 Goths depose Western Roman emperor, Romulas Augustus; Middle Ages begin.

A.D. 550 Justinian codifies Roman law in Corpus Juris Civilis.

A.D. 570 Muhammad is born at Mecca.

A.D. 620 Vikings invade Ireland.

A.D. 632 Muhammad dies.

A.D. 634 Muslims begin conquest of Near East and Africa.

A.D. 711 Moors invade Spain.

A.D. 768 Reign of Charlemagne begins.

A.D. 800 Charlemagne is crowned Holy Roman emperor.

A.D. 814 Arabic numerals are established.

A.D. 862 Viking Russ tribe seizes control of northern Russia.

A.D. 874 Vikings settle Iceland.

A.D. 900 Spain begins to drive out Moors.

A.D. 932 Printed books from woodblocks are developed in China.

A.D. 936 Otto I establishes Holy Roman Empire.

A.D. 981 Eric the Red begins settlement of Greenland.

A.D. 995 Fugiware Michiaga founds Japanese Golden Age.

A.D. 1000 Vikings begin exploration of North America.

Go to

"Significant Dates in the History of Religion" in chapter 9; "Philosophical Movements and Schools of Thought" in chapter 10

1021 Muslim Druse sect is founded by Caliph al-Hakim.

1054 Byzantine Empire breaks with Holy Roman Church; Abdallah ben Yassim spreads Islamic culture in Africa.

1066 Normans, led by William the Conqueror, conquer Britain.

1096 First Crusade is launched to oust Muslims from Holy Land.

1148 Second Crusade begins.

1156 Civil wars are fought in Japan.

1161 Chinese use explosives in warfare.

1162 Thomas à Becket becomes archbishop of Canterbury.

1189 Last recorded Viking voyage to North America.

1190 Genghis Khan begins conquest of Asia.

1204 Crusaders capture and sack Constantinople.

1210 Mongols invade China; Francis of Assisi founds Franciscan religious order.

1215 England's Magna Carta is signed by King John.

1228 Sixth Crusade results in capture of Jerusalem.

1240 Mongols capture Moscow, destroy Kiev.

1259 Thomas Aquinas develops official Roman Catholic philosophy.

1260 Kublai Khan founds Yuan dynasty in China.

1264 Simon de Montfort founds House of Commons in Parliament.

1270 Gregorius Bar-Hebraeus writes a history of the world.

1271 Marco Polo leaves for China to visit Kublai Khan.

1274 Mongols attempt invasion of Japan but fail.

1291 Crusades end as Muslims rout Christians in Palestine.

1295 King Edward I summons first representative Parliament.

1336 Civil war lasting until 1392 begins in Japan.

1337 Hundred Years' War between England and France begins.

The World

1347 Bubonic plague spreads from China to Cyprus.

1348 Black Death (plague) spreads to England.

1351 Plague reaches Russia; Europe's toll tops 25 million.

1363 Tamerlane begins conquest of Asia.

1368 Mongol dynasty ends in China; Ming dynasty begins.

1390 Turks conquer Asia Minor.

1402 Tamerlane conquers Ottoman Empire.

1419 Henry the Navigator begins period of African explorations.

1431 Jeanne d'Arc is burned as a witch at Rouen.

1453 Hundred Years' War ends; fall of Constantinople ends Byzantine Empire; Middle Ages end; Renaissance begins.

1454 Movable-type printing press is introduced.

1455 England's Wars of the Roses begins.

1478 Spanish Inquisition is begun by Ferdinand and Isabella; period of exploration by Europeans begins.

1482 Portuguese colonize African Gold Coast.

1488 Bartholomew Diaz sails around Cape of Good Hope.

1492 Christopher Columbus discovers West Indies.

1497 John Cabot discovers Newfoundland.

1498 Vasco da Gama sails around Cape of Good Hope to India.

1500 Pedro Cabral discovers Brazil.

1502 Columbus discovers Nicaragua.

1505 Portuguese colonize Mozambique.

1507 First world map showing "America" is produced.

1513 Vasco Núñez de Balboa discovers the Pacific Ocean.

1517 Martin Luther's Reformation begins.

1521 Hernán Cortés conquers Aztecs and claims Mexico for Spain.

1522 Crew under Ferdinand Magellan circumnavigates the world.

1531 Francisco Pizarro begins conquest of Peru.

1534 Henry VIII is excommunicated and founds Church of England; John Calvin begins Reformation program in Switzerland; Ignatius Loyola founds Society of Jesus (Jesuits).

1541 Hernando de Soto discovers Mississippi River.

1547 Ivan IV becomes first czar of united Russia.

1557 Portuguese establish colony at Macao.

1558 Elizabeth I becomes queen of England.

1582 Gregorian calendar is introduced.

1588 Spanish Armada is defeated by English fleet.

1595 Dutch colonize Guinea Coast.

1600 English East India Company is chartered.

1602 Dutch East India Company is formed.

1604 Russia begins settlement in Siberia.

1606 Willem Jansz discovers Australia.

1607 English found North American colony of Virginia.

1610 Hudson Bay is discovered.

1618 Thirty Years' War begins as a conflict between Europe's Protestants and Catholics.

1620 English Pilgrims reach Cape Cod, found Plymouth Colony.

1626 Dutch found New Amsterdam (New York).

1637 Russian explorers reach Pacific coast of Siberia.

1642 French found Montreal in Canada; King Charles I battles Parliament in English Civil War.

1652 English and Dutch begin series of wars; Dutch East India Company founds settlement on the Cape of Good Hope.

1654 Portuguese take Brazil from Dutch.

1655 England takes Jamaica from Spain.

1661 English take control of Bombay in India.

1664 England takes New Amsterdam from Dutch; Manchu dynasty is founded in China.

1683 Turkish army overruns Vienna.

1686 English establish Dominion of New England.

1696 Peter the Great leads Russian modernization program.

1704 English seize Gibraltar from Spain.

1733 John Kay starts Industrial Revolution with flying sewing shuttle.

1759 England captures Quebec in war with France.

1763 Peace of Paris gives Canada to England.

Go to "Art Movements and Styles" and "Architectural Styles and Movements" in chapter 7; "Literary Movements, Periods, and Styles" in chapter 8

1767 Townshend Acts tax American colony imports; Mason-Dixon line is established.

1770 Boston Massacre occurs; Townshend Acts are repealed except for the tax.

1773 Boston Tea Party occurs.

1774 First Continental Congress of American colonies is held.

1775 War of Independence begins in Massachusetts.

1776 Declaration of Independence is signed.

1781 English General Cornwallis surrenders at Yorktown.

1783 Treaty of Paris ends American War of Independence; India Act allows English control of India.

1788 First English convicts are transported to Australia; Sierra Leone is established as a refuge for blacks.

1789 George Washington is elected first U.S. president; U.S. Constitution takes effect; French Revolution begins.

1791 U.S. Bill of Rights takes effect.

1792 France is declared a republic; Denmark becomes the first country to ban slave trade.

1793 Maximilien Robespierre leads French reign of terror; Toussaint L'Ouverture leads revolt, ending French slavery in Haiti; first free settlers migrate to Australia.

1798 Napoleon Bonaparte invades Egypt, capturing Cairo; Thomas Malthus publishes essay on population explosion.

1803 Louisiana Purchase is completed.

1804 Lewis and Clark begin exploration of American Northwest; Bonaparte crowns himself Napoleon I, emperor of France.

1806 Napoleon dissolves Holy Roman Empire.

1807 England abolishes slave trade.

1809 David Ricardo develops modern concepts of finance.

1811 Simón Bolívar frees parts of South America from Spanish rule.

1812 War is fought between England and United States; Napoleon invades Russia, occupies Moscow.

1814 Napoleon is exiled to Elba.

1815 Napoleon is defeated at the Battle of Waterloo and exiled again.

"Significant Inventions, Technological **Go to** Advances, and Scientific Discoveries" in chapter 5

1819 Florida is ceded by Spain to United States.

1820 Missouri Compromise on U.S. slave states takes effect.

1821 José San Martín frees Chile and Argentina from Spanish control.

1823 Monroe Doctrine against foreign activity in America is adopted.

1833 England bans slavery and child labor in factories.

1836 Texas secedes from Mexico; battle of the Alamo is fought.

1846 War is fought between Mexico and United States; Irish potato famine occurs, with deaths reaching one million.

1848 Revolutions erupt throughout Europe; Marx and Engels produce *The Communist Manifesto;* Mexico cedes California and New Mexico to the United States.

1854 Crimean War is fought; Japan ends isolation, signs U.S. commercial treaty.

1860 Giuseppe Garibaldi begins nationalist movements in Europe.

1861 U.S. Civil War begins; British establish colonial presence in what is now Nigeria.

1863 Emancipation Proclamation declares abolition of slavery in part of the United States.

1865 U.S. Civil War ends; President Lincoln is assassinated.

1867 United States acquires Alaska from Russia; Dominion of Canada is established.

1868 Japan ends 700-year shogun rule, begins modernization.

1869 Suez Canal is completed.

1870 Franco-Prussian War is fought.

1883 Germany introduces health insurance.

1894 Sun Yat-sen begins move to end Manchu dynasty in China.

1898 War between Spain and United States is fought over Cuba; United States acquires Hawaiian Islands.

1900 Boxer Rebellion erupts in China, and hundreds of Europeans are killed; England and Germany begin arms race.

1902 Boer War ends; England acquires South African states.

1903 Panama, aided by the United States, secedes from Colombia.

1904 Russo-Japanese War is fought; Japan acquires Korea and Manchuria.

1908 William d'Arcy discovers oil in Persian Gulf region.

1909 England introduces old-age pensions; assembly line production is introduced in Detroit.

1912 Chinese revolution ends Manchu dynasty and republic is formed; passenger ship *Titanic* sinks, with 1,513 lives lost; Balkan wars begin.

1914 World War I follows assassination of Austrian archduke; trench warfare begins, and airplanes are used as weapons; Panama Canal opens.

1915 Poison gas is first used by Germany in warfare.

1916 Tanks are first used by England in warfare.

1917 United States joins Allies in European fighting; Bolsheviks led by Lenin seize power in Russia; Balfour Declaration urges Jewish state in Palestine.

1918 Russia withdraws from World War I fighting; Kaiser of Germany abdicates; Germany forms republic after revolt; armistice ends World War I.

1919 Treaty of Versailles causes heavy German economic losses; League of Nations is founded; Sinn Fein rebellion erupts in Ireland; Benito Mussolini introduces fascism in Italy; Gandhi begins passive resistance movement in India.

1920 Civil war is fought in Ireland; United States prohibits use of alcoholic beverages.

1921 Irish Free State is established.

1922 Union of Soviet Socialist Republics is established; Fascists march on Rome; Mussolini is named prime minister of Italy; Palestine becomes British League of Nations protectorate.

1923 Adolf Hitler forms National Socialist Party in Germany; Turkey becomes a republic after revolt that ends sultanate.

1924 Joseph Stalin succeeds Lenin as leader of Soviet Union; new Chinese government is formed with communist members.

1927 Purge of communists leads to civil war in China.

1929 U.S. stock market crash triggers worldwide depression; fighting begins between Jews and Arabs in Palestine.

1931 Japanese organize puppet state in Manchuria; Spain becomes a republic, and King Alfonso is deposed; British Empire status is changed to British Commonwealth.

1933 Adolf Hitler is named chancellor of Germany, and National Socialists (Nazis) purge opposition; Stalin purges opposition in Russia; United States ends prohibition experiment.

1934 Hitler assumes title of "Führer"; Mao Tse-tung starts "Long March" of Chinese communists.

1935 Italy invades Ethiopia; Hitler renounces Versailles Treaty and begins open rearmament; John Keynes publishes concept of government role in economy.

1936 Germany reoccupies Rhineland and forms "Axis" with Italy; General Franco begins Spanish Civil War; King Edward VIII of England abdicates to marry American Wallis Simpson.

1937 Japanese invade China, capturing Peking and Shanghai; German aircraft bomb Spain in support of Franco.

1938 Germany annexes Austria and gains Czechoslovakia's Sudetenland in Munich Pact.

1939 Germany annexes Czechoslovakia; Franco captures Madrid, and Spanish Civil War ends; Italy invades Albania; Germany invades Poland, triggering World War II; Russo-Finnish War ends in defeat in Finland.

1940 Germany invades France, Belgium, Denmark, and Norway; Battle of Britain prevents German invasion of England; Japan joins Berlin-Rome Axis; Italy invades Greece and joins war against England and France.

1941 Germany invades Russia; Italy and Germany invade Egypt; Japanese attack U.S. bases in Hawaii; U.S. joins Allies in war against Axis powers.

1942   Japanese capture Philippines and much of Southeast Asia; Battle of Midway alters naval balance in Pacific; Germans begin retreat in North Africa.

1943   United States begins recapture of Japanese Pacific bases; Allies invade Sicily; Italians surrender; Germans surrender to Russians at Stalingrad.

1944   Allies invade Normandy; German retreat begins; Allies liberate Rome, Paris, and Brussels; U.S. forces defeat Japanese navy in Leyte Gulf.

1945   Yalta Conference is attended by United States, Great Britain, and Soviet Union; Mussolini is assassinated; Hitler commits suicide; Germany surrenders; atom bombs are dropped at Hiroshima and Nagasaki; Japan surrenders, ending World War II; Potsdam Conference discusses postwar settlements.

1946   League of nations is replaced by United Nations; Ho Chi Minh begins war against French in Indochina; German war crime trials are held in Nuremberg.

1947   Marshall Plan aids European war recovery; Arabs reject plan for separate Jewish and Arab states; independent states of India and Pakistan are formed.

1948   Nation of Israel is established; war begins between Israel and Arab League; Gandhi is assassinated by a Hindu extremist; communists gain control of Czechoslovakia; Korea is divided into North Korea and South Korea; Berlin is blockaded by Soviet Union.

1949   Mao Tse-tung's communists gain control of China; Nationalist Chinese move government to Taiwan; South Africa establishes apartheid policy; Germany is divided into East Germany and West Germany; North Atlantic Treaty Organization (NATO) is formed.

1950   North Korean troops invade South Korea.

1951   Chinese communists occupy Tibet.

1952   Jawaharlal Nehru is elected first prime minister of India.

1953   Group of doctors in USSR tried for allegedly killing Politburo members; Stalin dies; USSR announces development of hydrogen bomb; Vietnamese Viet Minh forces invade Laos.

1954   Viet Minh troops defeat French at Dien Bien Phu; Vietnam is divided into North Vietnam and South Vietnam; South-East Asia Treaty Organization (SEATO) is formed; French-Algerian War begins.

1955   European communist states sign Warsaw Pact; Argentine President Juan Perón is exiled.

1956   Soviets crush anti-Russian uprising in Hungary; Egypt nationalizes Suez Canal, and British withdraw; Israel invades Egypt.

1957   Russia launches first artificial satellite, *Sputnik 1;* Fidel Castro begins revolution in Cuba; European Common Market is formed.

1958   Egypt, Syria, and Yemen form United Arab Republic States; Charles de Gaulle is elected president of France; United States launches an artificial satellite, *Explorer 1.*

1959   Fidel Castro overthrows Fulgencio Batista and becomes Cuban premier.

1960   Many European colonies in Africa gain independence.

1961   Bay of Pigs invasion of Cuba fails; Russian Yuri Gagarin is first man in space; communists build Berlin Wall; United States sends thousands of military advisers to Vietnam.

1962   John Glenn is first man to orbit space; Soviet missile crisis threatens in Cuba; Algeria votes for independence from France; Nelson Mandela imprisoned for antiapartheid activities in South Africa.

1963   Russian Valentina Tereshkova is first woman in space; President Kennedy is assassinated; United States, Great Britain, and Soviet Union sign nuclear test ban treaty.

1964   North Vietnamese boats attack U.S. Navy in Gulf of Tonkin; President Lyndon Johnson orders attack on North Vietnam.

1965   U.S. Marines are sent to Vietnam; U.S. aircraft begin air strikes against North Vietnam.

1966   China undergoes "Cultural Revolution."

The World

"Supreme Court Decisions" in chapter 21; **Go to**
"Important Dates in American History"
in chapter 25

1967 Six-Day War between Israel and Arabs is fought; Israel occupies Jerusalem and West Bank of Jordan River.

1968 Martin Luther King, Jr., is assassinated; U.S. senator Robert Kennedy is assassinated; Soviets invade Czechoslovakia to crush uprising; Vietcong stage Tet Offensive in South Vietnam; U.S. troop deployment in Vietnam passes 500,000; North Korea seizes U.S. Navy ship *Pueblo.*

1969 U.S. military begins withdrawal from Vietnam; U.S. astronauts land on the moon.

1970 U.S. troops invade Cambodia.

1971 Communist China replaces Taiwan in United Nations; Aswan High Dam completed in Egypt.

1972 President Nixon travels to China to renew relations; Great Britain takes over direct rule of Northern Ireland.

1973 Military coup in Chile overthrows Marxist government; Arabs attack Israel in October War; participants in Vietnam War sign peace agreements.

1974 Watergate scandal ends Nixon term in White House.

1975 Vietnam War ends with communist seizure of Saigon; communists take control of government of Cambodia; U.S. and Soviet spacecraft link up in space.

1976 Mao Zedong, architect of the Communist revolution in China and longtime party chairman and chairman of the People's Republic of China, dies. A nationwide purge of Orthodox Maoists was carried out and Mao's widow, Jiang Qing, and her radical associates, known as the Gang of Four, were arrested.

1978 United States votes to return Canal Zone to Panama in year 2000.

1979 Ayatollah Khomeini gains control of Iran; Shah of Iran leaves; Iranians seize U.S. Embassy in Tehran and hold hostages; Soviet Union invades Afghanistan; Israel

and Egypt sign peace treaty; Sandinistas force dictator Somoza to leave Nicaragua.

1980 War begins between Iran and Iraq; Solidarity trade union confronts communists in Poland.

1981 United States begins series of space shuttle flights; assassination attempt is made on President Ronald Reagan; assassination attempt is made on Pope John Paul II.

1982 Falklands War between Argentina and England is fought; Israel withdraws troops from Egypt's Sinai.

1983 Soviets shoot down South Korean airliner, and 269 are killed; Sally Ride is first U.S. woman in space; bomb kills 237 U.S. Marines in Beirut, Lebanon; U.S. forces invade island of Grenada.

1984 Marines withdraw from Beirut; Geraldine Ferraro is nominated as U.S. vice president.

1985 Mikhail Gorbachev becomes leader of Soviet Union.

1986 U.S. space shuttle *Challenger* explodes in flight, killing crew; Corazon Aquino is elected president of Philippines; U.S. aircraft raid Libya in retaliation for terrorism; nuclear accident occurs at Soviet Chernobyl power station.

1987 Palestinian *intifada* uprising begins in Gaza and West Bank; Iran-contra aid scandal involves U.S. officials; Gorbachev introduces program of extensive economic and social reforms; United States and Soviet Union agree to reduce nuclear arms; U.S. Navy ship *Stark* is attacked, apparently accidentally, by a missile from an Iraqi jet in the Persian Gulf.

1988 Cease-fire agreement is signed between Nicaraguan government and contra leaders; Iran accepts peace plan offer by Iraq; King Hussein abandons claim to West Bank territory and cedes authority to Palestine Liberation Organization; Palestine Liberation Organization recognizes Israel as a state and renounces terrorism; devastating earthquake in Armenia kills tens of thousands.

1989 Chinese military massacre protesters in Beijing's Tiananmen Square; U.S. troops invade Panama, driving General Manuel

1989 *cont.*

Noriega into custody; Berlin Wall is opened; Soviet army withdraws from Afghanistan; playwright Vaclav Havel is elected president of Czechoslovakia; Romanian leader Nicolae Ceauçsescu is overthrown and executed; opposition leader Patricio Aylwin is elected president of Chile, ending Pinochet military regime.

1990   Saddam Hussein's Iraqi army invades Kuwait, spurring international military buildup in the Persian Gulf; Germany is reunified; Soviet congress votes to begin popular elections for president; riots erupt in Britain over poll tax; Israeli police fire on Palestinians in Jerusalem, killing at least 17; Liberian president Samuel Doe is killed by rebels.

1991   U.S.–led multinational force attacks Iraq, freeing Kuwait; Soviet communists stage coup but are quickly rebuffed; Estonia, Lithuania, and Latvia declare full independence from USSR; the Soviet Union is dissolved, becoming the Commonwealth of Independent States; Haitian president Jean-Bertrand Aristide is exiled in a coup; Croatia and Slovenia declare independence from Yugoslavia; Communist government of Albania resigns; South Africa repeals the Population Registration Act, a fundamental apartheid law.

In Paraguay, dueling is legal provided both parties are registered blood donors.

1992   The Russian Federation drops price controls; South African whites vote to end white minority rule through talks with the black majority; Croatia, Bosnia and Herzegovina, and Slovenia are recognized by the European Community and by the United States; delegates from 178 countries attend the UN Conference on Environment and Development ("Earth Summit"); Salvadoran government and leftist Farabundo Marti National Liberation Front sign peace treaty ending 12 years of

civil war; Serbian nationalists lay siege to Sarajevo and begin campaign of "ethnic cleansing" of Muslims in Bosnia-Herzegovina; three nights of right-wing rioting against foreigners seeking asylum in Germany sets off wave of anti-foreigner violence and mass demonstrations against such violence; UN General Assembly ejects Yugoslavia for its support of Bosnian Serb militias; hundreds die in riots in India after Hindu extremists destroy a mosque in Ayodhya; UN authorizes U.S. troops to bring humanitarian aid to famine-stricken Somalia; Israel deports 400 Palestinians it believes to be members of militant Muslim groups.

1993   President George Bush and Russian President Boris Yeltsin sign START II accord to reduce nuclear arsenals; Czechoslovakia divides into two countries, the Czech Republic and Slovakia; U.S., France, and Britain conduct air raids on Iraq in response to Iraqi defiance of UN; Russian Congress of People's Deputies and President Yeltsin engage in struggle over whether executive or legislature should have more power; 200 killed by bombings in Bombay; troops loyal to Russian President Yeltsin put down takeover attempt by hard-line members of the Congress of People's Deputies; South Africa adopts a multiracial constitution, providing for majority rule and equal rights for black citizens; European Community's Maastricht Treaty, providing for an internal open market, takes effect, moving Europe closer to political, economic, and military integration; United States, Mexico, and Canada approve North American Free Trade Agreement (NAFTA), creating a free-standing trade bloc; 37 nations agree to halt dumping of nuclear waste into the oceans.

1994   African National Congress wins first universal elections in South Africa, and Nelson Mandela becomes the nation's first black president; Mandela forms multiracial government, stressing harmony and economic reform; civil war erupts in Rwanda, and members of the Hutu majority kill more than 500,000 Tutsi; more than 2 million refugees flee Rwanda to Zaire and Tanzania; Israel withdraws its forces from Gaza Strip and Jericho, paving the way for Palestinian self-rule in these regions; Bosnian Serbs end their artillery bombardments of besieged city of Sarajevo, and cease-fire in war between Serbs and Muslims follows; Israel and Jordan sign peace treaty, ending 46 years of hostility; civilian rule returns to Haiti as military government steps aside and Jean-Bertrand Aristide returns from exile to resume the office of president; Russian forces invade the breakaway republic of Chechnya, causing widespread destruction in the capital city, Grozny.

1995 United States intervenes to prevent collapse of the Mexican monetary system; earthquake strikes Kobe, Japan, killing 5,000; renewed fighting erupts in Bosnia, ending yearlong truce; Israeli and Palestinian leaders agree on further troop withdrawals from West Bank; truce between Russia and Chechen rebels ends fighting in Chechnya; NATO forces begin air strikes against Bosnian Serb positions; warring factions in Bosnia-Herzegovina agree to new peace plan; Israel agrees to second stage of withdrawal from Hebron; Jewish extremist assassinates Israeli prime minister Itzhak Rabin; France begins nuclear tests in South Pacific despite widespread international protest; voters in Quebec narrowly reject proposal to separate from Canada; four-year civil war ends in Bosnia with formation of Moslem-Croat federation and Serb republic.

1996 Leaders of Serbia, Croatia, and Bosnia agree to peace terms; fighting in Chechnya resumes; turmoil grips Middle East as Israel cracks down on terrorists in response to suicide bombings; UN tribunal indicts Serbs and Croats for war crimes; Russians and Chechens sign peace treaty; Boris Yeltsin is reelected as president of Russia, ending bid of Communists to resume control; Benjamin Netanyahu, Israel's new prime minister, opens the way to Jewish settlements on the West Bank, endangering peace process with Palestinians; violence erupts in Jerusalem as Israelis open archaeological excavation near Muslim holy sites; Tupac Amaru guerillas seize Japanese Embassy in Lima, Peru, during a diplomatic reception, taking 600 hostages; UN allows Iraq to resume oil exports for the first time since the Persian Gulf war; Kofi Annan is chosen as new UN secretary general.

1997 Israel and Palestinians agree on Hebron withdrawal; Peruvian troops end four-month standoff when they storm Japanese Embassy, freeing remaining 72 hostages and killing all 14 guerrillas; efforts to expand NATO into eastern Europe begin; Israeli-Palestinian peace talks break down over Israel's insistence on building Jewish housing in Arab-occupied East Jerusalem; scandal erupts over Switzerland's role in providing banking services for Nazi Germany and appropriating funds belonging to Holocaust victims; British voters return Labour party to power; rebel forces in Zaire oust longtime dictator Mobutu Sese Seko and change the name of country to Democratic Republic of Congo; Hong Kong reverts to Chinese control after 156 years as British colony.

1998 Pope John Paul II visits Cuba; UN inspectors clash with Iran's Saddam Hussein over weapons inspections; Isreal celebrates 50 years of statehood; Indonesian riots, sparked by monetary instability, result in the resignation of President Suharto and his replacement by B. J. Habibie; Asia's financial crisis deepens; Ireland votes yes on a peace agreement between Catholic and Protestant parties; an earthquake in central Afghanistan kills 5,000 people and makes 60,000 homeless; India and Pakistan test nuclear weapons for the first time; 96 people die in a German train wreck; Ethopia attacks Eritrea in a border dispute along the Red Sea; Serb forces massacre civilians in Kosovo.

MAJOR WARS, BATTLES, AND OTHER ARMED CONFLICTS

Simultaneous wars that were part of one general conflict but that had different names depending on the continent where they were fought are grouped together.

War, Battle, or Conflict	Date
Trojan War (Achaeans and other Greek peoples)	12th Century B.C.
Persian Wars (Persians vs. Greek city-states)	499–494, 490, 480–479 B.C.
Marathon, Battle of	490 B.C.
Salamis, Battle of (naval)	480 B.C.
Thermopylae, Battle of	480 B.C.
Plataea, Battle of	479 B.C.
Pelopennesian War (Athens vs. Sparta)	431–404 B.C.
Sparta-Thebes conflict in Greece	
Leuctra, Battle of	371 B.C.
Greece vs. Macedonia	
Chaeronea, Battle of	338 B.C.
Alexander the Great, conquests of	334–323 B.C.
Wars between Alexander's successors	315–280 B.C.
Punic Wars (Carthage vs. Rome)	
First	264–241 B.C.
Second (Hannibalic)	218–201 B.C.
Third	149–146 B.C.
Social War (Marsic or Marsian War) (Rome vs. Samnites and Marsi)	90–88 B.C.
Mithridatic Wars (Rome vs. Pontus)	88–84, 82–81, 74–63 B.C.
Gallic Wars (Julius Caesar's conquest of Gaul for Rome)	58–51 B.C.
Roman civil wars	49–31 B.C.
Pharsalus, Battle of	48 B.C.
Philippi, Battle of	42 B.C.
Actium, Battle of (naval)	Sept. 2, 31 B.C.
Rome vs. Germans (under Arminius)	
Teutoburg Forest, Battle of	A.D. 9
Rome vs. Visigoths	
Adrianople, Battle of	378
Rome vs. Franks	
Soissons, Battle of	486
Franks (under Charles Martel) vs. Saracen Muslims	
Tours, Battle of	Oct. 732
Normans (under William the Conqueror) vs. Saxons	
Hastings, Battle of	Oct. 14, 1066
Crusades (attempts by western Christians to free Holy Land from Muslims)	
First	1096–99
Second	1147–49
Third	1187–92
Fourth	1202–04
Fifth	1217–21
Sixth (Diplomatic)	1228–29
Seventh	1248–50
Eighth	1270
Genghis Khan, conquests of	c. 1200

War, Battle, or Conflict	Date
Scottish struggle for independence from England	
Bannockburn, Battle of	June 24, 1314
Hundred Years' War (France vs. England)	1337–1453
Crécy, Battle of	Aug. 26, 1346
Calais, Siege of	1346–47
Poitiers, Battle of	1356
Agincourt, Battle of	Oct. 25, 1415
Orléans, Siege of	1428–May 1429
Roses, Wars of the (English civil wars)	1455–99
Bosworth Field, Battle of	Aug. 22, 1485
Scotland and France vs. England	
Flodden Field, Battle of	Sept. 9, 1513
Spain and Venice vs. Turkey	
Lepanto, Battle of (naval)	Oct. 7, 1571
Spain vs. England	
Armada, The Spanish, defeat of (naval)	July 31–Aug. 8, 1588
Catholic League vs. France	
Ivry, Battle of	Mar. 14, 1590
Thirty Years' War (conflict between various European countries)	1618–48
English Civil War	1642–52
Edgehill, Battle of	Oct. 23, 1642
Marston Moor, Battle of	July 2, 1644
Dunbar, Battle of	Sept. 3, 1650
England vs. The Netherlands	1652–54, 1665–67
Devolution, War of (France vs. Spain)	1667–68
Dutch War (France and England vs. The Netherlands)	1672–78
King Philip's War (New England colonies vs. Wampanoag, Narragansett, and Nipmuck Indians)	July 4, 1675–Aug. 12, 1676
English Civil War	
Monmouth Rebellion	1685
Grand Alliance, War of the (War of the League of Augsburg) (France vs. England, Holy Roman Empire, Germany, Austria, Spain, Sweden, The Netherlands, and Brandenburg)	1688–97
King William's War (French vs. English colonies in America)	1689–97
Great Northern War (Sweden vs. Russia, Poland, and Denmark)	1700–21
Spanish Succession, War of the (France vs. England, Holland, Austria, Prussia, Portugal, and Savoy)	1701–14
Queen Anne's War (French vs. English colonies in America)	1702–13
Jenkins' Ear, War of (Great Britain vs. Spain)	Oct. 1739–41
Austrian Succession, War of the (Austria, England, The Netherlands, and Saxony vs. Prussia, Spain, France, and Bavaria)	1740–48
King George's War (British vs. French colonies in North America)	1744–48
Stuart attempt to regain the British throne	
Culloden Moor, Battle of	April 16, 1746
Seven Years' War (Prussia and Great Britain vs. Austria, France, Sweden, Russia, Saxony, Spain, and Kingdom of the Two Sicilies)	1756–63
French and Indian War (British vs. French colonies in North America)	1756–63
Cherokee War (Cherokee Indians vs. settlers on the western borders of Virginia and the Carolinas)	1759–61

The World

continues

Continued

War, Battle, or Conflict	Date
American Revolution	1775–81
Lexington and Concord, Battles of	Apr. 19, 1775
Fort Ticonderoga, Battle of	May 10, 1775
Bunker Hill, Battle of	June 17, 1775
Canada Expedition	Sept. 1775–June 1776
Long Island, Battle of	Aug. 27, 1776
Trenton, Battle of	Dec. 26, 1776
Princeton, Battle of	Jan. 2–3, 1777
Bennington, Battle of	Aug. 15, 1777
Saratoga, Battle of	Oct. 7, 1777
Brandywine, Battle of the	Sept. 11, 1777
Germantown, Battle of	Oct. 4, 1977
Monmouth, Battle of	June 28, 1778
Wyoming Valley Massacre	Summer 1778
Savannah, Battle of	Dec. 23–29, 1778
Bonhomme Richard and *Serapis,* naval battle between	Sept. 23, 1779
Savannah, Siege of	Sept.–Oct. 1779
Charleston, Siege of	Feb.–May 1780
Camden, Battle of	Aug. 16, 1780
Kings Mountains, Battle of	Oct. 7, 1780
Cowpens, Battle of	Jan. 17, 1781
Yorktown, Siege of	Sept.–Oct. 19, 1781
French Revolution (French civil war and war against most European countries)	1789–99
Bastille, storming of the	July 14, 1789
Reign of Terror	Sept. 1793–July 1794
Franco-American Naval War	1798–1800
Napoleon I, campaigns of and wars against	1796–1815
(France vs. various European countries)	
Italian campaign	Mar. 1796–Apr. 1797
Nile, Battle of the (naval)	Aug. 1, 1798
Marengo, Battle of	June 14, 1800
Hohenlinden, Battle of	Dec. 3, 1800
Copenhagen, Battle of (naval)	Apr. 2, 1801
Trafalgar, Battle of (naval)	Oct. 21, 1805
Austerlitz, Battle of	Dec. 2, 1805
Jena and Auerstädt, Battles of	Oct. 14, 1806
Eylau, Battle of	Feb. 8, 1807
Friedland, Battle of	June 14, 1807
Aspern, Battle of	1809
Wagram, Battle of	1809
Borodino, Battle of	Sept. 7, 1812
Leipzig, Battle of	Oct. 16–19, 1813
Waterloo, Battle of	June 18, 1815
Barbary Wars (United States vs. Morocco, Algiers, Tunis, and Tripoli)	1801–05, 1815
War of 1812 (United States vs. Great Britain)	1812–15
Detroit, Surrender of	Aug. 18, 1812
Frenchtown, Battle of	Jan. 22, 1813
Lake Erie, Battle of (naval)	Sept. 10, 1813
Thames, Battle of the	Oct. 5, 1813

The World

War, Battle, or Conflict	Date
War of 1812 (United States vs. Great Britain), *cont.*	
Chippewa, Battle of	July 5, 1814
Bladensburg, Battle of	Aug. 24, 1814
Lake Champlain, Battle of (naval)	Sept. 11, 1814
New Orleans, Battle of	Jan. 8, 1815
Creek War (United States vs. Creek Indians)	1813–14
Greek War of Independence (from Turkey)	1821–29
Navarino, Battle of (naval)	Oct. 20, 1827
Anglo-Burman Wars	1824–26, 1852–53, 1885
Java War (Java vs. the Netherlands)	1825–30
Russo-Turkish Wars	1828–29, 1853–56, 1877–78
Texas struggle for independence from Mexico	1836
Alamo, Siege of the	Feb. 23–Mar. 6, 1836
San Jacinto, Battle of	Apr. 21, 1836
Anglo-Chinese (Opium) War	1839–42
Anglo-Afghan Wars	1839, 1878–79
Sikh Wars (Great Britain vs. India)	1845, 1849
Mexican War (United States vs. Mexico)	1846–48
Taiping Rebellion (Chinese rising against Manchu Dynasty)	1850–64
Crimean War (Russia vs. Ottoman Empire, Great Britain, France, and Sardinia)	1853–56
Sevastopol, Siege of	Sept. 14, 1854–Sept. 9, 1855
Second Opium War (Great Britain and France vs. China)	1856–60
Sepoy Mutiny (revolt of Indian soldiers against British rule)	1857–59
Austro-Sardinian War (War of Italian Liberation) (Austria vs. France and Sardinia)	1859
Magenta, Battle of	June 4, 1859
Solferino, Battle of	June 24, 1859
Civil War, U.S.	1861–1865
Eastern Theater	
Fort Sumter, attack on	Apr. 12–14, 1861
Bull Run (Manassas), First Battle of	July 21, 1861
Ball's Bluff, Battle of	Oct. 21, 1861
Monitor and *Merrimack*, naval battle between	Mar. 9, 1862
Fair Oaks (Seven Pines), Battle of	May 31–June 1, 1862
Seven Days' Battles	June 25–July 1, 1862
Cedar Mountain, Battle of	Aug, 9, 1862
Bull Run (Manassas), Second Battle of	Aug. 29–30, 1862
Antietam, Battle of	Sept. 17, 1862
Fredericksburg, Battle of	Dec. 13, 1862
Chancellorsville, Battle of	May 1–5, 1863
Gettysburg, Battle of	July 1–3, 1863
Charleston, Sieges of	July–Aug. 1863
Fort Pillow Massacre	Apr. 12, 1864
Wilderness, Battle of the	May 5–6, 1864
Spotsylvania, Battle of	May 8–18, 1864
Cold Harbor, Battle of	June 1–3, 1864
Petersburg, Siege of	June 1864–Apr. 2, 1865
Cedar Creek, Battle of	Oct. 19, 1864
Sherman's March to the Sea	Nov. 15–Dec. 25, 1864

The World

continues

Continued

War, Battle, or Conflict	Date
Civil War, U.S., *cont.*	
Fort Fisher, Battle of	Jan. 15, 1865
Five Forks, Battle of	Apr. 1, 1865
Appomattox Court House	Apr. 9, 1865
Western Theater	
Boonville, Battle of	June 17, 1861
Fort Henry, Battle of	Feb. 6, 1862
Fort Donelson, Battle of	Feb. 13–16, 1862
Shiloh (Pittsburg Landing), Battle of	Apr. 6–7, 1862
Island No. 10, Battle of	Apr. 7–8, 1862
Corinth, Battle of	Oct. 3–4, 1862
Murfreesboro (Stones River), Battle of	Dec. 31, 1862–Jan. 2, 1863
Vicksburg, Siege of	May 19–July 3, 1863
Chickamauga, Battle of	Sept. 19–20, 1863
Chattanooga, Battle of	Nov. 23–25, 1863
Lookout Mountain, Battle of	Nov. 24, 1863
Missionary Ridge, Battle of	Nov. 24–25, 1863
Kennesaw Mountain, Battle of	June 27, 1864
Atlanta, Siege of	July 20–Sept. 2, 1864
Franklin, Battle of	Nov. 30, 1864
Nashville, Battle of	Dec. 15–16, 1864
Off Cherbourg, France	
Alabama and *Kearsarge*, naval battle between	June 19, 1864
War of the Triple Alliance (Brazil, Argentina, and Uruguay vs. Paraguay)	1864–70
Seven Weeks' War (Prussia vs. Austria)	June 14–July 1866
Ten Years' War (Cuba vs. Spain)	1868–78
Franco-Prussian War	July 19, 1870–Feb. 1, 1871
Gravelotte, Battle of	Aug. 18, 1870
Metz, Siege of	Aug. 19–Oct. 27, 1870
Sedan, Battle of	Sept. 1, 1970
Russo-Turkish War	1877–78
Zulu War (Great Britain vs. Zulus)	1879
First South African War (Great Britain vs. Transvaal)	1881
War of the Pacific (Chile vs. Peru and Bolivia)	1879–84
Mahdist War (revolt of followers of the Mahdi against Egyptian rule)	1881–90
Khartoum, Siege of	Jan. 1885
Sino-French War	1884–85
Sino-Japanese War	1894–95
Spanish-American War	1898
Manila Bay, Battle of (naval)	May 1, 1898
San Juan Hill, Battle of	July 1, 1898
Santiago, Battle of (naval)	July 3, 1898
Boer War (South African War, Anglo-Boer War, or Second War of Freedom) (Great Britain vs. Transvaal and Orange Free State)	1899–1902
Boxer Rebellion (China vs. foreign powers involved in the country)	1900–01
Russo-Japanese War	Feb. 5, 1904–Sept. 5, 1905
Japan Sea (Tsushima), Battle of the (naval)	May 27, 1905
Mexican Civil War	1910–20

War, Battle, or Conflict	Date
Balkan Wars	
First (Turkey vs. Serbia, Montenegro, Greece, and Bulgaria)	Oct. 8, 1912–May 30, 1913
Second (Bulgaria vs. Serbia, Greece, Turkey, Montenegro, and Romania)	June 29–Aug. 10, 1913
World War I (Austria, Germany, Turkey, and Bulgaria vs. Russia, France, Great Britain, Serbia, Italy, and United States)	July 28, 1914–Nov. 11, 1918
Charleroi, Battle of	Aug. 22, 23, 1914
Tannenberg, Battle of	Aug. 26–30, 1914
Marne, First Battle of the	Sept. 5–14, 1914
Ypres, First Battle of	Oct. 20 and 31, Nov. 11, 1914
Coronel, Battle of (naval)	Nov. 1, 1914
Falklands, Battle of the (naval)	Dec. 8, 1914
Dogger Bank, Battle of (naval)	Jan. 24, 1915
Ypres, Second Battle of	Apr. 22–May 24, 1915
Gallipoli Expedition (Dardanelles Campaign)	Apr. 25, 1915–Jan. 9, 1916
Verdun, Siege of	Feb. 21–Dec. 1916
Kut al Imara, Battle of	Apr. 1916
Asiago, Battle of	May 14–June 1916
Jutland, Battle of (naval)	May 31–June 1, 1916
Somme, Battle of the	July–Nov. 1916
Arras, Battle of	Apr. 4–May 4, 1917
Ypres (Passchendaele), Third Battle of	July 31–Nov. 10, 1917
Caporetto, Battle of	Oct.–Dec. 1917
Cambrai, Battle of	Nov. 20–Dec. 7, 1917
St. Quentin, Battle of	Mar. 21, 1918
Belleau Wood, Battle of	June 3–9, 1918
Chateau-Thierry, Battle of	July 15–21, 1918
Marne, Second Battle of the	July 18–Aug. 7, 1918
Amiens, Battle of	Aug. 8, 1918
St. Mihiel, Battle of	Sept. 12–21, 1918
Argonne, Battle of the	Sept. 26–Nov. 11, 1918
Vittorio Veneto, Battle of	Oct. 1918
October (Bolshevik) Revolution and counterrevolutionary movements (Russian civil war)	1917–20
Polish-Soviet War	1920–21
Greco-Turkish War	1921–22
Chinese Civil War	1927–36, 1946–50
Chaco War (Paraguay-Bolivia)	Dec. 1928–Nov. 1935
Japanese invasion of Manchuria and other parts of China	1931–37
Italian invasion of Ethiopia	Oct. 3, 1935–May 5, 1936
Spanish Civil War	1936–39
World War II (Germany, Italy, and Japan vs. numerous other countries)	1939–45
Western European Theater	
Poland, German conquest of	Sept. 1–17, 1939
Norway and Denmark, fall of	Apr.–June 1940
Western Europe, German conquest of	May–June 1940
Britain, Battle of (air)	June 19–Oct. 12, 1940
Bismarck, sinking of the (naval)	May 1941
Normandy invasion	June 6, 1944
Rhine River, Allied advance toward the (Operation Market Garden)	Fall 1944
Bulge, Battle of the	Dec. 16, 1944–Jan. 21, 1945

continues

Continued

War, Battle, or Conflict	Date
World War II (Germany, Italy, and Japan vs. numerous other countries), *cont.*	
Russian Front	
Finland, Soviet attack on	Nov. 30, 1939–Mar. 13, 1940
Soviet Union, initiation of German attack on	June 22, 1941
Stalingrad, Siege of	July 1942–Feb. 2, 1943
Kursk, Battle of	July 12–19, 1943
Dniepr River, Soviet offensive across the	Summer–Fall 1943
Ukraine, Soviet liberation of	Winter 1944
Berlin, fall of	Apr. 16–May 2, 1945
Mediterranean Theater	
Tobruk, Battles of	Dec. 1940, June and Nov. 1942
Greece, German conquest of	Apr.–May 1941
El Alamein, First Battle of	July 2–4, 1942
El Alamein, Second Battle of	Aug. 30–Nov. 4, 1942
North Africa, Allied invasion of (Operation Torch)	Nov. 8, 1942–May 11, 1943
Sicily, Allied invasion of	July 10–Aug. 16, 1943
Italy, Allied invasion of	Sept.–Oct. 1943
Anzio, operation at	Jan.–June 1944
Pacific Theater	
Pearl Harbor, bombing of (air/naval)	Dec. 7, 1941
Malaya and Dutch East Indies, Japanese conquest of	Dec. 7, 1941–Feb. 15, 1942
Philippines, Japanese conquest of the	Dec. 22, 1941–May 6, 1942
Burma, Japanese invasion of	Jan.–May 1942
Lombok Strait, Battle of (naval)	Feb. 19–20, 1942
Java Sea, Battle of the (naval)	Feb. 27, 1942
Tokyo, Doolittle bombing of	Apr. 18, 1942
Coral Sea, Battle of the (naval)	May 7–8, 1942
Midway, Battle of (naval)	June 4–5, 1942
Savo Sea, Battle of the (naval)	Aug. 1942
Guadacanal, Battle of (land/naval)	Aug. 7, 1942–Feb. 7, 1943
Eastern Solomons, Battle of the (naval)	Aug. 23–25, 1942
Santa Cruz Island, Battle of (naval)	Oct. 26, 1942
Gilbert Islands, conquest of the	Nov. 1943
Marshall Islands, invasion of the	Jan. 1944
New Guinea, conquest of	Apr.–July 1944
Leyte Gulf, Battle of (naval)	Oct. 24, 1944
Iwo Jima, conquest of	Feb. 19–Mar. 16, 1945
Okinawa, invasion of	Mar. 31, 1945
Hiroshima and Nagasaki, atomic bombing of	Aug. 6 and 9, 1945
Algerian war for independence from France	1945–62
Indonesian war for independence from The Netherlands	1945–49
Vietnamese war for independence from France	1946–54
Dien Bien Phu, fall of	May 7, 1954
Arab-Israeli War	1948–49
Korean War (North Korea and Communist China vs. South Korea and United Nations forces)	1950–53
38th parallel, initial North Korean attack across the	June 25, 1950
Inchon, UN landing at	Sept. 15, 1950
Manchurian border, Chinese Communist crossing of	Nov. 26, 1950

War, Battle, or Conflict	Date
Hungary, uprising in and Soviet invasion of	Oct. 23–Nov. 1956
Suez War (Israel, Great Britain, and France vs. Egypt)	Oct. 29–Dec. 1956
Revolutionary guerrilla warfare in Cuba (against Batista regime)	1956–59
Vietnam War (South Viet Nam and U.S. vs. North Vietnam)	1960–75
Tet Offensive, beginning of	Jan. 31, 1968
Bay of Pigs invasion (U.S. vs. Cuba)	1961
India-Pakistan war	1965
Six Day War (Israel vs. Egypt, Jordan, and Syria)	June 5–10, 1967
Nigerian civil war	1967–70
Bangladesh war (India vs. Pakistan)	1971–72
Yom Kippur War (Israel vs. Egypt and Syria)	Oct. 1973
Lebanon, civil war and Syrian and Israeli occupation of	1973–85
Soviet intervention in Afghanistan	1979–89
Persian Gulf War (Iran vs. Iraq)	1980–88
Salvadoran civil war	1980–92
Falklands War (Argentina vs. Great Britain)	Apr. 2–June 14, 1982
Grenada, U.S. intervention in	Oct. 25–27, 1983
Yugoslavian civil war	1987–95
Panama, U.S. invasion of	1989
Persian Gulf War (Iraq vs. U.S. and coalition of numerous countries)	1990–91
Rwandan civil war	1994
Chechnya, Russian invasion of	1994–96

WORLD EXPLORATION AND DISCOVERY

40,000 B.C. Cro-Magnons migrate to Europe from Near East.

28,000 B.C. Humans migrate from Asia to Americas over land bridge.

5000 B.C. Sumerians migrate to Mesopotamia.

2300 B.C. Semites migrate from Arabia to Mesopotamia.

2000 B.C. Israelites migrate from Euphrates Valley to Canaan.

1000 B.C. Phoenician sailors explore Britain and western Africa.

700 B.C. Central Asian tribes migrate to Persia.

640 B.C. Greek explorer Colaeus reaches Gibraltar and Spain.

600 B.C. Egyptian pharaoh Necho circumnavigates Africa; Greek explorer Midacritus finds tin in England or Brittany.

510 B.C. Greek traveler Scylax explores Indus River, Red Sea, and Arabia.

500 B.C. Bantu tribes migrate through eastern Africa; Greek explorer Hekataios travels to Spain and North Africa; Carthaginian explorer Himlico visits French Atlantic Coast.

480 B.C. Carthaginian admiral Hanno explores west coast of Africa.

424 B.C. Greek traveler Herodotus visits North Africa, Italy, and Arabia.

400 B.C. Greek explorer Ctesias travels to Ganges River in India.

345 B.C. Greek explorer Pythias explores northwest European coastline.

327 B.C. Alexander the Great leads army to Indus Valley of India.

325 B.C. Greek admiral Nearchus attempts to circumnavigate Arabia.

302 B.C. Greek traveler Megasthenes visits India, Tibet, and Ceylon.

218 B.C. Hannibal leads army with elephants from Spain to Italy.

138 B.C. Decimus Brutus becomes first Roman to reach west coast of Spain.

128 B.C. Chinese explorer of central Asia has contact with Greeks.

112 B.C.   Greek explorer Eudoxus sails to India and western Africa.

100 B.C.   Greek explorer Hippalus finds direct ocean route to India.

55 B.C.   Julius Caesar leads Roman army to Britain.

A.D. 20   King Juba of Morocco explores Canary Islands.

Cleopatra was part Macedonian, part Greek, and part Iranian. She was not an Egyptian.

A.D. 80   Gnaeus Agricola explores Atlantic coast of Britain.

A.D. 100   Roman explorer Julius Maternus crosses Sahara to Sudan; Alexander, Greek trader, sails to Vietnam and Cambodia; Chinese explorer Kan Ying reaches Black Sea and turns back.

A.D. 370   Huns, nomadic Mongols, invade Europe and reach Gaul.

A.D. 400   Chinese monk Fa Hsien visits India, Ceylon, and Java.

A.D. 407   Northern European Goths and Vandals spread to Mediterranean.

A.D. 431   Gunavarman, prince of Kashmir, travels to Java and China.

A.D. 570   Brendan, Irish monk, reportedly discovers America.

A.D. 620   Vikings explore Ireland.

A.D. 645   Chinese monk Yuan Chuang travels overland to India and returns.

A.D. 861   Vikings discover Iceland.

A.D. 872   Iraqi traveler Ibn Wahab visits China.

A.D. 900   Mayans migrate from Central America to Yucatan Peninsula; Arab traveler Ibn Rosteh explores Malay Peninsula and Java.

A.D. 921   Arabian diplomat Ahmad Ibn Fodhlan explores Russia and Poland.

A.D. 950   Maori sailors discover New Zealand.

A.D. 980   Arabs migrate to east coast of Africa.

A.D. 981   Eric the Red discovers Greenland.

A.D. 986   Viking sailor Bjarne Herjulfsson sights North America.

A.D. 1000   Leif Ericsson explores Atlantic coast of North America.

1002   Thorwald Ericsson explores American coast below New England.

1007   Viking Thorfinn Karlsefni establishes North American colony.

1150   Polynesian Toi Kai Rakan opens settlement of New Zealand.

1165   Spanish rabbi Benjamin visits synagogues of Asia and Near East.

1245   Franciscan monk Giovanni Carpini travels to Mongol capital.

1271   Marco Polo begins 24-year journey to Orient and Near East.

1291   Vivaldi brothers try sailing Atlantic from Genoa to India; Italian explorer Malocello discovers Canary Islands.

1337   Josef Faquin circumnavigates known world of 14th century.

1350   Polynesian chief Marutuahu established colony in New Zealand.

1419   Portuguese King Henry begins African exploration.

1431   Portuguese explorer discovers Azores.

1440   Italian explorer Niccolò Conti travels in Indonesia and Malaya.

1446   Portuguese explorer Nuno Tristao is lost on second trip to Africa.

1455   Venetian sailor Cadamosto discovers Cape Verde Islands.

1482   Portuguese navigator Diego Cao explores Congo River; Portugal establishes African Gold Coast settlements.

1488   Portuguese explorer Bartholomeu Dias sails around Cape of Good Hope.

1492   Christopher Columbus discovers the West Indies; German navigator Martin Behaim shows Earth is spherical.

1493   Pope Alexander VI divides New World between Spain and Portugal.

1494   Bartolome Colon, brother of Columbus, explores Haiti.

1495   Francisco de Almeida establishes Portuguese naval bases in eastern Africa.

1497   Italian John Cabot discovers Newfoundland for England.

1498   Columbus discovers South America and Trinidad; Portuguese navigator Vasco da Gama finds sea route to India.

1499   Spanish explorer Vincent Yañez Pinzon discovers mouth of Amazon River.

1500 Portuguese explorer Pedro Cabral discovers Brazil.

1501 Amerigo Vespucci explores coast of Brazil; Spanish explorer Rodrigo Bastidas discovers Colombia.

1502 Columbus discovers Nicaragua; Spaniard Alonso de Ojeda explores Haiti, Guiana, and Venezuela.

1504 Portuguese explorer Pacheco Pereira visits India.

1505 Portuguese establish settlements in Mozambique; Portuguese nobleman Tristão da Cunha leads expedition to India.

1507 German maps by Martin Waldseemuller identify New World as "America."

1510 Afonso de Albuquerque establishes Portuguese base in India at Goa.

1512 Spanish priest Bartolomé Las Casas is missionary to Cuban Indians.

1513 Balboa, in Panama, discovers Pacific Ocean; Ponce de Leon explores Florida and West Indies; Portuguese reach Canton, China.

1514 Spanish explorer Francisco de Montejo travels to West Indies.

1516 Spanish explorer Juan Diaz de Solís discovers Rio de la Plata, Uruguay.

1517 Spanish explorer Fernandez de Cordoba discovers Mayan ruins.

1518 Pedro Alvarado explores Southeast Mexico for Spain; Spanish conquistador Juan de Grijalva discovers Aztec Empire.

1519 Hernán Cortés conquers Mexico for Spain.

1521 Ferdinand Magellan dies in an attempt to circumnavigate Earth.

1522 Spanish navigator Juan Sebastián Elcano is first to circumnavigate Earth.

1524 Italian explorer Giovanni da Verrazano discovers New York harbor; Francisco Pizarro explores the west coasts of Panama and Peru.

1526 Italian Sebastian Cabot explores Rio de la Plata, Uruguay.

1527 Cabeza de Vaca begins trek from Florida to Mexican west coast.

1528 Spanish explorer Panfilo de Narvaez dies near mouth of Mississippi.

1530 German adventurer Nikolaus Federmann explores Venezuela, Colombia, and the Andes.

1533 Spanish conquistador Francisco Pizarro conquers Peru; Spanish conquistador Sebastián de Benalcázar conquers Ecuador.

1535 Jacques Cartier explores Saint Lawrence River; Spanish explore Chile; Spanish explorer Antonio de Mendoza establishes city of Buenos Aires.

1536 Spaniard Jiménez de Quesada explores Colombia and Orinoco River; Spanish conquistador Domingo de Irala explores Parana and Paraguay rivers.

1540 Vásquez de Coronado explores Arizona and New Mexico; Spanish monk Andres Urdaneta explores Philippine Islands.

1541 Hernando de Soto discovers Mississippi River; Francisco de Orellana travels Amazon River from source in Peru to mouth; Gonzalo Pizarro crosses the Andes from Ecuador to the Amazon River.

1542 Portuguese explorer Mendes Pinto is first European in Japan.

1544 Spanish conquistadors explore coast of Oregon.

1553 English explorer Richard Chancellor establishes Russian trade route.

1554 English explorer Sir Hugh Willoughby dies seeking Northeast Passage.

1557 Portuguese establish Chinese base at Macao.

1562 French explorer Jan Ribault establishes colony in South Carolina.

1564 Miguel López de Legazpe claims Marianas and Philippines for Spain and founds Manila.

1569 Spanish explorer Alvaro Bazan crosses Chaco of South America.

1576 English explorer Sir Martin Frobisher searches for Northwest Passage.

1581 Cossack Timofeevich extends Russian territory into Siberia.

1582 Cossack Koltso aids Timofeevich in exploration of Siberia; Spanish explorer Berrio navigates Orinoco River.

1584 Sir Walter Raleigh explores Virginia and North Carolina.

1592 Explorer Cornelis de Houtman discovers Dutch route to East Indies.

1594 Dutch explorer Willem Barents searches for Northeast Passage.

1595   Dutch establish settlements on Guinea Coast.

1598   Van Neck leads second Dutch expedition to East Indies; English explorer Will Adams travels to Japan.

1602   Englishman Bartholomew Gosnold explores New England coast.

1603   Samuel de Champlain explores Saint Lawrence River as "route to China."

1607   Englishman John Smith helps establish Jamestown, Virginia.

1608   Champlain founds city of Quebec; John Smith explores Cape Cod and Chesapeake Bay.

1610   Henry Hudson discovers Hudson Bay and River; Dutch navigator Willem Schouten sails around Cape Horn.

1613   Dutch colonist Jan Coen establishes factories in Indonesia; English explorer William Baffin discovers Baffin Bay and Island.

1614   Dutch captain Christianssen establishes fort at Albany, New York.

1615   Champlain explores lakes Huron and Ontario.

1617   Dutch explorers Jakob LeMaire and Willem Schouten start trip around world.

1618   French explorer Imbert finds Timbuktu in Africa.

1620   English Pilgrims reach Cape Cod.

1626   French establish settlements in Madagascar; Dutch settle New Amsterdam in North America; French missionary Jean de Brébeuf explores Lake Huron region.

1631   English captain Thomas James explores James Bay in Canada.

1637   Russian explorers reach Pacific coast of Siberia.

1642   French explorer Sieur de Maisonneuve founds city of Montreal; Dutch explorer Abel Tasman discovers Van Dieman's Land (Tasmania).

1645   Capuchin monks explore Congo River.

1646   French missionary Isaac Jogues discovers Lake George.

1649   Cossack Dezhnev explores Siberia and Alaska for Russia; Cossack Stadukhin explores the Lena and Kolyma rivers in Siberia.

1652   Dutch colonist Jan van Riebeek founds Cape of Good Hope settlement.

1659   French fur trader Pierre Radisson explores Minnesota.

1670   French fur trader Perrot explores upper Mississippi region.

1673   French explorers Louis Joliet and Jacques Marquette navigate the length of the Mississippi.

1675   Belgian explorer Louis Hennepin discovers Niagara Falls and Mississippi source.

1679   Frenchman Daniel Duluth explores Minnesota and Great Lakes.

1681   Sieur de La Salle explores Mississippi and names delta area Louisiana; English buccaneer William Dampier explores South Pacific islands.

1682   Buero da Silva explores Central Mountains region of Brazil; Pieres de Campos explores rivers of South America.

1683   Dutch explorer Aerssen establishes colony of Surinam; German naturalist Kaempfer visits Java, Thailand, and Japan.

1685   French missionary Claude Allouez explores western Lake Superior.

1697   Cossack Atlasov explores Kamchatka Peninsula for Russia.

1699   William Dampier explores northwest coast of Australia.

1721   Norwegian missionary Hans Egede is first European in Greenland in 200 years.

1723   Russian adventurer Fedorov explores northwest coast of America.

1732   Gvozdev explores Bering Sea and Alaska coastline for Russia.

1741   Russian explorer Chrikov discovers some Aleutian Islands.

1744   Frenchman Charles La Condamine measures arc of meridian in Andes.

1745   Basov explores Aleutian Islands for Russia.

1770   English navigator James Cook explores east coast of Australia.

1772   English explorer Samuel Hearne is first European to reach Arctic Ocean; Frenchman Yves Kerguélen-Trémarec discovers Antarctic islands; James Cook searches for possible continent of Antarctica.

1776 Cook searches for possible Atlantic–Pacific maritime passage.

1784 Daniel Boone explores Appalachian and Ozark areas.

1789 Scottish fur trader Sir Alexander Mackenzie explores western Canada.

Guam has no sand, only ground coral, which is used to make its roads.

1790 Russian fur trader Aleksandr Baranov explores Alaska; American explorer Robert Gray discovers Columbia River.

1797 German adventurer Hornemann explores caravan routes of Sahara Desert.

1798 British explorer George Bass circumnavigates Tasmania.

1799 German explorer Alexander von Humboldt tours North and South America.

1802 English explorer Matthew Flinders circumnavigates Australia; Portuguese explorers cross Africa.

1804 Lewis and Clark begin exploration of Louisiana Purchase; Russian Lisyanskii explores Pacific from Hawaii to Alaska.

1805 Canadian Fraser explores Canada west of Rocky Mountains; Russian navigator Adam Krusenstern maps Sakhalin, discovers Amur's mouth.

1815 Russian navigator Otto Kotzebue discovers many Pacific islands.

1818 French explorer René Caillé crosses Sahara, reaching Timbuktu.

1819 English explorer Sir William Parry finds Northwest Passage in Arctic.

1820 American Nathaniel Palmer discovers Palmer Peninsula of Antarctica.

1821 Russian Fabian Bellinghausen leads South Pole expedition.

1825 British explorer Sir John Franklin surveys Canadian Arctic region.

1828 German physicist Georg Erman circumnavigates Earth, studying magnetic fields.

1829 English explorer Freemantle founds West Australia colony.

1830 British Lander brothers explore Niger River and delta.

1831 American Benjamin Bonneville explores Rocky Mountains and California; British explorer James Ross finds North Magnetic Pole.

1835 British colonist Bourke explores new areas of Australia; American pioneer Jim Bowie explores U.S. Southwest.

1837 American trapper Joseph Walker explores Sierra Mountains.

1840 Frenchman Dumont d'Urville discovers Antarctic islands.

1842 John Fremont begins exploration west of Rockies.

1843 British colonist Edward Eyre explores South and West Australia; Scottish explorer Sir James Ross proves Antarctica has ice barrier.

1846 German explorer Friedrich Leichhardt disappears crossing Australia.

1847 French naturalist Comte de Castelnau crosses South America west to east.

1848 American explorer Elisha Kane surveys Gulf of Mexico.

1850 English naval officer Sir Robert McClure discovers Northwest Passage.

1851 German explorer Heinrich Barth crosses Sahara Desert twice; American explorer Savage rediscovers Yosemite Valley.

1853 Englishman Sir Richard Burton is first non-Muslim to visit Mecca and Medina; American explorer Elisha Kane leads Arctic expedition.

1854 U.S. Commodore Matthew Perry ends isolation of Japan; German Schlagintweit brothers explore Central Asia; Portuguese explorer Silva Porto crosses South Africa, west to east.

1855 Russian adventurer Nevelskoi explores Amur and proves Sakhalin is an island.

1856 Scottish missionary David Livingstone explores Africa; English explorers Richard Burton and John Speke discover Lake Tanganyika; English explorer Gregory crosses Australia east to west.

1857 English explorer John Speke discovers Lake Victoria.

1860 Irish explorer Robert Burke is first to cross Australia south to north; German explorer Karl Decken leads Kilimanjaro Mountain

1860   *cont.*
       expedition; John Speke and James Grant prove Lake Victoria is source of Nile; American Isaac Hayes searches for "open sea" above Arctic Circle.

1863   Frenchman Louis Faidherbe explores Senegal and Niger River in Africa.

1864   Hermann Schlagintweit is first European to cross Kuenlun range.

1866   Doudart explores Mekong River route to source for France.

1871   Russian naturalist Aleksi Fedchenko explores Asian mountain ranges; British journalist Henry Stanley finds missing Livingstone; American Charles Hall is first to explore above 82 degrees north latitude.

1872   French colonist Francis Garnier searches for China–Tibet river route.

1874   John and Alexander Forrest survey western Australia.

1878   German Eduard Schnitzer (Emin Pasha) explores African lake country; English explorer Sir George Nares surveys Magellan Strait; Russian Grigori Potanin explores Gobi Desert of Mongolia.

1879   Swedish explorer Nils Nordenskjöld discovers Northeast Passage; Russian Nikolai Przhevalski is first to cross Tibet's Humboldt Mountains; Joseph Thompson explores Great Rift Valley of Africa.

1880   French colonist Pierre Brazza explores African river routes to sea.

1882   French explorer Pierre Bonvalot discovers ancient cities of Asia.

1883   French officer Foucauld explores Algerian oases and Morocco.

1885   Portuguese explorer Capelo crosses South Africa.

1888   Norwegian Fridtjof Nansen explores Greenland ice cap; French explorer Louis Binger leads African scientific expedition.

1889   German explorer Hans Meyer is first to scale Kilimanjaro peak; Austrian Oskar Baumann explores African rivers and lakes.

1891   German Erich von Drygalski explores West Greenland.

1892   Scottish oceanographer William Bruce explores Antarctic coastline; Englishman William Conway is first to scale 23,000-foot Himalayan peaks; American Robert Peary explores Greenland and proves it is an island.

1893   Swedish engineer Andre explores Arctic by balloon; German explorer Goetzen crosses Africa east to west.

1894   Englishwoman Mary Kingsley explores Ogowe River in Africa.

1895   French explorer Charles Bonin crosses Tibet and Mongolia; Englishman Frederick Jackson explores Franz Josef Land in Arctic.

1897   Gerlache de Gomery leads Belgian Antarctic expedition.

1899   Sweden's Sven Hedin finds sources of Bramaputra and Indus rivers.

1900   Norwegian Carsten Borchgrevink is early Antarctic explorer.

1906   Norwegian Roald Amundsen is first to navigate Northwest Passage.

1908   British explorer Sir Ernest Shackleton nearly reaches South Pole.

1909   American explorer Robert Peary is first to reach North Pole.

1910   Bavarian officer Wilhelm Filchner leads German Antarctic expedition.

1911   Norwegian explorer Roald Amundsen reaches South Pole; American explorer Bingham discovers Machu Picchu in Peru; British explorer Sir Douglas Mawson leads Antarctic expedition.

1912   British explorer Robert Scott reaches South Pole.

1913   Theodore Roosevelt explores central Brazilian rivers.

1926   Americans Floyd Bennett and Richard Byrd fly over North Pole; American Lincoln Ellsworth flies over North Pole; Italian engineer Umberto Nobile flies over North Pole, from Norway to Alaska.

1927   American Charles Lindbergh is first to fly solo across Atlantic Ocean.

1929   American explorer Richard Byrd is first to fly over South Pole; German Hugo Eckener makes round-the-world flight.

1931   Eckener flies over North Pole.

1932   British explorer St. John Philby crosses Arabia's Rub-al-Kali Desert; French explorer Jean Piccard explores stratosphere in balloon gondola.

1935 Lincoln Ellsworth flies over South Pole.

1937 Russian aviator Valeri Chkalov is first to fly from USSR to America over North Pole.

1947 Norwegian Thor Heyerdahl sails balsa raft from Peru to Polynesia.

1953 British mountaineer Sir Edmund Hillary and Tenzing Norgay of Nepal scale Mount Everest.

1956 Heyerdahl explores Easter Island and eastern Pacific.

1957 (July 1957–Dec. 1958) As part of the International Geophysical Year, 67 nations cooperate in scientific exploration of the Earth and its environment.

1957 Soviet Union launches *Sputnik 1,* the world's first artifical earth satellite.

1958 *Explorer 1,* first U.S. satellite, is launched and discovers Van Allen radiation belts around Earth; U.S. nuclear submarine *Nautilus* passes under ice cap at North Pole.

1959 Soviet probes *Lunas 1, 2, and 3,* respectively, fly by, impact, and photograph the Moon.

1960 U.S. submarine *Triton* completes first circumnavigation of the globe under water; U.S. Navy Lt. Don Walsh and French explorer Jacques Piccard dive in the bathyscaph *Trieste* to a record 35,000 feet to the floor of the Mariana Trench, the deepest point in the Pacific Ocean; NASA weather satellite *TIROS 1* transmits television pictures of cloud cover.

1961 Soviet cosmonaut Yuri Gagarin, in *Vostok 1,* is first person to orbit Earth.

1962 John Glenn, in *Freedom 7,* is first U.S. astronaut to orbit around the Earth; NASA's *Mariner 2* becomes first space probe to fly by another planet (Venus).

1964 NASA's *Ranger 7* returns close-up photographs of the Moon just prior to impacting the lunar surface.

1965 NASA's *Mariner 4* space probe, as it flies by the planet Mars, transmits first close-up pictures of the planet's surface.

1966 Soviet Union's *Luna 9* and NASA's *Surveyor 1* make first soft landings on lunar surface.

1968 U.S. astronauts Frank Borman, James Lovell, and William Anders, in *Apollo 8,* are first persons to orbit around the Moon.

1969 U.S. astronauts Neil Armstrong and Edwin "Buzz" Aldrin, in *Apollo 11's* lunar landing module *Eagle,* are first persons to step onto the lunar surface.

1970 Soviet Union's unmanned probe *Luna 16* returns from the Moon with rock samples; its *Luna 17* mission lands a self-propelled vehicle on the Moon; its *Venera 7* space probe lands on Venus.

1971 NASA's *Mariner 9* becomes first space probe to orbit around another planet (Mars).

1973 NASA's *Pioneer 10* becomes first space probe to fly by the planet Jupiter.

1974 NASA's *Mariner 10* space probes takes first close-up photographs of the planets Venus and Mercury.

1976 NASA's *Vikings 1* and *2* become first spacecraft to land on surface of Mars.

1978 Italian Reinhold Messner and Austrian Peter Habeler make the first conquest of Mount Everest without artificial oxygen supplies; Japanese explorer Naomi Uemura becomes the first person to make a solo journey to the North Pole.

1979 NASA's *Voyager 1,* during flyby of Jupiter, discovers ring, erupting volcanoes on the Jovian satellite Io, and three new satellites; NASA's *Pioneer 11,* becomes first space probe to fly by the planet Saturn.

1980 *Voyager 1,* during flyby of the planet Saturn, discovers six new satellites.

1981 NASA scientists report that two meteorites found in the Antarctic may have originated on the planet Mars.

1982 Soviet space probes *Veneras 13* and *14* land on Venus and transmit first color photos.

1983 *Pioneer 10* becomes first spacecraft to leave solar system.

1984 Soviet engineers drill 7.5 miles to reach the Earth's lower crust.

1985 Deep oceanic vents are found in the Mid-Atlantic Ridge; U.S. oceanographer Robert Ballard leads French-American team, using

1985 *cont.*
sonar and a robot submarine, that discovers wreck of British ocean liner *Titanic* 13,000 feet deep in the North Atlantic.

1986 NASA's *Voyager 2* space probe flies by the planet Uranus and discovers 10 new satellites; European Space Agency's *Giotto* space probe photographs nucleus of Halley's comet; Dick Rutan and Jeanna Yeager, in experimental airplane *Voyager*, make first nonstop flight around the world without refueling.

1989 *Voyager 2* flies by the planet Neptune and discovers six new satellites and five rings.

1995 NASA's *Galileo* space probe releases entry probe into Jupiter's atmosphere and becomes first craft to orbit around the planet.

1997 NASA's *Pathfinder* space probe lands on the surface of Mars, and *Sojourner* rover carries out first mobile exploration of another planet.

1998 Thirty-five space missions have been launched in 1998. Eighteen involved the United States. China, Europe, and Israel. Japan and Russia also had missions. In January, the launch of the Lunar Prospector was the first NASA moon launch in 25 years. Later in 1998 Air Force Lt. Col. Eileen Collins, veteran of two previous shuttle flights, will become the first woman to command a shuttle mission.

POPULATION OF MAJOR WORLD CITIES

An asterisk (*) indicates that the population figure is for the metropolitan area.

City	Description	Population
Addis Ababa, Ethiopia	Capital since 1896	2,200,186
Ahmedabad, India	Founded in 1411	2,872,865
Alexandria, Egypt	Founded by Alexander the Great, 332 B.C.	3,382,000
Algiers, Algeria	Founded in 10th century on Roman site	1,507,241
Amman, Jordan	Site of biblical city of Ammonites	963,490
Amsterdam, The Netherlands	Founded in 1300	724,096
Ankara, Turkey	Capital of Galacia around 300 B.C.	2,719,981
Athens, Greece	Ancient Greek city-state in 700 B.C.	748,110
Auckland, New Zealand	Founded in 1840, original capital	336,500
Baghdad, Iraq	Center of Islamic culture since 813	4,648,609
Baku, Azerbaijan	Founded in 9th century	1,087,000
Bandung, Indonesia	Founded in 1810	2,026,893
Bangalore, India	Founded in 16th century	2,650,659
Bangkok, Thailand	Capital since 1782	5,572,712
Barcelona, Spain	Founded by Carthaginians around 300 B.C.	1,630,867
Barranquilla, Colombia	Inland seaport since 1935	1,064,255*
Beijing, China	Founded around 1122 B.C. as Peking; renamed in 1949	5,769,607
Beirut, Lebanon	Site of ancient Phoenician settlement	1,100,000*
Belgrade, Serbia	Site of Singidunum, ancient Roman camp	1,168,454
Belo Horizonte, Brazil	Cattle and cotton-trading center	2,600,000
Berlin, Germany	Founded in 13th century; capital of Germany 1871–1945, of United Germany since 1990	3,475,392*
Birmingham, England	Market town since before 13th century	1,009,100
Bogotá, Colombia	Founded by conquistadors in 1538	5,025,989*
Bombay, India	Established in early Christian era	9,909,547
Brisbane, Australia	Founded in 1824 as a penal colony	786,442
Brussels, Belgium	Capital since 1530	136,424
Bucharest, Romania	Capital since 1861	2,064,744
Budapest, Hungary	Site of Aquincum, 2nd-century Roman camp	1,996,000

City	Description	Population
Buenos Aires, Argentina	Settled by conquistadors in 1536	2,960,976
Cairo, Egypt	Site of 7th-century Arab military camp	6,849,000
Calcutta, India	Developed from 1690 English factory site	4,388,262
Calgary, Alberta, Canada	Originally (1875) Northwest Mounted Police post	710,677*
Cali, Colombia	Founded by conquistadors in 1536	1,718,871*
Cape Town, South Africa	Founded in 1652 as Dutch naval base	854,616
Caracas, Venezuela	Founded by conquistadors in 1567	1,822,465
Casablanca, Morocco	Site of ancient city of Anfa	2,943,000*
Chicago, Illinois, United States	Originally portage site for fur traders	2,731,743
Chittagong, Bangladesh	Portuguese trading post in 1600s	1,566,070*
Chongqing, China	Former capital of Nationalist China	2,266,772
Cologne, Germany	Site of Roman (A.D. 50) Colonia Agrippina	962,517
Copenhagen, Denmark	Capital since 1443	1,339,395*
Córdoba, Argentina	Founded in 1573; university founded in 1613	1,148,305*
Damascus, Syria	City of Egyptians and Hittites before 1000 B.C.	1,549,932
Delhi, India	Capital of northern India in 13th century	7,174,755
Dhaka, Bangladesh	Capital since 1971 secession from Pakistan	3,637,892*
Dnepropetrovsk, Ukraine	Founded in 1787 at Cossack village site	1,176,000
Donetsk, Ukraine	Founded in 1870, called Stalino until 1961	1,114,000
Dresden, Germany	Originally (A.D. 922) a Slavonic settlement	479,273
Dublin, Ireland	Originally a 9th-century Viking base	478,389
Düsseldorf, Germany	Rhine River port since 11th century	574,936
Edmonton, Alberta, Canada	Originally (1795) Hudson Bay trading post	616,741
Essen, Germany	Ruhr Valley city founded in 9th century	622,380
Frankfurt, Germany	Site of ancient Roman military camp	659,803
Fukuoka, Japan	Seaport on Hakata Bay founded in 13th century	1,275,165
Genoa, Italy	Roman settlement in 3rd century B.C.	659,754
Glasgow, Scotland	Founded by 6th-century missionaries	681,471
Guadalajara, Mexico	Originally founded in 1530	1,650,042
Guangzhou, China	Inland seaport since 3rd century B.C.	2,914,281
Guatemala City, Guatemala	Founded as capital in 1776	1,150,452
Guayaquil, Ecuador	Founded by conquistadors in 1535	1,508,444
Hamburg, Germany	Founded in 9th century by Charlemagne	1,702,887
Harbin, China	Village until linked by railroad in 1898	2,443,398
Havana, Cuba	Founded in 1519 as Spanish navy base	2,241,000
Ho Chi Minh City, Vietnam	Formerly Saigon, ancient Khmer village	4,181,600*
Hyderabad, India	Founded as Golconda; capital in 1589	2,991,884
Hyderabad, Pakistan	Founded in 1768 as capital of Sind	1,107,000*
Ibadan, Nigeria	Founded around 1830 as military camp	1,365,000
Istanbul, Turkey	Until A.D. 300, Byzantium; until 1930, Constantinople	7,331,927
Jakarta, Indonesia	Founded in 1619 as Batavia; renamed 1971	8,259,266
Jerusalem, Israel	Capital of ancient kingdoms of Israel and Judah	567,100
Johannesburg, South Africa	Founded as gold-mining camp in 1886	712,507
Kanpur, India	Village until ceded to British in 1801	1,958,000
Karachi, Pakistan	Founded in 1725 as Hindu trading center	9,863,000*
Kharkov, Ukraine	Founded in 1654 as outpost of Moscow	1,599,000
Kiev, Ukraine	"Mother of Russian Cities," founded A.D. 882	2,645,000
Kinshasa, Democratic Republic of Congo	Founded in 1881 as Leopoldville; renamed 1966	4,655,313
Kobe, Japan	Ancient fishing village until 1868	1,518,982

continues

Continued

City	Description	Population
Kuala Lumpur, Malaysia	Founded as tin-mining settlement in 1857	1,145,075
Lagos, Nigeria	Former slave trading center; now the capital	1,484,000
Lahore, Pakistan	Capital of Mogul sultans in 11th century	5,085,000*
La Paz, Bolivia	Founded in 1548; capital since 1898	713,378
Leipzig, Germany	Founded in 11th century; Bach was organist here	490,851
Lima, Peru	Site of oldest university in Americas (1551)	6,479,000*
Lisbon, Portugal	Ancient Phoenician, Carthaginian trading center	677,790
Liverpool, England	Chartered in 1207 by King John	479,000
Lodz, Poland	Founded in 1423; belonged to Russia until 1919	833,700
London, England	Established in A.D. 43 as Roman town of Londinium	6,679,699
Los Angeles, California, United States	Founded in 1781 as capital of Spanish colony	3,448,613
Madras, India	Founded in 1640 as British outpost	3,795,028
Madrid, Spain	A Moorish fortress until 932	3,041,101
Managua, Nicaragua	Established as capital in 1855 to end feud	1,195,000
Manila, Philippines	Founded by Spanish in 1571	1,599,000
Marseilles, France	Originally Massilia, Ionian Greek colony, in 600 B.C.	807,726
Mecca, Saudi Arabia	Birthplace of Muhammad in 570	550,000
Medellín, Colombia	Coffee, drugs, mining center founded in 1675	1,621,356*
Melbourne, Australia	Founded 1835 by Tasmanian settlers	3,198,200
Mexico City, Mexico	Aztec capital until captured by Cortés in 1521	9,815,795
Milan, Italy	Ancient Celtic town captured by Romans in 222 B.C.	1,334,171
Minsk, Belarus	City on Moscow-Warsaw rail link founded in 11th century	1,666,000
Monterrey, Mexico	Founded in 1579; invaded by U.S. troops in 1846	1,068,996
Montevideo, Uruguay	Settled by Spanish in 1726; capital since 1828	1,383,660
Montreal, Quebec, Canada	Site of Indian encampment, founded by French in 1642	3,172,242*
Moscow, Russia	Founded in 1147; became capital around 1340	8,792,000
Munich, Germany	Founded in 1158; birthplace of Nazi movement, 1923	1,255,623
Nagoya, Japan	Buddhist temple site in 2nd century; now an industrial city	2,153,293
Nanjing, China	Founded in 1368; twice capital in 20th century	2,090,204
Naples, Italy	Named Neapolis (New City) by Greek settlers around 600 B.C.	1,061,583
New York City, New York, United States	Founded in 1609 as New Amsterdam by Dutch; renamed 1664	7,333,253
Nizhni Novgorod, Russia	Founded in 1221; called Gorky after Maxim Gorky during Soviet era	1,424,600
Novosibirsk, Russia	"Chicago of Siberia," founded in 1893 on Trans-Siberian Railway	1,418,200
Odessa, Ukraine	Founded by Tartars in 14th century	1,073,000
Osaka, Japan	Founded in 16th century as capital city	2,575,042
Ottawa, Ontario, Canada	Selected as capital in 1858 by Queen Victoria	313,987
Palermo, Italy	Founded by Phoenicians in 8th century B.C.	694,749
Paris, France	Grew from pre-Roman settlement named Lutetia Parisiorum	2,175,200
Port-au-Prince, Haiti	Founded by sugar planters in 1749; capital since 1804	752,600
Pôrto Alegre, Brazil	Founded in 1742 by settlers from Azores	1,237,223
Prague, Czech Republic	Grew from 10th-century trading center	1,225,000
Pusan, South Korea	Originally a fishing village; opened to trade in 1443	3,798,113

City	Description	Population
Pyongyang, North Korea	Existed as Heijo, Korean cultural center, in 1100 B.C.	2,355,000
Quebec City, Quebec, Canada	Site of Indian settlement visited by Cartier in 1535	167,517
Quezon City, Philippines	Founded in 1940 as site of future capital	1,667,000
Quito, Ecuador	Originally Quito Indian camp; captured by Incas in 1470	1,100,847
Recife, Brazil	Settled by Portuguese in 1535	1,296,995
Rio de Janeiro, Brazil	Founded by Portuguese in 1502; capital since 1889	5,473,909
Riyadh, Saudi Arabia	Onetime center of classic Arabic architecture	1,800,000
Rome, Italy	According to legend, founded in 753 B.C. by Romulus	2,687,881
Rosario, Argentina	City in La Pampa region; founded in 1730	894,645
Rotterdam, The Netherlands	North Sea port chartered in 1328	598,521
St. Petersburg, Russia	Founded in 1703; named Leningrad from 1924 to 1991	4,882,600
Salvador, Brazil	Founded in 1549 as Bahia	2,070,296
Samara, Russia	Founded in 1586; formerly Kuibyshev	1,222,500
Santiago, Chile	Founded in 1541 by conquistadors	4,628,320
Santo Domingo, Dominican Republic	Oldest continuous European settlement in Americas, founded in 1496	2,100,000
São Paulo, Brazil	Founded in 1554 by Jesuit missionaries on Indian campsite	9,393,753
Sapporo, Japan	Founded in 1869 in government plan to develop Hokkaido Island	1,744,806
Seoul, South Korea	Originally named Keijo, a Korean capital since 1392	10,612,577
Seville, Spain	Originally Hispalis, a Phoenician trading center	714,148
Shanghai, China	Existed as Hu-tsen in Sung dynasty, 11th century	7,496,509
Shenyang, China	Formerly Mukden, capital city of 12th-century Tartars	3,603,712
Singapore, Singapore	Originally Singhapura, destroyed in 1365; refounded in 1819	2,989,300
Sofia, Bulgaria	Founded as Sardica by 2nd-century Romans; capital since 1879	1,113,674
Stockholm, Sweden	Originally a fishing village, founded in 13th century	703,627
Surabaja, Indonesia	Grew from 17th-century Javanese trading post	2,421,016
Sydney, Australia	First British settlement in Australia, 1788	3,738,500
Taipei, Taiwan	Settled in 18th century by Chinese mainland immigrants	2,652,685
Tashkent, Uzbekistan	Ancient central Asian city; existed in 1st century B.C.	2,106,000
Tbilisi, Georgia	Also called Tiflis; settled in 4th century B.C.	1,279,000
Tehran, Iran	Settled in 13th century by refugees from Mongol invasion	6,450,500
Tianjin, China	Also called Tientsin, ancient trading center	4,574,689
Tokyo, Japan	Founded in 12th century as fortress for warlord	8,021,943
Toronto, Ontario, Canada	Originally Fort Rouille, 1749; York, 1793; renamed 1834	3,893,046*
Tripoli, Libya	Founded as Oea by Phoenicians in 7th century B.C.	591,062
Tunis, Tunisia	Pre-Carthaginian city with access to Mediterranean	1,826,652*
Turin, Italy	Ancient Roman city of Augusta Taurinorum	945,551
Valencia, Spain	Former city of Romans, Visigoths, Moors	764,293
Vancouver, British Columbia, Canada	Originally settled in 1875 as Granville; renamed 1886	1,602,502
Vienna, Austria	Capital of the Austro-Hungarian Empire 1278–1918; now capital of the Austrian republic	1,539,848
Volgograd, Russia	Founded in 1589 as Tsaritsyn; later Stalingrad; renamed Volgograd in 1961	1,000,400
Warsaw, Poland	Settled in 11th century; capital since 1596	1,642,700
Washington, District of Columbia, United States	Founded in 1790 on site selected by George Washington	567,094

continues

Continued

City	Description	Population
Wellington, New Zealand	Founded in 1840; replaced Auckland as capital in 1865	153,800
Yangon, Myanmar	Existed as fishing village in 6th century	3,851,000
Yekaterinburg, Russia	Founded in 1721; called Sverdlovsk during Soviet era	1,347,000
Yokohama, Japan	Feudal fishing village until opened to foreign trade in 1859	3,300,513

THE UNITED NATIONS

The United Nations organization was established during World War II as an outgrowth of an agreement among 26 countries fighting the Germany-Italy-Japan Axis. It replaced the League of Nations as an instrument for the promotion of international peace and security.

The name was suggested by U.S. President Franklin D. Roosevelt in 1941 and was officially adopted the following year. The United Nations was formally organized on June 26, 1945, following an initial San Francisco conference to draft a charter.

The basic charter contains 19 chapters, divided into 111 articles, and provides for the support of a number of international organs and agencies (see chart).

THE SIX OFFICIAL LANGUAGES OF THE UNITED NATIONS

Arabic	French
Chinese	Russian
English	Spanish

SECRETARIES-GENERAL OF THE UNITED NATIONS

Name	Trygve Lie
Country	Norway
Term of Office	1946–1952

Name	Dag Hammarskjold
Country	Sweden
Term of Office	1953–1961

Name	U Thant
Country	Myanmar (formerly Burma)
Term of Office	1961–1971

Name	Kurt Waldheim
Country	Austria
Term of Office	1972–1981

Name	Javier Pérez de Cuellar
Country	Peru
Term of Office	1982–1991

Name	Boutros Boutros-Ghali
Country	Egypt
Term of Office	1992–1996

Name	Kofi Annan
Country	Ghana
Term of Office	1997–

THE UNITED NATIONS SYSTEM

Based on a chart from the *UN Chronicle*.

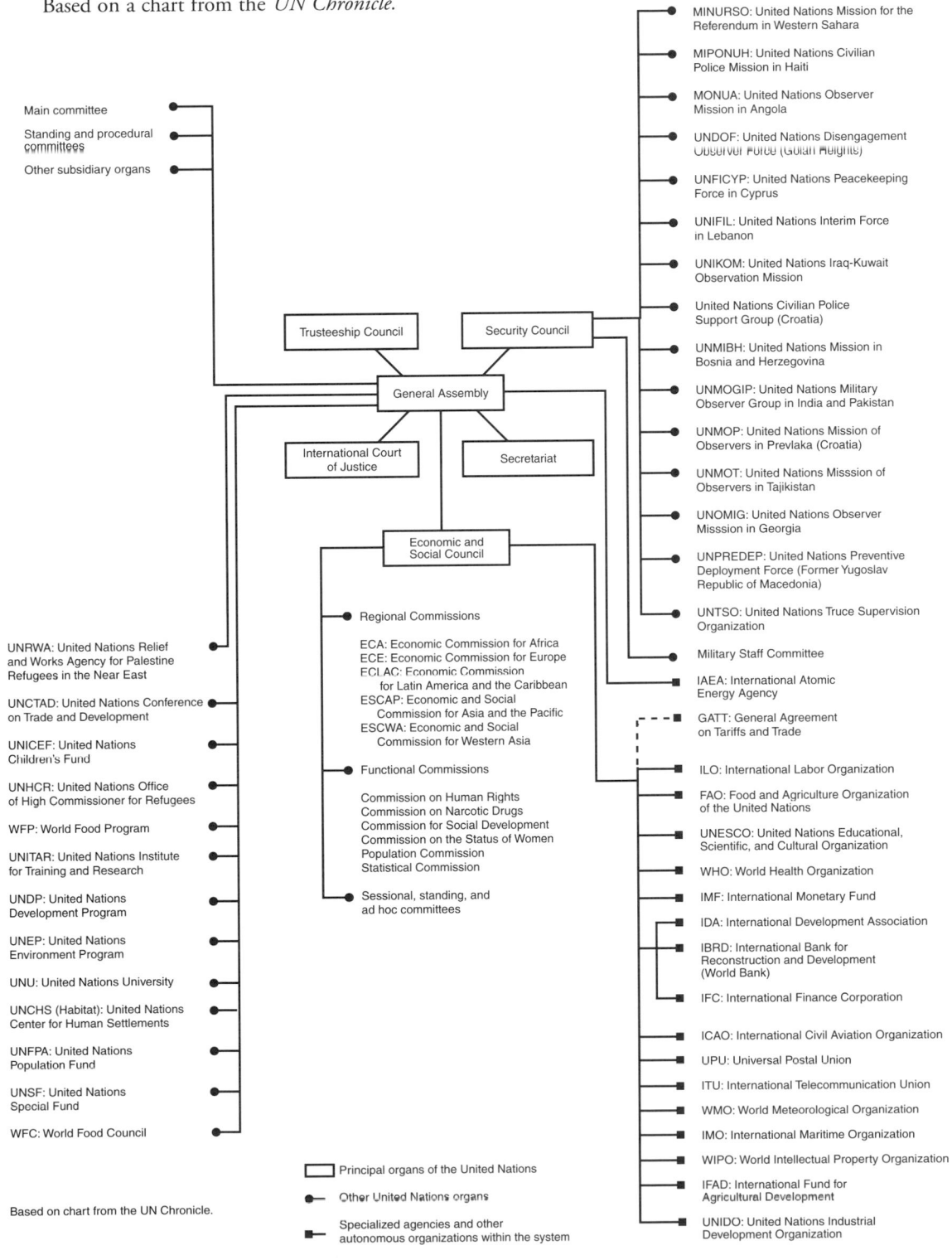

MINURSO: United Nations Mission for the Referendum in Western Sahara

MIPONUH: United Nations Civilian Police Mission in Haiti

MONUA: United Nations Observer Mission in Angola

UNDOF: United Nations Disengagement Observer Force (Golan Heights)

UNFICYP: United Nations Peacekeeping Force in Cyprus

UNIFIL: United Nations Interim Force in Lebanon

UNIKOM: United Nations Iraq-Kuwait Observation Mission

United Nations Civilian Police Support Group (Croatia)

UNMIBH: United Nations Mission in Bosnia and Herzegovina

UNMOGIP: United Nations Military Observer Group in India and Pakistan

UNMOP: United Nations Mission of Observers in Prevlaka (Croatia)

UNMOT: United Nations Misssion of Observers in Tajikistan

UNOMIG: United Nations Observer Misssion in Georgia

UNPREDEP: United Nations Preventive Deployment Force (Former Yugoslav Republic of Macedonia)

UNTSO: United Nations Truce Supervision Organization

Military Staff Committee

IAEA: International Atomic Energy Agency

GATT: General Agreement on Tariffs and Trade

ILO: International Labor Organization

FAO: Food and Agriculture Organization of the United Nations

UNESCO: United Nations Educational, Scientific, and Cultural Organization

WHO: World Health Organization

IMF: International Monetary Fund

IDA: International Development Association

IBRD: International Bank for Reconstruction and Development (World Bank)

IFC: International Finance Corporation

ICAO: International Civil Aviation Organization

UPU: Universal Postal Union

ITU: International Telecommunication Union

WMO: World Meteorological Organization

IMO: International Maritime Organization

WIPO: World Intellectual Property Organization

IFAD: International Fund for Agricultural Development

UNIDO: United Nations Industrial Development Organization

Main committee
Standing and procedural committees
Other subsidiary organs

Trusteeship Council

Security Council

General Assembly

International Court of Justice

Secretariat

Economic and Social Council

Regional Commissions

ECA: Economic Commission for Africa
ECE: Economic Commission for Europe
ECLAC: Economic Commission for Latin America and the Caribbean
ESCAP: Economic and Social Commission for Asia and the Pacific
ESCWA: Economic and Social Commission for Western Asia

Functional Commissions

Commission on Human Rights
Commission on Narcotic Drugs
Commission for Social Development
Commission on the Status of Women
Population Commission
Statistical Commission

Sessional, standing, and ad hoc committees

UNRWA: United Nations Relief and Works Agency for Palestine Refugees in the Near East

UNCTAD: United Nations Conference on Trade and Development

UNICEF: United Nations Children's Fund

UNHCR: United Nations Office of High Commissioner for Refugees

WFP: World Food Program

UNITAR: United Nations Institute for Training and Research

UNDP: United Nations Development Program

UNEP: United Nations Environment Program

UNU: United Nations University

UNCHS (Habitat): United Nations Center for Human Settlements

UNFPA: United Nations Population Fund

UNSF: United Nations Special Fund

WFC: World Food Council

Principal organs of the United Nations
Other United Nations organs
Specialized agencies and other autonomous organizations within the system

Based on chart from the UN Chronicle.

The World

UNITED NATIONS MEMBER STATES

Member	Year of Admission	Member	Year of Admission	Member	Year of Admission
Afghanistan	1946	Cyprus	1960	Korea, Republic of	1991
Albania	1955	Czech Republic	1993	Kuwait	1963
Algeria	1962	Denmark	1945	Kyrgyzstan	1992
Andorra	1993	Djibouti	1977	Lao People's	1955
Angola	1976	Dominica	1978	Democratic Republic	
Antigua and Barbuda	1981	Dominican Republic	1945	Latvia	1991
Argentina	1945	Ecuador	1945	Lebanon	1945
Armenia	1992	Egypt	1945	Lesotho	1966
Australia	1945	El Salvador	1945	Liberia	1945
Austria	1955	Equatorial Guinea	1968	Libyan Arab Jamahiriya	1955
Azerbaijan	1992	Eritrea	1993	Liechtenstein	1990
Bahamas	1973	Estonia	1991	Lithuania	1991
Bahrain	1971	Ethiopia	1945	Luxembourg	1945
Bangladesh	1974	Fiji	1970	Macedonia, the former	1993
Barbados	1966	Finland	1955	Yugoslav Republic of	
Belarus	1945	France	1945	Madagascar	1960
Belgium	1945	Gabon	1960	Malawi	1964
Belize	1981	Gambia	1965	Malaysia	1957
Benin	1960	Georgia	1992	Maldives	1965
Bhutan	1971	Germany	1973	Mali	1960
Bolivia	1945	Ghana	1957	Malta	1964
Bosnia and	1992	Greece	1945	Marshall Islands	1991
Herzegovina		Grenada	1974	Mauritania	1961
Botswana	1966	Guatemala	1945	Mauritius	1968
Brazil	1945	Guinea	1958	Mexico	1945
Brunei Darussalam	1984	Guinea-Bissau	1974	Micronesia	1991
Bulgaria	1955	Guyana	1966	(Federated States of)	
Burkina Faso	1960	Haiti	1945	Moldova	1992
Burundi	1962	Honduras	1945	Monaco	1993
Cambodia	1955	Hungary	1955	Mongolia	1961
Cameroon	1960	Iceland	1946	Morocco	1956
Canada	1945	India	1945	Mozambique	1975
Cape Verde	1975	Indonesia	1950	Myanmar	1948
Central African		Iran (Islamic	1945	Namibia	1990
Republic	1960	Republic of)		Nepal	1955
Chad	1960	Iraq	1945	Netherlands	1945
Chile	1945	Ireland	1955	New Zealand	1945
China	1945	Israel	1949	Nicaragua	1945
Colombia	1945	Italy	1955	Niger	1960
Comoros	1975	Jamaica	1962	Nigeria	1960
Congo, Democratic	1960	Japan	1956	Norway	1945
Republic of		Jordan	1955	Oman	1971
Congo, Republic of the	1960	Kazakhstan	1992	Pakistan	1947
Costa Rica	1945	Kenya	1963	Palau	1994
Côte d'Ivoire	1960	Korea, Democratic	1991	Panama	1945
Croatia	1992	People's Republic of		Papua New Guinea	1975
Cuba	1945			Paraguay	1945

Member	Year of Admission	Member	Year of Admission	Member	Year of Admission
Peru	1945	Slovakia	1993	Uganda	1962
Philippines	1945	Slovenia	1992	Ukraine	1945
Poland	1945	Solomon Islands	1978	United Arab Emirates	1971
Portugal	1955	Somalia	1960	United Kingdom of Great Britain and Northern Ireland	1945
Qatar	1971	South Africa	1945		
Romania	1955	Spain	1955		
Russian Federation	1945	Sri Lanka	1955	United Republic of Tanzania	1961
Rwanda	1962	Sudan	1956		
Saint Kitts and Nevis	1983	Suriname	1975	United States of America	1945
Saint Lucia	1979	Swaziland	1968		
Saint Vincent and the Grenadines	1980	Sweden	1946	Uruguay	1945
		Syrian Arab Republic	1945	Uzbekistan	1992
Samoa	1976	Tajikistan	1992	Vanuatu	1981
San Marino	1992	Thailand	1946	Venezuela	1945
São Tomé and Principe	1975	Togo	1960	Viet Nam	1977
Saudi Arabia	1945	Trinidad and Tobago	1962	Yemen	1947
Senegal	1960	Tunisia	1956	Yugoslavia	1945
Seychelles	1976	Turkey	1945	Zambia	1964
Sierra Leone	1961	Turkmenistan	1992	Zimbabwe	1980
Singapore	1965				

INTERNATIONAL ORGANIZATIONS

ADB	African Development Bank
AL	Arab League (League of Arab States)
ANZUS	ANZUS Council; treaty signed by Australia, New Zealand, and the United States
APC	African Peanut (Groundnut) Council
AsDB	Asian Development Bank
ASEAN	Association of Southeast Asian Nations
BENELUX	Belgium, Netherlands, Luxembourg Economic Union
CACM	Central American Common Market
CARICOM	Caribbean Community and Common Market
CCC	Customs Cooperation Council
CDB	Caribbean Development Bank
CE	Council of Europe
CEAO	West African Economic Community
CENTO	Central Treaty Organization
CFA	African Financial Community
CE	Council of Europe
CIS	Commonweath of Independent States (12 members of former Soviet Union)
CP	Colombo Plan
EC	European Community

ECA	Economic Commission for Africa (UN)
ECE	Economic Commission for Europe (UN)
ECLAC	Economic Commission for Latin America and the Caribbean (UN)
ECOSOC	Economic and Social Council (UN)
ECOWAS	Economic Community of West African States
ESCWA	Economic and Social Commission for Western Asia (UN)
EFTA	European Free Trade Association
EIB	European Investment Bank
ENTENTE	Political-Economic Association of Ivory Coast, Benin, Niger, Burkina Faso, and Togo
ESA	European Space Agency
ESCAP	Economic and Social Commission for Asia and the Pacific (UN)
EU	European Union
FAO	Food and Agriculture Organization (UN)
G-77	Group of 77
GA	General Assembly (UN)
GCC	Gulf Cooperation Council
IAEA	International Atomic Energy Agency (UN)

IBEC	International Bank for Economic Cooperation
IBRD	International Bank for Reconstruction and Development ("World Bank," UN)
ICAO	International Civil Aviation Organization (UN)
ICJ	International Court of Justice (UN)
IDA	International Development Association (IBRD affiliate, UN)
IDB	Inter-American Development Bank
IDB	Islamic Development Bank
IEA	International Energy Agency (associated with OECD)
IFAD	International Fund for Agricultural Development (UN)
IFC	International Finance Corporation (IBRD affiliate, UN)
IIB	International Investment Bank
ILO	International Labor Organization (UN)
IMF	International Monetary Fund (UN)
IMO	International Maritime Organization (UN)
INTELSAT	International Telecommunications Satellite Organization
IOC	International Olympic Committee
IOM	International Organization for Migration
ITU	International Telecommunications Union (UN)
LAIA	Latin American Integration Association
NAFTA	North American Free Trade Agreement
NAM	Nonaligned Movement
NATO	North Atlantic Treaty Organization
OAPEC	Organization of Arab Petroleum Exporting Countries
OAS	Organization of American States
OAU	Organization of African Unity
ODECA	Organization of Central American States
OECD	Organization for Economic Cooperation and Development

OIC	Organization of the Islamic Conference
OIEC	Organization for International Economic Cooperation
OPEC	Organization of Petroleum Exporting Countries
PAHO	Pan American Health Organization
SAARC	South Asian Association for Regional Cooperation
SADC	Southern African Development Community
SC	Security Council (UN)
SELA	Latin American Economic System
SPC	South Pacific Commission
SPF	South Pacific Forum
TC	Trusteeship Council (UN)
TDB	Trade and Development Board (UN)
UDEAC	Economic and Customs Union of Central Africa
UEAC	Union of Central African States
UNCTAD	UN Conference on Trade and Development
UNDP	UN Development Program
UNESCO	UN Educational, Scientific, and Cultural Organization
UNICEF	UN Children's Fund
UNIDO	UN Industrial Development Organization
UPU	Universal Postal Union (UN)
WEU	Western European Union
WFC	World Food Council (UN)
WFTU	World Federation of Trade Unions
WHO	World Health Organization (UN)
WIPO	World Intellectual Property Organization (UN)
WMO	World Meteorological Organization (UN)
WTO	World Tourism Organization
WTO	World Trade Organization

SEVEN WONDERS OF THE ANCIENT WORLD

Artemision at Ephesus This temple of the Greek goddess Artemis (also the Roman goddess Diana) was begun in 541 B.C. at Ephesus (now a site in Turkey) and completed 220 years later. The temple was 425 feet long and 220 feet wide with 127 marble columns, each 60 feet tall. The gates were made of cypress and the ceiling of cedar. The temple was destroyed by the Goths in A.D. 262.

The Colossus of Rhodes This 100-foot-tall bronze statue of the sun god Helios was erected between 292 and 280 B.C. in the harbor at Rhodes. According to legend, it appeared to stand astride the harbor but was actually on a promontory overlooking it. The statue was toppled by an earthquake around 224 B.C. and lay in ruins until A.D. 653, when the remains were sold as scrap metal.

The Hanging Gardens of Babylon This series of five terraces of glazed brick, each 50 feet above the next, was erected by King Nebuchadnezzar for

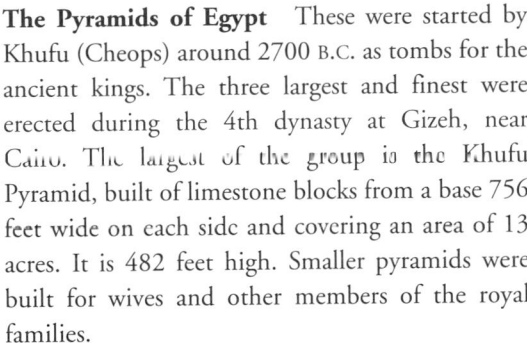

"Major World Philosophers" in chapter 10; "Cultural Symbols" in chapter 12

his wife, Amytis, in 562 B.C. The terraces, featuring rare and exotic plants, were connected by a winding stairway. A pumping device supplied water so the gardens could be irrigated by fountains.

The Mausoleum at Halicarnassus   This 140-foot-high white marble structure was built in 352 B.C. at Halicarnassus (now a site in Turkey) in memory of King Mausolus of Caria. Its massive base contained the sarcophagus and supported 36 columns crowned with a stepped pyramid on which was constructed a marble chariot. It was destroyed for the use of stone to build a castle for the Knights of Saint John in 1402.

Olympian Zeus   This statue of the supreme god in Greek mythology was executed in gold and ivory for the temple at Olympia. The figure of the seated Zeus was 40 feet tall and rested on a base that was 12 feet high. The portions of the statue representing the flesh of the god were covered with marble, and his cloak was made of gold. Golden lions rested near his feet.

The Pyramids of Egypt   These were started by Khufu (Cheops) around 2700 B.C. as tombs for the ancient kings. The three largest and finest were erected during the 4th dynasty at Gizeh, near Cairo. The largest of the group is the Khufu Pyramid, built of limestone blocks from a base 756 feet wide on each side and covering an area of 13 acres. It is 482 feet high. Smaller pyramids were built for wives and other members of the royal families.

The Tower of Pharos   This was a great lighthouse built on the island of Pharos, at Alexandria, Egypt, during the reign of Ptolemy Philadelphus, 285 B.C. Also called The Pharos, it was 500 feet tall with a ramp leading to the top. Light was produced with a fire, and reflectors and could be seen from a distance of 42 miles.

ROYAL RULERS OF EUROPE AND ASIA

CHINA

Major Chinese Dynasties

Shang	c. 1523–c.1027 B.C.
Zhou	c.1027–256 B.C.
Western Zhou	c.1027–771 B.C.
Eastern Zhou	770–256 B.C.
Spring and Autumn Period	722–481 B.C.
Warring States Period	403–222 B.C.
Qin	221–206 B.C.
Han, Former (Western)	202 B.C.– A.D. 8
Hsin	A.D. 9–23
Han, Later (Eastern)	25–220
Period of Disunion	220–589
Three Kingdoms Period	220–265
Wei	220–265
Shu	221–263
Wu	222–280
Jin	265–420
Western Jin	265–317
Eastern Jin	317–420
Southern Dynasties	420–589
Song	420–479
Ch'i	479–502
Liang	502–557
Ch'en	557–589
Northern Dynasties	386–581
Northern Wei	386–534
Eastern Wei	534–550
Northern Ch'i	550–577
Western Wei	535–557
Northern Zhou	557–581
Sui	581–618
Tang	618–906
Five Dynasties (Wu Tai)	907–960
Later Liang	907–923
Later Tang	923–936
Later Jin	936–946
Later Han	947–950
Later Zhou	951–960
Ten Kingdoms	902–979
Liao	947–1125

Major Chinese Dynasties, *cont.*

Western Xia	990–1227
Jin	1115–1234
Sung	960–1279
Northern Sung	960–1127
Southern Sung	1127–1279
Yüan (Mongol)	1260–1368
Ming	1368–1644

Qing (Manchu) Dynasty Rulers

Shun Chih	1644–1661
K'ang Hsi	1661–1722
Yung Cheng	1722–1735
Ch'ien Lung	1735–1796
Chia Ch'ing	1796–1820
Tao Kuang	1820–1851
Hsien Feng	1851–1861
T'ung Chi	1861–1875
Kuang Hsu	1875–1898
Tzu Hsi	1898–1908
P'u Yi	1908–1912

ENGLAND/GREAT BRITAIN

Saxon

Egbert	829–839
Ethelwulf	839–858
Ethelbald	858–860
Ethelbert	860–866
Ethelred I	866–871
Alfred	871–899
Edward (the Elder)	899–924
Athelstan	924–940
Edmund I	940–946
Edred	946–955
Edwy	955–959
Edgar	959–975
Edward (the Martyr)	975–978
Ethelred II	978–1016
Edmund II	1016

Danish

Canute	1017–1035
Harold I	1035–1040
Hardicanute	1040–1042

Saxon

Edward (the Confessor)	1042–1066
Harold II	1066

Norman

William I (the Conqueror)	1066–1087
William II (Rufus)	1087–1100
Henry I (Beauclerc)	1100–1135
Stephen	1135–1154

Plantagenet

Henry II	1154–1189
Richard I (Coeur de Lion)	1189–1199
John (Lackland)	1199–1216
Henry III	1216–1272
Edward I	1272–1307
Edward II	1307–1327
Edward III	1327–1377
Richard II	1377–1399

Lancaster

Henry IV (Bolingbroke)	1399–1413
Henry V	1413–1422
Henry VI	1422–1461

York

Edward IV	1461–1470

Lancaster

Henry VI (restored)	1470–1471

York

Henry IV (restored)	1471–1483
Edward V	1483
Richard III	1483–1485

Tudor

Henry VII	1485–1509
Henry VIII	1509–1547
Edward VI	1547–1553
Mary I	1553–1558
Elizabeth	1558–1603

Stuart

James I	1603–1625
Charles I	1625–1649
[Commonwealth,	1649–1653;
Oliver Cromwell, Lord	
Protector, 1653–1658;	
Richard Cromwell, Lord	
Protector, 1658–1659;	
military rule until the	
Restoration]	

The World

Charles II	1660–1685
James II	1685–1688
William III and Mary II	1689–1702
Anne	1702–1714

Hanover

George I	1714–1727
George II	1727–1760
George III	1760–1820
George IV	1820–1830
William IV	1830–1837
Victoria	1837–1901

Saxe-Coburg

Edward VII	1901–1910

Windsor

George V	1910–1936
Edward VIII	1936
George VI	1936–1952
Elizabeth II	1952–

FRANCE

Henri I	1031–1060
Philip I	1060–1108
Louis VI	1108–1137
Louis VII	1137–1180
Philip II	1180–1223
Louis VIII	1223–1226
Louis IX	1226–1270
Philip III	1270–1285
Philip IV	1285–1314
Louis X	1314–1316
John I	1316
Philip V	1316–1322
Charles IV	1322–1328
Philip VI	1328–1350
John II	1350–1364
Charles V	1364–1380
Charles VI	1380–1422
Charles VII	1422–1461
Louis XI	1461–1483
Charles VIII	1483–1498
Louis XII	1498–1515
François I	1515–1547
Henri II	1547–1559
François II	1559–1560
Charles IX	1560–1574
Henri III	1574–1589

Henri IV	1589–1610
Louis XIII	1610–1643
Louis XIV	1643–1715
Louis XV	1715–1774
Louis XVI	1774–1792
(First Republic)	1792–1804
Napoleon I	1804–1814
Louis XVIII	1814–1824
Charles X	1824–1830
Louis Philippe	1830–1848
(Second Republic)	1848–1852
Napoleon III	1852–1870

GERMANY

Frederick I	1710–1713
Frederick William I	1713–1740
Frederick II	1740–1786
Frederick William II	1786–1797
Frederick William III	1797–1840
Frederick William IV	1840–1861
William I	1861–1888
Frederick III	1888
William II	1888–1918

JAPAN

Tokugawa Shogun rule	1603–1868
(Meiji) Mutsuhito	1867–1912
Taishmo (Yoshihito)	1912–1926
Shomowa (Hirohito)	1926–1989
Heisei (Akihito)	1989–

RUSSIA

Ivan III	1462–1505
Vasilly III	1505–1533
Ivan IV	1533–1584
Theodore I	1584–1598
Boris Godunov	1598–1605
Theodore II	1605
Demetrius I	1605–1606
Basil IV	1606–1610
Wladyslaw (Polish Prince)	1620–1613
Mikhail Romanov	1613–1645
Alexia I	1645–1676
Theodore III	1676–1682
Ivan V and Peter I	1682–1689
Peter I (alone)	1689–1725
Catherine I	1725–1727
Peter II	1727–1730

The World

Russia, *cont.*

Anna	1730–1740
Ivan VI	1740–1741
Elizabeth	1741–1762
Peter III	1762
Catherine II	1762–1796

Paul I	1796–1801
Alexander I	1801–1825
Nicholas I	1825–1855
Alexander II	1855–1881
Alexander III	1881–1894
Nicholas II	1894–1917

ORDER OF BRITISH PEERAGE

Titles of nobility, or peerages, are granted by the king or queen of Great Britain upon the recommendation of the prime minister. In most *hereditary peerages,* the title passes on to a peer's oldest son, or to his closest male heir if the peer has no son (the other children are considered commoners). The title becomes extinct if there is no male heir. There are some ancient peerages that allow the title to be passed to a daughter if the holder leaves no male descendant. The last hereditary peerage was granted in 1964.

Life peerages are created each year by the British monarch for several distinguished persons. Life peers hold the rank for their own lives only; the titles do not pass on to their children. Both men and women may be granted life peerages, and the titles given to them are baron or baroness.

The following are the five grades of peers ranked from the highest to the lowest and the dates they were created. (Duke is the highest hereditary rank below that of prince.)

1. duke   *or*   duchess (1337)
2. marquess,   *or*   marchioness (1385)
   marquis
3. earl   *or*   countess (c. 800–1000)
4. viscount   *or*   viscountess (1440)
5. baron   *or*   baroness (c. 1066)

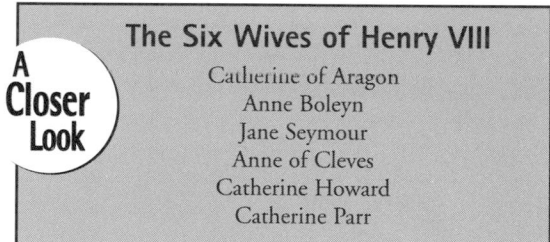

A Closer Look

The Six Wives of Henry VIII

Catherine of Aragon
Anne Boleyn
Jane Seymour
Anne of Cleves
Catherine Howard
Catherine Parr

GENEALOGY CHARTS OF THE BRITISH MONARCHY

Before the Conquest (827–1066)

Symbols

=	Marriage
|	Offspring
—	Siblings
Numerals	Order of rule

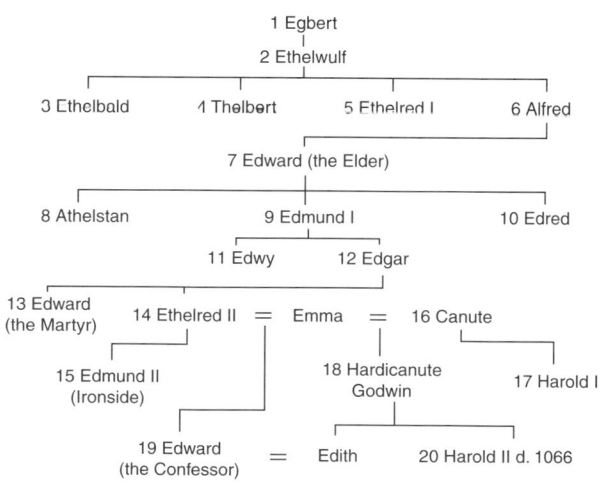

Norman Line (1066–1154)
Union of English and Norman Lines in Henry II

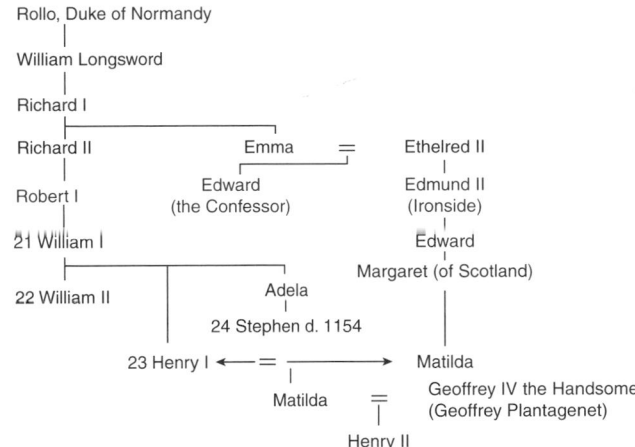

Plantagenet Line (1154–1399)

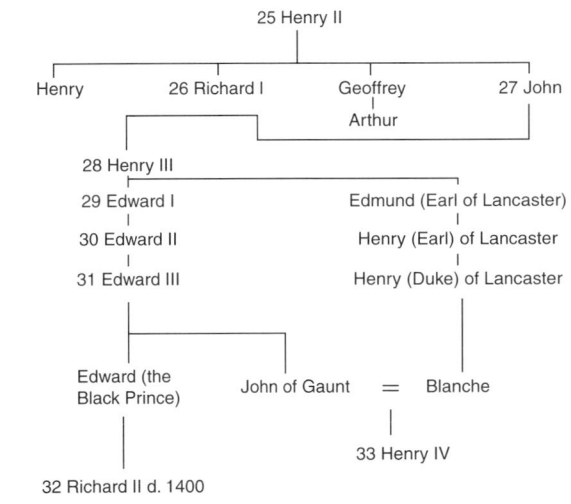

House of Lancaster (1399–1461)
House of York (1461–1485)

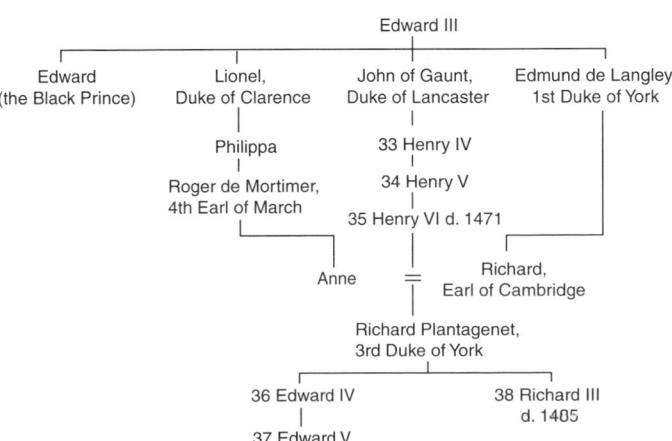

The World

House of Tudor (1485–1603)

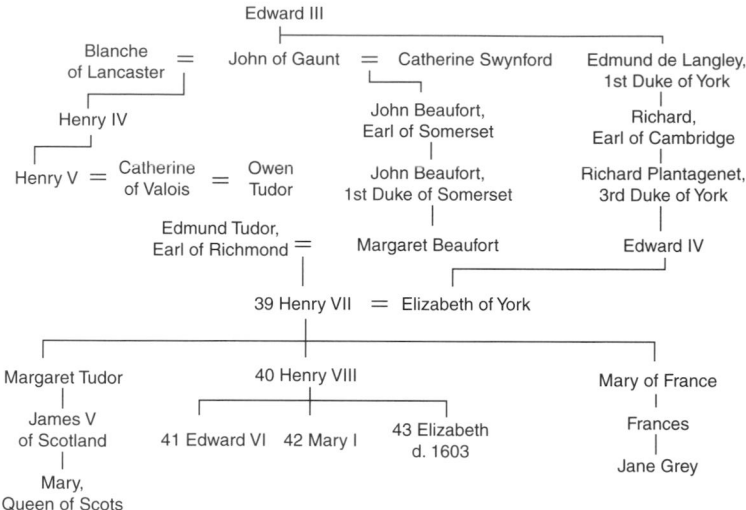

House of Stuart (1603–1714)

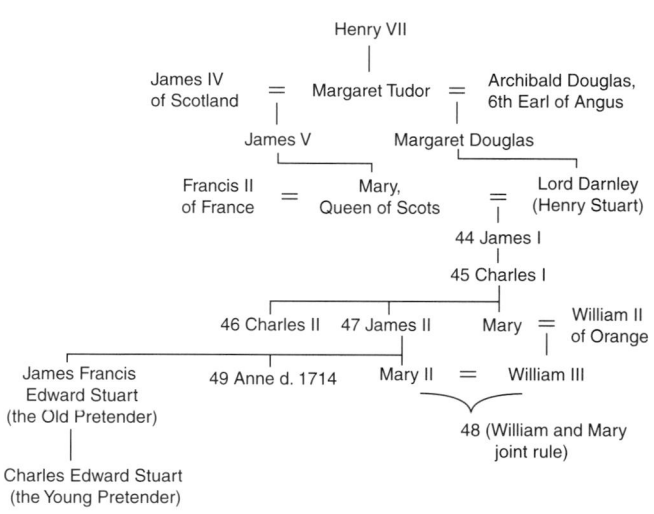

Houses of Hanover, Saxe-Coburg, and Windsor (1714–

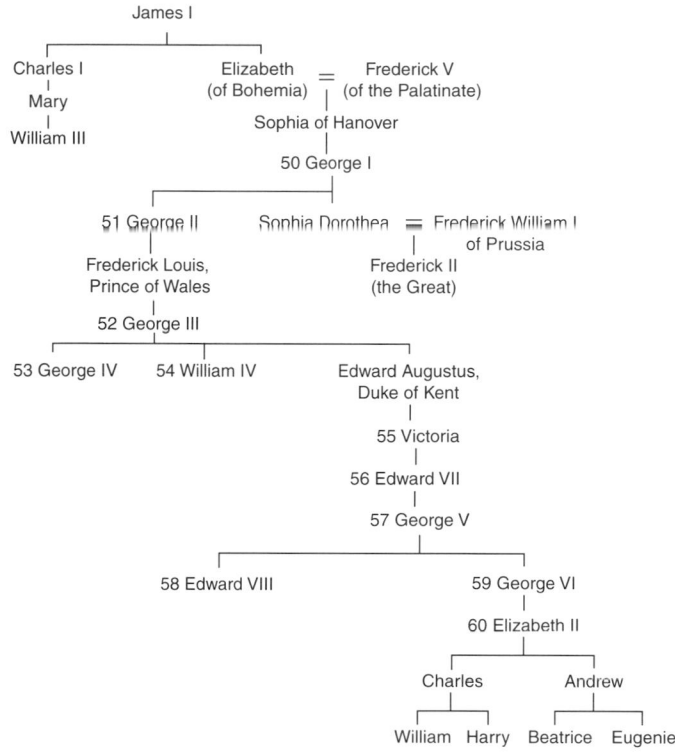

CONNECTIONS BETWEEN ROYAL FAMILIES

In the following charts, the notations (V1), (V2), and so on indicate the first, second, etc., child of Victoria, Queen of England.

ENGLAND, DENMARK, AND RUSSIA

Connections Between the Royal Families of England, Denmark, and Russia

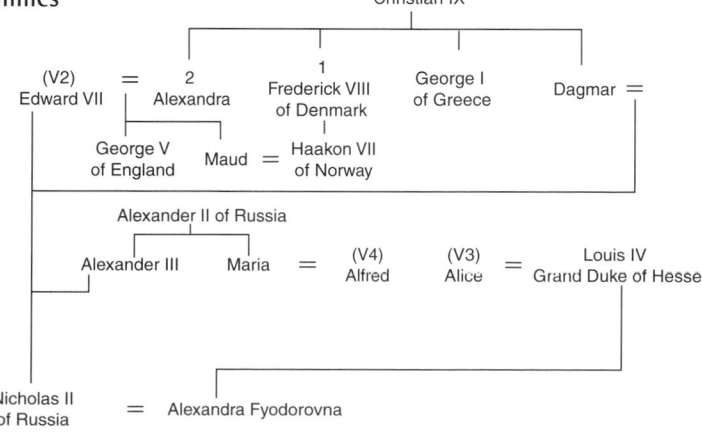

ENGLAND, GERMANY, AND SPAIN

Connections Between the Royal Families of England, Germany, and Spain

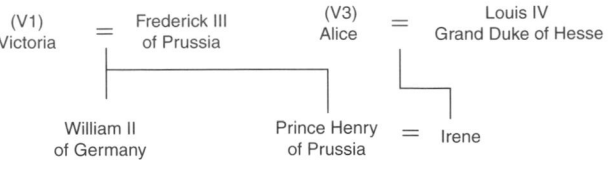

PRIME MINISTERS

AUSTRALIA

Sir Edmund Barton	1901–1902
Alfred Deakin	1902–1904
John Christian Watson	1904
George Houston Reid	1904–1905
Alfred Deakin	1905–1908
Andrew Fisher	1908–1909
Alfred Deakin	1909–1910
Andrew Fisher	1910–1913
Sir Joseph Cook	1913–1914
Andrew Fisher	1914–1915
William Morris Hughes	1915–1923
Stanley Melbourne Bruce	1923–1929
James Henry Scullin	1929–1931
Joseph Aloysius Lyons	1932–1939
Earle Page	1939
Robert Gordon Menzies	1939–1941
Arthur William Fadden	1941
John Curtain	1941–1945
Joseph Benedict Chifley	1945–1949
Robert Gordon Menzies	1949–1966
Harold E. Holt	1966–1967
John G. Gorton	1968–1971
William McMahon	1971–1972
(Edward) Gough Whitlam	1972–1975
Malcolm Fraser	1975–1983
Bob Hawke	1983–1991
Paul Keating	1991–1996
John Winston Howard	1996–

CANADA

John Alexander Macdonald	1867–1873
Alexander Mackenzie	1873–1878
John Alexander Macdonald	1878–1891
Sir John J. Abbott	1891–1892
Sir John S. D. Thompson	1892–1894
Sir Mackenzie Bowell	1894–1896
Sir Charles Tupper	1896
Sir Wilfrid Laurier	1896–1911
Sir Robert Laird Borden	1911–1920
Arthur Meighen	1920–1921
W. L. Mackenzie King	1921–1926
Arthur Meighen	1926
W. L. Mackenzie King	1926–1930
Richard Bedford Bennett	1930–1935
W. L. Mackenzie King	1935–1948
Louis Stephen Saint Laurent	1948–1957
John George Diefenbaker	1957–1963
Lester Bowles Pearson	1963–1968
Pierre Elliott Trudeau	1968–1979
Charles Joseph (Joe) Clark	1979–1980
Pierre Elliott Trudeau	1980–1984
John Napier Turner	1984
Brian Mulroney	1984–1993
Kim Campbell	1993
Jean Chretien	1993–

ENGLAND/GREAT BRITAIN

Sidney Godolphin (Earl of Godolphin)	1700–1701
Charles Howard (Earl of Carlisle)	1701–1702

Sidney Godolphin (Earl of Godolphin)	1702–1710
John Poulett (Earl Poulett)	1710–1711
Robert Harley (Earl of Oxford)	1711–1714
Charles Talbot (Duke of Shrewsbury)	1714
Charles Montagu (Earl of Halifax)	1714–1715
Charles Howard (Earl of Carlisle)	1715
Robert Walpole (Earl of Oxford)	1715–1717
James Stanhope (Earl Stanhope)	1717–1718
Charles Spencer (3rd Earl of Sunderland)1	1718–1721
Robert Walpole (Earl of Oxford)	1721–1742
Spencer Compton (Earl of Wilmington)	1742–1743
Henry Pelham	1743–1754
Duke of Newcastle (Thomas Pelham-Holles)	1754–1756
William Cavendish (Duke of Devonshire)	1756–1757
Duke of Newcastle (Thomas Pelham-Holles)	1757–1762
John Stuart (Earl of Bute)	1762–1763
George Grenville	1763–1765
Marquis of Rockingham (Charles Watson-Wentworth)	1765–1766
William Pitt (Earl of Chatham)	1766–1768
Augustus Henry Fitzroy (Duke of Grafton)	1768–1770
Frederick North (Earl of Guilford)	1770–1782
Marquis of Rockingham (Charles Watson-Wentworth)	1782
Marquis of Lansdowne (William Petty)	1782–1783
William Henry Cavendish Bentinck (Duke of Portland)	1783
William Pitt	1783–1801
Henry Addington (Viscount Sidmouth)	1801–1804
William Pitt	1804–1806
William Wyndham Grenville (Baron Grenville)	1806–1807
William Henry Cavendish Bentinck (Duke of Portland)	1807–1809
Spencer Perceval	1809–1812
Robert Banks Jenkinson (Earl of Liverpool)	1812–1827
George Canning	1827

Frederick John Robinson (Viscount Goderich)	1827–1828
Duke of Wellington (Arthur Wellesley)	1828–1830
Charles Grey (Earl Grey)	1830–1834
William Lamb (Viscount Melbourne)	1834
Sir Robert Peel	1834–1835
William Lamb (Viscount Melbourne)	1835–1841
Sir Robert Peel	1841–1846
Lord John Russell	1846–1852
Edward George Geoffrey Smith Stanley (Earl of Derby)	1852
George Hamilton Gordon (Earl of Aberdeen)	1852–1855
Viscount Palmerston (Henry John Temple)	1855–1858
Edward George Geoffrey Smith Stanley (Earl of Derby)	1858–1859
Viscount Palmerston (Henry John Temple)	1859–1865
Earl (formerly Lord John) Russell	1865–1866
Edward George Geoffrey Smith Stanley (Earl of Derby)	1866–1868
Benjamin Disraeli (Earl of Beaconsfield)	1868
William Ewart Gladstone	1868–1874
Benjamin Disraeli (Earl of Beaconsfield)	1874–1880
William Ewart Gladstone	1880–1885
Robert Arthur Talbot Gascoyner-Cecil (Marquis of Salisbury)	1885–1886
William Ewart Gladstone	1886
Robert Arthur Talbot Gascoyner-Cecil (Marquis of Salisbury)	1886–1892
William Ewart Gladstone	1892–1894
Earl of Rosebery (Archibald Philip Primrose)	1894–1895
Robert Arthur Talbot Gascoyner-Cecil (Marquis of Salisbury)	1895–1902
Arthur James Balfour	1902–1905
Sir Henry Campbell-Bannerman	1905–1908
Herbert Henry Asquith (Earl of Oxford and Asquith)	1908–1916
David Lloyd George (Earl of Dwyfor)	1916–1922
Andrew Bonar Law	1922–1923

Stanley Baldwin (Earl Baldwin of Bewdley)	1923–1924	Winston Churchill	1951–1955
James Ramsay MacDonald	1924	Sir Anthony Eden	1955–1957
Stanley Baldwin (Earl Baldwin of Bewdley)	1924–1929	Harold Macmillan	1957–1963
		Sir Alec Douglas-Home	1963–1964
James Ramsay MacDonald	1929–1935	Harold Wilson	1964–1970
Stanley Baldwin (Earl Baldwin of Bewdley)	1935–1937	Edward Heath	1970–1974
		Harold Wilson	1974–1976
Neville Chamberlain	1937–1940	James Callaghan	1976–1979
Winston Churchill	1940–1945	Margaret Thatcher	1979–1990
Clement Attlee	1945–1951	John Major	1990–1997
		Tony Blair	1997–

FOREIGN DIALING CODES

Note: For international telephone calls automatically routed through AT&T, dial "011" and then dial the code for that country, the city code if one is indicated, and the subscriber telephone number to be reached. Other long-distance telephone services may have other procedures and should be consulted for their specific instructions.

Algeria	213	Denmark	45	Greece	30
American Samoa	684	(Aalborg 8)		(Athens 1)	
Andorra	33	(Copenhagen 1 or 2)		(Rhodes 241)	
(all points 628)		Ecuador	593	Guam	671
Argentina	54	(Cuneca 7)		Guantanamo Bay	
(Buenos Aires 1)		(Quito 2)		U.S. naval base	53
Australia	61	Egypt	20	(all points 99)	
(Melbourne 3)		(Alexandria 3)		Guatemala	502
(Sydney 2)		Port Said 66)		(Guatemala City 2)	
Austria	43	El Salvador	503	(Antigua 9)	
(Vienna 1)		England. *See* United Kingdom.		Guyana	592
Bahrain	973	Ethiopia	251	(Georgetown 2)	
Belgium	32	(Addis Ababa 1)		Haiti	509
(Brussels 2)		Fiji	697	(Port-au-Prince 1)	
(Ghent 91)		Finland	358	Honduras	504
Belize	501	(Helsinki 0)		Hong Kong	852
Bolivia	591	France	33	(Hong Kong 5)	
(Santa Cruz 33)		(Marseille 91)		(Kowloon 3)	
Brazil	55	(Nice 93)		Hungary	36
(Brasília 61)		(Paris 13, 14, 16)		(Budapest 1)	
(Rio de Janeiro 21)		French Antilles	596	Iceland	354
Cameroon	237	French Antilles-Guadeloupe	590	(Akureyri 6)	
Chile	56	French Polynesia	689	(Reykjavik 1)	
(Santiago 2)		Gabon	241	India	91
Colombia	57	Germany	49	(Bombay 22)	
(Bogotá 1)		(Frankfurt 69)		(New Delhi 11)	
Costa Rica	506	(Munich 89)		Indonesia	62
Cyprus	357	(Berlin 30)		(Jakarta 21)	
Czech Republic	42	(other areas of former		Iran	98
(Prague 2)		East Germany 37)		(Teheran 21)	

Iraq	964	Netherlands Antilles-Aruba	297	(Madrid 1)	
(Baghdad 1)		(Aruba 8)		(Seville 54)	
Ireland	353	New Caledonia	687	Sri Lanka	94
(Dublin 1)		New Zealand	64	(Kandy 8)	
(Galway 91)		(Auckland 9)		Suriname	597
Israel	972	(Wellington 4)		Sweden	46
(Haifa 4)		Nicaragua	505	(Göteborg 31)	
(Jerusalem 2)		(Managua 2)		(Stockholm 8)	
(Tel Aviv 3)		Nigeria	234	Switzerland	41
Italy	39	(Lagos 1)		(Geneva 22)	
(Florence 55)		Norway	47	(Lucerne 41)	
(Rome 6)		(Bergen 5)		(Zurich 1)	
(Venice 41)		(Oslo 2)		Taiwan	886
Ivory Coast	225	Oman	968	(Tainan 6)	
Japan	81	Pakistan	92	(Taipei 2)	
(Tokyo 3)		(Islamabad 51)		Thailand	66
(Yokohama 45)		Panama	507	(Bangkok 2)	
Jordan	962	Papua New Guinea	675	Tunisia	216
(Amman 6)		Paraguay	595	(Tunis 1)	
Kenya	254	(Asuncion 21)		Turkey	90
Korea, South	82	Peru	51	(Istanbul 1)	
(Pusan 51)		(Arequipa 54)		(Izmir 51)	
(Seoul 2)		(Lima 14)		United Arab Emirates	971
Kuwait	965	Philippines	63	(Abu Dhabi 2)	
Liberia	231	(Manila 2)		(Al Ain 3)	
Libya	218	Poland	48	(Dubai 4)	
(Tripoli 21)		(Warsaw 22)		(Ras Al Khainah 77)	
Liechtenstein	41	Portugal	351	(Sharjah 6)	
(all points 75)		(Lisbon 1)		(Umm Al Quwain 6)	
Luxembourg	352	Qatar	974	United Kingdom	44
Malawi	265	Romania	40	(Belfast 232)	
(Domasi 531)		(Bucharest 0)		(Cardiff 222)	
Malaysia	60	Saipan	670	(Glasgow 41)	
(Kuala Lumpur 3)		San Marino	39	(London 71 or 81)	
Mexico	52	(all points 541)		Uruguay	598
(Mexico City 5)		Saudi Arabia	966	(Mercedes 532)	
(Tijuana 66)		(Riyadh 1)		(Montevideo 2)	
Monaco	33	Senegal	221	Vatican City	39
(all points 93)		Singapore	65	(all points 6)	
Morocco	212	South Africa	27	Venezuela	58
(Agadir 8)		(Cape Town 21)		(Caracas 2)	
Namibia	264	(Pretoria 12)		(Maracaibo 61)	
(Olympia 61)		Spain	34	Yemen Arab Republic	967
Netherlands	31	(Barcelona 3)		(Amran 2)	
(Amsterdam 20)		(Las Palmas, Canary		Yugoslavia	38
(The Hague 70)		Islands 28)		(Belgrade 11)	
Netherlands Antilles	599				

ADDITIONAL SOURCES OF INFORMATION

ORGANIZATIONS AND SERVICES

The Asia Foundation
P.O. Box 193223
San Francisco, CA 94119

Bureau of Public Affairs
U.S. Department of State
2201 C St., NW
Washington, DC 20520

Carnegie Endowment for International Peace
2400 N St., NW
Washington, DC 20037

Central Intelligency Agency
Public Affairs Director
McClean, VA 22050

European Community Press and Public Affairs
2300 M St., NW
Washington, DC 20037

Middle East Institute
1761 N St., NW
Washington, DC 20036

Organization of American States
17th Street and Constitution Avenue, NW
Washington, DC 20006

United Nations Headquarters
United Nations Plaza
New York, NY 10017

United Nations Information Center
1889 F St., NW
Washington, DC 20006

United States Mission to the United Nations
799 United Nations Plaza
New York, NY 10017

BOOKS

Central Intelligence Agency, *The World Factbook.* U.S. Government Printing Office, annual.

Grun, Bernard. *The Timetables of History.* Touchstone, 1991.

The Harper Atlas of World History. Rev. ed. Harper & Row, 1993.

Hoffman, Mark S. *The World Almanac and Book of Facts.* Pharos Books, annual.

Hulme, F. Edward. *Flags of the World: Their History, Blazonry and Associations.* Gordon Press, 1977.

Maps on File 1996. Facts On File, 1996.

The New International World Atlas. Rand McNally, 1995.

Schraepler, Hans-Albrecht. *Directory of International Organizations.* Georgetown University Press, 1996.

Simony, Maggy. *The Traveler's Reading Guide: Ready-Made Reading Lists for the Armchair Traveler.* Rev. ed. Facts On File, 1994.

Trager, James, ed. *The People's Chronology: A Year by Year Record of Human Events from Prehistory to the Present.* Rev. ed. Holt, Rinehart and Winston, 1994.

Wetterau, Bruce. *Macmillan Concise Dictionary of World History.* Macmillan, 1986.

Wetterau, Bruce. *The New York Public Library Book of Chronologies.* Prentice Hall, 1994.

The World

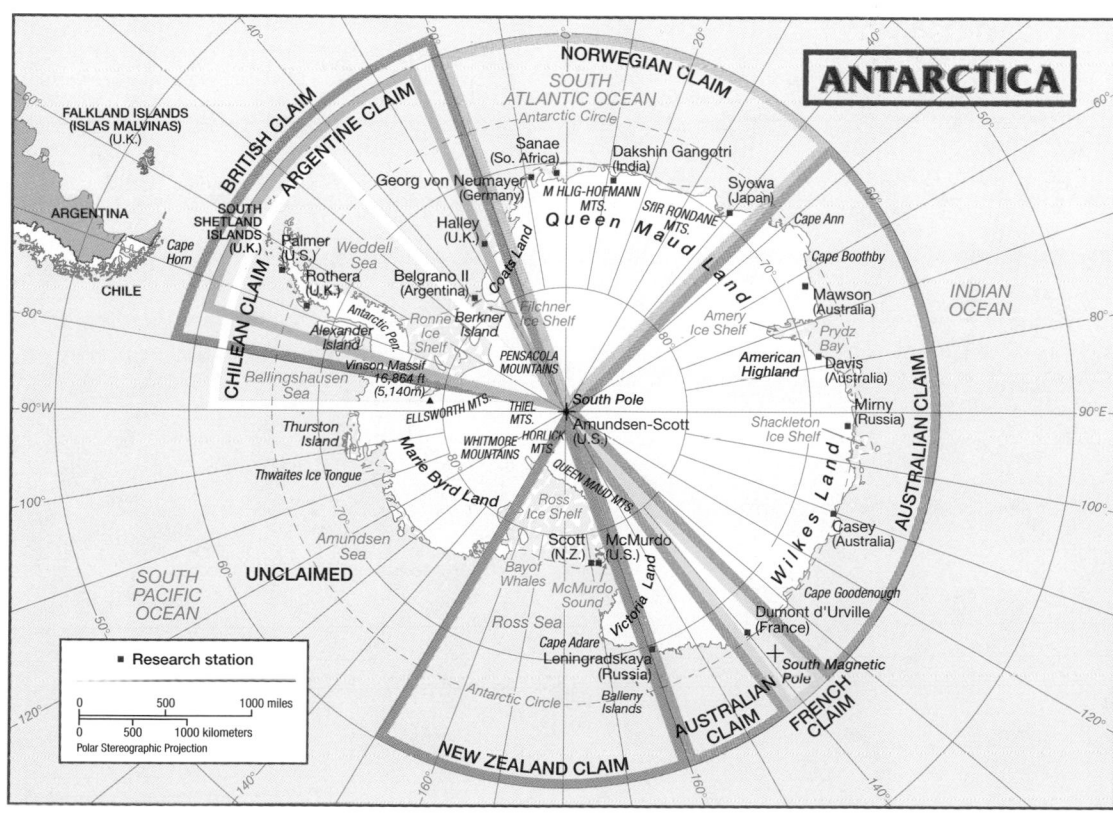

AFRICA

NORTH ATLANTIC OCEAN

North Sea

EUROPE

Baltic Sea

Black Sea

Aral Sea

ASIA

Caspian Sea

Strait of Gibraltar

Oran   Algiers   Tunis

Rabat   Fès

Casablanca   ATLAS MTS.

MOROCCO

TUNISIA

Tripoli   Banghazi

Misurata

Mediterranean Sea

Suez Canal

Alexandria   Port Said

Giza   Cairo

Persian Gulf

WESTERN SAHARA

ALGERIA

LIBYA

EGYPT

Tropic of Cancer

Nile

Red Sea

S   A   H   A   R   A

GUINEA-BISSAU

MAURITANIA

Nouakchott

MALI

TIBESTI MTS.

NIGER

CHAD

Port Sudan

North Khartoum

Omdurman

Khartoum

ERITREA

Asmara

DJIBOUTI

Gulf of Aden

Dakar

SENEGAL

Niger

BURKINA FASO

Niamey

SUDAN

Blue Nile

Djibouti

Banjul

GAMBIA

Bamako

Ouagadougou

L. Chad

N'Djamena

White Nile

Addis Ababa

Bissau

GUINEA

Conakry

TOGO

BENIN

NIGERIA

Abuja

ETHIOPIA

SOMALIA

SIERRA LEONE

Freetown

IVORY COAST

GHANA

Lome

Ibadan

Lagos

Porto-Novo

CENTRAL AFRICAN REPUBLIC

L. Turkana

Monrovia

Abidjan

Accra

CAMEROON

Bangui

UGANDA

KENYA

Mogadishu

LIBERIA

Malabo

Yaoundé

Congo

Kisangani

Kampala

INDIAN OCEAN

Equator

EQUATORIAL GUINEA

SÃO TOMÉ AND PRÍNCIPE

Libreville

CONGO

RWANDA

Kigali

L. Victoria

Nairobi

Mombasa

Victoria

SEYCHELLES

São Tomé

GABON

Brazzaville

DEMOCRATIC REP. OF CONGO

Kinshasa

Bujumbura

BURUNDI

Dodoma

Zanzibar

Dar Es Salaam

CAPE VERDE

Praia

CABINDA (ANGOLA)

Luanda

Kananga

TANZANIA

L. Tanganyika

L. Nyasa

COMOROS

Moroni

N

ANGOLA

Lubumbashi

MALAWI

Ilongwe

Blantyre

ZAMBIA

Lusaka

Zambezi

Harare

MOZAMBIQUE

Antananarivo

MAURITIUS

Port Louis

NAMIBIA

Windhoek

BOTSWANA

KALAHARI DESERT

Gaborone

ZIMBABWE

Beira

MADAGASCAR

St.-Denis

Réunion (Fr.)

Tropic of Capricorn

Johannesburg

Pretoria

Johannesburg

Maputo

Mbabane

SWAZILAND

SOUTH ATLANTIC OCEAN

Orange

Maseru

SOUTH AFRICA

LESOTHO

Durban

Cape Town

Port Elizabeth

⭐ National capital

0   350   700 miles

0   350   700 kilometers

Lambert Equal-Area Projection

EUROPE

ASIA

URAL MOUNTAINS

RUSSIA

Barents Sea

Murmansk

Perm'

Ufa

Orenburg

Izhevsk

Simbirsk

Saratov

Astrakhan'

Volgograd

Voronezh

Tula

Moscow

Yaroslavl'

St. Petersburg

Aral Sea

Caspian Sea

Baku

AZERBAIJAN

Grozny

Tbilisi

ARMENIA

GEORGIA

Yerevan

CAUCASUS MTS.

Krasnodar

Rostov

Black Sea

Bosporus

Constanta

Donetsk

Zaporozh'ye

Krivoy Rog

Odessa

Dnepropetrovsk

Khar'kov

Kiev

UKRAINE

MOLDOVA

Kishinev

Iasi

L'viv

CARPATHIAN MTS.

Gomel

Minsk

BELARUS

RUSSIA

Kaliningrad

LITHUANIA

Vilnius

LATVIA

Riga

ESTONIA

Tallinn

FINLAND

Helsinki

Turku

Baltic Sea

SWEDEN

Stockholm

Göteborg

Malmö

NORWAY

Oslo

Trondheim

Bergen

Norwegian Sea

ROMANIA

Bucharest

BULGARIA

Sofia

YUGOSLAVIA

Belgrade

MACEDONIA

Skopje

ALBANIA

Tiranë

Thessaloníki

GREECE

Athens

Aegean Sea

Crete

Mediterranean Sea

MALTA

Valletta

SLOVAKIA

Bratislava

HUNGARY

Budapest

Kraków

Łódź

Wrocław

POLAND

Warsaw

Gdańsk

CZECH REPUBLIC

Prague

Vienna

AUSTRIA

LIECHTENSTEIN

SLOVENIA

Ljubljana

CROATIA

Zagreb

BOSNIA AND HERZEGOVINA

Sarajevo

Adriatic Sea

ITALY

Rome

Naples

Bari

Palermo

Sicily

Sardinia (ITALY)

VATICAN CITY

Vatican City

SAN MARINO

MONACO

Monte Carlo

Corsica (FR.)

Florence

Genoa

Milan

Turin

Nice

Marseille

SWITZERLAND

Bern

Zürich

GERMANY

Berlin

Hamburg

Essen

Cologne

Frankfurt

Munich

DENMARK

Copenhagen

NETHERLANDS

Amsterdam

The Hague

BELGIUM

Brussels

LUXEMBOURG

Luxembourg

FRANCE

Paris

Strasbourg

Lyon

Bordeaux

Toulouse

Nantes

Bay of Biscay

PYRENEES

ANDORRA

Andorra

Barcelona

Valencia

Balearic Is. (SPAIN)

SPAIN

Madrid

Bilbao

IBERIAN PENINSULA

Seville

GIBRALTAR (U.K.)

Gibraltar

Strait of Gibraltar

PORTUGAL

Lisbon

Porto

AFRICA

ATLANTIC OCEAN

English Channel

UNITED KINGDOM

London

Liverpool

Birmingham

Edinburgh

Glasgow

Belfast

Northern Ireland

IRELAND

Dublin

North Sea

Faroe Islands (DENMARK)

Shetland Islands (U.K.)

Arctic Circle

ICELAND

Reykjavík

N

⊛ National capital

400 miles

400 kilometers

200

200

0

0

Lambe Equal-Area Projection

Atlas

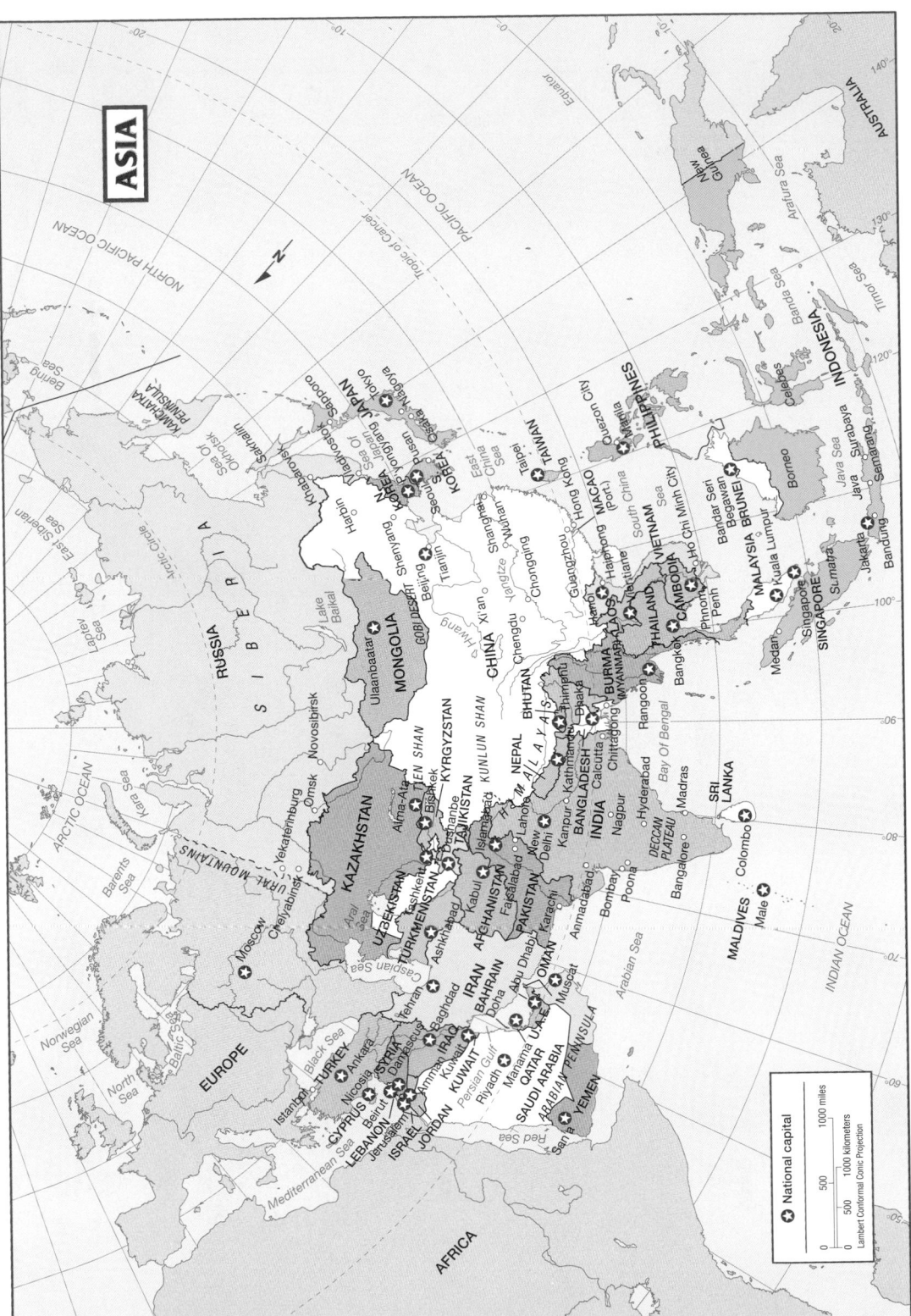

ASIA

National capital

1000 miles

1000 kilometers

500

500

Lambert Conformal Conic Projection

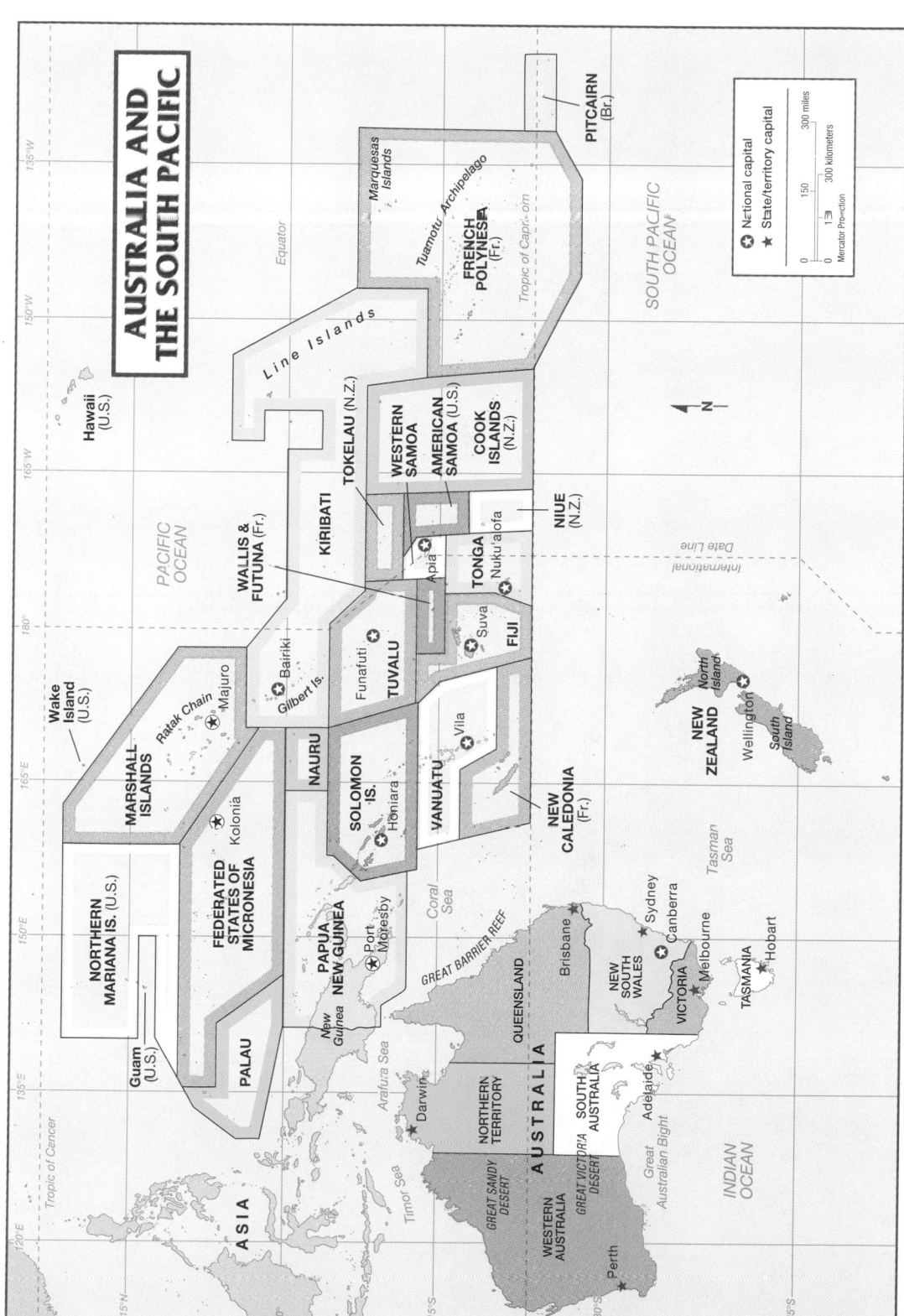

AUSTRALIA AND THE SOUTH PACIFIC

National capital
★ **State/territory capital**

0   150   300 miles
0 ╱ 300 kilometers
Mercator Projection

PITCAIRN (Br.)

Marquesas Islands

Tuamotu Archipelago

FRENCH POLYNESIA (Fr.)

Tropic of Capricorn

SOUTH PACIFIC OCEAN

Equator

Line Islands

Hawaii (U.S.)

TOKELAU (N.Z.)

WESTERN SAMOA

AMERICAN SAMOA (U.S.)

COOK ISLANDS (N.Z.)

KIRIBATI

Apia

NIUE (N.Z.)

WALLIS & FUTUNA (Fr.)

TONGA   Nuku'alofa

International Date Line

PACIFIC OCEAN

Bairiki

Funafuti

TUVALU

Suva

FIJI

Vila

Wake Island (U.S.)

Ratak Chain

Majuro

Gilbert Is.

NAURU

MARSHALL ISLANDS

Kolonia

SOLOMON IS.

Honiara

VANUATU

NEW CALEDONIA (Fr.)

Tasman Sea

NEW ZEALAND

North Island

Wellington

South Island

NORTHERN MARIANA IS. (U.S.)

FEDERATED STATES OF MICRONESIA

PAPUA NEW GUINEA

Port Moresby

New Guinea

Coral Sea

GREAT BARRIER REEF

Brisbane

Sydney

Canberra

NEW SOUTH WALES

Melbourne

VICTORIA

TASMANIA

Hobart

QUEENSLAND

Guam (U.S.)

PALAU

ASIA

Tropic of Cancer

Arafura Sea

Timor Sea

Darwin

NORTHERN TERRITORY

SOUTH AUSTRALIA

Adelaide

AUSTRALIA

GREAT SANDY DESERT

GREAT VICTORIA DESERT

WESTERN AUSTRALIA

Great Australian Bight

INDIAN OCEAN

Perth

N

SOUTH AMERICA

NORTH
AMERICA

CARIBBEAN SEA

ATLANTIC OCEAN

20°

10°

Barranquilla
Cartagena
Maracaibo
Caracas
Barquisimeto
VENEZUELA
Georgetown
Paramaribo
GUYANA
SURINAME
Cayenne
FRENCH
GUIANA

Medellín
Manizales
Bogotá
Cali
COLOMBIA

GUIANA HIGHLANDS

N

Quito
Guayaquil
ECUADOR

Equator

0°

Negro
Amazon
Belém
Fortaleza

AMAZON
BASIN
Manaus
Madeira
Tapajós
Xingu
Tocantins

Natal
João Pessoa
Recife

Trujillo

PERU
Lima
Callao

ANDES

São Francisco

Maceió
Aracaju
Salvador

BRAZIL

10°

BOLIVIA
La Paz
Cochabamba
Santa Cruz
Lake
Titicaca
Sucre

MATO GROSSO
PLATEAU
Brasília
Goiânia

BRAZILIAN HIGHLANDS

Belo
Horizonte

20°

M
O
U
N
T
A
I
N
S

GRAN CHACO

PARAGUAY

Campo
Grande
Campinas
Londrina

Ribeirão
Preto

Rio de Janeiro
São Paulo

Tropic of Capricorn

SOUTH PACIFIC OCEAN

Salta
San Miguel
de Tucumán
Resistencia
Asunción
Curitiba

Pôrto
Alegre

CHILE

Córdoba

Valparaíso
Santiago
Mendoza
Rosario
URUGUAY

30°

Concepción

ARGENTINA
Buenos Aires
La Plata
Bahía
Blanca
Mar del Plata
Montevideo

SOUTH ATLANTIC OCEAN

P
A
T
A
G
O
N
I
A

PAMPAS

Temuco

40°

Strait of
Magellan

Tierra del
Fuego

Falkland
Islands
(U.K.)

South
Georgia Island
(U.K.)

50°

Cape Horn

⊛ National capital

0   250   500 miles
0   250   500 kilometers
Lambert Equal-Area Projection

100°   90°   80°   70°   60°   50°   40°   30°   20°

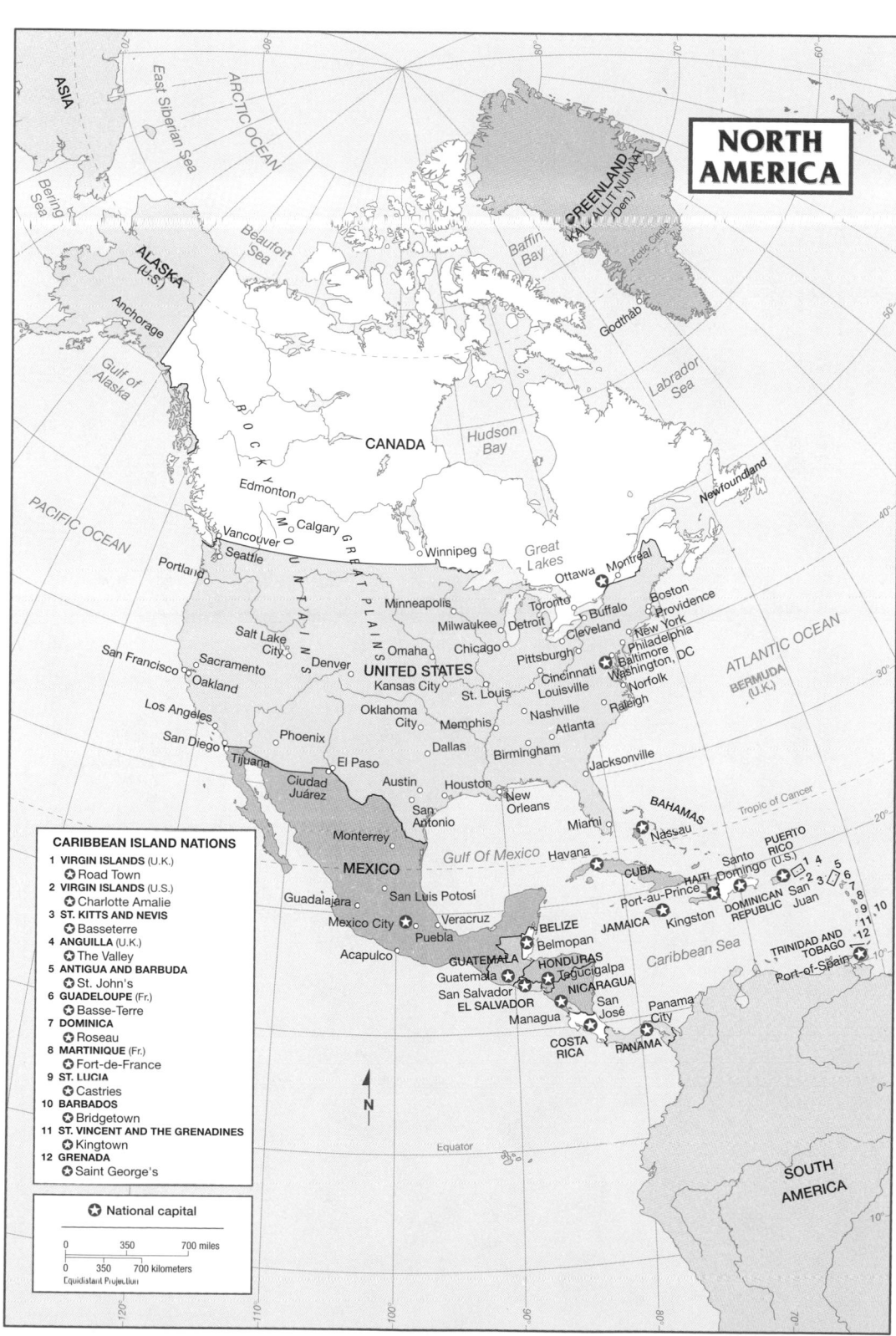

NORTH AMERICA

ASIA

ARCTIC OCEAN

East Siberian Sea

Bering Sea

Beaufort Sea

ALASKA (U.S.)

Anchorage

Gulf of Alaska

PACIFIC OCEAN

GREENLAND KAL./ALLIT NUNAAT (Den.)

Arctic Circle

Baffin Bay

Godthåb

Labrador Sea

Hudson Bay

CANADA

Edmonton

Calgary

Vancouver

Seattle

Portland

Newfoundland

Winnipeg

Ottawa Montreal

Great Lakes

Minneapolis
Milwaukee Detroit
Toronto
Buffalo
Cleveland
Boston
Providence
New York

ROCKY MOUNTAINS

GREAT PLAINS

Salt Lake City
Omaha Chicago
Pittsburgh
Philadelphia
Baltimore

San Francisco
Sacramento
Oakland
Denver
UNITED STATES
Kansas City
St. Louis
Cincinnati
Louisville
Washington, DC
Norfolk

ATLANTIC OCEAN

BERMUDA (U.K.)

Los Angeles

San Diego
Phoenix
Oklahoma City
Memphis
Nashville
Atlanta
Raleigh

Tijuana
El Paso
Austin
Dallas
Birmingham
Jacksonville

Ciudad Juárez
San Antonio
Houston
New Orleans
Miami

Monterrey
BAHAMAS
Nassau

Tropic of Cancer

MEXICO
Gulf Of Mexico
Havana
CUBA

PUERTO RICO (U.S.)

Guadalajara
San Luis Potosí
Santo Domingo
San Juan
1 4
5

Mexico City
Veracruz
Puebla
HAITI
Port-au-Prince
JAMAICA
Kingston
DOMINICAN REPUBLIC
2
3
6
7

Acapulco
BELIZE
Belmopan
8
9 10

GUATEMALA
HONDURAS
11
-12

Guatemala
Tegucigalpa
San Salvador
EL SALVADOR
NICARAGUA
Managua
Caribbean Sea
TRINIDAD AND TOBAGO
Port-of-Spain

COSTA RICA
San José
Panama City
PANAMA

Equator

SOUTH AMERICA

CARIBBEAN ISLAND NATIONS

1 **VIRGIN ISLANDS** (U.K.)
   ✪ Road Town
2 **VIRGIN ISLANDS** (U.S.)
   ✪ Charlotte Amalie
3 **ST. KITTS AND NEVIS**
   ✪ Basseterre
4 **ANGUILLA** (U.K.)
   ✪ The Valley
5 **ANTIGUA AND BARBUDA**
   ✪ St. John's
6 **GUADELOUPE** (Fr.)
   ✪ Basse-Terre
7 **DOMINICA**
   ✪ Roseau
8 **MARTINIQUE** (Fr.)
   ✪ Fort-de-France
9 **ST. LUCIA**
   ✪ Castries
10 **BARBADOS**
   ✪ Bridgetown
11 **ST. VINCENT AND THE GRENADINES**
   ✪ Kingtown
12 **GRENADA**
   ✪ Saint George's

✪ National capital

| 0 | 350 | 700 miles |
| 0 | 350 | 700 kilometers |

Equidistant Projection

N

Atlas

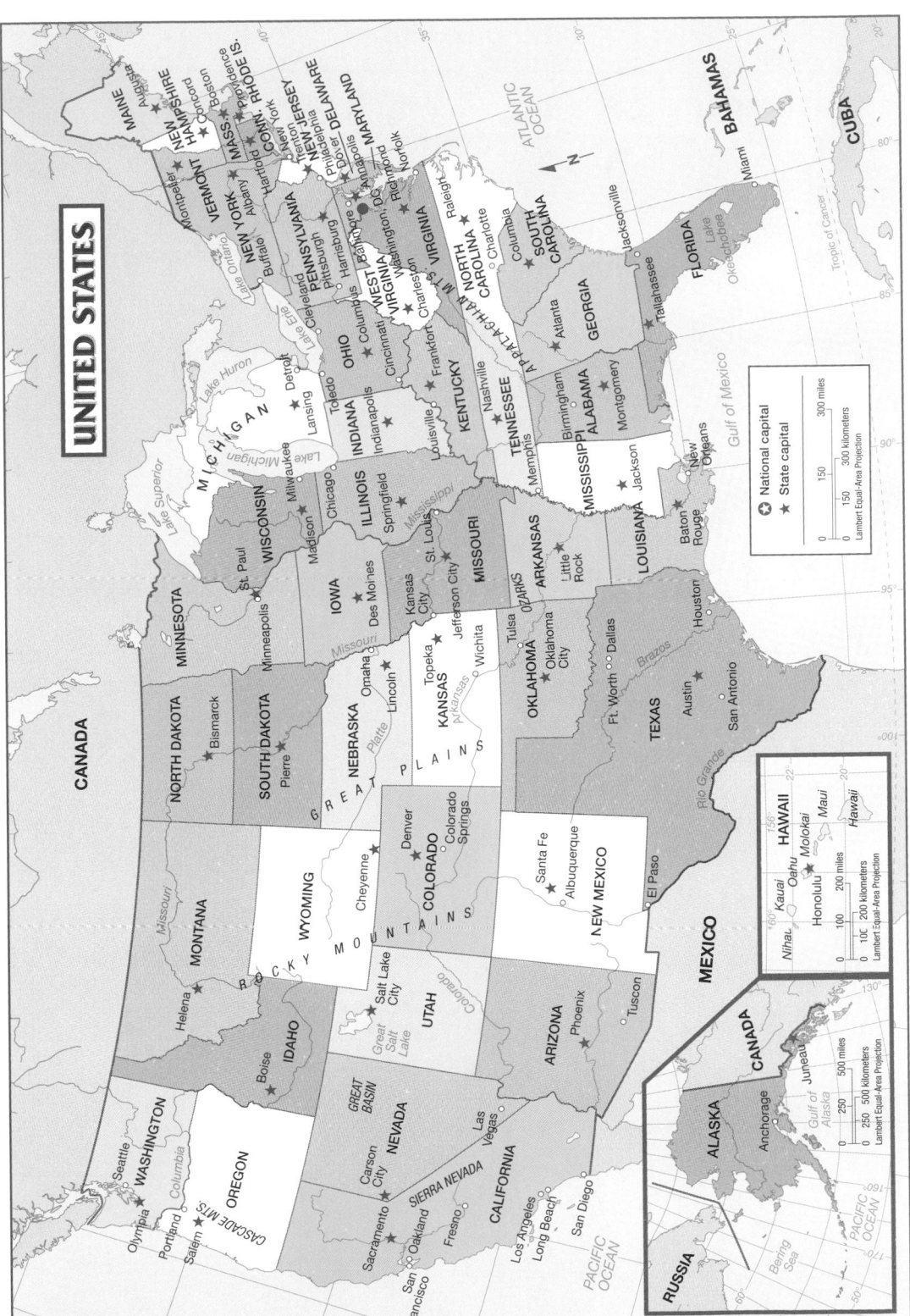

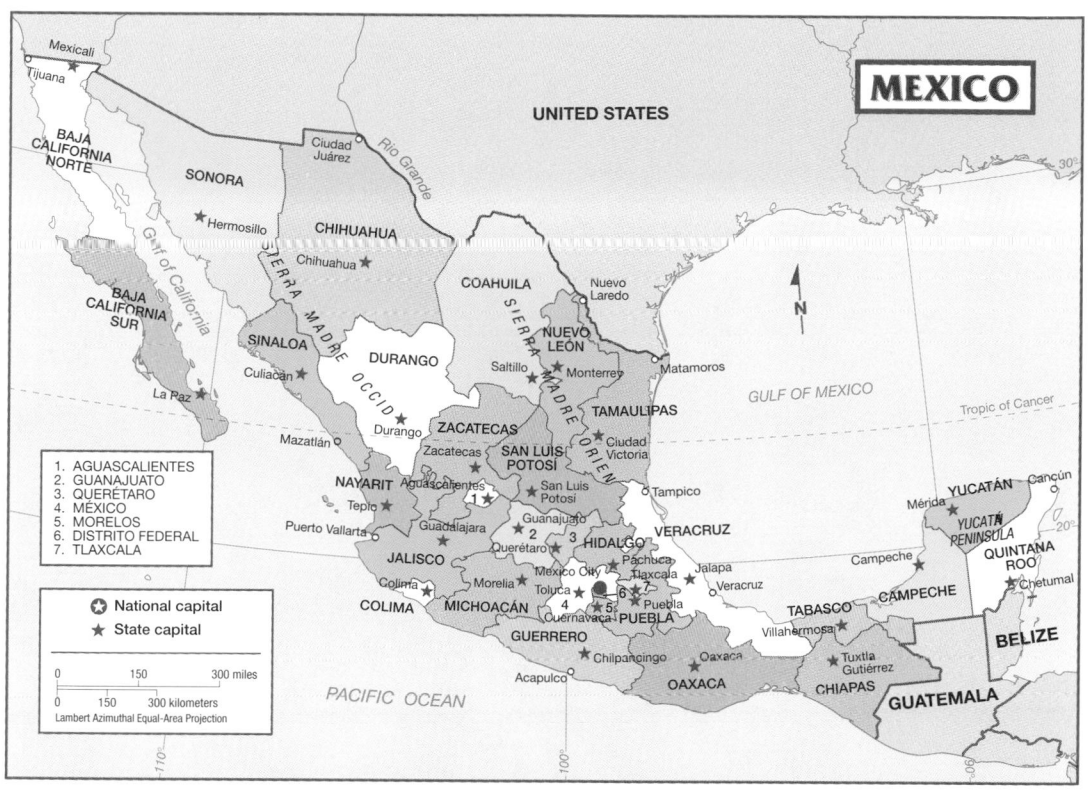

MEXICO

UNITED STATES

Mexicali
Tijuana
BAJA CALIFORNIA NORTE
SONORA
Ciudad Juárez
Rio Grande
CHIHUAHUA
Hermosillo
Chihuahua ★
COAHUILA
Nuevo Laredo
BAJA CALIFORNIA SUR
La Paz ★
Gulf of California
SIERRA MADRE OCCIDENTAL
SINALOA
Culiacán ★
DURANGO
Durango ★
NUEVO LEÓN
Saltillo ★ Monterrey
Matamoros
SIERRA MADRE ORIENTAL
GULF OF MEXICO
N
Tropic of Cancer
Mazatlán ★
ZACATECAS
Zacatecas ★
SAN LUIS POTOSÍ
Ciudad Victoria ★
TAMAULIPAS
1. AGUASCALIENTES
2. GUANAJUATO
3. QUERÉTARO
4. MÉXICO
5. MORELOS
6. DISTRITO FEDERAL
7. TLAXCALA
NAYARIT
Tepic ★
Aguascalientes
San Luis Potosí ★
Tampico
YUCATÁN
Cancún
Mérida ★
YUCATÁN PENINSULA
QUINTANA ROO
Chetumal
Puerto Vallarta ★
Guadalajara ★
Guanajuato
HIDALGO
VERACRUZ
Campeche ★
CAMPECHE
JALISCO
Querétaro ★
Pachuca ★
Tlaxcala ★ Jalapa ★
Veracruz
Colima ★
Morelia ★
Mexico City
Toluca ★
Cuernavaca ★
7
6
5
Puebla ★
TABASCO
Villahermosa ★
BELIZE
○ National capital
★ State capital
COLIMA
MICHOACÁN
4
PUEBLA
GUERRERO
Chilpancingo ★
Oaxaca ★
OAXACA
Tuxtla Gutiérrez ★
CHIAPAS
GUATEMALA
Acapulco
PACIFIC OCEAN
0   150   300 miles
0   150   300 kilometers
Lambert Azimuthal Equal-Area Projection

CANADA

ALASKA (U.S.)
Fairbanks
Banks Island
Victoria Island
Baffin Bay
Arctic Circle
GREENLAND (Denmark)
YUKON
Inuvik
Great Bear L.
Baffin Island
Godthåb
Whitehorse ★
NORTHWEST TERRITORIES
Yellowknife ★
Southampton Island
Igaluit (Frobisher Bay)
Narssarssuaq
N
Mackenzie
Hudson Strait
Labrador Sea
Great Slave L.
UNGAVA PENINSULA
ROCKIES
Peace
L. Athabasca
Reindeer L.
Hudson Bay
NEWFOUNDLAND
BRITISH COLUMBIA
Prince George
ALBERTA
Edmonton ★
Saskatchewan
Labrador
Goose Bay
Vancouver Island
Victoria ★
Calgary
SASKATCHEWAN
Saskatoon
L. Winnipeg
MANITOBA
QUÉBEC
Newfoundland
St. John's ★
PRINCE EDWARD ISLAND
Vancouver
Regina ★
Winnipeg ★
ONTARIO
Thunder Bay
L. Nipigon
Timmins
St. Lawrence
Québec ★
NEW BRUNSWICK
Charlottetown ★
Fredericton ★
Halifax
PACIFIC OCEAN
○ National capital
★ Province/Territory capital
0   250   500 miles
0   250   500 kilometers
Lambert Conformal Conic Projection
UNITED STATES
L. Michigan
L. Huron
Ottawa ●
Montréal ★
NOVA SCOTIA
Toronto ○
Hamilton
Windsor
L. Superior
L. Erie
L. Ontario
ATLANTIC OCEAN

Atlas

Atlas

INDEX

A

A.M. (ante meridiem), 5
Aalto, Alvar, 240
Aardvarks, 39
Aaron, Henry (Hank), 713
Abacus, 122, 243–244
Abbreviations, 413, 433. *See also*
  Acronyms
    common, 407–412
    cooking measurements, 536
    geographic directions, 904
    state, two-letter, 904
    street designators, 905
    territories, 904
    titles, 455
Abdul-Jabbar, Kareem [Lew
  Alcindor], 713
Abelard, Peter, 310
Abrasions, 480
Abstract expressionism, 230
Academy Awards, 209–215. *See also*
  Directors; Playwrights
Accured interest, 592
Acronyms, 404–406, 433
Act, 863
Actors/Actresses, 209–215
Acute accent ('), 415
Ad hominem fallacy, 313
Adam, Robert, 237
Adams, John Quincy, 861
Adams, John, 861
Additives. *See* Chemical additives
Adjective, 436–437
Adjustable life insurance, 580
Adjustable-rate mortgage (ARM),
  584–585
Adoption, 674
Advent, 306
Adverb, 436–437
Aerospace engineers, 141
Aeschylus, 203

Aestheticism, 261
Afghanistan
    currency, 789
    embassy, 801
    statistics, 914
    travel requirements, 796
Africa, map of, 976
Agassiz, Jean Louis Rodolphe, 146
Age of Reason (Enlightenment), 318
Agee, James, 248
Aging
    magazines, 678
    organizations, 638
    state commissions and aging, 642
    state commissions and offices,
      638–641
Agricola, Georgius (Georg Bauer),
  146
Agriculture Department, 671
Agriculture, 123
AIDS(acquired immune deficiency
  syndrome), 513
Aiken, Conrad, 248
Ailey, Alvin, 190
Air conditioning, 133
Air Force Academy, 677–678
Air mileage from New York City
    domestic flights, 758
    international flights, 788
Air safety hot line, 675
Airlines
    toll-free numbers, 738–742
    travel, people with disabilities, 734
    Web sites, 738–742
Airports, 742–747
Aisle, 243–244
Alabama
    botanical gardens, 380
    Commission on Aging, 638
    consumer affairs, 645
    crime statistics, 892–893,
      896–897

Alabama, *cont.*
　　domestic violence organizations,
　　　669
　　flower/bird/motto/nickname, 877
　　legislature, 876
　　name origin, 879
　　newspapers, 906
　　personal income per capita, 888
　　poison control centers, 489
　　population, 883
　　precipitation, 751
　　state tourism office, 747
　　temperatures, 753, 755
　　two-letter abbreviation, 904
　　wildlife refuges, 762–763, 778
　　zoos, 372
Alaska
　　Commission on Aging, 638
　　consumer affairs, 645
　　crime statistics, 894–897
　　domestic violence organziations,
　　　669
　　flower/bird/motto/nickname, 877
　　legislature, 876
　　name origin, 879
　　newspaper, 906
　　personal income per capita, 889
　　poison control centers, 489
　　population, 883
　　precipitation, 751
　　Standard Time, 8
　　state tourism office, 747
　　temperatures, 753, 755
　　two-letter abbreviation, 904
　　wildlife refuges, 763, 778
Albania
　　currency, 789
　　embassy, 801
　　statistics, 914
　　travel requirements, 796
Albee, Edward, 198
Albéniz, Isaac, 174
Albers, Josef, 218
Alberta, Canada
　　libraries, 344
　　museums, 369–371
　　zoos, 379
Alberti, Leone Battista, 239
Alcohol
　　champagne, 553
　　chemistry, 83
　　consumption, 531–532
　　during pregnancy, 501

　　mixed drinks, 553–556
　　serving amounts, 553
Alcoholism, 643–644. *See also* **Drug
abuse**
Alcott, Louisa May, 248
Alfalfa, 50
Algebra, 123
Algeria
　　Algiers, 954–955
　　currency, 789
　　embassy, 801
　　statistics, 914
　　telephone code, 972
　　travel requirements, 796
Algren, Nelson, 248
Ali, Muhammed [Cassius Clay], 713
All Saints' Day, 306
Allergies, 506–507
Alphabetization, 404
Alphabets
　　Arabic, 432
　　Braille, 400–401
　　Cyrillic, 432
　　commonly misspelled words,
　　　413–414
　　commonly misused words,
　　　412–413
　　consonants, 415
　　diacritical marks, 415
　　English, 404
　　Greek, 432
　　Hebrew, 432
　　Morse Code, 399
　　most recurring letters, 405
　　phonetic symbol, 415
　　pronunciation, 415
　　semaphore, 399
　　sign language, 400
　　vowels, 415
Altman, Robert, 205
Altocumulus (Ac) clouds, 96
Altostratus (As) cloud, 96
Alvarez, Luis Walter, 151
**Amendments to the Constitution,
849–854, 863**
America. *See* **North America; South
America; United States**
**American Bar Association (ABA),
633**
**American Civil Liberties Union
(ACLU), 634**
**American Crafts Council Library,
349**

American English, 415
**American flag, United States,
856–857**
**American Football Conference
(AFC), 698**
American League (AL) baseball, 688
**American Museum of Natural
History Library, 349**
American Revolution, 942
American Samoa
　　consumer affairs, 667
　　currency, 789
　　flower/bird/motto, 879
　　legislature, 877
　　telephone code, 972
　　Territorial Administration on
　　　Aging, 642
　　two-letter abbreviation, 904
American Sign Language. *See* **Sign
language**
**American Stock Exchange (AMEX),
592**
Amis, Kingsley, 255
Amish, 286
Amortization, 575, 585
Ampere, Andre Marie, 151
Amram, David, 164
Amusement parks, 779
Analects, The, 294
Analytical philosophy, 317
Anatomy. *See also* **Optic anatomy**
　　optic nerve, 124
Anaxagoras, 310
Anaximander, 310
Anaximenes, 310
Andersen, Hans Christian, 261
Anderson, Sherwood, 248
Andorra
　　currency, 789
　　embassy, 801
　　statistics, 914
　　telephone code, 972
　　travel requirements, 796
Angelico, Fra, 226
Angola
　　currency, 789
　　embassy, 801
　　statistics, 914
　　travel requirements, 796
Angry Young Men, 261–262
Anguilla
　　currency, 789
　　statistics, 914
　　tourist information, 780

Animals. *See also specific animals*
  bites, 480
  extinct, 40–42
  invertebrates, 40
  mammals
  marsupials, 37–38
    monotremes (egg-laying), 37
    placentals, 38–39
Anniversary gifts, 466
Announcements, wedding, 460–461
Annuities, 587
Anomalistic year, 10
Anouilh, Jean, 201
Anselm, St., 310
Ansky, Karl Guthe, 142
Antarctica
  map, 975
  statistics, 914
Antelope, 38
Anthropology, 352
Anthroposophy, 317
Antigua and Barbuda
  currency, 789
  embassy, 801
  statistics, 914
  tourist information, 780
  travel requirements, 796
Antioxidants, 547
Antiques, 352–353
Antonioni, Michelangelo, 208
Apollo moon missions, 115–116
Apostrophes (punctuation), 443
Appointments, business, 466
Appraisal, 585
Appreciation (investments), 592
Appropriate act, 863
Apse, 243–244
Aquariums, public
  California, 373
  Canada, 379
  Connecticut, 374
  Florida, 374
  Hawaii, 374
  Illinois, 374
  Louisiana, 375
  Maryland, 375
  Massachusetts, 375
  New York, 376
  Ohio, 377
  Tennessee, 378
  Texas, 378
  Washington, 378
Aqueduct, 122

Aquinas, St. Thomas, 310, 328
Arabic alphabet, 432
Arboretums, 380–384
Archimedes, 148
Architects
  American, 235–237
  Austrian, 240
  Brazilian, 240
  British, 237
  Dutch, 240
  Finnish, 240
  French, 238
  German, 240
  Italian, 239
  Spanish, 240
Architecture
  crossing, 244
  elements, 243–246
  movements and styles, 240–241
  reference works, 353–354
  Seven Wonders of the Ancient
    World, 931, 962–963
  skyscraper, 131
Architrave, 243–244
Argentina
  Córdoba, 955
  currency, 789
  embassies, 801
  major cities 955, 957
  standard time, 9
  statistics, 914
  telephone code, 972
  tourist information, 780
  travel requirements, 796
Aristophanes, 203
Aristotelianism, 317
Aristotle, 141, 310, 324
Arizona
  Aging and Adult Administration,
    638
  art museums, 362
  botanical gardens, 380
  consumer affairs, 645–646
  crime statistics, 894–897
  flower/bird/motto/nickname, 877
  legislature, 876
  libraries, 336
  name origin, 879
  newspapers, 906
  personal income per capita, 889
  poison control centers, 489
  population, 883
  precipitation, 751

  state tourism office, 747
  temperatures, 753, 755
  two-letter abbreviation, 904
  wildlife refuges, 763, 778
  zoos, 372
Arkansas
  consumer affairs, 646
  crime statistics, 894–895
  Division of Aging and Adult
    Services, 638
  domestic violence organizations,
    669
  flower/bird/motto/nickname, 877
  General Assembly, 876
  name origin, 879
  newspapers, 906
  personal income per capita, 889
  poison control centers, 489
  population, 883
  state tourism office, 748
  two-letter abbreviation, 904
  wildlife refuges, 764, 778
  zoos, 373
Armadillos, 39
Armah, Ayi Kwch, 253
Armed conflict. *See* Wars
Armenia
  currency, 789
  embassies, 801
  statistics, 914
  travel requirements, 796
Armstrong, Louis "Satchmo," 175
Arp, Jean (Hans), 223
Arpino, Gerald, 190
**ARPnet (Advanced Research
  Projects), 108**
Arrhenius, Svante August, 144
Art deco, 230
Art museums, 362–369
  Arizona, 362
  California, 362–363
  Canada, 370
  Colorado, 363
  Connecticut, 363
  Delaware, 364
  District of Columbia, 364
  Hawaii, 364
  Illinois, 364–365
  Indiana, 365
  Kansas, 365
  Kentucky, 365
  Maryland, 365
  Massachusetts, 365–366

Art museums, *cont.*
Michigan, 366
Minnesota, 366
Missouri, 366
New Jersey, 366
New Mexico, 366
New York, 367–368
Ohio, 368
Oklahoma, 368
Oregon, 368
Pennsylvania, 368–369
Texas, 369
Virginia, 369
Wisconsin, 369
Art nouveau, 230
Art terminology, 233–235
Artemision at Ephesus, 962
Arthropods, 40
Arthur, Chester, 861
Article, 436
Artificial insemination, 126–127
Artificial limbs, 124
Artists, visual
American, 218–221
Austrian, 230
Belgian/Flemish, 221
British, 221–222
Dutch, 222
French, 223–225
German, 225–226
Greek, 230
Italian, 226–228
Mexican, 228
Norwegian, 230
reference works, 353–354
Romanian, 230
Russian, 228–229
Spanish, 229
Swiss, 230
Aruba
currency, 789
embassy, 801
statistics, 914
telephone code, 973
tourist information, 780
travel requirements, 796
Ascension Day, 305
ASCII (American Standard Code for Information Interchange), 109
Ash Can School, 230
Ashe, Arthur, 713
Ashton, Sir Frederick, 192

Asia
holidays, 19–21
map, 978
Asimov, Isaac, 248
Aspects and nodes, 388
Aspirin, 133
Assessed valuation, 585
Assets, 592
Association of ideas (laws of association), 322–323
Assumable mortgage, 585
Assumption of the Blessed Virgin Mary, 305
Astaire, Fred, 190
Asteroids, 72, 77
Asters, 49
Asthma, 507
Astrology, zodiac signs, 395
Astronauts. *See* Space exploration
Astronomers, 74, 141–144
Astronomy
terminology, 76–80
aspects and nodes, 388
coordinates, 388
eclipses, 68–71, 78
Halley's comet, 125
magazines, 119
moon phases, 68, 388
orbital elements, 388
planets, 72, 388
reference works, 354
stars, 73–76, 80, 388
symbols, 388
units of measurement, 388
Atheism, 323
Atomic bomb, 137
Atomic clocks, 5
Atomism, 323
Atoms, structure concept, 122
Attire, etiquette, 469
Atwood, Margaret, 257
Auchincloss, Louis [Stanton], 248
Auden, W(ystan) H(ugh), 248
Audio books, 668
Audubon, John James, 143, 248
Augustine of Hippo, St., 310
Austen, Jane, 255
Austin, Mary, 248
Australia
currency, 789
embassy, 802
map, 979
standard time, 9

statistics, 914
tourist information, 780
travel requirements, 796
Austria
currency, 789
embassy, 802
standard time, 9
statistics, 914
telephone code, 972
tourist information, 780
travel requirements, 796
Vienna, 957
Authors. *See also* Literature; Playwrights; Poet laureates
African, 253–254
American, 248–253
Asian, 254
Australian, 254–255
British, 255–257
Canadian, 257–258
Czech, 261
Danish, 261
French, 258–259
German, 259
Greek, 261
Irish, 261
Italian, 259
Latin American, 259–260
Norwegian, 261
pseudonyms, 264–266
Roman, 261
Russian, 260
Spanish, 261
Auto racing, 684, 727, 730
drag racing, 684
flags, 684
Formula 1, 684
Foyt, A.J., 714–715
Indianapolis 500, 684–686
Petty, Richard, 717
stock cars, 684
Auto safety hot line, 675
Automobiles
insurance, 581–582
maintenance, 570
registration marks, international, 786–787
rental agencies, 736–737
safety, 675
road signs, 398
Autumn/fall season, 11, 60
Autumnal equinox, 11

Averroes, 310, 324
Avicenna, 149, 310, 324
Ayers, Alfred Jules, 310–311
Azerbaijan
    Baku, 954
    statistics, 915

B

Babbage, Charles, 146
Baby-sitters, 570
Bach, Johann Sebastian, 170
Bachelor dinner, weddings, 461
Back pain, 507
Backgammon, 719–720
Bacon, Francis (artist), 221
Bacon, Sir Francis, 311
Bacteria, 62, 544
Bad faith, 323
Bagpipe, 160
Baha'i religion, 284
Bahamas
    currency, 789
    embassy, 802
    statistics, 915
    tourist information, 781
    travel requirements, 796
Bahrain
    currency, 789
    embassy, 802
    statistics, 915
    telephone code, 972
    travel requirements, 796
Baker v. Carr, 624
Baking. *See* Food
Baku, 962
    currency, 789
    embassy, 802
    statistics, 923
    travel requirements, 796
Balanchine, George, 190
Baldwin, James, 248
Balloon payment, 585
Balzac, Honoré de, 258
Bandages, 479
Bangladesh
    Chittagong, 955
    currency, 789
    Dhaka, 955
    embassy, 802
    major cities, 955
    statistics, 915
    tourist information, 781
    travel requirements, 796

Bank accounts, 587
Bannister, Roger, 713
Baptists, 286
Baraka, Imamu Amiri, 248
Barbados
    currency, 789
    embassy, 802
    statistics, 915
    tourist information, 781
    travel requirements, 796
Barber, Samuel, 164
Barbizon School, 230
Barbuda
    statistics, 914
    travel requirements, 796
Baroque
    art movement, 231, 240
    musical style, 179, 262
Barrel vault, 243, 246
Barry, Philip, 198
Barth, John [Simmons], 248
Barthelme, Donald, 248
Bartlett, John, 248
Bartók, Béla, 174
Baryshnikov, Mikhail, 193
Base, 242
Baseball, 686–687, 727–728, 730
    Aaron, Henry (Hank), 713
    American League (AL), 688
    Cobb, Ty, 714
    DiMaggio, Joe, 714
    Gehrig, Lou, 715
    Griffey, Ken, Jr., 715
    Henderson, Rickey, 715
    Jackson, Reggie, 715
    Johnson, Randy, 716
    Mantle, Mickey, 716
    Maris, Roger, 717
    Mays, Willie, 717
    National League (NL), 688
    Rickey, Branch, 718
    Ripken, Cal, Jr., 718
    Robinson, Jackie, 718
    Ruth, Babe [George Herman], 718
    Ryan, Nolan, 718
    Stengel, Casey [Charles Dillon], 719
    World Series, 689–690
    Young, Cy, 719
Bashōmatsuo Munefusa, 254
Basie, William "Count," 175

Basketball, 690–691, 728, 730
    Abdul-Jabbar, Kareem [Lew Alcindor], 713
    Bird, Larry, 713
    Chamberlain, Wilt, 714
    Johnson, Earvin ("Magic"), 715–716
    Jordan, Michael, 716
    National Basketball Association (NBA), 691–692
    Rodman, Dennis, 718
    Smith, Dean, 719
    Wooden, John, 719
Bass drum, 162
Bassoon, 160
Bateson, William, 143
Bathroom fixtures, standard sizes, 567
Bats, 38
Batteries, 389
Battle of Hastings, 940
Battles. *See* War
Baudelaire, Charles Pierre, 258
Bauhaus, 240
Baum, L(yman) Frank, 249
Bay of Pigs, 947
Beach, Amy Marcy, 164
Beans, 50
Bear market, 592
Bears, 38
Beat Generation, 262
Beattie, Ann, 249
Beaumont, Francis, 199
Becker, Boris, 713
Beckett, Samuel, 201–202
Beckmann, Max, 225
Becoming, 323
Becquerel, Antoine Henri, 151
Beeches, 50
Beef. *See* Meat
Beethoven, Ludwig van, 170
Begonias, 49
Behrens, Peter, 240
Beiderbecke, Bix, 175
Being, 323
Béjart, Maurice, 193
Belarus
    currency, 789
    embassy, 802
    Minsk, 956
    statistics, 915
    travel requirements, 796

Belgium
  Brussels, 954
  currency, 789
  embassy, 802
  standard time, 9
  statistics, 915
  telephone code, 972
  tourist information, 781
  travel requirements, 796
Belize
  currency, 789
  embassy, 802
  statistics, 915
  telephone code, 972
  tourist information, 781
  travel requirements, 796
**Bellini, Jacopo, Gentile, and
  Giovanni, 226**
Bellini, Vincenzo, 171
Belloc, Joseph Hilaire Peter, 255
Bellow, Saul, 249
Belugas, 38
Benchley, Robert, 249
Benét, Stephen Vincent, 249
Benét, William Rose, 249
Benin
  currency, 789
  embassy, 802
  statistics, 915
  travel requirements, 796
Bentham, Jeremy, 311, 324
Berg, Alban, 166
Bergman, Ingmar, 205, 209
Berkeley, George, 311
Berlage, Hendrik Petrus, 240
Berlioz, Hector, 168
Bermuda
  currency, 789
  embassy, 802
  statistics, 915
  tourist information, 781
  travel requirements, 796
Bernard, Claude, 149
**Bernini, Giovanni Lorenzo
  (Gianlorenzo), 239**
Bernini, Giovanni Lorenzo, 226
Bernoulli, Daniel, 148
Bernstein, Leonard, 164
Beti, Mongo [Alexandre Biyidi], 253
**Better Business Bureau, United
  States, 645**
Beverages, serving sizes, 543
Bhagavad Gita, 294

Bhutan
  currency, 789
  embassy, 802
  statistics, 915
  tourist information, 781
  travel requirements, 796
Bible, 294–295, 360
Bicycle racing, 728, 731
  Tour de France, 693–694
Bicycle, 131
Bierce, Ambrose, 249
Bifocal lenses, 127
Big bang model, 77
Big Board, 592
Bill of sale, 598
Bill, U.S. Congressional 863–866
Binder, 585
Bioethics, 323
Biogradable materials, 569
Biography, 277, 351
Biologists, 143
Biology
  symbols, 389
  terminology, 62–65
Biondi, Matt, 713
Birches, 50
Bird, Larry, 713
Birds, extinct, 41–42
Birthstones and flowers, 396
Bison, 38
Bizet, Georges, 168
Black Death, 933
Black dwarfs, 73
Black holes, 73–74, 139
Blackjack, 724
Blackwell, Elizabeth, 149
Blair, Bonnie, 713
Blake, William, 222, 255
Blasco Ibañez, Vicente, 261
Blastomycosis, 513
Bleeding, stopping, 475–478
Blindness
  audio books, 668
  Braille, 400–401
  traveling, 734, 736
Blitzstein, Marc, 164
Bloch, Ernest, 164
Blok, Alexander Alexandrovich, 260
Bloomsbury Group, 262
Blue chip, 592
Blue Cross/Blue Shield, 579
Blue supergiants, 74
Boar War, 944

Board games, 729
  backgammon, 719–720
  checkers, 720–721
  chess, 721–722
  Monopoly®, 722–723
  Scrabble®, 723–724
Boccaccio, Giovanni, 259
Boccherini, Luigi, 171
Boccioni, Umberto, 226
Boethius, 311
Bohr theory, 100
Bohr, Niels Hendrik David, 151
Boils and blisters, first aid, 480
Boito, Arrigo, 171
Bolivia
  currency, 789
  embassy, 802
  La Paz, 956
  statistics, 915
  telephone code, 972
  travel requirements, 796
Böll, Heinrich, 259
Bonaire
  embassy, 802
  tourist information, 781
Bonaparte, Napoleon. *See*
  Napoleon I
Bond funds, 590
Bonds, finance, 588, 592–594
Bones
  animals, 45
  humans. *See* Skeletal system
Bonnard, Pierre, 223
Bontemps, Arna, 249
Book value, 592
Borg, Bjorn, 713
Borges, Jorge Luis, 259
Borlaug, Norman Ernest, 143
Borodin, Aleksandr, 173
Borromini, Francesco, 239
Bosch, Hieronymus, 222
**Bosnia and Herzegovina, Republic
  of**
  currency, 789
  embassy, 803
  statistics, 916
  travel requirements, 796
Boswell, James, 255
Botanical gardens, public, 380–384
  Kansas, 381
  Alabama, 380
  Arizona, 380
  California, 380

Colorado, 380
Connecticut, 380
Delaware, 380
District of Columbia, 381
Florida, 381
Georgia, 381
Idaho, 381
Illinois, 381
Indiana, 381
Louisiana, 382
Maine, 382
Maryland, 382
Massachusetts, 382
Michigan, 382
Missouri, 382
New Hampshire, 382
New Jersey, 382
New Mexico, 382
New York, 382–383
North Carolina, 383
North Dakota, 383
Ohio, 383
Oklahoma, 383
Oregon, 383
Pennsylvania, 383
Rhode Island, 383
South Carolina, 383–384
Tennessee, 384
Texas, 384
Washington, 384
Wisconsin, 384
Botany
ground covers, 56
plant names, 51–55
vine names, 56
Botswana, Republic of
currency, 789
embassy, 803
statistics, 916
travel requirements, 796
Botticelli, Sandro, 226
Botulism, 513
Boulanger, Lili, 168
Boulez, Pierre, 168
Bowed instruments, 159
Bowers v. Hardwick, 625
Bowling, 694–695, 728, 731
Bowman, Sir William, 149
Boxing
Ali, Muhammed [Cassius Clay], 713
Corbett, James J. ("Gentleman Jim"), 714
Foreman, George, 714

Leonard, Sugar Ray, 716
Louis, Joe, 716
Marciano, Rocky, 716
Tyson, Mike, 719
Boyle, Kay, 249
Boyle, Robert, 144
Boyle's law, 100
Brackets (punctuation), 442
Bradbury, Ray, 249
Bradstreet, Anne, 249
Brahe, Tycho, 141
Brahms, Johannes, 170
Braille alphabet, 400–401
Brain, 35
Bramante (Donato di Angelo di Antonio), 239
Brancusi, Constantin, 230
Braque, Georges, 223
Brazil
Belo Horizonte, 954
currency, 789
embassy, 803
Pôrto Alegre, 956
Rio de Janeiro, 957
Salvador, 957
São Paulo, 957
standard time, 9
statistics, 916
telephone code, 972
tourist information, 781
travel requirements, 796
Breast cancer, 511–513
Breathing, first aid, 474
Brecht, Bertolt, 202
Breton, André, 258
Breve, 415
Bridge (card game), 724–725
Bridges, suspension, 123
British Columbia (Canada)
aquariums, 379
libraries, 345
museums, 370
poison control center, 492
zoos, 379
British empiricism, 317
British English, 415, 443
British idealism, 317
British Virgin Islands
currency, 789
embassy, 803
statistics, 916
tourist information, 781
travel requirements, 796

Britten, (Edward) Benjamin, 167
Broca, Pierre Paul, 149
Broker, 585
Brongniart, Alexandre, 146
Bronté, Charlotte, 255
Bronté, Emily, 255
Brooks, Gwendolyn, 249
Brown v. Board of Education of Topeka, 624
Brown, Jim, 713
Browning, Elizabeth Barrett, 255
Browning, Robert, 255
Bruch, Max, 170
Bruckner, Anton, 166
Bruegel, Pieter, the Elder, 221
Brunei Darussalam, State of
currency, 789
embassy, 803
statistics, 916
travel requirements, 796
Brunelleschi, Filippo, 239
Bryant, Paul ("Bear"), 713–714
Buber, Martin, 311
Bubka, Sergei, 714
Buchanan, James, 861
Buchner, Georg, 202
Buck, Pearl, 249
Buddhism, 284, 292, 394
Budgets
personal, 575–576
government 179, 863
Bujones, Fernando, 190
Bulfinch, Charles, 235
Bulgakov, Mikhail, 260
Bulgaria, Republic of
currency, 789
embassy, 803
Sofia, 957
statistics, 916
tourist information, 781
travel requirements, 796
Bull market, 592
Bulletin board system (BBS), 110
Burbank, Luther, 143
Burgess, Anthony, 255
Burial, funeral etiquette, 472
Buridan's ass, 323
Burkina Faso
currency, 789
embassy, 803
statistics, 916
travel requirements, 796
Burma. *See* **Myanmar**
Burnham, Daniel Hudson, 235

Burns
    first aid, 480–481, 507
    pets, 45–46
Burns, Robert, 255
Burroughs, Edgar Rice, 249
Burroughs, William S., 249
Burundi, Republic of
    currency, 789
    embassy, 803
    statistics, 916
    travel requirements, 796
Buses, people with disabilities, 736
Bush, George, 862
Business
    appointments, 466
    directories, 351
    entertainment, 467
    gifts, 467
    letter writing, 446–447
    reference works, 354–355
    telephone, 467–468
Business symbols, 401
Butkus, Dick, 714
Button, Dick, 714
Buñuel, Luis, 209
Buys Ballot, Christoph Hendrik Diederik, 146
Byrd, William, 167
Byron, Lord [George Gordon], 255
Byzantine, 231, 240

C

Cacti, 50
Caffeine, during pregnancy, 501
Cage, John, 165
Calcium, 526–527
Calculators, 134, 136
Calculus, 391
Calder, Alexander, 218
Calderón de la Barca, Pedro, 204
Calendars, 124
    days, 10
    Egyptian, 931
    Gregorian, 12
    Jewish, 931
    Julian, 12
    lunar, 10–11
    perpetual, 13–17
    Roman, 12
    years, 10
California
    aquariums, 373
    botanical gardens, 380
    consumer affairs, 646–648

crime statistics, 894–897
    Department of Aging, 638
    domestic violence organizations, 669
    Families Anonymous, 643
    flower/bird/motto/nickname, 877
    legislature, 876
    libraries, 336–337
    Los Angeles, 956
    museums
        art, 362–363
        children, 372
    name origin, 879
    Narcotics Anonymous, 643
    newspapers, 906
    personal income per capita, 889
    poison control centers, 489
    population, 883
    precipitation, 751
    state tourism office, 748
    temperatures, 753, 755
    theme parks, 779
    two-letter abbreviation, 904
    wildlife refuges, 764–765, 778
    zoos, 373
Calories, burning, 530
Calvino, Italo, 259
Camargo, Marie, 193
Cambodia, Kingdom of
    currency, 789
    embassy, 803
    statistics, 916
    travel requirements, 796
Cambrian period, 93
Cambridge Platonists, 317
Camels, 38
Cameroon, Republic of
    statistics, 916
    telephone code, 972
    currency, 789
    embassy, 803
    travel requirements, 796
Camping, people with disabilities, 736
Campion, Jane, 205
Camus, Albert, 258
Canada
    Alberta
        Calgary, 955
        Edmonton, 955
        libraries, 344
        museums, 369–370
        zoos, 379
    British Columbia

        aquariums, 379
        libraries, 345
        museums, 370–371
        poison control center, 492
        Vancouver, 957
        zoos, 379
    currency, 789
    embassy, 803
    holidays, 19
    Manitoba, 379
    map, 983
    museums
    Nova Scotia, 493
    Ontario
        libraries, 344
        Montreal, 956
        museums; 370
        Ottawa, 956
        poison control center, 493
        Toronto, 957
        zoos, 379
    prime ministers, 970
    Quebec
        aquariums, 379
        Montreal, 964
        poison control center, 493
        Quebec City, 965
        zoos, 379
    standard time zones, 8–9
    statistics, 924
    time zones map, 8
    tourist information, 781
    travel requirements, 796
    statistics, 916
Cancer, breast self-examination, 511–512
Candela (cd), 26
Candlemas, 304
Canctti, Elias, 259
Cannizzaro, Stanislao, 144
Cannons, 123
Canonical hours, 294
Canova, Antonio, 226
Capacitors, 389
Capacity (dry and liquid) metric system, 24–25, 27
Cape Verde, Republic of
    currency, 789
    embassy, 803
    statistics, 916
    travel requirements, 796
Capek, Karel, 261
Capital, 242–243
Capitalization, 592

Capote, Truman, 249
Capra, Frank, 204
Caravaggio, Michelangelo Merisi da, 226
Carbon dioxide, 126
Card games, 729
  Blackjack, 724
  bridge, 724–725
  pinochle, 725
  poker, 725–726
  rummy, 726
  solitaire, 726–727
Cardiopulmonary resuscitation (CPR), 474–475
Carracci, Annibale, Agostino, and Ludovico, 226
Carroll, Lewis [Charles Lutwidge Dodgson], 255
Cars
  maintenance, 570
  registration marks, international, 786–787
  racing. *See* Auto racing
  rental agencies, 736–737
  safety hot line, 675
Carson, Rachel Louise, 146
Carter, Betty, 175
Carter, James (Jimmy), 862
Cartesianism, 317
Cartography
  Mercator projection, 94
  meridian, 94
  parallel, 94
  prime meridian, 95
  projection, 95
  relief, 95
  scale, 95
  symbols, 396–397
Carving turkey, 541
Cassatt, Mary, 218
Cassini, Giovanni Domenico, 141
Castanets, 162
Castle, Vernon, 190
Categorical imperative, 323
Cather, Willa, 249
Catholicism. *See* Roman Catholicism
Cats, 38. *See also* Pets
  diseases, 46
  immunizations, 44–45
  training, 43
  traveling with, 735
Cattle, 38
Catullus, 261

Cauchy, Baron Augustin Louis, 148
Caucus, 863
Cause, 323
Cavafy, C. P., 253
Cayman Islands
  currency, 789
  embassy, 803
  statistics, 916
  tourist information, 781
  travel requirements, 796
CD-ROM, 110, 140
Cedilla, 415
Ceilings, standard sizes, 566
Cellini, Benvenuto, 226
Celsius temperature scale, 29, 126
Celsius, Anders, 151
Cenozoic geological era, 85–86
Central African Republic
  currency, 789
  embassy, 803
  statistics, 917
  travel requirements, 796
Central America, holidays, 20–21
Central Standard Time (CST), 8
Certainty, 323
Certificate of Notary, 599
Cervantes Saavedra, Miguel de, 261
Cesaire, Aimé, 259
Cézanne, Paul, 223
Chad, Republic of
  currency, 789
  embassy, 803
  statistics, 917
  travel requirements, 796
Chadwick, Sir James, 151
Chagall, Marc, 228
Chain of being, 323
Chamber music, 180
Chamberlain, Wilt, 714
Chambers, Sir William, 237
Champagne, 553
Chandler, Raymond, 249
Chaplin, Charlie, 205, 207
Chardin, Jean-Baptiste Siméon, 223
Chatterje, Bankim-Chandra, 254
Chaucer, Geoffrey, 255
Chávez, Carlos, 174
Chayefsky, Paddy (Sidney), 198
Checkers, 720–721
Cheetahs, 38
Cheever, John, 249
Chekhov, Anton Pavlovich, 203, 260

Chelating agents, 547
Chemical burns, 481
Chemicals
  during pregnancy, 501
  food additives, 547–551
    outlawed, 552
  hazardous, disposal, 568–569
Chemistry
  terminology, 82–84
  elements, 80–81, 83, 126–127
  Periodic Table of the Elements, The, 81–82
  symbols, 389
Chemists, 144–145
Chen Kaige, 207
Cherubini, Maria Luigi, 171
Chess, 721–722
Chicken pox (Varicella), 513
  during pregnancy, 501
Chief executive. *See* Presidents
Children
  abuse, 644, 675
  adoption, 674
  babysitters, 570
  family planning, 671
  finances, 576
  gay/lesbian youth hot line, 675
  height, 506
  hot lines, 675
  immunizations, 502–503
  literature, 276
  museums
    California, 372
    District of Columbia, 371
    Massachusetts, 371
    Missouri, 371
    New York, 371
    Pennsylvania, 372
  parenting, 679
  pets, 44
  runaways, 644
  weight, 506
  with disabilities, 644
Chile
  currency, 790
  embassy, 804
  Santiago, 957
  standard time, 9
  statistics, 917
  telephone code, 972
  tourist information, 781
  travel requirements, 796
Chimpanzees, 39

China, People's Republic of
  Beijing, 954
  currency, 790
  dynasties, 963–964
  embassy, 804
  embassy, 804
  Great Wall, 122
  Guangzhou, 955
  Harbin, 955
  Nanjing, 956
  Shanghai, 957
  standard time, 9
  statistics, 917
  Tianjin, 957
  tourist information, 781
  travel requirements, 797
Chipmunks, 39
Chirico, Giorgio de, 226
Chiropractic, 514
Choir, 243–244
Choking, 481–482
Chopin, Frédéric François, 174
Chopin, Kate, 249
Choreographers
  American, 190–192
  Austrian, 195
  British, 192–193
  Cuba, 195
  Danish, 195
  French, 193
  German, 195
  Italian, 195
  Russian, 193–195
Christianity, 394
Christie, Agatha, 255
Christmas Day, 306
Christmas Island
  statistics, 917
Chromosome, 62 63
Church of Christ, 286
Church of England, 286
Church of Jesus Christ of Latter
  Day Saints, The (Mormons), 289
Churches. *See* **Religion;** *specific*
  churches
Churchill, Caryl, 199
Cinématographe, 205
Circle, 103–104
Circular cylinder, 105
Circulation, first aid, 474
Circumflex, 415
Cirrocumulus (Cc) cloud, 96
Cirrostratus (Cs) cloud, 96
Cirrus (Ci) cloud, 96

Cities, major world
  population, 962–966
  standard time zones, 9
Civets, 38
Civil Rights Commission, 671
Civil War (U.S.), 943
Clarinet, 160
Clarke, Arthur C(harles), 255
Classical music, 180, 262
  composers, 166, 168–169,
    171–175
    Albéniz, Isaac, 174
    Amram, David, 164
    Barber, Samuel, 164
    Bartók, Béla, 174
    Beach, Amy Marcy, 164
    Berg, Alban, 166
    Berlioz, Hector, 168
    Bernstein, Leonard, 164
    Bizet, Georges, 168
    Blitzstein, Marc, 164
    Bloch, Ernest, 164
    Boccherini, Luigi, 171
    Boito, Arrigo, 171
    Borodin, Aleksandr, 173
    Boulanger, Lili, 168
    Boulez, Pierre, 168
    Britten, (Edward) Benjamin,
      167
    Bruckner, Anton, 166
    Byrd, William, 167
    Cage, John, 165
    Chávez, Carlos, 174
    Cherubini, Maria Luigi, 171
    Chopin, Frédéric François, 174
    Clementi, Muzio, 171
    Copeland, Aaron, 165
    Copland, Aaron, 165
    Corelli, Arcangelo, 171
    Corigliano, John, 165
    Couperin, François, 168
    Cowell, Henry Dixon, 165
    Czerny, Karl, 166
    Dallapiccola, Luigi, 172
    Debussy, Claude, 168
    Delibes, (Clément Philibert)
      Léo, 168
    Delius, Frederick, 167
    Dello Joio, Norman, 165
    Donizetti, Gaetano, 172
    Dowland, John, 167
    Dukas, Paul, 168
    Dvořák, Antonín, 174

    Elgar, Sir Edward, 167
    Falla, Manuel de, 174
    Fauré, Gabriel, 168
    Franck, César, 169
    Gershwin, George, 165
    Gibbons, Orlando, 167
    Glinka, Mikhail, 173
    Gounod, Charles, 169
    Grainger, Percy Aldridge, 174
    Granados, Enrique, 174
    Grieg, Edvard, 174
    Handel, George Frideric, 170
    Hanson, Howard, 165
    Haydn, Franz Joseph, 166
    Haydn, Johann Michael, 166
    Hindemith, Paul, 170
    Holst, Gustav, 167
    Honegger, Arthur, 169
    Humperdinck, Engelbert, 170
    Ibert, Jacques François Antoine,
      169
    Ives, Charles, 165
    Janáček, Leos, 174
    Khachaturian, Aram, 173
    Kodàly, Zoltàn, 174
    Lasso, Orlando di (Roland de
      Lassus), 175
    Leoncavallo, Ruggiero, 172
    Liszt, Franz, 175
    Lully, Jean-Baptiste, 169
    MacDowell, Edward, 165
    Mahler, Gustav, 167
    Mascagni, Pietro, 172
    Massenet, Jules Emile Frédéric,
      169
    Mendelssohn, Felix, 171
    Menotti, Gian Carlo, 165
    Messiaen, Olivier Eug·ne Prosper
      Charles, 169
    Meyerbeer, Giacomo, 171
    Milhaud, Darius, 169
    Monteverdi, Claudio, 172
    Moore, Douglas, 165
    Morley, Thomas, 168
    Mozart, Wolfgang Amadeus,
      167
    Mussorgsky, Modest, 173
    Nielsen, Carl, 175
    Offenbach, Jacques, 169
    Orff, Carl, 171
    Paderewski, Ignace, 175
    Palestrina, Giovanni Pierluigi
      da (Johannes Praenestinus),
      172

Pergolesi, Giovanni Battista, 172
Piston, Walter, 166
Poulenc, Francis, 169
Prokofiev, Sergei, 173
Puccini, Giacomo, 172
Purcell, Henry, 168
Rachmaninoff, Sergei, 173
Rameau, Jean-Philippe, 169
Ravel, Maurice, 169
Respighi, Ottorino, 172
Rimsky-Korsakov, Nicolai, 173
Rossini, Gioacchino, 172
Rubinstein, Anton, 173
Saint-Saëns, Charles Camille, 169
Scarlatti, (Giuseppe) Domenico, 172
Scarlatti, Alessandro, 172
Schoenberg, Arnold, 166
Schubert, Franz Seraph Peter, 167
Schuman, William, 166
Schumann, Clara Josephine née Wieck, 171
Schumann, Robert, 171
Scriabin, Aleksandr, 173
Sessions, Roger, 166
Shostakovich, Dmitri, 173
Sibelius, Jean, 175
Smetana, Bedrich, 175
Strauss, Johann I, Johann II, Josef, and Eduard I, 167
Strauss, Richard, 171
Stravinsky, Igor, 173
Sullivan, Sir Arthur, 168
Tallis, Thomas, 168
Tartini, Giuseppe, 172
Tchaikovsky, Peter Ilyich, 174
Thomson, Virgil, 166
Var·se, Edgar, 166
Vaughan Williams, Ralph, 168
Verdi, Giuseppe, 172
Villa-Lobos, Heitor, 175
Vivaldi, Antonio, 172
Wagner, Richard, 171
Weber, Carl Maria von, 171
Webern, Anton von, 167
Wieniawski, Henri, 175
Zwilich, Ellen Taafe, 166
Classical revival, 241
Classicism, 231, 241, 262

Clause, 437–438, 441
Clavell, James [du Maresq], 254
Clavichord, 158
Clementi, Muzio, 171
Cleveland, Grover, 861
Clinton, William, 862
Clocks, 4
   atomic, 5
   computer, 110
   mechanical, 5, 123
   pendulum, 125
   portable, 123
   quartz, 5
   spring-driven, 5
   sundials, 5
   water, 5
Cloning
   animals, 141
   genes, 140
Closing (mortgage), 585
Cloth, woven, 122
Clothing
   cotton, 557
   linen, 557
   size conversions, 565
   stain removal, 559–564
   Synthetics, 557
   washing instructions, 557–559
Cloture, 863–864
Clouds, 96–97
Coalition, 864
Coast Guard Academy, 677
Coaxial cable, 135
Cobb, Ty, 714
Cocos Islands, 790
Coelenterates, 40
Coffee, 557
Cohen, Stanley H, 143
Colds, home rememdies, 507, 513
Coleman, Ornette, 175–176
Coleridge, Samuel Taylor, 256
Colette [Sidonie-Gabrielle Colette], 258
Collectibles, reference works, 352–353
Colleges, reference works, 356
Colombia
   Barranquilla, 954
   Bogota, 955
   Cali, 955
   currency, 790
   embassy, 804
   major cities, 956

   standard time, 9
   statistics, 917
   telephone code, 972
   travel requirements, 797
Colon (punctuation), 441–442
Colonialism, literature, 273
Color field painting, 231
Colorado
   art museums, 363
   Bacchus and Gamma, 643
   botanical gardens, 380
   consumer affairs, 648–649
   crime statistics, 894–897
   Division of Aging & Adult Services, 639
   domestic violence organizations, 669
   flower/bird/motto/nickname, 877
   General Assembly, 876
   libraries, 337, 350
   name origin, 879
   newspapers, 906
   personal income per capita, 889
   poison control centers, 489
   population, 883
   precipitation, 751
   state tourism office, 748
   temperatures, 753, 755
   two-letter abbreviation, 904
   wildlife refuges, 765, 778
   zoos, 373
Colossus of Rhodes, 962
Coltrane, John, 176
Column, 242–244
Comaneci, Nadia, 714
Comet, 77
Comma
   in grammar, 442
   in music, 180
Commerce Department, Consumer Affairs, 671
Commission, 585
Committee of the Whole, 864
Committee, 864
Commodity Futures Trading Commission, 672
Commonwealth of Independent States. *See* **Russia**
Communications, reference works, 355–356
Comoros Islands
   currency, 790
   embassy, 804

Comoros Islands, *cont.*
  statistics, 917
  travel requirements, 797
Compass, 123–124
Complex sentence, 438
Composers
  classical, 171–174
  jazz, 175–177
Composting, 569
Compound interest, 574
Compound sentence, 438
Compound-complex sentence, 438
Compress, 479
CompuServe, Inc., 347
Computer scientists, 146
Computers, 136. *See also* **Internet;**
  Netiquette; Web site addresses
  terminology, 169–115
  data banks for research
  PCs (personal computers), 107
  programming languages, 138–139
Comte, Auguste, 311
Conceptual art, 231
Conceptualism, 323
Concussions, 482
Condolences, 472
Condominium, 585
Conference committee, 864
Confucianism, 284
Confucius, 254
Congo, Democratic Republic of
  (formerly Zaire)
  currency, 790
  embassy, 804
  Kinshasa, 955
  statistics, 917
  travel requirements, 797
Congress, U.S.
  acts, 863
  amendments, 863
  appropriate act, 863
  bills, 863, 865–866
  caucus, 863
  cloture, 863–864
  coalition, 864
  committees, 864
  Conjunction, 436
  filibuster, 864
  impeachment, 864
  majority, 864
  majority leaders, 864
  minority leaders, 864
  minority party, 865
  override, 865

president pro tempore, 865
  quorum, 865
  reapportionment, 865
  referendum, 865
  riders, 865
  standing committee, 865
  United States, 862
Congressional Record, 864
Connecticut
  aquariums, 374
  art museums, 363
  botanical gardens, 380
  consumer affairs, 649
  crime statistics, 892–893
  Department of Social Services,
    Elderly Services Division, 639
  domestic violence organizations,
    669
  flower/bird/motto/nickname, 877
  General Assembly, 876
  libraries, 337
  name origin, 879
  newspapers, 906
  Odyssey Institute Corporation,
    644
  personal income per capita, 888
  poison control centers, 489
  population, 883
  precipitation, 751
  state tourism office, 748
  temperatures, 753, 755
  two-letter abbreviation, 904
  wildlife refuges, 765
  zoos, 373
Connor, Ralph [Charles William
  Gordon], 257
Connors, Jimmy, 714
Conrad, Joseph, 256
Consensus gentium fallacy, 313
Consonants, 415
Constable, John, 222
Constantine, 932
Constellations, 75
Constipation, 507–508
  pets, 46
Constitution of the United States of
  America, The, 842–848, 859–860
  Amendments, 849–854
Constructivism, 231
Consumer affairs
  Alabama, 645
  Alaska, 645
  American Samoa, 667

Arizona, 645–646
California, 646–648
Colorado, 648–649
Connecticut, 649
Delaware, 649
District of Columbia, 649
Florida, 649–650
Hawaii, 650–651
hot line, 675
Idaho, 651
Illinois, 651–652
Indiana, 652–653
Iowa, 653
Kansas, 653
Kentucky, 653
Louisiana, 653
magazines, 678
Maine, 654
Maryland, 654
Massachusetts, 654–655
Michigan, 655
Minnesota, 655
Mississippi, 656
Missouri, 656
Montana, 656
Nebraska, 656
Nevada, 656
New Hampshire, 656
New Jersey, 656–659
New York, 659–661
North Carolina, 661
North Dakota, 661
Ohio, 662
Oklahoma, 662
Oregon, 662
Pennsylvania, 662–663
Puerto Rico, 667
Rhode Island, 664
South Carolina, 664
South Dakota, 664
Tennessee, 664
Texas, 664–665
Utah, 665
Vermont, 665
Virgin Islands, 667
Virginia, 665–666
West Virginia, 666
Wisconsin, 667
Wyoming, 667
Consumer Information Center, 350,
672
Consumer Product Safety
  Commission, 672

Contact lenses, 132, 136, 138
mortgages, 585–586
Convulsions, 482
Conybeare, William Daniel, 146
Cook Islands
currency, 790
embassy, 804
statistics, 917
travel requirements, 797
Cooking. *See* Food
Coolidge, Calvin, 861
Cooper, James Fenimore, 249
Cooperative apartment, 586
Copeland, Aaron 165
Copernicus, Nicolaus, 141
Copper working, 122
Coppola, Francis Ford, 204–205
Copyrights, 618–620
Corals, 40
Corbett, James J. ("Gentleman Jim"), 714
Core of Earth, 84–85
Corelli, Arcangelo, 171
Corigliano, John, 165
Coriolis, Gustave-Gaspard, 147, 151
Corneille, Pierre, 202
Cornell, Joseph, 218
Cornice, 243–244
Corot, Jean-Baptiste Camille, 223
Correggio (Antonio Allegri), 226
Cosine (cos), 106
Cosmogony, 324
Cosmology, 77, 324
Costa Rica
currency, 790
embassy, 804
statistics, 917
telephone code, 972
tourist information, 781
travel requirements, 797
Cotangent (cot or ctn), 106
Cotton gin, 127
Cotton, 122, 557
Coulomb (C), 26
Coulomb's law, 27, 99–100
Counseling services
reference works, 361
Counterexample, 324
Couperin, François, 168
Coupon bonds, 592
Courbet, Gustave, 223
Cousteau, Jacques-Yves, 147
Coward, Noël, 200

Cowell, Henry Dixon, 165
CPR (cardiopulmonary resuscitation), 474–475
Crane, Stephen, 249
Credit ratings, 582–583
Crick, Francis Harry Compton, 149
Crime statistics, 894–895
areas, 898
city rankings, 891–897
types, 898
Croatia
currency, 790
embassy, 804
statistics, 917
travel requirements, 797
Crookes, Sir William, 144–145
Crossing, 243–244
Crossword puzzles
commonly used words, 425–431
Crusades, 932, 941
Côte d'Ivoire, Republic of (Ivory Coast)
currency, 790
embassy, 804
statistics, 929
telephone code, 973
travel requirements, 797
Cuba, 105
currency, 790
embassy, 804
Havana, 955
standard time, 9
statistics, 917
travel requirements, 797
Cubism, 231
Cultivation, plants, 58–60
Cultural symbols, 396
Cummings, e.e. [Edward Estlin], 249
Cumulonimbus (Cb) clouds, 96–97
Cumulus (Cu) clouds, 97
Cunningham, Merce, 190
Curaçao
embassy, 805
tourist information, 781
travel requirements, 797
Curie, Marie Sklodowska, 145
Curie, Pierre, 145
Currencies, international, 788–793
Customs information, 818–819
Cuvier, Baron, Georges Léopold Chrétien Frédéric Dagobert, 143–144

Cyberspace, 110
Cymbals, 163
Cynics, 317
Cyprus, Republic of the
currency, 790
Cyrenaics, 317–318
embassy, 805
statistics, 917–918
telephone code, 972
tourist information, 782
travel requirements, 797
Cyrillic alphabet, 432
Czech Republic
currency, 790
embassy, 805
Prague, 956
standard time, 9
statistics, 918
telephone code, 972
tourist information, 782
travel requirements, 797
Czerny, Karl, 166

D

D'Amboise, Jacques, 190
Da Vinci, Leonardo, 123
Dadaism, 231, 262
Dahlias, 49
Daisies, 49
Dalí, Salvador, 229
Dallapiccola, Luigi, 172
Dalton, John, 145
Dana, James Dwight, 147
Dance, 188.
choreographers, 190–196
Danilova, Alexandra, 194
Dante Alighieri, 259
Darwin, Charles Robert, 144
Darwin, Erasmus, 149
Dash (punctuation), 441–442
Dassies, 39
Dates, international date line, 8
Daumier, Honoré, 223
David, Jacques-Louis, 223
Davies, Arthur Bowen, 218
Davies, Robertson, 257
Davis, Miles, 176
Davis, Stuart, 218
Davy, Sir Humphry, 145
Daylight savings time, 9
Europe, 10
Days, 10

Daylight savings time, *cont.*
  hours, 4
  length, 5
  mean solar, 4
  sidereal, 4
  true solar, 4
De Broglie, Prince Louis Victor Pierre Raymond, 151
De Kooning, Willem, 218
De Mille, Agnes, 190
De Mille, Cecil B., 206
De Sica, Vittorio, 205, 208
De Vries, Hugo Marie, 144
deafness
  travel, 734, 736
  sign language, 400
Death penalty, 619
Death rates, causes, 516–518
Death. *See* Funerals
Debenture, 593
Debussy, Claude, 168
Decadence, 262
Decimal system, 123, 391
Declaration of Gift, 604
Declaration of Independence, The, 838–841
Deductive
  mathematics, 122
  reasoning, 324
Deed, 586
Deer, 38
Deficit, government, 864
Definite article, 437
Defoe, Daniel, 256
Degas, Edgar, 223
Deism, 318
Dekker, Thomas, 200
Delacroix, Eugène, 223
Delaware
  art museums, 364
  botanical gardens, 380
  consumer affairs, 649
  crime statistics, 892–893
  Division of Aging, 639
  domestic violence organizations, 669
  flower/bird/motto/nickname, 877
  General Assembly, 876
  name origin, 879
  newspapers, 906
  personal income per capita, 888
  poison control centers, 489
  population, 883

  precipitation, 751
  state tourism office, 748
  temperatures, 753, 755
  two-letter abbreviation, 904
  wildlife refuges, 765
Delibes, (Clément Philibert) Léo, 168
Delius, Frederick, 167
Della Robbia, Luca, Andrea, Luca II, Giovanni, and Girolamo, 227
Dello Joio, Norman, 165
DeMille, Cecil B., 205
Democratic Republic of Congo. *See* Congo, Democratic Republic of
Democritus, 311
Demography, reference works, 361–362
Demuth, Charles, 218
Denmark, Kingdom of
  Copenhagen, 955
  currency, 790
  embassy, 805
  royalty, 969
  standard time, 9
  statistics, 918
  telephone code, 972
  tourist information, 780, 782
  travel requirements, 797
Dennis et al. v. U.S., 624
Dental care, 514–515
  pets, 46
Deontology, 324
Deoxyribonucleic acid (DNA), 63, 137–138, 141
Derrida, Jacques, 311
Descartes, René, 311
Determinism, 324
Devers, Gail, 714
Dewey decimal system, 131, 345
Dewey, John, 311
Diacritical marks, 415
Diaghilev, Sergei Pavlovich, 194
Dialectic, 324–325
Dialectical materialism, 318
Dialog Information Services, Inc., 347
Diarrhea, pets, 47
Dickens, Charles, 256
Dickinson, Emily, 249
Dictionaries, 433
  foreign languages, 357
  references, 358
Diderot, Denis, 311

Didion, Joan, 250
Digestive system, 36
Dillard, Annie, 250
DiMaggio, Joe, 714
Dinesen, Isak [Karen Christence Dinesen, Baroness Blixen-Finecke, 261
Diogenes, 311
Diphtheria, 513
Diphtheria/tetanus/pertussis (DTP) immunization, 502
Directors, films
  Academy Award winners, 209–215
  American, 204, 206–207
  British, 207–208
  Chinese, 207
  French, 208
  German, 208
  Indian, 207
  Italian, 208–209
  Japanese, 207
  Latvian, 209
  Senegalese, 209
  Spanish, 209
  Swedish, 209
Disabilities
  airlines, 734
  alphabets, 400, 401
  organizations, 644
  physical, 668
  telecommunications device for the deaf, 668
  travel, 736
  visually impaired, 668
Disability
  Social Security benefits, 872–873
  Disability insurance, 580
Disciples of Christ, 286
Discovery and exploration time table, 122–129, 131–141, 628, 947–949
Diseases
  cats, 46
  dogs, 47
  humans, infectious, 513
  immunizations
Disk crash, 110–111
Dislocations, first aid, 483–484
Distress signals, 397
District of Columbia
  botanical gardens, 381
  consumer affairs, 649
  crime statistics, 892–895

D.C. Office on Aging, 639
domestic violence organizations,
 669
flower/bird/motto/nickname, 877
libraries, 337, 350
museums
 art, 364
 children, 371
 science and technology, 371
name origin, 879
personal income per capita, 888
poison control centers, 489
population, 883, 957
precipitation, 751
state tourism office, 748
temperatures, 753, 755
two-letter abbreviation, 904
zoos, 374
Dividends, 593
Diving
 Louganis, Greg, 716
Djibouti, Republic of
 currency, 790
 embassy, 805
 statistics, 918
 travel requirements, 797
**DNA(deoxyribonucleic acid), 63,
 137–138, 141**
Doctorow, E(dgar) L(awrence), 250
Dogs, 38
 diseases, 47
 immunizations, 44–45
 training, 43
 traveling with, 935
Dogwoods, 50
Dolin, Anton, 192
Dolphins, 38
Dome, 243–244
Domestic violence
 hot line, 675
 organizations, 669–670
Dominica, Commonwealth of
 currency, 790
 embassy, 805
 statistics, 918
 tourist information, 782
 travel requirements, 797
Dominican Republic
 currency, 790
 embassy, 805
 Santo Domingo, 957
 statistics, 918

tourist information, 782
 travel requirements, 797
**Donatello (Donato di Niccolo di
 Betto Bardi), 227**
Donizetti, Gaetano, 172
Donkeys, 39
Donne, John, 256
Doors, standard sizes, 568
Doppler effect, 77–78
Doppler, Christian Johann, 151
Dos Passos, John, 250
**Dostoyevsky, Fyodor
 Mikhaylovich , 260**
Doubt, 325
Dove, Arthur Garfield, 218
Dow Jones average, 347, 593
Dowland, John, 167
Doyle, Sir Arthur Conan, 256
Drag racing, 684
Drake, Edwin Laurentine, 147
Drama, playwrights
 American, 198–200
 British, 199–201
 French, 201–202
 German, 202
 Greek, 203
 Irish, 203
 Italian, 204
 Norwegian, 204
 Roman, 203–204
 Russian, 203–204
 Spanish, 204
 Swedish, 204
Dred Scott v. Sanford, 623
Dreiser, Theodore, 250
Dressing, first aid, 479
Drinks, alcoholic. *See* Alcohol
**Driving-while-intoxicated (DWI),
 531–532**
Drowning, 482
Drugs, illegal
 during pregnancy, 501
 hot line, 675
 organizations, 643–644
Drums, 163
Dryden, John, 256
**DTP (diphtheria/tetanus/pertussis),
 502**
Dualism, 325
Dubuffet, Jean, 223
Duchamp, Marcel, 223
Dufy, Raoul, 223–224

Dugongs, 39
Dukas, Paul, 168
Dumas, Alexandre, père, 258
Duncan, Isadora, 190
Dunham, Katherine, 190
Dürer, Albrecht, 225
Durrell, Lawrence, 256
Duty, 325
Dvořák, Antonín, 174
**DWI (driving-while-intoxicated),
 531–532**
Dynasties
 China, 963–964
Dystopias, literature, 275

E

Eakins, Thomas, 218
Ear, 34
Earth, 72
 core, 84–85
 crust, 84
 mantle, 84
 scientists, 146–147
Earthquakes. *See also* Geology
 map of zones, 88
 Richter Scale, 89, 136
 sea-floor spreading, 87
 subduction, 87
Easter Sunday, 305
Eastern Standard Time (EST), 8
Echinoderms, 40
Eclipses
 lunar, 68–69
 solar, 68 71
Economics, 275
Economy, United States
 household income-percent distribution, 890
 household median income by race,
  889
 personal income per capita,
  888–889
Ecuador
 currency, 790
 embassy, 805
 Guayaquil, 955
 Quito, 957
 statistics, 918
 telephone code, 972
 travel requirements, 797
Edel, Leon, 250
Ederle, Gertrude, 714

Edison, Thomas Alva, 205
Education Department, Consumer Affairs Staff, 672
Education, universities and colleges, 356
Educational Resources Information Center (ERIC), 350
Egg-laying mammals, 37
Eglevsky, Andre, 194
Egocentric predicament, 325
Egoism, 325
Egypt, Arab Republic of
  Alexandria, 955
  Cairo, 955
  calendar, 931
  currency, 790
  embassy, 805
  major cities, 954
  pyramids, 931
  standard time, 9
  statistics, 918
  telephone code, 972
  tourist information, 782
  travel requirements, 797
Ehrlich, Paul, 149
Eid-al Adha, 306
Eid-al-Fitr, 306
Eight, The, 231
Einstein, Albert, 151
Eisenhower, Dwight D., 861
Eisenstein, Sergei, 209
Élan vital, 325
El Greco. *See* Greco, El
El Salvador
  civil war, 947
  currency, 790
  embassy, 805
  statistics, 918
  telephone code, 972
  travel requirements, 797
Eleatics, 318
Electoral College, 863
Electric guitar, 163
Electric shock, 483
Electric, 133
Electron microscope, 135
Electronic instruments, 163, 165
Electronics, symbols, 389–390
Elements, chemistry, 80–81
Elephant shrews, 39
Elephants, 39
Elgar, Sir Edward, 167
Eliot, George [Mary Ann Evans], 256

Eliot, Thomas Stearns (T.S.), 200, 250
Elizabethan, 262
Elk, 38
Ellington, Edward Kennedy "Duke," 176
Ellipse, 104, 122
Ellipsis (punctuation), 441–442
Ellison, Ralph, 250
Elssler, Fanny, 195
E-mail, 111, 468. *See also* Internet; Netiquette; Web site addresses
Emancipation Proclamation, The, 854–855
Embassies, 801, 803–818
Emergencies. *See* First aid
Emerson, Ralph Waldo, 250
Emoticons, 402
Empedocles, 312
Empiricism, 317, 325
Employer-funded retirement plans, 591
Employment, federal government, 870–871
Emulsifiers, 547
Enamel, 124
Encephalitis, 513
Encyclopaedia Britannica, 351
Encyclopedias, 351
Encyclopedists, 318
Energy Department, 672
Engels, Friedrich, 312
Engineering terms, 117–118
Engineers, aerospace, 141
England
  Birmingham, 954
  Black Death, 933
  currency, 793
  embassy, 805, 817
  hereditary peerage, 966
  Liverpool, 956
  London, 956
  prime ministers, 970–972
  royal families, 966–968
  royalty, 964–965, 969–970
  standard time, 9
  statistics, 937
  telephone code, 972
  tourist information, 786
  travel requirements, 800
English language
  American, 415
  British, 415

  Greek prefixes/suffixes, 422–424
  Latin prefixes/suffixes, 425
Enlightenment (Age of Reason), 318
Ensor, James (Baron), 221
Entertainment
  attire, 469
  business, 467
  formal dinner parties, 469–471
  informal dinner parties, 470–471
  invitations, 468–469
  R.S.V.P.s, 469
  tableware, 469–471
Environmental Protection Agency, 672
Environmentalists, 146–147
Epictetus, 312
Epicureanism, 318
Epicurus, 312
Episcopal Church, 287
Epistemology, 325
Equal Credit Opportunity Act, 582
Equatorial Guinea, Republic of
  currency, 790
  embassy, 805
  statistics, 918
  travel requirements, 797
Equinox, 11
Equity, 586
Erasistratus of Chios, 149–150
Eratosthenes of Cyrene, 141–142
ERIC (Educational Resources Information Center), 350
Ericsson, Leif, 948
Eritrea
  currenty, 790
  embassy, 805
  statistics, 918
  travel requirements, 797
Ernst, Max, 225
Eschatology, 325
Escrow, 586
Essence, 325
Estonia
  currency, 790
  embassy, 805
  statistics, 918
  travel requirements, 797
Ethiopia, Federal Democratic Republic of
  Addis Ababa, 954
  currency, 790
  embassy, 806
  standard time, 9

statistics, 918
telephone code, 972
travel requirements, 797
**Ethnology, reference works,
352–353**
Etiquette
appointments, 466
gifts, 467
telephone, 467–468
business, 446–447
entertainment
attire, 469
formal dinner parties, 469–471
*informal dinner parties,
470–471*
invitations, 468–469
R.S.V.Ps, 469
tableware, 469–471
funerals
after burial, 472
arrangements, 471
burial, 472
condolences, 472
letter writing, 446–447
netiquette (Internet), 468
tipping, 594–595
weddings
anniversary gifts, 466
announcements, 460–461
bachelor dinner, 461
ceremony, 463
expenses, 465
gifts, 465–466
invitations, 460–461
reception, 463–465
rehearsal dinner, 461–462
shower, 461
thank-you notes, 465–466
Euclid, 148
Euler, Leonhard, 148
Euripides, 203
Europe
clothing size conversion, 565
daylight savings time, 10
holidays, 19–21
map, 977
European Union, 806
tourist information, 780
travel requirements, 797
Euthanasia. *See* Living wills
Evans, Bill, 176
Evans, Janet, 714
Evert, Chris, 714

Ewing, William Maurice, 147
**Excess interest whole life insurance,
580**
**Exclamation point (punctuation),
441**
**Executive branch of government,
859–860**
Exercise, caloric consumption, 530
Existentialism, 318
**Exploration and discovery,
947–949, 954**
Exponents, mathematics, 102
Expressionism, 231, 262
Extinct animals, 40–42
Eye, 34
Eyeglasses, 123
bifocal lenses, 127

F

Fabric care. *See* Clothing
**Fahrenheit temperature scale, 29,
125**
Fahrenheit, Daniel Gabriel, 151
Fair Credit Billing Act, 582
Faldo, Nick, 714
Falkland Islands
currency, 790
statistics, 918
Falklands War, 955
Falklands War, 947
Fall season, 11
Falla, Manuel de, 174
Fallacy, 313, 327
Families
planning, 670–671
single-parent, 674
Fannie Mae, 586
**FAQ (Frequently Asked Questions),
111**
Faraday, Michael, 151
Farm owners, Social Security, 874
Faroe Islands, 919
Farrell, Suzanne, 190
**Fassbinder, Rainer Werner, 205,
208**
Fatalism, 325
Fat-soluble vitamins, 520
Faulkner, William, 250
Fauré, Gabriel, 168–169
Fauvism, 231
**Feast of the Conception of St.
Anne, 306**

Feast of the Epiphany, 304
**Feast of the Immaculate
Conception, 306**
**Federal Communications
Commission, 672**
**Federal Deposit Insurance
Corporation (FDIC), 593, 672**
Federal government, U.S.
benefits, 872–875
budget, 863
civilian employment, 870–871
deficit, 864
finances, 866–870
forms of address, 449–450
judicial system, 622
statute of limitations, 618
structure, 859–860
surplus, 865
**Federal Home Loan Mortgage
Corporation, 672**
**Federal Housing Administration
(FHA), 586**
**Federal Information Centers (FIC),
673–674**
Federal Maritime Commission, 672
Federal Reserve System, 672
Federal Trade Commission, 672
Federated States of Micronesia
Legislature, 877, 904
Feininger, Lyonel, 218
Feld, Eliot, 190–191
Fellini, Federico, 205, 208–209
Feminism, literature, 275
Ferdinand, 149
Fermat, Pierre de, 148
Fermi, Enrico, 151
Feynman, Richard Phillips, 152
**FIC (Federal Information Centers),
673–674**
Fielding, Henry, 256
**Fifth disease (Erythema
Infectiosum)**
during pregnancy, 501
Figure skating, 714–715, 719
Fiji
currency, 790
embassy, 806
statistics, 919
telephone code, 972
tourist information, 782
travel requirements, 797
Filibuster, 864
Fillmore, Millard, 861

Films
Academy Awards, 209–215
cinématographe, 205
directors, 48–53, 205
history of, 205
invention of, 132
Kinetoscope, 205
reference works, 356
sound, 133
three-dimensional, 134
Finances
budgets, 575–576
child rearing, 576
credit ratings, 582–583
federal government, 866–870
finances, 584–586
insurance, 581–182
interest, 574, 586, 593
investments, 586, 594
   annuities, 587
   assets, 592
   bank accounts, 587
   bonds, 588, 590–594
   funds of funds, 590
   growth-oriented funds, 590
   hybrid funds, 590
   index funds, 590
   life insurance, 587
   money-market funds, 590, 593
   mutual funds, 589–591
   real estate, 588
   risk, 589
   small business, 589
   stocks, 588–594
   tax shelter, 594
   value-oriented funds, 590
loans, 582
mortgages
   adjustable-rate (ARM), 584
   affordability, 583–584
   amortization, 575
   assumable, 585
   balloon payment, 585
   binder, 585
   broker, 585
   calculating, 576
   closing, 585
   commission, 585
   condominium, 585
   down payment, 584
   Fannie Mae, 586
   Federal Housing Administration (FHA), 586
mutual funds, 593
net worth, 576–577

publications, 595
real estate, 583–584
retirement, 586, 591
Finland
currency, 790
embassy, 806
standard time, 9
statistics, 919
telephone code, 972
tourist information, 782
travel requirements, 797
Fire, 122
Fireplaces, 569–570
First aid
abrasions, 480
animal bites, 480
bandages, 479
black eyes and bruises, first aid, 480
boils and blisters, 480
breathing, 474
burns, 480–481, 507
   pets, 45–46
choking, 481–482
circulation, 474
concussions, 482
convulsions, 482
CPR (cardiopulmonary resuscitation), 474–475
dislocations, 483–484
drowning, 482
electric shock, 483
fractures, 483–484
frostbite, 485
head injury, 478
heart attack, 492
heat stroke, 485
insect bites, 485–486
kits, 479
neck or spine injury, 478
nosebleeds, 486
pets
   broken bones, 45
   cat diseases, 46
   constipation, 46
   dental disorders, 46
   diarrhea, 47
   dog diseases, 47
   parasites, 47–48
   rabies, 48
   respiratory infections, 48
   shock, 48
   skin problems, 48
   sprains, 49
   wounds, 49

poisoning, 486–492
preventing loss of blood, 475–478
preventing shock, 478–479
snake bites, 488
strokes, 492
travel kit, 734
First degree burns, 481, 507
Fiscal year, 10
Fish
cooking times, 542
extinct, 42
serving sizes, 543
Fitz, 176
Fitzgerald, Ella, 176
Fitzgerald, F. Scott, 250
Five Classics, 294
Five positions, ballet, 197
Flags, United States, 856–857
Flaubert, Gustave, 258
Flavor enhancers, 547
Fleming, Peggy, 714
Fleming, Sir Alexander, 150
Fletcher, John, 200
Floors, standard sizes, 566
Florida
aquariums, 374
botanical gardens, 381
consumer affairs, 649–650
crime statistics, 892–897
Department of Elder Affairs, 639
domestic violence organizations, 669
flower/bird/motto/nickname, 877
legislature, 876
libraries, 337
name origin, 879
newspapers, 907
personal income per capita, 888
poison control centers, 489
population, 883
precipitation, 751
state tourism office, 748
temperatures, 753, 755
theme parks, 779
two-letter abbreviation, 904
wildlife refuges, 765–766, 778
zoos, 374
Flourens, Jean Pierre Marie, 150
Flowers. *See also* **Plants;** *specific flowers*
cultivation, 58–59
for funerals, 471
germination, 61
Flu (influenza), 508, 513
Flute, 159

Flying buttress, 242
Flying lemurs, 38
Fokine, Michel, 194
Folacin, 524–525
Folk art, 231
Folklore, reference works, 359
Fonteyn, Dame Margot, 192
Food
    bacteria control, 544
    beverages
      champagne, 553
      coffee, 557
      mixed drinks, 553–556
      wine, 556–557
    chemical additives, 547–552
    cooking measurements, 536
    cooking times
      fish, 542
      fruit, 543
      meat, 539–541
      poultry, 541
      shellfish, 542
      vegetables, 542
    herbs and spices, 545–546
    pantry basics, 545
    phone hot lines, 545
    serving sizes, 543
    storage, 544
    substitutions
      herbal salt, 546
      ingredient, 538
      ingredients, 537
      kosher, 538
      low-fat, 538–539
    turkey, carving, 541
    weights and measurements,
      536–537
Food and Drug Administration, 672
Food poisoning, 486
Football, 694–695, 728, 731
    American Football Conference
      (AFC), 698
    Brown, Jim, 713
    Bryant, Paul ("Bear"), 713–714
    Butkus, Dick, 714
    Halas, George ("Papa Bear"), 715
    Lombardi, Vince, 716
    Marino, Dan, 716
    Montana, Joe, 717
    Namath, Joe, 717
    National Football Conference
      (NFC), 698
    Payton, Walter, 717
    Rice, Jerry, 718
    Rockne, Knute, 718

Shula, Don, 718
signals, 696–697
Simpson, O(renthal) J(ames), 718
Super Bowl, 698–699
Thorpe, Jim, 719
Ford, Gerald R., 862
Ford, John, 205–206
Foreign alphabets, 432
Foreign heads of state, forms of
    address, 450–451
Foreign languages
    alphabets, 432
    dictionaries, 351, 357
    frequently used words and
      phrases, 417–421
Foreman, George, 714
Form, 182, 325
Formal dinner parties, 469–471
Forms of address, 448
    business, 446–447
    foreign heads of state, 450–451
    government
      federal, 449–450
      United Nations, 450
    military, 454
    nobility, 452–453
    personal, 446
    religious officials, 451–452
    title abbreviations, 455
Formula 1, 684
Forster, E. M, 256
Fosbury, Dick, 714
Foucault, Jean Bernard Leon, 152
Foucault, Michel, 312
Four elements, 325
Four Horseman of the Apocalypse,
    294
Foxes, 38
Foyt, A.J., 714–715
Fractions, 102–103, 391
Fractures, first aid, 483–484
Fragonard, Jean-Honoré, 224
France
    currency, 790
    embassy, 806
    frequently used French words and
      phrases, 417–420
    Marseilles, 956
    Paris, 956
    Revolution, 950
    royalty, 965
    standard time, 9
    telephone code, 972
    travel requirements, 797
Franck, César, 169

Frankenthaler, Helen, 218
Franklin, Benjamin, 152, 250
Franklin, Miles [Stella Maria Sarah
    Miles], 254
Franklin, Rosalind, 150
Freddie Mac, 586
Free will, 325–326
French Revolution, 942
French Antilles, 972
French Guiana
    currency, 790
    statistics, 919
    travel requirements, 797
French Polynesia
    currency, 790
    statistics, 919
    telephone code, 972
    tourist information, 782
    travel requirements, 797
French West Indies, 797
Freud, Sigmund, 150
Frost dates, 60
Frost, Robert, 250
Frostbite, 485
Fruit
    botanical names, 51–55
    cooking times, 543
Fuentes, Carlos, 259
Fuller, (Richard) Buckminster, 235
Funds of funds, 590
Funerals
    after burial, 472
    arrangements, 471
    burial, 472
    condolences, 472
    flowers, 471
    letter writing, 446
    wakes, 471
Furman v. Georgia, 624
Futurism, 231
Futurism, 262–263

G

Gabo, Naum (Naum Neemia
    Pevsner), 229
Gabonese Republic (Gabon)
    currency, 790
    embassy, 806
    statistics, 919
    telephone code, 972
    travel requirements, 797
Gainsborough, Thomas, 222
Galapagos Islands. *See* Ecuador
Galaxy, 78, 141

Galen, 150
Galileo Galilei, 5, 142
Gallic Wars, 940
Gambia
    currency, 790
    embassy, 806
    statistics, 919
    travel requirements, 797
Gambler's fallacy, 313
Garciá Lorca, Federico, 204, 261
Garciá Márquez, Gabriel, 260
Gardening. *See* Plants
Gardner, John, 250
Garfield, James, 861
Garnier, Jean Louis Charles, 238
Gaudí y Cornet, Antonio, 240
Gauguin, Paul, 224
Gauss, Karl Friedrich, 149
Gay/lesbian youth hot line, 675
Gazelles, 38
Gehrig, Lou, 715
Gemini spacecraft, 115
Genealogy, 348
    British monarchy, 966–968
    libraries, 349
    Spanish monarchy, 970
General Agreement on Tariffs and
    Trade (GATT), 620
General assembly, states, 875–877
Genetic fallacy, 313
Geography
    charts, 122
    directional abbreviations, 904
    prime meridian, 6
Geology
    terminology, 92–95
    eras, 85–87, 93
    layers of the earth, 84–85
    magazines, 119
    maps, 88. *See also* Maps
    minerals, 90–92, 94
    plate tectonics, 87–90
    rocks, 91–92, 95
Geometry, 391
    symbols, 391
    three-dimensional shapes, 105
    triangles, 105
    two-dimensional shapes, 103–104
Geophysics. *See* Geology
Georgia
    botanical gardens, 381
    consumer affairs, 650
    crime statistics, 892–893, 896–897

domestic violence organization,
    669
flower/bird/motto/nickname, 877
General Assembly, 876
libraries, 337
name origin, 879
newspaper, 907
Office of Aging, 639
personal income per capita, 888
poison control centers, 489
population, 883
precipitation, 751
state tourism office, 748
statistics, 919
temperatures, 753, 755
two-letter abbreviation, 904
wildlife refuges, 766–767, 778
zoos, 374
Georgia, Republic of, 806
    currency, 790
    statistics, 919
    Tbilisi, 957
    travel requirements, 797
Georgian, 241
Geraniums, 50
Gerbils, 39
Géricault, Théodore (Jean Louis
    André Théodore), 224
Germany, Federal Republic of
    Berlin, 954
    Cologne, 955
    currency, 790
    Dresden, 955
    Düsseldorf, 955
    embassy, 807
    Essen, 955
    Frankfurt, 955
    frequently used German words
        and phrases, 417, 419–420
    Hamburg, 955
    Leipzig, 956
    Munich, 956
    royalty, 965, 969–970
    standard time, 9
    statistics, 919
    telephone code, 972
    tourist information, 782
    travel requirements, 798
Germination
    flowers, 61
    vegetables, 61
Gershwin, George, 165
Gerunds (part of speech), 440

Gettysburg Address, The, 855–856
Ghana
    currency, 790
    embassy, 807
    statistics, 919
    travel requirements, 798
Ghiberti, Lorenzo, 227
Giacometti, Alberti, 230
Giant telescope, 129
Gibbons, 39, 167
Gibraltar
    statistics, 919
    travel requirements, 798
Gibson, Althea, 715
Gide, André, 258
Gifts
    business, 467
    weddings, 465–466
Gilbert, Grove Karl, 147
Gillespie, John Birks "Dizzy," 176
Ginnie Mae, 586
Ginsberg, Allen, 250
Giorgione (Giorgione da
    Castelfranco), 227
Giotto (Giotto di Bondone), 227,
    239
Giraffes, 38
Girardelli, Marc, 715
Giraudoux, Jean, 202
Glinka, Mikhail, 173
Glockenspiel, 162
Gluck, Christoph Willibald von,
    170
Gnawing mammals, 39
Goats, 38
Godard, Jean-Luc, 205, 208
Goddard, Robert Hutchings, 141
Goethe, Johann Wolfgang von, 259
Gogol, Nikolai, 260
Gold mining, 122
Golden rule, 326
Golding, William, 256
Goldsmith, Oliver, 200
Golf, 699, 728, 731
    Faldo, Nick, 714
    Hogan, Ben, 715
    Masters, 700
    Nicklaus, Jack ("Golden Bear"),
        717
    Palmer, Arnold, 717
    Woods, Tiger, 719
    Zaharias, Babe Didrikson, 719
Gombrowicz, Witold, 261

Gong, 163
Gonorrhea, 513
Good Friday, 305
Goodman, Benny, 176
Googol, 106
Gordimer, Nadine, 253
Gorky, Arshile, 218
Gorky, Maxim (Alexei Maximovich
　Peshkov), 204, 260
Gothic revival, 241
Gothic, 231, 241, 263
Gounod, Charles, 169
Government
　agencies, 671–673
　executive branch, 859–860
　federal
　　budget, 863
　　civilian employment, 870–871
　　deficit, 864
　　finances, 866–870
　　legislative branch, 862
　　Medicare, 874–875
　　Social Security, 872–874
　　structure, 859–860
　　surplus, 865
　forms of address
　　federal, 449–450
　　foreign heads of state, 450–451
　　United Nations, 450
　judicial branch, 859–860
　legislative branch, 859–860
Goya y Lucientes, Francisco Jose de,
　229
Graduated payment mortgage
　(GPM), 584
Graf, Steffi, 715
Graham, Martha, 191
Grainger, Percy Aldridge, 174
Grammar
　adjective, 436–437
　adverb, 436–437
　American English, 443
　apostrophes, 443
　article, 436
　brackets, 442
　British English, 443
　clause, 437–438, 441
　colon, 442
　comma, 442
　conjunction, 436
　dangling participial phrases, 440
　dash, 442
　diacritical marks, 415

double negative, 440
ellipsis, 442
infinitives, 441
interjection, 436
modifier, 437
mood, 439
noun, 436–437
oxymoron, 427
palindromes, 428
parallel structure, 440
parentheses, 442–443
phrase, 437, 441
preposition, 436–437
pronoun, 436–437
punctuation, 441–443
quotation marks, 443
reference works, 357
semicolon, 442
sentence structure, 437–438, 441
spelling guidelines, 412–414
split infinitives, 440
subject, 439
tense, 439
verb, 436–439
voice, 439
Granados, Enrique, 174
Grant, Ulysses S., 861
Grass, Günter, 259
Grave accent, 415
Graves, Michael, 235
Graveyard School, 263
Great Books Foundation, 271–272
Great Pyramids of Egypt, 931
Great Wall of China, 122, 931
Greatest happiness principle, 326
Greco, El (Domenikos
　Theotokopoulos), 229
Greece
　Athens, 954
　currency, 790
　embassy, 807
　frequently used Greek words and
　　phrases, 417, 420–421
　prefixes/suffixes, 422–424
　standard time, 9
　statistics, 919
　telephone code, 972
　tourist information , 782
　travel requirements, 798
Greek alphabet, 432
Greek deities, 282–283
Greek language, 417, 420–421

Greenland
　currency, 790
　statistics, 919–920
　travel requirements, 798
Greer, Germaine, 254
Gregorian calendar, 12
Gregory, Cynthia, 191
Grenada
　currency, 790
　embassy, 807
　statistics, 920
　tourist information, 782
　travel requirements, 798
Gretzky, Wayne, 715
Grieg, Edvard, 174
Griffey, Ken, Jr., 715
Griffith, D.W., 206
Grimaldi, Francesco Maria, 152
Grimm, Wilhelm and Jakob, 259
Gris, Juan (José Victoriano
　González), 229
Grisi, Carlotta, 195
Groined vault, 243, 246
Gropius, Walter, 235
Grosz, George, 225
Ground covers, botanical names, 56
Growth-oriented funds, 590
Grünewald, Mathias (Mathis
　Gothardt Neithardt), 225
Guadeloupe
　currency, 790
　statistics, 920
Guam
　currency, 790
　flower/bird/motto, 879
　legislature, 877
　Office of Aging, 642
　telephone code, 972
　tourist information, 782
　two-letter abbreviation, 904
Guantanamo Bay U.S., 972
Guare, John, 198
Guatemala
　currency, 790
　embassy, 807
　Guatemala City, 955
　statistics, 920
　telephone code, 972
　tourist information, 782
　travel requirements, 798
Guernsey
　currency, 790
　statistics, 920

Guinea, Republic of
currency, 790
embassy, 807
statistics, 920
travel requirements, 798
Guinea-Bissau, Republic of
currency, 790
embassy, 807
statistics, 920
travel requirements, 798
Guinness Book of Records, 351
Guitars, 158, 163
Gunpowder, 123
Guyana, Co-operative Republic of
currency, 790
embassy, 807
statistics, 920
telephone code, 972
travel requirements, 798
Guzmán, Martín Luis, 260
Gymnastics, 714

H

Hadley, George, 147
Haiti
currency, 790
embassy, 807
Port-au-Prince, 956
statistics, 920
telephone code, 972
travel requirements, 798
Halas, George ("Papa Bear"), 715
Hale, George Ellery, 142
Hall, Sir James, 147
Halley, Edmund, 142
Halley's comet, 125
Hals, Frans, 222
Hamilton, Scott, 715
Hammered instruments, 158
Hammett, Dashiell, 250
Hamsters, 39
Hamsun, Knut, 261
Hancock, Herbie, 176
Handel, George Frideric, 170
Hanging Gardens of Babylon, 962
Hanson, Howard, 165
Hanukkah, 306
Harding, Warren G., 861
Hardouin Mansart, Jules, 238
Hardy, Thomas, 256
Hare, David, 200
Hares, 39
Harp, 158

Harris v. Forklift Systems, Inc., 625
Harrison, Benjamin, 861
Harrison, William Henry, 861
Harvey, William, 150
Hasek, Jaroslav, 261
Hawaii
aquariums, 374
art museums, 364
botanical gardens, 381
consumer affairs, 650–651
crime statistics, 894–895
Executive Office on Aging, 639
flower/bird/motto/nickname, 877
legislature, 876
name origin, 879
newspapers, 907
personal income per capita, 889
poison control center, 489
population, 883
precipitation, 751
state tourism office, 748
temperatures, 753, 755
time zone, 8
two-letter abbreviation, 904
wildlife refuges, 767
zoos, 374
Hawkes, John Clendennin Burne, Jr., 250
Hawking, Stephen William, 142
Hawkins, Coleman, 176
Hawks, Howard, 206
Hawthorne, Nathaniel, 250
Haydn, Franz Joseph, 166
Haydn, Johann Michael, 166
Hayes, Rutherford B., 861
Head sets, 389
Headaches, home remedies, 508–509
Health. *See also* First aid; Medicine
alcohol consumption, 531–532
breast cancer
breast self-examinatin (BSE), 511–513
mammograms, 513
chiropractic, 514
death rates, 503, 516–518
dental care, 514–515
exercise, caloric consumption, 530
height, 505
home remedies
allergies, 506–507
seasonal, 507
asthma, 507
back pain, 507

burns, 507
common cold, 507
constipation, 507–508
flu (influenza), 508
headaches, 508–509
hiccups, 508–509
hyperventilation, 509
indigestion, 509
insect bites, 509
insomnia, 509–510
premenstrual syndrome (PMS), 510
rashes, 510
sprains, 510–511
strep throat, 511
homeopathy, 515
immunizations, 496, 502–503
infectious diseases, 513
life expectancy rates, 504
living wills, 515–516
nonsurgical treatment, 496
nutrition
fat-soluble vitamins, 520
minerals, 521, 524–529
proteins, 520
vitamins, 522–525
water-soluble vitamins, 521
osteopathy, 514
patient's bill of rights, 498–499
pregnancy, precautions, 501–502
routine checkups, 496
surgery, 497–498
tests, 496
weight, 504–505
Health and Human Services Department, 672
Health insurance
Blue Cross/Blue Shield, 578–579
health maintenance organizations (HMOs), 579
private, 578
Hearing aids, 136
Hearing impaired, telecommunications device for the deaf, 668
Heart attacks, warning signs, 492
Hebrew alphabet, 432
Heat stroke, first aid, 485
Hedgehogs, 39
Hedonism, 318
Hegel, Georg Wilhelm Friedrich, 312
Hegelianism (neo-Hegeliansim), 318–319

Heidegger, Martin, 312
Heiden, Eric, 715
Height
    conversions, 505
    females, 506
Heimlich maneuver, 482
Heinlein, Robert A., 250
Helicopters, 127, 136
Heller, Joseph, 250
Hellman, Lillian, 198, 250
Hemingway, Ernest, 250
Hemorrhage, stopping, 475–478
Henderson, Fletcher, 176
Henderson, Rickey, 715
Henie, Sonja, 715
Henley, Beth, 198
Henri, Robert, 218
Henry, O. [William Sydney Porter],
    250
Hepatitis B immunization, 502–503
Hepatitis, 513
Heraclitus, 312
Hereditary peerage, 966
Hero of Alexandria, 149
Herophilus of Chalcedon, 150
Herpes simplex, 513
Herschel, Sir John Frederick
    William, 142
Herschel, Sir William, 142
Hersey, John [Richard], 250
Hertz, Heinrich Rudolf, 152
Hertzsprung-Russell diagram, stars,
    73
Herzog, Werner, 205
Hesse, Hermann, 259
Hewish, Anthony, 142
Hexagon, 104
Hiccups, home remedies, 508–509
Hindemith, Paul, 170
Hinduism, 284, 292–293, 394
Hines, Earl "Fatha," 176
Hipparchus, 142
Hippocrates of Cos, 150
Hippopotamuses, 38
Histoplasmosis, 513
History
    important world dates and events,
        931–939
    reference works, 357
    symbols, 396
    United States, 824–837
    world exploration and discovery,
        947–949

Hitchcock, Alfred, 207
HMOs (Health Maintenance
    Organizations), 579
Hobbes, Thomas, 312
Hobson's choice, 326
Hockey. *See* Ice hockey
Hodgkin, Dorothy Crowfoot, 145
Hoffmann, Josef Franz Maria, 240
Hofmann, Hans, 218
Hogan, Ben, 715
Hogarth, William, 222
Holbein, Hans, the Younger, 225
Holiday, Billie "Lady Day," 176
Holidays
    Asia, 20–21
    Canada, 19
    Central America, 20–21
    Europe, 20–21
    religious, 304–306
    South America, 20–21
    United States, 18, 304
Hollerith, Herman, 146
Holm, Hanya, 191
Holst, Gustav, 167
Holy books, 294–296. *See also*
    Religions
    Analect, The, 294
    Bhagavad Gita, 294
    Bible, 294–295
    Five Classics, 294
    Koran, 294
    New Testament, 294
    Old Testament, 294
    Talmud, 295
    Tao-te-ching (The Way and Its
        Power), 295
    Upanishads, 295–296
    Veda, 296
Holy Saturday, 305
Holy See, Apostolic Nunciature of
    the Vatican
    currency, 793
    embassy, 817
    statistics, 938
    telephone code, 973
    travel requirements, 798, 807
Home improvement
    chemicals, hazardous, 568
    exterior
        doors, 568
        siding, 567
        windows, 568
    fireplace maintenance, 569–570

    interior, 566–567
    Web site addresses, 571–572
Home ownership, 583
Home remedies,
    allergies, 506–507
    back pain, 507
    burns, 507
    common cold, 507
    constipation, 507, 508
    flu (influenza), 508
    headaches, 508–509
    hiccups, 508–509
    hyperventilation, 509
    indigestion, 509
    insect bites, 509
    insomnia, 509–510
    premenstrual syndrome (PMS),
        510
    rashes, 510
    sprains, 510–511
    strep throat, 511
Homeopathy, 515
Homer, 261
Homer, Winslow, 219
Honduras
    currency, 791
    embassy, 807
    statistics, 920
    telephone code, 972
    tourist information, 782
    travel requirements, 798
Honegger, Arthur, 169
Hong Kong
    currency, 791
    embassy, 807
    standard time, 9
    statistics, 920
    telephone code, 972
    tourist information, 782
    travel requirements, 798
Hookworm, 513
Hoover, Herbert C., 861
Hopkins, Gerard Manley, 256
Hopper, Edward, 219
Horns, 161
Horse racing, 700–702, 718, 728,
    731
Horses, 39
Horton, Lester, 191
Hospital insurance, 874–875
Hospital, Janette Turner, 254
Hot-air balloon, 127
Hot subdwarfs, 74

Hot tubs, during pregnancy, 501
Hotels
  people with disabilities, 736
  toll-free numbers, 737–738
Hot lines, 675
Hours, divisions of the day, 4
House of Representatives. *See*
  Congress
Housing and Urban Development
  Department, 672
Howells, William Dean, 251
Hoyle, Sir Fred, 142
Hubble, Edwin Powell, 142
Hughes, Langston, 251
Hugo, Victor Marie, 202, 258
Human anatomy
  brain, 35
  digestive system, 36
  ear, 34
  eye, 34
  muscle system, 35
  respiratory system, 36
  skeletal system, 34
Human beings (primates), 39
Humanism, 326
Humboldt, (Friedrich Wilhelm
  Heinrich) Alexander, Baron von,
  147
Hume, David, 312, 324
Humperdinck, Engelbert, 170
Humphrey, Doris, 191
Hundred Years' War, 941
Hungary, Republic of
  Budapest, 954
  currency, 791
  embassy, 807
  standard time, 9
  statistics, 920
  telephone code, 972
  tourist informaiton, 783
  travel requirements, 798
Hunt, Richard Morris, 235
Hurdy gurdy, 159
Hurston, Zora Neale, 251
Husserl, Edmund, 312
Hutton, James, 147
Hybrid funds, 590
Hydrogen bomb, 137
Hydrogen, 126
Hyenas, 38
Hyperbola, 122
Hyperventilation, 509
Hyraxes, 39

I

Ibert, Jacques François Antoine,
  169
  Ibsen, Henrik, 204
Ice hockey, 702, 729, 731
  Gretzky, Wayne, 715
  Lemieux, Mario, 716
  Messier, Mark , 717
  National Hockey League (NHL),
    703
  Plante, Jacques, 718
  Richard, Maurice ("Rocket"), 718
  Stanley Cup, 703–705
Iceland
  currency, 791
  embassy, 808
  statistics, 920
  telephone code, 972
  tourist information, 780, 783
  travel requirements, 798
Idaho
  botanical gardens, 381
  consumer affairs, 651
  crime statistics, 894–895
  domestic violence organization,
    669
  flower/bird/motto/nickname, 877
  legislature, 876
  name origin, 879
  newspaper, 907
  Office on Aging, 639
  personal income per capita, 889
  poison control center, 489
  population, 883
  precipitation, 751
  state tourism office, 748
  temperatures, 753, 755
  two-letter abbreviation, 904
  wildlife refuges, 767, 778
Idealism, 317, 326
Igneous rock, 91–92
Ignoratio elenchus fallacy, 313
Illegal drugs. *See* Drugs
Illinois
  aquariums, 374
  botanical gardens, 381
  Chicago, 955
  consumer affairs, 651–652
  crime statistics, 892–895
  Department on Aging, 639
  domestic violence organization,
    669

  flower/bird/motto/nickname, 877
  General Assembly, 876
  libraries, 337–338
  museums
    art, 364–365
    science and technology, 370
  name origin, 879
  newspapers, 907
  personal income per capita, 888
  poison control centers, 489
  population, 883
  precipitation, 751
  state tourism office, 748
  temperatures, 753, 755
  two-letter abbreviation, 904
  wildlife refuges, 767, 778
  zoos, 374
Imagism, 263
Immigration, admissions to United
  States, 884–887
Immortality, 326
Immunizations, 496, 503
  cats, 44–45
  dogs, 44–45
  travel requirements, 795–801
  vaccines, 502
Impeachment, 864
Impressionism, 231, 263
Indefinite article, 437
Indeterminism, 326
Index funds, 590
Indexing (mortgage interest), 586
India
  Ahmedabad, 955
  Bangalore, 955
  Bombay, 955
  Calcutta, 955
  currency, 791
  Delhi, 955
  embassy, 808
  Hyderabad, 955
  Kanpur, 955
  Madras, 956
  major cities, 954
  standard time, 9
  statistics, 920
  telephone code, 972
  tourist information, 783
  travel requirements, 798
Indiana
  Aging/In-Home Care Services
    Division, 639
  art museums, 365

botanical gardens, 381
consumer affairs, 652–653
crime statistics, 892–893
domestic violence organizaiton, 669
flower/bird/motto/nickname, 877
General Assembly, 876
libraries, 338
name origin, 879
newspapers, 907
personal income per capita, 888
poison control center, 489
population, 883
precipitation, 751
state tourism office, 748
temperatures, 753, 755
two-letter abbreviation, 904
wildlife refuges, 768
zoos, 374–375
Indiana, Robert, 219
Indianapolis 500, 685–686
Indigestion, 509
Individual retirement plans (IRAs), 587, 592–593
Indo-European languages, 416
Indonesia, Republic of
Bandung, 954
currency, 791
embassy, 808
Jakarta, 955
standard time, 9
statistics, 921
Surabaja, 957
telephone code, 972
tourist information, 783
travel requirements, 798
Inductive reasoning, 326
Inductors, 389
Indy cars, 684, 685–686
Infant, 629–630
Infectious, 513
Infinitives (part of speech), 440–441
Influenza immunization, 502–503
Informal dinner parties
etiquette, 470–471
Information, 629–630
Infrared light, 127
Infringement, 629–630
Inge, William, 198
Ingres, Jean-Auguste Dominique, 224
Initiative, 864

Injunction, 629–630
Innate ideas, 326
Inquest, 629–630
Insanity, 629–630
Insect bites, first aid, 485–486, 509
Insect-eating mammals, 39
Insomnia, 509–510
Inspector General's Hot line, 672
Instrumentalism, 326
Instruments, musical. *See* **Musical instruments**
Insulin, 134
Insurance
automobile, 581–582
disability, 580
health, 578–579
life, 579–580
investments, 587
Medicare, 874–875
property and liability, 580–581
Interest, 586, 593
accrued, 592
compound, 574
simple, 574
Interior Department, 672
Interjection, 436
International date line, 8
International organizations, 961–962
International style, 241
Internet, 112. *See also* **Computers**
browsers, 109
cyberspace, 110
e-mail, 111
home page, 112
Internet Service Providers (ISPs), 108, 112
listserv, 113
netiquette, 113
search engines, 108
spam, 114
Usenet, 115
Interstate Commerce Commission, 672
Intransitive verb, 437–438
Intuitionism, 319
Inventions, 122–129, 131–132, 134–141
discoveries, 130, 133
patents, 620
printing press, 941
wheel, 939

Invertebrates
arthropods, 40
coelenterates, 40
echinoderms, 40
mollusks, 40
sponges, 40
worms, 40
Investments, 586
annuities, 587
assets, 592
bank accounts, 587
bond funds, 590
bonds, 588, 592–594
funds of funds, 590
growth-oriented funds, 590
hybrid funds, 590
index funds, 590
life insurance, 587
money-market funds, 590, 593
mutual funds, 589–591, 593
puts and calls, 594
real estate, 588
red herring, 594
reference works, 355
retirement
employer-funded, 591
employer-sponsored, 591
Keogh plan, 591
profit-sharing plans, 591
simplified employee pension plans (SEP-IRAs), 591
Social Security, 591
retirement, 592
risk, 589
small business, 589
stock funds, 590
stocks, 588, 592–594
tax shelter, 594
value-oriented, 590
Invitations
parties, 468–469
wedding, 460–461
Iodine, 526–527
Ionesco, Eugene, 202
Iowa
botanical gardens, 381
consumer affairs, 653
crime statistics, 892–893
Department of Elder Affairs, 639
flower/bird/motto/nickname, 877
General Assembly, 876
libraries, 338

Iowa, *cont.*
name origin, 879
newspaper, 907
personal income per capita, 888
poison control center, 489
population, 883
precipitation, 751
state tourism office, 748
temperatures, 753, 755
two-letter abbreviation, 904
wildlife refuges, 768, 778
Iran
currency, 791
embassy, 808
standard time, 9
statistics, 921
Tehran, 957
telephone code, 972
travel requirements, 798
Iraq
Baghdad, 954
currency, 791
embassy, 808
standard time, 9
statistics, 921
telephone code, 973
travel requirements, 798
Ireland. *See also* **Northern Ireland**
currency, 791
Dublin, 955
embassy, 808
standard time, 9
statistics, 921
telephone code, 973
tourist information, 783
travel requirements, 798
Irish Renaissance, 263
Iron lung, 135
Iron, 526–527
Irrigation, 122
Irving, Washington, 251
Islam, 284–285, 292–293
lunar calendar, 11
symbols, 394
**ISPs (Internet Service Providers),
108, 112**
Israel
currency, 791
embassy, 808
Jerusalem, 931, 955
standard time, 9
statistics, 921

telephone code, 973
tourist information, 783
travel requirements, 798
Italy
currency, 791
embassy, 808
frequently used Italian words and
phrases, 418–419, 421
Genoa, 955
major cities, 956
Naples, 956
Palermo, 956
Rome, 957
standard time, 9
statistics, 921
telephone code, 973
tourist information, 783
travel requirements, 798
Turin, 957
Ivanov, Lev, 194
Ives, Charles, 165
Ivory Coast
statistics, 921
telephone code, 973
Ivory Coast. *See* **Côte D'Ivoire**

J

Jackals, 38
Jackson, Andres, 861
Jackson, Reggie, 715
Jackson, Shirley, 251
Jacobean, 263
Jacquard, Joseph Marie, 146
Jamaica
currency, 791
embassy, 808–809
statistics, 921
tourist information, 783
travel requirements, 798
James, Henry, 251
James, William, 312
Jamison, Judith, 191
Janácek, Leos, 174
Japan
currency, 791
embassy, 809
Fukuok, 955
Kobe, 955
Nagoy, 956
Osaka, 956
royalty, 965
royalty, 973

Sapporo, 957
standard time, 9
statistics, 921
telephone code, 973
Tokyo, 957
tourist information, 783
travel requirements, 798
Yokohama, 958
Jarrell, Randall, 251
Jazz composers, 175–178
Armstrong, Louis "Satchmo," 175
Basie, William "Count," 175
Beiderbecke, Bix, 175
Carter, Betty, 175
Christian, Charlie, 175
Coleman, Ornette, 175–176
Coltrane, John, 176
Davis, Miles, 176
Ellington, Edward Kennedy
"Duke," 176
Evans, Bill, 176
Fitzgerald, Ella, 176
Gillespie, John Birks "Dizzy,"
176
Goodman, Benny, 176
Hancock, Herbie, 176
Hawkins, Coleman, 176
Henderson, Fletcher, 176
Hines, Earl "Fatha," 176
Holiday, Billie "Lady Day," 176
Joplin, Scott, 177
Lewis, John A., 177
Miller, Glenn, 177
Mingus, Charli, 177
MIngus, Charlie, 177
Monk, Thelonious, 177
Morton, Ferdinand "Jelly Roll,"
177
Parker, Charlie "Bird," 177
Reinhardt, Django, 177
Smith, Bessie, 177
Tatum, Art, 177
Vaughan, Sarah "Sassy," 177
Waller, Thomas "Fats," 177
Williams, Mary Lou, 178
Young, Lester "Prez, 178
Jeans, Sir James Hopwood, 142
Jefferson, Thomas, 235, 861
Jehovah's Witnesses, 289
Jelly fish, 40
Jenner, Edward, 150
Jenney, William Le Baron, 235

Jersey, 921
Jiffy time, 18
Joffrey, Robert, 191
Johns, Jasper, 219
Johnson, Andrew, 861
Johnson, Earvin ("Magic"), 715–716
Johnson, Lyndon B., 861
Johnson, Philip Cortelyou, 236
Johnson, Randy, 716
Johnson, Samuel, 256
Joint committee, 864
Joliot-Curie, Frédéric, 152
Jones, Bill T, 191
Jones, Inigo, 237
Jong, Erica, 251
Jonson, Ben, 200
Jooss, Kurt, 195
Joplin, Scott, 177
Jordan, Hashemite Kingdom of
  Amman, 954
  currency, 791
  embassy, 809
  statistics, 921
  telephone code, 973
  travel requirements, 798
Jordan, Michael, 716
Joule (J), 26
Joule, James Prescott, 152
Joyce, James, 261
Joyner-Kersee, Jackie, 716
Judaism, 285, 292–293
  calendars, 931
  food, kosher substitutions, 538
  symbols, 394
  wedding ceremonies, 463
Judgment, 629–630
Judicial system, 859–860
  federal, 622
  Supreme Court
    decisions, 623–625, 627–628
    justice, 622
    justices, 623
Julian calendar, 12
Jung, Carl Gustav, 150
Jupiter, 72
Jury, 629–630
Justice, 326

K

Kafka, Franz, 259
Kahlo, Frida, 228

Kahn, Louis Isadore, 236
Kandinsky, Wassily, 229
Kansas
  art museums, 365
  botanical gardens, 381
  consumer affairs, 653
  crime statistics, 892–893, 896–897
  Department on Aging, 639
  domestic violence organization, 669
  flower/bird/motto/nickname, 877
  legislature, 876
  libraries, 338
  name origin, 879
  newspapers, 907
  personal income per capita, 888
  poison control center, 489
  population, 883
  precipitation, 751
  state tourism office, 748
  temperatures, 753, 755
  two-letter abbreviation, 904
  wildlife refuges, 768, 778
  zoos, 375
Kant, Immanuel, 312–313, 328
Karsavina, Tamara, 194
Kawabata, Yasunari, 254
Kazakhstan
  currency, 791
  embassy, 809
  statistics, 921
  travel requirements, 798
Keats, John, 256
Kelly, Gene, 191
Kelvin (K), 26
Kelvin, Lord William Thomson, 152
Keneally, Thomas (Michael), 254
Kennedy, John F., 861
Kentucky
  art museums, 365
  consumer affairs, 653
  crime statistics, 892–893, 896–897
  Division for Aging Services, 640
  domestic violence organizations, 669
  flower/bird/motto/nickname, 877
  General Assembly, 876
  name origin, 879
  newspapers, 907

  personal income per capita, 888
  poison control center, 490
  population, 883
  precipitation, 751
  state tourism office, 748
  temperatures, 753, 755
  two-letter abbreviation, 904
  zoos, 375
Kentucky Derby (horse racing), 701–702
Kenya
  currency, 791
  embassy, 809
  statistics, 921
  telephone code, 973
  tourist information, 783
  travel requirements, 798
Keogh plans, 591
Kepler, Johannes, 142
Kerouac, Jack, 251
Kettledrum, 162
Khachaturian, Aram, 173
Kierkegaard, Søren, 313
Killer whales, 38
Killy, Jean Claude, 716
Kilogram (kg), 26
Kilometers to miles, 28–29
Kinetic energy, 99–100
Kinetoscope. *See* Films
King Philip's War, 942
King, Billie Jean, 716
Kipling, Rudyard, 256
Kiribati, Republic of
  embassy, 809
  statistics, 921–922
  travel requirements, 798
Kirkland, Gelsey, 191
Kirstein, Lincoln, 191
Kitchen equipment, standard sizes, 567
Kites, 122
Klee, Paul, 230
Klimt, Gustav, 230
Kline, Franz, 219
Koalas, 37
Kodály, Zoltán, 174
Kokoschka, Oskar, 230
Kollwitz, Käthe Schmidt, 225–226
Koran, 294
Korea. *See* North Korea; South Korea
Korean War, 946

Kosinski, Jerzy, 251
Kubrick, Stanley, 205–206
Kuiper, Gerard Peter, 142
Kurosawa, Akira, 205, 207
Kuwait, State of
    currency, 791
    embassy, 809
    statistics, 914
    telephone code, 973
    travel requirements, 798
Kyd, Thomas, 200
Kyrgyz Republic (Kyrgyzstan)
    currency, 791
    embassy, 809
    statistics, 914
    travel requirements, 798

L

Labor Department, 673
Labrouste, Henri (Pierre François Henri), 238
Lamarck, Jean Baptiste Pierre Antoine de Monet, Chevalier de, 144
Lamps
    electronics, 390
Lang, Fritz, 206
Langmuir, Irving, 145
Languages
    American English, 415
    British English, 415
    computers, 113
    foreign words and phrases, 417–421
    game, 326
    Greek, 422–424
    Indo-European, 416
    Latin, 425
Lanthanoids, 81
Laos (Lao People's Democratic Republic)
    currency, 791
    embassy, 810
    statistics, 914
    travel requirements, 798
Lao-tzu, 254
Laplace, Marquis Pierre Simon de, 142
Lardner, Ring, 251
Lasso, Orlando di (Roland de Lassus), 174

Latin language
    frequently used words and phrases, 417–421
    prefixes/suffixes, 425
Latrobe, Benjamin Henry, 236
Latvia
    currency, 791
    embassy, 810
    statistics, 914
    travel requirements, 798
Laurels, 50
Lavoisier, Antoine Laurent, 145
Law
    bills, 865–866
    copyrights, 618–619
    death penalty, 619
    forms and contracts
        Agreement Between Owner and Contractor, 600–603
        bill of sale, 598
        Certificate of Notary, 599
        Declaration of Gift, 604
        lease agreement, 606
        lease agreements, 605–612
        Living Will, 613
        Power of Attorney, 614
        Privacy Act/Freedom of Information Act Request, 615
        Promissory Note, 616
        Request for Reason for Adverse Credit Action, 616
        Security Agreement, 617–618
    legal terms, 626–633
    medicine, patient's bill of rights, 498–500
    patents, 620
    reference works, 357
    wills
        living, 515 516
Lawn mower, 129
Lawrence, D(avid) H(erbert), 256
Laye, Camara, 253
Layer, Rod, 716
Le Corbusier (Charles Édouard Jeanneret), 238
Leacock, Stephen, 257
Leakey, Louis Seymour Bazett (1903–72) and Leakey, Mary Nichol, 147
Leakey, Richard Erskine Frere, 147
Lean, David, 207–208
Leap year, 10

Lease agreements
    "open" rental, 605–606
    seasonal, 607–608
    furnished, 607–608
    unfurnished apartment, 609–612
Lebanon
    Beirut, 954
    currency, 791
    statistics, 914
    travel requirements, 798
Ledoux, Claude Nicolas, 238
Leeuwenhoek, Anton van, 144
Léger, Fernand, 224
Legistlatures
    states, , 859–860, 862–865, 875–877
Leibniz, Gottfried Wilhelm, 313
Leibniz, Gottfried, 324
Lemieux, Mario, 716
Lemmings, 39
Length
    metric system, 27
    U.S., 24
Lenses
    bifocal, 127
    contact, 132
Lent, 304
Lento, 183
Leonard, Sugar Ray, 716
Leoncavallo, Ruggiero, 172
Leopards, 38
Leopold, Aldo, 147
Leonardo da Vinci, 227, 239
Lesotho, Kingdom of
    currency, 791
    embassy, 810
    statistics, 914
    travel requirements, 798
Lesotho, Kingdom of
Lessing, Doris, 256
Letter writing, 446
    business protocol, 446–447
    personal, 446
Letter-by-letter alphabetization, 404
Lewis, Carl, 716
Lewis, John A., 177
Lewis, Sinclair, 251
Lexis-Nexis, 347
Li Po, 254
Liberia, Republic of
    currency, 791
    embassy, 810

statistics, 914
telephone code, 973
travel requirements, 798
Libraries
Arizona, 336
California, 336–337
Canada
Alberta, 344
British Columbia, 345
Ontario, 344
Quebec, 345
Colorado, 337, 350
Connecticut, 337
Dewey Decimal System, 345
Distric of Columbia, 350
District of Columbia, 337, 350
Florida, 337
genealogy, 348–349
Georgia, 337
Illinois, 337–338
Indiana, 338
Iowa, 338
Kansas, 338
Library of Congress Classification
   System, 345–346
Maryland, 338
Massachusetts, 339
Michigan, 339–340
military, 351
Minnesota, 340
Missouri, 340
New Jersey, 340–341
New York, 341–342, 349–351
North Carolina, 342
Ohio, 342
Oklahoma, 342
online databases, 34–349
Pennsylvania, 342–343
reference works, 351
South Carolina, 343
Texas, 343
Utah, 344
Virginia, 344
Washington, 344
Web site addresses, 347, 349
Wisconsin, 344
**Library of Congress Classification
System, 345–346, 349**
Libya
currency, 791
embassy, 810
standard time, 9
statistics, 914

telephone code, 973
travel requirements, 798
Tripoli, 957
Lichtenstein, Roy, 219
Lie detectors, 134
Liechtenstein
currency, 791
embassy, 810
statistics, 914
telephone code, 973
travel requirements, 798
Lien, 586
Lifar, Serge, 194
Life expectancy rates, 504
Life insurance, 579–580, 587
Lifesaving procedures. *See* **First aid,**
475
Light-year, 31, 75
Limbourg, Herbert, Jean and Pol,
221
Limón, Jose, 191
Lincoln, Abraham, 861
Line-item veto, 864
Linguistics
philosophy, 319
phonetic symbols, 415
reference works, 357
Linnaeus, Carolus, 36, 144
Lions, 38
Lippi, Fra Filippo and Filippino,
227
Liszt, Franz, 175
Literature, 278
authors, 253–261
awards/prizes
   Pulitizer prize, 268–269
   National Book Award, 269-271
   Nobel prize, 267–268
books of the century, 272–276
Great Books Foundation,
   271–272
movements/periods/styles,
   261–264
poet laureates, 266–267
pseudonyms of, 264–266
terminology, 276–279
Lithuania
currency, 791
embassy, 810
statistics, 914
travel requirements, 798
Living wills, 515–516, 613

Llamas, 38
Loans, 582
Lobbyist, 864
Locke, John, 314, 324
Logic, 324, 326–327
Logical positivism, 319–320
Lombardi, Vince, 716
London, Jack, 251
Longfellow, Henry Wadsworth, 251
Lonline libraries, 346–348
Loos, Adolf, 240
Lorrain, Claude (Claude Gellé), 224
Lost Generation, 263
Louganis, Greg, 716
Louis, Joe, 716
Louis, Morris, 219
Louisiana
aquariums, 375
botanical gardens, 382
consumer affairs, 653
crime statistics, 894–897
domestic violence organization,
   669
flower/bird/motto/nickname, 877
Governors Office of Elder Affairs,
   640
legislature, 876
name origin, 880
newspapers, 907
personal income per capita, 889
poison control center, 490
population, 883
precipitation, 751
state tourism office, 749
temperatures, 753, 755
two-letter abbreviation, 904
wildlife refuges, 768–769, 778
zoos, 375
Lowell, James Russell, 251
Lowell, Percival, 143
Lowell, Robert, 251
Lowry, Malcolm, 251
Lubitsch, Ernst, 205–206
Lucas, George, 205
Lucretius, 314
Lully, Jean-Baptiste, 169
Lumière, Auguste and Louis, 205
Lunar calendar, 10–11
Lungs, 36
Lute, 158
Lutheran Church, 287, 292
Lutyens, Sir Edwin Landseer, 237

Luxembourg, Grand Duchy of
currency, 791
embassy, 810
statistics, 923
telephone code, 973
tourist information, 783
travel requirements, 798
Lyell, Sir Charles, 147
Lyme disease, 513
Lyre, 158

M

Macau
currency, 791
embassy, 810
statistics, 923
tourist information, 783
travel requirements, 799
MacDowell, Edward, 165
Macedonia, 806, 810. *See also*
Serbia and Montenegro; Yugoslavi
currency, 791
statistics, 923
Mach, Ernst, 152
Machado de Assis, Joaquim Maria,
260
Machiavelli, Niccolò, 314
Machine gun, 130
Macintosh computers, 107
Mackintosh, Charles Rennie, 237
MacMillan, Kenneth, 193
Macron (ø), 415
Madagascar, Democratic Republic
of, 923
Madison, James, 861
Magna Carta, 932
Magnesium, 526–529
Magnifying glass, 123
Magnolias, 50
Magritte, René, 221
Mahfouz, Naguib, 253
Mahler, Gustav, 167
Mailer, Norman, 251
Maillol, Aristide, 224
Maimonides (Moses ben Maimon),
314
Maine
botanical gardens, 382
Bureau of Elder and Adult
Services, 640
consumer affairs, 654
crime statistics, 892–893
domestic violence organization,
670

flower/bird/motto/nickname, 878
legislature, 876
name origin, 880
newspapers, 907
personal income per capita, 888
poison control center, 490
population, 883
precipitation, 751
state tourism office, 749
temperatures, 753, 755
two-letter abbreviation, 904
wildlife refuges, 769, 778
Majority leader, 864
Majority party, 864
Makarova, Natalia, 194
Malamud, Bernard, 251
Malaria, 513
Malawi
currency, 791
embassy, 810–811
statistics, 923
telephone code, 973
travel requirements, 799
Malaysia
currency, 791
embassy, 811
Kuala Lumpur, 956
standard time, 9
statistics, 923
telephone code, 973
tourist information, 783
travel requirements, 799
Maldives
currency, 791
embassy, 811
statistics, 923
travel requirements, 799
Malevich, Kasimir Severinovich,
229
Mali, Republic of
currency, 791
embassy, 811
statistics, 923
travel requirements, 799
Malory, Sir Thomas, 256
Malouf, (George Joseph) David,
254
Malraux, André, 258
Malta
currency, 791
embassy, 811
statistics, 923
tourist information, 783
travel requirements, 799

Mamet, David, 198
Mammals, 64
extinct, 42
marsupials, 37–38
koalas, 37
moles, 38
possums, 37
shrew opossums, 38
wombats, 37
monotremes (egg-laying), 37
placentals, 38–39
aardvarks, 39
bats, 38
dugongs and manatees, 39
elephant shrew, 39
elephants, 39
even-toed hoofed animals, 38
flying lemurs, 38
gnawing, 39
hyraxes and dassies, 39
insect eaters, 39
meat eaters, 38
odd-toed hoofed animals, 39
pandgolins, 39
primates, 39
rabbits and hares, 39
seals and walruses, 39
toothless, 39
tree shrews, 39
whales and porpoises, 38
Mammograms, 513
Man, Isle of, 923
Manatees, 39
Mandate, 864
Mandelstam, Osip Emilevich, 260
Manet, Édouard, 224
Manichaeanism, 320
Manitoba (Canada)
zoos, 379
Mann, Thomas, 259
Mannerism, 231
Manners. *See* **Etiquette; Netiquette**
Mantegna, Andrea, 227
Mantle, Mickey, 716
Manzoni, Alessandro, 259
Mapp v. Ohio, 624
Maps
crustal plates, 88
earthquake zones, 88
frost dates, U.S., 60
hardiness zones, U.S., 59
political
Africa, 976
Antarctica, 975

Asia, 978
Australia and South Pacific, 979
Canada, 983
Europe, 977
Mexico, 983
North America, 981
South America, 980
United States, 982
symbols, 396–397
time zones
   U.S. and Canada, 8
   world, 7
volcanic zones, 88
Marbury v. Madison, 623
Marciano, Rocky, 716
Marcus Aurelius, 314
Marigolds, 49
Marino, Dan, 716
Maris, Roger, 717
Markova, Dame Alicia, 193
Marlowe, Christopher, 200
Marmots, 39
Márquez, Gabriel García. *See* **García Márquez, Gabriel**
Mars, 72, 140
Marshall Islands, Republic of the
   embassy, 311
   Parliament and Council of Local
      Chiefs, 877
   travel requirements, 799
   two-letter abbreviation, 904
Marsupials, 37–38
   koalas, 37
   moles, 38
   possums, 37
   shrew opossums, 38
   wombats, 37
Martens, 38
Martinique (French West Indies)
   currency, 791
   embassy, 811
   statistics, 923
Martins, Peter, 191
Marvell, Andrew, 256
Marx, Karl, 314
Marxism, 320
Maryland
   Alcohol, Drug Abuse and Mental
      Health Administration, 643
   American Council on Alcoholism,
      643
   aquariums, 375
   art museums, 365

botanical gardens, 382
consumer affairs, 654
crime statistics, 892–895
domestic violence organization,
   670
flower/bird/motto/nickname, 878
General Assembly, 876
libraries, 338
name origin, 880
National Association for Children
   of Alcoholics, 643
newspaper, 907
Office on Aging, 640
personal income per capita, 888
poison control center, 490
population, 883
state tourism office, 749
temperatures, 753, 755
two-letter abbreviation, 904
wildlife refuges, 769, 778
zoos, 375
Mascagni, Pietro, 172
Massachusetts
   aquarium, 375
   botanical gardens, 382
   consumer affairs, 654–655
   crime statistics, 892–893,
      896–897
   domestic violence organization,
      670
   Executive Office of Elder Affairs,
      640
   flower/bird/motto/nickname, 878
   General Court, 876
   libraries, 339
   museums
      art, 365–366
      children, 371
      science and technology, 370
   name origin, 880
   newspapers, 907–908
   personal income per capita, 888
   poison control center, 490
   population, 883
   precipitation, 751
   state tourism office, 749
   temperatures, 753, 756
   two-letter abbreviation, 904
   wildlife refuges, 769, 778
   zoos, 375
Massenet, Jules Emile Frédéric, 169
Massine, Léonide, 194
Masters (golf), 700

Materialism, 327
Mathematical logic. *See* **Logic**
Mathematicians, 148–149
Mathematics
   algebra, 123
   calculus, 391
   constants, 391
   decimal system, 103, 123
   deductive, 122
   exponents, 102
   fractions, 102–103
   functions, 390
   geometry, 391
      triangles, 105
      two-dimensional shapes, 104
   googol, 106
   grouping, 390
   operation, 390
   relation, 390
   Roman numerals, 106
   set theory and logic, 391
   symbols, 390–391
   trigonometry, 122
      cosecant (csc), 106
      cotangent (cot or ctn), 106
      formulas, 106
      secant (sec), 106
      sine (sin), 106
      tangent (tan), 106
   unknown numbers, 102
Matisse, Henri, 224
Maugham, William Somerset, 256
Maundy Thursday, 305
**Maupassant, Henri René Albert Guy
de, 258**
Mauriac, François Charles, 258
Mauritania, Republic of
   currency, 791
   embassy, 811
   statistics, 923
   travel requirements, 799
Mauritius
   currency, 791
   embassy, 811
   statistics, 923
   tourist information, 783
   travel requirements, 799
Maury, Matthew Fontaine, 148
Mausoleum at Halicarnassus, 963
Maxwell, James Clerk, 153
Mayotte, 924
Mays, Willie, 717
McCarthy, Mary, 251

McCullers, Carson, 251
McCullock v. Maryland, 623
McCullough, Colleen, 254
McEnroe, John, 717
McKinley, William, 861
Mean solar day, 4
Measles
  during pregnancy, 501
  MMR, 502–503
  vaccine, 137
Measurements. *See* Weights and
  measurements
Meat
  cooking times, 539–541
  serving sizes, 543
Meat-eating mammals, 38
Mechanical clock, 5, 123
Mechanism, 327
Medical insurance, 875
Medical scientists, 149–150
Medicare, 874–875
Medications, 496–497
Medicine. *See also* Health
  artificial limbs, 124
  aspirin, 133
  medical terms, 519
  medications, 496–497
  professions, 122
  reference works, 358
  stethoscope, 128–129
  symbols, 391–392
Melville, Herman, 251
Mencken, H(enry) L(ouis), 251
Mendel, Gregor Johann, 144
Mendel's laws, 64
Mendeleev, Dmitri Ivanovich, 145
Mendelsohn, Erich, 240
Mendelssohn, Felix, 171
Mennonites. *See* Amish Mennonites
Menotti, Gian Carlo, 165
Mercator projection, 94
Merchant Marine Academy, 677
Mercury spacecraft, 115
Mercury, 72
Mesozoic geological era, 86
Messiaen, Olivier Eugène Prosper
  Charles, 169
Messier, Mark, 717
Metaethics, 327
Metamorphic rock, 91–92
Metaphysics, 327
Metempsychosis (transmigration of
  souls), 327

Meteorology
  Beaufort scale of wind force,
    97–98
  cloud types
    altocumulus (Ac), 96
    altostratus (As), 96
    cirrocumulus (Cc), 96
    cirrostratus (CS), 96
    cirrus (Ci), 96
    cumulonimbus (Cb), 96–97
    cumulus (Cu), 97
    nimbostratus (Ns), 97
    stratocumulus (Sc), 97
    stratus (St), 97
  symbols, 392–393
  windchill factor, 98–99
Meter (m), 26
Methodist Church, 287
Metric system, 127
  basic units, 26
  conversion, 28–29
  conversions, 505
  cooking measurements, 536
  decimals, 103
  derived units, 26
  prefixes, 27
  temperature, 29–30
Mexican War, 943
Mexico
  currency, 791
  embassy, 811
  Guadalajara, 955
  major, 956
  map, 983
  Mexico City, 956
  standard time, 9
  statistics, 924
  telephone code, 973
  travel requirements, 799
Meyerbeer, Giacomo, 171
Miró, Joan, 229
Michelangelo Buonarroti, 227, 239
Michener, James, 251
Michigan
  art museums, 366
  botanical gardens, 382
  consumer affairs, 655
  crime statistics, 892–895
  flower/bird/motto/nickname, 878
  legislature, 876
  libraries, 339–340
  name origin, 880
  newspapers, 908

Office of Services to the Aging,
  640
personal income per capita, 888
poison control center, 490
population, 883
precipitation, 751
state tourism office, 749
temperatures, 753, 756
two-letter abbreviation, 904
wildlife refuges, 769, 778
zoos, 375
Micronesia
  currency, 791
  embassy, 811
  travel requirements, 799
Microscopes
  compound, 124
  electron, 135
Middleton, Thomas, 200
MIDI (Musical Instrument Digital
  Interface), 163
Midway Islands, Administered by
  U.S. Navy, 877
Mies van der Rohe, Ludwig, 236
Miles to kilometers, 28–29
Miletian School, 320
Milhaud, Darius, 169
Military
  forms of address, 454
  libraries, 351
Military Academy, 677
Milky Way, 78
Mill, John Stuart, 314, 324
Miller, Arthur, 198
Miller, Glenn, 177
Miller, Henry, 252
Miller, Stanley Lloyd, 144
Millet, Jean-François, 224
Mills, Robert, 236
Milton, John, 256
Mind-body problem, 327
Minerals, 91–92, 524–529
  geology, 94
  nutrition, 90, 521
Mingus, Charlie, 177
Minimalism, 232
Minnesota
  art museums, 366
  Association of Halfway House
    Alcoholism Programs of North
    America, 643
  consumer affairs, 655
  crime statistics, 892–893, 896–897

Domestic Violence Organization, 670
flower/bird/motto/nickname, 878
legislature, 876
libraries, 340
Minnesota Board on Aging, 640
name origin, 880
newspapers, 908
personal income per capita, 888
poison centers, 490
population, 883
precipitation, 751
state tourism office, 749
temperatures, 753, 756
two-letter abbreviation, 904
wildlife refuges, 769–770, 778
zoos, 375–376
Minority leader, 864
Minority party, 865
MIR space station, 115
Miranda v. Arizona, 624
Mishima, Yukio, 254
Mississippi
consumer affairs, 656
Council on Aging, 640
crime statistics, 892–893
domestic violence organization, 670
flower/bird/motto/nickname, 878
legislature, 876
name origin, 880
newspaper, 908
personal income per capita, 888
poison control center, 490
population, 883
precipitation, 751
state tourism office, 749
temperatures, 753, 756
two-letter abbreviation, 904
wildlife refuges, 770, 778
zoos, 376
Missouri
American Council on Alcohol Problems, 643
botanical gardens, 382
consumer affairs, 656
crime statistics, 892–893, 896–897
Division of Aging, 640
flower/bird/motto/nickname, 878
General Assembly, 876
libraries, 340
museums
art, 366
children, 371

name origin, 880
newspapers, 908
personal income per capita, 888
poison control center, 490
population, 883
precipitation, 752
state tourism office, 749
temperatures, 753, 756
two-letter abbreviation, 904
wildlife refuges, 770, 778
zoos, 376
Mitchell, Arthur, 191
Mitchell, Margaret, 252
Mixed Drinks. *See* **Alcohol**
MMR(measles/mumps/rubella) immunization, 502–503
Modernism, 263
Modifier, 437
Modigliani, Amedeo, 227
Mohs, Friedrich, 148
Moldova, Republic of
currency, 791
embassy, 811
statistics, 924
travel requirements, 799
Mole (mol), 26
Moles (marsupials), 38–39
Molíre (Jean Baptiste Poquelin), 202
Molina, Tirso de (Gabriel Tellez), 204
Mollusks, 40
Monaco
currency, 791
statistics, 924
telephone code, 973
tourist information, 783
travel requirements, 799
Monaco, Principality of
embassy, 811
Monad, 327
Monarchy. *See* **Royalty**
Mondrian, Piet, 222
Monet, Claude, 224
Monetary
symbols, 401
Money-market funds, 590, 593
Mongolia
currency, 791
embassy, 811–812
statistics, 924
travel requirements, 799
Mongooses, 38

Monism, 327
Monk, Thelonious, 177
Monkeys, 39
Monopoly®, 722–723
Monotremes (egg-laying) mammals, 37
Monroe Doctrine, The, 854
Monroe, James, 861
Montage, 205
Montaigne, Michel de, 258
Montana
consumer affairs, 656
Coordinator of Aging Services, 640
crime statistics, 894–895
domestic violence organizations, 670
flower/bird/motto/nickname, 878
Legislative Assembly, 876
name origin, 880
newspapers, 908
personal income per capita, 889
poison control center, 490
population, 883
precipitation, 752
state tourism office, 749
temperatures, 753, 756
two-letter abbreviation, 904
wildlife refuges, 770–771, 778
Montana, Joe, 717
Montesquieu, Baron de (Charles-Louis de Secondat), 314
Monteverdi, Claudio, 172
Montgomery, Lucy Maud, 258
Montserrat
currency, 791
statistics, 924
Mood (verb), 439
Moon
Apollo missions, 116
lunar eclipses, 68–69
phases, 68, 388
Moore, Douglas, 165
Moore, G. E. (George Edward), 314
Moore, Henry, 222
Moorehead, Alan [McCrae], 254
Moose, 38
Morceli, Noureddine, 717
More, Sir Thomas, 314
Morisot, Berthe, 224
Morley, Thomas, 168
Mormons (The Church of Jesus Christ of Latter Day Saints), 289

Morocco
Casablanca, 955
currency, 791
embassy, 812
standard time, 9
statistics, 924
telephone code, 973
tourist information, 784
travel requirements, 799
Morrison, Toni [Chloe Anthony Wofford], 252
Morse code, 129, 399
Mortgages. *See also* **Real estate**
adjustable-rate (ARM), 584–585
affordability, 583–584
amortization, 575
assumable, 585
calculating, 576
contracts, 585
down payment, 584
Fannie Mae, 586
Federal Housing Administration (FHA), 586
Freddie Mac, 586
Ginnie Mae, 586
graduated payment (GPM), 584
indexing, 586
lien, 586
pledged-account (PAM), 584
points, 585–586
reverse, 585
shared-appreciation (SAM), 585
wraparound, 585
Morton, Ferdinand "Jelly Roll," 177
Moser-Proll, Annemarie, 717
Moses, Grandma, 219
Motels
people with disabilities, 736
toll-free numbers, 737–738
Web sites, 737–738
Mother Jones, 911
Motherwell, Robert, 219
Motion pictures. *See* **Films**
Mount Vesuvius, 924
Mountain Standard Time (MST), 8
Movies. *See* **Films**
Mozambique, Republic of
currency, 792
embassy, 812
statistics, 924
travel requirements, 799
Mozart, Wolfgang Amadeus, 167

Muir, John, 148
Muller v. Oregon, 624
Mumps, 513
Mums, 49
Munch, Edvard, 230
Munn v. Illinois, 623
Munro, Alice, 258
Murasaki, Shikibu, 254
Murillo, Bartolemé Estéban, 229
Murnau, F. W., 208
Muscles, 35
Museums
art, 362–369
Arizona, 362
California, 362–363
Colorado, 363
Connecticut, 363
Delaware, 364
District of Columbia, 364
Hawaii, 364
Illinois, 364–365
Indiana, 365
Kansas, 365
Kentucky, 365
Maryland, 365
Massachusetts, 365–366
Michigan, 366
Minnesota, 366
Missouri, 366
New Jersey, 366
New Mexico, 366
New York, 367–368
Ohio, 368
Oklahoma, 368
Oregon, 368
Pennsylvania, 368–369
Texas, 369
Virginia, 369
Wisconsin, 369
children, 371–372
California, 372
District of Columbia, 371
Massachusetts, 371
Missouri, 371
New York, 371
Pennsylvania, 372
science and technology, 370–371
Canada, 371
District of Columbia, 371
Illinois, 370
Massachusetts, 370
New York, 370
Pennsylvania, 370

Music
terminology, 178–187
classical composers, 166, 168–169, 171–175
jazz composers, 175–178
notation, 122
reference works, 359
symbols, 393–394
Musical Instrument Digital Interface (MIDI), 163
Musical instruments
bowed, 159
electronic, 163, 389
hammered, 158
orchestra, 163–164
percussion
definite pitch, 162
indefinite pitch, 162–163
plucked, 158
wind
brass, 161–162
open mouthpiece, 159–160
reed type, 160–161
Musk oxen, 38
Muskrats, 39
Mussorgsky, Modest, 173
Mutual funds, 589–591, 593
Myanmar, Union of
currency, 792
embassy, 812
statistics, 924
travel requirements, 799
Yangon, 958
Mysticism, 327
Myth of Er, 327
Mythology, 282–283

N

NAACP Legal Defense and Education Fund, 634
Nabis, 232
Nabokov, Vladimir Vladimirovich, 260
Naipaul, V. S., 260
Naive art, 232
Namath, Joe, 717
Namibia
currency, 792
embassy, 812
statistics, 924
telephone code, 973
travel requirements, 799
Nash, John, 238

National Archives, The, 350
National Basketball Association (NBA), 691–692
National Book Award
    fiction, 269
    nonfiction, 270–271
National Center for Missing and Exploited Children, 675
National Credit Union Administration, 673
National Football Conference (NFC), 698
National Health Information Center, 673
National Hockey League (NHL), 703
National Institute of Standards and Technology, 673
National Labor Relations Board, 673
National League (NL) (baseball), 688
National Organization for Victim Assistance (NOVA), 675
National parks, 758–762
National Runaway Switchboard, 675
Natsume Sōseki, 254
Natural law, 327–328
Natural rights, 327–328
Naturalism, 263, 327
Naturalistic fallacy, 327
Nature
    literature, 273
    symbols, 397
Nauru, Republic of
    currency, 792
    embassy, 812
    statistics, 924
    travel requirements, 799
Naval Academy, 678
Navratilova, Martina, 717
Nebraska
    consumer affairs, 656
    crime statistics, 892–893
    domestic violence organization, 670
    flower/bird/motto/nickname, 878
    legislature, 876
    name origin, 880
    Nebraska Department on Aging, 640
    newspapers, 908

personal income per capita, 888
poison control center, 490
population, 883
precipitation, 752
state tourism office, 749
temperatures, 753, 756
two-letter abbreviation, 904
unicameral government, 875
wildlife refuges, 771, 778
zoos, 376
Necessary and contingent truth, 328
Neoclassicism, 232, 263
Neoplatonism, 320
Nepal, Kingdom of
    currency, 792
    embassy, 812
    statistics, 924
    tourist information, 784
    travel requirements, 799
Neptune, 72
Neruda, Pablo [Neftali Ricardo Reyes Basoalto], 260
Net worth, 576–577
Netherlands, The
    Amsterdam, 954
    currency, 792
    embassy, 812
    Rotterdam, 957
    standard, 9
    statistics, 924
    telephone code, 973
    tourist information, 784
    travel requirements, 799
Netherlands Antilles
    currency, 792
    embassy, 812
    statistics, 924
    telephone code, 973
    travel requirements, 799
Netiquette (network etiquette), 113, 468. *See also* Internet
Networks
    computers, 113
    radio, 674–677
    television, 674–677
Neutering pets, 43
Neutron stars, 74
Neutrons, 139
Nevada
    consumer affairs, 656
    crime statistics, 894–895
    Division for Aging Services, 640

domestic violence organization, 670
flower/bird/motto/nickname, 878
legislature, 876
name origin, 880
newspapers, 908
personal income per capita, 889
poison control center, 490
population, 883
precipitation, 752
state tourism office, 749
temperatures, 753, 756
two-letter abbreviation, 904
wildlife refuges, 771, 778
Nevelson, Louise, 219
New Caledonia
    currency, 792
    statistics, 917
    telephone code, 973
New Hampshire
    botanical gardens, 382
    consumer affairs, 656
    crime statistics, 892–893
    Division of Elderly and Adult Services, 641
    domestic violence organization, 670
    flower/bird/motto/nickname, 878
    General Court, 876
    name origin, 880
    newspaper, 908
    personal income per capita, 888
    poison control center, 490
    population, 883
    state tourism office, 749
    two-letter abbreviation, 904
    wildlife refuges, 771
New Jersey
    botanical gardens, 382
    consumer affairs, 656–658
    crime statistics, 892–893, 896–897
    Division of Senior Affairs, 641
    Domestic Violence Organization, 670
    flower/bird/motto/nickname, 878
    legislature, 876
    libraries, 340–341
    museums, art, 366
    name origin, 880
    newspapers, 908
    personal income per capita, 888
    poison control center, 490

New Jersey, *cont.*
  population, 883
  precipitation, 752
  state tourism office, 749
  temperatures, 753, 756
  theme parks, 779
  two-letter abbreviation, 904
  wildlife refuges, 771, 779
  zoos, 376
New Mexico
  art museums, 366
  botanical gardens, 382
  crime statistics, 894–895
  domestic violence organizations, 670
  flower/bird/motto/nickname, 878
  legislature, 876
  name origin, 880
  newspapers, 908
  personal income per capita, 889
  poison control center, 490
  population, 883
  precipitation, 752
  State Agency on Aging, 641
  state tourism office, 749
  temperatures, 753, 756
  two-letter abbreviation, 904
  wildlife refuges, 771–772, 779
  zoos, 376
New Testament, 294
New York
  aquariums, 376
  botanical gardens, 382–383
  consumer affairs, 659–661
  crime statistics, 892–897
  domestic violence organizations, 670
  flower/bird/motto/nickname, 878
  legislature, 876
  libraries, 341–342, 349–351
  museums, 350
    art, 367–368
    children, 371
    science and technology, 370
  name origin, 880
  newspapers, 908–909
  New York, 956
  personal income per capita, 888
  poison control centers, 490–491
  population, 883
  precipitation, 752
  state tourism office, 749
  temperatures, 754, 756

  two-letter abbreviation, 904
  wildlife refuges, 772, 779
  zoos, 376
New Zealand
  Auckland, 954
  currency, 792
  embassy, 812
  statistics, 933
  telephone code, 973
  tourist information, 784
  travel requirements, 799
  Wellington, 958
Newlands, John Alexander Reina, 145
Newman, Barnett, 219
Newspapers, 906–910
  Alabama, 906
  Alaska, 906
  Arizona, 906
  Arkansas, 906
  California, 906
  Colorado, 906
  Connecticut, 906
  Delaware, 906
  District of Columbia, 906
  Florida, 907
  Georgia, 907
  Hawaii, 907
  Idaho, 907
  Illinois, 907
  Indiana, 907
  Iowa, 907
  Kansas, 907
  Kentucky, 907
  Louisiana, 907
  Maine, 907
  Maryland, 907
  Massachusetts, 907–908
  Michigan, 908
  Minnesota, 908
  Mississippi, 908
  Missouri, 908
  Montana, 908
  national, 906
  Nebraska, 908
  Nevada, 908
  New Hampshire, 908
  New Jersey, 908
  New Mexico, 908
  New York, 908–909
  North Carolina, 909
  North Dakota, 909
  Ohio, 909

  Oklahoma, 909
  Oregon, 909
  Pennsylvania, 909
  Rhode Island, 909
  South Carolina, 909
  South Dakota, 910
  Tennessee, 910
  Texas, 910
  Utah, 910
  Vermont, 910
  Virginia, 910
  Washington, 910
  Wisconsin, 910
  Wyoming, 910
Newsweek, 911
Newton (N), 26
Newton, Sir Isaac, 26, 153
Newton's second law, 99
Niacin, 522–523
Nicaragua
  currency, 792
  embassy, 812
  Managua, 956
  standard time, 9
  statistics, 917
  telephone code, 973
  travel requirements, 799
Nicklaus, Jack ("Golden Bear"), 717
Nielsen, Carl, 175
Niemeyer, Oscar, 240
Nietzsche, Friedrich Wilhelm, 314
Niger, Republic of
  currency, 792
  embassy, 812
  statistics, 917
  travel requirements, 799
Nigeria, Republic of
  currency, 792
  embassy, 812
  Ibadan, 955
  Lagos, 956
  statistics, 917
  telephone code, 973
  travel requirements, 799
Nihilism, 320
Nijinska, Bronislava, 194
Nijinsky, Vaslav, 194
Nikolais, Alwin, 191–192
Nimbostratus (Ns) cloud, 97
Nitrogen, 126
Niue
  statistics, 917
  travel requirements, 799

Nixon, Richard M., 862
Nobel Prize in Literature, 267–268
Nobel, Alfred Bernhard, 145
Nobility. *See* Royalty
Noguchi, Isamu, 219
Nominalism, 328–329
Non sequitur, 329
Nonrestrictive clause, 438
Nonsurgical treatment, 496
Norfolk Island
    statistics, 917
    travel requirements, 799
Norman, 241
North America. *See also* Canada;
    United States
    map, 981
    Vikings, 948
North Carolina
    botanical gardens, 383
    consumer affairs, 661
    crime statistics, 892–893, 896–897
    Division of Aging, 641
    domestic violence organization,
        670
    flower/bird/motto/nickname, 878
    General Assembly, 876
    libraries, 342
    name origin, 880
    newspapers, 909
    personal income per capita, 888
    poison control centers, 491
    population, 883
    precipitatin, 752
    state tourism office, 750
    temperatures, 754, 756
    two-letter abbreviation, 904
    wildlife refuges, 772, 779
    zoos, 377
North Dakota
    Aging Services, 641
    botanical gardens, 383
    consumer affairs, 661–662
    crime statistics, 892–893
    domestic violence organization,
        670
    flower/bird/motto/nickname, 878
    Legislative Assembly, 876
    name origin, 880
    newspaper, 909
    personal income per capita, 888
    poison control center, 491
    population, 883
    precipitation, 752
    state tourism office, 750

temperatures, 754, 756
two-letter abbreviation, 904
wildlife refuges, 773, 779
zoos, 377
North Korea
    currency, 791
    embassy, 809
    Pyongyang, 957
    statistics, 914
    travel requirements, 798
Northern Ireland
    embassy, 817
    standard time, 9
    tourist information, 784
Northern Mariana Islands
    Legislature, 877
    travel requirements, 799
    two-letter abbreviation, 904
Northern Securities Co. v. U.S., 624
Norway
    currency, 792
    embassy, 813
    standard time, 9
    statistics, 917
    telephone code, 973
    tourist information, 780, 784
    travel requirements, 799
Nosebleeds, first aid, 486
Noun, 436–437
Nova Scotia
    poison control center, 493
    standard time, 9
Novae, 74
Noverre, Jean Georges, 193
Nuclear fusion, 141
Nuclear Regulatory Commission,
    673
Numbers
    Braille, 400–401
Numerals
    Roman, 106
Nureyev, Rudolf, 194
Nurmi, Paavo, 717
Nutrition. *See also* Food
    food hot lines, 545
    low-fat substitutions, 538–539
    minerals, 521, 524–529
    pets, 44
    proteins, 520
    vitamins, 522–525
        fat-soluble, 520
        water-soluble, 521
Nutrition Information Center, 350

O

ø (macron), 415
O'Casey, Sean, 203
O'Keeffe, Georgia, 219
O'Neill, Eugene, 199
Oates, Joyce Carol, 252
Objectivism, 329
Obligation, 329
Oboe, 160
Ockham's razor, 329
Octagon, 104
October (Bolshevik) Revolution,
    945
Odets, Clifford, 198
Offenbach, Jacques, 169
Offset printing (web press), 130
Ohio
    aquariums, 377
    art museums, 368
    botanical gardens, 383
    consumer affairs, 662
    crime statistics, 892–897
    Department of Aging, 641
    domestic violence organization,
        670
    flower/bird/motto/nickname, 878
    General Assembly, 876
    libraries, 342
    name origin, 880
    newspapers, 909
    personal income per capita, 888
    poison control centers, 491
    population, 883
    precipitation, 752
    state tourism office, 750
    temperatures, 754, 756
    two-letter abbreviation, 904
    wildlife refuges, 773
    zoos, 377
Ohm, 26
Ohm's law, 27, 99, 153
Oklahoma
    art museums, 368
    botanical gardens, 383
    consumer affairs, 662
    crime statistics, 894–897
    domestic violence organization,
        670
    flower/bird/motto/nickname, 878
    legislature, 876
    libraries, 342
    name origin, 880

Oklahoma, *cont.*
newspapers, 909
personal income per capita, 889
poison control center, 491
population, 883
precipitation, 752
Special Unit on Aging, 641
state tourism office, 750
temperatures, 754, 756
two-letter abbreviation, 904
wildlife refuges, 773, 779
zoos, 377
Old Testament, 294
Oldenburg, Claes, 219
Olives, 51
Olympian Zeus, 963
Olympic Games, 729, 732
first games, 923
summer, 710–712
winter, 711–712
Oman, Sultanate of
currency, 792
embassy, 813
statistics, 917
telephone code, 973
travel requirements, 799
Omar Khayya'm, 149, 254
Ontario (Canada)
libraries, 344
museums, 370
poison control center, 493
zoos, 379
Ontology, 329
Oort, Jan Hendrik, 143
Op art, 232
Op, 124
Operating system (OS), 107,
113–114
Operationalism, 329
Ophüls, Max, 208
Oppenheimer, J. Robert, 74
Optic nerve, 124
Optimism, 329
Orangutans, 39
Orchestra, 163–164
Ordinary Language Philosophy, 320
Oregon
art museums, 368
botanical gardens, 383
consumer affairs, 662
crime statistics, 894–897
domestic violence organization,
670

flower/bird/motto/nickname, 878
Legislative Assembly, 876
name origin, 880
newspaper, 909
personal income per capita, 889
poison control center, 491
population, 883
precipitation, 752
Senior and Disabled Services
Division, 641
state tourism office, 750
temperatures, 754, 756
two-letter abbreviation, 904
wildlife refuges, 773–774, 779
zoos, 377
Orff, Carl, 171
Organizations
international, 961–962
Orozco, José Clemente, 228
Orthodox Church, 285
Orwell, George [Eric Blair], 257
OS (operating system), 107,
113–114
Osborne, John, 200
Oscars. *See* Academy Awards
Osteopathy, 514
Otters, 38
Override, 865
Ovid Technologies, 349
Ovid, 261
Owens, Jesse, 717
Owner and Contractor Agreement,
600–603
Ox-drawn plow, 122
Oxygen, 126
Oxymoron, 278, 427
Ozone, 129, 141
Ozu, Yasujiro, 205, 207

P

P.M. (post meridiem), 5
Pacific Standard Time (PST), 8
Paderewski, Ignace, 175
Paine, Thomas, 252
Painters. *See* Artists
Painting. *See* Art
Pakistan
cities, 963–964
currency, 792
embassy, 813
Hyderabad, 955
Karachi, 955
Lahore, 956

standard time, 9
statistics, 917
telephone code, 973
travel requirements, 799
Palau, Republic of
currency, 792
embassy, 813
Legislature, 877
statistics, 917
travel requirements, 799
two-letter abbreviation, 904
Paleozoic geological era, 86
Palestrina, Giovanni Pierluigi da
(Johannes Praenestinus), 172
Palindrome, 278, 428
Palladio, Andrea, 239
Palm Sunday, 305
Palmer, Arnold, 717
Panama
currency, 792
embassy, 813
standard time, 9
statistics, 917
telephone code, 973
travel requirements, 799
Pandas, 38
Pangolins, 39
Panpipes, 159
Pantheism, 330
Paper making, 123
Pappus of Alexandria, 149
Papua New Guinea
currency, 792
embassy, 813
statistics, 917
telephone code, 973
tourist information, 784
travel requirements, 799
Paraguay
currency, 792
embassy, 813
statistics, 918
telephone code, 973
travel requirements, 799
Parallel structure (grammar), 440
Parasites
external, 47
internal, 47–48
Parentheses (punctuation), 442–443
Parents, organizations for, 674–675,
679
Parker, Charile "Bird," 177
Parker, Dorothy, 252

Parks, people with disabilities, 736
Parmenides, 314
Parnassians, 263
Parrish, Maxfield, 219
Participles (part of speech), 440
Parties. *See* Entertainment
Parts of speech. *See* Grammar
Pascal, Blaise, 26, 146, 315, 324
Pascal's wager, 330
Passover, 305
Passports, 793–795
Pasternak, Boris Leonidovich, 260
Pasteur, Louis, 150
Pasteurization, 130
Patents, 620–621
Patient's bill of rights, 498
Paton, Alan Stewart, 253
Patron saints. *See* Saints
Pauling, Linus Carl, 145
Pause (punctuation), 442
Pavlov, Ivan Petrovich, 150
Pavlova, Anna Matveyevna, 194
Paxton, Sir Joseph, 237–238
Payton, Walter, 717
Paz, Octavio, 260
PCs (personal computers), 107
Peace Corps, 673
Peanuts, 50
Peccaires, 38
Peerage
    hereditary, 966
Pelé [Edson Arantes do
    Nascimento], 717
Pelopennesian War, 948
Penché, 197
Pendulum clock, 125
Pei, I(eoh) M(ing), 236
Pelopennesian War, 940
Pennsylvania
    botanical gardens, 383
    consumer affairs, 662–663
    crime statistics, 892–897
    Department of Aging, 641
    domestic violence organization,
        670
    flower/bird/motto/nickname, 878
    General Assembly, 876
    libraries, 342–343
    museums
        art, 368–369
        children, 372
        science and technology, 370
    name origin, 880

newspapers, 909
personal income per capita, 888
poison control centers, 492
population, 883
precipitation, 752
state tourism office, 750
temperatures, 754, 756
two-letter abbreviation, 904
wildlife refuges, 774, 779
zoos, 377
Pentacostal churches, 288
Pentagon, 104
Pentecost, 305
Percussion instruments, 163
Percy, Walker, 252
Performing Arts Library, The, 350
Pergolesi, Giovanni Battista, 172
Period (punctuation), 441
Periodic Table of the Elements, The,
    81–82
Periodicals, 352
Perpetual calendars, 13–17
Perrot, Jules, 193
Persian Gulf War, 947
Persian Wars, 940
Personalism, 320
Pertussis (whooping cough), 513
Peru
    currency, 792
    embassy, 813
    Lima, 956
    standard time, 9
    statistics, 918
    telephone code, 973
    travel requirements, 799
Pessimism, 330
Petipa, Marius, 194
Petit, Roland, 193
Petrarch, 259
Petronius, 261
Pets. *See also* Cats; Dogs
    with children, 44
    choosing, 42–43
    first aid
        broken bones, 45
        burns, 45–46
        constipation, 46
        dental disorders, 46
        diarrhea, 47
        parasites, external, 47
        parasites, internal, 47–48
        rabies, 48
        shock, 48

skin problems, 48
sprains, 49
wounds, 49
immunizations, 44
neutering, 43
nutrition, 44
spaying, 43
stain removal, 44
travel, 735
Petty, Richard, 717
Pharmacology, 391–392
Phases of the moon, 68
Phenomenalism, 330
Phenomenology, 320
Phidias (Pheidias), 230
Philipines
    currency, 792
    embassy, 813
    Manila, 956
    Quezon City, 957
    standard time, 9
    statistics, 918
    telephone code, 973
    tourist information, 784
    travel requirements, 799
Philosopher king, 330
Philosopher's stone, 331
Philosophers, 26, 310–317, 324,
    328
    Abelard, Peter, 310
    Anaxagoras, 310
    Anaximander, 310
    Anaximenes, 310
    Anselm, St., 310
    Aquinas, St. Thomas, 310, 328
    Aristotle, 310, 324
    Augustine of Hippo, St., 310
    Averroes, 310, 324
    Avicenna, 310, 324
    Ayer, Alfred Jules, 310
    Ayers, Alfred Jules, 311
    Bacon, Sir Francis, 311
    Bentham, Jeremy, 311, 324
    Berkeley, George, 311
    Boethius, 311
    Buber, Martin, 311
    Comte, Auguste, 311
    Democritus, 311
    Derrida, Jacques, 311
    Descartes, René, 311
    Dewey, John, 311
    Diderot, Denis, 311
    Diogenes, 311

Philosophers, *cont.*
Empedocles, 312
Engels, Friedrich, 312
Epictetus, 312
Epicurus, 312
Foucault, Michel, 312
Hegel, Georg Wilhelm Friedrich, 312
Heidegger, Martin, 312
Heraclitus, 312
Hobbes, Thomas, 312
Hume David, 324
Hume, David, 312
Husserl, Edmund, 312
James, William, 312
Kant, Immanuel, 312–313, 328
Kierkegaard, Søren, 313
Leibniz, Gottfried Wilhelm, 313
Locke, John, 314, 324
Lucretius, 314
Machiavelli, Niccoló, 314
Maimonides (Moses ben Maimon), 314
Marcus Aurelius, 314
Marx, Karl, 314
Mill, John Stuart, 314, 324
Montesquier, Baron de (Charles-Louis de Secondat), 314
Moore, G. E. (George Edward), 314
More, Sir Thomas, 314
Newton, Sir Isaac, 26
Nietzsche, Friedrich Wilhelm, 314
Parmenides, 314
Pascal, Blaise, 26, 315, 324
Phosphorus, 526–527
Plato, 315
Plotinus, 315
Pythagoras, 315
Quine, Willard Van Orman, 315
Rawls, John, 315
Rousseau,Jean Jacques, 315
Russell, Bertrand, 315
Ryle, Gilbert, 315
Santayana, George, 315
Sartre, Jean-Paul, 315–316
Schopenhauer, Arthur, 316
Scotus, John Duns, 316, 320
Smith, Adam, 316
Socrates, 316
Spinoza, Benedict (Baruch), 316
Thales of Miletus, 316
Unamuno, Miguel de, 316

Voltaire (François Marie Arouet), 316
Whitehead, Alfred North, 316
William of Ockham (Occam), 316
Wittgenstein, Ludwig, 316–317
Zeno (of Citium) the Stoic, 317
Zeno of Elea, 317
Philosophes, 320
Philosophy
movements/schools of thought, 317–322
terminology, 322–333
famous quotes, 319
Philosophy Documentation Center, 333
Phonetic symbols, 415
Phosphorus, 526–527
Photography
color, 134
Phrase, 185, 437, 441
Photorealism, 232
Physical disabilities, reading aids, 668
Physicalism, 330
Physicists, 151–153
Coulomb, Charles A., 27
Joule, James, 26
Ohm, Georg Simon, 27
Volta, Count Alessandro, 27
Physics
terminology, 99–101
magazines, 119
symbols, 392
Piazzi, Giuseppe, 143
Picasso, Pablo (Pablo Ruiz y Picasso), 229
Piccolo, 159
Pierce, Franklin, 861
Piero della Francesca, 227–228
Pigs, 38
Pinochle, 725
Pinter, Harold, 200–201
Pipe organ, 159
Pirandello, Luigi, 204
Piranesi, Giovanni Battista, 239
Pisano, Nicola and Giovanni, 228
Pissarro, Camille, 224
Pistol, 124
Piston, Walter, 166
Placental mammals, 38–39
aardvarks, 39
bats, 38

dugongsa and manatees, 39
elephant shrews, 39
elephants, 39
even-toed hoofed animals, 38
flying lemurs, 38
gnawing, 39
hyraxes and dassies, 39
insect eaters, 39
meat eaters, 38
odd-toed hoofed animals, 39
pangolins, 39
primates, 39
rabbits and hares, 39
seals and walruses, 39
toothless, 39
tree shrews, 39
whales and porpoises, 38
Planck, Max Karl Ernst Ludwig, 153
Planck's law, 101
Planets
diameters, 72
distance from sun, 72
Earth, 72
Jupiter, 72
Mars, 72
Mercury, 72
Neptune, 72
Pluto, 72
Saturn, 72
symbols, 388
Uranus, 72
Venus, 72
Plante, Jacques, 718
Plants. *See also specific plants*
alfalfa, 50
asters, 49
beeches, 50
begonias, 49
birches, 50
botanical names, 51–55
cacti, 50
cultivation, 58–59
dogwoods, 50
flowers, 61
frost dates, 60
geraniums, 50
germination, 61
ground covers, 56
laurels, 50
magnolias, 50
olives, 51
orders, 51

organizations, 65
perihelion, 10
poisonous, 57–58
primroses, 51
roses, 51
vegetables, 61
vines, 56
walnuts, 50
water lilies, 51
wild, 57–58
Plasma, 79, 101
Plate tectonics. *See* **Earthquakes;**
  Geology
Plath, Sylvia, 252
Platinum, 124
Plato, 315
Plato's cave, 330
Platonism, 320
Plautus, 203
Playfair, John, 148
Playwrights, 198–204
Pledge of Allegiance, The, 856
Plessy v. Ferguson, 624
Plisetskaya, Maya, 194–195
Plotinus, 315
Plows, 122–123
Plucked instruments, 158
Pluralism, 330
Plutarch, 261
Pluto, 72
Pneumonia immunization, 503
Pocket veto, 865
Poe, Edgar Allan, 252
Poet laureates. 266–267
Pointillism, 232
Points (mortgage), 585–586
Poisoning
  control centers
    Canada, 493
    United States, 489–490, 492
  corrosive, 486
  first aid, 486–488
  food, 486
  inhaled, 487
  noncorrosive, 487
  petroleum distillates, 487
Poisonous plants, 57–58
Poker, 725–726
Poland, Republic of
  currency, 792
  embassy, 813
  Lodz, 956
  standard time, 9

statistics, 918
telephone code, 973
tourist information, 784
travel requirements, 799
Warsaw, 957
Polio vaccine, 138, 502
Poliomyelitis, 513
Political action committee (PAC),
  865
Political philosophy, 330–331
Political science, reference works,
  359–360
Polk, James K., 861
Pollen, 125
Pollock, Jackson, 220
Polygon, 104
Pompeii, 924, 932
Pop art, 232
Pope, Alexander, 257
Popes, Roman Catholicism,
  297–304
Popular culture, literature, 274
Population. *See also specific coun-*
  tries
    United States, 881–883
    major world cities, 954–958
Porcelain, 123
Porpoises, 38
Porter, Katherine Anne, 252
Portugal
  currency, 792
  embassy, 813
  Lisbon, 956
  standard time, 9
  statistics, 918
  telephone code, 973
  tourist information, 784
  travel requirements, 799
Positivism, 331
Possums, 37
Post hoc ergo propter hoc, 313
Postal Rate Commission, 673
Postal service, U.S.
  state abbreviations, 904
  zip codes, 898–904
Postimpressionism, 232
Postmodernism, 241
Potassium, 528–529
Potter's wheel, 122
Poulenc, Francis, 169
Poultry
  cooking times, 541
  serving sizes, 543

Pound, Ezra, 252
Poussin, Nicolas, 224
Powell, Michael, 208
Power of Attorney, 614, 631
PPOs (Preferred Provider
  Organizations), 579
Pragmatism, 320–321
Pratt, E. J., 258
Praxiteles, 230
Pray/prey, 413
Precambrian geological era, 87
Predestination (fatalism), 331
Preferred provider organizations
  (PPOs), 579
Prefixes
  Greek, 424
  Latin, 424–425
Pregnancy
  alcohol, 501
  caffeine, 501
  chemicals, 501
  chicken pox (Varicella), 501
  drugs, 501
  fifth disease (Erythema
    Infectiosum), 501
  hot tubs, 501
  measles, 501
  radiation, 501
  saunas, 501
  smoking, 502
  steam baths, 501
  toxoplasmosis, 502
Premenstrual syndrome (PMS), 510
Premises, 313, 332
Prendergast, Maurice Brazil, 220
Prepayment penalty, 586
Preposition, 436–437
Pre-Raphaelite Brotherhood, 232,
  263
Presbyterian Church, 288
President pro tempore, 865
Presidents, U.S.
  bills, 866
  Electoral College, 863
  line-item veto, 864
  line of succession, 861–862
  overrides, 865
  pocket veto, 865
  veto, 865
Pre-Socratics, 321
Pressburger, Emeric, 208
Priestley, Joseph, 145
Primates, 39

Prime ministers
  Australia, 970
  Canada, 970
  England, 970–972
Primroses, 51
Principal, 586
Principle (or law) of noncontradic-
  tion, 331
Principle of sufficient reason, 331
Principle of utility, 331
Printing press, 123, 917, 941
  offset (web), 130
  rotary, 129
Privacy Act/Freedom of Information
  Act Request, 615
Product safety hot line, 675
Profit-sharing retirement plans, 591
Prokofiev, Sergei, 173
Promissory Note, 616
Pronoun, 436–437
Proofreaders' marks, 402
Property and liability insurance,
  580–581
Property crime. *See* **Crime**
Proteins, 520
Protest and progress, literature, 273
Protestants
  Amish Mennonites, 286
  Baptists, 286
  Church of Christ, 286
  Church of England, 286
  Disciples of Christ, 286
  Episcopal Church, 287
  Lutheran Church, 287
  Methodist Church, 287
  Pentecostal churches, 288
  Presbyterian Church, 288
  Reformed churches, 288
  Seventh Day Adventist Church,
    288
  United Church of Christ, 288
Protestantism, 285–287
  Reformation, 292
  wedding ceremonies, 463
Protons, 139
Proust, Joseph Louis, 145
Proust, Marcel, 258
Pseudonyms of authors, 264–266
Psychologism, 331
Ptolemy (Claudius Ptolemaeus),
  143
Puccini, Giacomo, 172

Puerto Rico
  consumer affairs, 667
  currency, 792
  flower/bird/motto, 879
  Legislative Assembly, 877
  Office of Elder Affairs, 642
  standard, 9
  tourist information, 784
  two-letter abbreviation, 904
  wildlife refuges, 775
Pugin, Augustus Welby Northmore,
  238
Pulitizer Prize in Letters, 268–269
Pulsars, 74
Punctuation, 441. *See also*
  Grammar
  American English, 443
  Braille, 400–401
  British English, 443
  letter writing, 446
  pause, 441–442
Punic Wars, 940
Purcell, Henry, 168
Purim, 304
Pushkin, Alexander Sergeevich, 260
Put down/put on, 413
Puts and calls, 594
Puzzles, crossword, 425–431
Pynchon, Thomas, 252
Pyramids, 122, 923, 963
Pythagoras, 149, 315
Pythagorean Theorem, 105, 321
Pytheas, 148

Q

Qatar, State of
  currency, 792
  embassy, 813
  statistics, 918
  telephone code, 973
  travel requirements, 799
QED, 331
Quakers (Religious Society of
  Friends), 290
Quarks, 138–139
Quartz clocks, 5
Quebec (Canada)
  aquariums, 379
  libraries, 345
  poison control center, 493
  zoos, 379
Questel-Orbit, 349

Question mark, punctuation, 441
Quine, Willard Van Orman, 315
Quorum, 865
Quotation marks (punctuation),
  443
Quotations, 351

R

R.S.V.P.s, 469
Rabbits, 39
Rabe, David, 199
Rabelais, François, 258
Rabies, first aid, 48
Raccoons, 38
Rachmaninoff, Sergei, 173
Radar (radio detection and rang-
  ing), 118, 136
  during pregnancy, 501
Radio alphabet (Morse code), 399
Radio stations, 118, 674–677
Radio telescope, 136
Railroad travel, people with dis-
  abilities, 736
Ramadan, 306
Rambert, Dame Marie, 193
Rameau, Jean-Philippe, 169
Rand, Ayn, 252
Raphael (Santi or Sanzio, 228
Rare earth series, 81
Rashes, home remedies, 510
Rationalism, 331
Rationalists, 321
Rauschenberg, Robert, 220
Ravel, Maurice, 169
Rawls, John, 315
Ray, Satyajit, 205, 207
RDA (recommended daily
  allowances). *See* **Nutrition**
Reagan, Ronald, 862
Real estate, 588. *See also* **Mortgages**
  decision tour, 583
  old vs. new home, 584
Realism, 232, 263–264, 331
Reapportionment, 865
Recall, 865
Receptions, wedding, 463–465
Recipes. *See* **Food**
Recollect/re-collect, 413
Recommended daily allowances
  (RDA). *See* **Nutrition**
Recorder, 160
Recreational symbols, 396

Rectangle, 104
Rectangular prism, 105
Rectifiers, 390
Recycling, 569
Red giants, 74
Red herring (investments), 594
Red supergiants, 74
Reed-organ instruments, 161
Reference works
  anthropology, 352
  antiques and collectibles, 352–353
  architecture, 353–354
  art, 353–354
  astronomy, 354
  business, 354–355
  communications, 355–356
  counseling services, 361
  dance, 361–362
  demography, 361
  dictionaries, 358
  encyclopedias, 351
  ethnology, 352–353
  folklore, 359
  foreign languages, 357
  grammar, 357
  history, 357
  investments, 355
  law, 357
  linguistics, 357
  literature, 357–358
  medicine, 358
  motion pictures, 356
  music, 359
  mythology, 359
  philosophy, 359
  political science, 359–360
  quotations, 351
  religions, 360
  science, 361
  social sciences, 361
  sociology, 361
  sports, 360
  statistics, 361–362
  taxes, 355
  technology, 361
  television, 355–356
  theater, 361–362
  travel, 356
  universities, 356
Referendum, 865
Reflecting telescope, 125
Reformation Sunday, 305
Reformed churches, 288

Refrigeration, food, 544
Refuges, wildlife, 762–777
Regular right pyramid, 105
Rehearsal dinner, weddings, 461–462
Reincarnation (transmigration of souls), 332
Reindeer, 38
Reinhardt, Ad (Adolph), 220
Reinhardt, Django, 177
Relative pronouns, 437
Relativism, 331
Religions
  Baha'i, 284
  Buddhism, 284, 292, 394
  canonical hours, 294
  Christianity, 394
  Church of Jesus Christ of Latter Day Saints, The, 289
  Confucianism, 284
  forms of address, 451–452
  Four Horsemen of the Apocalypse, 294
  Greek deities, 282–283
  Hinduism, 284, 292–293, 394
  holidays, 304–306
  holy books, 294–296
  Islam, 284–285, 292–293
  Jehovah's Witnesses, 289
  Judaism, 285, 292–293, 394
  Lutheran, 292
  Orthodox Church, 285
  Presbyterian, 288
  Protestant, 285–288
  reference works, 360
  Religious Society of Friends (Quakers), 290
  Roman Catholicism, 290, 292–293
  Roman deities, 282–283
  Rosicrucianism, 291
  Shinto, 291, 394
  Taoism, 291–292
  Ten Commandments, 293
  Twelve Apostles, 296
  Unitarian Universalist Association, 290
  Zoroastrianism, 291–292
Religious Society of Friends (Quakers), 290
Rembrandt Harmenszoon van Rijn, 222
Remington, Frederic, 220

Renaissance, 232, 241, 264
Renoir, Jean, 205, 208
Renoir, Pierre Auguste, 225
Rental agreements. *See* Leases
Reptiles, extinct, 42
Request for Reason for Adverse Credit Action, 616
Resistors, 390
Respighi, Ottorino, 172
Respiratory infections, pets, 48
Respiratory system, 36
Restrictive clause, 438
Résumés, 447–448
Retirement
  finances, 586
  investments, 591
  Social Security benefits, 591, 872
Reunion Island, 813, 918
Reverse mortgage, 585
Reynolds, Sir Joshua, 222
Rhinoceroses, 39
Rhode Island
  botanical gardens, 383
  consumer affairs, 664
  crime statistics, 892–893
  Department of Elderly Affairs, 641
  domestic violence organization, 670
  flower/bird/motto/nickname, 878
  General Assembly, 876
  name origin, 880
  newspaper, 909
  personal income per capita, 888
  poison control center, 492
  population, 883
  precipitation, 752
  state tourism office, 750
  temperatures, 754, 756
  two-letter abbreviation, 904
  wildlife refuges, 775, 779
  zoos, 377
Ribbed vault, 243, 246
Ribera, Jusepe de, 229
Riboflavin (Vitamin B2), 522–523
Rice, Jerry, 718
Richard, Maurice ("Rocket"), 718
Richardson, Henry Handel [Ethel Florence Lindesay Richardson Robertson], 255
Richardson, Henry Hobson, 236
Richler, Mordecai, 258
Richter earthquake scale, 89, 136
Richter, Charles Francis, 148

Rickey, Branch, 718
Rider, 865
Riefenstahl, Leni, 205
Rifles, 123
Right circular cone, 105
Rilke, Rainer Maria, 259
Rimbaud, Arthur, 258
Rimsky-Korsakov, Nicolai, 173
Ripken, Cal, Jr., 718
Risk of investments, 589
Rivera, Diego, 228
Rivers, Larry, 220
Road signs, 398
Robbins, Jerome, 192
Roberts, Sir Charles G. D., 258
Robinson, Bill (Bojangles), 192
Robinson, Jackie, 718
Rockets, 123
Rockne, Knute, 718
Rockwell, Norman, 220
Rococo, 232, 241
Rodin, Auguste, 225
Rodman, Dennis, 718
Roe v. Wade, 624
Roentgen, Wilhelm Conrad, 153
Roman calendar, 12
Roman Catholicism, 290, 292–293
    popes, 297–303
    saints, 296–297
    wedding ceremonies, 463
Roman deities, 282
Roman numerals, 106
Romanesque, 232–233, 241
Romania
    Bucharest, 954
    currency, 792
    embassy, 813
    standard time, 9
    statistics, 918
    telephone code, 973
    tourist information, 784
    travel requirements, 799
Romanticism, 233, 264
Roosevelt, Franklin D., 861
Roosevelt, Theodore, 861
Roses, 51
Rosetti, Dante Gabriel, 222
Rosh Hashanah, 305
Rosicrucianism, 291
Ross, Sinclair, 258
Rossellini, Roberto, 205
Rossini, Gioacchino, 172
Rostand, Edmund, 202, 258

Rotary printing press, 129
Roth v. U.S., 624
Roth, Philip, 252
Rothko, Mark, 220
Rouault, Georges, 225
Rousseau, Henri, 225
Rousseau, Jean Jacques, 315
Royalty. *See also* Monarchy
    Chinese dynasties, 963–964
    connections between royal fami-
        lies, 969
    Denmark, 969
    England, 964–965, 969–970
    forms of address, 452–453
    France, 965
    Germany, 965, 969–970
    Japan, 965
    Russia, 965–966, 969
    Spain, 970
Rubella immunization, 503, 513
Rubens, Peter Paul, 221
Rubinstein, Anton, 173
Rudolph, Wilma, 718–719
Rummy, 726
Runaways, organizations for chil-
    dren, 644
Rushdie, Salman, 254
Russell, Bertrand Arthur William,
    Earl, 149
Russell, Bertrand, 315
Russia, 19
    Black Death, 917
    currency, 792
    embassy, 814
    frequently used words and phras-
        es, 417, 420–421
    Moscow, 956
    Nizhni Novgorod, 956
    Novosibirsk, 956
    October (Bolshevik) Revolution,
        945
    royalty, 965–966, 969
    Samara, 957
    space exploration, 115
    St. Petersburg, 957
    statistics, 918
    time zone, 9
    tourist information, 784
    travel requirements, 799
    Volgograd, 957
    Yekaterinburg, 958
Ruth, Babe [George Herman], 718
Rutherford, Ernest, Lord, 153

Rwanda, Republic of
    currency, 792
    embassy, 814
    statistics, 918
    travel requirements, 800
Ryan, Nolan, 718–719
Rylc, Gilbert, 315

S

Saarinen, (Gottlieb) Eliel, 236
Saarinen, Eero, 236
Saba and St. Eustatius
    tourist information, 784
Sabin, Albert Bruce, 150
Sachs, Julius von, 144
Sagan, Carl Edward, 143
Sail/sale, 413
St. Helena
    currency, 792
    statistics, 918
St. Kitts and Nevis
    currency, 792
    embassy, 814
    statistics, 918
    tourist information, 784
    travel requirements, 800
St. Lucia
    currency, 792
    embassy, 814
    statistics, 918
    tourist information, 784
    travel requirements, 800
St. Maarten, 784
St. Martin, 785
St. Pierre and Miquelon, 918–919
St. Vincent and the Grenadines, 792
    embassy, 814
    statistics, 919
    tourist information, 785
    travel requirements, 800
Saint-Saëns, Charles Camille, 169
Saints
    Anselm, 310
    Aquinas, St. Thomas, 328
    Aquinas, Thomas, 310
    Augustine of Hippo, 310
    reference works, 360
    Roman Catholicism, 296–297
Saipan, 973
Salinger, J. D., 252
Salk, Jonas Edward, 150
Sallé, Marie, 193

Salyut space stations, 115
Samoan Standard Time, 8
Sampras, Pete, 718–719
San Marino, Republic of
  currency, 792
  embassy, 814
  statistics, 919
  telephone code, 973
  travel requirements, 800
Sand, George [Amandine Aurore
  Lucie Dupin], 258
Sandburg, Carl, 252
Santayana, George, 315
São Tomé and Principe
  currency, 792
  embassy, 814
  statistics, 919
  travel requirements, 800
  Sappho, 261
Sargent, John Singer, 220
Saroyan, William, 199, 252
Sartre, Jean-Paul, 202, 259,
  315–316
Satellites, 138
Satie, Erik, 170
Saturn, 72
Saudi Arabia, Kingdom of
  currency, 792
  embassy, 814
  major cities, 956
  Riyadh, 957
  standard time, 9
  statistics, 919
  telephone code, 973
  travel requirements, 800
Saunas, during pregnancy, 501
Saxhorns, 161
Saxophone, 161
Scarlatti, (Giuseppe) Domenico,
  172
Scarlatti, Alessandro, 172
Scarlet fever, 513
Schechter v. U.S., 624
Schenck v. U.S., 624
Schiaparelli, Giovanni Viginio, 143
Schiele, Egon, 230
Schoenberg, Arnold, 166
Scholasticism, 321
Schopenhauer, Arthur, 316
Schrodinger, Erwin, 152–153
Schubert, Franz Seraph Peter, 167
Schuman, William, 166

Schumann, Clara Josephine né
  Wieck, 171
Schumann, Robert, 171
Science. *See also* Technology
  aerospace engineers, 141
  astronomy, 141–144, 388
  biology, 143, 389
  chemistry, 126–127, 144–145,
    389
  computer scientists, 146
  earth scientists, 146–147
  environmentalists, 146–147
  magazines, 119
  mathematicians, 148–149
  medical scientists, 149–150
  museums, 370
  physicists, 151–153
  reference works, 361
Scorsese, Martin, 205–206
Scotland, 785
  embassy, 817
  Glasgow, 955
  standard time, 9
Scott, Sir Walter, 257
Scotus, John Duns, 316, 320
Scrabble®, 723–724
Screwdriver, 124
Scriabin, Aleksandr, 173
Sculptors. *See* Artists
Sculpture. *See* Art
Sea anemones, 40
Seals, 39
Search engines, 108
Seasonal lease agreement, 607–608
Seasons, 11–12, 60
Secant (sec), 106
Second-degree burns, 481
Secretaries-General, United Nations,
  958
Securities and Exchange
  Commission (SEC), 594, 673
Security Agreement, 617–618
Sedimentary rock, 91–92
Segal, George, 220
Selenium, 528–529
Seles, Monica, 718–719
Self employment, Social Security
  benefits, 874
Semaphore code, 399
Sembène, Ousmane, 209, 254
Semicolon (punctuation), 441–442
Senate, U.S. *See* Congress, U.S.
Seneca, 203–204

Senegal, Republic of
  currency, 792
  embassy, 814
  statistics, 919
  telephone code, 973
  travel requirements, 800
Senghor, Léopold Sédar, 254
Senior citizens
  Sensationalism, 331
Sense data, 331
Sentences, 437, 441, 442
  predicates, 438
  punctuation, 443
  subjects, 438
Serbia and Montenegro
  Belgrade, 954
  currency, 792
  embassy, 814
  standard time, 9
  travel requirements, 800
Serial processing
  computer, 114
  Server, 114
Sessions, Roger, 166
Seurat, Georges, 225
Seven Wonders of the Ancient
  World, 931, 962–963
Seventh-Day Adventist Church, 288
Sewing machine, 129
Sexton, Anne, 252
Seychelles
  currency, 792
  embassy, 814
  statistics, 919
  tourist information, 785
  travel requirements, 800
Shaft, 242–243
Shagley, Harlow, 143
Shahn, Ben, 220
Shakespeare, William, 201
Shapes
  three-dimensional, 105
  two-dimensional, 103–104
Shared-appreciation mortgage
  (SAM), 585
Shavuot, 305
Shaw, George Bernard, 201
Shawn, Ted, 192
Sheeler, Charles, 220
Sheep, 38
Shelley, Mary Wollstonecraft, 257
Shelley, Percy Bysshe, 257
Shepard, Sam, 199

Sheridan, Richard Brinsley, 201
Sherwood, Robert, 199
Shinto, 291, 394
Ships
    bell time signals, 6
    travel, people with disabilities, 736
Shock
    pets, 48
    preventing, 478–479
Shoemaker, Eugene, 143
Shoemaker, Willie, 718–719
Shostakovich, Dmitri, 173
Shotgun, 123
Showers, weddings, 461
Shrew opossums, 38
Shrews, 39
Shula, Don, 718–719
Shute, Nevil [Nevil Shute Norway], 255
Sibelius, Jean, 175
Side drum (snare), 163
Sidereal time, 4, 10, 79
Siding, standard sizes, 567
Sierra Leone
    currency, 792
    embassy, 815
    statistics, 919
    travel requirements, 800
Sign language alphabet, 400
Signal processor, 163, 165
Silk, 122
Simon, Neil, 199
Simple interest, 574
Simple sentences, 438
Simplified employee pension individual retirement plans (SEP-IRAs), 591
Simpson, O(renthal) J(ames), 718–719
Sine (sin), 106
Singapore, 957
    currency, 792
    embassy, 815
    statistics, 919
    telephone code, 973
    tourist information, 785
    travel requirements, 800
Singer, Isaac Bashevis, 252
Single-parents, 674
Single-word modifier, 437
Siquerios, David Alfaro, 228
Skating. *See* Figure skating; Speed skating

Skeletal system, humans, 34
Skepticism, 331–332
Skiing, downhill, 715–717
Skin problems, pets, 48
Skunks, 38
Skylab space station, 115
Skyscraper, 131
Sloths, 39
Slovak Republic
    currency, 792
    embassy, 815
    statistics, 919
    tourist information, 785
    travel requirements, 800
Slovenia
    currency, 792
    statistics, 919
    tourist information, 785
    travel requirements, 800
Small business, investments, 589, 673
Smetana, Bedrich, 175
Smileys, 402
Smirke, Sir Robert, 238
Smith, Adam, 316
Smith, Bessie, 177
Smith, David, 220
Smith, Dean, 719
Smoking, during pregnancy, 502
Snakebites, first aid, 488
Snyder, Hartland, 74
Soane, Sir John, 238
Soccer, 705, 729, 731
    Pelé [Edson Arantes do Nascimento], 717
    World Cup, 706
Social contract, 332
Social sciences, 361
Social Security
    disability, 872–873
    farm owners, 874
    retirement, 591, 872
    self-employment, 874
    survivor benefits, 873–874
Social Security, 873–874
Socialist realism, 264
Sociology, reference works, 361
Socrates, 316
Soddy, Frederick, 146
Sodium, 528–529
Solipsism, 332
Solitaire, 726–727

Solomon Islands
    currency, 792
    embassy, 815
    statistics, 919
    travel requirements, 800
Solstice, 11–12
Solzhenitsyn, Aleksandr I., 260
Somali Democratic Republic (Somalia)
    currency, 792
    embassy, 815
    statistics, 919
    travel requirements, 800
Sophists, 321
Sophocles, 203
Sore throats. *See* Colds
South Africa
    Cape Town, 955
    currency, 792
    embassy, 815
    Johannesburg, 955
    standard time, 9
    statistics, 919
    telephone code, 973
    tourist information, 785
    travel requirements, 800
South America
    holidays, 19–21
    map, 980
South Carolina
    botanical gardens, 383–384
    consumer affairs, 664
    crime statistics, 892–893
    Division on Aging, 641
    flower/bird/motto/nickname, 878
    General Assembly, 876
    libraries, 343
    name origin, 881
    newspapers, 909
    personal income per capita, 888
    poison control center, 492
    population, 883
    precipitation, 752
    state tourism office, 750
    temperatures, 754, 757
    two-letter abbreviation, 904
    wildlife refuges, 775, 779
    zoos, 378
South Dakota
    consumer affairs, 664
    crime statistics, 892–893
    domestic violence organization, 670

flower/bird/motto/nickname, 878
legislature, 876
name origin, 881
newspaper, 910
Office of Adult Services and
    Aging, 642
personal income per capita, 888
poison control center, 492
population, 883
precipitation, 752
state tourism office, 750
temperatures, 754, 757
two-letter abbreviation, 904
wildlife refuges, 775, 779
zoos, 378
South Korea
currency, 791–792
embassy, 809
Pusan, 956
Seoul, 957
standard time, 9
statistics, 914
telephone code, 973
tourist information, 783
South Pacific, map, 979
Soyinka, Wole, 254
**Space exploration, 115–116, 140,
    961–962**
Spain
Barcelona, 954
Civil War, 953
currency, 792
embassy, 815
Madrid, 956
royalty, 970
Seville, 957
standard time, 9
statistics, 920
telephone code, 973
tourist information, 785
travel requirements, 800
Valencia, 957
Spanish Civil War, 945
Spanish language, 417–421
Spaying pets, 43
Speaker of the House, 865
Speed skating
Blair, Bonnie, 713
Devers, Gail, 714
Heiden, Eric, 715
Spelling guidelines
American English, 415
British English, 415

commonly misspelled words,
    413–414
commonly misused words,
    412–413
Spenser, Edmund, 257
Sperm whales, 38
Sphere, 105
Spielberg, Steven, 205–206
Spinoza, Benedict (Baruch), 316
Spiritualism, 332
Spirituality, 274
Spitz, Mark, 719
Split infinitives (grammar), 440
Sponges, 40
Sports
auto racing, 684, 727, 730
    famous drivers, 714–715, 717
    Indianapolis 500, 685–686
baseball, 686–687, 727–728, 730
    American Leagues (NL), 688
    *famous players, 713, 714, 715,
        716, 717, 718.719*
    National League (NL), 688
    World Series, 688–690
basketball, 690–691, 728, 730
    *famous players, 713, 714,
        715–716, 718, 719*
    *National Basketball Association
        (NBA), 692*
    *National Basketball
        Association(NBA), 691*
bicycle racing, 693–694, 728, 731
board games, 719–724, 729
bowling, 694–695, 728, 731
boxing, 713, 714, 716, 719
card games, 724–727, 729
diving, 716
figure skating, 714–715, 719
football, 694–695, 728, 731
    *American Football Conference
        (AFC), 698*
    *famous players, 713, 714, 715,
        716, 717*
    *National Football Conference
        (NFC), 698*
    signals, 696–697
    Super Bowl, 698–699
golf, 699, 728, 731
    *famous golfers, 714, 715, 717,
        719*
    Masters, 700
gymnastics, 714

horse racing, 700–702, 718, 728,
    731
ice hockey, 702, 729, 731
    *famous players, 715, 716, 717,
        718*
    *National Hockey League
        (NHL), 703*
    Stanley Cup, 703–705
    Olympic Games, 729, 732
    summer, 710–712
    winter, 711–712
reference works, 360
skiing, 715–717
soccer, 705–706, 717, 729, 731
speed skating, 713–715
swimming, 713, 714, 719
tennis, 707, 729, 731
    *famouse players, 713, 714, 715,
        716, 717, 718*
    Wimbledon, 708–709
track and field, 729, 731
    *famous athletes, 713, 714, 716,
        717, 718*
volleyball, 709–710, 729, 732
Spotted fever, 513
Sprains
first, 483–484
home remedies, 510–511
pets, 49
Spring, 11, 60
Springboks, 38
Spring-driven clocks, 5
Square, 104
Squirrels, 39
Sri Lanka
currency, 792
embassy, 815
statistics, 920
telephone code, 973
tourist information, 785
travel requirements, 800
Stain removal
clothing, 559
combination, 560
pets, 44
specific stains, 561–564
**Standard Oil Co. of New Jersey et
al. v. U.S., 624**
Standard time, 6–7
Canada, 8
major world cities, 9
United States, 8

Standing committee, 865
Stanley Cup (ice hockey), 703–705
Starfish, 40
Stars, 80, 388
    binary, 77
    black dwarfs, 73
    black holes, 73–74
    charts, 122
    closest systems to earth, 76
    constellations, 75
    double, 78
    hot subdwarfs, 74
    life cycles, 73
    neutron stars, 74
    novae, 74
    pulsars, 74
    red giants, 74
    red supergiants, 74
    supernovae, 74
    variable stars, 74
    white dwarfs, 74
    white holes, 75
State government
    statute of limitations, 618
States, The United. *See specific*
    states
Stationary/stationery, 413
Statistics, reference works, 361–362
Steam baths during pregnancy, 501
Steam engine, 125
Stein, Gertrude, 252
Steinbeck, John, 252
Stella, Frank, 220
Stendhal [Marie-Henri Beyle], 259
Stengel, Casey [Charles Dillon], 719
Stethoscope, 128, 129
Stevenson, Robert Louis, 257
Stock cars, 684. *See also* Auto racing
Stocks, 588, 590–594
    dividends, 594
    splits, 594
    tender offer, 594
Stoicism, 321
Stokes, William, 150
Stoppard, Tom, 201
Stowe, Harriet Beecher, 252
Stratocumulus (Sc) cloud, 97
Stratus (St) cloud, 97
Strauss, Johann I, Johann II, Josef,
    and Eduard I, 167
Strauss, Richard, 171
Stravinsky, Igor, 173
Streets, designators, 905
Strep throat, 511

Strickland, William, 236
Strindberg, Johan August, 204
Stroke, warning signs, 492
Sturm und Drang, 264
Styron, William, 252
Subject, grammar, 186, 438–439
Subjectivism, 332
Substance, 332
Sudan, Republic of
    currency, 793
    embassy, 815
    statistics, 920
    travel requirements, 800
Suffixes
    Greek language, 424
    Latin language, 424–425
Sukkoth, 305
Sullivan, Louis Henry, 237
Sullivan, Sir Arthur, 168
Sully, Thomas, 220
Summer soltice, 11
Sun
    planets, distance from sun, 72
    solar eclipses, 68–71
Sundials, 5, 122
Sunflowers, 49
Super Bowl (football), 698–699
Superconductivity, 134, 138, 141
Supernaturalism, 332
Supernovae, 74
Supreme Court
    decisions, 623–625, 627–628
    justices, 622–623
Surgery, 497–498
Suriname, Republic of
    currency, 793
    embassy, 815
    statistics, 920
    telephone code, 973
    travel requirements, 800
Surplus, government, 865
Surrealism, 264
Survivor benefits
Suspension bridge, 123
Svalbard, 920
Swastika, 395
Swaziland, Kingdom of
    currency, 793
    embassy, 815
    statistics, 920
    travel requirements, 800
Sweden
    currency, 793
    embassy, 815

    standard time, 9
    statistics, 920
    Stockholm, 957
    telephone code, 973
    tourist information, 780, 785
    travel requirements, 800
Swift, Jonathan, 261
Swimming
    Biondi, Matt, 713
    Ederle, Gertrude, 714
    Evans, Janet, 714
    Spitz, Mark, 719
    Weismuller, Johnny, 719
Swinburne, Algernon Charles, 257
Switzerland
    currency, 793
    embassy, 815
    standard, 9
    standard time, 9
    statistics, 920
    telephone code, 973
    tourist information, 785
    travel requirements, 800
Sydenham, Thomas, 150
Syllogism, 332
Symbolism, 233, 264
Symbols
    astronomy, 388
    biology, 389
    birthstones and flowers, 396
    business, 401
    chemistry elements, 80–81, 389
    cultural, 396
    distress signals, 397
    electronics, 389–390
    emoticons, 402
    historical, 396
    literary, 279
    maps and charts, 396–397
    mathematics, 390–391
    medicine, 391–392
    meteorological, 392–393
    monetary, 401
    music, 393–394
    nature, 397
    pharmacology, 391–392
    physics, 392
    proofreaders' marks, 402
    recreational, 396
    religious, 394
    road signs, 398
    semaphore code, 399
    swastika, 395
    zodiac signs, 395

Synge, John Millington, 203
Synthesizer, 163, 165
Synthetic statement, 332
Synthetics
     washing instructions, 557
Syphilis, 513
Syrian Arab Republic (Syria)
     currency, 793
     Damascus, 955
     embassy, 815–816
     statistics, 920
     travel requirements, 800
Systematics (taxonomy), 36–37

T

Tableware
     etiquette, 469–471
     Tabula rasa, 332
Taft, William H., 861
Taglioni, Marie, 195
Tagore, Rabindranath, 254
Tahiti. *See* French Polynesia
Taiwan, Republic of China on
     currency, 793
     embassy, 816
     statistics, 920
     Taipei, 957
     telephone code, 973
     tourist information, 785
     travel requirements, 800
Tajikistan
     currency, 793
     embassy, 816
     statistics, 920
     travel requirements, 800
Talk to/talk with, 413
Tallchief, Maria, 192
Tallis, Thomas, 168
Talmud, 295
Tamayo, Rufino, 228
Tambourine, 163
Tangent (tan), 106
Tanizaki Jun'ichiro, 254
Tanzania, United Republic of
     (Zanzibar)
     currency, 793
     embassy, 816
     statistics, 920
     travel requirements, 800
Taoism, 291–292, 394
Tao-te-ching (The Way and Its
     Power), 295
Tapeworm, 513

Tarantino, Quentin, 205
Tartaglia (Niccolò Fontana), 149
Tartini, Giuseppe, 172
Tatlin, Vladimir Evgrafovich, 229
Tatum, Art, 177
Tautology, 332
Tax shelter, 594
Taxes, reference works, 355
Taxonomy (systematics), 36–37
Taylor, Paul, 192
Taylor, Zachary, 861
Tchaikovsky, Peter Ilyich, 174
Technology, 122–127, 131, 140
     computers, 136, 138–139
     literature, 275
     museums, 370
     reference works, 361
     satellites, 138
Telecommunications device for the
     deaf (TDD), 668
Teleogical ethics, 332
Telephone codes, international,
     972–973
Telephones
     business etiquette, 467–468
     hot lines, 675
Telescopes
     astronomical, 124
     binocular, 128
     giant, 129
     radio, 136
     reflecting, 125
     refracting, 126
Television, 118, 135
     reference works, 355–356
     stations, 674–677
Temperatures
     Celsius, 29, 126
     Fahrenheit, 29, 125
     food storage, 544
     frost dates, U.S.
     metric system, 29–30
     oven settings for cooking,
     water for laundry, 558
     windchill factor, 98
Ten Commandments, 293
Tender offer, 594
Tennessee
     aquariums, 378
     botanical gardens, 384
     Commission on Aging, 642
     consumer affairs, 664
     crime statistics, 892–897

flower/bird/motto/nickname, 878
General Assembly, 876
name origin, 881
newspaper, 910
personal income per capita, 888
poison control center, 492
population, 883
precipitation, 752
state tourism office, 750
temperatures, 754, 757
two-letter abbreviation, 904
wildlife refuges, 775, 779
zoos, 378
Tennis, 707, 729, 731
     Ashe, Arthur, 713
     Becker, Boris, 713
     Bjorg, Bjorn, 713
     Connors, Jimmy, 714
     Evert, Chris, 714
     Gibson, Althea, 715
     Graf, Steffi, 715
     King, Billie Jean, 716
     Layer, Rod, 716
     McEnroe, John, 717
     Navratilova, Martina, 717
     Sampras, Pete, 718
     Seles, Monica, 718
     Wimbledon, 708–709
Tennyson, Alfred (Lord), 257
Tenor drum, 163
Tense (verb), 439
Tetanus-diphtheria (Td) immuniza-
     tion, 503
Tetley, Glen, 192
Texas
     aquariums, 378
     art museums, 369
     botanical gardens, 384
     consumer affairs, 664–665
     crime statistics, 894–897
     Department on Aging, 642
     domestic violence organization,
     671
     flower/bird/motto/nickname, 878
     legislature, 876
     libraries, 343
     name origin, 881
     newspapers, 910
     personal income per capita, 889
     poison control centers, 492
     population, 883
     precipitation, 752

Texas, *cont.*
  state tourism office, 750
  temperatures, 754, 757
  two-letter abbreviation, 904
  wildlife refuges, 776, 779
  zoos, 378
Thackeray, William Makepeace, 257
Thailand, Kingdom of
  Bangkok, 954
  currency, 793
  embassy, 816
  standard time, 9
  statistics, 920
  telephone code, 973
  tourist information, 785
  travel requirements, 800
Thales of Miletus, 316
Thank-you notes, weddings,
  465–466
Tharp, Twyla, 192
The Nation, 911
The New Republic, 911
Theater, reference works, 361–362
Theme parks, 779
Theme, 279
Theophrastus, 144
Thermometer, 29, 125
Thermostat, 129
Thiamin (Vitamin B1), 522–523
Thickening agents, 547
Third-degree burns, 481
Thirty Years' War, 941
Thomas, Dylan Marlais, 257
Thomism, 321
Thomson, Virgil, 166
Thoreau, Henry David, 252
Thorpe, Jim, 719
Three-dimensional shapes, 105
Tilde, 415
Time sharing
  computers, 115
Time, 187, 911
  A.M. (ante meridiem), 5
  anomalistic, 10
  calendars
    Gregorian, 12
    Julian, 12
    perpetual, 13–17
    Roman, 12
    years, 10
  clocks, 4
  daylight savings, 9–10

days
  hours, 4
  length, 5
  mean solar day, 4
  sidereal day, 4
  true solar day, 4
descriptions of different time periods, 18
fiscal, 10
international date line, 8
jiffy, 18
leap year, 10
P.M. (post meridiem), 5
prime meridian, 6
seasons, 11–12
second (sec), 26
ship's bells, 6
sidereal, 10
standard, 6–8
tropical/equinoctial/solar, 10
universal, 6
zones, 7
Tintoretto(Jacopo Robusti, 228
Tipping etiquette, 594–595
Titian (Tiziano Vecellio), 228
Titles. *See also* **Forms of Address**
  abbreviations after names, 455
  mortgages, 586
TNT, 130
Tocks, dividends, 594
Tocqueville, Alexis de, 259
Togo, Republic of
  currency, 793
  embassy, 816
  statistics, 920–921
  travel requirements, 800
Tokelau, 921
Tolstoy, Leo [Count Lev
  Nikolayevich], 260
Tombaugh, Clyde William, 143
Tonga
  currency, 793
  embassy, 816
  statistics, 921
  tourist information, 785
  travel requirements, 800
Tools, 124, 566
Toothless mammals, 39
Torricelli, Evangelista, 148, 153
Toulouse-Lautrec, Henri de, 225
Tour de France, 693–694
Tourneur, Cyril, 201

Tower of Pharos, The, 963
Toxoplasmosis, 513
  during pregnancy, 502
Track and field, 729, 731
  Bannister, Roger, 713
  Bubka, Sergei, 714
  Fosbury, Dick, 714
  Joyner-Kersee, Jackie, 716
  Lewis, Carl, 716
  Nurmi, Paavo, 717
  Owens, Jesse, 717
  Rudolph, Wilma, 718
Transcendent, 332
Transcendentalism, 264, 321
Transformer, 118, 390
Transitive verb, 437–438
Transmigration of souls, 332
Transportation Department, 673
Travel
  air mileage from New York City
    domestic flights, 758
    international flights, 788
  airlines, 734, 738–742
  airports, 742–747
  automobiles
    registration marks, 786–787
    rental agencies, 736–737
  best vacation bets, 778
  buses, 736
  camping, 736
  checklists, 734
  disabilities, people with, 734, 736
  first aid kit, 734
  hotels, 736–738
  immunizations, 795–800
  international
    advisories, 801
    currencies, 788–793
    customs, 818–819
    embassies, 801, 803–818
    passports, 793–795
    tourist information, 780–786
    weather charts, 787–788
  magazines, 819
  motels, 736–738
  national parks, 758–762
  parks, 736
  pets, 735
  railroads, 736
  reference, 356
  ships, 736
  state tourism offices, 747–751

theme parks, 779
visas, 793, 795–800, 802
weather charts, 751–757
wildlife refuges, 762–777, 779–780
Treasury bill, 594
Tree shrews, 39
Trees
Triangle, 104, 163
    musical instrument, 163
    Pythagorean Theorem, 105
Trichomoniasis, 513
Trigonometry, 122
    cosecant (csc), 106
    cotangent (cot or ctn), 106
    formulas, 106
    secant (sec), 106
    sine (sin), 106
    tangent (tan), 106
Trinidad and Tobago
    currency, 793
    embassy, 816
    statistics, 921
    tourist information, 785
    travel requirements, 800
Triple Crown (horse racing), 701
Trochee, 279
Trojan War, 940
Trollope, Anthony, 257
Trombones, 161
Tropical/equinoctial/solar year, 10
True solar day, 4
Truffaut, François, 205, 208
Truman, Harry S., 861
Trumpet, 162
Trustees of Dartmouth College v. Woodward, 623
Ts'ao Hsueh-ch'in, 254
Tsiolkovsky, Konstantin Eduardovich, 141
Tuba, 162
Tubular bells, 162
Tudor, 241
Tudor, Antony, 193
Tull, Jethro, 144
Tunis, 965
Tunisia
    currency, 793
    embassy, 816
    statistics, 921
    telephone code, 973
    tourist information, 785
    travel requirements, 800
    Tunis, 957

Turgenev, Ivan, 261
Turing, Allan, 146
Turkey, Republic of
    Ankara, 954
    carving, 541
    currency, 793
    embassy, 816–817
    Istanbul, 955
    standard time, 9
    statistics, 921
    telephone code, 973
    tourist information, 786
    travel requirements, 800
Turkmenistan
    embassy, 817
    statistics, 921
    travel requirements, 800
Turks and Caicos Islands
    currency, 793
    statistics, 921
    tourist information, 786
Turks and Caicos Islands. See British West Indies
Turner, Joseph Mallord William, 222
Tuvalu Island
    embassy, 817
    statistics, 921
    travel requirements, 800
Twain, Mark [Samuel Langhorne Clemens], 253
Twelve Apostles, 296
Two-dimensional shapes, 103–104
Tyler, Anne, 253
Tyler, John, 861
Typewriter, 131
Typhus, 513
Tyson, Mike, 719

U

U.S. News & World Report, 911
U.S. v. E. C. Knight Co., 624
Uccello, Paolo, 228
Uganda, Republic of
    currency, 793
    embassy, 817
    statistics, 921
    travel requirements, 800
Ukraine
    currency, 793
    Dnepropetrovsk, 955
    Donetsk, 955
    embassy, 817

    Kharkov, 955
    Kiev, 955
    Odessa, 956
    statistics, 921
    travel requirements, 800
Ulanova, Galina Sergeyevna, 195
Ultraviolet light, 127
Umlaut, 415
Unamuno, Miguel de, 316
Undset, Sigrid, 261
Uniform Resource Locator (URL). See Web site addresses
Unitarian Universalist Association, 290
United Arab Emirates (UAE)
    currency, 793
    embassy, 817
    statistics, 921
    telephone code, 973
    travel requirements, 800
United Church of Christ, 288
United Kingdom (UK). See also England
    statistics, 921
    telephone code, 973
United Nations
    committees, 959
    forms of address, 450
    international organizations, 962
    library, 350
    members, 960–961
    Secretaries-General, 958
United States
    Better Business Bureau, 645
    Civil War, 943
    clothing, size conversion, 565
    Congress, 862
    Constitution, The, 842–848, 859–860
        Amendments, 849–854
    crime statistics, 891–895
    currency, 793
    death penalty, 619
    Declaration of Independence, The, 838–841
    economy, 888–890
    Electoral College, 863
    Emancipation Proclamation, The, 854–855
    flag, 856–857
    frost dates/zones map, 60
    Gettysburg Address, The, 855–856
    hardiness zones map, 59

United States, *cont.*
history
13 original states, 825
important dates and events,
824–837
holidays, 18, 304–306
immigration, 884–887
law-making bodies, 859–862,
876–877
legislative terms, 863–865
map, 982
Metric Conversion Act, 26
Military Academy Library, 351
Monroe Doctrine, The, 854
population, 882
postal service, 673, 898–904
presidents, 861
service academies, 677–678
Social Security, 872–874
space exploration, 115
State Department, 801
statistics, 921
Supreme Court
decisions, 623–625, 627–628
justices, 622–623
time, daylight savings, 9
time zones map, 8
Units of measurement
astronomy, 388
Universal time, 6
Universals, 333
Universe, 80
Universities, reference works, 356
**University of California v. Bakke,
625**
Upanishads, 295–296
Updike, John, 253
Uranus, 72
Urey, Harold Clayton, 146
Uruguay
currency, 793
embassy, 817
Montevideo, 956
statistics, 914
telephone code, 973
tourist information, 786
travel requirements, 800
Utah
consumer affairs, 665
crime statistics, 894–895
Division of Aging and Adult
Services, 642
flower/bird/motto/nickname, 878

legislature, 876
libraries, 344
name origin, 881
newspapers, 910
personal income per capita, 889
poison control center, 492
population, 883
precipitation, 752
state tourism office, 750
temperatures, 754, 757
two-letter abbreviation, 904
wildlife refuges, 776, 779
zoos, 378
Utilitarianism, 321
Utopianism, 333
Utopias, literature, 275
Uzbekistan, Republic of
currency, 793
embassy, 817
statistics, 914
Tashkent, 957
travel requirements, 800

V

Vacations. *See* Travel
Vaccines, 137–138, 502
Vacuum-tubed triudes, 390
Valéry, Paul, 259
Valois, Dame Ninette de, 193
Value-oriented funds, 590
Van Buren, Martin, 861
Van der Weyden, Rogier, 221
Van Dyck, Sir Anthony, 221
Van Eyck, Jan, 221
Van Gogh, Vincent, 222
Vanbrugh, Sir John, 238
Vanuatu
currency, 793
embassy, 817
statistics, 914
travel requirements, 800
Varèse, Edgar, 166
Vargas Llosa, Mario, 260
Variable life insurance, 580
Variable stars, 74
Varicella immunization, 502–503
Vatican City
statistics, 914
telephone code, 973
Vatican. *See* Holy See, Apostolic
Nunciature of the
Vaughan Williams, Ralph, 168

Vaughan, Sarah "Sassy," 177
Vault, 243, 246
Vaulted roof, 243
Veda, 296
Vega Carpio, Lope de, 204
Vegetables
botanical names, 51–55
cooking times, 542
cultivation, 58–59
germination, 61
serving sizes, 543
Vehicles, 122
**Velázquez, Diego Rodríguez de Silva
y, 229**
Venezuela, 817
Caracas, 955
currency, 793
embassy, 818
standard time, 9
statistics, 914
telephone code, 973
tourist information, 786
travel requirements, 801
Venturi, Robert, 237
Venus, 72
Verbs, 436–439
Verdi, Giuseppe, 172
Vermeer, Jan (Johannes), 223
Vermont
consumer affairs, 665
crime statistics, 892–893
Department of Aging and
Disabilities, 642
domestic violence organization,
671
flower/bird/motto/nickname, 878
General Assembly, 876
name origin, 881
newspaper, 910
Personal income per capita, 888
poison control center, 492
population, 883
precipitation, 752
state tourism office, 750
temperatures, 754, 757
two-letter abbreviation, 904
wildlife refuges, 776, 779
Vernal equinox, 11
Veronese, Paolo (Paolo Caliari), 228
**Verrocchio, Andrea del (Andrea di
Michele di Francesco di Cioni),
228**
Verse, 279

Vestris, Auguste, 193
Vestris, Gaetano, 193
Veterans Affairs Department, 673
Veto, 865
Vice presidents, United States, 861–862
Victorian, 264
Vienna Circle, 321
Vietnam
  currency, 793
  embassy, 818
  Ho Chi Minh City, 955
  standard time, 9
  statistics, 914
  travel requirements, 801
Vietnam War, 947
Vihuela, 158
Vikings
  exploration, 948
Vikings, exploration, 956
Villa-Lobos, Heitor, 175
Villella, Edward, 192
Vines, botanical names, 56
Viol, 159
Violent crime. *See* Crime
Violin, 159
Viral/virile, 413
Virgil [Publius Vergilius Maro], 261
Virgin Islands, 786
  consumer affairs, 667
  currency, 793
  flower/bird/motto, 879
  Legislature, 877
  two-letter abbreviation, 904
  Virgin Islands: Senior Citizens Affairs, 642
Virginia
  Al-Anon Family Group Headquarters, 643
  Alcohol and Drug Problems Association of North America, 643
  art museums, 369
  botanical gardens, 384
  consumer affairs, 665–666
  crime statistics, 892–893, 896–897
  Department for the Aging, 642
  domestic violence organization, 671
  flower/bird/motto/nickname, 878
  General Assembly, 876
  libraries, 344
  name origin, 881

  newspapers, 910
  personal income per capita, 888
  poison control center, 492
  population, 883
  precipitation, 752
  state tourism office, 750
  temperatures, 754, 757
  two-letter abbreviation, 904
  wildlife refuges, 777, 780
  zoos, 378
Visas, 793–800, 802
Visually impaired, audio books, 668
Vitalism, 333
Vitamins, 134–136, 522–525
  fat-soluble, 520
  shelf life, 497
  water-soluble, 521
Vivaldi, Antonio, 172
Voice (verb), 439
Volcanoes, 88, 95. *See also* Geology
Volleyball, 709–710, 729, 732
Volt (V), 26
Volta, Count Alessandro Giuseppe Antonio Anastasio, 153
Volta, Count Alessandro, 27
Voltaire [François-Marie Arouet], 259, 316
Volume, 24, 27
Volute, 246
Von Neuron, John, 146
Vonnegut, Kurt Jr., 253
Vowels, 415
Vuillard, Édouard, 225

W

Wagner, Otto, 240
Wagner, Richard, 171
Wake Island, Administered by U.S. Air Force, 877
Wakes. *See* Funerals
Wales (United Kingdom)
  embassy, 817
  tourist information, 786
Walker, Alice, 253
Wallace, Alfred Russel, 144
Waller, Thomas "Fats," 177
Wallis and Futuna, statistics, 914
Walls, standard sizes, 566
Walnuts, 50
Walruses, 39
Walter, Thomas Ustick, 237
Warhol, Andy, 220–221

Warren, Robert Penn, 253
Wars, 940
  American Revolution, 942
  Battle of Hastings, 940
  battle of Napoleon I (Bonaparte), 942
  Boer, 944
  Civil War (U.S.), 943
  Crusades, 941
  Falklands, 947
  French and Indian, 942
  French Revolution, 942
  Hundred Years', 941
  King Philip's, 942
  Koren, 946
  Mexican, 943
  October (Bolshevik) Revolution, 945
  Persian Gulf, 947
  Spanish Civil War, 945
  Thirty Years', 941
  Vietnam, 947
  War of 1812, 943
  World War I, 945
  World War II, 945–946
  Yom Kippur, 947
Washing instructions/stain removal, 557–564
Washington
  Aging and Adult Services Administration, 642
  aquariums, 378
  botanical gardens, 384
  crime statistics, 894–897
  domestic violence organization, 671
  flower/bird/motto/nickname, 878
  legislature, 876
  libraries, 344
  name origin, 881
  newspapers, 910
  personal income per capita, 889
  poison control center, 492
  population, 883
  precipitation, 752
  state tourism office, 751
  temperatures, 754, 757
  two-letter abbreviation, 904
  wildlife refuges, 777, 780
  zoos, 378–379
Washington, DC. *See* District of Columbia
Washington, George, 861

Wasserstein, Wendy, 199
Water clocks, 5
Water lilies, 51
Water mill, 123
Waterbucks, 38
Water-soluble vitamins, 521
Watson, James Dewey, 150–151
Watt (W), 26
Watt, James, 27
Watteau, Jean-Antoine, 225
Weasels, 38
Weather. *See also* **Meteorology**
  Celsius, 29, 126
  Fahrenheit, 29, 125
  frost dates, 60
  international cities, 787–788
  United States, 751–757
Web site addresses
  abbreviations, 433
  adoption, 674
  aging, 532–533, 639–642, 678
  airlines, 738–742
  alcoholism and drug abuse,
    532–533, 643–644
  aquariums, 372–375, 377–378
  autobmobile rental agencies,
    736–737
  Better Business Bureaus, 644
  botanical gardens, 380–383
  cancer, 532–533
  children, 644, 671
  consumer affairs, 678
  copyrights, 620
  databases, 347, 349
  diabetes, 532
  dictionaries, 433
  domestic violence, 669
  entertainment, 216
  exercise, 534
  family planning organizations, 670
  Federal Information Centers
    (FIC), 674
  financial publications, 595
  first aid, 493–494
  foreign consulate offices, 795
  genealogy, 346–348
  geology, 119
  government agencies, 671–673,
    677, 801, 898
  health and medicine, 493–494,
    532–533
  home and gardening, 571–572
  international, 796–801

  law, 516, 618, 634
  libraries, 346–349
  measurements, 32
  men's interests, 678
  newsmagazines, 911
  parenting, 674, 679
  patents, 621
  Philosophy Documentation
    Center, 333
  physics, 119
  radio stations, 674–677
  Social Security Administration,
    872
  sports, 727–729
  television stations, 677
  theme parks, 779
  travel, 737–738, 747–751, 795,
    818–819
  weights, 32
  Wisconsin, 384
  women's interests, 679
  zoos, 372–375, 377–378
Web stations, 674–676
Weber, Carl Maria von, 171
Webern, Anton von, 167
Webster v. Reproductive Health
  Services, 625
Webster, John, 201
Webster, Noah, 253
Weddings
  anniversary gifts, 466
  announcements, 460–461
  bachelor dinner, 461
  ceremony, 463
  expenses, 465
  gifts, 465–466
  invitations, 460–461
  letter writing, 446
  reception, 463–464
  rehearsal dinner, 461–462
  showers, 461
  thank-you notes, 465–466
Weeds, 50
Wegener, Alfred Lothar, 148
Weidman, Charles, 192
Weights and measurements, 101,
  504
  angle, 25
  area, 24, 27
  conversion, 505
  cooking abbreviations, 536
  dry and liquid measure capacity,
    24–25, 27

  females, 506
  food, 536–537
  historic, 31
  kilogram (kg), 26
  length, 24, 27
  liquid measure capacity, 25
  mass, 25, 27
  metric system, 26–29, 127, 505,
    536
  physics, 99
  special, 30–32
  volume, 24
Weir, Peter, 205
Weissmuller, Johnny, 719
Welles, Orson, 207
Wells, H(erbert) George, 257
Welty, Eudora, 253
Wenders, Wim, 205
Werner, Abraham Gottlob, 148
West Bank and Gaza Strip, statistics,
  914
West Virginia
  Commission on Aging, 642
  consumer affairs, 666
  crime statistics, 892–893
  domestic violence organization,
    671
  flower/bird/motto/nickname, 878
  Legislature, 877
  name origin, 881
  personal income per capita, 888
  poison control center, 492
  population, 883
  state tourism offices, 751
  two-letter abbreviation, 904
West, Benjamin, 221
West, Morris L(anglo), 255
Western Sahara, statistics, 914
Western Samoa
  currency, 793
  embassy, 818
  statistics, 914
  travel requirements, 801
Westwork, 246
Whales, 38
Wharton, Edith, 253
Wheels, 122
Whip, 865
Whipple, Fred Lawrence, 143
Whistler, James Abbott McNeill,
  221
White dwarfs, 74
White holes, 75

White, E. B., 253
White, Gilbert, 148
White, Stanford, 237
Whitehead, Alfred North, 316
Whitman, Walt, 253
Whooping cough (Pertussis), 513
Whose/who's, 413
Wieniawski, Henri, 175
Wigman, Mary, 195
Wilde, Oscar, 201, 261
Wildebeest, 38
Wilder, Billy, 207
Wildlife refuges, 762–777
Wilkins, Maurice (Hugh Frederick), 151
Will to believe, 333
Will to power, 333
Wills, 515–516, 613, 633
William of Ockham (Occam), 316
Williams, Mary Lou, 178
Williams, Tennessee, 199
Wilson, August, 199
Wilson, Charles Thomson Rees, 153
Wilson, Edmund, 253
Wilson, Lanford, 199
Wilson, Woodrow, 861
Wilsonline, 349
Wimbledon (tennis), 708
Wind instruments, 159–162
Wind, Beaufort scale, 97–98
Windchill factor, 98–99
Windmill, 123
Windows, standard sizes, 568
Wine service, 556–557
Winter solstice, 12
Wires, 390
Wisconsin
    art museums, 369
    botanical gardens, 384
    Bureau on Aging, 642
    consumer affairs, 667
    crime statistics, 892–895
    domestic violence organization, 671
    flower/bird/motto/nickname, 878
    legislature, 876
    libraries, 344
    name origin, 881
    newspapers, 910
    personal income per capita, 888
    poison control center, 492
    population, 883
    precipitation, 752
    state tourism office, 751

temperatures, 754, 757
two-letter abbreviation, 904
wildlife refuges, 777, 780
zoos, 379
Witt, Katarina, 719
Wittgenstein, Ludwig, 316–317
Wolfe, Thomas, 253
Wolfe, Tom [Thomas Kennerly Wolfe, Jr.], 253
Wolves, 38
Wombats, 37
Wood, Grant, 221
Wooden, John, 719
Woods, Tiger, 719
Woolf, Virginia, 257
Word-by-word alphabetization, 404
Wordsworth, William, 257
World Cup (soccer), 706
World history. *See* History
World leaders. *See* Monarchy;
    Presidents; Prime ministers;
    Royalty
World Series (baseball), 688–690
World War I, 945
World War II, 945–946
World Wide Web (WWW). *See*
    Internet; Web site addresses
Worms, 40
Wouk, Herman, 253
Wounds, pets, 49
Woven cloth, 122
Wraparound mortgage, 585
Wren, Sir Christopher, 238
Wrench, 124
Wright, Frank Lloyd, 237
Wright, Richard, 253
Wyeth, Andrew, 221
Wyoming
    consumer affairs, 667
    crime statistics, 894–895
    Division on Aging, 642
    domestic violence organization, 671
    flower/bird/motto/nickname, 878
    legislature, 876
    name origin, 881
    newspaper, 910
    personal income per capita, 889
    poison control center, 492
    population, 883
    precipitation, 752
    state tourism offices, 751
    temperatures, 754, 757
    two-letter abbreviation, 904
    wildlife refuges, 777, 780

X

X-Rays, 133–134
Xylophone, 162

Y

Yaks, 38
Year. *See* Time
Yeats, William Butler, 261
Yellow fever, 513
Yemen Arab Republic
    currency, 793
    embassy, 818
    statistics, 914
    telephone code, 973
    travel requirements, 801
Yiddish language, frequently used
    words and phrases, 417, 419–421.
    See also Hebrew alphabet
Yom Kippur, 305
Yom Kippur War, 947
Young Hegelians, 322
Young, Cy, 719
Young, Lester "Prez," 178
Your/you're, 413
Youskevitch, Igor, 195
Yugoslavia, Federal Republic of
    civil war, 947
    telephone code, 973
    statistics, 914

Z

Zaharias, Babe Didrikson, 719
Zaire. *See* Democratic Republic of
    Congo
Zambia, Republic of, 801
    currency, 793
    embassy, 818
    statistics, 914
    tourist information, 786
Zebras, 39
Zeno (of Citium) the Stoic, 317
Zeno of Elea, 317
Ziggurat, 246
Zimbabwe
    currency, 793
    embassy, 818
    statistics, 923
    tourist information, 786
    travel requirements, 801
Zinc, 528–529
Zinnias, 49

Zip codes, United States, 898–904
Zither, 158
Zodiac constellations, 75

Zodiac signs, 395
Zola, Émile, 259
Zoos, United States, 372–379

Zoroastrianism, 291–292
Zurbarán, Francisco de, 229
Zwilich, Ellen Taafe, 166

As the third consecutive Republican presidential term begins, some conservatives claim total victory. Robert B. Reich, Harvard political economist and one of America's leading thinkers, predicts the resurgence of liberalism instead.

In this collection of his finest essays, Reich confronts our most pressing political and economic dilemmas with characteristic wit and wisdom. He assails the fatuousness and fragility of America's paper economy; the damage wreaked upon business since management became a profession; the economy's disastrous failure to invest in the American worker; and the confusion surrounding our economic contest with Japan and our political contest with Russia. Reich offers pungent and revealing commentary on the evolution of the American presidency; on the faded belief in equal sacrifice; on the law and its loss of moral force; and on politicians who have set America on the road to Quayle.

Whether America will become a "kinder, gentler" nation remains to be seen; no one has argued for more humane policies than Reich. But soft-hearted liberals need hard heads, and Robert Reich's views speak ever more clearly to liberals, neo-liberals, left-of-liberals, and closet liberals — all of whom yearn for a powerful, pragmatic alternative to the prevailing dogma.

Also by the Author

MINDING AMERICA'S BUSINESS
(with Ira Magaziner)

THE NEXT AMERICAN FRONTIER

NEW DEALS: THE CHRYSLER REVIVAL
AND THE AMERICAN SYSTEM
(with John D. Donahue)

TALES OF A NEW AMERICA

THE POWER OF PUBLIC IDEAS
(editor and contributor)

THE
RESURGENT
LIBERAL
(And Other
Unfashionable Prophecies)

THE RESURGENT LIBERAL

(And Other Unfashionable Prophecies)

ROBERT B. REICH

TIMES BOOKS

RANDOM HOUSE

All rights reserved under International and Pan-American Copyright Conventions. Published in the United States by Times Books, a division of Random House, Inc., New York, and simultaneously in Canada by Random House of Canada Limited, Toronto.

All acknowledgments for permission to reprint material are found on the facing page.

Library of Congress Cataloging-in-Publication Data

Reich, Robert B.
  The resurgent liberal (and other unfashionable prophecies)/
Robert B. Reich.
     p.   cm.
  Includes index.
  ISBN 0-8129-1833-9
  1. United States—Economic policy—1981–   2. United
States—Politics and government—1989–   3. United States—
Social policy—1980–   4. Liberalism—United States.   I. Title.
HC106.8.R454   1989
338.973—dc19   89-4418

Manufactured in the United States of America

9   8   7   6   5   4   3   2
First Edition

PERMISSIONS
ACKNOWLEDGMENTS

Some essays in this work were originally published in the following publications: *Across the Board, The American Oxonian, Foreign Affairs, Harper's Magazine, The New Republic, The New York Times, The Washington Post, Working Mother,* and *Yale Journal of Law and Policy.*

"Toward a New Philosophy" ("The Once and Future Liberal"), April 1985, "The Rise of Techno-Nationalism," April 1987, and "The Corporation and the Nation," May 1988, were originally published in *The Atlantic Monthly.*

Grateful acknowledgment is made to the following for permission to reprint previously published material: *Harper & Row Publishers, Inc.:* Introductory essay from The *Power of Public Ideas* by Robert B. Reich. Copright © 1988 by Robert B. Reich. Reprinted by permission of the Ballinger Division, Harper & Row Publishers, Inc.

Harvard Business Review: "Regulation by Confrontation or Negotiation" ("The Origins of Red Tape") and "The Team as Hero" by Robert B. Reich from the May/June 1981 and May/June 1987 issues of *Harvard Business Review.* Copright © 1981, 1987 by the President and Fellows of Harvard College. Reprinted by permission of Harvard Business Review. All rights reserved.

National Education Association: "Education and the Next Economy" ("Dick and Jane Meet the Next Economy") by Robert B. Reich. Copyright © 1988 by National Education Association of the United States. Reprinted by permission of N.E.A.

The New York Times: "Entrepreneurialism" and "Loophole Mentalities" ("The Spirit of Law") by Robert B. Reich from the May 23, 1980, and September 13, 1987, issues of *The New York Times.* Copyright © 1980, 1987 by The New York Times Company. Reprinted by permission. All rights reserved.

Harcourt Brace Jovanovich, Inc.: Excerpts from *Revolution* by Martin Anderson. Copyright © 1988 by Martin Anderson. Excerpts from *For the Record* by Donald T. Regan. Copyright © 1988 Donald T. Regan. Reprinted by permission of Harcourt Brace Jovanovich, Inc.

For Sam

CONTENTS

Preface xiii

I THE PAPER ECONOMY
1 The Secret of His Success 3
2 The New American Entrepreneur 7
3 The Anthropomorphization of Wall Street
(Or Why the Market Crashed on October 19, 1987,
and Will Do So Again) 23
4 The Convenience of Banking 27
5 The Origins of Red Tape 34

II THE REAL ECONOMY
6 The Economics of Illusion and the Illusion of Economics 51
7 The Executive's New Clothes (I) 61
8 The Executive's New Clothes (II) 70
9 The Team as Hero 84
10 Dick and Jane Meet the Next Economy 96

III OF COLD AND TEPID WARS
11 The Rise of Techno-Nationalism 107
12 High-Tech Warfare 121
13 The Pentagon and the Gosplan 131
14 Beyond Free Trade 144
15 The Unspecial Relationship 160
16 Whose Cars? 166
17 The Corporation and the Nation 174

IV THE ROAD TO QUAYLE
18 The Redefined Presidency 189
19 The Spirit of the Law 192
20 A Sentimental Education 195
21 The Day I Became a Feminist 203
22 The Fourth Wave of Regulation 207
23 The Economic Theory of Politics 214

24 When the Women Returned Home 223
25 The Four Parables of American Politics 227

V THE RESURGENT LIBERAL
26 The Ideology of Survival 235
27 The Faded Ideal of Equal Sacrifice 242
28 The Liberal as Planner 247
29 How Not to Make Industrial Policy 255
30 Competence or Ideology? 258
31 Great Exhortations 268
32 The Once and Future Liberal 274

Index 291

PREFACE

MY REPUTATION AS A SOOTHSAYER BEGAN IN OCTOBER 1987, TWO WEEKS before the Dow Jones Industrial Average plunged five hundred points, when I appeared on a nationally televised talk show opposite a conservative economist who assured viewers that the bull market would continue. I demurred. My advice to viewers was to get out of the market before the coming crash. I had the temerity to predict that the crash would occur within the month. In the weeks following the crash I was inundated with letters from people wanting to subscribe to my investment letter. Politely but regretfully, I informed each of them that I did not publish an investment letter. I did not tell them, however, that I had been making precisely the same prediction for five years.

I have been predicting the resurgence of liberalism for many more years than that, and no doubt someday my clairvoyance will be appreciated in similar fashion. There are eventual benefits to tenacity. When the day comes, and my political prognostications are a valued commodity, you, dear reader, may justly share in the acclaim. After all, you were reading this before it became fashionable.

The following pages are especially designed for those who may feel the need for some companionship and fortification in the meantime. The true triumph of conservatism has come in making some of us feel defensive, even slightly embarrassed, about our liberal tendencies. (The most recent Democratic candidate for President tried for months to dodge the label, confessing to his liberal beliefs only under duress.) Under these circumstances, a firm assurance that such inclinations are essentially healthy, natural, and even socially beneficial may relieve the abashment and give courage to discuss them openly in mixed company.

Self-confidence is necessary but not sufficient. There must also be something to be confident about. Thus, a second purpose of this book. Modern liberalism should stand squarely for, and against, certain things. The following essays do not lack a point of view.

Conservative orthodoxy places great faith in the social utility of fear and avarice. Fear of unpleasant consequence, argues the conservative, keeps would-be criminals at bay, foreign aggressors in line, and the lazy and indolent off the streets. Avarice, meanwhile, inspires geniuses to new invention, mavericks and risk takers to new enterprise, and nations to new greatness. That few facts can be found to support these propositions is beside the point. They rest on faith, grounded in a mixture of strict child rearing, social Darwinism, and neoclassical economics.

Future historians who examine the late 1970s and 1980s will discover a different set of consequences flowing from the prevailing fear and avarice. They will find that excessive greed inspired clever criminals, on and off Wall Street, to ever more ingenious circumnavigations of law. Audacious displays of avarice also demoralized average working people who came to believe that the path to success lay in selfish opportunism rather than in loyalty to company and country. Greed on a grander scale led an entire nation into debt and thus into precarious financial dependence on foreign powers, oblivious to the burden placed on future generations. As lawfulness, loyalty, and national security so declined, society was forced to develop ever larger and more elaborate ways to deter criminality, opportunism, and foreign domination. This vicious spiral provoked conservative demands for even greater financial reward and more draconian punishment; if carrots and sticks failed to elicit the intended behavior, they argued, it was because the carrots were too meager and the sticks too frail.

What will history conclude finally reversed the trend? A financial crisis? A particularly revolting scandal? A generation of graying baby boomers, sated and sedated, despised by their children and grandchildren, who finally repented? The unanticipated bleeding heart of a President Quayle? My crystal ball fails me on these finer points. But of this I am reasonably certain: With the liberal resurgence will come a new appreciation of the importance to society of loyalty, collaboration, civic virtue, and responsibility to future generations. Such altruistic inclinations are unlikely to grow in a society organized around fear and greed. Resurgent liberals will adopt a different set of organizing principles. Avarice will be discouraged (there will be no shame, for example, in enacting a very high marginal tax rate on princely incomes). The pain and fear of economic dislocation will be eased (through extended unemployment insurance, job training coupled with day care, health insurance for the unemployed and working poor, and similar programs). American enterprises will become owned and controlled by all their employees (rather than solely by their overleveraged executives, per the latest fashion in corporate finance). And neither military jingoism nor economic mercantilism will any longer be the measure of patriotism. True patriotism will be founded instead on a common concern for, and investment in, the well-being of our future citizens.

A final prediction. As a by-product of the liberal resurgence, liberals will no longer feel embarrassed by their inclinations. In fact, fueled by renewed confidence and exuberance, liberals eventually will display the same grandiosity that got them into trouble last time. And the cycle will repeat.

*   *   *

The following ruminations span the decade or so before the coming liberal resurgence. The first set of essays concerns the rise of the paper economy—the substitution of paper for product in American managers' hearts and minds, and the attendant consequences for our politics and economics. A second group of essays deals with the larger incapacity of the economy to generate new wealth, due in part to the failure to invest in, and give meaningful voice and responsibility to, the American work force. I include here a summary of my ideas about the work force of the future and the challenge it poses to the American corporation and American education.

The next few essays are on economic nationalism. It is by now a commonplace that the nation is involved in two global contests—one, a political contest with the Soviet Union and its allies; the other, an economic contest with Japan. But there is confusion about which contest is the more important, how the two contests affect one another, and more generally, the appropriate role for economic nationalism in policy making. My arguments on these questions should be clear, if not convincing.

The final two sections are on American politics, social trends, and political thought. Economics cannot be divorced from politics (although many economists make valiant efforts in this direction). These essays seek some new connections, and directions.

In sum, as these essays reveal, the 1980s have provided abundant material for rumination. Nothing inspires the dissident imagination quite as well as prevailing orthodoxy; nothing emboldens it as well as excess in high places. In this respect I am deeply indebted to Ronald Reagan, George Bush, Ivan Boesky, Michael Deaver, Edwin Meese, George Steinbrenner, Donald Regan, Oliver North, Donald Trump, Frank Lorenzo, and many of the fine people who still inhabit the upper reaches of American business, finance, and government. Without their stout conviction and audacious conduct, these essays would not have been written.

Robert B. Reich
Cambridge, Massachusetts

I

THE
PAPER
ECONOMY

1

THE SECRET
OF HIS SUCCESS

GEORGE HAD BEEN ONE OF MY BEST STUDENTS WHEN I CAME TO HAR-
vard. I hadn't seen him since graduation. The wedding reception for one
of his classmates gave me a chance to catch up.

"What have you been up to, George?" I asked.

"Doing M and A deals," he said, a bit sheepishly.

"M and A deals?"

"Mergers and acquisitions," he explained. "You know—putting
them together, financing them, the whole bit. I'm an investment banker."

I tried to look enthusiastic. "Enjoying it?"

"Yeah. Made half a million last year. This year I'll top a million for
sure."

I was astounded, not only at the amount of money, but also at
George's overwhelming desire to tell me about it. "You mean, you actually earned half a million dollars?"

Now George became animated. "Base pay of one hundred and
twenty-five thousand dollars, bonus of three hundred seventy-five thousand dollars. There's no limit. I'll be earning two million dollars a year
by the time I'm thirty."

I remembered George equally animated, in the classroom six years earlier. It was a course on American political economy, and George had been an active contributor. He had the ability to get to the heart of the matter, to cut through conventional economic theory and its idealized view of markets, and to focus instead on the real frailties and foibles of the American system. Now I was going to find out what he had learned since then.

"Half a million dollars is a lot of money," I said with a smile. "You sure you're worth that much?"

George smiled back. "Of course not." Then he pointed to several of his classmates sitting at other tables. "And neither are Tim or Fred or Jane. They all made as much as I did last year, doing deals."

"How do you explain it, you and all the others pulling down that kind of money in your twenties?" I asked. "Economic theory says that people get paid according to their marginal product—what they contribute to society. You're earning more than most top executives of Fortune 500 companies, more than heart surgeons, nuclear physicists, more than university presidents, judges, the President of the United States. And much, much more," I added wistfully, "than Harvard professors. What gives?"

George's smile turned into a broad grin. His eyes lit up the way I remembered in the classroom. "Some say that we're worth every penny because we're restructuring America, making it more competitive." He laughed. "That's bull. We're just moving financial assets from one pocket to another. Unfriendly takeovers have been a big thing since the mid-1970s. What's happened with productivity growth since then? Zip."

"OK, OK. So tell me—why are you guys earning so much?"

"Look, there are two ways to make a bundle in this business," said George, his eyes narrowing in mock conspiracy. "The first is to move a huge sum of money. We work on a percentage basis, so the more money we move, the more we make."

George took out his pen and began drawing circles and numbers on a napkin. "Institutions like mutual funds, pension funds, bank trust departments, insurance companies—they're managing billion-dollar portfolios, more than a third of all the outstanding equity in the nation. And they're shifting big hunks of stock here and there at the slightest provocation."

George drew a line on the napkin, as if to add up the total. "The more action, the better for us. In 1980 the twenty biggest investment banks earned about eleven billion dollars. Last year, revenues topped thirty-five billion dollars."

George put down his pen. "Think about it—all this money moving around faster and faster. We grab a tiny piece of every dollar that's moved. The big institutions don't even miss it. I mean, what's a few million dollars when you're shifting billions every day?"

George grinned, eyebrows raised—the same mischievous expression I remembered from years before, when he was homing in on some core economic truth. "You have to remember that we're the ones who are advising the big institutions about whether they should move their money," he continued. "We're advising the corporate raiders about whether they should undertake a raid. We're advising everyone else about whether they should buy or sell or go private. And you know, it's just amazing how often our fancy analysis boils down to the same advice: Move your money! Quick!"

I was beginning to understand. "You said there were two ways to make a bundle. What's the second way?"

George paused, then leaned in toward me. "Remember, the first is to move a lot of money. The second way is to move it to where a lot of other money is heading, before the other money gets there." He lowered his voice. "You've been following the scandals—the insider-trading stuff?"

"George, I don't think you should tell me anything that . . ."

He stopped me. "No, no, no. Don't worry. I'm clean. Those guys that got indicted—they got greedy. They traded on inside information. They broke the law. My point is that you can move your money to where other money is heading without breaking the law."

George again picked up his pen and drew a big box on the napkin. "Let's call this an investment banking firm," he said. He divided the box into four squares. "Over here are the guys who help companies raise money. In the next box are the M and A specialists, the ones who do all the mergers and acquisitions and buyouts. In this third box are the guys who trade for the big institutions, the block traders. And in this last box are the guys who speculate on our own account, the arbitrageurs. In the gentlemanly days of investment banking most of the revenues came from the first box, from the guys who helped corporations get financing. But these days the really big earnings come from the other three boxes."

George drew dotted lines connecting the M and A specialists, the block traders, and the arbs. "Now, it would be illegal for us to trade on inside information; the arbs aren't allowed to buy into a company that's the target of one of our clients, for example. But you've got to remember how much information there is of a slightly more general character that's shared between these boxes all the time. I mean, you've got to talk about something at lunch, right?"

George again put on his mock conspiratorial expression. "Say the M and A guys have a client who's considering whether to take over CBS. Then they hear of another company that's interested in taking over ABC. Well, it doesn't take a rocket scientist to figure out that television networks are getting hot, so the M and A specialists tell the arbs to start buying NBC. Sure enough, network stocks take off, the firm makes a bundle. Illegal? Not at all. Done all the time."

George warmed to the topic. "Or suppose a prospective client comes in and says he's interested in taking over a car company, but the M and A guys have too much work and turn him down, and he goes to another investment bank. Still, you're pretty sure—given the client's size and history—that he's hot to make a bid for Chrysler. You also know that a lot of other investment bankers will soon figure out the same thing, as the client moves down the street trying to hire some muscle. So you tell the arbs to get into Chrysler fast. Sure enough, Chrysler's share price starts moving up in anticipation of a bid, and the firm makes a bundle. Illegal? No way. Done all the time.

"You see," he said, striking his pen on the table, "valuable information circulates all over every investment banking firm, all over Wall Street. It's not inside information, because it's not very specific, and nobody trades directly upon it. You profit indirectly from it. Call it *insidious* information." George laughed, proud of his neologism.

By now, the party was almost over. The bride and groom had already left. My wife mentioned something about baby-sitters and went to get our coats. I rose and extended my hand to George. "I'm afraid we have to get going, George. I would have liked to hear more, but I've got the idea. You've explained a great deal."

George gave me an iron grip. "It's all a big, speculative bubble," he said, rising. "I'm getting out before I'm thirty-five, before it bursts."

"That sounds wise," I said. "You'll be a rich man. What will you do then?"

George smiled broadly. "Politics."

2

THE NEW
AMERICAN ENTREPRENEUR

When the capital development of a country becomes a by-product of the activities of a casino, the job is likely to be ill-done. The measure of success attained by Wall Street ... cannot be claimed as one of the outstanding triumphs of laissez-faire capitalism.

—*John Maynard Keynes*
**General Theory of Employment,
Interest and Money** *(1936)*

THE PAPER ENTREPRENEURS ARE WINNING OUT OVER THE PRODUCT entrepreneurs.

Paper entrepreneurs—trained in law, finance, accountancy—manipulate complex systems of rules and numbers. They innovate by using the systems in novel ways: establishing joint ventures, consortia, holding companies, mutual funds; finding companies to acquire, "white knights" to be acquired by, stock-index and commodity futures to invest in, tax shelters to hide in; engaging in proxy fights, tender offers, antitrust suits, stock splits, leveraged buyouts, divestitures; buying and selling notes, junk bonds, convertible debentures; going private, going public, going bankrupt.

Product entrepreneurs—inventors, design engineers, production engineers, production managers, marketers, owners of small businesses—produce goods and services people want. They innovate by creating better products at less cost; establishing more-efficient techniques of manufacture, distribution, sales; finding cheaper sources of materials, new markets, consumer needs; providing better training of employees, attention-getting advertising, speedier consumer service and complaint handling, more-reliable warranty coverage and repair.

Our economic system needs both. Paper entrepreneurs ensure that capital is allocated efficiently among product entrepreneurs. They also coordinate the activities of product entrepreneurs, facilitating readjustments and realignments in supply and demand.

But paper entrepreneurs do not directly enlarge the economic pie; they only arrange and define the slices. They provide nothing of tangible use. For an economy to maintain its health, entrepreneurial rewards should flow primarily to product, not paper.

Yet paper entrepreneurialism is on the rise. It dominates the leadership of our largest corporations. It guides government departments and agencies. It stimulates platoons of lawyers and financiers. It preoccupies some of our best minds, attracts some of our most talented graduates, embodies some of our most creative and original thinking, spurs some of our most energetic wheeling and dealing. Paper entrepreneurialism also promises the best financial rewards, the greatest employment security, the highest social status.

The ratio of paper entrepreneurialism to product entpreneurialism in our economy—measured by total earnings flowing to each, or by the amount of news in business journals and newspapers typically devoted to each—is about two to one.

Our economic system has become so complex and interdependent that capital must be allocated according to symbols of productivity rather than according to productivity itself. These symbolic rules and numbers lend themselves to profitable manipulation far more readily than do the underlying processes of production. It takes time and effort to improve product quality, exploit manufacturing efficiencies, develop distribution and sales networks, thus enlarging market share and profitability. But through the strategic use of accounting conventions, tax rules, stock and commodity exchanges, exchange rates, and litigation, enormous profits are possible with relatively little effort.

Paper entrepreneurialism is also cleaner than product entrepreneurialism. The paper entrepreneur needs only a phone, a Telex, a fax machine, a good secretary. The product entrepreneur depends on a complex web of raw materials, suppliers, employees, machines, distributors, advertisers, consumers—any of which can cause unexpected problems, at any time.

When paper entrepreneurs look for solutions to America's slowing productivity and its loss of international competitiveness, they come up with paper remedies to stimulate capital investment: accelerated depreciation, tax credits, cuts in capital-gains tax rates, relaxation of antitrust laws. Product entrepreneurs focus on techniques for improving output: better quality controls, improved labor-management relations, more-effective incentives for managers and employees, more-aggressive marketing and sales.

We may need to choose from between both sets of strategies. But in evaluating them, we should consider carefully their likely effects. If we are to increase the economic pie, we will need to redress the balance of entrepreneurial effort. Which strategies will stimulate more paper and which more product?

* * *

The most obvious example of the dominance of paper over product is to be found in the continuing urge to merge and then unmerge. Over the last decade billions of dollars have been spent to acquire existing corporate assets. Only a small percentage of this sum was actually consumed in the takeover process, in the necessary costs of transacting the deals. Most of the money repeatedly circulated among investment bankers, arbitrageurs, portfolio managers, brokers, and other financial intermediaries, as they traded shares of stock in companies about to be taken over, or about to be disassembled, or they made bets on whether *other* financial intermediaries would expect such companies to be taken over or disassembled, and so on, in an almost infinite regression of trades and takeover bets, and bets on takeover bets, and trades on bets on takeover bets.

The language through which all this has been accomplished is colorful and childlike, featuring "golden parachutes," payments of "greenmail," "white knights," and poison pills of all hues. The bright colors mask darker realities, calling into question the purpose of the American corporation in the latter decades of the twentieth century. For at least fifty years it had been assumed that public ownership of stocks assured that America's major corporations were well managed and that public trading in such stocks guaranteed that investors received fair value. No longer.

Golden parachutes are nothing more than generous severance payments, often totaling large multiples of an executive's annual salary and bonus, which are awarded—the parachute automatically opens, as it were—when the takeover becomes successful. The proffered justification is dubious: Such insurance is thought essential to preserve the executive's impartial judgment about hostile takeover bids. Without the parachute, so the argument goes, the executive would be tempted to fight the takeover even if it were in the best interests of the stockholders. The logic suggests that the only way stockholders can trust corporate executives not to feather their nests at the stockholders' expense is to provide them a prefeathered nest at the stockholders' expense.

Greenmail is ransom, paid to those who are trying to take over the company, to get them to stop offering the company's stockholders high prices for their stock. The ransom is paid by corporate executives and directors, who presumably would lose their jobs if the predator succeeded. The ransom money comes ultimately from the same stockholders who are being courted by the predator. The justifications for greenmail are equally suspect: Executives and directors argue that predators don't understand the business and, once in control, would diminish its value. Alternatively, they argue that the stockholders don't know how much their stock is *really* worth, and they are being duped by the low bids of predators. Either way, the logic suggests that the current executives and directors are doing a superb job and only they are fit to judge how superb.

White knights, poison pills, and further exotica also help incumbent management ward off unfriendly predators. By the late 1980s managers who sensed the possibility of a hostile takeover employed a technique known as the "leveraged buyout." The financial complexities were dazzling, but the underlying principle was straightforward. The corporate managers borrow money, often at high interest rates, to buy up their company's stock. These loans are backed by the company's assets. The managers who now own the company thereupon make it more valuable, either by increasing its productivity or by selling off its divisions. They thus make a bundle. With high leverage, small improvements in operating performance can dramatically increase the value of a tiny equity base.

Here again, the proffered justification is oddly inconsistent with our inherited notions about the function and purpose of the corporation. The argument is that once managers' wealth is tied up in the company, they will become more efficient and improve the firm's performance; that is, managers who own their company work harder and better. But this logic suggests that the same managers have been grossly deficient in the past, failing to act in the stockholders' best interests.

All of these asset-rearranging techniques require the ubiquitous skills of accountants and lawyers. A new field of consultancy has grown up in recent years, euphemistically deemed "earnings management," which consists of the strategic use of accounting conventions—redistributing income from good years to bad, recognizing profits in advance of sales, and similar innovations. The leading edge of American jurisprudence is found in such fields as securities and tax law, where piles of arcane pleadings and truckloads of depositions now inundate our courtrooms and preoccupy squadrons of lawyers, overworked clerks, and despairing judges.

*   *   *

Apologists of such antics argue that they are justified by economic fundamentals. (When you hear an argument based on "economic fundamentals," you would be wise to place a hand firmly over your wallet and keep it there until the perpetrator has moved on.) Faced with the alternatives of investing in new plants, equipment, or research (risky propositions the payoffs of which are likely to be in the distant future), or of distributing the earnings to shareholders (who are immediately taxed on such largesse), corporate managers instead see considerable attraction in snapping up profitable, well-run companies with established market positions—even their own. They speak of wondrous gains from "synergy," the dynamic effects of pooled management on what were formerly independent firms, making the whole greater than the sum of the parts. They wax with equal enthusiasm over the gains to be had from disassembling and selling off piecemeal such parts, thus making the sum of the parts greater than the whole. And through it all, they exhibit faith—endless faith, indomitable faith—in the hidden, *potential* value of the assets being purchased, relative to the price they currently fetch on the stock market.

Most of this is nonsense, or worse. The record of the 1970s and 1980s is dismally clear. Acquiring companies rarely have done well for their stockholders. Despite all the claims for synergy, there is little evidence to suggest that mergers have on the average enhanced the basic profitability of merging enterprises. The subsequent rush to dismember suggests, in fact, just the reverse.

A case in point. R. J. Reynolds, the giant tobacco company, merged with Nabisco, the giant food processor, in 1985. The merger was then hailed as a brilliant strategy, through which the tobacco company would diversify into foods. Just three years later, the newly merged company became the object of a mammoth contest between armies of investment bankers pledging billions of dollars for the privilege of breaking it up once again.

Another. In the 1960s Avis Rent-A-Car was a part of ITT's conglomerate empire. Synergies notwithstanding, ITT sold Avis to Norton Simon. Norton Simon, in turn, was taken over by Esmark. One year later, Esmark succumbed to the blandishments of Beatrice Foods. In 1986 Beatrice itself was taken over by a group of investors that included several former Esmark executives. They promptly dismembered Beatrice, selling off Avis to its own managers. A mere fourteen months later, Avis's managers sold the erstwhile company to its employees. Over the years the only predictable aspect of Avis Rent-A-Car has been its penchant for changing hands.

Defenders of such escapades claim nevertheless that asset rearranging is no mere speculative game but a means by which the financial market ensures that resources are available for new enterprise. Close examination belies this comforting view. Wall Street's dynamism has little to do with the financing of new commercial venture. During most of the 1980s, new issues of common stock averaged only about 1 percent of the total stock outstanding. Ninety-nine percent of Wall Street's exuberance pertained to shares of stock already in circulation, which became objects of titillating rumor. Portfolio managers frantically bid against one another to take advantage of small upticks or downblips in this vast casino, betting pension funds or mutual funds in which Americans had placed their savings. In effect, most Americans unknowingly were engaged in continuous bidding against one another (and, if their money was entrusted to more than one fund manager, as was often the case, against themselves). It was exactly as if we had all crowded into Vegas for a long binge.

The American economy as a whole has not benefited demonstrably. Since the mid-1970s, when most of this began, productivity gains have slowed. Average real wages (controlled for inflation) have stagnated. Average stock prices have barely risen. And only the public-relations office of the United States Chamber of Commerce would contend that American firms have stayed competitive with those of Japan, West Germany, South Korea, and other places around the globe, where, incidentally, hostile takeovers and leveraged buyouts rarely if ever occur.

* * *

Then why did it happen? If there is no economic justification, why does it continue?

Let us go back to 1974. That year, the International Nickel Company decided to buy up enough shares in Electric Storage Battery Company to give International Nickel control over the board of directors of Electric Storage and thus allow International Nickel to run the company effectively. The managers of Electric Storage Battery did not want International Nickel to run the company, because they didn't believe that International Nickel could do a very good job of it, and they didn't want to lose their jobs. They thus regarded International Nickel's act as hostile, as it in fact was—the first in a long and not-so-distinguished line of such unfriendly initiatives.

Before International Nickel did this dirty deed, Wall Street had viewed such aggression as unseemly, if not unethical. One didn't just *take over* a company. A company was its managers and employees, its trademark and reputation. These attributes could not be purchased *against its will,* or so it was assumed. Besides, there was no reason for such shenanigans. The American economy, then run along more gentlemanly lines, had grown quite large, and at a rapid clip, without stooping to such behavior.

Then Wall Street's other shoe fell. In 1975 the Securities and Exchange Commission decreed that commissions paid on stock transactions were no longer to be based on fixed rates but were to be negotiable. Henceforth, brokers' commissions were to be subject to the free market, to ungentlemanly *competition*! Within a year revenues in Wall Street brokerage houses plunged $600 million. This was no time for squeamishness. Forget the niceties. The Street had to forage for new sources of earnings, and hostile takeovers looked like just the place to start.

The supply of investment bankers, as it were, created its own demand. There were twelve hostile takeovers of $1 billion or more in the remainder of the 1970s; between 1981 and 1984 there were forty-five. Then came the leveraged buyouts, culminating in the last days of the Reagan Administration, appropriately enough, with the $25 billion buyout of RJR-Nabisco. In 1978 mergers and acquisitions accounted for less than 5 percent of the profits of Wall Street brokerage houses. By 1988 the "M&A business," as it was affectionately called on the Street, accounted for more than 50 percent of their profits.

And profitable it has been. Over the decade the average incomes of paper entrepreneurs grew 21 percent, compared with a 7 percent rise in the incomes of everyone else.

The demand for paper entrepreneurs, in turn, generated more of a supply. Between 1977 and 1987 employment in the securities industry doubled—increasing by an average of 10 percent a year—compared to average yearly job growth of 1.9 percent in the rest of the economy. The stock market crash of October 19, 1987, slowed things down a bit. For several months there were poignant stories of $200,000-a-year investment bankers suddenly forced to sell their East Side duplexes. But within a year the forward thrust of the M&A business had been fully restored. By the end of 1988 one quarter of all new private-sector jobs in New York City, and more than a third of all the new office space in that industrious town, were devoted to paper professionals engaged in rearranging assets.

Deal making has proved particularly lucrative, because every time industrial assets are rearranged, paper professionals earn money. The larger and more complex the escapade, the more money they earn. If they handle the legal complexities, they are paid according to the amount of time they put in. If they manage the financial niceties, they are paid a small percentage of the deal. Thus, there has emerged a strong interest in doing deals.

And here, the most critical point: Paper entrepreneurs not only do the deals but also advise their clients (corporate directors, chief executives, pension-fund managers) about when and whether such deals *should* be done. Like doctors and automobile mechanics, who occupy equally enviable positions both of advising about the need for their services and supplying the needed services, paper entrepreneurs have discovered that there is no necessary limit to the amount of service they can urge on their customers and thereupon provide. Deals thus have become more plentiful, and larger.

More plentiful: In 1960 an average of three million shares of stock were traded daily on the New York Stock Exchange. During the entire year, some 12 percent of the listed shares were exchanged and, on average, held eight years before being resold. During an average day in 1988, by contrast, two hundred million shares exchanged hands. For the year as a whole, 95 percent of the listed shares were traded, and most remained with their owners for only a few hours. The dollar value of trading in stock-index options and futures—bets on how bundles of stocks will move—was five times that of the trades in shares of stock.

Larger: The RJR-Nabisco deal of 1988 generated close to $1 billion in paper-entrepreneurial fees. Like the obscure services listed on hotel bills and automobile stickers, those that comprised this sum were not self-evident: some $200 million for what was called a "buyout fee"; $400 million for "junk-bond underwriting and bank commitment."

"Merger and advisory fees" added another $150 million. The prospective sales of the food and tobacco businesses would earn investment bankers an additional $100 million. The platoon of lawyers and legal advisers reaped at least $50 million.

Deal making also has created abundant work for lawyers, especially when deals turn sour. Texaco and Pennzoil feuded over Getty Oil Company for almost three years. By the end, Texaco had paid over $60 million to lawyers; Pennzoil, $400 million.

Should the economy suddenly fall into recession or worse, no matter. By the close of the 1980s paper entrepreneurs were preparing to make money on the pending collapse. Investment banks had already amassed funds for "deleveraged buyouts," the purpose of which would be to do the reverse of what had been done during boom times—this time, reduce the debt load and increase the shares of stock. It was happily anticipated that the bonds of newly bankrupt companies could be purchased for a small fraction of their face values and new shares issued to the remaining creditors. The newly reorganized company could then be sold for a fat profit.

*   *   *

Through all this the historic relationship between product and paper has been turned upside down. Investment bankers no longer think of themselves as working *for* the corporations with which they do business. Corporations now exist for the investment bankers, who openly put them into play, buy and sell stock in them, initiate takeovers and leveraged buyouts. Whole departments of investment banks scan corporate America for businesses ripe for the plucking. It is as if doctors and auto mechanics went house to house, instructing the occupants on what they must do to aviod death or breakdown, and then ripping them and their cars apart to make the prescribed repairs.

Investment banks are replacing the publicly held industrial corporations as the largest and most powerful economic institutions in America. In 1987 Drexel Burnham Lambert, Wall Street's fastest-growing company, posted earnings of $500 million, putting it right up there with Xerox, Monsanto, and Kraft. After purchasing RJR-Nabisco, the firm of Kohlberg, Kravis, and Roberts controlled companies with total revenues of $50 billion, transforming KKR into the fifth-largest industrial company in the United States.

Twenty-five years ago the titans of American industry were chief executive officers of major industrial corporations. Today, as in the late nineteenth century, they are investment bankers. Each of the principal partners of KKR earns about $70 million a year. (One wing of the Metropolitan Museum of Art is named after its benefactor, Henry Kravis.) Michael Milken, the "junk bond king," was earning $550 million a year before his inconvenient clash with the federal government. Rarely have so few earned so much for doing so little. Never have so few exercised so much power over how the slices of the American pie are rearranged.

*   *   *

I do not want to suggest that all efforts directed at rearranging corporate assets are necessarily wasteful. To the extent that they allocate capital more efficiently to where it can be most productive, or smooth out what would otherwise be sudden changes in supply and demand, they make our economy perform better. But given the record of speculation and finagle, one must ask whether these benefits are worth what we're paying for them, in terms of both direct costs and future productivity.

The current obsession with asset rearranging harms productivity in four related ways:

1. Myopia Improvements in productivity often depend on investment strategies geared to the long term. Productivity gains come gradually. Research aimed at developing fundamentally new technologies is apt to go slowly, yielding little or no profit for many years. The development of the internal combustion engine, electronics, xerography, and semiconductors each depended on a quarter century or more of trial and error. Commercialization often requires the development of large production facilities, distribution and sales networks, and quality-control systems. All this demands a willingness to invest now for greater returns in a distant future.

But asset rearrangers typically require that investments pay off in the short term, at the expense of greater yields later on. General Electric's costly acquisition of RCA, for example, resulted in less research for both. In 1987 General Electric cut its research spending by 8 percent. Under new management RCA's famed David Sarnoff Research Center, for decades an incubator of television technology, slashed its staff by 25 percent. Or consider Borg-Warner, another company specializing in high technology. After a fierce takeover battle in the 1980s the firm gutted its research laboratory.

Truncated vision is due, in part, to the necessity of repaying huge loans used to finance such asset rearrangements. Nothing so focuses the corporate mind as threat of bankruptcy. Yet this is not a complete explanation. Asset rearrangers also have changed the pattern of stock ownership in ways that emphasize immediate gain. Not long ago the majority of stock on our exchanges was owned by individuals, many of whom remained with their companies for years. It was not unusual for such an investor to take a mildly proprietary interest in how his or her company was doing, and what it was planning to do. Today, 70 percent of corporate stock is bought and sold by professional portfolio managers of mutual funds, pension funds, and insurance companies. These managers must do more than invest for the future—they must also attract and keep clients. So they are under pressure to demonstrate the short-term earnings that potential clients demand. In the search for quick profits, they move in and out of large positions with little regard for the strengths of the underlying enterprise. Securities analysts and brokers likewise hope to show profits by correctly guessing the short-term fluctuation of price-earning multiples instead of the long-term potential for growth.

On the management side, the motivation is similar. The average corporate chief executive may have an even smaller stake in future growth than the average stockholder. The frenetic movement of corporate assets engenders a similar shifting of managerial talent. Top executives are fired, or they are lured to another newly rearranged corporation. They feel no loyalty to their present company, which, after all, is regarded by its directors and stockholders as little more than a collection of financial assets. Thus, the average term of office for today's chief executive officers is only four years.

Thanks to the high mobility of capital and management, those who have the strongest economic stake in the long-term health of an enterprise are apt to be its lower-level employees, whose mobility is more limited. Employees must live with the consequences of declining long-term productivity within an industry and a region; investors and managers often can bail out long before.

If you look at industries in which our competitive position continues to decline relative to that of Japan, South Korea, and West Germany—semiconductors, consumer electronics, machine tools—you will find the same pattern. The American companies have lower research and development budgets and older plants and equipment. This is the result of the precipitate balance sheet mentality, which translates into low investment in the research that may produce technological breakthroughs a decade from now, or in the modernized and expanded factories that may reduce costs and improve quality beyond the next turn in the business cycle.

2. *Wasted Talent* Asset rearranging also harms productivity by using up the energies of some of our most talented citizens. Paper entrepreneurs now embody the nation's most original economic thinking and energetic wheeling and dealing. The result is a "brain drain" from product to paper.

Today's corporate executives spend an increasing portion of their days fending off takeovers, finding companies to acquire, and responding to depositions in lawsuits instead of worrying about how their products can be made and distributed more efficiently, and with higher quality. More of our top corporate executives are trained in law and finance than in any other field—in contrast to three decades ago when most were trained in marketing, engineering, and sales.

There is a basic distortion here. The investment bankers and lawyers who helped RJR-Nabisco shift out of equities and into debt in November 1988 earned $1 billion for their efforts. This sum was double the amount devoted by the United States, in all of 1988, to the search for a cure for AIDS.

Our best minds (including my former student George) are increasingly drawn to the pie-dividing professions of law, finance, and accounting, and away from pie-enlarging professions like engineering and science. While graduate programs in law and accounting are booming, engineering and science programs are foundering—again in contrast with other industrialized nations.*

But I'm forgetting something, you might say—the recent boom in business-school attendance. Surely that reflects a shift toward hard-headed productive values? The most sought-after jobs among business-school graduates continue to be in finance and consulting, where the specialty is the shuffling of corporate assets. Out of a recent graduating class of 721 at the Harvard Business School, a grand total of 7 reported that they had gone on to start ventures of their own. "Independence" to

---

* In 1987, the majority of students graduating from American universities with doctorates in engineering were foreign nationals, most of whom would return to their home countries. Out of every ten thousand citizens in Japan, for example, only one is a lawyer and three are accountants. In the United States, twenty are lawyers and forty accountants. Out of the same group in Japan, four hundred are engineers and scientists; here, only seventy are engineers or scientists.

today's business graduate means working for the Boston Consulting Group instead of for General Motors. There, as the industrial equivalent of a lawyer, he can plot mergers and tax shelters without ever getting his hands dirty actually turning out a product.

3. *Debt* The money required to rearrange industrial assets—to mount hostile takeovers, to defend against hostile takeovers, to return a company to private ownership by repurchasing the publicly owned shares of stock—typically is borrowed. As has been suggested, high leverage creates extraordinary opportunities for profit. But it also creates substantial danger, should the economy sputter and interest payments be missed. This was, after all, the lesson we were supposed to have learned in the 1920s, when America last went on a speculative spree: There are few adventures more thrilling than gambling in the stock market with someone else's money, and few more dangerous to the overall economy.

Corporate debt in the 1980s has reached alarming proportions. Twenty-five years before, the average American corporation paid sixteen cents of every dollar of pretax earnings in interest on its debt. In the 1970s, it was thirty-three cents. Since 1980, the average corporation has been paying more than fifty cents of every dollar of pretax earnings in interest. The Brookings Institution, not known for its alarmist rhetoric, undertook to examine the effects on corporate America of a recession similar in severity to that which rocked the nation in 1974 and 1975. The Brookings Institution's computer simulation revealed that with the levels of debt prevailing in the late 1980s, one in ten American firms would succumb to bankruptcy.

Such fragility marks the triumph of private greed over social rationality. It may be in the self-interest of a lone paper entrepreneur to bet a giant American corporation against the odds. If he wins, he earns a fortune. If he loses, most of the loss is borne by those who lent him the money; and he can always make another bet. Eventually, he will win big. But if all paper entrepreneurs behave similarly, the entire economy is bet against the odds. This is precisely what has occurred.

4. *Divisiveness* An economy based on asset rearranging has a final disadvantage. It tends to invite zero-sum games, in which one group's gain is another's loss. As those engaged in rearranging the slices of the pie become more numerous and far more wealthy than those dedicated to enlarging the pie, social tranquillity is threatened. Trust declines. As trust declines, the pie may actually shrink.

There are signs that this vicious spiral has begun, as each corporate player seeks to preserve its standard of living by expropriating a portion of the declining wealth of another group. Corporate raiders expropriate the wealth of employees by forcing them to agree to lower wages and then passing the savings on to the new stockholders. Corporate borrowers using high-yield ("junk") bonds expropriate the wealth of other bondholders, and of employees, by suddenly subjecting the entire enterprise to greater risk. Executives expropriate the wealth of stockholders by paying greenmail to would-be acquirers or by undertaking a leveraged buyout and then reselling the company at a higher price. Investors expropriate other investors' wealth by trading on inside information.

The catch is that the groups seeking to grab assets from each other are often the very groups whose collaboration is necessary for real growth to occur. The clearest example is found in the field of labor-management relations. Here the portion of the pie shared by workers has been declining as inflation has outstripped wage hikes. Trying to recoup, unions demand catch-up raises, only to find that other unions do the same, which produces another round of inflation. And as corporate managers themselves become more militant in the face of declining profits, they are apt to resort to hostile counterstrategies—hiring consultants to bust the unions, moving factories to other states or countries. The result is a breakdown in cooperation between unions and management that will ensure even less product to spread around in the future. Only when an entire industry faces collapse, as in autos and steel, do labor and management begin to recognize their common interests—and by then it is usually too late to do anything other than seek protection from imports, thus expropriating the wealth of American consumers.

Blue-collar employees are still paying the heaviest price for America's competitive decline. Inner-city blacks and Hispanics have all but vanished from the productive economy. The gap between the nation's wealthiest 10 percent and poorest 10 percent has grown wider than at any time in the last fifty years. These divisions would not loom so large in an economy that was expanding rapidly. But the attempt to restore economic health will only be hobbled to the extent that citizens see themselves primarily as members of different warring factions, each seeking to exploit the other—blue-collar or white-collar, small business or big, investor or consumer, underclass or overclass.

* * *

How are we to break out of the downward spiral of asset rearranging? Defenders of free-market orthodoxy argue that nothing should be done, on the venerable principle that less government intervention is always preferable to more. What they fail to comprehend (or to admit) is that government already motivates paper entrepreneurs through tax and securities laws. The choice is not between more or less intervention but between different laws designed to motivate different behavior. When motivated by a desire to reallocate assets to their most productive uses, paper efforts can be beneficial. The goal is to reduce the incentive to speculate.

We could start with the incentives offered by our tax system. Paper entrepreneurs currently have an incentive to dedicate corporate earnings to speculative ventures—and to borrow to the hilt—because of two core features of our revenue code: First, stockholders pay income taxes on dividends they receive, but any increases in the value of their shares are taxed only when they sell their stock (and then, should George Bush get his way, at a lower tax rate). Second, the corporation can deduct from its taxable income interest payments on corporate debt but cannot deduct dividend payouts.

The bias against dividends would be less worrisome if corporations reinvested their earnings in new productive assets, rather than merely speculated on existing assets (like buying another corporation). Thus, one avenue of reform would eliminate the corporate income tax altogether and treat all corporate earnings as the direct income of stockholders—*unless* the corporation reinvested the earnings in new plants, equipment, research, or development. Corporate income thus "rolled over" into new productive investment would be taxable only to the extent that it caused share prices to rise, and then only as capital gains when the stockholder traded the stock.

A related reform would reduce the lure of debt. No longer would corporate raiders or leverage-buyout entrepreneurs be permitted to deduct interest payments on the large borrowings used to purchase corporate stock. If a prospective takeover or leveraged buyout promises new efficiencies, the deal should be sufficiently attractive to survive without the extra sweetener of a tax incentive. In addition, to deter dangerous levels of indebtedness, the Federal Reserve should establish guidelines discouraging banks from providing easy credit for such deals. (Commercial banks, still coping with precarious Latin American debtors, have been underwriting more than half of leveraged buyouts.)

A third reform would seek more *patient* capital. Stockholders who took a longer view would be rewarded; speculators, penalized. Thus, the capital-gains tax rate they paid on selling their stock would depend on how long they retained it. On assets held for a year or less, the capital-gains tax rate would be high (50 percent); on assets held for five years or more, the rate would be very low (10 percent). This scheme would result in no overall diminution of tax revenues, just a more beneficent allocation of incentives.

A fourth possibility is a national corporate stock sales tax. Pursuant to it, every sale of stock would be subjected to a small (one half of 1 percent) surcharge. This tax would be far more progressive than most sales taxes (the poor tend to gamble on things other than shares of stock). And it would actually raise $10 billion annually for the Treasury, as it reduced the speculative ardor of paper entrepreneurs.

Another set of changes would focus on the ownership of productive assets. Schemes of employee ownership and participation not only appear to improve productivity over the short term but may also improve prospects for long-run growth, since employees typically have a higher stake in the continuing viability of an enterprise than do either managers or investors. (Avis Rent-A-Car, now employee owned after fifteen years as a pawn of paper entrepreneurs, is showing record profits and productivity gains.) So why not employee-led leveraged buyouts? Employment stock option plans already offer generous tax incentives for employee ownership; these incentives might be rendered even more generous on condition that employees actually vote their own shares of stock rather than entrust them to management, as is now often the case.

Finally, the nation's securities laws would be amended to bar the more egregious forms of color-coded paper shuffling—golden parachutes and greenmail. Absent these innovations, speculation would be less attractive to all concerned.

*   *   *

These recommendations would help redress the balance between paper and product, but they are no cure for our nation's basic vertigo. The imbalance runs deep. A decade or more of legitimized greed has taken its toll on our collective capacity to produce high-quality goods and services. The assumption that we need only to alter tax and securities laws may be itself evidence of our paper habit. Perhaps our greatest challenge in the future is to redress the balance of paper and product within ourselves.

3

THE ANTHROPOMORPHIZATION OF WALL STREET

(Or Why the Market Crashed on October 19, 1987, and Will Do So Again)

ANTHROPOLOGISTS HAVE LONG KNOWN OF THE TENDENCY FOR PRIMI-tive civilizations to ascribe human attributes to animals, plants, and inanimate objects. Here in late-twentieth-century America we have gone a step further, attributing a range of emotions to a street. In fact, we worry incessantly about how the street is feeling. Is it confident? Hopeful? Despairing? Fearful? Much turns on its mood. Of late, government policy is hostage to the street's spirits.

The street in question is, of course, Wall Street. The policy in question is no less than the budget of the United States. If Wall Street likes a proposed budget, interest rates will fall, or so it is assumed. If interest rates fall, the U.S. government can borrow funds more cheaply to cover the budget deficit. Thus, the budget can be balanced sooner, and with less pain all around. The arithmetic underlying George Bush's artful "flexible freeze," his campaign promise to balance the budget in four years, relies on Wall Street's cooperation in reducing interest rates by at least two percentage points. On the other hand, if Wall Street dislikes a proposed budget, we have hell to pay.

The anthropomorphization of Wall Street is another product of the casual fiscal policies of the Reagan Administration. After eight years of ever deeper indebtedness, the Street's mood swings are now enough to send our entire federal government into paroxysms of self-doubt and sycophancy. "What can we do to regain the Street's confidence?" is the question heard most often in gilded offices on the Potomac. "What does the Street *want*?"

Washington's concern for Wall Street's happiness has had one particularly unfortunate consequence. It has rendered it awkward for policy makers to propose any substantial reforms in the way Wall Street conducts its business. Any reform that might diminish the flow of profits to the Street would, quite obviously, risk severe Street demoralization. A foul mood could settle in and, with it, a decline in stock values, higher interest rates, and other awful consequences.

The Crash of 1987 provided an example of the workings of this inhibitory mechanism. After October 19, when the Dow Jones Industrial Average plummeted more than five hundred points, Congress and the White House immediately sought to understand Wall Street's view of why the crash had occurred and what needed to be done to "restore confidence." Wall Street, not surprisingly, blamed it all on Washington: on the budget deficit, on protectionist trade legislation pending before Congress, and even more importantly, on a House Ways and Means Committee proposal to remove tax deductions for interest paid on loans used to take over a company. Investment bankers demanded an end to such pernicious policies. They filled the airwaves and op-ed pages with prescriptions for how Washington should mend its ways. Typical was the statement of Donald Drapkin, vice-chairman of Revlon, Inc., and a key figure in his company's effort to take over Gillette: "If you couldn't deduct interest incurred in an acquisition, it would be a disaster for the stock market and for American companies."

Washington, in its own plodding way, tried to oblige. The President and congressional leaders sought further cuts in the federal budget. The trade bill was rendered less objectionable to free traders. And—most telling—the Ways and Means Committee tax proposal was suddenly dropped. Chairman Dan Rostenkowski sought, as he put it, to "calm some of the apprehensions of a very nervous Wall Street."

Washington's solicitude was especially ironic in light of Wall Street's central role in the debacle. That stock prices were finally back to a realistic level after more than a year of frenzied speculation should have given Washington cause for relief, as if a fevered child had awakened from its hallucinations. That the Street was finally professing concern about the health of the American economy, after a decade of reckless disregard, should have provided further assurance.

The economic "crisis" that the Street discovered on that particular October day was no different from the slowly gathering crisis that existed before October 19. Some Americans felt poorer than they had before, no doubt, but their apparent prosperity in the halcyon days of the bull market was largely illusory—a paper prosperity. The real economy had been slowly unraveling for years while America busily consumed more than it produced. In 1986 the nation had generated some $800 billion more in goods and services than it had in the recession year of 1982, but it spent about $900 billion more—Mr. Micawber's recipe for eventual misery.

America had been able to ignore its profligacy only because foreigners were more than happy to lend us money, buy our corporations, and purchase our real estate. By the time of the crash, we were $350 billion in the hole, one third of downtown Los Angeles (among other U.S. cities) was in foreign hands, and our foreign creditors were growing distinctly nervous about our ability to repay our debts.

The anomaly through it all was the Wall Street bull market, which, beginning in 1983, surged upward in seeming disregard of the underlying decline. One big reason: Stock prices were responding not to the real economy but to takeovers, and/or threats of takeovers, which prompted corporations to do whatever was necessary to raise their share prices in the short term. Often this meant purchasing their own shares and thus going deeply into debt, and jettisoning long-term projects. New corporate debt ballooned by over $700 billion between 1983 and 1987, about the same amount by which share prices tumbled on that fateful day in October. The new debt made corporate America much more vulnerable to economic downturns. Interest payments soaked up an ever larger proportion of corporate earnings.

Wall Street's reverie could not go on forever, and it did not. The balloon was sure to burst eventually. It did.

In light of this history, there is something vaguely unseemly about the demands the Street still makes on Washington to clean up its act. Of course, the budget deficit needs to be tamed. But the deeper problem is not the budget deficit per se; it is the nation's chronic unwillingness to reduce total consumption and increase total investment—both public and private. In fact, hostile takeovers are themselves responsible for part of the debt problem. Likewise, America's drift toward protectionism is a symptom of a deeper economic malaise: the scarcity of new, well-paying jobs for industrial workers whose present jobs are threatened by cheap foreign goods and the unwillingness of American corporations—obsessively concerned with their immediate bottom lines—to invest for a future that would create such jobs.

Perhaps the most brazen demand is that Washington take no action to stem takeovers. In fact, the Street's assertion that the House Ways and Means Committee proposal was somehow responsible for the crash confirmed what many had suspected all along—that the takeover threats that had pushed share prices ever higher were largely motivated by the hidden tax subsidy to begin with. When it looked as if the subsidy was about to be taken away, stocks tumbled. The great takeover binge hadn't rested on the "economic fundamentals" at all, as Wall Street had repeatedly argued. It had been part of the tax game.

* * *

In the months following the crash, there was some tentative discussion about reforming Wall Street. President Reagan appointed a commission, headed by Nicholas Brady, himself a Wall Street financier (and future Treasury secretary), to examine the matter. The commission duly reported, suggesting a number of sensible and incremental legal and regulatory changes to avoid a subsequent crash. But none of the changes was implemented. A number of investment bankers, and not a few legislators, opined that such changes might "unsettle" the Street.

In the year following, takeovers and leveraged buyouts reached levels never before achieved. Once it was clear that nothing would change, nor that Mr. Rostenkowski would advance his proposal, the game was on again, with renewed relish. Wall Street's balloon began to refill and will continue to do so, until the next big pop.

4

THE
CONVENIENCE OF BANKING

RECENTLY, MY WIFE AND I TRIED TO GET A BANK LOAN. THE SUM WE sought was somewhat large compared to the salaries we earn but still safely within five figures. We are a good credit risk; we have always paid our bills on time; we live modestly.

I shared intimate details of our family finances with the bank. The lending officer had me fill out a long questionnaire. I had to supply him with three character references and find creditors who could vouch for my solvency and reliability. I even located a former landlord, who dimly remembered that I had once paid him rent on time. My file was then shifted to the manager of the bank's "disbursement services division," who subjected me to more detailed questioning and carefully scrutinized the project in which I was intending to invest. There followed another round of forms. An assistant treasurer of the bank's documentary control unit had a problem with one of the documents I supplied, which my lawyer solved. Another account officer wanted one of the forms notarized. A deputy credit supervising officer wanted more documentation. Then, after a month of waiting, I called the vice president for credit, who said that they were still reviewing my loan application but that no decision had been reached. He suggested I come in and fill out some more forms. Finally, after another month's wait, we got the loan.

I am a small customer. During the past decade or so, American banks have also lent several hundred billion dollars to the likes of Poland, Mexico, Brazil, Texas real-estate developers, Oklahoma energy moguls, takeover entrepreneurs, and leveraged-buyout moguls. Unlike my loan, however, many of *these* loans will never be repaid. And in contrast to the picayune and prolonged review of my little loan application, decisions to lend vast sums to such risky borrowers were made quickly, without extensive information or deliberation. There is, to put it mildly, a discrepancy here.

*　　*　　*

The American banking system is fundamentally oblivious to large risk. Small risks (that someone like myself might default on a relatively small loan) are well understood; they happen often enough that their probabilities can be measured, and standard precautions can be taken in advance. More to the point, loan officers know that their superiors also know these probabilities, so that any deviation from prudent lending practice is readily apparent. But a bank has little or no institutional memory of major defaults on a grand scale. These sorts of probabilities cannot be reduced to standard operating practice. The longer the interval since the last such disaster, the more likely it is that people will behave as if it could never happen again. Under these circumstances loan officers know only one thing: If they don't approve the giant loan, some other bank will. Prudence will be rewarded by conspicuous loss of business.

Moreover, loan officers are evaluated over relatively short time periods. Their performances are rated against quarterly earnings targets and loan quotas. Small run-of-the-mill borrowers who may default quickly thus present few attractions. Large bonuses come with the largest of borrowers whose huge defaults are likely to be years away, long after the loan officer has moved on to another job.

There is, in addition, the herding instinct that obtains whenever large sums of money are involved. As groups of American banks advanced credit to Poland or Mexico, to the purchasers of oil-drilling equipment or commercial real estate, or to the promoters of leveraged buyouts and other schemes, loan officers found safety in numbers. The mounting troubles of the Bank of the Commonwealth, First Pennsylvania, Continental Illinois, and countless savings and loans confirmed this pattern. Regardless of how risky the loans, the fact that other major banks committed their funds to the same class of borrowers lent credibility to the effort. Bank officials could claim that their decisions reflected the best wisdom at the time. Others, after all, had made the same mistake.

Then there is the omnipresent assumption that larger borrowers cannot default. They are thought to be too big and too established to do what small borrowers do all the time. Walter Wriston, former chairman of Citibank, lent billions to Latin American nations during the 1970s because, he confidently asserted at the time, "countries do not fail to exist." Yet ironically it is precisely because of their sovereign status that governments cannot always be relied on to exercise self-restraint in their borrowing.

Perhaps the most important factor explaining American banks' willingness to bear enormous risk is their justifiable confidence that the U.S. government will help them out in a pinch. This is particularly true of America's largest banks, which have taken on proportionately the largest risks. The fate of a large bank is too intertwined with the fates of numerous other, smaller lending institutions; its depositors' confidence is too important to the public's confidence in the entire banking system. The directors of the Federal Deposit Insurance Corporation decided to rescue the First Pennsylvania Bank of Philadelphia in 1980 because they feared that its collapse would also bring down hundreds of smaller banks that had its uninsured funds on deposit. Four years later, they decided that the pending collapse of Continental Illinois might lead to a national banking panic, since only 10 percent of its $39 billion in deposits was insured.

Having a relatively small percentage of insured deposits is not unusual for major American banks, since they pay no insurance premiums on deposits they accept from abroad—deposits that compose a significant portion of their overall liabilities. In effect, the Federal Deposit Insurance Corporation is prepared to rescue any failing multinational institution that cannot be sold to either a foreign or domestic suitor. With such a generous rule of thumb, it is small wonder that large American banks have been emboldened to risk their shareholders' money on questionable ventures. The risk is far less than it would otherwise seem.

*　　*　　*

International banking is never simply a commercial activity. American foreign policy is implicated whenever American banks do a sizable amount of business with other sovereign governments.

A telling example is the Polish debt crisis. During the era of détente, American banks were willing to lend large sums to the Soviet Union and its Eastern European allies, whose hard-currency indebtedness climbed from $7 billion in 1970 to nearly $66 billion by the end of the decade— significantly faster than these economies were growing. By 1980 Poland, in particular, was on the brink of defaulting on $26 billion of outstanding debt. With Poland's suppression of the Solidarity movement in 1981, the Reagan Administration was placed in a difficult bind. Efforts to pressure the Polish authorities into reversing their harsh policies were compromised by worries over the Poles' indebtedness to American banks. In the end the banks won. The Administration chose to rescue Poland and the banks—to the tune of $344 million in 1982 alone— rather than countenance a formal default.

Bank rescues have also been motivated by America's security interests in debtor countries. For example, Turkey's brush with financial collapse in 1979 summoned pledges of nearly $1 billion from the United States and other Western allies mindful of Turkey's strategic importance to NATO. Turkey was not the only beneficiary of this rescue, notably; the American banks, to which Turkey owed large sums, simultaneously profited.

The story has been similar in Latin America. U.S. banks, awash with Arab oil money throughout most of the 1970s, needed customers; oil-importing nations, particularly in Latin America, needed loans. Just as détente had signaled to the banks that large sums could be lent with impunity to the Soviet bloc, so too did the U.S. government's tacit acknowledgment of the importance of recycling petrodollars signal to them that there was relatively little risk involved in lending even larger sums to Latin American countries. By 1982 Argentina, Brazil, and Mexico together owed America's nine largest banks more than 140 percent of the banks' total capital. The process of rescheduling the debts and interest arrears gradually came to resemble default in all but name: It was default by attrition. By 1984 some $35 billion was flowing from the Latin American debtors to U.S. banks—a sum equal to 10 percent of these nations' aggregate export revenues and more than twice their hard-won trade surpluses.

At first the Reagan Administration left it to the International Monetary Fund (IMF) and the banks to work out austerity plans for the debtor nations. ("Austerity" was a nice way of saying lower living standards.) The plans were intended to clamp down on these countries' consumption and investment, to free resources for debt service. But the timing was unfortunate. Much of Latin America was just beginning to experiment with democracy. Beginning in 1980, generals had allowed power to pass to elected civilian presidents in several debtor nations. These newborn democracies were delicate things. Antidemocratic forces were waiting in the wings (the military in the right wing, the communists in the left) to pick up the pieces should democracy fail. High unemployment and collapsing living standards were not the most favorable accompaniments to democratic experimentation.

Latin American indebtedness has posed problems for the United States in other ways. As these southern economies faltered, a flood of illicit and dangerous drugs was released into the United States. By 1985 the sale of cocaine represented some 10 percent of Bolivia's gross national product and twice its legal export earnings. When ambitious Latin Americans were not turning to drug production, they were trying to find work in the United States. Illegal aliens constituted another flood, the intensity of which has been directly proportional to economic hardship at home.

In the fall of 1983 the United States contributed to a substantial increase in IMF funding in order to ease the debt crisis. In October 1985 Treasury Secretary James Baker formally proposed a program for sustained growth through which the World Bank (funded largely by the United States), regional development banks (also with U.S. funds), and U.S. banks would come up with some $29 billion over three years to help fifteen hard-pressed debtor nations. But by 1988 Latin American debtors were in even worse shape than before. U.S. banks hadn't fulfilled their part of the deal. Yet U.S. policy still placed the banks' interests over those of hemispheric peace and prosperity.

*　　*　　*

The Latin American debt crisis is not an entirely new phenomenon. U.S. bankers who claim they could not have foreseen the problems when they made the loans had only to examine history. In the late 1880s London's Baring Brothers Bank extended substantial loans to Argentina. When Argentina's pending default threatened to bring down the bank and undermine confidence in the entire British banking system, a rescue was organized by the Bank of England and the British Treasury, including a special commission to oversee a restructuring of the Argentina debt.

Government involvement was not always so mild. When Venezuela repudiated its debts in 1902, the Royal Navy blockaded Venezuela's harbors (giving rise to the term "gunboat diplomacy"). Concerned about the increased meddling of European powers in the hemisphere, Theodore Roosevelt pledged that the United States would henceforth assume responsibility for ensuring that the Latin American states fulfilled their financial obligations—thus committing the United States to subsequent interventions in the Dominican Republic, Haiti, Honduras, and Nicaragua, among others. The U.S. government became, in effect, a collection agency for the world's major banks. In the 1930s Britain's Royal Institute of International Affairs noted that "the history of investment in South America throughout the last century has been one of confidence followed by disillusionment, of borrowing cycles followed by widespread defaults."

*　*　*

What should be done to avoid more of the same in the future? If our biggest banks are prone to make large and dubious loans because of certain bureaucratic and political incentives built into the practice of large-scale banking, then no number of bank examinations or meetings between bank officers and government officials is likely to make much of a difference.

Most bank rescues are invisible. Decisions are highly technical, rendered by bureaucrats in the Federal Deposit Insurance Corporation, the Federal Savings and Loan Insurance Corporation, or the IMF and the World Bank. The avowed purpose is never to rescue a bank but to ensure the credibility of the banking system, protect unwary depositors, guard America's security interests, or stabilize debtor nations and improve the world economy. We seem to take for granted that achievement of these proximate goals necessarily entails saving a big bank—and the bank's shareholders—along the way. But so long as this assumption remains unquestioned, the internal incentives operating on bank officers will continue to lead them toward making big, risky loans. Why not, when the government will pick up the pieces?

A more lasting solution would seek to detach these other goals from saving the banks' shareholders. Many of our largest banks are still carrying mammoth loans on their balance sheets at face value, even though a significant portion of these loans are effectively in default. No one is prepared to blow the whistle and force the banks to write down the loans. Why not? Because this would impose enormous losses on the banks. Many would not have sufficient capital to meet the minimums required by law. It seems far safer to wait it out, to accept the charade of rescheduling the loans, all the while hoping that a government rescue will eventually put matters right.

But how disastrous would it really be to require that all loans be carried on the banks' books at market value? At worst, the banks would have to cut their dividends to build their capital back up to where it should be. Share prices would drop as a result. Perhaps shareholders would demand more prudence in the future; they might even vote out the old management, or tender their shares to somebody capable of doing a better job. Operating incentives would shift toward more care in lending large sums of money. As an added advantage, banks would be encouraged to sell the loans on the open market at a price reflecting their true, lower values. (That is something the banks dare not do now, for fear that the loans would then have to be entered on their books at the lower sale price.) This in turn would create a secondary market in such loans, allowing purchasers of the loans to swap them for equity in troubled debtor companies or in healthy companies within troubled debtor nations. Thus, the debts would be rescheduled in a way that would give debtors the freedom and incentive to restructure themselves. At the same time, bank shareholders would be deprived of their windfall.

American capitalism is premised on the comforting notion that public and private sectors are, and forever will remain, safely distinct. This prevailing view leads us to all sorts of policy prescriptions for tidying up the less desirable side effects of business activity. Occasionally, however, the veil is lifted and we are allowed to gaze in wonderment at a private sector whose largest institutions are guaranteed peace, safety, and profits by a public sector ever anxious to please them.

There are few callings more comfortable than commercial banking. Thus it has been for over a century, as the modern nation-state has quietly bailed out its bankers. But this tradition may be on the wane. After the binge of Third World lending in the 1970s, the thrift crisis of the 1980s, and what is likely to be the leveraged-buyout crisis of the 1990s, taxpayers may start resenting the fact that their tax dollars are used to cover the mistakes of these determinedly risky individuals.

5

THE
ORIGINS OF RED TAPE

ASK ANY BUSINESS EXECUTIVE ABOUT GOVERNMENT REGULATIONS, AND he will tell you a horror story of bureaucratic excess. But the executive will not, most likely, object to the *goal* of regulation. Most executives agree that the public deserves protection from toxic wastes, nuclear accidents, air and water pollutants, unsafe products, fraudulent claims, and monopoly. Even in such eras as the present, when business is ascendant and government suspect, the public supports these broad objectives. The complaints of American business center not on the purposes of regulation but on the ways they are designed and implemented: Statutes are overly complicated, and the rules devised to fulfill them are excruciatingly detailed, comprising voluminous rulings and interpretations, interpretations of interpretations, opinions and dissenting opinions of interpretations.

Even the simplest public goal spawns an imposing herd of rules requiring exhaustive filings, reports, nit-picking inspections, and picayune compliance with every jot and tittle of the law. And they are subject to constant alteration, elaboration, and ever-more-detailed explication. Under the spell of congressional committees, regulatory-agency officials, hearing examiners, administrative-law judges, appellate judges, and scores of zealous government lawyers, inspectors, and bureaucrats, regulations grow more complicated by the hour. They multiply in the *Federal Register*; they engorge the *Code of Federal Regulations*; they inundate companies with their petty requirements.

Tales of bureaucratic atrocities abound. The chairman of one large pharmaceutical firm complains that his company spends more hours filling out government forms and reports than it does on research for cancer and heart disease combined. Others tell of trivial, often silly requirements, such as giving loan applicants pages of detailed information that nobody ever reads or putting a toilet within one hundred yards of each employee. The laws are impenetrable: The Employee Retirement Income Security Act, which regulates private pension plans, runs to more than two hundred pages. It has been estimated that federal agencies require American business to fill out forty-four hundred different forms each year, together consuming 143 million hours of executive and clerical time, and costing $25 billion.

Nit-picking regulation has been blamed for slowing America's productivity and impairing the nation's competitiveness. But other advanced industrial nations require that their companies achieve similar regulatory goals. Environmental, health, and safety requirements in Japan and most of Western Europe are no less stringent than in the United States. There is one significant difference, however. Although the results of regulation are about the same among all advanced nations, the *means* of regulating are quite distinct. In other nations regulations are far less detailed than they are in the United States. They involve fewer rules and interpretations, impose less paperwork, entail only informal inspections and reports, and generate significantly lower compliance costs. If American business is conspicuously burdened by government regulation, it is not due to the ends that regulation seeks but to the means employed. Among advanced industrial nations, the regulation of American business is uniquely picayune.

* * *

Many who speak from or for American business attribute the trouble to the attitudes and values of the people who inhabit government regulatory agencies: These people want to be nettlesome. They compose a "new class" of college-educated social planners and public-policy professionals who disdain economic growth and abhor private enterprise. According to Irving Kristol, a principal exponent of such views, regulators "find it convenient to believe the worst about business because they have certain adverse intentions toward business to begin with." They seek "the power to shape our civilization—a power which, in the capitalist system, is supposed to reside in the free market." Their ambition is "to see much of this power redistributed to government, where *they* will then have a say in how it is exercised."

Kristol and his fellow travelers believe that denizens of the new class populate the staffs of regulatory agencies, surviving administration after administration. These individuals relish any chance to harass American business with endless, trivial commands, to clog the channels of commerce with their piddling requirements and endless forms. They take delight in transforming commonsensical regulatory goals into reams of nettlesome detail. According to Kristol and others who share his views, the new class is waging a war of attrition against capitalism. Paul H. Weaver, who wrote an article for *The Public Interest* entitled "Regulation, Social Policy, and Class Conflict," put it this way:

> The New Regulation [to protect the environment, safety, and health] is the social policy of the new class. . . . They have merely transferred power from those who produce material goods to those who produce ideological ones—to the intellectuals, policy professionals, journalists, and "reformers," who are arguably much less representative of the American people as a whole than those whose influence has been curtailed. . . . With each passing year it becomes clearer that the real animus of the new class is not so much against business or technology as against the liberal values served by corporate capitalism and the benefits these institutions provide to the broad mass of the American people.

This conspiracy has proved to be an oddly comforting phantom for American business. First, it provides a ready explanation for why business has felt so besieged. It is not any serious failing or erosion of legitimacy on the part of industry but rather the machinations of a group bent on undermining free enterprise. It is an enemy within that seeks to substitute centralized planning for free markets. Second, the story suggests a plan of action. All we need do is to expel from government these ideological traitors and put in their place teams of levelheaded and unbiased civil servants.

Finally, the story promises a happy ending. Once the saboteurs have been ejected, the present regulatory miasma will be transformed into simple, sensible rules. The public will continue to be protected—as it should be—from the irresponsible acts of a few misguided managers. The rest of American business will be freed of the nit-picking, the technicalities, and the meticulous excesses of the present system.

* * *

Unfortunately for those who find the story satisfying, it wilts in the face of the facts. To begin with, the "new class" of interventionist zealots who are supposedly responsible for the picayune character of so much modern regulation have been far harder to track down than expected. Both the Carter and Reagan Administrations were committed to reducing the burden of government regulation. Indeed, the latter installed its own counterzealots at the controlling levels of government agencies to track down the guilty parties. The Reagan Administration did succeed in abandoning some regulatory efforts. None other than George Bush himself was in charge of the effort. But—and here is the important point —it did nothing to change the *way* in which the remaining regulations were administered. The Administration's concerted efforts notwithstanding, the *Code of Federal Regulations* continued to swell with detail, the *Federal Register* bulged with new interpretations and elaborations, and American business continued to writhe under the burden of pettifogging directives from Washington.

The underlying problem had nothing to do with nefarious forces hidden within regulatory agencies; it was inherent in the American regulatory process itself. A probusiness administration might succeed in rescinding particular regulations but not in reducing the amount of niggling minutiae surrounding any regulatory goal.

In addition, it turns out that the vast majority of regulatory-agency lawyers and middle-level managers aspire not to undermine American capitalism but to live off it. After gaining experience in government, they move on to the private sector. They gain jobs in law firms, representing companies before regulatory agencies. They join consulting firms, accounting firms, research institutes, and public-relations firms. They move into government-affairs offices of large corporations and into trade associations. Some have even been known to join university faculties, from which they sell extracurricular insights to corporations. Their experience in government makes them valuable to the private sector, and they are not reluctant to trade on that value.

If America's regulatory miasma is not due to a covert war against capitalism waged within government agencies, then what is the real cause?

* * *

Unlike such capital cities as London, Paris, and Tokyo, which serve as national centers of trade, finance, education, and the arts, Washington, D.C., has only the federal government to give it prominence. Major business, intellectual, and creative enterprises are, for the most part, located elsewhere. Thus, although in other capitals government leaders meet frequently and informally with the leaders of other influential communities, no such easy communication takes place in Washington. (We owe this unique allocation of urban responsibility to Alexander Hamilton, who agreed to a plan to move the nation's capital city from New York to a swamp on the banks of the Potomac River in exchange for Thomas Jefferson's agreement that the federal government would absorb the Revolutionary War debt.) This fact, especially when coupled with the relatively short tenure of most U.S. regulatory officials, prevents federal policy makers and business executives from enjoying the same casual give-and-take, comfortable candor, and long-term familiarity that often characterize business–government relationships elsewhere.

Whatever dangers such frequent and informal contact may pose to the democratic control of the policy-making process, it does at least facilitate efficient communication between public and private sectors. Advanced industrial societies—with their complex technologies, intricate trading and financial arrangements, and labyrinthine government bureaucracies—require extensive internal coordination if they are to run smoothly, and such coordination requires, in turn, efficient communication. In Washington communication has come to depend on specialized professionals who act as intermediaries between government policy makers and business executives.

Who are these intermediaries? They are the approximately twelve thousand Washington-based lawyers who represent business before regulatory agencies and the federal courts, the nine thousand lobbyists who represent business before Congress, the forty-two thousand trade-association personnel who keep close watch on pending regulations and legislation, the eight thousand public-relations specialists who advise business executives about regulatory issues, the twelve hundred specialized journalists who report to particular industries on government developments that might affect them, the thirteen hundred public-affairs consultants who help business organize to deal with regulation, and the thirty-five hundred business-affairs consultants who provide regulatory officials with specialized information about particular industries.

Together with the 15,500 lawyers, lobbyists, and public-relations specialists within regulatory agencies and large corporations, these intermediaries comprise a virtual industry of their own.

Members of the industry usually work in Washington for several years in a variety of related positions—first, say, on a congressional staff, then on a regulatory-agency staff or a trade association, then in a Washington law firm or public-relations firm, then perhaps again in a senior congressional agency position, and then in a senior trade-association position. They circulate freely among the points of the Washington compass and change jobs frequently.

Their skills are for the most part strategic, not substantive. They know how to "position" a client to reduce unfavorable exposure, minimize risk, gain a positive image, fend off threats to its autonomy, enlarge its domain, reduce its vulnerability, or generally thwart its rivals. And though they may on occasion consult with economists or scientists, they are not so much interested in the truth or falsity of what these specialists have to say as in the tactical value of what they say—the extent to which it can bolster a client's argument or discredit the argument of a specialist on the other side.

Tension between business and government is necessary if intermediaries are to sustain or enlarge their economic base. This is not to suggest that intermediaries seek to foment business–government confrontation or that they do not often provide valuable help and information. Confrontation is, however, an unstated principle of their calling. It is their professional frame of reference, and it is within this frame that they measure their own success.

Several principles, therefore, can be observed to guide their actions:

1. SEEK TO ACHIEVE CLEAR CONTROVERSIES IN WHICH A CLIENT'S POSITION CAN BE SHARPLY DIFFERENTIATED FROM THAT OF ITS REGULATORY OPPONENT.

A sharply drawn regulatory dispute can be used to justify the services provided a client and perhaps even convince the client that still more resources are needed to carry on the battle. It can also be used to demonstrate to other potential clients the intermediary's virtuosity in mounting an aggressive campaign of legal maneuver, media management, and political pressure tactics. A dispute provides a standard by which an intermediary's services can be evaluated: A victory in the dispute strengthens the intermediary's reputation and thus provides a vehicle for self-promotion in the future.

This principle manifests itself in several ways. First, it encourages intermediaries to take extreme positions that tend to exaggerate the differences between the two sides. More important, it actively discourages intermediaries from heading off regulatory disputes—by engaging in informal problem solving at an early point, by seeking voluntary solutions that would prevent the necessity for regulation, by taking steps to avoid problems before they occur, or by seeking out areas of agreement on which compromise might be based.

Not long ago the National Highway Transportation Safety Administration (NHTSA) conducted tests of the crashworthiness of various automobiles. Afterwards, in an effort to obtain voluntary agreement about how the models could be made safer, NHTSA officials sought meetings with the manufacturers of cars, both domestic and foreign, that had failed the tests.

The U.S. manufacturers, represented at the meetings by their lawyers and government-relations staffs, refused to discuss possible improvements. They argued instead that the tests were flawed. The Japanese manufacturers, represented at the meetings by the engineers who had designed the cars in question, wanted to know precisely why their cars had failed. They brainstormed with NHTSA staff about the best means of increasing safety and, largely on the basis of those discussions, eventually devised low-cost improvements that enabled their automobiles to pass the test.

Several years ago, while serving as a Washington bureaucrat, I invited several corporate executives to a meeting to discuss a consumer problem that had arisen within their industry. The Federal Trade Commission (FTC) had been inundated with complaints for months, and it seemed clear that if the complaints were well founded, some sort of regulatory action would be necessary unless the industry took steps to mend its ways.

Each of the executives agreed to the meeting. Some expressed surprise and even gratitude that the agency was willing to talk informally about the problem and seek voluntary solutions to it before taking formal action. Within ten days of my invitation, however, each of the executives called back with a similar message: Each had been advised against attending such a meeting by legal counsel, a government-affairs vice president, or a trade-association representative.

A few of the executives were particularly candid about the advice they had received. It was not in their interest, so they were told, to "stick their necks out" by attending such a meeting at this early stage. The visibility could be dangerous. Moreover, it would, by lending credence to the agency's concerns, almost certainly encourage the agency to take some sort of regulatory action. Far better to wait until the issue became crystallized—that is, until they could get a clearer idea of what the agency was planning to do and how seriously the agency was taking the problem. I received a similar message from the FTC staff members responsible for regulating the industry. They were also opposed to such a meeting because, they argued, it might "tip our hand." The industry might learn what information we at the agency had about the problem, how far we were prepared to go in fighting it, and what strategies we might use in attempting to regulate against it. It would be preferable, they warned, to wait until we had more information about the problem —that is, until we had a much better idea of what we wanted from the industry—and until we could readily threaten the industry with a specific set of regulatory initiatives.

Both sets of advice came from people who believed they were acting in the best interests of their clients. Given the frame of reference in which these intermediaries work, their advice was probably correct. Regulatory battle could not be waged successfully if both sides talked candidly at an early stage about how to remedy the problem at issue. But their frame of reference was, of course, inappropriate. The proper goal was not to wage battle successfully but to remedy the problem quickly and efficiently.

2. WHEN INFORMING A CLIENT ABOUT ITS REGULATORY OPPONENT, EXAGGERATE THE DANGERS THAT THE OPPONENT'S ACTIVITIES AND DESIGNS IMPLY.

Providing the worst possible interpretation of an opponent's activities and motives often alarms a client and stiffens its resolve to fight. Such an extreme characterization may also elicit additional resources from the client and may even enable the intermediary to convince several other clients to join in the fray.

This principle is most evident in trade-association newsletters, bulletins, and conferences, which regularly excoriate regulatory agencies and caricature their activities.

Once, while still in Washington, I met with the editor of a trade-association newsletter who wanted a "background briefing" about the sorts of initiatives the FTC might undertake in the next few years. After explaining to him that my list of possibilities was extremely tentative (the five commissioners had not as yet approved any of them and comparatively few of them had any likelihood of reaching fruition), I let loose.

Three weeks later I was aghast, to put it mildly, to see the entire list printed in the trade-association newsletter under the headline FTC MAPS FUTURE POLICY. The article described the list as "what we can expect from FTC activists" and cautioned association members about the FTC's "ambitious designs" on their industry. The article ended with an ominous warning that "unless we take effective action now, these initiatives will be undertaken within the next two years."

Dire warnings are also sounded by legal counsel. Lawyers are, after all, trained to foresee the worst possible consequences stemming from any given situation and to prepare a client for them. This skill, when finely honed, necessitates not only a skeptical and somewhat pessimistic attitude toward all undertakings but also a degree of suspicion (occasionally bordering on paranoia) concerning the plans and motives of any potential opponents.

This kind of advice can be of enormous value, but it can also become dysfunctional when business executives and regulatory officials lose sight of the fact that legal counsel naturally conjures up worst-case scenarios. Their job is primarily to avoid such eventualities rather than to accomplish some positive goal.

Warnings of possible legal problems can intimidate all but the most fearless executive. Too often, the worst possible implications to be drawn from an opponent's actions or intentions are accepted as fact, and confrontation strategies are perceived to be the only rational means of dealing with them.

3. ONCE CONFLICT HAS BEGUN, PROLONG AND INTENSIFY IT.

A regulatory skirmish is by no means as useful a vehicle for advancing an intermediary's career as is an intense and protracted battle. Reputations of lawyers, lobbyists, and public-relations specialists have been established on the basis of such major conflicts as whether automobiles must be equipped with airbags, the requisite number of peanuts in an ounce of peanut butter, and the disclosure of health risks in certain foods and drugs.

Prolonged hostilities provide a continuing showcase for tactical acumen and warlike aggressiveness. They usually involve many parties—industries, corporations, trade associations, law firms, congressional committees, and regulatory agencies. Intermediaries who follow a typical career path often wish to demonstrate their political savvy and adversarial skill to as wide a range of potential employers as possible. I know of some successful intermediaries who, rising to ever more responsible positions as the original conflict grew and spread into new battles and second-order skirmishes, have worked on various sides of the same major issue for fifteen years in a half dozen different organizations.

Besides facilitating career advancement, these regulatory marathons can also provide intermediaries with a secure source of income for many years. Lawyers may spend a large portion of their working lives on a few such controversies, and public-relations specialists who represent clients in a protracted battle may gain semipermanent employment. For example, when in 1959 the Food and Drug Administration proposed a standard for the content of peanut butter, it launched a regulatory battle that kept a goodly number of intermediaries gainfully employed for twelve years.

Of course, their motives are not solely pecuniary. Pride in their work, a concern for punctiliousness, a desire to win for the sake of winning, and a limited understanding of the broad goals of business—government cooperation all play a part.

4. KEEP BUSINESS EXECUTIVES AND REGULATORY OFFICIALS APART.

Direct contact between business executives and regulatory officials, under any but the most formal circumstances, can jeopardize the intermediary's efforts to create and maintain regulatory conflict. Since these leaders, given a chance, are liable to discover their mutual interest in avoiding conflict and solving problems, they may also discover that they have little need for the elaborate infrastructure of intermediaries they support.

Intermediaries, therefore, usually seek to maintain a monopoly over the channels of communication between business executives and regulatory officials. They must be kept at a safe distance from each other, and on the few occasions when they do meet, intermediaries must be in attendance to ensure that tensions are sustained.

Washington lawyers, trade-association officials, and public-relations specialists usually advise business executives against meeting directly with regulators to discuss mutual problems. Their reasoning is that the executives are not sufficiently knowledgeable about issues that could arise and may, as a result, inadvertently say something prejudicial to their own interests. Not surprisingly, staff members of regulatory agencies proffer much the same advice to regulatory officials.

When one small Midwestern trade association asked me to set up a meeting between a dozen of its member executives and several FTC officials to discuss issues affecting the region's industry, a national trade association and its Washington counsel, which also represented several of the businesses, objected violently. They argued that such a meeting would jeopardize the delicate relationship they had established with the regulatory agency. The agency staff also objected on similar grounds.

A compromise of sorts was reached: A predictably useless meeting took place with 150 people in attendance, including all the Washington lawyers, trade-association staff, and regulatory staff whose "delicate relationship" could not risk a less formal setting.

5. ENGAGE IN ENDLESS ROUNDS OF DISCOVERING AND CLOSING LOOPHOLES.

This fifth and last rule is perhaps the most pervasive. It explains from whence regulatory "red tape" derives. So important is this principle, and so ubiquitous, that it deserves special attention.

Let us consider the case of an inventor named Henry and his turbocharged automatic vacuum cleaner. You just place Henry's vacuum on a shelf for five minutes, and—presto!—the room is spanking clean. Imagine that the product proves enormously popular and that Henry forms a major manufacturing company around his wonder vacuum. But Henry's brainchild suffers from one small flaw: It emits a roar something like a jet engine at full throttle, only louder. Every time the machine is switched on, the noise loosens tooth fillings and induces deep neurosis in dogs within a radius of two hundred yards. This flaw does not deter consumers from using the vacuum, however; following operating instructions, they simply set the timer, sedate the dog, and go off to the movies while the machine cuts loose. Soon, in neighborhoods all over America the vacuum's roar issues from empty houses, causing flocks of passing birds to fall stunned from the sky and neighbors at table to drop plates and fling drinks into the air. Henry would like to make a quieter version of the product, but adding an adequate muffler would triple the cost.

Now suppose that several years before all this, Congress had instructed the Environmental Protection Agency (EPA) to take steps to "ensure that no household appliance emits excessive noise." That was all the legislation said. Congress decided to leave it to the EPA to devise and enforce regulations concerning neighborhood noise pollution. Since then, the agency has issued only one broad rule: "No consumer product shall generate noise in excess of 110 decibels." That's it—nothing more specific than this, no reporting requirements, no interpretations, no elaborations. The EPA publishes the rule and considers the problem settled.

Henry has hired a Washington lawyer named Seymour, who informs him of the regulation. Worried about the threat to his company, Henry asks Seymour whether he can think of some legal way to continue selling the turbocharged vacuum cleaner. Seymour is a smart lawyer who specializes in federal regulations. "Not to worry," Seymour assures Henry, "I can think of two hundred ways to dodge this regulation."

Two months later, the EPA inquires about the vacuum. It seems they have been getting complaints about its noise. Seymour meets with the agency's attorney. "The regulation doesn't apply to the turbocharged automatic vacuum," says Seymour. "It says that no *consumer product* should emit a sound in excess of one hundred ten decibels, but this isn't a consumer product. It's designed for industrial applications, although consumers happen to use it. And it's not a product but a service, since under our unique payment plan it is leased rather than purchased outright." The attorneys silently take off their hats to Seymour and go back to their law books and word processors.

Two months after that, the agency announces a more detailed set of rulings, which define "consumer product" as "any product or service sold or leased to industrial or consumer users." They then return to Seymour's office. "Still doesn't apply," says Seymour calmly. "The regulation prohibits sounds in excess of one hundred ten decibels. But our automatic vacuum records only ninety-five decibels when we've tested it outside in the middle of a field during a hailstorm. Here's the proof." He hands the attorneys computerized results of the experiment. They take off their hats again, shake his hand, and drag back to the office.

Two months later, the agency announces precise specifications for how such products are to be tested to determine decibel levels—the kind of sound chamber in which testing is to occur, the type of testing equipment, scientific definitions for "decibel," and detailed requirements for when testing must be done and under whose auspices. The agency also announces that hereafter all manufacturers of a new product "designed for or adaptable to household use" must file a report with the agency stating its decibel level according to the prescribed test. All over America, developers of new cat beds, corn poppers, and sock matchers fume as they pay for the premarketing decibel tests Washington demands.

Over the next several years Seymour meets with the agency's attorneys innumerable times. Each time he claims that the burgeoning regulations, rules, and interpretations still do not apply. Each time thereafter, they become more detailed. Seymour disputes their applicability before administrative-law judges, and he appeals their rulings to the federal courts. He argues, as the occasion warrants and the spirit moves him, that the agency has exceeded its mandate from Congress, or that it has acted arbitrarily in singling out the turbocharged automatic vacuum, or that the company's constitutional rights have been violated. The administrative judges and appellate courts issue opinions that further elaborate on the agency's regulations and interpretations and its authority to regulate in this area. Meanwhile, the original statute has been amended by Congress to avoid the loopholes and ambiguities that Seymour (and others like him) have discovered. The new law is far more detailed and complex, spelling out in excruciating specificity what is required.

Five years later, Henry meets with Seymour. "I'm afraid," says Seymour, "we've reached the end of the line." Seymour points to a bookshelf sagging under the weight of statutes, regulations, rulings, advisory opinions, interpretations, court opinions, and appellate decisions, all concerning noise pollution. "But at least I got you more than five years of delay." Henry is downcast nonetheless. "Does this mean we have to stop selling the turbocharged automatic vacuum, or else install the muffler?" he asks. "Either that," Seymour warns, "or you'll have to pay the fine every year you violate the regulation." "How much?" Henry asks, trembling. "A full twenty-five hundred American dollars," Seymour says as he grins and takes off his hat to himself. Henry jubilantly goes back to his company, where he asks his secretary to organize a bake sale to cover the fine.

* * *

This example exaggerates, but not by much, the typical fate of a regulatory effort. It describes a familiar dynamic between American business and government. American corporations are not reluctant to test the limits of the law. They pay lawyers handsome sums to discover loopholes, technicalities, and elegant circumventions. In many instances the investment is worth it to the corporation. At least it buys temporary relief from a regulation, enabling the company to continue profitably doing what it was doing before. Each such maneuver generates a countermaneuver from within the regulatory bureaucracy and Congress; every feint and dodge, a more complicated prophylactic for the next encounter. The result, over time, is a profusion of regulatory detail that confounds and strangles American business.

There are no plotting villains in this tale. Seymour and lawyers like him have no intention of confounding American capitalism. Seymour does his job as he understands it and is good at what he does. Henry and other chief executives are not revolutionaries, either. Henry is trying to protect his company's interests. Indeed, Henry has a responsibility to his shareholders to do whatever he can, within the limits of the law, to maximize the firm's profits. If he did not hire good lawyers to maneuver around statutes and regulations that were open to such circumnavigation, Henry might be found liable for breach of fiduciary duty to his shareholders, or he might be taken over by someone with fewer scruples about exploiting every possible route to higher profits. Every actor in this sad and silly tale is simply carrying out the responsibilities assigned him within a set of rules that we all have accepted.

The story, exasperatingly, suggests no obvious plan of action. Any fundamental improvement would require a broader definition of responsibility by which businesses would not simply yield to the letter of the law but endorse its spirit, or else openly challenge the goals underlying the laws. And the story promises no happy ending, because such a change in attitude and practice will be difficult to achieve. Business executives like Henry, lawyers like Seymour, shareholders, and regulatory officials alike act on the expectation that American business will try to outmaneuver government. As thrust meets parry, the miasma of red tape thickens.

II
THE
REAL
ECONOMY

6

THE
ECONOMICS OF ILLUSION
AND THE
ILLUSION OF ECONOMICS

SOCIETIES, LIKE INDIVIDUALS, OFTEN WANT TO AVOID FACING THEIR
most pressing problems. Recognizing reality can be painful; addressing
it can be even more painful—requiring sacrifice and change. Thus, societies, like individuals, often deny that their problems exist. Or they erect
"straw men," which are not the real problems at all, and try to confront
them instead. Or they deny responsibility for problems, blaming others.
America has been using all these ploys to avoid coping with its economic
mess.

Some still deny a problem exists. Those who call themselves "supply-siders" claim, notwithstanding the nation's mounting indebtedness
to the rest of the world (estimated at more than $400 billion by the close
of 1988), that the economy is still buoyant, and we have only to keep
taxes down in order to reap the eventual rewards. Monetarists are somewhat less optimistic, but their solution is no less simple: The Federal
Reserve Board must exercise a steadier hand in controlling the money
supply. As reality has steadily intruded upon orthodoxy, however, these
two schools of denial have claimed fewer and fewer adherents. Both
supply-side economics and monetarism share a rare but unfortunate
distinction among economic theories: They have been tried in practice,
and they have failed.

*   *   *

If none of the other standard methods of denial work, there is always the possibility of blaming others for our economic problems—in this case, foreigners. Foreigners are the perfect foil. American politicians can talk tough without committing public money; foreigners cannot vote.

Consider, for example, America's recent "dollar diplomacy." In 1987 and 1988 the Reagan Administration insisted that it wanted to "coordinate" its economic policies with other advanced industrial nations but found the others resistant. The Louvre accord of February 1987, in which the major trading nations agreed to stabilize currencies and simultaneously reduce America's budget deficit while expanding their own economies, seemed a step in the right direction. But in the late summer and early fall West Germany had the temerity to raise its interest rates—prompting Treasury Secretary James Baker to announce on October 18, 1987, (the day before the Dow Jones Industrial Average dropped over five hundred points) that the United States would allow the dollar to fall in response to their uncooperativeness. In other words, the economic strain was *their* fault, and they were to be punished for it.

Left out of the Administration's calculation was Japan's and West Germany's understandable skepticism that the United States would fulfill *its* side of the bargain. Not even the flurry of postcrash negotiations between the White House and Capitol Hill produced much more than the already mandated Gramm–Rudman deficit reductions. The Japanese worried about their own large budget deficit and about the future needs of their rapidly aging population; the West Germans were, as usual, afraid of inflation and suspicious of Americans' spendthrift habits. From the viewpoint of these countries, the Reagan Administration was unreasonable, even hypocritical, in blaming them for the deteriorating economic situation. It was as if the town drunk were criticizing everyone else for excessive sobriety.

By the start of 1989 American officials were quietly predicting that the dollar would have to fall by another 20 percent or so to cure the U.S. trade imbalance. Yet a falling dollar would impose significant penalties on the likes of Japan and West Germany, whose exports to the United States would become correspondingly more expensive and thus fewer. Germany was already experiencing high unemployment; a further decline in exports would push unemployment perilously higher. Were the United States to balance its trade account by importing less or exporting more, four million additional Americans would be put to work, but approximately the same number of foreigners would become jobless—two thirds of them Japanese and Europeans. This was hardly a recipe for future coordination or cooperation.

* * *

A second means of blaming foreigners has also gained a certain cachet in recent years: our mounting economic problems attributable, at least in part, to our allies' insistence that we defend them from communists and terrorists, despite their unwillingness to pay a fair share of the cost of such defense. Were our trading partners to pay their due, our budget and trade deficits would shrink markedly, or so the argument goes.

It is true that the defense burden is unequally allocated. In 1983, for example, Americans produced a little over 40 percent of the combined gross national product of the United States, Japan, France, Great Britain, and West Germany yet provided almost 57 percent of the group's defense spending. By contrast, Japan's share of advanced-nation GNP was 14 percent, but its defense share was only 3.3 percent. But here again, the blame is not without a touch of hypocrisy. Our trading partners have never insisted that we bear this disproportionate share. It is, rather, a price we have been willing—even eager—to pay, in order to contain what we have perceived to be the spread of world communism (a concern shared by our allies, but rarely to quite the same degree) and to ensure our continued leadership in the defense of the free world. The Reagan Administration showed little reluctance in raising American defense spending from its low of 4.6 percent of GNP in 1979 to almost 7 percent in the 1980s—an explosion that partly accounts for America's mounting indebtedness—while simultaneously reducing foreign aid and support for international institutions.

Of course, it may be necessary in future years for all allies and trading partners to foot a larger part of the combined cost of defending us all. But such a move would not be without political consequence: America would no longer be in the same position of leadership; our allies would be more independent of us, able and perhaps willing to seek different accommodations with the Soviets and other perceived threats. In addition, a militarized Japan and more militarized West Germany would represent a substantial change in how we and they, and others, understand their power in the world. Amid growing fears of American abandonment in the face of Soviet conventional forces, West European leaders are already talking of defense cooperation among themselves and of a greater European role in NATO decision making. However the issue may be resolved, there is no basis at this juncture for arguing that our economic predicament is wholly or even mostly attributable to our allies' unwillingness to bear a fair burden of the common defense.

* * *

Congress, meanwhile, has been devising a third means of blaming foreigners for our economic problems and of deflecting costs on them. A mammoth new trade bill emerged from the House of Representatives in 1988 and was reluctantly signed into law as one of Ronald Reagan's last official acts. The trade law was designed, according to its progenitors, to ensure that American exporters competed on a "level playing field." Most of the law's provisions reduced presidential discretion over what to do about foreign nations found to have kept American goods out of their home markets, subsidized their exporters, or "dumped" their goods on American soil. Missouri Congressman Richard Gephardt, a Democratic presidential candidate, championed a provision that would have penalized imports from nations that maintained trade imbalances with the United States. He argued that his innovation was designed not to protect the American market but to open foreign markets. Even without the provision (which was left out of the final version), the trade law's focus was indisputably on the transgressions of foreigners.

In its waning months the Reagan Administration, not to be outdone, and perhaps to forestall even more extreme measures by Congress, vowed to "get tough on unfair foreign trade." First came a stiff duty on Canadian softwood shakes and shingles in response to alleged unfair subsidies, followed by 100-percent tariffs on $300 million worth of Japanese electronics products in retaliation for Japan's apparent dumping of semiconductors in Third World markets, a brief war with the European Economic Community over citrus and pasta, threatened tariffs on $100 million worth of Brazilian imports in response to Brazilian curbs on American computers and software products, talk of additional tariffs on $100 million worth of food imports from Europe in retaliation for bans on meat from animals treated with growth hormones, and a movement to withdraw special duty-free preferences for products from developing nations that have maintained substantial trade imbalances with the United States. Summarizing these and related developments, Special U.S. Trade Representative (soon to be Bush's secretary of agriculture) Clayton Yeutter touted what he terms the Administration's "extremely aggressive" approach to foreign trade. "Some of our trading partners have complained loudly about what they see as high-handed American practices," he said, proudly. "But that won't dissuade us from protecting our interests."

Here again, the responsibility for America's economic problems has been safely externalized. It is true, of course, that some nations subsidize their exports to us and hobble our exports to them. But absent international agreement on what sorts of subsidies and nontariff protections are unfair, America's responses merely reflect what the United States unilaterally deems to be unfair. The dominant metaphors create the impression of unsportsmanlike, if not indecent, behavior—"tilting the playing field," "dumping"—when in reality the playing field has always been as hilly as the Ozarks, and dumped goods are often known to American consumers by the less pejorative term "bargains."

* * *

Our trading partners may sense hypocrisy here as well. All told, by the start of 1989 fully 35 percent (by value) of the goods produced in the United States was protected by some form of nontariff barrier—including countervailing duties, antidumping levies, and so-called voluntary restraint agreements ("voluntary" only to the extent that our trading partner willingly accepted American demands to hold back exports under threat of more severe quotas should no agreement be reached). The comparable figure in 1980 had been 20 percent. Moreover, the U.S. government continues to subsidize American industry to a degree that makes most other nations seem like laissez-faire purists by comparison. Federally subsidized loans and loan guarantees, state and local tax abatements, and generous grants of "eminent domain" authority are routinely available to American businesses. Over one third of all the research and development costs of American corporations are now funded by the federal government.

The Defense Department and its sister agencies—the Department of Energy and the National Security Agency—have emerged as the most magnanimous and determined developers of American technology. The year 1988 marked something of a record. For example, in January the Administration formally approved a $4.4 billion plan for building a "superconducting supercollider," a fifty-two-mile underground racetrack for subatomic particles deemed by the Energy Department to be "critical" for America's international competitiveness in related technologies. Then in July the President announced that the Pentagon would lead a $150 million effort aimed at developing practical applications for "superconducting" materials—special alloys that when cooled lose all resistance to the flow of electric current. The National Security Agency, meanwhile, has been pouring $20 million a year into its Supercomputer Research Center, which is seeking to build the world's fastest computers. In October the Pentagon agreed to fund "Sematech," a research joint venture comprising America's leading semiconductor manufacturers, designed to improve their manufacturing competitiveness. And at the end of the year the National Aeronautics and Space Administration, whose mission has drifted steadily toward Defense Department needs, awarded $5 billion in contracts to design and build components for a space station —a project justified by NASA as having "potentially vital consequences for the nation's defense and its competitiveness."

In short, the Pentagon and its sister agencies have become the source of America's high-technology industrial policy—a policy that is more costly, complex, and intrusive upon the private sector than any ever imagined by our trading partners. The problem is not that they do it and we don't. The real problem for us is that we do it under the aegis of national defense—which is an exceedingly awkward and inefficient way to promote high technology—while they do it more openly and directly.

Blaming others for our economic problems may be reassuring but has two unfortunate consequences. It makes others angry and resentful and thus less inclined to cooperate over the longer term. And it makes us less inclined to take responsibility for what needs to be remedied in ourselves—the issue to which I now turn.

*　*　*

Our nation's growing economic problem is due neither to the federal budget deficit per se, nor to foreigners' unwillingness to treat us fairly. It is due to our overwhelming failure to invest in our collective productivity and the consequent decline in our capacity to add value to the world economy.

Indebtedness would be no cause for great alarm if the proceeds were invested in our future productivity. America's foreign debt is still small relative to its gross national product; Mexico has borrowed twice the amount as a proportion of its GNP. In the nineteenth century we borrowed far more, relatively speaking. But a century ago the loans were invested in factories, railroads, oil wells, inventions, and an array of other assets that produced future wealth. Not this time around. We are consuming our way into economic oblivion. Even Wall Street's reverie before Black Monday was based not on productivity gains but on threats of takeovers, which prompted corporations to do whatever was necessary to raise their share prices in the short term—often cutting back on long-term investment while purchasing their own shares and going deeply into debt.

Without a surge in productivity, the present debt cannot be repaid unless we drastically reduce our standard of living. Our predicament is analogous to that of any person living beyond his means, who must grow poorer unless he generates more wealth. The plot is familiar: As creditors realize that he is unlikely to be able to repay, his IOUs begin to decline in value, and new loans—if available at all—come only at exorbitant rates. To maintain present consumption, he begins selling off the contents of his house, including family heirlooms, and finally the house itself—which he thereupon rents from the new owners until he has no money left with which to pay the rent. So too with America; our failure to invest in future productivity is now reflected in a declining dollar, rising interest rates, and the steady sale to foreigners of shares in our companies and of our prime real estate. Trying to offset our trade imbalance by selling off our assets makes as much sense as selling the house to help pay future rent.

Most of the panaceas now being offered by politicians and economists provide alternative means of growing poorer—by, for example, allowing the dollar to continue to fall, cutting wages, reducing environmental and safety regulations, slashing public spending, even engineering a recession. While these strategies impose the burden of becoming poorer on different groups of citizens over slightly different periods of time, their overall effects are much the same. There is no secret to becoming poorer. Even if we did nothing, the becoming-poorer strategy would occur automatically as the dollar continued to slide. To repeat, the only becoming-richer strategy is to invest in our future productivity.

*   *   *

The current obsession with the federal budget deficit obscures an important point about the nature and purpose of productive investments. Popular wisdom holds that government expenditure "crowds out" private investment. But the reverse may now be closer to the truth. A significant portion of the investments undertaken by American corporations in recent years has been unrelated to the task of improving American competitiveness, while many of the most important types of productive investment can be undertaken only by the public sector.

Even as America's trade deficit has widened, American-owned corporations have continued to maintain their competitiveness by going overseas. Recent studies reveal that, while the percentage of world markets held by American corporations exporting from the United States has steadily declined during the last quarter century, such declines have been offset by the gains of American corporations exporting from other nations. As the dollar declines, some American corporations are coming back to America, and some foreign-owned corporations are joining them. Toshiba soon will be exporting to Japan microwave ovens and television sets made in its Tennessee plant, for example. But to the extent such corporations are being drawn to the United States by the relatively low costs of production here associated with a low dollar, their new investments in America are unlikely to be of a sort that will greatly enhance the value of what Americans contribute to the world economy. They are more likely to be in plant and equipment tailored to relatively low-skilled labor. Should the dollar hit sufficiently low depths, the United States may eventually become an attractive place to make things now produced in Southeast Asia and Latin America. But under these circumstances the real incomes of Americans—adding no more value to globally available plant and equipment than is added by any other low-skilled workers around the globe—would be very low indeed.

* * *

The only factors of production that are relatively immobile internationally, and thus on which depends uniquely the value that the nation adds to world commerce, are the skills of our citizens and their capacities to work together. To a significant extent, such assets represent returns on public investments—in education, training and retraining, research and development, and in all the systems for transporting our citizens and communicating among them—which comprise the nation's infrastructure. We do not commonly think of these sorts of expenditures as investments—the federal budget fails to distinguish capital expenditures, and the national income accounts treat all government expenditures as consumption—but they dramatically affect our future capacity to produce.

These public investments have either declined during the 1980s or, at best, remained at about the same level. Government spending on commercial research and development has declined 95 percent from its level two decades ago. (Even when added to private-sector research and development, the total is still less than 2 percent of GNP, lower than comparable research and development expenditures in any other advanced industrial nation.) Government spending to upgrade and expand the nation's infrastructure dropped from 2.3 percent of GNP two decades ago to 0.4 percent in the 1980s. Per-pupil expenditures on public elementary and secondary education have shown no gain in real terms; as a percent of GNP, they have declined—and this during an era in which demands on public education have significantly increased, due to the growing phenomena of broken homes, unwed mothers, and a rising population of poor. The federal government has retreated from the field of public education, leaving states and localities—many of them severely handicapped by low tax bases—with almost the entire job. Not surprisingly, an estimated 20 percent of American eighteen-year-olds are now functionally illiterate; one quarter of today's high school students drop out before graduation. This is not the sort of population likely to generate high productivity in future years.

We must do several things to reverse the trend. First, we must gradually scale back aggregate consumption by, for example, spurring the growth of personal savings through expanded Individual Retirement Accounts and Keogh plans, hobbling hostile takeovers and leveraged buyouts, and taxing more of Social Security benefits. Consumption might also be limited by reducing farm supports, jettisoning weapons projects that are of low priority or fail to perform as planned, and taxing consumption directly—through, for example, a progressive tax on a family's net spending.

But this is only half the agenda. We must *simultaneously* attend to the investment side of the ledger by, for example, inducing more private-sector spending on plant and equipment in the United States (restoring the investment tax credit and accelerated depreciation on investments made in the United States) and increasing government spending for education, retraining, child nutrition, prenatal and postnatal care, research and development, and infrastructure. These investment strategies may make it more difficult to reduce the federal budget deficit in the short term, but they are more important to our long-term economic health than any immediate fix. To focus singularly on reducing the federal budget deficit distracts us from this more fundamental agenda.

An additional aspect of our investment strategy should be to take the nation's research and development efforts out from under the Pentagon and its sister agencies and turn them over to civilian agencies whose explicit goal is to spur the nation's commercial competitiveness. As has been noted, we already have a bold industrial policy for high technology, but it is run out of the Defense Department. There are commercial spin-offs of course, but because the Pentagon's needs are quite different from what consumers need at a price they are willing to pay, the spin-offs are relatively few and far between. And defense projects are so enshrouded in secrecy that commercial entrepreneurs often cannot take advantage of the discoveries even if they want to. It is time we acknowledged our high-technology industrial policy—and, by implication, the legitimacy of other nations' similar programs—but undertook ours in a far more efficient and direct manner.

Reality can be painful. Denial, escapism, and self-righteous indignation toward others are common defenses against such pain, no less for a nation than an individual. But reality can become progressively more painful the longer it is avoided. Our immediate responsibilities are to accept the truth about ourselves—that we are falling behind in our collective capacities to add value to the world economy and that we must invest in one another to regain our stride—and to do something about it.

7

THE EXECUTIVE'S
NEW CLOTHES (I)

SINCE THE MID-1970S, AMERICA'S FIVE HUNDRED LARGEST INDUSTRIAL
corporations together have failed to generate a single new job. In fact,
their portion of the civilian labor force declined from 17 percent in 1975
to less than 11 percent in 1988. And their share of the nation's product
has declined as well: from 55 percent of GNP in the mid-1970s to just
over 40 percent in 1988.

True, not all of the problems were of their own making. During the
1970s, they had to contend with two oil shocks and a spate of new
regulations—all of which, in turn, required extensive new investments.
And the onslaught of foreign competition—much of it based on low-
wage labor—posed an unprecedented challenge. Still, large American
corporations proved themselves remarkably inept in responding to these
demands. After all, Japanese companies faced the same oil shocks, similar regulatory requirements, and an even more intensely competitive
environment, and did so without the American corporations' home-
player advantage of a huge and sophisticated domestic market.

Not even the current recovery has changed the picture dramatically.
America's biggest corporations continue their long downward slide, like
prehistoric beasts quietly expiring. Few have come even close to match-

ing their 1960s performance. The Dow Jones Industrial Average began its spurt in August 1982. But when adjusted for inflation, the peak reached in August 1987 was still below the old peak of January 1966.

The poor performance is all the more remarkable in light of the privileged position enjoyed by large corporations in Ronald Reagan's and George Bush's America. Not since the 1920s has big business been so unconstrained. Consider the extraordinary cut in corporate taxes that began with the Economic Recovery Tax Act of 1981. In 1965 corporate tax payments accounted for 26 percent of federal revenues; by 1986 the portion was down to 8 percent. "Safe-harbor leasing" and other similar devices built into the tax code allowed the biggest corporations to enjoy their lowest effective tax rates in fifty years. General Electric, for example, paid no taxes at all between 1981 and 1983, on profits of $6.5 billion. Since then, in the wake of the tax reforms of 1986, the corporate burden has inched upward, but only by inches, reaching 13 percent in 1988.

John Kenneth Galbraith once wrote reassuringly of the "countervailing power" within the American system, which offsets the influence of large corporations. But in the America of the 1980s, these counterweights were all but removed. Health, safety, and environmental regulations were deferred or cut back; consumers and environmentalists no longer claimed the media attention they once did. Organized labor was cowed; union membership was down to 17 percent of the private-sector work force, and wage concessions became the order of the day. Few voices any longer broached the subject of corporate responsibility to the poor or to the communities and nations in which they do business. In fact, the dominant issues on the public agenda in the 1980s were those over which American business itself is divided—how to simplify taxes, reduce the budget deficit, and get foreign nations to open up their markets to our goods and services. At the same time, and with increasing boldness, state and local officials—anxious to lure or keep major businesses—promised corporate leaders all sorts of special subsidies and tax breaks. Not even foreign competitors imposed an enduring constraint, as protectionism waxed.

*　*　*

Nothing so exemplifies the unfettered position of today's large corporations as the autonomous power enjoyed by their chief executive officers—"CEOs" in business-speak—notwithstanding the continuing poor performance of the companies they run. One measure is found in their salaries and bonuses, which have increased much faster than inflation, and twice as fast as the earnings of hourly workers. In 1988 CEOs of the one hundred largest publicly owned industrial corporations received raises averaging almost 12 percent, while the wages of hourly workers increased by less than 6 percent. Between 1977 and 1987 hourly wages barely kept up with inflation; but the salaries and bonuses of America's top CEOs rose three times faster than inflation. (Most top executives are less defensive about their remuneration than John Nevin, CEO and chairman of Firestone Tire and Rubber Company, who claimed, at Firestone's 1987 stockholder meeting, that his $5.6 million bonus that year had not "caused me to have any feelings of embarrassment and is not . . . a payment for which I believe I owe anyone any apologies." Nevin's stockholders were not convinced. The company had lost money and jobs. It employed half the people it had employed a decade before. Within months of Nevin's appearance, most of the company was sold to Japan's Bridgestone Corporation.)

We are faced with a paradox. Our major corporations are stewards for a sizable chunk of our national wealth. The long-term performance of these corporations is less than sterling and continues to worsen. But at the same time American citizens seem willing to grant these companies, and their CEOs, ever greater wealth and privilege. The only constraint is the possibility of an unfriendly takeover; but even this, as we have seen, leads only to a new round of musical chairs. The tune remains the same.

What will come of this? One possibility is that these divergent trends eventually will clash. At some point we can expect a resurgence of the sort of economic populism that periodically captures the American imagination. The large corporation and its leaders will be vilified in the media. This will be accompanied by a new round of regulatory restraints on corporate action. We may even get serious about proposals for economic democracy.

But a more likely possibility, at least in the short run, is that the United States will consider the twin problems of poor corporate performance and the privileged position of the CEO as challenges to managerial attitudes and techniques. (As a culture, we tend to prefer pep talks to social criticism—stories about what works to exposés about what doesn't—at least until the underlying problems loom so large that they can no longer be ignored.) Indeed, there is evidence that we have already embarked on this Panglossian path. It comes in the form of a new literary genre that has emerged during the last few years: the CEO success story.

*　*　*

The new genre has been enormously popular. *In Search of Excellence: Lessons from America's Best Run Companies* by Thomas J. Peters and Robert H. Waterman, Jr., first published in 1983, has sold six million copies to date. The celebrated book tells the stories of the best American companies and their leaders—Walt Disney Productions, Ray Kroc and McDonald's, Caterpillar Tractor, Texas Instruments, and so on—and suggests lessons to be learned from them. Not far behind in total sales is *The One Minute Manager* by Kenneth Blanchard and Spencer Johnson. This book is written as a fairy tale about a young man whose search for the perfect manager leads him to a guru—the One Minute Manager—who shares his great wisdom with the young man in a mere 106 pages of large-type text. Then come the autobiographies, among them *Iacocca,* the story of the irrepressible CEO of Chrysler, which held first place on *The New York Times* best-seller list for months, and *Managing* by Harold Geneen and Alvin Moscow, the tale of the erstwhile CEO of ITT. All of these CEO success stories have spawned imitations and variations. Bookstores are now bulging with new volumes of stories and anecdotes about creating, achieving, or becoming impassioned about "excellence"—preferably within one minute—and about tales of tough-minded CEOs who have overcome adversity to make millions.

I do not mean to tar with an overly broad brush. The books in this new genre vary substantially in quality and sophistication. *Iacocca,* for example, is a delight to read; the story he relates is charming, funny, in places quite poignant. On the other hand, Harold Geneen's attempt at self-revelation is ponderous and pedantic. Iacocca doesn't take himself too seriously; Geneen seems desperate to secure for himself a place in history. *In Search of Excellence* offers rare insights into motivating employees and satisfying customers; the authors skillfully weave their stories into memorable lessons. *The One Minute Manager,* by contrast, is a fatuous exercise in manipulative managerial techniques. But these important differences notwithstanding, the books share some features that help explain the popularity of the genre as a whole and shed some light on its significance in this era of repressed criticism.

The heroes of these stories are mavericks. They are crusty, strong-willed characters who have no patience for fools or slackers. They buck the system. They take no crap. They win. Iacocca's story really begins when Henry Ford fires him. The reason? "Sometimes you just don't like somebody," Ford explains. Iacocca then takes over Chrysler when the firm is at rock bottom. The rest of the take is about Iacocca's and Chrysler's joint comeback, and ultimate victory. The victory permits a bittersweet revenge on Henry Ford—and on all other autocrats and naysayers. Indeed, it is the American saga of the underdog who eventually makes it big—whose hard work, perseverance, and cunning finally prevail over the powerful elites that try to keep him down. The same story inspired Horatio Alger's novellas. It powers Rocky. It runs through *In Search of Excellence*—from Ray Kroc's hamburgers to the product champions at 3M.

Even Harold Geneen comes off as a maverick. As financial vice president of Raytheon in the 1950s, he refuses to report to the president through the president's staff. He tells the president: "Either I am running this company or they are. I want to get my orders directly from you and not from them. So, you think it over. And let me know Monday morning." When it looks like he won't be president, Geneen quits Raytheon to become CEO of ITT. At the time ITT is little more than a lackluster collection of overseas telephone companies that the Bell System has discarded. Over the next eighteen years Geneen builds it into a massive conglomerate with annual sales of $17 billion and profits of $550 million —the thirteenth largest company in the United States. He is tough as nails, True Grit.

*   *   *

Second, these CEOs are colorful and outspoken. They are the antithesis of the gray-flanneled professional manager of yore whose very blankness was his more distinguishing quality. Although many of them share a background in finance, they are contemptuous of the "bean counters" and the superanalytic MBAs, who in Iacocca's words "seem to think that every business decision can be structured and reduced to a case study." They eschew memorandums and elaborate procedures. They detest office politics. Geneen describes political maneuvering as "a form of unfair self-aggrandizement which, if not curbed, will destroy the morale and forward thrust of any company." In short, these heroes hate bureaucracy in all its many forms.

Third, they believe in "hands-on" management. They want to confront people directly, touch them, challenge them, and motivate them through the sheer force of personality. Geneen spends countless hours grilling his managers—demanding that they think through what they're proposing, that they get the facts exactly right, that they tell the truth.

Iacocca is a whirlwind of handshakes and inspirational talks—to employees, middle managers, shareholders, bankers, members of Congress, customers, anyone who will listen. General Electric's Reg Jones, portrayed in another of these tomes, personally meets all the company's new young managers, visits ailing employees in the hospital, asks that company technicians explain to him precisely what they are working on, in ways that he can understand. All the heroes of *In Search of Excellence* manage by walking around their offices and factories, talking to employees and customers, getting directly involved. Even the One Minute Manager puts his hands on employees' shoulders and gives them one minute of praise.

Finally, these CEOs are missionaries. Their stories take on an evangelical tone because these men have been inspired. They have found meaning and value in the services they provide. They manage their enterprises by ensuring that employees share those same meanings and values. The atmosphere in these companies is part religious revival, part pep rally. Personnel at Disney theme parks are trained to be "hosts," to think of visitors as personal guests. IBM is fanatical about customer service. Iacocca is a zealot, inspiring his followers with the Belief in Chrysler. Reg Jones effuses about "the distinctive spirit of G.E. . . . that intangible but ever-so-real amalgam of enterprise and loyalty and honor." These CEOs stage contests, award ceremonies, and celebrations; they foster myths, rituals, and legends. They love excitement and hoopla; they downplay cool rationality. In fact, their contempt for the abstractions of professional managers can be understood, in part, as a rejection of intellectualism—of the notion that knowledge and meaning derive from access to special expertise.

The evangelical message is that with enough guts, tenacity, and charisma you too—gentle reader—can be a great manager, a captain of industry. Geneen says, "Managers must manage!" Iacocca says, "You have to be a motivator!" The heroes of *In Search of Excellence* say, "Make the average Joe a winner and a hero!" *The One Minute Manager* says, "Invest in People!"

*   *   *

Considered together, these characteristics make popular heroes. In their contempt for bureaucracy, formal process, and intellectual abstraction—and their passion for outspoken independence, direct dealing, and charismatic leadership—these CEOs seem perfectly in tune with the antiestablishment tendencies now found on both the right and left of the political spectrum. They are cowboy capitalists.

These stories thus give comfort to Americans who harbor vague misgivings about the place of the large, sluggish corporation in American life—and about the faceless oligarchs who run them. The cumulative message of these books is that we are entering upon a new populist era in which the mavericks are in charge. They are shaking up torpid corporate bureaucracies, bringing forth a new sense of team spirit and entrepreneurship. The Henry Fords of the old world are being replaced by the Lee Iacoccas of the new. The imperious bean counters are on the run. There is no reason to question the fundamental legitimacy of big business in the United States, or to flirt with economic populism, because the populists already have taken over—from the inside. And they are wildly successful.

Surely the heroes of these books deserve our applause. They have brought a new dynamism to American enterprise and generated an aura of team spirit and collective commitment that is new to big business. They have properly shaken up encrusted bureaucracies—substituting charisma and zeal for standard operating procedures. But we should not be too quick to accept the comforting message these stories imply. The populism that these heroes evince may be relatively superficial. Beyond the new atmospherics, it remains unclear precisely what our heroes have accomplished. These books are strangely silent, for example, on precisely how corporate success should be defined or measured. The authors talk incessantly about "excellence," "top performance," and "winning"— and occasionally profitability. But for the most part the genre assumes away the central questions. How should we define corporate success? Have these mavericks really made a difference? Are the fundamental problems of big business susceptible to managerial solutions?

Consider the record. Harold Geneen writes that when he was CEO, he defined success as a 10-percent growth in earnings per year. He insisted that every one of ITT's far-flung divisions and subsidiaries attain at least this level of performance. "I used to say ITT was a 'lockbox' stock. That meant that shareholders, large and small, could put our stock on the bottom of the safe-deposit box and not have to look at it again. It would take care of itself." But ITT's actual performance during these years raises some doubts about Geneen's claims. Between 1959 and 1977 —Geneen's years at the helm—the firm's per-share earnings increased 117 percent. This just about matched the rise in the consumer price index. In fact, investors who took Geneen up on his "lockbox" notion —purchasing ITT stock when Geneen took over the company and selling it when he resigned—did less well than they would have done had they invested in a portfolio of all stocks on the New York Stock Exchange.

Geneen also asserts that in order to make money, you have to make a "contribution to society"—you must "create value." Geneen took this admonition seriously; during his tenure as CEO, he played an active role in politics. But one could question what sort of "contribution" this involvement represented. When the Brazilian government threatened to seize ITT's assets without adequate compensation, Geneen was instrumental in getting passage of the 1962 Hickenlooper Amendment, which barred U.S. economic aid to any government that seized American assets without adequate compensation; soon thereafter, Brazil improved its offer. Geneen and his corporation also sought to prevent the election of Salvador Allende to the presidency of Chile. During this same year, ITT paid millions of dollars in bribes to public officials in a number of countries. And according to an internal memo from ITT lobbyist Dita Beard, the company agreed to help finance the 1972 Republican National Convention in the expectation that Nixon's Justice Department would drop an antitrust suit against it.

Lee Iacocca's goal was less ambitious—to save Chrysler. He seems to have succeeded splendidly. But it remains unclear to what extent Chrysler's resurgence has been attributable to its management. In 1979 and 1980, when Chrysler plummeted into the red, Ford and General Motors were not far behind. In 1980 Ford lost about $1.5 billion—almost as much as Chrysler—and GM lost about $1 billion. Then, beginning in 1981, all three automakers rode the same wave upward, ultimately to new record profits.

What accounts for this almost identical pattern? In 1979 Paul Volcker and the Federal Reserve Board he chaired decided to "break the back of inflation" by squeezing the money supply. Interest rates skyrocketed, and Americans stopped buying cars. In 1981 the Reagan Administration got the Japanese to limit the number of cars they shipped to the United States, and in 1982 the Federal Reserve Board loosened the money supply. At that point Americans started buying American cars again. It seems likely that Chrysler—flush with a federal loan guarantee —would have bobbed back to the surface again even without the charismatic leadership of Chairman Lee.

In fact, one might ask whether the goal of "saving Chrysler" was all that important—to anyone other than Chrysler's beleaguered stockholders, that is. During 1979, when Congress debated whether to guarantee $1.2 billion of new loans to the ailing firm, there was a great deal of talk about the importance of Chrysler to the American economy. But by 1985 Chrysler employed one-third fewer people than it did six years before. And more and more of the components that go into the cars that

Chrysler assembles—indeed, more and more of the cars that Chrysler sells—are manufactured outside the United States. Some commentators have suggested that in a few years the firm will be more appropriately called Chrysler Imports. In short, while Lee Iacocca seems to be a man of extraordinary talents, it's difficult to gauge exactly how much credit is due him, and for what.

The same ambiguities about the meaning of "success" plague many of the other success stories. During the 1970s, when Reg Jones was CEO of GE, the firm's growth in sales and net income just about held even with the growth of the American economy. This was hardly a stellar performance. Other companies that were doing well a few years ago when these stories were being gathered are now foundering; their leaders evidently did not position them for sustained profitability. By 1985 Walt Disney Productions was plagued by takeover battles, management shake-ups, and strikes. Texas Instruments was fighting for its life. Apple Computer was losing key personnel. Caterpillar Tractor was sustaining losses and moving its production abroad. ITT was on the verge of being broken up.

If our maverick heroes have had little practical effect on the performance of their firms—if their actions have merely perpetuated corporate privilege, notwithstanding their fiery rhetoric—then these CEOs cannot be the agents of economic populism. If the lessons they preach come down to mere atmospherics—making employees feel like winners, but not fundamentally altering the structure of ownership and control; creating a team spirit, but reserving the option of moving production abroad—then their populism is a sham. If their "successes" are defined so narrowly as to be meaningless in an era when economic change often entails large social costs and benefits, then it is only a matter of time before the sham is discovered. When this happens, our CEOs will be roundly condemned.

There is an overwhelming tendency in American life either to lionize or pillory the people who stand at the helms of our large institutions—to offer praise or level blame for outcomes over which they may have little control. This tendency is particularly apparent in regard to the performance of large corporations, whose legitimacy in our political and economic system continues to be an open question. The current infatuation with successful CEOs offers an illustration. The unfortunate result is that we are distracted from deeper questions about the organization of our economic system. In personalizing these exciting tales, we overlook much bigger stories.

8

THE EXECUTIVE'S
NEW CLOTHES (II)

IN AMERICA BUSINESS MANAGEMENT IS A PROFESSION. IT HAS ITS OWN graduate schools and advanced degrees; its own professional associations, conferences, and conventions; its own books, magazines, and professional newsletters; and a professional culture that distinguishes it from the general culture by language, clothing, income, and style of work.

The professional manager in America exists above the industrial din, away from the dirt, noise, and irrationality of people and products. He (he is almost always a he) dresses well. His secretary is alert and helpful. His office is as clean, quiet, and subdued as that of any other professional. He plans, organizes, and controls large enterprises in a calm, logical, dispassionate, and decisive manner. He surveys computer printouts, calculates profits and losses, sells and acquires subsidiaries, and imposes systems for monitoring and motivating employees, applying a general body of rules to each special circumstance. Because the professional manager deals in abstractions, he can move from company to company with relative ease, manipulating people and capital as he goes.

This may be why American productivity gains have declined over the past fifteen years, while those of Japan—a country of the approximate size and topography of Montana, without any physical resources to speak of, and more dependent on imported oil than we are; a country with over half our population, aging more quickly than ours, whose workers now receive a slightly higher average wage than we do—continue to rise. The Japanese do not have professional managers. Nor, for that matter, do the West Germans, whose productivity also has burgeoned over the decade. They have managers, all right, but their managers get their hands dirty. They work directly with people and machines. They come up through the ranks after spending most of their working lives with the same company and are considered part of the production team. In America, by contrast, it is rare for a manager to spend his working life with the same company and even rarer for him to have started out on the shop floor.

*   *   *

Professional management is relatively new as professions go. The first graduate school of business administration was established in America in 1908. It came in the wake of a vast thirty-year wave of mergers creating the first large vertically integrated manufacturing corporations —controlled by a centralized cadre of administrators. The Administrative Management Association was founded eleven years later. Efficiency experts like Frederick Winslow Taylor, Henry L. Gantt, Frank Gilbreth, and Harrington Emerson were soon espousing progressivist notions of scientific management through which the workplace was to become a well-oiled machine and work was to be designed systematically to fit the aptitudes of workers. "Under scientific management," wrote Taylor, "arbitrary power, arbitrary dictation ceases. . . . [T]he man at the head of business . . . is governed by rules and laws which have been developed through hundreds of experiments."

Through scientific management each step of production was to be reduced to its simplest components and arranged in sequence to ensure the highest level of productivity consistent with reasonable levels of quality and fatigue. Jobs were to be uniform and specialized. Discretion and skill were to be minimized. Thus, the very process of production was to be removed from the province of workers. The first step of scientific management, according to Taylor, was "the gathering on the part of [management] of all knowledge which in the past has been kept in the heads of the workmen." The solution to quality control, for example, was to be mechanical—a system of inspectors, and inspectors over inspectors, combined with random sampling. It was no longer necessary for workers to think.

By the late 1920s the American business leader had been transformed from a person whose success was ensured by the Protestant virtues of prudence, punctuality, and perseverance to one whose rise depended on his ability to motivate and manipulate others. And the American worker was transformed into an object to be motivated and manipulated. The new bureaucratic enterprise required businessmen who could apply management techniques to large numbers of employees. Business leaders flocked to management courses in human engineering. Dale Carnegie's first book, *Public Speaking and Influencing Men in Business* (1926), became an instant best-seller. Researchers like Elton Mayo and F. J. Ruethlisberger instructed managers about human relations. A new branch of the profession appeared called "personnel management," replete with studies of industrial physiology and psychology to aid business leaders in getting the most out of their employees.

It was not until after World War II, however, that professional management came into its own. The spectacular performance of American industry during the war drew worldwide attention to American management techniques. Sir Stafford Cripps, chancellor of the exchequer in Britain's postwar Labour government, sent teams of British businessmen to America to learn our secrets. The Marshall Plan further exported American management ideas. But only in Britain did they take firm root, perhaps because the British class structure had already drawn a sharp distinction between white-collar and blue-collar, and the ideal of professional management fit neatly into this hierarchical scheme.

* * *

Even today no single word in French, German, Swedish, or Japanese conveys the general meaning of management as we know it. Indeed, the role of professional business manager is viewed with suspicion abroad, where most business administrators are trained instead in engineering or applied economics. To be sure, there are institutes of management training in Western Europe and Japan, but they exist outside the traditional educational system and are designed for mid-career executives who want specific training in particular aspects of management. They don't give degrees. Nor do they confer professional status. In continental Europe and in Japan business administration is a vocation rather than a profession.

The founding fathers of Japanese and continental European industry —the Yataros, Zenjiros, and Krupps of the late nineteenth century— were succeeded by a generation of business leaders who ascended to management from the factory floor. They intuitively understood the importance of worker participation and job security to productivity. By and large, they supported trade unionism. They accommodated a variety of schemes to ensure that workers were given responsibility for their work—codetermination on boards of directors, workers' councils, elaborate systems of consultation. And they built job security into their productive processes.

Moreover, by the time large, multidivisional corporations first appeared in these countries, government bureaucracies responsible for social welfare were already well established. Thus, business leaders tended to accept the legitimacy of welfare programs and to acknowledge the responsibility of the corporation to contribute to social welfare through the provision of some modicum of employment security. Full employment remains a national goal to which business leaders in these countries subscribe.

By contrast, our professional managers have been less than enthusiastic about social welfare. Perhaps this is because the rise of professional management here preceded the development of our welfare state or because few of our managers have had direct shop-floor experience. Whatever the reason, American managerial elites have fought unionization and opposed job security and worker participation and to this day view the welfare state as sharply antithetical to productivity.

Because the ideal of professional management never took firm root in continental Europe or in Japan, there was not the sharp division of labor between the planning and execution of work, which has characterized Anglo-Saxon enterprise. In recent years this bifurcated way of viewing production—separating thinkers from doers, corporate mind from corporate body, white-collar from blue-collar—has had unsuccessful results in America and Britain. It has spawned two distinct corporate cultures that communicate primarily through formal channels of management directives and union complaints. While U.S. and British companies typically are deeply concerned about the career advancement and job enrichment of their managers, they exhibit no such passion for their workers. The gap between the average blue-collar wage and top executive compensation is larger in America than in any other developed country. And blue-collar workers in America and Britain have little access to company data. They are kept in the dark about company plans and profits.

* * *

The costs of this artificial distinction between corporate thinkers and doers are by now obvious. White-collar strategists and planners often don't comprehend life on the production line, and in consequence their schemes are either impractical or irrelevant, either sabotaged or ignored by the work force. Meanwhile, workers who understand production and could improve it in countless ways don't give a damn. They have no institutional voice. Moreover, the insensitivity of professional managers to the everyday needs of employees has taken a toll. Many of our businesses are plagued by chronic absenteeism and work stoppages. In the mid-1980s the average number of days per year lost to industrial disputes for every one thousand employees was over 1,000 in the United States and over 800 in Britain, compared to 45 in Sweden, 250 in Japan, and 85 in West Germany. The quality of products made in America or Britain is widely considered to be inferior to those of West Germany or Japan. American and British employees are notoriously suspicious of automation, mechanization, or other innovations to improve productivity—and for good reason, since their jobs may be jeopardized as a result. For all these reasons American and British productivity has been increasing at a slower pace than elsewhere.

This is not to suggest that companies in continental Europe and Japan are models of labor-management harmony. On the contrary, Japanese labor unions annually mount a rhetorically threatening "spring offensive" against management. Swedish workers are proud of their militancy. Many French workers espouse socialist ideals. And West German labor unions periodically fulminate against their companies. The difference is that these adversarial contests take place within an institutional and political framework based on the premise of near-full employment and worker participation. Workers in these countries understand that their fates are tied to the profitability and competitiveness of their industries. They are the ultimate beneficiaries of productivity improvements. Adversarial contests are a means of reasserting this central fact. Militancy is thus highly symbolic—a periodic ritual through which all elements of the work force reestablish their social compact. Indeed, in many of these countries white-collar employees are themselves union members who duly participate in these rites. Nothing could be further from the bitter and continuous conflicts that have long separated professional managers from workers in America and Britain.

The first step toward revitalizing Anglo-Saxon economies will be to break down this artificial wall separating thinkers from doers and to render the workplace truly collaborative. This will happen eventually because we have no choice but to make it happen if we are to sustain our economic base. The transformation will not be couched in ideological terms but will be viewed simply as a means of increasing productivity. Our workplaces will become more equitable, secure, and democratic—notwithstanding the individualistic, social-Darwinist rhetoric of the Reagan, Bush, and Thatcher Administrations—because international competition will require that they be so.

The danger is that this transformation will occur later rather than sooner, by which time the road to economic renewal in America and Britain will be straight uphill. The ideology of professional management is by now so deeply embedded in Anglo-Saxon culture that our business leaders at first may seek to emulate the social reality of the Japanese or German workplace through the mere implementation of new management techniques. The sharp distinction between thinkers and doers will remain intact but will be camouflaged by cosmetic devices—quality circles, work groups, collaborative teams, encounter groups, meetings of all sorts and sizes—which serve to soften or blur the underlying structure of management control. Organization-development specialists and consultants will swarm over the workplace advising professional managers about how to improve the "quality of working life" without fundamentally altering the organization of production.

*   *   *

This silliness has already begun. America is awash with new managerial theories promising to transform miraculously the American workplace into its Japanese counterpart. *Theory Z: How American Business Can Meet the Japanese Challenge,* by William G. Ouchi, and *The Art of Japanese Management: Applications for American Executives,* by Richard T. Pascale and Anthony G. Athos, to take two notable examples, are both how-to books in the best tradition of professional management. Both exhort American business leaders to use management techniques that will, they allege, make American workers as dedicated as their Japanese counterparts. These techniques include giving workers more job security, developing nonspecialized career paths for them, providing them with gradual and standardized promotions that minimize competition among workers, undertaking collective decision making, and displaying a "holistic" concern for the welfare of workers. *Theory Z* provides managers with a step-by-step guide to implementing these techniques and includes several case histories of American firms that seem to have succeeded with them. *The Art of Japanese Management* contrasts the management style of ITT's Harold Geneen with that of Konosuke Matsushita, head of the Matsushita Electric Company (maker of Panasonic, Quasar, and Technics products). Where Geneen was tough and confrontational—driving his employees relentlessly, firing them if they didn't perform, and wielding almost despotic authority over ITT's vast organization—Matsushita used his authority in far more subtle and supportive ways. ITT's profitability dropped precipitously after Geneen's retirement, but Matsushita continues to prosper. To the authors, the moral is clear: American managers must strive to create an atmosphere of intimacy and trust in the workplace. Rather than terrorize their employees by using techniques of fear and control, managers should obtain their loyalty and devotion by tending to their needs.

These are worthy goals. If fully implemented, they surely would enhance American productivity. But they will not be fully implemented so long as the American corporation continues to be dominated by professional managers. Because the authors in no way challenge the dominance of professional managers, their prescriptions are mere management techniques to achieve short-term profitability. There will be no real job security because managers cannot justify the high short-term costs of keeping workers employed during economic downturns. There will be no genuine career paths or real prospects of promotion for most blue-collar workers, because it is cheaper for managers to hire mid-level employees who are already trained than to train blue-collar workers for mid-level jobs. And there will be no real collective decision making, because managers cannot afford to lose control. Moreover, collective decision making is extraordinarily time-consuming and costly in the short term. Thus, while it may be profitable in the short term to make employees *feel* as though they have job security, career prospects, and direct input into company decisions, it is not immediately profitable to restructure the corporation along these lines.

Since the authors studiously ignore the possibility of a reorientation of the American corporation and the financial institutions on which it relies, the issue becomes one of how business managers can create the impression of a collaborative workplace. Accordingly, when they get down to specifics, the authors of both books dwell on atmospherics and attitudes. They urge managers to give their employees "meaning," to transform the workplace from a setting in which work is merely performed to one in which employees are spiritually uplifted. Indeed, they go so far as to blame our economic problems in part on our historic insistence on separating church, state, and corporation—distinctions that have, they argue, led to a highly mechanistic view of production in which employees are viewed as interchangeable units. By way of contrast they offer Matsushita, who merged these separate institutions into one. His was the first company in Japan to have a song and a code of values. Each morning eighty-seven thousand Matsushita employees together sing the song and recite the code. By these and other devices they are inspired to be zealous.

¤   ¤   ¤

This emphasis on the atmospherics of intimacy and trust at the workplace is hardly new to professional management in America. In their attempt to stem the rising tide of trade unionism during the first decades of the century, American managers adopted "workplace cooperation" as their slogan and devised an elaborate system of committees to represent worker interest. By 1922 there were 385 different companies maintaining 725 plans of employee representation, which together involved 690,000 workers. Frederick Winslow Taylor, the founder of scientific management, declared that his whole object was to create a trusting relationship between worker and manager and thereby to "remove the cause for antagonism." By the mid-1930s the preeminent business journal, *Management Review,* was urging business leaders to give their employees "what every human being asks for in life: respect for his personality, his human dignity, an environment that he comprehends, and an assurance that he is progressing." The *Review* was adamant about the importance of collaboration: Workers want to be treated "not as servants, but as cooperators."

Such trust and collaboration was of course nothing more than a means of motivating and manipulating the work force while maintaining professional control. The new management theorists merely extend these devices by offering techniques designed to create spiritual togetherness. One is reminded of the Amana and Oneida utopian communities of nineteenth-century America that succeeded so well as commercial enterprises (making iceboxes and tableware, respectively) precisely because they had so thoroughly socialized their workers to share a single vision. Or the modern Amway and Shaklee soap and vitamin distributors, which periodically rev up their door-to-door sales forces through evangelical pep rallies. The logical ending point for psychological manipulation at the workplace is old-time religion, with professional managers as its priests. Management continues to be the applied science of short-term manipulation.

America's new management gurus' emphasis on the spiritual side of the Japanese company is misplaced. The religiouslike devotion of Japanese workers to their companies is the least appealing and least transfer-able feature of Japanese production. Do we want American workers to behave like the sales officer of a large Japanese company who in 1979 committed suicide after being caught in a scandal over aircraft imports from the United States? Does anyone believe that American workers would subscribe to the sentiments he expressed in his suicide note: "[T]he company is eternal. . . . I must be brave and act as a man to protect that eternal life"?

*   *   *

Potentially far more important and relevant to the American work-place is the Japanese organization of production, and the political and social context in which it exists—issues on which the new management theorists barely touch. Japanese workers enjoy a far higher degree of equity, job security, and responsibility than their American counterparts —and these features are real, not cosmetic. In Japan, unlike in the United States, the risk of severe economic downturns is borne by stockholders rather than by employees. Employees are not laid off when sales decline, because the company's major stockholders—banks and other companies with whom it does business—come to its aid. And its most senior man-agers take substantial cuts in pay rather than allow lower-level workers to bear a financial burden. One has only to compare how Mazda handled its huge deficit in the early 1970s—cutting the pay of senior managers by 20 percent, freezing the pay of middle-level managers, but maintain-ing cost-of-living increases for its low-level workers and keeping them all employed—with Chrysler's decision, when it faced a similar crisis, to lay off 28 percent of its blue-collar work force but fire only 7 percent of its middle-level managers and cut its white-collar salaries by an average of only 5 percent. Is it any wonder that Mazda's work force was com-mitted to restoring the company to competitive health? Could we expect the same enthusiasm from Chrysler's workers?

Japanese managers ascend the same company ladder as do all other employees; their training begins on the factory floor. A Japanese worker can look forward to becoming a subsection head or a section head in a few years, and with enough diligence may one day become a company director. Indeed, the directors of most Japanese companies come from the ranks of employees, after having worked their way up through the company for twenty or thirty years. Such directors are naturally more likely to identify with the interests of the employees with whom they've worked for decades than with stockholders. They are apt to encourage consultation with employees and to minimize distinctions between labor and management. They are likely to take the long view—investing in their employees' training, career advancement, and long-term welfare.

Perhaps most significantly, Japanese corporate executives draw substantially lower salaries than their American counterparts do: While it is rare for a top manager in Japan to earn more than six times the salary and benefits of the lowest-level workers in the company, it is hardly unusual for top American executives to earn fifteen times that of their company's lowest-level employees.

To an extent unprecedented in the United States, Japanese unions are company unions. Bargaining occurs almost exclusively at the company level; the unions are part of the company. In the largest firms employees are guaranteed employment until the age of fifty-five. Most employees of smaller subcontractors are also protected by the larger companies they serve. Job dismissals are rare. These relationships are codified in Japanese labor law: Japanese courts generally will not uphold a dismissal unless the employer can show that there was no less onerous alternative. Because unions are company unions and because workers expect to stay on forever, the interests of the company and those of the union tend to converge.

American labor law, by contrast, presumes fundamental conflict between managers and employees, as exemplified by the National Labor Relations Act. Supervisors are excluded from the act's protections because they represent management; union membership, it is assumed, would involve supervisors in a conflict of interest. Section 8(a)(2) of the act even makes it an unfair labor practice for employers to "dominate or interfere with the formation or administration of any labor organization or contribute financial or other support to it." It thus bars many management-initiated measures designed to increase union participation in the firm.

This assumed conflict of interest has influenced other areas of American labor-management relations. Under American labor law, employers have no obligation to reveal company finances to employees unless the employers claim an inability to pay the specific wages and benefits that the union demands. Nor do employers have a duty to bargain about decisions to scale back their operations. Nor, in general, must they bargain about investment, production, or site locations. The express logic of these and other related rules is that the National Labor Relations Act did not contemplate perfect equality between labor and management and that in fact managerial prerogatives must be preserved so that companies can maximize shareholders' return on investment. The act requires only that labor and management negotiate toward an agreement in good faith, not that they share the same goals. Indeed, the statute permits parties to employ sometimes debilitating economic weapons to induce the other side to come to terms.

*   *   *

In sum, the Japanese company exists primarily for its employees rather than for its senior managers or stockholders. It seeks to adapt itself to employee needs. In Japan one repeatedly hears the phrase "the enterprise and its employees share a common destiny." Japanese firms do not rely substantially on equity held by individual stockholders, institutions, or companies existing outside the industrial group to which the firm belongs. For the most part, their profit margins are small. Japanese companies aim instead to enlarge their market shares, influence, and dominance—and thereby to enhance the prestige and economic security of all the people associated with them. The network of economic relationships that define the enterprise gives it its value and social meaning. Instead of serving merely as a *means* through which various parties—including investors—make money, the enterprise has independent value as a system of relationships.

The law and ideology underlying American enterprise is fundamentally different. Companies compete for both consumers' dollars and investors' dollars. It is assumed that capital flows to where it can get the highest return and that the primary function of enterprise is to maximize that return. The enterprise is little more than a network of financial relationships within which managers must act on behalf of the investors of capital. Thus, in principle, there is an inherent clash of interests between managers and investors on the one side and employees on the other. Each group will inevitably seek to increase its own share of the firm's revenues.

Without such fundamental conflict, enterprise harmony is possible; with it, harmony is merely an armistice during the intervals between rounds of negotiation, a temporary cessation of reciprocal threat. Notwithstanding the quality circles and teams that are now all the rage in American factories, the basic reality of corporate life is not lost on American workers.

This is ironic, of course, because American workers are coming to own more and more of American industry. The growth in employee pension plans over the past twenty years has been no less extraordinary, now reaching over 50 percent of corporate equity. Indeed, pension funds are now America's largest single source of investment. Add to this the group health and life insurance funds of which American workers are the beneficiaries and you have a sizable chunk of all investment in American enterprise. Accordingly, it is becoming technically accurate to say that American companies do *in fact* exist primarily for their employees. But because the lines of responsibility from company to employee are so attenuated—through a maze of plans, trustees, institutional investors, and stock portfolios—most employees don't feel as if their companies exist for them, and American companies don't act as if they do.

* * *

Those who say that the Japanese form of enterprise capitalism cannot take root here because our culture is so different should consider how comparatively new this Japanese ideal is even in Japan. Industrial harmony is largely a postwar phenomenon. The prewar years were marked by bitter struggles between factions within the Army and Navy, between the military and the industrial groups, between tenant farmers and landlords. There were few large enterprises to confer benefits on those who worked for them. Company unions scarcely existed. Trade unions were suppressed by the authorities. Lifetime employment had little meaning in an industrial system in which nearly half the population consisted of impoverished peasants. Economic growth was elusive in the wake of the financial panic of 1927, the invasion of Manchuria in 1931, the fascist attacks on capitalism during the 1930s, the war with China from 1937 to 1941, World War II, the economic collapse of 1946, and the post–Korean War recession of 1954. In the decades ahead, as the Japanese economy and society become further integrated into a global capitalist system in which neither social harmony nor enterprise benefit is a central tenet, these premises may further evolve—or wither.

At the same time, the liberal individualism that infuses America's contractual approach to matters of economic organization is not the only tradition on these shores. There is also a deep strain of civic republicanism, of local political organizations, economic cooperatives, religious groups, and community associations, that has been as concerned with the moral quality of civic life and the relationships on which it is based as with the protection of individual liberties. It is to this tradition, which confers intrinsic value on economic and social relationships, rather than to the direct emulation of the Japanese, that we probably will owe our most enduring experiments with worker participation in management, employee profit sharing, and employee and community ownership of industry.

Of course, there is much about Japanese capitalism that one would not wish the United States to emulate. The job security enjoyed by employees of the largest firms and most of their suppliers is to some extent made possible by the *insecurity* of temporary workers—the vast majority of whom are women—who constitute about 20 percent of the labor force. Although unions comprise a larger percentage of the eligible workers in Japan than in the United States, union coverage does not extend to such temporaries or to the employees of small subcontractors, who typically absorb most of the unemployment during the slack periods. Moreover, several groups continue to be rejected from the Japanese economy. Social barriers have blocked the advancement of Japan's 1.2 million *burakumin* ("ghetto people"), descendants of the lowest social order in feudal Japan. The vast majority of them remain trapped in urban ghettos, working in menial jobs. Japan's seven hundred thousand Koreans and fifteen thousand Ainu—descendants of the country's earliest inhabitants—are also excluded. In addition, women in Japan face social barriers that effectively bar them from responsible positions in industry.

Another unattractive feature of Japanese enterprise is the belief that it is not *possible* for employees' interests to conflict with managers, because managers are working for the benefit of the employees. Employees may make suggestions, of course; they may even, on occasion, express anger over managers' actions. But ultimate responsibility for their well-being rests with those at the top of the management hierarchies. Such paternalism delegitimates employees' independent conclusions about their own needs and interests. Disputes are akin to family squabbles between children and parents; they are to be taken seriously, but everyone realizes that the parents really know best.

* * *

Moral exhortation, evangelical pep rallies, and quality circles are no substitutes for the identity of interest between labor and management that occurs within an organization existing primarily and directly for its employees. American managers who try techniques of psychological manipulation may be successful in the short run. But manipulation has no staying power. Workers are not stupid, nor are managers omnipotent. Psychological manipulation invariably breaks down over the long term, resulting in more distrust and higher levels of adversarial combat.

We need fewer managerial lessons in how to better manipulate employees that seek to make professional managers into better manipulators. Perhaps we need fewer professional managers. Instead, we need men and women who understand intimately the nature of work and the processes of production, and who thus can provide practical and effective leadership. And we need productive organizations that unequivocally exist for the benefit of those who work within them.

There is no art to Japanese management. There is no mystery about how to meet the Japanese challenge. While there is much about the Japanese company that we would find abhorrent if transplanted here, there is also much that we can learn from the Japanese about the effective organization of production. Put most simply, we can learn that people are motivated to be productive not because they are well manipulated but because they have a direct stake in future productivity.

9

THE TEAM AS HERO

"Wake up there, youngster," said a rough voice.

Ragged Dick opened his eyes slowly and stared stupidly in the face of the speaker, but did not offer to get up.

"Wake up, you young vagabond!" said the man a little impatiently; "I suppose you'd lay there all day, if I hadn't called you."

So begins the story of *Ragged Dick, or Street Life in New York*, Horatio Alger's first book—the first of 135 tales written in the late 1800s that together sold close to twenty million copies. Like all the books that followed, *Ragged Dick* told the story of a young man who, by pluck and luck, rises from his lowly station to earn a respectable job and the promise of a better life.

Nearly a century later, another best-selling American business story offered a different concept of heroism and a different description of the route to success. This story begins:

All the way to the horizon in the last light, the sea was just degrees of gray, rolling and frothy on the surface. From the cockpit of a small white sloop—she was 35 feet long—the waves looked like hills coming up from behind, and most of the

crew preferred not to glance at them. . . . Running under
shortened sails in front of the northeaster, the boat rocked one
way, gave a thump, and then it rolled the other. The pots and
pans in the galley clanged. A six-pack of beer, which someone
had forgotten to stow away, slid back and forth across the
cabin floor, over and over again. Sometime late that night, one
of the crew raised a voice against the wind and asked, "What
are we trying to prove?"

The book is Tracy Kidder's *The Soul of a New Machine*, a 1981
tale of how a team—a crew—of hardworking inventors built a computer
by pooling their efforts. The opening scene is a metaphor for the team's
efforts and treacherous journey.

Separated by one hundred years, totally different in their explanations of what propels the American economy, these two stories symbolize
the choice that America will face in the 1990s; each celebrates a fundamentally different version of American entrepreneurialism. Which version we choose to embrace will help determine how quickly and how
well the United States adapts to the challenge of global competition.

Horatio Alger's notion of success is the traditional one: the familiar
tale of triumphant individuals, of enterprising heroes who win riches and
rewards through the combination of Dale Carnegie–esque self-improvement, Norman Vincent Peale–esque faith, Sylvester Stallone–esque
assertiveness, and plain, old-fashioned good luck. Tracy Kidder's story,
by contrast, teaches that economic success comes through the talent,
energy, and commitment of a team—through *collective* entrepreneurship.

Stories like these do more than merely entertain or divert us. Like
ancient myths that captured and contained an essential truth, they shape
how we see and understand our lives, how we make sense of our experience. Stories can mobilize us to action and affect our behavior—more
powerfully than simple and straightforward information ever can.

To the extent that we continue to celebrate the traditional myth of
the entrepreneurial hero, we will slow the progress of change and adaptation that is essential to our economic success. If we are to compete
effectively in today's world, we must begin to celebrate collective entrepreneurship, endeavors in which the whole of the effort is greater than
the sum of individual contributions. We need to honor our teams more,
our aggressive leaders and maverick geniuses less.

* * *

The older and still dominant American myth involves two kinds of actors: entrepreneurial heroes and industrial drones—the inspired and the perspired.

In this myth entrepreneurial heroes personify freedom and creativity. They come up with the Big Ideas and build the organizations—the Big Machines—that turn them into reality. They take the initiative, devise technological and organizational innovations, discover new solutions to old problems. They are the men and women who start vibrant new companies, turn around failing companies, and shake up staid ones. To all endeavors, they apply daring and imagination.

The myth of the entrepreneurial hero is as old as America and has served us well in a number of ways. We like to see ourselves as born mavericks and fixers. Our entrepreneurial drive has long been our distinguishing trait. Generations of inventors and investors have kept us on the technological frontier. In a world of naysayers and traditionalists, the American character has always stood out—cheerfully optimistic, willing to run risks, ready to try anything. During World War II, it was the rough-and-ready American GI who could fix the stalled jeep in Normandy while the French regiment only looked on.

Horatio Alger captured this spirit in hundreds of stories. With titles like *Bound to Rise, Luck and Pluck,* and *Sink or Swim,* they inspired millions of readers with a gloriously simple message: In America you can go from rags to riches. The plots were essentially the same; like any successful entrepreneur, Alger knew when he was on to a good thing. A fatherless, penniless boy—possessed of great determination, faith, and courage—seeks his fortune. All manner of villain tries to tempt him, divert him, or separate him from his small savings. But in the end, our hero prevails—not just through pluck; luck plays a part too—and by the end of the story he is launched on his way to fame and fortune.

At the turn of the century Americans saw fiction and reality sometimes converging. Edward Harriman began as a $5-a-week office boy and came to head a mighty railroad empire. John D. Rockefeller rose from a clerk in a commission merchant's house to become one of the world's richest men. Andrew Carnegie started as a $1.20-a-week bobbin boy in a Pittsburgh cotton mill and became the nation's foremost steel magnate. In the early 1900s, when boys were still reading the Alger tales, Henry Ford made his fortune mass-producing the Model T and in the process became both a national folk hero and a potential presidential candidate.

Alger's stories gave the country a noble ideal—a society in which imagination and effort summoned their just reward. The key virtue was self-reliance; the admirable man was the self-made man; the goal was to be your own boss. Andrew Carnegie articulated the prevailing view: "Is any would-be businessman . . . content in forecasting his future, to figure himself as labouring all his life for a fixed salary? Not one, I am sure. In this you have the dividing line between business and nonbusiness; the one is master and depends on profits, the other is servant and depends on salary."

The entrepreneurial hero still captures the American imagination. Inspired by the words of his immigrant father, who told him, "You could be anything you want to be, if you wanted it bad enough and were willing to work for it," Lido Iacocca worked his way up to the presidency of Ford Motor Company, from which he was abruptly fired by Henry Ford II, only to go on to rescue Chrysler from bankruptcy, thumb his nose at Ford in a best-selling autobiography, renovate the Statue of Liberty, and gain mention as a possible presidential candidate. Could Horatio Alger's heroes have done any better?

Peter Ueberroth, son of a traveling aluminum salesman, worked his way through college, single-handedly built a $300 million business, went on to organize the 1984 Olympics, became *Time* magazine's Man of the Year and the commissioner of baseball. Steven Jobs built his own computer company from scratch and became a multimillionaire before his thirtieth birthday. Stories of entrepreneurial heroism come from across the economy and across the country: professors who create whole new industries and become instant millionaires when their inventions go from the laboratory to the marketplace; youthful engineers who quit their jobs, strike out on their own, and strike it rich.

In the American economic mythology these heroes occupy center stage: "Fighters, fanatics, men with a lust for contest, a gleam of creation, and a drive to justify their break from the mother company," says George Gilder. Prosperity for all depends on the entrepreneurial vision of a few rugged individuals.

*   *   *

If the entrepreneurial heroes hold center stage in this drama, the rest of the vast work force plays a supporting role—supporting and unheralded. Average workers in this myth are drones—cogs in the Big Machines, so many interchangeable parts, unable to perform without direction from above. They are put to work for their hands, not for their minds or imaginations. Their jobs typically appear by the dozens in the help-wanted sections of daily newspapers. Their routines are unvaried. They have little opportunity to use judgment or creativity. To the entrepreneurial hero belongs all the inspiration; the drones are governed by the rules and valued for their reliability and pliability.

These average workers are no villains—but they are certainly no heroes. Uninteresting and uninterested, goes the myth, they lack creative spark and entrepreneurial vision. These are, for example, the nameless and faceless workers who lined up for work in response to Henry Ford's visionary offer of a $5-per-day paycheck. At best, they put in a decent effort in executing the entrepreneurial hero's grand design. At worst, they demand more wages and benefits for less work, do the minimum expected of them, or function as blank bureaucrats mired in standard operating procedure.

The entrepreneurial hero and the worker drone together personify the mythic version of how the American economic system works. The system needs both types, it is assumed. But rewards and treatment for the two are as different as the roles themselves: The entrepreneurs should be disciplined through clear rules and punishments. Considering the overwhelming importance attached to the entrepreneur in this paradigm, the difference seems appropriate. For, as George Gilder has written, "All of us are dependent for our livelihood and progress not on a vast and predictable machine, but on the creativity and courage of the particular men who accept the risks which generate our riches."

* * *

There is just one fatal problem with this dominant myth: It is obsolete. The economy that it describes no longer exists. By clinging to the myth, we subscribe to an outmoded view of how to win economic success—a view that on a number of counts endangers our economic future.

In today's global economy the Big Ideas pioneered by American entrepreneurs travel quickly to foreign lands. In the hands of global competitors, these ideas can undergo continuous adaptation and improvement and reemerge as new Big Ideas or as a series of incrementally improved small ideas.

The machines that American entrepreneurs have always set up so efficiently to execute their Big Ideas are equally footloose. Process technology moves around the globe to find the cheapest labor and the friendliest markets. As ideas migrate overseas, the economic and technological resources needed to implement the ideas migrate too. Workers in other parts of the world are apt to be cheaper or more productive—or both—

than workers in the United States. Around the globe, millions of potential workers are ready to underbid American labor.

Some competitor nations—Japan, in particular—have created relationships among engineers, managers, production workers, and marketing and sales people that do away with the old distinction between entrepreneurs and drones. The dynamic result is yet another basis for challenging American assumptions about what leads to competitive success.

Because of these global changes, the United States is now susceptible to competitive challenge from two directions. First, from developing nations: By borrowing the Big Ideas and process technology that come from the United States and providing the hardworking, low-paid workers, developing nations can achieve competitive advantage. Second, from the Japanese: By embracing collective entrepreneurship, the Japanese especially have found a different way to achieve competitive advantage while maintaining high real wages.

Americans continue to lead the world in breakthroughs and cutting-edge scientific discoveries. But the Big Ideas that start in this country now quickly travel abroad, where they not only get produced at high speed, at low cost, and with great efficiency but also undergo continuous development and improvement. And all too often, American companies get bogged down somewhere between invention and production.

Several product histories make the point. Americans invented the solid-state transistor in 1947. Then in 1953 Western Electric licensed the technology to Sony for $25,000—and the rest is history. A few years later, RCA licensed several Japanese companies to make color televisions —and that was the beginning of the end of color television production in the United States. Routine assembly of color televisions eventually shifted to Taiwan and Mexico. At the same time Sony and other Japanese companies pushed the technology in new directions, continuously refining it into a stream of consumer products.

In 1968 Unimation licensed Kawasaki Heavy Industries to make industrial robots. The Japanese took the initial technology and keep moving it forward. The pattern has been the same for one Big Idea after another. Americans came up with the Big Ideas for videocassette recorders, basic oxygen furnaces, microwave ovens, automobile stamping machines, computerized machine tools, integrated circuits. But these Big Ideas and many, many others quickly found their way into production in foreign countries: routine, standardized production in developing nations or continuous refinement and complex applications in Japan. Either way, the United States has lost ground.

Older industrial economies, like our own, have two options: They can try to match the low wages and discipline under which workers elsewhere in the world are willing to labor, or they can compete on the basis of how quickly and how well they transform ideas into incrementally better products. The second option is, in fact, the only one that offers the possibility of high real incomes in America. But here's the catch: A handful of lone entrepreneurs producing a few industry-making Big Ideas can't execute this second option. Innovation must become both continuous and collective. And that requires embracing a new ideal: collective entrepreneurship.

* * *

If America is to win the new global competition, we need to begin telling one another a new story in which companies compete by drawing on the talent and creativity of all their employees, not just a few maverick inventors and dynamic CEOs. Competitive advantage today comes from continuous, incremental innovation and refinement of a variety of ideas that spread throughout the organization. The entrepreneurial organization is both experience based and decentralized so that every advance builds on every previous advance and everyone in the company has the opportunity and capacity to participate.

Although this story represents a departure from tradition, it already exists, in fact, to a greater or lesser extent in every well-run American and Japanese corporation. The difference is that we don't recognize and celebrate this story—and the Japanese do.

Consider just a few of the evolutionary paths that collective entrepreneurship can take: Vacuum-tube radios became transistorized radios, then stereo pocket radios audible through earphones, then compact discs and compact-disc players, and then optical-disc computer memories. Color televisions evolve into digital televisions capable of showing several pictures simultaneously; videocassette recorders, into camcorders. A single strand of technological evolution connects electronic sewing machines, electronic typewriters, and flexible electronic workstations. Basic steels give way to high-strength and corrosion-resistant steels, then to new materials composed of steel mixed with silicon and custom-made polymers. Basic chemicals evolve into high-performance ceramics, to single-crystal silicon and high-grade crystal glass. Copper wire gives way to copper cables, then to fiber-optic cables.

These patterns reveal no clear life cycles with beginnings, middles, and ends. Unlike Big Ideas that beget standardized commodities, these products undergo a continuous process of incremental change and adaptation. Workers at all levels add value not solely or even mostly by tending machines and carrying out routines, but by continuously discovering opportunities for improvement in product and process.

In this context it makes no sense to speak of an "industry," like steel or automobiles or televisions or even banking. There are no clear borders around any of these clusters of goods or services. When products and processes are so protean, companies grow or decline not with the market for some specific good but with the creative and adaptive capacity of their workers.

Workers in such organizations constantly reinvent the company; one idea leads to another. Producing the latest generation of automobiles involves making electronic circuits that govern fuel consumption and monitor engine performance; developments in these devices lead to improved sensing equipment and software for monitoring heartbeats and moisture in the air. Producing cars also involves making flexible robots for assembling parts and linking them by computer; steady improvements in these technologies, in turn, lead to expert production systems that can be applied anywhere. What is considered the "automobile industry" thus becomes a wide variety of technologies evolving toward all sorts of applications that flow from the same strand of technological development toward different markets.

In this paradigm entrepreneurship isn't the sole province of the company's founder or its top managers. Rather, it is a capability and attitude that is diffused throughout the company. Experimentation and development go on all the time as the company searches for new ways to capture and build on the knowledge already accumulated by its workers.

Distinctions between innovation and production, between top managers and production workers, blur. Because production is a continuous process of reinvention, entrepreneurial efforts are focused on many thousands of small ideas rather than on just a few big ones. And because valuable information and expertise are dispersed throughout the organization, top management does not solve problems; it creates an environment in which people can identify and solve problems themselves.

Most of the training for working in this fashion takes place on the job. Formal education may prepare people to absorb and integrate experience, but it does not supply the experience. (See "Dick and Jane Meet the Next Economy," which follows.) No one can anticipate the precise skills that workers will need to succeed on the job when information processing, know-how, and creativity are the value added. Any job that could be fully prepared for in advance is, by definition, a job that could be exported to a low-wage country or programmed into robots and computers; a routine job is a job destined to disappear.

* * *

In collective entrepreneurship individual skills are integrated into a group; this collective capacity to innovate becomes something greater than the sum of its parts. Over time, as group members work through various problems and approaches, they learn about each other's abilities. They learn how they can help one another perform better, what each can contribute to a particular project, how they can best take advantage of one another's experience. Each participant is constantly on the lookout for small adjustments that will speed and smooth the evolution of the whole. The net result of many such small-scale adaptations, effected throughout the organization, is to propel the enterprise forward.

Collective entrepreneurship thus entails close working relationships among people at all stages of the process. If customers' needs are to be recognized and met, designers and engineers must be familiar with sales and marketing. Salespeople must also have a complete understanding of the enterprise's capacity to design and deliver specialized products. The company's ability to adapt to new opportunities and capitalize on them depends on its capacity to share information and involve everyone in the organization in a systemwide search for ways to improve, adjust, adapt, and upgrade.

Collective entrepreneurship also entails a different organizational structure. Under the old paradigm companies are organized into a series of hierarchical tiers so that supervisors at each level can make sure that subordinates act according to plan. It is a structure designed to control. But enterprises designed for continuous innovation and incremental improvement use a structure designed to spur innovation at all levels. Gaining insight into improvement of products and processes is more important than rigidly following rules. Coordination and communication replace command and control. Consequently, there are few middle-level managers and only modest differences in the status and income of senior managers and junior employees.

Simple accounting systems are no longer adequate or appropriate for monitoring and evaluating job performance: Tasks are intertwined and interdependent, and the quality of work is often more important than the quantity of work. In a system where each worker depends on

many others—and where the success of the company depends on all—
the only appropriate measurement of accomplishment is a collective one.
At the same time the reward system reflects this new approach: Profit
sharing, gain sharing, and performance bonuses all demonstrate that the
success of the company comes from the broadest contribution of all the
company's employees, not just those at the top.

Finally, under collective entrepreneurship workers do not fear technology and automation as a threat to their jobs. When workers add
value through judgment and knowledge, computers become tools that
expand their discretion. Computer-generated information can give
workers rich feedback about their own efforts, how they affect others in
the production process, and how the entire process can be improved.
One of the key lessons to come out of the General Motors–Toyota joint
venture in California is that the Japanese automaker does not rely on
automation and technology to replace workers in the plant. In fact,
human workers still occupy the most critical jobs—those where judgment and evaluation are essential. Instead, Toyota uses technology to
allow workers to focus on those important tasks where choices have to
be made. Under this approach, technology gives workers the chance
to use their imagination and their insight on behalf of the company.

*   *   *

In 1986 one of America's largest and oldest enterprises announced
that it was changing the way it assigned its personnel: The U.S. Army
discarded a system that assigned soldiers to their units individually in
favor of a system that keeps teams of soldiers together for their entire
tours of duty. An Army spokesperson explained: "We discovered that
individuals perform better when they are part of a stable group. They
are more reliable. They also take responsibility for the success of the
overall operation."

In one of its recent advertisements BellSouth captured the new story.
"BellSouth is not a bunch of individuals out for themselves," the ad
proclaimed. "We're a team."

Collective entrepreneurship is already here. It shows up in the way
our best-run companies now organize their work, regard their workers,
design their enterprises. Yet the old myth of the entrepreneurial hero
remains powerful.

Bookstores bulge with new volumes paying homage to American
CEOs. It is a familiar story; it is an engaging story. And no doubt, when
seen through the eyes of the CEO, it accurately portrays how that indi-

vidual experienced the company's success. But what gets left out time after time are the experiences of the rest of the team—the men and women at every level of the company whose contributions to the company created the success that the CEO so eagerly claims. Where are the books that celebrate their stories?

If the United States is to compete effectively in the world in a way designed to enhance the real incomes of Americans, we must bring collective entrepreneurship to the forefront of the economy. That will require us to change our attitudes, to downplay the myth of the entrepreneurial hero, and to celebrate our creative teams.

First, we will need to look for and promote new kinds of stories. In modern-day America, stories of collective entrepreneurship typically appear in the sports pages of the daily newspaper; time after time, in accounts of winning efforts we learn that the team with the best blend of talent won—the team that emphasized teamwork—not the team with the best individual athlete. The cultural challenge is to move these stories from the sports page to the business page. We need to shift the limelight from maverick founders and shake-'em-up CEOs to groups of engineers, production workers, and marketers who successfully innovate new products and services. We need to look for opportunities to tell stories about American business from the perspective of all the workers who make up the team, rather than solely from the perspective of top managers. The stories are there—we need only change our focus, alter our frame of reference, in order to find them.

Second, we will need to understand that the most powerful stories get told, not in books and newspapers, but in the everyday world of work. Whether managers know it or not, every decision they make suggests a story to the rest of the enterprise. Decisions to award generous executive bonuses or to provide plush executive dining rooms and executive parking places tell the old story of entrepreneurial heroism. A decision to lay off 10 percent of the work force tells the old story of the drone worker. Several years ago, when General Motors reached agreement on a contract with the United Auto Workers that called for a new relationship based on cooperation and shared sacrifice and then, on the same day, announced a new formula for generous executive bonuses, long-time union members simply nodded to themselves. The actions told the whole story. It is not enough to acknowledge the importance of collective entrepreneurship; clear and consistent signals must reinforce the new story.

Under collective entrepreneurship all those associated with the company become partners in its future. The distinction between entrepreneurs and drones breaks down. Each member of the enterprise participates in its evolution. All have a commitment to the company's continued success. It is the one approach that can maintain and improve America's competitive performance—and America's standard of living —over the long haul.

10

DICK AND JANE
MEET THE NEXT ECONOMY

WHAT KIND OF EDUCATION WILL THE NEXT GENERATION OF AMERICANS
need? The conventional view is that they will need *more* and *better*
education, but there is surprisingly little agreement about what *more* and
better actually mean.

Education is one of those issues about which many people have
strong opinions. This is because almost everyone has been educated. Or
more accurately, almost everyone has been *subjected* to education. Those
with the strongest views on the matter tend to be those on whom the
experience has had the least lasting effect. The truly educated person
understands how ambiguous are the goals of education, and how complex the means.

By focusing on the relationship between education and the next
economy, I do not mean to suggest that education's only, or most important, purpose is economic. To the contrary: A truly educated person
is motivated by, and can find satisfaction in, a wide array of things that
are not traded in markets or that cost very little. A just and democratic
society depends on a citizenry educated in civic responsibility rather than
economic aggrandizement.

＊　　＊　　＊

In the early postwar years most young people could look forward to jobs requiring only that they be able to learn some relatively simple task that could be repeated, over and over. That's because the American economy was organized around economies of scale. The overarching goal was high-volume standardized production in which large numbers of identical items could be produced over long runs, allowing fixed costs to be spread as widely as possible. Whether it was wheat, steel, or even insurance, the same overarching rule prevailed: Every step along the production process was to be simple and predictable so that it could be synchronized with every other step. Productivity was a function of high volume and low cost.

There was little room or need for innovation. Once in a while some-one came up with a major invention—for example, continuous casters for making steel, automobile stamping machines, plastics—but these big breakthroughs were relatively rare. In fact, innovation often was seen as a problem rather than as a solution. Innovation meant changes in prod-ucts and production processes, and such changes cost money. If the changes happened too often, it was difficult to achieve the economies of scale necessary to pay for them and still make a profit.

In fact, competitors quietly agreed not to innovate very much for fear of rocking this profitable boat. These were the days when most industries were dominated by a few large companies—the Big Three automakers, a handful of steel producers, three or four major food pro-cessors—who quietly, but efficiently, coordinated prices and investments in order to achieve the stability and predictability necessary for vast economies of scale. The tail fins on our cars grew longer, but underneath the hoods the autos remained about the same year after year, and it did not matter very much which brand one bought.

Under high-volume standardized production, as has been noted in a previous chapter, a few people at the top made all the decisions. They designed the system and planned all the standard operating procedures by which it would run. Most people followed orders. Indeed, for the production system to be stable and predictable, the majority had to follow orders exactly. Rigid work rules and job classifications posed no challenge to this hierarchical system, because every job was rigid to begin with—like cogs in a giant wheel.

A primary goal of public education within this stable system was to prepare most young people for such "cog" jobs. They had to be trained to comprehend and accept instructions, and then to implement them conscientiously. Discipline and reliability were core virtues.

A much smaller number of young people had to be prepared to act as decision makers at the top. They needed to be trained to gather information, translate the information into abstract symbols, manipulate the symbols to find answers, turn the answers into operating instructions, and then communicate the instructions downward. Here, abstract logic, clarity, and firmness were the core virtues.

Our schools were reasonably effective at preparing Americans for these two kinds of jobs. Most children graduated from high school or vocational school ready to accept cog jobs. A few were set on an advanced track through high school and into colleges that prepared them either for careers as professional managers or for the related professions of law, banking, engineering, and consulting. Productivity soared.

*   *   *

Unfortunately, high-volume standardized production can no longer provide the productivity gains needed to maintain our standard of living. In a world where routine production is footloose and millions of potential workers are eager to work for wages far lower than Americans are willing to work for, we can no longer expect to be competitive simply by producing more of the same thing we produced before, at lower cost. As the production of commodities shifts to other nations, America's competitive advantage correspondingly must shift toward work the value of which is based more on quality, flexibility, precision, and specialization than on its low cost. For example, only a small fraction of the American work force is still employed on the farm. But the food industry nevertheless accounts for close to one quarter of the jobs in the United States. That's because most of what Americans and consumers in other advanced nations now spend for food goes to the people who process, package, market, and retail it, and to the agricultural epidemiologists, geneticists, international bankers, commodity traders, chemists, and process engineers who supply the technology and money for producing it, rather than to those who actually grow and harvest it. Similarly, most of what is spent on appliances, clothing, cars, computers, air travel, or a host of other things is for designing, engineering, fabricating, and advertising, rather than for standardized, routine work. In fact, much of the growth in what has been termed services within the American economy is attributable to just such businesses.

The older industrial economies like America thus have two options: (1) They can try to match the wages for which workers elsewhere are willing to labor, or (2) they can compete on the basis of how quickly and how well they can transform ideas into incrementally better goods and services. Both paths can boost profits and improve competitiveness in the short run, but only the second can maintain and improve the standard of living of most Americans over time.

The first path—toward stable mass production—relies on cutting labor costs and leaping into wholly new product lines as old ones are played out. For managers this path has meant undertaking (or threatening) massive layoffs, moving (or threatening to move) to lower wage states and countries, parceling out work to lower-cost suppliers, automating to cut total employment, and diversifying into radically different goods and services. For workers this path has meant defending existing jobs and pay scales, grudgingly conceding lower wages and benefits, shifting burdens by accepting lower-pay scales for newly hired workers, seeking protection from foreign competition, and occasionally striking.

The second path involves increasing labor's *value*. For managers this path means continuously retraining employees for more complex tasks, automating in ways that cut routine tasks and enhance worker flexibility and creativity, diffusing responsibility for innovation, taking seriously labor's concern for job security and giving workers a stake in improved productivity via profit-linked bonuses and stock plans. For workers this second path means accepting flexible job classifications and work rules, agreeing to wage rates linked to profits and productivity improvements, and generally taking greater responsibility for the soundness and efficiency of the enterprise. The second path also involves a closer and more permanent relationship with other parties that have a stake in the firm—suppliers, dealers, creditors, even the towns and cities in which the firm resides. On this second path, all those associated with the firm become partners in its future, sharing downside risks and upside benefits. Each member of the enterprise participates in its evolution. All have a commitment to its continued success.

The second path to the next economy relies, above all, on a work force capable of rapid learning. Many important skills will be transferred informally among workers as they gain experience on the job, rather than gleaned through formal education and training. But the ability to learn on the job will depend on learning skills and attitudes developed long before.

* * *

In some respects, the training of young people in the old economy resembled the system of high-volume standardized production in which they were to take part when their training was complete: Responsibility was exercised by a very few, at the top. The majority of students were pushed, as if on an assembly line, through a preestablished sequence of steps. Each step involved particular routines and practices. Teachers— the production workers—had little discretion over what they had to do to each batch that passed through; students passively received whatever was doled out. Inspectors tried to weed out the defects, sometimes returning them to an earlier step for reworking. Most students got to the end of the assembly line, more or less ready to take their places along real assembly lines somewhere in the economy.

The premises of education in the next economy must be quite different. Just as productivity can no longer be a matter of making more of what we already make at less cost per unit, productivity in education cannot be solely a function of the numbers of children who pass standardized examinations at a lower cost per unit. Because our future economy will depend to an ever greater extent on thinking, rather than repeating learned information, future reforms must motivate teachers and students alike to engage in the *process* of learning. Rather than prescribe exactly what should be learned and how and when the information should be doled out, reformers should aim at improving students' capacities to learn. Just as in the enterprise of the future, responsibility for education must be pushed downward, to students and teachers. They must be allowed and encouraged to take more initiative in deciding what is learned, and when and how it is learned. Education modeled around long lists of facts that "every adult should know" and standardized tests will produce robots adept at Trivial Pursuit but unable to think for themselves or to innovate for the future.

How can teachers better help students learn how to learn? First, instead of giving students information along a preestablished sequence of steps and then asking them to "play back" the information on tests, the emphasis in teaching should be on educating young people to formulate problems and questions for themselves. Thus, rather than teach students to assume that problems and solutions are generated by others (as they were under high-volume standardized production), students should be led to understand that problems and questions are created, that students can have an active role in creating them, and that such critical and creative approaches can guide them through their careers.

Second, instead of teaching through repetition and drill, the emphasis should be on allowing students to experiment for themselves with solving the problems they help define. Thus, rather than conveying particular pieces of information or imposing established routines—a type of teaching and learning relevant to high-volume standardized production —teachers must help students gain the experience of working through problems and thus discovering underlying principles that help define and solve related problems.

The difference between absorbing information and gaining understanding depends on how much responsibility students are taught to accept for their own continuing learning. It is like the difference between learning how to get from one location to another in a city by having someone drive you or by driving yourself with a guide sitting beside you. In the first instance you may eventually learn the way, but you probably will learn sooner by being in the driver's seat. Indeed, if your guide also allows you to experiment a bit, warning you only when you're going down blind alleys or heading in the wrong direction, you may gain even more understanding of the terrain and thus learn how to find other places as well.

An understanding of underlying principles and patterns allows discovery of other information and gives that new information added context and meaning. The new information, in turn, permits deeper insight into the principles and patterns. As Michael Polanyi has written, "[w]e cannot comprehend the whole without seeing its parts, but we cannot see the parts without comprehending the whole." *

The habits and techniques of experimentation—of iterative discovery of parts and wholes—will be critical in the next economy, where technologies, tastes, and markets are likely to be in constant flux. Informal, on-the-job education will be a central aspect of work. Formal education and training will no longer be limited to young people but will be available on a continuing basis to workers throughout their working lives—an accepted and expected aspect of one's career. A work force capable of taking responsibility for its own continuous learning will prove a more precious national asset than countless new factories and equipment.

*　　*　　*

In the old economy, a relatively few people at the top could analyze and plan the production process by themselves and then issue operating instructions to everyone else. So long as professional managers and their professional aides—bankers, lawyers, accountants, and engineers—got it "right" on paper, it was assumed that the rest would follow automat-

---

* *The Study of Man* (Chicago: University of Chicago Press, 1958), pg. 29.

ically. But paper professionals are far less relevant to the future economy. As has been noted, the weakest link in the American economy is between ideas and implementation, between paper and product. Thus, if our business enterprises are to be as flexible and innovative at all levels as they need to be, our youngsters must be prepared to work with and through other people. While there will always be a need for a certain number of solo practitioners, the more usual requirement will be that combinations of individual skills are greater than their sums. Most of the important work will be done by groups, rather than by individual experts.

Learning to collaborate suggests a different kind of education than one designed to prepare a relatively few talented young people to become professional experts. Instead of emphasizing the quiet and solitary performance of specialized tasks, a greater emphasis should be placed on interactive communications linked to group problem–definitions and solutions. Students should learn to articulate, clarify, and then restate for one another how they determine questions and find answers. Rather than be trained to communicate specialized instructions and requests—skills relevant to high-volume standardized production—students should learn how to share their understandings and build on each other's insights.

Communication skills are only one aspect of collaboration. Young people also must be taught how to work constructively together. Instead of emphasizing individual achievement and competition, the emphasis in the classroom should be on group performance. Students need to learn how to seek and accept criticism from their peers, to solicit help, and to give credit to others, where appropriate. They must also learn to negotiate—to articulate their own needs, to discern what others need and see things from others' perspectives, and to discover mutually beneficial outcomes.

The "tracking" system, by which students are grouped in the classroom according to the speed of their learning, is another vestige of high-volume standardized production—the deluxe models moving along a different conveyor belt from the economy cars. This may be an efficient way to cram information into young minds with differing capacities to absorb it; but tracking or grouping can also reduce young people's capacities to learn from and collaborate with one another. Rather than separate fast learners from slow learners in the classroom, all children (with only the most obvious exceptions) should remain together so that class unity and cooperation are the norm. Faster learners would thus learn how to help the slower ones, while the slower ones would be pushed harder to make their best effort.

In sum, it is not enough to produce a cadre of young people with specialized skills. If our enterprises are to be the scenes of collective entrepreneurship—as they must be—experts must have the ability to share their skills broadly and transform them into organizational achievement; and others must be prepared to learn from them.

III

OF COLD
AND
TEPID
WARS

11

THE RISE
OF TECHNO-NATIONALISM

ON OCTOBER 23, 1986, FUJITSU, LTD., THE LARGE JAPANESE ELECTRON-
ics company, announced that it would buy Fairchild Semiconductor Corporation, a Silicon Valley firm. (Fairchild had needed cash in order to
stay competitive; its executives had approached Fujitsu, which had been
seeking to acquire an American technology company.) The announcement of the proposed sale was greeted with dismay in Washington.
Fairchild produces high-speed electronic circuits on tiny chips of silicon,
which instruct all sorts of weapons systems in how they should operate.
Between a third and a half of Fairchild's production is sold to American
defense contractors. Pentagon officials worried that the proposed sale
would put critical technology into the hands of the Japanese. Officials in
the Commerce Department were concerned that the deal would give
Fujitsu control over related chip technologies that are used in many
American products, from automobiles to telecommunications equipment
—at a time when American competitiveness is thought to be in jeopardy.

The Reagan Administration never decided whether to ban the sale.
It didn't have to. Citing the "rising political controversy" in the United
States, Fujitsu finally decided to drop the deal on its own. But the concern
that the proposed deal aroused is itself noteworthy. Fairchild is not the

only American company producing such specialized chips. Technically, it is not even an American company; it was bought in 1979 by Schlumberger, the French oil-field-services firm. The proposed sale to Fujitsu would violate no American law. Nevertheless, the deal touched a raw nerve. All over America there is growing worry that the Japanese are running off with our technology.

This new concern is, I believe, misplaced. Americans are correct to worry about national technological prowess but not about Japanese access to our technology. The emerging debate over how to restore America's technological preeminence misconstrues the problem and thus advances the wrong solutions. The underlying predicament is not that the Japanese are exploiting our discoveries but that we can't turn basic inventions into new products nearly as fast or as well as they can. Rather than guard our technological breakthroughs, we should learn how better to make use of breakthroughs wherever they occur around the globe. In this, the Japanese may have much to teach us.

* * *

With the important exceptions of restrictions on the transfer of "sensitive" technologies to the Soviets and their allies, on the sale of major weapons systems, and on the pursuit of classified research by Eastern-bloc nationals, techno-globalism has been the norm in America. From the techno-globalist's point of view, it is meaningless to speak of America's discoveries and technological breakthroughs relative to those of Japan, West Germany, or any other friendly nation, because there is no way to separate "our" technological advances from "theirs." Technological development is a joint product of multinational institutions— universities, research laboratories, corporations, even defense programs —that link talented people from all corners of the globe through computers, satellite communications, and jet airplanes.

This organizing principle has taken deep root in America. Basic research is now a worldwide undertaking. The scientists and engineers who populate American universities and laboratories typically think of themselves as members of a global community of researchers who work jointly on projects, meet periodically at international conferences, exchange papers, and publish their findings worldwide. Their graduate students come from every nation on earth. Even the funding of American university research is now global. A substantial portion is sponsored by foreign companies, especially Japanese.

Foreign companies, meanwhile, are setting up research laboratories in the United States and staffing them with American scientists and engineers. American companies are doing much the same abroad—especially in Japan. More than 180 Japanese scientists and technicians now populate DuPont's Yokohama laboratory, where they develop new materials technologies. IBM is investing heavily in Japanese research: At IBM's Tokyo Research Laboratory, tucked away behind the far side of the Imperial Palace in downtown Tokyo, a small army of Japanese engineers is busy perfecting image-processing technology. At IBM's Kanagawa lab, in Yamato City, Japan, fifteen hundred researchers are developing hardware and software for the next generation of computers.

In 1988 Japanese companies placed more than $500 million in U.S. venture-capital funds. Rather than high financial returns, the Japanese want licensing, marketing, and joint-venture agreements with the companies they back. American companies likewise are buying some of their most complex technologies from foreign firms. West Germany's Siemens and Canada's Northern Telecom have become key suppliers of electronic components used by American makers of telecommunications equipment. West German and Italian companies are supplying other American manufacturers with precision castings, forgings, and ball bearings.

Even the Defense Department, which is responsible for funding about one third of all the research and development undertaken by U.S. corporations, has for the most part adopted an ecumenical attitude toward the advancement of new technologies. In 1983 it got Tokyo's agreement to allow Japanese companies to sell or license technology to American corporations working under contract to the Pentagon (marking the first time that the Japanese government had allowed Japanese companies to work even indirectly on American defense contracts). In 1986 the Pentagon secured West Germany's and Japan's cooperation on research for the Strategic Defense Initiative (unceremoniously dubbed "Star Wars"). Our allies remain skeptical that Star Wars will ever work as advertised. But they were seduced into joining the effort by the prospect of picking up expertise in the technologies involved—technologies that they believed would be important to their future economic competitiveness.

Techno-globalism, in sum, has come to be America's central, albeit tacit, organizing principle for developing new technologies. The notion of "American" technology has thus become a meaningless concept. Across a broad expanse of the globe (excluding little but the Soviet Union and its allies) national boundaries have in this respect become less and less relevant.

*   *   *

The principle of techno-globalism has helped American universities, corporations, and the Pentagon accomplish what each of these institutions has understood to be its primary goal: generating, respectively, new knowledge, high profits, and state-of-the-art weaponry. But other interests are at stake as well, and they appear to be in fundamental conflict with these more proximate goals. Increasingly, techno-globalism is being challenged by a different organizing principle, which looks to America's relative prowess—both military and economic—in the world of sovereign nations.

There is a new concern that as America becomes ever more dependent on "them" for advanced technologies, our economic leadership will be threatened and our national defense imperiled. Two related phenomena lie behind this anxiety. The first is America's trade balance in high-technology goods, like computers, communications equipment, and scientific instruments, which in 1986 turned negative for the first time ever. This negative balance is owing in part to the insatiable appetite of American consumers and government officials for all sorts of imports (of which high-tech products are a mere subset), and in part to the sluggishness of overall foreign demand. But the loss of competitiveness in high-technology products within our domestic markets is troublesome nonetheless. As our indebtedness to the rest of the world—particularly to Japan—steadily mounts, the loss of high-tech competitiveness threatens our standard of living. The only way to pay off the debt without dramatically lowering our standard of living sometime in the future is to achieve equally dramatic increases in productivity. To become that much more productive, we would need to perfect and apply the very technologies in which Japan is gaining dominance. The knowledge gleaned by perfecting each new generation of technology spills over into other areas of the economy, creating a national pool of talent and technological experience that can improve productivity overall. Because each new generation of technology builds on that which came before, once off the technological escalator it's difficult to get back on. At best, our standard of living would continue to fall relative to that of the Japanese.

The second phenomenon is our new commercial and military vulnerability to the Japanese, should they choose to hold back their high-tech gadgets from us. Japanese microelectronics, in particular, now lie at the heart of many American products—from telecommunications equipment to automobiles. They are also vital to our advanced weapons systems. Most primary defense contractors on advanced weapons systems are American firms, but more and more, their subcontractors supplying the most advanced electronic components are Japanese. On the basis of data supplied by the Board of Army Science and Technology and the International Trade Commission, I estimate that 40 percent, by value, of the advanced electronics finding their way into American weapons systems are now coming from Japan. If the present trend continues, the proportion will rise to 55 percent by 1992. A substantial portion of the advanced electronics for the Strategic Defense Initiative will be produced in Japan.

In many cases American companies that were on the leading edge of microelectronics several years ago have simply dropped out of the running. With the costs of perfecting each new generation of technology escalating rapidly, and the time interval during which the investment can be recouped growing shorter, the price of staying in the race has often become too high relative to the return. A world-class factory for fabricating semiconductors now costs around $200 million. By 1995, when X-ray lithography will be used to fabricate semiconductors, the cost will be $1 billion. Few firms will be able to afford to stay in the race. Monsanto used to produce "float-zone" silicon, a material used in fabricating high-power electronic switching devices, indispensable to space-based weaponry. But since Monsanto abandoned the market, in 1983, the Pentagon has been totally dependent on Japanese companies for it. In 1987 Intel announced that it would cease production of "bubble" memories, used primarily in fighter planes and communications satellites. This left the Pentagon dependent on Hitachi and Fujitsu. The National Security Agency, charged with electronic eavesdropping and communications security, buys almost all its ceramic packages (used to house and protect the chip circuits) from one Japanese company, Kyocera. Richard Reynolds, director of the Defense Sciences Office at the Defense Advanced Research Projects Agency, summed up the situation: "In some cases you either buy from Japan or you don't get it."

Most of the world's memory chips—the fingernail-size circuits that drive just about every electronic gadget you can name, including almost all of the electronics necessary for Star Wars—are now made in Japan, which is also their largest market. Japanese companies are on the way to dominating world production of gallium-arsenide computer chips (capable of processing data much faster than conventional silicon chips), on which Star Wars is particularly dependent. The innards of supercomputers, also vital to Star Wars, increasingly come from Japan as well. Cray

—the largest American manufacturer of supercomputers—must get its advanced memory chips from either Fujitsu or Hitachi. Japanese companies are even taking over the technologies needed to make advanced memory chips—everything from the microlithography that prints tiny circuits on slivers of silicon to the manufacture of the ceramic casings surrounding the circuits. Japanese companies are now the dominant producers of equipment for scrubbing and baking silicon wafers, for insulating the circuits, inspecting and testing them, and assembling and packaging them. The Japanese dominate world production of the materials of which chips are made, such as high-quality silicon and quartz glass. Japanese dominance extends even to the construction companies that produce "clean rooms," in which advanced chips are made.

In 1980 fifteen American companies, all of them profitable, were producing most of the world's memory chips, and American companies produced most of the components and equipment for making chips. By now, most American producers of chip-making equipment have closed up shop. Erich Bloch, the director of the National Science Foundation, said, "The [American chip] industry is going downhill at a faster rate than anybody ever thought possible."

*   *   *

The Pentagon's new vulnerability in microelectronics is now a subject of heated debate in Washington, particularly at the highest reaches of the Pentagon and the National Security Council (NSC). In 1987 the NSC circulated a draft report on the extent of American dependence on Japanese microelectronics. The report is notable not only for linking the two kinds of vulnerability—military and economic—but also for portraying America's interests in terms quite different from the prevailing globalism:

> Leadership in research and development in advanced (non-silicon) semiconductor materials and devices seems to already be passing to Japan, especially in the optical electronic fields which may be the basis of the highest performance end products of the future. . . . With some significant exceptions computer software R&D is still clearly an American strength, but the Japanese are becoming expert in the architecture of mainframes and supercomputers, and obviously in the manufacturing and engineering of personal computers. Telecommunications component research is becoming dominated by the Japanese, and while their strengths in downstream system and network

industries are more limited, the trend is toward Japanese leadership in some communication systems based on their advantages in semiconductor components. Industrial automation is a field where the Japanese not only already dominate the present market, but also research and development in most subdisciplines. Clearly the conventional model of U.S. technological leadership in basic research followed by more successful Japanese commercial exploitation is no longer accurate in many of the critical technologies targeted by the Japanese.

According to the NSC report, this trend threatens not only America's defense capabilities but also its standard of living:

> By the turn of the century, microelectronics will certainly have major direct effects upon the performance of industries which will directly account for perhaps a quarter of GNP, and which have powerful effects upon military capabilities, economy-wide productivity, and living standards. These include automobiles, industrial automation, computer systems, defense and aerospace products, telecommunications, and many consumer goods. . . . If the United States loses competitive advantage in these industries, its productivity, living standards, and growth will suffer severely. Moreover, these industries are dominated by a few nations and firms so that competitive advantage brings significant economic profits and political influence. Thus if the United States becomes a net importer and a technically inferior producer, it would also become a less independent, less influential, and less secure nation.

The immediate danger, according to the NSC report, is that Japanese high-tech firms could withhold their advanced chips and related technologies from American firms that have become dependent on them and could thus "impede the ability of the United States to compete in almost any area of manufacturing."

The report speaks of America's declining technological strength and of Japan's coming technological lead. The adjectives alone convey the critical difference between this view and that of techno-globalism.

*   *   *

New policies are being proposed to help America pursue advanced technologies. The policies take many forms and are being advocated, piecemeal, in many quarters. Their unifying characteristic is the unambiguously *national* orientation they would give to the development of new technologies. The goal is to keep technological knowledge *here*. In contrast to the prevailing principle of techno-globalism, this one might be called techno-nationalism.

Listen to the new voice of techno-nationalism: When asked whether he would support a proposal to boost federal research funds for American universities on the condition that the research be restricted to American citizens, Richard Cyert, the president of Pittsburgh's prestigious Carnegie-Mellon University (one of America's centers of research on advanced industrial processes), responded affirmatively. "I'm sure it would be unpopular, in the sense that we like to think of ourselves as world citizens. . . . But we want to have America get some temporary advantage from the research that we can do."

Watch Congress turn toward techno-nationalism: The Federal Technology and Transfer Act of 1986, quietly passed by the Ninety-ninth Congress, authorizes America's national laboratories to license their inventions to private firms—but not just to any company willing to pay the highest price. The legislation requires that preference be given to American firms. Watch American companies seek government's help in furthering techno-nationalism: The Semiconductor Industry Association, a trade group of American chip makers, has joined forces with a congeries of giant American computer firms to create an ultramodern chip-production facility. Known as Sematech, the plant is to be a proving ground for state-of-the-art equipment necessary for making the next generation of chips. "This is our last chance," the president of the trade group told me in late 1987. "If we lose the ability to make this equipment in America, we might as well fold up the tent." Every major American chip producer and computer manufacturer has signed up to participate in the project, the cost of which will exceed $1 billion over the next five years. The Pentagon has agreed to pay a substantial portion of the cost. But here's the condition: Whatever state-of-the-art devices emerge from this ambitious project must go only to American companies.

One of the strongest recommendations to emerge from all the policy panels, industry groups, and think tanks is to increase federal spending for American research and development. In a report to the secretary of defense, for example, the Defense Science Board recommended that the U.S. government spend roughly $2 billion over the next five years for semiconductor research and development. About half that sum would go to the above-mentioned project, from which foreign companies would be banned. The remainder would establish university "centers for excellence" in scientific and engineering research (open to American researchers) and directly fund semiconductor research by American firms.

We can expect more of the same in the future. Democrats in Congress are busily devising plans for spurring American technology by spending more on research and development by American companies. The White House, meanwhile, has been exploring ways to tap Star Wars research for American commercial technology and to ward off further Japanese takeovers of American companies in "strategic" industries. The Bush Administration wants to enlarge the budget of the National Science Foundation, sponsor science and technology centers in American universities, and fund giant research projects, such as a $6 billion particle accelerator.

The overriding goal of these initiatives is to protect future American technological breakthroughs from exploitation at the hands of foreigners, especially the Japanese. In contrast to techno-globalism, this new principle presumes the possibility—indeed, the necessity—of viewing American technology as a body of knowledge separate and distinct from that possessed by other nations. Technology is viewed as something that can be uniquely American—developed here, contained within the nation's borders, applied in America by Americans. It is like a precious commodity that we should save for ourselves rather than allow foreigners to carry off.

* * *

Techno-nationalism faces three formidable difficulties. First and most obvious is the logistical challenge of confining new knowledge within national borders. Modern technology typically doesn't leak out in boxcars or briefcases. Instead, blueprints and designs flow out over the airwaves, by satellite, from one computer to another.

The second challenge is more paradoxical. As we have seen, American universities, corporations, and even the Defense Department are now international endeavors. Their technological advances come by way of global projects that draw upon talented people the world over. To graft techno-nationalism onto these techno-global systems leads to absurd results.

The paradox becomes clear when considering how any of these initiatives might actually work in practice. How, for example, might an American university go about the task of excluding foreigners from major research projects? The first problem would be how to define who was foreign. A good many American university professors and graduate students are of foreign origin and only later become American citizens. Some are permanent resident aliens; some, here on temporary visas, hope and expect to remain in the United States. Some are American citizens who plan to teach and live abroad for long periods of time after they finish their research, and who will thus carry off whatever they learn. What about an American citizen employed by a Japanese company? Should he be excluded as well? Beyond the problem of deciding who should be excluded, there is the issue of what such people should be barred from doing. Should foreigners be permitted to talk with American researchers about what's being learned? May they assist the American researchers—as research assistants or as administrative, clerical, or maintenance workers?

The questions grow even more tangled when it comes to distinguishing between American and foreign companies. Only American firms will be allowed to participate in the Sematech project; American firms will get first crack at inventions coming from national laboratories; the Defense Department doesn't want foreigners owning American high-tech companies. But what's an "American" firm?

Suppose that most of the shareholders and directors of a company are foreign, but its headquarters is in the United States and most of its employees are American. (This describes Fairchild before Fujitsu sought to take it over.) Does this firm qualify? Or suppose that a large and growing portion of the firm's shareholders are foreign, and 40 percent of its employees live and work abroad. Does this firm qualify? (It's IBM.)

Or consider an American-owned and -managed firm that has factories and research laboratories around the globe. This firm continuously applies what it discovers in one country to new products and processes being developed in another and regularly shifts its scientists and engineers around the world. Should it be given special access to American technology? And what about an American-based firm that shares its technology with a Japanese firm and markets the Japanese-made products in the United States? In both instances American firms are apt to be exploiting American technology but using it elsewhere. Do these firms pass muster?

Most American high-tech companies are well along in the process of losing their uniquely American identities. Faced with Japanese competitors that have more money to spend on research and development, and better-trained employees, even the largest and most well-endowed American firms have concluded that joining them is a wiser strategy than trying to beat them. Motorola—one of America's leading electronics companies—is linking up with Toshiba to build a new chip-making factory in Sendai, Japan. Toshiba is supplying the technology needed for the next generation of memory chips, and Motorola the technology for the next generation of logic chips (Motorola still has an edge in this category of chip technology, which instructs computers in how to solve problems). AT&T has joined with Fujitsu to challenge IBM's dominance in computer systems. In both deals the American firms are sharing their latest technology with their Japanese partners, and vice versa. If the underlying purpose of techno-nationalism is to keep American technology here, then presumably Motorola, AT&T, and all the other American electronics firms now sharing technology with their Japanese counterparts should be excluded—lest the Japanese gain instant access to our technology. But by this criterion few "American" firms—if any—would remain eligible.

These paradoxes suggest an inconvenient truth: Techno-nationalism cannot be superimposed on institutions organized on the basis of techno-globalism. Even if it were clearly in the national interest to try to keep America's technological learning at home, this goal is too sharply at odds with the premises on which our universities and corporations are based for it to provide a meaningful guide for public policy.

* * *

The third challenge that the principle of techno-nationalism faces goes even deeper: It is not in America's interest to bar foreigners from the fruits of our research and development. Technology is not like a scarce commodity, to be hoarded up. Its real value to us is only indirectly related to the gadgets it spawns at any given time. Nor does its value lie in information that can be conveyed through data, blueprints, or instructions. The value of technological learning is a certain kind of knowledge, founded in shared experience. It exists in people's heads. Thus, the real worry is not that we are becoming dependent on Japan's high-tech gadgets but that we are losing the ability to transform new discoveries into gadgets nearly as efficiently as they can.

Most advances in technology build on what has come before—on prior technological experience. A dramatic discovery or ground-breaking invention may win a prize and bring fame to its progenitor. But such breakthroughs generally mean less to a nation's economic or military might than the speed and success with which they are absorbed, improved upon, and incorporated into new products and processes.

Scientists, engineers, and tinkerers of all sorts progress mostly by applying their understanding of technologies to new problems. They rearrange solutions in new ways, make incremental improvements in previous methods of doing things, and try out new variations on themes.

Experience—the breadth and depth of familiarity with technology—is what determines the technological fecundity of a society. Mere information, such as specific data about the latest discovery or blueprints of a new invention, is relatively useless for designing future generations of technology. It may solve an immediate technological problem, but it does not provide experience for solving the next one. It supplies answers but it does not teach. (Indeed, access to information may actually inhibit learning. As anyone knows who has tried to solve a puzzle with the answer book open, the ready availability of help can substitute for direct experience and thus make it more difficult to do it yourself the next time.)

What does it mean, then, to speak of America's (or any nation's) technological prowess? Basic inventions do of course yield improvements, but these are easily disseminated as information, in blueprints, codes, and instructions—which reach Seoul almost as soon as they reach St. Louis. What's crucial is the extent of American engineers' and production workers' technological experience—their cumulative insights into how technologies work and how they can be adapted and improved—for only prior experience enables one to absorb the new technological learning and translate it into new experience.

The warnings now issuing from Washington that Japan might hold back certain high-tech gadgets mistakenly assumes that high-tech gadgets are like strategic raw materials—the kind of thing that one shouldn't have to depend on a foreign power to supply. But the analogy is inapt. These days our security depends less on ready access to blueprints or materials than on our collective ability to apply knowledge quickly to solving new problems. What needs to be stockpiled is not gadgets or things but experience and competence. As long as our engineers and production workers have accumulated experience in the technologies on which the Japanese gadgets are based, they can easily contrive replacements. Indeed, because high technologies evolve so quickly, both our military security and our commercial competitiveness turn on how quickly we can transform emerging technologies into the *next* generation of gadgets.

Here we come to the nub of our problem. Americans continue to lead the world in scientific discoveries and Nobel laureates. But we have had difficulty turning our basic inventions into streams of commercial products. As I have emphasized before, we tend to get bogged down somewhere between the big breakthrough and its application.

Why have the Japanese been so much more successful than we have in turning basic inventions into new products? Because Japanese engineers and production workers have been getting more technological experience than Americans. Given a choice between buying a particular high-tech component off the shelf from the Japanese or spending more money to build it from scratch, most American executives opt for the former. Building the component would enable American engineers and production workers to learn the technology from the inside and thus to improve on it in the future. But American executives, it seems, cannot guarantee themselves any harvest from investing in the experience of their engineers and production workers. American engineers change jobs, on average, every two years. Their restlessness creates geographic centers of technology like Route 128 around Boston, and Silicon Valley. This is good for the engineers but bad for the firms that have invested in them. Why go to the expense of giving them valuable experience when they'll just walk off with it? Japanese engineers and production workers, in contrast, tend to stay put for life. Investments in their technological competence are more certain to reap returns to the corporation that makes them.

* * *

Investments in experience cannot be protected like investments in real estate or machinery. Investors can claim and defend their stake in tangible assets but not in value that resides in people's minds. American executives cannot force their workers to stay with the firm. Patents are no answer when the learning is cumulative, taking the form of increased intuition and judgment, and yielding a stream of innovations over a number of years. As global competition has intensified and profits have been squeezed, more and more American firms have chosen to buy from the Japanese or otherwise link up with Japanese firms rather than build for themselves. Accordingly, investments in Americans' technological experience have declined. Even Route 128 and Silicon Valley are showing signs of faltering.

The answer is not to hold back our basic inventions from the Japanese. It is to help corporations profit from investments in the technological competence of Americans and thus give American engineers and production workers experience in quickly turning basic inventions into first-class products. The nationality of the corporation's shareholders and directors—and whether the corporation goes by a Japanese or an American name—is irrelevant to the task. Today's corporations engage in research, fabrication, and production all over the globe. Their retained earnings are invested wherever they can get the highest return. Which nation's engineers and production workers will gain technological experience? Our national interest lies in ensuring that Americans get at least a fair share.

Applying this logic to Fujitsu's proposed purchase of Fairchild suggests a response quite the opposite of that evinced by Washington. Fujitsu is one of the world's leaders in the production of complex memory chips. Making advanced memory chips is a skill that Americans need. Rather than trying to prevent Fujitsu from buying Fairchild, we should have invited Fujitsu into America to design and produce its most complex chips here. If Fujitsu needed to be coaxed to do so, we should have subsidized it.

Japanese companies like Fujitsu can help American workers discover how to transform research findings into practical innovations of all kinds. Our national policy goal should be to ensure that they do indeed teach us and that we do in fact learn.

12

HIGH-TECH WARFARE

THE UNITED STATES IS ENGAGED IN TWO GLOBAL CONTESTS. THE FIRST IS a political contest with the Soviet Union. The second is an economic contest with Japan. The first began shortly after World War II; it requires complex weapons systems and rests on a delicate set of alliances and spheres of influence. The second began about a dozen years ago; it requires complex technologies and depends on an intricate set of trading relationships. Both contests are critical to the future of America—the second quite as much as the first. But Washington seems incapable of viewing international relations in any terms other than cold war diplomacy.

* * *

The fiasco over the Soviet gas pipeline in October 1981 illustrates the problem. After six years of negotiation, the Western European nations agreed to supply the Soviets with equipment to build a pipeline that would carry natural gas thirty-six hundred miles from the Siberian fields to Western Europe. The equipment was to include compressors, which would work like giant fans to push the gas along the pipeline, and some 125 turbines, which would supply the power to operate the compressors. The most intricate part of a turbine is the rotor—a collection of carefully shaped blades, arranged along a shaft. Their manufacture requires sophisticated casting techniques and exotic metals. The rotors were to be designed and supplied by America's General Electric Company; equipment for the compressors was to come from other American companies, such as Dresser, Caterpillar, and Cooper Industries. But citing the Soviet Union's "heavy and direct responsibility for the repression in Poland," the Reagan Administration abruptly barred American export of any high technologies to the Soviets, forcing the cancellation of these subcontracts, which were worth some $250 million.

The ban did not have much effect on the timetable for the pipeline, however, since several European companies, which hold licenses from the U.S. firms to manufacture American-designed equipment on their own, stepped in to fill the gap. Even this inconvenience appeared to be short-lived when, at the Versailles economic summit the following June, then Secretary of State Alexander Haig suggested to Western European leaders that the President would ease the pipeline restrictions if the Europeans would limit their practice of extending favorable credit terms to the Soviets. The Europeans accepted the bargain, agreeing to raise their interest rates on Soviet loans. But then the other shoe dropped: On June 18 President Reagan, apparently irked at statements by some Europeans that the limits on export credits were meaningless, extended the original pipeline ban to cover sale to the Soviets by foreign subsidiaries of American companies (technically, any firm in which an American company has a controlling interest, even if that means ownership of a comparatively small percentage of the foreign company's outstanding shares) and also to include sales by foreign firms of American-licensed technology. The reason given for this sweeping ban was that the Soviets had simply failed to respond to the earlier sanctions.

European reaction was swift. The French and Italian governments promptly instructed their companies to defy the American ban and fulfill the Soviet contracts. West German Chancellor Helmut Schmidt urged German companies also to flout the U.S. sanctions. Even Margaret Thatcher, Reagan's ideological soul mate, invoked Britain's 1980 law on trade, which limits the extraterritoriality of U.S. laws. On August 25 the French subsidiary of Dallas-based Dresser Industries began loading three large compressors onto a cargo ship bound for the Soviet Union. Other European companies followed suit.

The pipeline simply meant too much to the Europeans to bow to American pressure. It promised jobs for several thousand European workers (a weighty consideration with over ten million Europeans un-employed), orders worth at least $11 billion, and a source of energy from somewhere other than the Persian Gulf.

Even if the pipeline ban could have been enforced, it would not have seriously hurt the Soviets. At most, it would have postponed the building of the pipeline for one or two years while European companies rede-signed the turbines and the Soviets produced substitute rotors. In the meantime, the Soviets would have collected sizable penalties and perfor-mance bonds from the European companies in default. Ironically, the only internationally traded items that the Soviets really needed, and on which a widely observed trade embargo might therefore have had a noticeable effect on Soviet policy, had nothing to do with the pipeline. It was grain. For every $160 million in grain the Soviets buy abroad, they save enough resources to produce $700 million worth of oil. And yet, eager to placate hard-hit Midwestern farmers, the Reagan Administra-tion—at the height of the pipeline controversy—extended for another year the U.S. agreement to sell the Soviet Union up to twenty-three million tons of wheat and corn. In light of the grain agreement, Reagan's insistence that the nations of Western Europe must bear the cost of whipping the Soviets into line seemed churlish, if not duplicitous. The Administration's main argument, that Soviet gas sales would earn the Soviets hard currency while American grain sales to the Soviets would cost them currency, would have been stronger was not the currency earned by the Soviets on the gas sales merely passed on to American farmers in exchange for grain.

Even less convincing was the Administration's concern that the pipeline would make the Europeans overly dependent on the Soviets and therefore render them more vulnerable to Soviet power politics. By the most optimistic forecast, Soviet gas exports to Western Europe would account for less than one fourth of Europe's gas consumption by 1990 —with much of the rest still coming from the Middle East. And that fraction of Europe's gas needs would amount to a much smaller fraction —no more than 8 percent—of Western Europe's total energy bill. From the standpoint of Europe's vulnerability, it seemed wiser to diversify energy supplies than to continue to gamble on a steady supply from the Middle East. More to the point, with its missiles poised at Europe's major cities and its tanks amassed along Europe's borders, the Soviet Union had more effective means for twisting Europe's collective arm than sacrificing revenues on its sales of natural gas. The leaders of West-ern Europe may not wear Adam Smith ties, but they do understand that because trade generates benefits for both traders, it inevitably creates mutual dependencies, and this mutuality deters either side from doing anything that may displease the other. The Europeans saw the pipeline as a bulwark against Soviet power politics in the region.

Europe's open and noisy defiance of the pipeline ban was a blow to American credibility and a setback for the Atlantic alliance as a whole. But there was no serious danger that this break signaled the beginning of a gradual dissolution of NATO. Europe and America simply had too much at stake in their mutual security to let a pipeline come between them. The real damage of the imbroglio was to the American economy, and the real beneficiaries were the Japanese. To understand why this was so, it is necessary to look at the new global environment in which Japanese and American companies are now competing.

*   *   *

High-technology components are the fastest growing and most competitive segments of international trade. They are coming to be the building blocks for countless manufactured products. Precision gadgetry like semiconductors, microprocessors, lasers, fiber-optic cables, robots, turbines, and rotors are finding their way into all sorts of complex machines, from automobiles to guided missiles. Because semiconductors can store huge amounts of information on the miniature circuits that are etched onto them, for example, they are key elements in new computer, telecommunication, and aerospace technology. Dominance in technological building blocks like these will provide the same economic strength that steel production gave the United States in the first half of this century. The nation that can produce them cheaper and better than any other will have a huge advantage in producing and selling the advanced technologies of the future.

As noted, success in selling such components as miniature circuits and fiber-optic cable depends on experience and technological innovation. With experience in reducing the cost of material and overhead and in fabrication, the cost can drop while quantity improves. Even the production of precision products like rotors benefits substantially from know-how and experience.

The racecourse is worldwide. Japanese and American companies are competing to obtain experience by selling around the globe to manufacturers that use the technologies in their final products. These Japanese or American companies sometimes can gain more ground by licensing a foreign company to manufacture the equipment on its own, on the basis of Japanese or American designs; this is typically done when there are substantial costs to transporting the equipment or where a foreign country—anxious to preserve employment and gain technological know-how—has erected import barriers. The American or Japanese company that licenses the technology earns royalty fees that help it pay for further research and development and also gains potential customers for additional technology that complements the licensees' equipment. In this way, licensing often provides a foot in the door to obtaining experience and volume in a whole range of related components.

Viewed in this light, the pipeline ban was ominous. The real losers were American companies that supplied or licensed European manufacturers with high-technology components. These European manufacturers would think twice before again contracting with an American company. Who knows when another ban—tenuously related to American defense interests—would be invoked by the White House? Whenever possible, these European manufacturers would look to Japan for their high-technology needs. They have learned their lesson, and American companies—not just General Electric, Dresser, Caterpillar, and Cooper, but the whole array of American high-technology manufacturers—would suffer for it.

*　*　*

The same sort of economic myopia can be seen in Washington's policies toward Latin America. The Reagan and Bush Administrations have piously decried the use of foreign aid and export credits to bolster the economies of our southern neighbors, preferring to rely instead, in Ronald Reagan's memorable phrase, on "the magic of the marketplace." It was to be through trade, not aid, that Latin Americans would come to embrace the wonders of capitalism. In retrospect it is clear that this talk was aimed more at shoring up America's political and military influence south of the border than at bolstering the region's economies. While American arms sales to Latin America increased dramatically through the 1980s, the door to the promised U.S. market was slammed shut. The United States imposed quotas on sugar imports, costing Latin American and Caribbean exporters some $180 million annually—to say nothing of the extra $3 billion that American consumers would now be paying each year. The beneficiaries were fourteen thousand American sugar producers and processors—notably Gulf and Western Industries, the Hunt brothers' Great Western Sugar Company, and the Monitor Sugar Company, owned by Barlow Rand, Ltd., of South Africa.

Other Latin American industries were also denied access to the U.S. market. In what was ultimately a futile effort at protecting U.S. textile manufacturers from foreign competition, the United States signed bilateral deals with Mexico and Brazil designed to limit their textile exports to America to the same low levels as were permitted under the old Multifiber Agreement. And Brazilian steel makers came under fire for allegedly unfairly subsidizing its steel industry, resulting in duties against Brazilian steel makers.

Meanwhile, the Japanese have been busy building markets in Latin America for their high technologies. The Japanese understand that the demand for many products that incorporate high technologies is growing faster there than in industrialized countries. Sales of automobiles, television sets, and home appliances have been relatively sluggish in the United States and Western Europe because most Americans and Europeans already own these products. But in Latin America sales have mushroomed in recent years. By selling in these expanding markets, building manufacturing facilities there, licensing Latin American producers to manufacture Japanese-designed components, and providing Latin Americans with entire plants of their own, the Japanese have participated directly in that growth. Japanese companies thereby have gained the sales volume and experience they need to set a very low price for their high technologies, enabling them to undercut American competitors even in the U.S. market. At the same time, the Japanese are setting up channels to market their older technologies.

Meanwhile, Latin Americans are gaining the resources and skills necessary to make use of the new technologies. All this is made possible by the continual forward movement of Japanese industry. Collaborating with the government, Japanese companies are willing to discard older technologies as fast as newer ones can be developed, while financing the development of the new technologies by gaining strong and sometimes dominant positions in the world market for older ones. Japan's Overseas Economic Cooperation Fund provides very low interest loans to Latin Americans to finance large technological purchases, particularly of whole manufacturing plants (60 percent of Japan's Ex-Im Bank loans are aimed at selling whole plants). Japan's tax laws provide additional incentives for technological transfer. And Japan provides its companies with generous insurance against foreign losses. American foreign policy, obsessed with military and diplomatic advantage, is blind to this dynamic competitive process.

*　　*　　*

The same failure to understand international competition is affecting the very development of American high technology. The Pentagon now funds nearly one third of all the research and development undertaken by American corporations—almost twice the proportion funded by the Japanese government. For basic research, concerned with broad-based and theoretical experimentation that may have few immediate commercial applications, U.S. government funding exceeds two thirds of the total.

The Pentagon is now funding research and contracting for very large scale integrated circuits (the next major stage in the evolution of semiconductors), computer-aided manufacturing technologies appropriate to a "factory of the future," advanced fiber optics, lasers, supercomputers, superconductors, and new materials technologies. The Pentagon also has become the leading purchaser of many of these same technologies. As of 1988, the Pentagon employed more than 40 percent of the nation's scientists and engineers with advanced degrees. And since more than half of the Ph.D. engineers who now graduate from American colleges and universities are foreign nationals and thus frequently ineligible for employment by defense contractors, defense work actually commands an even larger share of American engineering doctorates.

Japan's Ministry of International Trade and Industry is pushing the same technologies. But unlike MITI, the Defense Department has no interest in the successful marketing of these new technologies. The Pentagon wants new and ever more advanced weapons systems. The two goals have begun to diverge sharply.

The marketing of new commercial products is stimulated by domestic competition, which forces firms to improve their performance and aggressively seek foreign outlets. Although MITI allows firms to cooperate on specific basic research projects, it ensures that they are fiercely competitive in marketing. For example, thirty-two Japanese companies now produce semiconductors, and the competition is intense. But the Pentagon is relatively unconcerned about competition within American industry. Over 65 percent of the dollar volume of U.S. defense contracts is awarded without competitive bidding. And even where competitive bidding occurs, the bids are often rendered meaningless by large cost overruns. The Pentagon seems most comfortable with large, stable contractors who are relatively immune to the uncertainties of competition.

Marketing new products successfully also requires long lead times, during which firms can apply new technologies and make sure they have adequate capital, labor, and productive capacity to meet anticipated demand. Many MITI projects span a decade or more. But Pentagon programs are subject to relatively sudden changes in politics and in perceptions of national security needs. The precipitous rise in U.S. defense spending during the 1980s created bottlenecks in the production of key subcomponents and capital goods, and shortages of engineers and scientists in advanced electronics and machinery.

Marketing of high technology requires a global strategy. MITI encourages exports through low-interest financing, subsidized insurance for risks overseas, and subsidies to international trading firms for establishing new markets. By contrast, Washington has imposed strict export controls on commercial high technology, requiring that purchasers ensure against transfer of their products to communist countries.

Finally, and most important of all, commercialization requires that new technologies be transferable to commercial uses at relatively low cost. MITI sees to it that new technologies are diffused rapidly into the economy and incorporated into countless commercial products. But the advanced designs required by tomorrow's elaborate military hardware —designs incorporated into precision-guided munitions, air-to-air missiles, cruise missiles, night-vision equipment, and missile-tracking devices —are not as easily applicable to commercial uses as were the more primitive technologies produced during the defense and aerospace programs of the late 1950s and early 1960s. Indeed, it is precisely *because* America's commercial high technologies are not likely to be adaptable to defense needs in the years ahead that the Defense Department has launched its own research and development programs to produce advanced gadgets designed expressly to meet its own needs. Rather than encourage American commercial development, defense spending on emerging high technologies has had the opposite effect over the long term, diverting U.S. scientists and engineers away from commercial applications. And Pentagon jitters about leaks to the Soviets have cast a veil of secrecy over commercial high-tech research.

Commercial spin-offs depend on quick, efficient access to new technology, but the door is rapidly closing. For example, during the 1980s, the Pentagon increased, from 13 to 20 percent, that portion of its research budget deemed so secret it won't even disclose what it is funding. Ever more research has fallen under a new executive order that makes it relatively easy to classify government documents without considering the public's need to know.

Even unclassified research has been controlled. The Pentagon routinely insists it has the right to review university-based research before the results are published and includes prepublication-review clauses in its research contracts. (Between 1980 and 1988 government officials pulled scientific papers from academic conferences a dozen times.)

In all these ways the United States is sacrificing the nation's high-tech future to the short-term exigencies of national defense and the parochial demands of domestic producers. America continues to regard the rest of the world through the foggy lenses of cold war diplomacy rather than through the clear glasses of commercial competition. Our international economic policies in the 1980s have consisted almost entirely of trade embargoes, tariffs, quotas, dumping complaints, antitrust challenges, and an occasional sensational arrest for alleged theft of trade secrets. And rather than encouraging our emerging industries and nurturing our high technologies, we are distorting their growth through exorbitant defense expenditures on esoteric military hardware.

* * *

It is ironic that the Reagan and Bush Administrations, whose laissez-faire rhetoric comes to us almost intact from the nineteenth century, should stymie free and robust international trade and cripple American industry in the process. But the conservative mind still sees the world as a vast chessboard on which subtle games of power politics are to be played—another vestige of the nineteenth century. The international economy is of secondary importance. Foreign policy is the bailiwick of the State and Defense Departments; the Commerce Department plays third fiddle. We have no equivalent of Japan's MITI, which is concerned primarily with the future of the national economy and its place in a changing world economy.

This international myopia is having grave consequences. America is losing the high-technology race. The nation's economy is not evolving rapidly enough for American companies to capture a significant share of the world's emerging markets. Already the Japanese have most of the world market in memory chips. They are gaining significant market shares in fiber optics, communications equipment, sensing devices, and composite materials. They are substantially ahead in robotics, computer-aided manufacturing, and photovoltaics. They completely dominate consumer electronics—videocassette recorders, camcorders, fax machines, and high-definition television. America's declining competitiveness in these emerging technologies will be accompanied by a decline in our relative standard of living. The decline has already begun.

Some will say that all this is well and good. Americans have lived too high on the hog for too long, and it is fitting and right that other industrialized nations should reach and surpass us. Who cares about high technology anyway? The problem is twofold. First and most obviously, if our national economy is no longer growing and many Americans therefore come to feel poor relative to what they once had and relative to what citizens in some other countries now have, it will be harder than ever to convince them to share their wealth with their less fortunate fellow citizens. All too often, history teaches us, a society's capacity for compassion and civic virtue exists in direct proportion to the rise in its citizens' real incomes.

The second problem with a declining position in international competition brings us full circle, back to national defense. For our ability to maintain peace and deter aggression depends on our overall prosperity; the resources and commitments that national defense requires over the long term can be sustained only amid a growing and buoyant economy. Perhaps even more to the point, America's best guarantee of national security over the long term is a buoyant world economy in which the fruits of prosperity are widely shared. Trade embargoes, tariffs, quotas, dumping complaints, arms sales, and all the other ways in which American foreign policy distorts international trade add nothing to the real wealth of the world. Unlike the military and diplomatic contest that has preoccupied the Reagan and Bush Administrations, the contest in commercial high technology at least in some respects pays a dividend to the rest of the world in the form of a higher quality of life.

The United States can meet the Japanese challenge in high technology only through policies calculated to spur American high-tech producers to commercial success in world markets: generous funding of commercial research and development; low-interest loans to less-developed nations to finance their technological purchases; education loans and grants to ensure an adequate supply of engineers and teachers; awards of defense contracts to smaller, innovative high-tech companies; more defense contracts channeled toward generic technologies with commercial applications; and an open world trading system that eschews embargoes and import barriers. In short, we need an affirmative industrial policy for American high technology. By taking precisely the opposite tack in each of these areas, the Reagan and Bush Administrations have threatened our economic future and, in the process, jeopardized our national security.

13

THE PENTAGON
AND THE GOSPLAN

I HAVE A FRIEND WHO CAN TALK NONSTOP FOR SEVERAL HOURS ABOUT computers without using a single word found in Webster's dictionary. Even verbs and gerunds are transmogrified into technicalese. I dimly understand him, but only because his highly animated hand and body movements communicate something of the functions and relationships he's describing; and the exercise is exhausting.

We live in a world where technical complexities and possibilities are advancing faster than is our ability to communicate about them. High technologies are shifting the ground on which our economy and our national defenses are built. They are altering relations among nations and tilting the balance of power. Most of us technological illiterates still think in terms of gross national products, numbers of missiles and divisions, and the extent of command over people and natural resources. But the real balance of power is coming to have less to do with these static aggregates than with a less tangible measure: the speed with which a nation's people comprehend and employ the latest technologies. And none has a greater stake in the potential of high technologies to shift the balance of power than three nations of remarkable technological prowess: the United States, the Soviet Union, and Japan. Each, in its own way, has been striving to match or exceed the technological eminence of the others.

The Soviet Union's successes in this competition among the technological superpowers should not be underestimated. The Soviets were the first to orbit unmanned and manned satellites. The Soviets' successful launch of the first Sputnik in 1957 stimulated America to equal, and eventually to greater, exertions: the Apollo program, the passage of the National Defense Education Act, the creation of the National Aeronautics and Space Administration, and so on. The Soviets also managed to produce a hydrogen bomb without direct assistance from anyone else. And in the intervening years they have created a broad range of highly sophisticated military weapons.

The Soviets' technological sophistication extends to industry as well. They were the first to invent continuous casting equipment for producing steel. They have pioneered new technologies for welding, electroslag remelting, cement making, aluminum casting, the coating of titanium nitrides, and the application of ultrathin diamond films to various materials. They invented the many-lined weaving machine and several advanced consumer products and processes. (They also invented anti-nicotine chewing gum.) And they have shown themselves capable of planning and implementing enormously complex technological projects, often spanning decades—like the recently unveiled Energia rocket, which is able to propel heavy loads into space. The Soviets will use the Energia for unmanned missions to Mars, and they are well on the way to launching orbiting platforms covered with solar cells for converting sunlight into electricity to be beamed back to earth.

*   *   *

All these technological achievements notwithstanding, the Soviets are behind in many areas. They produce more machine tools than any other nation on earth, but they have failed to incorporate into their production system computerized machine tools, industrial robots, and the computers and communications gear necessary to link them all up. They pump more petroleum and natural gas than anyone else, and they produce more steel, but they haven't yet ventured into either advanced drilling and exploration equipment or new material technologies. They are woefully behind in very large scale integrated circuits, supercomputers, biotechnology, personal computers, even copying machines. And the near meltdown at Chernobyl revealed a perilous shortcoming in the safe use of nuclear power.

Most important, the Soviets are losing ground in advanced technologies relative to Japan and the United States. And in terms of the balance of world power, relativity is everything. Although the Soviets have continued to maintain an average growth rate in gross national income about equal to that of the United States, the Soviet Union's real product per work hour is now about one quarter that of Japan and one fifth that of the United States. It is falling further behind every year. Thus, the average Soviet citizen has to work longer and harder just to stay put. The system's capacity to extract huge savings and apply them to new investment is no longer yielding the spectacular growth of decades ago.

Part of the problem is a depletion of natural resources. Energy supplies have become less plentiful and less accessible; the remaining stocks of oil and natural gas are at much deeper levels or in more remote regions. The Soviets are also up against a declining birthrate in European Russia, where most of the nation's industrial capacities are located. But the larger problem is the Soviet Union's inability to incorporate new technologies into its production system. Capital accumulation can only take the economy so far. Unless the Soviets do a better job utilizing technology, they will fall further behind, and they know it.

* * *

The modern Soviet economy owes much of its structure and philosophical underpinnings to Joseph Stalin's relentless drive toward modernization. Stalin's chief economic aim was to expand heavy industry. To do that, he had to expropriate massive amounts of capital from the agricultural sector and create a highly centralized planning system capable of directing the capital to large projects, such as steel mills, railroads, and factories. The objective was to produce high volumes of standardized goods so that the nation would both enjoy an adequate standard of living and be capable of meeting its military needs without undue dependence on imports. Such forced modernization required centralized direction. Ministries in Moscow set production targets and prices, allocated materials, and determined how the resulting goods were to be distributed.

Stalin's economic organization was remarkably successful. Right up until the mid-1960s, industrial production boomed. Steel production, for example, grew by about 9 percent a year throughout the 1950s. When Nikita Khrushchev visited the United States in 1959, he could credibly boast that—at the rates by which the two economies were growing— the Soviet Union would overtake the United States within twenty years.

But an economy that is planned at the center, and premised upon mass production and heavy industry, is an inflexible economy. It can generate large amounts of identical things, but it cannot shift easily into the production of new goods. Nor can it adjust for quality. As an industrial economy becomes more complex, the number of adjustments needed to ensure that the right things of the right quality are produced at the correct time in the right place increases logarithmically. Prices that are allowed to rise and fall with changes in supply and demand automatically signal to everyone how to make these sorts of adjustments. But central planning sends no such helpful instructions. Instead, planners drown in paperwork, and everybody else just drowns. According to 1988 calculations, Gosplan, the central bureaucracy responsible for most of the planning and allocation, handles about seven million documents and makes eighty-three million calculations each year. The State Price Committee sets two hundred thousand prices annually.

Even Khrushchev understood the limitations of central planning. In 1957, in an attempt to decentralize some of these adjustment decisions, he abolished most of the industrial ministries at the center. Many of the displaced Moscow bureaucrats migrated to the regional councils, or *sovarkhozy,* that were to take over from the center. But those who remained kept tight rein, and they never fully allowed the reforms to take effect. After Khrushchev's ouster in 1965 Alexei Kosygin restored much of the central bureaucracy. Not until almost two decades later did a Soviet leader again attempt decentralization, by which time the inefficiencies of central planning had taken a severe toll on the Soviet economy.

One of Khrushchev's reforms had a more lasting influence. In an attempt to spur productivity, he gave certain enterprise managers a bit more discretion over the assortment, the styles, and the prices of the goods their plants produced. The continued resistance of Moscow bureaucrats notwithstanding, this reform took root; by 1970 it was extended to all firms.

Still, Soviet planners have always resisted change. History has recorded few bureaucracies more entrenched than the bureaucracy that plans the Soviet economy. The *nomenklatura* comprises about four hundred thousand people, most of them in Moscow. Their livelihood and status depend on maintaining strict control over allocation and pricing decisions. They are conservative by belief and by instinct. Their deep-seated reluctance to experiment with economic reforms is shared by many other Soviet citizens: by minor bureaucrats in the fifteen republics and the 159 regions of the republics, by military officers, by Party officials, and by average workers, all of whom think they have little to gain and a great deal to lose by change, and many of whom have experienced the disruptions and the inconveniences brought on by previous efforts to alter the system.

*   *   *

Enter Mikhail Gorbachev. No other Soviet leader has ever been able to assume such extensive control of both the Party and the government in so short a time. Within one year of his election as Party general secretary, Gorbachev had removed almost half of the directors of ministries and state commissions and had altered the same proportion of top leaders in the Central Committee departments. He had extruded Party chiefs in one quarter of the republics and almost one third of first secretaries in the 159 regions of the republics and had shifted the membership of the Central Committee in his direction. He moved with equal speed in filling all these vacancies with people supportive of his reforms.

Can Gorbachev reform the system? More important, what does "reform" mean to Gorbachev? He is too wily a politician and bureaucratic infighter to define "reform" so radically that it cannot be accomplished. First, he wants to reduce the size of Moscow's top planning bureaucracy, thus cutting back the number of power centers with a vested interest in maintaining economic controls. He has announced his intention to halve the fifty-thousand-employee staff of Gosplan and to cut the number of Moscow ministries from eighty to twenty. Planning ministries would no longer have day-to-day responsibilities for prices and output. They would focus more of their efforts on planning new technologies, promoting foreign trade, and training personnel.

Second, Gorbachev would give enterprise managers more control over prices and output targets and more responsibility for the day-to-day implementation of plans. They would retain a share of the profits and use it for salaries or enterprise improvements. Unproductive enterprises would be shut down and unneeded workers laid off. In addition, managers would be elected by workers. Third, he wants to consolidate enterprises within larger, vertically integrated associations, thus enabling suppliers and their industrial customers to adjust to one another's needs directly, without too many external plans and directives. And fourth, he seeks a relaxation of tensions with the West so that more resources can be freed from military requirements and shifted to new investment and so that the Soviet Union can obtain credits, consumer goods, and technology from the United States and its allies.

Debate rages in the Soviet Union about whether these reforms go too far or not far enough. Top officials who have been Gorbachev loyalists in the past—Politburo member Nikolai I. Ryzhkov, who heads the Council of Ministers, and Gosplan chief Nikolay V. Talyzin—have spoken out against the bureaucratic cuts. Others say the reforms do not go far enough. Nikolai Shmelyov, a prominent Soviet economist, has proposed that subsidies and price setting be abolished, central planning be eliminated, the ruble be devalued to its real price in world money markets, and that the nation accept some unemployment as a natural by-product of a free-market economy. Shmelyov noted recently that Gorbachev's proposals were inadequate: "We are again dooming ourselves to halfhearted measures. And halfheartedness, as we all know, is often worse than inactivity."

The very fact of this debate—so much of it in public, within official publications—is remarkable. The Soviet Union is now openly arguing about the merits of capitalism. The debate illustrates the fifth plank in Gorbachev's reform strategy: getting the broader Soviet public involved in such deliberations, and thus gaining their support for whatever economic reform emerges.

* * *

Gorbachev the politician is likely to prevail over Gorbachev the economist. He is too cunning to push the bureaucracy too far too fast. Thus, the reforms that are actually put into effect during the next few years will, in all likelihood, be more modest than those many Soviet economists are now advocating. Initially, Gorbachev said that he was committed to "a profound transformation of the economy." But since then, his language has been more moderate. He has talked only of "perfecting the economic mechanism" and has gone out of his way to stress that his proposals signal no major change with the past. He was even quoted as telling a group of automobile workers of "the enormous advantages of a centrally planned economy." As if to reassure the bureaucrats, he added that "we will even have to strengthen the principle of centralization, where necessary."

But here's the rub: Improvements in productivity, in the form of greater quantities of goods, aren't enough to rescue the Soviet economy. These days an ever increasing proportion of the value of consumer products and military equipment alike derives from the application of advanced technologies. This trend is apparent in all advanced industrial nations. The world's leading economies are shifting out of jobs traditionally associated with heavy industries (such as steel making, large-batch chemical production, and assembly) toward jobs that require the manipulation and application of knowledge (making and marketing high-strength ceramics, new alloys, specialty chemicals, computers, and integrated circuits). These new products fulfill many of the same functions as the old, but with far greater efficiency and flexibility and thus at far lower cost. Most important, these new products, and the services related to them, continually change as technologies evolve.

At best, the reforms that Gorbachev is seeking will render the Soviet economy administratively more efficient. This is no small feat. Stories are recounted of new milk plants installed in areas where there are few cows, petrochemical plants where no oil pipelines reach. But Gorbachev's reforms will not fundamentally alter the incentives operating on workers and managers. In all likelihood, poor quality will continue to haunt the production system. Every Soviet manager and worker knows how easy it is to measure, and thus to be rewarded for, quantity—and how difficult it is to measure, and to be disciplined for, poor quality. Gorbachev hopes to reverse this by administrative fiat. He has announced a new bureaucracy, the State Acceptance Service, charged with quality control. But as long as the old incentives remain in place, there is no reason to suppose that quality will show much improvement.

A bigger problem is that a centrally planned economy, even one that allows local administrative discretion, creates no incentives to innovate. Every Soviet manager and worker is aware of the risk that an innovation might slow the flow of products and thus reduce the year's bonus, while a successful innovation is unlikely to have any effect other than to increase next year's production quota. The result, not surprisingly, is that Soviet enterprises are extraordinarily reluctant to try something new. Not even the proposed Law on State Enterprise will affect these incentives very much.

The Soviet Union is not without occasionally dramatic technological breakthroughs, but these typically occur in laboratories far removed from the workplace. Some of these new inventions eventually find their way into enterprise plans, financed by a central Fund for the Development of Science and Technology. But by the time bureaucrats in Moscow discover that a new invention might be useful and then decide precisely where it should go, years may have passed. None of Gorbachev's reforms will speed the pace of technology transfer from the laboratory to the factory.

* * *

There is a still more fundamental barrier to technological innovation in the Soviet Union. Technological innovation can thrive only in an environment that invites, or at least tolerates, dissent. Technological innovation is largely a process of imagining radical alternatives to what is currently accepted and sharing these new possibilities with others. Problems must be openly recognized, and ferment must be generated among creative minds to find solutions. These are, in effect, acts of subversion. They almost invariably stir things up. And no clear boundaries exist between different categories of imagination, between different realms of subversion. The scientific, the managerial, the economic, the philosophical, the cultural, the political: They have a way of running into each other. It is no accident, as the Marxists used to say, that many of the Soviet Union's most brilliant scientists and artists are also political dissidents.

Moreover, many of the new technologies are themselves subversive. Computers, word processors, and telecommunications equipment not only incite unorthodox ideas; they also allow them to be exchanged instantly. They inspire communities of dissent. Totalitarian regimes understand this; they monopolize the technologies of communication—the press, radio and television, telephones, and now the computer. Nothing threatens a police state's legitimacy more than private and robust debate; nothing ensures its survival more than the isolation and fragmentation of the citizenry.

These ironies lie at the core of Gorbachev's dilemma. For more than a half century the Soviet police state has maintained tight control over communications among Soviet citizens. Even today senior scholars and scientists are loath to use copying machines: In most enterprises and universities copying departments are staffed by the KGB. How, then, can the Soviet Union be expected to adapt technologies that will unleash so much communication? How could the Soviets embellish and improve the new technologies without simultaneously inviting political and social dissent? To gain technological sophistication, Soviet economics and politics would have to be transformed. This the Soviet bureaucracy will not allow. Technological sophistication is essential to the Soviet Union's economic and political survival. Technological backwardness is essential to the Soviet Union's system of government.

* * *

Not since Stalin forced the Soviet Union into becoming an industrial state has any nation sought economic development with as much determination—and achieved it with as much success—as Japan. Many people can remember a time, not so many years ago, when "Made in Japan" was synonymous with cheap, shoddy workmanship. (During the 1950s, American regulators filed charges against a toy manufacturer from the Japanese town of Usa whose products bore the label MADE IN USA.) During the past twenty-five years, however, Japan has concentrated almost exclusively on improving productivity and shifting production to more advanced goods. Rather than trying to preserve its industrial base, Japan has sought to propel it into the future, at the same time casting off older industries in which Japan's competitive position was declining.

Thus, the Soviet Union is not the only superpower now falling behind technologically. For Gorbachev, the technological challenge potentially implies a fundamental transformation in the Soviet economic and political system. What does the Japanese technological challenge imply for America?

There are interesting parallels. Both the Soviet and the American military bureaucracies are the major users of advanced technologies in their respective economies. Both initiate and sponsor vast programs of research and development. Neither military bureaucracy worries much about ensuring competition among suppliers.

The Pentagon is also America's largest purchaser of high technology. The means by which the Pentagon decides what technology it wants to buy and then goes about obtaining it bear remarkable similarities to the nightmarish planning and allocation system centered in Moscow. According to a 1987 study by the Center for Strategic and International Studies in Washington, each year the Pentagon undertakes fifteen million separate contracts, overseen in the first instance by 150,000 acquisition officers. On top of them are nearly twenty-five thousand auditors and inspectors. The Pentagon floats on a veritable sea of paper. Procurement regulations themselves total thirty thousand pages and are issued by seventy-nine different offices. The direct cost of monitoring all this flow of paper is approximately $10 billion annually.

The Pentagon, no less than the Soviet military bureaucracy, is subject to wondrous inefficiency, along with more venal intention. Few months elapse in America without another story about the apparent deceit or gross negligence of a defense contractor. In recent years General Electric admitted to defrauding the Air Force of $800,000 by forging workers' time cards on a contract for upgrading the warheads on Minuteman missiles. More recently, the company admitted that it had overbilled the Pentagon by $10 million. McDonnell Douglas produced fighter jets the tail fins of which develop unusual cracks. Hughes Aircraft's missiles were found to be faulty. Texas Instruments' semiconductors didn't work as they should. And then there were the $500 hammers and $7,000 coffee makers. Between 1986 and 1989, more than five hundred contractors were suspended or permanently barred from doing business with the Pentagon because of poor workmanship or questionable billings. Forty-five of the nation's one hundred largest military contractors have come under criminal investigation for kickbacks, illegal overcharges, and other nefarious activities.

Every major cost overrun, scandal, or mistake in military contracting has elicited two powerful political reactions. On the one hand, Congress and the public have been eager to identify wrongdoers. There are typically elaborate criminal investigations, grand jury indictments, and stories in the press suggesting egregious instances of venality and cupidity. Most of these end in charges being dropped for want of adequate evidence of criminal intent or in watered-down plea bargains that at least temporarily satisfy the public's desire to place blame.

On the other hand, with every new scandal or revelation, the Pentagon is pressured to add still more layers of checks, monitors, and inspectors—to clog the procurement process with more paperwork, red tape, bureaucracy. In the wake of disclosures that the Defense Department was paying $400 each for $8 claw hammers, for example, the military added seven thousand additional staffers to solve its spare-parts problems. This bureaucratic propensity, too, resembles the Soviet response.

Secrecy is an important aspect of high-technology development within both bureaucracies, the Pentagon's and Gosplan's. Some of America's most modern factories, outfitted by the Pentagon with computer-integrated manufacturing systems—such as LTV Corporation's Vought plant, which produces the B-1 bomber—are now shrouded in Pentagon secrecy. No commercial entrepreneurs are allowed in to see how to do it.

There are other parallels. Like the Soviet Union, the United States continues to excel at technological breakthroughs but finds it difficult to move them quickly from lab to factory. Unlike Japan and the Soviet Union, we are blessed with an army of technological entrepreneurs, concocting extraordinary inventions in their basements and attics. But a significant percentage of their inventions never make it into production on our shores. American manufacturers haven't been particularly interested in new technology. Having succeeded so well for over fifty years in large-batch and mass production, American manufacturers haven't wanted—or understood the need—to shift to more knowledge-intensive forms of production.

Of course, the technological parallels between the Soviets and us should not be overstated. American productivity continues to be the highest in the world—far higher than Soviet productivity, still a bit higher than Japanese productivity. But both the Soviet Union and the United States are slipping badly in the global technology race. The reason is simple. Success depends less on big discoveries than on a widely diffused, continuous, and incremental drive toward application and refinement.

* * *

Technology development in all three nations—the Soviet Union, the United States, and Japan—is, to a large extent, planned. It must be. Private enterprises, which depend on profits for their continued survival, are rarely in a position to experiment with radically different ways of doing things. The risks are too great; the costs of shifting over the production system are too high. At best, these enterprises will wait until some other company tries out the new technologies. But such caution will badly hobble the pace of technology development overall. Thus, every industrialized government is in the business of technology planning, development, and transfer. The critical question is not whether such planning occurs, but how it is carried out.

In the United States, as noted, the tasks of technology development and transfer have been consigned largely to the Pentagon, which, not unlike the Soviet system of central planning, is a bureaucracy, with a bureaucracy's rigidities and concealments. In Japan, by contrast, technology development and transfer entail a close partnership between profit-driven enterprises and a range of quasi-independent agencies halfway between public and private sectors. The notorious Ministry of International Trade and Industry (MITI) is more coordinator than planner: It establishes joint research ventures among private firms and convenes endless councils and conferences of engineers and managers to parcel out risks and responsibilities more efficiently. Of equal importance are financial institutions, like the Japanese Development Bank, that provide low-interest loans to enterprises seeking to experiment with new production technologies. And then there is the array of institutes and semiofficial laboratories that comb the world for new inventions and, after licensing them, organize groups of Japanese firms to find ways of utilizing them.

Of the three planning systems, Japan's is by far the most successful at transferring new technologies into the production system. It is the least bureaucratic and secretive, the most flexible. Consider, for example, the latest rage in high technology, superconductive alloys capable of transmitting electricity with virtually no loss of energy. If all the hoopla can be believed, these wondrous materials promise to revolutionize both goods and weapons. They are still in the labs, but they will find their way into production within the next few years. Which nation will take the lead? In Japan superconductive applications are now being pursued in dozens of institutes and joint research ventures, involving every major industry group and hundreds of smaller businesses and subcontractors. In the United States, by contrast, superconductive applications are being pursued within only three major institutions—IBM, AT&T, and the Office of the Strategic Defense Initiative in the Department of Defense—and most of the funding is coming from the Pentagon. Nobody knows exactly what the Soviets are now doing about superconductivity, but it's a fair bet that the central ministries and the military bureaucracies are in charge. We will have to wait for years to discover which of these three nations will prevail, but the odds strongly favor Japan.

*   *   *

If Darwinism could explain the evolution of political economies—such that the most successful economic organizations predominate until more adaptive, and thus more successful, ones come along—we might be able to predict the direction in which Gorbachev's reforms will eventually lead. We could make the same prediction about America's response to Gorbachev's reforms, indeed about the evolution of the American political economy itself. The prediction is that Japan will amass so much power that the United States and the Soviet Union will have no choice but to copy its decentralized, open planning system. The politics and the economics of the three superpowers would converge in a kind of managed, democratic capitalism.

But political economies don't follow Darwin's rules. Pesky things like culture, values, and beliefs intrude. It is here, perhaps, that Japan enjoys its most important advantage, for its political culture, institutions, and public values all tend toward the rapid utilization of new knowledge. By contrast, the military-encrusted bureaucracies of the Soviet Union and the United States tend toward the preservation of the economic status quo. As Gorbachev proceeds with his strategy and the United States responds, only one prediction seems reasonably safe. Increasingly, and in highly subtle ways, changes in these nations' relative technological prowess will lead to changes in the balance of world power and thus in the strategies employed by both the Soviet Union and the United States toward one another. But both nations' strategies will be affected by their technological prowess relative to Japan's. And more and more, the balance of power, at least as it is determined by technology, will tilt toward Japan.

14

BEYOND FREE TRADE

THE AMERICAN IDEAL OF FREE TRADE, WHICH EMERGED FULL-BLOWN IN the postwar era, assumed a steady expansion of capital-intensive standardized production within all industrialized nations. This was a heroic assumption. Comparative advantage among nations was perceived to depend on differences in the relative abundance of capital and labor, which in turn depended on national differences both in willingness to defer consumption and accumulate capital, and in the historic inheritance of capital stock. It was assumed that this comparative advantage would change over time; even less-developed nations eventually would adopt capital-intensive industries. But the process would be evolutionary —adjustments would be slow, regular, and predictable. It stood to reason that the best policy for ensuring both expansion and steady change would be a gradual reduction in trade barriers. That way, each nation could exploit large economies of scale in the type of production in which it currently enjoyed a comparative advantage, while incremental changes in investment and capital accumulation slowly altered the terms of trade.

Neoclassical trade theory itself was built on a much older, and even more heroic, assumption. Adam Smith and David Ricardo had based their potent arguments for free trade principally on geographic differences in *natural* endowments, implying a quite static distribution of advantages and disadvantages. A nation had no real choice but to realistically accept the economic station its land and climate had assigned it. As machine-based industry developed and spread, later theorists refined the model to accommodate the importance of physical capital. This "factor-proportions" model turned on the observation that some peoples were better than others at making and using machines for reasons that had little to do with natural resources. Comparative advantage became less a matter of given endowments, more a matter of chosen investments. Yet because it grew out of an era when technologies changed gradually, and when colonialism and devastating world wars stifled or distorted international economic adjustment, neoclassical trade theory never fully acknowledged the profound difference between comparative advantage as a fact of natural endowments and comparative advantage as an ever-changing product of social organization and choice. Until very recently, observing that the United States was rich in capital while Korea was rich in unskilled labor seemed as comfortably solid a basis for trade as observing that Portugal was sunny and suited for grapes while Ireland was verdant and suited for sheep. This was the theoretical basis of the free-trade principle that underpins American trade policy today.

Just as the Ricardian model had viewed world trade from the perspective of the textile industry—in which Britain then enjoyed a dominant position—so, by analogy, did the United States' postwar trade policy take the perspective of America's dominant industries: steel, chemicals, automobiles, rubber, and electrical machinery. Stability and predictability, to ensure that the fixed costs could be recovered, were the only principles of public policy necessary to spur further investment in these industries. Potential efficiencies in world-scale production promised to preserve American dominance of these industries, since the marginal costs of making the last mass-produced unit were quite low.

The postwar free-trade ideal was appropriate to its time, an era of unprecedented mass consumption of standardized goods. A new, relatively homogeneous generation of consumers was gorging itself on new homes, cars, and all sorts of steel and plastic gadgets. Throughout the 1950s and 1960s the American economy grew not by innovating but by expanding the scale of its basic production processes and thus reducing unit costs. Western Europe followed that lead. There were few breakthroughs in new products or processes and very little real competition. But prosperity reigned, as demand seemed insatiable. Free trade was a means both of enabling the rest of the world to partake in this bounteous expansion and of permitting the United States to preserve its economic preeminence.

The ideal was codified in the General Agreement on Tariffs and Trade, signed in 1947, and articulated in more detail in the subsequent rounds of tariff negotiations. It was expressed in principles of nondiscrimination (all nations to be treated the same), reduced government intervention, and the formal negotiation of trade disputes. The GATT structure succeeded reasonably well because all parties (except the less-developed nations) had a stake in making the system work so they could share in American-led prosperity and, not incidentally, because the United States possessed sufficient economic and political power to enforce its vision. The volume of world trade rose dramatically, exceeding gains in world production. Between 1913 and 1948 world trade had risen 2.5 percent per year on average; world production, only 2 percent; between 1948 and 1973 trade increased by 7 percent per year, and world production by 5 percent.

* * *

The principal departures from the free-trade ideal were agricultural commodities and textiles—largely because these two categories of trade threatened American producers from the start. United States representatives to GATT insisted on an exception for primary commodities. The United States already had restricted imports of dairy products, wheat, and peanuts. Sugar quotas went into effect in 1948. Later came "voluntary" agreements with Taiwan on mushrooms, with Australia and New Zealand on beef, and with Mexico on strawberries and tomatoes. Farm subsidies similarly were exempt: In 1955, when the contracting parties to GATT adopted provisions limiting the use of export subsidies, they effectively excluded primary commodities from coverage.

Policies to preserve the textile industry followed a related logic of escalating preservationism. In 1957 Japan agreed to limit its textile exports to the United States. This was followed five years later by a multilateral agreement (the Long Term Arrangement) designed to protect North America and Europe against cotton textiles from Japan and other developing nations; it has been extended and enlarged since then.

These two exceptions to the postwar ideal of free trade contained the seeds of its demise. Agriculture and textiles were the only significant sectors where genuinely free trade would threaten American producers. The world market for farm goods was limited. Competitors in Canada and Australia had not been crippled by war. And American agricultural interests expected that once the worst of the devastation was repaired,

Europe and Japan would soon become largely self-sufficient in food and even become exporters. Thus, American farmers saw little to gain and much to lose from free trade and simply rejected the principle. (There is an irony here. The potential world market and the American competitive edge have both proven greater than expected, and for decades the United States has tried unsuccessfully to recant its own exception and bring agriculture under the banner of free trade.)

In textiles the causes were different, but the effect was the same: Some American interests foresaw sizable immediate losses from free trade, and U.S. negotiators dutifully obtained exemptions from the rules. The world market for textiles, unlike the market for food, *was* expected to grow, but early in the postwar era it was clear that low-wage countries were better suited for most textile manufacturing.

In both cases, where free trade would have called for substantial immediate adjustment on the part of significant economic groups in the United States, the principle was unceremoniously abandoned. There were no public policies to guide adjustments of this magnitude. Nor were there mechanisms for international trade agreements to shape such policies. It was far easier—and more expedient—simply to declare each of these sectors to be special cases warranting unique decisions and relationships *outside* the framework of an open trading system. The ideal of free trade—and the codes and institutions that were growing up around it—had no response to the problem of structural adjustment. These early failures of the ideal foreshadowed its widespread breakdown today.

* * *

Even when the adjustment problems of the United States and Western Europe loomed larger in the 1970s, the United States continued to view the issues narrowly in terms of the free-trade ideal. Government interventions were seen as always regrettable but occasionally unavoidable concessions to buy off opposition to continued liberalization. At the instigation of the United States, the European (OECD) Council of Ministers in June 1978 adopted a hortatory document entitled "Policies for Adjustment: Some General Orientations," which emphasized that whenever governments intervened to ease the pain of trade adjustments, across-the-board policies affecting all industries were superior to targeted ones, and that in any event such interventions should be temporary. There was no mention of the importance of ongoing programs for stimulating emerging businesses, retiring excess capacity in older businesses, and retraining workers for new jobs.

During another round of negotiations in the late 1970s, the United

States continued to seek international agreements to limit government interventions that "distort" international trade. Several of the codes that emerged—governing public procurement practices and nontariff barriers—were informed by the free-trade ideal. But the subsidies code reflected no consensus on what sorts of subsidies were out of bounds; the code did little more than establish processes to ensure that one nation's retaliation against another for such subsidies was not disproportionate to the offense.

*   *   *

Trade accords became progressively less coherent and conclusive because the premises on which the postwar free-trade ideal had been founded were no longer applicable to large segments of industrialized economies. Comparative advantage was no longer a relatively static phenomenon based on slowly evolving capital endowments. The hourly output of workers in certain less-developed nations like South Korea and Taiwan was catching up to the output of workers in the United States and other industrialized nations because they were starting to use many of the same machines, purchased from international engineering and capital-equipment firms with money borrowed from international banks.

The pace of structural change was dramatic. As recently as the mid-1960s Taiwan, Hong Kong, Korea, Brazil, and Spain specialized in simple products that required large amounts of unskilled labor but little capital investment or technology—clothing, footwear, toys, basic electronic assemblies. Japan's response was to shift out of these products into processing industries like steel and synthetic fibers, which called for substantial capital and raw materials but still used mostly unskilled and semiskilled labor and incorporated relatively mature technologies not subject to major innovations. Ten years later, the newly industrialized countries had followed Japan into basic capital-intensive processing industries. Japan, meanwhile, had become an exporter of steel technology instead of basic steels and moved its industrial base into products like automobiles, color televisions, small appliances, consumer electronics, and ships—businesses requiring considerable investment in plant and equipment, as well as sophisticated new technologies.

By 1980 Taiwan and the other rapid industrializers had themselves become major producers of complex products like automobiles, color televisions, tape recorders, CB transceivers, microwave ovens, small computers, and ships. South Korea now has the largest single shipyard in the world; South Korea's Pohang steel mill is one of the most modern in the world. Almost all the world's production of small appliances is now centered in Hong Kong, South Korea, and Singapore. At the same time, Malaysia, Thailand, the Philippines, Sri Lanka, India, and other poorer countries are inheriting the production of clothing, footwear, toys, and simple electronic assemblies. India is fast becoming a center for computer programming.

Far from halting this migration of high-volume standardized production, automation actually has accelerated it. Sophisticated machines are readily transported to low-wage countries. Robots and computerized machines are substituting for semiskilled workers. Automated inspection machines are reducing the costs of screening out poor-quality components—and thereby are encouraging firms in industrialized nations to farm out production of standardized parts to developing nations.

* * *

In the face of this rapid movement into high-volume standardized production, Japan, and to a lesser extent West Germany, has sought to shift their industrial bases to products and processes that require skilled workers—precision castings, new materials, special chemicals, and sensor devices, as well as the design and manufacture of fiber-optic cable, fine ceramics, lasers, large-scale integrated circuits, advanced semiconductors, and advanced aircraft engines. Skilled labor has become the only dimension of production where advanced industrialized nations can create and retain an advantage.

These nations' governments are working with their businesses and labor unions to accomplish the shift. They are ensuring that managers obtain long-term capital and that workers obtain retraining. They are selectively raising entry barriers and reducing costs in an effort to alter the pattern of national investment, and thereby to accelerate structural change in their economies. They have undeniably made mistakes. On occasion, they also bow to the demands of older industries to maintain the status quo. Often they find it difficult to achieve consensus about the best strategy for adjustment. They are having problems coping with the current recession while trying to maintain flexibility. But these nations understand the inevitability and urgency of structural change, and the central importance of easing and accelerating the transition.

As the free-trade ideal has become hopelessly inadequate to guide these shifts, international economic agencies and formal trade processes sponsored by the United States have been progressively bypassed and enfeebled. Only the easiest of disputes are now settled within the GATT system; most major issues of global economic change are dealt with outside it. Bilateral export agreements have become the rule rather than the exception. Japan now "voluntarily" limits its exports to Western Europe of automobiles, machine tools, television tubes, and videocassette recorders; and its shipments to the United States of steel, automobiles, machine tools, semiconductors, and many other items. Western European nations limit their sales of steel to the United States. Quotas, tariffs, and other barriers are being imposed on a wide range of products. The European Economic Community maintains a tariff of 17 percent on integrated circuits. Australia, South Africa, Spain, Mexico, and twenty-six other nations require fixed percentages of domestic content in automobiles assembled within their borders. France is restricting imports of videotape recorders by subjecting them to detailed inspections and delays.

* * *

The free-trade ideal also has been crumbling within the United States. In many respects its erosion here has been more dramatic than elsewhere and has set a precedent for other nations. Since the late 1960s, the pattern has become well established: American industries suddenly faced with foreign competition have threatened to file complaints with the government alleging foreign "dumping" in the United States of goods priced lower than production costs, or foreign subsidies that render the imports "unfairly" cheap. Eager to avoid protracted litigation and the trade and diplomatic frictions accompanying it, the exporting nation often has responded by negotiating "voluntary" agreements with the United States, setting a limit to the volume of exports shipped to these shores. As structural changes continue and the exporter adapts by becoming more efficient, the drama repeats itself, with the resulting restrictions becoming even tighter than before.

In 1969 U.S. steel producers pressured the government to obtain voluntary limits on the tonnage of steel that could be exported to the United States from Western Europe and Japan. When these failed to stem the tide, the industry filed antidumping petitions. In 1978 the Carter Administration agreed to impose a "trigger-price" mechanism, which effectively barred imported steel at any price below the computed cost of production by Japan's most efficient producer plus transport charges, overhead, and a stipulated profit margin. After the steel industry filed new antidumping petitions in 1980, the trigger price was increased by 12 percent. After the steel industry *again* filed countervailing duty cases in 1982, alleging that steel-exporting nations were unfairly subsidizing their industries, the Reagan Administration negotiated a formal quota on steel exports from Western Europe, limiting sales to 5.44 percent of the U.S. market. Other steel-exporting nations received similar quota shares of the U.S. market.

In 1977 the U.S. government negotiated a marketing agreement with Japan, limiting Japanese imports of assembled color televisions to just under 1.6 million units annually. Similar agreements subsequently were negotiated with Taiwan and South Korea. In 1978 the U.S. government substantially increased tariffs on CB radio transceivers. In the 1980s the Reagan Administration forced Japan to limit its automobile exports to the United States to 1.68 million vehicles—a move that encouraged other importing nations to demand similar assurances from the Japanese. Meanwhile, American officials pressured Japanese electronic equipment manufacturers to limit their exports to the United States and to provide assurances about minimum prices.

American industries threatened by foreign competition also have been propped up by a wide assortment of government subsidies, special tax provisions, and subsidized loans and loan guarantees. These forms of assistance have mushroomed since the late 1960s, as global competitive pressures have increased. Finally, as has been noted, the United States continues to grant substantial subsidies and impose severe trade barriers under the pretext of national security.

Some connections to national defense are farfetched, but the connection continues to serve as a useful pretext. Merchant shipping is assumed to be a "strategic" industry in the United States; as a result, foreign merchant ships are barred from U.S. coastal trade, while the U.S. government spends approximately $500 million per year subsidizing the shipbuilding industry. Crude oil from Alaska's North Slope may not be shipped to Japan for fear that such trade will compromise America's "energy independence." Recently, the U.S. government pressured AT&T to award a large fiber-optics contract to a U.S. company rather than to Fujitsu, the lowest bidder, out of fear that the United States might otherwise grow too dependent on Japan for this strategically important product. (Protection of the U.S. watch industry was once defended on the ground that only watchmakers had the skills necessary for designing bomb sights, and recent demands for barriers against Chinese textiles warn of the danger of inadequate domestic capacity for making military uniforms.)

*   *   *

The practical choice facing the United States and every other indus-trialized nation is whether (and to what extent) to preserve existing jobs and industries *or* to help move capital and labor to higher value-added and more competitive production. The point is this: Both choices imply an active role for government. But the first is politically and administra-tively easier to accomplish than the second, at least in the short run. Most people are afraid of change, particularly when they suspect that its burdens and benefits will fall randomly and disproportionately. By the same token, many policies to preserve the status quo—policies like trade barriers protecting against foreign competition and special tax benefits propping up deteriorating balance sheets—do not entail active and visi-ble government interventions; no bureaucrats intrude on corporate dis-cretion; Congress votes no budgets. The costs do not appear on any national accounts, and those who bear them are seldom aware of the source or extent of the burdens.

On the other hand, policies designed to ease and accelerate an econ-omy's transition to higher value-added and more competitive production often necessitate that governments work closely with business and labor to ensure that the sharp changes required do not impose disproportion-ate costs on some or windfalls for others; that workers have adequate income security and opportunities for retraining; that communities on the rise have adequate public services and systems of transportation, communication, and energy; that declining communities have help in phasing down; that emerging industries have sufficient capital to cope with the high costs and risks of starting up, beyond the costs and risks that private investors are willing to endure; and that industries in diffi-culty have sufficient resources to reduce capacity in their least competi-tive parts and restructure their most competitive. All of these activities entail an active and explicit government role.

The more attractive option is obvious. The future standard of living of Americans depends on rapid adjustment both within the United States and among our trading partners. Preservationism, here or abroad, im-perils our future prosperity and that of the rest of the world. Efforts merely to preserve jobs and industries invariably give rise to "zero-sum" international games in which improvements in living standards for one nation come at the expense of another. Such zero-sum games are unsta-ble. They often deteriorate into trade wars, as each nation scrambles to maintain its own living standard by blocking others from exercising their own competitive strengths. Mounting import barriers and subsidies are obvious manifestations of this decline. More subtle are the situations in which poorer nations, whose expectations for higher living standards are dashed by the protectionist policies of industrialized nations, no longer can maintain their growth momentum and thereby stop importing complex products from industrialized nations; shrinking Third World markets in turn reduce the growth of the industrialized nations.

The international economy can be compared to a mill wheel driving the process of structural change in each national economy, pushing each into higher-valued production and generating, ultimately, an ever richer world. The current that propels the wheel is the flow of goods and services from country to country. Any attempt to dam up the current— say, to maintain jobs in the U.S. steel industry by blocking imports of Brazilian steel—reduces the current's force and slows down the wheel. Brazil has smaller earnings with which to repay its international loans, and its growth is stalled. It thus imports fewer U.S. products, and America's growth is slowed. Once the mill wheel begins to decelerate, it is difficult to restore the momentum short of unblocking all the dams and letting the current surge. But the sort of convulsive economic adjustments required to get the world economy moving again under these circumstances are far more difficult to arrange. In periods of slow growth and high unemployment, a progressively larger proportion of firms and workers become hostage to protectionist policies.

* * *

The United States' interest lies in promoting the rapid transformation of all nations' industrial bases toward higher value-added production, while discouraging zero-sum efforts to preserve the status quo. But this strategy requires that the United States abandon its condemnation of all government interventions as illegitimate departures from the free-trade ideal.

U.S. trade policies have had just the opposite effect—discouraging positive adjustments at home and abroad. Part of the problem is that America's failure to discriminate between desirable government interventions and undesirable ones—treating them all as somehow illegitimate and thereby forcing them outside the channels of international scrutiny and negotiation—has ceded much of the initiative to political coalitions bent on preserving the status quo. Informal, voluntary export agreements of the sort now covering substantial portions of the world market for steel, automobiles, textiles, and consumer electronics are almost certain to be undertaken as last-ditch efforts to save jobs. Negotiated piecemeal, without any overarching framework to guide them or any adjustment strategies against which to measure them, these agreements often fall prey to short-term political demands. One bilateral restraint provokes the next, as each nation feels itself progressively more endangered by the possibility that world output will be diverted toward it.

America's formal trade policies also have signaled to our trading partners that we reject the notion of active adjustment. For example, when the U.S. Commerce Department determined in the early 1980s that Britain was unfairly subsidizing British steel—but failed to consider that the subsidies were being used by British steel to reduce capacity and retrain redundant workers—the United States appeared to reject this adjustment strategy outright. Yet capacity reductions and retraining programs organized by affected industries with government help are among the most effective ways of easing the shift of capital and labor out of declining sectors. Indeed, the American steel industry itself stands to gain substantially from such reductions in world steel-making capacity.

Perhaps the saddest irony is that our formal machinery for responding to the allegedly unfair practices of our trading partners has tended perversely to block industrial change at home. America's primary instruments of trade policy have been antidumping levies and countervailing duties, both of which can only shield domestic producers from foreign rivals. As international competition has intensified in recent years, many U.S. firms have used these mechanisms to shield their domestic market and avoid the pressure to adapt. Congressional demands for "reciprocity" against foreign trade barriers and subsidies—and the Reagan Administration's "get tough" policies threatening retaliation against these allegedly unfair practices—suffer from the same perversity. Even if a foreign trade barrier or subsidy is patently a zero-sum attempt to preserve the status quo, it makes no sense for the United States to express its opposition in a way that retards industrial change in this country as well.

* * *

What sorts of principles might guide a new trade policy to encourage positive adjustment at home and among our trading partners? A new trade policy designed to accommodate structural change in the world economy would distinguish between two distinct categories of trade friction, each linked to a different type of business: low-skilled standardized businesses, or high-skilled emerging businesses. A strategic trade policy would be designed to facilitate adjustment within each category.

Low-skilled standardized businesses can be found in basic steel, cotton and simple synthetic textiles, metalworking, most shipbuilding, and basic chemicals. These businesses are characterized by long runs (or large batches) of fairly simple commodities, technologies that are evolving slowly, a relatively low level of skills demanded in the production process, and often intensive use of energy. Notwithstanding that capital costs may be high in some of these businesses, it is relatively easy for newly industrialized nations like South Korea, Taiwan, Hong Kong, Singapore, Brazil, and Mexico to pursue them and become strong competitors. Their labor costs are low, they often have access to cheap raw materials, and their markets for such standardized products often are growing rapidly.

The task for the United States and other advanced industrial nations is to ease the adjustment of their firms and workers out of these businesses as quickly as possible. The least competitive firms should be induced to close, thereby giving the more competitive firms time in which to consolidate operations and shift to higher value-added production. Underutilized plant and equipment should be scrapped or put to other uses. Workers should be retrained. New businesses should be encouraged to move into affected communities. All this often requires an infusion of extra resources, since distressed businesses and their communities are unlikely to possess the wherewithal to do it themselves.

Thus, government subsidies linked directly to these adjustments should be encouraged, both within the United States and in other advanced industrial nations. A similar case can be made for some protection from lower-cost imports for a limited time during the transition—but *only* if specifically linked to a plan for capacity reductions and retraining. Domestic consumers will pay higher prices for these goods in the interim, but the higher prices may be viewed as a justifiable tax to help finance the transition.

For example, Japan's recent efforts at redeploying people and capital out of low-skilled standardized businesses have been relatively successful. Since 1978, the government has helped businesses organize adjustment cartels to scrap excess capacity and find alternative employment for their workers. Other advanced nations are installing such adjustment mechanisms with varying degrees of success. If the United States is to have any workable alternative to protection, it must create similar instruments for easing the transition. At a minimum, the United States should refrain from countervailing against foreign subsidies or retaliating against foreign trade barriers, when these practices are directly tied to capacity reductions and retraining programs.

On the other hand, the United States can legitimately object to certain of our trading partners' practices—like subsidizing exports and setting prices below production costs—which merely retard the shift of capital and labor out of these businesses. Such preservationist policies complicate adjustment and concentrate its costs. They can make it harder to design and implement national transition strategies. Even more objectionable in terms of the goal of continuing economic advance, these policies often end up slowing economic growth within developing nations (which otherwise would shift into these low-skilled standardized businesses) and thus retard the expansion of export markets for more complex goods produced in advanced nations.

The United States should seek international agreements with other advanced industrial nations, establishing targets and timetables for capacity reductions, the scrapping or conversion of existing plant and equipment, and retraining of workers. America might go even further— initiating the creation of an international adjustment fund to help finance these transitions. Payments into the fund would be proportional to a nation's current employment in designated low-skilled standardized businesses; drawing rights would be proportional to a nation's agreed-upon capacity and employment reductions.

Agreements among advanced industrial nations to targets and timetables for phasing out low-skilled standardized businesses would need to be complemented by trade policies encouraging adjustments of developing nations into these same businesses. For example, while no legitimate function is served in advanced nations by granting these businesses export subsidies or in pricing these products below production costs, trade practices like these actually might help *developing* nations quickly gain the production scale necessary to become profitable. For developing nations shifting into standardized businesses, export subsidies and below-cost pricing policies are more accurately viewed as being analogous to investments in new plant and equipment. At the least, therefore, a trade policy geared to adjustment would not impose countervailing duties or antidumping levies on these developing-nation imports.

*   *   *

Emerging businesses in advanced industrial nations are characterized by rapid technological change. All depend largely on skilled labor. Examples include the design and fabrication of optical fiber cable, large-scale integrated circuits, advanced aircraft engines, complex polymer materials, and products derived from recombinant DNA. Many of these businesses are found in the higher-valued, more specialized segments of older industries—for example, automobile transaxles, aramid fibers, and corrosion-resistant steel. In many of these businesses the traditional line between goods and services is becoming blurred—for example, office communications and computer-aided manufacturing. In short, these are the businesses of the future on which our standard of living and that of every other industrialized nation is growing dependent.

Every industrialized nation is racing to gain scale and experience in these businesses; national strategy, not natural endowment, is the key to competitive advantage. Every nation—including the United States, through the back door of NASA and the Department of Defense—is subsidizing research, development, and commercialization. Some nations also are erecting import barriers on the theory that these businesses represent "infant industries" that must be temporarily sheltered. Finally, in anticipation of burgeoning markets, some firms are setting prices substantially below current production costs. Which of these practices should the United States oppose? Which should it emulate?

Subsidies to spur development should be welcomed. New, higher-valued products and new processes for generating them add to the world's wealth. Even if every nation aims for leadership in the same field, this will not become a zero-sum game, since an infinite range of variations and improvements can be achieved, and intense competition will spur even greater progress.

For emerging businesses even below-cost pricing should be welcomed as a positive-sum strategy. Such pricing is undertaken in anticipation of a substantial drop in prices with greater scale and experience. The producer thereby gambles that there will be sufficient demand for the product to generate a healthy return when and if the producer gains a dominant market position—a gamble made all the more risky by the possibility that a competitor will bring out a new product generation in the meantime. Because this form of competition keeps prices low, all consumers benefit. Moreover, given the dynamic nature of the market, below-cost pricing under these circumstances is not predatory—any competitor can leapfrog to a new and better product.

The United States has two handicaps in this race. The first is its significant spending on defense-related research and development, which leads only occasionally and by accident to commercially competitive products or processes. This problem, as I have already suggested, is best addressed by boosting support for nondefense research and development and by ensuring that to the extent possible, defense needs are met by technologies and products directly applicable to commercial, civilian markets. The second handicap takes the form of antitrust policies that discourage research joint ventures among domestic firms in international competition. This can be remedied by altering the antitrust laws explicitly to permit such joint ventures when the world market share of the relevant U.S. firms is under, say, 25 percent.

But there is no reason why the United States should erect trade barriers against foreign emerging businesses that enjoy targeted subsidies or set prices below production costs. Barriers only reduce domestic competition and thereby retard the shift of domestic producers into these businesses. So long as markets are growing and changing rapidly, the financial health of domestic firms in these businesses is not dependent on heavy investment in existing production capacity or on a stable pool of customers; it is dependent on rapid adaptation and quick exploitation of new opportunities—a set of organizational skills that can be honed best in a highly competitive global market.

Nor does the "infant industry" argument provide a reason to protect emerging businesses in today's global economy. Such protection rarely will help a domestic firm catch up to a foreign competitor enjoying a head start in scale and experience. Since technologies are changing rapidly, a better strategy for the domestic firm is to leapfrog to the *next* product generation and establish a leading position there. Domestic producers intent on making such a leap may need government subsidies but not protection from imports of the product they aim to surpass.

Import barriers also may jeopardize the international competitive positions of domestic industrial purchasers—who must now pay more for their components or settle for components of poorer quality. U.S. pressure on Japan to reduce exports of semiconductors surely placed American computer manufacturers at a competitive disadvantage relative to Japanese computer manufacturers, who have ready access to better and cheaper chips; similarly, were the President to disallow investment tax credits for the purchase of numerically controlled machine tools manufactured in Japan, as some American machine-tool manufacturers have urged, U.S. producers of automobiles and construction equipment no longer would have access to superior Japanese machine tools at a low cost.

For these same reasons the United States should strongly oppose the erection of foreign trade barriers that block U.S. exports of high-technology products. But because such tactics are apt to hurt these other nations at least as much as they do U.S. producers, the United States has an opportunity through international negotiations to convince these trading partners that the route to competitive success in emerging businesses lies more with subsidies than import barriers.

A final aspect of U.S. strategy for emerging businesses concerns investments in the education, training, and group learning that now define advanced nations' comparative advantage and determine their capacity to adopt emerging high-value businesses. This subject has been discussed. The quality of public education will continue to be critically important. But since many of the most relevant skills can best be learned on the job, it is becoming increasingly important to develop and attract emerging businesses that will invest aggressively in the training and development of their employees.

*   *   *

The goal is to change the nature of the debate and the focus of attention. Rather than preoccupy ourselves (and our trading partners) with endless and empty disputes over whether a particular practice constitutes an unwarranted subsidy, or a firm is engaged in "dumping," or a certain domestic industry has suffered an injury, or certain nontariff barriers are disruptive to free trade—these new trade strategies would focus the debate on the central question of whether the practices in question serve to accelerate adjustment *or* to maintain the status quo. And to answer that question, we would need to know how particular businesses fit within the evolving world economy.

The international economy is changing too rapidly to expect that we can discover any immutable principles to guide it automatically on its way. Structural changes are painful, and the vagaries of politics inevitably will play a larger role in setting trade policy in the United States and in every other nation in the years ahead. Thus, we need a set of strategic concepts that are consistently applied and that clearly alert our trading partners to what we conceive to be our interest. For the same reason a formal, courtlike apparatus for fact finding and disposition of trade disputes will prove to be less useful than an ongoing process of political debate and negotiation, in which all sides are permanently engaged.

The choice is clear. The forces of preservation will continue to gain ground without firm U.S. leadership in the opposite direction. The United States should approach our trading partners in full awareness that adjustment is inherently difficult, that active government intervention is inevitable and sometimes desirable, and that—through explicit strategies and an ongoing process of negotiation and compromise—we can change zero-sum international conflict into a positive-sum enterprise for world growth.

15

THE UNSPECIAL RELATIONSHIP

ON MARCH 5, 1946, WINSTON CHURCHILL, SPEAKING BEFORE A GROUP
of farmers and local businessmen in Fulton, Missouri, referred to the
"special relationship" between the United States and Great Britain—a
relationship that had led the allies to victory and would continue to lead
the world in the postwar era. Assuming without question Britain's continued status as a leading world power, Churchill regarded the alliance
as between equals; any shortfall in Britain's economic influence would
be compensated by its political skills and historic wisdom. Every subsequent British prime minister has expressed similar sentiments. Anthony
Eden likened the relationship to that between Austria and Britain after
1815. Harold Macmillan invoked a more classical analogy, somewhat
less flattering: "We . . . are Greeks in this American empire. You will
find the Americans much as the Greeks found the Romans—great big,
vulgar, bustling people, more vigorous than we are and also more idle,
with more unspoiled virtues but also more corrupt."

The idea of a "special relationship" between Britain and the United
States was from the start more a hope than a historical description. The
hope was largely Britain's—that America would accept and underwrite
Britain's status as a coequal world power in an era in which Britain's

actual power was waning. The idea never had the same appeal in the United States. Before the wartime alliance most Americans had regarded Britain as a quaint, or even occasionally menacing, imperial power. For more than a century, the deepest instinct of the United States in foreign affairs had been to isolate itself from Europe. America remembered, too, that Britain had been an enemy in two wars. The Irish who flooded into America in the mid- and late-nineteenth century did little to soften this hostile view.

* * *

From America's side the "special relationship" since World War II has been founded in mutual defense against the Soviet Union. The wartime alliance merely had shifted its concern from one common enemy to another. The Soviet Union's first atomic explosion in the autumn of 1949 hastened the process by which the postwar relationship was transformed into a military alliance supported by massive force. The special relationship thereafter took the form of efforts to contain Soviet aggression—through joint leadership of the North Atlantic Treaty Organization, coordinated action in the United Nations Security Council, the sharing of political and military intelligence, Britain's willingness to devote a high proportion of her national product to military purposes, and its acquiescence to American jet fighters based on British soil and nuclear submarines in British ports. Although the United States rarely treated Britain as an equal partner in making strategic decisions, American officials nevertheless consulted closely with their British counterparts during these early postwar years, and Britain was responsible for suggesting many of the initiatives that marked NATO's response to the Soviets.

Britain's enthusiastic cooperation in containing the Soviets was reciprocated by America's willingness to trust Britain with nuclear weapons and to subsidize their cost. In 1958 Britain became the only American ally (to the lasting distress of President De Gaulle) to receive technical information on the production of nuclear warheads and fissile material. Subsequently, the United States allowed Britain to buy the Polaris submarine and then, in 1980, the Trident. No other American ally was given access to these advanced nuclear systems.

This military and strategic relationship took root precisely as Britain's economic and political power in the world began to wane. The decline would, over time, both enhance Britain's dependence on the United States and reduce America's interest in Britain. Both consequences would be unfortunate. As the "special relationship" became increasingly one-sided, Britain grew ever more fearful of either becoming a pawn of or, alternatively, being abandoned by the United States. As America began losing interest in its foremost ally, American policy makers grew less sensitive to the needs and desires of all its allies.

* * *

World War II had set the two allies on different economic trajectories. While the war pulled America out of the Depression, instigating a production boom that lasted twenty years and extending America's economic influence around the world, it had had a very different effect on Britain. Britain sacrificed a quarter of its national wealth to the war and, ultimately, its economic hegemony over a significant part of the globe. The trend would not be apparent for a decade or more. In 1950 Britain's gross national product had just ceased to equal that of France and West Germany combined. As late as 1959, though far behind the United States, Britain still possessed the second-largest GNP in the world. But by 1970 Britain had been overtaken by West Germany and was easily matched by France. By 1985 Britain's GNP per capita was less than that of Italy.

Given how far Britain has fallen, it is easy to forget the extraordinary degree of economic power the nation exercised on the eve of the war. In 1939 the British Empire and the United States together accounted for about 60 percent of the world's industrial production and controlled roughly three quarters of the globe's military wealth. At the war's end the two were the only industrial economies still largely intact. It was natural that Britain and America would now take joint responsibility for redesigning the world economy—developing a system of fixed exchange rates to minimize currency fluctuations, an International Monetary Fund to ensure liquidity, a World Bank to aggregate and direct development finance, a General Agreement on Tariffs and Trade to ensure an open trading system. And it was by dint of their joint commitment to this system that it worked so well for a quarter of a century. The years 1945 to 1970 witnessed the most dramatic and widely shared economic growth in the history of mankind. World GNP grew from $30 billion to over $300 billion. Even allowing for inflation, real incomes tripled, world trade quadrupled.

Since the 1970s, Britain's decline as a world power has, in the eyes of American policy makers, begun to overshadow Britain's reliability as a military ally. Simultaneously over the last fifteen years, and especially during the 1980s, Britain has begun to view America as less the leader of the free world than a frustrated actor seeking to impose its will upon it. It is in this respect that the gradual undoing of the "special relationship" has had the most unfortunate of consequences, both for the United States and for the world.

* * *

Few nations in history have combined such raw military and economic muscle with so parochial a view of the rest of the globe as does modern America. The vast majority of the citizens of the United States speak no foreign language, read little or nothing about happenings beyond their borders, and are decidedly ignorant of the history, culture, or policies of the rest of mankind. In one recent survey 40 percent of American high school seniors had difficulty finding Canada on a world map. This attitude of benign neglect of the rest of the species is a luxury that only a large, naturally wealthy, and geographically isolated nation could have maintained for any length of time. Before World War II its consequences for the rest of the world were relatively harmless. Since then, American ethnocentrism has had more unfortunate effects. The biggest impediment to America's effective leadership of the free world has been its limited ability to understand and collaborate with the rest of the free world.

It is precisely here that the "special relationship" with Britain played such an important role in the quarter century after the war. In Britain the United States found another nation whose citizens spoke the same language, who shared similar legal and political institutions, not to mention many of the same ancestors, but who, by virtue of geography and history, possessed a different and perhaps broader vision of the world. Here was a people whom Americans could trust: friends and confidants in an unfriendly and confusing world, who provided another perspective, and thus helped America overcome its chronic tendency toward parochialism. Although the evidence is scattered and anecdotal, there is little doubt that during this era American officials often sought the counsel of their British counterparts and obtained the sort of frank and confidential advice that one can get only from an old and trusted friend whose judgment is deeply valued. To be sure, the two allies at times reinforced each other's delusions. But Britain's advice often comprised a different viewpoint, causing Americans to think again and to refine or abort a course of action that might not have been adequately thought through.

Yet as Britain's economic and political power has waned, each subsequent American administration has come to view Britain more as one among several constituents whose assent is sometimes necessary or useful to legitimize a policy, or who must be mollified and cajoled into accepting a particular American initiative, and less as a special counsel. (American culture has long tended to discount advice coming from the impecunious: As the Yankee homily goes, "If you're so smart, why ain't you rich?") Notwithstanding the personal friendship of Margaret Thatcher and Ronald Reagan, the generation of experts and bureaucrats that now populates the higher reaches of the White House, the National Security Council, the State Department, the Treasury, and the Defense Department has no direct experience and little memory of the "special relationship" in its golden days. To them, increasingly, Britain is just another pestering voice.

This gradual transformation from a special to a not-so-special relationship has in turn loosened the subtle constraints on American foreign policy, rendering it less sensitive to the needs and views of all of America's allies, with the result that the policies that have issued from Washington in more recent years have too often been unilateral, peremptory, and wide of the mark. And as American policy has appeared in Britain to diverge ever more from the judicious and responsible path, and American officials seem ever less inclined to consult seriously and in advance with their British counterparts, Britain has understandably begun to withdraw from the relationship, to distance itself from America.

The new and more popular form of anti-Americanism in Britain, as in the rest of Western Europe, is, I believe, attributable to what appears to be America's growing indifference to its European allies and to the effects of her policies on world politics and economics. Sadly, examples abound: The postwar system of international economic institutions set up by America and Britain is now coming apart, and U.S. economic policies are largely to blame. America refuses to tame its yawning budget deficit, which has undermined the stability of world currencies; it continues to contrive bilateral "voluntary restraint agreements" and "orderly marketing agreements" with trading partners, with the result that world markets for steel, automobiles, consumer electronics, and other goods are rapidly becoming cartelized; and it is unrelenting in imposing harsh conditions on the repaying of the Latin American debt to U.S. banks, thus drying up these potential markets while destabilizing their new democracies.

American defense policy reveals similar insensitivities. The Reagan Administration fluctuated between complete lack of interest in negotiating reductions in either strategic or intermediate-range nuclear weapons (the inclinations of allies notwithstanding) and then, as at the Reykjavik summit meeting in 1987, sudden—and shocking—willingness to eliminate offensive ballistic missiles altogether, without any advance warning to allies. Toward the Third World, the United States of the 1980s seemed to have adopted a strategy of supporting anticommunist rebels wherever they operated. And America chose to lead the free world against terrorism by solemnly instructing its allies not to bargain with terrorists while covertly sending arms to Tehran for the release of American hostages in Lebanon.

*　*　*

Ironically, the age-old American ideal of a pristine nation, separate from the rest of the world, which can either assert its will unilaterally upon the world or withdraw from it, has less relevance to the situation in which America finds itself today than at any time in the past. American unilateralism has boomeranged, setting off a series of reactions that have come back to where they began. When the United States has stimulated its economy while other nations have opted for restraint, it has summoned a flood of imports and risked inflation and unemployment. When the nation has unilaterally raised interest rates, it has ravaged debtor nations and invited a global recession. When America has closed its borders to foreign goods, it has crippled its debtors' efforts to pay back their loans. When it has lent support to any dictator or revolutionary distasteful to the Soviets, America has lost whatever moral advantage it possessed in the Third World.

Faced with these awkward realities, there has been a temptation in America to lash out—to be ever more assertive toward the rest of the world. American politicians increasingly describe international relations as a series of tests of America's credibility, determination, and resolve. They warn of becoming a "patsy." The assumption is that either we win or they win.

Britain's shift toward Europe, away from the "special relationship" with America, is understandable in this new context. So, too, are the doubts being expressed in Europe these days about the reliability of America's nuclear umbrella, and about America's willingness to maintain free trade and cooperate on macroeconomic management. By 1992 Europe will achieve a new economic identity; a new political independence cannot be far away.

Thus, as Britain moves away from America in response to America's having moved away from Britain and its allies, Britain will be leaving America more alone than this nation has been at any time over the last half century. It is a solitude that is at once poignant and dangerous.

16

WHOSE CARS?

ON FEBRUARY 17, 1983, GENERAL MOTORS AND TOYOTA ANNOUNCED plans for the joint manufacture of a subcompact car in the United States. General Motors would contribute its assembly plant in Fremont, California, and $20 million in cash. Toyota would kick in $150 million in cash. The car, a front-wheel-drive version of the Toyota Corolla, which Toyota already produced and sold in Japan, would be called, in its American version, the Chevrolet Sprinter. About 250,000 cars would be produced annually.

The only thing unusual about this arrangement was its two participants. These were not mom-and-pop operations. General Motors is the largest manufacturer of cars in the world. It sells 40 percent of the cars people buy in the United States. Toyota is Japan's largest carmaker and the third largest in the world. In the U.S. market Toyota ranks number four, just after Chrysler. In sales of subcompacts within the United States Toyota ranks number three, ahead of Chrysler. Both GM and Toyota have long set the pace for the other automobile companies in their home markets in prices, styling, and innovation. Not surprisingly, the two companies are the most profitable auto manufacturers on the globe.

For the past ninety-four years the U.S. government has enforced, with varying degrees of ardor, laws that prohibit companies from monopolizing or restraining trade. Antitrust concepts have a certain charming obscurity about them, and no two lawyers who specialize in this fascinating corner of the law share precisely the same notions about what is or is not permissible. But of this much we can be sure: When the largest and near-largest firms in a market comprising just a few large firms collude with one another, agreeing on a price at which to sell their goods and exchanging information about products and marketing strategies, something questionable is happening in the eyes of the law. At the very least, an arrangement has been made that might easily cause prices to rise.

And so the Federal Trade Commission spent a year investigating the planned joint venture between General Motors and Toyota. A majority of the commissioners then concluded that the plan (ever so slightly modified) was fine. Their logic, spelled out in a public statement, represented one of the first in government decisions expressly modifying traditional law in light of international competition. It marked the beginning of a more explicit national industrial policy. And sadly, it was wrong.

* * *

The commissioners were persuaded of the wisdom of the venture primarily on the grounds that it offered General Motors a "valuable opportunity" to learn firsthand about Japanese manufacturing and management. GM could thereby become a more efficient company. "If GM can learn how to build significantly lower-cost cars, as Japanese producers can now do, it will attempt to implement those lower-cost methods at its other plants," noted the commissioners. In recent years the interpretation and enforcement of antitrust laws have demonstrated increasing respect for whatever efficiencies might possibly be imputed to an agreement among firms, but this particular sort of efficiency—learning by colluding—has never before been thought of sufficient merit to pass even the mildest muster. Applied generally, this new principle of antitrust analysis would seem to permit any two companies to combine so long as one was better at doing something than the other.

But the commissioners had something rather more special in mind. The benefits of learning how to produce cars efficiently presumably would extend beyond General Motors. GM would show other U.S. automakers that "the Japanese system can work in America." This would lead inexorably to "a more efficient, more competitive U.S. automobile industry." At last, we get to the logical core of the argument, the new rule being enunciated. The real justification for allowing America's largest car company to team up with Japan's largest car company was to improve the international competitiveness of the U.S. automobile industry. According to the commission's majority, this long-term national benefit outweighed whatever risk that the arrangement might cause car prices to rise in the near term.

The commissioners' goal was unobjectionable. To be in favor of enhancing U.S. competitiveness is not exactly controversial. But to their real credit, these Republican appointees managed to transcend the White House's ideological revulsion toward industrial policy and accurately perceive that a decision either way would affect the structure of American industry for years to come. The question to be addressed in this case —as in countless government decisions about tax rules, tariffs and quotas, federal procurement contracts, loan guarantees, and research grants —was, What is our national competitive strategy to be?

They asked the right question. It was their answer that was wrong. To understand why, we have only to examine how the world automobile industry has been evolving.

* * *

The world automobile market was then a $250-billion-a-year business, not counting sales of parts, secondhand cars, repair, and service. World car production peaked in 1978 at 31.8 million vehicles and was inching back from the 1982 trough of 27.5 million. Japan then accounted for roughly 25 percent of this output; the United States, for 23 percent. (Since then, the percentages have changed only slightly, with Japan moving up and the United States moving down.) The industry is a major employer in all industrialized nations. If subcontractors, component manufacturers, dealers, advertisers, mechanics, and other related occupations are included, automaking still employs about 15 percent of all Japanese workers and 17 percent of Americans. Many of these jobs, moreover, pay quite well. Relative to other industrial workers worldwide, auto workers are highly productive.

The most dramatic development in the world automobile industry over the past decade, as in so many other industries, has been the success of the Japanese. But it would be wrong to conclude from this that Japan's national economic strategy turns on automobile production. The auto industry in Japan is no longer a particularly favored sector; it enjoys none of the special tax preferences, low-interest credit allocations, antitrust exemptions, or consumer subsidies that are had by fledgling companies in such fields as biotechnology or computers. Strength in the world automobile market is not an end in itself for the Japanese. Their long-term goal is not simply to sell more cars. It is to gain world dominance in the knowledge-intensive industries of the future. Automobile production—or more accurately, the design and fabrication of complex auto parts and the processes necessary to put them together—is a means toward that end. This point bears further elaboration.

Regardless of whose nameplates grace their exteriors, today's automobiles increasingly are multinational creations. Economies of scale and experience, together with political exigencies, are coming to require that parts be produced wherever on the globe they can be manufactured most cheaply and assembled in the region of the globe where the finished cars are to be sold. It is a safe bet that twenty years from now General Motors cars will bear no special relationship to the United States and Toyota no special connection with Japan. One no longer will be able to speak with pride (or derision) about an "American" automobile any more than about a "Japanese" or "West German" automobile. Regardless of where corporate headquarters is located, shareholders, lenders, managers, workers, and consumers alike will be drawn from all over the globe.

But there will be at least one important difference among nations. Workers' real wages—their standard of living—will depend on the *portion* of the production process for which they have responsibility. Since assembly operations will be highly automated worldwide, with robots handling most tasks, the critical distinctions among national work forces will depend on which components they specialize in producing. Workers engaged in making such relatively simple parts as seatcovers, windshield wipers, and dashboards, for example, will not command the same rewards in the global economy as those engaged in more complex tasks. Indeed, the proportional contribution of world auto sales to a nation's wealth will turn on the relative value added to automobile production by that nation's work force. National competitiveness in the automobile industry, as in many other global industries, will come to depend on national prowess in the higher-valued aspects of production.

The Japanese understand this prospect. They are bent on capturing the highest-valued portions of world auto production. They are specializing in such parts as engines, transaxles (front-wheel-drive transmissions and axles), electronic fuel injections and monitoring systems, precision ball bearings, and in such processes as robots and computer-controlled systems for putting all the parts together. These products and processes, in turn, rely on advanced microelectronics and on strong but lightweight synthetic materials and alloys. They thereby represent specific commercial applications of Japan's emerging knowledge-based industries.

The overall strategy is clear. It is the same strategy that underlies Japan's recent, rapid shifts into aircraft engines, videocassette recorders, telecommunications devices, and personal computers. These products are launchpads for gaining scale and experience in the world's newest technologies. Attaining immediate profits from these products is less important than becoming the largest and most experienced world practitioners of the advanced methods that lay behind them. A Japanese labor force so attuned will easily come to dominate the highest-valued portions of any global industry. There is nothing sinister about this; consumers all over the globe continue to benefit from Japan's advances, although Japan eventually will enjoy the world's highest standard of living. Viewed in this light, the Japanese automobile strategy is part of an overall national strategy by which the Japanese will become the design engineers for the world.

*　　*　　*

Japan's automobile strategy is by now well under way. GM buys its diesel engines from Isuzu; Chrysler, many of its transaxles and engines from Mitsubishi. Ford gets its complex parts from Mazda. In Ohio and Britain Honda is assembling cars, the designs and more sophisticated components of which come from Japan. Nissan is assembling trucks in Tennessee and cars in Britain and Spain; their designs and highest-valued parts also come from Japan.

This trend is particularly apparent in the production of the smallest cars, which must be designed and manufactured especially carefully in order to minimize costs and maximize comfort. As the Japanese have learned in producing everything from televisions to semiconductors, innovations in products and manufacturing processes often occur at the most compact end of a product line, where the engineering challenges are the greatest. For the same reason, development expenses often are highest at the compact end. If your strategy is to gain scale and experience in applying new technologies, then you will gladly bear these costs; the investment will pay off in a work force better able to innovate in the future. But if your strategy is to maximize profits over the next three or four years, you will buy the compact technology from someone else. Accordingly, the Japanese are developing it; the Americans are buying it.

Subcompact automobile technology—including the design, advanced parts, and machines for assembling the parts according to the designs—is being ceded to the Japanese. GM is importing subcompacts from Suzuki and Isuzu and assembling "R" cars produced by Isuzu; GM's futurist Saturn model is still on the drawing board. Chrysler has quietly abandoned its planned replacement for the Omni/Horizon family of cars and is looking to Mitsubishi to fill out its subcompacts. Ford has invested $500 million in Mexico, where it will assemble a Mazda subcompact.

*   *   *

The joint venture between General Motors and Toyota fits this pattern exactly. The cars that roll out of the Fremont, California, assembly plant are designed in Japan; their engines, transaxles, and other advanced components, manufactured in Japan; many of the robots and computerized machine tools used to assemble them, designed and produced in Japan. Left to American labor are the lower-skilled assembly tasks, production of the simpler parts, and of course, advertising, sales, and repair services to be offered in the United States.

GM, Ford, and Chrysler have grown more profitable largely by cutting their costs and selling bigger cars based on older models. During the past decade, the three companies have closed assembly plants, shut down vast networks of parts plants, and laid off a sizable portion of their work force. They have canceled or delayed at least a dozen new products. They are now "lean and mean," which is the way corporate managers in America like to describe the newly dismembered companies over which they preside. They are investing in new models only gradually, extending the lives of older models by making slight alterations.

General Motors leads this timid pack. Its costs are the lowest, its profits highest. But it worries about the next downturn in the business cycle. Its "planning horizon" is three years. If GM finds a new way to cut its costs, Ford and Chrysler must follow suit or else run the risk of losing even more of the market. GM has decided that it is cheaper to buy subcompact technology from Japan than to invest in it at home. And the cheapest way to buy subcompact technology from Japan is to get the Japanese to foot part of the bill for jointly assembling Japanese cars in America. That is what the joint venture with Toyota is all about. It is a white flag of surrender. Other U.S. automakers will see it and follow.

Joint ventures like this one fit nicely into Japan's automobile strategy, making it worth the extra cost. They create an immediate demand for Japanese designs, sophisticated components, and high-technology manufacturing systems. Yet because they appear to save American jobs, they also forestall mounting political pressures in the United States to protect against Japanese imports. Indeed, the United Auto Workers was quite supportive of the GM–Toyota plan. Never mind that the jobs preserved or created in America are lower skilled and routine, eventually to be replaced by robots and computers. In the immediate future at least, there are jobs. To American workers, the obvious alternative seems far less salutary.

*   *   *

Is there any other alternative? Surely not the proposal, touted by the United Auto Workers Union, that cars sold in the United States must contain a high percentage of components produced in America. Even if 90 percent of the value of cars sold here were produced here, Japan still would be supplying the most sophisticated 10 percent and simultaneously supplying the rest of the globe (including GM, Ford, and Chrysler operations abroad) with an even larger percentage—thereby maintaining superior scale and experience at the highest-valued end of world auto production. More to the point, the perennial "domestic content" proposal gives companies no real incentive to invest in advanced automobile technologies within the United States. When pressed, they can simply duplicate whatever technologies already have been perfected in Japan. Meanwhile, everyone who buys a car in the United States gets stuck with a huge price tag reflecting the higher cost of making cars in America. We lose both ways.

There is no simple solution. Japan's competitive strategy embraces its entire industrial base; America's strategy is the by-product of individual corporate strategies whose goals may have little to do with enhancing the standard of living of Americans. To reverse the present trend and gain predominance in the highest-valued portions of world auto production would require that auto companies operate under a very different set of incentives than they do today. At the least, such a reversal would entail changes in tax laws, international trade laws, and antitrust rules. For example, Congress or the special trade representative might have linked Japan's "voluntary" export restraint to explicit agreements by U.S. automakers to invest in advanced automobile technologies and to train their workers in these emerging fields. We missed this opportunity; the automakers got the benefits of the export restraint with no strings attached.

The GM–Toyota joint venture represented another small opportunity to move the auto industry in the right direction. To be sure, had the Federal Trade Commission rejected the proposed venture, that would not have stemmed the tide; at best, it might have slowed it down a bit. Antitrust law is a crude means of fashioning industrial policy. But the commissioners might have used the occasion to announce a different direction for antitrust enforcement in the future, perhaps encouraging joint research ventures among American companies and clearly signaling the strategic perils for the American economy that lay in the path GM and Toyota had chosen. If they in fact believed the dubious contention that the venture would help the entire U.S. automobile industry, moreover, the commissioners might have called GM's bluff and required the arrangement be a public "demonstration project" in which Ford and Chrysler were invited to participate. But the commissioners did none of these things. By approving the venture instead, and doing so on such broad grounds, they opened the floodgates.

17

THE CORPORATION
AND THE NATION

IF THE CORPORATIONS AMERICANS OWN AND WORK FOR SUCCEED, THE
American economy will too—or so we were brought up to believe. This
assumption was given its most brazen expression thirty-five years ago by
Charles Erwin Wilson, who was then the president of General Motors;
he was nicknamed "Engine Charlie," in order to distinguish him from
another Charles E. Wilson, "Electric Charlie," who was the president of
General Electric through the 1940s. During the Senate hearing on his
confirmation as Eisenhower's nominee for secretary of defense, Wilson
was asked whether he could make a decision in the interests of General
Motors' shareholders. Wilson said that he could but that such a conflict
would probably never arise. "I cannot conceive of one because for years
I thought what was good for our country was good for General Motors,
and vice versa. The difference did not exist."

Engine Charlie's statement was widely criticized at the time as an
example of corporate America's arrogance, but in fact it simply expressed principles already codified in American law and policy: The
corporation existed for its shareholders, and as they prospered, so would
the nation.

This root principle of our political economy is no longer valid. The corporations Americans own and work for are becoming disconnected from the national economy. The overall success of these corporations has less and less to do with America's continued growth and prosperity. Corporation and nation are growing apart, and American law and politics must adapt to this new reality.

*   *   *

When Engine Charlie uttered his dictum, it was easy to believe that what was good for corporations and their shareholders was also good for the national economy. At least, shareholders' interests were not so narrowly defined as to seem inconsistent with the nation's broader economic objectives. Shareholders were typically too widely dispersed to exert any real control over the corporation. Most shareholders faithfully held on to their shares, treating them as long-term investments and trusting that share values would continue to rise over time.

Top corporate executives thus enjoyed wide discretion to do whatever they pleased, including what they deemed to be socially responsible, as long as their expenditures could be justified as benefiting shareholders over the long term. This rationalization was capacious enough to encompass almost any activities that might improve the corporation's image. In fact, some of the expenditures they made—on basic research, the development of new products and technologies, employee training, various educational and philanthropic activities—had little positive effect on the corporation's bottom line, because the new knowledge easily spread to other firms. But these activities did help spur broader economic development within the regions the corporations inhabited. And many of the executives relished the role of the "corporate statesman," who mobilized private resources for further public gains.

These activities should not be romanticized. Managerial discretion was not always put to such noble purposes. But it could be, and the prevailing ideology held it to be an appropriate exercise of corporate power.

In the past few years, however, the stock market has become far more efficient at keeping the executives' attention fixed on the bottom line. First, the dispersed individual shareholders of yore have largely been replaced by a relatively few professional investment managers, who are responsible for investing enough billions of dollars of pension funds, mutual funds, and insurance funds to make up at least a third of all the equity in corporate America. These investment managers are responsible for some 70 percent of the trading on the New York Stock Exchange.

They compete against one another and are quick to shift funds from one corporation to another, depending on whose share prices are rising or falling at the moment. Second, the deregulation of brokerage fees and new technologies linking computers to trading floors have reduced the costs and increased the speed of such transactions; the computer linkages also give investment managers up-to-the-minute data on share prices. Third, financial entrepreneurs have refined techniques for acquiring controlling blocks of shares, sometimes even using the corporation's own assets as collateral. Because of these three developments, it has become relatively easy for an aggressive company or a few audacious individuals to seize control of even the largest of American corporations when they sense a failure by the corporation's executives to exploit some opportunity for increasing the value of their shares.

To deter raiders, every major American corporation is busily "restructuring" itself, to use the Wall Street euphemism. This has required eliminating or drastically cutting back on discretionary spending. "There are very few corporate statesmen anymore," laments James Joseph, the president of the Council on Foundations, which monitors corporate giving. "CEOs no longer want to spend their time on social issues." As one executive put it recently, "It becomes positively un-American to look at anything except their own bottom line."

*   *   *

Executives no longer argue that what is good for shareholders is necessarily good for the nation. In fact, many are now insisting that the stock market's unrelenting demand for higher share value is actually harmful to the nation and that raiders should be restrained. Their warnings are being heard. In one recent *Business Week*–Harris poll 64 percent of the people surveyed favored new government restrictions on hostile takeovers. States are taking the lead in protecting their corporations. Earlier this year Delaware—where almost half the firms on the New York Stock Exchange are incorporated—became the twenty-ninth state to limit takeovers, thus in one swoop effectively shielding half of corporate America. Congress is considering legislation to discourage hostile mergers nationwide.

What may have escaped notice by America's business leaders is the logical consequence of their new argument. One of the great advantages of the Engine Charlie principle to American business was its implicit rejection of any formal means of holding corporations accountable for the nation's continued prosperity. In benefiting shareholders, the corporation would necessarily spur the economy forward. But once it is granted, even by business leaders, that this is not always the case—indeed, that *too much* attention to shareholders' demands may in fact detract from the nation's long-term vitality—then the presumptive link between corporate executives' responsibilities to their shareholders and to the nation is severed. What is good for the shareholders is not necessarily good for the nation.

The question that in Engine Charlie's day had been submerged under the vague rubric of "long-term" shareholder interests thus arises: By what means should corporations be held accountable to the public for contributing to the nation's prosperity?

* * *

As ever more of corporate America is bought by foreign nationals, another divergence appears between the interests of the corporation and its shareholders and the interests of the nation.

In Engine Charlie's time virtually all major corporations doing business in America were owned by Americans. Thirty years later, this situation has changed. Other national economies are catching up with that of the United States; a few are on the verge of surpassing it. American-owned corporations are no longer the only global enterprises of significant power and scale, nor even the largest ones. And in a historic reverse, foreign ownership of American capital now stands at over $200 billion, more than double what it was in 1980, and it is rising rapidly.

The low dollar has made bargains of American corporations, as if corporate America were having a fire sale, with every company marked 35 to 50 percent off its regular price. The companies that have been bought include some sporting familiar names, like Doubleday, CBS Records, Purina Mills, Mack Truck, Allis-Chalmers, and Firestone. Foreign capital is also pouring into the American stock market. Major banks and investment houses—BankAmerica, Shearson Lehman, Paine Webber, and Goldman, Sachs—are now partly owned by Japanese banks intent on breaking into the American financial market.

The wave of foreign acquisition of corporate America is having an effect in the United States similar to that felt in other nations when they faced American investment years ago—when charges of American "imperialism" were in the air and fears that American multinational corporations would exploit host nations were acute. A trade bill passed in 1988 by the House of Representatives requires foreign investors to report to the government any "significant" interest they had acquired in an

American corporation. The version passed in the Senate authorizes the administration to review any proposed acquisition of an American corporation by foreigners. American business leaders, although delighted to have foreign investors bid up the prices of their own shares, have expressed mounting concern about the number of foreign-owned corporations popping up in their midst.

Here, too, the implication is that the interests of the shareholders of the corporations in our midst are no longer the same as the nation's. In this instance, it is not enough that a corporation produces goods and services within the United States and employs American workers. To guarantee that corporate success will translate into national success, the corporation must also be firmly under the control of *American* citizens —so the argument goes. American shareholders and executives, it is assumed, can be trusted to act in the nation's interest under circumstances in which foreign shareholders and executives cannot be trusted. But a step is missing from this argument, just as a step was missing from the previous argument, that corporations protected from takeovers will act in the long-term interest of the economy. Here the unanswered question is, Why and under what circumstances should American citizens be expected to forgo profits in pursuit of national goals?

* * *

In Engine Charlie's time almost everything that American-owned corporations sold here or abroad—particularly anything involving the slightest complexity in design or manufacturing—was produced in the United States. This is no longer the case. American-owned corporations are now doing all sorts of technologically sophisticated work outside the United States. A significant proportion of America's current trade imbalance is due to this tendency.

Look closely at almost any major American corporation that sells complex gadgets and you are likely to see a foreign producer in disguise: In 1986 IBM imported $1.5 billion worth of data-processing equipment and General Electric half a billion dollars' worth of cassette recorders, microwave ovens, room air-conditioners, and telephones. Apple Computer's Asian plants make all Apple II computers, which in 1986 accounted for more than half of the company's sales. Eastman Kodak now sells, under its own name, Canon photocopiers, Matsushita video cameras, and TDK videotape, and it has farmed out the production of its thirty-five-millimeter cameras to Haking Industries, in Hong Kong, and Chinon Industries, in Japan. And so on.

All such goods that American corporations buy or make abroad and then sell in the United States are counted as American imports. The current frenzy in Washington over allegedly unfair foreign trade practices has obscured this reality. Consider Taiwan, which now exports some $19 billion more to the United States each year than it imports from the United States. The imbalance has provoked the indignation of American politicians, some of whom are demanding that Taiwan take steps to improve the balance or incur stiff penalties. But on closer examination the real culprit emerges. Several of Taiwan's top exporters are American-owned corporations—RCA, Texas Instruments, and General Instruments. All told, more than 30 percent of Taiwan's trade imbalance with the United States, and more than half of its imbalance in high-technology goods, is attributable to American-owned corporations buying or making things in Taiwan and exporting them back to the United States. Taiwan's only sin is to have a highly skilled population that is willing to work for relatively low wages (Taiwanese engineers earn a quarter of the salary of American engineers, and Taiwanese technicians a fifth of their American counterparts' wages).

Even Japan's notorious trade surplus with the United States is in substantial part the handiwork of American-owned corporations. Fully $17 billion, or about 40 percent, of Japan's $39.5 billion trade surplus with the United States in 1985 (a year in which the trade imbalance surged) was the result of American corporations' buying or making things in Japan to be sold in the United States under their own brand names. One of the ironies of our age is that an American who buys a Buick or an RCA television is likely to get *less* American workmanship than if he had bought a Honda or a Matsushita TV.

Americans who live and work in the United States continue to consume more than they produce and to import more than they export—hardly the path to prosperity. But American-owned *corporations* are doing quite well, regardless. They are not only raking in nice profits by buying or making things abroad for sale here but also doing well by buying or making things abroad for sale everywhere else. In 1985 American-owned corporations sold the Japanese over $53 billion worth of goods that they made in Japan—a sum greater than the American trade deficit with Japan that year (Japanese companies, meanwhile, sold us only $15 billion worth of goods that they made in the United States). IBM Japan is huge and prosperous in its own right, with eighteen thousand employees, annual sales of $6 billion around the world, and research and production facilities that are among the most advanced anywhere.

In fact, American-owned corporations have remained competitive worldwide. A recent study by Robert Lipsey and Irving Kravis, of the National Bureau of Economic Research, suggests that while the fraction of world markets held by U.S. corporations exporting from the United States has steadily dropped during the past twenty-five years, such losses have been offset by the gains of American-owned corporations exporting from *other* nations.

*　*　*

One conclusion that might be drawn from all this is that America's competitive decline does not stem from any inherent deficiency in the top management of American corporations. The stream of books exhorting managers toward excellence notwithstanding, American managers have done well by their shareholders (although not so well by America). Unsurprisingly, this insight has been welcomed by American business leaders eager to shift the blame for our competitive woes onto someone else. Mobil Oil Corporation made the argument succinctly in a 1987 advertising pronouncement:

> American multinational companies can, and do, compete successfully all over the world. While the U.S. trade balance became a shambles, these companies continued to operate successfully in world markets. They did so by producing in those countries with the best business climates. . . .
>
> So to argue that American businessmen have lost their management and technological skills, or grown fat and lazy, is neither true nor relevant. We should be looking to ourselves to learn why this country has provided a less favorable business environment than some of our trading partners. And then we should act to improve the climate.

Stripped to its brutal essentials, Mobil's message is this: American corporations and their shareholders can now prosper by going wherever on the globe the costs of doing business are lowest—where wages, regulations, and taxes are minimal. Indeed, managers have a responsibility to their shareholders to seek out just such business climates. If America as a whole wants to be a successful exporter, it must compete with other nations to be the location where American corporations find it profitable to set up shop.

This lesson is well understood by state governments. Consider, for example, the Hyster Company, an American-owned corporation that makes forklift trucks used to shuttle things around factories and warehouses. In 1982 Hyster informed public officials in five states and four nations where it built trucks that some Hyster plants would close. Operations would be retained wherever they were most generously subsidized. The bidding was ferocious. Within six months Hyster had collected $72.5 million in direct aid. Britain is reported to have offered $20 million to ransom fifteen hundred jobs in Irvine, Scotland. Several American towns—including Kewanee, Illinois; Sulligent, Alabama; and Berea, Kentucky—surrendered a total of $18 million in direct grants and subsidized loans to attract or preserve around two thousand jobs.

The same underlying problem emerges. Subsidies and tax breaks are offered with no strings attached—no means of holding corporations accountable to the public. Executives of the Hyster Corporation are under no more legal obligation to direct corporate efforts toward spurring the American economy than are the executives of companies shielded from takeovers by recent state laws, such as those passed by Delaware, or than are the executives of American-owned corporations in general. Hyster can take the subsidies and tax breaks and do with them whatever it wants. Indeed, just last August Hyster announced another wave of closings. The Engine Charlie principle, as this example illustrates, is no longer valid, but nothing has replaced it to reestablish the link between corporation and nation.

*   *   *

The privileged place of the corporation in America has been justified for more than a century by the assumption that corporations automatically fuel the nation's economic growth—that what is good for shareholders is necessarily good for America. In the past few years, however, as corporate America has become simultaneously more attentive to the immediate demands of shareholders for high returns and more international in its ownership and operations, its links to the national economy have seriously weakened.

How *should* the corporation be bound to the nation in the future? Should it be bound at all? The struggle to define a new relationship between corporation and nation will be one of the central economic and political tasks of our era, and it will defy easy solutions. Only the contours of the emerging debate can be seen.

On the one side will be those who argue that any divergence between corporate strategies and national goals is perfectly OK. The world economy as a whole will be stronger if corporations are free to attract investors from anywhere and undertake production anywhere, with the sole objective of rewarding their shareholders with the highest possible returns. In this view, any special relationship between particular corporations and a particular nation will result in an inefficient use of resources overall. As the world economy grows ever more integrated, the nation-state is becoming outmoded and irrelevant anyway. A nation's only legitimate concern with corporations doing business within its borders should be to guard its citizens from harmful side effects of corporate activity, such as pollution, unsafe products, monopolization, and fraud.

But this view fails to take into account the positive side effects of corporate activity for a nation—in particular, the training of a nation's work force in new skills applicable outside the company, and technological discoveries with broader potential. Such corporate investments in the skills and knowledge of a nation do not necessarily benefit shareholders, as has been noted, because the benefits often leak out of the company as the new knowledge spreads and as employees take their skills elsewhere. But they are critical for moving an economy forward. Positive side effects like these are as relevant to the welfare of a nation's citizens as are the potential harmful side effects. In a world in which nation-states continuously compete for economic power and the influence that flows from it, decisions about where investments are undertaken, by whom, and of what sort can have profound political consequences as well.

On the other side of the debate will be those who argue that corporations should be tightly bound to the nation. In this view large corporations in particular should be firmly under public control. It will be urged, for example, that representatives of the public be placed on corporate boards; that some corporate shares be held by publicly appointed trustees or by public authorities; that American corporate investments in other nations, and foreign investments here, be reviewed to ensure compatibility with national economic goals; and that transfers of American capital or technology across the border be carefully monitored. But this view suffers from the opposite infirmity—it sacrifices market efficiency to public accountability. Without the hope of maximizing profits, the spur of competition, and the fear of loss, enterprises have a tendency to stagnate. Too much of this, and entire economies can decline. There is a growing consensus, now apparently extending all the way to the Kremlin, that public ownership and centralized controls are not the path to progress either.

*   *   *

The best solution would be to focus specifically on what things we want corporations to do that are apt to be unprofitable to shareholders and then to induce corporations to do them. What is it we want corporations to do? Not to preserve jobs in the United States that can be done far more cheaply by foreign workers eager to do them. The costs of trying to keep such jobs here—as reflected in higher prices for consumers and onerous burdens on Third World workers deprived of work—would far exceed the benefits. We should ask corporations instead to help propel the American economy forward by training American workers in new skills and investing in new knowledge. America's economic future depends not on the old jobs we used to do but on the new contributions we can make to an increasingly integrated world economy.

Our overriding goal should be to ensure that America is a place where enterprises of whatever nationality perform sophisticated tasks and thus give large numbers of Americans valuable experience. There are several ways of inducing corporations to undertake complex production in America. The first and most obvious is to ensure that our citizens are capable of learning quickly on the job so that Americans will be the kind of workers global corporations want to train. This will require that we as a nation invest more than we do now in education—in preschool programs, in basic literacy and numeracy, in scientific and technical competence, and in foreign-language training, to name only the most critical areas. Numerous recent studies reveal the ignorance of American schoolchildren relative to those in Japan and other industrialized nations, and the extent of illiteracy and innumeracy in the society. In recent years there has been much handwringing over reading and math scores in certain locales, and even some progress in raising them. The important point is that America's future productivity is directly related to our collective capacity to learn on the job, which depends in turn on how well we are prepared to learn. No corporation, however well intentioned, can afford to make up for a lack of basic education.

In addition to the general lure of a competent work force, however, we will need more-substantive inducements. They could take several forms. We might, for example, subsidize corporations that do certain kinds of advanced design and manufacturing in the United States, with the amount of the subsidy depending on the numbers of employees so engaged. Or the inducement might take the form of a tax credit, similarly structured.

Inducements like these would also be costly, resulting in higher taxes or prices for most Americans. But unlike the open-ended initiatives now commonplace, these inducements would feature a quid pro quo: Corporations receiving them would be delivering benefits to the American economy, through on-the-job training and new knowledge. And the greater the benefits to the economy, the greater the inducements to the corporation.

These inducements would not hobble international trade or shelter American corporations from competition. They would be made available to any corporation—headquartered anywhere, owned by anyone. Corporations would thus be held accountable for what we as a public sought from them yet would have a continued incentive to allocate resources to their most profitable uses. Such inducements would have the additional virtue of pushing us to clarify our long-term development strategy— forcing our government representatives to define the categories of experience and skills we think will be most important to the nation's future.

*   *   *

The difficulties in the way of administering such inducements, or even gaining sufficient political support to launch them, should not be underestimated. It has been hard enough to strengthen public education and ensure a minimal level of competence in the American work force; this program of on-the-job training and research is far more ambitious. Moreover, many Americans lack confidence in government's capacity to accomplish public purposes wisely and efficiently and already feel overwhelmed and overtaxed by public needs.

But the alternatives are even less attractive. Our national strategy for economic development clearly must be more than, and different from, the sum of the strategies used by the corporations our citizens own or work for. To repeat, this is not because these corporations are irresponsible or unpatriotic, but because their widening global opportunities for making profits—and shareholders' mounting demands that they exploit such opportunities—are coming to have no direct or unique bearing on the nation's continued growth. The direction in which we are heading —blocking takeovers, hobbling foreign owners, and granting tax breaks and subsidies indiscriminately—seems far riskier and costlier than the direction I have proposed.

The growing divergence between corporation and nation is part of a larger quandary. As our economy becomes so entwined with the world's that the nations' borders lose their commercial significance, Americans need to understand and recognize the subtle ways in which our citizens are connected to one another—not through the corporations we own but through the skills and knowledge we absorb. Without this understanding we cannot expect to elicit the sacrifices required to gain greater skills and knowledge. Corporations are no longer the building blocks of the U.S. economy; our citizens are.

IV

THE
ROAD
TO
QUAYLE

18

THE REDEFINED PRESIDENCY

WHY DID GEORGE WIN? JUST BECAUSE HIS CAMPAIGN WAS ESPECIALLY vicious? No. Michael Dukakis threw his share of mud. Because of peace and prosperity? No. The public knows the peace is fragile, and prosperity uneven and vulnerable. Because America has turned conservative? No. Most Americans still want government help with education, day care, health care, housing, and the environment.

Then why did it happen? Simply, George Bush was elected because he demonstrated during the campaign that he could better fulfill the role of President as that role is now understood by the American people. George Bush campaigned for Ronald Reagan's job, and that's what he got. Michael Dukakis campaigned for a job that no longer exists.

The President used to be the government's chief executive, responsible for solving problems and implementing laws. He had a symbolic function, to be sure, but we all understood that his primary duty was to run the executive branch of government. We held the President accountable for the decisions he made. We demanded that he respond to the press, tell the truth, and take responsibility for major decisions.

But under Ronald Reagan, the Presidency was transformed, and the press and the public gradually accommodated to the change. The President has become our nation's toastmaster, the host and narrator of our country's unfolding TV docudrama. As redefined by Reagan, the President's function is to welcome home brave soldiers, comfort the families of fallen heroes, celebrate the birthdays of national monuments, exult our friends, and condemn our enemies. He is the reflection of our preferred national self-image—bountiful, buoyant, effervescent. His chief function is to make us feel safe, proud, and happy.

Ronald Reagan rarely met with the press, since this isn't required of the redefined President. A 1989 report by the Commission on the Presidential News Conference notes that Reagan's two immediate predecessors averaged one press conference every month, but Reagan averaged only six per year. Instead, he sought carefully staged visuals, photo opportunities, ceremonial pageantry. According to the report, "[e]very morning Reagan's team would meet to determine what images of the President they wanted to get on the nightly news." Thus, with each passing night we grew more accustomed to seeing our President on television, with the stirring or soothing message of the day.

Nor, in the redefined Presidency, is the truthfulness of White House statements a matter of major concern. Truth or falsehood isn't the point of such pronouncements. At the start of the Reagan Presidency the press and the public were upset about gross inaccuracies. But most people now accept that the President needs a wide degree of factual latitude. Made-up facts are accepted as illustrations, useful for the President's broader messages of uplift and inspiration.

Nor, finally, do presidential decisions matter very much. The redefined Presidency is separate from the day-to-day business of government. Ronald Reagan allowed others to make the decisions of state. To this, we have also accommodated. The public now accepts that the President should attend to sculpting the larger vision, rather than the details of governing. Since he makes no decisions, the redefined President can make no mistakes—outside his realm of symbol and image.

George Bush campaigned precisely for the job that Ronald Reagan left. Bush's campaign was a microcosm of the redefined Presidency—insulated from the press, carefully staged and scripted for the evening news, wondrously immune to the confusion of real issues. Bush had few press conferences, for fear that he might say something silly or embarrassing. He did not anguish over the accuracy of his statements. His handlers met each morning to decide on the day's theatrical backdrop—a flag factory, a crowd of police chiefs, Boston Harbor. "We are running a campaign that is designed for network TV," said Roger Stone, a senior

Bush adviser, in the weeks before the election. "That means only one message a day. . . . It means not allowing anything unplanned."

It should come as no surprise that George Bush was better qualified than was Michael Dukakis to take on Ronald Reagan's job. Bush had the advantage of seeing Ronald Reagan do it, close up, for eight years. And most of the people who guided Bush through the campaign—who gave him the scripts, told him where to stand, what to do and say—were the same people who guided Reagan as he redefined the Presidency.

Michael Dukakis campaigned for the old job. Nobody told him such services were no longer required. So he spent too much time proposing policies for educating our kids, ensuring our health, or restoring our technological lead. He talked too much with the press, and he resisted the advice of his packagers. When he tried to drop substance for symbols —like the time he rode around in that tank—he just looked silly. When he tried to spin visions, his words fell flat. He is altogether too serious, too somber, too dull for the redefined Presidency.

The tragedy of Michael Dukakis is that he wanted to be the nation's chief executive, while the open job was as Ronald Reagan's replacement. When it came time for Americans to ask which one of the two candidates would be better at doing what we have come to expect of our President, the choice was clear. We couldn't possibly envision Michael Dukakis as our national toastmaster. But George had proven himself a natural.

19

THE SPIRIT OF THE LAW

"YOU KNOW THE RULE: NO SUGARY SNACKS BEFORE DINNER."

"But Daddy," my son said plaintively, chocolate all over his face, "it wasn't a snack. It was just a few cookies. It wasn't sugary. The package said it was natural. And besides, I didn't eat them before dinner. It's five o'clock and dinner isn't till half past six." Since then, the family snack rule has become more specific.

When the spirit of the law is disregarded, the letter of the law expands until it claims attention.

In recent years the same drama has been played out on a larger stage. Investigations into wrongdoing at the highest levels of American business and government are turned over to prosecutors and defense attorneys, who argue over narrow definitions, while Congress seeks to prevent recurrences by enacting ever more detailed constraints.

Item: A coterie of Wall Street bankers and their friends stands accused of insider trading. The Securities and Exchange Commission, charged with enforcing the law, has defined insider trading broadly as a type of fraud. But in response to elaborate arguments by the bankers, there is pressure on the SEC to be far more explicit.

So it now recommends to Congress a new law barring the use of insider information if "it has been obtained by, or as a result of, or its use would constitute, theft, bribery, misrepresentation, or espionage through electronic or other means, or a breach of duty to maintain such information in confidence or to refrain from purchasing, selling or causing the purchase or sale of, the security which duty arises from any fiduciary, contractual, employment, personal or other relationship with . . . " and so on, for five turgid pages.

Securities lawyers think this clarifies and closes loopholes in the old standard and thus will be easier for the SEC to enforce. Maybe. But there was never any doubt about the purpose of the former law: to make sure that no one profits from information unavailable to the public, lest investors eschew a market that seems rigged. And the bulwarks thrown up in the new version will pose little challenge to defense attorneys skilled in the art of legal circumnavigation.

Item: A gaggle of former presidential assistants stands accused of using public office for personal gain. The Ethics in Government Act of 1978—itself a post-Watergate effort to render explicit what had always been understood as inappropriate conduct—bars former officials from lobbying their old offices within a year of leaving them, especially on matters that were pending when they left.

But one of the accused—a former White House deputy chief of staff—says the law doesn't apply to what he did. He had a right to lobby the Office of Management and Budget on behalf of a private client as soon as he departed his office, he claims, since OMB is not technically part of the White House, where he worked.

Another recently indicted White House aide argues that he did no wrong even in lobbying the White House, since the White House isn't a place where matters are ever "pending" anyway; it's where they're decided. In response, Congress is now trying to tighten the lobbying law, no doubt rendering it as convoluted and picayune as the SEC's proposed ban on insider trading.

Item: A band of high-level military officers is suspected of having violated several laws in funneling money to the contras. In late 1985 Congress expressly barred "any agency or entity of the United States involved in intelligence activities" from doing so. (This law, by the way, was an effort to close loopholes in earlier laws intended to stop military aid to the contras.)

But the officers, who were then staff members of the National Security Council, argue in court that the NSC is an advisory body to the President, not an intelligence agency, and thus was not included in the ban. Next time, Congress will be sure to close this loophole.

*   *   *

Regardless of who wins in the courts, we all lose. When the law degenerates into cat-and-mouse games of discovering and closing ambiguities, it loses its moral force, without which no set of detailed proscriptions can ever be detailed enough.

The cumulative effect is to loosen the bonds of mutual trust and responsibility on which a free society depends. And this exacts a real cost from all of us, as our society becomes as rule bound as a potted plant no longer able to grow.

The solution is not to be found in more niggling rules, which even a small boy intent on chocolate cookies can elude. It lies in a society that focuses on why laws are enacted rather than how they are phrased and thus demands adherence to the law's purposes as well as to its literal constraints.

Fines or imprisonments, or even impeachments, are appropriately reserved for those who transgress the letter of the law. Those who violate its spirit deserve a less official but no less sure form of punishment: They should stand disgraced in the court of public opinion.

20

A SENTIMENTAL EDUCATION

THERE WAS A PARADOX AT THE HEART OF THE REAGAN ADMINISTRATION.

In his book* Martin Anderson, Ronald Reagan's first domestic policy adviser, portrayed a White House that was the very model of efficient and thoughtful policy making. "All major policy ideas had to pass through a gauntlet of committee meetings, ranging from formal meetings of the full Cabinet or the Cabinet councils, to smaller, more informal gatherings," he wrote. Each of the six Cabinet councils had jurisdiction over an area of policy that cut across departments—like trade, natural resources, and defense. In addition to the relevant Cabinet members, each had its own staff and executive secretary. Below these were a number of working groups, developing specific policy options in each area and tracking the implementation of decisions already made. The councils and working groups, in turn, were supported by "the best research facilities in the world," comprising a "level of available expertise, facts, and studies . . . [exceeding] that of even the most sophisticated research institutions," including an endless stream of classified information pouring in from the four corners of the globe.

* *Revolution* (New York: Harcourt Brace Jovanovich, 1988).

To say nothing of the talent. Anderson spared no superlative in describing most of his White House colleagues. David Stockman, then director of the Office of Management and Budget, had attracted "probably the most talented team to ever head the budget office . . . unrivaled in OMB's history." The White House speech writers were "the most talented group assembled since the days of Kennedy and Nixon." He even quoted Robert Strauss, who in a (characteristic) fit of nonpartisan enthusiasm called the White House staff "simply spectacular . . . the best I've ever seen."

For Anderson, moreover, this extraordinary system was a logical extension of Reagan's 1980 presidential campaign, in which "the largest and most distinguished group of intellectuals ever assembled for an American political campaign" had been organized into forty-eight policy task forces, each producing detailed reports on what the Reagan Administration should do once in office. George Shultz alone presided over six economic policy task forces, whose membership totaled seventy-four "highly talented" individuals. The subsequent transition to the White House was "the most carefully planned and effective in American political history." The personnel operation, through which two thousand gifted young men and women were chosen to fill the highest levels of the Administration, "was easily the best in the history of the United States."

Let us assume even a small element of truth to Anderson's hyperbole. Compared with other recent administrations, the one that came to office in January 1981 did appear to be unusually competent and well organized. It knew what it wanted to do, and it had thought about how to do it.

But, the paradox: How could such a beautifully designed policy process have generated the remarkable stream of blunders that marred the Reagan Administration? Why the unprecedented budget deficits, culminating in over $400 billion owed to the rest of the world? Why the foreign policy debacles—the disaster of the Marines in Lebanon, the Bitburg folly, the foolishness of the "disinformation" campaign, the Iran–contra fiasco, the humiliation by Noriega? Why the seemingly endless series of scandals, improprieties, forced resignations? Even the Administration's claimed successes, like the Soviet withdrawal from Afghanistan and the treaty on intermediate-range ballistic missiles, seemed to depend less on any carefully conceived strategy than on events and personalities over which the White House had no control, and on luck.

* * *

Donald Regan, the President's secretary of the Treasury during the first term and chief of staff for two years during the second, offered one explanation for this arresting divergence between input and output. In his titillating memoir,* he blamed Reagan's fantastic passivity. The book made headlines for its revelations that a clairvoyant in California determined Reagan's schedule, but Regan's criticism of the President was more fundamental than anything merely celestial. Regan wished to demonstrate that Reagan simply wasn't interested in the substance of policy.

The campaign task forces, the working groups, the talented advisers notwithstanding, when Regan took the Treasury job, he had no clue what he was supposed to do. After several months he confessed in his diary: "To this day I have never had so much as one minute alone with Ronald Reagan! Never has he, or anyone else, sat down in private to explain to me what is expected of me, what goals he would like to see me accomplish, what results he wants. . . . How can one do a job if the job is not defined?" Lacking any guidance from above, Regan felt it necessary "to figure these things out like any other American, by studying [Reagan's] speeches and reading the newspaper." Thus was the economic policy of the United States divined by the secretary of the Treasury.

What did the President want to do, for example, about taxes? Regan could only guess, based on the President's facial expression, on presidential fidgets, when the issue of taxes was raised. "I had the impression, based on observation of his body language rather than any words he had spoken in private, that he wanted to hold the line against new taxes." Should Regan and James Baker swap jobs? When they proposed it to the President, he simply smiled approvingly. "I did not know what to make of his passivity," Regan recalled. "He seemed to be absorbing a fait accompli rather than making a decision."

Regan was consistently stunned at the President's lack of involvement. Reagan never issued an order. He rarely asked a question. He provided no guidance at all. A Potemkin Presidency, according to Regan, all form and no substance. Reagan only acted the part of President; he wasn't really President at all. Regan tried to explain:

> As President, Ronald Reagan acted on the work habits of a
> lifetime: he regarded his daily schedule as being something like
> a shooting script in which characters came and went, scenes
> were rehearsed and acted out, and the plot was advanced one

* *For the Record: From Wall Street to Washington* (New York: Harcourt Brace Jovanovich, 1988).

> day at a time, and not always in sequence. The Chief of Staff was a sort of producer, making certain that the star had what he needed to do best; the staff was like the crew, invisible behind the lights, watching the performance their behind-the-scenes efforts had made possible. . . . Checking off each event with a pencil after it ended and preparing himself for the next gave [Reagan's] life a regularity and tangible measure of accomplishment that . . . was deeply pleasing to him.

The result was "an environment where there seemed to be no center, no structure, no agreed policy." The policy-making talent generated huge amounts of paper, but no final decisions ever seemed to emerge from all this apparatus. In Regan's account there was simply nobody at the top who made final decisions.

During his tenure at the Treasury, Regan found himself increasingly critical of the way the President's staff seemed to encourage such passivity in the chief executive. They wanted to protect Reagan from controversy and also to protect the public from the bold visions and the strong opinions that Regan felt certain burned deep inside the President. Regan agreed to become chief of staff because he wanted to allow Reagan to be more assertive, more decisive, more presidential: to "let Reagan be Reagan." And he tried. Regan reduced the number of Cabinet councils, centralized control over the chain of command, and sought to streamline the decision-making process so that the President could be more directly involved.

One of his first acts as chief of staff was to prepare a planning memorandum for the President on a range of controversial subjects that were likely to arise during the following year, including farm supports, protectionism, Social Security, and Western European defenses. The memorandum set forth overall priorities and included detailed policy recommendations, specific presidential actions, and timetables. "What do you think?" he asked the President, expecting a substantive dialogue about the complex and somewhat daring initiatives he was proposing. " 'It's good,' the President replied, nodding in approval. 'It's really good, Don.' " Nothing more.

In the end, as we all know, Regan was fired. And he is bitter about that. He blamed Nancy Reagan, other White House staffers, the news media, national security advisers McFarlane and Poindexter, and above all, Ronald Reagan. Regan's failed effort to get Reagan involved in the substantive choices facing the President of the United States resulted in Regan himself being made a target. Criticized by the media for his lax supervision of the National Security Council staff (over which, he protests, the chief of staff has no direct control) and detested by insiders who resented his assertive role, Regan was scapegoated for the inevitable failings of an indifferent president.

*   *   *

At least, that's his story. But his story doesn't ring true, exactly. We have heard similar complaints before, with the same self-serving, self-pitying quality about them. David Stockman, in his own memoir, sought to place blame for the Administration's mammoth budget deficits on Reagan's failure to get involved. "He conveyed the impression that since we all knew what needed to be done, we should simply get on with the job," Stockman chided. But there was more to it, according to Stockman, than simply getting on with the job. Cutting public spending or raising taxes required hard choices that the President was unprepared to make. Politics triumphed, because Ronald Reagan wouldn't take the lead.

It is worth remembering that Regan and Stockman were on opposite sides of the economic debate during Reagan's first term. Regan was a confirmed supply-sider who assumed that tax cuts would generate more tax revenues, as people began to work harder and earn more money. Stockman insisted that tax increases would be necessary. Reagan did not shy away from this debate, however. Most of the White House staff was on Stockman's side, but Reagan ultimately sided with Regan. In other words, here is one instance in which Reagan was an assertive—indeed, a bullheaded—president.

There is a natural temptation to attribute lassitude to superiors who disagree with one's own wisdom. (How could he have been paying attention if he failed to comprehend the obvious superiority of my argument?) And there is a natural temptation to impute indolence to a superior who agrees too quickly with one's recommendations, without fully acknowledging their brilliance. (How could he have been alert if he failed to discuss the finer points of my argument?) Regan and Stockman ultimately came to the same conclusion about Reagan, but from opposite poles. All that they possessed in common were raging egos, which demanded of Reagan both complete acquiescence and sparkling attentiveness. When they failed to receive one or the other, they grew bitter.

In fact, the record will show that Ronald Reagan was quite a decisive president and deeply concerned about a whole range of issues. The paradoxical disparity between inputs and outputs—between the elaborate systems of policy formulation in the White House and the often ill-conceived blunderbuss that emerged—was not due to Reagan's passivity. It was due, rather, to the peculiar character of Reagan's engagement. If anything, Reagan was too personally involved in decisions—too passionate, too caring, too sentimental. Time and again, he decided issues on the basis of emotion rather than reason.

Reagan's blunders owed to his failure to respect the process of policy making. And his staff swiftly grasped that lack of respect. Forget the Cabinet councils, working groups, panels of experts, the briefing books. When Reagan's advisers wanted him to decide something in a certain way, they circumvented these established channels and manipulated his feelings.

When Regan wanted the President's go-ahead to reform the federal income tax system, for example, Regan devised a way to play on Reagan's emotions. As Regan told it:

> As a way of introducing the subject, I asked him a question about his old employer, the General Electric company: "What does General Electric have in common with Boeing, General Dynamics, and 57 other big corporations?"
>
> Reagan's interest was immediately aroused. He had fond memories of his days as a television host and traveling goodwill ambassador for GE, and a large number of anecdotes and stories about this experience.
>
> "I don't know," he said, leaning forward in his chair and smiling. "What *do* they have in common?"
>
> "Let me tell you, Mr. President," I replied. "What these outfits have in common is that not one of them pays a penny in taxes to the United States government."
>
> "*What?*" the President said.
>
> His shock was genuine. A dumbfounded silence settled over his economic advisers. What unconventional idea was I trying to plant in the President's mind now?
>
> "Believe it or not, Mr. President," I continued, "your secretary paid more federal taxes last year than all of those giant companies put together."
>
> The President flushed, a sure sign of surprise and discomfort. "I just can't believe that," he said.
>
> "I don't blame you for doubting it," I replied. "But it's the truth. . . . It's perfectly legal, but it's wrong, Mr. President, when a hardworking secretary pays more to support her government than 60 of the richest corporations in the land. The time has come to do something fundamental about the tax system. It's too complicated, it's grotesquely unfair, and it's a drag on the economy because it discourages competition."

By now the President's cheeks were carmine and there was a spark of resolution in his eye.

He said, "I agree, Don, I just didn't realize that things had gotten that far out of line."

I interpreted his words as an instruction to go full steam ahead with a proposal to overhaul the entire federal tax structure.

Martin Anderson offered another example, in some ways more chilling, of the White House staff's shrewd tendency to bypass the normal channels of policy making through appeals to Reagan's emotions. When the Israelis began to bomb Beirut in June 1982, Michael Deaver, then deputy chief of staff, was upset. According to Anderson, Deaver lurched into the Oval Office, and the following exchange ensued:

"Mr. President, I have to leave."

The President was startled.

"What do you mean?"

"I can't be a part of this anymore," replied Deaver, "the bombings, the killing of children. It's wrong. And you're the one person on the face of the earth right now who can stop it. All you have to do is tell Begin you want it stopped."

Reagan stared at Deaver with a look, as Deaver later described it, of "My God, what have we done?" and then asked his secretary to get Menachem Begin, the prime minister of Israel, on the phone. . . .

When the call to Israel came through, Reagan told Begin bluntly that the shelling and bombing of Beirut had to stop. Reagan's last words were, "It has gone too far. You must stop it."

In 20 minutes Begin called back and said it was done. The shelling and bombing was stopped. Reagan was somewhat incredulous and said, "I didn't know I had that kind of power."

But the master of the emotional manipulation of the President was William Casey, the crumpled wizard of the CIA. According to Anderson, Casey never missed an opportunity to play upon Reagan's fears and Reagan's sympathies. And here lies a clue as to why Reagan agreed to sell arms to Iran, the protestations of his secretaries of defense and state notwithstanding. William Buckley was the CIA's station chief in Lebanon when he was kidnapped on March 16, 1984. Anderson tells us that Casey wanted Buckley freed at all costs. In order to wring concessions out of the United States, Buckley's kidnappers had sent the CIA a videotape of Buckley's brutal torture, complete with agonizing sounds. "Appealing deeply to Reagan's emotional anguish," Casey then arranged for

Reagan to see the sickening videotape. And thereafter Reagan would share Casey's intense commitment to free the hostages, almost regardless of the consequences.

* * *

The White House that emerges from these memoirs was a palace of intrigue, but it had its own unfortunate coherence. The intrigue consisted, to be precise, in the attempts of advisers to outmaneuver one another to capture the heart, not the mind, of the President. Every conversation was an opportunity to play to his emotions; every chance encounter, an opening for an evocative anecdote to convince him to decide this way or that. The people surrounding Reagan continuously sought to make use of his feelings for their purposes. They fed him vivid stories and letters to illustrate particular positions, they filled his schedule with emotionally charged events and meetings, they prevented him from being along with one of their competitors who might use the same tricks for opposite purposes, they planted pointed newspaper articles that he was sure to read.

Regan hated Nancy Reagan for the simple reason that she understood this game so well. After all, she had been playing it for decades. Her fascination with astrology was a minor irritant, really. What irked Regan most was that Nancy could outmaneuver him. She could orchestrate her husband's sentiments far better than Regan could. That, and not the zodiac, was how she could determine what Reagan would decide, far more effectively than could the President's chief of staff. And all the cabinet councils, the working groups, the experts, the briefing books were irrelevant to this larger, inner drama. Regan understood this, and so did Nancy. In the end, the two of them found themselves in a tug-of-war over the President's heart. Regan's biggest frustration was he was not the wife.

Historians of the Reagan Administration will certainly record a bold and decisive president—not the weak, indolent creature caricatured by Regan and Stockman. But history will also reveal a president without any appreciable capacity to make thoughtful decisions. The White House's sophisticated apparatus of policy development, of which Martin Anderson is so proud, was superseded by Ronald Reagan's boyish heart. Decisions *were* made, but as a result of the manner in which they were made, they bore little relation to the facts, the analysis, and the expertise on hand. America had eight years of government by sentimental education.

21

THE DAY
I BECAME A FEMINIST

"I LOST, BY FOUR VOTES," SHE SAID, SIMPLY. "I'LL BE HOME SOON." I
must have looked shaken as I put down the phone. Our precocious six-
year-old, who had been eyeing me, summed up the situation: "They fired
Mommy, didn't they?"

Sexism had always been something of an abstraction to me. I knew
it existed, but I assumed that it was the product of backward and parochial cultures. It might show up in entrenched corporate bureaucracies
dominated by old-boy networks, or in ethnic groups governed by male-
dominated traditions, or in working-class communities in which Rambo
still reigned. But surely no such noxious bias would be found in the
overwhelmingly liberal, intellectual, worldly, and high-minded university community that we safely inhabited.

Yet a string of white males had been voted tenure just before her.
Most had not written as much as she, nor inspired the same praise from
specialists around the nation as had her work. None of their writings
had been subjected to the detailed scrutiny—footnote by footnote—to
which her colleagues had subjected her latest manuscript. Not one of the
male candidates had aroused the degree of anger and bitterness that
characterized her tenure decision.

Why? At first I was bewildered. I knew most of the men who had voted against her. A few I knew to be narrow-minded, one or two I might have suspected of misogyny. But most were thoughtful, intelligent men. They had traveled widely, read widely, had held positions of responsibility and trust. I was sure that they felt they had been fair and impartial in judging her work. They would be appalled at any suggestion of sexual bias.

Gradually, I came to understand. They were applying their standard of scholarship as impartially as they knew how. Yet their standard assumed that the person to whom they applied it had gone through the same training and had had the same formative intellectual experiences as they. It assumed further that the person had gained along the way the same understandings of academic discipline, and the same approaches to core problems, as they had gained. In short, their standard was premised on the belief that the people they judged had come to view the modes and purposes of scholarship—of the life of the mind—in the same way they had come to view it.

Through the years she has helped me to see the gender biases of these assumptions. Her experiences and understandings, and those of other women scholars, have been shaped by the irrefutable reality of gender. The values and perspectives she brings to bear on the world —and in particular, the world of ideas—are different from theirs, because she has experienced the world differently. In fact, it is the very uniqueness of her female perspective that animates her scholarship, that gives it its originality and intellectual bite. They had applied their standard as impartially as they knew how, but it was a male standard.

Not that they were incapable of appreciating her scholarship simply because they were men: after all, the experts in her field whose opinions had been solicited during the tenure review, and who had overwhelmingly praised her work, had been male. And the majority of the men on her faculty had voted to grant her tenure; she had failed only to get the necessary two thirds. Presumably, the men who supported her had been able to imagine the life of the mind from a different perspective than their own. They had been able and willing to expand their standard— not to compromise it or to reduce it, but to broaden it to include a woman's way of knowing. I suspect that those who did not, did not care to try.

And why would they not have cared to try? Here again, I was momentarily stumped. Apart from the few diehards, they were kindly men, tolerant men. But perhaps they did not feel that she had invited them to try. Early on, her closest friends on the faculty were a group of young professors who took delight in challenging the sacred cows of prevailing scholarship. Her early articles openly proclaimed a feminist perspective. She had not played at being a good daughter to the older and more traditional men on the faculty, giggling at their jokes and massaging their egos. Nor had she pretended to be one of them, speaking loudly and talking tough. They had no category for her, and to that extent, she had threatened them, made them uncomfortable. So that when it came time for them to try to see the world from her perspective, they chose not to.

* * *

Since the vote, she has remained strong and as certain of the worth of her scholarship as before. Many women colleagues, and many men, rallied to her cause. There were student demonstrations. She pondered a lawsuit. She was offered a faculty position elsewhere and is happy with her new job.

But the experience has shaken me. First came the rage and confusion. Only later came insight into the insidiousness of sexism even in our most enlightened institutions. It has made me wary, in addition, of my own limited perspective—of the countless ways in which I fail to understand my female colleagues and students and their ways of knowing the world.

I have begun to notice small things. A recruiter for a large company calls to ask about a student who is being considered for a job. "Does she plan to have a family?" he inquires, innocently enough. "Is she really—er—serious about a career?" It is not the first time such a question has been put to me about a female student, but it is the first time I hear it clearly, for what it is.

A male colleague is critical of a young woman assistant professor: "She's not assertive enough in the classroom," he confides. "She's too anxious to please—doesn't know her own mind." Then, later, another colleague, about the same young woman: "She's so whiney. I find her very abrasive." It is possible, of course, that she is both diffident and abrasive. But I can't help wondering if these characterizations more accurately reflect how my two colleagues feel about women in general—their mothers, wives, girlfriends—than about this particular young woman.

At a board meeting of a small foundation on which I serve, the lone woman director tries to express doubts about a pending decision. At first, several loquacious men in the group won't give her a chance to speak. When finally she begins to voice her concern, she is repeatedly interrupted. She perseveres and eventually states her objection. But her concern goes unaddressed in the remainder of the meeting, as if she had never raised it. It seems to me that this isn't the first time she was ignored, but it is the first time I noticed.

In my class I present a complex management problem. An organization is rife with dissension. I ask, What steps should the manager take to improve the situation? The answers of my male students are filled with words like "strategy," "conflict," "interests," "claims," "trade-offs," and "rights." My female students use words like "resolution," "relationship," "cooperation," and "loyalty." Have their vocabularies and approaches to problems always been somewhat different, or am I listening now as never before?

The vice president of a corporation that I advise tells me he can't implement one of my recommendations, although he agrees with it. "I have no authority," he explains. "It's not my turf." Later the same day, his assistant vice president tells me that the recommendation can be implemented easily. "It's not formally within our responsibility," she says, offhandedly. "But we'll just make some suggestions here and there, at the right time, to the right folks, and it'll get done." Is the male vice president especially mindful of formal lines of authority and his female assistant especially casual, or do they exemplify differences in how men and women in general approach questions of leadership?

If being a "feminist" means noticing these sorts of things, then I became a feminist the day my wife was denied tenure. But what is my responsibility, as a male feminist, beyond merely noticing? At the least: to remind corporate recruiters that they shouldn't be asking about whether prospective female employees want to have a family; to warn male colleagues about subtle possibilities of sexual bias in their evaluations of female colleagues; to help ensure that women are listened to within otherwise all-male meetings; to support my women students in the classroom, and to give explicit legitimacy to differences in the perceptions and leadership styles of men and women. In other words, just as I seek to educate myself, I must also help educate other men.

This is no small task. The day after the vote on my wife's tenure, I phoned one of her opponents—an old curmudgeon, as arrogant as he is smart. Without the slightest sense of the irony lying in the epithet I chose to hurl at him, I called him a son of a bitch.

22

THE FOURTH
WAVE OF REGULATION

ONCE EACH GENERATION, AMERICAN BUSINESS HAS AN OPPORTUNITY TO
exert leadership—to set the public agenda rather than defend itself
against the public. And once each generation, the American business
community squanders the opportunity. It is doing so again, under the
benign aegis of Ronald Reagan and George Bush.

The first generation of American business leaders had an opportunity to exert leadership in the mid- and late-1880s, when mass-produc-
tion techniques began to transform the relationship of managers and
workers and the modern diversified corporation was born. But the business community's inability then to understand and respond to the public
responsibilities attendant upon large corporate size contributed to the
Populist and Progressivist agitation of the last decades of the nineteenth
century and the early decades of this century—to antitrust legislation
and the establishment of the Federal Trade Commission, to laws governing hours and working conditions, and to legislation protecting consumers from dangerous drugs and unwholesome meat.

American business had a second opportunity during the 1920s, after
joining in successful partnership with the government on the War Industries Board and thus earning a measure of public trust. Its failure then to

respond to the postwar demands of labor, investors, and consumers foreshadowed New Deal programs to protect these groups—legislation establishing a framework for labor-management relations, regulations governing the securities and banking industries, and laws further protecting consumers from unsafe foods, drugs, and cosmetics.

Business had a third opportunity in the 1950s and early 1960s, when government fiscal and monetary policies appeared to ensure steady economic growth, and Americans enjoyed the prosperity that business and government—working together—seemed able to provide. But the failure of American business once again to seize the initiative in anticipation of a new set of emerging public concerns about the environment, health, consumer safety, equal opportunity, and political corruption set the stage for a third wave of regulation, beginning in 1965. This wave was manifested in thirty-five separate regulatory programs covering everything from unsafe toys and flammable fabrics to unsafe mines and toxic chemicals. The third wave ended in 1978 with the defeat of several proposed pieces of legislation—to establish a consumer protection agency, enlarge protections accorded organized labor, eliminate certain special tax advantages enjoyed by business, and bar conglomerate mergers of firms above a certain size.

* * *

There are remarkable parallels among the three periods. Each successive wave was marked by a further extension of government control over business—either enlarging the jurisdiction of agencies already established or establishing new ones. Of the twenty-eight independent regulatory agencies founded between 1887 and 1980, all but seven were established during one of these three periods.

Each wave was immediately preceded by dramatic accounts in the popular press of public harms or dangers attendant upon business activity—Upton Sinclair's revelations of unsanitary conditions in the meatpacking industry at the turn of the century; Ida Tarbell's ringing indictment of the Standard Oil Trust; Louis Brandeis's exposé of the banking industry; more recently, Rachel Carson's stirring account of environmental decay; Jessica Mitford's revelations about the funeral industry; and Ralph Nader's string of exposés concerning dangerous cars, drugs, and food additives. Complementing these journalistic efforts (dubbed "muckraking" before World War I and "investigative reporting" in the 1970s) were public scandals and disasters, which lent credibility to the exposés and further undermined public confidence in business: the Triangle Shirt Waist factory fire, Jay Gould's Wall Street manipulations, the elixir sulfanilamide disaster, thalidomide deformities, fatalities in General Motors' Corvair and Ford's Pinto, scandals over union pension funds and foreign bribes, Allied Chemical's dumping of a toxic chemical into the Chesapeake Bay, mine cave-ins, leaks from nuclear reactors.

In each period dramatic events and revelations spurred middle-income citizens into political action. In the Progressive era organizations first sprang up at the local level, promoting the environment, consumerism, and better government. During the New Deal, middle-income groups formed antibusiness coalitions with urban ethnics, intellectuals, and organized labor. In the most recent wave middle-income groups joined with the organized poor on certain issues affecting business and with students and labor on others.

Each wave endured for about a decade before the interest of the middle-income groups waned and the antibusiness coalitions, of which they were a central part, began to disintegrate. In the first two periods the immediate cause of the decline was an international crisis, culminating in the buildup of military armaments, and the outbreak of global hostilities. The most recent wave ended with an international economic crisis spurred by an oil embargo, and the need for a national economic mobilization (or "revitalization" as it was termed). In all three periods middle-income groups, whose economic survival was suddenly at stake, quickly forsook their antibusiness activities and joined in an unstable coalition with business.

I have simplified, of course. Lines of cause and effect were more complicated than this. Business leaders sometimes sought regulations in order to protect themselves against competition. But I think it fair to say that embedded within much of regulatory history has been a pendulum-like cycle—an almost predictable waxing and waning of antibusiness political activity the momentum of which has been maintained from generation to generation in large part by the business community's own defensiveness or indifference to public concerns.

* * *

Instead of actively anticipating the *next* wave of public activism and exerting leadership in setting the future public agenda, America's business leaders have been content to enjoy their temporary respite from criticism. They have merely awaited the inevitable series of scandals, disasters, and exposés that signal a return to the politics of confrontation. At most, they have resorted to public-relations devices—expensive media campaigns designed to create a corporate image of social responsibility.

The business community has been unable to see below the surface of public activism. The waves of regulation have not reflected sudden shifts in public opinion about business as much as they have represented shifts in the public's willingness to engage in political activity.

Public opinion toward business has been remarkably stable over time. In survey after survey, a majority of the public has continued to support government regulation. This is true even in our current period of regulatory quiescence. In one recent survey 81 percent of the respondents felt that business had a responsibility to control pollution, but only 40 percent felt that business was fulfilling that responsibility; 80 percent thought that business had a responsibility to advertise honestly, but only 37 percent felt that business was fulfilling that responsibility. The responses were more favorable with regard to providing safe products of good quality—66 percent felt that business was fulfilling its obligations here. But that still left a large minority—34 percent—who disagreed. In another recent poll 80 percent of the respondents felt that government must ensure that business clean up its air and water pollution, provide safe products and services, and provide safe working conditions.* These results are not substantially different from those of similar polls undertaken over the last thirty years.

This underlying public distrust of business manifests itself in a variety of ways. Even when there is not political support for increased regulation, as now, the public vents its latent distrust in lawsuits and in market decisions to forsake American-made products.

Notwithstanding that case-by-case litigation over liability is cumbersome, costly, and extremely time-consuming, it has increased dramatically as the third wave of regulation has receded. Asbestos cases forced Johns-Manville into bankruptcy. Injuries resulting from the use of Firestone "500" steel-belted radials have given rise to millions of dollars in personal damage awards; injuries from the Dalkon Shield IUD have resulted in millions more; accidents related to an allegedly faulty gear shift in several Ford Motor Company models spawned hundreds of lawsuits and resulted in several large awards; the accident at Three Mile Island resulted in nineteen class actions for damages to personal property with an estimated total liability of $1.5 billion and earned lawyers over

* Harris and Roper polls, July and September 1987.

$7 million in legal fees; disorders arising in connection with the drug DES, used to prevent miscarriages, have resulted in a large number of class actions involving more than one thousand lawyers. The list goes on: toxic shock from tampons, cancer from benzene and vinyl chloride, birth defects from endrin, suspected cancer from trichloroethylene (TCE) and polychlorinated biphenyl (PCB). In addition to these specific liabilities, and partly because of them, American business paid over $8 billion in liability insurance premiums in 1988, up almost 300 percent from 1975 and still growing.

Even as more citizens seek legal redress, the courts are extending the limits of business liability. The California Supreme Court has ruled that plaintiffs in DES suits need not prove which manufacturer provided the specific brand of DES that caused the problem; instead, all manufacturers can be held liable, since they all produce the same drug. This is a potentially far-reaching doctrine, which could make entire industries liable whenever specific responsibility for damages is difficult to discern.

The courts are also looking more favorably on punitive damage awards, in which victims are not only compensated for the damages they endure but are also awarded an amount designed to punish the company for having inflicted the injury. For example, the Minnesota Supreme Court has affirmed a $1.8 million award against a textile manufacturer for producing cotton pajamas that caught fire and badly burned a young child; $1 million of that amount was punitive. A Florida jury has awarded a dealer in business machines $5 million, of which $3.3 million represented punitive damages for injuries resulting from defects in the manufacturers' plain-paper copiers.

Business executives are not fortune-tellers, and in many instances it is extremely difficult—if not impossible—to foresee potential dangers or injuries resulting from the use of certain products. But in reviewing these cases, one is struck by the abundance of early warning signals. The first cases of asbestos-related injuries, for example, were reported over sixty years ago. There was a major conference on asbestos dangers in New York almost twenty years ago. The first cases of DES malignancies were reported more than fifteen years ago. In almost every case of unsafe autos or tires, the companies involved received accident reports long before there were many injuries. Hooker Chemical Company could have spent $1.5 million in the early 1950s to build a landfill for its toxic wastes; its use of Love Canal, and subsequent sale to the City of Niagara Falls, ended up costing the company three or four times that amount in liability alone.

All too often, American business leaders have taken the short-term view, placing immediate profits above potential problems that may be years away. The easing of regulations during the 1980s has further encouraged this sort of myopia, making it that much more difficult for company employees who are concerned about these matters to be heard.

*   *   *

There is another way the public is expressing its discontent with American business. Consumers who find that a product is of poor quality, that it demands inordinate repairs, that it falls apart too quickly or appears to be dangerous have an easy option: to buy a *competitor's* product. Since the early 1970s, consumers have been exercising that option in large numbers, deserting American-made manufacturers for Japanese and West German producers. Surely, consumers are attracted by lower price tags on many foreign items; but quality continues to be a key reason for the desertion.

American business has deluded itself into spending millions of dollars to stall new regulations and fight product recalls. For example, some time ago the U.S. government levied a fine—the largest ever assessed under the Motor Vehicle Safety Act—against a major U.S. tire manufacturer for its failure to recall voluntarily tires that it knew did not meet federal safety standards. Not by coincidence, even before the government knew that the problem existed, a foreign tire manufacturer captured a $500 million share of the U.S. tire market.

The lesson should be clear. American business can no longer afford to wait for the next wave of regulation and then use the same stratagems of legal delay and obfuscation used too often in the past to block new rules. America has grown more litigious; our citizens are far more willing to seek damages in court than ever before. The world has become smaller; consumers here and abroad are more willing to buy another nation's products if they perform better. And the public side effects of business have grown more substantial, with large populations now suddenly endangered by leaks of toxic chemicals or malfunctions in nuclear reactors.

Should there be a fourth wave of regulation, it is likely to be no less onerous than previous waves. Perhaps more so. The irony is that unless American business actively seeks to anticipate and respond to emerging public concerns in advance of that wave, business already will have been seriously eroded by the time it breaks. For regulation is only the most visible expression of the public's discontent; animosity toward business is manifest in many other ways. American business leaders can discover the size and direction of the next wave by merely examining the causes of their mounting legal liability and declining profits.

23

THE ECONOMIC
THEORY OF POLITICS

IN RECENT YEARS ECONOMISTS HAVE CAST THEIR IMPERIALIST SIGHTS ON realms far removed from the seductive curves of supply and demand. One area in particular has captured their fancy, perhaps because the domain is large—stretching, as it were, across the globe. It is the domain of politics.

The modern economist's fascination with politics is not a new one, of course, nor is it especially surprising. The way people work together to produce goods and services is intimately tied to the way they set and pursue public goals. Indeed, the notion that the economic and political spheres of our life can be separated is of recent vintage. The very word "economics" was not firmly established until 1890, when Alfred Marshall wrote his *Principles of Economics*. Before then the term was "political economy"—with the adjective serving as a reminder of the "economy's" origins and effects. The entire field branched off in the late eighteenth century from moral philosophy, the study of citizens' rights, duties, and obligations. In earlier eras it seemed impossible to consider economic relationships in isolation from their specific political and social contexts.

The new attention given to politics by economists proceeds, however, from different premises. Rather than envision economic phenomena as outgrowths of political and social life, the new approach views political phenomena as outgrowths of economic life.

Not surprisingly, politics seen from this end of the telescope is even more dismal than the "dismal science" itself. In the marketplace personal demands are mediated through competition for scarce resources. But in politics the demands of special-interest groups are forwarded, often covertly, through exclusive channels to legislative committees, agencies, and bureaus. Politics becomes a pipeline to the public trough.*

As the American welfare state has burgeoned, the economic theory of politics has gained adherents. It seems to offer an explanation both for the failure of the Great Society to eradicate poverty and for the poor economic performance of the United States in recent years. According to this view, popular expectations and group demands on government have reached extraordinary levels, resulting in a vast expansion of government responsibilities; not all of these commitments can be fulfilled. The only way out of this morass is to reduce government responsiveness to these demands—to amend the Constitution to limit public spending and taxes, revert to the gold standard to discipline monetary policy, and devise new governmental arrangements like public corporations and independent authorities, which are less vulnerable to democratic politics. Democracy, in other words, must be saved from its own excesses by dramatically reducing access to state benefits or by reducing the discretion of public officials to respond to political demands—which amounts to the same thing.

*　　*　　*

One of the most recent, and most engaging, proponents of the economic theory of politics is Professor Mancur Olson, author of *The Rise and Decline of Nations.*† As the title implies, Olson sought to account for why some economies grow quickly, others slowly, and still others

---

* The economist Joseph Schumpeter, in some respects intellectual father of this school of thought, sought to dispense with the "classical doctrine" of democracy and its presumption that people are capable of acting with the common good in mind. Instead, Schumpeter saw democracy as "an institutional arrangement for arriving at political decisions in which individuals acquire the power to decide by means of a competitive struggle for people's votes." See his *Capitalism, Socialism, and Democracy* (New York and London: Harper and Brothers, 1942).
† New Haven: Yale University Press, 1982.

not at all. His answer: politics. Since broad and dispersed interests find it hard to organize for political action, the likelihood is that small narrow-interest groups will engineer a redistribution of benefits toward themselves and away from everyone else. Moreover, since people discover the benefits of such group action and organize themselves only gradually, a stable society will steadily accumulate more and more special-interest groups. After a long period of stability, such groups will have disproportionate political influence.

The means by which special-interest groups redistribute national wealth to themselves reduce a society's overall efficiency. If the special-interest group succeeds in raising some price or wage, or in taxing some type of income at lower rates than other income, the extra resources that are diverted into the favored area add less to society's output than they otherwise would. Or the special-interest group may seek to establish a cartel in order to reduce output and thereby enjoy a higher price, and in so doing it imposes additional inefficiencies on society as a whole. Such activities slow a society's growth by reducing the rate at which resources are reallocated from one activity or industry to another in response to new technologies and conditions. Indeed, special-interest groups may simply block technological change.

Olson employed these ideas to explain the postwar "economic miracles" in the nations that were defeated or occupied in World War II, particularly Japan and West Germany. In Germany Hitler did away with independent unions as well as other dissenting groups; immediately after the war, the Allies eviscerated German cartels and organizations with right-wing origins. Japan's militaristic regime had suppressed left-wing organizations; after Japan's defeat, American occupiers cracked down on Japan's monopolies and purged an entire generation of the business elite. Thus, in these nations violence and repression wiped the slate clean of special-interest groups by the end of the 1940s and thereby opened the way to rapid growth. On the other hand, the United States and Great Britain—countries with comparatively long and undisturbed histories of democratic freedom—have experienced slower growth in the postwar era. Both nations are rife with special-interest groups.

Professor Olson's answer? Rather than reduce political access generally, he would have us reduce the influence of special-interest groups on the political process. Violence and repression are one means of eliminating special-interest groups, at least for a time; but Olson was not so cynical as to conclude that economic growth requires a bloodbath. He sought instead a cultural and ideological transformation. He expressed the hope that the schools and the mass media would create a widespread public antipathy to special-interest groups. The remedy would follow quite naturally from this change in attitudes.

> A society with the consensus that has just been described might choose the most obvious and far-reaching remedy: it might simply repeal all special interest legislation or regulation and at the same time apply rigorous antitrust laws to every type of cartel or collusion that used its power to obtain prices and wages above competitive levels.

Then, presumably, society would alter irrevocably its political arrangements so that special interests would be prevented ever again from holding sway.

* * *

It is perhaps too easy to take issue with the evidence Olson invoked to bolster his thesis. For example, the eradication of special-interest groups is neither adequate nor indeed necessary to explain much of the postwar economic dynamism of Germany or Japan. The loss of physical capital (combined in Japan's case with relatively little to begin with) left these nations with very low productivity levels on which to build. Both countries thus could show enormous proportional strides as they caught up with other, less ravaged nations. Such advances were fueled by the shift of labor from agriculture to industry—a shift well under way in many other industrialized nations—and by the simple expedient of adopting technologies developed elsewhere. (The recent rapid growth of Southern and Western states within the United States can be similarly explained. Starting from a much lower level of productivity than Northeastern states, the Sun Belt has played catch-up to older industrial regions; this process of economic homogenization has been accelerated by generous defense spending and public-works projects during the postwar era.)

There is a more basic issue, however. Olson, like others of his persuasion, proffered the ideal of a democratic state devoid of special-interest politics. It is a state whose economy can be "naturally" adaptable and innovative. Olson did not discuss this vision in detail, but one can infer its key features: No organization stands between the individual and the government except perhaps large encompassing organizations that effectively neutralize partisan appeals. The only small groups are households and firms, which relate to one another almost exclusively through the market. Social relations are virtually coextensive with market relations. Workers no longer are organized in industry-wide unions; wage bargaining occurs instead at the level of the firm. A household's income depends on the market value of its members' labor. The government's chief responsibility, apart from providing for national defense and certain public goods like highways, is to police the market in order to guard against the possibility that any group of individuals, households, or firms might seek to distort it through collusion.

Some, no doubt, may find this sort of society attractive. But what about its economic neutrality? After all, there exists an infinite array of alternative market outcomes, each equally efficient, depending on the *initial* distribution of resources in the society. And that initial distribution is maintained and enforced not primarily by specific regulations blocking market entry into certain profit-making activities, nor by discrete price-fixing arrangements and restrictive practices within the private sector; it is maintained by determinations about the nature and form of rights in property, the allocation of public services, and the rules of liability and contract governing society as a whole.

These deeper judgments, framed by courts and legislatures, are conveniently neutral on their face. No special interests are explicitly deemed their beneficiaries. But their consequences are profoundly distributive. Different groups of people, facing different circumstances, are affected by them in different ways. One's access to clean air, police protection, and safe working conditions, for example, is apt to vary substantially, depending on one's geographic community, income, race, and other characteristics. While "membership" in a geographic community, racial group, or income class is not the sort of "membership" Olson had in mind, these less voluntary associations nevertheless shape the deeper pattern of rights and social privileges in modern societies.

As people experiencing similar disadvantages come to understand their common interests and exert their collective political power, these more fundamental rules, and the distributions to which they correspond, are sometimes amended through political action. Thus, to dismantle the system of interest-group politics is to freeze the particular distribution prevailing at the time that the dismantling occurs.

The mechanics of democracy, moreover, are at stake. By positing a society in which nothing mediates between state and individual but encompassing organizations, Olson would effectively cripple democratic institutions. Interest groups are conduits for democratic participation. They are seedbeds for democratic opposition. Because they create centers of power, influence, and mutual support that are independent of the state, interest groups help to check state power. Totalitarian regimes are quick to dismantle special-interest groups. Hitler banned independent unions, trade associations, professional associations, and civic groups; the Soviets cannot tolerate an independent trade union movement in Eastern Europe.

*　　*　　*

Is economic growth inconsistent with robust interest-group politics? It may indeed be, if politics is understood primarily as an instrument for appropriating shares of national income. The economic theory of politics, which attends only to the outcomes of self-interested actors' political behavior, ignores the effects of political action on the actors themselves. Yet it is precisely through broadly political activities—within local trade unions, civic groups, grass-roots political movements, town meetings, professional associations, parent-teacher associations, chambers of commerce, shop-floor organizations, charitable organizations, and election campaigns—that individuals discover the subtler dimensions of their own needs and learn about the needs of others. They begin to understand the relationship between self and society; the encounter itself shapes their social values. If political organization is understood as a source of social values as well as a conduit for political demands, there is no inherent conflict between interest-group politics and economic growth.

Economists generally decline to specify how preferences are formed. It is enough, for most analytical purposes, to assume that people simply have wants and display them through the choices they make. But what of those wants that people cannot or prefer not to express in market terms—patriotism, social justice, the well-being of family and friends, or certain aspects of the natural environment? Those who trumpet the economic theory of politics assume that such preferences, although perhaps difficult to identify and to measure, exist prior to and outside of any social interaction. Social institutions neither create nor alter them. The group interest is simply the sum of its individual members' preferences. Individuals engage in political activity precisely in order to maximize their preexisting self-interests.

*　　*　　*

A contrary view is that political preferences embody values that are conditioned by social experience. Within political organizations people reconsider and revise perspectives and opinions. Common interests are discovered. Disagreements and inconsistencies force individuals to balance and rank their wants. What previously had been assumed to be solely personal concerns are found to be shared ones, and this discovery often empowers participants to act on them. Thus, individual values are transformed into social values that extend beyond the confines of the group. Collective purposes are forged. Political movements are born. But even more important, through the group experience a social morality is defined and refined. Groups create citizens.

The economic theory of politics, which casts groups as mere aggregations of atomized individuals, posits no effective public restraint on selfish conspiracies of group members against the rest of us. The greater the number of special-interest groups, the more collusion against the common good. But the social theory of politics, which sees in these groups the vehicles by which citizens come to understand common interests, suggests that one of the most effective restraints on selfish demands against the state may be the understanding and sophistication that derive from political experiences within such groups. The wider and more active is the public's participation in politics, therefore, the sounder and deeper is the potential political commitment to the common good, including economic growth. The economist's ideal of a rationally self-interested individual enters politics only to further preexisting, strictly personal goals. But the goals of citizens are formed in part by their social experience. The economist's rational actor, if not restrained, inevitably exploits other individuals and stifles the economy; such a person cannot be trusted with real democracy. A virtuous citizen, on the other hand, can at least potentially embrace general prosperity as a common cause and lend energies to achieving it.

*   *   *

How can nations overcome the bias against economic change? One way is to reduce or eliminate political organization and political access, particularly for those who bear the brunt of the dislocations associated with economic change. Olson pointed to Taiwan as a "prototypical" example of fast growth and low inflation, due, he said, to "Taiwan's nearly complete absence of special-interest organizations." He also singled out South Korea and Singapore for special mention.

It is no accident that these nations lack special-interest organizations. The South Korean government periodically declares all political opposition to be illegal. Those outside the ruling coalition are effectively disenfranchised. Demonstrators expressing dissatisfaction have found themselves jailed or killed. The government of Singapore continues to bar most political opposition. Taiwan has no free press, and only a facade of multiparty representation; it periodically jails dissidents.

The alternative way to overcome a population's fear of economic change is to ensure that the burdens and the benefits of economic change are allocated in ways that most people deem to be fair. And to achieve this sort of consensus, a nation would have to democratize its system of economic planning. Economic democracy might take the form of devices like shop-floor participation in decisions governing plant and working conditions, labor-management committees to plot company investment strategies, community and regional planning boards to determine local development objectives, and national bargaining over wages and prices. The aim is not to politicize every economic issue, but to recognize that every important economic choice is by nature political, and therefore to open up political channels in which the substance of economic change can be debated explicitly.

No capitalist democracy has extended the concept of economic democracy very far, but several of the more successful trading partners of the United States have, over the past several decades, experimented with a wide variety of approaches. For example, the vast majority of workers in the United States have no financial stake in their companies nor any formal means of participating in company decisions. But in West Germany employees are represented on workers' councils and on supervisory boards. Even in Japan, whose formal politics is relatively insular, employees participate in companies through elaborate systems of consultation at all levels of the firm. (Indeed, in many respects, Japan's system of bottom-up economic planning is far more democratic than its top-down politics.)

This is not to suggest that companies in continental Europe and Japan are models of labor-management harmony; they are not. The difference is that workers in these nations understand that their fates are tied to the profitability and competitiveness of their firms. Therefore, they bargain for change—retraining programs, relocation assistance, new investment in plants and equipment. Their counterparts in the United States and Great Britain, meanwhile, seek to maintain the status quo, because change threatens their economic security. Similarly, while in Great Britain and the United States macroeconomic policies designed to restrain inflation impose unemployment on the segment of the population least able to cope with it, wage and price increases in many other industrial nations follow guidelines established in national negotiations.

Smaller-scale groups—local unions and industry associations—participate indirectly through their representatives.

One indication of the comparative effectiveness of these various participatory mechanisms is found in the distribution of national income and wealth. By 1985 (the latest year for which such data are available) the poorest 20 percent of the population in the fast-growing nations fared better than in the slow-growing ones. In Japan the poorest fifth received 7.9 percent of after-tax national income. In West Germany the comparable figure was 6.5 percent. In Great Britain the poorest fifth received 6.3 percent of national income, and in the United States the share was only 4.3 percent. Indeed, of twelve industrialized nations, the United States ranks tenth in posttax income equality. Of fourteen industrial nations, the United States ranks fourteenth in the extent of social insurance coverage.

Other data also tend to stand Olson on his head. For example, by comparison with other more vigorous economies, a very small proportion of the working population in the United States is unionized. In 1988 only 17 percent of private-sector wage and salary earners belonged to a union. The figure was 33 percent in Japan and 42 percent in West Germany. In certain respects, moreover, Americans appear to be *less* politically active than their counterparts in other industrial nations. Comparatively few Americans actually take to the polls during national elections. In 1988 George Bush won the Presidency with the votes of less than 28 percent of the potential electorate.

These data are only suggestive. Yet together they frame a picture of two nations, the United States and Britain, both of which have experienced comparatively poor economic performance over the last twenty years, and both of which possess relatively few democratic mechanisms for ensuring that the burdens and benefits of economic change are allocated in a politically acceptable way. Both nations draw a relatively rigid delineation between economic decision making—whether within the government or within large corporations—and democratic institutions. Mancur Olson correctly observed that both nations possess a wide array of legal impediments to economic change: licensing restrictions, professional associations, regulatory barriers, trade barriers. But if the argument developed here is correct, these various restrictions have grown up, not in *consequence* of long-standing democratic institutions in these nations, as Olson would argue, but because of the inadequacy of these democratic institutions to deal effectively with the social dimension of economic change.

24

WHEN THE
WOMEN RETURNED HOME

She was searching for something she believed in—and look *what she found. Her husband, her children, her home, herself. She's the contemporary woman who has made a new commitment to the traditional values that some people thought were "old fashioned." Researchers are calling it the biggest social movement since the '60s.*

—*Advertisement for* Good Housekeeping
January 1989

IT SEEMS LIKE YESTERDAY, BUT DEMOGRAPHERS TELL US THAT THE RE-action set in a full decade ago, around 1990. It was then that American women began going back home.

You remember: George Bush was in the White House. General Motors, Ford, and Chrysler were still making a few of their cars on American soil. It was after Wall Street's Black Monday but before Apocalyptic Tuesday. And more than half of all women with infants or school-age children worked outside the home.

And then, the big switch. By 1995 the vast majority of women with children were back in the home. Indeed, the latest survey shows that 85 percent of married women do not hold paying jobs.

Why the turnaround? Sociology professor Ernest Schwein of Harvard's Center for Gender Studies thinks that the "back to the home" movement came as a reaction to the earlier era. "Social changes occur in cycles," he says. "Look at how rapidly women had swarmed into the workplace! In 1950 only 11 percent of women with children under six years old held jobs outside the home. By 1986 it was 52 percent! Inevitably, there had to be a rebound, a backlash of some sort, a return to traditional values."

As evidence, Dr. Schwein points to the advertisements, articles, and TV talk shows that began to appear around 1989, extolling the virtues of home life for women and predicting the dire consequences for children of maternal employment. These pronouncements had a common theme: Women were fooling themselves if they thought they could "have it all" —a career, a family, and a well-run home. And they didn't need to. They could choose. One perfectly respectable choice was to withdraw from the world of paid work and become a "homemaker" like women of the 1950s.

In fact, says Dr. Schwein, the movement back to the home fit the tempo of the times. The 1990s resembled the 1950s in many ways. After more than a decade of hearing Ronald Reagan's homilies and George Bush's bromides, the average American had sunk into a nostalgic stupor. The older values of family, home, and neighborhood had become wondrously appealing. By the start of the decade it was once again acceptable for women to opt for homemaking. They were no longer embarrassed when people asked about their jobs or careers. "I stay home!" was said confidently, even with a smile.

What has been the aftermath of such a rapid about-face? Financial analysts point to the near collapse of many industries. Convenience businesses—take-out food stores, same-day laundries and dry cleaners— were the first to go. Now that women don't have to manage their careers and their homes simultaneously, saving time is no longer worth the price. Same with products like microwave ovens, frozen food, and giant freezers. Sales of all of these have plummeted in recent years. And the entire child-care industry is in disarray. Says an incredulous Sidney Hirsch, president and CEO of Toddlers-R-Us, a national day-care chain, "We never expected this." The firm has just filed for bankruptcy.

Home construction is down from previous levels, as are sales of new cars. Families can no longer afford large-ticket items. Indeed, average family income has dropped about 30 percent since women went back home. There has been a corresponding rise in mortgage foreclosures, personal bankruptcies, and the number of families living below or near the poverty line. Says Theodora Meadows of the Commerce Department's Bureau of Working Women (which is being disbanded next month), "Many women entered the work force twenty-five years ago to prop up family earnings. Now that they've gone home, there's no prop."

In general, American women are now far more dependent on their husband's income than they were a decade ago, and advertisers have stopped courting them. Remember those ads of the mid-1980s featuring women driving sports cars or carrying rawhide briefcases? No more. Nowadays, men make all the major family purchases. In ads women are back scrubbing bathroom bowls and eradicating ring around the collar.

Another interesting result: The Census Bureau reports that the divorce rate is half what it was in the 1980s. Yes, marriages are holding tight—and sales of tranquilizers are soaring.

The drop in the rate of divorce, according to Dr. Rex Tyranous of Columbia's Institute for Sexual Studies, has nothing to do with marital harmony. "Women are sticking to men because they have to. They gave up their careers, so they can't strike out on their own, can't escape from bad marriages. Economically, they're trapped."

Indeed, sociologists note that many of the old hierarchies have returned. The renewed financial dependency of women has placed them in a subordinate position. Dr. Tyranous again: "Ten years ago, men were just beginning to share responsibilities at home—taking care of the children, cleaning, cooking meals. Now it's back to Ozzie and Harriet. All across America, men come home from a busy day at the office, grab a beer, sit in their favorite chair, and are waited on. They don't even interact with the kids."

Even in affluent suburbs adult men are going out drinking together. Neighborhood bars have reemerged, as have "men only" clubs.

There is a noted upsurge in "momism" among children, particularly boys. Dr. Bruno Heifetz, a psychiatrist at Cornell's Childhood Sexual Disorder Clinic, puts it bluntly: "With mommy now back in the home full time, the attachments are simply too intense. We are seeing just what we saw in the 1950s—young men who can't form mature relationships with women because they lack the emotional integrity that comes with full separation from the mother. And we see all the symptoms back again as before—rage, depression, acute competitiveness. I thought we were on the way to licking this problem a decade ago."

But the loudest warnings are coming from economists who worry about the nation's external debt, now hovering close to the $3 trillion mark. "America's competitiveness has worsened dramatically," says Robert B. Reich, director of the American Academy of Economic Pontification. "It was bad ten years ago, of course. But since then, the private sector has lost a huge portion of its talent, its brains, its capacity to innovate. The precipitous decline in productivity gains really dates from the late 1980s, when women started staying home."

The experts are stumped for a solution. There's no easy way to lure women back into the paid work force. "Once a social backlash begins, you can't readily stop it," says sociologist Schwein. "It has a predictable momentum. You have to let it play itself out."

Nevertheless, several states have been experimenting with subsidies and tax incentives designed to encourage women to go back to work. Wisconsin, for example, now offers employed women a four-month paid maternity leave. Minnesota subsidizes day care and gives tax credits for transportation and service expenses in connection with the job. Lieutenant Governor Susan Fromidge—one of the last of America's women still holding high public office—says the benefits are necessary. "Every woman we can get back into the work force generates three more jobs, reduces medical and public health costs, improves the quality of our young people, and adds to productivity. Clearly the investment is worth it."

Not all agree. Mrs. Nadine Kornfalb, a young housewife in Skokie, Illinois, thinks that the "back to the home" movement is a good thing: "True, we now live in a one-bedroom apartment. When I worked, we could afford our own house with separate bedrooms for the kids. And we used to eat steak once in a while, go to the movies occasionally, and take vacations. Now we eat a lot of potatoes and watch more TV. But I don't mind at all. My life is so much easier than my mother's was. That generation of women tried to do too much—family, home, career, personal development. They made themselves miserable, and everyone around them. My generation—we just make everyone happy."

25

THE FOUR PARABLES
OF AMERICAN POLITICS

THE NEXT PRESIDENTIAL RACE WILL START REMARKABLY SOON. IN SHORT order, we will be treated to a new round of speeches, debates, and interviews concerning America's most pressing problems. Some of the proposals will be original, a few of the perspectives even novel. But underlying the rhetoric will be stories we have heard many times before. They are the same stories we tell and retell one another about our lives together in America; some are based in fact, some in fiction, but most lie in between. They are our national parables.

These parables are rooted in the central experiences of American history: the flight from an older culture, the rejection of central authority and aristocratic privileges, the lure of the unspoiled frontier, the struggles for social equality. One can distill four central themes:

1. The Rot at the Top This parable is about the malevolence of powerful elites, be they wealthy aristocrats, rapacious business leaders, or imperious government officials. It is the story of corruption in high places, of conspiracy against the public. At the end of the century, muckrakers like Upton Sinclair and Ida Tarbell uncovered sordid tales of corporate malfeasance; their modern heirs are called investigative reporters. The theme arises from the American detective story whose hero—such as Sam Spade, Serpico, or Jack Nicholson in *Chinatown*—traces the rot directly to the most powerful members in the community. The political moral is clear: Americans must not allow any privileged group to amass too much power.

2. The Triumphant Individual This is the story of the little person who works hard, submits to self-discipline, takes risks, has faith in himself, and is eventually rewarded with wealth, fame, and honor. Consider Benjamin Franklin's *Autobiography,* the first of a long line of American manuals on how to become rich through self-denial and diligence. The theme recurs in the tale of Abraham Lincoln, log-splitter from Illinois who goes to the White House; in the hundred or so novellas of Horatio Alger, whose heros all rise promptly and predictably from rags to riches, and in modern success stories, such as *Rocky* and *Iacocca.* Regardless of the precise form, the moral is the same: Anyone can "make it" in America through hard work and perseverance.

3. The Benign Community The third parable is about the American community. It is the story of neighbors and friends rolling up their sleeves and pitching in to help one another, or self-sacrifice, community pride, and patriotism. The story is rooted in America's religious traditions, and its earliest formulations are found in sermons like John Winthrop's "A Model of Christian Charity," delivered on-board ship in Salem Harbor just before the Pilgrims landed in 1630. He envisioned a "city set upon a hill" whose members would "delight in each other" and be "of the same body." Three hundred years later, these sentiments echoed in Robert Sherwood's plays, John Steinbeck's novels, Aaron Copland's music, and Frank Capra's films. The last scene in *It's a Wonderful Life* conveys the lesson: Jimmy Stewart learns that he can count on his neighbors' generosity and goodness, just as they had counted on him. They are bound together in a spirit of dependence and compassion. The principle: We must nurture and preserve genuine community.

4. The Mob at the Gates The fourth parable is about social disintegration that lurks just below the surface of democracy. It is the tale of mob rule, violence, crime, and indulgence—of society coming apart from an excess of democratic permissiveness. It gives voice to the fear that outsiders will exploit the freedom and openness of America. The story shows up in Federalist writings about the instabilities of democracy, in

Whig histories of the United States, and in the anti-immigration harangues of the late nineteenth and twentieth centuries. Its most dramatic appearance in recent years has come in fictionalized accounts of vigilante heroes who wreak havoc on muggers—like Clint Eastwood's Dirty Harry or Charles Bronson in *Death Wish*—and in Rambo's messy eradication of platoons of communist fighters. The lesson: We must impose social discipline, lest the rabble overrun us.

* * *

These four parables are completely familiar to most of us. They shape our political discourse. They confirm our ideologies. Every American retells and listens repeatedly to all four stories; every politician and social commentator borrows, embellishes, and seeks legitimacy from them.

But the parables can be linked together in different ways, each arrangement suggesting a distinct political message. At any given time in our nation's history one particular configuration has been dominant, eventually to be replaced by another. The art of political rhetoric has been to reconfigure these stories in a manner that affirms and amplifies the changes already occurring in the way Americans tell the tales.

In the early part of the century, for example, leaders of the Progressive era emphasized the link between the parables of Rot at the Top and the Triumphant Individual. Big business—the trusts—blocked worthy citizens from their rightful places in society; corruption at the top was thwarting personal initiative. Woodrow Wilson put the matter succinctly in a speech during the 1912 presidential campaign, promising to wage "a crusade against the powers that have governed us . . . that have limited our development . . . that have determined our lives . . . that have set us in a straitjacket to do as they please." In his view, the struggle against the trusts would be nothing less than "a second struggle for emancipation."

By the 1930s, the parables had shifted. Now the key conceptual link was between Rot at the Top and the Benign Community. The liberties of common people were under attack by leaders of big business and finance. In the 1936 presidential campaign, Franklin D. Roosevelt warned against the "economic royalists" who had impressed the whole of society into "royal service."

"The hours men and women worked, the wages they received, the conditions of their labor . . . these had passed beyond the control of the people, and were imposed by this new industrial dictatorship," he warned in one speech. "The royalists of the economic order have conceded that political freedom was the business of the government, but they have maintained that economic slavery was nobody's business." What was at stake, he concluded, was the "survival of democracy."

The shift from the Progressives' emphasis on the Triumphant Individual to the New Deal's Benign Community was more than an oratorical device. It represented a change in Americans' understanding of social life. The Great Depression had provided a national lesson in social solidarity; nearly every American family felt the effects of poverty. The Benign Community became intimately relevant as relatives and neighbors sought to help one another, as government became the insurer of last resort, and then as Americans turned together to winning the "good war" against fascism. The Benign Community embraced the entire nation.

In the decades following World War II, however, the Benign Community became a less convincing parable. Much of the country's middle class began to enjoy a scattered suburban affluence, far removed from the experiences of mutual dependence that had characterized American life a generation before. The prewar images of the common people and the forgotten man were less compelling now that most Americans felt prosperous and not at all forgotten; the story of Rot at the Top was less convincing now that life at the top was within plain sight.

* * *

The descendant of the Benign Community was a feeble impulse toward social altruism. Lyndon Johnson's War on Poverty was sold to the American public as being relatively costless. The idea was that proper Keynesian management of the economy required substantial public expenditures, which might as well be for the benefit of the poor. The economy was buoyant enough that America could afford to enlarge its welfare state; the "fiscal dividend" could be spent on the less fortunate. And in any event, "we" were only giving "them" and "equal opportunity," simply allowing the Triumphant Individuals among them to come forth and find their true potential. Under the banner of civil rights and social justice, Triumphant Individuals joined the nation's Benign Community.

Once again, the configuration of stories Americans told one another began to shift. As the economy slowed in the 1970s, a public tired of belt tightening became less tolerant of social altruism.

Enter Ronald Reagan, master storyteller. His parables drew upon the same four American tales, but substantially recast. This time the Rot at the Top referred to career bureaucrats in government and liberal intellectuals. The Triumphant Individuals were America's business entrepreneurs. The Benign Community comprised small, traditional neighborhoods in which people voluntarily helped one another, free from government interference. And the Mob at the Gates was filled with criminals, pornographers, welfare cheats, illegal immigrants, Third World debtors and revolutionaries, ornery trading partners, and communist aggressors—all of them encouraged by liberal acquiescence. The Reagan Revolution would discipline "them," to liberate the Triumphant Individuals in "us." Political choices in this story were cast as how "hard" or "soft" we should be on "them." Hard always emerged as the only decent American response.

In the 1988 election, both Michael Dukakis and George Bush tried to claim the American parables for themselves, but Bush wielded them far more effectively. Dukakis sought to portray Bush as a wealthy preppy —the Rot at the Top—and himself as a son of immigrants who had lived the American dream of the Triumphant Individual; Dukakis also warned America of the Japanese Mob at the Gates, and he called for a Benign Community that would ensure good jobs at good wages for every American. Bush, on the other hand, portrayed Dukakis as a member of the Harvard liberal intelligentsia—the Rot at the Top—and himself as a Triumphant Individual who had come to Texas as a young man to make his fortune. Bush accused Dukakis of letting criminals out of jail to rob and rape honest Americans (the Mob at the Gates), and he celebrated America's "thousand points of light"—the generous, Benign Community of America, which would help the less fortunate among us through acts of charity rather than through central government.

Inevitably, the configuration of stories Americans tell one another will change yet again. The "us" and "them" recountings of the present era eventually may be superseded by a new version that reflects a more complex, interdependent world. Perhaps, in the next version, the parable of the Benign Community will be expanded to include more of the earth's peoples, and that of the Triumphant Individual will embrace our collective aspirations for freedom and dignity. Indeed, it is just possible that Americans already are telling one another these sorts of stories, and are only waiting for a new set of political leaders to give them voice.

V
THE RESURGENT LIBERAL

26

THE
IDEOLOGY OF SURVIVAL

AT THIS WRITING, GEORGE BUSH'S "KINDER, GENTLER NATION" IS STILL rather callous. One in four of our nation's children is now born into poverty, up from one in five a decade ago. One in six has no health insurance. Following years of progress in preventing infant death, improvements in infant mortality have stopped; our rate is now worse than in nineteen other nations (a black baby born in Boston or Washington, D.C., is more likely to die before his or her first birthday than a baby born in Jamaica). Twenty million Americans remain hungry; a half million children, malnourished. The average American's real wages have declined since 1980. For the poor and near poor, the drop has been more severe. Meanwhile, the share of household income of the richest fifth of the American population continues to rise. The gap between the two groups is now wider than at any time over the last fifty years.

Those who inhabit the left of the political spectrum are tempted to view all this as evidence of the continuing triumph of wealth and privilege. They dream of a new politics that would unite the poor and near poor and restore the liberal agenda long ago lost to Ronald Reagan and his unkind, ungentle ilk. Such populist notions have romantic appeal. But they will fail unless they transcend class interest and come directly to terms with American ideology.

Political discourse in America rests on ideals so long established that they have become encoded onto American life. It is this emblematic battle, rather than a debate over class interests, that has been lost by those who place great value on social justice. The logic of self-interest has never been far away from this contest, to be sure, but neither has it been a primary motivating force. Indeed, direct appeals to class consciousness have never gained much political currency in America. America's emblematic battles have instead been over the nature and meaning of the public interest.

It is easy to dismiss supply-side economics as a pretext for securing the wealth of the rich at the expense of the poor. It is by now apparent that tax breaks for wealthy people and for giant corporations do not "trickle down" to anyone else, because the rich are prone to spend their extra income on yachts, real estate, or Oriental carpets rather than saving it, and because large corporations are apt to spend their extra income building foreign factories or buying up other companies rather than investing in new productive capacity in the United States. And one could be forgiven for viewing America's obsession with its national security as a manifestation of the same underlying class conflict—to protect the rich from the poor—this time played out on a global scale, in which the rest of the world is perceived as coveting America's riches.

But these mercenary assumptions underrate the continuing appeal, to a broad spectrum of Americans, of Reaganism and its kinder, gentler incarnation in Bushism. Both derive from a strand of conservative social philosophy that was last prominent in America one hundred years ago. Although it has lived on in our political culture, that strand has had little to do with the dominant tradition of American conservatism, founded on the inviolability of property and profound distrust of popular social change. Instead, it celebrates change and often fails to respect established boundaries. While the main line of American conservatism has looked to the likes of Edmund Burke and Alexander Hamilton for intellectual sustenance, this minor strand, from which Reaganism derives, looks to Herbert Spencer and William Graham Sumner. Its central organizing principle is social Darwinism.

* * *

Few Americans living today have read any of Herbert Spencer's writings, but they had an electrifying effect on America during the last three decades of the nineteenth century—a far greater effect than in Spencer's native England. Their influence was so great, in fact, that they worked themselves into the folkways of American political philosophy

—into the everyday assumptions that many Americans still carry around in their heads about how social life is and should be arranged.

To Spencer and his followers, the marketplace was a field for the development and encouragement of personal character. Work provided people with moral discipline, which was critical to survival. Life, after all, was a competitive struggle in which only those with the strongest moral fiber could survive. It was through this competitive struggle that societies became stronger over time. Only the fittest were able to prosper, because only they were able to muster the necessary resources to sustain themselves and their offspring.

Even before Darwin's evolutionary theories were presented to the world in 1859, Spencer had developed the idea that the pressure of subsistence on populations would have a beneficent effect on the human race. The miserable social conditions of the early industrial revolution had provided data for Malthus's grim essay on the principle of population, but Spencer saw in the thesis a cause for hope. For the very process of impoverishment would place a premium on skill, intelligence, self-control, and the power to adapt through technological innovation. The inevitable pressure of poverty would itself stimulate human advancement by selecting the best of each generation for survival. It was Spencer, not Darwin, who coined the phrase "survival of the fittest."

An inevitable correlate of this principle was that government should do little or nothing to eliminate poverty. Charity was permissible; if the "fittest" wished to bestow gifts on some of the less fit, that would not contravene evolutionary forces and might indeed enhance the moral character of the giver. But state intervention to improve the lot of the poor would have disastrous results. Not only were the effects of public programs for the poor often vastly different from their intended consequences (since poverty was an infinitely complex social phenomenon that could never be eradicated), but the programs themselves interfered with natural selection. Spencer's follower, William Graham Sumner, a professor of political and social science at Yale, writing three years after Ronald Reagan's birth, put the case succinctly: "[I]f we do not like the survival of the fittest we have only one possible alternative, and that is the survival of the unfittest. The former is the law of civilization. . . . [A] plan for nourishing the unfittest and yet advancing civilization, no man will ever find."

Spencer and his followers publicly deplored poor laws, state-supported education, regulation of housing conditions, and the protection of the consumer against dangers and deceptions. They also found anathema any state-enforced effort to achieve equality, even equality of opportunity, because evolution depended for its force on *inequality*. Those who could not adapt themselves to their environment for whatever reason should not be artificially helped, so they thought, because the survival of the species depended on the survival of people who could adapt. Without natural inequalities, the law of survival of the fittest would have no meaning.

*　　*　　*

If all this sounds impossibly cold-blooded to someone living in the last decades of the twentieth century, it may be more because these sentiments have been disguised within socially acceptable rhetoric than because they have been totally discredited in the popular mind. Consider the oft-repeated charge by conservatives that the nation's poor can find work if they really want to (why, just look at the help-wanted columns in your daily newspaper), or the circumlocutions surrounding proposals to develop urban "enterprise zones," return welfare responsibilities to the states, provide tax credits for private schools, and eliminate the progressive income tax. The party line is that our society has grown fat, flaccid, and careless. We are soft from too much coddling. Only by trimming the fat, going back to basics, and enhancing our vigilance can we hope to return America to its former position of prosperity and strength. This suggests that the government's withdrawal will release all sorts of energies among those best able to adapt and survive, while forcing less-able souls to work harder. Those least able to survive should not be nurtured by the state, lest the entire society become demoralized as a result and the wrong habits and qualities be thereby encouraged in our citizens. (An important image in this symbolic argument is the welfare mother who has more babies in order to get a bigger welfare check.)

The subtle allure of social Darwinism finds its way into other policy arenas. One can detect its presence in recent discussions about foreign aid. Apart from contributions to Israel and Egypt, America is now providing an infinitely tiny portion of its GNP in aid to poorer nations—the smallest percentage of any industrial nation. After all, so the argument goes, there is very little that we or anyone else can do to relieve human suffering in sub-Sahara Africa or the Indian subcontinent. It is tragic, of course, but it is a fact of life. If we fed them, that would only make them more dependent and prolong their agony.

*　　*　　*

America's tepid responses to Soviet proposals to dismantle weapons and reduce troops can also be viewed most clearly through the myopic lens of social Darwinism. Notwithstanding that Herbert Spencer was a pacifist and an internationalist, the ideas he fathered are easily transmuted into demands for more weapons, bigger bombs, and trade embargoes. If only the fittest will survive, we must ensure our national strength. If survival is a bitter contest, then surely the Soviets will bury us should our vigilance wane.

One can also see the underpinnings of social Darwinism in this decade's hands-off approach to corporate acquisitions and buyouts. Let RJR-Nabisco borrow to the hilt, regardless of consequence to the larger economy. Drop antitrust charges against behemoths like IBM, since their market power arises by virtue of inherent superiority. Let corporations gobble up smaller companies and drive rivals into the sea. Their successes are to be encouraged, and weaker companies must be weeded out; that is the law of natural selection. Our economy will be all the stronger for it.

Social Darwinism's underlying concern with the development of moral character—and with the survival of those with the strongest fortitude, ambition, and conviction—suggests a connection between these economic and military policies and the moral crusades of the New Right. If prayer in the public schools builds moral conviction in our young, if proscriptions on abortions make people more responsible for their actions, if the possession of firearms encourages people to defend themselves and their families, then the nation and its citizens will be so much the stronger. And such moral strength is necessary both to keep our economy virile and to defend ourselves against the godless Soviets.

These ideas are not unique to Ronald Reagan or to George Bush. They have been with us, in one form or another, for more than a century. They have been a minor strand in America's popular political philosophy, to be sure. But Reagan did not single-handedly bring them to renewed national prominence. The teachings of Herbert Spencer and William Graham Sumner no doubt helped shape the political consciousness of many youngsters born around the first decade of this century, particularly in America's heartland, and so it is not surprising that they colored Ronald Reagan's own instinctive ideology. But they have resonated in the America of the 1980s because issues of survival have once again taken a central place in the nation's consciousness.

* * *

The current preoccupation with survival has its roots in America's fallen hopes. In the decade of the 1970s Americans' expectations for ourselves and our nation were dashed in a rude series of shocks, symbolized by Vietnam, OPEC, and Watergate. Perhaps even more significant than these discrete setbacks was the fact that a large and pampered postwar generation reached adulthood within an economy that could not deliver. By 1978 the standard of living of most Americans was beginning to decline for the first time in forty years. Survival seemed to be at stake for the simple reason that so many trends all at once sloped downward. For Americans who were accustomed to seeing the future as a more bountiful and better version of the present, the decade of the 1970s presented an ominous prospect.

It is difficult to be precise about the beginnings of a zeitgeist, but there is little doubt that as a nation and as individuals we now ponder our survival with a degree of concern not felt since the early 1930s, perhaps not since the turn of the century. Questions of survival are everywhere: Can our cities survive? Can democracy survive? Will our economy survive? Politics and economics in America have grown deadly serious. The presidential campaign of 1988 was devoid of specific issues but replete with dark warnings and accusations. Polls revealed that Americans are worried about the future.

*   *   *

The ideology of survival is enormously powerful, and Ronald Reagan and George Bush have exploited it at every turn. Their happy talk about America's future is matched by dark forebodings, should we lose our way. Liberals must respond to the apprehension about survival if liberalism is to speak to its time. The question that must be addressed by those who still place great value on social justice and democratic processes is not what type of political program will appeal to the selfish interest of a majority of voters. Granted, we need a new agenda on the left; Great Society liberalism has run up against a bureaucratic wall. But reformers are wrong to focus entirely on programs and policies at a time when the real challenge for those on the left is to enunciate an ideology appropriate to an era haunted by fears of survival.

Since the middle decades of the twentieth century, American liberalism has been preoccupied with issues of income redistribution. How the pie is divided among rich and poor continues to be a vitally important question, of course, but it is far less compelling than survival. If we are forced to choose between a more equitable distribution of our wealth and the continued vitality of our society—and this is precisely the choice that has been posed by Reaganism and the New Right—there is little doubt which side most Americans will take, for survival is a precondition to everything else.

The politics of class only cuts us off from one another; a new ideology on the left must join us together as one people facing a common challenge. That new ideology must be premised on the importance of the values of conciliation and community to the continued survival of the nation and the planet. It can take as one of its starting points the threat of nuclear holocaust that imperils us all unless we reach global agreement on arms control. If the "fittest" is assumed to be the nation that can amass the greatest nuclear arsenal, then the process of natural selection will doom us all.

In the economic sphere as well, communitarian values can be shown to underpin future prosperity. Economic survival is coming to depend critically on how well people collaborate within large and complex organizations. By the same token, cynical indifference to public values is corrosive, as each person or group becomes less willing to bear any burden on the supposition that others are avoiding their fair share. We see the dark side of this paradox in the $90 billion in taxes that the Internal Revenue Service estimates were unpaid last year; in the dishevelment of our parks and public facilities; in the reluctance of many people to report crimes or corruption. A collective commitment to social justice and democratic processes helps assure everyone that benefits and burdens are allocated fairly, and this assurance in turn is the very foundation of future prosperity and social security. A collective cynicism about the fairness of the system perpetuates itself in the opposite direction, impoverishing our life together.

The coming ideological debate is not over how the pie is to be divided; nor is it the old contest between efficiency and equity, property and state-enforced charity. It has deeper roots, and the stakes are higher. As the economies of America and all other nations slow down, and some begin to decline absolutely, many people are tempted to maintain their standard of living by expropriating a portion of the declining share of everyone else. But these beggar-thy-neighbor strategies, already apparent in America, will undermine civic virtue and ultimately reduce the prosperity and security of everyone.

The coming debate is over the ideologies of survival. A central concern with fairness is the flip side of social Darwinism. Such a concern is patently more relevant to America's future survival than is an ideology that celebrates competitive struggle. Those who value social justice must spread the message that in the long run the dog-eat-dog world hailed by the new social Darwinists will lack even the memory of a bark.

27

THE FADED
IDEAL OF EQUAL SACRIFICE

WHAT DO CITIZENS OWE ONE ANOTHER? YOUR ANSWER MAY COMPRISE A longer or shorter list of civic obligations, depending on your ideological bent. But most people would agree to two minimal requirements: You should pay taxes to support the common good, and you should help defend the nation from its enemies.

There will be disputes about amounts, conditions, and definitions, but most Americans would agree that the two burdens—to support and defend the common good—should be shared by all adult members of our democratic community. These burdens should not only be shared, but be shared equally. Equality of sacrifice is important to society's general perception of fairness—the foundation on which our entire system is built.

This idea isn't new. The principle of equal sacrifice is a cornerstone of modern liberal political thought. John Stuart Mill proclaimed that "[w]hatever sacrifices [society] requires . . . should be made to bear as nearly as possible with the same pressure on all." In defending the nation, the wealthier should stand shoulder to shoulder with the poor. In paying taxes, the wealthier should bear a comparable financial pain by ceding a larger proportion of their incomes. Even Adam Smith, the progenitor of free-market conservatism, saw the wisdom of a progressive tax: "It is not very unreasonable that the rich should contribute to the public expense, not only in proportion to their revenue, but something more in proportion."

Yet in recent years America has retreated from this central creed of civic obligation in two important ways: (1) In June 1973 the draft was ended. We now have an all-volunteer armed service, whose members are somewhat more likely than the population as a whole to be minority (as 27 percent of the armed forces now are categorized) and to lack any college education (79 percent). (2) In November 1986 the progressive income tax was substantially ended. Beginning in 1988, the federal government claimed no more than 28 percent of the highest personal incomes in the land, giving us the lowest top tax rate of all industrialized Western nations.

*   *   *

America's surrender of the ideal of equal sacrifice has occurred without much public debate or even awareness that we were doing it. It has come rather as a by-product of specific policies that seemed otherwise perfectly sensible.

In both terminating the draft and retreating from income tax progressivity, the logic was much the same. Four basic arguments were made against the rhetoric of equal sacrifice:

It was hypocritical. First, it was noted that the prevailing reality fell far short of the ideal of equal sacrifice. By 1973, when the draft was ended, it was clear that wealthier citizens had managed to create or exploit loopholes in the Selective Service System. The eleven million men who had served in Vietnam were drawn disproportionately from lower-income families. Similarly, by 1986 tax progressivity was shown to be a similar sham. Despite a top personal rate of 50 percent, for example, families earning over $200,000 a year paid on average only 22 percent of their income in taxes.

It was wasteful and bred cynicism. The tactics wealthier Americans used to escape these obligations had wasted valuable resources and bred a cynical and contemptuous attitude toward the law. In the late 1960s many draft-age men who had no intention of becoming preachers, doctors, or teachers were flooding into graduate programs that offered them relief from conscription. One 1972 survey showed "avoiding the draft" to be among the three most important reasons cited for attending college. Others sought refuge in fatherhood, feigned illnesses, or various forms of legal and bureaucratic chicanery.

In a similar vein high-income taxpayers of the 1970s and 1980s sought investment—in railroad boxcars, office buildings, and cattle feeding, to name a few—the attractions of which had far more to do with avoiding tax payments than gaining direct economic returns. In seeking tactical advice and legal counsel for avoiding the draft or reducing their taxes, wealthier Americans spawned entire service industries dedicated to outwitting the government.

It was naive. It was assumed to be politically unrealistic to expect any greater degree of sacrifice on the part of wealthier citizens than the actual extent to which they willingly accepted the burden. No more than a relatively low percentage of their sons could be coerced into the military; no greater than a relatively low fraction of their incomes could be captured by the Internal Revenue Service.

It was inefficient. Finally, reform entailed a kind of exchange. In return for explicitly affirming and legitimating the relatively low burdens that wealthier citizens actually bore, the system for recruiting military personnel or for gathering personal tax payments could be rationalized and streamlined. Loopholes could be eliminated, waste and distortions removed; an unworkable and hypocritical process could be replaced by one capable of recruiting dependable soldiers or of efficiently garnering tax receipts.

Thus the President's Commission on an All-Volunteer Armed Force argued in its 1970 report that abandoning the draft would require that the government pay its recruits salaries competitive with the private sector. But these higher personnel costs would be offset by the benefits flowing from more professionalization and dedication among enlistees, less turnover, and a more "rational" process of selection.

Ten years later, the cause of tax reform appeared doomed until Senate Finance Committee Chairman Bob Packwood offered to lower the top rate to 28 percent, at which point the bill moved toward swift passage. Advocates of tax reform conceded that the only way to broaden the tax base, eliminating the welter of deductions and exemptions, was to reduce the top marginal rate until it approximately matched the effective rate that wealthier citizens actually paid.

*   *   *

The logic in both instances was the same, and reformers were drawn to similar conclusions: No purpose was served in continuing to maintain the fictions of universal conscription or of progressive taxation. By accepting political reality and making official what had become the norm, each system could be strengthened and rendered more efficient.

But in both cases the reformers failed to consider that the ideals of universal service and tax progressivity had moral value in *themselves,* as social aspirations. They symbolized the equal sacrifices that Americans believed in. They represented the goal of social solidarity. That the ideal was not achieved in practice did not mean that we should no longer seek to achieve it.

In both instances the gap between the ideal of equal sacrifice and the reality of evasion had widened only recently, in response to particular events, and might have closed again as quickly had the ideal not been abandoned.

The move toward an all-volunteer army occurred at the end of an unpopular war. Overall, only 20 percent of the troops we sent to Vietnam had been drafted, and the ability of the Selective Service System to compel young men to serve steadily declined during the course of the hostilities. In a 1972 poll only 13 percent of the public said they supported peacetime conscription. But the situation had been quite different before Vietnam.

More than 60 percent of the Americans serving in World War II had been drafted, and the Selective Service System had functioned relatively well. Peacetime conscription remained popular after World War II. Even in 1969 fully 60 percent of the population was in favor of it. Since Vietnam, popular support for the draft has bounced back somewhat. In a 1984 National Opinion Research Center survey 42 percent of adult Americans said they would favor a return to the draft. Forty-four percent favored a wider system of compulsory national service for both men and women even if "such a program made it necessary to increase your taxes by a small amount—for example, by 5 percent."

Our more recent retreat from tax progressivity also occurred in an era when the public was especially unsympathetic toward the purposes their sacrifices would serve. Beginning with Watergate, Americans' confidence in government had steadily declined. Jimmy Carter and Ronald Reagan both campaigned against Washington insiders, meddling bureaucrats, and chronic government inefficiency.

The late 1970s and early 1980s had been marked by tax revolts in the states. As public support for taxation waned, tolerance for tax avoidance increased. And as the loopholes widened, the actual rates paid by wealthier Americans sharply declined. Years earlier, when Americans had greater faith in government, the top tax rate was much higher and exemptions fewer, with the result that the tax code was far more progressive in actual effect: In 1944 a family of four with an income of $100,000 (in 1986 dollars) paid about $40,000 in taxes; in 1966 the same family paid $30,000; in 1980 just $24,000.

* * *

The surrender of the ideals of universal service and tax progressivity was not costless, as reformers had assumed. The shift to an all-volunteer armed force and to a low marginal tax amounted to a renunciation of social aspiration. The retreat signaled an abandonment of an important goal and our sense of mutual responsibility and interdependence. From here on, there would be less of a shared understanding of the principle of equal sacrifice, less striving to narrow the gap between aspiration and reality.

The failure of reformers to recognize what they were abandoning was linked to the way in which they had defined the problems to begin with. In both cases "reform" meant accomplishing specific common acts more efficiently, rather than reinforcing our capacity for common action.

The conferences and commissions convened in the early 1970s to study the possibility of an all-volunteer armed service understood the goal primarily as ensuring a reliable supply of military personnel. Richard Nixon's concerns about meeting our "manpower needs" were echoed by liberal reformers. Similarly, various liberal organizations like Citizens for Tax Justice and The New Republic, which called for tax reform in the late 1970s and early 1980s, for the most part saw the challenge as broadening the tax base and simplifying the code.

The tendency for reformers in America to focus on administration rather than principle has often reflected a healthy pragmatism. We fix what we can, when we can. But the same tendency also can blind us to the broader consequences of our efforts and the cumulative ways in which they reinforce or undermine social norms.

At a time in American history when prophets of the right are busily claiming the high moral ground, attributing the decline of character and civic virtue to the temptations of the welfare state, it is perhaps appropriate for liberals to resurrect the venerable ideal of equal sacrifice as a core principle of public philosophy.

28

THE LIBERAL AS PLANNER

GROVER CLEVELAND CALLED HIMSELF A LIBERAL AND SPENT MUCH OF his time as President defending American corporations and financiers against the fulminations and protestations of workers, socialists, and Populists. Herbert Hoover identified his cause as liberalism in the 1928 presidential campaign. Robert Taft called himself a liberal to the end of his life. To this day, many European intellectuals and American leftists continue to identify liberalism with its nineteenth-century quest for economic and civil independence from the ancien régime, for the freedom of individuals to contract with whomever they wish and for whatever purpose.

For most Americans, however, liberalism has come to stand for something quite different: big government. The shift in meaning began during the first decades of the twentieth century and culminated in the New Deal. It was fueled, in part, by the rise of the giant American corporation and by the view that such large concentrations of economic power were the natural and inevitable consequence of technological change. Big government was necessary to tame the giant corporation, to ensure that it functioned in the public's interest, to counterbalance its awesome power on the side of the individual American.

*   *   *

Adolf A. Berle exemplified this new thinking. Like Robert Moses (a Republican) and David Lilienthal, he belonged to a generation of planners. Their monuments—the SEC, the Triborough Bridge, the Tennessee Valley Authority—are still with us. So too is their vision.

Born at the end of the last century, Berle grew up in the Progressive era, when it was assumed that men of good sense and broad perspective could rise above the rapacity of big business and the corruption of politics to lead the nation toward greatness. His was the vision of a confident, powerful, assertive, expansive government that would function as the senior partner of corporate America. Berle the man was as assertive and expansive (and arrogant) as the government he envisaged. In his many writings and in his numerous public activities, he represented an American liberalism that was as idealistic as it was grandiose.

Pushed by an ambitious and imperious father, Berle entered Harvard College at the age of fourteen, graduated with honors from Harvard Law School, promptly and presumptuously became an adviser at the Paris peace talks after World War I, practiced law and lectured on corporate finance, and then in 1932 collaborated with a young economist named Gardiner Means to write a book that shook the nation, *The Modern Corporation and Private Property*. By that time America was mired in economic depression, Hoover and the Republican champions of Wall Street were on the run, and America wanted to understand what had happened and what to do about it.

Most of Berle and Means's book was dry, filled with lawyer's arguments and economist's data; but taken as a whole, it told a tantalizing tale about the increasing concentration of American economic power in the hands of a relatively few giant corporations and their managers, who were accountable neither to their shareholders nor to the public at large. The authors concluded by demanding that "the modern corporation serve not alone the owners or the [managers] but all the society." The federal government must rein in unbridled captains of industry and put the modern corporation to work for the nation. Neither laissez-faire nor socialism was the answer. The real answer was to be found in a partnership between business and government, in which government had the senior role. Although few people ever read the book (in its first twenty years only thirty-five thousand copies were sold), *The Modern Corporation and Private Property* became, in the indubitable words of *Time* magazine in the spring of 1933, the "economic bible of the Roosevelt administration."

* * *

Berle had been drawn into Franklin D. Roosevelt's "brain trust" even before the election. His ideas and his influence were evident during the campaign, especially in FDR's notable Commonwealth Club speech, given in San Francisco in the fall of 1932. Reviewing the history of the American economy, Roosevelt pointed out that "in many instances the victory of the central Government was a haven of refuge to the individual." Hoover's protective tariffs and government loans had benefited big business at the expense of the individual. Wealth in America was far more concentrated now in 1932 than it had been in 1912. Roosevelt then described the nation's challenge in words that echoed Berle:

> Our task now is not discovery or exploitation of natural
> resources, or necessarily producing more goods. It is the
> soberer, less dramatic business of administering resources and
> plants already in hand, of seeking to re-establish foreign
> markets for our surplus production, of meeting the problem of
> underconsumption, of adjusting production to consumption, of
> distributing wealth and products more equitably, of adapting
> existing economic organizations to the service of the people.
> The day of enlightened administration has come. . . . [We
> should not] abandon the principle of strong economic units,
> merely because their power is susceptible of easy abuse. . . .
> Today we are modifying and controlling our economic units.

It was to this job—of modifying and controlling economic units through enlightened administration—that Berle turned with relish. Berle's prescriptions for the federal regulation of securities became the Securities and Exchange Act. His influence was felt in the creation of the National Recovery Administration and in the Temporary National Economic Committee hearings later in the decade. He argued for a branch banking act, for the coordination of all federal credit agencies, such as home loan banks, for the consolidation of railroads, for a federal incorporation act, for a national program of sickness and unemployment compensation, for a public-works finance corporation. In much of this, he was prescient. He urged that "women performing [for] equal income . . . [is] a field we have not yet entered but it is plainly foreshadowed by the modifications going on."

For the next three decades Berle hopped from office to office, from project to project, like a gourmet cook in a soup kitchen, stirring pots, bringing issues to a boil, advising and scolding lesser mortals, everywhere imperious and often insufferable. No sooner had the New Deal been launched than he left it to become an adviser to Fiorello LaGuardia, then mayor of New York during one of the city's periodic financial crises. There he took on the role Felix Rohatyn was to play four decades later, devising financial schemes to save the city and then, without undue modesty, accepting full credit for having done so. Then back to Washington as a State Department assistant secretary, running Latin American affairs, dabbling in civil aviation, working on a host of other weighty matters. Then to Brazil as ambassador. Then back to New York, and so on, continuing through the Kennedy Administration, in which he was briefly in charge of a task force on Latin America.

* * *

Berle's pattern was to set himself up as a fount of ideas but to leave the work of implementation to others—and then to fulminate over how badly his ideas were handled. He bruised egos wherever he went, and his short tenure in any single job was as much a function of others' impatience with him as of his impatience with everyone else. It never occurred to him that policies that could not be administered well were probably bad policies to begin with. For those who worked with Berle, "enlightened administration" was synonymous with arrogance.

There was an arrogance, too, in Berle's ambitions for America. He espoused a foreign policy intellectually consistent with his view of government's purpose and role in the nation. Just as Americans needed a strong central government to liberate them from the predations of giant corporations, nation-states needed powerful international institutions to liberate them from the scourges of colonialism, nineteenth-century imperialism, and then—after World War II—from international communism. In the absence of powerful international institutions, however, the job of ensuring national self-determination naturally fell to America. Berle never came to terms with the possibility that America-as-global-policeman would exercise imperial power itself. He was certain that no state would willingly become communist; where communism existed, he assumed that it had to have been imposed from the outside.

Then Cuba turned communist, and revolution threatened in other Latin American nations. Berle urged American intervention. Years later, he was an advocate of America's role in Vietnam, and in 1969 he described an antiwar strike at Harvard as directed by "a small group of organizers working primarily as political warfare agents for Maoist communism." Berle's rhetoric became more strident. In the end he disavowed his earlier commitment to self-determination in favor of communist containment. Berle the Progressive liberal ended his days as Berle the anti-communist curmudgeon.

*　　*　　*

The Progressivist origins of Berle's ideas were never far below the surface. Berle's vision of a powerful national government, guiding American industry and protecting individual rights, was the direct descendant of that of Herbert Croly. Croly had been the first editor of *The New Republic* during its visionary days before World War I. Almost a quarter century before Berle and Means produced their tome, Croly had offered in *The Promise of American Life** a stinging critique of the reformers' infatuation with trust-busting.

Foreshadowing Berle, Croly argued that big businesses "contributed to American economic efficiency" and that civilized society should aim, therefore, to substitute cooperation for competition. Corporations should be able to fulfill their "natural" growth, so long as federal powers were used to bind their activities to the national interest. And wielding these new federal powers were to be wise public leaders free from selfish interest. What was needed, said Croly, was a "New Nationalism" to direct individual efforts away from selfish pursuits, toward collective solutions to the nation's problems. This was the logic of Alexander Hamilton applied to an industrial America.

Theodore Roosevelt took up Croly's ideas and placed them at the center of his 1912 Bull Moose platform, in opposition to Woodrow Wilson's call for stricter antitrust enforcement. These two visions of reform—a cooperative system of national planning, or a competitive system of atomized economic units umpired by trustbusters—faintly echoed the much older Hamilton–Jefferson debate. But this was also a completely new discussion about the role of private power in an industrialized economy, and its terms were to guide subsequent liberal debates. Two decades later, Berle offered his generation a forceful restatement of Croly's position, and he spent much of his intellectual life battling with those on the other side—Felix Frankfurter, Benjamin Cohen, Thurmond Arnold—who shared the Wilsonian view.

The New Deal never resolved the liberal debate. To the end, the planners and the atomizers fought one another for control of the ideological agenda. The National Recovery Administration marked the high

* First published in 1909; Harvard University Press edition, 1965.

watermark of the planners; Arnold's reign at the Justice Department, of the atomizers. Nor has the debate been resolved since.

* * *

How should the economy be reorganized, and who should do the organizing? Liberals have never come up with a coherent answer. The problem with the liberal planners' vision has always been arrogance. How are the planners to know what the economy needs or in what direction it should move? How can the public be assured of their knowledge and impartiality? The problem with the liberal atomizers' vision has always been sentimentality and naïveté. How can a complex industrial economy function with only small businesses and dispersed sources of capital? Is there, as a practical matter, really such a thing as a free market?

Liberals have tended to forget this debate when times are good and then indulge in it once again when the economy is threatened. The labels may change and the prescriptions may differ in specifics, but the underlying controversy survives. In this decade, for example, some thoughtful observers have argued that America needs an explicit industrial policy to encourage older industries to reduce outmoded technologies, to channel research and development funds into emerging industries, and to help workers retrain. Otherwise, the necessary shifts in the nation's industrial base will come more slowly and be more painful, and in the meantime the United States will have lost out to other nations that have made the transition more smoothly (notably Japan). These arguments have been greeted by the predictable Wilsonian response—recently emanating from such august liberal enclaves as the Brookings Institution—that all we need do is maintain free trade and free-floating currencies, and the economy will fix itself.

The two views battled for Walter Mondale's allegiance during the 1984 presidential campaign. Neither prevailed. Nor, for that matter, did Mondale. Liberals were again in disarray over how the economy should be organized, until the ensuing recovery seemed to render the problem irrelevant.

Through it all, conservatives have sounded like Wilsonian liberals but acted like planners. Herbert Hoover as secretary of commerce in the Coolidge Administration, and then as President, rhapsodized over the wonders of the free market, but he suspended antitrust enforcement and proceeded to organize American business into powerful trade associations to plan industrial growth with the "cooperation" of the federal government. Sixty years later, Ronald Reagan waxed equally enthusiastic over the magic of the market and the heroism of entrepreneurs but followed Hoover's well-worn path toward business planning.

*   *   *

It should be noted that Reagan's plan to shrink old-line basic industries—forcing radical cuts in employment and wage concession, busting the unions—was quite successful. Standardized goods, such as steel, autos, textiles, commodity chemicals, and others that rest on mass or large-batch production, are particularly vulnerable to price competition. Thus, the easiest way to reduce the size of these industries was to increase the prices of these goods in world markets, making it difficult for them to be exported and making it relatively easy for foreign producers to threaten them at home. And the fastest way to increase the price of these goods was to raise the value of the dollar by keeping interest rates high. Presto: These older industries were forced to contract. Between 1981 and 1985, as the value of the dollar soared, some two million jobs were lost in old-line manufacturing businesses. Membership in industrial unions shrank dramatically. Steel, autos, and others were forced to reduce domestic capacity, set up operations abroad, and diversify into specialized niches. By 1985, when the dollar started to decline, old industrial America was a pale shadow of its former self.

Reagan's plan to promote high technology was equally ambitious. Between 1981 and 1988 about $600 billion was channeled into new weapons, most depending on advanced technologies. This demand for state-of-the-art products pulled these emerging industries down the learning curve to the point where commercial spin-offs were attainable. By the mid-1980s well over 50 percent of all the research and development funding for America's high-tech industries was coming directly from the Pentagon. In 1987 the Pentagon launched a major effort to develop practical applications for superconductors, special alloys that lose all resistance to the flow of electric current when cooled; it agreed to fund Sematech, a research joint venture comprising America's leading semiconductor manufacturers, designed to improve their competitiveness; and the National Security Agency poured money into parallel processing, the most advanced computer architecture, which may produce the fastest computers in the world. The Strategic Defense Initiative aimed to extend the frontiers of lasers, fiber optics, new materials, and computer technologies into the twenty-first century.

Viewed as a whole, Reagan's economic policy and military buildup constituted an extraordinarily ambitious plan for shifting America's industrial base. This was planning with a vengeance. But because Reagan was an avowed defender of the free market from the depredations of big government, there were few voices to his right denouncing Washington's vulgar intrusion into the temple of the marketplace. As only Richard Nixon could open relations with Beijing, so only Ronald Reagan (and Hoover) could make economic planning respectable.

But there are important differences between conservative planning and liberal planning. The former is done far more quietly, and it tends to be run by large corporations and Wall Street. Neither Hoover's trade associations nor Reagan's Federal Reserve Board and Pentagon are exemplars of open, democratic accountability. Conservative planning also has an uncanny way of making the rich richer and the poor poorer.

Were he alive today, Adolf Berle would be incensed at the hypocrisy of the present planning system and dismayed at the cynicism with which the public has come to view the federal government. He would, no doubt, get on the phone to his favorite Democratic candidate and presumptuously instruct him to tell the American people exactly what was happening.

29

HOW NOT TO
MAKE INDUSTRIAL POLICY

"INDUSTRIAL POLICY" IS ONE OF THOSE RARE IDEAS TO HAVE MOVED swiftly from obscurity to meaninglessness without any intervening period of coherence. Blame it on the business cycle. Before the recovery commenced in late 1982, neoliberals, progressives, leaders of organized labor, Democrats, and others to the left of supply-side economics thought they had found in that term a simple answer to Reaganomics— an answer that promised growth, equality, and some degree of democratic planning. But the recovery intervened too soon. Most people stopped worrying about the economy (although they have every reason to continue to worry). And by the time the 1992 depression gets under way, it may be too late to worry.

What would have happened to "industrial policy" had the recovery not happened? At some point many supporters would have discovered that their own definition of "industrial policy" conflicted with that of many other supporters. How *much* growth? What *sort* of equality? And especially, *whose* planning? Alas, there are no simple answers, even to the vacuities of supply-side economics.

Rhode Island offered a test case. By 1983 the recovery had all but passed it by. Unemployment was still high, relative to the rest of New

England. Average manufacturing wages were the lowest in New England, forty-eighth among the fifty states.

So a small group of civic leaders got together to plan a new industrial policy for the state. The "Greenhouse Compact," as it was called, featured $750 million in public aid for business, designed to help older companies restructure and newer industries grow (hence the name). In addition, organized labor would support legislation to modify strikers' benefits, business leaders would overhaul the state's antiquated unemployment insurance system, the banks would invest more money in the state, and voters would approve a new bond issue. Every major group would kick in something and get back more—a larger version of the Chrysler bailout. The whole thing would be run by a "strategic" commission.

On paper, the plan was impressive. (I confess a slightly self-serving bias; the plan's principle author—Ira Magaziner—is an old friend and fellow intellectual traveler.) It was supported by virtually every leader of every interest group in the state.

But when it was put to a vote, the good citizens of Rhode Island rejected the Greenhouse Compact, four to one.

The most plausible explanation: Voters liked the plan but didn't trust their state government to implement it. Government in Rhode Island is roughly analogous to an old septic tank: Although necessary and surely useful, it periodically overflows in a most noxious manner and needs to be drained or replaced. At the same time they were being asked to approve the Greenhouse Compact, Providence voters were seeking a replacement for their mayor, who had been recalled from office after having been convicted of assault. The night before the vote Rhode Islanders were informed on the evening news that a Providence commissioner had been arrested in connection with a wide-ranging corruption probe.

But there may be a deeper lesson here for those who are readying a new version of industrial policy for the next downturn in the business cycle. My guess is that most Americans like the idea of more "cooperation" among business, labor, and government. They also support public financing of research and development, worker retraining, plant modernization, technical education, transportation, industrial parks, and export credits. They would like to ensure that industries that benefit from special tariffs, quotas, and tax breaks use the extra cash to retool their factories and retrain their workers. And they would like to see all these economic-development policies rendered more coherent, more "strategic." (Ubiquitous Harris and Gallup polls bear me out.)

But Americans *don't* like central planning, they don't like compli-
·cated plans, and they especially don't trust business, government, and
labor elites to do the planning. These predilections are as populist as
apple pie, running clear across the political spectrum and rooted deep in
our political history.

In other words, "industrial policy" is fine so long as it builds on
current policies and institutions. But wrap it in an elaborate plan and
assign it to a new "strategic commission" comprised of the Big Shots,
and you can stuff it.

Which is what Rhode Island did.

30

COMPETENCE OR IDEOLOGY?

"THIS CAMPAIGN IS ABOUT COMPETENCE, NOT IDEOLOGY," SAID MIchael Dukakis. George Bush, and apparently most Americans who exercised their right to vote, disagreed.

What, exactly, do we mean by "competence" when it comes to running the American government?

Beneath the daily activities of elected officials, administrators, and their advisers and critics, and beneath the public's tacit decision to accord legitimacy to specific policy decisions, exists a set of first principles that suggest what competent policy making is all about. They comprise a view of human nature, of how people behave as citizens. They also reflect a view of social improvements, of why we think that society is better in one state than another. And they offer a view of the appropriate role of government in society—given human nature, our aspirations for social improvement, and our means of defining and solving public problems.

These principles are often implicit in policy making. They may be invoked to justify a particular policy, but the ground from which these principles spring is usually taken for granted. To state them is to end the conversation, because there seems to be nothing left to say. Nevertheless, they draw on ideas that have been debated for centuries (later I will briefly place them in their historical context). The current incarnation of these principles is intimately related to America's present political culture. As it evolves, so will they.

The prevailing philosophy of policy making in America can be summarized as follows: People are essentially self-interested rather than altruistic and behave much the same way whether they are choosing a new washing machine or voting on a new board of education. The public good, or "public interest," is thus best understood as the sum of these individual preferences. Society is improved whenever some people's preferences can be satisfied without making other people worse off. Most of the time, private market exchanges suffice for improving society in this way; public policies are appropriate only when—and to the extent that —they can make such improvements more efficiently than the market can. Thus, the central responsibility of public officials, administrators, and policy analysts is to determine whether public intervention is warranted and, if so, to choose the policy that leads to the greatest improvements.

These principles are familiar, not because they describe how public policies are actually made in modern America but because they shape the way public policies are typically *justified* and *criticized*. They suggest what is and is not legitimate for government to do, how policy makers should act, how they and those who advise them should think about public problems. Importantly, these principles also sound a cautionary theme: The supposed tendency for individuals to use public policies to get what they want for themselves creates a danger that those who have the greatest stake in a given matter will collude against the rest of us, whose individual interests in any particular policy are apt to be small. This danger can be overcome if policy makers carefully ensure that everyone's preferences are objectively weighed, alternatives are fully considered, and net benefits are maximized.

The ubiquity and robustness of these principles in contemporary America is quite remarkable. They undergird the position papers that stream out of policy institutes and assorted think tanks. They serve as the basis for memorandums of policy analysts in government and academe, editorials in prominent newspapers and magazines, learned treatises on public policy, court opinions crafted by judges schooled in "law and economics," lobbyists' pleadings, and administrative hearings. You hear them even when politicians or administrators talk candidly about what they think they ought (but may not be able) to do. Whenever people who deal in public policy want to be (or to sound) objective and techni-cally rigorous in discussing solutions to public problems, they tend to employ these assumptions—sometimes tacitly, often without further ex-planation or rationale.

Such assumptions—about human nature, about social improve-ment, and about the proper role of government—have proven useful in several respects. First, they are appropriate to a heterogeneous society comprising a multiplicity of values and viewpoints, all of which need to be considered in making policy. Rather than assume a single, unifying "public interest," it is often more accurate—and safer—to assume that interests collide and thus trade-offs are inevitable. Second, these premises direct policy making to practical, answerable questions: Who wants this policy and why? How do we know? How much do they want it? Who will lose by it, and how much would it cost to compensate the losers? Why can't the market take care of this? What are the advantages and disadvantages of each alternative way of accomplishing the objective?

The prevailing assumptions also suggest ready means of answering the questions and reaching solutions. It is a matter of measuring what people want and analyzing the most efficient way of satisfying these wants, or of engineering compromises among competing groups pur-porting to speak for the self-interests of their members. Finally, the assumptions are sufficiently neutral and commonsensical that policies derived from them can gain broad assent, thus avoiding conflicts based solely on ideology or personal rancor. Compromises can readily be reached. For all these reasons, these principles together comprise what is taken for the policy-making ideal in present-day America. They offer a model for what politics should accomplish—would accomplish—if it were less corrupted by special pleadings, money, ideology, and bias.

*   *   *

But for all its virtues, the prevailing view of competent policy mak-ing ignores other important values. In particular, it disregards the role of ideas about what is good for society and the importance of debating the relative merits of such ideas. It thus tends to overlook the ways such normative visions shape what people want and expect from their govern-ment, their fellow citizens, and themselves. And it disregards the impor-tance of democratic deliberation for refining and altering such visions over time and for mobilizing public action around them.

The core responsibility of those who deal in public policy—elected officials, administrators, policy analysts—is not simply to discover as objectively as possible what people want for themselves and then determine and implement the best means of satisfying these wants. It is also to provide the public with alternative visions of what is desirable and possible, to stimulate deliberation about them, provoke a reexamination of premises and values, and thus to broaden the range of potential responses and deepen society's understanding of itself. And here, perhaps, is where ideology comes in.

Many of the most important policy initiatives of the last two decades cannot be explained by the prevailing assumptions about human nature or social improvement. Consider the civil rights laws and regulations of the 1960s; the subsequent wave of laws and rules governing health, safety, and the environment; and the reform of the tax code in 1986. These policies were not motivated principally or even substantially by individuals seeking to satisfy selfish interests. To the contrary, they were broadly understood as matters of public rather than private interest. And this perception gave them their unique authority. People supported these initiatives largely because they were thought to be good for *society*. Nor were public preferences with regard to these policies stable or preordained. Public support grew and changed as people came to understand and engage with the ideas underlying them. The official acts of policy making—enacting the laws, promulgating the rules, issuing the court opinions—were embedded within social movements and understandings that shaped them and propelled them forward. To disregard these motivating ideas is to miss the essential story.

There is ample evidence that the most accomplished government leaders—those who have achieved significant things while in office or at least set the direction of public action—have explicitly and purposively crafted public visions of what is desirable and possible for society to do. These ideas have been essential to their leadership, serving both to focus public attention and to mobilize talent and resources within the government. Ronald Reagan perhaps best exemplified this approach to policy making. His speeches, interviews, and press statements were not simply devices to muster public support behind a particular initiative or to glorify the accomplishments of his Administration. They were means of educating the public in an approach to governance, creating a framework through which the public would come to support a wide variety of initiatives and to understand public issues.

The act of raising the salient public question—how to overcome welfare dependency or Soviet aggression, how to improve American competitiveness or reduce the budget deficit—is often the key step in the formulation of policy, because it subsumes the value judgments that declare something to be a problem, focuses public attention on the issue, and frames the ensuing public debate. When questions "catch on" in this way, it is not because those who pose them are especially talented at manipulating public opinion or linking preconceived preferences to attractive agendas. The phenomenon is more interactive than that, and preferences are less defined, more fluid. Even before the question is asked, the public (or a significant portion of the public) seems already to be searching for ways to pose it—to give shape and coherence to events that seem random and unsettling—and thus to gain some measure of control. Rather than responding to preexisting public wants, the art of policy making has lain primarily in giving voice to these half-articulated fears and hopes and embodying them in convincing stories about their sources and the choices they represent.

The prevailing ideal of competent policy making casts government as problem solver, intervening when it can satisfy preexisting preferences more efficiently than the market can. Democratic processes, in this view, are primarily means for alerting policy makers to what people want for themselves. But if I am correct in seeing policy making, inevitably, as a process of posing questions, presenting problems, offering explanations, and suggesting choices, then the prevailing view seriously understates the responsibilities of policy makers, policy analysts, and citizens.

It is not difficult to tally preferences in this era of instantaneous electronic polling and of sophisticated marketing techniques for discovering what people want and how much they want it. It is a considerable challenge, however, to engage the public in rethinking how certain problems are defined, alternative solutions envisioned, and responsibilities for action allocated. The failure of conventional techniques of policy making to permit such civic discovery may suggest that there are no shared values to be discovered in the first place. And *this* message—that the "public interest" is no more than an accommodation or aggregation of individual interests—may have a corrosive effect on civic life. It may invalidate whatever potential exists for the creation of shared commitments and in so doing may stunt the discovery of public ideas. Such a failure may in turn call into question the inherent legitimacy of the policy decisions that result. For such policies are then supported only by debatable facts, inferences, and trade-offs. They lack any authentic governmental character beyond accommodation or aggregation. Those who disagree with the procedures or conclusions on which the policies are based have every reason to disregard them whenever the opportunity arises. Under these circumstances disobedience is not a social act reflecting on one's membership in a community but merely another expression of preference.

To the extent that deliberation and reflection yield a broader repertoire of problem definitions, solutions, and civic responsibilities, society is better equipped to cope with change and to learn from its past. The thoughtless adherence to outmoded formulations of problems, choices, and responsibilities can threaten a society's survival. Policy making should be more than and different from the discovery of what people want; it should entail the creation of contexts in which people can critically evaluate and revise what they believe.

*   *   *

This suggests a different role for policy makers and policy analysts than that of the prevailing ideal. The responsibility of government leaders is not only to make and implement decisions responsive to public wants. A greater challenge is to engage the public in an ongoing dialogue over what problems should be addressed, what is at stake in such decisions, and how to strengthen the public's capacities to deal with similar problems in the future. Such an explicative process, properly managed, can build on itself: As society defines and evaluates its collective goals, it examines its norms and beliefs; in defining its purposes, it becomes better able to mobilize its resources and achieve its goals.

By the same token, the responsibility of policy analysts is not only to choose the best means of achieving a given objective. It is also to offer alternative ways of understanding public problems and possible solutions and thus to expose underlying norms to critical examination. The analyst can provoke such examination in several ways: by juxtaposing widely accepted but morally or politically inconsistent assumptions about certain public problems and their solutions, by questioning the conventional metaphors and analogies used to justify and explain policies and offering new ones in their place, by providing plausible but novel interpretations of large events, by revealing underlying similarities and patterns in the public's approach to seemingly unconnected situations, and by advancing alternative future scenarios premised on how society might cope with certain problems.

Policy makers and analysts will not spend all their time in such explicative activities; there may be relatively few opportunities for effectively redefining and evaluating social norms. But these responsibilities should be understood as critically important to these jobs. The prevailing philosophy comprises a useful set of precepts for guiding much policy making, particularly where there is wide and enduring consensus about the nature of the problems to be solved, the range of possible solutions, and appropriate allocations of responsibility for solving them; and where solving the problems *as understood* is more useful than understanding them differently. The prevailing philosophy is less helpful—indeed, may forestall social learning—where these conditions are not met. My suspicion—difficult to document, hopeless to prove conclusively—is that many public issues, perhaps most of those considered important enough to be discussed in the newspaper or everyday conversation, fall in the second category, in which definitions, constraints, and responsibilities are centrally at issue.

* * *

In a sense, these differences are aspects of a broader debate that has raged for centuries over human nature and the purposes and methods of governance. Do we as citizens dare entrust our collective fates to a government reflecting the demands of self-interested individuals? If not, what is the alternative?

The modern debate had its origins in the Renaissance, in the first stirrings of humanist thought and the beginnings of the bureaucratic state. By the sixteenth century the monarchs of Europe had evolved administrative machinery capable of organizing finance, waging war, and issuing laws and regulations. These bureaucracies were populated by men who owed their positions to specialized training and administrative competence, not to feudal right. They were uniquely skilled in using organization to accomplish complex tasks efficiently. Bureaucratic absolutism was elaborated and refined in the seventeenth century by Louis XIV of France, whose specialized, hierarchical system provided a model for Prussia, Spain, Austria, and Russia. By the eighteenth century "enlightened despots" were firmly entrenched on the continent. Even with the advent of modern parliaments in the nineteenth and twentieth centuries the instruments of central authority and bureaucratic control continued to dominate the core functions of government in continental Europe. As the German sociologist Max Weber described it, "the bureaucratic type of organization . . . is, from the purely technical point of view, capable of attaining the highest degree of efficiency and is in this sense formally the most rational known means for carrying out . . . control over human beings."

The rise of this new, rationally authoritarian form of government paralleled a growing concern about the governability of the masses. By the seventeenth century many thinkers had concluded that moral exhortation and the threat of damnation could no longer be trusted to restrain people's destructive passions. Niccolò Machiavelli, for example, warned that men are "ungrateful, voluble, dissemblers, anxious to avoid danger, and covetous of gain." Thomas Hobbes foresaw the fragility of an order based on human passion and had concluded that the only alternative was a strong central government—a leviathan.

England, however, was evolving another alternative—deliberative government. Victory over the Stuarts had forestalled the kind of bureaucratic absolutism taking root across the Channel. In its place the House of Commons was elaborating what Edmund Burke would call a "deliberative assembly," guided by "the general reasons of the whole." It was through deliberation that common interests and attachments could be discovered and developed and passions thus be restrained. Burke recoiled from the egoistic philosophy animating the French Revolution, whereby

> laws are supported only by their own terrors, and by the
> concern which each individual may find in them from his own
> private speculations, or can spare to them from his own
> interests. In the groves of their academy, at the end of every
> vista, you see nothing but the gallows. Nothing is left which
> engages the affections of the commonwealth. On the principles
> of this mechanic philosophy our institutions can never be
> embodied, if I may use the expression, in persons; so as to
> create in us love, veneration, admiration, or attachment. But
> that sort of reason which banishes the affections is incapable of
> filling their place. These public affections, combined with
> manners, are required sometimes as correctives, always as aids
> to law.

The notion that democratic deliberation would inspire ideas about what was good for society, and thus instill common attachments and constrain selfish passions, was widely discussed in England and America during the late eighteenth and nineteenth centuries. John Stuart Mill saw in democracy a means of developing moral and intellectual capacities "by the utmost possible publicity and discussion, whereby not merely a few individuals in succession, but the whole public, are made, to a certain extent, participants in the government." American Federalists and Antifederalists alike worried about the instability of a society based on selfish passion and spoke of the need for citizens' "attachment" to institutions and "affection" toward one another. After touring America,

Alexis de Tocqueville mused that "the most powerful and perhaps the only means that we still possess of interesting men in the welfare of their country is to make them partakers in the government . . . civic zeal seems to me to be inseparable from the exercise of political rights." And by 1872 the English essayist and critic Walter Bagehot could conclude that "a policy of discussion not only tends to diminish our inherited defects, but also . . . to augment a heritable excellence. . . . No State can be first rate which has not a government by discussion."

* * *

A third alternative for dealing with the passions of a more worldly populace was also being advanced at about the same time. Rather than rely on bureaucratic absolutism to subjugate the passions or on deliberative government to civilize them, this alternative relied on calculated self-interest to constrain them. This third view emerged from the musings of eighteenth-century political economists of the "Scottish Enlightenment," like Adam Smith, Adam Ferguson, and Sir James Stuart, who regarded the discipline of the marketplace as the key to social stability. Stuart argued that a population governed by rational self-interest would be more stable than one susceptible to appeals to general interest, which were likely to ignite the passions. "[W]ere a people to become quite disinterested: there would be no possibility of governing them. Everyone might consider the interest of his country in a different light, and many might join in the ruin of it, by endeavoring to promote its advantages." The British utilitarians—Jeremy Bentham and his progeny—and the economists and sociologists who followed in their wake, shared many of these assumptions. Although, in their view, "every agent is activated only by self interest," egoistic behavior was entirely compatible with the general good. Indeed, they argued, each individual's rational pursuit of his own self-interest would yield the highest utility overall. Government was necessary only as a last resort, a night watchman to guard against encroachments on trade and the freedom to pursue self-interest. Its purpose was entirely instrumental—to help maximize individual utility.

The reigning American philosophy of policy making has drawn on these three currents of thought—bureaucratic expertise, democratic deliberation, and utilitarianism—but in equal parts. Especially in this century, beginning with the Progressives' efforts to insulate policy making from politics and continuing through the modern judiciary's oversight of policy making, there has been a tendency to subordinate democratic deliberation to the other two themes. As the "administrative state" has grown, its legitimacy has increasingly rested on notions of neutral competence and procedural regularity. The "public interest" has been defined as what individual members of the public want for themselves—as such wants are expressed through opinion surveys, data on the public's willingness to pay for certain goods, and the pleadings of interest groups. The ideal of public policy has thus become almost entirely instrumental designed to maximize individual satisfactions.

*   *   *

The tradition of democratic deliberation, with its emphasis on what is good for *society* and its concern for citizenship education and social understanding, has been subordinated in part, I think, because of our culture's understandable fear of demagoguery and intolerance. Particularly since the 1930s, we have had ample evidence of the dangers of totalitarianism—of moral absolutism and social engineering toward some monolithic view of the public interest. It seems far safer to assume that people *are* motivated primarily by selfish desires, that social improvement *does* require trade-offs and compromises among such goals, and that the purpose of government *is* instrumental—to accomplish such trade-offs and compromises, particularly when private transactions do not suffice. The great virtue of the American form of government has appeared to lie precisely in its pluralism and ethical relativism, its *lack* of any overarching public ideas about what is good for society.

But there may be greater dangers in failing to appreciate the power of public ideas and the importance of deliberation about them. In an era like the present one—when overall public purposes are less clear than during wars or depressions; when the ways public problems are defined, choices posed, and responsibilities tacitly allocated can make all the difference; when many issues are so technically complex that values are easily hidden with expert judgments; and when "great communicators" can hold center stage on national media geared to visionary appeals— our strongest bulwark against demagoguery is the habit of critical discussion about, and self-conscious awareness of, the public ideas that envelop us. Competence, as it has been understood, is not enough. We also need leadership.

31

GREAT EXHORTATIONS

THE START OF EVERY YEAR INVITES NEW RESOLVE ABOUT HOW WE WILL improve ourselves. The start of every fourth year invites new resolve about how we will improve the nation. With extraordinary regularity Americans begin new diets (having given up on the old one) and become enthralled with new political candidates (having given up on the old). Both recurring urges—toward self-improvement and public improvement—require persistent enthusiasm and unending hope.

To help us in these efforts, we turn to two kinds of improvement books that grace best-seller lists. One kind tells us how to improve ourselves—by losing weight, making money, enjoying sex, getting in contact with the cosmos, getting in contact with eligible members of the opposite sex, getting in contact with ourselves, becoming healthier and fitter, influencing people, managing a successful business, sounding intelligent at parties, and so on.

The other kind of improvement book tells us how to improve society —by cleaning up the environment, ending the arms race, shoring up American defenses, organizing higher education around great books, relieving poverty, and so on.

The two kinds of books begin from different premises. Self-improvement books assume that our private lives are unsatisfactory in some way and that by following some prescribed course of action we can achieve happiness and fulfillment. Public-improvement books assume that certain cherished values are being ignored by the public and that by mending our collective ways we can achieve a good society.

Most of us carry around both sets of aspirations—things we want for ourselves and our families on the one hand, and things we want for our society (or for mankind, future generations, the planet) on the other. The two categories—our personal wants and our public wants—are not always in perfect harmony. The public interest is different than the sum of our selfish wants, the musings of microeconomists and political power brokers to the contrary notwithstanding. The task of improving society involves something more than satisfying the personal desires of some people without making others feel worse off.

Research into political attitudes reveals the difference between the two realms. Although people sometimes vote on the basis of what's good for them personally, they also put aside personal interests to a surprising degree. People's views on busing to achieve racial integration have been shown to depend less on their own experience with busing (or the likelihood that their children will either be bused or go to school with children who are) than on their beliefs about the value of integration in general. People's ideas about the overall level of unemployment and about hardships it causes have more effect on their voting patterns than whether they are unemployed or in danger of becoming so. Attitudes toward the Vietnam War turned much less on whether one (or one's family members or close friends) had experienced it firsthand than on one's general views of American foreign policy. Attitudes toward government programs to provide universal health insurance or guarantee jobs are better correlated with one's general political views than with one's own health or employment status. And so on.

* * *

The two kinds of books that represent these two realms of aspiration are sometimes at war with one another, just as are our selfish and social inclinations. The authors of public-improvement books often decry the selfishness, acquisitiveness, narcissism, greed, and self-indulgence that divert our attention from more noble ideals. They admonish us, in effect, to stop being obsessed with self-improvement. (Professor Allan Bloom, author of a best-seller called *The Closing of the American Mind,* expressed outrage at what he considers to be a modern ethos that recognizes no right or wrong, only problems susceptible to personal counseling.)

Authors of self-improvement books, by contrast, often go to great lengths to reassure us that we shouldn't feel guilty, bad, or otherwise inadequate. We'd be far better off if we stopped listening to all the preaching that is imposed on us and responded instead to personal needs that arise from deep inside. By freeing ourselves from the "oughts," we can become more spontaneous, energetic, sexier, more popular, more influential—whatever we want to become.

(There is a hybrid genre of books whose authors advocate a society in which everyone seeks self-improvement—think of Charles Reich's *Greening of America,* on the left of the political spectrum, or Robert Ringer's *Looking Out for Number One,* on the right. But such antistatist, let-a-thousand-flowers-bloom tracts are less about public improvement than self-improvement. They use the language of public improvement therapeutically, to reassure us that our personal longings are justifiable: Don't feel guilty if you're not involved in political movements and social reform, they seem to say. It's fine to drop out, do your own thing, indulge yourself. Indeed, if everyone did that, we'd have a better society.)

Although most of us hold both self-improvement and public-improvement messages in our heads simultaneously, we tend to be more responsive to one of them at one time in our lives than at another. When we first reach political consciousness—typically between the ages of eighteen and twenty-one, or whenever we first leave home—the self-absorption of our teenage years gives way to a greater concern with the society around us, its aspirations and the inevitable gaps that lie between such aspirations and reality. Then, with the start of our own families, our individual concerns tend to take precedence once again. Our personal wants and public wants cycle back and forth in this way as we live out our lives.

So too with our society. As the historian Arthur Schlesinger, Jr., and the political economist Albert O. Hirschman have both noted, society's passion for public improvement seems to wax and wane over time, alternating with periods in which society is more preoccupied by selfish concerns. Periods of public improvement—like the Progressive era of the first decades of the century, the Depression and war decades, the reformist 1960s—eventually lead to exhaustion and disillusionment when the reforms fail to achieve the exaggerated hopes that fueled them, causing people to turn inward. Self-improvement eras (the 1920s, the 1950s, the 1980s) ultimately lead people to feel empty and disconnected from one another even when their personal ambitions are satisfied, causing a society to turn outward once again.

Not surprisingly, public-improvement eras are often marked by best-selling public-improvement books. America of the 1960s was inspired by the likes of Ralph Nader's *Unsafe at Any Speed*, Rachel Carson's *Silent Spring*, Michael Harrington's *The Other America*, Jonathan Kozol's *Death at an Early Age*, Betty Friedan's *The Feminine Mystique*, and John Kenneth Galbraith's *Affluent Society*. Progressive reforms had earlier been spurred by muckraking accounts like *The Jungle* by Upton Sinclair and Ida Tarbell's *History of the Standard Oil Trust*.

Perhaps society's shifting interests in public and then private improvement are related to our personal cycle. By force of sheer numbers, a huge generation like the postwar baby boomers can turn society inward or outward. It seems more than coincidental that the last great wave of best-selling public-improvement books appeared in the 1960s, just as the early baby boomers reached college age.

*   *   *

Sometimes we're attracted to public-improvement books not because we want to improve society but because we enjoy sharing in the author's indignation about how society has gone off track. Americans have always liked debunking our dominant institutions. (The verb "debunk" itself is as American as apple pie.) We relish exposés. There's nothing quite as much fun as kicking a sacred cow or two. The more venom and vitriol, the more we applaud. In this respect, public-improvement books are just glorified self-improvement books. They may have ponderous titles, but they might as well be hawked as cures for chronic exasperation.

Righteous indignation can also be seductive, however. When public-improvement books are taken too seriously, they can be more dangerous than self-improvement books. Bad advice for improving ourselves will, at worst, disappoint us and cause some of us to have wasted a bit of money. But bad advice for improving society can lead to all sorts of mischief.

What's more, there is a natural check on bad advice about self-improvement. We think we know if we're unhappy or unfulfilled, and if a book doesn't help us much, it won't even make it as a paperback. Self-improvement books are like new shampoos or deodorants. Success is proof enough.

But there's less of a check on bad advice for improving society. Most of us are not very confident about what society's core values really are, apart from high abstractions like freedom and equality (and even these have an annoying way of bumping up against each other when pushed too far). Nor can we simply try out what the author of a public-improvement book advises in order to test it for ourselves, the way we can a new diet or sexual technique.

Often authors of best-selling public-improvement books assert that some cherished value is being subverted and rely on exhortation to convince us they're correct. They scold us, shake us, implore us. They throw around words like "virtue," "honor," "nature," "truth," and "conscience" the way authors of self-improvement books throw around words like "feeling," "bliss," "wonderment," and "delight."

In making their case, public-improvement authors may expose startling facts that we hadn't known before but that run counter to what we have preferred to believe about some aspect of our society. Look at the corruption! Behold the poverty! Witness the ignorance, the cruelty, the decay! Or they may cite a wide range of troubling phenomena, of which we're already dimly aware but had not considered symptoms of the same fundamental crisis: It's all due to our loss of commitment! It's because of our lack of patriotism! It's capitalist greed!

But what often gives public-improvement books particular force—and what makes them especially dangerous—is their one-sidedness. The correctness of the cause is never in doubt. Their authors stand aligned with all that is right, good, and truthful in the world—against the forces of wrongheadedness, false consciousness, and evil. They admit to no shades of meaning, ethical dilemmas, trade-offs, possibilities for unintended consequences. They have no patience for relativism. There is no room for compromise. It is all or nothing: Either we create a perfectly clean environment, abandon all nuclear arms, completely democratize the corporation, eradicate communism, focus all of higher education on the values encoded in the great books of civilization—or we are doomed. Such moral absolutism is understandable. Public-improvement books wouldn't attract our attention unless they conveyed total conviction. The danger comes in treating these exhortations as if they were reasoned arguments for public-policy making, when they are nothing of the sort. They are polemics—single sides of often complex issues.

* * *

Provocation of debate about what is good for society can itself result in public good, of course. Democracy depends, after all, on public deliberation. And among the most important subjects we must repeatedly deliberate on are definitions of the problems we face together and under-standings of what we need to ask of one another in order to solve them. There is no better means of mobilizing a free people to collective action than through discussion. (Indeed, there's no better check on the bad advice contained in public-improvement harangues than the habit of democratic deliberation.)

Herein lies the real value of public-improvement books. At their best, they goad us into thinking, arguing, questioning our premises, reevaluating what we want society to be. They remind us that we have collective choices—and personal responsibilities for helping make and execute such choices. They inform and stimulate us—as *citizens*.

Beyond their specific admonitions, then, public-improvement books contain a more general but more enduring exhortation: that we become responsible citizens who continuously and conscientiously deliberate our collective future. Public-improvement books thus offer us another goal for our self-improvement—civic virtue, which holds out the possibility of peace between our warring sets of aspirations.

32

THE ONCE AND
FUTURE LIBERAL

IT IS WITH SOME PERSONAL ANGUISH THAT I CONFESS TO MY CLOSEST
friends (and now, dear reader, to you) that I spent six months of my life
advising Michael Dukakis in his dispiriting run for the Presidency. (I use
the term "advising" in the generally accepted sense that I wrote innumerable memos to the candidate, attended an endless series of meetings
with other advisers, chatted buoyantly on television and with reporters
about the candidate's "new" ideas, and spent hours on the phone, usually very late at night, advising campaign staffers who said they would
be talking with the candidate within the week. I actually spoke with
Michael Dukakis only twice, and on both occasions he gave a credible
performance of having better things to do than listen to my pontifica-
tions.)

The campaign was depressing for many reasons, not the least because my candidate lost. There was also "the vision thing," as George
Bush so eloquently described it. Bush, in case you have forgotten, accused Michael Dukakis of being a *liberal*. That is, Dukakis was a card-
carrying member of the ACLU, he despised the American flag, and he
wanted to release black murderers and rapists from prison, among other
things.

Dukakis responded less forcefully to these charges than one might have wished. At first, he told the American people that *he,* rather than George, was the real conservative. Not until the last ten days of the campaign, when it looked as though all was lost anyway, did he confess that, yes, he *was* a liberal. George had been right all along. Dukakis threw himself upon the mercy of the American electorate.

George Bush was able to define a *liberal* the way he wanted, because few Americans any longer know what a liberal is. American conservatives now have a clear public philosophy, whereas liberals do not. This chapter is about why that is so. It is also about the need for a new and more coherent liberal public philosophy and the difficulties that may frustrate the development of such a philosophy.

* * *

The new conservative public philosophy presents a coherent approach to the world. It proposes explanations for a great deal of our collective experience over the past twenty years, and it embodies these explanations in a vivid core parable about the perils of indulgence and permissiveness. The story line is familiar to postwar America; it is one of doting parents and their spoiled children, of public irresponsibility and social excess. But the parable also tells of a world "out there" grown more ruthless and sternly warns that as individuals and as a nation we are in danger of losing our way. We must impose discipline and responsibility. Through renewed fortitude we can triumph over the forces that threaten us. The parable's power lies in its simplicity and scope, and its evocation of unarticulated fears and hopes.

Consider the new conservative public philosophy's position on social welfare. First, the welfare system is riddled with waste and fraud. Second, when welfare *has* gone to those it was intended for, its effects have often been perverse. It has encouraged poor teenage girls to have babies and discouraged them from marriage and work, trapping children in a lifelong culture of dependency and irresponsibility. At the same time, criminal suspects now enjoy so many rights that our police are incapable of keeping order, so drugs and crime infest our cities. We have forbidden teachers to control their classrooms, so inner-city schools are failing to educate poor children. The three forms of laxness reinforce one another: The easiest path for inner-city youths is to drop out of school, and then for the girls to have babies and live off welfare, and for the boys to live off girlfriends on welfare and the proceeds of crime. The only solution is to reverse course. We should eliminate welfare (except to victims of sudden and unexpected hardships). We should allow our teachers to punish and expel. We should authorize our police officers and judges to mete out swift and certain punishment. In short, we should restore social discipline.

The conservative parable equally encompasses economic policy. For years, the story goes, America has been profligate. The liberal solution to the tendency of the economy to succumb cyclically to recession and underemployment was for the government to spend freely enough to take up the slack. But this Keynesian approach ultimately proved its own undoing. Government went on spending beyond its means, even during times of buoyant growth. Also, it bred expectations that it would always step in to snap the economy out of slumps and slowdowns. The result was a breakdown of social discipline. The lesson of this story, too, is clear. We must restore discipline to the economy. We had to "break the back" of inflation in the early 1980s through tactical unemployment, to remind workers of their vulnerability to joblessness should wage demands get too high, and we must stand ready to do so again. Future economic policy must take the control of inflation as its first priority and relegate unemployment to a lower priority. To control inflation is to impose discipline on the system; the attainment of every other economic goal depends on that basic discipline.

Other strands of the conservative economic philosophy hold that the only way to discipline government spending is to pass a constitutional amendment mandating a balanced federal budget. Others emphasize the discipline of the marketplace and the central importance of rewarding successful entrepreneurialism and punishing failure. According to this view, we should reduce taxes and forswear subsidies and bailouts. The market is *the* source of social discipline—rather than taxes or government regulations. There is a spirited debate between the conservative budget balancers and the supply-siders over whether we should increase taxes to narrow yawning budget deficits. But both sides diagnose our economic ills as the heritage of an overly permissive environment in which no one was held responsible for his economic actions.

* * *

Foreign policy makes up a third aspect of the conservative parable. For years liberals have sought to appease the Soviets, placate the less-developed nations of the Third World, and coddle our allies. As a result, the story goes, we became an easy mark. Our defenses were down; the Soviets surged ahead of us in armaments. Emboldened by our passivity, they viciously subjugated Afghanistan, cracked down in Poland, and expanded their influence in southern Africa, Southeast Asia, and Central America. Simultaneously, the United States was being taken for a ride by Third World nations that demanded our aid but persistently sided with our adversaries and voted against us at the United Nations. Other Third World nations have threatened default on loans from our banks. We were humiliated by Iran and have been easily victimized by international terrorists. In addition, Japan and our European allies have been unwilling to cooperate with us in restricting East-West trade. Worse, they have taken advantage of our open economy by dumping their subsidized goods here. Japan is strongly reluctant to import American goods.

The overarching lesson is the same. We must impose discipline, on adversaries and allies alike. We must regain our credibility, and the way to do that is to get tough. We should maintain a strong military defense, get the Soviets (and their Cuban allies) out of Central America, give aid to Third World nations only when they play on our side, and tighten up on East-West trade so that the Soviets cannot easily take advantage of our technology. The Soviets are ready to make concessions on armaments only because we held tough and built up *our* armaments. We should "play hardball" with our allies on trade and defense. We should threaten to retaliate against Japan if its markets are not fully open to our products. And we should impose austerity on Third World debtors, ensuring that they repay their debts and end their profligate ways.

What is so compelling about all these arguments—drawn from social welfare, economics, and foreign policy—is that they are mutually reinforcing. No conservative public philosopher, and certainly no politician, subscribes to the full complement of these views. But the details of these arguments are less important than the overarching parable. Liberal permissiveness has laid us open to exploitation. Without discipline, there has been no accountability. Without accountability, decadence has crept in, irresponsibility has become endemic, the system has lost its "moral fiber," and we have let ourselves become victims.

The conservative parable embodies a subtle but important distinction between two forms of social discipline—one applying to *us*, the other to *them*. *They* are the poor, the workers who demand unjustly high wages, our trading partners, Third World debtors, and the Soviets. We must discipline them. To do so, we will need to be strong and resolute.

In a curious way bundling such disparate issues together into a single parable of decadence, slackness, and assertiveness gives comfort.

The larger explanation suggests a way of comprehending, and thereby eventually reversing, the decay. Lessons can be learned, steps taken. It is simply a matter of recognizing the prevailing pattern and applying the moral. The new conservative public philosophy offers an easy formula.

* * *

The liberal response to the new conservatism has been unconvincing —and not because Walter Mondale, Tip O'Neill, John Kenneth Galbraith, or even Michael Dukakis has been lacking in imagination. Even in recent years liberals have shown no end of cleverness in devising new schemes and programmatic solutions to all manner of problems. Those who bemoan the liberals' dearth of "new ideas" have not been paying attention. The failure has lain deeper, with a liberal public philosophy that no longer embodies a story in which most Americans can believe. The liberal parable does not explain. It does not yield clear lessons. It does not ring true.

The prevailing liberal public philosophy rests on notions of altruism and conciliation. The parable is that of wise and generous parents who skillfully accommodate the conflicting demands of their children, help their poorer cousins, and seek reconciliation with wayward relations. The modern liberal hero is a combination of Jesus and Robert Young in *Father Knows Best.*

This parable generalizes across issues as easily as the new conservative fable does. It requires no great elaboration here, because it is so familiar to us. The needy should be helped. The less fortunate should have the opportunity to become as prosperous as the richest among us. Those who are members of groups that have been discriminated against in the past should be given special help. People who commit crimes should be rehabilitated, not merely punished. Economic policy should favor full employment even at the cost of some inflation, for joblessness is an awful burden to impose on anyone; inflation can be restrained by an incomes policy that will cause no increase in unemployment, unlike the conservative remedy. Taxes should be progressive. Poorer nations deserve our aid, to encourage land reform and the growth of democratic institutions. As to our allies, we should work in concert with them, all the while recognizing that their needs and priorities may be different from ours. And we should persistently seek a structure of peaceful coexistence with the Soviets, through trade, cultural exchanges, summit meetings, and arms control.

The liberal public philosophy has its own coherence. Only through altruism and conciliation can we maintain domestic tranquillity and global peace. Only through peace can we gain prosperity. Only through prosperity can we afford to be charitable and conciliatory. The logic is internally consistent. And this philosophy contains a moral vision no less compelling than that of the disciplinarians.

But the parable of the generous and wise parent seems to many Americans disconcertingly naive in a world grown colder and crueler. Popular wisdom now teaches that the welfare system does not reduce poverty, "full-employment" budgets cause inflation, Third World aid merely generates corruption and profligacy, détente merely promotes Soviet aggression. The new conservatives did not invent these relationships; they just pointed them out. Charity and conciliation are worthy goals for our personal lives, but such sentiments cannot sustain a nation in the world as it is. They are no longer reliable pillars for a public philosophy.

* * *

Yet the fact is that pure altruism never figured prominently in the liberal public philosophy of the period from the New Deal to the end of World War II—the gestation period of modern liberalism. The New Deal was concerned primarily with social insurance rather than with the redistribution of wealth. The stronger precept of social solidarity was born not of specific legislation or programs but of certain experiences— the Depression and World War II—that profoundly affected almost all Americans. The goals of reviving the economy and winning the war, and the sacrifices implied in achieving them, were well understood and widely endorsed. The public was motivated less by altruism than by its direct and palpable stake in the outcome of what were ineluctably *social* endeavors.

This distinction between social solidarity and altruism parallels the conservative penchant for disciplining others but not necessarily ourselves. The liberalism of the New Deal and World War II partook of an inclusive spirit of generosity toward ourselves. Society was not seen as composed of *us* and *them*; it was the realm of *we*. We were all bound together, fundamentally dependent on one another's compassion and common sense.

The liberal idea of common dependence even found its way into thinking about national defense and international trade. While conservatives sought to isolate America from the world, the liberals who emerged from the Depression and the war designed a system of "collective security" in which we and our allies would work collaboratively. These earlier liberals forged the United Nations and other structures for mediating international political disputes, and they created a parallel system for working out the rules of world trade.

*   *   *

The liberalism of the 1960s was quite different. By this time many Americans were experiencing the exhilaration of rapidly rising incomes, along with the new mobility and privacy that went with cars, highways, and suburban homes. There was less occasion in everyday life for social solidarity. Generosity still claimed the liberal conscience, but circumstances had transformed this sentiment into altruism. Thanks to liberal altruism, the hitherto ignored lot of the poor was brought to the public's attention. Gradually, however, our poorer citizens, and the inhabitants of other, poorer nations, became *them*.

The special conditions of the time allowed *us* to be generous to *them* with little identifiable sacrifice. The extraordinary growth of the American economy during the 1960s made it possible for the nation to wage a war on poverty, and then another on North Vietnam, and even enjoy a rise in living standards. Keynesianism, the dominant economic school of the time, asserted that such public spending, far from impoverishing the middle class, would serve to keep the vast economic machine going at full throttle. Extending civil rights to blacks also cost the majority of Americans relatively little. Segregation in Southern schools, luncheonettes, and hotels could be forcefully attacked without causing unpleasant side effects elsewhere. The United States was preeminent in the world economy, with no serious trade competition from overseas. So the nation could afford to indulge its allies and the Third World; boosting foreign purchasing power could only result in more American export sales. In short, the liberal public philosophy of the 1960s and early 1970s entailed a peculiarly low-cost form of charity.

This easy altruism was reinforced by prevailing pluralist ideas about American democracy. By the 1960s pluralism had come to serve both as a description of the American political system and as a prescription for its continued health. American politics was thought to be powered by shifting and overlapping groups whose leaders bargained with one another over the shape and purpose of public action. The result was assumed to be a stable but responsive political system. To many Americans, these features helped explain why democracy had continued to survive so well in the United States in contrast to its fate in other nations.

In the pluralist view, the "public interest" was nothing more (or less) than an accommodation among group leaders, with no substantive content apart from what these leaders sought. Policies that could placate a greater number of interest groups were by definition the most conducive to the public good. Pluralism thus contained no principled limits on what compromises should be reached or how far government should go to accommodate the various groups that made up the public.

These two intellectual currents—Keynesianism and pluralism—were easily combined. Just as Keynesianism legitimized the idea of activist government as a way to stabilize the economy, pluralism legitimized it as a way to stabilize politics. Both currents were ultimately propelled by the comforting notion that some people could be helped without imposing costs on others. Full employment in the economic sphere, coupled with the ongoing accommodation of interest groups in the political sphere, would ensure that everybody got his over the long term. Public issues were subtly transformed into private claims, all of which could eventually be satisfied. Hard choices and the setting of priorities could be avoided; the logic of public action could be left vague. Social altruism knew no bounds and had no strict definition. There was no finely honed and rigorous liberal public philosophy, because there seemed to be no need for one.

As a result, postwar liberalism was doomed to excess. Its fullest flowering, in the 1960s and early 1970s, occurred in an anomalous moment of history during which the United States was particularly unconstrained. It was a sheltered and rich environment, a cultural hothouse unlike anything America had experienced before or is likely ever to experience again.

* * *

Any public philosophy so germinated would be enfeebled once it left the hothouse. Liberalism was no exception. As the economy began to slow and American economic preeminence came under challenge, it was no longer possible for some groups to benefit without the burden manifestly falling on others. But because liberal pluralism lacked any definition of the public good apart from the sum of individual claims, and also lacked a system of principles for screening and balancing such claims, conflicts grew harsher and claims more insistent. By the late 1970s liberalism and, inevitably, the Democratic party, too, appeared less the embodiment of a shared vision and more a tangle of narrow appeals from labor unions, teachers, gays, Hispanics, blacks, Jews, the handicapped, the elderly, women. Of course, these demands were no more parochial than those from Republican claimants—bankers, oil companies, insurance firms, doctors, and corporate bureaucrats, among others. But the perception remained that the Democratic party was dominated by "special interests," because by the late 1970s the liberal public philosophy conveyed no central theme to organize and legitimate the claims of its diverse constituencies. It failed to explain the new reality in which we found ourselves and to prescribe clear lessons. It offered nothing but a feeble and unconvincing call to charity and conciliation. Without an integrating philosophy, these fractious Democratic constituencies, each promoting its own agenda, were all that liberalism had to show to the citizenry.

The philosophical watershed, where conciliation gave way to discipline, came with the Administration of Jimmy Carter—the Democratic President who carried into policy many of the central precepts of the new conservative public philosophy. Carter understood the public's growing disdain for Washington. He had campaigned as an outsider, against the Washington "insiders." He decried "fraud, waste, and abuse" in the burgeoning welfare system and sought its overhaul. (Carter's abortive reform effort adopted the model of the negative income tax, first proposed by conservative economists to minimize administrative complexity and purge the system of its presumed incentives against work and family.) Carter's conservative tendencies became particularly apparent in the last years of the Administration. He appointed Paul Volcker chairman of the Federal Reserve Board and supported the Fed's decision, in October 1979, to limit the nation's money supply in order to combat inflation, even though interest rates and unemployment were predicted to rise as a result. And it was Carter, and his national security adviser, Zbigniew Brzezinski, who ended détente with the Soviets. In the wake of the Soviet invasion of Afghanistan, in December 1979, Carter embargoed grain sales to the USSR; and in response to the Soviet deployment of SS-20 missiles in Eastern Europe, Carter moved to install U.S. missiles in Western Europe.

All these departures from liberal public philosophy were understandable: Many Americans resented the growth in welfare spending; inflation was soaring; the Soviets were becoming more aggressive. The point is that Jimmy Carter—and the American public—embraced the new conservative public philosophy because it seemed to offer the only comprehensible guide to what was happening and what to do about it. The world was already divided into *us* and *them*—that is, greedy workers, the poor, Soviets, and other foreigners. The choice was to be either charitable and conciliatory or assertive and tough. The first alternative had proved to be tragically misguided. That left only the second. Absent any other option, the public's efforts to discern what was at stake and the lessons to be learned inevitably began to be shaped by the conservative parable.

*   *   *

Every public philosophy that gains credence, every story about our lives together that strikes a chord of recognition among the public, contains some truth. If it did not, the parable would not resonate so powerfully in our collective consciousness. But a public philosophy is a simplification of reality. Without some simplifying fables, citizens would be awash in disconnected data. The world is too complex for wholly empirical politics.

The new conservative public philosophy contains an important element of truth. America's permissive policies of the 1960s and early 1970s, and the larger failure to define goals and limits, of which the permissive policies were a consequence, did contribute to the growing problems of welfare dependency, inflation and economic drift, and Soviet aggression. Permissiveness—that is, an overwhelming preference for smoothing over rather than settling conflict—contributed to an environment in which unaccountability flourished, both at home and abroad. In abdicating public authority, America issued an invitation to irresponsibility, at home and abroad.

But the skeins of cause and effect are far more tangled than anything dreamt of in the conservative parable. The 1960s liberal public philosophy can be faulted for ignoring the harsh realities of the late 1970s and the 1980s. But the new conservative public philosophy is open to criticism for denying their underlying causes. However much public laxity may have contributed to our troubles, it was not the principal culprit. A far deeper transformation was occurring across all three realms of immediate concern—domestic poverty, the national economy, and the Soviet threat. The transformation is still going on, even if we can discern only its outlines.

Before turning to first causes, consider some salient symptoms: By 1988 the average weekly earnings of American production workers, adjusted for inflation, were just about the same as they had been a full twenty years before. Women and baby boomers streamed into the workplace—some nineteen million of them over the 1970s, and millions more since then. But many of these new entrants have been driven by the need to prop up stagnant or declining family incomes. Young workers, in particular, have fallen behind. Many can no longer afford to buy their own houses nor aspire to the standard of living enjoyed by their parents.

The poorest among us have fared the worst. America's poverty rate —the fraction of the population officially listed as controlling too little cash to tend to their minimal needs—stopped declining in 1973 and then slowly began edging up again. When the income of the median American family stopped rising, so did that of the poorest.

The pernicious lure of welfare dependency cannot be blamed for the continuing plight of America's poor, as conservative sociologists would have us believe. Subtract payments to the middle class and the elderly from the nation's growing social-welfare bill and it becomes apparent that the needy have received surprisingly little public help during this long period of stagnation. In fact, from 1970 to 1980 annual case assistance for each nonelderly poor person in the United States rose by just ninety-three dollars—hardly a sum to tempt crowds of Americans away from honest labor. Adjusted for inflation, benefit levels for Aid to Families with Dependent Children, which is the largest cash-assistance program for the poor, actually declined during the decade, and they have continued to decline since 1980.

Most "welfare" has gone to the middle class, through programs like Medicare and Social Security, not to the poor. By 1980 the aggregate of these benefits was more than three times larger than that for programs based on need.

* * *

Just as conservative sociology provides the wrong explanation for the persistence of poverty, conservative economics gives the wrong explanation for our long-term industrial problems. Our economy has suffered less from inflation and underinvestment than from a long-term slowdown in productivity. For nearly two decades before 1970 the average working American had produced around 3 percent more goods and services at the end of each year than at the start. But in the 1970s the annual increase in the rate of productivity fell dramatically. Not even the 1980s economic recovery has returned productivity to its former level of growth. Almost no growth of productivity in America has meant almost no rise in the real incomes of Americans. This stagnation has been particularly apparent in comparisons between the United States and other nations. From 1973 to 1988, for example, while American productivity improved by an average of just 2 percent a year, the Japanese were producing 6 percent more each year. Even the troubled economies of Western Europe raised productivity more rapidly than we did.

No one can fully explain why our rate of productivity growth has declined, especially relative to that of other nations. But we know that productivity depends on social organization—on how our firms are managed and our workers motivated and trained, and on how quickly our enterprises adapt to new possibilities and challenges. Adaptation is the key, because the terms of global competition have changed dramatically.

And here we have come to the heart of the matter. The stresses Americans began experiencing in the 1970s are intimately connected with the transformation of the global economy. The two oil shocks of the 1970s, the flood of Japanese automobiles and consumer electronics into America, and the loss of American jobs in basic manufacturing— much of this story is painfully familiar. Other aspects of the transformation are less well understood. Our difficulties competing in the world actually became apparent in the early 1970s. American manufacturers were able to stay competitive during the 1970s only with the help of a drop in the value of the dollar, which produced a drop in the foreign prices of American exports. No degree of toughness with our trading partners would have altered this outcome much.

*   *   *

This transformation is not limited to the patterns of trade between the United States, Japan, and Western Europe; it is far more international than that. In fact, our economic fate is being played out ever more centrally in the Third World—in particular, Latin America, the Middle East, and Southeast Asia. The planet's population balance is tipping precipitously in the direction of the Third World. In 1950 two thirds of mankind lived in less-developed nations. By 2020 the proportion will be five sixths. The implications for our economy and our politics are profound.

Step by step, the nations of the Third World are climbing toward industrialization and a higher standard of living, though each one is pursuing its own path to development. Far from halting this migration of mass production to the Third World, automation is actually accelerating it. Sophisticated machines are readily transported to countries where wages are low. Robots and computerized machines are substituting for semiskilled workers. And all the while, ever greater numbers of Third World citizens are flooding into the work force. The vast majority will be willing to work for a small fraction of the wages of an American. More than two billion people now live in countries where the per capita income is the equivalent of $400 or less. Some of these nations are already stepping onto the first rungs of the industrial ladder.

While this transformation is causing strains in industrialized nations, as workers in basic industries face the loss of traditional jobs, it is leading to upheaval in much of the Third World. Some developing nations have sunk deeply into debt, and many are awash in severe inflation. Rapid industrialization has contributed to urban poverty, corruption, and social unrest; the unrest has encouraged extremist left-wing and right-wing regimes and, on occasion, religious zealotry.

This unrest brings us to the last realm of the new conservative public philosophy, which concerns the Soviet threat. There can be no doubt that the Soviet Union has taken advantage of Third World instability wherever possible. But these Third World tensions are manifestations of an economic and social transformation; their connection to the East-West rivalry is in most cases derivative and wholly secondary. Our national security is surely affected by religious fanaticism in Iran, sectarian violence in Lebanon and India, the ability of the oil-producing nations to raise oil prices, the flow of advanced weapons to all manner of semi-sovereign groups, South Korea's and Taiwan's advances in high technology, and China's convulsive drive toward modernization. But these developments are not the result of Soviet machinations, and to view them as such, to treat them as occasions for secondhand warfare between the United States and the Soviet Union, leads to tragically myopic prescriptions. Yet the conservative parable holds no other role for the poor majority of mankind than as a pawn in the East-West struggle.

The Soviet Union has been brought to the peace table, not because of American toughness, but because of the fragility of the Soviet economy, no longer able to support its huge military commitments. To this extent, America and the Soviet Union share a common problem, which, if unaddressed, will lead them to a common fate. The military machines of both nations are undermining their respective economies at a time when Japan, South Korea, and West Germany are surging ahead. The East-West struggle has not disappeared, but it is rapidly becoming a sideshow to a more profound realignment of world wealth and, accordingly, world power.

*   *   *

The new conservative philosophy is comforting to an America confronted by a newly intractable world—mostly poor and nonwhite—in which America is no longer preeminent. The parable of permissiveness and indulgence invites us to deny the wholly natural loss of an unnatural postwar economic and political supremacy and to reject our new interdependence. It lets us blame our trials on liberal indulgence and promises renewal if only we forswear the flabby principles of altruism and conciliation. It charges us to summon our power and exercise it boldly to reclaim our hegemony.

But the conservative parable virtually ignores the fundamental transformation of the world economy and society. It overlooks the key relationships between domestic poverty and the stagnation of family incomes, between this stagnation and changes in the global economy, between these changes and political instability around the globe, between this instability and Soviet opportunism, and between Soviet overextension and our own overextension. Its message of social discipline and pugnacity, in other words, does not so much seek preeminence as presume it. This is an invigorating but reckless vision.

The first objective of our public policy, and thus the first concern of a durable public philosophy, must be to redefine America's place in a transformed world. The overriding goal is not to resist change by clinging to dangerous notions of world mastery but rather to embrace change as inevitable and to ease the dislocations it causes. Our other goals— reducing domestic poverty, maintaining a buoyant national economy, and deterring Soviet aggression—are attainable only insofar as we achieve this basic reorientation to reality. But the new conservative public philosophy fails to comprehend the scope or importance of the global economic changes we have been discussing and the force they exert on our goals, and thus many of the policies that it inspires are being pursued without any attempt to assess their unintended effects. In being tough with the Soviets, with our trading partners, and with Third World debtors, therefore, we run the risk of frustrating global adjustment. The ironic result is that we also make worse the problems of domestic poverty, our national economy, and Soviet adventurism.

* * *

Whatever form it might take, a new, liberal philosophy would embrace a much more informed and strategic approach to global change. Its parable would evoke dynamism and diversity. Above all, the new philosophy would reject the notion—so deeply embedded within both liberal altruism and conservative pugnacity—that the central struggle of our age is over the division of a fixed quantity of global wealth. It would suggest instead the possibility of an enhanced quality of life for all, contingent on mutual adaptation. It is crucial to understand that such an approach would be neither a matter of charity nor a ploy in a competitive struggle for survival but an expression of a larger and more enlightened self-interest—akin to the ideal of social solidarity that modern liberalism abandoned for altruism. The easier the transition is for any one group or nation, the smoother and more rewarding it will be for everyone else.

The new public philosophy would lead to policies that embrace the reality of interdependence in all three realms—economics, foreign affairs, and social policy. Preceding chapters advanced a number of specific proposals. To summarize: Our trade policies would welcome the transfer of basic industries to poorer nations; we would reject the grim choice between deindustrialization and protection. Simultaneously we would relieve Third World debtors of their burdens and offer the Third World access to the kind of long-term financing they desperately need. So far as these measures ameliorated the trauma of global change, right-wing generals and left-wing revolutionaries would have fewer occasions to exploit despair. We thus could feel more secure about reducing our military support to Third World countries. And exquisitely mindful of the crippling effects on our economy of our military burden, we would respond to Soviet troop reductions and offers to reduce arms expenditures with bold reductions and counteroffers of our own.

A central domestic task would be to ease the transition of our own work force out of low-skilled standardized businesses of the sort that Third World nations are beginning to enter. This would require not only more money for education, but a different approach: Rather than stress routinized learning, which prepares our children for lives of routinized work, our schools would train young people to discover problems and solutions for themselves, and give them skills in collaborating with others. It would also require that, once prepared for a lifetime of learning, our workers be given on-the-job experience designing and producing complex technologies—regardless of whether the firm they work for is headquartered in New York, Tokyo, or Bonn. Thus it is that education, training and retraining, and the nurturing of technologically intensive businesses would become central goals of public policy.

Simultaneously, hostile takeovers, leveraged buyouts, and other feats of transactional daring would be curbed. Fewer of our young brains would gravitate to Wall Street and to corporate law; more would be attracted by the challenges of inventing, manufacturing, and marketing new products worldwide, and of discovering new cures for dread diseases, better ways of cleaning our environment, and improved means of delivering public services. Worker ownership would become commonplace, as everyone connected with the enterprise shared in its profits and bore the burdens of its losses. Government would help spur new technologies, but no longer through the Department of Defense; a civilian research and development agency would provide seed money to groups of firms willing to pool their efforts and put up the bulk of the funds.

A more adaptable national and world economy would help restore the long-term upward direction of American incomes, including those of poorer Americans. A new public philosophy would also embody the recognition that we have a direct stake in the poor themselves, in their increasing productivity and adaptability. In an era in which capital and technology flow around the earth at the speed of an electronic impulse, national economic vitality depends to an ever greater extent on the health and readiness of *all* our people. Domestic spending on the pre- and postnatal care of poor infants, and on the nutrition and preschool education of poor children, would come to be seen as an extension of policies for guarding our nation's long-term security and prosperity.

* * *

Clearly the transition to a new public philosophy will not be easy. We are entering a paradoxical era. At a time when technology is rendering geographic borders almost irrelevant, there is an upsurge in nationalism—in chauvinistic posturing and sectarian violence. At a time when global collaboration can yield huge benefits, we are witnessing a withdrawal from international institutions and multilateral negotiations, save for joint military commands and banking consortia. And just when we need bold leadership in Washington, we elect politicians who want to avoid hard choices and who regard government as fundamentally inept. In all these dimensions resistance to change is mounting precisely as— and largely because—the change is becoming more convulsive. The conservative mind wants to preserve and protect, to restore and to reclaim: back to traditional values, back to basics, back to old-fashioned patriotism and the simplicities of a local market economy. But there is no turning back, and efforts to cling to the past will only render change more painful.

If it is to be useful to us, a new liberal philosophy must explain reality and yield palpable lessons for the future. But if it is to be accepted, it must do so in a manner that simplifies and reassures. Sadly, these two conditions are sharply at odds in this age of turbulent change and baffling complexity. Hence, the resurgent liberal's greatest challenge.

INDEX

absenteeism, 74
Administrative Management
    Association, 71
aerospace program, 128
Affluent Society, The (Galbraith), 271
Afghanistan, 196, 282
AIDS research, 18
Aid to Families with Dependent
    Children, 284
Ainu people, 82
Air Force, U.S., 139
Alger, Horatio, 65, 84, 85, 86, 87,
    228
Allende, Salvador, 68
Allied Chemical, 209
Allis-Chalmers, 177
Amana community, 77
Amway, 77
Anderson, Martin, 195, 196, 201,
    202
anti-nicotine chewing gum, 132
antitrust laws, 158, 167, 172–73,
    207, 252

Apollo, 132
Apple Computer, 69, 178
arbitrageurs, 5
Argentina, 30, 31
armed service, all-volunteer, 243–44,
    245, 246
arms sales, 125
Army, U.S., 93
Arnold, Thurmond, 251
Art of Japanese Management, The
    (Pascale and Athos), 75–76
asbestos, 210, 211
asset rearranging, 12, 14, 16–22
    harm of, 16–20
    reform of, 20–22
astrology, 197, 202
AT&T, 117, 142, 151
Athos, Anthony G., 75
austerity plans, 30–31
Australia, 146, 150
Autobiography (Franklin), 228
auto industry, 20, 40, 68, 91, 151,
    166–73, 253

automation, 92, 93, 99, 149, 169, 172, 285
Avis Rent-A-Car, 12, 22

B-1 bomber, 140
Bagehot, Walter, 266
Baker, James, 31, 52, 197
balance of power, 142–43
balance sheet mentality, 17
BankAmerica, 177
Bank of England, 31
Bank of the Commonwealth, 28
bankruptcy, 19
banks, 27–33
    federal government and, 29
    Japan and, 177
    Latin America and, 28, 29, 30–32, 164
    loan policies of, 27–33
    reform of, 32–33
    savings and loans, 28
Baring Brothers Bank, 31
Barlow Rand, Ltd., 125
Beard, Dita, 68
Beatrice Foods, 12
Begin, Menachem, 201
Beirut, 201
BellSouth, 93
Bell System, 65
below-cost pricing, 156, 157, 158
Bentham, Jeremy, 266
Berle, Adolf A., 248–51
big business, 247, 251
Big Ideas, 88–89, 90
Black Monday (1987), 14, 24, 52, 57
blacks, 20, 235
Blanchard, Kenneth, 64
Bloch, Erich, 112
block traders, 5
Bloom, Allan, 269–70
blue-collar employees, 20, 73
Board of Army Science and Technology, 111
Bolivia, 31
Borg-Warner, 16
Boston, 119
Bound to Rise (Alger), 86

Brady, Nicholas, 26
"brain drain," 18
Brandeis, Louis, 208
Brazil, 30, 54, 68, 126, 149, 155
Bridgestone Corporation, 63
British Treasury, 31
brokers, 13
Bronson, Charles, 229
Brookings Institution, 19, 252
Brzezinski, Zbigniew, 282
"bubble" memories, 111
Buckley, William, 201
budget deficit, 23, 24, 25, 52, 59, 164, 199
bull market, 25
bureaucracy, 134–37, 138–39, 140, 245
Burke, Edmund, 236, 265
Bush, George, 21, 37, 62, 189, 190–91, 207, 222, 231, 258, 274–75
Bush Administration, 75, 115
    foreign trade policies of, 129–30
    laissez-faire rhetoric of, 129
    Latin America and, 125
Bushism, 236
Business Week, 176
buyouts, 5
    "deleveraged," 15
    leveraged, 10, 12, 13, 20, 59, 288

California Supreme Court, 211
Canada, 54, 109, 146, 163
capital gains, 21–22
Capitalism, Socialism and Democracy (Schumpeter), 215n
Capra, Frank, 228
Carnegie, Andrew, 86, 87
Carnegie, Dale, 72, 85
Carnegie-Mellon University, 114
Carson, Rachel, 208, 271
Carter, Jimmy, 245, 282
Carter Administration, 37, 150
Casey, William, 201–2
Caterpillar Tractor, 64, 69, 122, 125
CBS Records, 177
Center for Strategic and International Studies, 139

CEOs, 17, 62–69, 90, 93–94, 175,
176
  as mavericks, 65–66
  as missionaries, 66
  performance of, 67–69
  salaries and bonuses of, 63, 94
  success stories of, 63–65
  term of office of, 17
Chernobyl, 132
Chevrolet Sprinter, 166
Chile, 68
China, 151, 254
Chinon Industries, 178
Chrysler, 64–65, 66, 68–69, 78, 87,
  166, 170, 171, 172, 173
Churchill, Winston, 160
CIA, 201
Citibank, 29
Citizens for Tax Justice, 246
civic republicanism, 81
Cleveland, Grover, 247
Closing of the American Mind, The
  (Bloom), 269–70
cocaine, 31
Code of Federal Regulations, 35, 37
Cohen, Benjamin, 251
collective entrepreneurship, 90–95,
  98
  automation and, 93
  education and, 99–103
  need for, 90, 94–95
  organizational structure of, 92–93
  product development and, 90–91
  reward systems and, 93
  teamwork and, 92, 93–94
Commerce Department, U.S., 107,
  129, 154
Commission on the Presidential News
  Conference, 190
communism, 250
competition, 145, 182
  foreign, 12, 26, 150, 212
  global, 119, 127, 151, 154
  Japanese, 89, 212
  low-wage, 89, 98, 147, 179, 286
computers, 54, 56, 92, 109, 110,
  111–12, 138, 149, 176, 253
concessions, 20, 62, 99

Congress, U.S., 24, 54, 68, 114, 140,
  154, 176, 192–94
conservative public philosophy, 275–
  78, 282, 283, 286–87
consumer electronics industry, 17
consumption, reduction of, 59
Continental Illinois bank, 28, 29
Cooper Industries, 122, 125
Copland, Aaron, 228
corporations, 174–85
  debt of, 19, 21, 25, 57
  income tax of, 21, 62, 200
  interests of, 174–75, 178, 181,
    184
  international nature of, 116–17,
    119–20, 124, 177, 178–80
  Japanese and U.S. compared, 78,
    80
  lawsuits against, 210–11
  new policies for, 183–85
  privileged position of, 62, 181
  public ownership of, 182
  short-term view taken by, 171, 212
  side effects of activities of, 182
  social Darwinism and, 239
  stock sales tax of, 22
Council on Foundations, 176
Cray, 111–12
Cripps, Stafford, 72
Croly, Herbert, 251
Cuba, 250
currency levels, 52, 136
Cyert, Richard, 114

Dalkon Shield, 210
Darwin, Charles, 237
David Sarnoff Research Center, 16
Death at an Early Age (Kozol), 271
Death Wish, 229
Deaver, Michael, 201
debt:
  corporate, 19, 21, 25, 57
  Latin American, 21, 29, 30–32
  Polish, 28, 29, 30
  Revolutionary War, 38
Defense Advanced Research Projects
  Agency, 111

Defense Department, U.S., 55, 56,
  59–60, 107, 114, 116, 129, 157,
  164
  classified research and, 128–29,
    140
  contracting scandals of, 139–40
  high technology and, 127–28, 139,
    142, 253
  Japan and, 107, 109, 110, 111,
    112–13
Defense Science Board, 114
defense spendingg, 53, 128, 129, 157
de Gaulle, Charles, 161
Delaware, 176
Democratic party, 115, 282
DES, 211
détente, 29, 30, 282
Development Bank, 141
distribution of wealth, 20, 222, 240
dollar, U.S., 52, 57, 58, 177, 253, 285
"dollar diplomacy," 52
Dominican Republic, 32
Doubleday, 177
Dow Jones Industrial Average, 24, 52,
  62
draft, military, 243–44, 245
Drapkin, Donald, 24
Dressler Industries, 122, 125
Drexel Burnham Lambert, 15
Dukakis, Michael, 189, 191, 231,
  258, 274–75, 278
"dumping," 54, 55, 150, 159
DuPont, 109
duties, 54, 55

Eastman Kodak, 178
Eastwood, Clint, 229
economic fundamentals, 11, 26
Economic Recovery Tax Act (1981),
  62
economic theory of politics, 214–22
  economic change and, 220, 221–22
  economic democracy and, 221
  social experience and, 219–20
  special interest groups and, 216–
    19, 220–21
  weaknesses of, 217–19

economies of scale, 97, 144, 169
Eden, Anthony, 160
education, 59, 96–103, 130, 159,
  183, 288
  collective entrepreneurship
    economy and, 99–103
  economies of scale and, 97–98,
    99–100
  "tracking" system of, 102–3
Egypt, 238
election of 1988, 189–91, 222
Electric Storage Battery Company, 13
Emerson, Harrington, 71
employee ownership, 22
employment patterns, 13–14, 18, 61
Energia rocket, 132
Energy Department, U.S., 55
engineers, 127, 128, 179
entrepreneurs, paper and product, 7–
  9, 13, 14–15
equality of sacrifice, 242–46
Ethics in Government Act (1978), 193
European Economic Community, 54,
  150

Fairchild Semiconductor Corporation,
  107–8, 116, 120
Federal Deposit Insurance
  Corporation, 29, 32
Federalism, 228, 265
Federal Register, 35, 37
Federal Reserve Board, 21, 51, 68,
  254, 282
Federal Savings and Loan Insurance
  Corporation, 32
Federal Technology and Transfer Act
  (1986), 114
Federal Trade Commission, 40, 41–
  42, 43–44, 167, 173
Feminine Mystique, The (Friedan),
  271
Ferguson, Adam, 266
Firestone Tire and Rubber Company,
  63, 177, 210
First Pennsylvania Bank of
  Philadelphia, 28, 29
"flexible freeze," 23

Food and Drug Administration, 43
food industry, 98
Ford, Henry, 86, 88
Ford, Henry, II, 64, 87
Ford Motor Company, 68, 87, 170,
    171, 172, 173, 209, 210
foreign aid, 53, 238
foreign competition, 12, 26
foreign ownership, 57
foreign policy, 276–77
For the Record (Regan), 197–98
France, 53, 74, 122, 150, 162
Frankfurter, Felix, 251
Franklin, Benjamin, 228
free-market, 20–21, 24, 276
French Revolution, 265
Friedan, Betty, 271
Fujitsu, Ltd., 107–8, 111, 112, 116,
    120, 151

Galbraith, John Kenneth, 62, 271,
    278
Gallup Poll, 256
Gantt, Henry L., 71
gas sales, 123
Geneen, Harold, 64, 65, 66, 68, 75–
    76
General Agreement on Tariffs and
    Trade, 146, 150, 162
General Electric, 16, 62, 66, 69, 122,
    125, 139, 174, 178
General Instruments, 179
General Motors, 68, 93, 94, 169,
    170, 174, 209
    Toyota and, 93, 166–68, 171, 172,
    173
*General Theory of Employment,
    Interest and Money* (Keynes), 7
Gephardt, Richard, 54
Germany, Republic of (West), 52, 53,
    71, 74, 109, 122, 149, 162, 221,
    222
    competition from, 12, 17, 212
    postwar recovery of, 216–17
Getty Oil Company, 15
Gilbreth, Frank, 71
Gilder, George, 87, 88

Gillette, 24
give-backs, 20, 62, 99
global economy, 88, 124, 153, 158,
    159, 169, 182, 183, 285
    see also technoglobalism
GNP, 58–59, 61, 113, 162
    of other nations and U.S.
    compared, 53, 162
golden parachutes, 9–10, 22
Goldman, Sachs, 177
Good Housekeeping, 223
Gorbachev, Mikhail, 135–38, 139,
    142
Gosplan, 134, 135, 140
Gould, Jay, 209
government regulation, 34–47, 207–
    13
    as "antibusiness conspiracy," 35–
    37
    bureaucracy of, 34–35
    intermediaries and, 38–47
    in other countries and U.S.
    compared, 35
    public opinion of, 210
    red tape and, 44–47
    reduction of, 62
    three periods of, 207–9
grain sales, 123, 282
Gramm-Rudman deficit reductions, 52
Great Britain, 53, 74, 145, 154, 170,
    181, 216, 221, 222
    GNP of, 162
    management style of, 72, 73
    productivity gains in, 74
    U.S. and, 160–65
Great Society, 215, 240
Great Western Sugar Company, 125
Greenhouse Compact, 256–57
Greening of America (Reich), 270
greenmail, 9, 10, 20, 22
Gulf and Western Industries, 125
gunboat diplomacy, 31

Haig, Alexander, 122
Haiti, 32
Haking Industries, 178
Hamilton, Alexander, 38, 236, 251

Harriman, Edward, 86
Harrington, Michael, 271
Harris poll, 176, 210*n*, 256
Harvard Business School, 18
hero myths, 84–88, 93
Hickenlooper Amendment, 68
high-skilled emerging businesses, 148–49, 154, 156–59
high technology, 124–30, 131, 136
  Defense Department and, 127–28
  global nature of, 125, 126
  growth of, 124
  Japan and, 124–28, 129, 130, 131, 139
  marketing of, 126, 128
  Soviet Union and, 131–33, 136
Hirschman, Albert O., 270
Hispanics, 20
History of the Standard Oil Trust (Tarbell), 271
Hitachi, 111, 112
Hitler, Adolf, 216
Hobbes, Thomas, 265
Honda, 170
Honduras, 32
Hong Kong, 148, 149, 155
Hooker Chemical Company, 211
Hoover, Herbert, 247, 248, 252
hormones, 54
hostages, 165
hostile takeovers, 12, 13, 25, 26, 57, 59, 63, 176, 288
House of Commons, 265
House of Representatives, U.S., 54, 177
Hughes Aircraft, 140
human engineering, 72
Hunt brothers, 125
hydrogen bomb, 132
Hyster Company, 180–81

Iacocca (Iacocca), 64, 87, 228
Iacocca, Lee, 64–65, 66, 68, 69, 87
IBM, 66, 109, 116, 117, 142, 178, 179
ideology of survival, 239–41
illegal aliens, 31

improvement books:
  public, 268–73
  self, 268, 270
income tax:
  corporate, 21, 62
  1986 reforms of, 62, 243, 245–46
India, 149
industrial physiology and psychology, 72
industrial policy, 255–57
infant mortality, 235
inflation, 165, 220, 276, 282, 286
In Search of Excellence (Peters and Waterman), 64, 65, 66
insider trading, 5–6, 20, 192–93
Intel, 111
interest:
  payments, 21, 24, 25
  rates of, 52, 57, 68, 253
intermediaries:
  careers of, 39, 42–43
  conflict prolonged by, 42–43
  confrontation sought by, 39–41
  definition of, 38
  direct communication prevented by, 43–44
  exaggerations made by, 41–42
  loopholes and, 44–47
  motives of, 43
Internal Revenue Service, 241, 244
International Monetary Fund, 30, 31, 32, 162
International Nickel Company, 13
International Trade Commission, 111
inventions, 89, 108, 117–18, 119, 140
investigative reporting, 208, 227
investment bankers, 3–6, 14, 15–16, 18
  money earned by, 3, 16, 18
investment banks, 4–6, 15
  Japanese, 177
  money earned by, 4, 15
  structure of, 5
investment managers, 175
investment strategy, 56, 59–60
Iran-contra scandal, 165, 196, 201

IRAs, 59
Israel, 201, 238
Isuzu, 170, 171
Italy, 109, 122, 162
It's a Wonderful Life, 228
ITT, 12, 64, 65, 66, 68, 69, 75–76
IUDs, 210

Japan, 12, 17, 52, 61, 70–71, 74, 81,
    148, 149, 155, 221, 222
  auto industry of, 168–71
  balance of power and, 142–43
  competition from, 89, 107–8
  corporate structure of, 80
  defense spending of, 53
  employment patterns of, 18*n*, 82
  GNP of, 53
  government regulation in, 35
  high technology and, 124–28, 129,
    130, 131, 139
  job security in, 78, 79, 82
  Latin America and, 126
  management style of, 71, 72, 73,
    76, 77, 78–79, 80, 81, 82
  microelectronics industry of, 110–
    11, 112–13
  minorities in, 82
  organization of production in, 78
  paternalism in, 82
  postwar recovery of, 216–17
  product development in, 89, 108,
    118–19, 141, 170
  productivity gains in, 70, 141
  profit in, 80
  salaries in, 79
  standard of living in, 170
  stockholders' responsibilities in,
    78
  trade between U.S. and, 54, 68,
    146, 151, 179
  trade quotas and, 150–51
  unions of, 74, 79, 82
  U.S. techno-nationalism and, 110–
    13, 115–17
  women in, 82
Jefferson, Thomas, 38, 251
Jobs, Steven, 87

job security, 72, 73, 76, 78, 99
  in Japan, 78, 79, 82
Johns-Manville, 210
Johnson, Lyndon B., 230
Johnson, Spencer, 64
Jones, Reg, 66, 69
Joseph, James, 176
Jungle, The (Sinclair), 271
junk bonds, 16, 20
Justice Department, U.S., 68
Kawasaki Heavy Industries, 89
Keogh plans, 59
Keynes, John Maynard, 7
Keynesianism, 280, 281
KGB, 138
Khrushchev, Nikita, 133
Kidder, Tracy, 85
"kinder, gentler nation," 235
Kohlberg, Kravis, and Roberts, 15
Korea, Republic of (South), 12, 17,
    148–49, 151, 155, 220–21
Kosygin, Alexei, 134
Kozol, Jonathan, 271
Kravis, Henry, 16
Kravis, Irving, 180
Kristol, Irving, 35–36
Kroc, Ray, 64, 65
Kyocera, 111

labor, skilled, 149, 156
labor-management relations, 20, 70–
    83
  see also collective entrepreneurship;
    management
LaGuardia, Fiorello, 250
Latin America:
  debt of, 21, 29, 30–32, 164
  Japan and, 126
  U.S. and, 31–32, 125–26
law, spirit vs. letter of, 192–94
Law and State Enterprise, 137
lawyers, 15, 16, 18, 210–11
  as intermediaries, 38–39, 40, 42,
    43–47
Lebanon, 165, 196, 201
leveraged buyouts, 10, 12, 13, 20, 33,
    59

liberal individualism, 81
liberalism, 240–41, 246, 274–89
  big government and, 247
  conservative planning compared
    with, 254
  development of, 279–81
  new philosophy for, 287–89
  public philosophy of, 278–79, 283
  reorganizing the economy and, 252
Lilienthal, David, 248
Lincoln, Abraham, 228
Lipsey, Robert, 180
lobbyists, 38–39, 193, 259
"lockbox" stocks, 67
Long Term Arrangement, 146
Looking Out for Number One
    (Ringer), 270
Los Angeles, 25
Louis XIV, King of France, 264
Louvre accord, 52
Love Canal, 211
lower-level employees, 17
low-skilled standardized businesses,
    148–49, 154–56
LTV Corporation, 140
Luck and Pluck (Alger), 86

McDonald's, 64
McDonnell Douglas, 139–40
McFarlane, Robert, 198
Machiavelli, Niccolò, 265
machine tools industry, 17
Mack Truck, 177
Macmillan, Harold, 160
"Made in Japan," 139
Magaziner, Ira, 256
Malaysia, 149
Malthus, Thomas, 237
management, 63–69, 70–83, 180
  anti-unionism of, 73
  blue-collar-white-collar split, 73–
    74
  hands-on style of, 65–66
  Japanese and U.S., compared, 71,
    72, 73, 78–79, 82–83
  lack of practical knowledge of, 70–
    71, 73–74

  manipulation by, 70, 72, 76–77,
    82–83
  scientific, 71, 77
  superficial use of Japanese style by,
    75–76
Management Review, 77
Managing (Geneen and Moscow), 64
Man of the Year, 87
Mars, 132
Marshall, Alfred, 214
Marshall Plan, 72
Matsushita, Konosuke, 75–76, 77
Matsushita Electric Company, 75–76,
    77
Mayo, Elton, 72
Mazda, 78, 170, 171
MBAs, 65
Means, Gardiner, 248
Medicare, 284
merchant shipping, 151
mergers and acquisitions, 3, 5, 9, 14
  growth of, 13
  language of, 9
  R. J. Reynolds and Nabisco, 11–12
  value of, 11–12
Metropolitan Museum of Art, 16
Mexico, 30, 54, 89, 126, 146, 150,
    155, 171
microelectronics, 110–11, 112–13
Middle East, 123
Milken, Michael, 16
Mill, John Stuart, 242, 265
Minnesota Supreme Court, 211
Minuteman missiles, 139
Mitford, Jessica, 208
MITI, 127–28, 129, 141
Mitsubishi, 170, 171
Mobile Oil Corporation, 180
"Model of Christian Charity, A"
    (Winthrop), 228
Model T, 86
*Modern Corporation and Private
    Property, The* (Berle and Means),
    248
"momism," 225
Mondale, Walter, 252, 278
monetarism, 51
Monitor Sugar Company, 125

Monsanto, 15, 111
Moscow, Alvin, 64
Moses, Robert, 248
Motorola, 116–17
muckraking, 208, 227
Multifiber Agreement, 126

Nabisco, 11–12, 13
Nader, Ralph, 208, 271
NASA, 56, 132, 157
National Bureau of Economic
    Research, 180
national debt, 51
National Defense Education Act
    (1958), 132
National Labor Relations Act (1935),
    79–80
National Opinion Research Center,
    245
National Recovery Administration,
    249, 251–52
National Science Foundation, 112,
    115
National Security Agency, 55, 56,
    111, 253
National Security Council, 112–13,
    164, 194, 199
NATO, 30, 54, 124, 161
Nevin, John, 63
New Deal, 208, 209, 230, 247, 251,
    279
New Republic, 246
New Republic, 251
New Right, 239, 240
New York City, 38
New York Stock Exchange, 175, 176
New York Times, The, 64
New Zealand, 146
Niagara Falls, N.Y., 211
Nicaragua, 32
Nissan, 170
Nixon, Richard M., 68, 246, 254
nomenklatura, 134–35
nontariff protections, 54, 55, 148
Noriega, Manuel, 196
Northern Telecom, 109
Norton, Simon, 12

nuclear power, 132
nuclear weapons, 161, 164–65, 238–
    39

Olson, Mancur, 215–17, 218, 220,
    222
Olympics (1984), 87
Oneida community, 77
O'Neill, Thomas P. "Tip," 278
One Minute Manager, The
    (Blanchard and Johnson), 64, 66
Other America, The (Harrington),
    271
Ouchi, William G., 75
Overseas Economic Cooperation
    Fund, 126

Packwood, Bob, 244
Paine Webber, 177
Panasonic, 75–76
paper entrepreneurs, 7–9
    fees paid to, 14–15
    income of, 13
parables, 227–31, 275, 283
Pascale, Richard T., 75
Peale, Norman Vincent, 85
peanut butter, 42, 43
Pennzoil, 15
pension plans, 80–81
Peters, Thomas J., 64
petrodollars, 30
Philippines, 149
pluralism, 280–81
Poindexter, John, 198
poison pills, 9, 10
Poland, 122
    debt of, 28, 29, 30
Polanyi, Michael, 101
"Policies for Adjustment," 147
policy making, 258–67
    historical development of, 264–66
    new role of, 263–64
    private interest and, 259–60, 266–
        67
    public interest and, 260–61, 262,
        266–67

portfolio managers, 17
poverty, 59, 215, 230, 235, 237, 284
Presidency, transformation of, 189–91
President's Commission on an All-Volunteer Armed Force, 244
Principles of Economics (Marshall), 214
product development, 89, 90–91, 98–99, 108, 117–19, 137, 140, 170
product entrepreneurs, 7–9
productivity gains:
    in Great Britain, 74
    in Japan, 70, 141, 284–85
    in Soviet Union, 141
    in U.S., 12, 57, 74, 76, 98, 110, 141, 284–85
product quality, 74
profit, 67, 69, 80, 97, 119, 182
Progressive era, 207, 209, 229, 230, 248, 266
Promise of American Life, The (Croly), 251
protectionism, 24, 25, 62, 152–53, 158
Protestant virtues, 71
public and private sectors:
    cooperation between, 33
    movement between, 37
    spending of, 57, 59–60
public interest, 258, 259
Public Interest, 36
public investments, 58
Public Speaking and Influencing Men in Business (Carnegie), 72
Purina Mills, 177

quotas, import, 150

Ragged Dick (Alger), 84
Raytheon, 65
RCA, 16, 89, 179
Reagan, Nancy, 198, 202
Reagan, Ronald, 24, 26, 54, 62, 164, 195–202, 207, 230–31, 235, 245, 253–54, 261
    character of, 197–98, 199–200, 201–2
    Latin America and, 125
    Presidency transformed under, 189–91
    Soviet Union and, 122, 123
Reagan Administration, 75, 107
    blunders of, 196
    defense policies of, 164–65
    defense spending of, 53
    fiscal policies of, 23–24, 52
    government regulation and, 37
    laissez-faire rhetoric of, 129
    Latin America and, 125
    Poland and, 30
    policy-making process of, 195–96, 200–202
    Soviet Union and, 122–23
    trade policies of, 54, 68, 129–30, 151, 154
Reaganism, 236, 239, 240
Reaganomics, 255
recession, 15, 149, 165
    potential consequences of, 19
red tape, 44–47
Regan, Donald, 197–99, 200–201, 202
regional development banks, 31
"Regulation, Social Policy, and Class Conflict" (Weaver), 36
Reich, Charles, 270
Renaissance, 264
Republican National Convention (1972), 68
research, 21, 141
    classified, 128–29
    decline of, 16, 17–18, 58
    Defense Department and, 128–29
    global nature of, 108–9
    government funding of, 55, 58, 114–15, 127
"restructuring," 176
Revlon, Inc., 24
Revolution (Anderson), 195
Revolutionary War, 38
Reykjavik summit (1987), 164–65
Reynolds, Richard, 111
Rhode Island, 255–57

Ricardo, David, 144–45
Ringer, Robert, 270
Rise and Decline of Nations, The
  (Olson), 215–17
R. J. Reynolds, 11–12, 13
RJR-Nabisco, 13, 14–15, 18
robots, 89, 92, 132, 149, 169, 172
Rockefeller, John D., 86
Rohatyn, Felix, 250
Roosevelt, Franklin D., 229–30, 248
Roosevelt, Theodore, 31–32, 251
Roper poll, 210*n*
Rostenkowski, Dan, 24, 26
Royal Institute of International
  Affairs, 32
Royal Navy, 31
ruble, 136
Ruethlisberger, F. J., 72
Ryzhkov, Nikolai I., 136

safe-harbor leasing, 62
satellites, 132
savings and loans, 28, 33
scandals, 208–9
Schlesinger, Arthur, Jr., 270
Schlumberger, 108
Schmidt, Helmut, 122
Schumpeter, Joseph, 215*n*
scientists, 127, 128
Scottish Enlightenment, 266
Securities and Exchange Act (1934),
  249
Securities and Exchange Commission,
  13, 192–93, 248
securities industry, 13–14
securities laws, 11, 21
Selective Service System, 243, 245
Sematech, 56, 114, 116, 253
semiconductor industry, 17, 54, 56,
  107–8, 112, 114, 120, 127
Semiconductor Industry Association,
  114
Senate, U.S., 178
sexism, 203–6
Shaklee, 77
Shearson Lehman, 177
Sherwood, Robert, 228

shipbuilding industry, 151
Shmelyov, Nikolai, 136
Shultz, George, 196
Siemens, 109
Silent Spring (Carson), 271
silicon, 111
Silicon Valley, 107, 119
Sinclair, Upton, 208, 227, 271
Singapore, 149, 155, 220–21
Sink or Swim (Alger), 86
Smith, Adam, 144–45, 242–43, 266
social Darwinism, 75, 236–41
social disintegration, 228–29
Social Security, 59, 284
Solidarity, 30
Sony, 89
Soul of a New Machine, The (Kidder),
  84–85
South Africa, 125, 150
sovarkhozy, 134
Soviet Union, 53, 108, 131–38, 139,
  196
  balance of power and, 142–43
  central planning system of, 133–
    38
  dissent in, 138
  excluded from technoglobalism,
    109
  gas pipeline of, 121–24, 125
  high technology and, 131–33, 138,
    142
  loans to, 29–30, 122
  productivity gains in, 141
  reform in, 135–38, 142
  ruble of, 136
  technical achievements of, 132
  technical weaknesses of, 132–33
  U.S. and, 121–25, 135, 161, 165,
    282, 286
Spain, 148, 150, 170
Spencer, Herbert, 236–38, 239
Sputnik, 132
Sri Lanka, 149
Stalin, Joseph, 133
Stallone, Sylvester, 85
standard of living, 57, 95, 110, 113,
  129–30, 152, 157, 169, 170,
  172, 240

Standard Oil Trust, 208
State Acceptance Service, 137
State Department, U.S., 129, 164
State Price Committee, 134
Statue of Liberty, 87
steel industry, 20, 124, 126, 132, 145, 148, 150–51, 154, 253
Steinbeck, John, 228
Stewart, Jimmy, 228
stock-index options and futures, 14
Stockman, David, 196, 199, 202
stock market crash (1987), 14, 24, 52, 57
stock prices, 12, 24, 25, 26
Stone, Roger, 190–91
Strategic Defense Initiative (Star Wars), 109, 111, 115, 142, 253
Strauss, Robert, 196
Stuart, James, 266
Study of Man, The (Polanyi), 101
subsidies, 54, 55, 62, 146, 150–51, 155, 158, 159, 181
sugar, 125, 146
Sumner, William Graham, 236, 237, 239
Sun Belt, 217
Supercomputer Research Center, 56
superconducting supercollider, 55
superconductors, 56, 142, 253
supply-side economics, 51, 199, 236
survival of the fittest, 237, 238, 241
Suzuki, 171
Sweden, 74
synergy, 11

Taft, Robert, 247
Taiwan, 89, 146, 148, 151, 155, 179, 220–21
takeovers, hostile, 12, 13, 25, 26, 57, 59, 63, 176, 288
Talyzin, Nikolay V., 136
Tarbell, Ida, 208, 227, 271
tariffs, 54, 150
tax laws, 11, 21
tax revolts, 245
Taylor, Frederick Winslow, 71, 77
teams, 85, 93, 94

techno-globalism, 108–10, 114, 115, 117, 119–20
techno-nationalism, 110–120
    Congress and, 114, 115
    Defense Department and, 114
    goal of, 115
    problems of, 115–19
Tehran (Iran), 165
televisions, color, 89, 148, 151
terrorism, 165
Texaco, 15
Texas Instruments, 64, 69, 140, 179
textile industry, 126, 145, 146, 147, 151, 253
Thailand, 149
Thatcher, Margaret, 75, 122, 164
Theory Z (Ouchi), 75
Third World, 165, 276, 285–86, 288
3M, 65
Three Mile Island, 210
Time, 87, 248
Tocqueville, Alexis de, 266
Toshiba, 58, 116–17
Toyota, 93, 166–68, 169, 171, 172, 173
trade, 54–55, 57, 58, 123–24, 152–59
    agricultural, 146, 147
    free, 144–48, 149–50, 252
    growth of, 146, 162
    new policy for, 154–59
    wars, 152
trade associations, 38–39, 41–42, 43–44
transistors, 89
Treasury, U.S., 164, 197, 198
Triangle Shirt Waist factory fire, 209
"trigger-price" mechanism, 150
Trivial Pursuit, 100
trust, 76, 77
Turkey, 30

UAW, 94, 172
Ueberroth, Peter, 87
unemployment:
    foreign, 52–53, 123
    U.S., 165, 253, 255, 276, 282

Unimation, 89
unions, 62, 149, 222, 253
  Japanese, 73, 74, 79, 82
  in Western Europe, 73, 74
United Nations, 161, 280
United States:
  balance of power and, 142–43
  economic and military status of,
    110–11, 112–13, 125, 126,
    162–63
  fear of economic change in, 221
  foreigners blamed by, 52–55, 56
  foreign policy of, 164
  Great Britain and, 160–65
  high-technology industrial policy
    of, 56, 60, 253
  international institutions and, 53
  Irish in, 161
  Latin America and, 31–32, 125–
    26
  national debt of, 51
  national parables of, 227–31, 275
  parochialism of, 163, 165
  productivity gains in, 12, 57, 74,
    76, 98, 110, 141
  Soviet Union and, 121–25, 135,
    161, 165, 282, 286
  trade between Japan and, 54, 68,
    146, 151, 179
  trade imbalance of, 54–55, 57, 58,
    110, 178, 180
  universities of, 108, 110, 115, 117
Unsafe at Any Speed (Nader), 271
utilitarianism, 266

Venezuela, 31
Versailles economic summit (1982),
  122
Vietnam, 243, 245, 250, 280
Volcker, Paul, 68, 282

wages:
  of blue-collar workers vs.
    executives, 73

concessions of, 20, 62
growth of, 13
real, 12, 20, 162, 169, 235
Wall Street:
  anthropomorphization of, 23–26
  federal government and, 23–26
  hostile takeovers as viewed by, 13,
    56–57
  reform of, 26
Walt Disney Productions, 64, 66, 69
War Industries Board, 207
War on Poverty, 230
Washington, D.C., 38
Watergate, 245
Waterman, Robert H., Jr., 64
Ways and Means Committee, House,
  24, 26
Weaver, Paul H., 36
Weber, Max, 264
welfare state, 215, 246, 275
Western Electric, 89
Western Europe, 35, 74, 145, 150, 164
  management style of, 72, 73
  Soviet gas pipeline and, 121–24
  unemployment in, 123
wheat sales, 123
white knights, 9, 10
Wilson, Charles Erwin "Engine
  Charlie," 174, 175, 176, 181
Wilson, Woodrow, 229, 251
Winthrop, John, 228
women, 203–6, 223–26
  in Japan, 82
  sexism against, 203–6
  work and, 223–26
worker participation, 72, 73, 74, 75,
  76, 78
World Bank, 31, 32, 162
World War II, 162, 163, 245
Wriston, Walter, 29

Yeutter, Clayton, 54–55

zero-sum games, 19, 152, 153, 157